CONTEMPORARY BUSINESS LAW

Principles and Cases

CONTEMPORARY BUSINESS LAW

Principles and Cases

J. David Reitzel, M.S., J.D.
Professor of Business Law
California State University, Fresno

Donald P. Lyden, J.D.
Late Professor of Business Law
California State University, Northridge

Nathan J. Roberts, J.D., LL.M.
Emeritus Professor of Law
Loyola University, Los Angeles

Gordon B. Severance, J.D., Ph.D.
Professor of Business Law
University of Nevada, Reno

FOURTH EDITION

McGRAW-HILL PUBLISHING COMPANY

New York St. Louis San Francisco Auckland Bogotá Caracas Hamburg
Lisbon London Madrid Mexico Milan Montreal New Delhi Oklahoma City
Paris San Juan São Paulo Singapore Sydney Tokyo Toronto

CONTEMPORARY BUSINESS LAW

Principles and Cases

This book was set in Goudy Old Style by the College Composition Unit in cooperation with Monotype Composition Company.
The editors were Johanna Schmid and Karen Hughes;
the designer was Joan Greenfield;
the production supervisor was Janelle S. Travers.
Project supervision was done by The Total Book.
R. R. Donnelley & Sons Company was printer and binder.

1 2 3 4 5 6 7 8 9 0 DOC DOC 8 9 4 3 2 1 0 9

ISBN 0-07-051905-6

Library of Congress Cataloging-in-Publication Data

Contemporary business law: principles and cases/
J. David Reitzel
... [et al.].—4th ed.
p. cm.
Includes index.
ISBN 0-07-051905-6
1. Commercial law—United States—
Cases. I. Reitzel, J. David.
KF888.C62 1990
346.41'07—dc19
[344.1067] 89-2464

ABOUT THE AUTHORS

J. DAVID REITZEL is currently Professor of Business Law, California State University, Fresno, and was formerly Professor and Chairman of the Department of Business Law at The American College, Bryn Mawr, Pennsylvania. Before that he taught at St. Cloud State University, St. Cloud, Minnesota. Professor Reitzel holds a J.D. degree from Indiana University and B.S. and M.S. degrees from Purdue University. Admitted to the Indiana and federal bars in 1969, Professor Reitzel was Editor-in-Chief of the *American Business Law Journal* and is the author of numerous articles and papers, many dealing with business law education.

DONALD P. LYDEN (deceased) was Professor of Business Law, a former Acting Dean of the School of Business Administration and Economics, and a former Chairman of the Department of Business Law at California State University, Northridge. A member of the California Bar, Professor Lyden was active in several academic and professional organizations, maintained a private law practice in the Los Angeles area, and was a past President of the Pacific Southwest Business Law Association.

NATHAN J. ROBERTS, Professor of Law Emeritus, Loyola Law School, Los Angeles, received an A.B. degree from Syracuse University, a J.D. degree (with honors) from the University of Florida, an an LL.M. degree from George Washington University. He was a member of Phi Kappa Phi. Professor Roberts was Assistant Judge Advocate General for Civil Law of the Army and is a retired Brigadier General. He was also a member of the faculty of the Army Industrial College and later was in charge of the business courses of the Extension Division of the University of California, Santa Barbara. He was admitted to practice before the Supreme Court of the United States and in the courts of the States of Florida, North Carolina, and California. Professor Roberts was a contributing author to *Government Contracts Practice* and to *Basic Techniques of Public Contracts Practice,* both published by California Continuing Education of the Bar, and to *Business and the Law,* published by McGraw-Hill Publishing Company.

GORDON B. SEVERANCE is currently Professor of Business Law and former Acting Dean of the College of Business Administration, University of Nevada. He is Emeritus Professor of Law, California State University, Los Angeles. He also taught at Occidental College, California State University at San Diego, and the University of Southern California. He is a magna cum laude graduate of Stanford University where he received an M.A. degree. He also holds the J.D. and Ph.D. (economics) from the University of Southern California. A member of Phi Beta Kappa, Professor Severance is a past President of the Pacific Southwest Business Law Association. A specialist in real property and corporation law, he has maintained a private law practice for more than forty years. He is President and director of an international import-export corporation, and has authored numerous journal articles in the area of international business law. Professor Severance has been awarded a Fulbright grant to teach at The Makerere University School of Law in Uganda.

CONTENTS

Part Five
Property and Estates

Part Six
Debtor-Creditor Relations

Part Twelve International Business Law

Chapter 48 Legal Aspects of International Business Transactions 1053

TABLE OF CASES

PREFACE

Purpose

A business student needs two kinds of law courses, each giving attention to the internal and external environments of business:

(1) A broad introductory course revealing the general nature of law, its major elements and modes of operation, its facilitative and restrictive roles in business activity, and some of the dynamics of law, ethics, and business.

(2) Additional law study relevant to the student's business major and future roles as a business person and citizen—coursework building upon themes struck in the introductory course and enhancing one's ability to take law into account when making business decisions.

Our purpose has always been to provide material for both kinds of courses—material that, for each type of course, would contribute not only to business students' professional development, but also to their awareness of the fundamental, enduring, and universal aspects of the law.

In undertaking this, the fourth edition of *Contemporary Business Law,* our first concern was to improve the elements commonly used in the introductory course and to develop practical materials on business ethics (centered around a new chapter, Law and Business Ethics, by Geoffrey C. Hazard, Jr.) for use throughout the book as an integral part of the study of business law. We have updated the text where legal developments warrant, and we continue our efforts to streamline it, improve readability, and maintain a proper balance in meeting the immediate and long-term student needs that a comprehensive business law textbook should address. The result, we believe, is a book especially suited to business schools with a variety of degree programs and a corresponding variety of law courses.

Organization and Appendixes

Contemporary Business Law has the following twelve parts together with appendices containing the United States Constitution (excerpts), the Uniform Commercial Code, The Uniform Partnership Act, the Uniform Limited Partnership Act, and the Model Business Corporation Act:

Part One:	Law, Ethics, and the Legal System
Part Two:	Tort and Criminal Law
Part Three:	Contracts
Part Four:	Sales
Part Five:	Property and Estates
Part Six:	Debtor-Creditor Relations
Part Seven:	Insurance
Part Eight:	Commercial Paper
Part Nine:	Agency
Part Ten:	Business Organizations (including securities regulation and accountants' liability)
Part Eleven:	Government Regulation (including administrative law and process)
Part Twelve:	International Business Law (dealing with legal aspects of international trade)

The introductory and background chapters of Part One are followed by a wide variety of legal foundations chapters (Parts Two through Ten) relating to the functions, internal structure, and operations of business. Next are five chapters (Parts Eleven and Twelve) focusing on the external environment of business. As noted below, however, much material on the external environment appears in the legal foundations chapters; and three of the regulation and external environment chapters—Chapter 44 on administrative process, Chapter 47 on labor and employment law, and Chapter 48 on legal aspects of international trade—are recommended for use in the introductory course.

Approach

Law is a both a facilitator and a regulator of business activity. To develop these key relationships, a business law course should present the law in context and in sufficient depth to reveal its origins, functions, philosophic premises, evolutionary nature, major lines of growth, and its strengths and weaknesses as a method of social control.

Presenting law in its business context requires attention to business functions and activities and to the goals and aspirations of business people. What the law allows business people to do is a matter of values and policy. Consequently, as in prior editions, we have stressed the "why's" of the law as a basis for understanding the law-business relationship. As Lord Coke observed 400 years ago, "If by your studie and industrie you make not the reason of the law your own, it is not possible for you long to retaine it in your memorie." A mastery of the *reason* of the law, we believe, leads to understanding, evaluation, and appreciation of it and to a deeper understanding of the thing regulated. We continue in the fourth edition, therefore, to emphasize the development, the economic and social contexts, and the underlying policies of the law—and the evolutionary interaction among law, ethics, and business activity. This emphasis is consistent with the tenor of the AACSB curriculum guidelines pertaining to the legal, social, and ethical environment of business.

Contemporary Business Law also takes an integrative approach to the presentation of business law. The first seven chapters on the development and nature of law, the role of law and ethics in business decision-making, the courts, arbitration, torts, and the criminal law introduce topics that are referred to time and again in subsequent chapters on public and private law topics. And, although the book has five independent chapters on government regulation of business (those on securities regulation, administrative process, antitrust law, and the law of labor and employment), much regulatory material is worked into chapters on private law. The contracts chapters, for example, discuss government regulation affecting contracts generally, consumer protection law relating to unordered merchandise, state legislation on contract modifications involving no new consideration, statutory limits on minors' rights to disaffirm contracts, consumers' rights of avoidance under state and federal consumer protection statutes, and many similar topics.

Other integrative aspects include added emphasis in the contracts chapters on sales law concepts and their impact on the common law of contracts; discussions of the relationship between tort and contract and tort and agency law; a unifying presentation of secured transactions; a chapter relating state insolvency law to state and federal controls on debt collection activity and to federal bankruptcy law; a linkage in Chapter 28 between the law of assignments and commercial paper law; an introduction to arbitration in Chapter 3 and further discussion elsewhere; extensive reference to constitutional law and administrative process throughout; application in the chapter on international business transactions of public and private law topics presented earlier but relevant to world trade; and an integrated presentation of business ethics. Students are not likely to miss the point that the legal environment within which business operates is a "seamless web" of public and private law as affected by ethical, social, and political considerations.

Ethics and Business Law

At all levels of business activity, people face a variety of social pressures, temptations, and potentially corrupting influences that may overshadow the dictates of law and cloud their judgment in the conduct of business. Where norms of conduct collide, moral dilemmas arise. A course in business law provides an excellent opportunity for considering the ethical standards to which business conduct should conform and the role they should play in business decision-making. Our aim in providing substantial new materials on business ethics is to engage students actively in considering both legal and non-legal behavioral norms when charting a course of business conduct.

The keystone of our presentation is the new Chapter 2, Law and Business Ethics, by Geoffrey C. Hazard, Jr., Sterling Professor of Law at Yale University. A writer and authority on legal and business ethics and Chairman of the Permanent Editorial Board for the Uniform Commercial Code, Professor Hazard brings a wealth of scholarship and experience to the task of developing an analytical framework for the study of business ethics. The chapter, which identifies norms of conduct that might be in conflict and suggests a basis for resolving ethical dilemmas, can be used as part of any business law course, introductory or advanced.

The ethics chapter is supplemented by the following:

- In Chapter 1, a new introductory section entitled "Law, Morals, and Ethics."
- "Ethics in Practice" sections at the ends of Parts Two through Twelve. All the sections present ethical dilemmas in the form of case problems derived from news accounts and other sources. Many of the problems involve conflict-of-norms situations similar to those discussed in Chapter 2. Some of the sections open with a brief comment on aspects of business ethics relevant to that part—for example, the discussion of corporate social responsibility in the section for Part Ten.
- In many chapters, brief commentary and Review Questions on relevant ethical concerns.
- In the Instructor's Manual, supplemental notes on ethical implications of substantive law.

Major Changes and Additions

In addition to the ethics elements previously mentioned, changes and additions for the fourth edition include:

- In Chapter 1, a new section entitled "Law, Litigation, and Lawyers" (emphasizing the social and business functions lawyers serve).
- New treatment of contract law: More emphasis on its evolution and modern form—18th century just-price doctrine, 19th century "classical" period, and 20th century developments (e.g., nature and role of promissory estoppel, treatment of contracts of adhesion, impact of UCC Article 2 and government regulation, significance of the second Restatement).
- To streamline presentation of contract law without loss of content, combination of former chapters on offer and acceptance into one entitled Mutual Assent: Offer and Acceptance, and of former chapters on capacity and avoidance into one entitled Avoidance of Agreement.
- For flexibility in the presentation of the law of commercial transactions, a division of Chapter 17 into mini-chapters entitled Part One, Delivery and Storage of Goods; Documents of Title and Part II: Transfer of Title and Risk of Loss; Title of Good Faith Purchasers.
- Where relevant in the sales chapters, commentary on the new UCC Article 2A, Leases.
- In Chapter 43, discussion of mergers, leveraged buy outs (LBOs) and insider trading.
- In Chapter 48, overview of the Convention on Contracts for the International Sale of Goods (CISG).
- Numerous new cases and case problems.
- Many new illustrations and charts.
- In the contracts, sales, secured transactions, and commercial paper chapters, an expanded, integrated set of diagrams to aid comprehension of abstract concepts.

Course Formats

An eternal problem of business law instruction is how to structure and balance the first and subsequent courses in business law, giving proper attention in both to the external as well as the internal legal environments. The first course usually serves as an introduction to the legal aspects of business and legal process generally; as a basis for further business law study; and as general education for non-business students. Depending on the number and content of subsequent courses, the law content of first courses can vary considerably among universities.

One first-course format widely approved by AACSB accreditation teams emphasizes one or two fundamental business law topics (such as contract law) in a context of broad-ranging background material about law and business. The first 25-40% of the course commonly is devoted to the development of law and equity; business and the Constitution; courts, procedure, and arbitration; basic functions of criminal, tort, and contract law; introduction to administrative law and process; the general nature of government regulation of business; and the relationship between law and ethics. The middle part develops foundation topics such as contract and agency law (but with heavy emphasis of themes and interrelationships sketched in the early part of the course). The remaining 15-20% introduces topics such as the law of labor and employment and legal aspects of international trade. A course so structured has many advantages. It reveals the variety and interlocking nature of business law, pursues at least one foundation study in sufficient depth to give a realistic view of law and legal process, and consolidates foundation elements of business law into one prerequisite course.

Many chapters on introductory topics such as torts and business crimes can be assigned as outside reading (students being expected to raise questions in class). The chapter on contract remedies can receive similar treatment or even be omitted where, for example, remedies have been discussed in other parts of the course. Depending on the kind of instructional device used in class, the chapter on administrative law can be assigned as outside reading (a general understanding of administrative process being the object); or it can be made the focus of a more intensive in-class study. A four-unit, one-semester course will accommodate all the topics listed in the preceding paragraph. For the more common three-unit course, the content can be adjusted by, for example, pursuing the law of agency in another course.

Special Features

The mastery of basic legal terms, principles, and concepts underlies the ability to recognize law as a process and to explore it at a more sophisticated level. The end-of-chapter review questions provide students with an opportunity systematically to check their comprehension of the textual materials. Several other features of this book also facilitate learning. They include:

1. For student overview, a content outline at the beginning of each chapter.
2. A new case format, with facts, opinion, and judgment clearly labeled. Cases integrated with text material.
3. Key terms italicized in text and defined in understandable language.
4. An extensive glossary and index at the end of the book.
5. An abundance of examples illustrating the application of law, including some extended examples in particularly difficult areas.
6. Principles of law and underlying policies explained in sufficient depth for accurate understanding.
7. Diagrams and line drawings to help students visualize difficult abstract concepts.
8. Chapter summaries to aid review.
9. Review questions and case problems arranged in the order of the textual material, and worded to provide clues for locating material needed to answer the questions or solve the problems.

Supplementary Materials

Additional aids are available in three separate supplements: the Study Guide by James Highsmith, California State University, Fresno; the Test Bank by Joerg Knipprath, Southwestern University, School of Law, and Penelope Mercurio, California State University, Northridge; and the Instructor's

Manual, by the text authors, Penelope Mercurio, and Jeorg Knipprath.

The Study Guide provides general study help, including aid for reading and briefing cases; chapter review objectives and outlines; and independent study questions and case problems, with answers.

The Instructor's Manual features outline grids keying cases, review questions, and case problems to chapter topics; teaching and ethics notes; case briefs and comments; solutions to the case problems; commentary on the in-text Ethics in Practice sections; and transparency masters.

The Test Bank provides over 1750 test items in a chapter-by-chapter format that can be used easily with or without the aid of a computer. For adopters who use computers, the publisher will provide on request a computerized test generation system called EXAMINER, or MICROEXAMINER.

Acknowledgments

In preparing the fourth edition of *Contemporary Business Law,* we were aided by perceptive reviews—reviews which helped us greatly in revising and adding material. We acknowledge with gratitude the work of the following reviewers: Andrew L. Abrams, College of Charleston; William J. Day, Attorney, Cleveland; Howard C. Ellis, Millersville University of Pennsylvania; Frank S. Forbes, University of Nebraska—Omaha; Karla H. Fox, University of Connecticut; Janine S. Hiller, Virginia Polytechnic Institute; E. Clayton Hipp, Jr., Clemson University; Jack M. Hires, Valparaiso University; James M. Jackman, Oklahoma State University; Madeline Johnson, University of Houston; Andrew Laviano, University of Rhode Island; Avi Liveson, Hunter College; Arthur J. Marinelli, Ohio University; Donald O. Mayer, Western Carolina University; Michael J. Navin, Dickinson School of Law; Jan Neuenschwander, Attorney, Leagre and Barnes; Richard W. Perry, Santa Rosa Junior College; Carol D. Rasnic, Virginia Commonwealth University; Jean Margo Reid, New York University; Virgil J. Rhodes, Lincoln Land Community College; Ellen Blumberg Rubert, College of Lake County; R. Wayne Saubert, Radford University; W. Michael Seqanish, Towson State University; W. Richard Sherman, St. Joseph's University; S. Jay Sklar, Temple University; and James B. Zimarowski, University of Notre Dame.

Professor Gordon Severance gratefully acknowledges the contributions of Professor Jan Duffy (California Polytechnic State University, San Luis Obispo) to the chapter on the law of labor and employment, and the assistance of Laurence J. Severance, Ph.D., J.D., in preparing the chapter on the legal aspects of international business.

With sadness, we note the deaths of two esteemed colleagues: Ethel S. Hoeber in 1986, and Donald P. Lyden in 1988. Their contributions to *Contemporary Business Law* were many and valued.

J. DAVID REITZEL
NATHAN J. ROBERTS
GORDON B. SEVERANCE

CONTEMPORARY BUSINESS LAW

Principles and Cases

PART ONE

Law and the Legal System

CHAPTER 1

Nature and Development of Law in the United States

The law touches every aspect of business life. Each day millions of people work in business enterprises throughout the free world to produce goods and services. All of this activity flourishes against a background of law. Police and fire laws provide a security system within which business can operate. Millions of contracts, enforceable by courts of law, are made daily. Landlords contract with tenants. Businesses contract with employees for their services, with suppliers for raw materials, and with wholesalers for distribution of finished products. Billions of dollars of credit loans and cash payments are made each day by means of promissory notes or bank checks, both of which are legal concepts. Business machinery is property that is protected by criminal and civil laws. A complex structure of law regulates every aspect of business. Zoning laws dictate where a business can operate. Labor laws establish rules covering health and safety of workers and union-management relations. Other laws prohibit business from engaging in monopolistic practices or polluting water and air.

How did this law develop? How does it affect a person involved in business? Answers to these questions are what this book is all about. This chapter will: (1) discuss the meaning of law; (2) trace the historic development, philosophy, and functions of law; (3) outline the classifications of law; and (4) review the sources and trends of law in the United States.

Definition and Meaning of Law

Definition of Law

The word "law" has many meanings, and it is used in many disciplines. In physics there is the law of gravity; in economics there is the law of supply and demand. Even in the field of jurisprudence—which is the scientific study of law—scholars have offered dozens of different definitions of law. However, for purposes of this text, the term "law" denotes the results of an evolutionary lawmaking *process* whereby a government develops a system of rules and regulations, enforceable by penalties, to control the conduct of its people. Whenever a sovereign nation, whether democracy or dictatorship, uses the law as an instrument of social control to establish (posit) such rules and regulations, they are collectively referred to as *positive law.* Such law is positive because a government is telling its people to do, or not to do, certain acts.

In a democratic country such as the United States, the lawmaking process produces positive law that includes the development of federal and state constitutions and amendments, the enactment (passing) of laws by Congress and the state legislatures, and the delegation of legislative power to administrative agencies and to subdivisions of state governments such as counties and cities. Lawmaking as a process also includes court interpretations of state and federal laws by a judge who determines the meaning intended by the enactors of the law, and how that law applies to a particular case before the court. Thus "law" at any given moment is a body of rules and regulations that is the product of the lawmaking process. Since business, social, and political relationships are changing daily, a flexible legal system is needed to accommodate the new and unprecedented problems that are constantly arising. Therefore, it is important to view law as a dynamic and evolving system of social control and not as an unchanging body of "dos and don'ts."

Meaning of Business Law

The phrase *business law* does not refer to a single branch of law; rather, it describes those parts of the law most closely connected with typical business activities. Thus, in the public law area, chapters of this book furnish an overview of criminal law, administrative law, governmental regulation of labor relations, and the issuance of securities by corporations. Chapter 48 discusses international law as it affects transnational business. In addition, there is a chapter on the manner in which business is affected by bankruptcy law, and as the occasion warrants, throughout this book there is treatment of constitutional law as it affects business. However, most of the book is devoted to those branches of private law which might be considered the foundations of business: the law of torts, property, contracts, sales, secured transactions, commercial paper, agency, partnerships, and corporations.

Objectives of a Course in Business Law

The main general objective of a course in business law is to help students—business majors and nonmajors alike—to understand the legal aspects of common business activities. This goal can be broken down into six specific objectives.

Understanding and Applying Legal Principles. The first objective of most business law students is to learn the leading principles of business law and how to apply them to business problems. This skill can be developed by applying the legal rules and principles presented in each chapter to the solution of the case problems that appear at the end. The knowledge thus learned should enable the student to recognize situations in which it is not safe to proceed without competent legal help, and to communicate effectively with a lawyer if the need arises.

Understanding the Relationship between Law and Business. Business law students as well as business planners should develop an understanding of the relationship between law and business, which has at least three major aspects:

- How and why law facilitates business activities
- How and why law constrains business activities
- How law and business adjust to each other

Recognizing Business Law as Representative of Law in General. Every person should have some knowledge and appreciation of the law under which she or he lives. For many college students, a business law course is the best source of knowledge about the law as a whole. Although business law is only a sample of law, that sample is a fairly representative one. The history, philosophy, functions, sources, structure, and even the shortcomings of business law are typical of law in general. And business law is representative of other law with regard to how legal disputes are resolved; how values held by legislators, judges, and society affect the development of law; and how law grows to accommodate new needs.

Understanding Law as an Institution in International Relations. Since World War II, American firms have transacted a growing proportion of their business in foreign markets, and the amount of direct foreign investment in the United States has also steadily increased. These transnational business transactions can occur only because of the existence of a complex framework of internationally recognized legal principles that are a mixture of the law of contracts, negotiable instruments, and international trade treaties, as well as the domestic laws of the nations whose business firms are trading with each other. It follows that a solid grasp of American business law is an important foundation for understanding the more complex field of international business law.

Evaluating the Law. In a democratic society, a citizen has a right to comment on the quality of the law and to try to affect its content. To exercise this right responsibly, a citizen should learn how to evaluate the law. A course in business law provides an unusual opportunity to do so. Evaluating the law involves, among other things, identifying the functions and policy of the law; considering the social, economic, and ethical background of the law; perceiving trends in the law; and understanding the reasons for the trends.

Understanding the Roles of Participants in the Legal Process. A course in business law contributes directly and indirectly to an understanding of the roles of participants in the legal process. The major figures in that process include litigants, lawyers, judges, jurors, legislators, the heads and staffs of administrative agencies, personnel in the executive branch of government, and legal scholars. Three of these—lawyers, judges, and legal scholars—have significant developmental roles in the legal process as it pertains to the law presented in this book.

Law, Litigation, and Lawyers

We have previously defined law as the result of a process whereby a government develops rules and regulations that are enforceable by penalties, or *sanctions*. The machinery for imposing and enforcing sanctions is the court system, discussed in Chapter 3. The *need* to enforce a particular law, whether civil or criminal, is brought to the court's attention by the filing of a lawsuit. If someone steals a car, the district attorney files a criminal action. If a neighbor comes into your yard and cuts down your trees, you go to an attorney who files a civil trespass action for money damages. In both cases, litigation is commenced by lawyers. While it is true that in the drama of a lawsuit juries decide the facts and the judge interprets the law, it is the lawyers who are the principal actors. Let's focus briefly on the relation between law, litigation, and lawyers.

Litigation in the United States. The United States has the highest proportion of lawsuits to population of any industrial country in the world. There were more than 10 million lawsuits pending in state and federal courts of the nation in 1988. A recent news headline reads: "Everybody is suing everybody," and indeed they are! Parents sue children and children sue parents. A hospital employee seeks a court injunction against a compulsory AIDS test, claiming it invades his legal right of privacy. Another employee sues the hospital, claiming he is an AIDS victim as result of the hospital's negligence in *not* testing for AIDS. The huge volume of litigation is managed by 700,000 lawyers—more than two-thirds of all attorneys in the world. California alone has more lawyers (over 100,000) than are to be found in all of Great Britain.

Lawyers: Why Do We Need Them? Some critics contend that the plethora of lawyers is primarily responsible for stirring up the ever-increasing volume of litigation. Others say that since the pressures of modern-day living have made people more hostile and belligerent, more attorneys are needed to process legal actions. While there is some truth in these arguments, they ignore several significant reasons that explain the growing number of attorneys and lawsuits:

1 For more than 900 years, the Anglo-American legal system has encouraged the belief—which is widespread today—that court is the proper place to go for the settlement of disputes. Americans are culturally programmed to believe that litigation is an appropriate substitute for physical violence as

the final arbiter of disputes. In contrast, other cultures discourage litigation. For example, the prerevolutionary Chinese, with their background of Confucian, Taoist, and Buddhist traditions, espoused a morality that emphasized family values, respect for ritual and learning, and belief in a cosmic harmony. Going to court would run counter to a philosophy that has inner tranquillity and detachment as a primary goal. Similarly Japan, with one of the lowest litigation rates in the world, has a cultural background based on the belief that it is a bad reflection on one's honor to go to court instead of settling differences directly with an adversary.

2 The tremendous increase in the number of complex laws enacted by state and federal legislatures in recent years requires the skill and training of more lawyers to interpret and explain them. Since 1960, Congress has passed more laws than were passed in the entire previous history of the nation. In addition, each year there are hundreds of regulations adopted by federal administrative agencies, such as the Federal Trade Commission, that have the force of law. There are thousands of new laws enacted by state legislatures annually, and the number of ordinances (laws) adopted by counties and cities is measured in tens of thousands. Most of these new laws affect business, either directly or indirectly. Businesspeople, as well as others, increasingly need lawyers to explain the probable impact of a new law upon their business or their personal lives. For example, thousands of tax lawyers each day advise clients how the Tax Reform Act of 1986 affects their proposed business plans. Businesspeople need lawyers for three critical purposes: as *advocates,* as *advisors,* and as *negotiators.*

Lawyers as advocates. Lawyers are quick to devise new theories interpreting a statute so that it does not adversely affect their business clients. Often the "correct" interpretation (as ultimately determined by a court) can make a difference of thousands—or even millions—of dollars. For example, in *Berkey Photo, Inc. v. Eastman Kodak Co.,*[1] lawyers for Berkey, a photo-finishing company, contended that it was injured by production and marketing policies of Kodak which violated Sections 1 and 2 of the Sherman Act (a federal antimonopoly law). The trial court agreed, and entered judgment against Kodak for $41 million. Lawyers for Kodak appealed. The question was whether the Sherman Act prohibited Kodak's conduct. The court held that it did not, and reversed the judgment of the trial court. Kodak avoided a $41 million liability because it had a competent law firm serving as its *advocate* in court.

Lawyers as advisors. In addition to serving as advocates, lawyers function as *advisors,* another major role that is important to business. As advisors, lawyers counsel businesspeople about their legal rights and duties, and explain the legal consequences of alternative courses of action. When a lawyer or law firm gives such advice, it is often referred to as practicing *preventive law,* that is, guiding clients away from serious legal problems before they reach the point where litigation is necessary. The success of most businesses requires the use of preventive law. Retaining an attorney as advisor on preventive law policy decisions is usually a good bargain. Not only does it avoid costly judgments but it also maintains legal fees at a relatively low level. The same lawyer who charges $100 per hour for office consultation time usually charges $250 per hour for the time involved in trying a lawsuit in court. When litigation attorney fees, court costs, and expert witness fees are added, the total cost of a trial of even the most simple case can easily range between $5,000 and $20,000. In a number of suits brought by large corporations in recent years, attorney fees have exceeded $25 million. Recognizing the importance of preventive law, large companies often employ "in house" attorneys to write opinions on the legal implications of contemplated business decisions as well as to draft contracts and other legal instruments.

Lawyers as negotiators. Lawyers are qualified by training and experience to bargain effectively on behalf of their clients in deals involving sales contracts, leases, real estate, international trade agreements, and other complex transactions. They obviously have the skills necessary to negotiate compromises of pending lawsuits. Seasoned lawyers understand that a reasonable settlement benefits the client by avoiding the costly burden of further litigation as well as the uncertainty of the outcome. The wisdom of this approach is reflected in the old adage: "A bad settlement is better than a good lawsuit." Attorneys know the legal

[1] 603 F.2d 263 (2nd Cir. 1979).

strength and weakness of litigation and they are therefore competent to evaluate the merits of a proposed settlement.

There are two reasons why it is usually desirable to use an attorney to negotiate a settlement of business disputes. First, businesspeople are often emotionally involved in an issue and their tempers may flare to the point where differences are magnified rather than resolved. Attorneys, as "outsiders," tend to look at a controversy with greater objectivity, and their legal skill enables them to discard quickly unreasonable and emotionally charged arguments. Second, if two business opponents discuss a settlement without benefit of counsel, there is always the danger that if the dispute later goes to trial one of them will testify untruthfully as to the substance of the conversation. For example, suppose a seller says to the buyer: "I admit that some of the shoes I shipped to you were defective," but later at the trial of the issue the buyer falsely testifies that the seller also said: "And I know your damage is at least $25,000." If the buyer (who is lying) testifies in a convincing manner, the jury may believe him or her. Attorneys insulate their clients from this danger because (1) they are careful not to make any admissions against the interests of their clients, and (2) they customarily develop a letter or other documentary proof that the proposed meeting between clients is for the sole purpose of carrying out *compromise discussions.* This technique enables them to take advantage of the legal rule that statements made as part of a compromise discussion are not admissible at the time of trial. The rule exists because the policy of the law is to discourage litigation by encouraging settlements out of court. Without the rule, such agreements could not be reached because a party would be reluctant to discuss the issues openly for fear that the other party might later misrepresent the conversation to a court or jury.

Law, Morals, and Ethics

While law, morality, and ethics are interrelated and often parallel, there is an important distinction. Law at any given time consists of a government's rules and regulations that are enforced by penalties. In contrast, many widely accepted moral and ethical standards of conduct are observed voluntarily without enforcement. The law doesn't require Americans to be charitable, yet they give millions of dollars each year to the poor and hungry. Clearly this moral behavior is above and beyond the law. How do we account for it?

Morals. Most moral principles throughout the world find their origin in teachings of philosophers such as Plato, Aristotle, Socrates, Buddha, Moses, Christ, Mohammed, and Ghandi. Often these teachings are contained in sacred writings (ethical codes) such as the Bible or the Koran. In addition, national cultures and modern-day western humanistic movements have expressed moral standards and statements of ethical conduct. Philosophy and religious beliefs, then, contribute heavily to moral standards that are reflected in ethical codes of conduct.

Function of Ethical Codes. The often-heard saying: "You can't legislate morality" is not entirely true. As nations have developed, many moral precepts contained in ethical codes have been reflected in positive law. For example, most religio-ethical codes, as well as laws, condemn murder, rape, robbery, and adultery. Nevertheless, there remains a large body of moral and ethical precepts that, for two reasons, cannot be reflected in positive law. First, in a democracy (e.g., India), diverse groups with different beliefs are unlikely to agree which code of ethics should be adopted as law. Second, as one moves away from universally accepted standards of conduct (e.g., "Thou shall not kill") to precepts that call for highly subjective interpretation (e.g., "Love thy neighbor as thyself"), it becomes practically impossible to legislate those of the latter type because each person in society might interpret them differently. Nevertheless, despite our inability to reduce "Love thy neighbor as thyself" to a law on the statute books, millions of people seriously try to observe this precept because of their commitment to what they regard as a higher law arising from their religious or philosophical convictions.

Sometimes, however, even a vague ethical standard will be interpreted in a very specific way if large numbers of people or nations demand it. For example, the decision of the Allied Powers after World War II to prosecute the Nazis responsible for the Holocaust was grounded not on existing international law but on the view that such heinous mass murder was so shocking to the conscience of all humanity that it violated "higher law." This concept is often referred to as the "Nuremberg Principle."

How ethical principles improve law. Although law is intended to set a *minimum* standard of conduct, there has been a tendency throughout history for people to regard this minimum as the maximum, and to become apathetic about elevating the law to an even higher plane. Thus, at any given time, complacency with existing law has had a chilling effect on the desire for change.

But in every era, there have been counterforces at work. There have always been the trailblazers, motivated by ethical standards that were higher than existing law, who sought to elevate it to a new, higher plateau. Thomas Jefferson invoked this ethic when he said: "I have sworn upon the altar of almighty God, eternal hostility against every form of tyranny over the mind of man." Others followed: Harriet Beecher Stowe (abolition), Susan B. Anthony (women's suffrage), Mahatma Ghandi (an India independent of colonial rule), and Martin Luther King (civil rights). Clearly, laws don't create values, they reflect them. Thus, in a democracy such as the United States, ethical ideas serve the important function of stirring up the popular conscience to support new laws that generally promote a higher level of justice. The leaders who do the stirring are less concerned with "what is" and more concerned with "what ought to be."

How ethical principles influence legislators. The above discussion leads to an important conclusion: In a democracy, the ethical standards of voters and their elected representatives underlie virtually every law that is enacted, whether they realize it or not. For example, even a proposed 25-mph speed limit law presents subtle ethical considerations. Suppose the guiding ethic of Leon Legislator who is about to vote on such a measure is the golden rule ("Do unto others as you would have them do unto you"). Before voting, he will ask himself (at least subconsciously): "If I were driving through that congested area, what speed would I want others to maintain in order to protect my safety?" On the other hand, if the dominant ethic of the legislator is: "Vote for the view favored by your biggest campaign contributor" and a large corporate supporter opposes the speed limit because it will slow down the deliveries of its truck drivers, his vote will be slanted against the speed limit. The decision in both illustrations pivots on an ethical principle.

Business Ethics and the Law. Many business observers in the last decade have stressed a growing need to include individual ethics and corporate (group) social responsibility as an important part of a business education program. The need for ethical principles in business is illustrated by the wave of scandals arising from individual and corporate misconduct that has rocked the commercial world: government officials using their influence to secure lucrative contracts for incompetent manufacturers; profiteering in the millions by bribing stockbrokers to reveal confidential information about contemplated mergers; corrupt dealings with foreign officials to secure business; and false advertising, illegal discharge of toxic chemicals to pollute air and water, massive securities swindles, computer fraud, and other white-collar crime.

Most of the misdeeds that have fueled shocking newspaper headlines involve an individual violating an *ethical concept that is also reflected in existing law.* When this happens, harm to society is done, not because of the absence of a good ethical-legal standard, but because a recalcitrant individual chose not to follow it. The solution of the problem lies in (1) raising that individual's awareness of the law, (2) motivating compliance with the law by ensuring that the sanctions that are imposed for violating it are clear, and (3) creating awareness of the positive benefits (maximum freedom for everyone) that flow from observing the law.

A more troublesome question is: How can we increase businesspeople's awareness of those ethical principles that are *not* reflected in existing criminal or civil law? The search for the answer raises many personal questions: When there are so many conflicting ethical standards to choose from, which should I select and follow? I want to do what is "right" and "fair" but what do those words mean? "Right" and "fair" are fine for standard situations, but how do I apply them to complex moral struggles that elude easy categorization? Unfortunately, there are no objective answers to these questions. Each person has a value system that has been consciously or otherwise adopted from family or peers. Consequently, modifying one's value system to accommodate complex moral problems as they arise may as much involve the use of intuition and conscience as reason. Nevertheless, it is productive to think rationally about some of the different ethical systems and concepts such as those listed in Table 1.1. Chapter 2 discusses in greater depth the interrelation between law and business ethics and suggests an approach to resolving perplexing ethical dilemmas. In addition, at the end of most parts of this book are special sections entitled Ethics in Prac-

Table 1.1 Selected Ethical Systems and Concepts

Ethical System or Concept and Author or Supporters	Summary of Principal Features or Main Ideas
Golden Rule (Bible)	"Do unto others as you would have them do unto you."
Utilitarianism (Jeremy Bentham)	"Good" conduct is that which ensures the greatest good for the greatest number of people. We should maximize the good consequences of contemplated action over the bad consequences. In business, this is often done by cost-benefit analysis.
Communism (Karl Marx)	Evil is the result of "ruling class" exploitation of the working class proletariat. Law is an embodiment of ruling class interests (not morality). In the utopian communist society, the State will fade away, and the guiding ethic will be: "From each according to his ability, to each according to his need."
Self-interest (Adam Smith)	Each person, by seeking his self-interest will be led, as if by an unseen hand, to further the interests of all.
Traditional "Big Business" Ethic (Rockefeller, Carnegie)	"What is good for business is good for the country."
Absolute Ethical Standard (Immanuel Kant)	Follow universal imperatives, e.g., "Never cheat—not even to balance the score against a dishonest person who has cheated you."
Act Responsibly (Christopher Stone)	A responsible person, or corporate manager: (1) observes the moral implications of situations; (2) restrains the impulse to make a snap decision, and reflects upon alternate courses of action, and which is "right"; (3) recognizes accountability for the consequences of the action taken; and (4) acts reasonably in making a decision and is prepared to defend it, if challenged.

tice, which deal with the ethical problems that can arise from the business relationships discussed in that part.

Business Ethics and Consumer Protection. Consumer protection is another area where ethical standards are increasingly being reflected in new laws. Consumer protection law can be defined as those legal rules (legislative and judicial) modifying traditional commercial law so as to confer a more favorable remedy on a person injured by property or services purchased for personal, family, or household use. Consumer protection laws directly affect business by imposing new legal standards and duties upon it. Wherever appropriate throughout this book, the effect of consumer protection laws is pointed out; for example, Chapter 18 is devoted to a discussion of product liability; Chapter 44 discusses consumer protection activities of the Federal Trade Commission; and Chapter 43 reviews the manner in which the Securities and Exchange Commission protects the investing public. Warranties in the sale of real estate, fraud in the law of torts, and consumer fraud as an aspect of white-collar crime are additional examples.

Development of Anglo-American Law

Like most other aspects of society, law has evolved. An examination of how law has developed and how legal philosophy has contributed to that development will be helpful in understanding contemporary law. In general, business law in America has its foundations in the English legal system. It developed gradually in overlapping phases as summarized below.

Development of Law in England

Development of Common Law in England. After the Norman invasion of England in 1066, William the Conqueror and his successors moved rapidly to unite the country under a common rule. Under William, the Curia Regis (King's Court) developed into a system of royal courts throughout England. The legal principles expressed in the more important decisions of the justices of the King's Court were written in books called *reported cases,* which set out the key facts, the issue of law, and the decision as well as the reasons for it. These accumulated decisions, appropriate for all the nation, became known as the *common law* because of its acceptance countrywide—it was common to all the people.

Bringing suit under common law. Under the common law the *plaintiff* (a person with a grievance against another person) brought suit to recover money from the *defendant* (the one against whom the suit was brought). The only remedy that could be obtained by the injured party was a sum of money as recompense (damages). Court proceedings under the common law were very formal. An action could be brought only if there was a *king's writ,* that is, a letter bearing the seal of the king allowing a grievance of that kind to be heard. Such writs were limited to a small number of types of grievances. Actions for which writs existed included (1) money lent by the plaintiff to the defendant but not repaid, (2) money received by the defendant to be delivered to the plaintiff but not paid, (3) money owing for goods sold and delivered by the plaintiff to the defendant, and (4) injury to the plaintiff or his or her property by the defendant (called an *action in trespass*). If the reason for which the plaintiff demanded payment of money from another could not be fitted into the form of some recognized king's writ, no suit could be brought.

Stare decisis. The process of deciding new disputes by referring to earlier precedents in the reported cases is called the *doctrine of stare decisis,* literally "to stand on decided cases." This doctrine has influenced greatly the development of Anglo-American law for a number of reasons: (1) *Stare decisis* is an effective method of ensuring that the legal system is consistent, because issues involving similar circumstances will tend to be decided in the same way. (2) *Stare decisis* promotes efficiency for lawyers and courts by providing ready-made guidelines for deciding new cases, thus avoiding the need to rethink each rule of law every time a particular kind of dispute arises. (3) Because *stare decisis* produces a relatively uniform and consistent body of law, it avoids unnecessary litigation in the courts by enabling lawyers to research the case law and advise a client of the probable outcome of an unmeritorious case. (4) *Stare decisis* provides stability in the legal system by permitting courts to rely on decisions based upon the experience of the ages. However, although courts will usually follow an earlier case decision, they will not hesitate to overrule it when reversal is warranted by changes in commercial usage, society's notions of fairness, or practical necessity.

Development of Equity. The rigidity and inadequacy of the common law writ system led to the development of a supplemental court of *equity,* the origins of which date back to 1270. The limitations of the common law, permitting only recovery of land, personal property, or money, led disgruntled plaintiffs to petition the king for special relief. In response, the king established a Court of Chancery under a special judge called a *chancellor in equity.*

The meaning of equity can best be explained by an example. Suppose John wanted to stop Matthew from continuously grazing his cattle on John's pasture. The only remedy in the common law courts was money damages for trespass. However, money would not solve John's problem, because a money judgment for damages rendered by the court in a given year would not compensate John for damages to his grasslands in later years. To recover such damages, John would have to keep filing lawsuits. What John needed was someone in authority to order Matthew to keep his cattle off John's land. John had to petition the king to secure that relief. The king would then refer the matter to his chancellor, the next most important official, who issued the order in the king's name. In this way, the court of chancery (equity) developed. The chancellor, and later the justices of the chancery court, applied their own "discretion," their "sense of justice," and "conscience" to the facts stated in the petitions which reached them, and issued their decrees accordingly. The modern functioning of equity in the United States is discussed later in this chapter. Commencing in the early 1600s the court of equity became a substantial force in providing relief where the remedy at common law was inadequate. In addition, legislation by Parliament began to modify and supplement the common law.

Adoption of the Law Merchant. During the expansion of international trade in the seventeenth and eighteenth centuries, the "law merchant" was gradually blended into the common law of England. Beginning about 1756, the law merchant was eventually incorporated into the common law. The law merchant consisted of practical rules of trade and commerce developed over the centuries by European traders and enforced in local mercantile courts. These rules were based on the customs of merchants, were international in character, and were devised because no law suitable for trade then existed. The law merchant, as developed in the English common law, contributed substantially to our contemporary law of negotiable instruments, insurance, and sales of goods and, to a lesser extent, to our law of partnership and agency.

Development of Law in the United States

Adoption and Growth of Common Law in the United States. When the English colonists came to North America, they brought with them the system of common law supplemented by the more flexible system of equity. These systems were adopted, first in the colonies and then, after 1789, in each of the states except Louisiana, which derived its law from France. Some states adopted the systems by constitutional provision, others by statute, still others by judicial decision. Most states adopted the common law as it existed in England in 1776, the date of the Declaration of Independence. After the Constitution was adopted in 1789, American court decisions continued to develop the law and commenced to reflect theories of competition and individualism. Throughout the nineteenth century, courts often followed the laissez-faire views of Adam Smith's *Wealth of Nations*, and held that there should be minimal government interference with business and maximum freedom of businesspeople to contract.

The Era of Social Justice. Commencing about 1875 and continuing into the present, there has developed what is often described as an era of social justice. The emphasis has been to encourage the satisfaction of as many human wants as possible. In this era many new social interests have found protection through state and federal legislation and its interpretation by the courts. The focus has been on resolving conflicts between competing interests so that the more substantial and socially desirable interest will prevail. For example, in *Tennessee Valley Authority v. Hill*,[2] the Supreme Court balanced the interests of society in preserving the snail darter (a small fish) under the Endangered Species Act of 1973 against the need for a dam that was partially constructed at a cost of $100 million and held that the darter should be preserved. The court enjoined further construction of the dam on the grounds that the "plain intent of Congress in enacting this statute was to halt and reverse the trend toward species extinction, whatever the cost." In contrast with the earlier period of laissez-faire, the legislatures and courts have no hesitancy in placing limitations on the ability of individuals and businesses to use property or to contract in oppressive ways that might harm a substantial segment of society. There has also been a proliferation of state and federal agencies and commissions regulating virtually every aspect of business, particularly quasi-public corporations such as insurance companies, airlines, railroads, and public utilities.

Development of Equity in the United States. From the outset, the United States recognized the English system of equity. The Constitution (Art.

[2] 437 U.S. 153 (1978).

III, sec. 2) provides that "The Judicial Power shall extend to all Cases, in Law and Equity."

Merger of courts of law and equity. Originally courts of law and courts of equity in the United States were separate. However, although the distinction between the *functions* of law and equity are still maintained, almost all states now try equity cases and law cases in the same courts. Notwithstanding the *procedural* merger of law and equity, the two systems of legal theory retain distinctly separate identities.

Equity principles and maxims. A main historic function of a common law judge is to resolve disputes by applying existing law (e.g., statutes and prior decisions). Where the law is clear and not obviously outmoded or destructive, common law judges apply it as written. A similar approach is used in the interpretation and enforcement of contracts. Because common law judges look to contracts and to existing law for statements of substantive rights, they avoid deciding controversies merely on the basis of their own moral convictions, which might be too lax or too strict.

In contrast, the court of chancery was a "court of conscience" whose decision was not grounded on common law principles, but upon the use of wise discretion in deciding what was morally right, equitable, and just. Over the centuries, equity courts developed guidelines, or *maxims,* to assist the judge. For example, the "clean hands" doctrine is based upon the maxim: "He who comes into equity must do so with clean hands." A complainant in equity will be denied an equitable remedy (such as an injunction) if his or her own conduct is illegal or unethical. The overreaching complainant will have to settle for any remedy available in a suit at law for money damages. Other maxims used by equity courts today are:

- Equity regards as done that which ought to be done.
- Equity will not suffer a wrong to exist without a remedy.
- Equity regards the substance rather than the form.
- He who seeks equity must do equity.

Laches and statutes of limitations. Another maxim, "Equity aids the vigilant," underlies the equitable doctrine of *laches,* that is, unreasonable delay in asserting a legal right. At law and in equity, there is a need to encourage the bringing of lawsuits while evidence and memories are fresh, and to establish a time at which potential defendants and their business associates may conduct their affairs free from disruptive litigation. At common law a person has a fixed time within which to bring suit. The time is fixed by a "statute of limitations," and the time limit applies uniformly to all cases within the relevant class of lawsuit. For tort actions the statute of limitations period is usually 2 years; for contract actions, 4 to 6 years; for actions for the recovery of real estate, 10, 15, or even 21 years. In contrast, the equitable doctrine of laches imposes no fixed time limit. A person must bring a suit in equity within a *reasonable* time, which may vary according to the circumstances of the case. An equity judge may consider many factors in determining what is reasonable, including the complainant's inexcusable delay in asserting a right which causes undue harm to the respondent, or whether the complainant has impliedly waived the right to equitable relief by knowingly acquiescing in existing conditions or in the defendant's actions.

The foregoing phases in the development of law reveal a progression from the simple and primitive to the complex and civilized, but they also reveal that the Anglo-Saxon legal system has been flexible throughout the ages in changing the law in response to changing human and social needs.

Role of Legal Philosophy in the Development of Law

How can a legal system that reaches into all aspects of human affairs be given adequate direction in its development? Legal philosophy is part of the answer. Legal philosophy contributes to the coherence and refinement of law by expressing for lawyers, judges, legislators, legal scholars, and the public some general principles upon which the law has been or should be based. Although there have been many legal philosophies, four major schools of legal thought have been especially influential in the development of Anglo-American law.

Natural Law

In ancient times, thinkers such as Socrates, Plato, Aristotle, and Cicero believed that the physical world as well as humankind have inherent in them perfect and eternal laws which they obey, that these ideal *natural laws* can be discovered by reason, and that human (positive) law should conform to natural law. Cicero, Rome's greatest lawyer, summarized it this way:

> True law is right reason consonant with nature, worldwide in scope, unchanging and everlasting. The law does not differ for Rome or Athens, for the present and the future, but one eternal and unchanging law will be valid for all nature and for all times.

Some of the leaders of the American Revolution followed a school of thought known as Deism. The Deists adopted the theory of natural law and applied it to the struggle with England. They held that if the king was a tyrant, the people had the right to revert to the laws of nature, reassert their freedom through a natural "right of revolution," and establish a new order of laws consistent with natural rights. "Natural law" philosophy influenced Thomas Jefferson in writing the Declaration of Independence in such phrases as: "We hold these truths to be self-evident, that all men are created equal, and that they are endowed by their Creator with certain inalienable Rights."

Divine Law

Judeo-Christian tradition, reflected in the Mosaic Code and the canon law of the early Holy Roman Empire, held that all law is of divine origin. It follows that the early religious leaders of the church were regarded both as lawgivers and as interpreters of divine law. Most of the judges appointed to William the Conqueror's King's Court were bishops from the church, chiefly because of their scholarly learning. Hebrew and early Christian leaders developed rules of law that covered virtually all aspects of spiritual and temporal life, and many of these doctrines influenced the development of English law. In medieval times, the Church exerted a powerful influence over the secular kings in order to ensure that the laws of a country were consistent with theological doctrine. The king was viewed as holding office by divine right. Thus, the Stuart kings of England, in their unsuccessful struggle against the growing secular power of Parliament, vigorously asserted that since they were endowed with a divine right to rule, the king's decrees were superior to the laws of men enacted by a legislative body.

The influence of divine law philosophy has diminished significantly since medieval times. Yet even today the philosophy is invoked by diverse religious groups on a variety of controversial legal issues. However, the Constitutional principle of separation of church and state is firmly embedded in the American legal system.

Sociological Jurisprudence

The natural law and divine law philosophies contrast with the modern sociological school, which has provided a philosophical basis for the social control legislation that commenced after the Civil War and continues into the present. The sociological school uses the methodology of the social sciences to analyze the law. They hold that the immediate purpose of the law is to protect individual interests, but that the paramount purpose of law is to balance three kinds of competing interests for the ultimate good of society: the general public interest, particular group interests, and individual interests. The adequacy of the legal system is judged by how well it serves society in balancing these competing interests.

Legal Realism

The school of legal realism, an offshoot of the sociological school, was pioneered by Oliver Wendell Holmes (1841–1935). Like the sociological school, the realists utilize the social sciences to analyze the manner in which law functions, with emphasis upon discerning the policy underlying the law. However, believing that judges often obscure the true grounds for decision, the realists prefer to look at what officials actually do, rather than at what they say. Thus, the focus is on the true manner in which legal problems are resolved. For example, the law may fix the maximum speed limit at 55 mph, but if the highway patrol only issues citations to persons going over 65 and prosecutors only prosecute cases above that speed, the legal realists would say that the speed limit is 65 mph. Thus, what the law enforcers do is as much an indicator of law content as what the statutes actually say.

None of the foregoing legal philosophies has been totally abandoned. Just as contemporary law contains elements of ancient law, so contemporary legal philosophy contains echoes of the past. Just as the natural law philosophers searched for eternal principles underlying the law, the search for values continues, but today it concentrates primarily on furthering the interests of society. Contemporary legal and social issues will also continue to be fruitfully analyzed by applying competing philosophical theories of law and then weighing the alternative solutions that are dictated by those theories.

Nature of Contemporary Law in the United States

An understanding of the nature of our contemporary Anglo-American law requires examination of the functions and classifications of that law.

Modern Functions of Law

Most of the functions of law today are implied by the Preamble to the Constitution of the United States, which was adopted "to form a more perfect Union, establish Justice, insure domestic Tranquility... promote the general Welfare, and secure the Blessings of Liberty." For nearly two centuries, federal and state legislatures and the courts have reflected their perception of the popular will by translating these broad objectives into notions of due process of law, individual freedoms, and appropriate limits on those freedoms. What are the actual functions of law that have emerged, and how should an ideal legal system function? Four major functions of law will be discussed.

Preserving Domestic Tranquillity. Every day, conflicts develop over ownership of property, repayment of debts, or who is "to blame" in an auto accident. Internal peace depends upon a system of law that settles disputes fairly, so that self-help and violence are not necessary. Keeping domestic peace also requires maintenance of order. The legal system must protect its citizens from criminal conduct that threatens their property—or life itself. The civil law of torts together with criminal law seek to preserve peace and order by imposing penalties on those who would threaten to disrupt it. These penalties, called legal *sanctions,* are critical to the successful functioning of the law, because without them the law probably would not be obeyed. Sanctions commonly used by civil courts are: sheriff's levy of execution, which involves the seizure and sale of a debtor's real or personal property, and injunctions (ordering a defendant not to do a certain act) issued by courts of equity, which are enforceable by jail sentence. In addition, criminal court sanctions include punishment by fine or imprisonment and, in some states, the death penalty.

Expanding Individual Freedom. References in the Constitution to "the Blessings of Liberty," as well as the personal privileges contained in the Bill of Rights, reflect Constitutional concern for individual freedom. From the Magna Carta in 1215 to the decisions of the Supreme Court, the Anglo-American system of law has witnessed a steady expansion of individual freedom. The functioning of the law to increase personal freedom often conflicts with other functions and objectives of the law. For example, a local ordinance that requires school children to salute the flag conflicts with their freedom of religion when they belong to a religious sect that opposes such activity. The Supreme Court of the United States ultimately resolves such conflicts by balancing the individual freedom against the competing need of society to regulate for the general welfare.

Providing for Change. Revolutionary upheavals in the world today demonstrate that governments frequently collapse because their laws are too rigid to meet the changing needs of the people. Perhaps the most remarkable characteristic and function of the Anglo-American system of law is that it provides for gradual, orderly change as the social need arises. The provision in the Constitution for amendment, and the power of the courts to modify old common law precedents to fit new and changing circumstances are illustrative of the flexibility in the legal system. Another advantage of gradual change, as contrasted with abrupt revolution, is that the legal system provides stable legal rules. Such stability permits lawyers to advise clients such as business managers about the legal consequences of alternative business decisions.

Promoting the General Welfare. A major objective of contemporary law is to encourage the satisfaction of as many human wants as possible and to assure fair play between groups as well as between individuals. In the twentieth century, a principal function of law has been to promote the general welfare of the American people by focusing on greater economic, political, and racial equality for its citizens. The legal system has provided greater social justice through state and federal legislation, aided by liberal court interpretations. Income taxes have reduced inequalities in earnings, a social security system has provided retirement pensions, labor laws have reduced exploitation of workers, unemployment compensation laws have eased the plight of the jobless, and workers' compensation laws have provided health care for those injured in industrial accidents. The legal system has further functioned to promote the general welfare through legislation establishing health, safety, and pollution control laws. Many of these laws affect business directly, such as court enforcement of contracts and laws protecting consumers from exploitation and fraud.

Limitations on the Legal System

The successes of the Anglo-American legal system should not obscure the fact that there are limits to what the law can accomplish. For example, many states have determined that courts are not the best places to decide child custody issues and have opted instead for specialized tribunals to resolve such matters. Legal scholars have also criticized the practice of allowing traditional juries to determine the damage awards in large antitrust cases. Instead, a panel of experts schooled in economics has been proposed. An ancient rule: "*De minimus non curat lex,*" which means "the law doesn't care for trifles" is cited by courts today in dismissing suits that are so trivial it would waste the court's time to consider them. Likewise, courts will dismiss a dispute that is moot, for example, a case that presents no actual controversy or in which the issues have ceased to exist.

Ideal Characteristics of a Legal System

The Roman lawyer Cicero wrote: "It is our duty to aspire above our human nature." The evolution of Anglo-American law is a reflection of the aspirations of idealistic lawyers from Lord Coke to Chief Justice John Marshall, each striving in his own way toward the goal inscribed over the entrance to the United States Supreme Court: "Equal Justice Under Law." Perhaps ideal justice will never be attained, but it is important that the people of each generation continue the endless effort to improve the system. The evolution and functioning of law discussed above suggest at least some answers to the basic question: What are desirable characteristics of the law? There is reasonably widespread agreement that the following are desirable attributes of an ideal legal system:

1 The cornerstone of the system must be the consent of the governed. In a democracy, this means that the people must be informed and must communicate their views to their elected representatives, who then reflect their will in the laws that are enacted.
2 The system must strive for a fair balance between socially necessary laws and the individual's desire for freedom from excessive, burdensome, or oppressive controls.
3 The law must be administered evenly and equally to all persons in similar circumstances, without special favor or privilege to anyone. This ideal is reflected in the Constitution's guarantee of "equal protection of the law." In short, the system must be a "government of laws, not of men."
4 The laws should be clear enough so that people can understand them and should avoid vagueness, inconsistency, or incoherence. Laws should be fair and reasonable so that most people will observe and respect them voluntarily. Disrespect for some laws leads to disrespect of all laws. Hence, laws generally should not violate fundamental social customs, religious beliefs, or moral codes. The futility of laws that contradict social custom is demonstrated by the inability of the federal government to enforce the Eighteenth Amendment to the Constitution, which prohibited sale of alcoholic beverages.
5 Law, especially criminal law, should be within the people's capacity for obedience.
6 The law must be capable of flexibility to meet changing social needs.
7 The law should be enforced in a speedy and efficient manner, recognizing that "Justice delayed is justice denied."
8 Retroactive laws should be kept at a minimum. To limit despotism, the Constitu-

tion prohibits enactment of ex post facto laws, that is, laws imposing criminal sanctions upon persons for acts which, when committed, were not criminal. On the other hand, much nonpenal legislation confers remedial benefits on the population, and therefore retroactive application is not legally objectionable. Some judicial decisions create new law, and when they do, the retroactive effect can hardly be avoided.

Classification of Law

A perspective of the vast scope of law is to be gained by examining the broad categories into which law has been classified. The most common and convenient classification is: (1) substantive and procedural law; (2) public and private law; and (3) criminal and civil law.

Substantive and Procedural Law. *Substantive law* is concerned with the recognition of rights, duties, privileges, and immunities. The law of contracts, property, torts, and business relations are examples. *Procedural law,* on the other hand, specifies any formal steps to be followed in enforcing or asserting rights, duties, privileges, and immunities. Procedural law is discussed in Chapter 3.

Public and Private Law. *Public law* deals with the organization of government and with its relation to the people. It includes constitutional law, administrative law, and criminal law. *Constitutional law* prescribes generally the plan and method by which government conducts public affairs. In the American legal system, the important aspects of constitutional law include the allocation of powers between the federal and state governments; the distribution of powers among the executive, judicial, and legislative branches of government (both state and federal); and the rights guaranteed to the people. *Administrative law,* discussed fully in Chapter 44, is concerned with the regulatory activities of countless federal and state administrative agencies such as the National Labor Relations Board or a state public utilities commission. *Criminal law* consists of statutes that prohibit certain conduct under penalty of fine or imprisonment or both. Criminal law is discussed in Chapter 7.

Private law deals with the relationships among private persons and organizations. Of the many branches of private law, four are fundamental in the study of business law.

1 The *law of contracts* is concerned with the rights and duties arising out of such promises as the law will enforce or otherwise recognize. Related to the law of contracts is the law of *persons,* which deals with the extent to which various classes of persons (e.g., minors, mental incompetents) are subject to the rights and duties normally recognized in the law.
2 The *law of property* deals with the ownership, possession, use, and disposition of things. The law of sales, of secured transactions, and of commercial paper (negotiable instruments) is a blend of contract law and property law.
3 The *law of torts* obligates a person who has committed a private wrong other than a breach of contract to make compensation for the wrong.
4 The *law of business relations* includes the law of agency, of partnerships, and of corporations and deals with the relations between agent and principal, two or more partners, and persons participating in the operation of a corporation.

Criminal and Civil Law. The criminal law defines offenses against the state and prescribes punishment for their commission. Most crimes are defined by legislation, although some statutes merely refer to a crime by its common law name and thereby leave to the courts the task of applying the common (case law) definition of the offense. In the United States, the *civil law* is that law relating to private rights and remedies sought by plaintiffs in civil actions as contrasted with criminal proceedings. The usual remedy in a civil suit is a judgment for damages, often for breach of contract or commission of a tort.

Sources and Rank of Law in the United States

In the United States, the law must accommodate the diverse and often-opposing needs and desires of a huge population. The complex legal structure required for such a task can be understood by recalling certain basic facts about our system of government.

First, the Constitution of the United States recognizes two levels of government—federal and state. Consequently, we have 52 major governmental entities capable of making law. Through a process of delegation, thousands of smaller governmental entities and subdivisions (United States possessions and territories, cities, counties, towns, etc.) have the power to make law. Second, within each major governmental entity, law comes from judicial, legislative, and administrative sources.

Constitutional Sources of Law

The Constitution of the United States allocates governmental power in two principal ways: (1) between the federal and the state governments and (2) among the three branches of the federal government.

Federal-State Allocation of Powers. As between the federal and the state governments, the federal government has the powers enumerated (expressed) in the Constitution. Article I, section 8, gives Congress the power to legislate in several areas which affect business. Among the most important are the power to levy and collect taxes, to regulate interstate commerce, to provide for the general welfare, to enact a bankruptcy law, and to establish a patent and copyright system.

In addition, under the Constitution the federal government also has powers (called implied powers) which are not specifically named in the Constitution but which are necessary and proper for carrying out the enumerated powers. The federal government has, for example, the implied power to incorporate a national bank as a means of carrying out its express powers to impose and collect taxes, to borrow money, to regulate commerce, and to raise and support armies.[3]

On the other hand, "The powers not delegated to the United States by the Constitution, nor prohibited by it to the States, are reserved to the States respectively, or to the people."[4] The powers of a state include its "police power," that is, the power of the state, through its legislature, to limit the personal freedom and property rights of persons for the protection of the public safety, health, and morals and for the promotion of the public convenience and general prosperity. Although the police power of a state is quite broad, it is subject to constitutional limitations such as the due process clause of the Fourteenth Amendment which requires that there be a logical connection between a police regulation and the general welfare. State laws against crime, residential zoning ordinances, and the regulation of the manufacture and sale of intoxicating liquors are examples of the exercise by a state of its police power.

There is no police power expressly conferred on the federal government. However, the federal government is empowered to regulate interstate commerce, and in the exercise of its commerce and other powers, Congress indirectly exercises control over many of the social and economic problems that the states may attack directly under their police power. The federal antitrust laws, the Civil Rights Act of 1964 prohibiting racial discrimination in interstate commerce, and a variety of federal statutes pertaining to industrial safety are examples of congressional use of the commerce power to control problems which the states often attack directly under their police power.

Powers of the federal government frequently overlap the powers of state governments. Consequently, conflicts between state and federal law arise. How such conflicts are resolved is discussed in Chapter 3.

Although the federal and the state governments have broad regulatory powers, the federal Constitution prohibits the federal government, the state governments, or both, from engaging in certain activities. The first ten Amendments to the Constitution (called the Bill of Rights) protect individuals from governmental oppression. For example, the First Amendment guarantees individual freedom of religion. Other constitutional prohibitions help mark the boundaries between federal and state authority. For example, states may not coin money or enter into treaties with foreign countries. Such

[3]*McCulloch v. Maryland*, 4 Wheat. 316, 4 L. Ed. 579 (U.S. Sup. Ct. 1819).

[4]U.S. Constitution, amend. X.

activities are exclusively federal responsibilities. The federal government also has a broad power to regulate interstate commerce; but the federal government may not tax articles exported from any state or give preference to the ports of one state over the ports of another.

Distribution of Powers within the Federal Government. The federal Constitution distributes federal powers among three branches of government—the legislative, the judicial, and the executive. Each branch of the federal government thus has an area of primary responsibility. Congress has the power to make laws authorized by the Constitution. The federal judiciary has the power to decide cases and controversies. The President of the United States has executive powers and duties. The President is the Commander in Chief of the armed forces, has the power to make treaties (subject to the concurrence of the Senate), and is required to "take Care that the Laws be faithfully executed."

The distribution of powers among the three branches of government is known as the "separation of powers," and it serves two main purposes:

1 It enables each branch of government to exercise its constitutional prerogatives without undue interference by the other branches.
2 It prevents the excessive accumulation and unchecked use of power by a would-be dictator.

However, the separation of powers is not absolute. For efficiency of governmental operation, considerable overlapping of functions is necessary. The judicial power is vested in one Supreme Court and in such inferior courts as the Congress may from time to time establish. Yet, officers who hold hearings for administrative agencies decide controversies, and in so doing they carry out a "quasi-judicial" function. The power to make law is vested in Congress, but the courts frequently decide cases by applying common law principles to topics for which there is no statutory law. To the extent that such decisions are legal precedents, the courts which make them can be said to make law. In reality the federal government is one of separation and overlap of powers. Most state constitutions follow the model of the federal Constitution with regard to separation and overlap of powers.

As a further protection against the excessive accumulation of power, the powers of a branch of government are limited by powers possessed by one or both of the other branches. For instance, the Supreme Court has interpreted the Constitution as giving the judicial branch of the federal government the power to declare legislation and executive exercises of power unconstitutional. Subject to the approval of the Senate, the President fills vacancies in the Supreme Court, and the President may veto legislation. Congress may enact laws affecting the structure of the federal court system and the activities of the President; and by a process of impeachment (accusation), trial, and conviction, Congress may remove the President, the Vice President, and other civil officers of the United States (including members of the judiciary) from office for committing high crimes and misdemeanors. Similar checks and balances are found in the state governments, most of which pattern their constitutions after the federal Constitution.

Legislative Sources of Law

The word "legislation" is ordinarily used to refer to statutes passed by Congress and by state legislatures. But the legislative power of the United States and the various states may be exercised in more than one way. The phrase "enacted law" is usually used to designate the exercise of the legislative power in its broadest sense. Enacted law can be said to include the following classes of law:

1 Federal and state constitutions
2 Federal and state statutes (acts)
3 Federal treaties
4 Executive orders and proclamations issued by the President of the United States or by state governors when authorized by statute
5 Administrative rules and regulations when authorized by statute, which have the force and effect of law
6 Ordinances of the subdivisions of the states, such as cities and towns

Judicial Decisions as a Source of Law

Judicial decisions are a twofold source of law: (1) Courts, through their decisions, interpret and test the validity and application of enacted laws in the light of constitutional provisions and the intent of the Congress, legislature, local government, or agency that formulated them; and (2) in areas not covered by legislation, courts apply the common law and expand it with decisions that apply to new situations. Thus, courts play a major role in determining how laws may be applied, what restraints laws place upon individuals and businesses, and what privileges individuals and businesses can expect to enjoy under the law. To this extent, it is frequently said that, through their decisions that appear in the reported cases, courts *make* laws. Examples of how courts make law appear in the case decisions throughout subsequent chapters in this book.

Judicial Interpretation and Construction of Statutes. *Interpretation* of a statute is the process of discovering and explaining the meaning of any unclear language. *Construction* of a statute is the process of discovering and explaining the legal effect which the statute is to have. Construing a statute may involve interpreting unclear language, but it mainly involves such tasks as determining the purpose or policy of the statute, deciding how the provisions of a complex statute are related, and deciding to what specific people or things the statute applies. "Interpretation" and "construction" are often used interchangeably.

Determination of constitutionality. Sometimes a statute is alleged to be not only unclear but also unconstitutional. The courts have developed two main "tests" for determining the constitutionality of a statute: the "any-rational-purpose" test and the "compelling-interest" test.

Under the *any-rational-purpose test,* a statute is constitutional if it has some rational purpose, even though the purpose found by the court is not the purpose which may have been expressed by the legislature. The use of this test of constitutionality minimizes judicial interference with legislative activities by imposing a light burden of justification on the legislature, and this is the test usually applied.

The *compelling-interest test* is applied where legislation threatens individual rights, such as the right to vote or to exercise freedom of speech. Under the compelling-interest test, such legislation will be held unconstitutional unless there is a governmental interest sufficiently compelling to warrant curbing the right in question. Compared to the any-rational- purpose test, the compelling-interest test imposes a heavier burden of justification on the legislature and is therefore less compatible with the separation-of-powers doctrine. For this reason, the courts tend to limit application of the compelling-interest test to infringement of fundamental rights guaranteed by the Constitution.

Role of *Stare Decisis* in Judicial Decisions. In the United States, the rule of *stare decisis* applies in the following way: If a decision was rendered by a higher court of the state in which a case is being tried (or by the Supreme Court of the United States), and that decision can be applied to the case presently before the lower court, then the higher court's decision is binding upon the lower court and must be followed. However, if the decision emanated from the highest court of another state, it is taken into consideration by the judge but need not be followed. Thus, courts in different states sometimes express different views as to the principles of law involved and, on occasion, as to their applications. The result is that there is a "majority rule" that reflects the view of a majority of the states and, correspondingly, a minority rule.

There is a twofold difficulty in applying the doctrine of *stare decisis.* First, attorneys for the plaintiff or defendant can usually find *conflicting precedents* to support the position of their respective clients. For example, suppose Art is rowing a boat on his vacation in Utah and negligently injures Beth in the head by hitting her with his oar while she is swimming. Beth sues and obtains a judgment for personal injuries for $100,000. Art doesn't have any money or assets, but he does have an automobile insurance policy which says that the insurance company will pay up to $100,000 to any victim of Art's negligence "occurring while Art is operating a *vehicle.*" Beth sues the insurance carrier, claiming that it should pay her $100,000 under Art's policy because she was injured by Art's negligence *while he was operating a vehicle.* There are no case precedents in Utah on the meaning of the word "vehicle," but the insurance carrier's attorney finds several cases in other states where courts held that the word "vehicle" does *not* include a boat. Beth's attorney finds a case where the courts held the word "vehicle" in an automobile insurance policy includes a boat and that a boat is a "vehicle." The case precedents are clearly in conflict.

At this point, the second difficulty in applying *stare decisis* arises. *Courts are not bound to follow a pre-*

cedent case in which the key facts are distinguishable from those in the case under consideration. Since no two fact situations are identical, each attorney will try to persuade the court not to follow the precedent that is against his client's interest by distinguishing the facts in the precedent case from those before the court. Thus, the insurance company lawyer will argue to the court: "The case precedent Beth is relying on should not be followed because the *facts are different*—Beth's precedent involved a *motor* boat which is obviously more closely related to a motor vehicle than to a rowboat. Therefore, because the facts of the motor boat case are different from the facts before the court, the court should not follow the motor boat case precedent cited by Beth's attorney." Beth's lawyer will make a similar effort to convince the court that the facts in the precedent cases cited by opposing counsel are distinguishable, and therefore the court should not consider them as applicable to the case before it. In deciding the case, the judge will determine (1) which cases argued by counsel have substantially identical key facts as the case before the court and are therefore sound precedents, and (2) if the out-of-state case precedents are conflicting, which case precedent involves a desirable rule of law for Utah to adopt and follow. In this example, the judge is called upon to decide a "case of first impression" in Utah, that is, a case which raises a question of law that has not previously been ruled upon in that state. Conflicts between case precedents as well as differences in the underlying facts are a major reason for the uncertainty of the outcome of any lawsuit. Lawyers almost always have reasonable differences of opinion as to how conflicting precedents apply to the facts in their clients' case, and it is not predictable which precedent the court will choose in deciding the applicable rule of law.

In deciding a particular case, appellate courts generally follow their earlier case precedents. However, they will not hesitate to reverse a long-standing decision if warranted by changed economic and social circumstances. When the rule of law of an earlier case is reversed by a later decision, a new case precedent has been established which is then followed by the lower courts in resolving subsequent suits involving the same principle of law.

Modern Role of Equity in Judicial Decisions.

The primary focus of modern equity courts is on "balancing the equities" between the parties, relying upon equitable maxims and the court's sense of justice. An equity court wields broader powers than a court of law. The judge in an equity "court of conscience" is less restricted by case precedents than a court of law. In addition, the equity judge has wide discretion and only if it is clearly abused will a decision be reversed on appeal. Unlike the *judgment* of a court of law which is usually for money damages, the equity judge's decision, called a decree, may reserve for many years jurisdiction to resolve future issues that may arise between the parties. For example, an equity divorce decree may by its terms retain jurisdiction over the parties to later modify (up or down) the amount of monthly alimony initially ordered by the court. In recent years equity courts have significantly expanded their role as an instrument of social reform. For example, in an appeal from an equity court's decree in *Brown v. Board of Education,*[5] the U.S. Supreme Court held that separate educational facilities for blacks and whites are inherently unequal. The trial court retained jurisdiction to administer a far-reaching school bussing program. Because of the growing importance of equity courts in our judicial system, it is essential that businesspeople understand the basic differences between law and equity.

Differences between actions at law and actions in equity. The major differences between suits at law and in equity are set out in Table 1.2. The three most important distinctions are:

1 In an action at law the plaintiff generally is seeking only a money judgment for damages, whereas in an action in equity the relief sought is some equitable remedy plus money. Such remedy in equity that the plaintiff is seeking may be a *decree* declaring a status (such as a decree declaring the rights and duties of the parties to a business contract or one adjudging a person bankrupt) or an order prohibiting the defendant from engaging in an act (an *injunction*) or commanding the defendant to perform an act (mandatory *injunction*). Today, in order to persuade a judge in a court of law to "turn his hat around" and hear a case as an equity matter, a plaintiff must show: (*a*) that *great and irreparable damage* will result

[5] 347 U.S. 483 (1954).

Table 1.2 Major Differences between a Suit at Law and a Suit in Equity

	Action at Law	Action in Equity
Nature of relief sought by plaintiff	A money judgment for damages to compensate plaintiff for the loss sustained	A decree of an equity judge: (*a*) ordering defendant to do or not do an act (injunction), or (*b*) declaring a status (e.g., decree of divorce, bankruptcy, or quieting title to real estate)
Time within which suit must be filed	Plaintiff must file suit within the time period fixed by the state statute of limitations	Plaintiff must file within a reasonable time after the event which gave rise to the cause of action (doctrine of laches)
Jurisdiction of the court	Plaintiff must show injury from defendant's conduct arising out of facts containing all of the elements of a legal cause of action (e.g., negligence, fraud, trespass, etc.)	Plaintiff must show: (*a*) the law remedy is inadequate for any one of the following reasons: (1) There is a continuing wrong by defendant; (2) the law remedy would require a multiplicity of law suits; (3) if plaintiff obtained judgment in a suit at law, it could not be collected because of the insolvency of the defendant; (4) difficulty of measuring damages in money terms; *and* (*b*) Great and irreparable injury to property will result if equitable relief is not granted (e.g., a tenant wrongfully cutting down the landlord's forest)
Method of finding facts at trial	Plaintiff (or defendant) has the right to request a trial by jury; if no request, trial is by the judge.	The equity judge finds the facts as well as rules upon issues of law. (Some states permit an *advisory* jury to recommend findings of fact to the equity judge.)
Method of enforcing judgment or decree	Levy of execution; the sheriff seizes money of defendant or sells defendant's property to satisfy the judgment.	Contempt of court proceedings may be initiated by plaintiff against a defendant who disobeys an equity decree, and defendant can be fined or sentenced to a jail term, or both.

to a property interest if equitable relief is not granted and (*b*) that the *remedy in an action at law is inadequate.* The law remedy (a money judgment) might be inadequate because of insolvency of the defendant, which would make it impossible for the plaintiff to collect the judgment, or because of a continuing wrong. For example, if a defendant commits trespass by wrongfully using a landowner's private road each day, a money judgment for damages up to the date of the trial would not compensate the plaintiff for damages arising from such wrongful use in the future.

2 Law and equity differ with respect to the method of determining facts at the time of trial. The Constitution guarantees a jury

trial in most actions at law, whereas in equity there is no jury trial; the equity judge decides the facts.

3 Finally, law and equity differ also in the method of enforcing a judgment. To enforce a judgment at law, the person to whom a judgment was awarded must undertake a second legal process, called "execution." Execution of a judgment at law is the process of procuring a writ of execution from the clerk of the court and having the sheriff seize the defendant's property and sell it to satisfy the judgment. In contrast, decrees in equity are enforceable directly against the respondent (defendant) by means of a contempt-of-court proceeding. A respondent who refuses to obey a decree in equity can be sent to jail or fined until he or she obeys the decree or shows a willingness to obey.

Equitable remedies. The most familiar equitable remedies are the injunction, specific performance of a contract, rescission of a contract, an accounting for profits, and the imposition of a constructive trust. Specific performance, rescission, and other remedies applicable to contracts are discussed in subsequent chapters of this book. Two equitable remedies—injunction and specific performance—need special mention here.

An *injunction* is a judicial order to perform an act or, more commonly, an order to refrain from performing an act which threatens irreparable harm. Temporary and permanent injunctions may be issued in many situations: for example, in labor disputes; in situations involving a nuisance (a use of property in such a way as to harass, annoy, or harm neighbors); and in situations involving violations of civil rights.

Specific performance will be ordered where (money) damages are inadequate to compensate the nondefaulting party to a contract for the failure of the defaulting party to perform or to deliver the specific thing promised. Damages are inadequate, for example, where the thing to be delivered is unique. A work of art is considered unique, and its purchaser will usually be granted specific performance where the seller can deliver it but refuses to do so. However, a court will not order the specific performance of a contract for personal services even though those services are unique, as this would in effect impose involuntary servitude. Courts of equity also will not make orders whose enforcement is impractical; for example, many large-scale construction contracts would be impractical to enforce specifically.

Administrative Sources of Law in the United States

Day-to-day operations of government rest largely in the hands of administrative agencies such as the Internal Revenue Service, the Federal Trade Commission, and the National Labor Relations Board. The regulations of an administrative agency, when published in a government publication called the *Federal Register,* have the force and effect of law. Chapter 44 discusses administrative law emphasizing the authority of administrative agencies to regulate the conduct, scope, and size of business organizations.

Rank of Laws in the United States

Rank of Enacted Laws in Order of Authority. Our legal system would be unworkable if law were not ranked in some order of authority. Article 6 of the federal Constitution provides a framework for ranking enacted law. According to Article 6:

> This Constitution, and the Laws of the United States which shall be made in Pursuance thereof; and all Treaties made, or which shall be made, under the Authority of the United States, shall be the supreme Law of the Land; and the Judges in every State shall be bound thereby, any Thing in the Constitution or Laws of any State to the contrary notwithstanding.

By virtue of this Article, the federal Constitution heads all enacted laws in authority. Next below it are the statutes and treaties of the United States. United States statutes and treaties are of equal rank. When federal and state enacted law covers the same subject matter, the federal law prevails. When only state law is involved, the state constitution ranks highest, followed by state statutes. Below the statutes come the ordinances of the state's subdivisions. However, those constitutional federal statutes which carry out some federal power will take precedence over conflicting state statutes.

Even where a federal statute regulates a federal matter, much nonconflicting state law can coexist. For example, the federal Bankruptcy Code expressly looks to state law for the regulation of certain aspects of bankruptcy. Where federal statutes are silent as to the role of state law, nonconflicting state regulation is valid *except* in three situations: (1) where national uniformity of federal regulation is required, (2) where the federal government has "preempted" (taken exclusive control of) the field, and (3) where the state statute does not usurp federal authority but otherwise violates the Constitution.

Rank of Common Law in Relation to Enacted Law. In terms of substantive coverage, the common law ranks below all classes of enacted law. A rule of common law will be applied only where there is no valid enacted law. However, the fact that the common law ranks below enacted law should not lead us to minimize the role of the courts. They have the exclusive responsibility for determining the common law, and they have the ultimate responsibility for determining the constitutionality and the meaning of enacted law. Moreover, when courts interpret constitutions and statutes, their interpretations affect the content of the enacted law.

Rank of Administrative Rules. In addition to the great number of federal and state statutes there are the rules and regulations of federal, state, and local administrative agencies. These rules and regulations have the force and effect of law, and they rank ahead of common law decisions in approximately the way that federal and state statutes do.

Trends in the Law of the United States

Trend toward Greater Uniformity in State Law

Two approaches toward greater uniformity in state law are in progress in the United States, and each is achieving a considerable measure of success. One approach is that of encouraging state legislatures to pass uniform legislation. The other approach is that of encouraging courts to apply uniformly stated principles of the common (decisional) law.

Trend toward Uniform State Laws. The movement to encourage uniform legislation began in 1892 with the founding of the National Conference of Commissioners on Uniform State Laws. The national conference is a body of commissioners appointed by the governors of their respective states. Committees prepare tentative drafts of acts, sometimes employing legal experts for the purpose. Through a process of criticism and revision, each uniform act reflects the experience and judgment of lawyers from every part of the United States. When it is finally approved by the national conference, a proposed act is submitted to the American Bar Association for approval, and eventually the act is recommended for adoption by the state legislatures. Over the years, many uniform acts have been developed and adopted (e.g., the Uniform Partnership Act and the Uniform Consumer Credit Code). Those dealing with commercial subjects such as commercial paper and sale of goods were eventually incorporated into the Uniform Commercial Code.

In adopting uniform laws or codes, all states make changes in order to conform to local needs. To the extent of the changes, the uniform laws, including the Uniform Commercial Code, are different, but they are substantially uniform.

On certain subjects where uniformity does not seem practical, the national conference prepares "model acts" to guide state legislatures in the drafting of their own acts. Illustrative of model acts are the Model Business Corporation Act and the Model State Administrative Procedure Act.

Trend toward Uniform Statements of the Common Law. The movement to encourage courts to apply uniformly stated principles of common (decisional) law was initiated by the American Law Institute in 1923.

The object of the institute is "to promote the clarification and simplification of the law and its better adaptation to social needs, to secure the better administration of justice, and to carry on scholarly and scientific legal work." One method by which the institute seeks to attain its object is by preparing and printing a "restatement" of the common law covering each major branch of the law. For example, there is a Restatement of the Law of Contracts, a Restatement of the Law of Agency, and a Restatement of the Law of Torts. The American Law Institute is continually working on the updating of published restatements of the common law.

There is a growing tendency on the part of lawyers, judges, and authors of legal works to quote from the restatements and to view them as persuasive statements of legal principles. However, it should be noted that a restatement, unlike a uniform act which has been adopted by a legislature, is *not* an official statement of law. Its rules and principles are merely persuasive to a court until incorporated into official judicial opinions.

Summary

Law is defined as the result of a *process* whereby a nation adopts enforceable rules and regulations (positive law). *Business law* describes those parts of law most closely connected with business. These include aspects of public law such as criminal, administrative, and constitutional law, as well as statutory law regulating business. However, the basic foundation of business law is the law of torts, property, contracts, sales, secured transactions, commercial paper, agency, partnerships, and corporations.

A course in business law provides understanding of the legal aspects of business activities, how legal principles are applied to business problems, the relationship between law and business, how to evaluate law, and the roles of the participants in litigation, as well as a general understanding of the legal system.

The high volume of lawsuits in the United States results from the huge increase of federal, state, and local laws in recent years, as well as popular acceptance of litigation as a method of settling disputes. Lawyers are essential to the legal system because they are trained to function as advocates, advisors on preventive law, and as negotiators.

Moral and ethical standards throughout the world originate from teachings of philosophers and religious leaders. Although many moral standards are reflected in existing law, there is a large body of moral principles above the law. In a democracy, leaders in every era stir up the popular conscience to transform some of these ethical standards into positive laws, such as consumer protection statutes. There are subtle ethical principles (good or bad) that underlie all positive law—even a speed limit statute.

In the last decade, business and academic leaders have increasingly emphasized the study of business ethics. To the extent that business ethical principles are reflected in existing law, the goal is to increase awareness of such law. To the extent that ethical standards are not reflected in law, the problem is to educate people as to the various ethical theories and systems developed over the centuries so that each person can develop a sound and workable set of ethical principles.

Anglo-American law developed gradually in four overlapping stages. These stages of development reveal a progression from the simple law of ancient times to the complex law of today. A major objective of contemporary law is to encourage the satisfaction of as many human wants as possible and to assure fair play between groups as well as between individuals.

A number of legal philosophies have been influential in the development of Anglo-American law. These schools of legal thought have given direction to the development of law by expressing general principles upon which the law has been or should be based.

Most modern functions of law have their antecedents in the Constitution; these include: preserving internal peace, providing for change, and promoting the general welfare. Nevertheless, there are limits to what the law can accomplish. Judges lack time to be concerned with trifling matters or moot or hypothetical problems. An ideal legal system should be based upon the consent of the governed, achieve a fair balance between necessary laws and individual freedom, and be administered evenly and equally to all persons in similar circumstances. The laws should be clear enough that people can understand them. In addition, the laws should be flexible to meet changing needs, they should be enforced expeditiously, and retroactive laws should be kept at a minimum.

For purposes of analysis and study, the law has been classified as substantive and procedural, public and private, criminal and civil. Sources of law in the United States are constitutional, legislative, judicial, and administrative. The Constitution of the United States allocates governmental power between the federal and the state governments and among the three branches of the federal government. The federal government has the powers expressly conferred on it by the Constitution together with implied powers necessary and proper for carrying out the express powers. All other powers are reserved to the states or to the people. In accordance with the doctrine of separation of powers, the Constitution distributes federal powers among the legislative, judicial, and executive branches of the federal government. Most state constitutions and governments follow the federal model.

Within the framework established by the Constitution, each state is free to develop its own law. All states except Louisiana adopted some version of the English legal system—common law as supplemented by a separate system of equity.

In most states, common law and equity were merged into a single system as to procedure; nevertheless, the common law and equity retain separate identities. The common law and equity can be distinguished by: (1) the nature of the remedy being sought, (2) the manner of enforcement of judgments, and (3) the right to trial by jury in a court of law but not in equity.

The trend toward greater uniformity of state law is accelerated by uniform state legislation and by more uniform court decisions that use the restatements of law developed by the American Law Institute.

Review Questions

1 **(a)** In what ways is law a "process"? **(b)** Define the term "positive law."

2 Which objective or objectives of business law do you consider the most important? Why?

3 What functions do lawyers perform that are necessary to business?

4 **(a)** Throughout the world, what is the origin of most moral and ethical codes? **(b)** How do ethical principles improve law?

5 **(a)** What is meant by the term "common law"? **(b)** What was the original reason for the development of the common law? **(c)** How did the King's Court contribute to the development of law? **(d)** Explain the meaning and significance of *stare decisis.*

6 Why did the English develop a system of equity?

7 **(a)** What was the "law merchant"? **(b)** How is the law merchant related to contemporary business law in the United States?

8 How and to what extent did the English common law become a part of law in the United States?

9 To what extent have common law and equity merged in the United States?

10 Legal philosophy guides the development of law by expressing some general principles upon which the law has been or should be based. What main guiding belief or principle characterizes each of the following schools of legal thought? **(a)** Natural law; **(b)** divine law; **(c)** sociological jurisprudence.

11 **(a)** What are some of the functions of the law? **(b)** Give examples of some matters which lie outside the purview of the law.

12 **(a)** Of the eight attributes of an ideal legal system, which do you consider most important? Why? **(b)** Is complete attainment of one or more of the eight characteristics possible or desirable? Explain.

13 Explain the essential differences between **(a)** public and private law, **(b)** substantive and procedural law, and **(c)** criminal and civil law.

14 **(a)** What are the sources of law in the United States? **(b)** What method or means is used by each of these sources to express the law?

15 **(a)** How does the Constitution of the United States allocate power between the federal and state governments? **(b)** Define and illustrate the police power of the states. **(c)** Does the federal government have a police power? Explain.

16 **(a)** How does the Constitution distribute power among branches of the federal government? **(b)** Explain the meaning and purpose of "separation of powers." **(c)** Is the separation of powers complete? Why? **(d)** Illustrate the "checks and balances" of the federal government.

17 What is the role of *stare decisis* in judicial decisions in the United States?

18 **(a)** What are the chief differences between actions at law and actions in equity? **(b)** Describe or define the following equitable remedies: injunction and specific performance.

19 In legal effect, how does a uniform state law differ from a restatement of the common law?

20 P (plaintiff) observes D (defendant) digging a foundation for a barn which P knows is going to encroach 6 inches onto P's land. After the barn is built, P sues D in equity seeking a mandatory injunction ordering D to remove the encroachment. What will the equity court probably rule? Why?

CHAPTER 2

Law and Business Ethics

Geoffrey C. Hazard, Jr.

Ethical considerations affecting the conduct of business supplement business law. As part of the "rules of the game" to which business managers and employees must adhere in their work, the law operates alongside other rules, including nonlegal norms of fair dealing. These derive from personal beliefs and conscience, norms that prevail in the community at large, and norms of loyalty, responsibility, and integrity that prevail in a particular organization. Legal rules for the most part complement and sustain these other norms. However, sometimes there can be conflict between two or more of these sets of norms, resulting in serious ethical dilemmas. Study of legal rules raises awareness of possible ethical conflicts involving law and can help develop ways of thinking through such conflicts.

Difference between Philosophical and Applied Ethics

Law, community norms, and personal standards of morality are normative standards or general propositions that dictate how people ought to behave in various circumstances. Law consists of normative standards expressed in statutes, regulations, and court decisions based on the authority of government. Community norms are usually expressed through "ways of doing things" and are based on custom and tradition of a social group or set of interacting social groups. For example, whether adults in a particular group are strict or are permissive with small children, or with teenagers, is a community norm and can vary from one community to another. Personal moral standards usually reflect what an individual learns through a combination of interaction with family and friends and through exposure to more systematic thought in terms of religion and philosophy.

In modern academic life, *ethics* refers both to the content of normative standards and to the logic and psychology of normative standards, apart from their content. Studying the logic and psychology of normative standards involves such questions as "What is meant by saying that Jones has an obligation to do such and such?" and "Is a norm justified because it refers to conduct that is intrinsically good, or because following the norm will yield good results for society?" These two questions, important in philosophical tradition, concern (*a*) the theoretical nature of a duty or right, whether legal or moral, and (*b*) the different kinds of justification for a rule that creates a duty or right. The logic and psychology of ethics, which such questions pursue, is the central concern of traditional academic philosophy and religious philosophy. The classic works include Plato and Aristotle in the Greek tradition, the Old Testament in Jewish, Christian, and Moslem traditions as well as the Talmud, New Testament, and Koran in those traditions, respectively, and the works of such thinkers as Thomas Aquinas, Immanuel Kant, and Jeremy Bentham.

A different aspect of ethics (the aspect with which this chapter mainly deals) is the study of the content of normative standards and their significance in everyday life. This subject is usually called *applied ethics.* A subdivision of applied ethics is the study of normative problems arising in a business context, usually called *business ethics,* or *law and business ethics.* That is what is being addressed here.

In analyzing how law and ethics can interact to create ethical dilemmas in business settings, we first map out the relationship between law and other standards of conduct. We then take a look at the ethical standards of a particular workplace. We should then be able to see how law interacts with personal morals and the ethical standards of the workplace.

The Interaction of Law, Personal Morals, and Community Ethics

In general, legal rules are consistent with the personal moral standards that most people share. Certainly in the long run, rules of law reflect the sense of right and wrong prevailing in the general community. At the same time, community standards of right and wrong both reflect and influence personal moral standards. For example, most Americans now believe that men and women are equal in mental capability, capacity for work, and moral worth. The belief that men and women are equal in these respects is reflected in the position that women are now beginning to attain in American society, which contrasts with the position of women in many other cultures. For example, women as well as men serve as state governors, members of Congress, judges including a justice of the Supreme Court, and business leaders. Advertising is designed to appeal to both women and men as consumers. In addition, the law reflects this belief. There are legal rules prohibiting discrimination on the basis of gender regarding wages and other terms of employment, promotion, retirement benefits, etc.

Just as legal rules are the expression of aggregate personal beliefs, legal rules also influence personal moral values and community ethical standards. The fact that it is illegal to discriminate in employment on the basis of gender, race, or age does not mean that there is no such discrimination or that everyone agrees with the law prohibiting discrimination. However, the existence of such a law changes the standard operating procedures in employment relationships. For example, it used to be that classified ads for employment listed male and female jobs separately; such separate listings are no longer legal. Changes in standard operating procedures in business in turn affect everyday expectations about how women are to be treated in the workplace. And change in these expectations, over the course of time, changes the way the average person thinks about the role of women in the workplace in particular and in society in general.

The same principle can be seen at work in other areas of activity. For example, product safety laws provide forceful incentives to manufacturers to make and market products that are safe, and those laws both influence and are influenced by community standards concerning safety. The rules of civil procedure used in courts tend to be the standard by which the fairness of "private adjudication" is conducted. For example, employee disciplinary proceedings have tended to resemble court trials. Concepts of authority in corporation law can be used as a model for informal private associations.

On the other hand, if legal regulations that widely depart from community standards are ignored, cynicism about the law can result. A simple example, already alluded to in Chapter 1, is the 55-mph speed limit. Although this legal standard may have enjoyed general public support during the gasoline shortage of the early 1970s, it no longer does. Most drivers on the highway follow their own sense of safe speed or simply take the flow of traffic as their standard. The 55-mph rule is also ignored by law enforcement officials except as a legal basis for arresting people who exceed the informal speed limit of about 65, or when they make an arrest that they cannot otherwise justify. This law enforcement policy can be perceived as capricious and results in disrespect for the system's pretense concerning the traffic law.

Something like the same problem is widely believed to result from present laws on drug use. Thus, although the law generally conforms to community standards of right and wrong, it sometimes contradicts them. Another example is the requirement that strict bidding procedures be followed in competition for government contracts. The bidding regulations can become very complex as a result of the government's attempt to provide perfect protection against corruption and favoritism. If the rules get overly complicated, however, only those familiar with the technicalities will be able to bid. This defeats the original public policy of promoting competitive bidding.

Organizational Norms

In any business environment, the functioning norms include not only law, personal morals, and community standards, but also standards of the particular business and the particular industry. Some industries have generally high standards of craftsmanship, efficiency, and courtesy to customers and fellow workers. Many individual businesses have such standards, even though standards in the industry may be lower. By the same token, some companies are "bad actors," known to be hard to get along with in business dealings, to have contentious labor relations, and to cut corners in complying with the law. The same is true of nonbusiness organizations, including government agencies and bureaus.

The character of an organization in this regard is often referred to as its *ethical climate.* Sometimes an organization's ethical climate is distinct and easy to "read" for both an insider and an outsider. Sometimes it is very complex and ambiguous, seeming to say one thing and yet to allow something else. Some businesses have elaborate ethical codes that reinforce high standards of operating practice, for example, with respect to fairness in contracts with customers. Others have high standards of operating practice without any formal codes. Still others have high-sounding codes and statements of policy but deviate from those standards in actual practice. Thus, a business firm may say that "honesty is the best policy" but in fact be unfairly aggressive in dealing with customer complaints. Such a contradiction affects not only its customers but also puts its employees in an ambiguous situation. Is the customer to be treated generously, as the official policy says, or aggressively, as indicated by the company's actual general practice? A key problem in business ethics, whether for an employee or a customer, can be figuring out what is the real climate of an organization, and hence what is really expected in the way of conduct.

Some business organizations have the equivalent of 55-mph speed limits: They proclaim high-sounding rules but expect something else in practice. When discrepancies exist between professed organizational norms and "real" norms, very serious personal and management problems can arise. In mild forms, these discrepancies simply represent the difference between the ideal and the real. When the discrepancies are severe, however, a person who is in such an organization literally does not know what is expected. Often the only solution can be to avoid responsibility. "The boss told me that it has to be this way."

Legal Rules and Organizational Norms

Legal rules and organizational norms can diverge and inevitably do so to some extent. Legal rules are formulated by legislatures through statutes and by courts through decisions. Legislatures and courts stand outside any particular organization or part of the community and theoretically express the "public interest" as a whole. This is not the same perspective as that of an individual business or a particular local community.

For example, as we shall see in Chapter 44, the public interest as a whole may be served by rigidly requiring that all communities dispose of their garbage in a safe and sanitary manner, and by requiring similar standards for industrial effluents. From the point of view of a particular community or business, however, the standards established by law may seem hypersensitive and hypertechnical. A community or firm therefore may be inclined to cut corners, to completely ignore the legal rules, or even to conceal noncompliance and engage in a cover-up. From the viewpoint of the individual organization, these strategies for avoiding compliance are advantageous in the short run and may be so even in the long run, notwithstanding that they involve risk of violation. Compliance generally involves greater cost than noncompliance. In economic terms, compliance means "internalizing" costs that otherwise could be "externalized," that is, sloughed off on someone else. The classic case is dumping sewage into a river. Whether the dumping is done by a city or by an industry or firm, it saves that organization money but imposes costs on those downstream.

Thus from a societal viewpoint, noncompliance with law results in the unjust transfer of costs to some other sector of society or at least subjects others to unlawful risks—as when trucking companies schedule their trips on the assumption their drivers will average 70 mph, safe or not. Pervasive noncompliance, of course, can result in chronic disorder and anarchy, with adverse consequences for everyone but the very powerful.

Law sets general minimum standards of behavior. On the basis of such standards, law serves to compel individuals, business firms, and communities to internalize costs that they might otherwise impose on others. Legal standards also provide the basis for compensation to those who suffer injury when someone violates the standards, as when a firm that pollutes the air is required to pay damages to nearby landowners. Legal standards concerning contracts specify the conditions under which a promise or commitment is legally enforceable, and are the basis for enforcing contract rights. In these and myriad other respects the law supports conduct that takes account of the interests of others, and thus promotes security and predictability in personal, community, and business relationships. However, there is usually incentive to shirk obligations. Some obligations seem technical or unanswerable. Hence, individuals, communities, and firms are sometimes reluctant about or resistant to fulfilling their legal obligations.

Personal Morals and Organizational Norms

Similar conflicts can arise between personal moral standards and organization norms when the norms of business permit what most people consider to be wrongdoing. For example, some businesses use misleading and high-pressure sales techniques that are offensive to most people's personal standards. On the other hand, business ethics can legitimately require conduct that employees might find offensive if they were simply acting on their own account. For instance, a business can legitimately require a supervisor to discipline or even discharge an incompetent employee; indeed, an ethical business cannot function if it tolerates serious incompetence. Yet if the incompetent employee is the supervisor's close personal friend, the responsibilities a person owes toward a friend could lead the supervisor to ignore or cover up the incompetent performance. If the supervisor does so, he or she will violate the business "code" and transfer the cost of incompetence from the friend to the company.

Roles and Rules

Ethical conflicts of the kind described above are familiar in everyday experience. Yet our very familiarity with these problems may make it difficult to analyze them and to understand how they originate and how they may be controlled. We must examine the individual's multiple roles and the multiple normative systems in which these roles are embedded.

Everyone has multiple roles: Family member; resident of a neighborhood; citizen of a city or other community; citizen of a state and of the nation; employee or artisan or professional; perhaps member of religious affiliation or social club; member of informal circle of friends, etc. Each role involves a set of expectations that the person has for himself and that others have for him in the relationships arising out of that role. These expectations are not merely forecasts of how the person probably *will* behave; they are also more or less definite obligations as to how the person *should* behave. Thus, a family member is supposed to be protective of the welfare of his or her parents, brothers and sisters, and spouse and children. An employee is supposed to be competent and loyal in carrying out his or her responsibilities on the job. A neighbor is expected to be considerate of the interests of those nearby, as by avoiding loud parties at night, etc. A citizen is expected to obey the law when driving down the highway, computing income tax, etc.

Some role-governing rules are legal ones, some are organizational or community norms, some are personal or family standards. The rules governing driving on the highway and paying income tax are legal rules governing the role of citizens generally. Company rules governing employees are norms of the business organization. The rules governing courtesy to the neighbors are largely community norms.

However, most nonlegal ethical standards at some outer limit coincide with and are backed up by legal rules. Thus, the rule that one is to be protective of members of one's family is backed up by a legal rule governing extreme violations of that trust, by which a parent can be prosecuted for physical abuse of a child. The rule that an employee is supposed to be competent and loyal is backed up by the legal rule that allows an employer to fire someone who violates these duties. A neighbor who holds loud parties can be prosecuted for disturbing the peace.

Generally speaking, the roles we play and the rules that govern them are consistent. If they were not, the social fabric would pull apart. Communities would dissolve into feuding factions and businesses could not function as productive enterprises. A vivid example of this kind of internal conflict is found in South Africa, where blacks insist on full equality but the white minority insists on apartheid. At bottom, blacks and whites have radically different views as to the proper role of blacks in South African society and its economy.

One of the tasks of a viable legal system is that of continuously reconciling personal and community standards, on the one hand, with legal standards on the other. For example, it was formerly the legal rule that a buyer purchased a product on a "take it or leave it" basis. In the Latin phrase, the rule was *caveat emptor*—buyer beware. But business practice has changed. Manufacturers and retailers came to recognize that getting repeat business was good business and that business reputation was a valuable asset. Many of them came to act on the principle, "The customer is always right." This in turn led to a public expectation that goods usually were or ought to be of good quality, at least free from dangerous defects. The changed public expectation came to become a business standard, and as a business standard was absorbed into the law that dictates what is required in "reasonable" business practice. The end result of this process is that caveat emptor is no longer the rule. On the contrary, every product is required by law to be "reasonably fit for the purpose intended," unless there are effective contract provisions waiving this standard.

In a similar way, the law in every field, through the influence of community standards, evolves toward reducing the conflict between those standards and legal rules. But in any given situation at any given time, there is likely to be some discrepancy between legal standards and community ethical standards. As a result, there may be conflicting role expectations.

Role Conflict and Rule Conflict: The Structure of Ethical Problems

Most if not all ethical problems reveal themselves to be the result of conflicting rules emanating from conflicting role expectations. The plant manager who is tempted to let the factory effluent slip quietly into the river has a role as manager that commands loyalty to and efficient performance for the company. Yet she also has a role as citizen that commands loyalty and obedience to the law and a role as a member of the community that commands being a good neighbor. The supervisor who is confronted with inefficient or dishonest performance by an employee who is also his brother has a responsibility to the company arising from his role as supervisor and another responsibility to his brother arising from their family relationship.

Similar problems can arise within a business. A subordinate who discovers that his supervisor is fudging product test data, for example, occupies the roles of company employee, of departmental subordinate, of citizen, and perhaps of personal friend of the supervisor. As company employee, his duty is to see that the test data are not fudged. As an immediate subordinate, the employee has a special loyalty to his supervisor, a loyalty that may be partly coerced through the supervisor's power of retaliation. As a friend of the supervisor, the subordinate is expected not to get him into trouble. As a citizen, the employee may have a legal obligation, for example, if the tests are required by law.

As long as the supervisor directs that the tests be done honestly, and if that is the company policy, the rules of the various roles are consistent. The subordinate-employee-friend-citizen does not encounter conflict in the rules governing his various roles. But if the supervisor wants the tests done dishonestly, or in a way that distorts the test process so that the results are unreliable, then the subordinate-employee-friend-citizen faces a conflict as to the rules or expectation of role. This is the typical form of an ethical conflict. Similar conflicts can occur between one's roles as family member and citizen, or neighbor and citizen, or family member and neighbor.

Resolving Ethical Conflict

Ethical conflict is an unavoidable aspect of adult life. We have to support ourselves, which means we have jobs that can involve a role beyond "being yourself." We usually maintain family relationships, which also involve roles and rules. We have to live somewhere, so that we have a role as neighbor and are subject to the rules of that role. We drive cars, owe taxes, and have other responsibilities as citizens. Any of these circumstances may create ethical conflicts.

Ethical conflict occurs in business because it occurs in life generally. However, resolving ethical conflict in business is especially critical for at least three reasons. First, employment, whether in business or otherwise, is a major part of life in modern society. Very few people in modern society simply till the land, much less live off it. Roles at work, and the rules that go with them, are a major component of our daily existence. Second, many of the tasks in employment involve conflict or competition—who shall do particular work, who is responsible for particular problems, who will be promoted, etc. Major conflicts can be encountered concerning scope of responsibility and authority among levels and divisions in a business organization. Similar conflicts are encountered in relationships between firms, for example, between a supplier of parts and the manufacturer that assembles the finished product, or between a service business and the company that supplies its equipment. All such situations involve temptations to act covertly or deceptively. Third, the business organization can have the character of a socially isolated society. Membership in such a society can unduly dominate a person's other roles. When this happens, the organization's norms become laws unto themselves. People in the organization do what it wants more or less without regard to what may be required by the law, or, for that matter, by personal and community standards.

Keeping the risks of such conflict in reasonable perspective is a continual challenge to leading an ethical life. Being successful in this regard requires awareness of the nature and structure of ethical problems, as described above. It also requires a sense of self—a concept of one's *identity*—so as to resolve what role, and therefore what expectation, is to govern when a conflict is presented. That is one interpretation of the meaning of the old phrase, "to thine own self be true."

The inner self must analyze the structure of the work setting in which the individual finds himself or herself. The legal rules governing the situation can be absorbed and understood. The rules that operate in a particular firm or community setting can also be absorbed by observation, reflection, and interpretation. The individual can compare those sets of rules with his or her own personal moral code. He or she can locate the possibilities of conflict and visualize pathways for resolving them. The study of legal norms then can be a technique for learning to function effectively in a complex society.

Review Questions

1 In business settings, what is a common source of ethical dilemma?

2 **(a)** What is a "normative standard"? **(b)** How do legal norms differ from community norms? **(c)** What other norms or standards might be involved in an ethical dilemma?

3 This chapter focuses on an aspect of applied ethics called "business ethics." What is the general nature of the study of business ethics?

4 Illustrate one of the following: **(a)** How do aggregate personal beliefs influence legal rules? **(b)** How do legal rules influence personal moral values or community standards? **(c)** How do legal rules affect business practices?

5 **(a)** Why might a legal regulation be ignored by the people to whom it applies? **(b)** Illustrate how a law could be ineffective for accomplishing its intended purpose.

6 How are the "organizational norms" of a business firm related to its "ethical climate"?

7 **(a)** What is there about a law that can put it into conflict with a business firm's organizational norms? **(b)** Illustrate how law compels a business firm to internalize costs. **(c)** Why might the firm resist internalizing those costs?

8 How can business ethics legitimately require employees to act in a way that they would find offensive if they were simply acting on their own account?

9 Explain or illustrate how a person's multiple roles in society contribute to the existence of ethical dilemmas.

10 If an employee were confronted with on-the-job ethical conflict, what steps might the employee take in resolving it?

Discussion Questions

1 How would you define "personal morality," for example, in dealings with a supervisor at work?

2 How would you define "community standard"?

3 Identify some of the various communities of which you are a member.

4 Have you seen situations where there was a discrepancy between the "official rule" and the behavior actually expected by "the authorities" in charge of the situation?

5 Identify some legal rules other than the 55 mile per hour speed limit that do not seem to be seriously intended to be observed or enforced.

6 Have you been a member of a class or seminar where members of the class expected to copy from each other on papers or examinations? **(a)** Did this expectation "go against the grain" with you personally? With any other members of the class? **(b)** If it did "go against the grain," how should an individual act who feels that way?

7 In the situation described in question 6, suppose the teacher was aware that students were copying from each other. **(a)** What should the teacher, as the "authority," be expected to do? **(b)** Suppose the teacher said in a casual way that he or she knew a lot of people were copying from each other, but did nothing further? What message about copying would the teacher be communicating? **(c)** How should members of the class react if the teacher behaved as in (b) above? **(d)** How would you react in that situation?

8 Suppose you are working in a factory production line where some employees routinely engage in petty theft of company property. Would your answers to questions 6 and 7 above remain the same? (For question 7, substitute "your immediate supervisor" for "the teacher.")

CHAPTER 3

The Court System; Civil Procedure; Arbitration

Most people in the United States come in contact with the judicial system at some time during their lives. Almost everyone is called for jury duty as the volume of criminal proceedings and civil litigation in this country fills the courts with cases. It follows that the many cases engage time and attention of many plaintiffs and defendants, attorneys and witnesses. In addition to major crime cases, our news media daily report cases from constitutionality issues and ordinance violations through neighborhood and business torts and contract breaches. Beginning with Chapter 4 of this book, we present actual court cases for you to read. In order to understand each case, you must be familiar with the court system and the procedures involved in the trial and the appeal of a civil lawsuit. First we discuss the function and the jurisdiction of courts in the United States, the organization of the federal and state courts, and the work of the courts. The remainder of the chapter deals with procedures related to civil lawsuits and with arbitration as an alternative to litigation in resolving disputes.

The Court System

In most states the same court system handles both criminal and civil cases. To distinguish between criminal matters and civil, first realize that *crimes* are offenses against the state as the sovereign authority. Since such offenses are against the entire society, against *the public,* it is the state, i.e., government, that brings suit, not the victim of the crime, and it is the states' attorneys who prosecute in criminal cases, not private attorneys. Other functions and procedures unique to criminal law are discussed in Chapter 7, but as this book deals with commercial law, the discussion of the court system and procedure that follows will focus upon civil law matters.

Function of Courts

The word "court" has various meanings. At times it is synonymous with "judge," as when a judge tells an attorney to address his or her remarks "to the court and not to the opposing counsel." At other times it indicates the place where a judicial tribunal functions, as in the statement that *trials* must take place "in court," whereas *orders* may be signed "in chambers" (the judge's office). Usually, however, *court* means a tribunal established by the state or federal government for the administration of justice.

The main function of a court is to decide controversies between parties in a lawsuit, the *litigation,* which comes to us from Latin roots meaning *to dispute.* The parties in dispute are called *litigants,* and the court's decision is called a *judgment.* Since the court's main function is to resolve disputes, it ordinarily will not answer hypothetical questions; it will not advise, for example, what a person's rights would be under a *proposed* contract. But, if there is a real dispute to be decided, the courts may *declare the rights* of parties to a controversy even though no actual wrong has occurred. These judgments, called *declaratory judgments,* in which rights are declared without ordering the parties to do anything, are useful because they permit rights to be determined (as under existing leases, contracts, wills of deceased persons, statutes, etc.) before harmful action has been taken. Several cases presented in later chapters involve requests for declaratory judgments.

Jurisdiction of Courts

The word "jurisdiction" is used in different senses, but for our purpose *jurisdiction* means *the authority or power of a court to hear and decide controversies.* In order to process a case, a court must have two kinds of jurisdiction:

- Jurisdiction over the subject matter (type of case)
- Jurisdiction over the property or over the litigants

Jurisdiction over the subject matter in a case depends on hierarchy within the court system, and on limitations set within states and for federal districts. A court may have jurisdiction to hear breach of contract cases, for example, but be limited to suits in which no more than $10,000 is claimed for damages. Another court can hear divorce cases but not hear challenges to ordinances or statutes.

Jurisdiction over property is limited generally to a defined geographic area. Generally, a state court will have authority to handle cases involving lands lying within the state but not over lands beyond its borders.

Jurisdiction over the parties (called *personal jurisdiction*) is necessary when a party seeks to impose personal liability on another, such as an action for an injunction or for damages, or for alimony or child support. If both parties reside in the same community, the suit will be decided by the local courts. But a jurisdictional dispute can arise if one party's permanent home (called *domicile*) is in another state.

Two concepts—*implied consent* and *minimum contacts*—help a court decide if it has jurisdiction over persons domiciled elsewhere. An example would be a business based in California that regularly transports goods to Nevada, Utah, and Arizona; it has at least minimum contact in each of those states and can come under their courts' jurisdiction. Another example involves nonresident motorists. Most states have a statute under which an out-of-state driver is said to impliedly consent to the jurisdiction of the local courts over any lawsuit arising from use of the highways: Such driver can be held liable in these "foreign" (not home) states and be called to court there.

Because the United States Constitution established a dual system of government, two sets of courts—federal and state—have also been established. Where only one court has the authority to hear and decide a case, the court is said to have *exclusive jurisdiction*. Where two or more courts have authority, they have *concurrent jurisdiction* over the case. In some classes of cases the jurisdiction of the federal courts is exclusive; in other cases, federal and state courts have concurrent jurisdiction.

Exclusive Federal Jurisdiction. The United States Congress has given the federal courts exclusive jurisdiction over certain classes of cases where the subject of dispute is a federal statute or regulation. For example, cases involving antitrust laws, bankruptcy, patents, trademarks, copyrights, and suits to review decisions by federal administrative agencies may be brought only in federal courts. While cases within the exclusive jurisdiction of the federal courts often are complex and involve millions of dollars, Congress has specified no minimum amount for such cases; thus, a suit under the federal Internal Revenue Code to obtain a refund of tax must be filed in a federal court even though the amount sought is only a few dollars.

Concurrent Jurisdiction. The most common type of case involving concurrent jurisdiction is one where the parties to the lawsuit are citizens of different states or nations (referred to as *diversity of citizenship*). Under present law the federal courts have jurisdiction in diversity of citizenship cases only when the matter in controversy exceeds the sum or value of $50,000. Let us suppose that Peter, a resident of California, wishes to sue Diane, a resident of New York, for breach of contract and seeks $80,000 in damages. If Diane is subject to the jurisdiction of courts in California (based on implied consent, minimum contacts, etc.), Peter may sue in either a federal court or in the state court of California. If Diane is not subject to the jurisdiction of courts in California, Peter may sue in either a federal or state court in New York.

Exclusive State Jurisdiction. State courts have exclusive jurisdiction over certain obvious classes of cases such as divorce, child custody, and probate of wills of deceased persons. In addition, the most common types of civil lawsuits for damages, such as those resulting from automobile collisions, ordinarily involve parties living in the same state and come under the exclusive jurisdiction of state courts. When the parties to a lawsuit not involving federal law both reside in the same state or in different states but the sum involved is $50,000 or less, the state courts have exclusive jurisdiction. Thus, in the example above, if both Peter and Diane reside in California, the state court would have exclusive jurisdiction over the case regardless of the amount of damages asked. Or, if they resided in different states but Peter's damages were less than $50,000, he would have no choice but to sue Diane in a state court.

Federal Court System

The United States Constitution provides that the "judicial power of the United States shall be vested in one Supreme Court, and in such inferior [lower] courts as the Congress may from time to time ordain and establish."[1] At present the federal court system consists of district courts, courts of appeals, the Supreme Court, and various special courts. Figure 3.1 illustrates the federal court system.

[1]U.S. Constitution, Art. III, sec. 1, par. 1.

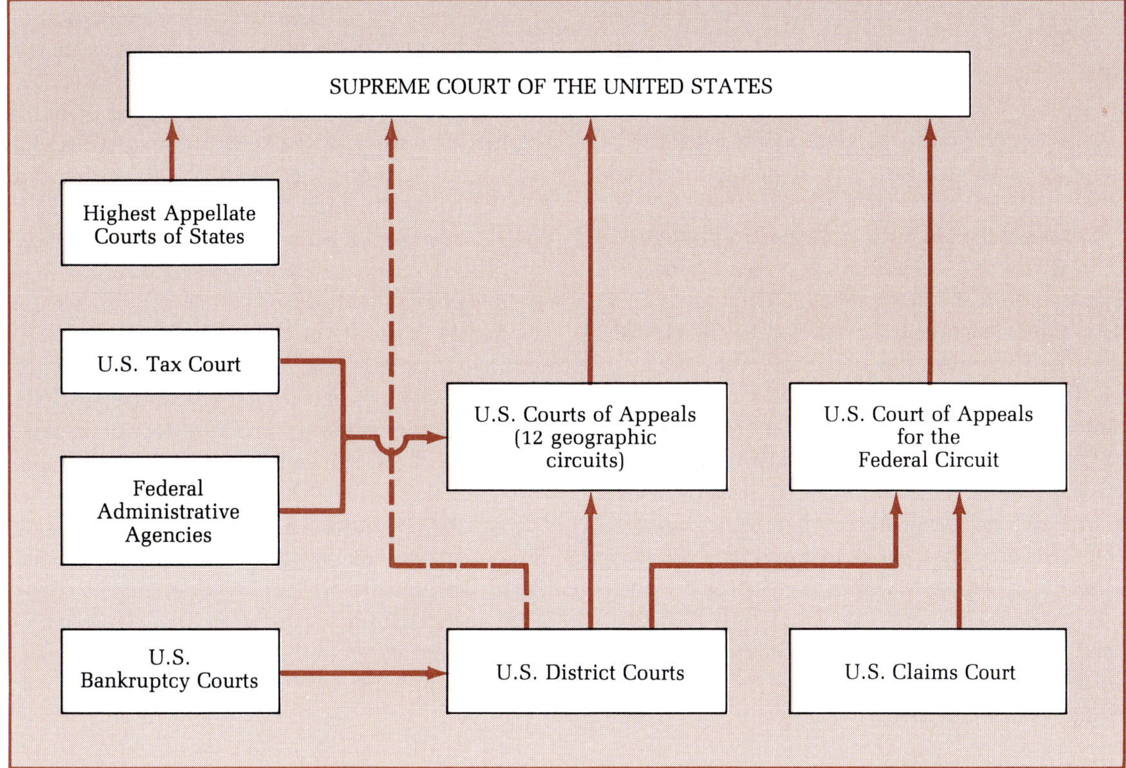

Figure 3.1 The federal court system.

The President of the United States, with the advice and consent of the Senate, appoints judges who serve on federal courts for the period of their good behavior.

District Courts. The district courts are the trial courts of the federal judicial system. Ordinarily, a litigant begins a federal lawsuit in a United States district court. There is one such court for each federal judicial district. In the less populous states a district covers the whole state; in the more populous states, such as California and New York, there are several federal districts.

Depending upon the volume of cases filed, the court may consist of one, two, or more judges. Most cases are tried before a single judge; a few types of cases are tried before a panel of three judges.

Courts of Appeals. If a litigant is dissatisfied with the judgment rendered by the district court, the party may file an appeal with a higher court. The courts of appeals hear all appeals from district courts except for a few classes of cases where appeals may be taken directly to the Supreme Court. They also review orders of federal administrative agencies, such as the Consumer Product Safety Commission, the Environmental Protection Agency, and the Federal Trade Commission.

Originally the judges of these courts traveled a circuit and the courts were called *circuit courts of appeals*. There are at present twelve geographic circuits serving the fifty states. Although judges of the courts of appeals no longer travel regularly, they are still referred to as "circuit judges."

A panel of three judges hears appeals. The court of appeals does not retry a case which has been tried in a district court. Instead, the judges review a stenographic record of the trial to determine if an error of law was made in the trial. For example, a litigant may file an appeal alleging that the district court judge improperly denied a motion or gave the jury an erroneous instruction.

The Supreme Court. The chief function of the Supreme Court is its appellate function. Most of the cases it reviews come from the courts of appeals, although a few come from other federal courts and even from the highest state courts. Even though the highest appellate courts of the states are not part of the federal court system *per se,* they may have their decisions appealed to the Supreme Court when the issue in the case involves a federal question. Accordingly, these courts are included in Figure 3.1.

A litigant is not entitled as a matter of right to be heard in the United States Supreme Court. This is true even if a case involves a federal question. The Supreme Court has discretion to choose only the cases it deems most important to hear.

The members of the Supreme Court are called "justices." The Constitution is silent about the size of the Supreme Court, and the number of justices has varied between six and ten. It is now, and for many years has been, nine. There is no constitutional requirement that a person be a judge, or even a lawyer, to be appointed to the Supreme Court.

Special Courts. From time to time Congress has created special courts for limited purposes or for certain geographic areas. The more important special courts, with their jurisdictions briefly indicated, are as follows: (1) United States Claims Court: to hear nontort claims against the United States; (2) United States Tax Court: to hear cases involving collection of federal taxes; and (3) miscellaneous courts, including territorial courts (e.g., Guam) and the United States Military Courts.

In 1982 Congress established the United States Court of Appeals for the Federal Circuit. This court is based in Washington, D.C. Its function is to review decisions of the U.S. District Courts involving customs and patents, and to review decisions of the U.S. Claims Court.

State Court Systems

The court systems of the states vary in details but are alike in fundamentals. Every state has a series of local trial courts of original jurisdiction and a court of appeals. The dissimilarities consist primarily in the variety of local courts, in the number of levels of appellate courts, and in the titles given to some of the courts. Figure 3.2 illustrates a typical state court system.

Judges of state courts are selected in various ways. In many states judges are elected by the citizens. In some states the governor appoints all judges. In a few states, there is a combination of appointment and election in which judges are appointed for their first term and then if a judge desires to continue in office after the expiration of his or her appointive term, he or she must stand for election. Often no other candidate's name appears on the ballot; the only decision the voters make is whether the incumbent shall be returned to office.

Election campaigns require the candidates to raise money from individuals and groups. If a candidate is elected to office, he or she is often presented with ethical questions—like conflict-of-interest—which have been the subject of legislation. Many states have passed statutes requiring candidates for public office to disclose the source and amount of campaign contributions they receive. Once elected, judges like other public officials, must file annual statements of their assets, such as stocks, bonds, and real estate holdings. These public disclosures are intended to deter public officials from making decisions that would result in personal gain (direct or indirect) to themselves or to a campaign contributor.

Trial Courts. In most states trial courts are divided into two groups—the minor judiciary and the higher trial courts.

Figure 3.2 A typical state court system.

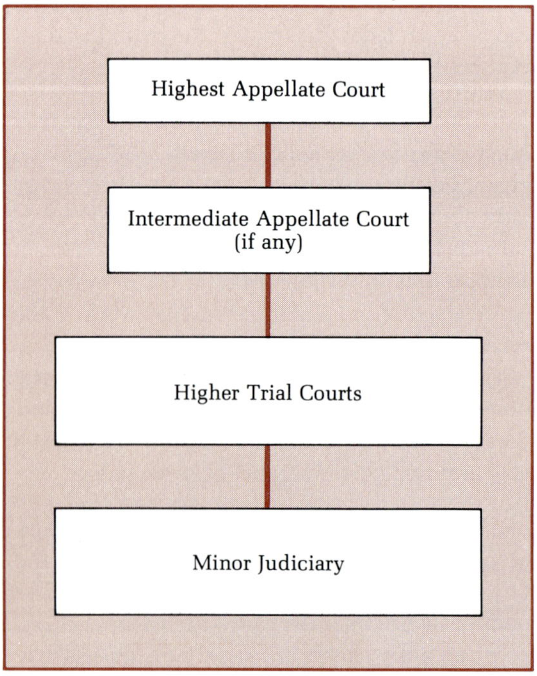

The Minor Judiciary. Traditionally, officers called "justices of the peace" handle legal cases of minor nature. A justice of the peace is not required to be, and usually is not, a legally trained person. Typically, he or she is elected by citizens in the local community. In many states the lowest trial court is called a city court, police court, or municipal court. The jurisdiction of such courts is limited. For example, in California, justice and municipal courts have jurisdiction over civil cases where the amount in controversy is $25,000 or less.

Most states have created a special tribunal called "small claims court." This court has very limited jurisdiction; the usual maximum in damages that a party in a civil action may ask for is $1,500 to $2,000. There are several benefits to filing a suit in small claims court: (1) There is very little cost to the parties, (2) a hearing is held to resolve the dispute very soon after suit is filed, and (3) the trial is held in an informal manner. In some states litigants may not be represented by lawyers. The major disadvantage of a small claims suit is the limited right to appeal. In California, for example, if the one who files the action loses, he or she has no right to appeal to a higher court. If the one who files the action wins the suit, the other party may appeal. In some states, such as Michigan, neither plaintiff nor defendant has the right to appeal.

Higher trial courts. In every state there is a court of general and original jurisdiction for each county. It may be called the district court, the superior court, or the circuit court.[2] In California, the jurisdiction of superior courts over civil suits is limited to cases involving an amount in controversy exceeding $25,000. The superior court, with a three-judges panel also acts as an appeals court to hear appeals from small claims, justice, and municipal courts.

In some states, and especially in the more populous counties of some states, the courts of *general jurisdiction* are supplemented by one or more courts of *special jurisdiction.* The most commonly found courts of special jurisdiction are criminal courts, equity courts, and probate courts. In Los Angeles County the superior court has over 200 judges and numerous special courts.

[2]In New York, strangely enough, it is called the "supreme court." In Ohio, it is called the "court of common pleas."

Appellate Courts. In most states the highest appellate court is called the supreme court.[3] Members of the court are usually called *justices.* The number of justices serving in the highest state court varies; usually the number is either five or seven. In most states the governor appoints all supreme court justices, although in a few states they are elected by the citizens.

Many states have an appellate court intermediate between the trial courts and the state supreme court. A dissatisfied litigant may appeal from the trial court to the court of appeals, alleging an error of law was made by the trial judge. In Texas there are two intermediate appellate courts: the court of criminal appeals and the court of civil appeals.

As in the federal court system, appeals are heard by a panel of three justices. No new evidence is allowed; the court simply reviews the trial procedure and evidence from the stenographic record of the trial. A litigant who is dissatisfied with the decision of a court of appeals may appeal to the state supreme court. In some states appeal to the state supreme court is allowed as a matter of right. In others, such as California, an appeal to the supreme court is largely a matter of privilege, and the practice is for the court to grant the privilege only in the most important cases.

Civil Procedure

When disputes between individuals or business firms cannot be resolved amicably, litigation often results. This part of the chapter discusses the steps in the trial of cases, from beginning to end. Knowledge of these steps, shown in Figure 3.3, and of the terms used in litigation will be of assistance in understanding the cases presented in the following chapters. Often, an appeal is based on a defect alleged to exist in one or more steps in the trial of a case.

Procedures Prior to Trial

Pleadings. Pleadings are the initial written statements presented to the trial court by each party to

[3]In New York the highest appellate court is called the court of appeals."

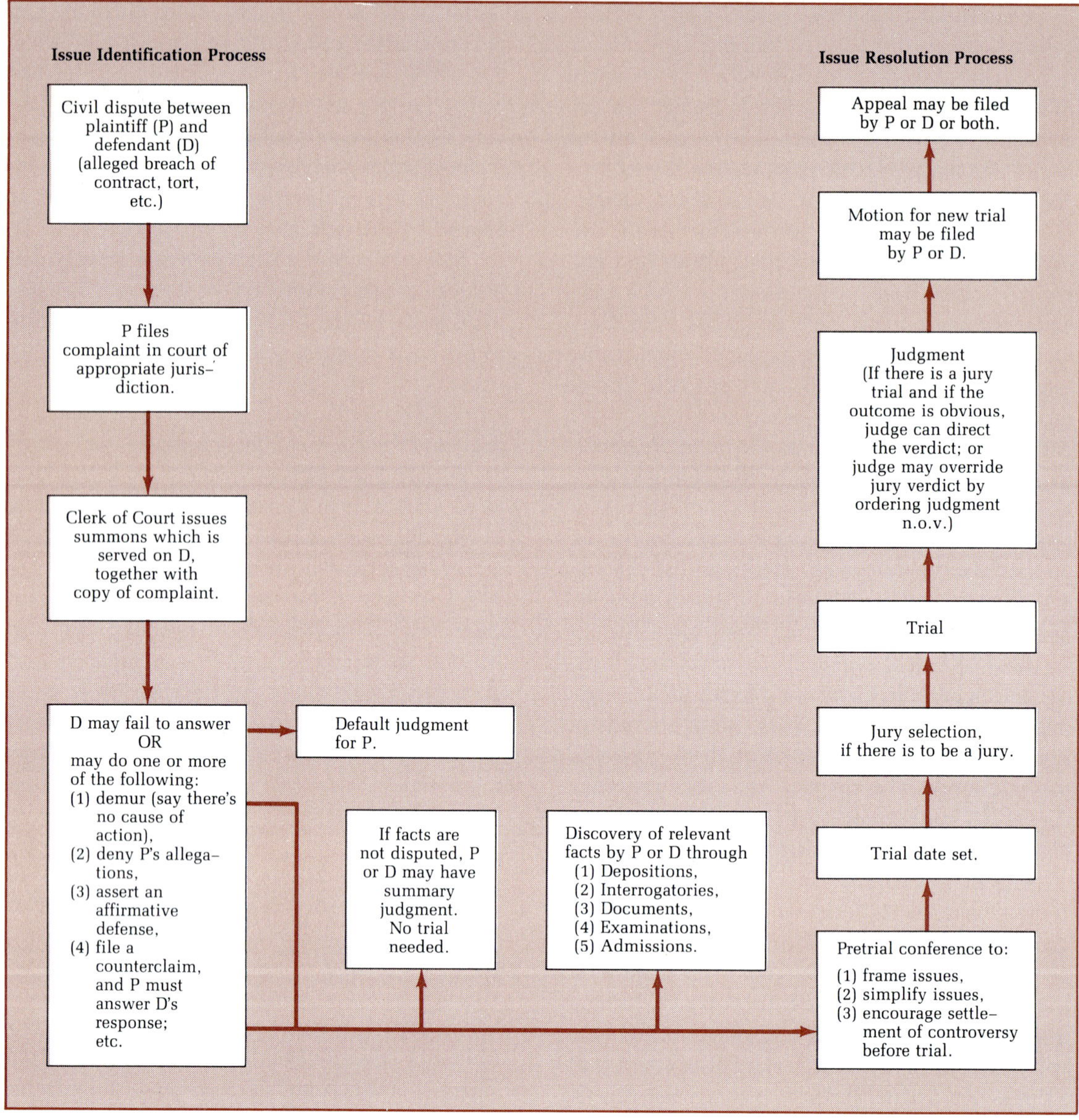

Figure 3.3 Flow of civil litigation.

a civil suit. The function of pleadings is to reduce the controversy to its essential issues.

Summons and complaint. The party who initiates a civil lawsuit is called the *plaintiff.* The party being sued is called the *defendant.* The plaintiff initiates a lawsuit by filing with the court a statement variously called a *complaint, petition,* or *declaration.* The requirements for a complaint in California are typical of those states which have modernized their pleadings. The complaint must contain a statement of the facts constituting the cause of action, in ordinary and concise language, and a demand of the relief which the plaintiff claims. For example, the plaintiff may state, "On January 1, the defendant drove his automobile in a negligent manner and collided with the plaintiff, causing great bodily injury." The plaintiff would then request damages in a certain amount, such as $100,000. This request, called the *prayer,* varies according to the nature of the action. For example, the plaintiff may pray that a tenant who has not paid rent be ordered to vacate an apartment owned by the plaintiff.

The plaintiff brings the defendant under the jurisdiction of the court by serving the defendant with a copy of the complaint and a document called a *summons*. A summons is, in effect, an order of the court directing the defendant to appear in court within a certain time period, usually 30 days. In the summons the defendant is advised that if no action is taken within the 30 days, the plaintiff may take a judgment against the defendant by default. A judgment by default means that the plaintiff receives what he or she asked for in the prayer (e.g., damages or equity remedy) without further court proceedings. Ordinarily, "serving" a copy of the summons and complaint (called *service of process*) is accomplished by handing the papers to the defendant in person. This may be done by a professional process server or a court official such as a sheriff or a marshal. However, when the defendant cannot be found, provisions in most states allow for "substituted" service. Such service may be accomplished by mailing or by advertising in a newspaper.

Demurrer. After the defendant is served the copy of the summons and complaint, the defendant must file with the court a responsive pleading within the required time in order to avoid a default judgment. There are several pleadings that a defendant may file. The defendant may challenge the court's jurisdiction or the legal sufficiency of the plaintiff's complaint by means of a document called a "demurrer," or in some states a "motion to dismiss." A demurrer to a complaint challenging its legal sufficiency says in effect: "Even if the facts alleged in the complaint are assumed to be true, still the complaint does not state a cause of action against the defendant." For example, suppose Peter alleges in his complaint that Donna promised to meet him at a certain movie theater at 7 P.M. on Saturday night and to attend the movie with him. Peter alleges that Donna failed to appear, breaching her promise, and this caused Peter great mental distress. He asks for $1000 damages. Donna would likely file a demurrer to the complaint, alleging that the complaint does not state a cause of action recognized at law.

A demurrer raises an issue of law which the court must decide. If the court *sustains* the demurrer, the judge is ruling that the plaintiff has failed to state a recognized cause of action. The plaintiff ordinarily is then given time to file an amended complaint. If the plaintiff fails to file an amended complaint, a judgment of dismissal will be filed against him or her. If the court *overrules* the demurrer, the judge is ruling that the plaintiff has stated a recognized cause of action. The defendant is then given time to file a further pleading. If the defendant fails to do so, a default judgment will be entered for the plaintiff. Whether the demurrer is sustained or overruled, the losing party has the right of appeal. Many cases in this textbook involve an appeal from a demurrer or motion to dismiss. On appeal the question is: Did the trial court correctly decide the issue of whether the plaintiff stated a recognized cause of action?

Answer and counterclaim. The defendant in a civil lawsuit most commonly chooses to file another type of responsive pleading called an "answer." An *answer* may contain a general denial, that is, the defendant denies everything contained in the complaint, or a specific denial, that is, the defendant denies the truth of one or more of the essential allegations of the complaint and admits the truth of the other allegations.

An answer may contain one or more affirmative defenses. An *affirmative defense* is an allegation of some new matter as a bar to plaintiff's recovery. For example, suppose that the plaintiff alleges in the complaint that on a specified date the plaintiff lent the defendant the sum of $1000 and that the defendant has failed to pay it or any portion thereof. If the money was indeed loaned but the defendant has received in bankruptcy a discharge from all debts, the defendant may file an answer admitting the debt, but alleging bankruptcy as an affirmative defense. Other examples of affirmative defenses are statute of limitations and statute of frauds. These and many other defenses are presented in various chapters later in this book.

In most states the defendant as part of the answer may assert a counterclaim. A *counterclaim* is an assertion that the defendant has a claim against the plaintiff. Such claim need not be related to the plaintiff's cause of action stated in the complaint. For example, suppose Paula sues Dennis alleging breach of a contract. Dennis may file a counterclaim alleging that Paula made defamatory statements about him which caused him to suffer damages. The plaintiff must file an answer, called a "reply" to a counterclaim or risk dismissal.

Summary Judgment. At various points during the pleading stage of litigation, either party to the lawsuit may make a motion for a *summary judgment.* The summary judgment procedure is designed to dispose of suits in which there is no genuine issue of fact for a judge or jury to decide. The judge conducts an informal hearing to review the pleadings. The parties may file affidavits (sworn statements) of witnesses who would be called by the parties to testify if a trial were held. If the pleadings and affidavits reveal no material issue of fact, the judge makes a ruling that no trial is necessary and enters a judgment for the plaintiff or defendant. Like the demurrer, the summary judgment procedure helps to avoid the expense of unnecessary trials. If a judge grants a motion for summary judgment, the losing party may appeal to a higher court.

Discovery. At one time there was a feeling in the legal profession that a lawsuit should be a battle of wits, with each side guarding its case jealously and making the adversary's trial preparations as difficult and onerous as possible. Often the parties did not know until the day of trial what witnesses the other party would call to testify. In order to minimize the element of surprise, to improve and speed up the trial of cases, and to encourage settlements before trial, all states today provide for and encourage the parties to learn as much as possible about the adversary's case prior to trial. There are five major devices for discovery of facts before trial:

- Depositions
- Interrogatories
- Inspection of documents and property
- Physical and mental examinations
- Request for admissions

Depositions. A *deposition* is a statement under oath made at a hearing held out of court and after due notice to the other side. Ordinarily, each party will request permission to take the deposition of the other party and the party's key witnesses. A hearing is arranged at the office of one party's attorney. A court reporter records the questions and answers and prepares a written transcript for the witness to sign. In recent years, many courts have encouraged the use of videotape depositions. The need for a written transcript is eliminated; and if the videotape is presented at trial, the judge or jury can view the witness and better evaluate the person's credibility.

Depositions serve various purposes: to discover what testimony to expect at the trial; to obtain testimony while it is fresh in the mind of the witness; to impeach (discredit) a person's testimony at the trial by showing that the testimony varies from the deposition; and to preserve testimony where there is danger that it may be unavailable at the trial. For example, a deposition may be desirable if a witness is elderly, has a serious illness, or is likely not to be available for the trial. Often, attorneys will take the deposition of an expert witness, such as a doctor or engineer, and use the deposition at the trial in place of actual testimony. Expert witnesses receive large fees for testifying at trials, and their schedules are often such that it may be difficult to secure their attendance at the trial.

Interrogatories. *Interrogatories* are written questions addressed by one party in a case to the other party to elicit information that can be used as a basis for further questions at a deposition hearing or at the trial of the case. An interrogatory may be used, for example, to demand a list of the other party's witnesses. Interrogatories are relatively inexpensive and can be served informally (usually by mail) and answered without the necessity of the presence of a court reporter or opposing attorney. Ordinarily, the answers must be given in writing, under penalty of perjury. As with depositions, the answers can be used for impeachment purposes at a trial.

Inspection of documents and property. Either party to a case may secure a court order permitting the party or an agent to inspect, copy, or photograph documents or tangible things in the possession or control of another. For example, in a case where the plaintiff alleges personal injury the defendant may wish to inspect medical or hospital records pertaining to the injury.

Physical and mental examinations. When the physical or mental condition of a party is in controversy, the court may issue an order requiring him or her to submit to an examination by a physician. In many lawsuits both parties will request an examination by physicians. Often, the doctors' opinions as to a party's condition are at odds with one another and the judge or jury must then weigh the credibility of each physician.

Request for admissions. Either party may serve upon the other party (usually by mail) a request that he or she admit the genuineness of some document or the truth of some assertion described or set forth in the request. Failure to deny in writing and under oath the genuineness of the document or the truth of the assertion constitutes an admission of its genuineness or truth. The admission relieves the requesting party of the burden of producing proof on that point at the trial.

In general, the information sought by discovery must be relevant to the subject matter of the lawsuit. For example, in most cases it would be improper to ask in a deposition hearing or in an interrogatory for a party or witness to disclose his or her social security number. But it is not required that the information sought be used in evidence at a trial nor that the information be admissible evidence. Thus, a plaintiff is entitled to discover the existence and scope of the defendant's insurance coverage, although such information is not admissible as evidence in a trial.

Pretrial Conference. In most states the courts require a pretrial conference in civil suits. A pretrial conference is a meeting of the judge and attorneys, and sometimes the parties, held usually two or three weeks before trial. The conference serves two purposes. One purpose is to shorten the time of trial by refining or narrowing the issues, clarifying the pleadings through amendments, and placing a limitation on the number of witnesses and exhibits. The second purpose of the pretrial conference is to encourage an out-of-court settlement. At the end of the conference, if no settlement has been reached, the judge sets a date for the trial.

Trial of Cases

Before the trial date, the plaintiff and defendant must decide whether the trial will be by judge or by jury. In some suits no jury is allowed, as in suits for equity relief. In other suits either party may request a jury but is not required to do so (i.e., they may *waive* a jury). If either side requests a jury, a deposit of jury fees ordinarily must be made in advance of the trial date. On the day of a jury trial, the first step is for the parties to select a jury. (The judge selects the jury in cases tried in federal district courts.) The remaining steps in a trial are substantially the same whether or not a jury is used.

Opening Statements of Counsel. Ordinarily, the next step in a civil trial with a jury consists of opening statements by attorneys for the plaintiff and for the defendant. The purpose of the opening statements is to outline the general nature of the case and to indicate the kinds of evidence to be offered, so that the judge or jurors may understand the significance of each item of evidence as it is introduced.

In some states the attorney for the defendant may elect to make an opening statement after plaintiff's evidence has been presented and before the defendant presents any evidence. In doing so, defense counsel attempts to confute testimony just given as he uses it as background for evidence that the defense will present.

Presentation of Evidence. The plaintiff proceeds next to introduce evidence to prove the allegations of the complaint. The word evidence is used in different senses. As used here, *evidence* means *anything presented at the trial for the purpose of inducing belief in the truth or falsity of some contention.* The two chief methods of inducing belief are testimony of witnesses and physical evidence. *Testimony* is secured by calling a witness, swearing the person in, and asking the person questions.

Degree of proof required. There is an important difference in the degree of proof required to win a civil lawsuit and the degree of proof required to win a criminal case. Most of us are familiar with the statement that in order to convict a defendant of a criminal offense, the prosecutor must prove the facts "beyond a reasonable doubt." In other words, if the judge or jury is not overwhelmingly convinced of the defendant's guilt, the defendant must be acquitted. In a civil lawsuit the plaintiff must prove his or her case "by a preponderance of the evidence." This ordinarily means that the plaintiff's evidence simply must be more credible than the defendant's evidence. Thus, the standard of proof is lower in civil cases and easier to achieve. This explains in part why a defendant may be acquitted of a crime (say, assault and battery) and yet be liable to a plaintiff in a civil suit based on the same set of circumstances.

Types and rules of evidence. The primary method of proving facts in a civil lawsuit is to present the testimony of witnesses. When a witness is put on the stand, the person is first examined by the attorney who called the person as a witness. This is called *direct examination* and is followed by a *cross-examination* conducted by the attorney for the other side. Ordinarily, the purpose of cross-examination is to show the witness's lack of credibility, by, for example, casting doubt on his or her powers of observation. The attorney may try to impeach the witness by showing that the witness's answers on the stand differ from those given in a deposition or interrogatories. The cross-examination may be followed by a *redirect examination,* in order to give the witness an opportunity to explain or modify answers given on cross-examination. The trial judge has discretion to allow the examination to proceed to a re-cross-examination, or even beyond.

In addition to presenting witnesses' testimony to prove facts, it may be necessary to present physical evidence. Physical evidence may consist of objects or documents which have been verified as authentic. Items of physical evidence are called *exhibits* and are tagged with a number for future reference (e.g., "Plaintiff's 1"). The rules of evidence governing the introduction of exhibits and the testimony of witnesses are numerous and technical. These rules may be the basis for a party to "object" to a question of a witness or to the introduction of physical evidence, the judge then either *sustaining* or *overruling* the objection. Many of the rules are designed to protect a jury of lay persons from irrelevant and prejudicial material.

Motions at close of evidence. After the plaintiff has called all witnesses for the plaintiff's side and has introduced all physical evidence desired, the plaintiff "rests." At this point the defendant may make a *motion for nonsuit* (in some states called *a motion to dismiss*). By such a motion the defendant contends that the plaintiff has failed to prove his or her case, as outlined in the complaint and opening statements. If the judge agrees, a judgment of nonsuit is entered in favor of the defendant. If the judge does not agree, the motion will be denied, and the defendant proceeds to introduce evidence to contradict the plaintiff's evidence. The defendant calls witnesses and introduces physical evidence in the same manner as the plaintiff did.

When there is a trial by jury, either party, or both, may make a *motion for directed verdict* at the close of defendant's evidence. By such a motion a party contends that the facts proved are so clear that reasonable people could not differ as to the outcome of the case. If the judge directs a verdict for a party, the judge thereby takes the case away from the jury and then enters a judgment for the party who made the motion. If neither party moves for a directed verdict, the judge may on his or her own motion order a directed verdict.

Closing Arguments of Counsel. After all evidence is presented, the attorneys for each party are allowed to make final or closing arguments. These usually take place before the judge's charge to the jury. In the final argument, each attorney will review the evidence produced by his or her side and emphasize its adequacy and credibility, discuss the evidence produced by the other side to show its inadequacy and lack of credibility, and indicate the conclusions of fact that may reasonably be drawn from the evidence.

Charge to the Jury. When there is a trial by jury, the judge instructs the jurors after closing arguments by both attorneys as to the law to be applied in their deliberations. Normally the judge instructs the jury that its duty is to determine the facts of the case; to accept the law as stated by the judge; and, by applying the law so stated to the facts so determined, to reach a decision for the plaintiff or the defendant. These instructions are a guide to assist the jury in reaching a verdict. For example, the judge may say, "Negligence means the failure to exercise reasonable care to prevent harm to others. If you find that the defendant drove his car 80 miles per hour in a residential area, you must find the defendant has committed the tort of negligence."

Attorneys may, and often do, submit to the judge written instructions which they request the judge to include in the charge to the jury. The refusal to include a requested instruction or to give the instruction in the wording requested is often the basis of an appeal to a higher court.

Verdict of the Jury. After receiving the judge's instructions, the jury retires to the jury room to consider the evidence and reach a verdict. In federal courts and in many state courts the jury verdict must be unanimous. Some states, such as California, authorize a verdict in a civil action to be reached by vote of three-fourths of the jurors. When the jury has reached its verdict, it returns to the courtroom and in the presence of the judge (and usually in the presence of the parties and their attorneys) announces its verdict.

The type of verdict just considered—that is, a verdict for plaintiff or defendant reached by applying the law as stated by the judge to the facts as found by the jury—is called a *general verdict.* If a general verdict is given for the defendant, the jurors' functions terminate; if the verdict is for the plaintiff in a civil action for damages, the jury must fix the amount of damages to which the plaintiff is entitled.

Another type of verdict is a *special verdict.* Such a verdict generally consists of answers to specific questions asked by the judge without any attempt to reach a decision for either party. The judge then decides the case by applying the law to the facts as given in the special verdict.

Judgment; Motions after Trial. The last step in the trial of a case is the judgment. A *judgment* is the decision of the court. The judge might simply state that the defendant is liable to plaintiff for $100,000. Often, after the judgment in a jury trial is entered in the court records, the losing party will make a *motion for judgment notwithstanding the verdict,* also called a judgment *non obstante veredicto* (n.o.v.). The judge will grant the motion and enter judgment for the losing party only if there is no substantial evidence to support the decision of the jury. In some states the judge on his or her own motion may reject the jury verdict and enter a judgment for the other party. The party whose verdict is overturned usually will appeal to a higher court.

After the judgment is entered, a *motion for a new trial* may be made by either party. There are several grounds upon which to make a motion for new trial. If the plaintiff has won the case, the defendant may move for a new trial on the grounds that the judge committed prejudicial error in the conduct of the trial or that the damages assessed are excessive. For example, the defendant may claim that the judge improperly refused to allow the defendant to introduce important evidence at the trial. A party may be granted a new trial if the other party, or the party's attorney, was guilty of prejudicial misconduct during the trial. However, a party is not entitled to a new trial if the party's own attorney was negligent or incompetent. A new trial may be granted where the losing party shows new evidence was discovered after the trial. However, the party must prove that the evidence is significant and could not have been obtained before trial by due diligence. The plaintiff, although the winner, may move for a new trial on the ground that the damages awarded are insufficient under the evidence.

If a motion for a new trial is granted by the judge, the case is again put on the trial calendar. Eventually it will be set for trial before another judge or jury. If the motion is denied, the moving party may appeal. In certain instances, the judge may order a denial of a new trial if the plaintiff consents to a reduction in the amount of the judgment (called a "remittitur"). Or the judge may order a new trial unless the defendant consents to an increase in the amount of the judgment (called an "additur").

Appeals

After the entry of judgment, the party who feels dissatisfied by the outcome may file an appeal. Normally the loser appeals; sometimes the winner appeals (e.g., the plaintiff may allege that the damages awarded were inadequate under the evidence); occasionally both parties appeal. The party who files an appeal is called the *appellant.* The other party is called the *appellee,* or the *respondent.*

In the cases you will be reading in the following chapters the appellant's name usually appears first (e.g., *Jekyl v. Hyde*). The order of the names probably will not be the same as appears in the trial court, and this may cause some confusion. Suppose, for example, that Hyde sued Jekyl in the superior court. The case would be entitled *Hyde v. Jekyl.* Hyde would be the plaintiff and Jekyl the defendant. If Hyde won the case and Jekyl appealed, the appeal case would usually be retitled *Jekyl v. Hyde.*

Review of the Case. The appellate court does not retry the case. No new evidence is allowed and there is no jury. The appellate court reviews the case as conducted in the trial court to see if any error of law or of conduct was committed. Usually the appellate court limits review to such questions as: Did the trial judge properly exclude or admit evidence, follow proper procedure, or state or apply the law accurately? If the trial judge committed error, was the error serious enough to warrant reversal of the judge's decision?

Sometimes an appellate court conducts a limited review of the facts found by the trial court. Such a review is necessary in deciding whether a summary judgment or a judgment n.o.v. was warranted. It should be noted, however, that an appellate court will not overturn a trial court's ruling unless the ruling is in serious disharmony with the evidence. The trial judge and jury, having the witnesses physically present, are in a better position than an appellate court to evaluate the credibility of witnesses. The appellate court therefore does not reweigh the evidence. The appellate court reviews the complete record of the trial of the case and listens to oral arguments by the attorneys for both parties, who also submit written "briefs" to support their arguments.

Decision and Opinion. After consideration of the record and the arguments made, the appellate court announces its decision (judgment) in writing. This decision is ordinarily accompanied by a written opinion in which the court explains the basis or reasons for its decision. If the appellate justices do not agree unanimously, a dissenting opinion may be written. Some cases presented in this text contain a majority opinion or "holding" of the case, followed by a dissenting or "minority" opinion.

The decision by an appellate court ordinarily takes one of three forms: (1) If the appellate court finds that no error of law has occurred, it will *affirm* the judgment of the trial court. (2) If prejudicial error is found, the appellate court may *reverse* or *modify* that judgment. (3) When the evidence does not clearly justify a decision for one party or the other, the appellate court may *reverse* and *remand* the judgment of the trial court. To remand the case means that the appellate court directs the trial judge to hold a new trial or to take other action regarding the case.

The opinions of the highest appellate courts of each state are published in two places: (1) in the official state reports, and (2) in a series of books called *The National Reporter System,* where opinions are grouped by geographic areas of the United States. For example, turn to page 54 where the first case in this book appears. The letters and numbers under the case name are called the *citation.* The citation 499 N.E.2d 678 means the full text of the case is printed in volume 499 of the *Northeastern (Second) Reporter* beginning at page 678. The words and numbers in parentheses following the citation show that the case was decided by the Illinois Supreme Court in 1986.

Arbitration as an Alternative to Civil Litigation

The courts in many states are crowded with cases, and there is a long wait for litigants to get to trial. The costs of civil litigation sometimes are staggering. Attorneys' fees, cost of depositions, and fees of expert witnesses are but a few of the items each party to a suit must pay for. Often, the parties to a dispute will avoid litigation by a process called *arbitration.*

Arbitration is a nonjudicial method of resolving civil disputes. Rather than file a lawsuit, the disputing parties agree to let a neutral third party decide who is right and who is wrong. The parties select an arbitrator or sometimes a panel of three arbitrators. The arbitrator may be a retired judge or a person who is skilled in an area that is the subject of dispute. For example, if two parties have a disagreement involving the performance of a construction contract, they may choose a licensed contractor as an arbitrator. An arbitrator's decision, called an "award," is binding on the parties and is subject to only a limited judicial review. Usually a party must show an illegal award, fraud, or gross mistake in order to obtain a judicial review. Absent such showing, the arbitrator's award has the force and effect of a judgment at law.

As an alternative to litigation, arbitration of disputes has a number of advantages. Usually it is less formal (e.g., the rules of evidence are greatly relaxed), is more efficient (e.g., the parties do not have to wait years for a courtroom), and is less expensive than litigation (e.g., there are no jury fees to pay, and attorney fees are much lower).

However, there are several disadvantages to arbitration. There is no right to a jury and only limited right to appeal an arbitrator's award. The presiding officer usually is not a judge trained in the law and rules of evidence, and evidence allowed may not be subject to the same strict rules of scrutiny as prevail in a court trial. For example, hearsay evidence which may be prejudicial to a party is not allowed in a court of law, but might be permitted at an arbitration hearing.

In rare instances and as a means of alleviating increasing court congestion, arbitration may be imposed by law (state or federal legislation) and is called *compulsory arbitration.* It is usually limited to public-interest emergency disputes between public employees—such as police officers, fire fighters, or teachers—and their employers. Compulsory *judicial arbitration* statutes provide that cases where the plaintiff is asking for damages under a certain amount, usually $20,000 to $25,000, shall be decided by arbitrators who usually are attorneys and who apply the same rules of evidence that are used in a judicial trial. A party who is not satisfied with the arbitrator's award may appeal and demand a judicial trial.

Although compulsory judicial arbitration is new and the right to appeal is liberal, the results thus far are positive. In most states arbitration has significantly reduced the number of cases awaiting judicial trial.

Summary

Courts are established to decide actual controversies between parties, not to answer hypothetical questions. In order to process a case, a court must have jurisdiction over the subject matter and jurisdiction over the property or the parties.

In our dual system of federal and state governments, there is a federal court system and a system of state courts. In some classes of cases the federal courts have exclusive jurisdiction, in others the state courts have exclusive jurisdiction, and in still others the federal and state courts have concurrent jurisdiction. The federal court system consists of district courts, courts of appeals, the Supreme Court, and various special courts. The state court systems typically include several types of trial courts, intermediate appellate courts, and a supreme court.

When a dispute is not settled by an agreement out of court and litigation results, the parties must follow a lengthy series of civil procedures before, during, and after a court trial. However, where there is no recognized cause of action or no material question of fact for a judge or jury to decide, judgment can be awarded in the pleadings stage of litigation. During a trial there are various times a party may make motions to terminate the proceedings without further action. After judgment the losing party may make a motion for judgment n.o.v. or may make a motion for new trial. Judgments at the various stages of litigation can be appealed to higher courts.

The function of an appellate court, state or federal, intermediate or supreme, is to review the case as conducted by the trial court to see if any error of law was committed. The appellate court may affirm the decision of the trial court, reverse the decision, or reverse and remand the case for a new trial.

Arbitration, an alternative to litigation with the force and effect of law, is a nonjudicial method of resolving disputes by private, disinterested persons. There are both advantages and disadvantages to arbitration. Compulsory arbitration is usually limited to public-interest emergency disputes and to cases filed where the plaintiff asks for damages below $20,000 to $25,000.

Review Questions

1 (**a**) What is the main function of a court? (**b**) What is the purpose of a declaratory judgment? (**c**) Explain how an action for declaratory judgment is consistent with a court's main function.

2 (**a**) What is the general meaning of jurisdiction? (**b**) Describe and give an illustration of jurisdiction over the subject matter. (**c**) Define personal jurisdiction and explain when it is required.

3 (**a**) List and explain the circumstances under which a court may exercise jurisdiction over a citizen of another state. (**b**) Explain the difference between a person's domicile and his or her residence.

4 (**a**) Give two examples of classes of cases over which the federal courts have exclusive jurisdiction. (**b**) What is required for a federal court to have jurisdiction over a case involving citizens of different states? (**c**) To what extent do the *state* courts have jurisdiction over cases involving citizens of different states?

5 **(a)** Describe the work of the following federal courts: district courts, courts of appeals, and the Supreme Court. **(b)** Explain who appoints federal judges and state the length of their terms of office.

6 **(a)** Describe the courts commonly found in a state court system. **(b)** How are vacancies filled? **(c)** What ethical question might a judge face who campaigns for election?

7 **(a)** What is the purpose of the pleading stage of litigation? **(b)** What is the "prayer"? **(c)** Describe how process may be served on a defendant.

8 Explain what happens after a judge: **(a)** sustains a demurrer: **(b)** overrules a demurrer.

9 **(a)** List the items a defendant may include in an answer. **(b)** What is a counterclaim? **(c)** What happens if a plaintiff fails to answer a counterclaim? **(d)** Why do you think states allow, or even encourage, counterclaims?

10 **(a)** What is the purpose of a summary judgment? **(b)** Describe a circumstance for which a judge will grant a motion for summary judgment?

11 **(a)** What is the purpose of discovery devices? **(b)** Explain the purpose and use of "deposition," "interrogatory," and "request for admission of facts."

12 What are the purpose of a pretrial conference?

13 **(a)** Briefly describe the difference between opening and closing arguments in a trial. **(b)** Explain the difference between the degree of proof required to win a civil lawsuit and the degree of proof required for a conviction in a criminal case. **(c)** What is a motion for nonsuit? **(d)** What is a motion for directed verdict?

14 **(a)** Explain the difference between a general verdict and a special verdict? **(b)** What is a judgment? **(c)** What is a "judgment n.o.v"? **(d)** What are the typical grounds for a motion for a new trial?

15 **(a)** Explain how a plaintiff becomes an appellant; an appellee **(b)** What is the function of an appellate court? **(c)** How does it perform this function?

16 **(a)** Define "arbitration." **(b)** List the advantages of arbitration. **(c)** List the disadvantages of arbitration. **(d)** Why do you think a party might wish to have a trial by jury rather than an arbitration proceeding?

PART TWO

Tort and Criminal Law

CHAPTER 4

Nature of Torts; Intentional Torts

Most torts are committed unintentionally, either because a person is not paying attention to what he or she is doing or because the person does not know that the particular act is a tort. The moral is clear: to avoid tort liability we need to acquire a basic knowledge of the nature of torts and of the law relating to the most important types of torts.

The law of torts is designed to give redress to individuals and business firms from civil wrongs other than breach of contract. It is especially important to the businessperson, who may become the victim of a tort at one time or another or may intentionally or unintentionally commit a tort. A businessperson may also be responsible to others for torts committed by employees and agents. The proprietor of a small business, as well as the multinational corporation, continually risks being sued in tort by a customer, a fellow businessperson, or a member of the public.

Nature of Torts

Meaning of Torts

A *tort* has been defined as "a civil wrong other than breach of contract, for which the court will provide a remedy in the form of an action for damages."[1] In each state the courts and legislatures determine which civil wrongs are actionable. New torts are recognized from time to time, existing torts are applied to new fact situations, and common law torts are abolished as social conditions change. That is, as social needs change, the law of torts changes. For example, invasion of privacy was not generally accepted as a tort until the 1930s. Also, a number of torts based on interference with family relations, such as breach of promise to marry and alienation of affections, are no longer recognized in many states.

Tort liability is based on conduct that is socially unreasonable, and because what is unreasonable depends on point of view, judges and legislators must strike a balance between an injured person's claim to protection (of person or property) and an accused person's claim to freedom of action.

[1] *Prosser and Keeton on The Law of Torts*, 5th ed., West Publishing Company, St. Paul, 1984, p. 2.

Crimes Distinguished from Torts

A crime and a tort are often similar, and the same act may constitute both a tort and a crime. For example, "unjustifiably confining another person within fixed boundaries" is both the tort and crime of "false imprisonment." In such a case the perpetrator may be prosecuted for criminal offense—in which the victim is only a state's witness—and at the same time be sued for damages in civil court by the victim.

To prevent confusion, remember the following:

1 A *crime* is an offense against the sovereign authority, i.e, against the state.
2 A crime is prosecuted by the local, state, or federal government.
3 A crime may involve harm to the person or property of another—similar to tort offense—or be violation of a statutory prohibition.
4 A crime is usually punished by fine or imprisonment or both.

In contrast, a *tort* is a civil wrong—an unreasonable interference with private rights—and suit is brought by the injured party. In a civil suit for tort the plaintiff may request both *compensatory damages*—to cover medical bills, lost wages, mental distress, other actual costs—and *punitive damages*. Punitive damages may be awarded if the defendant's conduct was willful, malicious, or particularly oppressive, and are imposed to punish a defendant and to set an example that will deter others from such extreme misconduct.

Until Chapter 7, when we discuss criminal activities involving business organization, our focus is solely on torts.

Classes of Torts

The civil wrongs recognized as torts in contemporary law are classified according to the nature of the wrongdoer's conduct and are grouped into two main classifications: *intentional* torts and *unintentional* torts. The major intentional torts, which will be discussed in this chapter, are:

- Intentional harm to the person
- Intentional harm to property
- Fraud as a tort

The major unintentional torts, to be discussed in the next chapter are:

- Negligence
- Liability without fault

Interference with commercial or business rights, called *business torts* and broadly grouped as "unfair competition," is discussed in Chapter 6.

Intentional Harm to the Person

Of the major intentional torts involving harm to the person, battery is the only one in which physical contact with the injured person's body is essential. The other intentional torts involve interference with the person's peace of mind or injury to reputation.

Battery

The tort of *battery* can be defined as the intentional, harmful or offensive touching of another person without consent or legal justification. The harm may range from permanent disfigurement to merely removing a person's hat without permission or grabbing a plate out of someone's hand. The degree of harm suffered by a victim will often determine the type of damages requested in a lawsuit. If the action of the defendant was willful, malicious, or particularly oppressive, the plaintiff may ask for punitive damages.

In an action for battery there are two major defenses available to the defendant: consent and privilege. The plaintiff's consent may be expressed by words or implied from conduct. Situations where implied consent occurs are in athletic contests, such as boxing, football, and baseball, where the participants are assumed to consent to the physical contact normally associated with the sport. However, whether the consent is express or implied, the tort of battery may occur if a party exceeds the consent given.

A common situation presented to the courts involves medical surgery. Let us suppose that Mrs. Abel consents to have Dr. Barr perform an operation on her nose. While Mrs. Abel is unconscious and under an anesthetic, Dr. Barr decides that she would look much better if her eyelids were also altered, and he performs this procedure. Dr. Barr may be held liable for the tort of battery.

A person's intentional touching of another without consent may be excused if such conduct is "privileged." The most common privilege asserted is self-defense, which allows one to use reasonable force to prevent personal harm. The privilege applies where the defendant is in actual danger of harm and also where there is no danger but the defendant reasonably believes there is. The privilege is limited to the use of force which reasonably appears to be necessary to protect against the threatened injury. In many states the privilege of using reasonable force extends to defense of a third person who is in immediate danger of attack. Deadly force may be used only when the defendant has reason to believe he or she is threatened with death or serious physical harm.

The privilege of using reasonable force may also extend to the protection of property where there is danger of immediate damage or wrongful appropriation. Ordinarily, there is no privilege to use deadly force in protection of property. For example, a landowner is privileged to install a spiked wall or fence to prevent trespassers but may be held liable in tort if a thief is injured or killed as a result of the landowner's setting a spring gun or keeping a vicious watchdog at large.

Assault

The tort of *assault* may be defined as intentionally causing another to be in apprehension of an immediate battery. A battery need not follow an assault in order for the assault to constitute a tort. The two torts are separate and distinct. In most states a plaintiff in a tort action for assault may not recover damages unless he or she was aware of the defendant's conduct and felt threatened. Thus, a defendant would not be liable for pointing a loaded pistol at a plaintiff who thought that the pistol was unloaded.

Generally, in order for a plaintiff to establish that he or she was apprehensive, it must be established that the defendant threatened to use force and had the apparent present ability to carry out this threat. For example, suppose Ann makes an oral threat to shoot Bill while pointing a pistol at him that he believes is loaded. Ann is liable for the tort of assault even though she knows the pistol is unloaded.

Apprehension is measured from the point of view of a reasonable person. No legal redress is given to the unusually timid, nor is recovery denied to the unusually brave.

In an action for assault the defendant may assert the defenses of consent and privilege. These defenses, discussed in connection with the tort of battery, are equally applicable here. In an action for assault the defendant may not be held liable if the defendant proves he or she acted under the reasonable belief that an attack was imminent even if the belief was mistaken. Bill, above, need not wait until Ann pulls the trigger on the pistol; he is privileged to threaten the use of reasonable force to protect himself.

False Imprisonment

The tort of *false imprisonment* may be defined generally as intentionally causing the confinement of another without consent or legal justification. Situations involving false imprisonment include confinement caused by: (1) physical restraint on a person's movement, (2) threat of force to one's person or to a member of one's immediate family, (3) force or threat of force directed against a person's property, and (4) refusal to release a person from confinement when there is a duty to do so. Confinement ordinarily means a person is restricted to a limited area and lacks knowledge of a reasonable means of exit.

A situation involving false imprisonment often presented to the courts is one in which a retail merchant detains a customer suspected of shoplifting. Where an action is filed against a merchant for false imprisonment, ordinarily the merchant asserts the defense of "shopkeeper's privilege," alleging he or she was justified in detaining the customer. In order to avoid liability, the defendant must prove that he or she had reasonable grounds to believe the plaintiff committed a crime (shoplifting, petty theft). This reasonable belief by the defendant is referred to as *probable cause.* Even with probable cause, the merchant may be liable if the customer is detained for an unreasonable length of time or in an unreasonable manner.

The defendant in a false imprisonment action may avoid liability by proving the plaintiff consented to restriction of his or her movement. For example, if a store customer, after being accused of committing a crime, voluntarily accompanies the merchant to his or her office in an attempt to clear up the matter, the merchant has not committed false imprisonment.

The following case illustrates a typical lawsuit between a department store and a customer suspected of shoplifting.

CASE 4.1 Adams v. Zayre Corp. · 499 N.E.2d 678 (Ill. App. 1986)

FACTS Mary Adams entered the Zayre store with her daughter and son. Terry Jo Buckner, the store's security manager, testified that she observed Mary pick up a pink radio, walk across two aisles and put it into her purse. She picked up some underwear and then went to the domestics department where she selected two blankets. Mary then went with her daughter to the checkout lanes and paid cash for the underwear and blankets. Terry, still watching Mary, checked the domestics department to see if Mary left the radio there; then Terry and three security personnel confronted Mary after she left the store but no one asked Mary for a receipt. Terry testified that nobody touched Mary and that she willingly returned to the store. Mary testified that she was held by the arm until she returned through the entrance of the store where she was released and escorted into the security room.

In the security room the Zayre employees searched Mary's purse and her daughter's purse and found nothing. After about 15 minutes a man came in with Mary's blankets and sales receipt. He gave her the receipt and stated that the pink radio was not in the blankets. Mary asked to leave but the employees ignored her request. They were writing up a report and told her she would have to wait until they were done processing. After another 15 minutes a man came in and told her she could leave. She asked to leave through a back door because people in the store had looked at her and laughed when she was brought in.

CASE 4.1 Continued

Mary sued Zayre for false imprisonment and after a trial received a judgment for $2,500 compensatory damages and $30,000 punitive damages. Zayre appealed.

OPINION

STROUSE, J. . . . False imprisonment consists of the unlawful restraint, against a person's will, of that individual's personal liberty or freedom of locomotion. . . . Defendant [Zayre] is, however, afforded protection by sections 16A-5 and 16A-6 of the Criminal Code. [The statute empowers a merchant who has reasonable grounds to believe that a person has committed retail theft to detain such person in a reasonable manner for a reasonable length of time.] A court of review will not set aside a jury verdict on the ground that it is contrary to the manifest weight of the evidence where there is sufficient credible evidence in the record to support the jury's verdict. . . .

A review of the record reveals that plaintiff's [Mary Adam's] case in chief presents a case of false imprisonment. She testified that the security guard grabbed her by the arm after she exited the store. A minor struggle ensued, after which she was forcibly led back into the store and ushered to a security area. Four witnesses testified that she was under their forcible control.

. . . The record reflects that the jury could have found defendant's actions to be unreasonable—both in manner of execution and time of detention. "The use of unnecessary force on suspected shoplifters by store personnel, as well as rudeness and harassment of the suspects, have been factors upon which the courts have determined either that the manner of detention was not reasonable as intended by the statute or that a finding to that effect was supportable." . . . There was also corroborated testimony that defendant detained plaintiff for one-half hour—15 minutes of which was after they had concluded their search and investigation and determined that there were no grounds to continue holding the plaintiff. Further, based on the disputed testimony, the jury could have found that no reasonable grounds existed for holding the plaintiff. We therefore cannot say that the jury's verdict as to general damages was against the manifest weight of the evidence.

We last address defendant's contention that punitive damages are inappropriate. Punitive damages are permitted where an arrest is effected recklessly, oppressively, insultingly or willfully, with a design to oppress and injure. . . . The manner of plaintiff's apprehension has already been described. This apprehension was conducted in violation of the store's own guidelines as to the manner in which a suspect is observed and detained. These guidelines provide that a store security officer making an arrest must have continual and unbroken surveillance of a subject after the alleged taking, up to the actual apprehension of the subject. The officer must follow the suspect in such a manner as to have "both the subject and the merchandise under observation at all times. If the subject gets out of sight even for a moment the apprehension cannot be made unless another theft act is witnessed." Since the security officers thoroughly searched the plaintiff and found no radio, it can only be concluded that even if plaintiff had taken a radio, it was not in her possession at the time she left the store and she should not have been detained.

Also, the store guidelines for approaching suspected shoplifters were violated. The store policy as to approaching suspects is as follows:

> "Again, when the suspect reaches the sidewalk (outside the store) and the officer is sure of his case, this approach is suggested: 'Excuse me, my name is Sandy Smith, Store Security (showing I.D.). May I examine your cash register receipt for (describe the article or articles concealed).' When identification of the article has been established and examination of the receipt shows no ring-up, ask the suspect to return to the store to privately discuss the incident. If at all possible avoid touching the suspect. There are circumstances where this is necessary, sometimes the person needs to be coached along with the hand placed under an arm for direction and guidance through the store, BUT ROUGH TACTICS MUST BE AVOIDED."

CASE 4.1 Continued

The testimony of plaintiff and others was that this apprehension was conducted in a reckless, oppressive, insulting, and willful manner.... Here, the jury found a factual basis for the punitive award and we cannot say that the jury's award of punitive damages was against the manifest weight of the evidence....

JUDGMENT Affirmed.

Infliction of Mental Distress

The tort of *infliction of mental distress* can be defined as intentionally or recklessly causing severe mental suffering in another by means of extreme or outrageous conduct or language. Generally, extreme and outrageous misconduct means exceeding all bounds of decent behavior. For example, collection agencies have been held liable to debtors for outrageous high-pressure tactics, and landlords have been held liable to tenants for similar conduct. A person has been held liable for falsely telling a woman that her husband was seriously injured and in a hospital, thus causing the woman to suffer emotional trauma and physical injury.

The courts have been reluctant to impose liability on a defendant who utters obscene or abusive language. There are two reasons for this reluctance: a high regard for freedom of speech and the danger of encouraging groundless or trivial lawsuits. Thus, the citizen in contemporary society usually must face insults, annoyances, profanity, and discourtesy without legal redress. Although obscene or abusive language ordinarily is not sufficient grounds for a tort action, special circumstances may result in a defendant's being held liable. Innkeepers (operators of motels or hotels), common carriers (railroads, bus lines, airlines, etc.), and public utilities (telephone companies, power companies, etc.) have been held liable to patrons for language of employees that is profane, indecent, or grossly insulting to people of ordinary sensibilities.

In most states the plaintiff need not suffer physical illness in order to recover damages for the tort of infliction of mental distress. In recent years large awards have been made to plaintiffs who suffered no physical injury.

A defendant may be held liable for mental distress inflicted recklessly. For example, a defendant who without excuse inflicts a serious beating on another person may be liable to a member of the person's family who is present and suffers emotional distress.

Defamation

The tort of *defamation* can be defined generally as the unjustified publication of a false statement that tends to hold a person up to hatred, contempt, or ridicule, or to cause him or her to be shunned or avoided. To hold a defendant liable in an action for defamation, the plaintiff must prove that the false statement was "published," that is, communicated to someone other than the plaintiff. The publication need not be to a large group. Communication to a single person may be enough. For example, delivery of a message to a telegraph company for transmission is a publication to the employee receiving it.

Defamation involves harm to a person's good name or reputation in the community. In order to constitute a tort, the statement published must be of a nature to reflect upon the defamed person's character or to disgrace him or her. For example, it is defamatory to say falsely that a person is a drunk, a liar, or incompetent at his or her job. The courts have awarded damages to one accused of being a member of the Communist party, to one accused of refusing to pay his just debts, and to a kosher meat dealer accused of selling bacon.

No tort is committed if a defamatory statement is published about a person who is dead. While kin of the deceased might be embarrassed—even suffer mental distress—the deceased cannot suffer defamation.

Defamation requires a statement of fact, and thus no tort is committed if one voices a derogatory "opinion" about another. For example, it is not tortious to engage in name-calling, such as making an insulting reference to another's ancestry, where it is clear that the defendant is not calmly and objectively asserting a fact.

Types of Defamation (Libel and Slander). Defamation includes two torts—libel and slander. *Libel* is defamation committed generally by means of written communication. Libelous matter may be published in a variety of forms such as newspaper articles, verses, pictures, signs, motion pictures, cartoons, and caricatures. Libel may also involve conduct conveying a defamatory message, such as one person hanging another in effigy or a bank dishonoring a customer's valid check.

Slander is defamation committed generally by means of oral communication. The defamatory matter is expressed in spoken words and may be communicated person to person or by radio or television.

Occasionally it is difficult to determine whether the tort is libel or slander. The courts have held that transcribing defamatory language dictated to a stenographer is libel rather than slander. A defamatory statement made in the sound track of a motion picture is also libel.

Defenses. There are two major defenses to the tort of defamation: truth and privilege. In most states *truth* is a complete defense to a defamation action. For example, suppose Andrea maliciously and in bad faith publishes the statement "Charles is a criminal," and Charles is a convicted embezzler. Charles could not recover damages from Andrea for defamation. In certain circumstances, he may have a cause of action against Andrea for the tort of invasion of privacy. That tort is discussed in the next section.

The defense of *privilege* is based upon the idea that the defendant should be allowed to publish a defamatory statement in order to further some interest of social importance. In some instances the interest is deemed to be of such great importance that the defendant is given complete or absolute immunity regardless of motive or the reasonableness of conduct.

Absolute privilege protects the following: (1) Statements made in a civil or criminal action or quasi-judicial proceeding by the parties, witnesses, lawyers, judges, and jurors, as long as the statements are relevant or pertinent to an issue in the proceeding; (2) statements made by federal and state legislators performing their duties and by witnesses in legislative and quasi-legislative hearings; (3) statements made by superior officers of the executive departments and branches of the federal and state governments in the exercise of their duties (in some states the privilege extends to lower level state officers and local government officials).

The defense of *qualified or conditional privilege* is available to a defendant under circumstances deemed to be of lesser importance than those above. To avoid liability, the defendant must prove the defamatory statement was published to protect some recognized interest in good faith and without malice. Recognized interests include one's own financial interest, membership in an organization, credit standing, and employment record. The following have been held to be proper purposes justifying defamatory communications: to warn someone of the misconduct or bad character of a third person where there is a legal or moral duty to speak, and to give information to public officials in the interest of crime prevention or detection. The defense of qualified privilege protects communications between persons with a common interest, such as partners, corporate officers, and members of professional associations.

If a defendant abuses his or her qualified privilege, the plaintiff may hold the defendant liable in an action for defamation. The qualified privilege is lost if the defendant communicates defamatory matter to a person who has no legitimate interest in it. For example, suppose that an employer discharges an employee and later is requested by a prospective employer to give a letter of reference. If, in the letter the employer stated falsely that the employee was incompetent, the defendant may assert the defense of qualified privilege. But, if the former employer publishes the letter in a newspaper, any qualified privilege is lost.

The qualified privilege also may be lost if the defendant acts with malice or improper purpose. Malice may be express or implied. *Express malice* means the defendant acted from spite or ill will, not from a legitimate desire to further a recognized interest. *Implied malice* means the defendant acted recklessly, i.e., he or she had no reasonable grounds for believing the statement. Mere negligence, however, is not sufficient to constitute an abuse of a qualified privilege.

A *qualified constitutional privilege* exists to publish defamatory statements about a public figure or public official. The privilege is based on the constitutional protection given to freedom of speech and freedom of press. A defendant who publishes a false defamatory statement about a public official or a public figure may not be held liable unless the defendant acts with "actual malice." *Actual malice* means that the defendant knows the statement is false or shows a reckless disregard of the truth.

The courts have held that public officials are those high-ranking government officers, whether executive, legislative, or judicial, who control the conduct of government. No complete definition has yet been given but it is clear that low-level and middle-level public employees are not public officials. Police officers, however, are held to be public officials.

Public figures include two groups of people: (1) persons who have achieved fame and notoriety, such as sports figures and well-known entertainers; and (2) persons who voluntarily thrust or inject themselves into the forefront of public controversy in order to influence the outcome of issues, such as consumer advocates and environmentalists. Persons who are involuntarily put in the public eye, such as criminals or attorneys defending persons accused of heinous crimes, are not public figures.

The rationale behind the qualified privilege concerning public persons is that they have greater access to the mass media than do private persons and thus can counteract the effects of defamation. Also, those who inject themselves into public controversies must expect to be the object of public discussion.

The following case involves multiple defendants who assert several privileges.

CASE 4.2 Burke v. Deiner · 463 A.2d 963 (N.J. Super. A.D. 1983)

FACTS Burke was the executive director of the New Brunswick Parking Authority. In June 1976 Burke's young daughter, who worked for the Authority as a parking attendant, confessed to having stolen two bank bags containing her shift's receipts for two days. It was part of her job to carry the bags to the bank and deposit them in a chute. The incident received considerable notoriety and enabled Burke's political foes to focus public attention on his stewardship of the Authority's operations.

The city director of finances engaged Rosenthal and Attinger, accountants, to conduct a detailed audit. They had been the city's accountants for many years and made annual audits for the Authority. Their special audit, submitted to the Authority August 10, 1976, itemized ten specific "weaknesses and deficiencies in internal control" and made ten recommendations for correcting them. On October 28, 1976 the mayor filled two vacancies on the Authority board of commissioners with Glaser and Buono. At a meeting held later that same day, Commissioners Glaser, Buono, and Deiner removed Burke from office. The resolution charged him with "negligent operation of the Parking Authority, which borders on misappropriation or misuse of the property of the Authority and... serious inefficiency in the discharge of his duties" for failing to follow the recommendations in the special audit. The resolution referred to "serious accounting and financial problems... uncovered by the Accounting Firm of Rosenthal and Attinger.... "

In a separate lawsuit Burke was reinstated to his job with back pay. Then, Burke sued the three commissioners and the accountants for defamation (libel). The accountants claimed qualified privilege and the trial judge dismissed the suit against them. At trial, the commissioners' claims of privilege were rejected and the jury awarded Burke $2,000 compensatory damages and punitive damages as follows: $2,000 as to Deiner, $5,000 as to Buono, and $11,800 as to Glaser. The commissioners and Burke appealed.

OPINION BRODY, J.... Given plaintiff's [Burke's] position as executive director, there is an unmistakable implication that the alleged deficiencies [in the special audit] reflected adversely on his office, business or employment, and are therefore defamatory as a matter of law.... If given the opportunity, a reasonable jury could have found from plaintiff's evidence that some of the criticized practices and omissions alleged in the report were knowingly false or deliberately put in a false light. For example, the first item of "weaknesses and deficiencies" is the alleged failure to deposit cash receipts daily. Plaintiff and

CASE 4.2 Continued

his expert testified that this statement is based largely on the fact that the bank did not record deposits made after banking hours until the following business day....

The trial judge had to identify and apply three qualified privileges and immunities that protect the commissioners and accountants from liability even though their statements are legally defamatory.

Plaintiff had or appeared to the public to have a substantial responsibility for the conduct of governmental affairs and was therefore a public official.... As a public official plaintiff cannot recover from the commissioners or the accountants for the harm caused by their defamatory statements relating to his official conduct unless he proves with convincing clarity that the statements were made with actual malice—that is, with knowledge that they were false or made with reckless disregard of the truth. *New York Times Co. v. Sullivan*, 376 U.S. 254, 84 S.Ct. 710, 11 L.Ed.2d 686 (1964). The judge carefully and correctly charged the jury as to this federal standard of proof and definition of malice....

The judge was also correct in noting that plaintiff's evidence *prima facie* met the federal definition of malice as to the accountants' statements. Their familiarity with the Authority's procedures over the years lends credence to the claim that their alleged distortions were made in deliberate or reckless disregard of the truth rather than through innocent misunderstanding of the operations of the garages and parking lots.

...We reject the commissioners' claim of absolute immunity. [Ed. comment: Parking Authority commissioners are not superior officers of an executive department of federal or state government. Thus, at most they could claim a qualified or conditional privilege.]

The third qualified privilege or immunity to be identified pertains to the accountants' audit. "A communication made *bona fide* upon any subject-matter in which the party communicating has an interest, or in reference to which he has a duty, is privileged if made to a person having a corresponding interest or duty...." The purpose of this privilege is to encourage free discourse, by reducing the risk of a defamation suit where public policy considerations especially favor the communication. The special audit is such a privileged communication. The accountants were engaged as experts to report the results of their investigation so that important managerial decisions could be made.

This privilege, however, is lost when the communication is not made in good faith.... We have held that such a defamer is only protected by an "honest good faith belief in the truth of the report...predicated on reasonable grounds, and in making that determination consideration will be given to whether the information reported has been obtained from reliable sources and the investigation and evaluation of such information were reasonable under the circumstances." *Krumholz v. TRW, Inc.*, 142 N.J.Super. 80, 89, 360 A.2d 413 (App. Div. 1976).

The status of plaintiff as a public official affords the accountants the benefit of two privileges. The protection for a qualifiedly privileged communication is lost if the statements are not made in "good faith" which *Krumholz* defines essentially as absence of negligence. However, the protection afforded the critic of a public official is not lost unless the statements are made with "malice," which *Sullivan* defines as made with knowledge that they are false or with reckless disregard of their truth or falsity. We need not decide the precise scope of the accountants' qualified privilege. It is enough to say that the protection afforded by the privilege rises no higher than the *Sullivan* standard of actual malice. Plaintiff must therefore be given the opportunity to meet the federal standard of proof and establish the federal definition of malice to overcome the privilege afforded the accountants as critics of a public official....

JUDGMENT Reversed as to the judgment entered in favor of defendants Rosenthal and Attinger and remanded for a new trial of plaintiff's defamation claim against them. In all other respects the judgment is affirmed.

Invasion of Privacy

The tort of invasion of privacy sometimes involves interference with a right to publicity, sometimes involves harm to one's physical or mental solitude, and occasionally involves harm to a person's reputation in the community.

Invasion of privacy usually occurs in one of four forms: (1) The wrongdoer uses a person's name or likeness without consent for business purposes. A typical example is using a public figure's name or picture without consent to advertise a commercial product. (2) The wrongdoer unreasonably intrudes upon a person's physical solitude. Examples include illegal entry of one's home, illegal wiretapping, and unauthorized investigation of one's bank account. (3) The wrongdoer makes public disclosure of private information about a person which is offensive and objectionable. An example is publishing the history and the present identity of a reformed criminal. (4) The wrongdoer publishes information which places a person in a false light. An example is using improperly a photograph of an honest taxi driver in connection with a magazine article on cheating taxi drivers. When the information published is false and defamatory, the injured person may have an additional cause of action for defamation.

Several defenses are available to a defendant in an action for invasion of privacy. The defendant may assert that the plaintiff has no cause of action because the one whose interest is invaded is dead. Consent, express or implied, is a defense to a suit for invasion of privacy. The courts have held that an individual has no right of privacy while in a public place, that one impliedly consents to intrusion upon personal solitude after leaving one's abode. Thus, in the absence of special circumstances no tort is committed if a person's picture is taken while walking along a sidewalk or while sitting as a spectator at a public event.

A defendant in an action for invasion of privacy may assert a constitutional privilege to give publicity to public figures or to publish news or matters of public interest. A public figure's right of privacy is not given the same protection as that of an ordinary person. A similar loss of privacy is suffered by a person who becomes involved in a matter of public interest. For example, one who is the victim of a crime or the witness to a crime has no cause of action if he or she is identified in the news media and the person's personal and family background is exposed to public view. The courts permit this invasion of a person's privacy because there is a legitimate public interest in newsworthy events.

In the following case the court discusses the defenses available in a suit for invasion of privacy.

CASE 4.3 Kinsey v. Macur · 165 Cal. Rptr. 608 (Cal. App. 1980)

FACTS While Bill Kinsey was in the Peace Corps in Tanzania in 1966, his wife died when they were on a picnic. Kinsey was charged with her murder and spent six months awaiting trial. He was subsequently acquitted. The case attracted some notoriety, including articles published in *Time* magazine. In December 1971, Kinsey met Mary Macur at a cocktail party in San Francisco. At that time he was a graduate student at Stanford University and she worked at a medical institute. For the next five months Kinsey and Macur had a love affair. On April 5, 1972, Kinsey told Macur that he would no longer be seeing her since a woman was coming from England to live with him.

In the fall of 1972, Kinsey accepted a job in Central Africa. He and Sally Allen went to Africa and were subsequently married. Shortly before they left the United States, each received a letter from Macur stating in graphic terms how Kinsey had mistreated Macur. During the time the Kinseys were in Africa they received more letters. Other letters were received by acquaintances of Bill Kinsey and forwarded to him. Some letters accused Bill of murdering his first wife, spending six months in jail for the crime, being a rapist, and other questionable behavior.

CASE 4.3 Continued

On July 9, 1973, Sally and Bill Kinsey filed a complaint for invasion of privacy. On June 28, 1977, after a trial without jury, judgment was entered for Bill Kinsey for $5,000. Macur appealed.

OPINION

MILLER, J. . . . Courts now recognize four separate torts within the broad designation of "invasion of privacy": (1) the commercial appropriation of the plaintiff's name or likeness, . . . (2) intrusion upon the plaintiff's physical solitude or seclusion; (3) public disclosure of true, embarrassing private facts concerning the plaintiff; and (4) publicity which places the plaintiff in a false light in the public eye. . . . In the present case, only the latter two forms of invasion of privacy are alleged.

. . . Except in cases involving physical intrusion, the tort must be accompanied by publicity in the sense of communication to the public in general or to a large number of persons as distinguished from one individual or a few. . . . The interest to be protected is individual freedom from the wrongful publicizing of private affairs and activities which are outside the realm of legitimate public concern. . . .

Appellant [Macur] first contends that her mailing of letters to "perhaps twenty [people] at most" was insufficient publicity to justify a finding that respondent's [Kinsey's] privacy had been invaded. Since these mailings were ostensibly to only a small select group of people, appellant argues that the requirement of mass exposure to the public as opposed to a few people has not been satisfied. Appellant's contention misstates the applicable law. . . .

In the instant case, appellant, in her professed attempts to "tell the whole world what a bastard he is," sought to reach a large group of people whom she knew had nothing in common except the possible acquaintance of Bill Kinsey. . . . Recipients of her letters included the Kinseys, their former spouses, their parents, their neighbors, their parents' neighbors, members of Bill Kinsey's dissertation committee, other faculty and the President of Stanford University. Since this court believes these recipients adequately reflect "mass exposure" we decline to yield to appellant's claim of insufficient publicity. . . .

Appellant next contends that, even if respondent's privacy had been invaded, the invasion was privileged since Kinsey was a public figure. This status, she contends, was achieved "by virtue of his entry into the Peace Corps and through his trial for the murder of his first wife." Given this "public figure" status, she asserts that she may exercise her constitutional privilege to disseminate critical material if done without malice. . . . It is difficult to see how respondent could become a public figure simply because of his participation in the Peace Corps or his employment with the United Nations.

With respect to Kinsey's notoriety by virtue of his trial, respondent was involuntarily thrust into the public limelight through the unfortunate death of his first wife. Offered the opportunity to be released on bail, he declined in favor of waiting some six months in jail for his trial at which time he was acquitted.

In the leading case of *Melvin v. Reid* 297 P. 91, plaintiff, a prostitute, was charged with murder and acquitted after a very long and very public trial. She abandoned her life of shame, married and assumed a place in respectable society, making many friends who were not aware of the incidents of her earlier life. The court held that she had stated a cause of action for privacy against defendants who had made a movie based entirely on Mrs. Melvin's life some seven years after the trial. . . . Since Kinsey, like Mrs. Melvin, had been acquitted of the murder charge, there is a strong societal interest in allowing him "to melt into the shadows of obscurity" once again.

Appellant argues that her First Amendment rights of freedom of speech has been cut off by respondent's right to privacy. She points out that the "only social sanction available to a person wronged is exposure" noting that "people do not always relate damaging information about others in a detached, rational manner, particularly when they feel they have been victimized."

CASE 4.3 Continued

"The right 'to be let alone' and to be protected from undesired publicity is not absolute but must be balanced against the public interest in the dissemination of news and information consistent with the democratic processes under the constitutional guarantees of freedom of speech and of the press. [Citations.]" A review of the contents of Macur's letters yields very little that may be considered to be of public interest....

Little of what Macur wrote in her letters to the Kinseys and their acquaintances could be considered "newsworthy."... She falsely accused him of murdering his wife and of having spent six months in jail for the crime.... The fact that appellant "believed her own allegations" is not relevant to the issue of newsworthiness. Her admission in her opening brief that she had described her experiences with respondent in "graphic, if hysterical detail" is a gross understatement of the truth.

JUDGMENT The judgment is affirmed.

Misuse of Legal Procedure

There are three intentional torts involving misuse of legal procedure:

- Malicious prosecution of criminal action
- Malicious prosecution of civil action
- Abuse of process.

Often there is overlap between one or more of these torts and other torts discussed previously. For example, the wrongful filing of criminal charges may result in the accused being falsely imprisoned. But a person who initiates civil or criminal proceedings against another is given a large degree of freedom to make mistakes without being liable for a tort, thus reflecting social policy that encourages use of the courts for resolution of legitimate disputes and for bringing criminals to justice.

Malicious Prosecution of Criminal Action.

The tort of *malicious prosecution of criminal action* can be defined generally as instigating or encouraging criminal proceedings against another when three elements are present: (1) the proceedings terminate in favor of the accused, (2) there is no probable cause for the proceeding, and (3) the instigator has acted maliciously. The student should note that two proceedings are involved. The first is a criminal proceeding in which the person accused of a crime is the defendant; a civil proceeding follows in which the person accused of a crime is the plaintiff, the defendant being the instigator of the criminal charges. If the accused is convicted of the crime charged, he or she may not recover damages in a tort action for malicious prosecution.

As a general rule, the plaintiff in a malicious prosecution action must prove that the prior criminal proceeding terminated in such a way that it cannot be revived, such as by acquittal after trial. The second element, lack of probable cause, may be proved by establishing (1) that the defendant instigator of the criminal proceedings did not honestly believe the accused was guilty, or (2) that the defendant's belief was not supported by facts sufficient to lead a reasonable person to begin criminal proceedings. "Malice" as used in malicious prosecution actions does not necessarily mean hatred, spite, or ill will. The plaintiff need prove only that the instigator's primary purpose in bringing the criminal proceedings was something other than bringing an offender to justice.

The defendant may defeat an action of malicious prosecution by proving that although the criminal proceeding terminated in favor of the accused, the plaintiff was in fact guilty of the offense charged.

Malicious Prosecution of Civil Action.

The majority of states today recognize as a tort the wrongful initiation of a civil suit, usually called malicious prosecution of civil action. The courts generally require the same three elements to be present as in malicious prosecution of criminal action. However, in an action for *malicious prosecution of civil action* there is a fourth element: The plaintiff must prove that he or she suffered actual harm, such as the expenses incurred in defending the civil action or a loss of business.

Abuse of Process. The tort of *abuse of process* can be defined as the use of legal process for an improper purpose. For example, suppose that Cedric files suit for breach of contract against Donna, asking $10,000 in damages, and secures from the court a writ of attachment instructing the sheriff to take possession of her business worth $50,000. A *writ of attachment* is an order of court issued at the beginning of a lawsuit which enables the plaintiff to take possession of one or more of the defendant's assets. Attachment is justified only if there is a legitimate fear that by the time the lawsuit is concluded the defendant will have dissipated or hidden his or her assets. Here, if Cedric has no justified belief that Donna's assets will be unreachable and merely takes these legal steps in order to force a settlement out of court, he may be liable to Donna for the tort of abuse of process. Such misuse of process is a form of extortion.

There is no requirement that the civil action terminate in favor of the injured party or that there be an absence of probable cause. The typical misuse of legal process occurs while litigation is pending and the outcome uncertain. The initiator may, in fact, have probable cause to begin the civil action.

Intentional Harm to Property

Property as used in this discussion refers to things people own, such as land, furniture, and accounts receivable. (The law of property is discussed in Chapters 20, 21, and 22.) The phrase "harm to property" can be used in two senses: in the sense of physical harm (i.e., injury) to the property, and in the sense of wrongful interference with the possession of property.

Trespass to Real Property

The tort of *trespass to real property* may be defined generally as intentionally, and without consent or legal justification, entering upon real property in possession of another or causing an object or a third person to enter the property. *Real property* includes the land and all things imbedded in it or firmly attached to it, such as minerals, trees, fences, and buildings. Thus, one may be held liable in tort for walking across another's lawn, cutting down a neighbor's tree, or painting someone's barn without permission.

Real property customarily includes the airspace above the surface of the land and materials below the surface. Thus, a person may be liable for trespass by causing an object to enter the airspace of another without permission. For example, if Arnold has a large tree planted on his land the branches of which extend over the boundary line of his property into the airspace above the land of his neighbor, Betty, Arnold may be liable to Betty in damages for trespass.

A defendant may be liable for trespass to real property even though he or she acts in good faith under the mistaken belief that the land belongs to the defendant, or that he or she has the consent of the owner.

Trespass to Personal Property

The tort of *trespass to personal property* (sometimes called "*trespass to chattels*") can be defined as intentionally and without consent or legal justification taking or damaging personal property in the possession of another. *Personal property* as used here means movable or portable things, such as appliances or furniture. Thus, a person may be held liable in tort for taking another's kettle or car without permission. The tort of trespass to personal property usually involves temporary use of an item or slight harm to the item. The plaintiff's damages ordinarily would be the value of loss of use of the item and any drop in value of the item caused by the defendant.

Conversion

The tort of *conversion* can be defined generally as intentionally and without legal justification seriously interfering with possession of the personal property of another. The essential difference between conversion and trespass to personal property is the degree of harm caused by the defendant. The following illustrate acts that give rise to a cause of action for conversion: (1) Wrongfully taking possession of another's property for an indefinite period, as by stealing (2) Improperly selling or transferring possession of one person's property to another person, as by delivering goods to the wrong person (3) Lawfully acquiring possession of someone's property and later upon demand wrongfully refusing to return the property to the one entitled, as by a repair shop keeping goods until an exorbitant repair bill is paid (4) destroying another's property or substantially altering it so as to make it unusable, as by killing or maiming someone's animal.

A converter will be liable in damages even though he or she acts in good faith or under a mistake of law or fact. In an action for conversion the plaintiff need not prove the defendant had an evil state of mind or an improper purpose in interfering with possession of the plaintiff's property. Thus, an innocent purchaser of stolen property may be liable for the tort of conversion. However, if one innocently receives lost or stolen property merely for purposes of storage or transportation, the courts would not hold the warehouser nor the carrier liable. In such a case the defendant is not asserting ownership of the goods.

As stated above, conversion differs from trespass to personal property in the degree of harm caused by the defendant. This difference is reflected in the theory of recovery. In an action for trespass the plaintiff is compensated for the harm to property or for loss of possession. In an action for conversion the owner recovers the full value of the property at the time of conversion. Upon payment of the judgment, the converter becomes the owner of the property. Thus, an action for the tort of conversion is appropriate only when the defendant has so seriously damaged or interfered with the plaintiff's possession as to justify a forced sale of the article. An action for trespass is the appropriate remedy for minor interferences resulting in little damage to the plaintiff's goods.

The owner of converted property may not wish to sue for the value of the property but may want the property returned. Possession may be recovered by filing a lawsuit and, without waiting for trial of the case, having the court issue an order called a "writ of replevin." In some states the procedure is called "'*claim and delivery*.'" The plaintiff must post a bond to protect any legitimate interests the defendant may have.

The following case provides an interesting and unusual illustration of the tort of conversion.

CASE 4.4 Quealy v. Paine, Webber, Jackson & Curtis, Inc. · 475 So.2d 756 (La. 1985)

FACTS William Quealy inherited 1500 shares of New England Gas and Electric Association (NEGEA) common stock. He kept the stock certificate in a suitcase in his hotel room. A fire at the hotel forced him to move to another hotel. Sometime later he noticed that he had not received his quarterly dividend on the stock and immediately contacted NEGEA. He was told that the shares had been surrendered. Apparently, the stock certificate had been stolen from Quealy's suitcase.

Shortly after the fire at the hotel a man claiming to be Quealy talked to Donald Castrone, sales manager of a new car dealership, about purchasing a car. During their negotiations, the imposter stated that he wanted to buy the car with cash and offered to sell Castrone 1,500 shares of NEGEA, at a price below market value. The imposter claimed that he did not want to sell the stock through a broker because he wanted to avoid the usual delays in receiving cash for the stock. Castrone contacted his attorney, William Ryan, who in turn called Paine, Webber, Jackson & Curtis, Inc., regarding the steps necessary for Castrone to purchase the stock by private sale and then to sell it for cash without waiting the usual period.

Charles Bailey, manager of Paine Webber, checked with NEGEA and determined that the stock had not been reported as lost, stolen, or missing. Paine Webber then advised Ryan that in order to transfer the stock, it would require a notarized bill of sale.

CASE 4.5 Continued

Castrone and the imposter went to Ryan's home the following evening. The imposter signed the back of the stock certificate and a bill of sale which Ryan then notarized. The following day Ryan and Castrone took the papers to Paine Webber, where Godchaux, the office manager, reviewed the documents. Bailey then placed on the stock certificate a guarantee that the signature was that of the person whose name appeared on the face of the certificate (William Quealy). NEGEA would not accept the shares without the signature guarantee. Castrone then sold the stock for $24,885 cash. Castrone paid the imposter $24,000. Paine Webber earned a commission of $390.

Quealy filed suit against Paine Webber and NEGEA for conversion. The trial judge gave him a judgment for $32,437 for the loss of his shares, based on their value on the day before trial, together with $15,840 for lost dividends, and $15,000 in general damages. Paine Webber appealed.

OPINION

MARCUS, J. . . . A conversion consists of an act in derogation of the plaintiff's possessory rights, and any wrongful exercise or assumption of authority over another's goods, depriving him of the possession, permanently or for an indefinite time, is a conversion. It is of no importance what subsequent application was made of the converted property, or that defendant derived no benefit from his act. . . .

Without Paine Webber's signature guarantee, NEGEA would not have accepted the stock and Quealy would have remained the record owner. Paine Webber's signature guarantee was therefore a necessary step in the transfer of ownership and was a contributing cause of Quealy's loss. Internal regulations (Internal Control Memo #50) circulated to Paine Webber employees required that signature guarantees be made only where the employee either knows the individual or takes steps to verify his identity, such as by making a comparison of the signature to a signature card or other similar records. As a member of the New York Stock Exchange, Paine Webber was bound by that association's Rule 405 (also known as the "Know Your Customer" rule) which obliged the brokerage firm to use due diligence in knowing with whom it does business. Godchaux and Bailey testified, however, that they merely relied on the notarized bill of sale as proof that the signature of Quealy was genuine. Bailey guaranteed that the signature was that of the person named on the face of the certificate, although Paine Webber personnel did not know Quealy nor have a record of his signature and the certificate was not signed in their presence. Moreover, . . . none of the personnel had previously known Castrone.

Under these circumstances, it was not reasonable for Paine Webber to rely on the notarized bill of sale and take no further steps to verify the authenticity of Quealy's signature. In guaranteeing the signature of a person they did not know, who did not sign in their presence, and whose signature they did not compare to other existing records, Paine Webber employees acted in a manner inconsistent with Quealy's property rights. Paine Webber wrongfully assumed control over Quealy's stock and contributed to depriving him of its possession and was liable for conversion. . . .

The traditional damages for conversion consist of the return of the property itself, or if the property cannot be returned, the value of the property at the time of the conversion. . . . Where a commodity which fluctuates in value is converted, its owners should be given the benefit of better prices that prevailed within a few months afterwards. . . . Every act whatever of man that causes damage to another obliges him by whose fault it happened to repair it. . . .

The value of Quealy's NEGEA shares on the date they were wrongfully transferred by Paine Webber to NEGEA (December 9, 1977) was $24,885. Rather than following the general rule in conversion cases and measuring the shares' value as of the date of conversion, the trial judge awarded Quealy $32,437 for the lost stock, which represented its market value on the day before trial (December 13, 1983). The general rule accomplishes the goal of fully compensating the conversion victim in cases where the converted prop-

CASE 4.5 Continued

erty depreciates over time. In such instances, the victim is made whole by returning to him exactly what was lost. In the case of stock, which fluctuates in value, applying the general rule of damages will not always accomplish the goal of making the victim whole. Such is the case here. In order for Paine Webber to fully repair the damage caused, it must reimburse Quealy in an amount sufficient to enable him to repurchase exactly what was lost: 1,500 shares of NEGEA stock. . . . The trial judge thus properly awarded Quealy an amount commensurate with the value of 1,500 shares of NEGEA stock as of the day before trial.

Damages for mental anguish and inconvenience arising from the loss of use of property have been allowed in tortious conversion cases. . . . The award of general damages in a conversion case, if proven, is clearly supported by the jurisprudence. Quealy testified that except for a small disability pension, the dividends from the converted stock constituted his main source of income and his living conditions were drastically impaired by the loss of those dividends. He was physically unable to work, and on December 14, 1983 (date of trial), he had been without the dividend income for six years. There was ample evidence in the record to support a finding that Quealy suffered mental anguish, humiliation and inconvenience from the loss of use of his property. Therefore, the trial judge did not err in awarding general damages.

JUDGMENT The judgment . . . is affirmed. . . .

Fraud as a Tort

Fraud, which usually inflicts harm of a monetary nature, will be discussed again in connection with the law of contracts, Chapter 11. Here fraud is examined as a misrepresentation sometimes leading to the two major intentional tort classifications discussed above: harm to the person and harm to property. For example, fraud may play a part in battery, a defrauder misrepresenting himself or herself in inducing another's consent to physical contact, which consent allows battery to occur. And we have seen harm to property in *Quealy v. Paine, Webber, Jackson & Curtis, Inc.* above as an imposter fraudulently claimed to be Quealy and sold Quealy's property; this fraud also caused mental distress as cited in the case study. Thus we see that fraud can be an important cause for action in the law of torts.

Elements of Fraud

To recover in an action for the tort of fraud, sometimes called "deceit," the plaintiff must prove five elements:

1 A false representation of material fact
2 Knowledge that the representation was false
3 Intent to induce another to act
4 Justifiable reliance on the representation
5 Injury resulting from such reliance

The first three elements focus on the defrauder, the last two on the victim. Some of the elements are modified in some states, and only the most common provisions of the contemporary law are presented here.

False Representation of Material Fact. A person may misrepresent overtly by words or actions or covertly by concealment. A representation includes making an oral or written statement of fact and making a statement by conduct. Turning back the odometer of a car is a misrepresentation by conduct.

Historically, silence, or failure to disclose facts of which one has knowledge, was not treated as a false representation. Today, however, a growing number of exceptions to this rule reflect increasing concern for the consumer's right to full and accurate information. In one sense, a *duty to disclose* is a principle of ethical behavior that has been adopted as a rule of law. Thus, today in a business transaction one party is not permitted to tell a half-truth.

For example, if the seller of a lot improved with a residence knows there are two engineer's reports regarding the condition of the soil, one favorable and the other unfavorable, and the seller informs the buyer only of the favorable report, the seller has made a false representation of fact. Another example of false representation by concealment is the following: John makes a statement while he is negotiating with Carol which he believes to be true. Later John obtains information which indicates that the statement he made was untrue or misleading. If John enters into an agreement with Carol without disclosing the new information received, many courts would hold that his concealment constitutes a false statement of fact.

Material facts are important facts that would affect the person's decision in a transaction. In recent years many states have imposed a *duty of disclosure* in sales transactions where one party has knowledge of material facts not available to the other party and is aware that the other party is under a misapprehension because those facts are unknown. For example, in negotiating for the purchase of a residence, the buyer's decision would be affected by the fact that the house is infested with termites. If the seller knows of the defect and the sale is completed without disclosure of this fact, the seller may be held liable for damages in tort. However, a party is not required to disclose facts that are obvious or that could be discovered by reasonable inspection.

Fraud, a misrepresentation or concealment of a material fact, does not include faulty opinionating. A fact is something that exists now or in the past. Thus, a prediction—such as "This business will be profitable"—is not a statement of fact. As a general rule a person is not liable in tort for misrepresentations of opinion, value, or law.

Sellers of goods often make statements such as "this is the best television on the market," or "this is the most economical car on the market." Such statements are called "puffing" and are regarded as the sellers's opinion only. Each party to a business transaction is presumed to be able to form personal judgments and may not rely upon those of an adversary in the bargaining process. Statements of value (e.g., "my house is worth $100,000") ordinarily are not treated as representations of fact, nor are casual statements of law treated as representations of fact.

A person may be held liable for misstatements of opinion, value, or law where the circumstances make it probable that the other party would rely on the statements rather than on his or her own judgment. One such situation is where the parties have a relationship of trust and confidence such as between a client and accountant or customer and banker, or between family members. Another such situation is where one party claims to have superior knowledge which is not available to the other party. Thus, the ordinary person may be expected to rely on the opinion of a real estate broker as to the value of land or the opinion of an attorney upon a point of law.

Knowledge of Falsity. Knowledge of falsity exists not only when a person makes a false representation of fact with knowledge of the falsity but also when one makes a statement without any belief as to its truth or with reckless disregard as to whether it is true or false. Thus, a person who represents something as being true of his or her own knowledge but who is in fact completely ignorant of the subject is reckless and is treated in the law as knowingly making a false statement. Negligent unintentional misrepresentation is further discussed in Chapter 5.

Intent to Induce Action. For a plaintiff to establish a cause of action for fraud it must be proved that the defendant intended the plaintiff, or a class of persons to which plaintiff belongs, to believe and act upon the false representation. There is a trend in contemporary law to expand liability and allow recovery to persons who did not deal directly with the defrauding person but whose reliance on his or her representation should have been anticipated. For example, a seller of a car may be held liable not only to an immediate purchaser but also to a remote purchaser for a deliberate misrepresentation concerning an important aspect of the car (e.g., "this car has never been in a wreck"). Automobiles are frequently resold, and the seller should reasonably have foreseen that subsequent purchasers would rely on the representation.

Justifiable Reliance. Simply put, justifiable reliance means that the plaintiff acted *because of* the defendant's misrepresentation, and that the reliance was "justifiable." It is not necessary to prove that the defendant's misrepresentation was the sole cause of the plaintiff's loss. It is sufficient for the plaintiff to prove that the misrepresentation was a substantial factor in influencing his or her decision. Thus, there may be justifiable reliance where a plaintiff's decision to buy or sell an article was based on information obtained from several sources, including the defendant's false representation.

In some situations one may have difficulty in determining whether reliance was justified. Reliance is said to be justifiable if the plaintiff has acted reasonably and prudently. As a general rule the ordinary person may justifiably rely on representations as to the quantity of land or the quality or authenticity of merchandise without making an independent investigation. However, a plaintiff of normal intelligence, ordinary experience, and average education may not justifiably rely on representations that the average person by reasonable investigation should discover are false (as by looking under the hood of a car to verify the condition of the engine).

A defendant may be held liable for fraud if he or she takes advantage of a plaintiff knowing that the plaintiff is illiterate or unusually gullible. On the other hand, a plaintiff who has special knowledge, experience, and competency may not justifiably rely on the defendant's statements but must exercise his or her own judgment. As stated earlier, the ordinary person is not justified in relying on a defendant's statement of opinion or representation of law unless special circumstances are involved.

Resulting Injury. The damage suffered as a result of a person's false representation in a business transaction may be slight (loss of a few dollars) or serious (loss of valuable property). In a tort action for fraud the plaintiff must prove that the misrepresentation was the cause of the loss. Thus, if a plaintiff is fraudulently induced to purchase stock as an investment and there is a general decline in the stock market, the loss in value of the stock may not be recovered. The loss was not caused by false representation which induced the plaintiff to purchase the stock.

In the following case the court discusses the elements of a tort action for fraud and the calculation of damages.

CASE 4.5 Village Toyota Co., Inc. v. Stewart. · 433 So.2d 1150 (Ala. 1983)

FACTS Mr. and Mrs. Stewart (plaintiffs) telephoned Village Toyota and said they were interested in buying a Toyota. The salesman quoted over the phone a price of $5,400. When they went to the dealership to look at the car the salesman said some additional accessories had been added to the car and that the total price now was $5,800. The Stewarts indicated that they also wanted air conditioning and an AM-FM stereo radio. The salesman said he would allow $1,700 for their 1976 Mercury as a trade-in. The parties dickered over this, and eventually $2,200 was agreed on. The salesman then filled out a buyer order form and indicated the total price of the car with air conditioning and radio would be $6,700. He asked if the Stewarts would like to purchase the "Tender Loving Care" (TLC) warranty package at a cost of $217. The Stewarts declined. They signed the order form and indicated thereon that they did not want to buy the TLC package .

After all these negotiations, the Stewarts went to the office of the business manager, where the business manager discussed the TLC warranty program in more detail with them, and subsequently the Stewarts agreed to purchase the warranty. The manager then filled out a document showing an additional charge of $217 for TLC. The Stewarts took their new car and left, taking no documents except the window sticker. The window sticker showed a total price of $5,400 for the car, including the TLC option. After receiving the sale documents in the mail, the Stewarts realized that they had been charged twice for the TLC option: once in the sticker price and a second time by the business manager. When Mr. Stewart went to the dealership the manager and the salesman told him that the reason the $217 on the window sticker was not subtracted from the original price was that they had allowed more than the true value of the Mercury as a trade-in

CASE 4.5 Continued

allowance. The manager said the Mercury was worth $1,800 or $1,900. The Stewarts sued for fraud. The jury found for the Stewarts and awarded $217 compensatory damages, plus $50,000 punitive damages. Defendant, Village Toyota, appealed.

OPINION

PER CURIAM . . . The elements of fraudulent misrepresentation under [Alabama] code provision are: (1) a false representation, (2) concerning a material existing fact, (3) which is relied upon by the plaintiff, and (4) damage to the plaintiff as a result of the false representation.

As to the first element, . . . defendant maintains the salesman never explicitly told the plaintiffs [Stewarts] that the sales price did not include the TLC package. Defendant maintains that the plaintiffs were given a *total* package price including air conditioning and radio of $6,700. Further, defendant argues that the sticker price, which included TLC, should not be considered as forming part of the basis of this transaction. We cannot agree.

When the plaintiffs initially called the dealership, they were quoted the sticker price for this particular car, which included the TLC package. When they arrived at the dealership the sticker price was again the initial price quoted. Plaintiffs told the salesman that they did not want TLC added into the price of the Toyota. However, neither the salesman, nor the business manager, subtracted the cost of TLC from the total sales price. . . . Thus there was sufficient evidence of a misrepresentation in this case.

The defendant also argues that the fraudulent misrepresentation must concern a material existing fact which supplies the inducement or motivation for plaintiffs' action. . . . The plaintiffs repeatedly indicated that they did not want the TLC package and it seems fair to presume that they would not have accepted the deal if they had been told they were paying for an option which, at that time, they did not want. . . .

Defendant also maintains that the plaintiffs were not damaged as a result of the misrepresentation. Again, we disagree. Initially, the plaintiffs signed an order form indicating they were not being given TLC although the sticker price included a charge for it. They later agreed to pay an *additional* $217 (over and above the "package price" of $6,700) in order to obtain this option. We are of the opinion that the jury could have found that the plaintiff's actual damages as a result of this transaction were $217.

Finally, defendant argues that even if there was a material misrepresentation, the plaintiffs' reliance must have been reasonable under the circumstances. If there is knowledge, or notice of facts which would have excited inquiry, or surrounding circumstances which would have aroused suspicion in the mind of a reasonable person, a plaintiff cannot be said to have relied upon a misrepresentation and cannot recover. . . .

We agree with the general propositions of law cited by the appellant; nonetheless, we conclude that in this case the evidence was sufficient to support a finding that the actions of the plaintiffs were reasonable. The plaintiffs saw the sticker, which included a charge for TLC. They subsequently told the defendant's salesman they did not want this option; however they did want air conditioning and a radio. The defendant then quoted a total price for the car, which should have reflected only the options the plaintiff wished to purchase. There was no price breakdown given for any of these options. Therefore, under the evidence presented, the jury could have found that the plaintiffs were justified in thinking that the defendant had subtracted the price of the TLC and added the price of the air conditioning and radio in arriving at the total price. Thus, the plaintiffs' reliance on the defendant's misrepresentation was reasonable under these circumstances. . . .

The defendant also maintains that an award of punitive damages in this case is not warranted. It states that in order to allow an award of punitive damages the fraud must be gross, malicious, oppressive, and committed with intent to injure. . . .

We are of the opinion that an award of punitive damages in this case was justified. . . . plaintiffs repeatedly stated they did not want an option, were led to believe

CASE 4.5 Continued

they were not purchasing that option, but were nonetheless charged for it. We find this type of fraudulent conduct sufficiently gross to merit an award of punitive damages.

Damages in these cases are allowed not only to punish the defendant, but also for the purpose of protecting the public by deterring the defendant and others from doing such wrong in the future.... The practice described in this case is a customary practice at Village Toyota, according to testimony by defendant's witnesses at trial. Conduct of this nature is simply dishonest. According to testimony at trial, this continues to be the custom and practice of the defendant. An award of punitive damages by the jury may in some way deter this conduct in the future....

JUDGMENT Affirmed.

Measure of Damages for Fraud

In the typical fraud case the plaintiff has been induced to exchange with the defendant items of value such as money for goods, money for services, or services for goods. The measure of the plaintiff's loss is called *direct damages.*

In the United States two methods are used to measure direct damages for the tort of fraud. The majority rule is called the *benefit-of-bargain* rule. Under this rule the successful plaintiff recovers the difference between the value of the property or service received and the value it would have had if it had been as represented. For example, suppose Mary, a professional antique dealer, falsely represents a desk to be a genuine antique worth $1,000, when in fact, the desk is a cheap replica worth only $150. John, the plaintiff-buyer, relies on Mary's representation. Believing the desk to be worth $1,000, John haggles with Mary over the price until she finally sells the desk for $600. John takes the desk home still believing Mary's representation that the desk is worth $1,000. Under the majority rule, John would get the full benefit of the bargain. He would recover $850 in damages—the difference between the represented value of $1,000 and the real value of $150. Under the minority *out-of-pocket* rule, plaintiff John would recover the difference between the value of what he transferred to defendant Mary ($600) and the value of what defendant transferred to plaintiff—a desk worth only $150. Thus, John would recover only $450 under the minority rule. The majority benefit of the bargain view is based upon the idea that the buyer who is victimized by fraud is not fully compensated by the mere return of out-of-pocket losses, but he is entitled to compensation for the full value of the bargain he believed he was getting. The benefit of the bargain rule also punishes the fraudulent wrongdoer by imposing liability for more than mere out-of-pocket losses of the plaintiff.

In appropriate cases the plaintiff may be entitled to *special damages* (also called "consequential damages") and punitive damages. Special or consequential damages include specific losses caused by the fraud that are reasonably foreseeable. Suppose, for example, that Frank is fraudulently induced to buy a defective car from Barbara. If the car breaks down and Frank is forced to rent a replacement car, he could assert as special or consequential damages the cost of the car rental. In addition, the plaintiff may be awarded punitive damages in order to punish the defendant (Case 4.5) when the tort is willful, malicious, or particularly oppressive.

Summary

Tort liability is based on conduct which is socially unreasonable. Important in determining of what is unreasonable is the balance between an injured person's claim to protection and the defendant's claim to freedom of action. Various kinds of civil wrongs are recognized as torts in contemporary law, and they are classified according to the nature of the wrongdoer's conduct. The two main classes are intentional torts and unintentional torts.

The major intentional torts involving harm to the person are battery, assault, false imprisonment, infliction of mental distress, defamation (libel and slander), invasion of privacy, malicious prosecution of criminal action, malicious prosecution of civil action, and abuse of process. Battery is the only one of these torts in which bodily contact is essential. The remaining torts generally involve interference with the other person's peace of mind or injury to reputation. A plaintiff may request compensatory damages to cover medical bills, lost wages, and mental distress. If the defendant was willful, malicious, or particularly oppressive, the plaintiff may recover punitive damages. In an action for tort the defendant may avoid liability by proving one or more defenses, such as consent or privilege.

To constitute the tort of defamation, a false defamatory statement must be communicated to someone other than the one defamed. Infliction of mental distress and invasion of privacy may occur without communication to a third person. Truth is an absolute defense to an action for defamation but is no defense to an action for infliction of mental distress or invasion of privacy.

The torts of malicious prosecution of criminal action, malicious prosecution of civil action, and abuse of process are related to one another and to the torts of defamation and invasion of privacy. These five torts ordinarily involve harm to a person's reputation. A major difference between malicious prosecution of civil action and abuse of process is that an action for abuse of process may be brought prior to the conclusion of the civil action filed by the instigator. There is no requirement that the original action terminate in favor of the injured party.

The major intentional torts involving harm to property are: trespass to real property, trespass to personal property, and conversion. In an action for trespass the plaintiff is compensated for the harm to property or for loss of possession. In an action for conversion, the owner recovers the full value of his or her personal property. Replevin and claim and delivery are remedies to secure the return of the property.

Fraud sometimes plays an important part in the commission of torts involving harm to the person, but it usually arises in connection with business transactions where money or property is exchanged. The tort of fraud involves intentional misrepresentation of a material fact, committed by means of one's words, actions, or concealment, justifiably relied on by another to his or her injury.

Review Questions

1 Explain the difference between compensatory damages and punitive damages.

2 **(a)** Define the tort of battery. **(b)** List and explain briefly the defenses available to a defendant in an action for battery. **(c)** How does the privilege of self-defense differ from the privilege of protection of one's property?

3 **(a)** What is an assault? **(b)** Explain the statement, "an attempted battery is not necessarily an assault." **(c)** Give an example of a battery that is not preceded by an assault.

4 **(a)** Define false imprisonment. **(b)** Why is it important for a business person to have some knowledge of this tort?

5 **(a)** Define the tort of infliction of mental distress. **(b)** How does this tort differ from other torts that involve mental distress, such as assault and false imprisonment?

6 **(a)** Define defamation. **(b)** Why do you think publication is required in order to recover for the tort of defamation? **(c)** Explain the difference between libel and slander.

7 **(a)** List and give examples of three types of absolute privilege. **(b)** Explain qualified privilege and how it may be lost. **(c)** Explain the difference between implied malice and actual malice.

8 **(a)** List and give examples of the four main forms of invasion of privacy. **(b)** List and explain briefly the defenses to an action for invasion of privacy. **(c)** Explain the legal protection given to a public figure's right of privacy.

9 **(a)** List the three torts involving misuse of legal procedure. **(b)** Explain each of the three elements required in an action for malicious prosecution of criminal action. **(c)** What additional element is required in an action for malicious prosecution of civil action?

10 Define abuse of process, and explain how it differs from malicious prosecution.

11 **(a)** Define trespass to real property. **(b)** Explain how a defendant may be liable for trespass to real property without actually going onto the plaintiff's land.

12 **(a)** Define the torts of trespass to personal property and conversion. **(b)** Explain the major difference between these torts.

13 **(a)** List the five elements of the tort of fraud. **(b)** Explain how fraud may be committed by concealment. **(c)** Give an example of an opinion that may be grounds for an action in fraud. **(d)** Explain how a defendant who misrepresents may be held liable to someone he or she has never dealt with.

14 Explain both the majority rule and minority rule of measuring direct damages in a fraud action.

Case Problems

1 Mrs. Rice, while in the Super X Drug Store, placed makeup, lipstick, and cologne in a Rose's Department Store sack. At the checkout counter Mrs. Rice did not remove the items from the sack or offer to pay for them. As she was preparing to leave the store, Mrs. Rice was stopped and escorted to the employees' lounge. According to witnesses she admitted taking the three items, but Mrs. Rice testified that she thought she had paid for the three items and in any event had no intent to steal. The store manager called the police, and Mrs. Rice was taken to the police station where she was arrested. She was detained at the drugstore for 25 to 30 minutes. The trip to the police took some 5 to 8 minutes, and she was served with an arrest warrant some 5 to 15 minutes later. Mrs. Rice filed suit for false imprisonment and the jury returned a verdict in her favor, awarding her $75,000 as compensatory damages and $75,000 as punitive damages. Should this verdict be upheld?

2 Stephen D. Bloomer was a resident of Kansas Neurological Institute (KNI) for 13 years. Stephen contracted bilateral pneumonia and died. The county coroner told Stephen's mother, Mary A. Burgess, that an autopsy would be required. Dr. Perdue, who worked for KNI and had treated Stephen, asked Mrs. Burgess for permission to perform the autopsy and stated KNI would want to examine the brain. Mrs. Burgess agreed to a partial autopsy but told Dr. Perdue that she would not allow KNI to examine Stephen's brain. Dr. Perdue failed to inform the county coroner that Mrs. Burgess had consented only to a limited autopsy. The coroner performed a full autopsy and Stephen's brain was removed and sent to KNI. Three weeks after Stephen's funeral Dr. Heeb at KNI discovered the brain and called Mrs. Burgess. Dr. Heeb said KNI "had her son's brain in a jar" and asked her what she would like to have done with it. Stephen's body was exhumed and his brain buried with his body. Mrs. Burgess sued Dr. Perdue and KNI for infliction of mental distress. Who should win the lawsuit?

3 Brown gave a check to Skaggs for groceries. Skaggs failed to endorse the check, and it was returned to the store unpaid. It was sent through again without being endorsed and was again returned unpaid. Brown received a letter saying that as a result of the return of the check Brown's name was to be placed on a list of problem checks circulated by an organization called Check Verification Association of Central Oklahoma (CVA). Member stores reported to CVA all checks returned to them and held for seven days. CVA printed a list and circulated it to the members. Skaggs sent a report to CVA mistakenly showing Brown's check had been returned because of insufficient funds. For a month Brown's checks were refused at Skaggs and other stores and Brown made purchases with cash. Brown sued Skaggs for libel. Skaggs alleged privilege. Who should win the suit?

4 In 1964 the Maricopa County Board of Supervisors appointed Dale Dombey the county's insurance agent of record for health and life insurance. Dombey implemented and serviced life and health insurance programs covering county employees. He lobbied for creation of group insurance for county employees and, after a plan was instituted, continued to push for improvements. Dombey was not a county employee and was not paid by the county. He received commissions from the insurance carriers, which by 1978 were in excess of $55,000 per year. He also received commissions on all contributions by employees to a deferred compensation plan he was successful in getting the board of supervisors to adopt. In March and April of 1979 a series of newspaper articles was published in *The Arizona Republic* falsely asserting that Dombey was the man in "control" of Maricopa County's life and health insurance programs. The articles implied that he had made excessive commissions from the various programs he administered (one article alleged he had earned $150,000 each year), that he had "kept" employees' investment funds, and that he was under investigation by a grand jury. Some of the articles were written without talking to Dombey. Calls were made to the reporters complaining of inaccuracies and a full report, detailing all of Dombey's accounts and commissions was made to the board of supervisors and to the reporters. The newspaper continued to publish articles containing false allegations. Later, a document, 3 inches thick, was given to the newspaper detailing all its alleged errors and supported by extensive records. The newspaper, relying on its own prior articles, ignored the document and printed another factually inaccurate article. Dombey sued for defamation. The trial court held that Dombey was a private figure and the jury awarded him $600,000 damages. On appeal the defendant argued that Dombey was a public figure and that a qualified constitutional privilege protected publication of the articles. Are the defendant's arguments correct?

5 Martinez was a junior high school student. The *Democrat-Herald*, a newspaper, published a story discussing drug use in the local junior high school. Included were several photographs of what were called "apparent drug transactions" between junior high school students. Martinez was one of the students in the photographs. She sued for invasion of privacy alleging (1) the defendant used her photograph without consent for commercial benefit and (2) the publicity put her in a false light. At trial, the court allowed evidence to be introduced that Martinez was a user of marijuana. Evidence also was introduced showing that the newspaper's circulation had been decreasing and that it had laid off several employees. The story about drugs appeared in the "People" section of the newspaper rather than in the "hard news" section. Should the newspaper be liable for either of the two types of invasion of privacy alleged?

6 In October 1984 Francis Heneghan brought his 1973 Cadillac to Cap-A-Radiator shop to have his radiator repaired. He told Jim Peister, manager of the shop, that his radiator was leaking and asked how much it would cost to repair. Peister told him $59.95. No written estimate was prepared and no inspection of the radiator was made. Later that morning Peister telephoned Heneghan's wife and told her that upon inspection the radiator should be replaced, not repaired, at a cost of approximately $200. Mrs. Heneghan called Peister back and advised him that Mr. Heneghan did not want the radiator replaced or repaired. Peister then told her that there would be a $25 service charge for checking out the radiator and removing it. When Heneghan returned to the shop to pick up his car Peister said that the radiator was not reinstalled and that Heneghan would have to pay $25 to have it reinstalled. Heneghan left and the vehicle remained on the premises. In January 1985 the shop told Heneghan to pick up his car or he would be liable for storage charges. Heneghan sued for conversion. Should he recover?

7 Barbara retained John, an attorney, to represent her in a proceeding to increase spousal support and child support granted her in a divorce. On two occasions she and John had sexual intercourse with each other. Before they did so, Barbara told John that she would not engage in sexual relations with him if there was any likelihood of her becoming pregnant. John told her not to worry, saying, "I can't possibly get anyone pregnant." She understood this to mean that he was sterile by nature or as the result of a vasectomy. As a result of sexual intercourse with John, Barbara became pregnant. The pregnancy was tubal, and in order to save her life, Barbara's fallopian tube was removed and she was rendered sterile. Does Barbara have a cause of action against John for one or more torts?

8 Reed purchased a house from King. Although they were aware of its history, neither King nor his real estate agents told Reed that a woman and her four children were murdered in the house ten years earlier. King and the agent represented the premises were in good condition and fit for an "elderly lady" living alone. After Reed moved in, neighbors informed her that no one was interested in purchasing the house because of the stigma. Reed paid $76,000, but the house was worth only $65,000 because of its past. Do these facts satisfy all the elements required for the tort of fraud?

CHAPTER 5

Unintentional Torts: Negligence and Liability without Fault

Most people do not intentionally inflict harm on others. However, an individual or business firm may unintentionally harm the person or property of another and become liable in tort for damages. The two major areas of liability for unintentional acts are liability for the tort of negligence and liability without fault. The first part of this chapter is devoted to a discussion of the major legal aspects of the tort of negligence and the major defenses available. The last part of the chapter is devoted to several areas of liability without fault and the major defenses available.

Negligence

Nature of Negligence

There is no universal definition of the tort of negligence although many definitions have been given by legal writers, judges, and legislatures. For our purposes *negligence* is failure to exercise due care when there is a foreseeable risk of harm to others. The tort of negligence may be illustrated by the following comparison. A person who intentionally drives a car into another's car is guilty of the tort of trespass to personal property. One who carelessly drives a car at an excessive rate of speed and cannot stop it in time to avoid a collision is guilty of the tort of negligence.

Elements of Negligence

In order to establish a cause of action for negligence, the plaintiff traditionally is required to prove four elements:

1 The defendant owed a duty to protect the plaintiff against harm.
2 The defendant failed to exercise due care.
3 The plaintiff suffered actual loss or damage.
4 The defendant's negligence was the cause of the plaintiff's injury.

The law of negligence continually changes, and many states have modified these elements. The most common provisions of the contemporary law are examined here.

Duty of Care. A duty to protect the plaintiff against harm is commonly called a duty of care. There are many views among legal writers and judges as to who owes a duty of care and when the duty arises. For our purposes it can be stated that a duty of care arises whenever a person should foresee that his or her conduct will create an unreasonable risk of harm to others. For example, driving a car on a deserted highway at an excessive speed does not create a duty of care. By contrast, such conduct in a populated area creates an unreasonable risk of harm to others, and the driver owes a duty of care.

An important question is: To whom does the defendant owe a duty of care? The narrow view is that in order to establish a duty of care, the plaintiff must be within the "zone of danger" created by the defendant's conduct. If the defendant should reasonably have foreseen a risk of harm to this particular plaintiff or to a class of persons to which the plaintiff belongs, then the defendant has a duty to exercise due care to avoid harm to the plaintiff. On the other hand, if the plaintiff was outside the zone of danger, the defendant is not held to a duty of care. Thus, the "unforeseen plaintiff" who is injured by the defendant's careless conduct has no cause of action. For example, a person who carelessly starts a fire is liable for damages to the owner on whose land the fire is begun but may not be liable to an owner whose land is burned an unforeseeable distance away.

The following case discusses whether several defendants owed duties of care to the plaintiff.

CASE 5.1 Becker v. Barbour Blvd. Equipment Rentals, Inc. · 726 P.2d 967 (Or. App. 1986)

FACTS Carolyn Becker rented a rooftop bicycle rack from Barbour Blvd. Equipment Rentals, Inc. The rack, manufactured by Schwinn Bicycle Company, was selected and installed on the

CASE 5.1 Continued

roof of Becker's van by Rentals' employees. Later the same day, while Becker was driving with four bicycles in the rack, it fell off and came to rest in the center lane of the highway. Becker stopped and walked back to the vicinity of the rack and, while standing at the side of the highway, was struck by an automobile driven by Ronald Olson. Becker sued Rentals and its employees claiming they negligently failed to furnish a bicycle rack of the correct size and failed to fasten straps of a sufficient length to permit safe and secure mounting on the roof of her van. She joined Schwinn as a defendant, alleging negligent manufacture of the rack. The trial court dismissed the complaint for failure to state a cause of action. Becker appealed.

OPINION

DEITS, J. . . . In order to state a claim for negligence, a plaintiff must allege facts showing that the defendant owed the plaintiff a *duty,* that the defendant breached the duty and that that was a substantial factor in causing damage to the plaintiff. The question of duty is a matter of law for the court to decide. . . . [T]he issue of duty is concerned, not with the particular case, but with "the question of whether as a matter of policy liability should be imposed in the class of case before the court. . . . " Here, the *class* of case involves the duty of those who manufacture, rent or install products for use on automotive vehicles to exercise reasonable care so that their conduct does not create a foreseeable risk of harm to users of the product. Defendants' duties . . . are drawn from the general duty recognized in *Kirby v. Sonville,* 594 P.2d 818 (1979):

> [I]n general one owes the duty to every person in our society to use reasonable care to avoid injury to the other person in any situation in which it could be reasonably anticipated or foreseen that a failure to use such care might result in such injury.

. . . [D]efendants cannot be held liable for harm that reasonable persons would not foresee to be a risk of their conduct. . . . [I]f a plaintiff's injury is not of the general kind to be anticipated from a defendant's conduct, or if a plaintiff is not one of the general class foreseeably threatened, a court must rule that the defendant is not negligent as a matter of law. . . .

We conclude that a jury could determine that injury to plaintiff [Becker] was foreseeable, because defendants ought reasonably to have foreseen that improper design, selection or installation of a rooftop bicycle rack would cause the rack to fall off a moving vehicle, posing a hazard to traffic. Further, a jury could also find that they should have foreseen that the user would try to retrieve the rack and its cargo and might then be struck by a vehicle that was attempting to avoid it. Plaintiff's injuries were not unforeseeable as a matter of law. . . .

These are not the sort of improbable events (or parties) involved in *Allen v. Shiromal Leathers,* 514 P.2d 545 (1973), where the plaintiff, who had volunteered his assistance at the scene of a collision caused by the defendant, was struck by his own car as it was being parked by an unlicensed, under-age driver. It was held that that plaintiff was not of the general class of persons foreseeably threatened by the defendant's collision. The user of a bicycle rack, on the other hand, might be expected to retrieve it from the road, both for salvage and for safety. . . .

JUDGMENT Reversed and remanded.

Failure to Exercise Care. The judge or jury in a lawsuit for negligence must determine if the defendant failed to exercise due care. To assist in this determination, the courts have established a standard of behavior as that of a hypothetical "reasonable person of ordinary prudence." The judge or jury compares the conduct of the defendant with the presumed conduct of the ordinary prudent per son under the same or similar circumstances. If the defendant's conduct does not measure up to the model standard of conduct, the defendant may be held liable for damages for the tort of negligence.

The ordinary prudent person standard. Negligence is often described as the failure to do what the ordinary prudent person would do under the same or similar circumstances. The ordinary prudent person has been described as "a personification of a community ideal of reasonable behavior, determined by the jury's social judgment."[1] When evaluating the defendant's behavior, allowances are made if the defendant is handicapped with blindness, deafness, or other physical disability. In evaluating the conduct of a defendant who is a minor, the judge or jury does not hold the child to the same standard of conduct as an adult. The judge or jury determines what is reasonable to expect from children of like age, intelligence, and experience to the defendant.

Presumed experience and knowledge. When the judge or jury applies the ordinary prudent person standard, the defendant is presumed to have knowledge of certain facts. Every adult with a minimum of intelligence is presumed to know such things as: the fact that fire burns and that flammable objects will catch fire; the principles of balance and leverage as applied to the person's own body; the limits of the person's own strength; the normal habits, capacities, and reactions of other human beings; and the dangers involved in explosives, electricity, moving machinery, and firearms. Ordinarily, a defendant will not be excused if he or she denies knowledge of these facts. The courts generally impose this minimum standard of knowledge based on what is common to the community. In addition, a defendant is presumed to know the limits of his or her own knowledge and in certain circumstances may be held liable for negligence for proceeding in the face of ignorance. For example, a lay person may be negligent in attempting to give medical treatment.

A person who possesses or claims to possess superior knowledge or skill is held to a higher standard of conduct than the ordinary prudent person. Physicians, dentists, attorneys, accountants, and other professional persons hold themselves out to the public as having specialized skill and knowledge. In a lawsuit for professional malpractice, the defendant is presumed to have the skill and learning commonly possessed by members of the profession in good standing in the same or a similar community. Failure to possess the presumed knowledge and skill is strong evidence of negligence.

Application of experience and knowledge. To exercise due care means to use one's presumed experience and knowledge in such a manner as to prevent an unreasonable risk of harm to others. To determine whether the defendant's conduct was unreasonable, that is, whether he or she breached the duty of care, requires a balancing of factors. The defendant's conduct is judged by (1) the severity of damage that might occur and (2) the probability that such damage will occur, compared with (3) the expense or inconvenience in taking precautions. The defendant is considered negligent if his or her conduct is such that factors (1) and (2) are greater than factor (3). For example, supplying gasoline to another in an open bucket is unreasonable conduct and thus negligent. The risk of probable injury if the gasoline is ignited outweighs the cost or inconvenience of supplying a closed container with a warning label.

The more probable and the more serious the harm, the greater the expense and effort that must be taken to prevent that harm. Thus, the courts have held that a great amount of care must be exercised in dealing with items that are known to be dangerous such as gas, electricity, or elevators. Great care is required when dealing with persons who are known to be irresponsible, such as insane persons or intoxicated persons. In many states the courts have held social hosts and sellers of alcoholic beverages negligent for furnishing alcohol to guests or customers who are obviously intoxicated. In those states the seller or host has been held liable to a third person who was injured by an intoxicated guest or customer driving a car.

Negligent misrepresentation. A person may commit the tort of negligence by misuse of language. For example, one may be liable for making a false statement of fact having failed to exercise due care to determine the truth. Most cases of negligent misrepresentation involve defendants in the business of supplying information for the guidance of others, such as accountants, attorneys, and real estate brokers.

[1] *Prosser and Keeton on the Law of Torts,* 5th ed., West Publishing Company, St. Paul, 1984, p. 175.

Injury to the Plaintiff. The harm suffered as a consequence of another's negligence may be physical (harm to the person or property) or mental (fright, pain). In most lawsuits for negligence, the plaintiff's injury is easily shown and the plaintiff recovers damages for any physical injury. In addition, an award may be made for mental suffering accompanying the physical injury, that is, for pain, suffering, fright, and humiliation. The courts have been reluctant to award damages where the plaintiff's injury is limited solely to fright, shock, or other mental distress. The major objection to recovery for mental distress unaccompanied by physical injury is the danger of fictitious claims. Mental distress is easily simulated and difficult to deny. In most states today, the plaintiff may recover damages only if the defendant caused immediate physical injury to the plaintiff or caused mental distress followed by physical harm. For example, a pregnant woman who suffers mental distress from a defendant's negligence may recover damages if the distress results in a later miscarriage.

One situation the courts have great difficulty in resolving is that of a bystander witnessing harm negligently inflicted upon another person. Ordinarily, the courts do not hold the defendant liable to the bystander for the tort of negligence, since the defendant could not reasonably foresee mental distress to that person. The bystander is "outside the zone of danger" created by the defendant's negligence. However, in a few states recovery has been permitted when four elements are present: (1) the injury inflicted on the third person is serious and of a nature to cause mental distress to the bystander; (2) the shock results in physical harm to the bystander; (3) the bystander is a close relative to the person injured; and (4) the bystander is present at the time of the injury to the third person or suffers the shock almost immediately after the accident. Suppose, for example, a mother appeared on the scene of an accident moments after her child had been seriously injured by the defendant's negligence. In some states the mother would be allowed to recover damages if she suffered mental distress and physical harm.

Negligence the Cause of Injury. In order to hold the defendant liable, the plaintiff must prove that the defendant's negligence was the cause of the injury. Sometimes the cause is obvious, as where the defendant carelessly drives a car and hits the plaintiff. At other times a remote event occurs that contributes to the plaintiff's injuries. For example, an architect designs stairs that are unreasonably steep, which cause the plaintiff to fall three years later.

Two questions are commonly used by courts to establish whether the defendant should be held liable for the plaintiff's injury: (1) Was defendant's conduct the actual cause of the plaintiff's injury? (2) Was there proximate cause?

Actual cause. The term *actual cause* (sometimes called *cause in fact*) in general means something without which plaintiff's injury would not have occurred. The test sometimes is referred to as the "but for" test—"but for the defendant's conduct the plaintiff would not have been injured." Actual cause may be a positive act or a failure to act. For example, a court would hold that failure of the defendant to fence his or her yard is a cause in fact of a child's drowning in the defendant's pool. If the plaintiff's injury would have occurred without the defendant's conduct, a court ordinarily will hold that the defendant's negligence is not the actual cause of the plaintiff's injury. For example, suppose that Daniel is driving his car knowing that it has defective brakes. A child suddenly darts into his path, and Daniel is unable to stop in time and injures the child. If Daniel probably would have hit the child even if the car had good brakes, his negligence is not the actual cause of the child's injury.

To be the actual cause does not mean that the defendant's conduct must be the *only* cause of the plaintiff's injury. There can be *concurring* causes. Suppose, for example, that two persons simultaneously drive loud motorcycles at high rates of speed so close to a pregnant woman that she suffers mental distress and has a miscarriage. In a lawsuit, the woman may hold both defendants liable. Neither person is allowed to argue that the identical harm would have occurred without their negligence (i.e., it would have happened anyway). In this special class of cases the courts use an alternate to the "but for" test, determining instead that the negligent conduct was a material or substantial factor in causing the injury.

Proximate cause. The second major test of causation is proximate cause. The purpose of proximate cause is to place a limitation on the defendant's liability; important in deciding this limit is the concept of foreseeability. While our ethical standards require responsibility for conduct—and liability for negligence—we also hold that legal responsibility should end when the results are extraordinary or unanticipated. For example, suppose a rental agency furnishes a negligently maintained car with smooth tires to a surgeon, not knowing he is driving to a rural town to perform emergency surgery. A blowout wrecks the car, preventing the doctor from operating with the result that the patient's arm has to be amputated. Many courts would hold that the rental agency is not liable to the patient because the particular results of its negligence were unforeseeable (i.e., surprising or improbable).

However, the defendant is liable where it is only the *extent* of the plaintiff's injury that is not reasonably foreseeable. For example, the defendant is liable where the defendant's negligence causes the aggravation of a plaintiff's unforeseeable previous condition, such as heart disease. It has been said that the defendant "takes his victim as he finds him."

Proximate cause also limits the extent of the defendant's liability when there is an intervening cause. An *intervening cause* is one that occurs after the defendant's negligence and alters the consequences. An infinite variety of possible intervening causes exist, and it is obvious that a defendant should not always be held liable for the plaintiff's injury. As a general rule the defendant is liable only if the intervening cause of plaintiff's injury is reasonably foreseeable.

A person may be liable for failing to foresee the negligence or intentional acts of others. For example, a landlord has been held liable for failing to protect against, or warn a tenant of, possible harm from criminal assault when the landlord knew of past similar incidents in the neighborhood and could reasonably foresee a future occurrence.

An intervening cause which is not reasonably foreseeable is called a *superseding cause*. If a superseding cause occurs, the defendant will not be held liable, since although the defendant's negligence is a cause in fact (actual cause), it is not the proximate cause of plaintiff's injury.

The following case illustrates the two tests of causation.

CASE 5.2 Stahl v. Metropolitan Dade County · 438 So. 2d 14 (Fla. App. 1983)

FACTS Andrew Stahl, a 13-year-old boy, was riding his bicycle to school on a bicycle path built by Metropolitan Dade County on the north side of S.W. 128 Street. Children regularly used the path, and this was known to Dade County. The path, built in 1971, was made of asphalt and was about 5 feet wide. It had never received maintenance and was very bumpy in places where tree roots had grown underneath. Seeking to avoid one such area, Andrew rode off the path onto a parallel grassy area which had trees growing in it, and into the adjoining street. He was immediately struck and killed by an oncoming car. Andrew would have struck a tree had he not headed into the street.

Andrew's father sued Dade County alleging negligence in the maintenance of the bicycle path. Dade County was granted summary judgment on the grounds that its negligence was not the proximate cause of the accident. Plaintiff (the father) appealed.

OPINION HUBBART, J. . . . It is the established law of this state that to maintain a cause of action sounding in negligence, as here, the plaintiff must establish three elements. These elements are stated in the cases in slightly varying language and have no particular canonical form; they amount in substance, however, to the following:

1. The existence of a duty recognized by law requiring the defendant to conform to a certain standard of conduct for the protection of others including the plaintiff;
2. A failure on the part of the defendant to perform that duty; and
3. An injury or damage to the plaintiff proximately caused by such failure.

In the instant case, all agree that for summary judgment purposes the first two elements of the plaintiff's negligence (wrongful death) action are shown on this record, . . . It is solely the third element of "proximate cause" which is in dispute in this case. . . .

CASE 5.2 Continued

The Florida courts, in accord with most other jurisdictions, have historically followed the so-called "but for" causation-in-fact test, that is, "to constitute proximate cause there must be such a natural, direct, and continuous sequence between the negligence act (or omission) and the (plaintiff's) injury that it can reasonably be said that *but for* the (negligent) act (or omission) the injury would not have occurred."...

Florida courts, in accord with courts throughout the country, have for good reason been most reluctant to attach tort liability for results which, although caused-in-fact by the defendant's negligent act or omission, seem to the judicial mind highly unusual, extraordinary, bizarre, or, stated differently, seem beyond the scope of any fair assessment of the danger created by the defendant's negligence.... The test most often employed by the courts is the so-called "foreseeability" test.... Plainly, the "foreseeability" test finds a particularly consistent application in that large group of cases where, as claimed here, a plaintiff's injury is caused-in-fact by the defendant's negligence and, in addition thereto, by other "intervening causes" independent of said negligence.... *If an intervening cause is foreseeable the original negligent actor may still be held liable.* The question of whether an intervening cause is foreseeable is (ordinarily) for the trier of fact....

Plainly, the defendant Dade County's negligence in failing to properly maintain the bicycle path in question at the point where Andrew Stahl, the plaintiff's decedent, departed from the path was a cause-in-fact of the said decedent's death. Utilizing the "but for" test of actual causation, it is clear that "but for" the defendant's negligence herein, Andrew would not have been forced off the bicycle path, would not have been propelled onto an adjoining grassy area where menacing trees were located, would not have driven onto the adjoining street to avoid hitting the said trees, and would not have been struck and killed by an oncoming car. "But for" the defendant's negligence in the maintenance of the bicycle path, this tragic sequence of events would never have occurred. At the very least, a genuine issue of material fact is presented making a summary judgment inappropriate here....

Given, then, a proper showing of causation-in-fact in this case, we move on to determine whether the car/bicycle collision herein was a reasonably foreseeable consequence of the defendant's alleged negligent maintenance of the bicycle path herein.... We think that a reasonable jury on these facts could find that the negligent maintenance of the bicycle path would likely force a young bicyclist such as Andrew Stahl off the path to avoid a spill, across an adjoining grassy area and onto the street where he might be hit by a car. Stated differently, we do not, as a matter of law, see this as a highly unusual, extraordinary or bizarre occurrence flowing from the negligent omission herein. From our common experience, we know that a bicyclist has a certain momentum as he travels along a bicycle path. Upon discovery of a hazardous condition on the path he, very likely, may be forced to detour off the path onto whatever adjoins the path without being able to stop. Where, as here, the adjoining strip is a grassy area approximately five feet in width with menacing trees growing therein, he may very well be forced to drive into the adjoining street to avoid hitting the trees and is likely thereafter to be hit and killed by an oncoming car. True, the child's action in this case in driving into the street and the oncoming car's action in striking the child represent intervening causes-in-fact of the child's death in this case. Neither of these causes, however, can be said to be unforeseeable as a matter of law because plainly they could be reasonably expected from the defendant's initial negligence herein. At any rate, we think this is a question of fact for the jury on this record and was not a proper basis for entering a summary judgment.

...In sum, then, we conclude that the "proximate cause" element of the plaintiff's negligence action herein was not negated on this record as a matter of law. The summary judgment under review is therefore reversed and the cause is remanded to the trial court for further proceedings.

JUDGMENT Reversed and remanded.

Proof of Negligence

In order to recover damages in a lawsuit, the plaintiff has the burden of proving the four elements of negligence. The task is difficult, but two procedural aids are available that help the plaintiff in meeting this burden of proof: The doctrine of negligence *per se* and the doctrine of *res ipsa loquitur.*

Negligence Per Se. *Per se* means "of itself" or "by itself." The doctrine of "negligence *per se*" permits the plaintiff to use the defendant's violation of a criminal statute as proof that the defendant committed the tort of negligence. A criminal statute establishes a standard of behavior for a community. Thus, if a defendant violates a criminal statute, his or her conduct automatically constitutes failure to live up to the standard of the ordinary prudent person and therefore is negligence.

Negligence *per se* applies only if the plaintiff is within the class of individuals intended to be protected by the criminal statute and if the harm suffered is of the kind which the statute is intended to prevent. Negligence *per se* is often utilized in a lawsuit resulting from an automobile accident. Suppose the plaintiff is injured by the defendant's driving a car in excess of the state speed law. State motor vehicle codes carry criminal penalties for violation and are enacted generally to protect users of highways and public streets. Thus, if the plaintiff is injured by the defendant's automobile on a public street, the plaintiff's is within the class of persons to be protected and suffers the kind of harm intended to be prevented.

The majority of states treat the defendant's unexcused violation of an applicable criminal statute as conclusive proof of negligence. Thus, in a lawsuit the plaintiff need not submit further evidence to prove the first two elements of a cause of action for negligence; the court ordinarily instructs the jury to find a verdict of negligence. However, to recover damages, the plaintiff must of course prove the last two elements of a cause of action for negligence: injury and proximate cause.

Res Ipsa Loquitur. Occasionally, there is no clear or direct evidence of the defendant's failure to exercise due care but there is circumstantial evidence of negligence. *Res ipsa loquitur* is a Latin phrase meaning "the thing speaks for itself."

The doctrine of *res ipsa loquitur* permits the judge or jury to draw from circumstantial evidence the inference that the defendant was negligent. For example, it is reasonable to infer from skid marks on a street that an automobile was driven at an excessive speed. But more than one inference may be drawn from circumstantial evidence, and *res ipsa loquitur* is merely a rule of evidence in a lawsuit; it does not ensure a verdict in favor of the plaintiff. The defendant may introduce evidence to contradict the inference of negligence or to prove a defense. It is only in the absence of evidence to the contrary that *res ipsa loquitur* would likely result in a verdict for the plaintiff.

In most states today to utilize *res ipsa loquitur,* the plaintiff must prove the existence of two elements: (1) the event which caused the plaintiff's injury is of a kind that ordinarily does not occur in the absence of someone's negligence; and (2) the accident was caused by an instrumentality within the exclusive control of the defendant at the time of the injury. The doctrine has been applied to a wide variety of situations. Some examples are: a falling elevator, the explosion of a boiler, an unexplained plane crash, and a sponge left in a patient following surgery.

When there is more than one explanation of the cause of the event resulting in plaintiff's injury, the plaintiff is not required to eliminate all possible causes or inferences other than negligence. In order to use the *res ipsa loquitur* doctrine in a negligence suit, the plaintiff need only present evidence from which reasonable people can say that on the whole it is more likely that there was negligence associated with the cause of the event than that there was not. However, the plaintiff must eliminate any doubt that the defendant was in exclusive control of the instrumentality causing the injury. Ordinarily, the defendant may not be held liable where the negligence can be attributable to another.

The following case illustrates the benefit of *res ipsa loquitur* to a plaintiff when the cause of injury cannot be explained.

CASE 5.3 Carranza v. Tucson Medical Center · 662 P.2d 455 (Ariz. App. 1983)

FACTS Antonia Carranza, a four-year-old child, was admitted to Tucson Medical Center (TMC) for heart surgery. The surgery was performed by Dr. Sabbagh. After the surgery Antonia's parents noticed a burn on their daughter's left leg. There was no explanation for the burn. Carranza sued Dr. Sabbagh and TMC for medical malpractice. The defendants' motions for summary judgment were granted, and Carranza appealed.

OPINION HATHAWAY, J. . . . In response to appellees' [Dr. Sabbagh and TMC] motions for summary judgment, the appellant [Carranza] argued that the doctrine of *res ipsa loquitur* should be applied in this case. Elements necessary to invoke the doctrine are: (1) The accident must be of a kind which ordinarily does not occur in the absence of someone's negligence; (2) the accident must be caused by an agency or instrumentality within the exclusive control of the defendant; (3) the accident must not have been due to any voluntary action on the part of the plaintiff; and (4) the plaintiff must not be in a position to show the particular circumstances which caused the offending agency or instrumentality to operate to his injury.

Appellee Sabbagh concedes that a burn did occur on the child's leg after the surgery and this would indicate "that something unusual occurred in the operating room." He argues, however, that appellants have failed to show that he caused the problem or that the problem was caused by an instrumentality under his control. Such contention is joined in by appellee Tucson Medical Center and in addition, it alleges that appellants failed to make any showing that the accident was caused by an agency or instrumentality within its exclusive control. . . .

Appellees maintain there is nothing to show that the accident which occurred was due to their negligence. The general rule is that in malpractice suits, negligence on the part of a physician or surgeon must be established by expert medical testimony. However, our supreme court noted:

> This rule is in accord with the weight of authority generally where the defendant's use of suitable professional skill is the subject calling for expert testimony only, or the question to be determined is strictly within special and technical knowledge of the profession and not within the knowledge of the average layman. But the force of the rule is broken when the omission comes within the realm of common knowledge and thus, there is an exception to the rule that is as well settled as the rule itself, and that is expert testimony is not required where ". . . the negligence is so grossly apparent that a layman would have no difficulty in recognizing it." [Citations.]

In *Beaudoin v. Watertown Memorial Hospital,* 145 N.W.2d 166 (1966), and *Wiles v. Myerly,* 210 N.W.2d 619 (Iowa 1973), both malpractice cases against hospitals and surgeons, patients received burns to their buttocks area after operations in other parts of their bodies. In *Beaudoin, supra,* the court found that the doctrine of *res ipsa loquitur* should apply since a layman was able to conclude as a matter of common knowledge that burns such as the plaintiff suffered were not directly related to the operative procedure and would not have resulted if due care had been exercised. And in *Wiles, supra,* the court sustained the *res ipsa loquitur* instructions also writing that common knowledge and experience would tell an ordinary juror that in the course of events, one undergoing surgery does not sustain an unusual injury to a healthy part of his body in an area other than the area of the operation in the absence of negligence. We therefore believe it was unnecessary for appellant to provide expert medical testimony to show that the accident could not have occurred in the absence of someone's negligence. Such is within the realm of common knowledge.

The second requirement for application of the doctrine is that the injury was caused by an agency or instrument within the exclusive control of the defendant. Appellees make

CASE 5.3 Continued

much of the fact that appellants have not sued the attending personnel who were in the operating room. In their complaint, plaintiffs alleged a principal agent relationship between the surgeon and the hospital. If a physician or surgeon is, in fact, an employee of a hospital . . . the hospital will be held liable for the tortious acts of the physician or surgeon which are done in the scope of his employment. . . . Therefore, there is a material dispute raised as to "exclusive control" which is incapable of being resolved by summary judgment.

. . . Based on the pleadings, we think a sufficient factual basis is raised as to Dr. Sabbagh's relationship to the hospital so as to preclude the granting of summary judgment in favor of appellee hospital. . . . The doctrine of *res ipsa loquitur* is particularly applicable to the injuries suffered by the Carranza child and in the absence of evidentiary support for their motions for summary judgment, the motions were inadequate to dispel the material issues of fact which were raised by the pleadings.

JUDGMENT The orders granting the motions for summary judgment are vacated and the matter is remanded for further proceedings.

Defenses to Negligence

There are three major defenses to the tort of negligence: contributory negligence, assumption of the risk, and comparative negligence.

Contributory Negligence. The defense of *contributory negligence* can be defined as failure by the plaintiff to exercise due care for his or her own safety, which failure is a contributing cause of the plaintiff's injury. To determine whether the plaintiff exercised due care, the model of the ordinary prudent person is utilized. However, there is a difference in approach between determining whether the defendant is negligent and whether the plaintiff is contributorily negligent.

In determining whether the plaintiff is guilty of contributory negligence, the judge or jury is concerned about a risk of harm created by the plaintiff himself or herself, i.e., the plaintiff is required to exercise due care to protect his or her own interest from harm by others. Some legal writers and judges have stated that the defense might better be called "contributory fault."

Much criticism has been leveled at the defense of contributory negligence because it is a complete bar to the plaintiff's recovery. Thus, a plaintiff who is slightly negligent may not recover from a defendant who is greatly negligent. Most states have developed exceptions and modifications to the defense of contributory negligence, but the defense still is recognized in a small number of states.

Assumption of the Risk. The defense of *assumption of the risk* may be defined generally as voluntary exposure to a known risk. A plaintiff's assumption of the risk may be express or implied. Express assumption of the risk generally results from negotiations for a contract. For example, an operator of a raceway may require contestants to sign an agreement in advance waiving any claims against the operator for negligence by the raceway.

A common activity involving implied assumption of the risk is attendance at a sporting event. Suppose that a spectator at a baseball game is injured by a flying baseball. The spectator files a suit for negligence against the owner of the stadium alleging that the owner failed to provide a protective screen for spectators. The stadium owner may assert the defense that upon entering the stadium the plaintiff assumed the known risk of being hit by a bat or ball, that all spectators at a baseball game impliedly consent to the ordinary risks of harm associated with the game. Occasionally the defense of assumption of the risk overlaps the defense of contributory negligence, since exposure to a known risk may also amount to failure to exercise due care for one's own safety.

The ordinary prudent person model is not used to determine whether the plaintiff assumed the risk of the defendant's negligence; the judge or jury applies a subjective test. The judge or jury considers the particular plaintiff's age, experience, and knowledge, since these are important factors affecting the person's ability to understand and consent to the danger involved in the particular situation.

The defense of assumption of the risk has been criticized because it too is a complete bar to the plaintiff's recovery. As with contributory negligence, the courts have developed exceptions and modifications to the defense in an attempt to reduce the hardship resulting to the plaintiff.

Comparative Negligence. The dissatisfaction of the courts with the absolute defenses of contributory negligence and assumption of the risk has led to the adoption of the defense of comparative negligence. For example, in 1984 the Kentucky Supreme Court replaced contributory negligence with comparative negligence. The defense of comparative negligence in various forms is now provided either by court decision or by statute in the great majority of states.

In a lawsuit where both the defendant and the plaintiff are negligent, the defense of *comparative negligence* requires the judge or jury to apportion damages between the plaintiff and the defendant according to the fault of each. Thus, for example, if the defendant is found to be 75 percent at fault and the plaintiff is found to be 25 percent at fault, the plaintiff's damages will be reduced by 25 percent. Suppose that the plaintiff sustained $10,000 worth of injuries. The jury would award the plaintiff $7,500. Comparative negligence means that where the defendant also suffers injuries in the same accident, the plaintiff must forfeit a percentage of his or her damages. For example, suppose that in the above illustration the defendant has sustained $5,000 worth of injuries. The jury would then award the plaintiff $6,250 ($7,500 less 25 percent of $5,000).

The effect of the adoption of the comparative negligence rule on the defense of assumption of the risk varies greatly among the states. In some states express assumption of the risk remains as a complete defense, but implied assumption of the risk is treated as a form of comparative negligence, and the plaintiff's damages are reduced. In a few states assumption of the risk, whether express or implied, is retained as an absolute defense.

In the following case the court discusses the impact which comparative negligence has had on the defense of implied assumption of the risk.

CASE 5.4 Gonzalez v. Garcia · 142 Cal. Reptr. 503 (Cal. App. 1977)

FACTS Plaintiff Juan Gonzalez, defendant Francisco Garcia, Jack Longest, and Weldon Roberts were coworkers at a power plant on the 10 P.M. to 6 A.M. shift. They were members of a car pool. One day the four men finished work and went to nearby Avila Landing where they drank beer, tequila, and other alcoholic beverages for 3 hours. The plaintiff drank about three beers, the others drank considerably more. About 9 A.M. Roberts went home, and the defendant drove the plaintiff and Longest to a liquor store where Longest and the defendant purchased a bottle of tequila. Plaintiff asked several times to be taken home. He phoned his wife to ask her to pick him up, but there was no answer. Garcia and Longest drank the tequila and drove to a bar for another drink, despite plaintiff's protests. Plaintiff had a glass of beer while defendant and Longest continued to drink tequila. A disturbance arose at the bar, and the police came to investigate. One officer suggested that since plaintiff appeared to be the least intoxicated of the three, he should drive the other two home.

Plaintiff then drove defendant's car to Longest's house. When plaintiff returned to the car after helping Longest inside, defendant was in the driver's seat and insisted on driving. The two argued, and plaintiff tried unsuccessfully to reach his wife again. Finally, plaintiff got into the passenger's seat and the defendant drove off. The plaintiff fell asleep. The defendant apparently lost control of the car and caused it to roll over, landing on its side on the median strip of the freeway. A test indicated the defendant's blood had an alcohol content of .20 and that therefore he was unquestionably intoxicated. Plaintiff sued for damages for negligence, and defendant asserted comparative negligence and assumption

CASE 5.4 Continued

of the risk as defenses. The trial judge refused to instruct the jury on assumption of the risk. The jury returned a verdict for plaintiff but found him to be 20 percent responsible for his injuries. Defendant appealed and contended the trial court should have instructed the jury on the defense of assumption of the risk.

OPINION

STEPHENS, J.... The defense of assumption of risk was a late development in the law of negligence. The elements most frequently cited as essential to find assumption of risk are that the plaintiff have actual knowledge of the specific risk, appreciate the magnitude of the danger, and freely and voluntarily encounter it.

Most commentators recognize at least three kinds of assumption of risk: (1) express—where plaintiff, in advance, gives consent to relieve defendant of a legal duty and to take his chances of injury from a known risk; (2) implied—where plaintiff acts reasonably in voluntarily encountering a risk with the knowledge that defendant will not protect him; and (3) implied—where the plaintiff acts unreasonably in voluntarily exposing himself to a risk created by defendant's negligence....

So long as contributory negligence and assumption of risk were both complete bars to recovery, the distinction between the two was never completely clarified, especially with implied assumption of risk. Usually, if a distinction was made, it was based upon the fact that assumption of risk requires knowledge of the danger and intelligent and deliberate acquiescence, whereas contributory negligence is concerned with fault or departure from the reasonable man standard of conduct, frequently inadvertently. Also the standard for determining whether the defense is available is different—assumption of risk using a subjective standard of the particular individual and circumstances, and contributory negligence using an objective, reasonably prudent man standard with which to compare plaintiff's conduct.

Assumption of risk has been rather unpopular due to the harshness of the "all or nothing" recovery, and there has been considerable effort to abolish it completely, particularly in view of the emergence of the comparative negligence doctrine. Nevertheless, where the doctrine of comparative negligence has been accepted, there have been three different approaches to assumption of risk—completely abolishing it as a defense,... maintaining it as a complete and separate defense,... or merging it to some extent with contributory negligence.... In those states which have merged the defenses, there has frequently been a complete merger of implied assumption of risk and contributory negligence, with express assumption of risk remaining as a separate defense.... We find this last approach to be the better view and to be the approach most in keeping with the Supreme Court's opinion in *Li.* [*Li v. Yellow Cab Co.*, 13 Cal.3d 804 (1975).]

In the instant case defendant's negligent driving was the direct cause of plaintiff's injuries, and plaintiff's only contributing negligence was in riding in the same car. Thus, in this case plaintiff's conduct is of the type which is a variant of contributory negligence which "exists when a plaintiff unreasonably undertakes to encounter a specific known risk created by defendant's negligence."

Regardless of the extent of assumption of risk which still exists as a separate defense and complete bar to recovery, in this case plaintiff's conduct clearly falls into the overlapping area, the area of choosing an unreasonable alternative when reasonable ones were available, thereby evidencing a lack of due care for his own safety. Plaintiff had actual knowledge that defendant was intoxicated, he had been advised by a police officer that he should drive, he demonstrated that he probably had knowledge of the risk by his attempts to contact his wife, he had alternatives of remaining at Longest's house or calling a cab and yet he chose to ride with defendant. Where there is a reasonably safe alternative open, the plaintiff's free choice of the more dangerous way is unreasonable and amounts to both contributory negligence and assumption of the risk. To that extent the doctrines are merged under *Li, supra,* into the doctrine of comparative negligence.

CASE 5.4 Continued

The facts do not justify even an inference that the acts of plaintiff included an element in addition to negligence such as waiver of duty, agreement, or other element not a variant of contributory negligence.

There was no error in the court's refusal to give the instruction on assumption of risk as requested.

JUDGMENT The judgment is affirmed.

Liability without Fault

The remainder of this chapter is devoted to a discussion of *liability without fault,* sometimes called *strict liability.* As the term implies, there are situations where a person may be held liable for injuring another even though the person has no intent to injure anyone and, in fact, acts with the utmost care to prevent harm to others. In such a situation the conduct of the one causing injury is blameless, yet for reasons of social policy the law requires him or her to compensate the injured person for the loss. The social policy is based largely on the notion that one person has caused injury to another and, although no one is at fault, a system of allocating losses must be developed. The courts reason that liability for the injury should be imposed on the party who can best bear the loss; that party usually is the one who caused the injury.

Liability without fault exists in a variety of areas of contemporary law. All individuals and firms should be aware that whenever their conduct results in injury to another, there is the possibility of being required to compensate the injured person. The law of strict liability for workers' compensation is discussed in Chapter 47. Here three areas of strict liability have been selected for discussion: liability for injuries by animals, liability for injuries from abnormally dangerous activities, and product liability.

Liability for Injuries by Animals

Several rules of law impose liability without fault on the owners of animals. In most states, the owner of an animal that is likely to roam and injure the person or property of another is liable without fault for damages inflicted when the animal enters upon another's land. Such animals include: cattle, horses, sheep, hogs, turkeys, chickens, and most wild animals, since their natural tendency is to escape.

Either of two rules may apply when the injury occurs on the land of the animal's owner. First, the owner may be liable without fault for injuries inflicted by an animal that is dangerous by its nature and incapable of being domesticated. Such animals include lions, tigers, bears, elephants, and wolves. As a general rule, liability is absolute though the owner has raised the animal as a pet and it has shown no outward signs of being dangerous. The second rule of law pertains to domestic animals and domesticated wild animals that normally are not likely to injure people. The owner is liable for injuries inflicted only if the owner knows, or has reason to know, of a dangerous propensity in the particular animal. Domestic animals include dogs, cats, sheep, horses, and cows. Some courts have held that deer and monkeys are wild animals capable of being domesticated. In many states the legislatures have enacted special statutes which hold an owner liable for injuries from a dog bite, regardless of the owner's knowledge or prior warning.

When sued for damages for injuries inflicted by an animal, the defendant may assert one or more defenses. The defendant may assert assumption of the risk and prove that the plaintiff voluntarily exposed himself or herself to a known risk. For example, a plaintiff may not recover for injuries sustained from teasing a leopard. To avoid liability for a vicious watchdog, a landowner must post *adequate warnings* of the dog's presence. A "Beware of Dog" sign may not be adequate to warn someone that the dog is vicious and not just a dog that barks at people.

In most states the defendant is not allowed to assert contributory negligence as a defense. In many states comparative negligence is allowed in defense, with consequent reduction in damages.

Liability for Injuries from Abnormally Dangerous Activities

As a general rule, one is liable without fault for injuring the person or property of another by a dangerous activity that is inappropriate to the particular locality. Typical examples of such an activity are: crop dusting near livestock, storing quantities of explosives in the heart of a city, and drilling an oil well in a populated area. The courts have held that the following are not considered "inappropriate to the locality": storing gasoline in a service station, maintaining an ordinary fire in a factory, and stocking a small quantity of dynamite for sale in a hardware store. A person who engages in these activities is not liable without fault for injuring another but may be liable for the tort of negligence if the person fails to exercise due care. In the early decades of the twentieth century, flying an airplane was considered an abnormally dangerous activity, and aircraft operators were held strictly liable for harm to others. Today, in most states, the owner or operator of an airplane is held liable only when negligence is proved. Also, statutes ordinarily protect persons and firms laying gas or electric lines in public streets or doing blasting for the state, provided they are not guilty of negligence.

The defendant may assert the defense of assumption of the risk and prove that the plaintiff voluntarily exposed the plaintiff's person or property to a known risk. The defendant may not assert the defense of contributory negligence, but comparative negligence may reduce the plaintiff's recovery.

Product Liability

The law of product liability is complex and has a long history of development. Chapter 18 discusses this history and presents various contemporary theories of liability. This section is devoted to one theory: tort liability for defective products.

The overwhelming majority of states today recognize tort liability without fault for defective products sold to the public. The general rule has been stated as follows: *One who sells a defective product that is unreasonably dangerous is liable to the ultimate user or consumer if the seller is engaged in the business of selling such a product and the product reaches the user or consumer without substantial changes in the condition in which it is sold.*[2]

Under this general rule the seller is liable though the seller exercises all possible care to prevent harm to others. A major reason for adopting this rule of liability without fault is social policy. The courts have repeatedly stated that the risk of injury from defective products should be borne by the manufacturer or seller, who can insure against losses and distribute the cost to the public as an expense of doing business.

The courts have had difficulty in defining *a defective product that is unreasonably dangerous.* The usual definition is a product that does not meet the reasonable expectations of the ordinary consumer as to its safety. The product may be a sophisticated aircraft or automobile or a simple glass door or paper cup. The cause of the defect may vary. The design of the product may be defective; the manufacturer may make an unintentional and unavoidable error in production; or there may be inadequate instructions or warnings.

Liability for a defective product includes the maker of a defective component part, the manufacturer of the product, the wholesaler, and the retailer. However, liability is not imposed upon a person who is not engaged in the business of supplying goods of the particular kind, as when a private owner sells a defective car to another. (In certain circumstances, a seller may be liable for the torts of fraud or negligence.) Courts recently have held that a business firm, such as a car or truck rental agency, that leases personal property to others may be held liable without fault for injuries caused by a defect in the goods leased.

The courts have allowed persons other than users and purchasers to recover damages for injuries resulting from defective products. However, an injured person must be within the zone of danger. The zone of danger includes all persons who may foreseeably be injured by the defective product, such as family members, guests, or mere bystanders. One may recover for physical injuries, damages to the

[2]Based on sec. 402A, *Restatement (Second) of the Law of Torts,* vol. 2, American Law Institute, St. Paul, 1965.

product itself, and damages to one's property in the vicinity.

Several defenses are available to a defendant in a product liability lawsuit. The defendant may assert that the plaintiff made an abnormal use of the product which the defendant could not reasonably foresee, such as using a glass bottle to hammer a nail. The defendant may assert assumption of the risk as a defense, but not contributory negligence. A number of states permit the defense of comparative negligence in a product liability case, with damages reduced by proportion of fault.

In the following case the court discusses the elements of a cause of action for product liability and the possible defenses to liability.

CASE 5.5 Smith v. United States Gypsum Co. · 612 P.2d 251 (Okla. 1980)

FACTS

James H. Smith (plaintiff) and his wife, intending to panel their bathroom, bought two gallon cans of Wal-lite, a solvent-based adhesive. The directions on the can were as follows:

DANGER
EXTREMELY FLAMMABLE
VAPORS MAY CAUSE FLASH FIRE
VAPORS HARMFUL
See cautions on back panel

The back label carried the following admonitions:

> CONTAINS HEXANE. Vapors may ignite explosively. Prevent buildup of vapors—open windows and doors—use only with cross ventilation. Do not smoke, extinguish all flames and pilot lights; turn off stoves, heaters, electric motors, and other sources of ignition during use and until all vapors are gone. Do not take internally. Avoid prolonged contact with skin and breathing of vapor. Keep away from heat, sparks, and open flame. Close container after each use.

Plaintiff turned off his hot water heater and the pilot light on his kitchen stove and opened the front and back doors. He opened a can of Wal-lite and started to apply the adhesive over the bathroom window which was closed and sealed. Mrs. Smith turned on a fan across the hall from the bathroom. As she reentered the bathroom a blue flame erupted under plaintiff's trowel and an explosion occurred, seriously injuring plaintiff. Plaintiff filed suit against the manufacturer, U.S. Gypsum Co., and the distributor, Chicago Mastic Co., for product liability. A jury trial was held and plaintiff received a judgment for $600,000 damages. Defendants appealed.

OPINION

DOOLIN, J. . . . In *Kirkland v. General Motors Corporation,* 521 P.2d 1353, 1363 (Okla. 1974) this court set out the elements of a cause of action in manufacturers' products liability.

> "*First* of all Plaintiff must prove that the product was the cause of the injury; the mere possibility that it might have caused the injury is not enough.
>
> *Secondly,* Plaintiff must prove that the defect existed in the product, if the action is against the manufacturer, at the time the product left the manufacturer's possession and control. [Citation omitted.] If the action is against the retailer or supplier of the article, then the Plaintiff must prove that the article was defective at the time of sale for public use or consumption or at the time it left the retailer's possession and control.
>
> *Thirdly,* Plaintiff must prove that the defect made the article unreasonably dangerous to him or to his property as the term 'unreasonably dangerous' is [herein] defined."

CASE 5.5 Continued

Unreasonably dangerous is defined as "dangerous to an extent beyond that which would be contemplated by the ordinary consumer who purchases it, with the ordinary knowledge common to the community as to its characteristics." Defendants claim proof of the third element of the cause of action was missing.

There is no question the Wal-lite exploded, probably due to ignition of the vapors by the electric fan. But was the proximate cause an unreasonably dangerous product due to defective design and inadequate warnings, or was it plaintiff's ignoring the warnings on the can?

. . . A manufacturer must anticipate all foreseeable uses of his product. In order to escape being *unreasonably* dangerous, a *potentially* dangerous product must contain or reflect warnings covering all foreseeable uses. These warnings must be readily understandable and make the product safe. . . . Defendants in the present case should have known that some users would install paneling in a room without a window. If the jury found Wal-lite was designed in such a way that the vapors ignited easily, and the warnings and directions did not adequately warn of the dangerous conditions created, it was justified in finding a defect in the product.

If jury found this defect made the product unreasonably dangerous to the consumer, *Kirkland's* third element is satisfied.

Expert testimony at trial indicated the hexane vapors contained in the adhesive were released at a rapid rate if applied as directed on the can. The label instructed the consumer to apply the adhesive with a saw-tooth trowel. The expert opined such use compounded the dangers as this type of application doubled the evaporative rate by making grooves in the mixture. He concluded the release of the vapors into an enclosed space was too rapid to be overcome or guarded against. Plaintiff and his wife both testified the instructions and warnings were read and followed to the best of their ability. They attempted to satisfy the "cross ventilation" instruction by opening the doors and using the fan.

Defendants claim the evidence shows plaintiff deliberately disregarded the instructions and warnings on the can, resting their case on the fact the bathroom contained no open window. This, they submit, caused the accident, not any defect in the Wal-lite. There is no evidence of such deliberate disregard of the instructions. To the contrary, testimony indicates every attempt was made to heed the warning.

We hold there was sufficient evidence the warnings on the Wal-lite did not prevent the product from being unreasonably dangerous. Proof of the third element was sufficient to send the case to the jury.

Defendants ask us to hold as a matter of law that plaintiff misused the product and voluntarily assumed the risk of a known defect, defenses to a manufacturers' products liability action under *Kirkland v. General Motors, supra.* Use of Wal-lite as an adhesive, its sole purpose, cannot be misuse of the product even if plaintiff used it carelessly as alleged. Evidence does not support defense that plaintiff knew the warnings were inadequate or that its application with a trowel would make the product more dangerous. The existence of the defenses is a jury question. Trial court properly overruled defendants' demurrers to the evidence and motions for directed verdict.

. . . Defendants objected to the testimony of one of plaintiff's expert witnesses, a chemical engineer, that warnings [on the label] appeared to him "to be inadequate," arguing this is testimony as to the ultimate fact. Also they objected to testimony of a psychiatrist [that the] warnings would be vague to a person such as plaintiff.

We feel this is well within permissible testimony of expert witnesses and is not reversible error. Defendants had ample opportunity for cross-examination. . . .

JUDGMENT Judgment affirmed.

Summary

There are two major areas of tort liability for unintentional harm to others: liability for the tort of negligence and liability without fault. Negligence may be defined as the failure to exercise due care when there is a foreseeable risk of harm to others. In order to recover damages in a lawsuit for negligence, the plaintiff must prove four elements: (1) The defendant owed a duty of care to the plaintiff; (2) the defendant failed to exercise due care; (3) the plaintiff suffered actual loss or damage; and (4) the defendant's negligence was the cause of the plaintiff's injury. A duty of care arises when one should foresee that his or her conduct will create an unreasonable risk of harm to others. Whether the defendant has exercised due care is determined by comparing the defendant's behavior to that of the hypothetical ordinary prudent person. The defendant will be held liable if his or her conduct is unreasonable. The harm suffered by the plaintiff may be physical or mental. As a general rule the plaintiff may recover damages for negligent infliction of mental distress only if the plaintiff suffers physical injury from defendant's conduct.

Cause, or "causation," is used to refer to the connection between the defendant's negligence and the plaintiff's injury. The plaintiff may recover damages if the defendant's negligence was an actual cause of the plaintiff's injury and there is no superseding cause. Proximate cause is a limitation on the defendant's liability based on foreseeability. Proximate cause includes an intervening cause that is reasonably foreseeable.

Two major procedural doctrines assist the plaintiff in proving that the defendant was negligent. Negligence *per se* permits use of the defendant's unexcused violation of a criminal statute to establish negligence. *Res ipsa loquitur* is used when there is no direct evidence of the defendant's negligence but there is circumstantial evidence from which an inference of negligence can be drawn.

Three major defenses are available to a defendant in a lawsuit for negligence: contributory negligence, assumption of the risk, and comparative negligence. Comparative negligence is provided in the great majority of states and has largely replaced the two other defenses.

There are three major areas of liability without fault (strict liability): liability for injuries by animals, liability for injuries from abnormally dangerous activities, and product liability. In a strict-liability lawsuit the defendant may be held liable though he or she exercises all possible care to prevent harm to others. The defendant may assert the defense of assumption of the risk but ordinarily may not assert contributory negligence of the plaintiff. Some states permit the defendant to assert comparative negligence as a defense and reduce the plaintiff's recovery.

Review Questions

1 (a) Define the tort of negligence. (b) List the four elements required to establish a cause of action for negligence.

2 (a) What is a "duty of care"? (b) Who owes this duty and when does it arise? (c) To whom is the duty owed?

3 (a) Explain how a judge or jury determines if a defendant has failed to exercise due care. (b) How does the age or condition of the defendant affect the determination?

4 Give examples of the types of injuries for which a plaintiff may recover damages in a negligence suit.

5 List the four elements required for a bystander to recover damages for the tort of negligence.

6 (a) Explain the purpose of proximate cause. (b) Define and give an example of each of the following terms: "concurring cause," "intervening cause," "superseding cause."

7 (a) Explain the doctrine of "negligence *per se.*" (b) Under what circumstances does the doctrine apply?

8 (a) Explain the doctrine of *res ipsa loquitur.* (b) What are the three elements required in order to utilize the doctrine in a lawsuit?

9 (a) Define contributory negligence. (b) How does this definition differ from the definition of the tort of negligence?

10 **(a)** Define "assumption of the risk." **(b)** Explain how the judge or jury determines if a plaintiff has assumed the risk.

11 Explain why the defense of comparative negligence is more beneficial to a plaintiff than either contributory negligence or assumption of the risk.

12 **(a)** Explain the social policy behind strict liability. **(b)** State and give examples of the three rules of law that may apply to injuries by animals.

13 In what circumstances may a person be held liable for injuring another by an abnormally dangerous activity?

14 **(a)** State the general rule of liability for injuries from defective products. **(b)** Who may be held liable for injuries from a defective product? **(c)** Who may recover damages for injuries from a defective product? **(d)** What defenses are available to a defendant in a product liability suit?

Case Problems

1 Johnson represented to the state of Indiana that he was interested in locating a laser research facility in the state but he would need $100,000 of local money to secure a federal grant. Hollis, a state official, assisted Johnson by mailing announcements throughout the state, referring responses to Johnson and arranging meetings with interested investors. Glick invested $25,000 before he discovered that Johnson was a "con man." Johnson was later apprehended and convicted of theft, but none of the money was recovered. Prior to Glick's investment, Hollis had become suspicious of Johnson because he refused to divulge the name of the company he represented. Hollis made numerous inquiries and requested a report from the state police but never told Glick of his suspicions. Glick sued the state of Indiana for the tort of negligence. Does Glick have a cause of action for negligence?

2 Julie Bowen went to the office of attorney David Arnold to discuss dissolution of her 11-year marriage to Ronald Bowen. Arnold explained dissolution procedures generally and discussed discovery devices available. About 2 months later Julie returned to Arnold's office with her husband, who was not represented by a lawyer. Ronald presented a written settlement proposal which gave Julie 12 percent of his 91.8 percent ownership in his landscaping business, Prairie Restorations. Ronald valued the business at $60,000. Julie received other assets in return for relinquishing her interest in the business. Arnold told her that in a contested proceeding she could receive anywhere from 0 to 50 percent of the value of her husband's interest in the business. He also told her that he did not have enough information to verify Ronald's valuation and that an independent appraisal could be performed. Julie said that she trusted her husband's valuation and declined to order an appraisal. Ronald offered to make his financial records available but Arnold did not ask to see them. Following court approval of the settlement and dissolution, Julie remarried. She later filed a legal malpractice action against Arnold, alleging that he was negligent in not conducting discovery and not informing himself and Julie completely and accurately of the financial assets of the couple. Julie's expert witness testified that the value of Prairie Restorations at the time of settlement was $103,447. Arnold's expert witness testified it was worth $48,740. (*a*) What standard of care should be used by the judge or jury to determine liability? (*b*) Who do you think should win the lawsuit?

3 Terri Ann Saucier was in the Winn-Dixie food store walking toward checkout counter number eight when she slipped on a milk puddle. She lost her balance and fell to the floor, injuring her lower back. Witnesses testified that a few small milk puddles of 2 or 3 inches in diameter pooled in the aisles near the checkout counter. No one saw the milk before the accident and the exact length of time that the milk remained on the floor could not be determined. Winn-Dixie testified that the entire store was swept and mopped each morning before opening. Cleaning during the day was performed on an "as-needed" basis. There were no periodic inspections for spills or other hazards, but all thirty-five employees were instructed to be on the lookout for dangerous conditions. Saucier sued Winn-Dixie for negligence and received a jury verdict of $20,000. Should this award be upheld?

4 Dr. Lhim, a staff psychiatrist, cared for John Patterson, an alcohol- and drug-dependent schizophrenic, at Northville State Hospital. Patterson had a long history of psychological disorder and had signed himself into Northville on six occasions between 1972 and 1975. On one occasion in 1973 Patterson had threatened his mother for money. In September 1975 Patterson asked to be released, and Dr. Lhim discharged him the next day into the care of his mother, Mollie Barnes. On November 2 Patterson was in his aunt's house where his mother was staying. Patterson took his aunt's shotgun and began firing it inside the house. His mother tried to restrain him and in the struggle Patterson killed her. Mollie Barnes's estate sued Dr. Lhim and Northville, alleging negligence in discharging Patterson and negligence in failing to warn Mollie Barnes that Patterson was a danger to her safety. The defendants argued that if there was any negligence it was not the proximate cause of Mollie Barnes's death. Can the estate establish all four elements of a cause of action for negligence?

5 Avis left a rental car unattended in the parking lot at the Miami International Airport with the key in the ignition, the door open, and the car lights flashing. The car was subsequently stolen. The thief operated the car negligently and collided with a car driven by Charlie Vining, severely injuring him. The area around the airport had the highest incidence of auto theft in Dade County. Avis had had vehicles stolen in the past. Vining sued Avis for negligence. The trial court dismissed the complaint, stating that even if Avis were negligent it was not liable because the criminal act of stealing the car broke the chain of causation. Is Avis's negligence the proximate cause of Vining's injuries?

6 Moughon was driving her car to the repair shop. As she came around a curve, the car went up over the right curb and out of control, and then came back into the street and across the center line into the left lane, where it collided with Wolf's car. Wolf sued Moughon, alleging negligence *per se* in failing to keep her vehicle on the right side of the road in violation of a Texas statute. Moughon claimed unavoidable accident and testified that she had had her brakes repaired two days before and that when she drove the car home the vehicle would pull to the right each time she applied the brakes. Who should win the lawsuit?

7 On March 23 a fire started in Peck's Steak House and damaged three neighboring buildings. The fire began in a locked storeroom in the rear of Peck's. The storeroom had no outside doors or windows. The room was always locked, and the only keys belonged to Mr. and Mrs. Gant, owners of the restaurant. On the day of the fire the only people in the restaurant were the Gants and two employees. Flammable substances were stored in the room, but because the room was so badly burned, it was impossible to determine which, if any, of these substances caused the fire. The owners of the damaged buildings sued Gant for negligence, alleging *res ipsa loquitur.* Gant argued that the doctrine should not apply since the fire could have started by spontaneous combustion. Are these facts sufficient to justify the use of *res ipsa loquitur?*

8 Richard, 19 years old, spent several hours drinking at the Caravan Restaurant and Lounge. He died shortly thereafter in a one-car automobile accident. His blood alcohol content was .21. It is unlawful in the state for a person under 21 to acquire, possess, or consume liquor. Richard's estate sued Caravan, alleging negligence in serving alcoholic beverages to a minor who was obviously intoxicated. Cindy, a cocktail waitress and Richard's girl friend, stated that his speech and ability to write were affected by the alcohol and that he was beyond the point of self-control. The state has a statue which prohibits the sale of alcoholic beverages to minors and intoxicated persons. (*a*) What theories could Richard's estate use to prove negligence? (*b*) Does Caravan have a plausible defense to assert in the lawsuit?

9 Koos produced grass seed on 55 acres of land. After the seed was harvested, Koos and a crew equipped with mobile water trucks burned the field by setting fire to dry straw. They first plowed a protective strip around the perimeter. While the field was being burned, Roth's adjoining field caught fire, causing $8000 of damage. No one saw how the fire on Roth's property started, but witnesses stated that probably a whirlwind carried burning material from Koos's field. Roth sued, and Koos defended that he should not be liable for an unintentional and nonnegligent injury to Roth's property. Who should win the lawsuit?

CHAPTER 6

Business Torts: Interference with Business Rights

The American concept of free enterprise is woven into the fabric of our economic life. Competition inspires innovation and progress, encourages efficiency, and is a basic ingredient not only of our expanding economy but also of our standard of living. At the same time, competition may open the way for unethical or illegal practices which could, unless restrained, stifle lawful business or ultimately cause financial loss to the general public.

In Chapters 4 and 5 we dealt with the tortious invasion of private rights. In this chapter we consider those torts which particularly interfere with commercial or business rights. For ease of discussion we call such business interferences *business torts.* This chapter does not treat a manufacturer's or distributor's tort liability arising out of the sale of an article which fails to meet the standards of quality or usefulness imposed by contract or by law. That subject is considered at length in the discussion of product liability in Chapter 18.

Nature of Business Torts

A firm that has been injured by a business tort is entitled to compensation (damages) for the losses it sustains. If the wrongdoing business does not stop its unlawful actions and the injured firm cannot be adequately compensated in money, a court may order an injunction (a prohibition or restraining order) against the continuance of the tortious activity. To illustrate, it is normal practice for a court to enjoin (that is, to stop) a business from using a name on its products which is so similar to a name used by a competitor that a purchaser cannot easily distinguish between the products of the two companies. Thus, the manufacturer of "M and M" candies could secure an injunction against a company selling a similarly packaged confection under the trade name "M and N."

Concepts and methods of doing business change to reflect shifting emphasis resulting from such factors as national advertising, the force of labor unions, and the economic pressures of foreign commerce. Likewise, the criteria as to what practices constitute business torts are not constant. In reaching its decision a court weighs the conflicting interests involved. It may, under appropriate circumstances, find that interests are present in a particular case which excuse or *privilege* an interference with another's business rights or are of such a slight degree as not to justify court action.

Most interferences with business rights may be included within the broad term "unfair competition." It would be impossible in a chapter of limited length to discuss all the devices considered by the courts to be unfair competition. Excluded from consideration here are such obviously improper acts as harassing a competitor's customers, blocking the ingress or egress of a competitor's delivery trucks, displaying a sign saying "Main Entrance" over one's own door adjacent to a competitor's entryway, threatening groundless lawsuits, and paying a competitor's employees to commit sabotage.

For simplicity, the wide scope of business torts is discussed in this chapter under four broad categories:

1 Entering wrongfully into business
2 Interfering with business relations
3 Disparaging reputation or property
4 Engaging in unfair trade practices

In each instance the facts must be examined and the interests of the respective parties viewed in the light of the ethical standards expected of businesspeople. These standards are expressed in statutes, such as those which prohibit combinations in restraint of trade (for example, the Sherman Antitrust Act, discussed in Chapters 45 and 46), in the decisions of the courts, and in codes of ethics of trade and professional associations.

Entering Wrongfully into Business

It is a cardinal principle of American free society that, in general, a person may engage in any business he or she chooses and may compete with other businesses for customers.

Unless a new enterprise stoops to improper business practices, it is not required to account for the losses a competitor may suffer if, because of the new enterprise's merchandising policies, the competitor can no longer operate at a profit and must close its doors. By way of illustration, there would be no violation of the rights of an old "corner store" forced out of business by a big new store which uses such competitive practices as selling at discount prices or threatening to discharge any of its own employees who trade in the old corner store. These practices would be among the legitimate weapons in the war for customers, and the possibility of their use is a normal risk of business life.

However, the right to engage in business is not without limitation. A business cannot be carried on for the sole purpose of driving some other firm out of business or out of the neighborhood. In that event there would be only a simulated competition. For example, suppose George runs the only barber shop in a certain small town. Because of his outspoken political views, the members of the Lodge decide the town would be better off without George. They therefore arrange to establish a competing barber shop and put one of their retired members in charge. The Lodge expects that when George feels the economic pinch he will move away. The Lodge will then advertise for another barber to open a shop in the town and will close its own shop. The action of the Lodge is clearly intended only as a personal action against George. It would be quite different if the Lodge had established its barber shop to make a profit, for that is a legitimate end.

The privilege to engage in business is curtailed whenever a governmental unit grants an exclusive franchise to an individual or firm. Thus, a state Public Service Commission may grant a franchise to Railway X to construct and operate a railroad line between two designated points within the state, and the Federal Communications Commission may grant to a certain broadcasting station the exclusive right to use a designated frequency upon which it may broadcast. Any attempt by another individual or firm to invade such an exclusive right is subject to a restraining order and a fine and possibly to a judgment for damages. Similarly, the privilege of engaging in a business or profession may be curtailed by a state statute which requires, as a prerequisite to engaging in business, the fulfillment of specific qualifications or approval of an applicant by an examining board. For example, proof of qualification is required before someone can practice medicine or law, or become a real estate broker, security salesman, or electrical contractor. In general, it is the responsibility of the state to take corrective action against a person who does business without the requisite permission. However, many courts permit a licensed member of a profession to bring an action on behalf of the entire protected group to restrain an interloper who wrongfully attempts to enter the field.

Interfering with Business Relations

There are two aspects of the tort of interfering with business relations: (1) interfering with contract relations, and (2) interfering with employer-employee relations.

Interfering with Contract Relations

The understandings of business people when they buy, sell, or undertake a business dealing are expressed either orally or in writing in *contracts* (agreements). Even where there is no explicit agreement, the existence of a contract frequently may be implied from the actions of the parties. The nature and elements of contracts are discussed in detail in Chapters 8 through 19.

The right to engage in a contract and the right to expect its performance are necessary to the orderly conduct of business affairs. These rights are considered in law to be property rights and the law looks with great disfavor upon any interference with them. A third party might wrongfully interfere with the contract relations of others at two stages of the contracting process: (1) in the initial stage, by interfering with the *making* of a contract; and (2) after the contract is in existence, by interfering with its *performance.*

Interfering with the Making of a Contract; Interfering with Economic Advantage. A tort is committed when an individual or a firm, acting with malice, induces another not to enter into a contract with a third party. As we have seen in Chapters 4 and 5, *malice* is a word not easily defined. It means here only that the interference was not justified or privileged or that illegal means were used to prevent the contract from coming into being.

The tort of "interfering in the making of a contract" is viewed in its broadest aspects to include liability for an *intentional* interference by a third party with present or potential economic or business relations or advantages when such interference is unjustified and without privilege. An unjustifiable or wrongful interference with another party's engaging in a contract or an interference with another's prospective economic advantage occurs when (1) the methods used are not within the privilege of fair competition, as is illustrated in Cases 6.1, *Wing,* and 6.2, *LaBar,* and (2) the purpose or motive is to divert or take business from another and the plaintiff suffers injury thereby. As was said by the court in *Lowell v. Mother's Cake & Cookie Co.*, 79 Cal. App.3d 13 (1978) "Whether an intentional interference by a third party is justifiable depends upon a balancing of the importance, social and private, of the objective advanced by the interference against the importance of the interest interfered with, *considering all circumstances* including the nature of the actor's conduct and the relationship between the parties."

If an inducement not to engage in a contract serves a legitimate end and no improper means is used (e.g., the interference was neither unjustified nor illegal), the action is said to be justifiable or privileged, and there is no tort. Competition carried on in an *acceptable manner* between businesses may result in one of them not receiving an expected contract. Under that circumstance, the interference with the making of the contract is simply a common instance of a *privileged interference.* Thus, wholesaler Whitehouse may with impunity offer a better discount to induce storekeeper Arnold to buy Whitehouse's merchandise rather than the merchandise of wholesaler Monroe, who supplied Arnold in the past; and Monroe cannot successfully complain that this is an improper interference with a contract of sale which had seemed assured.

Another example of bona fide competition might be this: assume that you damage your car in an accident. You get bids from Sam and from Yount, two body shop owners, to repair your car. The fact that Sam furnished the lower bid, thereby inducing you not to contract with Yount, was no more than fair competition.

Moreover, as revealed in the following case, an economic expectancy that has not yet reached the stage where the parties are about to engage in a contract is also protected from a *wrongful* interference by a third party.

CASE 6.1 Martin v. Wing · 667 P.2d 1159 (Wyo. 1983)

FACTS The Wings (the plaintiffs) owned certain property. The Martins (the defendants) lived next door. The Wings had their property up for sale. Mr. and Mrs. Thomson who were thinking about buying it, parked nearby to inspect the property. When the Martins saw the Thomsons viewing the land the Martins approached them. In the conversation which ensued, the Martins said that they were erecting a steel building next door to Wing's property; that there was a great deal of flooding of the land; that it was not accessible in the winter; and that the septic system for Wing's house had not been approved. Because of the Martins' statements, the Thomsons made no offer to buy the property and the Wings sued the Martins for interfering with their economic expectancy. After a judgment for the plaintiffs (the Wings), the defendants (the Martins) appealed.

OPINION ROONEY, C. J.... [Plaintiff] is seeking relief for "interference with prospective economic advantage," as opposed to "interference with contractual relations."... These separate causes of action tend to merge, except that the latter is aimed at the protection of the "probable expectancies" of life, such as future contractual relations.... The elements of the tort have been stated as:

1. the existence of a valid contractual relationship or business expectancy;
2. knowledge of the relationship or expectancy on the part of the interferor;
3. intentional interference inducing or causing a breach or termination of the relationship or expectancy; and
4. resulting damage to the party whose relationship or expectancy has been disrupted....

CASE 6.1 Continued

In *Martin v. Phillips Petroleum Company*, Tex. Civ. App., 455 S.W.2d 429 (1970), [the court said]:

> "...Our courts have also recognized a cause of action for tortious and wrongful interference with advantageous business relationships.... It need not be absolutely certain that the prospective contract would have been made were it not for such interference. A reasonable assurance thereof in view of all the circumstances, is generally sufficient.... A party does not have a right to be free from competition, but instead merely has the right to be free from malicious interference with the right to conduct negotiations that have a reasonable probability of resulting in a contract...."

Not only was there a "for sale" sign on the property for over a year, but appellants [the Martins] approached the Thomsons to initiate a conversation in which the Thomsons said they were considering purchase of the property. There was sufficient evidence of knowledge on the part of appellants of the relationship of the parties....

...[T]here was evidence that appellants approached the Thomsons and volunteered the information concerning flooding, the septic system and the problem of access in winter.... [T]here was evidence that this information was not accurate. Under the circumstances, we cannot disturb the findings of the trial court in this respect.

[T]he plaintiffs have] the right to be free from the intentional interference with the right to conduct negotiations that have a reasonable probability of resulting in a contract.

JUDGMENT Affirmed.

Thus far, the discussion has been limited to the interference by a third party with a prospective contract between other individuals. What of the situation where a person seeks to purchase from someone who refuses to sell? Such an occurrence, although technically not an interference with the making of a contract, is so closely akin to it that its brief consideration is appropriate here.

As a general rule, an individual is free to choose whether to sell or not to sell his or her products. However, at certain times, even though no third party is involved, this freedom is curtailed. Such curtailment may result directly from statutory mandate, as in the Civil Rights Act of 1964, or somewhat less directly from the requirement in a public utility franchise that the company must serve the public without discrimination. Even when no statute or franchise is involved, if a refusal to sell is for the purpose of creating an illegal monopoly, the refusal is improper. Moreover, although an individual acting alone may be privileged to refuse to deal with another, under certain circumstances the refusal is tortious because it is part of a concerted effort with others (a conspiracy). Thus, firms Ace Tire Co., Bill's Tire Co., and Carolina Tire Co., acting *independently of one another,* legally may refuse to deal with the Southern Tire Co.; but if the three firms enter into an agreement not to deal with Southern in order to force it out of business or to force it into a price combine, the refusal to deal constitutes a business tort.

Interfering with Contract Performance. As we have seen, the right of an individual *to enter* into contractual relations is protected by law. The right *to expect* performance under a contract already entered into is even more fully protected. In the event of breach of a contract (failure to perform the contract as agreed) by one of the parties to a contract in being, the other has a contract right of action to recover payment for the damages caused by the breach. This is called *an action in contract* (discussed at length in Chapter 15); it is not an action in tort.

Moreover, any unprivileged interference by a *third party* which retards, makes more difficult, or prevents performance of a contract between others, or makes its performance of less value to one of the contracting parties gives rise to *an action in tort* in which the plaintiff seeks compensation for the damages sustained. Inducing a breach of contract is the most common form of this type of business tort. Bona fide competition, as we have seen, may furnish legal justification for interfering with the *creation* of a contract; it does *not,* however, furnish legal justification for inducing *breach* of a contract.

An individual who intentionally induces a breach of contract is liable if the following conditions are present: (1) he or she knew of the existence of the contract and intended to bring about its breach, (2) the action was not legally justifiable, (3) the breach was the proximate result of the actions, and (4) damage to the plaintiff resulted.

A contract may provide that it is terminable at the will (i.e., at the election of) the parties to it. Notwithstanding this freedom, a third person is not privileged, without justification, intentionally to induce a termination of the contract.

The discussion of malice and legal justification with respect to interfering with the *making* of a contract is generally also applicable to the tort of *inducing a breach* of contract. Malice, in the sense of intentionally doing a harmful act without legal justification or excuse, is necessary to establish the tort of interference with contract performance. Whether malice is present depends upon the circumstances. The facts may be "so outrageous" that malice may be presumed.

The following case makes clear that the right to compete does not give license to interfere with another's business relationships.

CASE 6.2 Island Air, Inc. v. LaBar · 566 P.2d 972 (Wash. App. 1977)

FACTS Island Air, Inc., the plaintiff, operated an air service between the Anacortes Airport and the San Juan Islands in Puget Sound. On that route the plaintiff transported parcels for United Parcel Service, Inc. (UPS) under a contract which was terminable after 60 days notice by either of the parties.

Defendant LaBar, employed by another airline, told the plaintiff he was interested in purchasing the plaintiff airline if he could have figures as to Island Air's operations so that he could determine its value. Plaintiff furnished the information, including information about the UPS contract, with the understanding that the matters revealed were confidential; that the information would be used only to estimate Island Air's value to determine a fair purchase price; and that the information would not be used by LaBar for the purpose of competing with Island Air.

Later, LaBar told plaintiff he would not purchase the plaintiff's business. Instead, he submitted to UPS an offer to carry their parcels to the islands on more favorable terms than he had learned the plaintiff charged. UPS canceled its contract with Island Air and entered into a new contract with defendant.

Plaintiff sued LaBar, claiming, among other things, that LaBar had tortiously interfered in plaintiff's business relationship with UPS. LaBar answered that he had engaged in only a privileged competitive activity; that the UPS contract was terminable at the will of either of the parties to it after giving appropriate notice; that UPS voluntarily terminated the contract; and that no tort occurred. The lower court held for the plaintiff and the defendant appealed.

OPINION CALLOW, J. . . . Did the defendant tortiously interfere with the business relationship between Island Air and United Parcel Service or were the actions of defendant justified as permissible competition?

. . . [Defendant asserts] that his actions were justified because (1) the contract between the plaintiff and UPS was terminable at will; (2) UPS did not breach the contract with

CASE 6.2 Continued

plaintiff but terminated it according to its terms; [and] (3) public policy encourages and promotes competitive contract bidding;... We do not agree.

... Liability for the unjustifiable interference in another's commercial relations is not dependent on the existence of an enforceable contract... [nor does it] depend upon whether a contractual relationship was breached.... Further, the fact that a party's terminable at will contract is ended in accordance with its terms does not defeat the party's claim for damages caused by an unjustifiable interference....

We support the principles of free competition, but a claim of competition *alone* does not justify interference by a stranger to a contract....

... Further, it has been said: While a trader may lawfully engage in the sharpest competition with those in a like business, ... when he oversteps that line and commits an act with the *malicious intent of inflicting injury upon his rival's business,* his conduct is illegal, and if damage ensues from it the injured party is entitled to redress.

Self-enrichment... and not personal ill will, may well have been the motive; but it is malice nevertheless. While ill will toward a person is malice in its... popular sense, in the technical, legal sense it is the intentional doing of a wrongful act without justification or excuse.... And a "wrongful act," within the intendment of this definition, is any act which, in the ordinary course, will infringe upon the rights of another to his damage, *except it be done in the exercise of an equal or superior right*.... The weapons used by the trader who relies upon this right [of competition] for justification must be those furnished by the laws of trade, or at least must not be inconsistent with their free operation.

... Here, the means employed by the defendant to gain a competitive advantage involved... a violation of a covenant [the promise not to misuse the confidential information].

The role of the court is to raise the standard of business morality and care, not judicially to sanction tortious activities. Higher standards benefit and protect both the innocent members of an industry and the general public....

JUDGMENT The judgment is affirmed.

Perhaps the most sensational lawsuit for inducing a breach of contract culminated in 1986 in a $10.53 billion judgment in favor of the Pennzoil Company against the Texaco Company. Pennzoil alleged that in 1984 it offered to buy the Getty Oil Company; Getty's board of directors accepted the offer; representatives of both companies shook hands and toasted the agreement with champagne. Stories of the event were published in the newspapers. However, before their agreement was signed the Texaco Company offered Getty a higher price. Getty's directors accepted Texaco's offer and did not follow through with their Pennzoil agreement. After trial in a Texas court the jury found that Getty and Pennzoil had entered into a contract and that Texaco, with knowledge of the contract, had intentionally caused its breach. The Court of Appeals upheld the judgment but reduced the punitive damages by $2 billion and the Texas Supreme Court held there was no reversible error. Texaco subsequently paid Pennzoil $3 billion in settlement of the judgment.

A seeming exception to the rule that the law looks with disfavor upon inducing a breach of contract exists when the act involves peaceful persuasion and the objective sought to be accomplished results in benefit to the public. Assume, for example, that a labor union in furtherance of a strike pickets an employer's plant. Not wanting to cross the union's picket line, Gary's Trucking Company breaches its contract with the plant. Although the union had induced that contract breach, it will not be liable in tort because it is generally recognized that the public interest in improved working conditions transcends the right of a contracting party not to have a contract interfered with by a stranger to it. However, a labor union can be restrained and even held liable in damages if its action constitutes an unfair labor practice under applicable statutes, such as by engaging in a secondary boycott.

A *boycott* is a form of business coercion whereby two or more parties combine for the purpose of jointly refraining from (or preventing others from) having business dealings with some person or firm. A boycott may be either *primary* or *secondary.* For instance, if labor union members, in aid of their strike against the Heatherton Department Store, agree not to make purchases from that store until the strike is settled, the union is engaged in a *primary boycott.* This is a legal device to influence labor relations. However, if the union members picket the Spencer Company (a supplier to Heatherton) because Spencer continues to do business with Heatherton during the strike, the union is then engaged in a *secondary boycott.* This kind of boycott is an unfair labor practice and is illegal because it is directed to injuring the business of an innocent person or firm not involved in the basic labor dispute. It should also be noted that any kind of boycott is unlawful if it is executed with force, violence, or threats [*Smith v. Grady,* 411 F.2d 181 (5th Cir. 1969)].

The same act which gives rise to the business torts of interfering with the making of a contract and of inducing a breach of contract may also give rise to other tort actions. For example, suppose that Judy induces Craig to breach his contract with the Fortune Cookie Company by publishing disparaging statements about the quality of that company's products. Fortune would have two causes of action against Judy: one for inducing the breach of contract and one for trade libel, a business tort to be discussed later.

Interfering with Employer-Employee Relations

Interfering with employer-employee relations is an aspect of the broader business tort of interfering with business relations. A staff of trained employees is a most important element of any successful business organization, requiring time and money to develop. If a trained employee is induced to leave a company in order to work for a competitor, the new employer may reap a considerable economic advantage. Not only will the new employer be saved the expense of training the employee but it may also "inherit" some of the other company's manufacturing processes and customers and perhaps learn something of its trade secrets (trade secrets are discussed later in this chapter). A contract of employment, therefore, represents a valuable property right. The tort of wrongful hiring away another's employee is an aspect of the tort of inducing a breach of contract. Inducing an employee to change employment may be tortious whether the initial employment relationship was established in writing or orally and whether the initial employment was for a specified term or at will.

Newspapers and trade journals regularly carry advertisements of job opportunities, holding out attractive working and living conditions and favorable salary scales to induce qualified persons to apply. Suppose as a result of such an advertisement an individual leaves his or her current employment and goes to work for the company which placed the ad. Does this mean that the firm which advertised has committed a tort and so is liable in damages? Not necessarily, as the court said in *Sarkes Tarzian, Inc v. Audio Devices, Inc.* (166 F.Supp. 250, S.D. Cal. 1958): "In our free economy, social mobility is a chief characteristic. An employee who is dischargeable at will is under no obligation to treat his employer otherwise or with more consideration than he can be treated by [the employer]."

The privilege of an employee to change jobs is not, however, a license to an employer, *at its pleasure,* to entice an employee away from working for a competitor. If, for instance, the Brick Company induces Carl to leave his position with Aspen not only to gain an employee but also to *injure* Aspen, then the pirating away of Carl is *malicious.* Under such a circumstance the new employer, Brick Company, wrongfully interfered with the preexisting employer-employee relationship and committed a tort. In the context of this tort, *malice,* as in any other interference with business advantage, means that the wrongdoer intentionally and without cause or excuse interfered with the relationship.

The court, in the next case, clarifies what constitutes a wrongful pirating away another's employee.

CASE 6.3 Avtec Industries, Inc. v. Sony Corporation of America · 500 A.2d 712 (N.J. Super. 1985)

FACTS Plaintiff, Avtec Industries, Inc., installed and serviced video and audio systems and rendered engineering and maintenance service for such companies as AT&T and Georgia Power Company. In furtherance of its business, it had an agreement with defendant Sony which required Avtec, at its own expense, "to have at least one of its technically oriented personnel, with an electronic background, trained at a service school designated by" Sony, the defendant.

In March 1981 Avtec hired Serge Caleca, who was highly qualified, to work as a technician in its service department. Caleca was given additional on-the-job training by the plaintiff and was also sent to the Sony service school and seminars. While at the seminars Caleca expressed an interest in working for Sony. A job came open and Caleca applied for the position. In September he left Avtec and started to work for defendant Sony.

Avtec sued Sony, charging that as a result of its dealership agreement, it maliciously interfered with Avtec's contractual relationship with Caleca by hiring him away. The jury determined that Sony acted in good faith and without malice. However, the jury also found that Sony "acted in an unfair manner or violated generally accepted standards of common morality in hiring Mr. Caleca" and "used wrongful means in hiring [him]". It returned a verdict for the plaintiff. The judge granted the defendant's motion for a judgment notwithstanding the verdict and Avtec appealed.

OPINION BILDER, J. . . . Simply stated, we are asked to decide whether a manufacturer can be liable to one who is a nonexclusive dealer for a number of manufacturers when it hires away one of its key at-will service employees. Avtec says the hiring amounts to an intentional interference for which it is entitled to consequential damages. . . .

That Sony intentionally interfered with the employee-employer relationship between Caleca and Avtec is unquestionable. . . . The at-will nature of the relationship was irrelevant vis-à-vis Sony because Caleca's right to leave does not furnish Sony with a right to interfere. . . .

. . . The mere persuasion of an employee to change jobs is not wrongful; but if it is done to injure the employer, it is wrongful. . . . It is undisputed that Caleca was not hired to injure Avtec. And it would have been wrongful if done to benefit the "raider" at the employer's expense "unless done in the exercise of an equal or superior right" . . . The right to compete for employees is such an equal right provided it is not done by improper means. . . .

An examination of cases in which interference has been found discloses egregious conduct directed toward destruction of a competitor's business. Thus, in *Wear-Ever Aluminum Inc. v. Townecraft, etc., Inc.*, [75 N.J. Super. 135, 182 A.2d 387 (Ch. Div. 1962)] there was a deceit practiced in which the defendant secretly used Wear-Ever's zone manager to induce its entire Philadelphia sales force to desert the defendant-competitor. And in *A. S. Rumpell, Inc. v. Hyster Company*, 165 N.Y.S.2d 475 (Ct. App. 1957), 144 N.E.2d 271, . . . Hyster was charged with interfering with employment relationships in order thereby to destroy the existing manufacturer-dealer relationship and appropriate Rumpell's sales organization and goodwill. We have been shown no case in which the wrongfulness did not involve predatory conduct such as deceit or intended harm to the plaintiff. . . .

> In oft-cited *dicta*, [Judge] Learned Hand said: So far as we have found, it has never been thought actionable to take away another's employee, when the defendant wants to use him in his own business, however much the plaintiff may suffer. It is difficult to see how servants could get the full . . . [pay for] their services on any other terms; time creates no prescriptive right in other men's labor. If any employer expects so much, he must secure it by contract. . . .

The jury's finding that Sony acted in good faith, without malice and without exploiting a confidential relationship precludes liability.

JUDGMENT The judgment n.o.v. is affirmed.

Disparaging Business Reputation or Property

Any business is entitled to compete with other firms free from disparagement of its reputation and of the products it sells. This part of this chapter deals with business torts (1) involving disparagement of a firm's reputation, also referred to as "defamation," and (2) torts involving disparagement of its property.

Disparagement of Business Reputation

The disparagement of reputation through the publication of an injurious falsehood is a tort discussed in Chapter 4. Here, we need only recognize that a disparagement of a businessperson or firm, such as a corporation or a partnership, may be a damaging tort. The wrong occurs when an unprivileged communication of a derogatory statement adversely affects the credit rating of a businessperson or firm or otherwise deters a third party from doing business with the person or firm disparaged. For example, a supplier of ink to the Ace Printing Company learns that Ace will henceforth buy its ink from a different source. Angry at this development, the supplier parks a truck in front of the Ace building. On the side of the truck is a large banner which falsely proclaims: "Ace Printing does not pay its bills." As a result, other ink suppliers refuse to do business with Ace. The false publication by the supplier was tortious because it damaged the Ace Company.

To constitute a disparagement it is not necessary that the defamatory statement mention by name the party affected if it is reasonably understood to refer to that party. And although the words may be ambiguous, if they are used in a way which makes clear (1) that they are intended to be derogatory, (2) that they refer to a particular individual or firm, and (3) if they are understood in that light, a disparagement has occurred.

Unless state law dictates otherwise, in a case of disparagement of a business there are available to the defendant all the defenses which may be used in a suit involving personal defamation (see Chapter 4). Therefore, a defense of absolute privilege or of qualified privilege may be asserted by one accused of the tort of disparagement of a business.

Of the two forms of privilege, the more common type is *qualified* or, as it is sometimes called, *conditional* privilege. The defense is given this name because it may be asserted only on condition that the maker of the defamatory falsehood reasonably believes the statement to be true and, without malice, publishes it in furtherance of some recognized interest. For instance, a credit bureau, in response to a request from one of its members, furnishes a derogatory credit report on another firm based upon erroneous information. When sued for disparagement the credit bureau successfully may claim its action to be qualifiedly privileged because it received the erroneous information in good faith and published it only to the firm that requested the credit report. If, however, it circulates the derogatory report indiscriminately, the defense of privilege is absent.

Disparagement of Business Property

The term *disparagement of property* refers collectively to the common law torts of slander of title and slander of quality (usually called *trade libel*).

Slander of Title. This tort involves the unprivileged publication of untrue matter which casts doubt upon, or denies, the validity of another's title or interest in any kind of property and the publication causes financial loss. A disparagement of property may involve such actions as, for example, wrongfully filing for record a mortgage or claim of lien upon the property; wrongfully asserting that a third person has some interest in the property; wrongfully stating that the owner of the property cannot legally deliver its possession to another; or, in bad faith, claiming that use of a competitor's product will result in a patent infringement suit.

Slander of Quality (Trade Libel). Slander of quality, or trade libel, is the unprivileged publication of false matter which indicates that another's property lacks the *characteristics* its vendor claims for it or which indicates that the property is unfit for the purposes for which it is being sold or leased. This tort is akin to slander of title, but here the financial loss is caused by belittling the *quality* of another's property, rather than the *title* to it. Slander of title always involves a statement of fact, but trade libel may be either a false statement of fact or a dishonest expression of opinion made in such circumstances that the vendability of the property will probably be diminished. Following the passage of various federal and state laws requiring truth in advertising, there have been fewer incidents of trade libel.

It is not unusual for a single improper publication to constitute both a trade libel and a defamation. Such a situation would exist, for instance, when the statement not only disparages the quality of an article but also reflects upon the honesty of the owner or storekeeper who offers it for sale.

Defenses against Disparagement of Property. Just as truth of the statement and privilege of utterance are defenses in actions for defamation, so are they defenses in actions for disparagement of property. As in defamation, the privilege may be either absolute or qualified. Whether or not the defendant should be held to have a qualified privilege often presents a difficult problem to the courts. A qualified privilege exists when the publication is made in a reasonable manner or, as many courts say, without malice, and to satisfy a purpose which the law recognizes as justifiable.

The following illustrate the disparagement of another's property under qualifiedly privileged circumstances:

- In a dispute over the title to an automobile, one of the parties claims title to the vehicle honestly believing it to be hers.
- Although a storekeeper may exaggerate the benefits of his or her merchandise, even to claiming that it is "the world's best," (so-called "puffing"), no *untruthful direct attack* may be made on another's wares. Thus, the Emerald Soap Co. may advertise that its soap washes clothes brighter and cleaner than any other soap even though that statement impliedly disparages the soap manufactured by other companies. However, Emerald is not privileged untruthfully to say, "Our soap washes clothes brighter and cleaner than X's because their soap does not dissolve in water."

A disparaging statement made to a third party for the latter's protection is another example of qualified privilege. The privilege is present when (*a*) the person making the statement believes it to be true *and* (*b*) he or she is under a duty to inform the third party. That principle applies, for instance, in the following hypothetical situation: A real estate agent shows certain farmland to a potential purchaser. The agent knows that the well on the land is dry for 2 months each summer. The agent is obligated to tell a potential purchaser of that condition even though the agent thereby disparages the property and may lose the sale.

Engaging in Unfair Trade Practices

The most common business tort and the one under which the widest range of wrongs occurs, is that of engaging in unfair trade practices. This tort encompasses all interferences with the right of a business to enjoy the trade advantages it creates for itself and to profit from the goodwill and good reputation it earns. The wrong may be committed by a competitor, by someone not in competition with the injured business but within its merchandising chain from manufacturer to dealer, or even by an individual in an entirely unrelated business.

Unfair trade practices take many forms. Among them are fraudulent marketing; infringing another's trademark or trade name; infringing a patent or copyright; and unlawfully appropriating another's trade secrets. There have been unfair trade practices involving such disparate articles as drugs, liquor, brake linings, oil filters, bolts used in the assembly of aircraft, helicopter clutch plates, sunglasses, basketballs, fire doors, shoes, and credit cards. In response to what appeared to be a growing recourse to unfair trade practices, in 1978 the National Conference of Commissioners on Uniform State Laws presented to the states for adoption a Uniform Deceptive Trade Practices Act and a Uniform Consumer Sales Protection Act. These acts have been adopted by many states. Some unfair trade practices, such as an agreement among manufacturers to limit the territory in which each will sell its products (called a *combination in restraint of trade*) are prohibited by antitrust statutes. These statutes are discussed in Chapters 45 and 46. We will discuss unfair trade practices under two general headings: (1) fraudulent marketing, and (2) pirating intellectual property.

Fraudulent Marketing

The term *fraudulent marketing* refers primarily to falsifying the source or maker of an article or imitating the physical appearance or packaging of an article.

Falsifying Source or Maker. If a business concern intentionally misrepresents a product or article, and a purchaser relies upon that misrepresentation, the business tort commonly called "palming off" has been committed. For example, in each of the following scenarios customers believed that the articles were actually as represented:

- A store displays the sign "Arrow Shirts" above a stack of shirts on a counter in such a way as to indicate that all the shirts in the pile are Arrow brand, but actually only one or two are Arrow shirts.
- A dress store has a sign in its window falsely claiming, "Dress styles by Dior."
- A manufacturer falsely tells wholesalers that the motor in an electric tool was approved by the UL Testing Laboratory.

Such a false representation is a tort against the UL Testing Laboratory, which has been damaged by the accusation that it has approved what might be an inferior or dangerous product. Of course, the purchaser of the product is harmed because he or she has not received the tool with an electric motor that has been approved by the UL Testing Laboratory.

Imitating Physical Appearance or Packaging. Imitating the form or style of another's product or its distinctive wrapping is another form of "palming off" if a prospective purchaser is deceived by the imitation. An example of imitating the form of another's product would be if cheap imported dolls were made to look like Cabbage Patch dolls and sold under that name. An example of copying the wrapping of another company's product might be if a manufacturer wraps his candy bar in paper with printing that closely resembles the wrapper of a well-known candy bar. This tort also would occur when a company uses employees' uniforms or delivery vehicles so similar to those already used by another company that a customer is misled in distinguishing between the two and thereby is caused to deal with one firm believing it to be the other. However, it should be recognized that in order to retain the public benefit which free competition offers, the law allows considerable latitude to business concerns to copy the styles and designs of their competitors as long as no palming off occurs.

Although the copying and sale of a product may economically harm the originator, the courts generally will neither restrain nor cause the imitator to respond in damages as long as the imitator (1) does not resort to unfair methods in securing the copy, (2) does not use fraudulent marketing in introducing it to the public, or (3) does not make the imitation so similar to the original that the public would be misled as to the source of the article.

Assume that the High Fashion Store sends its buyer to Paris where she purchases expensive original couturier dresses to be sold in its dress salon. The dress styles are not copyrighted or patented. The Bargain Dress Store, which sells popular-priced dresses, reads in the newspaper that High Fashion has "original dresses fresh from Paris" for sale. The Bargain Dress Store sends its designer to High Fashion where she examines the Parisian dresses displayed there. She then returns to her own store and makes an excellent copy of one of them. Bargain puts the imitation on sale for one-fourth the price of High Fashion's original but does not advertise the dress as an original Parisian model. High Fashion has no basis for tort action against Bargain.

If we were to change the above hypothetical facts to say that Bargain secured the dress design by bribing one of High Fashion's employees to show the dress privately so that Bargain's designer could copy it, or if Bargain had promised not to make a copy of the dress but nonetheless did so, then Bargain would have secured its copy through improper means and its privilege to imitate would have been lost.

The next case illustrates how a court applied the rules pertaining to copying a design which is not protected by copyright or patent.

CASE 6.4 Polo Fashions, Inc. v. Craftex, Inc. • 816 F.2d 145 (4th Cir. 1987)

FACTS

Polo Fashions, Inc., the plaintiff, is a well-known distributor of clothing for men and women designed by Ralph Lauren. The company uses the trade names POLO and RALPH LAUREN. Either name appears on labels affixed at the back of the neck of each garment. Plaintiff also embroiders on the breast of its knitted sport shirts a fanciful representation of a polo player mounted on a horse.

Defendant, Craftex, Inc., manufactures knitted sport shirts. During 1982 and 1983 the company manufactured and the defendants sold 1,388 dozen knitted sport shirts bearing an embroidered emblem substantially identical to the plaintiff's polo player symbol. Craftex attached inside the back of the neck of each shirt a label bearing the words Knight of Armor.

Plaintiff filed action against the defendants alleging, among other causes of action, common law trademark infringement and unfair competition. The district court found that the defendants made a profit of $14,837.72 in the manufacture and sale of the sport shirts and that the plaintiff had suffered damages in that amount. The court then trebled the damages under North Carolina's Unfair Trade Practices Act and the defendants appealed.

OPINION

HAYNSWORTH, Cir. J. The North Carolina common law of unfair competition in the context of trademarks and trade names is similar to the federal law of trademark infringement. Unfair acts of a defendant are actionable when they damage a plaintiff's legitimate business. [Citation.] Such damages are suffered when a rival adopts for his own goods a sign or symbol in an apparent imitation of another's that would likely mislead prospective purchasers and the public as to the identity of the goods. [Citations.] Such damage was suffered by the plaintiff in this case when the defendants placed on the market demonstrably inferior goods bearing the polo player symbol.

The North Carolina unfair trade practices statute prohibits unfair methods of competition and unfair or deceptive acts or practices. [Citation.] As used in the statute, the words "unfair methods of competition," have not been precisely defined by the North Carolina courts, although it has been suggested that they encompass any conduct that a court of equity would consider unfair. [Citations.] A practice is unfair if it is unethical or unscrupulous, and it is deceptive if it has a tendency to deceive. [Citations.]

The defendants contend, however, that there is no likelihood of confusion because of a label affixed inside the back of the neck of each shirt bearing the words Knight of Armor. The plaintiffs never used such a mark as Knight of Armor, but even the most sophisticated purchaser, seeing the polo player symbol on the front of the shirt, might suppose the plaintiff had adopted another trademark in addition to POLO, RALPH LAUREN and POLO BY RALPH LAUREN. Moreover, in the after sale context, one seeing the shirt being worn by its owner would not see the label on the back of the neck. Seeing the polo player symbol, it is likely that the observer would identify the shirt with the plaintiff, and the plaintiff's reputation would suffer damage if the shirt appeared to be of poor quality. [Citations.]

On the facts of this case we think that the likelihood of confusion was so unassailably established as to warrant the district court's entry of summary judgment for the plaintiff as to liability....

It cannot be said that the defendants' infringement caused the plaintiff to lose the sales of the number of shirts sold by the defendants. Nor can it be said that the plaintiff lost sales equivalent to the total dollar sales of the shirts by the defendants. The retail price of plaintiff's shirts was several times the retail price at which the defendants' goods were sold. It is more than likely that some buyers of the defendants' shirts would not have been willing to pay the higher price necessary to purchase one of the plaintiff's shirts. That the

CASE 6.4 Continued plaintiff's sales were adversely affected, however, can hardly be denied.... [F]airness to the infringers suggests strongly that the plaintiff's damages should be limited to the defendants' profits, and that is what was done. The district court properly... trebled that amount under the North Carolina statute....

JUDGMENT Affirmed.

Pirating Intellectual Property

The intellectual property of a business is generally understood to mean its trademarks, trade names, patents or copyrights, and trade secrets. (For our present purposes we need not discuss specific products of the mind such as books, songs, or works of art.) A business has a property right in its intellectual property which can be of great value to the company which owns it. The piracy of intellectual property is a business tort. We shall discuss such piracy under five headings: (1) infringing a trademark; (2) infringing a trade name; (3) infringing a patent; (4) infringing a copyright; and (5) violating a trade secret.

Infringing a Trademark. A *trademark* is any word, symbol, device, or design adopted and placed on or affixed to an article offered for sale or to its container to identify its originator. A trademark belongs to and may be exclusively used by the firm which first employs it. A trademark need not be registered with a state or with the federal government in order to earn protection from infringement (its use by someone else without permission). If a trademark is not registered, the first user of that name or design has a common law property right in it and the mark is known as a *common law trademark.* However, registration extends its geographical effectiveness and furnishes proof of the date its use began. Registration may also prolong the life of a trademark and entitle its owner to additional legal remedies in the event of infringement.

Place or personal names or words normally descriptive of an article or of its use generally may not be trademarked, as such words should be available to anyone. However, if those words are used as part of a design or device or are so fanciful or uncommon as not normally to be identified with an article, they may then be subject to trademark. This distinction may best be explained by two illustrations. (1) "Swiss watch" may not be trademarked to describe a watch made in Switzerland, for all watchmakers in that country should be free to so describe their products. But if "Swiss Watch" is the name given to, let us say, a candy bar, it would be such a fanciful use of the words that it may be adopted as a trademark. (2) Manufacturer John Smith may not trademark that name, for any person by that name should be free to use it to identify his own product. However, if one of these John Smiths accompanies his name with his picture or other unique design, the entire device may be trademarked to identify the source of a product. Familiar to many generations of consumers is the trademark "Smith Brothers Cough Drops" with the picture of the two bearded Smith brothers on the box.

The business tort of *trademark infringement* is committed when there is an *intentional or unintentional* use of a trademark that is so similar to a previously established trademark of another firm that it is likely to confuse prospective purchasers as to the source of the product. In response to the "epidemic of commercial counterfeiting" the Trademark Counterfeiting Act of 1984 was enacted. Under it, a defendant, for a first offense, may receive a 5-year prison sentence and be fined $250,000. In addition, the aggrieved party can recover damages equal to three times the profits involved from the improper use of the mark, together with attorneys' fees.

Words or devices which have not been made the subject of a trademark may be protected from copying by an unauthorized person or firm if the words or devices have acquired a secondary meaning. A *secondary meaning* is acquired when the name or device connotes in the public mind a specific product or source. In that event, use of the name by another company in such a way as to deceive a purchaser constitutes unfair competition. The Supreme Court has said with respect to Coca-Cola:

> The name means a single thing coming from a single source, and well known to the community.... In other

words, "Coca-Cola" probably means to most persons the plaintiff's familiar product to be had everywhere rather than a compound of particular substances.... [It] has acquired a secondary significance and has indicated the plaintiff's product alone. (*Coca-Cola Co. v. Koke Co. of America*, 254 U.S. 143, 146 (1920).

In that case, it was found that unfair competition resulted when another company used a name so similar to Coca-Cola that it would probably deceive purchasers and cause them to buy a soft drink believing it to be the product of Coca-Cola Company when in fact it was manufactured by another company. A later federal appeals court followed the quoted *Coca-Cola* decision when it unanimously rejected a claim that "Coke" has become a generic name applicable to all cola drinks.

Infringing a Trade Name. The term *trade name* refers to a name or phrase used by a business concern by which it is generally known even though the trade name is not the firm's legal name. For example, "Sohio" is the trade name by which Standard Oil of Ohio is generally known, and "IBM" is the trade name for the company whose legal name is International Business Machines Corporation. The precise difference between a trademark and a trade name is usually immaterial, since the law affords protection against the wrongful appropriation of either where confusion or uncertainty results or may result.

Sometimes a trademark or trade name is so commonly used that it is understood as a generic or descriptive designation for that *type* of article. If that situation arises, the trademark or trade name no longer solely identifies a *particular* source or brand but describes the article in general. What was formerly a trademark or trade name may then be used by anyone to describe the article, provided, of course, there is no attempt to palm off the new product as the original. For example, the word "Vichy" was originally a brand name for a French mineral water. "Vichy" has now become a generic term and can be used by anyone to denote mineral water as long as the source of the product is made clear to the public. Similarly, the term "deep freeze," originally the trademark of a specific brand of freezer, has now become a generic term referring to any freezer.

A trademark of the word "LITE" to distinguish a beer a company brews is the subject of the case which follows.

CASE 6.5 Miller Brewing Company v. Heileman Brewing Company · 561 F.2d 75 (7th Cir. 1977)

FACTS Meister Brau, Inc., secured a trademark on labels containing the name "LITE" for beer that has no available carbohydrates. Meister Brau later sold its interest in "LITE" trademarks to the plaintiff, Miller Brewing Company. Miller used the term "LITE" upon labels for a beer lower in calories than Miller's regular beer but not entirely without available carbohydrates. Miller spent considerable money advertising the beer. Soon other brewers, including defendant, G. Heileman Brewing Company, marketed reduced-calorie beers labeled or described as "light." Miller filed a trademark infringement action. The district court enjoined Heileman from distributing beer anywhere in the United States under a brand name incorporating the word "light." Heileman appealed.

OPINION TONE, Cir. J.... The registrations are prima facie evidence of Miller's exclusive right to use the word "LITE" for beer with no available carbohydrates.... Inasmuch as the beer marketed [by Miller]... contains available carbohydrates, the registrations are not prima facie evidence of Miller's exclusive right to use the mark on that beer. Thus,... Miller's brand name "LITE" must be evaluated under the common law of trademarks without the benefit of registration.

The basic principles of trademark law which are applicable here... may be briefly summarized. A term for which trademark protection is claimed will fit somewhere in the spectrum which ranges through (1) generic or common descriptive and (2) merely descriptive to (3) suggestive and (4) arbitrary or fanciful....

CASE 6.5 Continued

A generic or common descriptive term is one which is commonly used as the name or description of a kind of goods [e.g., "Consumer Electronics"]. It cannot become a trademark under any circumstances. Using the phonetic equivalent of a common descriptive word, i.e., misspelling it, is of no avail. . . .

A merely descriptive term specifically describes a characteristic or ingredient of an article [e.g., "After Tan Lotion"]. It can, by acquiring a secondary meaning, i.e., becoming "distinctive of the applicant's goods," . . . become a valid trademark.

A suggestive term suggests rather than describes an ingredient or characteristic of the goods and requires the observer or listener to use imagination and perception to determine the nature of the goods [e.g., "gobble-gobble" for turkey parts]. Such a term can be protected without proof of a secondary meaning.

An arbitrary or fanciful term [e.g., "Q-Tips"] enjoys the same full protection as a suggestive term but is far enough removed from the merely descriptive not to be vulnerable to possible attack as being merely descriptive rather than suggestive.

"Light" has been widely used in the beer industry for many years to describe a beer's color, flavor, body, or alcoholic content, or a combination of these or similar characteristics. . . Indeed, state statutes even use "light beer" as a generic or common descriptive term. "Light" is clearly a common descriptive word when used with beer. . . . [E]ven if Miller had given its light beer a characteristic not found in other light beers, it could not acquire the exclusive right to use the common descriptive word "light" as a trademark for that beer. Other brewers whose beers have qualities that make them "light," as that word has commonly been used, remain free to call their beer "light." Otherwise a manufacturer could remove a common descriptive word from the public domain by investing his goods with an additional quality, thus gaining the exclusive right to call his wine "rosé," his whiskey "blended" or his bread "white."

The word "light," including its phonetic equivalent, "lite," being a generic or common descriptive term as applied to beer, could not be exclusively appropriated by Miller as a trademark. . . .

JUDGMENT [T]he preliminary injunction must be reversed.

Infringing a Patent or Copyright

The Constitution (Art. I, Sec. 8, Cl. 8) authorizes, and Congress has enacted, patent and copyright laws which give to inventors and authors for an extended period of years the exclusive right to market their "brain children." It is governmental policy to encourage the expenditure of time, energy, and resources upon discovery, scientific and mechanical inventions, and the advancement of the arts.

Infringing a Patent. A patent may be issued for a process (e.g., a way to bond cloth); a machine (e.g., an innovative sewing machine); a manufacture (e.g., a new toy); a composition of matter (e.g., a new plastic); or a plant (e.g., a novel hybrid rose). A normal patent lasts 17 years. A design patent may also be granted but it lasts a lesser period of years.

The Semiconductor Chip Protection Act of 1984 created a new form of intellectual property in "mask work" (the primary device used in the manufacture of a semiconductor chip). The creator of mask work is given the exclusive right for 10 years to reproduce and distribute the mask or chip. It is intended by the act to combat the unauthorized duplication of semiconductor chips used in a wide variety of products ranging from computers and sophisticated weapons systems to kitchen products and video games and thereby to encourage further research and investment in this high-tech field.

To acquire a patent, the applicant must demonstrate to the U.S. Patent Office that the invention or discovery is *useful, novel,* and *not an obvious variation* of some article already known or in existence. The patent holder gives notice to the public that the article is patented by placing on it the word "Patent" (or "Pat.") and the patent number.

It should be understood, however, that having a patent issued to you does not keep copycat products off the market. There may be a *patent infringement*. That is, an article embodying your patent may have been made, either intentionally or unintentionally by another, without your permission. Some foreign countries have no patent laws or, if they have them, they are inadequate or go unenforced. South Korea, for example, prohibits patenting any chemical compound and denies copyright protection to semiconductors and computer software. If a foreign firm, without permission, makes a product or article covered by a U.S. patent and brings it into this country to compete with the American invention, the foreign firm is subject to the same legal consequences as anyone else charged with patent infringement.

In the event of a patent infringement within the United States, the patent holder may bring suit to enjoin the infringement and also to ask for damages. Such suits are notoriously involved and costly. As the patent holder may be required to prove the validity of his or her patent as well as the fact of infringement, the litigation may place in jeopardy the very valuable property right that a patent represents. Therefore, not infrequently, a patent holder, instead of resorting to a lawsuit, sells to the infringer a license to use the patented product or design.

Infringing a Copyright. Copyright protection covers writings, recordings, and like intellectual property. To be copyrighted, a work must show certain minimum levels of creativity and originality. Although a work is copyrighted, the copyright is not infringed if a later work is substantially similar to it.

The courts have devised a "fair use" doctrine which permits a person, without the owner's consent, to copy excerpts from a copyrighted work if the copying is within the bounds of "fair use." Whether or not the use is "fair" depends upon such factors as: how much material is involved, the purpose for which the copy is made, whether the infringer seeks financial gain from the use of the copyrighted material, and what effect it has on the potential market for the original work. The courts are liberal in finding that a copying is "fair use" if it is for educational, historic, or scientific purposes.

A copyright is automatically acquired by placing upon all publicly distributed copies of the work a symbol such as ©, or an abbreviation meaning copyright, the year of first publication, and the name or abbreviation of the name of the owner. A copyright for work created subsequent to January 1, 1978, lasts for the life of the author plus 50 years after the author's death. In order for an action for infringement of a copyright to be instituted, the copyright claim (e.g., a written notice) must first be registered with the Copyright Office in the Library of Congress with payment of a small fee. As in the case of a patent, a copyright may be valuable and its infringement—a business tort—may be enjoined and made the basis of a suit for damages. In addition, the court may order the impounding and subsequent destruction of all copies of phonograph records and tapes made or used in violation of the copyright owner's exclusive rights. A person who infringes a copyright willfully may also be subject to fine and imprisonment.

Violating Trade Secrets

A *trade secret* is any information guarded by a firm because it furnishes the business with a peculiar economic advantage. Illustrative of trade secrets are: an engineering process, a formula, a method of utilizing a tool, a quality control procedure, a customer attitude study, or a delivery route. In certain instances, reliance upon a trade secret furnishes the owner with greater protection than does a patent.

Just as a firm is privileged as a normal incident of competition to copy the physical characteristics of a product, a firm is allowed to copy another's business methods and processes provided the information making such imitation possible comes into the copier's possession legitimately. Therefore, if a firm gains the knowledge of another's trade secret dishonestly, as through industrial espionage or commercial bribery, or through the abuse of a confidence, an unlawful interference with the business rights of another has taken place and a business tort has been committed. (A discussion of the violation of an employer's trade secret by an employee follows later in this chapter.)

Because of the importance to businesses of trade secrets, the National Conference of Commissioners on Uniform State Laws prepared a Uniform Trade Secrets Act. Thus far, it has been adopted by twenty states. In the prefatory note to the act, the commissioners said:

> A valid patent provides a legal monopoly for seventeen years in exchange for public disclosure of an invention. If, however, the courts ultimately decide that the Patent Office improperly issued a patent, an invention will have been disclosed to competitors with no corresponding benefit. In view of the substantial number of patents that are invalidated by the courts, many businesses now elect to protect commercial valuable information through reliance upon the state law of trade secret protection. . . .
>
> Notwithstanding the commercial importance of state trade secret law to interstate business, this law has not developed satisfactorily. . . . [E]ven in states in which there has been significant litigation, there is undue uncertainty concerning the parameters of trade secret protection, and the appropriate remedies for misappropriation of a trade secret. . . .

The next case gives us a broad analysis of the law pertaining to trade secrets.

CASE 6.6 Valco Cincinnati, Inc. v. N & D Machining Service · 492 N.E.2d 814 (Ohio 1986)

FACTS Valco Engineering, the plaintiff, manufactures equipment which automatically and at high speed applies industrial glue to containers to seal them for shipping. Each component of the equipment is critically designed to ensure that at precisely the right moment the glue begins to flow in a fixed volume through the applicator head and stops exactly when it is supposed to.

Over a period of more than 24 years and with much experimentation, Valco's engineering division developed and standardized unique materials, processes, tolerances, and dimensions. To keep its processes secret, Valco had locking devices on the doors of its factory; all visitors were screened; the general public was never taken through the plant; competitors were never allowed within it; and its design drawings, always bearing proprietary markings, were made available to its suppliers for only limited purposes. . . .

In 1976 Valco hired Draginoff, who had no prior experience in commercial glue application, as a machinist in charge of the machine shop. Later he progressed to production manager, thus becoming familiar with its processes and materials as well as its suppliers and customers.

Draginoff, with Valco's permission, set up a machine shop to do outside machine shop work. He conducted the business with his two brothers under the name N & D Machining Service, Inc. None of the Draginoffs had prior experience in the commercial glue application equipment field. N & D contracted with Valco to make certain parts for its applicator. For this purpose they were supplied with drawings and specifications.

In 1980 Draginoff resigned from Valco. Valco later learned that N & D (doing business as Superior Adhesive Equipment Co.), using Valco's process, was manufacturing and selling glue application equipment to a Valco competitor. Valco sued N & D and the Draginoff brothers for wrongfully appropriating its trade secrets and sought a temporary and a permanent injunction to prevent them from manufacturing replacement parts for Valco products. After trial, the court issued a permanent injunction. The court of appeals affirmed and N & D appealed to the State Supreme Court.

OPINION HOLMES, J. . . . Initially, the legal nature of the term "trade secret" must be analyzed. . . . As pointed out by Judge Black in his well considered appellate opinion below, . . .

> "A trade secret may consist of any formula, pattern, device or compilation of information which is used in one's business, and which gives him an opportunity to obtain an advantage over competitors who do not know or use it. It may be a formula for a chemical compound,

CASE 6.6 Continued

a process of manufacturing, treating or preserving materials, a pattern for a machine or other device, or a list of customers. . . . A trade secret is a process or device for continuous use in the operation of the business. Generally it relates to the production of goods, as, for example, a machine or formula for the production of an article. It may, however, relate to the sale of goods or to other operations in the business, such as a code for determining discounts, rebates or other concessions in a price list or catalogue, or a list of specialized customers, or a method of bookkeeping or other office management." . . .

The employer who has discovered or developed trade secrets is protected against unauthorized disclosure or use, not because he has a property interest in the trade secrets but because the trade secrets were made known to the employee in a confidential relationship.

. . . [A] proper means of obtaining the information [by a third party] contained within a trade secret may be by way of (1) discovery by independent invention; (2) discovery by "reverse engineering," that is, by starting with the known product and working backward to find the method by which it was developed, the acquisition of the product having been by a fair and honest means, such as purchase of the item on the open market; (3) discovery under a license from the owner of the trade secret; (4) observation of the item in public use or on display; or by (5) obtaining the trade secret from published literature.

Underlying almost every case in which a former employee is accused of the unauthorized disclosure . . . of trade secrets is . . . balancing or reconciling . . . the conflicting rights of an employer to enjoy the use of secret processes and devices which were developed through his own initiative and investment and the right of employees to earn a livelihood by utilizing their personal skill, knowledge and experience." . . . A balancing of these two interests may be facilitated by distinguishing between knowledge and skill that is general in the trade as a whole and "secret" knowledge which is acquired particularly and specifically from the employer.

. . . The trial court found, and the court of appeals affirmed that Valco's materials and manufacturing processes were unique to its products in that no competitor made products exactly like Valco's, and that such products were developed only after a great deal of experimentation, testing, and field experience.

. . . Under all the . . . evidence, we hold that the trial court quite properly concluded that, under the circumstances, Valco had taken reasonable precautions to protect the secrecy of its information and to prevent it from being made available to persons other than those permitted by Valco. . . .

JUDGMENT Judgment affirmed.

Business Tort as Unethical Conduct

Unethical conduct, whether directed against another business or against the public, underlies all actionable torts committed by businesspeople. That is not to say that every incident of unethical conduct is a tort. Sometimes unethical conduct is such a slight invasion of another's rights that it does not reach the status of a tort. For example, a visitor to an office without permission reads an open letter lying on an untended desk. That party certainly acted in an unethical manner but the damages are so slight that it can be assumed no actionable tort occurred. However, when unethical business conduct results in damage to another, it can be anticipated that such conduct will be recognized by the courts or by statute as tortious.

Summary

While the spirit of competition with its play of interest against interest is inherent in the business world, our free enterprise economy does not justify conduct which is contrary to the standards expected of businesspeople or contrary to public policy as determined by our courts and legislatures. Business practices which violate such standards or policy are business torts and may constitute criminal acts as well. A person harmed by a business tort may secure redress in damages and, if money damages cannot be determined or cannot give adequate relief, may secure a court order (called an injunction) directing the defendant to discontinue the tortious act.

The most frequently recurring business torts may be grouped into the following four broad categories: wrongfully entering into business; interfering with business relations; disparaging reputation or property; and engaging in unfair trade practices.

Entering into competition with an established firm is not normally a tort, even if it causes the established firm to lose customers and profits. However, under certain circumstances merely to engage in a business may violate the rights of others, as where the entry into business is for predatory purposes or is in violation of a franchise given to another concern by a governmental agency.

The basic right to contract is protected by law. It is therefore a tort for someone unjustifiably to induce another person to refrain from entering into a contract with a third party if that contract otherwise would have been consummated. The right to receive the performance of a contract already entered into is even more zealously guarded by the law. Although a breach of contract *by one of the parties* to the agreement gives rise only to an action *in contract,* and not to one in tort, different legal responsibilities arise if a *third person induces* another to breach a contract already in being. In that event, the wrongdoing party is liable in tort for the damages he or she has caused the injured party to suffer.

Everyone is entitled to compete in an orderly business world free from unprivileged disparagement of reputation, property, and product. Where the unprivileged dissemination of false and defamatory matter tends to injure the reputation of a business, it constitutes the tort of disparagement; where it casts doubt upon or denies the validity of title to property, it constitutes the tort of slander of title; where it indicates that a property or product lacks the characteristics claimed for it by its owner or producer, it constitutes the tort of trade libel.

Engaging in unfair trade practices may consist of "palming off" a product for that of another manufacturer by false advertising or by imitating its physical appearance or packaging. Or the practice may consist of the piracy of intellectual property involving the infringement of a trademark, patent, or copyright; the intentional or unintentional imitation of a trade name; or the unlawful use of another firm's trade secret. These wrongful practices cause an unlawful diversion of trade and thus constitute torts against the firms whose business has been diverted. Such actions may also constitute torts against the purchasers of the products involved.

Review Questions

1 Comment, from a business law standpoint, upon this statement: "Anyone with sufficient resources and know-how can engage in any business he or she wants. That's what freedom of competition is all about."

2 **(a)** Explain and give an illustration of the tort of interfering with another's economic advantage. **(b)** How does that tort differ from the tort of wrongfully inducing someone not to enter into a contract?

3 **(a)** What circumstances must be present to constitute the tort of inducing a breach of contract? **(b)** Why can a person be guilty of wrongfully inducing a breach of contract even though the contract provides that it may be terminated by either party at will?

4 What is meant by "malice" in the torts of wrongfully inducing someone not to engage in a contract and wrongfully inducing a breach of contract?

5 Felix, an accountant working for High Brothers, in response to an ad leaves his job with that company. High Brothers is now very shorthanded. Its personnel manager knows that George, who works for Pelican, a High Brothers competitor, is an excellent accountant. The manager telephones George at his place of work and offers to pay him a large salary if he will work for High Brothers. Despite Pelican's efforts to keep George as an employee, he accepts High Brothers' job. A Pelican officer tells you, its attorney, that Pelican would really suffer if George revealed to their competitor High Brothers information about Pelican's business. He instructs you to sue High Brothers for pirating away George and to prevent George from revealing to that company any of Pelican's business affairs. Discuss the issues you must consider.

6 Distinguish between an absolute privilege and a conditional privilege with respect to the disparagement of a business reputation.

7 Distinguish between "slander of title" and "trade libel."

8 Assume a jewelry store advertises that it specializes in "Mikimoto" pearls with the largest stock of such pearls in the state. You read the ad, go to the store, ask to see a string of pearls, and are shown several. At no time did you ask if they were Mikimoto pearls and at no time did the salesperson indicate whether they were or were not. You buy one of the strings of pearls assuming they are from Mikimoto. Later an expert sees the pearls and tells you they are not Mikimoto pearls. Discuss whether or not the store has been guilty of a business tort.

9 Beacon Company makes a very popular flashlight that is not patented. The Nite-Lite Company copies Beacon's design and sells an identical flashlight at a lower price than Beacon charges. Beacon sues Nite-Lite seeking damages for unfair competition and to enjoin Nite-Lite from selling its imitation flashlight. Explain the principles of law involved in the litigation.

10 **(a)** Distinguish between a "trademark," a "trade name," and a "patent." **(b)** When does a trademark have a "secondary meaning"?

11 **(a)** What constitutes a patent or trademark infringement? **(b)** Can an unintentional act amount to an infringement? **(c)** Since a patent may stifle competition, what is the public policy justification for granting a patent?

12 **(a)** What is a "trade secret"? **(b)** Through reverse engineering Baxter Ltd. learns how an article is made. What does that mean? **(c)** Did Baxter Ltd. thereby commit a business tort? Why?

Case Problems

1 With money borrowed from SIC Investment Company, Brock, the defendant, bought an automobile. As is customary SIC was given a lien on the car for the balance of the purchase price, and the insurance policy on it was made payable to both Brock and to SIC according to their respective interests in the vehicle. Brock had an accident and secured three estimates for the repair of the car. Brock told Lewis, the plaintiff, manager of one of the three body shops that had bid on the work, that his shop would get the job. However, before Brock entered into any contract, SIC told Brock to have the work done elsewhere because it had information that Lewis, when he repaired someone else's car, had charged for work that was not done. Brock took SIC's advice and had his car repaired by one of the other shops. Lewis sued SIC for interfering with his prospective contract relations. Although SIC admitted that because of its statements Brock was induced not to enter into the contract with Lewis, SIC claimed that it had not committed a tort. What should the court decide? Why?

2 AM International, the defendant, had a written contract with DP Service, the plaintiff, for the latter to exclusively distribute AM's products to wholesalers for a stated period of time. AM wanted to modify that agreement to permit it also to sell its own products to wholesalers. DM refused and before the contract came to an end, AM breached it. DP brought suit against AM for the tort of intentional interference with its prospective economic advantage under the contract. Did AM commit the alleged tort? Explain.

3 The GFC Corporation, the plaintiff, had a manufacturing plant near Dover, Maryland. The only railroad transportation to and from the plant was by means of the Penn Central Railroad bridge. The ship *SS Yorkmar,* while moving up the river that flows under the bridge, negligently collided with the bridge, damaging it to such an extent that no railroad traffic could move over the bridge for some time. As a result, GFC was unable to meet certain of its contract commitments, the contracts were canceled, and GFC suffered considerable damage. GFC therefore sued the owner of the *SS Yorkmar,* alleging tortious interference with the performance of GFC's contracts. Should GFC recover? Why or why not?

4 Wear-Ever Aluminum, Inc., the plaintiff, manufactures aluminum cooking utensils which it sells through house-to-house salespeople. The salespeople are independent contractors whose contracts are terminable at will. Townecraft Industries, the defendant, sells aluminum cooking utensils in competition with Wear-Ever. In order to build its sales organization and to increase its share of the market, Townecraft hired Daniel who had worked for Wear-Ever. Daniel then induced approximately thirty-five people, constituting practically the entire sales force of Wear-Ever's Quaker City Division, to leave that firm and to take jobs with Townecraft. Wear-Ever sought an injunction to prevent Townecraft from further recruiting Wear-Ever's employees. Should Wear-Ever be successful in its litigation? Why or why not?

5 Consumers Service, the defendant, was in the business of testing products and publishing for general distribution reports of their findings. Consumers included in one of its publications an evaluation of a Bose 901 series loudspeaker system. Among other things, the article said that the system used a "rather gigantic amount of power [and] . . . the panelists could pinpoint the location of various instruments much more easily with a standard speaker system than with the Bose. . . . Worse, individual instruments heard through the Bose system seemed to grow with gigantic proportions and tended to wander about the room. For instance, a violin appeared to be 10 feet wide and a piano stretched from wall to wall. . . ." Bose Corporation, the plaintiff, sued Consumer Service for falsely disparaging Bose's sound system, proved that a single individual, not a group of "panelists" had tested the system, and also proved that the individual who did the testing was biased. As a result, the plaintiff was damaged. Consumers Service defended on the ground that they were entitled to express an opinion upon a product for sale to the public. Should the plaintiff recover? Why or why not?

6 Henry Perky in 1895 secured a patent on a pillow-shaped biscuit cereal made of baked whole wheat which was called, in the patent, "shredded wheat." Perky was associated with the Natural Food Company. The name of that company was, in 1908, changed to the Shredded Wheat Company. In 1930 its business and goodwill were acquired by the National Biscuit Company, the plaintiff. Perky's patent would have expired in 1909 but in 1908 the patent was declared invalid because at least as early as 1894 shredded wheat had been manufactured although not patented. Registration of the name "Shredded Wheat" as a trademark was refused because those words described an article of food which had been produced and sold for more than 10 years. However, the National Biscuit Company continued to make and sell its shredded wheat.

The Kellogg Company, the defendant, since 1927 made and sold a shredded wheat breakfast food under the name "Kellogg's Shredded Whole Wheat Biscuit." Its product is also in pillow shape, although each biscuit is about two-thirds the size of those produced by the National Biscuit Company. In 1932 National Biscuit Company sued the Kellogg Company for unfair competition. The Supreme Court of the United States dismissed the bill of complaint. However, two of the justices in a dissenting opinion, held that ". . . It seems sufficiently clear that the Kellogg Company is fraudulently seeking to appropriate to itself the benefits of the goodwill" created by the National Biscuit Company.

Do you agree with the majority or with the opinion of the dissenting justices? What is the basis for your conclusion?

7 Klamath Lumber Co., the plaintiff, manufactures and sells at wholesale load binders (equipment used in handling logs and cut lumber). Klamath had expended much time and energy to secure creditworthy customers. Clarence Miller was employed as Klamath's shop manager and his wife, Hilda, worked in its office. While still employed there, the Millers, the defendants, secretly began the construction of a drill press similar to one used by Klamath. They later quit their jobs with Klamath and manufactured binders similar to those made by Klamath. The Millers created a customer list based almost entirely upon the names Hilda remembered were Klamath's customers. Klamath brought suit to enjoin the Millers from soliciting Klamath's customers. The Millers responded that they had not copied Klamath's customers' list but had merely relied on their memories to assist them in developing their own list of potential customers and that all those names could be found in business directories. Should the court grant the injunction? Why or why not?

CHAPTER 7

Criminal Law; Computer and Other White-Collar Crimes

Why is a chapter on criminal law included in a business law text? After all, business law is based upon the principles of *civil* law. The answer is that, unfortunately, we must recognize that some criminal activities are so closely linked with the conduct of business that they have become known as "business crimes," or "white-collar crimes." It is estimated that such crimes add about 15 percent to the price of all goods and services sold in the United States and that they cost the public more than do the crimes of larceny, robbery, burglary, and auto theft combined. Today, a rapidly growing number of business crimes involve the wrongful access to computer-stored information and the misuse of computer capabilities.

To understand the scope of business crime it is first necessary to have an understanding of what criminal law is and how the justice system operates. This chapter, therefore, begins by explaining what constitutes a criminal act, what are the different classes of crimes, and how a crime differs from a tort (a civil wrong). It then notes the primary differences between procedures for the trial of criminal offenders and the procedures in civil suits. Against that background, the chapter discusses individual business, or white-collar, crimes, focusing particularly upon computer crimes.

Criminal Law Principles

What Is a Crime?

A *crime* is either: (1) the commission of an act which the law forbids, or (2) the failure (omission) to perform an act which the law commands. A crime is a *public* offense committed against the state or against the federal government. It is punishable by the state or by the federal government in a criminal proceeding in its own name. State statutes express what actions are offenses against the state. Federal statutes, primarily the U.S. Criminal Code, express what actions constitute offenses against the United States.

As explained in Chapters 4 and 5, a single wrongful act may be at the same time both: (1) a wrong against an individual (a tortious act or a private wrong), which furnishes the basis for a *civil* suit in tort, and (2) a wrong against society (a crime or a *public* wrong), which furnishes the basis for a criminal prosecution. The recovery of damages from a defendant for a tort does not bar punishment for the criminal aspect of the same act. Thus, if Arthur steals six compact disk players from the Olympic Company warehouse, he has committed a private wrong (a tort) against that company, and Olympic may, in its own name, bring a civil action against Arthur to recover payment for the value of the sets. At the same time and without regard to the outcome of that tort action, the state may arrest Arthur and, in its name, prosecute him for the criminal offense of larceny (the wrongful taking of another's property with intent not to return it). Larceny is a *public* wrong.

Most acts recognized as crimes in today's society have been outlawed since ancient times. But as social standards and ethics change with the passage of time, our views as to what actions constitute offenses against society also change. Therefore, criminal law is never static. Society weighs the new and innovative schemes which people devise to gain profit or reward, and, if the public dictates, the state legislature or Congress enacts new criminal statutes to outlaw those schemes.

The rapidity of evolution in our criminal law system becomes evident when we recognize that not quite four hundred years ago in at least one American colony a man or woman could be charged with practicing witchcraft, tried for that offense, and, if found guilty, burned at the stake. Today, there is no such offense and no such punishment. Before the invention of commercial aircraft it naturally would have been impossible to commit the offense of hijacking a plane; and, until the relatively recent widespread use of credit cards, an offense grounded upon their misuse was, of course, unknown.

Elements of a Crime

A crime is a socially blameworthy act, committed by a mentally competent person, with the intent required by law.

The Act. To commit an offense, an act must take place which the law forbids or there must be the failure to do something which the law requires. For example, a person who steals another's property commits an act which the law forbids; a person who meets the minimum filing requirements yet fails to file an income tax return omits to do something the law requires.

For a criminal act to be committed, some physical act or breach of legal duty must occur. The mere *intention* to commit a crime, unaccompanied by any act in furtherance of that intention, is not a crime. Likewise, an act that is only *preparatory* to the commission of an unlawful act is not a crime. Any time during the preparation stage the individual may change his or her mind and commit no crime at all. Consider these facts: Ralph, a member of the computer programing staff of the New Bank, decides to program the bank's computer so as to credit other people's money to a hidden account he will establish for his own benefit. In his mind, Ralph works out the details of his scheme and the next day he opens an account under an assumed name at a branch of the New Bank where he is not known. Ralph still is only in the preparation stage. But later, when Ralph directs the computer to transfer funds from other depositors' accounts into the account he has opened, he passes beyond preparation and commits a criminal act. His theft will be dubbed a "white-collar crime" since it involves some kind of business transaction.

Mental Capacity. To be guilty of a crime, a person must have the mental capacity to understand: (1) the nature of his or her act and (2) that the act is wrongful. If an individual is so mentally unsound as not to have had the mental capacity to be responsible for a criminal act he or she committed, that person would be criminally insane and hospitalized rather than punished.

Youthful offenders. Most states, adopting the common law formula, hold that a child under 7 years of age at common law is conclusively presumed not to have the mental capacity to commit crime. A boy or girl between the ages of 7 and 14 years may be proved to have criminal capacity. A person more than 14 years of age is considered to have the same criminal capacity as an adult.

To protect people from having to bear the stigma of a criminal conviction for a youthful caper, however, all states have adopted some form of juvenile or youthful offender law. A youthful offender (the age depending on the state) who is accused of a criminal act normally is not charged with the commission of a specific crime but only with being a juvenile delinquent. If the charge is proved, the youth may be held in a juvenile detention center for a limited period of time and is usually treated as a person requiring help and guidance rather than punishment.

Insanity. An insane person is one who is so mentally unsound because of birth defect, disease, or accident as not to be legally responsible for what he or she does. It follows that if someone "goes out of his or her mind" simply because of having *voluntarily* ingested alcohol or drugs and, while in that condition, commits a criminal offense, that person may not successfully base a total defense upon insanity although his or her condition may be offered to negate the presence of so much of an offense as requires a criminal intent.

The court in the following case dealt with such a situation.

CASE 7.1 People v. Free · 447 N.E.2d 218 (Ill. 1983)

FACTS Free was charged with murder, attempted murder, and attempted rape. At the trial, Free testified that on the night the events occurred, "he had consumed a few beers, a marijuana cigarette and a 'mint leaf or, as it's called, dust'." The mint leaf was soaked in a PCP, or phencyclidine, compound and dried. Free testified that he had no actual recollection of what he did that night and claimed that he was not legally responsible for his actions. Witnesses on Free's behalf testified that he was suffering from a mental disease, "a toxic psychosis, secondary to some sort of chemical or drug intoxication." Free was found guilty of all of the charges and sentenced to death. Among the several issues raised by him on appeal was whether the court committed error by not instructing the jury on insanity.

OPINION RYAN, C. J. . . . The rule that a defendant who is legally insane will be relieved of criminal liability must be reconciled with the generally accepted rule that a defendant who is

CASE 7.1 Continued

voluntarily under the influence of intoxicants at the time of the crime will not be relieved of criminal responsibility. The essential consideration is not whether the medical profession characterizes the defendant's use of intoxicants resulting in a psychosis as a mental disease or defect, but rather whether society should relieve from criminal responsibility a defendant who voluntarily ingests such intoxicants and then commits criminal acts. It is obvious to us that an actor should not be insulated from criminal responsibility for acts which result from a temporary mental state that is voluntarily self-induced.

We therefore hold that toxic psychosis induced by voluntary intoxication on drugs, alcohol or both, is not a "mental disease or mental defect" which amounts to legal insanity under our statute.... A majority of jurisdictions agree....

Simply stated, a voluntary intoxication or a voluntary drugged condition does not raise the defense of insanity, but... it may be used to negate the existence of the mental state [e.g. specific intent] which is an element of the crime.... A voluntary intoxication or a voluntary drugged condition precludes the use of the insanity defense *unless* the mental disease or defect is traceable to the habitual or chronic use of drugs or alcohol... and such use results in a "settled" or "fixed" permanent type of insanity.... There is no evidence... that the... disease or defect [claimed by the defendant] was "settled" or "fixed."

JUDGMENT ...Affirmed.

Insanity under the criminal law is not the same as the "insanity" which causes a person to be legally incapable of entering into a contract or the "insanity" which causes a person to be legally incapable of making a valid will.

A frequently used criminal law test of insanity is the M'Naghten Rule, named after the accused person in an old English case in which his sanity was in question. The M'Naghten Rule (also known as the right and wrong test) is that an individual did not have the mental capacity to commit a crime if that person was suffering from such a defect of reason: (1) as not to know what he or she was doing, or (2) if, knowing what he or she was doing, nonetheless did not know that the act was wrong.

Any test of sanity cannot be applied with mathematical precision; expert witnesses in criminal trials all too frequently express opinions contrary to one another. Because of this uncertainty, it has been suggested that a jury should be authorized to return a verdict of "guilty but insane," or "guilty but mentally ill," or "guilty but mentally incompetent." Others object to such proposals because under our legal system an insane person cannot be guilty of a criminal offense. The Comprehensive Crime Control Act of 1984, an extensive revision of the U.S. Criminal Code, has addressed the problem by providing that a person who, in the federal courts, defends on the ground of insanity at the time of the offense has the burden to prove his or her insanity. Under the prior practice, when a person claimed not to be responsible for a criminal act because of insanity, the government had the burden to prove that the defendant was sane.

Diminished mental capacity. The presence or absence of mental capacity to commit a criminal act is particularly difficult to assess in those states which permit an accused person to show a diminished mental capacity. In those states, an accused may claim that he or she, *although not insane* at the time of the alleged offense, was not capable, because of diminished mental capacity, of entertaining the specific intent necessary to be guilty of the crime charged. This defense might be available, as mentioned in the *Free* opinion we have just considered (Case 7.1), to someone who was voluntarily intoxicated at the time he or she committed an offense which requires proof by the state of the accused's specific intent. If diminished mental capacity is established, the accused is not discharged from custody but normally would be found guilty of an offense that does *not* require proof of specific intent and is lesser than the crime charged. For example, for a person to be convicted of murder there must be proof that the homicide was intended. If diminished capacity is established, the accused may be found guilty, not of murder, but only of a lesser homicide in which intent is not an element.

Criminal Intent. For an act or omission to be criminal, it must have been committed with an evil purpose or with a blameworthy or person-endangering state of mind. This is called *mens rea* or *criminal intent.* Such an intent is identified in statutes by words such as "knowingly," "wrongfully," "corruptly," "willfully," "fraudulently," "intentionally," "maliciously," "feloniously," "negligently," or "wantonly." Criminal intent is almost always proven by inference, based upon the premise that *people are presumed to intend the natural consequences of their voluntary acts.* Thus, if Barry took a hand tool owned by his employer, Stark Co., and pawned it, the jury, in Barry's trial for larceny, may presume that he intended to deprive Stark Co. of its property permanently, a necessary ingredient of the crime of larceny.

A criminal intent should not be confused with the *motive* which induces an individual to commit a criminal act. The distinction between the two is explained in Case 7.2.

CASE 7.2 Cantrell v. Commonwealth of Virginia · 329 S.E.2d 22 (Va. 1985)

FACTS Cantrell, the defendant, told the police that when he came home about 6:40 P.M., December 8, 1981, someone hit him over the head with a hard object, knocking him to the floor; that he was tied hand and foot and again beaten; that he heard shots; and that he then passed out. He also reported that he regained consciousness about 9 P.M. and managed to untie himself. He found that his wife, Judy, had been shot and killed with his shotgun. He phoned his parents for help, "went into shock," and awoke at the hospital.

The police found Cantrell's house in disarray. Cantrell gave the police a list of items he claimed were missing. About 3 hours later a tracking dog led the police to a field on Cantrell's property where those articles were found. Apparently the only trail the dog discovered leading away from the field led back to the house. No fingerprints were brought to light by the police at the scene, on the shotgun, or on the items found in the field. During the succeeding 4 months the police gathered additional circumstantial evidence against Cantrell. As a result he was charged with, tried for, and found guilty of his wife's murder. He was sentenced to life imprisonment.

Cantrell appealed. He claimed the trial court had erred in not requiring the Commonwealth to prove that he (Cantrell) had a motive for the crime.

OPINION RUSSELL, J.... The defendant argues... that proof of motive is required in cases such as his, where the prosecution seeks to prove the identity of the criminal agent by purely circumstantial evidence, which does not completely exclude the possibility that another person was the perpetrator.

...As recently as *Bishop v. Commonwealth,* 313 S.E.2d 390 (1984), we said:

> We are guided by familiar principles. Where the evidence is entirely circumstantial, all necessary circumstances must be consistent with guilt and inconsistent with innocence and must exclude every reasonable hypothesis of innocence. The chain of necessary circumstances must be unbroken. The circumstances of motive, time, place, means, and conduct must all concur to form an unbroken chain which links the defendant to the crime beyond a reasonable doubt....

The defendant misapplies these principles by confusing the species of circumstances which may or may not be available for proof in any given case, with the elements of the crime, which must each be proved in every case if a conviction is to be had. Intent, for instance, is a requisite element in many crimes, but motive is not. Motive is merely a circumstance tending to prove the guilt of the alleged perpetrator, as its absence may tend to show his innocence. It is relevant and probative on the issue of identity of the criminal

CASE 7.2 Continued

agent, but it is not an element of any crime. "Motive and intent are not synonymous. Motive is an inducing cause, while intent is the mental state with which the criminal act is committed.... The prosecution is never required to prove motive, although it may do so."... Motive has never been a requisite element of the crime of murder in Virginia,... or in any other jurisdiction of which we are aware.... The crime may be clearly established and no motive ever discovered. We conclude that the jury was correctly instructed....

JUDGMENT The case was reversed on other grounds and remanded.

Classification of Crimes

Crimes may be classified in a number of ways. For instance, they may be seen from the point of view of the specific wrongs or injuries inflicted as: (1) crimes against the person, such as murder, rape, manslaughter, battery, and assault; (2) crimes against property, such as arson, larceny, and embezzlement; and (3) crimes against the government, such as treason, making a false official statement, and violating election laws. Crimes may also be classified within broader categories by their degree of wrongfulness and by their legally permissible punishments. These broader classifications are more appropriate for this book, which focuses on business law and not upon the anatomy of individual crimes.

Crimes Classified by Degree of Wrongfulness.

Crimes, when classified according to their degree of wrongfulness, are either: (1) those of moral turpitude, that is, offenses involving a base or depraved act (in legal terms, called "*malum in se* offenses"); and (2) those which do not involve moral turpitude but are wrong because prohibited by law (called "*malum prohibitum* offenses").

Malum in se offenses. Malum in se (bad in themselves) offenses include, but certainly are not limited to, the crimes of murder, rape, arson, robbery, and larceny. To be guilty of a *malum in se* offense, the person committing the wrongful act must have the specific intent identified with the crime charged.

It should be recognized, however, that under certain circumstances a negligent act or omission may also constitute a crime involving moral turpitude. For instance, when a careless act which results in injury or death is so reckless that it reflects a heedless indifference to the safety and rights of others, it is *criminal negligence.* Assume that an individual manufactures and sells babies' rattles without first being certain that they are not harmful to children; assume also that a number of babies are poisoned from their use. Clearly that individual is guilty of something more than the negligence discussed in Chapters 4 and 5.

The next case distinguishes between simple negligence and criminal negligence.

CASE 7.3 Commonwealth of Pennsylvania v. Heck · 491 A.2d 212 (Pa. 1985)

FACTS On a clear, dry day, defendant Heck was driving his automobile north on Route 141. He intended to turn left at the intersection of that route with Union Schoolhouse Lane. Heck reached the intersection and was in the process of making the turn when his right front fender was struck by a motorcycle being driven south on Route 141. Heck, who was exceeding the speed limit by about 15 miles per hour, did not see the motorcycle until almost the moment of impact. The motorcycle driver was thrown from his machine and died from the injuries he sustained. Heck had violated a Pennsylvania traffic law which required him to yield the right-of-way to the approaching motorcycle.

CASE 7.3 Continued

Heck was charged with, and tried for, the criminal offense of vehicular homicide, an offense involving moral turpitude punishable by 5 years incarceration and the revocation of the violator's driver's license.

Heck was convicted of the offense charged and sentenced only to probation and a fine. Heck appealed, asserting that, as his wrongful act involved only simple negligence, his conviction of a crime involving moral turpitude was a denial of the due process of law to which he was entitled.

OPINION CIRILLO, J. . . . The troubling questions raised on this appeal center on the level of culpability necessary to prove vehicular homicide. . . . The requirement that an underlying traffic violation be the cause of death does not necessarily supply any element of fault [to the crime charged]. The traffic violation does not inherently depend on culpable conduct. One may reasonably misjudge whether an approaching auto is so close as to constitute a hazard. . . .

. . . Although we find the evidence sufficient to uphold a finding that Heck *should* have known he was violating . . . the Vehicle Code (Vehicle turning left), we find it insufficient to establish any degree of culpability higher than ordinary negligence. Specifically, the evidence failed to prove that Heck *knew* when he began to make his turn that [the motorcycle] was so close as to constitute a hazard. Had this . . . been proven, it could be said that Heck proceeded in the face of a known illegal risk, and we could conclude that the . . . death was the result of greater than ordinary negligence. . . .

Moreover, we find the evidence insufficient to prove that Heck's failure to apprehend the hazard in time was a "gross" deviation from a reasonable standard of care. . . .

It is not all that difficult to harmonize the idea of criminal negligence with the dominant theme of the criminal law to punish only acts done with a guilty mind. We must remember that criminal negligence involves a *gross* deviation from reasonable care such that it would be shocking to allow the actor's lack of awareness to excuse his actions in the circumstances. The criminally negligent act has been done so heedlessly, so indifferently, and so grossly contrary to common experience that it becomes intolerable to reasoning minds that the actor did not perceive the risk of harm created by his conduct. In such cases the law presumes wantonness. . . . "Criminal negligence" is a breach of duty so flagrant . . . that we may safely indulge in the legal fiction that it was committed with actual intent to injure. . . . The judicial conscience therefore does not revolt at labeling it criminal.

. . . We are unable to conclude otherwise than that [defendant] was the victim of prosecution under a substantively irrational law. . . . [O]ur holding does not purport to decide the constitutionality of vehicular homicide prosecutions where the offender was conscious of wrongdoing or grossly deviated from a reasonable standard of care. . . .

JUDGMENT Reversed and appellant is discharged.

Malum prohibitum offenses. These are illegal acts (often relating to business conduct) which are not naturally evil but which are made criminal and prohibited because they violate laws enacted for the safety, health, or well-being of the community. A violation of a *malum prohibitum* offense generally does not involve moral turpitude; seldom may lengthy imprisonment be ordered, and offenders may be punished *without* proof of criminal intent. The penal provisions of the Federal Food, Drug and Cosmetic Act, illustrated by Case 7.5 on page 129, and of the truth-in-lending laws (discussed in Chapter 12) are examples. Another offense of this class involves the sale of intoxicating liquor to minors. Assume, for instance, that John owns a bar in a state which, as a matter of public policy, makes it a criminal offense to sell liquor to minors. John knows that his bartender, Bill, occasionally sells liquor to minors and has instructed Bill to stop doing so. Nevertheless, when John is away, Bill knowingly sells intoxicating liquor to a minor, thereby committing a *malum prohibitum* offense. Even though John was not present when the offense was committed, *both* he and Bill may be guilty of the offense arising out of the unlawful sale. The fact that John may be held guilty of something he did not do may seem harsh, but the law obligates him to make certain that his bar is run in a law-abiding manner. Our society takes this position because it is easier for the owner of a business to make sure that his or her employees abide by the law than for the police to keep a continuous watch over the manner in which the business is conducted. Note the similarity between *malum prohibitum* offenses and torts involving *strict liability* (discussed in Chapter 18).

Crimes Classified by Degree of Punishment

When classified according to degree of permissible punishment, criminal offenses may be broken down into two categories: felonies and misdemeanors. (Treason, a betraying or breach of allegiance, is a constitutional crime and is usually not included within the common categories of criminal acts.)

Felonies. Felonies, whether *malum in se* or *malum prohibitum* offenses, are all serious crimes for which society has authorized punishment: (1) under federal law by imprisonment for more than 1 year, and (2) in most states by incarceration in a state prison rather than in a county jail.

With conviction of a felony, a fine may also be imposed. In those jurisdictions which authorize the death sentence, certain felonies (called *capital offenses*) may be punishable by execution.

Misdemeanors. A *misdemeanor* is a lesser crime, such as stealing property worth an amount less than that required to constitute a felony (in some states $100). A misdemeanor is punishable by fine and possibly by imprisonment for no more than 1 year in an institution other than a state prison.

A misdemeanor should not be confused with an *infraction.* An infraction is a minor wrong and in most states is not considered to be a criminal offense. Infractions involve such departures from community standards as minor traffic offenses and parking violations. Punishment is normally a fine or the withdrawal of a privilege such as the right to drive a motor vehicle, or, in many jurisdictions, the optional requirement that the offender attend a course of instruction in a traffic school in lieu of a fine.

Unethical Conduct

As we have seen, a crime is an unethical act that is an offense against the sovereignty of the state, and it is subject to punishment by the state. However, many unethical acts which are contrary to the mores of the community have not attained the stature of a crime, and criminal penalties do not attach to them. Instead of being punished for a crime, the transgressor earns for such a reprehensible act the ill-will of the community and, if he or she is a business or professional person, the loss of customers and clients; perhaps he or she even is made the defendant in a lawsuit.

The following are examples of unethical acts which normally are not crimes:

1. A store owner, finding his grocery store to be the only one in town able to do business after a tornado, greatly raises the prices on all the food he sells.
2. A laboratory technician tells acquaintances about the secret experiments the laboratory in which he works is conducting, thereby breaching his obligation of secrecy.
3. The personnel officer employed by a corporation gives jobs to her relatives and to those to whom she "owes a favor" instead of to the applicants who could best serve the corporation.
4. An elderly woman gives money to a trusted friend, asking that he invest it for her. Without asking her permission, he lends her money to his own small business and he pays the woman interest on the money.
5. A maker of powdered milk induces third-world mothers to buy its product as an alternative to breast feeding, knowing that many illiterate mothers, unable to read the directions on the package and wishing to "stretch" the powder to make it last longer, very likely will so overdilute the product that it will be of slight nourishment to their children.

Businesspeople are becoming increasingly conscious that they owe special ethical obligations to the public they serve, and most strive to maintain high standards. In addition, business concerns and professional people attempt to police their industries, trades, and professions through their active trade and professional associations.

Criminal Procedure

Meaning of Criminal Procedure

The term *criminal procedure* refers to the various steps involved in bringing to trial (prosecuting) a person accused of having committed a crime. These procedures are different from the civil law procedures discussed in Chapter 3 for the enforcement of contract rights or for collecting damages for injuries resulting from a tort.

A criminal prosecution is brought by the *state* as plaintiff in an action in its own name. It is *not* an action by the victim of a crime. In a criminal case the victim will only be one of the witnesses for the prosecution.

Constitutional Guarantees

Throughout the entire process of initiating and carrying on a criminal prosecution, the accused person is presumed to be innocent until proven guilty. The courts carefully protect an accused's constitutional right not to be deprived of life, liberty, or property without due process of law. "Due process" means that an individual is free from unreasonable searches and seizures and that a warrant for arrest will not be issued except upon probable cause that the individual charged had committed a crime. With due process an accused is entitled: (1) to a speedy public trial by an impartial jury, (2) to be confronted by the witnesses for the prosecution, and (3) to compel his or her own witnesses to be present at the trial. In addition, an accused cannot be compelled to be a witness against himself or herself. The Constitution also assures an accused the right to have the assistance of counsel. If she or he cannot afford to hire a lawyer, the court assigns competent counsel whose fee is paid by the state. Most jurisdictions maintain a staff of *public defenders,* attorneys whose sole occupation is to defend those accused of crime who cannot afford to pay for legal counsel.

Arrest

An arrest, normally by a police officer, is the first step in criminal prosecution. The Supreme Court of the United States, in the landmark case *Miranda v. State of Arizona* [384 U.S. 436 (1966)], held that an arrested person must not be questioned by the police unless first warned of his or her right to remain silent, to be represented by an attorney, and to have the attorney present during questioning. If these so-called Miranda warnings are not given to an accused who is interrogated by the police after he or she is taken into custody, any statement (such as a confession) the accused makes to the police may not be used in evidence against that individual at trial.

Except in unusual circumstances, an arrested person is entitled to be released on bail or on his or her "own recognizance." *Bail* is a sum of money or other security, or the obligation of a bonding company, which guarantees that the accused will be present for trial. One's *own recognizance* is a personal assurance or promise to be present for trial. The Comprehensive Crimes Control Act of 1984 extends the conditions under which a judge may refuse to allow a federal prisoner to be released on bail.

Information or Indictment

An accused is formally charged with the commission of an offense by a document called an *information* filed by the prosecuting (district) attorney. However, if a felony is to be charged, the offense may, instead, be described in an *indictment* filed by a grand jury. The accused then, in a proceeding called an *arraignment,* enters a plea either of guilty, not guilty, or (as permitted in most states) *nolo contendere.* Nolo contendere means "I do not wish to contest" the accusation. Although not technically a guilty plea, it is an implied admission of guilt. This type of plea is frequently used by companies or by individuals prominent in public life because that plea is not such an unequivocal admission of guilt that it can be used against an accused in a subsequent civil suit.

A prosecuting attorney and the accused and his or her counsel may reach an agreement for the accused to plead guilty to a lesser offense than that charged in exchange for the assurance of receiving a substantially lesser punishment than might have been imposed had the accused been tried on the original charges. This is called a *plea bargain.* The state thereby is saved the time and expense of what might have been an extended trial, and the accused protects himself or herself from what could have been a very severe sentence. Many people do not agree that an accused should be able to so bargain with state prosecutors; others see plea bargains as necessary to save the court system from becoming so clogged with trials as to founder.

Trial

The Fourteenth Amendment guarantees an accused the right to a trial by a jury selected from a fair cross-section of the community. In a capital case (where the penalty may be death) the jury must consist of twelve persons; otherwise the jury need not exceed six people.

The jury in a criminal case must determine *beyond a reasonable doubt* that the accused is guilty. Contrast this degree of proof with that in a civil trial where the jury may reach a verdict based only upon a *preponderence* of the evidence, which is a lesser degree of proof. Also, in practically all states the jury must reach its verdict in a criminal case by a *unanimous* agreement of its members, while in a civil case the verdict may be reached by the agreement of three-fourths of the members of the jury; in some jurisdictions an even smaller majority is permitted.

Criminal Sentences

The sentencing process is far more flexible and is subject to fewer procedural requirements than is the trial of a criminal case. Some states have a schedule, fixed by statute, of punishments which must be imposed by the trial judge for an offense of which the accused has been found guilty. Other states have by statute fixed only the maximum periods of confinement and the maximum fines which may be imposed; the trial judge exercises a great deal of discretion in determining the sentence he or she believes is appropriate to the offense and to the convicted individual. Generally, the trial judge may order the sentence suspended in whole or in part and may place the prisoner on probation. With increasing frequency, courts include in sentences an order to perform a period of public service. Under procedures established in each state, a prisoner may be released from confinement on parole before completing the sentence imposed.

Let us return for a moment to Arthur and the Olympic Warehouse and assume that Arthur has been tried and found guilty of stealing the compact disk players. We can expect that he will be imprisoned and perhaps required to pay a fine. Arthur pays his fine (if one is imposed) *to the state,* not to Olympic. Whether he will be required to pay damages to Olympic is decided in a civil court if Olympic brings suit.

In order to bring about greater uniformity in sentences for federal offenses, the Congress, in the Comprehensive Crime Control Act of 1984, established the United States Sentencing Commission. That agency is charged with setting a narrow permissable sentencing range for each *federal* offense. After the sentence ranges are established, either the government or the defendant may appeal a sentence that departs from those guidelines. The Act also provides for a phasing out of the U.S. Parole Board. When that is accomplished, federal prisoners will no longer be released from confinement on parole.

An accused who has been found guilty in a state or federal court may, on the ground that the lower court committed an error in law, appeal to a higher court for reconsideration of the conviction, but a verdict of not guilty following a jury trial ends the case and there can be no appeal by the prosecution. (The defendant, of course, would not want to have the verdict reversed.) In a civil suit either the plaintiff or the defendant may appeal a judgment.

Computer and Other White-Collar Crimes

What Are White-Collar Crimes?

Neither federal nor state penal statutes characterize any particular criminal act as a "business" or "white-collar" crime. These terms are used by the Department of Justice to identify informally a wide range of specific crimes all of which are nonviolent and are committed for financial gain by means of deception, generally by persons who take advantage of their special occupational skills and opportunities.

The term "white-collar crime" was first used to characterize a crime committed by a person of respectability in the course of his or her occupation—someone who, figuratively, went to work wearing a white collar. However, that concept has since been broadened. In current criminal justice usage, the focus of the meaning of white-collar crime has shifted to the nature of the crime instead of to the persons or occupations involved. White-collar crimes cover a wide variety of offenses. They normally involve some sort of fraud, guile, misrepresentation, or evasion of statutory directions designed for the protection of the public.

A white-collar crime committed by a business is usually thought of either as a wrongful act committed by one business entity against another business, or as a rip-off by a business against the public, the government, or an individual. For example, a white-collar crime committed by a business might be a misrepresentation in its corporate financial statements to its stockholders; an unlawful manipulation of a publicly traded stock; false advertising; bribery of a public official; the sale of adulterated foods; or an illegal political contribution.

Certain crimes in which a business is the *victim* are also referred to as white-collar crimes. For instance, the unauthorized invasion of a company computer to secure stored secret data, the embezzlement or pilferage of money or supplies by an employee, the theft of securities by a broker, or a fraudulent insurance claim may all be considered to be white-collar crimes.

The losses suffered by business concerns that are victimized by white-collar crime, and the increased insurance premiums that businesses must pay to protect themselves from the possible losses they might suffer, are all passed on to the public in the form of higher prices. So it is we who pay!

Computer Crimes

Computer-related offenses have become a particularly troublesome type of white-collar crime. Today, computers process the financial transactions of government and of practically all business enterprises, large and small. Money circulates not physically but in the form of binary digital information. Computers perform the most intricate calculations and business tasks; some computers print out negotiable instruments; many write checks; others maintain inventories and place and fill orders. In addition, computer memory banks are repositories for trade secrets and other confidential business information such as customer lists and pricing formulas.

An unscrupulous individual who possesses the inventiveness to discover the required commands can, using his or her personal computer and telephone lines, unlawfully gain access to large corporation and government computers which are served by many terminals. Such an individual can unlawfully extract from the computer confidential information, rearrange its data, alter the accounts stored in its memory, or transfer money that the machine controls.

A number of computer programming whizzes, called "hackers," intrigued by the challenge, set out to discover how to gain access to computers of large corporations and of government agencies using only their own personal computers and telephone hookups. Many hackers, including high school students, have succeeded. For instance:

- Four teenagers, one of them only 13 years old, illegally gained access to two computers at NASA's Marshall Space Center. Their unauthorized entry destroyed records and blocked scientists from using the government computers.
- Two teenagers made more than $55,000 worth of telephone calls to other hackers around the country, charging the calls to a credit card number they had illegally gained via their personal computer.
- In 1985 a group of student hackers infiltrated the computerized files of the University of Southern California. They made unauthorized grade changes in computerized transcripts, and even created and sold phony degrees.
- More recently, a Cornell University computer whiz graduate student created a computer program which, by means of the electronic mail system, he entered into the unclassified nationwide Pentagon network called *Arpenet.* The program acted as an electronic "virus" which interfered with the operations of about 6,000

computers across the country until it was detected and removed. Fortunately, the virus caused no lasting damage.

Thefts running into millions of dollars have been committed by computer manipulation. Some experts estimate computer crimes cost the public at least $10 billion a year. The report of the legislative hearings upon the bill which became the Small Business Computer Security and Information Act of 1984 states in part:

> Many small businesses have yet to learn... how to protect their information, and how to safeguard their computers from accidental or deliberate misuse....
>
> The stakes are high. According to FBI statistics, the average bank robbery is $10,000. The FBI estimates that the average computer crime is over $400,000. According to one expert on computer crime, only one of the estimated 200,000 computer crimes committed each year is likely to be prosecuted. Few companies want to admit they were victims of computer theft because it would devastate a firm's image....

Kinds of Computer Crime. Businesspeople should know that a computer may be used for criminal purposes in many ways. For example, false information may be inserted into the machine to alter data in the computer memory; programming orders given to a computer may be wrongfully modified; or a wrongdoer may withdraw from a computer's memory and improperly use information stored within it. Illustrative of such computer crimes are the following actual occurrences:

1 A bank official introduced into a computer false debits and credits at such intervals that the bank's internal security system did not detect the fraud for a considerable time. As a result, the official succeeded in embezzling $21 million from the bank before he was caught.

2 By telephone, a man not connected with a company instructed its computer to deliver supplies of wire, cable, and other costly equipment to locations he selected. The deliveries were made, and he subsequently unlawfully sold more than a million dollars' worth of the company's products.

3 In the now famous Equity Funding case, the management of a large finance company which controlled a mutual fund and an insurance company inflated its assets by programming its computer to show ownership of about fifty thousand fictitious insurance policies reputed to be worth about $2 billion. Other insurance companies, in legitimate transactions called "reinsurance," purchased many of the fictitious policies. The purchasers relied upon computer printouts furnished them to establish the authenticity and current status of the nonexistent policies. Millions of dollars were lost through the far-reaching swindle.

4 An employee in the accounting department of a large company was authorized to "round out" employees' net salaries down to two decimal places. When he did so, using the computer, he wrongfully transferred the tiny remainder amounts to his own salary account. Over a period of time he thereby "earned" thousands of dollars.

5 An employee was convicted of the theft from his employer of fifty-nine computer programs which had a market value of approximately two and one-half million dollars.

Laws Applicable to Computer Crimes. Statutes which prohibit the theft and unlawful disposition of property belonging to another and frauds perpetrated by mail and telephone were enacted long before computers came upon the scene. Now, with the advent of the computer age, the question has arisen whether intangible computer data is "property" within the meaning of precomputer statutes which make criminal the stealing of any *thing* of value. That question has generally been answered in the affirmative.

To remove doubts as to whether "old" criminal statutes apply to computer activities, more than twenty states (led by Florida and California) have enacted laws specifically defining computer crimes. It is estimated that there are about forty provisions of the federal criminal code (Title 18, U.S. Code) which may be applicable to the misuse of computers. These are particularly 18 U.S.C. 641, which prohibits the theft of government property and related offenses; 18 U.S.C 1341, which prohibits mail fraud; and 18 U.S.C. 1343, which prohibits fraud by wire. Of importance, too, is the Electronic Funds Transfer Act (15 U.S.C. 1693), which concerns the making of payments and deposits electronically. In addition, the Comprehensive Crime Control Act of 1984 adds to the U.S. Code a specific provision which imposes penalties upon anyone who improperly accesses and discloses classified information stored in a federal computer.

A Sampling of Other White-Collar Crimes

Criminal acts which involve computers are not the only types of white-collar crimes. As Justice Phillips said in *American Cyanamid Co. v. Federal Trade Commission,* 363 F.2d 757 (6th Cir. 1966), "It is impossible to frame definitions which embrace all unfair [business] practices. There is no limit to human invention in this field. Even if all known unfair practices were sufficiently defined and prohibited, it would be at once necessary to begin all over again." Practically any offense related to business which can be committed without violence may be called a white-collar crime. We will consider by way of illustration such disparate offenses as bribery, violations of public health and safety laws, consumer frauds, violations of securities and antitrust laws, and larceny and embezzlement by an employee.

Bribery. Bribery is the illicit giving or promising to give something of value to another to induce that individual to take some desired action. Bribery may be: (1) of a public official; (2) of a businessperson (commercial bribery); or (3) of a foreign official.

An offer of a gift or a favor is a bribe if it is accompanied by a corrupt intent. If such an intent is present, the guise under which the offer or payment is made is immaterial. It may be, for instance, a donation to a police ball or to a political party. The bribe offer may be anything the receiver considers to be of value, such as money, clothing, a price advantage, inside information which might lead to financial gain, free travel, or sexual favors. However, it has been held that a corrupt intent is not present when a donor makes a gift merely to create a generally congenial business climate not conditioned upon the recipient's performance of any particular act.

Bribery of public officials. This offense is the effort to influence a public servant to handle an official matter in a way that serves a private interest. Such a private interest may be, for example: to thwart official interference with an illegal activity, to secure a building permit or business license, to defeat or effect passage of a statute or ordinance, or to forestall prosecution of a criminal act.

Illustrative of the bribery of public officials is a March 1984 case. There, in exchange for bribes, employees of the Philadelphia-based Defense Industrial Supply Center of the Department of Defense gave the defendants, Standard Air Parts and its president, confidential pricing information on bids made by the defendants' competitors for the sale of articles to the government. Having improperly received this information, Standard Air Parts was able to bid at prices which resulted in that company being awarded more than $2.3 million worth of defense contracts. The president of Standard and the company itself were charged with and found guilty of, among other offenses, ten counts of bribing public officials. The president was sentenced to 4 years in prison and fined $208,000. Standard Air Parts was fined an additional $159,000.

Commercial bribery. Commercial bribery does not involve a public official. It is the offense of unlawfully inducing a businessperson to take some particular action with respect to a business activity. Unfortunately, commercial bribery commonly occurs and its repercussions are widespread. In fact, the general counsel of one large company estimates that one of its former employees accepted as much as ten million dollars in bribes over a 5-year period. Among the objectives for which commercial bribes are given are:

- To secure new business
- To cover up inferior products or services
- To gain inside information concerning competing bids
- To secure preferential treatment above competitors
- To acquire proprietary information
- To prevent work stoppages

For example, to gain competitive advantage, a firm may offer to pay an employee of another company to commit acts of industrial espionage such as turning over his or her employer's pricing schedules, customer lists, or secret manufacturing processes. Or, among other examples, commercial bribery occurs when a wholesaler bribes a liquor store manager not to carry a competitor's product or to give that wholesaler preferred shelf space.

Commercial bribery is not recognized as a crime in all states. In those states where commercial bribery is not a crime, the aggrieved party has recourse only to the civil remedies of injunction (a court order against repetition of the act) and to an action for damages. There is no general federal law proscribing commercial bribery. However, the Sherman Antitrust Act, the Clayton Act, the Robinson-Patman Act (see Chapters 45 and 46), and the Federal Alcohol Administration Act may apply in particular situations.

The following case will help to clarify the meaning of commercial bribery.

CASE 7.4 N.J. Gendron Lumber Co. v. Great Northern Homes, Inc. · 395 N.E.2d 457 (Mass. 1979)

FACTS N.J. Gendron Lumber Co., the plaintiff, instituted a sales promotion program it called the "Acapulco Adventure." The promotion included form letters to each customer by business name but not to a particular employee of that customer. Included was an invitation to cocktails and dinner at which Gendron would introduce its "Great Escape" plan and literature inviting Gendron's customers to go to "fabulous Acapulco." For a given volume of purchases the customers would win a free trip to "frolic in the sun." Edmund Michalski, the plant manager of defendant, Great Northern Homes, Inc., received the promotional literature and he made purchases for his employer from Gendron.

Great Northern suffered reverses and failed to pay Gendron money due it. In the subsequent suit by Gendron against Great Northern, the defendant claimed that Gendron had wrongfully induced Michalski, its employee, to buy from Gendron for Great Northern's account—that is, that Gendron had committed the crime of commercial bribery. After a finding for the plaintiff, disallowing Great Northern's defense of commercial bribery, Great Northern appealed.

OPINION KASS, J. . . . There are not present in the record the elements of "commercial bribery" which is the advantage one competitor secures over fellow competitors "by his secret and corrupt dealing with employees or agents of prospective purchasers." . . . [The commercial bribery] statute requires the offer of a bribe to an employee with the intent that he promote the interests of the person offering the bribe over those of his employer. . . . In the instant case Gendron attempted no clandestine bonus agreement with Michalski. Rather the "Acapulco Adventure" promotion was attended with maximum drumbeats and song, and the hoopla was disseminated to all of Gendron's customers on a to-whom-it-may-concern basis, not to any individual employee. The secretiveness and intent to suborn, which are essential elements of commercial bribery, were absent in the "Acapulco Adventure."

"Wrongful inducement" may be related to the tort of wrongful interference with commercial relations. The very idea of inducement, however, implies that Gendron, in its promotion, acted for the purpose of bringing about a breach or, at least, acted with reason to know that, if Gendron attained its purpose, a breach of an employee's duty to its employer would result. . . . The judge, therefore, properly instructed the jury that it had to find a purposeful intent by Gendron to influence Michalski to buy from Gendron materials he would normally have ordered from other wholesalers. The jury apparently found that intent lacking. . . .

JUDGMENT Affirmed.

A *kickback* is a common form of commercial bribery. By way of examples, the following are two actual cases:

- In order to be hired, Ida secretly paid a part of her salary back to the company. The money that Ida secretly repaid to her employer was a kickback.
- Doe, a buyer for a large retail chain store, bought for his company a quantity of blue jeans from pantsmaker X, paying $9.75 per pair. The next year, Joe made a private arrangement that X would charge the store $9 per pair and would pay Doe, "under the table," 25 cents for each pair delivered.

One U.S. attorney has said that in the defense industry, unfortunately, "[m]any buyers are on the take and many suppliers are willing to make under-the-table payments to buyers in order to win subcontracts." Workers in more than twenty defense contractor and subcontractor concerns were defendants in one series of indictments for kickbacks and bribery schemes that a prosecutor called "a cancer on the defense industry."

Bribery of foreign officials. Bribes, kickbacks, and other forms of gratuitous payment to foreign officials are sometimes made to obtain new business, to avert expropriation or nationalization of property, to avoid the expulsion of an individual by a foreign government, or to expedite the performance of a routine service. Although payment in the form of bribes to officials may be a way of life in some countries, bribery of government officials is contrary to the law of practically every country. Because of the widespread bribery of foreign officials by U.S. businesses, brought to light during the Watergate investigations, Congress, in 1977, enacted the Foreign Corrupt Practices Act. That Act makes it illegal for a businessperson to give anything of value to any foreign government official to influence an official act. Severe penalties may be imposed for violation of the Act.

Offenses Violative of Public Health and Safety Laws. The Federal Food, Drug and Cosmetic Act is one of many laws enacted to protect the public health and environment. It established the Food and Drug Administration, authorizing it to publish regulations setting standards for the quality of the foods we eat and for the effectiveness of the drugs we buy. Violations of those regulations are examples of *malum prohibitum* offenses against public health and safety laws.

In order to convict a defendant of having violated the Federal Food, Drug and Cosmetic Act, the government need not prove that the accused had a specific intent to violate the Act or even that he or she had a specific knowledge of the commission of the offense. For instance, the manager in charge of a food freezing plant may be found personally guilty if the plant sells boxes of frozen vegetables that are short of the weight shown on the label, even if he or she had no specific knowledge of that misrepresentation.

A first conviction for a violation of the Federal Food, Drug and Cosmetic Administration regulations is punishable as a misdemeanor, but if the offender is again convicted of any violation of the Act, or if there was an intent to defraud or mislead, the crime is a felony.

The liberal interpretation given to the Federal Food, Drug and Cosmetic Act is demonstrated by the next case.

CASE 7.5 United States v. Hohensee · 243 F.2d 367 (3d Cir. 1957)

FACTS Adolphus Hohensee was the president of Scientific Living, Inc., and controlled El Rancho Adolphus Products, Inc. Both companies, located in Pennsylvania, manufactured and sold health foods. In January 1952, Hohensee told the proprietor of a health food store in Phoenix, Arizona, that he intended to lecture on health subjects there. He provided the store with El Rancho Adolphus brand products. During February and March 1952, Hohensee gave lectures and distributed literature recommending El Rancho Products for many chronic diseases and physical complaints. At the lectures peppermint tea "was recommended for gallstones, colic, flatulence, headache, rheumatism, high blood

CASE 7.5 Continued

pressure, arthritis, prostate trouble, lumbago, fits, convulsions, colitis, tuberculosis, asthma, pinworms and tapeworms." Similar fantastic representations were made for the curative properties of wheat germ oil and herb laxatives.

As to curative properties, the label of the El Rancho peppermint tea packet stated only: "Used as a delicious refreshing table beverage. Take one level teaspoon of Adolphus peppermint tea for each cup of water, steep for four minutes. Do not boil. Sweeten to taste."

Hohensee, who had been previously convicted of a violation of the Federal Food, Drug and Cosmetic Act, and his two corporations were indicted and convicted of again violating the Act. The three appealed.

OPINION

McLAUGHLIN, Cir. J.... The Supreme Court [in *Kordel v. United States,* 1948, 335 U.S. 345] reaffirmed its position... that [the Federal Food and Cosmetic Act] be given a liberal interpretation to effectuate its high purpose of protecting unwary consumers in vital matters of health. The intended uses of the products in the present issue (as in *Kordel*), were to cure, ameliorate, or prevent diseases. The evidence to prove their uses included both graphic materials distributed and testimony of oral representations to users and prospective users.... The crime is that the labels on the containers were insufficient for the purposes for which the products were to be used. The statute prohibits the shipment of any products that are to be used as drugs... [that] are inadequately labeled for that purpose.... It is argued that since the lectures occurred some weeks after the products were introduced into interstate commerce, there was no proof of a medicinal or curative purpose or use of the products at the time of the shipments from Scranton to Phoenix.... The Supreme Court specifically held [in *Kodel*] that:

> The false and misleading literature in the present case was designed for use in the distribution and sale of the drug, and it was so used. The fact that it went in a different mail was wholly irrelevant whether we judge the transaction by purpose or result. And to say that the prior or subsequent shipment of the literature disproves that it "is" misbranded when introduced into commerce, is to overlook the integrated nature of the transaction....

[Hohensee's] guilt falls into the felony category, not because of evil intent, but because of the maximum sentence of three years for second offenders provided by... [the Act]. The Act imposes criminal sanctions as a means of regulating activities so dangerous to the public welfare as not to permit of exception of good faith or ignorance. A person acts at his peril in this field....

JUDGMENT The judgments of the District Court will be affirmed.

Frauds. Fraudulent actions affecting business are patently white-collar crimes. We can view them in two categories: (1) business frauds and (2) consumer frauds.

Business frauds. Actual instances of white-collar crimes of this category are the following:

- A large stock brokerage concern was fined $2 million after pleading guilty to 2,000 counts of bilking banks out of several million dollars in interest payments.
- Through various schemes, certain individuals established MasterCard and Visa accounts in banks, representing themselves as legitimate businesses. They then submitted to the banks for payment records falsely purporting to represent credit card purchases by customers.
- Some of the largest suppliers of products used by the Department of Defense have been charged with inflating by millions of dollars the prices of products they sold to the government; others conspired to rig bids; and still others used false invoices and other documents to avoid competitive bidding or to secure payment of unincurred costs.

We should also recognize that most tax evasions can be considered to be white-collar crimes involving fraud against public taxing authorities. It is not possible in a book such as this, which views the entire spectrum of business law, to discuss the vast array of taxes that are imposed by federal and state governments and by subordinate taxing authorities upon business concerns. We should recognize, however, that here is a broad "playing field" for unscrupulous people. For example, a business may be carried on without paying a required license tax; attempt may be made to evade an inventory tax; a business may not record or report sales subject to sales tax or may fail to pay to the authorities the tax due; a business may fail to pay to the government sums required to be withheld from an employee's wages; and a business may fraudulently evade payment, among other tax obligations, of income taxes. If the employer does not do so, he commits a white-collar crime.

Consumer frauds. Consumers are so often victimized by the fraudulent acts of suppliers that such offenses have become known as *consumer frauds.* (See also Chapter 4.)

Increasingly, federal and state laws are enacted to protect the public from suppliers of goods and services who may take unfair advantage of their customers. Consumer protection divisions have been established in the offices of all state attorneys general and in many district attorneys' offices. These officials are helping the public to recognize consumer frauds and to guard against them. The following categories of consumer frauds illustrate the problem.

- *Appliance service rip-offs:* A customer is charged an exorbitant amount for the repair of an appliance when the price had not been agreed upon beforehand. The customer is forced to pay this exorbitant price in order to gain return of the appliance.
- *Automobile sales and repair frauds:* The mileage indicator (odometer) of a car is rolled back to conceal the extent of a secondhand vehicle's prior use.

  A commercial garage makes unnecessary repairs to a customer's vehicle, or the customer is billed for work that was not actually performed.
- *Home improvement frauds:* A salesperson for an unscrupulous company persuades a homeowner to sign a contract for the application of oil to the roof of a house "to protect it from the elements." In fact, oiling has no useful effect.

  A contractor is paid for remodelling a house and for all materials that were used in the work. He intentionally fails to pay the companies that supplied the materials, and the latter file liens against the property. The homeowner must then pay the suppliers to discharge their liens, thereby in effect, paying twice for the materials.
- *Merchandising frauds:* In addition to such obvious frauds as false or deceptive advertising, merchants sometimes take advantage of customers in other ways. Seconds may be sold as perfect merchandise; scales may be improperly balanced; gasoline pumps may incorrectly calculate gallonage and price; or articles of inferior quality may be "palmed off" as being those of a reputable well-known manufacturer.

  Particular advantage may be taken of a customer who signs a retail installment payment contract. The signed contract may have blank spaces which can be filled in later by the seller to his or her personal advantage. According to the Connecticut attorney general, more than one thousand Connecticut homeowners unknowingly signed second mortgages on their homes as a part of a scheme involving the purchase of home improvements.

Warranties may be expressed only orally and may be wrongfully omitted by the seller from the written contract, interest charges may be unreasonable, and there may be hidden finance charges. To protect the public against unconscionable retail installment contracts, "truth-in-lending" statutes have been enacted by Congress and by several states (e.g., Calif. Civil Code, Sec. 1801; Conn. Gen. Laws [1958], Sec. 36–393; N.Y. Con. Laws, Chap. 24A, Sec. 6–101). Violation of such statutes are white-collar crimes.

Salespeople may be instructed to "switch" customers from their interest in advertised "bait" items to other articles which return a greater profit. The following case provides an illustration of the "bait and switch" scam.

CASE 7.6 People v. Block & Kleaver, Inc. · 427 N.Y.S.2d 133 (N.Y. 1980)

FACTS Block & Kleaver, Inc., the defendant, sold bulk beef at retail. It advertised the meat at prices less than it had paid. Each customer who responded to the advertisement was shown beef that was fatty, discolored, and unappetizing. The customer was told that "about 54 percent of the weight" had to be trimmed away before it could be used. The customer was also shown more appetizing, pretrimmed meat that was more expensive. The defendant's employees represented that the amount of waste of the better beef would be only about 10 percent—although when tested by authorities it had an average waste of 31 percent. As a result, customers purchased the more expensive meat.

The defendant was charged with misleading advertising and consumer fraud. After a nonjury trial, the defendant was convicted of both offenses. Pertinent parts of the trial court's opinion follow.

OPINION MARK, J.... [T]he Penal Law... proscribe[s] the sale promotional practice known as "bait and switch advertising," "bait advertising," or "fictitious bargain claims."... This practice consists of advertising a product at a very low price; a pattern of conduct discouraging the purchase of the advertised article by disparaging the same and exhibiting a poor-appearing specimen of the advertised article; and the resulting switch to the purchase of a product costing more than the one advertised....

[In *People v. Glubo,* 158 N.E.2d 699 (N.Y. 1959)] the defendant advertised via television a sewing machine which cost $45, for the price of $29.50. A customer who responded was visited by a salesman who would undertake to prove the advertised machine was inoperable and point out that it was basically defective and inferior. The salesman would then attempt to persuade the customer to order a better machine at a much higher price.... The People's case rested on the fact that the defendant advertised for sale a sewing machine it did not intend to sell in order to obtain leads so that it might sell the higher priced machine. The defendant made no false representations concerning the machines they did sell and the sewing machines sold by the defendants were worth the money paid therefor.

The Court of Appeals held that the conduct of the defendant constituted false advertising and that it was properly convicted....

...[T]he defendant here [Block & Kleaver] was engaged in a scheme to defraud.... [It] cannot defend on the ground that the misrepresentations of its employees were mere seller's talk.... The federal courts have constructed two tests for distinguishing fraudulent representations from puffing.... Under the first test, a seller engages in a fraudulent representation when he actually invents non-existent attributes.... False declarations of value constitute fraud.... Under the second test the purchaser is entitled to receive a product conforming to his expectation, and he is defrauded if his expectation is not met.... When a buyer receives a product not meeting the specifications represented... or the value of the product is less than represented... he has been defrauded....

JUDGMENT Accordingly, the defendant is found guilty of the crime of Scheme to Defraud... in violation of... the Penal Law.

Securities Laws Violations. The laws and regulations governing the issuance and trading of corporate securities are discussed at length in Chapter 43. However, at this point it is important to recognize that the issuance, sale, and purchase of securities (stocks and bonds) furnish a fertile field for white-collar crimes.

Securities offenses involve fraudulent schemes for the purchase or sale of stocks or bonds or the intentional failure to disclose vital information which an average investor would want to know before entering into a transaction. For example, Isabel, a stockbroker, breaks the law if she fails to tell a prospective customer that she (or her firm) has a financial interest in the company whose stock she is "pushing." Or, assume that John, a company director, knows that a medicine his firm manufactures is about to be withdrawn from the market because it produces harmful side effects. Knowing that the price of his company's stock will fall when news of the withdrawal of the highly profitable product is released, John sells his own stock in the company. Such a stock sale, based upon "inside information," is illegal.

In 1986 the Securities and Exchange Commission (SEC) brought to light the illegal insider trading on the New York Stock Exchange by a group of young men, dubbed by the press "the Yuppie Five." Among them were analysts for two large investment-banking firms and two lawyers, members of most-respected New York law firms engaged in work for their clients involving corporate takeover activities. Based upon inside information acquired before the public had knowledge of an impending takeover attempt, the five bought shares of stock in the companies and then, after the public announcement, when invariably the price of the shares was higher, sold them for handsome profits. Substantial jail sentences and fines were imposed on the "Yuppie Five" for these criminal acts. In addition, they were required by the SEC to turn over to the government the profits they had made in the transactions. At the same time, among other unlawful insider trading cases, the SEC imposed a $100 million civil penalty upon Ivan Boesky, a well-known corporate takeover entrepreneur, who was also sentenced by a federal court to confinement for 3 years.

Antitrust Offenses. Congress has enacted various laws to prevent businesses from engaging in any activity considered to be in restraint of trade. Among these *antitrust laws* (the subject of Chapters 45 and 46) are the Sherman Antitrust Act and the Clayton Act as amended by the Robinson-Patman Act of 1936. Antitrust offenses are classic examples of white-collar crimes. Such laws are designed to prevent business concerns from, among other improper activities, fixing prices in agreement with their competitors or engaging in corporate mergers that would restrict free competition.

By means of restraints of trade, businesses can unlawfully charge the public prices that are not held down by market forces. For example, it would violate antitrust laws and constitute a white-collar crime if a number of competing toy manufacturers whose products dominate the toy market were to agree among themselves: (1) what prices they will charge, or (2) that each of those companies would sell its products only in a prearranged area of the country.

Penalties for violating the antitrust laws may be severe. In civil suits, injured parties may secure as much as triple damages and reimbursement for litigation costs. Fines may be levied not only upon the firms involved, but also upon the individual wrongdoers, such as company managers, and jail sentences may also be imposed.

Larceny and Embezzlement by Employees. Any consideration of white-collar crime must recognize that a business may also be the *victim*. Computer offenses, discussed above, often are committed by employees who victimize their employers. Larceny and embezzlement of an employer's property, by computer and other means, are all too common. *Larceny* is the wrongful taking of the property of another with the intent permanently to deprive the owner of its possession. *Embezzlement* is the wrongful withholding of the property of another by someone to whom that property has been entrusted.

In many firms the white-collar crimes of theft (larceny) or embezzlement by employees of cash, tools, spare parts, office supplies, and other materials are very real problems. Unfortunately, it is not uncommon for a salesperson to charge a friend an amount less than an article is marked; another salesperson may overcharge a customer and pocket the overage; an expense account may be inflated; and shipping clerks may steal racks of clothing and sides of beef.

Most of these activities are carried on by people with no criminal records. Detection is difficult, and criminal prosecution—when it is undertaken—furnishes but slight deterrence to others. Yet, the losses from this type of white-collar crime are greater than all the nationwide robbery and burglary losses combined. Such business crimes have a great impact on the economy of the country, since commercial enterprises include as a part of their overhead the losses they suffer from white-collar crimes—and thus these losses are ultimately charged to the consumer.

Punishment for White-Collar Crimes

A bulletin published by the Department of Justice in November 1986 reported that:

> . . . Generally speaking, the criminal justice agencies in the jurisdictions studied do not appear to have treated the 28,012 white-collar crimes differently than they did other types of crime. White-collar defendants were prosecuted and convicted at rates similar to those accused of violent, property and public-order crimes. . . .
>
> White-collar crimes . . . were prosecuted and resulted in convictions about as often as, or more often than, other felonies. Those convicted after arrest for white-collar crimes were sentenced to incarceration at a rate similar to the average for all offenders, but less than for violent and property offenders; and they received sentence lengths of more than 1 year much less often than either violent or property offenders, but about as often as public-order offenders. . . .

Summary

A crime is an unlawful act punishable by the state. For an act to be a crime, it must be committed by a mentally competent person who possesses the requisite criminal intent. A crime involves something more than a mere intention to do a wrong or to prepare to do one.

A person under 7 years of age or one who is insane, as defined by the criminal law, does not have sufficient mental capacity to commit a crime. The most widely used test of insanity under the criminal law is the M'Naghten Rule, also known as the right and wrong test.

To be convicted of a criminal act involving moral turpitude, the actor must have had a criminal intent. However, no proof of criminal intent is required to establish the commission of a *malum prohibitum* offense, that is, one which does not involve moral turpitude but is wrong only because it is prohibited. Any offense which is punishable by imprisonment for more than 1 year or by the imposition of a death sentence is a felony. All lesser offenses are misdemeanors. Some actions by businesspeople are not criminal, but they nevertheless are unethical.

"Criminal procedure" refers to the various steps involved in prosecuting someone accused of having committed a crime. The Constitution assures that an accused will not be deprived of life, liberty, or property without due process of law. An accused is presumed to be innocent until proved guilty. If the accused is convicted, he or she may appeal to a higher court, but after a verdict of not guilty the state may not appeal.

"Business crime," or "white-collar crime," is a name frequently given to a nonviolent criminal act related to business. Among such crimes are computer offenses; bribery; Federal Food, Drug and Cosmetic Act violations; securities law violations; antitrust offenses; consumer frauds; and larceny and embezzlement by employees.

Computers are becoming more and more the subject of criminal activity. A person is guilty of a crime if he or she intentionally: (1) inserts false information into a computer's memory, (2) wrongfully varies its programming, or (3) improperly appropriates information stored in the machine. Computer crimes presently cause losses of millions of dollars to American business each year.

Frauds related to business transactions, and frauds which take advantage of consumers are common white-collar crimes. Increasingly, federal and state governments are creating measures to protect consumers from these offenses.

Review Questions

1 (a) What is a criminal act? (b) What is the cardinal difference between a crime and a tort?

2 (a) What constitutes the mental capacity to commit a crime? (b) What is *mens rea?*

3 What is meant by the phrases *malum in se* and *malum prohibitum?*

4 Contrast a felony, a misdemeanor, and an infraction.

5 Enumerate four constitutional guarantees which apply to due process in a trial of a person charged with having committed a criminal act.

6 What is the Miranda rule? Who promulgated that rule?

7 In a criminal prosecution, what is the difference between an indictment and an information?

8 Contrast the degree of proof necessary to establish the existence of a fact in a civil suit with the degree of proof needed to find the existence of intent in a criminal prosecution.

9 Contrast the right to appeal a judgment in a civil suit with the right to appeal a verdict in a criminal prosecution.

10 **(a)** What is a white-collar crime? **(b)** Why was that name given to this facet of the criminal law? **(c)** How do such crimes differ from other crimes?

11 **(a)** Explain how a computer can be the instrument of a criminal act. **(b)** Why should computer crimes be of particular interest to businesspeople?

12 **(a)** What is a kickback? **(b)** How does a kickback affect the general public?

13 Give three examples of business frauds.

Case Problems

1 Gerdine had a used car lot from which he sold automobiles on commission. Reuben left his car with Gerdine to be sold. A week later Gerdine told Reuben that a purchaser had the car "on approval." Two weeks later, Reuben, not seeing his car on Gerdine's lot, demanded its return. Gerdine said that he would pay for it when he had the money. Reuben sued Gerdine for the value of his automobile. While that action was pending, Gerdine was arrested and charged with unlawfully taking Reuben's car. Gerdine filed a motion to dismiss the criminal action because a civil suit was already pending which, in effect, required Gerdine to pay for the car. What action should the court take?

2 Otto's girlfriend, Susan, refused to see him any more. Otto learned that, since breaking up with him, Susan was dating Felix, who shared an apartment with Otto. Otto bought a package of Rough-on-Rats, a rat poison which is also fatal to humans if ingested, intending to put some in Felix's breakfast coffee at his first opportunity. However, before the opportunity arose, Felix saw the Rough-on-Rats, and he asked Otto what it was for. Otto replied, "I'll tell you. You stole my girl, and I'm going to kill you." What offense did Otto commit?

3 Early in the morning of January 1, 1985, Jerry shot and killed his wife after he had been drinking, "cursing, talking crazy, doing stupid, foolish, and weird things, falling on furniture, hitting things with his fist, and getting the guns out." At the subsequent trial for the homicide, he claimed that he could not be convicted for his criminal actions because, due to the extent of his intoxication, he could not form a criminal intent. Is this a correct statement of the law? Discuss.

4 Hancock, an employee of Texas Instruments Automatic Computer Corporation, without authority, photographed fifty-nine computer programs belonging to his employer and attempted to sell them. He was tried and found guilty of the offense of stealing property of a value of more than $50. On appeal, Hancock contends that he was unlawfully convicted because no physical property or original documents were removed from his employer's premises and that, at best, he took only $35 worth of paper. How should the appeal be decided? Why?

5 The president of a bank, whose primary duties were to attract new business to the bank and to maintain its public relations, used bank money to do favors for public officials. The bank president thought that those officials might be influential in securing new deposits by the government in his bank. Based on these circumstances alone, the bank president was charged with the bribery of public officials. Should the bank president be found guilty of the offense charged? Explain.

6 The Brothers Food Corporation operated a warehouse where foodstuffs were stored. Starr, the secretary-treasurer of the corporation, was in charge of the sanitation of the warehouse. After fields surrounding the building were plowed for farming, mice infested the warehouse. Starr knew of the problem, and he instructed the janitor to get rid of the mice. The janitor failed to do so. When, later, the Food and Drug Administration inspector found many mice in the warehouse, he charged Starr with violating the Federal Food, Drug and Cosmetic Act. Was Starr guilty of the offense? Explain.

7 The Grand View Department Store advertises Levi jeans at half the price for which other stores are selling them. The only Levi jeans the store has are small children's sizes. When a customer comes into Grand View to purchase a pair of Levis for herself, she is told that the only Levi jeans the store has for sale are the children's small size, but that the store has a full range of Calvin Klein jeans. These jeans are not on sale, and though they are more costly, their price is fair and is no greater than the price of Calvin Klein jeans in other stores. Competitors of Grand View object to the manner in which that store carries on its business. Are the competitors justified in their objections? Explain.

ETHICS IN PRACTICE

"Ethics" has a variety of meanings. The academic discipline called "ethics" deals with the nature of moral duty and obligation and with the philosophy of what is good and bad. Sets of moral principles or values, also called "ethics," govern the conduct of individuals or groups. These principles, or rules of conduct, often are derived from the formal study of ethics but mostly develop over time as a matter of custom and usage. As noted in Chapter 2, people may find themselves faced with conflicting standards of ethical behavior and so may need to consider how to recognize, analyze, and resolve ethical dilemmas.

Ethics, as applied to business activities, has at least two major aspects—*business ethics* and *corporate social responsibility*. Business ethics focuses mainly on day-to-day business activities, especially on the way in which individuals deal with others within or outside the firm. Corporate social responsibility is more concerned with the extent to which a business firm should pursue social objectives beyond profitmaking. The "Ethics in Practice" sections in this book emphasize business ethics problems, but some deal also with corporate social responsibility.

Most of the "Ethics in Practice" problems involve ethical dilemmas of the kinds discussed in Chapter 2. Some problems are purely hypothetical. Some are based on news accounts of business activities, and a few are based on decided court cases. There may or may not be a violation of law. Resolving the problems will require identifying sets of norms that may be in conflict.

Problems in Ethics

1 Marvin placed a newspaper ad reading: "Government jobs in your area." The ad listed salaries ranging from $9,000 to $16,000 and gave a telephone number but no address. Bob called the number and was asked to give his Visa charge account number for a catalog that would explain details. The charge for the catalog was $29.95. Bob assumed that the catalog would list and explain specific jobs with specific salaries at specific locations. However, Bob received a brochure that merely listed names, addresses, and telephone numbers of government employment offices. Bob could have gotten the same material from the government printing office at no charge. The brochure offered a refund if the purchaser was dissatisfied, but it gave no return address. **(a)** Has Marvin committed any violation of law? **(b)** Has Marvin committed a breach of ethics by selling what was available to buyers free? Would your answer be different if Marvin had charged only $3?

2 Drugco, a 1,000-store chain of pharmacies operating in several states, loses about $20 million to shoplifters each year. To combat shoplifting, Drugco has instituted a new policy: Instead of routinely prosecuting alleged shoplifters under the criminal statutes, local Drugco stores may allow suspected shoplifters to buy their way out of trouble by paying the store $200. The procedure is as follows: When shoplifters are caught, the store manager is to have them arrested if they seem like professional criminals. However, if they seem to be amateur, casual shoplifters, the manager may let them go after verifying their names and addresses. In about a week, the freed suspects receive letters demanding payment of the $200. If they refuse to pay, Drugco sues them in small claims court for civil damages. Most persons accused of shoplifting have been paying up. **(a)** Given your understanding of "due process of law," is there anything about the new policy that makes you feel uncomfortable? **(b)** Suppose you are interviewing for a job as a Drugco manager and are asked your opinion of the new policy. Would your status as an applicant affect your evaluation? How? **(c)** If you are uncomfortable with the new policy, would you feel better knowing that it has the approval of authorities in twenty-six states? Why?

3 Jonesco, a construction company, builds houses. A couple of days before completing one project, Jonesco instructed the power company to disconnect temporary power poles, and told the subcontractors they would need portable generators to finish the work. Later, Susan, the owner of a nearby house, learned that instead of using a portable generator, one subcontractor entered her garage while she was at work and plugged his power tools into her garage outlets. Outraged, Susan called the police, the state contractors' license board, and the power company. All agreed that the subcontractor had made an illegal entry and had stolen electricity, and that she had a good claim against him and Jonesco. Upon being advised that the district attorney probably would not be interested in pursuing the matter as a criminal case, Susan decided not to bring criminal charges. Instead, Susan asked Jonesco to pay her September power bill as reparation for the subcontractor's illegal conduct. Jonesco apologized to Susan, told the subcontractors "Don't do this again," and offered her $10 for the electricity, the actual cost of which Jonesco estimated at about 46 cents. Susan rejected the offer and sued Jonesco in small claims court for $93—the amount of her September power bill plus 1 day's lost wages. **(a)** What violations of law did the subcontractor commit? Is there any ethical justification for his conduct? **(b)** Did Jonesco act ethically in offering Susan $10? To answer, would you need to know whether Jonesco had been involved in similar incidents in the past? **(c)** Did Susan act ethically in demanding $93? Would it be helpful to consider the kinds of harm that Susan suffered? Are other factors relevant?

4 Downtown merchants in Sonoma asked the city manager to do something to make more parking spaces available for shoppers. The city manager responded by hiring Ron, a new "meter man," and providing him with a new motorized cart. Ron tripled the average number of parking tickets—from 200 to 600 per month. Although virtually all the tickets were justified, the city clerk's office has been flooded with complaints. "I thought it was pretty Scroogey," complained Lydia, cited and fined $20 during the Christmas season for parking slightly into a red zone during a shopping trip. "It doesn't encourage you to come back for fear you're going to get zapped." Merchants now fear that strict enforcement of parking regulations will scare away customers. The police lieutenant has instructed Ron to be more lenient, for example by ticketing only cars parked halfway into an adjoining space. Should parking law enforcement policy be so easily influenced by downtown merchants and the volume of citizen complaints?

PART THREE

Contracts

CHAPTER 8

Introduction to the Law of Contracts

The contract is one of the most important legal devices ever developed in the quest for economic security and a stable society. Individuals enter into contracts when they buy a house, visit the dentist, or buy an automobile on the installment plan. Business firms enter into contracts with suppliers of raw materials, parts, and equipment; with banks, utility companies, and other service institutions; and with employees, investors, and customers. Although governments have considerable power to command obedience, much of their work is accomplished by means of contracts entered into voluntarily. It is largely by contract that the processes of production, exchange, and distribution are carried on in a free enterprise system such as ours.

Nature of Contracts; Importance of Contract Law

Meaning of Contract

A *contract* may be defined simply as a promise or set of promises that the courts will enforce. A contract may also be defined as an agreement enforceable at law. This agreement often consists of an exchange of promises between two persons, called "parties," whose object is to strike a bargain that is acceptable to each party. In exchange for Ann's promise to pay Ben $2,000, Ben promises to paint Ann's house. Under either of the above definitions, the transaction is a contract.

Since promises are a vital part of contracting, it is helpful to consider the legal meaning of promise and its contractual function. A *promise* is "a manifestation [showing] of intention to act or to refrain from acting in a specified way, so made as to justify a promisee in understanding that a commitment has been made."[1] The party who makes a promise is called the "promisor." The one to whom the promise is made is called the "promisee." The "commitment" is the promisor's pledge or assurance that he or she will perform in the way specified, and it ordinarily is made to induce the promisee into a contract. Because the ability to rely on commitments is essential for planning and carrying out business activities, the law protects promisees' expectations of performance by enforcing contractual and certain other kinds of promises.

A promise may be communicated in language or by nonverbal conduct. When communicating in language, a promisor need not use the word "promise." Expressions such as "I will pay" and "I hereby offer to pay" are promises to pay.

Often, promises are inferred from nonverbal conduct. For example, at an auction, a promise to pay may be inferred from the bidder's act of raising a hand or a card. This is so regardless of any secret intention of the bidder not to pay. Contracting parties such as the seller at an auction usually can rely on external (objective) manifestations of intention and are not bound by internal (subjective) intentions that contradict the outward manifestations.

Requirements for a Contract

The usual goal of contracting parties is an exchange of values: money for goods or for real estate, goods for services, and so on. There may be a period of negotiation or bargaining during which the parties "dicker" back and forth to establish the price and other terms. The resulting contract will call for one party to render a performance (or to make a promise to perform) in exchange for the other party's return performance or promise.

A contract for an exchange of values usually must meet the following requirements:

1. There must be an agreement, that is, a manifestation of *mutual assent* ordinarily arrived at by a process of *offer* and *acceptance* (which may or may not involve bargaining over terms).
2. The promises must be supported by *consideration.* Ann's promise to pay money is consideration for Ben's promise to paint her house. Ben's promise to paint the house is consideration for Ann's promise to pay money. (Thus, usually, each contracting party is both a promisor and a promisee.)
3. The parties involved must have *capacity* (mental or legal ability) to contract.
4. The agreement must have a *legal objective*—i.e., must be permitted by law.

[1] *Restatement (Second) Contracts,* Sec. 2(1).

For certain types of contracts, there is another requirement: a writing or a legally acceptable substitute. Each of these requirements is discussed further in the following chapters.

Significance of Contracts and Contract Law

Contract law is a body of rules governing the formation, performance, and enforcement of contracts. Its major purpose is to protect the reasonable expectations of individuals, businesses, and governments that contracts will be binding on and enforceable by the parties. Because contracts are enforceable, private parties can make personal and business plans of immense variety, confident of receiving the bargained-for exchange or a court-ordered equivalent (usually a money payment called "damages"). The large-scale, long-term business planning necessary for a modern industrial society would be difficult to achieve without the legal enforceability of contracts.

As a part of business studies, contract law is tremendously significant because it underlies or is related to all major areas of law affecting business. Chapters 8 to 15 deal mostly with the "common law" of contracts—i.e., the modern American version of its forerunner, the English common law of contracts. Common law contract principles appear throughout the law governing employment, labor-management relations, partnerships, corporations, antitrust and merger problems, secured transactions such as mortgages, insurance, and the landlord-tenant relationship. The law of contracts has been adapted to serve special needs. For example, we have a special body of contract law governing the sale of goods—Article 2 of the Uniform Commercial Code (UCC). An even more specialized body of contract law—Article 3 of the UCC—applies to commercial paper: the checks, notes, drafts, and certificates of deposit used in financial transactions. Even the law of bankruptcy requires attention to contract principles, since the courts must decide which of the troubled debtor's contracts are to be enforced and which are not. A study of the concepts, principles, and technical vocabulary of contract law will aid immensely in understanding most other business law.

Development of Contract Law[2]

Like law in general, the law of contracts has changed over the centuries in response to changes in social conditions, needs of the population, and philosophies of government. The development of American contract law during the eighteenth, nineteenth, and twentieth centuries presents a striking example of how law evolves to meet new needs.

As late as the eighteenth century, contract law in America reflected a frontier culture of small towns, farmers, and small traders, and an attitude, established in medieval times, that a thing had a fair or a "just" price that would change little over time. One role of this early contract law, especially as applied by the courts of equity, was to assure fairness of exchanges between individuals. So, if a contracting party was overcharged, the court would look into the equivalency of the exchange (adequacy of the consideration), at least to the extent of refusing to enforce a grossly unequal bargain. Thus, the courts of this period acted as monitors of contracts and awarded damages in accordance with a fair price standard that was independent of the agreement of the parties.

Classical View of Contract Law

Market Economy, Laissez-faire, and Freedom of Contract. As a result of the industrial revolution, the first large commodities markets appeared in this country early in the nineteenth century. With them came great changes in contract law and philosophy that caused the nineteenth century to be known as the "classical period" of contract. Influenced by laissez-faire economic theory (that the operation of the free market determines value) and the fact that market values fluctuate, legal writers and judges soon rejected the eighteenth century idea of a fixed just price that should be universally binding. Instead, value was now thought to rest on a

[2] The discussion of the development and nature of contract law is based largely on M. Horwitz, *The Transformation of American Law* (1977), L. Friedman, *Contract Law in America* (1965), R. Pound, *The Spirit of the Common Law* (1921), and C. Fried, *Contract as Promise* (1981).

host of variable, subjective factors which a court was in no position to evaluate—for example, supply and demand, the relative value of other investments, and, above all, the individual needs and preferences of the bargaining parties. Consequently, price and other terms of a contract could be properly determined only by the agreement of a willing buyer and seller, each acting in his or her own self-interest in a free market with a minimum of governmental interference.

During the nineteenth century, then, contract law came to reflect the following premises:

1 Contracting parties should have a broad freedom to contract as they like—to make economic decisions subject only to a few limitations imposed by law for the prevention of fraud, the protection of minors, and so on.
2 Parties dealing "at arm's length" (as wary strangers) are presumed equal in bargaining power and thus capable of protecting themselves from being taken advantage of: *caveat emptor* ("Let the buyer beware").
3 Contracts should be enforced because the parties, being creatures of free will, intend the consequences of their actions: promisees' reliance on the promised performances.
4 Since value is subjective (personal to the contracting parties), only the contracting parties are competent to judge whether the things exchanged are equivalent. Therefore, the bargain struck by the parties will not be overturned merely for inadequacy of consideration; indeed, harsh bargains are to be expected in a market economy and ordinarily will be enforced.
5 However, although the heart of contracting is the "meeting of the minds" (agreement) of the contracting parties, the interpretation and construction of a contract (determining what the parties meant) is a question of law for the court to decide. Thus, the court has the power to conform the parties' meaning to external rules of law with which their actual intent might otherwise conflict.

Role of Nineteenth-Century Contract Law.

In the eighteenth century, the usual function of a contract was to transfer ownership of an existing thing for an equivalent value, and an important objective of contract law was to assure equivalency of exchange between the individuals involved. But in the emerging market economy of the nineteenth century, people began using contracts to assure themselves of a *future* performance for an agreed future consideration—to reduce the risk of loss in an impersonal, fluctuating market. The function of contract became that of ensuring an expected future return, even if the bargain turned out badly for the other party. It was no longer the function of courts to assure equivalence of exchange; their function was now to enforce the legitimate agreements of contracting parties, and most agreements were considered legitimate even if one party could demonstrate that he or she had received the worst of the bargain. Contract rules based on the face-to-face dealings of the eighteenth century were on the way out. Replacing them were the uniform, consistent, abstract rules thought necessary for protecting expectations in the impersonal national markets of the nineteenth century.

Contemporary View of Contract Law

Many nineteenth-century contract principles apply today. For example, today's courts ordinarily do not look into the adequacy of consideration, preferring, as before, to leave economic valuation to the parties. However, the twentieth century has seen substantial developments in contract and contract-related doctrines and considerable movement away from nineteenth-century contract philosophy and practice.

Viewed broadly, the modern contract law of most states consists of three major, interrelated elements. They are:

1 The state's common law of contracts, which applies to contracts such as those for real estate and services.
2 The Uniform Commercial Code (UCC), another body of state law which applies to contracts more likely to be involved in interstate commerce—e.g., contracts for sales of goods. To foster efficient distribution of goods, many UCC contract rules differ substantially from their common law counterparts.
3 Government regulation (state and federal) affecting contracts.

Uniform Commercial Code. Mass production and the development of national markets led to a need for buyers and sellers of goods to do business across state lines. However, the law applying to contracts for the sale of goods (like the common law applying to other contracts) varied considerably from state to state. To facilitate interstate commerce in goods, legal scholars drafted a number of "uniform acts" for the individual state legislatures to adopt so that all states would be operating under the same commercial law. The Uniform Sales Act, adopted between 1907 and 1941 in thirty-six states and the District of Columbia,[3] introduced substantial uniformity into the law of sales. Eventually, the Uniform Commercial Code replaced the Uniform Sales Act and other uniform acts on related topics. The Code, now in effect in all states except Louisiana, has nine articles on topics of commercial law.[4] Article 2 governs sales of goods.

As noted in the sales chapters of this book, Article 2 provides flexible rules of contracting well suited to the vast numbers of fast-paced sales transactions occurring daily. Unlike the cumbersome common law rules governing real estate and services contracts in many states, Article 2 emphasizes ease of contract formation; judicial discretion in contract enforcement (but in light of actual business practices); ethical business conduct and fair dealing, especially by merchants; and, for breach of contract, practical remedies that permit business to continue with a minimum of interruption.

In every state, most people will contract for services or real estate, and also for goods. Consequently, the residents of all states (except perhaps Louisiana, where the common law of contracts was never adopted) will encounter two rather different bodies of contract law governing bargained-for exchanges: the common law of contracts and Article 2. Yet, these bodies of law are closely related. For example, where Article 2 does not provide a rule to cover a sales contract situation, the common law contract rules apply.

[3]Robert J. Nordstrom, *Handbook of the Law of Sales,* West Publishing, St. Paul, 1970, p. 4.

[4]Louisiana, being of French background, adopted Roman civil law in its French form as the basis of its legal system. Consequently, Louisiana has a civil code somewhat like the UCC. Although Louisiana has not adopted the UCC as such, its legislature has adopted in substance Articles 1, 3, 4, 5, 7, 8, and 9.

Restatement (Second) of the Law of Contracts. Early in the twentieth century, the American Law Institute (ALI), a group of leading legal scholars and practitioners, saw a need for more uniformity in the common law than then existed. The ALI published a number of works, called *Restatements,* on major law topics such as contracts, torts, and agency. Having examined thousands of often conflicting judicial decisions, the ALI presented (in the form of written rules, examples, and commentary) its best estimate of the common law for each area, stating the majority positions of the courts and a number of significant minority positions. Often criticized as creating an illusion of legal certainty when in fact law constantly grows and adjusts to social forces, the *Restatements* nevertheless have been influential guides to judges as they decide cases.

The *Restatement of the Law of Contracts,* published in 1932, reflected the nineteenth-century ideal for a law of contracts—precise, abstract, impersonal rules aimed at allocating risk in huge, impersonal markets. Nearly 50 years later, the ALI published the *Restatement (Second) of the Law of Contracts.* It reflects modern developments in and attitudes toward contract law. In particular, *Restatement (Second)* adopts and applies to the common law of contracts many flexible, discretionary UCC standards formerly limited to sales of goods, often in language nearly identical to that of the Code.

A *Restatement,* unlike a uniform act enacted into law by a legislature, is not an official statement of law. The rules and principles of a restatement are merely guidelines for the courts. However, over time, significant portions of the *Restatements* have become law in many states by a process of judicial incorporation. Some parts of *Restatement (Second)* have been adopted by many courts in the United States, while other parts have been ignored. As the provisions of *Restatement (Second)* are incorporated into the common law of contracts, there will be a narrowing of the differences between it and the law of sales, and a modernization of the common law.

Government Regulation Affecting Contracts. From early times, the government has placed limits on what people may do to each other through contract. The eighteenth-century court's limiting a seller to a "just price" is one example of judicial intervention into private agreements for the purpose of protecting a weaker party. Even in the nineteenth century when the parties' decision as to value was supposed to remain undisturbed, judges would intervene indirectly to remedy extreme cases of exploitation—for example, by interpreting vague contract language against the exploiter. As discussed later in the section entitled "Contracts of Adhesion," the twentieth-century courts have been considerably more active in coming to the aid of weaker parties.

Legislatures also have a fairly long history of regulating contractual relations. In 1921, Dean Roscoe Pound, in *The Spirit of the Common Law,* made note of "statutes requiring payment of wages in cash, statutes regulating conditions of labor, and legislation with respect to non-living wage, minimum wage, and the like." Today, state and federal regulation of employment contracts is pervasive, and other legislative and administrative agency limitations on freedom of contract abound. The UCC imposes an obligation of good faith on all parties to Code transactions, gives the parties a right to avoid (cancel) "unconscionable" (oppressively unfair) contracts or contract clauses, and imposes warranties (guarantees of quality) in the sale of goods if the seller does not take care to exclude them. In most states, legislatures or administrative agencies regulate, on behalf of customers, the terms of contracts for insurance, water and electricity, and the like. And there is a large and growing amount of federal regulation of private contracts, often in the form of disclosure statutes protecting consumers, such as the Truth-in-Lending Act, the Real Estate Settlement Procedures Act, and the Fair Credit Billing Act. Much of the legislation affecting the content of contracts will be discussed in later chapters.

Contracts of Adhesion. The "contract of adhesion" (a contract imposed by a party who enjoys overwhelming bargaining power) is the subject of much of the government regulation just discussed. A traditional assumption underlying contract law is that both parties negotiating a contract have sufficient bargaining power that one party cannot take undue advantage of the other. In many instances, the parties are indeed so well matched in terms of bargaining power that each can look out for his or her own interests. Large corporations, for example, usually can fend for themselves when dealing with one another, as can most people who negotiate the purchase of a used car from a neighbor. Often, however, one party, usually a borrower or a buyer dealing with a large firm, has no meaningful choice with regard to some or all of the contract terms; they are imposed by the stronger party against the weaker party's wishes, usually by means of a standard-form contract called a "contract of adhesion." Rather than permit the form to be varied, the firm or industry imposing it simply refuses to deal with anyone who will not accept its terms. Most contracts for consumer goods, insurance, mortgages, consumer credit, automobiles, and a host of other goods and services are contracts of adhesion.

Contracts of adhesion serve legitimate functions in our economy and usually are enforced despite the weaker party's lack of consent to the imposed terms. Many businesses could not function on a large scale if the terms of each transaction had to be negotiated individually. Transaction costs for sellers of inexpensive goods and services could become prohibitive. The insurance industry, which must be able to calculate and limit risk, would be unable to do so if insurance contracts varied with each customer. Yet, people upon whom contracts of adhesion are imposed are vulnerable to exploitation. Despite the presumption that all contracting parties are equals, even nineteenth-century courts took steps to remedy the worst abuses of superior bargaining power. Twentieth-century courts, legislatures, and administrative agencies have recognized the misuse of standard-form contracts as a major problem and have developed a variety of ways to combat it—e.g., by interpreting the contract in favor of the weaker party, by finding that the stronger party did not give consideration, by requiring disclosure of key information, or by applying the concept of unconscionability, discussed earlier.[5]

Classification of Contracts

The study of contract law often involves reference to particular kinds of contracts. The following paragraphs describe some common types of contracts and some of their characteristics. A given contract may fit into more than one category.

[5]Slawson, "Standard Form Contracts and Democratic Control of Lawmaking Power," 84 *Harvard Law Review* 529 (1971).

Express and Implied Contracts

An *express contract* is one in which the terms of the contract are stated in words. An *implied contract* is one in which the terms of the contract are wholly or partly inferred from conduct or from surrounding circumstances. When Jane, on passing a market where she has an account, picks up a bag of oranges marked "98¢," holds up the bag, and waits until the clerk nods, the promise to pay 98 cents (and, in fact, the whole contract) is implied by the conduct of the parties. In legal effect there is no difference between an express contract and an implied contract. They differ merely in the manner in which assent is manifested.

Unilateral and Bilateral Contracts

A *unilateral contract* is one in which only one party makes a promise. Ann tells Ben, "I'll pay you $10 to mow my lawn." This is an offer for a unilateral contract because Ann (the promisor) expects Ben (the promisee) to accept her offer by performing the requested act (mowing). In contrast, a *bilateral contract* is one in which both parties make promises. Ann says to Ben, "I'll pay you $10 to mow my lawn. Will you mow it Friday for that price?" Ann has made an offer for a bilateral contract because Ben is to indicate his acceptance by making a verbal response that either states or implies a promise to mow the yard on Friday ("Yes," or "Yes, I'll mow your lawn on Friday for $10").

In the situations described above, Ann is the "offeror" (the person making an offer) and Ben is the "offeree" (the person receiving the offer). A contract forms, or "arises," when the offeree (Ben) indicates agreement to, or "accepts," the offer.

In the bilateral contract situation involving Ann and Ben, a contract arises as soon as Ben communicates his acceptance to Ann. Consequently, as soon as Ben accepts the offer, he is obligated to mow the yard on Friday, and Ann is obligated to pay him $10 upon his completing the job.

In the unilateral contract situation, however, a contract does not arise until Ben completes his performance (or, in many states, begins it). Consequently, unilateral contracts tend to arise later than bilateral contracts, and there is more time for the offeror (Ann) to "revoke" (cancel) the offer. In states where the offeree (Ben) must perform completely to accept an offer for a unilateral contract, the offeree risks having the offer canceled after beginning the performance, but before completing it. Since, in those states, partial performance is not sufficient to create a contract, the offeree is not entitled to the contract price. However, as explained later in this chapter, the offeree (Ben) may be entitled to a lesser payment—for the reasonable value of his part performance—under the doctrine of "quasi contract."

Executory and Executed Contracts

An *executory contract* is one that is yet to be performed. Ann says to Ben, "I'll pay you $10 to mow my lawn. Will you mow it tomorrow?" and Ben says "Yes." Ann and Ben have entered into an executory bilateral contract. It is executory because neither party to it has rendered the promised performance.

An *executed contract* is one that has been performed. If Ben mows the lawn and Ann pays him $10, the contract is fully executed (performed). If Ben mows the lawn but Ann fails to pay, the contract is *partially executed.* It could also be said to be *partially executory,* since Ben has performed but Mary has not.

Enforceable, Unenforceable, Voidable, and "Void" Contracts

An *enforceable contract* is one for the breach of which the law gives a remedy. The usual remedy is a judgment for monetary damages. In appropriate circumstances (discussed in Chapter 15), the equitable remedy of specific performance is available.

An *unenforceable contract* is one meeting the basic requirements of mutual assent, consideration, legal object, and parties with capacity to contract, but which the law will not enforce because of the parties' failure to comply with some other legal requirement. For example, contracts for the sale of land must be in writing to be enforceable. An oral contract for the sale of land ordinarily is unenforceable.

A *voidable contract* is one which a party may either enforce or get out of (avoid) as that person chooses. For example, a person who was induced to enter a contract by the other party's fraud may avoid (cancel) the contract, or may enforce it and have damages for any loss caused by the fraud.

A *"void" contract,* if there can be such a thing, is nothing more than an attempt at contracting that never produced a contract because some essential contractual element (mutual assent, consideration, legal object, or capacity of the parties) was missing. A person who has been declared insane by a court lacks contractual capacity. That person's alleged contract is void.

Formal and Informal Contracts

A *formal contract* is one to which the law gives special effect because of the form or special language used in creating it. At common law, a written promise to which the promisor's seal (e.g., a wax emblem) was attached was enforceable because the sealed document complied with the formalities prescribed by law, and not because there was any consideration given for the promise. In most states, the legal effect of a seal has been abolished. Today, the most common formal contracts are *negotiable instruments* (commercial paper) such as checks. To create a negotiable instrument, a person must use a particular form or style of language. A negotiable instrument has legal characteristics that differ from those of ordinary contracts. How negotiable instruments differ from ordinary contracts is discussed in Chapters 28 to 32.

Informal contracts are those for which the law does not require a particular set of formalities or special language. The usual requirements for a contract (mutual assent, consideration, etc.) must be met, but the parties to an informal contract may use any style of language they please. The contract may be oral, or it may even be inferred from the parties' conduct, in the absence of a statute requiring a writing. Often, contracts result from an exchange of letters or telegrams between parties who did not know that such an informal exchange could be binding. Where the parties use language to create a contract, it can be as elaborate or as sketchy as they desire. Informal contracts are sometimes called "simple" contracts, although they may in fact be very complicated.

Doctrines Related to Contract Law

Two important doctrines—quasi contract and promissory estoppel—supplement modern contract law. Centuries old, quasi contract provides a damage remedy to prevent injustice where under the classical rules of contract formation no enforceable contract promise exists.

Promissory estoppel provides promise enforcement where classical contract rules would not. Largely a twentieth-century development, it is perhaps the most significant advance in contract law since the nineteenth-century movement away from the just-price doctrine.

Quasi Contract

Sometimes people deliver goods, improve real estate, or render services to others without benefit of an enforceable contract. They might have delivered goods by mistake to the wrong person or improved the wrong real estate. They might have thought there was a contract when in fact none arose. Or the contract that they did negotiate might have turned out to be unenforceable. These people are not entitled to a *contract* price, because their attempt to contract, if any, failed. But they might be entitled to an *alternative* remedy (an amount in lieu of contract damages) under the doctrine of quasi contract.

Quasi contracts (sometimes called "implied-in-law" contracts) are not contracts at all; they are obligations imposed by law *to prevent unjust enrichment* of one person at another's expense. The obligation is created by law, not by mutual assent, and in fact often is imposed contrary to one's wishes.

To recover damages in a lawsuit based on quasi contract, the plaintiff ordinarily must prove four things: (1) The plaintiff conferred a benefit on the defendant; (2) the plaintiff reasonably expected to be paid for the benefit, or at least did not intend it as a gift; (3) the plaintiff was not an "officious intermeddler" (a person who intrudes into affairs that are none of his or her business); and (4) allowing the defendant to retain the benefit without paying for it would unjustly enrich the plaintiff. The amount of recovery in quasi contract is the reasonable value of services rendered or property delivered, and *not* some contract price that might have been agreed to.

The following situations illustrate the nature of quasi contract and its relationship to contract law:

- Ann, a physician, discovers Ben unconscious by a roadside and renders emergency medical services. Ben dies without regaining consciousness, and Ann files a claim against Ben's estate for payment for her services. Ann had no contract with Ben because, being unconscious, he lacked capacity to contract and also was incapable of the assent necessary for a contract. Nevertheless, Ann has a remedy in quasi contract for the reasonable value of her services. Ordinarily, "reasonable value" is the rate customarily charged in the community for services of the kind rendered, without regard to what the claimant (Ann) would have charged.

- Before leaving for work, Art writes the following note to Betty and leaves it in her mailbox: "I'll pay you $20 to mow my lawn this afternoon." After Betty has mowed half the lawn, Art returns home and refuses to let her complete the job. Since the law of Betty's state requires that she complete the mowing in order to accept Art's offer for a unilateral contract, no contract arose, and Betty has no cause of action for the contract price of $20. However, she has a quasi-contract remedy for the reasonable value of her services. If the customary rate for mowing lawns the size of Art's is $30, Betty would be entitled to $15 for the half she mowed.
- Al agrees orally to sell his house to Bob for $50,000 plus 10 percent annual interest. Bob is to pay $400 per month until the purchase price is paid, and Al is then to transfer ownership to Bob by means of a document called a "deed." Bob moves into the house, and during the next 3 years replaces the roof and builds a garage. Seeing the improvements, Al cancels the oral contract and brings suit to evict Bob. Since oral contracts for the sale of real estate are not enforceable in Al's state, Al wins the eviction suit and moves back into the house. Bob had no contract with Al for the improvements, but under the law of quasi contract is entitled to their reasonable value.

In some situations, the courts deny quasi-contract recovery even though the defendant received a benefit. If the plaintiff did not reasonably expect to be paid, the court will deny recovery. For example, a physician who treats a member of his immediate family ordinarily would not be allowed quasi-contract recovery for services rendered. Nor would an intermeddler (a person who tries to force benefits upon another) be allowed a quasi-contract recovery. Suppose Ann leaves her car at a service station for an oil change. When she returns, Ben, the service station operator, demands payment not only for the oil change but also for a tune-up he gave the car without Ann's consent. Ben, an intermeddler, has neither a contract for the tune-up nor a right to a quasi-contract recovery. In contrast, the physician coming to the aid of an unconscious person in an emergency is not characterized as an officious intermeddler. Most courts reason that it is simply good public policy to assure physicians of reasonable payment as an inducement to aid helpless victims with whom contracting may be impossible.

Promissory Estoppel

Under traditional contract law, a party's promise is enforceable only when a contract arises, usually after a process of offer and acceptance establishing an exchange of consideration. But often the classical rules of contract formation are not compatible with reasonable business practices, and people rely on promises only to learn later that no enforceable contract arose. In such a situation, a court might apply the doctrine of *promissory estoppel* to enforce a promise that would be unenforceable under the traditional rules of contracting.

To say that a promisor is "estopped" means only that the person is prevented by law from avoiding liability for the consequences of his or her promise. Section 90 of both *Restatements* sets forth three elements, or requirements, of promissory estoppel:

1. There must be a promise that the promisor should reasonably expect to induce action on the part of the promisee.
2. The promise must induce such action. That is, the promisee must act in justifiable reliance on the promise to his or her detriment. (There is an exception for charitable subscriptions, discussed later.)
3. The situation must be such that injustice can be avoided only by enforcement of the promise.

Consider, for example, the dilemma facing Ben, a building contractor who wants to construct the new City Parking Garage. Before he can prepare his bid (offer) on the project, he must first collect price information from a host of subcontractors, each of whom will compete with others for the right to perform various parts of the work—concrete, electrical, plumbing, elevators, and so on. Al submits to Ben the lowest bid of $500,000 for the electrical work, and Ben incorporates it into his own offer to the City. City accepts Ben's bid, thus obligating him to build the garage for the price he promised. But before Ben can accept Al's offer to do the electrical work for $500,000, Al raises the price to $600,000. Since there is no contract between Al and Ben for the $500,000 price, Al has no obligation under traditional contract rules to perform as promised. However, Ben *relied* on Al's promise to do the work for $500,000, and under the doctrine of promissory estoppel Ben can enforce that promise. Ben's reliance is justifiable because, as Al surely had reason to know, there is no other practical way for building contractors to operate than by relying on unaccepted bids. Ben relied to his detriment by committing himself to a contract with City on the basis of Al's original price information.

Presentation of Contract Law in This Textbook

Chapters 9 to 15 deal mainly with common law principles governing contracts in general. Contract formation, the nature of consideration, writing requirements, grounds for avoiding contracts, the assignment of contract rights to third persons, and remedies for breach of contract are among the topics that apply to informal contracts of all kinds, including those for real estate, services, insurance, suretyship, and sales of goods. Since the UCC has affected the common law of contracts, relevant Code concepts such as unconscionability are referred to in Chapters 9 to 15 where appropriate. However, most of the contractual aspects of sales law are presented in Chapters 16 to 19, which highlight the substantial differences between the law of sales and the common law of contracts. Of course, the study of general contract principles also requires attention to promissory estoppel and quasi contract.

Many kinds of contracts—those concerning insurance, suretyship, employment, and the extension of credit, for example—are discussed in separate chapters throughout the book. Since such law topics present special questions of public policy, an important focus of those chapters is government regulation affecting the content of the contracts involved. Chapters 9 to 15 also illustrate how legislation affects contracts, and in those chapters there is considerable discussion of judicial limits on freedom of contract.

Finally, presented elsewhere in the book are some highly specialized adaptations of contract law such as the law of negotiable instruments (the most prevalent kind of formal contract), documents of title, and corporate securities. Understanding the concept of negotiability, for example, first requires an understanding of the law of assignments, a key topic presented in the general discussion of contract law.

Summary

A contract is a promise or an agreement that a court will enforce. Contract law governs the formation, performance, and enforcement of contracts. Its major purpose is to protect reasonable expectations that contracts will be binding on and enforceable by the parties.

The law of contracts has changed over the centuries in response to changes in social conditions. In the eighteenth century, its main goal was to transfer ownership of an existing thing and to assure fairness of exchanges between individuals. The nineteenth-century goal was to protect expectations of future performance in impersonal national markets.

In most states, twentieth-century contract law consists of three interrelated elements: the common law of contracts; Article 2 of the UCC, applying to sales of goods; and government regulation affecting contracts. Modern contract law continues many nineteenth-century principles, but there is more emphasis on flexibility of contracting, judicial discretion in contract enforcement, fair dealing, and practical remedies aimed at continuing business without interruption. There is also considerably more government regulation of contracting and a greater interest by the courts in coming to the aid of weaker parties who, for example, may be exploited by contracts of adhesion. Although such contracts ordinarily are enforced, twentieth-century courts, legislatures, and administrative agencies have developed a variety of ways to combat their misuse.

Contracts are classified in a variety of ways: as express or implied; unilateral or bilateral; executory or executed; enforceable, unenforceable, voidable, or "void"; and formal or informal.

Two important doctrines—quasi contract and promissory estoppel—supplement modern contract law. Quasi contract provides a damage remedy (reasonable value of a benefit conferred) to prevent unjust enrichment where a person conferred the benefit in the absence of a contract. Promissory estoppel, a most significant development in twentieth-century contract law, provides promise enforcement where classical rules of contract formation do not, on the basis of the promisee's justifiable reliance on the promise.

Review Questions

1 (a) What is the meaning of "contract"? **(b)** Explain the meaning of "promise" as used in the law of contracts. **(c)** What function do promises serve in contracting?

2 (a) Is bargaining an essential element of a contract? **(b)** What are the usual requirements for the creation of a contract for an exchange of values?

3 What is the major purpose of contract law?

4 (a) In general, how has contract law changed over the centuries? **(b)** What are the main features of nineteenth-century contract law? **(c)** Have these features been abandoned by twentieth-century contract law?

5 (a) In most states, what constitutes twentieth-century contract law? **(b)** In what ways, if any, has twentieth-century contract law departed from that of the nineteenth century? **(c)** What have the Uniform Commercial Code and the *Restatement (Second) of Contracts* contributed to present-day contract law?

6 Give five examples of how the government regulates contracting.

7 (a) What is a contract of adhesion? **(b)** Are such contracts enforceable? Why or why not?

8 On September 1, Seller and Buyer sign a written agreement which states that on September 20 Seller is to deliver 5 kilograms of a certain substance to Buyer, and that Buyer is to pay the specified price on or before October 10. Seller delivers the substance as promised. It is October 5, and Buyer has not yet paid for it. Is the contract: **(a)** Express or implied? **(b)** Unilateral or bilateral? **(c)** Executory or executed? **(d)** Formal or informal? **(e)** Enforceable or "void"?

9 (a) How is the doctrine of quasi contract related to the law of contract? Consider the underlying purpose of quasi contracts and the statement "quasi contracts are not contracts at all." **(b)** Give examples of situations where quasi-contract principles would apply and where they would *not* apply. **(c)** To what amount of damages is a winning plaintiff entitled under the doctrine of quasi contract?

10 (a) How is promissory estoppel related to the traditional law of contracts? **(b)** What circumstances must exist for the application of promissory estoppel? **(c)** Explain how promissory estoppel could be helpful to a building contractor.

CHAPTER 9

Mutual Assent: Offer and Acceptance

As noted in Chapter 8, a major use of contracts is to arrange an exchange desired by the parties—for example, money for real estate, goods, or services. For such contracts, there must be an agreement—a manifestation of mutual assent.

The process of reaching contractual agreement has remained mostly unchanged for centuries, but today, more than ever before, the context within which parties make agreements varies enormously. Two neighbors negotiate face to face for the sale of a used car; two giant corporations negotiate over great distances for the sale of a multibillion-dollar business; or an individual or small firm deals with a large corporation or a government agency. The parties may be equal in bargaining power; more often, they are decidedly unequal.

Despite these differences, contractual agreement ordinarily is reached by a process of offer and acceptance in which one person, the "offeror," makes an offer to another person, the "offeree." An offer is a communication that creates a "power of acceptance" in the offeree. If the offeree accepts the offer ("exercises" the power of acceptance), a contract arises and both parties are bound by its terms.

This chapter examines the process of offer and acceptance. First is a discussion of the offer: what is required to create it and how it may be terminated prior to an acceptance. The chapter then discusses the acceptance and closes with a brief comment on agreements looking forward to a writing.

Before turning to the offer, we should consider what an offeree may do in response to an offer. The offeree has the following choices:

1 To accept the offer as presented and thus make a contract
2 To reject the offer, thus terminating it and losing the power of acceptance
3 To make a counterproposal called a "counteroffer" in substitution for the offer, thus rejecting the offer by implication, but at the same time giving the offeror the power to accept the counteroffer. Often, by submitting a series of counteroffers to each other (or by using less formal negotiating techniques), the parties dicker back and forth over the terms of the proposed contract before reaching final agreement.
4 To remain silent. Here, the offer ordinarily expires automatically after the passage of a reasonable time.

Figure 9.1 lists the offeree's options upon receiving an offer. A is the offeror, B is the offeree, the arrow represents A's offer, and P/A represents "power of acceptance."

Offer

Nature of an Offer

Offer Distinguished from Nonoffer. An *offer* is a statement or other communication by which the offeror confers upon the offeree a legal power to accept the offer and thereby to create a contract. But how can one tell an offer from a communication that is not an offer? An offer normally does three things:

1 It *indicates the exchange of "consideration"* that the offeror has in mind.
2 It *identifies an offeree* (a person who is to have the power of acceptance).

Figure 9.1 Offeree's options upon receiving an offer.

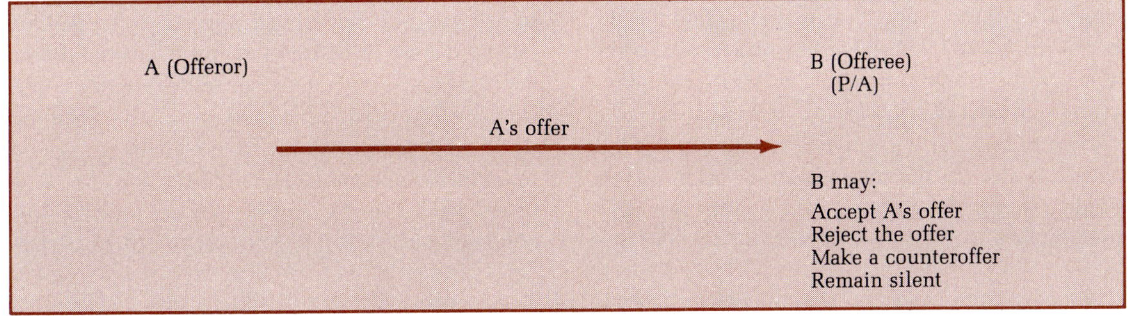

3 It reveals a *commitment* by the offeror to deal with the offeree.

Since each party to a contract expects to benefit from it, an offeror must give something to get something, and so will propose an exchange of consideration (legal value that each party expects to receive). Consequently, the offer ordinarily: (1) expresses or implies a promise by the offeror to do or refrain from doing some stated thing, and (2) requests from the offeree a return act or promise of performance. Since an offer by definition confers a power of acceptance on a specific person (or class of persons) called an "offeree," it necessarily indicates who is to be the offeree, i.e., who is to have the power of acceptance. Ann's statement, "I'll sell my horse Thunder for $5,000" reveals an exchange that Ann finds acceptable, but it is not an offer. Ann's statement made to Ben, "I'll sell Thunder *to you* for $5,000," is an offer because Ann, in addition to indicating the exchange she wants, has identified Ben as the offeree. And, by promising to sell Thunder *to Ben,* Ann has committed herself to dealing with him. So, while nonoffers may propose an exchange that the proposer finds acceptable, only offers *commit* the proposer to a contract with an *offeree.*

Where negotiating parties exchange communications over a period of time, it may be necessary to analyze each communication, or several communications together, to determine whether the qualities needed for an offer are present and, if they are, when the offer arose.

Language of Commitment. To determine whether a person has made the commitment required for an offer, one may need to distinguish language of commitment from statements of intention, negotiatory statements, and invitations to submit offers. Ann says to Bob, "I am going to sell my camera for $100," and Bob replies, "I'll take it; here's the $100." There is no contract; a reasonable observer would conclude that Ann's statement was not an offer (i.e., was not a promise to sell the camera to Bob). It was only a statement of her *intention* to deal in the future with a person as yet unidentified; it did not reveal the present commitment to deal with Bob needed for an offer. (In the situation just described, however, *Bob* has made an offer to Ann. How so? Consider whether the three qualities normally present in an offer are present here.)

Statements that are not in themselves offers but are preliminary thereto are called *negotiatory statements.* People use negotiatory statements for a variety of reasons—for example, to sound out the other party before making an offer, to maneuver him or her into making the first commitment, or to invite bids (offers). Thus, a person does not make an offer by saying, "My car is worth $3,000" or "I should get at least $3,000 for my car."

As usually worded, circulars, catalogs, and newspaper advertisements are not offers, but are mere *invitations* to submit offers. Consider, for example, the following newspaper advertisement: "FOR SALE—1986 Ford truck for only $9,000. Cash or trade." This ad can be understood to say, "I will sell my 1986 Ford truck for $9,000 or will trade it for another vehicle." The ad describes an exchange acceptable to the advertiser, and it implies a promise to sell. However, it is not an offer because it does not identify an offeree and thus makes no commitment to sell to any particular person. The ad is merely an invitation to interested persons to make an offer to the advertiser. Similarly, an L.L. Bean mail-order catalog is an invitation to make an offer. One who orders merchandise from the catalog is an offeror; L.L. Bean, the offeree, may accept or reject the offer.

Offerees like L.L. Bean and the owner of the Ford receive two important benefits from their offeree status: (1) They can reject offers if the number exceeds the quantity of goods available for sale. (2) They can reject the offers of customers whose creditworthiness is in doubt. However, it should be noted that twentieth-century law sharply limits the right of many sellers to reject offers. For example, merchants who refuse to sell goods at advertised prices may be in violation of state or federal laws prohibiting false or deceptive advertising, unfair trade practices, and the like. Many such laws require a seller to stock a sufficient supply of advertised goods to meet a reasonably expectable demand for them or to give "rain checks" if the supply runs out. And sellers covered by the Civil Rights Act of 1964 may not reject offers merely on the basis of race, color, religion, sex, or national origin. However, these laws do not change the fact that, ordinarily, the merchant-advertiser merely solicits or invites offers from customers and may reject offers for legitimate reasons.

Sometimes, though, whether by design or by accident, a newspaper advertisement *does* constitute an offer. Consider, for example, an ad reading, "To the first ten customers taking advantage of this offer we will sell a Model X Sure-View Television for $199.50 cash." Like most such ads, it identifies an exchange of consideration acceptable to the merchant—a television set for $199.50. But this ad has two features ordinarily lacking in advertisements for the sale of goods: (1) It identifies offerees—the first ten customers responding to the ad; and (2) it contains language of commitment—"We will sell . . . to" those first ten customers. The presence of this language makes the ad an offer and not merely a solicitation of offers. Incidentally, the use of the word "offer" in this ad is insignificant. All ads for the sale of goods are "offers" in the nonlegal sense of being announcements of their availability for purchase. But a *contractual* offer creates a power of acceptance in an offeree. To constitute that kind of offer, an ad must go beyond a mere announcement of availability and make a commitment to sell to whoever is identified as an offeree. That person could be a specific individual ("Tom Jones"), a member of a limited class of people ("the first ten customers who respond to this ad"), or anyone in an unlimited class of people ("the public").

Often it is not clear whether a particular proposal was an offer or merely an invitation or other preliminary negotiation. When called on to decide such issues, the courts will consider not only the language used but also the surrounding circumstances. Ordinarily, a communication addressed to a group or to the public at large is less likely to be held an offer than is one addressed to an individual. However, *notices of reward* (normally addressed to the public at large and not a specific person) are held to be offers. The notice may contain a promise to pay money (e.g., "$100 for safe return of my dog Charlie"), but lack an express commitment to pay it to a particular person. Yet, a court can usually infer from the surrounding circumstances the offeror's commitment to pay the money to the person who provides requested item or information.

Ordinarily, a statement on a price tag in a store is considered to be a *price quote* and not an offer. The reasons why newspaper advertisements usually are not offers apply equally here. Thus, "For Sale, $29.95" usually means no more than a willingness to consider an offer to buy at $29.95. The customer who wishes to purchase the item and tenders $29.95 to the store is the offeror. The store is the offeree and may accept or reject the customer's offer.

The question of who is the offeror and who is the offeree is often raised in deciding controversies arising out of the *public auction* of goods or other property. Auctions may be either "with reserve" or "without reserve." These terms indicate whether the auctioneer (who acts on behalf of the seller) has reserved (retained) the privilege of withdrawing the goods from sale during the bidding process. In an auction *with reserve* the auctioneer is the offeree and has the power of acceptance. As offeree, he or she may reject all bids. In an auction *without reserve* the auctioneer is much like an offeror, with the bidders competing to determine who will win the power of acceptance. After the auctioneer calls for bids in an auction without reserve, the property cannot be withdrawn unless no bid is made within a reasonable time. In either type of auction (with or without reserve), a bidder may withdraw his or her bid until the auctioneer announces the completion of the sale by the fall of the hammer or in some other customary way.

Unless an auction is expressly advertised to be without reserve, it is an auction *with* reserve. An auction with reserve tends to produce a fair market value because the seller, as offeree, may reject all bids and await a more favorable market. In contrast, an auction without reserve tends to produce lower prices because the seller, being the offeror, has no power to reject low bids. However, the auction without reserve may be useful for moving property quickly. Section 2-328 of the Uniform Commercial Code codifies the common law of auctions and applies it to sales of goods.

The following case involves the question of whether an informal letter is an offer or merely an invitation to submit an offer.

CASE 9.1 Southworth v. Oliver · 587 P.2d 994 (Or. 1978)

FACTS Joseph Oliver (defendant) and J. W. Southworth (plaintiff) had several discussions concerning the sale of a portion of land owned by Oliver in Bear Valley. On June 17 Oliver sent the following letter to Southworth and copies of the letter to three other neighbors: "Enclosed please find the information about the ranch sales that I had discussed with you previously. These prices are the market value according to the records of the Grant County Assessor. Please contact me if there are any questions." The following was enclosed on a separate letterhead: "Selling approximately 2.933 acres in Grant County in T. 165 S., R. 31 E., W.M. near Seneca, Oregon at the assessed market value of:

Land	$306,409
Improvements	18,010
Total	$324,419

Terms available—29% down—balance over 5 years at 8% interest. Negotiate sale date for December 1, 1976 or January 1, 1977. . . ."

Upon receiving the letter and enclosure, plaintiff immediately sent a letter to Oliver, dated June 21, as follows: "Re the land in Bear Valley near Seneca, Oregon that you have offered to sell; I accept your offer." Defendant then denied that his letter of June 17 was intended as an offer and claimed it was only a starting point for further negotiation with the four interested parties. Southworth filed suit for a declaratory judgment that defendant was obligated to sell the land to him. The court granted a decree in favor of plaintiff. Defendant appealed.

OPINION TONGUE, J. . . . The difficulty in determining whether an offer has been made is particularly acute in cases involving price quotations, as in this case. It is recognized that although a price quotation, standing alone, is not an offer, there may be circumstances under which a price quotation, when considered together with [other] facts and circumstances, may constitute an offer which, if accepted, will result in a binding contract. It is also recognized that such an offer may be made to more than one person. Thus, the fact that a price quotation is sent to more than one person does not, of itself, require a holding that such a price quotation is not an offer.

We agree with the analysis of this problem as stated in Murray on Contracts 37–40, Sec. 24 (1977), as follows:

> . . . The first and strongest guide is that the particular expression is to be judged on the basis of what a reasonable man in the position of the offeree has been led to believe. This requires an analysis of what the offeree should have understood under all of the surrounding circumstances, with all of his opportunities for comprehending the intention of the offeror, rather than what the offeror, in fact, intended. . . . The most important of the remaining guides is the language used. If there are no words of promise, undertaking or commitment, the tendency is to construe the expression to be an invitation for an offer or mere preliminary negotiations in the absence of strong, countervailing circumstances. Another guide which has been widely accepted is the determination of the party or parties to whom the purported offer has been addressed. If the expression definitely names a party or parties, it is more likely to be construed as an offer. If the addressee is an indefinite group, it is less likely to be an offer. . . . The guide operates effectively in relation to such expressions as advertisements or circular letters. The addressee is indefinite and, therefore, the expression is probably not an offer. . . . Finally, the definiteness of the proposal itself may have a bearing on whether it constitutes an offer. In general, the more definite the proposal, the more reasonable it is to treat the proposal as involving a commitment. . . .

That letter [dated June 17, 1976] did not come to plaintiff "out of the blue," as in some of the cases involving advertisements or price quotations. Neither was this a price quo-

CASE 9.1 Continued

tation resulting from an inquiry by plaintiff. According to what we believe to be the most credible testimony, defendant Joseph Oliver decided to sell the lands in question and defendant then sought out the plaintiff who owned adjacent lands. Defendant Oliver told plaintiff that defendant was interested in selling that land, inquired whether plaintiff was interested, and was told by plaintiff that he was "very interested in the land," after which they discussed the particular lands to be sold. That conversation was terminated with the understanding that Mr. Oliver would "determine" the value and price of that land, i.e., "what he wanted for the land," and that plaintiff would undertake to arrange financing for the purchase of that land. In addition to that initial conversation, there was a further telephone conversation in which plaintiff called Mr. Oliver "to ask him if his plans for selling... continued to be in force" and was told "yes"; that there had been some delay in getting information from the assessor, as needed to establish the value of the land; and that plaintiff then told Mr. Oliver that "everything was in order" and that "he had the money available and everything was ready to go."

Under these facts and circumstances, we agree with the finding and conclusion by the trial court, in its written opinion, that when plaintiff received the letter of June 17th, with enclosures, ... a reasonable person in the position of the plaintiff would have believed that defendant was making an offer to sell those lands to him.

This conclusion is further strengthened by "the definiteness of the proposal," not only with respect to price, but terms, and by the fact that "the addressee was not an indefinite group."...

The failure to add the word "offer" and the use of the word "information" are... not controlling, and, as previously noted, an offer may be made to more than one person. The question is whether, under all of the facts and circumstances existing at the time that this letter was received, a reasonable person in the position of the plaintiff would have understood the letter to be an offer by defendant to sell the land to him....

JUDGMENT For all of these reasons, the decree of the trial court is affirmed.

Serious Proposal. To constitute an offer, a proposal must be made with serious intent, or appear to be so made. The offeror's subjective intent is not important; the test is whether an ordinary reasonable person would consider the offeror's proposal to be a serious one. For example, suppose Bette attends an auction and bids $500 for an antique clock. It is irrelevant that she thinks to herself that she does not have $500 and that she secretly hopes someone else will make a higher bid and relieve her of her foolish commitment. The auctioneer is justified in treating Bette's bid as a serious proposal, that is, an offer.

Statements obviously or apparently made in jest or under the stress of great excitement or as bravado or bluff are not offers. If Adams makes a proposal to Brown, Adams's intention will be held by courts to be what a reasonable person in Brown's position would judge Adams's intention to be. Thus, if Brown should realize that a proposal by Adams was made in jest or under the stress of great excitement or as bravado or bluff, the proposal would not constitute a legally effective offer.

The classic case involving a proposal made under the stress of great excitement is *Higgins v. Lessig.*[1] An old harness worth about $15 had presumably been stolen. When the defendant, Lessig, discovered the loss, he became "much excited" and using "rough language and epithets" said he would give $100 to any person who found out who the thief was. Plaintiff, who had been present when Lessig made the statement, furnished the information and sought to recover the reward. The trial court found for the plaintiff. However, the appellate court reversed the judgment on the ground that the de-

[1] 49 Ill. App. 459 (1893).

fendant's language was not to be regarded as a serious proposal but "as the extravagant exclamation of an excited man."

Definite and Complete Terms. Courts often have said they are reluctant to "make a contract for the parties," and have stated that to be enforceable, a contract must contain reasonably definite and complete terms. The essential terms usually include the names of the parties, the subject matter involved (description, quantity), the price, and the time and place for performance. Sometimes the offer contains all the essential terms. If the offer by itself does not meet the requirements of reasonable definiteness but requires definite terms in the acceptance, the offer and acceptance together may meet the requirement that the terms of a contract must be reasonably certain.

An example of an offer requiring such "definite terms in the acceptance" was contained in the case of *Minneapolis & St. Louis Railway* (plaintiff) *v. Columbus Rolling Mill* (defendant).[2] The defendant, by letter of December 8, offered to sell plaintiff 2,000 to 5,000 tons of iron rails at a specified price. In its decision, the court said: "This offer would authorize the plaintiff to take at his election any number of tons not less than two thousand nor more than five thousand, on the terms specified." If the plaintiff had elected to take, say, 3,000 tons, there would have been a contract, although considered alone the offer was not even reasonably definite as to quantity.

It should be noted that the requirement is not one of absolute definiteness but only of reasonable definiteness. Promises of performance to be rendered "immediately" or "at once" or "as soon as possible" have been held to meet this requirement. Similarly, quantities and prices have been held to be reasonably definite even though qualified by such expressions as "about" or "more or less" or "approximately." But a proposal to pay "a fair share of my profits" was held to be conjectural, depending on personal views, and thus not reasonably definite.

Often the dynamics of business are such that a potential seller or buyer does not wish to specify or is unable to specify an exact quantity of goods to be sold or purchased. Instead, Fred may offer to sell to Grace all the oranges to be grown on Fred's citrus ranch during the next season; or Charles may offer to buy from Denise all the paint required for the next two years in the operation of Charles's automobile body shop. Upon acceptance, the first type of offer becomes an "output" contract; the second becomes a "requirements" contract. Although both appear to be rather indefinite as to quantity, the courts enforce them. Section 2-306 of the UCC continues the common law policy of enforcing output and requirements contracts, and requires the parties to act in good faith when establishing the amount of goods to be delivered. A seller may not force an unreasonably large output on the buyer; and a buyer may not demand an unreasonably large delivery under a requirements contract. What is reasonable is to be determined in light of any stated estimate contained in the contract. If there is no such estimate, the amount may be measured by prior dealings between the parties or by what is normal in the trade or industry in comparable circumstances. Thus, the law provides needed contract flexibility while protecting the parties from surprisingly large variations in outputs and requirements.

A proposal may not be reasonably definite and complete if a material (major) term has been omitted. In most contracts, material terms include the names of the parties, the subject matter involved, the price, and the time and place for performance. It does not follow, however, that all the terms of an offer must necessarily be expressed. Some of them may be *implied.* For example, if a contract fails to mention the time of performance, courts usually will hold that performance within a reasonable time is implied in the offer.

Whether material terms such as price will be implied depends greatly on the subject matter of the contract. Because land is such a valuable and limited resource and often is the major asset of its owner, the common law traditionally has required a high degree of definiteness in contracts for its sale. Accordingly, if an offer for real estate fails to state a price, the courts will not imply one and will hold that the offer is too indefinite to enforce. Even a slight vagueness in stating the price of land has been sufficient for some courts to refuse to "make a contract for the parties."

Article 2 of the UCC reveals a much different policy toward contract formation and the implication of missing terms. Traditionally, the common law has required a rather precise process of offer

[2] 119 U.S. 149 (1866).

and acceptance for a contract to arise—reflecting, perhaps, a preference for negotiating each deal carefully and deliberately, as is appropriate in real estate transactions. In contrast, contracts for the sale of goods are made with a minimum of formality by businesspeople in a hurry, often across state lines. To promote business efficiency, Section 2-204 permits a contract for the sale of goods to "be made in any manner sufficient to show agreement, including conduct by both parties which recognizes the existence of a contract... even though the moment of its making is undetermined." Moreover, nearly every term of a sales contract can be implied, including price, "if the parties have intended to make a contract and there is a reasonably certain basis for giving an appropriate remedy."

Suppose Sam delivers 300 gallons of heating oil to Betty without stating a price, and she uses or otherwise indicates a willingness to pay for it. Even though there might have been no clearly stated offer and acceptance, and no specifically identifiable moment of agreement, Sam and Betty's conduct reveals their intention to make a contract. But the price term has been left "open." Where nothing is said as to price, UCC Section 2-305 imposes "a reasonable price at the time for delivery." What is reasonable can be determined in a variety of ways. For example, if there is a market price, it probably will be taken as reasonable. There would be a market price for such mass-produced items as household appliances, lumber, or oil. Even for unique goods such as art objects or custom clothing for which there is no clear market price, there might be an alternative basis such as an expert's appraisal for establishing a reasonable price.

Contracts for services are governed by the common law. If the price has been left open, the courts will more readily imply a reasonable price than if the subject of the contract were real estate. Generally, however, the courts are not so liberal in supplying a price for services as they would be in a sale of goods, unless they have adopted the *Restatement (Second)* provisions on open terms (similar to those of Article 2).

The following case discusses the rule that the terms of an offer must be reasonably definite and complete.

CASE 9.2 Lessley v. Hardage · 727 P.2d 440 (Kan. 1986)

FACTS Samuel Hardage employed Dean Lessley as executive vice president of Hardage's real estate development business. The parties agreed that Lessley would receive an annual salary of $55,000, life and health insurance, and a company car. In addition, Hardage had a "golden handcuffs" plan by which key employees would share in company projects. Hardage promised that 10 percent of each project would be set aside for key employees. This would then be distributed to the key employees based upon a determination by Mr. Hardage of the percentage that each person would receive. This percentage was to be based upon the quantity and quality of each employee's work. After Lessley had been employed about 20 months, Hardage increased the "golden handcuffs" plan to the lesser of 25 percent of the total project or 50 percent of Hardage's interest in the project. Soon thereafter, a dispute arose concerning the plan, and Lessley was fired. He filed suit for breach of contract, and received judgment for $161,800, representing amounts due under the "golden handcuffs" plan. Hardage appealed, contending that the oral contract was not sufficiently definite and certain to create an obligation to pay bonuses.

OPINION MILLER, J.... The general rule for evaluating the sufficiency of the definiteness of contractual terms is stated in *Hays v. Underwood, Administrator*...:

> [I]n order for an agreement to be binding it must be sufficiently definite as to its terms and requirements as to enable a court to determine what acts are to be performed and when performance is complete. The court must be able to fix definitely the legal liability of the party. We have adhered to this general rule....
>
> Again, however, the courts generally have so far deviated from the general rule and set up so many exceptions that it is an exceptional case where the rule can be followed as a

CASE 9.2 Continued

complete guide to the determination of the sufficiency and the definiteness of the terms of a contract.

> The courts will so construe an instrument as to carry the intentions of the parties into effect where possible.... The law will favor upholding a contract against a claim of uncertainty where one of the parties has performed his part of the contract. A contract may contain imperfections or be lacking in detail but it will not be held void for uncertainty if the court, under the recognized rules of construction, can ascertain the terms and conditions by which the parties intended to be bound....

In the past, this court has required only reasonable certainty in contracts. In *Richards Aircraft Sales, Inc. v. Vaughn*...we said: "[A]bsolute certainty is not required—only reasonable certainty is necessary."

The basic issue in this case is whether the reservation of discretion by Hardage renders the contract so indefinite as to be unenforceable.... There is authority on both sides of this issue, and no Kansas case is directly on point.

In *Borden v. Skinner Chuck Co.* ... the court determined that a statement in a booklet issued by the employer that bonuses were customarily paid and were entirely within the discretion of the Board of Directors did not constitute a direct and enforceable offer to pay a bonus. In contrast, Hardage promised the plaintiff that 10% (later 25% or 50%) of equity or cash would be set aside from each venture for key employees. While the exact amount of each employee's share was to be determined later, there was a definite promise to give a particular group of employees a fixed share of the cash or equity.... The case most similar to the case at hand is *Hilgenberg v. Iowa Beef Packers, Inc.* ... *Hilgenberg* involved a bonus of indefinite amount—it was to be a percentage of the employee's salary, but no employee was told of the precise percentage. However, the employer had allocated, though not segregated, $14,175 for the payment of bonuses. The jury found that the bonus in *Hilgenberg* was supported by consideration, and it found that the plaintiffs were entitled to the money set aside by the employer. The court apportioned the amount set aside among the employees.

...Lessley argues, correctly, that the mere existence of a discretionary duty does not render a contract unenforceable. Typically, a good faith obligation is implied to limit the exercise of discretion....

The essential term claimed to be lacking in the employment agreement before us is the amount of the cash Lessley would receive. Hardage led employees to believe that they would be compensated in a manner commensurate with the work they did on each project—the quantity and quality of their work. This does not appear to us to be an immeasurable, indefinite compensation scheme. Hardage agreed to place a fixed percentage, readily ascertainable, aside, the same to be divided among key personnel. Once the total sum due the employees was fixed, the allocation of that amount among the key employees would seem here, as in *Hilgenberg*, a matter which a court or jury, upon proper evidence, may determine.

The trial court relied on *Heckard v. Park*... in denying Hardage's motion for summary judgment. In Syl. Par. 5 of that opinion, we said:

> The law implies that contractual provisions requiring the exercise of judgment or discretion will be honestly exercised and faithfully performed.

Lessley had fully performed the work required of him by the contract. We hold that the oral contract between Lessley and Hardage, as established by the evidence and found by the jury, was sufficiently definite and certain to create an obligation on the part of the employer to pay percentages of retained equity interest and cash to the key employees. We further hold that, while the precise amount of the cash award to which plaintiff is entitled was not fixed in the contract, it is easily determinable, and in this instance was properly determined by the jury upon the basis of the evidence before it. The obligation of honest judgment implied in contracts where the exercise of judgment or discretion is involved

CASE 9.2 Continued

cannot be used as a shield to prevent recovery by the plaintiff in this action. We do not regard the precise amount to which plaintiff is entitled to be an essential term of the agreement, where the amount can readily be determined by the jury.

JUDGMENT . . . [A]ffirmed.

Communication to Offeree. Ordinarily, the offeror states the terms of a proposal in person to the offeree or transmits them by telephone, letter, or telegram. The offer becomes legally effective when it is communicated to the person or persons for whom it was intended. "Communicated" literally means "brought to the attention of."

In some instances the courts hold that an offeree can assent to a proposal which he or she does not know about if, under the circumstances, the offeree should have realized that a proposal was made. For example, proposals sometimes are printed on signs at parking lots or on shop walls, or on claim checks (such as those issued in parking lots, checkrooms, or repair shops), and on invoices. In any such situation the test of whether communication has occurred is: Could the customer reasonably be expected to know that an offer was being made to him or her? If so, the offer has been communicated to him or her; if not, there has been *no* communication. For example, suppose you take your stereo set to a repair shop and you are given a claim check or receipt which contains provisions in small print or has provisions on the reverse side. A court would likely hold that (depending on the size of print, color, etc.) the ordinary person would not read such material and thus the proposed terms were not communicated to you.

Termination of Offers

Several things can happen in the period following communication of a legally effective offer. Sometimes the offeree accepts the offer immediately and an agreement is concluded. This most often occurs when parties negotiate face to face. At other times, usually when negotiations are conducted by mail, the offeree takes time to consider the offer and then replies to the offeror. When there is a delay by the offeree, several problems can occur. For example, suppose the offeree waits a length of time and then sends an acceptance. The offeror might assert that the offeree waited too long and that the offer expired before the acceptance occurred.

When an offer terminates, the offeree's "power of acceptance" terminates. An offer may be terminated in various ways, and we need to examine the most common methods. Four major methods of terminating an offer are by: (1) lapse of time, (2) revocation by the offeror, (3) rejection or counteroffer by the offeree, and (4) death of the offeror or offeree.

Termination by Lapse of Time

Specified time limitation. An offer may be so worded as to terminate on a specified date. An example is: "This offer will remain open until 5 P.M., October 10."

Difficulty arises when the limitation is worded ambiguously. Suppose that an offeror mails a letter which gives the offeree "ten days to accept or reject this offer." Is the offeror's intention to have the ten-day period measured from the date the letter is sent or from the date it is received? Although there is some conflict in court decisions, the usual ruling is that the time runs from the day of receipt by the offeree.

Implied time limitation. Where an offeror does not specify a time limitation, the offer remains open for a reasonable period of time. What constitutes a reasonable period of time is a question of fact to be determined on the basis of all relevant circumstances, including: (1) the subject matter of the offer, (2) the market price situation, (3) the distance between the parties, (4) any special objective the offeror had in making the offer where that objective is known to the offeree, and (5) the method of communication chosen by the offeror. Thus, an offer to buy or sell eggs terminates sooner than an offer to buy or sell land; an offer to sell gold or silver, which have rapidly fluctuating prices, terminates sooner than an offer to sell iron ore, which has relative price stability; an offer which the offeree knows has been made to meet an emergency situation terminates sooner than one not so made;

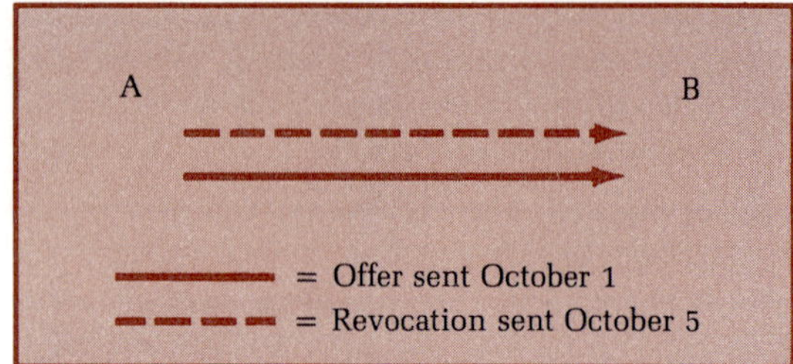

Figure 9.2 **Offer followed by revocation.**

and an offer sent by telegram normally terminates sooner than one sent by letter.

An attempt by the offeree to accept an offer after a specified time or a reasonable time has expired may be considered a counteroffer.

Termination by Revocation

Power of revocation. As a general rule, an offeror has the power to revoke (withdraw) an offer at any time before acceptance even though he or she has promised not to do so. For example, if the offeror states, "This offer will remain open until October 10," the offeror may revoke the offer on October 5. In doing so, the offeror may be acting unethically, but there is no violation of the law. Figure 9.2 illustrates an offer sent on October 1, followed by a revocation sent on October 5.

An offeror should know that the offeree is likely to take some sort of action in reliance on the offer. If the offer is suddenly revoked, the offeree may suffer hardship. To alleviate that hardship, the courts and legislatures have imposed limits on the ability of offerors to revoke offers.

1 *Irrevocable offers: options, promissory estoppel.* One such limitation is the irrevocability that results from an *option contract.* Ann says to Ben, "I'll sell you my horse Thunder for $5,000, and for $5 you have 30 days to decide." Ben pays the $5. For $5, Ben has purchased 30 days during which to consider Ann's offer. Under this contract ($5 for 30 days' time), Ben has the "option," or choice, of either accepting or rejecting Ann's offer to sell Thunder for $5,000. In essence, Ben has made a contract whose object is to make Ann's offer (to sell Thunder) irrevocable for 30 days.

2 *Promissory estoppel* (discussed in Chapter 8) is also used by some courts to limit the revocability of offers. As explained in Case 9.3, which follows, the offeree's (promisee's) reliance on the offer to his or her detriment is a sufficient basis for making the offer irrevocable. (Actually, promissory estoppel has a much broader application than just to make offers irrevocable. As noted in Chapter 10, promissory estoppel is an alternative to "consideration" as a basis for making promises enforceable. Some writers believe that promissory estoppel may be replacing contract as a basis for promise enforcement.)[3]

[3]E.g., G. Gilmore, *The Death of Contract* (1974).

CASE 9.3 Lyon Metal Products v. Hagerman Construction Corp. · 391 N.E.2d 1152 (Ind. App. 1979)

FACTS Hagerman Construction Corporation (plaintiff) was preparing a bid for the construction of a school. One of the items it was required to bid upon was athletic lockers. On February 12, 1974, Lyon Metal Products, Inc. (defendant) submitted a bid to Hagerman for the lockers in the amount of $16,824. The bid was on a Lyon quotation form. On the bottom of the form, in small print, was the following: "This quotation is subject to . . . the further condition contained on the reverse side hereof." On the reverse side, in yet smaller print, eight conditions were printed. One said: "This quotation may be withdrawn and is subject to change without notice after 15 days from date of quotation." The specifications for the project, which Lyon read, required that bids remain open for 120 days.

CASE 9.3 Continued

Lyon's bid for the lockers was the lowest of four received by Hagerman and was used by Hagerman in computing its bid. On February 12 Hagerman was informed that it was the lowest bidder on the school project. Lyon learned of this 3 or 4 days later. On March 1 Hagerman sent Lyon a letter of intent stating that a formal contract would be sent about June 10. Lyon did not respond to this letter. On June 5 a formal contract was sent but was never received by Lyon because of a wrong address. On September 6, 1974, Lyon withdrew its bid and submitted a new price of $28,750. Hagerman obtained the lockers from another supplier for $24,787. Hagerman filed suit against Lyon for damages. The trial court entered judgment for Hagerman in the sum of $7,963 based upon the doctrine of promissory estoppel. Defendant appealed.

OPINION

GARRARD, P. J. . . . The doctrine of promissory estoppel, embodied in Section 90 of the Restatement of Contracts, provides that:

> A promise which the promisor should reasonably expect to induce action or forbearance of a definite and substantial character on the part of the promisee and which does induce such action or forbearance is binding if injustice can be avoided only by the enforcement of the promise.

. . . Our task is to determine whether there was sufficient evidence of probative value in the case at bar to support each of the elements of promissory estoppel, viz: (1) whether Lyon made a definite promise to Hagerman with the reasonable expectation that the promise would induce action of a definite and substantial character on the part of Hagerman; (2) whether the promise induced such action; (3) whether Hagerman acted in justifiable reliance upon the promise to its detriment; and (4) whether injustice can be avoided only by enforcement of the promise. . . .

Lyon offered to supply a given quantity of specified kinds of lockers at a stated price. It realized that if its quote or bid was the lowest received by Hagerman that Hagerman would use the Lyon bid in computing its own bid. In fact, Lyon not only realized that its promise would induce action of a definite and substantial character, it was Lyon's express intention that this would occur. Hagerman did use the Lyon bid in computing its bid, which subsequently bound Hagerman to provide the lockers to the school corporation at the price quoted. Lyon was notified by the letter of intent that Hagerman intended to have Lyon supply the lockers at the quoted price. When Lyon refused to supply the lockers at the price quoted, Hagerman was forced to incur the loss of $7,963.

Lyon asserts that Hagerman could not have reasonably relied on its offer since the offer expressly stated that it was subject to withdrawal or modification 15 days after the date it was given. We acknowledge that several cases have stated in dicta that if the bid states that it was revocable or reserves a right of withdrawal or otherwise disclaims any intention to be bound, there could be no reasonable reliance by the general contractor. . . . However, we have determined that there was sufficient evidence of probative value from which the trial court could have found justifiable reliance notwithstanding the 15 day clause. The evidence established that the project specifications required that the bids be held open for 120 days. Lyon's attempted variation of this specification was printed in small letters on the back of its quote along with seven other conditions and the reference to the conditions on the reverse side was itself in small print. Hagerman's agent testified that he barely glanced at the conditions. Lyon made no special effort at any time to apprise Hagerman of the 15 day clause. After it had received the letter of intent which referred to "uncertainty of prices" and the reason for delay in sending the formal contract, Lyon did not inform Hagerman that its bid would be adjusted by increases in prices. Furthermore Langevin, Lyon's agent, testified that more than 120 days had elapsed when the bid was withdrawn in September. From this evidence, the trial court could have inferred that Lyon did not intend the 15 day clause to be the controlling time period but rather the

CASE 9.3 Continued

120 day period found in the specifications.... Lyon was aware that Hagerman was low bidder and that Hagerman was relying on it to supply the lockers at the quoted price. The project specifications... adequately informed [Lyon] of the extent of its obligations.

For these reasons, we conclude that the trial court did not err in finding that Lyon was liable to Hagerman under the theory of promissory estoppel.

JUDGMENT Affirmed.

3 *Other irrevocable offers.* Some types of offers are commonly made irrevocable by statute. Among such offers are bids made to governmental agencies (for example, to build a highway), and, under Section 2-205 of the Uniform Commercial Code, "firm offers" of merchants. A *firm offer* is a written and signed offer of a merchant to buy or sell goods, where the writing gives assurance that the offer will be held open. ("Goods" does not include real estate or services.) Such an offer is not revocable within the time-period provisions of Section 2-205, even though the offeror was not paid to keep the offer open.

In a unilateral contract situation, the offeree faces hardship where the offeror asks for an act that takes time to perform but then, after the requested performance has begun, serves notice of revocation. Under traditional rules of contracting, there was no acceptance of the offer (and no contract) until the requested act was performed. Suppose Clyde offers to pay Debbie $500 if she will wallpaper his apartment. If Clyde can revoke his offer when Debbie has papered half the apartment, Debbie will have no right to the contract price and will have to rely on a suit in quasi contract for the reasonable value of her services.

For the protection of offerees such as Debbie, the courts have developed three main approaches to the unilateral contract revocation problem:

1 If the offer permits Debbie to accept *only* by performance, her beginning the requested performance creates an *option contract.* Under it, she may continue to perform or not, as she chooses; having never promised a performance, she never became obligated to render one. However, to enforce the contract against Clyde, Debbie must complete the performance within the time stated in the offer, or if none is stated, within a reasonable time. If she chooses not to complete the performance, she may be entitled to a quasi-contract recovery for the reasonable value of her part performance.[4]

2 If the offer is worded in such a way that Debbie may accept either by *performing* the requested act or by *promising* to perform it, her beginning the performance is an acceptance *and* a promise to complete the performance. Thus, both she and Clyde are bound by the contract. As in the previous situation, Clyde is not liable for payment until Debbie makes a timely performance, but Debbie is liable here for breach of contract if she fails to perform as requested.[5]

3 Clyde may be prevented by the doctrine of promissory estoppel (Section 90 of both *Restatements*) from revoking his offer after Debbie begins performance. As Clyde could foresee, Debbie has relied to her detriment on his promise.

What constitutes revocation. The usual method of revocation is for the offeror to notify the offeree that he or she is withdrawing the offer. No special form of notice is required. Anything suffices which lets the offeree know that the offeror has reconsidered and no longer intends to enter into the proposed contract. The notice may be given face to face, over the telephone, or by letter or telegram. The general rule is that a revocation is effective when received by the offeree.[6]

[4]This is essentially the rule of Section 45 in both *Restatements.*

[5]This is essentially the rule of Section 62 of the *Restatement (Second)* and Section 2-206 of the UCC.

[6]By statute in California and a few other states, a written revocation becomes effective when posted or put into the course of transmission by any reasonable mode.

There is one situation in which revocation occurs even though the offeror's change of mind is not known by the offeree. Where an offer has been made to the public generally, as in an offer to pay a reward, the offer may be withdrawn by giving public notice of revocation. If the same amount of publicity is given to the revocation as was given to the offer, revocation is effective even against a member of the public who knew of the offer but does not know of the publication of notice of revocation.

Termination by Rejection or Counteroffer. A *rejection* is a manifestation by the offeree of his or her intention not to accept the offer. Rejection terminates the offeree's power of acceptance unless the offeror: (1) has indicated a contrary intention or (2) has been paid to keep the offer open for a fixed period that has not yet expired, as in an option contract.

A rejection may be express, or implied by words or conduct. Thus, the offeree may reject by saying, "Your offer is not acceptable," or by tearing a written offer to pieces and throwing them into a wastebasket in the presence of the offeror. At that point, the rejected offer ordinarily terminates and the offeree may not later change his or her mind and accept.

Usually, a rejection is effective when the offeror receives it. Until then, the offeree still has the power of acceptance (unless the offer has already been terminated in some way other than rejection). Therefore, the offeree can change his or her mind and accept the offer before the rejection reaches the offeror. Ben receives an offer from Ann and mails her a letter of rejection. Ben then changes his mind about rejecting. He could telephone Ann and accept the offer before she receives the letter of rejection.

A *counteroffer* is an offer made by the *offeree* to the offeror relating to the same matter as the original offer but differing from it in one or more particulars. Arnold offers to sell his car to Barbara for $1,500 and she replies, "I will give you $1,000 for the car." Barbara has made a counteroffer. Although Barbara's counteroffer impliedly rejects and therefore terminates Arnold's original offer, it differs from an outright rejection: Negotiations between the parties are still alive. Arnold now may accept the counteroffer, reject it outright, or make a counter-counteroffer to Barbara. Figure 9.3 illustrates the legal effect of a counteroffer and the options available to an offeror (*A*) who receives a counteroffer from the offeree (*B*).

Not all counteroffers impliedly reject the original offer. For example, in response to Arnold's offer to sell his car to Barbara for $1,500, Barbara says, "I am considering your offer, but I will buy immediately if you will take $1,000." Barbara has made a counteroffer, but she obviously has not rejected Arnold's original offer.

Rejections and counteroffers should be distinguished from mere requests for information. Ann offers to sell her house to Ben for $80,000. Ben says, "I am considering your offer, although I think the price is too high. Would you be willing to scale it down to $75,000?" Ben's response is not a rejection of Ann's offer; on the contrary, it tells her that her offer is still being considered. Neither is Ben's response a counteroffer. He has merely inquired about a price reduction and has not substituted an offer of his own for Ann's.

Figure 9.3 Counteroffer—offeror's options.

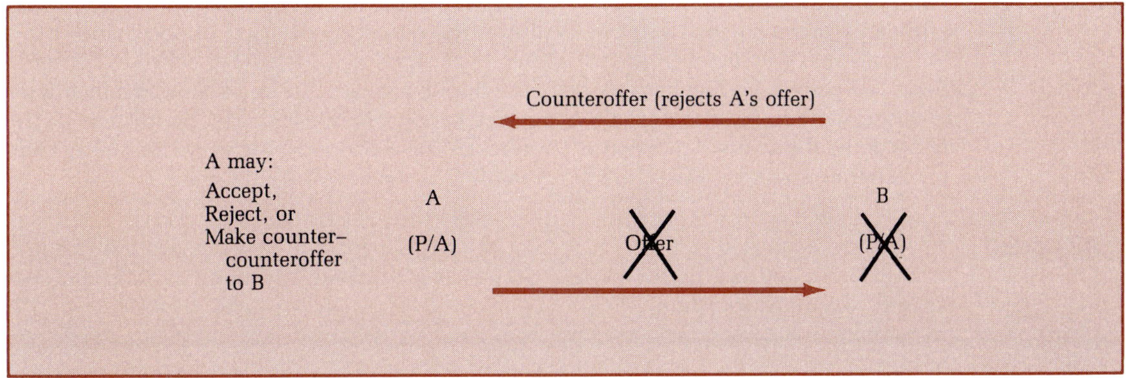

A *conditional acceptance* is a form of counter-offer. For example, Arnold offers to sell his car to Barbara for $1,500 in one cash payment, and Barbara says, "I accept your offer of $1,500 and I will pay you in three equal monthly installments." By departing from the payment terms of Arnold's offer, Barbara has made a conditional acceptance and has impliedly rejected the offer. To constitute an acceptance, the offeree's response must exactly match (be a "mirror image" of) the offer, and not include an additional or different term.

There is at least one exception to the mirror-image rule. An acceptance is considered unconditional if the offeree adds to the acceptance a condition which merely expresses that which would be implied in fact or by law. For example, an acceptance is unconditional though the offeree specifies that payment will be made within a reasonable time or requires a certificate of title from the offeror.

The following case involves the problem of an offeree's adding words to the offeror's proposal.

CASE 9.4 Panhandle Eastern Pipe Line Company v. Smith · 637 P.2d 1020 (Wyo. 1981)

FACTS Panhandle Eastern Pipe Line Company fired its employee, Nowlin Smith, Jr. After discussions with Smith's union representative, Panhandle sent a letter to Smith offering to withdraw the discharge if he would agree to certain terms and conditions. Smith signed the letter under the typewritten words, "Understood, Agreed to and Accepted," added some handwritten notations, and again signed his name. Panhandle claimed that Smith made a counteroffer by adding terms and conditions to the offer, and the company refused to rehire him. The notation added by Smith was a request to see his personnel file at the company and to contest any mistakes he found there. Smith sued for breach of contract and received a judgment of $40,000. Panhandle appealed.

OPINION BROWN, J. . . . The law of contract formation dictates that one who modifies an offer has usually rejected the offer and made a counteroffer, and that no contract exists unless the original offeror accepts the counteroffer. . . . An offer must be accepted unconditionally; but there is, as always, an exception to the rule. An acceptance is still effective if the addition only asks for something that would be implied from the offer and is therefore immaterial. . . . A Panhandle supervisor, Mr. Smith, and a company machinist, who was also a union representative, all testified that all Panhandle employees had the right to see their personnel files. Panhandle's offer to withdraw its discharge and eventually reinstate Mr. Smith carried with it the implication that he would be able to see his personnel record when he was once again an active employee.

Besides reserving the right to see his personnel file, Mr. Smith wrote that his personnel file contained mistakes, and that he was having financial problems, apparently as a result of the company's actions. Williston has described the kind of acceptance Mr. Smith made as one showing "an abundance of caution," and Corbin has called it a "grumbling acceptance," which in this case it certainly appeared to be. The acceptance was unenthusiastic to be sure, but it was an acceptance nevertheless. Mr. Smith signed his name under the words "Understood, Agreed To and Accepted." He wrote that he agreed to the terms and conditions. . . . His "grumbling acceptance" should stand. . . .

JUDGMENT The district court had jurisdiction to hear the dispute and correctly decided that a contract did exist and had been breached. Its damage award was supported by sufficient evidence. We therefore affirm.

Termination by Death or Incapacity of Offeror or Offeree. The death or incapacity of the offeree, and usually that of the offeror, terminates an ordinary offer (i.e., terminates the power of acceptance), regardless of whether the other party is aware of the occurrence. Incapacity is a lack of legal or physical ability to contract, usually resulting from a disability such as mental illness or defect, narcotics addiction, or extreme intoxication. For the offer to be terminated, the disability must be sufficiently serious to be considered permanent. People under lesser disabilities may have capacity to make or to receive offers; however, as discussed in Chapter 11, any resulting contract may be voidable by the person with the disability.

The death of the offer*ee* terminates the offer because only an offeree has a power of acceptance and the offeree's death makes acceptance impossible. However, the death of the offer*or* does not necessarily terminate the offer. In general, contracts are binding on the estates of deceased parties. So, an option contract (e.g., one in which the offeror is paid to hold the offer open for a fixed period) is binding on the estate of a deceased offeror. Ben pays Ann $10 for 30 days to consider her offer to sell him Blackacre, and she dies on the third day. Ben still has the power of acceptance. But if Ann's offer under the option contract was for her personal services (surveying Blackacre and drawing up plans for a housing development), her death makes her performance impossible and discharges the option contract, thus terminating the offer. Even ordinary offers could remain binding on a deceased offeror's estate if the circumstances required for promissory estoppel exist.

Termination by Loss of Subject Matter or Supervening Illegality. The loss or destruction of the subject matter of a proposed contract terminates the offer. Thus, if the offer concerns the purchase or sale of a horse and the horse dies before the offer is accepted, the offer is terminated.

If a proposed contract or performance becomes illegal after an offer has been made but before it is accepted, the offer is terminated by "supervening illegality." Eric offers to sell a ton of salmon to Row's Cannery. Before Cannery can accept the offer, the state legislature enacts a law, effective immediately, prohibiting further sales of salmon for the current year. The statute makes Eric's proposed performance illegal and terminates the offer.

Acceptance

Acceptance is the offeree's manifestation of assent to the terms of the offer. Under the common law rules of contract formation, the acceptance must exactly match (be a "mirror image" of) the offer, and not include a different or additional term. If Al says, "I'll sell my farm Blackacre to you for $300,000," and Betty replies, "I accept your offer, but you'll have to paint the front gate," Betty has not accepted, but has instead made a counteroffer to Al. This traditional mirror-image rule is still widely applied to contracts for real estate and services. However, the rule is inconsistent with modern business practices in the sale of *goods* and has been abandoned by Article 2 of the UCC.

Each day millions of contracts for goods are made by an exchange of preprinted forms, one prepared by the lawyer for the buyer and the other by the lawyer for the seller. Each lawyer serves the interests of his or her own client and will draft the form in a way that gives the client the most advantage. It is unlikely that the forms of buyers and sellers will match exactly. Consequently, if the mirror-image rule applied, the offeree could not be sure of a contract until the offeror actually performed by, for example, accepting goods that the offeree-seller sent. But one purpose of a contract is to assure the offeree at the earliest possible moment that the offeror will be bound if the offeree accepts. If the offeror may escape contractual liability just because the offeree's form departs from the terms of the offer, the offeree faces uncertainty as to whether a contract has arisen.

To reduce uncertainty in the formation of *sales* contracts, Section 2-207 provides that the offeree's expression of acceptance "operates as an acceptance even though it states terms additional to or different from those offered." Suppose Ann offers to buy a printing press from Ben for $50,000. Ann's order form says nothing about how a dispute between her and Ben will be resolved if the printing press is defective. She just assumes that she will have a right to go to court. But Ben's acceptance form says, "Disputes relating to this transaction shall be resolved by arbitration." Despite the fact that Ben's acceptance does not mirror Ann's offer, a contract arises because the two forms reveal agreement on the minimum terms necessary for a sales contract. Under the Code, the arbitration clause is merely a proposal for an addition to the contract contemplated by Ann. Whether the clause becomes a part of the contract depends on the application of Article 2 rules governing the fate of the proposed term. These rules are discussed in Chapter 16.

Acceptance of Unilateral Offer

An offer to enter into a unilateral contract (often called a "unilateral offer") requests from the offeree an *act* of performance in exchange for the offeror's promise. As noted earlier in this chapter, there was no acceptance of a unilateral offer (and no contract) under the traditional rules of contracting until the offeree performed the requested act. Today, where an offer permits acceptance *only* by performance and the requested act takes time to perform, the courts often hold that the offeree's *beginning* the performance or making a *substantial beginning* of performance is sufficient to create an option contract. This rule enables the offeree to continue the performance and to accept the offer.

In the unilateral contract situation just described, the mere beginning of performance, or even a "substantial" beginning, is *not* the performance required to accept the offer and earn the contract price. To accept, the offeree must perform the act completely or nearly so. Al writes to Beth: "I will pay you $1,000 to paint my house while I'm away on vacation beginning today. Since there's no phone or mail where I'm going, you'll have to accept my offer by doing the work." To earn the contract price, Beth must paint the entire house. However, the courts allow for minor imperfections in performance. If Beth fails to paint a small portion of the house, she nevertheless has "substantially performed" the requested act and is entitled to the contract price minus the cost to Al of having another painter finish the job. This *doctrine of substantial performance* is discussed in Chapter 15 and applies to unilateral and bilateral contracts alike.

Often it is not clear whether the offeror intended a unilateral or a bilateral contract. Where the wording of the offer permits the offeree to accept either by performing the act or by *promising* to do so, the beginning or a substantial beginning of performance constitutes an acceptance of the offer. Art says to Bill, "I'll pay you $100 to tear down that old shed by next Thursday." Bill can accept by saying "OK." Or Bill can accept by beginning the work. Either way, a court will imply Bill's promise to complete the job by Thursday. If he completely performs, he will be entitled to the contract price. If he substantially performs, he will be entitled to the contract price minus the amount Art must pay someone else to complete the work.

Acceptance of Bilateral Offer

An offer to enter into a bilateral contract (often called a "bilateral offer") is accepted by the offeree's communicating the return promise requested by the offeror. Usually bilateral offers are so worded or are made under such circumstances that the requested promise must be expressed in words. Sometimes, however, the requested promise is to be manifested by the performance of some act. In certain limited situations, acceptance of a bilateral offer takes place even though the offeree remains silent.

Acceptance by Words Expressing Assent. No particular words are required to express assent to a bilateral offer. The offeree may say simply, "I accept your offer," or use any other words indicating unequivocal acceptance. Ambiguous expressions such as "Your order will receive our prompt and careful attention," lead to controversy over whether there has been an acceptance.

Communication of acceptance. The general rule is that the offeree's acceptance of an offer for a bilateral contract must be communicated to the offeror. There is no acceptance if the offeree merely says "I accept" in a vacant room, utters the words to his or her own representative, or signs "I accept" on the offeror's written proposal without delivering it to the offeror. As noted later in this chapter, however, "communication" does not necessarily require that the offeror receive the offeree's message of acceptance. In the proper circumstances, it is sufficient that the offeree made a reasonably diligent *attempt* to communicate the message of acceptance by, for example, mailing a letter to the offeror.

Medium of acceptance; when and where acceptance becomes effective. Courts have often said that the offeror is "master of the offer." The offeror may specify (require) that acceptance is to be communicated face to face or by telephone, mail, telegraph, or some other medium. Steel Corporation in its offer to sell steel to a customer says, "You must accept this offer by letter received at our home office by June 1." The offeree may not accept by any other medium. Thus, an attempt by the customer to accept by telephone is ineffective as an acceptance but amounts to a counteroffer. Usually, however, an offeror makes no specification as to how acceptance is to be made or is to take effect. Consequently, the courts often have the problem of deciding when and where an acceptance becomes effective. Assume that two parties wish to contract by mail. Is the acceptance effective when mailed by the offeree or when received by the offeror? The answer depends on whether the offeree has complied with the "deposited acceptance rule."

Under the *deposited acceptance,* or "mailbox," *rule,* the acceptance is effective (i.e., a contract arises) at the point of dispatch if the offeree has used an *authorized medium* of acceptance while the offer is still open. Where the offeror stipulates that a particular medium of acceptance must be used (as Steel Corporation did in the preceding paragraph), only the stipulated medium is authorized. Where the offeror says nothing regarding the medium of acceptance, the offeree is impliedly authorized to accept by any *reasonable* medium. A medium of acceptance is reasonable if, for example, (1) it is the one used by the offeror, (2) it is customary in similar transactions, or (3) it is appropriate in view of the speed and reliability of the medium used, the prior dealings between offeror and offeree, or usage of trade.

The deposited acceptance rule places the risk of a lost or late acceptance on the offeror. One rationale is that the offeree assumes that by posting an acceptance, he or she has concluded a contract and makes commitments to others in reliance on that assumption. Another rationale given by courts is that the offeror is more likely to inquire if a reply is not received promptly, whereas the offeree is less likely to inquire and detect a loss because it is not customary to acknowledge receipt of an acceptance. An offeror who wishes to avoid the risk of a delayed or lost acceptance should specify that the acceptance must be received by the offeror at the offeror's place of business on or before a certain date.

The following case involves an offeree who first attempted to accept the offer, then changed her mind and rejected the offer.

CASE 9.5 Pribil v. Ruther · 262 N.W.2d 460 (Neb. 1978)

FACTS Bertha Ruther hired John Thor, a real estate broker, to sell 160 acres of land that she owned. On April 12, Lawrence Pribil presented a written offer to purchase the property for $68,000. Ruther signed an acceptance on the same day and handed a copy of the agreement to Thor for delivery to Pribil. Thor returned to his office and had his secretary write a letter to Pribil with a copy of the agreement enclosed, which the secretary then sent by certified mail. The letter was postmarked "April 15, 1976 P.M." and was received by Pribil on April 16, 1976. Ruther called Thor in the morning of April 15 and said she was going to "terminate the contract," because Thor had lied to her. Immediately after receiving the call, Thor telephoned Pribil and told him that Ruther was not going to sell the farm. Pribil sued for breach of contract. The trial court held in favor of Pribil. Ruther appealed.

OPINION BOSLAUGH, J. . . . The principal issue in this case is whether the defendant [Ruther] had effectively rejected the plaintifs [Pribil's] offer and revoked her acceptance of the offer before the acceptance had been communicated to the plaintiff. . . .

An express contract is proved by evidence of a definite offer and unconditional acceptance. Where the offer requires a promise on the part of the offeree, a communicated acceptance is essential. . . .

CASE 9.5 Continued

The signing of the acceptance on the Uniform Purchase Agreement by the defendant did not make the contract effective. It was necessary that there be some communication of the acceptance to the plaintiff. There must be some irrevocable element such as depositing the acceptance in the mail so that it is placed beyond the power or control of the sender before the acceptance becomes effective and the contract is made. Delivery to the agent of the defendant was not delivery to the plaintiff and did not put the acceptance beyond the control of the defendant.

The plaintiff contends that the deposit of the acceptance in the mail satisfied the requirement that the acceptance be communicated. Where transmission by mail is authorized, the deposit of the signed agreement in the mail with the proper address and postage will complete the contract. The difficulty in this case is that there is no evidence that the acceptance was deposited in the mail before Thor called the plaintiff and informed him that the defendant would not sell the property.

The evidence is that Thor handed the purchase agreement to Mrs. Kasebaum [his secretary] with instructions to send a copy to the plaintiff.... The postmark indicates only that the postage was canceled sometime during the afternoon of April 15, 1976. The telephone call from the defendant was received at 11:42 A.M. The call from Thor to the plaintiff was made immediately afterward.

If we assume that transmission by mail was authorized in this case, there is no evidence to show that the acceptance was deposited in the mail before the defendant's call to Thor, and Thor's call to the plaintiff notifying him that the defendant had rejected his offer. The evidence does not show that the acceptance was communicated to the plaintiff and thus became effective before the defendant changed her mind and rejected the offer....

JUDGMENT The judgment of the District Court is reversed and the cause remanded with directions to dismiss.

As a general rule, an acceptance by an *unreasonable medium* is not effective on dispatch but only upon *receipt* by the offeror (if the offer is still open). Thus, a contract may result though the offeree uses an unreasonable medium. Suppose, for example, that Harry sends by electronic mail an offer to sell perishable produce to Stella. Instead of replying by the same medium, Stella sends an acceptance by regular mail. Under the circumstances, the medium would be unreasonable. However, if the offer is still open when the acceptance is received by Harry, a contract would result.

As noted earlier, no acceptance occurs if the offeror has specified that a particular medium *must* be used by the offeree to communicate an acceptance and the offeree has used a different medium. The offeree's use of the different medium amounts to a counteroffer. Therefore, it is critical, when analyzing a factual situation, to determine whether the offeror has required (specified) a particular medium for acceptance or has merely suggested that a particular medium be used. In the absence of very strong, clear language, courts interpret offerors' statements as "suggestive." Accordingly, where the offeror has merely suggested the use of a particular medium, the offeree may accept by using any reasonable medium.

Occasionally a judge or jury must decide whether an offer is still open. If the offeror sent a notice of revocation (effective upon receipt) as the offeree attempted to accept the offer, the judge or jury faces a difficult factual determination: Did the offeree revoke the offer before the offeror accepted it?

Figure 9.4 involves an exchange of letters between A, the offeror, and B, the offeree. The offer was sent on May 1 and received on May 5. The revocation was sent on May 3 and received on May 6. The acceptance was sent on May 6 and received on May 9. Do A and B have a contract? Would the question be easier to answer if B had used an *unreasonable* medium of acceptance such as a carrier pigeon?

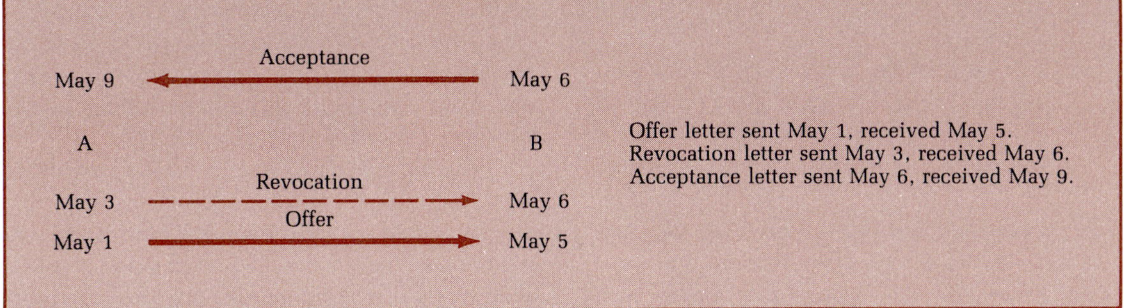

Figure 9.4 Exchange of communications.

Effect of acceptance plus rejection. There is an important exception to the general rule that an acceptance by any reasonable medium becomes effective on proper dispatch. The rule does not apply where the notice of acceptance was preceded by a notice of rejection. The reason for the exception is that the notice of rejection might be the first to reach the offeror, and the offeror should be entitled to act on it immediately—for example, by selling perishable goods quickly to another buyer. To protect the offeror, the law provides that an acceptance dispatched after a rejection has been sent is not effective until received. In short, when a notice of rejection is followed by a notice of acceptance, the first one to reach the offeror is the effective one.

Suppose that instead of sending a notice of rejection followed by a notice of acceptance, the offeree sends a notice of acceptance followed by a notice of rejection. Here, the courts apply the general rule that a notice of acceptance becomes effective when properly dispatched. However, if the notice of rejection reaches the offeror first, and the offeror changes his or her position in reliance on it, the offeree is estopped (barred) from enforcing the contract.

Acceptance by Act Indicating Assent. The acceptance of an offer to enter into a bilateral contract may at times properly be expressed by an act which implies a promise. A nod of the head, the raising of a hand, and the fall of an auctioneer's hammer are common examples. Similarly, taking possession of, or exercising dominion over, something may constitute acceptance. To illustrate: Curtis, a contractor, has a pile of lumber stored on a vacant lot. Curtis tells Donna to "take a look at the lumber. If it's worth $80 to you, haul it away." Donna hauls it away. The act of taking possession of the lumber is an acceptance of the offer and an implied promise to pay the $80. The offeree who objectively manifests an intent to accept is not permitted to testify that his or her secret intent was otherwise. In the above example, hauling away the lumber is held to be an acceptance, regardless of Donna's subjective intention.

Acceptance by Silence. The mere silence of an offeree in response to an offer does not constitute acceptance. Al says to Ben, "I'll sell you Blackacre for $200,000. If I don't hear from you by May 1, I shall assume that you accept my offer." Ben remains silent. There is no acceptance. Ben might not have heard the offer, or might have heard it but simply chose to ignore it. The law does not permit Al to force a contract on Ben without better evidence of his intention to contract.

However, if the offeree's silence is accompanied by other circumstances from which assent reasonably can be inferred, silence *can* constitute acceptance. Two examples follow:

1 Silence and inaction operate as an acceptance where the offeree takes the benefit of offered services with reasonable opportunity to reject them, and with reason to know that the offeror expects payment. Without Ben's request, Ann, a computer programming instructor, starts giving Ben's child lessons in computer programming on Ben's home computer. Ben has reason to know that Ann's intention is to give a course of ten lessons and to charge her usual price for it. But Ben does not object, and he silently allows the instruction to

continue. Ben is bound to pay the price of the course.

2 Silence operates as an acceptance where, because of previous dealings or otherwise, it is reasonable for the offeree to notify the offeror of the offeree's intention not to accept. Office Supply Co. sends out a salesperson to solicit orders (offers) for office supplies "subject to acceptance by the home office." If Office Supply's practice has been invariably to fill the customer's orders or to inform the customer promptly that it is unable to fill a particular order, the company's silence will be treated as an acceptance. Some courts hold that the firm has the duty of rejection even in the absence of a past course of conduct. These courts believe that the initiative taken by the firm in soliciting an order warrants any customer in believing that the order is accepted unless the customer is promptly notified to the contrary so that he or she may place an order elsewhere.

In the past, people received unordered merchandise in the mail (together with a letter seeking payment) and then used or otherwise benefitted from it. Many courts held that a contract resulted from such use, reasoning that the offeree's exercising dominion over the merchandise (acting like its owner) implied acceptance of the seller's offer. To prevent unscrupulous merchants from flooding consumers with unordered merchandise and harassing them with repeated billings and threats of lawsuits, the federal and state legislatures enacted a variety of consumer protection statutes. For example, a 1976 federal law makes it an unfair and deceptive practice for a seller to mail unsolicited merchandise to consumers. Under that law, the recipient of unordered merchandise may treat it as a gift, and so may use or dispose of it without liability for payment.

Agreement Looking Forward to a Writing

Often parties who are negotiating for a bilateral contract decide at some point in the negotiating process that when agreement is reached it will be put into writing and signed. If agreement is reached, does a contract come into being as soon as the agreement is reached or not until the agreement is put into writing and signed? The question is easily answered if the parties made clear what their intention was.

Where the parties have not made clear what their intention was and litigation ensues, the court will try to determine the intention from all the surrounding circumstances. The court would consider such factors as: (1) prior dealings between the parties, (2) the amount of money involved in the agreement, (3) the number and complexity of details, and (4) the amount of time required for performance. Hilton negotiates with Baron an oral contract to construct a hotel involving large sums of money, many complicated details, and a long time to complete performance. The parties agree to reduce their agreement to writing. A court would hold that the parties did not intend to be bound unless and until they signed a written agreement.

By contrast, if the parties orally agree on all the details and the transaction involves a small amount of money, the courts might conclude that the parties intended to be bound when the oral agreement was reached and that the writing was to serve merely as a "memorial" (record) of the agreement. Ken and Lisa negotiate for the sale of Ken's stereo. They orally agree on a price of $250, with delivery to take place in 1 week, and agree to reduce their agreement to writing. Ken refuses to deliver the stereo until a written agreement is signed by both parties. A court could hold that the writing is merely a memorial and that Lisa may enforce the oral contract.

Summary

The kind of contract used to arrange exchanges between the parties is based on an agreement—a manifestation of mutual assent reached through offer and acceptance.

An offer is a communication by which the offeror confers a power of acceptance on an offeree and thus the ability to accept the offer and make a contract. An offer normally indicates the exchange that the offeror has in mind, identifies the offeree (the person with the power of acceptance), and reveals a commitment by the offeror to deal with the offeree. To be a legally effective offer, a proposal must contain language of commitment (express or implied); be made with serious intent; be sufficiently definite and complete in its terms as to reveal the parties' rights and duties; and be communicated to the offeree. In general, offers involving real estate must be more detailed than offers involving services and goods.

A power of acceptance may be exercised any time before the offer is terminated. An offer may be terminated in a variety of ways, including lapse of time, revocation, rejection or counteroffer, and death of the offeror or offeree. Most offers are revocable any time before acceptance. Some are irrevocable for a fixed or a reasonable time if: (1) they are the subject of an option contract (including unilateral offers where the offeree begins performance), (2) the doctrine of promissory estoppel applies, or (3) a statute makes a class of offers irrevocable. Offers, including some irrevocable ones, are terminated when the offeror receives a rejection or a counteroffer or conditional acceptance. A counteroffer ordinarily is an implied rejection, but it does not terminate negotiations.

Acceptance is the offeree's manifestation of assent to the terms of the offer. Under the common law, the acceptance must be a mirror image of the offer, or there is a counteroffer. The mirror-image rule applies to contracts such as those for real estate or services, but it has been abandoned by Article 2 of the UCC, which applies to the sale of goods. Under Article 2, a contract usually arises even though the acceptance departed from the terms of the offer.

To accept a unilateral offer, the offeree must at least substantially perform the requested act. However, where the requested act takes time to perform, the offeree's beginning the performance or making a substantial beginning is sufficient to create an option contract that enables the offeree to continue the performance and accept the offer. Where the offeree may accept an offer by either performing or promising to perform, the beginning or substantial beginning of performance is an acceptance binding both offeror and offeree, but the offeree must at least substantially perform to be entitled to the contract price.

An offeree ordinarily uses words to accept an offer for a bilateral contract; sometimes the words are inferred from an act such as nodding at an auction. The acceptance must be communicated to the offeror, but "communication" does not necessarily require that the offeror receive the offeree's message. Under the deposited acceptance rule the sending of an acceptance by a medium invited by the offeror is sufficient as a communication. Unless the offeror requires the use of a particular medium, the offeree's use of any reasonable medium will do. The offeree's using an unreasonable medium amounts to a counteroffer.

Mere silence in response to an offer does not constitute acceptance. However, if the offeree's silence is accompanied by other circumstances from which assent reasonably can be inferred, silence can constitute acceptance, but such instances are rare. Consumer protection statutes permit consumers to treat merchandise as a gift when merchants mail it unsolicited in the expectation that the consumer will use and feel compelled to pay for it.

Parties negotiating a bilateral contract may decide that any agreement they reach will be put into writing and signed. Whether the agreement was binding while still oral, or only when reduced to writing, depends on the intent of the parties.

Review Questions

1 (a) What function does an offer serve? (b) What responses might an offeree make to an offer?

2 Alice says to Bob, "I'll sell my horse Jimbob for $1,000." Has she made an offer? Consider the three qualities that are normally present in an offer.

3 (a) Is a newspaper advertisement an offer? Why or why not? (b) Ordinarily, catalogs are considered merely invitations to make offers, with the sellers being offerees. What benefits do sellers receive from this offeree status?

4 In terms of offeror-offeree status, what difference does it make whether an auction is "with reserve" or "without reserve"? What difference does it make economically?

5 What test do courts apply in determining whether a proposal of conduct is seriously intended?

6 (a) Why would a person use a requirements contract or an output contract? (b) Is there any limit on the amount of goods that can be demanded from the seller under a requirements contract?

7 **(a)** "All material terms must be expressed for a proposal to be sufficiently definite to be an offer, but minor terms may be implied." Is this statement true? Why or why not? **(b)** Regarding contract formation and the implication of missing terms, how does the policy of Article 2 of the UCC differ from that of the common law?

8 Under what circumstances may an offer be irrevocable?

9 **(a)** Does a counteroffer reject the offer? **(b)** Does it suspend negotiations? **(c)** Amy offers to sell her car to Becky. Becky says, "I accept your offer on condition that you supply the title papers for the car." Is there a contract? Why or why not?

10 Under what circumstances will the death of the offeror *not* terminate the offer?

11 **(a)** What is the mirror-image rule? **(b)** For what reason does Article 2 of the UCC make it inapplicable to contracts for the sale of goods?

12 How do the terms "beginning of performance," "substantial beginning of performance," and "substantial performance" apply to the acceptance of a unilateral offer?

13 **(a)** Explain how the deposited acceptance rule works. **(b)** Under this rule, who bears the risk of a lost communication? Why does that person bear the risk?

14 If an offeree uses an unreasonable medium of acceptance, can there be an acceptance? If so, when and where?

15 **(a)** How might silence operate as an acceptance of a bilateral contract? **(b)** Where an agreement becomes legally effective before it is put into writing, of what value is the writing?

Case Problems

1 In 1973 Jonathan Abrams was admitted to the Illinois College of Podiatric Medicine. He failed Physiology 101. Abrams had a minor neurological disturbance resulting in a slow reading speed. He was placed on probation and told he must successfully pass a two-semester sequence, Physiology 101–203, in order to register for the 1974–1975 academic year. He failed the two courses and was dismissed from school. Abrams filed suit for breach of contract and sought reinstatement. He alleged that the college said he "should not worry . . . that everything would be done to assist him, including figuring out some way to help him." He also alleged that the college violated the *Student Handbook*, which provided: "Evaluation of the Student. It is desirable that the instructor should periodically inform the student of his progress. . . . The student should be informed soon after mid-term examinations of his standing with recommendations, if necessary, for improvement." Did the college make a legally sufficient offer to Abrams?

2 Phyllis Chaplin sued Consolidated Edison Company of New York, Inc. ("Con Ed"), alleging that Con Ed discriminated against epileptics in violation of federal law. In August 1981, Con Ed's attorney, Sheila Rosenrauch, sent a settlement proposal to Chaplin's attorney, James C. Francis IV. Francis replied that Chaplin had "a series of objections to the proposed settlement." Rosenrauch then stated in a letter of September 16 that Con Ed was still willing to settle on the terms stated, but "if this agreement is not satisfactory to your client in its present form, then I must withdraw all offers of settlement." Francis wrote on September 17 that he could not convince his client to accept the terms. Shortly thereafter the U.S. court of appeals decided a separate case in which it held that the federal law did *not* create a private cause of action for epileptics. On September 30, Francis wrote to Rosenrauch and said Chaplin had had "a change of heart" and decided to accept the offer. Rosenrauch replied by telephone that the settlement was no longer acceptable. Was there mutual assent (offer and acceptance) here?

3 Vincent Benya submitted a written offer to buy 5,243 acres of timberland from S&T Paper Co. The purchase price was $605,000, with a deposit of $5,000, an additional $146,000 at closing, and the balance to be paid in annual payments over 10 years with interest at 9 percent. Seller was to give buyer a warranty deed at closing, 60 days from date of agreement. S&T's attorney inserted several items into the letter: deposit of $10,000, an additional $141,000 at closing, the balance to be paid in quarterly payments with interest at 10 percent, and seller to give buyer a special warranty deed. A lawsuit resulted between the parties, and the trial court concluded that the changes made by S&T to Benya's offer were minor and did not constitute a counteroffer since the purchase price, closing date, and cash required were substantially the same. The court held there was a binding contract between the parties. Was the judgment of the trial court correct?

4 Carlton Vaulx insured his automobile with Cumis Insurance Society, Inc. Vaulx did not pay his premium, and Cumis sent him a notice that his policy had been terminated. They offered to reinstate the policy if they received Vaulx's premium by January 31. The offer was in bold type, all capitals, and contained a detachable portion at the bottom with the policy number and the insured's name. In smaller type, above the detachable portion, were the words "Please mail this copy with your remittance." On January 28, Vaulx mailed a money order for the full premium amount but did not send the lower detachable portion of the offer. Cumis received the money order on January 31. Cumis was unable to ascertain Vaulx's policy number or the purpose of the payment until February 11. In the meantime, Vaulx's policy was terminated. On March 5, Cumis issued a refund check to Vaulx. On March 7, Vaulx had an automobile accident and Cumis refused to insure Vaulx, claiming that he failed to comply with the terms of the offer of reinstatement and thus failed to accept. Did Vaulx accept the offer?

5 Braun owned a parcel of real estate and gave permission to Disner, a real estate agent, to show the property and receive offers. Disner received an offer of $165,000 from Froling and brought the offer to Braun. Braun rejected the offer and, through Disner, made a counteroffer of $185,000. Froling notified Disner that he accepted the counteroffer. Disner neglected to tell Braun of the acceptance, and Braun notified Froling that the deal was off. Froling sued for breach of contract. Was there a binding contract?

6 Crouch sent a letter to Purex inquiring about buying a building and its contents. Crouch received a letter from Purex signed by Frank Knox giving a price of $500. Crouch then sent a letter to Knox which read: "I guess we will buy the building for the amount you quoted, $500. I am sending you a personal check for this amount. . . ." The check was made out to Frank Knox and stated on its face that it was "For Silica building and equipment in and about that building." Knox endorsed the check to Purex, and Purex deposited it. Shortly thereafter, Knox sent Crouch a telegram stating that the check was deposited by mistake and Purex would issue a check to him. Purex then sent a letter to Crouch enclosing a $500 check and stated that they could not accept Crouch's offer because they had sold the building and machinery to someone else prior to receiving Crouch's check and letter. Crouch filed suit against Purex for breach of contract. Who should win?

7 Mosebach, a CPA, was president and secretary of Elberon Elevator, Inc., operator of a grain elevator in Iowa. Severson and Mosebach negotiated for the sale of the company, which owned land, several buildings, inventory, vehicles, and equipment. Ultimately, they arrived at a value of $50,000 for the physical assets, exclusive of inventory. Mosebach telephoned Blythe, the other major stockholder, informed him of the terms of the transaction, and then said to Severson, "Well, you have just bought an elevator." That evening Mosebach notified the elevator manager of the sale and told him he would not be employed by the new owner. Severson gave Mosebach a $5,000 check as earnest money, and they agreed to draw up a written agreement of sale. Before a writing was prepared, Mosebach refused to sell the company, contending that the parties did not settle all essential terms and that he contemplated further negotiations which would culminate in a written contract. Severson maintained that the written document was to be prepared merely as a memorial of the oral contract. Was there a binding oral contract?

CHAPTER 10

Consideration

Not all promises are legally enforceable. Purely social promises (e.g., to love someone or to attend a party given in one's honor) and most promises to make a gift are not enforceable. Yet, the courts will enforce many types of promises, especially those of commercial significance. What distinguishes enforceable promises from unenforceable promises?

To be enforceable under the early common law, a promise had to be in writing, and the writing had to bear the seal or insignia of the promisor. The writing then had to be delivered to the promisee or to the promisee's agent. Completing these steps was evidence to a largely illiterate population that the promisor took the transaction seriously and intended to be bound. Even a promise to make a gift was enforceable if sealed and delivered.

The sealed promise was an early type of *formal contract,* enforceable simply because the promisor had complied with formalities prescribed by law, and without regard to whether the promisor had received something in exchange for the promise. As literacy and the ability to make a signature increased, the ceremonial role of the seal diminished. Today, the UCC makes seals inoperative in sales of goods. A number of states have made seals inoperative for all contracts, and other states have reduced their legal effect. However, although the sealed promise is of relatively little importance in today's contract law, other kinds of formal contracts—negotiable instruments, letters of credit, and so on—are widely used. A promisor's use of legally required formalities, then, is one basis for enforcing promises.

But as trade and commerce developed in England, a need arose for a broader range of promise enforcement. The largely rural population of that era conducted most of its business informally and had little time for or understanding of ceremonial contractual formalities. By the early fourteenth century, courts were enforcing some kinds of unsealed promises and were seeking some basis—some underlying idea or theory—for determining which unsealed (informal) promises should be enforceable. The courts now recognize three bases for the enforcement of *informal* promises:

- Consideration
- Promissory estoppel
- Statutes and case law imposing liability where consideration or the justifiable reliance needed for promissory estoppel is lacking[1]

Promissory estoppel has grown dramatically in the twentieth century as a basis for promise enforcement. Yet, consideration remains the most common basis for enforcing informal promises. The first two parts of this chapter discuss consideration. The third part discusses promissory estoppel and other bases for promise enforcement.

The Requirement of Consideration

The doctrine of consideration arose out of a need to enforce informal promises made as a part of a bargained-for exchange. A person usually performed an act, or promised to do so, because some other person promised a return performance such as a payment of money. Each person's promise was made "in consideration of" (i.e., because of and in exchange for) the other person's promise, and each promise created an expectation of performance. To protect those expectations, the courts long ago began to enforce informal promises which had been induced by consideration.

Nature of Consideration

Meaning of Consideration. Like many complex legal concepts, consideration is viewed and defined in somewhat different ways by various judges and legal writers. There are, however, two major views or theories of consideration that together reveal its nature: (1) the bargained-for exchange theory, and (2) the legal detriment theory.

Bargained-for exchange theory; reciprocal inducements. Section 71 of the *Restatement (Second) of the Law of Contracts* provides in part:

> "(1) To constitute consideration [for a promise], a performance or a return promise must be bargained for.

[1]John E. Murray, Jr., *Murray on Contracts,* Bobbs-Merrill, Indianapolis, 1974, p. 125.

"(2) A performance or return promise is bargained for if it is sought by the promisor in exchange for his promise and is given by the promisee in exchange for that promise."

For example, suppose Ann said to Ben, "I'll pay you $20 to mow my lawn," and Ben responded by mowing Ann's lawn. Ann (the offeror-promisor) promised to pay Ben $20 in exchange for his services; and Ben mowed the lawn as a result of and in exchange for Ann's promise of payment. The prospect of Ben's mowing the lawn induced Ann to promise him the payment, and her promise of payment induced Ben to mow the lawn. This is the reciprocal bargaining relationship required for Ben's act to constitute consideration for Ann's promise to pay. Since Ann received consideration for her promise, it is enforceable.

In contrast, suppose Al says to his daughter Bea, "I am going to buy a new car next month. I promise to give you my old car at that time." Here, because Al seeks nothing in return for his promise, there is no bargained-for exchange. Al has merely promised to make a gift to Bea. Since Al has received no consideration for his promise, it is unenforceable.

Legal detriment theory. Consideration can also be thought of in terms of legal detriment to the promisee. Under this theory, a promisee gives consideration if she or he suffers a legal detriment in response to the promisor's promise.

To suffer a *legal detriment,* the promisee must: (1) do (or promise to do) something that he or she is not legally obligated to do, or (2) refrain from doing (or promise to refrain from doing) what she or he is legally privileged to do.[2] Ann says to Ben, "I'll pay you $20 to mow my lawn." If he mows the lawn, he suffers a legal detriment by performing an act that he was not legally obligated to perform—and thus gives Ann consideration for her promise to pay $20. As in the bargained-for exchange discussed earlier, there must be a cause-and-effect relationship between the promise and the detriment. This means essentially that the promise must induce the detriment, and that each must be given in exchange for the other.

Another way to understand legal detriment is in terms of the promisee's *giving up a legal right.* When Ann made her offer, Ben had no legal obligation to mow the lawn. He was free to use his time as he wished. But when he mowed the lawn, he gave up his right to use his time for other purposes and thus suffered a legal detriment. Or suppose Ann drove negligently and injured Ben, giving him a right to sue her for damages. Then she says to Ben, "I'll pay you $5,000 not to sue me for injuring you," and Ben accepts her offer. By agreeing not to sue her, Ben gives up a legal right, suffers a legal detriment, and so gives Ann a consideration that makes her promise enforceable.

When a promisee suffers a legal detriment, the promisor gains a corresponding legal benefit.[3] In the example just given, Ben suffered a legal detriment by agreeing to refrain from suing Ann. Ann received a corresponding legal benefit: a right, upon paying $5,000, not to be sued by Ben. (Some courts hold that consideration exists if the promisee suffers a legal detriment *or* if the promisor gains a legal benefit as a result of the promisee's performance or return promise. However, most courts limit their analysis to a search for legal detriment.)

There is an important distinction between *legal* and *actual* benefits and detriments. Most people enter into contracts expecting to gain something of real value. Since they ordinarily expect an actual, economic benefit for whatever they must give up in exchange, they naturally think in terms of actual benefits and detriments—money for services, money for real estate, and so on. But for consideration to exist (and for a promise to be enforceable), the promisee need suffer only a *legal* detriment. The often-cited case of *Hamer v. Sidway*[4] illustrates the point. There, an uncle promised to pay his nephew $5,000 if he would "refrain from . . . using tobacco" until he was twenty-one. The nephew refrained from doing so. The uncle did not pay, and the nephew sued. The court held that the nephew had a legal right to use tobacco, and by giving up that right he suffered a *legal detriment* even though abstaining probably was an *actual* physical *benefit* to him. Consequently, there was consideration for the uncle's promise to pay $5,000. (Furthermore, when the uncle received the performance for which he had bargained, he received a legal benefit—a restriction of the nephew's legal rights—even though

[2]John D. Calamari & Joseph M. Perillo, *The Law of Contracts,* West Publishing Company, St. Paul, 1987, p. 187.

[3]Ibid., p. 188.

[4]121 N.Y. 538 (1891).

the nephew's performance did not benefit the uncle economically.)

By defining consideration in terms of legal rather than actual benefits and detriments, courts accomplish two things: (1) in ordinary circumstances, the courts thereby leave the problem of economic valuation to the parties to the contract, and (2) the courts provide an abstract guideline that is applicable to an immense variety of contractual exchanges.

Most of the preceding examples involve *unilateral* contracts in which there is only one promisor (Ann) and one promisee (Ben). In a *bilateral* contract, both parties make promises and each party is both a promisor and a promisee.

For a typical *bilateral* contract to arise, each party must give consideration for the other party's promise—i.e., each party must suffer a legal detriment. Amy says to Bob, "I'll sell you my car for $10,000, delivery and payment to be made in 2 weeks. Is that satisfactory to you?" Bob says, "Yes, I'll pay you the $10,000 upon delivery." Amy has suffered a legal detriment by promising to deliver the car to Bob and thus giving up her right to do something else with it. Similarly, Bob has suffered a legal detriment by giving up his right to use his $10,000 in some other way. The parties have created an executory bilateral contract. As it happens, Amy and Bob will receive actual benefits and suffer actual detriments if they perform their contractual obligations in 2 weeks, but this fact is irrelevant to the existence of consideration. Because each party suffered a *legal* detriment, the consideration necessary for a contract exists immediately upon the exchange of promises, and the failure of either party to perform later as promised (or even a present *threat* not to perform later) entitles the other party to a remedy (e.g., damages) for breach of contract. Figure 10.1 shows the movement of consideration in a typical executory bilateral contract.

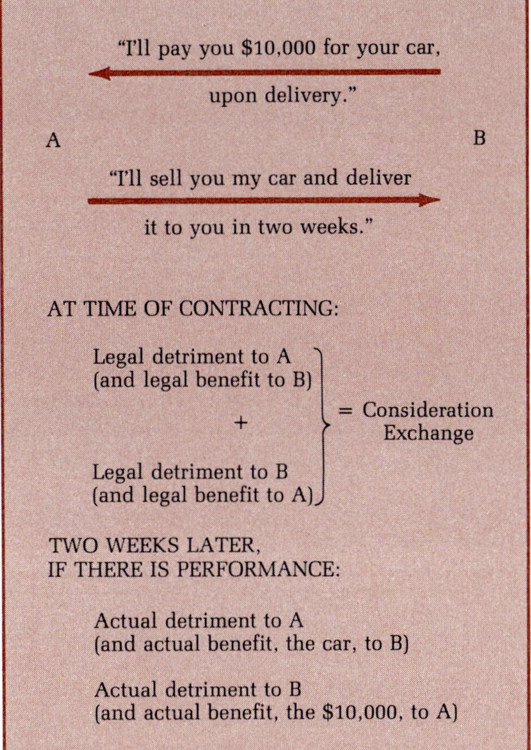

Figure 10.1 Consideration in bilateral contract.

The following case discusses the meaning of consideration.

CASE 10.1 In re Estate of Weinsaft · 647 S.W.2d 179 (Mo. App. 1983)

FACTS In 1972, Thomas L. Weinsaft signed a written agreement with his son, Nicholas L. Weinsaft. Thomas agreed that during his lifetime he would not transfer any interest in his 765 shares of stock of Crand Manufacturing Company unless he first gave Nicholas an opportunity to purchase it. Upon Thomas's death, Nicholas was to have the "option and right to purchase all of the . . . stock" from Thomas's estate. The agreement recited that it was entered into "in consideration of $10.00 and other good and valuable consideration, including the inducement of Second Party [Nicholas] to remain the chief executive officer of said company." Thomas died in 1980. Nicholas gave notice that he intended to buy the stock, but one of the beneficiaries under Thomas's will objected, contending

CASE 10.1 Continued

that Nicholas had given no consideration for Thomas's promises. Alleging that there was a binding contract, Nicholas brought suit to compel the estate to transfer the shares to him. The trial court granted judgment to Nicholas, and the beneficiary (here called "Intervenor") appealed.

OPINION

PREWITT, J. . . . Plaintiff as the one relying on the agreement had the burden [of proving] consideration. . . . However, that burden was met when the agreement was introduced in evidence and no evidence established that the recitals of consideration were erroneous. The recitation of consideration in an agreement . . . creates a presumption that the recitals are true, which presumption continues unless overcome by evidence to the contrary. . . .

Intervenor contends that the recitation of consideration was insufficient because the agreement "does not specify to whom the '$10.00 and other good and valuable consideration' flows" and the ambiguities in such a document should be resolved against the optionee [plaintiff Nicholas]. We see no merit in this contention. It is obvious that the consideration recited was to the decedent [Thomas] for the grant of the options contained in the agreement. If the consideration included the inducement of plaintiff to remain as chief executive officer as it stated, then that and the other considerations could . . . flow [only] to the decedent.

Plaintiff remained as chief executive officer, and this was sufficient consideration. Plaintiff was not legally obligated to work for the corporation and could have left, but did not do so. Consideration sufficient to support a contract may be either a detriment to the promisee or a benefit to the promisor. . . . The detriment to the promisee may consist of his doing anything . . . he is not [legally] bound to do or refraining from doing anything he has the right to do. . . . In addition, the $10.00 recited was sufficient consideration. Because an option contract may be of no benefit to the optionee, depending upon changes and circumstances which occur during the life of the agreement, little consideration is necessary to support it. Amounts as low as $1.00 have been held sufficient. . . .

Intervenor [also contends] that the contract is void because it purports to effect the disposition of property at death without complying with the statutory requirements for a will. That contention also must be denied. The agreement was not testamentary because it was a contract made and in force during the decedent's lifetime. . . .

JUDGMENT

. . . [A]ffirmed.

Movement of Consideration. The consideration (i.e., performance or return promise) demanded by a promisor usually moves from the promisee to the promisor—but it need not necessarily do so. The performance or the return promise may be given to some person other than the promisor if the promisor so requires. Ann promises to pay Bob $200 if he delivers a guitar to her son Tom. Bob delivers the guitar to Tom. Bob's act of delivery is consideration for Ann's promise even though Bob made no promise to Ann and did not deliver the guitar to her.

Because the contract between Ann and Bob is intended to benefit Tom, it is called a "third-person beneficiary contract." Such contracts (discussed further in Chapter 14) may be unilateral, as above, but often are bilateral. In a bilateral third-person beneficiary contract, the movement of consideration is different from that just described for a unilateral contract. Ann says to Bob, a guitar dealer, "I'll pay you $200 for this guitar if you'll promise to deliver it to my son Tom." Bob says, "OK, I'll deliver it to him." Bob's promise, made to Ann, is consideration for her promise to pay the $200. Here Ann immediately receives a legal benefit (Bob's promise to deliver the guitar to Tom), while Tom later receives an actual benefit, the guitar. Figure 10.2 illustrates the movement of consideration in a bilateral, third-person beneficiary contract.

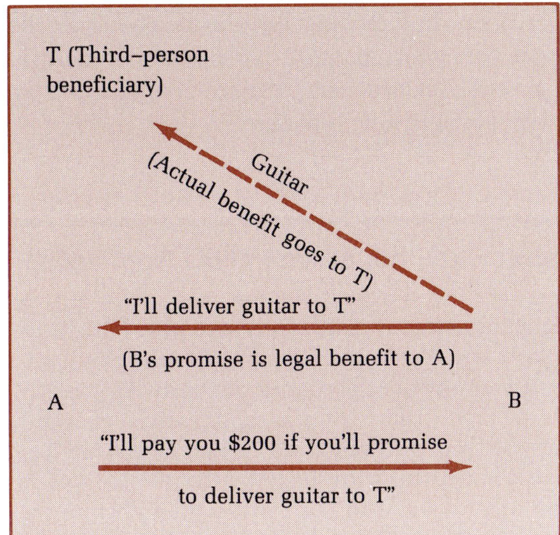

Figure 10.2 Movement of consideration in bilateral third-person beneficiary contract.

Consideration Distinguished from Motives.

Consideration should not be confused with the motive for giving it. "Love and affection" may be compelling motives for making a promise, but they do not reveal an act of bargaining. Thus, Alice might write to her daughter, "In consideration of my love and affection, I promise to send you a check for $1,000 on your twenty-first birthday." Alice bargained for nothing in exchange for her promise, which, being unsupported by consideration, is only a promise to make a gift.

In the case of *Hamer v. Sidway*, discussed earlier, the uncle made his promise to pay the nephew $5,000 in exchange for the nephew's giving up his right to use tobacco. The uncle's promise might have been motivated by a desire to protect or to improve his nephew's health, by a desire to impose his moral code on the nephew, or even by a desire to torment the nephew, hoping he would be too weak-willed to "kick the habit." Whatever a promisor's motive, the promise is not enforceable unless the promisee gives consideration, as the nephew did by not using tobacco.

"Past Consideration"—No Consideration.

Consideration is something given in exchange for a promise and to induce it. Accordingly, anything that occurred *before* a promise was made cannot be consideration. A father says to his son, "I am so happy you stayed in college and received your degree. In consideration of that fact, I promise to pay you $1,000 at the end of next month." Undoubtedly the father has a *motive* for his promise—his pride in his son's accomplishment. However, the promise is unenforceable—is only a promise to make a gift—because the son's graduation was not something bargained for or induced by the promise. The fact that a past event cannot be something bargained for has given rise to the statement, "past consideration is no consideration." Though sometimes used by judges, the expression "past consideration" is self-contradictory; that which occurred before the promise cannot be consideration at all.

Illusory Promise; Requirements Contract

Whether a promise can be consideration also depends on its *content.* Sometimes a statement seems to be a promise but does not obligate the "promisor" to any performance whatever. Such statements are called *illusory promises.* For example, Al says to Bess, "I'll deliver to you at $3.25 per bushel as many bushels of corn, not exceeding 5,000, as you may order within the next 30 days." Bess responds by saying, "I'll buy at that price as many bushels as I shall order from you within that period." Although Bess seems to have made a promise, in fact she has not committed herself to purchase any corn. Her promise is illusory, is not a legal detriment to her, and is not consideration for Al's promise. Moreover, because Al has made a commitment but Bess has not, their agreement *lacks* the *mutuality of obligation* required for a bilateral contract to arise.

In contrast, if Bess had promised to buy as many bushels (not to exceed 5,000) as she would *need in her business,* the promise would not be illusory. The arrangement is called a "requirements contract," and Bess's business needs provide an objective standard for determining some minimum amount of purchase. Because requirements contracts are useful and because the amount to be purchased does not depend solely on the whim of a party to the contract, courts routinely enforce them.

If a promisor has an unrestricted right to cancel an agreement—for example, to cancel it without notice—the promise is illusory. But if the right to terminate the agreement is restricted in any way, courts ordinarily will hold that the promise is not illusory.

Sometimes a right to cancel is conditioned on (is not to occur until) the happening of some event such as a strike or a war, or the agreement might require the promisor to give, for example, 30 days' notice of cancellation. In such instances, the promise is not illusory because the promisor is obligated to perform for some minimum amount of time. Case 10.2 discusses whether a promise is illusory.

CASE 10.2 Wright & Seaton, Inc. v. Prescott · 420 So. 2d 623 (Fla. App. 1982)

FACTS On May 1, 1979, Raymond Prescott signed an employment agreement with Wright & Seaton, Inc., an insurance agency. Prescott was to receive $20,000 per year plus commissions and was to perform executive, administrative, and sales duties as assigned by Wright & Seaton. Wright & Seaton was to employ him for 1 year, and reserved the right to terminate his employment at any time, with or without cause, upon written notice. Prescott agreed not to engage in a business competitive with Wright & Seaton for 3 years following termination of Prescott's employment. On April 16, 1980, 2 weeks before the expiration of the 1-year term, Prescott delivered a letter of resignation, effective at the end of the month, stating that the agreement was "void for failure of consideration, inadequate consideration, and lack of mutuality." That is, Prescott alleged that Wright & Seaton's promise of employment was illusory and could not be the basis for a contract. Prescott then went to work for a competing insurance agency in Wright & Seaton's area. Wright & Seaton filed suit to enforce the agreement not to compete. From a judgment for Prescott, Wright & Seaton appealed.

OPINION GLICKSTEIN, J. . . . We start out with the proposition that . . . the parties entered into a bilateral contract containing mutual executory promises. Appellant [Wright & Seaton] agreed to continue to employ and pay appellee [Prescott for 1 year]; appellee agreed to work for appellant and not to compete with it for a period of time in a certain area when his employment terminated. Appellant retained the right, however, to terminate the employment without cause. But this right could . . . be exercised [only] upon the giving of written notice. . . .

[Our supreme court has held,] "The detriment which will constitute a consideration for a promise need not be an actual loss to the promisee. It is sufficient if he does something that he is not legally bound to do."

In the absence of the parties' agreement, appellant was not bound to provide appellee with written notice. The requirement that it do so can be held to be sufficient consideration to support the promise of the other party. It is stated in 1 S. Williston, *A Treatise on the Law of Contracts, § 105* . . . :

> An agreement wherein one party reserves the right to cancel at his pleasure cannot create a contract.
>
> Since the courts, however, do not favor arbitrary cancellation clauses, the tendency is to interpret even a slight restriction on the exercise of the right of cancellation as constituting such legal detriment as will satisfy the requirement of sufficient consideration; for example, where the reservation of right to cancel is for cause, or by written notice, or after a definite period of notice, or upon the occurrence of some extrinsic event, or is based on some other objective standard. . . .

[Consequently, Wright & Seaton's promise to employ Prescott for a year was not illusory. Moreover, since there was a termination clause, the court treated the employment contract as terminable at the will of either party.]

Second, and more important, is the rule stated in 17 C.J.S. *Contracts § 100(3)* . . . :

> [If a contract lacks] mutuality at its inception such defect may be cured by the subsequent conduct of the parties. Want of mutuality is no defense in the case of an executed contract,

CASE 10.2 Continued

and a promise lacking in mutuality at its inception becomes binding on the promisor after performance by the promisee....

[T]hat rule... is applicable under the circumstances of this case.

If appellant continued to employ appellee, the latter promised that upon termination of his employment he would not compete with appellant. Even if we were to assume... an absence of mutuality of obligation at the inception [of the contract—and for sake of discussion we do because appellant retained the right to cancel the agreement], appellant completely performed its obligations to continue to employ and pay appellee for his services [for nearly the full year].... If appellant did not perform for the entire year, it was only because appellee made it impossible for appellant to do so. Under such circumstances there was complete performance by appellant of what it had promised to do in exchange for appellee's promise not to compete; as a result, appellee's promise not to compete became binding upon him and enforceable by injunction....

Additional reasons for enforcing appellee's covenant not to compete have been noted in at least three decisions applying Florida law. *Tasty Box Lunch Co. v. Kennedy*... said:

> Inasmuch as the employment was a continuing contract terminable at the will of the employer or the employee, the continued employment and agreement to pay commissions was consideration for the employee's agreement not to compete.

... Here, although the relationship between the parties was terminable at will,... appellant employed appellee for eleven months and sixteen days in reliance upon his promise not to compete; [this employment was consideration for appellee's promise not to compete].

JUDGMENT [We reverse and direct the trial court to fashion an appropriate injunction against Prescott.]

Adequacy of Consideration; Sham or Nominal Consideration

Ordinarily, any legal detriment, no matter how economically inadequate, may constitute consideration. If the courts were to substitute their ideas of relative values for those expressed by the parties in their agreement, endless litigation, delay, and uncertainty would result. Moreover, today's courts, like those of the nineteenth century, are reluctant to interfere with freedom of contract by relieving an adult party of a bad bargain. Mistaken judgments about value are likely in competitive markets, may be offset by gains in other transactions, and often are reasonably relied on by the other party. Accordingly, the economic decisions of contracting parties usually are binding even though one of them may suffer loss.

Nevertheless, gross inadequacy of consideration may be evidence that only a gift was intended, or it may be relevant in resolving other contract issues. Suppose Ann persuades Ben to pay her $10,000 for $3 worth of foreign currency. The gross disparity between what Ben gave and what he received may be circumstantial evidence of Ann's fraud, duress, overreaching, or undue influence, or of Ben's mistake or incapacity. These problems are discussed further in Chapter 11.

Often an agreement states that a promise was made "in consideration of $1," even though the $1 was neither bargained for by the promisor nor paid by the promisee. The pretended payment is called "sham" or "nominal" consideration and usually is not acceptable as consideration. Suppose that Alice, intending to give her new Cadillac to her son Bob, promises to deliver the car to him later in the month "in consideration of $1." Alice may have used this language in the mistaken belief that the law requires it for a gift, or because she wanted to disguise the gift as a sale. Whatever her reasoning, the "consideration" is a pretense, and in most states Alice's promise is not enforceable. In contrast, suppose Alice owes a large unpaid balance on the purchase price, and promises to deliver the car to Bob "in consideration of $1 and Bob's assuming my car debt." Even if the $1 was only a matter of form, his promise to assume Alice's debt, being a legal detriment to him and given in exchange for Alice's promise to deliver the car, is a consideration that makes her promise enforceable.

Problems Relating to Consideration

The courts must deal with a variety of problems relating to consideration. Many arise during the performance of a contract. For example, a buyer of goods that are rapidly falling in value might persuade the seller to accept a smaller payment than the buyer originally agreed to. A builder might run into unanticipated difficulties and pressure the client into a higher payment than specified by the contract. The creditors of a troubled debtor might agree to accept less than originally owed. Are such promises enforceable? In resolving these and other problems, the courts may have to decide whether consideration is present, and if it is not, whether the promise should be enforced anyway.

Performance of Existing Legal Duty

At common law, performing or promising to perform an act that one was already legally obligated to perform was not consideration for another person's promise. Still widely followed, this *pre-existing duty rule* applies: (1) where the existing duty is imposed by statute or by the common law, and (2) where a person is already under a contractual obligation to render a specified performance but later demands more for it (or insists on doing less than originally promised).

Existing Statutory or Common Law Duty. A person's performing an act already required of him or her by statute or the common law is not consideration. Ann and Ben, the county sheriff, see Tom steal Ann's car. Ann says to Ben, "I'll pay you $100 to arrest that man." Ben arrests Tom and later demands $100 from Ann. Ann's promise is not enforceable because Ben, as sheriff, already had a duty to arrest Tom. In making the arrest, Ben suffered no new legal detriment and conferred no new legal benefit on Ann who, as a citizen, was already entitled to have Ben perform his duty. Similarly, a promise to pay a witness to tell the truth in court is not enforceable. Witnesses are already required by law to tell the truth, and doing so cannot be a new legal detriment to them. Nor is it consideration for a person to refrain (forbear) from doing what he or she is not legally privileged to do. No one has a right to commit a tort or a crime. Without provocation, Bob threatens to hit Ann. Fearing harm, Ann promises to pay Bob $100 if he will not hit her. Bob does not hit Ann and later demands the $100. Bob had no right to hit Ann, and his refraining from doing what he had no right to do in the first place cannot be consideration for her promise.

Existing Contractual Duty. Like statutes and the common law, a contract establishes legal duties that are binding on the parties. Sometimes, however, the parties agree to modify the contract so that one party's obligation increases while the other party's duty remains the same. Does a promise to pay or to do more for the same return consideration bind the promisor? The question is troublesome to the courts.

Under the pre-existing duty rule, if the promisor receives no consideration for the new promise, the court is not supposed to enforce it. Yet many one-sided modifications of existing contractual obligations are quite reasonable even if the promisor did not receive consideration for the new promise. Where the benefiting promisee is acting fairly, some courts will enforce the new promise even though the existence of consideration may be arguable. In a few states, modifications made because of circumstances unforeseen by the parties, and modifications upon which the other party has reasonably relied, are enforceable even though consideration clearly is lacking. And under Section 2–209(1) of the UCC, which applies in virtually all states, "An agreement modifying a [contract for the sale of goods] needs no consideration to be binding." Nevertheless, for the modification of contracts covered by the common law, consideration for the new promise normally is required.

Understanding how the courts handle the pre-existing duty problem as it relates to modified contracts requires, first, an understanding of two basic contract situations:

1. In April, Amy hires Bill to work for her as marketing director for a 1-year term at $500 per week, the term to begin in July. In June, Amy and Bill agree to modify the contract so that Bill will receive $550 per week for the same work. Under the pre-existing duty rule, Amy's promise to pay the additional $50 is unenforceable. Having already contracted to work as marketing director for $500 per week, Bill suffered no new legal detriment for Amy's promise to pay the extra $50, conferred no new legal benefit on Amy, and therefore gave no consideration for Amy's promise.
2. Amy hires Bill as marketing director at $500 per week for the 1-year term as described above. Then in May, Bill receives an offer from another company, and Amy and Bill agree in writing to cancel (rescind) the April contract, each saying in effect, "I'll free you from your obligation under the April contract if you'll free me from mine." Because each party's promise is bargained for and given in exchange for the other's promise, both Amy and Bill receive consideration and the rescission agreement is a binding contract cancelling the April contract. Bill suffered the requisite legal detriment by giving up his right to receive $500 per week from Amy; Amy suffered a legal detriment by giving up her right to Bill's services as marketing director. Since neither Amy nor Bill has any further duty under the April employment contract, both are free to contract with whom they please. So, if in June Amy rehires Bill as marketing director at $600 per week for a 1-year term, Bill owes no pre-existing contractual duty to Amy that could prevent enforcement of her promise to pay $600.

Situation 1 above is relatively uncontroversial; i.e., most courts would find Amy's promise to pay the extra $50 unenforceable for lack of consideration. Situation 2 is likewise uncontroversial; most courts would find the contract of rescission sufficient to cancel the original contract and prepare the way for an enforceable later contract between the same parties.

However, many contract modification cases fall between these clear extremes. Ann hires Bob to build an asphalt road along one side of Ann's farm for a stated sum; after partial performance, Bob discovers he will lose money on the job and threatens to quit unless Ann agrees to pay more. To persuade Bob to continue, Ann promises to pay him an additional $3,000, and Bob completes the work. Is Ann's promise enforceable?

The answer may depend on the reason for Bob's underestimating the cost of the road. If Bob was negligent in preparing his bid—or if he intentionally underbid to get the job, expecting to raise the price later—nearly all courts would hold that Bob was under a pre-existing duty to build the road for the price originally agreed to and so gave no consideration for Ann's promise to pay more. Application of the pre-existing duty rule is common in circumstances such as these, to prevent contractors from extorting a higher price when they themselves caused or should have anticipated the loss.

Suppose, however, that Bob would lose money because of some *unforeseeable circumstance* such as an earthquake of unusual severity that destroyed part of the work, and Ann agreed to pay more than the original contract price to get Bob to continue. Some courts would enforce Ann's agreement to pay more, reasoning that the extra work, being unforeseeable, was not a part of the original bargain, and Bob's doing it was consideration for Ann's promise of extra payment. The courts differ on how unforeseeable the circumstance must be for the extra work to be new consideration. Some courts require a high degree of unforeseeability, ruling that labor disputes, most increases in the cost of materials, and most bad weather are foreseeable. A few courts accept a lesser degree of unforeseeability as sufficient, as long as the person seeking the extra payment was not negligent. Case 10.3 involves a contractor-promisee who encounters difficulties that he did not foresee.

CASE 10.3 Crookham & Vessels, Inc. v. Larry Moyer Trucking, Inc. · 699 S.W.2d 414 (Ark. App. 1985)

FACTS Crookham & Vessels, Inc., was the general contractor on a project to build an extension of a railroad. Crookham entered into a subcontract with Larry Moyer Trucking, Inc., to do the excavation and dirt work on the project in accordance with plans and specifications. Moyer started work and soon encountered a problem in constructing ditches. Water would not drain out of the ditches because the culverts through which they were to drain were clogged off of the jobsite. This caused the ditches to collapse, requiring Moyer to repeatedly have to redig the ditches. Moyer told Crookham that he would not continue to work without extra pay for redigging the ditches. Crookham agreed to this, but he later refused to pay. Moyer filed suit and received a verdict for $3,998.39 due on the contract and $12,095 for "extra ditching." Crookham appealed.

OPINION COOPER, J.... Under Arkansas law, there must be additional consideration when the parties to a contract enter into an additional contract....

> Mere performance of an existing contract or a part thereof, is of itself no consideration for a new promise to the party performing.... If, without legal justification, one party to a contract breaks it, or threatens to break it, and to induce performance on his part the adversary party promises to pay more than was provided for by the original contract, there is in principle no consideration for such promise, as the party who threatens to break the contract does, when he finally performs it, no more than he was bound in law to do.

Here, the contract admittedly required the appellee [Moyer] to dig the ditches so that he met the specifications at the time the project was approved, and it is undisputed that that is what the appellee did. Where the work performed is covered under the terms of the contract, as here, there can be no recovery for it as extra work.... Here,... the appellee had the duty to acquaint himself before bidding with the conditions, nature, and extent of the work to be performed, and the condition of the culverts in question could have been taken into account. In Arkansas, it is settled that "[i]nconvenience or the cost of compliance with the contract or other like thing cannot excuse a party from the performance of an absolute and unqualified undertaking to do that which is possible and lawful."... *Accord, Baton Rouge,* 304 F.Supp. at 585 ("Where one agrees to do, for a fixed sum, a thing possible to be performed, he will not be excused or become entitled to additional compensation because unforeseen difficulties are encountered."). Here the appellee did no more than was required by its contract; the unforeseen clogged culverts merely made it more difficult. The appellant has received no additional consideration for its alleged promise to pay extra, having gotten no more than it bargained for in the first place. Therefore, the jury verdict in the amount of $12,095.00 for the "extra ditching" must be overturned.

JUDGMENT There has been no appeal of the award of $3,998.39 for costs under the contract.... Therefore, we can, and do, modify the judgment by deleting the jury's award and affirming the award of $3,998.39 for contract costs and the prejudgment interest thereon.

Part payment of a liquidated claim. One variation of the pre-existing duty rule involves part payment of a liquidated claim. A debt (or claim) is said to be *liquidated* when there is no dispute about its existence or amount. Al agrees to repair Bev's bulldozer for $350, makes the repairs, and sends her a bill for that amount. Bev's debt is "liquidated" because Bev and Al have agreed on the price. If Bev (the debtor) can later persuade Al (the creditor) to accept part payment of the liquidated debt as payment in full, is Al's promise to do so binding?

Part payment of a liquidated debt, made when it is due or past due, is not consideration for the creditor's promise to accept the part payment as payment in full. Suppose Bev insists that Al's $350 charge is too high, and he agrees to accept $250 as payment in full but later sues Bev for an additional $100. Al will prevail. Bev's original agreement to pay $350 created a liquidated debt. Thus, Bev has a pre-existing duty to pay $350, and, having suffered no new legal detriment for Al's promise to accept $250, gave no consideration for that promise.

The part payment rule operates satisfactorily where the creditor's charge is reasonable, and especially where, in addition, the debtor is trying to take unfair advantage of the creditor. However, the rule has been criticized as tending to defeat the legitimate expectations of debtors who *in good faith* persuade creditors to reduce what may have been an exorbitant price. Consequently, the courts have been "astute to find consideration" if the debtor has done anything at all in connection with the payment that he or she was not originally obliged to do.[5] For example, suppose Bev is insolvent and on the verge of bankruptcy. If she agrees not to declare bankruptcy in exchange for Al's promise to accept $250 in full satisfaction of the debt, Al's promise is enforceable. This new agreement (if actually carried out) is an "accord and satisfaction" of Al's original claim against Bev. Their new agreement is the "accord," and its performance is the "satisfaction." The consideration needed for an accord and satisfaction can occur in many other ways—for example, where Bev (acting in good faith) pays Al $250 and, in addition, gives him a potato, or pays at a place other than that required by the contract, or pays before the due date of the original debt.

The courts are not the only protectors of debtors who have negotiated a lower payment in good faith. The undesirable consequences of the part payment rule to debtors has caused some state legislatures to modify or abolish it. For example, in California, New York, and Pennsylvania, a debtor may enforce a creditor's *written* release of a balance owed even though the debtor gave no new consideration. And under the UCC rule discussed earlier, many oral and all written sales contract modifications are binding without consideration.

[5]Murray, op. cit., Sec. 86.

Settlement of an unliquidated claim; payment-in-full checks. The part payment rule does not apply if the debt is *un*liquidated. A claim is unliquidated when there is an honest dispute about the existence of an indebtedness or, more commonly, about its amount. Al repairs Bev's bulldozer, saying nothing about the price, and he later sends her a bill for $350. Protesting that the bill is unreasonably high, Bev offers $250 as payment in full. Al reluctantly agrees to accept $250 as payment in full. Bev pays that amount, and Al later sues her for an additional $100. Al's promise to accept $250 is binding on him. Why?

In the absence of an agreement on price, Al is by law entitled to a reasonable price for his services. But by agreeing to accept the $250 that Bev offered, Al reached an accord with her—an agreement on price that replaces the reasonable price that a court would have imposed. What is reasonable is subject to dispute; consequently, Bev's debt is unliquidated. By giving up their respective rights to have a court decide what is reasonable, each gave consideration for the other's promise: Al for Bev's promise to pay $250, and Bev for Al's promise to accept it as payment in full. Bev's paying the $250 was a satisfaction of the accord.

The result would be the same if (with no prior agreement on price) Bev had sent Al a check for $250 marked "Payment in full of bulldozer repair bill," and Al cashed the check. Because Al knew or had reason to know the terms of Beth's offer of payment, his cashing the check is an acceptance that creates an accord. There is an accord even if Al crosses out the notation before cashing the check and later sues Bev for an additional $100. Obviously, Al has not in fact agreed to accept $250 as final payment, but largely to resolve disputes efficiently, the vast majority of courts treat check-cashing in these circumstances as conclusive evidence of the creditor's agreement to the terms offered. If Al wanted to pursue the $350, he should have returned Bev's "payment in full" check and brought suit for $350. He would, of course, run the risk that the court would find something less than $350 a reasonable payment for his services.[6]

[6]Can a person who receives a check marked "payment in full" nullify the effect of that language by adding a statement such as "This check is cashed under protest," and thus reserve a right to collect the balance allegedly owed? At least for the sale of goods, Section 1–207 of the UCC seems to permit such action, and the New York courts have so held. The states of Delaware,

What happens when a debtor owes an account that is partly liquidated and partly in dispute, and he or she offers a check made out for the liquidated amount but marked "payment in full" of the whole account? May the creditor cash the check and later collect the unliquidated portion of the debt? Some courts hold that the creditor may collect the balance of the claim. They reason that the debt is liquidated as to the amount admittedly due, the debtor has a pre-existing duty to pay it, and doing so therefore is not consideration for the creditor's promise (implied from cashing the check) to release the debtor from the balance of the claim. *Most* courts hold that the creditor cannot collect the unpaid balance. They reason that if any part of the claim is in dispute, the entire debt is unliquidated, and a payment offered and accepted as payment in full is a binding accord and satisfaction.

The case that follows involves an account that is partly liquidated and partly unliquidated. The debtor offers as full payment of the whole account an amount substantially less than the amount he admitted was due.

Florida, Massachusetts, and New Hampshire may be in agreement with the New York position. The courts of *most* states, however, hold that Section 1–207 does *not* replace the accord and satisfaction rule applying to payment-in-full checks. See Calamari & Perillo, op. cit., Sec. 4–11.

CASE 10.4 Field Lumber Co. v. Petty · 512 P.2d 764 (Wash. App. 1973)

FACTS Petty, a general contractor, made numerous purchases from Field Lumber Co. Field's ledger statement showed a balance of $1,752.21 in October 1970. Petty acknowledged a balance of $1,091.96 but disputed the difference of $660.25, which represented an allegedly unauthorized $292.60 purchase by an employee and a 1-percent-per-month finance charge. In early October 1970, Petty mailed a check for $500 to Field Lumber Co. with a letter—clear and definite in its terms—indicating that the check must be accepted in full settlement of the claim or returned. The letter also recited that the funds had been borrowed. In response, Field Lumber Co. notified Petty by telephone that it would require full payment but cashed the $500 check.

Field initiated action to recover the sum alleged to be due and owing. The trial court held that cashing the check under the circumstances discharged Petty from any further liability on the account. Field appealed.

OPINION FARRIS, J. . . . We reverse. We recognize the general rule that where a sum due is unliquidated or disputed and a remittance of an amount less than that claimed is sent to the creditor with a statement explaining that it is in full satisfaction of the claim, the acceptance of such a remittance by the creditor constitutes an accord and satisfaction.

However, this rule is not applicable where a portion of the alleged debt in excess of the amount paid is acknowledged and not in dispute. In such a case a debtor cannot unilaterally tender a lesser sum than that which it is agreed is due and owing and rely upon the retention of that sum as full settlement of the debt unless there is some additional consideration given therefor. An accord and satisfaction is founded on contract, and a consideration therefor is as necessary as for any other contract.

The recognition of a debt in a fixed amount and in excess of the $500 which was tendered under the circumstances here precludes the finding of an accord and satisfaction unless there is proof of new consideration. It has long been the rule in this state that payment of an amount admitted to be due can furnish no consideration for an accord and satisfaction of the entire claim.

Here we cannot find a scintilla of evidence indicating that any new consideration was given. Petty did not borrow the sum after agreeing with Field . . . that he would do so if it would be accepted as full settlement. He borrowed the money of his own volition and

CASE 10.4 Continued

then simply mailed the check with a letter after efforts had been made and were continuing to be made to recover the full amount. To find an accord and satisfaction here where a definite portion of the alleged debt was acknowledged to be due and owing and therefore liquidated and undisputed would place a creditor at a disadvantage in accepting partial payments from a reluctant debtor, since by doing so he would be jeopardizing his right to receive the balance, even though in law that balance was in fact due him. It is true that courts look with favor on compromise, but this means genuine compromise, arrived at through mutual agreement.

The payment of $500 here was a payment on account; whether the disputed sum of $660.25 is due and owing is a proper subject for litigation. The cause is remanded for determination of the question of the balance due on account.

JUDGMENT Reversed and remanded.

Composition Agreement

A *composition agreement* is an arrangement between a debtor and two or more creditors whereby the debtor, who is unable to pay the full amount owed, agrees to pay a smaller sum to each of the creditors, and they agree to accept their pro rata portions in *full* satisfaction of their claims. Don owes $6,000 to Al, $4,000 to Betty, and $2,000 to Carla. Unable to pay the whole amount because of business losses, Don offers his creditors a composition agreement under which each creditor is to receive 50 percent of his or her claim. If the creditors agree to cancel the balances owed, a composition results. In most states, Don will be discharged from his obligation to each of the participating creditors upon making the part payment he promised.

Sometimes the creditor tries to cancel the composition and collect the amount originally owed, arguing that the debtor gave no consideration for the creditor's promise to accept the smaller amount as full payment of the original, liquidated debt. The courts have found consideration in a variety of ways, some logical and some not. Some courts say, logically, that the legal detriment required to support the creditor's promise is the debtor's giving up his or her legal right to declare bankruptcy and thus have all the debts canceled in their entirety. Other courts say that a composition is really an agreement among creditors, with the debtor being a third-person beneficiary of their contract. Under it, each creditor incurs a legal detriment by giving up the right to force payment of the amount originally due, in exchange for the other creditor's promises to accept less as full payment.

Some courts do not attempt to justify enforcement of composition agreements on the basis of consideration. Instead, they base their decisions on the ground of public policy, reasoning that composition agreements settle a group of claims expeditiously at a minimum of expense to the parties, and that such out-of-court settlements lessen the ever-increasing volume of litigation.

A composition agreement applies only to the creditors who are parties to it. If Betty had refused to enter into the agreement discussed above, she would not have shared in the distribution of Don's assets; but neither would she be precluded from later attempting to collect the full $4,000 Don owed her.

Forbearance to Sue on a Claim

Every person has a right to litigate a valid claim. Giving up the right to do so is a legal detriment which, if bargained for, constitutes consideration. While driving their cars, Amy and Bob collide in an intersection. They are unsure who was at fault. However, thinking that Bob was more at fault than she was, Amy promises not to sue Bob if he agrees to pay her $2,500 (a reasonable estimate of her damages). Bob agrees but later refuses to make payment, and Amy sues him for breach of contract. Bob argues that his promise is unenforceable because Amy gave no consideration for it. Because Amy had a right to sue Bob for damages, she suffered a legal detriment when she promised not to sue him, and therefore gave consideration for his promise to pay the $2,500.

A person may believe that he or she has a valid claim (whether in tort or for breach of contract), when in fact it is invalid. Can a forbearance to sue be consideration if the forbearing person's claim turns out to be invalid? Because the courts favor out-of-court settlements, the answer usually is "yes," so long as the claim: (1) involves *uncertainty as to the facts or the law*, or (2) the promisor had a *good faith belief* at the time of contracting that the claim was valid. Al honestly believes that Bev has breached her contract with him, and he promises not to sue her if she will pay him $500. Although unconvinced that she breached it, Bev pays. Al's forbearance to sue is consideration for Bev's payment. This result seems sound because Al's belief in his claim is honest, Bev was uncertain, and out-of-court settlements ease the burden on the courts. Moreover, Bev could have refused to pay, thus forcing Al to decide whether it would be cost-effective to sue her.

In contrast, suppose that Al, knowing he has no contract with Bev, agrees not to sue her for its breach. Bev, erroneously thinking that she had contracted with Al (because she signed forty-three contracts last month), agrees to pay him $500. A person (Al) who agrees not to assert a clearly unfounded claim gives up nothing, incurs no legal detriment, and so gives no consideration for anything that might have been given in exchange for the alleged "forbearance."

Case 10.5 involves a person who agreed not to rescind (cancel) a contract.

CASE 10.5 Veilleux v. Merrill Lynch Relocation Management, Inc. · 309 S.E.2d 595 (Va. 1983)

FACTS Mary Veilleux entered into an agreement to purchase a residence from Merrill Lynch Relocation Management, Inc. for $126,000. Before the closing of the sale, Veilleux discovered the house had a leaky basement and she said that she did not want to purchase the house. The settlement date was imminent, and after some negotiations Veilleux agreed to sign the settlement papers in return for Merrill Lynch's promise to repair the basement. After the sale closed, work was done on the basement but it did not stop the leak. Veilleux then had the work done by a company known to her. Merrill Lynch refused to pay for the work, and Veilleux filed suit. The trial court held that there was no consideration for the promise to repair and gave judgment for Merrill Lynch. Veilleux appealed.

OPINION THOMAS, J. . . . In [its] opinion, the trial court stated the reasons for its ruling:

> Counsel for plaintiff [Veilleux] argued at trial that there were verbal contracts (i.e., assurances) made by the defendants [Merrill Lynch] that the water and water damage repairs would be made by the defendants. . . . Plaintiff's counsel argued at trial that the consideration for such verbal contracts was the plaintiff going to settlement on July 5, 1978. Case law in Virginia is clear that the mere act of going to settlement is not consideration for subsequent contracts where the party is performing an obligation that he is already obligated to perform. In this case the plaintiff had obligated herself to go to settlement since there was no basis for rescission of the contract to purchase the house. . . .

At the time the trial court ruled in this case, it did not have the benefit of our decision in *Pierce v. Plogger*. . . . *Pierce* is on all fours with the present case and controls its disposition. . . .

In disposing of *Pierce*, we addressed the question whether Pierce's forbearance to sue provided adequate consideration for the oral and written warranties. We held it did. . . . The trial court, in the instant case, was incorrect when it concluded that Veilleux had no cause of action in rescission. In our view, that erroneous conclusion was critical to the trial court's decision that there was a failure of consideration. Had the court been able to review *Pierce* it doubtless would have reached a different conclusion.

Counsel for Merrill Lynch attempts to distinguish *Pierce* on the ground that Pierce stated explicitly that he was bargaining for the oral and written warranties and that he

CASE 10.5 Continued

made an express agreement not to pursue a rescission claim. We think that attempted distinction is without merit....

The facts in this appeal do not, in our opinion, differ materially from those in *Pierce.* Veilleux refused to close until she received the oral promise to repair the basement. She did not say the words "I refuse to close until you promise to fix the basement." But her actions establish that refusal. Only after she received the promise did she sign the settlement papers. Prior to that time she made unmistakably clear that because of the leaky basement she did not want the house.... [W]hile... on cross-examination, she testified further as follows:

> If I had not been assured that the conditions on that house would have been put in order, I would have not signed the settlement papers. I would have gone, at that point, to get a lawyer who would protect me....

She could hardly have made her position any clearer. We have no doubt that had she not received the oral promise to repair the basement there would have been no settlement and she would have pursued her legal remedies against Merrill Lynch.

When she settled, she forbore to sue. She gave up a valuable right. What we said in *Hooff v. Paine*... applies with equal force here:

> The law is well settled that forbearance, or the promise of forbearance, to prosecute a well-founded or doubtful claim is a sufficient consideration for a contract.

Pierce establishes that she could have maintained a claim for rescission. *Pierce* also teaches that whether consideration is adequate is a question of law. In light of these authorities and upon our consideration of the facts we hold, as a matter of law, that there was consideration to support Merrill Lynch's promise to repair Veilleux's basement....

JUDGMENT Affirmed in part, reversed in part, and final judgment.

Promises Enforceable without Regard to Consideration

From the preceding discussion, it is fair to conclude that the concept of consideration is elusive and that the search for it is sometimes forced and arbitrary. Case 10.2 illustrates the point. There Prescott had promised not to engage in postemployment competition with his employer, Wright & Seaton. Later Prescott quit his job and worked for a competitor, contending that his promise was unenforceable for lack of consideration because Wright & Seaton's promise of employment was illusory. The court held that even though Wright & Seaton had a very broad right to terminate Prescott's employment, the promise of employment was not illusory. Wright & Seaton had agreed to give Preston *written* notice of termination, and incurring this small legal detriment was consideration for Prescott's promise.

Despite the triviality of the consideration in this case, the result seems sound because Wright & Seaton was performing its side of the bargain, while Prescott appears unreasonable in canceling the agreement late in the term of employment to avoid the noncompetition clause. But what if the *employer* had been the unreasonable one, intending, for example, to employ Prescott for a short time, fire him, and then invoke the 3-year noncompetition clause? If the court had mechanically applied the rule that "any detriment, no matter how small, constitutes consideration," injustice would result because the employer would be allowed to use a technical application of the consideration doctrine to impose hardship on the employee. Yet, if to avoid this injustice the court held that the requirement of written notice is *not* consideration, the resulting rule would be inconsistent with what had been decided before.

In fact, as many commentators have noted, the courts often have manipulated the doctrine of consideration to avoid injustice, thus creating confusion and inconsistency in the law. Whether a consideration requirement is needed at all has been questioned. Some commentators have urged that it be abandoned, and that contracting parties be required merely to indicate a "deliberate and serious intent" to make a contract. Most courts and legislatures, however, adhere to the traditional approach of creating exceptions to the consideration requirement. Some promises that are enforceable without consideration, such as modifications of sales contracts, have already been mentioned. The remainder of this chapter discusses other major exceptions to the consideration requirement.

Promises to Perform Prior Legal Duty

In most states, where a contractual duty has been terminated by operation of law, a subsequent promise to perform the terminated duty may be enforceable even if the promisor receives nothing in exchange for the new promise. Examples include a promise made: (1) following bar of the original duty by the statute of limitations, and (2) following a debtor's discharge in bankruptcy.

Promise Following Bar by Statute of Limitations. As noted in Chapter 1, all states have statutes of limitations prescribing time limits within which legal action must be started. A person who fails to bring his or her lawsuit within the time prescribed by the statute loses the right to do so. That is, the suit is "barred" by the statute. Ann contracts to pay Ben $500, Ann breaches the contract, and Ben fails to sue her within the time prescribed by the statute of limitations. Ann's contractual duty is discharged (extinguished), and Ben can never compel Ann to pay the discharged debt.

Suppose, however, that Ann later promises to pay Ben the discharged amount. Since Ben ordinarily will not have given any consideration for Ann's promise, is her promise to pay the barred debt enforceable? As a general rule, a debtor's written promise to pay a barred debt is enforceable without consideration. Moreover, in the absence of a writing, many courts treat a part payment by the debtor as an implied promise to pay the barred debt if the payment is voluntary and if the circumstances reveal an intention to pay the unpaid balance. Some judges say that the debt, together with "moral obligation," is sufficient "consideration" to support the new promise to pay. Other courts make clear that they are enforcing the new promise as an exception to the requirement of consideration, because they feel it is good public policy to do so.

Promise Following Discharge in Bankruptcy. Under federal bankruptcy law, a troubled debtor may receive a discharge in bankruptcy from his or her debts, and a financial "fresh start." Before 1978, debtors often "reaffirmed" one or more of the discharged debts and found themselves still obligated to pay even though they received no consideration for the new promise. Believing that many financial institutions were unfairly pressuring unwitting debtors into reaffirming their discharged debts and endangering their fresh start, the drafters of the 1978 Bankruptcy Code sharply limited the ability of debtors to make reaffirmation agreements. Today, no reaffirmation agreement is enforceable unless it: (1) was made *before* the discharge was granted, and (2) it complies with numerous Code-imposed rules designed to inform and protect the debtor. These rules are discussed in Chapter 26 under "Discharge Hearing; Reaffirmation; Protection of Discharge." If a reaffirmation agreement complies with them, it is enforceable even though the debtor receives no consideration for the new promise to pay.

Promises Enforceable Because of Promissory Estoppel

Promissory estoppel is an alternative to the doctrine of consideration as a basis for enforcing promises. As noted in Chapter 8, a promisor is "estopped" (prevented by law) from avoiding liability for the consequences of his or her promise if three circumstances are present:

1. There is a promise that the promisor should reasonably expect to induce action on the part of the promisee.
2. The promise induces such action—i.e., the promisee justifiably relies on the promise to his or her detriment. (Under *Restatement (Second)*, however, a charitable subscription, discussed later, is binding without proof that the promisee relied on it.)
3. Injustice can be avoided only by enforcement of the promise.

The doctrine of promissory estoppel originated as a basis for enforcing gift promises within the family (e.g., a promise to give land), charitable promises, and so on. Today it is a major basis for enforcing commercial promises as well—in particular, those anticipating a contract that never arose because there was no consideration or no acceptance of an offer. The construction industry provides an example. As noted in Chapter 8, it is impractical for a general contractor to make contracts with subcontractors before obtaining the prime contract. Yet, general contractors often rely on subcontractors' bids (promises) as a basis for preparing the prime bid and entering into the prime contract. If nothing more than traditional contract law were available for the protection of general contractors, they would face much uncertainty in their dealings. Promissory estoppel fills a gap in contract law.

The modern trend is to apply promissory estoppel even more broadly—for example, to promises made during the course of preliminary negotiations. In the case of *Hoffman v. Red Owl Stores, Inc.*,[7] the plaintiff sold his business, moved his family to another town, and purchased business property there in reliance on the defendant's assurances that the plaintiff would become the operator of one of the defendant's retail grocery stores. When the deal did not materialize, the plaintiff successfully invoked the doctrine of promissory estoppel, even though the defendant's representations were too indefinite to constitute a contractual offer. The elements of promissory estoppel were present: the promisor should have expected the action that the promisee took, and injustice could be avoided only by enforcing the defendant's promise. The court could not award damages for breach of contract, however, since there was no offer, no acceptance, and no consideration. Instead the court awarded plaintiff the amounts he had lost and expended in reliance on the promise.

Charitable Subscriptions

A *charitable subscription* is a promise to make a gift to a charity. "Charitable" refers not merely to institutions founded for the purpose of aiding people in unfortunate circumstances, but also to institutions such as churches, schools, colleges, libraries, museums, and hospitals. A "subscription" is usually a signed promise by each of several persons to contribute a sum of money specified on a subscription form. Are such gift promises enforceable?

Charitable subscriptions have been widely enforced in the United States, in keeping with the general feeling here that private philanthropy serves an important function in our society.[8] Some courts have purported to find consideration for charitable subscriptions in the exchange of promises among subscribers; other courts have found it in the implied promise of the charity to use the funds in accordance with the terms of the subscription agreement. The difficulty with these and other explanations based on the bargain theory of consideration is that in the typical charitable subscription the promisor does not have a bargaining intent, but intends only to make a gift. Consequently, modern courts tend to explain enforcement of such subscriptions on the basis of promissory estoppel instead of traditional consideration theory. However, because many charities could not show the detrimental reliance required by promissory estoppel, some courts have held that reliance is not required for the enforcement of charitable subscriptions. This is the position of Section 90 of the *Restatement (Second)*.

Summary

The courts enforce many types of promises. Formal contracts are enforceable because the promisor used legally required formalities. Informal promises may be enforced on the basis of:

1. Consideration
2. Promissory estoppel
3. Statutes and case law imposing liability for reasons of policy, where consideration or the circumstances required for promissory estoppel are lacking

Consideration may be defined as a legal detriment to the promisee, bargained for by the promisor. A legal detriment is the promisee's giving up a legal right. Usually a legal detriment to the prom-

[7] 133 N.W.2d 267 (Wis. 1965).

[8] Calamari & Perillo, op. cit., p. 280.

isee will be a legal benefit to the promisor, but benefit to the promisor is not required. For the detriment to be consideration, it must be induced by the promise and given in exchange for it. By defining consideration in terms of legal rather than actual benefits and detriments, the courts leave economic valuation to the contracting parties.

"Past consideration" is not consideration because the promise, having been made after the happening of the act for which it was given, did not induce the act. An illusory promise is not consideration because the promisor makes no enforceable commitment. Ordinarily, the courts will not look into the adequacy of consideration, except, for example, where inadequacy may be evidence of fraud or of intent to make a gift. Although consideration can have small economic value, sham or nominal consideration will not make a promise enforceable.

The performance of a pre-existing statutory or common law duty is not consideration for a promise. Nor is the performance of a pre-existing contractual duty consideration for a promise to pay or to do more than was originally agreed to. But if an existing contract is rescinded by mutual agreement, the parties are free to contract as they like.

Part payment of a liquidated claim is not consideration for the creditor's promise to accept the payment as payment in full. However, if the debtor makes a lesser payment and, in addition, does something he or she was not originally obligated to do, the creditor's promise to accept less is enforceable as an accord and satisfaction. Similarly, a creditor's cashing a check offered as payment in full of an *un*liquidated debt is an accord and satisfaction. A composition agreement is enforceable even though the agreement involves liquidated debts. A promise to forbear from suing another person is a legal detriment if the one forbearing had a valid claim, a doubtful claim, or an honest belief that his or her claim was valid.

Some promises are enforceable despite a lack of consideration—for example, modifications of sales contracts, a written promise to pay a debt that has been barred by a statute of limitations, and some bankruptcy reaffirmation agreements. Under the doctrine of promissory estoppel, a promise not supported by consideration may be enforceable if the promisee justifiably relied on the promise to his or her detriment.

Review Questions

1 (**a**) Briefly explain or describe four bases of promise enforcement used in our legal system. (**b**) As a basis of promise enforcement, how does consideration differ from promissory estoppel?

2 Explain the legal detriment theory of consideration.

3 Al insures his life for $100,000, naming his wife Tina as beneficiary. Diagram the movement of consideration.

4 Benita repairs the roof of her father's house. Pleased with her work, the father says, "Next week I'm going to pay you $300 for that job." Is the father's promise enforceable? Why or why not?

5 John agrees to sell his car to Hector for $2,000. The car has a market value of $4,000. Contending that the consideration is inadequate, John refuses to go through with the deal, and Hector sues John for breach of contract. (**a**) On these facts, will the court consider adequacy of consideration? (**b**) Under what circumstances, if any, would a court consider adequacy of the consideration?

6 Judge Sharp refuses to rule on Sue's case unless she agrees to pay him $100. Sue agrees, the judge rules, and Sue later refuses to pay the $100. Is Sue's promise enforceable?

7 Under what circumstances will a promise to accept part payment of a liquidated debt be binding on a creditor? Give examples.

8 Illustrate "accord and satisfaction" as it applies to: (**a**) a liquidated debt, and (**b**) an unliquidated debt.

9 Some courts hold that a composition agreement lacks consideration; yet such agreements are enforceable. On what ground are they enforceable?

10 Does forbearance to sue on a claim constitute consideration? Explain in terms of legal detriment.

11 A promise to pay a debt barred by the statute of limitations lacks consideration. Under what circumstances will such a promise be enforced?

12 To what kinds of promises was the doctrine of promissory estoppel originally applied? To what kinds is it applied today?

Case Problems

1 Boston Redevelopment Authority (BRA) purchased a building which housed the business of Graphic Arts Finishers. BRA promised to pay Graphic's relocation expenses if it would move out of the building. Graphic agreed to relocate and not to liquidate its business. BRA did not pay all of Graphic's moving expenses, and Graphic sued for breach of contract. BRA defended that there was no consideration for its promise. Who should win?

2 McIntyre entered into a contract (called a "listing agreement") with Century 21 under which McIntyre agreed to pay a 7 percent commission if Century 21 produced a buyer for his residence. A contract to sell the home was entered into shortly thereafter which contained a provision that the sale was contingent upon the buyers' acquiring a loan from the Veterans Administration. Before the V.A. makes a loan it inspects the property and specifies any needed repairs. The purchase agreement provided: "Any repair work necessary as a result of the inspection report may be done at Owner's expense, or at Owner's option this agreement may be terminated." McIntyre's home was inspected, but McIntyre elected not to pay for repairs specified by V.A. and gave notice that he was terminating the sale agreement. Century 21 then agreed to pay for the repairs from its commission. McIntyre again refused to complete the sale. Century 21 sued McIntyre for its commission, claiming it had produced a buyer for the residence. McIntyre defended that there was no enforceable contract of sale, that the owner's promise was illusory since he had the option to repair or to terminate the agreement. Was the owner's promise illusory?

3 Osborne had worked for 48 years for Locke Steel Chain Co. and was chairman of the board. He entered into an agreement with Locke whereby the company would pay him $15,000 a year for life. Osborne was to hold himself available for consultation and advice with the company and not to compete with the company in its domestic or foreign markets. The company paid Osborne for 3 years and then, after trying to reduce the payments, repudiated the contract. Locke claimed the consideration given by Osborne was inadequate to justify payment of $15,000 a year for life. Is this a sufficient reason to justify Locke's repudiation of the contract?

4 Argeros successfully bid on and entered into a contract with Pennsylvania to paint all metal surfaces on five bridges. The contract described bridge No. 4 as including an "open type steel beam bridge flooring." The weight of the bridge was shown as "approximately 180 tons." Argeros looked at the bridge prior to submitting his bid but did not calculate its dimensions. While painting bridge No. 4, he determined that it weighed 260 tons and requested extra compensation. The Pennsylvania Deputy Chief Engineer instructed Argeros to complete the work, which he did. Argeros then filed a claim for $6,900 for painting the surfaces represented by the additional tonnage. Argeros asserted that the engineer's instruction was an oral modification of the contract and that he performed extra work pursuant to the oral modification of the original contract. Should his claim be allowed?

5 In 1976 Ramona and Lee dissolved their marriage, and Ramona was granted $200 per month as a single sum for the support of two minor children. By 1981 Lee was behind $7,800 in payments. Ramona offered to settle the back child support for $4,500 and to amend the decree of divorce to provide for $100 per month after February 1, 1981. Lee agreed to pay $1,000 in cash and to give Ramona his note for $3,500 in full satisfaction of back child support. Ramona accepted the proposal and Lee, in reliance on the agreement, borrowed a substantial sum of money to meet business obligations. Ramona then secured a court order to attach $7,800 of the loan proceeds. Lee filed suit for the return of the funds, claiming there was an accord, which satisfied his obligation of back child support. Was there an accord?

6 Fred was driving an automobile owned by his employer when it was hit by a pickup truck insured by Aetna. Fred suffered personal injuries and filed a claim against Aetna. A claims adjuster contacted Fred and offered a settlement. She said that Aetna would pay him $184.25 for medical bills and $200 for his injuries. Aetna sent a check for $384.25 on the front of which was written in block letters "CLAIM SETTLEMENT." Fred endorsed the check on the back and wrote underneath "NOT A RELEASE OF ANY CLAIMS," and deposited the check. Fred sued Aetna for damages for his personal injuries. Aetna defended that there was an accord and satisfaction. Who should win?

7 Benjamin Ravelo was a police officer with the Honolulu Police Department. He applied for a position with the County of Hawaii Police Department and was accepted. A letter from the county stated that he would be sworn in as a police recruit on January 2, 1979. After receiving the letter, he resigned from the Honolulu Police Department, and his wife, Marlene, resigned from her job. They made plans to move from Honolulu to Hilo and to remove their children from private school. On December 20, 1978, Benjamin was informed by the county that he was not going to be hired after all. Mr.

and Mrs. Ravelo tried but could not get their jobs back. They both sued the county for breach of contract. The county defended that under the civil service law Benjamin would only have been a probationary employee whose employment was terminable without cause at any time during his probationary period. The trial court held that there was no basis for breach of contract and dismissed the complaint. Was the trial court correct?

CHAPTER 11

Avoidance of Agreement

If people could escape their contractual obligations for trivial reasons, our economic system could be seriously undermined. In the interest of economic stability, therefore, a court usually will enforce a contract without regard to whether a party made a good or a bad bargain. Even a contract of adhesion (standard-form contract) normally will be enforced, as long as the party with the superior bargaining power does not exercise it in an oppressive way.

Yet, where the circumstances warrant, the courts permit people to avoid (cancel) their contracts. For example, the law allows insane persons to avoid contracts for lack of capacity. Similarly, minors' contracts; contracts entered into by mistake; those induced by duress, undue influence, or fraud; and unconscionable contracts may be avoided.

A person may exercise the power of avoidance in a variety of ways. One might do so simply by returning unwanted goods and demanding his or her money back, or in some other way making clear to the other party that the contract is no longer in effect. This is called "rescinding" or "disaffirming" the contract. Or, if the other party brings suit to enforce the contract, the party wishing to avoid (disaffirm) it need only plead his or her right of avoidance as an affirmative defense. Sometimes a person will feel the need to go to court to exercise the power of avoidance, and so will seek the *equitable remedy of rescission.* To rescind the contract in this formal way, the plaintiff ordinarily must: (1) act promptly and fairly, (2) return or offer to return anything received from the other party, and (3) demand the return of whatever the rescinding party gave to the other party. As noted later in this chapter, the requirements for rescission are applied a bit differently to minors than to adults.

This chapter deals with four major bases for avoiding an agreement: (1) lack of (or limited) contractual capacity, (2) a defect in the assent required for a bargained-for exchange, (3) unconscionability, and (4) consumer protection statutes granting consumers a right of avoidance.

Avoidance on Ground of Incapacity

Capacity is the ability or power to do something. A person has *contractual capacity* if he or she: (1) is mentally able to understand the nature and consequences of making a contract, (2) is physically able to manifest assent to a bargain, and (3) is permitted by law to make the contract in question. A person who lacks or suffers an impairment of these abilities is under a *disability,* and so has a total or partial *incapacity* (lack of capacity). Most people have "full" contractual capacity; that is, they are capable of contracting on the full range of topics permitted by law to be the subject of contracts. A few (e.g., some insane persons) have no capacity to contract. Between these extremes are persons having "limited" contractual power. Minors, for example, are presumed to have a disability common to youth—immaturity and inexperience that make them vulnerable to exploitation by others. So, although minors generally are permitted to make contracts, the law protects minors from their disability by making most of their contracts voidable. In a few states minors cannot make certain kinds of contracts—for example, in California, a contract involving land.

When a person brings suit to enforce a contract, the court presumes that both parties possessed full contractual capacity when the contract was made. To counter this presumption, the defending party must allege that at the time of contracting he or she lacked contractual capacity. The following discussion deals first with the contractual capacity of minors, and then with the contractual capacity of mentally incompetent persons and persons temporarily under the influence of alcohol or other drugs.

Contractual Capacity of Minors

At common law, persons under the age of adulthood were called "infants." Today they are commonly referred to as "minors."

For centuries, the law has permitted minors to avoid or "disaffirm" most of their contracts. The reasons include:

- Minors need protection from their immaturity, inexperience, and tendency to buy impulsively.
- They are especially likely to be the victims of unscrupulous adults.
- Young minors may not understand the nature and consequences of their contracts.

The policy of protecting minors is very strong. In furtherance of that policy, the law gives minors a right: (1) to enforce contracts against adult parties or (2) to disaffirm such contracts without any showing of misconduct by the adult. However, the one-sidedness of the right to disaffirm has caused some people to refuse to contract with minors. Consequently, minors may be unable to acquire essential goods and services. To encourage businesses to supply such "necessaries," the law requires minors to pay for them to the extent discussed later in this chapter.

Within recent years, there has been growing concern that minors may be receiving too much protection at the expense of adults who treat minors fairly. Perhaps because of advances in education, older minors may be more sophisticated than they once were and thus more likely to take advantage of unsuspecting adults. In part to protect the legitimate interests of adults, the statutes and judicial decisions of most states impose limits on the right of minors to disaffirm contracts. These limits vary greatly from state to state. Some of the more common ones are discussed later in this chapter—for example, statutes making certain types of contracts enforceable against minors even though the thing supplied may not be a "necessary."

Period of Minority. The age at which the period of minority ends and the minor achieves full contractual capacity (that is, loses the right to disaffirm) does not necessarily correspond with the age or ages that a state sets for other purposes. Thus, a statute in a particular state may set one age at which a person has the capacity to make a will, another age for acquiring a driver's license, and still another for legally purchasing liquor. In the vast majority of states, the age of majority for most *contract* purposes has been lowered from 21 (the traditional common law age of majority) to 18.

In a few states a person becomes of age (acquires full contractual capacity) upon marriage prior to age 18, but in most states married minors retain their right of disaffirmance. At one time, some states had laws stating that only females become of age upon marriage. Thus, it was possible that when a couple married while under age, the husband remained a minor but the wife became an adult. The U.S. Supreme Court has now held that states may not establish one age of majority for males and a different age for females unless the classification by gender serves some important governmental objective and is substantially related to the achievement of that objective.[1]

A number of states have a statutory procedure for "judicial emancipation" of minors (i.e., for freeing them from legal restraints). The statutes require a petition by or on behalf of the minor and also a court hearing. The court investigates the facts, and if the judge finds that removal of disabilities is in the best interests of the minor and that the minor is capable of tending to his or her own affairs or business, the judge will sign an order of emancipation. The effect of the order is to enable the minor to enter into contracts as if the minor were an adult—that is, without benefit of a right to disaffirm on the ground of minority. Thus, adults are encouraged to do business with emancipated minors.

There is also a form of emancipation (sometimes called "parental emancipation") in which parents surrender their right to the care, custody, and earnings of their minor child and renounce their parental duties. Parental emancipation occurs, for example, where the minor is working and the parents consent to the minor's leaving home and establishing a separate residence. Parental emancipation has no effect upon the contractual capacity of the minor; the minor still may disaffirm his or her contracts.

Disaffirmance of Minors' Voidable Contracts. The general rule is that a minor's contract is voidable by the minor. Exercise of the power of avoidance is commonly referred to as the "disaffirmance" of the contract.

Nature of disaffirmance. The right of a minor to disaffirm a contract is absolute. Consequently, the minor needs no reason to disaffirm and may do so regardless of his or her personal experience, education, or sophistication. Thus, a minor who is 17 years and 11 months old and is well-versed in the law of minors' rights has the same right to disaffirm as does a child of 10.

Most courts hold that the power of disaffirmance is personal to the minor. This means that during the minor's lifetime, only the minor or a legally appointed guardian may exercise the power, and upon the minor's death only the minor's heirs or a personal representative may exercise it. An adult party to a contract with a minor has no similar power

[1]*Craig v. Boren*, 429 U.S. 190, 197 (1976).

of disaffirmance; the adult is bound to the contract unless the minor disaffirms it. Where both parties to a contract are minors, each has a power of disaffirmance.

Requirements for disaffirmance. A minor may avoid (disaffirm) a contract in any way that makes clear his or her unwillingness to be bound by the contract. The disaffirmance may be oral or written, and it may be accomplished with or without a lawsuit. If the other party sues the minor to enforce the contract, the minor may disaffirm by pleading minority as a defense. Or the minor may disaffirm by filing a suit to set aside the transaction. More commonly, a minor will disaffirm by, for example, simply returning unwanted goods and demanding the return of anything paid for them.

Whatever the method of disaffirmance, the law of most states requires the minor to: (1) disaffirm during minority or within a reasonable time after attaining majority, (2) demand the return of any consideration (e.g., money or goods) transferred to the other party, and (3) return or offer to return any consideration received if it is still in the minor's possession. What constitutes a reasonable time after attaining majority depends on the circumstances of the case. Suppose Mel, a minor, buys an expensive racing bicycle, uses it every day, and soon after his eighteenth birthday decides to disaffirm the contract. Mel will have relatively little time to disaffirm. His frequent use of the bicycle reduces its value. Allowing Mel to continue using it a long time after reaching majority and then to disaffirm the contract would be unjust to the seller. In contrast, if Mel had never used the bicycle, or if he had used it infrequently, the court might allow him a longer time after reaching majority to disaffirm.

Upon disaffirmance, a minor is entitled to the return of any property still in the hands of the other contracting party (or to its value if it cannot be returned). However, under Section 2-403(1) of the UCC, a minor may not recover *goods* from an innocent *third-person* ("bona fide") purchaser—that is, from a person who purchased them without knowing that the seller had purchased them from a minor. Suppose Mary, a minor, sells her car to Alice, an adult. If Mary disaffirms the contract while Alice still has the car, Mary is entitled to have the car back from Alice. But suppose Alice sells the car to Tom and delivers it to him before Mary disaffirms the contract with Alice. If Tom had no notice of Mary's minority, he is entitled to keep the car, and Mary's only recourse is against Alice for its value. Some states have enacted statutes extending this Code principle to contracts other than those for the sale of goods.

Upon disaffirmance, the minor must return whatever was received if it is still in his or her possession. The courts are not in agreement on whether the minor can disaffirm when unable to return the property received or when able to return it only in damaged condition. The majority view is that the minor may disaffirm even though the property received has been lost, destroyed, or damaged. One justification for this rule is that the same immaturity of judgment which causes minors to enter into improvident contracts causes them to be careless in using and guarding the property received. The minority view is that a minor is not permitted to disaffirm a contract unless he or she pays for benefits received, or accounts at least for depreciation not caused by negligence. Under either rule—majority or minority—if the minor has sold or exchanged property purchased from the adult and still has the proceeds of the sale or exchange, the minor must transfer the proceeds to the adult. Case 11.1 discusses the requirements for disaffirmance and applies the majority rule.

CASE 11.1 Star Chevrolet Co. v. Green · 473 So. 2d 157 (Miss. 1985)

FACTS Kevin Green was 16 years old on August 14, 1981, when he purchased a 1979 Camaro automobile for $4,642.50 from Star Chevrolet. The car became inoperable because of a blown head gasket. In November 1981, Kevin informed Star Chevrolet that he was disaffirming the contract, and he demanded the return of the purchase price. He offered to return the Camaro, but Star Chevrolet would not accept it unless it was restored to its original condition.

CASE 11.1 Continued

In January 1982, Kevin brought suit for the purchase price. The car sat for 4 or 5 months until Kevin finally replaced the head gasket himself and drove the car. In June 1982, the Camaro was heavily damaged in an accident, after which the car had a salvage value of $1,500. Kevin was credited with the salvage value in an insurance settlement, the proceeds of which he used to buy another car. Later Kevin received a judgment for the purchase price of the car, and Star Chevrolet appealed.

OPINION

SULLIVAN, J. . . . Upon disaffirmance of a minor's contract, he is required to return the consideration received by him if he still has such consideration in his possession, or if it is within his powers to do so. . . . This requirement can be complied with not only by an actual return of the consideration but also by a tender or offer to return it. . . .

From the time Kevin disaffirmed the contract in November, 1981, until suit was filed, Star Chevrolet refused to fully refund the purchase price unless the Camaro's blown head gasket was repaired. This position was erroneous. . . . Kevin's duty to tender the vehicle was not contingent upon its restoration to [its] condition at the time of sale. . . . We [also reject the contention] that Kevin's tender was inadequate because he failed to engage a wrecker to transport the vehicle . . . , when it appears that to do so would have been a vain or useless thing, since [Star Chevrolet] would not have [made] the full refund to which [Kevin] was entitled under law. Accordingly, we hold that the complaint for rescission, including [a copy of] the . . . letter of disaffirmance, sufficiently alleged an offer of tender. . . .

. . . [T]he right of a minor to disaffirm his contract is based upon sound public policy to protect the minor from his own improvidence and the overreaching of adults. . . . It is the policy of the law to discourage adults from contracting with minors, and the adult cannot complain if, as a consequence of his violation of this rule of conduct, he is injured by the minor's exercise of the right of disaffirmance, since this injury might have been avoided if the adult had declined to enter into the contract. . . . The general rule is that upon disaffirmance of a minor's contract, he is required to return the consideration only if it is still in his possession. The minor who disaffirms a contract is not obliged to return the consideration received by him or its equivalent where during his minority he has wasted, squandered, destroyed, used, or otherwise disposed of the consideration. . . .

Finally, depreciation in the value of the vehicle due to the minor's misuse or neglect, short of [an] intentional or grossly negligent act amounting to an independent tort, is not allowable by way of recoupment. In other words, the minor is not liable for damages [resulting from] the very improvidence and indiscretion of infancy against which the law seeks to protect him. . . .

Turning to the facts of this case, the minor clearly had the consideration, i.e., the vehicle, in his possession when he first notified appellant of the disaffirmance of the contract. Had appellant [Star Chevrolet] offered the minor, as the law required, a full refund of his purchase price, the minor clearly would have been required to return the vehicle. . . . Instead, the appellant did not, and while suit was pending the minor repaired the vehicle and began to use it. There is no hint in the record that the accident which destroyed the vehicle was the result of any deliberate design on the minor's part to fraudulently deprive appellant of that which would have placed him in status quo. For aught that appears in the record, the accident was caused by [ordinary] carelessness and improvidence [of the minor]. Disaffirmance at this point would have required the appellant to refund the full purchase price and the appellee, in turn, to return the damaged Camaro, since the law does not condition a minor's right to disaffirm a contract upon placing the other party in status quo, but . . . requires [only] the return of whatever consideration remains in the minor's hands. . . .

. . . We are urged to offset the minor's recovery by the $1,500 salvage value of the [Camaro] on the ground that the minor had the duty to tender this consideration to appellant in order to receive a refund of the full purchase price.

CASE 11.1 Continued

We are persuaded that the appellant's contention is sound. . . . Accordingly, the damages assessed against Star Chevrolet Company are reduced from $4,642.50 to $3,142.50.

JUDGMENT Affirmed as modified.

Effect of misrepresentation of age. Most courts hold that a minor who has intentionally misrepresented his or her age is not thereby prevented from avoiding the contract. However, there is a conflict of authority on whether the minor is liable in tort for that misrepresentation. It is well established that minors are liable for their torts generally, and most courts hold that a minor is liable for the tort of deceit (fraud). This majority view reflects a belief that the law's protection should not extend so far as to insulate minors from their intentional wrongdoing. The minority view is that the minor should *not* be held liable in deceit, because such liability enables the adult to enforce indirectly a contract that the law permits the minor to avoid. The minority view is based on the idea that lying about one's age is a folly of youth from which a minor should be protected.

Ratification of Minor's Voidable Contracts. In a broad sense, "ratification" means the confirmation of a previous act or promise. When used in connection with minors' contracts, ratification means a manifestation of an intention to be bound by a contract entered into during the period of minority. The minor cannot ratify a contract until he or she becomes of age. Any purported ratification during minority is ineffective.

A contract may be ratified in one of three ways: by express ratification, by implied ratification, or by failure to make a timely disaffirmance. An *express ratification* is one in which the intention to be bound by a contract previously made is expressed in words. Unless a statute provides otherwise, ratification may be made orally. No particular form of expression is required. Any wording suffices as long as it indicates an intention to be bound. Making a definite promise to perform a contract previously entered into is one way of expressing such an intention.

An *implied ratification* is one in which an intention to be bound is inferred from the person's conduct. For example, suppose that Brenda enters into a contract 3 months before reaching her majority. Under the terms of the contract she receives some diving gear for which she is to pay later. Two months after reaching her majority, she sells the gear. Disposal of the gear is an act inconsistent with an intent to disaffirm and thus may be held to constitute ratification. Other conduct from which ratification may be inferred includes using property purchased for more than a reasonable time after majority and part payment or other performance of contract terms after reaching majority.

As noted earlier, to disaffirm a contract, a minor must take action during minority or within a reasonable time after attaining majority. Failure to disaffirm within a reasonable time after attaining majority results in a ratification. In determining a reasonable time, some courts consider whether the contract is executory or executed. These courts permit a person to wait much longer to disaffirm an executory contract than an executed one, provided such delay does not prejudice the other party to the contract.

Contracts That Minors Cannot Disaffirm. The general rule that minors may avoid their contracts is subject to certain exceptions. Some of these exceptions have been created by statutes. Examples are a statute which provides that minors who are emancipated by court order cannot avoid contracts and a statute negating the right of minors to avoid the payment of student loans to pursue advanced education.

In some states there are statutes requiring a court to approve certain minors' contracts, such as contracts of employment as an entertainer or professional athlete. Many states have statutes providing that a court must approve a contract compromising a minor's tort claim, as for example a negligence suit for injuries sustained in an automobile accident. The minor may not later disaffirm a court-approved contract.

Other exceptions to the general rule have been created by court action. For example, minors generally cannot disaffirm their bailbond contracts, because permitting avoidance "would be contrary to sound public policy." Some of the court-created exceptions can be explained only on the ground that on entering into the contract, the minor had promised to do something which the law would require the minor to do even in the absence of a contract. For example, a minor father who contracted to support his illegitimate child was not permitted to avoid the contract, because in entering into the contract he promised to do only what he would be required to do under a rule of the common law.

Where a minor owns property, a court may, upon petition, appoint a guardian to manage the estate of the minor. The guardian may sell the minor's property when appropriate, and the sale is not subject to disaffirmance.

Liability of Minors for Necessaries. Ordinarily, a minor's parents or guardian will provide the minor with food, clothing, housing, and other necessities of life. If the parent or guardian is unable or unwilling to do so, the minor may purchase such "necessaries." May the minor later disaffirm the contract?

Nature of liability for necessaries. A minor who contracts for necessaries may disaffirm the contract in accordance with the general rule regarding minors' contracts. However, the minor may be liable *in quasi contract* to the provider of the necessaries, for their reasonable value. The law places this liability on minors mainly for their protection. If minors could avoid all obligation to pay, they might have difficulty in securing necessaries.

The quasi-contractual liability of minors for necessaries is their *reasonable value* only, and not the perhaps higher amount the disaffirmed contract might have imposed. Suppose Mary, a minor, signs a contract to lease an apartment for 1 year at a rental of $500 per month. Her contractual liability is $6,000. After 3 months, Mary disaffirms the contract and vacates the apartment without having paid any rent. By disaffirming, Mary avoids the duty to pay for the apartment for 12 months, and she is no longer bound to the $500 monthly rate specified in the now-ineffective lease contract. She is liable instead for the reasonable value of the 3 months' housing she actually received. That amount might be more or less than the rental amount stated in the lease. If a court decides that $300 per month is reasonable, Mary's former landlord is entitled to $900.

Goods and services recognized as necessaries. Since goods or services might be recognized as necessaries in one situation and not in another, "necessaries" is a relative term. One factor determining whether a good or service is a necessary is the minor's *station in life.* Clothing of high quality and fashion may be a necessary for a minor whose father is a diplomat, but not for one whose father is a factory worker. Another factor is whether the minor was *emancipated* at the time the contract was made. Parents are legally obligated to provide necessaries for their unemancipated children; a minor is not liable for necessaries so long as the minor's parent or guardian supplies them. Food, for example, is *not* a necessary for a minor whose parents provide an adequate supply. However, in many states, when a minor is emancipated the parents are relieved of the obligation to provide necessaries for the child. Consequently, after emancipation, a minor may be liable for the reasonable value of his or her own necessaries.

Courts have held that food, clothing, shelter, medical services, tools of a trade, and some degree of education are necessaries. Other goods and services have been so characterized by some courts. Examples are a reasonable fee for legal services for the enforcement of a tort claim and a reasonable fee paid to an employment agency for assistance in finding a job for a married minor.

Case 11.2 discusses the liability of the parents of an unemancipated minor for her necessaries.

CASE 11.2 Madison General Hospital v. Haack · 369 N.W.2d 663 (Wis. 1985)

FACTS Debra Hughes, then 16 years old, was admitted to Madison General Hospital on February 3, 1976, in order to have a baby. She was living with her parents and had no financial assets. The baby was delivered by caesarean section on February 16. On April 12, 1976,

CASE 11.2 Continued

Bruce Haack and Debra were married. The hospital attempted unsuccessfully to collect the unpaid portion of its bill and filed suit against Debra and Bruce Haack. The circuit court dismissed the claim against Debra and Bruce. Madison General Hospital appealed.

OPINION

ABRAHAMSON, J. . . . Emergency medical services are generally considered necessaries, and this point is not in dispute in this case. . . .

The essence of the hospital's argument is that Debra Haack is liable for the medical expenses under a theory of unjust enrichment, that is, a quasi-contractual obligation imposed by law. . . .

The hospital's theory of Debra Haack's liability under the doctrine of unjust enrichment, however, overlooks the fact that when a minor has not contracted for necessaries, the law has traditionally imposed a quasi-contractual liability on a minor's father, not on the minor, under the doctrine of necessaries. . . . A parent's quasi-contractual obligation, under the doctrine of necessaries, arises because a third party has fulfilled the legal obligation of the parent to support the minor. Traditionally the law imposed the duty of support for the minor on the male parent. Today the wife shares with the husband the legal duty of support of the family. . . . Under the common law doctrine of necessaries, the party or parties unjustly enriched by the medical care provided Debra Haack and liable for payment of the medical expenses appear to be one or both of Debra Haack's parents. . . .

The hospital, however, asserts that Debra Haack is liable for payment for medical services because her parents defaulted in paying for the medical services. . . .

Although courts suggest that a minor may be liable for necessaries if a parent defaults in payment, these courts frequently refuse to hold the minor liable, determining that the proof of the parent's neglect, failure, refusal, or inability to pay is insufficient.

Even if we were to conclude that a minor should be liable for medical expenses when a parent neglects, fails, refuses, or is unable to pay, we would conclude that the record in this case is insufficient to establish the parents' neglect, failure, refusal, or inability to pay. There is no evidence that the hospital ever sought payment from Mrs. Hughes. With regard to Mr. Hughes we know only that he apparently resided at the same address as Debra Haack at the time the medical services were rendered, that the hospital was unsuccessful in collecting payment from his health insurer, that the hospital may have mailed some bills to him, that he apparently left Wisconsin after the infant's birth, and that the hospital filed suit more than four years after the medical services had been rendered and failed to obtain service on him.

On the basis of this record, we conclude that Debra Haack is not liable to the hospital for the medical services furnished to her. . . .

There is a sense of uneasiness attached to following traditional common law and concluding that Debra Haack need not pay for the medical services she received. She appears to be profiting at the expense of the hospital, which did its best for her welfare. . . . We recognize that the laws relating to the capacity of infants to contract balance society's interests in protecting the minor and the family against interests in protecting innocent creditors. Similarly the doctrine of necessaries and the various exceptions thereto make this balance. We have been unwilling to modify the traditional rules governing infants' contractual liability, saying modification is best left to the legislature. . . .

We turn now to the question of Bruce Haack's liability for the medical expenses incurred by Debra Haack at the time of the birth of the infant. . . . In deciding this question we consider two fact situations that "might have occurred," and the legal consequences that would have followed from each of them. First, Bruce and Debra Haack might have married prior to the birth of their infant. In this event, Bruce Haack probably would have been liable for the expenses under the doctrine of necessaries. . . .

Second, Bruce Haack and Debra Hughes might not have married, in which case Debra Hughes could have instituted paternity proceedings against Bruce Haack. In 1976 the

CASE 11.2 Continued

circuit court would have been required to order Bruce Haack "to pay all expenses incurred for lying-in and attendance of the mother during pregnancy. . . ."

Considering the policies underlying both the doctrine of necessaries and the paternity statute, we conclude that it would be inequitable and against public policy to allow Bruce Haack to escape liability for Debra Haack's medical care arising from her pregnancy merely because the marriage took place after the birth of the infant instead of before the birth. . . . We also conclude that it is consistent with the doctrine of necessaries to hold Bruce Haack liable for the medical expenses in this case. Clearly a benefit has been conferred upon Bruce Haack. It would be inequitable if he were not obliged to compensate the hospital for the services rendered to the mother of his infant.

JUDGMENT For the reasons set forth, we affirm the judgment of the circuit court dismissing the claim against Debra Haack, and we reverse the judgment of the circuit court dismissing the claim against Bruce Haack. . . .

Contractual Capacity of Other Persons

Mentally Incompetent Persons. Ordinarily, a contract made by a person who is mentally incompetent is voidable, just as a contract made by a minor is voidable and for the same reason—to protect persons unable to protect themselves against imposition. In protecting the mentally incompetent, however, the law seeks also to protect the justifiable expectations of the other contracting party.

Test of mental incompetency. There are many types of mental incompetency. Among them are the traditional forms of mental illness or insanity, congenital deficiencies in intelligence, and mental disability resulting from old age, accidents, or organic disease. Mental incompetency may be mild or severe. The general test for determining whether a person should be allowed to avoid a contract on the ground of mental incompetency may be stated thus: Did the person have, at the time of entering into the contract, sufficient mental capacity to understand the nature and consequences of the transaction?

A person suffering from mental illness may have "lucid intervals," i.e., may from time to time regain the ability to understand his or her business affairs. A contract made during such an interval is binding on both parties. Where a mentally ill person has some understanding of a transaction, his or her right to avoid the contract will depend on whether the other party was aware of the mental impairment and on whether the impaired person received adequate consideration. Courts often grant rescission in these "gray-area" cases on the grounds of undue influence, fraud, or duress.

Effect of mental incompetency. The courts consider a number of factors when deciding what effect mental incompetency should have on the impaired person's agreements. Two key ones are: (1) Was the transaction executory or executed? (2) Before the transaction occurred, had a court declared the impaired person mentally incompetent and appointed a guardian for him or her?

A mentally impaired person may enter into a contract without having been diagnosed as mentally incompetent or declared so by a court. Such a person's *executory* contract is avoidable, either by the impaired person upon regaining mental capacity or by a legal representative who might later have been appointed to act on his or her behalf. If the contract was *executed,* however, and the other party had no reason to know of the mental incompetency, the contract is *not* avoidable if under the circumstances avoidance would be unjust to the other party.

Sometimes a court declares a person to be mentally incompetent and appoints a guardian (or conservator) to handle his or her affairs. After the adjudication of incompetency, only the guardian can make contracts for the incompetent, and any agreements made by the incompetent person after the adjudication are *void,* not voidable. This is significant where the incompetent party's property finds its way into the hands of a third person. Suppose a court declares Mel mentally incompetent and appoints a guardian for him, and later Mel sells his car to Brad for a tenth of its value. Then Brad sells the car to Cora for its full value and leaves the country. Cora knew nothing of the transaction between Mel and Brad. Since Mel's agreement was void, Brad did not receive ownership of the car, and neither did Cora. Mel is entitled to the car; Cora's only recourse is against Brad.

Like minors, mentally incompetent persons are liable in quasi contract for the reasonable value of necessaries.

Persons under the Influence of Alcohol or Other Drugs. In most respects, the law treats the contracts of persons who are acting under the influence of alcohol or other drugs the same way it treats the contracts of mentally incompetent persons. For example, where a guardian or conservator has been appointed to handle the property of a drug abuser or chronic alcoholic, any transaction entered into thereafter by the impaired person is void. Where no guardian or conservator has been appointed, an intoxicated person's transactions are usually held to be voidable.

As is true of mental incompetency, there are degrees of being intoxicated or under the influence of drugs. Relief will be granted if at the time of contracting the person is so intoxicated or so under the influence of drugs that he or she does not understand the nature and consequences of the transaction. Where the intoxicated person has some understanding despite intoxication, avoidance will depend on whether the other party was aware of the intoxication and whether the consideration for the intoxicated person's promise was inadequate.

A person who lacks understanding as a result of using alcohol or other drugs is liable in quasi contract for the reasonable value of necessaries.

Avoidance on Ground of Defective Assent

The bargain theory of contracts is fundamental to a free enterprise system. It was assumed in discussing offer, acceptance, and consideration that the parties acted freely in the marketplace so that genuine assent could be achieved. Occasionally that assumption of an environment of free exchange is put in question. One party may coerce the other by various improper means to assent to an agreement. A party may use a position of trust or confidence to unfairly persuade the other party to enter a contract. A party may even lie to induce the other to assent to a contract. At other times a party may innocently misrepresent an important fact, or both parties may enter a contract holding mistaken beliefs about important facts.

A party should not be held to a bargain made under any of the circumstances stated. Following is a discussion of five recognized grounds for avoiding a contract: duress, undue influence, fraud, misrepresentation, and mistake, each of which results in defective assent.

Duress

Meaning of Duress. As traditionally defined, *duress* is a a wrongful threat, by words or conduct, that induces such fear on the part of the person threatened as to overcome his or her free will. Many courts today view duress as a wrongful threat that induces assent on the part of a victim who has *no reasonable alternative* but to do what the threatening party demands, such as signing a contract very unfavorable to the victim. Typically, the threatening party gains money or property to which he or she is not entitled. The resulting contract is voidable by the victim.

Elements of Duress. The traditional elements of duress are: (1) a wrongful threat, and (2) fear that overcomes the victim's free will.

Wrongful threat. Much business conduct involves express or implied threats that are not wrongful. Threatening to deal with someone else if a supplier will not give one a better price is the essence of healthy competition, and in the absence of extraordinary circumstances certainly is not wrongful. Nor is it wrongful to threaten a civil lawsuit in a good-faith effort to reach an out-of-court settlement of a dispute. But many kinds of threats are wrongful and can lead to duress. They include threats to the person, threats to property, and threats to one's business or means of earning a living.

Threats to the *person* may take the form of:

1 A threat to injure the person being threatened; his or her spouse, child, or other relative; or any other person such as an em-

ployee, if the threat actually induces the threatened person's assent.

2 A threat of criminal prosecution (directed at the threatened person or at others such as his or her spouse or child) to force the threatened person to make a contract. Ann discovers that Ben, her employee, has stolen goods from her, and threatens him with criminal proceedings unless he agrees to pay her $3,000. Fearing he will be sent to prison, Ben agrees. He is under duress and may rescind the contract. The harsh sanctions of the criminal law are intended to promote the safety of the public, and Ann is misusing them to force the settlement of a private dispute. Furthermore, by agreeing to suppress prosecution if Ben will pay, and thus interfering with the state's ability to challenge criminal conduct, Ann acts contrary to the public good. Instead of using the criminal law for what it was not intended, Ann is expected to pursue her *civil* claim against Ben for the value of the stolen goods (or to *threaten* to pursue it to force Ben into an out-of-court settlement).

Threats to *property* may take the form of a threat to damage, destroy, or wrongfully seize or withhold real or personal property. Sam, a supplier negotiating with Ron at his retail store, threatens to smash Ron's expensive, uninsured plate glass window with a brick unless Ron signs a contract for goods. To save the glass, Ron may have no reasonable alternative to signing. Preventing Sam's action may not be possible or may pose an unacceptable risk to Ron; and the police may be too far away to help. Ron's contract is voidable for duress even though he might have needed the goods and the price was fair. Lenders commonly take mortgages on real estate to secure repayment of a loan for which the real estate is "collateral." Where the debtor fails to pay what is owed, the lender's threat to foreclose the mortgage is coercive, but rightful. The threat would be wrongful, however, if the lender made it to force a payment that is not due or that the lender knew to be excessive.

Threats to *a person's business* or to a person's means of earning a livelihood may, under certain circumstances, result in duress. This kind of duress by threat is commonly referred to as *economic duress,* or *business compulsion.* Ordinarily a court will not hold that there has been economic duress unless the plaintiff seeking to rescind can prove that irreparable injury to his or her business or to chances of gaining an adequate livelihood would result if the defendant were to carry out the wrongful threat.

As a general rule, threatening to file a civil action against someone is not duress. Thus, a party who agrees to pay a sum of money to avoid being sued may not rescind the agreement. However, if the circumstances are appropriate, a court may find economic duress. Suppose, for example, a large corporation threatens to sue a small business person unless the person transfers to the corporation a novel invention discovered by the person. The large corporation knows that by claiming patent infringement and filing an expensive lawsuit, it could cause irreparable injury to the businessperson. A court would find economic duress if the corporation is attempting to gain something to which it is not entitled. Of course, it would not be duress for the corporation to file a suit in good faith to protect its lawful rights.

Overcoming of free will. To constitute duress, the threat must produce fear sufficient to overcome a party's free will. The test in most states is the reaction of the particular individual threatened. Courts consider a party's age, sex, mental capacity, and other relevant circumstances. The particular individual need not be as brave as the "ordinary reasonable person." The law protects the unusually timid.

The following case involves economic duress.

CASE 11.3 Mancino v. Friedman · 429 N.E.2d 1181 (Ohio App. 1980)

FACTS In 1973 three painters filed mechanics' liens against an apartment house owned by Harry Friedman. The painters claimed they had not been paid for work performed at the apartments, and they retained an attorney, Paul Mancino, to file suit to foreclose their liens.

CASE 11.3 Continued

At the time, Friedman was attempting to obtain a bank loan, which required removal of the liens against the apartment property. A settlement was reached, Friedman paid the painters through Mr. Mancino, and the painters in return executed releases of their claims against the property. Subsequently, Friedman learned that the mechanics' liens had not been released as agreed and contacted Mancino. Mancino said that he had not been paid $350 in legal fees owed to him by his clients, the three painters, and that unless Friedman paid the $350 he (Mancino) would not file the releases of mechanics' liens. Friedman signed a promissory note payable to Mancino for $350 plus interest at 8 percent per annum. Mancino filed suit to enforce the note and Friedman defended by alleging he signed the note under duress. The court gave judgment for Friedman, and Mancino appealed.

OPINION

SILBERT, J. . . . Economic duress, often termed "business compulsion," is a species of duress recognized in modern practice by a majority of American courts. In Ohio, one court, while finding the concept inapplicable to the facts presented in the appeal before it, nevertheless, in so holding, had occasion to set forth the material elements of the defense:

> "*The fear of some impending peril or financial injury, or the mere fact that one acts with reluctance, does not constitute duress. Duress involves illegality, and implies that a person has been unlawfully constrained by another to perform an act under circumstances which prevent the exercise of free will,* and it can never constitute fraud or duress to do as and what a person has a legal right to do, whatever the pecuniary consequences may be to those with whom he deals." (Emphasis added.) . . .

Thus, the defense of economic duress, or business compulsion, arises where one individual, acting upon another's fear of impending financial injury, unlawfully coerces the latter to perform an act under circumstances which prevent his exercise of free will.

Here, the issue which this court must resolve is whether the pressure exerted upon appellee [Friedman] by appellant [Mancino], a licensed Ohio attorney, in refusing to file mechanics' lien releases, which were part of a settlement agreement between his clients and appellee, until appellee first agreed to sign a promissory note in the amount of the attorney's fees owed appellant by his clients, constituted business compulsion. . . .

We first observe that appellee's affidavit contained credible evidence that he indeed executed the note to appellant solely out of fear of impending financial injury, i.e., the immediate consequences of failing to secure a refinancing of his property. Second, under the surrounding circumstances evidenced within the affidavit, the trier of fact could reasonably have inferred that appellant, as an attorney, effectively prevented appellee from exercising his free will in this matter. Finally, the method of fee extraction utilized by appellant, while not technically unlawful, clearly constituted an abuse of the privilege to practice law which this state has granted appellant. Consideration for sound public policy, derived from various relevant precepts within our Code of Professional Responsibility, demands that we not countenance, in any manner, this type of predatory practice engaged in by an Ohio attorney to extract his fees from vulnerable non-clients.

We note that, but for the license which the state has permitted him to hold, appellant could not have successfully pressured appellee to execute the promissory note in question. We find this use of his license to practice law so antipathetic to the high standards of the legal profession, that, while not amounting to a violation of law, it, in our opinion, supplants the element of unlawfulness, by definition, needed to prove a defense of business compulsion.

JUDGMENT

Accordingly, we conclude that the facts within appellee's affidavit sufficiently demonstrated the merit of his claimed defense of economic duress. . . . [A]ffirmed.

Undue Influence

Undue influence occurs when one party overcomes the free will of the other party by *unfair persuasion.* Many cases involve persons making gifts of money or property, or making wills which include large bequests to persons outside one's immediate family. Thus, in the usual case of undue influence there is an unnatural enrichment of one party at the expense of the other party or the other's family.

Unfair persuasion is most likely to occur in either of the following situations:

1 A person is under the domination of another person
2 There is such a relationship of trust and confidence (called a "fiduciary relationship") between two persons that one of them is justified in assuming that his or her best interests will be protected by the other

In the first category, a person may be under the *domination of another person* because of mental weakness, ignorance, lack of experience, old age, poor health, physical handicap, emotional strain, or financial distress.

The second category embraces relationships of trust and confidence, called *fiduciary relationships,* such as parent and child, guardian and ward, husband and wife, physician and patient, attorney and client, and pastor and parishioner. Most courts take the position that if it is established that a confidential relationship existed when a transaction was entered into that benefited the trusted person, the burden of proof is on that person to prove the transaction was not procured by undue influence. Thus, for example, if an attorney prepares a will for a client in which the attorney is to receive a large sum of money in preference to the client's legal heirs, a court would require the attorney to prove that she or he did not exercise undue influence over the client.

In the following case the court discussed the defense of undue influence.

CASE 11.4 Cripe v. Atlantic First National Bank of Daytona Beach · 422 So. 2nd 820 (Fla. 1982)

FACTS Carrie Hare owned several apartment buildings in Daytona Beach, with a total of forty-nine units. Joe and Sereata Cripe were her tenants for 7½ months each year. They spent the remainder of each year in Michigan. In 1966 Mrs. Hare, then 80 years old, asked Joe Cripe to help her manage her rental business. The rental income was placed in joint accounts so that Joe could sign checks both for business expenses and for her personal expenses. In return for their services, the Cripes were given free rent and utilities year-round and, upon Mrs. Hare's death, Joe would receive the balances in the joint bank accounts. In 1969 part of Mrs. Hare's property was condemned by the state for the widening of a highway, and she received $31,000. On the suggestion of Joe, Mrs. Hare deposited the money in the joint names of herself and Mr. Cripe.

Mrs. Hare died in 1976 at the age of 90. There were three joint accounts containing $12,700, $10,900, and $32,000, respectively. Joe Cripe obtained the funds as survivor. Atlantic First National Bank of Daytona Beach, as representative of her estate, filed suit to recover the funds on the ground that Mr. Cripe obtained them by undue influence. The trial court held for the defendants (Mr. and Mrs. Cripe). On appeal, the district court of appeals held that the facts gave rise to a presumption of undue influence, that the burden shifted to the defendants to rebut the presumption and justify Mrs. Hare's gift to them, and that they had failed to rebut the presumption. The Cripes appealed to the Florida Supreme Court.

OPINION BOYD, J. . . . The [district] court said, there is a presumption of undue influence when the stronger party gains a financial benefit from the weaker, and burden is on the stronger party to rebut the presumption.

CASE 11.4 Continued

In the case of *In re Estate of Carpenter*... cited by the district court, it was held that when a person who is a primary beneficiary of a will had a confidential relationship with the testator and there was active procurement of the bequest, a presumption of undue influence arises....

We believe that the agreement between Mrs. Hare and the Cripes, pertaining to the management of her properties and the supervision of her personal care, in exchange for the remaining balances in the accounts maintained for meeting her business and personal expenses, must be considered separately from the transaction by which Mr. Cripe obtained permission to deposit the condemnation proceeds into a joint account. On appeal, the district court should have applied the *Carpenter* test to the two transactions separately.

The evidence showed that the Cripes began to manage Mrs. Hare's apartment business and to supervise her personal care in 1966. There was no evidence to establish that at the time this arrangement began by agreement of the parties, there was a confidential relationship between them. While the weakness or dependence of one party to an agreement is relevant to the question of undue influence once a confidential relationship exists, it does not in itself establish a confidential relationship. Therefore, with regard to the agreement for management services and personal care in exchange for an apartment and the remaining balances on the death of Mrs. Hare, the district court erred in holding that a presumption of undue influence was raised. Even if a confidential relationship had been shown, so that a presumption of undue influence was created, we believe the defendants' showing with regard to their agreement with Mrs. Hare rebutted the presumption. Therefore there was sufficient evidence for the trial court to conclude that the plaintiff bank was entitled to no relief with regard to the account balances that derived from the arrangement. The district court incorrectly substituted its judgment for that of the trial court.

With regard to the $32,000 certificate of deposit derived from the condemnation award, however, the considerations are different. By the time Mrs. Hare obtained the condemnation settlement award in 1969, a close and dependent relationship had developed between herself and Joe Cripe. There was evidence to show that after he had been managing her affairs for some time, she became dependent upon him for financial services and advice and that she placed her trust in him. A confidential relationship had developed. From that point forward, Joe Cripe was prohibited from using his position of trust and confidence for acquisition of personal gain or to acquire property without full, fair and adequate consideration. The condemnation proceeds were deposited in a joint account because Mr. Cripe asked Mrs. Hare to do so. Since there was a confidential relationship and active procurement of a financial benefit, a presumption of undue influence arose. This presumption placed upon the defendants the burden of providing a reasonable explanation of the gift.

In an attempt to carry this burden, Mr. Cripe explained that Mrs. Hare agreed to deposit the money in a joint account because he had handled the condemnation transaction and knew more about it than she did. There was no evidence, however, that Mr. Cripe provided anything more than routine administrative services in connection with the compensation award, services which he was already obligated to perform as Mrs. Hare's property manager. In return for some relatively insignificant paperwork, the Cripes received a sum of money out of all proportion to the services provided.

Petitioners argue that there was insufficient proof of active procurement with regard to the deposit of the condemnation proceeds into a joint account. There was evidence, however, that Mrs. Hare's mental condition had deteriorated and she had become totally dependent on the Cripes. Where there is such inequality of mental strength, active procurement can be shown by evidence, as there was here, of a request or suggestion by the dominant party.

CASE 11.4 Continued

Therefore with regard to the condemnation funds, the district court was correct in finding undue influence from the evidence....

JUDGMENT

The decision of the district court of appeal reversing the trial court with regard to the two joint accounts, referred to in the district court's opinion as containing $12,700 and $10,900 respectively, was in error and should be quashed. That portion of the district court's decision that reversed the trial court with regard to the $32,000 certificate of deposit, derived from a condemnation settlement, was correct and should be approved. Accordingly, the decision of the district court is quashed in part and approved in part.

Misrepresentation

A misrepresentation is an untrue statement of fact. It may be "innocent" or "fraudulent." A misrepresentation is *innocent* if it is made by a person who does not know the statement is false. If a person makes a misrepresentation knowing of its falsity and intending to deceive or mislead someone with it, the statement is *fraudulent.* Whether innocent or fraudulent, a misrepresentation that induces a person into a contract gives that party a right to rescind it, or to assert the misrepresentation as an affirmative defense if the misrepresenter tries to enforce the contract.

Intentional Misrepresentation (Fraud). Sometimes, however, where the misrepresentation is fraudulent, the defrauded person prefers to sue in *tort* for fraud damages. Alice, an art dealer, owns a forged painting. Knowing it is worth only $100, Alice tells Betty, a less experienced art dealer, that it is authentic. Betty knows that the painting, if authentic, is worth $10,000 in the retail art market. Consequently, she pays Alice's asking price of $5,000. Under the UCC loss-of-bargain rule for fraud damages (applicable to sales of goods), Betty is entitled to $9,900 to compensate her for the loss of her expected bargain.[2] If Alice's fraud was especially malicious or oppressive, Betty may also be entitled to punitive damages.

[2]UCC § 2–721. Under this loss-of-bargain rule (also in effect in a majority of states for *nonsales* transactions), Betty is entitled to the difference between the value of the forged painting ($100) and the value the painting would have had if it had been authentic as represented ($10,000). If Alice had defrauded Betty in a *nonsales* transaction—e.g., a sale of real estate—Betty might have been subject to the minority out-of-pocket rule for fraud damages. Under that rule, she could recover from Alice only the difference between the value of the thing received ($100) and the amount paid ($5,000).

As noted in Chapter 4, to hold a defendant liable for the *tort* of fraud, the plaintiff must prove the existence of the following elements:

1. A false representation (misrepresentation) of *material* fact by the defendant. A fact is material if it is important enough to affect the plaintiff's decision to enter a transaction.
2. Defendant's knowledge that the misrepresentation was false
3. Defendant's intent to deceive or to mislead the plaintiff (intent to induce the plaintiff to act)
4. Justifiable reliance by the plaintiff on the misrepresentation
5. Injury or loss to the plaintiff

There is considerable difference between what is required to win a suit for the tort of fraud and what is required to *rescind a contract* on the basis of fraud or to establish fraud as a *defense* in a breach-of-contract action. To rescind a contract or to defend on the basis of fraud, the victim is not required to show that the misrepresented fact was material or that the victim suffered injury. A major reason for the less demanding proof requirements for rescission or defense is that the defrauded person seeks only to be returned to the position he or she was in before the contract was made, and is not seeking compensation for a lost bargain (profit) or punitive damages. Suppose Betty bought the forged painting as discussed above but there is no established retail market value for it. In the absence of circumstances justifying punitive damages, Betty might be better off rescinding the contract (returning the painting and receiving her money back) than trying to prove a market value for authentic paintings where such values are in doubt.

Often, contracts contain exculpatory or disclaimer clauses such as, "It is agreed that there are no representations of any kind between the parties other than contained in this written contract." Courts commonly ignore such provisions and allow a party to introduce evidence that he or she was defrauded.

Innocent Misrepresentation. In nearly all states, innocent misrepresentation is not a tort. Therefore, a party who contracts in reliance on an innocent misrepresentation ordinarily is limited to rescinding the contract or to raising misrepresentation as a defense to enforcement. However, to be of legal consequence, an innocent misrepresentation must be of a *material* fact, whereas materiality is not an essential aspect of a rescission action based on fraud.

Mistake

Mistake is a belief that is not in accord with the facts.[3] Mistake as used in this discussion means an erroneous belief that is not induced by the fraud or misrepresentation of the other contracting party. Some frequently recurring kinds of mistakes are:

- Mistake in connection with words used
- Mutual mistake of fact
- Unilateral mistake of fact
- Mistake of law

Mistake in Connection with Words Used. We have seen that modern law usually takes an objective approach toward expressions of assent. If John, who owns a Ford and a Dodge, means to offer his Ford for sale but inadvertently says, "I'll sell you my Dodge for $495," and Bill replies in good faith, "I accept your offer," there is a contract for the sale of the Dodge. "In good faith" means that Bill must not know or have reason to think that John misspoke. If John's Dodge was reasonably worth $1,500, Bill's attempted acceptance of the offer may be ineffective. An offeree is not allowed to "snap up" an offer that is too good to be true.

Sometimes an offer contains a latent (not yet obvious) ambiguity. In the above illustration there was only one possible meaning of "my Dodge." Suppose, however, that John owned two Dodge automobiles, one a 1970 model and one a 1973 model. If John thought he was selling the 1970 Dodge and Bill thought he was buying the 1973 Dodge, there is no contract. Only if both parties actually intended the same subject matter (either car) of the sale would there be a contract.

Another type of mistake may occur in connection with words used and be of such nature that the court will correct the mistake. An error in transcription occurs where the parties have made an oral agreement and in the process of reducing the agreement to writing a mistake is made with the result that the writing does not correctly state the terms of the oral agreement. Suppose, for example, that Paula orally agrees to sell a parcel of land to Don. The legal description of Paula's land is "Lot 6 of the Blackacre Tract." When a written document is prepared to incorporate all the terms of sale, the parcel is described as "Lot 9 of the Blackacre Tract." In this situation either party may seek through court action the remedy of reformation. *Reformation* means that the court will order that the written document be corrected to conform to the terms of the oral agreement.

Mutual Mistake of Fact. At times both parties to a contract assume the existence of a vital fact and on the basis of that assumption enter into the contract. If they later discover that the assumption is false, either party may: (1) raise the mistake as a defense in a lawsuit filed by the other to enforce the contract or (2) rescind the contract.

A mutual mistake of fact usually means that the parties have a false assumption about some material aspect of the subject matter of the contract (identity or quality, quantity or extent). The existence or nonexistence of the aspect must be vital and basic to the parties' bargain and must not be a matter of opinion. For example, suppose a person buys a violin and both the seller and buyer believe it to be a genuine Stradivarius. The buyer later discovers the violin is an imitation and worth a fraction of the sale price. The buyer may rescind the contract on the ground of mutual mistake of fact. No rescission would be allowed if both parties expressed their ignorance about violins and simply guessed this one to be a genuine Stradivarius. Where there is "conscious uncertainty," both parties assume risks.

[3] *Restatement (Second), Contracts,* Sec. 151.

A mistake of opinion or judgment is not ground to avoid a contract. For example, if a person sells a horse because he or she believes the horse is not fast enough to race competitively, the seller may not rescind if the horse later does race successfully and the value of the horse rises.

The following case discusses mutual mistake of fact as a ground for rescission of a contract.

CASE 11.5 Beachcomber Coins, Inc. v. Boskett · 400 A.2d 78 (N.J. Super. 1979)

FACTS Beachcomber Coins, Inc. (plaintiff), a retail dealer in coins, purchased for $500 a dime purportedly minted in 1916 at Denver. It was later discovered that the "D" on the coin signifying Denver mintage was counterfeited. Boskett had acquired this coin and two others of minor value for a total of $450 and believed the dime to be a genuine rarity. A representative of plaintiff spent from 15 to 45 minutes in close examination of the coin before purchasing it. Upon discovery that the coin was a counterfeit, plaintiff brought an action for rescission, asserting mutual mistake of fact. The trial judge held for defendant (Boskett) on the ground that customary coin dealing procedures are for a dealer to make his or her own investigation of the genuineness of the coin and to "assume the risk" of the purchase if his or her investigation is faulty. Plaintiff appealed to the Superior Court, Appellate Division.

OPINION CONFORD, P. J. . . . The evidence and trial judge's findings establish this as a classic case of rescission for mutual mistake of fact. As a general rule,

> . . . where parties on entering into a transaction that affects their contractual relations are both under a mistake regarding a fact assumed by them as the basis on which they entered into the transaction, it is voidable by either party if enforcement of it would be materially more onerous to him than it would have been had the fact been as the parties believed it to be. . . .

By way of example, the *Restatement* posits the following:

> A contracts to sell to B a specific bar of silver before them. . . . The parties suppose that the bar is sterling. It has, however, a much larger admixture of base metal. The contract is voidable by B.

Moreover, "negligent failure of a party to know or to discover the facts as to which both parties are under a mistake does not preclude rescission or reformation on account thereof." . . . In the *Riviere* case . . . relief was denied only because the parties could not be restored to the *status quo ante.* In the present case they can be. It is undisputed that both parties believed that the coin was a genuine Denver-minted one. The mistake was mutual in that both parties were laboring under the same misapprehension as to this particular, essential fact. The price asked and paid was directly based on that assumption. [That] the plaintiff may have been negligent in his inspection of the coin (a point not expressly found but implied by the trial judge) does not, as noted above, bar its claim for rescission. . . .

Defendant's contention that plaintiff assumed the risk that the coin might be of greater or lesser value than that paid is not supported by the evidence. It is well established that a party to a contract can assume the risk of being mistaken as to the value of the thing sold. . . . The *Restatement* states the rule this way:

> Where the parties know that there is doubt in regard to a certain matter and contract on that assumption, the contract is not rendered voidable because one is disappointed in the hope that the facts accord with his wishes. The risk of the existence of the doubtful fact is then assumed as one of the elements of the bargain. . . .

CASE 11.5 Continued

However, for the stated rule to apply, the parties must be conscious that the pertinent fact may not be true and make their agreement at the risk of that possibility. In this case both parties were certain that the coin was genuine. They so testified. Plaintiff's principal thought so after his inspection, and defendant would not have paid nearly $450 for it otherwise. A different case would be presented if the seller were uncertain either of the genuineness of the coin or of its value if genuine, and had accepted the expert buyer's judgment on these matters. . . .

JUDGMENT Reversed.

Unilateral Mistake of Fact. Under a traditional rule of contract formation, when a party to a contract assents on the basis of his or her own mistake, the mistake is not a ground for relief unless the other party knows or has reason to know of it. Bob, a bidder for a subcontract on a construction project, makes a computational error so that his bid (offer) to George, the general contractor, is materially less than it otherwise would have been. George accepts the offer, and Bob later wants to rescind the contract. Under the traditional rule, whether Bob may do so depends on whether his error was obvious to George ("palpable"). If the bid was so low that George should have realized an error had been made, he will not be allowed to "snap up" Bob's offer. Otherwise, Bob is bound under the traditional rule, even though he might suffer a loss on the job.

When would Bob's error be palpable so that he could have rescission? Suppose that George received several bids around $750,000, his own estimates show that the lowest profitable bid is likely to be $700,000, and Bob's bid is $500,000. Under the "palpable error" test, George is on notice of Bob's error, and Bob may rescind. However, a substantial disparity among bids does not, by itself, necessarily put the offeree on notice that the lowest one was in error. It is not uncommon for intended, profitable bids to vary dramatically in size, especially those for smaller home repair contracts. The critical factor here is that George had information from his own sources about what the minimum profitable bid should be. The rule regarding palpable mistake does not apply to errors in judgment or opinion. If Roger offers to sell his car for $500 and Sally accepts, knowing that the car is a classic worth $5,000 and that Roger is unaware of this fact, there is a contract and Roger may not rescind.

Today a person is often granted rescission on the basis of his or her own mistake even though the other party had no reason to suppose that a mistake had been made. The conditions essential to such relief are:

1. The matter as to which the mistake was made must relate to a material feature of the contract.
2. The mistake must be of so grave a consequence that to enforce the contract would be unconscionable.
3. Generally the mistake must not be the result of gross negligence by the party making the mistake.
4. It must be possible to give relief by way of rescission without serious prejudice to the other party except the loss of the bargain. In other words, it must be possible to put the unmistaken party in *statu quo*.
5. The party seeking relief must give prompt notice when the mistake is discovered.

Relief from a contract entered into with unilateral mistake of fact usually takes the form of rescission. However, the mistaken party may raise mistake as a defense in a lawsuit filed by the promisee to enforce the contract.

Mistake of Law. Mistake of law means ignorance of law, or a wrong conclusion as to the effect of law upon a known set of facts. In the past the general rule was that no relief would be given to a contracting party for a mistake of law unaccompanied by a mistake of fact. Modern courts recognize that statutes and case law often are so complex, contradictory, or poorly stated that even skilled lawyers have difficulty interpreting them. The injustice of some of the results produced has led to an increasing number of exceptions and to much criticism. Today, in many states relief for mistake of law is placed on the same basis as relief for mistake of fact. Relief is granted if the mistake of law is either:(1) mutual or (2) unilateral but palpable.

Avoidance on Ground of Unconscionability

The courts and the legislatures have long been concerned with protecting weak, often uneducated contracting parties from overreaching by unscrupulous, stronger ones. The law of fraud serves this policy. Yet, many misleading and exploitive business practices fall short of established wrongs such as fraud, duress, and undue influence. High-pressure selling of shoddy goods while depriving the buyer of meaningful remedies by use of fine-print clauses is an example. Out of long-standing legal efforts to combat such practices has emerged the concept of "unconscionability" which appears in Section 2-302 of the UCC and Section 208 of the *Restatement (Second) of the Law of Contracts.*

Unconscionability is yet another basis for rescinding a contract or for defending against its enforcement. If a contract is unconscionable, a court may refuse to enforce it in its entirety. If some term of a contract is unconscionable, the court may enforce the remainder of the contract without the unconscionable term, or it may limit the application of the unconscionable term in such a way as to avoid any unconscionable result.

Because it can take so many forms, unconscionability has no rigid definition. Instead, the courts apply guidelines such as "oppression" and "unfair surprise" on a case-by-case basis. Any contract or contractual term that oppresses or unfairly surprises a contracting party may be unenforceable even though the practice involved does not constitute fraud or some other traditional variety of illegal conduct.

Over the years, the courts have identified a number of practices that may be held unconscionable if the circumstances warrant. These practices have been classified as either "procedural" or "substantive" unconscionability. The resulting buildup of case law provides specific guidance for the courts as they decide what new practices and variations of old ones should be declared unconscionable.

Procedural unconscionability has to do with an unfair or deceptive process of contract formation. Procedural unconscionability may occur, for example, where a seller uses high-pressure salesmanship or, by means of a clause in fine print placed near the end of a complex contract, seeks secretly to deprive a semiliterate buyer of rights which buyers normally would not wish to give up if the topic were discussed.

Substantive unconscionability has more to do with unreasonably harsh terms of a contract than with a deceptive process of contract formation. An excessively high price might be held unconscionable, as in *Jones v. Star Credit Corp.*[4] There, the plaintiffs, who were welfare recipients, agreed, after a visit from a salesman representing Your Shop At Home Service, Inc., to pay $900 for a home freezer unit with a maximum retail value of $300. With the addition of credit charges, credit life insurance, credit property insurance, and sales tax, the purchase price totaled $1,234.80. After paying $619.88, the plaintiffs sought to avoid the agreement. The defendant claimed that with various added credit charges, the plaintiffs still owed $819.81. Holding that the agreement was unconscionable, the court noted the exorbitant price, the high credit charges, the fact that the plaintiffs' very limited financial resources were known to sellers at the time of the sale, and the consequent probability that the sellers knowingly took advantage of the plaintiffs.

Substantive unconscionability also occurs where a seller-creditor in an installment sale of goods or services unduly restricts the buyer-debtor's remedies for breach of contract or unduly expands the creditor's own remedial rights. In *Williams v. Walker-Thomas Furniture Co.*,[5] the buyer, a welfare mother with seven children and a monthly income of $218, purchased items of furniture from the seller on credit over a period of 5 years. The contract of sale contained a provision giving the seller a security interest in all the items of furniture until the account was fully paid, instead of the more usual security interest in only the items not yet paid for. The buyer missed payments on the last item, a stereo set costing $514.95. Although she had previously made

[4] 298 N.Y.S.2d 264 (N.Y. Sup. Ct. 1969).
[5] 350 F.2d 445 (D.C. Cir. 1965).

payments of more than $1,400 on a total debt of $1,800, so that the balance due was less than the purchase price of the stereo, the seller sought to repossess all the furniture. The appellate court held, in effect, that the trial court could find the contract unconscionable if the circumstances surrounding the sale involved oppression and unfair surprise. These elements would be present if, for example, the buyer had no meaningful choice as to the terms of the contract and if it contained terms unreasonably favorable to the seller; if the buyer had no reasonable opportunity to understand the terms; or if important terms were hidden by the use of fine print and deceptive sales practices. If the seller kept the existence of the repossession clause unknown to Mrs. Williams, or upon her request for an explanation refused to explain the clause or gave misleading information, the transaction would have involved procedural unconscionability. Even if she understood the provision, however, it would be substantively unconscionable if unreasonably harsh.

Avoidance under Consumer Protection Laws

We have in this country a wide variety of federal and state "consumer protection" laws. The legislation is intended to protect people from deceptive advertising, hidden charges for loans, inaccurate credit reports, unfair billing practices, undue loss as the result of lost or stolen credit cards, and a host of other evils that befall consumers in their day-to-day transactions. Some of the legislation requires disclosure of interest rates, finance charges, and other contractual terms. A few consumer protection statutes are designed to combat high-pressure tactics and unfair business practices, and these statutes grant consumers a right to avoid (rescind) certain of their contracts.

The statutory right of rescission is associated mainly with consumer credit sales. Under the federal Consumer Credit Protection Act (also known as the Truth-in-Lending Act) a consumer, after entering into a consumer credit transaction involving a lien on the consumer's residence, has 3 business days to rescind the transaction. The 3 days are sometimes referred to as a "cooling-off period." A typical situation in which the consumer is given the right to rescind occurs when a creditor makes improvements (a new roof, aluminum siding, etc.) on the consumer's residence. If the consumer does not pay the creditor, or if subcontractors or suppliers are not paid in full, mechanics' liens are created. The consumer has 3 business days to rescind the transaction. A prerequisite to rescission is that the consumer must return or offer to return the consideration received from the creditor. No problem is encountered if the goods purchased are removable from the residence. Suppose, however, that the goods are custom-made or are permanently attached to the residence. The federal regulations provide that if return of the merchandise would be impractical or inequitable, the consumer must offer to pay its reasonable value. To avoid such problems, most creditors do not deliver goods or perform work until the 3-day rescission period has expired.

The right to rescind does *not* apply to a first mortgage or to a lien given to acquire or construct the residence. Nor does it apply to liens on property other than the consumer's principal residence, such as vacation property.

A regulation of the Federal Trade Commission grants a consumer 3 days to avoid a home solicitation sale in excess of $25. The purpose of the regulation is to give the consumer a cooling-off period to reflect on purchases made in the home. There are numerous instances of high-pressure salespeople inducing someone in the home to buy an expensive vacuum cleaner or set of encyclopedias. No reason need be given for rescinding the sale within the 3-day period. After the 3-day period expires, the consumer may rescind only if one of the traditional contract law defenses can be proved (duress, undue influence, fraud). The FTC rule applies to both cash sales and credit sales. The rule does not apply to transactions in which the consumer requests the seller to visit the home for the purpose of repairing the consumer's personal property, or to the sale of insurance.

Summary

The law protects persons vulnerable to exploitation by allowing them to avoid contracts for such reasons as minority, mental incompetency, duress, fraud, and unconscionability. A person may exercise the power of avoidance by rescinding the contract or by pleading the right of avoidance as a defense to contract enforcement.

The law seeks to protect minors from imprudence while also protecting the legitimate interests of adults who contract with them. As a general rule, minors' contracts are voidable. A minor ordinarily may disaffirm a contract while still a minor or within a reasonable time thereafter by demanding the return of the consideration given and returning whatever he or she received if still in possession of it. However, minors have a quasi-contractual liability for necessaries and in various states are not permitted to disaffirm certain types of contracts.

Mentally incompetent persons have a similar power of avoidance. A person is considered mentally incompetent if unable at the time of contracting to understand the nature and consequences of the transaction. Where a mentally impaired person's contract is executed, it is not avoidable if the other person had no reason to know of the incompetency and avoidance would be unjust to the other party. If a court declares a person mentally incompetent and appoints a guardian, any later contract attempt by the incompetent person is void. In terms of legal rights, intoxicated persons are treated much like mentally incompetent persons.

People also may avoid contracts on the basis of defective assent caused by duress, undue influence, misrepresentation, or mistake. Duress is the use of a wrongful threat to coerce a person into a contract by fear. Undue influence is the use of unfair persuasion to gain advantage over another person, as where a fiduciary takes advantage of a client to gain control of the client's property. Misrepresentation, whether innocent or fraudulent, gives the victim a right to rescind the contract or a defense to enforcement. To rescind on the basis of fraud, the victim is not required to show that the fraud was material or that it caused injury. For a person to rescind on the basis of innocent misrepresentation, however, the misrepresentation must be material.

Various types of mistake may give a contracting party a basis for rescission. They include mutual mistakes of fact and unilateral mistakes of fact. In the latter situation, the mistaken party is the one seeking relief. Under the older "palpable error" test, the mistaken party is held to the contract unless the error was obvious to the other party. Today there may be relief for unilateral mistakes that are not obvious to the other party if the mistake is serious, if the other party is not unduly harmed by rescission of the contract, and if the party seeking relief acts promptly.

Contracts may be avoided, in total or in part, for unconscionability, a concept developed to combat misleading and exploitive business practices falling short of traditional wrongs such as fraud. A few federal and state consumer protection statutes give consumers a right to avoid certain of their contracts. For example, the federal Truth-in-Lending Act gives consumers 3 days to rescind a consumer credit transaction involving a lien on the consumer's residence.

Review Questions

1 (a) For what reasons does the law permit people to avoid their contracts? (b) How might a person exercise the power of avoidance?

2 (a) Why are minors allowed to avoid their contracts? (b) What effect does judicial emancipation have on a minor's power of avoidance? What effect does parental emancipation have?

3 (a) Who may exercise a minor's power of disaffirmance? (b) What is required for a minor to make an effective disaffirmance?

4 (a) Upon disaffirmance, to what property may a minor be entitled? To what property may he or she not be entitled? (b) Must a disaffirming minor always return property received under the contract?

5 With regard to minors' contracts, explain the meaning and legal effect of ratification.

6 (a) What is the reason for holding minors liable for necessaries? (b) Is a minor liable for the retail price of necessaries? (c) Is an automobile a necessary? Why or why not?

7 (a) By what legal test is a person's mental competency determined? (b) What difference does it make that a mentally incompetent person's contract was executed rather than executory? (c) What is the legal effect of a court's adjudicating a person mentally incompetent and appointing a guardian? In what main situation is this effect especially significant?

8 Is it duress to use a threat of criminal prosecution to force a thief to pay for stolen property? Explain in terms of **(a)** the elements of duress, and **(b)** the purpose of the criminal law.

9 Give examples of two kinds of situations in which undue influence is most likely to occur.

10 **(a)** What must a person prove to rescind a contract on the basis of fraud? **(b)** How does this differ from what he or she would have to prove to win a suit for the tort of fraud? **(c)** What must a person prove to rescind a contract on the basis of innocent misrepresentation?

11 Illustrate how mutual mistake could be a basis for rescinding a contract.

12 Under what circumstances may a person rescind a contract on the basis of that person's unilateral mistake?

13 **(a)** How can one tell if a contract is unconscionable? **(b)** Illustrate "procedural unconscionability" and "substantive unconscionability." **(c)** Can a contract containing an unconscionable clause be enforceable? Explain.

14 Under some consumer protection statutes, a consumer has a 3-day "cooling-off period." **(a)** For what kinds of transactions is this period available? **(b)** What kinds of transactions are not covered by the 3-day right to rescind?

Case Problems

1 In July 1973, James Halbman, Jr., a minor, contracted to buy a 1968 Oldsmobile from Michael Lemke for $1,250. Halbman paid Lemke $1,000 cash and took possession of the car. Halbman agreed to pay $25 per week until the balance was paid. About 5 weeks later, after Halbman had paid a total of $1,100, a connecting rod in the vehicle's engine broke. Halbman had it repaired but did not pay the repair bill of $637.40. In October 1973, Halbman disaffirmed the purchase contract by letter, returned the certificate of title, and demanded the return of his $1,100. Lemke did not return the money. In the spring of 1974, in satisfaction of a garageman's lien, the garage elected to remove the vehicle's engine and transmission and towed the vehicle to the residence of Halbman's father. Lemke was asked several times to remove the vehicle, but refused. During this period the vehicle was vandalized, making it unsalvageable. Halbman filed suit for rescission and asked for the return of the $1,100. Lemke argued that he should be entitled to recover the amount of the repair bill. How should the trial court rule?

2 Steven Kiefer bought a 1960 Willys station wagon from Fred. At the time of sale Kiefer was 20 years old, married, and the father of one child. The age of majority was 21. Kiefer had difficulty with the car and returned it. He demanded return of the purchase price since he was a minor at the time of sale. Fred refused, alleging that Kiefer was emancipated and therefore was liable on the contract, and alleging that Kiefer had misrepresented his age by stating he was over 21 at the time of sale. If Fred can prove these allegations, is either one sufficient to deny Kiefer the right to disaffirm?

3 Vassyl Lonchyna was a minor in 1969 when he signed a contract enlisting in the U.S. Air Force. At the time, Lonchyna was a college student and wanted to become a medical doctor. The contract specified that the Air Force would provide him with undergraduate and graduate education, and in return Lonchyna would serve on active duty in the Air Force for a specified number of years. At age 21 Lonchyna accepted a commission in the Air Force as a second lieutenant. Later he accepted promotion to first lieutenant. Three times he applied to the Air Force for "educational delays" deferring the start of his active duty commitment. Lonchyna filed suit to avoid the enlistment contract on the ground that he was a minor at the time he signed. Should the court grant Lonchyna's request for avoidance?

4 On October 17, 1972, Kenneth, a minor, was in an accident and was admitted to Greenville General Hospital for emergency medical care. He was hospitalized 87 days, and the hospital bill totaled over $9,000. At the time of admission, Kenneth's mother signed the admission form as a responsible party. Kenneth's father was also listed as a responsible party, and all the bills were sent to him. Kenneth lived at home and was supported by his parents. The parents failed to make any payment on the hospital bill. Kenneth recovered a sum of money from the person responsible for the injuries he sustained in the accident, which sum was placed in a special account under the supervision of the probate court. Greenville filed suit against Kenneth's estate for the hospital bill. The probate court granted the hospital a judgment for $9,000. Was the trial court correct in granting judgment?

5 G.A.S. and S.I.S. were married in 1957 and subsequently had four children. In 1970 G.A.S. was hospitalized for 8 weeks for mental health problems. Similar illnesses occurred in 1972 and in early 1974. He was diagnosed as suffering from paranoid schizophrenia and was given drug therapy. In December 1974, G.A.S. suffered a recurrence and was committed again to the state hospital. At the time he was employed as a design engineer at a yearly salary of $21,000. The hospital allowed him to work during the day and return for treatment at night. S.I.S. filed for divorce and served G.A.S. with the summons on January 10, 1975, while he was in the hospital. S.I.S.'s attorney prepared a separation agreement which was signed by both parties on February 20, 1975, in the attorney's office. G.A.S. did not want the divorce and did not read the agreement before signing it. Throughout February 1975, G.A.S. was on extensive medication, and on February 20 he was given three drugs which adversely affected his reasoning powers. S.I.S. stated that the parties negotiated $750-per-month child support and that they together went over a draft of the entire separation agreement. G.A.S. denied setting the $750 monthly figure but stated that S.I.S. originally asked for $1,100 out of his $1,300 net monthly income. The agreement also provided that a parcel of land inherited by G.A.S. would be sold and the proceeds used to pay off the marital debts first and the balance then divided equally. There were other terms that were onerous to G.A.S. He filed suit to rescind the agreement. How should the court rule?

6 In November 1960, Logan Corporation agreed to buy two businesses owned by Litten. Logan promised to pay Litten's creditors, to employ Litten for 1 year at a stipulated salary, and to give Litten an option to buy 5,000 shares of Logan's stock. Litten transferred the businesses to Logan, but Logan refused to pay Litten's creditors in full. In January 1961, the creditors threatened Litten with bankruptcy. On January 9, Logan presented to Litten a new agreement which contained no stock option and no employment clause. Logan said the creditors would not be paid unless Litten signed the agreement. Litten signed the agreement and later filed suit to avoid the 1961 agreement and to enforce the terms of the November 1960 agreement. Should the court set aside the 1961 agreement?

7 Robert and Wendy Pfister owned 100 shares of Tracor Computing Corp., a stock no longer traded publicly. They asked Foster & Marshall, Inc., a stock brokerage firm, to evaluate the stock. They believed the stock to be of little value and were surprised when the broker told them that under its new name, Continuum Co., Inc., it was worth $4,950. The Pfisters asked the broker to recheck the figures, and, on its reassurance that the stock was worth $4,950, sold the stock to Foster & Marshall. A year later Foster & Marshall discovered that the Tracor stock had been exchanged for Continuum stock at a ten-to-one ratio and that the Pfisters owned only ten shares of Continuum. Foster & Marshall sued Mr. & Mrs. Pfister for $4,455 overpayment. The Pfisters claimed Foster & Marshall made a unilateral mistake and are not entitled to recover. Who should win?

CHAPTER 12

Illegal Agreements

Previous chapters in this series have dealt with four requirements for a contract—offer, acceptance, consideration, and legal capacity of the parties. Another requirement is that the agreement must not be illegal.

The first part of this chapter examines the nature and general effect of illegal agreements; the second part, some common types of illegal agreements. The final portion of the chapter discusses the limited circumstances in which the courts will aid a party to an illegal agreement.

Illegal Agreements in General

Nature and General Effect of Illegal Agreements

Meaning and Effect of Illegality. An agreement is illegal if it is made or performed in violation of law—e.g., a constitution, a statute, a rule or regulation of an administrative agency, or a principle or policy of the common law. Subject to exceptions discussed later in this chapter, the courts will not enforce illegal agreements or in any other way give aid to either party.

Some agreements are so obviously contrary to law that they are unenforceable in their entirety—for example, Jane and Joe's agreement to rob a bank. More often, contracts contain parts (called "clauses," "provisions," or "terms") that are illegal, as where Joe agrees to sell a car to Jane on credit but at a higher rate of interest than permitted by law. Depending on how the illegal part affects the whole contract, a court may refuse to enforce the contract, may strike out the illegal part and enforce what remains, or may limit the application of the illegal part to achieve legality and prevent serious injustice. An agreement need not involve a violation of the criminal law to be illegal. There is no criminal violation, for instance, where a contract clause denies a seller the right to sue the buyer if the buyer does not pay; but such a clause is likely to be held illegal and therefore unenforceable.

Significance of "Public Policy." When deciding whether agreements are legal, a court often must determine whether they are consistent with public policy. "Public policy" has been defined as: (1) "the principle of law which holds that no [person] can lawfully do that which has a tendency to be injurious to the public or against the public good," and (2) "the principles under which... freedom of contract or private dealings is restricted by law for the good of the community."[1] So, an agreement that is against the public good is "against public policy" and may be held illegal. Suppose, for example, that the three private trash-hauling firms operating in Metropolis agree to divide the market so that each can collect garbage in a certain geographic area free from the competition of the others. Each firm now has its own monopoly and can charge excessive rates that must be paid by the residents or passed along to others in the form of higher prices to their customers, to the injury of the whole community. A variety of statutes and judicial decisions forbid such agreements because they are in restraint of trade and thus against that element of public policy which approves of free competition.

Constitutions, statutes, and administrative rules and regulations are declarations of public policy. In the absence of legislation, courts may decide what the public good requires if called upon to determine whether an agreement is sufficiently threatening to the public to be declared illegal.

Every determination of public policy involves a value judgment—a balancing of competing interests, including the interests of the public—and such judgments may vary from state to state and change over time. For example, in the 1976 case of *Marvin v. Marvin*,[2] the California Supreme Court held for the first time that an agreement between an unmarried man and woman regarding property acquired while they lived together may be enforceable. Traditionally, such an agreement has been held against public policy and unenforceable, since to enforce the agreement might encourage people to live out of wedlock. As the California court's change of position indicates, notions of what constitutes sound public policy are affected by changes in what the public and the lawmakers consider ethical, moral, or tolerable.

Agreements Illegal by Constitution or Statute

An agreement may be illegal because it is not in compliance with a constitution or a statute. Lack

[1] *Black's Law Dictionary. See* "policy."

[2] 18 Cal. 3d 660, 557 P.2d 106.

of compliance may be evident because the enactment states that the agreement is "illegal," "unlawful," "void," or "against public policy." But many enactments do not express the legislative intent to make a particular agreement illegal. In such instances, the court will have to determine the implied intent by *construing* the statute or constitutional provision, i.e., deciding what its purpose is, what evils it seems intended to prevent, and whether it was therefore meant to apply to the agreement in question. In *National Labor Relations Board v. Bratten Pontiac Corp.*,[3] for example, Bratten induced its employees to agree not to unionize by offering them new benefits while they were considering whether to join the union. A provision of the National Labor Relations Act makes it an "unfair labor practice" for an employer to interfere with the employees' right to join a union. Although the Act does not list the giving of benefits as a type of interference, the court held that Bratten's doing so while the union election was pending constituted an interference that made the agreement between Bratten and the employees unlawful and unenforceable.

Constitutions, too, often make agreements illegal by implication. For example, it used to be a common practice for sellers of real estate to include in their sales contracts a clause (called a "restrictive covenant") prohibiting occupancy by or sale to black people or to other minorities. Although the U.S. Constitution does not expressly forbid such clauses, the Supreme Court held in the 1948 case of *Shelley v. Kraemer*[4] that enforcement of such a clause by a state court or other state officer is a denial of the equal protection of the laws required by the Fourteenth Amendment. Consequently, racially discriminatory restrictive covenants are unenforceable in any state. Similarly, in a 1981 case,[5] the court refused to compel a construction company to comply with a New Jersey statute requiring it to hire citizens of New Jersey before hiring persons from out of state. Requiring the firm to favor New Jersey citizens in employment contracts would violate the privileges and immunities clause of the U.S. Constitution and make the contracts illegal.

[3]406 F.2d 349 (4th Cir. 1969).
[4]68 S. Ct. 836.
[5]*Neshaminy Constructors, Inc. v. Krause,* 437 A.2d 733 (N.J. Super. Ct. Ch. Div. 1981).

The Civil Rights Act of 1964 as amended, the 1963 Equal Pay Act, the 1967 Age Discrimination in Employment Act, and the Equal Credit Opportunity Act as amended in 1976 (all federal legislation) prohibit a wide variety of discrimination on the basis of race, color, religion, sex, national origin, and age. Although aimed mainly at employers and others who practice illegal discrimination directly against individuals, these Acts would also be violated by agreements between, for example, a corporation and a labor union to practice the prohibited forms of discrimination.

That attitudes about public policy vary from state to state and change over time can be seen in two cases involving statutes prohibiting gambling agreements. In *Williams v. Weber Mesa Ditch Extension Co.*,[6] Williams purchased a $5 raffle ticket and was notified that he had won the prize, a 40-acre tract of land. Soon afterward, the defendant, a nonprofit corporation, nullified the raffle and held a new drawing because of the late arrival of tickets that had been delayed in the mails. Williams did not win the new drawing and brought suit to specifically enforce the first one. The supreme court of Wyoming held that the raffle was a gambling contract within the meaning of Wyoming's civil statute making gaming transactions "utterly void and of no effect." This case represents the traditional, still rather widely held view of lawmakers that gambling is so harmful to the public welfare that gaming contracts are not to be enforced.

Over the years, however, many state legislatures have decided that some forms of gambling such as lotteries and pari-mutuel betting on horse or dog races provide recreational and revenue-raising benefits that justify making them legal. With this change in attitude have come not only legalized gambling, but also changes in related law. Gambling on credit has long been viewed as very detrimental to the public good, leading as it may to excessive losses, borrowing from loan sharks, and impoverishment. In *Gottlob v. Lopez,*[7] Lopez, while gambling in the Tropicana Casino in Atlantic City, borrowed $5,500 from Gottlob to continue gambling. Lopez did not repay the loan, and Gottlob brought suit. In holding that the gambling debt was enforceable, the court stated, "The 1976 constitutional amendment [authorizing casino gambling

[6]572 P.2d 412 (Wyo. 1977).
[7]501 A.2d 176 (N.J. Super. Ct. App. Div. 1985).

in Atlantic City] and the enactment of the Casino Control Act altered our public policy regarding enforcement of gambling debts incurred while wagering in a licensed casino." Before 1976, all New Jersey gambling debts were "utterly void and of no effect." The Casino Control Act now regulates the extension of credit to gamblers by licensed casino operators such as Tropicana, but it is silent about loans from nonlicensees such as Gottlob. Nevertheless, the court held that all loans contracted to facilitate legalized gambling are enforceable, even those made by unregulated persons like Gottlob.

In Case 12.1, the court considers the legality of a doctor's agreement with a hospital administrator.

CASE 12.1 Mason v. Hosta · 199 Cal. Rptr. 859 (Cal. App. 1984)

FACTS As an independent contractor, Geoffrey M. Hosta (defendant), a licensed medical doctor, provided emergency room physician services to hospitals. He and his staff of doctors billed patients for emergency medical services and assigned the patient accounts to the individual hospitals for collection.

In 1974, Hosta entered into a contract with James J. Mason (plaintiff), a layperson hospital administrator. Mason was to persuade fellow hospital administrators to contract with Hosta for their emergency room services, and he would receive $250 per month for each hospital client for as long as it employed Hosta. Payments to Mason were to be renegotiated each 6 months and increased as Hosta's net receipts increased.

Mason referred several hospitals to Hosta and for about 3 years received referral fees. Then, upon being advised that the arrangement with Mason was illegal and unethical, Hosta ceased making payments. Mason brought suit for breach of contract. Holding that the arrangement violated Section 650 of California's Business and Professions Code, the trial court granted summary judgment to Hosta. Mason appealed.

OPINION MERRICK, A. J. . . . "The Business and Professions Code interdicts [prohibits] as a misdemeanor, and also as grounds for revocation or suspension of license, *the giving or receiving, by any person licensed to practice any of the recognized healing arts, of any . . . rebate, refund, commission . . . or other unearned consideration . . . as compensation or inducement for referring patients or customers to any person or firm.* . . . This interdiction *was designed to protect the public and prohibit all unearned rebates, refunds, commissions, and the like among licentiates* [licensees] *engaged in the healing arts for the referral of patients.* . . ."

. . . It is obvious [that] the . . . contract provided for payments to plaintiff by defendant as compensation solely for plaintiff's soliciting, referring, and procuring clients on defendant's behalf. Thus, the hospitals became the "clients" . . . of . . . Dr. Hosta as a result of plaintiff's "referrals," and, in turn, the emergency room patients of the hospitals contracted with, of necessity, became the referred "patients."

[Plaintiff] . . . contends that section 650 was designed to prevent patients from being charged excessive fees in order that a "kickback" could be made to [a doctor making a] referral. And, since there was no finding of such excessive fees, plaintiff could not be held to have violated the law. And, even if defendant doctor did pass on the expense of his referral fees to his emergency room patients, this is of little consequence like any other cost of the doctor's doing business.

. . . Certainly the referral fees paid to plaintiff by Dr. Hosta increased the doctor's overhead. Undoubtedly without this added expense the doctor could bill his services to the patients, the bearers of these health care costs, at proportionately lower rates. The effect of the . . . referral fees on the cost of health care to the ultimate patients is not just potential, it is clear.

We note [that the contract] provided for the renegotiation of the referral fee to be paid to plaintiff based on increases in the net receipts to defendant doctor. . . . Thus the "referral

CASE 12.1 Continued

fee" to be paid plaintiff was potentially directly related to the medical services rendered by defendant.

"In California alone, health care costs gross nearly $10 billion annually and undoubtedly constitute the largest single industry in the state, exceeding agriculture and aerospace in dollar volume."... Obviously a business of that scope... is susceptible of possible abuses and potential harm to the user public. The Legislature was aware of the reprehensible practices of some unethical licentiates who engaged in nefarious practices which resulted in "kickbacks," "rebates," and "hidden fees," and enacted section 650... to proscribe such activities.

The... contract provides for payments to appellant (non-licensee) by respondent (licensed doctor) as compensation for appellant's soliciting, referring and procuring clients on respondent's behalf. It is precisely this sort of referral fee to which the prohibition of... section 650 is directed. Performance of the... contract violates the statute.... *Civil Code section* 1550 provides that a lawful object is essential to the very existence of a valid contract.... [An agreement] in direct violation of... express prohibitions in a statute is void....

No matter how subtly disguised, or ingeniously interpreted, the... contract, by its terms and the performance required... violates section 650.... Further, it is an attempt to thwart the legislative design and public policy to proscribe illegal and unethical contracts providing for the payment by licensed physicians of consideration as compensation and inducement to non-licensees for the referral of patients....

JUDGMENT [The judgment of the trial court] is affirmed.

Agreements Which May Be Contrary to Public Policy

Some kinds of agreements are so threatening to the public welfare that virtually all agreements of the class, if challenged in court, would be held unenforceable as against public policy. Agreements to commit a crime or a tort are an example. Other kinds of agreements and clauses, such as contracts of adhesion and exculpatory clauses, are not necessarily harmful and will be denied enforcement only if misused.

Contracts of Adhesion. A *contract of adhesion* ("standard-form" contract) is one in which there is so great a disparity of bargaining power that the weaker party has no choice but to accept the terms imposed by the stronger party or forego the transaction. As noted in Chapter 8, contracts of adhesion serve legitimate functions in our economy and usually are enforced despite the weaker party's possible lack of consent to some or most terms. Yet, because of the great disparity of bargaining power that characterizes contracts of adhesion, people upon whom they are imposed are vulnerable to exploitation. In the absence of an effective bargaining power, what is their protection?

The first protection could be the sense of fairness and responsibility which most businesspeople bring to their business dealings. Should that fail, the next protection might be a vigorous competition among sellers. And sometimes the terms of a contract are monitored by an administrative agency for the benefit of individual consumers. The insurance commissions of most states, for example, require that insurance companies include in their policies certain clauses protecting the interests of those who purchase insurance coverage. Whether motivated by ethical considerations or merely by the pressures of competition, many businesses choose not to exercise their superior bargaining power in oppressive ways. If ethical and competitive protections fail, the courts and legislatures may intervene. The courts have invalidated contracts or clauses in a variety of ways—for example, by holding that an adhesive contract or clause is contrary to public policy.

Exculpatory Clauses. *Exculpatory clauses* are contractual provisions whose aim is to exempt a contracting party from the payment of damages for his or her own misconduct. Such clauses frequently are challenged in court as being contrary to public policy.

In many states, some types of exculpatory clauses are made illegal by statute. In the absence of a statute dealing with exculpatory clauses, the courts must decide whether to enforce them. Ordinarily, the courts will not enforce those that relieve a contracting party of responsibility for his or her own criminal conduct, intentional torts, or "gross" negligence. In such instances, the desirability of freedom of contract and the need of the public for stability of contracting give way to other interests. Among them is the need of the public for protection against contractual arrangements which, by protecting wrongdoers, tend to induce a lack of regard for the safety or rights of others. A clause that exempts a person from liability for his or her own "simple" negligence might or might not be upheld. If the clause is freely consented to by parties of substantially equal bargaining power, the court ordinarily will uphold it as an appropriate measure for shifting risk of loss. In contrast, if the clause is a part of a *contract of adhesion* so that the weaker party has no choice but to bear the consequences of the other party's simple negligence, the clause might be invalidated.

In Case 12.2, the California Supreme Court applied a state statute to a contract of adhesion containing an exculpatory clause. The case is especially noteworthy for its discussion of the circumstances under which such clauses will be held invalid.

CASE 12.2 Tunkl v. Regents of University of California · 383 P.2d 441 (Cal. 1963)

FACTS The University of California at Los Angeles Medical Center admitted Hugo Tunkl as a patient. Tunkl, in great pain, under sedation, and probably unable to read, signed a document containing the following clause: "RELEASE: The hospital is a nonprofit, charitable institution. In consideration of the hospital and allied services to be rendered and the rates charged therefor, the patient... hereby releases The Regents of the University of California and the hospital from any and all liability for the negligent or wrongful acts or omissions of its employees, if the hospital has used due care in selecting its employees." Alleging that personal injuries resulted from the negligence of two physicians employed by the Medical Center, Tunkl sued the Regents for damages. Mr. Tunkl died after suit was brought, and Mrs. Tunkl was substituted as plaintiff. She stipulated that the hospital had selected its employees with due care. The trial court entered judgment for the Regents, and plaintiff appealed.

OPINION TOBRINER, J. This case concerns the validity of a release from liability for future negligence imposed as a condition for admission to a charitable research hospital.... [W]e have concluded that an agreement between a hospital and an entering patient affects the public interest and that, in consequence, the exculpatory provision included within it must be invalid under Civil Code section 1668.... [Section 1668] states: "All contracts which have for their object, directly or indirectly, to exempt anyone from responsibility for his own fraud, or willful injury to the person or property of another, or violation of law, whether willful or negligent, are against the policy of the law."

...[T]he courts' interpretations of [Section 1668] have been diverse.... The court in *England v. Lyon Fireproof Storage Co.* ... categorically states, "The court correctly instructed the jury that—'The defendant cannot limit its liability against its own negligence by contract, and any contract to that effect would be void.'"... The recent case of *Mills v. Ruppert*..., however, apparently limits "[N]egligent... violation of law" exclusively to statutory law. Other cases hold that the statute prohibits the exculpation of gross negligence only; still another case states that the section forbids exemption from active as contrasted with passive negligence....

CASE 12.2 Continued

In one respect, [however,] the decisions are uniform. The cases have consistently held that the exculpatory provision may stand only if it does not involve "the public interest."* In *Stephens v. Southern Pacific Co.* . . . a railroad company had leased land, which adjoined its depot, to a lessee who had constructed a warehouse upon it. The lessee covenanted that the railroad company would not be responsible for damage from fire "caused by any . . . means." This exemption, under the court ruling, applied to the lessee's damage resulting from the railroad company's carelessly burning dry grass and rubbish. Declaring the contract not "violative of sound public policy," the court pointed out [that] "As far as this transaction was concerned, the parties, when contracting, stood upon common ground, and dealt with each other as A and B might deal with each other with reference to any private business undertaking." The court concluded that "the *interests of the public* in the contract are more sentimental than real" and that the exculpatory provision was therefore enforceable.

In applying this approach . . . some later courts enforced and invalidated such provisions under section 1668. Thus, in *Nichols v. Hitchcock Motor Co.* . . . the court enforced an exculpatory clause on the ground that "the public neither had nor could have any interest whatsoever in the subject-matter of the contract. . . . The agreement between the parties concerned 'their private affairs' only."

In *Barkett v. Brucato* . . . , which involved a waiver clause in a private lease, Justice Peters summarizes the previous decisions in this language: "These cases hold that the matter is simply one of interpreting a contract; that both parties are free to contract; that the relationship of landlord and tenant *does not affect the public interest;* that such a provision *affects only the private affairs of the parties.* . . . (Emphasis added.)

On the other hand, courts struck down exculpatory clauses as contrary to public policy in the case of a contract to transmit a telegraph message . . . and in the instance of a contract of bailment. In *Hiroshima v. Bank of Italy* . . . , the court invalidated an exemption provision in the form used by a payee in directing a bank to stop payment on a check. The court relied in part upon the fact that "the banking public, as well as the particular individual who may be concerned in the giving of any stop notice, is interested in seeing that the bank is held accountable for the ordinary and regular performance of its duties, and also in seeing that directions in relation to the disposition of funds deposited in the bank are not heedlessly, negligently, and carelessly disobeyed, and money paid out contrary to directions given." . . .

If, then, the exculpatory clause which affects the public interest cannot stand, we must ascertain those factors or characteristics which constitute the public interest. . . . [T]he courts have revealed a rough outline of that type of transaction in which exculpatory provisions will be held invalid. . . . [T]he attempted but invalid exemption involves a transaction which exhibits some or all of the following characteristics. It concerns a business of a type generally thought suitable for public regulation. The party seeking exculpation is engaged in performing a service of great importance to the public, which is often a matter of practical necessity for some members of the public. The party holds himself out as willing to perform this service for any member of the public who seeks it, or at least for any member coming within certain established standards. As a result of the essential nature of the service, in the economic setting of the transaction, the party invoking exculpation possesses a decisive advantage of bargaining strength against any member of the public who seeks his services. In exercising a superior bargaining power the party confronts the public with a standardized adhesion contract of exculpation, and makes no provision whereby a purchaser may pay additional reasonable fees and obtain protection against negligence. Finally, as a result of the transaction, the person or property of the purchaser is placed under the control of the seller, subject to the risk of carelessness by the seller or his agents. . . .

*The view that the exculpatory contract is valid only if the public interest is not involved represents the majority holding in the United States. Only New Hampshire, in definite opposition to [the] "public interest" test, categorically refuses to enforce exculpatory provisions. . . . [Court's footnote.]

CASE 12.2 Continued

While obviously no public policy opposes private, voluntary transactions in which one party, for a consideration, agrees to shoulder a risk which the law would otherwise have placed upon the other party, the above circumstances pose a different situation. In this situation the releasing party does not really acquiesce voluntarily in the contractual shifting of the risk. . . . Since the service is one which each member of the public . . . may find essential to him, he faces, despite his economic inability to do so, the prospect of a compulsory assumption of the risk of another's negligence. The public policy of this state has been, in substance, to posit the risk of negligence upon the actor; in instances in which this policy has been abandoned, it has generally been to allow or require that the risk shift to another party better or equally able to bear it, not to shift the risk to the weak bargainer.

In light of the decisions, we think that the hospital-patient contract clearly falls within the category of agreements affecting the public interest. To meet that test, the agreement need only fulfill some of the characteristics above outlined; here, the relationship fulfills all of them. Thus the contract of exculpation involves an institution suitable for, and a subject of, public regulation. . . . That the services of the hospital to those members of the public who are in special need of the particular skill of its staff and facilities constitute a practical and crucial necessity is hardly open to question.

The hospital, likewise, holds itself out as willing to perform its services for those members of the public who qualify for its research and training facilities. While it is true that the hospital is selective as to the patients it will accept, such selectivity does not negate its public aspect or the public interest in it. . . .

In insisting that the patient accept the provision of waiver in the contract, the hospital certainly exercises a decisive advantage in bargaining. The would-be patient is in no position to reject the proffered agreement, to bargain with the hospital, or in lieu of agreement to find another hospital. . . . [We must] conclude that the instant agreement manifested the characteristics of the so-called adhesion contract. Finally, when the patient signed the contract, he completely placed himself in the control of the hospital; he subjected himself to the risk of its carelessness.

[The court then rejected the defendants' arguments in support of their exculpatory clause. The court also pointed out that although the clause was invalid, the plaintiff must prove negligence on the part of the physicians.]

JUDGMENT The judgment is reversed.

Common Types of Illegal Agreements

As traditionally understood, "illegality" refers to conduct that is against the law each time it occurs, regardless of the circumstances. Suppose Joe hires Ann to steal Ben's property. The transaction and all others like it lack the legality required for a contract to arise; Joe and Ann have not created a contract—they have merely made an agreement that is "void," i.e., that creates no legal rights whatever.

Sometimes a contract or a contractual clause is permitted in some circumstances but not in others. For example, as noted later, a clause prohibiting competition might be wrongful or not, depending on the circumstances surrounding the contract. It cannot be said that the act of prohibiting competition is inherently evil, because the law sometimes permits it. Nevertheless, when done under forbidden circumstances, the act is wrongful and can be considered illegal to the extent, at least, of denying enforceability to the noncompetition clause.

The following pages discuss a few representative types of illegal agreements.

Agreements Not to Compete

Types of Agreements Not to Compete. Much of our law is aimed at preserving free trade and an active competition among sellers so that the public will have an abundance of goods and services without being forced to pay unreasonably high prices. In general, price fixing, monopolistic combinations of firms in restraint of trade, and other types of agreements not to compete are against public policy. Controlling large-scale restraints on trade is the purpose of the Sherman Act, the Clayton Act, and other antitrust law discussed in Chapters 45 and 46.

However, some agreements not to compete are beneficial and even necessary for businesses to operate efficiently. Two important examples are:

- An agreement by the seller of a business not to compete with the buyer.
- An agreement by an employee not to compete with the employer after the termination of the employment.

Because these agreements would prohibit a person from engaging in his or her livelihood, the courts are reluctant to enforce them except for compelling reasons. For what reasons and to what extent may such agreements be enforced?

Agreement by seller of a business. Where the owner of a business sells it as a "going concern," the buyer rightfully expects to receive all of the business assets—including the continued patronage of the seller's customers (their goodwill) free from the seller's interference until the buyer has had a reasonable opportunity to establish his or her own business reputation. To protect goodwill, the buyer might require the seller to sign an agreement not to compete with the buyer. The courts will enforce such an agreement if it imposes no more than a reasonable restraint on the seller. Usually a restraint is reasonable if it is so limited in duration and in territory covered as to protect only the goodwill purchased. The reasonableness of a restraint is a question of fact to be determined from all the circumstances. A covenant (promise) by the seller of a small store with a neighborhood trade not to compete for 6 months anywhere within the city might be unduly burdensome to the seller and unenforceable, whereas a covenant by the seller of a firm doing a statewide business not to compete for 3 years anywhere in the state might be a reasonable restriction.

Agreement by employee. Often employees must sign employment contracts that contain covenants not to compete with the employer upon termination of the employment. The covenant may purport to prohibit the employee from setting up a business in competition with the former employer, from entering the employment of a competitor, or from revealing the former employer's trade secrets. Even in the absence of a contractual provision, an employee has no right to reveal the employer's trade secrets, and so a contract provision prohibiting such conduct will be enforced.

An employee's agreement not to compete with the former employer, however, may or may not be enforceable. Enforcement of such an agreement may seriously hamper the employee in his or her efforts to earn a living, or it may deprive the public of the benefit that could result from competition between the employer and the former employee. To be enforceable, an employee's covenant not to compete must be reasonable in duration and territory covered. To determine whether the duration and territorial coverage of a particular covenant are reasonable, a court must consider the degree of hardship the covenant imposes on the former employee, the harm to the public resulting from the reduced competition, and the seriousness of the employer's need to prevent competition by the former employee.

Divisibility of Agreements Not to Compete. Suppose that Bob, the buyer of a small delicatessen store whose business extends for a twelve-block radius, requires Sue, the seller, to agree not to compete within a radius of 20 miles. Immediately after the sale, Sue announces that within the next few days she will open a new delicatessen store three blocks from her former location. Bob seeks an injunction restraining Sue from opening the store. Most courts would agree that Bob has demanded an unreasonably broad restriction on Sue's right to conduct a business. But they would also agree that Sue threatens to interfere unreasonably with the goodwill Bob thought he had purchased. Whom should the courts protect?

Some courts refuse to enforce overly broad restrictions, and thus would deny Bob injunctive relief. They refuse enforcement to encourage buyers to be cautious and to draft clauses that will be reasonable. In these jurisdictions, buyers who draft overly broad clauses do so at the risk of losing all protection. Other courts would hold that because a twelve-block limitation would have been reasonable, the restrictive agreement is enforceable at least to that extent. In granting the buyer injunctive relief, these courts treat overly broad agreements as "divisible," or "severable," (partially enforceable), especially where the overbreadth seems inadvertent or where the reasonableness of the restriction was difficult to estimate.

A similar problem arises—and a similar split of authority occurs—where an agreement not to compete specifies a time limit greater than necessary to protect the purchaser. Sometimes agreements not to compete mention no time limit. In such instances many courts enforce the agreement if the seller attempts to compete before the expiration of a reasonable time, but only if the agreement is otherwise reasonable.

The case that follows involves a franchise agreement. The validity of its covenant not to compete is governed by principles similar to those just discussed.

CASE 12.3 McCart v. H & R Block, Inc. · 470 N.E.2d 756 (Ind. App. 1984)

FACTS Robert McCart [defendant] operated a tax preparation service in Rochester, Indiana. In 1968 he signed a contract affiliating his tax service with H & R Block, Inc. [plaintiff]. In 1969 he became a district manager for Block, a position that prevented him from keeping the Rochester office in his name. Accordingly, on behalf of Block, he issued the Rochester franchise to June McCart, his wife, who in 1975 signed a new franchise agreement with Block. It contained a "franchisee's covenant not to compete," which prohibited her from competing with Block "for a period of two years after the termination...of this franchise...within 50 miles of the franchise territory...." On December 15, 1981, June terminated the agreement, saying she had arthritis. In 1979, Robert had begun working at June's franchise location, representing himself as the office manager, conferring with Block representatives, and doing tax work on Block forms.

Shortly after canceling the Block agreement, June sent a letter to former Block clients announcing that she was disassociating herself from Block and was joining her husband's tax service. She used Block envelopes with "H & R Block" blacked out, but with Block's slogan "The Income Tax People" remaining and the name "Community Tax Service" added. In each envelope, Robert enclosed a letter of his own announcing that he was opening an office at the old Block location under the new name.

Block opened a new tax service nearby. The new franchisee quickly learned that customers confused her office with the McCarts' and that even the telephone information operator thought there were two Block locations. Block was granted an injunction preventing the McCarts from operating their tax service within 50 miles of Rochester. The McCarts appealed, contending: (1) that Robert should not be enjoined from competing with Block, and (2) that the covenant in June's franchise agreement was an unenforceable restraint of trade.

OPINION GARRARD, J....*I. Propriety of injunction against Robert.* Robert contends that...the trial court erred by enjoining him from competing with Block. We disagree.

[The court held that] "the defendants,...acting together, have [endeavored] to trade upon the going concern value, goodwill, and national advertising efforts of the plaintiff, a valuable property right of the plaintiff[,] in violation of the terms of the...franchise agreement."

Robert's argument is a logical one: he did not sign the...agreement; he therefore should not be bound by its restrictive covenant....While we find no Indiana cases directly addressing this issue, our search of the law in other states reveals..."that the rule that a stranger to a covenant may be enjoined from aiding and assisting the covenantor in violating his covenant is supported by an overwhelming weight of authority"....

As the...cases amply establish, it is not necessary to show Robert's signature on the agreement before enjoining him from assisting the breach of the agreement by June. The

CASE 12.3 Continued

evidence supports the finding that Robert acted together with June to breach her agreement.... [As] stated by the trial court: "If this court were to enjoin June only and allowed Robert to continue the tax preparation trade at the same site and with the same customers the Court would be ignoring the business realities of the situation, frustrating the proper purpose of [the restrictive covenant], and [permitting June to compete indirectly] and benefit in specific violation of the contract terms. The McCarts treated the operation as their joint business...and held themselves out to the public that way."...Robert knowingly participated and aided June in the violation of her contract with Block. Their cooperative conduct amounted to mere subterfuge designed to avoid June's obligation under the contract. The court did not err by including Robert within the scope of the injunction.

II. Enforceability of the covenant not to compete.... June contends the covenant is void as a restraint on trade and unreasonable as to its territorial limitation. She contends that because she did not learn any of Block's trade secrets, confidential information, or customer lists during the term of the agreement, Block had no recognizable, protectible interest that could be covered by the covenant consistent with public policy.

It is true that a covenant in general restraint of trade is void as against public policy....The enforceability of the covenant depends upon the facts and circumstances surrounding each case[,] including the legitimate interests of the covenantee [Block] and the protection provided in terms of the duration and geographical limitation of the covenant. While most often the enforceability of a covenant not to compete arises in the context of a sale of a business or a contract between employer and employee, "The rule is well established that such a clause is good if it is ancillary to any lawful contract[,] subject, of course, to the test of reasonableness of the covenant and whether it is inimical to the public welfare."...

Before we can affirm the enforcement of this covenant not to compete, we first must determine the nature of Block's protectible interest. In the...franchise agreement, Block granted to June "exclusively, the right to operate an income tax return preparation service and to perform 'related services' under the name and service mark 'H & R Block'" in Rochester. A service mark is a form of property and has property rights associated with it....In exchange for the property right granted to her by Block, June agreed...to pay Block a percentage of the gross receipts from the preparation of income tax returns during the term of the agreement and to not compete with Block for two years thereafter.

The rationale for entering a contract for the use of a service mark is to draw on the reputation associated with the name in order to attract customers by identifying the services of one person and distinguishing them from services of another....Robert entered the initial agreement with Block because "there was money to be made in it." The use of the name "H & R Block" allowed June to take advantage of the public's recognition of that name.

June's argument is essentially that the customers at the...Block office in Rochester were hers, not Block's, and that...the courts should not enforce the covenant which would prevent her from providing services for her customers. Her argument must fail because it overlooks the value of the service mark for which she bargained.

Despite June's present contention to the contrary, at the time she entered the contract with Block, both parties understood that the bargain for use of the Block service mark was a bargain for customers who would be attracted to the Block name. She cannot now be heard to claim [that] Block has no protectible interest in [the] customers she gained while offering services under that name....

While we conclude [that] Block did have a protectible interest in the customers June serviced under the Block name, we still must determine the reasonableness of the covenant. The subject of area limitations has been discussed in this state in the context of employment contracts....Restrictive covenants in employment contracts are invalid if they restrict the employee from competing in an area greater than necessary to protect the

CASE 12.3 Continued

goodwill of the employer. . . . In *Frederick,* we reversed an order enjoining an ex-employee from engaging in the contract building maintenance business in an eight county area for ten years from the date he terminated his employment. The covenant was unreasonable because the employee . . . had operated in [only] two counties. Thus the covenant prohibited activity beyond the area within which [the employer had a protectible interest]. . . . In *Losure* . . . the employee of a coffee service agreed not to compete during his employment and for three years thereafter in any area he serviced during his employment. We held [that] this covenant, properly limited as it was to the employee's area of work, was enforceable to protect the business and goodwill of the employer.

The evidence here shows that 22 miles was as far as any customer had traveled to use June's services at the . . . office in Rochester. June argues that the 50 mile limitation imposed upon her is therefore unreasonable. However, focusing again on Block's protectible interest . . . we cannot agree with her. In the above cases, the employees would go to the customers to sell a product or provide a service[,] thus defining a specific area of activity. Here Block's protectible interest was the customer recognition of its service mark and the year to year affiliation those customers might develop with a particular office. Unlike the above cases, the nature of this business requires that the customers go to the . . . office to have their tax returns prepared. Thus the area [defined] by the customer affiliation is broader and less specific, depending as it must on where the competing office is established. . . . [T]he McCarts might open an office 44 miles from Rochester and still draw the same customers who previously had traveled 22 miles to have their taxes prepared in Rochester. Block has as much right to protect its interest in those customers as it did customers in Rochester. The McCarts had a list of all the customers who had used their service at the . . . Block office. . . . They used that list to take advantage of the customer affiliation they had built on the Block name during their combined thirteen years as Block franchisees. It was not unreasonable to recognize Block's protectible interest and to enforce the covenant against the McCarts as it was written[,] restricting competition for two years within a 50 mile radius of Rochester.

JUDGMENT Affirmed.

Agreements Involving Usury

Meaning and Effect of Usury. To discourage the charging of exorbitant interest, almost every state has a statute specifying the highest rate of interest that may be charged for a loan of money. *Usury* is the charging of any rate of interest in excess of that permitted by law.

Statutes usually specify a maximum rate of interest of general application for "normal" loans and a series of higher maximum rates for other kinds of loans, for example, loans by pawn brokers and small loan companies. Typically these latter kinds of loans involve small amounts of money and relatively high costs of collection. The bookkeeping expenses attending such loans, together with the doubtful creditworthiness of many of the borrowers, warrant higher maximum interest rates. The states differ in their treatment of usurious agreements. In some states usurious agreements are void, and the overreaching lender forfeits interest *and* principal. In other states a usurious agreement is voidable, but only as to the amount of interest in excess of the amount permitted by law. In still other states the agreement is voidable as to the usurious amount, and the injured party may recover a penalty of double or triple the usurious amount.

Effect of Usury Limits on Availability of Credit. Statutes imposed usury limits long before the need for massive amounts of credit developed. When the need developed, the market price of business and consumer credit was forced up, well beyond the limits imposed by the usury statutes, and lenders diverted their funds to more lucrative markets. To encourage lenders to provide businesses with an adequate supply of credit, the laws of many states now exempt loans to corporations from the limits imposed by the usury statutes. Other state laws encourage the extension of consumer credit by exempting certain types of consumer loans and lenders from the coverage of the usury statutes—for example, consumer real estate loans, car loans, and installment loans made by banks and credit unions. The courts, too, have recognized the need for more consumer credit and in a number of ways have contributed to its availability. Chief among these contributions was the development of the "time-price" doctrine. When a person makes immediate payment for goods at a store, he or she is charged a so-called "cash" price which supposedly represents the lowest price at which the seller is willing to do business. If the buyer is permitted to purchase the goods on a credit (e.g., installment payment) basis, the seller runs a higher risk of nonpayment. To compensate for the added risk, the seller may charge a higher price (called the time price) for the goods. Under the time-price doctrine (in those states which still impose it), the credit sale of goods is not a loan, and the difference between the cash price and the time price is not considered interest. This is so even though the difference is commonly expressed in terms of a percentage of the cash price. Thus, credit sales of goods are sometimes held not to be subject to the usury statutes.

Reform of Consumer Credit Extension and Usury Law. Legislatures typically have imposed flat limits on the rates of interest which can legally be charged, and they have left to the courts the task of deciding which methods of interest calculation violate the statutes. Some methods of calculating or expressing interest disguise the actual rate of interest being charged and were originally devised to circumvent the statutory limits on interest. Some of these methods are still in use. They tend to confuse borrowers and to make comparison shopping for credit difficult.

Within recent years there have been significant attempts to reform the law relating to credit extension and usury. The federal Truth-in-Lending Act[8] and the Uniform Consumer Credit Code (UCCC)[9] impose disclosure requirements on the lenders to whom the laws apply. Under both laws, lenders must disclose to borrowers the true cost of credit. Moreover, the cost of credit must be calculated and reported to borrowers in terms they can understand: specifically, in terms of an annual percentage rate as that rate is defined in the applicable law. The UCCC is more than a disclosure statute. It also provides maximum rates of interest which can legally be charged, prohibits false and misleading credit advertising, and imposes other restrictions on lenders. Both the Truth-in-Lending Act and the UCCC apply to all extensions of consumer credit: bank loans, credit sales of goods, and other forms of consumer credit.

[8]Officially known as Title I, Consumer Credit Protection Act.
[9]As of June 1987, adopted by Colorado, Guam, Idaho, Indiana, Iowa, Kansas, Maine, Oklahoma, South Carolina, Utah, Wisconsin, and Wyoming.

Agreements in Violation of Sunday-Closing Statutes

Many states have statutes prohibiting or regulating certain kinds of Sunday transactions. Such statutes are commonly referred to as Sunday-closing laws, or "blue laws," and in colonial times were intended to encourage the practice of religion. Today, the First and the Fourteenth Amendments of the United States Constitution forbid laws "respecting an establishment of religion, or prohibiting the free exercise thereof."

Nevertheless, Sunday-closing legislation will be upheld if the purpose for it is rational and nonreligious and if the legislation does not violate the due process or equal protection guarantees of the state or federal constitutions. Sunday-closing laws will be upheld, for example, where they have an economic justification or where they are merely an exercise of a state's police power to provide a day of rest, amusement, and family togetherness. In some states, Sunday-closing laws are generally enforced; in others, they are generally ignored.

Agreements in Violation of Licensing Statutes

All states have statutes requiring a person to obtain a license, certificate, or diploma before carrying on certain occupations. Licenses are required of doctors, dentists, lawyers, public accountants, and those engaged in other professions; of electricians, plumbers, contractors, beauty operators, barbers, and those engaged in other skilled occupations; and of pawnbrokers, wholesalers and retailers of liquor, operators of restaurants and hotels, and those engaged in other kinds of businesses.

Usually, licensing statutes provide that any person who carries on one of the designated occupations or businesses without obtaining the required license is subject to a fine. However, most licensing statutes do not state whether an unlicensed person may enforce his or her contracts with customers or clients. To decide this question, courts look to the character of the statute. Some licensing statutes are regulatory in character, designed to protect the public against unprincipled and unqualified persons. Other licensing statutes are revenue-raising measures that impose a license simply to collect a tax. If a statute is regulatory, unlicensed persons ordinarily cannot recover payment for services rendered or for goods delivered. Licensing statutes applying to building contractors usually are regulatory in nature. A building contractor who does not have the required license normally is not allowed to recover compensation for services performed in constructing improvements on someone's land. By denying compensation to violators of regulatory licensing statutes, the courts encourage unlicensed practitioners to withhold services until they have demonstrated (by compliance with the statute) possession of the minimum qualifications thought necessary for the safety of the public.

In contrast, city or county business licensing ordinances ordinarily are revenue-raising measures. A business that fails to acquire the required license may be fined by the taxing authority but may still enforce contracts and recover compensation for services rendered.

Whether a statute is of a regulatory or revenue-producing character may be the most important test in helping courts decide whether to award violators recovery of compensation, but it is not the only available test. Others include: Did the unlicensed person perform the contract fully and well? Did the performance endanger public safety, health, or morals? Would denial of recovery cause a substantial loss to the unlicensed person and an undeserved windfall to the other party?

As the following case illustrates, the fact that a licensing statute is regulatory does not necessarily require a violator to forfeit compensation for services rendered.

CASE 12.4 Thistle v. Englert · 479 N.Y.S.2d 921 (App. Div. 1984)

FACTS Thistle delivered her 1964 Chevrolet Corvette to Englert for modifications and repairs. Nearly 3 years later Thistle sued Englert for possession of the car and damages. Englert counterclaimed for $6,162.30 for repair services and sought to foreclose his alleged garageman's lien. Thistle contended that Englert was not licensed to repair motor vehicles and thus was not entitled to payment.

OPINION SCHNEPP, J. . . . The proof establishes that the defendant was engaged in the business of repairing motor vehicles and he admits . . . that he operated an unregistered motor vehicle repair shop [in violation of article 12-A of the Vehicle and Traffic Law].

. . . It has been held that an agreement to render services by one who is not licensed or registered, although required to be by statute, renders the contract illegal and unenforceable, even though fully performed. . . . As a general rule, however, the purpose of the Legislature in enacting a licensing statute controls in arriving at a determination of this issue. . . . Our task, therefore, is to ascertain whether the Legislature intended to require forfeiture of contractual rights as a means to further the purposes of the repair shop registration act. [If the statute] has a regulatory purpose to protect the public against fraud and incompetence, the conclusion that the Legislature intended to penalize the statute breaker by denying him enforcement is "much more likely". . . . This conclusion is tenable, however, only if the public interest in the enforcement of contracts is clearly outweighed by the public policy behind the regulation. "If the statute does not provide expressly that its violation will deprive the parties of their right to sue on the contract, and the denial of [a right to sue] is wholly out of proportion to the requirements of public policy or appropriate individual punishment, the right to recover will

CASE 12.4 Continued

not be denied." . . . Accordingly . . . the court must strike an appropriate balance which furthers the goals established by the Legislature without causing disproportionate and unintended hardship to the unregistered defendant. . . .

The purpose of the Motor Vehicle Repair Shop Registration Act is clearly regulatory. [Its purpose is to further] highway safety by promoting proper and efficient repair of motor vehicles, the protection of consumers from dishonest, deceptive and fraudulent practices, the elimination from business of persons who engaged in dishonest or fraudulent practices, and the setting of standards for quality repairs. . . . [T]he primary legislative intent was to promote safety and to protect consumers by regulating the fitness of repair shops. . . .

We [must] now examine the statute . . . in order to determine whether the Legislature intended to require forfeiture as a means to effectuate its regulatory purpose. . . . [T]he act itself is silent on the matter of the enforceability of contracts and does not expressly mandate forfeiture. Next, there is no doubt that the Legislature considered registration, not forfeiture, to be the linchpin of the entire regulatory scheme. Once a repair shop is registered, the commissioner has broad powers to investigate the quality of repairs, to regulate against fraudulent and deceptive practices, and to assess civil penalties, including fines and restitution. Registration is so important to the Legislature's purpose that [it] conferred on the commissioner and the Attorney-General authority to apply for injunctive relief to put unregistered repair shops out of business. . . .

As an alternative to the drastic remedy of injunction, the commissioner has the authority . . . to hear and determine charges of unregistered operation and to assess a civil penalty of $1,000, all but $50 of which may be avoided if the repair shop is registered within 10 days. . . . [T]hat the Legislature chose to impose only a civil penalty instead of criminal sanctions and to establish a minimum fine of just $50 [indicates] a legislative intent that in the first instance repair shops should not be severely punished for not registering. . . . The Legislature sought to accomplish [its] purpose with a nuisance penalty backed up with the *threat* of more severe punishment. . . .

. . . [T]he minor punishment of a $50 civil penalty distinguishes article 12-A from other licensing or registration statutes where the legislature has imposed greater penalties giving the offense of not registering a more serious character. [Often], where the Legislature has signaled that not registering is in . . . itself a serious offense, the courts have subsequently implied a legislative intent to deny enforcement of contracts as necessary to further the goal of the legislation. This is particularly true where failure to register is punishable as a criminal offense . . . and also where there is a sizable civil penalty. . . . Present in such statutes, but absent from article 12-A, is an indication from the Legislature that unlicensed persons pose such a significant threat to the public that they should immediately be put out of business.

That the Legislature did not intend to require the forfeiture of contractual rights under article 12-A may also be implied from the fact that only the Attorney-General is authorized to seek injunctive relief to put unregistered repair shops out of business. . . . Adding the penalty of forfeiture of contractual rights to the sanctions imposed by the Legislature would be inconsistent with the intent of that body to delegate authority only to the commissioner and the Attorney-General to deal with unregistered repair shops. . . . [I]n light of the *de minimis* $50 penalty for failure to register, the added . . . penalty of forfeiture would be unduly harsh and disproportionate and unnecessary to further the goals of the legislation. . . . Accordingly, defendant's operation of an unregistered motor vehicle repair shop does not preclude recovery for the [repair] services he performed . . . , and since the underlying claim is enforceable, he may assert a garageman's lien against the motor vehicle.

JUDGMENT The order of Special Term [is] affirmed.

Confession of Judgment Clauses in Promissory Notes

A person who borrows money or buys a house, car, or business on credit usually must sign a promissory note for the amount owed plus interest. Most note forms contain a number of clauses that specify the rights and duties of creditor and debtor. One often included is the "confession of judgment" clause. It is so named because, by agreeing to it, the debtor gives written permission for the creditor's attorney to go to court and "confess judgment" against the debtor for the full amount of the debt upon the debtor's failure, justified or not, to make payments as they fall due. A note containing such a clause is a "cognovit note." If a creditor can enforce a cognovit note, the debtor is not entitled to notice of the court action, cannot raise any defenses to payment that he or she might have, and cannot appeal the judgment.

Suppose Dora buys a flower shop from Carl and signs a cognovit note for the purchase price to be paid in monthly installments. Later, learning that Carl fraudulently overstated the accounts receivable, she withholds the next monthly payment in an attempt to force Carl to lower the purchase price to reflect the true value of the business. Carl can immediately go to court and confess judgment against Dora. Since Dora cannot raise her defense of fraud and cannot appeal the judgment, she is left in the uncomfortable position of having to bring an independent lawsuit to resolve the problem. In the meantime, Carl is free to execute the judgment.

Because of the misuses to which cognovit notes can be put, most states severely limit their use or enforcement. Many state statutes declare the confession of judgment clause void regardless of the kind of credit transaction. Others prohibit the use of such clauses in consumer credit transactions. Still others limit their enforceability—for example, by allowing the debtor to raise certain defenses. Only nine states permit the unrestricted use of cognovit notes, usually on the ground that they encourage the extension of credit by making debt collection easier and will not be abused by most creditors.

Agreements Involving Interference with Governmental Processes

An agreement that interferes with the orderly processes of government—federal, state, or local—is against public policy. The interference might consist of corrupting a public official (legislative, executive, or judicial) or misleading the official's judgment. Two kinds of forbidden agreements are: (1) those interfering with the legislative process, and (2) those interfering with the judicial process.

Interference with the legislative process sometimes occurs through lobbying, although most lobbying is legal. For example, everyone has the right to try, by the presentation of facts and arguments in an open and aboveboard manner, to persuade legislators to vote for or against proposed legislation. But no one has a right to persuade public officials by bribery, threats, or other improper means. An agreement with a public official that he or she will take action in exchange for an improper inducement is illegal and thus unenforceable, regardless of whether the aim is to influence the passage of a law, the content of an administrative rule or regulation, or the government's awarding a contract. Also illegal is an agreement with an agent that he or she will procure official action by improper means.

The most common form of *interfering with the judicial process* is the bribery of a witness, juror, or judge. Bribery takes many forms—e.g., money or an interest in a business in exchange for favorable action; or even, where a judge is up for reelection to office, a promise to swing certain votes in the judge's favor for deciding a case a certain way.

An indirect interference is just as illegal as a direct one. For example, a party to a lawsuit might agree to pay a witness who is in the jurisdiction and subject to subpoena a fee greater than permitted by statute. The agreement is illegal because the payment may predispose the witness to favor the party whose witness she or he is rather than to speak the truth. Witness-fee statutes commonly exempt expert witnesses from the fee limitation. An agreement to pay an expert any reasonable compensation is legal, provided the agreement does not make payment contingent on the outcome of the case.

The ban against agreements interfering with the judicial process applies not only to civil but also to criminal proceedings. Suppose Dan steals money from his employer and Dan's father agrees to repay the amount if the employer will not press charges against Dan. The agreement is contrary to public policy as an interference with the enforcement of the criminal law. The father's promise to pay is unenforceable, and so is the employer's promise not to press charges.

Case 12.5 involves an interference with the governmental contracting processes of a foreign country—an act of "influence peddling" contrary to the public policy of both that country and the United States.

CASE 12.5 Kashfi v. Philbro-Salomon, Inc. · 628 F.Supp. 727 (S.D.N.Y. 1986)

FACTS A.M. Kashfi (plaintiff) signed a written agreement with Lazar Beresiner, who allegedly was acting on behalf of Philbro-Saloman, Inc. (defendant) and its English subsidiary, Derby & Co., to arrange an oil barter agreement between Philbro and the Iranian government. The oil was to be sold and the proceeds used by the Iranian government to buy American-made military aircraft. According to Kashfi, an Iranian citizen residing in California, he set up a series of meetings between key Iranian officials and Philbro, a Delaware trading corporation that deals in oil, metals, and other commodities. Kashfi contends that in June 1976, the Shah of Iran approved the oil barter transaction, that the agreement resulted in the sale of $2.4 billion worth of Iranian oil, and that Philbro owes him $24 million, the 1 percent fee provided for in the written agreement. Kashfi brought suit for that amount, and Philbro, denying that the oil barter transaction was ever executed, moved for summary judgment.

OPINION TENNEY, D. J.... [Philbro] argues that the summary judgment should be granted... because the agreement is illegal under Iranian law and therefore is unenforceable. The Court agrees.

Summary judgment is... appropriate in this case because the contract sued on contravenes Iranian law and is therefore unenforceable.... A party to an illegal contract cannot ask a court of law to help him enforce that contract. Relief is denied to such a plaintiff, not because the court favors the defendant, but rather because the court will not aid a party whose claim arises out of his own immoral or illegal act....

The legality of a contract is ordinarily determined in accordance with the law of the place where the contract is performed.... In the case at bar, it is undisputed that performance was rendered in Iran. Iranian law, therefore, is controlling....

In the case at bar, the Court concludes that the contract is unenforceable because it violates Iran's penal statute—the Law for the Punishment of the Use of Influence Contrary to Justice and Legal Provisions... (the "Influence Law"). Articles One and Two of the Influence Law essentially prohibit an individual from being paid to exercise his good standing or influence with a public official.... Essentially, the plaintiff is seeking to be paid for having used his personal and political contacts for the defendant's benefit, which is precisely the type of conduct that is prohibited by the Iranian Influence Law.

The plaintiff himself admits that he is seeking compensation for exercising his influence. In his amended complaint, the plaintiff states that Beresiner wanted him to "use his contacts and influence in Iran to obtain meetings with... key cabinet members and the Shah of Iran himself, in order to present defendant's proposals".... In this... Statement, the plaintiff declares that he was an intimate friend of Alam, the Minister of the Imperial Court, and admits... that Alam facilitated business for him with the government of Iran based on the personal relationship between the plaintiff and Alam....

The... agreement... also contravenes the public policy of the United States. Exercising personal or political influence with government officials in order to obtain a government contract is expressly prohibited by [the federal Procurement Statute].... [Court's footnote: "In arguing that the contract is legal, the plaintiff relies on [the *Panelfab* case]. In that case, the court held that it is lawful for an individual 'to contract to use his influence [or] personal connections merely to gain access to a public official or even to urge an official to favor his client's proposal, as long as the persuasion is made on the merits of the proposal and not on any other basis.'... In the case at bar, the Court must apply the law of Iran, and the Iranian Influence Law would prohibit a contract such as the one

CASE 12.5 Continued

described in *Panelfab*. Moreover, the federal Procurement Statute would also prohibit such a contract, if the parties were attempting to procure a government contract. Thus the plaintiff's reliance on the *Panelfab* case is misplaced."]

Obviously the... agreement in the instant case is not invalidated by the federal Procurement Statute, since the United States government was not involved. However... [t]he Iranian Influence law is similar to the federal Procurement Statute, and... it appears that the objectives of both laws are the same. The purpose of the Procurement Statute is threefold: (1) to prevent the use of improper influence in connection with securing government contracts; (2) to eliminate arrangements which encourage inequitable and exorbitant fees that bear no reasonable relationship to the services rendered; and (3) to prevent contracts being awarded on a basis other than merit. *See*... *Quinn v. Gulf & Western*.... ("[Contingent fee] arrangements could easily result in higher prices for government goods and services as well as [in] contracts which would not have been awarded had all the potential contractors been afforded equal consideration.") These objectives can also be ascribed to the Iranian Influence Law. [Court's footnote: "It is interesting to note... that the plaintiff is seeking $24 million, a fee which... appears to bear little relationship to the value of the services actually performed. Moreover, the plaintiff stated... that Alam facilitated business for him based on their friendship, [a practice] which essentially undermines the policy of awarding a contract based on merit rather than personal contacts."] In order to enforce the [agreement] in this case, the Court would essentially have to disregard these objectives.

JUDGMENT Thus, for the reasons set forth above, the Court concludes that the... agreement is unenforceable.

Effect of Illegality

The General Rule

As a general rule, the courts will aid neither party to an illegal agreement. So, if the agreement is completely executory, neither party can tender performance and have performance or damages from the other party. If the agreement is completely executed, neither party can rescind it, tender the performance received, and compel the return of his or her own performance. Where one party has performed and the other party has not, the party who has performed cannot recover the performance or its value, and the other party cannot compel performance. Consequently, one wrongdoer may be unjustly enriched at the expense of the other.

Exceptions to the General Rule

To prevent the injustice that can result from a rigid application of the general rule, the courts recognize a number of exceptions to it. These exceptions, some of which are illustrated in the following paragraphs, involve circumstances in which a strict enforcement of the general rule would defeat other policies of the law.

Parties Not Equally at Fault. Where the parties to an illegal agreement are both blameworthy, but not equally so (not "*in pari delicto*"), and the party who was less at fault has rendered some performance, that party will be allowed to recover the performance or its value.

Courts frequently apply this principle where a person was induced to enter into an illegal agreement by the fraud, duress, or undue influence of the other party. Suppose that Ann, heavily in debt, fears that her creditors will seize all her property. Working on these fears, Ben, her lawyer, induces Ann to turn her property over to him on the promise that he will return it when her financial troubles are over. Ben subsequently refuses to perform his promise, and Ann sues. Although Ann's transfer of the property was for the illegal purpose of cheating her creditors, the courts will allow Ann to recover her property. To refuse to do so would be to reward the more blameworthy of the two parties to the illegal agreement.

Withdrawal from Illegal Agreement. Where an illegal bargain has been partly performed but the illegal part has not yet been performed, the party who has rendered performance can withdraw from the bargain and recover the performance or its value. The performing party is said to have a *locus poenitentiae*—literally, a place or opportunity for repentance. The opportunity to repent is not restricted to situations where one party is less at fault than the other. It applies also where the parties are equally at fault.

A common application of the repentance doctrine is a bettor's withdrawal from a wager in a state where bets are illegal. Suppose that each party to the wager deposited money with a stakeholder who has agreed to pay the winner of the bet. By depositing money, each party has partially performed the agreement. However, performance of the illegal part of the agreement does not occur until the money is paid to the winner. At any time before such payment occurs, either party is entitled to withdraw from the agreement by giving notice of repudiation to the stakeholder. If the stakeholder ignores a notice of repudiation and pays the wager, the stakeholder is liable for the amount of that party's deposit to the party who has given notice of repudiation.

Party Protected by Statute. Some statutes make a particular kind of agreement illegal to protect the members of a certain class of persons. For example, many statutes require the registration of corporate securities and the disclosure of financial information about the company before securities are sold. When a member of the protected class—here, potential purchasers of securities—agrees to buy unregistered securities, that person is usually entitled to some kind of relief despite the illegality of the transaction. The statute may state what relief is available. Where the statute does not specify a remedy, the court will grant an appropriate one—for example, rescission of the agreement if the purchaser of unregistered stocks or bonds wishes to cancel the deal. If the general rule of nonenforceability were applied, the purchasers for whose benefit the statute was enacted would be unable to get their money back and would be deprived of the protection that the legislature intended to provide.

Effect of Partial Illegality

Some agreements are illegal only in part. The general rule is that the illegal part taints the whole agreement and makes it void. However, where the agreement is "divisible," i.e., where the legal part of the agreement can be separated from the illegal part, most courts will enforce the legal part. Some kinds of agreements are clearly divisible—for example, an agreement to sell several articles at a designated price for each article. Even if one of the articles cannot legally be sold, the agreement could be enforced as to the other articles. However, if the agreement called for the sale of those same articles for one lump sum, the agreement would be indivisible and void.

Effect of Knowledge of Intended Illegal Use

A person who agrees to supply property or services, not knowing that the thing supplied will be used by the other party for an unlawful purpose, can enforce the agreement. Suppose that Ann agrees to rent a dock to Ben. Unknown to her, he intends to use it for smuggling goods into the country. If Ben finds another dock better suited for his purposes and refuses to pay the rent, Ann can recover damages for breach of contract; but if Ann changes her mind about renting the dock to Ben, he *cannot* enforce the agreement. A person who intends to accomplish an unlawful purpose may not enforce a "facilitating contract," that is, a contract made for the purpose of enabling him or her to accomplish the unlawful purpose.

Summary

An agreement is illegal if made or performed in violation of a constitution, statute, or other declaration of public policy. An agreement is against public policy if it tends to be injurious to the public.

Contracts of adhesion and exculpatory clauses may or may not be against public policy, depending on the circumstances. Agreements not to compete are restraints on trade, and the courts are reluctant to enforce them except for compelling reasons. Many such restraints are enforceable if properly limited. For example, an agreement by the seller of a business not to compete with the buyer is usually enforceable if so limited in duration and territory covered as to protect only the interest purchased. In contrast, a restriction that unreasonably deprives a person of the opportunity to engage in gainful employment will not be enforced.

Many other kinds of agreements are illegal. Among them are agreements to pay a usurious rate of interest and agreements involving interference with governmental processes. Many states prohibit the use of confession of judgment clauses in promissory notes.

Some classes of agreements present special problems. The law of usury must protect borrowers from overreaching lenders without unduly limiting the supply of consumer credit. A Sunday-closing law is unconstitutional if its purpose is to establish or prevent the free exercise of religion, but it may be constitutional if it has an economic or other nonreligious basis.

As a general rule, the courts will aid neither party to an illegal agreement. However, the rule is subject to many exceptions that give effect to various policies of the law. For example, where the parties to an illegal agreement are both blameworthy but the party who was less at fault has rendered some performance, that party may be allowed to recover the performance or its value. Similarly, a party protected by a statute may have a remedy despite the illegality of the transaction.

Review Questions

1 **(a)** An agreement is illegal if it is against public policy. Who has the authority to declare public policy? **(b)** Where a statute does not express any intention to make an agreement illegal, how do the courts determine whether the legislature had such an intention?

2 **(a)** Is a contract of adhesion void as against public policy? Explain. **(b)** Is a clause that exempts a contracting party from the payment of damages for her or his own negligence enforceable? Explain.

3 Even though there might be a justification for enforcing an agreement not to compete, the agreement will not be enforced unless the restraint it imposes is reasonable. In general, under what circumstances will the restraint be held reasonable?

4 **(a)** What is the legal effect of a usurious agreement? **(b)** What measures did the legislatures take to nullify the effect of the older usury limits on the availability of credit? **(c)** How might the judicial "time-price" doctrine contribute to the availability of consumer credit?

5 How do the Truth-in-Lending Act and the Uniform Consumer Credit Code affect agreements for the extension of credit?

6 Suppose a person is required to obtain a license before rendering services. Under what circumstances will a person who fails to obtain the required license be denied the right to enforce an agreement to compensate him or her for services rendered? Why?

7 Why do most states either declare confession of judgment clauses in promissory notes void or severely limit their enforceability?

8 An agreement involving interference with governmental processes is unenforceable. Give an example.

9 Give an example of a policy of the law justifying an exception to the general rule that a court will not aid either party to an illegal agreement.

Case Problems

1 Maura Wiscomb was seriously injured in a collision between the motorcycle she was operating and an automobile driven by her husband. She sued him in negligence. He turned the matter over to his insurance company (Mutual), which provided liability and uninsured motorist coverage for both Wiscomb vehicles. Seeking a declaratory judgment, Mutual denied liability, citing a family or household exclusion clause contained in the insurance policy: "Exclusions: This policy does not apply . . . (1) to bodily injury to the insured or any member of the family of the insured residing in the same household as the insured." The Financial Responsibility Act of the state of Washington requires drivers to demonstrate financial responsibility by filing a certificate of insurance, posting a bond, or depositing $60,000 worth of securities with the state. Few, if any, Washington insurance companies offered policies without the exclusion clause. The trial court held that Mutual was not liable. The court of appeals reversed, holding the clause void as against public policy. Mutual appealed to the Washington Supreme Court. Should the court hold the clause enforceable?

2 Wilcom operated a "drag strip" where, for a fee, persons could engage in automobile timing and acceleration runs (drag racing). Winterstein entered a race but was required to sign a document purporting to release Wilcom from liability for any injuries Winterstein might suffer while racing. Near the end of his run, his car hit a 100-pound cylinder head lying on the track. Winterstein sustained permanent injuries. The cylinder head was not visible to him when he commenced the race, but it was visible to Wilcom's employees who were stationed in a tower to watch for any hazards on the track. Alleging that Wilcom's employees were negligent and that the release was unenforceable, Winterstein sued Wilcom for damages. Was Winterstein entitled to damages?

3 Robins & Weill, Inc., an insurance agency engaged in the general insurance business, employed Mason and Hill to sell commercial insurance and to service the accounts. Both men signed employment contracts containing a covenant not to compete with Robins & Weill in the general insurance business for 3 years in Guilford County, where Robins & Weill did business. Several years later, Mason and Hill opened their own general insurance business, competing with Robins & Weill in Guilford County. Upon leaving Robins & Weill, Hill took with him a copy of its customer list. To enforce the covenant not to compete, Robins & Weill sought an injunction against Mason and Hill. The trial court granted a preliminary injunction against Mason and Hill. They appealed, and the court of appeals upheld the injunction to the extent that it prevented defendants from selling commercial property and casualty insurance, but stayed it to the extent that it forbade defendants from selling other lines of general insurance. Should the court of appeals have upheld the preliminary injunction in its entirety?

4 Delahunty performed repair work on Domizio's motor vehicle. Domizio was not satisfied with the result and refused to pay Delahunty for his services. Delahunty then sought to enforce the artificer's (mechanic's) lien he claimed to have on the vehicle. Domizio brought suit to enjoin Delahunty from enforcing the lien. At the hearing Delahunty admitted that neither he nor any of his employees had a license to repair motor vehicles. A state statute provided that "No person . . . shall engage in . . . the repairing of any motor vehicle without having been issued either a new car dealer's, a used car dealer's or a repairer's license." The fee charged for the license was small, and another state statute rendered violation of the licensing requirement criminal. Assume that Delahunty's services were competently performed. Was Delahunty entitled to compensation for his services and, consequently, to an artificer's lien?

5 Columbia Construction Co. hired Rapp Contracting Co. to install a water system in a townhouse complex being built for Highpoint Townhouses, Inc. Rapp completed the work and filed a mechanic's lien on the townhouse property. Highpoint did not pay, and Rapp sued to enforce the lien. Highpoint contended that the contract, and therefore the mechanic's lien, was unenforceable under a statute making it "unlawful for any person to engage in the work of plumbing . . . in the District of Columbia unless he is licensed [as] or is an employee of a licensed master plumber." The statute also provided that plumbing done by an unlicensed employee of a licensed master plumber "shall be done under the immediate personal supervision of the licensed man." Rapp admitted lacking a master plumber's license, but argued that Columbia had contracted with Federline, a master plumber, to acquire the permit required to tap into District water mains. According to Rapp, "we [did the installation] under their permit," but "I had no contact with the master plumber at all on the job, with regards to that permit." However, Rapp did do the work under the scrutiny of a District of Columbia inspector. The trial court ordered enforcement of the lien, and Highpoint appealed. Was the trial court correct in enforcing the lien?

6 The Interstate Commerce Commission (ICC) issued an order directing Southern Railway Co. to increase rates on grain shipments from the Midwest to the Southeast by approximately 16 percent. If allowed to stand, the order, Southern thought, would cause it to lose a $13 million investment in "Big John" railroad cars plus a "tremendous" loss of revenue in the future. Southern sought help from Robert B. Troutman, an Atlanta attorney. Troutman had no experience in ICC matters, but he was known as a personal friend and political ally of President John F. Kennedy. Southern told Troutman that it was filing a federal lawsuit to enjoin the order of the ICC. Southern asked Troutman to persuade the President and the Department of Justice to "ditch" the ICC and to enter the case on the side of Southern. Troutman did so, and the ICC order was struck down in court. Southern failed to compensate Troutman in the agreed manner, and he filed suit. A jury awarded him $175,000. Southern appealed, contending that the contract upon which Troutman sued was "to exert his personal and political influence upon the President of the United States" and that it was therefore in violation of public policy and unenforceable. Under what circumstances would Troutman's activities on behalf of Southern be legal so that he would be entitled to compensation?

CHAPTER 13

A Writing as a Requirement; the Parol Evidence Rule

To be enforceable, many informal contracts are required by the state "statute of frauds" to be in writing. The first part of this chapter discusses why and for what classes of contracts the statute of frauds imposes a writing requirement. It also discusses why the law sometimes permits alternatives to the normally required writing.

There is another question involving written contracts—one having nothing to do with the statute of frauds. A party to a written contract may contend that the writing (whether or not required by the statute of frauds) does not express the agreement of the parties. The dissatisfied party may wish to challenge the contents of the writing on the basis of prior inconsistent oral or written statements. That problem is considered in the second part of this chapter where the parol evidence rule is discussed.

Writing Requirements under the Statute of Frauds

In the 1300s the English courts began to enforce oral promises. In those days, parties to a lawsuit and anyone else with an interest in its outcome were incompetent as witnesses and were not allowed to testify. Instead, contract enforcement was based on the testimony of witnesses who were not parties to the contract. If they could be persuaded to testify falsely, a person could be held to a "contract" into which he or she had not entered. In 1677, to prevent such "frauds and perjuries," the English Parliament enacted the Statute of Frauds, which provided that a contract to which the Statute applied would not be enforced unless "the agreement . . . or some memorandum or note thereof shall be in writing, and signed by the person to be charged" with breach of the contract. Today, contracting parties in every state except Louisiana are subject to a statute of frauds (or, usually, an accumulation of statutes) similar in content to the English original.

The statute of frauds applies only to *certain* classes of contracts—those, such as contracts for the sale of land, thought to affect a vital interest of a contracting party. Except where a statute of frauds or some other special statute requires a writing for the formation or enforcement of a contract, an oral contract is as enforceable (though usually not so easily *provable*) as a written one.

Moreover, even for those classes of contracts covered by the statute of frauds, the writing requirement applies only to *executory* (unperformed) contracts, not executed ones. Suppose Alicia orally contracts to sell her house to Mario. As long as the oral contract remains executory, neither Mario nor Alicia can enforce it. But once Mario pays for the house and Alicia delivers a deed to it (a document transferring ownership to Mario), the oral contract, being executed, is binding on both. By performing the contract, Alicia and Mario have provided sufficient evidence that a contract was intended. In fact, as noted later in this chapter, the law accepts other substitutes, in addition to performance, for the writing normally required by the statute of frauds.

Classes of Contracts Covered by the Statute

Nearly every state statute of frauds requires a writing for the following six classes of contracts:

1. A contract of an executor or administrator to answer for a duty of the decedent (the executor-administrator provision)
2. A contract to answer for the debt or default of another (the suretyship provision)
3. A contract made upon consideration of marriage (the marriage provision)
4. A contract for the sale of goods worth more than $500 (the sales provision)
5. A contract for the sale of an interest in land (the land-contract provision)
6. A contract not performable within a year (the 1-year provision)

Many state statutes of frauds include additional classes of contracts. Examples are a contract to pay a commission for the sale of land and a contract of a person to leave property to someone else by will. The discussion in this chapter is limited mainly to the six basic classes of contracts.

Contract of Executor or Administrator. A promise of an executor of a will (or an administrator of an estate where there is no will) to pay the debt of the decedent out of the executor's own funds must be evidenced by a writing. Bereaved family members who happen to be executors are particularly vulnerable to pressures by the decedent's creditors for payment. The writing requirement gives executors a bit more time to consider whether to pay someone else's debt. Some states treat the executor-administrator situation as a form of suretyship, discussed in the next section.

Contract to Answer for Debt or Default of Another. Suppose Dan wants to buy a car, but Clara will not sell it to him unless Sam promises to pay the purchase price if Dan fails to pay. As a favor to Dan, Sam promises to pay if Dan does not. Sam is a *surety*, a person who, by contract or by operation of law, becomes liable for the debt or default of another person. In Figure 13.1, D represents Dan (the debtor), C represents Clara (the creditor), and S represents Sam (the surety). Sam's promise can be either oral or written.

Under the suretyship provision of the statute of frauds, Sam's promise to answer for Dan's debt or default is not enforceable unless evidenced by a writing. Sam has taken on a heavy burden—Dan gets the car, and Sam will have to pay even if Dan refuses to do so for no good reason. The writing requirement is especially for the protection of those who may be under social pressure to take on heavy obligations without considering the risks, and usually without receiving payment. Such burdensome promises often are made by family members and friends. But the writing requirement applies also to commercial suretyship transactions. An oral promise by a fidelity (bonding) company given to an employer to make good any embezzlement of company funds by an employee is not enforceable, nor (usually) is the oral promise of the president of a corporation to pay a supplier if the corporation doesn't.

Frequently, though, people promise to pay someone else's debt because they will themselves receive a substantial benefit. Because such promises are beneficial to the people making them, the courts have created an exception to the suretyship provision of the statute, called the "main-purpose" or "leading-object" rule: When the surety's main purpose is to obtain some personal pecuniary or business advantage, the promise is "not within" (is not covered by) the statute, and the surety's promise is therefore enforceable even though oral. Suppose Dan contracts to build a house for Sue, who has already contracted to resell it. Dan then contracts to buy the building materials from Cora, but gets into financial trouble and fails to pay for some of the materials furnished. Cora refuses to deliver any more materials until she receives payment for those already delivered. Sue, fearing that a delay may cause

Figure 13-1 Suretyship relationship.

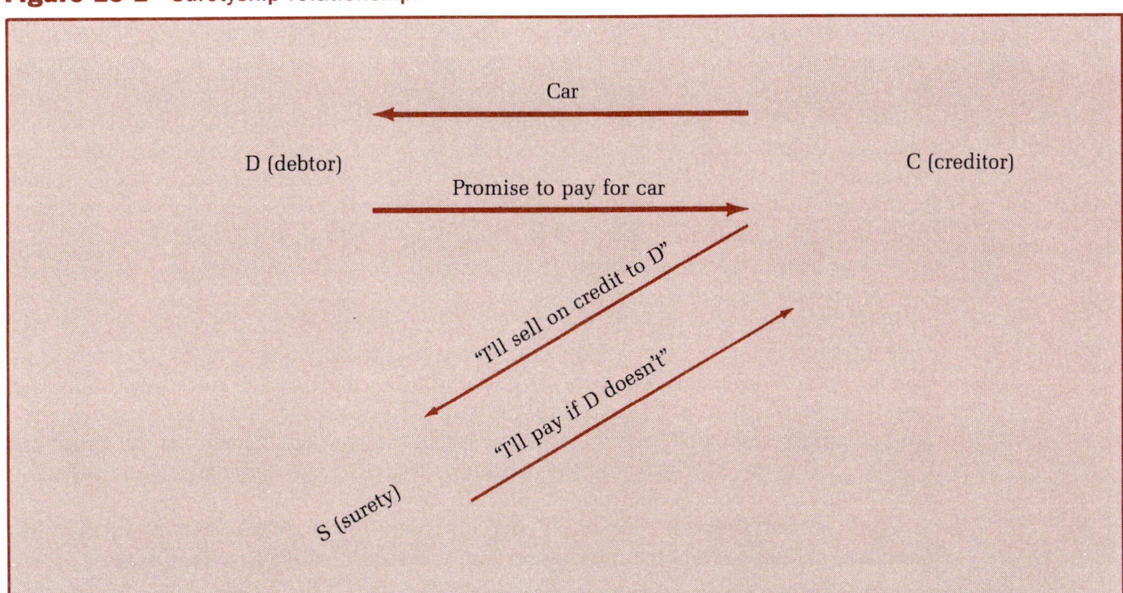

her to default on her contract to sell the house, orally promises to pay Cora for any materials furnished if Dan does not pay for them. Sue's oral promise is enforceable because her main purpose in making it was to get the house built on schedule for her own benefit.

Case 13.1 illustrates the application of the main-purpose rule to a major investor in a corporation.

CASE 13.1 Graybar Electric Co. v. Sawyer · 485 A.2d 1384 (Me. 1985)

FACTS For several years, Pine Tree Electric Co., an electrical contractor, bought equipment and supplies on credit from Graybar Electric Co. (plaintiff). When Pine Tree failed to pay its bills on time, Graybar cut off its credit. An owner of Pine Tree sought financial help from an employee who approached Sawyer, his father-in-law, about financing his contribution. Sawyer (defendant) invested $100,000 in the company himself and later lent Pine Tree an additional $300,000.

After investing, Sawyer required Pine Tree to hire a comptroller. In a reorganization of the company, Sawyer became the sole preferred stockholder with all the voting power and elected himself vice president. In July, 1980, Sawyer met with Graybar representatives, and Graybar reopened Pine Tree's credit account. When Pine Tree made no payment on its account in August and September, Graybar placed a hold on Pine Tree's pending orders, including a $30,000 telephone switch that Pine Tree was to install in Lewiston for the New England Telephone Company. At a second meeting called to straighten out the credit problem, Sawyer allegedly told Graybar representatives that if Pine Tree did not pay its account, he would arrange to have it paid. Graybar again reopened Pine Tree's line of credit and delivered the telephone switch to Pine Tree. Pine Tree never paid for it. Graybar and other creditors forced Pine Tree into involuntary bankruptcy. Contending that Sawyer had orally promised to pay the Pine Tree account if Pine Tree did not, Graybar sued Sawyer for the price of the switch. From a judgment for Graybar, Sawyer appealed.

OPINION McKUSICK, C. J. . . . [The Maine Statute of Frauds] provides that "no action shall be maintained in any of the following cases: . . . to charge any person upon special promise to answer for the debt, default, or misdoings of another . . . unless the promise, contract or agreement . . . is in writing and signed by the party to be charged therewith." This traditional component of the Statute of Frauds has, however, long been subject to an exception in a case where the promisor's main purpose in making his [oral] promise is to secure some benefit for himself. . . .

[R]ecent formulations of the rule [are based on] the idea that the promise, though collateral, is enforceable because the promisor does not need the protection against his own generous impulses afforded by the Statute of Frauds. *Restatement (Second) of Contracts* § 116 (1981). Where a surety's main objective is to serve his own pecuniary or business advantage, the gratuitous element of the suretyship is eliminated, the likelihood of disproportion in the values exchanged is reduced, and the context of commercial dealings provides evidentiary safeguards. . . .

Both the common law rule and the *Restatement* formulation focus on whether the evidence adduced at trial justifies the conclusion that the promisor's main purpose was to advance his own interests. The benefit that a promisor must expect to receive under the main purpose rule in order to be held to his [oral] promise must be substantial, immediate, and pecuniary, though it may flow to the promisor through benefit to the principal obligor. . . . The jury instruction in the present case gave a thoroughly adequate statement of the law on the main purpose rule. . . .

The evidence before the jury amply supports its finding . . . that Sawyer intended by his promise to procure an immediate and substantial benefit flowing directly to himself. Saw-

CASE 13.1 Continued

yer had outstanding loans to Pine Tree of almost $300,000. He admitted in testimony that he needed to keep the business going in order to be paid back. The activities he undertook to get the business back on its feet financially were extensive. He followed [up on] his initial loan of $100,000 by lending Pine Tree further large sums of money with the obvious purpose of keeping jobs going. He structured the loan transactions to give himself, as the sole voting stockholder, all of the authority formerly held by the board of directors. He reserved to himself the control of Pine Tree's borrowing. He guaranteed letters of credit necessary for Pine Tree to obtain two other jobs. . . . He received interest on his loans to Pine Tree through the fall and winter of 1980 and the spring of 1981. He also received $18,000 . . . in partial repayment of the principal amount of the loans. He testified at length about his desire to increase Pine Tree's profitability so that he could be paid back. . . .

In view of the necessity of maintaining the flow of supplies to Pine Tree in order to keep the business going, and the necessity of its staying in business if Sawyer was to be repaid, the jury could reasonably find that Sawyer's oral promise, given to avoid serious difficulties for Pine Tree, was intended to confer on him a direct and substantial benefit. . . .

The facts of the present case resemble closely those of the cited Maine cases and are well within the purview of the rule as contemplated in the *Restatement*. In the *Maine Candy* case, for example, the promisor gave an oral promise of payment of past debts to keep the business going so that he could recover his own investment. . . . Comparison of the present case with those authorities demonstrates that it falls within the accepted ambit of the main-purpose doctrine. . . .

JUDGMENT Judgment affirmed.

Contract upon Consideration of Marriage. The marriage provision in the statute of frauds applies to contracts or promises "in consideration of marriage." Usually the bargain involves a promise to give money or property in exchange for a marriage or a promise of marriage. Such bargains, known as property settlements, often are used as estate-planning devices by people with established families who wish, upon remarriage, to protect the interests of existing heirs. But prenuptial agreements and other property settlements are not enforceable unless in writing. Suppose Phil tells Miriam, "If you will marry me, I'll transfer to you my 5,000 shares of IBM stock." Phil's promise must be in writing to be enforceable. The same is true where Phil's father promises to give Miriam a house if she will marry Phil.

The marriage provision does not apply to mutual promises to marry. As stated in *Withers v. Richardson*, an 1844 Kentucky case, "It would be imputing to the legislature too great an absurdity to suppose that they had enacted that all our courtships, to be valid, must be in writing." Thus, in many states an exchange of oral promises to marry can create an enforceable contract. But sometimes people have falsely alleged the existence of such a contract in an attempt to extort payments of money or to embarrass a former lover, and there have been sensational "breach-of-promise" trials. To curb these and other abuses, the legislatures of some states have enacted statutes which provide that the breach of a promise to marry (in a situation involving merely mutual promises to marry) does not give rise to a cause of action.

Contract for Sale of Goods. Article 2 of the Uniform Commercial Code governs the sale of goods. Article 2 has its own statute of frauds, UCC § 2-201. Under that section, a contract for the sale of goods for a price of $500 or more is not enforceable unless the party against whom enforcement is sought has signed "some writing sufficient to indicate that a contract for sale has been made between the parties." This basic rule has a number of exceptions that are discussed in Chapter 16. For example, under the circumstances spelled out in § 2-201, a contract between merchants for goods worth more than $500 may be enforceable even though oral. Reasons for such exceptions are discussed later in this chapter.

Contract for Sale of Interest in Land. Under the statute of frauds, a contract for the sale of an interest in land must be evidenced by a writing to be enforceable. Such interests (discussed in Chapter 22), include contracts to sell or buy land; leases of land (unless the lease is within a statutory exception for short-term leases); real estate mortgages; and express easements (e.g., a right of way over land, granted by the owner to a utility company or to an adjoining landowner).

Statutes in most states exempt short-term leases (and contracts for them) from the land-contract provisions of the statute of frauds. A lease is usually called "short-term" if it is for a term of a year or less. In most states an oral lease for a 1-year term is enforceable without regard to when the term is to begin.

Contracts for the sale of *oil, gas, or other minerals* still in the ground at the time of contracting are contracts for the sale of goods (and are subject to the UCC statute of frauds) if the seller (landowner) is to "sever" the mineral from the land. If the buyer is to enter the seller's land and do the severing or extracting, the contract is one "affecting land" (is similar to a lease) and must conform to any statute of frauds provision pertaining to the sale of an interest in land. However, *growing crops* or other things attached to realty and capable of severance without material harm to the land are defined in the UCC as *goods,* regardless of whether the buyer or the seller is to do the severing. Contracts for growing crops and those other things (such as buildings or equipment to be salvaged) are subject to the UCC statute of frauds and its $500 rule.

The writing required by the statute of frauds for the sale or purchase of an interest in land should not be confused with the writing (called a "deed") commonly used for actually transferring the interest and having the transfer recorded in the public land records. A deed is a document signed by the "grantor" conveying (transferring) an interest in realty and may be used to make either a sale or a gift of the interest to the "grantee." The writing required by the statute of frauds merely provides evidence of an intention to enter a contract. Usually it is not adequate as evidence of a transfer of an interest in land. Case 13.2 involves the land-contract provision of the statute of frauds.

CASE 13.2 Peters v. Morse · 466 N.Y.S.2d 506 (App. Div. 1983)

FACTS Peters, a licensed practical nurse, commenced caring for Lyle and Harriet Nelson, an elderly couple, on October 10, 1976. She visited the Nelson home each day to attend to their medical needs and to do normal household chores. After Mrs. Nelson died in July, 1977, Peters continued to perform the same services for Mr. Nelson until his death on August 31, 1979. During Mr. Nelson's final illness, Peters moved into the Nelson residence to provide continuous care for him. Peters was never paid for her services but relied upon the Nelsons' repeated oral promises that they would convey their farm to her upon their deaths. In a will, executed just before his death, Lyle Nelson left Peters nothing. She then brought suit against the executor of Mr. Nelson's estate, seeking recovery in *quantum meruit* for the reasonable value of her services and, in a second cause of action, enforcement of an oral agreement by the Nelsons to devise (will) the farm to her. The trial court dismissed the complaint in its entirety, holding that the contract cause of action was barred by the statute of frauds provision requiring a contract to make testamentary disposition to be in writing. The court refused to allow the *quantum meruit* claim on the ground that allowing it would also violate the statute of frauds. Peters appealed.

OPINION KANE, J. P. . . . During appellate argument, plaintiff conceded that the contract cause of action had been properly dismissed, leaving for resolution only the *quantum meruit* ruling.

The fact that an express contract is unenforceable because of its failure to comply with the Statute of Frauds does not mean that quasi-contractual recovery for the reasonable

CASE 13.2 Continued

value of services rendered is, therefore, necessarily unavailable.... Indeed, the right to recover [in quasi-contract] has long been recognized in the specific circumstances presented, namely, when there has been an oral contract to make a bequest, and there is nothing in either [the statute of frauds or a cited case] which alters this durable rule. Special Term's fear of undermining the requirement that a contract to make a testamentary disposition be in writing is unfounded because the recovery afforded persons like plaintiff is limited to the reasonable value of services they performed; the consideration which would have been forthcoming had the terms of the oral agreement been enforced is irrelevant unless it can be helpful in determining the reasonable value of the services provided. That this distinction is real is evidenced by the fact that plaintiff can receive only the value of her services and not the property promised by decedents.

[In the Dombrowski case], *quantum meruit* was inappropriate because of the intimate relationship between the plaintiff and decedent, the compensation the plaintiff received from decedent during the latter's lifetime, and the complete absence of proof of the reasonable value of the plaintiff's services. In contrast, plaintiff in the instant case performed important services which are well documented; her relationship with the Nelsons was not one which would suggest that she aided them without expectation of pay, and she presented a bill for her services during Mr. Nelson's lifetime....

JUDGMENT ...[J]udgment modified... by reversing the dismissal of plaintiff's first cause of action for the reasonable value of her services....

Contract Not Performable within a Year. Like other classes of contracts covered by the statute of frauds, long-term contracts are considered sufficiently important to warrant a requirement that contractual intent be evidenced by a writing. The dividing line between a long-term and a short-term contract has been set at 1 year, but the distinction is not as simple as it might sound. Because courts prefer to enforce oral contracts that serve a useful social purpose, they have tended to interpret the class of long-term contracts narrowly and, consequently, to enforce a variety of oral contracts that seem long-term but are commonly held to be short-term.

So, most courts, interpret "*not* to be performed within a year" as "*cannot* be performed within a year." If performance of the contract could conceivably occur within 1 year, the contract is not covered by the statute and need not be evidenced by a writing. Suppose Annette contracts to support Ben for the rest of his life. Since the contract could conceivably be performed within a year because Ben might die at any time, the contract is enforceable even though oral. In contrast, full performance of a contract to support Ben for the next 4 years could not possibly occur in less than a year, and it is not enforceable unless evidenced by a writing.

Many oral contracts that specify a performance to be rendered for a term of more than 1 year are nevertheless terminable at any time for a variety of reasons such as the death or the bankruptcy of one of the parties. Such apparently long-term contracts might or might not be subject to the writing requirement. Many courts take the view that the words "not to be performed within a year" refer to actual performance, and that terminability of an oral multiyear contract for reasons other than a completed performance is an insufficient basis for interpreting the contract as short-term. Other courts take the opposite view and hold that the possibility of a rightful termination *is* a sufficient basis for holding that an oral multiyear contract is short-term and enforceable without a writing.

The critical 1-year period begins to run at the time of the *making* of the contract. But the time at which the law considers a contract to be made can differ from the time the contracting parties might have had in mind. Suppose that on January 1, Art and Beth enter into an oral personal services contract that is to run for "a year." Since the law does not usually count fractions of a day, the 1-year period does not begin to run until January 2. Consequently, the 1-year period ends January 1 of the following year, and the contract is short-term, enforceable though oral.

Suppose, instead, that Art and Beth's oral contract is for a term of nine months, that it is signed on January 1, and that performance is to begin on June 1 of the same year. This is a *long-term* contract (for which a writing is required), because performance cannot be completed until a year and 3 months after the January 1 making of the contract. (Recall, however, that an oral *lease* for a year *is* enforceable in most states even if the term of the lease is to begin sometime after the lease agreement was made.)

"Performed within a year" means fully performed within the year. Consequently, if either party to a contract promises a performance that cannot be fully completed within a year, all the promises in the contract are within the statute and must be evidenced by a writing. "But unlike other provisions of the Statute, the one-year provision does not apply to a contract which is performed on one side at the time [the contract] is made."[1] Thus, if Ben borrows $15,000 from Annette, and Ben promises to repay the loan in three semiannual payments of $5,000 each, Annette can enforce the contract against Ben even though the contract was oral, because Annette had completely performed her part of the contract at the time the contract was made.

Where one of the parties to an oral long-term contract later completes his or her performance, the statute does not prevent enforcement of the promise of the other party.[2] Most courts hold that full performance by the one party makes the contract enforceable against the other.

Case 13.3 involves an oral employment contract. The court goes beyond the statute of frauds issue to discuss the nature and varieties of "permanent" employment contracts, a subject of much confusion and concern to many people.

[1]*Restatement (Second) of the Law of Contracts,* American Law Institute, Philadelphia, 1981, sec. 130, comment *d.*
[2]Ibid., sec. 130(2).

CASE 13.3 Eklund v. Vincent Brass & Aluminum Co. · 351 N.W.2d 371 (Minn. App. 1984)

FACTS In 1977, Paul Vincent, president of Vincent Brass & Aluminum Co. (defendant), hired Clyde Eklund (plaintiff) as vice president of sales on the understanding that the position was permanent, as long as Eklund performed satisfactorily. The employment agreement was oral. In accepting Vincent's offer, Eklund, then a 47-year-old general sales manager for U.S. Steel Supply Corp., gave up a 26-year career with that company.

According to Mr. Vincent, Eklund understood his job, worked very hard, and developed sales and administrative programs that increased sales. Eklund received pay raises and bonuses. In 1980, Vincent retired, recommending Eklund, Mike White, and Norman Smith as potential successors. Smith was chosen to succeed Vincent as vice president and general manager of Vincent Brass.

Smith soon fired Eklund without warning or explanation, and a few months later fired White. Sales decreased after Eklund's termination. Eklund immediately sought comparable employment, but in 1983 accepted a job at less than two-thirds of his compensation at Vincent Brass. Eklund sued Vincent Brass for wrongful termination of the oral employment agreement. The trial court dismissed Eklund's claim for breach of contract, holding that (*a*) there was no written contract complying with the statute of frauds, and (*b*) an employment contract of indefinite duration is terminable at will. Eklund appealed.

OPINION FOLEY, J. . . . [The Minnesota statute of frauds states]: "No action shall be maintained, in either of the following cases, upon any agreement, unless such agreement, or some note or memorandum thereof, expressing the consideration, is in writing, and subscribed by the party charged therewith: (1) Every agreement that by its terms is not to be performed within one year [from] the making thereof. . . ."

CASE 13.3 Continued

"The test is simply whether the contract by its terms is capable of full performance within a year, not whether such occurrence is likely." *Martin v. Federal Life Insurance Co.*...; *see also Rowe v. Noren Pattern & Foundry Co.*... ("Where an oral contract may be completed in less than a year, even though... in all probability the contract will extend for a period of years, the statute of frauds is not violated."...)

The trial court relied on *Roaderick v. Lull Engineering Co.*... in holding that Eklund's alleged contract for permanent employment until retirement was not enforceable because it could not be performed within one year.

Roaderick can be distinguished by comparing it with *Bussard v. College of St. Thomas*.... In *Roaderick*, the employee's alleged oral contract called for a *minimum* of two years' employment. This contract literally could not be performed in less than one year. Even if the employee died within a year, the contract would not be performed in full. Therefore [its enforcement] was barred by the statute of frauds.

In *Bussard*, the employee's alleged oral contract for permanent employment had no minimum term but was to last so long as the employee wished. This contract could be fully performed within a year[;] therefore the court held: "The statute of frauds is clearly not an impediment to plaintiff's proof of an oral agreement. A contract of permanent employment is 'performable within a year' because of the possibility of death within a year. Numerous cases... so hold."...

Here, Eklund's alleged contract for permanent employment until retirement, so long as he performed satisfactorily, could have been fully performed within one year under any of the following circumstances: (1) Eklund's death, (2) Eklund['s voluntary departure], or (3) Eklund['s failure] to perform satisfactorily. The trial court erred in granting Vincent Brass summary judgment on the basis that the statute of frauds barred proof of Eklund's oral contract of employment.

The trial court held that even if Eklund could prove a contract for permanent employment, such an indefinite contract is terminable at the will of either party under the rule of *Skagerberg v. Blandin Paper Co.*,... and *Cederstrand v. Lutheran Brotherhood*....

Although generally an assertion of a permanent employment contract is interpreted as employment at-will, all the evidence must be evaluated, including the intentions of the parties, to determine whether the contract was in fact indefinite as to duration [i.e., for "permanent" employment].

If a jury determines [that] the parties intended an indefinite contract, Eklund may still overcome the presumption that his contract is terminable at-will. The "at-will rule"... is only a rule of construction—not one of substantive law. *Pine River State Bank v. Mettille*.... The Minnesota Supreme Court explains: "[T]he somewhat arbitrary rule of most jurisdictions that a contract for 'permanent employment' will be construed to be terminable at the will of either party... is... too mechanical an answer to the more basic issue of ascertaining the real intent of the parties.... The cases which reason that the at-will rule takes precedence over even explicit job termination restraints, simply because the contract is of indefinite duration, misapply the at-will rule.... It should not be necessary for an employee to prove a contract is [for] 'permanent' employment or for a specified term in order to avoid summary dismissal if the parties have agreed otherwise...."

In *Cederstrand*, the Minnesota Supreme Court recognized that an employee may prove he was to be "dismissed only for cause by proving a contract to that effect."...

[In *Pine River*, the court stated], "A terminated employee need not prove he provided additional consideration to assert an enforceable contract for permanent employment. Additional consideration merely gives a court 'better reason to believe that the parties... were referring to lifetime employment and were not, instead, simply making a distinction between temporary or seasonal employment and employment which is steady or continuing although nevertheless terminable at will.'... The [parties may agree] that the employment will not be terminable by the employer except pursuant to their agree-

CASE 13.3 Continued

ment, even though no consideration other than services to be performed is expected by the employer or promised by the employee."...

The trial court erred in granting Vincent Brass summary judgment on this claim for breach of contract. Eklund produced evidence which indicates his alleged contract may be enforceable despite the general presumption that an alleged permanent employment contract is not enforceable. At trial Eklund should be given an opportunity to prove [that his contract] included a job security provision, limiting his dismissal to unsatisfactory performance.

JUDGMENT Affirmed in part, reversed in part and remanded.

Requirements Regarding the Writing

The primary purpose of a statute of frauds is to require reliable evidence that an alleged contract was indeed entered into. To accomplish this purpose, the English statute relied mainly on a requirement that "the agreement...or some memorandum or note thereof, shall be in writing, and signed by the person to be charged" with breach of contract. Most states have adopted the same or similar wording. Certain questions arise regarding the statutory requirements:

1 What content must the memorandum have?
2 What form may it take?
3 What is a "signature," who must do the signing, and where may the signature be placed?
4 At what time may the memorandum be made and signed?

Content. To be sufficient evidence of a contract, the memorandum ordinarily must:

- Identify with reasonable certainty the subject matter of the contract and the parties to it.
- Sufficiently indicate that a contract with respect to that subject matter has been made between the parties.
- State with reasonable certainty the essential terms of the unperformed promises in the contract.

The subject matter and the parties do not have to be identified with precision—only with reasonable certainty. For example, a memorandum which describes the subject matter of a contract as "my lot on the corner of Grant Street and Fourth Avenue in the County of X, State of Y" is sufficiently definite if the seller owns only one of the four lots on the intersection of Grant Street and Fourth Avenue. Similarly, a party may be identified by name or initials, even though there may be other persons with the same name or initials. Where there is no dispute as to the parties, a person may be sufficiently identified as a party to the contract by being in possession of a memorandum signed by the other party.

Form. No particular form is required for the memorandum. It may be in the form of a letter, a receipt, an order blank, an invoice, a check, an entry in an account book, or an entry in a diary. It may consist of several writings if one of the writings is signed and the writings in the circumstances clearly indicate that they all relate to the same transaction.

Signature. The signature may consist of any symbol made or adopted with an intention to authenticate the writing as that of the signer—name, initials, rubber stamp, and so on. Most statutes of frauds state that the memorandum must be "signed by the party to be charged," meaning the party to be charged with breach of contract in any subsequent legal proceeding. Signatures need not appear at any particular place on the memorandum unless the statute provides otherwise.

Time. There is no requirement that the memorandum be made at the time the contract is made. Courts differ in their views as to the required time. One view is that a memorandum may be made and signed at any time before suit is instituted. Another is that the memorandum may be made or signed at any time before or after the formation of the contract.

Alternatives to the Writing

Sometimes a person knows about the statute-of-frauds writing requirement, but enters into an oral agreement intending later to use his or her own lack of compliance with the statute as a means of avoiding contractual liability. For example, Melissa might orally contract to sell her house on a privately financed basis, intending to collect a few monthly payments before using the lack of a writing as an excuse for repudiating the contract. Thus, the statute itself can be used as an instrument of fraud against persons ignorant of the writing requirement or too lacking in bargaining power to compel a writing. More frequently, neither contracting party knows of the writing requirement, or the parties find compliance with it inconvenient. To prevent the injustice that can arise from refusal to enforce an oral contract covered by the statute of frauds, the legislatures and the courts have developed alternatives that may serve as substitutes for the normally required writing.

Legislatively Developed Alternatives. Under the Uniform Commercial Code, a writing is only one of several ways to evidence a contract for the sale of goods. Other ways include part performance of an oral sales contract, admitting in court to an oral sales contract, and failure by a nonsigning merchant to respond to certain kinds of written communications. Often, these alternative kinds of evidence are just as reliable as a writing would be in revealing contractual intent. UCC § 2-201, the statute of frauds applicable to sales of goods, is discussed further in Chapter 16.

Sometimes statutory language is broad enough to encompass modern alternatives to the traditional writing. One court held that a tape recording of an oral agreement for the sale of corporate securities (e.g., stocks and bonds) complied with the writing requirement of UCC § 8-319, the applicable statute of frauds.[3] Noting that under the UCC the term "writing" includes "printing, typewriting, or any other intentional reduction to tangible form," the court held that the tape recording, agreed to by both parties, was a reduction of the oral contract to tangible form. There was no need for a signature here, the court added, because the identity of the oral contractors had been clearly established by other means. The purpose of the statute of frauds—preventing fraud and perjury by use of evidence more reliable than the unassisted memory of witnesses—had been accomplished by an alternative to the usual writing.

[3]*Ellis Canning Co. v. Bernstein*, 348 F. Supp. 1212 (D. Colo. 1972).

Judicially Developed Alternatives. Two judicially developed doctrines—the *doctrine of equitable estoppel* and the *doctrine of part performance*—provide ways of preventing injustice from the misuse of the writing requirement.

Courts have long held that if one party to a contract has misrepresented (or has concealed) a material fact and the other party has relied on the misrepresentation to his or her detriment, the party who made the misrepresentation is "estopped" (prohibited) from using the statute of frauds as a defense.[4] Suppose, for example, that Chuck tells Alice, "I have typed and signed a memorandum of our oral agreement and have just mailed it to you," when in fact Chuck had not done so. If Alice substantially changes her position in reliance on Chuck's statement and later sues him for breach of the oral contract, he probably will be estopped from setting up the defense of the statute of frauds.

The judicial doctrine of part performance is applied mainly to oral land contracts. Courts of equity have long held that an oral contract for the sale of land will be specifically enforced when the contract has been partly performed *if* the purchaser takes action which is "unequivocally referable to the oral agreement" and has reasonably relied on the agreement to his or her substantial detriment. Usually "it is necessary for possession of the land to be transferred to the purchaser plus either of the following elements: (1) payment of all or a substantial portion of the purchase price, *or* (2) the making of valuable improvements upon the land by the purchaser."[5] Case 13.4 discusses what is required for a sufficient part performance.

[4]John E. Murray, *Murray on Contracts*, Bobbs-Merrill Company, Indianapolis, 1974, sec. 333. See also, Cal. Civ. Code, sec. 163: "Where a contract which is required to be in writing is prevented from being put into writing by the fraud of a party thereto, any other party who is by such fraud led to believe that it is in writing, and acts upon such belief to his prejudice, may enforce it against the fraudulent party."

[5]*Restatement (Second), Contracts*, sec. 139.

CASE 13.4 Gegg v. Kiefer · 655 S.W.2d 834 (Mo. App. 1983)

FACTS Joseph Kiefer and his wife owned a 274-acre tract of land, approximately 70 acres of which was farm land. Francis Gegg farmed the 70 acres as a tenant on a "cash-rent" basis. He also cared for the rest of the property, maintaining the gravel road, cleaning out the creek bed, clearing brush and weeds, and improving the land's drainage system. Kiefer was pleased with his tenant's work and over the years told him, "Now, Franco, you take care of this land because someday it will be your own." After his wife's death in January 1979, Kiefer's health deteriorated. During Kiefer's illness, he and Gegg discussed the sale of the farm, apparently agreeing on a price of $45,000. In March or April, Gegg visited a local banker to arrange a $45,000 loan to buy the farm. On April 15, Gegg asked Kiefer whether he was ready to sell his property. Kiefer said yes, indicated that he "had turned everything over" to his nephew, William Kiefer, and asked if his nephew had brought the deed to Gegg. The nephew had not done so. On May 1, Kiefer died intestate, having made no plans with his nephew to transfer the land to Gegg. Gegg brought suit for specific performance of the oral contract. The trial court ordered specific performance, and William Kiefer, the administrator of Joseph Kiefer's estate, appealed.

OPINION PUDLOWSKI, Presiding Judge.... Respondent [Gegg] urges us to believe that the totality of the evidence supported the trial court's finding of an oral contract and was sufficient to overcome the bar of the Statute of Frauds.... An oral contract to convey land falls within the literal ambit of the Statute... and so will not be enforced at law.... However, equity will decree specific performance where a party has so far acted on the promise that to deny him the benefit of the agreement would be unjust. This resort to equity avails sparingly, and only upon clear and convincing proof of a definite agreement. The elements of proof required by equity for the specific performance of an oral contract to convey real estate were prescribed in [the 1912 case of *Walker v. Bohannan*] and have been uniformly followed since: [The court then listed eight requirements, including "(5) the proof of the contract as pleaded must be such as to leave no reasonable doubt in the mind of the chancellor that the contract as alleged was in fact made, and that the full performance... has been had...."]

More recent Missouri cases have recognized the legal principle that oral promises to convey real estate may be enforced where the plaintiff has partially performed.... These cases seem to support relaxation of "full performance," the fifth requirement set forth in *Walker* above.

Respondent's amended petition pleaded that the oral contract was consummated on or about March 6, 1979. However... respondent urges us to believe that the evidence supported the trial court's findings of a "two-part" contract. In the first part, respondent claims that the earlier statements made by Kiefer promising that the land would someday be his induced him to make improvements in it.... In the second step, respondent claims that Kiefer orally agreed to sell the property... for $45,000 and respondent's past services. Both of respondent's arguments fail.

In regard to Kiefer's early statements... such statements [as "someday it will be your own"] are too indefinite to constitute... a contract.... Normally, where time of performance is not [stated], it is implied that performance may be required in a reasonable time. However... in the case at bar, Kiefer's statements occur over a thirty year period. There was no intention by Kiefer to immediately convey the property or to convey it within a reasonable time. Rather his intention was to hold onto the land as long as possible. It is essential to an agreed oral contract subject to specific performance that there be a meeting of the minds upon terms so definite that promises and performances are reasonably certain.... The court cannot make a contract for the parties....

CASE 13.4 Continued

Further difficulty with respondent's position is that he attempts to establish the terms of the contract by evidence that he did perform additional services on the farm between 1947 and 1979 without receiving compensation. Performance of the services... however, is [as] consistent with... a landlord-tenant agreement as... with the expectation that decedent would sell his nearly 274 acre farm for a fraction of its value.... [T]he good land management by respondent benefited Kiefer, but it also [benefited] respondent as tenant. The arable acreage was landlocked. Had respondent not maintained and graveled a road, his access to the tillable tract would have been hampered. The drainage system, crop rotation, weeding, and use of lime, fertilizer and seeds improved not only the land's value, but also increased the farm's crop yield, again benefiting respondent.... Respondent's actions were not unequivocally and solely referable to an alleged contract for sale of realty.... [W]e are unable to conclude that prior to March 6, 1979, respondent and Kiefer contracted for the sale of Kiefer's farm.

[As to March 6 and afterward], the conversation relating to the selling of the farm was definite enough to form a contract... but in no way proved performance thereof.... We note that there is no showing of part performance by respondent to require enforcement of the contract. The initial occupancy of the farm by respondent was as a tenant under an oral agreement to pay an annual cash rental and with the obligation to maintain the property. Work performed on the property was necessary to make it productive.... The act of purchasing the corn planter was not [solely referable to] the agreement to purchase Kiefer's property. At the time of purchase, respondent was farming two additional parcels of land.... The evidence that he was arranging to borrow $45,000 from the bank was merely tentative. Anticipatory, preparatory, collateral and ancillary acts, performed in reliance on a verbal contract, generally are not sufficient part performance to call for an exception to the provisions of the statute of frauds....

JUDGMENT The judgment is reversed....

Modification or Rescission of Contracts Covered by the Statute

Modification of Contract. If a contract is modified by a subsequent agreement and the contract as modified is within the statute of frauds, the requirements of the statute must be satisfied. Suppose that Wilma orally contracts to employ Jennifer for a term of 6 months beginning the first of the next month. On the first of that month, on the recommendation of Jennifer's former employer, Wilma decides to employ Jennifer for 18 months, and she agrees. The oral agreement as modified exceeds 1 year and must be in writing to be enforceable.

Rescission of Contract. Suppose the parties to an enforceable contract (such as a written employment contract for a term exceeding 1 year) wish to rescind (cancel) it orally. Usually they may do so. However, not all courts agree that a land contract may be orally rescinded. The prevailing rule is that it may be rescinded orally just as other contracts within the statute may be. However, where land has been transferred by an effective deed, an agreement to rescind the transaction is a contract for the transfer of an interest in land and is required by the statute of frauds to be in writing to be enforced.

Effect of Adopting a Writing: Parol Evidence Rule

Often the parties to a contract make a variety of written and oral statements in the process of negotiating the terms of the contract, and then they sign a writing called an "integration" that supposedly represents their final decision as to the terms of the contract. What happens if one of the parties alleges that one of these prior statements (called "parol evidence"), and not the term that appears in the integration, truly states the parties' agreement? The court will apply the *parol evidence rule,* the purpose of which is to promote certainty and security of transactions by giving binding effect, as far as is reasonable, to a writing signed as the final expression of an agreement.

The Parol Evidence Rule

Two kinds of writings are of key significance in the application by the courts of the parol evidence rule. The first kind of writing, called a "partially integrated agreement," states something less than the totality of the parties' understanding, but as to the portion covered, the writing is complete. The second kind of writing, called a "completely integrated agreement," is regarded by the parties as being a *complete and exclusive* statement of all terms of the agreement.

Under the parol evidence rule, a partially integrated agreement may *not* be contradicted but *may be supplemented* by evidence of prior negotiations or agreements, oral or written. A completely integrated agreement may not be either contradicted or supplemented by evidence of prior negotiations or agreements. However, parol evidence *will* be admitted to resolve an ambiguity in an integration (whether partial or complete) and to resolve other questions such as the presence of fraud.

Even though the parol evidence rule does not permit an integrated agreement to be contradicted by prior agreements, the rule has no application to agreements entered into subsequent to the writing. Thus, where an integrated contract is modified or rescinded by a subsequent oral or written agreement, there is no violation of the parol evidence rule.

Determining Intention of Parties

The parol evidence rule applies only to writings that the parties intend as the final expression or integration of their agreement. Sometimes the parties declare in the writing that they intend it to be a complete expression of their agreement. The court will usually give effect to such a declaration of intention. Even if the wording of the contract omits a term such as price or time of performance, the court will usually hold that a reasonable price or a reasonable time was implicit in the writing and that therefore the writing was not necessarily incomplete. However, courts do not always give effect to declarations of completeness. If, for example, the declaration is a term of adhesion, or the writing is obviously incomplete, the court may set aside the declaration and admit parol evidence.

In the absence of a declaration that the writing is an integration, the court will examine the writing to see if it appears complete. If it appears complete on its face—i.e., if it contains the terms usually found in contracts that are considered to be complete—the court will treat the writing as an integration in the absence of contrary evidence.

It should be noted that the parol evidence rule serves to exclude evidence of prior negotiations only where there is a direct conflict between an unambiguous integration and the information sought to be presented to the court. For many purposes, parol evidence of prior negotiations is freely admissible even where there is an integration—for example, as we have seen, to clear up an ambiguity in the integration or to resolve an allegation of fraud. Parol evidence is admissible for other purposes: for example, to determine whether an agreement was illegal or lacked consideration or whether a writing constitutes a full or only a partial integration.

The case that follows involves an application of the parol evidence rule and an allegation of fraud.

CASE 13.5 Howell v. Oregonian Publishing Co. · 728 P.2d 106 (Or. App. 1986)

FACTS Howell and others (plaintiffs) were independent newspaper dealers who purchased newspapers from the Oregonian Publishing Co. (defendant) for resale to customers in the Portland area. The dealership system had operated for almost 30 years, and the dealerships had become valuable, several selling recently for $100,000 to $155,000.

CASE 13.5 Continued

The dealership contract form prepared by defendant and used before 1977 (the F-25 form) provided that the dealership agreement would expire on a specified date but would automatically be renewed each year unless either party gave notice of the desire not to renew. Defendant consistently told the dealers that the provision was in the form so that defendant could terminate contracts for unsatisfactory dealer performance. The criteria used to judge dealer performance included the quality of service, promotional efforts undertaken to increase circulation, and the number of customers served within a dealer's territory. Neither the criteria nor a specific description of each dealer's territory was specified in the written form contracts. Defendant also consistently represented to dealers that the agreements would be renewed as long as the dealers performed adequately.

In 1979, defendant introduced a new contract form (the F-25B form). It did not contain the automatic renewal clause, providing instead that "neither seller [defendant] nor Dealer [plaintiffs] shall have the right to insist on renewal of this agreement." Defendant assured dealers that the language in the new form was used only to avoid a new Federal Trade Commission regulation, that the change in language would not affect the value of their dealerships, and that their renewal rights had not been altered.

In 1980, defendant's president began discussing with the circulation manager a change from independent dealerships to an agency system for delivery of papers. Dealers were not told of these discussions, and defendant continued to assure dealers that their contracts would be renewed if their performance was satisfactory. In 1982, defendant announced its decision to change to an agency system and to eliminate the independent dealerships. Howell and other dealers filed suit seeking injunctive relief or, alternatively, damages. From a summary judgment for defendant, plaintiffs appealed.

OPINION

WARDEN, P. J. . . . A summary judgment may be granted only if no genuine issue of material fact exists and the movant is entitled to judgment as a matter of law. . . . Appellants [plaintiffs] first contend that the written renewal provisions are ambiguous and that there are issues of fact concerning the parties' intent in entering into them and concerning whether defendant's representations modified the written contracts. Defendant argues that the contracts are unambiguous and that the parol evidence rule prevents the admission into evidence of proof of its representations. . . .

Any contract term reduced to writing supersedes all prior and contemporaneous negotiations and oral understandings as to that term. . . . If the contract is either partially or fully integrated, the rule closes the door to parol evidence concerning the written terms of the contract. . . .

The written agreements were not fully integrated, even though they include an integration clause. It is undisputed that the specific geographical limits of each dealer's territory, a crucial provision of the agreements, were not reduced to writing. However, although the written contracts are not completely integrated, the partial integration doctrine applies. . . . Under that doctrine, a written agreement invalidates all prior and contemporaneous oral agreements that are inconsistent with the written agreement. . . . "To be 'inconsistent' within the meaning of the partial integration doctrine, the oral term must contradict an *express provision* in the writing." *Hatley v. Stafford*. . . . We now examine the respective renewal provisions of the agreements. . . .

[W]e agree with defendant that the clauses are unambiguous, because they are incapable of more than one sensible and reasonable interpretation. The clauses contain specific language that allows either party unconditionally to terminate the agreements on their respective expiration dates. Defendant's representations that the agreements would be renewed so long as the dealers performed adequately directly contradict that express language. The written renewal provisions of the agreements therefore supersede all prior and contemporaneous negotiations and oral understandings.

CASE 13.5 Continued

However, written contracts may be modified by subsequent oral agreements. . . . Because there are issues of fact concerning whether the representations were made subsequent to the execution of the written agreements, and if they were subsequently made, whether the representations modified the renewal provisions of the agreements, we reverse the summary judgment on appellants' breach of contract claims.

We next examine the fraud claims. Proof of fraud by evidence of prior or contemporaneous promises and representations is not prohibited by the parol evidence rule. . . . We therefore reverse the summary judgment on the fraud claims. . . .

JUDGMENT Judgment for defendant . . . reversed and remanded. . . .

Summary

The statute of frauds applies to classes of contracts thought to affect such important interests of contracting parties that writings should be required as evidence of contractual intent. Except where a statute of frauds or some other special statute requires a writing for the formation or enforcement of a contract, an oral contract is as enforceable as a written one.

The classes of contract commonly covered by a state statute of frauds are:

1 A contract of an executor or administrator to answer for duty of the decedent
2 A contract to answer for the debt or default of another
3 A contract made upon consideration of marriage
4 A contract for the sale of goods for a price of $500 or more
5 A contract for the sale of an interest in land
6 A contract not performable within 1 year

The primary purpose of a statute of frauds is to require reliable evidence that an alleged contract was indeed entered into. To accomplish this purpose, the statute requires that an agreement covered by the statute, or some memorandum or note thereof, shall be in writing and signed by the person to be charged with breach of contract in any subsequent legal proceeding.

The statute of frauds can itself be used as an instrument of fraud or oppression against persons ignorant of the writing requirement or too lacking in bargaining power to compel a writing. To prevent injustice which can arise from misuse of the writing requirement, the courts apply the doctrines of equitable estoppel and part performance in the enforcement of some oral contracts. Under some statutes of frauds, such as the one applicable to sales of goods, a writing is only one of the several ways to evidence a contract. Other ways include part performance and admitting to a contract in court. If a contract is modified and the contract, as modified, is within the statute of frauds, the modified contract must conform to the requirements of the statute.

A statute of frauds indicates what evidence is required for enforceability of a contract. The parol evidence rule indicates what evidence a court will consider in determining the content of a contract. The parol evidence rule does not, in litigation, permit admission of evidence of an oral or written agreement made prior to an integrated agreement if the prior agreement conflicts with the terms of the integration.

Review Questions

1 The statute of frauds does not apply to all contracts. State the criterion which is generally applied in determining which contracts should be covered by the statute of frauds.

2 **(a)** Why is a promise of an executor to pay the debt of the decedent out of the executor's own funds covered by the statute of frauds? **(b)** Under what circumstance would such a promise be enforceable?

3 A surety's promise to pay the debt, default, or miscarriage of another must be evidenced by a writing to be enforceable. **(a)** Illustrate a contract of suretyship. **(b)** Explain the operation and significance of the "main-purpose" rule.

4 **(a)** To what kinds of contracts involving marriage as consideration does the statute of frauds apply? **(b)** To what kinds of such contracts does the statute not apply? Why?

5 **(a)** Explain to which of the following contracts the land contract provision of the statute of frauds applies: Purchase of land. Lease of land. Mortgage. Contract for sale of oil. Contract for sale of growing crops. **(b)** Distinguish between a deed and the writing required by the statute of frauds for a land contract.

6 **(a)** How do the courts distinguish between contracts which are performable within a year and those which are not? **(b)** What is the significance of the distinction? **(c)** A makes an oral contract to support B for the rest of B's life. Under the statute of frauds, is the oral contract enforceable? Explain.

7 What kind of writing will satisfy the statute of frauds?

8 **(a)** How can the statute of frauds be used as an "instrument of fraud or oppression"? **(b)** Illustrate how *legislatures* have attempted to prevent the injustice which can arise from the misuse of the statute of frauds writing requirement. **(c)** Describe two ways in which the *courts* have attempted to prevent the injustice arising from the misuse of the statute of frauds writing requirement. **(d)** Under what circumstances might a court enforce an oral land contract?

9 Are oral modifications and rescissions of contracts covered by the statute of frauds? Explain.

10 **(a)** What is the purpose of the parol evidence rule? **(b)** Illustrate the operation of the parol evidence rule.

Case Problems

1 Holmdel Heights Construction Co. was developing some land for home building. Sugarman owned 18 percent of Holmdel's stock and, as its attorney, was owed $14,000 for legal services. Holmdel hired Schoor Associates to do engineering and planning work for the development, but failed to pay Schoor as agreed. Schoor ceased working. To secure additional financing, Holmdel needed more engineering work done at once. At a conference on financing, Sugarman orally agreed to pay all of Holmdel's outstanding and future bills, in the event of Holmdel's default, if Schoor would continue the engineering work. Schoor continued the work but received no further payment. Because Holmdel was insolvent, Schoor Associates sued Sugarman for the amounts due them. He contended that his promise was unenforceable under the statute of frauds. The trial court rendered judgment for Schoor, the appellate court reversed the judgment, and Schoor appealed. Should Sugarman be held liable on his oral promise to pay for the engineering work?

2 The Bank and Trust Company of Old York Road (Bank) held a mortgage on real estate owned by Eastgate Enterprises. Bank foreclosed the mortgage and, as permitted by statute, charged Eastgate for costs and attorney's fees. To obtain a release of the mortgage, Eastgate paid costs and fees totaling $9,455.36. Eastgate then brought suit to recover that amount from Bank, alleging that Bank had breached an oral agreement not to foreclose the mortgage. The trial court dismissed Eastgate's complaint on the ground that the oral agreement was unenforceable under the Pennsylvania statute of frauds. Eastgate appealed. Was the oral agreement enforceable?

3 In 1954, Allstate Insurance Co. orally agreed to employ Gilliland until his retirement age of 62, as long as he substantially complied with Allstate's lawful instructions. Allstate was to notify him if he was not fulfilling his duties so that he could correct any deficiencies. Gilliland soon began participating in profit sharing, pension, and savings plans and continued his participation until Allstate terminated his employment in 1972 without good cause or prior notice. As a result of the termination, Gilliland lost profits and earnings and the amount that would have accumulated in the pension fund had he remained employed until retirement. Gilliland sued Allstate for breach of the oral contract. From a judgment for Allstate, Gilliland appealed, alleging that the statute of frauds did not bar enforcement of the contract. Would enforcement of the oral contract violate the statute of frauds?

4 McMahan owned a 10-acre lot (the Bluff Road property) which he used as a source of fill dirt and gravel in the construction of an interstate highway. McMahan needed additional fill dirt, and Koch, McMahan's project manager, attempted to acquire it from Wegehoft's land located adjacent to the Bluff Road property. Wegehoft agreed to sell fill dirt to McMahan, but only if McMahan would sell Wegehoft the Bluff Road property. Koch drafted, and he and Wegehoft signed, a handwritten note containing the following provision: "F. McMahan Const. Co. will give Wegehoft the option to buy approximately 8½ acres located at 4404 Bluff Road for the price of $5,000. . . ." Koch said he would have an official contract prepared. Wegehoft never received such a contract. During the next three years, Wegehoft made repeated inquiries of Koch about a deed to the Bluff Road property. McMahan denied that there was an agreement for the sale of the property, and Wegehoft brought suit for specific performance. At trial, McMahan challenged the sufficiency of the memorandum to satisfy the statute of frauds. Was the memorandum sufficient?

5 Sylvia owned some mortgaged real estate. He was in default on mortgage payments, and to avoid foreclosure of the mortgage, he agreed orally to sell the property to Weale. Weale secured a bank commitment to finance the purchase, paid an attorney $150 for examining the title and doing other legal work relating to the property, and spent $2,860 for a survey of the land. In the meantime, Cole learned of the proposed sale, visited the property, and saw the survey work. He then offered to purchase the land, and he and Sylvia signed a contract of sale. Weale and Cole brought separate actions against Sylvia for specific performance. In a single hearing, the trial court granted specific performance to Weale and ordered Cole to file a release of his recorded written purchase agreement. Cole appealed. Was Weale entitled to specific performance?

6 Arlo Essex was a successful service station operator. In 1968, Skelly Oil Co. sought him out as a lease operator for a Skelly station then under construction. During negotiations Essex expressed concern about a clause in the proposed lease giving either party the option to cancel it on 30 days' notice. The Skelly representatives assured Essex that the language in the lease was merely a formality and that if Essex ran a good operation, he could remain in the location until he decided to retire. Essex then agreed to terminate his existing lease of an Apco station and to sign the Skelly lease. In 1973, Skelly canceled the lease and converted the station into a self-service operation called Surfco. Alleging fraud, Essex sued Skelly. One Skelly representative said he and others were instructed in Skelly training sessions to overcome prospective lessees' resistance to the cancellation clause by assuring them that the clause would not be used to terminate a lease except for unsatisfactory performance by the lessee. Essex won a jury verdict for actual and punitive damages. The trial court entered a judgment n.o.v. for Skelly, apparently on the ground that the written lease should prevail over the parol evidence concerning fraudulent misrepresentations. Essex appealed. Should the jury verdict for Essex be reinstated?

CHAPTER 14

Rights and Duties of Third Persons

Contracts are used in many different ways to accomplish a variety of business purposes. Often, only two contracting parties are involved, as when Al promises to work for Beth for an agreed wage, or Ann promises to sell a new car to Ben for a specified price. Frequently, however, contracts involve more than two persons. Al might promise to work for Beth if she will pay an agreed amount of money to Tina, a "third-person beneficiary" of the contract between Al and Beth. Or Ann might promise to sell a car to Ben on credit, intending to sell to Credit Corporation for immediate cash Ben's promise to make future payments for the car. Ann's sale of Ben's promise is an "assignment" of her contract rights.

This chapter focuses on contracts involving third persons. The first part of the chapter deals with *third-person beneficiary contracts* (sometimes called "third-party contracts"). The second and third parts deal with the *assignment of contract rights* and the *delegation of contract duties*.

Third-Person Beneficiary Contracts

Under the English common law, a person could not sue for breach of a contract unless he or she was one of the contracting parties—i.e., was "in privity of contract" with the person being sued. A mere contract beneficiary had no enforceable rights.[1] In 1859, the American courts broke away from the English view with the case of *Lawrence v. Fox.*[2] Defendant Fox had borrowed $300 from Holly, promising to repay the money not to Holly, but instead to Holly's creditor, Lawrence. Fox did not pay Lawrence, and Lawrence sued Fox for breach of the contract between Fox and Holly. Affirming the trial court's judgment for Lawrence, the New York Court of Appeals held that where a promise (Fox's) is "made for the benefit of another, he for whose benefit it is made [Lawrence] may bring an action for its breach." Today, most states recognize, as an exception to the "privity of contract" requirement, the right of a third person to sue for breach of a contract made for that person's benefit.

[1]John E. Murray, Jr., *Murray on Contracts*, Bobbs-Merrill, Indianapolis, 1974, secs. 276 and 277.
[2]20 N.Y. 268.

There are three kinds of third-person beneficiaries: creditor beneficiaries, donee beneficiaries, and incidental beneficiaries. Only the first two have rights of enforcement.

Meaning of Third-Person Beneficiary

To be a third-person beneficiary as the term is understood in the law (i.e., to have a right to enforce a contract made by others), the third person must be *intended by the contracting parties* to receive the performance that was the subject of their bargain. Figure 14.1 represents a third-person beneficiary contract. In it, A is the promisor (the person promising the performance that the third person is to receive), B is the promisee (the other contracting party), and T is the third-person beneficiary who is to receive A's performance.

There are two types of intended third-person beneficiaries—donee and creditor. Suppose Ben insures his life for $50,000 with Ace Life Insurance Co., and designates his wife Tina as the beneficiary of the policy. She is a *donee* beneficiary because Ben's purpose is to confer a gift upon her at his death. Suppose, however, that Ben buys an expensive car on credit, insures his life for the amount of the unpaid purchase price, and makes Tom, the car dealer, the beneficiary. Tom is a *creditor* beneficiary because Ben's purpose in naming Tom as beneficiary is to fulfill a legal obligation that Ben owes Tom—the duty to pay for the car.

Likewise, the so-called "assumption contracts" involve creditor beneficiaries. For example, Ann agrees to buy from Bill a house that he has been buying on credit; Town Mortgage Co. (Bill's lender) holds a mortgage on the house; and as part of the purchase price Ann agrees to assume (promises to pay) Bill's remaining mortgage debt. Town Mortgage is the third-person creditor beneficiary of the assumption contract between Ann and Bill. Most states classify donee and creditor beneficiaries as "intended beneficiaries" and allow any intended beneficiary to sue the promisor directly for breach of contract.

In contrast, a contract may benefit people who have no connection with it and whom the contracting parties had no intention of benefiting. Suppose Ben hires Ann to tear down a dilapidated tenement house he owns and to replace it with a beautiful apartment building. The contract, if carried out, may well enhance the value of all properties in the neighbor-

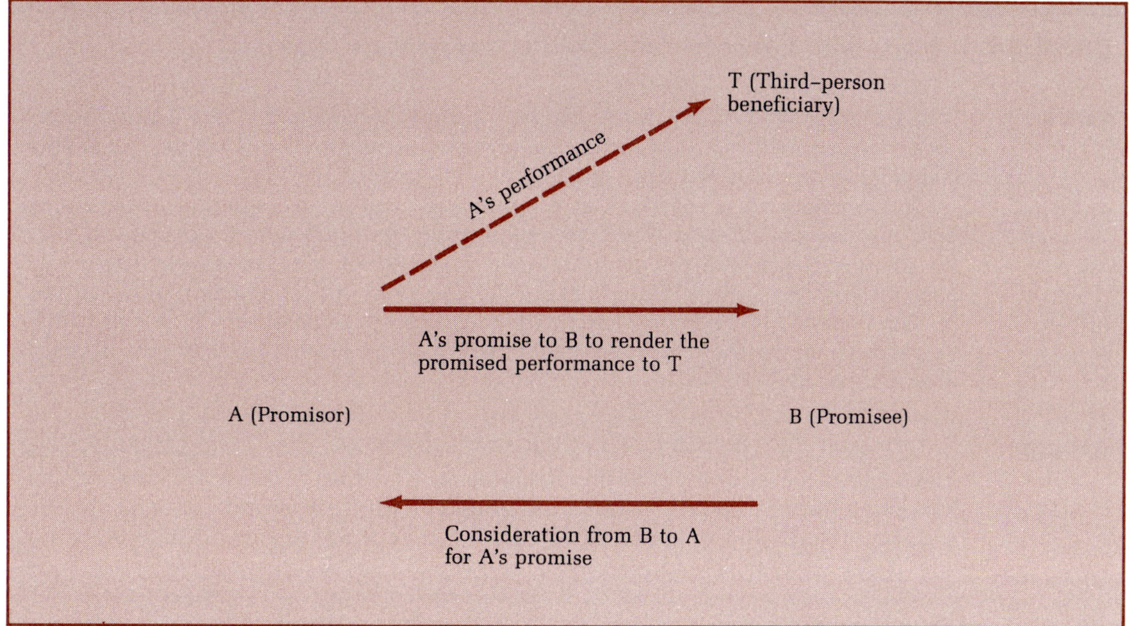

Figure 14.1 Third-person beneficiary contract.

hood, and their owners may benefit from Ann's promised performance. But at best those owners are *incidental* beneficiaries. As such they have no rights under the contract if it is performed, and no right to sue Ann if she breaches it.

To enforce a contract, intended beneficiaries do not have to be identified by name, nor do their identities have to be known at the time of contracting. It is sufficient that the beneficiary can be identified at the time performance is due. Suppose, for example, that an oil company contracts with a state to provide emergency roadside service to travelers on a freeway as a part of its duties under its exclusive service station franchise. A traveler injured because of the oil company's failure to provide emergency service is an intended beneficiary and has a cause of action for the oil company's breach of contract. Similarly, if Ace Life Insurance Co. contracts with Bob to pay $100,000 at his death to his "children" or to his "estate," the description of the intended beneficiaries is sufficient.

Reason for Recognizing Rights of Beneficiaries

One reason for allowing a donee beneficiary to enforce the contract is that often only the beneficiary can do so effectively. When Ben named his wife Tina as beneficiary of his $50,000 life insurance policy, Ben, the promisee, intended to confer a gift upon Tina and not to obtain personal benefit. Therefore, if Ace Insurance Co., the promisor, breaches the contract, Ben (who has personally suffered no substantial injury) would be entitled only to nominal damages and to restitution of any consideration given. Unless Tina has the eventual right to enforce the insurance contract for its face amount, Ben's purpose would be defeated. Moreover, life insurance policies would be of little worth if surviving beneficiaries could not enforce them.

Unlike a donee beneficiary, a creditor beneficiary (Tom, the car dealer) has a contract with the debtor-promisee (Ben) and certain rights of enforcement against him. The process of enforcement, however, may be cumbersome and may result in unnecessary litigation. Ben dies and Ace Insurance Co. refuses to pay Tom the amount still owed for the car. Because it is inefficient to require Tom to sue Ben's estate and to require the estate in turn to sue the promisor (Ace), the beneficiary can sue the promisor directly.

In Case 14.1, an insurance agent is an alleged promisor who encounters an unusual potential liability to an injured motorist.

CASE 14.1 Flattery v. Gregory · 489 N.E.2d 1257 (Mass. 1986)

FACTS William and Joalta Gregory owned two cars, a 1973 Mercury and a 1975 Toyota. Insurance coverage on the Mercury included a $100,000 amount for bodily injury. The Toyota bodily injury coverage was $20,000.

In December 1979 Douglas Flattery (plaintiff) was injured when his car collided with the Toyota. He sued William Gregory and won a judgment for over $118,000. Because Gregory's bodily injury insurance coverage for the Toyota was limited to $20,000, Flattery sued William Borhek, the Gregorys' insurance agent, alleging that Borhek (defendant) had contracted with the Gregorys to procure a $100,000 bodily injury coverage for the Toyota but had failed to do so. From a judgment for Borhek, Flattery appealed.

OPINION O'CONNOR, J. . . . [Borhek] can be liable to [plaintiff Flattery] on a contract theory only if he violated a duty to the plaintiff established by a contract between the Gregorys and himself. . . . Essential to the plaintiff's assertions of . . . third party contract liability to him is a claim that Borhek promised the Gregorys that he would procure liability insurance with bodily injury limits of $100,000 per person and $300,000 per accident on the 1975 Toyota. Our first inquiry, therefore, is whether the complaint gives sufficient notice of a claim of such a promise . . . to withstand Borhek's motion to dismiss. We conclude that the complaint adequately [states such a claim. The complaint] alleges that such a promise was implied from Borhek's earlier procurement of motor vehicle liability policies containing $100,000/$300,000 limits on other vehicles owned by the Gregorys. . . . Under the complaint, the plaintiff could prove sufficient prior dealings between Borhek and the Gregorys to warrant a finding of a promise implied from custom.

Of course, the plaintiff's complaint does not state a claim upon which relief can be granted unless, in addition to alleging Borhek's promise [to procure the higher] coverage, the complaint also permits proof of facts establishing a legally recognized duty which was owed by Borhek not just to the Gregorys but to the plaintiff as well. . . .

We turn to the question [of] whether recovery under the complaint is possible on the theory that the plaintiff is a third-party beneficiary of a contract between Borhek and the Gregorys. In *Rae v. Air-Speed, Inc.*, . . . we held that the plaintiff could recover . . . on a contract theory[,] announced in that case our adoption of Restatement (Second) of Contracts § 302[, and] impliedly adopted related sections too. . . . Quoting *Brewer v. Dyer*, . . . we "recognize[d] again the principle of law that, 'when one person, for a valuable consideration, engages with another, by simple contract, to do some act for the benefit of a third, the latter, who would enjoy the benefit of the act, may maintain an action for the breach of such engagement.'" . . .

We must inquire whether the plaintiff was "an intended beneficiary" of the service promised by Borhek as that term is used in the Restatement (Second) of Contracts § 302, and whether the promised service was "for the benefit of" the plaintiff as contemplated in *Brewer*. . . .

> Where performance [of a promise] will benefit a person other than the promisee, that person is a beneficiary. . . . A promise in a contract creates a duty in the promisor to any *intended beneficiary* to perform the promise, and the *intended beneficiary* may enforce the duty (emphasis added). . . . An *incidental beneficiary* acquires . . . no right against the promisor or the promisee" (emphasis added). . . . (1) Unless otherwise agreed between promisor and promisee, a beneficiary of a promise is an intended beneficiary if recognition of a right to performance in the beneficiary is appropriate to effectuate the intention of the parties and either (*a*) the performance of the promise will satisfy an obligation of the promisee to pay money to the beneficiary; or (*b*) the circumstances indicate that the promisee intends to give the beneficiary the benefit of the promised performance . . .

CASE 14.1 Continued

The standard Massachusetts automobile liability insurance policy in 1979 contained the following language relative to optional bodily injury coverage: "... [W]e will pay damages to people injured or killed in accidents if you or a household member is legally responsible for the accident.... The damages we will pay are the amounts the injured person is entitled to collect for bodily injury through a court judgment or settlement." It is clear that the plaintiff would have benefited from Borhek's performance of his alleged contractual obligation. In the ordinary course of events the plaintiff would have received $100,000 from the insurer. Thus, the plaintiff was a "beneficiary" as described in [the *Restatement*]. We also think that the plaintiff was an "intended" beneficiary.... If the allegations of the complaint are proved, recognition of the plaintiff's right to Borhek's performance is an appropriate way to effectuate the intent of Borhek and the Gregorys that the plaintiff receive the amount of his judgment against Gregory up to $100,000, thus discharging, to that extent, "an obligation of the promisee [Gregory] to pay money to the beneficiary."...

...[T]he fact that the Legislature's purpose in enacting the compulsory motor vehicle insurance law is to protect travelers does not warrant the conclusion urged on us by the defendant that "*the* [sole] purpose of noncompulsory coverage is to protect the insureds".... [A Massachusetts statute] gives an injured highway traveler who has recovered a judgment against the party responsible for his injuries the right to collect directly from the tortfeasor's insurer the amount of the judgment up to the limits of the...compulsory and optional insurance.... That provision displays the Legislature's view that injured highway travelers are intended beneficiaries of optional automobile liability insurance.

The more important question for purposes of our analysis here, however, is not whether the Legislature views injured travelers as beneficiaries of optional automobile liability coverage, but rather whether the contracting parties intend the injured party to be a beneficiary of their contract. Applying the Restatement... principles discussed above, we conclude that the plaintiff was clearly an intended beneficiary of the alleged contract between Borhek and the Gregorys. Logic alone argues to the same result. Although the owner of a motor vehicle may be motivated to obtain optional liability insurance coverage solely by a selfish interest to protect his assets, rather than by concern for the needs of parties negligently injured by him, the fact is that a motor vehicle owner achieves that protection by entering into a contract the very object of which is the payment, in whole or in part, of judgments against him. The parties to the insurance policy, or, as in this case, to a contract to procure such a policy, intend the injured third-party judgment holder to benefit from their contract. It makes no difference, therefore, whether the insurance is compulsory or optional....

JUDGMENT The judgment of dismissal is reversed....

Vesting of Beneficiary's Rights

A beneficiary has no cause of action against the promisor for breach of the beneficial promise unless the beneficiary's rights have "vested" (become established). Vesting can occur at a variety of times, depending on the circumstances. Most life insurance policies have a standard form clause permitting the insured party (the promisee) to change the beneficiary at any time. Under such insurance policies, the beneficiary's rights to the face amount of the policy do not vest until the death of the insured person. In contrast, if an insurance policy does *not* provide for a change of beneficiary, the beneficiary's rights vest when the beneficiary is named—usually when the insurance contract is made. In other situations—especially where a promisor has a right to revoke the beneficial promise—the beneficiary's rights may vest when he or she brings suit on the contract or materially changes his or her position in justifiable reliance on the promise.

Promisor's Defenses against the Beneficiary

Whether a beneficiary may enforce the beneficial promise also depends on the enforceability of the contract between the promisor and the promisee. The promisor may assert against the beneficiary any defense that the promisor could have asserted against the promisee if the promisee had sought to enforce the contract—fraud, mistake, absence of mutual assent or consideration, illegality, violation of the statute of frauds, lack of capacity, and the like. Suppose Bess hires Grace, a minor, to give guitar lessons to Bess's son Juan. If Grace refuses to carry out her part of the bargain and Juan sues Grace for breach of contract, Grace may assert her defense of infancy.

Assignment of Contract Rights

Meaning and Nature of Assignment

Al has just signed a contract in which Beth has agreed to install an electronic security system in Al's office building for $40,000, payment to be made when she finishes the work 3 months from now. Beth has Al's written promise of future payment, but she needs immediate cash to pay her employees. She can get it by selling Al's promise to Cora for, say, $37,000 so that Cora can collect the $40,000 from Al later. Or perhaps Beth does not need cash, but just wants Cora to have Al's promise as a birthday gift. Whether Beth's purpose is to obtain cash or to make a gift, she accomplishes it by transferring ("assigning") to Cora Al's promise to pay.

Meaning of Assignment. An *assignment* is the *present transfer* of an existing right (often, a contract right) by its owner (Beth) to someone else (Cora). Beth, the person doing the transferring, is the "assignor." Since the assigned right may consist of a promise made to the assignor, Beth may also be called the "promisee," "obligee," or "creditor." Cora, the person to whom the right (Al's promise to pay) is assigned, is the "assignee." In a sale or gift of a right, the assignor transfers ownership of it; consequently, when a right is assigned, the assignor's (Beth's) interest in the obligor's (Al's) performance ends, and the assignee (Cora) becomes the person entitled to Al's performance. Some attempts to make an assignment are legally ineffective. So, courts sometimes distinguish between "attempted" or "purported" assignments and "effective" assignments.

Figure 14.2 illustrates an assignment of a contract right. A, B, and C represent contracting parties such as Al, Beth, and Cora. B sells goods or services to A on credit; and A (the obligor) promises to pay B in the future, perhaps by making installment payments. At this time, B has a contract right against A, but no cash. To raise immediate cash, B assigns to C the obligor's promise to pay; and in exchange for the assignor's promise, C (the assignee) gives money (or other consideration) to B. Thus, in Figure 14.2, the assignee is a purchaser of the assigned right. If B had made a gift to C of the assigned right, there would of course be no arrow representing movement of consideration from C to B.

Requirements for Assignment. Ordinarily, an assignment may be made in any form. Any act or statement, written or oral, indicating an intention to make a present transfer of a right usually is sufficient. However, the assignment of some kinds of rights poses special problems that require statutory regulation. For example, wages often are the last asset that a struggling debtor may have available. Where assignments of wages are permitted, statutes commonly require a writing as evidence of a wage assignment.

Since a right may be assigned as a gift, an assignor's receiving consideration for a right obviously is not required for an assignment to be effective. But under the law of gifts, a gift is not effective until the property involved is delivered. So, the courts do not regard a *gift assignment* as having been made until the assignee-donee acquires a substantial measure of control over the property. If the property being assigned is a contract right represented by a document such as a life insurance policy or a bank savings account book, the gift assignment may be accomplished by, for example, the assignor's delivering the document to the assignee or the assignee's agent.

Effect of Notice of Assignment. Until the obligor (Al) receives *notice* of the assignment, he owes no duty to the assignee (Cora). Until then, Al's

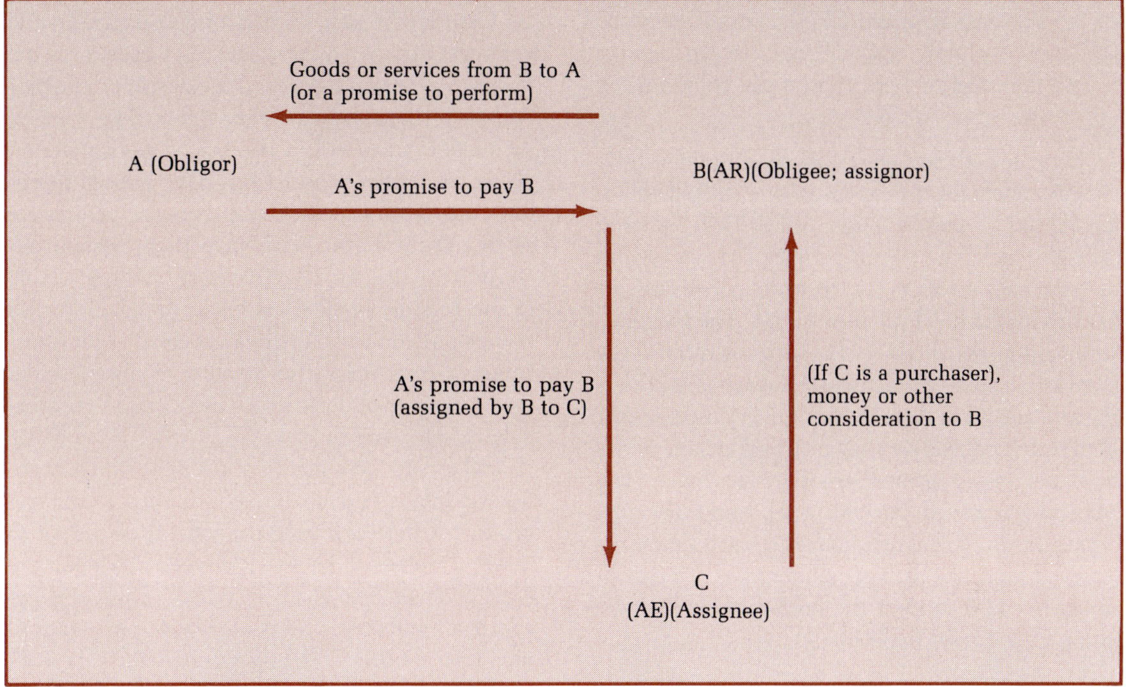

Figure 14.2 Assignment of contract rights.

only duty is to the assignor-obligee (Beth). When notified of the assignment, however, Al must render performance to Cora and not to Beth unless Beth has been authorized to receive payment for Cora. Commercial assignees often do authorize assignors to collect assigned customer accounts on behalf of the assignees. But an obligor without notice of assignment cannot be required to pay twice.

Legal Position of the Assignee. Al promises to pay Beth $40,000 for an electronic security system, payment to be made in 3 months. For $37,000, Beth immediately assigns to Cora the right to Al's payment. How does Cora determine that $37,000 is an appropriate amount to pay? She will consider a number of factors when negotiating the price—e.g., whether an alternative investment would be more profitable, and whether she faces a substantial risk of noncollection. Assessing the amount of risk requires Cora to consider what rights she acquires if she buys Al's promise, and what collection problems she might face if, for example, Beth's work is not satisfactory to Al.

An assignee "stands in the shoes" of the assignor. This statement means two things:

1 The assignee (Cora) acquires any *rights that the assignor (Beth) had* at the time of the assignment. These rights include the right to the obligor's (Al's) performance and any related right that Beth might have had, such as any priority of payment that the law gives her over Al's other creditors if Al becomes insolvent.
2 The assignee takes the assigned rights *subject to defenses* of the obligor. Al may assert against Cora any defense that he could have asserted against Beth (illegality of the contract, failure of the consideration that Beth was supposed to give for Al's promise, fraud by Beth, Al's infancy, and so on). Al may also assert any defense arising after the assignment was made but *before he received notice* of the assignment. Examples are: (1) Al paid Beth before receiving notice of the assignment. (2) Beth has released Al from any further obligation. (3) Beth and Al have rescinded or modified their contract so that Al now owes nothing or owes a smaller amount. Because Cora cannot enforce Al's promise if he has a good defense to payment,

she faces a substantial risk of noncollection. Accordingly, she will tend to pay less for the assigned right than if she could take it free from Al's defenses.

Suppose Beth defrauded Al by substituting a cheap security system for the expensive one she billed him for. Al has a cause of action against Beth for fraud damages, including punitive damages. Does he also have one against Cora for fraud when Beth assigns her rights to Cora? The answer is no. The assignee's "standing in the shoes" of the assignor means only that Cora acquires the rights of the assignor, and faces the same defenses that Al could have raised against Beth had there been no assignment. Al can use Beth's fraud as a *defense* against Cora if she sues him for the amount he promised. But under the common law rules of assignment, Al has no cause of action against Cora for fraud, since she did not commit fraud. And Cora would not have to bear the burden of *Beth's* fraud unless Cora agreed to do so.

Effect of Waiver-of-Defenses Clause. To reduce an assignee's risk of noncollection, and consequently to make assigned rights more valuable, assignors or assignees often insert "waiver-of-defenses" clauses into the contract forms to be signed by obligors such as Al. Under such a clause, Al "agrees" not to assert against an assignee (Cora) any claim or defense that Al may have against the assignor (Beth). If enforceable, the waiver-of-defenses clause would require Al to pay Cora despite a defective performance or other misconduct by Beth. For any redress, Al would have to seek out Beth, who might be insolvent, recalcitrant, or unavailable for suit.

Case law is in a state of disagreement on the enforceability of waiver-of-defenses clauses. Some jurisdictions have enforced such clauses because they enhance the value of assigned rights. The value of such rights increases as the risk of noncollection decreases. Other jurisdictions have refused to enforce waiver-of-defenses clauses because such clauses often surprise buyers and leave them without effective remedies for defective performances. A rule of the Federal Trade Commission renders invalid waiver-of-defenses clauses in *consumer credit* transactions.[3] As to transactions not involving consumer credit, waiver-of-defenses clauses remain enforceable in some states.

Subject to "any statute or decision which establishes a different rule for buyers or lessors of consumer goods," Article 9 [Section 9-206(1)] of the UCC makes a waiver-of-defenses clause enforceable as to some defenses, but not as to others. Thus, with regard to assertability of defenses, Article 9 treats a contract with a waiver-of-defenses clause much like a negotiable instrument. The law of negotiable instruments is discussed in Chapters 28 to 32.

Case 14.2 involves an obligor who does not want merely to assert a defense against an assignee and thus avoid paying the assignee. The obligor wants to go further and have damages from the assignee for the *assignor's* fraud. Can the obligor do so? The answer depends on the impact of the state Consumer Protection Act on the legal position of the assignee.

[3]*FTC Trade Regulation Rule*, Title 16, *Code of Federal Regulations*, Part 433 (amended and effective April 14, 1977).

CASE 14.2 Rosemond v. Campbell · 343 S.E.2d 641 (S.C. App. 1986)

FACTS Campbell (defendant), a building contractor doing business as Quality Construction Company, went to the home of the Rosemonds (plaintiffs) and solicited a contract for home repairs and improvements. The Rosemonds, persons of limited education, agreed to pay $3,236.69 for new roofing, storm windows, a storm door, porch screening, and a suite of living room furniture.

The next day, Campbell drove the Rosemonds to the office of Marion Harris (defendant), whose company had financed more than a thousand construction or home improvement jobs by Campbell over a period of 20 to 25 years. At Harris's office, the Rosemonds executed a second mortgage on their house to Campbell to secure payment of the contract price. They also signed a nonnegotiable promissory note made out to Harris for

CASE 14.2 Continued

the contract price plus 19.66 percent interest, and signed a disclosure statement and a security agreement in favor of Harris. Campbell immediately assigned his mortgage to Harris, who paid the loan proceeds directly to Campbell.

Campbell's work was done defectively or not at all. After trying for 4 years to persuade Campbell or Harris to complete the work and remedy the defects, the Rosemonds sued both. At the close of the Rosemonds' evidence, the trial judge granted Harris's motion for nonsuit. The jury returned a verdict for actual and punitive damages against Campbell. The Rosemonds appealed the judgment in favor of Harris, contending that he, too, had committed fraud and had liability under the South Carolina Consumer Protection Code.

OPINION

BELL, J. . . . A careful review of the record convinces us that the nonsuit [on the fraud cause of action] was properly granted.

In order to establish fraud on the part of Harris, the Rosemonds were required to prove, among other elements of the tort, that Harris made a false representation of a material fact, knowing of its falsity, with the purpose or expectation of having them rely on its truth. . . . There is no evidence in the record that Harris made any representations whatsoever to the Rosemonds concerning the work to be performed by Campbell on their house. . . .

[The Rosemonds also contend that] Campbell was the agent of Harris when [Campbell] induced them [into] the contract. . . . [T]he evidence falls far short of establishing that Harris was a principal to the [home improvement] contract [or] that Harris has a proprietary or other interest in Campbell's construction company. Although he did a continuous business with Campbell over many years, [nothing indicates] anything but an arm's length relationship between two separate and distinct enterprises. Campbell's company is only one of several for whom Harris provides financing on a regular basis. [There is no evidence that] Campbell was acting at the direction or in the interest of Harris when [Campbell] solicited the contract. [The Rosemonds] argue that Harris's status as a principal . . . is shown by the fact that all the documents were executed in his office. It is not uncommon, however, for a bank or other lender to prepare the documents in connection with a financing of this sort. The [home improvement] contract itself was filled out by Campbell [on] a standard printed form of Quality Construction Company. [T]here is no evidence from which a reasonable inference of agency can be drawn. . . .

The Rosemond's third cause of action sought to impose liability on Harris, as assignee of their contract with Campbell. [The South Carolina Consumer Protection Act] provides:

1. With respect to a consumer credit sale . . . , an assignee of the right of the seller . . . is subject to all claims and defenses of the consumer against the seller . . . arising from the sale . . . of property or services. . . .
2. A claim or defense of a consumer specified in subsection (1) may be asserted against the assignee under this section only if the consumer has made a good faith attempt to obtain satisfaction from the seller [assignor] with respect to the claim or defense and then only to the extent of the amount owing to the assignee with respect to the sale . . . as to which the claim or defense arose at the time the assignee has written notice of the claim or defense.

The circuit court was of the opinion that this statute merely . . . gives the consumer a right to assert any defense or setoff he has against the seller if the seller's assignee attempts to enforce the debt, but it does not give the consumer a right to sue the assignee on a claim against the seller. In other words, the court concluded the consumer may use the statute as a shield, but not as a sword against the assignee.

[On the basis of] this reasoning, the court granted Harris's motion for a nonsuit on the third cause of action, because the Rosemonds were asserting their claim of fraud by Campbell offensively rather than defensively against Harris.

CASE 14.2 Continued

The question presented for our decision is whether the Rosemonds are entitled to assert an affirmative claim against Harris for Campbell's fraud or whether the statute limits them to a defensive assertion of the claim.

At common law, an assignee's rights can be no greater than those of his assignor. . . . Consequently, the assignee of a debt takes the obligation subject to all claims and defenses the obligor may have against the assignor. However, absent an agreement to the contrary, the common law assignee takes only the benefits, not the burdens of the assigned obligation. . . . Thus, as against the assignee, the obligor can only assert a claim defensively when the assignee seeks to enforce the obligation; he has no common law right to sue the assignee affirmatively on a claim against the assignor arising from the underlying obligation. . . .

The Consumer Protection Act alters these rules with respect to consumer credit sales. [It prohibits] a "waiver of defenses" clause in consumer credit sales agreements and consumer loan agreements. [It] subjects an assignee of the seller's rights to all claims and defenses of the consumer against the seller, even though the . . . consumer has purported to waive his claims and defenses as against the assignee.

As originally enacted by the General Assembly, [the Act] permitted the consumer to subject an assignee to claims and defenses available against the seller only as a matter of defense in an action by the assignee. . . . There was no affirmative right to sue the assignee on claims against the seller. Thus, the assignee was in the same position under the statute as he was under the general common law rule.

In 1976, the General Assembly amended [the Act] by deleting the language which limits the consumer to defensive assertion of claims against the seller's assignee. . . . As amended, the statute subjects the seller's assignee to all claims of the consumer against the seller arising from the underlying credit sale. In effect, the amendment enlarges the consumer's rights. It permits him to assert any claim available against the seller offensively in a suit against the assignee as well as defensively as an offset or counterclaim in a suit by the assignee to enforce the obligation. . . . The assignee's liability under the statute is derivative: unless the consumer has a valid claim against the seller [assignor], he has no claim against the assignee. Moreover, when the consumer asserts such a claim offensively against the assignee, the statute limits his recovery to the amount due on the obligation at the time the assignee has written notice of the claim. . . . Any damages in excess of those recoverable against the assignee can, of course, be recovered from the seller, since he is liable on the underlying contract of sale. . . .

. . . Under the amended statute, the Rosemonds were entitled to assert an affirmative claim against Harris for Campbell's alleged fraud. If the Rosemonds presented sufficient evidence to send the question of Campbell's fraud to the jury, they were also entitled to have the jury consider Harris's derivative liability under the statute. . . .

JUDGMENT Reversed and remanded.

Assignments Which Are Not Legally Effective

The law allows most types of contract rights to be assigned. However, to protect the obligor (Al), the law does not recognize an assignment of a contract right where Beth's transferring it would materially change Al's duty; materially increase the burden or risk imposed upon him by his contract; or materially impair his chance of obtaining a return performance. Furthermore, there can be no effective assignment of contract rights where the assignment is forbidden by statute or is otherwise against public policy, or where assignment is validly precluded by contract. Some of these situations are illustrated in the following paragraphs.

Assignments Materially Varying the Obligor's Duty or Risk. The most obvious material change in an obligor's duty is a substantial variation in the nature or quantity of performance to be rendered. Suppose Al contracts with Beth to paint her portrait, and she attempts to assign her rights under the contract to Carl. Painting Carl's portrait is not the same as painting Beth's portrait. If assignment were permitted, the nature of Al's performance would be changed. The assignment is not effective unless Al consents to it. Or suppose that Alco, a small oil producer, contracts to furnish Bencorp all the oil it needs for its business, and that Bencorp sells the business and attempts to assign to the purchaser Alco's promise to supply oil to Bencorp. If the purchaser's needs for oil are materially greater than Bencorp's, the assignment will not be effective unless Alco consents to it, because of the unexpected burden Alco would otherwise face.

Some rights are of such a nature that their transfer causes no substantial change in the obligor's (Al's) performance. A common example is the right of a creditor (Beth) to a payment of money for her completed performance. All that remains is for Al to pay, and under the law it can make no difference to him who receives the money—Beth or her assignee. Therefore, a creditor ordinarily may assign the right to an earned money payment without the consent of the obligor.

However, an assignor may not unilaterally increase the obligor's risk. Suppose that Beth's house is insured by Allfire, a fire insurance company, and that Beth sells the house to Carl and assigns the fire insurance policy to him. The assignment is ineffective unless Allfire consents. Presumably one of the risk factors that insurance companies consider when setting their rates is the safety record of the insured person. Allowing insured persons to assign a policy without the consent of the insurer could result in increasing the insurer's risks and in impairing the insurer's ability to insure effectively.

Assignments Impairing Obligor's Return Performance. Nor may an assignment materially reduce the obligor's chances of obtaining the expected return performance. Al contracts with Beth, a famous race car driver, to manage her car leasing business for 10 percent of the net profits. The business is well known because of Beth's racing success. Then she sells her business to Carl, who intends to rename it, and assigns to him her rights to Al's services as manager. The assignment is ineffective without Al's consent, since he may be deprived of the special benefit he expected from Beth's racing reputation. Even in ordinary employment contracts, the employer may not assign the right to the employee's services without his or her consent. All such contracts are considered so personal in nature that any assignment would impose a material change on the employee.

In Case 14.3, a credit buyer of real estate wants to assign his rights to another person. Can he substitute another buyer for himself without the seller's consent?

CASE 14.3 Lancaster v. Greer · 572 S.W.2d 787 (Tex. Civ. App. 1978)

FACTS Greer (plaintiff) entered into an earnest money contract with Bates, agreeing to sell him 467 acres of land on credit. Bates, who planned to develop the land and resell parts of it from time to time, placed the required $2,000 earnest money in escrow. As part of the deal, Bates was to begin construction of an access road to the property.

Substantial development problems arose, and Bates decided to abandon the contract and forfeit the $2,000. He arranged for the money to be transferred to Greer, and without Greer's knowledge assigned to Lancaster (defendant) all rights Bates may have had in the contract. About a month later, Greer negotiated a resale of the property, only to discover on the day set for closing that Lancaster had earlier that day recorded the purported assignment in the county land records. Alleging that the recorded assignment document was void and constituted a "cloud" on his title to the land, Greer brought suit against Lancaster. Holding that the contract between Greer and Bates was nonassignable, the trial court entered a summary judgment in favor of Greer. Lancaster appealed.

OPINION MOORE, J. . . . On appeal Lancaster [argues that] the sales contract in question is assignable as a matter of law. In reply, Greer argues that the contract was not assignable because

CASE 14.3 Continued

it involved the extension of credit to Bates. The sole . . . issue to be determined is whether the contract is assignable.

Paragraph 1 of the . . . contract between Greer and Bates contains a description of the land in question as well as the method by which payment for the land shall be [made]. . . .

Paragraph 2 of the contract allows the purchaser to sell any or all of the said tracts of land and provides for the release of the vendor's lien and deed of trust lien affecting such tract provided $600 per acre is paid to the seller's escrow agent. Paragraph 2 provides in pertinent part:

> It is further agreed that the above described deed shall contain a provision to the effect that the Buyer will be permitted to sell tracts of any size, and the Seller will execute a release of the vendor's lien and deed of trust lien affecting such tract provided that the sum of $600.00 per acre in the tract to be released shall be deposited with the . . . escrow agent. The money . . . shall be used for the purpose of meeting the principal and interest payments. . . . It is further agreed that if there should be an accumulation in said escrow account sufficient to pay all of the unpaid principal and all of the interest to accrue according to the terms of said notes that the Seller will in writing request said escrow bank to remit to the Buyer any such excess. It is also agreed that . . . when said indebtedness . . . is fully paid the Seller will execute to the Buyer a release of said vendor's lien and deed of trust lien on all of the property. . . .

Nowhere does the contract authorize assignment, nor does the contract prohibit assignment. The present action turns on the question of the assignability of the earnest money contract. The general rule is that all contracts are assignable. . . . However, there are some well-recognized exceptions to the rule. One exception is that rights arising out of a contract which involve[s] an extension of credit between the parties to the contract are not assignable. . . . It has been held that contracts for the sale of real estate which provide for credit from the seller are not assignable. . . .

Appellant [Lancaster] concedes that paragraph 1 of the . . . contract which sets out the method of payment provides for an extension of credit, and that if this paragraph alone were in the contract, such contract, being one involving credit, could not be assigned. However, appellant takes the position that paragraph 2 . . . permits a one-time cash payment of the entire indebtedness without the extension of any credit and therefore is assignable as a severed portion of the contract. With this position we do not agree.

. . . [T]here is no provision in any paragraph of the contract which would allow for a total cash payment at closing or which allows for the consummation of the contract . . . unless vendor's lien notes and deed of trust liens are created. . . . Paragraph 1 makes it explicitly clear that the payment for the land is expected to be made in annual installments over a ten-year period. Paragraph 2 specifically states that the money deposited in the escrow account shall be used for the purpose of meeting the principal and interest payments. This money is not to be considered a cash payment for a tract of land, but rather a prepayment of the principal and interest on the notes. Obviously, credit must be extended before any notes could be executed in order to be prepaid.

The rationale underlying the exception to the general rule is that credit contracts by their very nature involve a relationship between the seller and the buyer of personal confidence and trust, such that the seller must have intended the rights conferred by the contract to be exercised only by him in whom he actually confided. . . . Whenever the contracting parties have relied on the skill, character or credit of each other, the law will not permit one of the parties to substitute for himself another person in whom the opposite party may not repose an equal trust or confidence. . . .

As the essential nature of the earnest money contract is one extending credit, a relationship of personal trust and confidence was intended and created between Greer and Bates such that the law will not permit in the absence of Greer's consent the substitution of another party for Bates. It is undisputed that Greer did not consent to the assignment.

CASE 14.3 Continued

This relationship of personal trust is not only borne out in paragraphs 1 and 2 of the contract but also in paragraph 4. The seller places reliance not only on the buyer's financial ability but also on their personal relationship of trust and confidence by obligating the buyer to commence the construction of an access road to the property in question. . . .

JUDGMENT We hold that the earnest money contract is not assignable in whole or part as a matter of law since it involves an extension of credit by the seller to the purchaser, and because of the personal confidence and trust involved in building an access road. . . . It follows that the instrument assigning the contract from Bates to Lancaster is null and void. . . . The judgment of the trial court is affirmed.

Assignments Forbidden by Statute or Public Policy. Federal and state statutes prohibit or regulate the assignment of certain types of claims. For example, a federal statute makes assignment of a claim against the federal government void except where the claim has already been allowed and a Treasury warrant for payment has been issued. This statute tends to minimize litigation against the government. Most states have statutes prohibiting the assignment of future wages or regulating in amount and method the assignment of future or earned wages, veterans compensation, old age and disability payments, and the like. These statutes ease pressures on debtors to commit their incomes far in advance of receipt.

In the absence of a regulatory statute, the courts will invalidate assignments that are against public policy. Suppose Betty is injured by Alicia's negligence but does not want to sue because the loss was small and she and Alicia are good friends. May Betty assign her cause of action against Alicia to Christine? Most courts would hold the assignment void. Christine's trading in other people's lawsuits is against public policy because it interferes with the tendency of many potential litigants to settle their claims out of court, or tends to stir up disputes and ill will where injured persons would not have thought to sue at all. However, if Betty herself brings suit and wins a judgment against Alicia, Betty *can* assign the judgment to Christine. Because the judgment has reduced Betty's unliquidated tort claim to a liquidated claim for money damages, it is now assignable like any other money debt.

Assignment Prohibited by Contract. Contracts often contain a "nonassignability" clause forbidding the obligee (Beth—B in Figure 14.2) from assigning his or her rights. In deciding whether to enforce the clause, the courts consider the principle of freedom of contract (which supports enforcement) and the policy of free alienation (transfer) of property (which justifies invalidating the clause).

Generally, nonassignability clauses are enforceable, since the obligor (Al—A in Figure 14.2) usually has a substantial interest to protect. But sometimes Al's need to prevent assignment is small whereas Beth's need to assign is great. Then the policy of free alienation may prevail. Most courts will not enforce clauses prohibiting Beth's assignment of money claims that have been earned by performance, e.g., the assignment of amounts owed to her for a house she recently painted or a claim under an insurance policy after loss has occurred. And in most states clauses prohibiting the assignment of rights under contracts for the purchase of real estate are against public policy. Suppose Art agrees to sell Becky his house in exchange for monthly payments for the next 10 years, and a contract clause says she cannot resell the house. Three years later, Becky sells the house to Connie and moves to another state. Most courts would uphold Becky's assignment of her rights to Connie, since, as discussed later in this chapter, Becky remains liable to Art for the unpaid debt, and Becky's need to assign is great. Note that the risk factors here differ from those in Case 14.3. There, Bates abandoned his contract with Greer before any performance—forfeiting the $2,000 as damages for his breach, effectively removing himself from any further liability, and putting Greer in a precarious economic position.

Like most courts, the Uniform Commercial Code invalidates nonassignability clauses that impose unreasonable restraints on the alienation of property. Though the Code gives effect to many nonassignability clauses, UCC § 2-210(2) permits a seller of goods to assign his or her right to damages for the buyer's breach of the whole contract, or any right to payment resulting from the seller's full performance, despite an agreement to the contrary. A similar provision in UCC Article 9 applies to assignments of accounts receivable. It makes "ineffective" any contract term prohibiting a creditor from assigning the account debtor's obligation to pay, even where the creditor has not yet fully performed. Ann hires Beth to install $3,000 worth of plumbing in Ann's house. Payment is due 60 days after Beth completes the work, and she is not to assign her rights under the contract. Before beginning work, she assigns the account to Carl for $2,700. The assignment is valid.

Successive (Dual) Assignments

Sometimes, through mistake, negligence, or fraud, a person sells the same right to two or more assignees. Which assignee has priority? The majority rule in the United States (the "American rule") is that as between successive assignees of the same right, the first in time has priority. The reasoning is that when an effective assignment is made, the assignor has no further rights that could be subject to a second assignment.

The majority rule is subject to some exceptions. For example, a subsequent assignee prevails where the prior assignee negligently failed to take possession of the documentary evidence of the assignment and thus enabled the assignor to transfer the document to a second assignee. Also, where the first assignment is revocable or voidable, as where a gift has been promised but not delivered, the second assignment reveals the assignor's intent to revoke or avoid the first assignment, and the second assignee wins.

The minority American rule (the "English rule") is that the assignee who first notifies the debtor of the assignment has priority. This rule encourages potential assignees to inquire of debtors as to the existence of rival claimants and to take prompt action in notifying debtors of assignments.

Warranties of the Assignor

Suppose that an assignee (Cora) tries to collect payment from the obligor (Al) but is met with a valid defense. What recourse has Cora against the assignor (Beth)? Where an assignment is made for value, Beth impliedly warrants that:

1. The right assigned actually exists.
2. It is subject to no limitations or defenses other than those stated or apparent to Cora at the time of assignment.
3. Beth will do nothing to defeat or impair the value of the assignment to Cora.

An assignment of a supposed but nonexisting claim is a breach of the first warranty listed above. Assignment of a claim that is subject to Al's defense of fraud is a breach of the second warranty. Beth's unauthorized collection of the debt from Al is a breach of the third warranty.

Cora does not receive an *implied* warranty (one imposed on Beth by law even without her knowledge) that Al, the debtor, is solvent. If Cora is unwilling to assume the risk of Al's nonperformance, she should require Beth to make an *express* warranty of performance. Where Beth receives consideration for such a warranty, she will be liable to Cora for Al's failure to perform.

Delegation of Contract Duties

Al contracts with Beth, agreeing to pay her $25,000 for a swimming pool to be built in his backyard. In setting up the contract, Al conferred on Beth a contract right to $25,000. But in exchange for Al's promise, Beth made a return promise to Al that created in her a *duty of performance*—to provide a swimming pool. Depending on the terms of the contract, Beth might perform her duty in any of several ways. She might, for example, build the pool herself, perhaps with the assistance of employees. Or she might do part of the job and subcontract other parts such as the electrical and concrete work. Or she might have an understanding with Al that she will not personally build the pool; instead, she will find someone else (Carl) to build it. To carry out the transaction, Beth will *delegate* to Carl her duty to build the pool and at the same time (for, say, $1,000) *assign* to Carl her rights against Al. Thus, for a $1,000 payment, Carl ends up with the duty to build the pool and the right to $25,000 from Al.

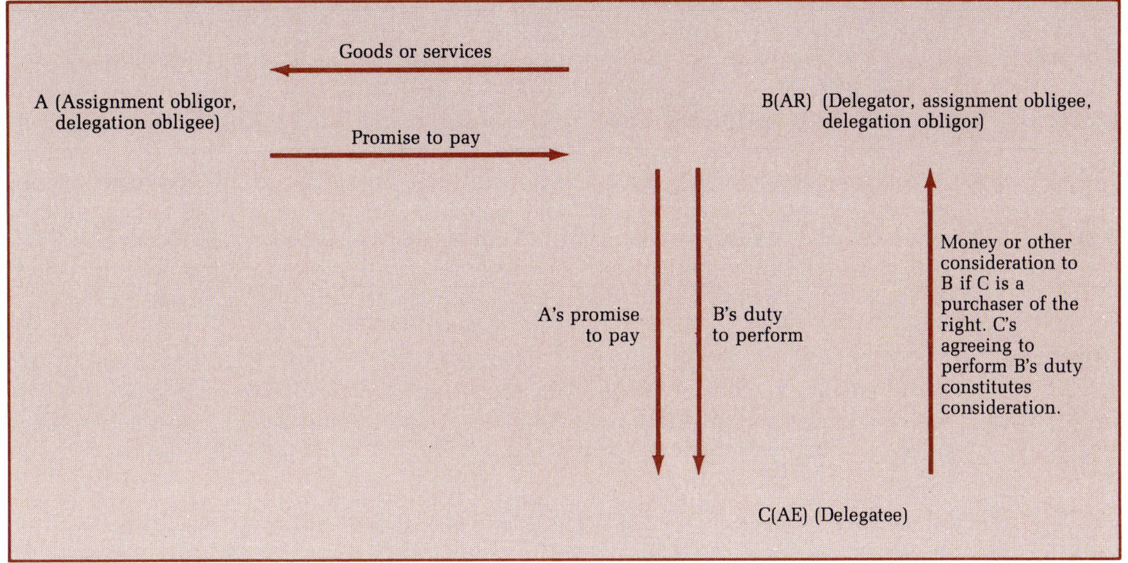

Figure 14.3 Assignment of rights and delegation of duties.

Meaning of Delegation

When a person assigns a right, the assignee receives ownership of it, and the assignor's interest in it ceases. But a contracting party who undertakes a *duty* is not allowed to put it aside casually. He or she is expected to perform the duty or to be responsible for its performance. Because assignment implies an absence of any further interest in or concern about the thing assigned, duties may not be assigned. Duties may only be delegated. *Delegation* means no more than that a person under a duty of performance (Beth) authorizes another person (Carl) to render the required performance. The person who delegates the duty is often called the *delegator,* and the person to whom the duty is delegated is called the *delegatee.*

Figure 14.3 illustrates an assignment of a contract right and a delegation of the assignor's duty of performance. In it, A, B, and C represent Al, Beth, and Carl. Note that Figure 14.3 is a modification of Figure 14.2 and that *for the purposes of delegation,* B is the obligor (person owing the delegated duty) and A is the obligee.

The delegator (Beth) remains liable to the contract obligee (Al) for any failure of the delegatee (Carl) to perform. Beth will be released from liability to Al only if Al consents to the release. (An arrangement totally releasing the delegator from liability is called a *novation.*)

Case 14.4 illustrates the continuing liability of the delegator of a contractual duty.

CASE 14.4 Contemporary Mission, Inc. v. Famous Music Corp. · 557 F.2d 918 (2d Cir. 1977)

FACTS Contemporary Mission, Inc. (Contemporary), a group of Roman Catholic priests who write, produce, and publish musical compositions and recordings, owned all the rights to a rock opera entitled *Virgin.* In 1972, Contemporary entered a contract with Famous Music Corporation (Famous) in which Famous agreed to manufacture, promote, and sell

CASE 14.4 Continued records made from the master-tape recording of *Virgin*. Tony Martell, the president of Famous, had successfully distributed the rock operas *Tommy* and *Jesus Christ Superstar*.

The following year, Contemporary entered another contract with Famous for the distribution of recordings of musical compositions other than *Virgin*. This contract was called the Crunch Agreement. In 1974, Famous's record division was sold to ABC-Dunhill Record Corporation (ABC Records). Contemporary was told that it would have to look to ABC Records for performance of the contracts. ABC Records refused to perform the contracts, and Contemporary sought to hold Famous liable for breach of contract. The trial court rendered judgment for Contemporary, and Famous appealed. The following excerpts from the appellate opinion pertain only to the Crunch Agreement.

OPINION MESKILL, Cir. J.... There is no dispute that the sale of Famous's record division to ABC constituted an assignment of the Crunch agreement to ABC. The assignment of a bilateral contract includes both an assignment of rights and a delegation of duties. The distinction between the two is important.

> Perhaps more frequently than is the case with other terms of art, lawyers seem prone to use the word "assignment" inartfully, frequently intending to encompass within the term the distinct concept of delegation....An assignment involves the transfer of rights. A delegation involves the appointment of another to perform one's duties. J. Calamari & J. Perillo, Contracts sec. 254 (1970).

Famous's arguments with respect to the Crunch agreement ignore this basic distinction, and the result is a distortion of several fundamental principles of contract law.

It is true, of course, as a general rule, that when rights are assigned, the assignor's interest in the rights assigned comes to an end. When duties are delegated, however, the [delegator's] obligation does not end.

> One who owes money or is bound to any performance whatever cannot by any act of his own, or by any act in agreement with any other person, except his creditor, divest himself of the duty and substitute the duty of another....This is sufficiently obvious when attention is called to it, for otherwise obligors would find an easy practical way of escaping their obligations. 3 Williston on Contracts sec. 411 (3d ed. 1960).

This is not to say that one may not delegate his obligations. In fact, most obligations can be delegated—as long as performance by the [delegatee] will not vary materially from performance by the [delegator]. The act of delegation, however, does not relieve the [delegator] of the ultimate responsibility to see that the obligation is performed. If the [delegatee] fails to perform, the [delegator] remains liable....

JUDGMENT The judgment of the district court is affirmed in all respects except as to its ruling with regard to lost royalties, and the case is remanded to the district court for further proceedings in accordance with this opinion.

Delegable and Nondelegable Duties

Beth contracts to build a swimming pool for Al, but Al and Beth say nothing about delegation. May Beth delegate her duty to Carl without Al's consent? The answer depends on whether the duty is delegable or nondelegable.

Unless a clause in the contract forbids delegation, a duty ordinarily may be delegated over the objections of the obligee (Al) where the delegatee's performance would be substantially the equivalent of the delegator's performance. Duties that normally may be delegated include the duty to:

- Pay money
- Deliver standard merchandise
- Manufacture ordinary goods

- Build according to a set of plans and specifications

In contrast, a duty is nondelegable if its performance requires special skill or the personal attention of the would-be delegator. Duties which may *not* be delegated without the consent of the obligee are the duty to:

- Support a relative
- Provide professional services (e.g., architectural services such as designing a swimming pool and supervising its construction)
- Farm "on shares" (tenant shares output of farm with landlord)
- Represent another as an exclusive sales agent
- Manufacture a special class of high-quality goods
- Render personal services to an employer

For the protection of obligees such as Al, the courts enforce contract clauses which forbid the delegation of duties, even where a duty would otherwise be delegable. Some delegations are forbidden by law, usually because the performance, if delegated, would vary materially from that contracted for.

Case 14.5 involves an attempted delegation over the objections of the obligee.

CASE 14.5 Macke Co. v. Pizza of Gaithersburg, Inc. · 270 A.2d 645 (Md. 1970)

FACTS The defendant Pizza Shops, retail outlets under common ownership, contracted with Virginia Coffee Services, Inc. (Virginia), to have cold-drink vending machines installed in each of their six locations. The machines were owned and serviced by Virginia.

In 1967, The Macke Company (Macke) purchased the assets of Virginia, and Virginia assigned the six vending machine contracts to Macke. The Pizza Shops attempted to terminate the contracts, and Macke brought suit against each of the shops for breach of contract. The court rendered judgment for the defendants, and Macke appealed.

OPINION SINGLEY, J. . . . In the absence of a contrary provision—and there was none here—rights and duties under an executory bilateral contract may be assigned and delegated, subject to the exception that duties under a contract to provide personal services may never be delegated, nor [may] rights be assigned, under a contract where *delectus personae* ["choice of the person"] was an ingredient of the bargain. *Crane Ice Cream Co. v. Terminal Freezing & Heating Co.* . . . held that the right of an individual to purchase ice under a contract which by its terms reflected a knowledge of the individual's needs and reliance on his credit and responsibility could not be assigned to the corporation which purchased his business. [In another case] our predecessors held that an advertising agency could not delegate its duties under a contract which had been entered into by an advertiser who had relied on the agency's skill, judgment and taste.

The six machines were placed on the appellees' premises under a printed "Agreement-Contract." . . . We cannot regard the agreements as contracts for personal services. They were either a license or concession granted Virginia by the appellees, or a lease of a portion of the appellees' premises, with Virginia agreeing to pay a percentage of gross sales as a license or concession fee or as rent, and were assignable by Virginia unless they imposed on Virginia duties of a personal or unique character which could not be delegated.

The appellees earnestly argue that they had dealt with Macke before and had chosen Virginia because they preferred the way it conducted its business. Specifically, they say that service was more personalized, since the president of Virginia kept the machines in working order, that commissions were paid in cash, and that Virginia permitted them to keep keys to the machines so that minor adjustments could be made when needed. Even if we assume all this to be true, the agreements with Virginia were silent as to the details

CASE 14.5 Continued

of the working arrangements and contained only a provision requiring Virginia to "install... the above listed equipment and... maintain the equipment in good operating order and stocked with merchandise."

We think the Supreme Court of California put the problem of personal service in proper focus a century ago when it upheld the assignment of a contract to grade a San Francisco street:

> All painters do not paint portraits like Sir Joshua Reynolds, nor landscapes like Claude Lorraine, nor do all writers write dramas like Shakespeare or fiction like Dickens. Rare genius and extraordinary skill are not transferable, and contracts for their employment are therefore personal, and cannot be assigned. But rare genius and extraordinary skill are not indispensable to the workmanlike digging down of a sand hill or the filling up of a depression to a given level, or the construction of brick sewers with manholes and covers, and contracts for such work are not personal, and may be assigned....

...[T]he difference between the service the Pizza shops happened to be getting from Virginia and what they expected to get from Macke did not mount up to such a material change in the performance of obligations under the agreements as would justify the appellees' refusal to recognize the assignment.... Modern authorities... hold that, absent provision to the contrary, a duty may be delegated,... and that the promisee cannot rescind, if the quality of the performance remains materially the same....

JUDGMENT Judgment reversed....

Assignment of "The Contract"

Sometimes a nonassignability clause prohibits the assignment of "this contract." Did the parties intend to prohibit the assignment of rights or to prohibit the delegation of duties or to prohibit both? The common law rule is that such ambiguous language bars only the delegation of the assignor's duty of performance, and *not* the assignment of rights. This rule has been adopted by Section 2-210(3) of the UCC and is consistent with the policy that rights should be more freely transferrable than duties.

The phrase, "the contract," or "this contract," is similarly ambiguous when used to *make* an assignment. Beth writes on the back of her contract with Al, "For value received, I assign this contract to Carl—(Signed) Beth," and hands it to Carl. Does Beth's language effect both an assignment of rights and a delegation of duties? As to contracts on subjects covered by the general law of contracts (real estate, services, etc.), the courts disagree. Some courts would hold that Beth has only assigned her rights; others would hold that she has both assigned her rights and delegated her duties. For the sale of goods, however, the UCC provides that language like Beth's effects both an assignment of rights and a delegation of duties.

Liability of the Delegatee

Carl, the delegatee, might promise to perform Beth's duty as a favor to her, for nothing. Because he has received no consideration for his promise, he has no contractual obligation to Beth and is not liable to either Beth or Al for failure to perform the delegated duty.

But where as a part of the deal Carl also receives an assignment of Beth's rights, he has received the required consideration and is liable to Beth for breach of his promise to perform her duty. Is he also liable to Al, Beth's obligee? If Beth's contract with Al was a sale of goods, the UCC applies. Under its provisions, Carl is liable to Al. If the Code does not apply (as in a sale of real estate or services), Carl is still liable to Al in all but a few states, because Carl's promise to perform Beth's duty is part of a third-person beneficiary contract, enforceable by intended beneficiaries like Al.

Summary

A person may acquire rights in someone else's contract in two ways—by being an intended third-person beneficiary or by the process of assignment.

The law allows any intended beneficiary (donee or creditor) to sue the promisor directly for breach of contract if the beneficiary's rights have vested. However, the promisor may assert against the beneficiary any defense that the promisor could have asserted against the promisee.

An assignment is the transfer of a right by its owner to a third person. The assignee acquires whatever the assignor had, and takes the assigned right subject to any defense that the obligor could have asserted against the assignor. A right is assignable unless its transfer would materially vary the duty of the obligor, increase the obligor's risk under the contract, or impair the obligor's chances of obtaining return performance; or unless assignment of the right is forbidden by law or by a valid nonassignability clause. A person who assigns the same right two or more times raises the question of who has priority. Under the majority rule, the first assignee in time prevails. Under the minority rule, the assignee who first notifies the debtor of the assignment prevails.

An assignor for value impliedly warrants that the right assigned actually exists, that it is subject to no limitations or defenses other than those stated or apparent at the time of the assignment, and that the assignor will do nothing to defeat or impair the value of the assignment.

Duties cannot be assigned, but can be delegated unless the delegatee's performance will differ materially from the delegator's, or unless delegation is forbidden by law or by the contract. Delegation of a duty does not relieve the delegator from his or her duty of performance unless the obligee expressly releases the delegator from the duty.

A valid prohibition of the assignment of "the contract" bars only the delegation of duties. Under the UCC and some case law, the assignment of "this contract" accomplishes both an assignment of rights and a delegation of duties. A delegatee who receives consideration for promising to perform a delegated duty is liable to the delegator, and usually to the obligee, for failing to perform the duty.

Review Questions

1 (a) Must a person be specifically named as a third-person beneficiary to be one? Explain. (b) For what reasons are third-person beneficiaries allowed to enforce the beneficial promises?

2 (a) When does a beneficiary acquire a cause of action for breach of a beneficial promise? (b) What defenses may the promisor assert against the suing beneficiary?

3 (a) For what reasons are assignments of contract rights made? (b) Define "assignment" and distinguish it from the creation of rights in a third-person beneficiary. (c) Is consideration required for an assignment to be effective? Explain.

4 What is the legal position of the person to whom contract rights have been assigned?

5 (a) What is a "waiver-of-defenses clause"? (b) Why do some jurisdictions enforce such clauses? Why do some jurisdictions not enforce them?

6 Give three examples of assignments that would not be legally effective.

7 What two policies might a court consider when deciding whether to enforce a "nonassignability clause"?

8 (a) Distinguish the "American rule" pertaining to successive assignments of the same contract right from the "English rule." (b) Which rule do you think is the more sound?

9 (a) Illustrate how the three warranties of the assignor can be breached. (b) How might an assignee be protected against the risk of the debtor-obligor's insolvency?

10 (a) For what reason might a business person delegate a contractual duty? (b) In terms of legal effect, what is the difference between an assignment of rights and a delegation of duties? (c) Under what circumstances may a delegator be released from liability to the person entitled to the delegator's performance?

11 (a) Where the parties to a contract say nothing about the delegation of duties, under what circumstances may the duties be delegated? (b) How will a court treat a contract clause that forbids delegation?

12 Under what circumstances will a delegatee be liable on his or her promise to perform the delegated duty?

Case Problems

1 Security Savings & Loan Association (Security) held a mortgage on the home of the Knickelbeins. According to them, their payments included monthly amounts to cover a homeowners' insurance policy to be procured by Security on their behalf, but because of Security's failure to make the premium payment, the insurance was terminated in 1971. In 1974, Mr. Schell was attacked by a dog owned by the Knickelbeins. Mr. Schell died, and Mrs. Schell sued Security for damages, alleging that she was a third-person beneficiary of the mortgage contract between the Knickelbeins and Security and so had a right to sue Security for its failure to provide insurance coverage. Security contended that she was not a third-person beneficiary. From a decision for Mrs. Schell, Security appealed. Should the trial court's decision be upheld?

2 The Harmans hired Hoosier Construction Co. to construct a building that would utilize a floating slab floor as opposed to a structural slab. Hoosier then contracted orally with C.E.&M., a professional engineering firm, for drawings for the portion of the building above the slab and for periodic inspections of the construction site to assure conformity with its plans. The contract between Hoosier and C.E.&M. specifically excluded any responsibility on the part of C.E.&M. for the slab or the foundation. The building conformed to C.E.&M.'s plans, but because of the highly compressible soil upon which the building was constructed, the floating slab floor sank 6 to 8 inches. The Harmans sued C.E.&M. for damages, alleging that state professional licensing statutes gave them a cause of action against C.E.&M. as third-party beneficiaries of the contract between Hoosier and C.E.&M. If the licensing statutes gave the Harmans status as third-person beneficiaries, were they entitled to damages?

3 Shapiro, the president of a lumber and supply corporation, obtained a loan on its behalf. As security for the loan, the corporation assigned to the bank the corporation's rights under construction contracts it was to perform. The corporation experienced financial difficulty, and Shapiro applied the proceeds of the contracts to other corporate debts. Upon failure of the corporation to repay the loan, the bank sued the corporation for the conversion of funds to which the bank was entitled. (Conversion is defined as an unauthorized exercise of the right of ownership over personal property belonging to another, to the exclusion of the owner's rights.) Did the corporation convert the bank's funds?

4 The Equitable Life Assurance Society, owner of the Decatur North Professional Building, hired Builders Glass to recaulk the exterior of the building. The contract stated that "all work done by [Builders] will hold a 10 year guarantee." About a year later, Equitable sold the building to Decatur North Associates, which soon discovered leakage problems that it attributed to Builders' deficient recaulking job. Later, Equitable assigned its recaulking agreement with Builders to Decatur North, including the 10-year guarantee. Decatur North then sued Builders Glass for breach of the guarantee. Builders contended that the guarantee was not assignable. Was it?

5 In 1968, Eastern Woodworking Co. bought eleven lots from Chimney Hill Corporation, a housing development consisting of over 900 lots and a large area of "common land" containing recreational facilities, roads, and a water system. A document filed in the public records stated that an annual charge would be imposed against each lot in Chimney Hill for the right to use the common lands and related facilities. The money was to be paid to Chimney Hill or its "successors" or "assigns." However, Eastern's purchase agreement stated, "There will be one annual charge . . . until one or more of the lots have been improved." In 1975, Chimney Hill conveyed the common land to the Chimney Hill Owners' Association, Inc. and assigned to the Association the right to collect the annual charge. The Association billed Eastern for the annual charge for each of the eleven lots. Arguing that none of its lots had yet been improved, Eastern paid only one assessment, and the Association brought suit for the additional amount allegedly owed. Must Eastern pay the charges for an additional ten lots?

6 Genessee Valley Medical Care, Inc., (Blue Shield) contracted with subscribers to provide surgical and other medical care to them and to eligible members of their families. The contract provided that payment for services provided by "participating" physicians would be made directly to them, payments to "nonparticipating" physicians would be made to the subscribers, benefits of the contracts (including payments to doctors) were personal to the subscribers and were not assignable, and "No action at law shall be brought hereunder against [Blue Shield] unless commenced within twelve months from the date when services were rendered." Robischon, a nonparticipating physician, rendered covered services. The patient assigned to him her right to payment from Blue Shield. Blue Shield refused to honor the assignment. More than a year later, Robischon sued Blue Shield, alleging that the nonassignability clause was void and unenforceable as between him and the assignor. Was Robischon entitled to payment from Blue Shield?

7 Petry contracted with Cosmopolitan Spa International, Inc., for a membership in its spa. The contract contained an exculpatory clause purporting to free Cosmopolitan from liability for "accidental or other physical injury." Cosmopolitan sold the spa to Holiday Spa of Tennessee, Inc. Then Petry injured her back when she sat on an exercise machine and it collapsed under her. Alleging negligence, she sued Holiday for damages. The trial court held that the exculpatory clause was enforceable and that as assignee of Cosmopolitan's rights, Holiday had the benefit of the clause. Should the trial court's decision be upheld?

8 Smith sold a taxicab company to Wrehe. Wrehe made a partial payment but still owed Smith $15,000 under the contract. With Smith's consent, Wrehe then assigned "the contract" to a corporation. The assignee-corporation made some payments but soon defaulted, and Smith sued Wrehe for the balance due under the contract. Wrehe contended that only the assignee was liable to Smith. Was Wrehe liable to Smith?

CHAPTER 15

Performance, Breach, and Discharge of Contracts; Remedies for Breach of Contract

Most contracting parties expect to give and receive the promised performances. But the circumstances surrounding a contract may change from what the parties originally contemplated. The performance agreed to may have become impossible, the parties might disagree as to the kind or degree of performance required by the contract, or the contract may have been superseded by a later one. In such situations the courts may be called on to decide whether a contract has been *discharged* (i.e., performed or in some other way terminated). If a contractual obligation has not been discharged, a failure or refusal to perform it is a *breach* of the contract for which the aggrieved (offended) party may have a *remedy* such as damages, rescission, or specific performance.

The first part of this chapter focuses on the performance, breach, and discharge of contractual obligations. The second part discusses (1) remedies that are available for breach of a contractual obligation that has not been discharged, and (2) the quasi-contractual remedy that may be available in the absence of an enforceable contract.

Performance, Breach, and Discharge of Contracts

Meaning of Performance, Breach, and Discharge

Performance is the carrying out of the obligations imposed by a contract. Al agrees to sell his car to Ben for $800, delivery and payment to be made 30 days from now. Al performs by delivering the car at the time promised; Ben performs by paying then.

The contract means the parties' agreement as supplemented or limited by law. Contracting parties often fail to state all the terms of the contract. Because a major goal of contract law is to foster performance, the law will supply many missing terms. Al and Ben forgot to specify the place for delivery. Under the Uniform Commercial Code (the law applying to sales of cars and other goods), the place for delivery is Al's business or residence. If the agreement contains an illegal term such as a usurious interest rate or an unconscionable clause, the courts will not enforce that term even though the parties might have agreed to it, but will limit enforcement to the remaining provisions if they are sufficient to constitute a contract.

Breach is any failure of a party to perform a duty imposed by the contract. Failure to perform constitutes a breach even though the aggrieved party might have suffered no harm as a result of it. A refusal *now* to perform an obligation scheduled for *future* performance is called an *anticipatory repudiation* or *anticipatory breach* of the contract.

Discharge is the termination of a contractual obligation. Performance is the usual method of discharge. Discharge may occur also where, for example, the parties to a contract agree to cancel it or the agreed performance has become illegal or impossible to carry out. As Case 15.1 illustrates, precisely what is required for performance is often a matter for a court to decide.

CASE 15.1 Koval v. Peoples · 431 A.2d 1284 (Del. Super. 1981)

FACTS Peoples [defendant] contracted to construct a house for the Kovals [plaintiff]. The lot was not serviced with public water, and the contract provided that Peoples would provide a well. Peoples delivered a house and a well, but the Kovals claimed that the water was polluted and unfit for domestic use. Alleging that Peoples breached his contract, the Kovals brought suit for damages, including the cost of installing a water purifier system. Peoples filed a motion for summary judgment.

OPINION TAYLOR, J. . . . [I]t is undisputed that [defendant] did provide a well which produced water. The issue is whether defendant's contractual obligation required him to provide a well whose water would comply with the water quality requirement of the building and

CASE 15.1 Continued

plumbing codes adopted by New Castle County and the drinking water standards found in the regulations of the State Board of Health.

In the law of contracts, it is a recognized principle that existing laws form a part of a contract. This principle was stated by this court in *Trader v. Jester*... in the following language:

> The rule is well established that the laws in force at the time and place of making the contract enter into and form a part of it as if they had been expressly referred to, or incorporated in, its terms. The obligation of the contract is measured by the standard of the laws existing at the time of the making of the contract.

This principle applies equally to municipal ordinances. Courts in various states have held that contracts for performance of work are controlled by governmental regulations relating to the manner in which the work may be performed or the quality of the work, in the absence of express contract provision to the contrary....

Courts have used different approaches in reaching the result that government regulations have an effect on contractual obligations and rights. In some cases the court has presumed that the parties intended to incorporate existing laws. Some courts have merely stated the proposition that in the absence of contrary provisions in the contract, existing laws are an obligation of the contract with the same effect as if expressly set forth in the contract. Other courts have held that existing law is an implied term of every contract. [Still others] have held that in the sale of a new house there is an implied warranty that the builder-vendor has complied with the building code....

The significance of the above cited decisions is their unanimity that a statute or ordinance which purports to impose a requirement or a restriction on a subject matter which is directly involved in a contract will be given effect in the application and enforcement of the contract unless the contract by clear language removes the contractual undertakings from the effect of the law or ordinance....

In this State, statutes and codes which are designed to protect the health...of the public establish a standard governing construction, equipping or use of facilities or property....I conclude that compliance with applicable laws and regulations is a requirement and condition of building contracts for work to be performed in this State unless the contract expressly provides for a different measure of performance....

[T]he building and plumbing codes applicable to New Castle County...require dwelling houses to be supplied with potable water. I conclude that a well provided under a contract for the construction of a dwelling house must meet the water requirements for the dwelling house as those requirements have been established by law....Here there is no contract language showing that the parties intended the contractual obligation to depart from the requirements of the law....

Regulations adopted by the State Board of Health...provide drinking water standards [that] apply to public water suppliers in Delaware. With respect to a dwelling unit, a public water supplier is a person who furnishes water for more than three dwelling units....In the absence of different water quality standards for single dwelling units, and recognizing that the water uses for dwelling units are likely to be the same regardless of the number of units drawing on the supply, I conclude that the water quality standards found in the State Board of Health regulations determine the requirements for potable water as that term is used in the Codes adopted by New Castle County.

JUDGMENT

...I find sufficient evidence that the well water did not meet the standards of the regulations to withstand defendant's motion for summary judgment...and the motion is denied.

Role of Conditions in Defining and Discharging Duty of Performance

A party to a contract might "condition" his or her performance on the occurrence or nonoccurrence of some fact or event. If the condition does not occur, then the party for whose benefit it was made is discharged from performance. Al, a resident of Minnesota, agrees to work at Beth's dairy in Nebraska on condition that he can find a place to live near the dairy at least 1 week before his employment is to begin. Al's duty to work for Beth in Nebraska will not become effective unless the condition is met or is waived by Al. If he cannot find living quarters within the agreed time, there has been a failure of the condition and he is discharged from his obligation. Or suppose that Buildo Corp. agrees to dig a tunnel to be completed within 18 months. The contract may include the condition that any time lost because of labor disputes will not be counted against the 18 months and the completion date will be extended accordingly. As these examples indicate, contractual conditions contribute to flexibility of contracting. They also help to establish the circumstances under which a contractual duty may be discharged.[1]

Discharge by Performance

A party to a contract discharges contractual obligations by performing them within the time established by the contract. If the contract does not specify a time for performance, it is due within a reasonable time after the contract is made. Sometimes, however, a party (1) offers a performance that is refused, (2) performs but fails to do so exactly as the contract requires, or (3) states in advance that he or she will not perform when the time for performance arrives. What are the rights of the aggrieved party?

Effect of Tender of Performance. A person may be able to discharge his or her obligations by making a *tender* (an offer) *of performance.* Al contracts with Beth to repair the roof of her house "in a good and workmanlike manner," i.e., according to the standard practices of the roofing industry in that locality. But Beth does not approve of the way Al is preparing to do the work and tells him that he "absolutely may not put a ladder against the house." Al replies that he is prepared to do the work in a way recognized by the trade as proper but that he cannot get onto the roof without using a ladder. Beth refuses to let him proceed. Al has made a tender of performance that not only discharges him from any further duty of performance but also entitles him to damages for profits lost as a result of Beth's unjustifiably preventing him from performing the contract.

Effect of Defective Performance (Breach) on Discharge. What kind of breach of contract by one party will discharge the other party from his or her duty to perform? Often discussed under the label of "doctrine of substantial performance," the problem can also be considered in terms of whether the breach of contract is material or nonmaterial.

A *material breach* is so serious that the nonbreaching party may be deprived of the benefit expected from the breaching party's performance. A material breach discharges the nonbreaching party from any duty to perform. In contrast, a *nonmaterial breach* does not deprive the nonbreaching party of the benefit of the bargain, and does not discharge that party, though the breach may cause inconvenience, annoyance, or extra expense for which the nonbreaching party may have damages. Ann contracts to build a house for Ben. She pours the foundation, but does nothing further and leaves town. Ann has committed a material breach of the contract and Ben is discharged from his duty to pay. In contrast, if Ann builds a house according to plans and specifications, except that she installs cheap door-knobs instead of the expensive ones called for by the contract, Ann has substantially performed. She has breached the contract, but the breach is nonmaterial. Ben is not discharged from his duty to pay Ann for the house, but because of Ann's nonmaterial breach, Ben may subtract from the contract price his cost of securing and installing the specified hardware.

So, a party to whom a contractual duty is owed has a remedy for any breach of that duty whether the breach is material or not. The availability of remedies for any breach tends to discourage people from treat-

[1]Traditionally, conditions have been classified as conditions "precedent," "subsequent," or "concurrent." These classifications have been challenged as unsound, and the *Restatement of the Law (Second) Contracts* has abandoned some of that terminology. John E. Murray, *Murray on Contracts,* Bobbs-Merrill, Indianapolis, 1974, sec. 141.

ing their contractual commitments lightly. A nonmaterial breach does not discharge the other party because such a breach is relatively insignificant and often occurs inadvertently. To discharge the aggrieved party despite the breaching party's substantial performance would upset the latter's legitimate expectation of performance (payment) and would enable the aggrieved party to escape contractual obligations on the basis of trivial deficiencies.

Although any material breach is cause for the discharge of the aggrieved party, there is a difference of legal opinion as to when the discharge should occur. Traditionally, the courts have held that a material breach immediately discharges the injured party, even though there is still time under the contract for a proper performance. Under a newer rule, an uncured (uncorrected) material failure to perform allows the injured party to suspend his or her performance while the breaching party uses any time remaining under the contract to cure the defective performance. If the breaching party cannot cure the defect within the remaining time, the injured party's performance is then discharged. This newer rule prevents the injured party from using a curable material breach as an excuse to escape a contract which, for some reason other than the breach, is no longer attractive to the injured party.

What breaches are material? The answer is for a court, and to some extent for the contracting parties, to determine.

Breaches made material by contract terms. Within limits, the courts permit the parties to a contract to determine by their agreement which duties imposed by the contract are material. Consider, for example, a contract for the sale of land. Usually such a contract specifies the day for "closing," that is, the day upon which the transaction is to be formally completed. Will failure of the seller to convey the land on that day discharge the buyer from the duty to pay? Will failure of the buyer to make the agreed payment on that day discharge the seller from the duty to convey the land? Delay of performance does not necessarily constitute a material breach of the contract. Unless the contract makes timely performance "of the essence" of the contract, a party's minor delay serves only to *postpone* and not discharge the other party's duty of performance. The aggrieved party does, of course, have a remedy for any loss caused by the delay.

The parties to a contract may make time of the essence, that is, state in the contract that a failure of one party to perform by the time stated is material and shall discharge the other party. However, the courts ordinarily will require that the parties have an actual agreement that time is to be of the essence. Time is not made of the essence merely by the presence in a contract form of a standard time-is-of-the-essence clause. The parties can also make other topics material. Examples are the use of certain materials or methods of manufacture, specific inspections or tests, or a special way of crating and shipping.

Breaches made material by court decisions. Normally, a court will find the following kinds of breach, among others, to be material: unreasonable delay in performance, delivery of seriously defective goods or the wrong goods, failure to deliver any goods, inability to deliver clear title to land, or substantial failure to render services bargained for.

Effect of Anticipatory Breach. Where a party makes a material *anticipatory* breach (e.g., states that he or she will not perform when the time for performance arrives), almost all courts allow the aggrieved party to suspend his or her own performance and either (1) await a change of mind by the breaching party or (2) take steps such as finding a substitute for the performance promised by the breaching party. If the aggrieved party chooses the latter course of action, he or she is discharged from liability to the breaching party and is entitled to damages for any higher costs encountered in acquiring the substitute performance.

Other Bases for Discharge

The kinds of discharge discussed so far result from performance, a failure to perform, or the occurrence or nonoccurrence of a circumstance specified in a condition. But there are other bases for discharging a contracting party.

Discharge by Subsequent Agreement. The parties to a contract may wish to end it without performing, or, with a view to performance, may wish to alter the performance obligations in some way. Subsequent agreements of the parties are useful for such purposes. The following paragraphs describe some common types of subsequent agreements and the extent to which they discharge the obligations imposed by the original contracts.

Mutual rescission. In general, *rescission* means cancellation of a transaction. A *mutual* rescission is the voluntary act of putting an end to an executory bilateral contract by means of an agreement to do so. Hal, a young professional athlete enjoying unexpected success, becomes more valuable to his employer. As a preliminary to negotiating a new personal services contract, Hal and his employer agree to rescind the old one. The agreement of rescission is itself a new contract, agreed to without going to court, in which each party discharges the other by surrendering the rights that were established by the old personal services contract. The mutual surrender of rights constitutes the consideration necessary for, and the performance of, the contract of rescission that clears the way for the new personal services contract.

Where one or both parties have *partially performed* an executory bilateral contract, does the law require compensation for or the return of the partial performances? Some courts treat mutual rescission as if it were the court-ordered equitable remedy of rescission (discussed later in this chapter) that must always be accompanied by restitution (compensation for or the return of partial performances), regardless of any agreement to the contrary. Most courts, however, hold that the mutual rescission of an executory bilateral contract is itself nothing more than a contract, and that the decision of the parties regarding partial performances will be enforced.

Accord and satisfaction; substitute contract. Instead of rescinding the original contract, the parties to it may wish to substitute a new set of *performance obligations* for those imposed by the original contract. So, they may resort to an *accord and satisfaction* or to the very similar *substitute contract.* Where the new agreement is not made until after the maturity or breach of the original contract, the new agreement is called an *accord* and the performance of it is called a *satisfaction.* Where the new agreement is made before the maturity or breach of the original agreement, the new agreement is usually called a *substitute contract.* An accord and satisfaction or a substitute contract discharges the original contract if the parties to the new agreement so intended.

Novation. A *novation* is used to accomplish the substitution of *parties* to a contract, with or without a change in the performance obligations. Suppose Ben has a contract with Ann, but Ben is unable to perform it. Then Ann agrees with Ben and Carol that (1) for the payment promised to Ben, Carol will perform Ben's duties under the original contract, and (2) Ben will be freed from any further liability to Ann. The resulting contract is a novation under which Ben is discharged from his duties under the original contract.

Release; contract not to sue. In its broad sense, a *release* is any discharge from liability. The release of a contractual obligation usually is accomplished by means of a writing. In some states a written release is effective without consideration, if sealed and delivered. In other states a release is invalid unless supported by consideration. Where one party to a contract promises never to sue the other for breaching it, the promise, if supported by consideration, constitutes a *contract not to sue* and discharges the other party.

Discharge by Impossibility, Frustration, or Impracticability. Sometimes the circumstances surrounding a contract change so drastically that the contract originally contemplated (1) cannot be performed, (2) is no longer of value to the obligee (party to whom performance is owed), or (3) can be performed only with great hardship or loss to the obligor. So, the party adversely affected might seek a discharge on the ground of impossibility of performance, frustration of purpose, or impracticability of performance.

Impossibility of performance occurs where a promised performance literally is no longer possible (or never was possible). Performance is impossible where, for example, Ann hires Ben to manage her business but he dies or becomes incapacitated before his performance is due or completed. Or impossibility may result from destruction of an object or a source of supply expressly required for performance, as where Ann sells her 1961 Corvette to John for a July delivery but the car is destroyed in May. Sometimes a performance is declared illegal after the contract was made. Although the act contracted for may still be physically possible, the performance may be declared "impossible" because performance would be against the law.

In situations involving *frustration of purpose,* performance is possible and legal despite the changed circumstances. But the performance is no longer of value to the frustrated obligee who once sought it. Suppose Art has an apartment that commands an excellent view of the Rose Bowl parade. He agrees to rent the apartment to Beth for the day of the parade so she can view it in comfort. If a disaster results in the cancellation of the parade, Beth's purpose in contracting for the use of the apartment is frustrated. Unless the contract expressly imposed the risk of cancellation on Beth, she may be discharged from the rental contract.

Where a contract involves *impracticability* of performance, the performance is possible and legal, but it has become so burdensome due to circumstances unforeseeable at the time of contracting (or reasonably unforeseen) that a court will not enforce the contract. Acme agrees to build a dam for City for $1,000,000. If the project costs an extra $100,000 to complete because Acme's engineers failed to detect ordinarily detectable geological formations, Acme will have to bear the extra cost even if the company sustains a loss on the contract. Because the geological formations were reasonably foreseeable, Acme's performance will not be held impracticable. In contrast, suppose an earthquake of record intensity opens a deep crack in the dam site that will cost $6,000,000 to fill before the dam can be constructed. Here the cost of performance is so great that, given the unforeseeability of the earthquake, a court is likely to hold performance of the contract impracticable.

As Case 15.2 illustrates, the courts are reluctant to discharge a contract on the ground of impracticability or frustration of purpose, even though the obligor might lose money in performing it. While obligors often face heavy competition, small margins of profit, and a variety of uncertainties of performance, obligees rely on agreed prices when seeking financing or setting up other contracts. So, in the absence of a contrary agreement, the obligor generally is considered to have assumed the ordinary risks and difficulties of the contract.

CASE 15.2 M & M Transport. Co. v. Schuster • 13 B.R. 861 (S.D.N.Y. 1981)

FACTS

M & M Transportation Co. (M&M), in the business of intra and interstate transport, was the owner of operating rights granted by the Interstate Commerce Commission. The longstanding practice of the ICC was to restrict entry into the trucking industry by stringently limiting the opportunity of a motor carrier to obtain operating rights from the ICC. Rather, a transport company ordinarily would have to purchase operating rights from a company that already owned them.

M&M [plaintiff] became financially troubled, and in a 1977 bankruptcy sale sold its operating rights to Schuster [defendant] for $650,000. Schuster made several payments on the purchase price. In 1980, Congress enacted the Motor Carriers Act. The Act "deregulated" the trucking industry, making entry into the trucking industry easy, and substantially lessening the value of Schuster's once-exclusive rights. Alleging that deregulation frustrated his purpose in buying the rights, Schuster refused to pay M&M the balance of nearly $300,000 due under the contract. M&M brought suit and moved for a summary judgment in its favor.

OPINION

ROY BABITT, Bankruptcy Judge.... There is no dispute that these defendants were represented at the sales by knowledgeable businessmen, all cognizant of the risks involved and mindful of the industry. A policy of deregulation was considered by the national legislature as far back as 1971.... That [the rights sold by M&M] were at all times subject to regulation by the ICC or by the legislature cannot be questioned....

Under the principle of commercial frustration, a party responsible for an otherwise lawful contractual obligation is discharged from performance, where that performance, although possible, is rendered undesirable or oppressive because of supervening events.... This principle is an offshoot of the twentieth century's rejection of a judicial hands-off policy towards contracts. It reflects increased judicial involvement in private contracts. It is an affirmation of the reality that there are situations where society's needs are best served by *not* enforcing the performance of senseless contracts.... Essentially, the principle of commercial frustration affords a means by which courts allocate risk in order

CASE 15.2 Continued

to decide who is to bear the burden of any event not provided for by the parties' agreement.... The basic test is whether the parties contracted on a basic assumption that a particular contingency would not occur....

With these guiding principles in mind, the court now turns to the law of New York, the governing law as the parties agreed. New York, to a large extent, follows the principle of commercial frustration, as outlined in the Restatement (Second) of Contracts § 285....

The Restatement breaks this rule down into three inquiries: (1) The purpose that is frustrated must have been a principal purpose of that party in making the contract. Here, there is no doubt that the defendants determined their bids and entered into these contracts in order to take advantage of the restrictive regulatory structure which made it virtually impossible for others to obtain operating rights from the ICC.... (2) The frustration must be substantial. This element is to ensure that the defense of commercial frustration will not be accepted in cases where performance has become merely less profitable.... [T]he change achieved by the 1980 law substantially lessened the value of the rights purchased.... [But the] lessened profitability occasioned by the 1980 statute is no different [from] a change in fashion and the impact of such change on the profits of the purchaser of... mini or maxi dresses.

The final element, (3), is that the non-occurrence of the frustrating event must have been a basic assumption on which the contract was made. This makes the foreseeability of the event a factor in the determination.... A careful reading of the record... discloses that [this factor] is fatal to defendants' defense.... Here, the defendants made their agreements knowing full well that the value of the rights they bought depended on an unchanged regulatory structure, but one that always was and remained subject to change....

Although defendants argue against the foreseeability of deregulation, the facts belie the premise. [Schuster's] affidavit... says:

> In June 1977, and for years previously thereto, the undersigned [was] aware that there had been discussions in Congress about the possibility of some changes in the Interstate Commerce Act, but these discussions had never materialized into any concrete proposal with any realistic prospect of adoption by Congress, and many of the proposals given the most serious consideration did not contemplate the substantial elimination of the limited entry into the marketplace which had always been incident to ICC operating rights.

This affidavit demonstrates ample knowledge of the possibility of deregulation. That defendants chose to disbelieve or to dismiss the possibility as a serious threat was a personal assessment. That defendants bid as they did with knowledge of a potential deregulation was a matter of their business judgment. For all that appears their bids might have been pitched not only to the possibility of diminished profits but to the judgment that their expectations would measure up to their investment even if deregulation, in fact, were to come.... [T]hese defendants could have insisted that if deregulation were to come within a set period, the sales would be nullified. They chose not to [do so]....

Here, the only frustration is the defendants' in that known risks they assumed have turned out to their disadvantage.... Commercial frustration is no defense where no unusual or unforeseeable event prevented performance and where provision could readily have been made for what actually occurred.

JUDGMENT ... [P]laintiff is entitled to the grant of summary judgment....

Discharge by Operation of Law. Sometimes contractual obligations are discharged by law, regardless of the will of the parties. Illustrations include discharges by merger, and by bankruptcy or the "running" of the statute of limitations.

Merger is the fusion or absorption of a lesser thing or right into one of a higher order. Under the parol evidence rule, for example, where the parties to a contract reduce it to writing in circumstances indicating that the writing is to be the complete and final expression of their bargain, all prior negotiations are merged into the final writing. By operation of law the final writing supersedes and discharges any conflicting prior agreements.

A *discharge in bankruptcy* is granted by a court and releases the debtor from the contractual obligations covered by the discharge. However, many debts are not dischargeable in bankruptcy (alimony, back taxes, and so on), and to be effective, the discharge must be pleaded as a defense to an action on a contract covered by it. The *"running" of the statute of limitations* (expiration of the time permitted for bringing suit) also bars enforcement of a contract.

Remedies for Breach of Contract; Quasi-Contractual Remedy

The remedies usually sought in a lawsuit for breach of contract are damages (the "legal" remedy discussed in Chapter 1), and rescission and specific performance ("equitable" remedies). The remainder of this chapter discusses some common kinds of contractual damages, three equitable remedies relating to contracts, and the quasi-contractual remedy that may be available where there is no enforceable contract.

Remedies for Breach of Contract

The "Legal" Remedy—Damages. A court awards *damages* by ordering a payment of money that compensates a plaintiff for harm caused by the defendant's breach of the contract. A judgment for damages (the traditional remedy "at law") is the sole remedy where a payment of money is an adequate substitute for the performance promised by the breaching party. Ben contracts to sell 5,000 tons of #1 wheat to Carl; the price of wheat then rises 5 percent above the contract price; and Ben breaches the contract by selling all his wheat to Sue. If #1 wheat is readily available from other sources, Carl's only remedy is a judgment for damages in an amount sufficient to cover the higher cost of substitute wheat and any extra expenses required to procure it.

Kinds of damages. A breach of contract can cause many kinds of loss to the aggrieved party, or no loss at all. Consequently, the courts award damages of various kinds, depending on the degree or kind of harm suffered by the aggrieved party. They include:

1 *Compensatory damages:* An award of money that will repay the injured party for loss caused by the breach of contract.
2 *Nominal damages:* An insignificant sum awarded to the aggrieved party where there is a breach of contract but no real injury, or where there is a real injury but the plaintiff's evidence fails to show the amount. An award of nominal damages entitles the aggrieved party to recover court costs (but, usually, not attorney's fees).

(*Punitive damages,* also called *exemplary damages,* are intended to punish or make an example of the defendant for malicious or fraudulent conduct. Punitive damages are above and beyond any compensatory damages that might be awarded. Since punitive damages are not compensatory in nature, they usually are not awarded for breach of contract.)

Liquidated damages clauses. A contract may contain a clause stipulating an amount of damages to be paid for breach of contract. Or the clause might provide a formula for calculating damages in the event of breach. Such liquidated damages clauses take the place of a judicial determination of damages and are enforceable if limited to compensating the injured party for loss. Liquidated damages clauses are *not* enforceable, however, if they are "penal" in nature—that is, if they merely penalize the breaching party, without regard to actual damages, for committing the breach. A liquidated damages provision that awards to the injured party an amount disproportionate to the actual damages sustained, or likely to have been sustained, will not be enforced.

Case 15.3 illustrates the position of most courts, that liquidated damages clauses are enforceable where two conditions exist at the time of contracting:

1 It appears to the parties that the harm flowing from the breach will be difficult to estimate accurately.
2 There is a reasonable relation between the damages agreed on and those expected to occur in the event of breach.

CASE 15.3 Zlotoff v. Tucker · 201 Cal. Rptr. 692 (Cal. App. 1984)

FACTS Zlotoff [plaintiff] owned two adjoining vacant lots and, in the same block, a skating rink and an adjoining parking lot next to E. R. Cota's office building. For several years Cota, his employees, and visitors used Zlotoff's parking lot without permission, angering Zlotoff. In 1977, Zlotoff listed his vacant lots for sale. Tucker [defendant] offered to buy them. During negotiations, Zlotoff told Tucker of his anger toward Cota over misuse of the parking lot and said he did not want Cota to become owner of the vacant lots. Zlotoff asked Tucker if he was related to Cota. Tucker said no. Tucker was in fact Cota's nephew.

Zlotoff then sold the lots to Tucker under a written contract of sale that expressed Zlotoff's reluctance to sell to Cota, that forbade Tucker to do so directly or indirectly, and that contained a clause requiring Tucker to pay $20,000 plus attorney's fees, costs, and interest in the event that Cota became owner of the lots, through Tucker, within 10 years of the sale to Tucker. Less than a year later Cota became owner of the lots in a transaction involving Tucker. Zlotoff sued Tucker for breach of contract and fraud. The trial court awarded Zlotoff $20,000 plus attorney's fees and interest, and $2,500 in punitive damages for Tucker's fraud. Tucker appealed.

OPINION GERALD BROWN, Presiding Judge. . . . [Under § 1671 of the California Civil Code], "The parties to a contract may agree therein upon an amount which shall be presumed to be the amount of damages sustained by a breach therefor, when, from the nature of the case, it would be impracticable or extremely difficult to fix the actual damage."

At the time Zlotoff sold Tucker the vacant lots it was reasonably foreseeable, given Zlotoff's anger toward Cota, [that] Zlotoff would suffer mental and emotional damages if Tucker breached the agreement by [conveying] the property to Cota. Zlotoff testified: "It was very difficult evaluating my pain and suffering and the inconvenience and discomfort I had with Cota all of these years." Under these circumstances the court properly found [that] such damages were difficult to ascertain when the parties entered into their agreement. Further, on this record the court could properly find [that] the $20,000 liquidated damages clause resulted from the parties' reasonable efforts to ascertain what damages Zlotoff would suffer if Tucker resold the vacant lots to Cota. Before accepting Tucker's offer, Zlotoff told Tucker about his feelings toward Cota and his desire [that] Cota not become owner of the vacant lots. . . . Zlotoff also told Tucker [that] $20,000 was the difference between the listing price and a price he had earlier quoted to Cota. Further, Tucker signed the $20,000 liquidated damages clause only after Zlotoff agreed to Tucker's requested modifications limiting the period of Tucker's liability for reselling the property to Cota. . . .

Tucker contends the court should not have enforced the parties' liquidated damages agreement because such agreement improperly restricted his right to dispose of the vacant lots Zlotoff sold him. . . . However, section 711 prohibits only unreasonable restraints on alienation. . . . [The trial] court said: ". . . I'm inclined to think that this restraint was a reasonable one, and I'm so finding for the reason that the feelings of Mr. Zlotoff which have been termed by the defense a vendetta were ones that a reasonable person can have, where his property is interfered with, trespassed upon and so forth, and where attempts to [resolve the dispute] by amicable discussions have been fruitless." Under the circumstances here the court properly found the limited restrictive clause was reasonable. . . . Any restraint on alienation under the parties' agreement . . . was minimal. . . . [T]he parties' agreement affected reconveyance only as to two specifically named persons and limited any restriction to the earlier of 10 years or the date Zlotoff sold the nearby skating rink. The court properly enforced the . . . agreement. . . .

Tucker contends the court erroneously awarded Zlotoff punitive damages for breach of contract. However, Tucker misconstrues the court's findings. Zlotoff pleaded [a cause

CASE 15.3 Continued

of action for fraud]. . . . After trial the court found Zlotoff proved his allegations of. . . fraud. The court properly awarded Zlotoff punitive damages under section 3294 after specifically finding Tucker committed "rather gross fraud."

JUDGMENT The judgment is affirmed.

"Equitable" Remedies. Often, a payment of money damages is not an adequate remedy for a breach of contract. Where the legal remedy is inadequate, the aggrieved party may be entitled to an equitable remedy: reformation, rescission, or specific performance of the contract.

Reformation. Sometimes, through mistake or fraud, a written contract does not express the actual agreement of the parties. For example, Art Gallery agrees to pay Maria $5,000 for her painting but the written contract shows the price to be $500. Maria may bring a suit in equity for the reformation (correction) of the contract so that it will express the true agreement of the parties.

Rescission. Sometimes a person has a valid reason for rescinding (canceling) a contract—fraud, mistake, duress, and the like—but is uncertain about his or her legal right to do so (or is unable to do so) without the aid of a court. The court-ordered equitable remedy of *rescission* is available. When seeking rescission, the plaintiff petitions the court to order cancellation of the contract and to restore what the plaintiff has parted with. Since the plaintiff must "do equity to receive equity," the plaintiff ordinarily must make or offer restitution (a return) of anything the plaintiff received from the defendant under the contract.

A plaintiff might be denied rescission even though the remedy at law is inadequate. Suppose that Anne, in negotiating the sale of her drugstore to Bill, fraudulently overstates the assets of the business by 20 percent. Bill learns of the fraud 2 weeks after taking possession of the store but continues to operate it for a year while the volume of business declines to almost zero due to his mismanagement. Bill then brings suit in equity to rescind the contract, expecting to return the now worthless drugstore to Anne and to receive from her the amount he paid for it. Bill will be denied the remedy of rescission. Under the equitable doctrine of *laches* (which forbids unreasonable delay in asserting one's rights), and under the principle that Bill must "do equity to receive equity," he must seek rescission (and make a good-faith attempt to return the business) within a reasonable time after learning of Anne's fraud. It would be unreasonable to permit Bill, who learned of the fraud early, to ruin the business over the course of a year and then to return to Anne the worthless remains. Despite being denied the equitable remedy of rescission, however, Bill may pursue his legal remedy of damages if the time specified in the applicable statute of limitations has not expired.

Specific performance. Specific performance is available where the remedy at law (damages) is inadequate to compensate for loss caused by a failure to perform a contractual duty. Art contracts with Roberto for a painting, but Roberto changes his mind and refuses to deliver it. Art must have the artwork itself to enjoy its special qualities. Roberto can be compelled by a court of equity specifically to perform the contract by delivering the painting to Art. Similarly, a contract for the purchase of land, or of some interest in it, is specifically enforceable, since each parcel of real estate is considered under Anglo-American law to have unique physical features or some special commercial value such as a good location that cannot be adequately compensated for by a payment of money.

Sometimes, however, a court will withhold specific performance even though the remedy at law is inadequate and will instead limit the plaintiff to his or her remedy at law. The courts prefer not to impose offensive personal relationships on contracting parties. So, a court will not compel the specific performance of a contract for personal services, for example. Nor will the court specifically enforce a contract to marry or, usually, a contract to enter into a partnership.

Courts also refuse to grant specific performance where judicial supervision of the performance is impractical or beyond the ability of the court. Some partnership agreements that do not impose an offensive personal relationship would nevertheless be impractical for the court to enforce specifically, as would some contracts to arbitrate and some construction or repair contracts. Large-scale construction contracts would be especially difficult to enforce specifically, and injured parties to such contracts often are left to their remedy at law.

Case 15.4 discusses what is necessary for a plaintiff to qualify for the remedy of specific performance.

CASE 15.4 First Nat'l State Bank of New Jersey v. Commonwealth Federal Savings & Loan Assoc. · 610 F.2d 164 (3d Cir. 1979)

FACTS Mathema Developers began construction of the Glen Oaks Shopping Mall. As in most real estate developments, financing was to take place in two stages: (1) a short-term construction loan from a commercial bank, and (2) a long-term "permanent" loan from a savings institution or an insurance company. Commonwealth Federal Savings & Loan Association [defendant] made to Mathema a commitment for $3,500,000 in permanent financing. A short time later, First National Bank of New Jersey [plaintiff] made to Mathema a $3,600,000 construction loan. In making the loan, First National relied on Commonwealth's earlier consent to Mathema's assigning to First National the long-term loan commitment made by Commonwealth. After First National disbursed the construction funds, it sought a closing of the long-term financing Commonwealth had promised. By this time, the shopping mall was in grave economic difficulties, and Commonwealth refused to make the loan. When the builder was unable to keep up its loan payments, First National foreclosed its construction mortgage, began operating the mall at a loss, and sued Commonwealth for specific performance of the commitment. The federal district court ordered specific performance. Commonwealth appealed, alleging that specific performance should not be granted to enforce mortgage loan agreements.

OPINION ADAMS, Circuit Judge.... We come now to what appears to be the most provocative issue on this appeal, namely whether the decree of specific performance was proper. Under New Jersey law, the "right to the equitable remedy of specific performance turns upon the existence of an adequate remedy at law; and the adequacy of the legal remedy of compensation depends upon the facts... of the particular case.... Generally, the remedy at law is said to be inadequate in two situations: (1) where damages would be insufficient because the subject matter of the contract is of such a special nature that it resists translation into [money]; or (2) where "damages are impracticable" because "it is impossible to arrive at a legal measure of damages at all, or at least with any sufficient degree of certainty."...

Traditionally, courts have been reluctant to grant specific performance of agreements to lend or borrow money, inasmuch as money is intrinsically fungible. The more recent cases, however, and especially those involving construction loans, have shown a greater recognition that specific performance may be justified in exceptional circumstances....

The district judge... found that New Jersey law supported the principle that a contract for the financing of a shopping center is unique, in the sense that the term has been used in cases granting specific performance, because the subject matter itself is "unavailable in similar form." Further, he ascertained that the damages suffered by First National were not susceptible to accurate calculation and that "an award of damages would fail to make plaintiff whole."

In so holding, the trial judge placed principal reliance on *Selective Builders, Inc. v. Hudson City Savings Bank*..., a case from a New Jersey trial court.... [Selective Builders, Inc. sought specific performance... against Hudson City Savings Bank, which had issued a permanent mortgage loan commitment on an apartment complex.... The [court] ordered specific performance of the loan.... Damages at law were held inadequate because

CASE 15.4 Continued

(1) it would be difficult to calculate damages, (2) a damage award would not make plaintiff whole, and (3) the rights of third parties would be prejudiced if only damages were awarded. . . . [court's footnote].]

Commonwealth attempts to distinguish *Selective Builders*. . . because the developer there had tried without success to secure other mortgage financing, while there is no evidence here that First National made any such effort. But the court in *Selective Builders* quoted approvingly from a decision . . . that emphasized the futility of seeking alternative mortgage financing for an obviously failed project: "The would-be permanent mortgage lender must contemplate that if, at the last minute, it cancels its commitment such action would be disastrous to the borrower; that in such event obtaining a new permanent mortgage loan would be well-nigh impossible [because] whatever brought about the cancellation would [surely] prevent another lender from entering the fray. . . ." We . . . reject Commonwealth's assertion that specific performance was improper because First National should have attempted to mitigate its damages by obtaining substitute performance at a higher interest rate.

[Since the estimated value of the shopping mall varied from a low of $1,070,000 to a high of $3,500,000], there is ample evidence in the record to support the district court's conclusion that accurate calculation of damages was impracticable in this case.

As between the construction lender and the permanent lender, it does not appear unreasonable to place the risk of the success or failure of a real estate venture on the latter. Real estate developments generally are riskier than other business investments, and therefore mortgage rates are significantly higher than interest rates on most other loans. If the permanent lender can escape its commitment when a project seems to have failed, that party will have achieved a significant shifting of risks without a corresponding shift in the returns on successful ventures. A permanent lender's primary security on such a venture is the capitalized value of the project, and so it is the permanent lender, not the construction lender, that has the responsibility and presumably the expertise to analyze the business risks. It is therefore appropriate to place the risk of the project's nonviability on the permanent lender. . . .

JUDGMENT The judgment of the district court will be affirmed.

Interests Protected by Contract Remedies. Remedies for breach of contract protect three interests of the nonbreaching party: the expectation interest, the reliance interest, and the restitution interest.

The expectation interest. The expectation interest is the interest that a party has in receiving the thing for which he or she contracted. The expectation interest usually is protected by an award of damages sufficient to put the nonbreaching party in as good a position as he or she would have been in had the contract been performed. Where the legal remedy of damages is inadequate to accomplish that result, the equitable remedy of specific performance may be available to the aggrieved party.

The measure of damages necessary to give effect to the expectation interest varies according to the circumstances surrounding the breach of contract. Consider three possible situations in which Sue, a dealer in construction equipment, contracts on January 1 to sell a tractor to Ben, a building contractor. The price of the tractor is $50,000, and Sue is to deliver the tractor on March 1.

1 In breach of the contract, Sue fails to deliver the tractor, and Ben must buy that kind of tractor from Sam for $55,000, the market price on March 1. The amount of damages necessary to give Ben the benefit of the bargain is $5,000. This amount is called "general damages." General damages are those that the law presumes to have resulted directly from the wrong complained of, without regard to any special circumstances of

the plaintiff. General contract damages usually consist of the difference between the contract price and the market price at the time performance is due. If the market price is lower at that time, Ben suffers no general damages (but may receive nominal damages).

2 At the time of contracting, Ben informs Sue that he needs the tractor by March 1 so he can avoid a penalty for breaching a construction contract with Cora. Sue promises but fails to deliver the tractor by that date. Ben buys a replacement tractor at a higher market price, but is not able to buy it in time to avoid the penalty. Sue is liable to Ben for the difference in the price of the tractors and might be liable for the amount of the penalty Ben had to pay Cora. That amount constitutes *consequential (special) damages* resulting from Sue's failure to deliver the tractor by the date promised. Sue is liable for such damages if they were within the contemplation of Sue and Ben when they made their contract.

3 Besides being a building contractor, Ben is also a retail dealer in construction equipment. At the time of the contract with Sue, Ben had a contract for the resale of the tractor. In breach of the contract with Ben, Sue fails to deliver the tractor. Sue is liable in damages to Ben for the amount of profit he would have made from the resale of the tractor.

If *Ben* were the breaching party in these situations, Sue, the seller, would have remedies that protect the seller's expectation interest.

The reliance interest. The reliance interest is the interest of the nonbreaching party in recovering costs of preparing for the hoped-for performance. The seller might have altered machinery or contracted for supplies to fill a special order for the buyer. The buyer might have made preparations to store, sell, or use goods that the seller promised to deliver. In either situation the nonbreaching party suffers a monetary loss which may be recoverable from the breaching party as reliance damages.

The restitution interest. The restitution interest is the interest of the nonbreaching party in recovering a benefit (amounting to less than full performance) that he or she conferred on the other party. A buyer might have made a partial payment for land promised but not conveyed. A seller might have made a partial delivery for which payment was promised but not made.

A party seeking restitution may wish to recover property delivered or, instead, to recover its value. A return of the property itself is called "specific restitution"; a payment of the value of a benefit conferred is called "substitutionary restitution"; a return of property together with compensation for a decrease in its value is called "mixed restitution."[2] Substitutionary restitution is necessary where the benefit cannot be returned—for example, where services were rendered or goods were consumed. Mixed restitution is useful where the property to be restored has been damaged or has depreciated.

Limits on Damage Remedies. A plaintiff's right to recover damages for breach of contract is limited. The principal limits on the recovery of damages are reflected (1) in rules concerning causation, certainty, and foreseeability of damages, and (2) in the requirement that a plaintiff minimize (mitigate) his or her damages where reasonably possible.

Causation, certainty, and foreseeability of damages. A plaintiff must prove the amount of loss with reasonable certainty. In a suit for general damages, the amount of loss may be determined by reference to market values. Where there is no established market, the amount of loss will be determined by other means such as an appraisal.

The recovery of *special (consequential) damages* is subject to more complex limits, mainly because special damages represent losses due to special or unusual circumstances surrounding the breach of contract. Art's new hair dryer short-circuits, causing a fire that destroys the hair dryer and Art's collection of rare books. The loss of the hair dryer constitutes *general* damages. The loss of the rare books constitutes *special* damages. Art sues the manufacturer of the hair dryer. Whether Art will be allowed to recover damages for all his losses is determined in part by rules governing causation, certainty, and foreseeability of special damages.[3]

[2]Dan B. Dobbs, *Handbook on the Law of Remedies,* West, St. Paul, 1973, sec. 4.4.

[3]The discussion that follows is based mainly on Dobbs, op. cit., sec. 12.3.

Causation of special damages. Special damages usually are not recoverable unless the defendant's breach was the *chief* cause of the loss. Some courts find causation present if the breach was a *substantial factor* in causing the loss.

Suppose Sue promises a March 1 delivery of parts to Ben so he can complete the assembly of machines to be shipped to his customers. Sue's failure to deliver the parts on time could upset Ben's production schedule, put him in breach of contracts with his customers, and thus cause him lost profits or other damages. But if Ben's employees go on an extended strike beginning April 30, his inability to meet his obligations to his customers would be attributable to the strike. If Sue breaches during the strike but performs before the strike ends, her breach will not be the cause of Ben's loss, even if Sue's performance is very late.

Certainty of special damages. Suppose Sue never delivers the parts and her breach causes Ben to breach his own contracts. What loss has her breach caused Ben? He might have suffered a loss of profits due to his customers' canceling their contracts with him, and his reputation as a supplier of machines might have been harmed. Most courts would consider proof of canceled contracts sufficiently certain to support an award of damages. Loss of commercial reputation (goodwill) is much more difficult to prove. Some courts refuse to allow damages its loss, reasoning that goodwill is too speculative and uncertain for adequate proof of loss ever to be made. However, most courts recognize loss of goodwill as a legitimate element of recovery, and they award damages where proof of loss is adequate.

Foreseeability of special damages. Suppose that Ben plans to assemble machines and to sell them to thousands of customers. Failure of a supplier to deliver commonplace parts could defeat Ben's expectations. Should the supplier be liable not only for general damages, if any, but also for special damages such as Ben's lost profits?

The main policy of the law of damages is to make the plaintiff "whole," that is, to protect his or her expectancy and reliance interests. Limiting this policy is the somewhat conflicting policy of protecting the defendant from unexpected and potentially ruinous awards of special damages, even though all the damages claimed flowed from the defendant's breach. To place a reasonable limit on "remote" damages, American courts have followed *Hadley v. Baxendale,* a famous English case decided in 1854.[4] Under principles developed from that case, the courts have refused to award special damages unless at the time of contracting they were "foreseen by" or were "within the contemplation of" the parties to the contract.

Some older courts would not hold a defendant liable for special damages unless the defendant had actually agreed to pay them, though a number of courts permitted the agreement to be inferred from the conduct of the contracting parties. Article 2 of the UCC (governing sales of goods) has rejected the so-called "tacit agreement rule," which required an actual agreement but permitted it to be inferred from conduct. Under the UCC, special damages can be within the parties' contemplation in the absence of any agreement to pay them. It is sufficient that the breaching defendant had at the time of contracting "reason to know" of potential special damages.

Mitigation of damages. A plaintiff may not recover damages for losses he or she could reasonably have avoided. This general rule of damages applies to breaches of contract. Suppose Ann is wrongfully discharged in breach of her 2-year employment contract. She has a damage remedy for that breach, but her recovery of damages may be reduced by amounts she could reasonably have earned by taking other suitable employment. A manufacturer who continues to manufacture goods after the buyer repudiates the contract may not be allowed the expenses of the continued manufacture as damages unless the continuation is a commercially reasonable attempt to avoid loss. These examples illustrate the *rule of avoidable consequences.* The rule is not meant to defeat legitimate claims for damages. Rather, in applying it, the courts intend to disallow damage claims only where (and to the extent that) a very modest effort by the plaintiff would have reduced the plaintiff's loss.

Quasi-Contractual Remedy

Suppose the following situations:

- Dr. X notices an unconscious stranger lying on a roadside and renders emergency medical services. The stranger dies without regaining consciousness.

[4] 156 English Reports 145.

- X makes improvements on a house under an oral purchase agreement that is not enforceable as a contract because of failure of the parties to comply with the statute of frauds.
- X transports her children to school because the school board refuses to perform its statutory duty to do so.

None of these situations involves a contract. Yet, in each one X has conferred a benefit on someone. To prevent the "unjust enrichment" of the person benefited (or in the first situation perhaps to encourage the rendering of emergency services), the law provides a restitutionary remedy called *quasi contract.* Under the law of quasi contract, the plaintiff may recover the thing conferred if it is specifically restorable. Otherwise, the plaintiff may recover the reasonable value of the property or services conferred.

A quasi-contractual remedy is available only where there is no enforceable contract. Mercedes has partly performed services called for by her contract with Rafael and has rightfully rescinded it on the ground that full performance has become impossible. The contract no longer exists and cannot be the basis for Mercedes' recovery of damages. However, she may be entitled to recover in quasi contract the value of her services. In quasi contract the measure of her damages is the reasonable value (ordinarily the market value) of her services and *not* the price established by the now-ineffective contract.

Summary

The duties of contracting parties are determined by their contract. A party discharges his or her duty by performance or, sometimes, by tendering the required performance.

A material breach of contract by one party may discharge the other, either immediately or when the material failure to perform cannot be cured. In addition to discharge by performance, by failure of a condition, and by material breach, there are other kinds of discharge. They include discharge by subsequent agreement; by impossibility, frustration, or impracticability; and by operation of law.

Money damages, the remedy at law, is the preferred remedy. Where the remedy at law is inadequate, the equitable remedy of reformation, rescission, or specific performance may be available. Liquidated damages clauses may be enforced if they are not penal.

Remedies for breach of contract protect three interests of the nonbreaching party. The expectation interest is the interest that a party has in receiving the benefit of the bargain. The reliance interest is the interest of a party in recovering costs incurred in preparing for the hoped-for performance. The restitution interest is the interest of a party in recovering his or her partial performance.

A plaintiff must prove damages with reasonable certainty. The principal limits on the recovery of special damages are reflected in rules concerning causation, certainty, and foreseeability of special damages. A plaintiff may not recover damages for losses which the plaintiff could reasonably have avoided. For many situations where there is no enforceable contract, there is a quasi-contractual remedy, provided by the law to prevent unjust enrichment.

Review Questions

1 Describe the relationship between performance, breach, and discharge.

2 Illustrate how the use of a condition may help establish the circumstances under which a contractual duty will be discharged.

3 **(a)** How may a party to a contract discharge his or her duty of performance? **(b)** Why are remedies available for nonmaterial breaches of contract? **(c)** What is the legal effect of a material breach? When will this effect occur?

4 **(a)** Must a mutual rescission involve a return of partial performances to be effective? **(b)** How does an accord and satisfaction differ from a novation?

5 How does discharge by impossibility differ from discharge by frustration? From discharge by impracticability? In your answer illustrate each kind of discharge.

6 Juanita signs a contract providing that she will pay $3,000 if she fails to render the services required of her by the contract. Under what circumstances might this provision be enforceable?

7 **(a)** Does being denied an equitable remedy affect the availability of the legal remedy of damages? **(b)** In what situations, and for what reasons, might a court refuse to order specific performance even though the remedy at law is inadequate?

8 Distinguish between general and special damages.

9 List three kinds of restitution and describe a typical use for each.

10 With regard to special damages, what is the purpose of the "foreseeability" requirement?

11 Explain the meaning and operation of the rule of avoidable consequences.

12 What is the relationship between quasi-contractual and contractual remedies?

Case Problems

1 Mahacek operated a trucking company. When his truck developed major engine problems, he took it to International Harvester Co. (IH) for repair. IH gave Mahacek a detailed price quotation of $4,469.58 for the repairs. When the repairs were completed, IH said the charges exceeded $6,900, and demanded payment in cash. In negotiations with IH, Mahacek made three offers—to pay $4,469.58 by charging it to his account, to pay $6,900 by charging it to his account, and to pay $4,469.58 in cash. Mahacek did not have the cash, but his brother had agreed to lend it to him. IH refused all three offers and retained the truck, claiming a common law artisan's lien in it to secure payment. IH brought suit for its charges, and Mahacek counterclaimed for damages for wrongful detention of the truck. A jury awarded Mahacek $16,500. IH was granted a judgment notwithstanding the jury's verdict on the ground that Mahacek had failed to discharge the artisan's lien. Assume that IH had agreed to repair the truck for $4,469.58. Was any of Mahacek's offers sufficient to discharge the lien and thus to make IH's retention of the truck wrongful?

2 The Warrens hired Denison to construct a house on their property. The contract price was $73,400. After the Warrens took possession of the house, a dispute arose over the quality of workmanship. Because of the dispute the Warrens withheld the balance of $48,000 due under the contract and brought suit for a declaratory judgment. In their suit they sought a discharge from their remaining obligations under the contract, alleging that Denison had failed to perform his obligations. The jury found that when the Warrens took possession of the house it was fit for the ordinary purposes for which houses are used. The jury also found that $2,000 in repairs would be required to correct defective workmanship. Did Denison's defective performance discharge the Warrens from their remaining obligations under the contract?

3 Oxford Funding Corp. agreed to purchase real estate from James H. Northrup, Inc., and made a down payment on the purchase price. Northrup was to deliver the property together with rental permits required under the Town Code. On the day before the date set for closing, Oxford canceled the transaction and demanded that Northrup return the down payment. Although the permits were easily obtainable, Northrup had not yet acquired them. Oxford contended that the lack of the permits constituted a title defect that justified the cancellation, and brought suit to recover the down payment from Northrup. Northrup argued that Oxford's cancellation was an anticipatory repudiation of the contract that entitled Northrup to keep the down payment. Who should prevail?

4 For several years, Lovorn was a sales representative for Iron Wood Products Corp. Then a dispute developed between them over the amount of commissions owed Lovorn by Iron Wood. After considerable correspondence between the parties, Iron Wood tendered to Lovorn a check for $7,707.87. On its reverse side the check read, "Endorsement constitutes acceptance of final payment in full and without recourse for the period ending December 27, 1975." Lovorn endorsed the check, cashed it, and sued Iron Wood for commissions allegedly still unpaid. Iron Wood contended that Lovorn's cashing the check constituted an accord and satisfaction of the dispute over commissions. Did the parties reach an accord and satisfaction?

5 D.H.M. Industries (plaintiff) leased a 500,000 square foot warehouse to Central Port Warehouses, Inc. (defendant) for a 20-year term at a total rental of $10.5 million. Defendant paid plaintiff a security deposit of $126,525 (about 2 months' rent). The lease provided that if the lease was terminated, plaintiff had the right to retain the security deposit and to collect damages from the defendant. Defendant wrongfully refused to take possession of the premises, thus breaching and terminating the lease. In plaintiff's suit for damages the defendant sought the return of the security deposit, alleging that the lease provision relating to the security deposit imposed a penalty. The trial court held that the amount of the security deposit had been agreed upon as liquidated damages. Was the trial court in error?

6 Sachs Electric Co. agreed to do electrical work for West Oak Developments. Learning of changes in the project that would affect the electrical work, Sachs reviewed the drawings and informed West Oak that the changes would substantially raise the cost of Sachs' work. The developer stated that "if that is your price for this job, then I will find someone else to do it." Sachs informed the developer of a $1,000 payment for temporary power, and the developer replied, "if you will send me your engineering drawings, I will return your $1,000." The general contractor (Bullen) hired another company to do the electrical work at a cost higher than Sachs' new bid. Then West Oak and Bullen sued Sachs for the difference between the Sachs bid and the amount paid to the other subcontractor. The jury found an agreement to rescind the Sachs–West Oak contract. The trial court entered a judgment for Sachs, and West Oak appealed. Should the judgment be upheld?

7 Dupre, a rice farmer familiar with internal combustion engines, hired Tri-Parish Flying Service to repair an irrigation pump engine that was using oil excessively. Tri-Parish installed new piston rings and said the excessive oil consumption would cease after the rings sealed. The condition persisted, and Dupre made numerous complaints. Tri-Parish assured Dupre that he could continue to use the engine until Tri-Parish could take it back to the shop for a check after the irrigation season. Before the end of the season the engine threw a rod and was a total loss. Dupre sued for damages for loss of the engine and for partial loss of his rice crop. The trial court held that Dupre was not entitled to damages because, by continuing to use the malfunctioning engine, he had failed to mitigate his damages. Dupre appealed. In a companion suit Tri-Parish sought payment for the repairs. **(a)** Did Dupre violate his duty to mitigate damages? **(b)** If not, to what damages was Dupre entitled? **(c)** Was Tri-Parish entitled to payment for the repairs?

ETHICS IN PRACTICE

Problems in Ethics

Consider the ethics of the following contract situations:

1 Mary hires Paul to remodel her bathroom for $5,000. Paul is to begin the work in 2 weeks, and in preparation draws up detailed plans for some of the installations. On the weekend before Paul is to begin the job, Mary learns that Pamela will do the same work for $100 less. When Paul arrives to begin the remodeling, Mary tells him that she has hired Pamela for the job. Paul protests, pointing out that his bid for the job was very low, that he has spent considerable time preparing for the job, that he will profit very little from it, and that he needs the work to keep his assistant employed. Mary says she is willing to pay any damages that Paul can prove in court. **(a)** Is Mary's conduct consistent with her rights and obligations under the law? **(b)** If her conduct is consistent with legal norms, is it ethical? Upon what factors do you base your response? Does it matter, for example, that Pamela is a woman? **(c)** Would your response in (*b*) above differ if Paul's assistant were a mentally retarded person with little chance of alternative employment?

2 Light & Power Co. (Lightco) plans to dam a stream and build a hydroelectric generating station there. The land needed for the project is worth about $250 per acre. Lightco instructs Fred, its employee, to dress up as a farmer, tell the present landowners that he wants to buy their land for a tree farm, and acquire it as cheaply as possible without revealing that he works for Lightco. Having been taught that it is a sin to tell a lie, Fred is uncomfortable with his assignment. However, he wants to move up in the Lightco organization. Knowing that other Lightco employees have been transferred or demoted for refusing similar assignments, Fred does as he is told. He pays some sellers $300 per acre, but is able to buy similar land of several elderly people for $100 per acre. Later, Fred unexpectedly receives a bonus of $50 for each acre of land bought for less than $150. He feels very guilty about the bonus. **(a)** Is Lightco's approach to acquiring the land legal? Ethical? **(b)** Is it legal for Fred to have paid the elderly people only $100 per acre when he paid others $300 per acre for similar land? Is it right for him to have done so? **(c)** What norms might be in conflict to cause Fred's feeling of discomfort with his assignment? **(d)** What should Fred do with the bonus? Does it matter that Fred's wife is seriously ill and will require expensive hospital treatment?

3 Dr. Smith, a general medical practitioner, receives free samples of drugs from a variety of drug companies. As part of his treatment of patients, he dispenses the drugs and bills the patients for them, charging about 10 percent less than the patients would have to pay at the local drugstore. **(a)** In terms of general contract law, is Dr. Smith's conduct legal? Assume that there is no special statute or professional regulation forbidding doctors from selling free samples. **(b)** Is Dr. Smith's conduct ethical? If not, would it be all right for Dr. Smith to give the free samples to patients without charge? **(c)** Suppose you are Dr. Smith's office manager and he instructs you to seek out large supplies of unused free samples from other doctors so that he can give all his patients free drugs. Would this be an ethical thing for him to do? **(d)** Suppose Dr. Smith instructs you to seek out unused free samples for him to sell to patients for 50 percent of the drugstore price. How would you feel about doing so? Why?

PART FOUR

Sales

CHAPTER 16

Introduction to the Law of Sales; the Sales Contract

People seek goods of immense variety: food, clothing, raw materials of every description, office equipment, inventory for resale—the list is endless. Each day, a department, grocery, or hardware store of modest size makes hundreds of sales, while nationally the number is in the billions. The principal means for channeling this vast bulk of goods from producers to consumers is the contract for the sale of goods, which has long been governed by a special body of law called the *law of sales.*

The common law of contract was never well suited to sales of goods. Early in English history, agriculture was the main enterprise, and the land-oriented contract law was too cumbersome for the needs of traders. So they developed their own commercial law, which was based on the customs of merchants, and enforced it in their own trade organizations.[1] International and unifying in character, this "law merchant," as it came to be known, was fairly well adapted to fast-moving transactions in goods.

As commerce assumed more importance in England, the law of sales emerged from the law merchant as one of many distinct bodies of commercial law, and judges began to incorporate the law merchant (and the law of sales) into the common law. In England the law of sales was put into statutory form by the enactment in 1893 of the Sales of Goods Act. That act formed the basis in the United States of the Uniform Sales Act, which was superseded by Article 2 of the Uniform Commercial Code (UCC).

The law of sales under Article 2 is a variation of the common law of contracts discussed in Chapters 8 through 15 of this book. The common law applies to contracts for real estate, personal services, and so on. In contrast, the contract rules of Article 2 apply only to contracts involving *goods*—office equipment, cars, boats, clothing, food, and similar things. Since some Article 2 rules differ greatly from their common law counterparts, businesspeople should keep in mind that contract rules applying to a sale of land may not apply to a sale of goods.

Furthermore, a business deal may involve a number of Code transactions, not just the law of sales. Suppose you sell office equipment at retail and need to purchase 100 floor lamps from a manufacturer. Article 2 governs the formation and performance of the sales contract. But if the lamps are delivered by a common carrier such as a railroad or a trucking company, ownership may be transferred to you by means of an Article 7 document of title called a "bill of lading." You might pay for the lamps with a check (governed by Article 3) that will be cashed by the seller in accordance with the banking rules of Article 4. Or, if you arrange a credit rather than a cash purchase, the seller probably will reserve an Article 9 "security interest" in the lamps so that the seller can repossess them in the event that you fail to pay for them. If you arrange a credit purchase from a foreign manufacturer, the seller might require you to provide an Article 5 "letter of credit." Subsequent chapters of this book discuss not only the law of sales but also documents of title, Article 9 secured transactions, letters of credit, and checks and other commercial paper used in payment and in financing.

The first part of this chapter deals with Article 2—its purposes, key concepts, and coverage. The second part deals with the sales contract itself.

[1] Theodore F.T. Plucknett, *A Concise History of the Common Law,* Little, Brown, Boston, 1956, p. 67.

Purposes, Key Concepts, and Coverage of Article 2

Purposes of the Law of Sales

Before the development of the UCC, the law governing commercial transactions varied considerably from state to state. These differences hampered interstate commerce. To facilitate a national trade in goods, the Code drafters simplified and modernized the law of commercial transactions; encouraged the expansion of commercial practices through custom, usage, and the agreements of contracting parties; and tried to make the law among the various jurisdictions uniform. Considerable uniformity has been achieved despite the fact that each state adopting the Code has a right to amend it as that state sees fit.

Actual performance of sales contracts is especially important for the smooth flow of our national and international commerce. Raw materials, equipment, and supplies must arrive on a schedule that permits a manufacturer to meet commitments to buyers who, in turn, may have made commitments

Table 16.1 Some Sections Having Special Application to Merchants

Section	Topic	Purpose of Section
2-103(1)(b)	Good faith	To provide a higher and more objective test of good faith for the merchant than for the nonmerchant
2-201(2)	Statute of frauds	To reduce compliance requirements between merchants; thus, to expedite contract formation
2-205	Firm offer	To protect offeree's expectation that certain offers by merchants will remain open without consideration
2-207(2)	Counteroffer	To expedite contract formation between merchants by reducing right to invoke common law counteroffer rules
2-209(2)	Modification of contract	To force evidence (nonmerchant's signature) that nonmerchant agreed to modification of the contract
2-509(3)	Risk of loss	To impose risk of loss upon merchant, in certain circumstances, until buyer receives the goods

to other buyers. For the distribution process to operate efficiently, each person in it must be able to rely on the performance of others, with little time to engage in an elaborate contracting process. As noted later in this chapter, Article 2 reduces the opportunities for a contracting party to delay his or her promised performance or to escape contractual obligations without good reason.

The emphasis of Article 2 on performance is but one aspect of a basic policy of the Code—to encourage sound business practices and to encourage *ethical* business conduct. That the Code stresses both the practical and the ethical will be apparent as we review some key concepts of the law of sales.

Key Concepts of the Law of Sales

Merchant. Article 2 applies to *sales transactions* without regard to whether the parties to the sales contract are merchants or nonmerchants. However, merchants are subject to special rules of Article 2. Some of these rules expedite sales by replacing common law rules that might impede the formation or performance of sales contracts. Others make clear the rights or duties of a merchant in transactions with other merchants or with nonmerchants. Table 16.1 shows the purposes of some key Article 2 sections applying to merchants.

In one sense, *merchant* means a person who deals in goods of the kind involved in the transaction [2-104].[2] This kind of merchant is the professional trader or dealer in goods so familiar to us in our day-to-day transactions, and is referred to later in this chapter as a "dealer-merchant."

But the meaning of merchant under Article 2 is not limited to dealers in goods. The word also applies to persons who, though not personally dealing in goods in the manner of a professional trader, nevertheless by their occupations are expected to have knowledge or skill peculiar to the business practices or goods involved. An insurance company that buys office equipment and supplies is a merchant as to the ordinary business practices (such as ordering and taking delivery of goods) that ought to be familiar to any person in business. Merchant also includes even those persons or organizations that *employ* someone to conduct business activities. Thus, a college or university can be classified as a merchant if it has a regular purchasing department or business personnel who are familiar with business practices [2-104, comment 3].

Dealer-merchants are subject to sales rules that do not apply to other merchants. For example, only dealer-merchants make certain warranties (guarantees) concerning the quality of the goods they sell. These and other warranties are discussed in Chap-

[2]The hyphenated numbers in brackets refer to sections of the Uniform Commercial Code reprinted in Appendix 1. The number 2-104 means "Article 2, section 104" and is commonly read as "Section 2-104."

ter 18. In contrast, *all* merchants are subject to those rules of Article 2 designed to make the contracting process more efficient and fair. And all merchants are subject to higher standards of commercial conduct than those that apply to nonmerchants. An example is found in the next paragraph, which deals with the good faith requirement.

Good Faith. All persons who engage in transactions covered by the UCC must use good faith in performing their contracts and in enforcing obligations owed to them. There are two meanings of "good faith." The first meaning is "honesty in fact" (actual honesty even though the person might have been careless) in the conduct or the transaction concerned [1-201]. This meaning applies to all persons subject to the Code. The second meaning, which applies to *merchants,* is "honesty in fact" *and* the "observance of reasonable commercial standards of fair dealing in the trade" [2-103]. Thus, merchants and nonmerchants alike must be honest in their dealings, but merchants must be especially careful not to take unfair advantage of those with whom they deal or to cause them loss. For example, sometimes a merchant-buyer has the right to reject delivered goods. If the seller has no agent or place of business where the rejection occurs, the merchant-buyer meets the obligation of good faith by disposing of the rejected goods in accordance with reasonable instructions of the seller or, *in the absence of instructions,* by selling *perishable* goods for the seller's account [2-603(1)]. A merchant-buyer who leaves rejected tomatoes on a loading dock to rot may be honest in fact but he or she would not be observing reasonable commercial standards of fair dealing with regard to the distant seller and therefore would not be acting in good faith.

Identification (of Goods) to the Contract. The parties to a sale may need to know precisely when the sale occurred, the earliest moment at which the buyer may insure undelivered goods against loss, or what rights the buyer has to demand the delivery of particular goods. The answers to such questions may depend in part on whether goods have been "identified" (i.e., designated) as the subject of a *particular* contract of sale.

The parties may make an "explicit" (clearly stated) agreement as to when the goods will be identified to the contract [2-501]. In the absence of an explicit agreement, Article 2 provides the rules. Where the contract is for the sale of goods "already existing and identified" (e.g., particular goods owned or possessed by the seller), identification *to the contract between the seller and the buyer* occurs as soon as the contract is made. If the contract is for crops or for the unborn young of animals, identification to the contract usually occurs when the crops are planted or when the animals are conceived. If the contract is for the sale of "future goods" other than crops or animals (e.g., goods yet to be manufactured or acquired by a supplier for a retailer), identification occurs when the goods are shipped, marked, or otherwise designated as the goods to which the contract refers.

One important consequence of identifying goods to a contract is that the buyer immediately obtains a "special property" (a limited right) and an "insurable interest"[3] in the goods even though the buyer might not yet be the owner. Suppose that Julien orders 1,000 radios from Gladys. Gladys then manufactures 2,000 radios and marks 1,000 of them as the radios to be shipped to Julien the next day. He does not yet have title to (ownership of) the radios. However, because the 1,000 radios have been identified to the contract, Julien has a Code-created "special property" in the radios and therefore may insure them against loss, as he may wish to do if he pays for them in advance or makes contracts for their resale before receiving them. Furthermore, if Gladys becomes insolvent before delivering the radios, Julien is entitled to those in which he has a special property *and* for which he has made arrangements for payment. Julien is thus protected from the claims of Sarah's creditors.

Other Key Concepts. Some Code concepts—unconscionability, course of performance, course of dealing, and usage of trade—are of ethical and practical significance in the law of sales and will be discussed later in this chapter. Others, such as commercial impracticability, appear in subsequent chapters. The case that follows illustrates the meaning of good faith.

[3]An *insurable interest* is a financial stake in property or in someone's life that will justify the person who has that stake in insuring the property or life against loss. If there never was an insurable interest, a contract of insurance is not enforceable against the insurance company.

CASE 16.1 Baker v. Ratzlaff · 564 P.2d 153 (Kan. App. 1977)

FACTS Ratzlaff contracted to sell to Baker the 1974 crop of popcorn grown on Ratzlaff's farm for $4.75 per hundredweight (cwt.). Under their written contract Ratzlaff was to deliver corn upon Baker's order within times specified by the contract; if Baker failed to pay for the popcorn at the time of delivery, Ratzlaff had the option of selling it elsewhere or otherwise disposing of it as he saw fit. Baker's practice in paying for delivered popcorn was to have his employee, Martin, forward weight tickets from the grain receiving station in Texas to Baker's business office in Garden City, Kansas, where checks were written out and mailed. During the week Martin would accumulate tickets and send them to Baker's office so that they would arrive on Monday mornings. Baker ordinarily made payment within a few days after delivery. Ratzlaff delivered two loads of popcorn but Martin did not offer immediate payment nor did Ratzlaff demand it or seek payment from Baker's business office, which had ample funds available and which was located on a direct route to Ratzlaff's Kansas farm. During the following week Baker requested more deliveries. Ratzlaff did not make the deliveries, saying his driver was ill and some equipment had broken down. A week after the first deliveries, Ratzlaff sent Baker a written notice of contract termination, alleging that Baker had failed to pay on delivery as required by their contract. Soon afterward Ratzlaff sold the undelivered popcorn to another buyer for $8.00 per cwt. Baker had to pay a higher price for popcorn needed to meet his own delivery commitments. Baker sued Ratzlaff for breach of contract and was awarded $52,000 in damages, the difference between the parties' contract price of $4.75 and the $8.00 Ratzlaff received. The trial court awarded judgment to Baker, and Ratzlaff appealed.

OPINION REES, J. . . . The trial court's findings were in part as follows:

> 3. That between the time that the contract for the production of the popcorn was entered into and the time for delivery the price of popcorn had risen sharply and that it was greatly to the defendant's financial advantage if he could in some way get out of his contract for the sale of popcorn. . . . The court concludes that the parties are under a duty to deal fairly with each other in good faith and that the defendant breached this duty by declaring a termination of the contract upon a technical pretense and that therefore as a matter of law the plaintiff is entitled to recover . . . damages. . . .

. . . Defendant . . . contends that the district court erred in finding that defendant's termination of the agreement was a breach of its duty to perform and enforce the contract in good faith. Defendant argues that it was under no good faith obligation in terminating the contract and, even if it was, the termination was made in good faith.

[UCC Section 1-203] provides as follows: "Every contract or duty within this act imposes an obligation of good faith in its performance or enforcement." [Section 1-201(19)] defines "good faith" as "honesty in fact in the conduct or transaction concerned."

Defendant maintains the good faith obligation . . . is not applicable because termination of a contract is not "performance" or "enforcement" of a contract. Under the facts of this case, we disagree. The termination clause . . . of the contract does not permit termination at will but only upon failure of plaintiff to pay on delivery. Defendant's right to terminate and retain or dispose of undelivered popcorn is an inseparable incident of enforcement of substantive provisions of the contract. We believe that only tortured reasoning could exempt defendant's exercise of the termination clause from the good faith obligation . . . and we decline to do so.

There was substantial competent evidence in the record to support the district court's finding that defendant had breached his obligation of good faith. His failure on delivery of either load of popcorn to the Stratford plant to demand payment, his failure in the subsequent telephone conversations with plaintiff and Martin to demand payment, and

CASE 16.1 Continued his hasty resale of the popcorn to another buyer at a price nearly double the contract price, provided the trial court with ample evidence upon which to find an absence of good faith....

JUDGMENT ...[T]he judgment is affirmed.

Transactions Covered by Articles 2 and 2A

Unless the context otherwise requires, Article 2 applies to *transactions* in goods [2-102]. By their express terms, many sections of Article 2 apply only to contracts for the sale of goods, and not to other kinds of transactions such as gifts or leases of goods. But the drafters of the Code intended to encourage the application of certain Code principles directly or "by analogy" to a wider range of transactions than just sales. For example, buyers injured by defective goods often have the benefit of an Article 2 warranty. In many states, the courts imply a similar non-Code warranty in a *lease* of goods because similar policy justifies the warranty. The courts of some states apply the Article 2 warranty provisions directly to nonsales transactions such as leases and bailments of goods.

Applying Article 2 to leases of goods has serious drawbacks. The law concerning such leases was derived from many sources—the common law of personal property, the law of real estate leases, and Articles 2 and 9 of the UCC. The result has been an uneven application of a body of law that imperfectly fits the lease transaction.

To remedy the situation, the drafters of the UCC developed Article 2A, which applies specifically to *leases of goods,* a wide variety of transactions ranging from a consumer's rental of a car or small tool to long-term commercial leases of aircraft or industrial equipment [comment, 2A-102].[4] Article 2A does *not* apply to a lease intended as a secured transaction; security "leases" (i.e., security interests "disguised as leases") are covered by Article 9.

In legal content, Article 2A closely resembles Article 2. Consequently, much of what is said in the sales chapters about Article 2 applies as well to Article 2A. There are differences, however, and to illustrate them, this and subsequent chapters will discuss key provisions of Article 2A where relevant. Until the states adopt Article 2A, Article 2 will continue in many states to apply directly or indirectly to leases of goods.

Still, Article 2 applies especially to the *sale* of goods. A sale is the passing of title to (ownership of) goods from the seller to the buyer, in return for a consideration called the price [2-106]. The price can be made payable in money, goods, or realty, *or in some other way* [2-304]. Thus, a legally binding *promise* to pay (whether with money, goods, realty, or otherwise) is another way of paying the price. As to the meaning of title, suppose you buy a used car and agree to make twelve monthly payments. The seller probably will retain a "security interest" (often called "title") so that the seller can repossess the car if you fail to make the payments. Yet, at the time of the sale, *you* receive basic ownership rights in the car—the right to use, enjoy, and sell it—subject only to your seller's right to be paid. These basic ownership rights constitute the kind of title referred to in the definition of "sale." In a *contract to sell* goods, the seller agrees to transfer title to the buyer at some future time. This kind of sales contract is used, for example, where the seller does not yet own existing goods or where the goods have not yet been produced.

Article 2 applies only to transactions *in goods.* In general, *goods* means things that are movable at the time they are identified to the contract for sale [2-105]. Although the primary focus of Article 2 is upon movable things, goods includes the unborn young of animals, growing crops or other things attached to realty and capable of severance without material harm to it, timber to be cut (by either buyer or seller), and minerals (including gas and oil) to be removed from realty by the seller [2-105(1); 2-107]. Goods also includes money *if* the money is a commodity. Thus, coin collections are considered goods. "Goods" does *not* include real estate, personal services, or intangible personal property such as corporate securities, patent rights, and bank accounts. Sales of such non-

[4]As of March 1989, Article 2A has been adopted by Oklahoma and, with extensive revisions, by California.

goods are subject to the common law of contracts, whose rules often differ from those of the law of sales.

Article 2 does not apply to any transaction that is intended to operate *only* as a security transaction, even though goods may be involved. *Pledges* and *chattel mortgages* (discussed in Chapter 26) are intended to operate only as security transactions. However, a *conditional sale contract* is meant to effect a sale of goods while creating a security interest for the seller, who retains the security interest until the goods are paid for. Article 2 governs the sale aspects of a conditional sale contract, and Article 9 governs the security aspects.

The courts do not agree on how to treat transactions involving a combination of goods and services. What is the nature of an automobile "tune-up" in which a mechanic replaces parts and adjusts the engine? Is it a sale of goods or a sale of services? The distinction is very important where the goods are defective and cause injury. If the transaction is classified as a sale of goods, an Article 2 warranty (assurance that the goods are not defective) often is available to the injured plaintiff as a basis for a lawsuit. If the transaction is classified as a sale of *services,* the common law of contracts applies, and under that law warranties often are *not* available where the service is improperly performed. Many courts settle the matter by deciding whether the sale is *predominantly* for goods or for services. Thus, if the amount or value of the goods is relatively insignificant in the transaction, these courts will hold that it is a sale of services for which a warranty might not be available.

But the relative amount or value of the goods is not the only factor that the courts consider in deciding how to treat mixed transactions. A court may place more importance on the question of who should bear loss resulting from the use of defective goods. A transfusion of contaminated blood usually is treated as an aspect of medical services and thus as not subject to sales warranties. Courts and legislatures adopting this position believe that persons who provide essential medical services should be held liable only for negligence or intentional misconduct. But the courts of some states hold that medical supplies (other than blood) are goods, and that Article 2 warranties should apply. These courts believe that a person injured by a defective product should not have to bear the loss, even where the service aspect of the transaction predominates. Have beauticians or electricians made a sale of goods to which Article 2 warranty or other rules should apply? Some courts recognize a sale (and a warranty) as to the goods. Other courts will consider the mixed contract to be one for services, but will recognize non-Code warranties. A few courts recognize non-Code warranties even in purely services contracts.

In Case 16.2, the Supreme Court of Alabama decides whether to apply the Code to a medical item that is not sold and that is used in the performance of a medical service.

CASE 16.2 Skelton v. Druid City Hosp. Bd. · 459 So. 2d 818 (Ala. 1984)

FACTS Mr. Skelton (plaintiff) suffered a hernia. During a hernia repair operation at the Druid City Hospital ("Druid City," defendant), a suturing needle broke off in his body, where part of the needle remains. The needles used by the hospital were designed for repeated uses, were sanitized between uses, and were replaced when bent or dull. Alleging that the broken needle was defective, Skelton sued Druid City for breach of a UCC warranty that the needle was fit for its intended use. From a judgment for Druid City, Skelton appealed.

OPINION EMBRY, J.... Druid City contends [that] no implied warranty arose from its transaction with Skelton for which liability can be asserted. It relies mainly on the language of § 2-315, which provides as follows:

> Where the seller at the time of contracting has reason to know any particular purpose for which the goods are required and that the buyer is relying on the seller's skill or judgment to select or furnish suitable goods, there is... an implied warranty that the goods shall be fit for such purpose.

CASE 16.2 Continued

Druid City successfully argued to the trial court that the Skeltons could not prevail under count III (alleging breach of implied warranty of fitness for particular purpose) because: (1) the hospital is in the business of providing a *service* to patients; it is not a "merchant" or "seller" such that an implied warranty could arise from any transaction in goods between that institution and a patient; and (2) the suturing needle which broke off during Mr. Skelton's surgery was merely equipment used incident to providing a "service"; there was no "sale" of that needle to Skelton from which an implied warranty could arise....

Druid City attempts to define that transaction as wholly consisting of a "service" to Skelton. We do not agree with that characterization. It can make no serious contention that Skelton did not pay for the *use* of the suturing needle, or that patients generally do not buy supplies and pay charges for equipment used in the course of their treatment.

Because of the nature of the re-use of the suturing needle at issue here, we... agree with Druid City that there was no "sale" of the needle to Skelton. Rather, the instant transaction is more akin to a *lease or rental* of equipment than a sale. That does not, however, preclude an implied warranty... from arising from the transaction.

Article 2 [of the UCC] applies, by its terms, to "transactions in goods." § 2-102. That phrase is left undefined by the Code, but a number of courts have held there is significance in the use of the term "transaction" rather than "sale." In light of the statement in the Official Comment to § 2-313, that the *warranty sections of Article 2* "need not be confined to sales contracts," we opine our legislature intended that § 2-315 be broadly interpreted to include transactions in which there is no actual transfer of title, such as rental and lease transactions. Numerous courts have so held....

Therefore, we conclude the transaction here involved is both a service transaction *and* a "transaction in goods." This court has previously addressed the issue [of] whether implied warranties arise from "mixed" or "hybrid" agreements, those that involve both a sale of goods and a rendering of services. In *Caldwell v. Brown Service Funeral Home*..., the plaintiffs sought the service of a funeral home for the burial of their eight-year-old son. They signed a statement for the services and for a casket and vault in the aggregate sum of $860. Because the vault provided by the funeral home was too small for the casket, graveside services had to be conducted twice.

The plaintiffs sued on a theory of implied warranty of fitness and the trial court granted summary judgment in favor of the funeral home.... The funeral home argued that it had merely provided a "service" for the plaintiffs and, therefore, no warranty could have arisen. Reversing that court's judgment, we stated:

> Here the funeral home knew that the Caldwells were purchasing a vault for the casket of their son, and that they were relying on the seller's judgment to furnish suitable goods. As a professional in this business, the seller could be expected to be aware of any size requirements for the vault to hold the casket which the seller also sold....

The *Caldwell* case cannot be distinguished from the present case regarding whether the provider of a service can be held liable under § 2-315. In both cases the plaintiffs went to the defendants seeking services and products necessary to those services; and in both cases the plaintiffs were submitted a total bill for the products and services. In both cases the plaintiffs were injured by the products sold with the services, and in both cases the plaintiffs relied upon the skills and expertise of the defendants in selecting the involved products. This same approach to "hybrid" transactions has been adopted by other courts....

Druid City further claims that, even if it is a "seller" of goods, because of its status as a hospital it is not a "merchant" as defined and required by provisions of the Code and has not held itself out as having "knowledge or skill peculiar to the practices or goods involved in the transaction." We find that claim untenable for several reasons.

First, the definition of "merchant" in the Code is [broad and] does not exclude institutions such as hospitals.

CASE 16.2 Continued

> "Merchant" means a person who deals in goods of the kind or otherwise by his occupation holds himself out as having knowledge or skill peculiar to the practices or goods involved in the transaction or to whom such knowledge or skill may be attributed by his employment of an agent or broker or other intermediary who by his occupation holds himself out as having such knowledge or skill....

We cannot ignore the fact that hospitals, whether profitable or not, are businesses. They are not merely buildings which provide housing for the seriously-ill patients or independent physicians.

In the course of their competition, hospitals certainly hold themselves out to the public as having special knowledge regarding the provision of medical services to patients. Inherent in this presentment is a warranty that the hospital will sell, furnish, or supply patients with goods for use in the provision of medical services which are fit for their intended purpose. For that reason, Druid City is clearly a "merchant," within the Commercial Code's definition of that word.

[Even if Druid City were] not a "merchant," it would still be liable under § 2-315 because of the nature of the patient's reliance on the skill and judgment of the hospital in [selecting] medical supplies used for the care of the patient.... Patients are rarely in a position to judge the quality of the medical supplies and other goods sold to them and used in their care; often, those supplies are of an inherently dangerous nature. The complete dependence of patients on the staff of a hospital to choose fit products for their care justifies the imposition of an implied warranty under § 2-315, whether the hospital is a "merchant" or not. [Moreover, Section 2-315 applies to "sellers," not just to merchant-sellers. Ed. note.]

Finally, we note that, were this court to exclude hospitals from the implied warranty provisions of the Code based on the arguments presented by Druid City, the effects would be far-reaching. The hospital's theory would, for example, create an exemption from § 2-315 for the *service* department of an automobile repair shop which installs defective brakes on a car. Assume that the same business had a *parts* department which sold a consumer defective brakes to be installed by the consumer. Under Druid City's rationale, it would be liable under § 2-315. We conclude the legislature [meant § 2-315 to apply to both situations]....

JUDGMENT The judgment [of the trial court on the warranty count] is... reversed.

The Sales Contract

Unless displaced by particular provisions of the UCC, rules of law that apply to contracts generally apply as well to contracts for the sale of goods [1-103]. So, a contract for the sale of goods must meet the usual requirements for the *formation* of a contract: mutual assent (offer and acceptance), an exchange of consideration, parties having legal capacity to contract, and a legal objective (purpose). Contracts for the sale of goods are also subject to many general legal principles relating to the *form* and *interpretation* of contracts. However, the UCC modifies most of these aspects of general contract law to adjust them to sales transactions and contemporary business needs.

Formation of the Sales Contract

Article 2 Standard for Contract Formation.

People create sales contracts in a wide variety of ways. Some spell out the terms of the contract in great detail, as in the purchase of a new car. Others say very little or nothing, as in the purchase of goods at a supermarket. On occasion, what is said or done is so vague and sketchy that no contract arises. Consequently, the courts sometimes are faced with the question of what minimum conduct is required to create a sales contract.

Under Article 2, a contract for the sale of goods may be made in any manner sufficient to show agreement, including conduct by both parties which recognizes the existence of a contract. The contract may arise even though the exact moment at which agreement arose cannot be determined. Furthermore, even though one or more terms are left open, there can still be a contract for sale if the parties have intended to make a contract and there is a reasonably certain basis for a court to give an appropriate remedy for breach of the contract [2-204].

Acts Required for Contract Formation. Specifically, then, what minimum acts of contracting does Article 2 require of the buyer and the seller? First, before there can be a sales contract, the *parties* to it must be identified. Suppose you have recently opened a bakery and need some flour. You phone a local supplier and say, without identifying yourself, "Please send some wheat flour right away." The supplier's employee says, "OK." As of this moment there is no contract because you and the supplier have not said enough to enable a court to give an appropriate remedy to either of you if called upon to do so. The supplier does not even know with whom it is dealing.

Suppose now that you identify yourself so that the supplier can make a delivery. There still is no contract because you have not said how much flour you want. To have an enforceable sales contract you ordinarily must specify the *quantity* of the goods you seek.[5] Must you specify the *kind* of wheat flour as well? A statement of kind would be helpful but is not always necessary for a contract to arise. If you have had prior transactions with this supplier, the supplier might know from this past experience what you mean by "wheat flour." As to *price*, the Code provides that the parties can make a contract even though the price is not specified. Where the parties intend to make a contract but state no price, the price is a "reasonable" price as of the time set for delivery [2-305]. A reasonable price might be the current market price if there is one. Thus, as a practical matter, no sales contract is likely to arise unless the *parties* to it and the *quantity* of goods have been spelled out somehow. The other term essential for a contract to exist, the *price*, may be supplied by law.

[5]Except, for example, in a "requirements" contract. An agreement to buy "all the wheat flour I shall need in my business next year" is a requirements contract whose quantity term has been left open to be filled in later as the buyer's needs dictate.

Where the parties to a contract fail to state a term such as price or time or place of delivery, the term is said to have been left *open*. Costs of production might not be known at the time of the sale, the market price might be subject to considerable variation, or the parties might simply have forgotten to state a price or some other term. The drafters of Article 2 recognized that it is normal and necessary for businesspeople to contract with a minimum of detail, often on the basis of a phone call. By permitting open terms, and by providing rules of law to "fill the gaps" left by the open terms, the Code accomplishes two things: It enables the parties to contract quickly where price or other information is not immediately available; and it fosters performance of agreements that under nonsales law might have been considered too indefinite to enforce.

We turn now to some particular aspects of contract formation under Article 2—the offer and the acceptance.

Offer under Article 2. Some of the common law rules governing contract offers in *non*sales transactions are unsuitable for sales of goods and have been replaced by Code rules. The common law rules governing offers for certain types of unilateral contracts, and offers promised to be held open for a fixed time, are examples. The law governing offers in auctions (discussed in Chapter 9) has not been changed but instead has been codified and made part of Article 2.

Offer seeking prompt or current shipment of goods. Suppose a retail fish dealer needs an emergency supply of sardines and places the following order: "Ship me 50 cases of X grade sardines at once." This is an offer for a unilateral contract because the dealer expects the sardine seller to accept the offer by performing the act requested by the dealer. Under the common law rules of offer and acceptance, such an offer can be accepted *only* by the seller-offeree's performing the requested act, here, a *shipment* made at once. An attempt by the offeree to accept by, for example, phoning or telegraphing an immediate *promise* to ship promptly would be ineffective, and the offeror would be free to revoke (withdraw) the offer. The ability to revoke gives the offeror the opportunity to "play the market," often to the surprise and injury of the shipper who is in fact making a prompt shipment just a few minutes or hours after the promise was sent. To prevent this kind of injurious surprise, Article

2 provides that an offeree may accept an offer for prompt or current shipment by making *either* a prompt shipment or a prompt promise to ship, unless the offeror has made it very clear that the offer can be accepted only by a prompt shipment [2-206].

Firm offer. Under the common law of contracts, a person who has promised to hold an offer open for a fixed time is not required to honor that promise unless he or she has received consideration for it. Suppose that Sarah offers to sell a certain piece of real estate to Bernie for $50,000, giving Bernie 10 days to decide whether to buy. Sarah will not be held to her promise to hold the main offer open unless she asked for and received consideration for that promise. In sales of goods, however, if a *merchant* states in a *signed writing* that the offer to buy or sell goods will be held open, this statement cannot be revoked merely because the merchant received no consideration for it [2-205]. The promise to hold the offer open is binding for the time stated or, if no time is stated, for a reasonable time not to exceed 3 months. Thus merchants who make firm offers can no longer upset the reasonable expectations of offerees that such offers will remain open for the promised time.

Acceptance under Article 2. Some UCC rules on the acceptance of offers are similar to the common law rules, but the UCC departs from common law acceptance rules that unreasonably obstruct the formation of sales contracts.

Authorized medium of acceptance. The UCC version of the "deposited acceptance rule" differs little from its modern common law counterpart. The mechanics of accepting an offer under the UCC rule may be summarized as follows:

1 The acceptance is effective at the point of dispatch if the offeree has used an *authorized medium* of acceptance.

2 Where the offeror stipulates that a particular medium of acceptance must be used, only the stipulated medium is authorized. Sam offers to sell goods to Brenda, stating in the offer that "This offer may be accepted only by a letter addressed to me at my place of business." Brenda immediately mails a letter of acceptance to Sam's business address. The acceptance is effective (i.e., a contract arises) when Brenda mails the letter. If she uses a medium other than the one Sam stipulated, there is no acceptance. Her use of a different medium does not necessarily destroy her power of acceptance, however, because unless otherwise indicated by the offeror (Sam), an offer is open for a reasonable time. Brenda therefore may have time remaining to use the required medium of acceptance, but runs the risk that Sam will revoke his offer (or that it will otherwise be terminated) before she can do so.

Under Article 2, the offeror will not be held to have required a particular medium of acceptance unless the requirement has been "unambiguously indicated" to the offeree [2-206(1)]. So, a court may hold that the words "Please respond by letter" do not make the letter the sole permitted medium of acceptance, but instead indicate that an acceptance by another medium may be effective, at least when received.

3 Where an offeror says nothing regarding the medium of acceptance, the offer may be accepted in any manner and by any medium reasonable under the circumstances [2-206]. Some courts applying the common law have ruled that offerors impliedly authorize only those acceptance media that are at least as fast as the medium used to make the offer. The Code position is that a slower medium may in some circumstances be reasonable and therefore effective upon dispatch.

Often the beginning of performance by the offeree is an appropriate method of acceptance, as where Ben Buyer (the offeror) telegraphs Sam Seller (the offeree) in a distant state to begin manufacturing and shipping goods immediately. If Sam begins the requested performance but does not inform Ben of that fact, Ben is faced with uncertainty. To reduce this uncertainty, Article 2 requires Sam to give Ben notice within a reasonable time that the performance has begun. If Sam does not give the notice, Ben (the offeror) may treat the offer as having expired before acceptance [2-206(2)]. Thus, Ben will be free to acquire the goods from another source without liability to Sam even though Sam may in fact have begun performance.

Article 2 counteroffer rules. The common law of contracts of most states requires that the offeree respond exactly to the terms of the offer. Under that law, an offeree who departs from the terms of the offer in even a relatively small way is held to have rejected the offer and to have substituted the offeree's own counteroffer. Thus, no contract will arise under the common law of contracts unless the original offeror (now the offeree of the counteroffer) accepts the counteroffer. This rule—that the original offeree's acceptance must be a "mirror image" of the offer for a contract to arise—is still widely applied in contracts for real estate and services, for example.

However, the "mirror image" rule is inconsistent with modern business practices in the sale of goods. Each day millions of contracts for goods are arranged by an exchange of preprinted forms, one prepared by the lawyer for the buyer and the other by the lawyer for the seller. Each lawyer is hired to serve the interests of his or her own client and will draft the form in a way that gives the client the most advantage. Since it is unlikely that the forms of buyers and sellers will match exactly, an offeree could never be sure that a contract arose until the offeror actually performed by, for example, accepting goods that the offeree-seller sent. But one purpose of a bilateral contract (one created by an exchange of promises) is to assure the offeree at the earliest possible moment that the offeror will be bound if the offeree accepts. If the offeror may escape contractual liability just because the offeree departed from the offer in some minor way as a result of the forms used, the offeree is faced with uncertainty as to whether a contract arose and with the expense of preparing to render (or receive) a performance that the offeror has a legal right not to accept (or deliver).

To reduce delay and harmful surprise in the formation of sales contracts, the drafters of Article 2 abandoned the "mirror image" rule. However, the offeree is still permitted under the Code to make a counteroffer by *stating* his or her intention not to be bound to a contract unless the offeror assents to whatever additional or different terms the offeree has introduced [2-207(1)]. Suppose Sam offers to sell Brenda a computer for $5,000, and Brenda responds with the statement, "I accept your offer, but only on condition that you agree to arbitrate any dispute arising out of this sale instead of going to court." Brenda has made a counteroffer, and there is no contract unless Sam accepts it.

But if Brenda makes a timely statement of acceptance that introduces different or additional terms, and does so without *expressly* conditioning her acceptance on Sam's assent to the new terms, they are to be treated by the court as mere proposals for addition to the contract [2-207(2)]. Suppose that Sam made his offer to Brenda on his preprinted sales form that said nothing about arbitration, and Brenda responded by using her acceptance form that contained on its reverse side a printed clause stating, "Disputes relating to this transaction shall be resolved by arbitration." Although Brenda's form contains an arbitration clause, Brenda has not used language expressly requiring Sam's assent to the clause. So, since the offer and acceptance forms reveal agreement as to enough terms for a contract (computer for $5,000, and identification of the parties to the sale), a contract arises despite the fact that the acceptance does not mirror the offer.

The proposed new terms may or may not become a part of the contract, depending on the application of Article 2 rules governing the fate of the proposed terms. Whether a proposed new term becomes a part of the contract depends, in part, on whether the term would "materially alter" the obligation that the offeror expected to undertake. The rules pertaining to proposed new terms may be summarized as follows:

1. If the new term is a major departure from or addition to the offer (i.e., if the new term "materially alters" the offer), the new term will not become a part of the contract unless the offeror actually consents to the (major) new term. Whether a term is material is for a court to decide. An offeree-buyer's substituting a lower price than the one offered would be a material alteration, no matter how slight the price change. Also, most courts consider the offeree's adding an arbitration clause to be a material matter. The reason is that offerors normally expect to have access to an impartial court if troubles develop rather than being forced into an arbitration proceeding that may occur in another state under law that favors the other party.
2. *Between merchants,* a *minor* new term (such as an insignificant variation as to method or time of delivery) *will* become a part of the contract *unless* the merchant-offeror does

one of two things to prevent the minor term from being included. (*a*) When first making the offer, the merchant-offeror *expressly limits* the offeree's acceptance to the terms of the offer. Or (*b*), having failed to so limit the offer, the merchant-offeror later gives the offeree *notice* of the offeror's objection to the minor new term and does so within a *reasonable time* after the term has been communicated to the offeror.

In summary, then, under Article 2 a sales contract arises if the parties agree on the basic terms necessary for a contract; and no major alterations may be imposed on any offeror (whether merchant or nonmerchant) without that person's consent. Nor can a minor new term be imposed on a *non*merchant-offeror without the nonmerchant's consent. However, a *merchant*-offeror must take action to prevent a merchant-offeree's proposed minor term from becoming a part of the sales contract. Figure 16.1 illustrates the UCC treatment of the offeree's additional terms. A is the offeror, B is the offeree, and AT is B's proposed additional term.

Consider now a situation somewhat different from the ones just discussed: Brenda and Sam are merchants. Brenda phones Sam an order for goods, Sam ships them, and Brenda receives and begins using them. *Later* Brenda sends Sam a letter confirming her order and Sam sends Brenda a letter correctly stating the terms of the oral agreement but adding a term stating that any dispute arising from the contract will be submitted to arbitration. The goods prove defective and Brenda sues Sam for damages. He asks the court to require Brenda to submit her claim to arbitration. Must she? Here we have a situation involving an agreement followed by "confirmatory memoranda," one of which adds a new term. The courts will treat the situation in the same way they treat an acceptance that departs from the terms of the offer. If the new term is material, it is not binding on Brenda without her consent.

Sometimes the writings of buyer and seller are so much in conflict that no contract results from the exchange of writings. Yet, because the seller shipped goods and the buyer accepted and paid for them, a contract of some sort arose. In the event of a dispute between buyer and seller about the quality of the goods, their price, or other matters, what are the terms of the contract? The contract actually arrived at will include any terms on which the writings of the parties agree, together with any terms that can be inferred from other conduct of the parties and any terms supplied by the UCC: delivery terms, warranties, and so on [2-207(3)].

Case 16.3 involves a material alteration of an offer, and a communication problem frequently encountered in dealing with a large, complex corporation.

Figure 16.1 UCC treatment of offeree's added term.

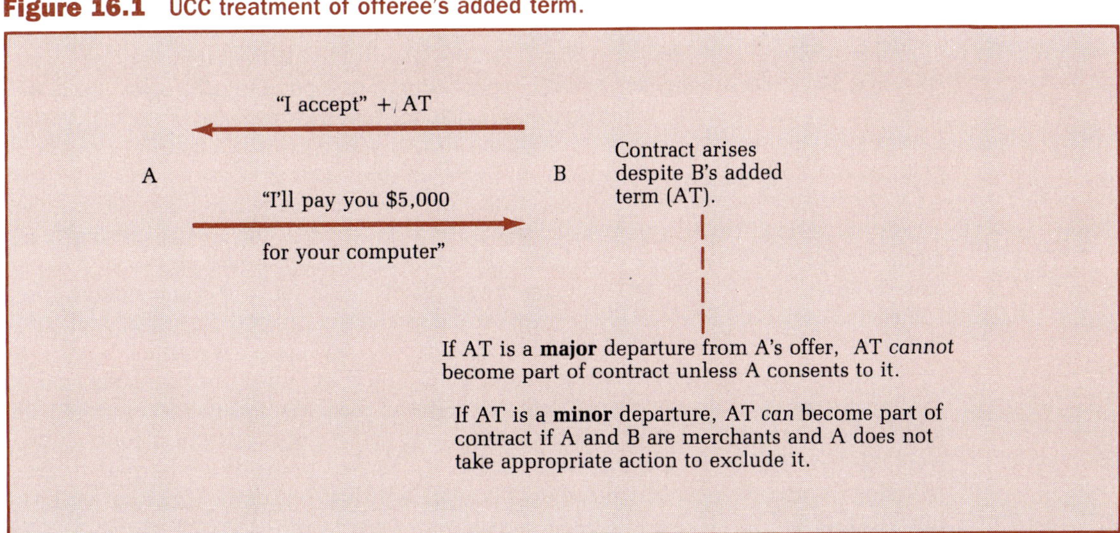
"I accept" + AT
A
B
"I'll pay you $5,000
for your computer"
Contract arises despite B's added term (AT).
If AT is a **major** departure from A's offer, AT *cannot* become part of contract unless A consents to it.
If AT is a **minor** departure, AT *can* become part of contract if A and B are merchants and A does not take appropriate action to exclude it.

CASE 16.3 Steiner v. Mobil Oil Corp. · 569 P.2d 751 (Cal. 1977)

FACTS Steiner (plaintiff), an independent service station operator, bought gasoline from Mobil Oil Corp. (defendant). Steiner's landlord decided to sell the service station property, and Mobil agreed to help Steiner buy it. Steiner worked out a proposal with Mobil's representative, Chenen. Mobil would supply the down payment of $30,000 in exchange for Steiner's entering a 10-year contract with Mobil. Mobil would treat the $30,000 as a prepaid competitive allowance to be amortized over the 10-year period through Steiner's purchase of 5.8 million gallons of gasoline. But Steiner determined that he could not pay Mobil's standard tank wagon price for gasoline and still have enough cash flow to meet the payments on the property. Accordingly, the proposal was modified to include a reduction of Mobil's tank wagon price by 1.4 cents per gallon for the duration of the contract. Steiner knew that Chenen did not have authority to accept the negotiated terms on Mobil's behalf.

Steiner and Chenen then prepared a proposal package for submission to Pfaff, the division general manager with authority to bind Mobil. It consisted of numerous separate standard Mobil forms, each modified as necessary. One form contained a clause stating that the 1.4 cents per gallon allowance "may be changed or discontinued by us at any time upon notice to you in writing." Upon receiving it, Steiner immediately phoned Chenen, telling him that he would not go ahead with the deal if Mobil could revoke the allowance, and demanding assurances that revocation would not occur. Chenen sent Steiner a letter acknowledging the demand and indicating that Mobil knew of it, but never sent a copy of the letter to Pfaff.

Instead, Chenen sent Pfaff a proposal package containing the provision for a revocable 1.4 cents per gallon allowance. Several months later, Pfaff approved it. Chenen phoned Steiner of Pfaff's approval and said he could proceed to purchase the property. Steiner did so. A Mobil employee later delivered the proposal documents to Steiner. Steiner did not reread them, and Mobil did not inform Steiner that the allowance Pfaff had approved was cancelable. For more than a year, Mobil granted Steiner the 1.4 cent discount. Then Mobil gave him written notice that the discount would be reduced to .5 cent per gallon. Steiner brought suit, seeking declaratory and monetary relief. The trial court held that transmitting Steiner's offer was part of Chenen's regular duties and that, through Chenen, Mobil had notice of Steiner's demand. From a judgment for Steiner, Mobil appealed.

OPINION TOBRINER, J. In this case, over one year after apparently accepting plaintiff's offer, the Mobil Oil Corporation sought to impose upon plaintiff the very contractual terms which [he] expressly rejected in his offer. As justification for its conduct, Mobil asserted that the crucial provision of plaintiff's offer was lost in the labyrinth of the Mobil bureaucracy, and thus that Mobil decisionmakers had no opportunity to pass on plaintiff's offer. . . . As we shall see, however, the trial court correctly concluded that section 2-207 of the California Uniform Commercial Code bars Mobil from in this way converting its own error into plaintiff's misfortune. . . .

Under traditional common law, no contract was reached if the terms of the offer and the acceptance varied. "In order to make a bargain it is necessary that the acceptor shall give in return for the offeror's promise exactly the consideration which the offer requests." . . . This "mirror image" rule of offer and acceptance was plainly both unfair and unrealistic in the commercial context. "The fact that the parties did intend a contract to be formed and both had a reasonable commercial understanding that the deal was closed, is ignored." . . .

Section 2-207 rejects the "mirror image" rule. "This section of the Code recognizes that in current commercial transactions, the terms of the offer and the acceptance will seldom be identical." . . . Under section 2-207 . . . the parties may conclude a contract despite the fact that, after reaching accord, they exchanged forms which purport to memorialize the agreement, but which differ because each party had drafted his form "to give him advantage." . . .

CASE 16.3 Continued

In place of the "mirror image" rule, section 2-207 inquires as to whether the parties intended to complete an agreement: "Under this Article a proposed deal which in commercial understanding has in fact been closed is recognized as a contract." . . . If the parties intend to contract, but the terms of their offer and acceptance differ, Section 2-207 authorizes a court to determine which terms are part of the contract, either by reference to the parties' own dealings . . . or by reference to other provisions of the code. . . .

Section 2-207 is thus of a piece with other recent developments in contract law. Instead of fastening upon abstract doctrinal concepts like offer and acceptance, section 2-207 looks to the actual dealings of the parties and gives legal effect to that conduct. Much as adhesion contract analysis teaches us not to enforce contracts until we look behind the facade of the formalistic standardized agreement in order to determine whether any inequality of bargaining power between the parties renders contractual terms unconscionable [or justifies interpreting the contract] against the more powerful party, section 2-207 instructs us not to *refuse* to enforce contracts until we look below the surface of the parties' disagreement as to contract terms and determine whether the parties undertook to close their deal. Section 2-207 requires courts to put aside the formal and academic stereotypes of traditional doctrine of offer and acceptance and to analyze instead what really happens. In this spirit, we turn to the application of section 2-207 in this case.

Section 2-207(1) provides: "A definite and seasonable expression of acceptance or a written confirmation which is sent within a reasonable time operates as an acceptance even though it states terms additional or different from those offered or agreed upon, unless acceptance is expressly made conditional on assent to the additional or different terms."

In this case, as the trial court found, Mobil provided "[a] definite and seasonable expression of acceptance." Steiner offered to enter into a 10-year dealer contract with Mobil only if Mobil . . . agreed to advance Steiner $30,000, and to give Steiner a 1.4 cents per gallon competitive discount on the price of Mobil gasoline for the duration of the contract. When Steiner telephoned Chenen . . . to inquire as to the fate of Steiner's offer, *Chenen told Steiner that Mobil had a check for him, that he should open an escrow account, and that he should go ahead with the purchase of the service station property*—in context a clear statement that Mobil had approved the deal.

Moreover, through . . . another Mobil employee, Mobil returned to Steiner various executed documents in an envelope unaccompanied by any cover [letter]. . . . The fact that Mobil returned the documents without in any way calling Steiner's attention to them is further evidence that Mobil regarded the process of negotiation as over and the deal as complete.

As the trial court also found, Mobil did not in any way make its acceptance "expressly . . . conditional" on Steiner's "assent to the additional or different terms." Chenen, in telling Steiner to go ahead with the purchase, did not suggest that Mobil had conditioned its acceptance. In returning the executed documents, Mobil enclosed no cover letter; again, it did not use the occasion in any way to condition expressly its acceptance.

Thus, neither of the restrictions which limit section 2-207(1)'s application [is] relevant in this case. Despite the fact that the terms of Mobil's acceptance departed partially from the terms of Steiner's offer, Mobil and Steiner did form a contract. To determine the terms of this contract, we turn to section 2-207(2). . . .

Subsection (a) [of § 2-207] provides that no additional term can become part of the agreement if Steiner's offer "expressly limit[ed] acceptance to the terms of the offer," [and Steiner's offer did so, because he expressed his intention not to go through with the deal if the 1.4 cents allowance were revocable].

Moreover, Mobil's acceptance falls within subsection (b) since without question the acceptance "materially alter[ed]" the terms of Steiner's offer. . . . The [UCC] comment notes that a variation is material if it would "result in surprise or hardship if incorporated

CASE 16.3 Continued

without express awareness by the other party. . . . " Here, Steiner clearly indicated to Mobil in the course of the negotiations that, without the 1.4 cents per gallon discount, he could not economically operate the service station. Mobil's alteration, therefore, amended the terms of the offer to Steiner's significant detriment; accordingly, the alteration was necessarily "material."

JUDGMENT . . . [T]he trial court correctly concluded that under section 2-207 the guaranteed discount included in. . . Steiner's offer, and not Mobil's standard revocable discount provision, became part of the agreement between Mobil and Steiner. Mobil cannot assert as a defense the failure of its own bureaucracy to respond to, or even fully recognize, Steiner's efforts to modify the standard Mobil dealer contract. The judgment is affirmed.

Shipment of nonconforming goods as an acceptance. Sometimes a seller fills an order by shipping goods that differ from what was ordered. The seller may have done so by accident or may have done so intentionally. If the nonconforming shipment was intentional, the seller's motive may have been bad, as when the seller attempts to substitute slow-moving goods in the hope that the buyer will not notice the substitution. Or the seller's motive may have been good, as when the seller knows that the buyer needs the goods immediately and, lacking the exact goods ordered, ships similar goods as an accommodation to the buyer.

Suppose Bob orders for prompt shipment 100 bolts of white silk cloth from Sue for manufacture into ladies' scarfs. Sue ships 100 bolts of white nylon cloth instead. Sue has not performed the requested act. At common law, a judge would have held that Sue has not accepted Bob's offer and therefore cannot be liable for breach of contract even though her shipping nonconforming goods might have caused Bob much inconvenience or loss. Under Article 2, if Sue ships the nylon *without giving Bob notice* that the goods are nonconforming, the shipment *is* an acceptance and at the same time a breach of contract. This rule will tend to discourage sellers from negligently filling orders or deceiving buyers by intentionally substituting nonconforming goods. However, where Sue gives Bob *timely notice* that the goods are nonconforming, the shipment is *not* an acceptance, and she will not be liable for breach of contract. This notice is especially important if Bob receives mail at his business office but the goods are delivered to employees elsewhere. If Bob has notice that the cloth is nylon but uses it anyway, there is a contract. If he decides not to use the goods, he may ship them back to Sue at her expense. This rule encourages sellers to accommodate buyers who may need substitute goods for maintaining production schedules, and to act reasonably in doing so.

Interpretation of the Sales Contract

Where a sales agreement is so sketchy or poorly worded that its terms are in doubt, a court may have to interpret it. Interpretation is a process by which a judge decides what legal obligations each party to the agreement undertook and whether the agreement amounts to an enforceable contract. A part of the judge's task might be to determine *which* of the parties' written and oral statements are included in the contract, and *what meaning* the parties' words should have. Contractual interpretation is largely beyond the scope of this book. However, businesspeople can benefit from knowing generally how the Code and the courts approach the problem of interpretation.

Meaning of "Contract." Since interpretation may be viewed as a judicial search for a contract, the meaning of "contract" becomes important. Under the Code, *contract* means the total legal obligation that results from the parties' agreement, as that agreement is affected by the Code and by any other applicable rules of law [1-201(11)]. *Agreement* means the bargain of the parties in fact, as found in their language or by implication from other circumstances, such as course of performance, course of dealing, and usage of trade [1-201(3)]. Since a sales contract includes obligations imposed by the Code and by other law, the parties must at least act in good faith and avoid unconscionable (harshly unfair) conduct. As was discussed earlier in this chapter, the Code and other law also fill in certain terms left open by the parties. Thus, the "sales contract" consists of the agreement of the parties as that agreement is limited and supplemented by law.

The Parol Evidence Rule. Often the parties to a sales contract make a variety of written and oral statements in the process of negotiating the terms of the contract, and then they sign a writing called an "integration" that supposedly represents their final decision as to the terms of the contract. What happens if one of the parties alleges that one of these prior statements (called "parol evidence"), and not the term that appears in the integration, truly states the parties' agreement? The court will apply the Article 2 *parol evidence rule.* Under that rule terms in a "writing intended by the parties as the final expression of their agreement with respect to such terms" are not to be contradicted by evidence of any prior agreement or by evidence of a contemporaneous oral agreement [2-202]. The same is true of terms agreed to by the parties in confirmatory memoranda (i.e., a memorandum from each party, with the memoranda agreeing on the term in dispute). However, agreed-to terms may be explained or supplemented by course of dealing, by usage of trade, or by course of performance. Agreed-to terms may also be explained or supplemented by evidence of consistent additional terms, unless the judge finds that the parties intended the writing to be not only a "final" but also a "complete and exclusive" statement of terms.

In summary, then, the court ordinarily will not admit into evidence any parol statement that directly contradicts an unambiguous term in an integration. The unambiguous term, and not the contradictory earlier statement, will be taken by the court as an accurate statement of the parties' agreement. But parol evidence *is* admissible to clear up vague or ambiguous language, to settle allegations of fraud, to supply missing terms where the final writing was not intended to be complete and exclusive, and so on. Thus the court sorts through the many conflicting statements that the parties might make and arrives at the selection of words that the court will hold to be the language of the contract.

Course of Performance, Course of Dealing, Usage of Trade. After deciding what statements are to be considered part of the contract, the court may have to determine the meaning of unclear language. The meaning intended by the parties is to be determined by their language and conduct, read and interpreted in light of commercial practices and other relevant circumstances [1-205, comment 1].

To aid interpretation, the Code gives special prominence to "course of performance," "course of dealing," and "usage of trade." *Course of performance* refers to how a particular transaction is carried out. There can be no course of performance unless there are repeated occasions for performance, such as several deliveries of coal to be made under a single contract of sale. Suppose that a contract for the delivery of coal says nothing about how large each delivery shall be. The buyer's acceptance of a series of small deliveries could establish a course of performance that would bind the buyer as to the next delivery [2-208(1)].

Course of dealing refers to a series of transactions, not just the performance of one transaction. A course of dealing (i.e., a pattern of prior contracts) can establish a background for the interpretation of the immediate transaction [1-205(1)]. Suppose that for each of five previous winters a buyer of home heating oil has always paid the delivery person in cash. The seller's acceptance of this practice establishes a course of dealing upon which the buyer may rely until notified differently, even if the driver absconds with the cash.

A *usage of trade* is any practice or method of dealing that is so regularly observed in a place, vocation, or trade that a party to a sales contract is justified in expecting that the practice will be observed in this contract too [1-205(2)]. It is a usage of trade in the seed corn business that sellers of seed corn make no guarantees of yield. A buyer who knew nothing of this usage of trade could nevertheless be bound by it.

Case 16.4 illustrates the application of the parol evidence rule to a dispute between contractors.

CASE 16.4 Rose Stone & Concrete, Inc. v. County of Broome · 429 N.Y.S.2d 295 (App. Div. 1980)

FACTS Rose Stone & Concrete (plaintiff) agreed with Triple Cities Construction Co. (defendant) to deliver gravel to a Broome County highway construction project. The contract stated that Triple Cities would make payment in accordance with "engineer's measure," i.e., the actual measurement of gravel compacted and in place at the job site rather than as loaded on trucks. Rose's president, unsure of how much weight loss would be involved, said he was assured that the weight reduction would not exceed 9 percent. Triple Cities said it told a Rose employee that the "engineer's measure" usually resulted in a 10–12 percent loss. When deliveries began, there were large discrepancies between Rose's cubic measurements of truck-loaded gravel and the amount Triple Cities calculated by applying the "engineer's measure." After failing to resolve the issue with Triple Cities, Rose brought suit for damages, seeking the difference between (a) the price based on the cubic weight of loaded gravel less a maximum shrinkage of 9 percent and (b) the smaller price for which Rose was given credit under the "engineer's measure." From a judgment for Triple Cities, Rose appealed.

OPINION MAHONEY, P. J.... The trial court found that "section 2-202 of the [UCC] prohibits the evidence that plaintiff offer(ed) to contradict the clear language of the contract." We disagree....

The parol evidence rule established by § 2-202... states that a contract "may not be contradicted by evidence of any prior agreement or of a contemporaneous oral agreement but may be explained or supplemented (a) by course of dealing or usage of trade... or by course of performance... and (b) by evidence of consistent additional terms unless the court finds the writing to have been intended also as a complete and exclusive statement of the terms of the agreement." The very technical nature of the term "engineer's measure" [requires] "explanation" or "supplementation" by use of extrinsic proof to determine the percentage of loss limitation the parties agreed to when they used the... phrase. It has been long settled that trade terms may be shown by parol evidence to have acquired a meaning by usage.... While it is clear that the parties had a common understanding that "engineer's measure" was a trade term characterizing the method of determining the actual weight of gravel when compacted for use, it is equally clear that there was a significant difference in their understanding of the degree or percentage of loss between loaded gravel and compacted gravel. Thus, since Rose continually disapproved of the disparities between truck measure and "engineer's measure" of gravel, it did not acquiesce to the high percentage of loss through the course of performance of the contract.... Accordingly, we conclude that it was error for the trial court to hold that the subject writing was "intended... as a complete and exclusive statement of the terms of the agreement."...

JUDGMENT Judgment [reversed on the first cause of action].

Unconscionability and Other Grounds for Avoiding the Sales Contract

As indicated in Chapter 11, a party to a contract may avoid (cancel) it because of wrongdoing by the other party such as fraud, misrepresentation, or duress. The UCC makes these and other common law grounds for avoidance available to the parties to a sales contract [1-103].

The elements of the common law grounds for avoidance have been rather clearly worked out in long lines of cases. However, the courts have had difficulty combating many harmful business practices that fall short of fraud and other established wrongs. So, to combat these harmful practices, the courts have developed the concept of *unconscionability,* which is specifically recognized by Article 2 as an additional ground for avoiding a sales contract.

A contract or a contractual clause is unconscionable if it is so one-sided as to "oppress" or "unfairly surprise" the party upon whom it is imposed. An unconscionable contract or clause is unenforceable even though the practice involved does not constitute fraud or some other traditional variety of wrongdoing. A court may refuse to enforce an unconscionable sales contract, may delete any unconscionable term and enforce the remainder of the contract, or may so limit the application of an unconscionable term as to avoid an unconscionable result [2-302].

As to what specific conduct will be declared unconscionable, the Code leaves that question for the courts to decide as a matter of law on a case-by-case basis. The courts have identified a number of practices that may be held unconscionable if the circumstances warrant. Suppose that a seller, by means of a clause in fine print placed in the middle of a complicated contract form, seeks secretly to deprive the buyer of a right that the buyer normally would not agree to give up if the topic were discussed, such as a warranty (guarantee) that the goods are fit for their ordinary purposes. Such a clause is unconscionable. High-pressure salesmanship may be a form of unconscionability. So may tricky or deceptive business practices. Furthermore, an excessively high price might be held unconscionable, as might a seller's unduly restricting the buyer's remedies for the seller's breach of contract or unduly expanding the seller's own remedies. For example, suppose that a furniture seller, by means of a clause in an installment-sale contract, retains for as long as the buyer's account is not fully paid a security interest in all items sold to the buyer over a period of years. Then the seller seeks to repossess the whole houseful of furniture because the buyer missed a payment on the last small item. If the value of the furniture to be repossessed greatly exceeds the amount of the unpaid debt, or the buyer did not understand the unusual consequences of missing a payment (losing all the furniture instead of only the item on which a payment was missed), the clause that provides for repossession is likely to be held unconscionable. However, while such a clause might be unconscionable in a contract between a merchant and a semiliterate customer, the same clause might be enforceable where buyer and seller are large corporations. This is so because people who have business experience presumably are in a better position to bargain with regard to contract terms, or at least to understand them and assess the risks.

In Case 16.5, the court discusses the circumstances required for a transaction to be held unconscionable.

CASE 16.5 Fotomat Corp. of Florida v. Chanda · 464 So. 2d 626 (Fla. App. 1985)

FACTS Plaintiff Chanda, a medical doctor, read a magazine article indicating that the deterioration of movie film could be avoided by transferring the film images onto videotape. After reading defendant Fotomat's flyer advertising the availability of such a service, Chanda delivered 28 rolls of developed Super-8 movie film for transfer to videotape. The order form contained the following language:

> By depositing film . . . with Fotomat, customer . . . agrees that Fotomat's liability for any loss . . . during the processing service will be limited to the replacement cost of a non-exposed roll of film . . . of similar size. Except for such replacement, Fotomat shall not be liable for any other loss or damage . . . arising out of customer's use of Fotomat's service.
>
> ______________________________
>
> Customer Signature

Dr. Chanda read this clause, asked the clerk about it, and signed it. The charge for processing the film was $31.00.

Fotomat lost the film. Dr. Chanda sued for damages, testifying that the film was of great sentimental value to him and his family because it recorded his honeymoon, the

CASE 16.5 Continued

graduation ceremony at his medical school, movies of his son's birth and early life, and many memorable vacations he and his wife had taken. The trial court held the loss limitation clause unconscionable and instructed the jury to ignore it. From a $9,500 judgment for Chanda, Fotomat appealed.

OPINION

ORFINGER, J.... [T]he court erred in holding the limitation of liability provision ... invalid....

The [UCC] does not attempt to define "unconscionability." Consequently, those courts which have dealt with the problem have often looked to the common law... because... [§ 2-302] is, [usually], a codification of the common law rules....

Florida has long recognized the principle that the courts are not concerned with the wisdom or folly of contracts,... but where it is perfectly plain to the court that one party has overreached the other and has gained an unjust and undeserved advantage which it would be inequitable to permit him to enforce, a court will grant relief even though the victimized parties owe their predicament largely to their own stupidity....

In *Kohl v. Bay Colony Club Condominium*..., the court [stated]: "The authorities appear to be virtually unanimous in declaring (or assuming) that two elements must coalesce before a case for unconscionability is made out." The first is... substantive... and the other [is] procedural unconscionability. A case is made out for substantive unconscionability by... proving that the terms of the contract are unreasonable and unfair. Procedural unconscionability, on the other hand, speaks to the... circumstances surrounding each contracting party at the time the contract was entered into [such as age, education, intelligence, business acumen and experience, relative bargaining power, who drafted the contract, whether the terms were explained to the weaker party, whether alterations in the printed terms were possible, and whether there were alternative sources of supply for the goods in question].

Most courts take a "balancing approach" to the unconscionability question[;]... to tip the scales in favor of unconscionability, [they] seem to require a certain quantum of procedural plus a certain quantum of substantive unconscionability.

This court has approved the "procedural-substantive" analysis in determining the question of unconscionability.... Applying the substantive prong of the test here, it cannot be said... that the limitation clause... was unreasonable, when viewed in its commercial setting, and when considering its purpose and effect....

Other courts have examined similar limitation clauses in film transactions and have refused to declare [them] unconscionable. In... *Posttape Associates v. Eastman Kodak Co.*, [the court] commented:

> It is the "unknown or undeterminable risks" which justify the utilization of a limitation in the film industry. Not only are the risks difficult to [assess] because of the latent nature of any film defect, but also because usually the seller is not aware of the scope of the film maker's undertaking....

[That the clause was reasonable] is demonstrated by the huge loss claimed by Dr. Chanda, compared to the cost of the service.... [T]he film had peculiar value to [him]. Some... was irreplaceable and all [had] great sentimental value, but that unknown [potential for loss] is the very reason for [including] the limitation of liability provision in the transaction. There is no way the processor can conceive of the risk it takes in accepting film for processing absent an explicit agreement to accept such risk. When the customer is made aware of the provision... and nevertheless proceeds with the transaction, he has assented to an agreement for which there is a commercial need, if the cost of the service is to be made reasonable.

Neither can we perceive that plaintiff satisfied the procedural prong of the test. The evidence reflects that Dr. Chanda saw and read the clause..., asked a question about it and was apparently satisfied with the answer because he signed it. He had previously suffered the loss of film at a different place of business, and it had been replaced by new

CASE 16.5 Continued

film. He was a doctor, well educated, experienced in business transactions, and well aware of what he was signing.... Thus the evidence falls short of showing procedural unconscionability. If, as indicated by the official comment to [§ 2-302], the principle involved... "is one of the prevention of oppression and unfair surprise... and not of disturbance of allocation of risks because of superior bargaining power," no such oppression or unfair surprise is shown here....

It is clear from the record... that the trial court refused to consider and apply the procedural/substantive test.... [I]nstead, the court appeared to view the unfairness of the agreement in retrospect, because of the result. The contract should have been reviewed in... light of the circumstances [existing] when it was made.

JUDGMENT The judgment for plaintiff is reversed, and the cause is remanded to the trial court with directions to enter judgment for plaintiff for the cost of 28 rolls of unexposed Super-8 movie film.

Form of the Sales Contract—UCC Statute of Frauds

The parties to a sales contract are not required to use any particular form of contract. As long as they provide the minimum amount of information required for a contract to arise, they may say as little or as much as they like about its terms, in whatever language and sequence of clauses they prefer. Yet, some rules of law do affect the form of some sales contracts. The Article 2 *statute of frauds* requires that specified kinds of sales contracts be evidenced by a *writing* or by some *legally acceptable substitute.*

The purpose of a statute of frauds is to require clear evidence—beyond mere oral statements of the parties—that a contract actually arose. This evidence is especially important where one person insists, but the other person denies, that a contract arose. As discussed in Chapter 13, statute-of-frauds requirements apply only to the more significant or more burdensome kinds of contracts. The Article 2 requirements apply only to sales contracts involving a price of $500 or more. (Some states specify a different amount.) Under Article 2A, a writing is required if rental payments total $1,000 or more.

Under the basic Article 2 rule, such a contract is not enforceable unless the party against whom enforcement is sought has signed some writing sufficient to indicate that a contract for sale has been made between the parties. Article 2 does *not* require that all the terms of the contract be stated. The writing is sufficient if it is signed by the party to be charged with breach of contract, specifies a quantity of goods, and indicates that the parties intended to enter into a contract [2-201]. The quantity need not be accurately stated, but the contract is not enforceable for more than the quantity stated in the writing.

Two classes of sales transactions are enforceable even though the party against whom enforcement is sought has signed nothing. Both classes of transactions involve situations where one party would be subjected to unfair surprise if the other party were permitted to cancel an agreement merely because the canceling party has signed nothing.

The first class consists of contracts "between merchants" in which a writing exists but has not been signed by the person against whom enforcement is sought. Suppose that merchant Brown telephones an offer to dealer Smith to buy a particular cash register for $1,000; that Smith replies over the phone, "I accept your offer"; and that Smith immediately sends Brown a written confirmation of the contract. Three weeks later, Brown, pointing out that she signed nothing, denies that the oral contract binds her. The statute of frauds is satisfied *without* Brown's signature if the following things happen: (1) Within a reasonable time after the oral transaction, Brown receives a writing confirming the contract and the writing is sufficiently detailed to be enforceable against the sender, Smith. (2) Brown has reason to know the contents of the writing. And (3) Brown does not give written notice of her objection to the contents of the writing within 10 days after receiving it.

In the second class of sales transactions there usually is no writing, but there may be convincing alternative evidence that the parties made a contract. If a party *admits in court* that a contract for sale was made, the oral contract can be enforced as to the quantity of goods admitted. If an oral contract has been *partially performed,* it is enforceable as to the goods for which the seller accepted payment, or as to goods that the buyer received and accepted. Oral contracts for goods to be *specially manufactured* for the buyer may also be enforceable—if the manufacturer has begun to make or procure them before notice of repudiation by the buyer and the goods are not suitable for sale in the ordinary course of the seller's business.

Alteration of the Sales Contract

After forming a sales contract, the parties may wish to modify it. They may want to change the time or place of delivery, specifications in the goods ordered, warranty obligations, or even the price. Under the general law of contracts, such modifications may not be enforceable unless both parties receive new consideration. Yet it is common practice for honest people to agree to, and to rely on, modifications that are not supported by consideration. Under Article 2, an agreement modifying a sales contract needs no consideration to be binding [2-209].

But sometimes a party to a sale forces a modification on the other party by, for example, threatening to withhold delivery of essential goods unless the purchaser "agrees" to pay more. Article 2 provides protections against such misconduct. One protection is the UCC requirement that any party to a Code transaction must act in good faith. In applying the good faith rule, a court may require the person seeking a modification to prove that there is a real need for it—for example, that the higher price to which the buyer agreed is justified by an actual increase in the price of raw materials. Another protection is the fact that the statute of frauds must be satisfied if the contract, as modified, will be for a price of $500 or more. Thus, there will be evidence (beyond the modification-seeker's allegations) that the other party actually agreed to the modification. There is a third protection. The parties to a signed agreement may require in their agreement that any modification or cancellation of the contract must be evidenced by a signed writing for the change to be enforceable, i.e., that there will be no oral modifications. However, where a "no oral modifications" clause is supplied by a merchant to a nonmerchant, the clause will not be binding on the nonmerchant unless he or she signs it separately.

What happens when the parties fail to provide a required writing and agree to an oral modification anyway? If one party *materially changes his or her position in reliance* on the oral modification, the other party has *waived* (given up) the protection of the required writing. Suppose Sam agrees in writing to sell Brenda a $1,000 copier to be delivered in 10 days, and the contract requires any modifications to be made in writing. On the third day Brenda phones Sam to tell him delivery will have to be postponed for another 15 days because she will not have room for the copier until then. Sam agrees to the postponement. At this point in the transaction, the 15-day oral postponement agreement is not binding on either party, since the contract requires that modifications be in writing. Now suppose that Sam has only this one copier in his store and will not receive another like it for 12 days. Believing he need not deliver a copier to Brenda for 15 days, Sam sells the copier to Tom. Because Sam has *relied* on the oral agreement, Brenda has lost (waived) her right to cancel the oral agreement, and she cannot insist on the original delivery date.

Summary

The general purpose of the UCC is to simplify, unify, and modernize the law of commercial transactions. The Code encourages sound business practices, ethical business conduct, and performance of sales contracts. Merchants generally have greater duties than do nonmerchants, and all parties to Code transactions must use good faith in carrying them out. The Code concept of identification of goods to the contract enables a party to know, for example, when the buyer may insure the goods.

Article 2 applies to present sales of goods and to contracts to sell goods at a future time. In general, *goods* means all things that are movable at the time of identification to the contract. Article 2 does not apply to contracts for such nongoods as real estate and personal services. Courts differ in their application of the Code to contracts for a mixture of goods and services.

A sales contract must meet traditional requirements for the formation of a contract, but most of these requirements have been modified by Article 2 to adjust them to contemporary business needs. A sales contract may be made in any manner sufficient to show agreement. Many terms may be left open, but ordinarily the parties and the quantity of goods must be identified.

Unilateral offers to buy goods for prompt shipment may be accepted either by a prompt shipment or by a prompt promise to ship. Certain firm offers made by a merchant are irrevocable even though the merchant receives no consideration for the promise to hold the offer open. Offers may be accepted by any reasonable means; and Article 2 treats some counteroffers as acceptances. Between merchants, minor new terms can become part of the contract, but a new term that materially alters the offer will not bind the offeror without his or her actual consent.

A shipment of nonconforming goods is both an acceptance and a breach of contract. However, if the shipper gives timely notice that the goods are nonconforming, the shipment will be considered an accommodation and not an acceptance and breach. Where a sales agreement is sketchy or poorly worded, a court may have to interpret it. The parol evidence rule helps a judge decide what statements should be held to be the language of the contract. The meaning of unclear language may be determined in part by reference to course of performance, course of dealing, and usage of trade.

A party to a sales contract may avoid it because of wrongdoing by the other party such as fraud, misrepresentation, or duress, or because the contract is unconscionable. The Article 2 and 2A statutes of frauds require that sales contracts involving a price of $500 or more, and lease contracts involving total rental payments of $1,000 or more, be evidenced by a writing or by some legally acceptable alternative such as admissions in court or part performance. An agreement modifying a sales contract needs no consideration to be binding.

Review Questions

1 A sale of goods may involve other UCC transactions too. Explain or illustrate.

2 Why is it necessary to have a body of sales law apart from the general law of contracts?

3 A basic policy of the UCC is to encourage sound and ethical business practices. Explain how the following Code concepts contribute to carrying out that policy: **(a)** merchant, **(b)** good faith, and **(c)** identification of goods to the contract.

4 **(a)** To what transactions does Article 2 apply? **(b)** How might a court treat a contract involving a mixture of goods and services? **(c)** To what transactions does article 2A apply? Not apply?

5 Explain whether the following statement is true: "Before there can be a sales contract, the parties, the price, and the quantity and kind of goods must be identified."

6 How and why does Article 2 depart from common law rules with regard to an offer for a unilateral contract? A firm offer?

7 **(a)** What is the effect of using a medium of acceptance that has been authorized by the offeror? **(b)** How does an offeree know what medium of acceptance has been authorized?

8 How and why does Article 2 depart from common law rules with regard to **(a)** counteroffers and **(b)** a shipment of nonconforming goods as an acceptance?

9 Explain generally how a court will interpret a sales contract whose terms are in doubt.

10 In what main way does unconscionability differ from other, traditional, grounds for avoiding a sales contract?

11 **(a)** How may the Article 2 statute of frauds be satisfied? **(b)** If a writing is used, what must the writing contain?

12 An agreement modifying a sales contract needs no consideration to be binding. How, then, may a buyer be protected if the seller forces the buyer to agree to a higher price by threatening to withhold delivery of essential goods?

Case Problems

1 Dr. Monteleone, a neurologist, leased a computer system from Neilson, receiving an option to purchase it at the end of the lease period for its fair market value. The agreement covered the computer and other hardware, software, and Neilson's services in customizing the system to meet Monteleone's needs. The system never worked properly. Monteleone canceled the contract and sued Neilson for damages for breach of UCC warranties. The trial court held that the lease was a transaction covered by the Code and that the transaction was for "goods" to which Code warranties apply. On appeal, Neilson argued that only the computer constituted "goods," and since it was not defective, Neilson had no Code liability for breach of warranty. **(a)** Was the lease transaction subject to UCC warranties? **(b)** If so, did those warranties apply to the software and to Neilson's services in customizing the system? Consider only Article 2 in your answer.

2 Alwinseal ordered goods from PPG for $65,000. PPG shipped them and sent Alwinseal an acknowledgment of the offer. PPG also sent a price list indicating a higher price than Alwinseal had offered to pay. PPG billed Alwinseal for $72,977.04, in accordance with PPG's new price list. Alwinseal paid the bill, claimed it had been overcharged by $7,977.04, and brought suit for the return of that amount. Was Alwinseal entitled to the amount it claimed?

3 Just Born, Inc., a candy manufacturer, purchased gelatin from Stein, Hall & Co. Just Born telephoned its orders and followed up with written purchase orders specifying terms such as price, quantity, and description of the goods. Stein, Hall responded by sending Just Born a "Sales Acknowledgment Agreement" and shipping the gelatin to Just Born's plant. Stein, Hall's agreement form contained an "Arbitration Clause" requiring any dispute to be settled by arbitration rather than in court. The gelatin was unfit for its intended use, and Just Born brought suit for damages. Stein, Hall insisted that the dispute be submitted to arbitration. Was Just Born bound by the arbitration clause?

4 Michel, Inc., made seven oral agreements to purchase yarn from Anabasis Trade, Inc. In each of the seven transactions, Anabasis (seller) sent Michel a written confirmation containing an arbitration clause. Michel signed and returned the first confirmation. Michel knew that the form contained the arbitration clause but never objected to it. Michel did object to the inclusion of a 30- rather than a 60-day credit term contained in the second and third confirmations, and these terms were changed to suit Michel. Later Michel discovered that the yarn did not conform to the contract specifications. Anabasis insisted that the dispute be submitted to arbitration. Michel brought an action to stay (stop) arbitration proceedings. The trial court held that the arbitration clause did not become part of the contract unless both parties explicitly agreed to it. Was the trial court correct?

5 Hoping to be admitted to the practice of law, Jaiswal, a certified public accountant, purchased over $1,400 worth of legal textbooks from Matthew Bender & Co. The invoices contained the names and addresses of buyer and seller, the date, the payment terms, descriptions and prices of the books, and a clause which entitled the purchaser to return the merchandise within 30 days for a full refund. Jaiswal was admitted to the bar, but several months after the sale refused to pay for the books, claiming they had been sold on approval and that the salesperson had assured him that he could return them if he decided they were not useful. Bender sued for the price of the books. Was Jaiswal liable for payment?

6 Sebasty, a farmer, made an oral agreement to sell 14,000 bushels of wheat to Perschke Hay and Grain for $1.95 per bushel. Perschke immediately sent Sebasty a written confirmation of the agreement, which Sebasty received. Under the agreement, Perschke was to pick up the wheat about 6 months later. In the meantime, the price of wheat rose, and when the time for performance arrived, Sebasty refused to provide the wheat. Alleging breach of contract, Perschke sued Sebasty for more than $14,000 in damages. Sebasty contended that the oral agreement was not enforceable because it did not comply with the statute of frauds. Part of Sebasty's defense rested on his allegation that he was not a merchant. **(a)** On what statute of frauds rule was plaintiff Perschke relying? **(b)** For the purpose of that rule, was Sebasty a merchant?

CHAPTER 17

Part One: Delivery and Storage of Goods; Documents of Title

Making a contract of sale is only the first step in what can be a complicated process of getting goods from seller to buyer. Often, they are put on a carrier for transport or in a warehouse for storage, their movement from buyer to seller being controlled by the use of documents of title. The goods may be lost or damaged in transit, and different people may claim ownership of the same goods. Under what circumstances is a carrier or a warehouse liable for lost or damaged goods? Who is entitled to the goods where ownership is disputed? These questions are the focus of Chapter 17, Part One. It deals first with the delivery and storage of goods and then with documents of title.

Delivery and Storage of Goods

Delivery of Goods

Delivery by Common and Private Carriers. A seller may ship goods by means of a carrier. A *carrier* is an individual or a business firm engaged in transporting passengers or goods for hire. A carriage contract for the transport of goods is a bailment[1] in which the bailor (the owner or another shipper) places the goods in the custody of the bailee (the carrier) for the purpose of safe transport to a person or a firm authorized by the shipper to receive them. Carriers of property include railroads, barge and ship lines, airlines, trucking companies, pipeline companies that transport oil or natural gas, and express companies whose business is the speedy delivery of small packages of goods or money.

A carrier has a "lien" on (claim against) goods in its possession for any unpaid transportation and related charges [7-307]. The carrier may enforce the lien by selling the amount of the goods necessary to pay its legitimate charges [7-308]. A carrier loses its lien on any goods that it voluntarily delivers or unjustifiably refuses to deliver.

[1]As noted in Chapter 20, a bailment is the legal relationship that results where one person (the bailor) transfers possession of personal property to another person (the bailee) under such circumstances that the bailee is under a duty to return the item to the bailor or to dispose of it as directed by the bailor.

Carriers are classified as "common" or "private." A *common carrier* offers its services to the public and must carry for all who apply, as long as there is room and no legal excuse for refusing to render the service. An express company, which by definition hauls only small packages, would have a legal excuse for refusing to haul passengers.

A common carrier has extensive liability for damage to or loss of goods being transported. Like any other bailee, a common carrier is liable for loss caused by its negligence and intentional torts such as *conversion* of the bailor's goods.[2] But in most states common carriers also are liable for loss due to causes beyond the carrier's control, such as fires, wrecks, theft, and violent mobs. The English courts began imposing this broader "insurer's" liability in the 1500s because common carriers or their employees could easily steal the goods, sell them, and pretend that the goods had been lost. Today the common carrier's liability as an insurer is based on additional factors: the great total value of the goods being shipped, the vast distances involved, and the difficulty a shipper would have in proving a carrier's negligence or fraud.

There are limits to the liability of a common carrier, however. It is not liable, for example, for losses caused solely by an "act of God" such as a tornado or an earthquake, an act or fault of the shipper, or the dangerous or perishable nature of the goods themselves. Furthermore, unless forbidden by law to do so, a common carrier may limit the amount of damages recoverable by the shipper where the carrier's rates are dependent on value and the shipper is given an opportunity to declare a higher value (probably for payment of a higher rate) [7-309]. The right to limit damages applies to the carrier's liability as an *insurer* (i.e., for loss from causes beyond the carrier's control) and to its liability for its own *negligence.* But a common carrier may *not* totally exempt itself from these liabilities, and it is not permitted even to limit its liability for *converting* the bailor's goods to its own use. Any other rule would reward wrongdoing by allowing

[2]As noted in Chapter 4, conversion is the act of taking or using someone else's personal property as one's own, without legal justification. A thief is a converter. So is a carrier or other bailee that delivers goods to the wrong person, uses the bailed goods as the bailee's own, or wrongfully refuses to release the goods to the bailor or to release them in accordance with the bailor's instructions.

the converter to keep the difference between the actual value of the converted property and any limited amount stated in the contract of carriage.

Figure 17.1 summarizes the liabilities of a common carrier.

Private carriers (including "contract" carriers) ordinarily are used to meet the special needs of shippers who find access to a common carrier lacking or its service unsatisfactory. An isolated rancher might hire a private carrier to haul cattle to market or to a loading yard to await the arrival of a common carrier. A manufacturer or a wholesaler might use a private carrier for deliveries to remote regions or to local areas not served by common carriers.

Private carriers differ considerably from common carriers. Private carriers do not hold themselves out as ready to serve the public generally and are not required to do so. Rather, they carry goods only for those persons with whom the carriers choose to contract. Unlike common carriers, private carriers are *not* liable as insurers of the goods. They are liable only as bailees, for loss caused by (1) their own negligence (including that of their employees), and (2) their intentional misconduct (and that of their employees), such as conversion of the goods. Thus, a private carrier would be liable for theft committed by its employees but would not be liable for thefts committed by strangers unless the carrier or its employees failed to use ordinary care to prevent the thefts. Private carriers are freer than common carriers to exclude liability for negligence. Private carriers usually may enforce contract clauses that exempt them from liability for ordinary negligence, but usually they may not enforce clauses that purport to exempt them from liability for "gross" negligence or for intentional misconduct.

Figure 17.2 summarizes the liability of a private carrier.

As the preceding discussion indicates, a common or private carrier may be liable for loss of goods in its custody, but sometimes the carrier is not liable. So, either the buyer or the seller must absorb the loss. The UCC provides "risk-of-loss rules," discussed later in this chapter, that determine who—the buyer or the seller—must absorb the loss or, if a carrier is liable, who must seek compensation from the carrier. UCC risk-of-loss rules apply also to the "noncarrier" and "pickup" deliveries discussed in the following paragraphs.

Common carrier IS LIABLE for loss caused by:

- Its (and employees') **intentional torts**—e.g., willful damage to goods, conversion of shipper's goods to carrier's own use
- Its (and employees') **negligence**

Common carrier IS LIABLE as **insurer** for losses beyond its control—e.g., loss caused by:

- fires
- wrecks
- theft
- violent mobs

BUT

Common carrier MAY LIMIT its insurer's and negligence liability if:

- shipping rates depend on value of the goods *and* shipper is allowed to declare higher value

Common carrier is NOT LIABLE for loss caused by:

- act of God
- act or fault of shipper
- dangerous or perishable nature of the goods

Figure 17.1 Liabilities of common carrier.

Noncarrier and Pickup Deliveries. Especially in the retail sale of bulky goods such as furniture, sellers commonly deliver the goods to the buyers by means of the sellers' own delivery vehicles. This kind of delivery is called a "noncarrier delivery"

Figure 17.2 Liability of a private carrier.

Private carrier IS LIABLE for loss caused by:

- Its (and employees') **intentional torts**
- Its (and employees') **negligence**

BUT

Private carrier usually MAY ENTIRELY EXCLUDE liability for its own ordinary negligence

Private carrier IS NOT LIABLE

- As insurer, or
- for loss caused by act of God, etc.

because the seller does not use a common or a private carrier. Sellers of many other kinds of goods—dairy products, fuels for home or commercial use, soft drinks, baked goods, small hand tools, and so on—make noncarrier deliveries to customers for resale or for the customers' own use.

Many buyers use their own vehicles to "pick up" the goods at the seller's premises. For example, a building contractor might have a fleet of trucks for pickup of gravel, lumber, and other building materials. Customers of local supermarkets and department stores ordinarily pick up the goods at the store rather than having the store make a noncarrier delivery. In the sale of automobiles and the like, the customer may visit the seller's premises several times to work out the terms of the sale and then return a few days later to pick up the automobile or other item after it has been prepared by the seller for use.

Storage in Warehouses

Often an owner of goods must store them in a warehouse until they are sold. A *warehouse* is a building or other enclosed area used to hold goods temporarily or for an indefinite time. When a person stores goods at a warehouse, a bailment relationship is created. The owner or other depositor of the goods is the bailor. The *warehouser,* a person or firm engaged in the business of receiving and storing goods for hire, is the bailee.

A warehouse may be "public" or "private." A *public* warehouse holds itself out as willing to store goods for any member of the public who seeks and pays for the storage service. Grain elevators buy grain from farmers willing to sell, but they also store grain for any farmer who wishes to wait for a higher price. Because they store for anyone seeking that service, grain elevators are public warehouses. In contrast, a *private* warehouse stores goods only for those persons with whom it chooses to contract.

A public warehouse is subject to more governmental regulation than is a private warehouse. Aside from this difference, the distinction between a public and a private warehouse is not very significant, since neither kind is liable as an insurer of stored goods unless by special agreement or under an occasional state statute imposing such liability on a public warehouse. Rather, public and private warehouses usually are liable only *as bailees* for loss of or damage to the goods during storage, i.e., for loss due to their negligence and their intentional misconduct in caring for the goods.

Like carriers, warehouses may limit their liability for negligence during storage. As noted in Case 17.1, this liability may be limited in the contract of storage to a specific amount per item, subject to the bailor's right to increase the valuation. If the bailor declares a higher value, the warehouse has a right to charge a higher rate for storage [7-204]. Like a carrier, a warehouse has a possessory lien on the goods for storage charges [7-209].

CASE 17.1 Western Mining Corp. v. Standard Terminals, Inc. · 37 UCC Rep. 1273 (D.C. Pa. 1984)

FACTS Western Mining, a seller of nickel products in North and South America, stored large quantities of nickel briquettes used in steelmaking at defendant Standard Terminals' warehouse facility in Arnold, Pennsylvania. The nickel came to the United States from Australia aboard ships in sealed containers delivered from the port of entry to the warehouse by common carrier. Standard Terminals (Warehouse) would store the nickel, advise Western Mining of the amount received, and issue warehouse receipts. Upon sale of the nickel, Western Mining would notify Warehouse of the amount and destination of the nickel to be delivered. Warehouse would then remove the nickel from storage, load it onto the carriers' vehicles, and prepare bills of lading and other shipping documents. Western Mining and Warehouse kept separate running paper inventories of the nickel and verified their records by physical inventories twice a year.

Twice in 1982 amounts of nickel totaling 8 metric tons valued at about $50,000 were discovered to be missing from the warehouse. Bailor and bailee reviewed their records

CASE 17.1 Continued

separately to determine if there was a bookkeeping error. The parties' accounts were in agreement and did not explain why the nickel was missing. Warehouse admitted the nickel was missing but denied any specific factual knowledge of what happened to it. A clause in the warehouse receipts issued to Western Mining reads as follows:

> 1. Limit of Bailee's liability [for] damage or loss is $200 a net ton. Should Bailor desire that side limit be increased, the storage rate shall be increased by three cents per month for each additional $100. Nothing herein contained shall preclude Bailor from taking out such insurance protection against fire or any other casualty as it may deem advisable.

Alleging that Warehouse had converted the missing nickel, Western Mining brought suit for its value.

OPINION

MENCER, D. J. This civil action for damages presents a number of somewhat unsettled questions of law in the . . . area of bailments with warehousemen. . . .

Under Pennsylvania law, a bailment for the mutual benefit of the bailor and the bailee requires the bailee to exercise reasonable and ordinary care. When a bailment is shown to exist, the bailor makes out a prima facie case against his bailee for hire for recovery of the value of the unreturned bailed goods by showing his delivery of the goods to the bailee and the latter's failure to redeliver them upon the bailor's demand. . . . Western Mining, the bailor, urges the extension of this rebuttable presumption of negligence to cover conversion of the bailed goods. The United States Court of Appeals for the Third Circuit had defined the Pennsylvania common law tort of conversion as ". . . an act of willful interference with the dominion or control over a chattel, done without lawful justification, by which any person entitled to the chattel is deprived of its use and possession." . . . The plaintiff urges our adoption of the reasoning of the Court of Appeals of New York in I.C.C. Metals, Inc. v. Municipal Warehouse Company. . . . The court there found that, where there was proof of delivery to a bailee and of a subsequent failure to return bailed goods coupled with the bailee's failure to adequately explain such failure, a presumption of conversion on the part of the bailee was appropriate.

The distinction between negligence on the part of a bailee as opposed to conversion . . . where, as here, the goods for all practical purposes no longer exist may seem inconsequential at first blush. The importance, however, relates to the measure of damages available to the bailor. The Uniform Commercial Code Section 7-204(2) . . . provides that a warehouseman's liability in the case of loss or damage may be contractually limited. Such a limitation is ineffective when the warehouseman converts the bailed goods "to his own use." Unless there is adequate justification [for our presuming conversion on the part of the defendant], any recovery to which the plaintiff is entitled will be limited to $200 per ton.

[Some courts have cited I.C.C. Metals with favor.] There is, however, case law which expressly rejects I.C.C. Metals. [An Illinois federal district court] found that conversion under Indiana law . . . requires some affirmative wrongful act and, because the bailor failed to introduce "'direct evidence of any positive wrongful act,'" granted summary judgment in favor of the bailee. . . . Pennsylvania, like Indiana, requires a willful interference with the dominion or control of a chattel in order to establish conversion. . . . There is no evidence in the record of any "positive wrongful act" by the bailee in its handling of Western Mining's nickel[;] therefore, a presumption of conversion by the bailee is inappropriate and we will not charge Standard Terminals with liability for the full value of the missing nickel on that basis.

Western Mining next argues, in effect, that even assuming no conversion by Standard Terminals[,] the actions of Standard Terminals were so egregious as to constitute gross negligence [and that] a finding of gross negligence is sufficient to defeat the applicability of any liability limitation. . . . [W]e find as a matter of law that the events surrounding the

CASE 17.1 Continued

disappearance of the plaintiff's nickel do not constitute gross negligence on the part of Standard Terminals.

The result of our ruling is that, because of the delivery of nickel to Standard Terminals by Western Mining, Western Mining's demand of return of the nickel and Standard Terminal's failure to return the bailed nickel, the loss of the nickel may be presumed to be as a result of Standard Terminals' negligence.

JUDGMENT Standard Terminals is, therefore, liable to Western Mining in the amount of $200 per metric ton as contracted for in the warehouse receipts covering this bailment agreement.

Documents of Title

Documents of title are an important part of the paperwork necessary for getting goods from sellers to buyers. A *document of title* is any writing that in the *regular course of business or financing* (i.e., in normal business transactions) is treated by the courts as adequate proof that the person in possession of it is entitled to receive and sell or otherwise dispose of the document and the goods it covers [1-201(15)]. To be a document of title, the writing must purport to be (must indicate that it is) issued by or addressed to a bailee (i.e., a carrier or a warehouseman), and must purport to cover identified goods in the bailee's possession.

A document of title serves three practical functions. First, it is a receipt: a written acknowledgment given by a bailee that the depositor or shipper left the specified goods with the bailee for storage or shipment. Second, it is a contract between the bailor and the bailee for the storage or the transport (carriage) of the goods. Third, as indicated in the previous paragraph, it is *evidence of title to (ownership of) the goods.*

Kinds of Documents

The two principal documents of title are the warehouse receipt and the bill of lading. A *warehouse receipt* is a writing issued by a warehouser to the person or firm that deposits the goods at the warehouse for storage. The depositor is the bailor; the warehouser is the bailee.

A *bill of lading* is a writing, issued by a carrier, evidencing the carrier's receipt of goods for shipment. The person delivering the goods to the carrier for shipment is the shipper and also the bailor; the carrier is the bailee. The shipper-bailor's act of delivering goods to a carrier for transport is called a *consignment.* The shipper (bailor) is the *consignor.* The person to whom the carrier is to deliver the goods at their destination is the consignee. Suppose Sam delivers goods to XYZ Railroad in Atlanta for transport to Brenda in Denver. Sam is the shipper, the bailor, and the consignor; the railroad is the carrier and the bailee; and Brenda is the *consignee.*

A *through bill* of lading is one issued by a carrier (to the shipper-bailor) for the transport of goods over the carrier's own lines for a certain distance and then over connecting lines to the destination. A through bill would be used, for example, where a railroad in the consignor's city does not go to the consignee's city but a connecting railroad does. A carrier that issues a through bill is liable not only for its own breach of the carriage contract, but also for any breach of the contract by the connecting carrier such as failure to deliver the goods to the proper person. The connecting carrier must honor the terms of the through bill even though the connecting carrier did not issue it [7-302].[3]

Where a seller ships goods by truck or air and then mails the bill of lading to the buyer, the goods often arrive at their destination before the bill of lading does. This is inconvenient for buyers who

[3]Article 7 of the UCC governs documents of title where the goods are shipped within a state. Where goods are transported in interstate or foreign commerce, federal law applies. For example, the federal Bills of Lading Act applies to interstate shipments of goods by common carrier. Although state law (Article 7) differs in some ways from the federal law governing documents of title, there is little difference as to the general principles discussed in this chapter.

need the goods right away and for carriers who have little storage space at the point of destination. So, the seller may use a *destination bill* of lading. A destination bill is issued *at the destination* by the carrier or its agent so that the buyer (consignee) may take possession of the goods immediately upon their arrival. Suppose that Sue, a Los Angeles seller, delivers goods to an airline for shipment to Ben, a New York buyer, and instructs the airline to issue the "airbill" (bill of lading) *in New York* to a bank named by Sue. The airline may issue the airbill to the New York bank even before the goods reach New York. In accordance with Sue's advance instructions, the bank collects payment from Ben and hands the airbill over to him. Ben can immediately use the airbill to get the goods from the airline rather than having to wait for the airbill to arrive in the mail while the goods remain in storage.

Principle of Negotiability

Documents of title may be either negotiable or nonnegotiable in form. The distinction can be of great importance to persons who use or are affected by such documents.

Negotiable Form; Its Effect on Who Is Entitled to the Goods. For a warehouse receipt or a bill of lading to be in *negotiable* form, the document must contain "order" or "bearer" language. That is, the document must *state* that the goods are to be delivered to the *bearer* of the document or to the *order* of a person named in the document to receive the goods. A document reading "Deliver five desks to bearer" or "Deliver five desks to Sam or order" is in negotiable form.

The form of a document, negotiable versus nonnegotiable, tells us *who* is entitled to have the goods from the bailee. A bailee who issues a negotiable document of title must deliver the goods described in the document to any "holder" who surrenders it to the bailee. A *holder* is any person, even a stranger to the bailee, who seems to be rightfully in possession of a negotiable document (one containing the required order or bearer language). Suppose that Sam, intending to sell certain goods when a buyer can be found, delivers the goods to Walt's Warehouse for storage. At Sam's request, Walt makes the warehouse receipt out to "Sam or [Sam's] order" and hands it to Sam. The receipt is negotiable in form and Sam is its holder. When Sam finds a buyer (Brenda), Sam needs merely to "indorse" the receipt (sign it on the back or in some other appropriate place, much as one would indorse a check) and deliver the receipt to Brenda. Brenda is now the holder and as such has the right, upon surrendering the document to Walt, to have the goods.

In contrast, a document that *lacks* order or bearer language is *nonnegotiable* in form. A bailee who issues a nonnegotiable document must deliver the goods only to the person specifically named in the document to receive them, or in accordance with that person's written instructions. Suppose that Sam in the preceding paragraph had instructed Walt to make the receipt out to Sam personally ("to Sam"). The receipt would be nonnegotiable in form. Such a receipt obligates Walt to deliver the goods to Sam and to no one else unless Sam gives Walt a contrary delivery instruction in writing. Sam might do this by means of a separate document called a "delivery order," or by writing on the warehouse receipt itself a statement of assignment ("I, Sam, hereby assign all my rights under this document to Brenda") and delivering the receipt to Brenda (the assignee).

Legal Rights Acquired by a Transferee of the Document. Whether a document of title is negotiable or nonnegotiable helps determine *what rights to the goods* a buyer (or other transferee) of the document acquires from the seller (or other transferor). The purchaser of a *non*negotiable document is merely an assignee and as such receives only the rights that the seller had. (The law of assignments is discussed in Chapter 14.) Suppose Tom delivers an antique desk to Walt's Warehouse, which issues to Tom a nonnegotiable warehouse receipt (one made out "to Tom"). Then Sam fraudulently induces Tom to assign the receipt to Sam. Sam sells the document (and, of course, the desk it represents) to Brenda, an antiques dealer who knows nothing of Sam's fraud. Brenda presents the document to Walt's and receives possession of the desk. Later, Tom demands the desk from Brenda. Brenda is merely Sam's assignee and, as such, has only the rights that Sam had. When Sam committed fraud, he became liable to Tom for the return of the desk or for its value. Brenda, Sam's assignee, is in no better position than Sam was, and Tom has a right to recover the desk or its value from her. If Tom chooses to hold Brenda liable, she will have to get the value of the desk from Sam, absorb the loss, or pass it on to others such as an insurance company. In Figure 17.3, Brenda receives a nonnegotiable warehouse receipt (WR) from Sam, but because of Sam's fraud she is not entitled to the desk.

In contrast, a good faith purchaser of a *negotiable* document may, in proper circumstances, take the document (and the goods) *free from* many defenses or claims of others to the goods. Suppose that Tom in the preceding paragraph had received a warehouse receipt made out to "Tom or order" and that because of Sam's fraud Tom indorsed and delivered the receipt to Sam, who then sold it to Brenda. Knowing nothing of Sam's fraud, Brenda is a "holder to whom the document has been duly negotiated" (Article 7's version of a good faith purchaser); as such she takes the document and the goods *free from* Tom's claim of fraud. Tom may recover the value of the goods from *Sam* (the defrauder), but Brenda (the good faith purchaser) keeps the goods and is not liable to Tom for their value. In this way, the law frees good faith purchasers from a variety of risks, and persons like Tom who are in a better position to protect themselves must pursue the wrongdoer, absorb any loss, or pass it on to others. The protection of good faith purchasers, widely known in the business community, encourages buyers to pay higher market values than they would if the chances of loss were greater.

In Figure 17.4, Brenda has received a *negotiable* warehouse receipt and therefore is entitled to the desk free from Tom's defense of fraud.

Good faith purchaser protection exists *only* where the transferee of the document takes it by a "due negotiation." For there to be a *due negotiation,* five requirements must be met [7-501]:

1 The document must be *negotiable* in form, i.e., issued "to bearer" or "to [Sam] or order."
2 The negotiable document must be in the possession of a *holder.* A holder is a person in possession of a bearer document, a person in possession of an order document issued to that person, or a person in possession of an order document issued to someone else and properly indorsed to the possessor. A document issued "to Sam or order" and

Figure 17.3 Nonnegotiable warehouse receipt.

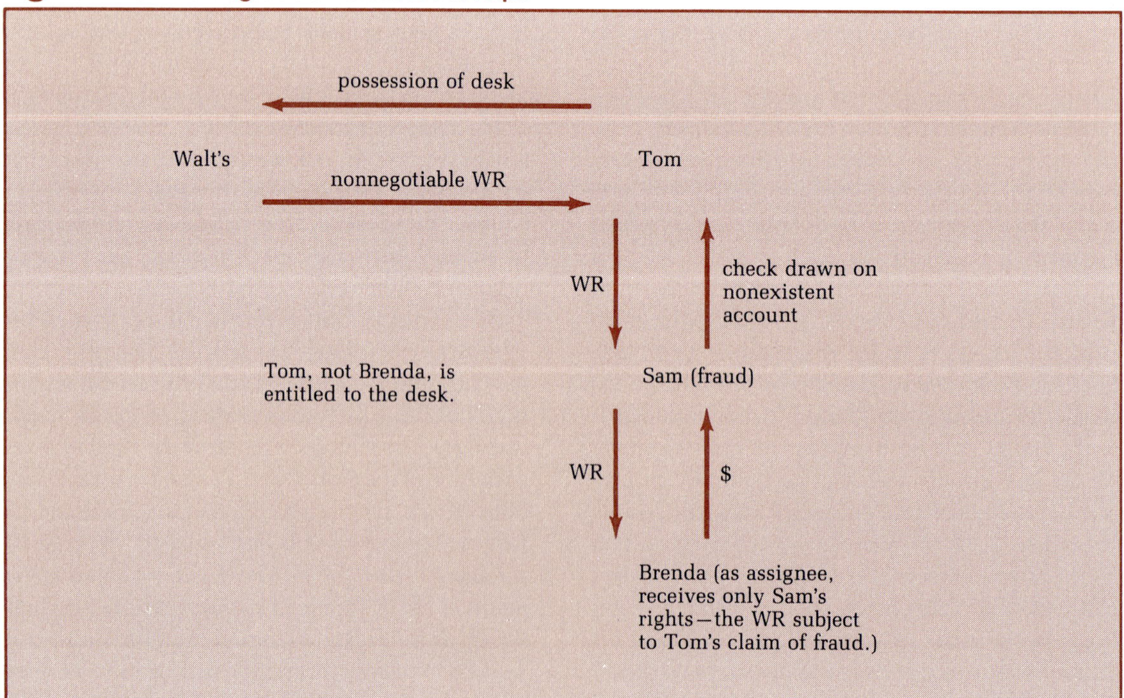

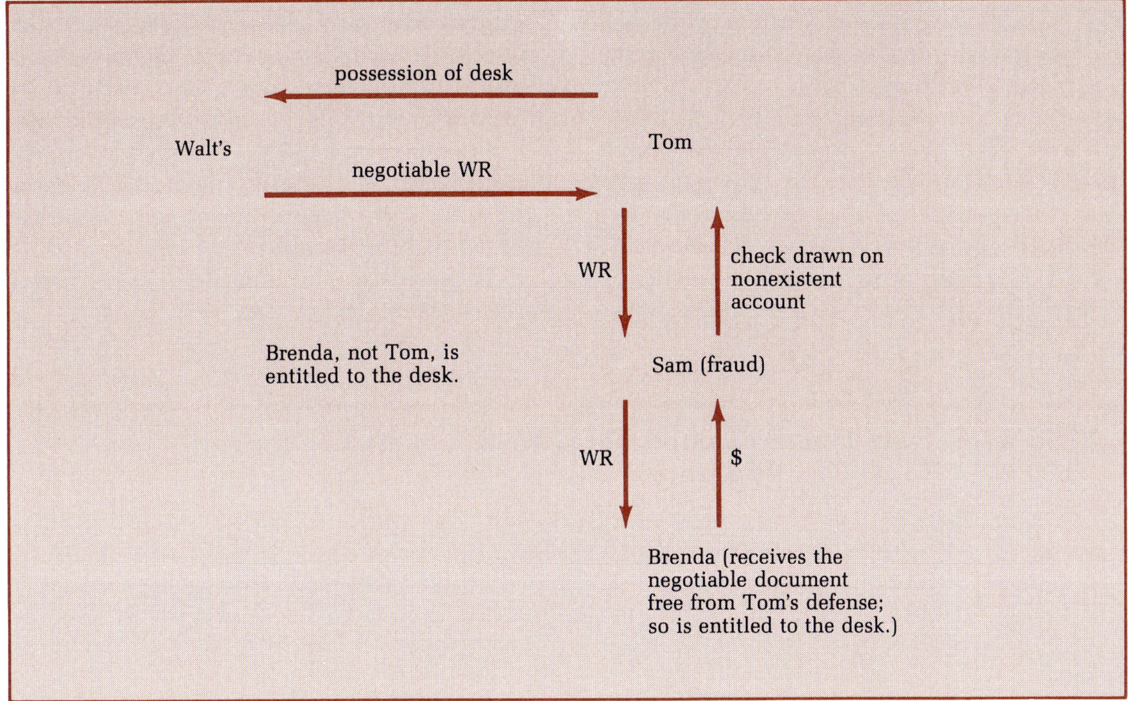

Figure 17.4 Negotiable warehouse receipt.

merely signed on the back by Sam is indorsed "in blank." By indorsing "in blank," Sam converts the order document into a *bearer* document. A *finder* or a *thief* of a bearer document is a *holder* and has the power to transfer it, because the finder or thief appears to be rightfully in possession of the lost or stolen document. If Sam indorses an order document by writing "Deliver to Brenda, (signed) Sam," the indorsement is "special," and Brenda must also indorse before another person can be a holder.

3 The holder must give *value* for the negotiable document, i.e., must *purchase* it. Under Article 7, "value" means any consideration sufficient to support a simple contract. This includes a binding promise to be performed in the future. Thus, executory (not-yet-performed) as well as executed (performed) promises constitute "value" under Article 7.

4 The holder must purchase the document *in good faith* and must be *without notice of any defense or claim* of another person to it. A thief (or finder) of a bearer document is a holder, but she cannot be in good faith (honest) because she knows that she is claiming someone else's property. Furthermore, the thief is on notice of the true owner's claim to the document. However, if a thief is a holder and sells the document to an innocent person, that person can be a good-faith holder who is without notice of the true owner's claim of ownership.

5 The negotiable document must be *negotiated* (transferred by delivery if it is a bearer document, or by delivery and indorsement if it is an order document) *in the regular course of business or financing* and not, for example, by someone who does not reasonably appear to be in the business of trading in goods. Suppose that Joe, a postal employee, finds a bearer document made out for "fifty boxcars of processed uranium" and sells the document to a metals dealer who knows that Joe is a mail carrier. It is not reasonable for the dealer to believe that Joe is the owner of the document. The dealer will be denied the benefits of a due negotiation by anyone (such as the true owner of the uranium) who

can prove that the negotiation by the mail carrier was outside the regular course of the metals-trading business.

What, again, are the benefits of a due negotiation? Essentially, there are two. First, the good faith purchaser receives from the *seller* of the document (a) title to (ownership of) the document and, consequently, the right to sell or to otherwise dispose of it, and (b) title to the goods themselves—both free from many defenses or claims of other persons, for example from a previous owner's defense that the seller acquired the document by means of fraud [7-502]. Second, the good faith purchaser receives, as a result of due negotiation, the direct obligation of the *issuer* (the warehouse or the carrier) to hold or deliver the goods according to the terms of the document.

The buyer's freedom from defenses of previous owners is illustrated by Case 17.2.

CASE 17.2 R. E. Huntley Cotton Co. v. Fields · 21 UCC Rep. 1157 (Tex. Civ. App. 1977)

FACTS Welton Fields and other plaintiff cotton farmers stored cotton at the warehouse of defendant, R. E. Huntley Cotton Co., and received warehouse receipts covering the stored cotton. Then plaintiffs sold 1,765 of the warehouse receipts to Vaughn B. Nowlin, a cotton buyer, who paid for them with checks drawn on First State Bank of Childress, Texas. The checks "bounced" (i.e., were dishonored when presented to the bank for payment). In the meantime, Nowlin sold the warehouse receipts to three cotton companies, also defendants in this case, and soon either sought or was forced into bankruptcy. Immediately, the plaintiffs brought suit seeking return of the warehouse receipts, damages from the bank, and an injunction restraining defendants from removing the cotton from the warehouse. The trial court granted a temporary injunction forbiddingdefendants from selling, encumbering, giving away, or otherwise removing the cotton from Cottle County. The defendants appealed, seeking to have the injunction dissolved.

OPINION ELLIS, C. J. [In seeking to have the injunction dissolved], the defendants... argued that the plaintiffs failed to demonstrate a probable right of recovery in the trial court. A basic question is whether the warehouse receipts were negotiable. If [they] were negotiable and [were] duly negotiated to the defendants, the plaintiffs failed to prove that they had a probable right of recovery, because the defendants would have received title to the cotton.... [I]f the warehouse receipts are negotiable instruments, there is no justification for a temporary injunction....

The... warehouse receipts... stated, "Upon return of this receipt and payment of all charges and liabilities due the undersigned Warehouseman as may be accrued at time of presentation, said One Bale of Cotton will be delivered to the above named depositor or its order, or bearer." The plaintiffs have argued that UCC Section 7-104 demands that a negotiable warehouse receipt be payable either to the order of a named person or to bearer. According to their interpretation, if both "order" language and "bearer" language appears on the face of the document, it is nonnegotiable. We cannot agree. [We believe] that the warehouse receipts the plaintiffs delivered to Vaughn Nowlin were negotiable as bearer documents of title.

A literal reading of Section 7-104(a)(1) seems to approve of warehouse receipts having terms "bearer or the order of a named person." Such a document would be negotiable. The warehouse receipts under consideration here contained exactly the same terms (although the terms are reversed). A literal reading of the statute, therefore, supports the defendants' position that the warehouse receipts were negotiable. Furthermore, while words of negotiability are certainly required, the Code authorizes negotiable warehouse receipts to be in any form.

CASE 17.2 Continued

The plaintiffs take the position that the "order" language in the receipts requires endorsement as a prerequisite to negotiation and that without endorsement the receipts were not duly negotiated. Although Section 7-501(a) states[,] "A negotiable document of title running to the order of a named person is negotiated by his indorsement and delivery," we note that Section 7-501(b)(1) states[,] "A negotiable document of title is also negotiated by delivery alone when by its original terms it runs to bearer." The exact language of the receipts is "to the named depositor or its order, *or bearer.*" (Emphasis added.) Thus, the receipts, by their original terms, run to "bearer," and there is no limitation on the bearer language. In this case none of the plaintiff-farmers endorsed any of their receipts but delivered them without endorsement to the purchaser. This is consistent with the testimony as to the practice in the cotton business whereby warehouse receipts are treated as bearer instruments [which need no endorsement for negotiation].... [W]e hold that the warehouse receipts... were negotiable as bearer paper.

The plaintiffs, however, have argued that even [if] the warehouse receipts were negotiable, they were not "duly negotiated" to the defendants.... At the temporary injunction hearing, no evidence was produced tending to prove that the cotton companies did not pay value for the warehouse receipts, or that the transaction was not in the regular course of business, or that they had actual notice of any claims to the warehouse receipts. Furthermore, there is no evidence that the defendants did not act in good faith. Although the plaintiffs presented some evidence that the defendants had access to information sufficient to put them on notice of claims to the cotton, that knowledge is immaterial unless defendants had actual knowledge of facts and circumstances that would amount to bad faith.... There is no evidence of such actual knowledge, and we have concluded that the plaintiffs failed to prove their probable right to relief....

JUDGMENT For the reasons above stated, the order of the trial court granting the temporary injunction is reversed and judgment [is] rendered that the injunction be dissolved.

Typical Uses of Negotiable and Nonnegotiable Documents. A businessperson needs to know how negotiable and nonnegotiable documents actually work in the physical distribution of goods in order to be able to choose between the two kinds on the basis of his or her business needs. Suppose that Sue, a wholesale seller of groceries, purchases 5,000 cases of canned sardines for resale to supermarkets in Sue's city. Having no storage facilities of her own, Sue deposits the sardines at Walt's Warehouse and is issued a nonnegotiable warehouse receipt (one made out "to Sue"). As a matter of routine recordkeeping, Walt retains a copy of the receipt so that his employees will know that the goods are to be delivered to Sue and to no one else. If Sue instructs Walt to deliver the sardines to her, Walt will do so *without* requiring Sue to surrender the warehouse receipt. To prove that he has delivered the sardines to the person entitled to them (here, Sue), all Walt needs to do is to have Sue "sign" for the goods when she receives them. Sue's signature together with Walt's copy of the warehouse receipt is proof of a proper delivery.

But Sue does not want Walt to deliver the goods to her. She wants to *control* their delivery to the supermarkets for which the sardines are intended. Suppose Bert's Supermarket orders ten cases of sardines from Sue. Sue will write out a "delivery order" instructing Walt to release ten cases of sardines to Bert. Bert will pay Sue for the sardines, take the delivery order to Walt, and receive ten cases of sardines. Walt will require Bert to surrender the delivery order and sign for the ten cases so that Walt will have evidence that Sue gave the instruction and that Walt made a proper delivery. Sue still has the nonnegotiable warehouse receipt and the ability, therefore, to control the delivery of the other 4,990 cases of sardines. Note, incidentally, that a delivery order is itself a document of title, and that Sue, not Walt, is its issuer. A delivery order is an example of a document of title that is "addressed to" a bailee.

Suppose instead that Sue had been issued a *negotiable* warehouse receipt (one made out "to bearer" or "to the order of Sue"). Sue could accomplish a delivery of the ten cases to Bert by means of the negotiable warehouse receipt, but the delivery process would be awkward and slower. The reason is that Sue must *surrender* a negotiable document of title to Walt in order to receive the goods (or to have Bert receive them). Even though Sue wants only a partial delivery of the 5,000 cases (here, ten cases), she still must actually deliver the document to Walt so that he can write on it that ten cases have been delivered. Thus, if Sue should later sell the negotiable document, a holder to whom it is duly negotiated will be on notice that he or she is entitled only to 4,990 cases. Negotiable documents are very suitable for transferring goods as a single unit to one buyer, but they are inefficient for making partial deliveries to many different buyers.

Bailee's Obligations and Liabilities under Document

Regardless of whether a document of title is negotiable or nonnegotiable, the bailee (the warehouse or the carrier) issuing it has certain obligations and liabilities. However, some of these obligations and liabilities do vary according to whether the document is negotiable or nonnegotiable.

Warehouser's Obligation to Keep Goods Separate; Fungible Goods Exception. Ordinarily a bailee has a duty to return to the bailor the specific thing bailed or to dispose of it as the bailor instructs. Since many warehouses are large and very crowded, goods can easily be misplaced, and the warehouser might be unable to make a prompt delivery. To make locating the goods easier and delivery more certain, the law requires that a warehouser keep separate from all other goods those covered by a particular warehouse receipt, unless the receipt provides otherwise [7-207].

There is an important exception for "fungible" goods. Goods are *fungible* if one unit (a bushel of grain, a barrel of oil, etc.) is, by nature or by usage of trade, the equivalent of any other unit of that size. Fungible commodities such as oil of a particular grade often are purchased from many sellers and stored and transported in bulk. Because it would be impractical for a warehouse to keep each lot of fungible goods separate, fungible goods may be "commingled" (mixed or stored in one mass). A mass of commingled fungible goods—e.g., a mass of wheat or corn in a grain elevator—is owned in common by all the persons who contributed to the mass or who have acquired a share in it. The warehouser—e.g., the owner of a grain elevator—is liable to each owner of the mass for that person's share.

Obligation to Deliver to "Person Entitled under Document"; Excuse for Nondelivery. Unless excused by law, a warehouser or a carrier must deliver the goods to the person entitled to them by the terms of the document, and not to someone else [7-403]. Under a *negotiable* document, the "entitled person" is the *holder.* Suppose Sam delivers goods he owns to Carla, a carrier; that Carla issues a negotiable bill of lading to Sam; and that Sam intends to travel to the destination and pick up the goods when they arrive there. The negotiable bill will be made out "to bearer" or "to Sam or order," as Sam chooses. In either event, Sam is the holder as long as he possesses the bill of lading, and Carla must deliver the goods to him if he surrenders the bill and satisfies the bailee's lien (pays the shipping charges owed to the carrier).

Suppose the bill is made out "to bearer" and Sam sells the goods to Ben and delivers the bill to him. Ben is now the holder because he is in possession of a bearer document, and he is entitled to the goods.

May a finder or a thief of a bearer document be entitled to the goods? Suppose Sam loses the bearer document, Joe (a dishonest person) finds it, and before Sam can notify Carla Carrier of the loss, Joe takes the document to her and asks for the goods. Joe is the holder because he is in possession of a bearer document, and he appears to be entitled to the goods. If Carla *in good faith* delivers the goods to Joe, Carla cannot be held liable to Sam [7-404]. Carla is in good faith if, as here, she lacks notice that Joe is not the true owner of the document. Joe's taking delivery will, of course, be wrongful as to Sam, and Sam will have a cause of action against Joe for damages or for the goods themselves.

Who is the holder of an *order* document of title? The answer depends on how the order document is indorsed. Suppose Sam's bill of lading is made out "to Sam or order." Then Sam sells the goods to Ben, indorses the bill "in blank" (i.e., merely signs Sam's name on the back of the bill without naming anyone as indorsee), and delivers the bill to Ben. Ben is the holder because he is in possession of a properly indorsed "order bill" of lading, and he is entitled to the goods.

Since Sam's in-blank indorsement converts the order bill of lading into a *bearer* document, any finder or thief will be a holder. By making a "special" indorsement ("Deliver to Ben, (signed) Sam"), Sam can preserve the order character of the document and thereby make sure that only Ben will be the holder. Because Sam has identified Ben in the indorsement as the person to have the document, only Ben can be its holder, and only Ben is entitled to the goods. Now Ben must indorse the bill before anyone else can become the holder.

Under a *nonnegotiable* document (one issued "to Sam") the "person entitled under the document" is the person named in the bill to receive the goods *or* is someone to whom that person has issued a delivery order. Suppose Carla issues Sam a bill of lading made out "to Sam." Sam is the only person entitled to the goods. However, Sam can issue to Ben a delivery order (or assign the bill) and thereby instruct Carla to make a full or partial delivery to Ben. Ben thus becomes the person entitled to the goods.

In a number of situations the bailee is *excused* for failing to deliver the goods to the person entitled to them by the terms of the document, regardless of whether the document is negotiable or nonnegotiable. Four excuses are illustrated in the following paragraphs:

1 Delivery of the goods to a person with "paramount title," i.e., with superior ownership rights. Sue steals goods from Tom; delivers them to Walt who issues Sue a negotiable warehouse receipt; and sells the goods to Brenda, indorsing and delivering the document to Brenda. In the meantime Tom, the true owner, learns where the goods are and talks Walt into releasing the goods to Tom. Then Brenda, a holder to whom the document was duly negotiated, presents it to Walt, who refuses to deliver any goods to her. Although Brenda is the person entitled *under the document* to receive the goods, Walt has no delivery obligation to Brenda because Walt has delivered the goods to Tom who, because he is the true owner, has paramount title. The result would be the same if Walt, not knowing the situation, had by blind chance delivered the goods to Tom.
2 Damage to or loss of the goods for which the bailee is not liable. A tornado destroys a freight train and all the goods in it. The carrier is not liable because the loss was due to "an act of God," a source of loss beyond even a carrier's liability as an insurer.
3 A valid limitation of the bailee's liability. Carla Freight Lines, a common carrier, imposes a liability limit of $7 per pound for cloth it transports. Without declaring a higher value, Sam ships cloth containing gold thread. The cloth, worth $50 per pound, is ruined due to negligence of Carla's employees. Carla's liability is $7 per pound.
4 Rival claims to the goods. Where two or more persons claim the same goods, the bailee is excused from delivery until the bailee has had a reasonable time to determine which of the rival claims is valid, or to bring a legal action to require the claimants to seek a court determination of their rights.

Liability for Bailee's Nonreceipt or Misdescription of Goods. Suppose that through mistake or fraud a warehouse (or a carrier) issues Sam a document of title without ever receiving the goods from him, or that it issues a document that misdescribes the goods, as where the document says, "5,000 pounds of lobster" but the warehouse (bailee) actually received 5,000 pounds of low-grade shark meat fit only for pet food. Then Sam sells the document to Ben, a good faith purchaser, who knows nothing of the warehouse's nonreceipt or misdescription. The warehouse is liable to Ben for any loss caused by the nonreceipt or misdescription [7-203; 7-301]. Good faith purchasers are protected in these circumstances *without regard* to whether the document is negotiable or nonnegotiable. However, if the document *conspicuously* and *truthfully* indicates that the issuer *does not know* whether the goods were received or whether they conform to the description, the issuer is *not* liable to Ben. If the document says, for example, "contents, condition, and quality unknown," "this package said to contain______," or "shipper's weight, load, and count," Ben is on notice of the nonreceipt or misdescription and should have looked into the situation before buying the document. Thus, the law protects warehouses and carriers who honestly do not know what was received and who give clear notice of that fact.

Liability Where Document Is Lost or Missing. Brenda purchases a properly issued document of title, but then it is lost, stolen, or destroyed. At Brenda's request, a court may order the bailee to deliver the goods to Brenda or to issue her a substitute document. The bailee may comply with the court's order without liability to anyone who might later present the missing document to the bailee and demand the goods [7-601]. If the missing document was negotiable, it might have been in bearer form when lost or stolen. To protect an innocent *purchaser* of a missing negotiable document, Brenda must "post security" (e.g., purchase a type of insurance) to indemnify (compensate) anyone who suffers loss as a result of buying the missing document. If the document was nonnegotiable, the court is permitted but not required to order Brenda to post security.

Conflicting Claims to the Goods

Occasionally, a consignee, transferee, or even a holder to whom a document has been duly negotiated is not entitled to receive the goods and must seek a legal remedy from the transferor or someone else, or absorb the loss. Two examples follow:

Unauthorized Bailment. Even good faith purchasers acquire no rights to goods that have been bailed with a carrier or a warehouse totally without the authority of the true owner [7-503]. Suppose Sue steals goods from Tom, stores them at Walt's Warehouse, and duly negotiates the warehouse receipt to Ben. Because a thief acquires no ownership rights in the stolen goods, Tom has "paramount title" and is entitled to the goods even if they have been delivered to Ben.

Change of Shipping Instructions under Nonnegotiable Bill of Lading. Unless the bill of lading states otherwise, a carrier may, upon receiving proper instructions, deliver the goods to a person or a destination *other than* that stated in the bill [7-303]. For example, a consignor on a nonnegotiable bill of lading is entitled to change the shipping instructions. Suppose Sam contracts to sell a printing press to Ben, delivers it to carrier Carla, and has the nonnegotiable bill made out "to Ben." Then Sam, in breach of his contract with Ben, sells the press to X and instructs Carla to deliver the press to X instead of to Ben. X, if a buyer of the press in the ordinary course of business (i.e., if a good faith purchaser), is entitled to the press, and Ben is left to pursue Sam for a remedy.

Summary

Goods may be transported by common or private carrier. A common carrier serves the public generally and has extensive liability for loss of or damage to the goods. A private carrier may choose with whom to contract and is liable as a bailee only, and not as an insurer.

Often goods are stored in a public or private warehouse. Warehouses are liable as bailees for loss of or damage to the goods during storage.

Documents of title are used to control the movement of goods from sellers to buyers. A document of title is a receipt, a contract of storage or carriage, and evidence of title to the goods. The two major kinds are the warehouse receipt and the bill of lading. Each may be negotiable or nonnegotiable.

Negotiable documents differ from nonnegotiable ones in two main respects: what person is entitled to the goods, and what rights are acquired by a transferee of the document. The transferee of a nonnegotiable document is an assignee and receives only the rights that the transferor had. A holder of a negotiable document can receive more rights than the transferor had, but only if the document has been "duly negotiated" to the holder.

A bailee has obligations and liabilities under a document of title, whether negotiable or nonnegotiable. For example, the bailee is required to deliver the goods described in the document, unless it contains a proper disclaimer of liability for misdescription of the goods. Sometimes the bailee's obligations are excused, as where the bailee delivered the goods to a person with paramount title.

Review Questions

1 How does the liability of a common carrier differ from that of a private carrier for loss of or damage to the goods?

2 To what extent, if any, may a carrier limit its liability for loss of the goods?

3 What liability does a warehouser have for loss of the goods?

4 **(a)** Define "document of title." **(b)** What are its functions? **(c)** Explain the difference between a through bill of lading and a destination bill.

5 **(a)** What language would you use to create a negotiable document of title? A nonnegotiable document? **(b)** What are the two main differences in legal effect between a negotiable and a nonnegotiable document of title?

6 **(a)** What is required for a "due negotiation" of a document of title? **(b)** Explain whether a person who finds or steals a document of title can be its holder. **(c)** Explain whether a person who buys a stolen document can be a person to whom a document has been duly negotiated.

7 **(a)** What are the benefits of a due negotiation? **(b)** Under what circumstances would a nonnegotiable warehouse receipt be preferable to a negotiable one?

8 **(a)** Suppose a carrier releases goods to a person who has stolen the bill of lading. Is the carrier liable to the true owner of the document? Explain. **(b)** An earthquake breaks valuable antique bowls stored in a warehouse. Is the warehouser liable to the bailor? Why or why not?

Case Problems

1 Mitchell stored her household furnishings with All American Van & Storage Co. (Storage). Under the written contract of storage, Mitchell was to pay all storage charges on a monthly basis. Also, Storage could exercise its warehouser's lien by selling Mitchell's goods if the storage charges remained unpaid for 3 months and if, in the opinion of Storage, such action would be necessary to protect its accrued charges. Over the next 8 months Mitchell failed to pay any of the charges. Her unpaid bill totaled $804.30. On October 20, Storage notified her that her goods would be sold on November 7 if she did not pay the charges by October 31. Despite her claim that she was soon to receive a substantial sum of money from the Social Security Administration—a claim substantiated by two attorneys—Storage sold the goods on November 7 for $925.50, an amount insufficient to cover the debt plus costs of sale. Three weeks later Mitchell received a Social Security disability payment of $5,500. Alleging that Storage had breached a duty of good faith by refusing to delay the sale, Mitchell brought suit for damages. The trial court entered summary judgment for Storage, and Mitchell appealed, contending she should have been allowed to go to trial on the question of good faith. Should Mitchell have been allowed to go to trial?

2 Sanfisket, Inc., stored 2,500 pounds of frozen shrimp with Atlantic Cold Storage Corp. Atlantic issued Sanfisket a nonnegotiable warehouse receipt containing a clause limiting Atlantic's liability to 50 cents per pound. Six months later Sanfisket demanded delivery, but Atlantic was unable to locate the shrimp. Alleging conversion, Sanfisket sued Atlantic for $8,000, the market value of the lost shrimp. The trial court held that the evidence permitted a finding of negligence but not conversion, and awarded Sanfisket $1,250, the limit of Atlantic's liability under the warehouse receipt. Sanfisket appealed. The appellate court upheld the trial court on the question of conversion. However, Sanfisket contended that it had not been notified of the clause of limitation, that the clause was not conspicuous, and therefore that Atlantic should be held fully liable for its negligence. Should the clause be enforced under Section 7-204(2) of the UCC?

3 Enroute to Florida, Kinloch and his wife stopped in Mobile, Alabama. While there, Kinloch stored personal property with Teague Brothers Transfer & Storage Co. He received a warehouse receipt from Teague, signed it as bailor of the goods, was listed on the receipt as owner of the goods, and paid the storage fee. A month later Kinloch and his wife separated. Then Mrs. Kinloch took the warehouse receipt to Mobile and requested and received the goods. When Kinloch later demanded delivery, Teague was unable to comply, and Kinloch sued Teague for the value of the goods. Teague contended that its good faith and the wife's possession of the warehouse receipt excused Teague for liability for misdelivery. Was Teague liable to Kinloch for the value of the goods?

4 Crawford sold two carloads of bulk fertilizer to Cunningham, who paid by check. Crawford delivered the fertilizer to M-K-T Railroad and received two nonnegotiable bills of lading. Cunningham promptly resold the fertilizer to Clock. A few days later Cunningham's bank returned Cunningham's check to Crawford for lack of sufficient funds to cover it. The fertilizer was still in transit. Crawford certified to the Railroad that he was the true owner of the fertilizer and reconsigned it to another customer. Having already paid Cunningham for the fertilizer, Clock sued the Railroad and Crawford. Is the Railroad liable to Clock? Is Crawford?

CHAPTER 17

Part Two: Transfer of Title and Risk of Loss; Title of Good Faith Purchasers

Part One of Chapter 17 focused on the physical movement of goods from seller to buyer, on the liability of carriers and warehouses for loss, and on how documents of title are used in the delivery process. This part, Part Two, focuses instead on the contractual relationship between the buyer and the seller and on the rights of third persons to whom the buyer may sell the goods. Here, three questions are of particular concern: (1) When does title to (ownership of) the goods pass from the original seller to the buyer? (2) When does the risk that the goods will be lost or damaged in transit pass from the original seller to the buyer? (3) Where goods are resold by the buyer to a third-person purchaser, under what circumstances does the third person take the goods free from the claims of others such as the original seller?

Transfer of Title and Risk of Loss

Transfer of Title

Accountants use the concept of title (ownership) as the basis for determining entries in the books of their clients. Consequently, the Article 2 title-passage rules are of special significance to accountants whose clients deal in goods. On rare occasions, the parties to a sales contract will themselves want to know precisely when title to the goods passes from seller to buyer. Suppose that a state taxes goods and other personal property owned by its citizens. A citizen of such a state is not required to pay the tax until he or she actually owns the goods, i.e., until title passes. The exact time that a buyer receives title is governed by general rules of title passage contained in Article 2 of the UCC and discussed in the following paragraphs.

When Title Passes from Seller to Buyer. Subject to two limitations, the parties to a sales contract may decide by explicit (clearly stated) agreement when and how title is to "pass" (be transferred) from the seller to the buyer. The limitations are: (1) The seller cannot pass title until the goods have been *identified to the contract.* That is, for title to pass, the goods must exist and must be designated as the ones intended for the particular buyer. (2) Any reservation of "title" by a seller who is extending credit to the buyer is to be considered as nothing more than the reservation of a "security interest" [2-401]. The unpaid seller's keeping such an interest does not prevent the passage to the buyer of basic rights of ownership commonly associated with the word "title."

Where seller and buyer do not state when title is to pass, rules stated in Article 2 apply. Under those rules, if delivery is to be made *by moving the goods,* title passes when and where the seller completes performance with reference to the *physical delivery* of the goods, even though a document of title is to be delivered at a different time and place [2-401]. So, if you order a sofa from a department store and the seller agrees to make a noncarrier delivery to you at your house, you get title to the sofa when the store completes the promised delivery.

But suppose you order a sofa from a manufacturer located in another state. Now the sofa will have to be delivered by a carrier; and the time at which the manufacturer "completes performance with reference to physical delivery" depends on whether you and the seller created a "shipment" or a "destination" contract. If, regarding delivery, the seller agreed merely to see to it that the sofa would be shipped, the seller has entered into a *shipment* contract, and title passes to you when the seller puts the sofa into the custody of the carrier. If, however, the seller specifically agreed to be responsible for actually getting the goods to the destination, the seller has entered into a *destination* contract, and title passes to you when the sofa actually arrives at the destination.

If delivery is to be made *without moving the goods,* other rules apply. Suppose you buy a sofa that the seller has stored in a warehouse in your city, and the seller is to make delivery by means of a document of title (warehouse receipt or delivery order). Title passes when and where the seller delivers the document to you. If no documents are to be delivered, title to identified goods passes at the time and place of contracting, as where you go to a department store, make a contract to purchase a sofa for cash or on credit, and take it home in your own vehicle.

When Title Revests in Seller. Normally a buyer has the right to inspect the goods and to decide whether to accept or reject them. If, as in a shipment contract, the buyer receives title before seeing the goods and later rejects them, title "revests in" (goes back to) the seller regardless of whether the rejection was rightful or wrongful. Once the buyer accepts the goods, however, title will revest in the seller only if the buyer justifiably revokes acceptance—for example, after discovering a hidden defect. These revesting rules are intended to make clear who owns the goods when there is a dispute about their quality.

Transfer of Risk of Loss

Sometimes goods are lost, damaged, or destroyed without the fault of either the buyer or the seller. Yet one or the other will have to absorb the loss or try to collect from the person responsible for the loss, usually a carrier, warehouser, or insurer. The parties to a sales contract may decide for themselves which one is to bear the risk of loss or how it will be shared. Where the parties remain silent as to risk, Article 2 assigns it by means of practical rules that tend to place the risk of loss upon the party (seller or buyer) who is likely to have actual control of the goods, who is likely to insure them as they move through the delivery process, or who is likely to be better able to prevent loss. Risk of loss is *never* assigned on the basis of who had title when the loss occurred, since a person can acquire title (legal ownership) long before learning of danger to the goods or acquiring sufficient control of them to take preventive measures.

The following rules apply where the parties to the sales contract are silent as to risk of loss. Some of the rules apply to situations involving a breach of contract; others apply to situations involving no breach.

Risk of Loss Where There Is No Breach of Contract. The risk-of-loss rules discussed here apply to situations involving goods shipped by carrier, goods held by a bailee, "pickup" and noncarrier delivery of goods, and goods subject to a right of the buyer to return them to the seller.

When goods are to be delivered by *carrier,* the assignment of risk depends on whether the parties have entered into a shipment or a destination contract. In a *shipment* contract, the risk of loss passes from the seller to the buyer when the seller properly delivers the goods to the carrier. In a *destination* contract, the risk passes to the buyer when the goods are presented at the stated destination in such a way as to enable the buyer to take delivery from the carrier [2-509(1)].

In commercial practice, the shipment contract, with its early risk-shifting feature, is considered the normal kind of contract for arranging a carrier delivery. A contract is a *shipment* contract where the buyer and seller agree merely that the goods are to be shipped, without stating that the seller is to be responsible for a safe delivery. For example, Ben telephones Sam the following order: "Please send five barrels of oil by express." Sam puts the barrels in the custody of a carrier. Ben and Sam have created a shipment contract because their words and actions have fallen short of putting the responsibility for a safe delivery on Sam. Sam is justified in feeling no further responsibility for the oil because, having put it in the custody of the carrier, he no longer controls it; his insurance probably no longer covers it; he might already have received payment; *and* he has no indication from Ben that Ben expects Sam rather than the carrier to guarantee the oil's safe arrival. For the less-usual *destination* contract to arise—the kind that imposes risk of loss on the seller for the entire trip—the contract must contain specific language requiring the seller to remain responsible for the goods until they actually reach the buyer: "Please send five barrels of oil by express. I, Ben, will pay for them only upon their safe arrival."

Seller and buyer can specify a shipment or a destination contract in another way, by using standard shipping terms or instructions whose risk-of-loss consequences have been spelled out by Article 2. A St. Paul book manufacturer promises to ship to a New York buyer 300 books "FOB [free on board] St. Paul." Use of this expression creates a shipment contract, and the risk of loss shifts to the New York buyer when the seller puts the books into the possession of the carrier at St. Paul [2-319]. In contrast, a promise by the St. Paul seller to deliver books "FOB New York" would create a destination contract under which "the seller must at his own expense and risk transport the goods to that place and there tender delivery of them." Similarly, "FAS [free alongside a vessel at] the port of shipment" creates a shipment contract; and "FAS the port of destination" creates a destination contract.

The term "CIF" means that the price includes in a lump sum the *cost* of goods and the *insurance* and *freight* to the named destination. The term "C&F," or "CF," means that the price includes the *cost* of the goods and the *freight* charges to the named destination. Despite the word "destination," these terms create a *shipment* contract [2-320]. If a New York buyer says to a St. Paul seller, "Ship 300 books CIF New York," the buyer in effect appoints the seller as an agent for the purchase of insurance and the payment of freight. By performing the CIF delivery obligations, the seller shifts the risk of loss to the buyer upon delivery of the goods to a carrier.

When goods are held by a *bailee* (a warehouse or a carrier) to be delivered *without being moved,* the risk of their loss may be passed from seller to buyer in any of three ways: (1) Risk of loss passes from the seller when the buyer receives a *negotiable* document of title covering the goods. (2) Where the buyer receives a *non*negotiable document of title, risk of loss does not pass to the buyer immediately. A buyer who receives a nonnegotiable document is only an assignee and so takes the goods subject to the rights of others who, for example, might claim the goods as collateral for a loan to the seller. To protect the buyer from claims of third persons, the Code leaves the risk of loss with the seller until the bailee receives notice of the buyer's right to the goods (or until the buyer has had a reasonable time after receiving the document to give the bailee that notice). Upon the bailee's receiving the notice (or upon the passage of the reasonable time), the risk of loss passes from the seller to the buyer. However, the buyer takes the goods *free from* all rival claims to them. Even so, a bailee who knows of a rival claim before receiving notice of the buyer's rights might refuse to honor the document. The bailee's refusal "defeats the [seller's] tender" of the document and thus makes the seller liable to the buyer. (3) Sometimes goods to be sold are stored with a bailee who does not issue a document of title, as where a boat is docked at a marina or a dog is housed in a kennel. Where there is no document of title, risk of loss passes from seller to buyer when the bailee is informed of *and acknowledges* the buyer's right to the goods [2-509(2)].

In *pickup* and *noncarrier deliveries,* the time that risk of loss shifts from seller to buyer depends on whether the seller is a *merchant* or a *nonmerchant.* Suppose that Bob, by telephone, buys a sofa from Sue. The parties are silent about risk of loss, but Sue says, "You may pick up the sofa any morning during the next 3 days." On the morning of the second day, Bob arrives to pick up the sofa only to learn that it was destroyed by fire the preceding night.

If Sue is a *merchant,* the risk is upon Sue, since the risk of loss does not pass from a merchant seller to the buyer until the buyer's *actual receipt* of the goods [2-509(3)]. This rule applies even though the buyer has made full payment and has been notified that the goods are at his or her disposal. The rule also applies where Sue is to make a noncarrier delivery to the buyer's premises. The reason for the rule is that a merchant is likely to have insurance coverage on goods as long as they remain in his or her possession, whereas the buyer is not likely to have insurance on goods not yet possessed.

If Sue is a *nonmerchant* seller, the risk is on Bob. Risk of loss passes from a nonmerchant seller to the buyer upon the seller's *tender* (offer) of delivery. The seller makes a tender of delivery by notifying the buyer that the goods are available to the buyer [2-503(1)]. Thus, where Sue is a nonmerchant, the risk of loss may pass to Bob *before* Bob actually receives the goods.

Case 17.3 involves a merchant seller.

CASE 17.3 Hughes v. Al Green, Inc. · 418 N.E.2d 1355 (Ohio 1981)

FACTS In 1977, Doris Hughes (plaintiff) agreed to purchase a new Lincoln Continental from Al Green, Inc. (defendant), for $12,490. She made a down payment of $1,490, the balance to be financed through a local bank, and signed a purchase contract and an application for a certificate of title. Under the agreement, she was to take immediate possession of the car but would return it to the dealership for completion of new-car preparations and installation of a CB radio. On the way home, Hughes was involved in a collision that damaged the car substantially. The car apparently was not insured against loss. Hughes

CASE 17.3 Continued

was not cited in connection with the accident. The car was towed to the dealership where it remained.

After learning of the accident, the dealership submitted the paperwork to the bank and received an $11,000 check for the balance of the purchase price. The bank forwarded the documents to the clerk of court's office, which issued a certificate of title to the damaged vehicle in Hughes' name. Later, Hughes filed a complaint against Green, alleging that the dealership was liable to her for breach of contract because the vehicle was transferred to her in a damaged condition. The trial court entered judgment for Green. The court of appeals affirmed, and Hughes appealed.

JUDGMENT

SWEENEY, J. . . . Appellant's argument is based upon the Ohio Certificate of Title Act [Title Act] and pre-U.C.C. case law. [The Title Act] provides: "No person acquiring a motor vehicle from the owner . . . , whether such owner is a manufacturer, importer, dealer, or otherwise, shall acquire any right, title, claim, or interest in or to said motor vehicle until such person has had issued to him a certificate of title to said motor vehicle. . . ."

[A]ppellant's argument is that the . . . dealer was in breach of contract because . . . when the certificate of title was issued in appellant's name and ownership of the automobile [was thus] transferred to her, [she] no longer possessed that for which she bargained, i.e., an *undamaged* 1977 Lincoln Continental. . . .

[To resolve this case, we must] determine whether the buyer or the seller bore the risk of loss or damage to the automobile at the time of the collision, for as summarized by White & Summers, . . . : "To say that buyer had the risk of loss at the time the goods were destroyed is to say that he is liable . . . for the price. To say that seller had the risk of loss at the time the goods were destroyed is to say that he is liable in damages to the buyer for nondelivery unless he tenders a performance in replacement for the destroyed goods."

[Section 2-509] provides that in any case where the . . . goods are neither delivered by carrier nor entrusted to a bailee, ". . . the risk of loss passes to the buyer on his receipt of the goods if the seller is a merchant; otherwise the risk passes to the buyer on tender of delivery."

This provision represents a significant shift away from the prior importance of title in determining [when] risk of loss passes from . . . seller to buyer. Under the common law, not only did title to the . . . goods determine risk of loss, but it also determined the issues of the buyer's right to [have] the goods . . . , the seller's right to the purchase price, and the right to proceed against tortfeasors. Under the U.C.C., however, "[e]ach provision of [Article 2] with regard to the rights, obligations, and remedies of the seller, the buyer, purchasers, or other third parties applies irrespective of title to the goods except where the provision refers to such title." . . .

Thus, as noted in Nordstrom, Sales, . . . : "No longer is the question of title of any importance in determining whether a buyer or a seller bears the risk of loss. It is true that the person with title will also (and incidentally) often bear the risk that the goods may be destroyed or lost; *but the seller may have title and the buyer the risk,* or the seller may have the risk and the buyer the title. In short, title is not a relevant consideration in deciding whether the risk has shifted to the buyer." (Emphasis added.)

Similarly, in 3A Bender's Uniform Commercial Code Service . . . , it is stated . . . that § 2-509: ". . . sets forth a contractual approach, as distinguished from the property concept of title, to solving the issues arising when goods are damaged or destroyed. The section focuses on specific acts [of control], such as tender of delivery by the seller, or receipt of the goods . . . by the buyer. Title is relevant under this section only if the parties provide that risk of loss shall depend upon the location of title." . . .

In the instant [case, the buyer] had received possession of the automobile as partial execution of a merchant-seller's obligations under a purchase contract. Thus, unless other statutory provisions make § 2-509 inapplicable, the appellant, as a buyer in receipt of goods identified to a contract, must bear the loss of the car's value resulting from the collision. [It

CASE 17.3 Continued

should be apparent that appellant is thus entitled to any proceeds payable under any insurance policies covering the third-party tortfeasor involved in the collision. (Court's footnote.)]

[Section 2-509] does not conflict with [the Title Act]. [Its] purpose . . . is to prevent the importation of stolen motor vehicles, to protect Ohio bona-fide purchasers against thieves and wrongdoers, and to create an instrument evidencing title to, and ownership of, motor vehicles. . . . The Act was not adopted to clarify contractual rights and duties as was [UCC Article 2].

As stated in *Grogan Chrysler-Plymouth, Inc. v. Gottfried* . . . , "[The Title Act] was intended to apply to litigation where the parties were rival claimants to . . . ownership of the automobile; to contests between the alleged owner and lien claimant; to litigation between the owner holding the valid certificate of title and one holding a stolen, forged or otherwise invalidly issued certificate. . . .

[True, i]n cases decided prior to the adoption of the [UCC, the Title Act] was properly consulted in determining whether a buyer or seller bore the risk of loss or could proceed against third-party tortfeasors because determination of those issues was dependent, under the common law, upon a finding of *ownership*. [However, w]ith ownership no longer being determinative, [the Title Act] is irrelevant to the issue of risk of loss and thus does not conflict with a U.C.C. risk of loss analysis.

It is apparent that allocating the risk of loss to a buyer of goods prior to the point at which legal title is vested in the buyer would be grossly unfair unless the buyer is able to procure insurance to cover such a risk. [But under § 2-501, the buyer obtains a special property and an insurable interest when, as here, the goods are identified to the contract.]

JUDGMENT . . . [T]he judgment of the Court of Appeals is affirmed.

Some sales contracts give the buyer the *right to return the goods to the seller* even though they conform to the contract. There are two kinds of such sales. A seller may find the first kind, the "sale on approval," useful in breaking down the sales resistance of reluctant consumers. Or, a seller who wants to induce a merchant to stock a new product might resort to the second kind, the "sale or return."

A contract that grants a right to return conforming goods might not make clear which of the two kinds of sales was intended. The distinction is necessary for assigning risk of loss. If goods are delivered primarily for the buyer's use, the transaction is a *sale on approval,* and the risk of loss rests on the seller until the buyer accepts (i.e., approves) the goods [2-327]. If the goods are delivered primarily for resale, the transaction is a *sale or return,* and the risk passes from seller to buyer in accordance with the rules that apply to the particular delivery situation involved. Thus, where goods are shipped by carrier, the risk of loss passes from the seller to the buyer either at the point of shipment or at the point of destination, depending on the kind of shipping terms used by the parties. If the buyer returns goods in accordance with the sale-or-return provision of the contract, the return is at the buyer's risk and expense.

Case 17.4 involves not only a risk-of-loss question between buyer and seller, but also a carrier's liability for the loss.

CASE 17.4 Sternheim v. Silver Bell of Roslyn, Inc. · 321 N.Y.S.2d 965 (N.Y. Civ. Ct. 1971)

FACTS Silver Bell, a Long Island jewelry retailer, ordered from Sternheim, a Manhattan-based jewelry wholesaler, an assortment of diamond rings to be exhibited to a customer of Silver

CASE 17.4 Continued

Bell. As instructed by Silver Bell (defendant), Sternheim (plaintiff) delivered five rings to defendant SS & K Jewelry Services, Inc., a jewelry area contract carrier, in a package addressed to Silver Bell. Silver Bell was SS & K's customer, and paid SS & K a uniform weekly fee for transporting all of Silver Bell's packages between it and Manhattan jewelry establishments. The rings, worth $3,700.85, were never delivered to Silver Bell and remain unaccounted for. Sternheim sued Silver Bell and the carrier for the value of the rings, and Silver Bell cross-claimed against the carrier.

OPINION

STECHER, J. SS & K, a bailee, has failed to offer any explanation for the disappearance of the rings and I, accordingly, find it guilty of negligence and liable to [Sternheim] for its loss. SS & K, however, seeks to limit its liability, by contract made part of a receipt, to the sum of $200. Its "receipt" was an acknowledgement stamped on plaintiff's memorandum which clearly expressed that limitation; and a large sign calling attention to this limitation was situated immediately over the counter where SS & K received the package. This evidence was sufficient to sustain the jury's conclusion that a reasonable business man should have been on notice of the limitation. It was acknowledged by the parties (and I find it to be a fact) that SS & K was not a common carrier..., and the contractual limitation will be upheld even though no choice of rates was offered....

The transaction between [Sternheim] and Silver Bell was a "sale or return"...and title remained in the plaintiff.... [However, a]lthough Silver Bell [buyer] had neither title nor actual possession, as between it and the plaintiff, Silver Bell must bear the risk of loss.

[Section 2-327 provides] that in a "Sale on Approval" (delivery for prospective use rather than resale) the risk of loss is the seller's "until acceptance." The section is silent concerning the risk of loss in a "Sale or Return" (except for loss in the process of return). It would thus appear that the intent of the statute is to impose the same risk of loss rule in sale-or-return situations as in other sales.

[The transaction here is a shipment contract under § 2-509, which provides] in part: "(1) Where the contract requires or authorizes the seller to ship the goods by carrier (a) if it does not require him to deliver them at a particular destination, the risk of loss passes to the buyer when the goods are duly delivered to the carrier...."

It thus appears to be the intent of the statute to shift the risk of loss to the purchaser when the seller has done all which is required of him under the contract....The jury found that the rings conformed to the order and that [the contract called for delivery] to be made to [the] carrier....Upon this delivery, [Sternheim's] obligation was discharged and the risk of loss passed to Silver Bell.

Silver Bell, however, cross-claims against the defendant carrier...and indeed, as between them, there is little doubt that SS & K, whose negligence caused the loss, should bear its consequences. SS & K, however, again raises the defense of limitation of liability.

SS & K and Silver Bell stood in the relation of carrier to customer for twelve years, having had numerous transactions between them every week during this period. In each case, SS & K called to Silver Bell's attention, by its receipt, the $200 limitation of liability, and Silver Bell's president acknowledged that at all times material to this litigation he was aware of this attempt by SS & K to limit its liability. On this statement of facts, the jury was justified in finding that "Silver Bell, in directing that delivery of the items be made through SS & K (assented) to [the] limitation...." And although I refused to allow proof of a trade usage...to establish a limitation of liability between SS & K and [Sternheim], it was perfectly proper for the jury, in adjudicating the cross-complaint between the defendants, to consider a twelve-year course of dealing between [them] and [to] read [into their contract] their unrelieved practice of limiting liability....

In the usual course of a sale-or-return transaction, it is the buyer's obligation to pay the price quoted or return the merchandise. Had Silver Bell retained the rings, it would have been obligated to pay the plaintiff's selling price. But liability was not occasioned

CASE 17.4 Continued by a sale or other retention of the merchandise. It was imposed on Silver Bell by the bailee's neglect[,] and damages should [therefore] be assessed as in any breach of bailment: the replacement value . . . $3,700.85.

JUDGMENT Judgment [is] entered in favor of [Sternheim] against [Silver Bell] in the sum of $3,700.85 and against [SS & K] in the sum of $200. . . . On Silver Bell's cross-claim, judgment [is] entered . . . against SS & K for $200. . . .

It is conceivable that SS & K may be required to pay as much as $400 in this action[,] and that is in keeping with this decision. Its obligations to the other parties are separate and distinct[,] and each limitation of liability was by a separate contract. . . .

Risk of Loss Where There Is Breach of Contract. The risk of loss usually falls totally or partially on the party who breaches a sales contract. Suppose a *seller* breaches by delivering defective goods. The risk of their loss remains on the seller until the *seller corrects* (cures) the defects (e.g., by replacing the goods) or until the *buyer accepts* them (takes them as his or her own) in spite of their defects [2-510]. Where the buyer accepts goods, later learns of hidden defects, and then rightfully revokes the acceptance because of the defects, the buyer may *to the extent of any deficiency in his or her effective insurance coverage* treat the risk of loss as having rested on the seller from the beginning.

If the *buyer* breaches the contract before the risk of loss has shifted to the buyer, the seller sometimes may, to the extent of any deficiency in his or her effective insurance coverage, treat the risk of loss as resting on the buyer for a commercially reasonable time before the risk normally would have shifted. Suppose Ben orders 500 radios from Sue for delivery by carrier at the end of 15 days, and Sue immediately *identifies* the 500 radios to be shipped to Ben. Ten days later Ben breaches the contract by canceling the order. Later on the day of the breach, the 500 radios are destroyed by fire, and just before the fire Sue's insurance expired. The risk of loss ordinarily would not pass to Ben until Sue puts the goods into the custody of the carrier for shipment to Ben. This has not occurred yet. However, because Sue *identified the goods to the contract* before Ben breached it, and because Sue had no insurance at the time of loss, the risk of loss is on Ben and Ben must pay for the radios in full. This is a much greater liability than the contract damages Ben would have had to pay if the radios had not been destroyed.

Title of Good Faith Purchasers

As indicated earlier in this chapter, the law protects good faith purchasers of property, including good faith purchasers of goods. A person who buys *stolen* property acquires no rights in it because the thief had none. The true owner may recover the stolen property or its value from the purchaser, who, by claiming it as the purchaser's own, has committed the tort of conversion. But in many other circumstances the purchaser acquires ownership of property despite claims of prior owners.

To be entitled to take goods free from claims of aggrieved prior owners, a person must (1) be a "purchaser," (2) receive the goods in good faith, and (3) give value for the goods [2-403]. *Good faith* means honesty in fact in the transaction. If the purchaser is a merchant, good faith requires, in addition, conformance to reasonable commercial standards of fair dealing in the trade. In the law of sales, as in the law governing documents of title, a person gives *value* by giving any consideration sufficient to support a simple contract. Value, therefore, could consist of an executory (unperformed) promise.

The requirement that the protected person be a "purchaser" can be a source of confusion. In its ordinary sense "purchaser" means a person who buys something, and buying implies the giving of value. But the UCC adopts a broader, technical meaning of "purchaser." Under the UCC, a *purchaser* is a person who takes property by sale, negotiation, mortgage, *gift*, or any other voluntary transaction creating an interest in property. Thus someone who receives a gift is a "purchaser" but is not a purchaser "for value"; consequently he or she may lose the property to an aggrieved prior owner.

In two basic situations, illustrated below, a good faith purchaser *for value* takes the goods free from the claims of prior owners: (1) where the seller acquired a "voidable" title from a prior owner, and (2) where a merchant seller had no title but sold goods that were "entrusted" to him or her.

Where Seller Had Voidable Title

Suppose that Jane, a dealer in new and used garden equipment, fraudulently induced Tom to sell and deliver to her his garden tractor at a ridiculously low price. Tom intentionally transferred the tractor to Jane, but because of her fraud, she received only a voidable title. Consequently, Tom has a right to rescind (avoid, cancel) the contract and to get the tractor back from Jane. However, if Jane had sold the tractor to a good faith purchaser for value, Tom's only recourse would be a lawsuit against Jane for damages, and the purchaser would be entitled to the tractor itself, free from Tom's claim of fraud [2-403]. Thus, Jane, a person with *voidable* title, can confer on a good faith purchaser for value a better title than Jane had.

Where Goods Were Entrusted to Merchant Seller

Suppose Jane's father lent his own tractor to Jane, and without his knowledge she sold it to Bob, one of her customers. Jane's father has "entrusted" his tractor to Jane, a merchant. Any entrusting of goods to a merchant *who deals in goods of that kind* gives the merchant power to transfer all rights *of the entruster* to a "buyer in the ordinary course of business" [2-403]. Such a buyer is similar to a good faith purchaser for value and receives the same kind of protection. Here Bob may keep the tractor even though Jane had no title at all but only possession resulting from the entrustment. Thus, the law puts the risk of an unauthorized sale on the entruster, who is in a better position than the innocent purchaser to prevent loss. (Note that if Jane's father had stolen the entrusted tractor, he would have had no rights in it, and Bob could lose the tractor to the true owner.)

Protection of good faith purchasers is found in many branches of the law besides the law of sales. For example, under Article 3 of the UCC, holders in due course (similar to good faith purchasers) take negotiable notes and checks free from many defenses of issuers. Similar treatment is accorded good faith purchasers of negotiable securities (Article 8); many retail purchasers of goods subject to security interests (Article 9); and holders of "duly negotiated" documents of title (Article 7). Market values are enhanced, and commerce is benefited, if the good faith purchaser's perception of risk is minimized. Reducing that perception of risk requires prior owners to take more care in their transactions, track down wrongdoers, or sometimes absorb loss.

In Case 17.5 the innocent purchaser of a car faces the possibility of losing it to a prior owner.

CASE 17.5 Carlsen v. Rivera · 382 So. 2d 825 (Fla. App. 1980)

FACTS Rivera, doing business in Quebec, Canada, as Empire Auto Leasing, Reg'd., leased a 1976 Mercedes-Benz to James McEnroe, who, Rivera knew, was the owner of an automobile dealership. Later, McEnroe fraudulently obtained title to the car in the name of his agency, Jimmy McEnroe Auto. McEnroe sold the car to Expo Rent-a-Car, Inc., in Fort Lauderdale, Florida. Expo sold the car to Marlin Imports, Inc., which sold it to Carlsen.

Rivera brought an action against Carlsen to recover possession of the car. The trial court held that Rivera leased the car to McEnroe as an individual, that McEnroe stole the car by fraudulently obtaining title, that McEnroe in fact had no title, and that Rivera was therefore entitled to the car or its value together with damages for its wrongful detention. Carlsen appealed.

OPINION HERSEY, J. . . . Initially, it is necessary to determine whether there was an entrustment of the automobile. Both under the Code and under prior case law McEnroe could not

CASE 17.5 Continued

convey good title or even voidable title if he had stolen the automobile. While it is true that McEnroe is said to have stolen the automobile, he acquired possession lawfully by virtue of the lease agreement. He then committed larceny by forging the title documents, and converted the automobile by selling it. . . . He obtained possession lawfully and could therefore convey a voidable title which could be perfected upon a sale to a buyer in the ordinary course of business. The statutes make it very clear that any delivery of possession and any acquiescence in retention of possession constitutes entrustment. . . . [T]his would obviously include a lease agreement.

Having concluded that there was an entrustment, the second question . . . is whether McEnroe was a merchant who deals in goods of that kind.

The record discloses that McEnroe was actively engaged in the business of selling automobiles. The trial court apparently considered the fact that the lease recited McEnroe's home address rather than his business address as conclusively establishing the intention of the lessor to lease the automobile to McEnroe the individual rather than to McEnroe the automobile dealer. Even assuming this was the intention of the parties to that transaction, the statute clearly does not look to intent but to effect. It is undisputed that McEnroe was in the business of selling cars. In our view that is determinative of this issue. The purpose of [Section 2-403(2)] is to protect the buyer in the ordinary course of business and thus to eliminate impediments to the free flow of commerce. . . .

Quite clearly, then, there was an entrustment of the automobile to a merchant who dealt in goods of that kind.

If McEnroe had sold directly to Carlsen for valid consideration and without notice of the defect in title, then Carlsen would prevail as against the interests of the owner/entruster. Should the result be any different because of the existence of intervening sales? We think not. Carlsen purchased the automobile from Marlin Imports, Inc., which was engaged in the business of selling automobiles. Carlsen had no notice of any defect in the title and in fact obtained a title certificate. Under these circumstances, Carlsen was clearly a buyer in the ordinary course of business. In pre-Code language, McEnroe conveyed voidable title to Expo, who conveyed voidable title to Marlin, who conveyed voidable title to Carlsen, a bona fide [good faith] purchaser for value without notice. The Uniform Commercial Code does not change the result. The buyer in the ordinary course of business obtains good title by virtue of [Section 2-403(2)]. . . .

JUDGMENT Reversed and remanded.

Summary

Sometimes a party to a sales contract needs to know when title to the goods passes from seller to buyer. If delivery is to be made by moving the goods, title passes when and where the seller completes the physical delivery of the goods. If delivery is to be made without moving the goods, title passes when and where the seller delivers a document of title or, if no document is involved, at the time of contracting.

Where goods are lost or damaged, someone must bear the loss. The person who bears the risk of loss must either absorb it (perhaps through his or her own insurance coverage) or take the initiative to collect from the person actually responsible for the loss, such as a negligent carrier.

Risk of loss is never assigned on the basis of who had title at the time of loss. Rather, rules of Article 2 assign the loss to either the buyer or the seller, mainly on the basis of who is in the better position to control or to insure the goods. The risk-of-loss rules apply to situations involving goods shipped by carrier, goods held by a bailee, pickup and noncarrier deliveries, and goods subject to a right of the buyer to return them to the seller. Some of the rules apply where there is a breach of the sales contract; others apply to situations involving no breach.

A good faith purchaser for value may take goods free from the claims of prior owners. Such a purchaser gets no rights in stolen goods, but he or she does acquire ownership where the seller had voidable title. Where the purchaser bought goods in the ordinary course of business from a merchant dealer to whom they had been entrusted, the purchaser acquires whatever rights the entruster had.

Review Questions

1 If you contract to buy goods, when do you receive title (ownership)? Why might you need to know?

2 **(a)** What is the basis upon which the law assigns the risk that goods will be lost or damaged during delivery? **(b)** Does risk of loss pass from seller to buyer when the buyer receives title? Explain or illustrate.

3 **(a)** When does risk of loss pass under a shipment contract? When does it pass under a destination contract? **(b)** How do you know whether a contract is a shipment or a destination contract?

4 When does risk of loss pass where the goods are to be delivered without being moved?

5 When does risk of loss pass in a pickup or a noncarrier delivery? Why then?

6 When does risk of loss pass under contracts that give a buyer a right to return the goods?

7 What effect does breach of contract have on passage of risk of loss?

8 In the expression "good faith purchaser for value," why are the words "for value" necessary?

9 Illustrate the two basic situations in which a good faith purchaser for value takes the goods free from the claims of prior owners.

Case Problems

1 Dana Debs, Inc., a dress and suit manufacturer in New York City, received a written order from Lady Rose Stores, Inc., Westbury, Long Island, for the purchase of 288 garments. The order was on Lady Rose's printed form, and it advised Dana Debs to "ship via Stuart, 453 W. 57th St., New York City." Stuart Express Co., Inc., picked up the shipment. Later Stuart wrote Dana Debs that the entire shipment had been lost and that Stuart's limit of liability was $1 per garment, as indicated in the bill of lading. Dana Debs, the seller, then informed Lady Rose Stores of the loss and presented a bill for $1,756.80, the amount of the loss. Lady Rose contended that a destination contract had been created, and that risk of loss therefore could not pass to Lady Rose until Stuart tendered delivery at the destination. Was this a destination contract?

2 Silver ordered custom furniture from Wycombe for delivery to Silver's home. Wycombe informed Silver in writing that the furniture was ready for shipment. Silver paid for it, telling Wycombe to ship one room of furniture but to hold the other until instructed further. Before Wycomb received further instructions, the remaining furniture was destroyed by fire. Wycombe was not at fault. Silver's insurance company paid Silver for the loss and sought reimbursement from Wycombe. Wycombe refused to pay, contending that Silver's instruction to hold the furniture created a bailment, that Wycombe's notice to Silver constituted an acknowledgment of Silver's right to the goods, and that Wycombe had thereby shifted the risk of loss to Silver. Was the insurance company entitled to reimbursement from Wycombe?

3 Mrs. Conway purchased a necklace from Larsen Jewelers on a "layaway plan" under which the seller sets aside the item in question until the full purchase price is paid. Conway paid a total of $265 on the purchase price of $450. Then a burglar broke into the store and stole the necklace from a locked safe. As between Conway and Larsen, who must bear the loss?

4 Klein, a wholesale jeweler, and Lopardo, a retail jeweler, had a longstanding business relationship. Klein would deliver jewels to Lopardo, who would sell them to retail customers and pay Klein the agreed price. If unable to sell the jewels, Lopardo would return them to Klein. Approximately 10 days after Lopardo received two diamonds, they were stolen from his jewelry store. Who should bear the loss?

5 Chyrchel purchased three mobile homes from Southland Mobile Home Corp. The price included installation of facilities. A service crew employed by Southland was to install a new gas range in one of the trailers, hook up electrical and gas lines, and complete similar work. During the installation, Chyrchel smelled gas and asked the crew to check for leaks. A few days later, before the installations were completed, an explosion and fire damaged the trailer and made it uninhabitable. Southland refused to refund the purchase price or to replace the trailer. Alleging breach of contract, Chyrchel sued Southland for damages. Southland defended on the basis that the sale was complete before the fire and that the risk of loss therefore had passed to the buyer. Had the risk of loss passed to Chyrchel?

6 Marcus agreed to buy a Mainship boat from Corrigan's Yacht Yard & Marine Sales, Inc., and delivered his Silverton boat to Corrigan's in part payment, but without delivering the certificate of registration. Later, Corrigan's contracted to sell the Silverton boat to Heiselman. When Corrigan's failed to deliver Marcus's new boat on the date promised, Marcus rescinded the contract and retrieved the Silverton boat from Corrigan's. Heiselman sued Marcus in conversion for damages. Marcus contended that he never lost title to the Silverton boat because title was to transfer only upon receipt of and as payment for the new boat. Was Heiselman entitled to damages?

CHAPTER 18

Product Liability

Of the billions of products sold worldwide each day, a small but significant number are defective. Some defects are the fault of negligent manufacturers or of retailers who negligently prepare goods for sale. But often manufacturers are not at fault. Because individual inspection of mass-produced goods is not feasible, defects may escape detection despite excellent quality control efforts. Occasionally a product is so new and complex that its defects are not readily apparent to the seller or the buyer.

Whatever the degree of fault on the part of sellers, defective products exact a heavy toll of economic loss and personal injury. How this loss should be distributed is of great concern to sellers, injured persons, insurance companies, and foreign and domestic governments. It is also the subject of a collection of legal rules called *product liability law.* That law defines the obligation of sellers to compensate buyers, users, and even bystanders for loss or injuries caused by defective products.

Product liability losses are of two basic kinds: direct and indirect (consequential). *Direct loss* consists of the decreased value of the goods themselves as a result of a defect. This kind of loss is compensated for by an award of *direct* or *general damages*—e.g., the cost of replacing or repairing the defective goods. *Indirect losses* are those caused by defective goods, in addition to the decreased value of the goods themselves—e.g., personal injuries, damage to the property of others, or business interruption caused by the defective product. This kind of loss is compensated for by an award of *consequential damages.* An illustration follows:

Ben, a commercial vegetable gardener, purchases a new garden tractor from Sue for $3,000 cash. Because of a manufacturing defect, the engine explodes without warning the second time Ben uses the tractor, injuring Ben and a neighbor passing by on the sidewalk, and causing a fire that destroys the tractor and the neighbor's house. As indicated in Chapter 19, Ben may revoke his acceptance of the tractor and recover the purchase price from Sue. If Sue is solvent, Ben is thus protected from the loss of the tractor itself. But what if Sue is insolvent? May Ben recover the value of the tractor from the manufacturer? Perhaps more important to Ben and his neighbor, whom, if anyone, may they hold liable for the consequential losses—the personal injuries to themselves and the loss of the neighbor's house? These losses are substantial and may be far beyond Sue's ability to pay. Under the modern law of product liability, both Sue *and* the manufacturer (among others) might be liable for the losses.

Product liability law is a good example of how law evolves in response to changing social conditions. Centuries ago, goods produced for sale were relatively simple products, and buyers usually purchased them directly from the makers. Buyers were expected to examine the goods and to judge for themselves whether the goods were free from defects and fit for the buyers' purposes—caveat emptor, "Let the buyer beware." Under the law of that era, a person injured by a defective product could not maintain an action for damages unless he or she was "in privity of contract" (had a direct contractual relationship) with the seller, and then only if the seller had expressly guaranteed the quality of the goods. If purchases were made directly from the maker, as was usual, the buyer would be in privity of contract with the maker. If the buyer purchased an article from someone other than the maker, the buyer had no right of action against the manufacturer.

Then, during the mid-1700s came the industrial revolution. Machinery and power tools replaced hand tools. Large-scale industrial production led to mass advertising and to complicated systems for distributing huge amounts of goods. Increasingly, goods were distributed in packaged form by "middlemen" who knew little about their quality. Products became vastly more complicated and dangerous. No longer could purchasers easily inspect the goods and judge for themselves the merits of what they had bought. A seller's "puffery" (exaggerations used to make a sale) became dangerous because purchasers of unfamiliar products were no longer able to question the manufacturer personally or to recognize false statements if made. As industry developed, the doctrine of caveat emptor and the privity requirement made less and less sense.

Despite increased danger to the public from defective products, the courts were slow to discard the privity-of-contract requirement. In keeping with the laissez-faire philosophy of the nineteenth century, the courts were reluctant to impose liability on a seller with whom an injured person had not contracted. Moreover, there was strong sentiment among the courts and legislatures for protecting industry from liabilities that might impede its growth. As the use of middlemen increased, the privity requirement became a substantial barrier to the recovery of damages by injured consumers. Their contracts normally would be with retailers, not with manufacturers, and without privity of contract there could be no recovery of damages from the manufacturers who had produced the defective goods. In Figure 18.1, B (buyer) is in privity of contract with R (retailer), but not with W (wholesaler) or M (manufacturer).

In the early 1900s, the courts began to discard the privity-of-contract requirement. In the leading case of *MacPherson v. Buick Motor Co.*, Justice Cardozo stated the principle that the manufacturer of a product had a duty to make the product carefully and that this duty would be owed even to users other than the purchaser; i.e., an injured person could have a cause of action against the manufacturer for negligence even though there was no contract between that person and the manufacturer.[1]

[1] 111 N.E. 1050 (N.Y. 1916). MacPherson had purchased a Buick from a retail dealer and was injured when a defective wooden wheel collapsed. MacPherson sued Buick Motor Co., alleging negligent failure to inspect the wheel. A judgment for MacPherson was affirmed by the New York Court of Appeals.

Figure 18.1 Privity of contract.

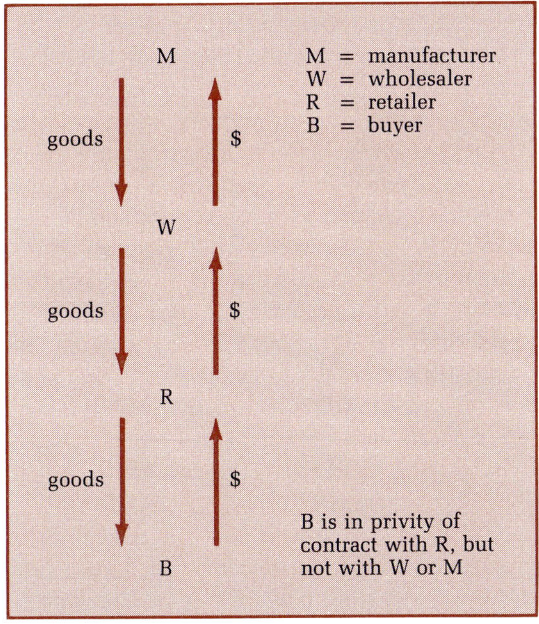

During recent decades, court decisions (like *MacPherson*) and legislation (especially the Uniform Commercial Code) have made dramatic changes in the law with respect to who should bear the cost of injury resulting from the use of defective products. The law has developed a number of theories of "product liability" that shift the burden of loss from the injured buyer, user, or bystander to the manufacturer, the wholesaler, or the retailer; and the privity requirement has been virtually abandoned. The most common causes of action available to the injured person are based on negligence, warranty, or "strict liability in tort." Frequently, the plaintiff alleges all three in the same complaint. If one cause of action does not fit the situation, the plaintiff might succeed with another.

The first part of this chapter is devoted to a brief discussion of negligence as a basis of product liability. The last two parts are devoted to warranties and strict liability as bases of product liability.

Negligence as a Basis of Product Liability

Elements of Negligence

A defendant is liable in negligence if the plaintiff proves four traditional elements of negligence:

1. A duty of care on the part of the defendant. The duty arises where the defendant should foresee a risk of harm to others from the defendant's conduct.
2. A failure of the defendant to exercise due care, i.e., a failure to act reasonably in light of the foreseeable risk of harm to others.
3. A reasonably close causal connection between the failure to exercise due care and the resulting injury.
4. Actual loss to the plaintiff. In negligence and other product liability cases, the defendant is usually a manufacturer, a distributor, or some other supplier of goods.

The courts have developed a number of tests for determining when a duty of care arises. A manufacturer producing "inherently dangerous" goods, such as explosives or poisons, has a duty to foresee possible dangers of various kinds and to take reasonable measures to prevent harm. Under the *MacPherson* decision a duty of care arises where a thing, if negligently made, may reasonably be expected to cause injury. Under other decisions, a duty of care arises if the goods are to be directly consumed, if the manufacturer can anticipate danger from the normal use of a product, or if the manufacturer can anticipate danger from the use that actually occurred. Under the latter two tests, a manufacturer of a caustic drain cleaner could be liable for failing to explain how to use the cleaning material safely, or for failing to provide a safety cap for the protection of children playing with the can. Retailers and other suppliers of goods have duties of care that correspond with the degree of danger they should foresee in their capacities as retailers or other suppliers.

Negligent conduct takes a variety of forms. Liability has been found for negligent design of a product; for negligent inspection or assembly of parts; for negligent inspection of a finished product; for negligent testing of a product before, during, or after production; and for negligent packaging. Other typical forms of negligence are failure to give adequate instructions for the use of a product, failure to warn of known dangers, and representations made negligently as to the effectiveness of a product.

Limited Usefulness of Negligence in Suits by Injured Plaintiffs

From the injured plaintiff's point of view, negligence as a theory of product liability may be useless in some situations. The plaintiff must prove that the defendant acted negligently. How could Bob Buyer prove that the defect in the garden tractor was the fault of the manufacturer? Acquiring proof of negligent design or of a negligent manufacturing process may require examination of the defendant's manufacturing facilities and processes. The defendant may be reluctant to provide the necessary information, and compelling the provision of such information or otherwise acquiring it, if possible at all, can be costly.

Sometimes the required causal connection between a particular defendant and the plaintiff's injury cannot be proved. Establishing that a soft drink bottle exploded and injured a shopper does not constitute proof that any act of the bottle manufacturer caused the bottle to explode. The injury-causing condition might have occurred while the bottle was in the custody of the wholesaler or the retailer. In a proper case, the doctrine of *res ipsa loquitur* ("the thing speaks for itself") may place upon a defendant the burden of proving that he or she was *not* negligent. However, the doctrine is not universally available. Where it is available, the plaintiff must show (1) that the thing causing injury was in the defendant's exclusive control at the time of the alleged negligent act, and (2) that the accident was one that ordinarily does not happen in the absence of negligence. Suppose an airliner crashes on a clear, calm day. A court might be persuaded to apply the doctrine of *res ipsa loquitur* on the theory that the plane and its maintenance were in the exclusive control of the airline, and that commercial airline crashes normally do not occur in the absence of negligence by airline employees. If *res ipsa loquitur* applies, the defendant is presumed negligent and must carry the burden of proving it was not negligent.

Plaintiffs in negligence cases face another difficulty. They must deal with a variety of defenses commonly raised by defendants. These include contributory negligence, comparative negligence, and assumption of the risk. *Contributory negligence* occurs where the plaintiff's own negligence in using the product contributes to his or her own injury, as where the instructions for using caustic drain cleaner are vague, but contrary to instructions that are given, the plaintiff causes an explosion by using five times the recommended amount in hot water. In its strictest applications, contributory negligence bars the plaintiff from any recovery of damages. Under the doctrine of *comparative negligence,* the plaintiff's own negligence is taken into account in determining how much damages the plaintiff may recover; the award to the plaintiff is reduced in proportion to the percentage of harm that is attributable to her or his negligence. Under the doctrine of *assumption of risk,* a plaintiff who knowingly and voluntarily confronts an obvious danger ordinarily may not recover damages for any resulting injury. Using a new but obviously frayed rope for mountain climbing in a nonemergency situation would constitute assumption of risk.

To avoid the defenses and the difficulties of proof that may be involved in a negligence suit, the law now permits a plaintiff to base product liability on theories other than negligence.

Warranties as a Basis of Product Liability

Much of the law of warranty is found in Article 2 of the UCC and in the federal Magnuson-Moss Warranty Act. The warranty provisions of Article 2 are limited by their terms to sales of goods, but have been applied "by analogy" to some transactions other than sales, such as leases of goods. The warranty provisions of Article 2A apply directly to leases of goods and are nearly identical to those of Article 2. As noted later in this chapter, the Magnuson-Moss Warranty Act applies only to sales of "consumer products," and with regard to such sales, the Act supersedes some provisions of the UCC.

Originally, the term "warranty" meant a promise or an agreement by the seller that (1) the thing sold had a certain level of quality, or (2) the seller had title to the thing and could confer ownership upon the buyer. Today, under the UCC, warranties created by the seller's promises (or *other* "affirmations" of fact) are called "express warranties." Article 2 of the UCC recognizes express warranties of title and express warranties of quality.

After the industrial revolution, courts began to impose warranty obligations upon the seller where, for example, the seller was *silent* about whether he or she intended to make a warranty. Warranties that are imposed by law are called "implied warranties." Under Article 2, a seller can be subject to implied warranties of quality (1) where the seller says nothing about warranties, or (2) where the seller attempts to exclude implied warranties but fails to use properly the methods of exclusion required by the Code. Implied warranties are *in addition* to any express warranty that the seller might have made. Article 2 also imposes a warranty of title on most sellers who are silent about what ownership rights the buyer is to receive; but for the reason stated later in this chapter, this nonverbal title warranty is not classified as an implied warranty.

The main function of a warranty is to establish the characteristics of a thing (the kind of ownership or the level of quality) to which the purchaser or another person is entitled as a result of the existence of the warranty. In a sale of goods, a warranty may be the only practical source of remedy for loss due to a defect in the title to or the quality of the goods. A plaintiff is entitled to damages upon proof that (1) a warranty was made (or imposed by law), (2) the product does not conform to the standard of title or of quality established by the warranty, and (3) the plaintiff suffered harm as a result of the breach of the warranty.

This part of this chapter discusses two overlapping bodies of warranty law: Article 2 of the UCC (state law), and the Magnuson-Moss Warranty Act (federal law). These bodies of warranty law are overlapping because although the federal Warranty Act applies to sales of "consumer products" and nullifies some warranty provisions of Article 2, the Warranty Act provides that other UCC warranty provisions continue to apply to sales of consumer products.

In the following discussion of UCC title and quality warranties, special attention is given to how warranties are made; what kind of ownership or level of quality is established by a warranty; how a seller may exclude warranties; and who, besides the buyer, is protected if a warranty is made.

UCC Warranties of Title

Nature and Scope of Title Warranties. If a seller says to a buyer, "I own these goods free and clear," the seller has made an express warranty of title [2-313]. But usually the parties to a sale are silent as to title. If the parties are silent, the Code imposes upon the seller a warranty that: (1) the title conveyed shall be good and its transfer rightful; and (2) the goods shall be delivered free from any security interest or other lien of which the buyer at the time of contracting has no actual knowledge [2-312].

Sometimes goods are manufactured and sold in violation of trademark or patent rights. To protect the buyer, the Code imposes upon a *merchant* seller *regularly dealing in goods of the kind* a warranty that the goods do not infringe upon the trademark or patent of any third person. However, if a buyer furnishes specifications for goods to be assembled, prepared, or manufactured by the seller, the buyer is responsible for avoiding infringement, unless the buyer and the seller have agreed to the contrary.

Exclusion or Modification of Title Warranties. Sometimes goods are sold "as is" or "with all faults." Section 2-316(3) permits sellers to disclaim "all implied warranties" by the use of such expressions. Are these expressions sufficient to exclude the nonverbal warranty of good title, rightful transfer, and freedom from liens? The answer is no. A person who buys something "as is" may be willing to take his or her chances as to the quality of the thing, but the buyer still expects to become the owner. To protect the buyer from an unexpected exclusion of the nonverbal warranty of title, Article 2 *limits the meaning of implied warranty to "implied warranty of quality."*

The nonverbal warranty of good title may be excluded or modified *only* by specific language or by circumstances that give the buyer reason to know that the seller does not have or claim ownership [2-312]. The "specific language" requirement could be met by the seller's statement that the seller does not warrant title, or that the seller warrants title only to a limited extent. However, the buyer is expected to recognize the fact that in certain circumstances sellers do not warrant title. For example, sales by sheriffs, executors, and foreclosing lienors are so out of the ordinary commercial course that their peculiar character is immediately apparent to the buyer. No warranty obligation is imposed upon such a seller.

UCC Warranties of Quality

A warranty of quality establishes a level of quality to which goods must conform if the seller is to avoid liability for breach of warranty. The level of quality established by an express warranty is determined by the seller's statements or other representations. The level of quality established by an implied warranty is measured by the concept of "merchantability" or of "fitness for a particular purpose."

The Code permits a seller to disclaim all implied warranties or, if the seller wishes, to substitute for an implied warranty a less burdensome express warranty. Yet the nature of the marketing process, certain features of the Code, the Magnuson-Moss Warranty Act, and the growing tendency of courts to resolve warranty doubts in favor of consumers limit the opportunities for a seller to escape warranty liability altogether.

Express Warranties of Quality. A seller may refrain from making express warranties, but express warranties can arise in ways that the seller might not anticipate. Under Section 2-313, *any affirmation of fact or promise made by the seller to the buyer which relates to the goods and becomes part of the basis of the bargain* creates an express warranty. Any seller who advertises goods is subject to having the advertising claims construed as factual, and some courts have held that a retail seller has adopted the statements made by the manufacturer, even though the retailer personally has said nothing concerning the goods.

Furthermore, under the Code an express warranty can arise without the use of words. *Any* description of the goods, including drawings and sketches, or *any sample or model* "which is made part of the basis of the bargain" creates an express warranty that the goods will conform to the description, sample, or model [2-313]. As long as businesspeople make normal use of advertising, models, samples, and diagrams, express warranties are likely to be made.

An express warranty must rest on some statement or other affirmation of *fact,* not on mere opinion or "sales puffing" of the seller. Despite the strong movement away from caveat emptor, the buyer is expected to detect and discount such nonfactual sales talk as "this is the finest stereo on the market." Statements made by sellers may range from those that are clearly opinion to those that are clearly fact. In the middle are statements that a court may have to interpret as either fact or opinion. The background against which a statement is made becomes important in interpreting it. Thus, a former garage mechanic who sold a used car to a nurse was held to have made an express warranty when he stated, "This is a car I can recommend. . . . It is in A-1 shape."[2]

Under the Code's "basis of the bargain" test, postsale talk may, and often does, create an express warranty. Even though an affirmation is made after a contract has been entered into, the affirmation may create expectations that the product will do what the seller promised. For instance, a person who buys a packaged product and later reads descriptive information contained within the carton may be led to make a use of the product that he or she would not have made if the seller had remained silent. The statement should be regarded as an indicator of quality level and as an aspect of the bar-

[2] *Wat Henry Pontiac Co. v. Bradley,* 210 P.2d 348 (Okla. 1949).

gain. Moreover, under the "basis of the bargain" test, assurances given when the goods are delivered and advertisements that are read after the sale could create express warranties.

Implied Warranties of Quality. Unless warranties are properly excluded, the Code imposes an implied warranty of merchantability, or an implied warranty of fitness for a particular purpose, or both. The warranties differ with regard to who makes them, how they are made, what quality level is established by each, and how they may be excluded.

Implied warranty of merchantability. A warranty that the goods shall be merchantable (fit for their *ordinary* purposes) is implied in a contract for their sale if the seller is a *merchant* with respect to goods of that kind [2-314]. A seller is a merchant if he or she deals in goods of the kind sold or gives the appearance of having knowledge of the goods. Normally, a person making an isolated sale of goods is not a merchant and therefore is not subject to the implied warranty of merchantability. However, the nonmerchant seller of goods is required by the good faith provision of the Code to disclose any material hidden defects of which he or she has knowledge.

To be merchantable, goods must meet the minimum standards of merchantability set by the Code. Fungible goods must be of fair, average quality within the description. All goods must pass without objection in the trade under the contract description; be fit for the ordinary purposes for which such goods are used; run of even kind, quality, and quantity within each unit and among all units; be adequately contained, packaged, and labeled as the sales agreement may require; and conform to the promises or affirmations of fact made on the container or label, if any [2-314(2)].

Other attributes of merchantability may arise by usage of trade or through the development of case law. Goods usually are not "fit" for their ordinary purposes unless they can be used safely. The degree of safety required for a product to be considered merchantable is developed in the case law. Some courts hold that goods may be fit for their ordinary purposes even though a few persons suffer allergic reactions or other isolated injuries not common to ordinary people.[3] The warranty of merchantability is not breached unless the goods fall below the required level of quality.

Implied warranty of fitness for a particular purpose. A warranty of fitness for a particular (special) purpose is implied where, at the time of contracting, three circumstances exist: (1) the seller has reason to know any particular purpose for which the goods are required, (2) the seller has reason to know that the buyer is relying on the seller's skill or judgment to select or furnish suitable goods, and (3) the buyer actually relies on the seller's skill or judgment [2-315]. Carl Customer tells the owner of a sporting goods store that he, Carl, will soon go on his first mountain-climbing expedition and needs some good climbing shoes. The owner says nothing but produces a pair of climbing shoes that Carl quickly examines and buys. The seller has made an implied warranty of fitness for a particular purpose. She knows the particular purpose for which Carl needs the shoes. Since she knows that Carl is a novice climber, she also has reason to know that Carl is relying on her to supply shoes that are suitable for that purpose. (The fitness warranty would be express if the owner had said, "These shoes are just what you are looking for.") The situation would be different if the owner had sold climbing shoes to "Cleats" Morton, a professional mountain climber with whom she had dealt many times before and who had always made his own choice of shoes, usually disregarding her advice. The seller would have no reason to believe that Cleats relied on her judgment. Therefore, an element necessary for an implied warranty of fitness to arise would be missing. Merchants and nonmerchants alike can be subject to an implied warranty of fitness.

An increasing number of judges hold that advertising can contribute to the existence of an implied warranty of fitness. A seller who advertises his or her product expects to persuade buyers that the product is suitable for a certain purpose or purposes. Many sellers also expect to create "brand loyalty" by convincing the buyer that the seller's product is superior to the products of competitors. Sellers who engage in brand-loyalty advertising may well have reason to know of the buyer's particular purpose and of the buyer's reliance on the seller to provide suitable goods. The warranty could be implied even though the seller never meets the buyer.

Under an implied warranty of fitness, the goods are defective if not fit for the particular purpose for

[3] *Robbins v. Alberto-Culver Co.*, 499 P.2d 1080 (Kan. 1972).

which they were furnished. But how is the minimum level of fitness for a particular purpose to be defined? Is a lotion unfit if one user out of millions is allergic to ordinarily safe ingredients? The difficult question, as yet unresolved, is how much harm is tolerable, given the general utility of a product. Most courts hold that a product is fit if it is safe for use by "normal" people. This approach works well enough when the number of unusually sensitive users is very small and their injuries are slight. If injury is widespread or severe, the court could find a breach of the warranty of fitness, find the seller negligent (e.g., for failure to provide conspicuous warnings), or impose strict liability. The problem of defining the minimum level of quality exists also with regard to the warranty of merchantability.

Case 18.1 discusses whether express and implied warranties were present in a contract to replace a roof.

CASE 18.1 Mennonite Deaconess Home & Hospital, Inc. v. Gates Engineering Co. · 363 N.W.2d 155 (Neb. 1985)

FACTS The Beatrice Community Hospital (hospital), owned by Mennonite Deaconess Home and Hospital, Inc. (plaintiff), discovered leaks in the roof over the geriatrics wing. After unsuccessful attempts to repair the roof, the hospital decided to replace it. One possibility was to replace it with a flat, layered roof of the type originally installed. Another option, the one chosen by the hospital, was a one-ply roofing system consisting of a rubber-like material attached to the outside perimeter of the building and rubber sheeting laid loose across the roof, sealed at the overlaps, and weighted down with rock ballast.

Hospital authorities met with Leonard Russell, an agent of Gates Engineering Co. (defendant), which manufactured a single-ply roofing system, and David Nece, president of Armstrong Construction Co., which was to install it. Russell said, "I came along with Mr. Nece to show and explain the Gates single-ply system." Russell also provided brochures describing the roofing system. One read in part, "WARRANTY PROVISIONS: Gates Engineering provides single source responsibility for roofing and flashing with each roofing system. Whether roofing new construction or re-roofing on existing structure, each GACOFLEX system requires consideration and approval by Gates' technical staff and installation by a registered system roofing contractor. Under these conditions a 10-year roof warranty is available." Gates's prior approval was required for a contractor to be a registered System I roofing contractor. A second brochure stated in part, "Each installation is carefully considered and approved by Gates's technical staff and installed by a Registered System I Roofing Contractor."

The hospital contracted with Armstrong and Gates for installation of the Gates roofing system and a 10-year warranty. Then representatives of all three inspected some roof projections and an expansion joint about which the hospital was concerned. The hospital was assured that the Gates system would handle the problem.

During installation, a field representative of Gates was present on the job for about two-thirds of the time. Later, Gates refused to issue the warranty because of numerous errors that Armstrong made in installing the roof. Soon after the Gates inspection, the roof began leaking. Gates and Armstrong refused to make repairs, and the hospital eventually replaced the entire roof with a system from another company. The hospital learned about a year after the installation of the Gates system that Armstrong had never been registered by Gates and had never installed a one-ply roof before. The hospital sued Gates for breach of express and implied warranties of the Gates roofing system. From a jury verdict for the hospital, Gates appealed.

OPINION KRIVOSHA, C. J. . . . [We first] turn to the question of whether the transaction upon which suit was brought was a "sale of goods" within the meaning of the Uniform Commercial Code or, rather, was a contract for the rendering of "services." If the transaction

CASE 18.1 Continued

was really a contract for services and not a sale of goods, the provisions of [Article 2 of the Code] do not apply.... The cases are uniform in holding that the U.C.C. applies where the principal purpose of the contract is the sale of goods, even though in order for the goods to be utilized, some installation is required....

We agree... with the following statement in *Bonebrake v. Cox*...:

> The test for inclusion or exclusion is not whether (goods and services) are mixed, but, granting that they are mixed, whether their predominant... purpose, reasonably stated, is the rendition of service, with goods incidentally involved (e.g., contract with artist for painting) or is a transaction of sale, with labor incidentally involved (e.g., insulation of a water heater in a bathroom)....

We believe that an examination of the contract, the brochures, and the evidence adduced at trial [make clear] that this contract had as its predominant factor the roofing material manufactured by Gates and only incidentally involved installation by a contractor approved by Gates. The evidence establishes that the hospital was not simply purchasing a new roof of any type or description. Quite to the contrary,... the hospital determined, after careful consideration, to use the one-ply system specifically manufactured and supplied by Gates. The contract specifically identified the type of roof to be installed and further identified it in such a manner that nothing other than the Gates material could be used. It is clear to us that what was being purchased here was a completed roof of the type manufactured by Gates, though installed by others approved by Gates.... [T]he provisions of the [U.C.C.] apply....

Gates agrees that an express warranty may be created in an advertising brochure, but argues that before such warranty may arise, the language in the brochure must evidence a clear intent to create the warranty. Gates then argues that because it was merely selling the roofing material, exclusive of installation, and that because the parties agree that the failure of the roof was the result of poor installation and not defective material, there is insufficient evidence in the record to sustain the verdict of the jury. We believe... [that] Gates simply misconstrues the nature of the transaction. The hospital was not contracting for the purchase and installation of any [common] roof. It was, in fact, purchasing a "roofing system," designed, manufactured, and supplied by Gates and installed by persons approved by Gates under its supervision....

...Gates attempted to explain away the language of the brochures by maintaining that the statements contained in [them] were the things that an architect or contractor was responsible to perform if a good job was to be accomplished and if the warranty was to be issued. The evidence simply does not support that view....

The evidence [revealed] that statements made by the Gates representative at the initial meeting were intended to be relied upon by the hospital. One of those statements was that before Armstrong would be permitted to install the roof, it would have to be a registered System I applicator.... [Another was that] the roof would be installed by a registered System I roofing contractor... in a manner conducive to good workmanship.... Further, the hospital was assured that someone from Gates would be on the roof during installation. Obviously, the point of having a representative of Gates on the roof during installation was... to ensure that the material was installed correctly. Yet, notwithstanding the presence of that representative, the record discloses that the installation was defective.... All of these statements constituted affirmations of fact or promises which constituted express warranties, breached by Gates....

We [now] turn to the question of whether there was a breach of [the] implied warranties... of merchantability [and] fitness [provided for in the Code]....

Once again, Gates argues that... the material itself was not defective and, in fact, the damage which resulted was caused by the defective installation and not by the condition of the goods.... [However, the] hospital was not purchasing raw material. It was purchasing a roofing system which was partially dependent upon proper installation....

CASE 18.1 Continued

To establish a breach of [the] implied warranty of merchantability, there must be proof that there was a deviation from the standard of merchantability at the time of sale and that such deviation caused the plaintiff's injury.... In order for the goods to be merchantable under § 2-314, they must be at least such as are fit for the ordinary purposes for which such goods are used.... The record is without dispute that Gates was to provide the hospital with a one-ply System I roof which would not leak when installed. That, they did not do. This, then, was evidence of a breach of [the warranty of merchantability].

The conditions under which a breach of [the] implied warranty of fitness exist[s] are also present in this case.... [T]o recover for a breach of an implied warranty of fitness, the purchaser must prove that (1) the seller had reason to know of the buyer's particular purpose, (2) the seller had reason to know that the buyer was relying on the seller's skill or judgment to furnish appropriate goods, and (3) the buyer... relied upon the seller's skill or judgment....

Once again, we believe that the evidence was sufficient to permit a jury to find... the necessary elements. Certainly, the jury could find that Gates had reason to know of the hospital's particular purpose for the roof. Likewise, the jury could find that Gates had reason to know that the hospital was relying on Gates' skill or judgment to furnish the appropriately installed roof. Indeed, the hospital told Gates it was. And, finally, the jury could... find that the hospital relied upon Gates' skill or judgment. It was only after the hospital was contacted by the representatives of Gates and assured of the quality of the roof that it purchased the Gates roof rather than another one-ply roof.

JUDGMENT ... [T]he verdict of the jury finding in favor of the hospital... must be affirmed.

Exclusion or Modification of Quality Warranties. Once made, an *express warranty* is difficult to disclaim. Section 2-316(1) states a general principle that words or conduct creating an express warranty, and words or conduct negating warranty, shall be construed wherever reasonable as consistent with each other, but that "negation or limitation is inoperative to the extent that such construction is unreasonable." Suppose that Sam, a used-car dealer, make an express oral warranty in the sale of a used car to Brenda. If the contract that Brenda signs contains a disclaimer of "all warranties, express or implied," the disclaimer will be unenforceable. Sam has taken the trouble to make an express warranty that is calculated to capture Brenda's attention. To give effect to Sam's disclaimer of his own express warranty would be an unreasonable action.

What if Sam makes an express oral warranty but the contract disclaims all warranties and further states that the writing is the final and exclusive expression of the agreement? Will the parol evidence rule of Section 2-202 prevent proof of the oral warranty? It might, but Brenda might be able to demonstrate that she did not agree that the writing should be considered final and exclusive. Under Section 2-202, the parties must agree. Litigation of the agreement issue is difficult because at its heart is the credibility of Brenda and Sam on a question of fact. The same is true about the question of whether Sam actually made the express warranty.

The *implied warranties* of quality may be excluded in either of two ways: (1) by the buyer's examining the goods or refusing to examine them, or (2) by the use of appropriate exclusionary language. If the buyer examines the goods (or a sample or model) before entering the contract, there is no implied warranty with regard to obvious defects. Nor is there an implied warranty as to obvious defects if the seller demands that the buyer examine the goods but the buyer refuses. Making goods available for inspection does not constitute a demand. The seller must make clear that the buyer is assuming the risk of defects which the examination ought to reveal. Exclusion by examination applies only to obvious defects, not to hidden ones; it also applies only to implied warranties, not to express warranties on which the buyer clearly indicates that he or she is relying.

Except in certain situations governed by the Magnuson-Moss Warranty Act, a seller who wishes to disclaim implied warranties by using exclusionary language may do so in either of two ways: (1) All implied warranties may be excluded by using expressions like "as is," "with all faults," or other language that, in common understanding, calls the buyer's attention to the exclusion of warranties and makes plain that there is no implied warranty [2-316(3)(a)]. (2) Implied warranties may also be excluded by complying with the provisions of Section 2-316(2). Under that subsection, an *implied warranty of merchantability* may be excluded orally or by a writing, but the exclusionary language must mention merchantability. If the disclaimer is written, the language of disclaimer must be conspicuous. Under the same subsection, an *implied warranty of fitness* can be excluded only by a conspicuous writing, but the exclusionary language may be general. A conspicuous general statement, such as "There are no warranties which extend beyond the description on the face hereof," is sufficient to exclude an implied warranty of fitness.

Strict compliance with the warranty exclusion provisions of the Code is not always sufficient to exclude an implied warranty. Some courts have held that certain attempts at exclusion are against public policy. In the pre-Code case of *Henningsen v. Bloomfield Motors,* 161 A.2d 69 (N.J. 1960), all automobile manufacturers doing business in New Jersey had adopted the same printed disclaimer of implied warranties and had substituted a "parts only" express warranty. Automobile buyers could not negotiate with the manufacturers for a more extensive warranty. The Supreme Court of New Jersey held that under these circumstances, an attempt by Bloomfield Motors to disclaim an implied warranty of merchantability was against public policy and was therefore invalid. As Case 18.2 illustrates, a few courts interpreting the Code have reached similar conclusions, usually on the ground that an attempted disclaimer is unconscionable. With regard to *consumer* products, the Magnuson-Moss Warranty Act, discussed later in this chapter, prohibits or limits the exclusion of implied warranties where a warranty has been made in writing.

CASE 18.2 A & M Produce Co. v. FMC Corp. · 186 Cal. Rptr. 114 (Cal. App. 1982)

FACTS A & M is a farming company owned solely by C. Alex Abatti. Abatti decided to grow tomatoes. Although an experienced produce farmer, he had never grown tomatoes or any other crop requiring a weight-sizer and was not familiar with weight-sizing equipment. When trying to locate the necessary equipment, Abatti first spoke with a salesman for Decco Equipment Co. The salesman recommended a hydrocooler in addition to a weight-sizer, and he submitted a bid of $60,000 to $68,000 for the equipment. Believing the bid was too high, Abatti next sought information from FMC Corporation. Isch, FMC's employee, did not say that a hydrocooler was required. According to Abatti, Isch recommended FMC equipment because it operated so fast that a hydrocooler was unnecessary, thereby saving A & M about $25,000. Abatti agreed to purchase FMC equipment for about $32,000 and signed a contract containing a disclaimer of warranties in bold print and a "Disclaimer of Consequential Damages" stating in somewhat smaller print that "Seller in no event shall be liable for consequential damages arising out of or in connection with this agreement. . . ." At harvest time A & M's troubles with the FMC equipment began. Tomatoes piled up in front of the singulator belt which separated the tomatoes for weight-sizing. Overflow tomatoes had to be sent through the machinery again, causing damage to the crop. The damage was aggravated because the tomatoes were not cooled by a hydrocooler, allowing a fungus to spread more quickly within the damaged fruit. FMC could not correct the problems. Abatti attempted unsuccessfully to get additional equipment from Decco and FMC. Because the FMC machine failed to work properly, Abatti lost most of the crop and had to close the packing shed.

Shortly thereafter, A & M offered to return the weight-sizer to FMC provided FMC would refund A & M's downpayment and pay the freight charges. FMC rejected this offer and demanded full payment of the balance due. A & M then sued FMC for damages, alleging breach of express warranties and breach of an implied warranty for a particular use. The trial

CASE 18.2 Continued

court awarded Abatti over $250,000 in damages on the ground that the disclaimers were unconscionable and that express or implied warranties had been breached. FMC appealed.

OPINION

WIENER, Associate Justice. . . . Acknowledging that a limitation on consequential damages may be unconscionable [under UCC § 2-719], FMC asserts [that] the trial court erred in applying [the doctrine of unconscionability] to the disclaimer of warranties. . . . [W]e conclude that an unconscionable disclaimer of warranty may be denied enforcement despite technical compliance with the requirements of § 2-316. . . . The policing provisions of § 2-316 are limited to problems involving the visibility of disclaimers and conflicts with express warranties. But oppression and unfair surprise, the principal targets of the unconscionability doctrine, may result from other types of questionable commercial practices. . . .

We now turn to the principal question involved in this appeal: Whether the trial court erred in concluding that FMC's attempted disclaimer of warranties and exclusion of consequential damages was unconscionable and therefore unenforceable.

. . . [U]nconscionability has both a "procedural" and a ["substantive"] element. The procedural element focuses on two factors: "oppression" and "surprise." "Oppression" arises from an inequality of bargaining power which results in no real negotiation and "an absence of meaningful choice." . . . "Surprise" involves the extent to which the supposedly agreed-upon terms of the bargain are hidden in a prolix printed form drafted by the party seeking to enforce the disputed terms. . . .

. . . No precise definition of substantive unconscionability can be proffered. . . . One commentator has pointed out, however, that "[substantive] unconscionability turns not only on a 'one-sided' result, but also on an absence of justification for it." . . . [T]he contractual term is substantively suspect if it reallocates the risks of the bargain in an objectively unreasonable or unexpected manner. But not all unreasonable risk reallocations are unconscionable; rather, enforceability of the clause is tied to the procedural aspects of unconscionability such that the greater the unfair surprise or inequality of bargaining power, the less unreasonable the risk allocation which will be tolerated. . . .

Both aspects of procedural unconscionability appear to be present on the facts of this case. Although the printing used on the warranty disclaimer was conspicuous, the terms of the consequential damage exclusion are not particularly apparent. . . . Both provisions appear in the middle of the back page of a long preprinted form contract which was only casually shown to Abatti. It was never suggested to him, either verbally or in writing, that he read the back of the form. Abatti testified [that] he never read the reverse side terms. There was thus sufficient evidence before the trial court to conclude that Abatti was in fact surprised by the warranty disclaimer and the consequential damage exclusion. How "unfair" his surprise was is subject to some dispute. He certainly had the opportunity to read the back of the contract or to seek the advice of a lawyer. Yet as a factual matter, given the complexity of the terms and FMC's failure to direct his attention to them, Abatti's omission may not be totally unreasonable. . . . In fact, one suspects that the length, complexity and [abstruseness] of most form contracts may be due at least in part to the seller's preference that the buyer will be dissuaded from reading that [to] which he is supposedly agreeing. . . . [The court then discussed the great difference in size and bargaining power between A & M and the much larger FMC and the probable inability of A & M to negotiate more favorable terms.]

[As to the substantive unconscionability of the disclaimer of warranties], the facts of this case support the trial court's conclusion that such disclaimer was commercially unreasonable. The warranty . . . went to the basic performance characteristics of the product. In attempting to disclaim [warranties], FMC was in essence [guaranteeing] nothing about what the product would do. Since a product's performance forms the fundamental basis for a sales contract, it is patently unreasonable to assume that a buyer would purchase a standardized mass-produced product from an industry seller without any enforceable per-

CASE 18.2 Continued

formance standards. . . . In this case, moreover, the evidence establishes that A & M had no previous experience with weight-sizing machines and was forced to rely on the expertise of FMC in recommending the necessary equipment. FMC was abundantly aware of this fact. The jury here necessarily found that FMC either expressly or impliedly guaranteed a performance level which the machine was unable to meet. . . . A seller's attempt, through the use of a disclaimer, to prevent the buyer from reasonably relying on such representations calls into question the commercial reasonableness of the agreement. . . . The trial court's conclusion to that effect is amply supported by the record before us.

As to the exclusion of consequential damages, several factors combine to suggest that the exclusion was unreasonable on the facts of this case. [The court emphasized the obviousness and severity of damage to A & M if the machine should fail; the fact that only FMC had the ability to prevent the loss; and the impropriety of shifting to one party a loss that only the other party can prevent.]

JUDGMENT [A]ffirmed.

Cumulation and Conflict of Warranties

In a sale of goods, a number of warranties may exist at the same time. For example, a *merchant* seller can be subject to a warranty of title, a warranty against infringement of a patent or a trademark, an implied warranty of merchantability, and an implied warranty of fitness for a particular purpose. In addition, any number of express warranties can be created, including express warranties of merchantability and fitness. To the extent that these express and implied warranties are consistent with one another, the buyer receives an accumulation of express and implied assurances. If a warranty of any kind is excluded, the seller remains subject to all other warranties that were made or imposed but that were not excluded.

Where there is a *conflict* of warranties, the intention of the parties to the sales contract determines which one is dominant. Section 2-317 states three tentative rules of construction for the guidance of the court: (1) exact or technical specifications displace an inconsistent sample or model or general language of description; (2) a sample from an existing bulk displaces inconsistent general language of description; and (3) express warranties displace inconsistent implied warranties other than an implied warranty of fitness for a particular purpose.

Suppose that a building contractor is interested in a new type of high-strength building block. The contractor inspects a sample, reads the results of a laboratory test conducted by the manufacturer, and purchases from the manufacturer a large quantity of the blocks. The blocks conform in strength to the sample but not to the laboratory test results supplied to the buyer as a part of the sales promotion. Which warranty prevails—the one arising from the sample, or the one arising from the test results? Under rule (1) in the preceding paragraph, the contractor is entitled to blocks that conform in strength to the specifications stated in the laboratory report.

Third-Party Beneficiaries of UCC Quality Warranties

Sometimes a defective product causes loss to someone other than the purchaser. The seller might admit making a warranty but may argue that the warranty should run only to the purchaser and not to others such as bystanders who might have been injured. Section 2-318 of the UCC gives certain "beneficiaries" the benefit of the same warranty or warranties that the buyer received in the contract of sale. Figure 18.2 shows the chain of distribution from manufacturer (M) to buyer (B), and it illustrates a spectrum of people who, in addition to the buyer, might be entitled to the seller's warranty.

There are three alternative versions of Section 2-318: Alternatives A, B, and C. Although they have a common purpose (to give beneficiaries the same warranty that the buyer received), they differ greatly as to who may be a beneficiary and as to the kinds of injury for which a beneficiary may receive a remedy.

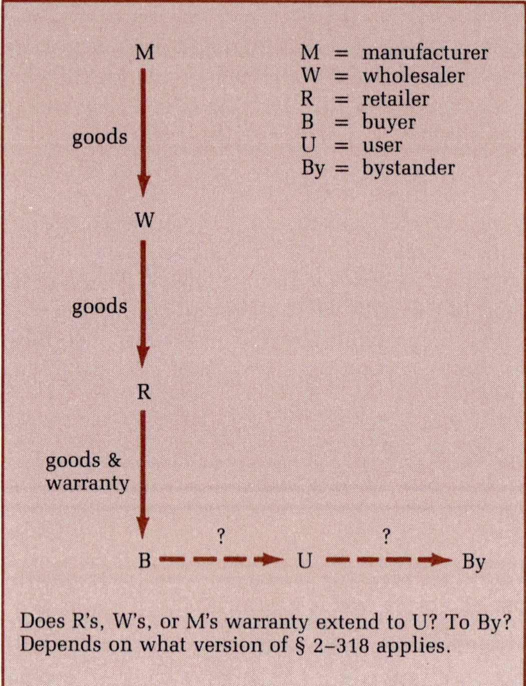

Figure 18.2 Third-party beneficiaries of buyer's warranty.

Recall the situation described at the beginning of this chapter. A defective garden tractor engine exploded, injuring Ben (the buyer) and his neighbor and causing a fire that destroyed the tractor and the neighbor's house. Suppose that neither the manufacturer nor the retail seller excluded the implied warranty of merchantability. To whom, besides Ben, does the warranty of each seller run? The answer depends on which version of Section 2-318 is in effect in the state whose law applies to the situation. Most states (over thirty) have adopted Alternative A or some version of it. Some states have adopted Alternative B or C or some variation. California has not enacted the section, relying instead on other consumer law.

Alternative A provides:

> A seller's warranty whether express or implied extends to any natural person who is in the family or household of his buyer or who is a guest in his home if it is reasonable to expect that such person may use, consume or be affected by the goods and who is injured in person by breach of the warranty.

This alternative is the most restrictive of the three. It permits recovery of damages only for personal injuries, not for injury to property. Bystanders, nonfamily members, and guests in automobiles are unprotected, unless the court is willing to include them in the protected class of beneficiaries by some process of interpretation. Ben's neighbor is not within the protected class. Moreover, if the language of Alternative A were applied literally (as the courts of a couple of states have done), even an injured member of Ben's family would be limited to a cause of action against the retail seller. The reason is that Alternative A extends the seller's warranty only to the beneficiaries of "his [the seller's] buyer." Since a manufacturer's immediate buyer ordinarily is a wholesaler, the manufacturer's warranty apparently would extend only to the beneficiaries of the wholesaler and not to beneficiaries of a consumer who buys from a retailer. However, a comment to Section 2-318 states that the section is neutral on the question of which sellers should be liable, and the courts of most states give a consumer-buyer's beneficiaries a cause of action against at least retailers and manufacturers.

Alternative B broadens the class of beneficiaries to whom a seller's warranty extends. The warranty "extends to any natural person [human being as opposed to a corporation] who may reasonably be expected to use, consume, or be affected by the goods and who is injured in person by breach of the warranty." Ben's neighbor could reasonably be expected to "be affected" by an exploding engine. Under Alternative B the neighbor would be entitled to damages for personal injuries but not for loss of the house.

Alternative C is a variation of Alternative B. It differs from Alternative B in two ways: (1) Alternative C extends a seller's warranty to "any person" (not merely to a "natural" person) who may reasonably be expected to use, consume, or be affected by the goods; and (2) Alternative C permits a beneficiary to recover damages for injury to property (as well as for injury to the person), unless the seller excludes or limits liability for injury to property. With regard to personal injury, a seller may not exclude or limit the operation of Alternative C. Under Alternative C, Ben's neighbor is entitled to damages for personal injuries and for the loss of the house if liability for property damage was not excluded by the sellers.

Case 18.3 involves Alternative A of Section 2-318, and the question of whether the court may go beyond Alternative A to extend warranty coverage to property damage as well as to personal injury.

CASE 18.3 Milbank Mutual Ins. Co. v. Proksch · 244 N.W.2d 105 (Minn. 1976)

FACTS Judelle Larson bought a Christmas tree at Charles Proksch's tree lot and set it up in her father's home, which was insured by Milbank Mutual Insurance Co. She paid $2 more than the regular price for the tree because Proksch's salesman said that it had been treated with fireproofing material. Normally, the Larsons took their tree down immediately after Christmas, but they decided to keep this tree up longer because of the fireproofing. At a New Year's party, two young people were throwing a pillow back and forth. It struck a lower branch of the tree, a small flame immediately appeared, and the tree went up in flames in a matter of seconds, causing over $9,000 in property damage to the house. Milbank (plaintiff) sued Proksch (defendant) for that amount in damages. The jury found that Proksch's employee had expressly represented the tree as fire-resistant. From a judgment for Milbank, Proksch appealed.

OPINION KELLY, J.... [D]efendant argues that recovery for property damage [suffered by a member of the buyer's family] is barred by [Minnesota's 1967 version of § 2-318], the law in effect at the time of the fire. We disagree. That statute was not intended to restrict the development of Minnesota common law relating to third-party beneficiaries of warranties. The statute provided:

> A seller's warranty[,] whether express or implied[,] extends to any natural person who is in the family or household of his buyer or who is a guest in his home if it is reasonable to expect that such person may use, consume or be affected by the goods and who is injured in person by breach of the warranty. A seller may not exclude or limit the operation of this section....

On its face, the above section *extends* the seller's warranty to an additional class of persons [beyond the buyer]; it does not restrict the warranty to [buyers] or impair the ability of courts to extend the warranty to other classes [such as people who have suffered only property damage] in appropriate cases. This interpretation is directly supported by the...Minnesota Code Comments to the section....The...comment [to § 2-318] provides:

> This section extends the seller's express and implied warranties to members of the buyer's family and household and to guests in his home. According to U.C.C. § 2-318, Comment 3, it does not limit the developing law to this extension, and the Minnesota courts are free to go beyond this section. At present, the law of privity in Minnesota is in a state of flux and already seems to go beyond the extension proposed in this section....

These comments make...clear that the...courts are free to continue the development of the common law of warranty.

This court recognized its ability to further that development in *Froysland v. Leef Bros. Inc.*... *Froysland* involved, in part, an action for breach of an express warranty made by a supplier to an employer with regard to the flame-resistant quality of clothing purchased by the employer for his employees. [One employee,] severely injured when the clothing caught fire,... brought an action against the supplier. Although an employee is not within the class of beneficiaries in [the 1967 version of § 2-318], we nonetheless allowed recovery[, stating]:

CASE 18.3 Continued

[The plaintiff] was the ultimate consumer of the treated garments and the intended beneficiary of the safety provisions provided by the express warranties in the agreement between his employer and defendant. To allow the employee to recover in such a situation is consistent with our prior decisions. We, therefore, hold that an employee may recover for breach of warranty by a supplier to an employer for a product used, as in this case, for the employee's safety. . . .

[T]he bulk of the cases and comments squarely support a court's authority to expand the class of third-party beneficiaries beyond the face of the section. . . . [One] court allowed recovery in a third-party beneficiary situation where leakage of an aerosol can caused property damage, but no personal injury. . . .

[T]he question remains whether [a further expansion of beneficiaries is appropriate in the instant case], in which a member of the buyer's family suffered serious property damage but no personal injury. Under the logic and policy underlying our prior cases, the answer is clearly yes. Prior to 1940, this court had not squarely faced the issue of whether lack of privity [of contract] should be a defense to breach-of-warranty actions, because our cases were most often decided on the alternative theory of negligence. . . . In the context of that theory, we have been liberal in allowing recovery in the absence of privity. For example, in [a 1929 case] we held that a poultry farmer could recover directly from a drug company for property damage to his flock caused by delivery of linseed oil instead of [cod] liver oil. We noted that the distinction between property damage and personal injury would not bar recovery. . . .

[The court then discussed a number of later negligence and warranty cases allowing plaintiffs to recover damages even though they had no contractual relationship with the suppliers of the defective goods.]

The *Froysland* case, discussed above, built on prior developments in holding that an employee was entitled to benefit from an express warranty to his employer when breach of that warranty had caused him to suffer personal injury. [On the basis of] *Froysland* and our other cases, we now extend the common law to allow recovery in this case. The destruction of a home and physical damage to personal property is no less an injury to one who sustains them than a bodily injury. When a seller offers a Christmas tree with an express warranty concerning its flame-retardant qualities, he has every reason to expect that all members of the buyer's household will enjoy the benefits of the tree and that a natural and probable consequence of a breach of his warranty is fire and consequent damage to their property. . . .

[Court's footnote: "A further persuasive reason for extending the common law is the current public policy of Minnesota, as embodied in [its 1969 adoption of Section 2-318's Alternative C, which allows] recovery to one "who is injured" by the breach of warranty and thus would cover the property damage sustained here.]

JUDGMENT [A]ffirmed.

Limits on Usefulness of UCC Quality Warranties

Like other bases of product liability, warranty may be of little or no value to some persons injured by defective products. The UCC does not require a seller to make an express warranty, and the UCC permits the seller to exclude those imposed by law. Indeed, in transactions covered by the Code it is common practice for a seller to exclude implied warranties entirely and to substitute a much narrower express warranty, one limited, for example, to the replacement of defective parts. Even where there is an implied warranty, the amount of damages recoverable may be sharply limited by the sales contract. In contrast, contractual disclaimers or limitations of strict tort liability or liability for gross negligence or for intentional torts ordinarily are not enforceable. Recall also that in many states an injured third party who is not a member of the buyer's family or a guest in the buyer's home has no warranty cause of action against the seller. And where a warranty cause of action exists, the plaintiff may be held to have assumed the risk of injury where the plaintiff knew of the defect and the risk was obvious.

Injured persons may face another problem when suing for breach of warranty: a surprise running of the UCC statute of limitations. A statute of limitations imposes a fixed maximum time within which person must bring suit, so that plaintiffs are encouraged to bring their suits promptly, while evidence is still fresh and available. The UCC provides a rather generous amount of time for bringing suit—4 years, and more in some situations. However, the time for suing may be reduced to as little as 1 year by the original agreement of the parties. Moreover, the period, whatever its length, begins to run when the sales contract is breached—by, for example, the seller's breaching a warranty. With one exception, breach of a warranty occurs when the goods are *tendered to the buyer* (offered for delivery), "regardless of the aggrieved party's lack of knowledge of the breach" [2-725(2)].[4] Goods such as Ben's garden tractor may have hidden defects that do not become apparent until after the limitation period has expired. In such a situation, injured persons would be barred from any warranty remedy. In contrast, the limitations period that applies to a cause of action in *negligence* or *strict liability in tort* (usually 1 or 2 years) begins to run when the injury-causing condition *was or should have been discovered.* In tort, then, the period for suing may extend indefinitely, because the time that the defect reveals itself, not the time that the product was tendered for delivery, usually marks the beginning of the period permitted for bringing suit. (For the protection of sellers, a few states specify that a suit in strict liability in tort must be brought within 6 to 12 years after the product was sold, regardless of whether the defect has been discovered by that time.)

[4]The exception is that where a warranty "explicitly extends" to the future performance of the goods (e.g., the seller warrants the goods for 2 years), the UCC limitations period (1 to 4 years) does not commence until the time during the 2 years that the defect was or should have been discovered.

"Consumer Product" Warranties under Federal Legislation

The UCC does not require warranties to be stated in language that is understandable by nonlawyers. Consequently, under the UCC many sellers have made warranties that are confusing, deceptive, or misleading, especially to consumers. To remedy the situation, Congress in 1975 enacted the Magnuson-Moss Warranty Act.[5]

Purpose and Scope of the Magnuson-Moss Warranty Act. The act has two broad purposes: (1) to improve the adequacy of warranty information available to consumers, to prevent deception, and thereby to improve competition in the marketing of consumer products; and (2) to encourage warrantors to establish procedures for the informal settlement of disputes with consumers. The Federal Trade Commission (FTC) has the duty of developing appropriate rules and putting the Warranty Act into effect.

The Warranty Act applies only to consumer products. A *consumer product* is any item of tangible personal property that is distributed in commerce and is normally used for personal, family, or household purposes. "Consumer product" includes items intended to be attached to or installed in real property, such as a water heater. Although the Warranty Act applies to consumer products costing more than $5, the act permits the FTC to impose its rules on consumer products costing some higher amount that the FTC selects. The UCC continues to apply to warranties in sales of goods to be used for purely *business* purposes. Furthermore, the UCC may continue to supply warranties in sales of *consumer products,* since a supplier who makes a written consumer product warranty may not exclude UCC or other implied warranties arising under state law.

Chief Requirements of the Act. The Warranty Act does not require that a consumer product or any of its components be warranted. However, sellers who make a *written* consumer product warranty must comply with Warranty Act disclosure and labeling requirements.

Disclosure requirements—contents and time of disclosure. The Warranty Act requires the maker of a written consumer product warranty to disclose

[5]15 U.S.C.A., secs, 2301–2312.

fully and conspicuously in a single document in simple, understandable language the items of information required by the FTC. The FTC requires the following information for products costing more than $15:

1. If the written warranty is not to be extended to every consumer who owns the product during the term of the warranty, the identity of the person or persons (such as the "original owner") to whom the warranty *is* extended.
2. A clear description of the parts or product characteristics covered by the warranty and, where necessary for clarification, what is excluded from the warranty.
3. A statement of what the warrantor (the maker of the written warranty) will do to correct a defect, malfunction, or failure of the product to conform with the warranty, including the items or services the warrantor will provide or for which the warrantor will pay. Also, where necessary for clarification, the items or services that the warrantor will *not* pay for or provide.
4. The time when the warranty begins (if at a time other than the purchase date) and the duration of the warranty term.
5. A step-by-step explanation of how the consumer may obtain warranty service. If a consumer must fill out and return an owner's registration card, a warranty registration card, or the like in order to qualify for warranty coverage or service, the warranty must disclose this fact.
6. Information about any informal dispute settlement procedure, such as arbitration, used by the warrantor.
7. Any limitations on the duration of *implied* (e.g., UCC) warranties, together with the following statement: "Some states do not allow limitations on how long an implied warranty lasts, so the above limitation may not apply to you." A limitation on the duration of an implied warranty must appear on the face of the written warranty.
8. Any limitations or exclusions of damages, together with a statement that some states do not permit such limitations.
9. The following statement: "This warranty gives you specific legal rights, and you may also have other rights which vary from state to state."

If a written consumer product warranty is made, its text must be made readily available to the prospective buyer *prior to sale.* A seller may use a variety of methods for making the text available, as long as the information is conspicuous and access to it is easy. The seller may, for example, prominently display the text of the warranty at a counter and clearly indicate the products covered, maintain a clearly labeled binder containing copies of warranties for products sold in a department, or display packages of consumer products in such a way that the warranties printed on them are clearly visible. The requirement of presale warranty availability applies to all sellers of consumer products, including catalog, mail-order, and door-to-door sellers. Any supplier (such as a manufacturer) who makes a written product warranty must provide the seller (e.g., a retailer) with warranty materials—tags, stickers, signs, appropriately printed packaging, etc.—necessary for the seller to make the required presale disclosure.

Labeling requirement—"full" v. "limited" warranty. In addition to the disclosures required by the FTC, the Warranty Act itself requires that any written warranty of a consumer product costing more than $10 must be clearly and conspicuously designated as either a "full warranty" or a "limited warranty," unless the warrantor is exempted from the designation requirement by a rule of the FTC.

A warranty is a "full warranty" (and can be so labeled) only if it meets four minimum standards or requirements imposed by the Warranty Act:

1. Where the product is defective or fails to conform to the written warranty, the warrantor must, without charge, remedy the product within a reasonable time.
2. Although a full warranty *may itself* be of limited duration (by use of language such as "full 12-month warranty"), it may *not* impose any limitation on the duration of any *implied* (e.g., UCC) warranty on the product.
3. To be effective, any clause purporting to exclude or to limit consequential damages for

breach of warranty must conspicuously appear on the face of the warranty.

4 If the product (or a component part) contains a defect or continues to malfunction after a reasonable number of attempts by the warrantor to remedy defects or malfunctions in the product, the warrantor must permit the consumer to elect either a refund of the purchase price or a replacement of the product or part.

If the warrantor replaces a component part, the replacement must include installation of the part without charge.

A full warranty (including one reading, for example, "full 12-month warranty") extends from the warrantor to any person who is a consumer with respect to the consumer product. The term "consumer" includes the buyer of a consumer product, any person to whom the product is transferred while its warranty coverage is in effect, and any other person, such as an injured bystander, who is entitled by the terms of the warranty or by state law to the benefit of the warranty.

A written consumer-product warranty that does not conform to the four minimum standards is a "limited warranty." A warranty is "limited" (and must be so labeled) if it, for example, requires the consumer (1) to fill out and return a warranty registration card in order to qualify for warranty coverage or service, or (2) to pay any costs of returning or remedying a defective product. A warranty that promises to replace defective parts but requires the purchaser to pay for installing them is a limited warranty. So is a 12-month warranty that protects the first purchaser but not a person to whom the product is transferred during the 12-month period.

Extent to Which the Act Supersedes the Code. The Warranty Act nullifies conflicting provisions of other warranty legislation. For example, the UCC permits the exclusion of implied warranties even where the seller has made a written warranty. Under the Warranty Act, a supplier who makes a written warranty may not disclaim or modify implied warranties. In two situations the act prohibits entirely the disclaimer or modification of implied warranties: (1) where the supplier makes a full warranty, and (2) where at the time of sale, or within 90 days thereafter, the supplier enters into a "service contract" with the consumer for the repair or maintenance of the consumer product. A service contract is a contract in writing to perform for a specified time services relating to the maintenance or repair (or both) of a consumer product. Where a supplier makes a *limited* warranty, implied warranties may not be disclaimed or modified as to content. But the supplier may limit the duration of implied warranties to the duration of a written warranty of reasonable duration, if the limitation is conscionable, is set forth in clear and unmistakable language, and is prominently displayed on the face of the limited warranty. In the sale of a consumer product, these Warranty Act provisions prevail over the conflicting provisions of the Code.

Enforcement of Warranty Act Provisions. A person who has the benefit of a consumer product warranty may, if injured by a defective consumer product, bring suit in any state or federal court having jurisdiction, and may recover actual damages or have other legal or equitable remedies. In addition, a consumer who wins the suit may be allowed by the court to recover as a part of the judgment the reasonable costs and expenses of suit, including attorney's fees based on actual time expended by the attorney. However, where a warrantor sets up an informal dispute settlement procedure (e.g., arbitration) that conforms to FTC regulations, and in the written warranty requires the consumer to use it before going to court, the consumer is bound by the requirement.

Some defects produce so little monetary loss that the individual consumer may not find it worthwhile to bring suit even though the product is useless or has caused injury. In such instances the consumer may choose to bring a class action against the warrantor, as is permitted by the Warranty Act, on behalf of all those harmed by the defective product.

To curb deception at the earliest possible moment, the Warranty Act empowers the Attorney General and the FTC to bring suit to enjoin (restrain) a warrantor from making a deceptive warranty or from violating any prohibition of the act. In addition, a warrantor is subject to a $10,000 civil penalty if found to be in violation of the Warranty Act or FTC regulations.

Case 18.4 involves an application of the Warranty Act.

CASE 18.4 Ventura v. Ford Motor Corp. · 433 A.2d 801 (N.J. App. 1981)

FACTS Ventura (plaintiff) purchased a new 1978 Mercury Marquis Brougham from Marino Auto Sales, Inc., an authorized Ford dealer. Ventura and his wife experienced engine hesitation and stalling problems early in their use of the car. The problems continued without interruption despite repeated attempts by Marino Auto to cure the problem. Bednarz, Ford's zone service manager and mechanical specialist, inspected the car and recommended certain repairs. Eventually, all attempts at repair failed and Ventura was forcibly removed from Marino Auto's premises. Alleging breach of warranty, Ventura sued Marino Auto and Ford Motor Company for damages. Marino Auto cross-claimed against Ford for indemnification. The trial court (1) granted plaintiff rescission of the contract and damages representing the purchase price less an allowance for plaintiff's use of the car, (2) awarded damages in favor of Marino Auto against Ford, and (3) awarded over $5,000 for attorneys' fees to plaintiff against Ford. Plaintiff's demands for interest, punitive damages in excess of $2 million, and treble damages were denied. Ford appealed.

OPINION BOTTER, P.J.A.D. . . . The [trial court's] findings that Ford breached its express warranty and that the car was substantially impaired were supported by sufficient credible evidence and must be affirmed on appeal.

Our reasoning through the body of law applicable to this commonplace contractual skein, which binds consumers, car dealers[,] and manufacturers together, differs from that of the trial judge. But we affirm plaintiff's recovery. We conclude that, despite Marino Auto's attempted disclaimer of all warranties, plaintiff can recover from Marino Auto for breach of [the] implied warranty of merchantability. We also uphold the award of counsel fees against Ford pursuant to the Magnuson-Moss Warranty Act.

The contract of sale between Marino Auto and plaintiff [contained conspicuous disclaimers of all warranties, express or implied]. On the back of [the] sales order-contract were the following terms which were made part of the contract:

> 7. It is expressly agreed that there are no warranties, express or implied, made by either the selling dealer or the manufacturer on the motor vehicle, chassis[,] or parts furnished hereunder except, in the case of a new motor vehicle[,] the warranty expressly given to the purchaser upon the delivery of such motor vehicle or chassis.
>
> The selling dealer also agrees promptly to perform and fulfill all terms and conditions of the owner service policy.

[The dealer also passed on to the purchaser a warranty from the manufacturer.] For the purpose of this opinion we will assume that the disclaimer of implied warranties of merchantability and fitness was effective under [UCC § 2-316]. The Magnuson-Moss Warranty . . . Act . . . enhances the consumer's position by allowing recovery under a warranty without regard to privity of contract between the consumer and warrantor, by prohibiting the disclaimer of implied warranties in a written warranty, and by enlarging the remedies available to a consumer for breach of warranty, including the award of attorneys' fees. The requirement of privity of contract between the consumer and the warrantor has been removed by assuring consumers a remedy against all warrantors of the product. . . . A "supplier" is defined as any person engaged in the business of making a consumer product directly or indirectly available to consumers, § 2301(4), and a "warrantor" includes any supplier or other person who gives or offers to give a written warranty or who is obligated under an implied warranty. § 2301(5). The term "written warranty" is defined in § 2301(6) to include . . . "(B) any undertaking in writing in connection with the sale by a supplier of a consumer product to refund, repair, replace or take other remedial action with respect to such product in the event that such product fails to meet the specifications set forth in the undertaking."

CASE 18.4 Continued

[Section 2308 of the Warranty Act] provides as follows:

> (a) No supplier may disclaim or modify (except as provided in subsection (b) of this section) any implied warranty to a consumer with respect to such consumer product if (1) such supplier makes any written warranty to the consumer with respect to such consumer product, or (2) at the time of sale, or within 90 days thereafter, such supplier enters into a service contract with the consumer which applies to such consumer product....

We will first consider the application of this act to the dealer, Marino Auto.... [P]aragraph 7 of the purchase order-contract provides that there are no warranties, express or implied, made by the selling dealer or manufacturer except, in the case of a new motor vehicle, "the warranty expressly given to the purchaser upon delivery of such motor vehicle...." This section also provides: "The selling dealer also agrees to promptly perform and fulfill all terms and conditions of the owner service policy." Ford contended in the trial court that Marino Auto had "a duty" to properly diagnose and make repairs.... The provision in paragraph 7 in these circumstances is a "written warranty" within the meaning of § 2301(6) (B) since it constitutes an undertaking in connection with the sale to take "remedial action with respect to such product in the event that such product fails to meet the specifications set forth in the undertaking...." In our view the specifications of the undertaking include, at the least, the provisions of the limited warranty furnished by Ford, namely:

> LIMITED WARRANTY (12 MONTHS OR 12,000 MILES/19,312 KILOMETERS) 1978 NEW CAR AND LIGHT TRUCK. Ford warrants for its 1978 model cars and light trucks that the Selling Dealer will repair or replace free any parts, except tires, found under normal use in the U.S. or Canada to be defective in factory materials or workmanship within the earlier of 12 months or 12,000 miles/19,312 km from either first use or retail delivery....

...For the purpose of this appeal we are satisfied that the dealer's undertaking in paragraph 7 constitutes a written warranty within the meaning of [the Warranty Act]. Accordingly, having furnished a written warranty to the consumer, the dealer as a supplier may not "disclaim or modify [except to limit in duration] any implied warranty to a consumer....

The result of this analysis is to invalidate the attempted disclaimer by the dealer of the implied warranties of merchantability and fitness. Being bound by those implied warranties arising under state law...Marino Auto was liable to plaintiff for the breach thereof as found by the trial judge, and plaintiff could timely revoke his acceptance of the automobile and claim a refund of his purchase price.

...The award of counsel fees fulfills the intent of the...Warranty Act. Without such an award consumers frequently would be unable to vindicate warranty rights accorded by law.

As to the amount of counsel fees allowed by the trial judge, we find no abuse of discretion. The allowance was for actual time spent at an hourly rate of $75....

JUDGMENT Affirmed.

Strict Liability as a Basis of Product Liability

If negligence cannot be proved and the seller has made no warranty, an injured plaintiff may wish to rely on strict liability as a basis for recovering damages.

Nature and Scope of Strict Liability

Courts use the expression "strict liability" in two senses. In one sense, *strict liability* means a liability that flows from a breach of a warranty of quality. In another sense, the sense in which the expression is used in this chapter, *strict liability* means a liability imposed by tort law. "Strict liability in tort" is imposed when a defective product has caused injury or when injury results from a justifiable reliance on a material misrepresentation of the quality of a product. The liability is called "strict" because the plaintiff need not prove "fault" (negligence or fraud) on the part of the defendant. The liability is "in tort" because the existence of the liability does not depend on the existence of a warranty. Strict liability in tort usually cannot be disclaimed. The ability of sellers to disclaim or otherwise to avoid warranty liability for serious loss explains in large measure the rapid development of strict liability in tort as a basis for lawsuits.

Strict liability in tort has had its greatest growth since the early 1960s, when the leading case of *Greenman v. Yuba Power Products, Inc.*, 377 P.2d 897 (Cal. 1963), was decided. In that case the plaintiff was injured while using a defective power tool that had been purchased by his wife. The court held, "A manufacturer is strictly liable in tort when an article he places on the market, knowing that it is to be used without inspection for defects, proves to have a defect that causes injury to a human being." Section 402A of the *Restatement of the Law (Second), Torts* contains similar language:

> One who sells any product in a defective condition unreasonably dangerous to the user or consumer or to his property is subject to liability for physical harm thereby caused to the ultimate user or consumer, or to his property, if (a) the seller is engaged in the business of selling such a product, and (b) it is expected to and does reach the user or consumer without substantial change in the condition in which it is sold.

This rule applies even though the seller has exercised all possible care in preparing and selling the product and even though the user or consumer has not bought the product from the seller.

Section 402B of the *Restatement* refers to situations not necessarily involving a defective product. By advertising, labels, or otherwise, a seller might make to the public "a misrepresentation of material fact concerning the character or quality of a chattel sold by him." A consumer of the chattel who justifiably relies on the misrepresentation and is thereby physically harmed may have a cause of action against the seller.

Reasons for Imposing Strict Liability; Procedural Benefits

The reasons most commonly offered for imposing strict liability include the following: (1) Users of complex or packaged goods are usually in no position to examine the goods at the time of purchase. Since much advertising is calculated to convince the public that goods may be used safely, users of defective goods are especially vulnerable to injury. So, when a defective product causes injury, the loss should be shifted from the individual to the manufacturer. (2) Manufacturers are in the best position to distribute loss due to defective products as a cost of doing business, either by raising prices or by procuring insurance. (3) Imposing strict liability will exert pressure on manufacturers to police their operations more carefully and to make fewer defective products. Also, some courts impose strict liability on everyone in the distribution chain so that the injured plaintiff will have a better chance of recovering damages. The manufacturer may be beyond the reach of the plaintiff but may be liable to a middleman who has been required to pay damages to the plaintiff.

Strict tort liability provides injured plaintiffs with procedural advantages similar to those of an action in warranty. The plaintiff may prevail essentially by proving (1) that the doctrine applies to the plaintiff's situation, (2) that the product had a defect when it left the defendant's hands and was unreasonably dangerous to the plaintiff (or that the plaintiff justifiably relied on the defendant's material misrepresentation), and (3) that harm to the plaintiff resulted. Ordinarily, contributory negligence of the plaintiff is not a defense to a suit based on strict liability in tort.

Case 18.5 involves the application of strict tort liability to a lease of goods.

CASE 18.5 Brimbau v. Ausdale Equipment Rental Corp. · 440 A.2d 1292 (R.I. 1982)

FACTS Marzano Construction Co. leased a backhoe from Ausdale Equipment Rental Corp. (defendant) for use on construction projects. While the backhoe was being used for digging,

CASE 18.5 Continued

the steel cable that supported the backhoe's boom and bucket snapped. There were no injuries, and the cable was replaced. Ten days later, Marzano used the same backhoe for laying concrete drainage pipe. While the backhoe was lightly supporting a pipe section in a trench so that Brimbau (plaintiff) could help secure it, the cable supporting the boom and bucket again snapped without warning. The bucket crashed to the ground, glanced off a section of pipe, and struck Brimbau, seriously injuring him. He based his suit on strict liability in tort and two other theories of liability. The jury returned a general verdict in favor of Brimbau, and the trial court entered judgment for him for $650,000. Ausdale appealed. Regarding strict liability in tort, the supreme court commented as follows:

OPINION

WEISBERGER, J. . . . Although the trial judge instructed in his charge . . . that strict liability applies to the leasing or rental of consumer products, this court has never considered that issue. Our cases adopting and applying § 402A of the Restatement (Second) *Torts* (1965) relate only to the sale and manufacture of defective goods. . . .

The doctrine of strict liability in tort originally developed in cases involving sales by manufacturers and retailers of unreasonably dangerous, defective products. . . . In fact, the rule enunciated in § 402A of the Restatement . . . , which has been instrumental in guiding the adoption of strict products liability by the majority of states in this country, expressly refers only to the liability of *sellers* of consumer products. Despite the early cases and the language of § 402A, however, the majority of jurisdictions that have considered the issue have extended the doctrine of strict tort liability to commercial lessors of personal property.

The policy considerations that impel imposition of strict liability upon manufacturers and sellers of dangerously defective goods apply with equal or greater force to lessors of potentially dangerous products or instrumentalities. Persons in the business of leasing, like manufacturers and sellers, continually introduce potentially dangerous instrumentalities into the stream of commerce and stand in a far better financial and technical position than lessees to insure against, prevent, and spread the costs of product-related injuries. Moreover, lessees of goods might have [less] opportunity to inspect a leased item than would a purchaser, and would rely to a greater extent upon an implied assurance by the lessor that the product is safe for its intended purpose. An additional consideration is that lessors put a given product to a more sustained use than do retailers, introducing and reintroducing the product into the consumer market with each new lease. One product may thus benefit a larger consuming public, but that same product may also expose a greater number of persons to potential injury. These factors support the imposition of responsibility on lessors to ensure that the used product is in a reasonably safe condition each time it is leased. We therefore join those courts that have held persons in the business of leasing personal property strictly liable in tort for injuries proximately resulting from products that they lease in a defective condition, which renders such property dangerous.

The defendant takes issue with the language of the trial justice's instruction on strict liability. Under the law of strict liability, a seller or lessor will be liable only if at the point of sale or at the commencement of the lease the product was already defective. Thus, to hold a seller or lessor liable, a plaintiff must prove that the product was defective at the time it left the control of the seller or lessor. . . . [T]he trial justice instructed the jurors that liability would attach [if] they found that the backhoe was defective "at the time of leasing." [T]his instruction was the substantial equivalent of the instruction urged by defendant. . . .

For the foregoing reasons, the defendant's appeal is denied and dismissed.

JUDGMENT The judgment of the Superior Court is affirmed. . . .

Limits on Usefulness of Strict Liability to Injured Plaintiffs

Strict liability, like the other bases of product liability, is not universally available to injured plaintiffs. The courts of a very few states have refused to adopt the doctrine of strict tort liability. Some of these courts have stated that the decision to adopt strict liability is for the legislature. The courts of certain other states will not impose that doctrine if the plaintiff has suffered only property damage. These courts reserve strict liability for situations involving serious personal injury, preferring to let most product liability matters be governed by warranty law. Moreover, the defendant in a strict liability suit usually may prevail by proving that the plaintiff knew of the defect, understood the danger, and voluntarily assumed the risk.

Summary

A person injured by a defective product may sue in negligence, warranty, or strict liability in tort. A defendant is liable in negligence if he or she is subject to a duty of care, violates it, and causes harm to the plaintiff. The duty arises and can be violated in a variety of ways. However, negligence can be difficult to prove.

Article 2 of the UCC provides for warranties of title and warranties of quality. Quality warranties are classified as express or implied. Any affirmation of fact or promise that relates to the goods and becomes a part of the basis of the bargain creates an express warranty. The implied warranty of merchantability entitles the buyer to goods that are fit for their ordinary purposes. An implied warranty of fitness for a particular purpose entitles the buyer to goods that will serve that purpose. A seller may refrain from making express warranties and may exclude implied warranties. A number of warranties may exist at the same time. A warranty of quality made to a buyer extends also to certain third-party beneficiaries.

The Magnuson-Moss Warranty Act establishes special rules for written consumer product warranties. The rules supersede conflicting rules of the UCC.

Strict liability in tort may be available to an injured person where the product is unreasonably dangerous to the user, or where the user has justifiably relied on the seller's misrepresentation of material fact concerning the nature of the product. One reason for strict liability is that sellers can best absorb loss and spread it as a cost of doing business.

Review Questions

1 Why has the privity-of-contract requirement been largely abandoned in product liability cases?

2 Why might the law of negligence be of limited usefulness to injured plaintiffs? Illustrate.

3 What must a plaintiff prove to obtain damages for loss due to a breach of warranty?

4 **(a)** What ownership attributes may a buyer be assured of under a warranty of title? **(b)** How may nonverbal title warranties be excluded?

5 **(a)** How may an express warranty of quality be made? **(b)** What would be the best way to avoid the liability that can result from an express warranty? **(c)** Is this method of avoiding liability compatible with normal business practices? Why?

6 Compare the implied warranty of merchantability with the implied warranty of fitness for a particular purpose with regard to **(a)** method of creation, **(b)** quality level assured, and **(c)** method of exclusion.

7 Suppose a seller orally states, "I do not warrant these goods." What warranties, if any, exist?

8 Compare Alternatives A, B, and C of Section 2-318 with regard to the class of people protected and the kind of injury protected against.

9 Why might the law of warranty be of limited usefulness to an injured plaintiff? Illustrate.

10 **(a)** What are the chief kinds of requirements of the Magnuson-Moss Warranty Act? **(b)** How does a full warranty differ from a limited warranty? **(c)** How does the Warranty Act limit the right granted by Article 2 to exclude implied warranties?

11 How may the provisions of the Warranty Act be enforced?

12 (a) What are the two main situations in which strict liability may be imposed? (b) For injured plaintiffs, what are the procedural benefits of strict liability in tort? (c) Why might strict tort liability be of limited usefulness to injured persons?

Case Problems

1 In 1980, Connie Daniell attempted to commit suicide by being locked inside the trunk of a 1973 Ford LTD automobile. Because the trunk latch did not have an internal release or opening mechanism, Daniell remained in the trunk for about 9 days. Later, Daniell sued Ford Motor Company for damages, alleging psychological and physical injuries resulting from a defect in the design of the trunk latch. Is Daniell entitled to damages? In your answer discuss all three of the product liability theories she relied on: (a) negligence, (b) warranty, and (c) strict liability in tort.

2 Tiderman bought a new mobile home manufactured by Fleetwood Homes. Shortly after occupying it, she experienced severe eye and throat irritation. Her allergist diagnosed her as suffering from asthma caused by exposure to formaldehyde fumes emitted from particle board in the mobile home. She moved out, but continued to suffer severe asthma attacks. Alleging breach of the warranty of merchantability, she sued Fleetwood for rescission of the contract and for damages for her personal injuries. At trial, expert testimony indicated that 20 to 25 percent of the population is allergic or potentially sensitive to substances such as formaldehyde. Fleetwood's defense experts diagnosed Tiderman as having a genetic predisposition to asthma. From a $566,500 jury award to Tiderman, Fleetwood appealed. Whether the trial court's decision should be upheld depended on whether there was a breach of the warranty of merchantability. Was the warranty breached?

3 Troy asked Swan Island Sheet Metal Works to manufacture a stainless steel crab cooker. The cooker was to be modeled after one that Troy already owned, and it was to use a gas burner. Bader, president of Swan Island, lacked knowledge of gas burners and so informed Troy, who agreed that Bader should seek expert advice on the design of the burner. Bader did so, and delivered the cooker. The burner never worked properly, and Troy ruined 1,200 pounds of crab while attempting to use the cooker. Troy refused to pay for it and sought damages arising from an alleged breach of the implied warranty of fitness for a particular purpose. The trial court awarded Troy $2,950 in damages. Swan Island appealed, arguing that since both Bader and Troy admitted ignorance of the design of gas burners, Troy could not have relied on Swan Island's expertise. Should the trial court's decision be reversed?

4 Mobley purchased a new car from Century Dodge and later discovered that the car had been involved in an accident. The contract of sale described the car as "new" and contained a disclaimer of all warranties, express or implied. Mobley sued Century Dodge for damages, alleging breach of an express warranty. Century Dodge contended that it had disclaimed any express warranty. Was Century Dodge's disclaimer effective to exclude an express warranty that the car was new?

5 Phillips purchased a horsewalker from Allen. A horsewalker is a device turned by an electric motor to exercise horses. The top is like an umbrella on a pole. Horses are attached to the arms of the umbrella which then is rotated in a circle at varying speeds. Upon delivery of the device, Phillips asked to see it work. Allen installed a temporary extension cord, cautioning Phillips that a permanent, grounded electrical connection was needed to prevent electrical shocks and injury. A few days later Phillips attached four horses to the walker by means of steel chains. After the walker had been in operation for a while, one of the horses was killed by an electric shock and the other three were injured. Alleging breach of the warranties of merchantability and fitness for a particular purpose, Phillips sued Allen for damages. The trial court held that Allen was not liable to Phillips, and Phillips appealed. Should the verdict of the trial court be upheld?

6 Bob Buyer, a stockbroker whose hobby is gardening, purchased a new garden tractor from Sarah Seller for $3,000 cash. Due to a manufacturing defect, the engine exploded without warning the second time Buyer used the tractor, injuring him and a neighbor passing by on the sidewalk and causing a fire that destroyed the tractor and the neighbor's house. By means of a full warranty the manufacturer promised to refund the purchase price or to replace the tractor if it proved to be seriously defective. Buyer and the neighbor seek compensation from the manufacturer for all their losses. The manufacturer contends that it is liable only to Bob Buyer and only for the value of the tractor. To whom is the manufacturer liable, and for what elements of damage?

7 Bullock, Inc., manufactured a deep-fat fryer. Hoping to convince Bennigan's Restaurant to buy it, Bullock placed the fryer in Bennigan's kitchen on a trial basis. Thorpe, an employee of Bennigan's, was burned by boiling oil from the fryer and sued Bullock for damages. A state statute imposes strict liability on manufacturers of defective products "sold as new." Assume that the fryer was defective. Should Bullock be subjected to a lawsuit based on strict liability in tort?

CHAPTER 19

Performance of the Sales Contract; Remedies for Breach of Contract

Many disputes between the parties to a sales contract concern the question of performance. Has the seller delivered what was promised? Has the buyer made the agreed payment? If either has failed to live up to the terms of the agreement, what remedy is available to the other? The first part of this chapter discusses the performance obligations of seller and buyer. The second part discusses their remedies for breach of the sales contract.

Performance of the Sales Contract

The physical acts required for the performance of a particular sales contract vary according to the kind of delivery process to which the parties agreed—delivery by carrier, seller's noncarrier delivery, buyer's picking the goods up at the seller's place of business, or delivery of a document of title without moving the goods. Yet, the legal principles governing performance are the same for all methods of delivery. Consider, for example, the steps normally taken in carrying out a sale involving a delivery by carrier:

1 Bob (the buyer) orders a desk from Sue.
2 Sue identifies the desk to the contract (e.g., marks it "for Bob").
3 Sue begins physical delivery by putting the desk in the custody of the carrier. How this is done is discussed later in this chapter.
4 The desk arrives, and Bob *inspects* it.
5 If the desk has obvious defects, Bob *rejects* it.
6 Upon Bob's rejection, Sue attempts to "*cure*" (correct) the defects. If cure is timely, Bob must "*accept*" the desk or be liable for breach of contract.
7 If the desk arrives undamaged, Bob accepts it.
8 Where Bob accepts the desk and later discovers hidden defects, Bob *revokes his acceptance* and returns the desk to Sue.
9 If there is no basis for rejecting the desk, Bob *pays* the price, less any proper deduc-

Figure 19.1 Performance of Sales Contract

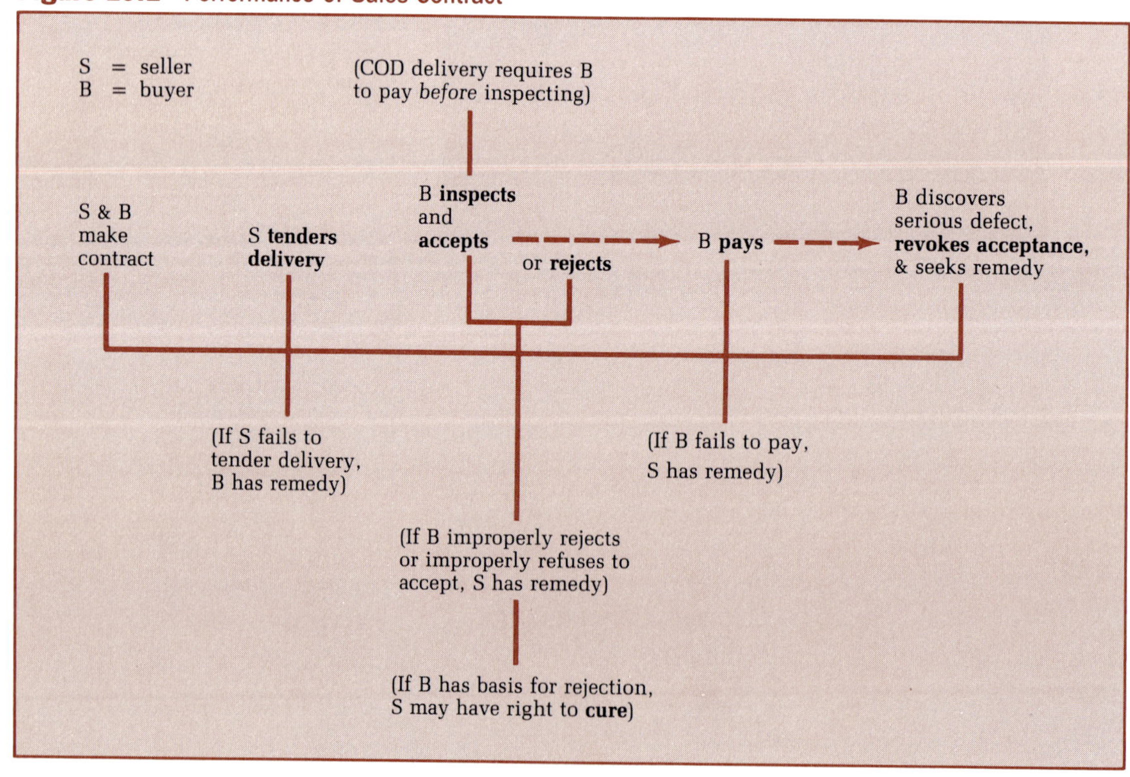

tions for minor damage or shortages such as a missing drawer pull.

Although the precise steps required for physical delivery vary from one method to another, the acts of inspection, rejection, cure, etc., are common to all types of delivery. Figure 19.1 shows the usual sequence of events that may occur during an attempt to perform a sales contract.

We turn now to the legal aspects of performance—the seller's obligation to deliver the goods, the buyer's obligation to accept and to pay for them, and certain excuses for nonperformance that relieve both parties of their obligations.

Performance: General Concepts

Obligations of the Parties. Sellers and buyers "perform" by meeting the obligations that they undertake by entering into a contract. In a sale of goods, the general obligation of the *seller* is to transfer ownership of the goods and to deliver them as required by the contract. The obligation of the *buyer* is to accept the goods and to pay for them as required by the contract [2-301]. The agreement of the parties, as supplemented or as limited by law, constitutes "the contract" by which the performance obligations of the parties are to be measured.

Meaning of "Tender." Sellers and buyers meet their performance obligations by making a "tender" of performance. A *tender* is an offer of performance by one party that, if unjustifiably refused, places the other party in default and permits the tendering party to have remedies for breach of contract. For example, Bill orders a swing set from Sue to be delivered to his house on Tuesday. Late Monday night Bill decides to cancel the contract. Early Tuesday morning, Sue's truck arrives at Bill's house with the swing set in good condition. Sue has made a tender of delivery. If Bill refuses to accept the swing set, he will be in breach of the contract.

The Perfect Tender Rule. If the goods or the seller's tender of delivery fails *in any respect* to conform to the contract, the buyer may reject the goods (or the tender) [2-601]. This rule, called the "perfect tender rule," protects the buyer from having to track down missing documents, from having to accept faulty documents (such as a warehouse receipt that lacks a necessary indorsement), or from having to argue with the seller about the sufficiency of an incomplete performance (such as a truckload of cotton that is missing one bale). The protection provided by this rule is especially important to buyers who are geographically distant from sellers. However, to prevent buyers from taking undue advantage of the right to reject, the perfect tender rule has certain exceptions or "relaxations" that are discussed later in this chapter.

Seller's Obligation to Deliver

How Seller Meets the Delivery Obligation. A seller meets his or her obligation to deliver the goods by making a tender of delivery. Tender of delivery requires that the seller (1) put and hold *conforming* goods at the buyer's disposition and (2) give the buyer any notification reasonably necessary to enable the buyer to take delivery [2-503(1)]. Goods are "conforming" when they are in accordance with the obligations under the contract, including any warranty (assurance) as to quality of or title to the goods. The seller's tender must be at a reasonable hour, and if the tender is of the goods themselves (as opposed to a tender of a document of title), the seller must keep the goods available for the period reasonably necessary to enable the buyer to take possession. Unless otherwise agreed, the buyer must furnish facilities reasonably suited to the receipt of the goods.

Tender Requirements for Common Types of Delivery. The specific acts required for an effective tender of delivery vary according to the kind of delivery agreed to by the parties to the sales contract or imposed by the UCC where the parties were silent as to delivery. Once the kind of delivery has been established, the specific acts required for an effective tender can be determined by applying the Code sections on tender. The tender requirements for some common types of delivery are discussed in the following paragraphs.

Delivery involving no carrier. Often delivery occurs at the seller's place of business. Suppose, for example, that Bob signs a contract to buy from Sue a particular motorboat from Sue's stock of boats, that the motorboat is to be specially equipped from Sue's stock of accessories, and that the contract says nothing about the time and place of delivery.

Sue must make delivery within a reasonable time [2-309]. Since Sue is a dealer who has a place of business, and since the boat and accessories are located there, the place for delivery is Sue's place of business [2-308]. Under Section 2-503(1), Sue may tender delivery by notifying Bob within a reasonable time that the boat is ready for pickup at Sue's place of business.

Delivery might involve a bailee such as a warehouse. Where goods are in the possession of a bailee and are to be delivered without being moved, the seller can fulfill the tender obligation by offering a negotiable document of title covering the goods or by procuring the bailee's acknowledgement of the buyer's right to have the goods [2-503(4)]. *If the buyer does not object,* the seller can make a tender by offering a *non*negotiable document of title or a written instruction (such as a delivery order) to the bailee to release the goods to the buyer. Recall from Chapter 17, however, that a seller who tenders a nonnegotiable document or a written instruction retains the risk of loss of the goods, and the risk that the bailee will not honor the document or instruction, until the buyer has had a reasonable time to present it to the bailee. Furthermore, the bailee's refusal to honor the nonnegotiable document or written instruction *defeats* the seller's tender (i.e., the bailee's refusal means that the seller has made no effective tender). All documents required for making a tender must be in correct form.

Delivery involving a carrier. Unless displaced by a contrary agreement, rules of Article 2 govern tender in common types of deliveries involving a carrier. Under a *shipment* contract (defined in Chapter 17), the seller fulfills his or her tender obligation by completing four steps: (1) putting conforming goods in the possession of a carrier, (2) making a reasonable contract for their transportation, (3) obtaining and promptly delivering or tendering in due form any document necessary to enable the buyer to obtain possession of the goods, and (4) promptly notifying the buyer of the shipment [2-504]. (The costs of shipping will be included in the price of the goods, or the buyer will pay the shipping charges separately.)

Except for installment contracts (discussed later), the perfect tender rule permits the buyer to reject nonconforming goods even for minor defects; and the seller's failing to provide a required document is always a basis for the buyer to reject a tender of delivery. Also, if the seller fails to notify the buyer of the shipment or fails to make a proper contract for the transportation of the goods, the buyer may reject the goods—*but only if the seller's failure causes the buyer a material delay or loss* [2-504]. These rules relating to shipment contracts thus place upon the seller the responsibility for arranging suitable transportation, but relax the perfect tender rule to protect the seller from harmless error in making the arrangements. Suppose Ben, a Michigan grocer, orders 500 crates of grapefruit from Sue, a Florida grapefruit seller. Sue properly ships conforming grapefruit by rail to Ben, but she forgets to notify Ben of the shipment. When the grapefruit arrives, the stationmaster immediately notifies Ben of its arrival. Ben suffers no harm from Sue's failure to notify him of the shipment and cannot reject the grapefruit. Figure 19.2 lists relaxations of the perfect tender rule.

Under a *destination* contract, the seller fulfills the tender obligation by completing three steps: (1) putting and holding conforming goods *at destination* for the buyer's disposition, (2) giving the buyer any notification reasonably necessary to enable the buyer to take delivery, and (3) tendering any required documents in correct form [2-503(3)].

Seller's Cure of Improper Delivery. A seller may have a right to "cure" (correct) an improper tender or an improper delivery. Suppose Sue sells a power saw to Ben, who requires delivery on or before June 1. Sue delivers the saw on May 25, but Ben rejects it because some parts are missing. Sue may give notice of her intention to cure the nonconforming delivery and then *within the time set by the contract for performance* may make a conforming

Figure 19.2 Relaxations of Perfect Tender Rule

A perfect tender is NOT required where:

1. The sales contract so provides.
2. Seller fails to notify seller of shipment or fails to make a proper transportation contract, but **no material delay or loss to buyer** results.
3. As discussed later in this chapter, seller has **time remaining** under contract **to cure** defects.
4. In installment contract (discussed later), **nonconformity** of goods is **minor.**

delivery [2-508]. Even where Sue has taken back the nonconforming goods and refunded the purchase price, she may effect cure if she can do so before the time for performance expires. The time for performance is the time stated in the contract (here, June 1); if no time was stated, the time for performance is a reasonable time.

Sometimes, to reduce the harmful effects of the buyer's surprise rejection of the goods, the UCC gives to the seller the right to cure a defective tender *after* the time set for performance. Where a buyer rejects a nonconforming tender that the seller had *reasonable grounds to believe would be acceptable* with or without money allowance, the seller may, upon notifying the buyer "seasonably" (in a timely manner), have a *further* reasonable time to substitute a conforming tender. For example, suppose Brenda orders Brand X galvanized pipe from Sam for delivery at noon on November 1. At the appointed hour Sam delivers Brand Y pipe of the same kind and quality for the same price. If Brenda rejects the Brand Y pipe, and if Sam reasonably believed that the delivery of Brand Y pipe would be acceptable, Sam is entitled to a further reasonable time to cure the nonconformity.

Buyer's Obligation to Accept and to Pay

Where the seller has properly tendered conforming goods, the buyer is obliged to accept them and to pay the price. However, the buyer's obligations are conditioned on a right to inspect the goods. Where a tender of delivery does not conform to the contract, the buyer may have a right to reject the goods or to revoke any acceptance (and to recover any payment) he or she might have made.

Meaning and Effect of Buyer's Acceptance. *Acceptance* of goods means that the buyer, in accordance with the contract, takes as his or her own the goods that the seller has appropriated (set aside) for the contract. The buyer may accept by words, action, or silence when it is time for the buyer to speak. Acceptance may occur in a variety of ways—for example, by the buyer's telling the seller that the goods are conforming or that the buyer will take or retain them in spite of their nonconformity; by the buyer's failure to make an effective rejection; or by the buyer's doing some act inconsistent with the seller's ownership, such as reselling the goods or incorporating building materials into a building [2-606]. If the buyer's act is wrongful, acceptance does not occur (and the buyer commits the tort of conversion) unless the wrongful act is ratified by the seller.

The legal effect of acceptance is that the buyer becomes obligated to pay the contract price [2-607]. Moreover, a buyer who has accepted a defective tender is *barred from any remedy,* including a remedy for breach of warranty, unless the seller is *notified* of the defect within a reasonable time after it has been or should have been discovered. Notice is required so that the seller may take steps to cure a defective performance or, where defective goods are alleged to have caused harm, so that the seller may adequately prepare for negotiation or defense of a lawsuit. What constitutes "reasonable" notice depends on the facts of the case. An injured consumer who is unaware of the requirement to notify the seller may be allowed more time to give notice than a merchant would be.

Buyer's Right to Inspect the Goods. The buyer may make a reasonable inspection of the goods to see whether they conform to the contract. Usually, the right to inspect may be exercised before payment or acceptance. Accordingly, when the seller is required or authorized to send the goods to the buyer, the buyer may take custody of the goods for the purpose of inspection without being considered to have accepted the goods. With rare exceptions, no agreement by the parties can displace the right of inspection [2-513, comment 1].

Even though the right to inspect usually may be exercised before payment, the buyer can be required by contract to pay first and inspect later. For example, unless otherwise agreed, CIF, COD ("collect on delivery"), cash against documents, and similar contract clauses require payment *before* inspection. Upon inspection after payment, the buyer may, of course, reject nonconforming goods and have appropriate remedies such as damages. And even where the contract requires the buyer to make payment before inspection, the buyer may withhold payment if the nonconformity is obvious without inspection [2-512]. The buyer is not required, for example, to pay for goods that obviously are not the goods ordered.

Sometimes a CIF contract contains a clause providing for payment *on or after arrival* of the goods.

The presence of such a clause gives the buyer the right to "such preliminary inspection as is feasible" *before* making payment [2-321(3)]. The clause merely postpones the time for payment. It does not, by itself, change the risk-of-loss consequences of a CIF contract. If the goods do not arrive, payment is due to the seller when the goods should have arrived.

Buyer's Options on Improper Delivery. Within limits imposed by the Code, a buyer may *reject* an improper tender or an improper delivery of goods. In some situations the buyer may *revoke acceptance* of defective goods.

Rejection of goods. In general, a buyer may reject goods that do not conform to the contract. Specifically, the buyer may "(a) reject the whole; or (b) accept the whole; or (c) accept any commercial unit or units and reject the rest" [2-601]. A "commercial unit" is an amount of goods that in business practice is treated as a single whole for purposes of sale, and whose division would materially impair its value or character (e.g., a machine, a bale of cotton, a carload of wheat).

The rejection must be made within a reasonable time after delivery or tender of the goods, and the buyer *must seasonably* (in a timely manner) *notify* the seller of the rejection [2-602]. In addition, the buyer must specify the defects upon which the buyer bases the rejection, if those defects are ascertainable by inspection [2-605]. The requirement that defects be specified is for the protection of the seller's right to cure any curable defects. A buyer who merely rejects a delivery without stating any real objections to it may be acting in commercial bad faith, seeking only to get out of a deal which has become unprofitable. Such conduct is not permitted. A buyer's failure to reject in accordance with Code rules *results in acceptance* and liability for payment.

The buyer's right of rejection is limited by important Code rules regarding installment contracts. An *installment contract* is one that requires or authorizes the delivery of goods in separate lots which are to be separately accepted. The buyer may reject a nonconforming installment (delivery of goods) *only if* the nonconformity *substantially impairs* the value of that installment *and cannot be cured* [2-612]. Suppose, for example, that Ben, a skilled furniture maker, uses 1,000 board-feet of high-quality walnut lumber each week. To meet his production needs he orders 10,000 board-feet to be delivered in ten weekly installments of 1,000 board-feet each at 8 A.M. sharp each Monday. Sue, the seller, delivers the first three installments, but the fourth lot, delivered at 7 A.M. Monday, is so knotty that Ben cannot use it. Ben may reject the fourth installment because the nonconformity substantially impairs its value to him—but *only if* Sue cannot make a substitute delivery of conforming lumber by 8 A.M.

The installment-contract restriction on a buyer's right to reject goods is a second exception to the perfect tender rule. The purpose of the exception is to prevent a buyer from, for example, seizing on a trivial defect as an excuse to reject goods that are, in fact, substantially what was ordered. In a shipment contract, the goods ordinarily will be at the buyer's place of business when rejected. The seller might be hundreds of miles away. If the seller had to prove that the goods and their tender were perfect, considerable expense could be involved, and the buyer would be in a position to threaten rejection to force a lower price. To protect the *seller,* the Code therefore prohibits the buyer from rejecting the goods unless the defect substantially impairs the value of the installment and cannot be cured. To protect the *buyer,* the Code permits the buyer to have damages for any defect, no matter how trivial.

Where one or more installments are so defective that they substantially impair the value of the *whole contract* (and cannot be cured), the buyer may cancel the contract (and have other remedies such as damages). However, if the buyer accepts a nonconforming installment without seasonably notifying the seller of cancellation, or brings suit as to past installments only, or demands performance of future installments, the buyer *loses* the right to cancel the breached contract (i.e., reinstates it).

An installment contract *may* require accurate conformity in quality as a condition to the seller's right to the buyer's acceptance, *but only if there is a real need* for such conformity. To be enforceable, a provision requiring accurate conformity in quality must have some basis in reason and must avoid imposing hardship by surprise. A requirement of strictly accurate conformity might be enforceable in a purchase of surgeon's tools or delicate parts for a space shuttle, but not in a purchase of waste logs to be processed into chipboard.

Case 19.1 discusses the right to reject nonconforming goods, and the difference between acceptance of goods and taking possession of them for the purpose of inspection.

CASE 19.1 Capitol Dodge, Inc. v. Northern Concrete Pipe, Inc. · 346 N.W.2d 535 (Mich. App. 1983)

FACTS Acting on behalf of defendant Northern Concrete Pipe, William Washabaugh investigated the purchase of a pickup truck with a snowplow attachment from Capitol Dodge, Inc. (plaintiff). During a test drive, the engine overheated. Washabaugh expressed concern about the overheating. Fuller, Capitol's salesman, said it resulted from an incorrect positioning of the snowplow blade in front of the radiator. Indicating his willingness to buy the truck if Fuller's assessment of the problem was correct, Washabaugh signed a contract of sale, and he gave Fuller a check for the purchase price.

The next day, LeFave and Reid, Northern's employees, arrived to pick up the truck, Fuller showed them how to position the blade, and they left for Northern's place of business. The engine overheated during the trip. Northern's mechanic called Capitol and was told to recheck the blade position, refill the radiator, and take the truck out for another drive. The engine again overheated. Capitol told LeFave to return the truck to Capitol's service department. Capitol replaced the radiator cap, LeFave again picked up the truck, and it continued to overheat.

On Washabaugh's orders, LeFave immediately notified Capitol by telephone that Northern was not taking the truck, that payment of the check was being stopped, and that Capitol should come get the truck. Capitol did so, and later had title papers issued in the name of Northern. Northern stopped payment on the check and tried to return the title papers to Capitol, but Capitol refused them and sued Northern for damages for breach of contract. From a district court judgment for Capitol, Northern appealed. The circuit court affirmed the judgment, and Northern appealed to the court of appeals.

OPINION PETERSON, J. . . . [The trial judge erred in concluding that Northern had accepted the truck.]

The Uniform Commercial Code, § 2-606, provides:

> (1) Acceptance of goods occurs when the buyer (a) after a reasonable opportunity to inspect the goods signifies to the seller that the goods are conforming or that he will take or retain them in spite of their nonconformity; or (b) fails to make an effective rejection. . . , but such acceptance does not occur until the buyer has had a reasonable opportunity to inspect them; or (c) does any act inconsistent with the seller's ownership. . . .

This language, in defining what constitutes an acceptance, clearly contemplates an act of the buyer beyond taking delivery or possession of the goods. Possession during the time necessary for the "reasonable opportunity" to inspect is contemplated prior to acceptance. Similarly, § 2-602 of the code allows a rejection of goods for nonconformance "within a reasonable time *after their delivery.*" Thus, while transfer[s] of possession or title may be acts bearing on the question of acceptance, they are not in themselves determinative thereof. . . .

In *Colonial Dodge, Inc. v. Miller*. . . , a majority of the Court adopted the holding in *Zabriskie Chevrolet, Inc. v. Smith*. . . , a case in which a newly purchased automobile became inoperable as the purchaser was driving it home from the dealer's showroom.

Zabriskie is pertinent for two reasons. In the first place, [with regard to] acceptance under the UCC, it speaks to the relationship between the manufacturer and seller of complex machines or devices on the one hand and the dependent buyer on the

CASE 19.1 Continued

other. . . . The buyer may be expert in the use of the machine or device[,] but he generally has no expertise as to the mechanical, electronic, chemical, and engineering components that combine to produce the intended performance. *Zabriskie* recognized this buyer dependency on the seller's expertise in holding that something more than a mere visual inspection is appropriate before the buyer can be held to have accepted the machine. We agree. A "reasonable time to inspect" under the UCC must allow an opportunity to put the product to its intended use, or for testing to verify its capability to perform as intended.

Zabriskie is also important for its holding that the adoption of [Section 2-601 of the UCC], which provides that the buyer may reject goods which "fail in any respect to conform to the contract," creates a "perfect tender" rule replacing pre-code cases defining performance of a sales contract in terms of [the seller's] substantial compliance. We agree with that construction of the code. . . .

In the instant case, there was no acceptance. Nothing that defendant did can be construed. . . as signifying, after a reasonable opportunity to inspect, that the truck conformed or that defendant would retain the truck in spite of its nonconformity. Defendant had the absolute right to reject the truck for nonconformity within a reasonable time, and to seasonably notify the plaintiff thereof. It did so.

JUDGMENT Reversed and remanded for entry of judgment in favor of defendant. . . .

Revocation of acceptance. Suppose Ben accepts goods that are defective. In two principal situations, Ben may have a right to revoke his acceptance of goods whose nonconformity *substantially impairs* their value to him [2-608]: (1) He may revoke where he knew of the substantial nonconformity but accepted the goods on the reasonable assumption that the defect would be cured and it has not been seasonably cured. (2) He may revoke where, *not* knowing of the substantial nonconformity, he *reasonably* accepted because of (a) the difficulty of discovering the substantial nonconformity before acceptance, or (b) the seller's assurances (express or implied) that the goods had no defects. Ben may revoke as to the entire lot of goods accepted or as to any subdivision of the lot that constitutes a commercial unit. Revocation of acceptance must occur within a reasonable time after Ben discovers or should have discovered the substantial nonconformity. Ben may *not* revoke if the goods have undergone substantial change for reasons *other than* their own defects, such as Ben's failure to store them properly. (Nor may Ben revoke his acceptance where he knew of the defects at the time of acceptance but had no reason to assume that the defects would be cured, as where an obviously damaged camera is sold "as is.")

As noted in Figure 19.3, although Ben may *reject* goods for even a trivial defect (where the perfect tender rule applies), he cannot *revoke acceptance* unless the defect in the goods is substantial. One reason is that rejection occurs when the goods are still new, or at least unused by the rejecting buyer, while revocation occurs after the buyer has taken possession of the goods and in all likelihood has used them. It would be unfair to sellers to allow buyers easily to revoke acceptance of depreciated goods.

The case that follows deals not only with revocation of acceptance but also with whether the seller has a right to cure after the buyer's revocation.

Figure 19.3 Rejection v. Revocation of Acceptance

Rejection: Available to buyer for ANY defect, no matter how minor, unless perfect tender rule does not apply.

Revocation of Acceptance: Available to buyer only if non-conformity is SUBSTANTIAL.

CASE 19.2 Gappelberg v. Landrum · 654 S.W.2d 549 (Tex. 1984)

FACTS Gappelberg purchased a large-screen Advent television set from Landrum, doing business as The Video Station. Gappelberg immediately experienced a variety of problems with the new set. After Landrum and the authorized repair agency made several house calls in unsuccessful repair attempts, the set totally ceased operating. Gappelberg allowed the television set to be removed from his home, but he refused offers of further repairs, saying he simply wanted his money and old set returned to him. Landrum felt he was in no position to return the old set, for which he had allowed $1,500 as a trade-in on the purchase price of over $3,700, since he had promised the old set as a prize for a promotional sweepstakes. Instead he offered Gappelberg another Advent as a replacement. Gappelberg refused to accept the substitute and brought suit against Landrum. The parties stipulated the following facts, among others: Gappelberg accepted the television set without knowledge of the defects; he revoked acceptance within a reasonable time after the defects were discovered and before any change in the condition of the set occurred because of circumstances other than the defects; he gave Landrum timely notice of revocation; and there were several major defects, any one of which substantially impaired the set. Nevertheless, holding that revocation of acceptance under § 2-608 of the UCC was subject to the seller's right to cure under § 2-508, the trial court rendered judgment for Landrum. The court of appeals affirmed the judgment, and Gappelberg appealed.

OPINION KILGARLIN, J. . . . The court of appeals, while affirming the judgment of the trial court, concluded that a seller did not have the right to cure by repair once there had been a revocation of acceptance, but the right to cure by replacement was not precluded.

The concept of revocation of acceptance is relatively new. . . . Early court decisions interpreting the Code confused the [term] "revocation" with "rescission" and "rejection." Gradually, however, the concept of revocation of acceptance has taken hold. Its principle is simple. The right of a buyer to revoke exists only when the buyer has initially accepted the goods in question. Rejection, however, is an initial act of the buyer, meaning there was never an acceptance.

The right of the seller to cure by repair or replacement clearly exists in instances of rejection. UCC § 2-508. This, of course, is not a rejection case. It is a case in which . . . the buyer was clearly entitled to revoke his acceptance. Revocation of acceptance is controlled by UCC § 2-608, which reads as follows:

> . . . (a) The buyer may revoke his acceptance of a lot or commercial unit whose non-conformity substantially impairs its value to him if he has accepted it (1) on the reasonable assumption that its non-conformity would be cured and it has not been seasonably cured; or (2) without discovery of such non-conformity if his acceptance was reasonably induced either by the difficulty of discovery before acceptance or by the seller's assurances. . . .

. . . [P]aragraph (a) (2) is applicable to this case. The only reference to cure in § 2-608 is in situations when the buyer knew of the defects at the time of acceptance of the goods. There is no reference to cure for our situation where Gappelberg accepted the television set without knowing of the defects. The court of appeals, in its opinion, has listed the numerous cases from other jurisdictions which hold that once a buyer properly revokes acceptance, the seller no longer has the right to cure by repair. . . .

The court of appeals in this case notes that in none of the cases in which a seller's right to cure has been denied once revocation of acceptance occurs was the buyer presented with such a generous offer as Landrum's offer to replace. The court of appeals concluded that "in the spirit of the Code," cure by replacement[,] even in revocation situations[,] should be authorized.

CASE 19.2 Continued

[However, in *Zabriskie Chevrolet, Inc. v. Smith,* a New Jersey rejection case,] the court observed that "for a majority of people, the purchase of a new car is a major investment, rationalized by the peace of mind that flows from its dependability and safety. Once their faith is shaken, the vehicle loses not only its real value in their eyes, but becomes an instrument whose integrity is substantially impaired and whose operation was fraught with apprehension." In *Zabriskie,* a new 1966 Chevrolet ceased to operate within one mile of being removed from the showroom, because of a faulty transmission. The buyer was not forced to take the Chevrolet with a different transmission in it, his faith in the whole automobile having been shaken. By the same token, Gappelberg had seen one Advent television perform, or fail to perform..., and there certainly is justification for his not wanting to go through experiences with another Advent. Professor Wallach states, "the seller is ordinarily in a better position to maximize the return on the resale of the goods, and his disposition of the goods eliminates the storage and other incidental expenses that may be involved in the unsatisfactory transaction."... This is probably the best policy reason of all for denying replacement after revocation—the relative position of the parties....

We are cited no good policy reason why different rules should [apply] to cure by replacement [than apply to] cure by repair.... Thus, we state that once a buyer has properly revoked acceptance of a product, the seller has [no] right to cure [either by repair or by replacement]....

JUDGMENT [T]he judgments of the courts below are reversed.

Buyer's Obligation to Pay for Goods Accepted. Bob Buyer meets his obligation to pay the price by making payment in accordance with the contract. If the parties have not stated how payment is to be made, Bob may pay in any customary manner, unless the seller demands payment in legal tender (money) and gives any extension of time reasonably necessary to procure it [2-511]. This rule protects Bob from a surprise demand for cash. For the protection of sellers who accept checks, however, a buyer's payment by check is only a conditional payment and is defeated by refusal of the bank upon which the check was drawn to pay it.

If the parties have not stated the time and the place for payment, either of the following rules applies: (1) Payment is due at the time and place at which the buyer is to receive the goods; or (2) where delivery is to be made by means of documents of title, payment is due at the time and place at which the buyer is to receive the documents, regardless of where the goods are to be received. Both of these rules are subject to any right of the buyer to inspect the goods before payment.

If the goods are lost in transit, and if the risk of loss has shifted to the buyer, the buyer is obligated to make payment at the time and place at which he or she was to receive the goods. Suppose that a foreign seller ships goods to a New York buyer under a CIF contract and the goods are lost at sea. A CIF contract places the risk of loss on the buyer when the seller properly puts the goods in the custody of the carrier. Because the buyer acquires the risk of loss when the carrier receives the goods, the buyer must pay for them despite their nonarrival and must rely on the insurance provided for in the CIF contract.

Where the parties have agreed to an extension of credit, the credit term governs the time, place, and manner of payment to the extent that the credit term discusses these matters.

Excuse for Nonperformance or Substitute Performance

If the performance of a contractual obligation becomes more burdensome than the obligated party anticipated, that party might ask to be excused from performance. In general, the parties to a contract are excused from their performance obligations when performance has been rendered impossible or unreasonably burdensome by circumstances beyond the contemplation of the parties at the time of contracting.

Excuse for Nonperformance. Article 2 adopts "commercial impracticability" as the main basis for excusing nonperformance of obligations under a sales contract. The article also provides rules that apply where an agreed method of payment or delivery fails and a substitute method is sought by the aggrieved (injured) party.

Commercial impracticability. Unless the seller has assumed a greater obligation, the seller is excused for delay in delivery or for nondelivery of goods *if* performance has been made *impracticable* by an unexpected occurrence of the type discussed in the next paragraph [2-615]. The seller is also excused if the agreed performance has been made impracticable because of an applicable foreign or domestic governmental regulation or order. Suppose that a manufacturer agrees to make and sell sophisticated electronics equipment to a buyer in a foreign country. If the foreign buyer's government later unexpectedly forbids the importation of such equipment, the manufacturer is excused from performance.

The drafters of Article 2 explain the meaning of *commercial impracticability* as follows:

> Increased cost alone does not excuse performance unless the rise in cost is due to some unforeseen contingency which alters the essential nature of the performance. Neither is a rise or a collapse in the market in itself a justification, for that is exactly the type of business risk which business contracts made at fixed prices are intended to cover. But a severe shortage of raw materials or of supplies due to a contingency such as war, embargo, local crop failure, unforeseen shutdown of major sources of supply, or the like, which either causes a marked increase in cost or altogether prevents the seller from securing supplies necessary to his performance, is within the contemplation of this section [2-615, comment 4].

Where commercial impracticability only *partially* impairs the seller's capacity to perform, the seller must *allocate* production and deliveries among his or her customers in a fair and reasonable manner. Regardless of the degree of impairment, the seller will *not* be excused from performance unless he or she seasonably notifies the buyer that there will be a delay or nondelivery. If there is a partial impairment, the seller must also inform the buyer of any production or delivery quota to which the buyer is entitled.

In response to the seller's notice of a material delay or an allocation of goods, the buyer may, by written notification to the seller, elect to do one of the following: (1) terminate (and thereby discharge) any unperformed portion of the contract or (2) modify the contract by agreeing to take the available quota [2-616]. The buyer may terminate the whole of an installment contract if the seller's deficiency *substantially impairs* the value of the whole contract. Where a seller is excused from performance because of unforeseen circumstances, the buyer is also excused, despite any agreement to the contrary.

Case 19.3 illustrates the general reluctance of the courts to discharge a contracting party on the basis of commercial impracticability unless the unexpected circumstance is truly unforeseeable and the loss so great as to lie beyond the reasonable expectations of the parties.

CASE 19.3 Maple Farms, Inc. v. City School District · 352 N.Y.S.2d 784 (N.Y. Sup. Ct. 1974)

FACTS In June 1973, the plaintiff (Maple Farms, Inc.) entered a contract with the defendant school district to supply it with milk for the school year 1973–1974. By December 1973, the price of raw milk was 23 percent higher than the price of raw milk in June. The plaintiff would lose $7,350.55 if required to supply milk at the December price. The defendant refused to relieve the plaintiff of its contract and to put the contract out for rebidding. Faced with losses on similar contracts with other school districts, the plaintiff brought this action for a declaratory judgment. The plaintiff alleged that the performance of the contract with the defendant school district has been made impracticable by the

CASE 19.3 Continued

occurrence of events not contemplated by the parties. The plaintiff requested (by means of a motion for summary judgment) that the contract be terminated.

OPINION

SWARTWOOD, J. The plaintiff [argues that the substantial increase in the price of raw milk] could not have been foreseen by the parties because it came about in large measure from the agreement of the United States to sell huge amounts of grain to Russia and to a lesser extent [from] unanticipated crop failure.

The legal basis of the plaintiff's request for being relieved of the obligation under the contract award is the doctrine known variously as "impossibility of performance" and "frustration of performance" at common law and as "Excuse by Failure of Presupposed Conditions" under the UCC, Section 2-615. . . .

Performance has been excused at common law where performance has become illegal; where disaster wipes out the means of production; [and] where governmental action prevents performance.

In *Mineral Park Land Co. v. Howard*, . . . the defendants agreed to take all the gravel from the plaintiff's land up to a certain quantity. The defendants took only half the agreed amount because the balance of the gravel was under the water level. The court relieved the defendants from the obligation to pay for the balance under water because it was not within the contemplation of the parties that the gravel under the water level would be taken and secondly because the cost of doing so would be ten to twelve times as expensive. The court stated the common law rule at page 460:

> "A thing is impossible in legal contemplation when it is not practicable; and a thing is impracticable when it can only be done at an excessive and unreasonable cost. . . . We do not mean to intimate that the defendants could excuse themselves by showing the existence of conditions which would make the performance of their obligation more expensive than they had anticipated, or which would entail a loss upon them. But, where the difference in cost is so great as here, and has the effect, as found, of making performance impracticable, the situation is not different from that of a total absence of earth and gravel."

. . . [W]here economic hardship alone is involved, performance will not be excused. This is so even where governmental acts make performance more expensive. Existing circumstances and foreseeability also play a part in determining whether a party should be relieved of his contracts.

The Uniform Commercial Code, Section 2-615, states in part:

> Except so far as a seller may have assumed a greater obligation . . . : (a) Delay in delivery or non-delivery in whole or in part by a seller . . . is not a breach of his duty under a contract for sale if performance as agreed has been made impracticable by the occurrence of a contingency the non-occurrence of which was a basic assumption on which the contract was made. . . .

[The case of *Transatlantic Financing Corp. v. United States** also involved the doctrine enunciated in Section 2-615, "Excuse by Failure of Presupposed Conditions." The court explained the doctrine in these words:]

> The doctrine ultimately represents the ever shifting line, drawn by courts hopefully responsive to commercial practices and mores, at which the community's interest in having contracts enforced according to their terms is outweighed by the commercial senselessness of requiring performance. When the issue is raised, the court is asked to construct a condition of performance based on the changed circumstances, a process which involves at least three reasonably definable steps. First, a contingency—something unexpected—must have occurred. Second, the risk of the unexpected occurrence must not have been allocated either by agreement or by custom. Finally, occurrence of the contingency must have rendered performance commercially impracticable.

CASE 19.3 Continued

Applying these rules to the facts here we find that the contingency causing the increase of the price of raw milk was not totally unexpected. The president of the plaintiff milk dealer has for at least ten years bid on contracts to supply milk for the defendant school district and is thoroughly conversant with prices and costs. The price from the low point in the year 1972 to the price on the date of the award of the contract in June 1973 had risen nearly 10%, and any businessman should have been aware of the general inflation in this country during the previous years and of the chance of crop failure.

However, should we grant that the first test had been met, and thus that the substantial increase in price was due to the sale of wheat to Russia, poor crops and general market conditions which were unexpected contingencies, then the question of allocation of risk must be met. Here the very purpose of the contract was to guard against fluctuation of the price of half pints of milk as a basis for the school budget. Surely had the price of raw milk fallen substantially, the defendant could not be excused from performance. We can reasonably assume that the plaintiff had to be aware of escalating inflation. It is chargeable with knowledge of the substantial increase of the price of raw milk from the previous year's low. It had knowledge that for many years the Department of Agriculture had established the price of raw milk and that that price varied. It nevertheless entered into this agreement with that knowledge. It did not provide in the contract any exculpatory clause to excuse it from performance in the event of a substantial rise in the price of raw milk. On these facts the risk of a substantial or abnormal increase in the price of raw milk can be allocated to the plaintiff.

. . . [W]here the circumstances reveal a willingness on the part of the seller to accept abnormal rises in costs, the question of impracticability of performance should be judged by stricter terms than where the contingency is totally unforeseen. . . .

There is no precise point . . . at which an increase in price of raw goods above the norm would be so disproportionate to the risk assumed as to amount to "impracticality" in a commercial sense. However, we cannot say on these facts that the increase here has reached the point of "impracticality" in performance of this contract in light of the risks that we find were assumed by the plaintiff.

JUDGMENT The plaintiff's motion is denied and the defendant is granted summary judgment dismissing the complaint.

*362 F.2d 312 (D.C. Cir. 1966).

Casualty to identified (specific) goods. Sometimes a contract is for a sale of a specific item or a lot of goods that is destroyed or damaged before the buyer actually receives the goods. Suppose Sarah Seller has on display a dozen Brand X refrigerators of a discontinued model. Eleven are green and one is yellow, and no others of that model are available to Seller. Bob Buyer makes clear that he needs the yellow refrigerator because it fits the color scheme of his kitchen. Buyer buys the yellow refrigerator, but before S can deliver it, it is destroyed by fire. Is Seller liable to Buyer for failure to deliver the yellow refrigerator?

The answer is "no." Where the contract requires for its performance specific goods that were identified when the contract was made, and the goods suffer casualty (damage) without fault of either party *before* the risk of loss passes to Buyer, then if the loss is *total,* the contract is *avoided,* i.e., neither Seller nor Buyer has any enforceable rights under the contract. If the loss is partial, Buyer may nevertheless demand inspection and at his option either treat the contract as avoided or accept the goods with due allowance from the contract price, but without any other right against Seller [2-613]. Here, since Seller is a merchant, the risk of loss does not pass to B until he actually receives the goods. Because the loss of the yellow refrigerator is total, S has no obligation to tender the refrigerator, and B has no obligation to pay for it. In contrast, if B had purchased *a* refrigerator of the discontinued model (instead of specifying the yellow one), Seller would be obliged to tender a Brand X refrigerator and B would be obliged to accept it and to make payment. However, if S's entire stock of the discontinued model had been destroyed, S would be excused from performance on the ground of impracticability.

Excuse for Substitute Performance. Sometimes the parties to a sales contract agree to a particular method of delivery or of payment. What happens if the *agreed method of delivery* fails—e.g., if an agreed type of carrier becomes unavailable without the fault of either party? The parties are required to use a commercially reasonable substitute carrier if one is available [2-614]. If there is no commercially reasonable substitute for the agreed method of delivery, both parties may be excused from their performance obligations on the ground of impracticability.

Where the *agreed means or manner of payment* fails because of domestic or foreign governmental regulation, the seller is required to make delivery only if the buyer provides a payment that is commercially a substantial equivalent. Sarah Seller contracts to sell refrigerators to a foreign buyer, and the buyer's government devalues its currency to one-tenth the value it had at the time of contracting. Seller is entitled to a payment substantially equivalent to the payment agreed upon and may refuse delivery if the substantial equivalent is not forthcoming. Where the buyer has already taken delivery of the goods, payment in accordance with the regulation discharges the buyer's obligation unless the regulation is discriminatory, oppressive, or predatory.

Remedies for Breach of Contract

A seller of goods expects to receive the price, and the buyer expects to receive goods that conform to the contract. If one party does not perform his or her contractual obligations, the other party may suffer inconvenience, monetary loss, or even a serious disruption of business. To minimize the difficulties that can result from a breach of a sales contract, Article 2 provides a number of remedies for the seller and the buyer. These remedies are available upon a breach or a threatened breach of the performance obligations discussed earlier in this chapter—the obligation of the seller to transfer and to deliver the goods and the obligation of the buyer to accept and to pay for them. The remainder of this chapter discusses the meaning of "breach of contract," the remedies of seller and buyer for breach of contract, and the extent to which the parties may limit remedies (e.g., the amount of damages) by means of the contract.

What Constitutes Breach of Contract

Failure of one party (upon tender of performance by the other party) to perform obligations imposed by the sales contract (including any warranty obligations) constitutes a breach of the contract. For example, the seller might deliver the wrong kind of goods, unmerchantable or stolen goods, fewer goods than specified in the contract, or no goods at all. Or the seller might deliver the goods later than required by the contract, perhaps too late for the buyer to use them. The buyer might default (breach the contract) by refusing to accept goods that conform to the contract or by refusing to pay all or part of the price. It should be noted, however, that unless the person entitled to performance *first tenders* his or her own performance, the other person's failure to perform is *not* a breach. Thus, the law of sales requires a positive indication from the person seeking a remedy for breach that that person had a real desire for performance and is not now merely seeking to enforce a contract that both parties had abandoned.

Often, the parties to a sales contract agree that their performances will be carried out at some future time, as where Sue sells Ben a car to be delivered and paid for 3 months from the date of the contract. But before the time scheduled for delivery, the buyer or the seller may express to the other party an intention not to go through with the contract. This refusal in advance to perform the contract is called a *repudiation* (or an *anticipatory breach*) of the contract. Such a repudiation gives the other party "reasonable grounds for insecurity," and the aggrieved (wronged) party has a right to "adequate assurance of due performance" [2-609].

The wrongdoer's failure to provide adequate assurance where such an assurance is warranted is also a repudiation of the contract. Upon a repudiation that will *substantially* impair the value of the contract to the aggrieved party, that party may suspend his or her own performance. Then the aggrieved party may await performance for a commercially reasonable time or take the remedial steps (such as canceling the contract) discussed later in this chapter [2-610]. However, the repudiating party (the wrongdoer) is free to retract the repudiation until the aggrieved party cancels the contract, materially changes his or her position, or otherwise indicates that he or she considers the repudiation final [2-611].

Suppose, for example, that Brenda has ordered 500 cabinets to be built by Sam and installed in Brenda's apartments before June 1, but on May 1 Sam's shop and many of the cabinets that have been built are seriously damaged by fire. Brenda has reason to doubt whether Sam can perform as promised, and she is entitled, upon making written demand, to an assurance of Sam's due performance. If Sam cannot make such an assurance—e.g., by providing reasonable evidence of ability to perform despite the fire—Brenda may treat the contract as breached and get cabinets elsewhere. Similarly, Sam might have agreed to extend credit to Brenda only to learn soon afterward that she has failed to pay other creditors. Brenda's ability to produce reasonable evidence of creditworthiness and to give valid reasons for failing to pay the other creditors might constitute an adequate assurance of due performance to Sam. The defaulting party has a reasonable time, not to exceed 30 days, to give the assurance.

Remedies of Seller and Buyer

The purpose of the UCC remedies for breach of contract is to put the aggrieved party in as good a position as that party would have been had the contract been fully performed [1-106]. More specifically, the remedies discussed in this chapter are intended to protect three main interests of seller and buyer: the expectation, the reliance, and the restitution interests. The *expectation interest* is the gain that the nondefaulting party expected to make had the defaulting party performed. The *reliance interest* is the interest of the nondefaulting party in recovering costs incurred in preparing for the hoped-for performance. For instance, the seller might have altered machinery solely to fill a special order for the buyer. The buyer might have made special arrangements to accommodate or sell goods that the seller promised but failed to deliver. The *restitution interest* is the interest of the nondefaulting party in recovering a benefit which that party conferred on the other party. The buyer might have made a prepayment on the price of the goods; the seller might have made a partial delivery.

Remedies of the Seller. Remedies are available to a seller where the buyer has breached the contract. The buyer breaches by (1) wrongfully rejecting the goods, (2) wrongfully revoking acceptance of the goods, (3) failing to make a payment due on or before delivery, or (4) repudiating as to all or part of the contract [2-703]. With respect to the goods affected by the breach, the seller may do one or more of the following.

1. The seller may *withhold delivery of the goods* where, for example, the buyer repudiates the contract or fails to make a payment due on or before delivery. Furthermore, where the seller learns before the buyer receives the goods that the buyer is *insolvent,* the seller may refuse to make delivery except for cash and, as noted in the next paragraph, may stop delivery of goods already on their way to the buyer [2-702].
2. The seller may *stop delivery of goods in the possession of a carrier or other bailee* [2-705]. If the reason for stoppage is the buyer's *insolvency*, the seller may stop the delivery, regardless of its size. But where the reason for stoppage is the seller's *insecurity* or something else not involving insolvency of the buyer, the right to stop delivery is limited to carload, truckload, planeload, or larger shipments. The reason for this limitation is to minimize the burden on carriers that would result if sellers were permitted to stop delivery of any shipment, no matter how small. A seller making a small shipment to a solvent

buyer of doubtful credit can avoid loss by shipping C.O.D. Moreover, where stoppage occurs for insecurity, the seller is merely suspending performance and awaiting the buyer's assurance of due performance. If the buyer makes the assurance, the seller is not entitled to resell or divert the goods.

3 As a preliminary to the remedy of resale or to an action for the price of the goods, the seller may *identify conforming goods to the contract.* If the goods are unfinished, the seller may either "complete the manufacture and wholly identify the goods to the contract, or cease manufacture and resell for scrap or salvage value, or proceed in any other reasonable manner" [2-704].

4 The seller may *resell the goods and recover damages* [2-706]. The resale must be made in good faith and in a commercially reasonable manner. Where the resale price is lower than the contract price, "the seller may recover the difference between the resale price and the contract price, together with any incidental damages . . . but less expenses saved in consequence of the buyer's breach." *Incidental damages* include (but are not limited to) any commercially reasonable expenses incurred in stopping delivery, transporting and caring for the goods after the buyer's breach, and returning or reselling the goods [2-710].

5 The seller may *recover damages for nonacceptance or repudiation by the buyer.* The usual measure of damages is "the difference between the market price at the time and place for tender and the unpaid contract price, together with any incidental damages . . . but less expenses saved in consequence of the buyer's breach" [2-708(1)]. Suppose that Betty Buyer contracts to buy a large car from Dan Dealer for $12,000. Shortly before the time scheduled for delivery, a severe oil shortage develops, and Betty cancels the contract because she thinks the car will use more gasoline than she will be able to obtain. Because of the oil shortage, and despite his best efforts, Dan can resell the car for only $10,000. Dan is entitled to $2,000 damages (the difference between the market price and the unpaid contract price), together with any incidental damages (such as interest or storage charges that accumulate while Dan attempts to find another buyer), but less any expenses that Dan saved because of Betty's breach (such as labor costs saved because the second buyer declined the undercoating and decorative painting ordered by Betty). Since the demand for large cars is weak, this measure of damages will "make the seller whole," i.e., will put the seller in as good a position as Betty's performance would have done.

6 When the buyer fails to pay the price as it becomes due, the seller may *recover the price of the goods.* This remedy is limited to (a) situations where the buyer has accepted the goods; (b) most situations where conforming goods have been lost or damaged after the risk of their loss has passed to the buyer; and (c) situations where goods identified to the contract cannot be resold at a reasonable price, e.g., where furniture designed in compliance with a customer's specifications is so ugly that it can be sold only as scrap [2-709].

7 To the extent justified by the buyer's breach, the seller may *cancel the contract.*

8 In a *few* situations the seller has a right to *reclaim delivered goods.* For example, the seller may reclaim the goods from the buyer where the contract requires payment on delivery, the goods were delivered, payment was demanded, and the buyer paid by a check that "bounced" [2-507]. However, the seller may *not* reclaim the goods where the buyer has already transferred them to a good faith purchaser for value.

The seller has a right of reclamation in another situation: Where the seller makes a credit sale and discovers that the buyer was insolvent when the goods were delivered, the seller may reclaim them from the buyer (but not from the buyer's good faith purchaser for value) *if* the seller makes written demand within 10 days after the buyer receives the goods [2-702].

Case 19.4 discusses remedies of the seller.

CASE 19.4 Servbest Foods, Inc. v. Emessee Industries, Inc. • 403 N.E.2d 1 (Ill. App. 1980)

FACTS Emessee contracted to buy 200,000 pounds of beef trimmings from Servbest at 52½ cents per pound, for delivery on February 22, 1974. On that date Servbest had 200,000 pounds of conforming beef trimmings in cold storage in lot 19700, and delivered to Emessee appropriate invoices and warehouse receipts covering that lot. The price of beef trimmings fell sharply. Emessee canceled the contract and returned the documents to Servbest. Instead of reselling lot 19700 to establish its damages, Servbest sold older trimmings at 20¼ cents per pound and sued Emessee for damages. Approximately 4 years after Emessee's breach and Servbest's resale of the trimmings, the trial court awarded Servbest $62,599.50 damages for breach of contract plus $727 as incidental damages and $13,152.46 in prejudgment interest. Emessee appealed.

OPINION CAMPBELL, J.... Emessee contends that the trial court erred in utilizing § 2-706 to calculate Servbest's contract damages because the sales accepted by the trial court as resales referred to sale of goods not identified to the contract, while a resale under § 2-706 must be of goods identified to the contract. Servbest denies the importance of identification to the resale remedy afforded by § 2-706.... Whether a resale under § 2-706 is limited to the goods identified to the contract where the goods are... fungible appears to be a question of first impression. While the language in § 2-706 to the effect that "the seller may resell the goods concerned" would appear to support Emessee's argument, we are required to reject Emessee's narrow reading of this section in light of the policy and intent underpinning the Code and the concept of "resale."

It is Emessee's position that the Code provides for fixing the identity of the "goods concerned" which are subject to resale under § 2-706 through the concept of "identification." Identification is that process by which goods are... set aside or otherwise designated as those to which a contract refers.... The function of identification in the Code is limited. Identification replaced passage of title as the condition precedent for attaining an insurable interest in goods which are the subject of a contract. Identification also plays a role in determining risk of loss. In each instance identification is related to the interest of a buyer in the goods and consequently his right to insure them and [the duty] to bear the risk of loss if they are damaged.

In determining whether identification is similarly linked with the right to resell under § 2-706, it is necessary first to explore the purpose of the [resale] remedy. It is a basic premise of any theory of contract damages that an aggrieved party should be placed in the position that he would have occupied but for the default. Section 2-706 also seeks to award damages based upon the protection of the seller's expectation interest....

From the foregoing references, it would initially appear necessary to restrict resales to goods identified to the contract in order to insure that the price received for the goods upon the resale accurately reflects the market value of the goods which are the subject of the contract, consequently guaranteeing the seller his expectation value. However, the Code embodies a retreat from the mechanical technicalities of prior commercial codes and dictates a liberal construction in order to provide a practical working tool for the commercial community.... Therefore, it is important to examine the necessity of identification in the context of fungible goods....

Fungible goods... are goods of which "any unit is, by nature or usage of trade, the equivalent of any other like unit." (Section 1-201(17).) Fungible goods, unlike other goods, are sold... in quantities by weight, measure, or count; the constituent parts making up the mass being indistinguishable from each other by any physical characteristic.... In the instant case Emessee has introduced no evidence to suggest that the goods which were the subject of the resales were not identical in quantity, quality and description [to] those

CASE 19.4 Continued

contained in lot 19700....[W]e find no basis upon which to conclude that the market value of the...trimmings sold from outside of lot 19700 was any different from the market value of the meat contained in lot 19700....Accordingly, we hold that the trial court's decision to employ the first sales of...trimmings after the breach...as a mitigating resale...was not erroneous.

...Emessee [next] contends...that the trial court's calculation of storage costs was improper in that the storage charges referred to the meat within lot 19700 while the deficiency award was based on the resale of different meat. We do not agree. Recovery of incidental damages should make the seller whole by returning him to the position he would have held were it not for the breach....[D]ue to the redelivery of the meat trimmings to Servbest by Emessee, Servbest had in its possession 200,000 pounds of meat it would not otherwise have had....Accordingly, it was proper for the trial court to reimburse Servbest for the cost of the storage....

JUDGMENT Affirmed.

Remedies of the Buyer. Remedies are available to a buyer where the seller has breached the contract. The seller breaches (1) by failing to make delivery or (2) by repudiating part or all of the contract. The seller is also in breach where (1) the buyer rightfully rejects the seller's tender or (2) the buyer justifiably revokes acceptance [2-711]. With respect to the goods affected by the seller's breach (including breach of a warranty), the buyer may do one or more of the following:

1 To the extent justified by the seller's breach, the buyer may *cancel the contract.*
2 The buyer may *recover so much of the price as has been paid* and, as explained later, *may have damages.*
3 The buyer may *"cover" and have damages as to all the goods affected,* whether or not the seller has identified them to the contract. The buyer *covers* by making or arranging in good faith a substitution of goods (from another source) for those due from the seller. The buyer may also recover from the seller, as damages, the difference between the cost of cover and the contract price, "together with any incidental or consequential damages...but less expenses saved in consequence of the seller's breach" [2-712]. *Incidental damages* resulting from the seller's breach include, for example, expenses reasonably incurred in inspecting, receiving, transporting, or caring for goods rightfully rejected, and expenses reasonably incurred in effecting cover. *Consequential damages* resulting from the seller's breach include "(a) any loss resulting from general or particular requirements and needs of which the seller at the time of contracting had reason to know and which could not reasonably be prevented by cover or otherwise; and (b) injury to person or property proximately resulting from any breach of warranty" [2-715].
4 The buyer may *recover damages for nondelivery* [2-713]. The measure of damages for nondelivery or for repudiation by the seller is the difference between the market price at the time when the buyer learned of the breach, and the contract price, together with any incidental and consequential damages, less expenses saved as a result of the seller's breach. This remedy applies only when and to the extent that the buyer has not covered.
5 Where an *insolvent* seller identifies goods to the contract but fails to deliver them or repudiates the contract, the buyer may *obtain the identified goods* from the insolvent seller [2-502].
6 The buyer may *obtain specific performance.* "Specific performance may be decreed where the goods are unique or in other proper circumstances" [2-716]. The drafters of the Code explain specific performance as it relates to Article 2: "Specific performance is

no longer limited to goods which are already specific or ascertained at the time of contracting. The test of uniqueness under this section must be made in terms of the total situation which characterizes the contract." Output and requirements contracts involving a particular source or market present the typical commercial specific performance situation. However, "uniqueness is not the sole basis of the remedy under this section, for the relief may also be granted 'in other proper circumstances,' and inability to cover is strong evidence of 'other proper circumstances'" [2-716, comment 2].

7 In a few situations the buyer may have a *right of replevin* [2-716]. *Replevin* is an action taken to acquire identified goods that the seller has wrongfully withheld from the buyer. Replevin is available (a) where the buyer is unable to effect cover after reasonable effort; (b) where the circumstances reasonably indicate such an effort will be useless; or (c) where the seller has shipped the goods and has kept a security interest in them, and the buyer has made or tendered satisfaction of the security interest. Replevin and specific performance are similar in that the buyer seeks the goods themselves. But replevin is available only where the goods are identified to the contract, while specific performance is available as to unidentified goods.

A buyer may have other remedies in addition to those listed in the preceding paragraphs. For example, upon rightful rejection or justifiable revocation of acceptance, the buyer has a security interest in goods in his or her control for any payments the buyer has made on their price, and for expenses of handling and resale [2-711]. A buyer who has accepted goods and given *timely* notice of defects may recover damages for loss due to any nonconformity of tender [2-714]. (Recall that a buyer who has accepted a defective tender is *barred from any remedy,* including a remedy for breach of warranty, unless the buyer *notifies* the seller of the defect within a reasonable time after it has been or should have been discovered.) Finally, upon giving proper notice to the seller, the buyer may "deduct all or any part of the damages resulting from any breach of the contract from any part of the price still due under the same contract" [2-717].

The case that follows discusses several remedies of the buyer.

CASE 19.5 McGinnis v. Wentworth Chevrolet Co. · 668 P.2d 365 (Or. 1983)

FACTS McGinnis purchased a new 1978 Chevrolet El Camino automobile from defendant Wentworth. Almost immediately, she had problems with the car, from cosmetic defects such as chipping paint and scratches to major mechanical problems such as a tendency for the engine to stall at intersections. After more than 3 months of unsuccessful repair attempts, McGinnis revoked acceptance of the car and requested either the return of her purchase price or a substitute El Camino. Upon defendant's refusal to recognize her revocation, McGinnis filed a complaint seeking return of the purchase price plus "incidental and consequential damages as follows: 1. Automobile storage fees... 2. Car rental fees and other incidental damages... [and] 3. Loan fees and interest charges."

At trial, defendant raised as a defense to the damages claim a limitation-of-liability clause in the purchase agreement stating that the seller "shall not be liable in contract, tort or otherwise for injuries to persons or property or for consequential damages or commercial losses." The trial court reserved judgment on the issue of the scope of damages, but it held that the car was a "lemon," that plaintiff's revocation of acceptance was justifiable, and that plaintiff was entitled to a refund of the purchase price less the value of her use of the car. The trial court denied her request for additional damages, evidently concluding that in a revocation-of-acceptance case a plaintiff's remedy is limited to a refund of the purchase price. The trial court did not rule on the effect of the contract's limitation-of-liability clause. Plaintiff appealed. The court of appeals held that she was entitled to damages for storage, insurance, and

CASE 19.5 Continued

the renting of a substitute automobile (as incident to "cover"). Defendant Wentworth appealed, objecting to the court's allowing rental costs as "cover."

OPINION

CARSON, J.... [Section 2-711 provides that]:

> (1) Where... the buyer rightfully rejects or justifiably revokes acceptance[,] then with respect to any goods involved... the buyer may cancel and whether or not he has done so may in addition to recovering so much of the price as has been paid: (a) "Cover" and have damages... as to all the goods affected... or (b) Recover damages for nondelivery....

Thus, a buyer in plaintiff's position is not relegated merely to cancellation of the contract and recovery of the [purchase price] (as apparently held by the trial court); rather, she also potentially is entitled to a catalog of other remedies, one of which is "cover." [Section 2-712 provides]:

> (1) After a breach within § 2-711 the buyer may "cover" by making in good faith and without unreasonable delay *any reasonable purchase of* or contract to purchase *goods in substitution* for those due from the seller.
>
> (2) The buyer may recover from the seller as damages the difference between the cost of cover and the contract price together with any *incidental or consequential damages* as defined in § 2-715, but less expenses saved in consequence of the seller's breach.
>
> (3) Failure of the buyer to effect cover within this section does not bar him from any other remedy. (Emphasis added.)

In an appropriate case, where a buyer does not "cover," she or he may recover damages for non-delivery [as described in Section 2-713]....

The question presented is whether plaintiff's claim for rental recompense falls within one of the classes outlined above. The Court of Appeals concluded that the renting of a replacement automobile was a reasonable way for plaintiff to cover[,] and thus the rental costs, as a cost in effecting cover, were recoverable as "incidental" damages.... Defendant, to the contrary, contends that these costs, if anything, are "consequential damages"... and are subject to the contract's liability exclusion.

The Court of Appeals' opinion evinces a misconception as to the purpose and function of the UCC's "cover" remedy. Where a seller breaches a contract for the sale of goods by failing to deliver the agreed-upon goods, the buyer's traditional pre-code contract remedy was to seek "loss-of-bargain" damages. The measure of damages was calculated as the difference between the contract price and the fair market value of the goods. This traditional remedy is reflected in the UCC's "market price" formula found in § 2-713 [which requires the court to determine the market price as of the "time when the buyer learned of the breach"—here a time difficult to pinpoint and which could involve different market values, depending on the time settled on by the court].

The UCC's "cover" alternative was intended to enable the buyer to "obtain the goods he needs" by allowing the disappointed buyer to reenter the market place and make a reasonable purchase of substitute goods.... This remedy also can obviate the often difficult calculation of the market price of the goods. When a buyer makes a reasonable "cover," the measure of damages is the difference between the actual "cover" purchased and the contract price. This formula results in a substantial departure from pre-code law where there was no assurance at what time or place the court would measure the market were the buyer to purchase substitute goods. Although § 2-712 makes it clear that the buyer is not obligated to "cover" (except insofar as she needs to mitigate her consequential damages...), if the buyer does not "cover," her loss-of-bargain damages, if any, will be computed under § 2-713, the market price provision.

We now focus on the question of whether the renting of a substitute automobile can be "cover" in these circumstances. Section 2-712(1)... describes "cover" [only] as "any reasonable purchase of or contract to purchase goods in substitution for those due from

CASE 19.5 Continued

the seller." A clear example of "cover" would be if plaintiff had purchased another 1978 El Camino or even a comparable automobile from another dealer. . . . [T]he official commentary to § 2-712 is not clear on whether the term "purchase" can include rentals. . . .

Given the "cover" remedy's purpose in providing certainty for the calculation of the buyer's loss-of-bargain . . . while also allowing the buyer to obtain the needed goods, we conclude that the . . . "cover" remedy generally is not intended to apply to a rental. Rather, the remedy is limited only to those situations where the buyer has purchased or contracted to purchase goods as an actual replacement for the agreed-upon goods. Rental costs are not readily translatable into a comparable value figure for computation of the loss-of-bargain[,] and, therefore, viewing temporary rentals as "cover" would defeat the remedy's intended purpose. . . . [T]he Court of Appeals erred in awarding plaintiff . . . rental fees as a cost "incidental" to "cover."

This does not end our inquiry, however. As stated above, where a buyer does not purchase substitute goods, her loss-of-bargain must be computed through the "market price" formula [of Section 2-712], and any additional losses are to be analyzed under [its] incidental and consequential damages provision.

Incidental and consequential damages are defined in § 2-715:

> (1) Incidental damages resulting from the seller's breach include expenses reasonably incurred in inspection, receipt, transportation and care and custody of goods rightfully rejected, any commercially reasonable charges, expenses or commissions in connection with effecting cover and any other reasonable expense incident to the delay or other breach.
>
> (2) Consequential damages resulting from the seller's breach include: (a) [a]ny loss resulting from general or particular requirements and needs of which the seller at the time of contracting had reason to know and which could not reasonably be prevented by cover or otherwise; and (b) [i]njury to person or property proximately resulting from any breach of warranty.

Whether a particular item of alleged damage is recoverable as incidental or consequential generally is not important[,] provided that it is recoverable as either. In this case, however, the distinction may be significant because of the contract's exclusion clause which precludes "consequential damages."

. . . [W]e conclude that plaintiff's rental expenses are not incidental damages. [The rental costs] relate to the particular circumstances of plaintiff relative to the goods, rather than being necessarily incident to a breach of this contract. Whether these expenses are recoverable as consequential damages . . . and the effect, if any, of the contract's limitation-of-liability clause, however, must be determined on remand. . . .

JUDGMENT Reversed and remanded.

Agreements Concerning Remedies; Limitation of Remedies

Under the UCC, reasonable agreements that modify or limit Code remedies will be given effect. Thus, seller and buyer may tailor their remedies to fit their special situation, as long as neither party takes undue advantage of the other.

Agreements Concerning Remedies. Like the general law of contracts, the UCC permits the parties to specify in the contract an amount of money (called "liquidated damages") that a defaulting party must pay for breaching the contract. A liquidated damages clause is enforceable only if the amount is reasonable in light of (1) the anticipated or actual harm caused by the breach, (2) the difficulty of proving loss, and (3) the impracticality of obtaining an adequate remedy without the clause [2-718]. A term fixing an unreasonably large amount as liquidated damages is void as a penalty. Similarly, a clause fixing an unreasonably small amount would probably be unenforceable because it would be considered unconscionable.

Suppose that Bob Buyer, a rice farmer, is contracting to buy a large irrigation pump from Dan Dealer. If the pump fails and the crop is damaged, Bob might have difficulty proving the exact extent of his loss, since no one can predict with certainty how many bushels of rice would have been produced if the pump had not failed. But Bob might be able to negotiate a liquidated damages clause stating that Dan will pay a certain amount per acre if the pump fails and causes damage to the crop. If the amount stated in the clause is a reasonable estimate of the anticipated loss, the clause will be enforceable. The amount will be reasonable if, for example, it is based on Bob's past rice production and if the clause gives Dan credit for any part of the crop that can be salvaged.

Suppose that Bob makes a down payment on the pump and the contract states that Dan may keep Bob's down payment as liquidated damages if Bob breaches the contract. Then Dan delivers a conforming pump and Bob wrongfully rejects it. Whether Dan may enforce the liquidated damages clause depends on whether the amount of the down payment is a reasonable estimate of Dan's loss. Dan is entitled to compensation for loss, but he is not permitted to penalize Bob by enforcing a forfeiture clause. If the down payment is very small compared to the loss, Dan may keep it and have further damages [2-718]. If the down payment is substantially larger than the loss, Dan will have to make a partial refund.

Suppose now that Bob makes a down payment but the contract says nothing about liquidated damages or how the down payment will be treated if Bob breaches the contract. Then Dan delivers a conforming pump and Bob wrongfully rejects it. Under a rule of the UCC, Dan may, *without having to prove damages,* keep some or all of Bob's down payment. Dan may keep 20 percent of the total value of the contract up to a maximum of $500. However, Dan must return to Bob any excess unless Dan can prove that the damages resulting from Bob's breach exceeded the amount of down payment Dan is entitled to keep [2-718]. Bob contracted to pay $5,000 for the pump, and he made a $1,000 down payment. Upon Bob's breach, Dan resold the pump for $5,000. Dan may keep $500 of Bob's down payment, but he must return the other $500. Note that the UCC itself, not a clause in the contract, permits the aggrieved seller to keep the money, perhaps because the seller may have minor losses and costs of resale that are difficult to calculate.

Limitation of Remedies. The remedies provided by Article 2 may be limited (or supplemented) by agreement of the parties. For example, the contract between Bob Buyer and the seller of the irrigation pump might have limited the seller's liability to the replacement of defective parts. However, if the limitation is unconscionable, it will not be enforced. In transactions involving *consumer* goods, the limitation of consequential damages for *personal* injury is presumed to be unconscionable [2-719]. In other transactions the limitation of damages is not *presumed* to be unconscionable, but the aggrieved person may prove that the limitation was in fact unconscionable.

Sometimes a clause of limitation appears to be fair and reasonable, but because of the circumstances that actually arose, it "fails of its essential purpose" so that the buyer is left without a remedy. In such a situation the limitation is ineffective and the general remedy provisions of the Code apply. In *Wilson Trading Corp. v. David Ferguson, Ltd.,*[1] for example, Wilson contracted to sell yarn to Ferguson. A clause provided that no claims would be allowed for defects discovered after weaving, knitting, or processing. Ferguson knitted a shipment of yarn into sweaters, washed them, and discovered that the color of the yarn had "shaded" (varied in color from piece to piece and within pieces), making the sweaters unmarketable. Ferguson gave Wilson prompt notice of the defect, which, Ferguson alleged, could not reasonably be discovered in the normal manufacturing process until after knitting and washing. The New York Court of Appeals held that if Ferguson could establish its factual allegations at trial, the clause of limitation would have "failed its 'essential purpose'" and would have deprived the buyer of the value of the bargain. Consequently, the clause would have to "give way to the general Code rule that a buyer has a reasonable time to notify the seller of breach of contract after he discovers or should have discovered the defect."

To the extent described in Chapter 18, the Magnuson-Moss Warranty Act prohibits the exclusion of implied warranties where a supplier of a "con-

[1]244 N.E.2d 685 (N.Y. 1968).

sumer product" has made a full warranty. However, a *conspicuous* exclusion or limitation of *consequential damages* will be enforced if it appears on the face of the consumer product warranty.

Summary

The obligation of the seller is to transfer and deliver the goods, and that of the buyer is to accept and pay for them. The seller meets the delivery obligation by making a tender of delivery. Tender requires that the seller put and hold conforming goods at the buyer's disposition and give the buyer any notice reasonably necessary to enable the buyer to take delivery.

Within limits imposed by the Code, such as the one pertaining to installment contracts, the buyer may reject a tender that fails in any respect to conform to the contract. The seller has a right to cure an improper tender before, and sometimes after, the time for performance has expired.

The buyer's obligation to accept and to pay is conditioned on the buyer's right to inspect the goods. Upon acceptance, the buyer is obligated to pay the contract price. In two main situations, the buyer may revoke acceptance of nonconforming goods. Unless otherwise agreed, the buyer may pay in any customary way. The seller may require payment in money but must give any extension of time reasonably necessary for the buyer to procure such a payment.

The parties may be excused from their performance obligations if the agreed performance has been made commercially impracticable by an unforeseen occurrence that alters the essential nature of the performance. Where an agreed method of payment or delivery fails, the aggrieved party may be entitled to a substitute performance.

A party to a sales contract is entitled to a remedy if the other party is in breach of the contract. The purpose of the UCC remedies is to put the aggrieved party in as good a position as the other party's full performance would have done. An aggrieved seller may, for example, withhold delivery of the goods, stop delivery of goods in the possession of a carrier, or have an action for the price; an aggrieved buyer may cancel the contract, "cover" and have damages as to the goods affected by the seller's breach, or have other remedies.

The remedies of Article 2 may be limited or supplemented by agreement of the parties to the contract. An unconscionable limitation of remedies will not be enforced. Where a supplier of a consumer product makes a full warranty, the Warranty Act requires that an exclusion or limitation of consequential damages appear conspicuously on the face of the warranty.

Review Questions

1 **(a)** In general, how does a seller fulfill the seller's tender obligation? **(b)** What specific acts are required for a seller to fulfill the tender obligation in a shipment contract?

2 In what kinds of situations may a seller "cure" an improper tender or delivery?

3 **(a)** What constitutes acceptance of goods? **(b)** What is the legal effect of acceptance?

4 **(a)** How is the buyer's right to inspect the goods related to the buyer's obligation to accept the goods? **(b)** How does a C.O.D. clause in a sales contract affect the buyer's right to inspect the goods?

5 **(a)** In general, under what circumstances may a buyer reject the seller's tender of delivery? **(b)** With regard to an installment contract, under what circumstances may a buyer reject an installment? Cancel the whole contract?

6 In what two main situations may a buyer revoke acceptance of goods?

7 Explain the meaning and legal effect of commercial impracticability as an excuse for nonperformance.

8 **(a)** Illustrate how a sales contract can be breached by the seller and by the buyer. **(b)** With regard to default, explain the significance of "reasonable grounds for insecurity." **(c)** What is "repudiation"? **(d)** Under what circumstances may an aggrieved party have a remedy for repudiation?

9 **(a)** Under what circumstances may a seller recover the price of goods when the buyer fails to make payment? **(b)** Describe three other remedies of the seller.

10 **(a)** Explain the meaning and significance of "cover" as a buyer's remedy. **(b)** Describe three other remedies of the buyer.

11 **(a)** Under what circumstances will a liquidated damages clause be enforceable? **(b)** May a seller keep a defaulting buyer's down payment? Explain.

12 To what extent may a sales contract limit the remedies provided by Article 2?

Case Problems

1 The Linscotts bought a double-width mobile home to be delivered and set up on a rural lot. Delivery and setup were completed in February, and the Linscotts moved in. They immediately encountered problems: The windows and storm windows were defective; the roof leaked; and the insulation was so inadequate that the furnace ran constantly without sufficiently warming the living areas. When spring arrived, the factory representative made some repairs. When summer arrived, he offered to install fiberglass insulation. The Linscotts refused to allow him to reinsulate unless he used foam core insulation. This request was refused, and Smith, the seller, made no further effort to repair the home. In the fall and winter other troubles developed. Copper water pipes froze and burst, electrical service went out, a hot water heater burned out, kitchen cabinets came apart, the floor cracked, and an oven malfunctioned. The Linscotts sued Smith for damages. The trial court held that the Linscotts were not entitled to damages because they had improperly prevented Smith from curing the defects. The Linscotts appealed. Was the trial court in error?

2 Oberg bought a new Chevrolet from Phillips and soon discovered numerous defects in engine performance, body, steering, paint, and accessories. During the first 3 months of Oberg's ownership, the car was in the seller's shop for 30 whole days and parts of 12 to 15 more days. After an unsuccessful repair session near the end of the first 2 months, Oberg gave Phillips a specific amount of time to repair the car. Phillips did not comply. Oberg then, in writing, revoked his acceptance of the car, and sued Phillips for breach of contract. Phillips contended that all of the defects were trivial and that Oberg therefore had no basis for revoking his acceptance. Did Oberg have a legal basis for revoking his acceptance?

3 Automated Controls, Inc. (ACI), agreed to design, manufacture, and sell to MIC Enterprises, Inc. (MIC), a system of solid-state electronic control boxes for use on center-pivot "Blu-Max" irrigation machinery made by RVC, Inc., and distributed by MIC. ACI was to deliver six control boxes and a timer by January 1976 for field testing. By February 16, 1976, ACI could deliver only one box. But, as ACI knew, timing was critical to MIC in coordinating the manufacture and the marketing of the Blu-Max machines. Consequently, MIC placed an order for a quantity of the untested control devices to be delivered in twelve monthly installments. ACI delivered some, and MIC paid for them. However, after several attempts, ACI could not make the control boxes work, and in June 1976 MIC canceled the contract. ACI sued MIC for breach of contract. Was MIC within its rights in canceling the contract?

4 Weller agreed to manufacture ice scrapers and snow brushes, place Talon's name on them, and ship them directly to Talon's customers. Under the agreement, Weller extended $47,000 credit to Talon. After checking Talon's credit record, Weller's president tried to locate Talon's president, but Weller's numerous phone calls were never returned. Weller became concerned about payment and demanded from Talon assurances of performance. Failing to receive them, Weller suspended shipments to Talon's customers for about 10 days. During this time Weller and Talon amended their agreement to give Talon more time to pay. Shipments resumed. Talon's debt increased to about $74,000. Weller sued for the amount owed. Talon argued that the amended agreement was not binding because Talon signed it under duress as a result of Weller's wrongful suspension of shipments. Weller contended that the suspension was rightful because Weller had reasonable grounds for insecurity. Was Weller's suspension of shipments to Talon's customers wrongful?

5 CIS, a computer broker, agreed to deliver a satisfactory computer to the Huntington Beach Union High School District, and to do so by the end of July. CIS was unable to make delivery. Because the offers of other bidders expired on July 12, School District had to rebid the contract and to pay a price almost $60,000 higher than CIS's contract price. School District sued CIS for $60,000 in general damages plus almost $10,000 in consequential damages. The trial court awarded School District the $10,000 in consequential damages, but it awarded only $12,000 in general damages on the ground that the second-lowest bid in the original bidding exceeded CIS's by only that much. School District appealed. Should the trial court's award of damages be upheld?

6 Begley was injured in an accident when the brakes on his Jeep failed. In 1976 Begley sued Reliable Motor Co. (the dealer) and American Motors Corp. (the manufacturer) for damages, alleging defects in the braking system and breach of warranty. Two years and five months later Reliable and AMC in turn sued the manufacturer of the brakes (Bendix Corp.) and the manufacturer of the brake fluid (Wagner Electric Corp.) for breach of warranty. Bendix and Wagner had no previous notice of Begley's suit. Bendix and Wagner denied liability, alleging unreasonable delay on the part of Reliable and AMC in giving notice of the breach of warranty. Should Bendix and Wagner be held liable to Reliable and AMC?

7 Brenda Buyer purchased two refrigerators, one for use in her home and the other for use in her business. On the face of each sales contract was the following clause in large type: "IF THIS REFRIGERATOR IS DEFECTIVE, SELLER'S LIABILITY SHALL BE LIMITED TO THE REPLACEMENT OF DEFECTIVE PARTS OR A REFUND OF THE PURCHASE PRICE AS THE SELLER ELECTS." The motors of both refrigerators were defective and shorted out, causing fires. The fire in Brenda's home damaged the kitchen and injured Brenda. The fire at Brenda's place of business destroyed an expensive copier and injured Brenda's employee. The seller agreed to refund the purchase price, but it refused to pay any other damages. Brenda sued the seller for all damages caused by the defective refrigerators. How should the case be decided as to (*a*) the refrigerator in Brenda's home, and (*b*) the refrigerator in Brenda's place of business?

ETHICS IN PRACTICE

It is difficult to think of a law that does not represent a value judgment on the part of the lawmakers. As noted in Chapter 1, even in setting speed limits, lawmakers must decide what conduct is appropriate (i.e., safe, efficient) and what is not. Some law promotes the values of special interest groups to the detriment of the public welfare. Most law reflects values that are consistent with the common good.

Problems in Ethics

1 The law of sales is an example of business law that reflects explicit value judgments of its drafters. In Article 2 (and, in fact, the whole Uniform Commercial Code), the drafters' basic concern is for efficiency of business transactions, itself a worthy economic goal. But as the comments to Code sections reveal, the drafters formulated many Code rules with the express purpose of fostering honesty and fair dealing—qualities that aid business efficiency but which most people would recognize as traditionally moral or ethical in tone. Explain how each of the following rules of sales law promotes honesty and fair dealing: **(a)** the rule concerning accommodation shipments; **(b)** the rule that an offeree's expression of acceptance acts as an acceptance even though it states terms additional to or different from those stated in the offer, and the additional terms are construed as proposals for addition to the contract; **(c)** the rule concerning unconscionable contracts.

2 In developing specific rules of law, the drafters of Article 2 might have been concerned mainly with the welfare of individuals and thus with imposing a standard of fair dealing to protect weak individuals from evils perpetrated by the unscrupulous. Or the drafters might have thought mainly of the market system as a whole, intending to provide the most healthy trading environment possible as a means of enhancing the confidence of traders and, consequently, economic values. Which of these possible general objectives—assuring contracting parties of a fair deal, or enhancing trader confidence and economic values—seems best to account for each of the following? **(a)** The Article 2 objective of encouraging actual performance, i.e., the Article 2 sales rules that (as compared to the common law rules of contracting) sharply limit the opportunities for a contracting party to escape from the contract on the basis of trivial defaults or insignificant errors of the other party. **(b)** The UCC requirement of good faith (honesty in fact) that applies to all Code transactions, including sales of goods; and in Article 2, the more stringent standard of good faith that applies to merchants. **(c)** The protections provided by the Code against extortionate modifications of a sales contract.

3 "Scentco" is a manufacturer of perfumes that it distributes in only the most exclusive stores. Scentco perfumes sell at retail for \$75 to \$185 per ounce, depending on the scent. Using a chromatograph in a process of "reverse engineering," Jane is able to develop a very close approximation of the secret formulas of Scentco, and begins production under her "Smellsco" label. Jane markets her line of perfumes in discount stores, drug stores, and groceries throughout the country for a retail price of \$7.50 per ounce. Cost of production, packaging, and distribution is about \$2 per ounce; Jane's price to her retailers is \$4 per ounce. Jane uses the same ingredients that Scentco uses, and she pays the same amount for them that Scentco does. In her advertising, Jane constantly challenges users of her perfumes to try to distinguish them from their Scentco counterparts, and she provides Scentco and Smellco samples so that prospective customers may try. Most people cannot tell the difference between Scentco perfumes and the "clones" that Jane produces. Scentco and others in the perfume industry are very angry with Jane and her Smellsco operation, but they have not been able to prove that she has violated the law. **(a)** Is Jane's conduct ethical? What about the way she acquired her perfume formulas? What about her marketing strategy and advertising technique? **(b)** Is Scentco acting ethically in the way it markets and prices its perfumes?

4 You are an electrical engineer working for a manufacturer of videocassette recorders (VCRs). The VCRs are among the cheapest on the market, selling at retail for $139. They break down early and often, and they carry a 30-day limited warranty. The average repair bill is $85. You know that by upgrading a few parts at the cost of $8 per unit, you can triple the life of the VCR and make it the most reliable, though still one of the least expensive, VCRs on the market. Your supervisor, however, wants you to continue building the VCR cheaply so that the company's repair subsidiary will have more repair business or buyers will purchase a replacement more often. Most people who purchase the VCR have annual incomes of less than $15,000. **(a)** Is the company acting legally in refusing to upgrade the VCR? Is it acting ethically? **(b)** Suppose you decide that the company is acting unethically. (1) What should you do to remedy the situation? Discuss the matter with top management? Secretly place an anonymous telephone call to a national consumer magazine to alert its testing staff to the problem? Take no action? (2) Would the fact that you are scheduled for a "performance review" in 3 weeks affect your decision?

5 "DrugInc" manufactures many lines of drugs and medicines for national distribution. Lately its heart disease drug, Hartheal, has been selling poorly. The main reason is that competing companies have developed much better heart medications. DrugInc's marketing manager devises a plan to give away millions of dollars worth of Hartheal to needy patients. Doctors will receive prescription certificates to pass on to the patients, who will redeem them at pharmacies. The plan is to be heavily advertised in the national news media. As a result of the plan, DrugInc salespeople will have unusual access to doctors for promoting its other lines of products, and DrugInc will be able to deduct the value of Hartheal from its income as a charitable contribution. A spokesperson for DrugInc issues the following press release: "We at DrugInc believe that no patient should be denied any life-saving medication because he or she cannot afford to pay for it." You have been asked to evaluate the ethics of DrugInc's Hartheal giveaway plan. **(a)** Does it matter that, although free to poor patients, Hartheal is an inferior medication that has serious side effects for a large proportion of the patient population? **(b)** Does it matter that other drug companies make drugs available free to doctors who request them for their indigent patients? Does it matter that these other free-drug programs are not as extensive or as well-publicized as DrugInc's will be?

PART FIVE

Property and Estates

CHAPTER 20

Nature and Importance of Property; Personal Property (Including Bailments)

Property law governs the ownership of *things*. More specifically, property law governs the *acquisition, transmission*, and *use* of things.[1] "Things" includes not only land, buildings, and other "real property," but also a huge variety of "personal property" such as automobiles, money, raw materials, factory equipment, trademarks, stocks and bonds, patents, franchises, and the "good will" of a business—anything, in short, that the law recognizes as capable of being owned.

Property is the foundation of any economic system. In a communist economy, state ownership and management of property is the norm; the communist state is especially interested in owning and controlling the "means of production." In contrast, a free enterprise "market" economy such as ours places high value on *private* property—ownership and management by private individuals—and on individual initiative as a major basis of production. In furtherance of these values, our law of property protects the individual's creations and acquisitions by giving him or her an exclusive right of ownership.

This chapter deals with the general nature and importance of property, especially private property, and with the law of personal property, including bailments. The next two chapters are devoted to real property.

Nature and Importance of Property

Meaning of Property

The word "property" is used in two different senses. In one sense, property refers to things owned, such as land, automobiles, and shares of stock in a corporation. Laypeople ordinarily think of property in this sense. Sometimes the law itself refers to things as constituting property. For example, a California statute defines property as "the thing of which there may be ownership."[2]

In its other sense, "property" means the exclusive right to use, possess, enjoy, and dispose of a thing. Used in this sense, property refers not to the *thing* but to a collection or *bundle of rights* in that thing—the rights to use, possess, enjoy, and dispose of it. This "bundle of rights" concept is a fundamental one; land and other physical objects can exist where there is no law (e.g., rocks on the moon), but property rights can exist only where there is law to define and enforce them. Moreover, by protecting people in the exercise of property rights, the law contributes to the value of things. Land, automobiles, and other things would not be valuable (that is, could not be exchanged in the marketplace) were it not for the owners' legally protected rights to use them freely, to sell them, or to give them to someone of their choice.

The bundle of rights is not always held by one person. Various property rights ("sticks out of the bundle") commonly are transferred to others such as creditors and tenants. Suppose that an owner of a house leases it to a tenant for a year. The tenant has the exclusive right to possess, use, and enjoy the house as a residence for the lease period. The landlord has temporarily given up one of the "sticks" in the bundle of rights (possession), but retains the others: the right to enjoy the house by receiving rental payments, the right to dispose of it, etc. If the landlord borrowed money to buy the house, he or she probably was required to give the lender a stick out of the bundle (a mortgage) as "security" for repayment of the loan—i.e., the right under a mortgage agreement to have the house sold if the landlord misses a payment, and to have the sale proceeds applied to the unpaid debt.

The word "title" appears frequently in discussions of property law. In its usual sense, "title" means "ownership"—basic ownership rights, including the right of disposal. But in secured transactions law (discussed later in this book), "title" sometimes is used in a more limited sense, to mean the "security interest" (such as a mortgage) that a creditor holds to secure an unpaid debt. In this narrower sense, "title" is nothing more than one stick out of the bundle of rights.

Classes of Property

Many laws are applicable only to certain specified classes or subclasses of property. The main classes of property are tangible and intangible, real and personal, and public and private.

[1] John C. Cribbet, *Principles of the Law of Property*, Foundation Press, Mineola, N.Y., 1975, p. 3.
[2] Calif. Civ. Code § 654.

Tangible and Intangible Property. Tangible property consists of things that have a physical existence, such as books, clothing, buildings, and land. Intangible property consists of things that do not exist in physical form but that have economic value, such as patents, copyrights, accounts receivable, and shares of stock.

To understand the concept of intangible property we need to observe an important distinction. We know, for instance, that a stock certificate is tangible personal property because it has a physical existence and can have value in and of itself as a collector's item. But the reason that an ordinary stock certificate has value in the commercial world is that the certificate *represents* an *intangible* property right—the right of ownership in a corporate entity. If the stock certificate is lost or destroyed (and the corporation still exists), the certificate can be replaced without the owner's loss of any rights in the corporation. The owner of a missing certificate remains a shareholder because the certificate is simply *evidence of ownership* and is not the corporate property itself.

Real and Personal Property. Real property consists of land, airspace above the land, and all things imbedded in the land or firmly attached to it, such as minerals, trees, fences, and buildings. Personal property is all property that is not real property and thus includes tangible things that are movable ("goods," "chattels") and intangible things that have economic value.

It is possible for items to be changed in their classification from real to personal and from personal to real. For example, a tree is real property until it is severed from the land—either by a person cutting it down or by an act of nature, as by wind or flood. When the tree is severed it becomes movable and is reclassified as personal property. The reverse of this situation occurs when personal property becomes attached to land. For example, a building contractor takes movable items, such as lumber and bricks, and firmly affixes them to the land in constructing a house. The items are thereby converted to real property.

Public and Private Property. All property, whether tangible or intangible, real or personal, can be characterized as public or private. The essential difference is in designating who has the right to use, possess, enjoy, and dispose of the particular thing. Private property is that held by an individual or a business entity primarily for personal or corporate benefit. Public property is that held by a governmental unit or agency, whether federal, state, or local. To illustrate: a national park and a city recreation center are classified as public property because a governmental unit holds the bundle of rights that constitute ownership of the park or recreational center. By contrast, many football and baseball stadiums are held as private property; i.e., a private individual or corporation holds the right to use, possess, enjoy, and dispose of the particular thing.

Legal Protection of Private Property

Private property is vital to the maintenance of a free, competitive society. For this reason, and for other reasons discussed below, governments have recognized the need for laws to protect private property.

Methods of Protecting Private Property. As we have seen, the concept of property embodies the idea of a bundle of rights, i.e., the exclusive right to use, possess, enjoy, and dispose of a thing. In regard to private property, an essential part of the definition is the word "exclusive": an individual holds the bundle of rights to the exclusion of the public at large and the government.[3] This concept of *exclusive* rights is deeply ingrained in our society.

The law provides protection from interference by others through the law of torts. (Much of the law covered in Chapters 4 and 5 is devoted to protection of private property.) For example, if someone intentionally enters your land without consent or legal justification, you may recover damages in a lawsuit for trespass. If someone takes or destroys your personal property, you may recover damages in a suit for conversion or trespass to personal property. In addition, if someone negligently harms your land or personal property, you may recover damages in a suit for negligence.

Private property is also protected against interference by the government. The U.S. Constitution provides in the Fifth and Fourteenth Amend-

[3]"Exclusive" does not mean unlimited. Restrictions on the use of private property are discussed on page 414.

ments that neither the federal nor any state government shall deprive a person of life, liberty, or *property* without due process of law. These provisions do not prevent the government from taking a person's property, but they do require the government to observe due process. We will discuss eminent domain and police power in Chapter 21.

In the following case the court faced a conflict between private property rights and the public's rights to free speech and assembly.

CASE 20.1 Cologne v. Westfarms Associates · 469 A.2d 1201 (Conn. 1984)

FACTS Westfarms Associates owned a large retail shopping center known as Westfarms Mall. The mall consisted of four connected buildings under one roof which housed 120 retail businesses. At each end there was a courtyard area, and in the center of the mall there was a grand court of 14,000 square feet. Westfarms permitted and sponsored various activities in the grand court, such as health clinics, volunteer tax assistance, fashion shows, and concerts. In July 1982 the Connecticut National Organization for Women (NOW) asked permission to solicit signatures on petitions in support of legislation pertaining to various social issues (sex discrimination, child support, etc.). The request was denied, and suit was filed by NOW and Christine A. Cologne, one of its members. On March 2, 1983, the trial court granted a judgment against Westfarms (defendant) enjoining them from prohibiting the plaintiffs' solicitation of signatures on various petitions. Due to an incident on May 22, when the Ku Klux Klan attempted to appear at the mall after being denied access by the defendants and there was a heated demonstration by anti-Klan demonstrators, the court modified the injunction by limiting the location for NOW's activities to the exterior of the building at one of the entrances. Both the plaintiffs [NOW and Christine A. Cologne] and the defendants appealed.

OPINION SHEA, J. . . . The issues presented by this appeal have an intricate background. In *Lloyd Corporation v. Tanner*, . . . the Supreme Court of the United States rejected the contention that a privately owned retail shopping center was the functional equivalent of the business district of a municipality upon which expressive activity protected by the first amendment to the federal constitution might be conducted as freely as upon a village green. . . . Federal law, whether based upon statute or constitution, establishes a minimum national standard for the exercise of individual rights and does not inhibit state governments from affording higher levels of protection for such rights. . . . In recognition of this principle, the Supreme Court of the United States in *Pruneyard Shopping Center v. Robins*, . . . although reaffirming its view that there was no federal basis for a right of access to a private shopping center for the purpose of expressive activity, held that the California courts were at liberty to construe that state's constitutional guaranty of freedom of speech to require such access, and that no violation of federally protected property rights or first amendment rights of the owners had occurred. . . .

The provisions of our Connecticut constitution upon which the plaintiffs rely are Sections 4 and 14 of article first, which is entitled "Declaration of Rights." Section 4 provides: "Every citizen may freely speak, write and publish his sentiments on all subjects, being responsible for the abuse of that liberty." Section 14 provides: "The citizens have a right, in a peaceable manner, to assemble for their common good, and to apply to those invested with the powers of government, for redress of grievances, or other proper purposes, by petition, address or remonstrance." A closely related provision of this article is Section 5: "No law shall ever be passed to curtail or restrain the liberty of speech or of the press." . . .

It is evident that the concern which led to the adoption of our Connecticut Declaration of Rights, as well as the bill of rights in our federal constitution, was the protection

CASE 20.1 Continued

of individual liberties against infringement by government.... Similarly, a review of their origin discloses no evidence of any intention to vest in those seeking to exercise such rights as free speech and petition the privilege of doing so upon property of others....

Despite the unqualified language of Sections 4 and 14, the plaintiffs do not maintain that the rights referred to therein are so absolute that they can lawfully be exercised anywhere, as a kind of public easement upon all privately owned realty for use as a political forum. Their claim is presently limited to the large regional shopping center operated by the defendants which, they contend, has assumed a uniquely public character by virtue of its great economic, social and cultural impact upon the community. We are unable, however, to discern any legal basis distinguishing this commercial complex from other places where large numbers of people congregate, affording superior opportunities for political solicitation, such as sport stadiums, convention halls, theatres, country fairs, large office or apartment buildings, factories, supermarkets or department stores.

...Property rights or economic interests have long been regarded as subject to reasonable regulation in promotion of the general welfare.... If, as the plaintiffs contend, the development of large suburban shopping centers has greatly diminished opportunities for political advocacy in the public streets of downtown areas and other public places, the problem should be presented to the legislature. We cannot presume that that body has any less concern for political liberty than this court.

As we have noted, the plaintiffs have not taken the extreme position which a literal reading of Sections 4 and 14 of article first might arguably warrant, that people seeking to exercise rights of free speech and petition have a constitutional right to do so wherever and whenever they please, but limit their claim to properties vested with a public character. Although we are under no legal constraint to follow *Lloyd Corporation v. Tanner*, ...we approve the rejection in that decision of such a claim as applied to a shopping center: "Nor does property lose its private character merely because the public is generally invited to use it for designated purposes.... The essentially private character of a store and its privately owned abutting property does not change by virtue of being large or clustered with other stores in a modern shopping center."

JUDGMENT ...[T]he case is remanded with direction to render judgment for the defendants.

Reasons for Protecting Private Property. The foundation of private property rests on protection of possession, a fact recognized in the familiar colloquialism "possession is nine-tenths of the law." There are good reasons to support legal protection of possession.

For many years it has been recognized that possession of property should be protected in order to avoid breaches of the peace. From earliest recorded history it has been apparent that one who possessed an object or a plot of land would instinctively fight to keep it from being taken by an aggressor. To avoid such fights, the notion of an intermediary to protect the owner became institutionalized in the form of laws to deter aggression. Today, the citizen's property rights are protected through these laws, enforced by means of a police force and a court system. We all benefit from avoiding the physical violence of "self-help" or vigilante groups associated with a more primitive society.

Another reason advanced for legal protection of possession is that society benefits when resources are developed, not left to lie fallow. Of course, there are limitations to development, such as zoning laws, that have been imposed for the protection of others. But, to the extent that we desire application of human knowledge and energy to natural resources, a choice of incentives to promote effective development is involved. The incentive to create, produce, and exchange is greatly increased when society gives protection to the possessor of private property and permits the possessor to retain the benefits of his or her labor. This rationale applies not only to utilization of physical objects but also to the area of intangibles. The law of patents and copyrights developed from the notion that intellectual effort that results in a valuable invention or creation should be protected from appropriation. This view is the proper response from a society that benefits from such creativity.

In sum, a market economy requires a framework of legal rules to avoid violence and to encourage individual effort by giving legal protection to possession of private property.

Legal Restrictions on Private Property

The concept of private property is not without limits. One who owns property must be aware of the rights of others. All states have health and safety laws regulating the use of property, motor vehicle laws, zoning ordinances, building codes, and the like. Federal rules and regulations prohibit undue pollution of the environment by property owners.

Part of the law of torts restrains an owner of property from using it in such a way that it harms others. An owner can be held liable in damages to a person who is injured on or near the property due to an intentional or negligent act, and in some instances, even if the owner is without fault. For example, a merchant may be liable in damages to a customer who slips and falls on a slippery floor, and the keeper of a pet lion may be liable without fault to one who is injured by the lion.

There are many other legal restrictions on private property, and new restrictions are being created at all levels of government. In Chapter 21 we will discuss legal restrictions placed on owners of real property. In today's world, the owner of private property must constantly keep abreast of new rules and regulations in order to plan his or her business transactions intelligently.

Personal Property (Including Bailments)

The most important aspects of the law of personal property involve the ownership and possession of such property. The rest of this chapter deals with the acquisition of ownership of personal property and with the temporary possession of it by someone who is not the owner.

Acquisition of Ownership of Personal Property

One may acquire ownership of personal property in various ways.

Acquisition by Purchase. Probably the most common method of acquiring ownership of personal property is by purchase from an owner. Sales of personal property are governed by the common law of contracts, or by specialized bodies of contract law, or both. For example, consumers and businesses purchase goods daily in the marketplace from a variety of sellers. Sales of goods are governed by Article 2 of the Uniform Commercial Code as supplemented by the common law of contracts.

Acquisition by Gift. Another way to become owner of personal property is to receive it as a gift. A gift is a voluntary transfer of property without consideration. The person making the gift is the "donor"; the person receiving it is the "donee."

Gifts may be classified as testamentary, inter vivos, or causa mortis. *Testamentary gifts* are those intended to take place at the death of the donor and ordinarily must be made by means of a will. Wills are discussed in Chapter 23. A gift *inter vivos* is one made between living persons; that is, the transfer takes place and the donor receives full ownership rights during the lifetime of the donor and donee. Except as noted later, a gift inter vivos is *irrevocable* by the donor.

A gift *causa mortis* is a transfer (of personal property only) by a donor in the belief that he or she will die as a result of existing illness or injury, or from an imminent peril such as a sinking ship. Because a gift causa mortis is made in contemplation of death and probably under emotional stress, it is revocable by the donor at any time. If the donor recovers from the illness or injury or escapes the peril, the gift is automatically revoked. The donee's dying before the donor also revokes a gift causa mortis.

Three elements are required for gifts inter vivos and causa mortis: (1) donative intent, (2) actual or constructive delivery of the property, and (3) the donee's acceptance of the gift.

Donative intent. To make a gift, the donor must intend for the donee to have the thing without paying for it, i.e., without giving consideration. Statements such as "Take it, it's yours" or "I want you to have this" are clear indications of the requisite donative intent. Where there is no clear indication of intent and a lawsuit results, the court must determine the donor's intent on the basis of whatever evidence is available.

The donor also must make a *present* transfer of all of his or her rights in the thing if there is to be a gift. John says to Mary, "I give you this horse, but you don't get ownership until the end of the fifth race tomorrow." Since John did not intend a present transfer of ownership, there is no gift. For the gift to be effective now, John must transfer ownership to Mary now.

Gifts, however, can be conditional. Suppose Fred says to his daughter Sue, "I give you this car, but if you drop out of school, I'll take it back." Fred then hands her the keys and gives her a certificate of title showing her as owner. Fred has made a present transfer of the car. If Sue violates the condition, Fred may revoke the gift. Note that for an inter vivos gift to be revocable, the right to revoke must be *expressed.*

Numerous courts have held that a gift made in contemplation of marriage is made upon an implied condition that it is to be returned if the donee breaks the engagement without legal justification. Consequently, the gift of an engagement ring is revocable under proper circumstances. But if the *donor* unjustifiably breaks the engagement, the donee ordinarily may keep the gift.

Sometimes the law's requirements result in the frustration of a donor's intention. Suppose that an elderly woman puts money in an envelope and writes on the outside, "To my nephew, John, upon my death." The woman's intent obviously was to retain control over the money until her death and to have the transfer occur at that time. However, there is no gift during the aunt's lifetime, because a gift requires an unconditional *present* transfer. The desire to retain control over the money and to have the transfer occur at the time of death could be effectuated only by a will. (*Note:* The words "To my nephew, John, upon my death" do not constitute a will. Under the statutes of most states, a will, to be valid, must meet certain formal requirements. One of these requirements is that the instrument must be signed.)

Delivery or satisfactory substitute. The requirement of delivery is usually met by physically handing the object to the donee and thereby giving up control and possession of it. No gift occurs if the donor does not give up complete control and possession of the object. For example, if one person says to another, "I want you to have my watch," but continues to wear the watch, no gift is made.

In some situations it is impractical to make physical delivery of an item, and the law allows a *constructive* (sometimes called *symbolic*) delivery. Giving the donee a key to a locker may, under some circumstances, be recognized as a delivery of the contents. Dan says, "I want you to have the jewelry in my locker," and gives Joan the only key. There is a delivery of the jewelry because Dan has given Joan, the donee, exclusive dominion and control over the jewelry. Since physical delivery of *intangible* property is impossible, delivery of a symbol will be sufficient to constitute delivery of the underlying interest. For instance, delivery of a savings account passbook is usually sufficient to pass ownership of the account to a donee. Even though the particular financial institution usually requires the donor to sign a withdrawal slip before the donee will be recognized as owner, courts would generally hold that title passed to the donee when the passbook was delivered. If the donor were to die or have a change of mind before signing anything, the donee could secure a court order forcing the institution to recognize the donee as owner. The donee's case is based not on mere oral words of intent, which could be subject to dispute, but on physical possession of a symbol, that is, the passbook.

In order to constitute a gift, delivery of an item need not necessarily be to the donee. Occasionally, a donor will turn over an item to a third person with instructions to deliver it to the donee or to hold it for the benefit of the donee. The question may then arise: Has the donor made a present transfer of his or her rights? The answer will depend upon the relationship of the third person to the donor.

Where the third person is an agent for the donor, there is no present transfer of rights. An agent owes a duty to follow the instructions of his or her principal. Thus, a donor who delivers an object to his or her own agent could have a change of mind at any time and get the object back. Where the donor delivers an item to an agent of the *donee,* the donor does not retain control, and there is a present transfer of rights.

Frequently, the donor will execute a written conveyance of an object—i.e., a letter or a document transferring ownership to the donee. The delivery of such a document is as effective in transferring ownership as is physical delivery of the object. For example, the gift of an automobile or a boat is usually accomplished by the donor's signing and delivering the certificate of ownership to the donee. Ownership of securities, accounts receivable, and other intangibles is often transferred by means of a written form of assignment.

Acceptance. There are few situations where an intended donee would not wish to receive a gift. However, it is fundamental that a person cannot be forced to accept something that he or she does not want. Some examples of items a person might not wish to accept as a gift are an automobile with an unpaid purchase price in excess of its current value, stock in a corporation on the verge of bankruptcy, and defective goods that require extensive repairs to be usable.

In a lawsuit in which the issue is whether the alleged donee intended to *accept* the gift offered, the alleged donee ordinarily will testify as to his or her subjective intent. Often, the court will draw inferences from the circumstantial evidence presented. If, for example, acceptance of the gift would impose undue burdens on the intended donee, the court may conclude that there was no acceptance. On the other hand, if the donee's conduct manifests ownership of the article, the court may infer an intent to accept. For example, riding a bicycle received as a birthday present is an act of ownership. It is not necessary for the donee to say, "I accept." In most instances, a gift will result in a benefit to the donee. Therefore, in the absence of contrary evidence, the courts ordinarily will *presume* acceptance by the donee.

The following case discusses the questions of intent and delivery.

CASE 20.2 McCune v. Brown · 648 S.W.2d 811 (Ark. App. 1983)

FACTS Billie Jean McCune leased a safety deposit box at a bank. On December 12, 1978, her father, W. G. Brown, Sr., placed in the box $250,000 worth of gold Krugerrands and Mexican pesos. Brown was involved in a divorce proceeding with his wife and transferred the gold to his daughter in an attempt to defeat his wife's rights to the property. Brown claimed that his daughter understood that the gold was to be transferred back to him some time after the divorce. McCune claimed that Brown made an unconditional gift to her and Brown filed suit to restrain McCune from removing any of the contents of the box. The trial court held that Brown had proved his right to possession of the gold, and McCune appealed.

OPINION CLONINGER, J.... The requirements for an effective inter vivos gift are:

1. The donor knew and understood the effect of his act, and intended that effect;
2. The donor made actual delivery of the chattel to the donee or his agent;
3. The donor[,] by delivery, intended to pass title immediately;
4. The donee actually accepted the chattel as a gift.

...These elements must be proven by clear and convincing evidence.... The rule with respect to delivery of gifts is not so strictly applied to transactions between members of a family.... However, even between family members, there must be an actual delivery of the subject matter of the gift to the donee with a clear intent to make an immediate unconditional and final gift beyond recall, accompanied by an unconditional release by the donor of all future dominion and control over the property so delivered....

In the instant case, we hold that there was evidence upon which the chancellor could find that there was no delivery of the gift with the requisite donative intent and unconditional release of all future dominion and control over the property. First of all, appellee

CASE 20.2 Continued

[Brown] paid no gift tax on the gold which was transferred to appellant [McCune]. Upon all the previous gifts which appellee had made to appellant, he had paid the gift tax. Secondly, appellee retained the keys to the safety deposit box which is some evidence of an intent not to give up an unconditional release of the gold. . . . Thirdly, there were other items in the safety deposit box which clearly belonged to appellee, including his will. Finally, appellee's grandson testified that appellee had first transferred the gold to a safety deposit box in his grandson's name. The grandson testified that he intended to give the gold back to his grandfather some time after the divorce. This gold was later transferred to a safety deposit box in the name of appellant, and the reason stated by the grandson was because appellant was to move back and live with appellee. This would make the contents of the box more easily accessible to appellee. This testimony corroborates the testimony of appellee. Therefore, we hold that the chancellor's decision on this issue is not clearly against a preponderance of the evidence. . . .

JUDGMENT The decision of the chancellor is accordingly affirmed.

Acquisition by Will or by Descent. When a person dies, with or without leaving a will, the decedent's property passes to others, called beneficiaries or heirs. As noted in Chapter 23, a common method of acquiring ownership of property is by inheritance—either under a will, or if there is no will, under the state's statute of descent and distribution.

Acquisition by Taking Possession. A person may acquire ownership of a movable object that is unowned by taking possession of it. *Possession* in its literal sense means control or power over an object. Taking possession of a movable object in today's world is not always sufficient to establish ownership of the object. In an urban, industrial society, few objects are unowned. As stated above, ownership of personal property is usually established in other ways, but one of the primary methods recognized historically was taking possession of something in its natural state.

Wildlife. Many early court cases involve the acquisition of ownership of wild animals, fish, and bees. Such acquisition often was necessary for survival in a frontier society. At times, more than one person claimed ownership of an animal. Obviously, some rule governing ownership rights in wild animals was required. The rule that emerged was that ownership of a wild animal was obtained by taking the animal into possession (as by trapping or netting). This rule is still part of our contemporary common law.

Today, a person's survival is seldom at stake, and there are many conservation laws protecting endangered species of animals and birds from capture. All states have established seasons for hunting and fishing, and there is a prerequisite license. Failure to comply with state or local laws usually is a criminal offense. Only within the legal limits outlined by the appropriate governmental unit can a person acquire ownership of wild animals today.

Abandoned property. A contemporary application of the acquisition-by-possession principle may occur today in regard to abandoned chattels. Ownership of an abandoned item may be acquired by taking possession of it with intent to exclude others. For example, if someone finds a broken watch lying in a trash barrel, the person may acquire ownership of it by picking it up and exercising control over it to the exclusion of others. The finder must proceed cautiously, however, and first establish that the article has truly been abandoned. "Abandonment" is the intentional relinquishment of all rights in an object without transferring ownership to another person.

Lost property. A different rule of law applies to *lost,* as distinguished from abandoned, property. One cannot become owner of lost property merely by taking possession of it. Suppose Alice's dog wanders away from home and Ben finds and takes care of it. As a finder of lost property, Ben acquires a legally protected right of possession against everyone except Alice, the owner. However, since the dog was *not unowned,* Ben does not acquire the rights of an owner.

The distinction between lost and abandoned property is not always easy to make. The test or guideline to apply is the intent of the owner. If the owner unconsciously or unintentionally gave up possession of the chattel, the item is said to be merely lost. If the owner has consciously given up possession, with the intent to relinquish ownership permanently, the item is thereby abandoned. A person's intent is not always obvious. Courts usually consider three factors in determining the intent of the owner in relinquishing possession: (1) the location of the item, (2) the value of the item, and (3) the utility of the item. Trash barrels, public dumps, and roadside areas are all repositories for abandoned items. However, if an item of great value is found in any such place, the item has probably been lost by the owner without any intent to abandon it. If the item is unusable without the expenditure of a large sum of money for repair, it is probable that the owner chose to relinquish possession and ownership permanently.

Mislaid property. Another distinction that sometimes is important in determining property rights is whether an item is lost or *mislaid.* An item is said to be lost when the disappearance is a result of something other than the owner's conscious conduct. For example, coins that fall through a hole in a person's pocket are not abandoned or mislaid, but lost. By contrast, an item is said to be mislaid if the owner intentionally placed it somewhere and later cannot remember, for the time being at least, where it was left.

In one respect, the law governing lost and mislaid objects is the same: in neither situation does a finder acquire ownership. The difference in legal effect concerns the right of possession. If the item was mislaid, the owner of the premises where the item was found is entitled to take possession. For example, suppose a customer places his or her sunglasses on a table while having a haircut and then leaves without them. The proprietor of the shop has a right of possession superior to that of a second customer who discovers the glasses. The rationale is that the owner logically can be expected to return to the premises as soon as he or she remembers where the item was left. On the other hand, if the item was lost, the finder is entitled to take possession and retain it against all persons except the rightful owner. For example, if sunglasses are found lying under a seat in a motion picture theater, the courts would most likely conclude that the item was lost, not mislaid, and the finder would be entitled to possession as against the theater owner.

In many states today the finder of a lost article can acquire full ownership of the item under proper circumstances. Usually, the statutes require the finder to turn the property over to local authorities while the county clerk advertises the loss. When a specified time has elapsed after the required steps have been taken, the statutes usually allow ownership to pass to the finder.

In the following case the court discusses the difference between lost and mislaid property.

CASE 20.3 Ray v. Flower Hospital · 439 N.E.2d 942 (Ohio App. 1981)

FACTS Karen Ray was employed as a receptionist by Flower Hospital. At the information desk where she worked there was a drawer for keeping lost and found property. The drawer was locked and under the control of the receptionist on duty. On the night of June 15, 1979, between 7:30 P.M. and 8:30 P.M., Karen noticed a soft-shell eyeglass case on the top of the information desk. Upon inspection, it was discovered to contain four diamond rings, a topaz pin, gold earrings, a diamond necklace, gold cuff links, and a gold coin. The property was placed in the hospital's safe, and the local police were notified. The newspaper lost and found column was checked for 30 days, but no one came forth to claim the jewelry. On December 13, 1979, Karen filed suit against Flower Hospital for declaratory judgment and return of the property to her. The trial court granted her motion for summary judgment, declaring the property to be lost and Karen to be the owner of the property. Flower Hospital appealed.

Appellant (Flower Hospital) made two arguments: (1) The eyeglass case, having been found on top of the information desk of defendant hospital, should be deemed to be mislaid property and by law remain with the owner of the premises, and (2) it would be

CASE 20.3 Continued

contrary to public policy to allow an employee, one of whose responsibilities is to accept custody of lost and mislaid property on behalf of the owner of the premises to claim ownership rights for "finding" property which has come into her possession during the course of her duties.

OPINION

CONNORS, P. J. . . . With respect to appellant's first argument, 1 Ohio Jurisprudence 3d 23, Abandoned Property, Section 13, defines "mislaid property" as follows: ". . . property which the owner voluntarily and intentionally *laid down* in a place where he could again resort to it, which location the owner then forgot. . . ."

In contrast, "lost property" is defined as follows: ". . . property which the owner has involuntarily parted with through neglect, carelessness, or inadvertence, that is, property which the owner has unwittingly suffered to pass out of his possession and the whereabouts of which he has no knowledge. . . . Articles which are *accidentally dropped* in any public place, public thoroughfare, or street, are lost in the legal sense."

The substance then, of this court's analysis, must be a determination of whether the property in question is legally "lost" or legally "mislaid." . . .

It is uncontroverted that the eyeglass case containing the jewels was found lying on the top of the information desk, not on the floor of the hospital in front of the information desk. Further, it cannot be presumed that the property was lost or abandoned from the mere passage of time, although this is another fact or circumstance to be taken into consideration in the particular case. . . . [T]he six months that elapsed . . . from the time of discovery until the time that the appellee [Karen Ray] filed suit to ascertain the ownership of the property, did not create a presumption that the goods were either lost or mislaid.

The location in which the property was found . . . however, does aid this court in its labeling the goods as lost or mislaid property. The jewels were secreted away in a soft-shell eyeglass case. They were not found strewn across the floor whereby anyone walking into the hospital could view them. Further, the eyeglass case containing the jewels in this case was laid down on the top of the information desk by someone, presumably the owner, or someone seeking their return to the true owner by turning the case in to the "lost and found" desk, and was not dropped by inadvertence, negligence or carelessness as would be the case of lost property. From all of the facts and circumstances of this particular case, this court finds that the property was mislaid, and, as such, should remain in the possession of the hospital.

As was stated by the Supreme Court of Texas in the case of *Schley v. Couch*, . . . :

> "Mislaid property is presumed to be left in custody of owner or occupant of premises upon which it is found and he is generally entitled to possession of such property as against all except the owner thereof."

Therefore, the appellant's first argument is found well taken, in that it was error for the trial court to award title to mislaid property to the appellee.

Turning now, to appellant's second argument, the Oregon Supreme Court, in deciding a case of lost-mislaid property, addressed the precise issue and stated that:

"The decisive feature of the present case is the fact that plaintiff was an employee or servant of the owner or occupant of the premises, and that, in discovering the bills and turning them over to her employer, she was simply performing the duties of her employment. . . ." . . . In a long line of cases where hotel chambermaids, bank janitors, bank tellers, grocery store bagboys and other employees have found property while in their employ, virtually every case has charged the employee with the duty to turn the found property over to the employer for safekeeping. . . . Therefore, this court finds that appellee owed a duty to both the rightful owner of the property and to her employer, to relinquish possession of the goods to the owner of the premises for gratuitous bailee purposes. Thus, the trial court was in error in awarding possession and control of the goods to the appellee. We find "appellant's second argument" well taken.

CASE 20.3 Continued

. . . this court enters the final judgment which should have been entered in the trial court and vests title to the property in question in the defendant-appellant, Flower Hospital, subject to the rights of the true owner.

JUDGMENT Reversed.

Acquisition by Accession. Often a person's property is improved or added to by the labor and materials of another person, as where Ralph's Auto Shop gives Ann's car a tune-up at her request. Under the legal concept of *accession* (addition, augmentation), Ann becomes the owner of whatever

Table 20.1 Classification of Bailments

Type of Bailment	Example (E stands for bailee; R stands for bailor)
Gratuitous bailments	
For bailor's sole benefit:	
Gratuitous storage of a thing	E allows a neighbor, R, to store his or her car in E's garage without charge
Gratuitous carriage of a thing	E transports R's sofa without charging R for the service
Receiving possession of a thing for the purpose of gratuitously performing work on it	E offers to sharpen R's lawnmower if he or she will bring it to E's basement: R brings it and leaves it in E's basement
For the bailee's sole benefit:	
Gratuitous loan of a thing	R lends his or her power saw to E
Mutual-benefit bailments	
Ordinary bailments for hire:	
Compensated storage of a thing	R stores his or her furniture in a commercial warehouse
Receiving possession of a thing for the purpose of performing compensated work on it	R leaves his or her typewriter with E to be cleaned and repaired
Hired use of a thing	E leases a car from the R Car Rental Co.
Pledge or pawn	R deposits stocks with his or her bank to secure a loan
Special bailments: bailments involving	
Innkeepers as bailees	R [hotel guest] leaves valuables in hotel safe
Common carrier of goods as bailees	R hires E [railroad] to transport merchandise

new value Ralph's efforts produced. That is, she is entitled to any parts that Ralph installed and to any new value to the car that resulted from his adjusting it during the tune-up. Ann has, of course, an obligation to pay for the tune-up.

Suppose, however, that Tom steals Ann's car, repaints it, and adds a clamp-on radio. Later Tom is apprehended, the car is returned to Ann, and Tom demands payment for the paint job and the radio. Under the law of accession, Ann is entitled to anything that Tom added that cannot be removed without damage to the car. Since removing the paint would damage the car, Ann acquires ownership of the paint job by accession and has no obligation to pay for it. However, because the clamp-on radio can be removed without damage to the car, Tom is entitled to the radio or to its value. The policy of the law of accession, where the improver added value wrongfully, is to protect the innocent owner from loss, and not to punish the wrongdoer.

Acquisition by Confusion. Sometimes goods belonging to different persons are so commingled or intermixed that the owners cannot identify their particular goods. The intermixing, called *confusion,* usually is rightful, as where several owners voluntarily permit the confusion of grain of a particular grade for storage at a grain elevator. Each owner remains owner of his or her proportionate share of the entire mass. But sometimes confusion is wrongful. Tim, the owner of an unmeasured quantity of salad oil, steals an unknown quantity of Mary's salad oil and mixes it with his own. Since it is impossible to determine the quantity of Mary's oil, ownership of the whole mass passes to her by confusion. As the innocent party, she has no obligation to pay Tim for his oil. Tim, however, has the right to try to prove how much he owns, though as a thief he may find it difficult to persuade a court that the amount he claims is accurate.

Bailments

The subject of bailments does not involve the acquisition of ownership of property. It concerns the temporary possession of personal property by one who is not the owner. We encounter bailments frequently in our daily lives, and a knowledge of the law concerning bailments may be helpful. For example, suppose you leave your stereo set with a merchant who agrees to repair the set, and while in his possession the set is damaged or stolen. The law of bailments determines your rights and the rights and duties of the merchant.

Meaning of Bailment. A bailment may be defined as the legal relation resulting from the transfer of possession of personal property from one person (called the "bailor") to another person (called the "bailee") under such circumstances that the bailee is under a duty to return the item to the bailor or to dispose of it as directed by the bailor. Two points should be emphasized concerning this definition: (1) A bailment involves the transfer of possession without the transfer of ownership; where possession and ownership are both transferred, the transfer constitutes either a sale or a gift; and (2) the bailor need not be the owner of the property. If Benita borrows Alejandro's book and lends it to Carmen, Benita is a bailor as to Carmen. Even a thief may be a bailor.

The transfer of possession of property referred to in the definition above implies voluntary acceptance of the property. Thus, where goods come into a person's possession without the person's knowledge, he or she is not a bailee of the goods. For example, if a person agrees to store an "empty trunk" for a neighbor, the person is not a bailee of an overcoat that the neighbor neglected to remove from the trunk.

Classes of Bailments. Bailments may be classified as gratuitous bailments and nongratuitous bailments. Nongratuitous bailments are usually called "mutual-benefit bailments" and are sometimes called "bailments for hire." A gratuitous bailment is one in which one of the parties receives a benefit in regard to the bailed article without being obligated to pay for the benefit. A mutual-benefit bailment is one in which each party is entitled to receive a benefit. Table 20.1 illustrates a variety of bailments.

A special bailment, as can be seen from the table, is one in which the bailee is an innkeeper (a hotel, motel, etc.) or a common carrier of goods (a railroad, an airline, etc.). The common law governing special bailments has been so affected both by federal and state statutes and by regulations of federal and state administrative agencies that it is not feasible to discuss in a volume of this size the contemporary law governing this type of bailment. Liabilities of carriers, common and private, are discussed in Chapter 17, Part One.

Creation of Bailments. A bailment is a simple relation, and its formation requires no ceremony. The relation may exist even though there is no contract between the bailor and the bailee. The mere act of one person's transferring possession of personal property to another may result in a bailment relationship between them (as, for example, leaving a stereo set at a repair shop). The law then imposes certain duties on the parties and gives them certain rights. These rights and duties may be supplemented or modified by a written or an oral agreement between the bailor and bailee.

One occurrence that deserves special attention is that of placing a car in a parking lot. Sometimes a bailment is created, while at other times a "lease" or "license" is created. The distinction between the two relations is important if the owner's car is stolen or damaged while in the parking lot. A bailee of goods assumes certain duties toward the goods. These duties are discussed in the next section. One who merely leases a parking space to the car owner does not assume the duties of a bailee. Since a bailment results from the transfer of possession, the test to be applied is whether the driver has given up control over the vehicle. For example, if a person drives a car to a parking garage, parks the car, locks it, and takes the keys, a *lease* of space, not a bailment, is created. The driver has not relinquished control over the car. On the other hand, if a person drives to a restaurant where an attendant parks the car, takes the key, and gives the owner a claim check, a *bailment* is created. The driver has given up control; possession has been transferred to the restaurant. Transfer of possession is all that is required: no formal documents need be signed and no particular words need be said.

Case 20.4 discusses some of the factors considered in determining whether a bailment exists.

CASE 20.4 Broadview Apartments Co. v. Baughman · 350 A.2d 707 (Md. App. 1976)

FACTS Glenn H. Baughman, plaintiff (appellee), was a tenant in the Broadview Apartments located in northwest Baltimore. He paid Broadview $15 a month to park his car in the Broadview Garage. The garage was beneath the apartment building and was an enclosed two-level garage, one level in the basement and one on the ground (lobby) floor. Each level had a separate entrance and exit. There was no attendant at the lobby level, but there was one on the basement level. There was a security guard on duty 24 hours a day, and each tenant had a key to the garage door.

On the night of November 23, 1966, appellee parked his car in his assigned spot on the lobby level, locked the car, and took the keys with him. When he returned the next day, his car was gone. It was never recovered. Mr. Baughman filed suit for the loss of his automobile. The trial court held that Broadview was a bailee of the car and, as such, was liable for the value of the missing car. Broadview appealed.

OPINION MELVIN, J. . . . A bailment is "the relation created through the transfer of the possession of goods or chattels, by a person called the bailor to a person called the bailee, without a transfer of ownership, for the accomplishment of a certain purpose, whereupon the goods or chattels are to be dealt with according to the instructions of the bailor.". . .

"To constitute a bailment there must be an existing subject-matter, a contract with reference to it which involves possession of it by the bailee, delivery, actual or constructive, and acceptance, actual or constructive.". . .

Once the bailment relationship is proven[,] certain responsibilities flow from the relationship. The bailee in accepting possession of the bailed property assumes the duty of exercising reasonable care in protecting it. . . . If no bailment is shown, and the owner of the property is a mere licensee or lessee of the storage space, then in order to recover against the defendant garage owner the plaintiff would have to prove specific acts of

CASE 20.4 Continued

negligence on the part of the defendant proximately causing loss or injury to plaintiff's property. . . .

The courts have uniformly found a delivery of possession to the parking lot operators, and therefore a contract for bailment, where the keys are surrendered with the car or where the car is parked by an attendant. . . . Some other factors which have been considered to be important are: (1) whether there are attendants at the entrances and exits of the lots, (2) whether the car owner receives a claim check that must be surrendered before he can take his car, (3) whether the parking lot is enclosed, and (4) whether the parking lot operator expressly assumes responsibility for the car. No single factor has been viewed as determinative of the issue. The law has probably been best stated in *Osborne v. Cline,* . . . where the New York Court of Appeals stated that

> Whether a person simply hires a place to put his car (licensor-licensee relationship) or whether he has turned its possession over to the care and custody of another (bailee-bailor relationship) depends on the place, the conditions and the nature of the transaction.

In the instant case we think the evidence is legally insufficient to establish that a bailor-bailee relationship existed. Appellee merely rented a parking space monthly: he parked his own car, locked the car and took the keys with him. There was no testimony that Broadview had a set of keys for the car or had any right or authority to move or exercise any control over the car. The parking garage was laid out in such a manner that it was possible for appellee to park his car without any attendant even being aware of his presence in the garage. Appellee entered into the monthly lease arrangement with full knowledge of how the garage operated. He was not required to check his car in or out, and there was no evidence whatsoever that control of the car was ever turned over to the operators of the garage, or that they ever accepted delivery or control. Nor was there any evidence that Broadview expressly contracted or asserted that the car would be safe from theft while in the garage. . . . The mere fact that he paid a monthly rent for an enclosed parking space . . . does not, standing alone, raise an inference of a bailment contract. . . .

JUDGMENT On the record before us, as we have indicated, there is insufficient evidence to warrant a finding of a bailor-bailee relationship between the parties. The trial court was wrong in finding there was such a relationship. . . . [R]eversed.

Bailee's Rights and Duties. In a bailment relation, possession of the bailed item passes to the bailee. Along with possession, the bailee acquires certain rights. In return, the bailee assumes certain duties for the protection of the bailor's interests.

Right to possess the bailed property. During the time that a bailment relation exists, the bailee has a right to the exclusive possession of the bailed property. The right of possession is protected by the law of torts, which gives the bailee a cause of action against any person who wrongfully interferes. For instance, if Andrews leaves his pedigreed dog with Happy Valley Kennel while on his vacation, and Brown steals the dog, Happy Valley has a cause of action for conversion against Brown to secure return of the animal or to recover damages.[4] The bailee's right of possession is protected even against the bailor. Suppose that Andrews rents his dog to Smith, to be used by Smith for hunting for a fixed period of time, and Andrews returns unexpectedly and wrongfully interferes by retaking possession. Smith has a cause of action against Andrews.

Right to use borrowed or rented property. Where the purpose of a bailment is the use of the bailed article, the bailee has the right to use the article in a fair and reasonable manner. For example, if George borrows his neighbor's drill and wood bit, he may use them to drill holes in wood. If

[4]See the discussion of the tort of conversion in Chapter 4.

George attempts to drill through metal or concrete, he is liable for any damage caused to the drill and bit. On the other hand, when the purpose of a bailment is for storage, the bailor does not contemplate any use of the goods, and the bailee would be liable for *any* use made of the goods. For example, if Charles boards his horse at a stable, and Deena, who works there, rides the horse in a parade, Charles has a cause of action against Deena.

Duty to exercise care. Every bailee owes to the bailor some degree of care in the custody of the bailed article. Under modern law, that standard is the degree of care that a reasonable person would exercise under all the circumstances of the case.[5] Among the more important circumstances are the value of the bailed article (jewelry, work of art); the nature of the article (whether easily portable or not, whether easily damaged or not); the facilities available to the bailee for taking care of the bailed article; the experience of the bailee (whether a professional bailee or not); the kind of community (metropolitan city or isolated rural town); and the presence or absence of any benefit to the bailee.

If the bailee is negligent, and if the negligence is a proximate cause of damage to the bailor's goods, the bailee may be held liable to the bailor. In the absence of fault, the bailee is not liable. Unless the bailment agreement so provides, the bailee is not an insurer. Thus, if an unexpected earthquake or flood occurs and destroys property in the possession of the bailee, the bailee cannot be held liable. Let us suppose, however, that a hurricane warning is announced. The bailee must now take reasonable precautions to protect the bailed property against this foreseeable, known risk, such as boarding up doors and plate glass windows. If the bailee does not do so and the goods are damaged, the bailee may be held liable for negligence.

In the event the bailor sues the bailee because goods were lost or damaged while in the bailee's possession, most courts would say that the bailee is *presumed* to be negligent and that the burden rests on the bailee to prove the precise cause of the loss or damage *and* to prove that he or she acted in a reasonable and prudent manner. For example, suppose someone leaves furniture in storage at a warehouse and thereafter a piece is stolen. The presumption is that the storage company was negligent in failing to prevent the theft and is liable. However, if the company can prove that the goods were packed safely and that a night watchman patrolled regularly, monitoring with closed-circuit television, a court might properly conclude that the company had exercised the degree of care expected from a reasonable person and therefore was not liable to the bailor.

It is not sufficient merely to show exercise of care. To avoid liability, the bailee also must explain the precise cause of the bailor's loss. The bailee may be held liable for an unexplained loss. There are several views by legal authorities to justify placing this burden on the bailee. One such view is that it is difficult for a bailor to obtain from the bailee or the bailee's employees the information needed to establish negligence. Usually, there are no independent witnesses to testify how a bailed article was lost or damaged. Therefore, the law assists the bailor by establishing a presumption that the bailee was negligent.

In the following case the court discusses the presumption of negligence when goods are damaged while in the bailee's possession.

[5]Many of the principles discussed in this section are discussed more fully in Chapter 5. See also Chapter 17 regarding duties of care by warehousers and carriers.

CASE 20.5 American Machinery Movers, Inc. v. Continental Container Service, Inc. · 436 So. 2d 1289 (La. App. 1983)

FACTS Continental Container Service, Inc., leased a 10-year-old diesel forklift from American Machinery Movers, Inc. About 1 month later, the forklift's engine failed. American sent a mechanic, Gerald Thomas, to the Continental yard, and he discovered that a piston had penetrated the side of the engine block, leaving a rather large hole in the motor.

CASE 20.5 Continued

Thomas noted there was insufficient oil on the dipstick. He told American that in his opinion the damage to the engine was caused by operating the diesel without the required amount of oil. American filed suit for the full cost of repairs, $7,579. Continental defended that the machine failed simply because of age, and that it had maintained the forklift properly throughout the lease (a mutual-benefit bailment).

The trial court held for the defendant, Continental. American appealed.

OPINION

AUGUSTINE, J.... American's claim against Continental is based upon these legal principles:

First, when the lessee [bailee] receives a leased thing in good order, he must return it in the same state.

Second, when damage occurs to the leased object while in the possession of the lessee, it is *presumed* that the damage has resulted from the lessee's negligence, and it is therefore his burden to exonerate himself from liability by proving his freedom from fault.... The reason for the presumption is that, having been in possession of the leased object, the lessee is more able than the lessor [bailor] to explain the cause of damage or loss....

The immediate issue is whether the lessee, Continental, discharged its burden to prove that the damage to the diesel forklift was not caused by its negligence.

As previously stated, Continental defended this action on the ground that the forklift was ten years old and failed simply because of its age. To prove this fact, the defendant offered the testimony of Mr. William Little, Continental's president, who testified that the average life expectancy of a machine such as American's is, at most, five years.... [W]e do not consider the foregoing evidence to be sufficient to carry the defendant lessee's burden of proof. First, Mr. Little's testimony concerning the work-life of a machine such as American's was based upon the performance of similar forklifts in Continental's yard, where forklifts are in constant, heavy toil over the course of a forty-hour week. But according to Mr. Dennis Scandurro, American's vice-president, the forklift in question was never subjected to such a rigorous work schedule. During the first seven years of the diesel's "life," it was not rented to anyone, but remained in the service of American Machinery Movers, where it was used primarily to unload other machines at various industrial locations around the city. Scandurro testified that such operations did not ordinarily require the forklift to be in operation for long periods of time, and consequently, the machine had relatively few hours on it as of the time it failed....

Moreover, even assuming that Little's testimony allows the inference that American's forklift had a life expectancy of only a *few* more years than those in Continental's yard, and therefore, that American's diesel had lived *beyond* its expected work-life, that fact merely warrants a finding that old age fatigue was among the many possible causes of breakdown. But having undertaken the burden to prove a specific cause of failure, it is not enough for defendant to prove the mere possibility of that cause.... Such evidence, utterly lacking in specificity, completely fails to educate us as to how or why the diesel might have been damaged. Accordingly, we hold that the defendant has failed to dispel the presumption that the damage to American's forklift was caused by Continental's negligence.

With respect to the plaintiff's specific allegation that Continental was negligent in not maintaining a proper level of oil in the diesel, and that this negligence caused the engine to fail, the defendant responds that it had maintained the forklift properly throughout the duration of the lease. The *only* witness who testified concerning this fact, however, was Kenneth Hemer, Continental's shop foreman, whose entire testimony on this point was hearsay:

CASE 20.5 Continued

Mr. Hemer:
"I went to each individual driver and asked him when he checked the oil last."

Mr. St. Pee:
"What did they say?"

Mr. Hemer:
"Mr. Jarreau did not have anything specific on that, and Mr. Mattix said that he hadn't checked it. Mr. Glenn said that a few days before (the breakdown) Delaney checked it."

This testimony cannot establish that the forklift was properly maintained, for even if Hemer's statements are accepted as true, the *only* person to check the oil within the week prior to the breakdown was Delaney. . . . If Delaney inspected the machine at all, it was probably on the *previous* Monday, a full week before the breakdown. Continental's policy with regard to its own machines, however, required inspection of oil and water levels every *two* days. But in testimony and in briefs to this Court, Continental admits that this policy was not followed with respect to the leased forklift. We therefore conclude that Hemer's testimony cannot carry the burden of relieving the defendant of its presumed negligence.

American, on the other hand, has affirmatively established that which it was under no burden to prove: first, that Continental did not maintain the machine with the frequency required by its own policy, and second, that at the time the engine failed, the oil was well below the required level. Finally, American's mechanic testified that the engine failed *because* of low oil, and although his testimony concerning the causal link between low oil and the subsequent engine failure was not as thorough as it might have been, his ultimate conclusion was not only reasonable, but also unrefuted.

JUDGMENT Accordingly, the judgment of the district court is reversed, and there is judgment herein in favor of American Machinery Movers, Inc. and against Continental Services, Inc. in the full sum of $7,579, plus legal interest from judicial demand and all costs.

Limitation of liability. In some situations the liability of the bailee may be limited or even eliminated by agreement of the parties. Common examples involve auto parking lots and checkrooms where claim checks or tickets are given to customers. The ticket usually contains language specifying a maximum amount of liability for damage to the bailor's property or disclaiming all liability. This situation is primarily one involving contract law, specifically the rules regarding communication of offers. Most courts hold that the bailee can limit liability only if the disclaimer is effectively communicated to the bailor. In contract law, a message is communicated if the recipient either knows or reasonably *should* know the information it contains. For instance, if a sign is posted with letters large enough for the ordinary person to see upon entering the establishment, the usual bailor may be chargeable with *notice* of the terms posted. Ordinarily, however, the bailor will not be chargeable with notice of terms contained in small print on the back of a ticket stub. In most states, even if the disclaimer is properly communicated, the bailee will be liable for *gross negligence* or for *willful* injury to the bailor's property. (See discussion of exculpatory clauses in Chapter 12.)

When a bailor transfers possession of an item of great value, such as jewelry or a work of art, he or she should notify the bailee of that fact. In some states, such as California, the statutes limit the bailee's liability in case of loss to the *apparent* reasonable value of the chattel, unless the bailor had specifically notified the bailee of its unusual worth. And, of course, a bailee is not liable for loss of an item within a bailed chattel if the bailee was not aware and had no reason to be aware of the presence of the item (such as valuable jewelry in an ordinary purse).

Duty to return the property. In a bailment relation the bailee is obligated to return the bailed property at the termination of the bailment or to dispose of it as directed by the bailor. If the parties have agreed to a specified time period for the bailment, the right to possession of the item automatically reverts to the bailor at the expiration of the period (as, for example, renting an automobile for 1 week). If the relation is a bailment at will (i.e., no term is specified), the bailor can request return of the goods at any time. In either situation, the bailee must promptly return the goods; if the bailee improperly withholds return of the bailor's property, the bailee may be liable to the bailor in tort.

A bailee may also be liable for wrongfully delivering goods to someone other than the bailor or a person designated by the bailor. A bailee who delivers the property to the wrong person is liable to the bailor for the tort of conversion. The bailee may have been induced to deliver the bailor's property to someone through trickery, fraud, or simple mistake. The bailee's liability for misdelivery, however, is *absolute* and is not based on negligence or bad faith.

Duty to compensate bailor in rental situations. In a mutual-benefit bailment of the type where the bailee hires the use of a thing, the bailee is obligated to compensate the bailor for that use. For example, a person who rents a trailer to haul goods must pay the bailor for the use of the trailer.

Bailor's Duties. When a bailment relation is created, the bailor has certain rights, namely, rights to performance of the duties listed in the preceding section, and the bailor owes certain duties with respect to the bailed property and to the bailee.

Duty to protect bailee from defects in the property. Where the bailor knows that the bailee will be using the bailed item and will be exposed to a risk of harm from such use, the bailor must exercise due care to prevent harm to the bailee, the bailee's employees, and the bailee's property from a defect in the bailed property. This is merely an application of the basic tort law of negligence. If the bailor knows of a defect, he or she must disclose it to the bailee. For instance, if a person knows there is a loose belt on a power mower that is being loaned to a neighbor, the owner must inform the neighbor of the defect.

Where great harm could occur from the use of a bailed item, the bailor is obligated to make an inspection of the article prior to relinquishing possession to the bailee. For example, a car rental agency should inspect a vehicle before it delivers the car to the customer-bailee. If the rental agency fails to make an inspection when an inspection would have disclosed a defect in the car, the agency may be held liable for an injury that later occurs as a result of the defect. Many states now have extended the law of product liability (discussed in Chapter 18) and hold commercial rental agencies liable without fault for injuries caused by a defect in goods leased.

Duty to compensate bailee in service situations. When the purpose of a mutual-benefit bailment is performance by the bailee of some service in connection with the bailed item, the bailor has a duty to compensate the bailee for the service. For instance, if a person leaves a car to be repaired at a commercial garage, and the mechanic properly performs the service requested, the bailor has a duty to pay for that service. If the bailor refuses to pay for the service, the bailee has a cause of action against the bailor for breach of contract.

Often, the bailee has the privilege of retaining possession of the bailed chattel until his or her just charges are paid. This privilege of retaining possession until compensation is received is called a "possessory lien." In most states there are statutory procedures that enable an unpaid bailee who has a lien on bailed goods to advertise and sell them at public auction, after waiting a specified period of time for payment. For examples, see Liens Imposed by Law on Personal Property, in Chapter 24.

Summary

Private property is an essential part of a market economy. In one sense, property refers to things owned. In its other sense, property means the exclusive right to use, possess, enjoy, and dispose of things. The main classes of property are: tangible and intangible, real and personal, public and private. Tangible property consists of things that have a physical existence; intangibles do not exist in physical form but have economic value. Real property is land, airspace above the land, and all things imbedded in the land or firmly attached to it. Personal property is all property that is not real property. Public property is held by a governmental unit or agency. Private property is held by an individual or business entity.

Personal property is of great commercial significance. A person or firm may acquire ownership of personal property in various ways—for example, by purchase or by gift. The elements of a valid gift are donative intent, a delivery or acceptable substitute, and an acceptance by the donee. To acquire ownership in an abandoned chattel a person must take possession of it—i.e., must exercise control over it. However, the finder of lost or mislaid property does not automatically acquire ownership rights. The finder of lost property is entitled to possession against everyone except the true owner. If the item was mislaid, the owner of the premises where the item was found is entitled to possession. If the owner does not appear, title to lost property may pass in accordance with local statutes.

A bailment results from the transfer of possession, but not ownership, of personal property by one person (the bailor) to another person (the bailee). There are two major classes of bailments: (1) gratuitous bailments, where only one party receives a benefit from the bailment relationship, and (2) mutual-benefit bailments, (sometimes called "bailments for hire"), where each party receives a benefit from the bailment relationship.

Both parties to a bailment relationship have certain rights and duties. The bailee has the right to possession of the bailed article and, when appropriate, the right to the use of the bailed article. The bailee has the duty to exercise reasonable care in the custody of the article, to return it to the bailor or to someone designated by the bailor, and, in one situation (hired use of a thing), to compensate the bailor. The bailor must exercise due care to protect the bailee from defects in the bailed item; and in commercial situations involving a service to the item, the bailor must compensate the bailee.

Review Questions

1 Discuss the two ways the word "property" is used in the law.

2 Define the following: tangible property; intangible property; real property; personal property; public property; private property.

3 How is private property protected under the law: **(a)** from interference by individuals? **(b)** from interference by the government?

4 **(a)** What are the reasons for the protection of private property? **(b)** Are these reasons valid in today's world? Why or why not?

5 **(a)** Give examples of legal restrictions that the law places on the use, possession, and disposition of private property. **(b)** Why do you think the law imposes these restrictions?

6 **(a)** Define "gift." **(b)** What are the requirements for a gift of personal property? **(c)** What does the term "donative intent" mean? **(d)** Indicate a method that a donor might utilize to make "delivery" of a musical composition. **(e)** Is acceptance of a gift by the donee always required? Explain.

7 **(a)** Give an example of how a person would take possession of a wild animal. **(b)** Do you think a person who traps a wild animal that has escaped from a circus acquires ownership of the animal? Why or why not?

8 **(a)** Distinguish between abandoned and lost property; lost and mislaid property. **(b)** Why is it important to determine whether an article is abandoned, lost, or mislaid?

9 **(a)** What is a bailment? **(b)** How does it differ from a gift?

10 State whether you agree, partially agree, or disagree with the following statements, and why: **(a)** A gratuitous bailment is one in which the bailor receives a benefit in regard to the bailed article without being obligated to pay for the benefit. **(b)** A mutual-benefit bailment is one in which the bailor receives a service for which he or she is obligated to pay.

11 **(a)** Explain the difference in legal consequences between a bailment of a car placed in a parking lot and a lease of space for that car. **(b)** What test is applied to determine which relation is created?

12 State whether you agree with the following statement and why. "The bailee's right to the exclusive possession of the bailed property is good against everyone except the bailor."

13 State and explain the duties a bailee owes to a bailor.

14 State and explain the duties a bailor owes to a bailee.

Case Problems

1 Dorothy had created three irrevocable trusts for her three children. In 1981 Dorothy and her husband, Joseph, commenced divorce proceedings in which Dorothy claimed that sixteen drawings by world-renowned artists belonged to the trusts, not to her. Joseph died and Dorothy then sought to reverse her position as to the drawings. She contended that she had constructed the appearance of gifts in order to keep the art works from her husband. The evidence showed that she had made unsolicited statements to her attorney, to her husband's attorney, to appraisers, and to others that the art works belonged to the trusts. The works were kept in a vault to which Dorothy had the only key. The drawings were of a delicate nature and of high value. Dorothy was experienced in conservation and security of art works, and the trustees of the trusts were not. Dorothy affixed labels to some of the drawings, indicating their ownership by specific trusts. She placed stamps on the mats of other drawings, and some drawings were placed in special boxes which were marked as property of specific trusts. In 1982 Dorothy had met with her son John and directed him to copy down the name of each artist and the title of each drawing so that ownership of each art work by a specific trust would be clear. Did Dorothy make a gift of the drawings to the three trusts?

2 Bernice, a safety deposit box subscriber at the Old Orchard Bank, found $6,325 in currency on the seat of a chair in an examination booth in the safety deposit vault. The chair was partially under a table. Bernice turned the money over to the bank. The bank wrote to everyone who had been in the safety deposit vault area either on the day of, or on the day preceding, the discovery. No one reported the loss of currency, and the money remained unclaimed for a year. The vault area was separated from a lobby by a gate, and entry was restricted to bank employees and customers. Under an Illinois statute, if any person finds lost money, the county clerk advertises for 3 weeks. If the owner does not appear within 1 year after the advertisement, ownership of the money passes to the finder. The advertisement was made, and 1 year elapsed. Is Bernice entitled to the $6,325?

3 Gullia landed his private airplane at Palm Beach International Airport and taxied it to Butler Aviation. He locked the plane and kept the key. The key opened the door locks and baggage compartments, but no key was necessary to operate the aircraft. The plane was logged on Butler's daily arrival sheet, and a Butler employee towed the plane to a parking area and tied it down. There was a fence around the airport perimeter. Butler controlled its area by stationing a security guard at its access gate and a dispatcher at a service counter at the other entrance. An employee checked nightly to see which aircraft were in the parking area. A week after Gullia's arrival an unknown person entered Butler's lot, paid the parking and refueling charges, and absconded with the plane. Did a bailment relationship exist between Gullia and Butler?

4 Before boarding a commercial airplane, Roger submitted to the usual airport security check. His hand baggage was placed on a conveyor belt and was rolled through the X-ray apparatus. At the same time, Roger was going through the magnetometer, from which he was unable to observe his baggage. Upon completion of the security check of his person, Roger went to the pickup end of the conveyor belt, grabbed the one and only bag there, which outwardly resembled his own bag, and proceeded to board the aircraft. Roger discovered that he did not have his baggage and reported the discovery to the airline agent. His baggage was never found. Should the operator of the security check apparatus be liable to Roger for the loss of the baggage and its contents?

5 Carr purchased Kodak Ektachrome-X 135 slide film and during August 1970 vacationed in Europe with his family. Carr took a great many photographs, and upon his return to the United States, took eighteen rolls of exposed film to Hoosier Photo Supplies to be developed. He was given a receipt for each roll. Hoosier sent the film to Eastman Kodak Company for processing. Only fourteen rolls were returned to Hoosier. Carr sued Hoosier and Kodak for $10,000 damages. Kodak defends that its film is distributed in boxes on which there is printed the following: "READ THIS NOTICE. This film will be replaced if . . . lost by us or any subsidiary company even though by negligence or other fault. Except for such replacement, the sale, processing, or other handling of this film for any purpose is without other warranty of liability." The receipt given to Carr by Hoosier contained similar language printed on the back side limiting liability to replacement of film. At the trial it was established that Carr did not read either the notice on the packages of film he bought or the notice on the receipts. However, because of years of experience as an attorney and as an amateur photographer he knew there was a limitation of liability printed on the boxes and on the receipts. Should Carr recover damages from Kodak or Hoosier?

6 In 1980 Mitchell was building a backyard fence, and a neighbor suggested he rent a post hole digger. He rented from Burke Rental Center a digger that was equipped with a slip, or centrifugal clutch, engineered to cause the auger to stop turning when it encountered an obstruction. The auger would resume operation when no longer in contact with the obstruction. Mitchell was unaware of this feature and Burke's employees did not explain the operation of the slip to him. Mitchell took the machine home and, after a minute or two of operation, the auger and pulleys quit running. He reached down to check the V-belt on the machine and it started running again. Mitchell's hand was sucked into it and was severely injured. There was no guard on the V-belt to prevent an unknowledgeable user from coming in contact with the hazard. Burke had purchased the digger in 1967 and in 1976 substantially altered it. What arguments could Mitchell advance to impose liability on Burke?

CHAPTER 21

Real Property: Nature, Acquisition, and Ownership

For obvious reasons, real property is the most important form of property. Most food comes from the land, as do the raw materials used in the production of almost everything: goods of infinite variety, housing, factories, public buildings, military equipment, dams and highways, electrical generators, transmission lines, earth satellites, ships at sea—the list is endless. Key to our survival, land is a major source of wealth and power. Its use and control are vital to every individual, business, and government. Because of its fundamental importance, land has been the subject of countless wars and private disputes.

A major concern of early Anglo-American law was the development of a law of real property to govern ownership of land and its transfer, taxation, and succession at death. Today's law emphasizes, in addition, responsible *use* of land in the context of a hugely expanding population. Anyone who contemplates the acquisition of real property should understand the various methods of acquiring ownership, the types of ownership available, and the rights and duties involved in owning real property.

The first part of this chapter is devoted to a discussion of the physical elements customarily included in the term "real property." Special attention is given to the subject of fixtures. The last two parts of the chapter are devoted to the acquisition and ownership of real property.

Physical Elements of Real Property

Land, Airspace, Subsurface

The term "real property" customarily includes the surface of the land, things attached to the land, the airspace above the land, and materials below the surface. The surface includes things found in nature, such as water and soil, and things added by human effort, such as buildings and crops. Below the surface are found such things as minerals, oil, and gas. The law pertaining to each of these elements is complex and too extensive to be covered in a business law text. However, certain fundamental rules and principles are presented to give a basic understanding of this area of law.

Airspace. The owner of real property has the right to the airspace above the surface of his or her land. An ancient rule of common law was that ownership extended to the "periphery of the universe." There was little need to question this rule prior to the invention of the airplane. Today, airspace is treated as an economic resource that should be available for public use, and the landowner's rights have been restricted. The general rule is that the landowner owns that portion of the airspace above the land that the owner can use in connection with the beneficial and convenient enjoyment of the land surface.

Ownership of airspace can be transferred with or without the transfer of the land surface. The transfer usually occurs automatically in connection with transfer of the land surface. However, the separate transfer of airspace is a growing phenomenon in the United States. Such transfer occurs, for example, when a person buys into a high-rise condominium. In effect, the purchaser buys a cube of airspace in the building. Some of the legal aspects of condominiums are discussed later in this chapter.

Crops and Timber. Items that grow on the land, such as trees, shrubs, corn, and potatoes, are considered to be part of the real property. Thus, when real property is transferred by a landowner, any trees and growing crops automatically pass to the transferee, unless the owner specifically reserves rights in them. Ownership of growing trees and crops may be transferred separately from a transfer of the land. Harvested crops and felled trees are classed as personal property and do not automatically pass to the transferee of the land.

Minerals. All materials below the surface of an owner's land are part of the real property. Minerals, such as gold, silver, and copper, can be of great commercial value. The landowner can transfer ownership of the subsurface separately or as part of a transfer of the real property. Separate ownership of the subsurface normally includes the right to enter upon the surface of the land to remove minerals. The prudent landowner will not transfer ownership of the subsurface without having given due consideration to how much the transfer would restrict use of the surface of the land. In cases involving conflict between owners of the surface and owners of the subsurface, courts ordinarily hold that the subsurface owner's right of entry may not be restricted unless it is shown that the surface will be irreparably harmed.

The following case discusses the relationship between the owner of the land surface and one who is entitled to take minerals from the subsurface.

CASE 21.1 Buffalo Mining Co. v. Martin · 267 S.E.2d 721 (W. Va. 1980)

FACTS In 1890 a mineral severance deed was executed which granted all coal and other minerals underlying certain real estate now owned by James and Toni Martin. Buffalo Mining Company acquired mining rights in a coal lease in 1969 from the owner of the mineral rights. Buffalo was involved in mining a large tract of coal, part of which was located under the Martins' property. In order to ventilate its coal mine, Buffalo erected an electric transmission line on the Martins' land. James Martin obstructed the project, and Buffalo filed suit to secure an injunction prohibiting the Martins from interfering with the erection of the line. The Martins contended that the power line constituted an unreasonable use of the surface and that the 1890 deed is silent as to the right to erect an electric power line. The trial court granted the injunction, and the Martins appealed.

OPINION MILLER, J.... It is generally recognized that where there has been a severance of the mineral estate and the deed gives the grantee the right to utilize the surface, such surface use must be for purposes reasonably necessary to the extraction of the minerals....

Appellants [Martins] rely heavily on three decisions in which this Court refused to interpret language granting surface rights in connection with deep mining as including the right to strip or auger the surface for coal.... These decisions were each based on two grounds. First, at the time of the original severance deed, neither strip nor auger mining was known and therefore could not have been within the contemplation of the parties. Second, and of even more importance, was the fact that these mining methods virtually destroyed the surface for its normal use,....

We do not believe that these three decisions are controlling in the present case. The issue here presented involves no claim of any widespread destruction of the surface, but whether the utilization of the surface for an electric power line can be inferred as a reasonable use within the context of the severance deed language....

It would appear from the foregoing cases that where the severance deed contains broad rights for utilization of the surface in connection with underground mining activities and these broad rights are coupled with a number of specific surface uses, courts will be inclined to imply compatible surface uses that are necessary to the underground mining activity....

Despite statements in *West Virginia-Pittsburgh Coal Co. v. Strong*, ... that the grant of express mining easements restricts or negates implied rights, we do not believe this principle to be controlling in the present case. First, in addition to a number of express surface rights, including the compatible use of telephone and telegraph lines, the severance deed sets forth the general grant of "all proper and reasonable rights and privileges for ventilating and draining the mines and wells." Moreover, we believe that *Strong* was correctly decided on the more fundamental principle that a right to surface use will not be implied where it is totally incompatible with the rights of the surface owner.

Our past cases have demonstrated that any use of the surface by virtue of rights granted by a mining deed must be exercised reasonably so as not to unduly burden the surface owner's use....

We conclude that where implied as opposed to express rights are sought, the test of what is reasonable and necessary becomes more exacting, since the mineral owner is

CASE 21.1 Continued seeking a right that he claims not by virtue of any express language in the mineral severance deed, but by necessary implication as a correlative to those rights expressed in the deed. In order for such a claim to be successful, it must be demonstrated not only that the right is reasonably necessary for the extraction of the mineral, but also that the right can be exercised without any substantial burden to the surface owner. . . .

JUDGMENT Affirmed.

Oil and Gas. Oil and gas occupy a unique position in the law because they are substances that flow from one place to another. The law regarding ownership of these physical elements differs in the various states. In most of the major oil-producing states, the landowner does not own any particular oil and gas below the land surface. The owner simply has the exclusive *right to drill* for oil and gas on his or her land and, if some is discovered, to extract it. The landowner may extract oil and gas from an underground pool, even if the boundaries of the pool extend under neighboring land. There are comprehensive state and federal laws restricting the amount of oil and gas that may be extracted. When the likelihood of an oil or a gas field exists, the usual practice in most states is for a group of landowners to grant the right to drill to one individual or firm, by means of leases. The typical lease provides that in the event oil or gas is found and is extracted by the driller, the payment that the landlord (or landlords) receives is a royalty based on the amount of oil or gas removed. For example, a common arrangement in oil leases is that the landowner (or landowners) receives the market value at the well of one-eighth of all oil extracted.

Water. Water on or below the surface of the land is real property. However, if the water is "severed" from the land and put in a container, its classification is changed to personal property. In arid parts of the western United States, local water agencies purchase water as they would purchase any commodity. The water is then transported by truck, pipeline, or canal and sold to farmers, ranchers, and consumers who may live hundreds of miles from the source of the water.

Water is a precious resource. The public policy of the federal and state governments is to preserve and protect that resource. Accordingly, statutes and court decisions restrict the water rights of landowners. In most states a landowner does not have the right to dig a well and take water from under the land in unlimited quantity. The owner may draw only the amount of water that he or she can reasonably and beneficially use. Likewise, a person who owns a parcel of land bordering on a stream or river has the right (called "riparian right") to take reasonable quantities of water from the stream or river, but she or he cannot dam up the stream or dig a channel and divert the entire water flow onto his or her land. Downstream owners also have riparian rights, and these rights cannot be unreasonably interfered with by an owner upstream.

There are many disputes over the appropriation, use, pricing, contamination, and discharge of ground and surface water. These disputes involve competing classes of water users (e.g., ranchers, industries, consumers), environmental protection groups, and city, county, state, and national governments.

Fixtures

General Nature of Fixtures. A fixture is personal property that later was attached to real property with the intent that it become permanently a part of the realty. An owner of land who uses building materials such as cement, lumber, and pipe to construct a residence clearly intends to convert these goods into real property. However, sometimes the affixing party's intent is not clear. If litigation results—e.g., between the buyer and the seller of real estate—the court has the difficult task of determining the probable intent.

Tests of a Fixture. To determine whether an item of personal property has become a fixture (and thus is to be treated as real property), the courts apply several criteria. The *intent* of the parties as expressed or as implied from their conduct is the most persuasive criterion. If Sam says to the buyer of his house, "This antique throw-rug is part of the house," a court will hold that the rug is a fixture even though in the absence of such a statement all courts might classify throw-rugs as personal property. But often people do not reveal their intention regarding such items, and the courts have to resort to other tests from which to infer the parties' *probable* intent. The usual tests (resorted to only in the absence of an indication of *actual* intent) are (1) the degree of attachment (annexation) of the personal property to the realty, (2) the degree to which the personal property is adapted to the use of the realty, and (3) the relationship of the competing parties. These three tests are not always given equal weight by the courts; the relative importance of each test depends on the circumstances of each case.

Degree of attachment. When an item is attached to realty in such a manner that removing the item would cause injury to it or to the realty to which it is attached, the courts consider such attachment strong evidence that the item is intended to be a fixture. One can reasonably infer that items attached by cement or by plaster were intended to remain permanently. Most heating and air conditioning systems are installed in buildings in such a way that to remove them would cause great injury, and therefore they usually are held to be fixtures.

The fact that an item is easily removable without injury to it or to the real property suggests that the affixing party intended for the item to remain personal property. However, ease of removal is not conclusive in determining whether an item was intended to be a fixture.

Adaptability to use. An item of personal property that is beneficial or necessary to the ordinary use of the real property to which the item is attached is likely to be held a fixture, even though the item may be easily removable. For example, doors, windows, and hot-water heaters are usually removable without injury, but courts normally hold such items to be fixtures. These items are necessary to the ordinary use of real property, and the courts infer that the affixing party must have intended the items to be permanently part of the real property. Items that are custom-made for the particular premises, such as wall-to-wall carpeting and built-in kitchen appliances, are also normally held to be fixtures.

The courts seldom hold an item to be a fixture if it is not beneficial or necessary to the ordinary use of the real property. For example, a large pipe organ installed in a home was held to be personal property because it was a musical instrument and not a necessary part of a residence.

Relationship of the parties. In order to determine the intent of a party who has attached an item to the realty, the courts also consider as evidence the relationship of the parties to each other. Thus, in litigation involving the right of a tenant to remove stereo speakers that the tenant has attached to the landlord's real property, the courts will presume that the tenant intended to remove the speakers at the end of the lease period. Such items are usually held not to be fixtures because a tenant seldom intends to make a gift of personal property to the landlord. In contrast, if the tenant replaced a wall-to-wall carpet without the landlord's knowledge, the carpet probably would be considered a fixture because of the attachment, adaptability, and damage-to-the-realty factors.

Disputes often arise between the buyer and the seller of real property as to whether certain items attached to the premises were intended to be removable by the seller or were intended to pass to the buyer as fixtures. Typical examples of items causing disputes are curtains, bookshelves, and television aerials. If the parties cannot agree and litigation results, the court will first apply the usual tests of method of attachment and adaptability to use. If doubt still exists, the court will generally favor the buyer and hold the disputed item to be a fixture. For example, a television aerial could be classed either as personal or real property, considering the method of attachment (easy to remove) and the adaptability of its use (very beneficial). Most courts would probably declare it to be a fixture and would not allow the seller to remove it.

In the following case the court applied the fixture tests to a common factual situation—that of placing a mobile home on a parcel of land.

CASE 21.2 Ford v. Venard · 340 N.W.2d 270 (Iowa 1983)

FACTS In 1973 Norman Van Sickle moved a double-wide mobile home to a plot of land owned by Luelia Jedlicka. Van Sickle had a foundation poured, removed the mobile home's hitches and wheels, and had it set on the foundation by crane. He believed that the house became part of Jedlicka's real estate when it was set down. Since 1973 Van Sickle welded the home into a single unit, put a roof over the entire building, and joined the exterior together with siding. There was no way the house could be disassembled without tearing it apart and no way it could be moved as one unit except by a house mover.

In 1977 Henry Edsel Ford bought the land from Jedlicka. The contract included all "attached fixtures" as part of the real estate included in the sale. William Venard had a judgment against Van Sickle, and in 1982 he attempted to enforce it by attaching and forcing an execution sale of the mobile home. Ford sued Venard, claiming that he, not Van Sickle, owned the home. From a judgment for Venard, Ford appealed.

OPINION HARRIS, J. . . . The first question is whether the mobile home was a fixture included under the terms of the land contract between Jedlicka and Ford. We think it plainly was. Under our common law rule personal property becomes a fixture when:

1. it is actually annexed to the realty, or to something appurtenant thereto;
2. it is put to the same use as the realty with which it is connected; and
3. the party making the annexation intends to make a permanent accession to the freehold.

See *Cornell College v. Crain*, ... The intention of the party annexing the improvement is the "paramount factor" in determining whether the improvement is a fixture. *Id.* "Physical attachment of the structure to the soil or to an appurtenance thereto is not essential to make the structure a part of the realty." *Id.* On the other hand, a building which cannot be removed without destruction of a substantial part of its value becomes "almost unavoidably an integral part of the real estate. . . ."

Venard argues that Van Sickle's home does not pass the *Cornell College* test. He argues the home was not physically annexed to the realty and that Van Sickle never intended, for purposes outside the present lawsuit, for his home to be permanently attached to the freehold.

Ford maintains, on the other hand, that Van Sickle's home passes the *Cornell College* test. He relies on the facts that the home's tongues and wheels have been removed; it was set on a foundation and girders; it has been extensively remodeled into a single unit; and its removal would be expensive and damaging. He points out that the home was used as a homestead, which is the use for which the realty had been appropriated. . . .

We have found buildings to be fixtures in a number of cases. See *Cornell College*, . . . (granary, corn crib and hog house, although built on removable skids); . . . We found buildings were not fixtures in *Durband v. Noble*, . . . (machine and feed sheds placed upon posts and "blocked up").

We are convinced the home became attached to the land. It could not be removed from its present location except in the sense that any permanent home could be. We hold that it has become an integral part of the real estate. . . .

JUDGMENT The trial court was right in ordering the issuance of the permanent injunction. Affirmed.

Acquisition of Ownership of Real Property

Acquisition by Private Individuals and Firms

Methods of Acquisition. There are various methods of acquiring ownership of real property. In some situations an individual (or a business firm) participates actively in a transaction to acquire ownership, as where a person contracts to purchase property. In other situations one acquires ownership without active participation, as where a person inherits property.

Acquisition by purchase. The most common method of acquiring ownership of real property is by purchase from an owner. The legal principles relating to a purchase are presented in the contracts part of this text. There is usually a period of negotiation during which one party makes an offer, the other party submits a counteroffer, the parties dicker over price and terms, and at the end an agreement is reached.

Under the statute of frauds, an agreement to purchase real property is generally not enforceable unless it is in writing. Almost invariably, a written contract is a part of the real property purchase transaction. The contract may be a standard printed form with blanks filled in, or it may be a lengthy, specially drawn instrument containing many terms and conditions. In either event, the actual transfer of ownership of the real property is accomplished by means of a written document, called a "deed," given by the seller to the purchaser. The various types of deeds and the requirements for a deed are discussed later in this chapter.

Acquisition by gift. Another common method of acquiring ownership of real property is by gift. The three elements required to establish a valid gift of personal property were discussed in Chapter 20. Similar elements (intent to make a gift, delivery to the donee, and acceptance by the donee) are required to establish a gift of real property. Since physical delivery of real property is impractical, the requirement of delivery is usually met by the owner's signing a deed and handing the deed to the donee or to an agent of the donee with intent to relinquish all dominion and control over the property.

Acquisition by will or by descent. An individual or a firm may acquire ownership of real property when someone dies. The owner of real property may have made a will, leaving the property to a named person or firm. If the owner dies without having made a will, the owner's real property passes to his or her heirs in accordance with the law of the state where the real property is located (see Chapter 23).

Acquisition by adverse possession. Occasionally, an individual or a firm acquires ownership of real property by adverse possession. The transfer of ownership occurs without the consent of the owner. Suppose, for example, that Gerard moves into an abandoned cabin located on Lillian's land. He plants a garden and farms two acres, all without permission of Lillian. If Gerard claims ownership of the land and occupies it for a specified period of years, he will acquire ownership of the land unless, within the period specified by the statute of limitations, Lillian takes legal action to protect her title. The rationale for allowing such an involuntary transfer of ownership is that historically the law favored productive use of land over nonuse. If the owner of land did not use it, or at least care enough to visit it, for a prolonged period of time and a trespasser made some visible use of the land, the law rewarded the trespasser with title to the property. Since the result is harsh—transferring ownership against the owner's wishes—the requirements are strict, and few cases reach the courts. Most often, the types of controversies that reach the courts involve mistaken boundary lines or one who occupies land under an invalid deed.

To acquire ownership of real property by adverse possession, the claimant must take possession of the property and must prove that the occupation of the property was (1) open and notorious, (2) exclusive and hostile to the owner, (3) under claim of right or color of title, and (4) continuous for the statutory period. In some states the claimant must also pay all property taxes levied against the property during the statutory period.

Open and notorious occupation means that the adverse possessor must actually use the real property in such manner as to make his or her presence known. For example, constructing a building, or enclosing land with a fence, or growing a crop would be visible signs of occupancy. Whether the owner observes the activities of the adverse possessor is immaterial. The law simply requires occupancy of such a nature that any reasonable person who cared to look would know that the occupant claimed some interest in the property.

To establish exclusive and hostile occupancy, the adverse possessor must be a trespasser. The possession must be without the permission of the owner and without recognition of the owner's rights. Obviously, such possession is dangerous, because it clearly gives the owner a cause of action against the adverse possessor. If the owner or others use the property at the same time as does the adverse possessor, the claim of adverse possession will fail because the occupancy has not been exclusive.

In most states, the adverse possessor must take possession of the real property either under claim of right or under color of title. Claim of right means the claimant knows that he or she is a trespasser committing a wrongful act but intends to establish ownership of the real property against all others. Color of title means the adverse possessor has some written document (usually a deed) or judicial decree that appears to transfer ownership but that is legally defective.

For an adverse possessor to acquire ownership of real property, the claimant must be in continuous possession for a minimum period specified by state law. The length of this period usually varies from 5 to 20 years.

There are certain situations in which an adverse possessor cannot acquire ownership of real property. For example, an adverse possessor usually cannot acquire ownership of real property held by a governmental agency for public use. Thus, ownership of land in a wilderness area held by the government cannot be acquired by an adverse possessor who meets all the requirements listed above.

In the following case the court discusses several of the elements required to establish title by adverse possession.

CASE 21.3 Chaplin v. Sanders · 676 P.2d 431 (Wash. 1984)

FACTS In 1957 or 1958, Mr. and Mrs. Hibbard cleared a parcel of land they owned of woods and overgrowth and set up a trailer park. To the east of the Hibbards' parcel was an undeveloped parcel of land owned by Mr. McMurray. There was no obvious boundary between the two parcels, and Mr. Hibbard cleared his land on the east up to a deep drainage ditch on McMurray's parcel. He then installed between the ditch and the western parcel a paved road which encroached some 20 feet onto the eastern parcel. In 1960 McMurray had a survey conducted and discovered the true boundary. He informed the Hibbards that their driveway encroached upon his land. In 1962 the Hibbards sold their land and trailer park to Mr. and Mrs. Gilbert. In the sale contract it was acknowledged that the blacktop road used by the trailer park encroached on the adjoining property. In 1976 Mr. and Mrs. Sanders purchased the western parcel and were given actual notice of the contract provision. Since 1958 the area between the road and the drainage ditch had been used by trailer park residents for parking, storage, garbage removal, and picnicking. Grass was mowed up to the ditch, and flowers were planted in the area. In the spring of 1978 the Sanders installed underground wiring and surface power poles in the area.

In May 1978, the Chaplins purchased the eastern (McMurray) parcel of land. They filed suit against the Sanders to quiet title to the area used in connection with the trailer park. The trial court found that the Sanders (and their predecessors) had satisfied each element of adverse possession with regard to the road and its three-foot shoulder but had not satisfied the open and notorious requirement with regard to the property between the roadway and the ditch. On appeal, the court of appeals held that, due to the Sanders' and their predecessors' actual notice of McMurray's ownership, the requirement of hostility had not been satisfied for either parcel. The Sanders appealed to the Washington Supreme Court.

OPINION UTTER, J. . . . In order to establish a claim of adverse possession, the possession must be: (1) exclusive, (2) actual and uninterrupted, (3) open and notoriousy and (4) hostile and under

CASE 21.3 Continued

a claim of right made in good faith.... The period throughout which these elements must concurrently exist is 10 years. Hostility, as defined by this court, "does not import enmity or ill-will, but rather imports that the claimant is in possession as owner, in contradistinction to holding in recognition of or subordination to the true owner." *King v. Bassindale*, ... We have traditionally treated the hostility and claim of right requirements as one and the same....

The doctrine of adverse possession was formulated at law for the purpose of, among others, assuring maximum utilization of land, encouraging the rejection of stale claims, and, most importantly, quieting titles. Because the doctrine was formulated at law and not at equity, it was originally intended to protect both those who knowingly appropriated the land of others and those who honestly entered and held possession in full belief that the land was their own. Thus, when the original purpose of the adverse possession doctrine is considered, it becomes apparent that the claimant's motive in possessing the land is irrelevant and no inquiry should be made into his guilt or innocence.... The "hostility/claim of right" element of adverse possession requires only that the claimant treat the land as his own as against the world throughout the statutory period. The nature of his possession will be determined solely on the basis of the manner in which he treats the property. His subjective belief regarding his true interest in the land and his intent to dispossess or not dispossess another is irrelevant to this determination....

In the present case, due to the contract language manifesting Hibbard and Gilberts' recognition of McMurray's superior title, the [appeals] court determined that their possession was not hostile to McMurray's interest. Under our holding today the contractual provision is no longer relevant. What is relevant is the objective character of Hibbard's possession and that of his successors in interest....

The trial court found the character of possession to have been hostile for at least a 10-year period. We agree. The Sanders and their predecessors used and maintained the property as though it was their own for over the statutory period. This was sufficient to satisfy the element of hostility.

The Sanders also appeal from the trial court's finding that Parcel B [the property between the roadway and the ditch] was not possessed in an open and notorious manner.

In *Hovila v. Bartek*, ... we stated that the requirement of open and notorious is satisfied if the title holder has actual notice of the adverse use throughout the statutory period. This is consistent with the purpose of the requirement, which is to ensure that the user makes such use of the land that any reasonable person would assume he is the owner....

Here the trial court found that McMurray knew of the Hibbards' encroachment in 1960. He was aware of these encroachments until he sold to the Chaplins in 1978. Although the trial court explicitly found that McMurray knew of the road's encroachment on his land, it did not explicitly so find with regard to the strip running between the roadway and the ditch (Parcel B). Mrs. Hibbard testified at trial that she and her husband consistently maintained and mowed Parcel B. It would have been so maintained in 1960 when Mr. McMurray informed the Hibbards that their road was encroaching on his land. We are compelled to conclude, from this evidence, that McMurray was aware of the Hibbards' use of the strip abutting the roadway. This conclusion is all the more compelling when the disparate condition of McMurray's undeveloped, overgrown property and the cleared, mowed and maintained strip of land separating the roadway and McMurray's land is considered....

In determining what acts are sufficiently open and notorious to manifest to others a claim to land, the character of the land must be considered. *Krona v. Brett*, ... "The necessary use and occupancy need only be of the character that a true owner would assert *in view of its nature and location*."...

...The residents of the trailer park mowed the grass in Parcel B and put the parcel to various uses: guest parking, garbage disposal, gardening and picnicking. Some residents

CASE 21.3 Continued used portions of Parcel B as their backyard. The trial court concluded that the contrast between the fully developed parcel west of the drainage ditch and the overgrown, undeveloped parcel east of the drainage ditch was insufficient to put the owners of the eastern parcel on notice of the Sanders' claim of ownership. We disagree.

JUDGMENT Accordingly, the case is reversed and remanded with directions to quiet title to the disputed property in the Sanders.

Transfer by Deed. Regardless of whether an owner of real property decides to sell it or to give it away, the actual transfer of ownership is accomplished by means of a document called a "deed." The person transferring ownership (title) is the *grantor;* the person receiving it is the *grantee.*

Types of deeds. Various types of deeds are used in the United States to transfer ownership of real property. The more common types are the quitclaim deed, the grant deed, and the warranty deed.

The language in *quitclaim deeds* varies, but a typical wording is "Grantor hereby transfers, releases, and quitclaims her interest to Grantee." The legal effect of a quitclaim deed is to transfer to the grantee whatever interest, if any, that the grantor may have in the property. If a defect is discovered that results in loss or reduction of ownership of all or part of the real property, the grantee will have no recourse *under the deed* against the grantor. (However, the grantee may have a cause of action on other grounds such as fraud.)

A *grant deed* contains wording such as "grantor hereby grants and conveys" certain real property to the grantee. The legal effect of such a deed is to transfer the grantor's ownership to the grantee and to give the grantee some protection if, later on, a defect is discovered in the grantor's title. In many states a statute imposes upon the grantor implied covenants (promises) that (1) the grantor has not transferred the same real property or any interest in it to another grantee and (2) the grantor has not encumbered the property. For example, if Carla grants to James the ownership of timber growing on her land and later, using a grant deed, sells Sally the entire real property, Sally would have a cause of action against Carla for breach of the first implied covenant. However, a grant deed does not protect the grantee against all possible defects. Suppose that before Carla acquired the property, it was subject to a right-of-way (easement) entitling a neighbor to use a 10-foot-wide strip of the land as a driveway. Carla's grant deed gives Sally no cause of action against Carla, because Carla did not grant the easement to the neighbor and so did not breach an implied covenant. In such a situation, the grant deed gives no more protection than does a quitclaim deed.

In most midwestern and eastern states, the *warranty deed* is the type commonly used for transferring ownership of real property. Warranty deeds are classified as general or special. In a *general warranty deed,* the grantor *expressly* warrants to the grantee that ownership is transferred free from *all* defects or claims, regardless of when they arose. Thus, in the previous example involving the easement, if Carla had given Sally a general warranty deed, Sally would have a cause of action against Carla (unless the existence of the easement had been specifically noted in the deed itself). In a *special warranty deed,* the grantor warrants against only those defects or claims arising *after* he or she acquired title. The special warranty deed is used mainly by trustees or by executors of deceased persons' estates who must transfer real property as part of their fiduciary duties. Tyrone holds real property in trust for Second Church, fails to pay taxes on it as they come due, and on behalf of the church sells the property to Jessie May by special warranty deed. The state's tax lien, which arose after Tyrone acquired ownership, violates his covenant against encumbrances, and Jessie May has a cause of action against him. Tyrone would not be liable, however, for unpaid tax liens arising before he acquired the property.

Requirements for a deed. As previously stated, a deed is a written document used to transfer ownership of real property. The requirements for a valid transfer of ownership by deed are (1) a competent grantor, (2) a capable grantee, (3) words of conveyance, (4) adequate description of the real property, (5) proper execution, (6) delivery, and (7) acceptance. The law relating to each of these requirements is extensive and varies somewhat among the states. A discussion of these requirements is beyond the scope of this text and is reserved for a course in real estate law.

Recording of deeds. Ordinarily, if all the above requirements are met, the grantor's ownership of the real property passes to the grantee. However, there is always a danger that a grantor may mistakenly or knowingly give a second deed to the same real property, or a portion of it, to someone else. In order to minimize disputes and hardships that could result from such occurrences, the states have enacted recording statutes.

The recording statutes differ among the states, but essentially the statutes allow a public record to be made of all deeds and other documents affecting real property. An individual or business firm can "record" a deed by filing it at the office of a designated local government official, usually called a county "recorder" or "registrar." The purpose of recording a deed is to put on notice potential subsequent grantees, and other persons interested in the real property, that ownership has passed to the grantee.

Many states have enacted what is called a "notice" or "pure notice" statute which provides that an unrecorded deed is void against a subsequent purchaser for value who had no notice or knowledge of the prior deed. Other states have enacted a "race-notice" statute which provides that an unrecorded deed is void against a subsequent purchaser for value who had no notice or knowledge of the prior deed *only* if the later deed is recorded first. This system thus results in "a race to the registry." For example, if Alma, the owner of certain real property, gives a deed to Bob and subsequently sells the same real property to Charles and gives him a deed, Charles will acquire the ownership of the real property if he had no knowledge of the deed to Bob and if he records his deed before Bob records his. In a race-notice state it is often said that "first to record is first in right." This is true, of course, only if the first to record has no notice or knowledge of a prior deed or claim to the property. In the above example, Bob would lose the ownership acquired from Alma but would have a cause of action against her for damages.

Acquisition by Governmental Units and Agencies

Acquisitions of property by governmental units (e.g., school districts, townships, counties, states, and state and federal administrative agencies) are of increasing significance in contemporary society. To meet the needs of a growing population, governmental units expand and new ones are created. They need to acquire real property to house personnel, equipment, and supplies, and to carry out a host of governmental functions such as the development of recreational areas and the building and improvement of libraries, hospitals, schools, highways, airports, waterways, and military facilities.

Usually, governmental units acquire property just as individuals and business firms do—by buying it. Occasionally, the government acquires ownership through adverse possession or by gift. Governmental units acquire ownership of real property in additional ways: through eminent domain, dedication, and escheat.

Acquisition through Eminent Domain. The government has a power of "eminent domain"—i.e., a right to take private property for public use without the owner's consent. This right is limited by the Fifth and Fourteenth Amendments to the U.S. Constitution, which require (1) that the property be taken only for a public purpose, and (2) that its owner be paid a just compensation. The legal procedure by which the power of eminent domain is exercised is called "condemnation."

Not all of the government's interferences with private property are "takings" (condemnations). For example, for the benefit of the larger community, zoning laws impose restrictions on the use of private property. These restrictions may substantially reduce the value of some realty, but they do not necessarily do so and may, in fact, increase value. Whatever the effect on property values, landowners are not deprived of ownership by zoning laws, and so they are not entitled to compensation for a "taking."

Suppose, however, that a city builds a new airport next to an established residential area. When the airport is in use, noise from jetliners makes living in the area unbearable. The houses near the airport lose much of their value, and the owners sue the city for damages. Although the city might argue that it did not "take" the houses, the court probably would rule in favor of the homeowners on the basis of "inverse condemnation." Under that doctrine, the city's building a noisy airport deprived the residents of the enjoyment of their property, an important "stick" in their bundle of ownership rights, and thus constituted a compensable taking of private property to the extent of the loss in value.

Before private property can be taken without the owner's consent, the acquiring agency must establish that the taking is for a public use. Early court cases recognized certain obvious public uses, such as streets, highways, military installations, public buildings, and reservoirs. The concept of public use has been steadily broadened over the years, and today courts rarely hold any contemplated use by a governmental unit or agency to be improper. Public use now includes urban renewal projects, automobile parking facilities, rapid-transit lines, and public recreational and entertainment facilities.

The right of eminent domain may be exercised not only by a governmental unit but also by a private corporation entrusted with performance of a public service. For example, public utility corporations supplying gas, electricity, and telephone service can condemn property for utility lines and poles. In such instances, the corporation acts under delegation of power from the state or federal legislature.

Acquisition through Dedication. Dedication of real property is a gift by the owner to a governmental unit or agency on the condition that the property be used for a designated public purpose. The designated purpose might be for a park, street, beach, or historical landmark. The gift can occur during the donor's life or upon his or her death. There is typically a statutory procedure to be followed. The owner makes a formal offer to give certain real property to a city, state, or federal governmental unit or agency, indicating the use or uses to which the property may be put and any other conditions the unit or agency must meet. If the appropriate governmental officials decide to accept the gift on the conditions stated, a statute or an ordinance is formally passed, and the owner transfers the property to the governmental unit or agency. Thereafter, the government is responsible for the maintenance and operation of the facility.

In certain situations, a "common law" dedication can occur. If an owner of real property makes an offer, express or implied, to give ownership to the public, and if there is evidence of acceptance by the public, a dedication may take place without formal action. For example, if an owner freely allows the public to do such things as drive across the land, park cars on it, or have picnics on the land, a court may find that a common law dedication has occurred.

Acquisition through Escheat. The state government may occasionally acquire ownership of real property by escheat. Earlier, it was pointed out that when the owner of property dies without making a will the decedent's property passes to his or her heirs. Let us suppose that a decedent has made no will and has no heirs, i.e., no spouse or blood relatives who can inherit the property under state law. When such a situation occurs, the ownership of the property passes to the state. Ownership is said to "escheat" to the state.

Types and Incidents of Ownership of Real Property

Types of Ownership of Real Property

Various types of ownership of real property are possible, but no state recognizes all of them. When given a choice, an individual (or a firm) must decide which of the available types of ownership will best serve the person's needs or legal position.

Sole Ownership. The simplest form of ownership is ownership by a sole individual, corporation, or governmental unit or agency. Where ownership is acquired by purchase or by gift, the grantee receives a deed. The deed often contains language that describes the grantee: "a married woman," "a single man," "a minor," "a Delaware corporation," etc. The presence or absence of such language does not affect the individual nature of sole ownership.

Tenancy in Common. Several types of *co-ownership* are available to people who wish to own property together or who want to confer co-ownership upon others. The most prevalent form of co-ownership is the *tenancy in common.* In it, two or more individuals or firms acquire ownership of the same property and thus become co-owners ("cotenants"). Each cotenant acquires an undivided fractional interest in the property and, as owner, can sell that interest, give it away, or leave it to someone by will. The fractional interests of tenants in common often are equal, but are not required to be. Thus, one of two cotenants could own an undivided two-thirds interest in a parcel while the other owns one-third. To say that a cotenant has an "undivided" interest means only that each cotenant has a fractional ownership of each portion of the property—of every rock, building, or tree. Consequently, no cotenant can claim the best land and force the others to take the worst. A major feature of tenancy in common is that when a cotenant dies, that person's interest goes to his or her heirs, and not to surviving cotenants.

To create a tenancy in common, a deed should say, "to A and B as tenants in common." However, in most states, it is sufficient that the deed say "to A and B," since, for the reason noted later, a conveyance to two or more persons will be *presumed* to create a tenancy in common (and not a joint tenancy) in the absence of an express indication otherwise.

Real property held under tenancy in common is subject to voluntary or court-imposed *partition.* Partition is a process of physically dividing the realty up between the cotenants so that each may have sole ownership of his or her share. Suppose that Ann, a cotenant, sells her undivided interest to Tom. He is entitled to partition so that he can manage his portion of the land as he likes.

Joint Tenancy. *Joint tenancy* is available in most states and often is selected by (or conferred upon) two or more purchasers who are closely related.

Nature of joint tenancy. In a joint tenancy, each cotenant (1) owns an *equal* undivided interest in the entire parcel of real property, and (2) is considered also to be the owner of the whole parcel. Ann and Ben own Blackacre as joint tenants. Each one owns an undivided one-half interest in Blackacre (which he or she can sell or give away during his or her lifetime), and each also owns the whole of Blackacre from the moment that the two of them became joint tenants, subject to the rights of the other person. To create a joint tenancy, the deed from the grantor typically would say, "to A and B as joint tenants." In some states, the law requires the deed to say, "to A and B as joint tenants *with right of survivorship.*"

A major feature of joint tenancy is its so-called "right of survivorship." If one of two joint tenants dies, his or her undivided fractional interest immediately ceases, and the survivor, already being an owner of the whole, simply remains as sole owner. If one of three joint tenants dies, that person's undivided one-third interest ceases, and the two survivors now have undivided one-half interests as joint tenants.

A person's will takes effect at the time of his or her death and serves to transfer ownership of the deceased person's estate to the people named in the will as heirs. Because a joint tenant's fractional interest ceases at his or her death, it never becomes part of his or her estate and therefore cannot be disposed of by will. Jason owns Whiteacre in joint tenancy with his second wife, Regina. He executes a will leaving all his assets to his children of a former marriage. Upon his death, his interest in Whiteacre ceases, and there is no interest in the real property to pass to the children under the will. (Many courts would say that Jason's interest passed to Regina by right of survivorship, but such statements are not technically accurate. Because Jason's fractional interest ceased at the time of his death, there was nothing of his to pass to Regina. She was an owner of the whole of Whiteacre all along and at Jason's death simply continued as owner.)

Where a joint tenant transfers his or her interest to another, the joint tenancy is said to be "severed" and becomes fully or partially a tenancy in common, depending on the number of joint tenants. Ann and Ben are joint tenants. Ann sells her one-half interest to Tom. Tom and Ben are now tenants in common. Upon the death of a tenant in common, that person's interest passes to his or her heirs, and not to the other cotenants. Suppose now that Ann, Ben, and Carl are joint tenants and Ann sells her one-third interest to Tom. He is a tenant in common as to Ben and Carl, but Ben and Carl continue to be joint tenants as to each other. As in a tenancy in common, the undivided interests are subject to partition.

Presumption of tenancy in common. Sometimes a grantee intends to confer co-ownership upon the grantees but the deed does not reveal what kind of co-ownership the grantor intended. Ann and Ben buy land from George, who gives them a deed saying, "to Ann and Ben" or "to Ann and Ben jointly." The deed is ambiguous. Were Ann and Ben intended to be tenants in common or were they to be joint tenants?

Under the early English common law, joint tenancy was presumed. The king granted land to his tenants in exchange for various kinds of service, including military service. To acquire sufficient military personnel, the king's tenants often granted rights in the land to subtenants who would serve as knights in the king's army. The presumption of joint tenancy was consistent with the English policy of preserving feudal property holdings (and the king's military power) until the death of the last survivor. In contrast, Americans have typically viewed land as a commodity that should be widely owned to remain productive. In the United States, therefore, a tenancy in common is presumed in the absence of evidence that a joint tenancy was intended. Because land held by a deceased tenant in common goes to his or her heirs, it tends to be dispersed among many users rather than consolidated into the hands of an aging, perhaps unproductive survivor.

The presumption of tenancy in common also applies when individuals acquire co-ownership by will or by descent. Charles dies, leaving land "to my children, Dora and Elliot, jointly." Dora and Elliot acquire ownership of the land as tenants in common. If Dora dies before disposing of her interest, her share of the land goes to her heirs and not to Elliot (unless he happens to be her heir).

Tenancy by the Entirety. Some states have a type of co-ownership called "tenancy by the entirety," which can exist only between husband and wife. Under the English common law, husband and wife were viewed as one person. Consequently, when land was conveyed to them as co-owners, they received only a single ownership interest, an "entirety," which they owned together. If one tenant by the entirety died, the survivor became the sole owner of the whole, as in joint tenancy. But because a married couple was viewed as one person incapable of having individual shares, neither one had an undivided one-half interest. Thus, neither husband nor wife could transfer a fractional interest (because neither person owned one). Nor could either of them transfer the whole without the consent of the other; they could transfer the whole property only by acting jointly. However, an absolute divorce converted the tenancy by the entirety into a tenancy in common.

In a few states, the tenancy by the entirety is much like the old English version. In some states, the tenancy by the entirety has been abolished. In over half the states, a conveyance to husband and wife creates a joint tenancy or a tenancy in common.[1]

Community Property. Community property is a type of ownership found in only nine states in the United States.[2] Historically, the area within eight of these states was owned by France and Spain, both of which had adopted the civil law system of community property. The system was continued in the states later created out of this area. The ninth state, Wisconsin, adopted a form of community property as of 1986, by enacting the Uniform Marital Property Act. Each of the nine states has developed its own laws regarding community property, and the subject is too extensive to be covered in a business law text. However, a few general observations can be made.

Community property is usually defined in such a way as to include property acquired by a husband or wife during their marriage, except property acquired by gift, by will, or by descent. This type of ownership is similar to both joint tenancy and tenancy in common in that each person (spouse) owns an undivided interest in a parcel of property. As with joint tenancy, the interests in community property are always equal. As with tenancy in common, either spouse may make a deed or a will disposing of his or her one-half interest in community property. If a spouse dies without a will, his or her community interest generally will pass under state statutes to the surviving spouse.

Any property owned by a spouse on the date of marriage and any property received by him or her thereafter by gift or inheritance is the *separate property* of that spouse. Separate property may be converted to community property by agreement of the spouses.

[1]John E. Cribbet, *Principles of the Law of Property,* Foundation Press, Mineola, N.Y., 1975, p. 96.

[2]Arizona, California, Idaho, Louisiana, Nevada, New Mexico, Texas, Washington, and Wisconsin.

Partnership Property. Often, two or more persons conducting business together form a partnership, which acquires property (land, equipment, etc.) that the partners use in the business to produce income. Each partner has an undivided interest (a *tenancy in partnership*) in this so-called "specific partnership property." At the death of a partner, his or her interest in the partnership itself (actually, the monetary value of that interest) passes to his or her heirs. However, the deceased partner's share of the *specific* partnership property automatically "passes" to the surviving partner or partners. Thus, although surviving partners must account to the deceased partner's heirs for the value of his or her share of the partnership itself, the heirs cannot disrupt the surviving partners' business by taking machinery or other assets that they need for operating the business. Tenancy in partnership is discussed further in Chapter 36.

Condominiums and Cooperatives. In recent years, there has been a tremendous increase in the number of condominiums in the United States. A *condominium* type of ownership is utilized most often for residential purposes, but its use is rapidly expanding to office buildings and commercial property. Briefly stated, condominium ownership involves separate ownership of a unit in a multiunit building, combined with an interest in the common areas and the land. For example, if a grantee acquires ownership of a unit in a high-rise building, the grantee becomes the sole owner of that unit. In effect, the person owns a cube of airspace. Along with the ownership of that unit, the grantee acquires an undivided interest as tenant in common in the ground on which the building stands and in the "common areas" within the building, such as elevators, stairways, hallways, and recreation areas. In some planned communities, a condominium development may consist of a "campus" of buildings. In such developments, the common areas may include a club house, swimming pool, golf course, and other recreational facilities.

The word "cooperative" is used in different senses. As used here, *cooperative* refers to a corporation that is organized for the sole purpose of owning and managing a multiunit building(s), such as an apartment house or an office building, and sells shares of stock in the corporation. A purchase of shares of stock carries with it the right to occupy a unit (an apartment or office) in the building. Thus, the shareholder, unlike the purchaser of a condominium unit, does not own the particular unit of the building he or she occupies; all the units are owned by the cooperative. In legal effect, a unit in a condominium is real property, whereas a shareholder in a cooperative owns personal property.

Incidents of Ownership of Real Property

When an individual, a firm, or a governmental unit or agency acquires ownership of real property, legal rights and duties accompany the ownership. These rights and duties exist regardless of the method of acquisition of ownership or the type of ownership acquired.

Rights of Owners. Ordinarily, an owner of real property has the exclusive right to use, possess, and dispose of the land. The owner's rights extend into the subsurface and the airspace above the surface. The owner can cultivate the land, grow crops, build a house, or install a swimming pool. An owner may give permission to others to use the property or to take minerals from the subsurface, either for temporary periods or for long durations. An owner may use real property as security for a loan or may dispose of the property by gift, by sale, or by will.

Duties of Owners. The rights of an owner of real property are not unlimited. There is a growing awareness of the rights of others, and the law imposes certain duties on every property owner. Occasionally some duties are assumed by property owners through agreements with others.

Duties imposed by law. One of the most pervasive of the duties imposed by law is the duty not to create a *nuisance*. For many years the laws of nuisance have prohibited landowners from maintaining anything on their premises that is injurious to the health of others, that is offensive to the senses, or that unreasonably interferes with the comfortable enjoyment of life or property. For example, the following things have been held to be nuisances under the circumstances involved: rock quarry, drop-forging shop, dilapidated wooden building, slaughterhouse, airport, emission of smoke or odors, obstruction of a street or river. In recent years, nuisance laws have been enforced more vigorously as a result of public demand to protect the environment from pollution. Liability generally is not based on intent or on negligence of the owner, but is imposed by the courts even though the owner is without fault.

Another duty of the property owner is not to *encroach* on a neighbor's property. For example, an owner must not allow the roof of his or her house or the limbs of a tree to overhang into a neighbor's airspace, nor may an owner allow the roots of a tree to extend into the neighbor's land and interfere with the comfortable enjoyment of the neighbor's property. Still another duty of the property owner is always to exercise *due care* in the use and maintenance of the person's property in order to prevent injury to others. For example, an owner who invites guests to his or her house should remove a child's skates from the entry walk before the guests arrive. This is an application of the tort law of negligence discussed in Chapter 4.

Many local government regulations impose duties on owners of real property. The power of local governments to impose these regulations is part of what is known as the "police power." *Police power* is the power to restrict the activity of persons in the interest of public health, safety, morals, and welfare. Such restrictions must not be unreasonable, arbitrary, or discriminatory. Zoning ordinances are enacted by city and county governments to regulate land use. These ordinances generally designate segregated zones or areas where land can be used for residential, agricultural, commercial, or industrial purposes. Zoning ordinances may also regulate the height, size, and appearance of buildings; the size of yards and open spaces; and the amount of off-street parking. Building and safety codes are enacted by city and county governments to regulate the construction, repair, or alteration of buildings. Most local governments have also enacted ordinances enabling the city or county to compel the owner of property to remove rubbish or weeds from his or her property, or to remedy unsafe or unsightly conditions on the property.

The following case discusses the power of a city government to regulate the location of specified businesses.

CASE 21.4 Dumas v. City of Dallas · 648 F. Supp. 1061 (N.D. Tex 1986)

FACTS The city of Dallas adopted a zoning ordinance that regulated the operation of all sexually oriented businesses in Dallas. The most important provisions were: (1) a business must be at least 1,000 feet from a church, school, residential area, park, or another sexually oriented business; (2) licensing and inspection are required for all regulated businesses; (3) all patrons in an arcade—even if within a closed booth—must be within the sight of a manager; and (4) various restrictions are to be imposed on layout, furnishing, hiring, and lighting. Each business in violation of the 1,000-foot prohibition was given 3 years to relocate. Sexually oriented businesses include adult arcades, adult bookstores or videostores, adult motels, adult theaters, and nude model studios. Numerous operators of these businesses joined in a lawsuit challenging the constitutionality of the ordinance.

The plaintiffs raised various objections, including the enormous cost of relocating. Many businesses had great investments in their locations—one had a parking lot valued at $1 million. Other plaintiffs faced economic hardship from the ordinance's restrictions. Adult motels, for example, were restricted to renting rooms for at least 10 hours, rather than the previous 2-hour period which was common, which resulted in an 80 percent reduction in income.

OPINION BUCHMEYER, J.... The law of zoning allows the will of a majority, expressed through a representative body, to control the evolution of a community and shape its character. The law of free speech, in contrast, prevents the majority will from suppressing minority expression that the majority finds intolerable. It is perhaps inevitable that the two values should clash, when a zoning ordinance attempts to limit the freedoms of those involved

CASE 21.4 Continued

in expressing unpopular views.... Divining the intent of a legislative body is inherently problematic, but the intent... in adopting the Ordinance is transparently clear.... [T]he Ordinance was concerned solely with controlling the secondary effects of sexually oriented businesses on surrounding neighborhoods.... [The City Council] stated that they were concerned not with the content of the speech associated with sexually oriented businesses, but with the crime, urban blight, and plummeting property values that inevitably seize the neighborhoods where such businesses locate.... The intent of the City in passing the Ordinance was solely to control the secondary effects of sexually oriented speech on the neighborhoods its purveyors inhabit, rather than to eliminate the speech itself....

Regardless of the Ordinance's focus on the secondary effects of sexually oriented businesses, there is no doubt that its terms have an incidental impact on expression that is protected by the first amendment. Because of this impact, it is appropriate to analyze the statute....

First, it is without doubt that the police power of the City encompasses the power to enact a zoning and regulatory ordinance such as that considered here.... The legislative response to the secondary effects of sexually oriented businesses evinced a clear intent to leave alternative avenues open for expression of that genre, while lessening the effects of such businesses on the surrounding community.... No doubt remains... that dispersed zoning of sexually oriented businesses is permissible, provided that "reasonable alternative avenues of communication" exist....

The land available for sexually oriented businesses under the Dallas ordinance is substantial.... The maps considered by the City upon enacting the Ordinance detail several areas that are open to sexually oriented businesses, and it cannot be said that a "reasonable" opportunity for such businesses does not exist under the Ordinance. The plan adopted by Dallas differs markedly from the Galveston plan rejected in *Basiardanes*, ... ; that plan incorporated an outright ban on 85–90 percent of the city's total area, and the remaining areas, located "among warehouses, shipyards, undeveloped areas, and swamps," were reached by "few access roads." The Dallas plan, in contrast, permits location in several areas stretching from the inner city area to the north and south suburbs, accessed by such major thoroughfares as Interstate 35, Interstate 30, Loop 12, Highway 183, and Harry Hines Boulevard. Eight to ten percent of the city's total area—21,000 acres—is available....

The three-year amortization clause is also challenged. Such clauses, however, are uniformly upheld.... The period allowed by the Ordinance is more generous than others that have been upheld; it is a valid mechanism used to enforce valid locational regulations....

The Ordinance requires various internal restrictions of regulated businesses—from major renovations in the design of adult arcades to the allowance of sofas in nude modeling studios. While such intrusions into the internal design of regulated businesses may seem unduly restrictive, they have consistently been upheld. See *Wall Distributors, Inc. v. City of Newport News*, ... (requiring closed viewing booths to be within view of management "falls within the broad general limits of the police power").... [M]oreover, recent pronouncements of state power to regulate morality and private consensual sexual activity are probably broad enough to encompass regulations on adult motels.... As the City has made the requisite findings, the various restrictions on the operation, layout, design, and furnishing of regulated businesses must be upheld....

Efforts to restrict the accessability of sexually oriented speech have long been part of Western legal tradition, as has the principle that expression should be free and unfettered. The reconciliation of the competing values implicit in these two long-standing concepts inevitably shifts over time, in response to technological change and evolving conceptions of the legality of legislating majoritarian conceptions of morality. Restrictions in the place and manner of sexually oriented expression through zoning regulation is the most recent

CASE 21.4 Continued jurisprudential attempt to allow majority community structure to coexist with minority expression. . . .

JUDGMENT [T]he sexually oriented business ordinance enacted by the City follows the substantive dictates of this body of law, and must be upheld.

Duties created by agreements. In some situations, duties are imposed on the owner of real property by deed or by contract. For example, when an individual acquires ownership of a parcel in a subdivision tract (including condominiums and cooperatives) the purchaser usually agrees as a condition of the purchase to assume certain obligations. These obligations are set forth in the deed executed by the subdivider and are imposed for the protection of all present and future owners in the subdivision tract. Thus, each owner might be required to maintain his or her premises in a neat and safe condition at all times. Types of construction and architectural design within the tract are often controlled.

When the purchaser of real property finances all or part of the purchase price by borrowing from a private or an institutional lender, certain duties are imposed for the protection of the lender. The borrower generally signs an agreement that includes, among other provisions, the obligation to pay all property taxes and assessments, maintain adequate insurance, keep the premises neat and sanitary, and not to resell the property without consent of the lender.

Summary

The term "real property" customarily includes surface of the land, things attached to the land, airspace above the land, and materials below the surface. Ownership of any of these physical elements of real property can be transferred separately.

A fixture is an article that was personal property but which has been attached to real property with the intent that it become permanently a part of the realty. Controversies arise because the intent of the attacher is not always clear. In such cases, the courts apply three tests: (1) degree of attachment; (2) adaptability of the item to the use of the real property; and (3) relationship of the parties.

Individuals and business firms can acquire ownership of real property in several ways. The most common ways are by purchase and by gift. In each such instance, the transfer of ownership is accomplished by means of a deed from the grantor to the grantee. The recording of a deed is not essential to the transfer of ownership from a grantor to a grantee; nevertheless, the deed should be recorded to protect the grantee from claims by third persons who may later acquire an interest in the property. Other methods by which individuals and firms may acquire ownership of real property include adverse possession; will; and, in the case of individuals, descent.

Governmental units and agencies—local, state, and federal—frequently acquire ownership of real property. In addition to acquiring ownership by the methods available to individuals and business firms, governmental units and agencies may acquire property by exercising the power of eminent domain. Under this power, private property may be taken for public use without the owner's consent. A governmental unit or an agency may receive ownership of property by statutory or common law dedication. A state may acquire ownership of real property by escheat.

Various types of ownership of real property are possible. The list includes: sole ownership, tenancy in common, joint tenancy, tenancy by the entirety, community property, partnership property, condominiums, and cooperatives. The right of survivorship exists in a joint tenancy and tenancy by the entirety, but not in the other types of ownership.

Ordinarily, an owner of real property has the exclusive right to use, possess, enjoy, and dispose of the land, airspace, and subsurface. These rights are limited by duties to others imposed by law and by governmental regulation under the police power. In addition, many duties are assumed by purchasers of real property as part of a contract of purchase in a subdivision tract, or as part of a finance agreement with a lender.

Review Questions

1 List the physical elements of real property.

2 What is the rule today regarding a landowner's use of airspace? What is the reason for the rule?

3 Explain how each of the following items might be classified as personal property: **(a)** trees; **(b)** coal; **(c)** oil; **(d)** water.

4 **(a)** Define "fixture." **(b)** What are the usual tests of a fixture? **(c)** Apply the tests to the following items: window screens; front door key; lawn statuary.

5 **(a)** List the four methods by which private individuals and firms can acquire ownership of real property. **(b)** What elements are required to establish a gift of real property?

6 **(a)** What must a claimant prove to acquire ownership of real property by adverse possession? **(b)** What suggestions could you make to a landowner to help prevent loss of ownership to an adverse possessor?

7 What are the essential differences between the following: quitclaim deed; grant deed; warranty deed?

8 **(a)** What are the requirements for a valid transfer of ownership by deed? **(b)** Should a deed be recorded? Why or why not?

9 Explain the difference between a "notice" recording statute and a "race-notice" statute.

10 List and explain the methods by which a governmental unit or agency can acquire ownership of real property.

11 **(a)** What are the distinctions between eminent domain and dedication? **(b)** What is the similarity between them?

12 Give an example of each of the two types of dedication.

13 **(a)** In which of the following types of ownership must the owners' interests be equal: joint tenancy; tenancy in common; community property? **(b)** If an owner died without making a will, who would acquire his or her interest in each of the three types of ownership listed?

14 List and give examples of several important duties of landowners imposed by law.

15 Discuss the justification, pro and con, of impositions of deed restrictions by subdividers.

Case Problems

1 In 1935, the United States acquired title to 121 acres of land for watershed protection and forestry purposes. The deed contained the following: "[Grantor reserves] all minerals in, upon, or under the above described real estate, together with the right to prospect for and remove said minerals. . . ." In 1980, Downstate Stone Company acquired the right to all minerals from the heirs of the parties that had reserved the mineral rights in 1935. The lands were composed principally of limestone, which lay both on the surface and under topsoil. The lands were acquired under the Forestry Act and were administered by the Department of Agriculture as national forest lands. Downstate filed suit to determine if it was entitled to quarry limestone under the mineral reservation. Downstate admitted that limestone quarrying would require almost complete surface destruction; would level and remove the face of a 900-foot forested hill; and would leave a large open quarry area where there had been rocks, trees, and soil. Should the court permit Downstate to remove limestone under the 1935 mineral reservation?

2 Wilmington Water Corp. furnished water for commercial and residential uses. It maintained various pipes, mains, and storage tanks used in its water distribution system throughout New Castle County. The county imposed a property tax on the items, contending they were taxable as real property. Wilmington contended the items were personal property and not taxable. The storage tanks were steel and stood on metal legs bolted to concrete foundations. Other tanks rested on the ground by force of gravity. Thus, Wilmington argued that the items were easily removable. The structures were large and were capable of being removed but with great difficulty. At least one tank had been removed after a useful life of 30 years. The County argued that removability was not important in this case because the items were to be used indefinitely or until the end of their useful life, since removal would affect the water supply. Should the items be taxed as real property?

3 The City of Oakland filed a lawsuit to acquire by eminent domain the Oakland Raiders professional football team, a franchise member of the National Football League. The Raiders argued (1) that the law of eminent domain does not permit the taking of intangible property (a football franchise) and (2) that the taking contemplated by Oakland could not be for any "public use" within the city's authority. Is either of these arguments valid?

4 Mike Zamiska executed a deed conveying title to certain land to himself and his son, George, "as joint tenants and as in common with the right of survivorship." Upon Mike's death, George claimed title to the land as surviving joint tenant. Other heirs of Mike claimed that the deed created only a tenancy in common and thus George was limited to ownership of an undivided one-half interest. Did Mike create a joint tenancy or a tenancy in common?

5 Mr. and Mrs. Herring acquired title to a parcel of land as joint tenants with the right of survivorship. Mrs. Herring executed a deed conveying to Clarence Carroll, her son by a previous marriage, all "her right, title, and interest" in the parcel of land. Upon her death, Mr. Herring claimed title to the land by right of survivorship. **(a)** Is his claim correct? **(b)** Would your answer be the same if Mr. and Mrs. Herring were tenants by the entireties?

6 The city of Scottsdale rezoned the area in and around the McDowell Mountains into the Hillside Conservation Area and the Hillside Development Area. No new development was permitted on land within the Conservation Area. Joyce Corrigan owned 4,800 undeveloped acres, 80 percent of which lay within the no-development line. The McDowell Mountains were unique, being the only hilly or mountainous terrain within the Scottsdale city limits. The primary purpose of the zoning ordinance was to preserve the mountains in their natural state for the benefit of all residents of the city. Corrigan filed suit claiming the ordinance was unconstitutional because (1) it was an invalid exercise of the police power, and (2) enforcement of the ordinance would amount to a "taking" of private property without compensation (i.e., a disguised exercise of eminent domain). Evidence showed that development in the mountains could result in unsightly scarring. Evidence also showed that under the Hillside Ordinance the land in the conservation area would have no monetary value, whereas without the ordinance the land would be worth from $1,250 to $4,500 per acre. Should the ordinance be declared unconstitutional?

CHAPTER 22

Interests in Real Property

A finite resource, land is much in demand for productive, residential, and public purposes. Ownership gives a person maximum control over the use of land, but ownership is not always possible or even economically advisable. So instead of buying it outright, many people, even the largest corporations, rent (lease) real property from its owners for a host of purposes, residential and commercial. Owners and nonowners alike often seek rights-of-way over (easements in) land owned by others, and taxation of realty provides state and local governments with vast amounts of revenue for public purposes. Consequently, the subject of interests in real property is important to almost everyone in contemporary society.

Three types of interests in real property are of special significance—estates, easements, and liens. Estates (ownership interests) in real property range from those conferring full ownership to those conferring considerably less than full ownership, such as a tenancy under a lease. Easements and liens are both interests in the real property of *another;* thus two persons are always involved, i.e., one who owns the real property and one who owns the easement or holds the lien.

The first part of this chapter deals with the nature of estates and the different types of estates, with emphasis on landlord-tenant relations. The last two parts of the chapter are devoted to easements and liens.

Estates in Real Property

Meaning and Classification of Estates

The meaning of estates in real property has been explained as follows:

> The ownership interest that a person has in land is called an "estate." This [interest] may vary in size from absolute ownership, which is called a fee simple estate, to a mere tolerated possession called an estate at sufferance. An estate in land gives the owner of such interest the right to enjoy and possess the land—presently or in the future—for a period of time that may be long or short, definite or indefinite, depending upon the interest owned.[1]

[1]Gerald O. Dykstra and Lillian G. Dykstra, *The Business Law of Real Estate,* Macmillan Company, New York, 1956, p. 82.

There are two classes of estates: "freehold" and "leasehold." *Freehold estates* include those in which the duration of enjoyment is potentially infinite and those in which duration is measured by the life of a person. *Leasehold estates* include those in which the enjoyment is for a specified period of time and those in which the enjoyment is for an unspecified period not intended to be infinite.

Freehold Estates

There are two major types of freehold estates: fee simple estates and life estates. In either type the owner of the interest normally has the present right to use, possess, and enjoy the property. If the owner is not to exercise these rights until some future time, he or she has what is called a "future interest." Although future interests are sometimes discussed independently of freehold estates, they are discussed in this chapter under freehold estates because they generally involve either a fee simple estate or a life estate.

Fee Simple Estates. The estate that owners usually acquire in real property is the fee simple, sometimes referred to as a fee simple absolute, or merely as a "fee." A person owning property in fee simple has the fullest type of ownership—the largest "bundle of rights" possible under the law. The owner has the exclusive right to possess and enjoy the property, sell it, give it away, lease it to another, or borrow against it. Upon the death of the owner, a fee simple estate passes to the beneficiary or beneficiaries designated in the owner's will, or to the decedent's heirs if there is no will. This process of passing on a fee simple estate from generation to generation may continue indefinitely. There are no technical words required to transfer a fee simple estate from a grantor to a grantee. In most states any properly executed deed is presumed to pass a fee simple estate, in the absence of specific words indicating that a lesser estate is intended. There are other types of fee estates, but complete coverage of this area is reserved for a course in real estate law.

Life Estates. A life estate is an estate the duration of which is measured by the life of a person. For example, a deed to "Alice for life" creates an estate that will automatically end when Alice dies. A deed to "Alice for the life of Ben" creates an estate that will end when Ben dies. In this latter example, if Alice dies before Ben, the unexpired portion of the life estate passes to Alice's heirs or to the beneficiaries under her will. During the existence of a life estate, the holder of the estate (called a "life tenant") has a great many rights. The life tenant can use, possess, and enjoy the property; sell his or her interest; give it to a donee; borrow against it; or lease it to someone and collect the rents. However, any lease given by a life tenant cannot continue beyond the duration of the life estate. For example, if Alice, a life tenant, leases the property to Don for 10 years, there is no certainty that Don will be able to remain in possession for the full 10 years. If Alice dies and the life estate ends before the 10-year lease expires, Don must vacate the property.

Although a life tenant has many rights, he or she also has certain duties and obligations. The life tenant must keep all improvements on the property in good repair and must not use or treat the property in such a way as substantially to diminish its value. Any such abuse of the property is called "waste." Specific examples of waste are permitting the house or fences to fall into disrepair and removing timber, earth, or minerals unnecessarily. Normally, the life tenant must pay the annual taxes assessed against the property and pay interest on any mortgage or other encumbrance on the property. The reason the law imposes these duties on the life tenant is to protect the value of the property for the person who will take possession at the termination of the life estate.

Future Interests. When a person's right to use, possess, and enjoy a parcel of property is to begin at some future time, he or she has a future interest. Of necessity, when a grantor creates a life estate a future interest is also created. Someone will succeed to the use and possession of the property upon termination of the life estate. The law recognizes several types of future interests. Two major types are reversions and remainders.

Reversions. When the owner of real property transfers a life estate to someone or leases the property to someone for a certain period, the owner gives up the present right of possession and enjoyment. When the life estate or lease terminates, someone will succeed to those rights. If the grantor will reacquire the right of possession and enjoyment, he or she is said to own a reversion. For example, if Paul makes a deed conveying certain property to Betty "for her life" and makes no mention of who shall have possession and enjoyment when Betty dies, the general rule of law is that full possession and enjoyment will revert to the grantor. Thus, Paul has a reversion and is referred to as a "reversioner." Paul can transfer his future interest to another. If he dies before Betty without transferring it, the reversion will pass to his heirs or beneficiaries. When a life estate or lease terminates, the owner of the reversion will have all the rights of an owner of a fee simple estate.

Remainders. A remainder is also an estate where possession and enjoyment of realty are to occur in the future, but the person who is to receive possession and enjoyment is someone other than the grantor or the grantor's heirs. For example, if Paul transfers certain real property to Betty "for her life, then to Carol," Carol acquires a remainder. She can transfer her interest in the property to another. If she dies before Betty without having transferred the remainder, it will pass to her heirs or beneficiaries.

In Case 22.1, the owners of the remainder sued to enforce duties allegedly owed by the life tenant.

CASE 22.1 Banaszak v. Banaszak · 395 N.W.2d 614 (Wis. App. 1986)

FACTS Leonard and Lillian Banaszak entered into a prenuptial agreement which provided that upon Leonard's death Lillian would receive a life estate in their homestead. Leonard's children were to have the remainder interest, and Lillian was obligated to maintain the property and pay the real estate taxes for the duration of the life estate. Leonard was ill. Before he and Lillian made the prenuptial agreement, his guardian (one of his children)

CASE 22.1 Continued

mortgaged the property to secure a loan for the payment of Leonard's medical expenses. After Leonard died, Lillian refused to pay the interest on the mortgage. Leonard's children filed suit to require Lillian to pay the interest and, as part of her duty of maintenance, to pay for insurance covering possible loss or damage to the homestead. The trial court granted a summary judgment to the children. Lillian appealed.

OPINION

SULLIVAN, J. . . . Lillian contends that she is not obligated to pay the interest on the mortgage obligation because the children mortgaged the property to pay a debt for which she is not liable. Her analysis is incorrect. The property was mortgaged, with court approval, by Leonard's guardian to pay Leonard's medical expenses. Merely because one of the children was the guardian does not change the fact that either Leonard or his estate, not the children, was obligated to pay the loan. Because the mortgage encumbered the property before the life estate was created, the life tenant is required by law to pay the interest unless the instrument creating the life estate reflects a contrary intent. . . . Because the prenuptial agreement does not specifically excuse Lillian from the duties of a life tenant, we conclude that Lillian is obligated to reimburse the children for past interest payments and to pay future interest payments attributable to the property subject to her life estate.

Lillian also contends that she should not be obligated to reimburse the children for amounts spent insuring the property or to pay future insurance premiums. No Wisconsin court has addressed this issue specifically. The general rule is that, in the absence of an express or implied provision in the creating instrument, a life tenant is under no duty to insure the property. . . .

The instrument creating a life estate may impose a duty to insure on the life tenant. The prenuptial agreement conditions Lillian's life estate on maintenance of the property and payment of real estate taxes. Construction of an unambiguous contract is a question of law which this court determines independent of the trial court's decision. . . . We conclude that the contract is not ambiguous. The word "maintain" has a well-defined meaning and includes "keeping up, preserving, and rebuilding in case of destruction." . . . While insurance is one means to finance rebuilding costs, it is not maintenance. Insurance is a means of risk allocation, and the life tenant may choose to risk having to finance rebuilding the structure from her own assets.

The money judgment entered against Lillian provided reimbursement of both interest and insurance. Accordingly, we modify the money judgment and reduce it to $6,434.80 plus costs of $225.06. We uphold the injunction insofar as it requires Lillian to pay . . . the interest on the mortgage. We reverse that portion of the injunction requiring Lillian to pay future insurance premiums.

JUDGMENT Judgment modified and, as modified, affirmed in part and reversed in part.

Leasehold Estates

As previously noted, a leasehold estate is an estate in real property having a duration of a specified period of time or an unspecified period not intended to be infinite. The holder of a leasehold estate (called a "tenant" or "lessee") is given the exclusive right to possess and use certain premises during the leasehold period, or term. The owner of the property (called a "landlord" or "lessor") retains a reversion. He or she has all the other rights of a full owner and will normally regain the right to possess and use the premises at the end of the term. "Premises" is a word used frequently in creating leaseholds and may mean land or a building or part of a building with or without the land.

There are four types of leasehold estates: tenancies for a fixed term, periodic tenancies, tenancies at will, and tenancies at sufferance. Each of these types is discussed below. The first three types normally come into existence by means of an agreement called a lease. The nature and requirements of a lease and the rights and duties of landlord and tenant are such important topics that they warrant special consideration. These topics are discussed in connection with tenancies for a fixed term because the reciprocal rights and duties of the parties ordinarily are fully spelled out in leases for that type of tenancy.

Tenancies for a Fixed Term. The most common type of leasehold estate is the tenancy for a fixed term, often referred to as an "estate for years," even though the duration of the tenancy may be for a single year or for a term shorter than a year. The lessor and lessee can agree upon a term of any length, unless a statute provides otherwise. Most states have a statute specifying maximum terms for certain kinds of leases. For example, in California the maximum term for leases on agricultural land is 51 years; for oil and gas lands, 99 years; for town and city lots, 99 years.[2] A lease for a term in excess of a statutory maximum is usually held to be invalid.

Nature and requirements of a lease. A lease has two aspects. In one of its aspects, a lease is a contract setting forth the reciprocal rights and duties of the lessor and lessee concerning the use and possession of certain property. In its other aspect, a lease is a conveyance of an estate in real property from one person to another.

Although most people think of a lease as a written document, a lease need be in writing only if a statute so requires. Most states have a statute requiring leases for more than 1 year to be in writing. Even when the law does not require a lease to be in writing, sound business policy may require a written lease.

No particular words are necessary to create a valid lease. However, certain items should be mentioned in any kind of a lease: (1) the identification of each of the parties; (2) a designation of the premises leased; (3) the rent to be paid, and the time and manner of its payment; and (4) the term of the lease, including a beginning and ending date.

Rights and duties of landlord and tenant. The most fundamental right of the *landlord* is the right to receive the rental payments provided for in the lease. If the tenant defaults in the payment, the landlord has a cause of action for the unpaid rent. If the tenant unlawfully remains in possession of the premises, the law provides remedies by which the landlord may regain possession.

At common law when leased realty was destroyed or damaged by fire or other cause, the tenant bore the risk of loss and so had to continue paying the rent. This rule made sense then because most leases were of land for agricultural purposes, and the tenant could continue to use the land. Today, tenants commonly lease buildings for residential and commercial purposes, and destruction of the building would deprive the tenant of the benefit of the lease. Consequently, the statutes of most states reverse the common law rule, at least for commercial or residential leases. Under these statutes, where residential or commercial buildings are rendered unfit for occupancy or destroyed without the fault of either party, the tenant is relieved from the duty to pay rent.

The most fundamental right of the *tenant* is to have the exclusive possession and quiet enjoyment of the premises for the agreed term, free from interference by the landlord. The landlord's unlawfully evicting the tenant would deprive the tenant of the quiet enjoyment of the premises. Eviction can be actual (a physical removal of the tenant from the property) or constructive. A *constructive eviction* occurs where the landlord's acts or omissions deprive the tenant of the beneficial use of the property. Tom leases an apartment from Lena for a year. Lena agrees to provide heat during the winter. She fails to do so, and the apartment becomes uninhabitable. Lena has constructively evicted Tom. Tom has a right to vacate the apartment without paying any more rent.

Written leases usually contain provisions concerning the rights and duties of landlord and tenant. Customarily included are provisions that the tenant is to pay all electric and gas bills accruing against the apartment during the term of the lease; that the tenant is not to sublet the apartment or assign the lease without the written consent of the landlord; that the tenant will deliver the premises at the expiration of the term in as good order and repair as when received, natural wear and tear excepted; and that the landlord or an agent shall have

[2]Calif. Civ. Code, secs. 717, 718, and 718f.

the right to enter the premises at any reasonable hour to examine them and to make repairs. Leases of commercial and industrial properties, involving long terms and properties of great value, usually contain more provisions concerning rights and duties than do leases of residential properties.

Landlords and tenants are subject not only to the rights and duties set forth in a lease but also to those declared by the courts and those specified in statutes. For example, at common law the landlord had no duty to repair or maintain the premises occupied by the tenant during the term of the lease. In recent years there has been an important shift in the attitude of the judiciary toward the rights of tenants of residential property, especially in large metropolitan communities. Many courts now hold that the lessor impliedly warrants (guarantees) the habitability of a dwelling. Thus, the landlord must maintain the premises in a habitable condition throughout the term of the lease. If the landlord fails to meet this obligation, courts stress the contract aspect of leases and hold that the tenant can stay in possession *without paying rent.*

A number of state legislatures, in response to demands of tenant groups, have enacted statutes requiring the landlord of a building intended for residency to keep it in habitable condition, except for waste or dilapidations caused by the tenant. Generally such statutes define "habitable" to include at least adequate plumbing, water supply, heating, and sanitation. These statutes often provide that if the landlord fails to make necessary repairs, the tenant may do so and deduct the cost from the rent.

In the following case the court discusses the obligation imposed upon a landlord to protect a tenant from assault by intruders.

CASE 22.2 Penner v. Falk · 200 Cal. Rptr. 661 (Cal. App. 1984)

FACTS Scott Penner was a tenant in an apartment building owned by Joe Falk and others. In 1980 Penner was assaulted by two intruders who were waiting in the common hallway of the premises. He was robbed and suffered physical harm. Penner filed suit against the owners of the building, alleging two causes of action. The first cause of action alleged negligence by the owners. Penner alleged that the defendants were aware of prior crimes in the building (trespass, robbery, physical assault, etc.) and were aware of tenant complaints and demands for improved security but refused to remedy the situation. The second cause of action alleged breach of warranty of habitability. Defendants filed a demurrer which the trial court sustained. Penner appealed.

OPINION AMERIAN, J.... [C]ases dealing with adequacy of pleadings sketch the current status in California of the duty of a landlord to residential tenants, for criminal acts of violence committed upon tenants on the premises.

O'Hara v. Western Seven Trees Corp. (1977)... involved a plaintiff-tenant who alleged that defendant-landlord knew that a male Caucasian, whose drawing had been furnished to defendant, had raped several tenants of the apartment complex. In spite of this knowledge, when plaintiff was a prospective tenant, defendant assured her that the premises were safe and were patrolled by guards. Relying on the representations, plaintiff rented an apartment from defendant. Three months later, she was raped in her apartment. The assailant was the same person who had committed the other rapes and whose composite drawing had been furnished to defendant.

The court held that a cause of action had been stated for negligence in failing to provide adequate security. In holding that demurrer to the negligence cause of action should have been overruled, the court stated, "It has been held that since only the landlord is in the position to secure common areas, he has a duty to protect against types of crimes of which he has notice and which are likely to recur if the common areas are not secure. Liability does not make the landlord an insurer of the tenants' safety; the duty is merely to exercise reasonable care."...

CASE 22.2
Continued

7735 Hollywood Blvd. Venture v. Superior Court (1981)...was a case in which a plaintiff-tenant alleged simply that the defendant-landlord had knowledge that violent crime had occurred in the general area and neighborhood within the previous six months and that the landlord had failed to replace a burned out light which lit the outside of plaintiff's apartment. Plaintiff was the victim of a forcible rape inside her apartment at 4:30 a.m. The court held that no cause of action had been stated, in part because there were "no factual allegations to support the claim that the owner of the apartment house possessed knowledge any more precise than the knowledge of any citizen in Los Angeles County that there are violent crimes committed in this county."...

In analyzing the pleading before us for review, we note that paragraphs 9(d) and 9(e) allege an awareness by respondents [owners of the building] of conditions which, under *O'Hara v. Western Seven Trees Corp.*...give rise to a duty on their part.

Among other things, respondents were aware of crimes in the apartment building and apartments therein caused by the condition of the premises....

We conclude that it was error to sustain the demurrers to the first cause of action....[The court then discussed the contention that a cause of action for breach of warranty of habitability had been set forth.]

Appellant [Penner] has not alleged in his second cause of action facts to show that the living quarters were not in a habitable state, that bare living requirements have not been maintained by respondents or that respondents have failed to comply with applicable building and housing code standards....

Further, this case is distinguishable from *Kline v. 1500 Massachusetts Avenue Apartment Corp.*,...cited by appellant in support of the proposition that alleged lapses by a landlord in security measures should support a cause of action for breach of implied warranty of habitability.

In *Kline*, the tenant was assaulted and robbed at 10 p.m. in the common hallway of a 585-unit apartment building....When the tenant first signed a lease seven years before the incident, "a doorman was on duty at the main entrance twenty-four hours a day, and at least one employee at all times manned a desk in the lobby from which all persons using the elevators could be observed....By mid-1966, however, the main entrance had no doorman, the desk in the lobby was left unattended much of the time, the [side entrances were unguarded]...The entrances were allowed to be thus unguarded in the face of an increasing number of assaults, larcenies, and robberies being perpetrated against the tenants in and from the common hallways of the apartment building..."

The tenant testified that she had initially moved into the building because she was interested in security. She had been impressed by the precautions taken at the main entrance.

On these facts the court found "implied in the contract between landlord and tenant an obligation on the landlord to provide those protective measures which are within his reasonable capacity."

Appellant here has not alleged that there existed a level of security of the premises which was relied upon by him in entering into the landlord-tenant relationship. Appellant has not alleged that respondents permitted or effected a reduction in that level of security which existed at the time he entered into the lease.

The general demurrer to the second cause of action was properly sustained.

JUDGMENT The judgment is reversed. The matter is remanded with instructions to the trial court to enter a new order sustaining without leave to amend the general demurrer to the second cause of action, overruling the demurrers to the first cause of action and denying the motion to strike.

Transfer of interests under a lease. The landlord can transfer his or her reversion to another. If the landlord dies without having transferred the reversion, it passes to his or her heirs or beneficiaries. Where the reversion is transferred, the transferee becomes the landlord and is bound by the terms of the lease.

Unless the lease prohibits or limits the right to do so, the tenant may transfer all or part of the leasehold estate to another. In an *assignment* of the lease, the tenant (assignor) transfers his or her total interest under the lease to the assignee, who now has whatever rights the former tenant had and is liable for payment of the rent. However, unless expressly released from liability for the rent, the assignor (former tenant) remains liable as a *surety* for any rent that the assignee fails to pay. In a *sublease,* the tenant transfers a part of his or her interest to a subtenant and retains a reversionary interest. Tom leases an apartment from Lena for 1 year. He immediately sublets the apartment to Tina for a term of 6 months. Tom thus becomes her landlord and is entitled to collect rent from her. However, Tom is still Lena's tenant and remains liable to her for the rent he agreed to pay. When Tina's sublease expires, Tom's reversionary interest takes effect, and Tom regains possession of the apartment for the balance of his 1-year term.

Periodic Tenancies. A periodic tenancy is an estate in real property that is created for a specified period of time and will continue for successive periods of the same length until the tenancy is terminated. The period may be week to week, month to month, or any term the parties agree upon. Frequently, a periodic tenancy arises by inference from the conduct of the parties. Suppose, for example, that a landlord agreed to rent certain premises to a tenant, that no specified term was agreed upon, but that the tenant agreed to pay rent monthly. In the event of litigation, a court would normally hold that a month to month tenancy had been created.

A periodic tenancy continues indefinitely until the parties agree to terminate the tenancy or one of the parties gives notice of termination. Requirements regarding the method and time of notice vary among the states. A common requirement is that the notice must be given in writing in the same amount of time as the period of tenancy, but not to exceed 30 days. Under such a statute, 1 week's notice would be sufficient to terminate a week to week tenancy; and 30 days' notice would be sufficient to terminate a year to year tenancy. Generally, no reason for termination need be given by either party. However, in many states a landlord may not terminate a tenancy because the tenant reported dilapidations and building or health code violations to the authorities. Such a termination is called "retaliatory eviction." Neither may a landlord terminate a tenancy because the tenant withheld rent or deducted the cost of needed repairs from the rent due.

In order to establish retaliatory eviction, the tenant must prove that: (1) the tenant's grievance was bona fide, reasonable, and serious in nature and had a foundation in fact; (2) the tenant did not create the condition complained of; (3) the grievance existed at the time the landlord commenced eviction proceedings; and (4) the overriding reason the landlord sought eviction was to retaliate against the tenant for exercising his or her constitutional rights.

Tenancies at Will. A tenancy at will is an estate in real property created by agreement of the parties that the tenant will have the exclusive right to possession for an indefinite period of time not intended to be infinite. Such tenancies arise only in limited circumstances. Two examples of the way in which tenancies at will arise are when the tenant is given possession under a void lease and when the tenant is given possession while negotiations take place for a sale of the property or for a comprehensive written lease.

Ordinarily, tenancies at will are of short duration, since the tenant does not pay rent. If the tenant continues in possession and begins to pay rent, a periodic tenancy is created.

A tenancy at will can be terminated by either party, but many states require a landlord to give 30 days' written notice. Such a tenancy is automatically terminated upon the death of either party. The tenant cannot assign a tenancy at will to another. Any attempt to do so would automatically terminate the tenancy.

Tenancies at Sufferance. A tenancy at sufferance typically arises when a tenant remains in possession after the expiration of a tenancy for a fixed term, without the landlord's consent. In most states the landlord can institute legal action to evict the tenant at sufferance without first giving notice of termination of the tenancy. The tenant would be liable for the reasonable rental value of the premises for the period the tenant remains in possession after expiration of the tenancy for a fixed term. If the landlord accepts rent from a holdover tenant, a court very likely would hold that a periodic tenancy was created by the conduct of the parties. A landlord should therefore consider carefully the legal consequences before accepting rent from a tenant at sufferance.

Easements

Meaning of Easement

An easement may be defined as the right to use, or to prevent the use of, the real property of another in a specific manner. For example, Edith grants to Fred, an adjoining landowner, the permanent right to drive his car over a designated portion of her land in order to get to and from the nearest public street. Fred has a right-of-way easement. His land is called the "dominant" tenement or parcel. Edith's land, the land that is subject to the easement, is called the "servient" tenement or parcel.

An easement is an interest in real property, but it is not an estate in real property. We have seen that an estate is an ownership interest. The owner of an easement does not own the servient tenement but merely has the right to use it, or to prevent the use of it, in a certain way. The easement for roadway purposes, mentioned above, entitles Fred to drive his car across Edith's land but does not entitle him to fence it, cultivate it, or exercise the usual rights of an owner of an estate in real property.

Methods of Creating Easements

Creation by Express Grant or Reservation. The most common method of creating an easement is by deed.[3] The owner of real property executes a deed that transfers to the grantee a limited right to use the property of the grantor. For example, Edith executes a deed transferring to her neighbor, Fred, a right of way over her land. In some instances, a grantor transfers ownership of the property to another but expressly reserves an easement in the property for the grantor's own purposes. For example, Agnes, the owner of a 10-acre parcel of land, executes a deed transferring to Robert the fee simple ownership in 5 acres but expressly reserves the right to use a 12-foot strip as a roadway for access to the land retained by her.

Creation by Implied Grant or Reservation. In some situations, an easement may be created by implied grant or reservation. For example, suppose that Andrew owns 100 acres of land on which he constructs an irrigation system with an open ditch running from the north portion to the south portion. After several years he transfers ownership of the south portion to Donna without making any mention of an easement. Under these circumstances a court very likely would infer that the parties must have intended Donna to have an easement in Andrew's land for irrigation purposes. Such an easement is known as an easement by implied grant. In a similar manner, if Andrew had sold the *north* portion of the land to Donna without mention of any easement, a court would be warranted in holding that Andrew has an irrigation easement by implied reservation. Several conditions must exist before an easement by implied grant or reservation will be recognized by the courts: (1) The owner of real property must have transferred a portion of it to another person; (2) at the time of the transfer, there must have been a long, obvious use of one portion of the property; and (3) the easement must be reasonably necessary to the beneficial use of the other portion of the property (the dominant tenement).

Creation by Necessity. In rare situations an easement may be created by necessity. Where an owner of real property transfers to a grantee a portion of the owner's property so that the grantee is left without a means of access, the parcel is said to be *landlocked.* Upon application to a court, the grantee may be given an easement for access to his or her parcel over the retained portion of the grantor's property. Such an easement must be absolutely nec-

[3]The types of deeds and the requirements for a valid deed were discussed in Chapter 21 under the heading Transfer by Deed.

essary for the grantee, and not just convenient or desirable. Thus, a grantee who has access to a parcel of land but complains that the only way to get to the parcel is by way of a steep, narrow, winding road cannot expect a court to give an easement by necessity over a flatter portion of the grantor's retained property. If a grantor transfers ownership of real property and retains a portion that is inadvertently landlocked, the grantor is entitled to an easement by necessity over the transferred property.

Creation by Prescription. An easement by prescription arises from a person's use of real property contrary to the wishes of the owner. In most states, one who claims such an easement must show use of another's property that is open and notorious, hostile to the owner (i.e., the user must be a trespasser), and continuous for the period specified in the state statute of limitations.

The requirements are very similar to those for adverse possession, discussed in Chapter 21. The difference is that adverse *possession* results in the acquisition of ownership, while adverse *use* results in the acquisition of a prescriptive easement. Mary and Tom are neighbors. Almost daily for many years Mary has walked across a corner of Tom's property, eventually making a visible pathway. Tom objected many times during those years but took no legal action to prevent her use of his property, and he did not physically interrupt her use. Mary has acquired a prescriptive easement (if the statutory period of time has elapsed) and now has a legal right to continue walking across Tom's property.

The statutes of some states provide a method for preventing prescriptive easements. Landowners may post signs stating, in effect, "Right to pass is by permission, and subject to control, of owner." In those states, such language makes an otherwise adverse use permissive and prevents the creation of a prescriptive easement. However, it does not destroy an existing easement.

Creation by Dedication. In Chapter 21 we discussed dedication as a method by which a governmental unit or agency may acquire ownership of real property. The process of dedication may also be used to create an easement. For example, an owner of land may offer a roadway easement to the local city government. If the city council passes an ordinance accepting the offer, the city acquires an easement by statutory dedication. The owner of the servient tenement retains the right to use the airspace above the roadway and the subsurface below the roadway as part of the fee simple estate.

In recent years, the creation of easements by common law dedication has been asserted in lawsuits between environmental groups and owners of recreational land. Some courts have found that common law dedications have occurred when the evidence showed that the landowners freely allowed the public to camp, picnic, or walk across their property. In some states the property owner can avoid such claims of dedication by posting an appropriate sign in plain sight.

Use and Maintenance of Easements

The owner of an easement may exercise the right to use, or prevent the use of, the servient tenement according to the purpose of the easement and the circumstances surrounding its creation. Where an easement is created by *express grant,* a properly drawn deed will indicate the specific purpose of the easement, such as use of the land for a roadway, or for installation of power poles. Where an easement is created by *implied grant* or by *prescription,* there has been an obvious, open use that determines the extent of the easement owner's right to use the servient tenement. He or she will be able to use the property in the same manner as it was used previously. Under an easement by *necessity,* the right to use the servient tenement is limited to the purpose that necessitated the creation of the easement, such as use for vehicular access to the nearest public street. An easement by *dedication* allows the servient tenement to be used by the government or the public for the purpose specified in the landowner's express or implied offer.

The owner of an easement has the right and the duty to maintain and repair installations connected with the easement. For example, an easement owner may grade and pave the surface designated in a roadway easement or, if the easement is for utility purposes, the easement owner may enter the servient property to repair and replace water lines or sewer pipes as needed. The owner of the servient tenement may do as he or she wishes with the property as long as he or she does not unreasonably interfere with the use, enjoyment, and maintenance of the easement created.

The following case involves an attempt by the easement owner to expand the usage of the easement.

CASE 22.3 Wright v. Horse Creek Ranches · 697 P.2d 384 (Colo. 1985)

FACTS Geyer Ranch, an 830-acre cattle ranch, lies to the east of three large parcels known as the Buchheim Ranch, the Bull Ranch, and the Cockcroft Ranch. These four ranches were accessible from a county road by means of a private dirt road which traversed the Cockcroft, Bull, and Buchheim Ranches before reaching the Geyer Ranch. The road was rocky, not suitable for passenger cars, and was passable only 6 months out of the year.

On July 20, 1978 the owners of the four ranches entered into an agreement which stated that for more than 20 years access to their respective properties had been provided by the dirt road. Each party acknowledged the right of all other parties to use and maintain the road as an access easement. In August of 1978 Horse Creek Ranches purchased the Geyer Ranch for the purpose of subdividing it into smaller parcels of no less than forty acres each, to be sold as recreation residential property. On July 3 and 4, 1979 Horse Creek substantially widened the dirt road, removed rocks, trees, and brush, and flattened the road bed. Richard Wright, owner of Buchheim Ranch, filed suit against Horse Creek to prohibit the allegedly unauthorized use of the access road. The trial court found that there was a trend in the area toward subdividing large ranches into smaller agricultural and recreational tracts, that Horse Creek's predecessors had established a prescriptive easement over Wright's ranch, and that Horse Creek's use to service owners of 40-acre tracts was reasonably foreseeable and not an unreasonable burden on the servient tenement. Wright appealed to the Court of Appeals. The court affirmed, but added that the 1978 agreement created an express grant of an easement and that the parties could be assumed to have contemplated a normal development of the use of the dominant tenement. Wright appealed to the Colorado Supreme Court.

OPINION KIRSHBAUM, J. . . . Because the range of permissible uses of any particular easement is in the first instance defined by the circumstances surrounding the creation of that easement, precise delineation of the means by which a particular easement is acquired is critical to any determination of the extent to which the owner of the dominant estate is entitled to burden the servient estate. Our initial inquiry, therefore, must focus upon the nature of the easement Horse Creek owns.

Although the trial court concluded that the easement owned by Geyer had been obtained by prescription, it also suggested that the July 20, 1978 agreement changed the nature of that easement—a suggestion apparently adopted by the majority of the Court of Appeals. The agreement contains no language, however, indicating that the parties thereto intended to create any new rights or privileges. It contains no terms of conveyance, grant or new entitlement; indeed, with the exception of the title, it does not refer to an "easement" at all. We conclude that, as both Wright and Horse Creek agreed at trial, the agreement merely reflects a legally significant circumstance which the signatories already understood—that between 1957 and 1978 all of them had acquired easements by prescription over so much of the other properties as was necessary to obtain access to their properties. To construe such document as granting new obligations or benefits does violence to its terms and contravenes the intent of those who executed it.

The conclusion that Horse Creek acquired an easement established by prescription, rather than one created by grant, is critical to the selection of the test to be applied to Wright's claim of unauthorized use of the easement. . . .

CASE 22.3 Continued

Section 477 of the *Restatement of Property* offers the following principle as a reasonable standard for determining the extent of easements established by prescription: "The extent of an easement created by prescription is fixed by the use through which it was created."... One justification for the principle that a non-owner may establish a legally protected right to burden property possessed by another is the theory that by not protesting the adverse use to which the non-owner has put the property, the property owner can be presumed to have agreed to burden the servient estate to that degree.... Such agreement can be presumed only if the adverse use is open as well as continuous.... No presumption of voluntary forfeiture of incidents of ownership can be premised on conduct not performed and, therefore, not amenable to protest by the owner of the servient estate.... [T]he beneficiary of an easement established by prescription will be permitted to vary the use of the easement to a reasonable extent.... [S]ection 479 of the *Restatement of Property*... states as follows:

> In ascertaining whether a particular use is permissible under an easement appurtenant created by prescription there must be considered... the needs which result from a normal evolution in the use of the dominant tenement and the extent to which the satisfaction of those needs increases the burden on the servient tenement....

Both the trial court and the majority of the Court of Appeals focused their attention almost exclusively on the "normal evolution" standard of section 479....

The use to which the private road was put during the relevant prescriptive period was described by Bob J. Cockcroft and by Darrel Geyer as use primarily for ranching purposes, and occasional traffic by hunters, loggers and water commissioners. When asked if the road had ever been used "for access to any residence or home on the Geyer property," Cockcroft answered "[d]efinitely not."...

The evidence is unchallenged that from 1958 to 1978, the road was not used for residential purposes. The only evidence remotely suggesting any residential use at any time consisted of testimony that the remnants of three or four old cabins had occasionally been used for ranching and hunting purposes. At best, such evidence may by inference indicate that at some time prior to the prescriptive period the road may have been used for residential purposes; it does not establish the open, notorious and continuous use essential to establish a use by prescription....

The use to which Horse Creek seeks to put the easement includes use for recreational residential purposes. This represents a change in kind of use. It is a change which by necessity will subject the servient estate to increased burdens. Both Cockcroft and Wright testified that any increased traffic on the road would impede their ranching operations, and their testimony was not contradicted.

The change in the dominant estate, of course, is the change from a single, large agricultural enterprise to a recreational development area consisting of several smaller tracts owned by several individuals. The physical character of the easement has been substantially altered from a ten-foot wide primitive road to a passageway which now is twenty-one feet wide and accommodates two vehicles simultaneously. The purpose of the new use has changed from permitting infrequent access for ranching needs to encouraging frequent use by owners and their guests for recreational residence purposes. Finally, uncontradicted evidence established that the Buchheim Ranch will be burdened by the new use. Considering all of these factors, rather than focusing exclusively on the fact that subdivision of ranch properties was an inevitable phenomenon, we conclude that the trial court erred in enlarging the permissible use of the prescriptive easement acquired by Horse Creek to include recreational residence purposes....

JUDGMENT The judgment of the Court of Appeals is affirmed with respect to its conclusion that the case must be remanded to the trial court with directions to specify the location of the easement, and is otherwise reversed.

Termination of Easements

There are various ways in which an easement may be terminated or extinguished. The most common method is by a deed from the owner of the easement to the owner of the servient tenement. Some of the other ways in which an easement may be terminated are by (1) abandonment; (2) merger, as where the same person becomes the owner of the easement and the servient tenement, for obviously a person cannot have an easement on his or her own land; (3) destruction of the servient property, as where the tenant in an apartment building has an easement in the common halls and stairways, and the building is destroyed by fire or earthquake; and (4) adverse possession, as where the owner of the servient tenement refuses to recognize the rights of the easement owner and, for the statutory period, occupies the property adversely to the easement owner's rights.

Liens on Real Property

Meaning and Classification of Liens

In general, a lien is a claim or charge on property as security for the payment of a debt or for the performance of some other obligation. In one sense, a lien is a contingent claim held by a creditor. If the obligation is satisfied, there will be no interference with the debtor's right to use, possess, and enjoy his or her property. On the other hand, if the obligation is not satisfied, the lien holder may take steps (called "foreclosure") to sell the property and to apply proceeds from the sale to the debt.

There are two main classes of liens on real property: *voluntary* liens, which are created with the property owner's consent (mortgages, for example); and *involuntary* liens, which are created without the property owner's consent (mechanics' liens, for example). Only the most important voluntary and involuntary liens are discussed on the following pages.

Voluntary Liens on Real Property

Mortgages. A mortgage is the most common type of voluntary lien on real property. The mortgage device is used in connection with many different kinds of credit transactions. Usually, the device is used for either of two purposes. (1) It is used by a property owner as a means of borrowing a substantial sum of money needed for some personal or business reason. The property owner borrows from a lender, signs a promissory note, and executes a mortgage on his or her home or business property to secure the repayment of the money borrowed. (2) The mortgage device is often the indispensable means of financing the purchase of real property. The person who desires to purchase the property has sufficient cash for a down payment but not enough to pay the balance of the purchase price. If the seller agrees "to carry the mortgage," he or she gives the buyer a deed to the property, and the buyer executes a mortgage on the property in favor of the seller. If the seller does not agree to carry the mortgage, the buyer borrows the money from a lender and executes a mortgage to the lender.

Nature and requirements of a mortgage. As implied above, a real estate mortgage is an interest in real property given to secure the performance of some obligation. The two parties to a mortgage are called the "mortgagor" (the borrower or debtor) and the "mortgagee" (the lender or creditor). Under the statute of frauds, a mortgage must be evidenced by a writing. There is no requirement that a mortgage instrument be recorded in order to create a lien on the property mortgaged. However, the mortgagee should have the instrument recorded at the local county recorder's office as a protection against a claim of any subsequent purchaser or any subsequent mortgagee or other lien holder. (Recording was discussed in Chapter 21.)

Rights and duties of the parties. The *mortgagor* of real property ordinarily owns a fee simple estate and retains the right to use, possess, and dispose of the property. The mortgagor can lease the premises to another and collect rent. He or she can borrow further sums of money from other creditors and give subsequent mortgages to them. If the mortgagor transfers ownership of the property during life or if the property passes at death to his or her heirs or beneficiaries, the transferee takes the property subject to the mortgage. The typical mortgage instrument contains a list of duties specified by the mortgagee to be performed by the mortgagor. Some of the duties customarily included are to repay money borrowed; to keep the premises in good repair; to refrain from committing waste; to pay annual real property taxes; to pay any prior mortgage that may be on the property; to maintain adequate fire insurance on improvements; and not to transfer ownership without approval of the mortgagee.

The *mortgagee* has the right to performance of all the mortgagor's duties. Under the typical mortgage instrument the mortgagee has several duties. The mortgagee has a duty to lend money in accordance with the agreement of the parties. When the mortgagor pays back the loan, the mortgagee owes a duty to execute appropriate documents to remove the lien from the mortgagor's property. In the event foreclosure becomes necessary, the mortgagee owes a duty to act fairly and to follow the statutory procedure of the state. A mortgagee can transfer the mortgage to a third person and assign to such person the right to collect the debt that is secured by the mortgage. Upon the mortgagee's death, the mortgage passes to his or her heirs or beneficiaries. The transferee would be obligated to perform the mortgagee's duties mentioned above.

The following case involves violation of a duty imposed on the mortgagor by a mortgagee.

CASE 22.4 Investors Savings & Loan Association v. Ganz · 416 A.2d 918 (N.J. Super. Ch. 1980)

FACTS Mr. and Mrs. Ganz [defendants] borrowed $50,000 from Investors Savings & Loan Association [plaintiff] to finance the purchase of a home. The loan was secured by a mortgage in favor of the plaintiff. In the mortgage loan application the defendants stated they would occupy the property. The mortgage contained the following condition:

> And it is further agreed that, if the mortgaged premises are not used as the primary place of residence and are not occupied by the Mortgagor during the term of the mortgage loan, then and in such event, the aforesaid principal sum with accrued interest shall, at the option of the Mortgagee, become due and payable immediately, . . .

In October 1979 plaintiff learned that the premises were not occupied by the defendants but were occupied by tenants. Plaintiff demanded that the balance due on the mortgage be paid in full. Defendants did not make this payment, and the premises continued to be tenant-occupied. Plaintiff brought suit to foreclose the mortgage. Defendants filed an answer alleging that the acceleration clause and mortgage requirement that defendants reside in the mortgaged premises were unconscionable and inequitable and created a forfeiture, and thus were of no force and effect. Plaintiff moves for an order granting summary judgment.

OPINION KENTZ, J. . . . Where an acceleration clause is express and certain in its terms, such a clause requiring the payment of the entire balance due on the mortgage upon default in the performance of any covenant or condition of the mortgage is held to be a legitimate contractual obligation for credit on condition and not a penalty or forfeiture clause. . . .

The only remaining issue is whether the enforcement of the acceleration clause because of the violation of the owner occupancy requirement would be unconscionable or inequitable. This question appears to be one of first impression in this State.

Defendants contend that before such a clause can be enforced there must be shown some jeopardy or threat to the plaintiff's security and that plaintiff has demonstrated none. Defendants argue that unlike cases in which the mortgagor has defaulted on payments due or in which the identity of the mortgagor changes, defendants here remain responsible for the payments and are ready, willing and able to pay. Thus, they maintain that there is no jeopardy to plaintiff's security in the mortgage by virtue of the fact that they are not living in the premises.

CASE 22.4 Continued

Plaintiff states by affidavit that historically the purpose of a savings and loan association has been to assist persons in acquiring a home in which to reside and that this has always been plaintiff's policy. . . . Plaintiff contends that from its experience nonoccupying owners tend to restrict and minimize property maintenance and upkeep in order to enhance their financial return. Plaintiff argues that such conduct leads to an unreasonable depreciation of the property and jeopardizes the security on which the loan was made. In order to prevent this result, the owner occupancy provision is made a condition of the loan. . . .

When a contract is clear and unambiguous a court is bound to enforce its terms as they are written and the court may not make a better contract for either of the parties. A court has no right to rewrite the contract by substituting new or different provisions from those clearly expressed in the contract. . . .

In applying the foregoing to the facts of this case, I do not find that the owner occupancy requirement is unconscionable or inequitable. Given plaintiff's purpose to promote home ownership, its policy of not making loans except for that reason, . . . it cannot be said that its requirement of owner occupancy as a condition for the granting of a mortgage loan is unjust. Defendants were fully aware of this condition when they freely and voluntarily entered into the mortgage transaction. Furthermore, plaintiff's fear that the lack of owner occupancy might jeopardize its security is not unreasonable.

JUDGMENT Since defendants have defaulted, plaintiff has the right to accelerate the due date of the unpaid balance of the debt and to require payment thereof. Such payment having not been made as demanded, summary judgment of foreclosure is appropriate.

Foreclosure of a mortgage; right of redemption. If the mortgagor fails to perform any of the listed duties, the mortgagee has the right to foreclose; that is, steps can be taken to have the real property sold and to apply proceeds from the sale to the debt. The mortgagee may initiate a court proceeding to secure an order of sale. The sheriff or other officer of the court then conducts a sale by auction. At any time prior to the court's entering a decree of foreclosure, the mortgagor can reinstate the mortgage by curing the default; ordinarily, that means making up installment payments that have been missed. Normally, the mortgagor also has a statutory *right of redemption* after a foreclosure sale takes place—i.e., a right for a limited time to repurchase the property by payment of the auction sale price to the high bidder.

Trust Deeds. About half the states recognize the trust deed as an acceptable security instrument in real estate transactions. To the creditor, a trust deed has several significant advantages over the mortgage, and in some states the trust deed has virtually replaced the real property mortgage. States that refuse to recognize the trust deed on real property base the refusal on the ground that in the event of foreclosure debtors should have the procedural advantages connected with mortgages.

Nature of a trust deed. A trust deed is a document by which a debtor transfers the title to real property to a disinterested person (called a "trustee") to be held in trust as security for the performance of an obligation, usually the payment of a debt. The trustee is typically given the power to sell the property if the debtor defaults, and to apply proceeds from the sale to the debt.

Since mortgages and trust deeds perform a similar function, they necessarily have many features in common. Most of the preceding discussion concerning mortgages is applicable to trust deeds. However, while there are only two parties to a mortgage, there are three parties to a trust deed: the *trustor* (the debtor), the *beneficiary* (the creditor), and the *trustee.* Although the trustee holds title to the real property, it is a bare legal title, not a true ownership interest. In legal effect, the trust deed is considered to be merely a lien on the real property. If the trustor meets his or her obligations, there will be no interference with the use and possession of the property. When the obligation is satisfied the trustee will execute the necessary documents to reconvey title to the trustor. However, if the trustor-debtor defaults on an obligation, the holding of the title to the real property by the trustee becomes important. The major difference between a mortgage and a trust deed relates to foreclosure, as indicated in the following discussion.

Foreclosure of a trust deed. Under the terms of the typical trust deed the trustee is given the power to sell the property upon default by the debtor-trustor and to apply proceeds from the sale to the debt. In most states that permit the trust deed device, the creditor-beneficiary may elect to have the trustee use the same judicial procedure as for foreclosing a mortgage. However, the creditor ordinarily will elect to foreclose by having the trustee use the power of sale granted in the trust deed. The nonjudicial "power of sale" foreclosure by the trustee has certain advantages for the creditor: (1) it avoids the delay involved in getting a court order for a sale and avoids the expenses of litigation; and (2) it allows the trustor no right of redemption after the sale.

To foreclose by power of sale, the trustee simply notifies all interested persons (the debtor, other lienholders) that the trustor has defaulted. After a short period of time allowed for reinstatement of the trust deed, the trustee advertises and conducts an auction sale. Since the trustor has no right of redemption, the purchaser can immediately take possession, make improvements, lease, or even sell the property.

Involuntary Liens on Real Property

There are several liens on real property that can be created without the consent or approval of the owner. The statutes relating to such liens are complex and vary widely among the states. Some general aspects of the more important involuntary liens are discussed below.

Mechanics' Liens. At common law, a person who was not paid for performing a service or supplying materials in the improvement of someone's real property had a cause of action solely against the person who requested the service or materials.

Occasionally this resulted in hardship to the person providing the service or material. Suppose, for example, that Helen hired George, a building contractor, to add a room to her house. George contracted with Norman to supply lumber for the project and the lumber was used to build the room. George declared bankruptcy and Norman was not paid. At common law Norman had no remedy. Today, nearly every state has a statute giving such a person a mechanics' lien on the property he or she helped to improve, provided the person takes the steps required to perfect a claim. Mechanics' liens and the steps required to enforce them are discussed further in Chapter 24 in the section entitled "*Liens imposed by law on real property.*"

Attachment Liens. In certain situations an unsecured creditor who has filed an action against a debtor may have the defendant's property seized by the sheriff under a *writ of attachment.* The purpose of the seizure is to hold the property pending the outcome of the suit. Where the property is real property, "seizure" consists of having the sheriff record the writ of attachment in the county recorder's office. Upon recording, a lien is created against the property. If the plaintiff-creditor obtains a judgment in the civil action, the plaintiff can have the property sold by foreclosure. If the defendant-debtor prevails in the action, the attachment lien terminates. The U.S. Supreme Court has severely restricted the creditor's right to attachment, because attachment interferes with the debtor's constitutional right to use and dispose of his or her property *prior* to a court trial.[4]

Judgment Liens. When one party to a lawsuit receives a judgment requiring the other party to pay a sum of money, the party receiving the judgment is thereafter called a *judgment creditor;* the party against whom the judgment is rendered is called the *judgment debtor.* If the judgment debtor does not voluntarily pay the judgment, the judgment creditor may, under modern statutes, record the judgment in the county or counties in which the judgment debtor owns real property. When the judgment is recorded, it becomes a lien on any real property owned by the judgment debtor in the county. A judgment lien remains a lien on the property until the judgment is satisfied or is rendered inoperative by the expiration of the statutory period. In several states a judgment is valid for a period of 10 years. In some states a judgment may be renewed

[4]*Sniadach v. Family Fin. Corp.*, 395 U.S. 337 (1969).

for one or more statutory periods. Any real property acquired by the judgment debtor during the statutory period or any extension of it would be subjected to the judgment lien.

Execution Liens. A judgment creditor often faces the need to take coercive measures to enforce collection of a judgment. One method that may be available is to have the court issue a *writ of execution*. Such a writ is directed to the sheriff, ordering the seizure and sale of certain specified property of the judgment debtor. Details of the procedure vary among the states, but usually the sheriff records a notice of execution in the county where the judgment debtor's real property is located. Recording the notice creates a lien on the described parcel of property. Unlike the judgment lien, recording a writ of execution does not create a lien on *all* the judgment debtor's real property in the county, just on the described parcel. The sheriff sets a time and place for foreclosure sale of the specific parcel, advertises, and conducts the sale in the same manner as that of a mortgage foreclosure sale. Some state statutes provide for a redemption period following the sale.

Tax Liens. A tax lien is a special type of involuntary lien against real property. It is a lien created by a governmental unit or agency to enforce collection of a tax. A wide variety of taxes exists in our contemporary society, imposed by various agencies ranging from local townships to the federal government.

The most common tax lien in the United States is the property tax lien. Generally, the taxing agency is given an *automatic* lien against the taxpayer's real property to secure the payment of real property taxes. The state or local government is not required to file suit or have a trial prior to foreclosure. If the taxes are not paid within the statutory time period, the government can simply publish a notice in the paper and conduct an auction sale. There is typically no redemption period after sale, and the high bidder receives a tax deed immediately.

When the federal government or a state or local governmental taxing agency is attempting to collect an unpaid income tax, employment tax, sales tax, or other nonproperty tax, a lien on the taxpayer's real property is not automatically created. The governmental agency is usually required to record some type of delinquency notice in the county recorder's office. A lien is created by the recording. In order to sell the taxpayer's real property, the taxing agency generally must follow a procedure similar to that for foreclosing a mortgage. Often the taxpayer is given a redemption period after sale to recover his or her property.

Summary

There are three main types of interests in real property: estates, easements, and liens. An estate in real property is an interest that is, or may become, possessory. Estates are either freeholds or leaseholds. The major freehold estates are fee simple estates and life estates. The owner of a freehold estate can sell it, give it away, lease it to someone, or borrow against it. The death of an owner of a fee simple estate does not terminate the estate. Upon the owner's death the estate passes to the owner's heirs or to the beneficiaries named in his or her will. A life estate automatically terminates at the death of the person whose life measures the estate.

If the owner of an estate in real property is not to exercise the right to use, possess, and enjoy the property until some future time, he or she has a future interest. There are two main types of future interests: reversions (where the right of future possession is retained by the grantor) and remainders (where the right of future possession is owned by someone other than the grantor). Leasehold estates are those in which a person acquires the right to exclusive possession of certain premises for a limited period of time. The four types of leasehold estates are tenancies for a fixed term, periodic tenancies, tenancies at will, and tenancies at sufferance.

An easement is the right to use, or to prevent the use of, the real property of another in a specific manner. Easements may be created by express or implied grant or reservation, by necessity, by prescription, and by dedication. Easements may be terminated by deed, by abandonment, by merger, by destruction of the property, and by adverse possession.

A lien is a claim or charge on property as security for an obligation. If the owner of the property does not satisfy his or her obligation to the creditor, the creditor can take steps to foreclose the lien. Foreclosure usually involves a sale of the property at auction and the use of proceeds to satisfy the creditor's claim. Two major voluntary liens are the mortgage and the trust deed. The major involuntary liens on real property are mechanics' liens, attachment liens, judgment liens, execution liens, and tax liens. The procedure for foreclosure of involuntary liens is similar to that for foreclosure of mortgages.

Review Questions

1 What is an estate in real property?

2 What is the essential difference between a freehold estate and a leasehold estate?

3 What is a future interest? Give an example of how a future interest might be created.

4 **(a)** Explain the two aspects of a lease. **(b)** What are the most important rights of landlord and tenant under a typical lease?

5 **(a)** What duties does a landlord incur under the typical lease? **(b)** What duties does the tenant incur? **(c)** What can a landlord or tenant do if either wishes to be freed from these duties?

6 Explain how the following tenancies are created and terminated: **(a)** periodic tenancy; **(b)** tenancy at will; **(c)** tenancy at sufferance.

7 **(a)** What is an easement? **(b)** How does it differ from an estate in real property? **(c)** Define or explain: dominant tenement and servient tenement. **(d)** Why might it be important for you to know whether an easement exists before acquiring ownership of real property?

8 **(a)** List and explain briefly the five methods of creating an easement. **(b)** If you were about to purchase a parcel of real property, what steps could you take to determine whether an easement had been created by any of the five methods?

9 Describe the ways in which you could terminate an easement that is no longer desired.

10 **(a)** What is the nature and function of a lien? **(b)** Explain and give examples of the two main classes of liens.

11 **(a)** What function does the mortgagee perform in a real estate transaction? **(b)** List the rights of each party under the typical mortgage. **(c)** List the duties of each party. **(d)** How can foreclosure of a mortgage be avoided if threatened?

12 **(a)** Who are the parties to a trust deed? **(b)** What functions does each perform in a business transaction? **(c)** Why would a lender rather have a trust deed than a mortgage?

13 **(a)** What is a mechanic's lien? **(b)** Why do you think the states enacted mechanic's lien statutes? **(c)** What remedy other than a mechanic's lien is available to an unpaid contractor, subcontractor, laborer, or material supplier who benefits someone's real property?

14 **(a)** Explain the differences between an attachment lien and an execution lien. **(b)** Give examples of common types of tax liens that the typical individual or business firm would encounter in today's world.

Case Problems

1 A landlord, Toms Point Apartments, sought to evict a month-to-month tenant, Goudzward. The tenant raised the affirmative defense of retaliatory eviction. She alleged that she complained to the Attorney General's Office regarding the failure of the landlord to pay interest on rent security deposits and that she appeared at a hearing concerning the dismissal of the landlord's custodian. Goudzward claimed that the landlord retaliated for these acts by attempting to evict her. At the time the landlord commenced eviction proceedings the tenants had collected the interest due them and the problem with the custodian had been resolved. Are these allegations sufficient to sustain the defense of retaliatory eviction?

2 In 1974 Thomas purchased from Vereen 53 acres of land which was separated from the public road by other lands owned by Vereen. Vereen granted to Thomas an easement for an access road from the 53 acres to the state road. Thomas then constructed a hunting and fishing lodge and a road to his property. Thomas encountered trespassers on his property and obtained permission from Vereen to place a cable across the easement near its entrance to the public road. The cable was locked and keys given to Vereen. Thomas later removed the cable and placed it on his property where it adjoins the end of the easement. In 1982 Vereen was plagued by trespassers, night hunters, and vandals who drove vehicles over his planted fields. He erected another cable across the easement near the public road and gave Thomas a key to the lock. Thomas filed suit to prevent Vereen from obstructing his easement, contending that having to unlock two cables before entering his land imposed an undue burden on him, and that Vereen's cable was not necessary to the use of Vereen's property. Should Thomas win the lawsuit?

3 Szaraz owned 37 acres of undeveloped land bisected into parcels on the east and on the west by railroad tracks of Consolidated Railroad Corporation. The original owner of the land, Lusk, had conveyed land to the railroad for its tracks prior to 1900 and reserved an easement across the tracks to afford access between the west and east parcels. A plank or board crossing was in existence over the tracks for many years. In the early 1950's the Ohio Turnpike was constructed to the south of Szaraz's property. During construction the railroad tracks were temporarily relocated. Upon completion of the toll road in 1955, the tracks were returned to their former location. However, the crossing was not replaced, and a fence was built along the tracks. In 1979 Szaraz filed suit to compel the railroad to reconstruct the crossing or to pay him compensation for appropriation of the right of way. The trial court found that the easement had been extinguished. Was the trial court correct?

4 Norton borrowed $82,000 from Tucker Federal Savings and Loan Association and to secure the debt gave them a mortgage on land in DeKalb County. The mortgage contained the following "due on sale" clause: "Should the title to the property become vested in any person or entity other than the mortgagor, the unpaid balance of the note shall become due and payable, at the option of the holder." Norton signed an installment contract agreeing to sell the land to Randall, and the contract was recorded. Under the contract Norton agreed to deliver a warranty deed upon either Randall's payment of the purchase price in full or Tucker Federal's approving Randall's assumption of the mortgage. The contract further provided that "no fee simple title passes upon execution of this agreement." The Randalls took possession of the property. Tucker Federal sued, claiming the due on sale clause was activated by the land sale contract. Did Norton violate the terms of the mortgage?

5 The Illinois Mechanics' Lien Act provided that "any person who shall by contract with the owner of a lot or tract of land fill, sod, or excavate such land, or do landscape work thereon has a lien" on such land. The Act also provides that the lien claimant must "within 4 months after completion" file a claim of lien in the county recorder's office. Foley entered a contract with Ballantrae to plant trees, grass, and other foliage on Ballantrae's land. After these were installed Foley was to provide maintenance services until May 29, 1981. By December 14, 1980, Foley had installed all trees, grass, and shrubs required. Thereafter, and until May 29, 1981, Foley mowed the grass, watered it, and provided other maintenance services. On July 2, 1981, Foley filed a claim of lien in the county recorder's office, asserting that it was filed within 4 months of completion of the contract. A mortgagee objected, asserting: (1) the claim of lien must be filed within 4 months of the completion of the work (i.e., 4 months from December 14, 1980), which was not done, and (2) the Mechanics' Lien Act does not allow a lien for maintenance services. Is either of these objections valid?

CHAPTER 23

Estates, Wills, and Trusts

A well-known radio talk show personality has said that to make a will is "an act of love" and that not to make a will is "an act of contempt." This chapter will, among other things, explain the meaning of this cryptic but very true statement.

When you die, what happens to the business you owned and operated? Who is entitled to the shares of stock and other property you accumulated during your years of successful business life? What arrangements can you make in your lifetime to direct the disposal after your death of those assets, called your "estate." You have two options, either: (1) to do nothing, in which event your estate will be distributed in accordance with the law of your state; or (2) to, by will, direct who is to receive (inherit) your possessions. If you follow the first course you are said to die *intestate*; if you choose to make a will you are a *testator* and are said to die *testate*.

This chapter first considers the state's distribution of an intestate's estate. Next, there follows a discussion of how a will is made, changed, or revoked and a summary of the process, called *probate*, by which the distribution of the estate of any deceased person (a *decedent*) is actually accomplished. Lastly, we consider briefly how a legal device called a *trust* may add flexibility to a will and may even permit a decedent, after death, to control or limit the use of his or her estate by the individuals who inherited it.

Inheritance When There Is No Will

Law Applicable to Intestate Succession

There are no federal inheritance laws other than taxing statutes, but with our English common law background, our state inheritance laws (except Louisiana, which has a civil law background) are similar to one another. In a move toward achieving still greater uniformity among the states, the National Conference of Commissioners on Uniform State Laws has prepared, and submitted to the states for adoption, the Uniform Probate Code (UPC). Because of its increasing popularity, reference is made throughout this chapter to the UPC.

Usual Order of Intestate Succession

The laws of descent and distribution are designed to assure that an intestate's estate will pass primarily to his or her surviving spouse (wife or husband) and surviving issue, that is, lineal descendants, i.e. children, grandchildren, great grandchildren.

Under the UPC an intestate estate, after all debts have been paid, passes to eligible heirs in the order shown on Table 23.1 on p. 472.

Representation, referred to in Table 23.1, means that when a person who would have inherited from an intestate has died before the intestate and that individual leaves issue (children, grandchildren, and so on), such issue share equally the inheritance their parent would have received.

Intestate descent and distribution can best be understood by analyzing two hypothetical situations. For the first, assume that David dies intestate. His estate, after all debts and taxes have been paid, is valued at $350,000. David is survived by his wife and three children as well as by his mother, a sister, and a brother (see Figure 23.1).

Applying the UPC to this state of facts, since David is survived by his widow and more than one child, the widow receives $50,000 plus one-half of the remainder of the estate, totaling $200,000, and

Figure 23.1 Distribution of Estate to Spouse and Children

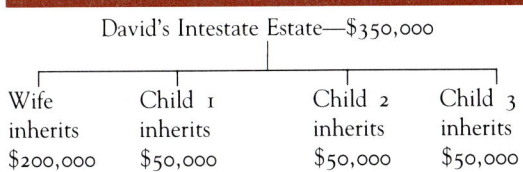

David's Intestate Estate—$350,000

Wife inherits $200,000	Child 1 inherits $50,000	Child 2 inherits $50,000	Child 3 inherits $50,000

Table 23.1 UPC Order of Inheritance of Intestate Estate

Eligible person	Entitled to
Surviving spouse:	
If no surviving issue or parent of decedent	Entire estate
If also surviving issue of decedent	$50,000 and one-half of balance of estate
If also surviving parent of decedent but no surviving issue	$50,000 and one-half of balance of estate
Surviving issue:	
If no surviving spouse of decedent	Entire estate in equal shares by representation
If also a surviving spouse of decedent	One-half of estate after spouse's $50,000
Surviving parent or parents of decedent:	
If also a surviving spouse	One-half of estate after spouse's $50,000
If no surviving spouse	Entire estate in equal shares
None of the above, but there are surviving brothers and sisters of decedent	Entire estate in equal shares by representation
None of the above, but there are surviving grandparents or issue of decedent's grandparents	Entire estate in equal shares by representation
None of the above	Entire estate escheats (becomes the property of) the state

the children equally divide the balance of the estate. David's mother, sister, and brother receive nothing because heirs in more preferred positions inherit the entire estate.

As another example, assume that Alice dies intestate, leaving no spouse or children. Alice is survived by her sister, Donna, who is married to Richard. She is also survived by a nephew and a niece, the children of her brother, Ben, who died some years ago. Ben's widow, Betty, is still living. Alice's estate of $360,000 will be distributed as shown in Figure 23.2.

As Alice is survived by no closer kin than her sister and the children of her deceased brother, Al-

Figure 23.2 Distribution of Intestate Estate to Immediate Family

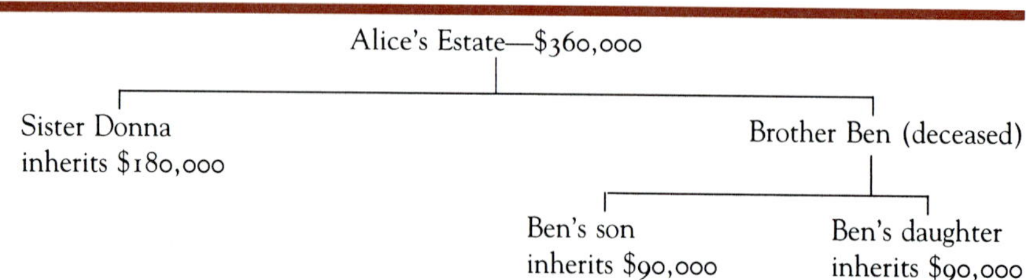

ice's estate is divided in half between them. The sister, Donna, inherits $180,000 and the brother's children, by right of representation of their father, Ben, inherit the remaining $180,000, dividing that sum equally between them, regardless of their ages. If Ben had been alive when Alice died, he would have inherited one-half her estate and his children would have inherited nothing. Although the sister's husband, Richard, and the brother's widow, Betty, were both alive when Alice died, they do not inherit from Alice because, not being her blood relatives, they are not in the inheritance chain.

Two of the more important differences between the UPC and the common law schemes for the distribution of intestate estates are:

1 Under the common law there is no preference of $50,000 to the surviving spouse. (See Table 23.1.)
2 Under the common law, when no spouse, child, or immediate family survive the decedent, the estate is divided among the closest blood relatives of the decedent even though those relatives may be so far removed that they did not share the same grandparents with the intestate. Such a distant heir has been labeled a "laughing heir."

Succession in Special Situations

Certain individuals to whom the regular order of distribution of intestate estates does not apply are: (1) an adopted child, (2) an illegitimate child, (3) a child who has received a substantial gift from an intestate parent in the parent's lifetime, and (4) an individual who becomes ineligible to inherit.

Adopted Child. Generally, an adopted child is in effect transplanted into the adopting family and out of the natural family. The adopted child acquires all the rights of a natural child of the adoptive parents and is entirely cut off from any right to inherit from a natural parent who dies intestate.

Illegitimate Child. In all states an illegitimate child is an heir of its mother. Although there is no uniformity among the states as to how an illegitimate child becomes the heir of its natural father, the more modern view is that such a child inherits from its intestate father if the parent-child relationship can be established according to the laws of the state having jurisdiction.

Advancements (Gifts) to Children. Practically all states apply the *principle of advancements* in intestate distribution. In determining each child's share of an intestate's estate, a probate court takes into account any substantial gifts (advancements) previously given by the parent to any of his or her children. In this way the total benefits the children receive are equalized. In some states, and under the UPC, for a gift to be considered an advancement against an inheritance there must be some written evidence that it was so intended.

Ineligible Heir. Under the UPC, an individual who "intentionally and feloniously killed" (the ingredients of murder) the decedent is ineligible to inherit from the victim. Accordingly, if someone normally eligible to inherit has been convicted not of *murder* of the decedent but of some lesser homicide (such as manslaughter), where there is no intent to kill, he or she may still be eligible to inherit.

Inheritance When There Is a Will

What Is a Will?

A will is a person's instructions for the disposition of his or her property after death. A will usually names an executor or executrix to administer the estate and may also appoint a guardian for minor children.

Why Make a Will?

If a decedent leaves no will, his or her heirs inherit according to state intestacy laws as above outlined. Why, then, should a person go to the trouble and expense of making a will? The answer is that the state distributes an estate in a cold and uncompromising manner while a will expresses personal desires as to who will inherit the property and how it will be divided among the beneficiaries. The state gives no consideration to the needs of those who inherit nor to whether the decedent and the heirs were on friendly terms. Moreover, no provision is made by the state for gifts to a church, to charity, or to close friends. A will is the means whereby the owner of property may make the ultimate demonstration of affection, compassion, and gratitude. Through a will a business person may direct how his or her business interests will be disposed of. A will also makes possible the settlement of an estate, particularly one of appreciable size, with a minimum of delay and expense to those left behind. Thus, meaning is given to the cryptic sentence that opened this chapter.

Requisites for a Valid Will

To be valid, a will must be in the form and executed in the manner prescribed by law. In addition, the *testator* (the person who executes the will) must have, when executing the will, (1) the requisite mental capacity (called *testamentary capacity*), and (2) the intent to make a will (called *testamentary intent*). If either of these requirements is absent, the purported will is void and the decedent died intestate. Until the maker of a will dies, it is not effective for any purpose and may be modified or revoked by the testator at any time.

Testamentary Capacity. Testamentary capacity has two elements: (1) the testator must have attained statutory age (usually 18 years) *before the will is executed (signed)* and (2) at the time of its execution must have had the mental capacity required by law.

Age. Pursuant to the above rule, if you made a will when you were 16 years old it is *not* a valid will. Nor does it become valid when you reach the statutory age. In order to have a valid will you must, after reaching statutory age, execute (sign) a new will (or re-execute your old will) in the manner required by the law of the state in which you live.

Mental capacity. Different courts apply different tests to determine whether or not a testator had the mental capacity to make a will. It can be said generally that you possessed the mental capacity to make a valid will if, at the time it was executed: (1) you knew you were signing a will, (2) you had the *capacity* to know the natural objects of your bounty and the nature and extent of your property, and (3) you were able to make an orderly disposition of it. A perfect memory is not an element of mental capacity. It is not necessary that you know who all your relatives are, nor must you remember all your property, its location, or its value.

Soundness of mind sufficient to make a will is not the same as the soundness of mind and mental capacity required to enter into a contract. Ordinarily, less mental capacity is required to make a valid will than to conduct regular business affairs. A testator need not be of or above average intelligence and, in fact, may have a very low I.Q.; may be very sick or very old; or may even be under a guardianship and still be legally competent to make a valid will.

Testamentary Intent. Testamentary intent is a necessary element of every will. It is present if the words of a will make clear that the instrument is intended to dispose of the signer's property effective *upon his or her death.* Although a will makes a gratuitous transfer of property, a transfer by will is not the same as an ordinary gift. To illustrate the difference, assume that Alice hands her ring to Marcy saying, "Here is my pearl ring. Take it; I'm giving it to you." Alice has made a gift to Marcy who now owns the ring. But if Alice includes in her will a provision stating, "I give my pearl ring to Marcy," this is not a gift at the present time but only the expression of an intention of what shall be done with the ring after Alice dies. Until that time (because a will does not become effective until the testator's death), Alice remains owner of the ring. At any time before her death Alice may change her mind and sell the ring, give it to anyone she chooses, or change her will and leave the ring to someone other than Marcy.

Fraud; undue influence. If a bequest in a will is made as a result of fraud, duress, or undue influence on the testator by another, or if the testator is mistaken as to the nature of the instrument he or she is signing, the will does not reflect the true intentions of the testator and testamentary intent is absent. The conditions which establish fraud, duress, and undue influence, discussed in contract formation, are equally applicable in the execution of a will.

The question whether undue influence was exercised arises most frequently when the person alleged to have so acted occupied a confidential relationship to the testator. Someone in a confidential relationship to a testator might be, for example, a close family member, friend, housekeeper, guardian, attorney, doctor, nurse, pastor, or financial adviser. If someone in such a close relationship is a beneficiary under a will, the probate court may *presume* that undue influence was exercised. In that event the person in the confidential position has the burden to prove that he or she did not, in fact, exert undue influence if that issue arises during the probate proceedings.

In the following case, an individual who was in a confidential relationship to a testator was presumed to have exerted undue influence.

CASE 23.1 Estate of Baker · 182 Cal. Rptr. 550 (Cal. App. 1982)

FACTS Dorothy Baker, an elderly woman, was told by her longtime friend Alta Potter that she (Alta) was in contact with the spirits of Dorothy's stepmother, Mary, and with a cousin, both of whom had died. Dorothy believed that Alta, a stockbroker, was a true psychic and medium. Dorothy's subsequent conduct, guided by the messages from her mother and cousin as communicated to her by Alta, was so bizarre (for example, she was prevailed upon to kill her pet cats) that Dorothy was alienated from her relatives and friends. In addition, she terminated her relationship with her own stockbroker and turned over her securities account to Alta.

At Dorothy's request, Alta recommended a lawyer to prepare Dorothy's will. The will was executed in 1977 in the lawyer's office but Alta was not present. In the will, Dorothy made small gifts to members of her immediate family but left the bulk of her estate to Alta, who was also named as executrix, and to Alta's grandson.

Alta told Dorothy that she (Dorothy) had to take a trip to Peru or her mother and cousin would be "earthbound" and Alta might not be able to communicate with them again. Dorothy hesitated about going because she was then 81 years of age, had had several heart attacks, and the doctor had warned her against going to high altitudes. However, Alta insisted and Dorothy and Alta went to Peru where Dorothy had another coronary attack. When she returned home she was hospitalized and died the following month.

Alta offered the will for probate. Clarence, Dorothy's brother, opposed probate of the clauses in the will in favor of Alta and Alta's grandson. Clarence alleged that Dorothy executed the will under the undue influence of Alta who stood in a confidential relationship to her. (Other issues raised by Clarence are not here discussed.) The lower court granted Clarence's petition and Alta appealed.

OPINION LILLIE, Acting Presiding Justice. . . . Undue influence consists of conduct which subjugates the will of the testator to the will of another and causes the testator to make a disposition of his property contrary to and different from that which he would have done had he been permitted to follow his own inclination or judgment. A presumption of undue influence arises when there is a concurrence of the following elements: (1) the existence of a confidential or fiduciary relationship between the testator and the person alleged to have exerted the undue influence; (2) active participation by such person in the preparation or execution of the will; and (3) undue benefit to such person or another person under the will thus procured.

. . . The evidence establishes the existence of the first element. . . . "Confidential and fiduciary relations are, in law, synonymous, and may be said to exist whenever trust and confidence is reposed by one person in the integrity and fidelity of another." . . . Nor can it be denied that Alta . . . unduly profited under Dorothy's will. . . . Dorothy believed Alta to be a true psychic and medium. . . . Alta thus obtained total control of Dorothy's mind.

Activity on the part of the proponent in procuring execution of the will may be established by inference, that is, by circumstantial evidence. . . . In determining whether undue influence was exerted by the proponent upon the testator in the execution of his

CASE 23.1 Continued

will, the jury is not limited to the actual time the will was executed, but may consider facts bearing upon undue influence both before and after execution so long as they tend to show such influence when the will was executed. . . . Nor need the one using the undue influence be present in person at the time of the execution of the document if the influence is present to constrain the party from exercising his free will.

. . . . Alta produced evidence that she was not present at the execution of the will; but that fact alone does not, as a matter of law, overcome the inference of undue influence. . . which may be drawn from other evidence. . . . On this record we must sustain the jury's implied finding that. . . [Alta] did not meet the burden of overcoming the presumption of undue influence. . . .

JUDGMENT The judgment is affirmed.

Mistake. If a person signs an instrument not knowing that it is a will, there is no testamentary intent and the purported will is void. A different rule is applied, however, where a testator knowingly makes a will and, based upon a mistaken belief, makes or omits to make a bequest. Such a mistake does *not* invalidate a will.

For instance, suppose that Cecile heard a false report that her friend Betty lost her house in a fire. Cecile then made a generous provision in her will for Betty. After Cecile's death any contest of that gift, based on the fact that Betty's house had not burned down, would fail because a court will not substitute itself for the testator and examine the testator's purpose in making a gift in a valid will. Such an activity would be tantamount to the court writing the testator's will. Or assume Cecile heard erroneously that her friend Henry, who lived in a distant city and to whom Cecile intended to make a bequest, had died. As a result, Cecile made no provision in her will for Henry. If after Cecile's death Henry should claim to be entitled to receive the gift Cecile had assured him would be his, the court will *not* change the provisions of the will to *create* a gift for Henry. The reason is obvious: to do so would amount to the court rewriting the testator's will. Such a court action would invite no end of litigation over the validity of bequests and the distribution of estates would be needlessly delayed. However, if Charlie had falsely told Cecile that Henry died in order that he (Charlie) would replace Henry in Cecile's will, then Charlie obtained his bequest through fraud. Henry, in an equity proceeding against Charlie, can have the court order Charlie to give up the amount of the bequest to Henry because Cecile left it to Charlie through Charlie's fraud.

Preparation of Wills

A will is a written instrument. It may be in any language as long as the testator understands what he or she is signing. A writing on paper purporting to be a will consists of all the sheets of paper intended by the testator to constitute the will and all the pages must be actually present when it is signed. Usually the pages are stapled or in some other way fastened together. If the sheets are not fastened together, those sheets which are found in proximity to each other and bear a logical continuity in the text constitute the will.

By a process called "incorporation by reference," the overwhelming majority of states permit a testator to make the contents of another document, even if not actually among the papers constituting his or her will, a part of a valid will. Although state rules for incorporation by reference may vary, it is generally required that the document must be in existence when the will is executed, the testator must intend the incorporation, and there must be appropriate reference within the will to the document to be incorporated.

Some states authorize only *formal* wills, others recognize both formal and *holographic* (handwritten), or *olographic,* wills. A few states also authorize oral, or *nuncupative,* wills. The latter involve personal property of limited value, usually made by soldiers or sailors under combat conditions. Because only formal and holographic wills are normally encountered, it is their execution we will now consider.

Formal Wills. Formal wills must be in writing, signed and witnessed. Some states require, in addition, that such wills be dated and published. In the law of wills "to publish" means to tell the witnesses that the paper being signed before them is a will.

Writing. While a formal will must be in writing, neither the kind of material upon which the writing appears nor the method of the writing is important. It may be handwritten, typed, printed, engraved, painted or otherwise recorded on any kind of material.

From the following case, it should be evident that the provisions of a will cannot be expanded by oral instructions of the testator.

CASE 23.2 In the Matter of the Estate of Reiman · 450 N.E.2d 928 (Ill. App. 4 Dist. 1983)

FACTS Paul Reiman executed in proper form a one-page will containing five paragraphs. Paragraph 1 directed the executor to pay all the testator's debts and the expenses of the administration of the estate. Paragraphs 2 and 3 made bequests of $10,000 each to Paul's mother and his sister. Paragraph 4 directed the executor to distribute the testator's remaining property "in accordance with the verbal guidelines given by me." Paragraph 5 nominates the executor. The heirs asked the court to strike out paragraph 4 as an improper testamentary direction. The court granted the heirs' motion and ordered the estate, except for the two $10,000 bequests, to be distributed according to the intestacy laws as there was no residual clause in the will disposing of any property remaining in the estate after all gifts described in the will were made. The executor appealed.

OPINION TRAPP, J.... No argument has been made by the executor that the direction to him to distribute in accordance with the testator's verbal guidelines as provided in paragraph 4 is a valid testamentary disposition. No such argument could, in fact, be made since it is fundamental that any disposition by way of verbal guidelines is prohibited by [law]....

...[A] bequest or devise... which is the subject of the testator's future directions, or directions which may be at any time changed after execution of the will, are void unless the directions are in writing and attested in conformity with the statute on wills....

Decedent's attempt to create an oral plan of testamentary devise by requesting the executor to follow "verbal guidelines" must fail....

[T]his court has no choice but to declare [paragraph 4 void].... As unfortunate as that result may be, it only underscores the necessity that a testator employ a knowledgeable scrivener to carry out his wishes.

JUDGMENT Affirmed.

Signing. A formal will must be signed by the testator in a manner that complies with state requirements. In most states, the law does not specify the particular place on a will where the testator's signature should be affixed. In some states, however, a will must be signed at the end to assure that no pages purporting to be part of the will are later added.

Under conditions established by state law, a testator may sign with a mark, such as "X," or the testator's name may be written as his or her signature by someone else at the testator's request and in the testator's presence. In this way an illiterate or paralyzed person may execute a valid will.

Dating. Generally, there is no requirement that a formal will be dated. However, if a testator executes several wills which contain contradictory provisions and none bears a date, the court would have great difficulty determining which was the most recent and therefore the effective will. To avoid what could be drawn-out and expensive litigation, any will should be dated when it is executed.

Witnessing. A formal will must be witnessed in the manner required by the state where the will is to be effective. If it is not properly witnessed the testator died intestate. A majority of the states (and the UPC) require two witnesses to the execution of a will but a few states require three witnesses. There is no requirement that a formal will be notarized, and if a will is not properly witnessed a notarization does not make it legally effective.[1]

Any person who, at the time of signing as a witness, is competent to be a witness in court may sign as a witness to a will. The witnesses must observe the testator sign the will or, in most states, if the will was signed outside the presence of the witnesses, the testator may show them the document and signature and acknowledge that it is his or her signature.

The UPC does not require the witnesses to sign in the testator's presence or in the presence of each other. Many states, however, do impose these requirements to achieve a legal execution of a will. In some states, and it is the better practice, the witnesses write their addresses as well as their signatures so that they can be located if needed to testify at the probate of the will. The contents of the will are not divulged to the witnesses.

Filing. A completed will is retained by the maker among his or her valuable papers or it may be held by an attorney or other person for safekeeping. Under the UPC, a will may be deposited in any court, according to its rules, for safekeeping. In that event it is kept confidential and may be withdrawn by the testator at any time. Upon the testator's death, the custodian of a will is required to file it with the appropriate court.

Figure 23.3 is a sample of a very short will. Note that despite its brevity it revokes all prior wills. To obviate any risk of pretermission the testator's family status is fully set out; it disposes of all the testator's property; in paragraph 4c it directs a "pour-over" to a trust; and it appoints an executrix. The attestation clause should satisfy the requirements of all states.

[1]However, the UPC provides that if the testator desires to have a "self-proved" will, the testator must attest to it before an officer authorized to administer oaths and there must be attached to the will an affidavit signed by the testator and two witnesses stating, in substance, that the testator was 18 or more years of age; that he or she voluntarily signed the will in the presence of the witnesses; and that the testator appeared to be of sound mind and was not acting under any undue influence. This type of will obviates the necessity of proof of execution during the probate proceeding.

Holographic Wills. Most states and the UPC recognize the validity of a handwritten, unwitnessed will, called a *holographic,* or *olographic,* will. In many states, a holographic will to be legally effective must be *entirely* in the testator's own handwriting. However, in some states and under the UPC, only the *material parts* of such a will need be in the testator's handwriting. In either event, it must be signed by the testator and, in some states, also dated. A holographic will is not witnessed, but if it is witnessed the validity of the will is not thereby effected.

Codicils to Wills

Assume that Agatha executed a valid will on March 15, 1980. Later, she decides to add to the will a gift to her niece, Cathy, who was born after the will was written. Must Agatha write a new will? She may if she wishes, but it is not necessary. Instead, she may add an amendment, modification, or addition to her will, called a "codicil." The codicil must be in the form required in that state for a valid will. A formal or a holographic will (in a state where holographic wills are recognized) may have one or more formal or holographic codicils. Agatha's codicil might read something like this:

> September 24, 1987. This is a codicil to my will executed by me on March 15, 1980. Paragraph 6(h) of that will is amended by adding, "I give $2,500 to my niece, Cathy." [signed] Agatha B. Doe.

A will, whether formal or holographic, and its codicils are read together. The date on which the last codicil was executed becomes the new date of the will to which it applies and the will is said to be "republished" as of that date. A valid codicil validates an invalid will or invalid provision in a will, and may revive a revoked will. For example, Tim threatened to tell Bob's employer that Bob had a criminal record unless Bob included a provision in his will leaving Tim $25,000. Bob, fearing that he would be fired, complied. This provision in Bob's will could be attacked because of the duress. But later, Bob wrote a legally valid codicil to his will

LAST WILL AND TESTAMENT

I, John Doe, a resident of the City of Miami, State of Florida, do declare this to be my last Will and Testament.

1. I revoke all previous Wills and Codicils heretofore made by me at any time.

2. I am married and the name of my wife is Jane Doe. All references in this Will to my wife are to her. I have never been previously married.

3. I have one child, Grace Doe, the issue of my marriage to my wife Jane. I have never had any other children.

4. I give, devise and bequeath all of my property, real, personal, and mixed, wherever situated as follows:

a. I give One Thousand Dollars to the American Cancer Society, to be used by it for research purposes.

b. I give One Thousand Dollars to my alma mater, The University of Florida, Gainesville, Florida, to be added to its general scholarship fund.

c. I direct my executrix to transfer out of any money or property within my estate, One Hundred Thousand Dollars to the trustee of the Grace Doe Trust, established by me prior to the execution of this Will, for the benefit of my daughter Grace, to be added to and administered as a part of that trust.

d. I give all the rest and residue of my property to my wife, Jane Doe, in fee simple. However, if she does not survive me then I give all of such property to the said Grace Doe Trust, to be administered as a part of that trust estate. And if my daughter, Grace Doe, does not survive both me and my wife, then I give all of said property to the American Cancer Society.

5. I nominate and appoint my wife, Jane Doe, as the executrix of this Will, to serve without bond. However, if she should predecease me or for any reason fails to qualify or declines to act as executrix, then I nominate and appoint Abner Archer, my attorney, as the executor of this Will, to serve with bond.

I subscribe my name to this Will this the first day of April 1985 in the City of Miami, County of Dade, in the State of Florida, in the presence of Mary Smith, Alfred T. Jones, and John P. Green, attesting witnesses, who subscribe their names hereto at my request and in my presence.

John Doe

ATTESTATION CLAUSE

On this the 1st day of April, 1985, John Doe, known to us to be the person whose signature appears at the end of this Will, declared to us the undersigned, that the foregoing instrument, consisting of two pages of paper, including the page on which we have signed as witnesses, was his Will. He then signed the Will in our presence and at his request, in his presence and in the presence of each other, we now sign our names as witnesses.

Mary Smith residing at 12 Main Street, Miami, Fla.

Alfred T. Jones residing at 44 Hope Road, Miami, Florida

John P. Green residing at 5 Seacoast Rd. Miami, Fla.

Figure 23.3 Form of a Short Will

leaving his automobile to his sister. Because of the codicil, after Bob's death Tim's duress can no longer be asserted to defeat the gift to Tim because the valid codicil updated and validated the will which contained Tim's gift.

Limitations on Disposition by Will

It is generally said that a competent testator may make any disposition by will that he or she chooses. However, the law makes exceptions to this rule for the protection of a surviving spouse and children. In some states the law also imposes limitations upon the gifts that witnesses may receive through wills they witness.

Protection of Surviving Spouse. All states have laws which are aimed at preserving to a surviving wife or husband some portion of the estate of his or her deceased spouse. These laws take one of three forms:

1 A few states apply the common law right of *dower.* Dower entitles a surviving wife to a life interest, free from her husband's debts, in one-third of the *real property* her husband had owned at any time during their marriage, and in which she did not, during the marriage, join in a deed conveying it to someone else. A surviving husband has a somewhat similar right called a *right of curtesy.*

2 Because estates today frequently consist of both real and personal property, the right of dower does not sufficiently protect a surviving spouse. Therefore, most states and the UPC have done away with dower and have substituted the right of a surviving spouse to elect to receive, instead of the inheritance provided by the decedent's will, a statutory *elective* (also sometimes called a "forced" share) of the deceased spouse's estate. Under the UPC the elective share is computed under rather complex rules established by the UPC. A surviving spouse who elects to take such a share is said to "take against the will."

3 Nine states (called community property states)—Arizona, California, Idaho, Louisiana, Nevada, New Mexico, Texas, Washington, and Wisconsin—protect the interests of a surviving spouse by providing that all property, real and personal, acquired *during* the marriage through the efforts of *either* spouse, and the income from such property, is *community property* owned by *both* the husband and the wife. All other property owned by either spouse is *separate property.* Thus, money and property owned by Margaret before her marriage to Jim is Margaret's separate property; and property Jim inherited from his parents after his marriage to Margaret is Jim's separate property.

A testator in a community property state may by will leave his or her *separate* property to anyone he or she chooses, but there are limitations upon the disposal of *community* property because each spouse owns an undivided one-half of that property. So if Jim after marrying Margaret starts a business with money he has earned since the date of that marriage, the business is owned by *both* Jim and Margaret. Jim may, by will, dispose of his half of the business to anyone he pleases. However, he cannot dispose of the other half because that half belongs to Margaret. At Jim's death she does not inherit her half from Jim because she already owns it by virtue of community property law. If Jim dies without leaving a valid will, under community property law and the UPC his half of the business and his share of any other community assets also belong to Margaret, his widow, who then owns all of their community property.

Protection of Surviving Children. A parent may, if he or she so chooses, completely disinherit a child. Instead of providing for a child by will, the parent may make gifts to more distant relatives, friends, charities, or even to strangers. However, for the disinheritance of a child to be legally effective it must be evident *in the will* that the testator *intentionally* gave the child nothing. Such an intention can be expressed by mentioning the child by name anywhere in the will and making no gift or only a nominal gift to that child, or it may be by a statement specifically disinheriting the child.

Generally, if it is *not* evident in the will that the parent intentionally omitted his or her child, regardless of the child's age, the child is said to be *pretermitted. A pretermitted child inherits as though its parent died intestate.* The will otherwise remains effective for all other beneficiaries.

Note that in the sample will (Figure 23.3), all the decedent's children are mentioned by name. This obviates any potential pretermission problem.

The case which follows illustrates pretermission.

CASE 23.3 Smith v. Crook · 206 Cal. Rptr. 524 (Cal. 1984)

FACTS Genevieve Rufran died on December 11, 1974, bequeathing her residuary estate to her three surviving children, the respondents in this action. A fourth child, June Smith, a daughter of Genevieve, had died before her mother. June had three children, the appellants, who were living when Genevieve, their grandmother, died. Genevieve's will mentioned her deceased child, June, but it made no mention of June's surviving children. Those children brought suit to establish their rights as pretermitted heirs. By deposition the lawyer who drafted Genevieve's will said she instructed him to exclude her daughter June as a beneficiary, stating that "she didn't want anything to go to June nor her issue."

The trial court found that decedent intentionally omitted the plaintiff grandchildren from sharing in her estate. The grandchildren appealed.

OPINION RACANELLI, P. J.... Under the provisions of section 90 of the Probate Code, a testator's children or children of a deceased child who are omitted from a will are entitled to share pursuant to the laws of intestacy "unless it appears *from the will* that such omission was intentional."...

The statutory purpose is to guard against the unintentional omission of the decedent's natural heirs from a share in the estate due to oversight, accident, mistake, or an unexpected change of condition... [T]he statute requires that in order for a testator to disinherit his lineal descendants, the intent to do so must be unmistakably expressed; it must appear on the face of the will.... extrinsic evidence may *not* be considered.... When such intent does not so appear, then the statutory presumption—that the failure to name a child or grandchild in a will was unintentional—must prevail....

.... There is no language in the will from which it appears that the testator had her grandchildren in mind and intentionally omitted them when she made her will;...

While extrinsic evidence is admissible to resolve ambiguities in a will... such evidence is inadmissible to explain or contradict an omission on the face of the will....

We conclude... there is nothing on the face of the will which demonstrates that the testator had her deceased daughter's surviving children in mind and intentionally omitted to provide for them. Under such circumstances, the presumption of section 90 stands unrebutted and entitles appellants as pretermitted heirs to share in the estate in accordance with the laws of intestate succession.

JUDGMENT Judgment reversed....

Witness as Beneficiary. Under the UPC a witness to a will, if named as a beneficiary, may inherit according to the will's terms. However, many states take a more restrictive attitude. Following the common law practice, in order to reduce the possibility of fraud, duress, or undue influence in the execution of wills, these states restrict a person who is one of a required number of witnesses to a will from inheriting any more than he or she would have received had the testator died intestate.

Revocation of Wills

A will is without legal effect until the testator dies. Until then, he or she may at any time *revoke* (cancel) the will. After a will has been revoked, it cannot be made effective again except by adding a codicil to it. Under certain circumstances, the revocation of a later will which revokes a former will revives the former one.

A revocation may be either (1) by the intentional act of the testator, or (2) by operation of law.

Revocation by Act of Testator

A will may be revoked by a testator either: (1) by a physical act to the document, or (2) by executing a later will.

Revocation by Physical Act. To revoke a will by physical act, the testator must, *with the intent to revoke,* do something physical to the will which the state says constitutes a revocation, such as burning, tearing, or obliterating it (making it unreadable), or drawing lines through the signature. Most states permit the *partial revocation* of a will by a physical act directed to the part the testator wants to revoke. No witnesses are required for the physical revocation (or partial revocation) of either a formal or a holographic will. State statutes establish conditions under which a physical act of revocation may be accomplished by another person under the testator's direction.

Revocation by Later Instrument. A testator may also revoke a will by executing a later will which either expressly or by implication revokes the earlier one.

Revocation by express words. To remove any doubt as to the testator's intentions, a will usually contains a statement such as this: "This will revokes all wills and codicils heretofore made by me at any time." A subsequent formal will may revoke a holograph and a subsequent holograph may revoke a formal will.

As is shown by the next case, the revoking words must be a part of a later will or codicil.

CASE 23.4 In re Estate of Harry Feir · 701 P.2d 3 (Ariz. App. 1985)

FACTS In 1979 the decedent, Harry Feir, then a resident of New Jersey, executed a will prepared for him at his request by attorney Kantor. On December 8, 1980, Feir sent a typewritten letter to the attorney in these words: "Plese be advised that I am VOIDING my will which you prepared for me on November 10, 1979. Thank you. Cordially yours, Harry Feir." The letter was signed before a notary public. Feir moved to Arizona in 1981 where he died in 1983. The original will and a copy of the typewritten letter of December 8, 1980, were found in the decedent's safe-deposit box.

Feir's sister, the appellee, made application for intestacy proceedings of the decedent's estate. Kantor, as executor, the appellant, opposed that application and filed petition for the probate of Feir's will. A judgment was entered in favor of Feir's sister and Kantor appealed.

OPINION HATHAWAY, J.... Appellant contends that the letter did not revoke the will. He argues that the court's ruling overlooks the similar statutory provisions of both New Jersey and Arizona... [that]:

> Revocation by writing or by act. A will or any part thereof is revoked by either: (1) A subsequent will which revokes the prior will or part expressly or by inconsistency. (2) Being burned, torn, cancelled, obliterated or destroyed, with the intent and for the purpose of revoking it....

This section is similar to § 2-507 of the Uniform Probate Code.... The official comment to [that] section explains that "revocation of a will may be by either a subsequent will or *an act done to the document.*" It is uncontested that the letter was not a subsequent will. It obviously does not comply with the statutory requirements for a will.

...The letter did not call for nor accomplish any act performed to the document. Although that letter may have expressed the testator's intent to revoke the will, the

CASE 23.4 Continued

omission of effecting a cancellation of the document is crucial and will not be overlooked... A will must be revoked in the manner prescribed by statute... The intent to revoke must be accompanied by an act which appears on the purported will...

JUDGMENT The judgment of the trial court is reversed....

Revocation by implication. A later will which is *entirely inconsistent* with an earlier one revokes the earlier instrument by implication even though no specific words of revocation appear in the later will. An example of two entirely inconsistent wills might be this: Peter's will names Arlene, Bess, and Carl as the sole beneficiaries; Peter's later will names three entirely different people the sole beneficiaries. The earlier will is revoked by implication. If the second will made Arlene, Eve, and Fred the sole beneficiaries, (that is, one of the original beneficiaries plus other new ones) the two wills would not have been *entirely* inconsistent. Both wills would be read together, possibly resulting in Arlene receiving two gifts—one under each will—a result which the testator really did not intend. The use of appropriate language could so easily have obviated the problem.

Revocation by Operation of Law

Under the UPC so much of a will as benefits a spouse is automatically, by operation of law, revoked when the parties are divorced or when their marriage is annulled. Unless the testator made a new will in favor of the divorced spouse, his or her property is disposed of as though the divorced spouse had predeceased the testator. As a mere separation of the parties is not a divorce, a separation does not revoke a will by operation of law. However, if the separation is accompanied by a complete property settlement, this constitutes a renunciation by the affected spouse of all benefits under a prior will. In some states which have not adopted the UPC, even a divorce with a property settlement does not cause a revocation of a will unless, in the settlement, the spouse expressly gives up the right to inherit by will.

Probate

Probate

Probate is the legal proceeding concerning the administration and disposition of both intestate and testate estates. During probate, an executor or administrator is appointed; will contests are tried in court; the decedent's assets are marshalled (gathered); the decedent's estate is inventoried; his or her taxes, other debts, and the costs of administration are discharged; and the remainder of the estate is distributed to the intestate heirs or to the beneficiaries under the will if the decedent died testate.

States have made many changes in their probate procedures in recent years. These changes were designed to obviate the need for the formal probate of small estates and to reduce the time required and the costs of securing court approvals for the various steps involved in formal probate proceedings. As an investigation of the details of probate administration would be far beyond the scope of a business law text, we need note merely that the UPC establishes an "informal" abbreviated probate procedure, available when the estate is small (one valued at not more than $5,000). It also provides for "formal" and more detailed "supervised" procedures in all other estates.

The UPC provides, in effect, that if someone dies intestate his or her real and personal property passes by operation of law to the heirs, subject to the rights of creditors. On the other hand, the title to any property passing by will cannot be established until the will is admitted to probate, that is, found by the court to be valid. Until that time the will has no legal effect.

Generally, a court applies the law of the state or states where the decedent's real property (land and buildings) is located to determine the validity and effect of a will upon that property. However, insofar as the personal property is concerned, a court generally applies the law of the state where the decedent was domiciled (his or her permanent home).

Will Contests. Any person who has a direct interest in a testate estate and who would be economically benefited if the will were set aside may contest its admission to probate. Contest may be based on any claim against the will's validity, such as that it was not properly executed or that the decedent was subject to undue influence. The issues raised are usually tried before a jury and the ordinary rules of evidence are applied.

Appointment of Personal Representative. Both intestate and testate estates are administered during probate by a *personal representative* of the decedent appointed by the probate court or by its registrar by an instrument called "letters of appointment," "letters of administration," or "letters testamentary." Although the UPC does not use such titles, in most states a personal representative of someone who died without a valid will is called an *administrator or administratrix;* if the decedent died testate, the personal representative, who normally had been designated in the testator's will, is called an *executor or executrix.*

Usually a personal representative is required to file a bond with the court to protect the estate against the possibility of its being improperly handled. In most jurisdictions, this requirement is waived where a will contains a provision stating that the executor (executrix) need not file a bond. Under the UPC no bond is required in an informal proceeding unless a special administrator is appointed.

Functions of Personal Representative. Personal representatives of testate and intestate estates have similar functions and obligations to their respective estates. Each represents the decedent. As such, he or she takes the following actions: (1) publishes notice to estate creditors of the need to file their claims within the time allowed by law; (2) gives required notices to heirs or beneficiaries; (3) takes possession of, inventories, and preserves the decedent's property; (4) pays taxes and allowable claims of creditors against the estate; and (5) distributes the remainder, if any, to the heirs or beneficiaries.

In addition, the UPC provides that "a personal representative has the same power over the title to property of the estate that an absolute owner would have, in trust however, for the benefit of the creditors and others interested in the estate." The Code then lists twenty-seven transactions which a personal representative, acting reasonably for the benefit of interested persons, may engage in. These include, among others, to perform, compromise, or refuse performance of decedent's contracts, manage and dispose of assets, make repairs, insure property, compromise claims, and employ necessary assistants. In states that have not yet adopted the Code, a personal representative may have less freedom of action.

Claims against Estates. A major purpose of probate administration is to protect the decedent's creditors and to settle all valid claims against his or her estate. "Nonclaim" statutes prescribe the time and manner in which claims against an estate must be filed. Usually claims must be filed within four months from the date of the first publication of notice to creditors (or within three years after decedent's death if there has been no notice by publication). Traditionally the notice must be published once a week for three consecutive weeks in a newspaper of general circulation. If a claim is not filed within the prescribed time, then payment is forever barred. Because of the especially short period of time within which claims must be filed against an estate, any businessperson who foresees the possibility that one of his or her customers may die owing the business money should ascertain the law as to how and when claims against an estate should be filed.

The personal representative receives and considers the claims that are filed and pays those determined to be valid. State statutes establish the order in which claims against an estate are paid. Costs of administration, funeral expenses, taxes, and reasonable and necessary costs of decedent's last illness take priority over other claims.

Distribution of Assets. After the costs of administration and all valid claims have been settled, the personal representative distributes the remaining money and property to the heirs or beneficiaries. An intestate estate is distributed in accordance with state inheritance laws discussed at the start of this chapter. A testate estate is distributed in accordance with the terms of the decedent's will and, if a will does not dispose of all the assets of an estate, inheritance (intestacy) laws then govern the distribution of the remainder.

In the case of a testate estate, there are four possible problem areas which can arise in its distribution. These are: (1) when there is ambiguity or mistake in the words of a will, (2) when there are insufficient assets in the estate to satisfy all the specified gifts, (3) when distribution to a named beneficiary is impossible because the beneficiary has predeceased the testator, and (4) when property described in the will is not in the estate.

Ambiguity or mistake in will. If more than one meaning can be given to a provision of a will, that provision is *ambiguous*. An example of ambiguity is a will which states, "I give my niece Sarah $100" and the testator has two nieces named Sarah—one Sarah Smith and the other Sarah Jones. Which Sarah inherits the $100? The court, after taking evidence to ascertain the testator's true intent, decides which of the girls inherits the $100.

In another will there may be a *mistake* in the description of the beneficiary or of the property covered by a devise (gift of real property). An example of mistake would be if Leo's will makes a gift of "my house at 684 Oxford Lane" but, in fact, the address of the house is 184 Oxford Avenue. Again, the court takes evidence to determine which house Leo owned and thereby meant in his will.

The following hypothetical case illustrates a type of mistake in a will which requires a different conclusion from that reached in the preceding paragraph. Alice asks her lawyer to draft her will, leaving, among other gifts, a diamond ring to Mary. The secretary's notes were garbled and she wrote, "I give my ______ to Mary," intending to ask her employer how the blank space should be filled. Unfortunately, the secretary forgot and the sentence was never completed. Alice, not noticing the omission, signed the will as it was written. Even though after Alice's death the lawyer clearly recalls her instructions, a court will *not* construe the will to make a bequest of the ring to Mary. Such a construction would mean the court is writing Alice's will, an undertaking beyond its power.

Insufficient assets in estate. It sometimes happens that the assets in an estate are insufficient, after all the estate taxes and debts are paid, to complete all of the gifts described in the will. The question then arises, which gifts must be cut down or go unsatisfied?

Courts settle the question by ordering the executor to *abate* (reduce or not pay) bequests in the following order: residual bequests abate first; general bequests abate next; and specific bequests abate last. Demonstrative bequests have characteristics of both general and specific bequests and, as such, abate with them. The following illustrations should make clear the distinguishing characteristics of each of those classes of gifts. A provision of a will states:

1. "I give my gold watch to Alfred P. Jones." This is a *specific* bequest (gift of personal property) because it refers to a certain specified object. A specific bequest or devise is usually identified by the word "my."
2. "I give $500 to my sister Dorothy." This is a *general* bequest of any $500 that can be found in the estate either in cash or through the sale of real or personal property not otherwise the subject of a gift.
3. "I give my sister Beatrice $500 payable from the money Tom Brown owes me, but if he does not pay his debt, then the $500 is payable from my general estate." A gift worded in this manner is called a *demonstrative* bequest. If it cannot be satisfied out of the particular source designated, it is treated as a general bequest.
4. "I give my good friend Joe Green all the rest and residue of my estate." This is called a *residual* devise or bequest. Joe is entitled to whatever remains in the estate after all specific, demonstrative, and general gifts have been paid.

As a general rule, all gifts within a class abate proportionately and the entire class abates before abatement applies to the next succeeding class.

If a will contains no residual clause (makes no residual gift) and some assets still remain in the estate after all gifts have been satisfied, those assets are distributed in accordance with applicable intestacy laws.

Named beneficiary predeceased testator. If a beneficiary predeceased the testator or renounces a gift, the gift *lapses,* that is, it is of no effect and the designated property or money may be applied to satisfy other gifts or, if there are no unsatisfied gifts it will become part of the residual estate. Under two circumstances, however, there is no lapse: (1) where the will makes an alternative disposition of the property, such as a gift "to my cousin Arthur, if he is living and, if not, then to my cousin Joe," and (2) when an "anti-lapse" statute applies. The UPC anti-lapse clause provides, in effect, that when a gift is made to a blood relative who had the same grandparent as the testator and that relative predeceased the testator, survived by issue, the gift does not lapse but the issue inherit it by right of representation. The anti-lapse statutes of many states are broader than the UPC version and apply to the issue of the nearest blood relatives of the testator even though they may not have had common grandparents.

Specific property not in estate. If property called for in a *specific* gift is not in the estate, the gift is of no effect. This is called an *ademption by extinction.* Thus, if a will makes a gift to Louis of "my Chrysler car," and the testator had sold the Chrysler but there is a Buick in the estate, in most states Louis will not inherit the Buick. Although the majority of courts mechanically apply ademption by extinction, a growing number apply the testator's intentions to the facts and do not impose ademption by extinction if the property described in the will can be followed into some other form of property. In those states, Louis will inherit the Buick.

Ethical Obligations of Personal Representative. A personal representative is a *fiduciary,* that is, a person upon whom a special trust and confidence has been imposed. He or she is expected to show more than ordinary candor, consideration, and honesty in dealings on behalf of the decedent's estate. The representative is required to act in its best interests without taking personal advantage of the business he or she conducts, exercising the same care in managing the estate's affairs as a prudent person would employ in managing his or her own affairs. Such fiduciary responsibilities are not present in ordinary business relationships where people deal with each other at arm's length. A personal representative is not permitted to purchase anything from the estate nor to make any personal gain from his or her conduct of its affairs. If the representative does make such a gain, the money must be turned over to the estate. The representative may also be liable to the heirs or beneficiaries of the estate for any losses it suffers because of his or her mismanagement, breach of duty, or bad faith actions.

A personal representative is entitled to a reasonable compensation. In some states compensation is upon a scale fixed by statute dependent upon the size of the estate; in other states compensation is fixed by the court; and in still others, following the UPC, it may be determined by the personal representative himself or herself. It is not unusual for a personal representative, particularly when a member of the decedent's family, to waive compensation.

Trusts

To complete a discussion of wills, recognition should be given to the relation of trusts to wills. However, trusts are generally so far removed from business law that no more than a brief explanation of their function is justified in a book of this scope.

Unlike ordinary business relationships where people deal with one another at arm's length, a trust is a fiduciary relationship. A trust comes into being when a *maker* (also called *settlor* or *trustor*) conveys property to another person or entity, called a *trustee,* to hold its legal title for the benefit of a third party, the *beneficiary* (also called *cestui que trust* (pronounced "seddy kay trust"), or *trustant.*[2]

Figure 23.4 is an example of a simple trust.

A trust makes it possible for someone to convey property to a trustee with directions to pay the income earned by investment of the trust funds as well as the trust property itself to designated people at times well after the maker of the trust has died. In this way a trust may act as a very effective substitute for or augmentation to a will.

[2]*Resulting trusts* and *constructive trusts* are not within the above definition and are not discussed here. These trusts are essentially equitable remedies designed to protect the interests of owners of property.

I, (the *maker*) by these presents convey to NATIONAL BANK (the trustee) $300,000 (the trust fund) to invest such funds and to pay annually the interest earned thereon to my daughter, Anna (the beneficiary), until she reaches 21 years of age at which time the trust fund is to be paid to her and this trust will terminate. If my daughter Anna dies before reaching 21 years of age, upon her death the entire fund is to be paid to the American Cancer Society.

[The trustee's powers and obligations are set out].

Signed this the 4th day of March, 1988, at Boise, Idaho.

John Donor

Figure 23.4 Form of a Simple Trust

Creation of Trusts

A trust involving personal property may be created orally although usually it is created by written instrument. A trust involving real property, to satisfy the Statute of Frauds, should be in writing. The UPC provides for the registration of trusts by filing with the appropriate court a brief statement identifying and giving information about the trust.

A trust may be established for private or charitable purposes.

Private Trusts. Any trust not established for charitable purposes is a *private trust.* Normally, a private trust is established for the care, health, maintenance, support, and education of some particular person or group of people or even for the trustor himself or herself. It need not be so limited, however, and may be for any purpose not contrary to public policy. Unlike a charitable trust, a private trust comes to an end when the purposes for which it was established have been accomplished or can no longer be attained. For example, a trust established to send John through college ends when John is accidentally killed in his freshman year. Under property law there is a rule, called the *rule against perpetuities,* that governs how long a private trust may last.

A private trust may be: (1) a living (inter vivos) trust or (2) a testamentary trust.

Living (inter vivos) trusts. A trust that comes into being during the trustor's lifetime is called a "living," or *inter vivos,* (pronounced vy-vos), trust. The National Bank trust illustrated in Figure 23.4 is a simplified example of a living trust.

The courts in most states hold that a living trust may not be revoked by the trustor unless, when creating it, he or she in its writing reserved the power to revoke it. The courts in other states hold that a living trust may be revoked by the trustor unless at the time of its creation he or she provided that it was irrevocable.

A living trust whose provisions continue to be effective after the death of its maker drastically lessens both the time and the cost of probate. There is normally a reduction in probate costs because the estate of the maker of the trust was reduced by the value of the property transferred to the trust. Therefore, there is less property in the maker's estate subject to probate administration and costs.

A person may, by a will executed subsequent to the establishment of a living trust, direct the will's executor to transfer assets from the estate into the trust, adding them to assets already in the trust. Such a direction in a will is called a "pour-over" provision, meaning that assets are poured over from the estate into the trust. The sample will in Figure 23.3 contains a pour-over provision.

Testamentary trusts. A testamentary trust is a part of a will and, like the will of which it is a part, does not become effective until the death of the testator; until that time it may be revoked or modified by the testator-trustor. When the testator-trustor dies the assets he or she has designated in the will are transferred by the personal representative of the testator to the trustee and the testamentary trust comes into being.

Discretionary trusts. A trustee of either a living or a testamentary trust may be given wide discretionary authority; in that event a living or testamentary trust may also be called a "discretionary trust." For example, a trustee may be given the power to determine how or to whom the trust assets will be paid. In this way the needs of beneficiaries can be reviewed and judged long after the trustor has died.

Spendthrift trusts. Most states allow the establishment of *spendthrift trusts,* which are set up primarily to protect individuals who are unable to manage their own finances. In such a trust, the trustor directs that the beneficiary has no rights whatever in the corpus (capital) of the trust nor to its income until the beneficiary actually receives it. Therefore, if a creditor secures a judgment against the beneficiary, the creditor is unable to levy execution against the debtor-beneficiary's interest *in the trust fund* as it has not yet been received by him or her.

Charitable Trusts. A charitable trust is the name given to a trust solely devoted to a purpose which serves or benefits the general public, such as for the promotion of religion, education, health, the arts, or to help the poor. The rules for the establishment and administration of charitable trusts are more liberal than those pertaining to private trusts. For example, a charitable trust can continue to exist indefinitely. In addition, a court of equity, applying what is called the *cy pres doctrine* (pronounced "sigh pray") may devote the trust to another generally similar charitable purpose when it is impossible or impracticable to carry out the original purpose for which the trust was established. No like rule is applicable to a private trust.

Ethical Obligations of Trustees

A trustee, whether serving with or without compensation, is a fiduciary and owes extensive obligations to the beneficiaries of the trust. Among the most important of those obligations is the duty of absolute loyalty. The trustee must administer the trust in accordance with its terms, exercising at least the degree of care and expertise which a reasonably prudent businessperson would exercise in dealing with his or her own property and affairs. The trustee must take care of and preserve the trust property, enforcing all rights and claims to which the trust is entitled and defending any action that is brought against it.

A trustee is required to use reasonable care and skill to keep the trust estate productive and may make only such investments with trust funds as a prudent person would make in the disposition of his or her own funds, taking into consideration the probable income and the probable safety of the principal. This is known as the *prudent investor rule.*

If a trustee makes a private gain through breach of trust, he or she must turn over those profits to the estate. For instance, assume that trustee Tom, exceeding his authority as trustee, "borrows" $5,000 from the trust fund he administers. He invests this money in the stock market and, through good fortune, makes a considerable profit. The money Tom borrowed and the profit Tom made belong to the trust estate.

Summary

Property may be inherited under the rules of descent and distribution (applicable when a person dies without a valid will) or through the provisions of a properly executed will. To make a valid will, a testator must have both testamentary capacity and testamentary intent. While a person must have a sound mind to make a valid will, it is not necessary that he or she have sufficient mental capacity to carry on business affairs. If a person, in making a will, is subject to the fraud, duress, or undue influence of another, the maker is not expressing his or her testamentary intent and the will (or the portion thereof affected) is void.

A formal will must be in writing, signed and witnessed by the number of witnesses (usually two) required by that state. A holographic will (not authorized in all states) must be entirely or in its material parts in the testator's own handwriting, signed and, in most states, dated. A holographic will is not witnessed.

The rule that a testator may make any disposition of his or her property the testator wishes is subject to certain exceptions to protect a surviving spouse and children.

A testator may revoke a will by a physical act the state recognizes as a cancellation. A will may also be revoked by a later will which specifically revokes the earlier one or is entirely inconsistent with it. Depending upon state law, a divorce of the parties may also revoke a will.

In the absence of a will, the state, in laws of descent and distribution, fixes who is entitled to inherit from a decedent. Primarily, a surviving spouse and children inherit an intestate's property. If the intestate left no surviving spouse or children, those laws determine which of the blood relatives of the decedent are entitled to inherit the decedent's estate.

Both testate and intestate estates are administered by a personal representative in a proceeding called "probate." The personal representative (generally called "administrator" or "administratrix" in an intestate probate and "executor" or "executrix" when a testate estate is in probate) takes charge of and inventories the assets of the estate, gives notice to creditors to file claims, pays valid claims filed within the period established by law, and then distributes the remaining assets among the beneficiaries.

A trust is a fiduciary relationship wherein the maker of the trust conveys property to a trustee who holds legal title of the property for the benefit of another (the beneficiary). The trustee may make only such investments with trust funds as a prudent person would make in the disposition of his own funds. A trust created in the maker's lifetime is a living or inter vivos trust. A trust incorporated in a will is a testamentary trust. A trust that is solely for the benefit of the public is a charitable trust and is subject to more liberal rules for its formation and administration than apply to private trusts. A trust can add great flexibility to a will and is a major tool in estate planning.

Review Questions

1 In a community property state which has adopted the UPC, if one spouse dies without having made a will, leaving a mother, a surviving spouse, and two children, who inherits the decedent's estate and in what shares?

2 John, a widower, dies without having made a will, survived by **(a)** both his parents, **(b)** Agnes, his childless daughter, and **(c)** two grandchildren, Richard and Sonny, the children of his daughter Becky, who predeceased John. Applying the UPC, how is John's estate distributed?

3 At age 17 Susan makes a will dividing the estate she inherited from her grandmother in equal shares between the charity Recording for the Blind, her parents, and her sister. Susan becomes a well-known novelist. She dies at 35 years of age, having never married or changed her will. Susan's two parents and her sister and the charity all survive her. How is Susan's estate distributed?

4 Comment upon this statement: If a person has the capacity to enter into a contract, he or she has the capacity to make a will.

5 Contrast a gift by will and one by the physical act of giving.

6 Contrast fraud and duress in contract law with fraud and duress in the law of wills.

7 **(a)** Distinguish between a holographic will and a formal will. **(b)** Is it correct to say that in most states a person who has a large estate, consisting of both real and personal property, must make a formal will rather than a holographic will? Explain.

8 **(a)** How many witnesses must there be to a formal will? **(b)** To a holographic will?

9 How can a will be revoked?

10 Contrast the duties of an administrator with those of an executor.

11 **(a)** In the law of wills, what is meant by abatement? **(b)** How does it arise? **(c)** How does it operate?

12 **(a)** Distinguish between and give examples of residual, general, and specific legacies. **(b)** If a decedent dies intestate, does the same classification apply? Explain.

13 What is meant by the legal device called a trust?

14 Explain how a trust can add flexibility to a will.

15 Why is an executor, an administrator, or a trustee subject to special ethical obligations in the performance of his or her duties?

Case Problems

1 Charles suspected that his wife, Nora, was having an affair with Fred. Charles warned Fred to stay away from his house. One evening, Charles saw his wife come into the house with Fred. Charles pointed a loaded shotgun at Fred. In the struggle that followed, the gun was discharged and Nora was killed. Charles was found guilty of manslaughter. Nora left no will. The probate court held that because he had intentionally brought about the armed confrontation resulting in Nora's death, Charles could not inherit from her. Do you think an appellate court would reverse the probate court's decision? Why or why not?

2 In 1975 a conservator was appointed over Hazel's person and estate. It had been alleged that, because of senile dementia, she was unable to care for herself both financially and personally; she was not eating properly and was unclean and incontinent; her home was unkempt and filthy; she seemed "kind of dreamy"; she had lent large sums of money to friends without taking any note or promises to repay; and she was easily confused and occasionally forgot dates, the time of the year, and what she was eating. Sometimes Hazel appeared extremely senile and at other times she seemed more normal and better oriented. In 1976 Hazel, then 89 years old, executed her formal will. The two witnesses to it testified she was mentally competent and knew that she was signing her will. Others testified that in the 1975–1977 period she was alert and able to carry on a coherent conversation. Hazel died in 1981. When her will was offered in probate, her competence to execute the will was questioned. How should the question be answered? Give the reasons for your answer.

3 Zech, who was 90 years old and infirm, lived with his friend Mary Tesch and her husband. At Zech's request, Mary called a lawyer who came to the house, and Zech had him prepare a will leaving all his property to Mary. Zech signed the will in the presence of the lawyer and his assistant. Later, Zech was moved to a nursing home and a bank was named as the conservator of his affairs. Mary and her husband often went to visit him but his relatives seldom did. After Zech died, his relatives objected to probate of his will, claiming (1) that because his affairs had to be handled by a conservator Zech was not competent to make a valid will; (2) that Mary had exercised undue influence upon Zech because he lived with the Tesch's, who had every opportunity to sway him at the time he made his will; and (3) that Mary continued to "butter him up" later by visiting him often, thus influencing Zech to make her his sole beneficiary. Therefore, they contended, Zech should be considered to have died intestate. The lower court allowed the will to be admitted to probate. How do you think the case was decided on appeal? Why?

4 Elizabeth Hall was terminally ill in the hospital. A will was written according to her directions and brought to her to be signed. She executed the will before the proper number of witnesses. Two days later, it was discovered that the papers she signed were only pages 1, 2, 3, and 5 of a purported 5-page will. The lawyer who prepared the will produced the missing page 4. That page set out the duties of the executor. All of the provisions disposing of her estate happened to be contained in the four pages that were before Mrs. Hall when she signed the will. What pages should be admitted to probate as Mrs. Hall's will? Why?

5 Jerry and Lela were husband and wife, having been married in North Dakota in 1970. Later that year Jerry executed a will, one article of which provided, "I give, devise, and bequeath to my wife Lela Margaret Knudsen, all my estate both real and personal." In 1982 Jerry and Lela were divorced. In 1983 Jerry married Susan. He neglected to revoke or modify his 1970 will. Susan now asks you whether she would be entitled to any of Jerry's estate in the event of his death, or would it all go to Lela? North Dakota has adopted the Uniform Probate Code. What would your answer be? Explain.

6 Kirk was the owner of a store which sold motorcycles. Kirk died intestate, survived by his wife, Emma, and by Kirk's two children by a former marriage. Emma was appointed administrator of Kirk's estate, which was then worth about $50,000. As required by law, she furnished a bond guaranteeing proper performance as administrator. Believing that she had inherited the business, Emma took over and ran it. She had no business experience and by the end of a year it was practically worthless. Emma ceased to pay rent on the business premises, locked the door, and left a few motorcycles in the building. In all that time Emma did nothing to administer her deceased husband's estate. A year later Kirk's children petitioned the court to appoint a new administrator. Should a new administrator be appointed even though there are no apparent assets in the estate? What should be done?

7 Lesher, in November 1987, ordered from and paid to his school $200 for four tickets to the Green Bowl football game. When he received his tickets just before game time in 1988 he claimed that his advance payment had established a living (inter vivos) trust between the school and himself. Accordingly, he said he was due the money the school, as trustee, had earned while his deposit money was in their possession. He therefore demanded an accounting from the school. Do you concur in Lesher's novel demand? Why or why not?

ETHICS IN PRACTICE

The laws pertaining to real and personal property and to the related subjects of estates, wills, and trusts are clearly defined. But here, as in most areas of law, ethical considerations may be as important as legal ones when deciding what course of action to take. To illustrate:

Problems in Ethics

1 Charles recently moved into the house next door to John. When Charles and his family are away for the weekend, John sees a new model power lawn mower in Charles's backyard and would like to see how it works. If he likes it, he intends to buy one for a $100 discount at a 1-day sale that will end before Charles is likely to return. John knows that if he borrows the machine without Charles's permission, he will be committing a trespass. However, although he has not met Charles, John doubts that Charles would sue him for using the mower. Other than the violation of trespass law, are there ethical factors that John should consider?

2 For many years Gladys has owned a six-family apartment building in a good neighborhood of Springfield. The apartments are continually rented for $500 per month and provide Gladys with a very satisfactory income. Recently, several new manufacturing plants have been built in Springfield, and housing is now in very short supply. Gladys's friends tell her that during the last 3 months rents for apartments like hers have jumped to $800 per month and that when her leases come up for renewal she should raise her rents to match those of other landlords. Gladys knows that four of her tenants cannot afford more than $500 and will have to move to a dangerous part of town if she raises the rent. There is no rent control law in Springfield. Should Gladys follow the advice of her friends?

3 You are the manager of an apartment building. The owner, Leo, leases a unit to Sam and Sue on a month-to-month basis. Leo prefers this type of lease because either he or the tenant can terminate the lease upon 30 days' notice. Sam and Sue have always paid their rent on time, are quiet, hardworking, and pleasant to all the neighbors, and attend church regularly. Recently, however, Leo has learned that Sam and Sue are not married. Leo's religion teaches that living out of wedlock is a mortal sin. Leo wants you to help him decide whether to terminate the lease. **(a)** What factors should you ask Leo to consider? **(b)** Will your personal belief about the propriety of living out of wedlock affect your advice? **(c)** Would it matter that five of Sam and Sue's immediate neighbors consider Sam and Sue's living arrangements scandalous and unacceptable? **(d)** Would you lean more toward termination if the five neighbors had young children? **(e)** What if Sam and Sue were late with their rent once, and on two occasions complained to a neighbor about his loud stereo? Would these facts make termination easier? **(f)** If Sam and Sue were of different races, would this fact affect your advice to Leo?

4 Mary owns and operates a large real estate office. As a result of her services as a realtor, her close friend Caroline made a considerable amount of money over the years in real estate transactions. Caroline died, and Mary was appointed as the executrix of her estate. Soon after Caroline's death, Mary was offered a large commercial property at a price well below its market value, but she had to act immediately to take advantage of the bargain. Not having sufficient funds available to make the required down payment, and believing that Caroline, if alive, would have lent her the money, Mary withdrew from the executrix account the required funds and gave Caroline's estate her (Mary's) personal promissory note in return. The note was payable with interest at the legal rate within six months, a date well before the estate was due to be closed. Is there an ethical problem here?

PART SIX

Debtor-Creditor Relations

CHAPTER 24

Purpose and Types of Secured Transactions; Suretyship

The willingness of a creditor to lend money allows people to engage in transactions they might otherwise have to postpone or forgo entirely, such as making a large consumer purchase or expanding a business operation. One can receive credit in a variety of ways. If you want to buy a car but do not have the cash, you might get a loan from a bank. Or you might persuade the dealer to sell you the car "on time," on the understanding that you will make installment payments until the price is paid. Many credit purchases of goods and services involve the use of a credit card. Often people will simply deliver goods or render services and bill you later. In all these instances there has been an extension of credit.

But credit extension involves a risk that the debtor will *default:* fail to repay a loan or fail to pay for property or services bought on credit. To reduce the risk of loss due to a debtor's default, a creditor may demand, or the law may provide, some sort of *security*—i.e., some backup source of payment that will be available to the creditor if the debtor fails to pay.

This chapter discusses the kinds of security devices or arrangements commonly used in business, with major emphasis on the secured transaction. As used here the term "secured transaction" means any contract between a creditor and a debtor that provides the creditor with a backup source of payment should the debtor break his or her promise to pay. Secured transactions are of two basic types: (1) Those in which the creditor's backup source of payment is real or personal property called "collateral security" or, simply, "collateral"; and (2) those in which the creditor's security is the promise of some third person (a "surety") to pay the debt. The surety's promise is given or imposed by law *in addition to* the debtor's promise to pay.

Some forms of security, such as the *mechanic's lien* discussed in the first part of this chapter (see also Chapter 22), are not contractual. Rather, they are *imposed by law* in favor of certain creditors and therefore may exist without the knowledge of the debtor or the creditor. The first part of this chapter briefly surveys the kinds of security devices—noncontractual and contractual—commonly associated with credit extension. The second part focuses on suretyship, one kind of secured transaction.

Purpose and Types of Secured Transactions

Purpose of Secured Transactions

As already noted, a secured transaction (or other security device) reduces the risk of nonpayment faced by a creditor who has made a loan or who has delivered property or rendered services expecting an agreed payment to be made later. How a secured transaction does so can be seen by comparing an unsecured transaction with a secured one.

An *un*secured creditor (one who extends credit without receiving any security) faces the maximum risk of nonpayment. Suppose Carl sells goods to Donna solely on the basis of her promise to pay later. Carl is an unsecured creditor and consequently has no right to repossess the goods if Donna fails to pay. Instead, to enforce his right to payment, Carl will have to sue Donna and obtain a judgment against her. If Donna refuses to honor the judgment, Carl will have to seek execution of it. To obtain execution, Carl must get a writ of execution from the court. The writ orders the sheriff or other proper officer to seize and sell any of the debtor's property located within the jurisdiction of the court and to apply the proceeds of the sale to the debt. Carl's obtaining judgment will be of little value if Donna has no assets, leaves the jurisdiction, or is discharged from her debts in a bankruptcy proceeding. Carl could "garnishee" (lay legal claim to) Donna's wages, but garnishment laws limit the percentage of wages he may take, and Donna might be unemployed or earn little.

Carl would substantially reduce his risk of nonpayment by insisting on a *secured* transaction—one that provides him with a backup source of payment that he may resort to if Donna breaks her promise to pay. Suppose the contract of sale states that if Donna fails to make timely payment, Carl will have the right to repossess and sell the goods he sold her. Carl has reserved for himself a "security interest" in the goods. Upon Donna's default, Carl, as a secured creditor, will have not only a claim against Donna's *general* assets, but also first rights, as against Donna's other creditors, to *take possession of and to sell,* in satisfaction of the debt, the specific goods that are the subject of the secured transaction.

The main purpose of a secured transaction is to protect the creditor, but the debtor is to be treated fairly too. Under modern security law, a defaulting debtor may lose the collateral and remains personally liable for any deficiency if the collateral is not valuable enough to cover the debt. But if the collateral is worth more than the amount of the debt, the debtor is entitled to surplus proceeds realized upon the sale or other disposition of the collateral.

Types of Secured Transactions

Secured transactions can be classified in terms of the source of the backup payment that is available to the creditor upon the debtor's default. So, there are (*a*) secured transactions in real estate, (*b*) secured transactions in personal property, and (*c*) suretyship transactions.

Where *property* is the collateral, the creditor acquires a *lien* (charge or claim) against the property. Some liens are imposed by law. Others are created by contract. Security devices can therefore also be classified in terms of how they arise—by law or by contract.

Liens Imposed by Law

Liens imposed by law on personal property. Often a person (the bailor) hires someone (the bailee) to repair, ship, or store the bailor's personal property. Under court decisions or statutes, the bailee has a *possessory lien* on the property for the amount the bailor agreed to pay for the service, or, in the absence of a stated price, for the bailee's reasonable charges. The lien exists only as long as the bailee keeps possession of the property. If the bailee voluntarily gives the thing back to the bailor without receiving payment, the lien is lost and the bailee becomes an unsecured creditor. Suppose that Donna delivers her antique clock to Carl for him to clean and repair, agreeing to pay him $50 for the work. Carl performs as agreed, but Donna refuses to pay the bill. Carl has a lien on the clock for $50, as long as he keeps the clock in his possession. Many state statutes permit Carl to enforce his lien by selling the clock in the manner prescribed by the statute—usually by giving Donna notice of the sale and advertising it. If no such enforcement provision exists, Carl may have to "foreclose" his lien. To *foreclose,* Carl must get a judgment against Donna for the amount owed and have the clock sold at a judicial sale.

Suppose that Donna, having refused to pay for the repair work, sneaks into Carl's shop after hours and takes the clock. Because Carl did not voluntarily give up possession, he still has his lien. The result would be the same if Donna had by fraud or duress induced Carl to give up possession of the clock.

Suppose instead that Carl, having agreed to clean and repair the clock for $50, presents Donna with a bill for $200 when she arrives to pick the clock up. Donna "tenders" (offers) the $50 she agreed to pay, but Carl insists on $200. Carl's lien is terminated, his possession is now wrongful, and he is liable to Donna for conversion of her property.

Suppose now that Donna calls Carl to her house to repair a grandfather clock. He repairs it there and later sends Donna a bill that is reasonable in amount. Donna refuses to pay Carl's reasonable charges. Since Carl never acquired possession of the clock, he has no lien on it and is therefore an unsecured creditor.

Possessory liens are classified as "specific" or "general." A *specific* lien entitles the creditor to retain possession of the property as security for only the one debt involved in the immediate transaction. A *general* lien entitles the creditor to keep the property until the debtor has paid all debts owed to the creditor as a result of the general course of business between the creditor and the debtor. For example, suppose Carl repaired Donna's watch last week and delivered it to her, but she has not yet paid the $40 they agreed to. Now she tenders (offers) the $50 she agreed to pay for today's clock repair, but Carl wants to keep the clock until she also pays for the watch repair. Unless Carl and Donna agreed otherwise, Carl's lien on the clock is "specific" and therefore is not effective as to the earlier debt. Donna's tender of the $50 terminates the specific lien, and she is entitled to possession of the clock. As to the $40 for the watch repair, Carl is an unsecured creditor. If Carl's lien against the clock had been "general," Carl would have been entitled to hold the clock until Donna also paid for the watch repair.

General liens are available only to a few groups of businesspeople. Attorneys-at-law, bankers, and factors (selling agents to whom their principals entrust goods for sale in the regular course of business), and sometimes a few others such as accountants, are granted general liens by law. Under a general lien, an attorney, for example, could hold the client's papers or other property that comes into the attorney's possession until all amounts owed the attorney are paid, even if for a variety of separate debts. In contrast, most bailees have only a specific possessory lien. These people include repairpersons and other artisans, common carriers, innkeepers, warehousers, finders of property for the return of which a specific reward is offered, a landlord who holds the property of a defaulting tenant, and agisters (bailees who take possession of cattle for the purpose of feeding them).

Liens imposed by law on real property. Real estate can be subjected to a variety of liens—judgment liens, tax liens, and mechanics' liens, for example. A landowner who is a losing defendant in a lawsuit may have his or her property subjected to a judgment lien in favor of the winning plaintiff. Land is also subject to a lien in favor of the state or other governmental unit for unpaid taxes. The *mechanic's lien* is imposed in favor of a person who *under a contract* has performed labor or furnished materials for the improvement of the landowner's real estate. The lien itself is involuntary (because imposed on the debtor by law rather than being contracted for), but it provides the mechanic with a backup source of payment (the improved real estate) in the event of the landowner-debtor's failure to pay the debt.

The term "mechanic" is broader than it sounds. The statutes of most states grant a mechanic's lien to anyone who, under contract, furnishes labor, services, or materials for the improvement of land. Thus, carpenters, electricians, landscapers, concrete workers, brickmasons, lessors of equipment, general contractors, subcontractors, surveyors, suppliers such as lumberyards (often called "materialmen"), and many others fall within the meaning of mechanic. Ordinarily, labor and services must be performed, and materials must be delivered *and incorporated into the improvement,* before the mechanic, artisan, or supplier has a right to a lien against the property.

The procedure for obtaining and enforcing a mechanic's lien is governed by statute and varies from state to state. In general, however, the mechanic must give written notice (by certified mail, for example) to affected persons—e.g., landowner, general contractor, construction lender—that the mechanic has furnished labor, services, or material for the improvement of the land. Then, after the mechanic completes the work, he or she must record a "claim of lien" (illustrated in Figure 24.1) in the courthouse of the county in which the improved land is located. The lien must be recorded within the time specified by the statute, e.g., 60 or 90 days after the work or contract has been completed. Upon complying with the statutory requirements, the mechanic has a lien against the property for the amount of the debt. Failure to comply means only that the mechanic is an unsecured creditor; the debt is still enforceable against the person who contracted for it.

Ordinarily, a mechanic has only a limited time to bring suit to enforce his or her lien—90 days after its creation, for example, or a longer time if the mechanic has extended credit. The time for enforcement is relatively short so that the landowner's title (ownership) will not be "clouded" (impaired) by the lien for an unreasonably long time. Mechanics' liens are enforced by a process of foreclosure. To foreclose, the mechanic must get a judgment for the amount due and a judicial order for the sale of the property.

Case 24.1 concerns the validity of a mechanic's lien.

RECORDING REQUESTED BY

WHEN RECORDED MAIL TO

NAME
STREET ADDRESS
CITY
STATE
ZIP

(SPACE ABOVE THIS LINE FOR RECORDER'S USE)

MECHANIC'S LIEN
(Claim of Lien)

The undersigned, ______________________________, referred to
(Full name of person or firm claiming mechanic's lien)

in this Claim of Lien as the Claimant, claims a mechanic's lien for the labor, services, equipment and/or materials described below, furnished for a work of improvement upon that certain real property located in the County of ______________________________, State of California, and described as follows: ______________________________
(Description of property where the work and/or materials were furnished. Although the street address is sufficient, it is advisable to give both the street address and the legal description.)

____

After deducting all just credits and offsets, the sum of $______________________________, together with interest thereon at the rate of
(Amount of claim due and unpaid)

______________________________ percent per annum from ______________________________, 19____, is due Claimant
(See note on reverse side) (Date when amount of claim became due)

for the following labor, services, equipment and/or materials furnished by Claimant: ______________________________
(General description of the work and/or materials furnished)

____

The name of the person or company by whom Claimant was employed, or to whom Claimant furnished the labor, services, equipment and/or materials is

____
(Usually name of person or firm who ordered from, or contracted with Claimant for the work and/or materials)

The name(s) and address(es) of the owner(s) or reputed owner(s) of the real property is/are: ______________________________

____
(This information can be obtained from the County Assessor's office where the real property is located)

SEE REVERSE SIDE FOR ADDITIONAL INSTRUCTIONS

Name of Claimant ______________________________
(See instructions on reverse side for proper signing)

By: ______________________________
(Signature of Claimant or authorized agent and title)

VERIFICATION

I, the undersigned, declare: I am the ______________________________ of ______________________________, the Claimant
(Title) (Name of Claimant)

named in the foregoing claim of mechanic's lien; I am authorized to make this verification for the Claimant; I have read the foregoing claim of mechanic's lien and know the contents thereof, and the same is true of my own knowledge.

I declare under penalty of perjury under the laws of the State of California that the foregoing is true and correct.

______________________________, 19____ ______________________________
(Date of signature) (Signature of the individual who verifies that the contents of the claim of mechanic's lien are true)

WOLCOTTS FORM 1024—MECHANIC'S LIEN (Claim of Lien)—Rev. 5/82
(price class 3)

Figure 24.1 "Claim of Lien" Form (*Reprinted by permission of Wolcotts Legal Forms, Inc.*)

CASE 24.1 Johnson v. Smith · 276 P. 146 (Cal. App. 1929)

FACTS Smith (defendant) had a house built by a contractor. The task of furnishing hardwood flooring and laying it in the building was subcontracted to a third person who purchased the flooring from Johnson (plaintiff). The subcontractor did not install it properly, and the Smiths' architect ordered it removed and other flooring laid in its place. Upon failure of the subcontractor to pay for the flooring, Johnson brought suit to foreclose a mechanic's lien he had acquired on the Smiths' house to secure payment. From a judgment for Johnson, the Smiths appealed.

OPINION HOUSER, Acting P.J.... Appellants [the Smiths] urge that the claim of lien was invalid because it failed to comply with the requirement of the statute that... it contain "a general statement of the kind of work done or materials furnished."... [T]he claim of lien upon which the action depended [states] that it was for "materials furnished." [The Code of Civil Procedure provides] that:

> No mistake or errors in the statement of the demand... shall invalidate the lien, unless the court finds that such mistake or error... was made with the intent to defraud, or the court shall find that an innocent third party, without notice, direct or constructive, has since the claim was filed become the bona fide owner of the property liened upon, and that the notice of claim was so deficient that it did not put the party upon further inquiry in any manner.

[Even if] it be conceded that the claim of lien for "materials furnished" was defective in that it contained no specification of the "kind" of materials, since... the findings of the trial court [do not reveal] that the error was made with "intent to defraud," or that an innocent third party suffered by reason of such error, it is clear that the defect is not of vital importance.... [I]n construing an earlier and somewhat similar lien statute, the rule had been announced... that "it was unnecessary to state specifically the kind of materials furnished or the prices of the several items."... In [Davis v. Livingston] it is said: "The second of the three notices is claimed to be defective [because] it does not state of what the 'materials' named therein consisted. [This objection is not] well taken. The particular character of the materials need not be stated in the notice. The statute does not expressly require it, and the 'nature and extent of the claim' may as well be understood without the aid of such detail as with it"....

Appellants contend [also] that, because the "materials" furnished by plaintiff were not finally used by the defendants in the construction of the building for which [the] materials were originally purchased, plaintiff was not entitled to maintain a lien on the premises....

...[T]o become entitled to a lien, a materialman who furnished material to a contractor to be used in the construction of a building is under no obligation to the owner of the premises to see that the contractor complies with the terms of his contract with the owner.... The syllabus in the case of Howe v. Schmidt,... which is sustained by the text of the opinion... [states] that: "A materialman is not required to ascertain whether or not material ordered by a building contractor for use in a building conforms to the requirements of the agreement between the contractor and the owner. His contractual relations are solely with the contractor dealing with him and he simply furnishes material as directed by the party with whom he contracts. He is under no legal obligation to the owner to see that the contractor complies with his contract, and so far as his right to a lien is concerned, is warranted in assuming that the contractor is fulfilling his contract with the owner. This is true, in the absence of bad faith on his part, notwithstanding he may know that material ordered may not be in all respects as provided by the written contract on file."...

CASE 24.1 Continued

In the instant case apparently the fault of the flooring lay entirely with the manner in which it was laid—not with the boards or material of which it was constructed. [The flooring was laid] not by plaintiff or...his employees, but was done by the defendants or their...employees. The fact that by the act of the owner of the building the "materials furnished" may have been rendered useless should not defeat the rights of an innocent materialman, who had no...notice of defective [installation].

JUDGMENT [The decision of the trial court is affirmed.]

Liens Created by Contract. Because so widely used, the security devices of greatest commercial significance are those created by contract in favor of lenders and sellers. Where real or personal property is the source of backup payment, the secured transaction creates a contractual lien against the property, in favor of the lender or credit seller.

Secured transactions in personal property. Vast amounts of consumer and business credit are secured by an interest in consumer goods, accounts receivable, negotiable instruments, inventory, equipment, and other forms of personal property. Secured transactions in personal property are so important commercially that they are the subject of Article 9 of the Uniform Commercial Code. These secured transactions are discussed in Chapter 25.

Secured transactions in real estate. Few people have enough cash to buy houses, land, or commercial properties outright. In fact, it often is economically unwise to do so, since a cash purchase of real estate would divert financial resources that could be better applied to other consumer purchases or to other aspects of a business operation such as product development or the purchase of equipment. Three security devices are commonly used to finance the purchase of real estate—the mortgage, the trust deed, and the land contract. Mortgages and trust deeds are discussed in Chapter 22.

The *land contract,* called in some states a *contract for deed* or *installment land contract,* is a long-term credit arrangement under which the seller commonly transfers some ownership rights to the buyer but retains a security interest in the property until it is paid for. By means of a land contract, Carla sells her house on credit to Don. Don will acquire the right to possess, use, and perhaps even sell the house, subject to a duty to pay Carla the agreed price plus interest as prescribed by the contract. However, Don will not receive a deed (document signifying full ownership) from Carla until he makes the final payment, perhaps several years later. In the meantime, Don is the "equitable" or "beneficial" owner, while Carla retains a sufficient interest, called "legal title," to enable her to have the property sold if Don defaults.

Suretyship

Nature, Creation, and Kinds of Suretyship

Nature of Suretyship. A *surety* is a person who, by contract or by operation of law, is liable for the debt, default, or miscarriage of another. Suppose, for example, that Dan wants to start up a small retail business but lacks sufficient funds. He seeks a loan from a bank, but the bank refuses to make the loan unless Dan finds a creditworthy person to cosign the promissory note that Dan will give to the bank in exchange for the loan. Dan's wealthy cousin Sam is willing to cosign the note. It reads in part, "We, or either or us, agree to pay $10,000 to First Bank or its order one year from the date of this note. (Signed) Daniel Debtor and Sam Smith." Sam is a *surety* because, by cosigning the note, he contracted to be responsible for the debt of Dan. When the note comes due, First Bank has the right to sue Sam for payment without first seeking payment from Dan.

Although the bank can look either to Dan or to Sam for payment, as between Dan and Sam, *Dan* is the person with ultimate liability. Thus, the definition of suretyship found in the *Restatement of the Law of Security* applies: One person (Dan) has undertaken an obligation (debt to First Bank), and another person (Sam, because he cosigned) is also under an obligation to the obligee (Bank) who is entitled to only one performance. And as between the two who are bound (Dan and Sam), one (Dan) rather than the other (Sam) should perform. Thus, if Sam is required to pay First Bank, Dan is liable to Sam.

In Figure 24.2, First Bank is the *creditor* (C), also known as the *obligee.* Dan is the *principal debtor* (D), also known as the *obligor.* Sam is the principal debtor's *surety* (S) and can also be viewed as First Bank's debtor.

Note that in Figure 24.2, two contracts are involved: (1) the main contract between the principal debtor and the creditor, and (2) the "collateral" (backup) contract between the surety and the creditor. Furthermore, the surety's liability can be either "primary" or "secondary." A cosigner of a note such as Sam has *primary* liability because First Bank has the right, when the note comes due (or upon Dan's default), to sue the surety without first seeking payment from Dan. But suppose that Dan is the only signer of the note, and that Sam signs a separate document reading, "If Daniel Debtor defaults in making scheduled payments on the $10,000 debt he owes First Bank, I will, upon notice of such default, pay any amount that Daniel Debtor still owes. (Signed) Sam Smith." Since Sam need not pay unless Sam first receives notice of Dan's default, Sam's liability is *secondary.* As illustrated later in this chapter, a surety's promise of secondary liability ("to pay if Dan doesn't") is not enforceable unless in writing.[1]

A surety may be liable for the principal's *debt* (usually understood to mean an obligation to pay money). But a surety can be liable, too, for the principal's *default* (failure to perform a nonmoney obligation), as where Sam promises to make good any loss resulting from Dan's failure to perform Dan's contract to deliver coal; or for the principal's *miscarriage* (tort or crime), as where Sam agrees to make good to Dan's employer any losses resulting from Dan's embezzlement or other mishandling of the employer's funds.

Creation of Suretyship. Usually suretyship is created by express contract, at the request of the creditor or the principal debtor. But suretyship can arise without the knowledge of the parties, by operation

[1]Technically, Sam is a *guarantor* here. However, most states have abolished the distinctions between suretyship and guarantyship, preferring to treat all such contracts as surety arrangements regardless of whether the backup promisor signed a separate document, and regardless of the kind of liability (primary or secondary) he or she undertook. Like the *Restatement of Security,* this chapter treats suretyship and guaranty as the same thing, although some of the guaranty terminology is defined because it is still used in some states.

Figure 24.2 Parties to a Suretyship Transaction

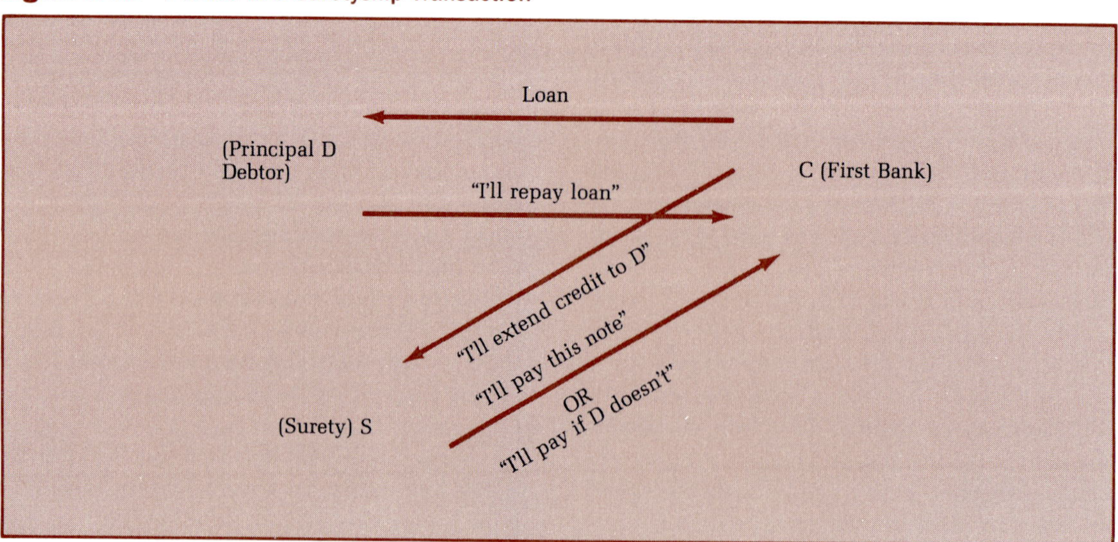

of law. Recall from Chapter 14 what happens when a person assigns his or her rights under a contract and also delegates the duties he or she is required by the contract to perform. The delegator remains responsible as a surety for the performance of those duties in the event that the delegatee fails to perform, unless the obligee (person to whom the duty is owed) releases the delegator.

Suppose you are buying a house financed by Second Bank and want to sell it to Dora before you have paid off the debt. She agrees to a purchase price of $50,000. You have a $30,000 mortgage indebtedness to the bank remaining. Dora pays you $20,000 and "assumes" the mortgage. Since you have delegated to Dora your duty to pay Second Bank the $30,000, you are a surety for the $30,000 unless and until the bank releases you from liability. Your suretyship liability arises even though the bank might not know that Dora has assumed the mortgage and even though you might not realize that you are still liable to the bank. Upon assuming the mortgage, Dora becomes the principal debtor. So, if you must pay because she refuses or fails to pay, she is liable to you. The same principles apply to assignments of leases. Suppose you assign to Dan the unexpired portion of your 2-year apartment lease because your employer transferred you to another city. Although Dan receives all your remaining rights under the lease and becomes the landlord's principal debtor, you remain liable as surety to your former landlord for any unpaid rent.

Suretyship can arise by operation of law in other unexpected ways. Suppose you drive negligently and injure Millie, another motorist. You have no insurance, but Millie is insured by Town Insurance Company. Both you and the insurance company are liable to Millie. The insurance company is liable on the basis of its contract to indemnify her for loss, and you are liable because of your negligence. Probably the insurance company will pay Millie immediately and seek payment from you, since you are ultimately liable. Under the law you are the principal debtor and the insurance company is, in this instance, a surety. As such the insurance company has, like any other surety, a right of reimbursement against you, the principal debtor.

Kinds of Suretyship. The precise obligation that a surety has will be determined in part by the kind of suretyship that the surety undertook.

Gratuitous v. compensated suretyship. Some sureties are paid for their services and some are not. Those who are not paid are called "gratuitous," "voluntary," or "accommodation" sureties because their main purpose in undertaking the surety obligation is to help out a relative or friend and not to profit personally. Gratuitous (accommodation) sureties *are* in fact contracting parties and are bound by their promises, but the consideration they receive consists of a "legal" benefit only—e.g., the creditor's promise to the surety to deal or to continue dealing with the principal debtor. Any monetary or other actual benefit goes to the principal debtor and not to the accommodation surety.

Suppose, for example, that you make an installment purchase of a car, and at the request of the seller a friend or relative cosigns or guarantees your note without being paid to do so. The surety had made a contractual commitment that is binding on him or her. The consideration necessary for the contract of suretyship to arise is the seller's promise (made to the surety) to sell the car to you, in exchange for the surety's promise to pay if you do not. However, despite the fact that the surety receives consideration, the suretyship is called "gratuitous" because while you receive the car and the extension of credit in exchange for your own promise to pay, the surety receives only a "legal" benefit (the creditor's promise to deal with you) in exchange for the surety's promise to pay. Since a gratuitous surety receives little or no actual benefit from the contract, most courts will resolve any ambiguities, vagueness, or other doubts about the scope of the undertaking in favor of the gratuitous surety and against the creditor.

The opposite is true for a *compensated* surety, sometimes called a "corporate" surety. A person or firm that undertakes a surety's obligation for hire usually will be held strictly to the contract, and any ambiguities, vagueness, or doubts as to the scope of the undertaking will be resolved in favor of the creditor and against the surety. This makes sense because the compensated surety usually is a company that, like an insurance company, estimates risks on an actuarial basis and charges the principal debtor a fee ("premium") that reflects the degree of risk.

The promise of a compensated surety to pay if the principal debtor does not is often called a "bond." There are many types of surety bonds, among them the following:

1 Bail, appearance, appeal, or judicial bond—various surety bonds associated with criminal or civil legal proceedings. A *bail* or *appearance bond* is the surety's promise to pay a specified sum to the court in the event that the criminal defendant covered by the bond fails to show up for legal proceedings. An *appeal bond* is a surety's promise to cover the costs of appeal in a civil case. *Judicial bond* is a general term for any bond required by a court to guarantee, for example, the payment of costs connected with an appeal or the availability of a fund needed to satisfy a judgment.
2 Bid bond—a surety bond used in connection with public construction projects to protect the public agency (creditor) from loss if the bidder (principal debtor) withdraws the bid or, upon winning the right to the contract, refuses to enter into it.
3 Completion, contract, payment, or performance bond—a surety bond guaranteeing, for example, that a contractor will complete a construction contract or pay for labor and materials.
4 Fidelity bond—a surety bond protecting an employer against loss due to embezzlement, larceny, or gross negligence by an employee.
5 Fiduciary bond—a surety bond required by a court to be provided by a trustee, executor, guardian, or other fiduciary to ensure proper performance of his or her duties.
6 License or permit bond—a suretyship bond required by state law before the state will issue a license or permit. The bond guarantees payment to an obligee for loss or damage resulting from operations of the licensee or permit holder.

Unconditional v. conditional suretyship. Surety relationships can be classified according to the nature of the surety's promise or undertaking. In a traditional suretyship arrangement, e.g., the cosigning of a promissory note, the surety-cosigner makes an unconditional promise to pay and, like the principal debtor, is immediately liable to the creditor when the note is *due.* There is no requirement that the creditor first seek payment from the principal debtor. In another kind of unconditional suretyship called an *absolute guaranty,* the surety promises to pay or to perform *upon the default* of the principal debtor. Here, the surety has no liability until the principal debtor defaults, but if the debtor defaults, the surety is immediately liable. In a *conditional guaranty,* however, the creditor must do more than merely show that the principal debtor is in default. To hold the surety liable, the creditor must first make a reasonable attempt to exhaust the creditor's remedies against the debtor, for example by suing the principal debtor and having the judgment returned unsatisfied.

Cosuretyship. Sometimes two or more sureties will bind themselves on behalf of a single principal debtor as *cosureties.* Cosureties must share the burden of the principal debtor's default, because although each has contracted to pay the full debt, a court would have no basis for imposing the whole loss on one while freeing the others.

Suppose Dan borrows $100,000 from Carla, and Sylvia cosigns the note at Dan's request. At the same time, at Carla's request, Sam (in writing) guarantees Dan's debt. Sylvia and Sam are cosureties. If Dan defaults, Sylvia and Sam must share the loss equally, unless they have agreed to share it in some different proportion. So, if Dan defaults and Carla compels Sylvia to pay the $100,000, Sylvia is entitled to a $50,000 payment, called "contribution," from Sam. Similarly, two or more accommodation signers of a note ordinarily are cosureties, and any one of them who pays more than his or her share is entitled to contribution.

Liability, Defenses, and Discharge of Surety

Liability of Surety. The liability that a surety faces upon the default of the principal debtor is determined by (*a*) the contract between the creditor and the principal debtor, (*b*) the contract between the creditor and the surety, and (*c*) other factors such as whether the surety has the benefit of any defenses when called upon to pay.

Usually the surety is responsible for precisely the performance, or any unperformed part of it, that the principal debtor promised the creditor in the debtor-creditor contract—for example, to pay $10,000 plus 12 percent interest on July 17, or to deliver 50 tons of coal at the rate of 1 ton per week. Where the seller of mortgaged real estate becomes a surety by operation of law because the buyer assumed the seller's mortgage, the seller-surety is liable to the creditor for the amount of the assumed debt that remains unpaid. However, the contract between the surety and the creditor can *limit* the surety's liability, as where the surety promises, "If Dan defaults on his $10,000 obligation to you, I will pay $5,000."

The *surety-creditor* contract determines the time of the surety's liability. As noted earlier, because the cosigner of a note has primary liability, the creditor may take the cosigner to court immediately upon a default of the debtor or as soon as the note comes due. In contrast, where a surety says, "I will pay Dan's debt if it is uncollectible," the surety has no liability until the creditor demonstrates that the debt is uncollectible. The creditor ordinarily will do this by getting a judgment against the debtor, attempting to collect on it, and having the judgment returned unsatisfied.

The case the follows addresses the problem that exists where the surety's maximum liability is less than the debt owed, and numerous creditors contend for the limited amount.

CASE 24.2 Homewood Investment Co. v. Moses · 608 P.2d 503 (Nev. 1980)

FACTS Home Lumber and Supply Co. furnished over $16,000 worth of materials to Homewood Investment Co. Homewood never paid, Home Lumber sued for the amount owed, and judgment was entered for Home Lumber against Homewood and others, including United Pacific Insurance Co., which had undertaken a $5,000 contractor's surety bond. United appealed from the judgment, alleging that since there were several other unpaid suppliers, Home Lumber was entitled to only a portion of the $5,000 bond amount.

OPINION BATJER, Justice.... [W]e agree with United that Home Lumber is not entitled to the full amount of the surety bond.... United correctly asserts that Home Lumber is entitled to only a pro rata share of the $5,000 surety bond. [A Nevada statute] states that "[e]ach bond or deposit... shall be in favor of the State of Nevada for the benefit of any person who:... [a]s a supplier or materialman furnished materials or equipment for the construction contract." Subdivision 5 of that provision states that "[c]laims, other than labor claims, against a bond or deposit shall have equal priority... and if the bond or deposit is insufficient to pay all such claims in full, they shall be paid pro rata." There is evidence in the record that other claims against United have been asserted.

JUDGMENT Therefore, the case is remanded to the trial court for a determination of Home Lumber's pro rata share of the bond....

Defenses and Discharge of Surety. A surety may have the benefit of three kinds of defenses: (1) the surety's own contractual defenses, (2) some of the contractual defenses available to the principal debtor, and (3) special suretyship defenses that usually arise after the surety undertakes the obligation.

Surety's own contractual defenses. A person has no suretyship liability if no contract arose or if, where one did arise, the surety exercises a right to avoid it. No contract *arose* if, for example, the person alleged to be a surety lacked capacity to contract or received *no* consideration for his or her promise. (Recall that even a so-called "gratuitous" surety receives consideration—the promise of the creditor to deal with the principal debtor.) A surety may *avoid* his or her contract where, for example, the creditor procured the surety's promise by means of fraud. Suppose First Bank seeks a fidelity bond to protect it from loss due to embezzlement of customers' funds by the bank's employees. First Bank knows but does not reveal to the surety that three of the bank's employees have been convicted of embezzlement. First Bank's fraud in concealing or knowingly failing to reveal material information gives the surety a ground for avoiding the contract.

Sometimes a surety may assert the statute of frauds as a defense. The statute of frauds comes into play where a surety agrees to answer for the debt, default, or miscarriage of another. Such an agreement is not enforceable unless it is in writing. Suppose Delbert is building himself a house on his own lot and is purchasing materials from Lumber Supply. Halfway through, Delbert fails to pay for some materials and Lumber Supply refuses to deliver any more until Delbert persuades some creditworthy person to guarantee payment. At Delbert's request, Susan promises Lumber Supply on the phone that "If Del does not pay for materials when they are delivered, I will." Lumber Supply makes further deliveries, Del does not pay, and when called upon for payment Susan refuses. Her oral promise is not enforceable. However, if Susan's "main purpose" in making the promise had been to benefit herself, her oral promise would have been enforceable. Suppose Del, as a general contractor, is building the house for Susan on her lot. Here, Susan's main purpose in promising to pay Del's debt is to get her house built. Her oral promise to pay Del's debt is enforceable.

Principal debtor's contractual defenses. With some very important exceptions, the surety may assert as against the creditor the defenses that the principal debtor could have asserted had there been only the contract between debtor and creditor. The defenses that the surety *may* assert usually arise out of situations involving wrongdoing or default by the creditor. Suppose that the creditor fraudulently tricks or by duress forces the principal debtor into the contract of indebtedness. Most courts hold that a surety who did not know of the fraud or duress when agreeing to be a surety may assert the principal debtor's defense. Some courts hold that the surety may not do so unless the principal debtor first repudiates the contract because of the fraud or duress. Similarly, if the principal debtor received no consideration (e.g., the creditor did not make the promised loan or deliver the promised materials), the surety may assert that defense of the debtor and escape liability to the creditor.

In some situations the principal debtor has a defense that is unavailable to the surety. Suppose Sam cosigns a note so that his minor daughter Dora can buy a car. Dora wrecks the car and, as permitted under state law protecting minors, rescinds the contract. Sam does *not* have the benefit of Dora's defense of infancy. The fact that Dora might rescind and cause loss to the creditor-seller was the main reason for the creditor to require a surety in the first place, and Sam understood or should have understood this when he became surety. However, if Dora, instead of wrecking the car, had simply returned it the next day unused so that the creditor suffered no loss, Sam *would* be discharged from his suretyship obligation. In a few other situations the surety is not protected by the debtor's defenses. Ordinarily the surety will be liable to the creditor despite the debtor's defense of insanity, bankruptcy, lack of corporate capacity to undertake the debt in question, or (where the debtor is a public agency) the debtor's assertion of sovereign immunity. Again, these are the kinds of risks that surety and creditor probably contemplated as the main reason for the suretyship. Case 24.3, however, illustrates a defense of the principal debtor that the surety *may* assert.

CASE 24.3 Domingues Motors, Inc. v. Lalonde · 417 So. 2d 900 (La. App. 1982)

FACTS Deborah Lalonde bought a new 1978 Chevrolet from Domingues Motors. She made a down payment of $171.40 on a purchase price of $8,576.13, leaving a total of $8,404.73 to be financed over a 4-year period. By means of a chattel mortgage, Domingues retained a security interest in the car, but since the financed debt totaled more than $11,000, Domingues required additional security. Deborah offered, and Domingues accepted, a continuing guaranty agreement from Deborah's father, John A. Lalonde. Domingues assigned Deborah's promissory note, the chattel mortgage, and the surety agreement "with recourse" to General Motors Acceptance Corporation (GMAC). About a year later Deborah filed for a discharge in bankruptcy, leaving over $9,000 of the debt unpaid. The

CASE 24.3 Continued

trustee in bankruptcy sold Deborah's interest in the car to GMAC in full satisfaction of its claim against the debtor's estate. Since GMAC had recourse against Domingues, GMAC sold the car back to Domingues, which in turn sold it at private sale for $5,200. Domingues then sued John Lalonde, on the basis of his guaranty agreement, for the amount of the debt remaining unpaid. The trial court sustained Lalonde's motion for summary judgment and dismissed Domingues' suit. Domingues appealed.

OPINION

GUIDRY, J.... [C]ounsel for plaintiff-appellant has devoted his entire argument to the [proposition] that the liability of a surety under a third party guaranty contract is unaffected by the principal debtor's discharge in bankruptcy.... Although we concede the correctness of [this] legal [principle], we find that the judgment of the trial court does [no] violence to [it]....

...[T]he record reflects as undisputed the fact that the mortgage creditor, GMAC, provoked a sale of the movable property, which secured the debt, to it without the benefit of appraisement.... It is well settled law that a mortgage creditor is absolutely barred from a deficiency judgment against the principal debtor where he provokes a sale, *judicial or private,* without the benefit of appraisement [citing a Louisiana statute and cases].... [S]ale... of mortgaged property without appraisement likewise bars a deficiency judgment against the debtor's surety, notwithstanding the surety's contractual stipulation that his liability "shall not be affected... by the discharge or release of the [principal debtor]... by operation of law or otherwise." [As the court stated in GMAC *v. Smith,* another Louisiana case]:

> The public policy of [the Louisiana statute] is so strong and unwaivable that it prevents even a judgment by default for the deficiency in the absence of allegation and proof of sale with appraisal....
>
> Plaintiff argues..., however, that the surety's contractual agreement was that his liability 'shall not be affected' by discharge of the debtor and that therefore... the ordinary rule of law that the discharge of the debtor [for lack of appraisement] discharges the sureties... does not apply.
>
> [But under Louisiana law, a surety has a] personal right to reimbursement from the debtor (apart from simple subrogation to the creditor's now-extinguished right). The consequence would thus be that the principal debtor would be liable to the surety if the creditor obtains a judgment against the surety.
>
> That consequence is inconsistent with [the statute requiring appraisement]. The debtor cannot himself waive the public policy of [the statute]... and the creditor cannot be allowed to defeat that public policy by the simple device of obliging the debtor to provide a surety who can then collect from the debtor. The provision of the surety's contract making his liability unaffected by the discharge of the debtor is inconsistent with the unwaivable public policy of [required appraisal] and is therefore unenforceable...

We are in total agreement with the holding in [GMAC *v. Smith*], and find the principles of law announced therein to be dispositive of the issue presented in the instant case....

JUDGMENT Affirmed.

Special suretyship defenses. The purpose of the special suretyship defenses is to protect the surety where acts of others increase the surety's risk or reduce the likelihood that the surety can recover the amount that will have to be paid on behalf of the principal debtor. The existence of a special suretyship defense in a particular instance, or the extent of it, depends on a number of factors: (*a*) Did the surety consent to the change that affects the surety's liability? If so, the surety remains liable. (*b*) Was the harm (e.g., an increased chance that the surety will have to pay) "material"? If not, a compensated surety remains liable. The more common special suretyship defenses are discussed in the following paragraphs.

1 Performance of the principal debtor's duty. If the principal debtor, the surety, or some third person performs the debtor's duty, not only the debtor but also the surety is discharged from any further liability.

2 Release of the debtor by the creditor. Where the creditor releases the debtor from the debtor's duty, the surety is also discharged. A *release* is a legally binding contract to give up a right that the releasing person has against the person to be released.

3 A tender (offer) of performance. The surety is discharged where the principal debtor or the surety makes a proper tender of performance which the creditor wrongfully refuses. However, the principal debtor is *not* discharged, because he or she has received the benefit of the contract with the creditor and should have to perform by, for example, repaying a loan. But in fairness to the debtor who is trying to perform, the creditor's wrongful refusal of tender immediately stops the running of interest.

4 Alteration of principal debtor's duty. A surety is entitled to rely on the original terms of the contract between the principal debtor and the creditor. If those terms are changed without the consent of the surety in a way that increases the surety's risk, an uncompensated (accommodation) surety will be completely discharged. However, a compensated surety will be discharged only if the increase in the surety's risk is material. If the risk increases, but not materially, the compensated surety is not discharged but the surety's obligation is reduced to the extent of the loss resulting from the change in the contract between the debtor and the creditor. No surety is discharged where the unconsented-to modification can only benefit the surety.

Suppose Dan leases a building from Carmen for a period of two years at a monthly rental of $500, and Sam agrees to pay the rent if Dan does not. Then Dan and Carmen agree to reduce the rent to $450 per month. Sam is not discharged even if he is an uncompensated surety, since the change in Dan and Carmen's contract can do nothing but benefit Sam. Sam is liable, of course, only for the lesser amount. But suppose that instead of changing the monthly rental, Dan and Carmen agreed to extend the 2-year term by 1 hour. If Sam is an uncompensated surety, he is discharged because there is an increase, though a small one, in his potential liability for the rent. If Sam is a *compensated* surety, he will not be discharged as to the 2-year term unless the court holds that the 1-hour extension is material, a highly unlikely holding. Now suppose Dan pays the rent for the full 2 years but fails to pay the rent for the extra hour. Sam, though a compensated surety liable for the rent attributable to the 2-year term, is not liable for the hour's rent resulting from the minor modification.

Another type of alteration occurs where debtor and creditor make a legally binding agreement to extend the time for payment of the debt. Such an agreement immediately and completely discharges an *uncompensated* surety who did not consent to it. However, a *compensated*, unconsenting surety is discharged only to the extent that he or she is harmed by the extension. Suppose Dora borrows $5,000 from Calvin, Dora signs a promissory note to repay the amount at the end of 6 months plus 10 percent interest, and Sally guarantees Dora's note. Without Sally's consent Dora and Calvin then enter into a binding contract to extend the time of payment for 3 more months. If Sally is an uncompensated surety, she is immediately and completely discharged from liability. If Sally is a *compensated* surety, she is discharged only to the extent that she is harmed by the extension. Sally would be harmed if called upon to pay the additional 3 months' interest that Calvin and Dora agreed to without Sally's consent. Moreover, if Dora became insolvent during the 3 month extension, Sally (even if she were a compensated surety) would also be discharged from liability to Calvin for the principal amount, because Sally agreed to bear the risk of Dora's insolvency for only 6 months, not 9.

Ordinarily, a legally binding agreement between debtor and creditor to increase the interest rate on a debt discharges an unconsenting surety. An agreement to *lower* the interest rate does not discharge the surety, who remains liable for the lowered amount.

5 Surrender or impairment of collateral. Sometimes a creditor has the benefit of a surety's obligation but also receives real or personal property from the debtor to secure the debt. The surety has a right to the benefit of the collateral. Therefore, where the creditor knows of the surety's obligation, the surety is discharged to the extent of any loss caused by the creditor's giving up the collateral or mishandling it in such a way as to reduce its value. Suppose Sarah is a surety where Clara lends $5,000 to Dale who pledges (temporarily transfers possession of) 100 shares of his stock to Clara as additional security. The stock is worth $2,000. Then, before Dale's debt is due and without Sarah's consent, Clara returns the stock to Dale. Sarah is discharged as to $2,000 but remains liable as a surety for $3,000.

Table 24.1 summarizes the defenses of the surety.

Rights of Surety and Cosurety

Upon the default of the principal debtor, the surety becomes obligated to perform—e.g., pay the creditor—if there are no defenses the surety can assert. If required to perform, the surety has certain "rights" against the principal debtor. The surety may be entitled to exoneration, reimbursement, or subrogation, or to some combination of these. If there are cosureties, the surety who pays may be entitled, in addition, to "contribution" from the others.

Rights of Surety. *Exoneration* is the right of a surety to have a court of equity compel a capable but reluctant principal debtor to pay. The rationale for exoneration is that the surety should not have to suffer the inconvenience and expense of having to pay out of the surety's own assets and then sue the principal debtor when the debtor has sufficient resources. The surety might choose exoneration rather than a suit for reimbursement where, for example, the surety's assets are real estate whose liquidation to pay the debt would cause undue hardship to the surety.

Upon the default of the principal debtor, the surety might simply pay the creditor and then sue the debtor for *reimbursement* (repayment). In general, a surety who has an obligation to perform for the debtor is entitled to be reimbursed by the debtor, but only after the surety actually pays the debt. The right of reimbursement exists regardless of whether the surety

Table 24.1 Examples of Surety's Defenses to Payment

S's Defenses to Surety-Creditor Contract	S's Defenses Derived from Debtor-Creditor Contract	Special Suretyship Defenses:
S's lack of capacity	C's fraud against D	Performance of D's duty
No consideration to S	C's duress	C's release of D
C's fraud against S	No consideration from C	S's tender of performance
	But not, usually, D's infancy, D's insanity, D's bankruptcy, D's other lack of capacity	Increase of gratuitous S's duty
		Material increase of compensated S's duty
		C's surrender or impairment of colateral

is a compensated or uncompensated one, and often the duty of reimbursement exists even though the principal debtor did not consent to the suretyship.

Where the debtor has not consented to the suretyship, the debtor nevertheless has a duty to reimburse the surety if the debtor is unjustly enriched because of the surety's performance. The unconsenting debtor will be unjustly enriched by the surety's performance where the debtor is bound to perform, has not performed, and has no defense. Suppose Dan signs a note for $5,000 payable to Clara, for the purchase of an antique rug. At Clara's request but without Dan's knowledge, Shirley guarantees the note. The note falls due, Dan cannot pay, and Clara receives payment from Shirley because the rug was stolen from Dan months ago and was not insured. Dan has a duty to pay Clara the $5,000. Shirley, by making payment for Dan upon his default, has enriched him by discharging his duty to Clara, and Shirley is entitled to reimbursement despite the fact that Dan did not consent to the suretyship.

Sometimes the principal debtor has *no* duty to reimburse the surety. For example, if the debtor has a defense that is good against the creditor, and the surety pays, the surety (having no *legal compulsion* to pay) is a mere volunteer and is *not* entitled to reimbursement. Suppose Cora fraudulently induces Dan to sign a note for $10,000. Then, without Dan's knowledge Sue guarantees his note. The note falls due, Dan does not pay, and Cora receives payment from Sue who knew nothing of Cora's fraud. Sue is not entitled to reimbursement from Dan because he, as a result of his fraud defense, was under no obligation to pay and therefore could not have been enriched by Sue's payment. Her payment to Cora was simply unnecessary and cannot be charged to Dan. However, Sue may be able to recover her payment from Cora on the ground of Cora's unjust enrichment.

In a number of other situations the surety is not entitled to reimbursement from the principal debtor. For example, if the debtor has received a discharge in bankruptcy as to the creditor's claim, the discharge serves also to bar the surety's claim for reimbursement. If the debtor were required to pay the surety despite the discharge in bankruptcy, the discharge would not give the debtor the protection intended by the drafters of the bankruptcy law. Similarly, for the protection of persons who lack capacity to contract, a surety may not have reimbursement from a debtor whose obligation is void or has been avoided because of the debtor's lack of capacity.

A surety who satisfies the principal debtor's duty to the creditor acquires a right of *subrogation,* i.e., a right to be substituted for or to take over the rights of the creditor as against the principal debtor. The creditor might hold stock or other property as collateral security for the debt. The surety, as subrogee, is entitled to the collateral. Or the creditor might have obtained a judgment against the debtor and received payment of the judgment amount from the surety instead of having to execute the judgment. The surety, as subrogee, is entitled to stand in the shoes of the creditor and enforce the judgment against the debtor.

Rights of Cosurety. A cosurety who performs the principal debtor's duty is entitled to *contribution* from the other cosureties. Suppose Dan defaults on his obligation to pay Candice $300,000 and there are three cosureties. If there was no agreement among the three as to how much each would be liable for upon Dan's default, the three must share the loss equally. If Simon, the first cosurety, is required to make full payment to Candice, Simon is entitled to a $100,000 contribution from each of the other two cosureties.

Suppose now that there are two cosureties. Simon agrees to be liable for $200,000 of Dan's debt, while Sheila agrees to be liable for $100,000. Then Dan pays $150,000 and defaults as to the other $150,000. Simon and Sheila must contribute in accordance with the proportion established by their agreements. Simon is responsible for two-thirds of the loss and Sheila for one-third. If Sheila must pay Candice the whole $150,000, Simon must contribute $100,000.

Suppose Dan owes Cora $60,000, and Sid, Sue, and Saul are equal cosureties. Dan is in default, and Cora releases Sid from liability. Sue and Saul are thereby discharged from liability as to the share of loss Sid would have had to absorb. Cora is entitled only to $40,000—$20,000 from Sue and $20,000 from Saul.

Like sureties, cosureties have rights of subrogation and exoneration. Cosureties are entitled to be subrogated to collateral held by the creditor, in proportion to the amount of their individual liabilities.

Case 24.4 discusses a number of issues, including the right of reimbursement, contribution, and subrogation. The following diagram represents the facts of that case.

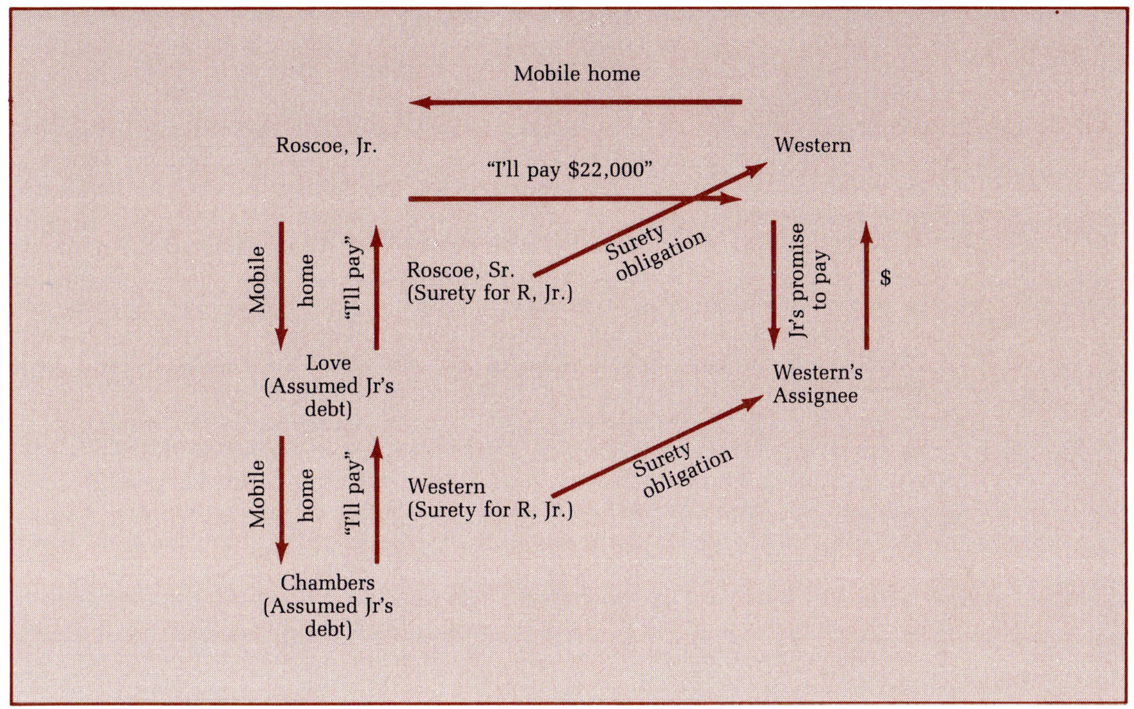

CASE 24.4 Western Coach Corp. v. Roscoe · 650 P.2d 449 (Ariz. 1982)

FACTS Roscoe, Jr. bought a mobile home on credit, for about $22,000. Roscoe, Sr. guaranteed Jr.'s performance. Western Coach, the seller, immediately assigned its rights under the sales contract to the first in a series of subsequent transferees collectively referred to here as "Western's assignee." As part of the assignment, and unknown to the Roscoes, Western also guaranteed Roscoe, Jr.'s performance. Roscoe, Jr. sold the mobile home to Love, and Love sold it to Chambers. Upon each sale, Western's assignee consented to the transfer of Roscoe, Jr.'s interest; each new transferee (Love and Chambers) assumed the obligation to perform; and each transferor (Roscoe, Jr. and Love) agreed to remain liable as a "primary obligor." Chambers defaulted on the payments. At Chambers' request, Western repossessed the home, which had been vandalized and stripped of its furnishings. Western repaired and refurbished the home, made the delinquent payments on the home, and paid back taxes that had accumulated. Western then sued Roscoe, Jr. and Roscoe, Sr. to recover the sums it claimed were spent on their behalf. The court directed a verdict for the Roscoes. After hearing more argument, the court granted Western's motion for a new trial, and the Roscoes appealed.

OPINION FELDMAN, J. . . . After reviewing the record, we find that the trial [court was correct in ordering a new trial].

The Roscoe, Jrs. were the principal obligors for performance of the buyers' obligations of the contract. Western was a guarantor of their performance. Western's suit against the Roscoe, Jrs. for reimbursement of payments made [by Western] under the retail installment contract was based on the theory that a guarantor who has paid his principal's debt is entitled to reimbursement from the principal. This is a correct statement of the law. . . .

The trial judge apparently believed that in order to recover under this theory Western had to prove that the Roscoe, Jrs. had agreed that Western would act as guarantor. This

CASE 24.4 Continued

element, however, is not necessary in order to establish a right to subrogation. The principal is liable to the guarantor even though the contract of guaranty was executed at the request of the creditor and without the knowledge of the debtor....

Western's suit against the Roscoe, Srs. was based upon the theory that as co-guarantor under the retail installment contract, the Roscoe, Srs. were liable to contribute a pro rata share of the amount that Western was required to pay under the installment contract. This is a correct theory of law....

[The Roscoes] contend that the evidence presented at trial establishes that a novation occurred when the mobile home was sold to the Loves, thus releasing... the Roscoe, Jrs. and their guarantors from liability.... Therefore, appellants argue, when Western made the default payments to the bank it acted gratuitously and is not entitled to reimbursement.

We recognize that if a novation had in fact occurred... the Roscoe, Jrs. and their guarantors [the Roscoe, Srs.] would have been released from liability.... However, to constitute a valid novation, there must be... an agreement of all parties to a new... contract. The novation agreement may be express or implied. In this case, there was... a factual question whether the Roscoe, Jrs. had been released from their obligations under the... contract when they sold the mobile home to the Loves. Mrs. Roscoe, Jr. testified... that it was her understanding that their obligation was extinguished when the Loves agreed to assume the payments under the contract. On the other hand, [the president] of Western testified that he had explained to the Roscoes that even though they sold the mobile home to the Loves, they remained liable.... Since there was a factual question whether a novation had occurred, the Roscoes were not entitled to a directed verdict on that basis.

In the alternative, the Roscoes seem to contend that, as a result of the sale from Roscoe, Jr. to Love, the Loves became the principal obligors on the debt by implication of law, so that, as between the parties to that sale, the Loves were principal obligors and Roscoe, Jrs. were sureties. Arguably, then, when [Western's assignee] learned of the transaction and of Roscoe Jr.'s implied suretyship relation with Love, it was legally required to refrain from doing anything which would adversely affect Roscoe, Jr.'s rights as surety by either impairing security for payment of the debt or the ability of the principal obligor [Love] to pay that debt. The Roscoes urge that when [Western's assignee] consented, without the Roscoes' knowledge, to the transfer of ownership from Love to Chambers, it committed an act which adversely affected the surety and thus released the Roscoes from their suretyship obligations.

Even assuming that... the Roscoes were converted to sureties by reason of the sale to Love and Love's assumption of the payments [an assumption requiring us to ignore the contract clause stating that the Roscoes remained liable as "primary obligors"], we disagree with the Roscoes' position.

By consenting to the sale from Love to Chambers, [Western's assignee] did nothing that would release Roscoe, Jr. from a suretyship obligation. [An] obligee's consent to the principal's [Love's] transfer of property which is security for the debt does not ordinarily release the surety [Roscoe, Jr.], unless the [transaction alters] the obligation, as, for example, by releasing the... obligor [Love. Here,] despite the transfer of the right of ownership in the trailer, the Loves remained primarily liable on the debt.... [T]he assumption agreement between Love and Chambers... provided that the "ORIGINAL PURCHASER [Roscoe, Jr.] or SUBSEQUENT TRANSFEREE [Love] agrees" that he/she would not be relieved from any of his/her responsibilities under the agreement. Thus, there was evidence which permitted the finder of fact to conclude that the Roscoes' rights against Love were unaffected by Love's sale to Chambers, with the result that the Roscoes were not released from their obligations whether they were principal debtors or sureties for Love's... performance....

Western contends that under the theory of unjust enrichment, it is entitled to be reimbursed by the Roscoes for the sums it paid.... It is well established that a person who

CASE 24.4 Continued

has been unjustly enriched at the expense of another is required to make restitution to the other. The principle is applicable, however, only if the person conferring the benefit is not an "officious intermeddler." [According to the *Restatement of Restitution*], "Officiousness means interference in the affairs of others not justified by the circumstances. . . ."

[Here] Western has established facts from which the jury could conclude that Western was not an "officious intermeddler." When the Chambers' defaulted. . . Western became liable [to Western's assignee] under its guaranty contract for the remaining amount due. . . . [A]t the time Western took possession of the mobile home and made the alleged repairs, the payments were in default. Thus. . . [Western's assignee] could have insisted that Western pay the debt. Had Western done so, it would have become entitled to be subrogated to [the assignee's] rights under the retail installment contract and to possession of the security. Thus, Western had an interest in seeing that the security for the debt was preserved and was therefore not an "officious intermeddler."

JUDGMENT The order granting a new trial is affirmed.

Summary

The purpose of a secured transaction is to reduce the creditor's risk of nonpayment. Some security devices give the creditor a lien on real or personal property as the backup source of payment. The lien may be imposed by law or it may be created by contract. In suretyship, the source of backup payment is the surety's promise to pay if the debtor does not.

The law imposes mechanics' and other types of liens on personal and real property in favor of persons who repair, store, improve, or otherwise render services in connection with the property. Liens created by contract include secured transactions in personal property; secured transactions in real estate such as mortgages and land contracts; and contracts of suretyship. Contractual security devices are used to secure repayment of a loan or the purchase price of property or services.

A surety is responsible for the debt, default, or miscarriage of the principal debtor. The surety is liable for precisely the performance, or any unperformed part of it, that the debtor promised the creditor—unless the surety agreed to be liable only for a lesser amount, or unless the surety has a defense to payment. The surety may have the benefit of the surety's own contractual defenses, some contractual defenses that are available to the debtor, and special suretyship defenses such as an alteration of the debtor's obligation not consented to by the surety. If the surety is called on to perform, the surety may be entitled to exoneration, reimbursement, or subrogation. A cosurety who pays more than his or her share of the debt may be entitled also to contribution from the other cosureties.

Review Questions

1 What practical advantage is there to being a secured creditor rather than an unsecured one?

2 **(a)** Under what circumstances will a bailee of personal property be entitled to enforce a possessory lien? **(b)** How does a "specific" possessory lien differ from a "general" one?

3 Under what circumstances may a person enforce a mechanic's lien against real property?

4 How does a "land contract" function as a security device?

5 Illustrate how suretyship can arise by operation of law.

6 How does a gratuitous surety differ from a compensated one? Is there any difference in legal liability? Explain.

7 What is a cosurety?

8 In defense to a claim that a surety is liable to the creditor, the surety may assert the surety's own contractual defenses. Give an illustration of such a defense.

9 A surety may assert some of the principal debtor's defenses but not all of them. Which ones may the surety *not* have the benefit of? Why?

10 Explain the purpose and give two illustrations of the special suretyship defenses.

11 What is "exoneration," and where is it likely to be sought?

12 **(a)** Under what circumstances may a surety have reimbursement from the debtor? *Not* have reimbursement? **(b)** Illustrate subrogation and contribution.

Case Problems

1 Just before the beginning of the irrigation season Larry brings three portable irrigation pumps to Carl for their annual cleaning and repair. Carl completes the work and presents Larry with a bill for $150, the reasonable value of Carl's services. Larry is short on cash and needs the pumps right away. Carl releases two of them to Larry but holds the third one as security for payment of his bill. Larry contends that by releasing the first two pumps, Carl has lost his possessory lien on the third one as well. Does Carl have a lien on the third pump? Explain.

2 First National State Bank (Bank) made a large personal loan to Recklitis, president of SCA Corp. Recklitis pledged his SCA stock as collateral for the loan. When the value of SCA stock declined, Bank sought additional security. Steir, chairman of the SCA board of directors, pledged his own SCA stock as collateral for the Recklitis loan. Steir later asked Kurzman, SCA's vice-president, to do likewise "for the good of the company." Kurzman did so. Later, Recklitis defaulted on the loan. Although Steir's shares were sufficient in value to satisfy the loan deficiency, Bank sold shares of Steir and Kurzman in proportion to the number of shares pledged by each. Kurzman protested, arguing that because he pledged his stock at Steir's request and subsequent to Steir's pledge, Bank should have taken only Steir's stock and not Kurzman's. Contending that Steir had no right of contribution from Kurzman, he sued Steir for the value of Kurzman's shares taken by Bank. Whether Kurzman should prevail depended on whether he was a cosurety. Was Kurzman entitled to the value of the shares?

3 Lloyd Corporation leased restaurant premises to Karafume Tempura, Ltd. O'Connor, a shareholder, director, and corporate secretary of the lessee, received thirty-five additional shares for signing a document guaranteeing payment of the rent. The lease provided that "no typical American food will be offered for sale in or from [the restaurant] at any time during the life of this lease." The restaurant's business was poor; Lloyd later agreed, through a modification of the lease, to permit the restaurant to serve American food in addition to Japanese-style food. O'Connor knew of the change. Eventually, the restaurant failed, and Lloyd sought unpaid rent from O'Connor. O'Connor refused to pay, contending that he was a gratuitous surety, that the change in the lease increased his risk, and that he had not consented to the change. Should O'Connor be held liable for the rent?

4 To induce Joe Caldwell to sign a contract to play professional basketball, Munchak signed a guarantee of salary payments. During the 1974–75 season Caldwell was suspended by his team, the Spirits of St. Louis, for violating the terms of his contract. One reason for Caldwell's suspension was his alleged interference with the contractual relationship between the Spirits and another player, Barnes. Barnes left the team. Spirits' representatives inquired of Caldwell as to Barnes' whereabouts. Caldwell said he did not know where Barnes was. In fact, Caldwell knew that Barnes had been at LaGuardia Airport several hours earlier, though Caldwell did not know where Barnes was going. Caldwell was never paid his salary for $220,000 for that season although he played in twenty-three games. He brought suit against Munchak on the basis of the guarantee. Munchak denied liability, alleging that by refusing to reveal Barnes' whereabouts Caldwell violated a contract provision that required him "not to do anything which is detrimental to the best interests of the CLUB." Did Munchak have a good defense against his liability as a surety?

5 Malibu Pools, Inc., borrowed money from and signed two promissory notes in favor of Western Bank. Barnhart signed an agreement guaranteeing payment of the notes. Rankin was a co-guarantor. Later, without the prior consent of Barnhart, Western Bank released Rankin from liability as co-guarantor. Malibu defaulted on the notes and was placed in bankruptcy. Aqua Leisure purchased Malibu's assets, agreeing to assume Malibu's debt (the notes). Barnhart signed an agreement stating that his guaranty was to "remain in place as [it] then currently applied." Since Malibu had not repaid the loan before the bankruptcy, Western Bank sued Barnhart for the unpaid amount. Barnhart contended that he had been discharged from liability because Western had released Rankin, and because Aqua Leisure had assumed Malibu's debts. Was Barnhart discharged from liability to Western Bank?

6 Coffey and Sawyer worked for Applied Systems as program writer and computer operator, respectively. They left Applied Systems to go into business for themselves, converting to their own use several of Applied Systems' computer tapes and programs. In subsequent legal proceedings, Applied Systems was awarded a $25,000 verdict against Coffey and Sawyer; Applied Systems was awarded $25,000 against National Surety on its indemnity bond covering Coffey and Sawyer; and National Surety was awarded $25,000 against Coffey and Sawyer on its claim for reimbursement. Coffey and Sawyer appealed, arguing that the verdicts made them liable twice for the same wrong, since they would be liable to both Applied Systems and National Surety. Are Coffey and Sawyer correct?

CHAPTER 25

Secured Transactions in Personal Property

As noted in the preceding chapter, vast amounts of consumer and business credit are secured by an interest in personal property—consumer goods, accounts receivable, inventory, equipment, and other "collateral"—possessed or owned by the debtor. Article 9 of the Uniform Commercial Code (UCC) governs secured transactions in personal property.[1] This chapter discusses (1) how, under Article 9, a creditor may acquire a security interest in personal property and make that interest enforceable against the claims of rival creditors, (2) who is entitled to the collateral (who has "priority") when two or more persons claim it upon the debtor's default; and (3) the rights of the secured party to dispose of the collateral if the debtor fails to pay.

Most rules of Article 9 apply without regard to whether the secured transaction involves consumer goods or business property. However, secured transactions in consumer goods (goods that are used or bought primarily for personal, family, or household purposes) are subject to a few special rules that are noted throughout the chapter.

Purpose and Coverage of UCC Article 9

Purpose of Article 9

Article 9 is a complicated body of law. Why it was needed, and how it operates, can be better understood by a brief look at the historical development of secured transactions in personal property.

Before the industrial revolution, demand for credit was relatively small, and the *pledge* was the main security device involving personal property. To obtain a loan, the debtor (pledgor) gave possession of the collateral to the creditor (pledgee). Today, one might pledge a ring or a violin to a pawnbroker or 100 shares of stock to a bank as collateral for a loan of cash. The pledgee-creditor will possess the collateral until the loan is repaid. If the loan is not repaid when due, the pledgee has a right to sell the collateral to cover the amount of the loan.

The industrial revolution dramatically increased credit needs and forced the invention of secured transactions that would allow the debtor to possess the collateral while paying for it. The most important pre-Code security devices were the chattel mortgage and the conditional-sale contract. Under the *chattel mortgage,* the debtor retained possession of the goods ("chattels") used as collateral, but temporarily transferred title to (ownership of) the chattel to the creditor or, in some states, granted the creditor a lien on the chattel. Upon payment of the debt, title reverted (went back) to the debtor or the lien was discharged. Under the *conditional-sale contract,* the buyer-debtor received possession of the goods from the seller, and the seller-creditor retained title until the buyer made the agreed payments. Like the pledge, these two devices are widely used today.

The pre-Code law of secured transactions had many short-comings that made credit extension expensive and risky. Among them were (1) a variety of security devices—chattel mortgages, trust receipts, factor's liens, etc.—each with its separate public-notice filing system, (2) courts that insisted on invalidating a security transaction if it did not fall into the category the lender thought it did, (3) the expense of multiple filings in the various public-notice filing systems as a hedge against the lender's wrong guess, (4) inadequate inventory and accounts receivable financing, and (5) different treatment by courts and legislatures of similar security devices, and even of devices of the same name.

To correct these problems, the drafters of the UCC developed, in Article 9, a legal framework for making the law of secured transactions more uniform, predictable, and useful. This framework has four main features:

1 The substitution of the single term *security interest* for the variety of expressions that had been used in the past to describe the property right that the creditor holds as security. Article 9 does not abolish the old security devices nor prohibit the use of the old terminology, but the old devices are no longer viewed as inherently different from each other. Instead, they are considered as variations of the same thing: an Article 9 secured transaction whose consequences are spelled out in the Article. Thus in the *pledge,* possession of the debtor's property by the creditor is the UCC security interest. In a

[1]All states except Vermont have adopted the 1972 version of Article 9, which is discussed in this chapter.

conditional-sale contract or a *chattel mortgage,* the creditor retains or receives "title" as the UCC security interest.

2 The substitution of a simplified public-notice *filing system* for the confusing and expensive pre-Code jumble of different files, records, and indexes for each type of security device.

3 A *single system of priorities* for resolving disputes where there are two or more conflicting interests in the same collateral, to replace the widely varying older state systems.

4 A *uniform method of liquidating collateral* (converting it into cash) after default, based on a commercially reasonable liquidation rather than the forced-sale provisions of many pre-Code statutes that caused economic loss to both creditor and debtor.

With regard to the nature of the UCC security interest, note that the word "title" has two legal meanings that can be confusing. In the law of property, title often means full ownership of a thing—the right to possess, use, enjoy, and dispose of a thing by selling it, giving it away, or destroying it. But in the law of secured transactions, the "title" that a creditor holds to secure payment of a debt is of a very limited nature. Under UCC § 1-201(37), "The retention or reservation of title by a seller of goods notwithstanding shipment or delivery to the buyer. . . is limited in effect to a reservation of a 'security interest.'" Like any other security interest, the creditor's "title" gives the creditor a *limited* right to control or dispose of (e.g., sell) the collateral—a right that can be exercised only upon the debtor's default, and then only as to the amount of the debt still owed. Table 25.1 illustrates the interests held by debtor and creditor in three common types of secured transactions.

Coverage of Article 9

Security Transactions Covered. Except for certain classes of excluded transactions discussed later, Article 9 applies (*a*) to any transaction (regardless of its form) that is intended to create a security interest in *personal property* or *fixtures,* and (*b*) to any *sale* of accounts or chattel paper [9-102]. "Personal property" includes not only goods, but also a wide variety of intangible property—stocks, bonds, goodwill, trademarks, accounts receivable, rights to refunds, etc.—and to any other personal property that is or "may become customarily used as commercial security" [9-106, comment].

The statement of Article 9's coverage raises two questions: (1) Fixtures are normally considered part of the real property to which they are annexed and for most purposes are subject to the local real estate law. Why, then, does Article 9, which deals mainly with transactions in *personal* property, apply to the security aspects of fixtures? (2) Why does Article 9, which applies mainly to *credit* transactions, apply also to *sales* of accounts and chattel paper?

Fixtures begin life as goods and often move in interstate commerce until annexed to realty. If the security aspects of fixture transactions were governed by real estate law, fixture creditors who sell nationally would be uncertain of their rights to the collateral in the event of the buyer's default, since the real estate laws of the states vary greatly as to creditors' rights. Article 9 reduces the uncertainty by providing a single set of rules that govern those rights, both

Table 25.1 Interests of Debtor and Creditor in Collateral

Security Device	Debtor's Interest	Creditor's Security Interest
Pledge	Title (basic ownership rights)	Possession
Chattel mortgage	Possession and other ownership rights	"Title" (the limited UCC variety)
Conditional-sale contract	Possession and other ownership rights	"Title" (the limited UCC variety)

before and after the fixture is annexed to the real estate.

The answer to the second question requires a look at the nature of chattel paper and accounts and how their owners typically use them to raise money. *Chattel paper* is a writing, or writings, evidencing (1) a debtor's obligation to pay for goods that he or she is buying on credit and (2) the seller's security interest in those goods [9-105]. Suppose you make a credit purchase of a home freezer from West Store, signing a promissory note for the purchase price and a conditional-sale contract giving West a security interest in the freezer. Together these two documents constitute chattel paper. In contrast, an *account* (often called an "account receivable") is any right to payment for goods sold or leased, or for services rendered, that is *not* evidenced by an instrument (e.g., a promissory note) or chattel paper [9-106]. A charge account at West Store is an example. If you buy a camera at West's and simply "charge it," West is an unsecured creditor as to the resulting account.

Both the chattel paper and the account are property rights owned by West that it can either *sell* or *use as collateral* for a loan. Suppose West has $100,000 worth of chattel paper from 100 customers, but none of it is due for several months. To raise money for current business needs, West might discount (sell) the paper for $90,000. The buyer will receive the paper and collect the face amount (plus any interest) from each West customer. Or, instead of selling the paper, West might pledge it to a bank as collateral for a loan, intending to repay the loan, get the paper back, and itself collect the face amount. In both transactions—sale and pledge—West receives money and gives up possession of the chattel paper. Because the transactions look so much alike, third persons such as West's other creditors or potential lenders may not know whether West still owns the paper. The difficulty is even greater where West sells the paper and is permitted to retain custody of it for collection.

To give fair warning to those third persons, the UCC drafters decided that Article 9 should apply to sales and secured transactions alike. Consequently, a *buyer* of West's chattel paper must comply with the rules of Article 9—i.e., like a lender, West's buyer must notify others who may later claim an interest in the chattel paper that the buyer, not West, owns it. The required notice may be given by filing a financing statement in the appropriate public records, or the buyer may accomplish the same result by taking possession of the chattel paper. A buyer of *accounts* ordinarily must file a financing statement since there is little or no paper for the buyer to possess.

To permit the use of old security devices and the development of new ones, *security interest* is defined broadly as "an interest in personal property or fixtures which secures payment or performance of an obligation" [1-201(37)]. However, it is not always clear whether a transaction such as a sale, lease, or consignment (an entrustment of property by the owner to a bailee for care or sale) is a *secured* transaction. Under the Code, the intention of the parties determines whether a transaction is secured or not. For example, sellers of goods, in attempts to protect themselves from the claims of buyers' creditors, often characterize sales of goods as "leases." In a true lease (e.g., lease of a computer) covered by UCC Article 2A, the lessor retains title (ownership) and grants possession and usage rights to the lessee. The lessor intends to remain owner. In a security "lease" covered by Article 9, however, the intention of the "lessor" is not to remain the owner, but to sell the goods and reserve a right to retrieve them if payment is not made. Since the "lease" is intended to secure payment of an obligation, the seller must follow the rules of Article 9 to prevail over creditors of the buyer-"lessee." The Code provides that a lease is one intended for security if the parties agree that at the expiration of the lease the lessee shall become the owner of the property for no additional consideration or for only a nominal (insignificant) consideration [1-201(37)].

Security Transactions Excluded. Twelve kinds of transactions are excluded from Article 9 coverage [9-104]. For example, assignments of wages as security for debts are excluded because such assignments present important social problems whose solution should be a matter of local regulation. Although most sales of accounts receivable are covered by Article 9, some are excluded because they have nothing to do with commercial financing—e.g., sales of accounts or chattel paper as a part of a sale of the business out of which they arose. In other instances, such as in the use of life insurance as collateral, or in the creation and enforcement of mechanics' liens, the transaction is excluded because it is adequately covered by non-Code law.

Table 25.2 (on page 520) lists some key terms relating to secured transactions.

Table 25.2 Secured Transactions Key Terms

Chattel paper: Document or documents evidencing (1) buyer-debtor's obligation to pay for goods and (2) seller-creditor's security interest in them.

Account: Any right to payment (for goods or services) not evidenced by an instrument or chattel paper. An account receivable.

Security interest: Any interest in personal property or fixtures that secures payment or performance of an obligation. Usually, possession (as in a pledge) or "title" (as in a chattel mortgage, conditional-sale contract, or "lease" intended for security).

Security lease: Lease intended for security. It is so intended where the lessee has the right, for a nominal or no additional consideration, to become owner of the property when the lease expires.

Acquiring and Perfecting a Security Interest

A businessperson's interest in the topic of secured transactions may center around what must be done to acquire a security interest or to grant one. Article 9 speaks in terms of "attachment" and "perfection." *Attachment* is the name of the process by which the debtor and the creditor create a security interest and make it enforceable as between themselves. *Perfection* is the process by which the creditor ("secured party") makes the security interest enforceable against third persons such as other creditors of the debtor who also claim an interest in the collateral.

Attachment of a Security Interest

Attachment Events. A security interest does not "attach" (arise), and therefore is not enforceable against the debtor, unless four attachment "events" have occurred:

1. The debtor and the creditor must *agree* that a security interest is to be created [9-203]. Ordinarily, this "security agreement" will be in writing.
2. The *creditor must possess* the collateral *or* the *debtor must sign* a security agreement that "reasonably identifies" the collateral [9-203; 9-110].
3. The *secured party must give value.* Otherwise there will be no debtor's obligation to be secured. The secured party usually gives value by making a loan, by selling goods on credit, or by making a binding commitment to extend credit.
4. The *debtor must have rights* in the collateral. Under the terms of the security agreement, some or all of the debtor's rights are held by the secured party as the security interest.

The attachment events may occur in any order. Attachment itself cannot occur earlier than the completion of the last event, but the parties to the security agreement can postpone the time of attachment.

The *security agreement* lays out the contract between the secured party and the debtor, often in considerable detail. In addition to the required description of the collateral, the security agreement usually includes at least the following:

- Statement that the creditor has a security interest in the described collateral.
- Description of the loan or other value given by the creditor.
- Debtor's promise to maintain the collateral in good condition.
- Debtor's promise to insure the collateral.
- Debtor's promise not to sell the collateral to someone else or otherwise impair the creditor's security without the creditor's prior written consent.
- Statement that the debtor must provide additional collateral if the original collateral declines in value.
- List of events that constitute "default": debtor's failure to repay the debt or any installment, death of the debtor, failure of the debtor's business, etc.

- Debtor's promise to deliver the collateral to the creditor upon debtor's default in paying the debt.
- Statement of creditor's right to repossess the collateral upon debtor's default.

Attachment Involving After-Acquired Property Clauses and Future Advances Provisions. Article 9 permits the use of an "after-acquired property clause" in commercial secured transactions [9-204] (but sharply limits its use when the collateral is consumer goods). For example, a bank might lend you $25,000 to expand your business and take a security interest in all your business assets and "any business assets [you] may hereafter acquire." By using such a clause, the creditor obtains a security interest in both present and future assets of the debtor instead of a security interest only in specific assets on hand at the creation of the secured transaction. If the other attachment events have occurred, the after-acquired property is subject to the security interest as soon as the debtor acquires rights in the property. Such a security interest is called a "floating lien." The floating lien is especially useful in inventory and accounts receivable financing because only one security agreement is needed to grant the creditor a security interest in a shifting mass of collateral.

The Code also permits the use of a "future advances" provision in the security agreement, so that the collateral put up by the debtor can secure future loans. Thus, without having to enter into a new security agreement for each new loan, the creditor safely and automatically gives value each time he or she extends new credit. Future advances provisions are especially useful where a creditor has agreed to make a large loan but the debtor needs the money only a bit at a time.

Table 25.3 (below) lists some key terms relating to attachment.

Perfection of a Security Interest

Entering into a security agreement with the debtor may not be sufficient, in itself, to protect the secured party fully. For the secured party to receive maximum protection from rivals who might claim the collateral, the security interest must be *perfected*. Ordinarily, these competing claimants will be other creditors of the debtor (as where several different banks might have lent the debtor money to begin a business), a buyer of the collateral from the debtor (as where the debtor sells encumbered inventory to customers), or a mechanic or other artisan who has repaired or improved the collateral. Timely perfection of a security interest gives the secured party *priority* over most, but not all, of these competing claimants, i.e., first claim to the collateral if the debtor defaults.

Methods of Perfection. Perfection may be accomplished in three ways: (1) automatically at the completion of the attachment events, (2) by the secured party's taking possession of the collateral, or (3) by the filing of a financing statement in the public records. Table 25.5 on p. 527 indicates which types of perfection may or must be used for partic-

Table 25.3 Key Terms Relating to Attachment

Attachment: Process by which debtor and creditor create a security interest and make it enforceable as between themselves. Involves four attachment events.

Security agreement: An agreement between debtor and creditor that creates or provides for a security interest.

Secured party: A creditor who receives a security interest.

After-acquired property clause: Clause in a security agreement granting the creditor a security interest in any property the debtor now owns or may later acquire.

Floating lien: A security interest, created by an after-acquired property clause, in a changing mass of collateral.

Future advances provision: A clause in a security agreement permitting the collateral to secure future loans.

ular types of collateral. A general discussion of perfection follows. A few specialized perfection rules are introduced later, in the section on priorities.

Perfection by attachment only. Article 9 grants the status of perfection to a few security interests even though nothing more than attachment has occurred. For example, the Code exempts a *purchase-money security interest (PMSI)* in most *consumer goods* from the general filing requirement. (A *purchase money security interest* is one taken or retained by a seller of the collateral—or, sometimes, one taken by a bank or other lender—to secure all or part of the purchase price [9-107].) Credit sales of consumer goods are so numerous that to require sellers to file a financing statement for each sale would impose an unreasonable burden on the market system. Since no physical notice-giving step, such as the secured party's taking possession, is required, the debtor-purchaser can, because of the seller's attachment-only perfection status, possess the consumer goods without endangering the seller's priority as against third persons who might claim the goods. However, as will be noted later in this chapter, the creditor-seller who perfects by attachment only is not fully protected and may lose the goods to a person who buys them from the debtor.

Motor vehicles and fixtures often are consumer goods, but attachment-only perfection usually is *not* available for them. Filing a financing statement (or compliance with a certificate of title statute) is required to perfect a security interest in a motor vehicle that is required to be registered; and in many states boats, trailers, and mobile homes also are subject to such a requirement [9-302]. A "fixture filing" (discussed later) is required for perfecting a security interest in a fixture.

Perfection by secured party's having possession. For most types of collateral, a security interest is perfected if the secured party possesses the collateral or if a third person bailee possesses it on behalf of the secured party. The pledge (discussed earlier) and field warehousing involve perfection by possession. In *field warehousing,* inventory used as collateral is segregated in a fenced-off area of the borrower's—e.g., a manufacturer's—premises and placed under the control of an independent warehouser who acts on behalf of the lender (creditor). As the debtor sells the inventory being used as collateral, the field warehouser releases the needed amounts and makes sure that the creditor-lender receives proper payment from the proceeds of the sale.

Usually possession is an alternative to filing, but for some collateral, possession is the required perfection method. For instance, because the public expects the possessor of money to own it, a security interest in money can be perfected only by the secured party's taking possession [9-304]. A similar rule applies to instruments (documents) such as checks.

Perfection by filing a financing statement. Security interests in most kinds of property may be perfected by filing a *financing statement* in the public records. The financing statement gives notice to the public that the secured party claims a security interest in the collateral. A major reason for the use of public-notice filing is to allow debtors such as purchasers of business equipment to use the collateral while paying for it. Filing has other advantages that make it the most commonly used perfection method with regard to business goods used as collateral: (1) Sellers give notice of their security interests quickly and easily by filing in only one or two places. (2) Persons contemplating buying expensive goods or accepting them as collateral for a loan can easily check the public record to determine whether they are encumbered. For some classes of collateral, such as accounts and general intangibles, filing is the required method of perfection because the property cannot be physically possessed by the secured party in such a way as to give notice to the public of the secured party's interest. To be legally effective as a notice to the secured party's rival creditors, the statement must be *signed by the debtor* and must include at least the following information: (*a*) the *names and addresses of the debtor and the secured party,* and (*b*) a *description of the item* (such as "one Buick auto, serial # 17") or *a statement of the type of collateral* (such as "all of the men's clothing at Holiday Clothiers, 44 State Street, Your City"). Where the collateral is closely identified with a particular parcel of land (e.g., crops, timber, minerals, fixtures), the financing statement must also contain a *description of the land concerned* [9-402(1)]. Figure 25.1 illustrates a typical financing statement form.

The amount of information required in the financing statement has been kept to a minimum because the reason for filing it is merely to give notice that the secured party may have a security interest in the collateral described. Potential rivals of the secured party, being able to see the financing statement in the public records, are expected to

STATE OF CALIFORNIA
UNIFORM COMMERCIAL CODE - FINANCING STATEMENT - FORM UCC-1 (REV. 12/87)
IMPORTANT - Read instructions on back before filling out form

QUAD
38601

This FINANCING STATEMENT is presented for filing pursuant to the California Uniform Commercial Code.

1. DEBTOR (LAST NAME FIRST - IF AN INDIVIDUAL)		1 A. SOCIAL SECURITY OR FEDERAL TAX NO.
1 B. MAILING ADDRESS	1 C. CITY, STATE	1 D. ZIP CODE
2. ADDITIONAL DEBTOR (IF ANY) (LAST NAME FIRST - IF AN INDIVIDUAL)		2 A. SOCIAL SECURITY OR FEDERAL TAX NO.
2B. MAILING ADDRESS	2C. CITY, STATE	2D. ZIP CODE
3. DEBTOR'S TRADE NAMES OR STYLES (IF ANY)		3A. FEDERAL TAX NUMBER
4. SECURED PARTY NAME MAILING ADDRESS CITY STATE ZIP CODE		4 A. SOCIAL SECURITY NO., FEDERAL TAX NO. OR BANK TRANSIT AND A.B.A. NO.
5. ASSIGNEE OF SECURED PARTY (IF ANY) NAME MAILING ADDRESS CITY STATE ZIP CODE		5 A. SOCIAL SECURITY NO., FEDERAL TAX NO. OR BANK TRANSIT AND A.B.A. NO.

6. This FINANCING STATEMENT covers the following types or items of property **(include description of real property on which located and owner of record when required by instruction 4).**

7. CHECK IF APPLICABLE ☒	7A. ☐ PRODUCTS OF COLLATERAL ARE ALSO COVERED	7B. DEBTOR(S) SIGNATURE NOT REQUIRED IN ACCORDANCE WITH INSTRUCTION 5(A) ITEM: ☐ (1) ☐ (2) ☐ (3) ☐ (4)
8. CHECK IF APPLICABLE ☒	☐ DEBTOR IS A "TRANSMITTING UTILITY" IN ACCORDANCE WITH UCC § 9105 (1) (N)	

9. DATE: ▶ SIGNATURE(S) OF DEBTOR(S)	CODE	10. THIS SPACE FOR USE OF FILING OFFICER (DATE, TIME, FILE NUMBER AND FILING OFFICER)
TYPE OR PRINT NAME(S) OF DEBTOR(S)	1 2	
▶ SIGNATURE(S) OF SECURED PARTY(IES)	3 4	
TYPE OR PRINT NAME(S) OF SECURED PARTY(IES)	5 6	
11. Return copy to: NAME ADDRESS CITY STATE ZIP CODE	7 8 9 0	
(1) FILING OFFICER COPY — FORM UCC.1 - FILING FEE $5.00 Approved by the Secretary of State		

Figure 25.1 Financing Statement Form

Table 25.4 Key Terms Relating to Perfection

Financing statement: A brief notice, intended to be filed in the public records, of the secured party's claim to the collateral described in the statement.

Perfection: Process by which secured party makes the security interest enforceable against third persons such as debtor's other creditors. Ordinarily accomplished by creditor's filing a financing statement or taking possession of the collateral. In some situations, Article 9 grants an "attachment-only" perfection status.

Purchase-money security interest: A security interest held by a seller of goods (or, sometimes, by a bank or other lender) to secure the purchase price.

Fixture filing: A financing statement covering goods that are or will be fixtures. Document must describe the fixture and the real estate involved and must state that the document is to be filed in the real estate records.

make further inquiry to determine the exact state of affairs between the secured party and the debtor.

The financing statement is not to be confused with the security agreement. A security agreement creates the security interest and usually spells out the duties that the secured party and the debtor owe each other. It is part of the attachment process and does not, by itself, make the security interest enforceable against anyone other than the debtor. In contrast, the financing statement, when filed in the public records as part of the perfection process, gives third persons notice of the secured party's claim to the collateral. However, if a security agreement is in writing, contains the minimum information required for a financing statement, and is signed by the debtor, the security agreement itself may serve as a financing statement (i.e., may be filed), as may a *signed copy* of the security agreement.

The proper place to file a financing statement can be determined only by reference to the relevant state's version of Section 9-401. A state's filing system may be "central" (e.g., one main office located in the state capital) or "local" (e.g., offices located in each township or county). Usually the filing system is some combination of central and local files, with security interests in such collateral as farming equipment and consumer goods to be filed locally, and security interests in inventory, industrial equipment, and accounts to be filed in the office of the secretary of state. Thus, users of the filing system who normally need to acquire credit information on a statewide basis can do so efficiently, while credit information about purely local businesses can normally be found in the county or township where the debtor resides or, sometimes, where the goods are located.

If goods are or are to become fixtures, a *fixture filing* is required, and the proper filing place is the office where a mortgage on the real estate concerned would be filed or recorded. The fixture filing must describe the fixture, must describe the real estate to which the fixture is to be annexed, and must say that the fixture filing document is to be filed in the real estate records.

Table 25.4 lists some key terms relating to perfection.

Case 25.1 discusses what constitutes a security agreement, and whether a failure to perfect a security interest affects the validity of the interest as between debtor and creditor.

CASE 25.1 Lojek v. Pedler · 42 UCC Rep. 1448 (Ohio 1986)

FACTS Lojek (plaintiff) owned several corporations that were in financial difficulty. To salvage them, Lojek and Pedler set up a plan of reorganization. During the financial dealings,

CASE 25.1 Continued

Lojek agreed to lend Pedler $300,000, with which Pedler was to buy 3,000 shares of stock in a corporation formed to carry out the reorganization. Under the terms of a "Trust Agreement" signed by Lojek and Pedler, Pedler would pledge the shares as collateral for the amount he owed Lojek, and Rondy would hold the shares until the debt was repaid. The agreement further provided that:

> In the event of the death of... [Pedler]... prior to the delivery of said shares to TRUSTEE [Rondy], then said stock certificates shall be immediately the property of... [Lojek], in full satisfaction of said note.

Lojek paid Pedler $300,000 and Pedler received the stock, but Pedler died before delivering the shares to Rondy. Lojek demanded the stock from Pedler's estate (defendant). The executor refused Lojek's demand. Lojek brought suit, seeking a declaratory judgment to determine ownership of the shares. From a judgment for Lojek, Pedler's estate appealed. The court of appeals reversed the judgment of the trial court, and Lojek appealed.

OPINION BROWN, J.... The court of appeals held that, rather than creating a trust, "the parties intended to pledge the shares to secure Pedler's debt to Lojek." We agree. We also agree that "[s]ince the shares were never delivered either to Lojek or to Rondy as Lojek's agent, the security interest was not perfected pursuant to [§ 9-304]. However, the court of appeals erred in its conclusion that Lojek lost all rights granted by the Agreement because of his failure to perfect his security interest....

[Sec. 9-105(1) (1)] defines "security agreement" as "an agreement which creates or provides for a security interest." The Agreement in this case refers to Lojek's security interest as a "present assignment" of the stock "pursuant to a pledge of said stock" as collateral for Lojek's loan to Pedler. Thus, the Agreement in this case clearly meets that statutory definition. Further, the security interest attached to the collateral as provided by [§ 9-203]: (1) the debtor signed a security agreement which contained a description of the collateral (the Agreement); (2) value was given (Lojek's transfer of $300,000 to Pedler; and (3) Pedler, the debtor, had rights in the collateral....

The parties agree that Lojek failed to perfect his security interest in the stock according to the terms of [§ 9-304]. To so perfect his security interest, either Lojek or Rondy on Lojek's behalf would have had to take physical possession of the shares. By the terms of the Agreement, the parties intended that Pedler would deliver physical possession of the shares to Rondy who would act as Lojek's agent for purposes of perfection. However, "...a security agreement is effective according to its terms between the parties,..." [§ 9-201]. Therefore, as between Lojek and Pedler (and, by extension, Pedler's estate),... the terms of the Agreement governed Lojek's rights in the collateral.

The Agreement contemplated the very situation which eventually occurred: "In the event of the death of... [Pedler] prior to the delivery of said shares to... [Rondy], then said stock certificates shall be immediately the property of... [Lojek], in full satisfaction of the note." Thus, for purposes of the Agreement, Pedler's death became a default-like event which triggered Lojek's legal right to take immediate possession of the collateral....

JUDGMENT Accordingly, we hereby reverse the judgment of the court of appeals, and enter final judgment in favor of plaintiff Lojek....

Grace Periods. Frequently, practical business needs require that a secured party have extra time, called a "grace period," to file or otherwise perfect a security interest, or have the benefit of a temporary "attachment-only" perfection status. Suppose, for example, that First Bank has a field ware housing arrangement with Martha Manufacturer and Martha receives an order for warehoused goods to be specially processed by Martha and shipped immediately to the buyer. Normally, a secured party who perfects by taking possession of the collateral (or, like First Bank, has a field warehouser do so) *loses* perfected status upon *releasing* the collateral to the debtor. However, where, as here, collateral must be released to the debtor for storage, further processing, shipping, or similar routine business purposes, the secured party's security interest *remains* perfected for up to 21 days without filing [9-304(5)]. This rule causes the least disruption of ordinary business activities, minimizes filing fees for the secured party, and eases the burden of paperwork for the filing system. If the secured party needs a longer period of perfection, he or she must, before the 21 days expires, either file a financing statement or take possession of the collateral.

Likewise, a security interest in the *proceeds* of a debtor's disposition of collateral remains perfected for a short time. Suppose Sue sells Dora a lathe on credit and files a financing statement. If Dora sells the lathe to Terri, Sue's security interest in the lathe *continues for 10 days* in any identifiable cash or noncash proceeds of Dora's sale [9-306]. After that time Sue's security interest becomes "unperfected" unless Sue, within the 10 days, makes a special filing with respect to the proceeds or takes possession of them.

Sellers often make credit sales of and retain purchase-money security interests (PMSI's) in *fixtures* or *collateral other than inventory* (e.g., business equipment such as a copier). Such sellers have 10 days after the fixture is annexed or the equipment is delivered to the debtor to perfect their PMSI's by filing a financing statement [9-313(4); 9-312(4)]. In the meantime their PMSI's are perfected by attachment only. Thus, suppliers may safely make early delivery and do the paperwork later.

Table 25.5 (on page 527) summarizes the methods of perfecting security interests.

Priorities among Conflicting Interests

Sometimes a debtor becomes insolvent and the collateral is not valuable enough to satisfy the claims of all creditors who allege an interest in it. Suppose, for example, that Dan wants to open a hardware store. To finance the business, he gets a $50,000 start-up loan in January from First Bank. Dan's security agreement with First Bank has an after-acquired property clause granting First Bank a security interest in "all business assets that Dan presently owns and in any that he may hereafter acquire." In February Dan gets $20,000 additional start-up financing from Second Bank. Dan's security agreement with Second Bank also has an after-acquired property clause. In March, Dan buys a $3,000 computerized cash register on credit from Computocash, and $10,000 worth of inventory on credit from Hardware Suppliers. Then, in late March, Dan's business fails. First Bank immediately claims all of Dan's business assets, which now consist of the unpaid-for cash register, the $10,000 worth of inventory bought on credit from Hardware Suppliers, and $5,000 worth of shelving and other business equipment. Second Bank claims the same assets; Computocash claims the cash register; and Hardware Suppliers claims the inventory that it sold to Dan on credit.

We obviously have a dispute among Dan's creditors over who gets the collateral. The priorities provisions of Article 9 settle the dispute by spelling out who is entitled to the collateral. Most conflicts over the collateral fall into one of the five categories discussed below.

Priorities among Conflicting Security Interests in the Same Collateral

Where two or more secured parties claim the same collateral, which one will prevail depends on a number of factors. Of special importance are: (1) The *nature of the conflicting security interests.* Is one a purchase-money security interest (PMSI), or are all of them of the same kind? (2) If one of the conflicting security interests is a PMSI, *what kind of collateral* is involved?

Priorities among Security Interests: General Rule. The general Code rule is that (*a*) conflicting security interests rank according to priority in time of filing or other perfection, and (*b*) if the conflicting security interests are unperfected, the first to attach has priority [9-312(5)]. Suppose Ron owns an antique chest worth $5,000. Then he gets a $5,000 loan from Cora, who plans to take possession of the chest next week as security for the loan. In the meantime Ron

Table 25.5 Methods of Perfecting Security Interests

Type of Collateral	Where Defined	Perfection Method	Where Indicated
Account (receivable). Example: A buys goods or services, promising to pay later. The promise is an account if not evidenced by an instrument or chattel paper.	9-106	Filing required, but casual or isolated assignments need not be filed. See Section 9-104(f) for assignments not subject to rules of Article 9.	9-302(1)(e) and (g)
Chattel paper. Example: A buys goods from B and signs a promissory note and security agreement. The note and agreement constitute chattel paper.	9-105(1)(b)	Filing or possession by secured party.	9-304(1); 9-305
Document (of title). Example: warehouse receipts, bills of lading, dock warrants, etc. May be negotiable or nonnegotiable.	1-201(15), (45) 7-201(2) 9-105(1)(f)	Filing or possession for negotiable documents. 21-day perfection status is available.	9-304(1) 9-304(5)
		For nonnegotiable documents, other rules apply.	9-304(3) and (5)
Instrument. Example: Checks, drafts, notes, whether or not negotiable; investment securities (stocks & bonds).	9-105(1)(i)	Possession only, except where temporary perfection status is granted.	9-304(1), (4), (5)
General intangibles. Example: Patents, copyrights, liquor licenses in some states.	9-106	Filing only.	9-302(1)
Goods:	9-105(1)(h)	In general, filing or possession; 21-day perfection status is available.	9-302(1)(a); 9-305 9-304(5)
Consumer goods	9-109(1)	Usually attachment is sufficient for purchase money security interests in consumer goods. Filing or compliance with a certificate of title statute is required for motor vehicles, boats, trailers, etc. For other security interests in consumer goods, general rules apply.	9-302(1)(d) 9-302(3) 9-302(4); 9-305
Equipment	9-109(2)	Filing, usually.	9-302(1)(a);9-305
Farm products	9-109(3)	Filing.	By implication from 9-109(3)
Inventory	9-109(4)	Filing, usually.	9-302(1)(a)

gets another $5,000 loan from First Bank, which takes and files a security interest in the chest before Cora takes possession of it. Since First Bank perfected its security interest first, First Bank is entitled to the chest upon Ron's default. If Cora and First Bank both fail to perfect their security interests, Cora will prevail because her interest attached first.

Priority of a Purchase-Money Security Interest. The after-acquired property clause so often put into security agreements by commercial lenders can cause serious difficulty for persons who sell goods to debtors on credit. Suppose Third Bank makes a start-up loan to New Corporation, Bank includes an after-acquired property clause in the security agreement and files a financing statement, and Northside Business Machines later sells New Corp. a cash register on credit. According to the terms of Third Bank's security agreement, the cash register, being after-acquired property, would now be subject to Third Bank's security interest. To protect sellers such as Northside who extend credit and retain a security interest in the goods sold, and thus to encourage them to extend credit, Article 9 gives first priority to the seller's PMSI *if it is properly perfected.* By following the perfection rules (discussed later) for particular types of collateral, Northside will prevail (have first claim) as to the goods sold on credit, *despite* the bank's *earlier* filed security interest in after-acquired property. If Northside does not comply exactly with the PMSI perfection requirements, Third Bank has priority as to the cash register.

Recall that a PMSI arises where a *seller* of goods retains a security interest in them to secure their purchase price. But *others than sellers* can also have a PMSI. Suppose you tell Second Bank you need a loan for new office furniture, the bank makes the loan and files a financing statement covering the furniture, and you actually use the loaned money to buy office furniture. Second Bank has a PMSI in the furniture even though Bank is not the seller, because Bank advanced you the purchase price [9-107]. Note, however, that the bank would *not* have a PMSI (and would not have the priority over other creditors that results from a PMSI) if you had used the loaned money for some other purpose such as buying a sports car. A *nonseller* who advances money to enable the debtor to purchase the collateral gets a *purchase-money security interest* only "if such value is in fact so used" [9-107(b)].

Special rules for perfecting PMSIs are found throughout Article 9. These rules vary according to whether the PMSI is in consumer goods, inventory, collateral other than inventory, or fixtures. Purchase-money perfection rules of major importance are discussed in the following paragraphs.

1. *Consumer goods.* The PMSI is perfected (and the credit seller gets priority over the buyer's other creditors) as soon as the PMSI *attaches.*
2. *Collateral other than inventory,* e.g., equipment for a retail store or a machine for a factory. The PMSI must be perfected by filing no later than 10 days after the debtor *receives possession* of the collateral.
3. *Inventory.* The purchase-money secured party (e.g., the creditor-seller) must do *two* things *before* the debtor receives possession of the inventory. *One,* the purchase-money secured party must perfect the PMSI by filing a financing statement. *Two,* the secured party must give written notice, to record holders of conflicting security interests in the inventory (such as a bank with an after-acquired property clause), that the purchase-money secured party "expects to acquire a purchase-money security interest in inventory of the debtor" [9-312(3)].

   Suppose Fifth Bank, under the future-advances provision of a filed loan agreement, grants Doris loans for the purchase of inventory. If Doris is fraudulent or careless, she might keep the money she borrowed from the bank for inventory and purchase the inventory on credit, granting to her inventory seller a PMSI in the inventory. The requirement that the inventory seller give advance notice to Fifth Bank enables the bank to police Doris's inventory purchasing activities and thus to avoid possible loss. And the inventory seller, by complying with the Code requirements (filing to perfect and giving the required notice before delivering the inventory to Doris), gets protection from previously filed security interests of other secured parties and will therefore be more willing to extend credit.

4 *Fixtures.* The requirements for perfecting a PMSI in a fixture are discussed later under "Priorities of Security Interests in Fixtures."

Case 25.2 discusses the kind of filing needed to give a PMSI in business equipment priority over a bank's earlier perfected security interest.

CASE 25.2 Greg Restaurant Equip. & Supplies, Inc. v. Valway · 472 A.2d 1241 (Vt. 1984)

FACTS Valway (defendant), a restaurant owner doing business as Ricardo's, received a loan for restaurant equipment from Burlington Savings Bank (Bank). The security agreement signed by Valway gave Bank a security interest in "all equipment and machinery... now owned or hereafter acquired" as collateral for the loan. Bank's financing statement, filed on June 8, 1981, described the debtor as "Richard M. Valway d/b/a Ricardo's." In August, 1981, Valway purchased restaurant equipment on credit from Greg Restaurant Equipment & Supplies (plaintiff). Greg retained a purchase-money security interest in the equipment and filed a financing statement 2 days later. Greg's financing statement listed the debtor as "Ricardo's."

Valway defaulted on his debt to Greg, and Greg filed suit to repossess the equipment. Because of its security interest in the same equipment, Bank opposed Greg's claim. The trial court held that Greg had perfected a valid PMSI in the equipment and was thus entitled to priority over the Bank's earlier perfected security interest. Bank appealed.

OPINION PECK, J.... Under the Vermont Uniform Commercial Code, a PMSI in collateral other than inventory gives its holder priority over conflicting security interests under certain conditions.... One reason for this special status is to encourage the infusion of new capital into a business when existing creditors are reluctant to advance more funds.... To effectuate this purpose, the Code gives the PMSI priority even over pre-existing security interests in after-acquired property....

The priority that PMSI holders enjoy, however, is not given lightly.... The Code generally requires that creditors file a financing statement to perfect their security interests.... This rule is subject to the exceptions... for consumer goods,... for collateral subject to temporary automatic perfection, and... for security interests perfected by possession. Because none of these exceptions [was] applicable in the present case, Greg must show... that it properly filed a financing statement within ten days after Valway received possession of the equipment.... There is no dispute that Greg meets the requirements for *attachment* of a purchase money security interest under § 9-107(a). The only question here is a narrow one: whether Greg's use of Valway's trade name "Ricardo's" rather than Valway's own name as debtor in the financing statement was sufficient to *perfect* the interest that had attached.

Greg advances two reasons why its filing was proper. First, Greg contends that because the Bank knew about Greg's security interest, the error was not seriously misleading and, therefore, the statement was effective under § 9-402(5). Second, Greg argues that the Bank was not a subsequent creditor, and therefore [was] not prejudiced by the error regardless of how misleading it was.

The lower court apparently agreed with Greg's arguments.... The flaw in the court's reasoning is that notice to the Bank of Greg's attempt to create a PMSI and the Bank's status as a prior creditor are inconsequential. Unless a security interest falls under one of the exceptions to the general requirement of filing,... the creditor aspiring to perfect a PMSI must file a financing statement properly. Knowledge of a third party is not a substitute for compliance with the Code's filing requirement, and will not serve to salvage an otherwise unperfected security interest. To hold otherwise would be to reword § 9-301(1) (a) to read:

CASE 25.2 Continued

"(1)... an unperfected security interest is subordinate to the rights of (a) persons entitled to priority under section 9-312, *unless those persons had knowledge of the unperfected security interest*."... Such an exception to the filing requirement does not appear in the statute.

The Code instead manifests a strict policy of relying solely upon proper filing to settle questions of perfection. The vagaries of determining factual issues of knowledge are thus avoided. For example, as between two conflicting security interests of equal status, § 9-312(5) (a) directs that the first interest to be perfected by proper filing will achieve priority. That section operates in favor of the first to file properly, regardless of a party's knowledge of prior security interests in the same collateral....

Because the purchase money priority is an exception to the Code's first-to-file rule, it should be allowed only when the creditor has shown compliance with the rules for perfection.... This approach is virtually required by § 9-303(1)....

Having determined that proper filing was required to perfect Greg's PMSI, regardless of the Bank's knowledge, we now turn to whether the filing made by Greg was adequate.

A financing statement that complies substantially with § 9-402 may be "effective even though it contains minor errors which are not seriously misleading."... The formal requisites of a financing statement are found in § 9-402.... Although no specific mention is made of the debtor's name..., it is no less a vital part of the filing procedure [than the listed items]. In Vermont, financing statements are indexed by the debtor's name... so that they may enable creditors to determine whether certain collateral is encumbered by pre-existing secured interests. The name under which a financing statement is filed is therefore essential to the "notice filing" system adopted in this state.... Failure to file under the correct name would make it impossible to find a financing statement. Although business creditors may be aware of a debtor's trade name in many instances, private creditors may not. This lack of notice to the public could result in... extended factual disputes on the issue of knowledge....

The Washington Court of Appeals... held that the only acceptable method of filing is under the debtor's name where he is doing business as an unincorporated proprietorship under a different name.... We concur... and we so hold. The extra burden that trade name filing would put on creditors searching the record is contrary to the implied policy of the Code, which contemplates that those wishing to perfect a security interest bear the burden of proper filing....

For these reasons we conclude that filing under the trade name "Ricardo's," since it is materially different from the name Valway, was seriously misleading, not a minor error, and therefore [was] ineffective to perfect Greg's claimed PMSI....

JUDGMENT Reversed and remanded.

Priority between a Security Interest and the Interest of a Third-Person Purchaser

Sometimes the conflict is between the secured party and a purchaser of the collateral from the debtor. A buyer of goods in the ordinary course of business (e.g., a person who in good faith buys goods from a wholesale dealer or a retail store) takes the goods *free of* a security interest created by the seller in favor of the seller's creditor even though the security interest is perfected and even though the buyer knows of its existence [9-307(1)]. This rule applies primarily where the dealer has granted to his or her lender a security interest in inventory and then makes sales from the inventory. The rule is intended to encourage buyers to pay full market values by minimizing the buyers' fear of loss at the hands of unseen creditors. To be protected, however, the "buyer in ordinary course of business" must, by definition, be in good faith. If the buyer knows that the terms of the security agreement between the seller and the seller's creditor are being *violated,* the buyer does not come within the meaning of buyer in ordinary course of business, and he or she takes *subject to* the security interest of the seller's creditor. Most good faith purchasers of chattel paper, negotiable instruments, and documents of title receive similar protection [9-308].

A dealer in consumer goods faces a serious problem when a consumer purchases the goods on credit and resells them to another consumer before paying the dealer for them. Suppose Camera Shop sells an expensive camera on credit to Joan for her personal use, that Joan sells the camera to her neighbor Fred before making any of the payments, and that Joan immediately spends the money and is now insolvent. If Camera Shop has retained a PMSI in the camera and has perfected the interest by *attachment only,* Camera Shop's PMSI gives Camera Shop priority (first claim to the camera) over Joan's other creditors, but it provides *no* protection against Fred (and Fred may keep the camera) if he bought the encumbered camera "without knowledge of the security interest, for value and for his own personal, family or household purposes" [9-307(2)]. However, if Camera Shop had perfected the PMSI *by filing* before Joan resold the camera to Fred, Camera Shop would be protected from a claim of ownership by Fred or any other subsequent purchaser. Whether a seller of expensive consumer goods should rely on attachment-only perfection or should instead undertake the extra expense of a filing is, of course, a matter of business judgment and risk assessment.

Priorities of Liens Arising by Operation of Law

Sometimes goods that are subject to a security interest are sent out for repairs or improvements. What if the repair-person (bailee) remains unpaid? Will the bailee's lien have priority over the security interest? Section 9-310 gives priority to *common law* possessory liens for materials or services furnished with respect to goods subject to a security interest, even though the security interest is perfected. Section 9-310 gives similar priority to *statutory* possessory liens *unless* the statute granting the lien expressly subordinates it to a prior security interest. Thus, most workers who repair or improve goods in the ordinary course of their business have the traditional mechanic's or artisan's lien on goods in their possession, until their just charges have been paid.

Priorities of Security Interests in Fixtures

Article 9 governs the creation and priority of security interests in fixtures, but leaves the definition of "fixture" largely up to non-Code real estate law. However, "no security interest exists under the Article in ordinary building materials incorporated into an improvement on land" [9-313(2)]. The rights of materials sellers are governed by local real estate mechanics' lien laws.

The fixture priority rules are so numerous and complex that only some major ones are discussed here. The rules are best understood by examining the conflicts that they are intended to resolve. The usual conflict is between purchase money fixture financers and real estate financers. Real estate financers (mortgagees) argue that to offset building depreciation or otherwise to encourage real estate financing, the law should give real estate mortgagees first claim to any fixtures that are later annexed to the real estate. Fixture financers argue that unless they are allowed to repossess unpaid-for fixtures, fixture credit will diminish and the improvement of real estate will be slowed.

It is common for a fixture seller to have to contend with real estate claimants whose interests in the real estate arose *before* the fixture was annexed, as well as with real estate interests that arose *afterward.* As the following illustrations indicate, the sequence of events is one of several factors to consider in determining who has priority in a fixture.

Suppose Oscar buys a house or a commercial building and soon afterward discovers that he must replace the worn-out furnace. Oscar buys an expensive furnace "on time" from Frank, who reserves a PMSI in it. Then Frank installs the furnace in Oscar's building, which is subject to a recorded real estate mortgage in favor of Rachel. For Frank's PMSI in the furnace to prevail over Rachel's earlier recorded mortgage on the real estate, Frank must perfect his PMSI by a *fixture filing within 10 days* after the furnace is annexed [9-313(4)(a)].

Now suppose that the furnace is to be installed in a *new* house that Oscar is having built, and that Rachel is the construction financer. Rachel's *construc-*

tion mortgage will prevail over Frank's PMSI in the furnace if Rachel takes two steps: (1) She must be sure that the furnace is installed (annexed) before the house itself is completed, *and* (2) she must record (file) the construction mortgage before the furnace becomes a fixture [9-313(6)]. By completing these two steps, construction financers who may have advanced money for major appliances as well as for the basic building can protect themselves from a surprise PMSI held by a fixture seller.

In many other fixture priority situations, the first creditor to make a fixture filing prevails. Suppose Bank makes a loan to Oscar and secures it by taking a mortgage on his house and its built-in air conditioner. Then Oscar buys goods on credit from Sam Seller and gives Sam not only a purchase-money security interest in the goods but also a security interest in the air conditioner. If Sam makes a fixture filing before Bank records its mortgage, Sam's security interest in the air conditioner prevails. If Bank records (files) first, *it* wins.

Priorities of Security Interests in Accessions and Commingled Goods

Accessions are goods that are installed in or affixed to other goods. For example, Orville owns a delivery truck, its engine burns out, and Orville's mechanic installs a replacement engine. The engine is an accession.

The following priority rule applies to accessions. If a security interest in an accession (Orville's replacement engine) *attaches before* the accession is installed or affixed, the security interest in the *accession* usually takes priority over the claims of all persons to the *whole* (Orville's truck) [9-314]. To prevail over subsequent purchasers and lenders, the accession financer must *perfect* the security interest in the accession, or the holder of the subsequent interest must have knowledge of the accession financer's interest, before the subsequent interest arises.

Suppose, for example, that Orville gives Thrifty Loan a security interest in the truck to secure a loan, and Thrifty files a financing statement. Then the engine burns out, Orville buys a replacement engine from Sam on credit, and Sam retains a PMSI before delivering the engine to Orville. Since Sam's PMSI attached before the engine was installed, the PMSI prevails over Thrifty's earlier perfected security interest. Now suppose that Thrifty made the loan and took its security interest in the truck *after* Orville replaced the engine. To prevail over Thrifty, Sam must have *perfected* his PMSI in the engine (or Thrifty must have received knowledge of it) *before* Thrifty's interest arose (attached). This rule is for Thrifty's protection, since unless Thrifty has notice of the accession financer's (Sam's) claim before extending credit, Thrifty would extend credit believing that the new engine is part of its collateral.

Commingled goods are those that are combined with others to form a single mass or product. For example, flour, sugar, and eggs may be commingled into cake mix, or component parts may be assembled into a machine. Where goods subject to a perfected security interest are commingled with other goods so that the identity of the commingled goods is lost in the mass, the security interest continues in the mass or product [9-315]. Where several such security interests continue in the mass, each of the various secured parties is entitled to a pro rata share of the mass. Suppose Egbert, Wheatley, and Sugarman sell eggs, flour, and sugar to Cake Mix Corp. and perfect their security interests. Then Cake Mix commingles the goods into a batch of cake mix. If Cake Mix fails to pay the suppliers, they have equal priority as to the mass, and each is entitled to share the batch of cake mix to the extent of that supplier's contribution to the mass.

Where component parts are assembled into a machine, a person who has a security interest in them must elect at the time of filing whether to treat them as accessions or as commingled goods. The difference is important, because upon the debtor's default a secured party may remove accessions (repossess them).

Default and Foreclosure

Meaning of Default

Since "default" is not defined in the Code, the common law meaning of failure to perform a legal duty applies. Nonpayment by the debtor is the most common default, and the security agreement may identify additional events that constitute default. Examples are: the debtor's unauthorized removal or sale of collateral, the debtor's failure to insure the collateral, the debtor's failure to furnish additional collateral if the value of the original collateral declines, the debtor's insolvency or bankruptcy, and loss or destruction of the collateral.

Rights and Duties of Secured Party upon Debtor's Default

When the debtor is in default, the secured party may enforce the security interest by taking possession of the collateral and (*a*) under certain circumstances *keeping* it in satisfaction of the debt or (*b*) *disposing* of the collateral in some commercially reasonable way, e.g., by sale [9-501]. The secured party may also use any judicial procedure available under non-Code law (e.g., state execution or foreclosure laws).

Acquiring Control of the Collateral. If the secured party does not already possess the collateral, he or she will need to acquire control of it. This can be done in a variety of ways. To collect accounts, the secured party may notify the debtor's account debtor (usually a purchaser from the debtor to whom the debtor has extended credit) to make payment directly to the secured party [9-502]. As to collateral in possession of the debtor, the secured party has two basic options. One, unless otherwise agreed, the secured party may simply take possession of the collateral after default, if he or she can do so without breach of the peace [9-503]. Two, the secured party may go to court to acquire possession (and *must* do so where a breach of the peace is threatened). In lieu of removing heavy equipment, the secured party may render it unusable (e.g., by removing a control device) and dispose of (e.g., sell) it on the debtor's premises.

What constitutes a breach of the peace varies according to the circumstances. Ordinarily, an objection by the debtor or a third party such as a custodian of the property involves a breach of the peace, since physical violence is a possible outcome. Breaking into the debtor's premises to get the collateral or posing as a police officer is also forbidden. But removing the collateral from a public street, a parking lot, or even the open parts of the debtor's premises is permitted, if done without objection by the debtor or a third party. As suggested by Case 25.3, mere lack of consent is not necessarily a peace-threatening objection.

CASE 25.3 Marine Midland Bank-Central v. Cote · 351 So. 2d 750 (Fla. App. 1977)

FACTS Marine Midland Bank had a purchase money security interest in a car sold to Cote. Cote was in default, and Altes or his employee, acting on behalf of the bank, entered Cote's private property early one morning and removed the car from the open carport. Cote sued Altes and the bank for trespass and was awarded $2,500 in compensatory and $2,500 in punitive damages. Altes and the bank appealed.

OPINION SMITH, J. . . . [Florida decisions] approved repossessions in similar situations. But appellees [the Cotes] argue those cases involved security agreements which explicitly authorized the creditor to enter upon the debtor's premises to repossess the security. Here the security agreement stated only

> . . . that when the Buyer is in default under this Contract . . . the Holder shall have all the rights and remedies of a secured party when a debtor is in default under a security agreement as provided under the Uniform Commercial Code, [appellees] hereby . . . agreeing that such rights and remedies include the Holder's right to take possession and dispose of the vehicle after default. . . .

We must decide whether the secured party's right to repossess collateral provided by the Florida UCC in § 9-503 includes a right to enter upon private property, or whether the statute simply authorizes creditors to contract for that right.

CASE 25.3 Continued

In Northside Motors... the Supreme Court held [that] § 9-503 "is no more than a codification... of a common law right and a contract right recognized long [ago] and creates no new right." The Restatement (2d) of Torts, § 183 states that at common law:

> (1) Except as otherwise agreed, a conditional vendor or lessor of a thing who is entitled to immediate possession thereof... is privileged, at a reasonable time and in a reasonable manner, to enter land in possession of the vendee or lessee, for the purpose of taking possession of the thing and removing it from the land.

Our Supreme Court recognized this privilege in Percifield v. State.... Courts in other jurisdictions have held a secured creditor privileged, under the UCC or the common law, to peacefully enter on the debtor's land when the security agreement authorizes repossession but does not specifically authorize entry.... While many of the cases approving entry by a creditor have involved a contract clause specifically authorizing entry, we have not found or been directed to any case holding a creditor liable because a security agreement lacked such a clause. Cases holding creditors liable for trespass or conversion have involved entry in to a dwelling, removal of collateral from an enclosed and secured garage, or some fraud or other misconduct by the creditor....

We hold that, absent a contrary agreement, when a security agreement provides [that] the secured party has on default the rights and remedies provided by the UCC, the right of repossession stated by § 9-503 implies, just as it did at common law, a limited privilege to enter on the debtor's land. The privilege may be exercised only "without breach of the peace."...

We do not undertake to define the limits of the privileged entry accorded a creditor under § 9-503. We hold simply that, unless the parties otherwise agree, when a vehicle is covered by a valid security agreement providing the creditor has a right to repossess the vehicle upon default, repossession of the vehicle from the debtor's unenclosed carport without threat or use of force is not trespass, regardless of whether the security agreement specifically authorizes entry upon the debtor's premises.

JUDGMENT [The judgments are reversed.]

Disposing of the Collateral. After obtaining the collateral, the secured party will want to keep or dispose of it. The secured party's keeping it in satisfaction of the debt and thereby terminating the debtor's interest in it is called "strict foreclosure" and is appropriate where the value of the collateral is equal to or less than the amount of the debt. However, strict foreclosure is permitted only where the secured party gives written notice of intention to keep the collateral and the debtor does not object in writing [9-505(2)]. If the debtor makes timely objection to strict foreclosure, the secured party *must dispose* of the collateral. Disposal is required also where the collateral is *consumer goods* and the debtor has paid 60% of the purchase price or loan [9-505(1)].

The secured party may dispose of collateral in any *commercially reasonable way,* whether by sale, lease, or otherwise [9-504]. A foreclosure sale may be public or private, as long as it is commercially reasonable. In any sale or other disposition, the secured party receives the amount of proceeds necessary to cover the debt and foreclosure expenses. Any surplus goes to the debtor. However, the debtor remains liable for any deficiency unless otherwise agreed, or unless the secured party is denied the right to the deficiency because of the secured party's misconduct (such as making a commercially unreasonable disposition).

Largely to protect the debtor, Article 9 imposes disposition rules that cannot be changed by the security agreement [9-501(2)&(3)]. For instance, the secured party must exercise reasonable care to preserve the collateral in his or her possession; the debtor has a right to redeem (buy back) repossessed collateral before it is disposed of [9-506]; and the debtor is entitled to appropriate remedies if the secured party fails to comply with Article 9. However, after default, the debtor may waive some of these rights.

Prior dealings between the debtor and the secured party may affect the secured party's right to repossess and dispose of the collateral. Suppose Dom is late with some of his payments and Candace accepts them without protest. Candace's conduct could cause Dom reasonably to believe that delay in making a future payment will not result in seizure of the collateral. Many courts will deny Candace the right to repossess the collateral unless, after permitting late payments, she notifies Dom that late payments will no longer be tolerated.

Case 25.4 involves a sale of repossessed collateral and alleged misconduct of both creditor and debtor.

CASE 25.4 Contrail Leasing Partners, Ltd. v. Consolidated Airways, Inc. · 742 F.2d 1095 (7th Cir. 1984)

FACTS In 1976, Consolidated Airways (defendant) sold a Grumman Gulf Stream commercial aircraft on credit to Contrail Leasing Partners (plaintiff) for $575,000, taking back a chattel mortgage on the plane. In 1978 Contrail defaulted. Consolidated repossessed the plane, made a deal to sell it to Emerald Airlines for $675,000, and notified debtor Contrail of the pending sale. Even though Contrail had referred Emerald to Consolidated in the first place, Contrail notified Emerald that it objected to the sale. Fearing that the sale would become entangled in legal proceedings, Emerald backed out. Later Consolidated paid over $26,000 for substantial maintenance work and notified Contrail that it planned to sell the plane at a public auction in two and a half weeks. Three days before the sale, Contrail sued Consolidated and moved for a preliminary injunction to prevent the sale. The motion was denied, and Contrail then filed a notice of lis pendens (litigation pending) with the Federal Aviation Administration. At the sale, Consolidated, the only bidder, purchased the plane for $515,000. Debtor Contrail got nothing because the proceeds of the sale were less than the unpaid mortgage debt plus various expenses that Consolidated claimed. At trial, the judge found that Consolidated's sale was commercially unreasonable and that on the day of the sale the plane was worth $625,000. From a judgment for Contrail, Consolidated and Contrail appealed, each alleging that the judge's calculations were erroneous.

OPINION POSNER, Circuit Judge.... A creditor who, having repossessed the debtor's goods, sells them to satisfy his debt is entitled to retain so much of the proceeds of the sale as is necessary to pay off the debt. See UCC § 9-504. If he has incurred reasonable expenses in preparation for the sale he is entitled to deduct those as well. The district judge recognized this principle and therefore allowed Consolidated to deduct various expenses, but he misapplied the principle in two respects:

1. He did not allow Consolidated to deduct the interest that had accrued on the note secured by the chattel mortgage between the date of default... and the date of the sale.... The unpaid principal... was $403,056.90, and the note called for interest at the rate of one percent a month.... [The judge's] opinion offers no ground for lopping off part of Consolidated's claim. His action is made more difficult to understand by the fact that he (quite properly) credited Contrail with the $38,000 that Consolidated had earned from leasing the plane during the period of repossession. Consolidated was able to generate that income for the debtor only because it had possession of the plane, and one of the costs of possession to Consolidated was going without the $403,000 that the debtor owed it. It was an opportunity cost, which is a real cost in law as in economics. Consolidated is entitled to recover that opportunity cost by charging interest for the period of repossession....

Though we have treated the interest as an expense of the creditor, it is more appropriately regarded as a part of the underlying debt.... The debt was unpaid principal plus

CASE 25.4 Continued

one percent interest for every month the principal was unpaid; and it was the principal plus accrued interest that Consolidated was entitled to keep along with expenses when it sold the plane. . . .

2. Another cost incurred by Consolidated during the period of repossession was the money that it spent to rebuild the propellers. . . . A prudent expenditure could be expected to be reflected in the value of the plane at the date of sale. . . . Since Contrail was the beneficiary of the expenditure, Consolidated was entitled to deduct it from the proceeds [of the sale].

[The court then considered other claims and expenses and calculated $557,245.99 as the net amount of unpaid debt and expenses owed by the debtor Contrail to Consolidated.]

. . . [I]f the sale was commercially reasonable, then since it yielded proceeds ($515,000) smaller than the amount due Consolidated, Contrail is entitled to nothing and Consolidated is entitled to the deficiency judgment it sought in a counterclaim that the district judge dismissed. But if the sale was commercially unreasonable, it becomes necessary to calculate the fair market value of the plane on April 9, 1979, and if that fair market value was more than what is due Consolidated, Contrail is entitled to the excess, plus . . . interest since [that date].

"A sale is commercially reasonable where it is done in public, during business hours, upon adequate notice within a reasonable time of repossession, and under conditions reasonably calculated to bring a fair market price." . . . The judge was entitled to find that the sale on April 9 . . . was not commercially reasonable because adequate notice was not given. Although Consolidated offered testimony that it gave notice of the sale orally to all major airplane brokers in the United States, the judge disbelieved this testimony, and we cannot say he was clearly wrong to do so. So far as appears, all Consolidated did in the way of notice was to place an inconspicuous ad in one publication of the used-aircraft trade (the second ad in that publication, which ran *after* the sale, does not count). . . . The fact that no one showed up for the sale except Consolidated is consistent with the fact that Consolidated made little effort, on this occasion anyway, to sell the plane. It may have been quite content to buy the plane from itself at a bargain price that would wipe out Contrail's equity in it.

. . . [C]onsolidated argues that Contrail should be estopped to protest the sale because of its having broken up the first sale to Emerald at a much higher price and having filed a notice of lis pendens on the eve of the second sale. But whether or not Contrail acted unreasonably on either occasion, its conduct could not justify Consolidated in not conducting a fair sale. . . . [Consolidated's] argument implies that if Consolidated at the "public" auction had sold the plane to itself for one cent, Contrail still could not protest. Consolidated did not do that, but it did set a price that wiped out Contrail's entire equity in the plane. So drastic a forfeiture . . . is not necessary to protect the creditor from misbehavior by the debtor. By breaking up the sale with Emerald . . . and then filing a lis pendens calculated to reduce the competition that Consolidated would face in buying in at the second sale, Contrail . . . hurt [only] itself . . . provided it did not drive the market value below the debt (plus expenses) [owed] to Consolidated. . . . If the costs of the debtor's misconduct fall on the debtor, it is not necessary also to decree forfeiture of his entire equity, which is the sanction that Consolidated is proposing.

Although the sale was unreasonable . . . we do not think the district court's valuation of $625,000 can be sustained. . . . [T]he testimony showed that the market for used Grumman Gulf Stream commercial aircraft is rather thin, and the fact that Emerald was willing to pay a high price in 1978 doesn't prove that anyone would have been willing to pay as high a price a year later. . . . [The $625,000 valuation] has three problems:

1. We cannot ignore Consolidated's argument that the relevant value is that of a plane against which a lis pendens has been filed. . . . Contrail cannot walk away from the consequences of having filed [the notice] on the eve of sale. . . . [O]n remand, the district judge must

CASE 25.4 Continued

make findings on the effect of the lis pendens on the plane's fair market value on the date of sale.

[The court then discussed other factors to be considered in estimating the value of the plane.] To sum up, a remand is necessary to permit the district judge to clarify his findings. He must... re-estimate the value of the plane (with the lis pendens)...; specify whether that is a retail or a wholesale price; [and] subtract from that price [the debt and] all pertinent expenses of sale, which we said earlier amounted to $557,245.99—but the figure may have to be adjusted [to reflect brokerage commissions as an expense of sale] if the judge estimates a retail rather than a wholesale price; and award Contrail what is left after the subtraction, plus interest from April 9, 1979.

JUDGMENT ...Affirmed in part, reversed in part, and remanded....

Summary

To make credit extension easier and safer, Article 9 substituted the term "security interest" for the variety of pre-Code descriptive terms, developed a simplified public-notice filing system, established a system of priorities for the states to use in common, and set up a uniform method of liquidating collateral after default.

The secured party receives maximum protection if the security interest is attached and perfected. Attachment is the process of creating a security interest and making it enforceable against the debtor. Perfection is the process of making the security interest enforceable against others than the debtor. Perfection occurs sometimes upon completion of the attachment events, but more commonly occurs by the secured party's taking possession of the collateral or filing a financing statement.

A perfected purchase-money security interest (PMSI) usually prevails over earlier perfected security interests. In most other conflict situations, the first to perfect or, if there is no perfection, the first to attach prevails. Similar priority rules apply to fixtures.

Upon the debtor's default the secured party has liberal repossession and disposition rights. However, the debtor is entitled to a commercially reasonable disposition of the collateral. The debtor is entitled to any surplus realized from disposition of the collateral, but remains personally liable for any deficiency unless freed from that liability by the secured party's misconduct.

Review Questions

1 **(a)** Why are security interests in fixtures covered by Article 9 rather than by real estate law? **(b)** Why does Article 9 cover sales of accounts and chattel paper?

2 **(a)** What is the Code definition of "security interest"? **(b)** Distinguish between a true lease and a "lease" that creates a security interest.

3 What must be done for a security interest to attach?

4 **(a)** What is a floating lien? **(b)** What is the purpose of an after-acquired property clause? Of a future advances provision?

5 Explain the legal consequence of perfecting a security interest.

6 **(a)** Why is a PMSI given priority? **(b)** How may a PMSI in inventory be perfected? Why is the procedure relatively complex?

7 Naming the usual participants, illustrate each of the following: **(a)** Conflicting security interests in the same collateral. **(b)** Conflicting security interests in a fixture.

8 What is the meaning of default?

9 How may the secured party repossess collateral upon the debtor's default?

10 Is a sale required for a disposition of collateral to be commercially reasonable? Explain.

Case Problems

1 Raat, doing business as Garden Construction and Landscape Co., did some work for the City of Westminster. In compliance with a statute intended to protect persons who supply labor or materials to public works contractors, the City withheld $5,000 from the amount owed Raat, subject to final settlement on October 20, 1980. Earlier, Raat had borrowed $20,000 from First National Bank and had signed a security agreement granting Bank a security interest in "all accounts receivable, whether now owned or hereafter acquired." The security interest was perfected in November, 1979. Raat defaulted on the loan. Consequently, on October 17, 1980, Bank notified City of the security agreement covering Raat's accounts receivable, and made a claim for the $5,000 that had been withheld. However, Heinrichsdorff, one of Raat's suppliers, also claimed the $5,000. The trial court held that Bank's security interest prevailed over Heinrichsdorff's claim. Heinrichsdorff appealed. Whether the trial court was correct depends on whether Bank's security interest attached to the $5,000 at the time it was withheld. Did Bank's security interest attach?

2 S & J Holding Corp. was in the business of operating video games. In S & J's bankruptcy proceeding, June, Inc., one of S & J's creditors, claimed not only S & J's video and vending machines but also the cash revenues generated by them. June's perfected security agreement covered "all of the assets of Shazamm Enterprises, Inc., including all equipment, inventory, accounts receivable, contract rights, intangibles, video games, cigarette machines, coin changers, and any and all other personal property or assets owned and used by the debtor in its business wherever located as well as any and all personal property hereinafter acquired. Products of collateral are covered." Did June have a valid, perfected security interest in the cash?

3 Financed by First of American Bank, Pierce bought a new van on credit. The security agreement described the van as a "new Chevy Delta Van," and listed its vehicle identification number. Pierce had the van customized after it left the manufacturer. The customizer gave the van a new serial number. The new number and the name of the Bank were noted on the van's certificate of title. Pierce paid Bank $5,000, and Bank released its lien on the van. Soon afterward, Pierce filed for bankruptcy. The trustee in bankruptcy claimed the $5,000 payment, alleging that because the security agreement did not accurately describe the collateral, Bank's security interest never attached. **(a)** Did Bank's security interest attach? **(b)** If it did attach, did it "unattach" as a result of the customizer's modification of the collateral?

4 Fowler, doing business as White Oak Lawn & Garden Center, borrowed $25,000 from White Oak State Bank, which, on December 5, 1975, perfected its security interest in Fowler's inventory, equipment, accounts receivable, and life insurance. Fowler sold the Center to Winslow, who had borrowed $51,500 from the same bank and granted it a security interest in the Center inventory. Winslow paid off Fowler's $25,000 debt to Bank. On December 22, 1977, Bank marked Fowler's note "paid." In the meantime Winslow borrowed $20,000 from Barr and signed a security agreement covering Center inventory. On December 27, the Barrs filed their financing statement. On the 28th, Bank filed its financing statement. In 1978 Winslow defaulted on the notes to Bank and Barr. Bank repossessed and sold the inventory without notifying Barr of the foreclosure. Later, alleging that he was entitled to the inventory and that Bank had wrongfully disposed of it, Barr sued Bank for damages. Was Barr entitled to the collateral?

5 Mishkin's 125th St., Inc., sold its drug business to Aberdeen Drugs Co. To secure the purchase price, Mishkin's took back a chattel mortgage and filed a financing statement, both of which covered the contents of the premises. Then Aberdeen signed a conditional sales contract with National Cash Register (NCR) for the purchase of two new cash registers. Seven days after delivering the cash registers to Aberdeen, NCR filed a financing statement in the proper offices. On both the conditional sales contract and the financing statement, NCR mistakenly designated the purchaser as "Mishkin's Drug, Inc.," instead of Aberdeen. When Aberdeen defaulted on its contract with Mishkin's, Mishkin's foreclosed on its chattel mortgage, selling the contents of the premises, including the two new cash registers. Alleging that it was entitled to priority over the buyer, NCR brought suit to recover possession of the cash registers. Should NCR prevail?

6 Fredrickson, a Ford dealer, received financing from Ford Motor Credit Company (Ford Credit), which, on August 16, 1977, filed a financing statement covering "inventory and equipment" and "replacement parts of or for any of the above." Later, First State Bank of Smithville lent Fredrickson money for the purchase of inventory. On September 26 (before Fredrickson received the inventory), Bank filed a financing statement covering it. On August 11, Bank had sent a letter to Ford Motor Company (FMC) advising it that Bank was committed to making a "capital loan" for the "operation" of the Fredrickson dealership. Sometime before September 14,

FMC forwarded a copy of the letter to Ford Credit. Fredrickson defaulted on the loans, and both Ford Credit and Bank claimed the inventory. From a decision that Bank's purchase-money security interest had priority over Ford Credit's security interest, Ford Credit appealed. Should the decision of the court below be upheld?

7 Deephouse Equipment Co. sold a backhoe to Knapp Construction Co., which resold it to Capitol City Construction Co. The machine "blew a rod" and needed extensive repairs. Before it was repaired, Capitol defaulted in payments. As required by the original financing agreement, Deephouse paid the finance company the amount of Capitol's remaining debt and repossessed the machine. More than 3 years later, having made no serious effort to sell the unrepaired backhoe, Deephouse sued Capitol for the amount Deephouse had paid. Capitol contended that Deephouse's nonaction with respect to the backhoe was commercially unreasonable and barred Deephouse from any recovery on the debt. Deephouse, who was facing bankruptcy, responded that the market for the inoperable backhoe was poor and that he had retained it hoping to find a used or rebuilt engine to make the backhoe salable. **(a)** Was Deephouse's conduct commercially unreasonable? **(b)** If so, should Deephouse be denied any recovery from Capitol?

CHAPTER 26

Bankruptcy

Anyone, even the largest corporation, can experience financial difficulty. If a business becomes so unprofitable that it cannot pay its debts, creditors naturally become concerned and can be expected to try to collect the amounts owed. Often, however, the debtor has so few assets that the claims of creditors cannot be paid, or can be paid only in part. Thus, several legal questions arise: (1) What may an unpaid creditor do to enforce his or her right to payment? (2) Where the debtor's assets are too few to pay all claims of creditors, how should those assets be distributed among the unpaid creditors? (3) Should the debtor be discharged (freed) from liability for debts remaining after existing assets have been distributed? Depending on the circumstances, either state or federal law or some combination of the two provides the answers.

Under state law, a creditor has a variety of ways to enforce the obligation of a *solvent* debtor, i.e., one who *can* pay but "defaults" (fails or refuses to pay a valid debt). These enforcement methods are largely beyond the scope of this chapter. Rather, the emphasis in on the rights of creditors and debtors where a defaulting debtor is *insolvent* (unable to pay his or her debts when they become due). *State insolvency law,* discussed in the first part of this chapter, permits the debtor to make some arrangement with unpaid creditors for full or partial payment. Or the insolvent debtor or the creditors may be entitled to the benefits of *federal bankruptcy law,* which, when resorted to, prevails over or displaces state insolvency law. *Bankruptcy* is the process by which (1) a financially troubled debtor is declared by a bankruptcy court to be incapable of paying his or her debts, (2) the debtor's available assets are distributed to creditors as required by bankruptcy law, and (3) the debtor, if honest, is granted a discharge from liability for most or all of the remaining unpaid debts. The second part of the chapter discusses the nature of bankruptcy law and the administration of debtors' estates. The third and fourth parts focus on the three major kinds of bankruptcy proceedings: liquidation, business reorganizations, and repayment plans for debtors with regular income.

Creditors' Rights and Debtor Relief

The process of bankruptcy, and the need for bankruptcy law, can best be understood by examining briefly how financial difficulty can develop and how the rights of creditors and the needs of debtors may collide. Consider, for example, the history of Joe's financial failure.

Joe's Financial Failure

Upon his graduation from State University, Joe and his wife set up a retail art supply store. Having no funds of his own, he borrowed $100,000 from First Bank as a start-up loan for renting a store building and purchasing equipment and inventory. Needing more start-up financing, Joe borrowed an additional $20,000 from Second Bank; purchased a copier, a cash register, and a computer on credit from Bud's Business Machines; and purchased $5,000 worth of art supplies on credit from Al's Art Supplies. Business was good. Joe opened several personal charge accounts with local department stores; bought a $100,000 home which he financed with a $90,000 mortgage from Third Bank at 15 percent annual interest; and opened two new stores that he financed in part with the profits from the first store and in part from unsecured loans from relatives. By now, Joe had 15 employees, two children in private schools, and a new Mercedes-Benz that he had bought on credit. Then, as a result of a widespread economic recession, many businesses in Joe's city laid off their employees and schools cut back on their art programs. Joe's art supply sales dwindled to almost nothing. Within weeks, Joe's creditors—secured and unsecured—were seeking immediate payment, but Joe could not pay. Some of his creditors began calling him at odd hours of the night. One creditor, the veterinarian who had performed surgery on Joe's dog, repeatedly phoned Joe and his relatives, demanding immediate payment of Joe's account and threatening to inform Joe's country club that Joe was a "deadbeat" who should have his membership canceled. Bill collectors constantly hounded Joe, his wife, and even their children while at school. One night a bill collector accosted Joe in a parking lot and beat him, inflicting serious injuries. Attempting to check into a nearby hospital, Joe was turned away because he could not demonstrate ability to pay for medical services. The next day Joe sought financial counseling.

Carla, the financial counselor, pointed out several things to Joe about his financial difficulties:

1 Joe's plight was caused in part by his own mismanagement of his financial affairs and by a too-rapid business expansion, but there were other causes more or less beyond his control: for instance, the economic recession and the willingness of some lenders to extend credit without adequately checking Joe's ability to repay.
2 Nevertheless, all Joe's creditors have valid claims against Joe for payment. None had committed fraud or other wrongdoing when extending credit to Joe, and all are entitled to payment in full.
3 However, despite their valid claims, Joe's creditors are limited by law in what they may do by way of debt-collection activities. As discussed in Chapter 25, a secured creditor may peacefully repossess collateral and make a commercially reasonable disposition of it in satisfaction of the debt it secures, and usually may hold the debtor liable for any deficiency. As discussed in Chapter 24, unsecured creditors such as Joe's credit card and open account creditors must rely on Joe's promises to pay, since unsecured creditors have no claim to any specific property of Joe's. If Joe does not pay, an unsecured creditor must bring suit, receive a judgment for the amount owed, and rely on Joe's general assets, if any, as the source of payment.

   But no creditor, secured or unsecured, may take debt-collection action that violates the debtor's rights under the law. For example, creditors who engage in overly vigorous collection activity risk liability to the debtor for defamation, invasion of privacy, intentionally causing emotional distress, or other torts discussed in Chapters 4 and 5. Under Article 9 of the Uniform Commercial Code, secured creditors must avoid a breach of the peace when repossessing collateral. Additional laws apply to *debt collectors* hired by Joe's creditors. Debt collectors may not engage in debt-collection activity that violates laws like the federal Fair Debt Collection Practices Act [15 U.S.C. § 1692 et seq.]. The Act prohibits a wide variety of objectionable collection practices: for example, threats of violence; the use of abusive language when trying to collect a debt; harassment by means of repeated telephone calls, or deception; and unfair methods of collection such as threatening to deposit a postdated check before the date of the check (and thereby intentionally causing other checks of the debtor to be dishonored).
4 Joe has a variety of options under state and federal law for attempting to pay his debts in full or in part, and under bankruptcy law may escape them altogether so that he can reenter business with a "fresh start."

How Joe May Settle His Unpaid Debts

Arrangements under State Law. Some of Joe's creditors received security interests in Joe's property when extending credit to Joe; but, as discussed in Chapter 25, if the collateral they claim is not sufficiently valuable to cover the amounts Joe owes them, even Joe's secured creditors will be unsecured in part. The temptation is great for unsecured creditors to protect themselves by exercising their rights under the state's "grab law"—i.e., law permitting an unsecured creditor to obtain a judgment against

Joe for the amount owed and to "execute" the judgment by having Joe's unencumbered property, if any, seized and sold without regard to the welfare of Joe's other creditors. However, execution sales often produce low prices. Joe's creditors might be willing to forgo the cumbersome and wasteful execution process and to consider alternative ways of receiving payment. Joe might suggest a composition or extension agreement. Or Joe might make an assignment for the benefit of creditors.

Composition and extension agreements. Composition and extension agreements are contracts between a debtor and some or all of his or her creditors, by means of which debtor and creditors agree to substitute a less burdensome obligation for the debts originally undertaken. In a *composition* agreement, the debtor agrees to pay the creditors some fraction (e.g., 20 percent of the amount the debtor owes, in full settlement of the creditors' claims). Usually each creditor will receive the same percentage that all other creditors receive, in what is called a "pro rata" (equal percentage) distribution. However, the agreement may provide that some creditors—for example, those owed small amounts—will receive 100 percent of their claims. A creditor who chooses not to participate in a composition is not bound by it. Instead, the nonconsenting creditor may pursue the usual collection process and execute against the debtor's unencumbered assets even though such action prevents the debtor from carrying out the composition agreement.

In an extension agreement, the debtor agrees to pay the full amount of all debts (with or without interest), but the creditors agree to allow the debtor to pay over a greater time than originally agreed. Often, creditors grant extensions of from 1 to 3 years. Nonconsenting creditors are not bound by an extension agreement and may pursue the usual collection process as to the amounts owed them.

Assignments for the benefit of creditors. A troubled debtor might choose to make a general assignment for the benefit of the debtor's creditors. A *general assignment* (also called an *assignment for the benefit of creditors*) is a voluntary transfer by the debtor of all of his or her available property to a person (the *assignee* or *trustee*) named by the debtor to (*a*) receive the debtor's property, (*b*) liquidate it (convert it into cash), and (*c*) distribute the cash to creditors in exchange for their promises to release the debtor from further liability. Under the terms of the assignment, each creditor covered by the assignment may receive a pro rata (equal percentage) distribution, or some creditors may receive a larger proportion of their claims than other creditors receive. Once a general assignment is made, no unsecured creditor may execute on or otherwise obtain rights to the assigned property, but is instead limited to whatever distribution the assignment document provides. However, creditors who did not assent to the assignment are not bound by its terms; consequently, the debtor's future earnings will be subject to the claims of unpaid nonconsenting creditors. Furthermore, as noted later in this chapter, a creditor who is unhappy with a general assignment may be able to upset it by commencing federal bankruptcy proceedings against the debtor.

Use of Federal Bankruptcy Law. Instead of using procedures available under state law for resolving financial difficulty, Joe (or his creditors) might seek the aid of federal bankruptcy law. The main advantage to Joe of a bankruptcy proceeding is the *discharge* from remaining unpaid debts that is available to him under the federal law. In contrast, under state law Joe remains liable to creditors (and subject to continuing executions against his property) unless contractually released from liability by, for example, a composition agreement. For Joe's creditors a main advantage of a bankruptcy proceeding is the more evenhanded treatment they receive under federal law than they might receive under state law. For example, under federal law, creditors of a given class are entitled to a pro rata distribution. By contrast, under the insolvency laws of some states debtors like Joe may "prefer" some creditors over others by paying the preferred creditors a larger percentage of their claims.

Federal Bankruptcy Law and Administration

For most people, bankruptcy is a most unpleasant fact of business life. A person with a bankruptcy discharge on his or her credit record may have difficulty obtaining new credit. If a bankrupt business must close down, employees lose their jobs and may lose back wages and pension benefits. General (unsecured) creditors may be unable to collect unpaid debts. Tax authorities lose a source or revenue and may be unable to collect unpaid taxes. Customers must look elsewhere for goods and services, suppliers lose a customer, and proprietors and shareholders may lose all or most of their investment.

Yet, bankruptcy does have its positive aspects. Freed by their bankruptcy discharges from impossible burdens of debt accumulated for reasons beyond their control, competent businesspeople may once again be good credit risks and productive citizens. Bankruptcy law also preserves employment by providing opportunities for a troubled business to stay in operation while it regains its financial health. And bankruptcy law reduces the potential for wasteful conflict among creditors by providing for an orderly and fair distribution of the debtor's remaining assets in the event of a liquidation proceeding. The nature of federal bankruptcy law and how its purposes are carried out are the subjects of the paragraphs that follow.

Purposes of Federal Bankruptcy Law

The United States Constitution gives Congress the power to regulate bankruptcies; and over the years since 1800, five different federal bankruptcy statutes have been in effect. The most recent one is the Bankruptcy Reform Act of 1978, referred to in this chapter as the Bankruptcy Code. The Bankruptcy Code (as amended in 1984 and 1986), together with interpretive court decisions (and procedural bankruptcy rules and standards published by the United States Supreme Court), constitutes our national bankruptcy law.

Federal bankruptcy law has two main purposes: (1) to provide a fair and evenhanded basis for distributing a debtor's available assets among creditors, and (2) to free debtors from impossible burdens of debt and thus to give debtors a fresh start so that they may more quickly return to productive business activities. One aspect of the fresh-start policy is the practice permitted by the Bankruptcy Code of allowing some firms to stay in business while they attempt to recover their financial health. Permitting financially distressed firms, especially large ones, to reorganize and stay in business tends to minimize the disruption of employment and to maintain the flow of goods and services to the public.

Basic Bankruptcy Procedure

Like any other judicial proceeding, bankruptcy follows a procedure specified by law. Although the procedure varies somewhat depending on who initiates it (debtor or creditors) or on the kind of relief sought (liquidation, reorganization, or repayment plan), the basic steps are as follows:

1 A person entitled to do so files a *petition* (in a federal bankruptcy court) requesting the bankruptcy judge to grant an "order for relief" with respect to a particular debtor alleged to be insolvent. An *order for relief* is a formal court ruling or declaration that the alleged debtor is insolvent (bankrupt). The filing of the petition results in an *automatic stay* (suspension) of most other legal action and nonjudicial collection activity affecting the debtor's estate (property), until the bankruptcy case is over or until the bankruptcy court vacates (terminates) the stay.

2 The debtor files with the bankruptcy court a listing of the debtor's assets and creditors.

3 Promptly upon entry (recording) of the order for relief, the bankruptcy judge appoints an *interim* (temporary) *trustee* to investigate the financial affairs of the debtor, to take control of the debtor's estate, to notify creditors of the bankruptcy proceeding, and to collect and distribute the debtor's *nonexempt* property to the creditors as required by the Bankruptcy Code. *Exempt* property is property such as clothing and tools that an individual debtor may keep free from the claims of creditors.

4 Within a reasonable time after entry of the order for relief, the bankruptcy judge calls the *first meeting of creditors* (but is not allowed to preside at or attend it). The creditors may elect a permanent trustee. If they fail to do so, the interim trustee serves as permanent trustee. *The debtor must attend the creditor's meeting and submit to examination (questioning) under oath.*

5 Depending on the honesty of the debtor and on the kind of bankruptcy proceeding involved, the court grants the debtor a discharge from most debts remaining unpaid, approves a plan of business reorganization,

or approves the debtor's plan for repayment of debts.

Role of State Law

Under the supremacy clause of the Constitution, the federal bankruptcy law prevails over conflicting state law. However, although Congress probably could preempt (displace) all state insolvency law, it has chosen not to do so. The Bankruptcy Code looks to state law for the resolution of a number of bankruptcy issues. Usually, the state law of property and of contracts will be followed for the purpose of determining, for example, what property the debtor owns. By express provision of the Code, state law may govern what property of the debtor (residence, tools, clothing, and so on) is exempt from the claims of creditors. State insolvency law that does not defeat the purposes of the Bankruptcy Code will usually be allowed to stand.

Functions of Trustee and Judge

Bankruptcy is not merely a judicial proceeding. It also involves the administration of the debtor's "estate," i.e., the debtor's property, for the benefit of the debtor and the creditors. Two officials have major responsibility for administering the estate: the trustee in bankruptcy and the bankruptcy judge.

The *trustee in bankruptcy* is responsible for collecting, liquidating, and distributing the debtor's estate. These tasks require the trustee to inspect the property and business of the debtor, to decide whether to adopt or reject executory (yet to be performed) contracts and leases, to operate the business of the debtor under certain circumstances, and to perform a variety of routine tasks relating to the administrative process. One of the trustee's major duties is to act on behalf of the general (unsecured) creditors. To discharge that duty, the trustee must guard the estate against unfounded claims of creditors, resist doubtful exemption claims of the debtor, and avoid (set aside) various transactions by means of which the debtor or others may have dissipated the estate. The trustee possesses extensive legal powers for carrying out these tasks. Many of the trustee's powers, especially the powers of avoidance, are discussed later in this chapter.

The *bankruptcy judge* has the usual judicial function of deciding any disputes that may arise during the bankruptcy process. Ordinarily the dispute will be between the trustee and a person affected by some act of the trustee in collecting and distributing the debtor's estate. The judge also has a number of administrative duties—e.g., appointing trustees and supervising their activities in the administration of debtors' estates.

Kinds of Bankruptcy Proceedings

The Bankruptcy Code[1] has eight odd-numbered chapters and, since 1986, a Chapter 12. Chapter 7 deals with liquidation, also known as "straight" or "ordinary" bankruptcy. Chapter 11 deals with corporate reorganizations, and Chapter 13 covers plans for the adjustment of debts of individuals with regular income. Chapter 12, entitled "Adjustment of Debts of a Family Farmer with Regular Annual Income," is similar to Chapter 13, but addresses financial problems peculiar to family farmers. Chapter 12 is beyond the scope of this book. Liquidation, corporate reorganizations, and Chapter 13 plans are discussed later in this chapter.

Most debtors—individuals, partnerships, or corporations—may *voluntarily* seek relief from debts or may be subjected to *involuntary* bankruptcy proceedings initiated by creditors. *Not* covered by the Bankruptcy Code are insurance companies, banks, savings and loan associations, credit unions, and similar organizations. Such businesses are regulated by federal or state administrative agencies, which are thought better equipped than the courts to handle their financial failure.

Railroads may be reorganized or liquidated under Chapter 11 of the Bankruptcy Code, but they are not otherwise eligible for bankruptcy. Municipal corporations are not liquidated, but may seek "adjustment" of their debts under Chapter 9 of the Code if state law authorizes them to do so. Stockbrokers and commodity brokers may be liquidated under Subchapters III and IV of Chapter 7. Railroad reorganizations, the adjustment of municipal debt, and the liquidation of stock and commodity brokers are beyond the scope of this book.

Chapter 1 of the Code contains various general provisions such as definitions and rules of

[1] 11 U.S.C. sec. 101 et seq. Citations to the United States Code are to titles and their sections; thus, here, Title 11, sec. 101 of the U.S.C. In this chapter, only the section numbers are given, in brackets: e.g., [101], which means "Section 101 of the Bankruptcy Code."

construction, and says who may be a debtor (i.e., who is eligible for relief from debts) in different kinds of cases under the Code. Chapter 3, entitled Case Administration, indicates how a case is begun and deals with the administrative powers of bankruptcy officials. Chapter 5 contains much of the substantive law of bankruptcy. It deals, for example, with (*a*) what property constitutes the debtor's estate, (*b*) the powers of the trustee to avoid (set aside) transactions that would diminish the debtor's estate, (*c*) the order (priority) in which distributions from the estate will be made to creditors, and (*d*) the duties and benefits of the debtor. Chapters 1, 3, and 5 apply to any kind of case under the Code.

Liquidation (Straight or Ordinary Bankruptcy)

The purpose of a Chapter 7 liquidation proceeding is to convert the debtor's nonexempt assets into cash, to distribute it as dictated by the scheme of distribution provided in the Bankruptcy Code, and to grant the honest debtor a discharge from most of the remaining debts.

Commencement of Straight Bankruptcy

Any "person" except a railroad or a regulated business of the type discussed earlier may file a *voluntary* petition to liquidate under Chapter 7 [109(b)]. *Person* includes individuals, partnerships, and corporations, but not governmental units [101(35)]. Therefore, municipal corporations may not file under Chapter 7 and cannot be liquidated (but *can* have their debts adjusted under Chapter 9 if state law permits). The filing fee is $60 and may be paid in installments. No one is exempted from paying the fee.

Most persons who qualify for a voluntary liquidation may be subjected instead to an *involuntary* liquidation proceeding [303]. However, farmers, including "family farmers" as defined in section 101(17) & (18), and charitable corporations may not be subjected to any kind of involuntary bankruptcy proceedings. A *farmer* is a person (individual, partnership, or corporation) whose gross income in the taxable year prior to bankruptcy was more than 80 percent from a farming operation owned or operated by that person [101(19)].

A person cannot be declared an involuntary bankrupt unless three requirements or conditions have been met.

1. The petitioning creditor or creditors must have claims totaling at least $5,000 in unsecured debts.
2. Where the number of creditors is twelve or more, three of them must join in the involuntary petition; otherwise, only one petitioning creditor is required.
3. The alleged debtor must have given the creditor or creditors a *ground for relief.* Under the Code there are two grounds for relief. One is that "the debtor is generally not paying such debtor's debts as such debts become due." The other is that the debtor has, within 120 days of the filing of the involuntary petition, made a general assignment (transfer of the debtor's property) for the benefit of creditors [303(h)].

These requirements serve several purposes. They provide specific, numerical guidance to the court and thus facilitate the administration of bankruptcy law. They also identify the level of financial ill health at which creditors may seek protection against the wishes of the debtor. And they serve, in part, to protect the debtor from unfounded, trivial, or harassing claims. The debtor has another important protection. If the allegations for an involuntary petition are not proved, the court may grant court costs to the debtor; and, if a trustee was appointed and took possession of the debtor's property, the court may award damages to the debtor. A bad faith petitioner may be liable for both compensatory and punitive damages even though no trustee was appointed [303(i)].

Collection and Liquidation of Debtor's Estate

The collection and liquidation of the debtor's estate can involve considerable litigation. Issues for the court to decide may include what property belongs to the debtor's estate, what powers the trustee has to set aside transactions in order to acquire property for the estate, and what exemption claims by the debtor the trustee should honor.

Property of the Debtor's Estate. The debtor's estate consists of a broad range of property interests either owned by the debtor as of the commencement of the bankruptcy case or recoverable for the estate by the trustee from someone other than the debtor [541]. Included in the estate are the following:

1 All legal and equitable interests of the debtor in property as of the commencement of the bankruptcy case, *except* (*a*) certain powers over property exercisable by the debtor solely for the benefit of others, and (*b*) the debtor's beneficial interest under a spendthrift trust which is valid under state law. A spendthrift trust is one set up to protect the beneficiary from his or her improvident spending habits. Where state law recognizes such a trust, creditors may not reach trust funds, and the beneficiary may dispose of funds only as they are received. The Bankruptcy Code makes spendthrift trust provisions that are enforceable under state law effective also against the trustee in bankruptcy.

   It should be noted that a secured creditor's security interest does *not* become a part of the debtor's estate. A security interest in collateral is by its nature the property of the creditor. Unless the secured transaction can be set aside under the trustee's avoiding powers, only the debtor's "equity" in the collateral is included in the debtor's estate. The trustee does, however, receive the collateral itself for purposes of administration.

2 All interests of the debtor and the debtor's spouse in community property *if* the community property is under the sole, equal, or joint management or control of the debtor.

3 Any interest in property held by others than the debtor and recoverable by the trustee for the debtor's estate under various provisions of the Bankruptcy Code. The powers of the trustee to recover property for the estate are discussed later in this chapter.

4 Certain property acquired by the debtor within 180 days after the date of the filing of the petition. This property includes inheritances, property acquired as a result of a divorce decree or a property settlement with the debtor's spouse, and property acquired by the debtor as a beneficiary of a life insurance policy or of a death benefit plan.

5 Income and other proceeds from property of the estate, and any interest or property that the estate acquires after the commencement of the case. (Earnings from services performed by an *individual* debtor after the commencement of the case are *not* included in the debtor's estate.)

Trustee's Power to Collect and Liquidate the Estate. To administer the debtor's estate properly, the trustee in bankruptcy must gain possession, custody, or control of the property, regardless of who actually has it. In carrying out his or her duties, the trustee has the benefit of (*a*) powers to use, sell, or lease property and to borrow money, (*b*) powers to assume or reject executory contracts and unexpired leases, and (*c*) powers to avoid a variety of transactions.

In exercising these powers, the trustee is aided by the "automatic stay" and the "turnover" provisions of the Code. A *stay* is a halting or a suspension of legal action. The filing of a petition in bankruptcy automatically stays the commencement or continuation of other legal proceedings affecting the debtor's estate until the bankruptcy case is over or until the stay is vacated by the bankruptcy court [362]. Thus, the trustee may preserve and administer the estate without undue interference. Some nonbankruptcy actions, such as criminal actions against the debtor, are excluded from the operation of the automatic stay.

The *turnover* provisions require holders of property to which the debtor's estate is entitled to deliver it to the trustee [542; 543]. The estate is entitled, for example, to any property that the trustee may use, sell, or lease in the administration of the case, including property subject to a security interest. The estate is also entitled to any property that the debtor is permitted later to exempt from the estate.

In Case 26.1, the trustee seeks turnover of real estate.

CASE 26.1 In re Olson · 39 B.R. 872 (D. Kan. 1984)

FACTS Mona Olson (debtor) inherited a one-third interest in 160 acres of unirrigated farm land from her grandmother. The will was admitted to probate on January 9, 1981. On January 21, Mona contracted to sell her interest in the real estate to her daughter Tammy for $5,000. On March 2, Tammy received a warranty deed to the property and made the final payment. On May 26, 1981, Mona and her husband filed a petition in bankruptcy.

In the fall of 1981, the trustee in bankruptcy filed a turnover complaint in the bankruptcy court, requesting that the court order the executor of the grandmother's estate to pay to the trustee all proceeds of the estate in which the debtors or their daughter Tammy had an interest. In April, 1982, the complaint was dismissed for lack of prosecution. A successor trustee filed another turnover complaint, other successor trustees became involved in the bankruptcy proceeding, and on September 13, 1983, trustee Kunce filed a complaint to set aside the debtors' conveyance to their daughter as a fraudulent transfer. The debtors opposed the turnover and the fraudulent transfer complaints.

OPINION FRANKLIN, B. J. . . . As defined by § 541, the bankruptcy estate is comprised of all legal or equitable interests held by the debtors when they filed their bankruptcy petition. Under the provisions of [that section, certain] property acquired by the debtors after the filing of their petition may also be included in the estate[, i.e., any property] "*that the debtor acquires or becomes entitled to acquire within 180 days after such date—(A) by bequest, devise, or inheritance. . . .*"

Therefore, the real estate devised to debtor Mona Olson, by her grandmother, is subject to the trustee's turnover complaint only if it was part of the estate at the commencement of the bankruptcy case or became part of the estate within 180 days after the petition was filed.

It is a fundamental principle of bankruptcy law that the property rights which form the estate under § 541 are defined by state law. . . . Therefore, the Court must look to Kansas law to determine the property interest Mona Olson acquired from her grandmother.

Under [a Kansas statute], "*No will shall be effectual to pass real or personal property unless it shall have been duly admitted to probate.*" Since the will . . . was duly admitted to probate . . . , that will was capable of passing a one-third interest in real property to Mona Olson.

. . . The law of Kansas [favors] the earliest possible distribution [of] inherited property consistent with the proper administration of the estate. . . . [T]he interest in real property [that debtor] Mona Olson inherited under her grandmother's will vested in her when the will was admitted to probate. Since it [apparently was not subject to administrative expenses or claims], Mona Olson acquired the entire one-third interest her grandmother had devised. . . . This Court finds . . . that the property passed to the debtor on January 9, 1981, when the will was admitted to probate [and that] the debtor [therefore] acquired her interest *before* the filing of the petition, not *within* 180 days *after* that date. . . .

The Court must next evaluate the effect of debtors' transfer of property to their daughter Tammy Olson. . . . The effect of [the March 12, 1981] transfer was to convey a fee simple interest to Tammy Olson and to divest Mr. & Mrs. Olson of their interest in the property. Accordingly, when the debtors filed their bankruptcy petition on [May 26], the one-third interest . . . did not become property of the estate under § 541, because debtors no longer held either equitable or legal title to it. Whether debtors transferred the property with the intent to hinder, delay or defraud their creditors is not an issue before this Court. The trustee had notice of the transfer when debtors filed their bankruptcy petition and described the conveyance in their answer to question 12b. Neither Trustee Clotfelter nor his numerous successors alleged that this was a fraudulent transfer until Trustee Kunce filed a complaint under § 548 on September 13, 1983. That complaint was dismissed on

CASE 26.1 Continued

April 11, 1984, because it was barred by the [two-year] statute of limitations set out in § 546(a).... Having found that this real property vested in Mona Olson when her grandmother's will was admitted to probate...; that debtors transferred their interest to... Tammy Olson prior to filing their bankruptcy petition, for apparent sufficient consideration; and that the 180-day provision of [§ 541(a)] is not applicable to the facts of this case, this Court finds the property was never part of the bankruptcy estate and therefore finds that the Motion for Turnover should be denied....

JUDGMENT [The motion] is... denied.

Power to use, sell, or lease property. Often the trustee needs to use, sell, or lease property (of the debtor's estate) that is subject to the claims of persons such as secured creditors, or to borrow money in a manner that might threaten existing security or other interests. These acts may be necessary to preserve valuable property or to keep a business operation going. The trustee may use, sell, or lease encumbered (mortgaged) property, but only if the security interest or lien is adequately protected [363(e)]. Encumbered property may not be sold free and clear of the encumbrance unless, for example, the holder of the security interest consents or the price received for the property is greater than the value of the interest [363(f)].

Before the enactment of the Bankruptcy Code, holders of "floating liens" under Article 9 of the Uniform Commercial Code often refused to extend further credit to a troubled debtor or to subordinate their liens to lenders who might be willing to extend additional credit to the failing business. Since floating liens ordinarily encumber all or most of the debtor's business property, their holders thus could force liquidation of the debtor's business even though liquidation might be ill-advised. Under the Bankruptcy Code, a trustee who is authorized to operate the business of the debtor may obtain unsecured credit or, if necessary, secured credit despite existing liens. Where property of the estate is already encumbered, the trustee may grant a junior lien on that property. Where new lenders refuse to extend credit on an unsecured or a junior lien basis, the court may authorize the trustee to grant a lien equal in priority or senior to existing interests, *if* there is adequate protection of the holders of existing interests [364].

Power to assume or reject debtor's contracts. Subject to court approval, the trustee may assume, reject, or assign executory contracts and unexpired leases of the debtor [365(a)]. This power enables the trustee to reject improvident or burdensome transactions, to retain for the estate any beneficial transaction that is assumable under state law, and to assign (sell) any contract or lease that is assignable under state law. The trustee's rejection of an otherwise binding contract or lease constitutes a breach of it and gives the aggrieved party a claim against the debtor's estate.

Some contract clauses or provisions of state law are intended to prevent the trustee from assuming contracts upon the debtor's bankruptcy or insolvency, even though the contract would otherwise be assumable. The Bankruptcy Code invalidates such clauses and provisions of state law [365(e)]. Consequently, the parties to a contract can no longer use the mere fact of bankruptcy or insolvency to deny to the trustee the debtor's rights and benefits under a contract or lease.

Power to assert debtor's defenses. To preserve the debtor's estate, the trustee may need to avoid contracts made by the debtor. To that end, the trustee may assert any personal defense or basis for suit that the debtor could have used against the other contracting party: duress, undue influence, fraud, statute of limitations, statute of frauds, usury, and so on [558]. Suppose Dan Debtor was induced by Sara's fraud to trade his $10,000 business computer for a defective one worth only $2,000. On the ground of Sara's fraud, Dan could have rescinded the contract and recovered his computer. Likewise, upon Dan's bankruptcy, the trustee may use Sara's fraud as a basis for avoiding the contract and recovering Dan's computer for the debtor's estate. A waiver of a personal defense by the debtor after the commencement of the case does not bind the debtor's estate.

Power of avoidance based on lien creditor or bona fide purchaser status. A *lien creditor* is a person whose debt or claim is secured by a lien on particular property. Suppose Sam sells a copier to Bob, retains a purchase-money security interest (PMSI) in the copier, and delivers it to Bob for use in his business. But at the time of the sale, Cora Creditor has a perfected security interest in Bob's business property and in "any business property which Bob may hereafter acquire." As discussed in Chapter 25, to perfect his PMSI in the copier, and thus to acquire priority over Cora's security interest, Sam must file a financing statement within 10 days after Bob receives possession of the copier. Sam fails to do so. Bob fails to pay the debt he owes Cora; she brings foreclosure action against Bob; and the court renders judgment for Cora. As a result of the judgment against Bob, Cora has a *judicial lien* on so much of Bob's property as was covered by Cora's perfected security interest. Because Sam failed to perfect his PMSI in the copier, Cora's security interest prevails and the copier, like the rest of Bob's business property, is subject to Cora's lien. Cora is a *judicial lien creditor.* As a creditor with a perfected security interest, Cora will prevail even as against Bob's trustee in bankruptcy (unless, as discussed later, the secured transaction constitutes a "preference" that is voidable by the trustee).

The Bankruptcy Code gives the trustee the *status* of a judicial lien creditor such as Cora whether or not such a person exists [544(a) (1)]. Suppose Sam sold the copier to Bob; Sam failed to perfect his PMSI; there was no such person as Cora; and a month after receiving the copier Bob filed a petition in bankruptcy. The trustee, having the status of a judicial lien creditor, has the power to defeat Sam's *unperfected* PMSI and to acquire the business equipment for the debtor's estate. (Sam would, of course, have a claim as an unsecured creditor for the price of the copier.)

The Code confers upon the trustee other statuses—for example, that of a hypothetical bona fide purchaser of real property from the debtor [544(a) (3)]. Thus, the trustee may acquire the debtor's real estate free from whatever competing claims a real bona fide purchaser would have taken the property free from. In addition, the trustee succeeds to the rights of certain *actual* creditors, that is, those who hold *unsecured,* allowable claims [544(b)]. The trustee may avoid any transfer by the debtor that such existing, unsecured creditors could have avoided but did not.

Power to avoid fraudulent transfers and preferences. The trustee has the power to avoid fradulent transfers and preferential transfers (preferences). Such transfers are wrongful and avoidable because they deprive the debtor's estate of assets to which it is entitled, or because they undermine a fundamental bankruptcy policy—equality of distribution among creditors.

The trustee may avoid any *fraudulent transfer* of the debtor's property made within 1 year before the filing of the petition in bankruptcy, regardless of who made the transfer [548]. Suppose, for example, that Dan is in financial difficulty and intends to file a voluntary petition in bankruptcy. But a week before doing so Dan transfers title to his $100,000 house to his sister for "safekeeping" until he receives a discharge in bankruptcy. Dan's transfer of the house is fraudulent as to his creditors. (The trustee may also avoid any fraudulent obligation incurred by the debtor within the 1-year period, such as the debtor's contract to pay someone for services, performance of which the debtor at the time of contracting intends not to require.)

The fraud may be either actual or constructive. The fraud is *actual* if the transfer or obligation involved an intent to hinder, delay, or defraud creditors. The fraud is *constructive* (involving no specific intention to defraud) if the debtor received less than a reasonable equivalent value for the transfer or obligation *and* (1) the debtor was insolvent or became insolvent as a result of the transaction, or (2) the debtor was engaged in business, or was about to engage in a business or transaction, for which any property remaining with the debtor was an unreasonably small capital, or (3) the debtor intended to incur, or believed that the debtor would incur, debts that would be beyond the debtor's ability to pay as the debts matured. Case 26.2 discusses whether a mortgage foreclosure sale involves constructive fraud.

CASE 26.2 Reinboldt v. Travelers Ins. Co. · 39 B.R. 678 (D. Minn. 1984)

FACTS The Reinboldts operated a dairy and grain farm in Minnesota. As security for a loan of $260,000, they signed a mortgage giving Travelers Insurance Co. a first lien on about 440 acres of their farmland. The Reinboldts defaulted on the note secured by the mortgage. In accordance with Minnesota law, Travelers foreclosed the mortgage by advertisement and purchased the property for about $221,000—the amount of the debt plus statutory costs and fees. During the 1-year redemption period provided by Minnesota law, Norwest Bank (the holder of a second mortgage on the farm, securing a $100,000 debt) redeemed (paid) the first mortgage held by Travelers, thus succeeding to Travelers' rights in the Reinboldts' land. In the meantime, the Reinboldts filed a Chapter 11 bankruptcy proceeding. As "debtors-in-possession" (Chapter 11 trustees), the Reinboldts brought suit to set aside the foreclosure sale as a fraudulent conveyance, alleging that the amount paid was not reasonably equivalent to the value of the property. The bankruptcy court denied debtors' request to set aside the foreclosure sale, and debtors appealed.

OPINION MacLAUGHLIN, District Judge. A debtor in possession . . . may recover for the benefit of the estate, property which has been fraudulently conveyed out of the estate. . . . The Debtors argue that the mortgage foreclosure sale constituted a fraudulent conveyance . . . because [Travelers] purchased the property for less than half of the fair market value. . . . [Bankruptcy Code § 548(a) (2) (A) provides that "the trustee may avoid any transfer of an interest of the debtor in property . . . that was made . . . within one year before the date of the filing of the petition, if the debtor . . . received less than a reasonably equivalent value in exchange for such transfer . . . and . . . was insolvent on the date that such transfer was made. . . .]

. . . Norwest argues that [for a number of reasons] the mortgage foreclosure sale should not be set aside. . . . First . . . the sale was completed in accordance with the Minnesota statute governing foreclosure by advertisement, and [in Minnesota] a debtor may not contest a foreclosure sale . . . for inadequacy of price. Next, . . . section 548 was intended only to avoid transfers effectuated by a debtor's own action, and accordingly, a validly conducted foreclosure sale is not a transfer within section 548. Finally, . . . adequate consideration was given at the mortgage foreclosure sale because the one-year redemption period provided by Minnesota law substantially lowered the fair market value of the property.

The Debtors' position is based on *Durrett v. Washington National Insurance Co.* . . . In *Durrett,* the court held that a foreclosure sale occurring within a year prior to bankruptcy is a transfer subject to avoidance as a fraudulent conveyance if the sale price is not reasonably equivalent to the value of the mortgaged property.

The United States Court of Appeals for the Ninth Circuit recently reached the opposite conclusion. . . . After examining the statutory and legislative history of section 548(a) (2) (A), as well as the policy considerations of setting aside a validly conducted mortgage foreclosure sale, the court concluded that lien enforcement actions such as mortgage foreclosure sales were not intended to be treated as constructive[ly] fraudulent conveyances. . . .

This Court . . . agrees with the Ninth Circuit's conclusion that a validly conducted mortgage foreclosure sale was not intended to be treated as a constructive[ly] fraudulent conveyance. . . . The Court also agrees with the bankruptcy court's conclusion that the foreclosure sale cannot be set aside, because under Minnesota law inadequacy of price is an insufficient ground for challenging an otherwise validly conducted foreclosure sale. . . .

JUDGMENT . . . [T]he order of the bankruptcy court . . . dismissing the debtor's claim . . . is affirmed.

CASE 26.2 Continued

[In a footnote the court stated, "[T]he very nature of a foreclosure proceeding, coupled with the equity of redemption under state law, lowers the fair market value of foreclosed property.... However, if the Court were to base its decision on this ground, a hearing would be necessary to establish if fair market value was paid."]

The trustee may also avoid *preferential payments or transfers* (preferences). A transaction is a *preference* (and is therefore avoidable by the trustee) if the transfer (1) was made to a creditor in settlement of an *antecedent* debt (a debt owed before the debtor made the transfer), (2) was made "on or within" 90 days before the filing of the bankruptcy petition, (3) was made when the debtor was insolvent, and (4) conferred upon the creditor more than the creditor would have been entitled to receive in a Chapter 7 liquidation case [547].

Preferences occur in a variety of ways. Sometimes, for example, a debtor faced with bankruptcy voluntarily pays a favorite creditor-supplier in full and leaves other creditors to share whatever remains. Sometimes a creditor pressures a debtor into making a preferential payment. Frequently, the preference takes the form of a security interest given just before bankruptcy for an unsecured debt incurred much earlier and originally intended to be unsecured. Preferences made within the 90-day period (*and, under the 1984 amendments, all other preferences*) are vulnerable to the trustee's attack regardless of whether the creditor had reasonable cause to believe that the debtor was insolvent.

The trustee has additional powers to avoid preferences made to "insiders" (i.e., the debtor's relatives, partners, directors, controlling persons, and so on). Preferences made to insiders within the 90-day period before bankruptcy are avoidable under the rule stated in the preceding paragraph. The trustee may also avoid preferences made to insiders between the beginning of the 90-day period and 1 year before bankruptcy.

Some transactions that appear technically to be preferences are not, and therefore they are not avoidable by the trustee. Suppose a supplier of inventory delivers goods to an insolvent retailer 30 days before the retailer's bankruptcy and, a few days later, receives full payment out of the proceeds from the resale of the goods. The supplier has extended unsecured credit and could be said to have received a preferential payment on account of an antecedent debt. However, the payment is not so treated under the Bankruptcy Code. The trustee cannot avoid an otherwise preferential payment of a debt incurred in the ordinary course of the debtor and creditor's business or financial affairs where the payment was made in the ordinary course of business according to ordinary business terms [547(c) (2)].

A similar rule applies where a lender intends to make a secured loan to an insolvent debtor, but the execution of the security documents occurs a few days after credit is extended. Since the debtor actually received cash at nearly the time the documents were signed, the debtor's giving the lender a security interest is not a preference, and the trustee may not avoid it. Such rules encourage suppliers and lenders to continue to do business with insolvent persons while there is a chance that they might recover their financial health. The rules do no harm to the general creditors because the protected suppliers and lenders have not depleted the debtor's estate.

Limits on avoidance powers. Since the trustee's main function is to protect the interests of general (unsecured) creditors, the trustee's powers to avoid transactions that dissipate the estate are necessarily quite broad. However, there are limits to those powers. For example, the trustee cannot avoid *all* preferential transfers, since Section 547 prohibits the trustee from avoiding an individual debtor's preferential transfer where the debts are primarily consumer debts and the value of the property affected by the transfer is less than $600. Many of the limits on the trustee's avoidance powers are left for the court to develop, as in the determination of what defenses of the debtor the estate may assert against others.

Additional limits are imposed by Section 546, among them the following:

1 The trustee's right to bring suit to avoid a transaction expires 2 years after the trustee's appointment or at the termination of the case, whichever occurs first.

2 Sometimes a person sells goods on credit only to discover after delivery that the buyer is insolvent. Under UCC § 2-702, the seller has 10 days to reclaim them from the insolvent buyer. The trustee's power of avoidance is subject to the seller's UCC (or other statutory or common law) right of reclamation if (*a*) the goods were sold in the ordinary course of the seller's business, and (*b*) the seller demanded reclamation in writing within 10 days after the debtor received the goods [546(c)].

3 Producers of grain sometimes deliver it (in the ordinary course of their business) to a grain storage facility owned or operated by an insolvent debtor. The trustee's power of avoidance is subject to any right that the producer has to reclaim the grain, if the producer demands reclamation in writing within 10 days after the debtor received the grain [546(d)]. Fishermen have similar rights regarding fish delivered to a processing facility owned or operated by an insolvent debtor.

The Debtor's Exemptions. As a part of the fresh-start policy, the Bankruptcy Code permits an *individual* debtor to exempt certain property from the debtor's estate, i.e., to have it free from the claims of creditors. The Bankruptcy Code gives an individual debtor a choice between two exemption systems—state and federal—unless, as is permitted by the Code, the debtor's state has denied its citizens the right to elect the federal exemptions. States that choose to do this are said to have "opted out" of the federal exemption scheme. Well over 30 states have opted out, limiting their citizens to whatever exemptions the state laws provide.

Some states limit exemptions to no more than about $5,000 worth of property. In other states the exemptible amount can exceed $100,000. Under California law, for example, an individual debtor may exempt up to $45,000 equity in a residence and have many other exemptions. The dollar value of the federal list lies between these extremes. The federal exemptions include $7,500 equity in a residence; $1,200 equity in one motor vehicle; $4,000 in ordinary household furnishings and personal apparel, no single item to exceed $200 in value; $500 in family jewelry; $400 in any property (including cash) plus any unused portion of the residential equity exemption to a maximum of $3,750; $750 in books and tools of the debtor's trade; any unmatured life insurance contract owned by the debtor (other than a credit life insurance contract); up to $4,000 cash surrender or loan value of an unmatured life insurance contract on the life of and owned by the debtor; alimony and child support; certain rights in pension or profit sharing plans; and awards from personal injury causes of action [522]. Many of the "opt-out" states grant exemptions in a similarly broad range of property interests, but usually in smaller amounts. Regardless of whether the debtor chooses the state or the federal exemptions, waivers of exemptions in favor of unsecured creditors are unenforceable.

A consumer-debtor may redeem exempt property that is subject to a security interest by paying to the secured creditor the amount of the allowed secured claim [722]. The right to redeem applies to tangible personal property intended primarily for personal, family, or household use. The debtor could, for example, redeem an automobile that would otherwise be repossessed.

A debtor may avoid certain liens to the extent that they impair the debtor's exemptions. The debtor may avoid any judicial lien that does so. The debtor may also avoid a nonpossessory, nonpurchase-money security interest that impairs an exemptible interest in such personal or family items as household furnishings, wearing apparel, tools of the debtor's trade, or professionally prescribed health aids [522(f)].

In Case 26.3, the debtor claimed as exempt property some real estate he had transferred to the creditor.

CASE 26.3 In re Huizar • 71 B.R. 826 (W.D. Tex. 1987)

FACTS Huizar, a dealer in motor homes, was heavily indebted to the Bank of Robstown. In January 1985, Huizar refinanced the debt, signing promissory notes and Deeds of Trust to 5 tracts of land as security. One of those tracts was the "Harpers Ferry" property that

CASE 26.3 Continued

Huizar later claimed as a homestead. Owing Bank over $425,000, Huizar defaulted on the notes. Bank granted a 90-day renewal loan in exchange for warranty deeds to the five parcels of land, the value of which was to be credited against the amount Huizar owed the bank. Bank recorded its deed to the Harpers Ferry property on September 4, 1985. On January 7, 1986, Huizar filed a voluntary Chapter 11 petition for relief from his debts.

During the bankruptcy proceedings, Bank alleged that Huizar, although having deeded the Harpers Ferry property to it, refused to vacate. Accordingly, Bank filed a Motion for Relief from the automatic stay in order to pursue state action to obtain possession of the property. Huizar claimed the property as his homestead, and Bank filed an objection to his Claim of Exemption. Huizar then brought suit to have the deed to the Harpers Ferry property set aside as a preferential transfer. Thus, the court was faced with two questions: (1) Did Huizar have a legitimate homestead claim as to the Harpers Ferry property? (2) If so, should the transfer to Bank be set aside as preferential so that Huizar could exempt the property?

OPINION

KELLY, B. J.... Upon filing his bankruptcy petition, all property interests of the Debtor entered the bankruptcy estate... subject to being withdrawn by the Debtor as exempt property.... Section 522(b) allows a Debtor to use applicable state law exemptions, as the Debtor did in this case....

Claiming an exemption does not... establish that the property in question is in fact exempt.... [A] bankruptcy court must turn to state law [to determine] state exemption rights.... In Texas a homestead is defined by... the Texas Constitution which... provides in pertinent part:

> The homestead, not in a town or city, shall consist of not more than two hundred acres of land, which may be in one or more parcels with the improvements thereon; the homestead in a city, town or village, shall consist of lot or lots amounting to not more than one acre of land, together with any improvements on the land....

Absent actual occupancy, some overt act of preparation is required to establish a homestead right in order to corroborate claimant's testimony that he intended to occupy the property as his homestead.... The evidence in this case was uncontroverted that the Debtor extensively remodeled the house and spent $12,000 to $15,000 before January 1985. In disputed testimony the Debtor stated that he had vacated a rented apartment and began moving into the Harpers Ferry house in December 1984. [There was evidence] that notice was given to Debtor's landlord of his intention to move out in February 1985.... [T]he Court finds... that the Debtor established a homestead interest in the Harpers Ferry property as of January 3, 1986.

A debtor's right to exemptions is determined as of the date the bankruptcy petition is filed.... [T]he Harpers Ferry property was conveyed to the Bank [before the petition was filed]. Thus, the Debtor may not exempt this property unless it can be recovered under an avoidance power and returned to the estate.

...The [Debtor alleges] that this transfer is voidable as... preferential.... [T]he evidence established... September 4, 1986, [as the date of transfer].... This date was more than 90 days prior to the filing of the bankruptcy petition. Thus, for the Debtor to establish that the transaction was a preferential transfer, he must also establish that the Bank was an insider.... Huizar has failed to meet this test.

The definition of "insider" is not limited to the examples given in the Code. Debtor contends that the Bank exercised such control or influence over him... that the Harpers Ferry transactions were not arms-length, and thus [were] voidable.... The purpose of the insider provisions of the Code is to protect general creditors from overreaching by those with special power or influence over the debtor.

...The only credible evidence on the point... shows that the current president of the Bank had been a close friend of the Debtor when the president was a loan officer at [another] bank. When he moved to Bank of Robstown, the president solicited Huizar's

CASE 26.3 Continued

business and became Huizar's primary lender. Over the years Huizar referred customers to the Bank, paid one or more unrelated loans which his employees owed the Bank, had loans aggregating two or three million dollars owing to the Bank, and took at least one vacation with the Bank president. The Debtor testified that he considered the Bank president to be his closest friend.

There was no credible testimony... that any of the transactions were other than properly negotiated loan[s].... All were evidenced by executed notes and the September 1985 agreement was in writing and signed by both parties.

Many courts have considered the issue of insider preferences and the amount of control necessary to support a finding of an insider relationship between the debtor and its creditor. The cases... have routinely held that a bank's financial power over the debtor does not by itself render the bank [an] "insider" for purposes of § 547 of the Code. *In re Jefferson Mortgage Co., Inc.*, ... [involved] an attempt by a trustee to avoid certain transfers of security interest[s] to the bank on the basis of insider control. The court held that "... this control was merely incidental to their creditor-debtor relationship. The creditor had only financial power over the debtor, and the debtor could have terminated the relationship at any time and looked for another creditor."... *See also In re Belco, Inc.*, ... (refusing to find insider control by a creditor-bank, stating that the bank possessed no stranglehold on the debtor so as to render the debtor powerless to act independently of the bank)....

As demonstrated by the existing case law, courts which have considered the insider preference issue as between a debtor and a creditor-bank have adopted a view that a creditor-lending institution must be able to exercise... reasonable debtor control without fear of being labelled an insider. This Court agrees.... In the case at hand, there [is] no credible evidence... that the Bank of Robstown held... actual or unreasonable control over the Debtor.... For this Court to find the existence of an "insider" relationship between the creditor-bank and the Debtor..., solely based upon the admitted personal relationship... between the Debtor and the president of the Bank of Robstown, would call into question virtually every lending transaction between a debtor and its longstanding lending institution and would result in the unreasonable conclusion that borrowers could [deal only] with bankers that were not friendly or understanding.

JUDGMENT ... [T]he Court finds that the Debtor... is not entitled to relief on the issue of preference....

Distribution of the Estate

Three kinds of creditors may be involved in the distribution of the debtor's estate: secured creditors, unsecured creditors called "priority" creditors, and other unsecured creditors called "general" creditors. The rights of the various kinds of creditors depend on rules governing proof of claim, allowability of claims, and priority of payments.

Proof of Claim. The distribution process begins with the filing of a document called a "proof of claim." A proof of claim is prima facie evidence of the validity and the amount of the claim [Bankruptcy Rule 301]. Only unsecured creditors are required to file proofs of claim. A secured creditor whose secured claim exceeds the value of the collateral is an unsecured creditor as to the amount of the deficiency, and a proof of claim is required for the recovery of the deficiency. Where a proof of claim is required, it ordinarily must be filed within 6 months after the first meeting of creditors [Bankruptcy Rule 302(e)]. Unless a proof of claim is timely filed, a claim cannot be "allowed" even though the claim is otherwise valid.

Allowability of Claims. Only "allowed" claims are eligible for payment out of the debtor's estate, and then, of course, allowed claims will be paid only to the extent that funds are available. What claims are allowed?

Upon the filing of a proof of claim the claim is "deemed allowed" unless an interested party such as a creditor or the trustee objects to the allowance of the claim. If there is an objection, the bankruptcy court must decide whether the claim is to be allowed. Claims filed after the 6-month limit will not be allowed. Where the debtor has a defense to an alleged debt (e.g., fraud or failure of consideration), a claim for payment of the debt will not be allowed. The Code lists other claims that will and will not be allowed [502; 503]. Where a claim is valid but contingent or unliquidated, the court must estimate the amount of the claim for purposes of allowance so that the closing of the case will not be unduly delayed.

Some otherwise allowable claims are disallowed, at least temporarily, to foster efficient administration of the bankruptcy case. Suppose Christine made a large, unsecured loan to Bernie 18 months before his bankruptcy; that 30 days before his bankruptcy she received a preferential payment for a small part of the loan; that the trustee had the preference set aside; and that Christine has not yet paid the preferential amount to the debtor's estate. She files a proof of claim for the difference between the preferential payment she received and the amount of the loan. Christine's claim will not be allowed unless she makes to the estate a timely payment of the preferential amount [502(d)]. Thus, the trustee has leverage to collect preferential and other improper payments.

Suppose, in contrast to the situation just described, that Christine made a $10,000 loan to Bernie 18 months before his bankruptcy, and that in the same week he sold to her, on credit, $1,000 worth of goods. This situation involves mutual debts, and Christine has a right of "set-off" that entitles her to reduce her $10,000 claim against Bernie by the $1,000 that she owes Bernie [553]. Thus, instead of having to pay the estate the $1,000 (which might be distributed to creditors of higher priority than herself) and then filing a claim for $10,000 (which might not be paid for lack of funds), Christine has only $9,000 at risk.

Priority of Payments. *Secured* creditors have property rights (security interests) that the trustee does not acquire. Consequently, secured claims are paid in full if the collateral is sufficiently valuable. If the collateral is not sufficiently valuable, the claimant is a general creditor as to the deficiency.

Next in line are the *priority* creditors, so called because the Code gives them priority of payment over the claims of the general creditors. The principle of pro rata (equal percentage) distribution is applied throughout the Code's general scheme of distribution. So, if funds are sufficient, the "first priority" claims are paid in full, and any excess is applied to the "second priority" claims. This process is repeated until the money runs out or all unsecured creditors are paid. Where funds are not sufficient to pay a class of claims in full, each claimant of that class receives the same percentage of his or her claim that the other claimants of that class receive, e.g., 10 percent. Seven classes of priority claims receive pro rata payments in the following order [507]:

1. Claims for administrative expenses and expenses incurred in preserving and collecting the debtor's estate.
2. Claims of tradespeople who extended unsecured credit to the debtor in the ordinary course of business after the filing of an involuntary petition but before the appointment of a trustee. Priority status for such claims tends to forestall the cutting off of goods, services, and operating credit at the slightest hint of financial difficulty, and therefore to give the debtor an early opportunity to escape bankruptcy.
3. Claims of the debtor's employees for up to $2,000 each in wages earned within 90 days preceding bankruptcy or preceding the cessation of the debtor's business, whichever occurs first.
4. Some claims of employee benefit plan administrators for contributions owed by the debtor to the plans.
5. Claims of grain producers and fishermen for up to $2,000 each for grain or fish deposited with the debtor but not paid for or returned.
6. Claims of consumers for the return of up to $900 each in prebankruptcy deposits paid to the debtor for services not rendered, or for the purchase or rental of property not delivered, where the services or property were for personal, family, or household use.
7. Claims for federal, state, and local taxes.

Finally, if any funds remain, the *general* creditors and a few other claimants receive a share of the debtor's estate [726].

Discharge; Nondischargeable Debts

Debtors who seek liquidation under Chapter 7 or 11, or who propose a Chapter 13 repayment plan, may receive a discharge from most debts that remain unpaid after the distribution of the debtor's estate or the performance of the plan. Most debtors are eligible for a discharge only once every 6 years. However, a wage earner or other debtor who is carrying out a Chapter 13 repayment plan may be eligible for discharge more frequently. The 6-year bar does not apply to a Chapter 13 debtor who pays 70 percent of the unsecured claims under a repayment plan that was proposed by the debtor in good faith and that represents the debtor's best efforts [727(a) (9)].

A discharge in bankruptcy is intended for *honest* debtors. Certain kinds of debtor misconduct will result in the debtor's being denied a discharge altogether. Some misconduct affects only a particular debt and results in a denial of discharge for that debt only. For a few debts the debtor remains liable on public policy grounds in the absence of wrongdoing.

Grounds for Denying Discharge. The grounds for denying discharge altogether include the debtor's fraudulent transfer or concealment of property (within 1 year before filing a bankruptcy petition) with intent to hinder, delay, or defraud a creditor or an officer of the estate; unjustifiably concealing or destroying business records or failing to keep adequate business records; making a false oath, a fraudulent account, or a false claim in connection with the bankruptcy case; failing to explain satisfactorily any loss of assets or deficiency of assets to meet the debtor's liabilities; and refusal of the debtor to obey lawful orders of the court [727]. Case 26.4 illustrates a variety of such misconduct.

CASE 26.4 In re Mazzola · 4 B.R. 179 (D. Mass. 1980)

OPINION LAVIEN, B. J. The plaintiffs in this proceeding, Wayne and Gayle LaVangie, seek to bar the discharge of the debtors . . . pursuant to . . . provisions of . . . the Bankruptcy Code. The plaintiffs allege the debtors made false oaths on their petition and transferred and concealed property within one year preceding the filing of the petition. . . .

The debtors filed a joint petition under Chapter 7 of the Bankruptcy Code on October 15, 1979. At the time of filing, the debtor Dennis Mazzola was the sole stockholder of the Dennis M. Construction Co., Inc., and was engaged in the home construction industry. Just prior to the filing of the bankruptcy, the plaintiffs had been involved in bitter litigation with the debtors . . . over a claim of faulty home construction. In fact, in August of 1979, the plaintiffs obtained an attachment on two parcels of property owned by the debtors jointly. In early September of 1979 the debtors accomplished the dissolution of the attachment, sold the properties speedily, deposited the $14,000 received from the sale in the checking account of Dennis M. Construction Co., Inc., and used the proceeds to pay the corporation's creditors. The debtors then abandoned their defense [of the litigation with the LaVangies] and filed a petition in bankruptcy on October 15, 1979. The testimony adduced at trial revealed several false answers in the debtors' schedules and statement of affairs. . . .

The purpose of section 727(a)(4)(A) [barring a discharge if the debtor knowingly and fraudulently, in or in connection with the case, made a false oath or account] is to ensure that dependable information is supplied for those interested in the administration of the bankruptcy estate on which they can rely without the need for the trustee or other interested parties to dig out the true facts in examinations or investigations. The trustee and creditors are entitled to honest and accurate signposts on the trail showing what property has passed through the bankrupt's hands during a period prior to his bankruptcy. A false statement in the schedules or statement of affairs due to mere mistake or inadvertence is insufficient for the denial of a discharge; fraudulent intent is necessary to bar a discharge. A reckless disregard of both the serious nature of the information sought and the necessary

CASE 26.4 Continued

attention to detail and accuracy in answering may rise to the level of fraudulent intent necessary to bar a discharge. . . .

There is no question in the present case that the schedule and statement of affairs filed by the debtors contained numerous false statements. The debtors concede the false statements exist. The determinative issue with regard to the ultimate granting or denial of discharge is whether those false statements were knowingly and fraudulently made so as to fall within the prohibition of section 727(a)(4)(A).

After hearing and observing Mr. Mazzola at trial, the court finds the explanations offered by Mr. Mazzola for the false statements in the documents not credible. The present facts do not reflect mere mistake or inadvertence but rather are indicative at the very least of such a cavalier and reckless disregard for truthfulness as to cause the court to find fraudulent intent. The court finds Mr. Mazzola's explanation for the false answer to question 12b on the statement of affairs to be particularly disturbing. Question 12b clearly asks the debtors whether they have transferred any real or tangible personal property during the year immediately preceding the filing of the petition. . . . The debtors answered "No" to the question. Mr. Mazzola stated at trial, under oath, that he interpreted the question to ask if he currently owned any property. The court cannot accept this explanation as credible. Mr. Mazzola is not an unintelligent individual inexperienced in real estate transactions as is evidenced by the fact that for many years he made his living building homes and buying and selling real estate. Mr. Mazzola's alleged interpretation of question 12b cannot be deemed a reasonable and honest misinterpretation of the question. The question is entitled, in bold face, "Transfers of property." There is nothing that could justify any genuine belief that "transfer" meant "present ownership." In fact, the entire page of the statement of affairs asks questions *only* about transfers. The pleadings further belie the credibility of this explanation, as the debtors' answer to the plaintiffs' complaint states that the debtor simply overlooked these properties. Indeed, even this contradictory explanation leaves much to be desired in the area of credibility inasmuch as these properties were subject to a controversial attachment obtained by the plaintiffs during the state court litigation between the parties and had been sold only one month prior to the filing of the bankruptcy petition.

None of this even attempts to explain why the transfer of the $14,000 from the sale of these properties to the corporation was not mentioned in the answer. Likewise, the explanations of the other false statements fall short of being credible. Mr. Mazzola claimed he failed to disclose the sole ownership of the corporation's stock because he believed it to have no value and that he failed to list the attachment because he considered it to be illegal and because it was dissolved approximately two weeks after it was granted. Individually any one of these explanations might appear plausible in the abstract, but when combined with the fact of the existence of the bitterly contested state court proceedings, the speed of the conveyances when the attachment was dissolved, the immediate transfer of the sale proceeds to the corporation which was not a party to the lawsuit, the subsequent abandonment of the state court proceeding, and the almost simultaneous filing [in bankruptcy] coupled with the blatantly false answers, there is simply too much self-serving "misunderstanding" and "mistake." . . .

I find that the statements were made with a calculated disregard for the importance of documents which were signed under penalty of perjury and on which a determination on the request for a discharge would be made. This reckless disregard for the truth is the equivalent of the fraudulent intent necessary to bar a discharge. . . .

JUDGMENT It is hereby ordered that the debtors Dennis Joseph Mazzola and Anne Tresa Mazzola be denied discharges in bankruptcy due to their false oaths in violation of 11 U.S.C. Section 727(a)(4)(A). . . .

Nondischargeable Debts. Although an individual debtor may receive a discharge, certain debts are not covered by it and therefore remain binding on the debtor [523]. Nondischargeable debts include the following:

1. Debts for certain taxes, e.g., where the debtor made a fraudulent tax return or a willful attempt at evasion of taxes. (In general, tax debts more than 1 to 3 years old, depending on the kind of tax, *are* discharged in the absence of fraud, late filing, and the like.)
2. Debts contracted on the basis of the debtor's false pretenses, false representations, or actual fraud. A materially false written financial statement can be the basis for denying discharge of the debt for which it was given (but not for denying a discharge altogether) where the debtor issued the statement with *intent to deceive* and the creditor *reasonably relied* on it.
3. *Presumed* nondischargeable under the 1984 amendments are: (*a*) consumer debts of $500 or more owed to a single creditor for luxury goods or services, incurred on or within 40 days before the order for relief, and (*b*) cash advances aggregating more than $1,000 that are extensions of consumer credit under an open-end credit plan, obtained by an individual debtor on or within 20 days before the order for relief. The purpose of the presumption is to discourage the practice of "loading up" on luxury items in anticipation of bankruptcy and later claiming them as exempt property.
4. Debts not scheduled by the debtor or others in time to permit a creditor without notice of the case to make a timely filing of a proof of claim.
5. Debts resulting from the debtor's embezzlement, larceny, or violation of a fiduciary duty.
6. Debts arising from alimony, maintenance, or child support awards.
7. Debts arising from the debtor's willful and malicious injury of another entity or willful and malicious injury to or conversion of an entity's property.
8. Debts arising from certain educational loans made, funded, or guaranteed by a governmental unit.
9. Governmental fines and penalties, except, for example, those relating to dischargeable taxes.
10. Debts arising from the debtor's liability for operating a motor vehicle while legally intoxicated.

Discharge Hearing; Reaffirmation; Protection of Discharge. Before an individual debtor may receive a discharge from unpaid debts, he or she must attend a *discharge hearing.* The Code requires the hearing primarily to protect the debtor; therefore, he or she must appear in person before the court to receive the discharge and to be informed of the consequences of any reaffirmation agreement (discussed below) that the debtor might have made, or to hear the reason why a discharge has not been granted [524(d)].

A discharge in bankruptcy is not an automatic protection against having to pay the discharged debts. As many debtors have been shocked to learn, the discharge must be pleaded by the debtor as a defense to any action subsequently brought to enforce a discharged debt.

Discharged debtors often are pressured to pay (reaffirm) discharged debts. Under prior bankruptcy law, reaffirmation agreements were routinely enforced. To protect debtors from creditor abuses in obtaining such agreements, the Code changed the rules for enforcing them. Now such agreements, if enforceable under nonbankruptcy (e.g., state) law, must also conform to requirements imposed by the Code: The agreement must be made before the discharge is granted; the agreement must clearly and conspicuously advise the debtor that he or she may rescind it any time before discharge or within 60 days after the agreement is filed with the court, whichever is later; the agreement must be filed with the court, together with an affidavit by the debtor's attorney that the agreement represents the debtor's informed and voluntary consent and does not impose undue hardship on the debtor or the debtor's dependents; and the court must have held the discharge hearing and warned the debtor of the consequences of reaffirmation [524(c)&(d)]. If an *individual* debtor was not represented by an attorney, the debtor's agreement to reaffirm a *consumer* debt (other than a consumer debt secured by real property) must be approved by the court to be effective. The court is to approve the agreement only if it does not impose an undue hardship on the debtor or the debtor's dependents and will be in the best interests of the debtor.

The laws of some states seek to penalize discharged debtors for exercising certain of their discharge rights. In the case of *Perez v. Campbell*, 402 U.S. 637 (1971), for example, an Arizona financial responsibility law permitted suspension of the driver's license of an uninsured driver who failed to pay an automobile personal injury judgment that had been discharged in bankruptcy. The United States Supreme Court held, by a 5 to 4 vote, that the suspension provision of the Arizona law was in conflict with bankruptcy law and therefore was void under the supremacy clause of the United States Constitution. The Bankruptcy Code follows and expands on that case by providing, in essence, that no governmental unit *or private employer* may penalize or discriminate against a debtor or the debtor's associates solely because of the debtor's failure to pay a discharged debt or because of the debtor's status as a debtor under bankruptcy law [525]. Thus, the fresh-start policy of the Code prevails over a state's policy of protecting favored creditors.

Business Reorganizations and Repayment Plans

Business Reorganizations

The main purpose of a Chapter 11 reorganization proceeding is to allow a financially troubled firm to stay in business while it undergoes a process of financial rehabilitation. Reorganization is essentially a process of negotiation in which the debtor firm and its creditors develop a plan for the adjustment and discharge of debts. The plan may provide for a change of management and even for the liquidation of the firm. However, a continuation of the business is the usual goal.

In a business reorganization case, the judge has a limited power to appoint a trustee. If requested to do so by a "party in interest" (e.g., a creditor or a shareholder or a committee of such persons), the judge may appoint a trustee "for cause," i.e., because of dishonesty or incompetence of the debtor or, where the debtor is a corporation, because of dishonesty or incompetence of its management [1104]. Unless the court orders otherwise, the debtor may continue to operate the business. Such a debtor, called a "debtor in possession," has most of the powers, rights, and duties of a reorganization trustee [1107(a)]. The word "trustee" includes "debtor in possession."

Most of the rules of bankruptcy law that apply to Chapter 7 liquidations apply also to Chapter 11 reorganizations. Most individuals, partnerships, and corporations that are eligible for Chapter 7 liquidation are eligible for Chapter 11 reorganization. Like Chapter 7 cases, reorganization cases may be voluntary or involuntary. And the requirements for forcing a debtor into involuntary liquidation apply to involuntary reorganizations as well. The trustee's powers, the law of fraudulent and preferential transfers, the grounds for denial of discharge, and many other aspects of bankruptcy law are the same or nearly the same for Chapter 11 cases as for Chapter 7 cases. Consequently, the discussion here is limited to topics of special significance to reorganization cases.

Role of Creditors' Committee. As soon as practicable after the court enters an order for relief under Chapter 11, the court must appoint a committee of unsecured creditors to recommend a plan for reorganizing the debtor. Ordinarily, the committee will consist of the seven largest unsecured creditors willing to serve. At the request of a party in interest, the court (1) may change the composition of the committee to make it representative of the various claims against the creditor, and (2) may appoint additional committees such as a committee of equity security holders (owners of stocks and bonds of the debtor if it is a corporation) [1102].

The principal tasks of the committee are to investigate the financial affairs of the debtor; to determine whether the business should continue to be operated; to determine whether to request the appointment of a trustee to displace the debtor-in-possession; and to consult with the debtor or trustee in the administration of the case [1103]. If no trustee is appointed, the debtor-in-possession continues the business as trustee under court supervision.

Plan for Satisfaction of Creditors' Claims. The plan of reorganization determines how much creditors will be paid, whether owners such as shareholders will retain any interest in the company, in what form the business will continue, and similar questions. To become effective, the plan ordinarily (*a*) must be *accepted* (consented to) by a certain percentage of persons whose rights as creditors or owners have been "impaired" and (*b*) must be *confirmed* (approved and put into operation) by the bankruptcy court.

The claim of a creditor or interest of an owner is *impaired* where the plan alters the legal, equitable, or contractual rights of its holder; where the plan fails to cure a pre-reorganization default by the debtor; or where the plan provides for payment of less than the full amount or value of a claim or interest [1124]. A class of *creditors* (secured or unsecured) has accepted the plan when holders of a simple majority in number and two-thirds in dollar amount of allowed claims approve the plan. A class of *ownership interests* has accepted the plan when holders of two-thirds in dollar amount of allowed interests approve the plan [1126].

Confirmation makes the plan binding not only on the debtor but also on creditors, equity security holders, and others, whether or not their claims are impaired, and whether or not they have accepted the plan. Consent of an *impaired* class of claimants is not necessary for confirmation if the plan treats the impaired class in a manner that is "fair and equitable" [1129(b)]. A plan may be fair and equitable if, for example, the members of the impaired class receive under the plan (1) the present value of the amount of their allowed claims, or (2) a pro rata share of their claims in a situation where junior classes of claims or interests receive nothing. The consent of an *un*impaired class is not necessary for confirmation. Confirmation ordinarily *discharges* all debts except, for example, nondischargeable debts of *individual* debtors [1141(d)].

However, dissenting minorities of impaired accepting classes receive protection. The Code requires that all members of a class, dissenters and nondissenters alike, receive at least the value that they would obtain as a result of a Chapter 7 liquidation [1129(a)]. That value will, of course, be zero if funds are exhausted by claims of higher priority.

Continuing the Business. While the plan of reorganization is being developed and put into effect, the trustee (or debtor-in-possession) continues the business and tries to reduce business losses by selling unprofitable divisions of the company, reducing the workforce, closing plants or stores where necessary, or rejecting or renegotiating burdensome contracts. Often these activities meet with strenuous objection, as where Continental Airlines sought in the early 1980s to reject its union contract with the Air Line Pilots Association in an effort to lower salaries and bring the company back to profitability. The bankruptcy court upheld the trustee's rejection of the union contract despite the union's contention that the rejection was an unwarranted interference with collective bargaining rights protected by the National Labor Relations Act.

The conflict between bankruptcy and collective bargaining policy has been governed by varying judicial standards. In the 1975 *REA Express* case, 523 F.2d 164 (2d Cir.), the court held that the trustee may reject a collective bargaining agreement only if it is so burdensome to the debtor that rejection is required for the reorganization to be successful. In *NLRB v. Bildisco & Bildisco,* 104 S. Ct. 1188 (1984), the Supreme Court held that (1) the trustee does not commit an unfair labor practice by unilaterally modifying or terminating a collective bargaining agreement before the bankruptcy court rules on the propriety of rejection, and (2) the trustee's rejection of a union contract is permissible on a showing merely that the contract burdens the debtor's estate and the equities balance in favor of rejection. After the *Bildisco* decision, Congress, in the 1984 amendments to the Bankruptcy Code, imposed an intermediate standard. Now the trustee may not reject a collective bargaining agreement until after a court hearing and ruling on the propriety of the rejection. In the meantime, the trustee must make a proposal to union representatives as to what modifications of employee benefits are necessary to accomplish a reorganization that is fair to all affected parties. Then, in its ruling, the bankruptcy court may approve rejection of the union contract *only if* the court finds that (1) the trustee has made a proper proposal and has provided the union with information necessary to evaluate it, (2) the union has, without good cause, refused to accept the proposal, and (3) the balance of the equities clearly favors rejection of the contract [1113].

Repayment Plans for Debtors with Regular Income

Chapter 13 of the Code permits an *individual* debtor to develop a repayment plan and, upon completion of payments under the plan, to receive a discharge from most remaining debts [1328]. Chapter 13 is available (on a voluntary basis only) to any individual (except a stockbroker or a commodity broker) who has a regular income, unsecured debts of less than $100,000, and secured debts of less than $350,000. The debts must be owing and unpaid at the time of the debtor's application for relief.

Much of the bankruptcy law previously discussed applies to Chapter 13 cases. Especially notable are those provisions of the Code that prohibit discrimination against debtors, restrict the enforceability of reaffirmation agreements, and provide exemptions for an individual debtor. Chapter 13 provides additional benefits that make it very appealing to overburdened consumer-debtors and sole proprietors. For example, the filing of a Chapter 13 petition stays actions against not only the debtor, but also his or her codebtors on consumer debts [1301]; and creditors cannot file an involuntary petition against the debtor [303(a)]. Other benefits unique to Chapter 13 are discussed later.

Typically, the debtor will propose either a composition or an extension plan. In a *composition* plan the debtor pays creditors less than 100 percent of their claims, on a pro rata basis for each class of claims. In an *extension* plan the debtor pays the full amount, but over a longer period than originally agreed. Payments under a plan (whether composition or extension) must be completed within 3 years after the court confirms the plan, or within 5 years if the court permits [1322]. Regardless of the kind of plan, the debtor must give the trustee control of the debtor's future income [1322], the trustee makes payments of claims [1326], and the debtor has the benefit of injunctive relief against creditors while the plan is being carried out.

Unsecured creditors do not vote on Chapter 13 plans; but for such a plan to be confirmed, unsecured creditors must receive at least what they would receive in a Chapter 7 liquidation. Priority claims must be paid in full (so long as funds are available), unless particular priority claimants agree otherwise [1322(a) (2)]. The plan may unilaterally modify the rights of most other claimants (secured and unsecured), so long as all claims in a class receive the same treatment. The right of the debtor to modify secured claims applies even to those secured by an interest in real estate [1322(b) (2)]. However, the plan cannot modify the rights of a creditor whose claim is secured by the debtor's principal residence.

A plan may be confirmed without the consent of a secured creditor where (1) the creditor retains his or her lien and the collateral is worth at least the amount of the claim, or (2) the debtor surrenders the collateral to the claimant [1325(a) (5)]. However, if the trustee or a holder of an allowed unsecured claim objects to confirmation of the plan, the court may not confirm it unless (*a*) there is sufficient property in the estate to cover the claim or (*b*) all of the debtor's disposable income for three years will be applied to payments under the plan [1325(b)].

To protect creditors, the court may, on request of a party in interest, dismiss a Chapter 13 case or convert it to a Chapter 7 case. Grounds for dismissal or conversion of the case include unreasonable delay by the debtor that is prejudicial to creditors; failure of the debtor to file a plan or to make timely payments under a plan; and a material default by the debtor in carrying out a term of a confirmed plan [1307(c)]. The debtor, too, may at any time convert to a Chapter 7 case or have the Chapter 13 case dismissed [1307(a)].

If the plan was a composition, the Chapter 13 discharge upon completion of the plan bars another discharge for 6 years unless the debtor has made 70 percent of the payments under the plan, the plan was proposed in good faith, and the plan was the best effort of the debtor [727(a) (9)].

Summary

Under state insolvency law, an insolvent debtor may make an arrangement with unpaid creditors for full or partial payment of the debts. Or, the insolvent debtor or his or her creditors may be entitled to the benefits of federal bankruptcy law which, when resorted to, prevails over state insolvency law.

Federal bankruptcy law has two main purposes: (1) to provide for a fair treatment of competing creditors, and (2) to give overburdened debtors a fresh start in business. The trustee in bankruptcy is responsible for collecting, liquidating, and distributing the estate. The bankruptcy judge supervises the activities of trustees and renders judicial decisions as the need arises.

The purpose of a Chapter 7 liquidation proceeding is to convert the debtor's nonexempt assets into cash, to distribute the cash in accordance with the scheme of distribution provided by the Bankruptcy Code, and to grant the honest debtor a discharge from most of the remaining debts. An individual debtor is entitled to exempt certain property from the estate. The claims of secured creditors are paid in full if the collateral is sufficiently valuable. To the extent funds permit, the remaining money is distributed to priority unsecured creditors and then to general creditors.

There are several grounds for a general denial of a discharge; and certain kinds of debts, such as alimony, are excepted from the discharge.

Business firms may be discharged from debts under Chapter 11, but its main purpose is to allow a financially troubled firm to reorganize and to stay in business while it undergoes a process of financial rehabilitation. Chapter 13 permits individual debtors to develop a repayment plan and, upon completion of payments under the plan, to receive a discharge from most remaining debts.

Review Questions

1 (a) What limits on debt-collection activity does the law impose on creditors? (b) How may an insolvent debtor settle his or her debts under state law?

2 To a debtor, what is the main advantage of federal bankruptcy law as opposed to state insolvency law? A main advantage of bankruptcy law to a creditor?

3 (a) What are the purposes of the federal bankruptcy law? (b) What are the basic steps involved in a bankruptcy proceeding? (c) How is federal bankruptcy law related to state law?

4 What are the main duties of the trustee in bankruptcy? Of the bankruptcy judge?

5 (a) What is the purpose of a Chapter 7 liquidation proceeding? (b) Who is eligible for a voluntary Chapter 7 proceeding? (c) Who may be subjected to an involuntary Chapter 7 proceeding? Under what circumstances?

6 (a) What two broad classes of property become part of the debtor's estate? (b) Does a secured party's security interest become part of the debtor's estate? Explain.

7 What fraudulent transfers may a trustee avoid?

8 Define "preference" and give an example.

9 Give an example of a claim that will not be allowed.

10 Illustrate the principle of pro rata distribution as applied to priority of payments.

11 List two grounds for denial of a discharge.

12 May a state suspend a driver's license because the driver failed to pay an automobile personal injury judgment that had been discharged in bankruptcy? Explain.

13 (a) What is the main purpose of a Chapter 11 business reorganization proceeding? (b) Explain the function of the creditor's committee. (c) How is the plan of reorganization made effective?

14 (a) With respect to Chapter 13 repayment plans for debtors with regular incomes, explain how a composition plan differs from an extension plan. (b) What is the source of funds for carrying out a repayment plan?

Case Problems[2]

1 Franklin filed a voluntary petition in bankruptcy. At that time she had debts of $100,000, and had the following property interests: (a) business equipment worth

[2]These problems are hypothetical cases that should be resolved by applying the Bankruptcy Reform Act of 1978 and its 1984 amendments.

$5,000, which was subject to a $3,000 chattel mortgage in favor of her bank, and **(b)** an automobile worth $1,000 that she intended to claim as exempt property. Five months after filing the petition, Franklin inherited $25,000 from her uncle. Three months later, at the death of another uncle, she received $50,000 as the beneficiary of an insurance policy on that uncle's life. In the meantime, after the filing of the petition, Franklin's business realized a net profit of $10,000, and Franklin earned $8,000 as a consultant to another firm. The trustee in bankruptcy claimed for the debtor's estate all the property described above. To what property was the trustee entitled?

2 Bago Corporation, a manufacturer of industrial packaging, experienced financial difficulty as the result of a strike by its employees and eventually could not meet its debt service charges and other expenses. In an attempt to keep the company afloat, Thomas, its chief financial officer, made an unsecured loan of $10,000 to the company. The strike soon ended, but by then the market for industrial packaging had softened. Fearing that the company might fail, Thomas sought repayment of the loan. In settlement of the loan, the president of Bago Corporation paid Thomas $10,000 out of the proceeds of recent bag sales.

Six months after repayment of the loan, creditors of Bago filed a Chapter 7 petition and forced the company into bankruptcy. Liquidation of company assets produced sufficient funds to pay priority claims, but only enough to pay 10 percent of the claims of general creditors. Consequently, the trustee brought suit to avoid as a preferential transfer Bago's repayment of the $10,000 to Thomas. He defended on the ground that the repayment of the loan did not occur on or within 90 days before the filing of the bankruptcy petition and therefore could not be considered a preference. Was the repayment of the loan a preference?

3 In the bankruptcy situation described in the preceding problem, Bagging Suppliers, Inc., delivered on credit to Bago a load of packaging materials 60 days before the filing of the petition in bankruptcy. Ten days later, Bago paid Bagging Suppliers in full for the materials. The trustee sought to avoid the payment as a preference. Was the payment of Bagging Suppliers a preference?

4 Jones owned an apartment building worth $100,000. Having recently suffered serious business reverses and needing immediate cash to pay creditors, Jones sold the building to his brother-in-law, Frampton, for $50,000. That amount was not enough to pay Jones's debts. Ten months later Jones's creditors forced Jones into involuntary bankruptcy. The trustee brought action against Frampton to recover the apartment building for the debtor's estate. Frampton defended on the ground that the sale of the building was not a fraudulent conveyance, as the trustee contended, but was rather a legitimate business transaction that produced for Jones much needed cash at a time when Jones had no knowledge that creditors would eventually force him into bankruptcy. Was the sale of the apartment building a fraudulent conveyance?

5 In the liquidation of Blotto, Inc., the following creditors filed timely proofs of claim: **(a)** three employees who had not been paid their wages of $1,000 each for 1 month preceding Blotto's bankruptcy; **(b)** 100 customers of Blotto, each of whom, prior to Blotto's bankruptcy, had paid Blotto a $50 unsecured deposit on pen and pencil sets that Blotto never delivered; **(c)** Second Bank, to which Blotto owed $8,000 secured by a valid, perfected security interest in collateral worth $4,000; **(d)** various administrative officials, lawyers, and accountants whose claims for their services totaled $5,000. The trustee realized $14,500 upon liquidation of the debtor's estate. How much of its claim does each creditor or class of creditors receive?

6 In a Chapter 7 proceeding, Swanson received a discharge from her debts. General creditors received only 12 percent of their allowed claims. A week before the discharge was granted, Swanson signed a reaffirmation agreement with one of the general creditors, Hayes, a plumbing contractor who had sold Swanson an air conditioning unit on open account for Swanson's business. The agreement required Swanson to pay, in monthly installments, $3,000 still unpaid for the air conditioner, a debt that was covered by the discharge. A week after signing the agreement, Swanson had second thoughts and sought to rescind the agreement. Hayes pointed out that the agreement was enforceable under state law. May Swanson rescind the reaffirmation agreement?

7 Sadiron Corp. was undergoing a Chapter 11 reorganization. The debtor proposed a plan that called for all classes of creditors to receive 50 percent of their claims. There was one class of bonds (secured by the total assets of the corporation) and one class of debentures (unsecured debt). Most of the bondholders objected to the plan, and the requisite majority could not be persuaded to vote for it. May the plan be confirmed without the consent of the bondholders?

8 Jones, the sole proprietor of a small business, encountered financial difficulty and sought relief under Chapter 13 of the Bankruptcy Code. In developing her repayment plan, she proposed to pay all creditors in full, but to extend the time for payment and to deprive secured creditors of their contractual rights to repossess collateral or to foreclose mortgages. Two secured creditors objected to the plan: Jones's major supplier of inventory, and the bank that held the mortgage on Jones's residence. May the repayment plan be confirmed over their objections?

ETHICS IN PRACTICE

When a debtor fails to repay a loan, the ethical character of applicable law becomes most evident. Formerly, the law of debtor-creditor relations heavily favored the creditor by permitting harsh loan terms and collection practices. The law has evolved from this creditor-oriented laissez-faire approach to a modern emphasis on fair dealing between the parties. Yet, despite extensive state and federal regulation of debtor-creditor relations, the law does not reach all lending and borrowing practices that may be ethically suspect. Consider the ethical implications of the following:

Problems in Ethics

1 Bigbank wants to expand its highly lucrative credit card business. Mary Jones is in charge of the project. She proposes the use of "preauthorized" credit extension. It works this way: Bigbank will buy customer lists from a number of credit bureaus; will identify the people who are making minimum payments on credit cards they already own; and, without requiring a credit check of individuals, will send them unsolicited Bigbank credit cards carrying a $5,000 line of credit. The alternative, which Mary does not favor, is the use of "prescreened" credit extension, in which each candidate must first apply for a Bigbank card and then pass a credit check (paid for by Bigbank) that will reveal whether the applicant's income is sufficient to support Bigbank's additional line of credit. Mary knows that preauthorized credit will produce more defaults than will prescreened credit, but she believes that the savings on credit checks will more than make up for the defaults. **(a)** Smith, a member of Bigbank's board of directors and a recovering "spendaholic," is concerned about preauthorized credit and hires you, an outside consultant, to evaluate the ethics of the practice. What ethical problems, if any, do you see? **(b)** Would your report on the practice differ if you worked for Mary Jones and *she* was the one who asked you to evaluate it? **(c)** Would the content of your report to Mary Jones, your supervisor, be affected by your knowledge that she very much favors the extension of preauthorized credit?

2 *Timemag,* a weekly news magazine, mails renewal solicitations six months before current subscriptions expire. A customer who checks the "bill me" box soon receives a bill for the next year's subscription. If the customer does not pay promptly, he or she may receive the following communications: a "Payment Due" notice, a "Payment Overdue" notice that threatens to surrender the account for collection action, and a letter from a collection agency informing the recipient of his or her rights as a debtor and demanding a response before the "matter becomes any more delinquent." All this usually occurs while the old subscription has several months yet to run. **(a)** Why would *Timemag* engage in such a billing practice? **(b)** Is this billing practice ethical? **(c)** *Timemag* says it usually sends the customer 8 bills and then reviews the situation before turning the account over to a collection agency. Is this practice more acceptable ethically than the other one? Why? **(d)** Evaluate the ethics of the following billing practice: Subscribers receive renewal notices that look like bills; subscribers who ignore them receive follow-up "overdue" notices that sometimes threaten collection agency action; if a subscriber ignores the second notice, the sender merely quits sending magazines when the subscription expires.

3 Mike and Sara Smith own a house in Oklahoma. They move to Virginia and buy a new house there. Because of the depressed housing market in Oklahoma, they cannot sell the old house for enough to cover the mortgage debt on it, nor can they rent it. When the bank approved the loan on the old house, it was worth much more than the amount of the debt, and no one could foresee the economic downturn that depressed the Oklahoma housing market. Now the mortgage payments on the two houses are a serious financial burden to the Smiths. They are considering just "walking away" from the Oklahoma house and letting the bank have it, hoping that the bank will absorb any loss. They know that it is difficult for banks to collect deficiency judgments from out-of-state debtors. They also know that while some lenders always pursue defaulting debtors for deficiencies, some lenders don't because they blame themselves for approving a loan that turns out badly. The Smiths seek your advice on the ethics of their "walk-away" plan. How would you respond if you were **(a)** a banker? **(b)** a CPA? **(c)** a lawyer? **(d)** a member of the clergy?

4 For decades, Asbesco manufactured insulation material containing asbestos fibers. Then, over 30 years ago, medical evidence indicated that the inhalation of asbestos fibers causes lung cancer. Thousands of workers and others who came into contact with insulation made by Asbesco developed lung cancer and related diseases. Many sued Asbesco for damages, alleging that their health problems resulted from their contact with Asbesco products. Although Asbesco is a very profitable corporation, its lawyers and accountants fear that liability resulting from present and future lawsuits may be so great that the company may eventually face dissolution under the bankruptcy law. To protect against that possibility, company lawyers recommend that Asbesco immediately file for protection under Chapter 11 of the Bankruptcy Code. Under a Chapter 11 reorganization plan, Asbesco can sharply limit its liability to winners of product liability lawsuits and thus stay in business. Many of those suing are former employees of Asbesco whose efforts made Asbesco wealthy. Assume that it is legal for Asbesco to receive Chapter 11 protection. **(a)** Is it ethical for Asbesco to use Chapter 11 this way? **(b)** Does it matter that Asbesco has long known of the medical evidence linking asbestos fibers to lung disease?

PART SEVEN

Insurance

CHAPTER 27

Insurance

Everyone faces a risk of business or personal loss from negligence, theft, vandalism, disease, labor disputes, war, floods, or earthquakes. Economic loss takes many forms: loss of or damage to physical assets such as household furnishings, real estate, and business equipment; a decrease in the value of corporate stock and other intangible personal property; loss of income, future productive capacity, and business reputation (goodwill); the loss of any accumulated assets needed to pay court judgments or expenses attending illness, injury, and death; and the loss to a family or business of valuable personal services. Risk management and the prevention of loss are of obvious concern to businesspeople.

To limit possible economic losses, people use several techniques of risk management. Among them are *risk control* (by, for example, installing smoke alarms and other safety devices), *risk transfer and distribution* (commonly done by means of an insurance contract), and *self-insuring,* (a planned absorption of loss, usually engaged in by companies large enough to take protective measures such as the funding of a special loss account). This chapter deals with insurance, the principal means of transferring and distributing the risk of financial loss. The first part of the chapter discusses the nature of the insurance mechanism. Subsequent parts discuss insurance against personal risk (life and health insurance), insurance against property risks (property and liability insurance), the regulation of the insurance business, and the roles of insurance agents.

How Insurance Works

Purpose of Insurance

Transfer of Risk; Meaning of "The Insured." A main function of insurance, the transfer of risk, is accomplished by means of a two-party contract called an "insurance policy." In a typical insurance policy, for a payment called a "premium" an insurance company (the insurer) agrees with another party (usually, the insured) to assume a *named* risk that otherwise would have to be borne by the insured or by others such as the insured's family or business associates. The transfer of the risk from the insured to the insurer ordinarily occurs when the insurance contract arises. If the insured suffers a loss covered by the policy, the insurer makes payment in accordance with its terms, usually to the insured or to a third-person beneficiary. This payment, a compensation or reimbursement for actual loss, is called "indemnity." Suppose Alice pays an insurer $100 to insure her expensive sports car against fire or theft. If the car is destroyed by fire, the insurer will indemnify Alice by paying her the value of the car as of the time of the loss. Thus, by means of insurance, Alice has traded off the possibility of heavy loss for a certain but more moderate cost.

In insurance terminology, "the insured" has two basic meanings—one for property and liability insurance and another for life insurance. In property and liability insurance, "the insured" is any person who is protected by a policy from risk of loss. Suppose Alicia purchases automobile insurance covering liability for personal injuries resulting from negligent operation of her car. The insurance policy, if typical, will protect Alicia and other licensed drivers to whom she might occasionally lend the car. All such persons are "insureds" under the policy and have a right to reimbursement from the insurer for amounts they are obliged to pay in settlement of claims covered by the policy. Suppose Alicia's employee, Carlos, drives Alicia's car with her consent and negligently injures Bernardo. Carlos is "an insured" under Alicia's policy. Bernardo has a claim against Carlos for hospital bills, loss of income, and so on. As an insured under Alicia's policy, Carlos may look to the insurance company for reimbursement for any amount he is required to pay Bernardo. The insurer might even make payments directly to Bernardo without litigation. However, Bernardo is not himself an insured under Alicia's policy; he is only a *claimant* against one.

In *life* insurance, "the insured" is the person whose life is the subject of the insurance contract. The death benefit specified by the policy will be paid to someone *other than* the insured—directly to a named third person called the "beneficiary" or to the insured's estate for distribution to others. In life insurance, as in other kinds of insurance, "the insured" will often not be a party to the insurance contract. Suppose that Alicia and Bernardo are business partners and that Alicia insures the life of Bernardo and names herself as beneficiary of the policy. Alicia and the insurance company are the contracting parties; Bernardo is "the insured" (meaning here "the person whose life is the subject of the insurance policy"); and Alicia is the beneficiary as well as the "policyholder" and the "policyowner."

Distribution of Risk; Pooling and Reinsurance. Insurers distribute risk of loss mainly by use of two risk-spreading techniques: pooling and reinsurance. *Pooling* is a process of treating as a single group a large number of individual risks of a certain kind so that the *total* loss likely to be sustained by the group of insureds can be accurately estimated. Then individual losses are distributed among all in the pool by requiring all insureds in the pool to pay the same premium per unit of coverage regardless of the amount of loss sustained by any one individual. The premium paid by an individual insured covers the insured's share of predicted *pool* loss, an amount for administrative costs, and insurance company profit (if the insurer is one for profit).

Reinsurance is a contractual arrangement in which an insurance company transfers (cedes) a part of the group risk it has assumed to another insurance organization, a reinsurer. The ceding company is somewhat like an individual who buys insurance; i.e., the ceding company pays the reinsurer to assume part of a risk that the ceding company believes might be too great for it to bear alone. By a process of pooling or of further reinsurance, the reinsurer distributes the ceded risk. An individual who buys insurance from a ceding company never becomes a party to a reinsurance contract. Reinsurance agreements are strictly between insurance organizations.

Indemnity; Insurable Interest

Indemnity Principle. The principle of indemnity is based on the idea that insurance is a system for distributing losses and not for generating a profit for the insured. Therefore, in the event of casualty an insured person should be limited to reimbursement (indemnity) for loss actually suffered. Suppose that Pam has identical medical insurance policies with two different insurers, that each policy will reimburse her for up to $5,000 in hospital expenses in the event of her illness, that she becomes ill and incurs $5,000 in hospital expenses, and that each policy has a "coordination-of-benefits" clause (a clause permitting an insurer to pay only a portion of a loss if other insurance covers the same loss). Pam may collect only the amount of her loss ($5,000) and, moreover, under the coordination-of-benefits clause, *only a proportion* of her loss from each of the companies with which she has a policy. Since she has policies with two companies, she will collect $2,500 from each one, and since neither company is liable for the whole loss, she will receive back from each company an appropriate proportion of the premiums she paid.

Coordination of benefits is consistent with the principle of indemnity. If Pam were allowed to collect the $10,000 she sought, she would receive $5,000 profit, and premiums charged to all insureds would have to be large enough to provide the profit. Not all insurance policies have coordination-of-benefits clauses, however. Some insurers believe that such clauses impede sales of insurance and create disputes between insurers that delay the settlement of claims.

The principle of indemnity underlies many legal rules governing the interpretation and enforcement of insurance contracts, such as the prohibition against using insurance contracts as gambling devices. The application of such rules helps minimize the cost of insurance by reducing the opportunities for a person to make a net gain from the insurance system. However, the indemnity principle of "reimbursement for actual loss only" is less often applied to life insurance than to other kinds such as property, liability, and health insurance.

Insurable Interest Requirement. The principle of indemnity is the source of the general requirement that a person who procures insurance must have an insurable interest in the property or the life insured. An *insurable interest* is the financial stake that a person has in property or in someone's life or health. For example, you have an insurable interest in your car but not in your neighbor's car. In property insurance, many circumstances give rise to an insurable interest. They include (1) ownership of and other rights in property; (2) contract rights, as in a contract for the sale of goods; and (3) potential legal liability to others. In a contract for the sale of goods, a buyer obtains an insurable interest in the goods when they are *identified to the contract* (marked or otherwise designated as the subject of a particular contract of sale) even though the buyer might not yet own or have possession of the goods. Thus, the buyer may insure against preacquisition risks of loss. In property and liability insurance, the insurable interest need exist only at the time of loss. This rule permits a person to make arrangements for insurance before acquiring property or being otherwise exposed to risk.

Ordinarily, a person may obtain insurance on his or her own life without regard to insurable interest, but to obtain valid insurance on the life of another, the person procuring the insurance must have an insurable interest—i.e., a financial stake—in the other's life. This requirement will usually be met where there is a close family relationship, as where a person seeks insurance on the life of his or her spouse or minor child to cover the expenses resulting from that person's untimely death. Where an adult seeks insurance on a parent's life, however, or where a person seeks insurance on the life of a sister, uncle, niece, or other such relative, the courts tend to require a showing of something more than the family relationship itself before holding that there is an insurable interest. The courts differ, however, as to whether an *existing* financial interest must be shown in such instances. Often much less will do, as where an aunt who had supported her niece from infancy was held to have an insurable interest in the niece's life on the basis of an expectation that the aunt might eventually receive a return benefit from the niece. Where there is no family relationship, an actual financial interest is required. A creditor has an insurable interest in the life of his or her debtor; a business entity has an insurable interest in the life of a key employee; and a partner may have an insurable interest in the life of his or her partner.

In life insurance, the insurable interest need exist only when the policy is taken out. By preserving the validity of the policy even where the insurable interest ceases, this rule helps preserve any cash values that might have accumulated, reduces the barriers to free assignability of cash-value policies, and enhances the marketability of life insurance by making clear to the public that policies will be honored. Cash values accumulate in policies where the premium charged exceeds the amount needed for immediate claims, administrative expenses of the insurer, and any profits that might be payable. Assignability of life insurance is discussed later in this chapter.

The requirement of an insurable interest is useful in at least three ways: (1) The existence of an insurable interest is evidence that personal or business economic loss is reasonably anticipated and that the insurance contract is not just a gambling device for making a speculative gain. Insuring the life of a total stranger in the hope of making a large gain from a small investment in premiums involves no insurable interest and results in an unenforceable wagering contract. In contrast, insuring the life of one's business partner may involve an expectation of economic loss to, and consequently an insurable interest in, the partner procuring the insurance. (2) The existence of an insurable interest helps pinpoint a specific property right or economic relationship and thus contributes to the proper reimbursement of the person or firm suffering loss. (3) The existence of an insurable interest tends to limit the operation of "moral hazard." *Moral hazard* is any characteristic of a potential recipient of insurance proceeds that will increase the frequency or severity of loss—e.g, poor health habits and tendencies toward fraud, arson, murder, accident-proneness, and exaggeration of claims. Thus, if A insures B's car but has no insurable interest in it, A might be tempted to destroy the car to collect the insurance.

Case 27.1 involves the questions of whether an insurable interest existed and who may complain of its absence.

CASE 27.1 Secor v. Pioneer Foundry Co. · 173 N.W.2d 780 (Mich. App. 1969)

FACTS Pioneer Foundry (defendant) employed Secor for 9 years. In 1960, Pioneer obtained a $50,000 ordinary life insurance policy on Secor's life. Pioneer was the applicant, owner, and beneficiary, and it paid the premiums, which were $5,625 annually because of Secor's unfavorable medical history. Secor's employment terminated in July 1963. Pioneer paid

CASE 27.1 Continued

the March 1964 annual premium, and Secor died the following month. The insurer paid $50,000 to Pioneer. Secor's widow (plaintiff), arguing that Pioneer had lost whatever insurable interest it had in Secor's life, sued to recover the policy proceeds from Pioneer. From a judgment for Pioneer, plaintiff appealed.

OPINION

LEVIN, J. . . . A preliminary issue—whether the plaintiff has standing to complain—is dispositive of plaintiff's contention that Pioneer Foundry no longer had an insurable interest after Secor left its employ. In *Hicks v. Cary* . . . , on facts similar to those before us, the Michigan Supreme Court declared that the insurer alone may assert that the beneficiary of a life policy does not have an insurable interest. . . . The rule . . . appears to be well supported in other jurisdictions. In the present case, the insurer . . . paid the proceeds of the policy to Pioneer . . . without asserting this possible defense.

The plaintiff argues that, apart from whether she has standing to raise the insurable interest defense, the underlying premise of the insurable interest requirement—the public policy against speculation on the life of another—is so pervasive that Pioneer . . . could not lawfully retain insurance on Secor's life after the termination of his employment. . . .

The purchaser of ordinary life insurance, as distinguished from [the purchaser of] casualty or property insurance, buys not only indemnification . . . against . . . potential loss, but also makes an investment. To terminate the rights of the owner or beneficiary of ordinary life insurance because the relationship to the . . . insured has changed, perhaps after many years of . . . premium payments . . . , would not only adversely affect this investment quality of life insurance but would also confer an unanticipated and unwarranted windfall on the insurer.

In recognition of these considerations the almost universal rule of law in this country is that if the insurable interest requirement is satisfied at the time the policy is issued, the proceeds of the policy must be paid upon the death of the . . . insured without regard to whether the beneficiary has an insurable interest at the time of death. It has, accordingly, been held that an employer who is the beneficiary of a policy insuring the life of one of his employees may collect [the] proceeds . . . even though the employee's death occurs after the termination of his employment.

The . . . policy issued to the defendant . . . is referred to . . . as "keyman" life insurance. The plaintiff emphasizes that the typical life . . . policy is purchased to provide for . . . family members who may be expected to suffer a personal as well as a financial loss upon the death of the . . . insured. From this she argues that keyman life insurance should not be governed by the same rules as apply to life insurance generally. The . . . distinction is not, in our opinion, meaningful. Life insurance is not meant to assuage grief; its primary function is monetary. It serves fundamentally the same purpose whether the beneficiary is a widow or a business; it seeks to replace with a sum of money the earning capacity of the . . . insured. . . .

We . . . decline to limit [Pioneer's] recovery to the amount of its investment in the policy and its financial loss . . . upon Secor's death. [Pioneer's] investment . . . was large. . . . It chose to make the [March 1964] payment . . . to preserve recovery of its prior expenditures. It did this in its own interest; it has not been suggested that it was acting for . . . Secor or his family. . . .

We can understand plaintiff's feeling that it is unseemly for Pioneer . . . to continue to own insurance on Secor's life after the termination of his employment and that since the plaintiff, not Pioneer . . . , suffered a financial as well as a personal loss upon Secor's death, the plaintiff has a greater moral right to . . . at least so much of the proceeds as exceeds the cost of the insurance. It has been suggested that upon the termination of employment an employer owning insurance should give the employee an opportunity to purchase it. . . . We are not aware, however, of any principle of law, apart from an obligation assumed under a contract, which obliges an employer . . . to offer to sell the policy to the employee. . . . [Given] the regularity

CASE 27.1 Continued with which insurance is now being purchased by businesses on the lives of employees, this might be an appropriate subject for legislation.

JUDGMENT Affirmed. Costs to defendant.

The Insurance Contract

An insurance policy is a contract subject to the general principles of contract law discussed in Chapters 8 to 15. Because the contract of insurance is so common in daily life, we now review some aspects of contract law as they apply to the insurance contract.

Contract of Adhesion. An insurance contract is usually one of adhesion, because the typical purchaser has little or no power to negotiate the price or other terms. The purchaser may choose the kind and amount of coverage, the beneficiary designation, and so on, but otherwise the purchase of insurance is basically a "take it or leave it" proposition in which the terms of a very complex standard form contract are imposed by the seller.

Contracts of adhesion have legitimate uses, however, and the insurance contract is an example. If all terms of an insurance coverage had to be bargained individually, transaction costs would be prohibitive. If insurers could not use standard forms, the limits of an insurer's liability would be uncertain, insurance companies would face tremendous difficulties in predicting loss, and the price of insurance would be difficult to determine. Yet, the adhesive nature of an insurance contract exposes purchasers to exploitation by unscrupulous insurance companies. To preserve the advantages of standard-form insurance contracts while curbing their abuse, administrative agencies control the content of insurance contracts, and the courts construe ambiguous policy terms against their preparers.

Offer and Acceptance. An insurance policy is complex and detailed, in part because the insurer must carefully control the nature and extent of liability. Attempts to control liability extend to all aspects of the insurance contract, including the contract formation process. Since the insurer's liability under an insurance policy *usually* arises immediately upon contract formation and can greatly exceed amounts paid in premiums, both the insurer and the insured have a strong interest in how the rules of offer and acceptance will be applied to the question of when an insurance contract arises.[1]

Ordinarily, insurance policies are sold by a representative of the insurer, called an "agent." The extent of the agent's authority to make insurance contracts on behalf of the insurer depends greatly on the kind of insurance involved. In property and liability insurance, the insurer may cancel a policy by giving a legally prescribed amount of notice to the insured and refunding any unearned premiums. Because the property and liability insurer may thus free itself from risks that have become unacceptable, the insurer gives its agents the authority to enter into binding contracts without consulting the company in advance about the merits of each individual contract. Often the agent may orally accept an applicant's offer and bill the applicant later, and the property or liability applicant thereby acquires immediate coverage subject to possible cancellation.

In contrast, the right of a life insurance company to cancel life insurance policies is sharply limited by law. Life insurance companies therefore prefer to check an applicant's health, determine whether there is an insurable interest, and inquire about moral hazard before issuing a policy. To give themselves time to make a proper investigation and to reserve to themselves the decision of whether to grant insurance coverage, life insurers often restrict their agents' authority to accept offers.

In life insurance, the rules of offer and acceptance can be applied to four common situations that might lead to the formation of a life insurance contract.

1 A person fills out an application for insurance but does not pay the first premium. At this

[1] In most health and disability insurance, and in some life insurance sold to older people, there is a "probationary" period specified, during which benefits are limited or excluded.

time the applicant is considered merely to be inviting the insurer to make an offer. The company then proffers a policy (presents it for acceptance). The company is the offeror. The applicant pays the first premium. The applicant has accepted the offer.

2 A person pays the first premium upon completing the application. The applicant is the offeror. The insurer delivers the policy to the applicant or to the insurer's agent for unconditional delivery to the applicant. The insurer, by making delivery, has accepted the applicant's offer.

3 A person applies for insurance and pays the first premium. The applicant is the offeror. The agent immediately gives the applicant a "conditional receipt" which specifies that the insurance is effective immediately (or as of a certain date) if the applicant is found to be insurable. The insurer has accepted the applicant's offer. If the applicant is not insurable, there is no insurance coverage and the premium will be refunded. If the applicant turns out to have been insurable, coverage occurs at the time specified by the conditional receipt, even though the applicant might, for example, be struck by lightning and die before insurability is determined.

4 The insurance company gives its agent authority to make temporary binding contracts. The agent accepts the applicant's offer by issuing a "binding receipt" or by issuing a temporary insurance policy. The applicant has insurance coverage while the company decides whether or not to grant the requested coverage. The temporary coverage ceases when the company issues a policy (whether or not for the amount originally requested), when the applicant is notified of denial of insurance coverage, or at some other time specified by the company or determinable by law.

Assignability of Contract. For many reasons, people attempt to assign their insurance policies. A purchaser of real or personal property might seek an assignment of the seller's fire insurance. A person might wish to sell or give away a policy of insurance on his or her life, or might wish to use the policy as collateral security for a loan. Some assignments of insurance are permitted and some are not.

As a general rule, contracts of property and liability insurance are not assignable without the consent of the insurer. If, for example, a homeowner with a good safety record had an absolute right to assign his or her fire insurance policy to a homeowner with a record of serious fires, the assignor could, by assigning the policy, impose a heavier risk on the insurer than warranted by the premium paid by the assignor. To allow the insurer to better screen out unacceptable risks, the law therefore treats most property and liability insurance as a "personal" contract that is not assignable without the consent of the insurer. However, *marine* insurance (essentially, insurance on a ship and its cargo while at sea) usually *may* be assigned without the consent of the insurer. Marine insurance is not so clearly subject to "moral hazard" as other forms of property insurance are, and there is a need in the transshipment of goods to have a type of insurance that is readily transferable. The language of marine insurance policies often implies free assignability, and the law will give effect to an assignment over the objections of the insurer unless the policy contains a clause restricting or prohibiting assignment.

Life insurance is more freely assignable than property and liability insurance, but assignability of life insurance depends very much on the kind of situation involved. *After the death of the insured,* a life insurance policy is a promise by the insurer to pay money and as such is freely assignable (e.g., by a policyowner such as the insured's creditor). The law favors free alienability (transferability) of property, and an obligation merely to pay money usually involves no personal considerations that would warrant enforcing a nonassignability clause.

An assignment of a life insurance policy by the policyowner *during the lifetime of the insured* may or may not be enforceable. Some life insurance policies contain clauses prohibiting assignment by the owner. Although the courts favor free transferability of property, they tend to give effect to nonassignability clauses during the lifetime of the insured, in part because such clauses protect the rights of creditors where insurance is used as security. But many policies contain no prohibition of assignment. Ordinarily a person who has such a policy on his or her own life may assign it and thus make use of the property rights represented by the policy. These rights consist mainly of (1) any cash values that might accumulate before the death of the insured and (2) the face amount of the policy that will be available upon the death of the insured (i.e., the "death benefit").

Where an insurance policy names a beneficiary to receive the death benefit, the rights of an assignee to the cash value may conflict with the rights of the beneficiary, since a main function of the cash value is to provide funding for a continuation of the death benefit that the beneficiary expects to receive. If the designation of beneficiary is *irrevocable* (as where no right to change the beneficiary has been reserved by the policy), the rights of the beneficiary prevail over those of the assignee. Where the beneficiary designation is *revocable,* the law varies. In some states the (revocable) beneficiary's rights are considered to be vested (absolute) subject to being divested (taken away). In those states the beneficiary's rights will prevail unless the beneficiary agrees to the contrary or unless the rights of the beneficiary are divested. Divestment can occur only where the change-of-beneficiary procedures outlined in the policy have been followed. In most states, however, the assignee's rights are superior to those of a revocable beneficiary. This majority rule, by protecting the assignee, enables the policyowner to make effective use of the policy as collateral for a loan.

Pricing of Insurance

In deciding what premium (amount) to charge for insurance coverage, an insurance company must estimate the cost of providing the insurance before knowing what the actual losses and the expenses of administration will be. The premium charged is an estimation of the company's actual cost of providing the insurance. The actual cost is determined after the company has accumulated data about actual losses. If the actual cost is less than the amount of premiums collected from all insureds, the company may "adjust" the premium downward and pay the policyowner a "dividend."

As normally understood, a dividend is a share of corporate profits paid to a shareholder. In insurance, the meaning of dividend is quite different. An insurance "dividend" may be viewed as a refund of a part of the price initially charged for the insurance. The dividend reflects the difference between (1) the premium charged plus earnings from investing the premium and (2) the lower premium required by the actual loss and expense experience and the profit structure of the insurer. Under the federal income tax law, a policyowner dividend is treated not as income but as a nontaxable refund of an "overcharge."

Duties, Defenses, and Rights of Insurers and Others

Duties of Insurer and Insured. An insurer has a *duty to make prompt payment* of valid claims. The statutes of several states provide special remedies to aggrieved persons for unjustified nonpayment or late payment of valid claims. These statutes typically impose on insurers liability for claimants' attorney's fees together with a monetary penalty. The statutes are especially useful in encouraging prompt payment of small claims. In states without such statutes, claimants may be at a decided disadvantage. Under common law principles of the United States, litigants generally must pay their own attorney's fees regardless of the outcome of the litigation, and the use of an attorney for a small claim may be impractical.

Liability insurers also have a *duty to defend* suits against insureds and, where circumstances warrant, a *duty to settle claims* out of court. The insurer's duty to defend arises, for example, where an injured person files a lawsuit alleging a claim within policy coverage. The insurer's duty to settle claims out of court arises especially where (1) the facts reveal a claim greatly in excess of policy limits, (2) the validity of the claim is not in serious doubt, and (3) the claimant is willing to accept the policy maximum and to release the insured from liability for the excess. Where the validity of the claim is doubtful, the insurer is not required to settle out of court.

The duties of insureds and other claimants relate primarily to the prompt presentment of claims and to the assistance and cooperation of the insured in lawsuits against the insured. *Prompt presentment* of claims is a requirement that must be met before the insurer can be held liable for payment of claims. Many policies require that claims be presented within a specified number of days after a loss. *Reasonable* policy provisions requiring notice and proof of loss are enforced by the courts because of the general benefit to the insured public that flows from prompt investigation and settlement of claims. A claimant who fails to make a timely claim or proof of loss will lose the right to a benefit unless there is a valid excuse for delay, as where a person is incapacitated or reasonably believes he or she was not at fault in an automobile accident and chose to rely on the other driver's insurance instead of on his or her own.

The *duty of assistance and cooperation* arises frequently under policies of liability insurance that impose on the insurer a duty to defend the insured against tort claims. The insured is expected to notify the insurer promptly if suit is filed against the insured, and to attend hearings and trials, give evidence, help arrange a settlement, help obtain the attendance of witnesses, refrain from interfering with legitimate defense and settlement efforts, and give any other reasonable assistance and cooperation connected with the trial of the case. However, the insured may not be imposed on unreasonably. The insured does not breach the duty of assistance and cooperation by, for example, refusing to make an expensive trip unless reimbursed for travel expenses.

Case 27.2 involves a statute giving an insured a remedy for the insurer's failure to pay a valid claim.

CASE 27.2 Fresh Meadows Medical Associates v. Liberty Mutual Insurance Co. • 400 N.E.2d 303 (N.Y. 1979)

FACTS Janina Tokarz was injured in an automobile accident. At the time she was a passenger in an automobile operated by a driver insured under a liability policy issued by Liberty Mutual Insurance Company (defendant). Tokarz thereafter incurred a $70 bill for X-ray services rendered by Fresh Meadows Medical Associates (plaintiff). She assigned her claim for payment of this bill to Fresh Meadows, which presented the bill to the insurance carrier. When the carrier declined to make payment, Fresh Meadows submitted its claim to arbitration under section 675 of the Insurance Law, demanding payment by the carrier of the $70 (called "first-party benefits") and associated attorney's fees. Initially the attorney for Fresh Meadows sought a fee of $1,650. Liberty Mutual challenged the amount. The attorney conducted further legal research to substantiate the fee and sought an additional $1,200 for a total fee of $2,850. The arbitrator awarded Fresh Meadows $70 for the X-ray bill and $2,850 for attorney's fees. Liberty Mutual appealed. The supreme court (a first-level appellate court in New York) upheld the award. Liberty Mutual appealed, and the Appellate Division reduced the award of attorney's fees to $1,650. Fresh Meadows appealed.

OPINION JONES, J. . . . [Only one] issue is presented for our resolution—in awarding an attorney's fee incident to determination of a claim for first-party benefits, did the arbitrator have authority to include services rendered by the attorney in substantiating the claim for counsel fees? We hold that he did.

The relevant provision of section 675 as applicable to this case was found in subdivision 1: "the claimant shall also be entitled to recover his attorney's reasonable fee if a valid claim or portion thereof was overdue and such claim was not paid before the attorney was retained." The insurance carrier contends that the arbitrator had no authority under this section to direct payment of counsel fees for services rendered in justifying the claim for the attorney's fee, that to the extent this arbitrator directed payment for such services he exceeded his authority and that the disposition at the Appellate Division should be upheld.

In enacting section 675 the Legislature reversed the traditional principle in our jurisprudence that each litigant is expected to bear the cost of his attorney's services. In granting the arbitrator authority under the new so-called No-Fault Insurance Law to make an award to the claimant for "his attorney's reasonable fee" if the underlying claim for first-party benefits was valid in whole or in part and had not been paid before the attorney was retained, the precise extent of such authority was not otherwise delineated. It is not disputed that the arbitrator was given authority to award counsel fees for services rendered in proving entitlement to first-party benefits. There is no explicit address in the statute, however, by way either of inclusion or of exclusion to whether the authority extends to

CASE 27.2 Continued

the category of services necessarily rendered by the attorney in substantiating his entitlement to an attorney's fee—an issue sometimes referred to by use of the phrase, "a fee on a fee." The statutory provision does not preclude allowance for such services. Nor did the regulations originally issued by the Superintendent of Insurance speak to this issue. . . .

The carrier asserts that the authority exercised by the arbitrator in this instance in granting the supplemental layer of allowances is so contrary to normal jurisprudential principle[s] that it may not be implied in the absence of express statutory provision. Claimant rejoins that the grant of any authority to make the carrier pay the fees of the claimant's attorney represents an abrogation of the principle on which the carrier would rely, and argues persuasively that the intent of section 675 was, in cases in which an insurance carrier refused to pay a valid claim for first-party benefits and forced the claimant to retain an attorney to take his claim to arbitration, to indemnify the claimant against economic loss in exacting payment from the recalcitrant carrier. To achieve that objective the arbitrator must have authority to direct the carrier to pay all attorney's fees; to the extent that any portion thereof [was] excluded, and thus left for payment by the client, the purpose of the statute would be frustrated.

We agree with claimant and hold that in exercising the authority conferred on him under section 675 to direct payment by insurance carriers of reasonable fees of claimant's attorneys, the arbitrator in making his determination may include services rendered by the attorney in substantiating the claim for counsel fees, including efforts expended in addressing any legal issues which may be involved as well as time spent in assembling and presenting factual data to support the claim.

JUDGMENT Accordingly, the order of the Appellate Division should be reversed, with costs, and the judgment of Supreme Court confirming the award, reinstated.*

*In announcing our decision we note . . . that pursuant to legislative authority the Superintendent of Insurance has now issued regulations limiting the amount of fees which may be awarded by an arbitrator in a section 675 arbitration. To the extent that there may previously have been anxiety in some quarters that arbitrators were being accorded unbridled authority to fix unreasonably high legal fees this anxiety should now be allayed. [Footnote by the court.]

Defenses of Insurer. Within limits, an insurer may invoke certain defenses to avoid paying a claim that would otherwise be valid. The defenses of concealment, breach of warranty, or misrepresentation might be available.

Concealment. Intentional failure by an insurance applicant to disclose a material fact constitutes concealment and is a good defense if the insurer granted coverage while unaware of the concealed fact. Examples are a driver's failure to reveal convictions for drunken driving when applying for automobile liability insurance, and a homeowner's failure when applying for fire insurance to reveal illegal storage of large amounts of gasoline in the basement.[2] The essence of concealment is (intentional) nondisclosure of a material fact.

Breach of policy warranties. A "warranty" in an insurance policy is a written statement, a description, or an undertaking by means of which an applicant for insurance assures the insurer of the literal truth of certain facts. Suppose that Don seeks to insure the contents of his warehouse against theft. The statement in the policy that "A watchman will be on duty at all times" is a warranty. At common law, breach of a warranty was a complete defense for the insurer regardless of the materiality of the breach. Thus, if on a Monday night there was no watchman on duty, the warranty was breached. If goods were stolen on Tuesday night after the watchman returned to work, the insurer had a good defense despite the probability that the breach on Monday had nothing to do with the theft.

[2]If the insurer's application form specifically addressed such questions to the applicant, a false answer would constitute misrepresentation.

Many insurers took advantage of this common law treatment of warranties by drafting complex and detailed warranty clauses that often deprived insureds of the coverage they expected. Over time, the courts began to construe insurance policies so as to minimize, where possible, the number and scope of warranties made. Today many states have a statute providing that a breach of a warranty is a ground for avoiding the policy only if the breach is *material,* i.e., if it contributes significantly to the loss. In marine insurance and in states not having a warranty statute, the strict law of warranty (as modified by the courts) is still in effect. However, for the reason noted in the following discussion of misrepresentation, *life* insurance has by statute been largely removed from coverage by the law of warranty. Consequently, life insurers no longer have breach of warranty as a defense to payment of claims.

Misrepresentation. In the law of insurance, a "representation" is an oral or a written statement of fact made by an applicant for insurance for the purpose of inducing an insurer to extend coverage. A misrepresentation (i.e., a false representation) upon which an insurer relies in issuing a policy is a ground for avoiding the policy, *but only if the misrepresentation is material.* An applicant for life insurance who states that she is in perfect health when in fact she has recently received hospital treatment for a severe heart attack has made a material misrepresentation. If the insurance company relied on the misrepresentation in issuing a policy, the company may rescind (cancel) the contract. If through its own investigation the insurer learned the true state of the applicant's health before issuing the policy, the insurer has not relied on the misrepresentation. But where there was no investigation, or where the insurer investigated but did not learn the truth, the insurer usually will be held to have relied on the applicant's misrepresentation. In the majority of states the defense is good even though the misrepresentation was unintentional.

Only a *material* misrepresentation will give the insurer a defense. In contrast, at common law, even an *immaterial* breach of *warranty* provided a defense. To mitigate the harshness of the common law warranty doctrine, most states today by statute require that statements made in an application for *life* insurance shall be considered representations and not warranties. Under such statutes, therefore, the inaccuracy of a statement must now be material for a life insurer to have a defense.

Incontestability. Most life and some health insurance policies contain a clause stating that the policy is "incontestable" after the passage of 1 or 2 years. Incontestability means that the insurer may not avoid the policy for concealment, breach of warranty, or misrepresentation. Statutes requiring the inclusion of incontestability clauses in life insurance policies are in effect in most states and were enacted in part to counter the harshness of the common law doctrine of insurance warranties. Today incontestability clauses are commonly used in life insurance policies, even where not required by law, since the protection afforded to purchasers of life insurance enhances its marketability.

Rights Contrary to Policy Provisions. Insureds and other claimants may have rights that are inconsistent with the language of their policies. So may insurers.

Rights of claimants. As indicated earlier in this chapter, the older law of insurance enabled insurers to draft insurance policies in such a restrictive way that insureds and other claimants often were deprived of expected benefits. Many denials of benefits were so surprising and harmful to claimants that the courts developed interpretive techniques as a means of controlling abuse and overreaching by the insurers. For instance, instead of interpreting a description of insured property as a warranty (to which the property had to conform exactly to remain covered by the insurance), the courts came to treat a mere description as no more than an identification of the covered property, with no warranty significance. Thus, today a 1979 car might be inaccurately described as a 1980 model and yet be covered.

The courts today use many legal doctrines—such as the doctrines of waiver and election—to recognize rights that are inconsistent with policy language. A *waiver* is a voluntary relinquishment of a known right. An insurer might, for example, pay a claim even though the insured failed to give the insurer notice of loss within the time prescribed by the insurance policy. If the insurer later seeks to retrieve the payment because the notice was late, a court is likely to hold that the insurer waived its right to insist that the notice be given within the prescribed time.

Election is a doctrine under which an insurer, by taking one course of action, is held to have disqualified itself from taking another course of action. Suppose Maria is late in paying her automobile insurance premium. Failure to pay a premium on time normally results in termination (lapse) of insurance coverage. However, some courts hold that an insurance company, by accepting late payment, has "elected" to accept the late premium; consequently, the company becomes liable for any covered claim arising during what would have been the lapse period. In applying the doctrines of waiver and election, the courts seek to give effect to broader principles of law: (1) An insurer will be denied any unconscionable advantage in an insurance transaction. (2) The reasonable expectations of applicants and intended beneficiaries will be honored.

Rights of insurers. Where defenses such as concealment and misrepresentation are not expressly provided for in an insurance policy, they are nevertheless available to an insurer as rights at variance with policy provisions. Also, like any other contracting party, an insurer may have the insurance contract "reformed" by a court to correct errors. An error may occur, for example, in the preparation of the policy or it may arise from a mutual mistake about some matter such as the age of the insured.

Personal Risks: Life and Health Insurance

Life and health insurance policies protect against risks such as premature death, disability, unemployment, and outliving one's financial resources. In a family context, insurance can provide reimbursement for medical expenses, a replacement for income lost due to disability, and, at death, funds to cover the cost of the last illness, burial, unpaid debts, taxes, and similar expenses. Insurance can also provide surviving family members with funds for maintaining their standard of living or adjusting to a lower one if necessary, for supporting minor children, and for meeting special needs such as education and paying off a mortgage on the family residence. In a business context, a firm can insure the lives of key personnel whose untimely death would create great financial hardship for the firm. Firms can also use insurance to enhance the availability of credit to the firm, to assure the continuation of business (e.g., where surviving partners need a large fund with which to discharge their obligation to the heirs of a dead partner), and to fund employee benefit plans in an effort to attract and hold talented employees. Determining how (or whether) to meet these family and business needs with insurance requires familiarity with the basic features of life and health insurance.

Life Insurance

Types of Life Insurance. There are four basic classes of contracts sold by life insurance companies: term life insurance contracts, whole-life insurance contracts, endowment life insurance contracts, and annuities.[3] The first three classes enable a person to provide or accumulate a fund for use or for investment and are associated in varying degrees with the risk of premature death. When people refer to "life insurance," they usually mean term insurance, whole-life insurance, or endowment insurance—or one of the many combinations or variants of these three basic types. The fourth class of contract, the *annuity*, is a device for systematically *using up* (liquidating) an existing fund. An annuity protects against the risk of outliving one's financial resources and is similar in principle to a life insurance "settlement option" providing a periodic income. The topic of annuities is beyond the scope of this book, but settlement options are discussed later in this chapter.

Term life insurance is a contract that furnishes life insurance protection for a fixed period ("term of years," commonly 1 or 5), for an annual premium that remains the same throughout the term. The face value of the policy is payable only if death occurs during the term, and nothing is paid if the insured survives beyond the term. The premium is increased at each renewal because more benefits are paid out by the insurer as the age of insured persons increases and more insured persons die. The purchaser of term insurance receives insurance protection only, and there usually is no buildup of cash

[3]The discussion of life and health insurance is based on S. S. Huebner and Kenneth Black, Jr., *Life Insurance*, Prentice-Hall, Inc., Englewood Cliffs, N.J., 1976.

values. The premium for term insurance is relatively low when compared to the premiums for other types of life insurance for a given age and face amount, because term insurance does not provide coverage past a given age, usually 65 or 70. However, term insurance often is renewable until that age without proof of insurability. Where a person requires substantial amounts of "pure protection" and is not interested in maintaining coverage beyond retirement, term insurance may be the best choice.

Whole-life insurance (also called "straight," "ordinary," or "lifetime" insurance) is a contract of "permanent" insurance, so called for two reasons. First, the insured is permitted (but not required) to pay premiums throughout life and thereby to keep the policy in effect for life. Second, even if the insured eventually quits paying premiums, there is a buildup of cash values that can be applied to keep the policy in effect for a period of time after the insured quits paying premiums. How long the policy will remain in effect after premium payment ceases, or at what face value, depends on the amount of the cash-value buildup.

Paying for whole-life insurance is almost always accomplished by means of the "level-premium" technique. Suppose Mei Ling pays a $500 annual premium for her whole-life insurance. The premium is "level" because the amount is fixed at $500 for the duration of the contract. In the early years of the policy, the premium amount paid by Mei Ling and the others in her mortality grouping is far more than is needed to pay claims and expenses that will arise during the early years. The excess amount is retained and invested by the insurer. The resulting fund, called a "legal reserve fund," is the source of the "cash surrender value" that a whole-life policy accumulates. The legal reserve fund will be sufficient to pay the increasingly frequent claims that will arise in future years. In a sense, the legal reserve fund is intended to be exhausted. If there were a million insureds in a particular mortality grouping and no persons were added to the group, all of the premiums and earnings paid into the legal reserve fund would eventually be paid out as claims, administrative expenses of the insurer, and profits if the insurer is one for profit. Thus, a whole-life policy is basically insurance with a forced-savings feature that finances, in advance, long-term insurance benefits for the policyowner and any beneficiary.

There are many varieties of whole-life policies. One, the *limited-payment life policy,* is especially attractive to people who prefer to have a whole-life policy that is "paid up" by the end of their working lives. A paid-up policy is one on which no future premium payments are due, but under which the insurance company is liable for the full benefits specified by the contract. In a limited-payment life policy, premium payments are made for a limited number of years—20, for example—but are larger than where premiums are payable throughout life. These larger payments may be viewed as payment in advance for whole-life coverage.

Because of the cash-value feature, a whole-life policy can be used as collateral for a loan (as can an endowment policy). Or, where the policyowner wishes to quit paying premiums before the policy is fully paid up, the cash value can be applied in a variety of ways to preserve a lesser degree of insurance coverage.

Endowment insurance is a contract under which the insured pays premiums for a specified number of years, called the "endowment period," and at the end of that time *receives the face amount of the policy.* If the insured dies before that time, the face amount is paid to a beneficiary, as in other types of insurance.

An endowment policy has two basic elements: a savings fund resulting from the accumulation and investment of a portion of the premium, and term insurance whose face amount decreases as the endowment policy savings fund increases. To provide sufficient funds to pay the face amount due at the end of the endowment period, the insurer must build a large savings element into the premium. Consequently, an endowment policy premium for a given face amount is higher than is the premium for any other type of insurance. Where protection from premature death is the main concern, as in a young family with limited finances, endowment insurance would not be suitable. In the event of early death, term or even whole-life insurance would provide much more insurance proceeds per premium dollar than endowment insurance would.

Settlement Options. A life insurance policy "matures" when the insured dies or when the insured survives the endowment period of an endowment policy. At the maturity of the policy, the "proceeds" (the face amount of the policy) are available to the person entitled to them under the terms of the policy, usually a beneficiary. Exactly how the beneficiary will receive the proceeds depends on what "settlement option" (way of receiving the proceeds) was chosen. The typical life insurance contract provides the following basic settlement options: (1) a right to receive a lump-sum settlement in cash; (2) a right to leave the proceeds (principal) with the company, to receive the interest in periodic payments, and to withdraw principal from time to time or to specify how the principal is to be disposed of; (3) a right to have principal together with interest paid in equal installments over a fixed number of years; (4) a right to have payments of a specified amount until principal and interest are exhausted; and (5) any of a variety of life income options that serve the same function as an annuity.

Health Insurance

Health insurance protects mainly against the risk of temporary and permanent disability resulting from injury or illness. Policies and plans of health insurance are so varied in their provisions that we can pursue only a general discussion of health insurance.

Basic Coverages. The expression "health insurance" encompasses two major categories of insurance protection: (1) disability income insurance and (2) medical expense insurance. *Disability income insurance* provides periodic payments to the insured as a substitute for income lost as a result of illness, disease, or injury. Some disability income policies cover only those disabilities resulting from *accidental injury*. Others cover disabilities resulting from both *accidental injury and sickness*. Usually, payments under such policies do not begin until the expiration of a stated period after the disability occurs. *Medical expense insurance* provides payments for medical care. "Medical care" includes hospital expenses, surgical expenses, nonsurgical expenses, and nursing expenses. As in disability insurance policies, medical benefits are limited in amount and duration.

Health insurance policies typically contain exclusions from coverage. Some policy provisions exclude risks that the insurer considers too great to cover, such as those encountered in military service. Some clauses exclude coverage of preexisting disabilities or health conditions in an attempt to limit "adverse selection" (the greater-than-normal tendency of poor risks to seek insurance). The desire to limit adverse selection also accounts in part for the exclusion of suicide and self-inflicted injuries. And, to prevent duplication of coverage and benefit payments, virtually all policies exclude coverage where the insured receives workers' compensation or other medical insurance benefits.

Types of Policies and Plans. People can acquire health insurance in so many ways that they may unwittingly have overlapping coverage and a higher than necessary health insurance cost. Health insurance can be acquired by means of individual health insurance policies, group health insurance policies, social security, and private noncommercial health insurance plans such as Blue Cross and Blue Shield. Other sources of health insurance coverage include life insurance disability "riders" (supplemental agreements that expand coverage) and even automobile insurance policies that provide medical expense coverage (limited, of course, to medical expenses relating to covered automobile accidents).

Group health insurance is widely used and should be distinguished from *individual* health insurance. Normally a person seeking individual insurance must provide evidence of insurability, whereas a company that issues group insurance (e.g., life or health) undertakes to insure every person in the group without regard to the insurability of individuals. In group insurance, the insurer issues one detailed *master contract* to the group policyholder (e.g., an employer) but only brief certificates to individual insureds such as employees. Also, many group policies are "experience-rated"; i.e., the premium charged depends to some extent on the claims record of the group. Experience rating gives a group an incentive to keep claims at a minimum.

Property Risks: Property and Liability Insurance

Property Insurance

Nature of Property Insurance. Property insurance indemnifies a person who has an insurable interest in physical property (real or personal) for its loss or for the loss of its income-producing ability. Property insurance protects against loss from certain "perils." A *peril* is a cause of loss such as fire, flood, theft, or vandalism.

Property insurance may be provided by means of either a "specified-perils" or an "all-risk" ("all-perils") contract. In a *specified-perils contract,* the insurer will make indemnity only for losses resulting from the particular peril or perils specified in the contract. A farmer's insurance against hail damage to crops is an example of a specified-perils contract. In an *all-risk contract,* the insurer will indemnify the insured for loss resulting from any peril except those specifically excluded by the contract. A homeowner's "personal property floater" is an all-risk contract because, despite certain exclusionary clauses and other limitations of liability, covered losses will be compensated for even though the particular peril was not spelled out in the contract. All-risk contracts are useful where the exact nature of the peril is difficult to predict.

The risk undertaken by a property insurer is subject to limits imposed by the policy. Many policies impose a "deductible," and all policies contain clauses of exclusion. A deductible is an amount of loss, specified in the policy, that the insured must absorb before he or she is entitled to payment from the insurer. Deductible amounts are common in automobile and homeowners' insurance. They serve to minimize insurance costs (and premiums) by eliminating small claims and claims that are particularly susceptible to moral hazard. Clauses of exclusion serve in property insurance, as in other kinds, to confine the insured risk to manageable proportions. Damage resulting from an act of war is a typical exclusion.

A property loss may be "direct" or "indirect." A *direct loss* is one resulting from damage to the physical property itself. Collision damage to a taxicab is an example. An *indirect loss* is one that occurs as a *consequence* of a direct loss. Loss of income while a taxicab is out of service because of collision damage is one kind of indirect loss. The extra expense of renting a car as a substitute for a taxicab that is temporarily out of service because of collision damage is another.

Types of Property Insurance. The following list is representative of the kinds of property insurance available for protection against personal or business losses. Most or all coverages are available on a single-peril, multiple-peril, "package," or all-risk basis. Some coverages are limited to direct losses, most encompass indirect losses, and a few (such as business interruption insurance) protect primarily against indirect losses.

1 *Fire insurance.* Provides indemnity against losses to insured buildings, contents, ships in port, and so on, due to accidental fire. Loss due to a "friendly" fire may not be covered as where, for example, a valuable object is accidentally tossed into the firebox of a furnace. If a friendly fire escapes and becomes "hostile," the resulting damage is covered.

2 *Automobile collision insurance.* Covers loss to the insured vehicle from its collision with another object. Does *not* cover bodily injury or liability arising from the collision; separate coverages are required for noncollision losses.

3 *Crime insurance.* Pays for losses caused by the criminal acts of others, such as burglary and other forms of theft.

4 *Inland marine insurance.* Originally provided protection for goods transported other than by ocean. Now it is often used to cover a variety of transportation and nontransportation losses, whether or not incurred on waterways.

5 *Accounts receivable insurance.* Protects against an inability to collect an account because of damage to records that prove the existence of the account.

6 *Business interruption insurance.* Protects against losses due to an inability of a business to operate because of fire or other hazards such as a flood.

Case 27.3 discusses whether a fire was friendly or hostile.

CASE 27.3 Engel v. Redwood County Farmers Mutual Ins. Co. · 281 N.W.2d 331 (Minn. 1979)

FACTS Engel (plaintiff) built a hog barn on his Minnesota farm for use in farrowing hogs. A furnace located just outside the barn heated it by means of a thermostat-controlled fan that blew hot air inside.

CASE 27.3 Continued

In the winter of 1976, Engel discovered that fifteen sows in the barn had died from an inadequate oxygen supply resulting from high temperature caused by an electrical malfunction in the thermostat. Although the temperature inside the barn reached 120 degrees, the fire inside the furnace burned and produced heat at its usual rate and was confined within the furnace, causing no damage to it and producing no soot or other foreign material. Engel filed a claim under his fire insurance policy with Redwood County Farmers Mutual Insurance Co. (defendant). Redwood rejected the claim on the ground that the loss was caused by a "friendly" rather than a "hostile" fire, and thus was not covered by the policy. Engel brought suit against the insurer. From a judgment for Engel, Redwood appealed.

OPINION

KELLY, J. . . . [In the early English case of *Austin v. Drew*], sugar being refined in plaintiff's factory was damaged by excessive heat and smoke. The sugar was contained in various rooms of an 8-story building through which ran a flue supplying the heat necessary for the refining process. At the top of the flue was a register which was normally kept open when the fire was high. An employee started the fire without opening the register. As a result, the fire overheated, smoking up the rooms containing the sugar and causing the damage complained of. The court, in denying recovery, stated:

> I am of the opinion that this action is not maintainable. There was no more fire than always exists when the manufacture is going on. Nothing was consumed by fire. The plaintiff's loss arose from the negligent management of their machinery. The sugars were chiefly damaged by the heat; and what produced that heat? Not any fire against which the company insures, but the fire for heating the pans, which continued all the time to burn without any excess. The servant forgot to open the register by which the smoke ought to have escaped and the heat to have been tempered. . . .

From this opinion has emerged a rule of law known as the hostile fire doctrine. It is recognized in a majority of jurisdictions where the issue has been raised, . . . although it has been criticized by many commentators. . . . In brief, the rule . . . states that a fire which is intentionally kindled and which remains at all times confined to the place where it was intended to be will be characterized as friendly and will not subject the insurer to any liability for the resulting loss. . . . [However, when] an insured buys a fire insurance policy which "covers all losses or damage by fire," his expectation is that it will cover all unintentional losses from fire, except listed exclusions, regardless of the nature or character of the fire. The doctrine thus seems to protect the insurer at the expense of the unwitting insured.

In Minnesota, this problem is avoided because of the judicially created limitations on friendly fires. In [the *L.L. Freeberg Pie Co.* case], we joined a minority of courts which require that a friendly fire, in addition to the elements listed above, be non-excessive. . . . Under the *Freeberg* case, a fire may be found to be hostile[,] although it was intentionally kindled and never escaped its confines, if it was excessive or uncontrolled. . . .

In the case before us defendant argues that even under the minority rule it should not be held liable because the fire was in no way excessive. . . . Defendant reasons that if the furnace burned only at its usual rate it could not possibly be excessive. We disagree. A fire which causes damage by burning for a greater length of time than intended is no less controlled merely because it continues to burn at its usual rate. . . .

Returning to the facts before us, the malfunctioning thermostat caused the furnace to burn continuously until the temperature reached 120 degrees—well beyond the preset temperature of 75 degrees. We do not believe that under these circumstances this fire can be described as controlled. It burned for an excessive period of time[,] resulting in temperatures much greater than those intended, causing the loss complained of. By characterizing this fire as hostile we are in no way departing from our prior decisions. We merely

CASE 27.3 Continued hold that a fire may be hostile although burning at its usual rate if it burns substantially longer or in some fashion other than expected. For the above reasons, we affirm the decision of the trial court.

JUDGMENT Affirmed. . . .

Liability Insurance

Nature of Liability Insurance. A person or a firm faces two broad types of liability for damages—liability for breach of contract and liability for a wide variety of torts. Liability insurance does *not* cover liability for breach of contract, nor does it cover losses resulting from other speculative activities such as trading in the stock market. Liability insurance protects only against *tort* liability, including, however, tort liability assumed by contract.

The sources and types of tort liability fall into several somewhat overlapping categories. They include:

1 Liability for one's own torts—negligent driving, professional malpractice, false imprisonment of a suspected shoplifter, libel and slander, etc.

2 Liability of an employer for torts committed by employees in the course of their employment, including many intentional torts.

3 Liability for loss resulting from defective products, whether based on negligence, breach of a warranty, or strict liability in tort.

4 Liability resulting from ownership of property—e.g., the strict liability attending the ownership of hazardous property such as a reservoir, and liability to guests, business invitees, and certain classes of trespassers for losses resulting from the negligent maintenance of one's home or business premises.

Types of Liability Insurance. Most of the tort exposures listed above may be insured against, although insurers commonly exclude from coverage some intentional torts committed by the insured. A policy might exclude assault and battery committed by the insured; but where the insured is a journalist, the policy might cover libel, since a charge of libel is a normal risk of journalism.

The following list is representative of liability coverage:

1 *Employer's liability insurance.* One type provides coverage for workers' compensation claims. Another protects the employer against claims of persons other than employees—e.g., business invitees.

2 *Errors and omissions insurance.* Protects the insured from liability to a customer resulting from the insured's error or oversight. An insurance salesperson, for example, might forget to include a requested coverage, or an architect might fail to provide adequate roofing material.

3 *Malpractice insurance.* Protects professionals such as doctors, lawyers, and accountants from liability for negligence in the practice of their professions.

4 *Fidelity (guaranty) insurance.* Protects against loss due to embezzlement and other dishonesty of employees and other persons holding positions of trust.

5 *Automobile liability insurance.* Protects a motor vehicle operator or owner from liability to third persons as a result of the operation of the vehicle. About half the states have some form of "no-fault" automobile insurance law under which claims for personal injury (and, in Massachusetts, for property damage) must be made against the claimant's own insurance company, regardless of who was at fault. The aim of such laws is to reduce the cost of automobile insurance by reducing litigation and other expenses, but many no-fault laws are ineffective for this purpose because the right to litigate to establish fault has been preserved even for rather small claims.

6 *Homeowners' liability insurance.* A coverage protecting a homeowner from damage claims of invitees and others.

Subrogation and Coinsurance

Two concepts have special significance in property and liability insurance. The first, an insurance company's right of *subrogation* (right to be substituted as a claimant against a person responsible for loss), applies mainly to liability insurance. Suppose that a teller in a bank embezzles funds from a customer's account and that the bank must make good the loss. At this point the bank has a right to recover the amount of the loss from the teller. Suppose now that the bank has a policy of fidelity insurance and that the insurance company rather than the bank must make good the loss. Upon payment of the bank's claim, the insurer acquires the right of the bank (is "subrogated to" the right of the bank) to collect the amount of the loss from the teller.

The second concept, *coinsurance,* applies to the insuring of commercial property.[4] A coinsurance clause is used by property insurers to prevent customers who underinsure commercial property from taking "unfair" advantage of a common method of setting rates for property insurance. Property rates are fixed at a certain amount per $1,000 of coverage on the preliminary assumption that all customers will carry their full share of the group risk by insuring their property for substantially full value. But if Webster and Smith own identical office buildings worth $100,000 each, and Webster insures hers for $20,000 while Smith insures his for $100,000, Smith pays a total premium that is five times larger than Webster's. This difference in premiums would be "fair" if large and small claims were in the equal balance implied by the flat premium rate per $1,000 of coverage. In fact, however, there are more small claims than large ones because there are more partial than total losses. If all claims were paid in full, the group of insureds that pays less in premiums would receive proportionately more in claims "payout" than would the group that insures for full value. Rather than reduce the premium rate when a person insures for full or nearly full value, the insurer uses the coinsurance clause to reduce the claims payout to the group that underinsures. Coinsurance is used in lieu of a reduced-premium ("graded-rate") system because such a system would require an expensive property appraisal each time a policy is issued or renewed. The coinsurance technique is statistically fair because it assures a rough equality of payout per premium dollar to all groups of insureds, but it creates a trap for unwary underinsureds who expect their losses to be fully covered.

A coinsurance clause works as follows: The clause provides that if the owner insured his or her property for at least a given percent of its value (usually 80 percent), then any loss will be paid in full up to the face amount of the policy. In contrast, if the owner insures the property for less than the required percentage, the owner must bear part of the loss and will recover from the insurance company only the amount indicated by the following formula, which is one of several that have been developed for different situations.

$$\text{Recovery} = \text{Actual loss} \times \frac{\text{Face amount of insurance}}{80\% \times \text{"actual cash value" of property}}$$

Webster in the preceding paragraph insured her $100,000 office building for only $20,000. Suppose she sustains a fire loss of $20,000. She will recover only $5,000 from the insurer, since recovery ($5,000) equals:

$$\text{Actual loss (\$20,000)} \times \frac{\text{Face amount of insurance (\$20,000)}}{80\% \times \text{\$100,000, the actual cash value of the property (\$80,000)}}$$

Suppose now that Smith insures his $100,000 office building for $80,000. The coinsurance requirement is met. If Smith sustains a $20,000 fire loss, it will be paid in full. However, if the value of the building increases and there is no corresponding increase in the amount of insurance, Smith will not be in compliance with the coinsurance requirement and will have to bear part of the loss. People who insure *residential* property often are subject to a "replacement cost clause" whose purpose is similar to that of a coinsurance clause.

Regulation of the Insurance Business

Insurance is aggressively marketed. The persuasion of sellers, the financial significance of insurance to buyers and sellers, the confusing complexity of insurance contracts, and the ignorance of much of the insuring public make insurance an obvious subject of abuse and, consequently, of governmental regulation. As noted earlier in this chapter, the courts try to strike a fair balance between insureds

[4] "Coinsurance" has other meanings that are beyond the scope of this chapter. One applies to reinsurance and another to health insurance.

and insurers by denying any unconscionable advantage to insurers and attempting to honor the reasonable expectations of insurance purchasers and beneficiaries. But the judiciary is only one component in the web of federal and state insurance regulation.

Federal Regulation

In 1944, the Supreme Court held that an insurance company that conducts business across state lines is engaged in interstate commerce and is therefore subject to the regulatory power of the federal government, specifically to the requirements of the Sherman Antitrust Act.[5] Prior to that decision, insurance regulation had largely been the responsibility of the states. After the decision, Congress enacted the McCarran-Ferguson Act to clarify the regulatory situation, especially as to the applicability of antitrust law to the insurance industry.

Under the McCarran Act, the regulation and taxation of insurance is left mainly to the states. However, the McCarran Act only partially exempts the insurance industry from the federal antitrust laws. Those laws (the Sherman Act, the Clayton Act, and the Federal Trade Commission Act) apply to the "business of insurance" *to the extent that the business of insurance is not regulated by state law.* "Business of insurance" means essentially the relationship between an insurance company and its policyholders. Where a state *fails* to regulate a harmful business practice falling within the meaning of business of insurance, federal law applies. And, since the McCarran Act exempts only the business of insurance from antitrust coverage, federal antitrust law applies to any aspect of an insurance company's business that lies outside the relationship between the company and its policyholders (if there is a sufficient jurisdictional relationship to interstate commerce). For example, an insurance company that conspired with an automobile glass franchisor to fix the price of replacement glass was subject to Sherman Act liability. Moreover, under the McCarran Act, all boycotts and acts of coercion and intimidation that might be engaged in by insurance companies remain subject to federal antitrust regulation regardless of whether that kind of misconduct is subject to state regulation.

[5]*United States v. South-Eastern Underwriters Association,* 322 U.S. 533.

State Regulation

At the state level, insurance regulation is carried out mainly by a state administrative agency usually known as the "insurance commission." One goal of the insurance commission is to ensure the financial soundness of insurance companies so that they can carry out their obligations. Therefore the insurance commission regulates insurance company investments and takes other measures intended to assure preservation of capital and reserves.

Another major regulatory goal is the reasonable and fair treatment of policyholders, insureds, and beneficiaries. This goal accounts for regulatory measures such as the licensing of agents and brokers and the requirement that insurance contracts contain a variety of protective provisions such as nonforfeiture clauses in cash-value life insurance policies. The insurance commissions also prohibit the inclusion of certain particularly burdensome contractual provisions, such as one requiring any suit against an insurer to be commenced within a period shorter than that provided for in the applicable statute of limitations.

Roles of Insurance Agents and Brokers

Under the law of agency, an agent is a person who makes contracts on behalf of another person, the "principal," and is subject to the principal's instructions and control. An "insurance agent" represents an insurance company (the principal) by selling insurance to third persons and acting as the insurer's agent in the process of contract formation. An "insurance broker" does not represent a company but, rather, places an order for insurance on behalf of the buyer and is therefore the *buyer's* agent. The rights and duties of principals, agents, and third persons are discussed in the agency chapters of this volume.

The primary job of an insurance agent is to sell a financial product. Whether out of a desire to sell more product or to be of greater service to clients, many insurance agents have in recent years taken on the role of financial adviser, and many have enrolled in courses of study designed to sharpen their advising skills. But insurance agents face special problems when they serve as both sellers and advisers.

A seller who avoids deception and other illegality is free to advertise the product and to engage in a variety of promotional practices, including those calculated to induce purchases on the basis of emotional appeals. Despite the prevalence of consumer protection law, the buyer bears considerable responsibility for judging the suitability of the product, or of the amount of the product, for his or her need. Unlike a seller, a financial adviser may be a fiduciary, and therefore subject to a more stringent standard of professional conduct than a seller. Financial advisers tend to work in areas of technical complexity. They usually undertake to analyze a client's personal problem and to offer a reasonable solution. A client uninformed about technical matters tends to defer to the judgment of the adviser who, because of that deference, is in a position to take advantage of the client or to harm him or her through negligence or incompetence. A client may reasonably expect the financial adviser to possess some minimal level of analytical ability and technical knowledge, to be open and honest in making recommendations, to proceed with care and discretion in the best interests of the client, and to reveal conflicts of interest. Where an insurance agent gives planning advice and also sells a financial product that he or she recommends for putting the plan into effect, a conflict of interests is evident. Such conflicts of interest do not go unnoticed by the courts when someone alleges overreaching in the sale of insurance.

Summary

Insurance is a contractual method of transferring risk from an insured to an insurer who distributes it by means of pooling and reinsurance. Since insurance is a system for distributing loss, an insured should be limited to indemnity for loss actually suffered. The principle of indemnity underlies the requirement of an insurable interest, a financial stake that a person seeking insurance has in property or in someone's life or health.

An insurance policy is a contract of adhesion. As such it is subject not only to ordinary rules of contract law, but also to legal controls commonly imposed on contracts of adhesion. Depending on the circumstances, an insurance contract may or may not be assignable. An insurer has a duty to make prompt payment of valid claims, and liability insurers may have a duty to defend the insured in a lawsuit. Insureds have a duty to make prompt presentment of claims and sometimes to give assistance and cooperation in lawsuits. Within limits, the insurer may invoke the defenses of concealment, breach of a policy warranty, and misrepresentation.

Policies of life and health insurance protect against the risks of premature death, disability, unemployment, and outliving one's financial resources. The three basic types of life insurance contracts—term, whole-life, and endowment—provide or help a person accumulate a fund, whereas the annuity contract is used to liquidate an existing fund. Health insurance provides disability income and medical expense reimbursement.

Property insurance protects against the loss of physical property or its income-producing ability. Liability insurance protects against tort liability. Subrogation, the right to be substituted as a claimant against a person responsible for loss, applies mainly to liability insurance. Coinsurance is used to prevent persons who underinsure their property from receiving disproportionate benefits.

Insurance is subject to federal and state regulation. Most insurance regulation is carried out by administrative agencies at the state level. Their goals are to ensure the financial soundness of insurers and to assure fair treatment of policyholders, insureds, and beneficiaries.

An insurance agent is a salesperson working on behalf of an insurer. An agent who adopts the role of a financial adviser might also acquire the liability of a fiduciary.

Review Questions

1 What are the two basic meanings of "the insured"?

2 Explain how insurers distribute risk of loss by **(a)** pooling and **(b)** reinsurance.

3 Explain how a coordination-of-benefits clause is consistent with the principle of indemnity.

4 What circumstances give rise to an insurable interest **(a)** in property insurance? **(b)** In life insurance?

5 If an insurance policy is a contract of adhesion, how does that fact affect its enforceability?

6 In insurance usage, what is the meaning of "dividend"?

7 What are the general duties of the insurer? What are the general duties of the insured or other claimant?

8 **(a)** In life insurance, what is the significance of treating statements made in an application as representations and not as warranties? **(b)** What is the significance of incontestability?

9 In function, how does an annuity differ from a contract of life insurance?

10 Explain the meaning and use of a "level" premium.

11 Why are settlement options necessary? Name some.

12 **(a)** What exclusions from coverage do health insurance policies typically contain? Why? **(b)** How does a group health (or life) insurance policy differ from an individual policy?

13 Distinguish between a specified-perils and an all-risk (all-perils) contract of property insurance.

14 **(a)** What kind of liability does liability insurance cover? Not cover? **(b)** Explain the meaning and purpose of subrogation. Of coinsurance.

15 What potential liability confronts an insurance agent who takes on the role of financial adviser? Why is there a problem?

Case Problems

1 Ryan and Tickle, both morticians, went into business together in 1971. Ryan Funeral Home, Inc., had 477 shares of stock distributed among twelve shareholders. Ryan owned 50 shares, Tickle bought 25 shares, and Ryan and Tickle had a 5-year option to buy the remaining stock from the other shareholders. Ryan and Tickle also purchased the Mullen Funeral Home, arranging to finance the unpaid balance over a period of 5 to 6 years. In 1972, to provide a fund by which the survivor could acquire ownership in the funeral homes, they purchased insurance on their joint lives. In early 1973, Ryan learned he had cancer. He died in 1975. Tickle collected the proceeds of the insurance policies and bought the outstanding interests in the two funeral homes. Alleging that Tickle did not have an insurable interest in Ryan's life, Ryan's widow brought suit to recover the insurance proceeds for Ryan's estate. If she had standing to sue, was she entitled to the insurance proceeds?

2 Butler purchased an Austin-Healy for $3,500. He was unaware that the car had been stolen. Two years after the purchase, the police seized the car and returned it to its lawful owner. Butler filed a claim with his insurer for the value of the car. Alleging a lack of insurable interest, the insurer refused to reimburse Butler for the loss, offering instead "$55 to $56" as a return of premiums paid. Did Butler have an insurable interest in the stolen car?

3 Wicker, seriously injured while helping trim a tree on Walker's farm, sued Walker for negligence. Walker's insurer denied liability because a clause in the policy excluded liability for bodily injury to "any farm employee arising out of and in the course of his employment by [the] Insured." The policy defined "farm employee" as "an employee ... whose duties are principally in connection with the farming operations of the Insured." Wicker worked only a few days a year for the Walkers. He was usually paid, but not always. There was no express contract as to terms of payment, hours to be worked, and the like. Under insurance law, an unclear or ambiguous exclusion clause will be construed against the insurer. Consequently, if the term "farm employee" was ambiguous, Wicker's injuries would be covered by the policy. Was the exclusion clause effective to deny coverage to Wicker?

4 Chadwick's car was badly damaged in a collision. Its precollision fair market value was $1,650. Immediately afterward, the salvage value was $100. Chadwick sought reimbursement from his insurer. The insurer's adjuster made five offers of settlement ranging downward from $1,250 to $800. Chadwick then submitted a written demand for $1,450. The insurer did not answer the letter or make a counterproposal. Chadwick sued the insurer for $1,450 plus an amount for rental of a replacement car, storage costs for the damaged car, a "bad faith" penalty, and attorney's fees. The jury returned a verdict in favor of Chadwick for $1,550 in damages plus $387 as a bad faith penalty and $800 for attorney's fees. The insurer appealed. Should the verdict for Chadwick be upheld?

5 Brown sought recovery from his insurer for the loss of his car, which had been destroyed by fire. The insurer's adjuster recommended a settlement of $3,200. In the meantime, Brown's attorney demanded $4,500, considerably more than the price of a comparable vehicle located by an adjuster. About 2 months before suing the insurer, the attorney demanded $5,400. Brown rejected a pretrial settlement of $3,800. Some 18 months after the loss, an independent appraiser engaged by the insurer estimated the loss at $3,363. The jury returned a verdict in favor of Brown for $3,950, and the trial judge awarded Brown an attorney's fee of $1,316.66. The insurer appealed the award of the attorney's fee. Should the award be upheld?

6 Phillips's application for life insurance asked the question, "Have you ever been told you had any of the following" listed diseases? Phillips answered "no" for each of the illnesses in the list. Phillips died, his widow sought payment of the policy amount, and the insurer refused to pay. The widow sued the insurer, which proved that Phillips had been treated for pulmonary emphysema, hemotysis, chronic brain syndrome associated with the consumption of alcohol, hypertension, and epilepsy, along with other long-standing physical problems for which he had been hospitalized. The trial court awarded the insurer judgment on the ground of material misrepresentation. The widow appealed, contending that Phillips spoke truthfully because he had never been told the names of any of the illnesses. Should the judgment for the insurer be upheld?

7 Schulze and Burch Biscuit Co. used several large gas ovens to bake crackers and related products. The ovens operated continually at 450 degrees Fahrenheit. At the end of a working shift, one of the ovens was accidentally left without any product on the conveyer belt running through the oven. Consequently, the temperature reached approximately 1,600 degrees, seriously damaging the oven and causing a loss of about $150,000. Schulze filed a claim for the loss, but its insurer, American Protection Insurance Co., denied the claim on the ground that the fire was "friendly." Schulze brought suit for the amount of the loss. Should Schulze prevail?

ETHICS IN PRACTICE

Insurance is a very sensitive industry ethically. Customers pay billions of dollars annually for various kinds of insurance coverage and expect insurance companies to invest the proceeds properly and to pay claims quickly and fairly. Because insurance companies are in business to make a profit, the interests of insurers obviously conflict with those of their customers and claimants: payouts reduce profits. Thus, there is pressure on insurance companies to market aggressively and to limit payouts whenever possible. Moreover, salespeople receive much larger commissions for some kinds of insurance than for other kinds, and to increase earnings they may act contrary to the interests of their customers. Then there are the customers and claimants who file false claims against the insurers. Money, it is said, "is the root of all evil," and insurance companies, which handle so much of it, are at the center of temptation. State insurance commissions and the civil and criminal law are available to help control abuses. Yet, as the following problems indicate, many practices involving insurance present ethical as opposed to purely legal questions.

Problems in Ethics

1 Credit-life and credit-health-and-accident insurance policies are sold to borrowers to cover the amount of the loan should the borrower die or become disabled. Credit insurance is very profitable to companies that sell it because they typically pay out a small percentage of premiums in claims; yet it is priced many times higher than standard term insurance of the same face amount. Compared to the commissions that salespeople receive on other types of insurance, credit-insurance commissions are very high. Loan companies and installment-plan sellers such as car dealers receive commissions on credit insurance they sell. Some sellers and lenders "pack" various credit-insurance policies into consumer-loan or installment-sales agreements, often without the customers' knowledge or consent. **(a)** Is it ethical for a lender (or an installment-plan seller) to require its customer to purchase life or health-and-accident insurance as a condition of the loan? To include credit-insurance charges without notifying the debtor? To require the customer to purchase credit insurance through the lender or seller? **(b)** Carsco advertises 4.9 percent financing on new cars, which is half to a third the rate charged by other new-car dealers: "Friday and Saturday only—instant financing." Unknown to customers who do not read the fine print in the ad, the low interest rate is contingent on the purchase of credit-life and credit-health-and-accident insurance. The credit insurance charges will add over $500 to the price of a $10,000 car, but the ad does not point this out and Carsco salespeople are instructed not to discuss the insurance charges unless asked. Is tying low interest rates to the sale of credit insurance in this manner ethical? If not, could "tying" somehow be made ethical? **(c)** You work for Lifeco, a credit insurance company. Its sales manager proposes the following sales plan: To gain access to customers, Lifeco employees will take jobs in car dealerships as finance or business managers. In their dealership positions, these employees will push Lifeco credit insurance policies and will receive commissions on all policies sold. Is this sales practice ethical?

2 In the insurance industry, "rebating" is an insurance agent's paying part of his or her commission to a customer as an inducement to purchase the policy the agent is selling. Many agents and insurance companies view rebating as unfair competition and have vigorously supported laws against it. The legislatures of most states have made rebating illegal. Yet, California's recently passed Proposition 103 permits consumers to seek rebates and other discounts from insurance brokers and agents. **(a)** Is rebating unethical? What factors are relevant to your answer? **(b)** If rebating is ethical, are laws against rebating unethical? Are the factors relevant to your answer different from those pertaining to rebating itself?

3 Healthco, a large health-and-accident insurer, routinely delays for several months the payment of small claims, collects interest on the unpaid amounts, and keeps the interest as company income. Is this practice ethical?

4 A number of insurance companies contribute substantial sums of money to Mothers Against Drunk Driving (MADD). The leaders of the California chapter endorse voters' initiatives aimed at reforming California insurance law and reducing auto insurance premiums. Despite vigorous opposition by the insurance companies, the voters adopt one of the initiatives. Soon after the election, and allegedly at the insistence of the insurance companies, the national MADD directors fire the California MADD officials for endorsing the initiatives. **(a)** Was it ethical for the national MADD directors to fire the California officials? **(b)** If the insurance companies forced the firings, was their conduct ethical?

PART EIGHT

Commercial Paper

CHAPTER 28
Nature of Commercial Paper; Negotiable Form

CHAPTER 29
Personal and Real Defenses; Negotiation of Commercial Paper

CHAPTER 30
Holder-in-Due-Course Status; FTC Limits

CHAPTER 31
Liability of the Parties; Discharge

CHAPTER 32
Checks; Relationship between Bank and Customer; Electronic Funds Transfer

CHAPTER 28

Nature of Commercial Paper; Negotiable Form

Businesspeople use many kinds of commercial documents daily. They include, for example, warehouse receipts, delivery orders, bills of lading, and other documents of title (discussed in Chapter 17) used in the distribution of goods; security agreements, financing statements, and certificates of title to motor vehicles, needed to create and enforce secured transactions (Chapter 25); and corporate securities such as stocks and bonds (Chapter 40), sold to raise funds for business activities. These various documents serve primarily as evidence of ownership or of indebtedness. We turn now to another class of commercial documents, called *commercial paper* or *negotiable instruments,* used mainly as a *substitute for money* or as a *means of extending credit* in terms of money. This chapter discusses the types and nature of commercial paper, the language ("form") required for an instrument (document) to be negotiable, and the main benefit that a purchaser of commercial paper receives: the right to have payment free from personal defenses of the person or firm that "issued" it (put it into circulation).

Nature of Commercial Paper

Centuries ago merchants began to devise ways of paying for property and services without having to carry large sums of money. The *bill of exchange* (nowadays called a "draft") was used in Europe for that purpose as early as the fourteenth century. With the growth of banking, a special kind of draft called a "check" came into wide use. Today most business transactions are settled by check. Checks and other drafts serve as a temporary, safe, and efficient substitute for money. Another kind of commercial paper, the *promissory note,* is used primarily as a means of extending credit. In its simplest form, a promissory note is the written promise of a person (a borrower or buyer) to pay a sum of money to another person (a lender or seller) at some future date. Article 3 of the Uniform Commercial Code governs commercial paper.

Types of Commercial Paper

Although all commercial paper may be classified as either a draft or a note, Article 3 lists four varieties of commercial paper: notes (often called "promissory notes"), certificates of deposit, drafts, and checks [3-104]. A certificate of deposit is a specialized type of note. A check is a specialized type of draft.

Promissory Notes. Notes are the simplest kind of commercial paper because they involve only two parties. A note is a writing in which one party (the *maker*) promises to pay a sum of money to another party (the *payee*). A note may be either a *demand* note (i.e., payable on demand of the payee or some other possessor called a "holder") or a *time* note (payable at a definite time after it is issued). A note may or may not bear interest, depending on the agreement of the parties. The principal and any interest may be payable in installments (e.g., a specified amount per month), or principal and interest may be due all at once in a single payment. Figure 28.1 shows a simple form of a "single payment" time note.

Certificates of Deposit. A *certificate of deposit* (CD) is an acknowledgment by a *bank* of receipt of money with an engagement (promise) by the bank to repay it, plus interest. The bank (broadly defined to include savings and loan associations and other business organizations legally empowered to engage in the banking business) is the maker. The payee, ordinarily an individual or a business firm, deposits money with the maker and receives the CD which, because of the interest, may be attractive as an investment. There are two classes of CDs: *demand certificates* (payable on demand of the payee or another holder) and *time certificates* (often referred to as TCDs because they are payable at a definite time after they are issued). Figure 28.2 illustrates a TCD.

Drafts. Drafts involve three parties. A *draft* is an order (command) by one person (the *drawer*) given to another person (the *drawee*) to pay a sum of money to a third person (the *payee*). The drawee can be any person or organization willing or obliged to obey the order. Suppose Tony's Pizza Parlor owes Anna $500 for a new oven she delivered, and Anna owes Cora $500. When Cora demands payment, Anna might not have the cash, but if Cora agrees, Anna might "draw" a $500 draft on (write out a draft directed to) Tony's Pizza Parlor with Cora as

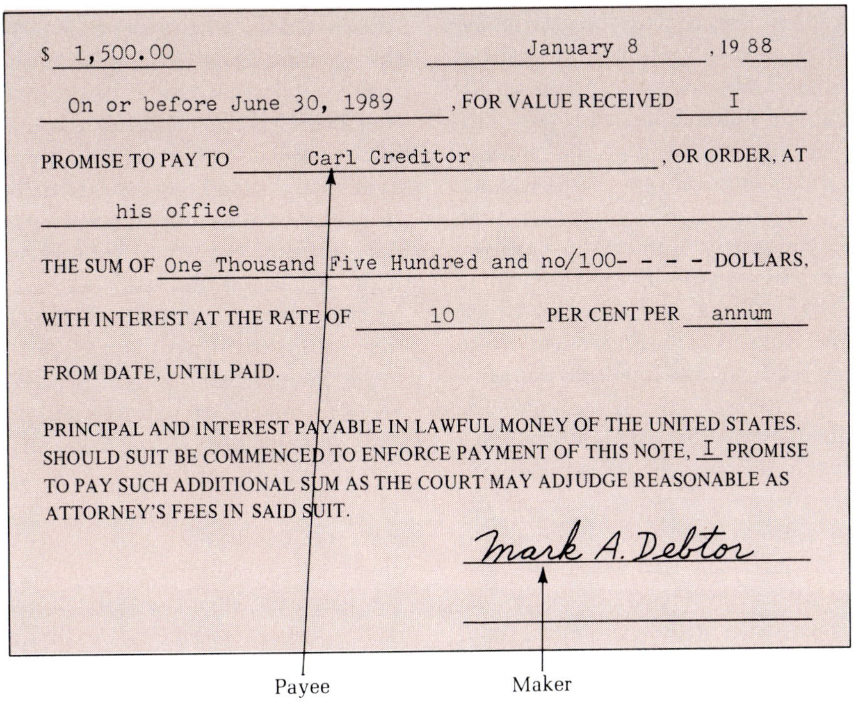

$ 1,500.00 January 8 , 19 88

On or before June 30, 1989 , FOR VALUE RECEIVED I

PROMISE TO PAY TO Carl Creditor , OR ORDER, AT

his office

THE SUM OF One Thousand Five Hundred and no/100- - - - DOLLARS,

WITH INTEREST AT THE RATE OF 10 PER CENT PER annum

FROM DATE, UNTIL PAID.

PRINCIPAL AND INTEREST PAYABLE IN LAWFUL MONEY OF THE UNITED STATES. SHOULD SUIT BE COMMENCED TO ENFORCE PAYMENT OF THIS NOTE, I PROMISE TO PAY SUCH ADDITIONAL SUM AS THE COURT MAY ADJUDGE REASONABLE AS ATTORNEY'S FEES IN SAID SUIT.

Mark A. Debtor

Payee Maker

Figure 28.1 Promissory note

payee. Thus, Anna (the drawer) orders Tony's Pizza (the drawee) to pay $500 to Cora (the payee). Cora may now present the draft to Tony's Pizza for payment, and if Tony's Pizza "honors" (pays) it, two debts are settled at one time. A draft may be made out to the payee in a variety of ways—e.g., to the order of "bearer," some designated third person such as Cora, the Internal Revenue Service, First Church, or even the drawer herself. An interest-bearing draft is illustrated in Figure 28.3.

Figure 28.2 Time certificate of deposit (by permission of Security Pacific National Bank)

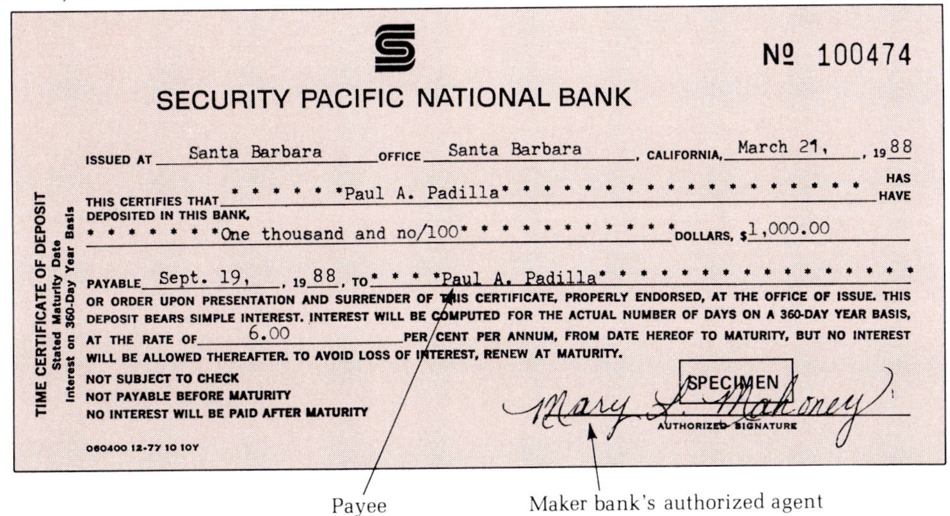

No 100474

SECURITY PACIFIC NATIONAL BANK

ISSUED AT Santa Barbara OFFICE Santa Barbara , CALIFORNIA, March 21, , 19 88

THIS CERTIFIES THAT * * * * * *Paul A. Padilla* * * * * * * * * * * * * * * * * * * HAS/HAVE DEPOSITED IN THIS BANK,

* * * * * * *One thousand and no/100* * * * * * * * * * *DOLLARS, $1,000.00

PAYABLE Sept. 19, , 19 88 , TO * * * *Paul A. Padilla* * * * * * * * * * * * * * * * * OR ORDER UPON PRESENTATION AND SURRENDER OF THIS CERTIFICATE, PROPERLY ENDORSED, AT THE OFFICE OF ISSUE. THIS DEPOSIT BEARS SIMPLE INTEREST. INTEREST WILL BE COMPUTED FOR THE ACTUAL NUMBER OF DAYS ON A 360-DAY YEAR BASIS, AT THE RATE OF 6.00 PER CENT PER ANNUM, FROM DATE HEREOF TO MATURITY, BUT NO INTEREST WILL BE ALLOWED THEREAFTER. TO AVOID LOSS OF INTEREST, RENEW AT MATURITY.

NOT SUBJECT TO CHECK
NOT PAYABLE BEFORE MATURITY
NO INTEREST WILL BE PAID AFTER MATURITY

SPECIMEN

Mary L. Mahoney
AUTHORIZED SIGNATURE

TIME CERTIFICATE OF DEPOSIT
Stated Maturity Date
Interest on 360-Day Year Basis

080400 12-77 10 10Y

Drafts are either demand drafts or time drafts. A *demand draft* is payable literally on demand of the payee or other holder any time after issue. Although demand drafts often begin with the words "on demand pay" or "at sight pay," the language "pay to . . ." is sufficient to indicate a demand draft. A *time draft* is one that is payable at a specified time after issue. The time might be indicated merely by writing the date of issue on the draft and then filling in another blank with the future date on which payment is to be made, as in the draft illustrated in Figure 28.3. Or the time draft might say, instead, "sixty days after date pay." A draft reading "sixty days after sight [by the drawee] pay" is a time draft, but it requires the "acceptance" of the drawee to fix the maturity date of the instrument. *Acceptance* is the drawee's written engagement (promise) to pay the draft when it falls due. Suppose Anna's draft drawn on Tony's Pizza Parlor reads, "Sixty days after sight pay to the order of Cora Creditor $500." Cora then presents the draft to Tony's Pizza for acceptance. Tony, the owner of Tony's Pizza, will write "accepted" across the face of the draft and will add the date and his signature. These acts constitute Tony's acceptance. Sixty days after acceptance, Cora is entitled to payment from Tony's Pizza.

From the time a draft is drawn, the drawee is customarily referred to as a "party" to the draft (a person with contractual liability for the face amount of the draft). However, a drawee is not truly a party unless and until he or she *accepts* the draft—i.e., by signature agrees to pay it. Until then the drawee has no obligation "under the instrument" (i.e., is not bound by the terms of the draft)[3-401]. A drawee who accepts a draft is called the "acceptor" and at that time becomes personally liable to the payee (or to some other holder) for payment of the face amount. So, when Anna issued the draft to Cora, Anna was the only signer and therefore the only person liable to Cora for the face amount in the event that Tony's Pizza refused to accept the draft. Then, when Tony's Pizza accepted the draft, Tony's Pizza also became liable to Cora as a signer (i.e., as a true party to the draft), and Cora has two sources of payment instead of one. If Cora decides to sell the draft now instead of waiting 60 days to collect it herself, the acceptor's signature gives the draft a greater value because, having two sources of payment, the purchaser faces a reduced risk of noncollection. The nature of a drawer's and an acceptor's liability is discussed further in Chapter 31.

Checks. A *check* is a draft drawn on a *bank* and payable on *demand* [3-104(2)(b)]. The drawer is a customer who has an account at a drawee bank. The payee may be any individual, firm, or organization named on the face of the check whom the drawer wishes to receive payment. Typically, checks are made out on printed forms having blank spaces for the date of the check, the payee's name, the amount to be paid, and the drawer's signature, as

Figure 28.3 Draft

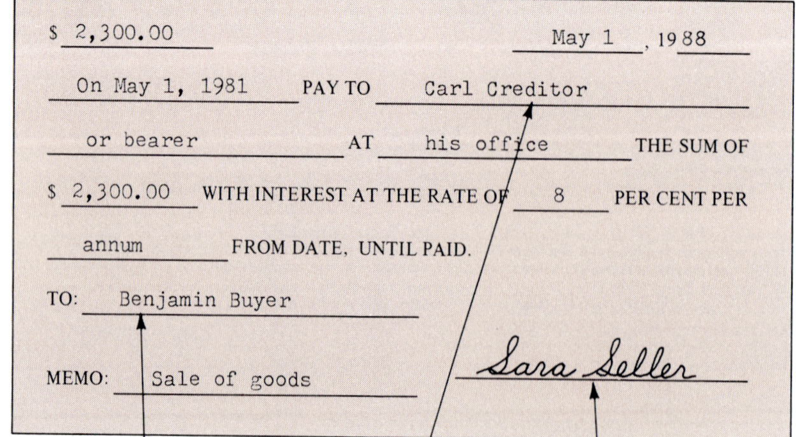
$ 2,300.00 May 1, 1988

On May 1, 1981 PAY TO Carl Creditor

or bearer AT his office THE SUM OF

$ 2,300.00 WITH INTEREST AT THE RATE OF 8 PER CENT PER

annum FROM DATE, UNTIL PAID.

TO: Benjamin Buyer

MEMO: Sale of goods

Sara Seller

in Figure 28.4. Checks are especially useful because they enable the drawer to make distributions from a single fund (the drawer's bank account) for paying debts and making gifts and purchases. And, because the checks issued by the drawer eventually "clear" the bank collection process and are returned to the drawer's bank and then to the drawer, the drawer has a record of expenditures.

Although frequently issued as gifts, checks usually are issued as part of an "underlying" contract—e.g., as payment for goods or services. Thus, there usually are two contracts: the check and the underlying transaction. Suppose Ann buys a typewriter from Typeshop and issues a check in payment. The check is one kind of "formal" contract discussed in Chapter 8, and Ann, as a signer, is liable for the face amount to the payee (Typeshop) or to some other holder such as a business firm where Typeshop might have cashed Ann's check. Ann is also a party to the underlying "informal" contract (discussed in Chapter 8) between herself and Typeshop for the sale of the typewriter. Ann will be liable in damages to Typeshop if she breaches the underlying contract by, for example, stopping payment of the check without good reason.

Ordinarily, a check operates as only a conditional (not yet final) payment of the underlying obligation. The check does not become final payment until honored (paid) by the bank on which it was drawn. Until the check is honored, its issuer remains liable on the underlying transaction. However, the seller's taking a check as conditional payment *postpones* the seller's right to sue on the underlying obligation [3-802(1)(b)]. If the drawee bank dishonors the check, as where the drawer has insufficient funds or orders the bank to stop payment, the right of the seller to sue on the underlying obligation is "revived." Thus, where Ann pays by check and the drawee bank dishonors it, Ann is in breach of the underlying contract, and Typeshop now may sue Ann for damages.

When a bank draws a check on itself, the instrument is called a "cashier's check." When a bank draws a check on another bank in which the first bank has money on deposit, the check is referred to as a "bank draft."

A *traveler's check* is a three-party instrument purchased from a bank or other firm and carried instead of cash by travelers. The traveler is the drawer, and for purposes of identification he or she must sign the traveler's check twice—once when the seller issues it and a second time when the traveler cashes it. The bank or other issuing firm is the drawee. When the drawee is a nonbanking firm such as American Express, the so-called traveler's "check" is not a check at all, but is a draft subject to the Code rules relating to drafts.

Negotiable Character of Commercial Paper

Understanding the negotiable character of commercial paper requires a preliminary look at some basic commercial paper concepts and practices, with a

Figure 28.4 Check (by permission of Security Pacific National Bank)

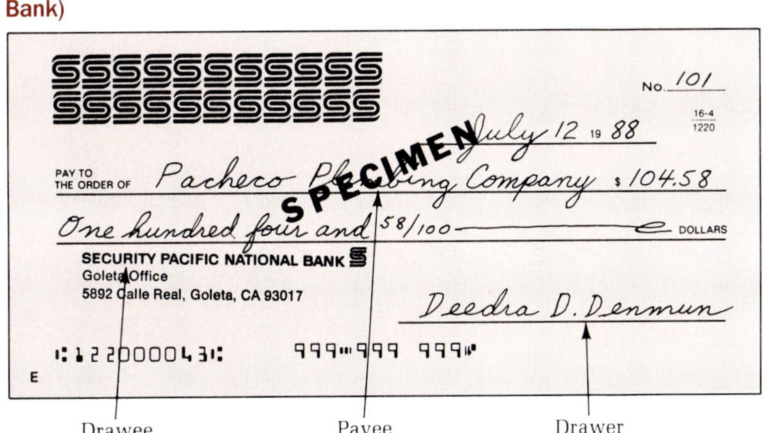

more detailed examination being reserved for later parts of this chapter and for subsequent chapters. Three expressions are of special significance in the law of commercial paper: (1) "negotiable form," (2) "holder in due course," and (3) "personal and real defenses."

Meaning of Negotiable Form. To say that an instrument (a note or draft) is "negotiable" or "negotiable in form" means simply that the writer of the instrument has used the language required by law for creating a negotiable instrument. For example, certain "magic words," called "language of negotiability," are required for an instrument to be a negotiable one. Precisely what those words are and why they must be used are discussed later in this chapter. It is sufficient, for now, to know that a note or draft is either negotiable or nonnegotiable, depending on its *wording;* and that in certain situations, soon to be illustrated, a negotiable instrument can confer *greater rights* on its owner than a nonnegotiable instrument can. Why a negotiable instrument confers greater rights requires a brief look at the meaning of "holder in due course" and "personal and real defenses."

Meaning of Holder in Due Course. Checks circulate from hand to hand as a substitute for money. Often, a check comes into the hands of a stranger to the drawer, as where the payee of a payroll check cashes it at a supermarket or liquor store. Similarly, *notes* may circulate among strangers. Notes (which usually bind their makers to a *future* payment) often are sold by their payees for *immediate* cash, as where you buy a car on credit and the dealer discounts (sells) your note to a buyer of commercial paper. Thus, commercial paper—issued by a maker or drawer to a payee—frequently comes into the hands of third persons who have no knowledge of the transaction between the original parties to the instrument. But sometimes the payee failed in the underlying transaction to perform a promised service, delivered defective goods, or in some other way gave the maker or drawer a *defense* to (a legal reason for not making) payment. If proven in court, the defense will be good against the payee. But what are the rights of the innocent third person who cashed the check or bought the note? Here, holder-in-due-course status becomes important.

Negotiable instruments are useful in business primarily because innocent third persons, *if they qualify as holders in due course,* ordinarily may collect from the maker or drawer (or from others to be discussed in later chapters) the amount specified in the instrument *even though* the drawer or maker has a valid reason not to pay the payee. The third person qualifies as a holder in due course if the instrument is in *negotiable form,* if the payee *properly transferred ("negotiated")* the negotiable instrument (as discussed in Chapter 29), and if the third person receiving it has the *personal characteristics* required by law for holder-in-due-course status. Basically, the third person is a holder in due course if he or she took the negotiable instrument *for value, in good faith,* and *without notice of defenses.* These and other personal characteristics required for holder-in-due-course status are discussed in Chapter 30. However, whether a holder in due course takes a negotiable instrument free from a defense depends, also, on the *kind* of defense it is: "personal" or "real." A holder in due course takes a negotiable instrument *free from personal* defenses but *subject to real* defenses.

Meaning of Personal and Real Defenses. A personal defense is one involving wrongdoing or some other circumstance that the law says must remain a private matter between the immediate parties to a negotiable instrument (e.g., between the drawer of a check and the payee) instead of becoming a source of loss to a (third-person) holder in due course. The payee's delivering defective goods is a personal defense. In contrast, a *real* defense involves wrongdoing or some other circumstance of so serious a nature that the (real) defense is good against even a holder in due course. The bankruptcy of the maker or the drawer is a real defense. Personal and real defenses are discussed further in Chapter 29.

Significance of It All: Cashing a Check; Buying a Note. Commercial paper is useful to the business community because holders in due course (and most of their transferees) can purchase it in relative safety, confident that it will usually be collectable despite disputes between the parties to the underlying transaction. Two examples follow:

1 John cashes his negotiable payroll check at a supermarket. Then Sam, the owner of the su-

permarket, presents John's check to the employer's bank for payment, only to learn that the employer has stopped payment of the check because John lied about the number of hours he worked during the week covered by the check. Sam immediately takes the dishonored check to the drawer (John's employer) for payment. The employer's *personal* defense to payment of the check (John's fraud) would be good against *John*, the payee, if John had kept the check and had himself sought payment from the employer after the bank dishonored the check. *Sam*, however, to whom John negotiated the check, is a holder in due course because he (Sam) paid for the check (by cashing it) and knew nothing of John's fraud when doing so. Therefore, Sam took the check free from the employer's personal defense. Accordingly, the employer must pay Sam the amount of the check and seek from John, the defrauding payee, any reimbursement (repayment) that might be due. The *legal* significance to Sam of holder-in-due-course status is that Sam takes the check free from the employer-drawer's personal defenses. One *practical* significance of Sam's holder-in-due-course status is that Sam, being free from personal defenses, will be more willing to cash checks for strangers than he would be if he had to absorb all losses.

2 You buy a car from Joe for use in your business. Joe expressly warrants that the car is in perfect running condition. Lacking cash, you pay for the car with your single-payment negotiable promissory note for $4,000 plus 10 percent annual interest. The note is due 1 year from now. You will have to pay, in principal and interest, a total of $4,400. Joe, the payee, could hold the note for a year and collect the $4,400 from you; but he needs cash now, so he immediately discounts (sells) the note to Brenda, a buyer of commercial paper, for $4,000. Thus, Joe has the $4,000 he needs now, and Brenda has a chance to make a profit by collecting the $4,400 in principal and interest from you when the note comes due.

A few days after these transactions, fire destroys your car because of a serious defect in its electrical system. The presence of the defect is a breach of Joe's warranty. You try to locate Joe but learn that he has left town permanently for parts unknown. At the end of the year, Brenda presents the note to you for payment. You refuse to pay because Joe's breach of warranty caused you the loss of the car. Unfortunately for you, the breach of warranty is a personal defense. Because Brenda became a holder in due course when she bought your note, she took it free from your personal defenses and is entitled to payment. You, the maker of the negotiable note, will have to absorb the loss if you cannot find Joe and make him pay.

As the preceding examples illustrate, a *negotiable* instrument can confer upon a holder in due course *more* than the usual contract rights, since unlike a transferee (assignee) of an ordinary contract, a holder in due course of a negotiable instrument is free from personal defenses when attempting to collect payment. If an instrument is *not* negotiable in form, its purchaser is merely an *assignee* (as opposed to a holder in due course) and therefore takes the instrument subject to *all* defenses, personal *and* real. (The law of assignments is discussed in Chapter 14.) Even a person who acquires a *negotiable* instrument from the payee might be only an assignee—e.g., where the negotiable instrument was not transferred properly (i.e., was not "negotiated" as described in Chapter 29), or where the acquiring person does not qualify as a holder in due course.

A major practical significance of negotiability in the discounting of notes is that a holder in due course, being free from personal defenses of the maker, will tend to pay more for the note than if the purchaser were merely an assignee. Brenda in the previous example 2 probably would have paid Joe much less for your note if it had not been in negotiable form, because as an assignee she would be subject to *all* of your defenses, personal as well as real, and therefore would face a much greater risk of noncollection.

Figure 28.5 shows a typical sequence of events in which (1) the maker and the payee enter into an underlying contract, (2) the payee sells the negotiable note to a holder in due course (HDC), and (3) HDC presents the note to the maker for payment. If the maker has a personal defense, HDC is nevertheless entitled to payment from the maker. If the maker has a real defense, HDC is not entitled to payment from the maker; however, as noted in Chapters 31 and 32, HDC may be able to go back to the payee for payment.

Some people wrongly believe that a *non*negotiable instrument may not be transferred from one

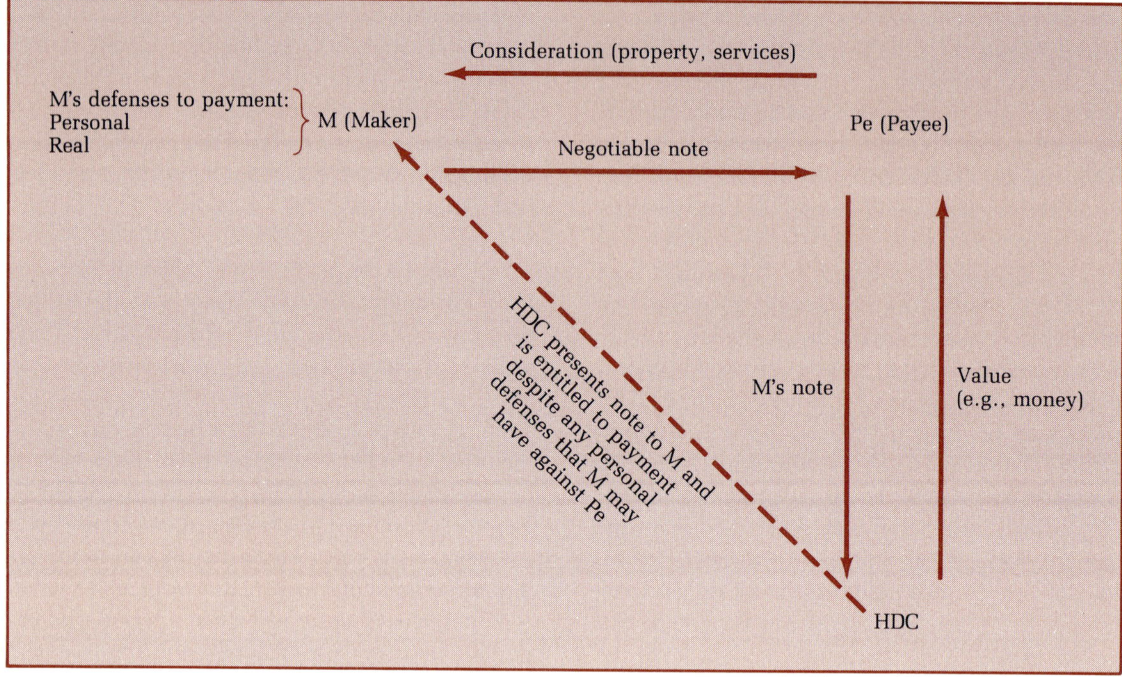

Figure 28.5 Legal significance of negotiability

person to another. However, the fact that an instrument is *negotiable* has relatively little to do with its *transferability*. True, a negotiable instrument is easy to transfer because, as the next chapter reveals, the mechanics of a "negotiation" (the special kind of transfer applicable to a negotiable instrument) are simple. But under the law of assignments discussed in Chapter 14, many ordinary contract rights are freely assignable (transferable), especially the right to a money payment. The main difference between a negotiable document and a nonnegotiable document lies in the *number of defenses* a good faith purchaser must face when seeking payment. A holder in due course of a negotiable instrument faces fewer defenses to payment than an assignee of a nonnegotiable instrument faces.

Dual Nature of Commercial Paper

Commercial paper is, simultaneously, a contract and a type of property.

Commercial paper is a contract because Article 3 imposes on *any signer* an "engagement" (promise) to pay the face amount, regardless of whether the signer knew that he or she was making such a promise. People who indorse (sign) their payroll checks when cashing them probably do not realize that, by indorsing, they have *contracted* to pay the face amount if the drawer (employer) does not; but indeed they *have* so contracted—because Article 3 says so [3-413; 3-414].

As we have seen, the negotiable instruments that constitute commercial paper are not ordinary contracts. They are "formal" contracts that by law have been given special qualities so that they can serve better as a *substitute for money* (the main use of a check) and as a *means of extending credit* (the main use of a note). Negotiable instruments are "formal" because they conform to a particular form or style of language required by the law. One of the special qualities resulting from their formal character is that the purchaser of a negotiable instrument can be a holder in due course, free from personal defenses of, for example, the maker or the drawer. The purchaser of a nonnegotiable instrument (an ordinary, "simple," or "informal" contract) can *never* be a holder in due course but is always a mere assignee, subject to all defenses.

Commercial paper is also a type of property that can be bought and sold. Recall from Chapter 25 that chattel paper, which consists of a promissory note and a security agreement, can itself be sold or pledged so that the business generating it can raise money before the note comes due. Also, many corporations issue commercial paper, in the form of promissory notes, for short-term financing. A person who buys such paper from the corporation may, in turn, sell it like any other property. Since commercial paper is property, it is subject to some rules of property law. For example, delivery of a negotiable instrument is a requirement for conveying ownership of it to a donee (a recipient of a gift) or to a buyer. And, as in the sale of goods, the law imposes warranties that may be available to a purchaser if the paper turns out to be defective in some respect. Warranties as they relate to commercial paper are discussed in Chapter 31.

Some Business Uses of Commercial Paper

Businesspeople use commercial paper in numerous ways. For example, a person or a firm usually buys a CD as an investment, to collect the interest. While holding the CD, however, the person or firm might pledge it as collateral for a loan (Chapter 25 discusses the pledge) or might simply sell it to raise immediate cash for some personal or business purpose. The bank that issues a CD does so, of course, to attract funds to lend to its customers.

Often, the creation of commercial paper is only one step in a complex transaction involving many other documents. The following paragraphs describe some common business uses of notes and drafts and the role of negotiable instruments in complicated transactions.

Uses of Notes. Promissory notes are used mainly as evidence of indebtedness in loan transactions and in credit sales of property or services. Typically, a borrower signs a note that bears interest on the principal amount. The principal and interest may be due in one lump sum at a fixed future time (or on demand), or principal and interest may be payable in installments, often equal monthly installments. Sometimes the maker agrees to pay the interest in installments and to make a final "balloon" (large) payment consisting of not only the final installment of interest but also repayment of the principal. Frequently, lenders are willing to extend unsecured credit, solely on the basis of the borrower's personal note. Often, however, they will insist that some third person co-sign the note as *surety* (discussed in Chapter 24), or that the note be secured by real estate or other property that the lender may sell if the borrower fails to repay the loan. (Secured transactions are discussed in Chapters 24 and 25.)

Notes frequently are used in financing the sale of goods on a secured basis. As indicated in Chapter 25, the *conditional sale contract* and the *chattel mortgage* are commonly used for this purpose. They consist essentially of a promissory note signed by the buyer as maker, together with a security agreement giving the seller the right to repossess the goods upon the buyer's default. Usually the notes are interest-bearing installment notes.

Uses of Drafts. Businesses use drafts most often in financing the sale of goods. Drafts are especially useful for this purpose when buyer and seller are strangers, are located some distance from each other, and make use of a reliable intermediary to handle the transaction. Suppose that Sally Seller is in Boston, Bob Buyer is in San Francisco, and Seller has agreed to extend 60 days' credit to Buyer for the purchase of a machine to be used in Buyer's business. This transaction will require the use of a 60-day time draft. When Seller ships the machine, she obtains from the carrier a bill of lading. She then draws a time draft reading, "To: Bob Buyer. Sixty days after sight pay to the order of Sally Seller $8,200." This amount covers the price of the machine plus shipping costs. Seller attaches the bill of lading, an invoice (itemized account of the goods), a security agreement, and a financing statement to the draft and takes it to her bank in Boston. The Boston bank forwards the draft with the attached documents to its correspondent bank in San Francisco. The San Francisco bank notifies Bob Buyer that the draft has arrived. He accepts the draft and signs the security agreement and the financing statement. The bank then delivers the bill of lading to Buyer so he can claim the machine when it arrives. The bank arranges to have the financing statement filed and, depending on Sally Seller's instructions, either holds the time draft for collection at the end of the 60 days, sells the draft to a buyer of commercial paper, or sends it to Sally. Time drafts such as the one drawn by Seller on the purchaser of goods (here, Bob Buyer) and accepted by the purchaser are called "trade acceptances," and they can be sold or pledged as collateral for a loan.

Negotiable Form

No purchaser of a note or a draft can be a holder in due course unless the instrument is in negotiable form. If the instrument lacks negotiable form, even an innocent purchaser will be merely an assignee, subject to all defenses of the maker or drawer.

The UCC sets forth eight requirements that must be met for a note or draft to be in negotiable form. The instrument must:

1 be in *writing,*
2 be *signed by the maker or drawer,*
3 contain a *promise or order* to pay that is
4 *unconditional* in character,
5 be *payable in money,*
6 be made out for a *sum certain,*
7 be *payable* either *on demand* or *at a definite time* after its issue, *and*
8 be *payable to the order of the payee* or *to bearer* [3-104].

If any one of these eight requirements is not met, the instrument is not in negotiable form, and all transferees are assignees only.

Some types of commercial paper, such as checks, are extremely simple and easy to use. Other types, such as notes, can be quite complicated and lengthy because of the many protective clauses that a lender or seller will demand as a condition to making the loan or selling on credit. Sometimes the added language destroys negotiability, and sometimes even a preprinted check form is altered in such a way as to destroy negotiability. Thus we have two questions: (1) What minimum language is required for the creation of negotiable form? (2) Once negotiable form is created, what clauses or language may be added to the instrument without destroying negotiability?

Minimum Language Required for Negotiable Form

The minimum language required for an instrument to be negotiable varies somewhat according to whether the instrument is a demand or a time instrument; however, some wording is common to all commercial paper:

Unconditional Promise or Order to Pay. To be negotiable, an instrument must contain language that clearly reveals the issuer's intention to be bound personally to make payment or to have a drawee pay. So, if the instrument is a note, it must contain the maker's *promise* to pay (e.g., "I promise to pay"; "I undertake to pay"). If the instrument is a draft, it must contain the drawer's *order* (command or instruction) to the drawee that the *drawee* is to pay (e.g., "Pay..."; "Pay to..."). A mere acknowledgment of debt ("IOU $50") is not a promise because there is no expression of the debtor's intention to pay the amount owed. The *intention to pay* must be *expressed.* Likewise, language such as "I wish you would pay" is not an order to pay but is merely an authorization or a request.

The promise or order must be clear and definite; but for the instrument to be negotiable, and thus to circulate most freely or to bring the highest possible price, the promise or order must also be *unconditional* (without reservations; absolute). John's language, "I promise to pay Eva or order $100 *if* I receive from her one used typewriter by 5:00 P.M. Friday" is conditional (and the note in which the language appears is nonnegotiable) because John has made his obligation to pay $100 depend on Eva's delivering the typewriter. If Eva puts the note into circulation, every potential purchaser will have to investigate the underlying transaction to determine whether Eva delivered the typewriter. This burden of investigation is inconsistent with a major aim of commercial paper law: to remove as many doubts as possible about the collectability of drafts and notes. The requirement that the promise or order be unconditional is discussed further in the part of this chapter entitled "Language That Destroys Negotiability."

Order or Bearer Language ("language of negotiability"). To be negotiable, an instrument must contain language expressing the issuer's intention (actual or presumed) that the instrument circulate freely. This language of negotiability can be either *order* language or *bearer* language, depending on the wishes of the parties. By using *order* language (e.g., "Pay *to the order of* Juan Jimenez" in a draft; "I promise to pay *to the order of* Juan Jimenez" in a note), the drawer or maker expresses a willingness for the payee to specify who will have the right to collect payment. By using *bearer* language (e.g., "Pay *bearer*" in a draft; "I promise to pay *bearer*" in a note), the drawer or maker expresses a willingness to pay *anyone* who is *in possession of* the instrument. The presence of bearer or order language assures any transferee (person who receives the instrument from the payee or other holder) that the issuer is willing to pay even a stranger.

In contrast, language such as "Pay Juan Jimenez" *lacks* the required order or bearer language (the instruction does not include the words "to the order of" or the word "bearer") and can cast doubt on whether the instrument was intended to circulate among strangers. The absence of order or bearer language results in a *non*negotiable instrument. While a nonnegotiable instrument is collectable under the law of assignments (if there are no real or personal defenses), not only the payee but also every transferee is subject to *any* defense, including any *personal* defense, that the maker or drawer has. So, if a drawer strikes out the words "to the order of" on a preprinted check form, the drawer has created a nonnegotiable check. In doing so, the drawer has preserved all personal defenses, but also has increased a purchaser's risk of noncollection and thus may have reduced the willingness of strangers to cash the check or to pay the full face amount for it.

Usually order or bearer language appears in a negotiable instrument because the issuer has simply filled out a preprinted form (such as a blank check) containing the language. Probably, most people neither know what language of negotiability is nor understand its significance. Nevertheless, language of negotiability is required by law for an instrument to be negotiable and, consequently, for a holder in due course to have the special benefit of being entitled to payment despite the personal defenses of the maker or drawer (or of other persons discussed in subsequent chapters).

Wording Indicating That the Instrument Is for a "Sum Certain" Payable in Money. An instrument is *payable in money* if it gives the payee the right to have payment in the currency of any domestic or foreign government: dollars, marks, rubles, pesos, etc. So, an instrument payable in wheat or corn cannot be negotiable. However, if the payee is given the option of demanding wheat *or* money, the instrument is payable in money. If the *drawer* or *maker* has the option of providing wheat or money, the instrument is *not* payable in money. The payment-in-money requirement enables a purchaser of the instrument to determine easily how much to pay for it, since calculations are made in some commonly accepted medium of exchange.

The requirement of a *sum certain* serves a similar purpose. If the sum is certain, a purchaser can determine quickly how much the maker or drawer owes, and therefore how much the purchaser should pay for the instrument. The sum is certain if the *purchaser* (or the payee) can, *at the time set for payment,* determine *from the instrument itself without reference to any outside source* the amount then payable. Suppose Sue signs a note reading, "I promise to pay the bearer of this note, on demand, $500 plus 10 percent annual interest," and delivers the note to Joe, who discounts it to Ann. Since Sue cannot predict when Ann will demand payment, Sue has no way of knowing how much interest she will owe Ann. Despite this, the sum is certain because *Ann,* the purchaser, will be able to compute exactly how much Sue, the maker, owes at the moment that Ann decides to demand payment. A provision in a note imposing a charge for late payment does not make the sum uncertain. Neither does a provision requiring the maker to pay reasonable attorney's fees for a collection suit upon the maker's default [3-106].

Signature of Maker or Drawer. The signature of the maker or drawer is required for the obvious reason that payees and other holders must be able to prove whose legal commitment the instrument represents. A signature is any symbol used or adopted by a party (e.g., a maker or drawer) with the present intention to authenticate the writing [1-201(39)]. So, a signature can be handwritten or typed, or it can be made by an agent for the agent's principal (and adopted by the principal), or it can consist of a trade name, an assumed name, a mark such as "X," or even a thumbprint.

The signature of a drawer or maker may appear in the body of the instrument. However, it normally appears at the end of the document. It is possible for the signature of the drawer or maker to appear on the reverse side of the instrument, but since such a placement is usually reserved for indorsements, it should be avoided for makers' and drawers' signatures because doubts could arise about who issued the instrument.

Language Making the Instrument Payable on Demand or at a Definite Time [3-109]. To be negotiable, an instrument must be payable on demand or at a definite time so that a purchaser can determine with ease and certainty two things: (1) when the purchaser will have a right to payment, and (2) how much the drawer or maker will owe if the instrument bears interest. However, whether a *date* is required for negotiability depends on the other (nondate) language of the instrument, since definiteness can be provided in a variety of ways. Some *time* instruments do need a date for negotiability, as where the instrument reads, "60 days after *date* pay. . . ." No date is required, though, for a time instrument reading "60 days after *sight* pay" or "I promise to pay 60 days after *demand*." In these instances, payment is at a definite time because the payee or another holder knows from the wording exactly when he or she will be entitled to payment. *Demand* instruments, including checks, need no date to be considered payable at a definite time. The payee or other holder of a demand instrument knows when she or he will demand payment and thus can compute with precision how much the drawer or maker will owe if the instrument bears interest. The blank for the date in a check form is used by the drawer to record the date that the drawer *issued* the check; the blank is *not* used to set a date for payment, since the payee or other holder can demand payment of the check for a substantial time after the date of issue. Usually, where no date for payment is stated, the instrument is a demand instrument, as where it reads, "I promise to pay . . . $100" [3-108].

Where payment is linked to an event that is uncertain as to time of occurrence, the instrument is not negotiable, and it does not become negotiable even though the event has occurred [3-109]. For example, a note reading "payable 30 days after the death of my Uncle Abner" is nonnegotiable because the time of Uncle Abner's death is uncertain.

In Case 28.1 a document lacks two of the qualities necessary for negotiable form.

CASE 28.1 Branch Banking & Trust Co. v. Creasy · 269 S.E.2d 117 (N.C. 1980)

FACTS Thomas Creasy, an attorney, was separated from his wife Margaret; Miller, one of Creasy's law partners, was representing her in the negotiation of a marital settlement. Thomas owed Branch Banking and Trust Co. (Bank) $35,000. Just before the note came due, Bank agreed to renew it on condition that Margaret sign an agreement guaranteeing Thomas's debts, present or future. At Thomas Creasy's request, Miller took Bank's guaranty form to Margaret and asked her to sign it. She did so reluctantly. Miller then returned to his law office and placed the guaranty agreement in the Creasy file. Thomas defaulted on a later note for $35,000, and Bank, which somehow had come into possession of Margaret's guaranty agreement, sued Margaret for the amount due. Margaret denied liability on the ground that the guaranty agreement had never been delivered to Bank, but only to her attorney, Miller. The trial court granted Bank's motion for summary judgment. The court of appeals reversed, holding that summary judgment in favor of Bank should not have been granted. Bank appealed.

OPINION BRITT, J. . . . The Court of Appeals held that the materials which were before the trial court were insufficient to establish as a matter of law that [Bank] was a holder in due course of the [guaranty] agreement and was entitled to take it free of the defense of nondelivery. . . .

The Court of Appeals was in error in treating this document as a negotiable instrument. To be a negotiable instrument, a writing must be signed by the maker or drawer, must contain an unconditional promise to pay a sum certain in money, . . . must be payable on demand or at a definite time, and must be payable to order or bearer. The "continuing guaranty" which was signed by defendant does not meet these requirements.

First, the document which was signed by defendant does not have the attribute of certainty [of sum]; it provides that: "The aggregate amount of principal of all indebted-

CASE 28.1 Continued

ness, obligations and liabilities at any one time outstanding for which the undersigned shall be liable shall not exceed the sum of $35,000." For the requirement of a sum certain to be met, it is necessary that at the time of payment the holder is able to determine the amount which is then payable from the instrument itself, with any necessary computation, without any reference to an outside source.... It is necessary for a negotiable instrument to bear a definite sum so that subsequent holders may take and transfer the instrument without having to plumb the intricacies of the instrument's background. The document in question calls for a ceiling on the amount of defendant's liability. It does not specify the amount of the liability that is to be paid. That data may be obtained only after resorting to sources of information which are external to the agreement itself. Such an absence is enough by itself to foreclose any finding that the paper... is negotiable.

The document upon which plaintiff relies is inadequate as a negotiable instrument in one other respect: At no place in the agreement is there any provision that it is "payable to order or bearer." For an instrument to be... negotiable... it must be "payable to order or bearer."... [The paper lacks words of negotiability, stating instead] that... "the undersigned hereby absolutely and unconditionally guarantees to you and your successors... the due and punctual payment of any and all notes, drafts, debts, obligations, and liabilities...."

JUDGMENT For the reasons stated, the decision of the Court of Appeals is reversed.

[The court of appeals erroneously assumed that to enforce Margaret's agreement, Bank had to be a holder in due course of the agreement and had to take it free from Margaret Creasy's personal defense of nondelivery. In reversing the court of appeals, the Supreme Court pointed out that Margaret had signed a contract of suretyship in favor of Bank that, if properly delivered to Bank, imposed primary liability upon Margaret for payment of her husband's debt. So, holder-in-due-course status of the bank was simply irrelevant to the issue of Margaret's liability to the bank. However, even a contract of suretyship must be delivered to be effective, and here there was delivery. Miller was acting as Thomas Creasy's agent in procuring Margaret's signature. Consequently, whoever transmitted the document to Bank under Thomas's instructions had a right to do so.]

Language That Destroys Negotiability

A note reading "On demand I promise to pay the bearer the sum of 50 dollars" is negotiable in form if signed by the maker—because the note contains an unconditional promise to pay and language of negotiability (the word "bearer"), and it states a sum certain that is payable on demand. Often, however, an instrument such as the note just described contains additional language. The additional language might have no effect on the negotiability of the instrument, or the additional language might deprive the instrument of negotiability. For example, additional language that *renders the sum uncertain* or the *time of payment indefinite* deprives the instrument of negotiability and limits its purchaser to the rights of an assignee. Likewise, although they are perfectly legal, words that *condition* the promise of the drawer or maker destroy negotiability because they may create doubts in the mind of a purchaser about the collectability of the instrument or they may require a time-consuming investigation by the purchaser of the circumstances surrounding the transaction between the maker and the payee. Some common situations involving additional language are discussed in the following paragraphs.

Express Conditions. If the promise or order is expressly conditioned on the happening or nonhappening of an event, the instrument is nonnegotiable. For example, a promise to pay "if the typewriter is delivered before June 4" is expressly conditioned on the happening of an event, and an instrument containing such a promise is nonnegotiable. The promise or order must be to pay in all events, not just on the occurrence of one event.

Words Referring to Another Agreement. The terms of the promise or the order are to be determined solely by what is expressed on the instrument. If the instrument states that it is "subject to" or "governed by" another agreement, the promise or order is conditional. Suppose a note reads, "Subject to the terms and provisions of chattel mortgage #17 on file in the Amos County courthouse, I promise to pay bearer the sum of $1,000." This note is nonnegotiable because the holder must look to another agreement to learn the scope of the maker's promise. Placing such a burden on holders is contrary to the idea of free circulation and efficient collection. So, the mere fact of subjecting the promise or order to the contents of an outside document destroys negotiability, regardless of what the outside document says.

People, however, often make a notation on the face of a negotiable instrument for recordkeeping purposes. If a check, draft, or promissory note merely *refers* to an underlying transaction without making payment depend on the maker's or drawer's satisfaction with the underlying transaction, the reference does not make the order or promise conditional. Thus, a promise is not made conditional, and negotiability is not destroyed, by the statement, "This note is given for the purchase of goods as per contract of June 4, 19xx." Nor is a check rendered nonnegotiable by the notation, "For one red sofa."

Case 28.2 discusses whether assigning a nonnegotiable conditional sales contract together with a negotiable note destroys the negotiability of the note.

CASE 28.2 Northwestern Bank v. Neal · 248 S.E.2d 585 (S.C. 1978)

FACTS Neal (defendant) purchased a boiler from Thomas Equipment & Supply Co. on credit, signing a conditional sales contract and a promissory note for $8,714.72. Thomas immediately assigned the documents for value to Northwestern Bank (plaintiff). Alleging that the boiler was defective, Neal refused to pay the balance due on the note. Bank brought suit against Neal for the unpaid balance. From a judgment for Neal, Bank appealed.

OPINION NESS, J.... [T]he trial court ruled as a matter of law that the note and conditional sales contract merged and therefore were nonnegotiable, and [that] the bank was not a holder in due course.... The jury received the case on the [theory] that the appellant bank stood in the shoes of the original seller, Thomas, and was subject to any defenses that might be asserted against the seller. This was clear error. A suit by a holder in due course was improperly converted into a suit on a sales contract with the quality of the merchandise being an issue.... [Section 3-104 of the UCC] provides:

> (1) Any writing to be a negotiable instrument... must (a) be signed by the maker or drawer; and (b) contain an unconditional promise or order to pay a sum certain in money...; and (c) be payable on demand or at a definite time; and (d) be payable to order or to bearer.

The instant note clearly meets the above requisites of negotiability. The trial court held that... the note merged with the conditional sales contract and could not be negotiable because [the contract] required certain conditions. While it is true that the conditional sales contract may not have been a negotiable instrument because it failed to meet the [unconditional language] requirement of [§ 3-104(1) (b)], that does not render the promissory note nonnegotiable.

We reject the single contract theory embraced by the trial court. The Bank of Commerce case, relied on by the lower court, is inapplicable because it involved a conditional sales contract with an attached note; here, the contract and the note were two separate documents. [Under § 3-119(2)], "A separate agreement does not affect the negotiability of an instrument."

We conclude that the trial court erred in holding that the two documents integrated into one writing.... The official comment to [§ 3-119(2)] illustrates the trial court's error in adopting the single contract theory:

CASE 28.2 Continued

Subsection (2) rejects decisions which have carried the rule that contemporaneous writings must be read together to the length of holding that a clause in a mortgage affecting a note destroyed the negotiability of the note. The negotiability of an instrument is always to be determined by what appears on the face of the instrument alone, and if it is negotiable in itself a purchaser without notice of a separate writing is in no way affected by it. If the instrument itself states that it is subject to or governed by any other agreement, it is not negotiable under this Article; but if it merely refers to a separate agreement or states that it arises out of such an agreement, it is negotiable.

[Although] the appellant bank [possessed] a negotiable instrument, the question remains whether the bank is a holder in due course. . . . The bank paid value in good faith for the note on the day it was executed. It is undisputed that the assignment preceded any notice [to the bank about the quality of] the merchandise sold. Accordingly, the bank qualifies as a holder in due course.

The trial court erred in concluding that the note was nonnegotiable, and that the buyer's claims could be asserted against the bank. The very essence of a holder in due course is that he takes free of [the maker's personal] defenses against the seller.

JUDGMENT Reversed.

Words Limiting Source of Payment. For an instrument to be negotiable, the maker or drawer must subject his or her *general credit* (total wealth) to liability for payment, as opposed to limiting payment to some fraction of his or her assets. This requirement is consistent with the idea of giving a holder maximum assurance of collectability. A note reading "I promise to pay to the order of First Bank $3,000 out of this year's wheat crop" is nonnegotiable because the source of payment is a particular fund rather than the total assets of the maker. In contrast, an instrument reading "Pay $100 to the order of Paul Payee and charge the merchandise account" is negotiable. The instruction to charge the merchandise account is merely a bookkeeping instruction. The drawer has not expressed an intention to make the merchandise account the sole source of payment. If the drawer had said, "Pay *only out of* the merchandise account," the order would be conditional and the draft would be nonnegotiable.

There are two exceptions to the rule that for an instrument to be negotiable, payment cannot be limited to a particular fund. First, short-term instruments issued by a government, or by a governmental agency or unit, are *not* rendered nonnegotiable merely by the fact that payment is limited to a particular fund or to the proceeds of particular taxes or other sources of revenue [3-105]. Second, an instrument issued by a partnership or an unincorporated association limiting payment to "the entire assets" of the association is not rendered nonnegotiable, despite the fact that the limitation is intended to protect the partners or members from their usual personal liability. The general credit of the association is still available for payment.

In Case 28.3, the court decides whether payment of a note has been limited to a particular fund.

CASE 28.3 Barnett Bank v. Regency Highland Condominium Assoc. · 38 UCC Rep. 1289 (Fla. App. 1984)

FACTS The Regency Highlands Condominium Association ("Condo," defendant) borrowed money from the condominium developer, Regency Highlands Associates, to pay for improvements that benefited Condo. The promissory note that Condo gave for the loan stated,

CASE 28.3 Continued

"Payment to be made as Capital Contributions are received from each apartment closing." The developer assigned the note to Barnett Bank (plaintiff) as collateral for the bank's loan to the developer. When the developer defaulted on that loan, Bank sought payment of Condo's note. Condo refused to pay, alleging that the developer had obtained the note from Condo by "fraud and trickery." Bank brought suit to enforce the note. From a judgment for Condo, Bank appealed.

OPINION DOWNEY, J. . . . [T]he trial court found that . . . the collateral note was not negotiable because it was conditional on its face. . . . The issue . . . is whether the statement on the note that "Payment to be made as Capital Contributions are received from each apartment closing" [makes the promise to pay conditional]. If it [does], the note is nonnegotiable and subject to any defenses the maker may have against the payee. . . .

. . . [F]or an instrument to be negotiable it must contain an unconditional promise to pay a sum certain in money. . . . However, an otherwise unconditional promise to pay is not made conditional by the fact that the instrument "indicates a particular account to be debited or any other fund or source from which reimbursement is expected. . . ." §3-105(1)(f). The law favors negotiability and is reluctant to adopt rules that burden transferability of negotiable paper. . . . The terms of the instrument itself determine negotiability. . . . Furthermore, the Uniform Commercial Code comment to § 3-105 makes it clear that the conditional character of a promise to pay is not determined by matters [outside] the instrument, but by the instrument itself. [The comment] states: "So far as negotiability is affected, the conditional character of the promise or order is to be determined by what is expressed in the instrument itself. . . . In addition, § 3-105(2)(b) suggests that in order for a promise to be conditional, the restrictive language must be express because that section provides: "(2) A promise or order is not unconditional if the instrument . . . (b) states that it is to be paid only out of a particular fund or source. . . ." In our view, the legend appearing on the face of the . . . note does not make the promise to pay conditional, since the legend contains no words explicitly limiting payment to a particular fund or source. . . .

[The court then held that Bank was a holder in due course and so took the note free from Condo's defenses.]

JUDGMENT Reversed and remanded. . . .

Table 28.1 gives examples of language that does and does not destroy negotiability.

Language and Omissions Not Affecting Negotiability

If a promise or order is unconditional, the sum is certain, and the time of payment is definite, an instrument that has the minimum required language of negotiability may be negotiable despite the presence of certain additional language. Sometimes the added language *does* in fact affect time of payment or other qualities pertaining to negotiability, but it is so beneficial that the UCC permits it and provides that it does not destroy negotiability. Other added language may or may not destroy negotiability. Some notable illustrations follow.

Acceleration Clauses. Often the parties to a negotiable instrument provide for acceleration (early payment) of the instrument. The maker of a note might want to pay it early to save on interest charges. The note might therefore read, "I promise to pay $1,000 to First Bank or order, together with 12 percent annual interest, on or before May 1, 19xx." The "on or before" language is an acceleration clause favoring the maker. Because the *maker* may choose when to pay the note, the time of payment could be considered indefinite from the viewpoint of the holder. However, the acceleration

Table 28.1 Commercial Paper Language

Destroying Negotiability	Not Destroying Negotiability
Pay to the order of Typeshop $700 *if I receive from Typeshop one Magic X Typewriter before June 1, 19xx.*	Pay to the order of Typeshop $700. (*For one Magic X Typewriter.*)
This note is *subject to* the terms of contract 117, dated June 4, 19xx.	This note is given for the purchase of goods *as per* contract of June 4, 19xx.
Pay $500 to the order of Jones *only out of* the merchandise account.	Pay $500 to the order of Jones, *and charge* the merchandise account.

clause is so beneficial to the maker, and it causes the holder so little difficulty, that under the UCC its presence does not destroy negotiability [3-109].

The payee or other holder might also have the benefit of an acceleration clause, as where a holder is permitted to require early payment "if I deem myself insecure" (i.e., "if I come to doubt the ability of the maker or drawer to pay") or the instrument provides that it "shall become immediately due and payable upon any default in payment of interest or principal." The presence of such a clause does not affect negotiability. However, a holder who exercises an option to accelerate because of the holder's insecurity (fear of nonpayment) must have a good faith belief that the prospect of payment is impaired [1-208].

Confession-of-Judgment Clauses. Sometimes an instrument contains a clause that authorizes the holder to have an attorney "confess judgment" (enter a judgment in court) against the maker or drawer if the instrument is not paid when due, even though failure to pay may be justified. The judgment cuts off every defense that the maker may have, and it also cuts off the maker's right to appeal the judgment. Confession-of-judgment clauses are so harsh that in most states they are void. However, the presence of such a clause in a negotiable instrument does *not* destroy negotiability *if* the clause can be exercised only after the maker's default [3-112]. If the clause can be exercised at *any* time, its presence *does* destroy negotiability.

Other Language and Omissions. Like the clauses just discussed, the following terms (provisions) do not affect the negotiability of an instrument:

1 A statement that collateral has been given as security and that in case of default the collateral may be sold.

2 A promise to maintain or protect collateral or to give additional collateral. For example, a note may state that it is secured by a deposit of securities having a current market value of $4,800 and that on written demand from the holder, the maker agrees to deposit such additional collateral satisfactory to the holder as may be necessary to maintain the value of the collateral at $4,800. Normally, such a note would contain a provision that if the maker fails to provide the additional collateral, the holder may sell the collateral previously deposited and apply the proceeds of the sale to the debt owed.

3 A term purporting to waive the benefit of any law for the advantage or protection of the obligor (e.g., a maker), as, for example, a waiver of a homestead exemption. (A homestead is the land and buildings occupied by the owner as a home and in most states is at least partially exempted from seizure or sale for debts.)

4 A term in a draft that provides that by indorsing or cashing the draft the payee acknowledges full satisfaction of an obligation owed to the payee by the drawer.

Antedating or *postdating* has no effect on the negotiability of an instrument [3-114(1)]. However, these practices may affect the time of payment if the instrument is payable on demand or at a fixed period after date. Thus, if a demand instrument is issued May 20 but is dated June 1, payment cannot be demanded until June 1, and if an instrument that is payable "30 days after date" is issued on May

20 but is dated June 1, it is not payable until 30 days after the stated date.

Certain *omissions* do not affect negotiability. Commercial paper sometimes contains a reference to the consideration for which the instrument was given. Though useful as a record of the transaction, such a reference is not essential for negotiability and is not required. Nor is a statement of the place where an instrument is drawn or payable required for negotiability.

It is customary and advisable for a maker or drawer to date a negotiable instrument. However, many instruments meet all the requirements for negotiability, including that of being payable on demand or at a definite time, even though undated. An ordinary check, for example, is a demand instrument which can be cashed immediately upon being issued. Since a date of issue is not required for establishing the time that payment is due, a date is not required for the check to be negotiable in form. The date line on a blank check has been provided for the convenience of the drawer in maintaining his or her records.

Rules for Interpreting Common Ambiguities

Like any other contract, a negotiable instrument may be so poorly worded that it requires interpretation. The UCC states a number of rules of interpretation that the courts are to apply [3-118]. These rules include the following:

1 Where there is doubt whether the instrument is a draft or a note, the holder may treat it as either. A draft drawn on the drawer is treated as a note.

2 Where there exists a discrepancy between handwritten terms and typewritten or printed terms, the handwritten terms control (prevail). Where there exists a discrepancy between typewritten terms and printed terms, the typewritten terms control.

3 Where the sum payable is expressed in words and also in figures, and the two expressions of amount differ, the sum payable is that expressed in words. However, if the words are ambiguous, the sum payable is that expressed in figures. (*Note:* A discrepancy between words and figures does *not,* by itself, render the sum uncertain.)

4 Where a provision for interest does not specify the rate of interest, the rate is the "judgment" rate at the place of payment. (A "judgment rate" is a rate of interest established by a state statute to be applied by the courts to judgments for damages where interest is an element of the damage award. The UCC adopts this rate for convenience and certainty.) If the instrument is dated, the interest will run from the date of the instrument; if it is undated, the interest will run from the date the instrument was issued.

Summary

Commercial paper serves as a substitute for money and as a means of extending credit because a holder in due course, unlike the purchaser of an ordinary contract, takes commercial paper free from personal defenses of makers and drawers and other parties to it. Commercial paper is both a formal contract that imposes liability on any signer for the face amount, and a type of property that can be bought and sold. Whether in the form of a three-party draft or a two-party note, commercial paper has a variety of business uses.

For a person to have the favored status of a holder in due course, commercial paper must be negotiable in form. An instrument will be negotiable if the maker or drawer uses certain minimum language prescribed by the UCC and avoids using additional language that renders the promise or order conditional or otherwise destroys negotiability. A number of contractual provisions in an instrument have no effect on its negotiability. Likewise, many omissions and the practice of antedating or postdating have no effect on negotiability.

Review Questions

1 What are the two main functions of commercial paper?

2 What is the main function of a note?

3 How does a promissory note differ from a certificate of deposit?

4 (a) What is the basic function or use of a draft? (b) How does a demand draft differ from a time draft? (c) What is the meaning of "drawee"? "Acceptor"?

5 (a) What is the main use or practical value of checks? (b) What is the relationship between a check and an "underlying transaction"? (c) Explain or illustrate the meaning of the statement, "A check operates as only a conditional payment of the underlying obligation." (d) Explain whether a traveler's check is a check or a draft.

6 A negotiable instrument can confer upon a holder in due course more than the usual contract rights. Using the expressions "negotiable form," "holder in due course," and "personal and real defenses," explain or illustrate how this is so.

7 A negotiable instrument is, simultaneously, a contract and a type of property. Explain.

8 Explain how a draft may be used, together with other documents, in financing the sale of goods.

9 What minimum language is required for an instrument to be in negotiable form? Is a date required? Explain.

10 (a) Give two illustrations of language that will destroy negotiability. (b) Give two illustrations of language that does not affect negotiability.

Case Problems

1 Herb bought, on credit, a large-screen television set for use in the lobby of his motel. In payment he gave Mary, the seller, a negotiable promissory note for $3,000. She negotiated it to First Finance Corp., a holder in due course. When the note came due, First Finance sought payment from Herb, but he refused to pay on the ground that Mary had lied to him about the performance characteristics of the TV set and that it had never worked satisfactorily. Assume that Mary had lied as Herb said and that the TV set was worthless. Is First Finance entitled to payment from Herb? Why or why not?

2 Shortly before her death, Ruby Eubanks received the following document from Mechanics Bank: "April 6, 1973. Mrs. Ruby Eubanks has deposited in this Bank $14,000 payable to the order of herself or Doyle Thomas in current funds 12 months after date on the return of this certificate properly endorsed with interest at 5 percent, per annum. (Signed) Mechanics Bank." The document was in her possession when she died. Both Doyle Thomas and the administratrix of her estate claimed the $14,000. If the document represented an ordinary bank deposit, Doyle Thomas would be entitled to the money under state banking law, which grants ownership of a joint bank account to the survivor. However, if the document was a negotiable certificate of deposit, it was Mrs. Eubanks' property at her death and became an asset of her estate. Was the document negotiable and thus an asset of Mrs. Eubanks' estate?

3 Is the following installment note negotiable? Which two of the eight requirements for negotiability are in doubt?

> May 5, 1977
>
> I promise to pay to the order of Dr. Richard Rowe the sum of twenty dollars ($20.00) each month, beginning June 5, 1977, until I have paid four hundred and eighty dollars ($480.00). In case of death of maker, all payments not due at date of death are canceled.
>
> *John Doe*

4 Holly Hill Acres purchased real estate from Rogers and Blythe. In payment, Holly Hill delivered its promissory note to them, together with a mortgage on the land to secure the note. The note stated: "This note . . . is secured by a mortgage on real estate . . . made by the maker [Holly Hill] in favor of the said payee [Rogers and Blythe]. The terms of said mortgage are by this reference made a part hereof." Rogers and Blythe transferred the note and mortgage for value to Charter Bank. When Bank tried to collect the amount of the note, Holly Hill refused payment, alleging that agents of Rogers and Blythe had committed fraud in inducing it to purchase the real estate. Whether Bank was entitled to payment depended on whether the note was negotiable. Was it?

5 A contractor's note, properly dated and signed, read: "I promise to pay to the order of Paul Payee within the next 60 days the sum of five thousand dollars ($5,000) from the jobs now under construction." Is the note a negotiable instrument? Which of the eight requirements may be in doubt?

6 Hank borrowed $50,000 from Jane so that he could establish his own hardware store. Jane required that Hank sign a promissory note for $50,000 payable to her order in ten annual installments plus 12 percent annual interest on the unpaid balance. The note stated, "This note shall immediately become due and payable with accrued interest whenever holder deems himself or herself insecure." Is this note negotiable? Which of the eight requirements may be in doubt?

CHAPTER 29

Personal and Real Defenses; Negotiation of Commercial Paper

As noted in the preceding chapter, a holder in due course has a favored status in the law. Unlike an ordinary holder or other assignee, a holder in due course takes commercial paper free from (1) rival claims of ownership and (2) many defenses of parties such as makers and drawers. For a person to be a holder in due course, three circumstances must exist. He or she (1) must receive an instrument that is negotiable in form, (2) must take the instrument by a method of transfer called "negotiation," and (3) must possess the personal qualities required by law for holder-in-due-course status (must be a good faith purchaser). However, once the rights of a holder in due course have been established, they can be assigned to (and enforced by) persons who lack some of the qualities of a holder in due course. The next chapter discusses the required personal qualities and how a person may acquire the rights of a holder in due course without personally being one. This chapter deals first with personal and real defenses, and then with the process of negotiation.

Personal and Real Defenses

Most commercial paper is issued as payment by the maker or drawer for property or services received from the payee, or as evidence of a loan made by the payee to the maker. In many of these underlying transactions, disputes arise about the quality or sufficiency of the payee's performance. Even where the payee *performs* his or her part of the underlying transaction, the maker or drawer may nevertheless have a legal right, because of some other circumstance such as the maker's minority, to cancel the underlying contract. Thus, the maker or drawer of the negotiable instrument given in payment may acquire *defenses* against having to pay the payee. But the payee might have transferred the instrument to a holder in due course, who, having paid for it, naturally wants to collect from the maker or drawer. So the question is: Must the maker or drawer pay the holder in due course even though the maker or drawer has a right to cancel the transaction with the payee? The answer depends on whether the defense of the maker or drawer is *personal* or *real.* A holder in due course takes a negotiable instrument free from personal defenses but subject to real defenses of all parties (signers).

Although the following discussion emphasizes the defenses of makers and drawers, any party to a negotiable instrument (maker, drawer, acceptor, or indorser) can have a real or personal defense to payment. Moreover, some conditions such as insanity and wrongful acts such as fraud or duress can be either a personal or a real defense, depending on circumstances noted later. (The "rival claims" [of ownership] that a holder in due course also takes free from often arise when an instrument is stolen or obtained by fraud. Such claims are illustrated in the part of this chapter dealing with negotiation of commercial paper.)

Personal Defenses

As noted in the previous chapter, a *personal* defense is one that the law says must remain a private matter between the immediate parties to a negotiable instrument, e.g., between the maker and payee, instead of causing loss to a holder in due course. So, where a holder in due course seeks payment and the maker or drawer has only a personal defense, the maker or drawer must pay the holder in due course and initiate legal action against the payee for breach of the underlying contract, seek from the payee a voluntary repayment, or absorb the loss.

The personal defenses include the following:

1 The payee's fraud, misrepresentation, duress, or undue influence in inducing the maker or drawer into the underlying transaction. These defenses are discussed in Chapter 11, but one, fraud, needs special mention here. There are two kinds of fraud: *fraud in the inducement* (always a *personal* defense), and *fraud in the execution of the instrument* (which *can* be a *real* defense under the circumstances described later in this chapter).

Fraud in the inducement gets its name from the fact that the payee induces (lures) the maker or drawer into voluntarily signing a negotiable instrument on the basis of the payee's lie about the nature of the underlying transaction. For example, Sue fraudulently represents herself to John as a member of First Church seeking contributions for the church's missionary work. In fact, Sue does not belong to the church, and it has no missionary program. Not knowing this, John makes out a $100 check to Sue, who tells John she will indorse (sign) it over to the church. Instead, she cashes the check at a local supermarket and disappears with the money. The supermarket, a holder in due course, is entitled to payment from John free from his defense of fraud in the inducement.

The key factor in John's liability to the supermarket is that John *knew he was signing a check, signed it voluntarily, and put it into circulation.* John's negligence (failing to investigate Sue's representations and issuing the check to Sue instead of to First Church) was great. A judge ruling in favor of the supermarket might point out that John was in a better position than the supermarket to detect the fraud and prevent loss. But some fraud in the inducement is so skillfully committed that it is undetectable; therefore, its victims are blameless. Nevertheless, it is at least arguable that even blameless victims are in a better position than the holder in due course to prevent loss. This possibility of self-protection, together with the policy of enhancing the marketability of commercial paper, is the basis for the rule that all forms of fraud in the inducement, detectable or not, constitute merely a personal defense.

2 Mistake (discussed in Chapter 11) of the kinds that would justify the maker or drawer in rescinding (canceling) the underlying contract.

3 Breach of warranty (discussed in Chapter 18), especially in sales of goods.

4 Failure of performance (also called "failure of consideration") such as the inability or refusal to deliver property, discussed in Chapter 15.

5 Nondelivery of the instrument. Suppose that near the end of the month Dora makes out a payroll check to her employee Paul, intending to deliver it to him after the first of the next month. Before then, Paul obtains possession of the check without Dora's knowledge and indorses it to Harry, a holder in due course. When Dora discovers that the check is missing, she stops payment on it. Then Harry presents the check to the drawee bank for payment. The bank refuses to pay, and Harry sues Dora, who contends that she is not liable to Harry because she never delivered the check to Paul. If Paul himself had tried to cash the check at the bank, Dora's defense of nondelivery would be good. However, since nondelivery of a signed instrument is a *personal* defense, it is not good against Harry, the holder in due course.

Occasionally a maker or drawer delivers a negotiable instrument to the payee on the understanding (*not* expressed in the instrument) that the delivery will not become effective unless a specified event occurs (e.g., unless a particular service is performed), or on the understanding that the instrument is to be used for a special purpose. While the defenses of conditional delivery and delivery for a special purpose are good as between the immediate parties, they are personal defenses and, as such, are not good against a holder in due course.

6 Unauthorized *completion* of a signed instrument. Suppose May signs a check naming Paul as payee but leaves the amount blank, instructing Paul to fill in the amount later for an amount not to exceed $100. He fills in the amount for $500 and negotiates the check to Harry, a holder in due course. Harry is entitled to $500 from May, free from her personal defense that Paul lacked authority to complete the check for $500. By signing a check and permitting someone else to fill in the amount, May has created a trap for holders in due course and therefore should absorb any loss.

Case 29.1 discusses whether the fraud involved constitutes a real or a personal defense.

CASE 29.1 Mellon Bank v. Donegal Mutual Ins. Co. · 29 UCC Rep. 912 (Pa. Ct. C.P. 1980)

FACTS McConnell made a claim against a person insured by Donegal Insurance Co. In settlement of the claim Donegal drew a check for over $3,700 on Farmer's First Bank, with which Donegal had an account, naming McConnell as payee. McConnell cashed the check at Mellon Bank where he had an account, and he received the proceeds in cash. Mellon Bank presented the check to Farmer's First Bank for payment, but Farmer's refused to

CASE 29.1 Continued honor the check because Donegal Insurance Co. had ordered Farmer's to stop payment on the ground that McConnell's insurance claim was fraudulent. Not being able to collect from the drawee because of the stop order, Mellon Bank sued Donegal, the drawer, for payment.

OPINION DOYLE, J. . . . [P]laintiff's motion for summary judgment [is] before us for disposition.

Defendant [Donegal] asserts that the deceit allegedly practiced by McConnell on defendant infects the instrument itself, viz.: it is a fraud and a "real" . . . defense available against anyone who asserts a claim on the instrument. Defendant's argument is based on a defense set forth in [Section 3-305(2)(b) of the UCC]. The commission's comment to the cited section states: "If under [local] law the effect of the . . . illegality is to make the obligation entirely null and void[,] the defense may be asserted against a holder in due course. Otherwise it is cut off." Defendant is bound by its pleadings and the defense which is *pleaded,* viz.: "fraudulent insurance claim." [Such a claim] is not the species of fraud in *esse contractus,* which renders an *instrument* void—it is only a deceit, a misrepresentation which induced the drawer to draw and deliver the instrument to malefactor McConnell. It is not a "real" defense available against a holder in due course. . . .

We find that there is no substantial issue of fact regarding plaintiff's status as a holder in due course. . . . We find that plaintiff is a holder in due course. We find that the defenses raised by defendant are not "real" defenses. [Although defendant must pay plaintiff, defendant] may recover from McConnell in a trespass action for deceit or may waive the tort and sue *in assumpsit.*

JUDGMENT Ergo, we must . . . grant plaintiff's motion for summary judgment. . . .

Real Defenses

As noted in the previous chapter, *real* defenses involve circumstances of such serious consequences to makers, drawers, and other signers of commercial paper that the policy of protecting holders in due course must yield to the need to protect signers. Unlike a personal defense, a real defense is good against any person, even a holder in due course. Article 3 identifies a number of real defenses [3-305]:

1 *Infancy (minority).* Infancy is a defense against a holder in due course "to the extent that it is a defense to a simple contract" under the law governing the underlying transaction. Recall from Chapter 11 that state law varies on matters such as the kinds of contracts a minor may rescind (cancel) and what the minor must do to be entitled to rescind. If state law permits a minor to rescind his or her contract (e.g., for the purchase of goods), minority (infancy) is a real defense as to any negotiable instrument the minor gave in payment. Suppose that the law of Mel's state permits minors to rescind their contracts for luxuries merely by returning the goods even though damaged. Mel, a minor, buys a camera (a luxury) and issues to Camera Shop a check for $500 in payment. A short time later Mel damages the camera, rescinds the contract, and places a stop-payment order on the check. In the meantime, Camera Shop has negotiated the check to Harriet, a holder in due course, who presents the check to Mel's bank and is refused payment. She then sues Mel for payment of the check. But because state law permits Mel to rescind the underlying transaction, Mel has, under the UCC, a real defense to payment of the negotiable instrument. By denying the holder in due course payment of the check, the UCC supports the local policy of protecting minors who elect to rescind the underlying contract. (As indicated in Chapter 31, Harriet may be able to compel Camera Shop to make good her loss, on the ground that Camera Shop breached a transfer warranty. Thus, as the law intended, Camera Shop ultimately would bear the risk of dealing with minors.)

2 *Incapacity other than minority; duress; illegality.* The defense of "other incapacity [than minority]" refers to incapacities such as insanity, drunk-

enness, and lack of corporate capacity to do business. They and the defenses of insanity and duress are described in Chapter 11. The defense of illegality is discussed in Chapter 12. Illegality occurs most often where a maker or drawer issues an instrument to pay a gambling debt in violation of a law prohibiting gambling or has signed a note carrying an interest rate that exceeds the rate permitted by the usury laws. All of the defenses just mentioned *may be real or personal, depending on state law.*

State law often distinguishes between instances of relatively minor wrongdoing that render an obligation merely *voidable* (rescindable at the option of an affected party such as the maker of a note) and those instances of serious misconduct that render the obligation *void* (of no legal effect whatever). The defenses of illegality, duress, and nonminority incapacity are *real* defenses *only if* state law, because of the seriousness of the circumstance involved, "renders the obligation of the party a nullity" (*void*) [3-305(2)(b)]. Duress provides an example. Forcing a person to sign a negotiable instrument at the point of a gun is in all states the kind of duress that renders the transaction void; the act of signing, though apparently creating a contractual obligation on the part of the signer, created no obligation at all because of the duress. In such a situation the drawer or maker has a *real* defense. In many states, however, forcing a person to sign a negotiable instrument under threat to prosecute the son of the maker for theft is a less serious form of duress that renders the maker's obligation under the instrument merely voidable and thus provides the maker with only a *personal* defense: one good against the wrongdoing payee should that person seek payment, but not good against a holder in due course seeking payment.

3 *Fraud in the execution.* Fraud in the execution (signing) of a negotiable instrument occurs, for example, where a payee persuades a person to sign a negotiable instrument by misrepresenting it as some other kind of document, or by indicating that the paper being signed is a negotiable instrument but misrepresenting its contents. Sometimes called "fraud in the essence" or "fraud in the factum," fraud in the execution may be either a real or a personal defense, depending on the circumstances surrounding the signing. Fraud in the execution is a *real* defense if the payee or another wrongdoer "has induced the party to sign the instrument with neither knowledge nor reasonable opportunity to obtain knowledge of its character or essential terms" [3-305(2)(c)]. Suppose a trusted and faithful ex-employee of a blind person asks the former employer to sign a "letter of reference" that is in reality a check for $1,000 made out to the ex-employee. Probably the ex-employee's fraud constitutes a *real* defense, good against even a holder in due course to whom the defrauder might negotiate the check. Only a court, however, can say with authority whether the blind drawer's defense is real or merely personal. If the drawer had reason to suspect wrongdoing by the ex-employee and had an opportunity to investigate but failed to do so, the defense is only a personal one even though the fraud concerned the nature of the document or its essential (important) terms.

4 *Bankruptcy.* One purpose of federal bankruptcy proceedings is to provide a hopelessly overburdened debtor with a "fresh start," by means of a formal release from debt called a discharge in bankruptcy. To give effect to the federal policy of debtor relief (and to the similar policy of state insolvency laws), Article 3 makes any discharge in insolvency proceedings (state or federal) a real defense, good against even a holder in due course of a negotiable instrument issued by the debtor [3-305(2)(d)].

5 *Unauthorized signature; material alteration. Unauthorized signature* includes both a forgery and a signature made by an agent exceeding his or her actual *or apparent* authority. The defense is good even against a holder in due course, unless the alleged signer ratified the signature (approved the signature as his or her own after the signing) or is precluded (prevented) by law from denying it. For example, suppose the Drew Candle Company employs Anna as a bookkeeper. Ordinarily a bookkeeper has no authority to write checks for his or her employer, but Anna *is* authorized to draw checks on Drew's bank account provided they are cosigned by the controller. Anna draws a check payable to her friend Pablo without securing the signature of the controller. Even if the check is negotiated to a holder in due course, Drew Company may assert the defense of unauthorized signature. However, Drew Company may be precluded from denying Anna's authority if it is careless in the handling of its checks, for example, if they are not kept in a secure place under proper supervision.

A *material alteration* (an unauthorized, significant change in the wording of a negotiable instrument) may be a partial real defense or no defense at all. It is no defense where the issuer assented (agreed) to the alteration or contributed to its making through negligence or other fault. For example, if the payee raises the amount of an instrument while the maker or the drawer looks on, a holder in due course may collect the increased amount. Where the maker or drawer did not assent and was not at fault, that person has a real defense good against a holder in due course, but only to the extent of the alteration, since "a subsequent holder in due course may in all cases enforce the instrument according to its original tenor" [3-407]. Suppose Donna draws a check for $200 payable to Pam. If Pam, without Donna's knowledge or negligence, raises the amount of the check to $1,200 and negotiates it to a holder in due course, Donna may be held liable only for the original amount, $200.

In Case 29.2, the court decides whether commercial bribery is a personal or a real defense.

CASE 29.2 Bankers Trust Co. v. Litton Systems, Inc. · 26 UCC Rep. 513 (2d Cir. 1979)

FACTS Litton Systems and Royal were divisions of Litton Industries. Defendant Litton Systems (Litton) decided to purchase photocopiers for use in its branch offices. Royal's salesman, Buquicchio, persuaded Litton Systems to lease copiers from Regent Leasing Corp. Unknown to Litton and Royal, Regent paid "service fees" to Buquicchio for "pushing" leases, especially Regent's leases, instead of sales.

To finance the purchase of copiers to be leased to Litton, Regent assigned the Litton leases to two banks for value. The leases contained a "waiver of defenses" clause stating that the assignees' rights would be independent of any claims of Litton as against Regent. Under Section 9-206(1) of the UCC, such leases have the effect of a negotiable instrument. Litton failed to make the payments due under the leases, and the banks brought suit. Litton denied liability, alleging that Regent's bribery of Buquicchio made the lease with Regent void and gave Litton a good defense against the banks. From a judgment for the banks, Litton appealed.

OPINION MORE, Circuit Judge.... Buquicchio's conduct was arguably illegal under New York Penal Law § 180.00... which declares commercial bribery to be a criminal offense. Litton claims that the bribes were such "illegality of the transaction, as renders the obligation of the party a nullity" and that, therefore, the leases were unenforceable even by a holder in due course....

The court... concluded that [although] "such payments could constitute a defense as against Regent... the making of such payments could not be asserted against a holder in due course...." Accordingly, it granted the banks' motions for summary judgment [stating,]

> [I]n using the term "nullity" the Legislature intended to provide a defense against a holder in due course only in cases where the obligation sued upon is void on its face (e.g. a wagering contract or a contract to perform an illegal act), and [did not intend] to provide a defense against such a holder where one of the parties to the original contract might have had an option to declare it void because of some illegal conduct [by] the other party....

...The illegality defense under § 3-305(2)(b) is available only if under the applicable state law the effect of the illegality is to make the obligation entirely null and void; the defense is ineffective against a holder in due course if the illegality causes the contract to be merely voidable.... An examination of the language of the New York decisions on the enforceability of bribery-induced contracts suggests that New York holds such contracts to be "void."... Nonetheless, upon further analysis, we conclude that [New York courts may hold a] contract induced by illegal bribery... merely voidable.

CASE 29.2 Continued

The problems and consequences of using the terms "void" and "voidable" were recognized by [Section 475 of] the *Restatement of Contracts:*

> Confusion in the use of the words "void" and "voidable" is common, chiefly because it frequently makes no difference whether a contract is void or voidable. In either event the injured party can usually escape liability, and in most cases that is the only question involved. The difference becomes important, however, where property is transferred and subsequently passes to a bona fide purchaser for value....

Since the New York cases on illegal contracts induced by commercial bribery do not involve holders in due course, one could reasonably assume that the authors of those opinions were using the term "void" loosely, without regard to its importance when a holder in due course enters the picture....

It is necessary...to consider the basic policy supporting the New York cases....Comment (a) to § 598 [of the *Restatement*] states that when a plaintiff sues to recover on an illegal bargain, courts deny relief because the *plaintiff* is a wrongdoer, not because they favor the defendant. Courts will not aid a person "who founds his cause of action upon his own immoral or illegal act."...This rationale is precisely the policy articulated in the New York decisions....The well-known maxim that no one shall be permitted to profit by his own fraud summarizes the policy....Where an innocent third party, such as a holder in due course, is suing upon an illegal contract, the policy argument is inapplicable because the plaintiff has done no wrong for which it should be penalized....

[In a footnote, the court quoted a New York holder-in-due-course decision on illegality as follows: "[W]here the statute itself does not make a contract void but simply prohibits the act,...the usages of trade and the necessity for [protecting] negotiable instruments require that the contract should be enforced....In order to make contracts void *ab initio,* a statutory declaration to that effect is necessary; and, without that statutory declaration...the note is good in the hands of a bona fide purchaser." Here, no statute made void a contract induced by bribery.]

Bribery which induces the making of a contract is much like a fraud which has the same result. The bribery of a contracting party's agent or employee is, in effect, a fraud on that party....Inasmuch as the [New York UCC] allows a holder in due course to enforce a contract induced by fraud..., the same treatment should be given to a contract induced by bribery. The result ought not be changed by the additional fact that commercial bribery is a criminal offense in New York.

Finally, it would be poor policy for courts to transform banks...into policing agents charged with the responsibility of searching out commercial bribery committed by their assignors....The holder in due course is protected...[so] that commercial transactions may be engaged in without elaborate investigation of the process leading up to the contract or instrument....Abrogation of the rights of a holder in due course is not warranted in this case.

JUDGMENT ...[T]he decision of the district court is affirmed.

Negotiation of Commercial Paper

"Issue" and "negotiation" are parts of the process of putting commercial paper into circulation. Ordinarily the maker or drawer will issue the paper to a payee. The payee may keep the instrument and later collect payment, or may instead negotiate the instrument to a third person. The third person becomes a *holder* if all requirements for a negotiation are met, and can be a *holder in due course* by meeting, in addition, the requirements for holder-in-due-course status.

Issue of an Instrument

Issue means the first *delivery* of an instrument by its maker or drawer to another person, usually the payee, with the intention of granting the payee rights in the instrument [3-102]. Upon issue, the payee is a holder of the instrument. So, when you make out a check and mail it to the gas company, you are *issuing* the check. The gas company becomes a *holder* when it receives (possesses) the check.

With respect to negotiable instruments, *delivery* means a voluntary transfer of possession [1-201(14)]. Where Dora makes out a check to Paul, and Paul picks it up from Dora's desk without authority while Dora is out of her office, there is no delivery. Neither is there a delivery if Dora merely hands the check to her *own* agent with instructions to take the instrument to Paul. Delivery does not take place until the agent gives *control* of the instrument to Paul. Where a drawer or a maker turns over an instrument directly to an *agent of the payee,* however, there is a delivery of the instrument.

An instrument can be issued even though the signer leaves lines blank for someone else to fill in [3-115]. Suppose Dora draws a check naming Paul as payee, leaves the lines for the amount blank, and gives the check to Paul with instructions to "fill in the amount I owe you." Because Dora signed the check and delivered it to Paul, it is issued even though it is an *incomplete instrument.* Issuing incomplete instruments is dangerous, but the practice is convenient and relatively frequent. Not to give effect to instruments completed by others than the issuers would unnecessarily raise doubts in the minds of holders in due course about the collectability of such paper. However, an incomplete instrument cannot be enforced until completed [3-115(1)]. Sometimes the instrument is filled out for more than the amount authorized. The extent to which an unauthorized completion is binding on the issuer is discussed in Chapter 31.

Negotiation of an Instrument

Negotiation can occur in a variety of ways, depending on the kind of paper involved (bearer or order) and the wishes or needs of the parties. A surprising variety of people have the *power,* though not always the *right,* to negotiate commercial paper. Where commercial paper is negotiated by indorsement, the indorser has several types of indorsement from which to choose. These topics relating to negotiation are discussed in the following paragraphs.

Meaning and Methods of Negotiation. *Negotiation* is the transfer of a negotiable (properly worded) instrument in such a way that the transferee becomes a holder [3-202]. (There can never be a negotiation unless the document is in negotiable form.) Ordinarily, a *holder* is a person *in possession* of *bearer* paper or *in possession* of *order* paper *that has been* (1) *issued* to him or her or (2) *transferred* to him or her *properly indorsed* (signed by the transferor). Thus, there are two methods of negotiation: (1) If the instrument is payable to *bearer,* it is negotiated by *delivery alone.* (2) If an instrument is payable to *order* (e.g., if the drawer or maker has made the instrument out to a named payee), the holder (e.g., the payee) negotiates it by *delivery together with any necessary indorsement* (here, the payee's signature).

The term "order paper" refers not only to an instrument made out to the order of a named payee but also to an instrument that is *indorsed* by a holder such as the payee *to* a named transferee. For example, Paul Payee indorses his payroll check (signs it on the back) as follows: "Pay John Jozinski, (signed) Paul Payee." The check, which was order paper when issued to Paul, continues to be order paper because Paul, the transferor, named John as the transferee. Now, for John to negotiate the check to someone else, John too must indorse it.

What happens if the holder of order paper, wanting to negotiate it, delivers it but forgets to add his or her indorsement? In that event, there has been a mere *transfer* of the instrument, not a negotiation. The transfer constitutes an *assignment* of the transferor's rights. Until the indorsement is supplied, the transferee is merely an assignee and is subject not only to real defenses but also to *any personal defenses learned of before the indorsement is supplied.* However, a transferee *for value* (i.e., a purchaser) is better off than an ordinary assignee. A transferee for value has "the specifically enforceable right to have (may have a court compel) the unqualified indorsement of the transferor" [3-201], and thus may become a holder in due course when the indorsement is supplied (if the transferee has the other qualities, such as good faith, necessary for holder-in-due-course status).

Who May Negotiate an Instrument. Any *holder* of commercial paper or a person acting on behalf of the holder can negotiate it *and thereby enable a properly qualified transferee to become a holder in due course* (the type of good faith purchaser who takes a negotiable instrument free from personal defenses). With one exception discussed in Chapter 31, a person who lacks holder status cannot negotiate commercial paper. A transfer by a nonholder ordinarily is merely an assignment of whatever rights the nonholder may have. However, if a transferor *is* a holder, that person has the *power* to negotiate the instrument even though the negotiation may be wrongful. This is because "holder" is defined broadly enough to include any person who is *or appears to be* the rightful owner of the instrument, as far as a prospective purchaser can tell from what is written on the face and on the back of the instrument. For example, any person *in possession* of paper made payable "to bearer" is a holder and can negotiate it, even though the possessor has stolen or found it. Order paper (such as a check made out to a named payee) that has been indorsed by the payee's merely signing it on the back (making an "in blank" indorsement) is another form of bearer paper. Anyone in possession of it, even a finder or a thief, is a holder and can negotiate it [3-301].

Recall that lack of delivery is a personal defense of the *drawer, maker, or acceptor* that is not good against a holder in due course or an assignee who has received the rights of a holder in due course. As illustrated below, the same principle operates to deprive *payees and others in the chain of transfer* of the personal defense of nondelivery when a holder in due course seeks payment. However, where a negotiation was wrongful, whether for lack of delivery or for some other reason, the wronged party has a cause of action against the transferor who committed the wrong. Some illustrations of rightful and wrongful negotiations follow.

1 Dora draws a check payable "to bearer" and delivers it to Paul. Paul, the payee, is a holder because he is in possession of bearer paper. Paul is the rightful owner and may negotiate the check. Paul's transferee will be a holder in due course if the transferee has the required qualities.

2 Dora draws a check payable "to bearer" and delivers it to Paul. Paul is a holder. Then Paul loses the check and Alfredo finds it. Alfredo is a holder because he is in possession of bearer paper. Alfredo has the *power* to negotiate the check and does so, even though Paul is the true owner and Alfredo's negotiation is wrongful as to Paul. Alfredo's transferee, Hanna, a holder in due course, takes the check free from Paul's personal defense of nondelivery (and Paul's claim of ownership). Paul's only recourse is against Alfredo for the tort of conversion.

3 Dora draws a check payable "to the order of Paul" and delivers it to him. Paul is a holder because he is in possession of an instrument drawn to Paul's order. Then Paul indorses the check by writing his name on the back (thereby converting the check to *bearer* paper) and lays the check on his desk, intending to take it to the bank the next day. That night Tom sneaks into Paul's apartment and steals the indorsed check. Although Tom is a thief, he is a holder because he is in possession of properly indorsed order paper (which, because of the in-blank indorsement, is now bearer paper). As far as a prospective purchaser can tell from what is written on the check (Paul's name in the "payee" blank and Paul's name on the back as indorser), Tom is the rightful owner. Tom negotiates the stolen check to Hanna, a holder in due course who takes it free from Paul's personal defense of nondelivery and claim of ownership. Paul's only recourse is against Tom, for the tort of conversion.

Legal Requirements for Indorsement. An *indorsement* is a signature, customarily found on the back of commercial paper, and made by or on behalf of a person *other than* a maker, a drawer, or an acceptor—e.g., made by a payee or other transferor [3-402]. Like any other signer, an indorser is, in circumstances discussed later in this chapter, liable contractually for the face amount of the instrument. Often, the payee *must* indorse to negotiate the instrument, as where a check is made out to a named payee; and thus the payee-indorser will be liable for the face amount (unless she or he excluded contractual liability by using the "qualified" indorsement discussed later in this chapter). Where an instrument is made out "to bearer," an indorsement is not required by law as a part of the negotiation process. However, the *transferee* might insist on an indorsement anyway out of habit or because the transferee knows that the indorser, as a signer, has liability for payment. The contractual liability of indorsers and other parties to a negotiable instrument is discussed in Chapter 31.

To be effective, an indorsement must be written by or on behalf of the holder, since the holder is the proper person to transfer the instrument [3-202(2)]. An unauthorized signature, whether by a forger or by an agent exceeding his or her actual or apparent authority, is wholly inoperative as that of the purported indorser [3-404]. A person who takes an instrument indorsed by an agent runs considerable risk unless there is assurance that the agent has the requisite authority. An unauthorized indorsement provides the purported indorser (*and* the maker, drawer, or acceptor from whom payment is sought) with a *real* defense to payment—one that is good even against a holder in due course.

An instrument payable to the order of Al, Bob, *and* Cora is payable to all of them and may be negotiated only by the indorsements of all of them. An instrument payable to the order of Al, Bob, *or* Cora is payable to any one of them and therefore requires the indorsement of only one of them [3-116].

Often, negotiable instruments are made payable to a named person with the addition of words describing the person as agent or officer of a specified individual or organization, or as a fiduciary for a specified person or purpose. For example, a check might be made out to to the order of "Jane Doe, Attorney for Rachel Roe"; "Carlos Cash, Treasurer of the Country Club"; or "Fritz Fine, Trustee of the Smithers Trust." In all such instances, the agent, officer, or fiduciary may indorse the check by signing his or her name alone [3-117]. The descriptive words make clear that the check is issued to the principal or to the organization, or on behalf of the beneficiary of the fiduciary relationship, and that the agent, officer, or fiduciary is named as payee only for convenience in cashing the check for the person for whom it was intended.

When an instrument is made payable to a person under a trade name (e.g., a check made payable to the order of "Tony's Pizza"), the holder may indorse by using the trade name, by using his or her own name, or by using both [3-203]. A person paying the instrument (e.g., a maker or a drawee) or giving value for it (e.g., the payee's transferee) may require indorsement in both names. The same rules apply where the payee's name is misspelled. That is, the payee may indorse with either spelling or both spellings; a transferee for value may require the payee to indorse by using both spellings.

Where an instrument is payable to the order of a corporation, the name of the corporation should appear in the indorsement. Under case law interpreting the UCC, however, an indorsement such as "John Doe, Secretary-Treasurer" is legally sufficient as the indorsement of the corporation.

Types and Uses of Indorsements. The indorsements used to negotiate commercial paper can be described by the application of three sets of terms. An indorsement is either "in blank" or "special"; it is also either "unqualified" or "qualified"; it is also either "nonrestrictive" or "restrictive."

In-blank or special indorsement. An indorsement *in blank* is so called because it does not specify who the transferee is to be. The payee or other indorser merely signs his or her name. Suppose a check is issued to the order of John Doe, and John signs it on the back as in Figure 29.1 The check is indorsed "in blank." The legal effect of an indorsement in blank is to convert *order* paper to *bearer* paper. So, the check can now be further negotiated by delivery alone [3-204].

Mailing or keeping possession of bearer paper (such as a check indorsed in blank) involves serious risk because, as noted earlier in this chapter, any *possessor* of bearer paper, even a finder or a thief, can negotiate it [3-301]. If John indorses his check in blank and a thief negotiates it to a holder in due course, John is deprived of all rights in the instrument, since a holder in due course takes it *free from all rival claims of ownership* [3-305(1)]. John's only recourse is to track down the thief.

John could protect himself from loss by using a "special" indorsement. A *special indorsement* specifies a person to receive payment. In Figure 29.2, the words "Pay Jane Doe, (signed) John Doe" is a special indorsement. Its legal effect is to continue the "order" character of the check, Thus, Jane's indorsement is required for further negotiation of

Figure 29.1

John Doe

Figure 29.2

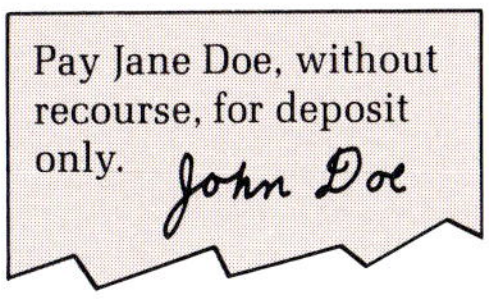

Pay Jane Doe, without recourse, for deposit only. *John Doe*

the check. If it is lost or stolen before Jane indorses it, neither she nor John has much cause for worry. The drawee bank must follow John's instruction as to whom to pay. By his special indorsement John instructed the bank to pay Jane. If the drawee disregards that instruction by paying a forger, the *drawee* must absorb the loss and attempt to track down the person to whom payment was made. (Note that a thief who steals the check and *forges* Jane's indorsement is *not* a holder and cannot negotiate the check [3-404]. The thief's transferee is merely an assignee who acquires no rights in the instrument because the thief had none.)

Although words of negotiability must appear on the *face* of an instrument to make it negotiable in form, their presence in or absence from an *indorsement* has no effect on the negotiability of the instrument. Indorsements simply give evidence of proper transfer and create liability on the part of indorsers; they neither create nor destroy negotiability of the instrument itself, no matter how they are worded.

Where an instrument is bearer paper on its face and carries no indorsement, the holder can protect against loss by using a special indorsement to convert the instrument into order paper. Suppose Jane draws a check payable to bearer and delivers it to Ann. Ann can protect herself against loss or theft by immediately naming herself the indorsee in a special indorsement: "Pay to the order of myself, (signed) Ann."

A holder may convert a blank indorsement into a special indorsement by writing appropriate words above the signature of the indorser. Suppose Rachel receives the instrument shown in Figure 29.3. It is payable to bearer because the last indorsement, that of John Doe, is in blank. Figure 29.4 shows how

Figure 29.3

Figure 29.4

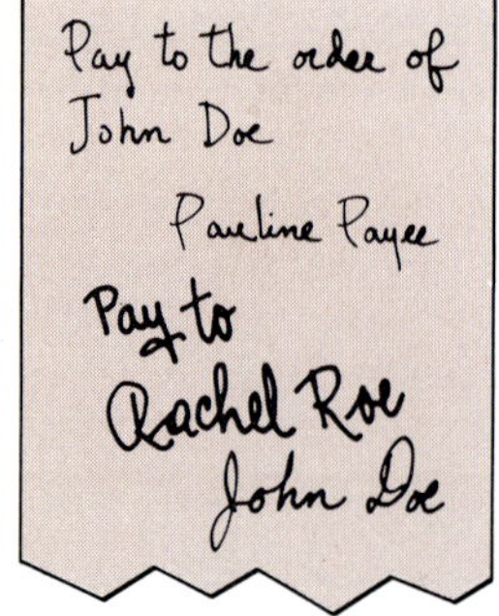

Rachel can convert the blank indorsement shown in Figure 29.3 into a special indorsement and can therefore acquire the protection of order paper.

Unqualified or qualified indorsement. One of the consequences of indorsing a negotiable instrument is that the indorser (the payee of an order instrument or some other holder who signs an instrument to negotiate it) may be liable for the face amount of the instrument if others fail to pay. To escape the contractual liability for the face amount that the UCC imposes on a signer, the indorser must make a "qualified" indorsement. In Figure 29.2, by the use of the words "without recourse," John Doe makes a *qualified indorsement.* Unless an indorser qualifies his or her indorsement by use of "without recourse" or words of similar meaning, the indorsement is *un*qualified; and the indorser has the usual indorser's liability for the face amount of the instrument if it is not paid by the maker, drawer, acceptor, or some other indorser [3-414]. However, an indorser who routinely uses qualified indorsements (or conditional indorsements, discussed later) may undermine the marketability of his or her paper by suggesting the existence of more risk than there is.

Nonrestrictive or restrictive indorsement. A *restrictive* indorsement specifies a particular use to which the indorsed instrument is to be put, or in some other way limits the way in which the indorsee may deal with the instrument [3-205]. If no restriction or limitation is stated in the indorsement, it is nonrestrictive, as in Figure 29.1. Most restrictive indorsements are enforceable, but some are not [3-206]. The following paragraphs illustrate the various kinds of restrictive indorsements.

1 *Indorsements purporting to prohibit further transfer of an instrument.* John Doe, a payee, indorses his paycheck as follows: "Pay Jane Doe only, and no one else. Further transfer is hereby prohibited, (signed) John Doe." This restrictive indorsement is *unenforceable.* Commercial paper cannot serve its function as a substitute for money if indorsers can prevent further negotiation. Jane may negotiate the check despite John's limitation, and so may Jane's transferee.

2 *Indorsement for deposit or collection.* John Doe, the payee of a check, indorses it "For deposit only, (signed) John Doe," delivers it to Ann, his bookkeeper, and tells Ann to deposit the check in Doe's

bank account. This restrictive indorsement is enforceable. Any person to whom Ann transfers the check, e.g., a bank or a supermarket at which Ann might attempt to cash the check, must pay or apply "consistently with the indorsement" any value given for the instrument [3-206(3)]. To the extent that Ann's transferee does so (i.e., sees to it that the funds are deposited in John's account), the transferee becomes a holder for value and may become a holder in due course by meeting the other requirements for holder-in-due-course status (such as good faith). If Ann's transferee does not make the payment in accordance with the instruction given in the restrictive indorsement, the transferee is liable to the indorser for any loss resulting from the transferee's failure to heed the restriction.

Suppose, for example, that Ann takes the check to Doe's bank, where Ann too has an account, and instead of following Doe's instructions, she has the bank apply the proceeds of the check to a debt that Ann owes the bank. Ann is acting wrongfully, and so is the bank. In ignoring Doe's restrictive indorsement, the bank has failed to apply payment consistently with Doe's indorsement, is not a holder for value, and cannot become a holder in due course of the check. Moreover, the bank has converted Doe's property and is liable to Doe for the amount of the check. The same would be true if the bank had disregarded an indorsement reading "For collection," "Pay any bank," or other words signifying a purpose of deposit or collection.

Any nonbank transferee would be required to observe Doe's restrictive indorsement, but not all banks within the banking system are required to do so [3-206(3)]. The bank where Ann deposited the check is a "depositary" bank. Depositary banks must obey restrictive indorsements (if they are enforceable). But other banks could be involved. If the check was drawn on a bank in another state, the depositary bank would have to forward the check to the out-of-state bank (called the "payor" bank) for collection, perhaps through one or more "intermediary" banks. Because intermediary and payor banks must handle checks in bulk, it is impractical for them to determine whether all restrictive indorsements have been heeded. Therefore, *intermediary and payor* banks are permitted to ignore all restrictive indorsements except those of the immediate transferors of such banks and those of persons presenting instruments for payment. In Case 29.3, the court discusses the nature of a payee's indorsement.

CASE 29.3 Walcott v. Manufacturers Hanover Trust · 507 N.Y.S.2d 961 (N.Y. Civ. Ct. 1986)

FACTS Kenneth Walcott's monthly mortgage payment was $610.59. Walcott (plaintiff) alleged that to cover his November 1985 payment, he mailed his paycheck plus a money order to Midatlantic Mortgage Co., using a United States Postal Box for the mailing. He said that he wrote his name and mortgage number on, and affixed the Midatlantic mailing sticker to, the back of the check. Upon being notified that he was late with the November payment, Walcott learned that his check had been cashed by Bilko Check Cashing Corp. and deposited in Bilko's account with Manufacturers Hanover Trust (defendant). The check eventually was cleared through Citibank and charged to the account of the drawer, New York City Transit Authority. Alleging that a thief had stolen his paycheck and that Manufacturers Hanover (Bank) had wrongfully credited it to Bilko's account, Walcott sued Bank and Bilko for the amount of the check.

OPINION HARKAVY, J.... The copy of the check... shows Mr. Walcott's indorsement and the mortgage number..., but shows no sign of the sticker....

The store manager of Bilko... testified that in order for a government check to be cashed, two pieces of identification are required.... She further testified that the person presenting the check in question must have had such identification since the notations as to the calculation of the check cashing fees on the front of the check indicate that

CASE 29.3 Continued

identification was shown. This identification procedure creates doubt as to whether the check was actually stolen.

The issue presented to this court is whether plaintiff's indorsement of his paycheck was such as to be a special or restrictive indorsement, thus limiting the negotiation of the instrument[,] or did it have the effect of creating a bearer instrument. . . .

[Section 3-204(1) of the UCC] defines a special indorsement as . . . one that "specifies the person to whom or to whose order it makes the instrument payable. Any instrument specially indorsed becomes payable to the order of the special indorsee and may be further negotiated only by his indorsement."

Examination of the back of the check . . . reveals that Mr. Walcott did not specify any particular indorsee. In order for the alleged attached sticker to have served that purpose it must have also complied with UCC § 3-202(2): "An indorsement must be written by or on behalf of the holder and on the instrument or a paper so firmly affixed thereto as to become a part thereof." The back of the check shows no sticker attached at all. Even if it had originally been affixed . . . as plaintiff claims, it obviously became detached easily, thus failing to meet the . . . requirements under the UCC to constitute a special indorsement. . . .

As to the numbers written under . . . plaintiff's signature, they did not have the effect of restricting [his] indorsement.

> An indorsement is restrictive which either (*a*) is conditional; or (*b*) purports to prohibit further transfer of the instrument; or (*c*) includes the words "for collection," "for deposit," "pay any bank," or like terms signifying a purpose of deposit or collection; or (*d*) otherwise states that it is for the benefit or use of the indorser or of another person. (UCC § 3-205)

This section of the [UCC] is very specific. The series of numbers representing plaintiff's mortgage account was insufficient to restrict negotiation of plaintiff's check. . . .

Plaintiff's indorsement had the effect of converting the check into a bearer instrument. The series of numbers having no restrictive effect, Mr. Walcott indorsed the check in blank, or otherwise stated, he simply signed his name. A blank indorsement under UCC § 3-204 (2) "specifies no particular indorsee and may consist of a mere signature." Additionally, "An instrument payable to order and indorsed in blank becomes payable to bearer and may be negotiated by delivery alone. . . ." Consequently, since plaintiff failed to limit his blank indorsement, the check was properly negotiated by delivery to . . . Bilko and properly cashed by them.

JUDGMENT Judgment for . . . Manufacturers Hanover . . . and Bilko. . . .

3 *Conditional indorsement.* Occasionally, a holder of an instrument will indorse it over to a merchant as payment for goods or services on the condition that the merchant-indorsee deliver the goods or render the services before receiving payment. Suppose Jane Doe, the payee of a check, indorses it "Pay to Able Typewriters provided they deliver a typewriter to me as per contract dated June 4." This is a conditional indorsement because of Jane's expressed intention that Able will not collect payment unless Jane receives the typewriter. As is true of an indorsement for deposit or collection, transferees must make payment consistently with the indorsement. So, when Able presents the check to the drawee bank, that bank must determine whether Able delivered the typewriter to Jane. If the bank ignores the condition—i.e., makes payment to Able even though Jane received no typewriter—Jane may compel the bank to pay her the amount of the check even though the bank has already paid Able.

4 *Trust indorsement.* Sometimes an indorser wants the indorsee to hold or to manage the proceeds of an instrument for the benefit of the indorser or someone else. Suppose Jane Doe is the payee of a note for $10,000 and wants that amount collected and held by Harriet for the benefit of Jane's daughter,

Judy. Jane indorses the note thus: "Pay Harriet Holder in trust for Judy Doe." Harriet is a "fiduciary" and as such has a duty to collect payment and to hold or manage it for the benefit of Judy. To qualify as a holder in due course, the *first taker* of the note from Harriet must be sure that Harriet applies the proceeds consistently with the indorsement [3-206(4)]. If Harriet transfers the note to Sam in payment of a debt that Harriet owes Sam, there are two bad results for Sam. First, he is not a holder in due course (and takes the note subject to all defenses) because he knows that Harriet is applying the note to her own debt instead of collecting the amount for the benefit of Judy. Second, Sam is liable to the trust for the amount of the note.

But Sam's *transferee* can be a holder in due course even though the transferee makes payment to Sam personally and not for the benefit of Judy. Fiduciaries such as Harriet often have broad powers to sell assets of the trust for management purposes, and this fact is well known in business circles. Suppose Sam sells the note to Sara. Although *Sam* is liable to the trust for the proceeds of the sale (since he is the first taker from Harriet and knows she received his payment for her personal use), Sara is not prevented from being a holder in due course just because she knows Sam bought the note from a fiduciary. Such sales usually are legitimate. However, if Sara knows at the time she buys the note that its sale to Sam was in *violation* of Harriet's fiduciary duties, Sara cannot be a holder in due course.

Case 29.4 illustrates the consequences of a depositary bank's failure to observe a restrictive indorsement.

CASE 29.4 Rutherford v. Darwin · 29 UCC Rep. 899 (N.M. App. 1980)

FACTS Darwin was a general partner of two partnerships: Rancho Village Partners (Village) and The Settlement, Ltd. (Settlement). Darwin had full authority to manage the funds of both partnerships with his signature alone. In 1977 he made a "draw" against a construction loan made by a bank to Village, receiving the $300,000 amount in the form of a money order made out to Village as payee. Darwin indorsed it, "Deposit to the account of Rancho Village Partners, Ltd." Then he took it to First National Bank in Albuquerque (FNBIA) where both Village and Settlement had accounts, and had the amount deposited in Settlement's account despite the indorsement, which directed otherwise. Within 2 weeks of the deposit, Darwin wrongfully took most of the $300,000 for his own use. The other Village partners sued FNBIA for the embezzled amount and won a summary judgment. FNBIA appealed.

OPINION ANDREWS, J. . . . The words "Deposit to the account of Rancho Village Partnership, Ltd." clearly constitute a restrictive indorsement under [Section 3-205 of the UCC]. Section 3-206 imposes upon FNBIA the duty to pay consistently with the restrictive indorsement, and this duty gives rise to liability for the bank if it fails to do so. . . .

FNBIA contends that Darwin "waived" the restrictive indorsement, and thus released it from its duty to pay as directed by the indorsement. We conclude, however, that New Mexico does not recognize any doctrine of the waiver of restrictive indorsements, and thus we cannot accept FNBIA's theory.

[S]everal cases decided in other jurisdictions under the Uniform Negotiable Instruments Law (NIL) suggest that the doctrine [of waiver] was once generally recognized. . . . We are aware of no case decided since the Uniform Commercial Code [superseded] the NIL as the law governing negotiable instruments which has recognized the doctrine, and thus the dispositive issue is whether the doctrine survives as part of the common law under the UCC.

The NIL was silent on the key issue of this case; both the bank's duty to pay as directed by a restrictive indorsement and the waiver exception to that rule were matters of common law under the NIL. With the adoption of the UCC, the rule as to the duty of the bank was codified in § 3-206.

CASE 29.4 Continued

Courts have frequently given effect to common law limitations and exceptions to newly codified common law rules. For example, many jurisdictions have held that a murderer may not take from the estate of his victim even where the general law of descent and distribution of the jurisdiction has been codified without the inclusion of that sensible and time honored common law limitation. However, the general rule is that:

> general and comprehensive legislation, prescribing minutely a course of conduct to be pursued and the parties and things affected, and specifically describing limitations and exceptions, is indicative of a legislative intent that the statute should totally supersede and replace the common law dealing with the subject matter. 2A Sutherland, Statutory Construction § 50.05. . . .

We hold that the codification of the law of restrictive indorsements contained in the UCC is sufficiently comprehensive and detailed to exclude common law exceptions which are not mentioned. Section 3-206 . . . sets forth with particularity when and by whom restrictive indorsements must be observed; it must be inferred that if the legislature had intended that restrictive indorsements would become ineffective for some other reason, such a direction would have been included in this section or elsewhere in the UCC. . . .

FNBIA further argues [that] the indorser of an instrument should be allowed to waive the indorsement by analogy to § 3-208, which states that one who reacquires an instrument may cancel [mark out] any indorsement which is not necessary to his title. . . . The section is not applicable because the instrument was not reacquired and because Darwin did not strike [cancel] the restrictive indorsement.

This second distinction is particularly important. The presence of an uncancelled restrictive indorsement on a negotiable instrument creates the legitimate expectation [in subsequent holders] that it was negotiated in accordance with the restriction, and thus it would, at least in some cases, tend to conceal embezzlement or misappropriation to allow such indorsements to be waived without being physically struck from the instrument. . . .

The circumstances of the transaction cry out for attention on the part of the bank. We hold, as a matter of law, that the bank had a duty to refuse to deposit the money to the account of The Settlement. The money order was restrictively indorsed to the account of an entity entirely different from that named on the accompanying deposit slip. The trial court observed that, particularly in light of the sum involved, the bank had an obligation to be sure that the money went into the proper account.

We adopt the reasoning of the New York Court of Appeals:

> The presence of a restriction imposes upon the depository bank an obligation not to accept that item other than in accord with the restriction. By disregarding the restriction, it not only subjects itself to liability for any losses resulting from its actions, but it also passes up what may well be the best opportunity to prevent the fraud. The presentation of a check in violation of a restrictive indorsement is an obvious warning sign, and the depository bank is required to investigate the situation rather than blindly accept the check. . . .

JUDGMENT . . . The decision of the trial court is affirmed. . . . [Dissenting opinion omitted.]

Special Rules on Effectiveness of Indorsement. Sometimes a payee presents an instrument to his or her bank for deposit but forgets to make a necessary indorsement. The depositary bank may supply the missing indorsement and immediately credit the customer's account, unless the instrument contains such language as "payee's indorsement required." If the instrument contains such language, the bank must return the instrument for the payee's actual indorsement [4-205].

Sometimes a person negotiates an instrument in circumstances giving that person a right to rescind (cancel) the negotiation and to get the instrument back from the transferee [3-207]. Examples are:

1 A negotiation by a minor or other person having a right to rescind for lack of capacity. For example, Dora, an adult, makes a check out to Paul, a minor. Paul cashes the check at a supermarket or indorses it over to a friend as a gift. *As long as the check remains in the possession of Paul's immediate transferee* (the supermarket or friend), Paul may rescind the negotiation and get the instrument back from the transferee.

2 A negotiation obtained by fraud, duress, or mistake. The wronged person may rescind the negotiation and retrieve the instrument from the immediate transferee.

3 A negotiation made by a trustee in breach of a fiduciary duty owed to the beneficiary of the trust. The beneficiary (or his or her legal guardian or other legal representative) may rescind the negotiation and retrieve the instrument from the immediate transferee.

However, although the transferor has a right to *rescind* the negotiation as to the immediate transferee, the negotiation *is effective* to transfer title to (ownership of) the instrument to the transferee [3-207(1)], and the transferee, even if a wrongdoer, has the power to negotiate the check further. So, if the instrument reaches the hands of a holder in due course *before* the aggrieved person (Paul in example 1 above) exercises the right to rescind, the aggrieved person *loses* the right to rescind the negotiation. Being thus freed from most claims and defenses of transferors, holders in due course are encouraged to accept and to pay maximum value for commercial paper.

Suppose, for instance, that Paul, a payee-minor, negotiates his paycheck to Tom and that before Paul can rescind the negotiation on the ground of minority, Tom cashes the check at Ferndale Auto Supply, which knows nothing of the transaction between Paul and Tom. Paul has lost the right to rescind the negotiation; Ferndale, a holder in due course, may keep the check and enforce it against Dora, the drawer. Paul is limited to a cause of action for damages against Tom.

Note that minority (infancy) is a complete (real) defense to payment where the minor is *the maker or drawer* of an instrument; but (for the protection of holders in due course) minority is, in effect, only a personal defense where a minor is *negotiating* an instrument issued by a person of full capacity. Yet, even a holder in due course cannot hold a minor *contractually* liable on his or her indorsement; so minority remains in some respects a real defense even in the process of negotiating instruments.

Summary

Most personal defenses, which are not good against a holder in due course, arise out of disputes about the quality or sufficiency of the payee's performance of an underlying transaction with the maker or drawer. The personal defenses include fraud in the inducement, breach of warranty in a sale of goods, nondelivery of the instrument, and unauthorized completion of a signed instrument. Real defenses, which are good even against a holder in due course, include infancy to the extent that it is a defense to a simple contract, serious forms of duress and illegality, fraud in the execution of the instrument, and unauthorized signature and material alteration.

Any holder of commercial paper can negotiate it and thereby enable a properly qualified transferee to become a holder in due course. Bearer paper is negotiated by delivery; order paper, by delivery plus any necessary indorsement. Depending on the needs of the parties, indorsements may be in blank or special, unqualified or qualified, and nonrestrictive or restrictive. A transferor of commercial paper may have a right to rescind the negotiation, including any indorsement, but if the paper first gets into the hands of a holder in due course, the transferor cannot have the instrument itself back.

Review Questions

1 What is the difference between a personal defense and a real defense? Illustrate each kind.

2 Who can have a personal or a real defense?

3 Is minority a personal or a real defense? Explain.

4 Is duress a personal or a real defense? Explain.

5 How could a negotiable instrument be put into circulation without being delivered by the maker or drawer to the payee?

6 **(a)** How may negotiation of a bearer instrument be accomplished? How may negotiation of an order instrument be accomplished? **(b)** What is the legal significance of negotiation? (For the answer, see the section entitled "Who May Negotiate an Instrument.")

7 Suppose a person buys a negotiable order instrument but the transferor forgets to indorse it. What is the legal position of the buyer?

8 Illustrate how a person can have the power, but not the right, to negotiate commercial paper.

9 For what purpose is each of the following indorsements used: **(a)** special, **(b)** qualified, and **(c)** restrictive?

10 Explain whether all banks are required to heed an indorsement for deposit or for collection.

11 What might be the economic consequence of a person's always using qualified or conditional indorsements when indorsing checks or notes?

12 Often a person who negotiates commercial paper has a legal ground for rescinding the negotiation. If such a ground exists, may the wronged person retrieve the negotiated instrument? Explain.

Case Problems

1 Paul fraudulently induced Mary to issue him a note reading: "July 2, 19xx. Sixty days after date I promise to pay Paul the sum of seven hundred dollars ($700.00), together with interest at the rate of 8 percent per annum. Value received. (Signed) Mary." The day after Paul received the note, he indorsed and sold it to Albert, who took it without notice of the fraud. Is Albert subject to Mary's defense of fraud?

2 To cover gambling losses incurred during private "freeze out" games of "21," Sandler drew checks in favor of Hutchings. Hutchings negotiated the checks to Nevada National Bank and received payment. When Nevada National presented the checks to the drawee bank for payment, that bank refused to honor them. Nevada National then sued Sandler for the unpaid amounts. Although gambling is legal in Nevada, a Nevada statute provides that all "notes drawn for the purpose of reimbursing or repaying any money knowingly lent or advanced for gaming are 'utterly void, frustrate, and of none effect.'" Sandler alleged that the statute gave him a good defense against payment. Was Nevada National, a holder in due course, entitled to payment from Sandler?

3 Nancy Hook was the guardian of Norman and Karen Bruner, both minors. Hook, who managed the trust estates of the children, purchased two negotiable certificates of deposit with fiduciary funds and transferred (pledged) them to Trenton Trust Company as collateral for loans to Hook and her husband. Each certificate was made out to Hook and to one child jointly, with no indication of Hook's fiduciary status. Lewis replaced Hook as guardian and brought suit against Trenton Trust to recover the certificates of deposit for the children's estates. Under state law, a guardian's contract pledging assets of a minor ward is not binding on the minor's estate without the approval of the probate court, and Hook had no such approval. The trial court granted judgment in favor of Lewis. Alleging it was a holder in due course of the certificates, Trenton Trust appealed. If Trenton Trust was a holder in due course, was it entitled to the certificates of deposit?

4 The Silver Slipper Gambling Hall and Saloon issued a payroll check to an employee, Mrs. Reggie Bluiett. She indorsed the check in blank and left it on a dresser in her home. The following day, she discovered that the check was missing. On that day, Freddie Watkins purchased two tires from Western Auto and paid for them with Mrs. Bluiett's payroll check, receiving the tires and a balance of about $112 in cash. Later, Watkins was charged with having obtained money under false pretenses from Western Auto. An essential element of the offense is that the person from whom the money is obtained must suffer injury or damage. Watkins was convicted of the charge and appealed. Should the conviction be upheld?

5 On May 16, 1969, the Bank of Hollywood Hills of Hollywood Hills, Florida, issued a cashier's check for $2,000 payable to "Richard and Grace Grimaldi." Four days later Richard indorsed the check "Grace Grimaldi by Richard Grimaldi" and presented it to a teller of the Beach National Bank located at Fort Meyers, Florida, where the Grimaldis had a joint account. The teller cashed the check and paid the full amount to Richard. On May 20 the cashier's check routinely arrived at the Bank of Hollywood Hills for payment. That bank refused to honor the check. Was it justified in refusing to honor the check? Explain.

6 Bruce Baglio died of personal injuries for which the City of New York was found liable. In settlement of the judgment against it, the city issued a check drawn on Manufacturers Hanover Trust Co., payable "to the order of Joseph Baglio as Administrator of the Est. of Bruce Baglio Dec'd." Joseph Baglio indorsed the check "Joseph Baglio" and presented it to the National Bank of North America for deposit in his personal account. Joseph Baglio then converted the proceeds of the check to his personal use. Baglio was dismissed as administrator, and Bates, his replacement, sued National (the depositary bank) for the face amount of the check. Should National Bank be held liable to the estate for the amount of the check?

CHAPTER 30

Holder-in-Due-Course Status; FTC Limits

To take a negotiable instrument free from personal defenses and rival claims of ownership, a holder must possess the personal qualities required for holder-in-due-course status *or* must receive the rights of a holder in due course by assignment under the "shelter provision" of the Uniform Commercial Code. However, in certain consumer credit transactions, holders have been deprived of holder-in-due-course status by a rule of the Federal Trade Commission. The first part of this chapter deals with the requirements for holder-in-due-course status. The second part notes how a person may acquire the rights of a holder in due course without personally being one. The third part discusses the FTC limits on the availability of holder-in-due-course status.

Holder-in-Due-Course Status

Requirements for Holder-in-Due-Course Status

A holder (a possessor of bearer paper or of properly indorsed order paper) may become a *holder in due course* by doing three things: (1) giving *value* for the instrument, (2) taking it in *good faith,* and (3) taking it *without notice* of (a) defenses to payment, (b) rival claims of ownership, or (c) the fact (if true) that the instrument is overdue when received or has been dishonored [3-302(1)].

Giving Value. To qualify as a holder in due course, the holder must give *value* for the instrument. So, if the payee of a negotiable instrument indorses and delivers it to a transferee as a gift, the transferee is not a holder in due course.

The meaning of "value" in the law of commercial paper differs sharply from its meaning in the law of sales and secured transactions. In sales and secured transactions, "value" means any consideration, including an executory (unperformed) promise, sufficient to support a simple (informal) contract. In the law of commercial paper, "value" means *performed* consideration [3-303(a)]. Suppose Maria Maker issues a negotiable note to Paula Payee, and Paula transfers it to Hal Holder in exchange for his promise to paint Maria's house *next week.* Hal has given consideration for the note (has "bought" it), but Hal has not yet given the required value for it because his promise has not yet been performed. When Hal does the painting, he will be a holder *for value.* If at that time he possesses the other qualities necessary for holder-in-due-course status, he will then be a holder in due course.

Suppose a different situation: Maria's note has a principal (face) amount of $2,000 and Paula agrees to sell the note to Hal in exchange for $1,000 to be paid at the time Hal receives the note, plus a used car to be delivered next week. Upon payment of the $1,000, Hal is a holder for value (and perhaps a holder in due course) to the extent of the *performed* consideration ($1,000). Hal will become a holder for value as to the rest of the note upon delivery of the used car.

As indicated in the preceding illustrations, value can take the form of money, services, goods, or other property such as real estate. But value takes other forms as well. Some common business examples follow:

1 *A bank's permitting a customer to withdraw money before a deposited item clears.* When a customer of a bank deposits for collection an "item" (a check or some other negotiable instrument), the bank credits the customer's account with the amount of the item. Ordinarily the customer has no *right* to draw against the item until it "clears" (e.g., is collected by the bank). The bank's act of crediting the customer's account is, in effect, only a *promise* to give value—when the item clears. However, if the bank permits the depositor to draw against the item *before* it is collected, the bank gives value (and becomes a holder for value of the deposited item) to the extent to which the bank permits a precollection withdrawal of money [4-208(1)(a)].

Where a customer deposits checks from time to time and from time to time makes withdrawals *before the deposited checks clear,* when are the proceeds of a particular check withdrawn? The UCC requires the application of the "first in, first out" rule. Suppose a customer opens a checking account on March 1 by depositing a check of $400; deposits similar checks on March 2 and on March 3; and withdraws $400 on March 5 and $400 on March 6. Under the "first in, first out" rule, the bank has given value on the check deposited March 1 at the time of the first withdrawal (March 5) and on the check deposited

March 2 at the time of the second withdrawal (March 6) [4-208(2)].

Where a customer deposits an item and does not make a withdrawal, the bank is automatically a holder for value when the customer acquires a *right* to withdraw the amount of the item—i.e., when the item is collected or otherwise "clears" [4-208(1)(b)].

2 *Paying for commercial paper with a negotiable instrument.* A holder takes an instrument for value by giving (in return for the negotiable instrument he or she receives) an entirely different negotiable instrument from the one the holder received. John sells Mary his certificate of deposit. Mary pays for it with a check. Mary is a holder for value.

3 *Making a loan and receiving a negotiable instrument as security.* Paul, the payee of a $5,000 note, wants to borrow $2,000 from Harriet. They agree that if Paul will indorse and deliver the note to Harriet for her to hold as security for the loan, Harriet will lend him the $2,000. The parties carry out the agreement. Harriet has given value for the note (to the extent of $2,000) by making the loan.

Often a buyer of commercial paper pays the face amount of the instrument as value. If you cash your payroll check at a supermarket, you ordinarily will receive the face amount because the check is a demand instrument that the supermarket can immediately convert into cash. But to give value, a buyer of commercial paper *need not necessarily pay the face amount.* The seller of a *time* instrument (such as a time draft or a note payable at a future date) wants cash now for an instrument that cannot be collected until later. Because the purchaser expects a profit and faces a risk of noncollection, the seller ordinarily will have to accept a "discounted" (reduced) amount for the instrument—i.e., something less than its total "yield" (face amount plus any interest). By paying a discounted amount, the purchaser of a time note can profit by selling it or by personally collecting the total yield when the note comes due.

For example, Maria issues a note for $100 plus 15 percent annual interest to Pearl, payable 1 year from date. Then Pearl immediately sells the note to Hal for $95. Here the total yield is $115. Hal's payment of $95 will give him a profit of 21 percent. However, he must wait a year to collect and must take the chance that Maria will refuse or be unable to pay. In the meantime, any inflation will erode his profit. All courts are likely to hold that Hal has given value. If he otherwise qualifies as a holder in due course (e.g., takes Maria's note without notice of her personal defenses), he is entitled to collect $115 from Maria when the note comes due, unless she has a real defense.

What minimum amount must Hal pay before a court will hold that he has given value for Maria's note? Under the general law of contracts, adequacy of consideration is an economic issue for the contracting parties to decide, and the courts will not make the decision for them. However, the main object of commercial paper law is to confer greater-than-usual rights upon a holder in due course to induce that person to pay *full market value* for the instrument. Theoretically, the discounting process by which a buyer of commercial paper determines how much to pay for a negotiable instrument involves an assessment by the buyer of the risk factors pertaining to the instrument being purchased. Therefore, the amount paid would constitute *full market* value only if the payment were reasonably related to the amount of risk attending the issuance and selling of the negotiable instrument. Suppose Hal pays only $20 for Maria's note. If Maria seldom pays her debts, Hal's paying $20 for her note could be a realistic assessment of risk, and Hal would be a holder in due course entitled to collect the $115 from Maria when the note comes due. But if Maria has a good credit rating, Hal's $20 payment for a note apparently worth $95 would not constitute full market value. Hal would be a holder in due course as to $20 and only an assignee as to the rest.

Even under the law of commercial paper, however, many courts are reluctant to analyze the risk factors and decide whether full market value was given. Rather than rule that Hal's $20 payment did not constitute full value, courts often will consider instead whether Hal acted in good faith in making such a small payment.

Acting in Good Faith. To be a holder in due course, the holder must act in *good faith* when purchasing commercial paper. Under commercial paper law, "honesty in fact" [1-201(19)] is all that is required for a person to be in good faith. A holder will be considered dishonest (and lacking good faith) only if he or she (1) has *actual knowledge* of wrongdoing or defects concerning the paper, or (2) *consciously ignores* suspicious circumstances. The test of good faith that applies to commercial paper is "subjective." This means that a court will look at the actual experience, intelligence, and judgment of each individual when deciding whether that individual has acted honestly. An inexperienced person of low intelligence may be held to have acted in good faith in circumstances that should have aroused suspicion in a professional buyer of commercial paper.

Because good faith is a matter of individual honesty, it cannot be described fully. However, the following illustrations suggest the general nature of good faith.

1 Maria issues a check for $800 to Paul. Paul negotiates it for $50 to Hal, a person of normal intelligence and experience. *Hal* lacks good faith even though he knows of no actual wrongdoing or defect concerning the check. Hal should wonder why Paul, the payee, would accept $50 for a check that Paul could cash for $800 merely by presenting it to the drawee bank.

2 Paul is the payee of a payroll check that he procured from Maria, his employer, by fraudulently overstating the number of hours he worked during the pay period. Maria instructs her bank to stop payment. Paul negotiates the check to his own bank in another town. Paul's bank knows nothing of the stop order and pays him the face amount without making inquiry of the drawee bank. Paul's *bank* is acting in good faith despite its failure to inquire. If Paul's bank were required to inquire about stop orders in each of its thousands of daily transactions, there would be intolerable delays in processing checks and other commercial paper. Paul's bank is permitted to assume that a person who negotiates an instrument is acting honestly, unless the bank has knowledge of additional facts that should arouse its suspicions.

3 Paul's Roofing does repair work on apartment buildings, receives promissory notes from its customers, and discounts the notes to Paul's Finance Co., a financial subsidiary of Paul's Roofing. Paul is president of both companies. Paul's Roofing consistently defrauds its customers and does shoddy work, but Paul's Finance Co. denies knowledge of these practices and insists it is a holder in due course of the notes. In deciding whether *Paul's Finance Co.* has the good faith necessary for holder-in-due-course status, a court will consider the extent of the finance company's knowledge of the transactions that gave rise to the notes, as well as the closeness of the relationship between the finance company and the payee (Paul's Roofing) from whom it purchased the paper. A finance company that is controlled by (or that controls) the payee or that buys great numbers of instruments from the payee at unusually large discounts is likely to be aware of questionable trade practices of the payee. Failure to investigate obviously suspicious circumstances can amount to bad faith.

In Case 30.1 the court discusses whether a close relationship between the transferor and transferee of a check reveals, by itself, a lack of good faith.

CASE 30.1 Bankers Trust Co. v. Crawford · 42 UCC Rep. 801 (3d Cir. 1986)

FACTS Jules Kutner owned Kutner Buick, and his son Jerome owned Chalfont Industries, the manufacturer of an automotive product called "Stop-A-Flat." Jules provided the initial capital for Jerome to establish Chalfont and lent him additional amounts for business purposes. Chalfont also used Kutner Buick for banking services. Kutner regularly cashed Chalfont checks and established a system of writing Kutner checks in exchange for Chalfont checks. Once, Chalfont used a Kutner Buick "exchange" check to meet its payroll, and at least twelve checks from Chalfont to Kutner "bounced" due to insufficient funds.

In 1982, Stuart Crawford purchased a Chalfont distributorship. During the negotiations, Chalfont made a number of false representations to Crawford and promised him that his distributorship would be at no risk because Chalfont would buy back any product that Crawford could not sell. The contract form had no clear buy-back provision. Crawford's lawyer redrafted the form to include one. At the signing, Chalfont, without Crawford's knowledge, substituted a form that did not contain the provision. As part payment on the contract, Crawford wrote a personal check for $42,023. Chalfont indorsed and delivered

CASE 30.1 Continued

it to Kutner Buick, which deposited it and immediately issued checks to Chalfont for about the same amount. Chalfont indorsed these checks over to its creditors. Crawford stopped payment on his check. Because of the stop-order, Kutner Buick was out-of-pocket $42,056.

After further discussion with Chalfont, Crawford requested Bankers Trust Co. (Bank) to issue a cashier's check for $50,023 to Chalfont. Crawford again became concerned about Chalfont and tried to intercept the check at Chalfont's office. However, Chalfont indorsed the check over to Kutner Buick, which returned $8,000 to Crawford and applied the rest to the $42,023 due it as a result of Crawford's stop-payment order.

In the meantime, Crawford's lawyer obtained a court order blocking Bank from making payment on the check. Bank (plaintiff) filed an interpleader naming Crawford and Kutner Buick as defendants. Kutner argued that it was a holder in due course and thus entitled to the check without regard to Chalfont's fraud. Crawford contended that Kutner, because of its close relationship with Chalfont, was not a holder in due course. From a judgment for Kutner, Crawford appealed.

OPINION

ROSENN, Circuit Judge . . . Crawford raises two primary issues. . . . First, he argues that the district court erred in refusing to apply the "close-connection" doctrine to defeat Kutner Buick's claim to "holder in due course" status. Second, he argues that Kutner . . . was under a "duty to inquire" into the transactional circumstances surrounding the receipt of the check and, because it failed to do so, did not take the check in good faith. . . .

> . . . The close connection doctrine . . . provides that: A transferee does not take an instrument in good faith when the transferee is so closely connected with the transferor that the transferee may be charged with knowledge of an infirmity in the underlying transaction. . . .

The doctrine

> was developed in part because of the difficulty of proving the transferee's actual knowledge of problems in the underlying transaction. The doctrine allows the court to imply knowledge by the transferee when the relationship between the transferee and the transferor is sufficiently close to warrant such an implication. . . .

The district court [held] that the [close connection] doctrine is not the law in Pennsylvania. . . . Crawford argues that the Pennsylvania Supreme Court, if presented with the opportunity, would adopt the doctrine. . . . Crawford, however, is unable to present a persuasive argument that Pennsylvania would [do so]. That six scattered states have adopted the close-connection doctrine does not suggest that Pennsylvania would adopt it. The district court's holding that [it] does not apply in Pennsylvania is not erroneous. [The court noted that "the desirability of solving such proof problems is undeniable, but Pennsylvania attempts to do so in another manner. It follows the rule that a duty to inquire may arise when circumstantial evidence shows that the holder did not exercise good faith."]

. . . The district court held that the proper test for determining good faith is to ascertain whether the transferee exhibited willful dishonesty or actual knowledge, and that the evidence did not demonstrate that Kutner Buick was guilty of either.

[Crawford, however,] asserts that Pennsylvania courts have consistently held that the good faith requirement [demands that a transferee] make an inquiry when he takes an instrument under circumstances that suggest the existence of a defect or defense thereto. [W]e cannot agree that [Crawford's cases] support his proposition that the holder here had a duty to inquire. . . . The mere taking of a check under suspicious circumstances is not sufficient to invalidate it in the hands of the holder, "unless there is proof of such fact from which bad faith may be reasonably inferred." . . . Good faith, in contrast with bad faith, is defined by the [UCC] as "honesty in fact in the conduct or transaction concerned." . . .

Bad faith may be established by circumstantial evidence and each case must depend upon its peculiar facts. Therefore, in *In re Stroudsbury Security Trust Co.*, . . . the appellate

CASE 30.1 Continued

court held that the bank there did not meet its burden of proving that it was a bona fide holder[,] because it accepted corporate bonds from a corporation's treasurer as a pledge for his personal debt without inquiry. The bank, therefore, had actual notice in the bonds themselves that the bonds were not owned by the treasurer[,] and this imposed a duty to inquire. . . .

Hanley v. Epstein. . . concerned a stolen check. The Hanley court ruled that sufficient suspicious circumstances surrounded the transfer of the check to enable the jury to properly conclude that the holder refrained from making further inquiry as to the identification of an indorsee "due to his fear that it would disclose a defect in his title.". . . In [the present] case, however, the district court made. . . findings of fact that are supported by the record and are not clearly erroneous.

21. There is no evidence that [Kutner] knew or had reason to know of Crawford's attempt to stop or reclaim the cashier's check.
22. There is no evidence that [Kutner] knew or had reason to know of the occurrence or substance of any conversations between Crawford and [employees] of Chalfont.
23. There is no evidence that the failure of [Kutner] to make any inquiries about the cashier's check stemmed from any desire to evade knowledge of Crawford's efforts to stop the check.

. . . [I]t appears. . . that Pennsylvania consistently follows the common law rule adopted by. . . the [UCC] that there is no affirmative duty of inquiry on the part of one taking a negotiable instrument, and there is no constructive notice from the circumstances of the transaction, unless [they] are so strong that if ignored they will be deemed to establish bad faith on the part of the transferee.

. . . The district court. . . found no evidence from the circumstances of the negotiation of the [cashier's] check or from the face of the instrument as would impose an affirmative duty on [Kutner] to inquire into the underlying transaction. [Kutner] apparently received the cashier's check in substitution for the check. . . on which Crawford had stopped payment. . . . We. . . conclude that under Pennsylvania law Kutner Buick accepted the cashier's check as a holder in due course.

JUDGMENT The judgment of the district court will be affirmed. . . .

Having No Notice of Defects. To be a holder in due course, a good faith holder for value must also take the instrument *without notice* (1) that it is overdue, (2) that it has been dishonored, or (3) that there is a defense to payment or a rival claim of ownership [3-302].

In contrast to the subjective test of good faith, the Code test for notice is *objective*. Under the UCC, a person has notice of a fact when he or she has *actual knowledge* of it; receives *a notice such as a letter* in time to take action or avoid loss (even though the letter remains unread); or from all the facts and circumstances known to him or her at the time in question has *reason to know* that the fact exists [1-201(25)]. For a person to lack good faith, mental awareness of wrongdoing or suspicious circumstances is required. But to be *on notice* of a defense or another difficulty surrounding commercial paper, a person need only possess relevant information, whether or not that person has actual mental awareness of the difficulty.

Notice that instrument is overdue [3-304(3)]. A negotiable instrument is *overdue* when the day of its maturity has passed and the instrument remains unpaid. An overdue instrument carries an increased risk of nonpayment, and a person who takes an instrument with notice that it is overdue falls short of the innocence required of holders in due course.

Whether a person has notice that an instrument is overdue depends greatly on whether the instrument is a time or a demand instrument, or on the terms (contents) of the instrument. The following illustrations involve *time* instruments.

1 In January, Maria issues Paula a note for $1,000. The note states that it is payable on May 1. On May 20 Paula sells the note to Hal for $900. Hal

can read and is mentally alert. Because the due date (May 1) appears on the note, and because Hal should know he is buying it on May 20, Hal is on notice that the instrument is overdue and should wonder why Paula is selling the note to him instead of collecting the amount from Maria. Hal cannot be a holder in due course.

2 In January, Maria issues Paula a note for $1,000. The note states that it is payable on May 1. It contains an acceleration clause which Paula may exercise "if Paula deems herself insecure." On April 3, Paula learns that Maria might not be able to pay the note on May 1. Feeling insecure, Paula exercises the clause (requires Maria to pay the $1,000 early, on April 3); but after paying the note, Maria leaves it in Paula's possession. On April 16, Paula sells the note to Hal. If Hal knows or has reason to know that acceleration has occurred, he has notice that the instrument is overdue [3-304]. If he is without such notice, he can be a holder in due course entitled to Maria's payment even though Maria has already paid the note.

The purchaser of a *demand* instrument such as a check or a demand note has notice that it is overdue (and cannot be a holder in due course) if at the time of purchase the purchaser has reason to know that *demand has already been made,* or that the purchaser is taking the instrument more than a *reasonable time after* its issue. For *checks* drawn and payable within the United States and its territories, this reasonable time is *presumed* to be 30 days [3-304(3)(c)]. So, if Mary *issues* Paula a check on June 1, and Paula *negotiates* it to Hal on July 5, Hal has taken an overdue instrument and cannot be a holder in due course—unless he can "rebut" the presumption (prove that a longer time than 30 days was reasonable, given the circumstances in which he found himself).

Notice that instrument has been dishonored. Dishonor is (1) a refusal by the maker of a note or the drawee of a draft to *pay* the instrument when it is due, or (2) a drawee's refusal to *accept* a *time* draft [3-307; 3-501, comment 3]. A holder who purchases an instrument with notice that it has been dishonored is taking risks beyond those normally associated with the taking of commercial paper, and does not deserve to have the special status enjoyed by a holder in due course. A holder could receive notice of dishonor by means of the letters "NSF" (meaning nonsufficient funds) stamped on the face of a check, or by information about dishonor received from some other source.

Notice of a defense or a rival claim. A holder who takes an instrument with notice of a *defense to payment* or of a *rival claim of ownership* cannot be a holder in due course. Examples follow:

1 Maria issues a check to Paula in payment for defective goods that Paula delivered to Maria. Hal, Paula's employee, knows of the defects. Paula later negotiates Maria's check to Hal in lieu of his regular paycheck. Hal is on notice of Maria's defense (failure of consideration or breach of warranty) and cannot be a holder in due course.

2 Paul indorses his paycheck in blank and places it on the dashboard of his car. On the way to the bank the check blows out the window. Hal sees the check land on the ground and sees Fay Finder pick it up. Soon Fay negotiates the check to Hal. Hal is on notice of Paul's claim of ownership and cannot be a holder in due course.

A person can be on notice of a maker's or a drawer's defenses even though he or she is not aware of any particular wrongdoing by the payee. A purchaser cannot be a holder in due course if the instrument is *incomplete,* if the instrument is *irregular* on its face, or if there are *other defects.* Examples of these sources of notice follow:

1 Maria signs and issues a check to Paul, but she leaves the line for the amount blank. As Paul knows, she intended to fill the check out for $100. Paul so informs Hal and, without filling out the amount, negotiates the check to Hal for $100. Because Hal is the taker of an incomplete instrument, he is automatically on notice of any defenses Maria might have (e.g., failure of consideration or Paul's fraud), even though he has no knowledge of any particular defense [3-304(1)(a)].

2 Suppose that Hal, in the preceding illustration, fills in the amount of $100 in Lisa's presence and negotiates the check to her for $100. Lisa has taken a completed instrument. Her knowledge that an incomplete instrument has been completed does *not,* by itself, charge her with notice of a defense or claim. She must also have notice that the completion was *improper* [3-304(4)(d)].

3 Maria issues a note to Paul for $100. Paul crudely alters the amount to read $1,000. The alteration is so obvious that it can be readily detected. This is an example of "irregular" paper. Because of

the obvious irregularity, a purchaser is on notice of wrongdoing and cannot be a holder in due course. An instrument stamped "NSF" or "Payment stopped" also is irregular.

4 Paula is trustee for Judy. Maria issues a check for $1,000 "to the order of Paula for the benefit of Judy." Paula owes Hal a $1,000 payment on Paula's car and negotiates the check to Hal in payment of Paula's personal debt. Because the check reads "for the benefit of Judy," Hal is on notice that Paula has negotiated it in breach of her fiduciary duty. This is one of those "other defects," notice of which prevents Hal from being a holder in due course [3-304(2)].

Payee as Holder in Due Course

A payee ordinarily is not a holder in due course. To be a holder in due course, the holder must, for example, take the instrument without notice of any defense. Where there is a defense, the payee will usually know of it, since normally the payee deals directly with the maker or drawer. Thus, if Paul fraudulently induces Dora to draw a check payable to his order, Paul, the payee, knows of the fraud.

Under the proper circumstances, however, a payee can be a holder in due course [3-302(2)]. A payee will not necessarily have notice of a defense where the payee and the maker or drawer deal with each other through an intermediary. Suppose, for example, that Don draws a check payable to Pam's Drugstore but leaves it blank as to amount and gives it to his agent, Arnold, telling him to buy some merchandise and fill the check out for the amount of the purchase. Instead, Don's agent fills the check out for more than the amount authorized, and Pam's Drugstore takes it for value, in good faith, and without notice of Don's lack of authority. Pam's, the payee, is a holder in due course.

Case 30.2 discusses the effect of taking a year-old check on the alleged holder-in-due-course status of a transferee who was also a payee.

CASE 30.2 American State Bank v. Northwest South Dakota Production Credit Assoc. · 404 N.W.2d 517 (S.D. 1987)

FACTS Fort Pierre Livestock Auction, Inc. (Auction, plaintiff), sold cattle for Gene Hunt. In payment, Auction issued check 19074 for $31,730.23, payable to Hunt and two other payees, one of which was Hunt's creditor, the Northwest South Dakota Production Credit Association (PCA, defendant). Then Auction discovered that it had miscounted the cattle, and issued check 19331 for $36,343.95 to the same payees as a replacement for check 19074. Auction did not ask Hunt to return check 19074, but it did attempt to stop payment on it. Its bank, American State Bank, denied receiving the stop-payment order.

A year later, on October 26, 1984, a PCA representative met with Hunt to arrange repayment of a delinquent loan. Hunt delivered checks 19074 and 19331 to PCA in exchange for the forgiveness of his remaining debt. PCA did not know that one check replaced the other or that Auction had attempted to stop payment on check 19074. PCA's agent telephoned Auction's manager and told him "a couple of old [Hunt] checks were going to be deposited."

Both checks cleared through Auction's account with American State Bank. Upon discovering that the bank had debited its account for both checks, Auction informed PCA that one check was meant to replace the other and demanded repayment for check 19074. Alleging it was a holder in due course, PCA refused Auction's demand. Auction sued PCA to recover the amount of the check. The trial court held that Auction had the defense of lack of consideration because check 19331 replaced check 19074, but it also ruled that PCA was a holder in due course and therefore took check 19074 free from that defense. Auction appealed.

OPINION KONENKAMP, Circuit J. . . . To be [a holder in due course], a party must take the instrument for value, in good faith, and without notice that it is overdue, or dishonored,

CASE 30.2 Continued

or of any defense against or claim to it by any person. . . . The fact that PCA was a payee does not [in itself] disqualify [PCA as a holder in due course. However, *as payee*, PCA never became a holder in due course because PCA never received possession of the check and therefore never became a holder]. If a party fails to qualify as [a holder in due course], then . . . he takes the instrument subject to:

> (*a*) All valid claims to it on the part of any person; and (*b*) All defenses of any party which would be available in an action on a simple contract; and (*c*) The defenses of want or failure of consideration, nonperformance of any condition precedent, nondelivery, or delivery for a special purpose. . . .

[In the October 26, 1984, transaction,] PCA took check 19074 for value and in good faith, but knew it was a year old; therefore, the only issue is whether PCA had notice [that] check 19074 was overdue. Under [Section 3-304(3) of the UCC]:

> The purchaser has notice that an instrument is overdue if he has reason to know . . . (*c*) That he is taking a demand instrument after demand has been made or more than a reasonable length of time after its issue. A *reasonable time for a check drawn and payable within the states and territories of the United States and District of Columbia is presumed to be thirty days*. . . .

This presumption is rebuttable . . . and we can envision instances where a delay of more than thirty days may be legitimate in the ordinary course of commerce, but PCA offered no justification for a year's delay. At the trial, PCA's representative testified he obtained the year-old check when Hunt simply pulled it out of his briefcase and handed it to him.

PCA concedes that it knew the check was a year old, but argues its telephone call to [Auction] warning of its imminent deposit of old Hunt checks along with [Auction's] apparent acquiescence overcomes the [presumption] that check 19074 was overdue. . . .

When a holder has no notice of a defect in an instrument at the time it comes into his hands, later events will not alter his HDC status. . . . If knowledge acquired after the taking of an instrument [will not undo HDC status], then logically, a holder with notice that an instrument is overdue at the time it is taken should not be able to undo that notice except in the most extraordinary circumstances. . . . When PCA's agent called [Auction,] he made no mention of the check numbers, their amounts, or dates; and [Auction's] manager made no comment which would lead the agent to believe the checks were not overdue, but only acknowledged the agent's intention to deposit them.

PCA's warning to [Auction] that it was about to deposit Hunt's "old checks" was insufficient to negate what was plainly visible on the check's face: a year-old date. Since it had notice that check 19074 was overdue, PCA was not a holder in due course. The trial court's finding to the contrary was clearly erroneous.

JUDGMENT Reversed. . . .

Rights of Transferees; Shelter Provision

The transfer of an instrument "vests in the transferee such rights as the holder has therein" [3-201(1)]. This rule states the general rule applying to assignments, that an assignee gets whatever rights the assignor had. Suppose, for example, that Maria buys from Paul three carts for use in her business and pays for them with a demand note made out to the order of Paul. Paul delivers two carts, which Maria uses, but he never delivers the third cart. In the meantime Paul has negotiated the note to his daughter Harriet as a gift. Although Maria has the defense of nondelivery as to the one cart, Paul is entitled to payment for the two carts he delivered. Harriet, who has not given value for the note, takes it subject to Maria's defense of nondelivery; but since Paul's transfer of the note vests in Harriet the rights that Paul had, Harriet is entitled to collect on the note to the extent justified by Paul's partial performance.

The same principle applies to the rights acquired by a holder in due course. When a holder in due course negotiates commercial paper, the transferee ordinarily acquires the *rights* of a holder in due course even if the transferee personally cannot qualify as one. Suppose Hal, a holder in due course of a note, negotiates it to Arnold as a gift. Since Arnold did not give value, he cannot qualify as a holder in due course. But, as assignee of Hal's rights, Arnold acquires whatever right Hal had—in this case, Hal's right as a holder in due course to have payment free from personal defenses and rival claims of ownership. Arnold is a holder "through" a holder in due course.

Section 3-201 of the UCC, which gives holders through a holder in due course the same freedom from claims and defenses that a holder in due course enjoys, is often referred to as the "shelter" provision." The policy behind it is to provide the holder in due course a free market for the paper. Providing a free market is accomplished by allowing most holders who are merely assignees to collect payment free from claims and personal defenses, since those assignees will thus be inclined to pay full value to the holder in due course. Figure 30.1 represents a series of negotiations (in the figure, from Pe to H_1; from H_1 to HDC; and from HDC to H_2) in which H_2, though not personally a holder in due course, takes M's note from HDC *free from* M's personal defenses. However, *some* transferees of a holder in due course are *disqualified* from receiving holder-in-due-course rights. A transferee who has been a *party to* (a participant in rather than merely on notice of) any fraud or illegality affecting the instrument, or who as a *prior* holder had notice of a defense or claim, cannot improve his or her position by taking from a later holder in due course. Attempts by prior holders to improve their positions by selling paper to a holder in due course and then receiving it back will be of no avail. In Figure 30.2, H_1 was not a holder in due course when he or she received M's note from Pe. H_1 is prohibited from improving his or her position by selling the

Figure 30.1 Shelter provision

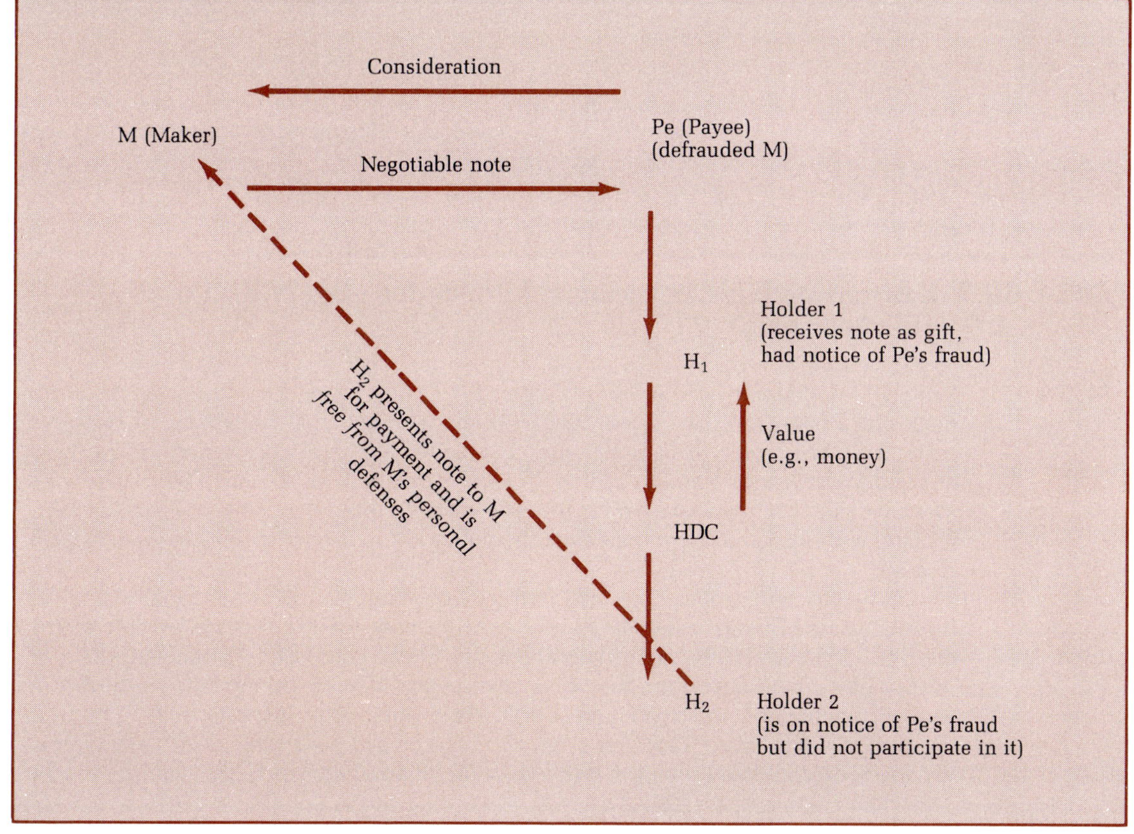

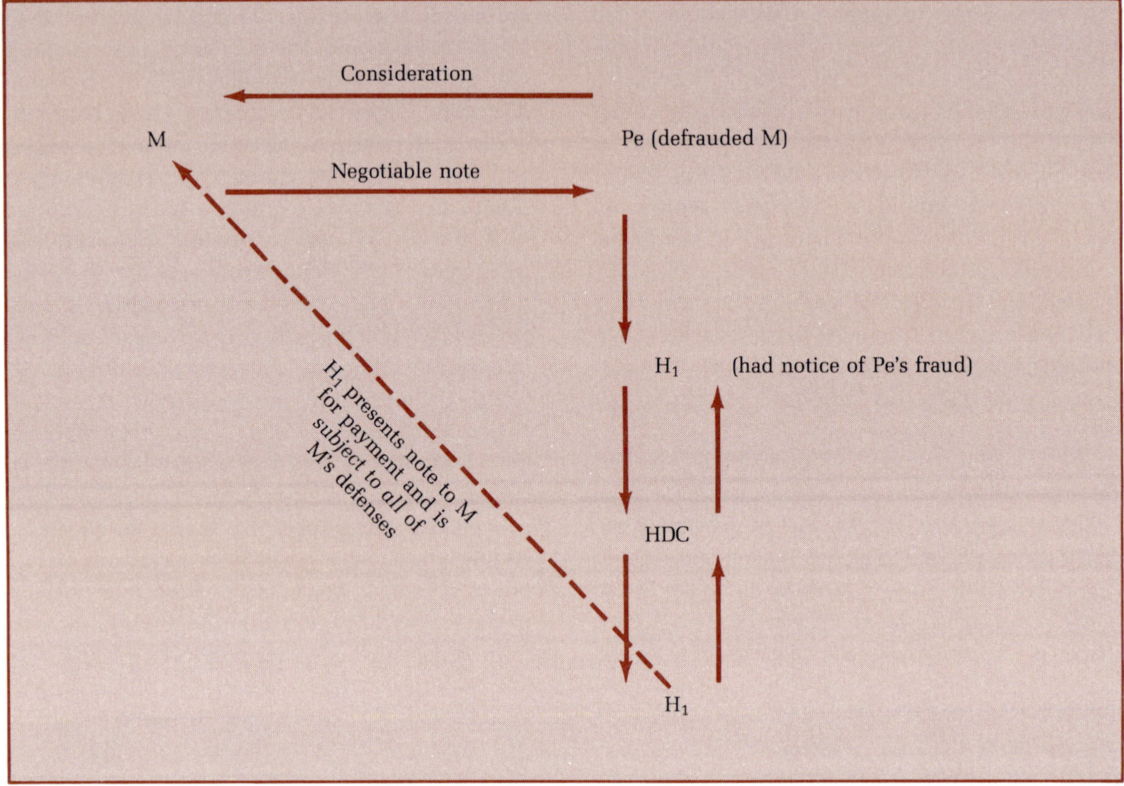

Figure 30.2 Shelter provision—a variation

note to HDC and buying it back. Consequently, H_1 takes the note *subject to* M's personal defenses.

Case 30.3 illustrates the operation of the shelter provision.

CASE 30.3 Canyonville Bible Academy v. Lobemaster · 247 N.E.2d 623 (Ill. App. 1969)

FACTS Samuel D. Lobmaster, the owner of Lobmaster Trailer Sales, Inc., owed the Jefferson Bank and Trust Co. (Bank) over $600,000. His practice was to discount to Bank his customers' notes representing trailer sales. Lobmaster also personally guaranteed payment of the discounted notes and as additional security made Bank the main beneficiary of a $200,000 policy of insurance on his life. Canyonville Bible Academy, a secondary beneficiary, was entitled to any proceeds of the policy not needed to cover Lobmaster's debt to Bank.

On February 18, 1964, Louis and Bernice Lobemaster (defendants) bought a trailer from Lobmaster Trailer Sales (LTS) and signed a note for $12,694.22, payable to the order of LTS in eighty-four monthly installments. On February 20, LTS endorsed the note over to Bank. Five days later, Samuel Lobmaster was killed in an airplane crash. About a year later, the Lobemasters defaulted in their payments on the note.

After notes owed to LTS were paid, Samuel Lobmaster's estate owed Bank approximately $200,000. Bank used the proceeds of the life insurance policy to set up a reserve

CASE 30.3 Continued

fund and charged defaulted obligations of LTS customers against it. On June 16, 1966, Bank assigned the Lobemasters' note to Canyonville Bible Academy (plaintiff). Thus, the Academy received the defaulted note instead of the insurance proceeds that Samuel Lobmaster had intended the Academy to have as a gift. The Academy sued the Lobemasters for payment of the note. From a judgment for the Lobemasters, the Academy appealed.

OPINION

TRAPP, P. J.... No question is raised by the defendants as to the following: (1) the validity of their signatures, (2) the acquisition of the note by the Bank prior to the date of the first installment, for value and in good faith in the regular course of business, and (3) the actual assignment of the note by the Bank to plaintiff on June 16, 1966....

The second affirmative defense is that... there was never a valid assignment or purchase of the note for value. [The defendants argued that under the Negotiable Instruments Law, the predecessor of the UCC in Illinois, a transferee had to give value before he or she could receive the rights of the transferor.]

Under [Section 3-201 of the UCC,] transfer is provided for as follows:

> (1) Transfer of an instrument vests in the transferee such rights as the transferor has therein, except that a transferee who has himself been a party to any fraud or illegality affecting the instrument or who as a prior holder had notice of a defense or claim against it cannot improve his position by taking from a later holder in due course.

...[A UCC comment states] the following:

> 2. The transfer of rights is not limited to transfers for value. An instrument may be transferred as a gift, and the donee acquires whatever rights the donor had.

Under [Section 3-201], it is quite clear that any transfer of an instrument transfers all rights of the transferor, except in the specific case[s] noted as... exception[s]. Since the Bank was a holder in due course and plaintiff was not a prior holder, the plaintiff by transfer from the Bank acquired the rights of a holder in due course irrespective of the question of value....

We conclude that the transfer of the defendant[s'] note by the Bank to plaintiff gave plaintiff the Bank's [rights] as holder in due course, and the note is enforceable by plaintiff against defendant[s].

JUDGMENT

The cause is reversed and remanded with directions to enter judgment in favor of plaintiff....

FTC Limits

Reasons for FTC Limits

In recent years, consumer groups have voiced strong opposition to holder-in-due-course status. They object to the idea that a maker or drawer of an instrument is not permitted to assert a legitimate defense—e.g., fraud in the inducement or breach of warranty—simply because the payee transfers a negotiable instrument for value to a third person. Especially upsetting is the impression that the courts have tended to resolve doubts against consumers and in favor of finance companies whose relationships with payees are clearly suspect, thus permitting, if not encouraging, widespread fraud, shoddy work, excessive finance charges, etc. Unsophisticated consumers are especially vulnerable to being exploited by unscrupulous sellers of goods and services who set up a financing subsidiary as a holder in due course to receive consumer notes that the sellers know are likely to be subject to personal defenses of the consumers.

The courts have, of course, allowed consumers to assert personal defenses where the holder could be shown to lack holder-in-due-course status. Some courts have gone so far as to find a lack of good faith, for example, on the basis of such facts as the holder's probable awareness of suspicious circumstances surrounding the seller-payee's, or industry-wide, business practices. The close business relationship between a seller and its financing subsidiary, unusually deep discounting of consumer notes, very speedy transfers of consumer notes from payee to transferee, and the fact that the transferee prepared note forms and other documents for the consumer to sign—the courts have considered all these factors and more when deciding whether a person is a holder in due course. In many close cases, judges have felt required to rule that a person was a holder in due course, even while expressing serious doubts about the transferee's status.

Because of inadequate or uneven protection of consumers by the courts, some state legislatures enacted statutes that deprived transferees of holder-in-due-course status or in some other way allowed consumers to assert their personal defenses. But only a few states enacted such statutes. So, in 1976, the Federal Trade Commission put into effect its Trade Regulation Rule 433 [16 C.F.R. § 433].

The FTC Rule

In the typical consumer credit transaction, the consumer's installment note is promptly transferred to a finance company, which purchases the note at a discount. FTC Rule 433 protects consumers by requiring a seller or a lessor of consumer goods or services to include in a consumer *credit* contract a prominently printed notice as follows:

NOTICE

ANY HOLDER OF THIS CONSUMER CREDIT CONTRACT IS SUBJECT TO ALL CLAIMS AND DEFENSES WHICH THE DEBTOR COULD ASSERT AGAINST THE SELLER OF GOODS OR SERVICES OBTAINED PURSUANT HERETO OR WITH THE PROCEEDS HEREOF. RECOVERY HEREUNDER BY THE DEBTOR SHALL NOT EXCEED AMOUNTS PAID BY THE DEBTOR HEREUNDER.

Failure of the seller to provide the required notice constitutes an unfair and deceptive practice within the meaning of Section 5 of the Federal Trade Commission Act. The notice requirement applies to all consumer credit contracts in or affecting commerce, including three common types: (1) a negotiable promissory note signed by the consumer, (2) an ordinary (nonnegotiable) consumer credit contract containing a waiver-of-defenses clause, and (3) a consumer credit loan arranged by the seller for the consumer-buyer.

The presence of this notice preserves all claims and defenses that a consumer may have, even against a good faith purchaser for value without notice of any defenses. A *consumer* is a person who acquires goods or services (e.g., automobiles, home improvements, and health spa memberships) for personal, family, or household use. Rule 433 does not cover purchases of real estate or securities, or purchases over $25,000; nor are contracts for public utility services affected by the rule. The rule cover a purchase in which the consumer pays by check. A check is not a credit instrument and need not contain the notice.

A merchant may not circumvent the FTC rule by arranging for the consumer to borrow money from a lender and pay cash to the merchant. The rule provides specifically that when the merchant arranges for the loan, the credit instrument must contain the specified notice, and the lender has no greater rights against the consumer than the seller does. However, the rule does not apply to all lenders. A lender is required to include the notice (and is therefore deprived of holder-in-due-course status) only where the merchant *refers* consumers to the lender or *is affiliated* with the lender by control or by business arrangement.

Rule 433 puts upon purchasers of commercial paper (and other consumer credit contracts) the burden of "policing" consumer financing. If those purchasers are careful to check for fraud and other misconduct of their transferors, consumers will receive a protection not formerly available to them—i.e., the scrutiny by commercial paper buyers of business practices the consumer once had to combat alone. If the policing activities are not effective, finance companies may pay less for consumer obligations since the risk of nonpayment would be greater. Ultimately, the seller of goods or services may raise the price to the consumer to compensate for a higher discount rate. To date, however, there is little evidence that prices have increased for this reason.

Rule 433 limits the protection that a consumer receives. The maker or drawer who has a defense may refuse to pay further sums on the instrument and may recover amounts previously paid. However, the consumer may not assert a claim against the holder of the instrument for damages in excess of the amount the consumer paid. If the consumer seeks a larger award for consequential damages, for example, he or she must institute an action in state court against the merchant who sold the goods or services.

Summary

Any holder of commercial paper can negotiate it and thereby enable a properly qualified transferee to become a holder in due course. The transferee, if he or she is a holder, may become a holder in due course by giving value for the instrument, taking it in good faith, and taking it without notice of defenses to payment, rival claims of ownership, or other problems surrounding its issuance, transfer, or collection.

A transferee of commercial paper receives whatever rights the transferor had. A holder who does not personally qualify as a holder in due course may receive the rights of one by assignment, under the shelter provision, the purpose of which is to assure a holder in due course of a market for the paper. However, a prior holder with notice of defenses cannot improve his or her position merely by selling an instrument to and repurchasing it from a holder in due course. Nor can a transferee who has been a party to any fraud or illegality affecting the instrument acquire the rights of a holder in due course.

FTC Rule 433 has, in effect, abolished holder-in-due-course status as to holders of certain consumer credit contracts, by imposing a notice requirement that preserves claims and defenses of consumers-makers. The rule puts the burden of policing consumer credit transactions on the purchasers of consumer credit contracts rather than on consumers alone.

Review Questions

1 Explain whether the following statement is accurate: "A holder in due course is a holder who takes the instrument for value, in good faith, and without notice of any defense against it."

2 **(a)** Explain the following statement: "In the law of commercial paper, value is not the same thing as consideration." **(b)** John Doe deposits a check in his bank. Under what circumstances, and to what extent, does the bank become a holder for value of that item? **(c)** Explain the "first in, first out" rule.

3 Is the following statement accurate? "A holder lacks the good faith necessary to be a holder in due course only if the holder has knowledge of actual wrongdoing concerning the instrument."

4 **(a)** When is a check overdue? **(b)** When are other varieties of commercial paper overdue?

5 **(a)** What is "dishonor"? **(b)** How may a holder be on notice of dishonor?

6 Can a holder be on notice of defenses of a maker or a drawer even though the holder is not aware of any particular wrongdoing by the payee? Explain.

7 Ordinarily, the payee of a negotiable instrument is its holder. How might the payee also be a holder in due course?

8 **(a)** What is the purpose of the "shelter provision"? **(b)** What kinds of transferees may not benefit from the shelter provision?

9 **(a)** What is the justification for FTC Rule 433? **(b)** To what transactions does it apply? Not apply?

Case Problems

1 Wesley Heights Realty drew a check for $1,400, payable to the order of a customer of Falls Church Bank. The customer deposited the check in his account, was given a provisional credit of $1,400, and was permitted to withdraw $140 immediately, before the bank discovered that Wesley Heights had stopped payment on the check. By the time the bank received the dishonored check, its customer had "skipped," leaving no credits in his account against which to charge the $140. Bank demanded $140 from Wesley Heights, which refused to pay because it had a personal defense against the customer. The trial court granted judgment to Wesley Heights, holding that the bank was only an agent for collection and "not a holder in due course for value." Bank appealed. If the bank gave value, the decision of the trial court should be reversed. Did the bank give value?

2 Girner issued a negotiable $5,000 promissory note to First Realty Corp. on September 25, 1980. A payment schedule was printed on the back of the note. Monthly payments were to begin on January 15, 1981. First Realty assigned the note to Bohra for value. On July 27, 1981, Bohra transferred the note to his attorney, Richardson, in payment for legal services. At that time, no payments had been recorded on the payment schedule. When Richardson tried to collect on the note, he learned that Girner had a personal defense. Girner refused to pay. Richardson, alleging that he was a holder in due course, sued Girner for the amount of the note. Was Richardson a holder in due course?

3 The drawer of two checks signed them in blank and delivered them to her husband. Kilroy allegedly stole the checks from the husband. Kilroy completed the checks (inserting his name as payee) and indorsed and cashed them at Central Savings Bank where he had an account. Central presented the checks to the drawee bank for payment, but the drawee dishonored them for insufficient funds. Central then sued the drawer for the amount of the checks. In opposing Central's motion for summary judgment, the drawer alleged that Central had notice of a possible defense as to the second check because before cashing it Central had received notice that the first check had been dishonored. As to the second check, was Central on notice of the drawer's personal defense of nondelivery to Kilroy?

4 Cochise College Park, Inc., sold an Arizona lot to Vanotti, who signed a promissory note and mortgage for the purchase price of about $4,400. Three weeks later, Cochise sold the note and mortgage to Salter for $2,760. Earlier, Salter had purchased from Cochise seven notes similar to Vanotti's and purchased three others with Vanotti's. Salter received Vanotti's original mortgage; the original Purchase and Sale Agreement; a copy of the Property Report required by a federal agency for interstate land sales; and a photocopy of a warranty deed executed by Cochise to Vanotti. However, no deed was ever delivered to Vanotti or recorded in Arizona. The Property Report granted Vanotti a 6-month period of inspection and a money-back guarantee. Federal law required that the purchaser receive a copy of the Property Report at or before the time of sale. Vanotti had not signed the Property Report and denied receiving a copy of it. After inspecting the property, Vanotti attempted to revoke the contract but could not locate any representative of Cochise, which was now in bankruptcy. Vanotti ceased making the monthly payments on the note, and Salter sued him for the balance due. Holding that Salter was not a holder in due course, the trial court dismissed the action. Salter appealed. Was Salter a holder in due course of Vanotti's note?

5 Impact Marketing, Inc., issued six postdated checks to Barry E. Bell for legal services to be performed in the future. Knowing that the checks were postdated and that the legal services had not yet been performed, Financial Associates purchased the checks from Bell at a discount. Impact paid four of the checks but stopped payment on the other two because Bell's services had been terminated. Financial sued Impact for the amount of the two dishonored checks. Is Financial entitled to payment?

6 Graff issued two promissory notes to Fred Klomann as payee. By special indorsement, Klomann gave the notes to his daughter, Candace. She examined the notes and handed them back to Fred for collection. Some time later, Fred scratched out Candace's name in the special indorsement, inserted the name of his wife, Georgia, and delivered the notes to Georgia. When she brought suit to collect on the notes, the maker, Graff, defended on the ground that Georgia had no right, title, or interest in the notes and therefore had no standing to sue for collection. From a summary judgment for Georgia, Graff appealed. Was Georgia entitled to payment of the notes?

CHAPTER 31

Liability of the Parties; Discharge

If you sign a promissory note in payment for goods, you expect to be (and are) liable for payment of the note in the absence of defenses assertable by you against the person presenting the note for payment. If you indorse your payroll check when cashing it, you might—to your surprise—be liable for the face amount if your employer's bank (the drawee) does not honor (pay) the check. You might receive a check containing a forged in-blank indorsement and make a gift of the check *without* signing it, and still have liability if the check proves uncollectable. Liability on a negotiable instrument, or in connection with its transfer and collection, can arise in a number of ways, both expected and unexpected.

A person who signs, transfers, or seeks payment of commercial paper may be subject to two kinds of liability: contractual liability and warranty liability. The Uniform Commercial Code (UCC) imposes *contractual* liability on most *signers* of commercial paper for the face amount of the instrument (including any interest). For example, if you issue a check, accept a draft in which you are named as drawee, or sign a promissory note, you will be liable contractually ("on the instrument") for the amount stated in the instrument. Likewise, when you indorse your paycheck to cash it, your indorsement, if unqualified, makes you contractually liable to the indorsee (e.g., a bank or supermarket) and to any other transferee for the face amount in the event that the drawee (your employer's bank) does not pay. Because commercial paper is not only a contract but also a type of property, the UCC imposes *warranty* liability too, on *nonsigners as well as on signers.* Breach of a warranty may occur when a person *transfers* or *presents for payment* an instrument (the property) that is defective in some respect, as where a signature has been forged. The UCC classifies commercial paper warranties as *transfer* or *presentment* warranties.

A person who pays the amount specified in a negotiable instrument, or who otherwise fulfills the contractual obligations imposed by the Code, is *discharged* (freed) from liability. A person may also be discharged from liability by the actions of others. The contractual liability of the parties, their discharge from liability, and liability for breach of warranty are the topics of this chapter.

Frequently, a person who comes into possession of a negotiable instrument faces liability for the tort of conversion. *Conversion* is the wrongful exercise of dominion and control over the personal property of another to the exclusion of the rights of the owner, or in a manner inconsistent with those rights. As noted in the preceding chapter, a person who steals or who finds and sells bearer paper is a converter. A person who steals or finds order paper and forges an indorsement also commits conversion; so does a person who pays or buys an instrument containing a forged indorsement, even if this person has no knowledge of the forgery. And, as is noted in the next chapter, banks can commit conversion in a number of ways. In all instances of conversion, the converter is liable to the true owner for the face amount of the instrument [3-419]. However, although conversion is an important source of legal remedy for persons who have been wrongfully deprived of negotiable instruments, the main focus of this chapter remains the contractual liability of signers (and its discharge), and warranty liability. These latter two are the kinds of liability that contribute most to the value and usefulness of commercial paper.

Contractual Liability of the Parties

In commercial paper law, contractual liability is of two basic types—primary and secondary. So, a signer of commercial paper may be a *primary party* or a *secondary party.* The ultimate liability of primary and secondary parties is the same: to pay the face amount of the instrument. But, as is discussed below, the *timing* of primary liability differs markedly from that of secondary liability. Other circumstances than type of liability (primary versus secondary) affect the existence or order of contractual liability as among various signers. These include whether the signer is an accommodation party, whether the signer is a guarantor, and whether a signature was made by an agent or was forged.

Recall from Chapter 28 that a "maker" is a person who issues a note or a certificate of deposit. A "drawer" is a person who issues a check or a draft. An "acceptor" is a drawee of a draft who signs the draft across its face and thereby agrees to pay it. As noted in Chapter 29, a "holder" is a person who is in possession of bearer paper or properly indorsed order paper, and who therefore appears to be the rightful owner, entitled to payment or acceptance.

In commercial paper law, "maker" always refers to the issuer of a *note* (or a certificate of deposit). Therefore, it is not correct terminology to call the *drawer* of a draft or check its "maker." Even so, this book uses the popular expression "to *make out* a check" (meaning "to write or to *draw* a check").

Liability of Primary Parties

The *maker* of a note or certificate of deposit (CD) and the *acceptor* of a draft or check are primary parties. Primary liability is unconditional; i.e., a primary party is liable to the holder of the instrument for the face amount, and can be sued for it immediately when the instrument comes due, without the need for any further action by the holder [3-122]. Consequently, when sued, a primary party cannot delay the lawsuit on the ground of the holder's failure to make presentment (demand) for payment. As a practical matter, however, holders normally try to collect payment from the primary party before bringing suit, even though they are not required to do so.

When a draft or check is *issued,* there is no primary party (i.e., no maker or acceptor). The drawer is a signer, but for the reason discussed in the next section of this chapter is a *secondary* party. The drawee is not a signer, and unless and until there is acceptance, the drawee is not liable "on the instrument" (i.e., is not contractually liable for the face amount) to anyone. Of course, if the drawee accepts a draft, the drawee *becomes* an *acceptor* and is then a primary party. "Certification" of a check by a drawee bank is a type of acceptance. Upon certifying a check, a drawee bank becomes a primary party, fully liable "on the instrument" without need for any further action by the holder. Other consequences of certification are discussed in Chapter 32.

Liability of Secondary Parties

The *drawer* of a check or draft and the *indorser* of any commercial paper are secondary parties. The liability of secondary parties differs from the liability of primary parties mainly in the events that "trigger" liability and, as to indorsers, in how long the liability lasts. How long liability lasts is discussed later in this chapter, in the section on discharge.

A primary party is immediately and unconditionally liable for the face amount when the instrument comes due. In contrast, a secondary party is liable (when the instrument is due) only if certain additional triggering "conditions" or events take place: *presentment* (demand) for payment or acceptance; *dishonor* (refusal to pay an instrument or to accept a time draft); and, especially for indorsers, *timely notice of dishonor.* For instruments accepted or payable outside the United States—i.e., in international trade—a fourth triggering event, called "protest," may be required. A *protest* is a document or certificate of dishonor signed and sealed by a public official such as a U.S. consul or a notary public authorized to certify that the instrument was dishonored.

The fact that secondary liability is conditional can be seen in the following illustrations:

1 You *issue* (make out and deliver) a check to Paula in payment for a tennis racket. As drawer of the check, you are a signer, but the understanding between you and Paula is that Paula (or some transferee of the check such as Paula's bank) will present the check to your bank (the drawee) for payment, not to you. Paula understands that she will be entitled to have payment directly from you only if the bank does not pay. You, as a drawer, are a secondary party because Paula (or a transferee) must *present* the check to the drawee for payment, undergo the unpleasant experience of having the check *dishonored,* and give you *notice of dishonor* before having the right to payment from you personally.

2 You work for Orange Groves, Inc., *receive* a paycheck for $300, indorse it in blank, and cash it at Ned's Supermarket. The understanding between you (the payee-indorser) and Ned is that Ned (or some transferee) will present the check to your employer's bank (the drawee) for payment. Ned can have payment from you only if (*a*) he *presents* the check to the drawee bank, (*b*) the bank *dishonors* the check, and (*c*) Ned gives you timely *notice of dishonor.* Thus, like the drawer of a check or draft, an indorser is a secondary party and is not liable for the face amount unless the conditions of presentment, dishonor, and notice of dishonor have been met.

The obligation of an indorser to pay upon the happening of the required conditions results from the indorser's "engagement" (promise) to pay imposed by the UCC [3-414(1)]. The *holder* of a dishonored instrument is entitled to payment from *any* indorser who has received timely notice of dishonor. But where one of several indorsers has paid, there may be a question as to whether the one who paid the holder may, in turn, have payment from some other indorser. Unless otherwise agreed among indorsers, the promise of an indorser is made only to *subsequent* indorsers (those signing later) and to the holder [3-414(2)]. Thus, liability of indorsers *to one another* is in relation to the order of signing. For example, Paul, the payee of a check, indorses and delivers it to Ben, who in turn indorses and delivers it to Cora. If Cora is unable to collect from the drawee bank, she may collect from Ben, and Ben in turn may collect from Paul. But if Cora had skipped Ben and had received payment from Paul, Paul could not collect from Ben because Ben's engagement as an indorser is made to *subsequent* indorsers (Cora), not prior ones (Paul). Paul's only recourse is to the drawer of the check.

Presentment, dishonor, and notice of dishonor are so important in the collection of commercial paper that they require further discussion.

Requirement of Presentment. *Presentment* is a demand for acceptance or payment of a negotiable instrument [3-504]. The demand is made *by* a holder *upon* the party expected to *pay* (i.e., the maker of a note or the drawee—including an acceptor—of a draft) or the party expected to *accept* (i.e., the drawee of a draft). Presentment may be made *in person* (e.g., by the holder's taking a check directly to the drawee bank), or *by mail,* or *through a clearinghouse.* A *clearinghouse* is a place where banks exchange checks and drafts drawn on each other and thereby settle their daily balances. A clearinghouse would be involved where, for example, the holder and the drawer of a check do their banking business at different banks. The holder takes the check to his or her own bank for collection; the holder's bank sends the check to a clearinghouse; and the clearinghouse presents the check to the drawee bank (which also deals with that clearinghouse). If presentment is made by mail, the time of presentment is the time that the party who is to pay or to accept receives the mail.

If a holder is slow to make presentment, secondary parties (indorsers and drawers) may be discharged (freed) from liability. As is discussed later in this chapter, a delay in presentment will discharge a *drawer* only in very rare circumstances. But unexcused delay always discharges *indorsers.*

Some instruments specify a date for presentment. A presentment after this date may discharge secondary parties. If no date is specified, the holder must make presentment within a "reasonable" time to avoid discharging secondary parties [3-503]. Where the holder of a draft seeks to avoid discharging the *drawer* (in those rare circumstances, discussed later, where discharge of a drawer is possible), the reasonable time for presentment is measured from the *date of the draft or its date of issue, whichever is later.* Where the holder seeks to hold an *indorser* liable, the reasonable time is measured from the *time of his or her indorsement.* What constitutes a reasonable time varies according to the circumstances. A court might allow more time if great distances or unreliable communications are involved than if distances are short and communication easy.

For an *uncertified check*—a check that has not been accepted ("certified") by the drawee bank—the reasonable time for presentment is *presumed* to be 30 *days* with respect to the drawer's liability and 7 *days* as to an indorser's liability [3-503(2)]. These time limits are intended to encourage prompt presentment of checks so that the check clearing process will remain efficient. However, a holder may "rebut" (demonstrate the impropriety of) the presumption by proving that under the circumstances a longer time for presentment was reasonable.

Recall from the preceding chapter that a person who takes a check for value more than 30 days after issue is presumed to be on notice that the check is overdue. A slow taker therefore cannot be a holder in due course. The 30-day limit for *presentment* just discussed in this chapter is different. Here we are talking about a *timely* taker but a slow *presenter.* A person who takes a check for value *within* 30 days after its issue usually is a holder in due course. If that holder in due course fails to make timely *presentment,* the holder loses the liability of indorsers and *may* lose the liability of the drawer. But if the drawer remains liable, as is usual, the holder in due course takes the check free from the drawer's personal defenses despite the loss of indorsers' liability due to slow presentment by the holder in due course.

Requirement of Dishonor. *Dishonor* is a refusal or failure to pay or to accept an instrument that the holder has properly presented for payment or acceptance [3-507]. Dishonor of a note or certificate of deposit occurs if the maker refuses to pay on the due date. Dishonor of *any* draft or check occurs if the drawee or acceptor refuses to *pay* on the due date. A *time* draft (e.g., one payable at a specified date after issue, or one payable "60 days after sight") is dishonored if the holder presents it *for acceptance* before the due date and the drawee refuses to accept it [3-507(1)]. The holder of a time draft has a right to the drawee's acceptance so that the holder can know early whether the drawee is willing to pay when the due date arrives. However, a drawee's refusal to accept a *demand* draft (or to certify a check, which also is a demand draft) is *not* a dishonor, because the holder of a demand draft (one payable upon the holder's demand) is already entitled to payment in cash and does not face the uncertainty of payment facing the holder of a time draft that is not yet payable [3-501, comment 3]. Of course, a drawee's failure to *pay* a demand draft upon presentment *is* a dishonor.

A party to whom presentment is made does have a right to assurances that the presentment for payment or for acceptance is proper, though. So, return of an instrument for lack of a proper indorsement is not a dishonor [3-507(3)]. Likewise, a refusal to pay or to accept for reasons such as an illegible signature, postdating, alteration of a payee's name, or evidence of forgery is not a dishonor. Moreover, it is not a dishonor for the person to whom presentment is made to require exhibition of the instrument, reasonable identification of the presenter, evidence of the presenter's authority to make presentment for another person, and presentment of the instrument at the place, if any, specified in the instrument for payment or acceptance [3-505(1)]. If a required place for presentment has not been stated, the holder ordinarily must present the instrument at the business location or residence of the party who is to accept or pay.

Failure of the presenter to comply with presentment requirements (exhibition of the instrument, reasonable identification, and so on) invalidates the presentment; but the presenter has a reasonable time to comply, and the time for acceptance or payment runs *from* the time of the presenter's compliance [3-505(2)]. Thus, the person who is to accept or pay has the full time allowed by the Code to investigate the situation. Deferring *acceptance* of a time draft until the close of the next business day is not a dishonor [3-506(1)]. Nor is it a dishonor to defer *payment* of most commercial paper pending a reasonable examination to determine whether it is properly payable. However, if payment is not made by the close of business on the day of presentment, the instrument is dishonored [3-506(2)].

Requirement of Notice. After an instrument has been dishonored, secondary parties (drawers and indorsers) must be given timely *notice of dishonor* if the holder (presenter) is to avoid discharging them from liability. Notice of dishonor must be given within time limits prescribed by the Code, usually 3 business days [3-508(2)]. Collecting banks have a shorter time to give notice of dishonor, up to 2 business days. The notice may be given in any reasonable manner, either orally or in writing. Unlike a presentment, a notice of dishonor sent by mail is given when *sent*, even though it may never reach the secondary party.

A person who is attempting to collect the amount of a dishonored check from an indorser must keep *two* time limits in mind: (1) the presumed 7-day limit on the indorser's liability (which begins to run at the *time of indorsement*), and (2) the 3-day *maximum* time for giving notice of dishonor (which ends at *midnight* of the third business day following the day of dishonor or receipt of notice of dishonor). The following examples illustrate the interplay between the two time limits.

1 On Monday, May 1, the following events occur: Dora makes a check out to Paul, Paul indorses it over to Hal at 10:00 A.M., Hal presents it to Dora's bank for payment, and Bank dishonors the check for insufficient funds. Paul is liable as indorser for 7 calendar days from the time he indorsed the check—until 10:00 A.M., Monday, May 8. But Hal has only 3 business days after the day of dishonor (or after the day he received notice of dishonor) to notify Paul of it, i.e., until midnight of Thursday, May 4. If Hal waits until Friday to give notice, he is too late to have payment from Paul.

2 Hal receives the indorsed check on May 1. Suppose he waits until Friday, May 5, to present it for payment, and Bank dishonors it then. Hal's 3 business days for giving notice (ending at midnight Wednesday, May 10) will be cut short because Paul's 7-day indorser's liability expires at 10:00 A.M., Monday, May 8.

Case 31.1 illustrates an important difference between primary and secondary liability.

CASE 31.1 Tepper v. Citizens Federal Savings & Loan Assoc. · 38 UCC Rep. 528 (Fla. App. 1984)

FACTS Rose Tepper was adjudicated an incompetent in December, 1982. On examination of her personal effects, a court-appointed guardian discovered a check for the sum of $6,068, dated January 4, 1974, made out to Rose Tepper as payee by the drawer, Citizens Federal Savings and Loan Association. The drawee was Jefferson National Bank, in which Citizens Federal had an account.

On December 20, 1982, Tepper's guardian presented the check to the drawee, which refused payment. The guardian then notified the drawer, Citizens Federal, of the dishonor. Citizens Federal refused to pay, and on July 12, 1982, Tepper's guardian sued the drawer for the amount of the check. From a judgment for Citizens Federal, Tepper's guardian appealed.

OPINION FERGUSON, J. The sole question presented is when does the statute of limitations begin to run against a drawer in an action for wrongful dishonor of a check—on the date of issuance of the check or the date of presentment and dishonor?

[The trial court held that the 5-year statute of limitations began to run on the date the check was issued, and that the guardian's suit was therefore barred.] We reverse [and hold] that the statute of limitations begins to run against a drawer of a check on the date of presentment and dishonor. . . .

A draft is a three-party instrument whereby the drawer orders the drawee to pay money to the payee. . . . A draft is also called a check when the drawee is a bank and the instrument is payable on demand. A drawee is not liable on the instrument until there has been an acceptance. . . . The act of accepting the instrument renders the drawee primarily liable as an acceptor. Because there are no conditions precedent to its liability, a cause of action accrues against an acceptor in the case of a demand instrument on the date of the instrument or date of issue. . . .

The drawer, on the other hand, is only secondarily liable on the instrument, in that there are conditions precedent to liability. The normal conditions precedent include presentment to the drawee, dishonor, and notice of dishonor. Therefore, a cause of action against the drawer of a draft accrues only upon demand following dishonor of the instrument. Notice of dishonor constitutes a demand. [A] cause of action against the drawer. . . Citizens Federal thus did not accrue until [Tepper's guardian] received notice of dishonor from the drawee, Jefferson National Bank.

Florida case authority for the proposition that the statute of limitations begins to run against an issuing bank on a *cashier's check* at the moment of issuance. . . is distinguishable. A cashier's check is a check on which the issuing bank acts as both the drawer and the drawee. Its own act of issuance renders the bank a drawee who has accepted the draft; thus the issuing bank becomes primarily liable [on a cashier's check] as an acceptor. Presentment of a negotiable instrument is not necessary in order to establish liability against parties who are primarily liable. In such a case the statute of limitations begins to run on a demand instrument at the moment of issuance. As to parties secondarily liable, however, such as the drawer herein, there is no [immediate] liability and thus no cause of action until demand following presentment and dishonor. . . . [Since Citizens Federal] was

CASE 31.1 Continued the drawer of the [check and was] therefore only secondarily liable, a cause of action did not accrue against it until after demand following presentment and dishonor on December 20, 1982. The action for wrongful dishonor of the instrument was commenced timely.

JUDGMENT Reversed and remanded.

Liability of Accommodation Parties

An *accommodation party* is a person who signs an instrument for the purpose of lending his or her name (credit) to another party to the instrument [3-415]. For example, suppose a person wishes to buy goods on credit and to give a promissory note in payment. The seller may refuse to extend credit if the buyer is a minor or has a poor credit rating. The seller may agree to sell the goods if another person (with good credit) will sign the note as an accommodation party.

Usually an accommodation party signs as either comaker or indorser, but he or she may sign in any other capacity, including co-drawer or acceptor. The contractual liability of an accommodation party to a holder and to others depends on the capacity in which the party signs. A person signing as maker or acceptor has primary liability; a person signing as drawer or indorser has secondary liability (i.e., presentment, dishonor, and notice are required to establish liability).

An accommodation party has a signer's usual liability to a holder and to others even though the accommodation party received no consideration for signing; however, an accommodation party has no liability on the instrument to the party accommodated [3-415(5)]. An accommodation party who pays the instrument has a right of recourse against the party accommodated. For example, a father who cosigns a note so his son may buy a car, and who pays the note when the son defaults, may recover the amount from his son. Whether a person signs as an accommodation party or, instead, as a co-obligor (a person equally liable) depends on the intention of the signers. An accommodation party is not liable on the instrument to the party accommodated; a co-obligor is liable (to the other co-obligor) for his or her share of the debt.

Liability of Guarantor

A *guarantor* is a signer of commercial paper who adds "payment guaranteed" or equivalent words to the signature. By such language a guarantor promises that if the instrument is not paid when due, he or she will pay it without the holder's having to resort to (make demand on) any other party [3-416(1)]. A *secondary* party who guarantees payment *waives* (gives up the right to) presentment and notice of dishonor, and thus acquires a liability that is indistinguishable from that of a co-maker.

A signer who adds "collection guaranteed" or equivalent words to the signature promises that if the instrument is not paid when due, he or she will pay it, but only if (1) the holder has first taken legal action to collect from the maker or acceptor, or (2) the holder can show that such legal action would be useless—e.g., because the maker or acceptor is insolvent. A secondary party (an indorser or a drawer) who guarantees collection waives presentment and notice of dishonor [3-416(2)].

Accommodation parties and guarantors are *sureties*. Suretyship is discussed in Chapter 24.

Effect (on Liability) of Signatures by Agents and Forgers

Signature by Authorized Agent. Agents frequently are authorized to sign commercial paper on behalf of their principals. Suppose that Andy Agar is authorized to sign a negotiable instrument on Pam Pell's behalf and wishes to bind her as maker, drawer, acceptor, or indorser without binding himself on the instrument. The best way for Andy to do this is to sign the instrument

> Pam Pell
> By Andy Agar, Agent

Andy escapes liability as a signer because he has (1) named the person represented, and (2) shown that he signed his own name in a representative capacity [3-403].

If Andy uses forms of signature that do not do *both* of these things, he may be held personally liable for the face amount of the instrument. The following examples illustrate the dangers of an agent's signing incorrectly. In the examples Andy is authorized to sign a check for Pam, made out to Paul Payee in payment for goods delivered to Pam.

1 Andy merely signs his own name: "Andy Agar." Andy is liable on the instrument. If Paul sues Andy for payment of the check, Andy will *not* be permitted to use parol evidence (discussed in Chapter 13) to show that he intended to sign as agent for Pam. Pam is not liable to anyone *on the instrument* because her name does not appear on it. However, under agency law (discussed in Chapters 33 to 35), Pam may be liable to Paul on the underlying transaction since she authorized it, as where Andy cannot pay the amount of the check.

2 Andy signs the check "Andy Agar, Agent." Andy is liable on the check. However, parol evidence *is* admissible between the immediate parties (Andy and Paul) to prove that Andy was not intended to be liable. Andy's parol evidence is *not* admissible against a holder in due course; therefore, Andy is liable to any holder in due course for the face amount. Pam is not liable on the check to anyone, since her name is not on it, but she may be liable to Paul on the underlying transaction, as in example 1 above.

3 Andy signs both names as follows:

Pam Pell
Andy Agar

Andy is liable on the check because he signed it. Pam is liable on the check because she authorized Andy to sign her name. Parol evidence is admissible between the immediate parties (Paul and Andy) to show that Andy was not intended to be liable, but parol evidence is not allowed to defeat Andy's liability to a holder in due course.

Case 31.2 discusses liability to the payee of a person who signs a note as both a representative and an individual.

CASE 31.2 First Safety Fund National Bank v. Friel · 3 UCC Rep. 2d 1021 (Mass. App. 1987)

FACTS Upon the death of her husband in 1981, Janet M. Friel (defendant) became president of New England Office Products Co. Although Mrs. Friel kept the company checkbook and signed all checks, the business was managed by her brother-in-law, David Friel.

In 1982 and 1983, he negotiated loans for the company and accompanied Mrs. Friel to First Safety Fund National Bank (plaintiff) to sign the notes. A bank officer presented prepared loan documents. As instructed, Mrs. Friel wrote "Janet M. Friel President" directly under the typed name of the corporate borrower, and on the line below that signature she wrote, "Janet M. Friel." She asked no questions about why she was asked to sign twice. She glanced over the papers but did not read them. When the company became insolvent in 1984, Bank sued her for payment of the notes. She contended that she was not to be personally liable on them. From a judgment for Friel, Bank appealed. The Appellate Division affirmed the judgment, and Bank appealed.

OPINION KASS, J. . . . Even an authorized representative, e.g., the president of a corporation, who signs his own name to an instrument is personally obligated if the instrument does not show that the signature is made in a representative capacity. . . .

. . . Mrs. Friel's difficulty is that [although] one signature [reveals representative capacity, the other] denotes personal obligation. . . . Dual obligations on the parts of a corporate borrower and its principal officers or stockholders are not unusual when small, closely held corporations borrow money. Reaching by lenders for the additional [security] is the norm. . . . Although the dual signature point has not arisen in the Massachusetts cases, other jurisdictions have held a corporate officer personally liable when he or she has signed twice [as here].

That does not, however, end the inquiry. The person who signs a note in an apparent individual capacity may escape personal liability by establishing that the immediate par-

CASE 31.2 Continued

ties to the note—here, the bank, the company, and Mrs. Friel—had [agreed] that personal obligation was not to attach. UCC § 3-403(2)(b). [The Appellate Division] concluded...that the bank and Mrs. Friel had [so agreed].

...We may accept as a fact that Mrs. Friel's subjective understanding that she was signing for a purely corporate loan but, in order for her to prevail, the bank must either (1) have given her to understand that it was not looking to her [for security] or (2) it must appear that the bank's intent was not to look beyond the company's assets. Neither proposition finds support in the facts found [in the evidence].

...Mrs. Friel did not negotiate the terms of the loans, she asked no questions, and the bank said nothing one way or the other about requiring her to become personally obligated on the loans. All that falls well short of an affirmative showing [required of the signer by law] that the parties had agreed that the corporation was to be solely liable.... An undisclosed intention by a maker to sign only in a representative capacity does not establish the understanding required by § 3-403(2)(b).

[The] Appellate Division appears to have relieved the defendant of liability on the basis of... mutual mistake.... There was, however, no finding—nor would the evidence have supported it—that the bank was mistaken about Mrs. Friel's personal obligation. ...Mrs. Friel may have been mistaken as to the consequences of her second signatures, but the mistake of one party to the transaction is not sufficient to invoke the principle of mutual mistake.... [Under limited circumstances,] a party may avoid a contract on the basis of a unilateral mistake.... [However,] a note of a close corporation indorsed by a principal officer is a commercial commonplace, hence scarcely unconscionable. The record does not suggest that the bank knew or had reason to know about Mrs. Friel's ignorance of the consequences of her second signature. Section 3-402 of the [UCC] places the risk of mistake on the signer....

One might wish that a conscientious loan officer would explain the consequences of documents and signatures to a borrower not represented by counsel, but the law, in a commercial transaction context, imposes no duty so to do. In the instant case...the record does not permit us to suppose that the bank officer was aware of the defendant's commercial naivete. The bank officer may well have felt no call to [explain] what he would have thought a quite routine transaction....

JUDGMENT The judgment [of] the trial court is reversed....

Unauthorized Signature. *Unauthorized signature* includes both a forgery and a signature by an agent without actual, implied, or apparent authority to sign the principal's name. An unauthorized signature is not binding on the person whose name is signed without authority, unless that person *ratifies* (later approves) it or *is precluded* (prevented) by law from denying it—e.g., where the "signer's" negligence substantially contributes to the making of the unauthorized signature [3-404]. An unauthorized signature *is* effective, however, to impose on the actual signer (a forger or an agent) liability to persons who in good faith pay the instrument or take it for value.

How can a person be so negligent that his or her unauthorized signature will be binding? Many business people sign commercial paper by means of a rubber stamp or a check-writing machine. If the owner of such a stamp or machine negligently gives unauthorized persons access to it, and if the negligence substantially contributes to the making of an unauthorized signature, the owner will not be permitted to claim lack of authority as a defense when a holder in due course demands payment. The same is true where a drawee or another payor pays the instrument in good faith and in accordance with reasonable commercial standards of the drawee's or payor's business. If there is *no* negligence, the usual rule continues to apply—an unauthorized signature provides the "signer" with a real defense that is good against even a holder in due course.

Effect of Indorsement by Imposter or Dishonest Agent

As noted in Chapter 29, a person ordinarily must be a *holder* to negotiate commercial paper, but there is one exception to this rule. The exception applies where, for example, a principal has been induced by the fraud of a dishonest agent to sign a negotiable instrument made out to a fictitious payee. Suppose that an employer is induced by a dishonest agent to sign a payroll check made out to a nonexistent worker. Then the agent gets possession of the check, signs the name of the fictitious payee on the back of the check, and cashes it at a supermarket. The dishonest agent is not the payee. Ordinarily the agent would not be a holder, and the indorsement would be a forgery. However, UCC Section 3-405 specifically provides that the indorsement of such a dishonest person *is* effective as that of the payee. Thus, the dishonest agent has a Code-conferred holder status, and the supermarket can be a holder in due course entitled to payment. A similar principle applies where an imposter (a person pretending to be someone else) tricks the issuer of a negotiable instrument into thinking the imposter is the intended payee.

Why should these particular dishonest people be given holder status? The reason is that the issuer of an instrument is in a better position than is a subsequent holder or a drawee to prevent the padding of payrolls and similar dishonesty, and to check the identity of imposters. An employer is expected to take reasonable care in supervising employees or to cover any loss by fidelity insurance. Although Section 3-405 may seem to encourage dishonesty, the persons who do the defrauding are still subject to criminal penalties for their dishonesty, to civil suits for damages, and, as signers, to liability on the instrument.

Discharge from Contractual Liability

As a negotiable instrument is transferred from hand to hand, the liability of various signers—makers, drawers, acceptors, and unqualified indorsers—may be discharged (terminated) by a variety of methods. A signer may assert discharge as a defense in a lawsuit brought to compel the signer to pay the instrument. Most discharges are personal defenses, but a few are real defenses. This part of the chapter describes some common methods of discharge and the effect of discharge on the rights of a holder in due course.

Common Methods of Discharge

Payment or Tender of Payment. A party who pays the amount of the instrument to a holder (and removes the instrument from circulation or cancels it by, for example, marking it "Paid") is completely discharged from liability on it [3-603(1)]. Discharge will not result, however, if the payment was made in bad faith, as where the person making payment knows that the holder acquired the instrument by theft. Nor will a payment that is inconsistent with a restrictive indorsement ordinarily discharge the person making payment.

The discharge of a party who has no recourse on the instrument (no valid claim against any other party) usually results in the discharge of all other parties [3-601(3)]. Thus, if a maker or drawer pays a holder and is thereby discharged, all others such as indorsers and accommodation parties are discharged too.

Usually an instrument is given for the purpose of discharging some underlying obligation. For example, a tenant mails the landlord a check for a month's rent. Unless otherwise agreed, the underlying obligation (here, to pay rent) is not discharged until the check is actually paid [3-802]. The landlord's taking the check, however, suspends the landlord's right to sue for nonpayment until the check is overdue or dishonored.

If a party *tenders* (offers) full payment to the holder at or after the maturity date of the instrument, and if the holder improperly refuses the tender, the tendering party is discharged to the extent of all subsequent liability for interest, costs, and attorney's fees [3-604(1)]. However, the tendering party is not discharged as to the principal (the face amount of the instrument), nor as to the interest accrued to the date of the tender.

Although improper refusal of a valid tender does not wholly discharge the party making the tender, it does wholly discharge any party who has a right of recourse against the tendering party [3-604(2)]. For example, assume that Martin executes a note payable to the order of Paula, who indorses it to Harriet; that at the maturity of the note Martin properly tenders to Harriet the amount of principal and interest due; and that Harriet, being mistaken as to the amount of interest due, improperly refuses the tender. Harriet's refusal of Martin's tender wholly discharges Paula from her secondary liability on the instrument. The result is that if Harriet later is unable to collect from Martin, she may not collect from Paula, because Paula (having been discharged) is lost to Harriet as an alternative source of payment. (However, Paula remains secondarily liable to *subsequent* holders in due course who take the instrument without notice of the discharge.)

Fraudulent and Material Alteration. After an instrument gets into circulation, it might be altered by a holder or by some other person. An *alteration* may consist of a deletion, an addition, or a substitution; or it might consist of the *completion* of an incomplete (but signed) instrument "otherwise than as authorized" [3-407].

An alteration may or may not discharge the party affected by it, depending on the circumstances surrounding the alteration. *No* alteration results in discharge of the affected party unless the following circumstances exist:

1 *The alteration was made for a fraudulent, or dishonest, purpose.* There is no fraudulent purpose where a holder fills in a blank under the honest but mistaken belief that the act is as authorized. Nor is there likely to be a fraudulent purpose where a holder substitutes a lower interest rate, intending to benefit the maker.

2 *The alteration was made by a holder of the instrument or by the holder's authorized representative.* An alteration made by a "stranger" to the instrument has no effect on the liability of the parties. A holder who has not misbehaved should not be penalized for the misconduct of a stranger.

3 *The alteration must be material.* It is material if it changes the *contract* of a party *in any respect.* The addition of 1 cent to the amount payable, or an advance of 1 day in the date of payment, is material and will operate as a discharge *if* it is fraudulent. A change that does no more than correct an obvious error is not material.

The extent to which a party is discharged from liability on the ground of a fraudulent and material alteration (referred to hereafter as "material alteration") depends on the nature of the person seeking payment from the offended party. A party whose contract is changed by a holder's material alteration is completely discharged from liability to (1) the holder who made the alteration, and (2) any other person who is merely an assignee of the altered instrument—*unless,* for example, the affected party assented to the alteration [3-407(2)(a)]. However, even though material alteration is a real defense (one good against a holder in due course), material alteration is at most a *partial* real defense, and it may be no defense at all. A holder in due course always may enforce the altered instrument against the affected party according to the *original tenor* (terms) of the instrument. And, where a *signed* but *incomplete* instrument has been completed, the holder in due course may enforce the instrument *as completed* [3-407(3)]. Furthermore, a holder in due course is entitled to enforce an instrument *as altered* (e.g., for a fraudulently raised amount) where the affected party's negligence (here, the maker's negligence) made alteration easy [3-406].

Suppose, for example, that Maria makes and delivers to Paul a note for $100, payable to Paul's order. Paul negotiates it to Art, who fraudulently raises the amount to $2,100 and then negotiates the note to Ben. Maria and Paul are discharged from any liability to Art because Art's alteration was fraudulent and material. If Ben is *not* a holder in due course, Maria and Paul are liable to Ben for $100, the amount originally specified in the note. But if in preparing the note Maria negligently left spaces in which additional words or figures could easily be inserted, or if she consented to the alteration, Ben, if a holder in due course, may recover the full $2,100 from Maria. Art, the defrauder, is liable to Ben for $2,100, regardless of whether Ben is a holder in due course.

Where a holder makes an unauthorized *completion* of a signed, incomplete instrument and transfers it, the signer is discharged as to a mere holder, but is liable to a holder in due course for the amount of the instrument *as completed.* The loss should fall on the signer whose conduct (i.e., issuing a signed but incomplete negotiable instrument) has made the holder's fraud possible, rather than on the innocent purchaser. Suppose Dora issues a paycheck to Paul but leaves the line for the amount blank for Paul to fill out for the amount she owes him, $200. Paul completes the check for $500. Dora is not liable on the instrument to Paul; but as to any holder in due course, Dora will be liable for $500.

This principle applies also where a thief or a "faithless employee" makes an unauthorized completion of a signed instrument and transfers it. Suppose Donna, an employer, signs forty payroll checks, otherwise leaves them blank for her agent to fill out later, and places them in her office safe. That night a thief breaks open the safe, takes the signed checks, fills them out for $100 in the names of fictitious payees, and negotiates them. As to any holder in due course, Donna will be liable for the amount stated in the completed instrument. The fact that Donna was careful to safeguard the signed checks does not alter the fact that by signing the checks and leaving them blank she has made the thief's fraud possible.

Unexcused Delay. The liability of a secondary party (a drawer or an indorser) is conditioned on presentment, dishonor, and notice of dishonor, unless one or more of these acts is *excused.* Presentment or notice of dishonor might be excused where, for example, the secondary party from whom payment is sought waives (gives up the right to) presentment or notice, or where the holder by reasonable diligence cannot make presentment or give notice. Any *un*excused delay in making presentment or giving notice of dishonor, however, *completely* discharges an *indorser* from liability on the instrument [3-501(1)]. In *Hanes v. Exten,*[1] for example, Mr. and Mrs. Exten were indorsers of an installment note which by its terms became due 30 days after a default by the maker. The maker defaulted. Hanes then acquired the note, held it for almost 18 months before demanding payment, and sued the Extens in their capacities as indorsers. The appellate court affirmed the trial court's holding that presentment and notice are required to charge an indorser with liability on the instrument, that the 18 months far exceeded the "reasonable" time allowed by the Code for presentment in the kind of situation here involved, and that Hanes had not given the Extens timely notice of dishonor. The indorsers were discharged from liability.

Though unexcused delay in making presentment completely discharges an *indorser,* it does not necessarily discharge a *maker, a drawer, or an acceptor.* Suppose, for example, that Dora, the drawer of a check made out to Paul, has on deposit with the drawee bank an amount sufficient to pay the check; that the drawee *bank* fails (becomes insolvent) 32 days after the check is issued; and that Paul presents the check for payment on the thirty-third day after its issue. Thirty days after issue is presumed to be a reasonable time within which to present an uncertified check for payment [3-503]. Ordinarily, Paul's delay in presenting the check will be unexcused. In such a situation Dora, the drawer, may discharge her liability to Paul by *assigning in writing* to the holder (Paul) whatever rights regarding the deposited amount Dora might have against the insolvent bank [3-502]. Thus, where funds were available during the 30 days and the bank later failed, the holder must absorb any loss caused by the holder's unexcused delay in presenting the instrument for payment.

But a holder's delay in presenting commercial paper for payment is not enough, in itself, to discharge the liable party. If the bank (or other custodian of funds meant for payment) remains solvent, as most do, the maker, drawer, or acceptor remains liable on the instrument for the full time prescribed by the applicable statute of limitations, despite the holder's delay in seeking payment. The purpose of this rule is to avoid imposing loss on holders whose delay is harmless and to avoid unjustly enriching the drawer or other party who normally has received goods or other consideration for issuing the instrument.

Case 31.3 discusses the rights of a holder seeking payment from a drawer 3 months after its check was dishonored.

[1]259 A.2d 290 (Md. App. 1969).

CASE 31.3 First American Bank v. Litchfield Co. • 353 S.E.2d 143 (S.C. App. 1987)

FACTS Litchfield Co. (defendant) drew a check on Bankers Trust payable to the order of Jensen Farley Pictures. Jensen Farley negotiated the check to First American Bank (plaintiff) for value, and First American forwarded the check to Bankers Trust for payment. Unknown to First American, Litchfield earlier that day had stopped payment on the check. Bankers Trust dishonored the check and returned it to First American. Three months later, after several attempts to collect the amount of the check from Jensen Farley, First American learned of Jensen Farley's pending bankruptcy and sought payment from Litchfield. Alleging that it had defenses against Jensen Farley, Litchfield refused to pay, and First American brought suit. From a judgment for First American, Litchfield appealed.

OPINION BELL, J. . . . The drawer of a check engages that upon dishonor he will pay the amount of the draft to a holder in due course. . . . The drawer has the right to stop payment, but remains liable on the instrument to a holder in due course. . . . Since Litchfield has conceded [that] First American was a holder in due course, Litchfield remains liable on the instrument unless it can establish a valid defense. . . .

Litchfield argues [that] its liability was discharged by First American's failure to give timely notice [that] the check had been dishonored. This defense is unavailing for two reasons.

First, failure to give notice of dishonor discharges a drawer only to the extent [that] he is deprived of funds maintained with the drawee bank to cover the check because the drawee bank became insolvent during the delay. . . . A drawer is not otherwise discharged. In this case, Litchfield was not deprived of any funds in its account with Bankers Trust nor did Bankers Trust become insolvent during the delay. Thus, Litchfield is not discharged.

Second, notice of dishonor is excused when the party to be charged has himself countermanded payment. [Section 3-511(2)(b).] Since Litchfield ordered payment stopped, it was not entitled to notice of dishonor. . . .

Litchfield argues strenuously that it is unfair to apply § 3-511(2)(b) to the drawer of a check who has no means of knowing whether the check has been negotiated to a holder. This reasoning misses the mark. The maker of an outstanding negotiable instrument is presumed to know [that] the instrument is subject to transfer to a holder in due course. . . . The drawer is often without actual knowledge that his check has been negotiated, but that ignorance in no way diminishes the rights of a holder in due course. To hold otherwise would, as a practical matter, destroy the negotiability of a check.

For these reasons, we hold [that] First American's delay in giving notice of dishonor does not discharge Litchfield's liability on the check.

JUDGMENT . . . Affirmed. . . .

Cancellation or Renunciation. Perhaps to make a gift or to pay a creditor, the holder of an instrument may discharge any party (e.g., an indorser or accommodation maker) by canceling the instrument (i.e., by destroying or mutilating it) or by canceling the party's signature (i.e., by crossing out the signature) [3-605]. The holder's canceling a signature discharges the liability of the favored person, but the holder still owns (has title to) the instrument and may negotiate or collect it.

A holder may also renounce his or her rights in an instrument by signing and delivering a written renunciation, or by surrendering the instrument itself, to the party to be discharged. Unlike a cancellation, a renunciation usually does not appear on the instrument itself; it appears instead in a separate letter or another document. Because a cancellation appears on the instrument, subsequent holders are on notice of it. But since evidence of a renunciation normally does not appear on the instrument, a renunciation is ineffective against a holder in due course without notice of it.

Impairment of Right of Recourse; Impairment of Collateral. Unless unqualified indorsers agree to the contrary, their liability is established by the order in which they indorse. That order is presumed to be the order in which their signatures appear on the instrument [3-414]. Thus, an indorser who pays a dishonored instrument has a right of recourse (a right of payment) not only against the drawer, maker, or acceptor, but also against any prior unqualified indorser who has received timely notice of dishonor. However, if the holder of an instrument impairs the right of recourse of an indorser or some other party, that party is discharged to the extent of the impairment.

Impairment of recourse takes many forms—e.g., a cancellation of a signature or an agreement not to sue. A holder's granting an extension of time for payment is also an impairment of recourse, because the extension prevents collection on the date originally contemplated by the various parties to the instrument.

Suppose that Martha issues a note to the order of Peter; that the note is successively indorsed to Agnes, Ben, Carlos, and Harold; and that Harold discharges Carlos from liability by canceling Carlos's indorsement. Harold's discharge of Carlos does not impair the right of recourse of Ben or Agnes because neither person had a right of recourse against Carlos, a *subsequent* indorser.

But suppose that, instead of discharging Carlos, Harold discharged Agnes by canceling her indorsement. Later, when Ben and Carlos indorsed the instrument, they might have done so expecting Agnes to pay if others did not. If Harold canceled Agnes' indorsement without the consent of Ben and Carlos, Harold has (by discharging Agnes) impaired their right of recourse against Agnes and has discharged them from liability too [3-606(1)]. Had Harold discharged Martha (the maker), he would thereby have discharged all other parties. This follows from the fact that an Article 3 discharge of Martha, a party who has no right of recourse on the instrument, discharges all other parties [3-601(3)(b)].

The impairment-of-recourse principle applies also to parties who are not indorsers but who have a right of recourse. For example, an accommodation maker has a right of recourse against the party accommodated. If the holder of a note *knows* that comaker A signed it for the accommodation of comaker B, and the holder releases comaker B without the consent of comaker A, the release discharges comaker A.

An unjustifiable impairment of collateral has the same effect as impairment of recourse. It discharges the party whose rights against others are jeopardized. Suppose that when Martha issued the note to Peter, she also pledged shares of stock to Peter as "collateral" (security) for payment of the note; that Peter indorsed the note and transferred the collateral to Agnes; and that Agnes indorsed the note to Ben but, without Peter's consent, returned the collateral to Martha. By returning the shares to Martha, Agnes has prevented Peter from having access to the collateral in the event that Peter must pay the note. Peter's collateral is thereby impaired, and Peter is discharged, to the extent of the impairment, from liability to Agnes and Ben [3-606(1)(b)].

Reacquisition of Instrument. An instrument is sometimes acquired by a person who was a prior holder. When such a reacquisition occurs, any intervening party is discharged as against the reacquiring party and subsequent holders not in due course [3-208]. For example, suppose that Paul indorses a note to Andrew, who indorses it to Brent, who indorses it back to Paul. The reacquisition of the instrument by Paul discharges Andrew and Brent as to Paul. Were this not true, Paul would have recourse against Andrew and Brent if the note was not paid when due, and then Andrew and Brent each would have a cause of action against Paul on his original indorsement. The purpose of the rule discharging intervening indorsers is to prevent such circular legal actions.

After reacquisition, the reacquirer (Paul, in the example) may keep the instrument until maturity and then seek to collect on it, or he may decide to negotiate it again before maturity. If the reacquirer

(Paul) decides to negotiate it, he may cancel (strike out) the intervening indorsements. Where the reacquirer negotiates the instrument after striking out the intervening indorsements, the intervening indorsers (Andrew and Brent in the example) are discharged *even against* subsequent holders in due course. The reason for this result is that physical cancellation of a prior indorsement is notice to all subsequent takers that the prior indorser has been discharged.

Other Methods of Discharge. There are numerous other methods of discharging a party from liability on the instrument. These include the methods discussed in Chapter 15 that are recognized by the general law of contracts and that apply to negotiable instruments as well: mutual rescission, novation, accord and satisfaction (discussed in Case 31.4), etc. So, a maker and a payee of a note may simply agree that the maker is no longer liable for payment. Other examples include a discharge in bankruptcy and, as noted in the next chapter, the discharge that may result from the certification of a check.

Effect of Discharge on Holder in Due Course

Generally, discharge of a party (a maker, an indorser, etc.) is a personal defense that is not good against a subsequent holder in due course who is without notice of it [3-602]. Suppose, for example, that Marty Maker pays Paul Payee the amount of a note before its maturity date and does not compel surrender of the note (remove it from circulation) or cancel it (e.g., by marking it "paid"). A subsequent holder in due course to whom Paul sells the note may require Marty to pay again. However, as noted in Chapter 29, a few discharges, such as a discharge in bankruptcy, are real defenses and are good even against a holder in due course.

In Case 31.4 a payee cashes a check marked "paid in full" but first writes "without prejudice" on it. The payee argues that under UCC Section 1-207 the use of those words prevents the cashing from becoming an accord and satisfaction. The court's response to that argument has been accepted by many other courts.

CASE 31.4 Chancellor, Inc. v. Hamilton Appliance Co., Inc. · 418 A.2d 1326 (N.J. Dist. Ct., Small Claims Div., 1980)

FACTS Hamilton Appliance Co. (defendant) purchased from Chancellor, Inc., a wholesale distributor, twelve Pioneer home stereo systems for a total of $2,785.64. A dispute arose as to the quality of the merchandise, the wholesale price as of the time of sale, the goods that could be returned to the plaintiff seller, and the total amount actually owed by the defendant buyer. Plaintiff issued the defendant a credit of $1,805.76, leaving a balance due of $979.88. The defendant mailed a check to plaintiff in the amount of $734.88 with a notation on the front, "paid in full." The check was accompanied by a letter that summarized the dispute and explained how the amount was calculated. Plaintiff indorsed the reverse side of the check with the words "without prejudice," deposited it, and advised the defendant that the check was accepted without prejudice to the plaintiff's rights. Plaintiff then brought suit for $245.

OPINION SAUNDERS, J. S. C. This contract action raises the novel issue whether Section 1-207 of the UCC has altered the common-law principle of accord and satisfaction affecting "full payment checks." More specifically, the question is whether a disputed claim is extinguished when the debtor tenders to the creditor a check marked "paid in full" and the creditor deposits the check after endorsing it "without prejudice" and notifies the debtor he is reserving his right to contend for the balance of the claim....

The court finds that there was a genuine dispute between the parties as to the amount of money due from defendant to plaintiff.... The New Jersey rule has been that when a check is tendered as payment for an unliquidated claim on the condition that it be ac-

CASE 31.4 Continued

cepted in full payment, the creditor is deemed to have accepted this condition by depositing the check for collection notwithstanding any obliteration or alteration....

Plaintiff argues that Section 1-207 alters the common-law accord and satisfaction principle and permits the creditor to accept and cash the check offered and to sue the debtor for the balance if the creditor explicitly reserves his rights.

Section 1-207 states:

> A party who with explicit reservation of rights performs or promises performance or assents to performance in a manner demanded or offered by the other party does not thereby prejudice the rights reserved. Such words as "without prejudice," "under protest" or the like are sufficient.

There are no cases in New Jersey interpreting this section of the Code.... The reported decisions in other jurisdictions interpreting Section 1-207 and discussing its effect on the common-law rule of accord and satisfaction have not been in agreement.

Only New York has held that Section 1-207 has altered the common-law rule.... Four courts have acquiesced to this view in dicta. Conversely, two courts have held specifically that Section 1-207 does not change existing law....

The New York cases which have concluded that Section 1-207 permits a party to reserve his rights while cashing a check offered in full payment are distinguishable [from the case before this court]. [They] were decided on the strength of the New York Annotations to the Code.... The New York annotation clearly deals with the effect of Section 1-207 on the "full payment check" and concludes that the rule of accord and satisfaction has been changed [in New York]. However, ... the New Jersey Study Comment did not adopt the New York Study Commission's report and conducted its own analysis of the Code. It gave no indication that, in adopting Section 1-207, the New Jersey Legislature would change the common-law rule....

The plaintiff argues that the legislature intended Section 1-207 to redefine the law of accord and satisfaction and to restrict the use of the "full payment check." A review of the Comments to Section 1-207 and its legislative history reveals no such intent. The New Jersey Study Comment does not mention the rule on accord and satisfaction. The Comment only states that Section 1-207 is in accord with its predecessor statute, Section 49 of the Uniform Sales Act. Section 49 did not purport to alter the rule of common-law accord and satisfaction. Its language spoke only to the acceptance of goods, not payments.... It would appear that the legislature adopted Section 1-207 presupposing that it reflected existing law.

Similarly, the UCC Comments to Section 1-207 do not reflect a legislative intent to change the common-law rule. Comment One states that "This section provides machinery for the *continuation of performance along the lines contemplated by the contract* despite a pending dispute..." [Emphasis supplied.] An accord and satisfaction involves a new contract, not the contemplated performance of the original contract. By using the "full payment check" the buyer is seeking to fulfill [discharge], not continue, its duty to pay....

The court does not find any evidence in either the legislative history of the commentaries to Section 1-207 supporting the plaintiff's position that the law of accord and satisfaction has been altered [in New Jersey].

If the court were to conclude that a creditor could reserve his rights on a "full payment check," a convenient and informal device for the resolution of disagreements in the business community would be seriously impeded. The court is hesitant to impair such a valuable, informal settlement tool where there is no indication that the legislature intended that result. I find that the acceptance by the creditor of a check offered by the debtor in full payment of a disputed debt is an accord and satisfaction of the debt and no condition of protest or attempted reservation of rights can affect the legal quality of the action. I hold that Section 1-207 has not altered the common-law rule of accord and satisfaction.

JUDGMENT Judgment for the defendant.

Warranty Liability

Because commercial paper is a type of property, the UCC imposes warranties (guarantees of the absence of certain defects) on sellers and other transferors of commercial paper. Sellers of commercial paper (transferors who receive consideration) make "transfer" warranties. Persons who present commercial paper for payment or acceptance make "presentment" warranties, and so does *any prior transferor* (e.g., a person who negotiates the instrument to the presenter), whether or not the prior transferor received consideration for the instrument.

Importance of Warranties

Warranty liability is important mainly because it often exists in the absence of contractual liability. The following, for example, have no contractual liability (i.e., no liability "on the instrument"): a qualified indorser; a person who negotiates an instrument without indorsing it; and an indorser who has been discharged because of the holder's unexcused delay in making presentment. But signers and nonsigners alike have some degree of warranty liability and are liable for any actual damages resulting from their breach of the warranties discussed later in this chapter.

For wronged persons, warranty liability has several practical advantages over contractual liability. Among them are:

1. Presentment, dishonor, and notice of dishonor are not required for a suit in warranty.
2. The right to sue for breach of a warranty arises immediately upon discovery of the breach, even though the time for payment may not yet have arrived.
3. Upon discovering breach of a warranty, a transferee may, if the transferor is willing to cooperate, simply rescind the transfer by returning the instrument to the transferor and receiving back anything paid for it. Even where the transferor has contractual liability for the face amount, voluntary rescission may be more useful to the transferee than enforcing the transferor's contract. A transferor who, like the transferee, is a victim of someone else's wrongdoing might voluntarily return the transferee's consideration but balk at paying the face amount of the instrument.

Warranties of Sellers (Transfer Warranties)

Any person, including a thief, who transfers a negotiable instrument *and receives consideration for it* makes the five warranties listed in Table 31.1 and discussed in the following paragraphs. If the seller transfers the instrument *without signing it* (as in the transfer of bearer paper), the warranties run only to the nonsigning seller's *immediate* transferee, if that person takes the instrument in good faith. If the transfer is by indorsement, the warranties run to *any* subsequent holder who takes the instrument in good faith [3-417(2)].

Table 31.1 Transfer Warranties

Person Making Transfer Warranties	Person Receiving Transfer Warranties	Warranties Received
Any transferor *receiving consideration*	Where transferor *does not indorse* but receives consideration, only the *immediate transferee*	1. Title 2. Signatures 3. Against alterations
	Where transferor *indorses* and receives consideration, *any subsequent transferee*	4. Against insolvency 5. Against defenses

Warranty Concerning Title. A seller of a negotiable instrument warrants that he or she has good title to (ownership of) it or is authorized to obtain payment or acceptance on behalf of one who has a good title, and that the transfer is otherwise rightful. The warranty is breached in the following circumstances:

1. When a finder or a thief of a bearer instrument sells it.
2. When there is a sale of an order instrument on which a necessary indorsement has been forged.
3. When the transferor purports to act on behalf of another person but is unauthorized to do so.
4. When the transferor has authority to act on behalf of another, but the person for whom the transferor acts does not have a good title to the instrument.

Warranty Concerning Signatures. A seller of commercial paper warrants that all signatures are genuine or authorized. Thus, a seller's transferee may sue the seller or rescind the transfer if the signature of a maker, a drawer, an acceptor, or an indorser is forged or unauthorized.

Warranty Concerning Alterations. A seller of commercial paper warrants that the instrument has not been materially altered. Suppose that Dan drew a check for $100 payable to the order of Pam; that Pam indorsed the check in blank and delivered it to Amy; and that Amy raised the check to $2,100 and then negotiated it by delivery to Ben for $2,100. As indicated earlier in this chapter, if Ben is a holder in due course, Pam and Dan are liable to Ben for $100, the original tenor of the instrument. But Ben also has a cause of action for breach of warranty against Amy. When Amy transferred the check to Ben and received consideration, she warranted that the check had not been materially altered. Amy's breach of warranty entitles Ben to a recovery of actual damages: here, $2,000 plus cost of litigation.

Warranty Concerning Insolvency Proceedings. A seller of a negotiable instrument warrants that she or he has no knowledge of any insolvency proceeding instituted with respect to the maker, drawer, or acceptor.

Warranty Concerning Defenses. The warranty concerning real and personal defenses—infancy, fraud in the inducement, etc.—varies according to the type of seller. A seller who transfers a negotiable instrument and makes an *unqualified indorsement,* or who transfers without indorsement, warrants flatly that no defense of any party is good against him or her. But a seller who makes a *qualified* indorsement (one "without recourse") warrants only that he or she has *no knowledge* of a defense of any party. This less burdensome warranty is consistent with the qualified indorser's freedom from *contractual* liability, yet it imposes warranty liability if the seller acts in bad faith—e.g., by failing to reveal knowledge of some party's fraud.

Warranties of Presenters and All Prior Transferors (Presentment Warranties)

Presenters' warranties (Table 31.2) run only to persons who pay or accept an instrument, i.e., only to makers, drawees, or acceptors [3-417(1)]. These "presentment" warranties concern (1) title, (2) signatures, and (3) alterations. The presentment warranties are made by the person actually presenting the instrument for payment or acceptance *and* by *all prior* transferors (sellers and nonsellers) of that

Table 31.2 Presentment Warranties

Persons Making Presentment Warranties	Persons Receiving Presentment Warranties	Warranties Received
Actual *presenters* *All prior* transferors	Maker, drawee, acceptor	1. Title 2. Signatures 3. Against alterations

instrument. Thus, if there is a breach of a presentment warranty, as where there is a forged indorsement, a payor (including an acceptor who pays) may have recourse against a rather large number of persons in addition to the actual presenter. For example, suppose Dan issues a check to the order of Pam. Then a thief steals it, forges Pam's in-blank indorsement, and transfers the check to Amy as a gift. Amy transfers it without indorsement to Ben, who presents it to and receives payment from Dan's bank (the drawee). As noted in the next chapter, upon Dan's timely discovery of the forged indorsement (and his reporting it to the bank), the bank must recredit Dan's account with the amount of the check. Having paid Ben, however, the drawee bank has a warranty cause of action against Ben, Amy, and the thief as a basis for recovering whatever money it paid out to Ben. Because of the forged indorsement, each of the three has breached the presenter's warranty that he or she "has good title to the instrument or is authorized to obtain payment or acceptance on behalf of one who has good title." A thief acquires no title by stealing and therefore cannot confer title on anyone else.

In the preceding example, no one has breached the presentment warranty concerning signatures—not even the thief who forged Pam's signature. Unlike the *transfer* warranty concerning signatures (that "*all* signatures are genuine or authorized"), the corresponding *presentment* warranty is only that the presenter (or a prior transferor such as a thief) has no knowledge that the *maker's* or *drawer's* signature is unauthorized. Here, the unauthorized signature was that of Pam, the *payee.* The presentment warranty concerning signatures has a further limitation. A holder in due course acting in good faith does *not* warrant an absence of knowledge that the maker's or drawer's own signature is unauthorized. As between the two innocent parties, the maker or drawer is in the better position to verify his or her own signature before payment.

The case that follows explains why an accommodation indorser may have no warranty liability.

CASE 31.5 Oak Park Currency Exchange, Inc. v. Maropoulos · 363 N.E.2d 54 (Ill. App. 1977)

FACTS John Bugay possessed a check drawn to the order of Henry Sherman, Inc., and fraudulently indorsed "Henry Sherman" on the reverse side. Bugay sought the assistance of defendant, James Maropoulos, in cashing it. Defendant took Bugay to the plaintiff, Oak Park Currency Exchange, Inc., where defendant was known. At the currency exchange, defendant identified himself, and the exchange agreed to cash the check if defendant would indorse it. He indorsed the check, received the money, and gave it immediately to Bugay.

Plaintiff indorsed and deposited the check in Belmont National Bank. The indorsement "Henry Sherman" was subsequently found to be a forgery. The bank sought and received payment back from plaintiff. Plaintiff, in turn, sought payment from defendant on his indorsement and for breach of warranty and filed this suit. The trial court directed a verdict in favor of defendant, and plaintiff appealed.

OPINION GOLDBERG, P. J. . . . In this court, plaintiff urges that defendant breached his warranty of good title when he obtained payment of a check on which the payee's indorsement was forged and that there was sufficient evidence to support a directed verdict in favor of plaintiff. Plaintiff's contentions are based exclusively on Section 3-417(1) of the Code. Defendant contends that an accommodation indorser does not make warranties under Section 3-417(1) and that the trial court properly directed a verdict for the defendant.

A party who signs an instrument "for the purpose of lending his name to another party to. . ." that instrument is an accommodation party. Section 3-415(1). Such a party "is liable in the capacity in which he has signed. . ." Section 3-415(2). Therefore defendant

CASE 31.5 Continued

is an accommodation indorser and would be liable to plaintiff under his indorser's contract, provided that he had received timely notice that the check had been presented to the drawee bank and dishonored. Section 3-414. Because these conditions precedent to the contractual liability of an indorser have not been met, defendant is not liable on his contract as an accommodation indorser.

Furthermore, the drawee bank, American National, did not dishonor the check but paid it. This operated to discharge the liability of defendant as an accommodation indorser.

The portion of the Code upon which plaintiff seeks to hold defendant liable is Section 3-417 entitled "Warranties on Presentment and Transfer."... Section 3-417(1) sets out warranties which run only to a party who "pays or accepts" an instrument upon presentment. We note that presentment is defined as "a demand for acceptance or payment made upon the maker, acceptor, drawee, or other payor..." Section 3-504(1). As applied to the instant case, the warranties contained in Section 3-417(1)... run only to the payor bank and not to any other transferee who acquired the check. In the case before us, plaintiff is not a payor or acceptor of the draft.... The case before us involves a transferee, not a party who paid or accepted the instrument. Thus it appears that reliance by plaintiff upon subsection 3-417(1) was misplaced....

An additional theory requires affirmance of the judgment appealed from. Subsection 3-417(2) of the Code provides that one "who transfers an instrument and receives consideration warrants to his transferee..." that he has good title.... The evidence presented in the case at bar establishes that defendant received no consideration for his indorsement. Though Mrs. Panveno [plaintiff's employee] testified that she saw Bugay hand defendant some money as the two left the currency exchange, she also testified that defendant stated that he was doing a favor for his friend; that she was not paying close attention to the two men and that she did not watch them as they walked away from her. Thus her testimony was considerably weakened by her own qualifying statements[,] and it was strongly and directly contradicted by the positive and unshaken testimony of defendant that he received nothing in return for his assistance. The simple fact standing alone that this witness saw Bugay hand some money to defendant, even if proved, would have no legal significance without additional proof of some type showing that the payment was consideration for defendant's indorsement.

JUDGMENT Judgment affirmed.

Summary

Most signers of commercial paper have contractual liability for the face amount of the instrument. The liability of makers and acceptors is primary; that of drawers and indorsers is secondary. A primary party is liable immediately and unconditionally when the instrument is due. A secondary party is liable only if the triggering events of presentment, dishonor, and notice of dishonor take place or are excused. The nature of an accommodation party's liability depends on the capacity in which the party signs—as a maker, an indorser, etc. A secondary party who guarantees payment has a liability like that of a comaker.

To avoid liability as a signer, an agent should name the person represented and show that the agent has signed in a representative capacity. Ordinarily an unauthorized signature has no effect as that of the person whose name is signed, but it does serve as the signature of the person acting without authority. An indorsement made by an imposter or by a dishonest employee in a "padded payroll" case *is* effective to negotiate the instrument.

The liability of signers may be terminated by a variety of methods, including fraudulent and material alteration and unexcused delay in making presentment. Generally, discharge is a personal defense, but a discharge in bankruptcy is a real defense.

Since commercial paper is property, there can be warranty liability. The UCC imposes transfer and presentment warranties.

Review Questions

1 **(a)** Distinguish between primary and secondary liability on an instrument. **(b)** Do all instruments have primary parties? Explain.

2 Explain the meaning and purpose of **(a)** presentment, **(b)** dishonor, and **(c)** notice of dishonor.

3 How long, and why, may acceptance or payment be delayed without the delay's being considered a dishonor?

4 What two things must an agent's form of signature do if the agent is to avoid liability on the instrument?

5 John Doe receives a check made payable to his order. A thief steals it, indorses it in Doe's name, and transfers it for value to Holder. **(a)** Is Doe liable on the instrument? Why or why not? **(b)** Is the thief? Why or why not?

6 Who is liable on an instrument made out to and indorsed by an imposter? Why?

7 **(a)** Under what circumstances will payment not discharge a maker, an acceptor, or an indorser of an instrument? **(b)** What effect does a person's taking a check have on the underlying obligation?

8 If an alteration discharges a party to the instrument, against whom will the discharge be effective? Against whom will it *not* be effective?

9 **(a)** Whom does unexcused delay in making presentment discharge completely? **(b)** Under what circumstances will unexcused delay discharge a maker, a drawer, or an acceptor?

10 Explain or illustrate how the following transfer warranties are breached: warranty of title, warranty concerning signatures, and warranty against alterations.

11 How does a qualified indorsement affect the warranty concerning defenses?

12 How do presentment warranties differ from transfer warranties with regard to **(a)** who makes them and **(b)** who receives them?

Case Problems

1 Marc Eliot, an officer of Impact Marketing, Inc., issued on behalf of Impact two postdated checks to Barry E. Bell for legal services to be performed in the future. The checks were drawn on Chemical Bank; "Impact Marketing, Inc." was printed on the checks; and they were signed "Marc Eliot." After Financial Associates purchased the checks at a discount, Impact terminated Bell's services and stopped payment on the checks. Financial Services, a holder in due course, sued Marc Eliot for the amount of the checks. Eliot defended on the ground that he had signed the checks on behalf of the corporation and should not be held personally liable. Was Eliot liable for the amount of the checks?

2 Snug Harbor Realty Co., a construction company, employed Magee as its superintendent. One of his duties was to inspect work in progress and be sure that work was done or materials delivered before Snug Harbor issued checks in payment. On the basis of Magee's investigations and accurate reports, Snug Harbor issued a number of checks to various suppliers and subcontractors. Magee was to deliver the checks to the people entitled to them, but instead he forged the indorsements of 132 payees and cashed the checks himself. Snug Harbor brought suit against the drawee bank to recover from it the amounts of the checks. From a judgment for the bank, Snug Harbor appealed. Should the bank be required to recredit Snug Harbor's account?

3 Two employees of the state of New Mexico created a fictitious entity, the Greater Mesilla Valley Sanitation District. They fraudulently induced a state official to issue to the district a warrant (an order to pay money) for $395,000. They then indorsed the warrant and presented it to the drawee—Citizen's Bank—which accepted and forwarded it to the Bank of New Mexico for payment. That bank, the fiscal agent for the state, honored the warrant. Having suffered the loss of the $395,000, the state called on Western Casualty, its surety on an employee bond, for payment. Western Casualty reimbursed the state, acquired any rights the state might have against the banks, and sued them for $395,000, arguing that because the employees' indorsements were forgeries, the banks wrongfully debited the state's account. From a judgment for the banks, Western Casualty appealed. Was the state, and thus Western Casualty, entitled to payment from the banks?

4 In exchange for merchandise, Florida City Express, Inc. (Express), signed two negotiable promissory notes totaling about $7,000, payable to Latin American Tire Co. Latin American indorsed and discounted the notes to the Bank of Miami (Bank), which took them before maturity, for value, and without notice of any defenses to payment. Before and after Latin American negotiated the notes to Bank, Express paid all the amounts due to Latin American, but did not require that Latin American display or surrender the notes or make any notation on the notes of payments made. At the maturity date of each note, Bank, after making unsuccessful demands on Latin American, sought but was refused payment from the maker, Express. Bank sued Express on the notes. Express raised the defense of payment. From a judgment for Express, Bank appealed. Should the judgment of the trial court be upheld?

5 Martin Maker executed and delivered to Paula Payee a 30-day note in the amount of $195 payable to the order of Payee. Payee indorsed the note in blank and "without recourse" and sold it to Alfred Anderson. Anderson indorsed the note in blank and "without recourse" sold it to Betty Brown. Brown, without indorsing the note, sold it to Harold Holder. After the due date of the note, Holder presented it to Maker for payment. Maker refused to pay, correctly stating that he had given the note to Paula Payee for a gambling debt and that a state statute made gambling instruments null and void. **(a)** Assume that Holder sued Brown for breach of warranty. Judgment for whom? **(b)** Assume that Holder sued Anderson for breach of warranty. Judgment for whom? **(c)** Assume that Holder sued Payee for breach of warranty. Judgment for whom?

6 Martin Maker executed a note payable to the order of Paula Payee. Payee lost the note. Fred Forger, the finder, forged Payee's indorsement and sold the note to Georgia Goodenough, who indorsed and sold the note to Harold Holder. Neither Goodenough nor Holder was aware of the forgery. Holder presented the note at maturity, and Maker paid it. Later Maker discovered that the signature on the instrument was a forgery. **(a)** Assume that Maker sued Holder for breach of warranty. Judgment for whom? **(b)** Assume that instead of suing Holder, Maker sued Goodenough for breach of warranty. What would be the judgment?

7 The Georgia Farm Bureau Mutual Insurance Co. (MIC) issued a check for $685.28 to Willie Mincey and itself (MIC) as copayees. Without indorsing it, MIC forwarded it to Mincey. He indorsed it and tried to cash it at First National Bank (FNB). Because Mincey was not known to FNB personnel, FNB refused to cash the check. Mincey returned to the bank with his uncle, Montgomery, who was known to FNB. FNB agreed to cash the check if Montgomery would indorse it. He did so, and Mincey received the cash. Eventually the check was returned to FNB for lack of MIC's indorsement. Mincey apparently was not entitled to payment and may not have been available for suit. FNB sued Montgomery for the amount of the check. Was Montgomery liable to FNB?

CHAPTER 32

Checks; Relationship between Bank and Customer; Electronic Funds Transfer

Millions of business firms and individuals have a checking account and, consequently, a continuing business relationship with a bank. They issue checks drawn on accounts in their banks; and they deposit for collection not only the checks they receive, but also drafts, matured bonds, interest coupons, and other instruments calling for payment in money. Banks refer to such instruments as "items."

Previous chapters dealt with many important aspects of checks—negotiable form; the liability of drawers and indorsers; the requirements of presentment, dishonor, and notice of dishonor for triggering the liability of secondary parties; etc. As noted in Chapter 28, a check performs a currency function; it is a substitute for money. Although a check is not normally used as a credit instrument (it cannot be payable in installments), it is freely transferable, and a transferee may purchase it (by "cashing" it for the holder) and become a holder in due course. Thus, the topics covered in Chapters 28 through 31, which apply to all negotiable instruments, govern the relationship of the parties to a check.

Additional laws, however, apply to checks and banks. For example, Article 4 of the Uniform Commercial Code (UCC), entitled "Bank Deposits and Collections," deals with the contractual relationship between a bank and its customers, especially its checking account customers. And federal law applies to the computer-controlled "electronic funds transfer" (EFT) systems now widely used as a substitute for paper checks. The first part of this chapter discusses the special nature of checks and the uses of certified checks. The remainder of the chapter discusses (1) the rights and duties of banks and their checking account customers, and (2) the nature of computer-controlled EFT systems.

Checks

Special Nature of Checks

As noted in Chapter 28, a check is a particular kind of draft. Two features distinguish checks from other kinds of drafts: a check is always drawn on a bank, and a check is always payable on demand of the payee or other holder [3-104(2)].

Even a *postdated* check (one issued, say, on May 1 but dated May 5) is a demand instrument—but one that does not become effective (payable) until the stated date arrives [3-114(2)]. The postdating simply postpones the time at which the holder may demand payment. For the reason discussed later in this chapter, the drawee bank may not safely honor (pay) a postdated check until the stated day arrives, but then it must honor the check upon the holder's demand unless there is some reason for dishonor such as insufficient funds in the drawer's account.

Figure 32.1 illustrates the relationship among the persons normally involved in issuing and cashing a check. Usually the drawer (Dr in Figure 32.1) issues a check to the payee (Pe) in payment for consideration such as goods or services sold to Dr by Pe. The exchange of the check for consideration is the "underlying" transaction (here, a contract) discussed in Chapter 28. After receiving the check from Dr, Pe may, for example, cash the check at a supermarket, cash it at Pe's own bank, or present it directly to the drawee bank for payment. Figure 32.1 shows Pe cashing the check at Pe's own bank (*selling* it, in effect) so that Pe's bank becomes a holder in due course (HDC), which takes the check free of the drawer's personal defenses. HDC will present the check (perhaps through a clearinghouse) to the drawee bank (De) for payment. In accordance with the contract of deposit between Dr and De, De will pay HDC the amount of the check, take possession of the check, cancel it by marking it "paid," and return it or otherwise make it available to Dr as a part of Dr's financial records.

A check is a depositor's order or instruction to the drawee bank to pay a specified amount from the drawer's (depositor's) account. Unless otherwise agreed, a check does *not* operate as an assignment (present transfer) of funds in the account [3-409]. Rather, the check is the customer's instruction to the bank to pay *when the payee or some other holder presents* the check to the bank. Since a check does not by itself transfer funds at the time of issue (and therefore does not confer on the payee or other holder any property right in the funds on deposit), the drawee bank is not liable *to the holder* for refusing to pay the check. However, the bank may be liable to the *drawer* (may be in breach of the contract of deposit) for refusing to pay. The bank's liability for wrongful dishonor (refusal to pay) is discussed later in this chapter.

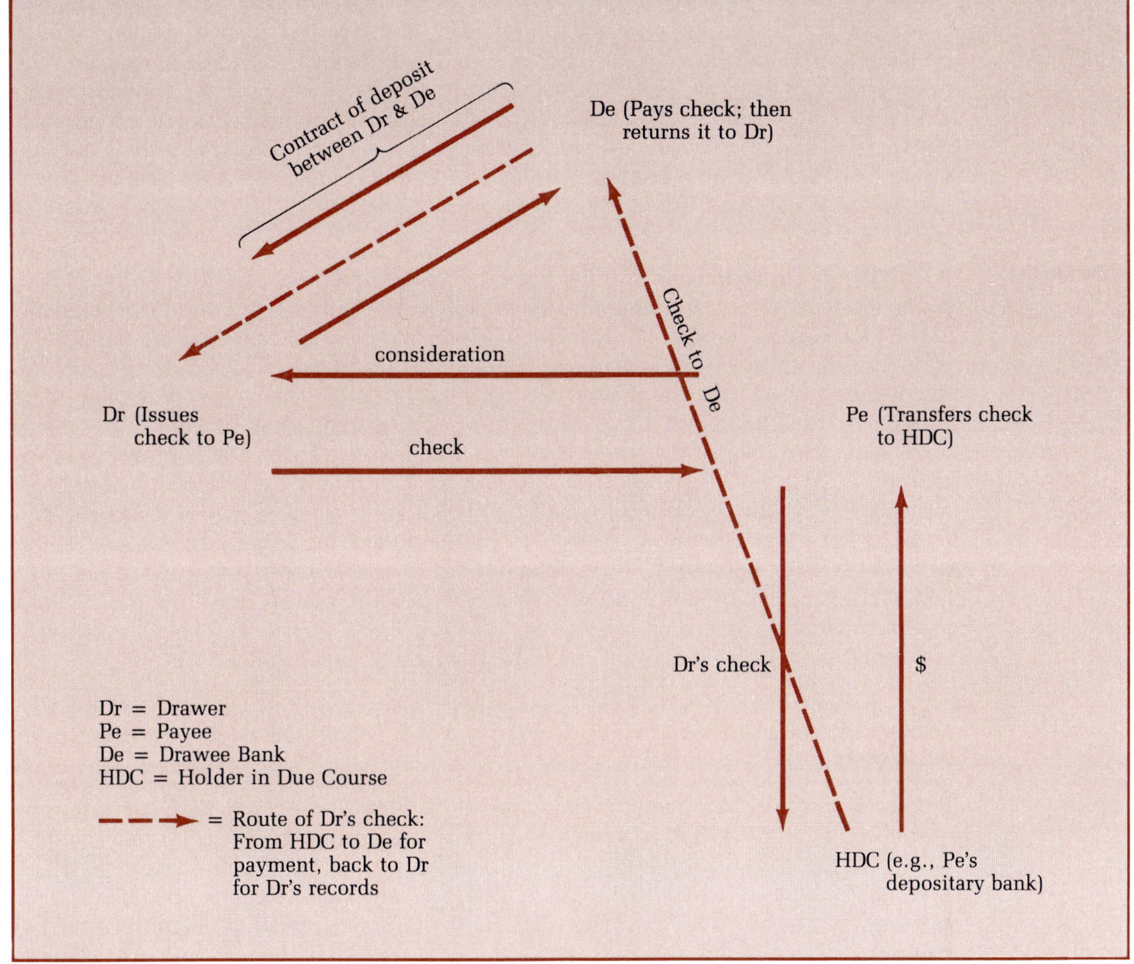

Figure 32.1 Issue, transfer, payment, and return of check

In Case 32.1, whether plaintiff Ward has insurance coverage depends on who has control of the funds represented by an uncashed check.

CASE 32.1 Ward v. Federal Kemper Insurance Co. • 40 UCC Rep. 753 (Md. Ct. Spec. App. 1985)

FACTS On May 19, 1981, Federal Kemper Insurance Co. (defendant) issued an automobile liability insurance policy to Aaron Ward, who paid the premium in full. The policy was to expire on November 17, 1981. On August 4, because of a change of vehicles owned by Ward, Kemper sent him a check for $12, drawn on Citizens National Bank. The check represented a refund of overpaid premium. Ward received the check but never negotiated it.

Soon after sending the check, Kemper discovered that the proper refund should have been $4.50 rather than $12. On August 18, it billed Ward for the difference, $7.50. Ward

CASE 32.1 Continued

never paid the $7.50, and pursuant to provisions of the policy, Kemper mailed Ward a notice of cancellation effective October 11. Ward had changed his address and apparently never received the notice. On November 15, Ward was involved in an accident while driving his car. Ward and others involved in the accident sustained personal injuries and property damage. Ward filed a claim with Kemper, but Kemper denied liability under the insurance policy. Ward sued Kemper, seeking a declaratory judgment as to coverage. From a judgment for Kemper, Ward appealed.

OPINION

ADKINS, J. The issue... is whether appellee Kemper properly cancelled an insurance policy for nonpayment of a premium. The question is whether Ward owed the premium at the time of cancellation. The answer to this seemingly simple question is complicated by a problem in the law of negotiable instruments: [I]n whose hands are the funds represented by a check that the drawer (Kemper) has mailed to the payee (Ward) but that is never paid by the drawee bank because never negotiated by the payee?...

...The parties agree that the real issue is who had the $7.50 premium-due balance that was included in the unnegotiated $12 check. If this money was Ward's by virtue of his possession of the check and his ability to negotiate it, then Ward owed Kemper the $7.50 and the cancellation was proper. If, on the other hand, the $7.50 was still under Kemper's control, because the check had not been negotiated when the policy was cancelled, the cancellation was improper. To resolve this question we must turn to the Uniform Commercial Code....

Ward points to § 3-409(1) of the [UCC], which provides that:

> A check or draft does not of itself operate as an assignment of any funds in the hands of the drawee available for its payment, and the drawee is not liable on the instrument until he accepts it."

Because of this rule, he argues, his mere possession of the... check did not have the effect of transferring the $12 to him. Kemper could have stopped payment or, for that matter, closed its account at the drawee bank prior to presentment of the check. In either of these events, he would have had nothing more than a claim against Kemper for the $4.50 in fact due him; the $7.50 overpayment would at all times have remained under the insurer's control, as it in fact did....

Kemper counters that by virtue of § 3-413 the drawer of a check "engages that he will pay the instrument according to its tenor..." and further "engages that upon dishonor [as through a stop-payment order] and any necessary notice of dishonor... he will pay the amount of the draft to the holder...." According to Kemper, a stop payment order may be effective to prevent payment of a check by the drawee, but that does not affect the drawer's liability to a holder in due course. Section 3-305. Had Ward negotiated the [check] to a holder in due course, thereby receiving value for it, Kemper would have been liable to the holder in due course despite any stop payment order.... When Kemper billed Ward for the $7.50 and when it issued the cancellation notice, it had no way of knowing whether a holder in due course had entered the picture. Thus, the argument continues, by issuing the check to Ward, Kemper obligated itself to pay $12. And since that obligation was $7.50 more than its actual premium refund debt to Ward, Ward was obligated to pay Kemper the difference. Therefore, Ward owed Kemper a premium of $7.50, a sum that has never been paid.

We think Kemper misapprehends the nature of a check and the relationships of the parties to it. A check is... an order by a drawer... to a drawee... to pay money to a payee.... As between drawer and drawee, the relationship is one of creditor and debtor. The drawer does not "own" the funds it has on deposit with the drawee. Its balance on the drawee's books represents a debt owed [to] the drawer by the drawee. The funds are "owned" by the drawee.

CASE 32.1 Continued

When the drawer draws a check on the drawee and delivers the check to the payee, the check ordinarily is regarded as only a conditional payment of the underlying obligation.... The conditions are that the check be presented and honored. Until those conditions are met, no one is directly liable on the check itself.... The underlying obligation represented by the check is similarly suspended until those conditions are met [Section 3-802(1)(b)]. If they are not met (if, for example, the check is dishonored)[,] an "action may be maintained either on the [check] or the obligation...."

The point is that the drawer is only secondarily liable on the check when he issues it.... As Ward correctly asserts, the delivery of Kemper's check did not operate as an assignment to him of any funds in the hands of the drawee.... Ward, when he received the check, acquired no proprietary interest in the fund on deposit.

The $12 check involved in this case was, of course, never dishonored. Thus, Kemper never became liable directly on the check, nor was its underlying obligation (to refund $4.50 to Ward) ever actually discharged. The check was never presented to the drawee and, therefore, [was] never paid, so the funds it represented were never transferred to Ward.... Under these circumstances, we do not think that Ward owed any premium to Kemper.... When Kemper attempted to cancel the policy[,] the entire premium was in its bank account; Ward owed it nothing at that time.

Accordingly, we hold that the [trial court] correctly concluded that "at the date the [premium-due] bill was sent in the amount of $7.50 on August 18, 1981, [the premium] was not due." That being so, Kemper could not lawfully have cancelled Ward's policy for nonpayment of that premium. Ward is entitled to a declaratory judgment to the effect that his Kemper policy was in full force and effect when the accident occurred....

JUDGMENT ... [R]eversed.... Appellee to pay the costs.

Certified Checks

Recall that no one is contractually liable for payment of a negotiable instrument unless that person has signed the instrument. Therefore a drawee bank has no liability on a check when it is issued, and the payee or other holder must rely mainly on the creditworthiness of the drawer (and of any indorser whose secondary liability has not been discharged) when deciding whether to cash a check or to receive it as payment for property or services. To reduce doubts of payees and subsequent holders about the collectability of a check, the drawee bank may be willing to *certify* it.

Certification is the *acceptance* of a check by a drawee bank [3-411(3)]. A bank official certifies a check by stamping the word "accepted" or "certified" on its face and adding the date of certification and the official's signature. Upon certifying a check, the drawee bank becomes *primarily* liable for the face amount of the check [3-409(1); 3-413(1)]. Because the bank ordinarily charges (debits) the drawer's account for the amount of the check before certifying it, the certification is an assurance to the person seeking certification and to subsequent holders that the bank holds money to pay the check. But regardless of whether the bank actually debits the drawer's account, the bank, by certifying the check, makes an *independent* engagement (promise) to pay. Thus, the holder may rely on the credit of the drawee bank instead of the credit of individuals such as the drawer.

Unless otherwise agreed, a bank is under no obligation to either a depositor (drawer) or a third person (such as the payee) to certify a check [3-411(2)]. Usually, however, a bank is quite willing to certify a check, provided the drawer has sufficient funds to cover it. A bank may certify a check at the request of the bank's customer (the drawer) or at the request of the payee or other holder.

A *drawer* may, before issuing a check, seek certification at the request of the payee who is unwilling to rely on the credit of the drawer alone. For example, a transport company that moves household furnishings interstate usually insists on being paid with a certified check before unloading the furnishings. A drawer can use a certified check for moving personal funds too, by having the drawee bank certify a check made out to the drawer or to a bank at a new location. Because of the certifying bank's primary liability, a bank at the new location ordinarily will allow the drawer to make withdrawals from the new account immediately instead of requiring the drawer to wait until the certified check "clears." Where a bank certifies a check at the request of the drawer, the certification *adds* the primary liability of the certifying bank to the usual secondary liability of the drawer.

Sometimes the *payee or other holder* receives a check and then seeks certification from the drawee. This might happen, for example, where the payee or holder would like to transport the check to a distant location and cash it there rather than cash it locally and carry the money. Where a bank certifies a check at the request of the payee or holder, the drawer and all prior indorsers are *discharged* from liability on the check [3-411(1)]. Thus, the certifying bank is *substituted* as the party liable for payment. The reason for discharging the drawer and prior indorsers is that the holder could have had cash merely by presenting the check for payment, and upon the holder's receiving cash the drawer and prior indorsers would have been discharged. The holder's act of procuring certification should not, and under the UCC does not, increase the liability of the drawer and prior indorsers beyond that which they originally had.

Relationship between Bank and Customer

Contract between Bank and Customer

By opening a checking account, an individual or a business firm enters into a contract with the bank (the "contract of deposit" noted in Figure 32.1). This contract imposes duties on the bank and on the checking account customer (the depositor). As indicated in Table 32.1 a major duty of the *bank* to the depositor is to make payments out of the depositor's account *only* in strict accordance with the depositor's *genuine* orders. Thus, the bank has absolute liability to the depositor for paying a forged or an altered check and ordinarily may not charge (debit) the drawer's account for the amount of a forged check or for the amount by which an altered check has been raised. If the bank does charge the drawer's account under such circumstances, it usually must recredit the drawer's account for the amount of the improper payment. The *depositor* owes two major duties to the bank: (1) to avoid negligence when drawing and issuing a check, and (2) to examine bank statements and canceled checks with reasonable care and to report forgeries and alterations promptly. If the depositor-drawer fails in these duties, the bank may be relieved of liability for an otherwise improper payment out of the drawer's account.

The technical complexities of banking operations are so great that it is not feasible to include in a printed contract all the rights and duties of the parties. Instead, many of these rights and duties are governed by provisions of the UCC. However, the bank and customer are free to vary by contract the effect of a Code provision, except that no agreement can disclaim a bank's responsibility for its own lack of good faith or its failure to exercise ordinary care [4-103].

Although it is not feasible to include in a printed contract all the terms of the contract, most banks require their checking account customers to sign a form, called a "signature card," that includes some of the principal contract provisions. Often the printed form deals with such matters as the bank's handling of items received from the customer for deposit or for collection, the depositor's responsibility when the depositor requests the bank to stop payment on a check, and the service charges to which the account will be subject. If litigation involves a problem that is not governed by specific contract provisions or by statute, courts look to the common law and to banking usage for the solution.

Nature of Bank-Customer Relationship

There is a dual relationship between a bank and its checking account customer: that of debtor and creditor, in which the customer is the creditor; and that of principal and agent, in which the bank is the agent. When the customer makes a deposit of *money* in his or her account, the bank becomes the customer's debtor. In the event of the bank's bankruptcy, the customer is a general creditor of the bank. If a cus-

Table 32.1 Major Duties of Bank and Checking Account Customer

Duties of Bank	Duties of Customer
To make payment out of customer's account strictly according to customer's orders	To use reasonable care in drawing and issuing checks
To honor customer's timely stop orders	To examine bank statements and canceled checks with reasonable care; to report forgeries and alterations promptly
To act in good faith and with ordinary care in the handling of customer's account	To pay the bank's service charges
Other duties as imposed by contract of deposit, the UCC, and other banking law	Other duties as imposed by contract of deposit, the UCC, and other banking law

tomer deposits a check or another item *for collection* (for the bank to present on behalf of the customer for payment), the bank is temporarily the customer's agent as to the particular item, until the bank collects the amount of the item for the customer. Then, upon collection of the item, the bank ceases being the customer's agent and becomes the customer's debtor as to the amount collected. A bank also acts as an agent for the customer in honoring checks that the customer has drawn against funds on deposit in her or his account.

Check Collection Process

Usually, a person initiates the check collection process by depositing a check with his or her bank. Suppose, for example, that Paul works in Fresno, California, for Dora, who owns a nationwide auto parts business. Paul receives his paycheck in Fresno, but it is drawn in Massachusetts on Boston Bank, where Dora has her payroll account. Paul has an account with Fresno Bank and deposits his paycheck there.

Fresno Bank has no direct dealings with Boston Bank. To collect the check for Paul, Fresno Bank will send it through a series of banks that collect checks for other banks. Paul's check may travel from Fresno Bank through some California state banks and the Federal Reserve Bank of San Francisco to the Federal Reserve Bank of Boston, which will present the check to Boston Bank for payment. A *clearinghouse* (a place where banks exchange checks and settle their daily balances) may be involved.

In Figure 32.2, the banks between Fresno Bank and Boston Bank are referred to collectively as "Fed Bank." Fresno Bank is the "depositary bank," Fed Bank is the "intermediary bank," and Boston Bank is the "payor bank." Depositary and intermediary banks are also called "forwarding" or "collecting" banks, and payor banks are the drawees of the checks being cashed. An intermediary bank dealing directly with the payor is called the "presenting" bank. Ordinarily, a collecting bank must forward a check no later than midnight of the banking day following the day of receipt—e.g., by midnight Tuesday for a check received on Monday [4-202]. This time limit is called the bank's *midnight deadline* [4-104].

Collection is accomplished by debiting and crediting accounts that banks maintain between themselves for collection purposes. Collection is based on a system of "provisional" (reversible) credits that Paul and the collecting banks expect to become "final." When a provisional credit becomes final, the bank becomes accountable to its customer for the amount [4-213(3)]. A bank may allow a depositor to withdraw funds against a provisional credit, and by doing so becomes a holder for value of the deposited item (to the extent of the value given). But if the provisional credit never becomes final, the bank has the right to recover the credited amount from the depositor.

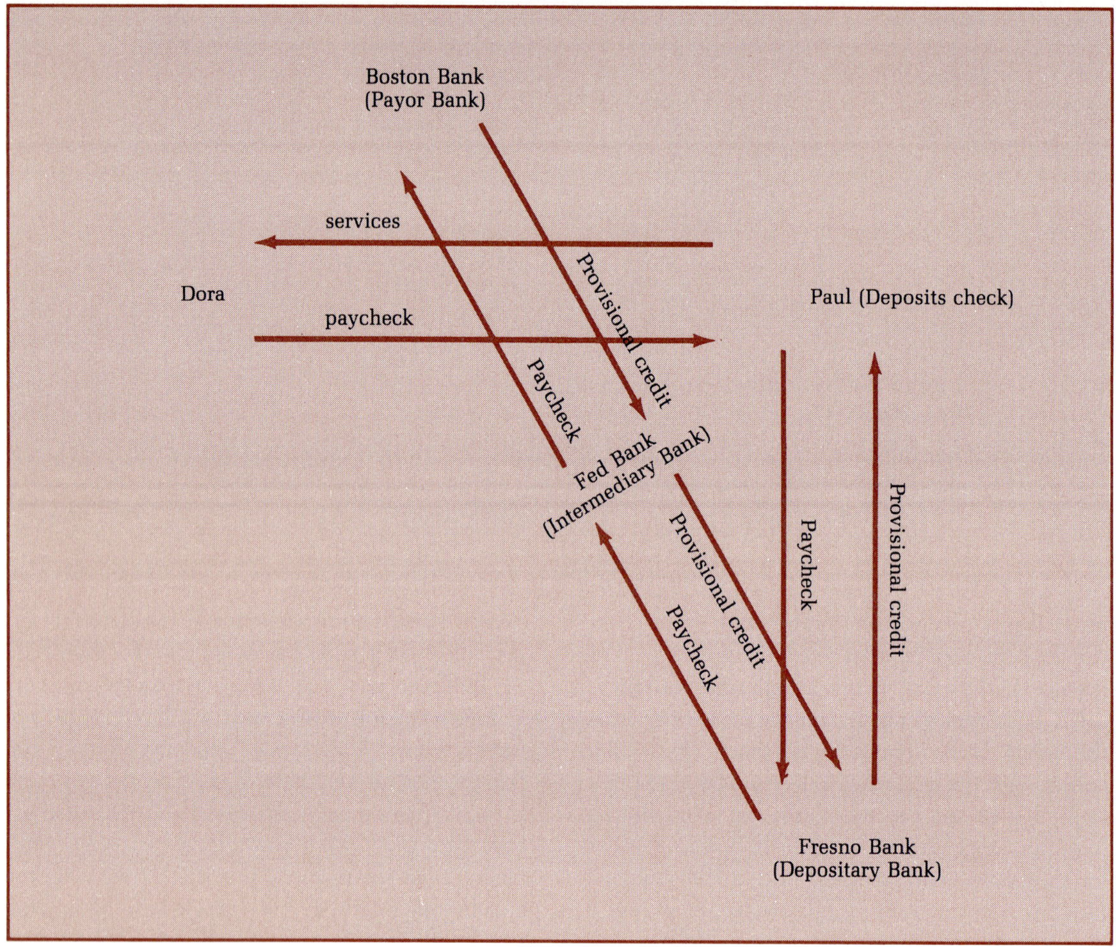

Figure 32.2 Banks in collection process

Provisional credits become *final* when the *payor* bank takes any of a variety of actions, whichever happens first [4-213]. Chief among them are:

1. *Paying the item (check) in cash.*
2. *Completing the process of posting the item to the drawer's account. Posting* is the payor bank's act of deciding to pay an item and recording the payment in the account to be charged. Ordinarily, the process involves the verification of signatures, determining that the drawer has sufficient funds available, marking the check "paid," and debiting the drawer's account.
3. *Failing to revoke a provisional credit within the time allowed by law.* To enable payor banks to distribute their workloads efficiently, the UCC permits them to engage in *deferred posting.* In deferred posting, a bank gives a provisional credit on the day a check is received and has until midnight of the following banking day (its midnight deadline) to complete the posting process. If the bank decides to revoke the provisional credit, it must do so (*by returning the check or by sending written notice of dishonor if the check is unavailable*) before the midnight deadline; otherwise, the provisional credit becomes final [4-301].

As soon as Fresno Bank has had a reasonable time to learn that settlement for Paul's paycheck has become final, Paul has a right to withdraw the funds (although the bank could permit earlier withdrawal). But suppose Paul deposits an "on us" check (a check drawn in his favor by another customer of Fresno

Bank) and receives a provisional credit. If the bank fails to dishonor the check by its midnight deadline (midnight Tuesday for a check deposited on Monday), payment is final and Paul therefore has a right to withdraw the funds when the bank opens on Wednesday, the second banking day following the bank's receipt of the item [4-213(4)].

When Bank May Charge Customer's Account

When a bank honors a check properly drawn on the customer's account, or certifies a customer's check, it *debits* (charges) the customer's account for the amount of the check. However, there are several situations where the bank's right to charge the customer's account may be questioned.

Payment of Overdraft. In the absence of some arrangement with the bank for permitting an overdraft (a check written on a checking account containing less funds than the amount of the check), the customer has no right to overdraw an account; and the bank has no obligation to pay an overdraft. If the bank chooses to honor an overdraft, it has a right to do so [4-401]. If the bank pays the overdraft, the customer must reimburse the bank.

In the ordinary checking account, the customer's obligation to repay an overdraft is not subject to interest charges. For the benefit of both customer and bank, many banks offer a special kind of checking account ("ready reserve checking account") that allows the customer to overdraw an account by a stated number of dollars. The amount of the overdraft in a "ready reserve" account is considered a loan, and the customer is charged interest.

Payment of an Altered Check. Where a holder in due course takes an instrument that has been altered, the holder may enforce the instrument according to its original tenor, i.e., for its original amount. The Code gives parallel protection to a drawee bank by providing that if the bank in good faith makes payment of an altered check, it may charge the customer's account according to the original tenor of the check [4-401(2)]. For example, if a customer issues a check in the amount of $100, a holder raises the amount to $2,100, and the drawee bank pays the check in good faith, the bank may charge the drawer's account, but with only $100. The bank may charge the drawer's account with the *raised* amount, however, if (1) the drawer's *negligence substantially contributed* to the alteration, and (2) payment by the bank was made in good faith and in accordance with reasonable commercial standards in the banking business [3-406].

Payment of Check Incomplete When Issued. A check containing a material omission, such as lack of an amount or lack of a named payee, will not be honored by the bank. However, the payee or holder of an incomplete check may fill in the missing information and present the check for payment. The UCC provides that if a bank in good faith makes payment of a completed item, the bank may charge the customer's account according to the manner in which the item has been completed [4-401]. Suppose that a customer signs a blank check and delivers it to the payee, telling that person to "fill it in for the amount I owe you," and the payee fills it in for twice the amount. If the bank in good faith pays the check, it may charge the drawer's account with the amount of the check as completed. Thus, the risk of loss is on the signer who, by issuing an incomplete instrument, made loss possible. The bank is protected even though it has knowledge of the completion—where, for example, the payee fills in the amount in the presence of a bank employee. The bank, however, is *not* allowed to charge the customer's account if the bank is on notice that the completion was improper.

Payment of a Stale Check. Banks generally call checks that are outstanding for 6 months or more "stale" checks. The drawee bank is not obligated to pay a check, other than a certified check, that is presented to it more than 6 months after the check is issued. If the bank chooses to honor a stale check (as where the bank knows its corporate customer wants all dividend checks honored), it may charge the customer's account, provided the payment is made in good faith [4-404].

A "stale" check is not necessarily "overdue." Recall that a check purchased ("cashed") more than 30 days after its issue is presumed overdue, and its purchaser cannot be a holder in due course. If Hal purchases a check *within* 30 days of issue, he *can* be a holder in due course; but if he holds the check for 6 months before cashing it, it has become stale. Thus, although Hal may hold the check free from the drawer's personal defenses, the drawee bank has a right to dishonor it by refusing payment.

Payment of a Postdated Check. Postdating a check has no effect on its negotiability [3-114]. A taker of a postdated check therefore may be a holder in due course. However, if a holder presents the check to the drawee bank for payment before the specified date, the bank may properly refuse payment, and there is no dishonor to trigger the liability of secondary parties. The bank's refusal to pay before the stated date is proper because the bank could be held liable to its customer for paying a postdated check early, charging the customer's account, and thereby reducing the balance in the account to a point where currently payable checks are dishonored. A bank will *not* be held liable for paying a postdated check if the drawer's own negligence is the cause of the drawer's loss or if the drawer postdated the check for a fraudulent purpose.

Bank's Liability for Wrongful Dishonor

A bank is liable to its customer for damages caused by the *wrongful dishonor* of (refusal to pay) the customer's check [4-402]. Since a bank is liable only for a *wrongful* dishonor, it is not liable where it dishonors a check for the drawer's lack of funds, or for lack of a necessary indorsement, or for other good reasons such as staleness. A bank is liable for wrongful dishonor only to the drawer-customer, for breach of the contract of deposit. A *payee or other holder* of a check who is harmed by the drawee-bank's wrongful dishonor has no right of recovery against the bank.

Wrongful dishonor includes intentional refusal to pay a check, brought about by mistake. Where the dishonor occurs through mistake, the bank's liability is limited to "actual damages proved." The Code *rejects* the view that the wrongful dishonor of a check automatically defames the drawer by reflecting badly on the drawer's credit and therefore entitles the drawer to an award without proof that damage has occurred. The Code recognizes, however, that actual damages may include damages caused by an arrest or prosecution of the customer or, as Case 32.2 illustrates, other circumstances directly resulting from the wrongful dishonor.

CASE 32.2 Twin City Bank v. Isaacs · 672 S.W.2d 651 (Ark. 1984)

FACTS On Sunday, May 13, 1979, Kenneth and Vicki Isaacs discovered that their checkbook was missing. On Monday, May 14, they reported the loss to Twin City Bank (Bank), with which they had a checking account. Later they learned that two forged checks totalling $2,050 had been written on their account and honored by Bank on May 11 and 12. Bank decided to freeze the Isaacs' account, which had contained approximately $2,500 before the forgeries occurred. A few valid checks cleared Monday morning before the hold order was issued, leaving a balance of about $2,000. After the freeze, Bank dishonored the Isaacs' checks. In mid-June 1979, the Isaacs sued Bank for wrongful dishonor of their checks and wrongful withholding of their funds.

Bank froze the account because Mr. Isaacs had been convicted of burglary and Bank suspected that the Isaacs were somehow involved in forging the checks. The forger was charged and convicted soon after the forgeries occurred. On May 30, 1979, the police told Bank there was nothing to connect the Isaacs with the person arrested. Two weeks later the police notified Bank a second time that they could not connect the Isaacs to the forgeries. Nevertheless, Bank continued the freeze, denying the Isaacs their funds for some 4 years. At trial, the jury awarded the Isaacs $18,500 in compensatory damages and $45,000 in punitive damages. The trial court denied Bank's motion for a new trial, and Bank appealed.

OPINION STEELE HAYS, Justice.... [B]ank maintains there was insufficient evidence to support the $18,500 award for mental anguish... [and] loss of credit and loss of the bargain on a house, [and] that the award of punitive damages should not have been given at all[,] as there was not only insufficient proof of actual damages but insufficient evidence of malice

CASE 32.2 Continued

or intent to oppress on the part of the bank. The bank does not challenge the sufficiency of the evidence of its wrongful dishonor, but contends only that there was no evidence to support an award of damages. These arguments cannot be sustained....

...[T]here can be no serious question as to certain losses: the $2,000 wrongfully withheld by the bank for four years, and the value of two vehicles repossessed because the Isaacs did not have access to their funds, resulting in a loss of approximately $2,200. Additionally, after the account was frozen the bank continued to charge the account a service charge and overdraft fees on checks written before the forgeries but presented after the account was frozen. The bank does not refute these damages but argues [that] there is no showing of any financial deprivation from loss of credit or loss of the bargain on a house the Isaacs wanted to buy, and insufficient proof of mental anguish. We find, however, that... there was sufficient evidence to sustain damages for mental suffering, loss of credit, and sufficient demonstration of some loss attributable to the inability to pursue the purchase of a home.... In general, the type of mental anguish suffered under § 4-402 does not need to rise to the higher standard of injury for intentional infliction of emotional distress. Wrongful dishonors tend to produce intangible injuries similar to those involved in defamation actions....

Decisions upholding recovery for mental suffering under the code have found injury resulting from circumstances comparable to this case. In Northshore Bank v. Palmer..., for example, a $275 forged check was paid from Palmer's account. After the bank knew or should have known the check was forged, it charged Palmer with the $275 check and later wrongfully dishonored other checks. Part of the actual damages awarded was attributed to mental suffering for the "embarrassment and humiliation Palmer suffered from having been turned down for credit for the first time in his life."... And in Farmers & Merchants State Bank of Krum v. Ferguson..., the plaintiff's account in the amount of $7,000 was frozen for apparently one month for reasons not stated. The plaintiff was awarded $25,000 for mental anguish, $3,000 for loss of credit based on a denial of a loan, $5,000 for loss of time spent making explanations to creditors, and $1,500 for loss of use of his money. The court justified the mental suffering award because the dishonor was found to be with malice—the bank had failed to notify Ferguson that the account was frozen, some checks were honored while others were not, and the bank continued to withdraw loan payments due it during the entire time.

In this case, prior to the forgery incident the Isaacs' credit reputation with Twin City Bank was described by the bank as "impeccable" and the freezing of their funds had a traumatic effect on their lives. They obviously lost their credit standing with Twin City, and were unable to secure credit commercially at other institutions because of their status at Twin City. The Isaacs had to borrow from friends and family, and were left in a precarious position financially. They did not have the use of their $2,000 for four years. The allegation relative to the loss of a house resulted from the dishonor of an earnest money check for a home they were planning to buy, ending prospects for the purchase at that time. Though there may have been insufficient proof of loss of the bargain on the house, as the bank argues, nevertheless this evidence was admissible as an element of mental suffering.... There was also testimony that the financial strain contributed to marital difficulties leading at one point to the filing of a divorce suit.... Finally, the Isaacs lost equities in two vehicles repossessed as a result of the withholding of their funds. One of these, a new van, was repossessed by Twin City in June, 1979, before a five day grace period for a current installment had expired.

...We recognize that our holding today presents some conflict with pre-code law by allowing recovery without exactness of proof as to damages.... However... § 4-402, although similar to its predecessor, has additional language which impliedly recognizes mental suffering and other intangible injuries... as recoverable under this statute....

[Bank objected to the award of punitive damages.] [W]e address only the question of the excessiveness of the verdict.... In Holmes v. Hollingsworth... we noted the elements

CASE 32.2 Continued

that may be considered in assessing the amount of punitive damages, recognizing that the deterrent effect has some correlation to the financial condition of the party against whom punitive damages are allowed. In view of the circumstances in their entirety presented by this case, we cannot say the amount awarded was grossly excessive or prompted by passion or prejudice. . . .

JUDGMENT Affirmed.

Stop-Payment Order

Customer's Right to Stop Payment. Because a check is not an assignment of funds, but is a mere order to pay, it is subject to countermand by the person who ordered the payment. The Code recognizes the right of the customer to instruct the drawee bank not to pay a certain check by issuing a stop-payment order [4-403], commonly called a "stop order." However, a drawer's stop order affects only the relationship between the drawer and the drawee. The stop order *does not* cancel the check itself. The check is a contract that binds the drawer, and the holder may bring suit on the check, against the drawer, when the bank dishonors the check by giving effect to the stop order. Whether the holder will prevail depends on the usual factors—e.g., whether the holder is in due course or, if not, whether the drawer has a personal defense. Thus, as further explained later in this chapter in the section entitled "Bank's Rights of Subrogation after Improper Payment," a stop order will protect the drawer in certain situations but not in others. Ordinarily there is a small charge to the customer for the bank's services in stopping payment.

Under the UCC, a stop order may be given orally or in writing. Most states have adopted the UCC rule permitting oral stop orders. In those states, an oral order is binding on the bank for 14 calendar days (1 day in the District of Columbia) but to be binding for a longer time the order must be confirmed in writing within the 14-day period [4-403]. A written order is effective for 6 months, but it may be renewed by the customer, in writing. In some states (Arizona, California, Florida, Texas, and Utah), a stop order is not binding on the bank unless it is in writing (although the bank may honor an oral stop order if it wishes to do so). To bind the bank, the stop order must be received in time and must contain sufficient information to give the bank a reasonable opportunity to act on the order before the bank has either certified or paid the check.

After the bank has certified a check (having in the process charged the customer's account), the *drawer can no longer stop payment.* A certification is the bank's own engagement (promise) to pay, and the bank is not required to impair its own credit by refusing payment for the convenience of the drawer [3-403, comment 5]. Neither may a bank stop payment of its own cashier's check. Certified checks and cashiers' checks are readily accepted as substitutes for money because banks rather than individuals stand behind them. To allow drawers to stop payment on such checks would undermine public confidence in them and thus would impair their utility.

Bank's Liability for Paying a Stopped Check. The drawee bank may be liable to the customer (the drawer) for the loss resulting from the payment of a check contrary to a binding stop order. It is no defense to the bank that it paid the check by mistake. Often a bank, by agreement with its customer, tries to limit or to disclaim liability for paying a check contrary to a stop order. However, a bank may not by such an agreement absolve itself from liability for bad faith or for *negligently* paying a check contrary to a stop order [4-103].

Bank's Right of Subrogation after Improper Payment. Suppose a bank pays a check contrary to a drawer's (customer's) stop order and charges the drawer's account. Then the drawer demands that the bank recredit his or her account for the amount of the check. The bank may or may not be required to do so. If the drawer's stop order has a valid basis, the drawee bank must recredit the drawer's account and seek payment from the person who in justice should make payment. If there was no legitimate basis for the stop order, the drawee is not required to recredit the drawer's account. These results follow from the fact that the drawee bank has a right of "subrogation" that at least partially protects the bank from loss due to its failure to honor the drawer's stop order. Consider the following examples of subrogation:

1 Maria issues a check to Pam in payment for totally defective goods that Pam delivered. Maria issues to her bank (the drawee) a timely stop order, but when Pam presents the check to Maria's bank for payment, the bank ignores the stop order and pays Pam the amount of the check, charging Maria's account. Since Maria has a defense to payment that is good against Pam (Pam delivered defective goods), the bank must recredit Maria's account. But under the UCC the bank is "subrogated" to (i.e., succeeds to or takes over) the rights of the *drawer* against the payee [4-407(c)]. This means that the bank "inherits" Maria's right to sue Pam for breach of the underlying transaction.

2 Suppose that, in the situation just described, Pam transferred Maria's check to Hal, a holder in due course; and that Hal, not Pam, received payment despite Maria's stop order. Under the UCC the bank also is subrogated to the rights of any *holder in due course* against the drawer [4-407(a)]. If the bank had honored the stop order, Hal (because he is a holder in due course) would still have a right to payment from Maria. She had only a personal defense against Pam, and a holder in due course takes free of personal defenses. Because the bank acquires Hal's rights by subrogation, the bank too would be entitled to payment from Maria free of her personal defense. So, the bank, having already charged Maria's account, need not recredit it; Maria's only remedy is against Pam.

3 Suppose Maria issues a check to Pam in payment for goods that Maria *wrongly* believes are defective. Maria issues her bank a timely stop order, but when Pam presents the check to Maria's bank for payment, the bank ignores the stop order and pays Pam the amount of the check, charging Maria's account. Maria demands that her bank recredit her account. The bank refuses. The bank is within its rights, since it, in paying despite the stop order, acquires any rights that the *payee* (Pam) has against the maker or drawer [4-407(b)]. Here, the goods are not defective and Maria has no valid defense against the payee. Thus, Pam has the right to Maria's payment and, by subrogation, so does the drawee bank. The bank, having already charged Maria's account, need not recredit it.

Effect of Unauthorized Signature or Alteration

As noted earlier in this chapter, a bank ordinarily may not charge a customer's account for the amount of a check or other item containing an unauthorized signature or for the amount by which an altered check has been raised. A bank that pays (or certifies) such an item may be required to recredit the customer's account for the amount of the improper charge and to absorb any loss or collect the amount from someone else. However, the bank's liability may depend on whether the customer gave timely notice of unauthorized signatures or alterations.

Banks generally furnish their checking account customers with monthly statements of account accompanied by canceled checks and other items in support of debit entries. Upon receiving such an account and supporting items (or being given reasonable access to them), the customer is under a duty to examine them promptly and carefully, and to give the bank *prompt* notice of any unauthorized signature or alteration [4-406(1)]. If the customer does not comply with the duties of inspection and prompt notice, and if the bank consequently suffers loss, the customer may not assert against the bank the customer's own unauthorized signature or any alteration [4-406(2)]. The bank would suffer loss, for example, where the customer's failure to give prompt notice of a forgery enabled the forger to "skip town" and avoid payment, or prevented the bank from suing the forger until he or she became insolvent.

If the customer can prove that the *bank* was negligent in not discovering an unauthorized signature or an alteration, the bank must recredit the customer's account for the amount of the unauthorized payment *even though the customer does not act promptly or is negligent* [4-406(3)]. The bank's liability, however, even for its own negligence, is subject to strict time limits. The customer must report *his or her own* unauthorized signature or *any alteration* within 1 year (60 days in the state of Washington) from the time the customer's statement is available to the customer. The customer must report an unauthorized *indorsement* within 3 years (1 year in California and Ohio) [4-406(4)]. Note that the times just mentioned are outer limits on the bank's liability for an improper charge. In reality, *unless the bank was negligent,* the customer has only a *reasonable* time to discover alterations and unauthorized signatures—not necessarily the full 1 or 3 years just discussed [4-406, comment 5].

Where a series of checks containing unauthorized signatures or alterations made by the *same wrongdoer* is paid by a nonnegligent bank and charged to the customer's account over a period of time, the customer has less time than usual to detect and report the wrongdoing. Where the same wrongdoer makes a series of forgeries or alterations, the customer has a reasonable time *not exceeding 14 calendar days* to report the wrongdoing [4-406(2)(b)]. If the reasonable time (up to 14 days) expires, and if the bank pays an unauthorized or altered item before receiving notice of earlier wrongdoing, the bank is not liable for the improper payments that occurred *between* the expiration of the reasonable time and the time that the bank received notice of the earlier wrongdoing.

Suppose, for example, that Carl's employee Amy skillfully forges Carl's signature on the twenty-fifth of each month to an extra monthly paycheck for 5 months in a row: May, June, July, August, and September. The bank pays all five checks in good faith, without negligence; and in late September Amy leaves town for parts unknown. On June 1, Carl received his bank statement and canceled checks for the month of May. They reveal the first forgery. The statements and canceled checks for the following months reveal the other forgeries. However, Carl, waits until December 1 before inspecting any of the records. Then, on December 1 Carl discovers all five forgeries, reports them to the bank immediately, and demands that the bank recredit his account for the amount of all five checks. What are the rights of Carl and the bank?

1 As to the first check, Carl has a *reasonable* time to discover the forgery of his signature—up to the outer limit of 1 year. Six months might or might not be a reasonable time within which to discover the forgery. Whether Carl was reasonable in waiting that long is a question for a jury. If Carl's inspection and notice to the bank were "prompt," the bank must recredit Carl's account for the amount of the first check.

2 As to the other four checks, Carl is not entitled to a recredit. Because the five forgeries were made by the same wrongdoer (Amy), Carl is subject to the 14-day limit. Since he did not discover and report the first forgery within 14 calendar days after receiving the May statement, and since he did not give the bank notice of the first forgery before the bank paid Amy the amounts of the other forged checks, Carl must absorb the loss or take action against Amy for the amount of the last four checks.

Suppose now that Carl notified the bank of the first (the May) forgery on August 26, immediately after the fourth (the August 25) forgery, but the bank paid the fifth (the September 25) forged check anyway. If Carl's August 26 notice was prompt as to the May forgery, the bank must recredit his account for the May check, is not required to recredit the account for the next three checks (because Carl violated the 14-day rule), but must recredit the account for the fifth check because Carl gave notice of the earlier wrongdoing before the bank paid the fifth check, and gave the notice in time for the bank to act on it.

If a customer promptly discovers and reports an *altered* check on which the amount has been raised by a wrongdoer and paid in good faith by the bank, the customer is entitled to, at most, a *partial* recredit. A bank that makes a good faith payment of an altered check always may charge the customer's account according to the original tenor of the altered item [4-401(2)(a)]. And, where the customer has signed and issued an *incomplete* item, the bank may charge the account according to the tenor of the item *as completed,* unless the bank has notice at the time of payment that the completion was improper [4-401(2)(b)]. Moreover, a bank may charge a customer's account for the whole amount of an altered item if the *customer's own negligence* substantially contributed to the alteration *and* if the bank paid the check in good faith and in accordance with the reasonable commercial standards of the bank's business [3-406]. The customer-drawer's leaving open spaces on the face of the check so that alteration is easy is one example of such negligence. Similarly, in situations involving indorsements by imposters or faithless employees (discussed in Chapter 31), a drawee bank that pays in good faith may charge the customer's account for the amount of the check and is not required to recredit the customer's account even after prompt discovery and notice [3-405].

Case 32.3 discusses whether a drawee bank observed reasonable commercial standards in paying forged checks by means of a computer without reviewing signatures individually.

CASE 32.3 Medford Irrigation District v. Western Bank · 676 P.2d 329 (Or. 1984)

FACTS The bookkeeper for Medford Irrigation District forged the name of its manager on several checks drawn on its account with Western Bank (defendant). (Apparently the bookkeeper made the checks payable to herself or to a fictitious payee, forged the name of the manager as drawer, and cashed them at various places by providing the indorsement required by the particular forged check.) Western Bank, the drawee, paid the checks and debited the District's account. District (plaintiff) brought suit to recover the face value of the checks. From a summary judgment for District, Western appealed.

OPINION RICHARDSON, P. J.... It is conceded for the purposes of the summary judgment motion that plaintiff was negligent in not supervising the bookkeeper and in not auditing the accounts and reviewing the bank statements. It is also conceded that plaintiff's negligence substantially contributed to the forgeries. Plaintiff argues that Western did not follow reasonable commercial banking standards, and failed to exercise ordinary care, in paying the forged checks.

Ordinarily the law places the risk of loss from forgeries on the bank. Any unauthorized signature is generally "wholly inoperative as that of the person whose name is signed." UCC 3-404. Because a forged signature is wholly inoperative, a forged check is not "properly payable," UCC 4-401, and a bank cannot debit the depositor's account. If, however, the depositor's negligence substantially contributes to the forgery, the depositor is precluded from asserting the improper payment against a bank which pays the check in good faith and in accordance with reasonable commercial standards of the banking industry. UCC 3-406. Also, if the depositor fails to exercise reasonable care in examining its bank statement and promptly reporting any unauthorized debits to the bank, the depositor is precluded from asserting the unauthorized payment unless it establishes lack of ordinary care on the part of the bank in paying the check. UCC 4-406.

Western... argues that there is a genuine issue of material fact as to whether it exercised ordinary care and whether its procedures comported with reasonable commercial banking standards. Western utilizes a computer check payment system. Checks for a face amount under $5,000 are paid without human intervention or "sight review" of the signatures. Checks are received for payment at Western's data processing center in Portland, and, unless there is a "hold" or a "stop payment" order for a check, it is paid automatically by computer. The canceled checks are ultimately forwarded to the customers along with the bank statement. The computer is programmed to "kick out" checks with a face amount of $5,000 or more. Absent specific instructions from a customer, only checks of $5,000 or more are individually reviewed for authorized signatures or alterations.

Western... concluded that the cost of reviewing checks for unauthorized signatures greatly exceeded the benefits.... [A] small number of forgeries was detected by individual review of checks, while the cost of that review was approximately $200,000 per year. Western contends that the procedure it [uses conforms] with methods used by most banks of its size throughout the United States. It argues that it is a fact question whether its procedures comport with reasonable commercial standards and whether it exercised ordinary care....

The reasonableness of commercial banking standards must be analyzed in the context of a bank's duty in relation to the depositor's account. Although a procedure may be

CASE 32.3 Continued

common throughout the banking industry, it is not, by that fact alone, a reasonable procedure. Implied in the relationship between a bank and its checking account depositors is a contractual undertaking on the part of the bank that it will . . . discharge its obligation [only] on an authorized signature. Section 3-404 specifies that an unauthorized signature is wholly inoperative, and a check with an unauthorized signature is not properly payable by the bank. UCC 4-401. The responsibility of the bank is to use ordinary care in paying only checks with authorized signatures. Thus, the procedure utilized must reasonably meet that responsibility to be considered due care or reasonable commercial banking standards in the context of UCC 3-406 or 4-406.

The [UCC] does not set out particular procedures or standards that the banking industry must follow, or attempt to define what ordinary care or reasonable commercial standards are [because, according to a comment to Section 4-103, due to the technical complexity of the field of bank collections, "it would be unwise to freeze present methods of operation by mandatory statutory rules"]. We do not hold that a bank must adopt a particular procedure, such as "sight review," in order to comply with the statutory mandate. We do hold that the procedure used must reasonably relate to the detection of unauthorized signatures in order to be considered an exercise of ordinary care or reasonable commercial banking standards. Western's approach is automatically to pay all checks under $5,000 without any procedure to detect unauthorized signatures on those items. While that approach, based on considerations of cost and efficiency, may be a prudent business decision and followed by most banks, it does not meet the bank's responsibility under the statutes. . . . We hold as a matter of law that the bank failed to exercise ordinary care and that the procedures adopted are not reasonable commercial practices.

Western contends that . . . there remain issues of fact as to causation and damages. This argument is premised on UCC 4-103(5):

> The measure of damages for failure to exercise ordinary care in handling an item is the amount of the item reduced by an amount which could not have been realized by the use of ordinary care, and where there is bad faith it includes other damages, if any, suffered by the party as a proximate consequence.

Western [contends] that the forgeries were so well done that they would not have been detected by individual scrutiny. Western argues that it is entitled to a fact determination [of] whether an exercise of ordinary care would have resulted in rejection of the checks. It contends that a fact finder could conclude that some or all of the checks would have been paid even with the use of sight review and that therefore it would not be liable for those checks under UCC 4-103(5).

[The UCC] creates a contractual arrangement between a bank and a depositor to the effect that the bank will pay only items which are properly payable. UCC 4-401. An item with an unauthorized signature is not properly payable. If the customer's negligence substantially contributes to the making of the unauthorized signature, it cannot assert that the item is not properly payable unless the bank is also negligent. If it is determined that the bank is negligent, the defense of the customer's negligence is not available, and the bank is strictly liable for improperly debiting the customer's account. There is thus no issue as to the causal relationship between the bank's lack of due care and the customer's loss if the loss is established. . . .

We conclude that, because Western failed to exercise ordinary care or to follow reasonable commercial banking practices, it is foreclosed from asserting plaintiff's negligence and is liable for paying the face amount of the forged checks. There is no issue of fact as to Western's liability or the amount. The court did not err in granting summary judgment for plaintiff. . . .

JUDGMENT Affirmed.

As indicated in Chapter 31 in the section on presentment warranties, a drawee bank is not obliged to pay a check containing a forged signature, even to a holder in due course. If the bank *does* make payment, the bank normally may not charge the customer's account. Nor may the bank retrieve the payment from a holder in due course, since payment to a holder in due course is final [3-418]. Instead, the bank must collect the amount of the mistaken payment from someone else or absorb the loss itself. From whom may the bank collect? The answer depends in large part on whose signature was forged.

Suppose that X forges Drawer's signature to a check made out to X; that X indorses the check to Hal Holder (a holder in due course); and that the drawee by mistake makes a payment to Holder that is "final" as the word "final" is defined in Section 4-213. Despite the forgery of the drawer's signature, the drawee bank cannot recover from Holder the money paid by mistake unless Holder breached a presentment warranty. This he did not do, since a holder in due course does not make the presentment warranty relating to the drawer's own signature. Neither did Holder breach the presentment warranty of title, since that warranty pertains only to forged indorsements. However, the bank may collect the amount from X. The forger X has knowledge that the drawer's signature is unauthorized. As a prior transferor, X has therefore breached a presentment warranty.

Suppose now that Drawer issues a check to the order of Payee, that X steals the check from Payee and forges Payee's indorsement, and that X sells the check to Watkins who presents it to and receives payment from the drawee bank. Watkins cannot be a holder (and therefore cannot be a holder in due course) because Payee did not *negotiate* the instrument; negotiation requires Payee's signature and delivery of the instrument. The bank may have payment from either Watkins or X. Since there was no negotiation, Watkins did not acquire title and is in breach of the presentment warranty of title. X (the forger and thief) lacks title and therefore is also in breach of the presentment warranty of title.

Effect of Customer's Death or Incompetence

As stated earlier in this chapter, the bank acts as the agent of its customer in two ways: (1) When a customer deposits an item such as a payroll check for collection, the bank collects the amount on behalf of its principal, the customer. (2) When a customer deposits funds that the bank is to pay out on the customer's behalf, e.g., by honoring checks drawn by the customer, the bank acts as an agent in paying those funds. It is the general rule in agency law that the principal's death, or the adjudication of his or her incompetency, terminates the agency relationship and, consequently, the authority of the agent, even before the agent learns of the death or incompetency. If this rule were applied to banks, however, it would be completely unworkable. In view of the tremendous number of items handled, banks acting as agents could not possibly verify the continued life and competency of their customers. Accordingly, the UCC provides that neither the death nor the incompetency of a customer revokes a bank's authority to pay or to collect an item, or to account for the proceeds of the collection, until the bank knows of the fact of death or of an adjudication of incompetence and has reasonable opportunity to act on it [4-405].

Furthermore, even though a bank knows of its customer's death, it may for 10 days after the date of death pay or certify checks drawn on or prior to that date. If there is any reason that such a check should not have been paid (such as fraud in the inducement), the executor or the administrator of the decedent's estate may recover the payment from the payee or other holder of the check or, if there is a real defense, from a holder in due course. There is one *exception* to the provision that a bank may pay or certify a check within 10 days after the drawer's death. A bank may not do so if it was ordered to stop payment by a person claiming an interest in the account, such as the executor of the decedent's estate or a person with whom the decedent had a joint account.

Bank's Liability for Conversion

A bank can become liable for the tort of conversion in a variety of ways. *Conversion* is the act of handling or using someone else's property in a manner inconsistent with that person's ownership. A bank converts a negotiable instrument, and becomes liable to the wronged person for the face amount, in the following ways [3-419]:

1 Refusing, on demand by the rightful owner (usually, the holder), to return a draft (or check) presented for acceptance.

2 Refusing, on demand by the rightful owner, to pay or to return to the owner an item presented for payment.
3 Paying an instrument on the basis of a forged indorsement.

Suppose Dora issues a check to the order of Paul. Then Tom steals the check, skillfully forges Paul's indorsement, and cashes the check at Dora's bank. Tom is both a thief and a converter. As a converter, Tom is liable to Paul for the amount of the check. Dora's *bank* is also a converter because it paid Tom on the basis of the forged indorsement and thereby acted in a manner inconsistent with Paul's ownership.

Case 32.4 discusses the liability of a depositary bank that cashes unindorsed checks for a person not authorized by the payee to receive payment.

CASE 32.4 Mid-Atlantic Tennis Courts, Inc. v. Citizens Bank · 658 F. Supp. 140 (D. Md. 1987)

FACTS Mid-Atlantic Tennis Courts, Inc. (plaintiff), hired Loy Smith to sell tennis court construction jobs and authorized him to deliver the executed contracts and any customer deposits to Mid-Atlantic's business office. Smith entered into a number of contracts with potential customers without informing Mid-Atlantic. Instead, he received deposit checks made out to Mid-Atlantic only or made out jointly to himself and Mid-Atlantic, opened checking accounts in his own name with Citizens Bank (defendant), and deposited the checks in those accounts. The checks were deposited with the indorsement "for deposit only" or with no indorsement. Eventually, Smith withdrew the funds from the accounts and disappeared. When Mid-Atlantic discovered the fraud, it sued Citizens Bank for the amount of the checks.

OPINION SMALKIN, D. J. . . . [T]he plaintiff seeks summary judgment for the checks in question. . . .

[I]t is clear that the plaintiff was the payee and "owner" of the checks . . . , and that they have been converted in the common law sense, viz., that Mid-Atlantic, as the true owner, has been deprived of the checks or the proceeds thereof. . . . The UCC, in § 3-419, applies conversion principles to negotiable instruments. . . .

It is axiomatic that an item is converted when it is paid on a forged indorsement, because the payment is made to one who has no good title. . . . This is just as true in the case where an indorsement necessary to transfer title is missing, because, without the necessary indorsement, there can be no negotiation of the order paper (such as all this paper was) . . . , and the taker is not a holder. . . . Although a bank is privileged in some circumstances to supply a missing indorsement, the only indorsement that it can supply is that of *its customer,* UCC § 4-205(1), and it is clear that Mid-Atlantic was not defendant's customer, because it had no account with defendant. . . . Until the bank supplies the missing indorsement of its customer, usually with a rubber stamp, it is not a holder of the item. . . . In this case, . . . the depositary bank never became the holder of the checks because of the absence of any indorsement whatever, a deficiency that it could not remedy by a stamp indorsement. . . . Because the depositary bank never became a holder in its own right, and because it took items as to which there was no indorsement whatever, it did not have good title to these items, and, therefore, it converted them when it eventually paid the proceeds over to Smith. . . . Although UCC § 3-419(3) usually protects depositary banks which have no proceeds of the items remaining in their hands . . . , that protection is unavailable where, as here, the depositary bank has not adhered to reasonable commercial banking standards. UCC § 3-419(3). . . . [Earlier, the court held that Bank's cred-

CAS 32.4 Continued

iting Mid-Atlantic's unindorsed checks to Smith's personal account was contrary to reasonable commercial banking standards.]

JUDGMENT Thus, the court concludes that... plaintiff is entitled to summary judgment against the defendant for all the items deposited bearing no indorsement or the "indorsement" of "for deposit only." The damages are the face amounts of the items. UCC § 3-419(2)....

Electronic Funds Transfer

To reduce the daily burden of processing billions of paper checks and deposit transactions, most banks use computerized electronic funds transfer (EFT) systems. EFT has several aspects: Intrabank processing; transfers of funds between banks; the "automated clearinghouse" (ACH); and the consumer elements—automatic teller machines, point-of-sale terminals, and pay-by-phone billing systems.

Intrabank Processing

Before funds can be transferred electronically, daily account activity must be recorded on magnetic tape or disks. Once, every deposit, withdrawal, or posting transaction was recorded laboriously by hand. Now, magnetically encoded checks and deposit slips enable computers to record account numbers, amounts of checks, and other information instantly; store it in its memory; enter daily account information into individual customer accounts; and print out balances and statements. Checks must be physically sorted as a part of the posting process. Computerized sorters process thousands of checks per hour.

Interbank Transfers; Automated Clearinghouses

EFT, which serves as a *substitute* for paper checks, has two major nonconsumer uses. The first, and oldest, is the electronic transfer of funds between banks. The Federal Reserve System, for example, has a central computerized switching center that enables its thousands of member banks to transfer funds between and within banks almost instantly.

A second EFT application is the use of the "automated clearinghouse" to facilitate direct deposits. Instead of sending thousands or millions of paper paychecks to employees, for example, large employers such as state governments send a magnetic tape containing payments information to an ACH. The ACH sorts the information according to the financial institutions in which the employees have accounts and, by electronic signals between computers, credits employee accounts. ACHs are now widely used for such recurring payments as private and governmental payrolls, social security payments, mortgage payments, and insurance premiums.

Consumer EFT Applications

Most familiar to many bank customers are the automated teller machines, point-of-sale terminals, and pay-by-phone bill-paying systems used in many parts of the country.

Automated teller machines, commonly located at banks, are operated by the customer's electronically encoded "debit card." When activated by the card, the machine will dispense specified amounts of money and will debit (charge) the customer's account for the amount withdrawn. The card can also be used to transfer funds between the customer's savings and checking accounts. Teller machines accept deposits for the customer's account, but the actual crediting of the account is done after bank personnel have verified amounts, reviewed indorsements, etc.

Point-of-sale terminals, similar in operation to automatic teller machines, are found in supermarkets and other businesses. Customers pay for purchases by using their debit cards to charge their bank accounts and credit those of the merchants. *Pay-by-phone* bill-paying systems require the bank customer to authorize, in advance, a list of payees and amounts to be paid. Then the customer need only pick up a telephone, enter the proper identification data, and give payment instructions to the bank's computer. This kind of bill-paying system operates without the use of a debit card.

As in the use of paper checks, there are many opportunities for an unauthorized person to make improper use of a customer's debit card or to order improper payments by phone. There is also the problem of errors in recordkeeping. Under the federal law governing EFT transactions, users of debit cards receive somewhat less protection from the wrongdoing of unauthorized persons than do users of paper checks. If a debit card is lost or stolen and used without the customer's permission, the customer is liable to the bank for a maximum of $50 worth of unauthorized use. The customer's loss is limited to $50 *only if* the customer gives the bank notice of the theft or loss within 2 business days. The customer's liability is a maximum of $500 if the 2-day notice requirement is not met; and if the customer does not give notice within 60 days, the customer's liability is unlimited. As to errors by the bank, they must be reported to the bank within 60 days after the customer receives a statement of account. Then the bank has 10 days to investigate and correct any errors.

Summary

Since a check does not by itself transfer funds at the time of issue, the drawee is not liable to the payee or holder for refusing to pay it, but the drawee may be liable to the drawer for refusing to pay. A bank is not required to certify a check, but a certification at the request of the payee or a holder discharges the drawer and any prior indorsers.

A bank is the debtor of the customer as to money on deposit. But the bank is the agent of the customer for purposes of collecting items and paying checks drawn by the customer. Many difficulties confront banks as they honor checks of their customers. These difficulties usually involve the payment of overdrafts, altered or forged checks, checks that were incomplete when issued, stale checks, and postdated checks. A bank is liable to the customer for damages caused by a wrongful dishonor, but in many situations a bank may charge the customer's account even though there was a valid stop-payment order. Where a bank has no right to charge the customer's account, the bank may have a right of subrogation against the payee or a holder.

The bank may not charge the customer's account where there is an alteration or an unauthorized signature, but the customer must inspect bank statements and promptly notify the bank of any improper charges if the bank is to be held liable. A bank can be liable for the tort of conversion in a variety of ways. Where electronic funds transfer systems are in use, bank customers are liable in varying degrees for unauthorized used of lost or stolen debit cards. Banks are fully liable for their own EFT errors, however, if properly notified of them.

Review Questions

1 What is the difference in legal effect between certification of a check at the request of the *holder* and certification at the request of the *drawer?*

2 **(a)** When and why is the relationship between a bank and its checking account customer that of principal and agent? **(b)** What is the significance in the collection process of a payor bank's midnight deadline? **(c)** How does a provisional credit become final? With what legal effect?

3 Under what circumstances may a bank that has paid a raised check charge the customer's account with the altered amount?

4 Explain why a bank may be liable to its customer for paying a postdated check before the specified date.

5 **(a)** Explain and give an example of a wrongful dishonor. **(b)** How are damages measured when a check is dishonored by mistake?

6 **(a)** How may a stop-payment order be made? **(b)** When must the order be received to be effective?

7 Explain in what way the following statement is inaccurate. A bank by agreement with its depositor may absolve itself from liability for paying a check contrary to a stop order.

8 Suppose that a bank has paid a check over a stop order and must recredit the drawer's account. Illustrate how the bank may be subrogated to the rights of the drawer.

9 List and give examples of situations where a payor bank may properly charge its customer's account for a check containing an unauthorized signature.

10 Where a customer's EFT debit card was lost or stolen and used without authorization, what is the customer's liability to the bank?

Case Problems

1 Dixon issued a check for $1,868.15 to Lloyd's Chevrolet-Olds. Later that day, Dixon called First State Bank, the drawee, to stop payment on the check. He gave Hargis, Bank's employee, the correct account number, check number, date, and payee of the check, but misstated the amount of the check as $1,828.73. When Dixon received his bank statement, he discovered that Bank had paid the check despite the stop order. Upon Bank's refusal to recredit his account, Dixon sued Bank for the amount of the check. At trial, Hargis testified that Bank's stop-payment requests were computerized, and Bank had to have the exact amount of a check in order to stop payment. From a judgment for Dixon, Bank appealed. Should the judgment be affirmed?

2 Giordano agreed to purchase two trucks for use in his business. National Newark & Essex Bank lent Giordano $9,500 for the purchase and drew a cashier's check on itself payable to the order of Fiero, the seller. Shortly after delivering the check to Fiero, Giordano discovered that the trucks were defective and asked Bank to stop payment on the check. Bank refused to do so. When Giordano later refused to repay the loan, Bank sued him for the amount. Whether Giordano should be held liable depended on whether Bank had a duty to stop payment on the check. Was Bank required to stop payment?

3 Atlantic Telec, Inc., made out a check to Genesis as payee, in payment for "soil inoculant" that Atlantic intended to resell to farm operators. Alleging that Genesis had breached its contract with Atlantic, Atlantic ordered Bank to stop payment of the check. Genesis presented the check for payment. Despite the stop order, Bank paid the check; and Atlantic sued Bank for $13,000, the amount of the check. From a judgment for Atlantic, Bank appealed. Bank also appealed the trial court's dismissing Bank's third-party complaint against Genesis, which Bank wished to pursue if found liable to Atlantic. **(a)** Was Bank liable to Atlantic? **(b)** If so, did Bank have a cause of action against Genesis?

4 Marlow crashed his car into the drive-in window facility of the Bank of Hartshorne, causing $1,200 damage to the facility. Marlow issued to Bank his check in payment for the damage. On May 30, Marlow died. On May 31, Cirar, Marlow's daughter, personally informed an official of Bank that her father had died. Although on notice of Marlow's death, Bank negotiated the check to The National Bank of McAlester on June 1, received the check back from the McAlester bank on June 3 for collection, and on June 4 paid the amount of the check to the McAlester bank, debiting Marlow's account. Alleging that Bank had made an improper payment from Marlow's account, Cirar, administratrix of Marlow's estate, sued the Bank of Hartshorne to recover the $1,200. Was the Marlow estate entitled to the $1,200?

5 United Account Systems (UAS) was employed by Refrigerated Transport Co. (RTC) to collect overdue accounts owed by RTC's customers, who made their checks out to RTC as payee. Without having authority to do so, UAS indorsed RTC's checks, deposited them in UAS's corporate checking account with National Bank of Georgia, and withdrew some of the funds. RTC won a judgment against the bank in conversion for the amount of the checks. Bank appealed, contending that its liability should be limited to the amount of money remaining in UAS's account at the time of suit. Bank relied on the following language of UCC § 3-419: "...[A] representative, including a depositary or collecting bank, who has in good faith and in accordance with the reasonable commercial standards applicable to the business of such representative dealt with an instrument... on behalf of one who was not the true owner is not liable in conversion or otherwise to the true owner beyond the amount of any proceeds remaining in his hands." Was RTC entitled to the face amount of the checks?

ETHICS IN PRACTICE

Like the insurance industry, commercial paper is rife with temptation for people who would part others from their money. Practices that are obviously illegal, such as forgery and the fraudulent alteration of checks, are discussed in the preceding chapters on commercial paper. The following problems focus more on ethical concerns than on the obviously illegal.

Problems in Ethics

1 Angela, a foreign student unfamiliar with banking law, has her checking account in a large American bank near campus. Angela's roommate steals Angela's checkbook from her desk, forges a check for $50, and cashes it at Angela's bank. Distressed by her roommate's dishonesty, Angela goes to the bank to close her account. Mary, Bank's employee, asks, "Why do you want to close your account? You just opened it." Explaining that her roommate forged Angela's name to a check and Bank cashed it, Angela replies, "I am from a very poor family. What else can I do?" Mary says, "Well, we can close your account as you ask and open a new one for you. Are you sure that's OK?" Angela says "Yes." Mary knows that Bank has a duty to recredit Angela's account for the $50, but she does not so inform Angela and Angela does not ask. **(a)** Has Mary committed a breach of ethics by not informing Angela of Bank's duty to recredit her account? **(b)** Has Bank itself acted unethically? What factors would bear on your answer?

2 Under UCC Section 4-403, an oral order stopping payment of a check is binding on the drawee bank for 14 calendar days. Most states have adopted this rule, but five states require stop orders to be in writing to be enforceable. In those five states, therefore, a person who attempts to stop payment of a check by phone can be required to go to the bank to sign the stop order. In the meantime, the bank can legally honor a check, even if it knows that the customer wants the check dishonored. **(a)** What would cause a legislature to require stop orders to be in writing? **(b)** Does the law requiring a stop order to be written seem consistent with sound business ethics?

3 Under UCC Section 4-103, a bank may not avoid liability for its own bad faith or for its negligence in the handling of its customer's account. Yet, the signature cards and stop order forms of many banks contain clauses stating, in effect, "Bank shall not be liable for oversight or accident in making payments from this account." This clause, if enforceable, would protect a bank from the consequences of its own negligence. Assume that banks know that such clauses are not enforceable. **(a)** Why would a bank use a clause that it knows is not enforceable? **(b)** Is it ethical for banks to use such clauses?

4 In 1985, John worked for Bank, which would not allow customers to draw against deposited checks for 15 business days after the day of deposit even though most checks took a maximum of 2 business days to clear. Bank learned that the House of Representatives was considering a bill that, if enacted into law, would eventually require banks to make customers' funds from local checks available to them on the second business day after the day of deposit, and within 5 business days for nonlocal checks. Bank sent John to Washington, D.C., to argue against the bill. In 1988, the bill was enacted into law. **(a)** Before passage of the new law, was Bank's practice of holding the funds for 15 days ethical? Would the size of Bank's fees for processing "bounced" checks be relevant to your answer? Would the number of bad checks Bank received be relevant? **(b)** If Bank's practice was unethical, was it also unethical for Bank to send John to Washington to lobby in favor of the practice? **(c)** If Bank's practice was ethical, did the law making it illegal also make it unethical?

PART NINE

Agency

CHAPTER 33

Creation of Agency; Contract Rights and Obligations of Principal and Agent

What does the term *agency* mean? To answer that question it would be helpful to go back into history. Years ago business was carried on by individual artisans in their homes and by small family-owned and operated shops. With the coming of the industrial revolution commerce vastly expanded and became more and more complex. The public wanted and expected an ever-increasing diversity of merchandise and services. Manufacturers and shopkeepers, in order to keep up with demand, stepped up production and hired others to work for them. As the size and complexity of commerce continued to grow, it became common practice for business owners to delegate responsibilities to others, sometimes conferring on subordinates the right to make managerial decisions. Very soon, as a result of this practice, many new kinds of legal problems arose. For example:

1 Under contract law, a contract must have the personal agreement of the parties who engage in it; but the world of commerce demands that others besides business owners be allowed to enter into binding contracts on the owner's behalf. How does the law permit Steve, the owner of a business, to give Jane the authority to bind the business by contract?
2 Under tort law, a person is not, except under unusual circumstances, responsible for a tort committed by someone else; but social justice demands that an employer be responsible for a tort committed by an employee in the course of employment. On what basis can store owner Ralph be held liable if employee Dudley, while working in the store, commits a tort such as punching a customer in the nose?

To reach practical solutions for such problems, contract law and tort law are supplemented by the law of agency, which derives its name from the concept that one person may act as the legal *agent*, or representative, of another. Agency law is summarized in the *Restatement of the Law of Agency, Second,* formulated and published by the American Law Institute.

Most agency rules are merely special applications of contract and tort law considered in earlier chapters. However, where a principal-agent relationship is involved, some agency law is unique and appears to be inconsistent with the basic rules of contracts and torts. Such departures from normal legal principles are recognized by the courts as desirable allocations of the risks arising in the normal conduct of business.

The law of agency is the subject of this and the two chapters which follow. This chapter discusses (1) the establishment of an agency relationship, (2) the circumstances under which an individual (a *principal*) may be bound to a contract entered into by someone else (an *agent*) acting on the principal's behalf, and (3) the contract rights and obligations which arise out of a contract entered into by an agent on behalf of a principal. Chapter 34 takes up the circumstances under which a principal may be liable for an agent's torts. The last chapter in this part, Chapter 35, examines the duties that a principal and an agent owe to each other and explains how an agency relationship is terminated.

Establishment of an Agency

The Principal-Agent Relationship

A principal-agent relationship exists when two persons or entities agree that one—the *agent*—will perform work or services for and under the direction or control of the other—the *principal.* Under certain circumstances to be later discussed, an agent may be called an employee or servant and a principal may be called an employer or master.

Through a principal-agent relationship, a principal may empower an agent to perform on the principal may legally engage. Therefore, the work that an agent may be empowered to carry on for the principal is practically without limit. It may range from a menial task in which no discretion is exercised by the agent to affairs in which the agent must exercise a great deal of discretion, such as carrying on negotiations, entering into contracts and other agreements, and buying and selling property on the principal's behalf.

To establish a principal-agent relationship, four elements must be present: (1) parties competent to be principal and agent, (2) who mutually agree, (3) that the agent will act for or on behalf of the principal, and (4) that the agent will be subject to the principal's direction or control.

Parties to an Agency

The Principal. Any person capable of entering into a contract may be a principal; likewise, a corporation or a partnership, or a federal, state, city, or other governmental entity may be a principal.

Generally, an unincorporated association, club, or society, not given by law the right to contract in its own name, is not a legal entity and cannot appoint an agent. The courts get around this by holding that the individuals within the organizations who actually engage the services of agents and those members who concur in that action are the principals.

A minor who under state law may legally engage in a contract may be a principal; but just as a minor (generally someone under 18 years of age) may disaffirm his or her contracts (see Chapter 11), a minor may disaffirm an agreement he or she has made to employ an agent. However, a nonminor agent does not have the right to disaffirm his or her agreement with a principal who is a minor.

There are three kinds of principals: (1) a disclosed principal, (2) a partially disclosed principal, and (3) an undisclosed principal.

Disclosed principal. A *disclosed principal* is one whose role as principal is known to the third party at the time of the transaction. In common practice the word "principal," unaccompanied by the qualifying adjective "undisclosed" or "partially disclosed," refers to a disclosed principal. Assume that John Smythe is employed to purchase horses for Purebred Farms. Smythe's business card looks like this:

John Smythe
Horse Buyer for
PUREBRED FARMS, INC.
Lexington, Kentucky.

When Smythe gives his card to Adams, who sells horses, Adams knows that Smythe is acting for Purebred Farms. Therefore, Purebred Farms is a disclosed principal and Smythe is an agent for a disclosed principal.

Partially disclosed principal. A *partially disclosed principal* is one whose existence, but not whose identity, is known to the third party at the time of the transaction. Assume that John Smythe's card reads as follows:

John Smythe
Purchasing Agent
144 High Street
Lexington, Kentucky

When Adams reads this card he knows that Smythe is acting as an agent for someone but Adams does not know who the principal is. In other words, only the fact that some principal stands behind Smythe is disclosed; the principal's identity is not revealed. In such a circumstance, Smythe is an agent for a partially disclosed principal. A principal legitimately may instruct an agent not to reveal his or her identity. Doing business in this way many times has kept a wealthy principal from being unjustly gouged. As an example, the Rockefeller family bought property in the heart of New York City through agents who did not disclose to the sellers the name of their famous principal. That property was then donated to the United Nations as the site for its headquarters.

Undisclosed principal. An *undisclosed principal* is one whose very existence is not known to the third party at the time of the transaction. Smythe's business card may read like this:

John Smythe
Horses Bought and Sold
144 High Street
Lexington, Kentucky

If Adams is handed this kind of card, he is led to believe that Smythe is acting for himself although Smythe may actually be acting for a principal. If Smythe is, in fact, acting for another, the principal is undisclosed and Smythe is an agent for an *undisclosed principal.*

The Agent. Someone who agrees to perform work or services under the direction or control of another (a principal) is an agent. The work or services may be quite simple, such as running an errand. Or the work or services may involve the exercise of a great deal of discretion and judgment affecting the principal's relations with third parties by contract or otherwise. An agent need not be an individual; for example, a corporation or a partnership may be an agent.

Any person who is able to comprehend the duties to be performed may be an agent. However, an agent need not be legally capable of entering into a contract for himself or herself. Assume a mother tells her 11-year-old son to go to the pet store, buy some dog food, and charge it to the parent's account. The boy, although too young to enter into a contract for himself, can legally carry out the instructions as his mother's agent. He may make a binding contract of purchase between his mother and the storekeeper because a contract made by an agent on behalf of a principal is considered to be the contract of the principal and not that of the agent.

An agent may be a general agent or a special agent.

General agent. An agent whose duties involve a continuity of service is a *general agent.* For example, John Smythe, permanently employed to seek out and buy good horses for Purebred Farms, is a general agent of Purebred Farms. Similarly, a woman permanently employed by a big chain store such as J. C. Penney to find good locations in shopping centers where new stores can be opened is a general agent.

Special agent. A person who is employed to conduct a single transaction or a small group of related transactions is a *special agent.* The realtor whom you engage to sell your house is a special agent. The distinction between a general agent and a special agent rests upon the degree of continuity of the relationship rather than upon the extent of the agent's powers. The terms "general agent" and "special agent" are also in common usage in some businesses; the meaning given to these titles depends upon the particular business involved. For instance, in the insurance industry a general agent sells insurance policies of many different companies, while a special agent represents a single company.

Gratuitous agent. It is not necessary for an agent to be compensated for his or her services. An agent who receives no compensation is a *gratuitous agent.* Such an agent may affect the legal relations of the principal with third parties to the same extent as an agent who is paid for his or her services.

Agreement between Principal and Agent

Mutual Assent. One party alone cannot establish a principal-agent relationship; both parties must in some way assent. To illustrate, assume that Arthur, formerly in the roofing business but now unemployed, wants very much to get a job with the Tip-Top Roofing Company. Without Tip-Top's knowledge or consent, Arthur goes around town telling building owners that he represents Tip-Top and attempts to sell them new roofing. He takes several orders which he brings to the Tip-Top Roofing Company. Is Arthur Tip-Top's agent? Because Tip-Top had not assented to the arrangement, no agency relationship at that time existed. However, if Tip-Top accepts the orders, then Arthur is held to be Tip-Top's agent. We will shortly meet this concept again when *ratification* is discussed.

Likewise, a principal-agent relationship would *not* be established if a store that sells computers, endeavoring to borrow money from a bank, asserts that it expects an increase in business because it has hired Charles, a computer programming expert. However, Charles has not yet agreed to take the job. The store's statement to the bank has not created an agency between itself and Charles. There must first be an assent by the agent. Mutual assent is required to create an agency.

Form of Agreement. Except in the special circumstances later discussed, no particular formality is needed to establish a principal-agent relationship. Usually, an agent is hired or employed by an informal oral understanding—for example, a storekeeper asks, "Can you start on Monday as a salesperson at $100 a week?" Fred answers, "Yes, that's fine." An agency contract has been created. However, when an important position is involved, it is common for the parties to enter into a written agreement formalizing the contract of employment and setting out the agent's duties and the benefits to which the agent will be entitled.

Sometimes an agency is created by an oral request of the principal followed not by verbal assent but by action of the agent which demonstrates assent. For instance, Henry tells his neighbor, "Bob, when you go to the hardware store, I'd appreciate your buying me a garden hoe. Charge it to my account." Bob does not reply but he buys the hoe. By his action, Bob became Henry's agent for that transaction and Henry is obligated to the hardware store to pay for the hoe.

Special Circumstances Requiring Written Agreement. Commonly, when a principal authorizes an agent to enter into a *written* contract on behalf of the principal, the agent's authority to do so must also be in writing. That is, it is necessary that an agent's authority be expressed with at least the same formality (dignity) as is prescribed for the act the agent is directed to undertake for the principal. This is called the *equal dignities rule.* The rule applies particularly when the type of contract which the agent is to negotiate for the principal is required by the statute of frauds to be in writing (see Chapter 13). The statute of frauds of many states requires that, to be enforceable, contracts for the sale of goods above $500 must be in writing. For example, in those states if you, an artist, make an arrangement with Fred that he will sell one of your paintings for $1,000, your agreement with Fred—that he will be your agent to represent you in the sale—must be in writing for Fred to make a binding sale.

It is common for states to require certain particular types of agency contracts to be in writing even though neither the statute of frauds nor the equal dignities rule applies. In many states (e.g., California) a real estate agent who represents a seller of property is not entitled to a commission for finding a buyer unless the agreement between the agent and his or her principal (the seller) is in writing.

A principal may give an agent a *power of attorney,* i.e., a written instrument by which the principal appoints an agent to carry on some important activity or to execute for the principal an instrument to be recorded as a public record. The power of attorney defines the duties and activities of the agent and the length of time the power of attorney is to be effective, and may itself be recorded. A *general power of attorney* authorizes the agent to do anything that may be necessary to transact the principal's legal affairs. A *special power of attorney* gives the agent power to carry out only some particular duty or duties and normally is limited in time or in place. An individual who is designated an agent by a power of attorney is called an *attorney in fact* and, despite the name given to the instrument, he or she need not be an attorney at law. A form of power of attorney appears in Figure 33.1.

Principal's Direction or Control of Agent

As we have seen, an agency agreement involves the mutual understanding of a principal and agent that the agent will act for the principal under the principal's direction or control. The words "direction" and "control" describe the degree of power that a principal may exercise over an agent.

Under agency law, *direction* means a principal's right to dictate to the agent what he or she is to do for the principal but *not how* the task will be accomplished. *Control* embodies the right of a principal to tell an agent not only *what* work or services to perform but also *how* the physical task is to be accomplished. A person or organization to whom a principal may give *only* directions normally is called, in agency law, an *independent contractor* or simply *agent;* an agent over whom a principal may exercise control is called an *employee* or *servant.*

Although in broad terms independent contractor and agent characterize one who performs services for another, each term has acquired a more specialized meaning over the years of the developing agency law. This is illustrated by Figure 33.2.

To clarify further, the paragraphs which follow will detail the differences between the terms "independent contractor," "agent independent contractor," and "employee" (or "servant").

Independent Contractor. Some of the characteristics of an independent contractor are that he or she:

- Carries on a distinct occupation or employment independent of the principal, normally with a separate place of business and business name

State of ______________

County of ______________

Know all men by these presents, that I, __________, the undersigned, of __________ *[address]*, City of __________, County of __________, State of __________, hereby make, constitute, and appoint __________, of __________ *[address]*, City of __________, County of __________, State of __________, my true and lawful attorney in fact for me and in my name, place, and stead, giving unto said __________ full power to do and perform all and every act that I may legally do through an attorney in fact, and every proper power necessary to carry out the purposes for which this power is granted, with full power of substitution and revocation, hereby ratifying and affirming that which ______________ or his substitute shall lawfully do or cause to be done by himself or his substitute lawfully designated by virtue of the power herein conferred upon him.

__________ *[If period of power of attorney is to be limited, add:*

This power ends ____________, 19____________ *]*

Dated __________, 19__________

[Acknowledged] *[Signature]*

Figure 33.1 Power of attorney—short form

- Has other customers or clients
- Supplies his or her own tools required in the work
- Is hired by the principal to perform only a particular work for a limited time and is not on the principal's permanent payroll
- May delegate to other people any duties except those which require the exercise of the contractor's personal judgment. For instance, assume that attorney Maxine is hired to try Ida's law suit. Maxine may delegate to her clerks the task of writing pleadings, briefs and memoranda and may permit clerks to assist at the trial of the case, but Maxine must herself conduct her client's case at the trial, as that is a duty involving the exercise of her personal judgment.

An independent contractor may be either not an agent of the principal or an agent of the principal.

Nonagent independent contractor. Most independent contractors are nonagent independent contractors. Their function can best be explained by illustration. For instance, assume that pursuant to your request a doctor gives you a physical exami-

Figure 33.2 Connotation of independent contractor; of agent

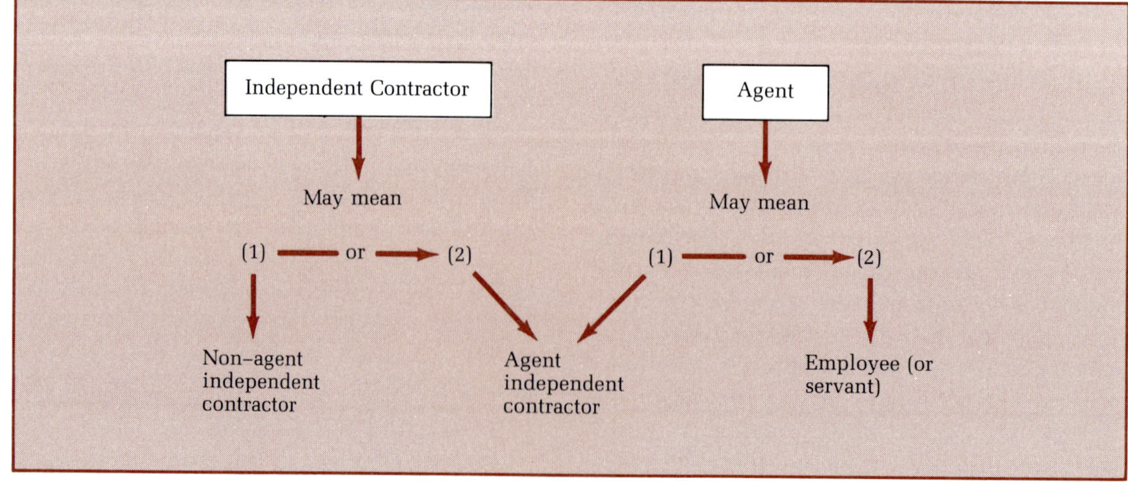

nation, or an architect prepares a set of plans for a house you intend to have built, or a builder erects the house in accordance with the architect's plans and specifications, or an accountant prepares your tax return in accordance with the information you furnish. Each of these individuals has undertaken to deliver a service or end product in accordance with your demands but, unless there are special arrangements, you have no authority to direct or order exactly how the doctor will conduct the examination, the architect will study the project and draw lines on his or her paper, the builder will physically build the house, or the accountant will make his computations.

Of course you may, either directly or inferentially, give a nonagent independent contractor general directions, such as, "in accordance with approved medical or accounting practices," "in a manner approved by the A.I.A.," or "in a good and workmanlike manner." But these general instructions are a far cry from the explicit direction or control an employer may exercise over an employee.

These nonagent independent contractors have undertaken merely to furnish a particular service or end product; they do not represent or act for the principal in relation to third parties. They are not your agents and the law of agency does not apply to them.

Agent independent contractor. Many independent contractors *represent their principals to third parties,* thereby becoming agents of their principals. The following are examples of the wide spectrum of *agent independent contractors:*

- Real estate agent: Joanne (the principal) employs Parkway Realty (the agent) to sell her house to a purchaser (the third party) whom Parkway will find.
- Auctioneer: Paul (the principal), owner of a fine painting, places it in the hands of auctioneers Park-Bernet (the agent) to sell it (to a third party), stating the minimum acceptable price.
- Attorney at law: Ida (the principal), after recounting certain facts, asks Maxine, an attorney (the agent), to sue someone (the third party) who damaged her car.
- Accountant: Bruce (the principal), who in a previous example employed an independent contractor accountant to prepare his income tax, later employs the same accountant to be present and represent him before an IRS agent (the third party), who is auditing Bruce's books. The accountant is now Bruce's *agent* because he is representing his principal to a third party.
- Purchasing Office in New York City (the agent) is hired to buy clothing from wholesalers (third parties) for retail clothing stores (the principals). The stores give Purchasing Office general directions as to the kind, style, quantity, and price range of the articles they require.
- Literary, theatrical, and athletic agents: Agents are employed by many authors to sell their literary works to publishers. Other agents are employed by actors to place them in moving pictures, plays, and commercial advertising, and still other agents are employed by professional athletes. Each of these agents represents many clients, discussing with third parties the terms and conditions under which their clients (their principals) will accept employment, and they also assist in the preparation of their clients' contracts.

In each of these situations, the independent contractor has been given general directions and guidelines but the principal has no right to control the details of the work. For convenience an independent contractor of this type is called simply an "agent" rather than the descriptive but unwieldy "agent independent contractor."

In the next section we consider the type of agent over whom the principal does have the right to exercise both direction and control. In that relationship the principal is called an "employer" or "master," and the agent is called an "employee" or "servant."

Employee (Servant). Examples of the type of agent over whom an employer (master) has the right to exercise both direction and control over the manner in which the work is to be done are:

- Bank teller: Marge (the agent), is a teller in the City Bank (the principal). Everything Marge does in her job must conform to the explicit procedures set forth by the bank.
- Salesperson: Edith (the agent), a travelling salesperson, has a defined territory and has been given explicit instructions as to what procedures to follow in selling the products of her employer (the principal).
- Computer operator: Donald, who works for a wholesale grocer, must keep records exactly as instructed by his supervisor.

- Factory worker: Leslie has specific tasks to perform.

From the above examples you will note that an employee (servant), while under the direction and control of the employer (master), may or may not represent that employer to third parties. In either case, agency law applies.

Normally, an employee is given a salary, is employed for a considerable period of time, and uses the employer's tools or equipment in furtherance of the employer's business. An employee is expected to perform personally the work or service for which he or she was hired and cannot delegate those duties to some other person except in an emergency when the principal cannot be reached.

The creation of an employer-employee relationship depends upon the right of the principal (the employer) to control the physical activity of the agent (the employee). That concept is at the heart of the following case.

CASE 33.1 Hanson v. Kynast · 494 N.E.2d 1091 (Ohio 1986)

FACTS Kynast was a student at Ashland University. He was a member of the university lacrosse team. The players were furnished game shirts displaying the name of the university, were given transportation when they played at other schools, and were furnished overnight lodging when the game was away from Ashland. Kynast used his own lacrosse stick and other equipment while playing. He was not compensated for his participation nor did he have a scholarship from the university.

In May 1982 the Ashland and Ohio State University (OSU) lacrosse teams were playing against each other at Ashland. During the game Allen, an OSU player, intercepted an Ashland pass and as he was scoring a goal was body-checked from behind by Ashland defender Kynast. Allen fell to the ground and Kynast stood over him taunting him. Concerned for Allen's welfare, Hanson, another OSU player, grabbed Kynast around the body. Kynast threw Hanson off. Hanson's head struck the ground and he was severely injured, resulting in his permanent paralysis.

Hanson sued Ashland University, Kynast, and others, alleging, among other causes of action, that the university was liable because Kynast was Ashland's agent. The trial court entered a summary judgment for Ashland; the Court of Appeals reversed, and appeal was taken to the Supreme Court of Ohio.

OPINION PARRINO, J. The first issue to be decided is whether the relationship of principal and agent existed between Kynast and Ashland.

This court has held that the relationship of principal and agent ... exists only when one party [has] ... the right of control over the actions of another, and those actions are directed toward the attainment of an objective which the former seeks.... Therefore, a principal-agent relationship can be found in the instant case only if Kynast was under the control of Ashland, and if he took some action directed toward the attainment of Ashland's objective.

... Students evaluate and determine which university best meets their needs, and then pay a fee to attend that university.... This relationship does not constitute a principal-agent relationship. The student is a buyer of education rather than an agent.... [A] buyer retains goods primarily for his own benefit, while an agent is one who retains goods primarily for the benefit of the one who delivers those goods. In the instant case, the "goods" to be delivered is an education and the university delivers the education to the student for a fee.

The degree of control necessary to establish agency has not been clearly defined. ... Instead, courts have generally examined various factors in determining whether the

CASE 33.1 Continued

requisite amount of control exists. One such factor is whether the individual is performing in the course of the principals' business rather than in some ancillary capacity. . . . In the case at bar, Kynast was not performing in the course of the principal's business, i.e., he was not educating students. On the contrary, he was participating in one of the educationally related opportunities offered by the university. Another factor to be considered is whether the individual was receiving any compensation from the principal. . . . It is undisputed that Kynast was never compensated for playing on the Ashland team. [Compensation is a normal indicia of agency; however, agency may be present although the actor is not paid.] A third factor is whether the principal supplied the tools and the place of work in the normal course of the relationship. . . . Kynast supplied his own equipment in order to play lacrosse.

A review of these factors clearly shows that Kynast was not controlled by Ashland for the purpose of establishing an agency relationship. The control exerted over Kynast by the university, i.e., the Ashland coach running the lacrosse teams, was merely incidental to the educational opportunity in which Kynast *voluntarily* participated. A limited amount of control is necessary to insure that each student is afforded a fair opportunity to benefit from the activity. The athletic guidance that was exercised by Ashland in this case does not satisfy the control element required to establish agency. . . .

Thus the trial court properly entered summary judgment for appellant on this issue.

JUDGMENT Judgment [of the Court of Appeals] is reversed.

Power of Agent to Bind Principal in Contract

A principal may authorize an agent to engage in a contract for the principal with a third party. When the agent, purporting to act for the principal, enters into a contract, it is a contract of the principal just as though the principal himself or herself personally engaged in it. The principal, not the agent, is the contracting party, is entitled to the benefits of the contract, and may enforce its performance. Likewise, it is the principal who must perform in accordance with the contract terms. This unique characteristic of an agency relationship is illustrated in Figure 33.3

The concept depicted in Figure 33.3 is the essence of the court's opinion in the following case.

Figure 33.3 Principal–agent–third person relationship

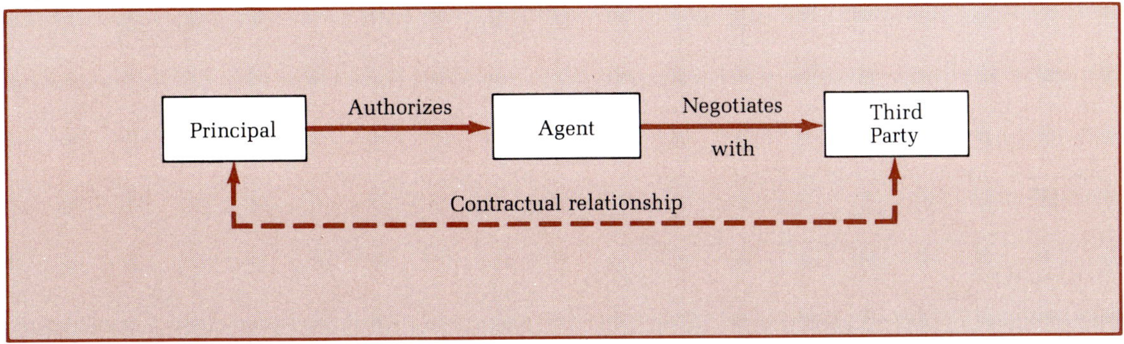

CASE 33.2 Pfluger v. Colquitt · 620 S.W.2d 739 (Tex. Civ. App. 1981)

FACTS Pfluger, the plaintiff, owned two antique Cadillac automobiles. The cars were displayed by Classic Cars, an antique automobile restoration business and museum. Colquitt, a customer, offered to purchase Pfluger's two cars for $14,500. Williams, the owner of Classic Cars, telephoned Pfluger who agreed to the sale of the cars at that price. Colquitt gave Williams his check payable to Classic Cars, received Williams's bill of sale, and took possession of the two cars. Pfluger still had the certificates of title but Williams assured Colquitt that Pfluger would send him (Colquitt) those papers as soon as Colquitt's check cleared the bank.

After Colquitt's check cleared, Williams failed to give Pfluger the money from the sale. Pfluger therefore refused to deliver the certificates of title to Colquitt and demanded the return of the cars. Colquitt refused to return them and Pfluger sued both Williams and Colquitt. Colquitt counterclaimed for title to the cars. The jury found that Williams was acting as Pfluger's agent when he sold the cars. Judgment was rendered for Colquitt for title to the vehicles and for Pfluger against Williams for the purchase money. Pfluger was not satisfied; he wanted his cars back and appealed so much of the judgment as vested their title in Colquitt.

OPINION GUITTARD, C. J. . . . [T]he jury found that Williams was acting as Pfluger's agent in selling the vehicles, and since there is no attack on this finding, the transaction had the same effect as if Pfluger had dealt personally with Colquitt, because one who acts through a duly authorized agent is bound as if he had acted in person. . . . Therefore, Colquitt is entitled to demand a proper transfer of the title from Pfluger.

This result is not affected by Colquitt's payment of the purchase price to Williams. Since Williams was found to be Pfluger's agent in making the sale, when Williams accepted the check, he did so as Pfluger's agent and became responsible to Pfluger for the money; thus, the payment had the same effect as a payment directly to Pfluger. . . . Williams's subsequent conversion of the money . . . could not adversely affect Colquitt's right to demand a proper transfer of the certificates from Pfluger . . .

JUDGMENT Affirmed.

An agent's authority to bind a principal in contract arises in various ways: (1) by *actual authority:* it is communicated or otherwise made known by the principal to the agent; (2) by *apparent authority:* it is made known *by the principal* to the third party in the transaction in which the agent is engaged; or (3) by *ratification:* it is evidenced retroactively by the principal giving approval to an agreement which had been entered into by someone who, without prior authority of the principal, purported to act as an agent of that principal.

Power of Agent Arising from Actual Authority

Actual authority may be conferred by a principal on an agent either expressly or impliedly.

Express Authority of Agent. If a principal tells an agent, either orally or in writing, what to do, this is the agent's *express authority* to act for the principal in accordance with those instructions. For example, Sunrise Stables tells Brent, a horse trainer, to purchase for the stables a sound five-gaited horse less than 3 years old and to pay no more than $2,500 for it. What Brent is told to do and the limits of his authority have been clearly stated by the principal. Brent has express authority to buy the horse within the limits of his instructions, and when he has done so Sunrise must pay for the horse.

Implied Authority of Agent. Instructions, particularly if the agent's services will continue over an extended period of time, are usually expressed in general terms such as, "O.K., you're hired as our football coach." When the agreement is in such general terms, it implicitly includes inferences that the agent may reasonably draw from (1) the principal's words and actions, (2) the circumstances surrounding the agency, (3) the customs of the trade or profession as well as of the community where the service is to be performed, and (4) the relations of the parties.

The authority an agent reasonably infers from a principal's express words constitute an agent's *implied authority.* The law presumes that an employer intends his employees to have such powers as are reasonably necessary for him or her to carry on work for the employer and such other powers as are reasonably necessary to carry into effect the powers thus implied.

The powers that are "reasonably necessary" for an agent to carry on his or her authorized work are not, however, without limitation. For example, an attorney employed to carry on a lawsuit has the implied authority to agree with opposing counsel on routine or procedural matters affecting the trial of the case. But the attorney may not, without the specific consent of his or her client, bind the client to an arbitration agreement in which there is no right to a later court trial because such an agreement affects the client's important substantial rights.

The following is an example of implied authority: Clarice hires Bess, instructing her "to manage my ladies' dress store in Newton." From that simple expression of authority, Bess may reasonably imply the power to do everything ordinarily required to operate a dress store in Newton, consistent with the location, size, and general character of the store and of the community it serves. These reasonable implications constitute Bess's *implied authority.* She would be empowered, among other things, to contract for newspaper and radio advertising, to hire and fire employees, to make emergency repairs to the store windows and fixtures, and to order and pay for merchandise that a store of that kind usually sells in that community. However, Bess does not have the implied authority to contract for all new carpeting and fixtures in the store, nor to move the store into a different building, nor to order men's clothing to be sold in the store. To have power to do these things that are not part of the normal management of the store, Bess must first secure express authority from Clarice.

Implied authority may also arise in another way. If some unforeseen emergency occurs with respect to a matter covered by the agency and it is impracticable for the agent to communicate with the principal, the agent is authorized to do whatever he or she reasonably believes to be necessary in order to prevent the principal from suffering a substantial loss. For example, Bruce, who drives a large refrigerated truck for Paul's trucking company, suffers a breakdown in the night out in the country. If the truck cannot immediately be repaired the meat it carries will spoil. Bruce tries to phone his boss but Paul cannot be reached. Bruce has an emergency service tow the truck to a garage where it is repaired and he instructs the tow-truck driver and the mechanic to send their bills to Paul. Bruce has implied authority to do these things because of the emergency and Paul must pay the bills.

Power of Agent Arising from Apparent Authority

When a *principal* leads a third party to believe that a certain person is his or her agent, or that an agent has a particular degree of power, the authority the *third party is led to believe the agent possesses* is called *apparent* or *ostensible authority.* The important factor in apparent authority is that it originates with, or, as might be said, is "set up" by the principal; it does not spring from the statements of the agent alone. One court has expressed it in this fashion: "Apparent authority can bind a principal only where there was some misleading conduct on the part of the principal. The actions of the agent cannot suffice." [*UA-Columbia Cable Television of Westchester, Inc. v. Fraken Builders, Inc.*, 464 N.Y.S.2d 814 (1983).]

A principal may manifest (make known) apparent authority in a variety of ways such as (1) by a direct statement to the third party, or (2) by permitting someone to have a business title, to occupy a position, or to perform duties which lead a third party reasonably to believe that the individual has power to act for the principal.

In the example in the previous subsection it would *appear* to a wholesale dress salesperson who sees Bess in the store acting as its manager that she has the authority to make purchases of women's clothing for the store. Bess's principal, Clarice, because of that apparent authority is bound by any contract Bess makes with the wholesale representatives within the scope of that authority.

If an agent really has the authority the third party reasonably believes the agent possesses, then apparent and actual authority are both present. The agent's authority is merely seen from two points of view: (1) the agent (Bess, in the above example) knows both her actual and implied authority, while (2) the third party (the wholesale salesperson in the example) observes only the agent's apparent authority.

However, it is not necessary that there exist an actual authority before there can be apparent authority. In two situations there may be apparent authority without a parallel actual authority:

1 An agent's apparent authority may be more extensive than his or her actual authority. This can best be explained by illustration. Assume that Joe is a salesperson in a hardware store. It is customary for salespeople to describe the merchandise they sell. One day Joe is told by his employer, "A representative from High-Klass Cookware is in town to demonstrate the new line of High-Klass products we have just received, so if any customer asks anything about those pots and pans, don't answer but refer the customer to the representative." Despite that limitation upon his authority, when customer Shirley asks Joe if the pots are nonstick, Joe, eager to make a sale, replies that they are, although in fact they are not. It reasonably appeared to Shirley, who had no knowledge of the limitation placed upon Joe's authority, that Joe was authorized to describe the pots he was selling. Joe, therefore, had the apparent authority to make the representation, and the store is liable to Shirley for his misrepresentation. This example illustrates the rule that secret limitations placed upon the authority of an agent by a principal are not binding upon third parties.

2 An individual who is not an agent at all may be given by someone the apparent authority to act as agent for that person. In that event, the individual who acts as an agent is said by some courts to possess *ostensible authority*. Such a situation brought about the dispute considered in *Hoddeson v. Koos Brothers*, 135 A.2d 702 (N.J. 1957). In that case, an imposter went through the motions of making a sale of furniture to an unwary customer in a department store. He accepted the money but, of course, the customer never received the furniture. The Supreme Court of New Jersey said that:

> Our concept of the modern law is that where a proprietor of a place of business by his dereliction of duty enables one who is not his agent conspicuously to act as such and ostensibly to transact the proprietor's business with a patron in the establishment, the appearance being of such a character as to lead a person of ordinary prudence and circumspection to believe that the imposter was in truth the proprietor's agent, in such circumstances the law will not permit the proprietor defensively to avail himself of the imposter's lack of authority. . . .

Whether or not apparent authority is conferred depends upon the facts in any particular case. Frequently, when there is apparent authority, a principal is *estopped* from denying (may not deny) the authority of the individual was has acted for the principal. Estoppel arises when a third party, relying upon apparent authority, changes his or her position, that is, does something that he or she would not otherwise have done. In the *Koos Brothers* case just cited, the customer would not have paid money to the "salesman" had she known that he was not a salesman at all. The department store was estopped from denying that the imposter had apparent authority to act for it and the store was obliged to deliver the furniture to the customer even though it received no payment for it.

The liability of the defendant in the next case rests upon the apparent authority of its agent.

CASE 33.3 Bolus v. United Penn Bank · 525 A.2d 1215 (Pa. Super. 1987)

FACTS Robert Bolus, the plaintiff, was in the trucking business. In 1976 he decided to expand the business by buying a tract of land in Bartonsville and building a truck repair facility there. Bolus contacted the defendant, United Penn Bank, to obtain financing for the project. He was referred to Emmanuel Ziobro, an Assistant Vice-President of the bank and a co-defendant. Ziobro orally agreed that the bank would fund the project. A loan of $135,000 from the bank was arranged and Bolus purchased the land and began construction. A few months later Bolus

CASE 33.3 Continued

changed the building plans to accommodate a new truck dealership and he told Ziobro the Bartonsville project required an additional loan of more than $100,000. The bank refused to make the loan but later did lend Bolus an additional $75,000.

In 1978 Bolus' business collapsed. He lost his truck dealerships and was forced to sell his properties to raise funds with which to satisfy the bank's loans. Bolus brought suit against the bank and Ziobro alleging that the bank had breached an oral contract to fund the Bartonsville project. Bank representatives testified that Ziobro had no authority to promise that the bank would finance the Bartonsville project and that his authority was limited to make only $5,000 unsecured and $10,000 secured loans. The jury returned a verdict in favor of the plaintiff and the defendants appealed, alleging, among other things, that the agency relationship between the bank and Ziobro had not been established. The portion of the court's opinion addressed to the agency issue follows.

OPINION

BECK, J. . . . [T]he Bank argues that there was no evidence to show that Ziobro had express, implied or apparent authority to bind the Bank to a lending commitment of the size Bolus alleged that Ziobro made to Bolus on behalf of the Bank. . . .

[T]here are four grounds upon which a jury can conclude that an agency relationship exists. . . .

1. express authority directly granted by the principal to bind the principal as to certain matters; or
2. implied authority to bind the principal to those acts of the agent that are necessary, proper and usual in the exercise of the agent's express authority; or
3. apparent authority, i.e. authority that the principal has by words or conduct held the alleged agent out as having; or
4. authority that the principal is estopped to deny. . . . .

Without reviewing the evidence in its entirety, we point out that it clearly established that Ziobro was employed as an officer of the Bank authorized to make loans. Although there was testimony that his individual lending authority was limited in amount, there was no evidence that this fact was communicated to Bolus or that Bolus should have concluded that Ziobro authority was limited. In addition, certain facts of record indicate that one other employee of the Bank himself apparently thought that Ziobro was in charge of all commercial lending at the Bank. When Bolus initially contacted the Bank for financing on the Bartonsville project, the employee told Bolus to speak to Ziobro because he was in charge of commercial lending.

Thus, the Bank itself held Ziobro out to Bolus as being clothed with authority to commit the Bank to provide whatever financing Ziobro reasonably determined to be appropriate under the circumstances. . . . Since in determining the apparent authority of an agent we must look to the actions of the principal, not the agent, we decide that the foregoing adequately established Ziobro's apparent authority as to this transaction. . . . A principal's limitation on the agent's authority in amount only that is not communicated to the third party does not limit the principal's liability. [Citations.]

Although a third party cannot rely on the apparent authority of an agent to bind a principal if he has knowledge of the limits of the agent's authority, without such actual knowledge, the third party must exercise only reasonable diligence to ascertain the agent's authority. [Citation.] The third party is entitled to believe the agent has the authority he purports to exercise only where a person of ordinary prudence, diligence and discretion would so believe. [Citation.] Thus, a third party can rely on the apparent authority of an agent when this is a reasonable interpretation of the manifestations of the principal. [Citation.]

Given the evidence reviewed above, we conclude the jury here could have decided that Bolus acted reasonably in relying on Ziobro's representations as to his authority. We

CASE 33.3 Continued

reiterate that Bolus was never required to deal with any other representative of the Bank, that the loan for the purchase of the land and construction of the Bartonsville project that Ziobro promised to Bolus did in fact come through, and that several witnesses testified that Ziobro repeatedly represented his authority and made commitments on behalf of the Bank which proved to be binding without first obtaining the approval of other Bank representatives. . . .

JUDGMENT Accordingly, we affirm. . . .

Ratification of Agent's Acts

Because an agency is a consensual arrangement between a principal and an agent, an individual who (1) exceeds his or her authority or (2) *without actual or apparent authority* claims to be acting for another, does not bind the principal for whom the act was undertaken. However, the party for whom the act was undertaken (the principal) can agree to it or, to use the legal term, affirm it. An act of affirmance is called a *ratification.* A transaction that has been ratified is treated as though it had been authorized originally. No new consideration need move to the principal and the ratification may be without the knowledge or assent of the third party to the transaction.

As an illustration of ratification consider this: Agnes, the office manager of a power tool company, has no authority to make any purchases for the firm. Nevertheless, learning that a computer she believes the company needs can be bought at a very special price, she orders it for her company and tells its purchasing agent that she has done so. The purchasing agent approves the purchase and pays for the computer, thereby ratifying Agnes's act.

Requirements for Ratification. In order to effect the ratification of an agent's act the principal must (1) have knowledge of all material facts involved or consciously ratify without such knowledge, and (2) affirm the act in its entirety or not at all. For example, let's say Fred, purporting to act for John but without John's authority, enters into an agreement to sell 500 chickens raised by John. Upon learning of the transaction, John cannot ratify the sale of only 200 chickens as that would be an attempt to ratify only a part of the transaction. John must ratify the agreement in its entirety or not at all.

While a ratification can come about by the principal specifically stating "I ratify the act," or words to like effect, usually ratification is expressed by implication. This comes about when a principal, with full knowledge of all the material elements of a transaction, (1) accepts any performance under the agreement which the agent, without authority, entered into with the third party, or (2) fails in a timely fashion to repudiate the agent's act, or (3) brings a legal action to enforce it.

Responsibilities of Principal and Agent after Ratification. Ratification brings about some interesting changes in the relationship of the parties and in their respective rights and obligations. Until the act is ratified, the "purported agent" has acted without authority. Therefore, the purported agent, having misrepresented his or her authority, may be liable in tort to the third party for the misrepresentation. As the agent acted without authority, neither the principal nor the third party is bound or required to perform the agreement made by the purported agent. After ratification, however, the situation changes. The purported agent is now established as the agent of the principal for the purpose of the transaction, the agent's liability to the third party disappears, and the principal and third party are bound to each other under the agreement made by the agent and are required to perform according to its terms. In addition, the agent may now be entitled to compensation for his or her services if compensation is a condition of the agency.

The following case illustrates ratification.

CASE 33.4 Progressive Casualty Ins. Co. v. Ehrhardt · 518 A.2d 151 (Md. App. 1986)

FACTS

Robert Ehrhardt had a motorcycle liability insurance policy issued by the Progressive Casualty Insurance Company. The policy provided that its coverage would cease at 12:01 A.M. May 19, 1983 if the premium of $70.40 was not paid by that time. If Ehrhardt tendered payment after the expiration date, the policy would be renewed effective on the postmark date the premium was mailed.

Ehrhardt failed to pay his premium and his policy automatically lapsed on May 19, 1983. Six days later (May 25) he was in a motorcycle accident in which he and Judith Penn, his passenger, suffered injuries requiring their hospitalization. That evening Robert asked his father to pay the overdue premium for the renewal of the policy. The next morning (May 26) the elder Ehrhardt paid the premium to the V. W. Brown Agency, the insurance company's agent. On that same day Judith Penn's mother by telephone informed Progressive Casualty that its insured, Robert Ehrhardt, had been in a motorcycle accident on May 25, 1983 in which her daughter suffered injuries. On May 31 Robert Ehrhardt notified Progressive that he had had an accident on May 26, 1983.

Upon receiving Ehrhardt's renewal premium on May 26, the Brown Agency immediately forwarded it by mail to Progressive's Richmond office. There the renewal was marked effective May 26, 1983, the date on which the envelope in which it was enclosed was postmarked. On June 2, 1983, Progressive's lead underwriter backdated its renewal from May 26 to May 19, 1983, and Robert Ehrhardt received in the mail from Progressive a renewal policy effective May 19, 1983.

Judith Penn filed a tort action against Ehrhardt for the personal injuries she sustained. At trial, Progressive asked the court to declare that it had no duty to defend or indemnify Ehrhardt because its insurance policy was not in effect at the time of the accident. The court concluded otherwise and Progressive appealed.

OPINION

BISHOP, J.... This case... need not turn on the issue of whether Progressive's underwriter acted with apparent authority [when he backdated the renewal of the policy, an argument made by the appellee]. Even if the underwriter acted completely without authority, Progressive can nevertheless become liable if it ratifies the agent's conduct. [Citations.] Ratification requires an intention to ratify, [citations], and knowledge of all material facts. [Citations.]

Intention to ratify may be inferred by words, conduct or silence on the part of the principal that reasonably indicates its desire to affirm the unauthorized act. [Citations.] Circumstances that suggest an intent to ratify include: receipt and retention of the benefits of the unauthorized transaction, [citations], and a failure to make a timely disaffirmance of the unauthorized acts.

Applying these factors to the case at hand, the telltale signs of ratification are apparent. There is no doubt that Progressive received a benefit when it backdated Ehrhardt's policy from May 26 to May 19, 1983. As Judge Fischer correctly noted,

> [t]he practice of backdating policies results in financial gain to the insurer by creating a shorter period of coverage [because the policy will terminate at an earlier date but the insurance carrier will be paid for the entire period.] While the amounts in any individual case are minor, if practiced on a larger scale, the financial gain can be significant. The practice, however, does have its perils as evidenced by the factual situation in this case.

Moreover, it is undisputed that Progressive retained the benefit and did not attempt to disaffirm the allegedly unauthorized act of its lead underwriter for over six months.

As to the second requirement [for ratification], we hold that Progressive acted with full knowledge of all material facts. The trial court explicitly found, and we affirm, that

CASE 33.4 Continued

Progressive was on notice that a loss to its insured occurred during the defaulting period. Because of that knowledge, Progressive is in no position to deny the legal implications of its retention of the benefits of the transaction. Accordingly, we hold that Progressive's actions retroactively conferred authority on its agent, subjecting it to whatever liability that backdating the policy entails.

JUDGMENT Judgment affirmed.

Contractual Rights and Obligations of Principal, Agent, and Third Party

The contractual rights and obligations of the parties to an agency transaction differ depending upon whether the principal is disclosed, partially disclosed, or undisclosed.

When Principal Is Disclosed

Agent Acting within the Scope of Authority. As we have already seen, when an agent acting within the scope of authority from a disclosed principal contracts with a third party the contract is as much a contract of the principal as it would have been had the principal personally entered into it. The principal and the third party may each require performance of the agreement by the other; the agent is only a go-between and, not being a party to the contract (see Figure 33.3), is not liable to the third party.

Since an agent for a disclosed principal is not a party to a contract between his or her principal and a third party, the agent can neither require performance nor be forced to make good a failure of the principal to perform. An exception would, of course, occur if the agent had agreed that he or she could be held responsible.

If principal Able claims that purported agent Baker had no authority to enter into an agreement for him (Able), then third party Charles who asserts Able's obligation has the burden of proving that Baker did have authority or that Able ratified the contract.

Agent Acting outside the Scope of Authority. When an agent of a disclosed principal acts *outside* the scope of his or her authority and the principal does *not* ratify the unauthorized act, the principal is not bound by it and is not obligated to the third party. Accordingly, if the purchasing agent for Agnes's company in the example on page 706 did not ratify Agnes's purchase of the computer, her company would not be obligated to pay for it and the computer company must look to Agnes herself for payment.

If a third party, before engaging in a business transaction and in order to avoid the risk of dealing with an agent who is acting without authority, had to demand and receive proof of the agent's authority, there would be a monumental impediment to the free and rapid conduct of business. To discourage such an impediment, the law presumes that a purported agent impliedly warrants (guarantees) that he or she has the authority to obligate the principal in the transaction. If that authority is absent and the transaction is not ratified by the principal, the third party may seek damages from the purported agent for breach of the implied warranty.

When Principal Is Partially Disclosed

When the principal is partially disclosed, both the agent and the partially disclosed principal are liable to the third party on a contract. An agent for a partially disclosed principal *is a party to the contract* because it is likely that the third party is relying on the reputation and credit of the agent as well as upon the possible financial resources of the unknown principal. Accordingly, absent an agreement to the contrary, the partially disclosed principal *and* the agent may be required to perform the contract and both are liable for its breach. For example, assume that Central Purchasing Agency (CPA) buys a carload of tires from the Firestone factory without disclosing that Brown is the purchaser (the principal) in this transaction. Firestone knows that CPA is buying the tires for a customer but does not know who that customer is. Brown receives the tires, but Firestone is not paid.

Firestone, in making the sale, relied upon the good credit rating of CPA as well as upon the assumption that the unknown partially disclosed principal would also be responsible. Therefore, CPA and Brown are each liable for the bill. Firestone can collect the amount of its bill only once, of course.

If a third party fails to perform an agreement entered into with an agent acting for a partially disclosed principal, the rights of the parties are reversed and either the agent or the partially disclosed principal can require the third party to perform its part of the agreement. Thus, if in the above example Firestone failed to deliver the tires, CPA or Brown could demand that Firestone deliver under the terms of the contract.

When Principal Is Undisclosed

Rights of Undisclosed Principal against Third Party. Even though the third party to the agent's contract has no idea someone else is involved in the transaction, agency law allows that unknown "someone" (the undisclosed principal) to disclose himself or herself and to require contract performance by the third party. There are four exceptions to this rule, however:

1. When performance to the principal would impose a greater burden upon the third party than if the contract were to be performed as originally agreed by the agent, the third party need not undertake the additional performance. For example, you (the principal) instruct me (your agent in this transaction) to buy 100 railroad ties for you but to spend no more than $500 which you give me. Hiram sells me the ties for that amount and agrees to deliver them anywhere within the town where his business is located. If you (the undisclosed principal) now reveal yourself to Hiram as the purchaser and demand delivery of the railroad ties in another town, Hiram is not required to transport them there unless you pay him for the extra distance involved.
2. When an undisclosed principal reveals himself or herself, the third party is entitled to assert any defense that the third party could have asserted against the agent if the agent had been the principal. To clarify this concept, suppose that I (your agent in the railroad tie purchase from Hiram) personally owe Hiram $100. Hiram does not deliver the ties. You, as the true purchaser, sue him for the return of the $500. Hiram can *set off* my debt of $100 to him against the money he received for the ties. Therefore, Hiram need return to you only $400, keeping the other $100 as repayment of my debt to him. This comes about because if I, the apparent purchaser of the railroad ties had demanded the refund, Hiram could have set off my debt by retaining the amount I owed him.
3. A third party will not be required to perform a contract entered into by an agent for an undisclosed principal if the existence of the agency was fraudulently concealed from the third party prior to entering into the agreement. A fraud may be perpetrated: (1) if the agent, when asked by the third party, denied the existence of the agency, or (2) if a principal, knowing that a third party does not want to deal with him or her nevertheless attempts to deal with that third party through an agent. For example, if I know that Fred does not want to have any business dealings with me, I cannot force him to perform if I got Henry to enter an agreement with Fred on my behalf without disclosing that I am the principal.
4. When personal performance by the agent is required by the contract (as when an agent promises as a condition of the contract to oversee the work), that agent must personally perform.

Rights of Agent for Undisclosed Principal against Third Party. An agent for an undisclosed principal occupies a different legal status from that of an agent for a disclosed principal with respect to rights against a third party. We saw that an agent for a *disclosed* principal is not a party to the contract and that if such an agent acts within the scope of his or her authority, the agent has no rights under the contract and cannot require its performance. However, an agent who acts for an *undisclosed* principal *is* a party to the contract, with all the rights of a principal. Therefore an agent for an undisclosed principal can enforce performance of the contract, including the right to bring suit against the third party for its breach.

Rights of Third Party against Undisclosed Principal or Agent of Undisclosed Principal. It would be unfair to give an undisclosed principal a right against a third party without giving a parallel right to the third party against the undisclosed principal. The common law therefore gives the third party the right, when the identity of the principal is revealed, to seek performance from *either* the agent *or* from the previously undisclosed principal, whichever one he or she chooses to hold responsible. The exercise of this choice is called an "election." Thus, under the common law, if Anne contracts with Burt, and Burt turns out to be an agent for undisclosed principal Xavier, Anne can demand performance from Burt and she is in no worse a position than if the contract had been with Burt alone; *or* Anne may elect to hold Xavier alone responsible for performance when Xavier's identity is revealed.

Many courts are moving away from the common law principle of election and instead give the third party to a transaction in which there was an undisclosed principal remedies against *both* the agent and the undisclosed principal, but permit only one satisfaction of the claim.

The case which follows is illustrative of this modern but yet minority view of a third party's rights against an agent for an undisclosed principal and against that principal when he or she becomes known.

CASE 33.5 Crown Controls, Inc. v. Smiley · 737 P.2d 709 (Wash. App. 1987)

FACTS Jim Smiley was a manufacturer's representative and distributor. Identifying himself as an agent of Industrial Associates, he purchased from Crown Controls certain industrial equipment. At no time did Smiley disclose that he was acting in behalf of a corporation. Crown later learned that Industrial Associates was a trade name of North American Drill Supply, Inc. (NADS), a corporation of which Smiley was the president. Crown sued NADS and Smiley individually for the cost of the materials purchased. Crown secured a partial summary judgment against NADS and attempted to garnish its bank account, but the account had been closed. Trial of the action against Smiley continued. The court permitted Crown to vacate its partial summary judgment against NADS and to enter a judgment solely against Smiley. Smiley appealed, claiming he had disclosed the name Industrial Associates, which was a trade name of NADS, his principal, and that Crown, in its action against NADS, had elected to hold that company rather than Smiley liable for the purchase.

OPINION CHAN, J. . . . Smiley . . . contends Crown Controls' efforts to collect its partial summary judgment against NADS constituted an election of remedies. . . . We agree that Crown Controls' . . . garnishing NADS' bank account constituted an election by Crown . . . to hold NADS liable of Smiley. However, we believe the election rule pertaining to agents and undisclosed principals is illogical and contrary to the policy of favoring full compensation of wronged parties. We therefore hold, for the reasons that follow, that Crown . . . may have judgment against both NADS and Smiley, although it may only have one satisfaction. . . . [Much dicta] recites the common law rule that, upon learning all the facts, a creditor who elects to hold the previously undisclosed principal liable thereby discharges the agent . . . even if the creditor thereafter discovers the principal is insolvent. . . .

This court may abandon or modify a common law rule if, in the light of current conditions and thinking, the rule's precepts are incompatible with present-day society. . . .

A leading case abolishing the rule of alternative liability in the undisclosed principal context is *Grinder v. Bryans Road Bldg. & Supply Co., Inc*, 290 Md. 687, 432 A.2d 453 (1981). . . . The *Grinder* court adopted the law of Pennsylvania as the better reasoned rule and the one endorsed by the legal commentators. Under that rule, the liability of the agent and previously undisclosed principal is joint and several rather than alternative.

> Undoubtedly an agent who makes a contract in his own name without disclosing his agency is liable to the other party. The latter acts upon his credit and is not bound to yield up his

CASE 33.5 Continued

right to hold the former personally, merely because he discloses a principal who is also liable.... But it does not follow that the agent can afterwards discharge himself by putting the creditor to his election. Being already liable by his contract, he can be discharged only by satisfaction of it, by himself or another....

When it is recognized that the third person acquires several rights against the principal and agent, there does not seem to be any reason...why he should not have every advantage that accrues to any one else who has more than one right. Specifically, his attempt to hold one obligor should not exonerate another obligor. And a merger of his claim against one into a judgment against that one should not take away his right against the other obligor. The several rights of a third person who has contracted with the agent of an undisclosed principal are comparable to the several rights acquired by a "creditor-beneficiary" for whom a contract has been made....

We agree with this analysis and hold that a creditor is entitled to take judgment against both an agent and his previously undisclosed principal, although the creditor may have only one satisfaction....

JUDGMENT The judgment is affirmed....

Summary

Agency is a consensual agreement whereby one person (the principal) authorizes another (the agent) to act on the principal's behalf and subject to the principal's direction or control. Depending upon the degree of control a principal exercises, an agent may be an independent contractor or an employee.

Anyone may be appointed an agent, but only an individual capable of entering into a contract may be a principal. The principal-agent relationship may be established in writing or, unless a statute provides otherwise, may be established orally or implied from the conduct of the parties.

An agent has the power to bind a principal to legal obligations when acting within the scope of authority established by the principal. Authority may be vested in an agent by a principal either directly (actual authority) or indirectly (apparent or ostensible authority). Actual authority arises expressly from the written or spoken words of the principal to the agent or implicitly from the agent's reasonable inferences therefrom. Apparent authority results from a manifestation *by a principal to a third party* that causes the third party reasonably to believe that an individual has authority to act for the principal. An agent's apparent authority may be greater or less than his or her actual authority. When a person without authority purports to act for another, the person for whom the unauthorized agent acts may affirm (ratify) the act.

If a party to a transaction knows that it is being conducted by an agent for a principal and the identity of such principal is revealed, the principal is a *disclosed principal;* but if the principal's identity is not revealed, the principal is a *partially disclosed principal.* When a transaction is conducted by an individual who purports to be acting for himself or herself alone when, in fact, that individual is acting for another, that individual is an agent for an *undisclosed principal.*

An agent acting within the scope of authority incurs no obligation on a contract entered into on behalf of a disclosed principal. The principal alone is responsible and may require performance by the third party.

When an agent acting within the scope of authority engages in a contract for an undisclosed principal, both the principal and the agent are parties to the contract. Upon the third party discovering the identity of the undisclosed principal the third party can, with few exceptions, hold the principal to the contract. However, since the liability of an agent and his or her undisclosed principal is not a joint liability, the third party must choose (elect) from which of the two he or she will require performance. Either the principal or the agent can require performance from the third party unless the agent fraudulently concealed the fact that he or she was acting for a principal or unless the third party had a right to expect performance by the agent personally. In that event, only the agent can be required to perform.

Review Questions

1 **(a)** Define "agency." **(b)** Indicate, in general terms or by specific examples, the importance of agency to the business community.

2 **(a)** What must the parties do to create a principal-agent relationship? **(b)** Is an individual who is qualified to be an agent also qualified to be a principal? Explain.

3 Distinguish between an independent contractor and an employee.

4 **(a)** In the law of agency, what does the term "right to control" mean? **(b)** How does this differ from the right of a principal to direct an agent?

5 Can a person who is hired as an employee bind his or her employer in contract? Explain.

6 **(a)** Distinguish between actual authority and apparent authority. **(b)** In what factual circumstances would one kind of authority exist without the other?

7 **(a)** What is meant by "ratification" in the law of agency? **(b)** What conditions must exist before it can be said that an act was ratified? **(c)** Does a third party have any recourse against either the principal or the agent if the principal does not ratify an agent's unauthorized act? Explain.

8 **(a)** Distinguish between a disclosed principal, a partially disclosed principal, and an undisclosed principal. **(b)** Does an agent for an undisclosed principal have a greater or lesser degree of apparent authority than an agent for a disclosed principal? Why?

9 **(a)** Where an agent, acting within the scope of his or her authority for a disclosed principal, enters into a contract for the principal, who are the parties to the contract? **(b)** If the third party fails to perform according to the contract terms, does the agent or the principal, or both, have a right of action against the third party? **(c)** If the principal fails to perform according to the contract terms, does a third party have a right of action against the principal, or against the agent, or against both? Give reasons for your answers.

10 **(a)** Why does the law permit a third party who dealt with an agent for an undisclosed principal to hold the undisclosed principal liable on a contract when the third party, at the time of entering into the contract, had no idea that he or she was dealing with anyone other than the agent? **(b)** Under what circumstances would an undisclosed principal have a right of action against a third party who had entered into a contract with an agent for the undisclosed principal?

Case Problems

1 Douglas, dressed in a doorman's uniform, was standing in front of the Directoire Restaurant when Weingart stopped his car in front of the restaurant. Weingart gave Douglas his car keys so that the car could be parked and Douglas gave him a claim check. When Weingart came out of the restaurant some time later, Douglas could not find Weingart's car. Weingart demanded that the restaurant pay him the value of the car. The restaurant owner refused, saying that Douglas was not an employee of the restaurant although he (the owner) was aware that Douglas was working on his own parking cars for Directoire Restaurant as well as for three or four other establishments on the block. What would be the result of the suit Weingart brought against the Directoire Restaurant for compensation? Why?

2 Charles wanted to buy a harvester from the Farmall Company but he knew that Farmall would not do business with him because of past unpleasant business relations between them. Charles therefore arranged for Warren, for a small fee, to make the purchase for him without disclosing the agency. Charles agreed to give Warren the full purchase price and the promised fee as soon as the harvester arrived. Warren ordered the machine. A month later, when the machine was delivered to Warren, he received from Charles the money to send to Farmall plus his fee. At this point, however, Warren began using the machine himself and did not turn it over to Charles, nor did he pay Farmall. Farmall learned that Charles was the undisclosed principal in the transaction and sued him for the purchase price. What should be the outcome of the litigation?

3 Viti put Quinn in charge of a filling station which Viti owned. Viti directed Quinn to buy all gasoline for the station from Newport Oil Company but, because of the fluctuating prices, never to buy more than one week's supply at any time. Viti told Newport to make sure to collect from Quinn, the station's manager, for all purchases made each week as Viti did not want bills to accumulate. Viti received weekly reports showing the business condition of the station. Despite Viti's direction to Quinn and the admonition to Newport, Quinn, instead of paying each week, ran up a sizable bill. Newport demanded payment from Viti who sent a check for one week's gasoline purchase and refused to pay anything more. Does Newport have a cause of action against Viti? Explain.

4 Valley Corp., a building contractor, was an authorized distributor of Bonanza Prefabricated Farm Buildings. Bonanza's brochures said, in part, "We back our buildings with a Local Independent Builder." Herman contracted with Valley for the erection of a Bonanza building. Because of Valley's poor workmanship, the building leaked when it rained. Herman sued both Bonanza and Valley for the money he expended to repair the leaks. What should be the result of the litigation? Why?

5 Perry was running for public office. He talked to Meredith, a printer, about printing some campaign material for him but Perry did not order the printing. Later, Perry's campaign director, who had charge of all expenditures for the campaign, knowing that Perry had discussed the matter with Meredith and believing that more campaign material was urgently needed, ordered the material from Meredith without first checking with Perry even though Perry had given him specific instructions not to place further printing orders without his (Perry's) personal approval. The material was printed, was returned to Perry's campaign headquarters, and was used by Perry in the campaign. Perry refused to pay Meredith for the printing, pointing out that he did not authorize the work to be done. Is Perry obligated to pay for the printing? Why or why not?

6 Grinder purchased building material from Road Building & Supply Company, Inc. Grinder did not pay for the material he purchased. When the supply company was preparing to sue Grinder, it learned that Grinder had purchased the material for a corporation in which Grinder had an interest. If the supply company files suit to force payment of the debt, should it sue Grinder, Grinder's corporation, or both? Why?

CHAPTER 34

Principals' Liability for Agents' Torts

Suppose a truck driver for a local department store collides with your car, damaging it and injuring you. You learn that the driver had been drinking. Do you have any right to expect payment for your damages from the department store or must you look only to the truck driver? The law upon which the answer to that question is based is outlined in this chapter. It examines the circumstances under which principals, such as the department store in the example, are liable for the torts of their servant and nonservant agents.

At the outset, it should be borne in mind that an individual who is injured or who sustains damage through the tort of an employee may have a cause of action against *both* the employer (principal) and the employee (agent). The employee is liable because each person is accountable for his or her wrongful actions. Depending upon the factual situation, an employer may also be liable for an employee's tort by application of tort law or the law of agency. Because an employee may not have the financial resources or insurance coverage with which to satisfy a judgment for damages, a person injured by an employee therefore usually attempts to force the agent's employer to pay for the injuries sustained.

How this dual liability may arise may be illustrated by the following two hypothetical incidents.

1. Thomas, the owner of a store, directs William, his employee, to "throw out" a disagreeable customer. William, being very literal minded, physically throws the customer out of the store and onto the sidewalk and the customer is injured.
2. The same employer, Thomas, without making any attempt to find out if Eddie is an habitual drinker of alcohol, hires Eddie to drive the company truck. Someone is injured when Eddie, after several drinks, drives the truck into another car.

Because each individual is personally liable for his or her own wrongs, William and Eddie, Thomas's employees in those illustrations, may each be required to pay damages for the tortious injuries they caused. In both these situations the employer, Thomas, also has a liability. In the first instance Thomas is *directly* liable under *tort* law because he *ordered* the wrong to be done when he told William to "throw the customer out"; and in the second he *negligently* put someone in charge of a vehicle whom he should have known might cause injury to others. In addition to this tort liability, Thomas is *vicariously* liable under agency law for the damages the third parties sustained because the injuries resulted from the actions of his employees who were acting within the scope of their employment. In this context, *vicarious liability* means that the employer, although neither present nor directly involved in the incident, is responsible for the acts of his or her agent. In either illustration the injured person normally would seek recovery by going against the employer (Thomas in this instance), anticipating that he would be covered by insurance and, in any event, would have the "deeper pocket" from which to pay a money judgment.

This chapter does not deal with an employee's own liability in tort; it deals solely with an employer's indirect (vicarious) liability for the tortious actions of an agent.

Liability for Torts Resulting in Physical Injury

Torts Resulting in Physical Injury Caused by Independent Contractor Agents

We noted in the previous chapter that a principal does not have the right to exercise control over how an independent contractor agent performs his or her assigned tasks. Because of this absence of control, agency law holds that generally a principal is *not* liable for a tort resulting in physical injury to a third party committed by an independent contractor agent. For instance, you would not be liable if a carpenter, an independent contractor who is working on your house, carries a large board on the sidewalk in front of your property and negligently swings it, striking and injuring a passerby. However, there are certain types of activities which cast a strict liability upon a principal regardless of whether the work is performed by an agent or a nonagent. These exceptions are discussed at page 728.

Torts Resulting in Physical Injury Caused by Employees

We also observed in Chapter 33 that if an agent is not an independent contractor the employer *has the right to control the manner* in which the agent performs his or her duties. Therefore, under agency law, an employer *is* liable for the tort of an employee who, acting within the scope of employment, causes physical injury to a third party. If we change the above illustration of the carpenter who is working on your house and assume that the carpenter is your *employee* rather than an independent contractor, then you *are* liable for damages if he or she injures someone. It was under this principle of agency law that, in the examples in the introduction to this chapter, Thomas was liable for the injuries incurred by his employees, William and Eddie.

The actual *exercise* of control by an employer is not essential to establish the employer's liability. An employer's *right* to exercise control, whether or not the control is in fact exercised, is the determining factor. To illustrate: Let's say that Henry is employed as a janitor by Archer, the owner of a four-story building. Archer has never given Henry instructions as to where to hang his pail while washing the windows. One day Henry drops a pail out of a fourth floor window and it injures Lisa, walking below. Archer, the employer, is liable to Lisa for the injury Henry, his employee, caused while acting within the scope of his employment even though Archer did not personally participate in the accident. It is immaterial that Archer did not exercise his right to control Henry's performance by giving specific safety instructions about hanging his pail. The important factor is that Archer had the *right* to do so because Henry was in Archer's employ.

"Master" and "Servant" Defined. Since a principal is liable for the physical torts of agents who are not independent contractors, that is, employees, but is *not* liable for the physical torts of independent contractor agents, it is helpful to adopt some simple terminology to identify each of the two types of agents. The common law, court decisions, the *Restatement of the Law of Agency, Second,* and authoritative treatises on agency law call employee-type agents "servants." *Their* principals (employers) are called "masters." Independent contractor agents and their principals are called simply "agents" and "principals."

While today it is appropriate to use the modern term "employee," as was done in Chapter 33, to identify agents over whom a principal may exercise control, rather than the archaic term "servant," most courts have not yet taken this step. Accordingly, in this chapter we follow court terminology and call employees servants and their principals masters.

***Respondeat Superior* Defined.** The liability of a master for loss or harm caused by his or her servant acting within the scope of employment is called *respondeat superior,* a Latin phrase meaning "Let the master respond." It is a shorthand method of saying that a master must respond in damages for the physical torts his or her servant commits within the scope of employment even though the master may have been personally free from fault. The tort may have been (1) the *negligent act* of a servant which results in physical harm or loss to a third person, or (2) an *intentional act* of a servant in connection with his or her employment which results in physical injury to another. *Respondeat superior* does *not* apply to an independent contractor agent.

Reasons for *Respondeat Superior*. The doctrine of *respondeat superior* was first expressed in an old English case in which Judge Holt said, ". . . whoever employs another, is answerable for him. . . . The act of a servant is the act of his master, where he acts by authority of the master." [*Jones v. Hart,* Holt, K.B. 642(1698).] The judge in that case gave no reasons for the conclusion he expressed, yet the doctrine of *respondeat superior* has become firmly fixed in our law. It is unique to the law of agency. The courts and legal writers over the years have given many reasons to justify this rule which makes an otherwise innocent person pay for another's fault. Among those reasons are:

1. A party who has the power to control another's acts should be held responsible for the results of those acts.
2. Since a master gets the benefits of a servant's acts, the master should bear the burden of them.
3. Although a master may be without fault, the injured person may also be without fault, and as between two people equally free of fault, an employer who places an employee in a position to cause injury in connection with that employment should bear the loss.

4 Wrongful acts of servants in the course of employment are a cost of conducting business.
5 This liability is imposed on masters for the privilege of using the services of others.
6 To make masters liable tends to make them more careful in selecting and supervising their servants and the public is benefited.
7 The master has the "deeper pocket" out of which to pay damages to a third party for an injury the latter sustains.

Whatever justification is adopted for casting the responsibility upon the master, the costs which a master is required to bear are normally represented by insurance premiums. These premiums become an element calculated in the cost of the services or articles a master sells. The ultimate result is that in every purchase the consuming public pays some portion of a master's protection against tort liability.

Application of *Respondeat Superior*

While the definition of *respondeat superior* may be simple, complex legal questions arise in its application. For example, it is necessary, on a case by case basis, to decide:

1 Was the wrongdoer a servant or a nonservant agent?
2 Who is the responsible employer when an injury is caused by a servant who, with the permission of his or her master, is borrowed by another employer and is temporarily working for that employer?
3 Was the servant acting within the scope of employment when the injury occurred?
4 Can a tort committed outside the scope of employment be ratified by a master?

Each of these questions will now be considered.

Was the Wrongdoer a Servant? As an employer need not actually exercise his or her right of control over an employee's physical actions in order to establish employer responsibility, frequently it is not clear whether a master-servant or a principal–independent contractor relationship is present. The courts must therefore consider all the circumstances surrounding the employment in order to reach a decision.

In Chapter 33 we considered some of the characteristics of an independent contractor agent. Although the presence of these criteria do not necessarily prove that such an agency exists, they furnish useful guidelines. Some of the factors which normally, but again not necessarily, indicate that an employee *is a servant* are:

- The work is closely supervised.
- The tools used in the work are supplied by the employer.
- Payment is made to the employee daily, weekly, or monthly.
- The work involves regular hours and the employee may not delegate his or her work to someone else without the employer's permission.
- The work the employee does is part of the employer's regular business.
- The parties believe that a master-servant relationship is present.

It must be emphasized that absence of one or more of these factors does not necessarily prove that the employee is not a servant nor does the presence of one or more of these factors necessarily prove that the employee is a servant. For example, the Bar-Bell Company hires Strong as a full-time salesperson to sell its exercise equipment throughout the western half of the state. Their agreement specifies that Strong is an independent contractor. Despite that contractual provision, a court may find, as in Case 34.1 which follows, that, under the particular facts before it, the salesperson was a servant, not an independent contractor, and Bar-Bell is therefore liable for Strong's negligent actions. Usually, when a court is required to determine whether someone is an independent contractor or a servant, conflicting factors must be considered. The court must weigh these factors in the light of the entire enterprise. It is not surprising, therefore, that different courts sometimes reach opposite conclusions when considering substantially similar facts.

How a court weighs the facts to determine whether a master-servant relationship exists and therefore *respondeat superior* applies, is demonstrated in the following case.

CASE 34.1 Mustang Transp. Co. v. Ryder Truck Lines, Inc. · 523 F.Supp. 1097 (1981); Aff'd 688 F.2d 823 (1982)

FACTS Henry Crowder operated a tractor-trailer truck under a lease agreement with Mustang Transportation Company (Mustang). The agreement described Crowder as an independent contractor. Crowder owned the tractor portion of the truck and Mustang owned the trailer. On behalf of Mustang and himself, Crowder entered into a one-way lease agreement with Ryder Truck Lines (Ryder) to transport a load of freight from New York to Michigan. Ryder paid Mustang for the use of the tractor-trailer in accordance with the lease agreement. In turn, Mustang paid Crowder in accordance with the terms of their agreement.

While carrying Ryder's goods, Crowder negligently caused his truck to collide with an automobile. As a result of the accident, one passenger in the car was killed and the driver and another passenger were injured. Dispute arose between Mustang's and Ryder's insurance carriers as to which was obligated to pay the damages occasioned by the accident. The matter was submitted to the court for trial without a jury. Pertinent portions of the court's findings of fact and conclusions of law, required by the Federal Rules of Civil Procedure, follow.

OPINION CLIFFORD SCOTT GREEN, J. . . . The first issue to be resolved is the nature of the relationship of Henry Crowder to Mustang and to Ryder at the time of the accident. Disclaiming liability for the acts of Crowder, Mustang and Ryder each denies that he was its agent or employee (servant) at the time of the accident. In fact, each contends that the other was his principal or employer (master). . . .

The *Restatement (Second) of Agency* characterizes a servant as "a species of agent" (Comment (a) to § 2) and defines it as:

> . . . an agent employed by a master to perform service in his affairs whose physical conduct in the performance of the service is controlled or is subject to the right to control by the master.

An agent who is not a servant is an "independent contractor." An independent contractor is one who "contracts to act on account of the principal." (Comment (b) to § 2 of the *Restatement, Second.*) The distinction between the relationship of master/servant and that of principal/independent contractor, according to the *Restatement,* is that in the former situation, the master is responsible to third persons for the physical conduct of the servant. . . .

[A]t the time of the accident, the relationship between Mustang and Crowder was defined by a lease agreement. Under Georgia law [applicable to the agreement] . . . [i]f the employer has or assumes the right to control how the work shall be done, as distinguished from the mere right to require certain definite results in conformity to the contract, the relation is that of employer and servant rather than that of employer and independent contractor. [Citation.] . . .

If a written contract describes a party as an independent contractor, it is presumed that he is as designated. [Citation.] However, if other provisions of the agreement reveal that the employer has retained control over the time, manner and method of execution of the work, this presumption will not apply. [Citation.]

An examination of the lease agreement, which was drafted by Mustang, reveals that despite the description of Crowder as an independent contractor, Mustang maintained sufficient control over the execution of Crowder's work to establish a relationship of master and servant. For example, paragraph 10 of the agreement states: "The owner [Crowder] agrees that the vehicle(s) shall be operated in accordance with the rules, policies and practice of Mustang." Paragraph 2 provides in relevant part: "Any driver (including the owner if he shall drive himself) shall comply with all the safety regulations of Mustang . . ." Similarly, Paragraph 5 states:

CASE 34.1 Continued

> Owner [Crowder] hereby agrees that no freight will be transported on said vehicle(s) while being used in the transportation of freight other than at the direction of Mustang, or with the knowledge and consent of Mustang, and that all freight transported therein will be transported pursuant to freight bills and bills of lading made out by or for and in the name of Mustang. . . .

While Mustang may have wished to limit its liability by describing Crowder as an independent contractor, these provisions show that it maintained too much control over the manner in which Crowder operated the tractor trailer and transported freight to create a relationship of principal and independent contractor. . . .

Having determined that Crowder was the servant of Mustang, I now must decide Crowder's relationship to Ryder. . . . The lease agreement entered into by Crowder on behalf of Mustang and himself with Ryder . . . does not give Ryder any control over the manner in which Crowder was to operate the truck. . . . [T]he language focuses on Ryder's control over the shipment and not over the driver. . . . Because Ryder merely had the "right to require certain definite results under the contract" [citation] at the time of the accident Crowder's relationship with Ryder was that of independent contractor and principal under Georgia law. Thus no basis for liability of Ryder for the negligence of Crowder arises under state tort law.

JUDGMENT . . . . Having found that Mustang was the employer of Crowder and thus vicariously liable for his acts . . . I will enter judgment [accordingly].

Many times, particularly when a franchise arrangement is involved, it can be very difficult to determine whether it is proper to apply *respondeat superior*. Under a franchise arrangement such as a Chicken Delight or Taco Bell store or an Arthur Murray Dance Studio, a local firm pays a fee to a nationally operated organization, takes its name, and does business under its rules. Whether such a business stands in relation to the franchising company as an independent contractor or as its servant raises many problems which have been the subject of much litigation.

Whose Servant Was the Wrongdoer? For the doctrine of *respondeat superior* to apply, not only must the tort feasor (the one who commits the tort) be a servant, but he or she must also, at the time of the wrongful act, be a servant of the master who is to be charged with the dereliction. Liability may depend upon (1) whether the servant was temporarily borrowed by another employer and while working for the temporary employer committed the tort which injured a third party, or (2) whether the servant had temporarily employed someone else (called a *subservant*) to do the servant's work and that subservant committed the tort.

The borrowed servant problem. Because businesses and trades are becoming increasingly specialized in today's world of commerce, employees of different principals often work on the same premises at the same time. When the Jones Company lends its employee, Tom, to the Smith Company to do temporary work for the latter, the Jones Company is said to be Tom's *general employer*, the Smith Company is Tom's *special employer*, and Tom is called a *borrowed servant*.

The courts have not articulated a uniform test for determining whether the general or the special employer is liable under *respondeat superior* for the tort of a borrowed servant. Some courts state that the special employer, being the one benefited, is the one liable for the wrongful act. Other courts find a general employer liable if the servant (1) is paid by and can be discharged by the general employer, (2) is a skilled worker who has control over the operational details of the work, (3) is not engaged in the borrower's usual business, (4) is employed by the special employer for only a brief period of time, and (5) is using tools and equipment furnished by the general employer. Still other courts, perhaps the majority, when presented with a borrowed servant problem, look to see whether an employee who is loaned to a special employer continues to further the interests of the general employer. If so, the general employer remains liable under *respondeat superior.*

The two following hypothetical situations illustrate the problem of the borrowed servant.

1 Smith Company, located next door to the Jones Moving Company, asks Jones to lend it an unskilled worker for 1 day because, due to the illness of one of its own employees, Smith is shorthanded on an important job. Jones (the *general employer*) agrees and directs Mark, its employee, to go to the Smith Company (the *special employer*) and "do whatever they ask you to do." Jones Moving Company continues to carry Mark on its payroll. While temporarily working for Smith, Mark negligently injures a third party. When the tort was committed, Smith had control over Mark's physical actions in the performance of his work, all of the tools and equipment belonged to Smith, and the work was entirely for Smith's benefit. Therefore, Smith, the special employer, is the responsible master.

2 The problem becomes more complicated where heavy equipment, such as a tractor with an operator or an airplane with a pilot, is rented out. The equipment is of considerable value and the operator or pilot, a servant of the equipment owner, is specially trained. He or she is required to take care of the equipment and to operate it in the manner established by the general employer. The party who rents the equipment (the special employer) directs the tractor operator where the machine is to be used, what earth to move, and where it should be piled, or directs the pilot what time to take off, where to go, and when to return. If, while complying with those directions, the tractor driver or the pilot operates the equipment negligently and injures someone or destroys property of a third party, the general employer would be liable under *respondeat superior.* This is because the borrowed servant (tractor operator or pilot) was still working for the benefit of the general employer, was doing his or her job in the manner required by the general employer, and was charged with the care of the equipment.

The following case presents an unusual factual situation in which the borrowed servant question arose.

CASE 34.2 Green v. United States · 709 F.2d 1158 (7th Cir. 1983)

FACTS Dr. Stanford had been since 1969 Chief of the Cardiothoracic Surgery Service at Lackland Air Force Base Hospital. In 1976 and 1977 his colleagues became concerned that his surgical skills were inadequate. The mortality rate for his patients was approximately four times the average mortality rate for the patients of the other surgeons at that hospital. To retrain himself in surgical procedures, Dr. Stanford applied for and received a temporary fellowship with Cardiovascular Surgery Associates (CVSA) in Milwaukee, Wisconsin. He remained on the Air Force payroll and received no pay from CVSA.

In 1978 Dr. Mullen of CVSA performed a coronary bypass operation on the plaintiff Takuye Green. Dr. Stanford acted as Dr. Mullen's first assistant, being responsible for opening the patient's chest and connecting the lines between the patient and the heart-lung machine. In the course of preparing the patient for surgery, a physician's assistant (William Signorini) negligently reversed the arterial and venous lines that were to be inserted into the patient's chest. When the heart-lung machine was turned on irregularities in the arterial and venous pressures were noted but it took 15 or 20 minutes before the error in the lines was discovered. As a result of the improper connection to the heart-lung machine, Mrs. Green suffered extensive, irreversible brain damage and is now a blind quadraplegic.

All the parties who participated in the surgery were made defendants in a malpractice suit that ensued. The United States was joined as a defendant under the authority of the Federal Tort Claims Act. The district court found that Dr. Stanford was 62% negligent in causing Mrs. Green's injuries, Dr. Mullen was 16% negligent, and Signorini was 22%

CASE 34.2 Continued

negligent. The court held that, by application of the Federal Tort Claims Act, as supplemented by the Medical Malpractice Immunity Act, the United States, Dr. Stanford's general employer, was liable for the negligence attributed to him. The Federal Tort Claims Act (FTCA) is a law by which the United States consents to be sued for damages arising out of torts caused by the negligent or wrongful acts of employees of the Government while acting within the scope of their employment. The United States contends that it cannot be held vicariously liable for Dr. Stanford's negligence because at the time of the operation he was a borrowed servant of CVSA.

OPINION

BAUER and COFFEY, Circuit Judges and BONSAL, Senior District Judge.... The FTCA requires us to apply the law of Wisconsin in deciding this issue, as the accident occurred in that state....

Wisconsin law, following the approach taken by the *Restatement of Agency*, ... starts with the inference that the employee remains in the employ of the general employer.... The mere fact that Dr. Stanford was working under the supervision of other physicians at CVSA at the time of the accident did not make him the borrowed servant of CVSA. Under Wisconsin law, the government must also show that the work done by Dr. Stanford was primarily for the benefit of CVSA, the special employer, rather than the Air Force. "... [T]he important question is not whether or not [the employee] remains the servant of the general employer as to matters generally, but whether or not, as to the act in question, he is acting in the business of and under the direction of one or the other...." However, even if it were true that Dr. Stanford was acting both "in the business of" and "under the direction of" CVSA, the evidence simply does not support the conclusion that his work—however narrowly defined—was of primary benefit to CVSA.

While CVSA may have decided to offer Dr. Stanford a fellowship with the expectation that he would contribute something to the group's medical practice in exchange for the training provided him, it is clear that the fellowship was intended to benefit the government and Dr. Stanford more than CVSA.... Dr. Stanford himself sought the unpaid fellowship at CVSA in order to improve his surgical skills. While at CVSA he continued to receive his salary from the Air Force. While this... does not necessarily show that the Air Force benefited more from Dr. Stanford's work in Milwaukee than did CVSA, it strongly suggests that this was the case. There can be no doubt that Dr. Stanford's fellowship suited the government's needs; it had the immediate advantage of forestalling an even greater controversy at [the Air Base] than has already arisen concerning his competence as a surgeon, and it had the long-term advantage of improving his skills....

Dr. Stanford himself was a board-certified thoracic surgeon; he went to CVSA as a fellow, not an employee; he was to remain there only a limited time and was not to be compensated by CVSA for his work; and the government, as distinguished from a private business enterprise, is not accustomed to loaning its employees to other employers.

We agree with the district court that Dr. Stanford's work at CVSA was not primarily for the benefit of CVSA. Therefore, under the law of Wisconsin Dr. Stanford was not the borrowed servant of CVSA and the United States remained liable for his negligence during the operation on Mrs. Green. [The court then discussed the appropriate division of damages.] For the aforementioned reasons, the decision of the district court is...

JUDGMENT Affirmed.

The subservant problem. An important characteristic of a servant's employment is that he or she has no authority to delegate the work to others without the master's permission. If, without that permission, a servant gets someone else (a *subservant*) to perform his or her work, the servant is the master of the subservant and, being so, the servant has a master's liability under *respondeat superior* for any wrongful act the subservant may commit in the course of the work. The reason for this is that the servant has the *right to control* the subservant in the performance of his or her work. To illustrate, suppose Harry is employed to drive a delivery truck for the Apex company. Harry, an avid baseball fan, without Apex's permission asks his brother, Bob, to drive the truck for him the next day because he (Harry) is going to the ball game. Bob accommodates his brother but unfortunately drives negligently and injures a pedestrian. Harry, as Bob's master, is liable under *respondeat superior.*

If, however, the servant was *authorized* by his or her employer to employ a subservant as, for instance, in an emergency, only the original master is responsible under *respondeat superior* for a tort committed by the subservant.

Was the Servant within the Scope of Employment? In order for a master to be liable for the tort of a servant, the tort must occur while the servant is acting within the scope of his or her employment. It is generally held, following section 228 of the *Restatement of the Law of Agency, Second,* that the phrase *in scope of employment* means that an act: (1) is of the same general nature as, or is incidental to, the authorized work; (2) has a reasonable connection in time and place with such work; and (3) is intended by the servant, at least in part, to serve the master. Stated negatively, a servant is not acting within the scope of employment where the act is greatly different from that authorized, or is far beyond the time and place limits, or is too little motivated by a purpose to serve the master. A growing number of courts have simplified the test of scope of employment to this: a servant's actions are within the scope of employment if they can reasonably be foreseen by the employer.

General nature of the work. A servant is acting within the general nature of his or her employment when engaged in any activity that can reasonably be regarded as incidental to the work that the servant was authorized to perform. Suppose that a debt collector uses abusive language and threats in order to intimidate an old lady into paying a bill. As a result, she suffers emotional distress and sues the employer. A court would consider whether the act was incidental to the servant's employment; whether or not the act was commonly done by the servant or by others in the master's employ; whether or not the act was within the master's business and, if so, whether the master had ever permitted such an act to be performed by a servant; whether or not the harm caused by the servant was done by an instrumentality furnished by the master; and whether or not the master could have reasonably anticipated that the servant would act as he or she did.

We have been considering acts that are or may be incidental to a servant's employment. Under some circumstances the *failure* of a servant to act may constitute conduct within the scope of employment for which the master is liable. For example, because a railroad guard neglects to lower a barrier at a railroad crossing a motorist is struck by a moving train. Since the guard failed to perform his required work the railroad is, of course, liable for the injury that was sustained.

Time and place of the act. For the doctrine of *respondeat superior* to apply, a servant's tortious act must have a reasonable connection in time and place with authorized work. Generally, a tort that occurs going to and from work (the so-called "going and coming rule") is not within the scope of employment. Therefore, when the employee is not being compensated for the journey, the master is not liable if the servant drives negligently and has an accident while rushing to get to work on time, or if he or she falls asleep at the wheel while driving home after a hard day's work.

But, as with many rules, there are exceptions to the going and coming rule. The fact that the act occurs before or after normal working hours does not necessarily preclude the master's responsibility. For instance, an employer asks Bob, an employee, to mail a package at the Post Office on his way home from work. While driving to the Post Office Bob has an accident. Because he was then acting in the dual purpose of serving the master as well as going to his home the "dual purpose rule" applies and he was within the scope of his employment. Had the accident occurred after Bob left the Post Office he would no longer have been serving a dual purpose and he would not have been within the scope of employment.

Under the so-called "lunch hour rule," if, while strictly on his own business, Bob is away from his employer's premises for lunch, he is not within the scope of employment. However, if Bob takes his lunch or coffee break upon his employer's premises (or if he goes to a restroom provided by the employer), Bob remains within the scope of his employment.

Even though a servant's act may have occurred outside working hours, if the employer is being served it may still be within the scope of employment. For example, assume that Eunice, a store employee, is directed by her employer to close the store at 5 P.M. and not to admit any more customers after that hour. A short time after the store is closed, Eunice responds to a knock on the door and allows a late-arriving customer to enter. Eunice may be within her scope of employment if, in an ensuing argument about merchandise the customer wants to return, she assaults the customer. The store may be liable for Eunice's tortious act even though it was outside her regular duty hours.

The time and place of a tort are important considerations in the application of *respondeat superior.* This is reflected in the series of cases which hold that an employee is within the scope of employment on the way home from an office party he or she was expected to attend. When an office party is held after working hours and away from the regular place of work, the fact that the employer mandated the employee's presence removes the circumstances from the going and coming rule and *respondeat superior* applies.

The next case applies the *foreseeability test* to a servant's incidental personal acts.

CASE 34.3 Lazar v. Thermal Equipment Corporation · 195 Cal. Reptr. 890 (Cal. App. 2 Dist. 1983)

FACTS Lanno was employed by the Thermal Equipment Corporation as its project engineer. Sometimes he went from his home directly to the company offices and at other times, both outside of normal working hours and on weekends when he was troubleshooting, he would go from his home to wherever an emergency called him. To facilitate his work, Thermal allowed him to take the company truck home at the end of each day and to use it for personal purposes.

On March 5, after he had finished his work, Lanno drove the truck from Thermal's plant in a direction away from his home, intending to purchase something at a store and then to drive home. Before reaching the store, Lanno struck a vehicle owned by Lazar, who sued Thermal for the injuries he sustained. The jury found that Lanno was not acting within the scope of his employment at the time of the accident. The judge determined that, as a matter of law, Lanno *was* acting within the scope of his employment and so entered a judgment for the plaintiff notwithstanding the verdict. Thermal appealed.

OPINION SCHAUER, P. J.... Under the doctrine of *respondeat superior* an employer is responsible for the torts of his employee if these torts are committed within the scope of employment....

The modern justification for the doctrine of *respondeat superior*... "is a rule of policy, a deliberate allocation of a risk. The losses caused by the torts of employees, which as a practical matter are sure to occur in the conduct of the employer's enterprise, are placed upon that enterprise itself, as a required cost of doing business.... It is just that [the employer] rather than the innocent injured plaintiff should bear the [losses]... because [the employer] is better able to absorb them, and to distribute them, through prices, rates or liability insurance, to the... community at large...." Categorization of an employer's action as within or outside the scope of employment thus begins with the question of foreseeability, i.e., whether the accident is part of the inevitable toll of a lawful enterprise.

> ...If the main purpose of [an employee's] activity is still the employer's business, it does not cease to be within the scope of the employment by reason of incidental personal acts, slight delays, or deflections [the *dual purpose rule*].... The fact that an employee is not engaged in the ultimate object of his employment at the time of his wrongful act does not preclude attribution of liability to an employer.... For example, acts necessary to the

CASE 34.3 Continued

comfort, convenience, health, and welfare of the employee while at work, though strictly personal to himself and not acts of service, do not take him outside the scope of employment.

... The evidence showed that Lanno planned a minor errand to be carried out, broadly speaking, on the way home.... [This] was foreseeable.... [W]here the servant is combining his own business with that of his master or attending to both at substantially the same time, no nice inquiry will be made as to which business the servant was actually engaged in when a third person is injured.... Where, as here, the deviation is insubstantial and foreseeable, the doctrine of *respondeat superior* will apply.

JUDGMENT The judgment is affirmed.

Often an employee is required to drive a company vehicle on a prescribed route or between specific locations. If the servant does not follow instructions a deviation has occurred. Whether a master will be liable for a tort committed by a servant while engaged in a deviation will depend upon whether the deviation is considered a "detour" or a "frolic" on the part of the servant.

- *Detour:* If a deviation is slight, it is said that an employee is only on a *detour* and is still within the scope of employment. Suppose Tom, a delivery driver, is directed not to drive the company pickup on Main Street but to use a nearby parallel road because his boss does not want the vehicle to add to the congestion downtown. Tom disregards the instruction and drives down Main Street in making his rounds. Tom's deviation from the prescribed route would be but a slight departure from his assigned duties. He would therefore be considered to have been on a detour and still within his scope of employment.
- *Frolic:* If a deviation from an assigned route is great, a servant may be said to be on a *frolic* of his or her own and outside the scope of employment. For example, Tom, instead of delivering packages, goes to the racetrack to see his favorite horse run, intending to resume his work immediately after the race. His driving to the racetrack constitutes a frolic, and if he has an accident on the way he will not be within the scope of employment.

The courts have given no clear rule to tell us where a detour ends and a frolic begins. However, most courts hold that a servant reenters scope of employment when he or she is again reasonably near the authorized route and the servant, within the time limits of the employment, again acts with intent to serve the master. The following situations which could arise illustrate the problem.

1 Tom, a servant, is directed to take the company truck and deliver a crate to the freight office. Tom takes the normal or authorized route and on the way to the freight office he has an accident. At the time of the accident Tom was within the scope of his employment. If his negligent driving caused the accident the master is liable.
2 Tom delivers the freight. He then, without his employer's permission, drives 15 miles farther away from his place of employment to visit his sister. He has an accident while turning into her driveway. At the time of the accident Tom is serving entirely his own purpose; it is unrelated to his employment, it is more than a slight deviation and it is one that was not foreseeable. Accordingly, the driver is on a frolic of his own and the master is not liable.
3 After a short visit with his sister, Tom begins to drive back to his place of work. But before reaching the vicinity of the freight office he has an accident. As Tom is not far from his authorized route, intended to return to his place of work and obviously is within his work hours, a court would most likely hold Tom to be within his scope of employment and the master liable.

The next case deals with the problem of smoking on the job as a deviation from scope of employment.

CASE 34.4 Edgewater Motels Inc. v. A. J. Gatzke · 277 N.W.2d 11 (Minn. 1979)

FACTS Gatzke, a district manager for the Walgreen Company, was in Duluth, Minnesota, to supervise the opening of a new Walgreen restaurant. While there, he stayed at the Edgewater Motel. His company, Walgreen, paid all his motel, laundry, living, and entertainment expenses. While in Duluth Gatzke worked about 15 hours each day and remained on call 24 hours per day to handle problems arising in other Walgreen restaurants in his district. On August 23, 1977, Gatzke worked at the restaurant for about 17 hours. About midnight, he, together with his regional supervisor and a manager from another district, left the restaurant and went to the vicinity of the Edgewater where they each had rooms. Before turning in, Gatzke and the other manager went across the street to a bar where they talked about company business. Gatzke had four brandy Manhattan cocktails and talked with the bartender about mixing drinks to gather information for the new Walgreen restaurant which also served liquor. About an hour later they returned to their rooms at the Edgewater. Gatzke smoked a cigarette while filling out his expense account and then he went to bed. A fire soon broke out and the motel was extensively damaged. Later investigation determined that the fire started in the wastepaper basket in Gatzke's room. Edgewater sued Walgreen claiming that Gatzke was within the scope of his employment when he negligently started the fire. After a verdict for the plaintiff, the court granted Walgreen's motion for a judgment in its favor notwithstanding the verdict and Edgewater appealed.

OPINION SCOTT, J. . . . The question raised here is whether the facts . . . reasonably support the imposition of vicarious liability on Walgreen's part for the conceded negligent act of its employee. . . . To support a finding that an employee's negligent act occurred within the scope of employment, it must be shown that his conduct was, to some degree, in furtherance of the interests of his employer. . . . Other factors to be considered are whether the conduct is of the kind that the employee is authorized to perform and whether the act occurs substantially within the time and place restrictions [of the employment]. . . . No hard and fast rule can be applied to resolve the "scope of employment" inquiry. Rather, each case must be decided on its own individual facts. The initial question . . . is whether the employee's smoking a cigarette can constitute conduct within his scope of employment. . . . A number of courts . . . have ruled that the act of smoking, even when done simultaneously with work-related activity, is not within the employee's scope of employment because it is a matter personal to the employee which is not done in furtherance of the employer's interests. . . . Other courts . . . have reasoned that the smoking of a cigarette, if done while engaged in the business of the employer, is within an employee's scope of employment because it is a minor deviation from the employee's work-related activities, and thus merely an act done incidental to general employment. . . .

. . . [W]e are persuaded by the reasoning of the courts which hold that smoking can be an act within an employee's scope of employment. It seems only logical to conclude that an employee does not abandon his employment as a matter of law while temporarily acting for his personal comfort when such activities involve only slight deviations from work that are reasonable under the circumstances, such as eating, drinking, or smoking. We . . . hold that an employer can be held vicariously liable for his employee's negligent smoking of a cigarette [if] he was otherwise acting in the scope of his employment at the time of the negligent act.

The record indicates that Gatzke was an executive type of employee who had no set working hours. . . . It was therefore . . . reasonable for the jury to determine that the filling

CASE 34.4 Continued out of his expense account [and the smoking] was done within the authorized time and space limits of his employment. . . .

JUDGMENT [W]e set aside the trial court's grant of judgment for Walgreen's and reinstate the jury's determination that Gatzke was working within the scope of his employment at the time of the negligent act.

Was the Act Intended to Serve the Master?

The last requirement for *respondeat superior* is that a servant's act must be undertaken with the intent, at least in part, to serve the master or that the act, if negligent or intentional, must be connected with and grow out of the employment.

Negligent act. Generally, a negligent act is considered to be within the scope of employment when (1) it occurs during working hours at the prescribed place of work or (2) while away from the workplace in the course of a servant's employment or pursuant to the employer's directions, unless the servant is on a frolic of his or her own. But even where a servant is on the employer's premises, a servant is outside the scope of employment if the act is undertaken *solely* to satisfy the servant's own purpose. For instance, assume that a factory maintains a parking lot for its visitors but factory employees are not permitted to park in that lot. One day Cy arrives late to work, parks his car in the lot, punches the time clock, and returns to the parking lot to move his car to a street near the factory. In the process of moving his car and while still on the factory grounds, Cy drives his car negligently and runs into a visitor's parked car. At that time Cy was moving his car solely to satisfy his own purposes and *respondeat superior* does not apply.

Intentional act. Thus far, we have considered torts arising from the *negligence* of a servant. A tortious act committed *intentionally* by a servant may also be within the scope of employment if it (1) was intended to serve the master or (2) was connected with and grew out of the employment in a sudden outburst of anger due to the frustrations and and pressures of the job as long as, in either event, the tortious act was not so violent as to be outrageous. If a servant's intentional tortious act can be said to be reasonably within the authorized duties of a servant, the action is within the scope of employment and the master is liable.

The following examples, taken from actual cases, will illustrate intentional torts in which *respondeat superior* applies.

1 King parked his truck at a shopping center to load empty Coca Cola bottles. Campanale drove up in another truck and asked King to move out of the parking space so that he (Campanale) could park there and make an urgent delivery. King refused to move his truck and Campanale punched him in the face. The act, although clearly wrongful and unauthorized, was committed by Campanale in an effort to overcome an obstacle in the way of his performance of his master's work. The wrongful act was not considered so "outrageous" under the circumstances as to take Campanale out of his scope of employment and his employer was liable to King.
2 Paul played center field for the Double Play Tavern's semiprofessional baseball team. In the ninth inning of the championship game the score was tied. The ball was hit to Paul in center field. Paul extended his glove to catch the ball and missed. A run scored and the championship was lost. Paul, in disgust, threw the ball out of the ballpark and it struck a young woman walking on the street. The court found that even though Paul was not then engaged in playing the game, the Double Play Tavern was liable for the resulting injury because Double Play Tavern received benefit by being represented in the semiprofessional league and Paul hurled the baseball out of the field in his utter frustra-

tion while acting for Double Play Tavern. His actions were not so unreasonable or outrageous under the circumstances as to take him out of his scope of employment.

Quite a different legal conclusion results when a servant's act bears no relation to his or her duties but takes place only because of personal animosity. Such a situation might be if Bill, a lathe operator at the Square Deal factory, without the knowledge of his employers; runs a football pool. During working hours he makes collections and pays off the winners. Jim, employed at a factory next door, invests in Bill's pool. One day, during working hours, Jim comes to Bill's workplace and claims that Bill is withholding winnings that should be paid. In the ensuing fight Bill fractures Jim's jaw. *Respondeat superior* does not apply and the Square Deal factory is not liable.

Can a Willful Tort Committed outside the Scope of Employment be Ratified?

Just as a principal can make himself or herself liable by ratifying an unauthorized *contract* entered into by an agent, a master can make himself or herself liable by ratifying a *willful tort* committed by a servant outside the scope of employment. An example, taken from an actual case, occurred when Fred fraudulently acquired money from Sarah and turned it over to his employer as a credit against a shortage in his (Fred's) accounts and the employer retained the money after learning that it had been fraudulently acquired. The employer was held to have ratified Fred's tort and was liable to Sarah for the money.

In the case that follows the court was faced with an account executive who unlawfully and for his own benefit traded with funds in a customer's account.

CASE 34.5 Pusateri v. E. F. Hutton & Co. · 180 Cal. App.3d 247 (Apr. 1986)

FACTS Francis and Jenny Pusateri deposited $196,000 with an office of E. F. Hutton & Co., a stock brokerage firm. Johnson was their account executive. The Pusateris told him they wanted to maintain a conservative account from which they would receive a monthly income of $2,000 to $2,500 and agreed that Johnson would manage their account. The Pusateris signed a standard Hutton form indicating they wanted to maintain a conservative investment program. Later Johnson had the Pusateris sign margin authorization and stock option forms but did not explain the meaning of those forms to them.

From October through December 1981, Johnson, without the Pusateris' knowledge, engaged in more than 130 transactions involving purchases and sales for their account, thereby generating sizeable monthly commissions for himself. Such an activity, called "churning," violates the rules of the stock exchange and is illegal. Nee, the office manager, when going over the monthly reports of his account executives, noted that Johnson was averaging commissions of more than $2,000 per month from the Pusateri account. This indicated that the account was not being handled conservatively. Nee conferred with Johnson about the account and asked Pusateri only if he was satisfied with his account executive, but Nee did nothing more about Johnson's handling of the account.

Johnson left Hutton's employ in February 1982 and the account was assigned to another account executive. In March 1982 the Pusateris, in reading their income tax return prepared by their accountant, first learned that they owed Hutton $3,600 on a margin account and that the value of their original investment of $196,000 had shrunk to $96,800.

Shortly after this discovery, Pusateri confronted Nee, the office manager, and his account was assigned to Gordon, another account executive. Gordon told Pusateri that his account had been badly mismanaged and that he should consult an attorney. Pusateri did so; the account was closed and the Pusateris filed suit against E. F. Hutton and Johnson.

CASE 34.5 Continued

The jury awarded the plaintiffs $45,000 in compensatory damages against both defendants and $160,000 in punitive damages against Hutton. Hutton appealed the punitive damage award.

OPINION RACANELLI, P. J.... In applying the standard for awarding punitive damages against employers, courts have generally required a showing that a corporate defendant either itself committed acts of oppression, fraud or malice, or that it authorized or ratified such acts on the part of its employees. [Citation.]....

Failure to dismiss an employee after the commission of oppressive acts is evidence of ratification if the managing agent has knowledge of, or the opportunity to learn of, the misconduct and fails to investigate. [Citation.]....Nee was aware of the excessive activity in plaintiffs' account and their conservative investment goals, yet he failed to inspect the Pusateris' portfolio....Nee admitted the large number of trades and amount of commissions prompted his November contact with Pusateri and his discussion of the account with Johnson. In thirteen months over $47,000 in interest and commissions was generated. ...Nee also admitted that he never mentioned [to Pusateri] the condition of the account or the fact that [at one time] nearly $200,000 was owed to Hutton on margin purchases. Nee agreed that the level of activity in the account indicated a need for his review.... In the succeeding months that Johnson continued to mishandle the account, Nee—inexplicably—did nothing to determine whether the unsuspecting clients were even aware of what was happening. Thus, although Nee did not testify directly that he knew of Johnson's activity and nonetheless approved it, there was sufficient circumstantial evidence from which the jury could conclude that this was true. From the sum of such persuasive evidence, together with Nee's direct knowledge of the status of the account, the jury was entitled to find that Nee consistently ratified Johnson's outrageous and oppressive conduct justifying the award of punitive damages against his corporate employer.

JUDGMENT The judgment and order...are affirmed in all respects.

Strict Liability of Principal

Near the beginning of this chapter we said that "there are certain types of activities which cast a strict liability upon a principal regardless of whether the work is performed by an agent or a nonagent." A principal is held to strict liability if a third party suffers injury or damage when work is performed by an agent (1) for a principal who is the holder of a license from a governmental instrumentality, such as a gas company which digs a ditch along a street in order to lay its gas lines, or (2) for a principal who is required by statute to maintain precautions for the protection of the public, such as a railroad company at its crossings, or (3) when the work involves inherently dangerous or ultrahazardous activities, such as blasting in a populated area or fumigating with a deadly poison. In those situations the duty of care is nondelegable. The Missouri Court of Appeals in the case of *Hofstetter v. Union Electric Company*, 724 S.W.2d, 527 (1986), gave meaning to the phrase "inherently dangerous" when it pertinently said:

> To be inherently dangerous, the work being done must, by its very nature, involve some "peculiar risk" of physical harm. A peculiar risk is differentiated from a "common risk" in that common risks are those to which persons in general are subjected by the ordinary forms of negligence which are typical in the community....The theory of liability for an inherently dangerous activity is not applicable where the negligence of the independent contractor creates a new risk, not intrinsic in the work itself, which could have been prevented by routine precautions of a kind which any careful contractor would be expected to take.

The next case deals with a principal's liability when inherently dangerous work is performed by an independent contractor.

CASE 34.6 Erickson v. Monarch Industries, Inc. • 347 N.W.2d 99 (Neb. 1984)

FACTS Monarch Industries, Inc., a defendant, was the general contractor which constructed a facility for the storage, drying and processing of grain. Walters-Heiliger Electric, Inc. was its subcontractor and also a defendant. It performed electrical work at the facility, furnishing and installing a large transformer.

After the facility's completion, Loyal Erickson was employed as one of its night operators. On October 5, 1977, he was found dead near the transformer installed by the subcontractor, killed when an explosion occurred in the transformer. Erickson's personal representative sued the defendants for his wrongful death, claiming that the transformer did not have capacity to carry the load placed upon it and that it had been improperly connected. As a result, the transformer became overheated and caused resinous material which surrounded its wiring to melt, forming a flammable gas which exploded and which, in turn, caused the doors of the cabinet housing the transformer to be blown out, striking and killing Erickson. Among other issues raised was whether the general contractor was responsible for negligence of his subcontractor. The lower court entered a verdict for the plaintiff against both defendants and they appealed.

OPINION BOSLAUGH, J.... Monarch contends that it cannot be held liable for the negligence of Walters-Heiliger. Monarch relies on the general rule that the employer of an independent contractor is not liable for physical harm caused to another by the acts or omissions of the contractor or his servants....

There are exceptions to this rule of nonliability. The general contractor remains liable for the negligence of the subcontractor "if he retains 'control' of the work—or if, by rule of law or statute, the duty to guard against the risk is made 'nondelegable.'"

...In the present case Monarch had a nondelegable duty to provide a facility which was safely wired. "The nondelegable duty exception is based upon the theory that certain responsibilities of a principal are so important that the principal should not be permitted to bargain away the risks of performance."

> "We believe that an essential element of the doctrine [of nondelegable duty] is the failure of the principal to see that all appropriate precautions are taken by the one to perform the inherently dangerous task. The doctrine, in short, says that the principal is negligent, and hence liable, because it has allowed the independent contractor to be negligent in performing the job. There is a nondelegable duty to see that the work is done with the requisite degree of care; when the contractor fails in fulfilling its duty of care, the principal has breached its own precautionary duty."... "The person on whom the duty devolves is not excused from taking the necessary precautions by contracting with or relying on others to take necessary precautions."...

In the present case Monarch entered into an agreement to construct the grain drying facility. Monarch employed Walters-Heiliger to perform the necessary electric wiring. W-H was required to exercise utmost care and skill in providing the proper components and in wiring the facility, as it was providing a dangerous commodity.... Monarch could not delegate its duty to provide a facility that was wired safely.... Moreover, the installation of the electrical transformer was an inherently dangerous task such that the law will not relieve the contractors' liability for their negligence....

JUDGMENT The judgment of the district court in favor of the plaintiffs and against the defendants Monarch and Walters-Heiliger is affirmed....

Liability for Torts Not Resulting in Physical Injury

Thus far in this chapter, we have considered a principal's liability for the torts of servant and nonservant agents which result in physical injury to third parties. We will now consider a principal's liability for those torts which do not result in physical harm—torts such as fraud, deceit, and defamation. As to these torts, a principal is liable when they are committed either by a servant or nonservant agent who is acting in the course of a transaction authorized or apparently authorized by the principal.

Liability is not restricted to situations where an agent commits a tort for the principal's benefit but may extend to a situation where the agent, in conjunction with the employment, commits a nonphysical tort for his or her own benefit. For example, assume that the Tent City Company manufactures tents and has been selling them through a sales agency. The agency, in order to earn quick commissions after learning that Tent City will soon use a different sales agency, falsely represents to purchasers that the material of which the tents are made is fireproof. Tent City had not authorized the sales agency to make such a representation and, in fact, the material was not fireproof. However, Tent City must bear responsibility for the agency's false statements.

Basis of Principal's Liability

When no physical harm results from an agent's tort, the basis of the principal's liability rests upon ordinary rules of actual and apparent authority. Thus, when a principal appoints an agent and clothes him or her with authority, the principal is liable for any loss to a third party caused by the agent's nonphysical tort occurring in the exercise of such authority. The reasoning behind this is that public policy dictates that a loss should be borne by the one who made the tort possible (the principal) as well as by the one who committed it (the agent), rather than be borne by the victim of the tort. As the U.S. Court of Appeals said in *Gilmore v. Constitution Life Ins. Co.*, 502 Fed.2d 1345 (10 Cir. 1974), "A principal may not accept the benefits of its agent's endeavors and reject out of hand detriments arising therefrom. A principal may not turn loose his agent on the general public, and then merely sit back and exercise little or no supervision [over the agent]."

Remedies of Principal against Agent

Being anxious to make a sale or to carry a transaction to a successful conclusion, an agent, consciously or unconsciously, may misrepresent some element of the transaction and, as pointed out above, the principal may be bound to the third party by those misrepresentations. It is therefore common practice for principals, in order to protect themselves from liability to third parties for their agents' deceit, to insert protective clauses in the contracts or order blanks furnished for their agents' use. Such a provision, called a *disclaimer* or *exculpatory* clause, is designed to put the third party on notice that the agent has no authority to make any representations other than those stated on the printed contract or order blank. A disclaimer clause might read as follows: "There are no understandings, agreements, or representations between the parties other than those stated in this written contract."

If improper actions of an agent cause his or her principal to suffer a loss, the latter has a right of action against the agent to secure reimbursement for the loss sustained. Whether the principal will collect on the judgment depends, of course, upon the financial resources of the agent.

Summary

A principal who has the *right to control* the manner in which an agent performs his or her duties is, in agency law, called a "master" and the agent is called a "servant." A master is liable for physical harm to third parties caused by a servant who is within the scope of employment even if the servant is acting contrary to instructions. This rule is called "*respondeat superior.*"

In general, a servant is acting within the scope of employment if the act (1) is of the same general nature as, or is incident to, the authorized work; (2) is reasonably connected with the work in time and place; and (3) is intended by the servant to be a part of the work. A servant does not necessarily leave his or her scope of employment when there is a slight departure from the prescribed work or specified route. Accordingly, a master is liable if a deviation from a specified route is slight (then it is called a "detour"), but is *not* liable if a deviation is substantial (then it is called a "frolic"). If a servant leaves a specified route to such a degree that he or she can be said to have engaged in a frolic, the courts are not agreed as to when the servant reenters the scope of employment. The majority view is that reentry occurs when the servant reaches a point reasonably close to the authorized route intending to reengage in the work.

If a servant is engaged in an activity in which the interests of the master are being satisfied to some substantial degree at the same time that the servant is acting for himself, the servant is still considered to be within the scope of employment.

Courts recognize that a master may be liable for an intentional tort of a servant which results in physical injury to a third party if the tort is not outrageous and is committed within the agent's scope of employment or occurs as a result of job frustration bearing a reasonable relationship to authorized work.

There are certain situations which impose upon a principal a strict liability for an injury or damage to a third party regardless of whether the tort was committed by an agent or by a nonagent independent contractor.

A principal is also liable for a tort which does *not* result in physical injury to a third party if the tortious act is committed by either a servant or nonservant agent within the scope of the agent's authority. Among such torts are fraud and defamation. To protect themselves from liability for agents' frauds, many principals include exculpatory statements on their order blanks and contract forms. They thereby give notice that the agent has no authority to make representations other than those printed upon the order or contract form.

Review Questions

1 Under what circumstances can both a principal and an agent be liable for a tort committed by the agent?

2 An employee works in a city far removed from the "home office." Is the employer liable for a physical tort committed by the employee in the performance of her duties? Why or why not?

3 **(a)** What is meant by "*respondeat superior*"? **(b)** What are some important reasons for the doctrine of *respondeat superior?* **(c)** What problems are commonly associated with the application of that doctrine?

4 How can you tell whether a person is a servant or an independent contractor agent?

5 Comment upon this statement: "To protect himself or herself from vicarious liability, an employer should have a standard clause in all employment contracts saying, 'it is agreed that the parties hereto have established a principal-agent relationship and not that of master and servant.'"

6 A servant is lent by her employer to another employer for one day, being subject to the temporary employer's orders. While working for the "temporary boss" the servant commits a tort. What tests will determine which employer is liable for the tort?

7 **(a)** What is meant by "scope of employment"? **(b)** How is "foreseeability" related to scope of employment?

8 Mabel gives explicit directions as to the care John, her servant, must exercise. Does this affect Mabel's liability for John's negligent act in the course of his work?

9 Why are the time when and the place where a tort is committed important factors in determining scope of employment?

10 What is the "lunch hour rule"; the "going and coming rule"; the "dual purpose rule"?

11 **(a)** Distinguish between a detour and a frolic. **(b)** Joe installs and repairs televisions for Circuit City, a large TV store. One afternoon, before going to his next installation job, Joe drops in for half an hour at a nearby playground to watch his son play in a little league baseball game. In attempting to get his car out of the playground's parking lot Joe runs into your car and damages it. To whom can you look for compensation? Why?

12 **(a)** Mike is a "bouncer" in a nightclub. He uses force to eject an unruly patron, injuring the patron in the process. Is the master liable? **(b)** Agnes sells shoes. She has shown a customer innumerable pairs of shoes and the customer has tried them all on but fails to buy. Agnes gets so exasperated that she uses insulting language to the customer who complains that she was defamed. Would the master be liable for Agnes' tort? Why or why not?

13 **(a)** Under what circumstances can a principal be liable for a tort resulting in physical injury to a third party caused by an independent contractor? **(b)** For a tort not resulting in physical injury?

14 Under what legal theory can an employer be liable for fraud or misrepresentation by a nonservant agent who personally benefited from the tort?

15 **(a)** What is meant by an exculpatory clause in a sales contract? **(b)** In what way and to what extent does such a clause protect the principal?

Case Problems

1 Tilley Steel Co. was a subcontractor working on a bridge abutment. Maxwell Construction Co. was the general contractor. The work required close coordination between the two companies. Their forepersons agreed that if either company required the use of a crane but did not have one available, the other company would make a crane, with its operator, available to the other without compensation.

One day, Wynn, who operated one of Tilley's cranes, was told by his supervisor to move the crane to Maxwell's work site and to help the Maxwell people place some concrete forms. While doing that work Wynn obeyed signals and directions given him by Maxwell's foreperson as to the placing of the forms. In the process, Marsh, one of Maxwell's workers, was injured by the crane's swinging boom. Does March have a cause of action against Tilley or must he look only to his employer, Maxwell, for compensation? What is the reason for your answer?

2 Dolores, who worked for a concern that cleaned offices, was driving home from work at a high rate of speed. Because of traffic congestion, the car in front of her slowed down but Dolores did not immediately reduce speed. When she applied the brakes, the car skidded across the road, striking another car and severely injuring its occupant. The injured person sued Dolores' employer, claiming it was liable because she was within the scope of her employment at the time of the accident as (1) she was going home from work and (2) she was carrying cleaning materials in her car which she intended to use in her work the next day. Is the employer liable? Why or why not?

3 The Ideal Heating Corp. had a rule that no employee could smoke in the work area. It was the practice of Lupella, an employee, to go to the washroom four or five times a day to smoke. On one of his trips to the washroom, he passed a large drum of highly flammable paint thinner outside the painting area (his work did not involve painting). Seeing an opportunity to fill his cigarette lighter, he opened the spigot of the drum, holding his lighter under it. Lupella was not able to turn off the spigot and a fire ensued. The Ideal plant and that of the Art Company next door were severely damaged. Art Company sued Ideal for the losses it sustained. Should the Art Company prevail? Why or why not?

4 Lambert was an installer-repairperson for the Telephone Company. After installing a telephone in the residence of the plaintiff, Lambert physically attacked her. Plaintiff sued the Telephone Company on the theory of *respondeat superior*. Lambert had never previously been charged with having committed any crime and no complaint had ever been lodged by a customer against him. Is the Telephone Company liable? What are the reasons for your answer?

5 McCutcheon was a police officer on the City of Philadelphia police force. One day he had just gone off duty and was still in uniform when he got into an argument with his neighbor, Fitzgerald. The argument got hot; McCutcheon drew his service revolver and shot and wounded Fitzgerald. Fitzgerald sued Philadelphia for compensation for the injuries its agent, McCutcheon, had inflicted on him. Should Fitzgerald recover? Why or why not?

6 A family of beavers had built a dam in a stream alongside a road. The county engineer decided the dam should be blasted open to prevent erosion of the roadbed by water backed up by the dam. An independent contractor was hired by the county to open the dam. As a result of the blasting, a good deal of mud was deposited on the road. The contractor did not remove the mud or put warning signs on the road. Westby, who was driving his car along the road, suddenly came upon the muddy surface. He was unable to slow the car down; it skidded, turned over, and was severely damaged. To whom might Westby successfully turn for compensation for the damages he suffered? Why?

7 Gilmore was employed by Beacon Kitchenware Products to sell its "No Stickum" pots and pans. Gilmore was supposed to send his orders to the company, which would ship the merchandise to the purchaser C.O.D.

On one occasion Gilmore sold a large order of kitchenware to Agnes, telling her that he could allow a 25 percent discount if she paid in advance. Agnes paid Gilmore the full purchase price less the discount. Gilmore, instead of sending the order and the money to Beacon, kept the money and destroyed the order form. When Agnes failed to receive the kitchenware she demanded that Beacon either deliver the merchandise or refund the money she had paid for it. Beacon replied that Gilmore no longer worked there; that Gilmore had acted illegally and outside the scope of his employment when he took Agnes's order; that Beacon never allowed discounts of the kind Gilmore had promised; that *respondeat superior* did not apply; and that Beacon was not obligated to Agnes in any way. Why would a court nevertheless hold Beacon responsible?

CHAPTER 35

Obligations of Principals and Agents to Each Other; Termination of Agency

The very nature of the principal-agency relationship imposes financial risks on a principal. An agent may act unwisely or may fail to follow instructions and cause his or her principal to be bound by a burdensome contractual obligation; or an agent may, whether intentionally or negligently, commit a tort that obligates the principal to pay damages. Since an agent can place such unexpected and unwanted obligations on a principal, the law of agency imposes a range of obligations upon agents toward their principals. Conversely, since the principal is normally the source of the agent's livelihood, the law also places definite obligations upon principals toward their agents. Thus, an ethical foundation underlies the entire principal-agent relationship.

A gratuitous agent is under no legal obligation to perform a promised act, but once performance is undertaken, he or she is subject to the same obligations as a paid agent.

This chapter examines (1) the obligations of principals and agents to one another and the remedies available if those obligations are violated, and (2) the termination of the agency relationship. In this chapter, for the most part, we need not distinguish between servant and nonservant agents because the obligations existing between servant and master are essentially the same as those which exist between principal and nonservant agent. Accordingly, we will generally use the all-inclusive terms principal and agent.

Obligations of Agents to Principals

An agent who undertakes to perform work or services assumes the duty (1) to use at least normal care and skill, (2) to obey the reasonable instructions of the principal, (3) to perform personally the work or services, (4) to communicate pertinent information, (5) to account to the principal for money the agent receives for the principal's account, and (6) to act with loyalty toward the principal.

Duty to Use Care and Skill

An agent impliedly assures the principal that he or she has the knowledge and skill to do the work to be undertaken and will use reasonable care and diligence in its performance. An agent does not guarantee (unless that guarantee is a part of the agency agreement) that he or she possesses and will exercise the *highest* degree of skill and diligence or will make *no* mistakes in the work. The law contemplates only that a principal is entitled to expect from an agent (1) the exercise of reasonable care and skill and (2) the degree of ability that is standard in the locality for the kind of work the agent undertakes to perform. For example, if Helen accepts a job requiring her to operate a computer, she impliedly represents that she has at least the average understanding of the language of the computer she will be using. Helen also impliedly represents that she will use the care and diligence of other computer operators in that locality. Similarly, in applying for a job in a machine shop, Henry impliedly represents that he can operate the machines on which he will work with the same proficiency as other operators in that job market.

An individual may hold himself or herself out as an expert in some field. If so, he or she must have the additional knowledge and will use the care and diligence usually possessed by such an expert in that or in a similar community. Someone practicing a profession which requires extensive education and special license from the state is generally considered to be an expert. Therefore an accountant who gives a client advice on tax matters impliedly represents that he or she is conversant with applicable tax law and regulations.

The court in the following case imposed fiduciary obligations upon a licensed real estate broker to accord with the high standards of competence expected of someone in that profession.

CASE 35.1 Perkins v. Thorpe · 676 P.2d 52 (Idaho App. 1984)

FACTS Betty Thorpe owned a 600-acre farm. A salesperson who worked for Perkins, a real estate broker, brought to Mrs. Thorpe a customer's offer to pay $273,000 for the property. She asked the salesperson if that was a fair price. He replied it was "high considering the condition of the ranch." However, Mrs. Thorpe turned down the offer because the purchase terms were not satisfactory to her. The salesperson returned with a modified purchase offer at the same price but with better terms. The offer was contingent upon the prospective buyers being able to sell certain other property they owned. Mrs. Thorpe accepted the offer. Mr. Perkins then prepared, and Mrs. Thorpe signed, an "exclusive listing agreement," thus making him her agent and agreeing to pay him a broker's commission if he found a buyer for the property or if she sold it herself during the period of the agreement.

Some time later Perkins' salesperson informed Mrs. Thorpe that the sale of her ranch was progressing toward a closing and that the buyers had obtained financing. However, several weeks later the people whose purchase agreement Mrs. Thorpe had accepted told her that they had been unable to sell their other property and therefore they could not complete the purchase of her ranch. Having no other potential buyer, and not having done any seasonal work on the farm because she anticipated closing the sale, Mrs. Thorpe became desperate. Fearing she would lose the property for failure to make her mortgage payments, she offered the farm to the same buyers at a reduced price. They accepted the new offer and bought the property for $265,000. A few months later an independent appraiser valued the property at $392,000.

When Mrs. Thorpe refused to pay Perkins a broker's commission he brought suit. Mrs. Thorpe counterclaimed, saying that Perkins, through his salesperson, had breached his duty to her by misrepresenting the farm's value. Summary judgment [that is, rendered without a jury] was entered for Perkins, the plaintiff, and Mrs. Thorpe appealed.

OPINION BURNETT, J. . . . In this case it is clear that . . . the salesman . . . solicited and established an agency relationship between the broker and Thorpe concerning the sale of the farm. . . . Her allegation that the broker—again through his salesman—misrepresented the value of her farm implicates the element of honesty if he intentionally understated the value, or the elements of due care and diligence if the statement was negligent. A broker is obligated to employ the degree of skill in his calling usually possessed by others in the same business. . . . The broker's conduct is required to meet a standard of competence because he is "issued a license and permitted to hold himself out to the public as qualified by training and experience to render a specialized service in the field of real estate transactions." The law requires that he perform to a certain level of skill; for if he failed to do so, "instead of being the badge of competence and integrity it is supposed to be, the [broker's] license would serve only as a foil to lure the unsuspecting public in."

Here, a trier of fact [a jury] . . . also could infer, from the difference between the earnest money price of $273,000 and subsequent appraisal of $392,000, that the value of the farm had been intentionally or negligently understated. Accordingly, we hold that the record contains a genuine issue concerning breach of . . . duty [which should have been referred to a jury for decision].

JUDGMENT . . . The judgment is reversed and the cause remanded.

Duty to Obey Reasonable Instructions

An agent is under a duty to obey the reasonable instructions of his or her principal. As a corollary to this rule, an agent is also required to refrain from doing acts that the principal has not expressly or impliedly authorized. For example, if a sales agent is instructed to accept only cash payments, acceptance of a check violates the duty of obedience to reasonable instructions. This would be so even if the agent is convinced the check is good and, in good faith, believes its acceptance would bring about a sale in which the principal would profit handsomely, whereas if the check were not accepted a valuable sale would be lost. Because an agent is liable to his or her principal for any loss which results from a failure to obey reasonable instructions, if the salesperson in the above example accepts the customer's check and it "bounces," the agent is personally liable to reimburse the principal for its amount.

There is an exception to the rule that an agent has a duty to obey reasonable instructions. In an emergency situation an agent legally may deviate from instructions to the extent that he or she in good faith believes deviation is necessary to protect the principal's interests. An emergency situation is one that the agent reasonably believes was unforeseen by the principal and which requires action before the agent has the opportunity to inform the principal and to ask for revised instructions. For instance, suppose John, the manager of a grocery store, instructs his employees that he (John) is the only person who can authorize the expenditure of the store's money and that the clerks are not to obligate the store for payments of any kind. On a hot August day, when John is out of town for 24 hours and cannot be reached, the store's freezer containing ice cream breaks down. Mary, one of the clerks, calls in a repairman to fix the freezer immediately—before the ice cream melts away. The store must honor that contract and pay for the repair.

Duty to Perform Service Personally

Unless a servant-type agent (an employee) has the express or implied assent of the principal to delegate work to a subservant, the employee must personally perform the work he or she was hired to do. This principle is expressed in the Latin phrase *Delegatus non potest delegare* (A delegate cannot delegate). The reason for this rule is obvious: Since the risks of agency are substantial, a person should be subject to these risks only when represented or served by someone of his or her own choosing. However, under situations such as the following, an employee may delegate his or her duty (1) when in a transaction the act that the employee seeks to delegate is purely clerical as, for instance, filing papers or filling in the blanks of printed purchase order forms with data furnished to the delegate by the employee, or (2) when the employer knows or has reason to know that it is impractical for the employee to perform the duty personally, as where the nature of the work is such that it must be carried on by a crew of people.

A *nonservant agent* (an independent contractor) has a much greater authority to delegate, having the implied authority to delegate to others the performance of so much of the work as does not involve the exercise of discretion. If the work does involve the exercise of discretion, a nonservant agent has the duty to perform it personally.

The following example should make clear the distinction between duties of a nonservant agent that are delegable and those that are not delegable. Assume that you hire Dorothy, a prominent real estate agent (a nonservant agent) to make an offer to purchase for you Green Acres, a large country estate. Dorothy may delegate to subagents such jobs as attempting to find out how much the current owner paid for Green Acres, whether there have been any recent offers for its purchase and, if so, for how much, and for what prices comparable properties have recently been sold. However, Dorothy may *not* delegate to others the right to decide the price she will recommend that you offer for the property nor the terms of payment. Likewise, Dorothy may not delegate to subagents the conduct of the actual negotiations leading to the purchase. These duties involve the exercise of discretion and require the judgment and decision of the agent herself.

If Dorothy, without your consent, gives Vernon (her subagent) the task of negotiating for the actual purchase, you can, when you learn of the improper delegation, repudiate responsibility for any of Vernon's acts and may refuse to honor any agreement Vernon negotiated. In addition, if you suffered damage because of Dorothy's breach, you may look to her for reimbursement. On the other hand, if you knew of Vernon's activities and permitted him to carry on the negotiations, or if you accept the terms Vernon arranged, then you ratified Vernon's actions and you are bound by Vernon's agreement with the seller of the property.

Duty to Communicate Pertinent Information

An agent, whether servant or nonservant, has the duty to keep his or her principal fully and promptly informed of all facts that are relevant to the subject matter of his or her agency. In agency law, this information is classed as either "knowledge" or "notice."

Knowledge is any information of importance which an agent acquires concerning a matter in which the agent has the power to bind his or her principal. For instance, assume that Hiram, who owns Clearview Farm, instructs Mike, his foreperson, to buy a used tractor for the farm. George, the owner of a nearby farm, offers to sell Mike a tractor, saying, "It's as good as new." When testing the tractor Mike discovers that it does not run well in reverse gear. However, believing that the machine is a "steal" at the price George asks and that it can easily be repaired, Mike buys it for the farm. After the tractor is delivered to Clearview, Hiram calls George on the phone and demands that George take back the machine and return the money paid for it because "its reverse gear doesn't work." However, since Mike, Hiram's agent, in the course of his duties acquired knowledge of the defect before buying the machine, the law assumes that Hiram, Mike's principal, had the same information. As a result, Hiram cannot use the tractor's defect as a basis for backing out of the purchase.

Notice is knowledge that a third party communicates to a principal through an agent. The law assumes that an agent does his or her duty and conveys to the principal all notices received for the principal. This assumption is binding upon the parties even if, in fact, an agent neglects to convey to the principal the notice the agent received. As a result the rights and liabilities of a principal with regard to a third party are the same as if the principal had *personally* received the notice.

To illustrate notice, assume that Ben owns an apartment building. He leases an apartment to Agnes for one year. The lease, which expires on August first, states that Agnes may extend it for another year at the same rent if she notifies Ben to that effect before June 30. On June 25, Agnes, when paying her rent to Fred, the agent in charge of managing Ben's apartment building, tells him that she is extending her lease for another year. Although Fred neglects to give Ben the message, the law assumes that Ben, Fred's principal, did, in fact, receive the notice. As a result, Agnes's lease is extended even though Ben had intended to rent the apartment to someone else at a higher rental.

The following case illustrates how a principal may be bound by an agent's knowledge.

CASE 35.2 Gering v. Smith Company · 337 N.W.2d 747 (Neb. 1983)

FACTS The City of Gering awarded a contract to the Smith Company for the construction of Phase IV of a gravity-flowing sewer system. Schaff, an employee of the City and the City's engineer on the project, designed the system. During the work it was observed by at least one construction engineer working on the job under Schaff that the sewer line had a "sag" in it. The sag was noted on a set of "as-built plans" drawn up by the Schaff organization but not shown to the city officials.

In November 1976 work upon the sewer line was finished. The next month Schaff filed a certificate of completion stating "I hereby certify that Outfall Sewer-Phase IV... has been fully completed according to the terms and conditions of the contract, and I recommend that the work be accepted." The City of Gering accepted the work and Smith was paid. It later became evident that further work would be required to correct the sag in the line. The City sued Smith for the cost of the corrective repair work. Smith appealed from a judgment for the City, maintaining that the City, through its engineer, accepted the work with knowledge of its defect and that therefore the City had waived any right to damages.

OPINION KRIVOSHA, C.J.... Knowledge of the agent Schaff was knowledge of the principal, City of Gering.... It is the duty of an agent to communicate to his principal all the facts

CASE 35.2 Continued

concerning the service in which he is engaged that come to his knowledge in the course of his employment, and this duty, in a subsequent action between the principal and a third person, he is... conclusively presumed to have performed. This is the foundation of the doctrine, necessary to the public safety, that notice to an agent is notice to his principal. Thus, in the instant case, the knowledge of the engineer, acting as agent of the City, is knowledge to the City....

The finding of the trial court... that the officials of the City did not see the "as-built plans" or have actual knowledge of the sag does not affect the matter of waiver where the uncontroverted evidence is that with knowledge of that fact the engineer for the City executed the certificate of completion, certifying that the work had been "fully completed according to the terms and stipulations of said Contract" and that [he] recommended that the work be accepted. The purpose of having such a certificate, according to the contract, is both to advise the City that the work it sought to have done was properly completed and to advise the contractor that the work as done was acceptable. If the City intended to object to the work because of the sag, a fact known to the City's engineer, it had to do so before accepting the work in reliance upon its engineer's certificate. The City has neither pled nor attempted to prove that acceptance by the City was induced by fraud.... The City may have some quarrel with its engineer, a fact we do not decide. What is clear, however, is that there was acceptance with knowledge and therefore waiver....

JUDGMENT Judgment reversed....

There are two exceptions to the rule that an agent is presumed to have given the principal all notices and information pertinent to an agency:

1. A principal is not presumed to have knowledge of any information the agent acquires in confidence. For example, if attorney Ruth, in the course of representing her client Fox learns from him in confidence that he contemplates going out of business, attorney Ruth may not reveal this information to Vortex, another of Ruth's clients, even though that information would be valuable to Vortex.
2. A principal is not presumed to have knowledge that an agent is acting adversely to the principal. For instance, if agent Con steals from his principal, the principal is not presumed to know of the embezzlement. The principal will be charged with knowledge of the wrong only after he or she actually learns of it.

Duty to Keep and Render Accounts

If an agent's duties require him or her to receive any money or other property for the principal, the agent is obligated to keep accurate records of those receipts. All such money or property must be turned over to the principal in accordance with the agency agreement or, if the agreement does not so specify, then within a reasonable time. Furthermore, a careful agent will not mix the principal's funds with his or her own money. A lawyer, for example, normally establishes a "Trustee Account," or a "Clients' Account," or some other special account, separate from the lawyer's personal account, where he or she deposits all collections or other moneys held for clients.

If an agent fails to account, the principal has a right of action against the agent in accordance with the agency agreement or may take other action authorized in that jurisdiction to recover money received by the agent and wrongfully withheld. In addition, the principal may recover from the agent any profit the agent personally made from the use of the money or property.

Duty to Be Loyal

The most far-reaching obligation of an agent to a principal is the duty to be loyal. The duty to be loyal is an aspect of the fiduciary relationship between a principal and an agent. The term *fiduciary* comes from the Latin word *fides,* meaning trust or confidence. A principal places trust and confidence in his or her agent and relies upon the agent to act solely for the principal's benefit in all matters connected with the agency. At the same time, the agent should refrain from placing himself or herself in a position that would encourage a conflict between the agent's own interests and those of the principal.

For convenience, an agent's duty of loyalty will be treated under three general headings:

1. The duty not to take any secret benefit in connection with a transaction the agent undertakes for the principal
2. The duty not to act adversely to the principal's interests
3. The duty not to use or reveal the principal's confidential information

Duty Not to Take Any Secret Benefit. To minimize the dangers that may arise from divided loyalties, the law directs that an agent may not (1) make a secret profit on a transaction conducted for a principal or (2) accept payment of any kind from anyone who might influence the agent's actions in the transaction. For example, Frank authorizes Carlos to sell Frank's car for $1,000, telling him that he will give Carlos a commission of $100. Carlos sells the car for $1500 and gives Frank only $900 (Frank's asking price minus the $100 commission). Carlos has wrongfully made a secret personal profit out of the transaction. He must turn the extra $500 over to Frank and he must also turn back his commission because he violated his fiduciary duty to his principal. However, as we shall see in Case 35.3, if Frank had told Carlos that the price of the car was $1,000 and that Carlos could keep anything above that, Frank would have established a net price. In that event, Carlos could have kept the $500 extra the purchaser had paid and also his commission of $100.

Government agencies and most companies employ purchasing agents. Some purchasing agents place orders with suppliers who give the agent an illegal kickback in order to get the order. (The magnitude of this wrongdoing and its cost to the public was discussed in Chapter 6.) The money or other consideration the agent secretly receives belongs to his or her principal and the agent may be discharged from employment. Under certain circumstances, the agent and the individual or business concern which gave the kickback may be subject to criminal prosecution.

It is the practice of some firms to give presents or token gratuities to people with whom they do business. *If the principal consents,* an agent may keep a gratuity from someone with whom the agent conducts the principal's business.

Duty Not to Act Adversely to Principal. An agent who acts adversely to his or her principal by simultaneously acting for a third party or by secretly buying from or selling to the principal is disloyal and violates an obligation basic to the principal-agent relationship. An agent, believing in good conscience that he or she must take an action adverse to the principal, is required first to inform the principal and, if the latter's consent is not forthcoming, the agent's only recourse is to resign from the agency.

Not to act for third party. It would be adverse to the principal if his or her agent were to act simultaneously for the principal and for the third party in a transaction. If an agent does so, he or she is acting for two principals who have conflicting interests. In this situation the agent would be under the same obligation to each of the principals as though acting for either one of them alone, and it would be impossible to be equally fair to both. Although intending to be absolutely fair, the agent might favor one of the principals over the other. Accordingly, an agent may not act for principals on both sides of any transaction *unless both* principals have knowledge of the fact and actually or impliedly consent to the dual representation.

Dual representation should be distinguished from the situation where an agent "stands in the middle" between potential contracting parties, speaking for neither of them to settle price or terms. In that position, the agent does not violate any confidences and does not represent conflicting interests because, by merely "standing in the middle," he or she takes no position for or against either of the principals. There is extensive case and statutory law affecting real estate agents who frequently are "in the middle" between the buyer and seller in a transaction involving the purchase or sale of a property.

In the event an agent represents principals on both sides of a transaction without making full disclosure and without obtaining the consent of both principals, either principal may do one or more of the following: (1) refuse to pay the agent or, if compensation has already been paid, secure its return regardless of the fairness of the agreement the agent negotiated, (2) rescind any agreement negotiated by the agent, (3) recover from the agent any damages suffered because of the transaction, and (4) terminate the agency.

If one of the principals knew of the dual representation, then the enumerated remedies are available only to the nonconsenting principal who may also have an action for damages against the other principal who acted in conjunction with the agent.

Not secretly to sell or to buy from principal. Corollary to the rule that an agent is duty bound not to act adversely to his or her principal is the rule that an agent may not, without the consent of the principal, play the dual role of agent and third party. It is not material that the agent innocently believes he or she is acting in the best interests of the principal.

Accordingly, an agent who buys for a principal may not, without the principal's full knowledge, sell his or her (the agent's) own property to the principal. If the agent were to do so, he or she would be acting as a third party and could take an unreasonable advantage of the principal. For instance, the agent could deliver an inferior article or cause the principal to pay an inflated price, or the agent might buy on the open market with his or her own money and then sell to the principal at a profit.

Likewise, an agent who is engaged in selling for a principal may not himself or herself, without full disclosure to the principal, buy an article the principal wants to sell unless the principal had placed a firm price upon the article. And because it is a legal principle that a person may not do indirectly what may not be done directly, an agent may not buy from his or her principal indirectly by having a friend or family member make the purchase.

The following case reflects the strict interpretation the courts give to the rule that an agent may not secretly buy property the agent has agreed to sell for the principal.

CASE 35.3 Sierra Pacific Industries, Inc. v. Carter • 163 Cal. Rptr. 764 (Cal. 1980)

FACTS Sierra Pacific, the plaintiff, owned certain real property it desired to sell. Carter, the defendant, was a real estate agent who was acquainted with the property. Relying on Carter's representations as to the value of the property, the plaintiff orally commissioned him to sell it for $85,000, for which Carter would receive a fee of $5,000. Carter showed the property to various people but was not successful in making a sale. After several months, Carter sold the property for $85,000 to his daughter and son-in-law. Carter retained his agreed $5,000 commission and turned the balance ($80,000) over to the plaintiff. Carter did not tell plaintiff his relationship to the buyer.

When Sierra Pacific discovered that Carter's daughter and son-in-law were the purchasers, it brought suit against Carter alleging that he had breached his fiduciary duty as agent and sought recovery of the $5,000 commission retained by him. After a verdict for Carter, the court granted Sierra Pacific's motion for a new trial. Carter appealed that order.

OPINION RHODES, Assoc. J.... An agent bears a fiduciary relationship to his or her principal which requires, among other things, disclosure of all information in the agent's possession relevant to the subject matter of the agency.... An agent may not compete with the principal, nor may he or she act as agent for another whose interests conflict with those of the principal....

In the context of an agreement to sell land on another's behalf, the general duties inherent in every agency become more specific. A real estate agent must refrain from dual representation in a sale transaction unless he or she obtains the consent of both principals after full disclosure.... This means under most circumstances that if the agent is related to the buyer in a way which suggests a reasonable possibility that the agent... could indirectly be acquiring an interest in the subject property, the relationship is a "material fact" which must be disclosed....

CASE 35.3 Continued

There is no question that Carter concealed information material to this transaction from his principal, Sierra Pacific. He claims that he was exempted from the disclosure requirement, however, on the basis of a so-called "net listing." Under a net listing agreement the seller agrees to take a fixed sum of money for his property and the broker is entitled to all additional sums as his commission. It is true that under this type of arrangement, a broker may not be obligated to disclose any relationship he has to the buyer....

In order to exempt a broker from the strict requirement of disclosure a real estate sales agreement must include a net sale price determined by the seller *without influence by the agent*....

Here, uncontradicted evidence shows that Sierra Pacific officials agreed to the $85,000 figure based on an estimate Carter made at their request. It is irrelevant whether $85,000 represented a fair price, or whether the officials also relied in part on their own recent experience in acquiring property.... It cannot be overemphasized that the key factor in permitting the real estate broker this relief [provided under the net listing exemption] is the independent and completely uninfluenced determination of the net sales price by the seller....

It is thus evident that Carter owed a duty of disclosure to his principal, Sierra Pacific. It is equally evident that the duty was breached.... Sierra Pacific was entitled to recover the commission it paid to Carter.... By misconduct or willful disregard in a material respect of an obligation imposed upon him by the law of agency, he may forfeit his right to compensation....

We thus are led to the inescapable conclusion that Carter is liable to Sierra Pacific as a matter of law for a minimum of $5,000 and that the jury's verdict to the contrary is in error....

JUDGMENT The order granting a new trial is therefore affirmed.... The only triable issue remaining concerns the extent of plaintiff's damages....

Duty Not to Use Confidential Information.

The law is well settled that an agent, whether servant or nonservant, is subject to the obligation not to use for his or her own benefit or for the benefit of someone else, confidential information the agent gains in the course of employment unless the consent of the principal is first obtained. Unlike an agent's obligations already discussed, this prohibition continues even after the agent ceases to work for the principal.

The duty not to use confidential information, like the other duties we have considered, is imposed by law as an adjunct of the agency status. Therefore it is not necessary that it be spelled out in an employment contract. However, it is normal practice for any firm which is working upon a defense contract or upon any other confidential matter to have its agents, as a condition of their hiring, sign a "Secrecy Agreement." The purpose of this procedure is (1) to call to their employees' attention their obligation not to disclose confidential matter, (2) to make the duty a contractual obligation for which the remedy of breach of contract would be clearly available, and (3) to make proof of the extent of the obligation easier to establish in the event of suit.

Duty not to use trade secrets. "Trade secrets" is the term applied to the confidential information of business concerns. Trade secrets take the form of, but are not limited to, formulas (chemical or otherwise), manufacturing processes, and customer and pricing lists. They consist of any information which may give a firm some advantage over its competitors (see also Chapter 6). To be able to characterize some particular information as a trade secret, a business concern must reasonably protect the information from the knowledge of its competitors and from the public. For a company merely to say, for instance, that one of its industrial processes is a trade secret is not sufficient to make it one. The company must also take steps to guard the secret of the process and keep the information confidential.

An employee has no right to use or to disclose trade secrets learned in any employment, past as well as present. It is inevitable, however, that when an employee changes his or her place of employment the employee will bring to the new job some knowledge gained from the former one. Though an employee may not disclose to the new employer trade secrets previously learned, the employee does have the right to use the skills and knowledge he or she has acquired. The line of demarcation between a learned skill and a former employer's trade secret is often difficult to draw. In such situations the difficulty must be resolved on a case by case basis.

Duty not to use customer lists. A customer list is a compilation of the names and addresses of potential purchasers of particular services or articles. For example, department stores keep lists of their charge account customers, banks have lists of Visa card holders, stockbrokers compile lists of people interested in financial matters, and the life blood of a mail order firm is its customer list. Customer lists are developed through the expenditure of time, money, and advertising effort and they are valuable products which may be sold.

An individual who goes into business for himself or herself using a former employer's confidential list to solicit customers may face a problem. A court presented with a case involving the alleged misuse of a customer list by a former employee must weigh the right of the former employee freely to work in a business of his or her own choice against the right of the former employer to protect its property. Generally the courts permit an individual to solicit the customers of a former employer if the names of such customers were known to the employee from having personally dealt with them during the course of the employment. As a New York Appellate Court has said, "Equity has no power to compel a man who changes employers to wipe clean the slate of his memory" (*Peerless Pattern Company v. Pictorial Review Co.*, (1911) 132 N.Y.S. 37, 39). Customers of a former employer may also be solicited if they are openly engaged in business or if their names can be discovered through examination of business directories such as the Yellow Pages of the telephone book.

It is important to note, however, that the privilege of an employee to solicit certain customers of a former employer does not give the employee a license to attempt to move to a new employer a partially completed contract on which the employee has been working.

In cases where an agent improperly reveals or wrongfully uses confidential information of his or her employer or former employer, the principal may sue the agent and the third party who knowingly uses that information to recover any profits made from such misuse. The principal may also be able to secure an injunction against both the agent and third parties to prevent them from further using the information. (See also Case 6.6, Chapter 6.)

The shop-right privilege. The *shop-right privilege* is a variant of an agent's obligation to pass along to his or her employer all information pertaining to the agency. The shop-right privilege arises in the following manner: An employee whose duties do not include research or invention conceives and perfects an invention while using the employer's facilities, materials, or equipment. The employee is the owner of the invention but the employer has a *shop-right* interest in it. This means that the employer has the right to use the invention without paying a royalty. However, if the duties of the employee are to conduct research or to invent, then the product of the employee's labors *belongs* to his or her employer, who is entitled to own any patents which may be issued on it.

Duty Not to Compete with Principal. Unless precluded by the agency agreement, an agent is free to act as he or she wishes in any matter that is not within the scope of the agency. That is not to say, however, that an agent may engage in an activity which is antagonistic to the principal's interests. For example, it would be an obvious breach of the duty of loyalty for a computer salesperson, in off-duty hours, to attempt to sell a rival brand of computers to a potential customer of the principal.

The obligation not to compete may also be seen from another point of view. If an agent learns that an economic opportunity exists in which his or her principal may be interested, the agent must bring that opportunity to the attention of the principal. If the agent does not do so but, instead, takes personal advantage of the opportunity, then the agent has improperly competed with the principal. An *economic opportunity* is the chance to engage in a transaction or series of transactions upon which a potential profit may be made. The following hypothetical situation should make this obligation clear.

Abner is an advance scout for a popular recording company. His duty is to discover new performers and arrange for their auditions at his employer's recording studio with a view to possible recording contracts. Abner, hearing Lena sing, is certain that the young soprano can become a very popular performer. Instead of sending her to his principal's studio, Abner becomes Lena's manager and sells her services to another recording company. Clearly, Abner has seized for himself an economic opportunity that rightfully belonged to his principal. However, if Abner had told his principal about Lena and the principal had decided not to offer her a contract, then Abner would have been free to do so himself, for if a principal does not take advantage of a known economic opportunity an agent is free to appropriate it to his or her own benefit.

An agent who improperly takes advantage of an economic opportunity that should have been offered to a principal is subject to a court order, secured by the principal, which (1) directs the agent to turn the opportunity over to the principal, (2) enjoins the agent from continuing to compete with the principal, and (3) requires the agent to turn over to the principal any profits made by the agent through his or her improper actions.

Obligations of Principals to Agents

Just as agents owe duties and obligations to their principals, principals have parallel obligations to their agents. The agency agreement may spell out some of those obligations; others are implied. Among the principal's obligations are: (1) To compensate the agent for work or services performed (unless otherwise agreed), (2) to keep and render accounts, (3) to continue the employment of the agent for such period of time as had been agreed between them, and (4) to provide the agent with means to accomplish the work. If the agent is a servant (employee), then the principal has two additional obligations: (5) to provide a safe workplace, and (6) to ensure that the employee will be compensated for injuries sustained in the course of the employment.

Duty to Compensate Agent

A principal's obligations to an agent primarily center around the duty to compensate the agent for services rendered (unless the agent had agreed to serve gratuitously). Normally the rate of compensation is understood before an employee begins the work. If a servant-type agent is employed and the rate of compensation is not specified, then the employee is entitled to the reasonable value of his or her services based upon the customary pay scale within the community for the work or service performed. All states have laws which impose penalties upon employers who are delinquent in paying wages owed to their employees or who pay less than the minimum wage established by federal law.

Compensation to be paid to a nonservant type agent is established by contract between the parties. However, if no agreement had been made, then the agent is due the reasonable value of his or her services. Compensation to the agent may be dependent upon the result attained. In that event, the agent earns a commission, fee, or bonus. In the real estate business, unless some other specific agreement is made, a real estate broker employed by an owner to sell a property undertakes to find a buyer who is ready, able, and willing to purchase the property at the price and terms specified by the owner. If the agent finds such a buyer (and if, as required in some states, the owner had employed the agent by a written agreement), the agent is entitled to a commission even if the owner has a change of mind and decides not to go through with the sale.

A principal is also obligated to compensate or indemnify an agent for any costs or expenses the agent incurs on the principal's behalf in accordance with the terms of the agency.

In the following case a principal who caused an auctioneer to make misrepresentations in an auction sale was required to reimburse the auctioneer for the damage assessed against him because of those misstatements. It could be called a case of an unprincipled principal.

CASE 35.4 Castille v. Folck · 338 So.2d 328 (La. 1976)

FACTS Navarre, the owner of a mare named Flying Cobre, consigned the horse to auctioneer Folck for sale at auction. Navarre told Folck the horse had "a negative Coggins Test" and that a laboratory certificate would be given the purchaser attesting that the horse did not have swamp fever. Folck, relying on Navarre's representation, repeatedly told the bidders during and after the sale that Flying Cobre had been tested and had a favorable Coggins Test certificate. Navarre attended the auction but did nothing to contradict Folck's assertion of the existence of the certificate. Relying on Folck's representations while conducting the sale, Castille, the plaintiff, bid $4,000 and bought the mare. In fact, Flying Cobre had not had a Coggins Test and Castille was not given the promised certificate. Castille therefore brought suit against Folck for rescission of the sale, return of the sale price, and damages.

Folck deposited into court the purchase price (which had not yet been paid to Navarre) and he brought Navarre into the suit as a third party defendant, claiming that, as Navarre was the principal and Folck was his agent, Navarre was responsible for any judgment which might be rendered against Folck growing out of the transaction. The trial court ordered the sale rescinded and Folck was directed to compensate the plaintiff Castille for the damages he sustained. In addition, Navarre was ordered to reimburse Folck. Navarre appealed.

OPINION GUIDRY, J. . . . The trial court determined that a principal-agent relationship existed between Folck and Navarre. . . . The only issue for determination by this court is the correctness of that portion of the trial court judgment which awards . . . Folck judgment over against third party defendant Navarre. . . .

Prior to and up until the time of sale Navarre assured Folck that the brood mare "Flying Cobre" had been Coggins tested and that a Coggins certificate would be furnished to the purchaser. . . .

Folck must be held to compensate plaintiff [Castille] for the damage caused by his deliberate misrepresentation. . . .

It is generally held that a principal is under a duty to reimburse his agent for payment of damages which the agent is required to make to third persons on account of the authorized performance of an act which constitutes a tort or breach of contract. . . .

The trial court found, and we believe correctly so, that although Mr. Folck did misrepresent to prospective purchasers before and at the time of sale that the broodmare Flying Cobre had been Coggins tested, he did so based upon assurances to that effect from his principal. As stated by the trial judge in his written reasons for judgment:

> Mr. Navarre continuously represented to Mr. Folck that the horse had been Coggins tested and he continued to represent this even after the sale was completed. . . . He, no doubt, approved of this representation [by Folck] for he made no outward attempt to halt it. . . .

. . . [W]e conclude that third party defendant, Navarre, is obligated to reimburse his agent, Folck, for the amount of damages finally determined to have been incurred by plaintiff. . . .

JUDGMENT Judgment affirmed.

Duty to Keep and Render Accounts

A principal is obligated to keep whatever accounts are necessary to establish the amount of money due an agent for services rendered. In the event a principal fails to keep or to render proper accounts, the agent may bring a legal action against the principal called an *action for accounting.* The amount that is due is thereby established and the court directs the principal to make payment.

If the agent is an employee, the principal must make deductions from the employee's salary for Social Security, disability insurance, income tax, and any other deductions that may be required in that state, and augment these deductions with employer contributions as required by law.

Duty to Continue Employment of Agent

Among a principal's obligations to an agent is the duty to retain the agent in employment for the period understood between them when the agent is hired. This is called an *agency for a term.* If there is no understanding as to the length of the employment, an *agency at will* is established.

The tenure of a *nonservant* type agent is generally established by his or her oral or written agreement with the principal. The employment period of a *servant-type* agent is generally determined (1) by an oral understanding, or (2) by the time interval for which the employee is to be paid, as, for example, if payment is to be by the week it is understood the employee will be retained for at least that length of time, or (3) by the established employment practices of the employer, or (4) by the completion of the work the employee was hired to perform.

A promise by an employer to give an employee "permanent employment" generally means only that the employment is not a temporary, short-term job but one that may be expected to continue for a reasonable period and that the employee may be discharged after timely notice if he or she fails to perform satisfactorily or conditions dictate a reduction in force.

As stated by an Alabama court in 1986 (*McCluskey v. Unicorn Health Facility, Inc.*, 484 So.2d 398), "The general common law rule is that an [at will] employee is terminable at will. . . . An employment contract at will may be terminated by either party with or without cause or justification. A party may be discharged for a good reason, a wrong reason, or for no reason at all."

In recent years the once dominant rule that employers could "at will" dismiss workers not protected by union agreements has been softened in varying degrees by the courts of at least forty states. With increasing frequency courts are limiting an employer's unrestricted right to fire an at-will employee. Courts find that procedures established by personnel directives and handbooks or through an extended course of conduct may establish an implied agreement that an at-will employee may be discharged *only for cause* and, in many cases, that the decision to fire an employee must be arrived at after some impartial hearing. It has been held that a representation in a job advertisement which says, "This position offers a career opportunity," or "This position offers excellent pension benefits" is a sufficient inducement to an applicant for the job to limit the employer's right to fire him or her only for cause. Some courts go further and impose upon the employer the obligation to act with good faith and fair dealing before it can effectively discharge an employee.[1]

As a result of the inhibitions courts are placing on the firing of employees, disgruntled former employees with increasing frequency are charging into court to demand huge awards, not only for lost wages but also for emotional distress and punitive damages. Six-figure judgments are common in some states.

Employers are now turning to their state legislatures for relief. The State of Montana, for example, has enacted a law which provides nonunion employees with basic protections against arbitrary dismissal but it also limits the award a court may impose in the event a former employee is successful in his or her suit against a former employer.

The case which follows reflects the developing extension of the obligation of an employer to retain an employee in his or her employment.

[1] The effect of Title VII of the 1964 Civil Rights Act upon discrimination in hiring, promotion, and firing is taken up in Chapter 47.

CASE 35.5 Wagner v. City of Globe · 722 P.2d 250 (Ariz. 1986)

FACTS Wagner, the plaintiff, was hired in May, 1974, by the City of Globe as a police officer. The first six months of his employment were probationary. About two months after Wagner joined the force, he learned that an individual named Hicks was in jail for violating a city vagrancy

CASE 35.5 Continued

ordinance that had been repealed more than a year before. Although Hicks had been sentenced to 10 days confinement (apparently without trial), 21 days had gone by and he was still in jail. Wagner told the local magistrate that Hick's arrest and confinement were illegal. The magistrate talked to the Chief of Police who told Wagner he did not appreciate "big city cops coming to Globe to tell me how to run my department." In a few days Wagner received a notice from the Chief of Police that his employment was terminated. In May 1975 Wagner brought suit against the City for wrongful discharge. The trial court granted summary judgment for the defendant and Wagner appealed.

OPINION

GORDON, C. J. . . . Every employment contract for an indefinite term is presumed to be terminable at will. . . . All parties have agreed that Wagner was an "at-will" employee; that is, his employment was for an indefinite term, at sufferance, and the employment could be terminated by either party, at will, for no cause or any cause. . . . The principle, generally referred to as the employment-at-will doctrine, is uniquely a product of the American common law traced to an 1877 treatise. . . . The doctrine of employment-at-will found fertile ground in the laissez-faire climate of the nineteenth century and thrived until very recently. Increasingly, however, the doctrine is under attack . . . Today three-fifths of the states have some form of cause of action for "wrongful discharge." . . . The trend has been to modify the at-will doctrine by creating exceptions to its operation. Three major exceptions have been developed: the "implied contract" exception, which relies upon proof of an implied promise of continued employment absent just cause for termination to protect the legitimate expectations of workers; . . . the "public policy" exception, which permits recovery upon a finding that the employer's conduct undermined some important public policy; and the implied covenant of "good faith and fair dealing," which protects employees from termination for bad cause. . . .

The at-will employment relationship, despite its limitations, is nonetheless contractual. . . . [I]t can be modified by the parties at any time just as other contracts can be modified. Accordingly, the presumption that employment contracts of indefinite duration are terminable at will can be modified by the parties. . . .

One widely accepted means of modifying the at-will contract is use or publication of personnel manuals, guides, or rules by employers. An employer's representations contained in a personnel manual "can become terms of the employment contract and limit an employer's ability to discharge his or her employees". . . .

Employees should not have to choose between their jobs and the demands of important public policy interests; thus courts have developed the public policy exception to the at-will doctrine. Actions for wrongful discharge in breach of public policy are essentially breaches of duties imposed by law, and are best characterized as actions in tort rather than contract. . . .

The public policy exception defies easy application because different factual patterns have been collected under the same general rubric of "public policy." Perhaps the easiest and least controversial pattern involves an employee's refusal to participate in illegal behavior. . . . Another category encompasses those cases where an employee is discharged for performing an important public obligation (e.g., employees discharged for accepting jury duty). . . . A third type of case involves the discharge of employees who exercise a legal right or privilege. For example, numerous states have held that the termination of an employee because he had filed a workers compensation claim violates public policy. . . . [or] for signing a union membership application. . . . The fourth type . . . [of] case involves the employee "whistle-blower" who exposes wrongdoing on the part of his employer and is then discharged. . . .

We believe that the petitioner's behavior is best characterized as whistle-blowing behavior. Wagner took affirmative steps to investigate and rectify the illegal detention and called it to the attention of the police chief and city magistrate. . . . We believe that whistle-

CASE 35.5 Continued

blowing activity which serves a public purpose should be protected. . . . [A]ctions which enhance the enforcement of our laws or expose unsafe conditions, or otherwise serve some singularly public purpose, will inure to the benefit of the public. . . . There is no public policy more important or fundamental than the one favoring the effective protection of the lives, liberty, and property of our people. . . . The petitioner's successful attempt to free Hicks from illegal confinement was a refreshing and laudable exercise which should be protected, not punished. . . .

JUDGMENT Consequently the trial court should not have granted summary judgment against the petitioner. . . Reversed.

Duty to Provide Means to Accomplish the Work

Normally, a principal need not furnish a nonservant agent with the means to accomplish the agent's task. However, a principal (employer) is obligated to furnish a *servant-type agent* (an employee) with the means necessary to accomplish the task for which he or she was hired if the agent's compensation is dependent upon the results to be accomplished. For example, a salesperson on commission should usually be furnished samples or descriptive literature; and a brickmason who is paid by the number of bricks laid in a day should be supplied with the bricks, mortar, and scaffolding required to do the job. An employer who does not furnish an employee with the means to do the work breaches the employee's contract of employment and is liable for any damages the employee suffers.

A principal must not place any agent (either servant or nonservant) in a position that jeopardizes the agent's future employment. For instance, a principal may not require an agent to perform an illegal or unethical act. If the principal attempts to do so, the agent may refuse to obey such instructions without violating his or her contractual or agency obligations to the principal.

Duty to Provide Safe Workplace

Not only must an employer furnish an employee with the means to accomplish the work for which he or she was hired, but of even greater importance is the requirement that all employers must furnish their employees with a safe place in which to work. National interest in working conditions led to the enactment of the Occupational Safety and Health Act of 1970. Under the authority of that act, the Secretary of Labor, through the Occupational Safety and Health Administration (OSHA), promulgates safety and health standards which must be adhered to by all employers. These standards are designed to assure that places of employment are free from hazards likely to cause death, injury, or sickness to employees.

Duty to Compensate Agent for Injuries

In discussing the right of an agent to be compensated for injuries suffered in the course of employment, we must again make the distinction between nonservant agents and servant-type agents. Unless a specific understanding to the contrary exists, a *nonservant* agent is *not* entitled to compensation for injuries sustained while performing services for a principal because the principal does not have the right to control the physical activities of such an agent. A servant-type agent is, however, entitled to compensation for injuries sustained while in the scope of employment because the principal (master) has the right to control the physical activities of such an agent (a servant). The right of a principal to control an agent's physical activities is discussed at length in Chapters 33 and 34.

This distinction might be clearer with illustrations. (1) Assume that you employ a real estate agent, Ruth, to sell your house. She is injured in an automobile accident while taking a prospective customer to view your property. Ruth is a nonservant type agent and you are not liable for Ruth's injuries. (2) Assume that a teacher, in the course of conducting a physical education class on a concrete playground, fractures his kneecap. The teacher is a servant-type agent and he or she may look to the school authorities for compensation.

Under the common law, a servant-type agent injured in the course of employment had great difficulty in securing compensation for work-related injuries. If the claim went to trial the worker had two almost insurmountable obstacles to overcome—the fellow-servant rule and the assumption-of-risk rule. Under the former, a worker could not recover if the injuries were caused by another worker (a fellow servant). Under the latter rule, a worker was held to have assumed all risks of the place of employment and of the tools and machinery upon which he or she worked. Therefore, if an injury was, for example, sustained because a drill press did not have a guard rail, if a workroom was poorly lit, or if protective clothing was not furnished, the worker was presumed to have assumed the risks of injury that might flow from that employment.

All states now have workers' compensation laws which supplant the common law, do away with the fellow-servant and assumption-of-risk defenses, and assure without a law suit that a worker will be compensated for injury or disease growing out of his or her employment. Special commissions decide the degree and permanency of an injury and apply an established compensation schedule. However, compensation under that schedule does not include payment for pain and suffering and the amounts allowed are less than could have been expected if recovery followed a successful law suit. Chapter 47 discusses workers' compensation in detail.

Remedies of Principals and Agents for Breach of Obligations

When the obligations owed by agents to principals and by principals to agents were discussed on earlier pages, the remedies for breaches of those obligations were noted in general terms. Many remedies are available and often several may be applied at the same time. An agent's recourse against a principal who does not properly fulfill his or her obligations depends, in large part, upon the contractual understandings between them and, if the agent is a servant, upon applicable statutory law designed to protect employees.

The remedies of a principal and of an agent may be grouped in the following manner:

Remedies of Principal

For breach of obligations by an agent, a principal may, under appropriate facts:

- Discharge the agent
- Withhold compensation
- Recover any secret profit made by the agent
- Recover, or impose a trust upon, any money or property gained or held by the agent to which the principal is entitled
- Restrain the agent by court injunction from continuing to breach his or her agency obligations
- Recover damages from the agent for breach of the contract of employment
- Secure reimbursement from the agent for any damages owing to a third party assessed against the principal because of the agent's wrongdoing
- Rescind a contract entered into by an agent for the principal in which there was a bribe or other improper inducement offered or paid to the agent by a third party

Remedies of Agent

For breach of obligations by a principal, an agent may, under appropriate facts:

- Refuse to continue his or her employment
- Bring legal action to force his or her reinstatement in employment
- Recover damages for the principal's breach of the employment contract
- Rescind the employment agreement and recover the value of any services rendered
- Bring an action for an accounting
- Secure reimbursement for payments made by the agent for the principal
- Secure indemnity for or exoneration from personal liability sustained while performing an authorized act for the principal
- Enforce a lien if authorized by statute
- Seek administrative or statutory relief from appropriate government agencies

Termination of Agency

Methods of Termination

An agency relationship may terminate (1) by reason of some limitation within the agency agreement, (2) by subsequent mutual assent, (3) by decision of one of the parties, or (4) by operation of law.

Termination by Provision in Agency Agreement. Where an agency is created for a specified purpose, the agency terminates automatically when that purpose has been accomplished. If John is hired to work on the construction of a building, his employment ends when the building is completed. Similarly, if the agreement states that the agency is to exist for a specified period of time, the agency terminates automatically when that time has run.

Termination by Mutual Assent. Since an agency is created by mutual assent, it can be terminated by mutual assent even if the parties may have originally agreed that the agency would continue for a longer time.

Termination by Decision of One Party. Because an agency is a consensual arrangement, either a principal or an agent may terminate it either orally or in writing or through actions which demonstrate that the agency relationship no longer exists. However, if one of the parties terminates the agency before the agreed time, he or she is liable to the other in damages. If a servant improperly terminates the agency relationship, the employer cannot force the employee to continue to perform his or her work, as that would be tantamount to involuntary servitude and therefore unconstitutional. However, if *an employer* improperly terminates the employment, he or she may be required to continue the employment of that agent.

Termination by Operation of Law. The phrase termination by operation of law denotes a termination which does not result from a decision of one or both of the parties. Termination by operation of law occurs in the following ways:

Death of principal or agent. The general rule is that the power of an agent to act for a principal ceases when his or her principal dies. As it is impossible for there to be an agent without a principal, if an agent enters into an agreement with a third party on behalf of a deceased principal, the agreement is void even if the agent had no knowledge of the death. The termination of an agency under these circumstances may adversely affect both the agent and the third party because (1) the agent had impliedly warranted that he or she (the agent) had authority so to act, but since that authority ceased with the death of the principal the agent may be liable on that warranty and (2) since no agreement between the third party and the principal came into being, the third party has no right of action against the principal's estate to enforce performance of the agreement. In addition, even though the agent may be liable on his or her warranty, the third party cannot force the agent to perform the contract for the now deceased principal. Because these hardships may result, some state laws now provide that if neither the agent nor the third party knew of the principal's death when they entered into their agreement, the estate of the deceased principal may be required to perform.

Permanent disability of principal or agent. If a permanent disability prevents either a principal or agent from being able to function as such, the agency terminates.

Loss of qualification of principal or agent. The failure of a principal or agent to obtain or retain a required franchise or license may result in the termination of the agent's authority. For instance, if Alice employs Hortense as her lawyer and Hortense is later disbarred, the disbarrment terminates Hortense's authority to represent Alice.

Impossibility of performance. The authority of an agent is terminated when the accomplishment of the agency purpose becomes impossible. Thus, if Carl is employed to sell Dan's automobile, the destruction of the automobile terminates Carl's authority.

Subsequent illegality. A change of law that makes performance of an agent's duties illegal also terminates the agency relationship. Suppose that the Axis Company manufactures and sells slot machines. Hazel is an independent out-of-state distributor for the company's slot machines. Subsequent enactment of a federal law making the interstate shipment of slot machines illegal would terminate the agency relationship.

Important change of circumstances. The authority of an agent also terminates when there is such a change in the affairs of the principal, or in the subject matter of the agency, or in external events, that the agent should reasonably infer that the principal would not desire the agent to act under the changed circumstances. Suppose a farmer employs an agent to sell his farm because he cannot borrow enough money to pay his taxes and buy needed farm machinery. If the agent learns that oil has been discovered on the farmer's land, the changed circumstance results in revocation of the agent's authority.

Notice to Third Parties of Termination

Notice When Termination Is by Act of Principal or Agent. When an agency is terminated by one or both of the parties to an agency agreement, the principal should give prompt notice of the termination to all persons who did business with the agent or who may have known of the agency. Failure to do so may leave the agent with *apparent authority* to continue to represent the principal. (Apparent authority is explained in Chapter 33.) If an agent, after termination of the agency still retains apparent authority, he or she continues to have the *power* (though not the *right*) to bind his or her principal contractually to a third party who acts in reasonable reliance upon that apparent authority.

To illustrate: Angus is employed by Prime Foundry to sell its widgets. Angus has sold widgets to the Jones Company in the past and Prime has always shipped the widgets in accordance with the orders Angus secured. Prime thereby clothed Angus with apparent authority to act for it in transactions with Jones. If Prime discharges Angus and terminates the agency, Angus still has the *apparent authority* to act as Prime's agent and to bind Prime in transactions with the Jones Company unless Jones in some way learns or is notified that the agency no longer exists. Thus, if Angus, after being fired, and with no notice being given to Jones, takes orders for widgets from Jones and unscrupulously pockets a cash down payment, Prime is legally bound to ship the widgets to Jones. Of course, Prime can bring suit against Angus to recover the money he took, but how much simpler it would have been for Prime to have notified all Angus's customers, including Jones, that Angus was no longer representing the firm.

In order to bring an end to an agent's apparent authority when an agency is terminated by the parties, the principal should give *actual* notice of the termination to all persons who had purchased Prime's products through the agent's solicitation. *Constructive* notice should be given to those parties who might have known of the agency but who had not previously done business with the principal through the agent. *Constructive notice* is brought about by placing a notice in the "Legal Notices" column of a newspaper of general circulation where the agency business is regularly carried on. The notice states that the named agent is no longer employed by the principal. Interestingly enough, a constructive notice is binding upon even those third parties who did not read the notice carried in the newspapers.

Notice When Termination Is by Operation of Law. The general rule is that when an agency terminates by operation of law, apparent authority automatically ceases without the need for any notice being given to third parties.

Summary

In return for the trust and confidence a principal reposes in an agent, an agent owes fiduciary duties to the principal. Among those obligations are the duty (1) to use ordinary care and skill in the work or service unless the agent obligates himself or herself to a higher standard, (2) to obey reasonable instructions given by the principal, (3) to perform the work or service personally, (4) to communicate to the principal any notice received for the principal or any knowledge of matters concerning the agency which the agent ought reasonably to know would be of interest to the principal, (5) to keep and render such accounts as the work or service requires, and (6) to be loyal to the principal.

In essence, the duty of loyalty means that an agent may not act adversely to the principal's interests. Pursuant to that obligation, an agent must pay to the principal any secret profit or other benefit he or she may have obtained above his or her regular salary or commission. As an agent may not act adversely to a principal, an agent may not at the same time represent both a principal and a third party to a transaction unless both those parties consent. Furthermore, an agent may not become the third party to a transaction carried on for a principal without the latter's consent for otherwise the agent would be representing conflicting interests. It follows that an agent whose duties involve selling something for a principal may not, without the principal's consent, buy the article; and an agent whose duty it is to buy, may not sell his or her own property to the principal. It is also axiomatic that an agent cannot use for his or her own benefit confidential information, such as trade secrets, belonging to a principal.

When an agent violates fiduciary duties, a principal may (1) terminate the agency, (2) withhold compensation that would have been due the agent had there been no violation of duties, and (3) recover such damage as the agent may have caused the principal. A principal may also rescind a contract an agent made with a third party where that party used illegal means such as paying a bribe to the agent to induce him or her to enter into the contract on behalf of his or her principal.

A principal's obligations to an agent involve the duty (1) to pay the agent compensation expressly or tacitly agreed between them, (2) to keep and render accounts, (3) to continue the agent in employment as agreed, (4) to provide a servant-type agent with the means to accomplish the work, (5) to provide a servant-type agent a safe workplace, and (6) to compensate a servant-type agent for injuries sustained while performing the job.

An agency agreement, being personal to the parties, terminates at the will of either of them or when its purpose is accomplished. It is terminated by operation of law when either of the parties dies or becomes permanently incapacitated, or when either party ceases to be qualified to act, or when the purpose of the agency becomes impossible or illegal.

An agent's apparent authority to act may sometimes continue after his or her actual authority has ceased. To terminate a continuing apparent authority, actual notice must be given to third parties who did business with the agent and notice by publication (constructive notice) must be given to those who may have known of the agency but had not previously done business with the agent.

Review Questions

1 **(a)** Why is the distinction between servant and nonservant agent, which was so important in the previous agency chapters, relatively unimportant in the context of obligations of principals and agents to one another? **(b)** Why does the law hold principals and agents to high ethical standards toward one another?

2 What is meant by a "fiduciary relationship" between principals and agents?

3 Distinguish between the degree of care owed by an agent who is an expert and an agent who is not an expert.

4 Discuss the authority of **(a)** a servant and **(b)** a nonservant agent to delegate his or her duties.

5 **(a)** What is the difference between "knowledge" and "notice" in the law of agency? **(b)** Do you think the duties owed by an agent concerning the communication of information to his or her principal are fair and reasonable? Why or why not?

6 **(a)** What is meant by an agent's duty of loyalty to his or her principal? **(b)** Is the duty of loyalty consistent with arms-length bargaining by employees with their employers for higher wages and improved work conditions? Give reasons for your answer.

7 Assume that an agent who is attempting to sell certain property for her principal, without the principal's knowledge also gives advice to the buyer, suggesting a price the buyer might offer for the property. The owner accepts the buyer's offer. The principal later discovers that the agent had also acted for the buyer. Would the principal be acting both legally and ethically if he refused to pay the agent the commission she expected on the sale? Why or why not?

8 Can an individual apply in his or her own business any information gained while working for someone else? Explain.

9 What is meant by a "trade secret"? by the "shopright privilege"?

10 **(a)** Give an illustration of an "economic opportunity." **(b)** Comment upon this statement: "The essence of free trade and of a free society is that every individual is free to take advantage of any opportunity he or she discovers and can afford."

11 What obligations does a principal owe to his or her agent?

12 **(a)** May an agency created by a *written* instrument be terminated before its normal conclusion by an *oral* notice of revocation of one of the parties to the other? **(b)** What might be the consequences?

13 You have a jewelry store in Chicago. Chris, who lives in Florida, has left with you a valuable necklace to sell on commission. You sell it to Mrs. Richards, who pays in cash and you deliver the necklace to her. You then send the money you received, less your commission, to Chris. However, unknown to you or to Mrs. Richards, Chris died 3 days before the sale. **(a)** Is the sale of the necklace binding on Chris's estate? **(b)** If the executor of her estate is displeased with the sale and offers to reimburse Mrs. Richards when the necklace is returned, what are the rights and liabilities of all of the parties?

14 When a principal gives notice to a third party that an agent is no longer employed by the principal, how is the notice given?

15 How do ethical standards in business, discussed in Chapters 1 and 2 of this book, apply to the principal-agent relationship?

Case Problems

1 Tom, employed as a driver by the Tanksley Trucking Company, was driving a company truck behind a car driven by Garcia. Tom repeatedly blew his horn, in effect asking Garcia to move to his right so that Tom could pass him. After a considerable interval, Garcia drove his car to the right, giving Tom room to pass. Tom, quite angry by this time, passed Garcia's vehicle so closely that it touched the vehicle and damaged it. Garcia sued Tanksley Trucking Company and secured a judgment. Thereupon, without Tom's consent, Tanksley withheld a portion of Tom's pay each week in order to secure reimbursement for the sum it was required to pay to satisfy the judgment. After several weeks, Tom gave up his job and sued to recover the amounts withheld from his pay. Should Tom succeed? Why or why not?

2 So that Miles could buy a house, he arranged to borrow money from the Perpetual Savings & Loan Association and for Perpetual to handle the closing (consummation) of Miles's purchase of the property. As one element of the closing, Perpetual secured a termite inspection of the property. It showed that the house was infested with termites and that their eradication would cost $450. Perpetual's representative attempted unsuccessfully to have the seller of the house pay for the termite eradication but did not bring the report to Miles's attention. After Miles moved into the house he discovered the termites and he spent $450 for the necessary corrective action. He sought reimbursement from Perpetual. The association replied that its duties were only to handle the "closing" of the sale of the property and that it performed these duties. Perpetual further stated that if Miles wants repayment for the costs of the termite work he should look to the seller of the property. Was Perpetual correct? Why or why not?

3 Burg was the manager of the molding department of the Precision Tool Company; his employment was at will. Burg was authorized, in an emergency, to buy production parts from outside manufacturers. Without his employer's knowledge, Burg organized a small machine shop with Horace as its manager, from which Burg bought needed supplies for Precision Tool. When his employers learned of this they discharged him. Burg sued Precision, saying that he was wrongfully fired because he never charged Precision more than the going market price for any supplies he purchased from his company for Precision. Should Burg recover? Discuss.

4 Green, a property owner, contracted with Smith, an architect, to draw plans for a building on the land and to supervise its construction. Kirkpatrick was the electrical contractor on the job. The construction was regularly inspected by Smith and when the work was finished he gave Green a "Certificate of Completion" certifying that all work had been done in accordance with the plans and specifications. About a month later a fire, determined to have been caused by faulty electrical work, broke out in the building. Do you concur that Green should sue Kirkpatrick to recover the resulting loss?

5 Orly was a director of the MAI Corporation. At a director's meeting Orly learned that, because of snow storms, the corporation had lost a good deal of money. He knew that when the next financial statement of the corporation was published, the price of its shares of stock would go down. Orly therefore sold 1,000 shares of MAI stock that he owned. The next month the financial report of the corporation was published and, as Orly had anticipated, the price of its stock fell. Orly then bought back 1,000 shares of MAI stock at $5,000 less than he had sold his stock for, thereby making a profit of that amount on his transactions. When the treasurer of MAI learned of Orly's maneuver, MAI sued Orly for the profit he had made. Should the corporation win the lawsuit? Why or why not?

6 Colquin sold insurance for Group Association Plans, Inc. The sale of group insurance requires a good deal of effort, time, and many conferences. Colquin asked for a raise in salary but when Group Association refused, he quit and went to work for a competitor insurance agency. Colquin continued his sales efforts among a number of companies with whom he had negotiated partially completed contracts for his former employer, but now he carried on the negotiations with the objective of selling those customers his new employer's policies. He was successful and consummated several contracts for his new company. Group Association Plans brought suit against both Colquin and his new employer to enjoin Colquin from soliciting his former clients and for damages. Should Group Association succeed? Why or why not?

7 Jose Davos was the grounds keeper of the newly remodeled Bay View Golf Club. He had so improved the course that he was given a new 3-year contract of employment with a raise in pay. The contract stated that the golf club would not, during the life of the contract, reduce or otherwise modify Jose's authority and he, in turn, agreed to continue in Bay View's employ for the full 3 years. Jose's reputation had so spread that 6 months after signing the new employment contract he was offered the grounds keeper's job at the exclusive Queen's Golf Club at a much higher salary. Jose left Bay View and went to work for Queen's. What should be the outcome of Bay View's suit to enjoin Jose's breach of his employment obligation? Why?

ETHICS IN PRACTICE

Like other areas of law, agency law reflects ethical norms. For example, a master's liability for the servant's torts is consistent with the widely held belief that a person should refrain from harming others without justification. The law of labor and employment (a close relative of agency law, discussed in Part Eleven) also reflects ethical concerns. Worker's compensation acts; federal labor legislation; the Civil Rights Act; legislation concerning equal pay for equal work, occupational health and safety, and pension reform; and other statutes express or imply value judgments about what is right and appropriate for mitigating the harshness and inequities of the workplace.

Agency law not only reflects ethical norms; it incorporates them as part of the law. For example, parties to ordinary business transactions deal with each other "at arm's length," i.e., as wary strangers. In arm's length transactions, a party sometimes can act unethically without violating the law. In contrast, in agency law a fiduciary relationship exists between principal and agent. Ethical and legal obligations merge, and conduct that breaches ethical standards—especially those pertaining to the agent's duty of loyalty and the principal's duties of fair dealing—also violates the law.

The following problems deal with conflicts-of-interest typical of principal-agent relations. Ethical concerns relating to labor and employment law are addressed in Part Eleven.

Problems in Ethics

1 You are a financial planner who advises a number of unsophisticated investors of modest means. Your main source of income is the commissions you receive from the sale of financial products that you recommend to your clients, who never inquire about commission rates. Commissions vary considerably among the products you sell. On a client investment of $10,000, you would receive the following commissions: Limited partnership, $600–$1,000; common stock newly issued to the public, $300–$1,000; annuities and life insurance products, $400–$600; common stock traded on the New York Stock Exchange, $200–$250; U.S. government securities, $50. Risk of loss is greatest for limited partnerships and least for government securities. **(a)** Does this commission structure pose an ethical problem for you? **(b)** If so, how would you resolve it?

2 Certified public accountants customarily charge clients an hourly rate for financial planning and other services. Recently, some CPA financial planners have wanted to quit charging by the hour and to rely instead on commissions for the sale of financial products to their clients. This practice is prohibited by the profession's code of ethics and frowned on by a majority of accountants. However, arguing that the ban on sales commissions is anticompetitive, the Federal Trade Commission is pressuring the AIPCA, the accounting profession's national association, to revise its code of ethics to permit the practice. At the urging of its state board of accountancy, California recently passed a law prohibiting accountants from receiving commissions or referral fees. The FTC cannot overturn this law. Five states permit accountants to accept sales commissions. Furthermore, the National Association of State Boards of Accountancy has proposed a new model code for state boards to adopt. Under the new code, an accountant can charge a sales commission on financial products that he or she advises a client to buy and can accept a referral fee for sending a client to another adviser, but must tell the client in writing that the accountant is collecting commissions or referral fees. You are a new CPA in a state that does not prohibit such compensation. You are unsure whether to charge an hourly rate for financial planning advice or to rely on sales commissions and referral fees. How will your decision be affected by the following? **(a)** Commissions and fees will produce substantially greater revenues for you than will the hourly rate that you can charge for financial planning services. **(b)** Financial planning will constitute about 50 percent of your business. **(c)** Accountants traditionally have been conservative in their investment advice, generally recommending liquidity, debt avoidance, and low-risk investments. **(d)** The highest commissions are paid on the riskiest investments. **(e)** Most accountants prize their professional objectivity and consider it a major reason for the good public image accountants enjoy. **(f)** There is a marked difference of opinion among legal authorities and within the accountancy profession about the propriety of commissions and fees for CPAs.

3 Bob is employed as a salesperson for the Best Electrical Company. He is told by his superior that Best Electrical is working on an electric light bulb which will have a practically indestructible lighting element. Although the new bulb has not yet reached the testing stage, Bob is given literature and told to take orders for the bulb and to receive a 10 percent deposit with each order. Bob knows that Best Electric is undercapitalized and is asking for the deposit money in order to secure funds with which to complete the bulb's development. Bob is instructed not to reveal this to his customers. Bob has reason to believe that the bulb cannot be perfected and that the customers who have paid deposits will most likely not be able to get refunds. What should Bob do? Why?

PART TEN

Business Organizations

CHAPTER 36

Introduction to Business Organizations; Formation of Partnerships; Rights and Duties of Partners

If you decide to start a business one of the first steps you must take is to determine what kind of business organization you will adopt. For all practical purposes there are four different types of business structures to choose from. The degree of personal control you will be able to exercise over your business and the extent to which you will be personally liable to its creditors will be dictated by the form of organization you use. The more control you retain, the greater will be your personal liability; diminishing control and diminishing personal liability go hand in hand with increasing complexity of the business structure.

In this and the succeeding seven chapters we will examine the four most common forms of business organizations and discuss the rights, obligations, and liabilities of the members of those firms.

Forms of Business Organizations

In ascending order of complexity but, at the same time, in descending order of owner control and personal liability for company debts, the four common forms of business organizations are: (1) sole proprietorship (the simplest form with the owner's greatest degree of personal control and liability), (2) general partnerships (including joint ventures), (3) limited partnerships, and (4) corporations (the most complex form with the least degree of personal control and liability).

Sole Proprietorship

When you are the sole owner (proprietor) of a business, the state exercises a minimum of control over how you operate that business. But since you have the maximum personal control over the enterprise, you are subject to full personal responsibility for all its debts.

Under most circumstances you may, as a sole proprietor, engage in any type of business you choose. You will merely be obligated to pay a license fee required of all businesses and to comply with any laws that may be applicable to the type of business you operate. Such applicable laws are, for example, zoning ordinances, laws governing advertising signs and store closing hours, and employee wage, hour, and compensation laws. As sole proprietor, you are in complete charge of your company's operations. If you require additional funds to carry on the business, you may be able to borrow from a bank or elsewhere and you may pledge the assets of the business as security for repayment of your loans or you may be required to pledge your house or other personal assets. You are entitled to all the profits the business makes and these profits are your personal earnings. You may dictate who will inherit your business in the event of your death by provisions in your will or trust unless you prefer to allow state laws of descent and distribution to apply to your estate (see Chapter 23).

A primary drawback to doing business as a sole proprietor is that, as sole owner, you alone are personally liable for all debts the business incurs and you may not have the resources or credit required by an expanding business.

Partnership

If you elect to establish a business in which you share ownership and control with one or more person(s), you can form either a *general partnership,* a *joint venture,* or a *limited partnership.* With more than one person involved in the ownership of the business, the organization is more complex than that of a sole proprietorship. Duties and obligations are assumed by you and your partners which are not present in a sole proprietorship.

If you form a *general partnership,* you and your copartner(s) may carry on almost any kind of business activity that you wish with only a minimum of government control. This type of organization is particularly appropriate for a small business which is owned by two or more people, each of whom desires to have a voice in its management. Usually, each member contributes, as his or her investment in the enterprise, money, property of some kind, work, or service. Like a sole proprietorship, each partner is personally liable for all the company's debts and each partner owes special legal obligations to his or her copartners.

A *joint venture* differs from a general partnership in that its business is of a more narrow scope and duration, usually being organized to carry out a single undertaking or a series of related undertakings expected to have a fairly short life span. The laws governing general partnerships generally apply equally to joint ventures.

Limited Partnership

In this form of organization, one or more of the partners (the general partners) manage the business while the the others (the limited partners) merely invest in the enterprise and have very limited rights in its management. If you become a general partner in a limited partnership you will be personally liable for the firm's debts just as is any partner in an ordinary partnership. If you become a limited partner, however, you have no personal liability. You will be essentially only an investor in the enterprise with but slight voice in its management. Limited partnerships are discussed at length in Chapter 38.

Corporation

Instead of establishing a sole proprietorship or a business in one of the partnership forms, you may find that a corporation best suits your needs. Of the four types of business organizations, the *corporation* has the most complicated structure. A corporation is established by a charter from the state and is a separate legal entity apart from its owners. This form of organization is particularly suited to large and complex enterprises. It may also be the organization of choice if the parties recognize they are starting a business whose success may be problematic and who do not want to place their personal resources at risk in the event the business should fail. The shareholders of a corporation, who may number in the thousands, are its owners. They have no voice in its day to day management and they have no liability for its debts, but they do share in the company's earnings.

This chapter discusses the organization of general partnerships (including joint ventures) and the rights and duties of partners; Chapter 37 deals with the dissolution and termination of partnerships; limited partnerships are described in Chapter 38; and Chapters 39 through 43 discuss corporations.

Formation of Partnerships

Partnership Law

The partnership form of business organization has an ancient legal lineage, having been used in classical Greek and Roman days. Partnership law is a part of the common law. In the United States partnership law has been modernized and codified in the Uniform Partnership Act (UPA). As the chapter progresses you will occasionally notice section numbers within parentheses; these refer to sections of the UPA which is reprinted in the appendix.

The UPA has been adopted in almost all the states. However the UPA does not completely cover all aspects of partnership law. On questions where the Act is silent and there is no applicable state law, the common law still governs. For instance, the UPA makes no provision for suit either by or against a partnership and state laws control.

What Is a Partnership?

A general partnership is a voluntary association of two or more persons to carry on, as co-owners, a business for profit (UPA 6). (Henceforth in Chapters 36, 37, and 38, the single word "partnership" will denote a general partnership.)

Under the common law a partnership is considered to be only a group or aggregate of people who constitute the firm. A partnership is not of itself a legal entity. Because of this concept:

- A partnership comes to an end when one of its members dies. If the surviving partner or partners continue to carry on the business, the new organization is either a sole proprietorship (if only one of the former partners continues the business) or a new partnership (if more than one of the former members continue it).

- Only in states where there exists specific statutory authority may a partnership sue or be sued in its own name (rather than in the names of its members personally).
- Each partner is personally liable for the firm's debts.

Requirements for Establishing a Partnership

A partnership comes into being when two or more persons associate together (1) to carry on as co-owners a business, (2) for profit. If their arrangement does not satisfy those two requisites then they have not formed a partnership even if it had been their intention to do so. Conversely, if their arrangement does fulfill those two requisites then they *have* formed a partnership and are subject to partnership obligations and liabilities even if they did not so intend.

To illustrate this rule, assume that Ben's father owns a vacant lot. He wants to help Ben get established in business. The two decide to operate an automobile wrecking business on that lot. Ben, who has the necessary tools, will do all the work. Ben's father puts up the necessary money to begin the business and they agree to divide whatever profits the enterprise earns. Although both Ben and his father contend that they are not partners, nonetheless they have formed a partnership.

Or suppose you and Harry organize an enterprise which you name Mariner's Partnership. Your stated purpose is to encourage the development of the city marina as a recreational area. Since your association is not a business for profit, you have not formed a legal partnership and partnership law is not applicable to it even though you have given it that name.

Because a partnership may be implied from the actions of the parties involved, immersing them in legal problems they did not anticipate, it is good practice that when people do business together as a partnership they should have a firm agreement setting forth the respective rights, duties, and obligations of each of them. There is no particular form in which a partnership agreement must be expressed. Although it may be either oral or written, individuals who form a partnership should, in their own best interests, reduce their agreement to writing. A well-drawn partnership agreement describes the activities the firm will carry on, how it will be conducted, the functions of each of the partners, the money, property, or work contributions each of them will make to the enterprise, and the circumstances under which the partnership will come to an end. The agreement will also describe how the partnership's assets and property will be disposed of when the business comes to an end or in the event one of the partners retires, becomes permanently incapacitated, or dies. Since a partnership agreement can be lengthy and complex, it should be prepared with the assistance of a lawyer.

Partners to Be Co-owners. For a business to be a partnership, the members must have agreed that all of them are co-owners of the business. Co-ownership involves (1) sharing the profits and losses of the enterprise [UPA 7, 15, 18(a)], and (2) sharing the right to engage in its management unless the partners agree otherwise. The receipt of a share of the profits of a business is prima facie evidence that the individual is a partner in the business, but such an inference cannot be drawn if the profits were received in payment of a debt, wages, rent, or interest on a loan [UPA 7(4)], or if the person receiving a share of the profits is not responsible for the concern's debts and obligations. Two examples will give meaning to these rules. Suppose Mary's father lends Mary and Jim, who are partners, $5,000 for their business. They all agree that no interest will be paid on the loan but, instead, Dad will receive a percentage of the profits the business earns until the loan is repaid. Dad is not a partner in the business; he is merely a *creditor*. By way of another example, say Mary and Jim hire Mabel to manage the store owned by their partnership. They agree that Mabel will receive 25 percent of the store's profits as her compensation. Mabel is an *employee* of the store and not a partner. In each of these illustrations there is no community of ownership by Dad or Mabel in the business itself and they are not personally responsible to the creditors of the firm. Therefore, neither Dad nor Mabel is a partner in the business.

A Business for Profit. The second leg upon which a partnership rests is that the partners intend their business to make a profit [UPA 6(1)] even if, in fact, no profit is earned. The UPA includes within "business" every trade, occupation, or profession (UPA 2). Therefore, any profit-oriented enterprise undertaken jointly by two or more parties is subject to partnership law. Certain organizations, such as a religious community, a patriotic or civic society, a college fraternity, or a fraternal order, are not organized for profit. These, therefore, are not partnerships.

A partnership may begin business with any amount of capital or with no capital at all. Contributions of the partners may vary widely: for example, a contribution may consist of money, services, property of any kind, a patent, a license, some kind of skill or know-how, the value of a person's name or credit standing, or merely the joint desire of the members. However, the law does not dictate that an individual must make any contribution to a partnership at all in order to become a partner.

The partnership business may be for some particular term stated in the partnership agreement or it may be a *partnership at will,* meaning one in which the length of the life of the partnership is unspecified.

Partnership Name

There is no legal requirement that a partnership adopt a name but frequently a partnership does business under some made-up or fictitious name. For example, it may adopt a name such as the "Tasty Food Coffee Shop." Doing business under a firm name rather than in the name of one of the partners permits the organization to create an identity which may be economically advantageous. In addition, a firm name tends to minimize questions as to whether an act or property is that of the partnership or of the partner in whose name the act is undertaken or in whose name property is held.

It should be recognized, however, that the use of a firm name is not conclusive evidence a partnership exists or that the individual whose name appears as part of a firm name is a partner. There is a possibility that the business is a sole proprietorship operating under a fictitious name. Also, partnerships, such as well-known law firms and brokerage houses, frequently continue to use within the firm name the name of a partner long since dead.

When a fictious name is adopted, the so-called fictitious name statutes (also called "doing business as," or DBA statutes) present in practically all states must be complied with. These laws require the registration of fictitious business names so that creditors can discover the identity of the individuals who are responsible for the firm's debts and upon whom service of legal process may be secured.

Who May Be a Partner?

In General. Any person who has the legal capacity to enter into a contract may enter into a partnership agreement. "Person" includes an individual, a partnership, a corporation (if authorized by its charter), and any other association (UPA 2). Therefore, a partnership may be one of the partners in another partnership.

No one can become a member of a partnership that is being organized or one that is already in being without the consent of *all* the members of the organization. This is called the principle of *delectus personae,* a Latin phrase meaning "choice of person." The reason why consent of all partners is required is, as we will see, that in a partnership each partner may become obligated to third parties by the actions of any of the copartners and so each member must place great trust and confidence in his or her copartners. Each partner, for his or her own protection, is therefore given the right to refuse admission to the partnership of any proposed new member.

Minors As Partners. Under ordinary contract law, minors may enter into contracts. It follows that a minor can enter into a valid partnership agreement either with adults or with other minors. A minor has the same rights as the other partners in the management of the business, including the right to incur debts for the partnership and to share in its profits.

Recognition must, however, be given to the contract law rule that a minor may, during minority, disaffirm ("get out of") his or her ordinary contracts. Thus, a minor who joined a partnership may, at any time during minority, disaffirm his or her agreement to be a member of the firm and may withdraw from it without being liable for breach of contract. However, any contributions the minor may have made to the partnership assets remain subject to the claims of those creditors who extended credit to the partnership during the minor's association with the firm. In some states, after disaffirmance any money a minor had contributed can be used by the partnership to pay for any losses it suffered during the time the minor was a member; in other states the minor's capital contribution must be returned to him or her without deducting for such losses. After disaffirmance, if the minor had not contributed the full amount of money or property he or she was supposed to put into the firm, the minor need not pay the balance.

A minor who does not disassociate from a partnership upon reaching the age of majority is personally bound for all liabilities incurred by the firm during the entire time he or she is a member.

Dormant Partner. Just as partners may, in their agreement, assign different duties and managerial functions to different partners, they may also agree that a partner may be dormant. A *dormant partner* (sometimes called a *silent* or *secret partner*) is a true member of a partnership with all rights and liabilities as such. However, a dormant partner's name is not used in the partnership business and his or her membership in the firm is not generally known by persons who do business with it. A dormant partner might elect this role, for example, if he or she is employed by another business in the town and wants to participate in the partnership but prefers that, for personal reasons, the community not know of this second financial venture.

Partners by Estoppel. Under certain circumstances an individual may have partnership liabilities as a partner by estoppel (UPA 16). A *partner by estoppel* (also called an *ostensible partner*) is really not a partner at all. He or she is an individual who, although not a member of a partnership, (1) represents himself or herself to a third party as being such a member, or (2) consents to a member of that partnership making such a representation. If, based upon that representation, a third party extends credit to the partnership both the partnership and the partner by estoppel are liable to the third party who extended credit to the firm in reliance upon the misrepresentation.

The following case shows how a problem involving a partner by estoppel may arise.

CASE 36.1 Springer v. Opsahl · 744 P.2d 884 (Mont. 1987)

FACTS The defendants, Harry Opsahl, Ray Ingalls, Walter Deines, Alan Hart, and Caroll Hart entered into a partnership named "Crosswinds Enterprises" to own and operate restaurants. Later, the five defendants formed a corporation under the name "Crosswinds Enterprises."

In July of 1979, Ingalls met with Springer, an architect. Ingalls said that he and his associates, whom he referred to as his partners, intended to build about forty-two restaurants. Ingalls, without disclosing the name of the contracting party for whom he was acting, entered into an oral contract with Springer for the design of two prototype buildings. Springer was to receive an agreed fee for each of the buildings erected based upon those designs. Later Springer received a retainer check for $1,000 drawn on the account of "Crosswinds of Dillon," signed by Alan Hart and Ray Ingalls. The check did not indicate whether that entity was a partnership or a corporation.

Three buildings were built using Springer's designs but he received no further payment. Springer filed suit against the five named defendants as partners. The lower court entered judgment against the defendants and they appealed, asserting, among other things, that the evidence did not establish that Crosswinds Enterprises was a partnership or that Springer relied on any such representation. The portion of the appellate court's opinion that discussed partnership by estoppel follows.

OPINION HARRISON, J. . . . Partnership by estoppel is controlled by § 35-10-308, MCA [UPA 16] which states in part:

> (1) When a person by words spoken or written or by conduct represents himself or consents to another representing him to anyone as a partner in an existing partnership or with one or more persons not actual partners, he is liable to any such person to whom such

CASE 36.1 Continued

representation has been made who has on the faith of such representation, given credit to the actual or apparent partnership.... When a partnership liability results, he is liable jointly with the other persons, if any, so consenting to the contract or representation....

At the time the contract was negotiated and entered, Ray Ingalls did not specifically state he represented either a partnership or a corporation. However, Springer testified that Ingalls did refer to the other individuals involved as his "partners." This representation could lead a reasonable person to believe he was dealing with a partnership. After the contract was entered, Springer received a retainer check drawn on the account "Crosswinds of Dillon." The check fails to classify the business entity, and it would not have been unreasonable for Springer to continue to believe he contracted with a partnership. The defendants do not contend there was a corporation organized under that name and the retainer check failed to notify Springer he was dealing with a corporation. Regardless of their intentions the record clearly indicates that they would have benefited financially by having the plaintiff perform the contracted work.

A similar issue was presented to the Supreme Court of Wisconsin in *Phillip Lithographic Co. v. Babich (1965)*, 27 Wis. 2d 645, 135 N.W.2d 343. In determining whether certain partners were individually liable upon a contract, the court stated:

> The general rule is that partners who continue to hold themselves out as such after the formation of a corporation cannot escape responsibility for contracts entered into after the change in business status without adequate notice that the partnership was dissolved. This is especially true when the corporation operates under the same name and circumstances as the partnership.

... Defendant Harry Opsahl testified he believed Springer worked for the partnership entity.... Additionally, Springer's subsequent efforts and work demonstrate he relied on this "holding out" to his detriment.... We therefore agree with the result of the District Court's conclusion and will not reverse on this issue....

JUDGMENT For the foregoing reasons, the District Court's decision is affirmed....

Partnership Property

Any overview of partnership law requires examination of the peculiar legal status of partnership property. The UPA was designed, among other things, to make it possible for a partnership, as a legal entity, to take title to and to convey property by instruments in its own name. The UPA does this by viewing a partner's interest in a partnership as distinct from his or her rights in the firm's property (UPA 25, 26). We will discuss these in turn.

Partner's Interest in the Partnership

Each partner's *interest in the partnership* consists of his or her share of the profits the firm earns and of its surplus when the business comes to an end (UPA 26). Stated another way, a partner's interest in a partnership is his or her ownership share of the partnership and in the net worth of all its resources, including the value of its goodwill.

Assignment of Interest in a Partnership. A partner's interest in a partnership is his or her personal property (UPA 26). A partner may sell or otherwise dispose of that interest (1) to the partnership itself, (2) to another partner in the firm, or (3) to a third party. Many partnership agreements provide that the partners have the right, either collectively or individually, to buy a partner's interest that is offered for sale (a *right of first refusal*) before the interest may be sold to a third party.

Assume that partner Ann desires to raise some money. She may temporarily assign her partnership interest as security for a loan—a temporary assignment. Or, if she decides to leave the partnership permanently, perhaps to retire or to go into some other business, she may sell her partnership interest outright—this would be a permanent assignment. In the first instance the temporary assignee is entitled to receive the profits which Ann would have received from the partnership until the loan is paid off and the assignment is canceled. In the second instance the permanent assignee will receive Ann's share of the profits until the dissolution of the partnership. At dissolution the permanent assignee is also entitled to receive the then value of Ann's interest. However, under the principle of *delectus personae* (see page 763), unless *all* the other partners agree to accept the assignee as a new partner, the assignee does not become a partner in the firm. And if the assignee is not made a member of the firm, he or she has no right to participate in its management nor to inspect the partnership books.

Heirs' Rights against Partner's Interest. When a partner dies, his or her *interest in the partnership* is part of the deceased partner's estate. Since a partnership interest is personal property (UPA 26), it is inherited according to the provisions of the deceased partner's will or, if there is no valid will, according to the inheritance laws of the state (see Chapter 23). Whoever inherits the partnership interest does not automatically become a partner in the firm but is an assignee with the rights set out in the preceding paragraph. The agreements of many partnerships provide that upon the death of a partner the surviving partners or the partnership itself will have the right of first refusal to buy the deceased partner's interest.

Creditors' Rights against Partner's Interest. If Sam is a partner in a business and he owes you money on a *personal* debt in a state that applies the UPA, there is only one way you can reach his partnership interest to enforce payment of his debt. You must secure a *charging order* (in the nature of an attachment) from the court (UPA 28). On the basis of that order, you then petition the court to appoint a receiver who will collect and turn over to you whatever partnership profits would otherwise be paid to Sam. If you are not repaid the debt owed by Sam, you may foreclose the charging order (an action similar to the foreclosure of a mortgage) causing Sam's interest in the partnership to be sold at a judicial (public) sale. The proceeds of the sale will be applied to pay off his debt to you and, if any sum remains, it will be paid to him. However, at any time before the sale Sam or his copartners, or the partnership itself, can redeem (buy back) his partnership interest by paying off his debt. If Sam's interest in the partnership is not redeemed, anyone may purchase it at the judicial sale. Of course the purchaser of Sam's interest does not thereby become a partner in the firm. He or she becomes only an assignee of that interest with the limited rights of an assignee described above.

Partner's Rights in Specific Partnership Property

What Is Specific Partnership Property? Partnership property under the UPA consists of (1) the real and personal property contributed by the partners to the firm's capital assets, (2) property acquired with partnership funds, (3) property created or manufactured by the partnership business, and (4) the profits the partnership earns (UPA 8). *Specific partnership property* means any *particular* property owned by a partnership such as a bank account, a building, an automobile, a crane, a computer, and so forth.

The UPA radically departs from the common law in its treatment of specific partnership property. Under the common law, that property is *directly owned* by the partners but under the UPA the *partnership* owns the property and a partner only *indirectly* owns specific partnership property by owning *an interest* in the firm. However, it is not always clear whether the partnership or an individual partner is the true owner of property in the firm's possession because the UPA allows such property to be held either in the partnership name or in the name of one or more of the partners (UPA 8, 10) and it is not unusual for a partner to permit the partnership to use his or her property without transferring its title to the firm. Whether the partnership or one of its partners owns specific partnership property is particularly important when (1) a partnership is dissolved and its assets are being divided; (2) a partner dies and his or her estate claims to be the owner of the property; (3) a creditor attempts to attach or to levy upon the property; or (4) when a partner is adjudged a bankrupt and his or her property must be made available to creditors.

The difficulty of settling a partnership property dispute can be visualized through the following illustration. Assume that the CTS partnership paid one of its partners, Charles, the full market price for the car he owned. Charles neglected to transfer the title of the car to the partnership. With the consent of his partner, Charles kept the car at his home and, when it was not used for business purposes, Charles used it for his own pleasure. Charles dies and his widow claims that the automobile is part of his estate—that the partnership paid Charles only for the right to use the vehicle and did not purchase it from him. Is Charles's estate or the partnership the true owner of the car? In a situation such as this the determining factor is the *intent* of the partners. In the absence of a definite understanding between them, their intent can be demonstrated by such factors as:

- On whose books the property is carried
- How the property is used
- Who pays the state and federal taxes, insurance premiums, and upkeep charges on it
- Who, if anyone, has made insurance claims if the property was damaged

A most important but not absolutely controlling factor is who provided the funds to acquire the property. If the property was acquired with partnership funds, it is rebuttably presumed to be partnership property and not the personal property of an individual partner (UPA 8).

Nature of Partner's Rights in Specific Partnership Property. As has already been noted, none of the partners directly owns any specific partnership property. The property is owned by the partnership as though the firm were itself a legal entity. An individual partner is only a tenant in partnership in the property with his or her copartners. *Tenancy in partnership* is a new form of legal interest created by the UPA [25(1); see also Chapter 21]. Under such a tenancy, a partner's rights in any particular item of partnership property are sharply limited. He or she has almost no right personally to use, control, or sell partnership property. If a partner wants to make personal use of any specific partnership property, the consent of the other partners must first be obtained. For instance, assume that a partner has the right to use the firm's executive aircraft to call on customers and to inspect the firm's distant operations. That partner has no right, without the consent of the other partners, to use the aircraft to take his or her family to a vacation resort even when the plane is not otherwise needed for company business.

Partner's Right to Sell or Assign Specific Partnership Property. Under a tenancy in partnership, a partner has no right to sell or assign any particular item of partnership property unless (1) all partners consent, or (2) the sale or assignment is simply carrying on the partnership business in the usual way [UPA 9, 25(2) (b)]. For instance, say that a partnership buys six tickets to the Super Bowl Game, intending to give them to six of the firm's best customers for public relations purposes. Ross, one of the two partners in the firm, believing that as a partner he owns one-half of all partnership property, gives three of the tickets to his children. Ross did not own the tickets; they were partnership property and he had no right to appropriate any of them for his own use, and he must account to the partnership for them.

Heirs' Rights in Specific Partnership Property. A partner's tenancy right in specific partnership property is not a part of a deceased partner's estate and is not subject to a claim by his or her spouse, heir, or other beneficiary [UPA 25(2) (e)]. When a partner dies, all partnership property remains part of the firm's assets. However, the *value* of that property is taken into consideration in determining the value of the deceased partner's interest in the partnership.

Creditors' Rights against Specific Partnership Property. Obviously, a creditor of a partner can have no greater right to specific partnership property than the debtor partner possesses. Therefore, because a partner has no *personal* right to specific partnership property, his or her creditors cannot reach specific partnership property by a charging order against the partner. A charging order can reach only a partner's *interest in the partnership.*

Rights and Duties of Partners

A member of a partnership has well defined legal rights and duties with respect to his or her copartners, to the partnership, and to third parties who do business with the firm. Partners may include in their agreement limitations upon the exercise of the partnership rights to which they are entitled by law, and they may delineate the duties all or any of them will be required to perform. However, neither the partners nor the partnership can modify or diminish any obligations to third parties that the law imposes upon them.

Fundamental to a partner's rights and duties is the fact that he or she owns an undivided interest in the partnership business and is a *principal* in the enterprise (UPA 18). Accordingly, the partnership is a business organization in which each partner personally is liable for the contract and tort obligations incurred by the partnership. At the same time, since more than one individual owns the partnership business, each partner as well as being a principal is also an *agent* of the partnership and of his or her copartners with the duties and obligations the law imposes upon all agents (UPA 9).

Rights of Partners among Themselves

Each partner has the right (1) to participate in the management of the firm, (2) to have access to its books, (3) to share in its profits, and (4) to be repaid for personal expenditures made on its behalf.

Right to Participate in Management. Unless otherwise agreed, each partner has an equal right with his or her copartners to manage the firm's business (UPA 18). If there is an odd number of partners, ordinary business problems are settled by decision of the majority. If there is an even number of partners they must have an understanding as to how they will settle their differences, for it is not the practice of the courts to hear suits involving mere disagreements between partners concerning ordinary business affairs.

When a question not ordinarily connected with the partnership business is in issue, such as a proposed change in the partnership agreement or whether a new partner should be admitted to the firm, the partners must arrive at a unanimous decision (UPA 9). If this is impossible, any of the partners can bring a lawsuit to secure a court order to dissolve the partnership. The grounds for dissolution of a partnership are discussed in the next chapter.

The right to participate in the firm's management is not determined by the value or kind of contribution each partner makes to the enterprise. For example, assume that a partnership consists of three people: Steve, who contributes $10,000 as his share, Edith, who contributes $2,000 and her business contacts, and Frank, who contributes only the use of a building he owns. Each of the partners, *unless the partnership agreement provides otherwise,* is entitled to an equal voice in the management of the business. They may, however, agree among themselves to limit the sphere in which each will work. Thus, they may agree that Steve will be in charge of the engineering activities, Edith will be the firm's purchasing agent, and Frank will be in charge of its sales department. Such an internal arrangement will, of course, limit the managerial authority of each of the partners. But an agreed limitation on a partner's *functions* does not diminish his or her legal *power to act* for the partnership if a third party has no knowledge of the limitation. What if Frank usurps Edith's function and, without her knowledge, purchases material that is needed and normally used by the firm and the party from whom the purchase is made does not know that Edith is the only partner authorized to buy for the partnership? Frank's act, although contrary to the partners' internal division of authority, is nevertheless binding upon the partnership; if his act damages the partnership he is liable to his copartners for whatever loss it sustained.

Right of Access to Partnership Books . Each partner has the right to look over the partnership books at any reasonable time and to copy from them (UPA 19). The books should be kept at the firm's principal place of business unless the partners agree to keep them at some other location. As has already been noted, an assignee of a partner's interest in the firm, having no right to participate in the management of the partnership, has no right to inspect its books.

Right to Share in Profits. In the absence of an agreement to the contrary, each partner is presumed to have an equal share in its profits [UPA 18(a)]. This presumption of equality exists even though the individual contributions to the firm may have differed considerably in amount and in character.

Therefore, in the above example of a partnership consisting of Steve, Edith, and Frank, they are not due differing shares of the firm's profits based upon the disparate contributions each made to their joint enterprise. Of course, Steve, Edith, and Frank may agree upon other criteria for the distribution of the partnership profits which could result in the partners receiving unequal shares. If they have such an understanding, it would be well for them to reduce it to writing.

Right to Be Compensated for Services. The UPA provides that "no partner is entitled to remuneration for acting in the partnership business." The compensation each is to receive is his or her share of the profits. But again, a partnership agreement may establish any desired exceptions to this general rule. Therefore, where one or more partners is expected to devote more time to the firm's business than the others, it is normal for their agreement to provide that the more active partner(s) will be compensated at some fixed rate for their additional services.

Right to Be Repaid Personal Expenditures. A partner may expend personal funds beyond the amount he or she agreed to contribute to the partnership's capital in order to pay a partnership debt or to satisfy an obligation in aid of the business. A partner who makes such a payment is entitled to repayment *with interest* from the partnership's assets. The following hypothetical case will demonstrate the basis for this rule. Let us assume that a partnership in order to complete a large order must purchase a quantity of a special chemical. Because its credit is poor, a bank will not finance the purchase, so the firm must pay for the supplies on delivery. The partnership agreement makes no provision for forcing any partner to make a contribution to the firm's capital in addition to that promised by each partner when the firm was organized and all promised contributions have long since been made. Now one of the partners, out of her own funds, pays for the necessary supplies. She has, in effect, made a loan to the partnership to enable it to carry on its ordinary business. If she had not done so it could not complete the important order. Accordingly, she is entitled to indemnification (repayment) with interest before any other payments are made to the partners out of the firm's capital [UPA 18(b); 40(b)].

The landmark case most frequently cited by the courts to illustrate the application of UPA 18 follows:

CASE 36.2 Levy v. Leavitt · 178 N.E. 758 (N.Y. 1931)

FACTS Levy, the plaintiff, joined with Leavitt, the defendant, in the purchase of a large quantity of bacon from the government, expecting to sell it overseas at a substantial profit. Leavitt was in sole charge of carrying out the enterprise; Levy was only an investor in it. After the bacon was purchased, the government at first would not allow its export and by the time the export was allowed, the bacon had spoiled and had to be destroyed. Leavitt induced Congress to pass a special act allowing him to sue the government for the loss. Leavitt won the suit and the government paid the claim. In all the above activities Leavitt expended his personal funds.

Levy brought an action for an accounting of the joint venture's affairs. Leavitt asserted he was entitled not only to repayment, with interest, of personal funds he had advanced, but also to payment for the reasonable value of his extraordinary services in preventing the venture from being a total loss. The referee refused to allow these claims and Leavitt appealed.

OPINION LEHMAN, J. . . . The partnership agreement was oral and informal. There is nothing to show that the parties considered or discussed whether the defendant should be entitled to compensation for his services or to any interest for moneys he might furnish. . . .

CASE 36.2 Continued

. . . In the case of joint partners, the general rule is, that one is not entitled to charge against another, a compensation for his more valuable or unequal services bestowed on the common concern, without special arrangement;. . . In the business of a partnership the services of a partner are rendered for the common benefit in the performance of an obligation created by the partnership agreement, and the resultant benefit is divided pro rata as provided in the partnership contract. Those profits constitute, in the absence of other agreement, the stipulated reward for services to be rendered, and there is no right to other compensation based on the reasonable value of services actually rendered. Inequality in the value of services rendered, even the fact that the services were extraordinary and that, at the time the contract was made, the parties did not contemplate that such services would be required in the course of the partnership business, would not alone justify the award of compensation outside the share of profits accruing to the partner rendering the services. . . . Though the evidence shows that unexpected obstacles called forth extraordinary exertions by the defendant in attempting to sell the bacon, nevertheless his services at that time were performed in compliance with the obligation he assumed when the partnership was formed, to devote his efforts to the resale of the bacon. There are no circumstances which would support an inference . . . that the partners agreed to pay compensation for such services. . . .

[As to] the defendant's right to charge against the plaintiff's share in the partnership funds, interest on moneys furnished by the defendant, . . . the Partnership Law . . . provides: . . . "A partner, who in aid of the partnership makes any payment or advance beyond the amount of capital which he agreed to contribute, shall be paid interest from the date of the payment or advance." . . . Where the express contract of partnership fails to provide for payment of special compensation for services rendered, the burden of proving that the parties intended such payment rests upon the person claiming such compensation. Where the express contract fails to provide for payment of interest on moneys furnished by a partner beyond the amount which he agreed to contribute, the burden of proving that the parties intended that no such interest should be paid rests upon the other partners. . . . The distinction . . . rests upon an inherent difference between the obligation of a partner to render services in the partnership business and the obligation to provide capital. . . . Therefore, where a partner pays money to the partnership beyond his partnership obligation, it is a reasonable inference that the parties intended that such payment should be a loan and should bear interest.

JUDGMENT The judgment should be modified in accordance with this opinion and as modified affirmed.

Duties of Partners

Each partner undertakes (1) to serve the partnership according to the terms of the agreement, (2) to share in the losses of the enterprise, and (3) to discharge fiduciary duties owing to his or her copartners. However, any obligation or duty owing between partners may be limited by the terms of their partnership agreement.

Duty to Serve Partnership. The partnership agreement generally defines the amount of time each partner is expected to devote to partnership affairs and the particular duties each will perform. All partners have the right to expect that any member of the firm who is actively running the business will devote full time to the enterprise and will apply his or her best efforts.

When a partner fails to perform his or her agreed duties or otherwise acts contrary to the partnership agreement there may be varying consequences depending upon the provisions of the agreement and whether the breach is or is not intentional.

Duty to Share in Losses. We have seen that each partner has a right to share with his or her partners in the profits of the business either equally or according to whatever ratio is established by the partnership agreement. Further, unless the agreement specifies otherwise each partner has the parallel duty to share in whatever losses the business may sustain in the same ratio as he or she had agreed to share in its profits [18(a); 40(d)]. Therefore, if the partnership does not have enough funds with which to cover all its losses, the partners may be required to cover the losses from their personal funds. How losses are distributed among partners when a partnership is dissolved is discussed in detail in Chapter 37.

Duty to Furnish Information. The UPA provides that each partner is required to render *on the demand* of any other partner true and full information concerning all things affecting the partnership (UPA 20). However, because of the high order of fiduciary duty that each partner owes to copartners, ethical business standards demand that a partner should *voluntarily* disclose to the others *any* information pertaining to the partnership business. As co-managers, all partners are entitled to equal knowledge of partnership affairs.

The following case illustrates the duty of partners to share information affecting their firm.

CASE 36.3 Marsh v. Gentry · 642 S.W.2d 574 (Ky. 1982)

FACTS Marsh, the plaintiff, was in partnership with Gentry, the defendant, in the business of buying and selling race horses. The partnership owned a mare named Champagne Woman, for which the partnership had paid $155,000, and her foal, named Excitable Lady. They agreed to sell Champagne Woman at auction. Both Gentry and Marsh were at the auction. Champagne Woman was sold at the auction for $135,000. Gentry did not tell Marsh and Marsh did not know that the horse had been purchased by Gentry's agent. Marsh discovered this 11 months later.

Marsh consented to Gentry's proposal that he (Gentry) sell Excitable Lady by private sale. Subsequently, Gentry told Marsh that the horse had been sold to someone in California at the price he and Marsh had established. Gentry gave Marsh his proper share of the sale price but Gentry refused to reveal the name of the purchaser. More than a year later, when Excitable Lady won a race at Churchill Downs, Marsh discovered that Gentry was the owner of the horse.

Marsh brought suit against Gentry for an accounting based upon Gentry's breach of his partnership obligation to make full disclosure to his copartner concerning both sales. The trial court held for the defendant (Gentry) and Marsh appealed.

OPINION O'HARA, J. . . . The controlling statute which is dispositive of this case is . . . [UPA 21], a codification of the common law . . . :

> Every partner must account to the partnership for any benefit and hold as trustee for it any profit derived by him *without the consent of the other partners from any transaction connected with the formation, conduct, or liquidation of the partnership or from any use by him of its profit.*

Applying the clear and unambiguous language of the statute to the facts of this case, it becomes instantly apparent that Gentry did not comply with the evident intent of the law when he withheld [information about the sale of the horses] and misled his partner concerning the two "transactions." . . .

We look first to the sale of Champagne Woman at auction. . . . The actual bidding was done by a secret agent of Gentry without the knowledge of Marsh. In addition, when the auction was completed, the sale was listed in the name of a third party. . . . As it turns out, the purchaser was Gentry himself. Admittedly, at an auction sale, the specific identity of the purchaser cannot be ascertained before the sale, but the [Partnership Act] . . . required a full disclosure by Gentry to Marsh that he would be a prospective purchaser.

CASE 36.3 Continued

As to the private sale of Excitable Lady, ... [e]ven though Marsh obtained the stipulated price, a partner has an absolute right to know when his partner is the purchaser. Partners scrutinize buy-outs by their partners in an entirely different light than an ordinary third party sale....

...The requirement of full disclosure among partners as to partnership business cannot be escaped.... Had Gentry made a full disclosure to his partner of his intentions to purchase the partnership property, Marsh would not later be heard to complain of the transaction.

Finally, Gentry maintains that it is an accepted practice at auction sales of thoroughbreds for one partner to secretly bid on partnership stock to accomplish a buy-out.... [T]he truth behind this statement is not at issue here. We would emphatically state, however, for the benefit of those engaged in such practices, that where an "accepted business practice" conflicts with existing law, the law whether statutory or court ordered, is controlling. To hold otherwise would be chaotic.

JUDGMENT Accordingly, the judgment... is reversed... and this cause is remanded... to determine ... [the sum due Marsh].

Fiduciary Duties. Because of the close personal nature of a partnership and the dual capacity in which each partner functions, that is, as both a principal and an agent, each partner has the duty to act with the highest degree of good faith and loyalty to the other partners and owes fiduciary obligations to them (UPA 21).

Among the most important fiduciary duties are (1) the duty not to profit secretly from any business with which the partnership is connected, and (2) the duty not to compete with the partnership of which he or she is a member.

Duty not to profit secretly. A partner must not secretly use partnership property or funds for private benefit or for payment of personal debts. If he or she wrongly uses partnership money or property, not only must the value of the "borrowed" item (or the value of the use to which it was put) be accounted for and repaid to the partnership, but the partner must also account for and pay to the partnership any profit made through its use. Thus, if partner Tom "borrowed" the partnership's company airplane and used it to take his family plus a couple of paying passengers on a weekend jaunt, not only must he pay the partnership for rental of the aircraft but he must also turn over to the partnership the money received from the paying passengers.

If a partner makes a secret profit in any transaction undertaken for the partnership, he or she is acting contrary to the firm's interests. In that case the partnership may secure payment from the dishonest partner in the amount of that extra profit and the circumstance could be cause for a dissolution of the partnership.

Duty not to compete. Similar to a partner's fiduciary duty not to make a secret profit is the duty not to compete with the partnership of which he or she is a member unless first receiving the consent of his or her copartners. Thus, a partner may not take personal advantage of an economic opportunity that he or she should know is within the ambit of the partnership business. For instance, in the landmark case of *Meinhard v. Salmon* [164 N.E. 545 (N.Y. 1928)], it was held that a partner could not take or renew in his or her own name a lease to property occupied by a partnership even though the new lease was not to begin until after the partnership agreement terminated. In his now famous opinion in this case Judge Cardozo said:

> Many forms of conduct permissible in a workaday world, for those acting at arm's length, are forbidden to those bound by fiduciary ties. A... [partner] is held to something stricter than the morals of the market place. Not honesty alone, but the punctilio of an honor the most sensitive, is the standard of behavior. As to this there has developed a tradition that is unbending and inveterate.

Fiduciary obligations do not preclude a partner from engaging in an activity that is separate and distinct from partnership affairs. For example, assume that Bill and Ray, as partners, operate the Wholesome Fruit Arcade. When Bill has no duties to perform at the Arcade, he may work at a neighboring shoe repair shop without accounting to the partnership for his salary from that employment. In fact, he may be a partner in the shoe repair business at the same time that he is a partner in the Fruit Arcade because the two firms are in no way in competition with one another.

The following case is an example of how a court will view a partnership's claim to the "moonlight" earnings of one of its partners when that moonlighting was, without his partner's consent, in competition with the business of the partnership.

CASE 36.4 Veale v. Rose · 657 S.W.2d 834 (Tex. App. 1983)

FACTS Rose, Veale, and others formed a partnership of certified public accountants. Their written agreement allowed the partners to pursue and receive pay for other business activities so long as those activities were not in conflict with the partnership practice and did not materially interfere with the partners' duties to the firm. Except with the expressed approval of the other partners, no partner could engage in the practice of public accounting other than on behalf of the partnership.

Partner Rose was an officer in Right Away Foods and he received compensation for performing accounting services for that company which did not require that the accountant be certified. He also performed accounting services "after hours" for another concern for which he personally received payment.

Rose left the partnership. Upon his departure, he and the others were unable to agree upon the amount due him from the firm. Rose therefore sued the partners for an accounting and for the money due him under the partnership agreement. Veale and the other partners counterclaimed, demanding the money due them for the accounting services which Rose carried on in competition with the partnership. The jury found that Rose had not performed accounting services in competition with the partnership while he was a member. Veale and the partners appealed.

OPINION NYE, J. . . . Partners may be said to occupy a fiduciary relationship toward one another which requires of them the utmost degree of good faith and honesty in dealing with one another. . . . Breaches of a partner's duty not to compete with the partnership are compensable at law by awarding to the injured partners their proportionate share of the profits wrongfully acquired by the offending partner. . . .

It is undisputed that while a partner of Paul G. Veale and Company, Rose rendered accounting services for Right Away Foods for which he billed and received payment personally. It is also undisputed that the partnership did not share in the proceeds of these private billings. . . .

Rose also admitted that he performed [other] accounting services during his tenure as a partner at Veale for which he billed and received payment personally. . . . His later testimony that he performed these services, in effect after hours, or in addition to his duties to the partnership, is of no value in light of the obligation imposed by the partnership agreement and by the common understanding of the term "competition."

The misappropriation by one partner to his own use of property of the partnership is considered in law as constructive if not actual fraud on the partnership, and is actionable. . . . Again the record is replete with Rose's admissions that he used employee and computer time and that he had not billed [his private client] for those services. . . . [T]he jury's responses were against the great weight of the evidence. . . .

JUDGMENT [W]e reverse and remand that portion of the trial court's judgment. . . . [The appellants were upheld in their counterclaim.]

The breach by a partner of his or her partnership duties gives a copartner a right (1) to recover from the wrongdoing partner any monetary losses sustained, (2) to secure an injunction when the circumstances so indicate, and (3) to use the breach as a basis to secure the dissolution of the partnership.

Power of Partners to Obligate Partnership and Copartners

We have already seen that each partner acts concurrently both as (1) a principal in and an agent for the partnership, and (2) as an agent of his or her copartners. Accordingly, when a partner appears to a third party to be carrying on the business of the partnership in the usual way, or when a partner is authorized by the other partners to take an unusual action, that partner has the power to obligate the partnership and his or her copartners. This power to obligate the partnership may involve: (1) engaging in a contract for the partnership, (2) making admissions or representations against the interests of the partnership, (3) receiving information or notice binding on the partnership, and (4) committing tortious or criminal acts for which the partnership is liable.

Power to Obligate by Contract

A partner may obligate his or her partnership and copartners by contract (1) when specifically authorized by the partnership agreement to do so, (2) when the other partners either actually or impliedly consent to the action, or (3) when the partner is apparently carrying on the business of the partnership in the usual manner.[1] The following two examples illustrate when a partner has authority to engage in a contract for the firm.

For example, assume that four physicians in partnership own a building in which their offices are located. Normally, no one of the physicians would have authority to sell the building as that authority was neither conferred by the partnership agreement nor would the sale of a building be in the usual course of business of a medical practice. But if the other three copartners authorize the fourth to sell the building, a contract of sale entered into by that physician is binding upon all the partners.

For a second example, assume that John and Harry own and operate a commercial fishing boat. The fish they catch are sold to wholesale fish dealers. If John contracts with a dealer for the sale of a catch of fish, John is carrying on the routine partnership business in the usual way and John has the authority to sell the fish. If, however, John contracts for the sale of the boat he is acting so far outside the way the partnership business is usually conducted that the consent of his copartner is required to make the sale of the boat a legal, enforceable transaction.

When partners have an agreement among themselves which limits the authority of a partner to act for the firm, a third party who has no notice of that limitation is not bound by the restriction on the partner's authority. For example, let's say that it is agreed among the partners who own a store selling office equipment that Jayson, one of the partners, will make no purchases for the firm. Nevertheless, Jayson contracts in the firm name to buy ten word processors that he is convinced he and his partners can sell at a profit. If the wholesaler of the word processors has no notice of the limitation on Jayson's authority and he appears to be carrying on the partnership business in the usual manner, then the contract of purchase is binding upon the partnership and upon all of the partners. If the partnership fails to sell the word processors and the store suffers a loss, Jayson must reimburse the partnership in the amount of the loss because he breached his partnership agreement.

Power to Obligate by Statement against Interest

A statement by a partner against the interest of the partnership may be used against the firm if it is made while he or she is carrying on the business of the partnership (UPA 11). To illustrate: Partner John, while using the partnership delivery van to make a delivery, negligently drives into Andy's auto. John admits that he caused the accident. That admission may be used as evidence against the partnership if it later denies liability.

[1] In Chapter 33 we examined at length the meanings of "apparent authority" and "implied authority."

Power to Obligate by Notice or Knowledge

All partners are charged with notice of any matter relating to partnership affairs that comes to the attention of *any* of its members (UPA 3, 12). For example, the city of Broadview sends a notice to Arnold, a member of the New Horizon partnership, warning the firm that if a drain pipe which allows water to flood city land is not repaired within 30 days, the city will take action against the partnership. That notice is effective upon the partnership and all its partners when it is delivered to Arnold, notwithstanding the fact that he ignores the notice and neither takes action to correct the defective drain nor informs his copartners of the notice. Arnold has violated his duty to keep his partners informed. If the partnership suffers loss because of Arnold's inaction, Arnold may be required to compensate the partnership and his copartners for the loss sustained and the failure of Arnold to take appropriate action after receiving the notice may be a ground for the dissolution of the partnership.

Parallel with a partner's duty to share receipt of a *notice* with his or her partners is the duty to share any pertinent *knowledge*. Thus, if a partner acquires knowledge pertinent to partnership affairs, that knowledge is imputed to the partnership and to all of its members. For example, the SB Company manufactures skate boards. One day, while testing some of the boards, partner Felix learns that one wheel has a tendency to lock, creating a hazard to anyone using the product. That knowledge is imputed to all members of the partnership.

There is one exception to this principle of imputation of knowledge, however. Partners are not assumed to know when a copartner *acts adversely to* (that is, against the interest of) the partnership. Thus, if a partner steals partnership money, the copartners are not presumed to have knowledge of the theft.

Power to Obligate by Tortious Act

Suppose Fred, one of three partners who own and operate the Beauty Shop, while giving a permanent wave to customer Virginia carelessly mixes and applies the wrong chemicals and thereby injures Virginia's scalp. Fred has committed a tort and is liable to Virginia because everyone is liable for his or her own torts. The partnership and Fred's copartners are also liable because each partner is liable for the tort of a copartner committed within the scope of the partnership business (UPA 13). If the partnership is ordered by a court to pay damages to Virginia, it can, of course, secure indemnification from wrongdoing partner Fred.

The following case illustrates a situation in which a partnership, being sued for a tort, was not liable because the partner's act was not in the ordinary course of the partnership business.

CASE 36.5 Investors Title Insurance Co. v. Herzig · 350 S.E.2d 160 (N.C. App. 1986)

FACTS Herzig, a member of the law firm of Everett, Creech, Hancock & Herzig, applied for a bank loan using his property as security. Before making him the loan, the bank required that Herzig obtain a title insurance policy. In order to secure the policy, Herzig submitted to the insurance company an "attorney's final title certificate" signed by himself beneath the words, "Everett, Creech, Hancock & Herzig" and above the words, "Member of the firm." In that certificate Herzig stated, in effect, that the title to the property was clear. The insurance company issued the policy and the bank made the requested loan. In fact, however, there were certain violations of restrictions in the title which could result in forfeiture of the property to the city of Henderson. Herzig subsequently defaulted on his bank loan.

The insurance company brought an action against Herzig for fraud and against the law firm of Everett, Creech, Hancock & Herzig for negligence and breach of warranty arising

CASE 36.5 Continued

out of the actions of its agent, Herzig. The lower court granted the defendant partnership's motion for summary judgment in its favor and the plaintiff insurance company appealed.

OPINION EAGLES, J. . . . Plaintiff . . . contends that because Herzig acted within "the ordinary course of the business of the partnership," the partnership is liable in tort. . . . [UPA Sec. 13] provides:

> Where, by any wrongful act or omission of any partner acting in the ordinary course of the business of the partnership or with the authority of his copartners, loss or injury is caused to any person . . . or any penalty is incurred, the partnership is liable therefore to the same extent as the partner so acting or omitting to act.

. . . Plaintiff contends that defendant Herzig had apparent authority to bind the partnership. . . . The apparent scope of partnership business depends upon the conduct of the partnership and its partners and what, by that conduct, they cause third persons to believe about the authority of the partners. The existence or nonexistence of apparent authority is determined from the standpoint of the third person. . . . If the facts and circumstances reveal that an ordinary prudent person in the plaintiff's position would have been put on notice that the alleged agent was not acting within the apparent scope of his authority then the principal is not bound. . . .

> It would seem to be clear that if the agent is purporting to act as an agent and doing the things which such agents normally do, and the third person has no reason to know that the agent is acting on his own account, the principal should be liable because he has invited third persons to deal with the agent within the limits of what, to such third persons, would seem to be the agent's authority. To go beyond this, however, and to permit the third persons to recover in every case where the agent takes advantage of the standing and position of his principal to perpetuate a fraud would seem to be going too far.

Applying these principles, it is clear . . . that Herzig certified title to his own property to obtain a personal loan and not to further any partnership business. The only connection between Herzig's actions and the partnership is the manner in which Herzig signed the title certificate. . . . [T]he firm received no compensation, . . . received none of the proceeds or any other benefit . . . and had no knowledge Herzig had certified title to his own property in the name of the partnership. More importantly though, the title certificate showed on its face that Herzig owned the property individually. No client of the firm appeared in the transaction. The title insurance policy states that a deed of trust from "David F. Herzig (single)" secures the [loan]. The purpose of the transaction was personal . . . and not for the purpose of furthering any business of the partnership.

. . . [W]e believe that under these facts . . . an ordinary prudent person in plaintiff's position as a title insurance company would have been put on notice that Herzig was acting on his own account, in his individual capacity and for his own benefit and hence not within the scope of his apparent authority . . . in furtherance of partnership business.

JUDGMENT Affirmed.

Actions to Enforce Partnership Obligations

Under the common law, as a partnership is only an aggregate of individuals, a suit against a partnership must be brought against the members of the firm personally and not against the partnership as such. However, many states now permit a partnership to be sued directly as though it were a legal entity.

At common law and under the UPA all the members of a partnership are: (1) *joint* obligors of a partnership obligation arising out of contract, and the third party's suit must be brought against *all* the partners by name; (2) *jointly and severally* liable for a tort committed by a partner acting within the scope of the business (UPA 15). "Jointly and severally" means that the suit may, at the plaintiff's election, be brought against all of the partners or against any one or more of them. Many states either by statute or by judicial interpretation make no distinction between actions in tort and actions in contract and all actions are considered joint and several.

It is generally not the practice of the courts to hear disputes between partners arising out of their business affairs unless the dispute rises to the level where it is the cause for a dissolution of the partnership by court order (see Chapter 37). In that event, the rights and liabilities of the several partners are determined in a proceeding called an *accounting.*

Summary

The most common types of business organizations are: (1) a sole proprietorship, (2) a general partnership (or joint venture), (3) a limited partnership, and (4) a corporation.

In a sole proprietorship, a single individual owns the business. There is a minimum of government control over it, and the business owner is personally liable for all the firm's debts. In a general partnership the business is owned by more than one person. Each has the right to manage the business and each is personally liable for the firm's debts. A joint venture is the same as a general partnership except that it is organized to conduct a single business transaction or a few related transactions. In a limited partnership the general partners manage the enterprise and are personally liable for the firm's debts. The other partners in the enterprise, called limited partners, have few managerial rights and no personal liability for the firm's debts. A corporation is the most widely used form of large business organization. Its owners, called shareholders, have no direct control over the management of the business and they have no personal liability for its debts.

A partnership is an association of persons who either formally or informally agree that as co-owners they will carry on a business for profit.

Any person who is legally competent to enter into a contract may, subject to the law of the state concerned, become a partner. However, no one can become a member of a partnership without the consent of all the partners in the firm.

The UPA specifies the rights and obligations of partners but they may, by agreement, establish rights and obligations among themselves that differ from those set out in the UPA. They may not, however, diminish the obligations owed by the partnership or by a partner to third parties. Unless the partnership agreement provides otherwise, partners (1) share equally in the profits of their enterprise; (2) are each obligated to pay, in the same proportion as they share in the profits, any losses the firm sustains; and (3) receive no compensation for their services to the firm, their remuneration being their share of the profits.

Each partner is both a principal in the firm and an agent of his or her copartners. Therefore, in the absence of an agreement to the contrary, all partners have equal rights in the management and conduct of the business and each is personally liable for its debts. A partner, like any other agent, may bind the partnership and his or her partners if the partner has express or apparent authority so to do. A partner has apparent authority if he or she reasonably appears to be carrying on the business of the partnership in the usual way.

Each partner reposes great trust and confidence in his or her copartners and therefore each is obligated to serve the partnership faithfully, to share in its losses, and to furnish to the others all information concerning matters which might affect the partnership. In addition, a partner owes his or her copartners fiduciary duties, among which are the duty not to profit secretly from any partnership transaction and not to compete with the partnership without first receiving the consent of the copartners.

Review Questions

1 **(a)** What are the principal forms of business organizations? **(b)** What are some advantages and disadvantages of each form?

2 What is the difference between a general partnership, a limited partnership, and a joint venture?

3 **(a)** What is a general partnership? (Hereafter a general partnership is called merely "partnership".) **(b)** How many people constitute a partnership? **(c)** What is the maximum length of time a partnership can exist?

4 **(a)** How is a partnership established? **(b)** What constitutes a "capital investment" in a partnership? **(c)** How much of a capital investment is required to form a partnership?

5 **(a)** Comment upon this statement: "A partnership can exist even though the parties do not know they are doing business as a partnership." **(b)** Why is it important that people doing business know whether or not they have formed a partnership?

6 Is the following statement true or false? "A person may participate in the profits of a business without being a partner in the business." Explain the reasons for your answer.

7 Why is it that a person cannot become a partner in a business unless all the partners already in the business give their consent.

8 Explain what is meant by a partner by estoppel.

9 **(a)** Distinguish between an interest in a partnership and a partner's rights in specific partnership property. **(b)** How does a judgment creditor of a partner reach a partner's interest in a partnership to obtain payment of the judgment debt?

10 When a partner dies what rights does the surviving spouse have regarding the deceased partner's interest in the partnership?

11 How do partners share in the profits of their enterprise? Explain.

12 How do partners share in the losses their partnership suffers? Explain.

13 Comment upon the following statements, giving reasons for your opinions: **(a)** Any partner, without the consent of his or her copartners, has authority to borrow money to carry on the partnership business. **(b)** If a partner, contrary to the instructions of the copartners, purchases on credit articles normally used in the partnership business, he or she alone is obligated on the contract of purchase. **(c)** Any partner has apparent authority to sell merchandise the partnership makes.

14 **(a)** Give several examples of the fiduciary duties of a partner? **(b)** Why does a partner have fiduciary duties?

15 Under what circumstances can a partnership be liable for the tort of one of the partners?

Case Problems

1 Arthur was opening his new accounting office. The only well-located office he could find was too large for his needs. He therefore asked Bryan, a lawyer who was also looking for office space, to share the offices and "split" the rental charges and secretarial costs with him. Bryan agreed. Arthur signed a lease for the rooms and they established their respective practices there. Bryan won a lawsuit, earning a large fee. Arthur claims a share of that fee, asserting that they had, by their arrangements, established a partnership. Was he correct? Why?

2 Able and Baker were partners, engaged in building a prototype of Baker's invention. Being short of working capital, they asked Oscar to invest $10,000 in the enterprise, telling him that he would have a 25 percent interest in the venture and that "there was no telling how much money he would make." Oscar gave Able and Baker the money. Although Oscar was told that he had nothing to do with the management of the enterprise, he frequently helped out in the work. He offered some of his own employees and drill presses to do rush jobs on the invention, and he helped prepare a brochure to be used in the sale of the device when completed. He cosigned with Able and Baker an application for a loan which unfortunately was not granted. Able then told Oscar that more money was required to develop the invention and, being told that the profits would be split three ways, Able invested an additional $10,000. Considerable more time and energy were expended on the project but no progress was made. Able and Baker spent most of the partnership funds for secondhand equipment which did not function properly. Finally, Oscar sued Able and Baker for return of his investment claiming that it was because of Able and Baker's negligence that the venture did not succeed and that, because he was merely a passive investor and not a partner in the enterprise, he was entitled to the return of his money. Should he recover? Why?

3 Rice and Smith, by written agreement, formed the R & S Partnership in which they each held a 50 percent interest. The partnership owned and operated a large apartment building in New York City. Their agreement said in part:

> Art. 12. It is agreed that neither partner shall have the authority to sell or assign any interest in this partnership before offering the said interest to the other party for purchase, except that either party may

assign a part or all of his share to a member of his immediate family who attains the age of 21 years.

In December 1983, Rice transferred one-half of his partnership share to his daughter, Alice, then 22 years of age. Rice said that Alice was now a partner in their enterprise, holding a 25 percent interest. Smith stubbornly refused to treat Alice as a partner. Was Rice or Smith correct? Why?

4 Welch acquired a concession stand at a racetrack. He did not have sufficient capital to operate the concession and he asked his friend Dunn to endorse a note which would make possible Welch's borrowing money at the bank. Dunn endorsed the note and, to be sure that payments on the note were made as they became due, Dunn took control of the accounting records of the concession, maintained its inventory controls, and, with Welch, signed checks on the concession bank account. Dunn periodically ordered supplies and paid concession bills by checks he signed. An order for grain was placed by Dunn with Anderson Grain Co. Anderson extended credit to the concession because of Dunn's financial responsibility. Anderson, when not paid, would contact Dunn, who immediately paid the bill out of the concession's bank account. Ultimately Anderson's bills were not paid and Anderson sued both Welch and Dunn as partners for the amount due. Dunn contends that he is not a partner; that his controls over the business were only his protection against his endorsement of the note. What would be the legal basis for Anderson's claim? Explain.

5 Dorothy, Ethel, and Sarah owned and operated in partnership the Hi-Time Liquor store. Dorothy and Ethel each had a 10 percent interest in the partnership and Sarah had an 80 percent interest. A personal creditor sued and obtained a judgment against Sarah. A charging order was entered against her partnership interest and the court appointed a receiver to do everything necessary to collect the judgment. The receiver sold Sarah's partnership interest at judicial sale and Audrey bought the interest. Soon thereafter it became time to renew Hi-Time's liquor license. Audrey, as owner of 80 percent of the partnership, applied for a renewal of the license. Dorothy and Ethel maintained that Audrey had no authority to make the application and they applied for the renewal. The State Liquor Authority was in a quandary. To whom should the license be issued? Why?

6 Martin suffered stomach pains. He consulted Dr. Barbour, who, after an examination, performed an operation. Martin's postoperative care was handled by Dr. Egle, who was Dr. Barbour's partner. Dr. Egle had not seen Martin before the operation and was not present at the operation. Because Dr. Barbour had, in the course of the operation, unnecessarily severed one of Martin's muscles, Martin became permanently disabled. Martin sued both Dr. Barbour and Dr. Egle for malpractice. Dr. Egle asks the court to dismiss the action against him as he was not a surgeon and he had nothing to do with the operation. Should Dr. Egle's motion be sustained? Explain.

CHAPTER 37

Termination of Partnerships

The life of a partnership, being an association of people closely engaged in business together, is largely dependent upon the continuance of the personal interrelationship of its members. The occurrence of a variety of events may bring about a change in that relationship and thereby cause the partnership to end. When circumstances are present which cause a partnership to end, its termination comes about through a three-step process. The first step is its *dissolution;* the second is the formal *winding up* of its business; and the third is its *termination.* Sometimes it is not necessary to undertake a formal winding up; instead, after an accounting of the interests of the partners and the settlement of its affairs, the *business* is continued by a remaining partner as its sole proprietor or by a new partnership consisting of the remaining partners either with or without new members.

The first part of this chapter considers the circumstances which bring about the dissolution of a partnership. The second part deals with the circumstances under which the business of a dissolved partnership may be continued without a winding up.

Dissolution of Partnerships

Section 29 of the Uniform Partnership Act (UPA) defines *dissolution* as "the change in the relation of the partners caused by any partner ceasing to be associated in the carrying on . . . of the business."[1]

Dissolution must not be confused with termination. When a partnership is dissolved it is not at that time terminated (ended), but it cannot continue to carry on its business in the normal way. A dissolved firm generally enters into a winding up stage during which the partnership is liquidated. Its current contracts are completed; debts due it are collected; its bills are paid; and the partnership's remaining assets, if any, are distributed among the partners. Only then is the partnership terminated.

Dissolution may be: (1) not in violation of the terms of the partnership agreement, (2) in violation of the partnership agreement, (3) by operation of law, or (4) by court decree.

Dissolution Not in Violation of Partnership Agreement

A dissolution that is not in violation of the partnership agreement may arise in several ways.

Dissolution Pursuant to Terms of the Agreement. It is common practice for partners, when they organize their business, to limit its life to some fixed term. For example, they may agree that their partnership will continue for 5 years. If the partners do not by some subsequent agreement before 5 years go by agree that the firm will continue until some later date or indefinitely, when the fifth year ends, the partnership is automatically dissolved. Partners may also condition the life of their partnership, either with or without a time limitation, upon the consummation of a stated purpose or upon the occurrence of a particular event. For example, if a partnership (or joint venture) is formed to race Golden Eagle, an outstanding horse, and if Golden Eagle breaks down and can no longer race, the partnership is dissolved.

Since the partnership association is a product of the voluntary agreement of its members, the partners may by unanimous assent at any time dissolve their association without regard to the term or purpose for which they had originally established it. Also, a partner, under conditions specified in their partnership agreement or concurred in by all the partners, may retire from the firm and thus, without violating the agreement, dissolve the partnership.

Older cases considered a partnership dissolved when the partners added a new member on the the-

[1]The Uniform Partnership Act is reproduced in Appendix 3.

ory that by unanimous agreement the partners had terminated the first firm and established a new one with the new member. More recent cases hold that a partnership agreement may permit the admission of a new partner without dissolution of the firm. These cases reflect the better view inasmuch as the original partners have not ceased to be associated together in the business.

Dissolution by Act of a Partner in a Partnership at Will. A partnership at will is one in which the partnership agreement does not specify any date or circumstance for its dissolution. Since the partners have not agreed to continue the partnership for any fixed period of time, each of the partners has the right to withdraw from it at any time. The withdrawing partner does not breach the partnership agreement even if the firm is operating profitably and its dissolution results in a monetary loss to the other partners.

Dissolution by Expulsion of a Partner. A partnership agreement may specify conditions under which a partner may be expelled from the firm. Among the reasons may be, for instance, that the partner has failed to pay his or her share of a partnership obligation, that the partner is bringing discredit upon the firm, or that the partner has failed to perform his or her agreed duties. But note that if the agreement does not make provision for expulsion, the other members of the firm are without authority to expel a wrongdoing partner; to free themselves from the unwelcome association they must seek a judicial dissolution of the partnership.

If the partnership agreement makes provision for the expulsion of a partner and the majority of the partners decide to take that action, they must follow the procedures established by their agreement. They must act in good faith, intending to serve the best interests of the partnership and not to injure or "get even" with the expelled partner.

Partners cannot, by expelling a member of the firm, cause the expelled partner to lose the value of his or her investment in the firm. Section 38(1) of the UPA provides that the expelled partner should be "discharged from all partnership liabilities ... [and] receive in cash ... the net amount due him from the partnership." As each partner is personally liable for partnership debts incurred while he or she was a member of the firm, unless some special action is taken an individual who is expelled from a partnership remains subject to the demands of entities who were then the firm's creditors. How these obligations may be discharged is discussed on page 790.

In the following case the court clarified the right of members of a partnership of doctors to expel, against his wishes, one of the partners.

CASE 37.1 Gelder Medical Group v. Webber · 363 N.E.2d 573 (N.Y. 1977)

FACTS The Gelder Medical Group was a partnership of several doctors who practiced medicine in Sidney, New York. In 1974 Dr. Webber joined the partnership. The partnership agreement provided that by majority vote of the partners any member could be requested to withdraw from the group and that such notice would be effective immediately. The expelled member would be paid his share of the profits to the date of termination and that he "will not for five years after any [voluntary or involuntary] termination ... practice his profession within ... thirty miles of the Village of Sidney, ... without the consent ... of the Gelder Medical Group."

After a few months, the majority of the doctors in the partnership reached the conclusion that Dr. Webber was an embarrassment to them. They asked him to withdraw from the partnership and he refused. Following the procedures specified in the partnership agreement, Dr. Webber was formally notified that effective immediately his association with the partnership was terminated and, after an accounting, he was paid $18,568.41. Soon thereafter, disregarding the provision in the partnership agreement prohibiting his practicing medicine in the vicinity of Sidney, he opened a medical office there. The

CASE 37.1 Continued

medical group brought suit to enjoin Dr. Webber from practicing medicine in Sidney. In reply, Dr. Webber claimed he was wrongfully expelled from the partnership because the group had acted in bad faith. The trial court held for the medical group; the Supreme Court affirmed and Dr. Webber appealed to the Court of Appeals which in New York State is the highest appellate court.

OPINION

BREITEL, C.J. . . . Covenants restricting a professional, and in particular a physician, from competing with a former employer or associate are common and generally acceptable. . . . [I]f they are reasonable as to time and area, necessary to protect legitimate interests, not harmful to the public, and not unduly burdensome, they will be enforced. . . .

Similarly common and acceptable are provisions in a partnership agreement to provide for the withdrawal or expulsion of a partner. While there is no common-law or statutory right to expel a member of a partnership, partners may provide, in their agreement, for the involuntary dismissal, with or without cause, of one of their number. . . .

. . . [N]o acceptable reason is offered for limiting the plainly stated provisions for expulsion, freely subscribed to by Dr. Webber when he joined the group, and none is perceived. When, as here, the agreement provides for dismissal of one of their number on the majority vote of the partners, the court may not frustrate the intention of the parties at least so long as the provisions for dismissal work no undue penalty or unjust forfeiture, overreaching, or other violation of public policy.

. . . Embarrassing situations developed, affecting the physicians and their patients, as a result of Dr. Webber's conduct, however highly motivated his conduct might have been. It was as important, therefore, in the group's eyes, as anything affecting survival of the group that it be disassociated from the new member's conflict-producing conduct. Indeed, at the heart of the partnership concept is the principle that partners may choose with whom they wish to be associated. . . . As with any contractual agreement, in the time-honored language of the law, there is an implied term of good faith. . . . In his affidavits Dr. Webber has not shown even a suggestion of evil, malevolent, or predatory purpose in the expulsion. Hence, he raises no triable issue on this score. . . .

JUDGMENT

Accordingly, the order of the Appellate Division should be affirmed.

Dissolution in Violation of Partnership Agreement

Because a partnership is a voluntary association of its members, any partner has the *power* to dissolve the association at any time. The agreement merely contractually puts limits on the *right* of a partner to exercise that power. When a partner exceeds those limits he or she is said to dissolve the partnership in violation of the partnership agreement. Such a dissolution occurs most frequently when a partner withdraws from the firm before the expiration of the agreed term. As noted on page 782, in a partnership at will the withdrawal of a partner is not in violation of the partnership agreement.

When a partner assigns his or her interest, whether the partnership is for a definite term or is a partnership at will, dissolution does not *automatically* result unless there is some evidence that the assigning partner intends to leave the firm. Normally, that intent is expressed by the departing partner in either an oral or written statement to the remaining partner(s).

Suppose that partner Howard assigns his partnership interest to a bank as security for a loan but continues to perform all his partnership duties. It is obvious that Howard has not evidenced any intention to withdraw from the partnership and automatic dissolution has not come about. However, if after assigning his interest to the bank, Howard tells his partners that he is leaving the partnership and wants to be paid for the value of his interest in the firm, he has caused a dissolution. Under less positive circumstances, a partner who withdraws in contravention of the partnership agreement does not bring about an *automatic* dissolution of the partnership, but such an act may be a basis for dissolution by court order under UPA 32, which we will soon consider.

When a partner causes a dissolution in contravention of a partnership agreement, the remaining partners have the privilege of continuing the partnership business or of winding it up. In either event, the withdrawing partner is entitled to receive payment of the value of his or her interest but that value is diminished by whatever damages the innocent partners may have suffered. For instance, assume that Bob was a partner in the Atlas Advertising Agency under a partnership agreement that still had 8 years to run. Before the expiration of the 8 years Bob left Atlas to join another agency and three of Atlas's clients withdrew their accounts and placed them with the agency Bob joined. The losses Atlas suffered may furnish the basis for a damage claim against Bob in the computation of the value of his interest in the Atlas firm.

The following case concerns the notice which must be given to effect a dissolution of a partnership by the exercise of the express will of a partner.

CASE 37.2 Thomas v. American National Bank · 694 S.W.2d 543 (Tex. App. 13th Dist. 1985)

FACTS Gonzalez, Porter, Rogers, and Dahlman, collectively held a one-third interest, and McCombs and Thomas each held a one-third interest in Southwestern Cinema, a joint venture. Gonzalez was the "Managing Venturer." Gonzalez negotiated a loan in the name of the joint venture with the American National Bank sufficient to pay off a loan the venture had previously made with another institution. Southwestern Cinema failed to make timely payment to the bank, which sued and secured a summary judgment against the venture and each of its members. McCombs and Thomas appealed, claiming that before the bank note was executed they had transferred their interests in the venture to Gonzalez and that they had relied upon Gonzalez' law firm to do whatever was necessary to terminate their partnership interests.

OPINION KEITH, J. . . . It is undisputed that all the participants intended to establish and maintain a joint venture. . . . A partnership, once proved, presumptively continues until the contrary appears. . . . Each partner is personally . . . liable for the partnership debts. "This personal liability . . . continues until the partnership is legally dissolved or until the withdrawing partner or partners gives notice of such withdrawal to third parties dealing with the . . . partnership."

. . . At common law, a partner could dissolve the partnership by giving "explicit notice" to the other partners . . . §31(1)(b) [of the UPA] codifies this common law rule by providing that dissolution can be caused by the "express will" of any partner. . . . Absent communication or notice of a desire to dissolve or terminate the partnership, there can be no dissolution by the "express will" of a partner. . . . Thomas and McCombs contend that [their] private agreement [with Gonzalez] constituted a transfer of interest such that they ceased to be partners prior to the time Gonzalez refinanced the partnership's debts with the loan from American Bank. . . . It is . . . undisputed that as of [the date the bank loan was executed] neither McCombs or Thomas had communicated with or given notice to any of the remaining partners [other than Gonzalez] or [to] American Bank that they had sold or transferred their interest in the partnership to Gonzalez. . . . Thomas and McCombs contend that this private agreement . . . constituted a transfer of interests such that they ceased to be partners prior to the [date of the American Bank loan]. . . . A private agreement between partners will not limit their liability to third parties without first giving notice of such withdrawal to third parties. . . .

JUDGMENT . . . The judgment of the trial court is affirmed.

Dissolution by Operation of Law

Dissolution by Death of a Partner. The death of a partner automatically causes the dissolution of a partnership of which the deceased was a member. This is because partners mutually rely upon the performance of copartners and upon the continued use of their contributions to the capital of the firm for the operation of the partnership business.

Some partnerships, particularly those in the accounting, finance, or legal fields, may have several hundred partners in a single firm. To forestall the possibility of forced dissolution and frequent reference to the law courts, these large partnerships, as well as many smaller firms, have buy/sell arrangements. These are agreements executed by each partner or clauses in their partnership agreements which provide for the purchase of the partnership interest of a member who dies, retires, or otherwise leaves the firm. In that fashion the dissolution of the firm is not automatic upon the death of a partner. Such a clause adds flexibility to a partnership organization, and there is basis for it to continue under its original firm name even when the partners whose names the firm bears are no longer alive. Recent cases are giving effect to such partnership agreements, and in several states laws have been passed which give those agreements clear legal foundation.

Dissolution by Bankruptcy. Dissolution also automatically results from the bankruptcy of a partnership or of an individual partner. A partner in a successful partnership might incur large personal debts, such as medical bills or credit card purchases, and see no way out but to go through personal bankruptcy. Unfortunately for his or her partners, bankruptcy results in the automatic dissolution of the partnership. As explained in Chapter 26, where the bankruptcy law was reviewed, if the partner's assets are not sufficient to discharge his or her debts, the partner is nevertheless relieved from any additional obligations, including those arising out of membership in a partnership. This protection afforded by the bankruptcy act takes precedence over the fundamental partnership concept that all partners are equally responsible for their firm's obligations.

Dissolution by Subsequent Illegality. Any event which makes it unlawful for a partnership business to be carried on or unlawful for any of its members to engage in the business causes an automatic dissolution of the firm. This can be illustrated by two examples.

- A partnership is in the business of selling intoxicating liquor at retail. A newly enacted state law makes the retail sale of intoxicating liquor illegal. Upon the effective date of that law the partnership is dissolved.
- Several individuals are partners in a law firm. One of its members is named to a judicial position which precludes the incumbent from practicing law. When the member assumes the judicial position, the partnership is dissolved.

Dissolution by Court Decree

Courts are reluctant to settle disputes between partners concerning the company's business affairs. Furthermore, partners have the power to dissolve a partnership without recourse to court assistance. Accordingly, usually court action to bring about partnership dissolution is not only unnecessary but also expensive and time-consuming. However, there are several circumstances which may justify a court to decree dissolution upon application of a partner when the other partners are unwilling for the firm to be dissolved. Among such circumstances are (1) the incapacity of a partner to perform his or her duties, (2) the misconduct of a partner, (3) the fact that the continuation of the business will result only in a financial loss, or (4) any other circumstance which justifies a court in finding dissolution to be equitable.

Dissolution for Incapacity of a Partner. The temporary incapacity of a partner does not cause a dissolution of a partnership nor does it furnish grounds for the member to be expelled from the firm. However, a partner's continuing mental or physical incapacity to perform partnership duties is a basis for a court to order dissolution.

If a partner is declared by a competent court to be so mentally unsound as not to be able to carry on business affairs there is clear ground for dissolution by court order. However, if a partner has not been judicially declared mentally unsound or if a partner suffers a physical disability which prevents him or her from performing partnership duties, the question whether the incapacity is sufficiently permanent to justify the dissolution of the partnership may not be easy to answer. It would be unfair to the other partners to require them to retain in the partnership a member who, over an extended period of time, is incapable of carrying on his or her agreed partnership functions. It would be equally unfair to force a partner to leave a profitable business organization because of a temporary disability or a disability that is more permanent but does not prevent the performance of partnership duties. If the parties cannot amicably resolve the matter, the competency of a partner to continue as a member of the firm must be presented to a court for decision. Problems such as these are usually anticipated when a partnership is organized. Partners do this by including in their agreement a provision which defines permanent disability and establishes a procedure whereby the interest of all members are equitably protected, generally by a "buyout" of the incapacitated partner's interest.

Dissolution for Misconduct of a Partner. Upon proper application, a court will order the dissolution of a partnership when it has been established that (1) one of the partners has been guilty of conduct which tends to prejudice the carrying on of the partnership business, (2) one of the partners willfully or persistently breaches the partnership agreement, or (3) when one or more of the partners find(s) it is not reasonably practicable to continue in business with another one (or more) of the other partners.

Because it is judicial policy not to interfere in minor internal partnership affairs, the intervention of a court is not warranted if financial loss to the partnership results from an incident in which a partner made an honest error in judgment (such as extending credit to an unworthy purchaser), or if the objectionable conduct is only trifling (such as the fact that a partner has a habit of losing his or her temper when discussing partnership matters). But if the wrongful action of a partner is fundamental to the partnership business, there is a valid basis for the firm's dissolution by court decree upon application by the innocent members of the partnership. Examples of fundamental wrongful conduct might be that a partner:

- Deals fraudulently with purchasing agents
- Refuses to explain or justify checks drawn against the partnership account
- Persists in dealing with customers in a manner that results in permanent injury to the partnership business
- Causes the firm to be brought into such public disrepute or ridicule that its credit and goodwill are impaired

Dissolution for Unprofitable Business. Since a partnership is an association designed to carry on a business for profit, one that can only be carried on at a loss is usually dissolved by agreement of the partners. However, it may be that one of the partners believes that the firm's success lies "just around the corner" and that therefore the partnership should not be dissolved. Or a partner might insist that an attempt should first be made to sell the business while it is a going concern. In either event, if the partnership is not one "at will" and the other partners still want to dissolve the firm, they must seek a court-ordered dissolution.

Dissolution for Other Circumstances. If it is equitable (fair) to all parties concerned, a court may order the dissolution of a partnership under a number of circumstances other than those discussed above. Dissolution may, for instance, be ordered because irreconcilable differences as to the running of the business exist between the partners or because a partner has taken personal advantage of an opportunity desirable to the partnership. Illustrations of such situations might be:

- Partners Jean and Tom cannot agree as to the amount of money their firm should spend on advertising or how its merchandise should be priced.
- Partner Smith of the Smith-Jones partnership, secretly, in his wife's name, purchases a wholesale oil business which sells large quantities of petroleum products to the Smith-Jones partnership. If Smith had told Jones, as he should have, that the oil business could be purchased, Jones would have wanted the partnership, which was capable of doing so, to purchase it. Smith's action was a breach of his fiduciary responsibility to his partner, warranting dissolution of the partnership.

The basis for a court-ordered dissolution for irreconcilable differences between the partners is discussed in the following case.

CASE 37.3 Cooper v. Isaacs · 448 F.2d 1202 (D.C. Cir. 1971)

FACTS Cooper and Isaacs were partners in Lesco Associates, which sold and distributed janitorial supplies. Their partnership agreement provided that it might be terminated by (1) the sale of the business, (2) mutual consent, (3) the retirement of a partner, (4) the death of a partner, or (5) the incompetency of a partner. Cooper filed a complaint asking for a dissolution of the partnership because there were irreconcilable differences between the partners regarding matters of business policy. Isaacs answered, alleging that as irreconcilable differences was not an agreed reason for the termination of the partnership, Cooper's complaint itself constituted a wrongful dissolution in contravention of the partnership agreement and therefore, he, Isaacs, was entitled to continue the partnership business alone. The District Court denied Isaacs' motion and appointed a receiver *pendente lite* [during the suit] to run the business. Isaacs appealed.

OPINION TAMM, J. . . . Since a dissolution based upon irreconcilable differences is not one of [the] events [enumerated in the partnership agreement], the filing of a complaint seeking this relief is, according to Isaacs, a dissolution in contravention of the partnership agreement. . . .

[UPA 32] provides:

On application by or for a partner the court shall decree a dissolution whenever . . .

(c) a partner has been guilty of such conduct as tends to affect prejudicially the carrying on of the business;

(d) a partner willfully or persistently commits a breach of the partnership agreement, or otherwise so conducts himself in matters relating to the partnership business that it is not reasonably practicable to carry on the business in partnership with him; . . .

(f) other circumstances render a dissolution equitable.

Courts interpreting these provisions have consistently held that serious and irreconcilable differences between the parties are proper grounds for dissolution by decree of court. . . . Since the Act provides for dissolution for cause by decree of court and Cooper has alleged facts which would entitle him to a dissolution on this ground if proven, his filing of his complaint cannot be said to effect a dissolution, wrongful or otherwise, under the Act; dissolution would occur only when decreed by the court or brought about by other actions. . . .

A partnership agreement can presumably change this result, but the terms of the agreement must be quite specific to effect such a change. This is so because the provisions of the Act regarding dissolution by decree of court were clearly designed to allow partners to extricate themselves from business relationships which they felt had become intolerable without exposing themselves to liability in the process, and this sound policy should apply unless expressly negated, and perhaps even then.

We do not believe it can be said at this time, with the case in its present posture, that the partnership agreement involved here was clearly meant to exclude the possibility of dissolution of the partnership by decree of court. . . .

We thus conclude that without further inquiry into the claims made by the parties, it is impossible to say that the mere filing of the complaint by Cooper constituted a wrongful dissolution.

. . . In circumstances similar to these, several courts have held the appointment of a receiver to be proper, and we find the reasoning of these decisions persuasive. Accordingly we affirm the District Judge's appointment of the receiver *pendente lite*.

JUDGMENT Affirmed.

Winding Up of Partnerships

The dissolution of a partnership brings to an end the normal working relationships of the partners. However, as already noted, a partnership does not cease to exist when it is dissolved. Except under circumstances later to be discussed, it must first go through another step—its winding up—before the partnership comes to an end.

Who Conducts the Winding Up; Compensation

If a partnership is dissolved because its agreed term has ended or its purpose has been accomplished or because the partners agree to its dissolution, all the partners are entitled to participate in the winding up. However, they usually entrust that function to one of their number or to some third party they designate. If the partners cannot agree upon who will conduct the winding up or a dissolution is ordered by judicial decree, a court will appoint a receiver to take charge of the winding up.

Neither a partner who has wrongfully withdrawn from a partnership and thereby caused its dissolution nor a partner whose bankruptcy caused the dissolution may conduct the winding up.

If a dissolution comes about because a partner has died and the surviving partners have decided not to continue the business, the winding up is undertaken as described above *except* that some states' laws dictate that, for the protection of the estate of the deceased partner, the winding up must be performed by his or her personal representative.

Because sooner or later every partnership business must be wound up, the winding-up process (except if a partner dies) is considered to be a normal partnership function and the partner or partners who conduct it are not entitled to compensation for that activity unless the other partners agree to pay. However, if the dissolution occurred because of a death, the winding-up partner(s) are entitled to compensation. A court-appointed receiver who conducts a winding up is entitled to be paid.

The Winding-Up Process

Winding up means the liquidation of the partnership business. During this process (1) the partnership's assets are preserved, (2) its unfinished business is completed, (3) money owing to the partnership is collected, (4) its debts are paid, (5) the person who conducts the winding up makes a full accounting, and (6) after the contributions made by the partners have been repaid, any remaining assets are distributed among the partners. If there are not enough assets to satisfy all creditors and to return the partners' contributions, each partner is obligated to contribute sufficient money so that they all suffer the same ratio of loss as the ratio in which each was entitled to receive profits (UPA 18(a), 34, 40).

Any debts incurred in the winding up or to complete any business unfinished at the time of dissolution are proper charges against the partnership and all of its members (UPA 35 (1) (a)).

Preserving Assets. The individual who conducts the winding up takes all actions necessary to preserve the firm's assets so that they continue as a source from which the partnership's creditors may be paid, the contributions made by the partners may be returned to them, and the profits of the business may be shared between them. Accordingly, any perishable assets should be guarded and protected from spoilage. All assets should be adequately insured.

Completing Unfinished Business. Because a partnership upon its dissolution ceases to be a going concern, the individual who conducts its winding up, unless specifically authorized by the agreement of the partners, judicial order, or statute, has no authority to bind the partners or the partnership by taking on *new* business. However, a dissolution does not discharge a partnership's executory contracts. The other parties to existing contracts continue to have the right to expect performance. Therefore, all unfinished business should be completed during the winding-up process.

If a contract is one of purchase by the partnership, the person in charge of the winding up uses partnership funds to pay for the purchase. If the contract is one of sale by the partnership, the property is delivered to the purchaser and payment is received in accordance with the contract terms.

To illustrate, assume that you, Ted, and Craig were in partnership building houses under contracts with property owners. Craig dies suddenly, thus dissolving the partnership while your firm has three houses under construction. Some materials are lying at the sites, other materials are on order, and additional materials will be needed to complete the buildings under contract. You and Ted agree that you will wind up the partnership. As the winding-up partner, you continue construction until all the existing contracts are fulfilled. To do so you may hire the necessary workmen, use the materials on the sites, and order the additional materials required. While you *may use* partnership funds to pay for all these costs, you are *not* authorized to bind the dissolved partnership by entering into any new contracts to perform *additional* construction. If you do enter into a new contract, you alone (not the dissolved partnership) will be obligated to fulfill it.

During the winding up of a partnership the completion of existing contracts and payments to employees may make it necessary to borrow money in the name of the partnership to gather sufficient funds with which to meet these needs. The partnership and its members are liable for any debts contracted in the performance of this kind of necessary borrowing.

If a tort is committed by a winding-up partner as a part of the winding-up process, the partnership and the partners will be liable to the same extent they would have been liable if the partnership had not been dissolved.

Collecting Debts and Discharging Liabilities. The person who conducts the winding up must exert his or her best efforts as a fiduciary to collect all debts due to the partnership. If necessary, a debt may be compromised, that is, a lesser amount may be accepted in full payment; and if all other collection methods fail suit may be filed against the debtor. Partnership funds may be used to pay the necessary legal and accounting fees and court costs.

Incident to the winding-up process, all valid partnership debts must be paid and other liabilities discharged.

Converting Assets into Cash. An important task in the winding-up process is the conversion into cash of all partnership assets to fulfill outstanding contractual obligations and to pay debts. How assets can best be turned into cash depends upon the circumstances. Important considerations are whether the property is perishable, the season of the year, the warehousing charges that would be incurred if the property were to be held for any length of time, and so on.

After all partnership debts have been paid, the partners are entitled to have the remaining partnership property converted into cash and applied to the payment of whatever amounts may be owing to each partner. However, the most ready buyers of partnership property are often the partners themselves. Therefore, the remaining partnership property may, with the consent of all the partners, be sold to one or more of the partners; or the property may be transferred to one or more of the partners to satisfy a partnership debt owing to such member or members. Whatever partnership property remains may be equitably distributed among the partners.

Making an Accounting. As related to a partnership winding up, an accounting (or an account) is a statement by the individual who conducts the winding up which reveals all the transactions that were involved in that process. It shows the total assets, debts, and equity of the firm at the date of the dissolution and at the conclusion of the winding up. If, after taking into consideration all receipts and disbursements, partnership assets are exhausted and claims against the partnership still remain unsatisfied, the accounting will indicate how much each partner is required to pay the remaining creditors. On the other hand, if all partnership obligations have been paid and partnership assets yet remain, the accounting will disclose how those assets will be distributed among the partners.

Partners' Powers Not Incident to Winding Up

Except in matters connected with winding up a partnership, its dissolution terminates the authority of all partners to act for it. However, although after dissolution a partner may have no *actual* authority, he or she may still have *apparent authority* to bind a dissolved partnership. Apparent authority exists when (1) the nature of the transaction is such that the partnership would be bound if the dissolution had not taken place, and (2) the third party had no knowledge or notice of the dissolution. To illustrate the application of this rule, let us return to the example where Craig, one of your partners in the construction business, died and you have been designated the winding-up partner. Assume that Capital Supply Company in another city, from which your other partner, Ted, regularly purchased hardware for your partnership, does not know of Craig's death. The partnership does not require any additional hardware to complete its contracts, but Ted, mistakenly believing that more doorknobs are needed, orders two dozen from Capital. Because of Ted's apparent authority to do business on behalf of the partnership, the contract is binding upon it.

In order to protect themselves against the possibility of being made liable on unauthorized transactions, partners should give third parties prompt notice of dissolution. With respect to third parties such as merchants and tradespeople who had extended credit to the partnership prior to the dissolution, "notice" means actual notice. This entails actually informing the former creditor that the partnership is dissolved or delivering to it a written notice of the dissolution, generally by sending a a return-receipt registered or certified letter to the former creditor.

As to a third party who knew of the partnership but had not extended credit to it prior to the dissolution, constructive notice is sufficient. What constitutes constructive notice may differ from state to state. Generally publication of a notice (in some states on more than one occasion) in a newspaper of general circulation serving the area or areas where the partnership did business, stating that it had been dissolved, constitutes constructive notice even if the third party did not see the notice.

Settlement of Partnership Accounts

Order of Payment. The ultimate objective of the winding-up process is to pay all partnership debts and then to repay to the partners the capital contributions they made to the firm together with their respective shares of any assets that remain. The liabilities of a dissolved partnership are paid in the following order:

1. Those owing to partnership creditors other than to the partners themselves
2. Those owing to partners for loans or advances made to the partnership
3. Those owing to partners as repayment of their capital contributions
4. Those owing to partners as their share of the profits, if any

The partners may, by agreement, change the order of payment among themselves of items 2, 3, and 4.

Settlement of Accounts among Partners Unless a partnership agreement provides otherwise, partners share equally in the *profits* of the business even if their investments (capital contributions) in the partnership were unequal amounts (see Chapter 36). If a dissolved partnership does not have enough assets with which to pay all creditors or to return to the partners their contributions to the firm's capital, then all the partners must contribute toward paying off those losses. Unless the partnership agreement provides otherwise, the partners' contributions are in the same ratio they established for the sharing of the firm's profits. If one of the partners is unable to discharge his or her obligation to the creditors, then the other partner or partners who are financially able are required to make up the deficiency.

The computation of how much each partner must contribute when partners who are entitled to *share equally* in profits have *contributed different amounts* to the capital of the firm can best be explained by illustration. Assume that partner Arnold made a capital contribution of $10,000; partner Baxter made a contribution of $5,000 and services; and partner Clara's contribution was her expert knowledge, which was extremely important to the firm. It was understood that the three partners were to share equally in the profits. Assume further that upon its dissolution the partnership was able to pay all its bills except two bills still outstanding: $2,500 to creditor Judith and $1,100 to partner Clara, who had loaned that amount to the business. The firm has no more money or property with which to meet these obligations. Most courts would compute the partnership accounts of this firm as follows:

Obligations of the firm:

To Judith	$ 2,500	(for amount due)
To Clara	1,100	(for loan to partnership)
To Arnold	10,000	(for return of capital contribution)
To Baxter	5,000	(for return of capital contribution)
To Clara	—	(no contribution made)
	$18,600	Total obligations

Contributions required:

Since the partners had agreed to share equally in the profits, they must contribute equally to cover the losses. Therefore, Arnold, Baxter, and Clara must equally share the loss of $18,600, or $6,200 each, distributed as follows:

Arnold	$ 0	no new contribution (original contribution $10,000; loss $6,200, balance due Arnold $3,800)
Baxter	$ 1200	additional contribution (original contribution $5,000; loss $6,200; balance due $1,200)
Clara	$6,200	(no original contribution)
	$7,400	Contributions required

Distribution of total contributions of $7,400:

To Judith	$2,500	(to pay creditor's bill)
To Clara	$1,100	(to repay loan)
To Arnold	$3,800	(partial return of contribution)

Therefore all partners share equally the loss of $18,600:

Arnold loses	$6,200	($10,000 original contribution less $3,800)
Baxter loses	$6,200	($5,000 original contribution plus new contribution of $1,200)
Clara loses	$6,200	($6,200 new contribution)

A few courts (e.g., California) would distribute the loss only among partners Arnold and Baxter and assess no monetary contribution against Clara, because Clara contributed services but no money to the partnership.

Settlement of Accounts with Creditors. Each partner is personally liable for all partnership obligations, that is, its debts, unperformed contracts, and tort claims (UPA 15, 36). Each partner also probably has debts of his or her own for such things as credit card purchases, house mortgage payments, car payments, and so on. If a partner does not have sufficient resources with which to pay both the partnership debts and his or her own debts, and legal actions are brought against the partner, the question arises whether the personal creditors of the partner or the partnership creditors are entitled to be paid first out of the partner's funds. Here a formula informally called the "jingle rule" applies. Under that rule, a partner's *personal assets* are first used to pay *personal debts*, while *partnership assets* are first used to pay *partnership debts*.

Under the Bankruptcy Reform Act of 1978, the jingle rule does not apply when a partnership is in bankruptcy. In that event, partnership creditors can recover payment from the individual partners at the same time as the partners' personal creditors. To illustrate, assume that a partnership of Aaron and Ben is in bankruptcy and it does not have assets with which to pay $6,000 owing its creditors. Partner Aaron has no personal assets but partner Ben has personal assets of $4,000 and he owes Doris a personal debt of $2,000. Since Aaron has no assets, Ben's $4,000 must in some way be applied toward both the partnership debt of $6,000 and his private debt to Doris of $2,000. As these two debts are treated equally, Ben's $4,000 is divided between the partnership creditors and Doris in the proportion each of their claims bears to the $8,000 *total* debt. Therefore, the partnership creditors receive $3,000 (six-eighths of Ben's $4,000) and Doris receives $1,000 (two-eighths of the $4,000).

Partners' Fiduciary Responsibilities during Winding Up

A partnership in the winding-up stage is still an existing business organization and the partners owe to one another the normal fiduciary obligations of partners. (Partners' fiduciary obligations are discussed in Chapter 36.)

The most common fiduciary problems which arise during the winding-up process concern (1) the improper exercise of winding-up duties, (2) the improper purchase by a partner of partnership property, and (3) the seizure for personal gain of partnership legal rights or opportunities. For example:

- A partner who conducts the winding up must use his or her best efforts in that endeavor. This involves the protection of partnership assets, the collection of moneys due the partnership without making private gain in the process, the settlement of the debts and obligations of the partnership to the extent possible, and the proper distribution to the partners of any profits which remain after its liquidation is completed. If the winding-up partner improperly performs these duties and damage to the copartners results, the winding-up partner is liable to them in an *action for an accounting.*

- Many times one of the partners desires to acquire partnership property being liquidated. He or she must deal fairly with the other copartners, disclosing everything he or she knows about the property bearing upon its value. If the purchasing partner fails to disclose all such facts or fails to reveal that he or she is directly or indirectly the purchaser, then there has been a breach of fiduciary duties and the sale may be voided by the other partners.
- A partner may not, during the winding-up process, seize for himself or herself partnership legal rights or opportunities which should be considered among the partnership's assets. The value of any such wrongful seizure must be accounted for in the final computation of the amounts of money owing to or by the partners.

The following case deals with a partner's fiduciary responsibilities during the winding up of a partnership.

CASE 37.4 Hooper v. Yoder · 37 P.2d 852 (Colo. 1987)

FACTS Steven Hooper and David Yoder formed a partnership for the manufacture and sale of frozen yogurt bars. They agreed to share equally in the financial risks, the work load, and the potential profits of the business, but no formal written partnership agreement was drawn up. In 1977 they formed Beautiful Daydreams, Inc. (hereafter Daydreams), to take over the partnership business. Hooper was named president and treasurer of the corporation and Yoder its vice president and secretary. The two men, who composed its board of directors, agreed to defer the issuance of stock in the corporation.

Market West, a food brokerage firm, agreed to accept stock in Daydreams in part payment of a loan Market West had made to Daydreams and, in October of 1978, Hooper and Yoder elected Brian Bradley of Market West a Daydreams director. The next month Hooper scheduled a meeting of the board of directors of the corporation. Yoder, who had gone to a business convention, was unable to attend the meeting. Nevertheless, Hooper and Bradley held the meeting and, without Yoder's knowledge, authorized the issuance of 95 shares of the corporation's stock to Hooper and 5 shares to Market West. In exchange, Hooper agreed to cancel a $9,500 debt owed to him by Daydreams and Market West agreed to cancel $500 of the debt owed to it. At a directors' meeting the following month, Hooper and Bradley told Yoder that because of the financial condition of the corporation, no more money would be taken out of it and Hooper and Yoder would not receive a salary.

On January 15, 1979 Hooper and Market West, the sole shareholders of Beautiful Daydreams, Inc., without notifying Yoder, removed the entire board of directors of the company and elected Hooper and Bradley as its only directors. Hooper and Bradley were also named, respectively, the corporation's president and vice president. On February 1, 1979, Yoder received notice from Hooper that his services with the corporation were terminated.

Later, Yoder learned that corporate stock had been issued to Hooper and to Market West, that he (Yoder) was no longer an officer of the corporation, and that Hooper received the sum of $141,500, as salary, from 1979 into 1982.

Yoder filed action against Hooper and Daydreams. The trial court entered a judgment in favor of Yoder for $70,750 (one-half of the salary paid Hooper beginning in 1979) and directed Hooper to transfer to Yoder 47½ shares of the stock held by him in Daydreams.

CASE 37.4 Continued

The court of appeals affirmed the judgment. Hooper than appealed to the Colorado Supreme Court.

OPINION

LOHR, J.... As a general rule, when partners organize a corporation to operate the business of the partnership and transfer the assets to the corporation, the partnership is dissolved. [Citation.] This is because such action usually reflects the express will of the parties that the partnership be dissolved....

The dissolution of a partnership, however, does not automatically terminate the existence of the partnership. The Uniform Partnership Act provides that "[o]n dissolution the partnership is not terminated but continues until the winding up of partnership affairs is completed." [Citations.] The winding up includes the entire process of settling the partnership affairs after dissolution. [Citations.]

When partners organize a corporation to continue the business of the firm, the winding up of the partnership includes the transfer of the partnership assets to the corporation in exchange for corporate stock. [Citations.] Here the winding up of the partnership remained incomplete pending issuance of corporate stock to Hooper and Yoder in equal amounts pursuant to the agreement they made as partners prior to incorporation. Because there were no shares of stock issued upon incorporation of Beautiful Daydreams, it cannot be said that the property of the partnership was exchanged for stock in the corporation and that the stock was then distributed to the partners, thereby winding up the partnership affairs. The circumstances of this case bring us to the conclusion that the winding up of the partnership was not accomplished upon incorporation and, therefore, the partnership continued to exist.

Because the partnership continued to exist, so did the fiduciary duties that one partner owes to another. Partners in a business enterprise owe to one another the highest duty of loyalty; they stand in a relationship of trust and confidence to each other and are bound by standards of good conduct and square dealing. [Citations.] Each partner has the right to demand and expect from the other a full, fair, open and honest disclosure of everything affecting the relationship. [Citations.] During the winding up of partnership affairs, the partners continue to owe to each other the same duty of loyalty and fair dealing. [Citation.]

...Hooper's actions in causing the issuance of 95 shares of stock to himself and none to Yoder and in drawing a salary from the business without the assent or knowledge of Yoder are the very antithesis of the type of fair dealing required between partners in winding up a partnership....

The trial court provided appropriate remedies for [Hooper's] breaches by... requiring Hooper to share the stock and salary equally with Yoder in accordance with the partnership agreement between them.

JUDGMENT Judgment affirmed.

Continuation of Partnership Business without Winding Up

The dissolution and winding up of a partnership involves some measure of forced sale at which it is highly probable that some or all of the partnership property will be sold for less than its true value. Liquidation of a partnership business may also result in the loss of the value of the firm's goodwill. Therefore the innocent partner or partners who did not cause the dissolution are likely to be faced, through no fault of their own, with financial loss if there is a winding up and forced liquidation of the business. To protect innocent partners, the law therefore allows a partnership business to be continued without a winding up when (1) there has been a wrongful withdrawal of a partner, or (2) after the expulsion of a partner, or (3) after the retirement or death of a partner.

If a partnership business is to be continued in place of a winding up, instead of the physical liquidation of its assets, there is an accounting of its affairs as of the date of the dissolution. In the accounting all the assets and liabilities of the partnership including the value of its goodwill are comprehensively reviewed and evaluated, and the value of each partner's interest is mathematically determined *as of the date of the dissolution.* Note that when there is a winding up, the value of each partner's interest is determined *at the end of the winding up* when the liquidation of the business has been completed (not the date of the dissolution).

When a partnership business is continued it is not the dissolved partnership that is the owner of the continuing business unless the original partnership agreement specifically so provides and state law so permits. Absent that rather unusual circumstance, the partner or partners who carry on the business do so either (1) as a sole proprietorship if only a single partner remains to operate the business or (2) as a new partnership if more than one of the partners of the dissolved partnership business carry it on.

If the business is to be carried on without a winding up after a wrongful withdrawal or the expulsion of a partner, different rules will apply than if there had been a retirement or death of a partner. Accordingly, the effect of continuing a dissolved partnership business without a winding up will be discussed under those two general headings.

Continuation after Wrongful Withdrawal or Expulsion of Partner

When a partnership is dissolved because a partner has wrongfully withdrawn from the firm or when a member is expelled as authorized by the agreement, the remaining partners must elect between (1) winding up the partnership business, or (2) continuing the partnership business. Neither the wrongdoing partner nor the expelled partner has a voice in that decision. If the remaining partners elect to wind up the partnership then the partnership is wound up in the manner outlined in the first portion of this chapter. If they elect to continue the business, the value of the withdrawing or expelled partner's interest is computed by deducting the firm's total liabilities from the value of its total assets. The departing partner is then due his proportionate share of the computed value of the partnership less, however, any damage he or she may have caused the partnership. In the computation of the value of a *withdrawing* partner's interest, no credit is given for the value of the partnership goodwill for he or she has, in effect, "walked away" from that partnership asset. If there is no provision in the partnership agreement to the contrary, it is generally held that when a partner is expelled, the value of the partnership goodwill is included in the computation of the value of his or her share.

A partner who wrongfully withdraws or is expelled is entitled to be paid in cash the computed value, as explained above, of his or her interest unless the partnership agreement provides otherwise. If full payment in cash is not made to the departing partner, he or she is entitled to have the balance due secured by a court-approved bond.

A wrongfully withdrawing partner or an expelled partner ceases to be a member of the partnership and is not liable for any obligations *thereafter* incurred by the partnership.

Continuation after Retirement or Death of a Partner

Effect of Partnership Agreement. Partners may agree, either when the firm is organized or at some later time, that if one of their members retires or dies, the surviving partner(s) may, *at that time,* decide whether to continue the business without going through a winding up, or to wind up and liquidate it. Typically, such an agreement will give the remaining partners the right to buy the interest of the member who retires or dies, setting out the method for determining the purchase price. If no such formula had been established and the remaining partners want to continue the business, an accounting of the partnership affairs must be conducted, including its goodwill, as of the date of the dissolution. The retired partner or the deceased partner's estate is entitled to be paid his or her share as determined by that accounting.

A different situation exists if the partners had not previously agreed that the remaining partner(s) may continue the business without a winding up. In that event, when a partner retires or dies, the surviving or remaining partner(s) must secure the consent of the retiring partner or of the personal representative of the deceased partner to continue the business without a winding up. If that request is refused, then, despite the wishes of the remaining partners, the partnership must be wound up.

Payment of Value of Partner's Interest. When a partnership business continues without a winding up following the retirement or death of a partner, the departing partner or the representative of the deceased partner is entitled to receive in cash his or her share of the computed value of the partnership, including the value of its goodwill. However, it may be that the remaining partners are unable immediately to pay the retiring partner or the estate of the deceased partner the value of his or her interest. Or it may be that instead of receiving payment, the retiring partner or the deceased partner's representative may want to leave all or part of that share in the partnership business as an investment. In that event, if the continuing partners agree to that course of action, the retiring partner or the representative of the deceased partner must, under UPA 42, elect whether to receive *either* (1) interest upon the share left in the firm, *or* (2) so much of the profits of the continuing business as that share earns. This election to receive interest or profits may be made only one time.

To illustrate this principle, assume that Hazel retires from the Babcock Press partnership. She leaves her share in the firm and elects to receive the profits her investment earns. The following year the country is in a deep recession and Babcock Press makes no profit. Hazel may not then change her election and opt to receive interest on the money she has invested. Her election to receive profits instead of interest is binding for as long as her share remains in the firm.

When a retiring or deceased partner's share is left in the business, he or she becomes an ordinary creditor of the partnership in that amount, but the other creditors have priority on any claim against the partnership.

The next case illustrates the application of UPA 42 to the rights of retired and deceased partners when a partnership business continues.

CASE 37.5 Matter of Trust Estate of Schaefer · 283 N.W.2d 410 (Wis. 1979)

FACTS Ben Schaefer owned thirteen parcels of real estate in partnership with Arthur Schaefer. Ben died in 1969. Arthur, the surviving partner, began to wind up the partnership. Ben's widow brought suit challenging the existence of the partnership, claiming that all the property belonged to Ben's estate. Because of the suit, Arthur attempted to keep the partnership affairs unchanged. He ceased liquidating its assets, incurred no new debts, and bought no new properties. About eight years later the Supreme Court of the state decided that the property was held by the partnership. Thereupon, the co-executor of Ben's estate and the trustee under Ben's will brought this action for a declaration whether the interest of Ben's estate in the property is (1) 50 percent of its valuation at the date of his death plus 50 percent of the profits from the date of death until final settlement of the partnership, or (2) 50 percent of its valuation at the final settlement of the partnership accounts, which has not as yet occurred. Since Ben's death, the property has appreciated in value and the second method of valuation would be more beneficial to the estate. The probate court determined that Section 42 of the Uniform Partnership Act controlled and therefore the trustee's interest is limited to 50 percent of the partnership assets valued at the date of death plus the interest or profits accruing since then until the date of final settlement. The trustee appealed.

OPINION BROWN, Presiding Judge. . . . When a partner dies, the partnership is dissolved. . . . On dissolution, however, the partnership is not terminated; it continues until the wind-up of the partnership affairs is completed. . . . Winding up is the process of settling partnership affairs after dissolution. Partners, or those claiming through a deceased partner, may agree

CASE 37.5 Continued

to settle the partnership affairs without a liquidation of the assets (by agreeing to a cash settlement or in-kind distribution). However, absent an agreement, winding-up involves reducing the assets to cash (liquidation), paying creditors, and distributing to partners the value of their respective interests. . . .

Ordinarily, upon distribution due to death of a partner, it is the duty and responsibility of the surviving partner to wind up the partnership with due diligence and pay the estate of the deceased partner the value of his interest in the partnership. . . . The surviving partner, however, need not wind up the partnership if he has a right to continue the business. . . . [when] the legal representative of the deceased partner consents to the continuation without liquidation of the partnership affairs. . . . The record is clear that the legal representative did not consent to or acquiesce in the continuation of the business. . . .

Therefore, . . . the business was not continued . . . but was instead a slow wind-up due to the pending litigation [brought by Ben's widow]. . . .

If a partnership is seasonably wound up after dissolution, *profits and losses* during liquidation are shared by the partners in proportion to their predissolution ratios unless they have agreed otherwise. . . .

Where the business is continued, the value of the deceased partner's interest may be different. Under Section 42 of the Uniform Partnership Act . . . the non-continuing partner (or his representative) has a *first election* between two basic alternatives, either of which can be enforced in an action for an accounting. He can force a liquidation, taking his part of the proceeds. . . . Alternatively, he can permit the business to continue (or accept the fact that it has continued) and claim as a creditor (though subordinate to outside creditors) the value of his interest at dissolution. This gives him a participation in all values at dissolution. . . . If he takes the latter route, he has a *second election* to receive in addition either interest (presumably at the local legal rate) or profits from date of dissolution.

Where the business is wound-up, the deceased partner's interest is not determined until the wind-up is complete. After the creditors have been paid, all profits are shared by the surviving partner and the deceased partner, as well as losses based on their predissolution ratios (in this case 50%). Therefore, where the business is wound up rather than continued under the conditions set forth in [UPA §42], the deceased partner's interest is the value of his interest at the date of liquidation (when wind-up is complete). This value includes assets appreciation during the winding-up period and is subject to any losses incurred during that time. . . .

In the present case, . . . there was no agreement to continue the business. . . . Therefore, Section [UPA 42] does not apply. Section [UPA 38] applies and the estate is entitled to 50% of the proceeds, including asset appreciation, at the time of liquidation or final settlement. . . .

JUDGMENT Decree reversed and case remanded for liquidation of all assets and distribution of the surplus, after payment to creditors, to the deceased partner's estate and the surviving partner, 50% to each, unless otherwise agreed.

Creditors' Rights When Partnership Business Continues

Rights against Original and Continuing Partnerships. When the business of a partnership is continued without a winding up of its affairs, the creditors of the dissolved (original) partnership become creditors of the new (continuing) partners and partnership, standing in an equal position with the new creditors of the continuing partnership.

If a new member is added to the continuing partnership, his or her contribution to its capital may be used to pay partnership debts incurred *before or after* he or she joined the firm. The new member is *not*, however, liable *personally* for any partnership debts which were incurred *before* he or she joined the firm.

Rights against Departed Partners. After dissolution each partner remains personally liable for all partnership obligations incurred while he or she was a member. For example, Tom, a partner in the Acme Partnership, died last April and the partnership was wound up. His estate (along with the other Acme partners) remained legally liable to pay partnership creditors for all debts that were incurred up to the time the winding up was concluded.

When there is a dissolution *without* a winding up, a partner who leaves the firm may be subjected twice to the same partnership debt if circumstances such as the following arise: suppose that at the time of Jim's retirement from the SITCO partnership, consisting of Jim, Perry, and Todd, the firm's only debt is $3,000 to Brown. Assume further that were it not for that debt, the value of Jim's interest in the partnership would be $11,000. However, taking that $3,000 debt into consideration, the value of Jim's interest at his retirement is reduced by $1,000, being one-third of the amount of the Brown debt. Accordingly, when he leaves the partnership, Jim is paid $10,000. Now, let us assume further that the partnership does not pay the Brown debt and a year after Jim's retirement Brown demands payment of his $3,000. If the SITCO partnership cannot pay him, Perry and Todd (the partners who have continued the business) *and Jim* (because the debt existed while Jim was still a partner) must each contribute one-third ($1,000) out of their own personal resources to discharge the Brown debt. Furthermore, in the event Perry or Todd (or both of them) cannot pay their own shares, Jim may find himself liable for the entire debt of $3,000.

To offset the possibility of the liability which Jim now faces, partners generally enter into what is called an "indemnification agreement" when a partner leaves the firm. By such an agreement the continuing partners agree to reimburse a departing partner for any amount he or she is later forced to pay to a creditor of the dissolved partnership. Sometimes a different device, called a "novation," is used. Under a novation agreement the creditor agrees not to hold the departing partner for the debt but to hold only the continuing partners responsible, and they agree to pay the creditor.

Summary

When partners no longer carry on a business *together,* their firm is automatically dissolved. Following dissolution, either the partnership may be wound up, that is, liquidated, or the partnership business may be continued by the remaining partner(s) after an accounting of the interest of each partner. A partnership is dissolved (1) by the agreement of all the partners, as expressed in the partnership agreement or at a later date, (2) by the withdrawal of a partner in a partnership at will, (3) by an act in violation of the partnership agreement, such as by the wrongful withdrawal of a partner, (4) automatically by operation of law, as when a partner dies, or (5) by court decree for any reason a court finds proper.

A partnership does not cease to exist when it is dissolved; its existence ends when the winding up is complete—that is, when all money owing to the partnership has been collected, all its debts have been paid, partnership contributions have been returned, and any remaining assets have been distributed among the partners in the same ratio as they share in the profits. If there are insufficient assets to pay all obligations, the partners must contribute from their own personal resources to share in the losses in the same ratio that they would have shared in the profits.

Depending upon the manner in which a partnership was dissolved, the winding up may be carried out by all the partners, by one or more of them, by someone designated by them, or by a receiver appointed by a court. In some states the law dictates that if the partnership has been dissolved because of the death of a partner, the winding up must be performed by the deceased partner's personal representative. If one of the partners caused the dissolution by an act in violation of the partnership agreement or because of personal bankruptcy, he or she may not conduct the winding up.

The person who conducts the winding up continues to carry out the terms of the firm's ongoing contracts but may not make any new contracts on behalf of the partnership except in connection with the winding up itself. During the winding up the partners still owe fiduciary obligations to each other.

A retiring partner or the personal representative of a deceased partner must give his or her consent if the remaining partners want to continue the business after dissolution without a winding up. The departing partner (or personal representative of a deceased partner) must then elect whether to receive his or her share in the firm in cash or to leave that share in the business as an investment. If it is left in the business, he or she must make a further election whether to receive interest on the money left in the business or to receive a share of the firm's profits.

Dissolution of a partnership for any cause does not free a withdrawing or retiring partner or a deceased partner's estate from liability for debts of the firm which existed when that partner was still a member of the firm.

Review Questions

1 Distinguish between "dissolution," "winding up," and "termination" of a partnership.

2 Does the addition of a partner to an existing partnership dissolve the partnership?

3 What is a partnership at will?

4 When a partner wrongfully withdraws from a firm, what happens to the capital contribution he or she made?

5 What is meant by the dissolution of a partnership by operation of law?

6 Assume a partner suffers a stroke and as a result is unable to walk. Discuss the effect of this unfortunate event upon a partnership of which this person is a member.

7 What effect, if any, does the dissolution of a partnership have on **(a)** its rental obligation under an unexpired lease, **(b)** a debt that is owed to the partnership, and **(c)** a contract to build a house which the partnership has half completed?

8 **(a)** At the conclusion of a winding up, what is the order in which partnership assets are distributed? **(b)** What action is taken if the assets are not sufficient to pay all the partnership debts?

9 When can a partnership business be continued without a winding up?

10 If the business of a dissolved partnership is continued without a winding up, does this mean that the original partnership is continuing the business? Explain.

11 When a partnership is continued without a winding up, what rights do the creditors of the dissolved partnership have?

12 How do ethics in business standards, discussed in Chapters 1 and 2 of this book, apply to a partnership relationship?

Case Problems

1 Stark and Henning, as partners, operated a sales agency. One of their accounts was the Utica Screw Company. Stark left the partnership, thereby causing its dissolution, and went to work for a former client, Utica Screw Company. Henning claimed that Utica Screw still owed the former partnership commissions for sales the partnership had made and therefore Henning, in the partnership name (permitted in that state), sued the Utica Screw Company. Stark did not join in the suit and Utica claims the suit should be dismissed because both partners did not bring the action. Discuss the issues involved.

2 Jerry, Nick, and Lorenzo owned the Juicy Orange Squeeze factory in a partnership which still had 4 years to run. Their agreement contained no provision for the expulsion of a partner. Lorenzo's outspoken political views became so distasteful to Jerry and Nick that, in Lorenzo's absence, they changed the locks on the factory doors and did not permit him to enter the factory. They told Lorenzo they had dissolved the partnership, that the two of them were going to carry on the business, and that they would pay him "every penny he had coming to him from the business." Lorenzo brings an action to secure a judicial termination of the partnership. He also seeks a court order directing him, Lorenzo, to wind up the partnership business. How should the court rule?

3 Deckard and Treadaway were partners trading under the name Deckard & Treadaway Electric. The partnership was dissolved by their mutual agreement. It was agreed that Deckard would conduct the winding up and that he could, if he wished, continue to operate the business as a sole proprietor. No notice of the dissolution was given to any supplier. A week after the dissolution and before the termination of the partnership, Deckard bought a supply of electric wire from Hecla Wire Company. Some of the wire was necessary to fill an order the partnership had received prior to its dissolution and the remainder of the wire Deckard planned to put in stock after he became the sole owner of the business. Hecla Wire was not paid and it sued the Deckard and Treadaway partnership and the partners individually. Treadaway claims that he is not obligated to pay for any of the wire. Is he correct? Explain.

4 Axel and Leonard, by an oral partnership at will, established a restaurant business. They made equal contributions to the firm's capital; each agreed to work full time and to share equally in the profits of the restaurant. After about a year, it was evident that the two men could no longer work together and Axel, on January 5, ceased to go to the restaurant. Leonard continued to operate the business, retaining the profits that were made. Several times Axel asked when the business was going to be wound up. On August 16 Leonard sold the restaurant to the Homelike chain. Axel immediately filed suit for an accounting in which he asked for one-half of the money Leonard had received on the sale. Leonard offered to pay Axel one-half the value of the restaurant as of January 5 when the partnership was dissolved, but Axel refused to accept that sum. Was Axel or Leonard correct? Why?

5 Arthur, Ben, Charles, and Doris conducted an at-will partnership law practice called ABCD. Arthur and Ben were handling for the partnership a multimillion dollar action on behalf of the Pluto Company. The ABCD law firm was entitled to a fee of 35 percent of any money judgment in favor of the client. Of this, under arrangements established by ABCD for the conduct of its business, Arthur and Ben would each be entitled to 15 percent of the amount of the partnership's fee. Shortly before the case was to come to trial, Arthur and Ben asked for 25 percent each. The other partners, Charles and Doris, were not willing to modify their office practices. Arthur and Ben thereupon left the partnership, thereby dissolving it, and formed a new partnership of their own. A few days later and before any winding up of ABCD had begun, Pluto discharged ABCD as its lawyers and hired the new partnership of Arthur and Ben to handle the litigation. Shortly thereafter and before ABCD had been wound up, the court entered a substantial judgment in Pluto's favor.

Arthur and Ben maintain that because ABCD was dissolved and the client had discharged that partnership, that ABCD was not entitled to any part of the fee. Were Arthur and Ben correct? Explain.

6 Turner, Kaplan, and Hoffman were partners. When Turner retired in 1980, Kaplan and Hoffman asked Turner to leave his partnership interest, amounting to $35,000, in the business, which they continued to operate. It was mutually agreed that Turner would receive annual payments representing the profits his share earned. During the next year Turner received a sizable return on his investment but thereafter the partners paid him nothing, saying that they would pay him his share of the profits "as soon as they had cleared up the old bills of the partnership." Turner complained that if they paid those creditors before paying him, they would be acting illegally. Comment upon Turner's position.

CHAPTER 38

Limited Partnerships

Perhaps a good way to begin an explanation of the organization and functions of limited partnerships and the difference between them and ordinary partnerships is by illustration.

Julie breeds race horses. She learns that Flasher, a very desirable colt, is for sale, but she lacks funds with which to buy him. Julie secures an option to buy Flasher and then she sets out to raise the purchase price of $20,000 and an additional $10,000 to cover the initial costs of raising and training the horse. Julie forms a limited partnership. She is the general partner and she sells limited partnership interests in units of $3,000 to ten investors, thereby raising the necessary $30,000. As the general partner in the enterprise, Julie will run the business and make all required decisions; the limited partners will have no managerial responsibilities. If the colt lives up to Julie's expectations the limited partners stand to earn back many times their investments by sharing with Julie the income from winnings, stud fees, the sale of Flasher for a high price, or from all these sources. Of course, the limited partners' profits will depend upon the success of the venture.

Julie buys the colt, hires a trainer, and pays all the bills. But alas, shortly after his first race, which he wins handily, Flasher falls, breaks a leg, and must be destroyed. Julie has used up all the capital investment obtained from the limited partners and still has many unpaid bills from the feed store, the veterinarian, the trainer, the blacksmith, and others. Because the enterprise was a limited partnership, Julie, the general partner, is personally responsible for all the debts. But although the limited partners risked and lost their investments, they have no personal liability to any of the creditors.

The limited partnership form of business organization was devised to satisfy the need of businesspeople and investors for some type of organization that would be similar to a partnership and yet would not subject an investor to the possibility of personal liability for the debts of the enterprise. Although the corporation form (discussed in the next five chapters) also invites the investment of funds without the exercise of management responsibilities and the investor is free from the possibility of personal liability for the firm's debts, an enterprise of limited scope or duration operated by a single person or by very few people may find the corporation form of organization too unwieldy and subject to too many administrative controls to be adopted.

A limited partnership fills the business organizational gap between a general partnership and a corporation and it has characteristics of both types of organization. Limited partnerships are extremely popular with investors because they can furnish very attractive returns and sometimes provide tax savings as well. In addition, this type of business organization is a vehicle which encourages investments in new and sometimes novel ventures. A limited partnership may be organized for any lawful business purpose. The illustration that opened this chapter might be one; others could be, for example, the purchase of a herd of young calves to be fattened and then sold as beef cattle, the drilling of wildcat oil wells, the ownership and rental of such things as railroad boxcars, locomotives, computers, or ice vending machines, the filming and distribution of a motion picture, or the purchase of undeveloped suburban land which is then divided, prepared, and sold as building lots.

The first portion of this chapter describes the organization of a limited partnership; the latter portion discusses its termination.

Limited Partnerships as Legal Entities

What Is a Limited Partnership?

A limited partnership is a partnership formed by two or more persons in the manner prescribed by law, which has one or more general partner(s) and one or more limited partner(s). The general partners conduct the business of the venture and have unlimited personal liability to creditors for its obligations; the limited partners have a very limited right to participate in the management of the business and the extent of their personal liability lies only in the risk of loss of their investments. The profit to which a limited partner will be entitled is set forth in the agreement of the partners. For instance, the agreement might stipulate that 80 percent of the profits will be divided among the limited partners and the remainder of the profits will be divided among the general partners.

Legal Basis of Limited Partnerships

Limited partnerships developed in the middle ages to enable the nobility and clergy to make quiet investments without being criticized for engaging in trade. The untidy business of commerce was left to the general partners who were of the merchant class. But the concept of limited partnerships never became a part of the common law, and within the United States they are solely the creatures of statute.

Because limited partnerships had no foundation in the common law, the statutes authorizing this organizational form usually were very strictly construed, some courts holding that even minor or trivial departures from the statutory requirements subjected the limited partners to the same personal liability as that of general partners. This strict construction tended to inhibit the effective accomplishment of the liberal purposes intended by these laws. Therefore the National Conference of Commissioners on Uniform State Laws in 1916 prepared a Uniform Limited Partnership Act. That act was adopted by all the states except Louisiana, which has its own form of limited partnership. Over the years, through experience with that Act, it was found that a limited partnership organization could operate more effectively if the limited partners were permitted to exercise a circumscribed degree of control in its management. To implement this change the original ULPA was superseded by the Revised Limited Partnership Act of 1976 which, in turn, was amended in 1985. This most recent version is the one cited in this chapter as ULPA and is reprinted as Appendix 4.

Application of Uniform Partnership Act to Limited Partnerships

While a limited partnership is distinct from an ordinary partnership, the two have many characteristics in common. In fact, the Uniform Partnership Act (UPA) is applied to limited partnership matters wherever the ULPA is silent. The UPA states in Section 6(2), "... this Act shall apply to limited partnerships except in so far as the statutes relating to such partnership are inconsistent herewith"; and ULPA Sec. 1105 states, "... In any case not provided for in this Act the provisions of the Uniform Partnership Act govern." Accordingly, if a question of law arises as, for example, to the powers and liabilities of a general partner, reference must be made to the UPA for answer.

Formation of Limited Partnerships

Requirements for Formation

To establish a limited partnership the ULPA dictates that the firm must consist of at least one general partner and at least one limited partner and that a *certificate of limited partnership* must be filed with the Secretary of State of the state in which it is organized (ULPA 201).

Certificate of Limited Partnership. In Chapter 36 we saw that in order to organize an ordinary business partnership all that is required is the oral or written agreement of two or more people to be associated together as co-owners to carry on a business for profit. The organization of a limited partnership is more formal. It comes into existence only when a proper certificate, signed by all of the firm's general partners, is filed as a public record. In addition, all the parties (the limited partners as well as the general partners) become bound by an *agreement of limited partnership*, but that agreement is not made a public record.

The Uniform Limited Partnership Act and state laws dictate that a certificate of limited partnership must contain (1) the name of the limited partnership, (2) the address of its office and the name and address of its agent for service of process, (3) the name and address of each general partner, (4) the latest date upon which the limited partnership is to dissolve, and (5) any other matters the general partners include in the certificate. Figure 38.1 is an example of a Certificate of Limited Partnership.

Filing of Certificate. It is required that the Certificate of Limited Partnership and any amendments to it, signed by the general partner(s), be filed in the office of the secretary of state in the state where the partnership is formed. Should the partnership desire to do business in any other state, it is required to register as a foreign limited partnership with the secretary of state of that state (ULPA 902).

If parties engage in a business which purports to be a limited partnership without signing and filing

Figure 38.1 Form of certificate of limited partnership

We, the undersigned, desiring to form a limited partnership pursuant to the Uniform Partnership Act as set forth in ________________ (cite the statute) of the State of __________, do hereby certify:

1. The name of the limited partnership is ____________________

____

2. The address of the office of the limited partnership is ____________

____

City of ______________ County of ______________

State of ________________ Zip ______________

3. The name and address of the agent for the service of process on the limited partnership is:

____

____

4. The name and the business address of each general partner in the limited partnership is:

Name	Business Address
____________________	______________________________
____________________	______________________________

5. The latest date upon which the limited partnership is to dissolve is ________________ . [insert terminating date or event]

In Witness Whereof the undersigned have executed this certificate this the _______ day of 19____ .

____
General Partner

____
General Partner

(Notary acknowledgment optional)

a certificate, a limited partnership is not formed but, instead, the organization is treated as an ordinary business partnership. In that event all its members—those designated limited partners as well as those designated general partners—are personally liable for the debts and obligations of the enterprise as though they were all general partners.

Thus, if you purchase a limited partnership interest in a nonexistent limited partnership (because a certificate was not filed), believing that you have no personal liability, you could find yourself responsible as a general partner for obligations the organization incurs.

To protect yourself from this liability you should either (1) cause an appropriate limited partnership certificate to be filed, or (2) in writing withdraw from (renounce) any future participation in the profits or income of the enterprise and file in the office of the secretary of state a certificate declaring such withdrawal (ULPA 304). But you cannot thus free yourself from liability to a creditor who had already transacted business with the firm believing that you were a general partner.

The potential liability of all partners, limited as well as general, when there is a failure to file a certificate of limited partnership is illustrated by the next case.

CASE 38.1 Deporter-Butterworth Tours, Inc. v. Tyrell · 503 N.E.2d (Ill. App. 3 Dist. 1987)

FACTS The American Professional Football Tour of Europe (Football Tour) was organized as a limited partnership in Iowa, filing its certificate of limited partnership on June 22, 1979. After some uncertain date in June of 1979 the plaintiffs sold goods to and performed various services for Football Tour for which they were not paid. On August 15, 1980, the plaintiffs brought action against Football Tour and "Unknown Owners" individually and as partners upon the contracts entered into by Football Tour. The trial court dismissed the action before trial and gave judgment to the defendants on the pleadings, holding that, among other reasons, the defendants were limited partners of a business entity and therefore were not personally liable to the plaintiffs. The court did not consider whether the debts were incurred before or after Football Tour filed its certificate of limited partnership. The plaintiffs appealed the trial court's refusal to reconsider its judgment.

OPINION SCOTT, J. . . . The final issue [raised by the plaintiffs in their appeal] is whether the status of certain defendants as limited partners limit their liability to the extent of their capital contribution in the event that the partnership is liable under the contracts alleged. The rules governing the status and liability of limited partners in Illinois is governed by the adoption of the Uniform Limited Partnership Act, (Ill. Rev. Stat. 1983, ch. 106–1/2, par. 44 *et seq.*) [U.L.P.A. §201(b)]. The same is also true of the Iowa partnership organized in this case. (*See* I.C.A. sections 545.1–545.58.) The rule, as established by the Act is that the certificate required by the Uniform Limited Partnership Act is a statutory prerequisite to the creation of a limited partnership. Until it is filed, the partnership is not formed as a limited partnership and all partners will be treated as general partners. (Citation.) Therefore any contracts entered into prior to June 22, 1979, the date on which the limited partnership certificate was filed and made of record, would be contracts entered into by a general partnership and all partners involved would be liable as general partners.

JUDGMENT For the foregoing reasons, the judgment of the circuit court of Rock Island County is reversed and this case is remanded for trial on its merits [to determine if any of the debts were incurred by Football Tour prior to June 22, 1979].

Limited Partnership Agreement

Form of Agreement. In addition to the certificate of limited partnership which the ULPA directs must be signed by the general partners, all the partners, limited as well as general, either expressly or impliedly, join in a limited partnership agreement covering the operations of the enterprise. The ULPA does not prescribe either its form or content nor is the agreement required to be in writing. However, because the agreement may be quite involved, a well-organized limited partnership will have its agreement in writing, prepared by a lawyer, and signed by all of the partners. Normally, each partner is given a copy of the agreement when he or she secures an interest in the firm.

Content of Agreement. A partnership agreement covers matters concerning the conduct of its business and the relationship of the partners, both general and limited, to the firm. It could be expected to include such information as (1) a description of the business to be conducted by the partnership, (2) the functions and duties of the general partner(s) and whether or not they may engage in competing enterprises, (3) the contributions to be made by any partner, (4) restrictions upon the business general and special partners may transact with the partnership (for example, whether or not a partner may sell something to the partnership), (5) the conditions under which an investor may acquire a limited partnership interest after the organization has been established, and (6) the rights of limited partners to vote on partnership matters.

Important to the agreement are provisions governing the conduct of the business if a general partner dies or ceases to perform his or her duties and how the profits earned by the partnership will be allocated (divided) among the general and the limited partners. The allocation may be (1) on the basis of the value of each member's contribution to the firm (not including promises of future contributions), or (2) by some other formula established in the agreement.

Business of a Limited Partnership

A limited partnership may carry on any business that a partnership without limited partners may engage in unless the statute under which it is organized provides otherwise. Many states require that certain regulated industries, such as banking, may be carried on only by entities organized under special statutes and a limited partnership may not qualify under such laws.

A limited partnership terminates at the time and/or under the conditions specified in its certificate. However, if the date of its termination is approaching and the objective of the business has not yet been reached, the partners may file an amended certificate establishing a new termination date.

Name of a Limited Partnership

Every limited partnership must have a name which, without abbreviation, includes the words "Limited Partnership" (ULPA 102). The name may not be deceptively similar to the name of any other firm organized under the laws of that state.

In addition, a limited partnership may not have the same name as the surname of one of its limited partners unless one of the *general* partners bears the same surname. For instance, if Henry Osborne is to be a limited partner, the business may not be named "Osborne Properties, a Limited Partnership," unless at the time the firm is organized one of the general partners is also named Osborne. Without this rule a third party who does business with the firm might improperly have the impression that Henry Osborne is actually a general partner and rely upon his financial resources (which might be considerable) in extending credit to the firm.

Should a limited partner knowingly permit his or her name to be used in the partnership name, he or she is liable to creditors who extend credit to the partnership in the belief that the limited partner is a general partner.

If a general partner's name is a part of the partnership name and he or she leaves the firm which then continues in business, the firm name need not be changed unless the partnership agreement so dictates.

Contributions to Limited Partnership

A partner's *contribution* to a limited partnership may be in the form of cash, property, services performed, a promissory note, or a written obligation to make a future contribution (ULPA 101(2)).

The following two examples illustrate how services may be treated as contributions to capital.

- Peter decides to form a limited partnership, does all the work required to bring a viable business into existence, and is its sole general partner. He lists the value of those services as part of the firm's capital. Although Peter could arbitrarily place a very high value upon those services, he is not likely to do so because, if he does, he would be entitled to such a large share of the profits that potential investors would not be attracted to purchase limited partnership interests in his firm.
- In the organization of his enterprise Peter asks Ethel, a lawyer, to perform all the legal services involved. She agrees to accept a limited partnership interest as her fee. The value of her services becomes her contribution to the firm.

As to a contribution in the form of a promise, if a partner fails to make a promised contribution of cash or property or services the partnership may, by legal action, force that partner (or his estate, if the partner has died), to pay the value of the promised contribution in cash (ULPA 502(b)). If a partner defaults in meeting that obligation, his or her debt may, by consent of all the partners, be compromised, that is, a smaller sum may be accepted in full payment. However, notwithstanding the compromise, a creditor who extends credit to the partnership may force the defaulting partner to pay the full value of his or her original obligation to the partnership.

As shown by the following case, a limited partner may not lightly refuse to fulfill his or her promise to make a capital contribution.

CASE 38.2 Partnership Equities, Inc. v. Marten · 443 N.E.2d 134 (Mass. App. 1982)

FACTS Columbia-Heather, Ltd., a limited partnership, was engaged in the construction of a large apartment project. Partnership Equities, Inc. was one of the general partners and Amin Khoury and James Marten, the defendants, were two of the limited partners in Columbia-Heather. Khoury and Marten had each obligated himself to contribute $83,750 to the partnership capital. The contribution payments were to be made in installments of $2,750 initially, and $20,250 annually for the succeeding four years. Khoury and Marten each made two $20,250 annual payments but both men refused to make the next two annual payments of the same amounts, claiming that the general partners had breached the partnership agreement by prematurely reimbursing themselves for certain development costs they had advanced.

The general partners sued Khoury and Marten to recover the unpaid contributions. The trial court ruled that the alleged breach by the general partners did not excuse the payment of the capital contributions to which Khoury and Marten had subscribed. The defendants appealed.

OPINION KASS, J. . . . Section 17 of the ULPA [to the same effect as Sec. 502 of the Revised ULPA] provides that, ". . . A limited partner is liable to the partnership . . . for any unpaid contribution which he agreed . . . to make in the future. . . ."

It is the defendants' position that . . . it is an inherent condition of further capital contributions that there be no material breach by other partners of the partnership agreement at the time the additional money is due. . . . [T]he circumstances in which payment of further capital contributions are excused are few and they are narrow. Payment may be excused when there has occurred a failure to meet a condition expressed in the certificate of limited partnership or when there has been a profound failure of consideration such as a repudiation of, or fraud incident to, the essentials of the venture to which subscription was made.

If their enrollment in the partnership were merely a bilateral agreement between the defendants and the general partners, the principle of contract law upon which the defendants

CASE 38.2 Continued

rely, that a material breach excuses performance, might well apply. . . . Relations of a limited partner to the partnership, however, are more complex in that other limited partners . . . rely on an expressed obligation . . . to contribute resources to the partnership. Taking the instant case as an example, the party providing the mortgage financing may well have depended in part on [knowledge of] capital subscriptions in appraising resources of the partnership to meet project expenses in excess of mortgage financing. Similarly, prospective investing limited partners may have calculated the aggregate capital to be invested in judging whether they should invest in the transaction being undertaken by the partnership. . . .

In the instant case the project has been built and is being operated. The defendants . . . have already received tax benefits, and they have offered no evidence that the general partners will cause the partnership not to pay a return on investment. . . . [The facts do not] suggest the general partners had either repudiated the deal or defrauded the limited partners. . . . [For] mismanagement, negligence, diversion of some assets, action beyond authority, or failure to perform certain elements of an agreement, . . . derivative suits are the appropriate remedy. [A derivative suit would be an action by a limited partner in the partnership name against the general partner(s).] If conditions are to be placed on the payment of future installments [of capital contributions], it is only necessary to articulate them in the limited partnership agreement.

OPINION Judgment affirmed.

Members of Limited Partnerships

General Partners

Who May Be a General Partner. Any person legally capable of engaging in a contract who meets the qualifications stated in the limited partnership agreement may be a general partner. A corporation (if its charter permits), or even another partnership may be a general partner in a limited partnership.

While there is no limitation upon the number of general partners there may be in a limited partnership, usually there are fewer than four. A general partner may make contributions to the limited partnership and he or she may also make contributions to it (invest) as a limited partner. Thus, a person may be both a general partner and a limited partner in the same partnership. He or she then has the powers and is subject to the liabilities of a general partner and, except as may be provided in the partnership agreement, also has the rights of a limited partner.

Admission of Additional General Partners. Partners may find it desirable to admit an additional general partner or partners into an existing limited partnership. This is accomplished in the manner set forth in the partnership agreement. If the agreement does not provide *in writing* for the admission of additional general partners, the written consent of all partners, limited as well as general, is then required (ULPA 401).

Powers of General Partners. A general partner in a limited partnership has all the powers and is subject to all the same rights, restrictions and liabilities as a partner in an ordinary business partnership (ULPA 403). He or she is the manager of the enterprise, conducting its business and executing, in the partnership name, any instrument necessary to carry on partnership affairs. Accordingly, a general partner may buy and sell partnership property without the knowledge or consent of the limited partners if such actions are in furtherance of partnership purposes and are in accord with the partnership agreement. If the general partner wishes to act beyond that limitation of authority, then all the partners (both general and limited) must first give their written consent. Thus, Steve, a general partner in an enterprise engaged in building a boating marina, has authority to purchase appropriate building materials, but if he wishes to buy a medical building in the partnership name he must first obtain written consent from all the other partners.

A general partner may *personally* do business with his or her firm or lend the firm money if the transaction does not violate the partnership agreement and does not violate any fiduciary duty owing by the general partner to the partnership. For example Sue, a general partner, may contract with the partnership to run its public relations campaign and to be paid for that service.

Fiduciary Obligations of General Partners to Limited Partners. A general partner, being in full charge of the partnership business, must act with the highest good faith toward the limited partners as the latter have no option but to rely upon the integrity of the general partner. That individual, therefore, owes a range of fiduciary duties to the limited partners. Among these obligations are:

- The duty to serve the partnership to the best of his or her ability in an effort to accomplish the purposes for which the limited partnership was formed.
- The duty to devote the partnership funds to the purposes for which the partnership was organized and to render to all the limited partners, on demand, full information about the financial condition and affairs of the partnership.
- The duty to comply with all applicable state and federal securities laws.
- The duty, in the event of a purchase of a limited partner's interest by a general partner or by the partnership, to make full disclosure to the seller of all information pertaining to the value of the interest, of the means whereby the purchase will be effected, and, if payment is not to be made in cash, of the value of the offered consideration.
- The duty not to acquire for himself or herself a business opportunity which rightfully should be taken for the partnership. The following scenario illustrates this last duty: Hal is a general partner in the Deep Gold Limited Partnership which is acquiring sources of gold ore. He learns that Jim, a prospector, has filed a claim to mine land close to the Deep Gold properties. Hal purchases the claim from Jim and then sells it to his partnership, making a handsome profit on the transaction. If Hal had not been a general partner of Deep Gold, the sale to the partnership would have been perfectly acceptable, but because he is a general partner Hal should not buy the claim and then sell it to his partnership. He has a fiduciary obligation to give his firm the right to purchase it directly from Jim at the lower price.

A general partner's fiduciary obligation does *not* include any guarantee that the limited partnership will be financially successful. That concept is the essence of the following case.

CASE 38.3 Wyler v. Feuer · 149 Cal. Rptr. 626 (Cal. App. 1978)

FACTS Cy Feuer and Ernest Martin and their corporation, Feuer and Martin Productions, Inc., the defendants, had been outstandingly successful producers of Broadway musical comedies for many years. Among their productions were "Where's Charlie," "Guys and Dolls," and "How to Succeed in Business Without Really Trying." Their first motion picture, "Cabaret," received eight Academy Awards. Martin became interested in and acquired worldwide picture rights to a book about the early life of the famous French singer, Edith Piaf. Feuer and Martin formed a limited partnership in which they were the general partners and Wyler (who had no previous movie experience) was a limited partner. The sole purpose of the enterprise was to make and distribute a film based on the book.

Wyler contributed the entire $1,512,000 it cost to produce the motion picture. When released, the film was not a success. It was evident that the partners had overestimated the public's interest in the subject matter and should not have employed an unknown French actress as the lead. Wyler sued the defendants for, among other causes of action,

CASE 38.3 Continued

the mismanagement of the business of the limited partnership. The trial court entered a nonsuit on that cause of action. The plaintiff appealed.

OPINION

FLEMING, Assoc. J. . . . [Under the mismanagement cause of action] Wyler alleged excessive costs of production for the French version of the motion picture, failure to produce a marketable English version, improvident selection of actors, unseasonable scheduling of photography, failure to obtain production financing, and procurement of disadvantageous distribution contracts.

A limited partnership affords a vehicle for capital investment whereby the limited partner restricts his liability to the amount of his investment in return for surrender of any right to manage and control the partnership business. . . . In a limited partnership the general partner manages and controls the partnership business. . . . In exercising his management functions the general partner comes under a fiduciary duty of good faith and fair dealing toward other members of the partnership. . . .

Three characteristics—limited investor liability, delegation of authority to management, and fiduciary duty owed by management to investors—are similar to those existing in corporate investment where it has long been the rule that directors are not liable to stockholders for mistakes made in the exercise of honest business judgment. . . . By this standard a general partner may not be held liable for mistakes made or losses incurred in the good faith exercise of reasonable business judgment.

According all due inferences to plaintiff's evidence, . . . we agree with the trial court that plaintiff did not produce sufficient evidence to hold the defendants liable for bad business management. Plaintiff's evidence showed that the Piaf picture did not make money, was not sought after by distributors, and did not live up to its producers' expectations. The same could be said of the majority of motion pictures made since the invention of cinematography. . . . The good faith business judgment and management of a general partner need only satisfy the standard of care demanded of an ordinary prudent person, and will not be scrutinized by the courts with the cold clarity of hindsight. The trial court correctly granted a nonsuit on the mismanagement cause of action.

JUDGMENT

The judgment is affirmed.

Liability of General Partner to Third Parties. Each general partner is personally liable to third parties for the debts and obligations of the firm. This liability is similar to the personal liability of partners in an ordinary business partnership (ULPA 403(b); UPA 15). A third party can reach a general partner's interest in the firm only by a charging order. A general partner is also liable to anyone who suffers a loss as a result of having relied upon a statement, known by the general partner to be false, in the certificate of limited partnership. For instance, you, as the general partner in a limited partnership, are *personally* liable to pay back a loan made by the National Bank to your partnership if, at the time the bank made the loan, it relied on a false statement in the partnership certificate which you signed.

Compensation of General Partner. A limited partnership agreement may provide for compensation to a general partner (in addition to a share of the profits) for managing the firm's affairs. There is no standard formula by which the rate of compensation to a managing general partner is determined. It may be fixed in a number of different ways. Among them are (1) a management fee representing a certain percentage of the partnership's annual income, (2) an agreed percentage of the total capital of the firm, (3) a reimbursement of money for reasonable expenses incurred in the management, (4) a salary or a fixed fee, or (5) some other formula. Whatever the arrangement, general partners, in establishing their business, try to arrive at compensation for themselves which will seem reasonable to investors.

Termination of General Partner's Status. Section 402 of the ULPA enumerates a number of events which cause a general partner to cease to be a member of the partnership. Among them are when the general partner (1) withdraws from the partnership, (2) assigns his or her interest, (3) is removed from that position by the limited partners in accordance with the partnership agreement, (4) files a petition in bankruptcy, (5) is adjudged incompetent to manage his or her affairs, or (6) dies.

Withdrawal. A general partner may at any time withdraw from the partnership by giving written notice to all the other partners (ULPA 602). Unlike the withdrawal of a partner in a partnership organized under the Uniform Partnership Act (in which event the partnership is dissolved), the withdrawal of a general partner from a limited partnership does not necessarily cause a dissolution of the firm. As we will soon see, normally the limited partnership agreement states that the limited partners may designate a new general partner to serve in place of the withdrawing general partner.

The wrongful withdrawal of a general partner may subject him or her to a claim for damages by the remaining partners. For instance, say that Phyllis, a general partner in the Rainbow Limited Partnership, originally agreed to remain in that capacity for one full year. However, at the end of three months she withdrew from the firm. Because her withdrawal was in violation of the limited partnership agreement, the partnership may recover from her whatever damages resulted.

Assignment of interest. A general partner who assigns his or her general partnership interest to someone else ceases to be a general partner in the firm. The assignee does not thereby become a new general partner unless all the limited partners consent thereto in writing or unless so authorized in writing or unless so authorized by the limited partnership agreement. If the assignee is not admitted as a partner, he or she is merely entitled to receive that portion of the profits or assets to which the assigning partner would have been entitled. A general partner who also owns a limited partnership interest in the firm may assign that interest without affecting his or her general partnership interest or status.

Removal. A general partner may be removed if the limited partnership agreement sets out the conditions under which that action may be taken. For example, if a partnership agreement states that the sole general partner can be removed if he does not sell the firm's building within 18 months and he fails to do so, then the limited partners may take advantage of that clause in the agreement and oust him.

Limited Partners

Who May Be a Limited Partner. Any "person" which, as used in the ULPA, means an individual, a partnership, a limited partnership, a corporation if its charter permits, an estate, association, or a general partner, may be a limited partner. In every limited partnership there must be at least one limited partner, but the law sets no limit on the number there may be. The number of limited partners in a firm depends primarily upon the financial needs and the character of the business in which the partnership is engaged. Some limited partnerships, such as one that is organized to drill for oil or to trade in real estate on a large scale, have been given the popular name of *master limited partnerships* because they have hundreds of limited partners (investors) scattered all over the country. These interests are traded on financial stock exchanges and thus there is a ready market for their purchase and sale. By way of example, the following four are master limited partnerships: Mesa Limited Partnership and Apache Petroleum Company Limited Partnership, both of which explore and drill for oil; Allstar Inns Limited Partnership, which owns and operates motels; and Maritrans Partners Limited Partnership, which transports petroleum products by sea. Considerable thought is currently being given by many corporations to change their form of business organization to that of master limited partnership, generally for tax reasons.

Most limited partnerships are not nearly so huge or ambitious as master limited partnerships. Usually, no more than thirty-five limited partnership interests are offered for sale in any one enterprise because when that number is exceeded the firm is required to comply with stringent federal securities laws. Each state also imposes restrictions on the sale of limited partnership interests. For example, in order to protect financially insecure investors from being imposed upon by promoters, a limited partnership interest may not be sold to anyone who does not possess the minimum financial worth specified by the state in which the limited partnership is organized.

Admission of Additional Limited Partners. After a limited partnership has been organized, a person may be admitted to the partnership in either of two ways (ULPA. 301; 704):

1 By acquiring an interest in it directly from the firm in the manner provided in the partnership agreement. If there is no such provision, the written consent of all the partners is then required before an additional limited partner may be admitted into the firm, or
2 By assignment of the interest from a limited partner if, under the provisions of the partnership agreement, he or she has the power to give an assignee the status of a limited partner

Powers of Limited Partners. While a limited partner is a *member* of a limited partnership, he or she is not a *partner* in the full sense in which that word is usually used. A limited partner is only an investor in the firm, receiving (if the firm is successful) income from that investment while having but slight authority to participate in the management of the enterprise. Like any stranger to the firm, a limited partner may be hired by the partnership as an employee or independent contractor. For example, Arnold, a limited partner, may be paid to be superintendent of a construction job being carried on by the partnership, and Susan, another limited partner, may be hired as the chief of its accounting department. Unless prohibited by the partnership agreement, a limited partner may also transact business with the partnership as though he or she were not a member of the firm (ULPA 107). So Ted, a limited partner whose own company sells air conditioning equipment, may sell his products to the partnership, and Lloyd, still another limited partner, may lend the firm money at interest. None of these or similar transactions will affect the limited partner's contribution to or status in the firm.

Likewise, a limited partner, unless specifically designated to act as an agent of the partnership, has no authority to bind the partnership either by contract or by tortious conduct. Thus, Ann, a limited partner, cannot obligate the partnership to pay a roofer to fix a leak in the firm's roof unless she is authorized by a general partner to hire the roofer. Similarly, Henry, who is not employed in any capacity by the limited partnership in which he holds a limited partnership interest, does not make the firm liable for a slander he commits against a competitor of the partnership unless he was specifically authorized by a general partner to make the slanderous statement.

Rights of Limited Partners. The principal rights of a limited partner fall within three general categories:

1 To share in the firm's profits and distribution of assets (ULPA 503; 504)
2 To secure information about the business (ULPA 105)
3 To participate to a *limited* extent, as set forth in the partnership agreement and the ULPA, in the control of the partnership (ULPA 302)

Right to share in profits and distribution. A limited partner is entitled to share in the firm's profits and in the distribution of its assets as provided in the partnership agreement.

Right to secure information about partnership business. A limited partner has the right to inspect and copy any partnership books. In addition, a limited partner may obtain from the general partner from time to time upon reasonable demand (1) information regarding the state of the partnership business and its financial condition, (2) copies of its federal, state, and local income tax returns, and (3) other information regarding its affairs.

In the case which follows the court had to decide a conflict between a general partner and limited partners as to the latter's entitlement to obtain partnership information.

CASE 38.4 McCain v. Phoenix Resources, Inc. · 185 Cal. App.3d 575 (Cal. 1986)

FACTS The Valley Investors was a limited partnership formed to own and develop land in California. Phoenix Resources, Inc., the defendant, was its managing general partner. McCain and Howell, the plaintiffs, were the limited partners. The plaintiffs, in questioning the manner in which the Phoenix Corporation was conducting the partnership affairs, sought to examine the partnership's books and records. Phoenix consented to the inspection of only the firm's accounting and financial records, legal documents such as contracts, and the minutes of limited partnership meetings. The plaintiffs demanded to see additional partnership records and Phoenix refused. The plaintiffs brought suit to have the court order Phoenix to make all partnership information available. The trial court enjoined [prohibited] the defendant from refusing to make all partnership records available for inspection and copying and the defendant appealed.

OPINION LOW, P. J. . . . It should be noted that a partner's statutory right of inspection can be exercised *without* a showing of either good cause or proper purpose. . . .

. . . A managing partner has a legal duty to disclose to copartners "matters affecting their business relationship" . . . [including] a duty to make a full disclosure of all matters substantially affecting the value of the partnership. . . . Because of their fiduciary relationship, the records sought by plaintiffs herein were not the private property of defendant, but were subject to the rights guaranteed to the other partners to have access to all information pertaining to partnership affairs.

Although a partnership should be protected from harassment by placing reasonable time, place, and manner restrictions on a partner's right of inspection, the statutory language demonstrates that a partner is entitled to have broad access to partnership information. . . .

Defendant also resists disclosure of any information [concerning the partnership] in the possession of the two law firms [employed by Phoenix]. . . . Defendant argues that "the right of inspection applies only as against partners" and alleges there is "no authority that would support a right of inspection against a law firm or any other third party as an adjunct of [plaintiffs'] right of inspection. . . ." A partnership can be a client of a law firm and a lawyer may transact business on behalf of the partnership. . . . Under such circumstances, it is foreseeable that a law firm would have information in its possession relating to partnership affairs. If, on the other hand, the law firm holds records which represent purely private or personal interests of one of the partners, the attorney-client privilege can be asserted to resist production of the records. . . .

We hold defendant was not justified in refusing to allow plaintiffs access to "true and full information of all things affecting the partnership" on the ground that the requested information did not come under the limited purview of financial records and legal documents. . . .

JUDGMENT The . . . order granting application for preliminary injunction is affirmed. . . .

Restricted right to participate in control of the partnership business. The philosophy underlying the limited partnership concept is that an investor, i.e., a limited partner, in exchange for his or her freedom from personal liability for the debts and obligations of the firm gives up the right to participate in its management. In the original (1916) version of the ULPA, if a limited partner took part in the management of the firm, then he or she lost that immunity and became subject to the same liability for all its obligations as that of a general partner.

However, over the years business experience has demonstrated that a limited partner should have a restricted right to participate in some elements of control of the business without being subjected to personal liability. The drafters of the later versions of the ULPA held to that concept, determining that it is contrary to sound public policy to hold a limited partner, who is not also a general partner, liable for any of the firm's obligations in the creation of which he or she did not participate. However, it was determined that a limited partner should be liable to persons who in the course of transacting business with the firm reasonably believe, based upon the limited partner's conduct, that he or she is a general partner.

To illustrate this concept: John, a limited partner in the Otis Limited Partnership, is an engineer. The partnership has been considering the purchase of a new piece of equipment from the Henry Company. He helps the general partner decide upon the equipment to buy. John does not have the liability of a general partner. However, in helping the general partner to decide what equipment the partnership should buy, John meets with Henry's salespeople on a day-to-day basis, discussing the merits and drawbacks of various models. Finally, when he is satisfied that he has selected the most suitable model for the Otis partnership to buy, John says to the Henry Company, "O.K., that one looks best; go ahead and ship it to us." Later, when Otis fails to pay the bill, Henry may hold John personally liable for its payment along with Otis's general partners.

The following case deals with a situation in which a limited partner, while not actively participating in the day-to-day management of the partnership affairs, so acted in a transaction that a third party extended credit to the partnership relying on the belief that the limited partner was a general partner in the firm.

CASE 38.5 General Electric Credit Corp. v. Stover · 708 S.W.2d 355 (Mo. App. 1986)

FACTS The Linnane Magnavox Entertainment Center was a limited partnership with one general partner, Paul Linnane, and one limited partner, Richard Stover. Their partnership agreement stated: "The general management, control and conduct of the business shall be vested in the general partner only and the limited partner shall have no power or authority to bind the partnership." Stover took no part in the firm's management.

Linnane Magnavox entered into two agreements with General Electric Credit Corp. (hereafter GE Credit), the plaintiff, under which GE Credit agreed to finance Linnane's purchase of inventory. Under the agreements Linnane Magnavox promised to repay GE Credit the advances it made to Linnane Magnavox to enable the partnership to procure the equipment. The agreements were signed by both Linnane and Stover as partners in Linnane Magnavox. Linnane Magnavox failed to repay GE Credit the amounts due under the financing agreements and GE Credit sued the partnership and the two partners to recover the advances made. Stover claimed that he was not liable because he was only a limited partner in the enterprise and that he signed the agreements as a limited partner without intending to assume any personal liability. However, the agreements did not show that Stover was only a limited partner and his intention was never communicated to GE Credit. The parties stipulated that if Stover had not signed the agreements, GE Credit would not have furnished the financing. Judgment was entered for the plaintiff and the defendants appealed.

OPINION SHANGLER, J. . . . The degree of control a limited partner may exercise without risk of liability as a general partner has been enlarged with the promulgation of each successive Uniform Limited Partnership Act prototype. . . . [T]he limited partner is allowed a list of business activities—described specifically [in ULPA 303(b)]—that will not constitute control of the business so as to expose the limited partner to liability as a general partner. . . .

CASE 38.5 Continued

...The control which exposes a limited partner to liability as a general partner... [under the law] is activity which causes the creditor the mistaken belief that the limited partner is a general partner—and that, usually upon evidence that the participation in control by the limited partner was substantially equivalent to that of a partner.

A limited partner, therefore, who induces a third party to believe that *for that transaction,* he would be personally bound, becomes liable for the loss incurred by that reliance.... The question for decision was whether... *for the purpose of the two agreements* Stover put his personal assets at stake and GE Credit was thereby induced to extend its credits to the partnership.

...Thus, it is quite irrelevant that the certificate of limited partnership on file with the Secretary of State of Kansas may have imparted constructive knowledge to GE Credit that Linnane was the designated general partner and Stover the limited partner....

Stover argues that the term [Linnane Magnavox "by Stover" on the agreements], signifies agency and hence an intention not to be personally bound.... The Stover signature was either to vouchsafe the contract obligations or else it was of no purpose. Linnane had already bound the partnership credit to the undertakings by his signature as general partner. Another signature on behalf of the partnership would have been superfluous.... The court could have determined that GE Credit was not willing to extend credit under the agreements to an undercapitalized limited partnership unless the investor—the limited partner—bound his personal assets to the undertaking. To that end, they... secured his commitment to be personally bound and only then, commenced to... extend credit for the inventory.

JUDGMENT The judgment... is affirmed.

As mentioned by Judge Shangler in the foregoing case, there are specific circumstances enumerated in ULPA 303(b) in which a limited partner is not to be construed to be liable as a general partner when the limited partner acts for the partnership. These activities are:

When a limited partner

1 Acts as a contractor for, or an agent or employee of, the limited partnership
2 Advises a general partner with respect to the business of the firm
3 Acts as surety for the partnership... or
4 Votes upon such matters as the dissolution and winding up of the partnership, or a change in the nature of its business, or the admission or removal of a general or limited partner, or an amendment to the partnership agreement

In their comments concerning this section, the drafters of the ULPA revision stated that they had extended the enumeration to assure that limited partners would not be subjected to general liability where such liability is not appropriate.

A limited partner is also allowed to bring a derivative action in behalf of the partnership without thereby participating in the management of the firm. In the case of a limited partnership, a *derivative action* is a lawsuit in the partnership name brought by one or more of the limited partners in order to protect or enforce a partnership right when the general partner(s) refuses to take appropriate action (ULPA 1001–1004).

A derivative action may, under appropriate circumstances, be brought against a third party, a general partner, or a limited partner. Such a suit would be appropriate, for instance, if the general partner(s) refused (1) to force a landlord to comply with his promise to extend a lease on premises occupied by and necessary for the continuation of the partnership business, (2) to force a general partner to turn over to the limited partnership moneys collected by him that rightfully belong to the partnership, or (3) to force a limited partner to pay a long past due promissory note given to the partnership as his or her contribution to the firm. A derivative suit may be a useful tool by which limited partners can protect their interests in the enterprise.

Liability of Limited Partners. The only financial risk an individual assumes when becoming a limited partner is the possibility of losing his or her investment in the firm (ULPA 303). The example at the opening of this chapter, in which Julie formed a limited partnership to own a race horse, illustrates this principle. There are three situations, however, in which a limited partner's risk is extended and he or she may incur personal liability for the firm's debts:

1. When a limited partner participates in the firm's control of the business beyond the boundaries permitted by the ULPA or the partnership agreement (such as in the *General Electric Credit Corp. v. Stover* case, above)
2. When no limited partnership certificate has been filed with the secretary of state
3. When a limited partner knowingly permits his or her surname (a different name from that of any of the general partners) to be used as part of the name of the limited partnership

Fiduciary Duties of Limited Partners. Unlike a general partner, a limited partner does not owe the partnership and the other partners any fiduciary duties. For instance, John, a limited partner in the Evergreen Trucking Company Limited Partnership, is not barred from attempting to take a client away from Evergreen by offering one of its clients a better price to do its trucking. But Fred, Evergreen's *general* partner, may not do that.

Action by Third Party against Limited Partner. A creditor who has a judgment against a limited partner arising out of a personal obligation can reach the limited partner's interest only after securing a charging order issued by a court. If the charging order is foreclosed, the purchaser at the foreclosure sale becomes an assignee of that portion of the partner's interest so purchased.

Assignment of Limited Partnership Interest. A limited partner, being only an investor in the firm, may at any time assign (sell or give away) all or a portion of his or her partnership interest without causing a dissolution of the firm. The assignee becomes entitled to receive any distribution to which the assigning partner would have been entitled on the assigned interest.

A person who acquires either all or part of a limited partner's interest does *not* automatically become a limited partner. If the partnership agreement permits, the one who assigns his or her interest may designate the recipient as a limited partner. If there is no such provision in the agreement, then the consent of all the limited partners is required before the assignee becomes a limited partner. An assignee who has become a limited partner is subject to the restrictions and liabilities imposed by the partnership agreement upon limited partners. However, the assignee is not obligated for liabilities unknown to him or her when the assignee became a limited partner.

Withdrawal or Death of a Limited Partner. A limited partner may withdraw from the partnership of which he or she is a member at the time and under the circumstances specified in writing in the partnership agreement. He or she is then entitled to receive whatever distribution the partnership agreement provides. If the agreement contains no provision for withdrawal, a limited partner may withdraw after giving at least 6 months written notice to each of the general partners and is entitled to receive, within a reasonable time after the withdrawal, the fair value of his or her interest as of the date of withdrawal.

If a limited partner dies, his or her personal representative may exercise all the rights to which that limited partner was entitled.

Termination of Limited Partnerships

A limited partnership, similar to an ordinary business partnership, goes through the process of dissolution and winding up before it is terminated.

Bases for Dissolution

A limited partnership is dissolved upon the happening of any of the following events:

1. The time or the event specified in writing in the limited partnership agreement occurs.
2. All the partners, in writing, agree to the dissolution.

3. A general partner dies or withdraws from the partnership, *unless* (*a*) the written provisions of the agreement permit the business to be carried on by the remaining general partners (if any), or (*b*) if there is no remaining general partner, the limited partners, within 90 days, agree in writing to continue the business and appoint one or more new general partners.
4. The partnership is dissolved by court order. Any general or limited partner may apply to a court for an order to dissolve a limited partnership whenever it is no longer reasonably practicable to carry on the business of the partnership. Among the reasons for a court to act may be, for example, (*a*) there is no profitable market for the products or services of the firm, (*b*) a limited partner has discovered that a general partner is acting fraudulently or in violation of his fiduciary obligations to the partnership, or (*c*) the general partner is not properly managing the partnership property, allowing it to deteriorate and to lose its rental value.

Winding Up

After its dissolution, a limited partnership is wound up by a general partner who has not caused the dissolution. If there is no general partner to conduct the winding up, then it may be performed by the limited partners or by some person, usually a receiver, designated by a court.

As in the winding up of an ordinary business partnership, the individual who conducts the winding up collects all debts owing to the partnership, sees that the partnership's existing contracts are performed, and turns its assets into cash.

At the conclusion of the winding up, any remaining assets are distributed in the following order (ULPA 804):

1. To the firm's creditors, including partners who are creditors.
2. To partners and former partners for distributions previously due them and unpaid, except as otherwise provided in the partnership agreement.
3. To the partners for the return of their contributions, except as otherwise provided in the partnership agreement.
4. Any remaining balance is distributed among the partners according to the partnership agreement formula.

The completion of the distribution terminates the limited partnership.

Summary

A limited partnership (authorized by the ULPA) is a business organization distinct from an ordinary business partnership although the two have many elements in common. A limited partnership is composed of at least one general partner and at least one limited partner. The general partner or partners manage and operate the partnership business. They have all the rights and liabilities of partners in an ordinary business partnership. The limited partners are investors in the firm; normally exercising no control over the management of its affairs. A limited partner is not personally liable for the firm's debts unless he or she participates in the control of the business.

A limited partnership may carry on any lawful business except as it may be restricted by state law. A limited partnership comes into existence when a certificate of limited partnership is filed in the office of the secretary of state where the partnership is organized. In addition, the parties either orally or in writing enter into a partnership agreement. The ULPA does not prescribe the content of the agreement. It deals with the authority of the general and limited partners and the distribution of the income and assets of the partnership between them.

Each limited partner and general partner may make a contribution of cash, property, or services to the capital of the partnership. If their agreement states no formula for the allocation of income, then the profits and losses are distributed in the same ratio as each partner's contribution bears to the total contributions received by the partnership.

Either a general partner or a limited partner ceases to be a member of the partnership upon assigning (selling or giving away) his or her entire partnership interest. In the event a general partner withdraws, the remaining general partner(s), if any, may continue to carry on the partnership business if the partnership certificate so provides. In the absence of such a provision, the limited partners may agree to a continuance of the business by the remaining general partner(s). If no general partner remains, the limited partners may either appoint a new general partner or dissolve the partnership.

When a limited partnership is dissolved, it goes through a winding-up process similar to the winding up of an ordinary business partnership. After the assets have been gathered together and turned into cash and all the creditors have been paid, the remaining assets are divided among the partners according to the formula set forth in the partnership agreement, and the partnership terminates.

Review Questions

1 Why would a businessperson want to invest in a limited partnership?

2 **(a)** How is a limited partnership formed? **(b)** How does its formation differ from that of a general partnership? **(c)** What limitations are there upon a name a limited partnership may adopt?

3 **(a)** What is a certificate of limited partnership? **(b)** What, in general terms, does this document contain?

4 If a required certificate of limited partnership is not filed, what is the result?

5 **(a)** What is a limited partnership agreement? In general terms, what might such an agreement contain? **(b)** If there is a limited partnership agreement, must there also be a certificate of limited partnership? Explain.

6 If a limited partner promises to make a contribution of $5,000 to a limited partnership and fails to do so, **(a)** what rights, if any, does the partnership have with relation to that promise? **(b)** What rights, if any, does a creditor of the partnership have with respect to the contribution?

7 **(a)** May a new general partner be admitted into a previously organized limited partnership? **(b)** May a new limited partner be admitted? How is each of these accomplished?

8 What powers does a general partner exercise in a limited partnership?

9 What are the obligations of a general partner to a limited partnership and its limited partners?

10 What are the duties and obligations of a limited partner in a limited partnership?

11 Discuss a limited partner's participation in a limited partnership business.

12 Compare the liability of general partners and that of limited partners to third parties.

13 **(a)** What is meant when it is said that a limited partner has filed a derivative suit? **(b)** What could be the purpose of such a suit?

Case Problems

1 Betz and Kinn were the general partners, and Twitchell and seven others were, in varying degrees of ownership, the limited partners in "Chena Springs Resort, a Limited Partnership." Twitchell owned only a 5 percent interest in the partnership and was entitled to 5 percent of its profits. The general partners neglected to file in the office of the Secretary of State a certificate of limited partnership for the enterprise. The Fox Trap Company, a creditor of Chena Springs, sued all the general and limited partners for the amount of a purchase made by Chena Springs which was unpaid. Twitchell maintains that the creditor's suit should have been directed against only the general partners or, in the alternative, against the general and limited partners in the proportions of their interests in the limited partnership. Was Twitchell correct? Explain.

2 In February, Graybar Electric Company extended credit to Blomquist Electric, a limited partnership in which Blomquist and Preston were the general partners and Lowe was the sole limited partner. Blomquist Electric had not filed the required certificate of limited partnership, but Graybar did not know this. Graybar knew, however, that Lowe was only a limited partner. In April, by letter to Graybar, Lowe renounced any interest in Blomquist Electric. Almost a year later Graybar, not having been paid and ascertaining that no limited partnership certificate had been filed, sued Preston, Blomquist, and Lowe for the unpaid bills. Graybar claimed that Lowe was liable as a general partner because no certificate was on file. Is Lowe liable to Graybar? Explain.

3 Spira-Mart was a limited partnership. Its partnership agreement showed that the limited partners were to contribute to the partnership capital various sums totaling $250,000. In fact, however, they contributed a total of only $74,000. A creditor of the partnership brought suit to collect from the delinquent limited partners an amount sufficient to discharge the creditor's judgment against Spira-Mart. Is the creditor entitled to this remedy? Explain.

4 The Meadows Project was a limited partnership engaged in developing 65 acres into an industrial park. Each of the thirty-two limited partners had contributed $50,000 to the enterprise. The limited partnership agreement contained no provision directing what portion of the enterprise's net profits would be distributed to the limited partners each year. However, the general practice of other successful limited partnerships in that city was to distribute each year all their net profits. At the end of the first year of the Meadows Project operation the general partner distributed to the limited partners as dividends only 50 percent of the net profits the partnership had earned, telling the limited partners the balance was being retained against the possibility of future partnership needs. As a result, each limited partner's dividend was equal to a return of only 5 percent on his or her investment. The limited partners petitioned the court to force the general partner to make a supplemental distribution. Will the limited partners be successful in the litigation? Why or why not?

5 Alice was the general partner in the Seaview Boutique, a limited partnership. Larry and Winnie were the limited partners, each having contributed $10,000 to the enterprise. After several months Larry decided that he would rather invest his money in another business, and he asked Alice to buy him out. Alice said she would pay Larry $10,000, the amount he had invested. He agreed, was paid, and withdrew from the partnership. About two months later Larry learned that the boutique was a very successful business and that his interest was worth at least double what he had sold it for. When he complained to Alice that he had sold too cheaply, she said that the selling of his interest was his own idea, she did not induce him to sell, and he had the privilege of refusing to accept her offer if he had wanted to. Does Larry have any legal cause of action against Alice? Explain.

6 Ozark Skyrise was a limited partnership organized for the purpose of operating a resort at Lake of the Ozarks. Seymour was the general partner and six individuals were the limited partners. Seymour learned that there was an opportunity to purchase at a most attractive price a motel near Kansas City, about a hundred miles away from the partnership's resort. Seymour thought that the purchase of the motel would be an excellent investment for the partnership and, as the partnership had sufficient funds in its bank account to make a down payment on the purchase, he bought the motel in the partnership name. When the limited partners learned of the purchase they demanded that Seymour dispose of the motel and reimburse the partnership for the funds he had expended. Were the limited partners legally justified to make that demand? Discuss.

7 Block and Dardanes entered into a limited partnership to operate a restaurant. Dardanes was the general partner and Block the limited partner. The restaurant was opened May 1, 1980, and Dardanes put his son in charge of it. Dardanes himself seldom went to the restaurant. A year went by and Dardanes told Block that the restaurant had not made any money but that he thought it would show a profit the next year. Block asked for an accounting of the business; Dardanes procrastinated, and Block sued for the dissolution of the partnership. Was such an action properly brought by Block, who was merely a limited partner? Explain.

CHAPTER 39

Nature and Formation of Corporations

The corporation-for-profit is the most important form of business organization in the United States. Since World War II, corporations have proliferated five times faster than have partnerships. The corporation form is ideally suited both to complex multimillion dollar enterprises and to small ventures whose members fear risk of personal liability.

This chapter briefly traces the development of corporation law and discusses important legal principles relating to the nature and formation of modern business corporations. Subsequent chapters in this series deal with the financing, management, and regulation of business corporations.

What Is a Corporation?

A corporation is an artificial being created by the state. It is an invisible, intangible legal entity that is independent of its owners—that is, those who own its shares. A corporation conducts business, enters into contracts, buys and sells property, and sues and is sued as though it were a living, breathing person. It pays taxes and, although it cannot be imprisoned, a corporation is subject to criminal prosecution and fine. Its debts are the obligations of the corporate entity and not of its individual owners, the shareholders.

Being a legal entity, a corporation is entitled to the equal protection of the laws assured by the Constitution. Among other constitutional rights, a corporation is protected from unreasonable searches and from having its property seized without due process of law.

The structure or anatomy of a corporation can best be understood by the diagram appearing in Figure 39.1.

Development of Modern Corporation Law

State Incorporation Laws

The idea that the Federal or state government can breath life into a fictitious legal person known as a "corporation" originated in ancient Rome and spread to England and thence to the American colonies. Initially, U.S. corporations were formed by special acts of the various state legislatures to carry on projects having some public purpose such as the building of canals or toll bridges. As the industrial revolution advanced, businesses of every description sought special legislative action to allow them to incorporate. In response to this pressure all the states, beginning with New York in 1811, enacted general incorporation laws called "enabling acts." These laws established restrictive procedures which, when followed, permitted any lawful business to be incorporated, thereby doing away with the necessity for special legislative acts. The general corporation laws also established guidelines for

Figure 39.1 The anatomy of a corporation

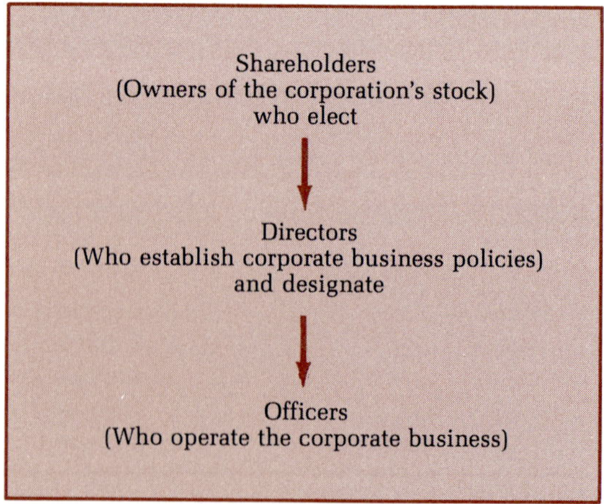

financing and dissolving corporations and the rights and duties of directors and shareholders. These statutes varied in detail from state to state.

In the course of the 19th century the restrictions on incorporation were relaxed as the states began to compete for the taxable income and employment opportunities generated by the larger companies. In 1899 the *Delaware General Corporation Law* was revised so as to offer corporations a maximum degree of freedom from restriction. As a result, today about half of the nation's Fortune 500 companies and fully 40 percent of the companies listed on the New York Stock Exchange, attracted by that state's corporate laws and court system, have been incorporated in Delaware.

In 1950 the American Bar Association published the Model Business Corporation Act as a guide for the revision of general corporation statutes to meet the needs of both large and small corporations and to encourage uniformity in state corporation laws. The 1984 revision of the act, the Revised Model Business Corporation Act, as further amended, is referred to here as the Revised Model Act and is reproduced as Appendix 5.

Each state also has a variety of regulatory statutes that govern and often restrict the business activities of corporations. Among those statutes are "blue sky" laws that establish criteria for the issuance and sale of corporate securities; laws that regulate particular kinds of corporations, such as banks and public utilities; corporate tax laws; and laws that regulate the activities within a state of corporations organized in another state or foreign country.

Federal Laws Affecting Corporations

There is no federal general law under which business people can incorporate although the Congress from time to time organizes a corporation to carry out some governmental objective, such as the Federal Deposit Insurance Corporation. Therefore, if you wish to form a corporation, you cannot apply to any agency of the federal government to secure a certificate of incorporation. You must secure your charter from the secretary of state of the state in which your company will be organized. Nevertheless, the federal government freely regulates the manner in which state chartered corporations operate. Those federal regulations and their accompanying case law have burgeoned into what is loosely referred to as "federal corporation law."

Nature of Modern Corporations

Characteristics of Corporations

Many characteristics set corporations apart from other types of business organizations. Briefly, those characteristics are:

Legal Entity. A corporation is a legal entity, also called an artificial person, created by the state as evidenced by its *articles of incorporation,* also called its *charter* and is subject to corporation law.

Perpetual Existence. A corporation continues in existence indefinitely unless it is given a shorter life by its articles of incorporation or is dissolved by action of the state for the reasons and under the procedures prescribed by state law. The death, illness, or withdrawal of a shareholder, officer, or corporation director does not affect the life of a corporation. Statutes in most states set out procedures (which are far from uniform) by which shareholders can force a corporation's dissolution. This action, however, is rarely taken.

Wide Purpose and Powers. It was formerly the practice of the states to require incorporators to fully state in the articles of incorporation the purpose for which it was being formed and it could not carry on any different or additional business. This limitation was later modified so that articles of incorporation could state multiple purposes. As a result, incorporators began to list every conceivable activity as a possible purpose of the corporation. In fact, so many purposes might be stated in the articles of incorporation that the actual business in which the corporation intended to engage was not discernible. The next liberalizing step, and one which is currently expressed in most state statutes and in the Revised Model

Act, allows the articles of incorporation to state merely that the purpose for which the corporation is being organized is to engage in "any lawful business."

The Revised Model Act also provides that a corporation has the same powers as an individual to do anything necessary to carry on its business and affairs. However, the states reserve the power to amend or repeal the Act at any time and thereby may limit or withdraw powers previously granted to a corporation. This is discussed more fully in Chapter 41.

Limited Liability of Shareholders. One of the primary characteristics of a corporation is that normally its shareholders, like limited partners in a limited partnership, are not personally liable for the company's debts and obligations. Therefore, except in unusual circumstances, the only financial risk someone undertakes upon becoming a corporation shareholder is the risk of loss of his or her investment in the enterprise. It is for this reason that the ownership of corporate shares is a most attractive investment vehicle. Unlike the general partner(s) in a limited partnership, neither the officers nor directors of a corporation are personally liable for the company's debts and obligations. This feature of the corporation causes it to be the preferred form of organization for people who are about to start a new and perhaps risky venture.

Free Transferability of Shares. A share of stock is a proportionate ownership interest in a corporation. Some corporations issue millions of shares, others may issue fewer than a dozen. Table 39.1 lists the number of shares issued by four representative giant American corporations.

The owner of shares of stock, unless restricted by contractual agreement, may freely transfer the shares to anyone he or she chooses, and it is not necessary to secure the permission of the corporation or of other shareholders to do so. Transfer of share ownership in no way affects the legal existence of the corporation. The free transferability of shares has been a major factor in the development of the national stock exchanges and in the prodigious expansion of industry in the United States.

Centralized Management. The management and control of a corporation is centralized in its shareholder-elected board of directors and in the officers who are appointed by and act under the board's authority. This centralized management enables a huge corporation to act with maximum efficiency to the benefit of its owners, the shareholders. Although the shareholders elect the board of directors, in an ordinary publicly held corporation they do not dictate the board's decisions and activities. However, as we will soon see, in a small, closely held corporation the shareholders also generally serve as its directors. Especially in publicly held corporations, the members of the board of directors are selected for the diversified business experiences they can bring to the company.

Corporations, Partnerships, and Limited Partnerships Contrasted

Now that we have examined the principal elements of corporations and in previous chapters

Table 39.1 Number of Shares of Common Stock Issued by Representative Corporations

Company	No. of Shares
American Telephone & Telegraph Co. (as of 31 Oct. 1988)	1,073,750,000
Exxon Corp. (as of 31 Dec. 1988)	1,289,000,000
General Electric Corp. (as of 30 Sept. 1988)	900,544,000
General Motors Corp. (as of 31 Dec. 1988)	612,913,342
Class E	50,646,603
Class H	128,388,969

looked at partnerships and limited partnerships, the essential characteristics which distinguish these three business organizational forms are summarized in Table 39.2.

Kinds of Corporations

Corporations may be classified in several ways. They may be seen as (1) corporations organized for public or private purposes, (2) corporations organized for profit or not for profit, (3) publicly or privately held corporations, and (4) domestic or foreign corporations. But such classifications should not be thought of as mutually exclusive because a corporation may be at the same time, for example, private, for profit, publicly held, and domestic.

Corporations Organized for Public or Private Purposes. A *public corporation* is one that is created by a state legislature or by Congress for governmental purposes. Clearly, an incorporated city or town, generally referred to as a municipal corporation, is a public corporation. A state may also create other types of public corporations, such as a state hospital for the insane, a state bar association, a sanitation, flood control, or irrigation district so common in the western states, or a publicly owned utility such as the electric generating plant owned by the City of Jacksonville, Florida.

From time to time the Congress of the United States itself creates a corporation to satisfy some public need. For instance, in 1823 it created a corporation familiar to us as the Smithsonian Institution. In 1932, to combat the depression, Congress created the Reconstruction Finance Corporation (RFC), and in 1933 the Tennessee Valley Authority was incorporated by Congress for the integrated development of the Tennessee River basin. More recently Congress created as corporate entities the United States Postal Service, Comstat (establishing a communications satellite system), and Amtrak (to operate a passenger railroad service).

A *private corporation* is one that is organized by private individuals for private purposes, usually to earn profits, but it may also be organized for nonprofit purposes.

Corporations for Profit or Not for Profit. Most corporations are *for profit.* That is to say, they are organized with the intent (1) to engage in a business which earns a profit, and (2) to distribute to the shareholders, as dividends, as much of those profits as the board of directors declares. Private for-profit corporations are with increasing frequency being constrained and regulated by state and federal laws and regulations. For example, regulations control the sale of corporate securities and regulate the manner in which a corporation may carry on its business. In succeeding chapters these laws and regulations are discussed in detail.

State statutes prescribe how *nonprofit* corporations may be organized, and there is a Model Nonprofit Corporation Act which may be used as a guide. A nonprofit corporation is similar to a corporation-for-profit in that both have boards of directors and officers, but normally the nonprofit corporation has members rather than shareholders. Many state laws direct that not more than one membership may be held by any individual member in a nonprofit corporation. Such a corporation receives special treatment under the Internal Revenue Code when it uses its profits in charitable, religious, educational, or fraternal activities.

The tax laws have encouraged the formation of a large number of nonprofit corporations. This is not to say that the organizers of these corporations did not intend them to make a profit. It means only that this class of corporation, which may be very profitable, does not distribute its profits in the same manner as do ordinary for-profit corporations. Instead of being distributed to the members, the profits are spent to further the corporation's stated purposes and its assets can be distributed to its members only when the corporation is dissolved. A nonprofit corporation such as, for example, a mission for the homeless that qualifies as a charitable corporation under the Internal Revenue Code, generally must, upon its dissolution, provide for the distribution of its assets to another charitable tax-exempt corporation rather than to its members.

Some of the very wealthy nonprofit corporations are organized as *foundations,* such as the Ford Foundation, the Rockefeller Foundation, and the Hughes Medical Foundation. An interesting transaction of the Hughes Medical Foundation is worthy of mention. Howard Hughes established and owned all the shares of stock of the Hughes Aircraft Corporation. In his lifetime he gave those

Table 39.2 Corporations, Partnerships, and Limited Partnerships Contrasted

Organizational Characteristics	Corporations	General Partnerships (Chapters 36 and 37)	Limited Partnerships (Chapter 38)
Entity	A separate legal entity and taxed as such.	Not a legal entity but has certain characteristics of one; consists of two or more partners who share equally in profits unless otherwise agreed.	Has many characteristics of a legal entity; partnership income belongs to its members in agreed percentages. Has two classes of partners: general and limited.
Creation	Created by the state upon application in required legal form; creation evidenced by charter or articles of incorporation.	Created by formal or informal agreement of its members; no state action involved.	Created by filing Certificate of Limited Partnership with state; also has, but not filed, a formal or informal Limited Partnership Agreement.
Duration	Perpetual corporate life unless limited by articles of incorporation or by law but life may be terminated by state or by shareholders as provided by law.	Life limited to term set by partnership agreement but is dissolved before expiration of term if for any reason partners cease to be associated in business together.	For the time or purpose specified in Agreement, but may be dissolved earlier as specified therein.
Purposes and powers	Limited as stated in Articles and state law; under Revised Model Act may engage in any lawful business with same powers as an individual.	To carry on any legal business agreed to by partners; generally state approval not necessary.	To carry on the business specified in the Certificate and Agreement.
Ownership of	By shareholders evidenced by shares of stock held.	By individual partners in proportions agreed.	By general and limited partners as specified.

Transfer of ownership	Shares normally transferred at will of shareholder; consent of corporation or of other shareholders not necessary; transfer has no effect on corporation.	Partnership interest may be transferred at will of partner but assignee does not become a partner unless all partners agree; transfer of entire interest dissolves the partnership.	General partner may transfer interest with effect specified in Agreement. Limited partner may transfer all or part of interest at any time; assignee becomes a limited partner only as specified in Agreement.
Liability of owners	Shareholder has no personal liability for corporate obligations; only risk is loss of investment.	All partners personally liable for partnership obligations; liability not limited to investment in partnership.	General partner has all the liability of a partner in a general partnership. Limited partner generally has no personal liability for partnership obligations.
Management	By board of directors and officers acting under it; shareholder generally limited to voting in election of directors and on amendments to articles and certain extraordinary matters.	All partners have right to manage the business; each is the agent of partnership and of his or her copartners.	General partner(s) manage the business; limited partners have only a limited right to assist management or to vote on changes of partnership organization.

shares to the Hughes Medical Foundation, which had been established some time earlier. After Mr. Hughes's death the Foundation sold those shares to the General Motors Corporation for $5 billion—considerably more than the shares were worth when the Foundation received them. Because of the nonprofit status of the Foundation, it was not required to pay a tax on the gain it made on the sale of the shares to General Motors.

Publicly Held or Closely Held Corporations. A *publicly held corporation* (also called a *publicly traded corporation*) is one whose shares are held by a large number of people—just how large a number is not defined—and whose shares are traded on the New York or American Stock Exchanges or in over-the-counter markets, or whose share price quotations are regularly published. As of April 21, 1989, 1,648 companies were listed on the New York Stock Exchange; as of December 31, 1988, 895 on the American Stock Exchange; and the shares of 4,402 companies, as of March 31, 1989, were traded in the national over-the-counter market (called NASDAQ, the acronym for National Association of Security Dealers, Inc. Automatic Quotation).

Publicly held corporations are vastly outnumbered by the multitude of small businesses whose shares are owned by a single individual, by family members, or by only relatively few people. These corporations are called "close corporations," or "closely held corporations," or "closed corporations." The shareholders of practically all these small corporations do not adopt that form of business organization to be merely passive investors as are the shareholders in publicly held corporations. Their primary purpose is to establish a business in which, either alone or in conjunction with a few close associates (1) they have personal control of the corporation's policies and operations, (2) they can enjoy some of the pension and tax benefits available to corporations, and (3) under the mantle of a corporation they are free from personal liability in the event the business is not successful.

A close corporation exhibits many characteristics of a sole proprietorship or of a partnership. Typically, in a close corporation:

- There are relatively few shareholders.
- Most or all its shareholders participate in the management of the company.
- Its shares are not listed or traded on any stock or over-the-counter market.
- There may be company-imposed restrictions on the transferability of its shares and on the admission of new shareholders.

Although the Revised Model Act is written in sufficiently broad language to accommodate both publicly held and closely held corporations, many states still have no statutory provisions for closely held corporations; however, a body of case law has arisen which specifically responds to the needs of such corporations. The American Bar Association in 1982 published a Supplement to the Model Business Corporation Act applicable to close corporations which is designed to be integrated with the Revised Model Act. Increasingly, states are following the Supplement or otherwise enacting laws which provide rules similar to those of the Supplement.

S Corporations and Professional Corporations. S or small business corporations are ordinary corporations which meet certain special requirements that entitle them to certain tax advantages under the Internal Revenue Code. An S corporation is a domestic corporation with no more than 35 shareholders, none of whom is a nonresident alien. A husband and wife are counted as a single shareholder. Among other technical requirements it may not be part of an affiliated group of corporations and must have only one class of stock, but the shareholders may have different voting rights. (Classes of stock and voting rights are discussed in the next chapter.) If the shareholders unanimously elect to be an S or small business corporation, it then comes under Subchapter S of the Internal Revenue Code and the Subchapter S Revision Act of 1982 (26 USC 1371 et seq.). For *federal* (not state) income tax purposes an S corporation is generally treated as though it were a partnership and its shareholders were partners. As a result, the corporation's profits are considered to have been allocated to the shareholders whether or not they actually received them, and the shareholders are taxed individually on that allocation. If the corporation loses money the shareholders are entitled individually to account for the losses allocated to them in their tax returns.

The *professional corporation* has arisen in response to the demand of professional people such as physicians, lawyers, architects, surveyors, and accountants, for permission to enjoy those corporate fringe benefits allowed a corporation employee not generally available to the proprietor of a business. Most states have responded to that demand by superimposing upon their business corporation statutes rather brief authorizations that establish professional corporations. Accordingly, it is now common to see on an office door a sign reading, for example, "Jane Doe, M.D., a Professional Corporation," or "Joe Dokes, a Law Corporation." When a professional person such as Dr. Jane Doe incorporates, she becomes an employee of the corporation and, as such, becomes entitled to whatever employee benefits the corporation may provide, such as participation in a pension or profit-sharing plan. In addition, under certain circumstances she may gain tax advantages. The statutes usually limit share ownership to duly licensed professional persons and they retain personal liability for professional acts they perform or those that are performed under their supervision.

Domestic or Foreign Corporations. A corporation is described as *domestic* within the state of its incorporation regardless of the residence of its shareholders. In any of the other forty-nine states where it may be doing business it is referred to as a *foreign corporation.* Thus, if the Magic Corporation is chartered in Delaware but does business in another state (for example if it maintains a factory and/or a sales office in New York), it is a domestic corporation in Delaware but in New York it is viewed as a foreign corporation.

When a state charters a corporation, say, a savings and loan or a utility company or just a single store, it creates a legal entity which is authorized to carry on within that state the business or businesses set forth in its charter. But the charter does not grant rights or privileges that are effective in another state without that other state's permission. A foreign corporation is required to obtain a *certificate of authority* from the secretary of state of each state (called a "host" state) in which it proposes to do business [Revised Model Act 15.01(a)]. If the foreign corporation fails to do so, it may not maintain a proceeding in any court of that state until it obtains the required certificate and it may also be liable to civil penalties. In addition, a foreign corporation that is authorized to transact business in a host state may have its certificate of authority revoked if it fails to maintain a registered office and a registered agent there, or if it fails, within 60 days after it becomes due, to file an annual report or to pay franchise taxes.

Many foreign corporations do business with suppliers and customers within states in which they have not obtained certificates of authority or they transit supplies and equipment through such states and frequently questions arise whether they are subject to that state's laws and regulations. The Supreme Court of the United States, in *International Shoe Co. v. State of Washington,* 326 U.S. 310 (1945) extended state jurisdiction over foreign corporations whenever there are "certain minimum contacts" of the corporation within the host state and the foreign corporation receives the "benefits and protection" of that state. It is natural that much case law has subsequently arisen under the facts in particular cases as to whether the foreign corporation maintained such contacts and received such business benefits and protection in the host state that it is subject to its taxes or regulations; whether it was "doing business" in the state; or whether the state was attempting an unwarranted interference with interstate commerce.

Formation of Corporations

Let us now turn to the steps required to form a corporation. In general, three steps are involved: (1) preincorporation activities, (2) filing articles of incorporation, and (3) the organizational meeting.

Preincorporation Activities

A business corporation originates as an *idea.* Preincorporation activities transform that idea into a reality. The individual who carries on these activities is called a *promoter.* In corporation law that word does not connote involvement in some sort of scam; rather, a promoter is an organizer engaged in a legitimate activity. An individual, a partnership, another corporation, or some other entity may be the promoter of a new corporation.

Assume that David, an engineer with only meager finances, has secured a patent on a superconductor manufacturing process. He wants to form a corporation which will use the patent in manufacturing electric motors. He knows that a lot of money must be raised through the sale of shares in the corporation. David therefore entrusts to a promoter the task of getting the enterprise underway. The promoter may be one of David's associates or friends or David may hire a promoter to do whatever is necessary. Among the promoter's multitude of functions may be:

- To verify the economic feasibility of the enterprise
- To bring together incorporators who will sign the certificate of incorporation
- To find subscribers who undertake to purchase the new corporation's shares of stock, and
- To arrange for necessary financing

In addition, the promoter may be required:

- To find and contract for factory space, manufacturing equipment, and materials necessary for the corporation to begin to work, and
- To recruit people to serve as the officers and key employees of the company

On the other hand, preincorporation activities may be far simpler than those in the above illustration. Assume that Richard Rover, as the sole proprietor, runs a bicycle sales and repair shop in Missouri. He decides to expand his business and thinks that he should operate as a corporation. Richard therefore talks to his lawyer, who prepares articles of incorporation furnishing all the information required by Missouri law. The articles are signed by Richard, the lawyer, and the lawyer's secretary as the original incorporators. The articles are sent to the Secretary of State of Missouri with the required filing fees. In a few days Richard is informed that the corporation has been formed. Thus, although Richard has done little in the foregoing process he has been the promoter of his new corporation.

Liability for Preincorporation Contracts. After the new corporation is organized, one of its first problems will be to decide what to do about preincorporation contracts the promoter may have entered into but which have not been fully performed. The promoter or the corporation, after it comes into existence, or both, may be liable upon contracts entered into by the promoter on the corporation's behalf before it was chartered.

Promoter's liability for preincorporation contracts. If a promoter makes a promise to personally pay the supplier of a service or article on a contract for the benefit of a future corporation, the promoter is, of course, liable. But even if the promoter made no such promise, if payment is not made by the corporation after it comes into existence the promoter must pay for the service or product he or she ordered (Revised Model Act 2.04). This is because at the time the order was given or the contract was entered into, the promoter was purporting to act for a principal, but that principal—the corporation—was not yet in existence. It is basic agency law that one who acts for a nonexistent principal is personally liable on the contract. Of course, a promoter and third party may have an understanding that the promoter binds only the proposed corporation and that the other party to the contract will look only to the corporation for performance. However, it is unlikely that many suppliers would enter into such a risky undertaking.

The following case deals with a promoter's liability on a contract made in the name of a corporation before the corporation was chartered.

CASE 39.1 Ratner v. Central National Bank of Miami · 414 S.2d 210 (Fla. App. 1982)

FACTS Appellant, Joel Ratner, was the promoter of The Stereo Corner, Inc. Ratner signed a merchant's Mastercharge agreement with the appellee, Central National Bank of Miami. The agreement was signed, "The Stereo Corner, Inc., by Joel Ratner." Stereo Corner, Inc. was not incorporated by Ratner, its promoter, until eight months later although it was doing business in the interim. Both before and after Stereo Corner was incorporated,

CASE 39.1 Continued

one of its employees forged a series of sales drafts (Mastercharge customer vouchers) which were deposited and credited to Stereo Corner's account. The Mastercharge agreement provided that the company warranted each sales draft and agreed to be liable for any of them that were improperly or fraudulently executed. When the bank was unable to collect on the forged vouchers, it charged Stereo the amounts due. Stereo became insolvent and the bank sued Ratner, claiming that he was individually liable on the Mastercharge agreement. Ratner claimed the bank intended to contract with The Stereo Corner as a corporate entity and not with him individually. Ratner also claimed that Stereo Corner ratified the agreement thereby making it its own. After summary judgment for the bank, Ratner appealed.

OPINION

FERGUSON, J. . . . The Florida law and general rule is that the promoter of a corporation is liable on his contract although the contract was made on behalf of the corporation to be formed, unless the other party agrees to look to another fund for payment. . . . The later formation of the corporation and subsequent adoption or ratification of the contract by the corporation does not necessarily release a promoter from liability, but may result in joint liability of the promoter and corporation, absent a novation or express release by the other party to the contract. . . . Moreover, where the promoter does not make it clear that he is acting as a promoter and misrepresents—even if unintentionally—that the corporation is already in existence, thereby causing the other party to enter the contract without knowledge that the entity has not yet been incorporated, the later formation of the corporation and subsequent ratification of the contract, will not by itself, relieve the promoter of liability.

In this case . . . there is no evidence that Central [Bank] agreed to look solely to the corporation. . . .

JUDGMENT

Affirmed.

Corporate liability for preincorporation contracts. A newly formed corporation does not *automatically* become a party to a preincorporation contract made on its behalf by a promoter. The legal reasoning behind this is twofold: (1) The promoter, when engaging in the contract, could not act as the agent of the corporation because the corporation had not yet come into existence and therefore could not have been a principal, and (2) the corporation, once organized, is a legal entity separate from its promoter, with independent rights and duties. Accordingly, generally a newly formed corporation is privileged to choose which of the preexisting contracts it will assume and which it will reject. However, some states require its corporations to adopt promoter's contracts made on its behalf.

A corporation adopts a preincorporation contract either expressly or impliedly. It *expressly adopts* by passing a resolution to that effect at a director's or shareholders' meeting. It *impliedly adopts* a preincorporation contract by accepting its benefits or by performing according to its terms. In either event, the promoter remains liable jointly on the contract unless the newly incorporated company enters into a *novation* agreement with the creditor. Under such an agreement the creditor accepts the corporation as a contracting party in place of the promoter, who is then released from liability under the contract.

Fiduciary Duty of Promoters. A promoter is not the agent of the corporation he or she is forming nor is the promoter the agent of individuals brought into the venture. Nonetheless, the promoter owes a fiduciary duty to the future corporation, to the subscribers of its shares, and to its future shareholders. This fiduciary duty requires fair dealing, the exercise of good faith, and the disclosure of all material facts concerning transactions he or she makes on behalf of the future corporation.

Typically, the duty of disclosure comes into play when a promoter sells to the corporation his or her own property, or exchanges it for shares of the corporation's stock.[1] Suppose Alfred, a promoter, owns property which he wants to sell to the new corporation, either for cash or for shares of its stock. For Alfred legally to make the sale or exchange he must make full disclosure to the board of directors of all elements of the transaction. If, however, the directors are controlled by Alfred, he is required to make the disclosure to all the then shareholders. Such a procedure protects the newly formed corporation from paying Alfred an exorbitant price for his property. If Alfred fails to make the required disclosure, the corporation may rescind the transaction or may keep the property and recover any secret profit Alfred may have made.

Subscription to Shares of Stock. Unless a corporation is to be closely held, part of a promoter's duties is the recruitment of investors in the new enterprise. The promoter does this by securing from potential investors a *subscription,* that is, an offer to purchase shares of stock of the prospective company at an agreed price, payable at an agreed future time. The issuance of shares is discussed in Chapter 40, which concerns the financing of corporations. At this point we merely note that anyone who offers to purchase shares of stock is called a *subscriber.*

Special problems arise in determining a subscriber's liability to a corporation when the subscription is entered into before the corporation has come into legal existence. A majority of courts treat a subscription as a continuing offer to purchase the shares and hold that the offer (subscription) may be revoked by the offeror at any time before acceptance. Other courts regard a subscription as a contract among the subscribers which is irrevocable unless all the subscribers consent. The Revised Model Act provides a compromise: it states in Section 6.20(a) that a subscription for shares of a proposed corporation is irrevocable for 6 months unless the subscription agreement provides otherwise or unless all the subscribers consent to the revocation.

There is conflict also as to what constitutes acceptance of a preincorporation share subscription. The majority view is that completion of the incorporation process amounts to an automatic acceptance of the subscriber's offer. The minority view is that there must be some act of acceptance on the corporation's part, such as listing the subscriber as a shareholder in the corporation records.

A subscription agreement obligates the subscriber to pay cash at the time stated in the agreement or, if the time is not stated, at such time as is fixed by the board of directors. If the subscriber defaults on a payment, the corporation may proceed to collect the amount due in the same manner it collects other debts. If the subscription is payable in installments, the subscriber is not a shareholder until the full amount is paid.

Creating the Corporation

Selection of State of Incorporation. If a corporation is to operate chiefly within one state, the business normally is incorporated in that state. But because corporations may operate in a number of states, and a great many do, important factors must be taken into account in selecting the state in which to incorporate a new enterprise. The selection might depend on the relative flexibility and freedom from restrictions offered by the corporation statutes in the various states. It is also desirable to select a state in which the courts have thoroughly interpreted the corporation statutes. A well-developed body of appellate case law eliminates uncertainty as to the meaning of those statutes.

If the corporation will operate in more than one state, the organizers should also consider the relative impact of fees and taxes levied by the several states. The states vary greatly in the amount of organization fees, franchise taxes, income taxes, and stock issuance and transfer taxes they impose. In addition, there is a difference in the legal cost and in the degree of difficulty encountered in complying with varying statutory incorporation requirements for qualifying the corporation to do business in foreign jurisdictions. As noted earlier, because the corporation laws of Delaware are especially sensitive to the organizational needs of corporate enterprises, about half the publicly traded corporations have been incorporated in that state.

Preparation of Articles of Incorporation. Incorporation requirements differ from state to state

[1]The leading cases on this problem are *Old Dominion Copper Mining & Smelting Co. v. Bigelow,* 89 N.E. 193 (Mass. 1909) and *Old Dominion Copper Mining & Smelting Co. v. Lewisohn,* 210 U.S. 206 (1908).

but the first step always is to draft and file *articles of incorporation*. The promoter prepares or has a lawyer prepare the articles. They may be likened to a self-imposed constitution. The articles, together with the applicable statutes of the state of incorporation, provide the legal framework within which the corporation must operate.

The Revised Model Act (2.02) requires articles of incorporation to state:

1 The corporation's name
2 The number of shares of stock it is authorized to issue
3 The street address of its initial registered office and the name of its initial registered agent at that office
4 The name and address of each incorporator

In addition, the articles may set out other pertinent corporate information such as the names and addresses of the individuals who are to serve as the initial directors, the purpose(s) for which the corporation is organized, and provisions regarding managing the business and regulating its affairs.

Some states require the articles to set out the powers to be exercised by the corporation and the term of its existence.

Corporate name. The corporation name must contain the word or the abbreviation for "corporation," "incorporated," "company," or "limited" (Revised Model Act 4.01). The name chosen must be distinguishable from the name of any domestic or foreign corporation authorized to transact business within the state. Care must be taken in the choice of name if it is expected that the corporation will transact business in states other than the state of its incorporation. In that case, the name selected should not be so similar to the name of any corporation already doing business in those other states that confusion in the sources of their respective products or services may arise. If the names are similar, the new corporation may be faced with an action for injunction brought by a previously established corporation. To illustrate, say that Tiny Tots Toys are sold extensively throughout the midwestern states but they have not yet been introduced into the New Jersey market. You form Tiny Kids Toys and incorporate in New Jersey. If you attempt to sell your product under that name in a state where Tiny Tots Toys are sold, very likely Tiny Tots will bring an action to enjoin you from selling your toys under your corporate name in that area.

Incorporator(s). An incorporator's sole function is to sign the articles of incorporation, usually before a notary public. The promoter may, if he or she so desires, sign the articles as incorporator—or may be one of the incorporators if more than one is required in that state. As a general rule, an incorporator who takes no part in company management is not exposed to legal liability.

Some states require three incorporators, but a majority of states require only one (Revised Model Act 2.01). The statutory qualifications for incorporators also vary. Some states impose citizenship or residence requirements or require incorporators to subscribe for shares. Many states permit a domestic or foreign corporation to be an incorporator, and Delaware even extends the privilege to a partnership or association.

Registered office and agent. A corporation must have, within the state of incorporation, a registered office with a registered agent (Revised Model Act 5.01). That office is not necessarily the corporation's business office although frequently it is. The registered office and agent must be maintained so that there is always someone available upon whom legal process may be served and to which official state notices may be sent.

Filing Articles of Incorporation. The signed articles of incorporation together with the required filing fees are forwarded to the designated state official, usually the secretary of state. The articles are there reviewed and if for any reason they do not conform to state law or regulations, or if the name selected is too similar to a name already in use, the articles are returned to the sender.

When the articles of incorporation have been found by the appropriate official to fully conform with statute, they are then officially "filed." *Filing* is a technical word which means state approval of the articles as evidenced by some state action—it may be by the issuance of a formal charter or certificate of incorporation, by the affixing of an official stamp acknowledging the filing, or by the mere issuance of a dated receipt of the filing fee. Normally, a corporation's life begins when the articles are filed with the secretary of state. Some states require additional filing in designated coun-

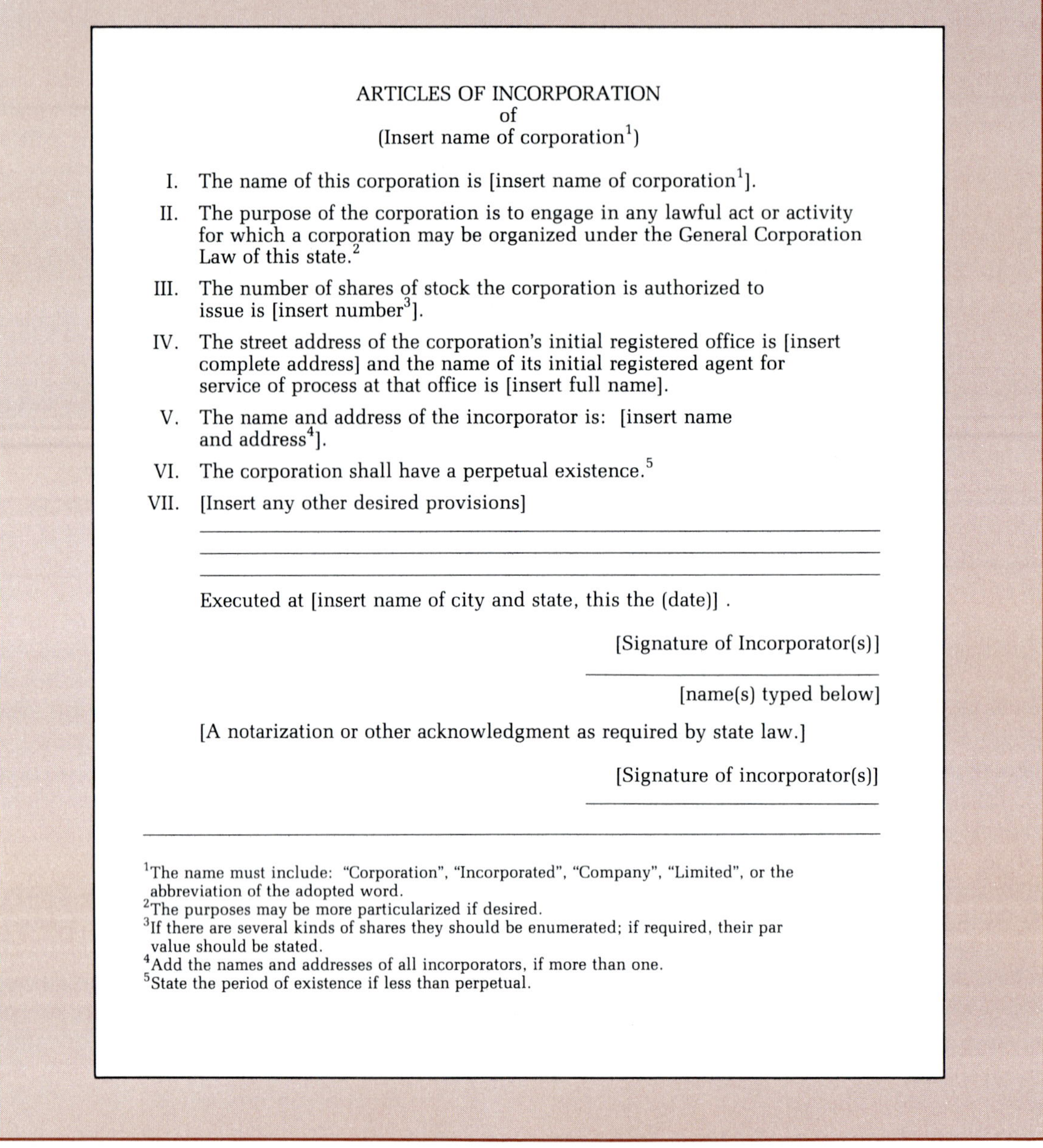

ARTICLES OF INCORPORATION
of
(Insert name of corporation[1])

I. The name of this corporation is [insert name of corporation[1]].

II. The purpose of the corporation is to engage in any lawful act or activity for which a corporation may be organized under the General Corporation Law of this state.[2]

III. The number of shares of stock the corporation is authorized to issue is [insert number[3]].

IV. The street address of the corporation's initial registered office is [insert complete address] and the name of its initial registered agent for service of process at that office is [insert full name].

V. The name and address of the incorporator is: [insert name and address[4]].

VI. The corporation shall have a perpetual existence.[5]

VII. [Insert any other desired provisions]

Executed at [insert name of city and state, this the (date)] .

[Signature of Incorporator(s)]

[name(s) typed below]

[A notarization or other acknowledgment as required by state law.]

[Signature of incorporator(s)]

[1]The name must include: "Corporation", "Incorporated", "Company", "Limited", or the abbreviation of the adopted word.
[2]The purposes may be more particularized if desired.
[3]If there are several kinds of shares they should be enumerated; if required, their par value should be stated.
[4]Add the names and addresses of all incorporators, if more than one.
[5]State the period of existence if less than perpetual.

Figure 39.2 Form of articles of incorporation

ties. For example, Delaware requires the filing of a certified copy of the articles in the county in which the corporation's registered office is located even though the corporation has come into legal existence upon the filing with the secretary of state. A few states condition corporate existence upon completion of all such subordinate filing requirements.

The Organizational Meeting

Once the corporation has been chartered, if its board of directors had not been named in the articles of incorporation, the initial incorporator(s) elect the members of the board and then the incorporators resign. The directors then hold an organizational meeting to get the newly formed corporate entity underway (Revised Model Act 2.05). At the organizational meeting the board of directors:

- Adopts bylaws which will govern the internal management of the corporation
- Elects officers, generally a president, a vice president, a secretary, and a treasurer and by resolution fixes their salaries
- Transacts other necessary business such as the adoption of resolutions authorizing the rental or purchase of an office, factory building, or other appropriate place where the company will carry on its business
- Selects the corporation's bank and designates who is authorized to draw checks upon the account
- Considers each of the preincorporation contracts or commitments made by the promoter on the corporation's behalf and either adopts or rejects them
- Adopts the form of certificate representing shares of the company's stock which will be issued to shareholders
- If applicable, the board may also direct the appropriate corporate officer to take action to call for payment of preincorporation subscriptions
- Adopts a corporate seal to be affixed to or impressed upon corporate documents required by law to be under seal, such as a transfer of title to real property. Banks and government agencies traditionally require that the corporate seal be affixed to certified copies of board resolutions. The seal is customarily kept in the possession of the corporation's secretary.

Bylaws got their name from the fact that in early England a little village was called a bye. Bye laws were the laws of the bye, and the term, made into one word, has come down to us from that time. Corporate bylaws are rules for the conduct of the company's operations. They must not be inconsistent with state law or with the articles of incorporation. They are, in effect, private laws which govern its internal affairs. The bylaws are binding upon the directors, officers, and shareholders even though they may not have been read by those individuals. However, *the bylaws are not binding upon persons outside the corporation.* For example, the bylaws of The John Doe Company, Inc., might provide that any purchase order over $500 must be approved by the company's treasurer. However, the Doe company is obligated to pay for an unapproved purchase amounting to $501 or more made by its purchasing office if the seller had no knowledge of the limitation on the buying agent's authority.

The following case illustrates how a bylaw functions as a rule for the governance of an organization.

CASE 39.2 Orchard Ridge Country Club, Inc. v. Schrey · 470 N.E.2d 780 (Ind. App. 3 Dist. 1984)

FACTS Orchard Ridge Country Club, the appellant, is an Indiana not-for-profit corporation. Its articles of incorporation provide in part that the board of directors may amend or repeal any of the bylaws. In July 1979 the board amended the bylaws to provide that members aged 65 and over who had paid dues for at least 20 years could opt to be called "honorary members" and pay only one-half the regular club dues.

In 1982 the board of directors, by a new amendment to the bylaws, abolished the one-half dues privilege. A group of honorary members 65 years of age or older who had paid active membership dues for at least 20 years and had opted to pay only one-half the regular dues, contend that the 1982 amendment is contrary to their contract with the club. The trial court held, in effect, that the bylaw amendment was beyond the authority of the board. The club appealed that decision.

OPINION HOFFMAN, J. . . . The board of directors of a corporation may adopt bylaws to govern matters of internal discipline, policy and management, and these bylaws constitute a contract between the corporation and its members. . . . In promulgating or amending by-

CASE 39.2 Continued

laws, the board of directors is given broad discretion to fix membership qualifications, rights and duties.... Where, as here, there is an express and clear reservation of the right to amend, [a member] is bound to take notice of the existence and effect of that reserve power. The power to enact bylaws is inherent in every corporation as an incident of its existence. This power is a continuous one.... No one has a right to presume that bylaws will remain unchanged.... Corporations have a right to change their bylaws when the welfare of the corporation... requires it and it is not forbidden by the organic law....

The duly chosen and authorized representatives of the members alone are vested with the power of determining when a change is demanded, and with their discretion courts cannot interfere. Were it otherwise, courts would control all benevolent associations, all corporations, and all fraternities....

...Under the bylaws, the Board of Directors retained the power "to fix the membership fees and dues and the times for the payment thereof...." The rights of membership were qualified from the outset such that any right granted could be revoked or changed.... The [honorary members] received the right to obtain Club benefits so long as they paid dues and complied with membership rules and regulations. The trial court erred in finding members entitled to continuing status as... honorary members.

JUDGMENT The judgment of the trial court is reversed.

Liability of Corporate Members

The freedom from liability or the liability of the shareholders of a corporation for its debts depends upon whether the statutes governing its incorporation were complied with and whether or not a court could legally ignore the corporation as a legal entity.

If a corporation is organized in full compliance with state laws, its "corporateness" is impregnable. Its shareholders are not liable for the debts of the corporation (Revised Model Act 6.22) unless, as will be subsequently discussed under the heading *Piercing the Corporate Veil,* a court disregards the claim of a corporation that it is, in fact, a legal entity separate from its shareholders.

A defectively formed corporation is open to attack on all sides. Creditors may contend that the business does not exist as a corporation and that its shareholders are partners with unlimited personal liability for the debts of the enterprise. Debtors who are sued by a defective corporation may challenge its capacity to contract or to sue. Subscribers to the corporation's shares may seek to escape liability on their subscription contracts by asserting that the proposed corporation never came into existence. The corporation itself may deny its own "corporateness" in order to avoid liability to creditors. Lastly, the state may cite failure to comply with statutory requirements for incorporation as the basis for a court order requiring the corporation to forfeit its charter or to cease operations.

The Revised Model Act (2.03(b)) and many state statutes now provide that the secretary of state's filing of the articles of incorporation is conclusive proof that the incorporators satisfied all conditions necessary to incorporate except in a proceeding by the state to revoke the incorporation or to dissolve it. Accordingly, in those states where that rule applies, once articles of incorporation are filed in the office of the secretary of state, the question of corporate existence should seldom arise. However, because opinions of the courts relating to the validity of a corporation continue to refer to *de jure corporations, de facto corporations,* and to *corporations by estoppel,* we should recognize the meaning of those terms.

De Jure Corporations

A de jure (meaning "according to law") corporation is one organized in compliance with state laws. It is a legal fortress which shields its shareholders from personal liability for corporate obligations. In states following the Revised Model Act, a de jure corporation is formed upon the filing of its articles of incorporation.

Some courts hold that all the provisions of the incorporation statute are mandatory and must be strictly complied with in all particulars in order to establish a de jure corporation. Other courts take a more liberal view and consider some of the statutory requirements to be *directory,* meaning that only substantial compliance is necessary. Whether substantial compliance will suffice and what constitutes substantial compliance, are questions decided on a case by case basis, the answer depending upon the circumstances in issue. For instance, articles of incorporation must be signed and the address of the individual who signs must be stated. The signing of the articles is a mandatory requirement which must be strictly complied with. If a signature is lacking, a de jure corporation is not formed. The address of the incorporator may be treated differently. If an incorrect address is stated in the articles a court may hold there has been a substantial compliance with the statute since some address is given. However, if no address at all has been stated, there was no compliance, the articles are defective, and a de jure corporation was not formed.

Defective Corporations

De Facto Corporation. What happens if the organizers of a business association do not comply with the law to the extent required to create a corporation de jure? Innocent shareholders may be personally liable for corporation debts. To protect them, a court may recognize the association as a corporation de facto—that is, a corporation actually existing. A de facto finding is based on the idea that injustice should not result from honest mistakes or omissions. That conclusion is often applied to prevent creditors from holding innocent shareholders liable because an incorporation attempt, made in good faith, falls short of the mandatory requirements in the statute.

There are two divergent rules, either of which may be applied to de facto corporations. It has generally been held that a de facto corporation exists if three prerequisites are present:

1. That there is a statute under which the association could have been validly incorporated.
2. That there was a good faith attempt to comply with the mandatory provisions of the statute.
3. That there was also a "corporate user"—that is, the association must in fact have exercised or attempted to exercise corporate powers.

However, as explained in Case 39.3, in those states which have adopted and strictly follow the Model Act, the de facto corporation concept is no longer recognized.

The legal existence of a de facto corporation can only be challenged by the state, not by a creditor of the corporation. The state may initiate a *quo warranto* proceeding which, literally, asks the corporation: "By what *authority* are you doing business?" However, it is improbable that the state would attempt to take the life of a de facto corporation unless its operations adversely affected the public interest.

The following case discusses the problem of the effect of the Revised Model Act upon the de facto concept.

CASE 39.3 Bowers Building Company v. Altura Glass Co. · 694 P.2d 876 (Colo. App. 1984)

FACTS Bowers Building Company was a general contractor. A company called Division 8, Inc. agreed to fabricate and install aluminum windows in a construction project for Bowers. On January 8, 1981, Division 8, Inc. assigned the contract to Altura Glass Co., Inc. Altura was unable to complete the work and Bowers was forced to hire another subcontractor to do the window work.

When John Crownover, the president of Altura Glass, accepted the assignment of the subcontract from Division 8, Altura did not have a corporation charter, although on that

CASE 39.3 Continued

day the necessary documents had been mailed to the secretary of state. The certificate was issued four days later, on January 12, 1981.

Bowers sued both Altura Glass and Crownover for breach of contract. The court held that because Crownover had acted as an officer of Altura Glass throughout the transaction and because the articles of incorporation had already been executed and delivered to Altura's attorney for filing, Altura had attained a de facto status and Crownover was not personally liable on the contract. The plaintiff, Bowers, appealed.

OPINION TURSI, J.... In *Bonfils v. Hayes,* 201 P. 677 (1921), Colorado recognized that de facto status exists when there is (1) a law under which a corporation can be formed, (2) a bona-fide attempt to form a corporation under that law, and (3) an exercise of corporate powers. Then, even though there are defects in compliance with the governing statute, the corporate status cannot be attacked collaterally....

In 1958 the General Assembly adopted a new corporation code based on [Section 2.03(a) of] the Model Business Corporation Act.... Under that act a corporation comes into existence upon the issuance of the certificate of incorporation.... At the time of the Bowers assignment, §7-2-104, Colorado Revised Statutes, provided that:

> Upon the issuance of the certificate of incorporation, the corporate existence shall begin, and each certificate of incorporation shall be conclusive evidence that all conditions precedent required to be performed by the incorporators have been complied with and that the corporation has been incorporated under this code.

Although this section was amended in 1981, the pertinent language here was unchanged.... Whether §7-2-104 abrogates the de facto corporation doctrine prior to the issuance of the certificate of incorporation has not been addressed. However, the comment to the Model Business Corporation Act Annotated... states:

> Under the unequivocal provisions of the Model Act, any steps short of securing a certificate of incorporation would not constitute apparent compliance. Therefore, a de facto corporation cannot exist under the Model Act.

Also,... *Cyclopedia of the Law of Private Corporations* §3762.1 (1982) states that under the Model Act "A corporation comes into existence only when the certificate of incorporation has been issued and, until issuance of the certificate, there is no corporation de jure, de facto, or by estoppel...."

Further, courts that have directly addressed the issue have concluded that there can be no de facto corporate existence prior to the issuance of the certificate of incorporation under statutes similar to ours....

...Therefore, we conclude that prior to the issuance of a certificate of incorporation there is no de facto status regardless of a substantial or colorable attempt to comply with the law effecting the creation of a corporation [and Crownover is personally liable].

JUDGMENT ...The cause is remanded....

Corporation by Estoppel. Under certain circumstances a party in a law suit is estopped, that is prevented, from claiming that a corporation does not exist as a legal entity even though the purported corporation does not meet either the de jure or de facto tests. A *corporation by estoppel* is then said to exist. A court may so conclude where, for example, (1) innocent shareholders face personal liability for the debts of an improperly organized corporation, (2) an improperly organized corporation attempts to escape contractual liability by denying its own corporateness, or (3) a person contracting with such a corporation tries to avoid liability by claiming that the corporation does not legally exist. For a corporation by estoppel to arise there must be:

- A representation by an enterprise that it is a corporation, followed by
- A reasonable reliance on that representation by another party, and
- Fair and equitable conduct by the party asserting the estoppel

The following two examples are illustrative:

1 John purchased a television set from a purported corporation. The company seeks to secure payment for the TV. John denies his obligation on the ground that the company was defectively formed and is not a corporation. In appropriate circumstances the court may hold that a corporation by estoppel exists and John is obligated to pay.
2 The ABC company, a defectively formed corporation, purchases a boat from the Windward Company but fails to pay for it. When Windward sues ABC, the latter denies liability, asserting that it is not a corporation. Unless fairness demands otherwise, the court will not allow ABC to deny its existence as a corporation.

The essential difference between a de facto corporation and a corporation by estoppel is that a court's finding of a de facto corporation recognizes its corporate existence. That finding is binding upon everyone, except the state, who does business with it. On the other hand, a court's finding that a corporation by estoppel exists affects only the parties to that suit.

Liability of Members of Enterprise Improperly Labeled a Corporation

No corporate legal entity is present when an incorporation effort is so defective that neither a de jure nor a de facto corporation is established, or when the business associates operate as a corporation without any intention of complying with the incorporation statutes. In either of these situations, and if corporation by estoppel does not apply, the purported corporation form under which the association is doing business does not shield its members against personal liability from third party claims arising out of transactions with the association. Most courts will subject each member of the purported corporation to personal liability as though the enterprise is a general partnership and all its "shareholders" are partners within it. Other courts, however, will impose partnership liability only on those who are *actively* involved in the promotion or management of the business and will limit the liability of the *inactive* members to their capital investments.

Piercing the Corporate Veil

We have seen that in order to do justice and to preserve the concept that an enterprise holding a certificate of incorporation is a legal entity separate from its shareholders, the law imposes a protective wall or veil between innocent corporate shareholders and the claims of third parties arising out of transactions with their corporation. On the other hand, under certain circumstances a court may look behind that wall and *pierce the corporate veil,* holding that the shareholder(s) are liable notwithstanding their claim that corporation law shields them from liability. The corporate veil may be pierced when a court finds (1) that the corporation is merely the *alter ego* or extension of a shareholder (usually a controlling shareholder active in the management of a close corporation), or (2) that two or more enterprises are parent and subsidiary corporations in which the subsidiary does not maintain an independent existence, or (3) that the corporation had been inadequately capitalized to carry on its intended business. In any of these events, the court, in order to do justice or to prevent the consummation of a fraud, may pierce the corporate veil and disregard the corporate legal entity concept.

The Alter Ego Doctrine. Under this concept a court may ignore the legal fiction that a corporation is an entity separate from its shareholder(s) when (1) there is such a unity of interest and ownership between the shareholder(s) and the corporation that, in practice, the separateness is not maintained or the corporation is used merely as a front for controlling interests behind it, *and* (2) fraud or injustice would be sanctioned if the corporation were allowed to be used as a shield to protect the shareholder(s) from liability.

In other words, the corporation is merely the *alter ego* or vehicle of the dominant shareholder or shareholders concerned and therefore creditors may hold the shareholder(s) liable for the debts and torts of the business. That unity may be evidenced in the following ways:

- The assets of the corporation and of a shareholder are commingled, no adequate record is kept to distinguish between the two, and corporate funds are used for the payment of private debts or for other private purposes.
- No minute book or other record of corporate activities is maintained, no directors are elected, and other corporate formalities are ignored.
- The shareholder uses the corporation as the instrument by which he or she can engage in economic ventures without risk, taking personal advantage of the gains which accrue and leaving to the corporation the payment of debts incurred.
- The corporation was established for a sham purpose.

Abuse of the corporate privilege arises most frequently when a close corporation is involved. However, it does not always follow that where one individual has absolute control of a corporation and owns all its shares that the corporate entity may be automatically disregarded. To pierce its corporate veil there must be some element of fraudulent purpose in its organization or an injustice resulting from its operations.

Since under the alter ego doctrine a shareholder may be liable for a corporation's debts and torts, similarly, under certain circumstances the debts and torts of a shareholder can be recognized as those of the corporation.

In the following case the court analyzes the requirements that must be met in order to find a corporation the alter ego of a shareholder.

CASE 39.4 Almac Inc. v. JRH Development, Inc. · 391 N.W.2d 919 (Minn. App. 1986)

FACTS Almac, Inc. owned a tract of land it wanted to develop for housing. To attract possible purchasers to the site, Almac, Inc. induced James Hill, a builder, to erect a speculation house on the the land by offering to sell a building lot to him on very easy terms. Hill organized JRH Development, Inc. to make the purchase and build the house.

JRH, with money borrowed from a savings and loan association and with personal funds advanced by Hill, built the house and made mortgage payments to the savings and loan and to Almac, Inc. Three years went by without a purchaser being found for the property and Hill stopped making the mortgage payments. The savings and loan association foreclosed and Almac sued JRH and Hill, seeking to hold him personally liable on JRH's debt to Almac. The trial court held that JRH Development Inc. was the alter ego of Hill, pierced the corporate veil of the company, and held Hill personally liable. Hill appealed.

OPINION CRIPPEN, J. . . . A creditor will be allowed "to pierce the corporate veil" of protection from liability and hold shareholders liable only when a two-prong test is met. . . . A court will first consider whether the corporation was formed either as the shareholders' "alter ego" or as their "mere instrumentality." If that prong is met, the court will allow the corporate veil to be pierced if there exists an element of injustice or fundamental unfairness. To determine whether the first prong is met, a court will consider several factors, including the sufficiency of capitalization for the purposes of the corporate undertaking, whether the directors failed to observe corporate formalities, whether the corporation failed to pay dividends, whether the corporation was insolvent at the time of the transaction, whether the dominant shareholder siphoned corporate funds, whether other officers and directors were nonfunctioning, whether corporate records were absent, and whether the corporation existed merely as a facade for individual dealings. . . . If "a number

CASE 39.4 Continued

of these factors are present," this first prong is met and the court will then consider whether the "injustice or fundamental unfairness" prong is met. . . . If both prongs of the test are met, the creditor will be allowed to pierce the corporate veil and hold the shareholders liable. . . .

. . . [In this case JRH's] total equity kept pace with the corporate liabilities until appellant [Hill] could no longer bear to plow any more of his personal funds into the corporation. . . . [T]he mere fact that the corporation became insolvent does not mean the corporation was initially undercapitalized. . . Appellant did not siphon funds from the corporation initially but instead pumped his own money into the corporation to keep it afloat. . . .

It is equally evident that the second prong is not met. . . . The evidence does not support the finding that the transaction here contains elements of injustice or unfairness such that the corporate entity should be disregarded. Although proof of "strict common law fraud" is not required to prove the second prong of the test, there must be proof that the corporation was operated "as a constructive fraud or in an unjust manner." . . . Appellant did not operate the corporation unjustly or fraudulently.

The trial court erred in determining that appellant was individually liable . . . to Almac, Inc. . . .

JUDGMENT Reversed.

Parent and Subsidiary Corporations. By applying the alter ego doctrine courts may pierce the corporate veil of a wholly owned subsidiary and impose on its more affluent parent corporation liability for the subsidiary's obligations if there is:

- Unity of interest and ownership between the parent and its subsidiary
- Use of the subsidiary to promote fraud, sharp practice, unfair advantage or illegality, or to evade a statute or contractual obligation, or
- Inadequate capitalization of the subsidiary to meet its normally anticipated business needs

The following facts would be evidence establishing the above requirements: intermingling of funds and accounting records; interlocking directorates; failure to observe separate corporate formalities; domination by the parent to an extent that makes the subsidiary a mere agent or instrumentality of the parent; the subsidiary does not, in its business operations, maintain a separate existence, e.g., the employees of the subsidiary are subject to direction by the personnel of the parent corporation; or the two corporations are essentially only parts of a single business enterprise.

However, because a corporation is the subsidiary of another does not, of itself, establish the propriety of piercing the corporate veil of the subsidiary and casting upon the parent liability for either a tort or contract obligation incurred by the subsidiary. The following case makes clear that there must be a domination of the finances, policies, and practices of the subsidiary.

CASE 39.5 Miller v. Dixon Industries Corp. · 513 A.2d 597 (R.I. 1986)

FACTS Robert R. Miller owned the majority of the shares of Dixon Industries Corporation and was an executive in that firm. After lengthy negotiations, Miller sold Dixon Industries to Bundy Corporation. As a part of that transaction Bundy agreed to continue Miller in Dixon's employ for five years and further agreed that Miller would continue his entitlement to receive the employee fringe benefits offered to company executives. Because he

CASE 39.5 Continued

was not offered certain stock option plans he claimed due him, Miller sued Dixon Industries, the company he formerly controlled. Miller joined Bundy Corporation as a party defendant, claiming that the employment contract he had entered into, although ostensibly with Dixon, was executed in furtherance of Bundy's interest and therefore he (Miller) was entitled to pierce Dixon's corporate veil.

The trial court, among other things, held Bundy Corporation and Dixon Industries Corporation jointly and severally liable. The following portion of the appellate court's opinion is limited to piercing the corporate veil of Dixon Industries Corporation.

OPINION

WEISBERGER, J.... Bundy asserts that the trial justice lacked an evidentiary basis for piercing the corporate veil.

The trial justice found that Miller negotiated with Bundy's representatives regarding the terms of the employment contract... and that Bundy controlled the Dixon Corporation following the purchase.

The standards for piercing the corporate veil vary with the circumstances. Generally, where a parent-subsidiary relationship is involved, it must be demonstrated that the parent dominated the finances, policies, and practices of the subsidiary.... The mere fact that there exists a parent-subsidiary relationship between the two corporations is insufficient reason to impose liability on the parent for the torts of the subsidiary.... A similar principle should be applied to liability for breach of contract.... Absent a showing of inequity, fraud, undercapitalization or domination by the parent corporation, separate corporate identities must be observed.... We believe it was error for the trial justice to elect to pierce the corporate veil. A careful review of the record discloses no evidence that Bundy perpetrated fraud or acted inequitably in negotiating the employment contract.... Bundy's involvement in the contract negotiations would seem to be an ordinary consequence of its impending purchase of the Dixon Corporation.

... Moreover, ... there is nothing on the record to suggest that Bundy and Dixon are anything other than distinct and adequately capitalized incorporated financial units.

JUDGMENT

For the reasons stated, the judgment of the superior court is... reversed....

Undercapitalized Corporations. Although a corporation's undercapitalization is not, in itself, sufficient to support a disregard of the corporate entity, it is a factor that a court may consider in deciding whether or not to pierce the corporate veil. If the corporation's capitalization is very small in relation to the business it intends to carry on and to the risks that the business necessarily entails, a court may find that the corporation was organized and carried on its business with a capital investment far less than its shareholders should reasonably have anticipated as necessary to meet its obligations. Under the circumstances, to protect creditors, a court may find it proper to go behind the corporate form. For instance, assume that Sue organizes a corporation with capital of only $500, intending to secure on credit goods worth several thousand dollars and to pay for them from the profits she expects to make on their sale. She says to herself that if the business is not successful, she will simply "walk away from it," free from any liability because the purchase was made in the corporation's name. If she succeeds in securing the merchandise on credit but the sales are not sufficient to pay for her purchases, it is only fair that Sue's creditors should be able to pierce the corporate veil and force her personally to pay their bills.

Summary

The corporation-for-profit is the form of business organization adopted not only by practically all the large companies in the United State, but also by most of the small ones.

State corporation statutes have been influenced in varying degrees by the Model Business Corporation Act and by the revision of that act. The chief characteristics of a business corporation are its: status as a legal entity, wide purpose, perpetual life, centralization of management in a board of directors elected by the shareholders, free transferability of its shares of stock, and limitation of each shareholder's liability to the amount of his or her capital investment.

There are various kinds of corporations: corporations organized for public or for private purposes, for profit or not for profit, those publicly held or closely held, S corporations, professional corporations, and domestic and foreign corporations.

A promoter is the moving force in the creation of many corporations. He or she finds people to subscribe to shares of the new company's stock, secures necessary financing, sees to the preparation of the articles of incorporation, and secures personnel necessary for the new corporation to begin business. The promoter owes a fiduciary duty to the subscribers, the shareholders, and to the corporation itself.

A corporation is not automatically liable on a promoter's preincorporation contract made in the name of a future corporation. The corporation may adopt such contracts expressly or impliedly but if it does so, the promoter remains liable unless the creditor agrees to hold only the corporation. Following the Revised Model Act, to incorporate, the state official designated by law, usually the secretary of state, is furnished signed *articles of incorporation*. These must contain the information required by state law, such as (1) a proposed corporate name which must not be too similar to the name of any other corporation already chartered or qualified to do business in the state, (2) a statement of the powers and purposes of the proposed corporation and of the number and kind of shares of stock authorized to be issued, (3) the name and address of the original incorporator(s), (4) the address of the corporation's registered office, and (5) the name of its registered agent. If the articles satisfy the legal requirements, the secretary of state issues a certificate of incorporation which constitutes the new corporation's charter and marks its birth.

The directors then hold an organizational meeting. At this time they adopt bylaws for the internal governance of the corporation, appoint officers, and take other necessary steps to get the enterprise in motion.

A corporation may be de jure, that is, one that fully complies with the requirements of the incorporation statutes, de facto, meaning that it sufficiently satisfies those statutes that it is not vulnerable to attack by anyone except the state; or a corporation by estoppel, which is neither a de jure nor a de facto corporation but an organization recognized as a corporation by the court in a particular lawsuit in order to do justice.

Under certain circumstances a court may disregard the accepted concept that a corporation is a separate legal entity. Among those circumstances may be that the corporation is the alter ego of a controlling shareholder or parent company or because the corporation was insufficiently capitalized. In that event the court may cause its shareholders or a parent corporation to be liable for its debts. Courts take such actions particularly in order to prevent sharp practice, fraud, or the evasion of contractual obligations.

Review Questions

1 Distinguish between state and federal corporation laws.

2 Explain the origin and meaning of the term "federal corporation law."

3 **(a)** What are the chief characteristics of a business corporation? **(b)** Explain the advantages that arise from each characteristic.

4 What are the chief differences between a corporation, a partnership, and a limited partnership?

5 Would you say that there is no longer a place for either a partnership or a limited partnership in our economy? Discuss.

6 Distinguish between the following kinds of corporations: **(a)** private and public; **(b)** publicly traded and closely held; and **(c)** domestic and foreign.

7 Explain the meaning of the term "close corporation."

8 **(a)** In the formation of corporations, who or what is a promoter? **(b)** Discuss the chief functions of a promoter. **(c)** In what way does a promoter owe fiduciary duties to future shareholders of the corporation?

9 Is a corporation privileged to deny responsibility on a preincorporation contract entered into by its promoter on its behalf? Give examples to explain your answer.

10 **(a)** What is a share subscription? **(b)** Under what circumstances, if any, may a share subscription be revoked? **(c)** How does a corporation accept a share subscription?

11 Discuss factors to be considered in selecting the state in which incorporation will be sought.

12 What basic information is generally required to be included in articles of incorporation?

13 **(a)** What is a corporation organizational meeting? **(b)** Who holds it? **(c)** What resolutions would normally be adopted at such a meeting?

14 **(a)** What is the difference between a de jure and a de facto corporation? **(b)** What is a corporation by estoppel?

15 **(a)** What is meant by piercing the corporate veil? **(b)** Why would a court take such action?

Case Problems

1 The Rippee brothers, who purported to act for Northwest Tech-Manuals, Inc., signed two 2-year leases for commercial space with Heintze Corp. as lessor. Heintze was unaware that Northwest was not incorporated when the first lease was signed on May 1. Northwest completed its incorporation on June 17, and the second lease was signed July 15. Northwest paid rent on both leases for a year and then abandoned them. Heintze sued Northwest and the Rippee brothers individually to recover unpaid rent. **(a)** Is Heintze entitled to recover from Northwest on either or both leases? **(b)** Are the Rippee brothers personally liable on either or both leases?

2 Emmick was the promoter of O.K. Enterprises, Inc. The corporation's organization meeting was attended by Emmick and Fosdick, his engineer, who was the initial incorporator. At that time Emmick exchanged a farm that he owned for 2,000 shares of the corporation's stock. Thereafter, individuals who had subscribed to the purchase of shares of the corporation were issued their shares. Several of those shareholders, upon learning of the consideration paid by Emmick for his shares, were of the opinion that his farm had been grossly overvalued. They want to compel Emmick to return to the corporation some of the shares issued to him. Have those shareholders a cause of action? Explain.

3 The general corporation law of Kansas provided that corporate existence commences after (1) filing articles of incorporation with the secretary of state and (2) filing a certified copy of the articles with the local county register of deeds. Allen, an officer and organizer of Construction Enterprises, Inc., filed proper articles with the secretary of state but never filed a copy with the county register of deeds. The state of Kansas sued the corporation for delinquent unemployment taxes and also sued Allen for personal liability as the operator of a defectively formed corporation. Allen claimed (1) that there had been substantial compliance with the statute so that a de jure corporation was formed and, alternatively, (2) even if Construction Enterprises Inc. was not de jure, it was a de facto corporation so that he was shielded from personal liability for the company's taxes. Was the corporation either de jure or de facto so as to insulate Allen from personal liability?

4 Baker owned a farm that had financial problems. He agreed to form a corporation with two investors who were to buy stock for cash sufficient to pay off the debts that Baker owed. As his capital contribution, Baker agreed to deed the farm to the corporation, and recorded the deed *before* the articles of incorporation had been filed with the secretary of state. Thus, at the time of the deed, the corporation was neither de jure nor de facto. After the corporation was formed, Baker participated in corporate business involving the farm and was active as an officer, director, and stockholder. He later claimed that since the corporation did not exist at the time of the deed, it was a nullity and that title to the farm remained in him. The corporation claimed that Baker should be estopped to deny the corporate existence because before and after the corporation was formed, Baker dealt with it as a corporation. Should Baker be estopped to deny corporate existence at the time he deeded the farm?

5 Kep, Inc., was organized in 1971 as a farming corporation. The initial capitalization, over $500,000, was adequate for the startup of the business, with Ingram and Piercey each owning 50 percent of the stock. Bad weather and crop failures caused financial losses in 1978, 1979, and 1980, and commencing in 1979 the farmland was mortgaged for the first time to secure loans to cover the deficit. In 1978, Kep, Inc., began purchasing fertilizer from Chemical Co. on an open account. Although Kep, Inc., paid an average of $55,000 per year on the account from 1978 to 1981, there was a growing indebtedness to Chemical Co., which sued Kep, Inc., for the unpaid balance of $54,000 and sought to pierce the corporate veil and hold Ingram and Piercey individually liable on the theory that the corporation was undercapitalized. The trial court held Ingram and Piercey personally liable for the debt, and they appealed, claiming that if the initial capitalization was adequate, the corporate veil should not be pierced because of financial deficits arising at a later time when the purchases were made from Chemical Co. on credit. Should the corporate veil of Kep, Inc., be pierced so as to hold its two stockholders personally liable?

6 All the stock of the Long Island Railroad (LIRR) was owned by the Metropolitan Transportation Authority (MTA), a public corporation. One of LIRR's trains struck and killed a man. The administrator of the decedent's estate sued MTA for the wrongful death which was caused by LIRR's negligence. There was no evidence that MTA and LIRR had commingled their corporate business. Is MTA liable to plaintiff?

CHAPTER 40

Financing Corporations

A corporation, like a business run by a sole proprietor or a partnership, requires working capital in order to grow and to compete in an expanding marketplace. How a corporation gets the money it needs is called "corporate financing," or "corporation financing." The two means by which a corporation raises those funds is through debt financing and equity financing, explained in the first portion of this chapter. The latter portion deals with the transfer of corporation securities and the distribution of dividends.

Debt Financing

Debt financing simply means borrowing money. As a general rule, state statutes give corporations the power to borrow money, to issue notes, bonds, and other obligations; no special enabling provision in a corporation's articles of incorporation is necessary. (See, for example, Section 3.02 of the Revised Model Business Corporation Act.) For convenience, we will treat corporate debt financing as either short-term or long-term.

Short-Term Financing

Short-term financing may take many forms—e.g., securing favorable bank credit, assigning accounts receivables, pledging some or all of the corporation's properties, and issuing promissory notes.

A promissory note is an instrument by which a corporation expresses its promise to repay, with interest, a sum of money it borrows. Promissory notes, as a form of commercial paper, are explained in Chapter 27.

When a corporation is newly formed or does not have well-established credit or sufficient collateral to secure the loan, a lender may require a corporate officer or major shareholder personally to guarantee its repayment. If the corporation does not pay the agreed-upon principal or interest on the due date, the lender may, either directly or through legal process, take possession of the collateral, sell it, and apply the proceeds to the debt. If the debt is personally guaranteed, the lender may, of course, go against the guarantor.

Long-Term Financing

A corporation accomplishes long-term financing through the sale of bonds. A bond is, in effect, similar to a note; however, each bond, generally in the sum of $1,000, is a part of a large corporation bond issue sold to financial institutions and individuals through stock and bond brokers. A *bond* is a negotiable security expressing the promise of the corporation to pay the bondholder (1) the amount of the bond at a distant future date, perhaps 10, 20, 30, or 40 years from the date the bond is issued, and (2) at a fixed rate of interest, typically payable semiannually.

The many possible combinations of bond provisions often result in varieties of bonds that defy easy classification. The major types of bonds issued by corporations are (1) registered bonds, (2) bearer bonds, (3) redeemable bonds, and (4) convertible bonds.

Registered Bonds. Most corporate bonds are registered. The term *registered bond* has several meanings, but in this context it means a bond issued to an owner whose name is stated on the face of the bond; the owner is thus registered on the records of the issuing corporation. The corporation undertakes to pay the stated principal and interest to the registered owner.

Bearer Bonds. A bearer bond has no registered owner, the corporation agreeing to pay anyone who has possession of the instrument (i.e., the bearer) the bond's stated interest and principal as they become due. In 1983, the Internal Revenue Code was amended to impose severe penalties for the further issuance of bearer bonds, and since that date all new bond issues are registered. The Congress took this action so that the IRS would henceforth be advised by the issuing companies of the recipients of bond interest and principal payments, thereby closing a possible income tax escape hatch.

Interest on a bearer bond is paid by an unusual procedure. Coupons, each representing 6 months' interest, are affixed to the bond. The holder of the bond detaches (clips) each coupon as it becomes due and deposits the coupon to his or her bank account. The bank then forwards the coupon to the appropriate paying agent for collection.

The holder of a bearer bond assumes the risk of its loss or theft. If a bearer bond is lost or stolen, the rightful owner may not require the corporation to issue another bond in its place, and the thief or finder may sell it to an unsuspecting purchaser. On the other hand, if a registered bond is lost or stolen, the owner may require the issuing corporation to replace it.

Redeemable Bonds. Bonds typically are redeemable (also said to be "callable"); i.e., the issuing corporation has the option of paying the principal of the bond before its due date. In the late 1970s and early 1980s, interest rates were very high and corporations that issued bonds obligated themselves to pay the high interest. In the late 1980s, interest rates fell and many corporations issued new bonds or otherwise borrowed money at the lower rates. Then, with the proceeds, they redeemed the high interest–rate bonds they had earlier issued.

Convertible Bonds. A convertible bond is convertible into a share or shares of stock of the issuing corporation based upon some formula stated on the face of the bonds. Typically, the bondholder is given the option of exchanging the bond for a predetermined number of shares of the corporation's common stock or other class of stock specified. A holder of a convertible bond can properly anticipate that a market value of his or her bond will parallel the rise in value of the corporation's shares. Meanwhile, the corporation remains obligated to pay the bondholder the face amount of the bond, together with periodic interest, when it matures.

Equity Financing

A corporation's initial stock issue usually provides most of the capital needed for it to commence business. The sale of additional stock or the issuance of a new series of stock may be required to provide the additional capital needs of the business. Because shares of stock represent an equity *ownership* interest in the corporation, corporate financing through the issuance and sale of stock is called "equity financing."

Nature of Shares of Stock

Shareholders, as *owners* of a corporation, have a significantly different relationship to the issuing corporation than do its bondholders, who are *creditors* of the company. As we have observed, even if the corporation is not profitable, a bondholder is entitled to repayment of the face amount of the bond as well as the stated interest. The owners of shares of stock, on the other hand, are entitled to receive dividends as declared by the corporate board of directors. If no dividends are declared, the shareholders receive no income from their ownership. If voting shares are involved, shareholders are entitled to vote for the election of the corporation's directors and upon other matters of extraordinary importance, such as the merger of the corporation with another company or the determination of whether or not the corporation should be dissolved. Bondholders, however, receive no dividends and they have no voting rights.

A share of stock does not confer upon the holder a vested title to any specific property owned by the corporation. Rather, a share of stock represents a proportionate ownership interest in the net worth or equity of the corporation. Net worth and equity are used here in the accounting sense to mean assets minus liabilities. In the event of bankruptcy or liquidation, creditors and bondholders have first claim on corporate assets. If there is any surplus remaining, it will be distributed to the shareholders.

A shareholder's interest is generally evidenced by a *stock certificate* for a stated number of shares of a designated type. The Revised Model Business Corporation Act (Sec. 6.26) provides, however, that "unless the articles of incorporation or bylaws provide otherwise, the board of directors of a corporation may authorize the issue of some or all of the shares of any or all classes or series without certificates. . . . " A few states, following this section of the Revised Model Act, have enacted statutes which permit the issuance of uncertificated shares, i.e., shares not represented by stock certificates. Instead, the shareholder's record of ownership is held by a bank, stock brokerage house, or registrar of the stock.

Issuance of Shares

Authority to Issue Shares. A business corporation can only offer and sell the classes of shares, up to the maximum number of shares of each class, that are authorized in its articles of incorporation (Revised Model Act, Sec. 6.01). An overissue is void. Each proposed issue must also satisfy state and federal statutes designed to protect the public from fraudulent stock schemes.

Issuance for Cash. Generally, shares of stock are sold by a corporation for cash at par or at their stated value. If a stock subscription is payable in installments, a certificate cannot be issued and delivered to the subscriber until the shares represented by the certificate are fully paid.

Issuance for Property. Tangible or intangible property may be accepted by a board of directors as adequate consideration for the issuance of shares of the corporation's stock; e.g., a person may offer to transfer to the corporation such tangible property as a parcel of land, a piece of machinery or equipment, or a vehicle in return for a certain number of its shares of stock. Intangible property, such as trade secrets, goodwill of a going business, accounts receivable, and patents, may also be used as consideration for the purchase of shares.

In some states, a corporation is precluded from issuing its stock in exchange for an unsecured promissory note, since such a note basically is a promise to pay money in the future. Let us suppose, however, that Charles gives Betty his promissory note for $10,000, due in 6 months. Betty wishes to buy shares of stock in the Ajax Corporation, but she has no cash. She offers to transfer Charles's note to the corporation in return for $10,000 of its stock. Under some state laws, a third-party note (such as Charles's note in this transaction) may be legal consideration for the issuance of stock. The Revised Model Act (Sec. 6.21(b)) goes further and permits a board of directors to authorize a corporation to issue stock in return for an individual's own unsecured note.

Issuance for Services. In most states, a corporation may issue its stock in return for *past* services that were rendered to the benefit to the corporation. Such an event would occur when a corporation issues stock to a promoter for services rendered in organizing the corporation. Many states, on the other hand, prohibit the issuance of stock in consideration of *future* services, even though the obligation to perform is evidenced by a contract. However, the Revised Model Act provides that a board of directors may authorize a corporation to issue stock in return for a contract for services to be performed.

Valuation of Consideration. The board of directors fixes the value of the consideration offered to the corporation in exchange for shares of its stock. Problems may arise in determining the valuation when the consideration is property or services. Opinions regarding the value of intangible property or of the services of a promoter may differ. A shareholder of a corporation may contend that its directors issued an excessive amount of stock in exchange for the consideration received and thus violated their fiduciary obligations owed to the corporation. In order to avoid expensive and time-consuming litigation, many states have enacted statutes stating that the determination by the board of directors of the value of consideration accepted for shares of stock shall, in the absence of fraud, be conclusive. The Revised Model Act (Sec. 6.21) also takes a liberal stance and requires only that if the directors determine that the consideration received or to be received for its shares is *adequate,* their determination is conclusive.

Illegal Issuance. If a corporation issues its stock in violation of state corporation laws, the issuance is illegal. Interestingly enough, the illegal stock issuance is voidable at the option of the shareholder who received the shares. Thus, the purchaser may choose to either keep the stock and comply with the terms of his or her agreement or rescind the transaction, return the shares, and recover the consideration given to the corporation.

The problem of whether shares of common stock issued for unsecured promissory notes, due on demand, are void or only voidable is the subject of the following case.

CASE 40.1 Kirk's Auto Electric, Inc. v. Kirk · 728 S.W.2d 529 (Sup. Ct. Ky. 1987)

FACTS Kirk's Auto Electric, Inc., issued eleven shares of its common stock to Billy Bone. Six years later, it issued ten shares of its common stock to André Bone and five shares to Joe Bone. In exchange for these shares, the Bones each delivered to the corporation unsecured interest-bearing promissory notes payable on demand. At the time the shares were issued, Billy Bone was a director and president of the corporation and Kirk was a director and its secretary. Billy Bone and Kirk each signed the certificates on behalf of the corporation. No payment was made upon the notes, and Kirk brought action to have the court declare void the shares of stock issued in exchange for the notes. The lower court held the notes to be voidable but not void, and Kirk appealed.

OPINION LAMBERT, J.... Section 193 of the constitution of Kentucky states:

> No corporation shall issue stock of bonds, except for an equivalent in money paid or labor done, or property actually received....

...In 1972 the General Assembly adopted the "Kentucky Corporations Act"... as follows:

> 271A.095. Payment for shares. (1) The consideration for the issuance of shares by a corporation may be paid only by an equivalent in money paid or labor done, or property actually received and applied for the purpose for which such corporation was created, and neither labor nor property shall be received in payment of consideration for the issuance of shares at a greater value than the market price at the time such labor was done or property delivered....
>
> (2) In the absence of fraud in the transaction, the judgment of the directors or the shareholders, as the case may be, as to the market price of the consideration received for shares shall be conclusive unless the person questioning the market price shall by a clear preponderance of the evidence establish a different market price.

This statute applies to stock issued to appellees, André Bone and Joe T. Bone. [Another statute, replaced by 271A.095, essentially to like effect, applied to the shares issued to Billy Bone.]

The constitutional and statutory provisions quoted herein evince a strong policy in this commonwealth toward protecting corporations, shareholders, and corporate creditors from the dissipation of corporate assets. The issuance of shares must be attended by good faith and the corporation must receive value not disproportionate to the value of the shares issued....

The promissory notes received by Kirk's Auto Electric, Inc. were unsecured and were payable only upon demand. The only persons eligible to demand payment from the makers of the notes were the members of the board of directors, appellant, Kirk, and appellee, Billy H. Bone, the same persons who authorized issuance of the shares and acceptance of the unsecured notes. Appellee, Billy H. Bone, was himself maker of one of the notes.

Therefore, appropriate vigilance would be less than assured. This transaction well illustrates the need for strict enforcement of the constitutional and statutory requirements.

Our holding in this case may appear to be too restrictive and represent an interference with the power of a corporation to conduct its business affairs. In ordinary commercial transactions, unsecured promissory notes are essential and undoubtedly constitute valuable consideration. Nevertheless, "[t]he (constitutional and statutory) provisions are impressed with a public interest and their primary purpose is to prevent fraud and to protect creditors or purchasers of stock or securities of corporations." *Mazer et al. v. Hazard Realty Corporation et al.*, 283 Ky. 283, 140 S.W.2d at 1037. If the public interest is to be protected, strict adherence to the law must be required.

CASE 40.1 Continued

We believe Section 193 of the constitution of Kentucky is plain and unambiguous. Stock issued by a corporation must be "for an equivalent in money paid or labor done, or property actually received." Otherwise, stock issued by a corporation is a "fictitious increase" which is void. . . .

JUDGMENT The judgment of the Court of Appeals is reversed. . . .

LEIBSON, J. Dissenting. . . . I would adopt [the] Court of Appeals' opinion to the effect that the stock issued to the Bones' was voidable, but Kirk has *no standing* to have the stock declared void because he actively participated in causing it to be issued.

Classes of Shares

Shares of stock may be issued as one class or may be divided into two or more classes. The two principal classes of stock are common and preferred, but there are many kinds of common and preferred shares. Articles of incorporation set forth the designations, preferences, limitations, and relative rights of each class of authorized stock.

Common Stock. Common stock is the basic stock issued by a corporation. Such shares represent an ownership interest in the corporation. If a corporation has only one class of stock, it is held to be *common stock,* even if the articles of incorporation do not use that term. State statutes typically permit corporations to issue classes of common stock with different rights or privileges. For example, a corporation may issue *Class A common stock* with voting rights and *Class B common stock* with no voting rights. A corporation may also issue one class of common stock with multiple votes per share (to be held by key officers and directors of the corporation) and another class with but one vote per share (to be held by the public). However, if only one class of common stock is issued, each common share must be treated equally with every other share issued.

In the next case, the court struck down a preference given to some holders of common shares over other shareholders.

CASE 40.2 Mullins v. 510 East 86th Street Owners, Inc. · 483 N.Y.S.2d 631 (N.Y. City Civ. Ct. 1984)

FACTS 510 East 86th Street Owners, Inc., owned a cooperative apartment building at that address. The corporation contended that its bylaws imposed, during the first 3 years of the cooperative's existence, a transfer fee of $60 per share for each sale, *regardless of how repetitive,* of its shares originally owned by a subscriber to the cooperative. Although the cooperative had only one class of common shares, the $60-per-share fee was imposed only one time if the shares had been originally purchased with the acquisition of an apartment after the subscription period ended. The board of directors gave the most confusing and inappropriate name of *unsold shares* to those later-acquired shares.

An original subscriber, in 1981, sold to the plaintiffs ninety-eight shares allocated to apartment 6B of the cooperative. In conjunction with the sale, the original subscriber paid the cooperative a transfer fee of $60 for each share sold. Before the 3-year period had expired, the plaintiffs (purchasers from the original subscriber) sold the shares and the right to the apartment to a third party. The plaintiffs were required to pay the cooperative another $60 per share transfer fee in order to effect the sale. The plaintiffs paid the fee

CASE 40.2 Continued under protest and brought suit to recover it. The defendant filed a motion to dismiss.

OPINION LEHNER, J. . . . To require that a purchaser from an original subscriber pay the transfer fee when he sells, but not require the purchaser from a holder of unsold shares to pay same under similar circumstances obviously results in shareholders, all of whom own the same class of shares, possessing different rights. This unequal treatment of shareholders the court finds to be in contravention of § 501(c) of the Business Corporation Law [BCL], which provides that "[s]ubject to the designations, relative rights, preferences and limitations applicable to separate series, each share shall be equal to every other share of the same class."

Although BCL § 501 permits the certificate of incorporation to provide for several classes of shares possessing different rights and preferences, the statute does not authorize the board of directors to enact by-laws creating preferences among shareholders, all of whom own the same class and series of shares. Unless the certificate creates preferences, then the rights and preferences of shareholders as such should be equal.

To effect a just result as a consequence of such invalidity, the court believes that plaintiffs should be treated the same as transferees from holders of unsold shares, with the consequence that no fee may be collected on their transfer. . . .

JUDGMENT Thus the complaint states a valid cause of action and the motion to dismiss is denied. . . .

Preferred Stock. Preferred stock gains its name because these shares have preferential rights over other classes of stock. Generally, the preference is the right to receive (1) dividends at a specified rate stated on the face of the shares, such as a stated number of dollars or a stated percentage of the par value of the shares, before any dividends are paid to the common stockholders, and (2) distribution, in the event the corporation is liquidated, ahead of any distribution to the common stockholders.

Despite the preferences given to preferred shares, they represent a *nonvoting* ownership interest in the corporation and are not considered to be a part of the company's debt. To designate shares as *preference* is without legal effect unless the articles of incorporation authorize the preference.

If a board is authorized to issue such shares, their issuance is optional and many corporations have chosen not to issue them. If the board decides to issue preferred shares, it may establish different classes or series of such shares, fixing their terms and assigning to each series independent rights, dividend rates, and redemption prices (Revised Model Act, Sec. 6.01).

The common types of preferred shares are (1) cumulative, (2) participating, (3) convertible, and (4) redeemable preferred shares.

Cumulative preferred stock. Dividends on preferred shares may be *cumulative* or *noncumulative.* Cumulative shares give the holder the right to receive the stated dividend in full each year. If there is a nonpayment in any year, that right is not lost but the unpaid cumulative preferred dividends cumulate and must be paid in full to the holders of such shares in the future before any dividends may be paid to the holders of the corporation's common shares. This inherent characteristic of cumulative preferred shares prevents directors (who are elected by the common shareholders) from intentionally failing to declare preferred dividends for several years and then declaring a large dividend payable to the common shareholders.

Holders of *noncumulative* preferred shares are not entitled to payment of past-due dividends, and any unpaid dividends need never be made up. To avoid the danger of a board of directors intentionally failing to declare dividends on the corporation's noncumulative preferred stock in order to create a greater fund for its common shareholders, articles of incorporation often provide that if preferred dividends are not declared for a specified period of time (e.g., eight quarters), the preferred shareholders have the right to replace a majority of the board of directors.

Participating preferred stock. If a corporation has unusually high earnings, owning *participating preferred* shares may be quite beneficial because the holder of such preferred shares has two "bites" at the dividend "apple." In addition to being entitled to the stated dividend before any dividend can be paid to the common shareholders, the holders of participating preferred shares participate with the common shareholders in the receipt of any remaining funds that are set aside for dividend purposes. Because such participation reduces the dividends that otherwise may be paid the common shareholders, most corporations do not give their preferred shares the right to participate.

Convertible preferred stock. Convertible preferred shares are similar to convertible bonds in that the holder of these shares has the option of converting them into shares of another class of stock of the corporation (usually common stock) at a predetermined ratio. If the shares to which they may be converted rise in value, the convertible preferred shares ordinarily would also rise in value.

Redeemable preferred stock. Redeemable preferred shares are issued with the condition that they may be repurchased (i.e., redeemed) by the issuing corporation at a stated price and time. It is not unusual for the issuing corporation to establish a sinking fund, separate from funds available for dividends, for redemption purposes. If the market value of the redeemable preferred shares rises above the redemption price, the directors can be expected to exercise the corporation's right of redemption. When a corporation repurchases its preferred stock, the common shareholders benefit because stock with a priority claim on dividends and liquidation proceeds have been canceled or returned to the corporation's treasury.

Par and No-Par Stock. Articles of incorporation may allow a company to issue shares with a par value or without a par value. *Par value* is a dollar amount below which the shares may not be sold by the issuing company. It is an arbitrary price set by the promoters or by the corporation's board of directors as the price the corporation expects to receive for fully paid shares. After a corporation's shares have been issued and sold, their par value becomes irrelevant, as the share price will be fixed by the marketplace.

If shares are sold by a corporation as fully paid but the consideration received by it was less than their stated par value, the shares are said to be *watered* to the extent the par value was not received by the corporation. For example, assume that shares have a stated par value of $100. In order to sell them to the public, the corporation accepts $75 for each share. Thus, each share is watered to the extent of $25. In most states, ordinarily neither the corporation nor minority shareholders may complain of stock watering. But if the corporation becomes insolvent, creditors may have a right of action against the shareholders to recover the amount that their shares were watered.

Stock that is issued without a stated value is said to be *no-par value* stock. All states authorize the issuance of no-par value stock which is sold by the issuing company at whatever price the board of directors determines is reasonable. In the absence of fraud or self-dealing, the board's determination of the reasonableness of the consideration—i.e., the *stated* value of the shares—will be upheld.

Thin Corporation

As we have observed, a corporation's financial structure usually includes both equity financing and debt financing. A *thin corporation* is one financed with a relatively high ratio of debt compared to its equity. In other words, it has an excessive amount of debt in its capitalization. What is considered an excessive amount of debt depends upon the facts in the particular case. In most cases, when debt equals or exceeds four times equity it is a thin corporation. In order to understand the concept of the thin corporation, we will visually use a hypothetical skeletonized corporate balance sheet, represented by Table 40.1.

For convenience, we have skeletonized the items presented in Table 40.1. Let us suppose for illustrative purposes that liabilities total $90,000 and that stockholders' equity is $10,000. The debt-equity ratio of our hypothetical corporation is therefore 9 to 1, and it is a thin corporation.

Particularly in close corporations there are at least two incentives for shareholders to thinly incorporate. The first involves the natural desire of investors in a close corporation to get their money

Table 40.1 Hypothetical Skeletonized Balance Sheet

BALANCE SHEET	
Assets:	Liabilities:
Plant	(Debt financing)
Equipment	Notes payable
Patents,	Bonds payable
etc.	
	Stockholders' equity
	(Equity financing)
	Common stock
	Retained earnings

back without giving up control of the business. Let us suppose that in our hypothetical corporation $100,000 was needed for start-up capital. If the investors put in that sum in cash and took back common stock, the only way they could get their capital back would be to sell their stock, assuming a purchaser could be found. This would be undesirable, as the shareholders do not want outsiders to become owners of the business and also do not want to give up their positions in the corporation. If, on the other hand, the investors (as in Table 40.1) are issued stock of the stated value of $10,000 and notes or bonds for $90,000, the latter amount is a debt the corporation owes. The corporation can repay the $90,000 debt, and the investors will still retain their full interest in the corporation.

The second incentive may be the possibility of reducing the corporate federal income tax by creating a thin corporation. This comes about because a corporation may deduct on its income tax returns interest payments to creditors but may not deduct dividends paid to shareholders. Thus, if the hypothetical thin corporation declares a dividend of 6 percent upon the $10,000 stock issue, that dividend of $600 is not tax-deductible. If that corporation also pays 6 percent interest on the $90,000 loan, it can deduct $5,400 on its income tax return because it has made a debt payment.

Since the government stands to lose possible tax revenue from thin corporations, the Internal Revenue Service is careful to search out abuses in the capitalization of corporations. Thus, if, as in the hypothetical case, the debt-equity ratio is too thin, tax authorities may (1) treat the loans from the shareholders as *contributions* to shareholder equity and (2) disallow the interest payments by the corporation to its shareholders and treat those payments as dividends. As a result, the corporation would be required to pay income tax on those payments. Thus, the degree of "thinness" of a corporation can be an important factor.

On the other hand, two dangers of incorporating a thin corporation can be recognized. One was discussed in Chapter 39, where it was observed that the inadequate initial equity capitalization and the *alter ego* doctrine may entitle creditors to pierce the corporate veil and hold the shareholders personally liable for the company's debts.

The second possible danger facing the shareholders of a thin corporation arises if the business becomes insolvent or declares bankruptcy and it has liabilities owing both to shareholders and to outside creditors. Under an equitable principle known as the *deep-rock* doctrine [the name derived from *Taylor v. Standard Gas and Elec. Co.*, 306 U.S. 307 (1939)], the court may refuse to treat those liabilities equally but instead may give to the outside creditors first claim against the corporate assets. In applying the deep-rock doctrine, the court considers, among many factors, the debt-equity ratio of the corporation.

Transfer of Securities

Every investor has a right to transfer his or her securities by sale, by pledge, by gift, or by the terms of a will. A bearer bond is transferred by mere delivery of the instrument. The transfer of registered securities (stocks and bonds) requires indorsement as well as delivery of the certificate to the new owner. In this context, "registered securities," as we have already discussed, means that the owner's name appears on the face of the security and is registered on the corporate books. The new owner of a security in registered form should register the transfer on the books of the issuer, but failure to do so will ordinarily not affect the new owner's title to the transferred shares. However, until a transfer is recorded, the corporation continues to recognize the transferor when it pays dividends, sends notices of meetings, or determines voting eligibility.

Indorsements Required

Indorsements of securities can be made on an assignment form printed on the reverse side of the certificate or on a separate document called a "stock power or bond power" which must then be delivered with the certificate. In either event, the transferor may indorse in one of two ways: in blank or special. Indorsement *in blank* occurs when the transferor simply signs his or her name without any additional language. For example, the owner may sign his name "Charles Smith" on the back of the certificate or on a stock or bond power. The effect of such a blank indorsement is to make the security into "bearer paper"; i.e., anyone who has possession of the instrument may exchange it for cash.

A *special* indorsement occurs when the transferor signs his or her name and also names a specific transferee. For example, the owner may sign the back of the certificate or the stock or bond power, "I hereby assign and transfer to Thomas Malone my 100 shares of Ajax Corporation common stock. (Signed) Christine Smith." The effect of a special indorsement is that in order to further transfer or sell the securities, the signature of the named transferee is required. Thus, in this example, if the stock is lost or stolen, a finder or thief would have to forge the signature of Thomas Malone in order to sell the 100 shares of Ajax. As a matter of business practice, most corporations customarily require the transferor's signature to be guaranteed by a bank or trust company. This procedure discourages forged or unauthorized indorsements.

The following case illustrates the legal necessity of *delivery* of the certificates representing shares in order to transfer legal title to them.

CASE 40.3 Bankwest, N.A. v. Williams · 347 N.W.2d 163 (S.D. 1984)

FACTS In January 1981, Tane Williams was divorced from his wife, Pamela. Several weeks later, in lieu of alimony payments for the year, Tane, by a separate written assignment, transferred to Pamela 317 shares of stock. However, the share certificates were not delivered to Pamela because Tane had previously signed them in blank and delivered them to Bankwest as collateral for a loan. Pamela did not notify the bank of the assignment nor ask it to transfer the stock to her. When Tane defaulted on the loan, the bank sold the shares at private sale. The proceeds were then applied to pay off the loan for which the shares were pledged as collateral, and the bank paid the surplus into court for distribution. Bankwest asserted it could levy execution upon the surplus to satisfy a judgment the bank had on two other notes executed by Tane that were unsecured. Pamela claimed she had sole right to the proceeds of the sale of the certificates over the amount canceling the indebtedness on the one loan for which they were held as security. The trial court gave judgment for Bankwest, and Pamela appealed.

OPINION HENDERSON, J. . . . As these stock certificates are negotiable instruments, resolution of this matter is governed by . . . the [South Dakota] U.C.C. Sections 8-102(1) and 8-105(1). "Delivery" with respect to instruments . . . means voluntary transfer of possession. Section 1-201(14).

> (1) Delivery to a purchaser occurs when (a) He or a person designated by him acquires possession of a security; or . . . (d) With respect to an identified security to be delivered while still in the possession of a third person when that person acknowledges that he holds for the purchaser; or (e) Appropriate entries on the books of a clearing corporation are made under 8-320. . . .

Pamela did not acquire possession of the security, for it was being held by . . . [the bank]; thus there was no delivery under item (a). Neither did the bank acknowledge it was holding the certificates for Pamela. In point of fact, it was never notified of the agreement transferring the stock. Pamela also testified that she did not notify . . . [the

CASE 40.3 Continued

corporation that had issued the stock] of the agreement, nor did she request a change of name on its books. There was, then, no delivery under provisions (d) and (e).

Without delivery, the agreement, in itself, could not act to validly transfer ownership of the stock. When a transfer is by separate document, Section 8-309 specifically states: "An indorsement of a security whether special or in blank does not constitute a transfer until delivery of the security on which it appears or if the indorsement is on a separate document until delivery of both the document and the security."...

The execution of the... 1981 agreement between Tane and Pamela did not constitute an effective delivery transferring ownership of the 317 shares of stock. The stock remained in the name of Tane. Bankwest, having a valid judgment against Tane, could lawfully execute upon the proceeds arising from the sale of the stock to satisfy its claim.

JUDGMENT ... Affirmed.

Lost or Stolen Certificates

Suppose Alice loses her certificate and Carol purchases it from the finder or a thief. What are the rights of the parties?

Under Article 8 of the Uniform Commercial Code (the law governing the transfer of securities), a bona fide purchaser acquires ownership of a security free from any adverse claim—for example, a claim that someone else is the owner. A *bona fide purchaser* is essentially a good-faith buyer who takes delivery of a bearer certificate (or of a properly indorsed registered certificate) without notice of an adverse claim. Bill steals Alice's bearer certificate (or her registered certificate that she has indorsed "in blank") and sells it to Carol, who has no knowledge of the theft. As a bona fide purchaser, Carol acquires the certificate free from Alice's claim of ownership. Carol also has a right to have the securities transferred into her name on the books of the corporation, and to receive a new certificate in her own name.

The situation is quite different where Bill steals Alice's *un*indorsed registered certificate and forges her indorsement. Only Alice or some authorized person can make an effective indorsement. Because Bill's forgery is ineffective to confer ownership rights on Carol, Alice is entitled to recover the certificate from Carol. Or, Alice may have a new certificate from the corporation by following the procedure set out in Article 8 for lost, destroyed, or stolen certificates. To obtain the new certificate, Alice must, for example, notify the corporation of the loss within a reasonable time after she has notice of it.

What happens if Alice properly obtains a substitute certificate, but in the meantime the corporation mistakenly issues a new certificate to Carol on the basis of the forged indorsement? The corporation must honor both certificates. Since both Alice and Carol are entitled to the shares specified in their certificates, the corporation must supply the required number of shares or absorb any loss, e.g., by pursuing the thief (Bill) or anyone, such as a transferring broker, who guaranteed the forged signature.

Restrictions on Transfer

A corporation has a duty to transfer into the name of a new owner a registered security upon request of the new owner. The corporation must record the transfer on the corporate books, cancel the surrendered certificate, and issue and deliver a new certificate registered in the transferee's name. If the corporation fails to do so, the new owner may recover damages for conversion or, in some instances, may obtain a decree compelling transfer. The new owner may also hold the corporation liable for unreasonable delay. Nevertheless, the corporation has a duty to inquire into any adverse claim if timely written notice is received before the transfer is recorded. This duty of inquiry may be discharged by any reasonable means.

As a general rule, securities are freely transferable. However, when stock of a corporation is closely held, the shareholders often wish to restrict the transfer of stock to others. Restrictions on future dispositions of stock are necessary to preserve continuity of control, an important factor in close corporations.

Three conditions must be met in order to restrict the transfer of stock:

1 The restriction must be *reasonable.* For example, sales of close-corporation stock to outsiders are usually restricted by providing that each shareholder must first offer his or her stock to the corporation or to the remaining shareholders or both. Such a provision is reasonable and is called a "right of first refusal." If the offer is refused by the corporation and other shareholders, the person may then sell to an outsider. Ordinarily such restrictions do not prohibit a shareholder from transferring shares by gift or by will. The beneficiary will take the shares subject to the same restrictions. In addition, the shareholders of a close corporation sometimes decide to create a mandatory buy-sell provision by mutually agreeing to buy the shares of persons who die or who may simply desire to cash out their investment.
2 Restraints on transfer must be contained in the articles or bylaws, or in an agreement among stockholders.
3 Reference to the restrictions on transfer must be noted "conspicuously" on the stock certificate.

Unless conspicuously noted on the certificate, any restriction imposed by the issuing corporation is ineffective "except against a person with actual knowledge of it" [UCC, 8-204). Generally, the full terms of the restriction do not appear on the face of a certificate, but a statement is printed in distinctive type that indicates where the full provision may be found.

Dividends and Other Corporate Distributions

Dividend Distributions

A corporation for profit is distinguished from a nonprofit or a public corporation by the fact that it has shareholders who expect to receive dividends. New corporations usually reinvest most of their earnings in the business, but more mature publicly held corporations generally distribute quarterly much of their profits to the shareholders as dividends. In fact, under the Internal Revenue Code a corporation may be subject to severe penalties if it attempts to retain too great a portion of its earnings rather than to distribute them to its shareholders.

Cash and Property Dividends. Dividends usually are paid in cash or in property. A corporation sends cash dividends each quarter to the shareholders registered on its books. On rare occasions a corporation will make a distribution of its assets, for example a portion of its inventory or shares of stock it owns in another corporation. Such a dividend is called a "property dividend," or a "dividend in kind."

Authority to Declare Dividends; the Business Judgment Rule. Most state statutes give corporate directors the exclusive power to declare dividends as long as they, in good faith, exercise sound business judgment. This is called the "business judgment rule." A court will not substitute its own judgment for that of directors unless the boards on which they sit clearly act arbitrarily, fraudulently, or in bad faith. The business judgment rule also applies to the declaration of dividends on preferred shares. Directors may, acting reasonably and in good faith, decide not to declare a dividend at a time when it would normally fall due. The board's business judgment will be upheld in the event a shareholder sues to compel declaration of a dividend.

The following case illustrates the rare situation where the court found that a corporation's board of directors did not exercise sound business judgment when it refused to declare a dividend. In this unusual case, earnings were amassed by a corporation far beyond expected business needs to the point where the court compelled payment of a dividend.

CASE 40.4 Dodge v. Ford Motor Co. · 170 N.W.668 (Mich. 1919)

FACTS The Ford Motor Co. in 1903 issued 1,000 of its authorized $100 par-value shares. In 1908, 19,000 shares were distributed to the shareholders as a stock dividend, thereby increasing the company's stated capital to $2 million. From 1911 to 1916, the Ford company paid dividends equal to 5 percent of its stated capital each month and also paid twelve special dividends totaling $41 million (a return of $410 to $1 on the original shares). The directors continued to declare regular monthly dividends of 5 percent, but in 1916 they discontinued the special dividends. In that year, the company had $53 million cash on hand. Total liabilities were $18 million, there was a surplus of $112 million, and anticipated annual profits were $60 million.

Originally, the Ford car sold for $900, but by 1916 the price had been reduced to $440. The directors justified their refusal to declare further special dividends by stating that they wished to lower the price of Ford cars to $360 and that they intended to construct a smelting plant and a steel plant to produce steel products to be used in manufacturing their cars. The cost of these facilities was estimated to be $24 million. John F. Dodge and Horace E. Dodge, owners of 2,000 shares of Ford Motor Co. stock, objected to the expansion of the business as unwise and to the absorption of profits which should be distributed to the company's shareholders. They filed an action to compel the Ford directors to declare a special dividend.

The trial court ordered the directors to pay a special dividend of $19 million. Ford appealed.

OPINION OSTRANDER, C. J.... The case for... [Dodge] must rest upon the claim... that... the withholding of the special dividend... is [an] arbitrary action of the directors requiring judicial interference.... This court in *Hunter v. Roberts, Throp & Co.*, 83 Mich. 63, 71, 47 N.W.131, recognized

> it is a well-recognized principle of law that the directors of a corporation, and they alone, have the power to declare a dividend. Courts of equity will not interfere unless [the directors] refuse to declare a dividend when the corporation has a surplus of net profits which it can, without detriment to its business, divide among its shareholders, and when a refusal to do so would amount to such an abuse of discretion as would constitute a fraud, or breach of that good faith which they are bound to exercise towards the stockholders.

Mr. Henry Ford is the dominant force in the business of the Ford Motor Company.... The record... convinces that he has the attitude towards shareholders of one who has distributed to them large gains and that they should be content to take what he chooses to give. His testimony creates the impression also that he thinks the Ford Motor Company has made too much money, and that, although large profits might be still earned, a sharing of them with the public, by reducing the price of the output of the company, ought to be undertaken....

There should be no confusion.... of the duties which Mr. Ford conceives that he and the stockholders owe to the general public and the duties which in law he and his codirectors owe to protesting, minority stockholders. A business corporation is organized and carried on primarily for the profit of the stockholders. The powers of the directors are to be employed for that end. The discretion of directors is to be exercised in the choice of the means to attain that end, and does not extend to a change in the end itself, to the

CASE 40.4 Continued

reduction of profits, or to the nondistribution of profits among stockholders in order to devote them to other purposes.... [N]o one will contend that, if the avowed purpose of the defendant directors was to sacrifice the interests of the shareholders, it would not be the duty of the courts to interfere....

Assuming the general plan and policy of expansion... [to be] for the best ultimate interest of the company and therefore of its shareholders, what does it amount to in justification of a refusal to declare and pay a special dividend or dividends?... If the total cost of proposed expenditures had been immediately withdrawn... from the cash surplus... on hand... there would have remained nearly $30,000,000.... Moreover, the contemplated expenditures were not to be immediately made. The large sum appropriated for the smelter plant was payable over a considerable period of time. So that, without going further, it would appear that, accepting and approving the plan of the directors, it was their duty to distribute on or near the 1st of August, 1916, a very large sum of money to the stockholders.

JUDGMENT The decree of the court below fixing and determining the specific amount to be distributed to stockholders is affirmed....

Persons Entitled to Dividends. The directors ordinarily close the stock transfer books for a stated period and fix a future "record date" to determine which shareholders are entitled to receive a dividend. The corporation may pay dividends to shareholders "of record" on that date without liability to transferees whose interests are unknown to the corporation [UCC, 8-207(1)]. Nevertheless, the recipient may be required to pay the dividend to others who have purchased the shares. A seller and a buyer can contractually agree to the disposition of a particular dividend. If there is no agreement to the contrary, the seller (transferor) is entitled to dividends declared before the transfer. The buyer (transferee) is entitled to dividends declared after the transfer. However, listed stock purchased during the 5 business days prior to the record date is *ex dividend* (without dividend) to the buyer.

For example, suppose that on May 1 (the declaration date), Ajax Corporation declares a dividend payable on June 15 to shareholders of record on June 1 (the record date). On June 3, Maria sells her 100 shares of Ajax stock to Larry, but Ajax had already closed its shareholders' ownership books. Because Larry was not an owner of record on June 1, Ajax will pay the dividend to Maria, the record holder, and not to Larry. In these circumstances, doubtless Maria and Larry had adjusted the selling price of the shares to take account of the dividend (the shares being sold *ex dividend*).

Directors of closely held corporations often do not fix a record date for dividend distribution. In that event, the date the dividend is declared is treated as the record date for determining which shareholders are entitled to the dividend. The entitlement of a shareholder to receive a declared dividend on the record date and not on the date of declaration is explained in the opinion in the next case.

CASE 40.5 Caleb & Co. v. E. I. Du Pont de Nemours & Co. · 615 F. Supp. 96 (D.C. N.Y. 1985)

FACTS E. I. Du Pont de Nemours and Co. ("Du Pont") made a tender offer for the shares of Conoco, Inc., agreeing to pay for all of the Conoco shares tendered through First Jersey National Bank before August 17, 1981.

CASE 40.5 Continued

On July 31, Conoco declared a 65-cent-per-share dividend, payable on September 14 to stockholders of record August 14. On August 5, Du Pont accepted the shares that had been tendered to the Bank. Plaintiff filed suit to bar the takeover, complaining, among other things, that the First Jersey Bank improperly permitted Du Pont to acquire the shares prior to paying for them, thereby improperly becoming entitled, as the shareholder of record on August 14, to the dividend on those shares.

OPINION SWEET, D. J.... Du Pont's acceptance of tendered shares on August 5 vested in Du Pont the right to be considered the record owner on August 14, even though payment for the shares post-dated August 14. The principle was explained and held to be uniformly applicable by Professor Williston, who stated:

> ... the purchaser of shares, absent any agreement to the contrary, is generally entitled to dividends, rights, and all the privileges of a shareholder, except voting power, from the time he makes the purchase contract *whether or not he has made payment,* has taken legal title or has been registered on the corporation records as a shareholder. 8 Williston on Contracts §953 at 320–321....

An examination of the Delaware authorities... establishes that an owner as of the record date but not the declaration date is the beneficiary of the dividend. A sale between the declaration and record dates causes the dividend to inure to the benefit of the purchaser.

> ... Before the record date problem arose the courts with very few exceptions held that dividends belonged to the owner of the stock on the date the dividend was declared. However, the practice of most corporations today is to declare the dividend to be payable to shareholders on a date of record between the declaration date and the date set for payment. The original purpose of such a practice was undoubtedly to protect the corporation, so that when it paid a dividend to the person registered on the books on the record date, no liability would fall on the corporation if such person were not the actual owner on that date.... [The numerical majority of the] courts have held that the record date is the effective date of the dividend and the actual owner on the date of record is entitled to the dividend even though he may not be the owner registered on the books of the corporation....

When there is both a declaration date and a record date, the declaration of the dividend creates a debtor-creditor relationship between the corporation and the owner of the stock on the date of declaration.... And if such dividend is not paid when due it may be recovered in an appropriate action by the shareholders.... However, the ultimate beneficiary of the dividend will still be controlled by the owner of the stock on the record date. As the court explained in *Wilmington Trust,* 25 Del. Ch. 193. 15 A.2d 665, 667 (1940), the debtor-creditor relationship between the corporation and stock owner arising at the time of declaration of the dividend [is] not ultimately controlling.

JUDGMENT I conclude that [the] clear implication [of the Delaware Code and of the majority of the decided cases] is that the owner as of the record date is the proper recipient of the dividend. Caleb's final cause of action is therefore dismissed....

IT IS SO ORDERED.

Legal Restrictions on Dividend Declaration. While the declaration of dividends is essentially the responsibility of a corporation's board of directors in the exercise of good business judgment, sometimes because of legal restraints they may not do so. Such restraints may be found in

- Its articles of incorporation
- Its preferred-share agreements
- Its bond indentures and loan contracts that prohibit dividends until the corporation repays the lender
- SEC rules that bind the corporation

The directors must also comply with statutory restrictions on payment of dividends imposed by the state of incorporation. These statutes are designed to protect the interests of creditors and shareholders by preserving the capital strength required by a corporation to carry on its business. Although these rules essentially present accounting rather than legal problems, we should recognize the direction in which the states are moving. The primary statutory restrictions are:

- All states provide that a dividend may not be paid if the corporation is insolvent or, as a result of the payment, would become insolvent.
- The majority of states say that dividends must be paid out of surplus—i.e., out of the excess of total assets over total liabilities—and that dividends may not be paid out of a corporation's stated capital.
- The minority have adopted a more liberal stance and permit payment of dividends (sometimes called "nimble dividends") out of current net profits, regardless of its effect on the corporation's capital account. Such dividends may be paid even if there was an earnings deficit in prior years.

  A variant of that flexible approach is the California rule that permits a corporation to pay a dividend as long as (1) its total assets, after the dividend payment, are at least equal to 125 percent of its liabilities, and (2) its current assets are at least equal to its current liabilities.
- The Revised Model Business Corporation Act [Sec. 6.40 (c)], in substance, precludes the payment of dividends, subject to further restrictions in a corporation's articles of incorporation, if (1) as a result of the payment the corporation would not be able to pay its debts as they become due in the usual course of business, and (2) the corporation's total assets would then be less than its total liabilities.

Other Corporate Distributions

Stock Dividends. A corporation may issue new shares of its stock to its existing stockholders as a "share" or "stock" dividend. The dividend shares are usually of the same class as the shares entitled to the dividend and are distributed in a fixed ratio. For example, if a 5 percent stock dividend is declared on common stock, one share of common will be issued and distributed for each block of twenty shares owned by holders of common stock. Dividend shares may be of another class or series if authorized by the articles or by the holders of a majority of outstanding shares of the same class as the proposed dividend.

The shareholders receive certificates evidencing the dividend shares, but the corporation does not, in fact, distribute any of its cash or assets. Stated capital is increased in the corporate books by the total amount of the stock dividend, and retained earning is reduced by the same amount. The shareholder's proportionate ownership interest in the corporation is unchanged. Stock dividends are not taxable as income by the recipients until the shares are sold. A stock dividend, therefore, may be considered to be merely a psychological dividend, but such dividends are gratefully received by the shareholders, being viewed as a substitute for a cash dividend which may be sold for cash at whatever price is established by the marketplace.

Stock Splits. A stock split is the division of each share of a class of stock into two or more parts. For example, if you hold ten shares of Ajax stock, and the stock is split two for one, the corporation will send you one additional share of stock for each share you hold. It will follow that the market price of each share will be adjusted accordingly. A stock split resembles a stock dividend in that the new shares do not increase a shareholder's proportionate ownership. However, a stock split does not increase the corporation's stated capital. Moreover, to effect a stock split, a corporation need not have retained earnings or meet any of the other statutory dividend tests. In addition, a change in the dividend rate per share usually accompanies a stock split. Typically, a stock dividend does not bring about a change in the per-share dividend rate.

A stock split is accomplished in a manner that is completely different from a stock dividend. The directors propose to the shareholders a stock split in some ratio, such as two-for-one or three-for-two. The shareholders then must vote to amend the articles of incorporation to reduce the par value of the shares being split. If 100 shares of $100-par stock are split into 200 shares of $50-par stock, the total stated capital ($10,000) remains the same but more shares are outstanding. The chief purpose of a stock split is to reduce the market price of shares to the customary price range of $20 to $75 per share. If the market price of a stock falls below that range, a *reverse stock split,* in which two or more shares become one, may be employed to increase the market price of the shares.

Redemption or Repurchase of Outstanding Shares. A corporation may reacquire shares of its stock in two ways: (1) by redemption and (2) by repurchase. We discussed redeemable preferred stock earlier in this chapter. In order to create a right of *redemption* of a class of stock in the corporation, the articles of incorporation must authorize the corporation to redeem the designated class of shares (usually preferred stock). The corporation's right of redemption is exercisable at the option of the directors and initiates an *involuntary* sale by the shareholders. The price and terms are fixed in the articles.

A repurchase, on the other hand, is a voluntary sale to the corporation by holders of the class of shares repurchased. Price and terms are not fixed, but they are negotiable between the corporation and the selling shareholder. The corporation may repurchase its preferred stock as well as its common stock.

In order to reacquire stock by redemption or purchase, the corporation ordinarily pays cash to the shareholder. It follows that a corporation's power to reacquire shares is restricted by statutes similar to those discussed above which limit dividend distributions. Thus, the corporation must have sufficient retained earnings, current earnings, or balance sheet surplus, and it must remain solvent after the acquisition.

A corporation may cancel repurchased shares or may hold them as treasury stock. Treasury shares cannot be voted and are not entitled to dividends. The benefit to the corporation of treasury shares is that they can be sold below par. The Revised Model Act [Sec. 6.31(a)] and several states no longer recognize treasury shares but provide that reacquired shares revert to the status of "authorized but unissued" shares. In contrast to purchased shares, redeemed shares cannot be reissued and must be canceled.

Summary

Corporations raise capital by selling shares (equity financing) and by borrowing funds from traditional business sources and by issuing and selling bonds (debt financing). In order to raise money for short periods of time (e.g., a few months), corporations normally issue *promissory notes;* for long periods of time they issue *bonds.* A bond is a corporate obligation which creates a debtor-creditor relationship between the corporation and the bondholder. There are many types of bonds. Unsecured bonds are called *debentures.*

A share of stock is a proportionate ownership interest in a corporation. Before the corporation can issue a stock certificate to a prospective shareholder, payment in full for the shares must be made in cash, usually in property other than promissory notes, or in services. There are two principal classes of stock: *common* and *preferred.* Common stock is subordinate to the liquidation and dividend preferences of preferred stock. Common stock ordinarily gives the holder the right to vote. Preferred stock has no voting rights except in extraordinary situations. There are many types of preferred stock.

Common stock may be issued with a par value or without a par value (no-par stock). The *par value* is the minimum price at which shares may be sold by the corporation. The par value of shares (fixed in the articles of incorporation) or the stated value of a no-par share bears no relation to the market value of the share which is determined by the marketplace. The Revised Model Act and the statutes of many states have done away with the concept of par-value stock.

Thin incorporation refers to a high debt-equity ratio. Tax authorities will disallow interest deductions on debts owed to shareholders if the corporation's debt-equity ratio is "too thin." In addition, a creditor may pierce the corporate veil if the corporation is too thinly incorporated. Moreover, the *deep-rock doctrine* ranks the claims of outside creditors ahead of debts owing to controlling shareholders of thin corporations.

The transfer of securities issued in "bearer" form is completed by their delivery to the transferee, but the transfer of "registered" securities (i.e., stocks or bonds having the owner's name on the certificate) requires indorsement and delivery of the certificate by the registered owner. If a certificate is lost or stolen, there are various legal consequences. Under the Uniform Commercial Code, if the owner promptly notifies the corporation when the loss becomes apparent and satisfies other requirements, the corporation will issue to the original owner an equivalent number of shares.

The courts will enforce agreements restricting share transfers if three conditions are met: (1) the restriction is reasonable, (2) the restriction is set forth in the articles or bylaws or in a contract between the shareholders, and (3) the restrictions are noted conspicuously on the certificates.

Typically, subject to certain statutory restrictions, directors have the discretion to declare dividends and may not be forced to pay dividends unless they act arbitrarily, fraudulently, or in bad faith.

A *stock dividend* creates the illusion of a property distribution but is not a true dividend. Retained earnings are reduced, and stated capital is increased without altering the shareholders' proportionate interests, which are merely represented by more shares. A *stock split* reduces the par value of outstanding shares and increases their number proportionately so that total stated capital is unchanged. No dividend test need be met in order to declare a stock split.

The use of corporate funds to redeem or to repurchase a corporation's own stock is restricted by statutes similar to those governing dividend distributions. Redeemed shares must be canceled, but in most states repurchased shares may be either canceled or held as treasury stock. Treasury stock held by the corporation has no dividend or voting rights, but it may be resold below par.

Review Questions

1 Explain the difference between a secured note and an unsecured note.

2 Distinguish between a registered bond and a bearer bond as to: **(a)** payment of interest, and **(b)** the impact of theft or loss of the bond.

3 Explain a bond that is **(a)** redeemable, and **(b)** convertible.

4 **(a)** What is a share of stock? **(b)** In what ways does a shareholder's relation to the corporation differ from that of a bondholder?

5 Explain why you agree or disagree with the following statement: "A corporation may issue its stock in return for services to be rendered in the future."

6 **(a)** What are the major advantages of owning common stock? **(b)** Does common stock always have voting rights? Explain.

7 Distinguish between **(a)** cumulative and noncumulative preferred stock, and **(b)** participating and nonparticipating preferred stock.

8 **(a)** Explain the meaning and purpose of stock with par value. **(b)** What is the benefit to directors of having no-par stock?

9 **(a)** Explain the term "thin incorporation." **(b)** In what ways might it be dangerous to the members of a corporation? **(c)** State and explain two incentives for thinly incorporating.

10 **(a)** What is required to transfer a "bearer" instrument? **(b)** What is required to transfer registered bonds and shares?

11 Why is it important for a new owner to record the transfer of registered shares on the books of the corporation?

12 What three conditions must be met in order to restrict the transfer of shares of stock?

13 **(a)** Explain the primary purpose of statutory restrictions on dividends. **(b)** Discuss the four major statutory tests of a valid dividend.

14 Why is a "record date" important in connection with the declaration of a dividend? In your answer, discuss the rights of transferees who are not of record when the dividend is paid.

15 Explain the similarities and the differences between a stock dividend and a stock split.

16 Discuss the similarities and the differences between a redemption and a purchase of shares by a corporation.

Case Problems

1 Haselbush agreed to buy 10,000 shares of X corporation's stock for $20,000 and gave a promissory note to the corporation for that amount. The purchase of the shares was entered on X Corporation's books, but the stock certificate was not issued to Haselbush pending payment of the note. When Haselbush failed to pay the note, X Corporation sued to collect. Haselbush asked the court to cancel the note because the transaction was illegal and thus voidable. Should the court order cancellation of the note?

2 Realty Co. was incorporated by eight doctors to build a medical building. Each of the doctors purchased common stock and bonds of the corporation. The bonds had a fixed maturity date, and no provision was made for their earlier redemption. If the corporation were to default on its bond payments, individual bondholders could not enforce payment without the consent of a majority of the bondholders, i.e., a majority of the eight doctors. In addition, the rights of the bondholders were subordinate to the rights of outside creditors. For 7 years Realty Co. deducted on its income tax return the accrued but unpaid interest on the bonds. The IRS construed the bonds as shares and disallowed the interest deductions. Was the IRS correct in treating the bonds as shares?

3 The certificate of incorporation of Spaziani Bakeries, Inc., states in part, "No certificate of stock of this corporation shall be transferred to any person or corporation until it has first been offered for sale to this Corporation." Vincent Spaziani, one of the original incorporators, died. His two heirs demanded that Spaziani's shares be distributed to them. The corporation contends that it must first have the opportunity to purchase the shares. Is the corporation correct?

4 On December 6, 1986, Zobrist delivered two stock certificates, each for 100 shares of KFC stock, to Schwabacher, a stockbroker, for him to sell. Schwabacher sold the shares. The sale of 100 shares was registered on KFC Corporation's books immediately, but the sale of the remaining 100 shares was not recorded until January 3, 1987. On December 5, 1986, KFC declared a two-for-one stock split effective on December 15, 1986, the record date. On December 16, 1986, Zobrist received a certificate for 200 new shares of KFC stock which he held until the following September, at which time he sold them for $14,797. Schwabacher discovered what had happened and, on behalf of the buyer of the stock, sued Zobrist for the $14,797. Should Zobrist be forced to give up the money?

5 In July 1977, plaintiff, Wright, became a marketing consultant for Anacomp, Inc. It was understood that in September 1977 the parties would reach a definitive agreement whereby Wright would be employed as an Anacomp executive for 5 years. As a part of the original understanding **(a)** Wright paid Anacomp $26,625 and received 3,060 shares of that company's common stock, and **(b)** it was understood that, if no definitive employment agreement were reached, the 3,060 shares of Anacomp's stock would be repurchased from Wright by the company at the price he had paid for them. Negotiations for the definitive employment agreement continued until 1979, when the parties realized that they could not come together on terms and Wright ceased to work for Anacomp. In accordance with their original understanding, the company repaid Wright the $26,625 he had paid for the 3,060 shares and asked for their return together with the additional 3,603 shares of Anacomp's common stock Wright had received as stock dividends and stock splits on the 3,060 shares. Wright brought suit for an accounting to determine his obligation. Is Wright required to return the 3,603 shares?

CHAPTER 41

Management of Corporations

The management authority of a corporation may be seen as a pyramid. At the broad base of the pyramid are the state *statutes* which define the outer limits of the powers that may be exercised by any corporation chartered within the state. Next, moving upward, each corporation's powers are made more definite by the *charter* issued to it when the state gives life to the corporation. At the next higher level of the pyramid are the corporation's *bylaws,* a set of self-developed rules for the governance of the corporation's directors and officers. At the apex of the pyramid are the *policies* established by the board of directors who were elected by the corporation's owners, its shareholders, to govern the translation of the corporation's powers (bestowed by the lower levels of the pyramid) into what is hoped to be a viable economic enterprise.

Because a corporation is an inanimate entity, it must, in order to utilize and implement its powers, act through living individuals, its officers appointed by the board of directors. The officers, in turn, hire employees to carry on the business of the corporation within the limits of its powers and policies fixed by the board of directors.

This chapter first discusses the powers under which a corporation operates. We next examine the managerial roles of corporate directors and officers and the liabilities to which each may be subjected. The final portion of the chapter deals with the special management problems that arise in close corporations.

The Corporate Entity: Powers and Liabilities

Sources of Corporate Powers

The term "corporate powers" refers to a corporation's legal capacity to carry out its business purposes defined in its certificate of incorporation. A corporation's powers may be express or implied.

Express Powers. The powers granted in state statutes to corporations and set forth in its charter are the corporation's express powers. Some states, particularly those which follow the Revised Model Business Corporation Act, give corporations very broad powers. The certificates of incorporation issued in those states grant a corporation the same powers as an individual possesses in order to do all things necessary and convenient to carry out its business affairs. In most states, corporations are given the power to exist in perpetuity; to sue and to be sued; to acquire or transfer real and personal property; to have a seal; to make bylaws; to make gifts for charitable or educational purposes; to adopt profit sharing, pension, or stock option plans as incentive compensation for directors, officers, or employees; to be a partner or joint venturer; and to guarantee obligations of others.

All states require the articles of incorporation to set forth the corporation's business purposes, but they may usually be stated in broad terms such as "to engage in any lawful business" without restating all the powers listed in the incorporation statute. Some businesses, such as banks, savings and loan associations, insurance companies, and utilities, have such close ties to public interest that their powers are subject to special limitations. For instance, laws provide that these businesses may not engage in manufacturing, retail sales, and other "commercial enterprises." Likewise, because of the unique character of professional corporations, the business in which such a corporation may engage is limited to rendering the professional service for which it was incorporated.

Implied Powers. The courts generally give broad effect to the powers stated in a corporation's charter. They hold that a corporation has, in addition to its expressly stated powers, *implied power* to perform all acts reasonably necessary to accomplish the purposes stated, provided of course, they are not unlawful or otherwise prohibited to the corporation. For example, Smith organizes a corporation. Its charter states simply that the corporation has the power to operate gasoline filling stations. The corporation has the implied power to buy and to install equipment, to buy and sell supplies for cash or on credit, to hire mechanics who will repair cars, and to operate a towing service.

What can be construed as an implied power depends upon the wording of the corporation's charter and the pertinent statutory provisions under which the corporation is organized. For example, in *Blue Cross and Blue Shield of Connecticut v. Mike,* 439 A.2d 1026 (Conn. 1981), the court held that the charter of Blue Cross and Blue Shield empowered it to establish and maintain a comprehensive health plan but that basic authority did not include as an implied power the right to own and operate an insurance company.

Ultra Vires Acts

Because the powers of a corporation may be limited, it is possible that the corporation itself, or an officer or employee in the scope of his or her employment, will exceed the corporation's express or implied powers. Such an action is said to be *ultra vires* (literally, "beyond strength"), meaning an act beyond the purposes or powers of the corporation. Thus, an *ultra vires* act would take place where a corporation's purchasing agent engages in a contract beyond the scope of its articles or implied powers, or if in the scope of employment a sales clerk negligently injures someone, or—and in this the *ultra vires* act is also a crime—if the corporate officers were to engage in a price-fixing scheme.

As demonstrated by the following case, a corporation may not claim that an action, merely because it more conveniently accomplished its corporate purposes, was within its implied powers and thus was not *ultra vires.*

CASE 41.1 Lovering v. Seabrook Island Property Owners S.C. · 352 S.E.2d 707 (S.C. 1987)

FACTS The Seabrook Island Property Owners Association (Association) assessed its members to pay for bridge repairs and improvements to the beach within the association's property. The petitioners, members of the association, relying upon applicable corporate law, challenged the validity of the assessment as an *ultra vires* action. The trial court granted summary judgment for the association, and the property owners appealed. The court of appeals reversed the trial court, and the association and the Seabrook Island Company, which owned the bridges and the beach, appealed to the supreme court of South Carolina.

OPINION PER CURIAM [opinion by the whole court]... It is undisputed that the Association had no express power to impose the assessment in issue. The Association and the Company argue, however, that the power to levy this special assessment was an implied or incidental power of the Association's authority under its By-laws to maintain and preserve the amenities and values of the development.

Implied or incidental powers are those which are reasonably necessary to the exercise of the corporation's express powers, not those which are merely convenient or useful. [Citations.]

Assuming, without deciding, that the Association had the responsibility of maintaining the streets and the beach, the By-laws provided the mechanism of an annual maintenance charge to finance the necessary repairs. Furthermore, the Association could have financed the repairs by use of its statutory authority to borrow funds under [the] S.C. Code..., a course of action the Association apparently considered and rejected. Since the power to levy a special assessment was not *necessary* for the Association to carry out its express powers, even if more convenient than the available fund raising methods, it could not be an implied or incidental power....

Based on the foregoing, the Court of Appeals correctly held that the imposition of the special assessment was *ultra vires.*...

JUDGMENT AFFIRMED....

Two question may be asked: (1) May anyone take action against a corporation because it committed an *ultra vires* act? (2) May a corporation successfully assert as a defense to liability for an *ultra vires* act that it cannot be held responsible because the act was beyond its legal authority? We will now examine those questions.

Ultra Vires as a Basis of Action against a Corporation. In rare situations, *ultra vires* may be used as a ground for suits against corporations. The attorney general of the state of incorporation may sue in a *quo warranto* action to enjoin or dissolve a corporation engaged in exercising powers beyond those stated in its charter. Suppose a bank opens a retail store. A shareholder may, by means of a derivative suit on behalf of the corporation, seek to restrain the *ultra vires* act of its directors and officers and to recover, on behalf of the corporation, damages from them. For example, *Lovering* (Case 41.1) was a derivative suit brought by a shareholder to restrain a corporate *ultra vires* course of action.

Ultra Vires Defense by a Corporation. A corporation may not successfully assert that it is not liable on a contract on the ground that its charter did not allow it to engage in such a contract—in other words, that it was an *ultra vires* act. The practical result is that a corporation may enter into valid contracts in excess of its powers. For example, if the president of a corporation should, in the corporation's name and beyond its express or implied powers, cosign a note for a friend, the corporation is liable to the creditor, and *ultra vires* is not a defense. However the president may, of course, be liable to the corporation for his or her improper action.

Liability for Torts and Crimes. *Ultra vires* does not furnish a defense by a corporation against an action in tort committed by its employee in the scope of his or her employment or against a corporate criminal act. The laws of agency (discussed in Chapters 33 and 34) are applicable to the torts of corporation employees who act within the scope of their employment. Under the agency law doctrine of respondeat superior, an injured party may hold a corporation liable for the wrongful acts of servant-type employees acting within the general scope of their employment, even if the corporate employer had instructed the employees not to commit the tort. The rule of respondeat superior imposes liability upon a corporation for the unintentional tort of negligence as well as for intentional torts—such as trespass, fraud, or conversion—committed by its employees. The wrongful intent of the employee is imputed to the corporation as a matter of law.

Whether a corporation can be liable for punitive (exemplary) damages for a willful, wanton, or malicious tort of an employee within the scope of his or her authority or employment has led to some confusion. Corporations have contended that they cannot be liable for such acts because they did not intend the wrong. A growing number of courts, as in *Robinson v. Winn-Dixie Stores, Inc.*, 447 So.2d 1003 (Fla. App. 1984), hold that if there was *some fault* on the part of the corporate management which foreseeably contributed to the plaintiff's injury, the corporation is liable for punitive damages. This conclusion is reached even though the corporation's fault was merely the result of negligence and was not willful or malicious. The majority view, however, as to whether punitive damages may be assessed against a corporation is expressed in the following case.

CASE 41.2 Smith v. United Technologies, Essex Group · 731 P.2d 871 (Kan. 1987)

FACTS Donald Smith, the plaintiff, sued his former employer, United Technologies, Essex Group, seeking damages arising from his discharge from employment. He alleged, among other things, that he had been discharged in retaliation for having filed a complaint with the Kansas Commission on Civil Rights. The jury found that he had been wrongfully discharged and awarded him $30,000 in actual damages and $25,000 in punitive damages. The defendant appealed that verdict.

OPINION McFARLAND, J. [As to the issue of punitive damages the court said] . . . In *Smith v. Wade*, 461 U.S. 30, . . . the U.S. Supreme Court held . . . that:

CASE 41.2 Continued

[A] jury may be permitted to assess punitive damages... when the defendant's conduct is shown to be motivated by evil motive or intent, or when it involves reckless or callous indifference to the federally protected rights of others. We further hold that this threshold applies even when the underlying standard of liability is one of recklessness....

In the case before us there was evidence of a concerted effort by defendant's managerial personnel to harass and terminate plaintiff in retaliation for his having filed civil rights claims....

...Further, punitive damages are allowed not because of any special merit in the injured party's case, but are imposed by way of punishing the wrongdoer for malicious, vindictive, or a willful or wanton invasion of the injured party's rights, the purpose being to restrain and deter others from the commission of like wrongs....A corporation is not liable for punitive damages awarded for an employee's tortious acts within the scope of employment unless (*a*) a corporation or its managerial agent authorized the doing and manner of the act; (*b*) the employee was unfit and the corporation or its managerial agent was reckless in employing or retaining him; (*c*) the employee was employed in a managerial capacity and was acting within the scope of employment; or (*d*) the corporation or its managerial agent ratified or approved the act of the employee....Against this standard there appears to be sufficient competent evidence to support the award of punitive damages....

JUDGMENT ...[A]ffirmed.

Corporation Directors and Officers

Directors

A corporation, being an inanimate entity, cannot itself utilize its powers nor can it establish or implement policy. All this must be accomplished by people who act for the corporation. The powers of a corporation, set forth in statutes and in its charter, are exercised by or under the authority of its board of directors which is charged with the management of the corporation's business affairs. The board is the source of overall corporation policy—policy that is implemented by its officers and other employees.

Ten states require a minimum of three directors,[1] and twelve states follow the Revised Model Act (Sec. 8.03), which requires only one director.[2] The remaining states offer a compromise, particularly to accommodate close corporations with but a single shareholder. These states provide that although there is a general requirement of three directors, the number of directors need not exceed the number of shareholders. Thus, if there is only one shareholder, there may be a single director. A company's articles of incorporation or its bylaws must fix the number of directors but need not set out their qualifications.

Election and Removal of Directors. Prior to the annual meeting of the shareholders, the directors present to them the names of nominees whom the directors recommend for membership on the board of directors. The shareholders may, if they wish, submit the names of their own nominees. Unless a corporation's articles or bylaws provide otherwise, a director need not be a shareholder. The directors are elected by the plurality vote of the corporation's owners, the shareholders.

[1]The ten states which require a minimum of three directors are Alabama, Colorado, Hawaii, Maryland, Mississippi, Montana, New Hampshire, North Dakota, Oklahoma, and Utah.

[2]The twelve states which require only one director are Arizona, Delaware, Florida, Michigan, Missouri, New Jersey, New Mexico, Oregon, South Dakota, Texas, West Virginia, and Wisconsin.

Typically, a director serves a 1-year term, although a corporation's articles or the bylaws may specify a longer period. If a director dies or resigns, the board of directors can elect a director to fill the vacancy, thus obviating the necessity of calling a special meeting of the shareholders.

A corporation's articles or bylaws may also give the board of directors the power to increase the size of the board. If the directors do so, they can temporarily fill "vacancies" created by this action until the next election of directors by the shareholders.

Most statutes permit the board to remove a director who has been declared insane or convicted of a felony. Seldom do a corporation's articles or bylaws permit the board of directors to remove a member of the board for any other reason. To permit such action would tend to encourage a majority faction of the board to stifle contrary opinion being expressed by a member not within that faction. The shareholders, however, as discussed in the next chapter, have the inherent power at any time to remove a member of the board for cause or without cause. In many states, following appropriate legal action, a member of the board may be removed by court order (Revised Model Act, Sec. 8.09).

Authority of Directors. The board of directors manages the business affairs of the corporation. To understand the broad scope of this responsibility, some of its functions may be noted:

- It establishes and reviews the company's principal goals, objectives, and policies.
- It reviews and approves major programs, budgets, and plans, and it monitors the financial and operating functions of the company.
- It can authorize the issuance of shares of stock and, in the name of the corporation, it can repurchase shares already issued.
- It elects directors to fill vacancies on the board, to hold office until the next annual meeting of the shareholders.
- It appoints and removes the corporation's officers, authorizes important actions by the officers, and oversees their performance.
- It may acquire the business of another corporation.
- It declares dividends and fixes the dates for their payment to the shareholders.
- It may adopt, amend, or repeal bylaws, unless the articles of incorporation reserve this power to the shareholders.
- It may recommend to the shareholders the dissolution of the corporation.

Compensation of Directors. Historically, most directors were shareholders and were not entitled to compensation unless they performed extraordinary services for the corporation. Today, however, particularly in publicly held corporations, most members of boards of directors are neither officers nor employees of the company but are knowledgeable, competent businesspeople outside the company who are asked to serve on boards to bring them unbiased expertise in particular fields. A director who is not an officer or another employee of the corporation is called an "outside member" of the board. An outside member does not necessarily own any shares of the corporation's stock. In order to encourage highly experienced women and men to accept the responsibilities of directorship, it is common practice for corporation boards of directors to authorize their companies to pay their outside board members substantial remuneration. This is usually done in the form of an annual cash retainer plus a per diem payment for attendance at board or committee meetings. In addition, some large firms give stock options or other innovative compensation packages to their outside directors.

Actions by Boards of Directors. A board of directors generally must assemble in a formal meeting in order to take action in behalf of the corporation. Such meetings are held at fixed intervals established in the bylaws or in a standing resolution. Special meetings may be held after notice (given as prescribed in the bylaws) to all the directors.

There is a growing authority for state statutes, articles of incorporation, and bylaws to permit boards to act not only through formal meetings but also through simultaneous telephonic conference calls, by video teleconference or, without a meeting, by giving their unanimous written consent to the transaction. Unless specified in statute or bylaws, there is no requirement that a board of directors meet at the corporate offices or even in the state of incorporation. Accordingly, it is not unheard of that a board of directors holds its meeting aboard a cruise ship or at an attractive resort.

The actions taken by a board of directors are expressed in formal resolutions adopted by a majority of the board during a meeting at which a quorum is present. A *quorum* is the minimum number of persons required to be present in order to legally transact the board's business. Statutes and bylaws may differ as to the basis upon which a quorum is computed—it may be the *authorized* number of directors or the number of *current* board members when vacancies in the board exist. Generally, a quorum consists of a majority of the members of the board [Revised Model Act, Sec. 8.24(a)]. A director is not allowed to vote by proxy and must attend the meeting in person in order to be counted for quorum purposes. A *proxy* is a person authorized to vote someone else's shares, or, according to the context, the word may also refer to the document granting authority to a specified individual to vote in someone's stead. For a resolution to be adopted, ordinarily a majority of those present must concur. Thus, assume that the board of directors has eleven members and that only six members attend a properly called meeting to name a new treasurer for the company. Let us say that four out of the six present elect Roberto as treasurer. Roberto is the new treasurer even though he was elected by the vote of only four members of an eleven-member board.

If directors deadlock in a vote and no majority emerges, most likely the issue will be held over until a meeting of the full board. If the full board is deadlocked on an important issue, such as the election of a new treasurer in the above illustration, courts in some states may appoint a provisional director to serve until the deadlock is broken.

Committees of Boards of Directors. As a company grows in size and complexity, the responsibility of its board of directors increases apace. Therefore, so that the board may most efficiently carry out its duties and responsibilities, it may create committees composed of its members and these committees give special attention to specific areas of concern. The committees bring reports and recommendations before the board of directors, and the board may delegate to one or more of these committees authority to act for the board in the intervals between meetings. While the committees can exercise such board powers within the limits of the resolutions by which they are established, they may not initiate extraordinary transactions.

New York Stock Exchange rules require every listed corporation to have an audit committee consisting of outside directors. They are charged with the duty of reviewing with an independent public accounting firm the annual and special audit reports and the internal accounting and financial controls of the company, and recommending any action deemed necessary. Large corporations have gone beyond the New York Stock Exchange direction that there be an audit committee; they normally establish additional committees in other areas of responsibility. By way of illustration, Table 41.1 lists the committees of the boards of directors of four large representative corporations.

Officers

The officers of a corporation actively control and manage the company's business activities. They act under the authority given them by the board of directors and are charged with carrying out its announced policies.

Election. The officers of a corporation are elected by the board of directors, and they hold office at the pleasure of the board, which also fixes their salaries. If the board by contract establishes the tenure of an officer, he or she still holds that office only at the pleasure of the board. However, if the officer is discharged before the end of the contract period, he or she may have an action against the corporation for breach of contract.

As a general rule, the bylaws provide for a president, one or more vice presidents, a secretary, and a treasurer. The bylaws also describe the general duties and authority of each officer; specific duties and responsibilities are assigned to the officers by the board. One person may hold more than one office, but in most states the same person cannot be both president and secretary. However, a growing minority of states have eliminated this prohibition to accommodate the needs of close corporations. Particularly in large, publicly held corporations, the board of directors may designate, in addition to the normally named officers, a *chief executive officer* (familiarly known as the CEO). If such office is created, it is generally filled by the president or by the chairperson of the board of directors, in addition to his or her other duties.

Table 41.1 Sampling of Committees of Boards of Directors

Corporation	Committees of the Board
Exxon:	
18 board members	Audit Committee
7 company officers	Board Advisory Committee on Contributions
11 outside members	Board Compensation Committee
	Executive Committee
	Finance Committee
	Nominating Committee
General Electric:	
19 board members	Audit Committee
3 company officers	Finance Committee
16 outside members	Management Development and Compensation Committee
	Nominating Committee
	Operations Committee
	Public Responsibilities Committee
	Technology and Science Committee
General Motors:	
22 board members	Audit Committee
9 company officers	Executive Committee
13 outside members	Finance Committee
	Incentive and Compensation Committee
	Nominating Committee
	Public Policy Committee

Authority of Officers. Corporate officers are employees of the corporation and, as its agents, may bind the corporation in contract and in tort when acting within the scope of their authority. Directors, on the other hand, are *not* agents of the corporation which they serve.

The authority of an officer may be express, implied, or apparent. An officer's *express authority* arises out of statements of authority set out in the company's bylaws and in specific directions given him or her by the board of directors. The officer's *implied authority* may stem from his or her reasonable understanding of the meaning and application of that express authority, from the powers previously exercised by an occupant of that office, or from the powers generally exercised by the incumbent of a similar office in another corporation in that general region. *Apparent authority* of an officer is the name given to the authority, whether or not there is express authority, which from the corporation's actions a third party is led to believe the officer possesses. For example, a vice president in charge of rocket booster development would appear to third parties to have authority to approve contracts for the purchase of rocket fuel even though, by the internal rules of the corporation, he or she had no such authority. Therefore, by apparent authority, a contract entered into by the vice president for rocket fuel binds the corporation.

Under agency law (see Chapter 33) an unauthorized act of an officer binds the corporation if it later ratifies the act.

Duties Owed by Directors and Officers

In the exercise of their management functions, directors and officers of a corporation owe their company the exercise of due care in the performance of their duties and loyalty with respect to the corporation [Revised Model Act, Secs. 8.30 (a), and 8.42 (a).]

Duty to Act with Due Care. Directors and officers may be liable to the corporation and to its shareholders if they do not exercise the proper degree of care in the performance of their duties. The test of what constitutes due care has been stated in several ways. The Revised Model Act (Sec. 8.30) provides that a director shall discharge his or her duties

- In good faith
- With the care an ordinarily prudent person in a like position would exercise under similar circumstances
- In a manner he or she reasonably believes to be in the best interests of the corporation

Some courts express the duty of care somewhat more strictly by holding that the care and skill must be what ordinarily prudent persons would exercise had they been *acting for themselves* at the time. Either standard of care may be difficult to apply to a business risk, so frequently taken by a director, where there is no known precedent to apply. For instance, imagine a board of directors of which both Jones and Smith are members. Director Jones introduces a resolution authorizing the corporation to market a new product which he has researched and is certain will be successful. It will cost several million dollars to test-market the product. Smith was absent from the previous directors' meeting when the product was fully discussed and the resolution was argued. In a subsequent meeting, Smith cast the determining vote in its favor because she is a personal friend of Jones. Let us now assume that the introduction of the product is a failure, the corporation loses several million dollars, and its shares go down in value. Are directors Jones and Smith, or either of them, liable to the corporation and to its shareholders for the losses sustained on the ground that a prudent person would have voted against undertaking the project?

In the event Jones and Smith are sued, it could be anticipated that each would deny liability, claiming he or she had exercised the due care required of a director, citing the business judgment rule in a matter in which no one could guarantee either success or failure. The *business judgment rule* is a basic principle applicable to directors and officers who must make business decisions. In essence, the rule is that a director or an officer who acts in good faith is not liable for a business decision which causes loss to the corporation if (1) the decision was not induced by any element of fraud, conflict of interest, or other illegality, and (2) he or she had not been guilty of gross negligence in reaching that decision.

As a member of a policymaking board, a director must be fully cognizant of the company's affairs and make decisions rationally, founded upon reasonable information. The information may be furnished by other directors, officers, or employees of the corporation, by its legal counsel, by accountants or other professional experts, by committees of the board of directors, or by his or her own independent reasonable investigation to discover the relevant facts. A director has not exercised the required care if, for example,

- He or she repeatedly fails to attend meetings of the board
- In preparation for a meeting, he or she fails to analyze the corporation's latest financial statements prepared by in-house and independent auditors or to review legal opinions of its attorneys pertinent to the corporation's activities
- He or she does not become conversant with available information relevant to his or her duties

If, because of such omissions the corporation suffers financial loss, the director may become liable in damages to the corporation or to its shareholders, but the negligent director is not liable to creditors of the corporation who are only indirectly injured.

From the foregoing, it could be concluded that director Jones in the previous hypothetical corporation may be able to take advantage of the business judgment rule to shield himself from liability, but director Smith may not be so fortunate.

The Supreme Court of the State of Delaware considered the use of the business judgment rule in the following landmark case.

CASE 41.3 Smith v. Van Gorkum · 488 A.2d 858 (Del. Supr. 1985)

FACTS Van Gorkum was the chairperson of the board of directors and the chief executive officer of Trans Union Corporation, a publicly traded company. Trans Union had a cash flow of hundreds of millions of dollars annually, but it had difficulty in generating taxable income.

Van Gorkum, without advice from outside financial consultants or auditors, approached Jay Pritzker, a man who was known to buy corporations, saying that Trans Union was a candidate for purchase at $55 per share—that being the price suggested to Van Gorkum by Trans Union's chief financial officer. Pritzker replied that he would buy Trans Union's shares from its shareholders in a "cash-out" merger into one of his corporations at the suggested $55 per share. Among his conditions was that Trans Union would have 90 days within which to receive a better offer, and if none were received, the sale to Pritzker would be concluded. Pritzker demanded a decision within 2 days.

Despite the negative reaction of Trans Union's senior management, Van Gorkum called a meeting of the board of directors for the following day. At that meeting, based primarily upon Van Gorkum's presentation, the directors approved the offer. No better offer was received within the succeeding 90 days; the directors again approved the merger and recommended to the shareholders that they authorize the proposed merger of Trans Union into Pritzker's corporation. They approved, and the merger was carried out. Dissident shareholders, headed by Smith, brought suit against the Trans Union board of directors for breach of their duty as directors in approving the merger. They asked for damages representing the difference between the $55 per share paid by Pritzker and the fair value of their shares.

The lower court granted judgment for the defendant, Trans Union's board of directors, holding that they were protected by the business judgment rule. Smith appealed.

OPINION HORSEY, J. . . . [W]e reverse and direct that judgment be entered in favor of the plaintiffs and against the defendant directors for the fair value of the plaintiffs' shareholdings in Trans Union. . . .

The business judgment rule exists to protect and promote the full and free exercise of the managerial power granted to Delaware directors. . . . The rule itself "is a presumption that in making a business decision, the directors of a corporation acted on an informed basis, in good faith, and in the honest belief that the action taken was in the best interests of the company. . . ."

The determination of whether a business judgment is an informed one turns on whether the directors have informed themselves "prior to making a business decision, of all material information reasonably available to them."

. . . Since a director is vested with the responsibility for the management of the affairs of the corporation, he must execute that duty with the recognition that he acts on behalf of others. Such obligation does not tolerate faithlessness or self-dealing. But fulfillment of the fiduciary function requires more than the absence of bad faith or fraud. Representation of the financial interests of others imposes on a director an affirmative duty to protect those interests and to proceed with a critical eye in assessing information of the type and under the circumstances present. . . .

Thus, a director's duty to exercise an informed business judgment is in the nature of a duty of care, as distinguished from a duty of loyalty. . . .

. . . We think the concept of gross negligence is . . . the proper standard for determining whether a business judgment reached by a board of directors was an informed one. . . .

CASE 41.3 Continued

The directors (1) did not adequately inform themselves as to Van Gorkum's role in forcing the "sale" of the Company and in establishing the per share purchase price; (2) were uninformed as to the intrinsic value of the Company; and (3) given these circumstances, at a minimum, were grossly negligent in approving the "sale" of the Company upon two hours' consideration without prior notice and without the exigency of a crisis or emergency.

... [W]e must conclude that the Board of Directors did not reach an informed business judgment in voting to "sell" the company for $55 per share....

JUDGMENT Reversed and remanded....

As shareholders become ever more aware of the obligations directors owe to their corporations and to the shareholders, as reflected in the *Van Gorkum* case, and as our society becomes increasingly one in which litigation is commonplace, more and more suits are being filed against directors on the ground that they failed to exercise requisite care, alleging that the business judgment rule was not satisfied. It is the general practice of the states to allow corporations based within them to indemnify (reimburse) directors for the expenses, settlement payments, and other costs the directors have paid in defending themselves in this type of litigation. Corporations generally purchase insurance as protection against such expenses. However, because of the difficulty in procuring adequate insurance and because of the increase in premium costs when coverage is obtainable, Delaware, effective July 1, 1986, amended its General Corporation Law in Section 102(b)(7). That section allows a certificate of incorporation to contain a provision eliminating or limiting the personal liability of a director to the corporation or to its shareholders arising out of breach of his or her duty of due care. As a result, insurance coverage should be more procurable. In addition, the Delaware law broadens a corporation's authority to indemnify its directors for damages imposed upon them by third-party suits arising out of their performance of corporate duties. The limitation on liability does *not*, however, apply to

- A breach of duty of loyalty to the corporation
- Acts or omissions not in good faith
- Intentional misconduct or a knowing violation of law
- Paying a dividend or making a stock purchase in violation of law
- A transaction from which the director derived an improper personal benefit

Other states are fast following Delaware's lead, and corporations are hastening to amend their articles of incorporation accordingly, stating in their annual reports, in substance, "the Board of Directors believes that in order to continue to attract and retain qualified directors, the Company must take some action to reduce the personal risk of service as a director."

Duty of Loyalty. Directors and officers stand in a fiduciary relationship to the corporations they serve. As was observed in Chapter 35 in the discussion of an agent's responsibility to his or her principal, the Latin root of the word "fiduciary" is *fides*, meaning faith, trust, or public confidence. Investors who buy shares of stock place trust and confidence in the directors and officers of the corporations that issue them, expecting them to manage and work for the corporation to make it profitable and to be socially responsible. This involves the duties of due care and loyalty on the part of those directors and officers. In essence, if a director or an officer acts in such a way as to create a conflict of interest between himself or herself and the corporation, a breach of fiduciary duty has occurred. In the case of closely held corporations being operated much like partnerships and where the shareholders, directors, and officers are usually all the same individuals, there exists an even higher degree of trust and confidence.

A breach of duty of loyalty may be manifested in many ways.

Doing business with a corporation. If a director or an officer sells her or his property to the corporation, the possibility exists that the director or officer has improperly induced the corporation to enter into a disadvantageous transaction. Some courts follow the common law view that such a purchase is *voidable* at the option of the corporation. The more modern view, however, is that the transaction is *not* voidable if (1) the contract is fair to the corporation, *or* (2) the conflict is fully disclosed or known to the *disinterested* directors or to the shareholders, and without counting the vote or consent of the *interested* parties, either body approves or ratifies the transaction (Revised Model Act, Sec. 8.31). However, some courts are more strict in applying this rule and require that to validate the purchase the transaction must be just and reasonable in addition to being fully disclosed by the interested party.

Any contract between a director or an officer and his or her corporation that is neither fair nor approved by directors or shareholders who have no personal interest in the transaction may be rescinded by the corporation. Alternatively, the contract may be affirmed, and the self-serving director or officer may be required to pay the corporation any damages it sustained.

Fixing one's own compensation. In large corporations, the salaries of officers are fixed by a committee of outside directors; therefore, although the entire board approves the salaries, a director who is also an officer of the corporation is protected from the charge of self-dealing. Inside directors who are also officers of the corporation receive no additional compensation because of their directorship duties. However, self-dealing is unavoidable in a case where the majority of the board of directors are outside members who fix their own compensation for their services as directors. If the directors' compensation does not bear a reasonable relation to the services they are required to render, a shareholder's suit to limit or deny that amount may be successful. Court rulings in these suits are often based upon the premise that directors do not have unlimited freedom to give away corporate property against the protest of the shareholders.

In closely held corporations, since the directors and shareholders are usually one and the same, there is generally no legal problem in this respect. However, a minority member of the board may bring action if the compensation bears no reasonable relation to the services the individuals are to perform.

Competing with a corporation. A director or an officer of a corporation who either personally or through another business competes with the corporation he or she serves may or may not be breaching a fiduciary duty, depending upon the facts in the particular situation. For example, it would be bad faith and a breach of duty if a director or an officer used influence to prevent the corporation from competing with a private business concern in which the director had a personal interest, or used corporate employees in a personal venture in which the corporation had no interest, or accepted secret profits or commissions on corporate transactions, or disclosed trade secrets to an outside business.

A similar type of conflict of interest may arise where an individual sits as a member of the board of directors of two corporations which contract with each other. This is called "interlocking directorates." In that circumstance, the director is, in effect, acting as an advisor to competing entities. Therefore, because a conflict of interest is presumptively present, interlocking directorates are viewed with suspicion, and the same criteria of fairness apply to them as in the case where a director acted for his own personal interest.

Seizing corporate opportunity. A director or an officer improperly competes with the corporation when he or she personally takes advantage of an economic or a business opportunity which rightfully belongs to the corporation. For instance, Perry, a director of the Marine Deep-Sea Fishing Company, Inc., learns that a particularly desirable new deep-sea fishing boat is for sale at a low price. The boat may be an economic opportunity which Marine could well use by adding it to the company's fleet. If Perry purchases the boat for himself to use for weekend excursions, he would be seizing an economic opportunity that rightfully belongs to his company and would be breaching his duty of loyalty to it.

Pursuant to this *corporate opportunity doctrine,* the director or officer must give the corporation the right of first refusal to act upon a business opportunity which comes to the director's or officer's attention. It is generally held that the corporate opportunity rule applies when

- A director or an officer becomes aware of the opportunity in his or her corporate capacity

- The corporation customarily deals in such an opportunity
- The opportunity is developed with corporate capital, facilities, or personnel

A corporate opportunity is *not* usually held to exist if

- The corporation cannot obtain necessary financing despite the directors' best efforts
- Involvement by the corporation would be *ultra vires*
- The director or officer who discovers the opportunity discloses it to his or her company and a majority of the *distinterested* directors votes against the proposal

The breadth of the corporate opportunity doctrine is brought out in the case which follows.

CASE 41.4 Comedy Cottage, Inc. v. Berk · 495 N.E.2d 1006 (Ill. App. 1986)

FACTS Hellenbrand and his wife were the sole shareholders in Comedy Cottage, Inc., which operated a club in Illinois. In 1979 or 1980, Berk, the defendant, was made the vice president of the corporation and given 10 percent of its shares. Berk became general manager and operated the club for the next 5 or 6 years while Hellenbrand was living in Nevada. In 1984, the club lease expired and the club became a month-to-month tenant. Hellenbrand directed Berk to obtain a new lease. The building owner on March 30, 1985, gave notice to Berk that the month-to-month tenancy was terminated. Berk immediately telephoned Hellenbrand, gave him this information, and resigned as an employee of the corporation. Hellenbrand phoned the building owner who said he did not wish to rent to Hellenbrand any longer.

Berk formed a new corporation named Comedy Company, Inc., and began to negotiate for a lease to the premises. On April 5 or 6, 1985, Berk, in the name of his new corporation, entered into a lease for the building. Hellenbrand immediately filed suit, alleging Berk had breached his fiduciary duty. The trial court held for the plaintiff, and Berk appealed.

OPINION O'CONNOR, J.... The principal issue before us is whether defendant breached his fiduciary duty of loyalty to the Comedy Cottage. Defendant asserts that he did not breach his fiduciary duty because (1) he resigned his position with the corporation before entering into competition; and (2) any corporate opportunity regarding a lease of the premises was terminated by the owner.... In determining whether an officer may take advantage of a business opportunity in which a corporation is interested, courts consider whether the corporation had an interest... in the opportunity and whether the acquisition thereof by the officer would hinder or defeat plans and purposes of the corporation....

The acquisition of a lease of the premises by Berk hindered the plaintiff's corporate plans to utilize the goodwill... built up during its many years of operation at the same location. Thus, Berk had a duty to refrain from acquiring the lease at the expense of the corporation.

...[T]he resignation of an officer will not sever liability for transactions completed after the termination of the party's association with the corporation if the transactions began during the existence of the relationship or were founded on information acquired during the relationship.

...In particular, Berk was still general manager when he received notice of termination of the corporation's lease. Berk then used the knowledge gained as a result of his position with the corporation as an opportunity to resign and obtain a lease for himself without competition or disclosure. Even assuming *arguendo* the defendant did not begin

CASE 41.4 Continued

competing for the lease until after his resignation, defendant remained bound by his fiduciary duty because his acquisition of the lease was based upon knowledge acquired during his employment....

In addition, Berk contends that because the corporation sought to obtain the lease without success, he could acquire the lease even though the corporation was more or less interested in it.... [However,] the corporation remained interested in the property acquired by its former officer, and no evidence indicated that he acquired the lease for a price higher than the corporation was willing to pay.

Defendant claims that any opportunity for the corporation to obtain a renewal of the lease was eliminated when the owner of the premises terminated the prior month-to-month lease and announced that he would no longer deal with Hellenbrand.... It appears from the record... that the personality conflict between Hellenbrand and the owner arose, in part, because Berk failed to clarify his actions to his employer or the owner of the premises.... [H]e did little or nothing to rectify the situation despite his special responsibilities in this matter.

JUDGMENT ...For the reasons stated above, we affirm the judgment....

Statutory Obligations. Statutes direct that all dividends or distributions to shareholders must be paid out of corporate earnings and not out of corporate capital. In addition, the Revised Model Act (Secs. 6.40 and 8.33) and state statutes prohibit distributions or dividends to shareholders if, as a result, the corporation would not be able to pay its debts as they became due. In the event directors declare dividends or distributions in violation of such statutory limitations, they, personally, and the corporation are liable for any illegal portion of the dividend or distribution that may have been made.

Directors are also subject to a number of statutory restraints which bear on their management functions. Those statutes are the subject of Chapter 43.

Protection against Takeover

Up to this point we have looked at the functions of directors as managers of the business activities of a corporation. There is another side of management that has become very important in recent years. This involves making decisions as to (1) the terms and conditions under which the corporation should accede to a friendly takeover by another entity, (2) what actions the corporation should take to frustrate an unwelcome takeover of the corporation, and (3) whether to provide some special financial protection to the corporation's principal officers in the event the company is taken over. Many of these decisions require reference to and approval by the shareholders at a special shareholders' meeting. A takeover means that an entity, by itself or with others, acquires control of a corporation by purchasing or otherwise controlling sufficient shares of its stock to take over its management.

Directors who believe that their corporation may be a takeover target may modify the corporation's financial structure in such a way as to ward off the takeover attempt. This restructuring has been given the name *poison pill.* The usual restructuring device is the issuance to its shareholders of a new class of preferred shares which must be repurchased from the shareholders by the corporation at a high price in the event the corporation is subjected to an unfriendly takeover. As a result, the cost of an unfriendly acquisition is increased to such a degree that the corporation is "poisoned" and its takeover becomes economically unattractive.

Instead of attempting to fight an unfriendly takeover, the directors may decide to seek a friendly sale of the corporation to another company on terms and conditions more agreeable to them than those offered by the unfriendly suitor. If a suitable purchaser can be found, the directors come into agreement with that company, whimsically called a *white knight,* and arrange for an amicable takeover.

There is yet another management ploy to defeat an unwelcome takeover by the holder of a block of the corporation's shares who is threatening to gain control. This is for the directors to authorize their corporation to purchase the shares held by the aggressor at a premium price in exchange for the aggressor's agreement not to continue with his or her takeover attempt. This, appropriately enough, is called *greenmail.*

The top-echelon officers of large corporations hold very lucrative positions. If a company is taken over by another corporation, there is a good possibility that there will be a change in personnel at that top level. To protect a key executive against that eventuality, a board of directors may give the executive a contract called a *golden parachute,* which provides special benefits if the corporation is taken over and the executive is either forced out or voluntarily leaves the corporation. It is common for the extra benefits to be in the form of a sizeable severance fee, usually two or three times the individual's annual salary.

Directors may be personally liable to the corporation and to its shareholders if they authorize the payment of greenmail or a golden parachute under such circumstances or in such an amount as not to be protected by the business judgment rule.

Unique Management Problems of Close Corporations

The nature of close corporations was discussed in Chapter 39. There it was observed that the management of a closely held corporation strongly resembles that of a partnership, and shareholders in a close corporation owe to their coshareholders fiduciary obligations similar to those of partners. If irreconcilable differences arise within a partnership as to how it will be operated, a partner, as a last resort, may cause its voluntary dissolution. But a minority shareholder cannot as readily secure the dissolution of a profitable close corporation, particularly in the absence of fraud by its majority shareholder or shareholders. Because of the difference in structure between publicly held corporations and close corporations, unique management problems may arise in close corporations. The principal differences in shareholder rights and management policies between publicly held corporations and closely held corporations are summarized in Table 41.2.

Management Problems of Close Corporations Analyzed

The management problems unique to close corporations can best be understood by examining the troubles of Hi-Tech, Inc., a hypothetical company.

Alejandro, Bob, and Carol formed Hi-Tech, Inc. They were its only shareholders, each holding an equal number of shares. The three were also the corporation's directors and officers. Each was employed by the corporation: Alejandro in production, Bob in sales, and Carol in accounting. Hi-Tech, Inc., was very successful. In 5 years each shareholder's equity had grown to $50,000, and the present problems had developed.

Voting Control Problem. Alejandro and Bob have consistently outvoted Carol on policy matters in directors' meetings. Alejandro, with Bob's concurrence, has given Alejandro's cousin, Horacio, a job as Carol's assistant. Carol maintains she needs no assistant. She is certain that Alejandro and Bob intend to ease her out of her job and to promote Horacio into the job of chief accountant. She has suggested long-term employment contracts for each shareholder, but the two men keep postponing that action. Carol is told by her attorney that a majority of shares elects the board, and that a majority of the board makes corporation policy. He says there is nothing he can do to assure her job security, as the facts do not reveal fraud or breach of fiduciary duty by the other directors.

Marketability-of-Shares Problem. Bob's wife holds a very lucrative position with another company. She believes she will be transferred to another city. Bob, in anticipation of the move, asks his banker and his stockbroker if they can sell his Hi-Tech shares. They tell him there is no ready market for them, that his best bet is to sell the shares to Hi-Tech, Inc., or to the other two shareholders. Bob lays his problem before Alejandro and Carol and asks them if they or the corporation would buy his shares if he has to move. They refuse to give definite answers.

Declaration-of-Dividend Problem. Alejandro is contemplating retirement and has been sure his

Table 41.2 Contrast between Shareholder Rights in Publicly Held Corporations and Shareholder Rights in Closely Held Corporations

	Publicly Held Corporations	Close Corporations
Transferability of shares	Most shares are freely transferable with little or no impact on the control of the corporation. No permission to effect transfer is required from the other shareholders.	The transfer may seriously disturb the balance of management control. To preserve such continuity, restrictions upon share transfer to outsiders are usually imposed by the bylaws or by agreement of the shareholders.
Marketability of shares	Shares can be readily sold on a securities exchange or in the over-the-counter market.	Because of the restrictions on share transferability, minority interests often cannot be sold except at a price far below their true going-concern value.
Shareholder control of corporation	Normally, a majority of the owners of outstanding shares elects the board of directors who, by majority vote, manage the corporation.	Shareholders normally are also the directors and officers. The majority shareholders may adopt policies which would work to the disadvantage of the minority.
Dividend policy	A majority of the board determines when to declare a dividend and the amount of any dividend. A decision not to declare a dividend will generally not be disturbed by the courts.	Majority shareholders may vote themselves disproportionately large salaries and not declare dividends. They may also attempt to freeze out a minority shareholder.

two co-owners would assist him in his retirement years by adopting a liberal dividend policy and a program for the firm's purchase of his shares over a period of time. Bob and Carol have ignored his proposal. They fear that if dividends are raised, they will be required to pay more personal income taxes, and they want to continue the directors' policy of using profits to encourage company growth. Bob does not agree to the corporation's buying Alejandro's shares. That arrangement would block Bob's plan to have the company buy his own shares. Alejandro is angry and threatens to sell his shares to Horacio.

Interruption-of-Continuity-of-Control Problem. Meanwhile, Alejandro and Bob have good reason to suspect that Carol has a serious health problem and they fear this might result in an interruption of control of the corporation's affairs. With increasing frequency, Carol has talked of making a gift of some of her shares in the company to relatives, and she says she has provided in her will for the remainder of her shares to go to her husband. Alejandro and Bob do not relish a business association with Carol's husband. They are also concerned about company shares falling into the hands of Carol's relatives who, they believe, would be neither cooperative nor competent businesspeople.

Freeze-out Problem. Carol's freeze-out problem worsens. She knows that if Alejandro sells his shares to Horacio, Bob and Horacio will then control the board of directors, and she fears that they will freeze her out of the company altogether. She expects that they will terminate her employment and then, knowing she might be in need of funds and that there is no ready market for her shares, will offer to buy her shares only at a price far less than they are worth.

The following case illustrates how a shareholder in a closely held corporation may be damaged when the other shareholders attempt a freeze-out.

CASE 41.5 Wilkes v. Springside Nursing Home · 353 N.E.2d 657 (Mass. 1976)

FACTS Wilkes, Quinn, Connor, and Riche were the sole shareholders, directors, and officers in the Springside Nursing Home, Inc. Each actively participated in the management of the corporation and received weekly salaries.

Friction developed between Quinn and Wilkes. At a directors' meeting, new weekly salaries for Quinn, Riche, and Connor were established, but no provision was made for a salary for Wilkes. A short time later, at the annual shareholders' meeting, Wilkes was not reelected a director or an officer of the corporation. He was then told by the other three that his services and his presence were no longer desired at the nursing home.

Wilkes brought suit for damages in the amount of the salary he would have received had he continued as an officer and director of the corporation. A judgment was entered dismissing Wilkes's action. He appealed, alleging that the majority shareholders had frozen him out, thereby breaching their fiduciary duty to him as a minority shareholder.

OPINION HENNESSEY, C. J. . . . Wilkes's claim for damages [is] based on a breach of the fiduciary duty owed to him. . . . In light of the theory underlying this claim, we do not consider it vital to our approach to this case whether the claim is governed by partnership law or the law applicable to business corporations. This is so as, all the parties agree, Springside was at all times . . . a close corporation. . . . In *Donahue v. Rodd Electrotype Co. of New England, Inc.*, 328 N.E.2d 505 (Mass. 1975), we held that "stockholders in the close corporation owe one another substantially the same fiduciary duty in the operation of the enterprise that partners owe to one another." [They must exercise] utmost good faith and loyalty. . . . "They may not act out of avarice, expediency or self interest in derogation of their duty of loyalty to the other stockholders and to the corporation." In the *Donahue* case, we recognized that one peculiar aspect of close corporations was the opportunity afforded to majority stockholders to oppress, disadvantage, or "freeze out" minority stockholders. In *Donahue* itself . . . the net result . . . was that the minority could be forced to "sell out at less than fair value," . . . since there is by definition no ready market for minority stock in a close corporation.

"Freeze outs," however, may be accomplished by the use of other devices. One such device which has proved to be particularly effective in accomplishing the purpose of the majority is to deprive minority stockholders of corporate offices and of employment with the corporation. . . .

The denial of employment to the minority at the hands of the majority is especially pernicious in some instances. A guarantee of employment with the corporation may have been one of the "basic reasons why a minority owner has invested capital in the firm. . . ." The minority stockholder typically depends on his salary as the principal return on his investment, since the "earnings of a close corporation . . . are distributed in major part in salaries, bonuses and retirement benefits." . . . In sum, by terminating a minority stockholder's employment or by severing him from a position as an officer or director, the

CASE 41.5 Continued

majority effectively frustrate the minority stockholder's purposes in entering on the corporate venture and also deny him an equal return on his investment.

...[I]t must be asked whether the controlling group can demonstrate a legitimate business purpose for its action....

...[I]t is apparent that the majority in Springside have not shown a legitimate business purpose for severing Wilkes from the payroll...or for refusing to reelect him as a salaried officer and director....There was no showing of misconduct on Wilkes's part as a director, officer, or employee of the corporation which would lead us to approve the majority action as a legitimate response to the disruptive nature of an undesirable individual bent on injuring or destroying the corporation. On the contrary, it appears that Wilkes had always accomplished his assigned share of the duties competently, and that he had never indicated an unwillingness to continue to do so.

It is an inescapable conclusion...that the action of the majority stockholders here was a designed "freeze out" for which no legitimate business purpose has been suggested. Furthermore, we may infer that a design to pressure Wilkes into selling his shares to the corporation at a price below their value may well have been at the heart of the majority's plan.

JUDGMENT ...So much of the judgment as dismisses Wilkes's complaint...is reversed.

Some Solutions to Close-Corporation Problems

The major concerns of close corporation owners, illustrated in the hypothetical case history of Alejandro, Bob, and Carol and in the *Wilkes* case reveal that all close corporation shareholders have conflicting but related goals. On the one hand, they want their shares to be readily marketable at a fair price, and on the other, they do not want the harmony and continuity of control of the corporation to be disturbed by other shareholders transferring their shares to outsiders. Several devices are used to reconcile these objectives.

First Refusal Agreements. In Chapter 40 we discussed restrictions on transfer of shares of stock. A first refusal agreement gives the corporation (and then the other inside shareholders) the right to purchase shares of a withdrawing shareholder at the same price and on the same terms as those offered to the sellers by a legitimate outside purchaser of those shares. Such an agreement preserves continuity of control among the insiders, but for one or more of the following reasons it may not furnish the expected solution.

- The selling shareholder would most likely get only a very low price offer from an outsider. The outsider would not be willing to pay much for a minority interest in a closely held corporation whose majority shareholders might effectively engage in freeze-out tactics. Therefore, the low matching price the corporation could rightfully offer would probably be unsatisfactory to the selling shareholder.
- As noted in Chapter 40, most states do not permit a corporation to repurchase its shares from any funds other than retained earnings. Therefore, if a corporation has insufficient retained earnings, it is not able to buy the shares.
- If the corporation cannot purchase the shares, there is no assurance that the inside shareholders who have the opportunity to do so will have the money to make the purchase or will want to add to their shares if they already have effective control of the corporation.

Thus, a first refusal agreement may be effective in assuring continuity of control, but it does not assure a would-be seller a market for his or her shares.

Offer to Sell and Obligation to Purchase. This solution resembles the one just discussed except that an obligation is placed upon the corporation or continuing shareholders to purchase the leaving shareholder's shares. As illustrated in Case 40.4 in the previous chapter, the price is usually established annually according to a formula agreed to by the shareholders rather than by an offer by some outsider. As the shareholders' obligation to buy may present difficulties for them because they would have to raise the necessary funds to do so, the purchase formula normally establishes a reduced price for the shares, such as their book value, without allowance for goodwill. It follows that if there is such an agreement, a shareholder who desires to sell his or her shares has the benefit of having a ready purchaser at a reasonable price. The corporation and the continuing shareholders, for their parts, are assured that the shares will not fall into the hands of outside individuals and that the shares will cost a reasonable amount.

Transfer of Shares upon Death. With the agreement that upon withdrawal of a shareholder from the corporation the remaining shareholders will buy his or her shares, often comes the provision for the same arrangement when one of the parties dies. Because the shareholders do not know which one of them will die first, each one is willing to accept an arrangement which obligates the survivors to pay a price per share closely approximating its market value. Therefore, the pricing formula generally includes the value of the firm's goodwill.

A surviving spouse or an heir may elect not to sell to the remaining shareholders the shares he or she has inherited, preferring to receive dividends on those shares and possibly to benefit from an anticipated increase in their value. To obviate such a situation, some agreements impose an obligation upon the estate of a deceased shareholder to sell the shares to the corporation or to the surviving shareholders with the correlative obligation upon the corporation or the surviving shareholders to buy them.

Countering Freeze-out Tactics

It is possible that the majority members of a board of directors may take advantage of their position and attempt to freeze out minority shareholders. They can do this by adopting corporation policies which are more agreeable to themselves than to the minority; for example, they may have the corporation employ themselves at high salaries while refusing similar employment to other shareholders. Or they may institute a policy to retain earnings in the corporation rather than to pay dividends, and they may lease or sell to the corporation their own property at high prices but still not at levels which could be characterized as fraudulent.

The ability of a majority of a company's board of directors to adopt such tactics can be circumscribed by the insertion in the articles of incorporation or bylaws, or in a shareholders' agreement, of technical provisions which limit the authority of a majority of the members of a board of directors. If such provisions fail to have the desired effect, the ultimate recourse is (1) to dissolve the corporation if it is so provided for in the firm's articles, (2) to seek a judicial dissolution of the corporation (dissolution is discussed in Chapter 42), (3) to seek, in the states which so allow, the appointment of an additional director to resolve the deadlock, (4) to resort to arbitration if that procedure is authorized in the corporation's articles or bylaws, or in a shareholder agreement, or (5) to agree that one group of shareholders will buy out the other.

Summary

The management of a corporation is dependent upon its powers (its authority to act). The corporation's express powers are derived from the statutes of the state where it is incorporated and its articles of incorporation. In addition, a corporation has implied powers to do all things reasonably necessary to carry out its express powers.

A corporation and its officers may be liable in damages for acts which exceed its corporate powers. Such acts are called *ultra vires.* A corporation is also liable as employers, under agency law, for the wrongful acts of the corporation's employees in the scope of their employment or authority. Similarly, vicarious liability may be imposed upon a corporation for crimes committed by its high managerial agents in the course of authorized corporate business.

Corporate affairs and policies are controlled by a board of directors. In publicly held corporations, the boards of directors consist of some individuals who have no other connection with the corporation (outside directors) and some who are primary officers within the corporation (inside directors). In closely held corporations, the directors are also shareholders and usually officers of the corporation. In both kinds of corporations, the directors are elected by the shareholders. The number of directors is fixed in the articles of incorporation. A board of directors acts by formal resolution adopted by a majority voting at a regular or special meeting at which a quorum is present, or by unanimous written consent without a meeting. The board may also act in special areas through committees composed of board members. The board of directors establishes the policies under which the corporation will be operated by its officers whom the board elects.

Directors must act with due care, exercising good business judgment in accord with the *business judgment rule,* after becoming reasonably acquainted with all the facts involved in the particular matter. A director also owes the corporation the fiduciary duty of loyalty. This restricts a director from entertaining a conflict of interest with the corporation. A conflict of interest may involve doing business with the corporation, competing with it, or seizing an economic opportunity which rightfully belongs to the corporation. A director *may,* however, contract with the corporation if the contract is fair and reasonable or if the conflict of interest is known to the disinterested directors or to the shareholders and either body approves the transaction.

A close corporation has few members, and its directors and officers are also shareholders. Because of this joinder of management and ownership, a close corporation very much resembles a partnership, and thus management problems not found in publicly held corporations may result. Those problems usually center around conflict in voting control, lack of marketability of shares, and the interruption of continuity in control of the business. In addition, a shareholder who is employed by the corporation is in danger of being frozen out of his or her job, of losing a voice in control, and ultimately of being forced to sell his or her shares at an unreasonably low price. Several devices, centering around prior agreements of the parties, are employed to counter these negative aspects of a close corporation.

Review Questions

1 **(a)** What are the sources of a corporation's powers? **(b)** May there be any limitation upon those powers?

2 Distinguish between a corporation's express powers and its implied powers.

3 What is meant by *ultra vires* with respect to a corporation's actions?

4 Can a corporation be liable for a tort or crime? Explain.

5 Distinguish between the shareholders, directors, and officers of a corporation.

6 **(a)** How does an individual become a corporation director? **(b)** How does she or he become a corporation officer? **(c)** What is the function of a committee of a board of directors? **(d)** Who serves on such a committee?

7 Are either directors or officers agents of the corporations they serve? Explain.

8 Distinguish between the authority of a director and that of an officer of a corporation.

9 Who fixes the salaries of corporation officers? of corporation directors?

10 **(a)** What is necessary for a board of directors to take an official action on behalf of its corporation? **(b)** Director X, sick in the hospital, gives his proxy to another member of the board to vote for him at a directors' meeting. What effect does this have on the actions the board takes at the meeting?

11 **(a)** What is the standard of care that must be exercised by a director in the performance of her duties? **(b)** of an officer of a corporation? **(c)** What is the business judgment rule? **(d)** Why, in your opinion, is there such a rule in corporation law?

12 **(a)** What is meant by the duty of loyalty? **(b)** In what way does a director or an officer owe a duty of loyalty to the corporation with which he or she is connected? **(c)** Does this duty exist in publicly held corporations as well as in closely held corporations? Explain.

13 **(a)** What is meant by interlocking directorates? **(b)** What is the doctrine of corporate opportunity? **(c)** Give an example of the application of that doctrine.

14 **(a)** What is the management function of a board of directors in the event some individual or entity attempts to buy out or take over a corporation? **(b)** What is meant by a poison pill, greenmail, a white knight, and a golden parachute in corporation parlance?

15 **(a)** Why is it that a closely held corporation may have management problems not present in a publicly held corporation? **(b)** Discuss at least four such areas of potential problems.

16 Recalling the discussion in Chapters 1 and 2 of the application of ethical principles to business law, discuss a director's obligation to the shareholders of his or her corporation, to the business community, and to the public at large.

Case Problems

1 The Howard Young Medical Center was a not-for-profit corporation. The board of directors, acting under their authority to amend the bylaws, radically changed the voting qualifications both for board membership and for the period during which the incumbent board could remain in office. The plaintiffs, representing a class of members, brought suit to set aside those amendments to the bylaws, alleging that its purpose was to entrench the present directors and their chosen successors in power. Can shareholders interfere with the directors' functions in this manner? Why or why not?

2 The bylaws of American Insurance, Inc., provided for a board of eight directors and a quorum of at least five directors. A contract with Management Corp. was reviewed and approved by a unanimous vote of six directors, the total number present at a meeting of American's board. Three of the directors who voted were also on the board of Management; two of the three were the president and secretary, respectively, of both corporations. Upon further review, American found the contract to be against its best interests and served notice of termination on Management. Management sued American for breach of contract and $180,000 in damages. American claimed that the contract was voidable because it had not been authorized by a quorum of disinterested directors. Is Management entitled to recover from American?

3 Ed Ash and his wife, Fay, owned 74 percent of Lumber Corporation's stock. The corporation borrowed $240,000 in exchange for demand notes payable to Ed, who was board chairman and president of the corporation. Ed was very wealthy and never required substantial payments on the notes, but when Fay filed for divorce, Ed stated: "I'll run the corporation into the ground as long as Fay has an interest in it." That year, Ed enforced payment of $140,000 on the notes. He then used his influence to cause the corporation (which was left with a deficit of $120,000) to file a notice of election to dissolve. Fay filed a shareholder's derivative suit against Ed for breach of his fiduciary duty to the corporation and its shareholders. Is Fay entitled to judgment on behalf of the corporation?

4 Arn and Ball organized Supply, Inc., and served as its directors and officers. Arn was the sole stockholder and personally guaranteed a $20,000 loan made to the corporation. No capital was invested by Ball. The corporation wanted to buy a building but it did not have the required cash or credit, so Arn bought the building for its benefit. He obtained financing and "temporarily" took title in his own name. Ball knew that the corporation was making the monthly loan payment of $500 and entering it in the books as "rent." The payments were shown as income on Arn's tax return. He also took the depreciation and listed the building as a personal asset on his financial statements. After 2 years, the corporation went into receivership. The receiver sued Arn, alleging his building purchase to be a breach of his fiduciary duty to the corporation. Should the court order Arn to deed the property to the corporation subject to the existing mortgage?

5 Emory, Arnold, Rose, and Sam each hold an equal number of shares in a closely held family corporation. They constitute the directors and officers of the corporation and are employed by it. It had been the practice of the board to retain all earnings in the business rather than to distribute profits as dividends. Arnold resigned from his positions as an officer, director, and employee of the firm, but he retained his shares in the company. He impressed on the board of directors his need for an income and asked that the corporation begin to pay reasonable dividends. The directors declared very small dividends. Arnold contends that the dividends thereafter paid were not established by the directors in good faith but only to "get even" with him, and that thus the directors breached their fiduciary obligations. He alleged that the dividend scale represents a concerted effort by the directors to deprive him of his right to a fair proportion of the profits of the business. Based on these facts, should Arnold expect to recover?

CHAPTER 42

Shareholders' Powers, Rights, and Liabilities

Although the preceding three chapters have focused on the nature and development of corporations, their financial structure, and the function of directors and officers, there has been an underlying theme: The role of the investing shareholders is of central importance in a corporation for profit. Shareholders are the ultimate owners of a corporation, but if shares are publicly held, the shareholders have only limited power to control the management of the corporation. In closely held corporations, the shareholders are also directors and officers and by virtue of those offices are active in daily management. People become shareholders in publicly held corporations because of the prospect of a return on investment and the assurance that if they need to liquidate their investment, there is a ready securities market for their shares—one hopes at a profit.

As we discussed in the previous chapter, directors and officers manage corporations daily without consulting shareholders. State and federal laws, however, do require approval by shareholders of various extraordinary proposals. Such proposals typically are of major importance to the corporation, such as electing and removing directors, amending the articles of incorporation, or approving a merger. This chapter will review how shareholders function in a corporation, and will discuss their rights, powers, and liabilities.

Powers of Shareholders

Election and Removal of Directors

Shareholders meet annually and elect directors by a majority of the shares voted. The directors hold office until the next such meeting or until their successors are elected and qualified. If the directors serve staggered terms, the shareholders vote on the directorships that are vacated as of each annual meeting. For example, if there is a nine-person board, with three directors elected each year for a 3-year term, at each annual meeting there would be three vacancies which the shareholders would fill by election.

Shareholders have the power to remove any or all of the directors (Revised Model Act, Sec. 8.08). In most states, the holders of a majority of the voting stock may remove a director at any time and need not show a reason for doing so. Thus, in a closely held corporation one or two persons may effectively control the directors and thus have *indirect* influence on corporate policy. In publicly held corporations, one or two persons may accomplish the same result by acquiring sufficient proxies from other shareholders to constitute a majority.

If a majority of shareholders do not desire removal of a director, many states provide an alternative for minority shareholders (see Revised Model Act, Sec. 8.09). The shareholders have the power to remove a director "for cause"—such as dishonesty or gross abuse of discretion. The statutes require the holders of a specified percentage of outstanding shares to vote for the director's removal. The holders of 10 percent of the shares of a New York or California corporation may petition the court to remove a director for cause if the required majority of shareholders are unwilling to act.

Amendment of Articles

Articles of incorporation and state statutes establish how those articles may be amended (see also Revised Model Act, Sec. 10.01 *et seq.*). A few examples of reasons to amend them are (1) to change the name of the corporation, (2) to change the number or par value of authorized shares, (3) to change the relative rights and preferences of issued or unissued shares, (4) to create new classes of shares, and (5) to deny or grant shareholders the right to acquire additional shares.

Shareholders must approve amendments to the articles, but ordinarily they do not initiate an amendment. Typically, a board of directors recommends to shareholders all proposals to amend the articles of incorporation. The board itself has limited power to adopt an amendment. In most states, a majority of the holders of the corporation's voting stock must approve an amendment to its articles. In addition, if an amendment will adversely affect a particular class of outstanding shares, a majority of that class also must approve the amendment.

Acquisitions by Merger or Consolidation

In the 1980s, the number of mergers and consolidations of major American corporations increased dramatically. Such amalgamations were encouraged by the structure of the U.S. income tax laws and by major financial considerations. During this period, the antitrust laws were interpreted by courts and federal regulatory agencies in such a manner that few mergers were prohibited. The laws concerning the mechanics of mergers and consolidations are complex and vary greatly from state to state. We will present here only a few common provisions.

A *merger* occurs when an existing, usually a large, corporation acquires all the assets and assumes all the liabilities of another, smaller corporation which then ceases to exist. The *surviving* corporation usually exchanges its securities or cash for the outstanding shares of the *disappearing* corporation, whose shareholders in turn receive cash or shares of the survivor. For example, in 1987 Chrysler Corporation by merger acquired the American Motors Corporation. If you had owned shares of American Motors stock, you would now own shares of Chrysler Corporation.

A *consolidation* occurs when a new corporation is created for the express purpose of consolidating the assets and liabilities of two or more constituent corporations which then cease to exist. Their outstanding shares are usually exchanged for securities issued by the consolidated corporation. For example, X Corp. and Y Corp. exchange their stock for stock in Z Corp.

Both mergers and consolidations require shareholder approval. In many states, such as California, a majority of shareholders of each class of stock of both corporations must approve the amalgamation. Approval is difficult when giant corporations, such as General Electric and RCA, seek to merge, because their shareholders number in the millions.

Sale of All Assets of a Corporation

Under the statutes of most states a proposal by the directors to sell, lease, or exchange all, or substantially all, of the corporation's assets must be approved by a majority of the voting shares. The directors have the power to sell, lease, or exchange corporate assets in the ordinary course of business. But, when the corporation owns only one major asset, the directors may no longer act alone. For example, suppose that the Bates Corporation's only asset is a hotel and that Hilton, Inc., agrees to buy it. The sale is not in the ordinary course of business, and it must be approved by the shareholders of Bates.

Typically, in a "sale of assets" transaction the purchaser does not assume any of the liabilities of the selling corporation. For this reason, a major corporation might choose not to acquire a small corporation by merger or consolidation; instead it might choose to purchase its prime asset with cash or stock. Another advantage of avoiding merger or consolidation is that no approval is required by the shareholders of the acquiring corporation. Following a sale of all its assets, the selling corporation may dissolve and distribute to its shareholders its cash or stock received from the purchasing corporation. In the alternative, the selling corporation could use its cash or stock to reactivate and begin a new business.

Appraisal Rights of Dissenting Shareholders

If a shareholder objects to a merger, a consolidation, or an extraordinary sale of assets and is outvoted by the majority, he or she can sell the stock on the open market. If there is no market because the corporation is closely held, the stockholder can accept his or her share in stock in the acquiring or surviving corporation when there is a merger or consolidation. When the majority votes to sell all the assets of a closely held corporation, a minority shareholder has no opportunity to sell or exchange his or her stock. However, most states today provide a remedy for the objecting shareholder, called *appraisal rights.* The Revised Model Business Corporation Act [Sec. 13.02(a) (4)] also extends appraisal rights to shareholders adversely affected by amendments to the articles of incorporation.

In the exercise of appraisal rights a dissatisfied shareholder who objects to a proposed merger, a consolidation, or an extraordinary disposition of corporate assets has a right to demand in writing that his or her shares be appraised and purchased by the corporation at a fair value. The corporation responds by making a written offer to purchase the shares. If the offered price is unacceptable to the shareholder, the corporation or dissenting shareholder may file suit for a judicial appraisal of the value of the shares. The court then appoints an appraiser who determines the fair value of the shares. The valuation approved by the court is binding upon the parties.

Corporate Dissolution

A corporation may dissolve (sell its assets, pay its debts, and terminate business) either (1) voluntarily, or (2) pursuant to court order. In most states, a majority of a corporation's voting shares has the power to voluntarily dissolve the corporation at any time. Thus, a majority of shareholders may choose to dissolve a corporation that is profitable and paying dividends.

An involuntary dissolution is more difficult to achieve. A shareholder must petition a court and set out facts which would justify a judicial dissolution. The Revised Model Act, Section 14.30(2), sets forth several grounds, also found in typical state statutes, which would justify a court dissolving a corporation upon a shareholder's petition:

- The directors are deadlocked in the management of corporate affairs, and irreparable injury to the corporation is threatened or corporate business can no longer be conducted to the advantage of shareholders.
- Those in control of the corporation have acted in a manner that is illegal, oppressive, or fraudulent.
- Corporate assets are being misapplied or wasted.

As a general rule, if the court grants a petition for involuntary dissolution, it will appoint a receiver to take over the management of a corporation. The receiver will proceed to sell all the assets of the corporation, pay its creditors, and distribute any remaining funds to shareholders.

The following case discusses the grounds for involuntary dissolution of a corporation.

CASE 42.1 Matter of Villa Maria, Inc · 312 N.W.2d 921 (Minn. 1981)

FACTS John Mondati and James Sheehan formed Villa Maria, Inc., to construct and operate a nursing home. Each owned 50 percent of the outstanding stock. The board of directors consisted of Mondati and his lawyer and Sheehan and his brother. The two Sheehan brothers secured, and personally guaranteed, a $650,000 loan for construction of the home. Mondati secretly caused a corporation that he owned to purchase land next to the home and then, as president, arranged for Villa Maria to lease the property as a parking lot. Mondati refused to call special board meetings when the Sheehans requested them, and refused to attend meetings when the Sheehans called them, thus preventing action because of lack of a quorum. Mondati received offers to purchase the home but never communicated them to the Sheehans, nor did he ever furnish them with a financial statement of the corporation. Although requested to declare dividends, Mondati refused to do so. A shareholder agreement between Mondati and Sheehan provided that if either shareholder wished to sell his stock, the other had the right to buy the shares at book value.

Sheehan brought suit in equity for a statutory dissolution. The trial court ordered dissolution and liquidation of the corporation's assets or, alternatively, gave Mondati the option to buy Sheehan's shares at appraised fair market value—not book value as provided in the shareholder agreement. Mondati appealed.

OPINION OTIS, J. . . . The power of the courts to grant an involuntary dissolution of a corporation is governed by Minn. Stat. § 301.49 (1980), which states in part:

> A corporation may be dissolved by involuntary proceedings in the discretion of the court when it is made to appear: . . .
>
> (3) that the directors or those in control of the corporation have been guilty of fraud or mismanagement, or of abuse of authority, or of persistent unfairness toward minority shareholders; or
>
> (4) that there is internal dissension and that two or more factions of the shareholders in the corporation are so deadlocked that its business cannot longer be conducted with advantage to its shareholders; . . .

CASE 42.1 Continued

The law is clear that "one entrusted with the active management of a corporation, such as an officer or director, occupies a fiduciary relationship to the corporation and may not exploit his position as an 'insider' by appropriating to himself a business opportunity properly belonging to the corporation."... By purchasing the land and then arranging for the terms of the lease between two companies in which he had an interest, Mondati breached his fiduciary obligation....

We cannot escape the conclusion that Mondati used his position as president to run Villa Maria as he pleased and that in doing so he acted unfairly toward the Sheehans. The Sheehans personally guaranteed the loans which made it possible to build Villa Maria. They have seen no return on an investment they made in 1965 and have never received financial statements indicating the corporation's status. There have been no meetings, no consultations, and Mondati has refused to consider issuing dividends. The district court has the equitable power to adjudge the dissolution of a domestic corporation where there is prejudicial mismanagement by those in control....

The court was fully justified in ordering dissolution and therefore appellant's [Mondati's] rights were no longer governed by contract but were limited to the liquidation assets available under the statute.... Mondati's high-handed manner in running Villa Maria as though it were his own business and his failure to consider the interests of the other shareholder justifies Sheehan's avoiding the agreement.

JUDGMENT Affirmed.

Shareholders' Meetings

Annual and Special Meetings

State statutes provide for two types of shareholder meetings: annual and special. A corporation's bylaws fix a time for the *annual shareholders' meeting,* the primary purpose of which is to elect the board of directors or to fill a vacancy in the membership of the board, and to review corporation operations of the previous year. Annual meetings tend to be routine and boring. Only occasionally will a meeting become lively by a shareholder questioning management's expenditure of funds or offering a resolution concerning the effect of the corporation's business on current social or political issues. If a place is not designated in the bylaws, meetings are held at the corporation's principal place of business. Any shareholder may seek a court order to compel the holding of an annual meeting if none is called by the board of directors after the lapse of a period of time stated in the articles, bylaws, or statute—e.g., 13 months after the last annual meeting or, if the Revised Model Act, Section 7.03(a)(1), is applied, the earlier of 6 months after the end of the corporation's fiscal year or 15 months after its last annual meeting.

As a general rule, a *special shareholders' meeting* may be called by holders of 10 percent or more of the shares entitled to vote, or by the president of the corporation. Special meetings are called infrequently, usually to consider matters that require action before the next annual meeting, e.g., to consider a merger, to remove a director, or to change company auditors.

Notice of Meetings; Waiver of Notice

Most states require that the shareholders who are eligible to vote at an annual or a special meeting must receive timely written notice of the place, day, and hour of the meeting and of the proposals which the shareholders are to consider. *Timely notice* usually means at least 10 days prior to the date of the meeting. At an annual meeting, shareholders may consider matters outside the scope of proposals stated in the notice. However, a different rule exists with regard to special meetings. Any action on a proposal not listed in the notice of a special meeting is void. Thus, for example, if a special meeting is called to approve a new stock option plan for key officers, there may not be presented to the shareholders for their approval or disapproval a resolution increasing the number of members of the corporation's board of directors.

Many states and the Revised Model Act, Section 7.04, permit shareholders to take corporate action under certain circumstances without strict compliance with all the procedural requirements of a formal meeting:

- Lack of notice or defective notice may be waived if (1) all the shareholders attend the meetings in person or by proxy, and no one objects; or (2) not all shareholders attend the meeting but the absent shareholders, before or after the meeting, sign a written waiver of notice.
- Shareholders may take action *without a meeting* if all shareholders entitled to vote on the action sign written consents which are filed with the corporate minutes or records.

Obviously, these methods of informal action are not suited to publicly held corporations. They are especially useful to closely held corporations with few shareholders.

Proxy Voting

A shareholder may vote his or her shares in person or appoint another to do so. The appointee and the authorization which the shareholder signs are both referred to as a *proxy*. Most statutes require a proxy to be in writing, and, unless the proxy declares otherwise, its duration is limited to 11 months. Proxies can be limited to a particular transaction, but most proxies authorize the appointee to vote on all matters submitted to the shareholders. Most publicly held corporations send a proxy form with the notice of annual or special meeting and ask the shareholder to mark "yes" or "no" in regard to specific issues and to return the completed proxy before the announced date of the meeting. Solicitation of proxies by contending groups often is expensive and involves professional consultants skilled in the strategies of vote accumulation.

Since a proxy is fundamentally an agency relationship for the purpose of casting a vote, proxies are governed by agency law rules. Unless a proxy is "coupled with an interest," it is revocable at any time. Revocation occurs if the shareholder (1) dies, (2) attends a shareholders' meeting in person and votes the shares, or (3) signs a later proxy for the same shares. The rule that the last proxy signed is the one that is counted is important in the strategy of proxy fights for control of a corporation. A proxy is *coupled with an interest* if, for example, a shareholder pledges his or her shares as security for a loan and, in conjunction with the loan, gives a proxy to the lender. The proxy is coupled with an interest because it is part of the lender's property interest in the shares, and, as long as the loan is unsatisfied, it cannot be withdrawn by the borrower without the lender's consent.

Quorum and Voting Requirements

A quorum is the minimum number required to conduct a meeting. Most states provide that a majority of the outstanding shares constitutes a quorum in the absence of some other figure specified in a corporation's articles or bylaws. A quorum may be achieved by shareholders attending the meeting in person or by proxy. In many major corporations it would be impossible to achieve a quorum without proxies because so few shareholders attend meetings in person.

Once a quorum is present, proposals may be approved by a simple majority of the voting shares present. Of course, the articles or bylaws may specify that certain actions (e.g., a corporate purchase of real estate) require the approval of more than a simple majority of voting shares. In addition, many statutes require that certain actions—e.g., mergers and amending the articles—must be approved by a majority of *outstanding* voting stock.

Voting Eligibility

Only holders of voting shares as of the record date fixed by the bylaws or by the board of directors have the right to vote at shareholders' meetings. In most states the corporation can establish a record date any time between 10 and 70 days prior to the meeting. The record date serves the dual purpose of determining those to whom the corporation will mail a notice of the meetings and those who are eligible to vote at the meeting. If you buy stock *after* the record date, you cannot vote unless you get a proxy from the seller.

Election of Directors; Cumulative Voting

An annual meeting of shareholders is held to elect the corporation's directors who generally serve 1-year terms. Voting may be either *straight* or *cumulative*. Most corporations adopt a straight voting system whereby the holder of each share is entitled to one vote in filling each vacancy on the board. Thus, if you hold 100 shares of Ajax stock and there are several nominees for two director openings, you may cast your 100 votes for each of the two nominees you desire to serve on the board. Normally, a simple majority of the shares voting at a meeting at which a quorum is present can elect all the directors.

Under the *cumulative voting* system, shares may be bunched together and the total votes can be cast for a single director. For instance, assume that there are 100 voting shares at the meeting and that two slates of five directors each are nominated for five directorships. Assume further that the holders of 70 shares want one slate and the holders of 30 shares want the other slate. Under cumulative voting, each shareholder may cast his five votes (five directors × one vote per share) in any manner he wants, such as one vote for each of five nominees, or a shareholder may cast all five of her votes for a single nominee, or any other desired division of his or her votes. If straight voting is used the 70-share majority will elect its entire slate of directors. But if cumulative voting is used and the majority spreads its 350 votes (70 shareholders × 5 votes each) evenly over its slate of five directors, each nominee receives 70 votes. The minority shareholders can "single shot" their slate and cast their 150 votes (30 shareholders × 5 votes each) cumulatively for just one of their nominees or they may divide their cumulative vote among two of their nominees, giving each 75 votes. In this way the minority is assured of at least some representation on the board of directors.

Often, "special interest" groups attempt to buy or secure proxies for sufficient shares to elect a representative to the board of large, publicly held corporations. Sometimes several such groups are contending for votes and the strategies become extremely complex.

Corporations that are subject to cumulative voting often diminish its effectiveness by permitting directors to be elected for longer, staggered terms. Suppose, in the above illustration, the articles are amended to provide for 3-year staggered terms, two directors to be elected in the first and second years, and one director in the third year. In the years two directors are to be elected, if the minority cumulates its votes, it has sixty votes (2 × 30). The majority has 140 votes (2 × 70). Even if the minority casts all its votes for one candidate, the majority is able to cast 70 votes for each of two candidates and defeat the minority. With staggered terms the minority is frozen out and could never gain representation on the board.

Shareholders' Rights

Shareholders have several rights given to them in state statutes. In the preceding section we discussed the most important right of a shareholder: the right to vote. We now discuss two other rights that may be of great benefit to shareholders.

Preemptive Rights

Preemptive rights mean that shareholders have a right to preserve their proportionate stock interests by purchasing shares of a new issue ahead of others. The use of preemptive rights is designed to prevent the dilution of the existing shareholders' equity in a corporation when additional shares are issued. For example, suppose you own 15 percent of the XT Corporation and the board decides to issue 10,000 new shares to Dodd. Your 15 percent will be diluted and you will have a smaller percent of the total outstanding shares, say, 5 percent or 10 percent. A *preemptive right* means that you have first option to buy up to your percentage of the new issue (15 percent). If you decide not to, then Dodd can buy the shares.

All states, except New Hampshire, recognize preemptive rights, but most states permit the articles to limit or deny such rights. In some states, including California, Delaware, New Jersey, Michigan, Massachusetts, and Pennsylvania, preemptive rights are recognized only if they are established in the articles. There are several exceptional situations where courts will not apply preemptive rights, the most important being the reissue of treasury stock.

The size of a corporation often determines whether its charter should authorize preemptive rights. Shareholders of closely held corporations may find that preemptive rights are crucial to voting control. On the other hand, most shareholders of publicly held corporations own only a very small proportion of outstanding shares and are, therefore, unconcerned about preemptive rights.

Large corporations sometimes protect their shareholders in a manner which is similar to preemptive rights by issuing to their shareholders options to buy its shares at a stated price. Sometimes such options are issued as a substitute for a dividend. The options may take the form of *stock rights* or *warrants.* The option under a stock right expires within a relatively short time if it is not exercised. A warrant is a long-term option to buy a certain number of the corporation's shares at a stated price. Warrants are freely transferrable and are frequently traded. Their value depends upon the option price specified compared to the market price of the corporation's shares.

The following case discusses the rights of shareholders in a closely held corporation when treasury shares are reissued.

CASE 42.2 Schwartz v. Marien · 373 N.Y.S.2d 122 (N.Y. App. 1975)

FACTS Smith, Marien, and Dietrich each owned one-third (fifty shares) of the outstanding stock of Superior Engraving Co. When Smith died in 1959, the corporation purchased his shares as treasury stock. When Marien died in 1961, his shares passed to his wife and three sons. Thereafter, Dietrich, his daughter Margaret Schwartz, and two of Marien's sons constituted the four-member board. When Dietrich died in 1968, the Mariens called a special board meeting and the third Marien son was elected to fill the Dietrich vacancy. The three Marien directors then voted to have the corporation sell one share of treasury stock to each of them. The three treasury shares gave voting control of the corporation to the Marien family. Margaret Schwartz was denied the right to buy treasury shares to equalize Dietrich holdings.

Schwartz sued the Marien brothers for breach of their fiduciary duty as directors and controlling shareholders. Schwartz's motion for summary judgment was denied, and she appealed.

OPINION JONES, J..... While preemptive rights as such do not attach to treasury stock in the absence of specific provision in the certificate [articles] of incorporation, members of a corporate board of directors nevertheless owe a fiduciary responsibility to the shareholders in general and to individual shareholders in particular to *treat all shareholders fairly and evenly.* [Emphasis added.]

Departure from precisely uniform treatment of stockholders may be justified where a bona fide business purpose indicates that the best interests of the corporation would be served by such departure. The burden of coming forth with proof of such justification shifts to the directors, where, as here, a prima facie case of unequal stockholder treatment is made out. Particularly is this so, when it appears that the directors favored themselves individually over the complaining shareholder. Additionally, disturbance of equality of stock ownership in a corporation closely held for several years by the members of two families calls for special justification in the corporate interest; not only must it be shown that it was sought to achieve a bona fide independent business objective, but as well that such objective could not have been accomplished substantially or effectively by other means which would not have disturbed proportionate stock ownership.

JUDGMENT [The case was remanded to the trial court with instructions to proceed in accordance with the above opinion.]

Right to Examine Corporate Books

Shareholders, as ultimate owners of the corporation, have the right to inspect corporate records. However, since undue demands could be made on the corporation, limitations may be imposed on the exercise of the right. The records which shareholders most often wish to inspect are minutes of meetings, books of account, corporate contracts, correspondence, and lists of shareholders. As a general rule, shareholders may inspect these records, subject to two conditions: (1) the inspection must be at the corporation's home office during usual business hours, and (2) the inspection must be for a proper purpose. The latter requirement has caused considerable litigation. A proper purpose would include the right to inspect the records in order to determine the corporation's financial condition or the propriety of dividends, and to discover mismanagement. Some courts limit inspection rights by holding that a proper purpose must be related to the shareholder's economic interest in the corporation. In many states the rule is that if the shareholder alleges a proper purpose, the burden shifts to the corporation of proving the shareholder has an improper purpose. Thus, a denial of inspection rights will be upheld only if the corporation proves that the shareholder has an ulterior motive, such as to aid a competitor, to discover trade secrets, or simply to harass management.

Management often tries to deny a shareholder a list of names and addresses of all other shareholders in the corporation, citing as an excuse the expense of preparation. The real reason may be self-defense, i.e., to protect the position of incumbent directors and officers. Courts have upheld the right of a shareholder to secure a copy of a shareholder list even if the avowed purpose is to start a proxy fight. A proper purpose does not include developing a mailing list of well-to-do persons to sell to mail solicitation firms. Some statutes attempt to reduce capricious demands by limiting the right of inspection to shareholders who have owned their shares for 6 months or to holders of 5 percent of outstanding shares. However, Delaware gives shareholders the right of inspection regardless of the size or duration of their holdings.

An inspecting shareholder may bring with him or her an attorney, an accountant, or another agent. The shareholder is entitled to copies of documents for which the corporation may make a reasonable charge.

The following case illustrates a request for a shareholder list for the purpose of soliciting proxies.

CASE 42.3 Hatleigh Corp. v. Lane Bryant, Inc · 428 A.2d 350 (Del. Ch. 1981)

FACTS Hatleigh Corporation owned over 15 percent of the outstanding common stock of Lane Bryant, Inc. On November 5, 1980, Hatleigh requested Lane Bryant to provide a stockholder list because it wished to communicate with other stockholders to solicit proxies in connection with the next annual shareholders' meeting and to elect members to the board of directors. Lane Bryant refused the request, stating that (1) Hatleigh was seeking the shareholder list for a purpose other than soliciting proxies, and (2) the request was premature since the next annual shareholders' meeting was in May 1981.

Hatleigh filed this suit requesting a court order to require Lane Bryant to supply a list of shareholders.

OPINION HARTNETT, J.... 8 *Del.C.* Sec. 220 provides in part:

> (b) Any stockholder, in person or by attorney or other agent, shall, upon written demand under oath stating the purpose thereof, have the right... to inspect for any proper purpose the corporation's stock ledger [and] a list of its stockholders... and to make copies or extracts therefrom. A proper purpose shall mean a purpose reasonably related to such person's interest as a stockholder....

At... trial Hatleigh showed it sought stockholder proxies for use at the next annual stockholders meeting of Lane Bryant. Testimony was also adduced which showed that

CASE 42.3 Continued

on October 8, 1980, a final effort was made to compromise Hatleigh's differences with Lane Bryant but that it was a failure....

Lane Bryant...claims that the...demand for a stockholder list was invalid because it was premature. It was made on November 5, 1980, and the next annual meeting is not scheduled until May of 1981. The lack of imminence of a stockholders' meeting is, however, irrelevant to the issue of whether a stockholder has a right to inspect and copy a stockholder list if a proper purpose for the inspection exists....If a demand for the inspection of a stockholder list is made for the purpose of soliciting proxies and there is a bona fide intent to solicit proxies at the time of the demand, there is no reason why the demand must be made within a certain number of days of the next scheduled stockholders' meeting....

Having decided that Hatleigh is entitled to a reasonable inspection of the list of stockholders of Lane Bryant, a question arises as to the scope of the inspection. A number of shares of Lane Bryant are listed on the books of the corporation as being held by "CEDE & CO." This denotes a recognized central certificate depository system whereby various brokerage firms hold stock that is actually owned by their customers in the name of CEDE & CO. or in the name of other similar firms organized to hold shares of stock for others. Lane Bryant claims that it has no obligation to furnish Hatleigh with a breakdown of the CEDE & CO. listings to show the names of the various brokerage firms holding Lane Bryant stock for clients in that name....

This mechanism of convenience for the brokerage firms, however, prevents the stock ledger from revealing to one examining it just which brokerage firms hold shares and the number of shares held by each. This information, or "breakdown", of shares can be provided to the corporation at its request....[T]his can apparently be accomplished in a matter of minutes. When the breakdown is disclosed the identity of the brokerage firms holding stock under the name of "CEDE & CO.", can be learned and contact can then be made with them in order to ascertain the number of beneficial owners on whose behalf they hold stock in street name so that a proper amount of informational materials may then be forwarded to the brokerage firms for distribution to the beneficial owners. Plaintiff [Hatleigh] seeks this "breakdown" list as to CEDE in order that he too may get his proxy solicitation materials into the hands of the beneficial owners in ample time for the annual meeting....

I therefore find that Hatleigh is entitled to a breakdown of the CEDE & CO. listings and other similar listings generally recognized as indicating the shares of stock are being held for brokerage firms and similar financial institutions.

Hatleigh also seeks certain other materials relating to the stockholder list of Lane Bryant which are available to Lane Bryant such as magnetic computer tape and daily transfer sheets reflecting transactions in Lane Bryant stock.

Once having established a proper purpose, a stockholder is entitled to the same lists and data relating to stockholders as is available to the corporation....To hold otherwise would be to give the corporation an unfair advantage in a proxy solicitation battle. The best interest of the stockholders requires that they quickly receive all the information generated by the competing interests. Lane Bryant, however, is under no obligation to prepare for Hatleigh lists, data, or computer tapes which are not readily available to it and, of course, Hatleigh must pay any costs involved....

JUDGMENT Plaintiff may submit a proposed order.

Rights of Action

Individual Suits and Class Actions. An *individual* shareholder may sue a corporation to enforce preemptive rights, inspection rights, or other rights to which the shareholder is entitled. Individual suits are also filed to recover dividends declared but unpaid, or to enjoin *ultra vires* acts. A group of shareholders may collectively pursue individual causes of action arising out of the same transaction by bringing a *class* action against the corporation. The individuals joining in the suit commence the action in their own names and on behalf of "all others similarly situated." There are two major requirements for a class action: (1) a common question (e.g., to force directors to pay a dividend to all shareholders of a class); (2) the class is so large as to make it impractical for the courts to handle multiple individual suits (e.g, a million shareholders in General Motors suing for $10 dividend each). Other members of the class must usually be given notice of the pending suit and may elect to benefit from the judgment by paying a pro rata share of litigation costs.

Shareholders' Derivative Suits. If a third party or an insider wrongs a corporation and the value of its shares is depreciated, each shareholder suffers a pro rata share of the damage. If the corporation does not file an appropriate action, a shareholder may file a *derivative suit,* which is a legal action to recover for the wrong done to the corporation. The wrong may have been committed (1) by a third party, as, for instance, a customer who has failed to pay money owing to the corporation or who has infringed its patents, or (2) by a corporate insider, as, for instance, an officer who has looted the corporation treasury, has seized for himself or herself a corporate opportunity, or has violated federal security laws to the damage of the corporation. The suit is for the benefit of the corporation, and the recovery belongs to it and not to the shareholder who brings the action. Therefore, a derivative suit protects the corporation and its creditors and equally benefits all shareholders because a recovery brings about an appreciation in the value of all the corporation's shares.

At times shareholders have used derivative suits to harass directors and officers with unwarranted accusations of mismanagement. These tactics have been used to intimidate management into making a lucrative out-of-court settlement or purchasing the complaining shareholder's stock at a favorable price. Abuse arising from such "strike" suits has led to restrictive statutes and court rules. Today, in most states in order to file a derivative suit, a shareholder must meet several prerequisites. He or she must (1) own his or her shares at the time of the wrongdoing; (2) show that a demand was made on the directors (and in some states, the shareholders) to commence suit on behalf of the corporation; (3) show that the directors refused to sue; and (4) show that the directors' refusal was in bad faith. If steps 2, 3, and 4 would be futile, the courts often waive them. If no demand has been made on the board for action, the burden is on the shareholder to prove that such a demand would have been futile. For instance, a demand would be futile if one or more members of a board were involved in an alleged wrong to such an extent that the board's interests were antagonistic to those of the corporation. It is not sufficient for a shareholder to allege that directors were negligent or even reckless in their actions.

In the event of a favorable judgment, a shareholder can generally recover reasonable litigation expenses from the corporation, but not anything for his or her time. Thus, a shareholder bringing a derivative suit must be a "crusader" type. Derivative suits and class actions are both initiated by stockholders, but there is an important difference: A derivative suit is commenced *for* the corporation, and the judgment recovered is the property of the corporation. A class action is a direct suit *against* the corporation for invasion of its shareholders' rights, and if a judgment is recovered, it directly benefits the shareholders.

The following case involves a derivative suit filed to recover "greenmail" paid to a well-known corporate raider.

CASE 42.4 **Samuel M. Feinberg Testamentary Trust v. Carter · 652 F. Supp. 1066 (S.D.N.Y. 1987)**

FACTS In 1984, Carl Icahn informed the directors of B. F. Goodrich Company that he had acquired 1,171,700 shares, or 4.9 percent, of Goodrich's common stock and that he planned to acquire control and obtain seats on its board of directors. Icahn also offered to sell to the corporation

CASE 42.4 Continued

his stock at $35 per share. The market price was then about $28 per share. On November 5, the directors accepted Icahn's offer and purchased his stock. Icahn agreed to abstain from acquiring any Goodrich stock for 5 years and agreed not to disclose the repurchase unless required by law. Goodrich announced the repurchase of stock in very general terms, but it did not disclose that the shares were purchased at a price significantly above the market price or that the shares were purchased from one individual. A similar general notice was given to the Securities and Exchange Commission in March 1985.

Two shareholders filed a derivative suit against the board of directors and Icahn, asking for various remedies, including rescission of the $41-million payment for Icahn's shares. The defendants moved for a dismissal of the suit on the ground that the shareholders failed to make a demand on the directors to take appropriate action. The plaintiff shareholders contend that such demand would have been futile.

OPINION

WALKER, J. . . . "[T]he . . . purpose of the 'demand' rule is to give the derivative corporation itself the opportunity to take over a suit which was brought on its behalf in the first place, and thus to allow directors the chance to occupy their normal status as conductors of the corporation's affairs" . . . However, "[s]uch a demand is excused if the demand would be 'futile,' 'useless' or 'unavailing;' if the directors are 'antagonistic, adversely interested, or involved in the transaction attacked, a demand on them is presumptively futile and need not be made.'" . . .

The Defendant Directors posit no proper business justification for their purchase of Icahn's stock at $35 per share, when this stock possessed a market value of $28 per share. This repurchase cost Goodrich a total of $41 million, or about $8 million more than a purchase of the same volume of stock in the open market. In return for this $8-million premium, Goodrich received nothing more than the 4.9 percent shareholder interest in Icahn's hands, his promise that he would not acquire shares of Goodrich stock for five years, and his promise of silence about the transaction.

. . . [Defendants] have pointed to no evidence indicating that elimination of Icahn as a shareholder would so improve the company's financial position to justify an $8-million premium. . . .

However, while the removal of Icahn as a potential Goodrich stock purchaser at an $8-million premium could only be accomplished at the expense of the individual shareholders, the same transaction would significantly benefit board members by securing the continued possession of their director positions. For, if Icahn in fact had consummated his proposed takeover, a change in Goodrich management, including the board of directors, was possible. With such a turnover, board members would lose the benefits they receive as Goodrich directors. Not only did such directorships carry with them an intangible benefit of prestige, they included significant financial rewards as well. Each of the directors received more than $20,000 in annual salary, with Defendants Carter and Patrick Ross receiving more than $300,000, and Defendant Ong receiving more than $500,000. If any director served on the board for five years, he was entitled to receive a yearly pension equaling at least half of his compensation during his final year on the board. The directors' desire to retain their positions furnishes the requisite "adverse interest" indicating that any plaintiff demand on the Goodrich board of directors would have proven futile. . . .

The adverse interest of the Goodrich directors is further indicated by their subsequent failure to disclose the Icahn transaction to the public and the shareholders. . . .

. . . The Court views the instant case as an atypical situation where the self-interest of corporate directors may well have dominated other considerations.

JUDGMENT

For the reasons set forth above, this Court finds that any plaintiff attempt to make demand in the instant case would prove futile. Defendants' motion to dismiss for failure to make demand is denied. . . .

Shareholders' Liabilities

The fact that a shareholder's liability is limited to his or her capital investment is perhaps the most important reason businesspeople form corporations instead of partnerships. However, shareholders may become personally liable if, as discussed in Chapter 38, creditors prove an abuse of the corporate privilege and "pierce the corporate veil." Other liabilities which frequently arise are discussed in the following paragraphs.

Liability for Unpaid Subscriptions

Stock subscriptions were discussed in Chapter 39. Some subscriptions provide that the subscriber will pay for the stock by making installment payments. If the corporation becomes insolvent or bankrupt, the subscriber remains liable for the unpaid balance owing on the subscription. If the subscriber dies, his or her estate is liable for the balance due.

Liability for True Value of Shares

Shares are sometimes issued for overvalued property. If the facts show fraud on the part of the shareholder or bad faith on the part of the directors, the shareholder is liable for the amount of any underpayment that results. In such cases the stock is called "watered stock." Courts have used a variety of theories to impose liability on the stockholder but the end result, in most cases, is to hold the shareholder liable to the corporation (or to its creditors) for the difference between the inflated value and the true value of the property, that is, for the "water." Stated another way, the shareholder must pay the difference between the true value of the property and the issuance price of his or her shares.

We stated in Chapter 40 that a corporation is not permitted to issue stock (otheı than treasury stock) at a price below par value. Thus, for example, if stock has a par value of $10 per share, the corporation should receive for each share $10 in cash, property, or services. In many states an exception is made where the directors in good faith attempt to but are unable to find anyone who will pay the full par value. In such a case, the corporation may issue shares at a "discount," show them as fully paid, and disclose both the discount and the value of the consideration on its balance sheet. This is not a watered stock transaction, and the shareholder is not liable to the corporation or its creditors even though he or she pays less than par value.

In any case, whether the sale was fraudulent or made in good faith, an innocent purchaser from the initial shareholder is not liable for any deficiency.

Liability for Unlawful Dividends and Distributions

Many states permit a corporation to recover from shareholders who know that a dividend or another corporate distribution is unlawful. Rules governing the declaration of dividends by directors were discussed in Chapter 40. Of course, the obvious problem is proving that a shareholder *knows* of the illegality. In a closely held corporation, the corporation (or creditors) might have a chance to prove such knowledge, since shareholders in a closely held corporation typically are active in the business as officers and directors.

A shareholder with knowledge may be held liable for unpaid debts of the corporation, up to the amount received as an illegal dividend or distribution. For example, suppose Maria knowingly receives an illegal dividend of $1,000 and the corporation becomes insolvent with $50,000 of unpaid liabilities. Maria may be compelled to return the $1,000. However, she is not liable for the remaining corporate liabilities.

Liability of Controlling Shareholders

We have been discussing liability of shareholders to the corporation or creditors. Now we turn to shareholders' liability to one another. Normally, one shareholder is not liable to another shareholder. But if a shareholder owns enough stock to control the corporation (either by outright ownership or by proxies), a fiduciary or "quasi-fiduciary" duty may be owed. The courts have not clearly defined the duties that controlling shareholders owe to minority stockholders. One problem that arises frequently, especially in closely held corporations, involves the injuries suffered by minority shareholders as the result of the sale of controlling shares. In a number of cases, the selling price of controlling shares is in excess of their fair market value because the price includes a premium to obtain voting control of the corporation. A growing number of courts will compel majority shareholders to disgorge the premium paid to them for control and will redistribute the amount of the premium ratably among *all* shareholders. In the following case, the court discusses the fiduciary duty owed by a controlling shareholder to the minority shareholders.

CASE 42.5 DeBaun v. First Western Bank & Trust Co. · 120 Cal. Rptr. 354 46 Cal. App. 3d, 686 (1975)

FACTS In 1955, Johnson formed Alfred S. Johnson, Inc. Johnson initially owned all the corporation's outstanding stock (100 shares), but he later sold 10 shares to Stephens and 20 shares to DeBaun. When Johnson died in 1965, he left his 70 controlling shares to first Western Bank & Trust Co. (Bank) as trustee of a trust created by his will. DeBaun and Stephens continued to run the business, and profits rose steadily. By 1968, Alfred S. Johnson, Inc. (hereafter called Corporation), had $198,000 of liquid assets and a net worth of $220,000.

Raymond Mattison owned S.O.F. Fund, Inc., and offered to have it purchase the Johnson shares, which bank held as trustee. The down payment was to be $50,000. The balance of $200,000 was to be paid over 5 years, and payment was to be secured by Corporation's assets. Bank's decision to accept the offer was based on Mattison's "friendly reception by fellow Jonathan Club members." A Dun & Bradstreed report suggested that S.O.F. Fund no longer existed and indicated that Mattison and his other entities had a history of financial failures and legal troubles. Bank held an unsatisfied judgment against Mattison, and it asked Mattison's attorney about pending litigation. His attorney referred Bank to courthouse records. The courthouse records, which Bank failed to check, showed that Mattison and his entities had potential liability exceeding $1 million under thirty-eight unsatisfied judgments, twenty-two recorded abstracts of judgment, fifty-four pending suits, and eighteen tax liens.

Bank's staff doubted that it was legal to permit Mattison, as a shareholder, to secure his personal obligation which arose from the purchase of Johnson's stock with Corporation's assets. However, Bank concealed these facts to induce DeBaun and Stephens (as stockholders and directors) to approve the sale to Mattison. Bank then gave Mattison a proxy to vote the 70 shares held by it in trust but retained them as additional security. Bank soon learned that Mattison was looting the corporation but took no action until the corporation was hopelessly insolvent. Pursuant to the security agreement, Bank sold Corporation's remaining assets for $60,000. After tax liens were satisfied, only $35,000 remained in the Johnson trust.

DeBaun and Stephens brought a derivative action on behalf of the Corporation against Bank to recover damages resulting from its sale of controlling shares to Mattison. The trial court held Bank liable to Corporation for $473,836 in damages (the corporation's net worth as of transfer date plus 10 years of projected, after-tax earnings). Bank appealed.

OPINION THOMPSON, J.... "In any transaction where the control of the corporation is material," the controlling majority shareholder must exercise good faith and fairness "from the viewpoint of the corporation and those interested therein." *Remillard Brick Co. v. Remillard-Dandini Corp.*, 109 Cal. App. 2d 405, 420; 241 P.2d 66. That duty of good faith and fairness encompasses an obligation of the controlling shareholder in possession of facts sufficient "to awaken suspicion that a potential buyer of his shares may loot the corporation,...to conduct a reasonable and adequate investigation of the buyer." (*Insuranshares Corp. v. Northern Fiscal Corp.*, 35 F. Supp. 22, 25 (E.D. Pa. 1940).)

CASE 42.5 Continued

[As trustee of Johnson's shares] Bank was the controlling majority shareholder. It became directly aware of facts that would have alerted a prudent person that Mattison was likely to loot the corporation.... Armed with knowledge of those facts, Bank owed a duty to Corporation and its minority shareholders to act reasonably with respect to its dealings in the controlling shares with Mattison. It breached that duty. Knowing that the information could be discovered from the public records, Bank closed its eyes to that obvious source.... Had Bank investigated, as any prudent man would have done, it would have... precluded its dealings with [Mattison].

Bank, however, elected to deal with Mattison in a fashion that invited his looting of Corporation's assets.... By fraudulently concealing its nature from DeBaun and Stephens, Bank obtained corporate approval of a security agreement which hypothecated corporate assets to secure Mattison's obligation to it. Thus, to permit it to sell its majority shares to Mattison, Bank placed the assets and business of Corporation in peril....

JUDGMENT The judgment is affirmed.

Summary

The shareholders exercise indirect control over corporate policies by electing or removing directors. Directors are elected for designated terms, but they may be removed with or without cause by a majority of the shares voted at a meeting called for that purpose. The shareholders may also amend articles in order to change the corporate name or to alter the number, par value, rights, or classes of authorized shares. Other extraordinary transactions which require shareholder approval include merger, consolidation, sale, or lease of substantially all corporate assets *not* in the ordinary course of business, and voluntary and involuntary dissolutions.

Shareholders exercise their powers by voting in annual or special meetings. Shareholders may vote in person or by proxy. Proper notice of shareholders' meetings must be given, but in closely held corporations there are several methods of *informal* shareholder action. With certain statutory exceptions, actions are usually effected by majority vote of the shares represented at any meeting in which a quorum (a majority of outstanding voting shares) is present.

A shareholder is entitled to one vote for each voting share held as of a fixed "record date" preceding a shareholders' meeting. Cumulative voting for directors is allowed in most states and required in a few. Cumulative voting gives minority shareholders greater influence by permitting their votes (shares owned × directors to be elected) to be cumulated for a single candidate.

Shareholders possess several rights in addition to the right to vote. Among them are preemptive rights which entitle a shareholder to preserve his or her proportionate stock interests and voting rights by buying shares of a new issue; these rights may be limited or denied in the articles. In addition, shareholders have a right to

- Inspect corporate books and records
- Institute individual suits and class actions
- Initiate derivative suits in the corporation's name to enforce its rights against third parties (if directors fail or refuse to do so)

Under certain circumstances, a shareholder may be held liable for unlawful dividends or distributions and for the "true value" of shares acquired in exchange for overvalued property. Controlling shareholders of close corporations may also be liable for the sale of controlling shares in situations involving fraud or wrongful purpose.

Review Questions

1 How do the shareholders exercise their managerial power?

2 Give two reasons directors might have for amending the articles of incorporation.

3 Explain the difference between a merger and a consolidation.

4 Why would an acquiring corporation purchase all, or substantially all, of another corporation's assets rather than consummating a merger?

5 **(a)** Under what circumstances do dissenting shareholders have appraisal rights? **(b)** Why are such rights important?

6 Distinguish between voluntary dissolutions and involuntary dissolutions and give one example of each.

7 Statutory provisions covering annual shareholders' meetings generally require a time for such meetings to be fixed. **(a)** How are shareholders advised of where and when such meetings will be held? **(b)** These provisions also permit shareholders to compel the calling of such meetings. How and under what circumstances can a shareholder do so?

8 **(a)** What would be the result if shareholders were given notice 8 days prior to a meeting? **(b)** What are the three methods of informal shareholder action?

9 **(a)** What is a proxy? **(b)** How long does a proxy last? **(c)** Under what circumstances may a proxy be revoked?

10 At shareholders' meetings, what is the usual minimum statutory requirement: **(a)** for a quorum? **(b)** for an affirmative vote of shareholders?

11 **(a)** How are the voting rights of shareholders determined? **(b)** What is meant by "record date"?

12 How does cumulative voting benefit minority stockholders?

13 Define the following terms: **(a)** preemptive right, **(b)** stock right, **(c)** warrant.

14 **(a)** State two limitations on a shareholder's right to inspect corporate books and records. **(b)** Why would a corporation want to deny a shareholder a copy of its list of shareholders?

15 State the major requirements for: **(a)** a class action, and **(b)** a derivative suit.

16 Under what circumstances is a shareholder personally liable for: **(a)** the difference between the par value of his or her stock and the value placed on property given as consideration for that stock? **(b)** an unlawful dividend?

Case Problems

1 Mardikos, Jerry Arger, and Andrew Arger each contributed $500 to the organization of Whale Chemical Company, a closely held corporation. Each owned one-third of the company's shares and each performed defined duties for the company; there were no other shareholders. Fifteen years later, the corporation was worth several million dollars. In 1980, the Arger brothers told Mardikos that he had undertaken too much work based on oral approvals from shipyards and that their company might not get paid for the work performed. A loud argument ensued. The brothers, for the first time asserted their formal corporate positions and said, in effect, "Since we are all here, this is a directors' meeting and we are removing you from managing this job and placing Jerry in charge." A few months later, another argument erupted when Jerry Arger fired Mardikos's son. Later, another shouting session arose in a dispute over how a bookkeeper was handling an invoice. Clearly, the parties ceased to get along in business with one another.

Mardikos brought suit to secure the dissolution of the corporation. Should the court order its dissolution?

2 Baggs formed Auto West, Inc., to operate a Volkswagen automobile dealership. Auto West encountered serious financial difficulties, and Baggs sold to Bryan and Graff 80 percent of the stock of Auto West. They became the officers and directors of the corporation. Baggs retained 20 percent of the stock and remained as general manager. Volkswagen would not agree to the change in ownership of Auto West unless Baggs had a majority of the voting rights. To satisfy Volkswagen, Graff and Bryan executed irrevocable proxies to Baggs for an indefinite period. The parties subsequently had disagreements over Baggs's operation of the dealership, and the board of directors fired him. Graff and Bryan, together with Auto West, filed suit to terminate the proxies. Baggs claimed that the proxies were irrevocable and that he still had majority voting rights. Was Bagg's contention correct?

3 Bruce Stancil and his brother Howard each owned 12,500 shares of the common stock of Stancil Refrigeration, Inc. An annual shareholders' meeting was conducted to elect members of the corporation's board of directors. The bylaws provided for cumulative voting. Three directors were to be elected, and Bruce Stancil nominated himself, Sarah Barnes, and Eva Stancil. Howard Stancil nominated himself, Clara Stancil, and Henry Babb. As cumulative voting was authorized, Bruce cast 12,500 votes for each of his nominees, thus casting a total of 37,500 votes. **(a)** How would you advise Howard to cast his votes? **(b)** Why?

4 Pillsbury, who had no interest in Honeywell, Inc., learned that Honeywell was manufacturing bombs to be used in the Vietnamese war. Pillsbury was opposed to the war and bought one share of Honeywell stock in order to make his views known to its management and stockholders. Pillsbury demanded shareholders' lists and all corporate records dealing with munitions and weapons produced by the company. When Honeywell failed to comply, Pillsbury sued. Should the court compel Honeywell to make the records available for inspection?

5 Harff owned convertible debentures of MGM, Inc. The board of directors declared a large cash dividend on the corporation's common stock. Harff filed a derivative action against the directors to recover for the corporation the amount of the dividend. The complaint alleged that the dividend was self-serving by the directors, who owned common shares, and that it impaired the value of the corporation's debentures by reducing the market value of the common stock into which the debentures could be converted. Do these facts satisfy the requirements for a derivative action?

CHAPTER 43

Securities Regulation and Accountants' Liability

A corporation must have money with which to acquire real property, supplies, and the means of production so that it can make products and offer services for sale. As stated in Chapter 40, corporations raise these necessary funds mainly by selling shares of stock and issuing bonds to the public. People who buy these securities could be victimized if corporations and securities dealers were permitted to engage in the sharp practices to which these activities are, unfortunately, particularly susceptible. Both the federal and state governments, therefore, have enacted laws and regulations that control the issuance of securities and the ways in which they may be traded. Among other things, those laws and regulations require that any corporation which offers to sell its stock must publish information about itself, its operations, and its financial structure. With that information, members of the public should be able to make informed judgments whether to buy or otherwise to trade in that corporation's securities.

This chapter examines federal regulations governing the issuance of securities, the requirements for trading in them, the regulation of state securities, and the responsibilities of accountants under the securities laws.

Purposes of Securities Laws

Federal Securities Laws

The primary federal securities laws are the Securities Act of 1933 and the Securities Exchange Act of 1934. They were enacted to ensure that: (1) accurate information is available to financial institutions and to potential investors about the financial stability and prospects of any company that issues a security and about the risks involved in its purchase, (2) the market for the security is not manipulated at the expense of an unwary investor, (3) individuals and firms engaged in the business of selling and making a market in securities maintain appropriate business standards, and (4) those who violate the rules are subject to penalties.

The Securities Act of 1933 was designed to regulate the *issuance* of new securities. The Securities Exchange Act of 1934 was designed to regulate the *trading,* i.e., the purchase and sale of existing securities. Both acts contain registration and antifraud provisions. The two acts are meant only to furnish a potential investor with information from which he or she can, after the exercise of mature judgment, determine whether or not to purchase a security. Neither of the acts guarantees a potential investor that the security is a sound investment or that no loss of money will result from its ownership.

Because shares of stock of corporations are bought by the general public throughout the country, almost without exception their issuance and sale affects interstate commerce. Therefore, the federal government, pursuant to its constitutional authority to regulate commerce among the states, has the right to regulate the issuance and sale of securities. Nevertheless, the federal government recognizes that the states also have jurisdiction over securities. As a result, the issuance of securities are subject to control by both state and federal agencies.

State Securities Laws

State laws that regulate the issuance of securities are known as *blue-sky laws* because in a 1917 case the court said that the state has an interest in preventing "securities schemes which have no more basis than so many feet of blue sky."

Blue-sky laws lack uniformity among the states, and their differences impose problems upon corporations desiring to qualify securities issues to be sold in more than one state. Some states, such as Delaware and Connecticut, have opted for minimal blue-sky regulation. Others, such as New York and California, exert a great degree of regulatory authority. Most blue-sky laws contain provisions that

- Require the corporate issuer to register proposed securities with a designated state agency
- Require brokers and others who deal in securities to register and obtain a license
- Impose severe penalties for fraud in the sale of securities or for submitting false or misleading data in state registration statements

One difference between state and federal securities laws is that most states require that the security be qualified, generally by proof that it is something more than "blue sky," while the federal acts only require disclosure of information to enable an investor to make an informed decision.

Securities and Exchange Commission (SEC)

To administer both the Securities Act of 1933 and the Securities Exchange Act of 1934, the Congress, as part of the latter act, created the Securities Exchange Commission (SEC). It consists of five members appointed by the President, no more than three of whom may be from the same political party. Today, with its principal office in Washington, D.C., and regional offices in Atlanta, Boston, Chicago, Denver, Fort Worth, Los Angeles, New York City, Philadelphia, and Seattle, the SEC staffs more than 5,000 people.

The SEC has broad power to make rules in implementation of the statutes it administers. These rules, like those of other governmental administrative agencies, have the force and effect of law. The Commission issues three kinds of rules: (1) those which are procedural, such as what forms are to be prepared, when they are to be filed, etc.; (2) those which define the terms used in the substantive regulations and pertinent statutes; and (3) substantive rules, such as Rule 10b-5 which makes it unlawful, by the use of the mails or by any other means of interstate commerce, in connection with the purchase or sale of any security to make any untrue statement of a material fact, or to omit to state a material fact, or to engage in any act or course of business which operates as a fraud.

The Commission regulates the various stock exchanges (New York, American, etc.) and over-the-counter markets (NASDAQ) as well as the issuance of new securities. It requires the registration of securities and of broker-dealers in securities, and also requires every issuer whose securities are publicly traded to file reports at stated intervals. We will examine these rules in detail in this chapter.

Securities Defined

Both the Securities Act of 1933 and the Securities Exchange Act of 1934 define a *security* as "... any note, stock, treasury stock, bond, debenture, evidence of indebtedness, certificate of interest or participation in any profit-sharing agreement, ... pre-organization certificate or subscription, transferable share, investment contract, ... fractional undivided interest in oil, gas, or other mineral rights, or, in general, any interest or instrument commonly known as a 'security,' or any certificate of interest or participation in, ... receipt for, ... or right to subscribe to or purchase any of the foregoing."

Cases hold that a security is involved even where the investor takes a limited role in the enterprise if the essential management efforts are in the hands of a third party.

In the following case, the U.S. District Court of Oregon clarified the circumstances under which a *note* is a security.

CASE 43.1 Ahern v. Gaussoin · 611 F. Supp. 1465 (D.C. Or. 1985)

FACTS Tradex, Inc. was an association of freight carriers. Tradex purchased at a discount the freight bills owed to its members and then itself collected the bills. Tradex at first financed its operations through loans from the Seattle First National Bank (SeaFirst), and later it borrowed from individuals and others connected with the trucking industry who were given promissory 30-day demand notes in return. In 1982, Tradex reorganized and filed a registration statement with the SEC covering the issuance of $30-million worth of 30-day demand notes. In 1983, SeaFirst declared Tradex in default of its loan agreement with the bank; payment on the demand notes was "frozen"; and the holders of the demand notes were unable to secure payment.

Ahern and other noteholders, the plaintiffs, filed suit against Tradex and its officers, directors, accountants, and attorneys, alleging, among other things, that the registration statement contained fraudulent representations and omissions in violation of the 1933

CASE 43.1 Continued

and 1934 securities acts. The defendants denied that the notes were securities within the purview of those laws. Plaintiffs made a motion for summary judgment.

OPINION

REDDEN, J.... The threshold issue is whether the notes constitute securities. All defendants contend they do not.

The Securities Exchange Act of 1934 [and the 1933 Act] define a security as "any note... or... any investment contract...."

Plaintiffs contend that what they hold are securities, either as "notes" or as "investment contracts" [as defined in *Securities and Exchange Commission v. W. J. Howey Co.*, 328 U.S. 293... (1946).] The critical question is whether there has been a necessary *investment* of money. The question is answered by applying the risk capital test [which] distinguishes investment transactions,... covered by the 1933 and 1934 Acts, from routine commercial transactions, which are not [covered].... Thus, even though notes are specifically included within the definition of a security, the court must look to the "economic realities" underlying the transaction....

In determining whether these notes are "risk capital" or merely "risky loans," I consider the [following] factors: (1) time; (2) collateralization; (3) the form of the obligation; (4) the circumstances of the issuance; (5) the relationship between the amount borrowed and the size of the borrower's business; and (6) the contemplated use of the proceeds.... No one of these factors compels a decision that the notes are or are not securities....

A demand or short-term note is seldom a security unless payment is "dependent upon the success of a risky enterprise, or the parties contemplate indefinite extension of the note or perhaps conversion to stock" [*Great Western Bank & Trust v. Kotz,* 532 F.2d 1252, 1257 (1976)].

The name given to the instrument by the parties is not controlling... but must be considered.... Beginning with Tradex's reorganization, it treated the notes as securities and those associated with Tradex referred to them as securities. Tradex's SEC registration statement identified the notes as securities....

In *Kotz,* the court stated that "[w]hether the obligations were issued to a single party or to a large class of investors sheds light on the nature of the financing."... The relationship between the amount borrowed and the size of Tradex's business is important because the larger the relative amount, the greater the noteholders' stake in the business and the greater their risk....

Whether a particular instrument is a security is ultimately a question of law, but where there are disputed facts, the issue [is] one for the jury....

JUDGMENT

... Plaintiff's motions for a summary judgment denied... [and case proceeded to trial].

Securities Act of 1933

Registration Requirements

The Securities Act of 1933 requires that no security may be offered for sale to the public unless it is first *registered* by filing with the SEC a registration statement containing detailed data sufficient to enable the investing public to judge the financial soundness of the issuer and the quality of the proposed security. The SEC staff has 20 days to analyze the registration statement and, if no objections are made, at the end of that period the issuer may proceed to sell its securities to the public. It is important to note that registration does not mean that the SEC has determined that the security is a risk-free investment, that it is fairly priced, or that the purchaser will not suffer a loss on his or her investment. The SEC simply ensures that sufficient disclosure is made.

Content of Registration Statement. A registration statement is in two parts. The first part is the *prospectus,* which contains information in summary form, including a balance sheet and statement of income and expenses. A copy of the prospectus must be furnished to every purchaser of the security. The second portion, *Part II,* contains detailed information not furnished in the prospectus. Part II is available for public inspection at the SEC office in Chicago, New York, or Washington, D.C. Among the information required to be included in Part II are

1 The plan for distribution of the security, sales, and underwriting costs; the proposed use of the proceeds anticipated from the sale; and a description of the rights and limitations which attach to the security
2 The names of and compensation to the issurers' directors and principal officers; the names of persons who control the company and who own 10 percent or more of its securities; and details about material transactions between any such persons and the company
3 Information about pending legal proceedings involving the company
4 Three years' detailed financial statements, certified by an independent public accountant

That a registration statement must not contain false statements or material omissions, and the liability of those responsible for its content, is the subject of the next case.

CASE 43.2 Escott v. BarChris Construction Corp. · 283 F. Supp. 643 (S.D.N.Y. 1968)

FACTS BarChris Construction Company built and equipped bowling alleys. In 1961, the company filed with the SEC a registration statement for the issuance of convertible debentures. The company was unable to pay the interest which became due on the bonds, and it filed a petition in bankruptcy.

The plaintiffs, Escott and sixty other debenture holders, sued under Section 11 of the 1933 Act to recover damages from BarChris, its directors, officers, attorneys, public auditors (Peat, Marwick, & Mitchell & Co., hereafter Peat, Marwick) and underwriters, alleging that the registration statement contained false statements, omitted material facts and was misleading. Each defendant claimed that he had used due diligence in ascertaining the facts set out in the registration statement. All the defendants were found guilty. The court's opinion, with reference to the underwriter and the public auditors, follows.

OPINION McLEAN, J.... It is a prerequisite to liability under Section 11 of the [Securities Act of 1933] that the fact which is falsely stated in a registration statement, or the fact that is omitted when it should have been stated to avoid misleading, be "material."... "[Therefore] the information required is limited to those matters as to which an average prudent investor ought reasonably to be informed before purchasing the security registered."

Judged by this test, there is no doubt that many of the misstatements and omissions in this prospectus were material.

Section 11(b) of the Act provides that: "... no person, other than the issuer, shall be liable... as regards any part of the registration statement not purporting to be made on the authority of an expert... [if] he had, after reasonable investigation, reasonable ground to believe... that the statements therein were true and that there was no omission... [and] as regards any part of the registration statement purporting to be

CASE 43.2 Continued

made on the authority of an expert . . . [if] he had no reasonable ground to believe . . . the statements were untrue. . . . " [This is called the "due diligence" defense.]

The *underwriters* [of the debentures] . . . say that the prospectus is the company's prospectus, not theirs. Doubtless this is the way they customarily regard it. But the Securities Act makes no such distinction. The underwriters are just as responsible as the company if the prospectus is false. And prospective investors rely upon the reputation of the underwriters in deciding whether to purchase the securities. . . . The purpose of Section 11 is to protect investors. To that end the underwriters are made responsible for the truth of the prospectus. If they may escape that responsibility by taking at face value representations made to them by the company's management, then the inclusion of underwriters among those liable under Section 11 affords the investors no additional protection. . . . In order to make the underwriters' participation in this enterprise of any value to the investors, the underwriters must make some reasonable attempt to verify the data submitted to them. They may not rely solely on the company's officers or on the company's counsel. A prudent man in the management of his own property would not rely on them. It is impossible to lay down a rigid rule suitable for every case defining the extent to which such verification must go. It is a matter of degree, a matter of judgment in each case. In the present case, the underwriters' counsel made almost no attempt to verify management's representation. I hold that was insufficient. . . . Hence they have not established their due diligence defense.

Peat, Marwick [the independent auditor]. . . . Section 11(b) provides . . . "no person shall be liable [for violating this Section] as regards any part of the registration statement purporting to be made upon his authority as an expert . . . [if] he had, after reasonable investigation, reasonable ground to believe and did believe, at the time such part of the registration statement became effective, that the statements therein were true and that there was no omission to state a material fact required . . . to make the statements therein not misleading."

This defines the due diligence defense for an expert. Peat, Marwick has pleaded it. . . .

Peat, Marwick's work was in general charge of a member of the firm, Cummings, and more immediately in charge of Peat, Marwick's manager, Logan. Most of the actual work was performed by a senior accountant, Berardi, who had junior assistants.

Berardi was then about thirty years old. He was not yet a C.P.A. He had no previous experience with the bowling industry. This was his first job as a senior accountant. . . .

[Berardi failed to discover that certain of BarChris's bowling allies had been sold; he made errors in calculating BarChris's current assets and in computing its contingent liabilities, its 1960 sales figures or cash position, and its contingent liabilities; and he did not follow the written program prepared by Peat, Marwick for the review].

In substance, he asked questions, he got answers which he considered satisfactory, and he did nothing to verify them. . . . Berardi had no conception of how tight the cash position was. He did not discover that BarChris was holding up checks in substantial amounts because there was no money in the bank to cover. He did not know of the loan from Manufacturers Trust Company or of the officers' loans. . . . As far as results were concerned, his review was useless.

Accountants should not be held to a standard higher than that recognized in their profession. I do not do so here. Berardi's review did not come up to that standard. He did not take some of the steps which Peat, Marwick's written program prescribed. He did not spend an adequate amount of time on a task of this magnitude. Most important of all, he was too easily satisfied with glib answers to his inquiries. . . .

This is not to say he should have made a complete audit. But there were enough danger signals in the materials which he did examine to require some further investiga-

CASE 43.2 Continued

tion. Generally accepted accounting standards require such further investigation under these circumstances....

Here again, the burden of proof is on Peat, Marwick. I find that that burden has not been satisfied. I conclude that Peat, Marwick has not established its due diligence defense.

JUDGMENT Defendant's motions to dismiss this action... are denied.

Activities before, during, and after Registration. *Before* filing the registration statement (including the prospectus) with the SEC, the issuer may contract with an investment banking concern to handle the distribution of a proposed issue. However, at this stage the issuer may not make any public statements about the securities or offer to sell them to the public.

During the waiting period following the filing of the registration statement, the issuer and interested investors may exchange oral offers to buy and sell the proposed securities, but no sale may be consummated. Written advertising is generally limited to a sketchy preliminary "red herring" prospectus, so-called because it bears a red legend stating that a registration statement has been filed with the SEC but has not yet become effective.

After the effective date of the registration the securities covered in the registration statement may legally be offered and sold to investors. In the typical situation, any sale of the securities must be accompanied (or preceded) by delivery to each investor of a copy of the prospectus. During the period of distribution, written advertising is usually limited to the publication of *tombstone ads,* given that name because of the sparseness of its message and its format. Such an advertisement is limited to a description of the securities and a statement of where and how the prospectus may be obtained. A typical tombstone advertisement, appearing in *The Wall Street Journal,* is reproduced in Figure 43.1.

Under the 1933 Act, other advertising is prohibited in order to protect the investing public from being influenced by slanted publicity initiated by the issuer. Investment decisions are thus encouraged to be based on the information contained in the formal prospectus.

Offer and Sale of Securities

What constitutes an offer or a sale of a security that must be preceded by a registration statement is broadly defined by the courts and the SEC. An *offer* of a security includes any attempt or proposal to dispose of a security for value. Solicitation of an offer to buy a security is also included within the meaning of the term. A *sale* of a security includes every contract for the sale or disposition of a security for value. A pledge of shares as collateral for a loan is within the definition of an offer or a sale.

A *public offering* involves a *distribution* of securities to the general public. It is generally made in either of two ways: (1) the issuer sells the securities directly to the public, or (2) as noted above, the issuer enlists the services of an investment banking firm, called an *underwriter.* An underwriter, either alone or in conjunction with other underwriters, usually sells the securities *for* the issuer on a "best efforts" basis, incurring no liability for unsold shares. However, an underwriter may contract to *purchase* the securities from an issuer in order to resell them to the investing public at a fractionally higher price.

An underwriter should be distinguished from a securities dealer (broker) who executes orders to buy or sell securities on a commission basis for the account of others. A dealer or broker may also act as an underwriter for particular shares. For example, in the Figure 43.1 tombstone advertisement Drexel Burnham Lambert, Inc., and Dean Witter Capital Markets are the lead underwriters, and the other listed brokers participate to a lesser extent in the underwriting.

Exemptions

The Securities Act of 1933 sets out two categories of exemption from its registration requirements: (1)

This announcement is neither an offer to sell nor a solicitation of an offer to buy these securities.
The offer is made only by the Prospectus.

1,600,000 Shares

Operating as

UNITED EXPRESS®

Common Stock

Price $9½ per Share

Copies of the Prospectus may be obtained in any State from such of the undersigned and such other dealers as may lawfully offer these securities in such State.

Drexel Burnham Lambert INCORPORATED   **Dean Witter Capital Markets**

Bear, Stearns & Co. Inc.	**The First Boston Corporation**	**Alex. Brown & Sons** INCORPORATED
Dillon, Read & Co. Inc.	**Hambrecht & Quist** INCORPORATED	**Lazard Frères & Co.**
Merrill Lynch Capital Markets	**Montgomery Securities**	**Morgan Stanley & Co.** INCORPORATED
PaineWebber Incorporated	**Prudential-Bache Capital Funding**	**Salomon Brothers Inc**
Shearson Lehman Hutton Inc.	**Smith Barney, Harris Upham & Co.** INCORPORATED	**Wertheim Schroder & Co.** INCORPORATED
Bateman Eichler, Hill Richards INCORPORATED	**Birr Wilson, Inc.**	**Boettcher & Company, Inc.**
Cable, Howse & Ragen INCORPORATED	**Crowell, Weedon & Co.**	**Morgan, Olmstead, Kennedy & Gardner** INCORPORATED
Seidler Amdec Securities Inc.	**Sutro & Co.** INCORPORATED **Van Kasper & Company**	**Wedbush Securities, Inc.**
L. H. Alton & Company	**Pacific Securities, Inc.**	**Volpe & Covington**

October 27, 1988

Figure 43.1 Sample of a tombstone advertisement

exempted securities which are not required to be registered at any time, and (2) *exempted transactions* wherein registration is not initially required but is required upon a subsequent transfer of the security.[1]

The practical significance of an exemption is (1) the cost of registration is avoided, and (2) the issuer is not subject to the onerous reporting requirements of the 1934 Act (discussed later in this chapter). There are no exemptions from the SEC's antifraud laws and regulations.

Exempted Securities. In general terms, the following principal categories of securities are exempt from registration:

- Securities issued or guaranteed by the U.S. government or by state or local governmental agencies
- Securities issued by banks and savings and loan associations
- Securities issued by religious and charitable organizations
- Insurance policies and annuity contracts
- Commercial paper (see Chapter 28) not advertised for sale to the public that (*a*) arises out of current business transactions and (*b*) has a maturity of not more than 9 months
- Under certain circumstances, offerings solely to residents of the state in which the entity is incorporated

The last exception is rarely used because of its technical nature and burdensome requirements; most local offerings qualify as exempted transactions under Regulation D, discussed in the next paragraph.

Exempted Transactions. The most widely used transactional exemption is SEC Regulation D, which exempts so-called *private offerings* or *private placements.* Regulation D contains several rules, the most important of which are Rules 505 and 506.

Rule 505 of Regulation D allows an issuer to sell no more than $5 million worth of securities in any 12-month period to (1) accredited investors and (2) to no more than thirty-five nonaccredited investors. *Accredited investors* include six groups: (1) institutional investors such as banks, insurance companies, and pension funds; (2) charitable or educational institutions with assets of more than $5 million; (3) key employees, directors, or executive officers of the issuing company; (4) any person with a net worth of more than $1 million; (5) any person with an annual income of more than $200,000; and (6) any person who purchases at least $150,000 of the securities, provided the purchase does not exceed 20 percent of his or her net worth. *Nonaccredited* investors have lesser financial worth and experience. For example, under Rule 505 an issuer may sell shares to up to thirty-five of its employees or members of the employees' families, even though the purchasers do not have sufficient financial knowledge or experience to evaluate the merits and risks of the investment.

Rule 506 allows an issuer to sell an *unlimited* amount of its securities to accredited investors and, at the same time, to no more than thirty-five other purchasers.

The chief differences between Rules 505 and 506 are: (1) Rule 505 limits the issue to $5 million, whereas Rule 506 has no limit on the dollar amount of securities offered; and (2) Rule 505 permits sale to thirty-five nonaccredited investors who probably lack financial background and knowledge to evaluate the merits and risks of the investment, but it requires that any nonaccredited investor be furnished certain information about the issuer normally contained in a registration statement. Rule 506, in contrast, requires that the nonaccredited investors be "sophisticated" enough to judge the merits and the risks of the investment.

Normally, the issuer qualifies investors by asking them to answer a questionnaire concerning their financial worth. A lawyer, a banker, or an accountant, for example, might not be in the accredited investor category, but she or he could be classified as a sophisticated investor.

Under Rules 144, 505, and 506, securities acquired through a private offering without registration bear the legend "Restricted." Some restrictions are that (1) the issuer may not advertise the offering, and (2) purchasers are prohibited from immediately reselling the securities, agreeing in writing to hold the shares for at least 2 years before selling them. After the 2-year waiting period, the holder may sell no more than a limited number of shares each calendar quarter, and the sale must be made through a broker. Because the securities may be

[1]The regulations defining exempted transactions are technical and have gone through repeated changes. Therefore, for a definitive enumeration of the exemptions and the application of the applicable rules, reference must be made to the U.S. Code and to the regulations published by the SEC.

sold only gradually, Rule 144 is popularly called the "2-year and dribble rule." However, the rule permits a resale during the 2-year holding period if the issuer files a registration statement with the SEC or if the resale otherwise qualifies for exemption under Rule 505 or Rule 506.

Securities Exchange Act of 1934

The Securities Act of 1933, which monitors the *issuance* of securities, is augmented by the Securities Exchange Act of 1934, which regulates the *trading* in securities after their initial issue. The 1934 Act contains reporting requirements as well as standards for fair dealing in the securities marketplace. After discussing the reporting requirements under the Act, we will focus upon three aspects of fair dealing in securities: (1) prohibitions against trading based upon inside information, (2) prohibitions against short-swing profits, and (3) fair practices in the takeover of a company by a corporate raider.

Reporting Requirements under the 1934 Act

Companies whose securities are registered with the SEC and traded on national securities exchanges, and corporations that have 500 or more shareholders and assets exceeding $3 million (even if their securities are not registered under the 1933 Act) are required to file three reports:

- Form 10-K. An annual report about the corporation's current management, outstanding securities, and business operations, including a certified financial statement for the preceding fiscal year.
- Form 10-Q. A quarterly operating statement and a certified statement of financial condition, together with disclosure of recent stock sales and purchases by officers and directors of the corporation.
- Form 8-K. An early warning report to be filed within 15 days of "any materially important event" affecting the corporation, such as a change of auditors, an offer to take over the corporation, or a major write-off of bad debts.

The foregoing reports are public records and are available for analysis by potential purchasers before buying a stock. In addition, the SEC examines the reports to discover whether any violations of security laws have occurred.

The 1934 Act requires securities exchanges, national securities associations, and brokers and dealers to register with the SEC. However, a broker or dealer may be exempted if his or her business is exclusively intrastate and if the facility of a national exchange is not used.

Prohibition against Insider Trading

A major purpose of the 1934 Act is to establish a "level playing field," i.e., equality of opportunity for everyone who engages in the buying or selling of corporation shares. SEC Rule 10b-5, implementing Section 10(b) of the 1934 Act, makes it unlawful, in connection with the purchase or sale of any security, to act fraudulently or deceitfully. *Insider trading* is a type of fraud covered by Rule 10b-5. It is the name given to the purchase or sale of shares of a publicly held corporation *based upon material inside or advance information* when (1) the public disclosure of that information could lead to an immediate rise or fall in the price of the shares, *and* (2) the inside information is not available to the other party to the transaction or to securities' traders generally. Several aspects to this rule must be closely examined.

Persons Covered by Rule 10b-5. The SEC Rule is not restricted to corporation directors, officers, or major shareholders who have inside information that could affect the price of the corporation's shares. The courts have extended the rule to include

- An employee of the corporation
- An outside attorney, accountant, or investment banker; his or her employees; and others who have access to inside information
- A person who acts on a tip (a *tippee*) from a corporate insider (a *tipper*), knowing that the information is not available to the investing public

The Insider Trading Sanctions Act of 1984 supplements Rule 10b-5. That Act empowers the SEC to bring a civil penalty suit against anyone who purchases or sells securities based upon material nonpublic information. The Act confers discretion on the court to assess a penalty payable to the United States of up to three times the profit gained (or the loss avoided) as a result of the unlawful purchase or sale.

Elements of Rule 10b-5. To constitute a violation of the proscription against insider trading, (1) the information which is the basis of the action must be material; (2) the accused must have had a duty to disclose the information or to refrain from trading based on that information (i.e., he or she must be shown to have breached a fiduciary duty); and (3) the accused must have acted with scienter. Each of these elements are defined and explained in the following case.

CASE 43.3 Securities and Exchange Commission v. Fox · 654 F. Supp. 781 (N.D. Tex. 1986)

FACTS Texas Instruments (TI), headquartered in Dallas, Texas, manufactures computers and other electronic products. Fox and three others, the defendants, were employed at the Consumer Products Group (Consumer Group), a division of TI at Lubbock, Texas. The various TI divisions annually forecast the business each anticipates for the year ahead. On February 22 and March 1, 1983, TI announced there was a defect in the computer's transformer, and in the latter part of May sales of its computer and related products fell sharply. Notwithstanding this, as late as June 8, 1983, the Consumer Group forecast the sale of 3-million consoles and 15-million software cartridges in 1983. On June 9 or 10, 1983, senior corporate management in Dallas rejected the Consumer Group forecast and instead reduced the production plan for 1983 to 2.3-million consoles and 12-million software cartridges. On June 10, 1983, this plan was reviewed and approved by TI's board of directors, and on that day it was publicly announced to the press. The new production plan resulted in an estimated corporate loss of $100 million for the company's second quarter. The market value of TI's shares lost approximately $1.4 billion in a week.

Prior to the June 10 announcement, Fox and his co-defendants purchased puts (a form of option contract) on TI stock and sold them later in the month. Fox made a profit of more than $500,000. The other defendants made lesser profits. The SEC sued the defendants under Section 10(b) and Rule 10b-5 for dealing in securities while in possession of nonpublic corporate information.

OPINION WOODWARD, C. J. . . . By alleging that the defendants traded on inside information, plaintiff must prove . . . (1) that the defendants were insiders; (2) that the information in defendants' possession was material; (3) that the defendants had a duty to disclose the alleged information or to abstain from trading; and (4) that the defendants acted with scienter.

A. *Definition of Insider*

. . . The term "insider" is far-reaching. It refers to corporate directors and management officers, but also includes "anyone in possession of material inside information." *SEC v. Texas Gulf Sulphur,* 401 F.2d 833 (2d Cir. 1968). Insiders are individuals "who are in a special relationship with a company and privy to its internal affairs, and thereby suffer correlative duties in trading in its securities." . . .

B. *Definition of Materiality*

The test for materiality is an objective one. . . . A fact is material under Rule 10b-5 if "there is a substantial likelihood that a reasonable shareholder would consider the omitted information important in deciding upon his course of action."

C. *The Duty to Disclose or to Abstain from Trading*

Because an insider has access to material inside information, he has a duty to disclose or to abstain from trading when in possession of such information. . . . The United States Supreme Court examined and discussed this duty in *Chiarella v. U.S.,* 445 U.S. 225

CASE 43.3 Continued

(1981), and *Dirks v. S.E.C.*, 463 U.S. 646 (1983). The Court stated that the duty to disclose or abstain rests upon two principles:

> (1) the existence of a relationship affording access to inside information intended to be available only for a corporate purpose, and (2) the unfairness of allowing a corporate insider to take advantage of that information by trading without disclosure.

...These principles are also the elements necessary to establish a Rule 10b-5 violation. ...The court held in *Chiarella* that the duty to disclose arises "when one party has information that the other party is entitled to know because of a fiduciary or other similar relation of trust and confidence between them.... There can be no duty to disclose where the person who has traded on inside information...was not a fiduciary or was not a person in whom the sellers of the securities had placed their trust and confidence." Therefore, only those persons who have such a duty commit fraud if they trade without disclosing material information.

D. *Scienter*

...In *Aaron v. Securities and Exchange Commission*, 446 U.S. 680 (1980), the Supreme Court held "that scienter is an element of a violation of §10(b) and Rule 10b-5, regardless of the identity of the plaintiff or the nature of the relief sought."....Scienter is defined as the "intent to deceive, manipulate, or defraud." *Ernst & Ernst v. Hochfelder*, 425 U.S. 185 (1976).

...Although defendants worked with sensitive information, the court finds that they were not insiders with respect to the material information that plaintiff alleges they used to purchase TI puts....Upon review of the evidence, this court cannot find that the defendants had inside information relating to the June 10 announcement...[which was] an unexpected event for TI employees....

The decision to reduce Consumer Group's plan for production of home computers... was not made until the meeting of the members of the board of directors of TI on June 10, 1983. [None of the defendants] was involved or participated in the discussions at TI corporate headquarters in Dallas on June 9 and 10, 1983, concerning the decision to reduce Consumer Group's production....

The plaintiff argued that the defendants acted with scienter, but scienter requires a high showing of misconduct....

Although the defendants' actions may appear suspicious or sinister in hindsight, whether the defendants acted with scienter "is a question of fact to be determined as of the time of the actions upon which the plaintiff is complaining."...As stated above, the defendants did not have material inside information and therefore, they were under no duty to disclose same.... Based upon the evidence the court cannot find that the defendants acted with scienter....

JUDGMENT ...The plaintiff's prayer for injunctive relief and disgorgement [of the profits the defendants made] is denied.

As pointed out by the U.S. District Court in Case 43.3, citing the Supreme Court of the United States, the offense of insider trading involves the breach of a fiduciary duty. The Supreme Court has also said that "a tippee's use of material nonpublic information does not violate §10(b) and Rule 10b-5 unless the tippee owes a...duty to disclose the information....That duty typically is derivative from...the insider's [the tipper's] duty....In other words, the tippee's obligation [arises] from his role as a participant after the fact in the insider's [tipper's] breach of a fiduciary duty toward corporate shareholders...." [*Bateman Eichler, Hill Richards, Inc. v. Berner*, 472 U.S. 299 (1985).]

Another aspect of breach of fiduciary duty is whether an employee who *misappropriates informa-*

tion from his or her employer and uses that information to trade in the securities market violates Rule 10b-5. The U.S. Court of Appeals for the Second Circuit in *SEC v. Materia,* 745 F.2d 197 (1984), answered that question in the affirmative. The U.S. Supreme Court on November 16, 1987, had before it a similar question when it considered the appeal of the convictions of Carpenter, Winans, and another [*Carpenter v. U.S.*, 484 U.S. ___, 108 S. Ct. 316 (1987)]. In that case, Winans, a reporter for *The Wall Street Journal,* wrote a column entitled "Heard on the Street" in which he gave positive and negative information about selected stocks. Winans, in violation of the *Journal*'s policy that prior to publication the contents of its paper is confidential information and should not be revealed, tipped off Carpenter and others about what would appear in his column. Over a 4-month period the defendants earned net profits of about $690,000 in stock trades on the basis of the information that was about to appear in Winans' "Heard" columns. Based upon the misappropriation of confidential information, the defendants were convicted of violating the securities laws and of mail and wire fraud. The defendants appealed. The Supreme Court was *evenly divided with respect to the convictions under the securities laws* but was unanimous with respect to the determination that the defendants had fraudulently misappropriated the *Journal*'s confidential information, and the Court affirmed the convictions under the mail and wire fraud statutes.

During 1986 and 1987, as a natural consequence of the flood of corporate takeovers and the rising prices of shares, the SEC's attention was directed to ferreting out insider trading. From information acquired from New York Stock Exchange computers and other sources, unusually heavy trading in the shares of companies rumored to be takeover targets were identified by the SEC. Resulting investigations led to the arrest of individuals who, on the basis of insider information, were active traders of shares of corporate targets. Among the arrested individuals were members of prestigious law, investment banking, and stock exchange firms. One particularly large trader was Ivan Boesky. He was fined $100 million by the SEC and was sentenced by a federal court to 3 years' confinement.

Congressional committees held extensive hearings on the insider trading problem and, to discourage insider trading, formulated the Insider Trading and Securities Fraud Enforcement Act, which became law on November 19, 1988. The Act authorizes a criminal court to confine an insider trader for up to 10 years and to impose a fine of up to $1 million. A corporation or partnership may be fined up to $2.5 million. In addition, the SEC may impose *civil* fines against an insider trader and against a company that knowingly or recklessly fails to detect or prevent insider trading by an employee. The Act also makes clear that a firm employed to carry on confidential matters regarding a corporation or its securities must establish procedures which insulate the portion of its office dealing in such matters from other sections of its office. As a further sanction, the Act authorizes the SEC to establish a bounty program to reward an informer whose assistance leads to the imposition of insider trading penalties and gives a victim of insider trading the right to take legal action against the violater.

Short-Swing Transactions

Sections 16(a) and 16(b) of the Securities Exchange Act of 1934 are insider trader sections which are not based on fraud but on the length of time a security is held. The sections provide that a director, an officer, or a beneficial owner of more than 10 percent of any registered security of a corporation is liable to the corporation for the profit she or he realizes on any purchase and sale of a security within a period of less than 6 months.[2] Such individuals are required to file with the SEC, and with the national exchange upon which the stock is traded, reports showing the number of the corporation's shares directly or beneficially owned as well as any change in those holdings.

These short-swing reports are public records and may be inspected by the SEC staff or corporate gadflies searching for violations. If a violation is discovered, and if the corporation fails to take action to recover the short-swing profit, a shareholder may file a derivative action to recover such profits on behalf of the corporation.

As a general rule, a short-swing trader must forfeit the profit even if he or she acted in good faith, did not possess or use inside information, and did not intentionally violate the statute. For this rea-

[2]A beneficial owner in this context is a person who owns the legal or equitable title to shares registered in another's name, including a parent whose securities are in a child's name or a spouse who pays for securities held in his or her spouse's name.

son, Section 16 on short swings may be viewed as more onerous than the insider trading Rule 10b-5, discussed previously. Another burdensome aspect of Section 16 is that short-swing profits are computed by matching the highest sale with the lowest purchase in a 6-month period. To illustrate, let us assume that Lee, president of Ajax Corporation, whose stock is registered with the SEC, on March 1 buys 100 shares of Ajax at $50 per share. On April 1, he sells the 100 shares at $40 per share, and on May 1 he buys another 100 shares at $30 per share. It would seem that over the period from March 1 to May 1 Lee suffered a loss of $10 per share, or $1,000. However, under Section 16 the sale of April 1 at $40 is matched against the purchase on May 1 at $30 per share, since they occurred within a 6-month period, and Lee is held to have made a *short-swing profit* of $1,000.

Corporate Takeover

Throughout the 1980s, corporate takeovers were very much in the news. Because shares of any publicly held corporation are available for purchase on the open market, they may be bought by anyone in a quantity sufficient to gain control of the corporation's board of directors and thereby to control its policies. This is called a "takeover." It may be for several purposes and in several forms. For example: (1) One corporation may take over another to enhance its business by acquiring the other corporation's skilled personnel and management, its patents, secret processes, its share of the market, etc; (2) The takeover may be a *leveraged buyout.* This involves the purchase of all of the corporation's shares of stock generally by some members of the top management of the company together with others. The transaction is involved, entailing the purchasers borrowing the necessary funds and pledging, as security for the loan, all of the assets of the corporation purchased; (3) The purchase of a company called the "target company" by a "corporate raider." The raider may intend to continue the corporate business under his or her own control, to merge the corporation into another corporation, or even to dismantle the corporation and sell its component parts, distributing the proceeds to all the shareholders (including himself or herself).

Whether a takeover or a merger of a corporation into another is beneficial to the target company's shareholders is debatable. Some raiders, such as the well-known T. Boone Pickens, claim they are acting in the best interests of the target company's shareholders, bringing a greater degree of efficiency to the company and raising the value of its shares. Some shareholders agree, feeling that the process permits them to sell their shares to the corporate raider at a price higher than that prevailing in the open market. Others, however, feel more economic harm than good comes of a takeover or merger; they see it as a prelude to the permanent closure of plants and the elimination of jobs.

Tender Offer. A corporate raider often seeks to gain control of a target company by soliciting proxy approval from its shareholders for the election of the raider's own slate of directors or for the merger of the target company into a company controlled by the raider. As an alternative, the raider may make a *tender offer,* i.e., an offer to the shareholders of the target company to buy their shares at a price the raider establishes. If the attempt succeeds, the raider acquires controlling interest in the target corporation. In order to induce the target company's shareholders to sell their shares, the raider offers to pay a price well above the market price of the shares. This anticipated spread between the offered price and the market price induces many people to buy the shares of a company they believe is a possible target for takeover, in the expectation of selling the shares to the offeror (raider) or on the open market at a profit when a tender is made.

Neither the Securities Act of 1933 nor the Securities Exchange Act of 1934 requires a corporate raider to give the shareholders of the target company any advance information about the proposed takeover. To forestall typical abuses that arose from this oversight, Congress in 1968 enacted the Williams Act as an amendment to the 1934 Act and enacted still further amendments in 1970. These amendments and SEC Rules 13(d) and 14(d) require that any entity acquiring beneficial ownership of more than 5 percent of a corporation's securities must, within 10 days, file a report with the SEC and with the corporation whose securities are being purchased. Among other things, the report must include

- The purchaser's name(s) and background
- The source of the funds used for the acquisition
- The purpose of acquiring the shares

If the purchasing entity intends to make a tender offer, he or she must, in addition to the foregoing information, also file with the SEC and with each offeree a report containing

- Details of any planned merger or other disposition of the target company's assets
- Information as to past dealings among the offeror, the target corporation, and those holding important positions in the target corporation
- Financial statements
- Any special agreements made with shareholders to obtain their support for the tender offer

To be sure that all shareholders are treated alike and that panic acceptance is not generated when there is a tender offer, shareholders' tenders are not accepted on a first-come, first-served basis. Instead, if more shares are tendered than the raider offered to purchase, the raider must purchase the tendered shares on a pro rata basis, paying the same price for all purchases. To illustrate this procedure, let us suppose that Ray Raider offers to buy 100,000 shares of Target Corporation at $25 per share. One thousand of Target's shareholders tender a total of 300,000 shares. Because Raider offered to buy only one-third the number of the total shares tendered, Raider, in order to treat all shareholders equally, may accept only one-third the number of shares tendered by each shareholder.

The Williams Act also prohibits the omission or misrepresentation of any fact likely to influence a reasonable shareholder's decision in connection with a proxy or tender offer solicitation. The offer to pay holders of large amounts of shares a higher price for their shares than is offered to other shareholders is specifically prohibited.

A tender offer to buy enough shares of a corporation to constitute a controlling interest may be either friendly or hostile. If the target corporation has no objection to a takeover by that offeror, then there is no problem—friendliness reigns. But if the board of directors of the target company concludes that it is in the best interests of the corporation and of its shareholders *not* to sell the offeror a controlling number of shares and if the offeror persists, then the tender offer is considered hostile. In that event, the directors of the target company may take a number of defensive actions.

Corporate Defenses against Takeover. As long as all the information required under the Williams Act is furnished, the Act is not a bar to a hostile takeover. As explained in Chapter 41, corporate management may adopt various devices to ward off a hostile takeover of their company such as restructuring the corporation to make it unattractive to a raider (the "poison pill"), paying "greenmail" to the raider, or finding a "white knight" to make a friendly takeover of the company.

The shareholders in the following case claimed that the directors of their corporation had violated the 1933 and 1934 securities laws when it did not publicize the fact that it was seeking a white knight after an attempted hostile takeover.[3]

[3]The most recent decision of the Supreme Court concerning the liability of companies for issuing misleading statements with regard to merger talks is *Basic, Inc. v. Levinson*, decided March 7, 1988 (108 S. Ct. 978).

CASE 43.4 Flamm v. Eberstadt · 814 F.2d 1169 (7th Cir. 1987)

FACTS On December 2, 1975, General Cable Corporation announced it intended to make a tender offer of $17 per share to the shareholders of Microdot, Inc. The shares were then being traded on the New York Stock Exchange at $11.75 per share. On December 5, Microdot issued a press release stating that the proposed offer was totally inadequate and that "[w]e will employ all resources at our disposal to defeat the offer." Other communications from Microdot advised its shareholders not to sell their stock either on the open market or to General Cable even though the share price had risen to more than $18 and then settled back to $17. Without publicly announcing its action, Microdot directed Goldman, Sachs, & Co., its investment bankers, to search

CASE 43.4 Continued

for a white knight to secure a better bid than that offered by General Cable. Northwest Industries expressed an interest in Microdot. On January 24, 1976, Microdot's board agreed to accept $21 per share if Northwest made such an offer. On January 26, Northwest's board of directors approved the purchase, General Cable dropped out of the picture, and Northwest acquired Microdot's stock.

Plaintiffs Ann and Arnold Flamm, knowing nothing about the search for a white knight, had sold their Microdot shares on December 29, 1975, for about $17.38 per share. Plaintiffs filed a class action against Microdot on behalf of all shareholders similarly circumstanced, maintaining that the company's search for a white knight was material information that was withheld from its shareholders in violation of Section 10(b) of the Securities Exchange Act of 1934 and SEC Rule 10b-5. Judgment was rendered for the defendants, and the plaintiffs appealed.

OPINION

EASTERBROOK, J.... The [trial] court told the jury that unless Flamm showed that the failure to disclose the search was material, and unless Flamm "justifiably relied" to his detriment on Microdot's statements and omissions, the [plaintiffs] could not recover....

Several courts of appeals have held that efforts by public corporations to arrange mergers are immaterial... as a matter of law, until the firms have agreed on the "price and structure" of the deal.... Microdot and Northwest did not agree on the price and structure of a deal until January 24, 1976, at the earliest, the day after the period in which the last plaintiff member of the class sold [his or her] shares. On December 29, 1975, when Flamm sold, Microdot was forlornly looking for a rescuer; the most that can be said is that Microdot had authorized an investment bank to send distress signals.

...Our colleagues on other courts of appeals have suggested two reasons why the disclosure of ongoing negotiations may "accomplish more harm than good." One is that disclosure of ongoing negotiations may befuddle the investors, leading them to think the outcome more certain than it is.... The other reason is that premature disclosure may frustrate the achievement of the firm's objective, destroying the source of the value sought to be disclosed....

Some potential acquirers may demand that negotiations proceed in secrecy. They may fear that premature disclosure may spark competition that will deprive them of part of the value of their effort, so that bids in a world of early disclosure will be lower than bids in a world of deferred disclosure.... [S]ilence during negotiations may be beneficial for investors.... Both the New York and the American stock exchanges suggest that listed firms postpone announcements until definitive agreements have been reached....

Premature disclosure could have reduced the chances of an acquisition by a White Knight and therefore reduced the bids made in the market for Flamm's stock.... Rule 10b-5 is about *fraud,* after all, and it is not fraudulent to conduct business in a way that makes investors better off....

The only concrete advice Microdot gave its investors was not to sell, because $17 was too low.... Flamm is hardly in a position to contend that because he rejected this advice he has been deceived.... Flamm's errors are not grounds on which to force other investors to pay damages (which is the effect of awarded damages against Microdot).

JUDGMENT

We therefore affirm the judgment.

State Laws Affecting Corporate Takeovers. In addition to actions by corporation management to stem the tide of takeovers, legislation has been considered by several states to control corporate raiders. A statute to that effect enacted by the State of Illinois was declared unconstitutional in 1982 (*Edgar v. MITE Corp.*, 457 U.S. 624) as being in conflict with the Williams Act. In 1987, the Supreme Court held constitutional an Indiana statute sharply restricting hostile takeovers of Indiana corporations; since then many other states have enacted similar laws.

Following is the case in which the Supreme Court upheld the Indiana law.

CASE 43.5 CTS Corporation v. Dynamics Corp. of America · 107 S. Ct. 1637 (1987)

FACTS On March 4, 1986, the Control Share Acquisition Chapter, applicable to Indiana corporations, was added to the Indiana Business Corporation Law. Under that Chapter, an entity that acquires 20 percent or more of the shares (called "control shares") of an Indiana corporation gains the right to vote those shares *only if* a majority of all *disinterested* shareholders (i.e., shareholders other than the acquiring entity) voting at a shareholders' meeting, approve.

Six days after the Indiana law went into effect, Dynamics Corp., which owned 9.6 percent of CTS Corporation's common shares, offered to purchase additional shares. If the purchase came about, Dynamics would own 25.7 percent of CTS's shares, and the provisions of the new restrictive law would be applicable. Dynamics filed suit, alleging that the new law conflicted with the congressionally enacted Williams Act, that the Chapter was violative of the commerce clause of the Constitution, and that there should be applied the former Indiana law which allowed an unrestricted stockholder vote on an acquiror's offer. The U.S. District Court held for Dynamics, the court of appeals affirmed, and CTS lodged appeal with the U.S. Supreme Court.

OPINION POWELL, J.... The Williams Act, backed by regulations of the... SEC, imposes requirements in two basic areas. First, it requires the offeror to file a statement disclosing information about the offer, including the offeror's background and identity; the source and amount of the funds to be used in the purchase; the purpose of the purchase, including any plans to liquidate the company or make major changes in its corporate structure; and the extent of the offeror's holdings in the target company. [Citations]

Second, the Williams Act, and the regulations that accompany it, establish procedural rules to govern tender offers.... The offer must remain open for at least 20 business days. [Citation] If more shares are tendered than the offeror sought to purchase, purchases must be made on a pro rata basis from each tendering shareholder. [Citations] Finally, the offeror must pay the same price for all purchases....

The Indiana Act operates on the assumption, implicit in the Williams Act, that independent shareholders faced with tender offers often are at a disadvantage. By allowing such shareholders to vote as a group, the Act protects them from the coercive aspects of some tender offers. The desire of the Indiana Legislature to protect shareholders of Indiana corporations from this type of coercive offer does not conflict with the Williams Act. Rather, it furthers the federal policy of investor protection.

The Act does not impose an absolute delay on tender offers, nor does it preclude an offeror from purchasing shares as soon as federal law permits. If the offeror fears an adverse shareholder vote under the Act, it can make a conditional tender offer, offering to accept shares on the condition that the shares receive voting rights within a certain period of time. The Williams Act permits tender offers to be conditional on the offeror's subse-

CASE 43.5 Continued

quently obtaining regulatory approval. . . . The regulatory conditions that the Act places on tender offers are consistent with the text and the purposes of the Williams Act. Accordingly, we hold that the Williams Act does not pre-empt the Indiana Act. . . . Because nothing in the Indiana Act imposes a greater burden on out-of-state offerors than it does on similarly situated Indiana offerors, we reject the contention that the Act discriminates against interstate commerce.

It. . . is an accepted part of the business landscape in this country for States to create corporations, to prescribe their powers, and to define the rights that are acquired by purchasing their shares. A State has an interest in promoting stable relationships among parties involved in the corporations it charters, as well as in ensuring that investors in such corporations have an effective voice in corporate affairs.

There can be no doubt that the Act reflects these concerns. The primary purpose of the Act is to protect the shareholders of Indiana corporations. It does this by affording shareholders, when a takeover tender is made, an opportunity to decide collectively whether the resulting change in voting control of the corporation, as they perceive it, would be desirable. A change of management may have important effects on the shareholders' interests; it is well within the State's role as overseer of corporate governance to offer this opportunity. The autonomy provided by allowing shareholders collectively to determine whether the takeover is advantageous to their interests may be especially beneficial where a hostile tender offer may coerce shareholders into tendering their shares. . . . [E]ven if the Act should decrease the number of successful tender offers for Indiana corporations, this would not offend the Commerce Clause.

JUDGMENT Accordingly, we reverse the judgment of the Court of Appeals.

Accountants' Responsibilities

Throughout the foregoing consideration of federal securities laws, and particularly in cases that augment the text, a continuing thread reveals the reliance the SEC places upon public accountants as the watchdogs of corporate compliance with the securities acts.

The SEC requires that *independent auditors* verify that companies maintain proper internal safeguards against corrupt practices. In addition, Section 13(b) of the Securities Exchange Act of 1934, as amended by the Foreign Corrupt Practices Act of 1977, prohibits keeping inaccurate books or maintaining off-the-book accounts and related improper practices. It requires reporting companies to make and keep books, records, and accounts that, in reasonable detail, accurately and fairly reflect the transactions and dispositions of the corporation's assets and to devise and maintain a system of internal accounting controls sufficient to ensure

- That corporate payments are made only with the specific authorization of management
- That all transactions, including payments made abroad, are accurately recorded so as to permit preparation of financial statements in accordance with generally accepted accounting principles
- That accountability is maintained for the corporation's assets, including cash payments made
- That access to assets is permitted only in accordance with management authorization
- That recorded accountability for assets is compared with existing assets at reasonable intervals and appropriate action is taken with respect to any differences

In addition to internal accounting safeguards, the Foreign Corrupt Practices Act of 1977 prohibits American companies from paying bribes to obtain business from foreign governments and requires internal accounting controls designed to prevent violations by directors and officers.

The National Commission on Fraudulent Financial Reporting in April 1987 recommended that when a company changes auditors or shifts accounting practices, it freely disclose its disagreements with outside auditors. The Commission urged that all audit committees of corporate boards of directors be given more authority in accounting, auditing, and disclosure areas and that outside auditors become more involved with corporate quarterly financial statements.

Civil and Criminal Liabilities under Federal Securities Laws

The 1933 and 1934 Acts impose civil and criminal liabilities on directors, officers, and others, including lawyers and accountants who participate in deceptive or manipulative practices or who commit fraud in connection with securities transactions. One who aids and abets such a wrongdoing or who knowingly benefits from a securities violation is subject to civil penalty.

Following an administrative hearing, the SEC may impose civil penalties such as denying a lawyer or an accountant the privilege of appearing or practicing before it, the revocation of registration, and the imposition of a civil fine. As earlier noted, a civil penalty of $100 million was imposed upon Ivan Boesky for massive insider trading. Those whose wrongs were on a lesser scale are generally required to disgorge any profits they made from the insider trading. The SEC may also file a civil suit in the courts for injunctive relief.

The registration provisions of the 1933 Act create a statutory cause of action in favor of any purchaser who relies upon materially false or misleading data in a registration statement. He or she can recover losses up to the full purchase price paid for the securities from (1) the issuer; (2) every signer of the registration statement; (3) anyone who was a director or who had consented to be named as such when the registration statement was filed; (4) every accountant, engineer, appraiser, or other expert who prepared or bore responsibility for a report or valuation statement which, with his or her consent, was used in the registration statement; and (5) every underwriter of the security. However, an expert is liable only with respect to so much of the registration statement as he or she prepared or certified.

A person who willfully violates any federal statute administered by the SEC is also subject to criminal penalties of fine and imprisonment.

Perhaps the most significant decision in the last decade involving criminal penalties for violations of the securities laws was handed down in the following case, *United States v. Weiner*, which arose out of the notorious Equity Funding frauds. The case is particularly important because it involves the criminal liability of public accountants. The court held that consistent departure from generally accepted accounting principles and auditing standards can be considered by the jury in determining whether there is criminal intent to violate the securities laws.

CASE 43.6 United States v. Weiner · 578 F.2d 757 (9th Cir. 1978)

FACTS Equity Funding Corporation of America (Equity Funding) sold mutual funds, life insurance, and equity funding programs. In a massive fraud, Equity Funding's officers, directors, and other personnel fabricated fictitious insurance policies in the names of people selected at random from telephone directories, creating on paper $62-million worth of nonexistent corporate assets. Securities registration statements filed by Equity Funding with the SEC included those nonexistent assets, and the registration statements also vastly inflated the company's income.

Weiner, Lichtig, and Block were independent public accountants who audited Equity Funding's books during the entire period of the frauds. Weiner was in charge of the audits of its financial statements, while Lichtig and Block supervised the audit field work. Among other irregularities, an account called Funded Loans and Accounts Receivable (FLAR)

CASE 43.6 Continued

used as an umbrella for falsified entries. Lichtig was present at a meeting when a company employee was directed to prepare a reconciliation for a $10-million improper entry in the FLAR account. When Block, while conducting an audit, questioned some accounting procedures, Equity's controller offered him a trip to Rome in exchange for his cooperation. No further questions were raised by Block, although a check of the schedules supplied to him would have revealed the falsity of the claimed assets.

Equity acquired Investors Planning Corporation for $10 million; however, the financial statement showed the value of the acquisition at about $27,800,000, based on an improper write-up of future commissions.

Various Equity Funding officials admitted that unsupported and false entries appeared in the financial statements and that defendants Weiner, Lichtig, and Block were involved. All three defendants were charged with and convicted of having willfully made or caused to be made untrue statements of material fact in various registration statements filed by Equity Funding with the SEC. They appealed their convictions, contending that they were the victims of the frauds perpetrated by the officers of Equity Funding and that, although they might have been to some degree negligent or might have erred in their judgment as auditors, they had committed no crimes.

OPINION

CHOY, GOODWIN, AND THOMPSON, J.... [I]t is undisputed that the financial statements of Equity Funding failed to reflect the actual condition of the company [and]... contained false statements of accounts. The connection of the defendants with the statements was shown by their individual responsibilities in relation to the audits....

The remaining inquiry is whether defendants approved of and concurred in the grossly misstated reports in the good faith belief that the statements were accurate representations or whether they knowingly and willfully acquiesced in the dissemination of false statements....

Various Equity Funding officials testified to the falsity of the figures that appeared on the financial statements and to the fact that in many instances no back-up papers supported the entries. Therefore, if the auditors had attempted to confirm the information given to them[,] they would have been unable to do so. The lack of back-up and supporting schedules would have been a clear indication that something was wrong. Since such back-up often was not even fabricated, the jury could infer that the auditors either completely failed to audit the areas in disregard of GAAS [Generally Accepted Auditing Standards], or consciously failed to audit in "cooperation" with the Equity Funding officials, thus purposely avoiding the false entries....

There is no question about the inaccuracy of the figures contained in the financial statements. The necessary determination is whether there was sufficient evidence to support the jury's verdict that the underlying [implied] finding that defendants had acted willfully and with knowledge in filing the incorrect data and certifying its reliability.

... Even if they [the defendants] did not initially know or indeed learn the step-by-step fictitious entries and improper manipulations, their consistent failure to apply GAAS and GAAP [Generally Accepted Accounting Principles] after they knew some kind of a major fraud was afoot provided a basis from which the jury could reasonably infer defendants' knowing and willful participation in the fraud....

... In our case, failure to apply generally accepted auditing standards is relevant to the issue of knowledge and willfulness.

... The judge's instruction, which stated that evidence regarding compliance with GAAS and GAAP was not conclusive, but was relevant, was a proper statement. The weight to be given the evidence was for the jury's determination.... The jury was instructed that proof of negligence was insufficient to support a conviction, and that proof of good faith constituted a complete defense to the charges. The court went on to instruct the jury that, in determining intent, the jury could consider whether defendants acted in

CASE 43.6 Continued

"reckless, deliberate... disregard for truth or falsity," and could infer from proof of such acts that defendants acted willfully and knowingly.

... [I]n *United States v. Jewell,* 532 F.2d 697 (1976), ... we held:

> ... to act 'knowingly'... is not necessarily to act only with positive knowledge, but also to act with an awareness of the high probability of the existence of the fact in question. When such awareness is present, 'positive' knowledge is not required....

JUDGMENT ... The jury instruction was proper. [Convictions] affirmed.

Summary

Both the federal and state governments have enacted laws which control the issuance and sale of securities. The federal Securities Act of 1933 establishes rules governing the registration of securities proposed to be sold. The Securities Exchange Act of 1934 establishes rules controlling the sale of securities after they are issued. The latter act also established the Securities Exchange Commission (SEC), which administers the federal securities laws. State laws, commonly called "blue-sky laws," augment the federal laws and the rules promulgated by the SEC.

The Securities Act of 1933, the Securities Exchange Act of 1934, and the rules promulgated by the SEC are intended to reduce the possibility of fraud and unfair dealing in the issuance and sale of securities in the United States and to preserve orderly markets for the ready purchase and sale of corporate securities. The federal and state laws and regulations furnish no guarantee that any security which has gone through the registration process or satisfies a state's blue-sky laws is a wise investment, will pay interest or dividends or will otherwise make money for the purchaser, or ultimately will not be worthless.

A wide range of instruments which represent the investment of money rather than ordinary commercial transactions between debtor and creditor are considered to be securities subject to the rules and regulations of the securities laws.

Before a security may be offered for sale it must first be registered with the SEC. The registration statement is in two parts: (1) the prospectus, which presents all material facts needed by an investor to make an informed decision about the security, and (2) a section labeled "Part II," which contains additional detailed information. If the registration statement contains any false statements or material omissions, those responsible, including the company's directors, officers, attorneys, public auditors, and underwriters, may be criminally and civilly liable. A purchaser of the security may also have a cause of action for damages. In addition to filing a prospectus, all companies that issue securities are required to file with the SEC periodic reports detailing their financial condition and other pertinent matters.

There are two classes of exemptions from the registration requirements: (1) exempted securities, and (2) exempted transactions. Securities that are part of an exempted transaction are "restricted" and may not be resold readily.

A major purpose of the 1934 Act is to assure that all would-be traders of securities have equal opportunity to ascertain the current value of the security. Accordingly, an inside trader—i.e., anyone possessing material corporate information not yet made public—commits a crime when he or she, with scienter, violates a fiduciary duty and trades on the basis of that information. A tippee who trades on the basis of information from such an insider (the tipper) is also liable.

The 1934 Act also requires anyone who owns more than 10 percent of any registered security to pay to the corporation any profit he or she makes as a result of a short-swing transaction (a purchase and sale within a 6-month period), even though no misuse of inside information is involved.

Accountants have a particular responsibility under the federal security acts. They are experts who are accountable, both civilly and criminally, for their errors or omissions in registration statements.

Review Questions

1 What are the essential differences between the Securities Act of 1933 and the Securities Exchange Act of 1934?

2 What controls do states exercise over the sale of securities?

3 **(a)** What is the Securities Exchange Commission? **(b)** What is its function?

4 What is a prospectus? a registration statement? a tombstone advertisement? an underwriter?

5 **(a)** What kinds of securities must be registered? **(b)** What information should be included in a registration statement?

6 Explain what activities are permitted with reference to a proposed sale of securities **(a)** prior to filing a registration statement; **(b)** during the waiting period after the registration statement is filed; and **(c)** subsequent to the effective date of registration.

7 What is the difference between an exempted security and an exempted transaction?

8 **(a)** What is meant by an accredited investor? a sophisticated investor? **(b)** What effect do these characterizations have on the purchase of securities? **(c)** Why should such characterizations be made?

9 **(a)** How does Rule 10b-5 affect insider trading? **(b)** Under what circumstances is a tippee precluded from trading in a security? **(c)** Why does the SEC endeavor to prevent insider trading?

10 **(a)** Who is affected by Section 16(b) of the Securities and Exchange Act of 1934, which proscribes short-swing trading? **(b)** What is the reason for the rule? **(c)** Who is entitled to the profit made on a short-swing trade?

11 **(a)** What or who is a corporate raider? **(b)** If a corporate raider makes a tender offer and management concludes that it is not in the best interest of the corporation to approve the offer, what options are open to the corporation?

12 A corporate raider purchases 7 percent of a company's outstanding shares. What notices must be given and to whom?

13 **(a)** What, in general, are the responsibilities of accountants regarding the issuance of securities? **(b)** Why are they subject to this responsibility?

14 Recall the discussion in the two opening chapters of this book concerning ethics and the law. What ethical considerations do you perceive in the issuance of securities? in their sale?

Case Problems

1 Rubin, the president of a mining company, secured a loan from the bank based upon his pledge of shares of stock in six companies. Through fictitious backup material, he represented the shares to be worth more than $1 million, but they were actually worthless. When charged with violating the antifraud provisions of the Securities Act of 1933, he denied liability, claiming that his pledge of the shares, which the bank did not transfer into cash, was neither a sale nor an offer to sell securities and therefore was not a transaction within the Act. Should the defense be sustained? Why or why not?

2 In April of 1981, Oryx Co. was incorporated. On June 30, 1981, Oryx filed with the SEC a registration statement for the sale of its common stock at $4.75 per unit. Akerman, the plaintiff, purchased 200 units at that time. Shortly thereafter, the price of Oryx units began to decline. Prior to November 10, it had fallen to $3.25 per share; from November 10 until late February 1982, the price remained steady. This represented a decline of about 24 percent. During the same period, the Over-the-Counter Composite Index declined only 7.3 percent.

On November 10, 1981, Oryx announced, both by letter to its shareholders and by newspaper articles, that its June 1981 registration statement had erroneously shown certain transactions to have occurred in the month of March which had actually taken place in April. As a result, its sales and earnings were overstated in the registration statement. Immediately prior to and subsequent to November 10, Oryx was selling at about $3.25.

Akerman sued both Oryx and the broker through whom he had purchased the shares for the loss in value of his shares, alleging a violation of the Securities Act of 1933 because the registration statement was erroneous.

Based solely on these facts, should Akerman recover? Why or why not?

3 Fond Hope Genetic Corporation manufactures and sells sophisticated pharmaceuticals. Arthur, a biologist, is the company's Vice President for Blood Pressure Research. Fond Hope has three other vice presidents, each of whom oversees a specialized area of scientific research. Arthur occasionally buys and sells shares of Fond Hope's stock, which is actively traded on a stock exchange. On January 12, 1988, Arthur borrowed some money and bought 1,000 shares of Fond Hope stock. On June 1, 1988, he sold 500 of those shares and made a profit of $10,000. The company treasurer says that since Arthur is an officer of the company he must turn over to it the profit he made in the stock trade. Arthur is incensed. He says that the rise in price of the Fond Hope shares was not related to any research carried on by his department and that he had no knowledge of the status of the company's other research activities nor why the shares rose in price. Must Arthur accede to the treasurer's demand? Why or why not?

4 Burlington Northern, Inc., made a hostile tender offer for 25-million El Paso Gas Co. shares at $24 per share. A majority of El Paso's shareholders subscribed to the offer. Burlington, taking advantage of the terms of its offer, withdrew its offer and announced a new and friendly takeover agreed to by the El Paso directors. By that understanding, Burlington agreed to purchase 21-million shares at $24 per share and, among other things, recognized "golden parachute" contracts between El Paso and four of its senior officers. The new offer was oversubscribed, and the takeover was completed. Burlington, however, bought a lesser number of the plaintiff's shares than it would have purchased under the original tender offer. The plaintiff and other similarly situated shareholders brought suit, alleging that Burlington, El Paso, and El Paso's board of directors had violated Section 10(b) of the Securities Exchange Act of 1934, which prohibits "fraudulent, deceptive, or manipulative acts... in connection with any tender offer," because Burlington had bought fewer of the plaintiffs' shares than it would have purchased under the original tender offer. The district court dismissed the suit because no misrepresentation was involved, the court of appeals affirmed, and appeal was taken to the Supreme Court.

The Supreme Court sustained the lower courts. What would be the basis for its decision?

5 Buckley, a securities broker, without any special knowledge or investigation of Company X, recommended to Allen that he should buy X's stock because its price was certain to rise. Relying on Buckley's representations, Allen, the plaintiff, purchased the stock. The price of the stock declined drastically, and Allen sued the broker who said that Allen's loss was due to a general decline in market prices. Does Allen have a cause of action against Buckley under Section 10(b) of the 1934 Act and SEC Rule 10b-5?

6 Berner and other investors, the plaintiffs, traded through Charles Lazzaro, a registered securities broker employed by Bateman Eichler, Hill Richards, Inc., a large stock brokerage organization. Lazzaro told them that he knew insiders of the T.O.N.M. Oil & Gas Exploration Corporation (TONM) who had told him that TONM had discovered vast amounts of gold in Surinam where it had thousands of acres of gold-producing land under option. Lazzaro also said that when the information becomes public, TONM's shares, then selling for $1.50 to $3.00, would go up to $10 or $15 and might increase to $100 a share within a year. Some of the plaintiffs asked Leslie Neadeau, TONM's president, whether Lazzaro's tip was accurate. Neadeau stated that the information was "not public knowledge" and that he "would neither confirm nor deny these claims," but allegedly he said, "Lazzaro is very trustworthy and a good man."

The plaintiffs bought TONM's stock, which declined substantially below the price paid by the plaintiffs. They sued, seeking capital losses and lost profits, claiming that Lazzaro and Neadeau, in violation of Section 10(b) of the Securities and Exchange Act of 1934, made untrue representations or expressed half-truths, intending that the plaintiffs would purchase the stock. The district court dismissed the complaint, reasoning that trading on inside information is itself a violation of Rule 10b-5 and that, as the plaintiffs were themselves wrongdoers, they were barred from recovery. The court of appeals reversed, and appeal was taken to the Supreme Court. Did the Supreme Court concur with the trial court? Why or why not?

7 Smith & Smith, certified public accountants, performed audits on the XYZ Corporation. The corporation's controller fraudulently concealed kickbacks given by the corporation to foreign purchasers. A shareholder brought suit against Smith & Smith for aiding and abetting the fraud, alleging that its failure to discover the fraud in the course of the audit was negligent and violated SEC Rule 10b-5. Are the accountants liable under that rule? Why or why not?

ETHICS IN PRACTICE

Although partnerships and corporations differ structurally, many ethical norms apply to both types of organization. For example, partners in an ordinary partnership are agents of one another, and each has fiduciary obligations to the others. Similarly, corporate officers, as agents of their corporations, have fiduciary obligations to their corporate employers; and corporate directors, although not agents of the corporations they serve, owe fiduciary obligations to their corporations and to the shareholders.

Under classical economic theory, the main obligation of corporate management (officers and directors) is to maximize profits for the shareholders. As noted economist Milton Friedman put it, "[T]here is one and only one social responsibility of business—to use its resources and engage in activities designed to increase its profits so long as it stays within the rules of the game, which is to say, engages in open and free competition without deception or fraud."[1] Commenting later on the role of the corporate manager, Dr. Friedman said, "That responsibility is to conduct the business in accordance with [the owners'] desires, which generally will be to make as much money as possible while conforming to the basic rules of the society, both those embodied in law and those embodied in ethical custom. . . . [T]he manager is the agent of the individuals who own the corporation . . . and his primary responsibility is to them."[2] Thus, the traditional agency-law standard of devotion to the principal's interests (so long as the agent acts within the law and ethical custom) would seem to mark the boundaries of ethical managerial conduct under classical economic theory.

But many commentators, including a number of business leaders, believe that corporations and their managers have broader responsibilities. As corporations have grown over the years, they have had great impact, for good and for ill, on the users of their products and services worldwide, and on the economic, social, and physical lives of the communities in which their plants and offices are located. To restrain the negative forces that corporations have the power to generate, new ethical norms have arisen, contributing to a body of ethical thought called "corporate social responsibility."

"The essence of the corporate social responsibility concept is the notion that business organizations have societal obligations that transcend economic functions of producing and distributing scarce goods and services and generating a satisfactory level of profits for their shareholders."[3] Proponents of corporate social responsibility argue that corporations are more than just privately owned economic entities—they are also citizens with rights and duties, and social actors whose conduct can affect millions of people. Consequently, managers have responsibilities, not only to shareholders, but also to other stakeholders such as employees, consumers, and the communities where the corporation resides. Corporate managers, then, are not only *agents of shareholders;* they are in a sense also *agents of society.* As such, they should do more than lawfully generate profits; they should spend corporate time and money on social concerns such as environmental pollution, unemployment arising from plant relocation, industrial hazards to employee health, and improvement of the quality of life in the host communities.

Within recent decades, many ethical norms, such as those condemning the pollution of the environment, racial discrimination in employment, and unwarranted threats to employee safety and health, have been incorporated into statutory law or administrative regulation and have become le-

[1]Milton Friedman, *Capitalism and Freedom* (1962).
[2]Friedman, "The Social Responsibility of Business Is to Increase its Profits," *New York Times Magazine,* Sept. 13, 1970, p. 33.
[3]Edwin M. Epstein, "The Corporate Social Policy Process and the Process of Corporate Governance," 25 *American Business Law Journal,* 361, 373 (1987).

gal norms as well. Other concerns, such as improving the quality of life in the host community, remain largely if not exclusively a matter of moral obligation. One key question is the extent to which a nonlegal ethical concern must be business-related to fall within a firm's corporate social responsibility.

An increasing number of large corporations accept the idea of corporate social responsibility (often seen as a desirable alternative to governmental regulation) and have taken steps to implement it systematically. Recently, the term "corporate social responsiveness" has been used to describe the implementation process—a process of strategic management by which a corporation may "anticipate and respond to rapidly changing and escalating social expectations" in its decision-making.[4] The emphasis is on *how,* not whether, the corporation should address the concerns of the broader society. Socially responsive management (1) selects appropriate ethical standards, (2) evaluates competing claims for societal improvement, and (3) allocates personnel and funds to those projects with the highest priority. Social auditing and accounting, the development of corporate codes of conduct, the adoption of industrywide ethical standards, and an ongoing involvement with the community are activities characteristic of corporate social responsiveness.

The problems that follow present a number of ethical dilemmas relating to internal or external corporate operations, or to both.

Problems in Ethics

1 BusyCorp has had a financially successful year. Its board of directors is considering whether to **(a)** give each of BusyCorp's employees a bonus based on length of service, **(b)** give very sizeable bonuses to each of the four senior corporate executives, **(c)** increase the dividend payable to shareholders, or **(d)** reduce to consumers the price of the company's highly profitable line of products. Assume that the board can choose only one of the alternatives. Does the choice of actions raise ethical questions?

[4]Ibid., p. 375.

2 A corporate raider is threatening to take over BusyCorp by acquiring a majority of its shares. The raider's practice is to dissolve the target corporation after the takeover and to divide its net assets among its shareholders (including the raider). As a result, it is common for some corporate divisions to be liquidated, their plants closed, and employees discharged. Civic leaders protest such actions. The raider responds that any legal entity has a right to convert its assets into cash and even go out of business if it so wishes. Does the raider's plan raise ethical questions?

3 A corporate raider has made an unfriendly offer to take over BusyCorp. Its board of directors is considering whether to adopt a poison pill plan and to establish golden parachutes for BusyCorp's four top officers. Some shareholders argue that the directors' actions present ethical problems. Are they correct? Would your answer be different if the four top officers were also directors?

4 Joe is engaged to Jane and loves her madly. He discovers that she is amassing a fortune in the stock market by trading in Megacorp stock, using insider tips furnished by Joe's boss, Megacorp president A. Crook. Joe knows that the Supreme Court has adopted the "misappropriation" theory. Under that theory, federal securities law makes it a felony for a corporate officer to steal (misappropriate) inside information, and persons who knowingly take advantage of it may be liable as coconspirators. Joe fears that if he reveals his knowledge, his climb up the corporate ladder may be blocked because top managers will not want to promote a person who may later "blow the whistle" on them. Joe also fears that Jane will be implicated as a coconspirator and will break their engagement. On several occasions, Joe has caught Jane telling little "white lies," and he has overheard Crook misrepresenting facts in order to gain an advantage in business transactions. Accordingly, Joe fears that Jane and Crook will implicate him in the crime by falsely testifying that he received inside information from Crook and repeated it to Jane. **(a)** What conflicting social pressures does Joe face? Are any ethical norms in conflict here? **(b)** What should Joe do to resolve the dilemma?

5 Fifteen major producers of foam cups, plates, and sandwich cartons (used by fast-food chains to package hamburgers) all use chlorofluorocarbons (CFCs) to make their foam containers. CFCs can destroy the Earth's protective ozone layer, which screens out the sun's ultraviolet rays that cause skin cancer, eye ailments, and environmental damage. The Environmental Defense Fund, Friends of the Earth, and the Natural Resources Defense Council requested the container manufacturers voluntarily to switch to a substitute compound (HCFC-22) that is 5 percent less destructive than CFCs to the ozone layer. Switching to HCFC-22 would involve a small increase in production costs which would be passed on to consumers. There is no law requiring container producers to switch. Foam packaging accounts for about 3 percent of the CFC used in the United States. **(a)** Under classical economic theory, would it be right or wrong for the fifteen companies to continue using CFCs in the production of foam containers? **(b)** Would a believer in corporate social responsibility have a different answer? Why or why not?

6 You are president and chairperson of the board of directors of Packco. You own none of its stock but control 51 percent of the voting shares. Twelve percent of Packco's business is the manufacture and sale of foam packaging. Congress enacts a law forbidding the use of CFCs. The sole supplier of HCFC-22 (the use of which is permitted) is a South African company owned by whites and employing whites only. Firms in the United States constitute 90 percent of the South African HCFC-22 market. You are being urged by opponents of South Africa's apartheid policy to refuse to buy South African products. You dislike apartheid and believe that a nationwide boycott of HCFC-22 will help end it. If you boycott HCFC-22, Packco will have to close a plant employing fifty people and reduce shareholders' dividends by 12 percent. **(a)** Does Packco have a corporate social responsibility to quit buying HCFC-22 from the South African company? **(b)** How would the race, ages, and economic circumstances of your employees affect your answer?

7 The following has been proposed by the American Law Institute as a principle of corporate governance that would be binding on corporate officials:

> "A business corporation should have as its objective the conduct of business activities with a view to enhancing corporate profit and shareholder gain, except that, whether or not corporate profit and shareholder gain are thereby enhanced, the corporation, in the conduct of its business (a) is obliged, to the same extent as a natural person, to act within the boundaries set by law, (b) may take into account ethical considerations that are reasonably regarded as appropriate to the responsible conduct of business, and (c) may devote a reasonable amount of resources to public welfare, humanitarian, educational, and philanthropic purposes."

(a) Where does this statement fit in the spectrum of opinion about the nature of a corporation and its social responsibility? **(b)** What *individuals* within the corporation will decide which ethical considerations can be "reasonably regarded as appropriate" for corporate action? Directors? Officers? Production workers? **(c)** What *standards* will be applied to competing ethical concerns for choosing which are "appropriate" for corporate response? Availability to claimants of aid from the government? Degree of benefit to the local community? Political acceptability of taking the requested action? Nature of aid sought—e.g., toys-for-tots versus scholarships for needy students versus an endowment for the arts? **(d)** What *guidelines* will management use to evaluate whether a particular course of action squares with "responsible conduct of business"? Amount of tax benefit? Extent to which governmental regulation might be avoided? Image of the corporation that results?

PART ELEVEN

Government Regulation

CHAPTER 44

Role of Administrative Law in the Regulatory Process

In the twentieth century, the United States has emerged as a huge industrial society of giant corporations, powerful labor unions, and complex social and economic problems such as unemployment, racial and sexual discrimination, costly and inefficient health care, pollution of the environment, and retirement income for the elderly. Early in this century, it was recognized that the three-branch government provided by federal and state constitutions (legislative, executive, and judicial) could not address issues of such magnitude by the traditional method of enacting laws that were enforceable only in the courts. Instead, state and federal legislatures increasingly delegated to the executive branch and to "independent" administrative agencies the right to exercise discretion by (1) making rules having force of law and (2) conducting trial-like hearings to adjudicate disputes over application of those rules.

Because of their power to make rules and regulations, administrative agencies are like legislatures. Yet they are also like courts, because they have authority to conduct trial-type hearings and to decide particular controversies. They also perform functions traditionally performed in the executive branch of government—for example, processing applications for social security benefits. In a well-known dissenting opinion, Justice Jackson described the importance of administrative agencies:

> The rise of administrative bodies probably has been the most significant legal trend of the last century, and perhaps more values today are affected by their decisions than by those of all the courts.... They also have begun to have important consequences on personal rights.[1]

Many people never go before a court of law, but every day their lives are affected by the decisions of state and federal administrative agencies that seek to prevent public harm by enforcing rules against unfair competition, unsafe automobiles, unsanitary food and meat, industrial accidents, unhealthy working conditions, employer discrimination against unions, dangerous nuclear waste disposal—and more. The list of activities regulated by administrative agencies is almost endless.

Much of this regulation applies to small business firms; but large firms doing interstate business may be subject to a staggering amount of administrative regulation from federal to local level. For example, suppose the hypothetical firm of Gardner Company, Inc., is engaged in food processing and does business in two states. In the establishment and conduct of its business, the Gardner Company has been subject to a number of agency requirements. It has had to (1) file articles of incorporation with the secretary of state of the "domicile" (home) state; (2) qualify to do business in every "foreign" state (any state other than the domicile state); (3) acquire a permit to sell a public issue of stock in the home state, and also from the federal Securities and Exchange Commission; (4) acquire licenses for food processing activities from federal, state, and local authorities; (5) file returns for: state sales and use taxes, state and federal income taxes, state and federal unemployment taxes, and social security taxes; withholding of income, unemployment, and social security taxes from employees' wages—and make the firm's pension plan conform to state and federal laws; (6) appear before the National Labor Relations Board regarding a union demand for an election; (7) defend its testing program for prospective employees against charges of violating the antidiscrimination provisions of the Equal Employment Opportunity Act; (8) cease certain advertising practices as required by the FTC, and conform its labeling and packaging to state and federal standards; (9) defend its procedures for discharge of food-processing wastes into a nearby river against objection from local, state, and federal agencies, including the Environmental Protec-

[1] *FTC v. Ruberoid,* 343 U.S. 470, 487 (1952).

tion Agency; (10) justify a contemplated purchase of a rival company before the antitrust division of the Justice Department; and (11) obtain a special import license from the U.S. Customs Service in order to import raw materials from Russia.

We see that some understanding of administrative law is essential in the conduct of modern business affairs. In this chapter we trace the development and scope of administrative regulation in the United States and consider the principal legal and business problems growing out of such regulation.

Development and Scope of Administrative Law

Meaning of Administrative Law, Administrative Agency, and Administrative Process

Administrative law is any law concerning the powers and procedures of administrative agencies, including the rules under which agencies create regulations, and the rules that permit a party aggrieved by an agency decision to petition for judicial review by a court. Administrative law is found in constitutions, statutes, and court decisions, as well as agency decisions, rules, and regulations. Administrative law normally does not include the substantive law produced by agencies. The substantive output of an agency is classified as tax law, labor law, antitrust law, or the like, since it becomes part of an existing body of substantive law.

The term *administrative agency* is used to mean any public officer, board, bureau, authority, or commission—other than legislatures and courts—having power to determine private rights and obligations by making rules and rendering decisions. The term refers equally to agencies organized within a department of government (e.g., the Patent and Trademark Office in the Department of Commerce) and those organized independently of any such department (e.g., the Federal Trade Commission). Administrative agencies have been characterized as "independent" if organized outside the executive departments of government. However, traditionally, an agency is said to be independent if the President lacks power to discharge its head without cause.

Administrative process in this chapter means the procedure through which administrative agencies carry on their work.

Rise of Administrative Regulation

Resorting to the use of administrative agencies as a means of social control in the United States goes back almost to the founding of the nation. The first Congress created agencies to implement laws regulating coastal trade, collection of customs, and the payment of veterans' bonuses.

During the eighteenth and until late in the nineteenth century, federal agencies played a minor role in the regulation of business. In 1887, Congress established the first major regulatory agency, the Interstate Commerce Commission (ICC). In 1913, the Federal Reserve Board was created, followed in 1914 by the Federal Trade Commission (FTC). The growth of aviation and radio resulted in the Federal Aviation Authority (FAA) and the Federal Communications Commission (FCC). In 1934, in the wake of the stock market crash of 1929, the Securities and Exchange Commission (SEC) was established to regulate the issuance and exchange of stocks and bonds in the capital markets of the nation.

Labor strife during the Great Depression brought the National Labor Relations Board (NLRB) to encourage collective bargaining between union and management and to prosecute unfair labor practices. The Food and Drug Administration (FDA) was reorganized and strengthened in 1938. Beginning in the 1960s, a number of new agencies were created: the Consumer Product Safety Commission (CPSC), Environmental Protection Agency (EPA), Equal Employment Opportunity Commission (EEOC), Nuclear Regulatory Commission (NRC), the National Highway Traffic Safety Administration (NHTSA), and the Occupational Safety and Health Administration (OSHA). Approximately sixty independent agencies now exist. In addition, the *United States Government Manual* lists several hundred agencies that operate under the Executive Office of the President, among which the Departments of State, Defense, and Labor are well known.

The growth of state and local governmental agencies has paralleled the federal trend. Today, thousands of state and local agencies regulate public utility rates; settle workers' compensation claims; issue and revoke drivers' licenses; administer welfare and medical benefits; and license hundreds of businesses and professions such as banks, insurance companies, beauty operators, construction contractors, doctors, real estate brokers, and marriage counselors. In addition, local county and city governments have established administrative agencies. For example, most cities and counties have planning commissions to administer zoning laws and grant building permits. The creation, structure, and functions of these state and local agencies are governed by the same general principles of administrative law that apply at the federal level.

Today, administrative agencies affect individuals and businesses more often, and with greater economic impact, than the decisions of all the courts in our judicial system. The explosive growth of administrative regulatory agencies has many causes, in particular the following:

1. The increasing complexity of life requires the services of legal experts in every field regulated by government. Legislators and judges generally are not experts in such technical and diverse fields as utility rates, security issues, public health, labor relations, and social insurance.
2. Legislators desire to free themselves, as far as possible, from enacting detailed legislation in order to focus on legislative policy. Similarly, legislators seek to free courts from a myriad of small cases so that judges will have more time for cases requiring the formulation of fundamental legal principles.
3. Effective regulation often requires greater uniformity of approach, supervisory continuity, and flexibility of action than could be achieved through traditional legislative and judicial patterns.
4. Many legislatures create agencies because they believe that court enforcement of regulatory laws is too costly, slow, and cumbersome; and that the public is better served by a cheaper, quicker system that minimizes the need for lawyers.
5. Most of the great regulatory statutes departed fundamentally from the substantive law evolved by the courts, and proponents of such statutes often feared that conservative courts would construe (interpret) away some of the legislative changes. The desire to have sympathetic agencies administer reform legislation is a major reason for the growth of the administrative process.
6. When legislators decide to regulate a new industry or to embark upon some program of social control for which there is no adequate basis of experience, they may resort to the administrative process as a means of coping with the problem on an experimental basis. For example, the Environmental Protection Agency was created in 1969 to establish and enforce standards for quality air and water—a task that initially required development of regulations on an experimental basis.
7. In the states there is a continuing need to regulate public utilities such as railroads, electric power, gas, and telephone companies. Often referred to as "natural monopolies" because the initial capital investment is so enormous that more than one company cannot operate profitably, such utilities receive monopoly privileges from the states. To protect consumers against excessive charges, legislatures established public utility commissions to regulate rate structures and other company policies that affect the public interest.

Legislative Delegation of Lawmaking Power to Agencies

State and federal administrative agencies are created by an act of the legislature called an "enabling statute." Typically, a federal enabling statute establishes a board or commission with a chairperson and four to six members, defines the subject matter jurisdiction of the agency, and delegates to it three kinds of powers:

1. A broad quasi-legislative rulemaking power
2. A quasi-judicial power to adjudicate whether an individual or business has violated statutory law or agency rules
3. A quasi-executive power to perform such functions as licensing, investigating and prosecuting violations, and advising the

public by interpreting agency rules to parties affected by them

The scope of an administrative agency's discretion to make and enforce rules is determined by the express or implied powers delegated to the agency by the enabling statute. An agency cannot legally exercise any power or discretion in excess of that which has been constitutionally delegated to it by the legislature.

The French philosopher Montesquieu influenced the fathers of the Constitution to provide in Articles 1, 2, and 3 for a separation of powers between the legislative, executive, and judicial branches of government. For example, Article 1 states: "All legislative Powers herein granted shall be vested in a Congress of the United States. . . ." Since the Constitution does not mention administrative agencies, let alone whether Congress can delegate its lawmaking power to them, two serious questions have arisen: (1) How can the concentration of legislative (rulemaking), executive (prosecuting violations of law), and judicial (adjudication of disputes) powers in the hands of a single official or administrative agency be justified under the separation-of-powers doctrine? (2) By what right, or at least to what extent may a legislature delegate to an agency the power to make rules that have the force of law? State constitutions also provide for separation of powers and likewise are generally silent about delegations of rulemaking power to administrative agencies.

Separation of Powers

Distributing powers among the three branches of government was meant to prevent the tyrannical concentration of power in any one authority. The concentration of legislative, executive, and judicial powers in one agency as illustrated in Figure 44.1 could be viewed as a violation of the separation-of-powers doctrine. Indeed, in the early days when commissions regulated railroads and utilities, the question was often before the courts. However, for more than half a century, the courts have generally refused to rule that administrative agencies or their activities are an unconstitutional violation of the separation-of-powers doctrine. Instead, courts have found agencies to be necessary and useful, and have let their work stand despite frequent challenge on constitutional grounds.

In holding that agencies exercising multiple powers are not in violation of the separation-of-powers doctrine, the courts have emphasized several arguments. First, courts have concluded that agencies do not, in fact, exercise legislative and judicial power, but only "quasi-legislative" and "quasi-judicial" power, i.e., power to make rules and to decide disputes only within the narrow jurisdiction delegated to them. For example, a state legislature may delegate to an Industrial Accident Commission power to make rules concerning workers' compensation and to adjudicate whether a particular worker is entitled to benefits. Although the Commission's rules *resemble* legislation

Figure 44.1 Powers of administrative agencies

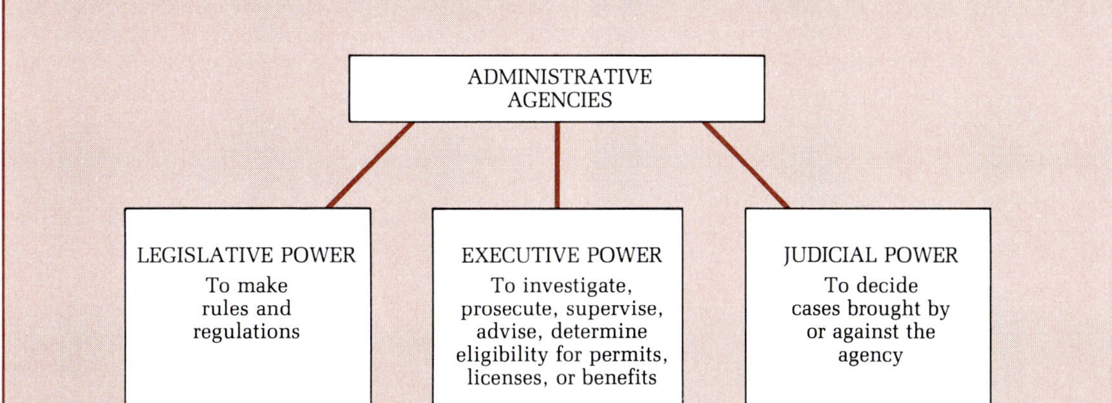

and its hearings *resemble* court trials, these activities are so narrow in scope that the agency cannot be said to be using the same kind of plenary power that the legislative, executive, and judicial branches of government exercise. Therefore, since legislative, executive, and judicial powers, in the true sense of those terms, have not been delegated to agencies, there is no violation of the constitutional doctrine of separation of powers.

Second, courts have frequently noted that there are checks and balances built into the administrative agency structure that function as safeguards against abuse of power. Unlike the legislature, which is independent of the other branches of government, an agency is at all times under the control of the legislature, which can always limit its activities by cutting its budget appropriations, by passing laws further restricting agency activity, or by abolishing it altogether. Similarly, in exercising their quasi-judicial function, agencies are not like courts that try cases and render judgments. Instead, agencies hold hearings and issue orders which are subject to review by the courts. Court review of agency orders provides an independent check by the judiciary on the abuse of the power of agencies, which technically operate under the executive branch of government. The Supreme Court has held that this judicial check is sufficient to meet the traditional requirement that the powers of the three branches of government should be separate.

Legislative Delegation of Power to Agencies

Early in this century, utility companies adversely affected by rate regulations imposed by public utility commissions questioned their regulatory authority as an unconstitutional *delegation* of legislative power. Responding to these challenges, courts developed the *primary standard* doctrine. Under it, a delegation of rulemaking power to an agency is not unconstitutional if the legislature establishes primary standards or guidelines to govern and limit the agency's exercise of power. Such a standard helps the courts, when reviewing the delegating statute, to decide whether the agency's power is sufficiently limited. Case 44.1 illustrates judicial recognition of the need for delegations of power to administrative agencies and the tendency of courts to accept even a very general guideline as sufficient to uphold the constitutionality of the enabling statute.

CASE 44.1 Village of Saratoga Springs v. Saratoga Gas, Electric Light & Power Co. · 83 N.E. 693 (N.Y. 1908)

FACTS Village of Saratoga Springs (plaintiff) sued the Saratoga Gas, Electric Light & Power Company (defendant) to enforce a rate-fixing order of the state commission of gas and electricity. The order limited the maximum price that the company could charge for gas and electricity. The company claimed that the rates were unlawful because the commission lacked the constitutional power to fix them. The trial court and intermediate appellate courts upheld the constitutionality of the commission's rate-fixing power.

OPINION CULLEN, C. J. We are now brought to the consideration whether... the power to prescribe the particular rates to be charged by public service corporations is so inherently and exclusively a legislative power that it is impossible of delegation to other branches of the government.... We see no reason why such power should be denied to the legislature.... There are in this state approximately four hundred and fifty gas and electric light companies. They are located in nearly every portion of the state, which contains within its bounds not only cities varying in population from ten thousand to four millions, but villages, agricultural communities, and the wild forests of the Adirondacks. It is plain that no uniform rate of charges could be established that would be just and reasonable. Besides, the difference in the output of the several companies, varying with the size of the communities they respectively supply, as well as the difference in the cost of material to the various companies, dependent on their location with reference to the cost of transportation of coal, oil and the like, would make a

CASE 44.1 Continued

rate that was fair in one place unreasonable in another. Therefore, any close approximation to a reasonable tariff would require special rates to be prescribed for many different localities. To do this properly would involve an investigation into the particular facts in each case. There was a time in the history of this country when carriers and public service corporations were so few that the legislature itself might have performed that labor. But by reason of the rapid growth of population and the great increase in the number of such corporations it has become impracticable for the legislature to discharge that duty. Moreover, many rates may require alteration from time to time. That the most appropriate method . . . is the creation of a commission or body of experts to determine particular rates has been said several times in the opinions rendered by the Supreme Court of the United States in the various railroad commission cases and in those of the state courts. . . . It cannot be said that in any real sense the legislature has delegated its power to the commission. The statute is complete. The legislature, not the commission, has enacted that there shall be maximum rates for the charges of gas and electric light companies, that light shall be furnished to consumers at those rates. . . . What is intrusted to the commission is the duty of investigation of the facts, and after a public hearing, of ascertaining and determining what is a reasonable maximum rate. . . .

It is contended that conceding that the legislature may commit to an administrative board the power to determine a tariff of rates, the statute must prescribe some standard by which the action of the board is to be governed; that otherwise the whole plenary power of the legislature is intrusted to the board, whose action may be arbitrary, and it is urged that the statute before us provides no such standard. We think otherwise. The statute provides that the commission shall fix the rates within the limits prescribed by law. This includes both statute law and common law. . . . The common law prescribes the rule that the rate should be reasonable. But it is said that "reasonable" is really no standard but a mere generality. Again, we are of a different opinion. Indeed, if the statute assumed to fix any other standard for rates than that they should be reasonable, we think it would be much more open to attack than in its present form. A lawmaker might exhaust reflection and ingenuity in the attempt to state all the elements which affect the reasonableness of a rate only to find that in a particular case he had omitted the factor which controlled the disposition of that case.

JUDGMENT The court upheld the constitutionality of the statute that delegated ratemaking authority to the utility commission.

At the federal level, the question of an unconstitutional delegation of legislative power to an agency was raised in the mid-1930s, when Congress enacted the National Industrial Recovery Act to deal with the problems of the Great Depression. In one of the broadest delegations of power in history, the act created the National Recovery Administration (NRA) and gave it authority to establish price-setting boards composed of representatives from firms in private industry. Violators of the minimum prices thus fixed by the NRA were subject to legal fines. In *A.L.A. Schechter Poultry Corp. v. United States,*[2] the Supreme Court struck down the act as an unconstitutionally broad delegation of law-making power that failed to set any standards to guide the agency created. Since *Schechter,* the Court has consistently upheld narrower Congressional delegations of rulemaking authority to administrative agencies. The modern view is that delegations of some power are "necessary in order that the exercise of legislative power does not become a futility."[3]

The Supreme Court accomplished the transition from the early to the modern view by resort to two theories: (1) Congress may enact legislation to

[2] 295 U.S. 495 (1935); but see, *Yakus v. United States,* 321 U.S. 414 (1944).

[3] *Sunshine Anthracite Coal Co. v. Adkins,* 310 U.S. 381, 398 (1940).

become operative upon the happening of some event or state of facts and may leave to others the responsibility of determining when the event or state of facts occurs; (2) Congress may declare a policy or determine a standard and may empower some officer or agency to fill in the details needed for implementation. The courts have taken a liberal view of what constitutes a declaration of policy or determination of standard. Such phrases as "public convenience, interest, or necessity," "just and reasonable," "fair and equitable," and "excessive profits" have been held to meet constitutional requirements. Similarly, the expression "unfair methods of competition" was held to be an adequate standard for the guidance of the Federal Trade Commission in carrying out duties delegated to it.[4]

In recent years, Congress has tended to specify in detail the procedures that the agency must follow in rulemaking and adjudications, tailoring such procedures to meet the particular needs of the agency. For example, in creating the Occupational Safety and Health Administration, it was recognized that OSHA would be establishing a wide range of safety rules on an industry-by-industry basis. Consequently, in the enabling statute, Congress provided for "informal notice-and-comment rulemaking," a speedy procedure that would simplify OSHA's task of drafting hundreds of regulations as quickly as possible. Generally, if the enabling statute is silent concerning rulemaking, adjudication, and judicial review procedures, then the provisions of the APA are applicable.

Lawmaking, Adjudication, and Other Agency Functions

This section discusses the day-to-day operations of federal administrative agencies in their legislative (rulemaking), judicial (adjudicating), and executive (e.g., prosecuting) functions. These activities are carried on within a framework of laws that apply generally to administrative agencies. The major general laws are discussed next.

Laws Affecting How Administrative Agencies Function

Administrative Procedure Act (APA). In the 1930s many of the new agencies that were created to administer economic recovery and reform tended to expand power and to act arbitrarily. Often there was public confusion about procedure because each agency developed its own system for making rules and for enforcing them in adjudication hearings. In 1946, Congress enacted the Administrative Procedure Act (APA) to establish more uniform agency procedures for rulemaking and adjudications in order to minimize agency misuse of power. The APA also set out specific grounds for judicial review, that is, appeal to the courts by any party adversely affected by agency action.

[4] *Atlantic Ref. Co. v. F.T.C.*, 381 U.S. 357 (1965).

The Federal Register Act. Another statute that affects all agencies is the Federal Register Act. Enacted in 1935, the Act created the Federal Register system which publishes three important references: (1) the *United States Government Manual,* (2) the *Federal Register,* and (3) the *Code of Federal Regulations* (CFR). The *Manual* lists the address of each federal agency and its regional offices. The purpose of the *Federal Register* is to provide notice in a single source of agencies' official acts. Published each business day, it gives notice of an agency's public hearings, including "formal rulemaking-on-the-record" as well as informal "notice-and-comment" rulemaking. In addition, the *Federal Register* publishes both proposed rules and adopted rules. The APA provides that most agency rules (also referred to in this chapter as "regulations") cannot be enforced until they have been published in the *Register.* Section 553(b) of the APA provides that such publication is constructive notice that makes a rule binding on all persons affected by it, regardless of whether they had actual knowledge of it.

When an agency such as the FTC has adopted and published a final rule in the *Federal Register,* it is republished in the *Code of Federal Regulations* and appears in the same section as all other current FTC regulations. Thus if the FTC adopted a new regulation within the last few days, one would be likely to find it in the *Federal Register,* along with any new regulations that OSHA or the NLRB might have adopted. However, in order to have access to all current regulations of the FTC, one would ordinarily turn to the FTC section of the *Code of Federal Regulations.*

Freedom of Information Act (FOIA). The Freedom of Information Act (FOIA) was enacted in 1966 as an amendment to the APA.[5] It requires that information in the possession of federal agencies be made available to the public upon request. The Act commands federal agencies to adopt rules specifying when, where, and how to request information under the FOIA, and the fees that are charged for compiling and copying. The request for information must describe it with reasonable certainty, and the agency must respond within ten working days. A party whose request has been denied may appeal the decision by filing an action in the federal district court; if he or she prevails, the court may award such party attorney fees.

Agencies are *not* required to disclose information if it is:

1 A classified secret involving national defense or foreign policy
2 An internal personnel rule or practice
3 Exempted from disclosure by other statutes
4 A trade secret, or commercial or financial information obtained from a person, which is confidential or privileged
5 Interagency or intraagency memoranda or letters
6 Personnel, medical, and similar files the disclosure of which would be an unwarranted invasion of personal privacy
7 Investigatory records gathered for law enforcement purposes
8 A report from an agency that regulates or supervises financial institutions such as banks
9 Geological and geophysical information, maps, and data concerning wells

Whenever there is doubt, courts construe all the above exemptions strictly against the agency and in favor of the party seeking information.

Government-in-the-Sunshine Act. In 1976, Congress took a further step toward the goal of making agency information and activities available to public scrutiny by enacting the Government-in-the-Sunshine Act,[6] sometimes referred to as an *open-meeting law.* The Act provides that whenever an agency is headed by two or more persons, a majority of whom are appointed by the President and confirmed by the Senate, it cannot act upon agency business unless every portion of every business meeting is "open to public observation." The ten exceptions to this rule are substantially the same as those of the FOIA listed above.

Most states have passed similar open-meeting laws which usually apply not only to agencies but also to subdivisions of government such as cities and counties. However, the specific provisions and exemptions of these open-meeting laws vary from state to state.

Federal Privacy Act of 1974 (FPA). In contrast to the FOIA and open-meeting laws, the Federal Privacy Act of 1974[7] restricts agencies from disclosing to any person or agency a record of an individual that is part of a system of records, without the individual's prior written consent. The term "record" refers to such matters as a person's education, financial transactions, medical history, and criminal or employment history. Eleven exceptions permit agencies to release such records. For example, they can be released to another agency for law enforcement purposes. The Act also permits individuals to examine and copy their own records and to request that the records be amended to correct factual errors. If the request is refused, a person may sue in federal court to require the records to be corrected and, if the action is successful, may recover attorney fees.

Quasi-Legislative Rulemaking

The broad discretion that the legislature delegates to agencies gives them a variety of regulatory choices. At one end of the spectrum, an agency can decline to regulate a significant segment of business that is properly within its jurisdiction. For example, the National Labor Relations Board (NLRB), shortly after its creation, issued rules narrowly defining business in interstate commerce so that millions of employees were excluded from its regulatory function of conducting elections among workers to choose a union

[5] 5 U.S.C.A. Sec. 552.

[6] 5 U.S.C.A. Sec. 552b.
[7] 5 U.S.C.A Sec. 552a.

to represent them. The NLRB also decided to establish relatively few rules and, instead, prosecuted "unfair labor practice" violations of the National Labor Relations Act in adjudication hearings, thus developing its unfair labor practice policy with case-by-case decisions over a period of years. At the other extreme, an agency such as the Federal Trade Commission may initiate a vigorous rulemaking program, promulgating (publishing) rules that regulate as many industries and businesses as possible. Increasingly Congress has mandated in its enabling legislation the type of regulatory technique that an agency will use. Thus, the enabling statute creating OSHA required it to promulgate rules establishing standards of health and safety in industry, and even spelled out the procedures to be used in rulemaking.

There are advantages and disadvantages to rulemaking by agencies as compared to the slower system of case-by-case adjudication. Rulemaking is costly and time-consuming, a disadvantage, and formulating a rule applicable to an entire industry is more difficult than adjudicating a single case. In addition, an agency that is proposing a rule often encounters powerful organized opposition from an entire industry. On the other hand, rulemaking offers distinct advantages: (1) It ensures sounder rules because affected persons and industries have an opportunity to contribute their expertise and criticism before a rule becomes law. (2) A single rulemaking proceeding may accomplish industry compliance with a clear set of rules that otherwise might require years if individual business were prosecuted on a case-by-case basis. (3) It is easier to understand and comply with rules than with a particular case decision that other businesses might view as irrelevant to their situation. (4) The growing complexity of matters being regulated, for example air pollution, requires that minimum standards be defined by scientific measurements that can be set forth easily in a clear set of rules.

Rulemaking Procedure. An agency's rules are the administrative equivalent of a statute and have the force of law. An agency can make rules only within the scope of power delegated to it by the legislature, and then only in accordance with the primary standards established by the legislature to guide it in its rulemaking. In order to survive judicial scrutiny of the courts, discussed later in this chapter, procedural fairness must be established in the rule. Under the Administrative Procedure Act (APA), which governs a federal agency's rulemaking procedures unless Congress provides different procedures in the enabling statute, there are two types of rulemaking—informal and formal.

Informal rulemaking. Most agencies use "informal" or "notice-and-comment" rulemaking provided for in Section 553 of the APA. This simple procedure involves three steps: (1) Notice of a proposed rule must be published in the *Federal Register.* (2) Interested persons must be given an opportunity to participate through submission of written comments containing data, views, and arguments, and although the agency is not required to provide an opportunity for oral testimony and argument, it has discretion to decide whether to do so. (3) After considering public comments, the agency must publish its final rule in the *Federal Register* (at least 30 days after the initial publication of the proposed rule in step 1 above) together with a concise general statement of the "basis and purpose" of the rule.

If informal rulemaking is judicially reviewed, the court will apply the most lenient standard under the APA and will set the rule aside only if it is "arbitrary and capricious, or an abuse of agency discretion." Although useful and relatively inexpensive, informal rulemaking has been criticized as unfair because parties opposed to a rule are neither informed of the factual basis underlying it nor given the opportunity (that a trial-type hearing would afford) to challenge the facts upon which the agency is relying and to attack the credibility of agency experts by cross-examination or by introduction of contradictory evidence.

Formal rulemaking. Section 553(c) of the APA states that "when rules are required by statute to be made on the record after opportunity for an agency hearing," the APA's *formal* procedures, set out in Sections 556 and 557, must be used. Therefore, if the statute which delegates rulemaking authority commands a hearing "on the record," with an opportunity for interested persons to testify and cross-examine witnesses before a rule is announced, the agency must comply. Such a hearing is often described as a trial-type hearing because it resembles a federal nonjury trial. After the hearing, the agency makes formal findings of fact, conclusions of law, and its decision adopting a final rule. These documents, together with the transcript of the proceedings, constitute "the record." The final rule must be supported by *substantial evidence* on the record taken as a whole. This means that a reviewing court applies a stricter standard than the "arbitrary and capricious" test that is applied to rules issued under informal rulemaking. Formal rulemaking is also called "rulemaking-on-a-record" because there is a formal transcript of the proceedings.

Although formal rulemaking permits effective use of cross-examination and presentation of testimony to test the factual basis of a proposed rule, it is costly and time-consuming. For example, in *National Nutritional Foods Association v. FDA,*[8] the Food and Drug Administration conducted formal rulemaking hearings for 18 months on a proposed rule regulating vitamin supplements. The entire effort became futile when an appellate court set aside the final rule on the ground that the agency had improperly limited the industry's cross-examination of a key agency expert witness. Because of the excessive time and expense required in formal rulemaking, Congress rarely mandates its use. For the same reasons, most agencies elect to use informal rulemaking unless a statute requires the formal model.

Hybrid rulemaking. In the last two decades, there has been growing discontent with the APA's informal-formal procedural dichotomy. Informal rulemaking, although efficient, may unduly limit the rights of the regulated to know or challenge a proposed rule; while formal rulemaking ensures trial-type rights to cross-examine and present testimony, it is often at great expense and intolerable delay. By the early 1970s, although federal courts continued to uphold the constitutional adequacy of informal rulemaking under the APA, they began requiring that such rulemaking (APA 553) contain some of the safeguards of formal rulemaking (APA 556, 557) such as oral hearings, cross-examination, and the right to present rebuttal witnesses. The resulting fusion is called *hybrid rulemaking.*

In *Mobil Oil Corp. v. FPC,*[9] the Natural Gas Act delegated rulemaking authority to the Federal Power Commission to fix rates for liquefiable hydrocarbons. The statute neither mentioned "on-the-record" proceedings nor indicated whether the formal or informal procedure should be used. However, Congress did provide that the rules adopted should be supported by "substantial evidence"—the standard used in formal rulemaking. Instead of interpreting the statute to require formal rulemaking, the court held that the ambiguity should be resolved by a hybrid arrangement. The agency could use informal rulemaking, but was required to provide a trial-type evidentiary hearing on some, but not all, of the factual issues. The court said:

> The APA may be viewed as providing the outer boundaries of administrative procedures. Congress has determined that the procedures outlined in section 553 will be the minimum protections upon which administrative action may be based, [granting] to interested parties a simple notice and right to comment. At the opposite end of the spectrum lie the requirements of sections 556 and 557. Those may be viewed as representing the highest degree of administrative protection that Congress believed would be necessary to protect interested parties. There is no reason, however, to conclude that Congress in establishing these limits intended to preclude all the possible formulations that might lie in between the two extremes.

In *United States v. Nova Scotia Food Products Corp.,*[10] the court interpreted informal rulemaking so as to *enlarge* public participation beyond the narrow right of written comment specified in the APA. The court held that even this narrow right had been nullified because the FDA did not disclose to interested parties the scientific study upon which it based its proposed rule. The court said:

> When the basis for a proposed rule is a scientific decision, the scientific material which is believed to support the rule should be exposed to the view of interested parties for their comment. One cannot ask for comment on a scientific paper without allowing the participants to read the paper.... To suppress meaningful comment by failure to disclose the basic data relied upon is akin to rejecting comment altogether.... The inadequacy of comment in turn leads in the direction of arbitrary decision-making.

Apparently concerned with the readiness of the lower courts to graft additional procedural safeguards onto informal rulemaking (as the lower court did in *Mobil Oil* above), the Supreme Court sharply criticized the practice in *Vermont Yankee Nuclear Power Corp. v. Natural Resources Defense Council, Inc.*[11] There the Court rejected the *Mobil Oil* argument that APA Section 553 merely established *lower* procedural bounds and that lower courts should be permitted to require *more* than the APA minimum where issues of great public import are

[8] 504 F.2d 761 (2nd Cir. 1974), cert. denied, 420 U.S. 946 (1975).
[9] 483 F.2d 1238 (D.C. Cir. 1973).
[10] 568 F.2d 240 (2nd Cir. 1977).
[11] 435 U.S. 519 (1978).

involved. Tracing the legislative history of Section 553, the Court concluded that Congress intended the discretion of the *agencies,* and not that of the courts, should be exercised in determining when extra procedural devices are needed. It held that "administrative agencies should be free to fashion their own rules of procedure." Although the decision in *Vermont Yankee* restricted the lower federal courts from developing further hybrid rulemaking procedures, they will probably continue to flourish for two reasons: (1) The Court's decision clearly permits the *agencies* to develop their own hybrid procedures, and (2) Congress has increasingly granted rulemaking authority based upon hybrid models that the earlier court decisions had developed.

Quasi-Executive Functions

The major executive functions of agencies are:

1. Issuing licenses and permits and determining eligibility of applicants for governmental benefits such as welfare payments
2. Investigating violations of statutes or administrative rules
3. Prosecuting such violations
4. Supervising industry activities such as banks
5. Advising the legislature of agency activities as well as giving advice to individuals or businesses concerning how they are affected by agency rules and how to comply with them

Most agencies perform all these functions but in varying degrees. For example, the National Labor Relations Board spends much of its time prosecuting unfair labor practices, whereas the Securities Exchange Commission concentrates a large part of its time on granting permits to corporations to issue and sell new securities. State licensing boards direct most of their efforts to testing applicants and issuing licenses to doctors, accountants, building contractors, drivers, and other persons.

Agency Investigations, Searches, and Inspections. Agencies investigate individual and corporate members of a regulated industry to obtain "legislative facts" (statistical data) needed for rulemaking and to obtain evidence necessary to prosecute violations of statutes or agency rules. The extent of an agency's power to compel disclosure of information depends upon the legislative delegation to the agency. For example, Congress has granted power to the FTC to inspect records of businesses, issue subpoenas, and "report orders" and "civil investigative demands" requiring businesses to submit information. Such inquiries, however, must be for a lawful purpose, must be relevant to the agency's mission, and must not seek information that is privileged because of the Fifth Amendment's guarantee against self-incrimination. Indeed, the most significant limitations on agencies' investigative powers are the constitutional prohibitions of the Fifth Amendment against compelling testimony involving self-incrimination, and the Fourth Amendment against unreasonable searches. These liberties have been vigorously guarded by the Supreme Court in recent years. Thus, *Camara v. Municipal Court*[12] held that an administrative agency must obtain a search warrant for a health or safety inspection of an apartment house. Similarly, *See v. Seattle*[13] required a warrant for inspection of a warehouse as part of an area search to enforce regulatory standards. In the case that follows, the Supreme Court established the general rule that the Fourth Amendment protects businesses against warrantless administrative agency searches.

[12] 387 U.S. 523 (1967).
[13] 387 U.S. 541 (1967).

CASE 44.2 Marshall v. Barlow's, Inc. · 436 U.S. 307 (1978)

FACTS The Occupational Safety and Health Act of 1970 (OSHA) authorizes the Secretary of Labor's inspectors to search the work area of any firm subject to OSHA's jurisdiction for

CASE 44.2 Continued

the purpose of discovering work hazards or violations of OSHA regulations. The act does not require a search warrant. In 1975, an OSHA inspector entered the customer service area of Barlow's, Inc., showed his credentials, and advised Barlow, the president, that he wanted to search the working areas of the business. After asking, and being advised that the inspector had no warrant and that OSHA had received no complaint about Barlow's, Inc. but was merely inspecting the firm as the result of a random selection, Barlow refused permission to inspect the working area. Barlow based his refusal upon his Fourth Amendment rights under the Constitution. OSHA then petitioned the U.S. District Court and obtained an order compelling Barlow to admit the inspector to the work area. The inspector again went to Barlow, presented the order, and was refused admission. Barlow's, Inc., then brought suit in the Court for an injunction restraining the Secretary from conducting warrantless inspections, claiming that they violated Fourth Amendment rights against unreasonable searches. The court held that the Fourth Amendment required a warrant for the type of search involved, and issued an injunction restraining warrantless inspections. The Secretary appealed.

OPINION

WHITE, Judge. . . . The Warrant Clause of the Fourth Amendment protects commercial buildings as well as private homes. To hold otherwise would belie the origin of that Amendment and the American colonial experience. . . . The general warrant was a recurring point of contention in the colonies immediately preceding the Revolution. The particular offensiveness it engendered was acutely felt by the merchants and businessmen whose premises and products were inspected for compliance with the several Parliamentary revenue measures that most irritated the colonists. . . .

The businessman, like the occupant of a residence, has a constitutional right to go about his business free from unreasonable official entries upon his private commercial property. The businessman, too, has that right placed in jeopardy if the decision to enter and inspect for violation of regulatory laws can be made and enforced by the inspector in the field without official authority evidenced by a warrant. . . . A warrant showing that a specific business has been chosen for an OSHA search on the basis of a general administrative plan for the enforcement of the Act derived from neutral sources such as, for example, dispersion of employees in various types of industries across a given area, and the desired frequency of searches in any of the lesser divisions of the area, would protect an employer's Fourth Amendment rights. We doubt that the consumption of enforcement energies in the obtaining of such warrants will exceed manageable proportions. . . .

The authority to make warrantless searches devolved almost unbridled discretion upon executive and administrative officers, particularly those in the field, as to when to search and whom to search. A warrant, by contrast, would provide assurances from a neutral officer that the inspection is reasonable under the Constitution, is authorized by statute, and is pursuant to an administrative plan containing specific neutral criteria. Also, a warrant would then and there advise the owner of the scope and objects of the search, beyond which limits the inspector is not expected to proceed. These are important functions for a warrant to perform, functions which underlie the Court's prior decisions that the Warrant Clause applies to inspections for compliance with regulatory statutes. . . .

JUDGMENT

We hold that Barlow's was entitled to a declaratory judgment that the Act is unconstitutional insofar as it purports to authorize inspections without warrant or its equivalent and to an injunction enjoining the Act's enforcement to that extent. The judgment of the District Court is therefore affirmed.

So ordered.

Of course, a warrant is not necessary if the owner of property consents to a search, or in case of emergencies such as putting out a fire. In addition, the Supreme Court has held that warrantless searches are permissible in certain businesses that are subject to licensing and intensive regulation such as selling retail liquor[14] or firearms.[15]

Nine years after the decision in *Barlow's*, a vendor of used auto parts, Joseph Burger, was asked by New York police officers to show his license and parts records that were required by state law. Burger replied that he had neither. Inspecting the premises without his objection, the police found stolen vehicles and arrested him. The appellate court reversed Burger's conviction, finding that the statute violated his Fourth Amendment rights because it authorized searches solely to uncover evidence of criminality. The U.S. Supreme Court reversed, holding that this type of warrantless search falls within the exception to the warrant requirement. The Court said that warrantless searches do not violate the Fourth Amendment where, as here: (1) there is a pervasively regulated industry, (2) the inspections are necessary to further the regulatory scheme, and (3) the statute appropriately restricts the scope of warrantless searches and the discretion of the inspecting officers.[16]

Prosecuting Violations. Millions of applications, claims, or tax returns are filed each year with agencies such as the Veterans Administration, Social Security Administration, and the Internal Revenue Service. If an agency decides to take adverse action, it serves a formal complaint upon an individual or business. This commences an adjudication proceeding involving a trial-type hearing under APA Sec. 554, discussed later in this chapter.

[14] *Colonnade Catering Corp. v. United States*, 397 U.S. 72 (1970).
[15] *United States v. Biswell*, 406 U.S. 311 (1972).
[16] *New York v. Burger*, 96 L. Ed.2d 601 (1987).

However, APA Sec. 554(c) requires agencies to provide an opportunity for settlement and most agencies have established rules governing settlement negotiation procedures. Agency prosecutors have almost unlimited discretion to settle cases, and most disputes are resolved through informal compromises. Often a respondent is asked to sign a "consent order," which reflects the terms of a compromise settling the dispute but which generally does not constitute an admission of violation of a statute or agency rule.

Many agencies have statutory power to take extraordinary action in emergency situations involving public health or safety. For example, the Consumer Product Safety Commission can remove a dangerous product from the market, the Federal Deposit Insurance Corporation can take over an "unsafe and unsound" bank, the Food and Drug Administration can seize property such as contaminated food, the Securities and Exchange Commission can suspend trading of a company's stock in the securities market, and the Federal Aviation Administration can suspend an airline pilot's license *before* an adjudication hearing is commenced. Statutes prescribe safeguards against the abuse of such power by requiring prior court approval of the action proposed by some agencies, or by providing that the agency must conduct a trial-type hearing immediately after the emergency action is taken.

Some agencies, such as the Federal Trade Commission and the National Labor Relations Board have statutory power to issue cease-and-desist orders prohibiting unlawful activity. In addition, many statutes provide for the imposition of civil penalties or fines each day such an order is disobeyed. Alternatively, in more serious cases, many agencies can apply directly to a federal court for an injunction restraining conduct that endangers the public health, safety, or economic interests. The following case is illustrative.

CASE 44.3 FTC v. Pharmtech Research Inc. · 1983-2 Trade Cases 69, 767

FACTS Pharmtech manufactured Daily Greens, a dietary supplement tablet, and in television ads stated:

CASE 44.3 Continued

> The following message concerns a revolutionary new concept in diet and nutrition. According to this report, commissioned by the National Cancer Institute, a combination of chrysoferous and carotene rich vegetables, have been proven to help our bodies build certain important biological defenses. Of course, to get the most benefit from any vegetable, you should eat them raw. But that's difficult to do every day. So I'd like to introduce you to Daily Greens. Daily Greens are not just another vitamin pill. They're natural, fresh, chrysoferous and carotene rich vegetables, dehydrated and compressed, to give you the important nutritional supplements, that could be so vital to your future health.... So, if you're not getting enough raw vegetables every day, rely on Daily Greens... To help your body defend itself.

In making these claims, Pharmtech relied solely on a report published by the National Academy of Sciences that reflected results of a study by the Committee on Diet, Nutrition, and Cancer. The committee report cautioned that its recommendations applied only to foods as sources of nutrients—*not to dietary supplements.*

FTC applied to the District Court in Washington, DC, for a preliminary injunction to restrain Pharmtech from falsely or deceptively advertising Daily Greens, pending the outcome of an FTC complaint against the firm, claiming that Pharmtech's ads violated both Sections 5 and 12 of the FTC Act. The question was whether the injunction should be granted.

OPINION

PARKER, D. J. An injunction may be issued under section 13(b) [of the act]... for the violation of any provision of law enforced by the FTC, including both false advertisements and misleading and deceptive advertisements.... A preliminary injunction under this section is proper if, after "weighing the equities and considering the Commission's likelihood of ultimate success, the Court determines that such action would be in the public interest."

Here, it is undisputed that Pharmtech's advertisements represent that the use of Daily Greens is associated with a reduction in cancer risk.... An advertisement is false if it fails to disclose sufficient facts to counter any false assumptions created by the advertisement, including omissions of any negative material facts.... The advertisements are false because the Report does not refer to a positive correlation between the use of a dietary food supplement such as Daily Greens and a reduction in the risk of cancer or the building of biological defenses. On the contrary, the Report expressly denies that its findings apply to the consumption of dietary supplements.

Section 5 of the Act declares that unfair or deceptive acts or practices in or affecting commerce are unlawful. [The] capacity of an advertisement to deceive consumers is judged by the impression conveyed by the entire advertisement, and not by the impact of isolated words and phrases.... Pharmtech's representations that the Report supports a finding that Daily Greens reduce the risk of cancer are unfair and deceptive because they convey a misleading impression. Pharmtech has played on the average consumer's well-founded fear of cancer, as a vehicle for the sale of its product.... The FTC has also established that it is likely to prevail on its claims that the defendant lacks a reasonable basis for its claims that the use of Daily Greens reduces the risk of cancer....

JUDGMENT

The Court, in balancing the equities, concluded that the deception was harmful to the public because (1) it played on consumer fear of cancer, (2) it tended to discourage consumers from eating vegetables instead of supplements, (3) Daily Greens cost nearly $15 a bottle, whereas fresh vegetables are readily available to consumers at a lower cost. Accordingly, the court issued a preliminary injunction against the use of the deceptive advertising. The Court also held that First Amendment free speech rights do not permit false advertising that will harm the public.

In addition to civil fines and penalties, many regulatory statutes provide for criminal sanctions against violators. For example, a person who willfully files fraudulent financial statements with the SEC can be prosecuted for a felony under the criminal provisions of the Securities Act, or can be sued in a civil action. If an agency decides to pursue criminal liability, the matter is referred to the Department of Justice for prosecution in the courts, since agencies are not equipped to provide the jury trials that criminal defendants have a right to demand.

Because of the expense and delay of criminal trials, most agencies prefer to pursue civil penalties. Thus, in *United States v. Ward,*[17] the U.S. Coast Guard, pursuant to the Clean Water Act, imposed a "civil penalty" of $5,000 on L.O. Ward for permitting oil to leak into a tributary of the Arkansas River. Immediately upon discovering the leak, Ward had reported it as required by the Act. He then filed suit to enjoin the Coast Guard from collecting the fine, arguing that the penalty was criminal in nature and that therefore the reporting requirements of the Act violated his right against compulsory self-incrimination. The Supreme Court held that where Congress has indicated an intention to establish a civil penalty, it is only when the statutory scheme is so punitive in nature as to negate that intention that the statute will be held unconstitutional as a violation of the right against self-incrimination. Since the Clean Water Act called for a maximum civil penalty of $5,000 for each offense, the Court held it was not sufficiently punitive to be considered criminal in nature, and therefore the Fifth Amendment privilege against self-incrimination did not apply. The decision would seem to uphold the right of most agencies to impose statutory civil penalties on violators.

Supervising and Advising. Where pervasive regulation is required, some agencies devote most of their time to informal supervision. For example, the Federal Home Loan Bank has a large staff of examiners that conducts regular audits of the nation's savings and loan associations. Administrators license new associations and branches, issue rules setting reserve requirements, and require periodic reports. Formal proceedings are rarely used, as most of the agency's business is conducted by informal conferences.

Most agencies expend considerable time in giving advice to individuals and businesses. For example, the IRS has hundreds of employees who answer the public's questions concerning taxes. Formal advice may be given in the form of: (1) a "no-action" letter indicating an agency will not prosecute a borderline violation, (2) a "private letter ruling" on a tax matter, or (3) a "declaratory order" under APA Sec. 554(e), permitting the agency to terminate a controversy or remove uncertainty about the issues. APA Sec. 554(e) also gives assurance that such order is binding on the agency. Agencies also educate the public on new rules and warn consumers about dangerous products. Threat of adverse publicity is sometimes used to induce a violator to comply with agency rules. However, the trend is for agencies to adopt internal rules that restrict comment to the media on pending cases, or that require advance notification to the business affected, so that it can prepare a response.

Quasi-Judicial Adjudication

Under APA Secs. 551(6) (7) every final agency action resulting in an order other than rulemaking is called an *adjudication.* Since agencies adopt comparatively few rules, it is clear that most agency decisions are adjudications that affect the rights and interests of individuals or businesses. However, only a very small proportion of these adjudications involve a formal trial-type hearing. Such evidentiary hearings are guaranteed under APA Sec. 554(a) only in those few adjudications where the enabling statute requires the agency decision to be determined "on the record" after hearing. Although the proportion of formal hearings is small compared to informal adjudications, each year over a thousand administrative law judges decide approximately 250,000 cases at formal hearings, exceeding by far the total number of cases decided by all the federal courts. However, the total number of *informal* adjudications decided by federal agencies each year is estimated in the millions.

[17] 448 U.S. 242 (1980).

Informal Agency Adjudications—Due Process. The vast majority of administrative adjudications involve informal action in which only minimal statutory safeguards protect the rights of the individual. Becauses the APA makes no provision for informal adjudications, agencies lack a uniform procedure for making decisions. The Freedom of Information Act and Privacy Act guarantee the right to notice of the rules, orders, or policy statements that the agency will use against an individual as well as access to agency documents needed to support a claim or defense. However, the most significant protection for the individual respondent is the Fifth Amendment restraint on the federal government that no person shall be "deprived of life, liberty, or property, without due process of law." State administrative agencies are restricted by a similar provision in the Fourteenth Amendment. The U.S. Supreme Court has interpreted this phrase to include the right to *procedural fairness,* that is, reasonable notice that an individual's rights are about to be affected by agency action, and an opportunity to be heard before final action is taken.

In recent years, two troubling questions have arisen: (1) At what stage of informal proceedings is a respondent entitled to a hearing? (2) Where the enabling statute fails to specify informal adjudication procedures, what type of hearing should be provided? The U.S. Supreme Court has ruled on these questions, but the decision spelling out what due process requires for one agency is often not applicable to another. Two cases in which the Court considered the claim that the Social Security Administration had not observed procedural due process will illustrate. In *Goldberg v. Kelly,* the Supreme Court held that termination of welfare benefits without first holding an evidentiary hearing was a denial of procedural due process. The decision emphasized that since Goldberg's livelihood was at stake, a hearing before cutting off his benefits was justified. Six years later in the case below, again involving termination of social security benefits without a hearing, the Supreme Court held that procedural due process was *not* violated. What factors distinguish the two cases?

CASE 44.4 Mathews v. Eldridge · 424 U.S. 319 (1976)

FACTS In 1968 the Social Security Administration (SSA) awarded disability benefits to Eldridge. In 1972 he completed a questionnaire forwarded by SSA representatives to determine if he continued to be eligible for disability payments. The agency, after reviewing current medical reports from Eldridge's physician and psychiatric consultant, notified Eldridge of their decision that he was no longer suffering a disability and that he had 6 months to request reconsideration of the decision. Instead of requesting this, Eldridge commenced suit in the federal district court, asking it to order immediate reinstatement of disability benefits. He argued that he had been deprived of procedural due process, because his benefits were terminated solely on the basis of his questionnaire and the medical reports which the agency had obtained and acted upon without first holding a hearing to afford him the opportunity to present rebuttal evidence. The District Court held that the agency had abridged Eldridge's right to procedural due process, and the Court of Appeals affirmed. The Supreme Court granted certiorari.

OPINION POWELL, Justice. . . . The issue in this case is whether the Due Process Clause of the Fifth Amendment requires that prior to the termination of Social Security disability benefit payments the recipient be afforded an opportunity for an evidentiary hearing. . . .

The Secretary moved to dismiss on the grounds that Eldridge's benefits had been terminated in accordance with valid administrative regulations and procedures and that he had failed to exhaust available remedies. In support of his contention that due process requires a pretermination hearing, Eldridge relied exclusively upon this Court's decision in *Goldberg v.*

CASE 44.4 Continued

Kelly, 397 U.S. 254 (1970), which established a right to an "evidentiary hearing" prior to termination of welfare benefits. The Secretary contended that *Goldberg* was not controlling since eligibility for disability benefits, unlike eligibility for welfare benefits, is not based on financial need; and... [that] issues of credibility and veracity do not play a significant role in the disability entitlement decision, which turns primarily on medical evidence....

Procedural due process imposes constraints on governmental decisions which deprive individuals of "liberty" or "property" interests within the meaning of the Due Process Clause of the Fifth or Fourteenth Amendment. The Secretary does not contend that procedural due process is inapplicable to terminations of Social Security disability benefits. He recognizes, as has been implicit in our prior decisions... that the interest of an individual in continued receipt of these benefits is a statutorily created "property" interest protected by the Fifth Amendment.... Rather, the Secretary contends that the existing administrative procedures, detailed below, provide all the process that is constitutionally due before a recipient can be deprived of that interest.

This court consistently has held that some form of hearing is required before an individual is finally deprived of a property interest.... The dispute centers upon what process is due prior to the initial termination of benefits, pending review.... More precisely, our prior decisions indicate that identification of the specific dictates of due process generally requires consideration of three distinct factors: First, the private interest that will be affected by the official action; second, the risk of an erroneous deprivation of such interest through the procedures used, and the probable value, if any, of additional or substitute procedural safeguards; and finally, the Government's interest, including the function involved and the fiscal and administrative burdens that the additional or substitute procedural requirement would entail....

Whenever the agency's tentative assessment of the beneficiary's condition differs from his own assessment, the beneficiary is informed that benefits may be terminated, provided a summary of the evidence upon which the proposed determination to terminate is based, and afforded an opportunity to review the medical reports and other evidence in his case file. He also may respond in writing and submit additional evidence....

The state agency then makes its final determination, which is reviewed by an examiner in the SSA Bureau of Disability Insurance.... If, as is usually the case, the SSA accepts the agency determination it notifies the recipient in writing, informing him of the reasons for the decision, and of his right to seek de *novo* reconsideration by the state agency....

If the recipient seeks reconsideration by the state agency and the determination is adverse, the SSA reviews the reconsideration determination and notifies the recipient of the decision. He then has a right to an evidentiary hearing before an SSA administrative law judge.... If this hearing results in an adverse decision, the claimant is entitled to request discretionary review by the SSA Appeals Council... and finally may obtain judicial review....

Since a recipient whose benefits are terminated is awarded full retroactive relief if he ultimately prevails, his sole interest is in the uninterrupted receipt of this source of income pending final administrative decision on his claim. His potential injury is thus similar in nature to that of the welfare recipient in *Goldberg*....

> the crucial factor in this context—a factor not present in the case of... virtually anyone else whose government entitlements are ended—is that termination of aid pending resolution of a controversy over eligibility may deprive an eligible recipient of the very means by which to live while he waits.

Eligibility for disability benefits, in contrast, is not based upon financial need. Indeed, it is wholly unrelated to the worker's income or support from many other sources, such as

CASE 44.4 Continued

earnings of other family members, workmen's compensation awards, tort claims awards, savings, private insurance, public or private pensions, veterans' benefits, food stamps, public assistance, or the "many other important programs, both public and private, which contain provisions for disability payments affecting a substantial portion of the work force. . . ."

An additional factor to be considered here is the fairness and reliability of the existing pretermination procedures, and the probable value, if any, of additional procedural safeguards. . . . In short, a medical assessment of the worker's physical or mental condition is required. This is a more sharply focused and easily documented decision than the typical determination of welfare entitlement. In the latter case, a wide variety of information may be deemed relevant, and issues of witness credibility and veracity often are critical to the decision-making process. *Goldberg* noted that in such circumstances "written submissions are a wholly unsatisfactory basis for decision."

The decision in *Goldberg* also was based on the Court's conclusion that written submissions were an inadequate substitute for oral presentation because they did not provide an effective means for the recipient to communicate his case to the decisionmaker. Written submissions were viewed as an unrealistic option, for most recipients lacked the "educational attainment necessary to write effectively" and could not afford professional assistance. . . .

In striking the appropriate due process balance the final factor to be assessed is the public interest. This includes the administrative burden and other societal cost that would be associated with requiring, as a matter of constitutional right, an evidentiary hearing upon demand in all cases prior to the termination of disability benefits. The most visible burden would be the incremental cost resulting from the increased number of hearings and the expense of providing benefits to ineligible recipients pending decision. . . .

We reiterate the wise admonishment of Mr. Justice Frankfurter that differences in the origin and function of administrative agencies "preclude wholesale transplantation of the rules of procedure, trial and review which have evolved from the history and experience of courts."

The judicial model of an evidentiary hearing is neither a required, nor even the most effective, method of decision-making in all circumstances. The essence of due process is the requirement that "a person in jeopardy of serious loss [be given] notice of the case against him and an opportunity to meet it." . . .

JUDGMENT We conclude that an evidentiary hearing is not required prior to the termination of disability benefits and that the present administration procedures fully comport with due process.

The judgment of the Court of Appeals is Reversed.

Other decisions have applied procedural due process principles to a variety of different agencies and situations. In *Bell v. Burson*[18] the Court held that temporary suspension of a driver's license was a critical threat to a property interest and required a prior hearing because the respondent might otherwise be denied a livelihood due to his inability to drive to work. Similarly, revocation of doctors' and other professionals' licenses have been held to require a prior hearing. In *Goss v. Lopez*,[19] the Court ruled that a high school student's education is sufficiently critical that before suspension he should have at least an informal prior hearing.

But in *Board of Curators of the University of Missouri v. Horowitz*,[20] the Court held that periodic faculty review and notice to a medical student of her unsatisfactory grade record was procedurally fair

[18] 402 U.S. 535 (1971).

[19] 419 U.S. 565 (1975).

[20] 435 U.S. 78 (1978).

and justified expelling her without a prior hearing. The Court ruled that such expulsion was not a denial of due process. In cases where the issue of fact is whether the student has earned passing grades, it is useful to ask: What would a hearing accomplish? Since grades have previously been determined by an almost universally recognized procedure, no issue of fact remains to be determined at a hearing. Oral hearings are for the purpose of settling issues of fact; therefore, courts generally hold that if the only issue in an adjudication is a question of law, there is no right to a hearing.[21]

Formal Adjudications. Formal adjudications are also referred to as "trial-type" or "evidentiary" hearings. They are required by the APA only when a statute calls for adjudication "on the record after opportunity for an agency hearing." As noted earlier, they constitute only a small proportion of total adjudications. However, statutes increasingly are commanding agencies to conduct formal adjudications.

Notice. Procedural due process spelled out in the APA gives a respondent the right to timely notice of agency charges as well as the time of the hearing. Such notice is given when an agency issues and serves a respondent with a complaint setting forth its factual contentions. If the outcome of an adjudication will affect other parties, such as competitors, an agency may notify interested parties and provide them with an opportunity to participate in the hearing. Upon a showing of good cause, an interested party who has a vital interest in the outcome of the adjudication may be permitted to intervene in the case as a respondent. In licensing cases, if there are two applicants where the rules permit only one license to be granted, a "comparative hearing" must be held in which both applicants have an opportunity to demonstrate the strength of their claims and the weaknesses of the competing application.

Discovery. In court, litigants have the right to pretrial discovery by means of depositions or written interrogatories (questions) which enable them to know the evidence of the adverse party well ahead of trial. However, in agency adjudications discovery rights are extremely limited. The APA confers no discovery privileges upon a respondent, but under the FOIA, a respondent has access to relevant, unprivileged information contained in agency files. In addition, under the *Jencks* doctrine,[22] after an adverse government witness has testified, a respondent can require disclosure of all prior statements made by the witness to government officials.

Trial: presenting evidence and cross-examination. A formal adjudication case is tried before an administrative law judge (ALJ), who conducts an evidentiary hearing similar to a federal nonjury trial. When authorized to do so by a statute, such as the National Labor Relations Act, the ALJ may issue subpoenas requiring witnesses to appear and testify. Otherwise Section 556(d) of the APA seriously limits the right to a full hearing, since the agency can require that all or part of the evidence be submitted in written form. Under this procedure, witnesses' verified written statements are submitted to the opposite party, who then is given time to reply with written rebuttal statements. The APA also gives agencies wide discretion to limit cross-examination. Since cross-examination is used to test a witness's memory, bias, logic, accuracy, expertise, and perception, prohibiting or restricting cross-examination may seriously affect the quality of an agency decision. Regardless of the method used to admit evidence, agency prosecutors must ordinarily prove their case by a "preponderance of the evidence."

Admissibility of hearsay: the "substantial evidence rule." Administrative treatment of the rules of evidence further illustrates the agency approach to procedural due process. Courts refuse to admit certain kinds of "hearsay" evidence (statements made by a witness on the authority of another, and not from personal knowledge or observation). The reason for excluding hearsay evidence is that the maker of the statement is not available in court for cross-examination to test his or her credibility. Therefore, exclusion of hearsay testimony is traditionally viewed as necessary to avoid the danger that a jury will base its findings of fact upon unreliable evidence.

In an administrative hearing, there is no jury—an administrative law judge makes the findings of

[21]*Mackey v. Montrym*, 443 U.S. 1 (1979).

[22]*Jencks v. United States*, 353 U.S. 657 (1957). This rule was codified as 18 U.S.C.A. Sec. 3500.

fact. Because parties to an administrative hearing often cannot afford an attorney and the hearsay rule is too complex for lay persons to understand and apply, administrative agencies almost universally admit hearsay evidence. This practice increases the risk that the ALJ may believe the hearsay and make findings of fact against a party who has presented highly credible contradictory evidence. However, it is now well settled by reviewing courts that permitting hearsay evidence in administrative hearings is justified on two grounds: (1) Unlike trial by a lay jury that doesn't understand the unreliability of hearsay, the trier of fact in an administrative hearing is an ALJ who, as a trained lawyer, has the expertise to readily recognize hearsay and to give it little or no weight. (2) On appeal to a reviewing court, the APA provides an additional safeguard against reliance on hearsay by requiring that the agency's findings of fact may be set aside unless there is *substantial evidence* to support such findings in the record of the proceedings. Since "substantial evidence" means direct testimony, not hearsay, agencies must be careful not to base findings of fact on hearsay evidence because of the likelihood that such findings would be reversed on appeal to the courts.

The *substantial evidence rule* prevents an appellate court from conducting a new trial (trial *de novo*) by requiring the court to accept agency findings of fact when they are based upon substantial evidence in the record. In determining whether there is substantial evidence, federal courts must consider the whole record and not just the evidence presented by one party. The reviewing court's function is to enunciate and apply the law. The practical result of the substantial evidence rule is that a party appealing an agency decision into the courts will rarely succeed in reversing the agency's findings of fact.

Even though administrative hearings present the risk of "rough justice" as opposed to the more precise fairness of courts of law, they can be upheld as socially necessary, particularly in matters involving small sums of money coupled with the need for a quick determination. For example, in a workers' compensation hearing, the risk of an unfair evaluation of the evidence may very well be outweighed by the urgency for a speedy decision.

Separation of functions. Just as the Constitution requires separation of *powers* between the legislative, executive, and judicial branches of government, an administrative agency must draw a clear line between its *quasi-executive* power to investigate and prosecute violations of agency rules, and its *quasi-judicial* responsibility to conduct adjudication hearings. This distinction between these activities is called *separation of functions.*

The Fifth Amendment restrains the federal government, and the Fourteenth Amendment restrains the states, from denying personal or property rights "without due process of law," that is, a fair hearing. Our traditional standards for a fair trial make it unthinkable for a judge to assume the role of prosecutor or for the lawyer for one of the parties to act as judge. Therefore, strict separation of the investigatory, prosecutorial, and judicial functions is required by the judicial system.

Administrative law, on the other hand, generally requires only the degree of functional separation which is needed to produce fair decisions. The combination of investigation with judging may be bad in such prosecuting agencies as the National Labor Relations Board and the Federal Trade Commission, but may be harmless and even desirable where claims are being processed by agencies that are as much interested in making payments to the deserving as in withholding payments from persons whose claims lack merit.

Decision and appeal. At the conclusion of the hearing, the ALJ prepares findings of fact and conclusions of law, and makes an *initial* decision, which becomes final unless the agency or commission modifies it. In contrast, a *recommended* decision *must* be acted upon by the agency before it becomes final.

In formal adjudications, agencies cannot rely on evidence that is not a part of the record. Section 556(d) of the APA provides that the "exclusive record for decision" consists of the transcript, exhibits, and other documentary evidence introduced at the hearing. In *Seacoast Anti-Pollution League v. Costle,*[23] after a hearing but before decision, the Environmental Protection Agency Administrator consulted a panel of agency scientists to assist him in analyzing the record. However, the panel furnished the administrator with additional scientific material, thereby *supplementing* the record. The court set aside the decision on the ground that the

[23] 572 F.2d 872 (1st Cir. 1978).

administrator had relied on data that was not a part of the record.

Judicial Review

Previous discussion in this chapter contains many illustrations of administrative agency abuse. Some agencies have attempted to expand their power beyond appropriate limits. Others, under time pressure to process thousands of decisions, have adopted procedural shortcuts that have denied due process of law to individuals and businesses. These shortcuts have steadily chipped away at the right to have unlimited discovery and cross-examination, to subpoena witnesses and present oral testimony, or to exclude hearsay evidence. Informal rulemaking has even failed in many cases to guarantee a hearing before adverse action is taken.

During the last half-century, many counter forces have developed to retard or limit agency abuse of power. Newspaper and television media can quickly expose agency misdeeds to public view, often triggering action by elected representatives in the legislature. Legislatures, in turn, have an impressive array of weapons at their disposal for curbing agency abuse. They can enact laws limiting the powers of an agency, or even abolish it. They can signal an agency to institute reforms by drastically limiting its budgetary appropriations and by conducting investigative hearings to expose agency irregularities . Individual legislators are generally very effective with "casework," that is, assisting constituents by means of friendly but authoritative direct contact with agencies. When an agency receives a letter with a "Member of Congress" tag, it is given priority attention. In addition, agency leadership is appointed by the President with the "Advice and Consent" of the Senate—a further source of legislative influence on agencies.

Notwithstanding the techniques legislators use to limit agency power, the most important continuing restraint against abuse by the administrative bureaucracy is *judicial review*. While media publicity or legislative investigations may eventually change unfair policies or rules, judicial review usually offers the only opportunity for immediate relief to a private party who has been arbitrarily mistreated by an agency.

Judicial review is the process by which the legality of agency action is scrutinized by state or federal courts. This section will discuss (1) the scope of judicial review, (2) how agency decisions come before an appellate court for review, and (3) the standards and principles which reviewing courts apply in ruling on the legality of agency actions.

Philosophically, the most important function of judicial review is to improve the entire administrative process. As one circuit court has said:

> Judicial review must operate to ensure that the administrative process itself will confine and control the exercise of discretion. Courts should require administrative officers to articulate the standards and principles that govern their discretionary decisions in as much detail as possible. Rules and regulations should be freely formulated by administrators, and revised when necessary. Discretionary decisions should more often be supported with findings of fact and reasoned opinions. When administrators provide a framework for principled decisionmaking, the result will be to diminish the importance of judicial review by enhancing the integrity of the administrative process, and to improve the quality of judicial review in those cases where judical review is sought.[24]

The power of courts to review administrative action has developed from three sources: statutes, the Constitution, and judicial decisions. Our discussion begins with cases in which court review is prohibited.

Nonreviewable Matters

Some laws specifically deny the power of judicial review. For example, one statute provides that the decisions of the Administrator of Veterans' Affairs on *any* question of law or fact regarding benefits for veterans and their dependents or survivors is not reviewable "by any court of the United States."[25] In *Agent Orange Product Liability Litigation*,[26] the court interpreted the statute, and ruled that the administrator's alleged failure to provide adequate

[24]*Environmental Defense Fund, Inc. v. Ruckelshaus*, 439 F.2d 584 (D.C. Cir. 1971).
[25]39 U.S.C.A. Sec. 211(a).
[26]818 F.2d 194 (2nd Cir. 1987).

medical treatment to servicemen exposed to Agent Orange in Vietnam was not subject to judicial review. The court reasoned that under the Constitution, Congress raises armies and the President commands them, and military decisions should not subject the government to liability as the result of "second guessing" by the courts.

Section 701(a)(1) of the APA prohibits judicial review of federal agency decisions when it is precluded by statute. Thus, in *United States v. Erika, Inc.*,[27] the statute establishing Medicare authorized the *Secretary of Health and Human Services,* or his agent, to reimburse persons over 65 for 80 percent of amounts they expended on medical supplies. Although the statute provided for an oral hearing if the supplier's request for reimbursement was refused, it did not provide for judicial review. Erika, Inc., a supplier of kidney dialysis equipment, objected when the secretary refused reimbursement based upon catalog price increases. After denial of relief at an oral hearing, Erika petitioned the Court of Claims for judicial review. The Supreme Court held that there was no jurisdiction to review determinations of the amounts payable under Medicare; that in light of the precise provisions of the statute, the omission of authorization of judicial review provided "persuasive evidence that Congress deliberately intended to foreclose further review of such claims."

Section 701(a)(2) of the APA precludes judicial review where agency action is "committed to agency discretion by law," but it is for courts to determine what this phrase means. In *Cuyahoga Valley R. Co. v. United Transp. Union,*[28] the Supreme Court held that the Secretary of Labor has an unreviewable discretion to withdraw a citation charging an employer with violating the Occupational Health and Safety Act (OSHA). The authority of OSHA's Review Commission was not extended to overturning the secretary's decision to withhold a citation, or to withdraw one. The Court said that permitting the Commission to review the secretary's decision would "discourage the secretary from seeking voluntary settlements with employers in violation of the Act, thus unduly hampering the enforcement of the Act"; and would "allow the Commission to make both prosecutorial decisions and to serve as the adjudicator of the dispute, a commingling of roles that Congress did not intend."

[27]456 U.S. 201 (1982).
[28]88 L. Ed.2d 2 (1985).

Reviewable Agency Decisions

Section 706 of the APA provides that the reviewing court shall decide all relevant questions of law, interpret constitutional and statutory provisions, and determine the meaning or applicability of the terms of an agency action. The reviewing court shall:

1 Compel agency action unlawfully withheld or unreasonably delayed and
2 Hold unlawful and set aside agency action, findings, and conclusions found to be
   - arbitrary, capricious, an abuse of discretion or otherwise not in accordance with law...
   - contrary to constitutional right, power, privilege or immunity
   - in excess of statutory jurisdiction...
   - without observance of procedure required by law
   - unsupported by substantial evidence...

Cases 44.2 and 44.5 (below) illustrate Supreme Court review under these APA provisions. The Model State Administrative Procedure Act contains similar provisions for review at the state level.

In a few limited situations, federal district courts can review agency actions. Since these are trial courts, testimony and additional evidence can be received to supplement incomplete or inadequate agency findings of fact.[29]

The federal Hobbs Act[30] grants judicial review in the U.S. Courts of Appeal from all *final* administrative orders which include decisions in formal and informal rulemaking as well as adjudications. However, because Courts of Appeal are not equipped to conduct trials or to receive testimony, and must rely on the evidence developed at the agency rulemaking or adjudicatory hearing, rarely is a de novo review permitted, that is, an entire new trial on the issues of fact. The appellate courts will simply apply one of the various tests discussed

[29]APA Sec. 706(2)(F); *Citizens to Preserve Overton Park, Inc. v. Volpe*, 401 U.S. 402 (1971).
[30]28 U.S.C.A. Sec. 2341-51.

in the next section to determine if the agency findings of fact are properly supported by the evidence. Since most agency records on appeal satisfy the evidentiary test that is used, agency findings of fact are seldom set aside by the reviewing court. However, reviewing courts have full jurisdiction to rule on issues of law, including matters of statutory or constitutional interpretation.

The substance of the foregoing discussion is illustrated by the following case in which (1) the initial review was by a federal district trial court, (2) the court interpreted the enabling statute, (3) the findings of fact were found to be inadequate, and (4) an agency decision was set aside as "arbitrary and capricious" under the APA.

CASE 44.5 Dunlop v. Bachowski · 421 U.S. 560 (1975)

FACTS After running for a union office and losing, Bachowski exhausted his union remedies under the union bylaws and then filed a complaint with the Secretary of Labor. He claimed a violation of the Labor-Management Reporting and Disclosure Act of 1959 (LMRDA). The purposes of this act are, among others, to prevent individuals from filing suits to block union elections by authorizing the Secretary as the *exclusive* plaintiff to file a court action *after* an election to set it aside in those cases where the law governing union conduct was violated. As required by the LMRDA, the Secretary conducted an investigation of Bachowski's complaint and decided not to challenge the validity of the election. The Secretary notified Bachowski of his decision but gave no reasons for it. Bachowski then filed suit in the Federal District Court for a writ of mandamus to compel the Secretary to file suit, claiming that the Secretary's decision not to do so was arbitrary and capricious. The Court of Appeals reversed the District Court's decision that it did not have jurisdiction to review the Secretary's decision, and the Supreme Court granted certiorari.

OPINION BRENNAN, J. . . . LMRDA contains no provision that explicitly prohibits judicial review of the decision of the Secretary not to bring a civil action against the union to set aside an allegedly invalid election.

In the absence of an express prohibition in LMRDA, the Secretary therefore bears the heavy burden of overcoming the strong presumption that Congress did not mean to prohibit all judicial review of his decision. The question is phrased in terms of "prohibition" rather than "authorization" because a survey of our cases shows that judicial review of a final agency action by an aggrieved person will not be cut off unless there is persuasive reason to believe that such was the purpose of Congress. . . .

Two conclusions follow from . . . our decisions: (1) since the statute relies upon the special knowledge and discretion of the Secretary for the determination of both the probable violation and the probable effect, clearly the reviewing court is not authorized to substitute its judgment for the decision of the Secretary not to bring suit; (2) therefore to enable the reviewing court intelligibly to review the Secretary's determination, the Secretary must provide the court and the complaining witness with copies of a statement of reasons supporting his determination. When action is taken by the Secretary it must be such as to enable a reviewing Court to determine with some measure of confidence whether or not the discretion, which still remains in the Secretary, has been exercised in a manner that is neither arbitrary nor capricious. . . .

The necessity that the reviewing court refrain from substitution of its judgment for that of the Secretary thus helps define the permissible scope of review. Except in what must be the rare case, the court's review should be confined to examination of the

CASE 44.5 Continued

reasons statement, and the determination whether the statement without more evinces that the Secretary's decision is so irrational as to constitute the decision arbitrary and capricious. . . .

JUDGMENT Thus, the Secretary's letter of November 7, 1973, plainly did not suffice as a statement of reasons required by LMRDA. For a statement of reasons must be adequate to enable the court to determine whether the Secretary's decision was reached for an impermissible reason or for no reason at all. For this essential purpose, although detailed findings of fact are not required, the statement of reasons should inform the court and the complaining union member both the grounds of decision and the essential facts upon which the Secretary's inferences are based. . . .

Reversed and remanded.

Evidentiary Standards that Restrict Agency Factfinding

The APA provisions for judicial review, discussed in the preceding section, contain two different tests of the adequacy of agency factfinding. First, the "substantial evidence" test is used in "on-the-record" *formal* rulemaking or adjudication. It requires that the reviewing court should set aside agency action which is unsupported by substantial evidence from the record as a whole. This means that there must be enough evidence in the record that a reasonable person could reach the same conclusion as the agency. For example, in *Wirtz v. Baldor Elec. Co.*,[31] the Secretary of Labor's rule established a minimum wage for government electrical contractors based on its industry survey which differed significantly from the contractors' data. Moreover, the Secretary had refused to submit for cross-examination the data he had obtained from each company in the industry. On review, the court was in doubt concerning the reliability of the Secretary's data, and set the rule aside because it was not supported by substantial evidence.

The second and more lenient standard is the "arbitrary and capricious" test, which applies to *informal* rulemaking or adjudications. It requires only that the informal agency rule or decision have some rational factual basis. The Supreme Court has said that the arbitrary-capricious standard requires a reviewing court to determine that (1) after considering *all of the relevant factors,* (2) the agency did not make a "clear error of judgment."[32] However, in applying the test, courts will not substitute their judgment for that of the agency so long as there is a factual basis for the ruling and a rational link between the facts and the informal rule or decision.

The practice of the courts in deferring to an agency's interpretation of facts—particularly in matters involving technical expertise—is called "agency deference." Courts will also grant considerable deference to an agency's interpretation of its own enabling statute. Thus, in *Chemical Mfrs. Assn. v. NRDC,*[33] the manufacturers advanced an interpretation of the Clean Water Act markedly opposed to that which the Environmental Protection Agency had consistently followed for a decade. The Supreme Court affirmed the EPA's interpretation, finding that it was logically consistent with the Act and reflected the will of Congress, and said: "We do not sit to judge the relative wisdom of competing statutory interpretations."

Standing, Exhaustion, and Ripeness Doctrines

Other standards and principles are applied by courts of appeal when reviewing agency actions. These include the standing, exhaustion, and ripeness doctrines.

Standing. Article III, Section 2 of the Constitution extends the judicial power of the courts only to "cases" and "controversies," that is, disputes in which the adversaries are genuinely opposed to each other. Thus, under APA Sec. 706 only a party "adversely affected or aggrieved by agency action" has the right (standing) to obtain judicial review. The

[31] 337 F.2d 518 (D.C. Cir. 1963).

[32] *Citizens to Preserve Overton Park, Inc. v. Volpe,* 401 U.S. 402 (1971).

[33] 470 U.S. 116 (1985).

Supreme Court has held that to have standing, the complainant must show (1) that he or she is aggrieved in fact, that is, has suffered substantial direct—not remote—injury as the result of agency action, and (2) that the interest an aggrieved party seeks to protect is within the range of interests that are arguably protected by the Constitution, statute, or regulation. For example, in *Sierra Club v. Morton,*[34] the U.S. Forest Service granted a contract to Walt Disney Enterprises to construct a ski resort in Sequoia National Forest. The Sierra Club, an environmental protection organization, sought to appeal the decision. The Supreme Court held that it did not have standing to sue because the Club had merely alleged a "special interest in conservation," but had failed to claim that any of its members actually used the Sequoia area. A plaintiff whose economic or property interests have not been injured nevertheless has standing to sue if First Amendment, Fifth Amendment, or other constitutional rights have been abridged. For example, in Case 44.2, although Barlow's economic or property interests had not been injured, he had standing to sue because his constitutional Fourth Amendment right of freedom from an unreasonable warrantless search was affected.

Exhaustion and Ripeness. Even though an injury is sufficiently direct to give a complainant standing to obtain judicial review, the *exhaustion* doctrine permits the court to dismiss the appeal where it appears that a party has not first exhausted all available administrative remedies. The underlying reason for the doctrine is that since most agencies have internal procedures for reconsideration and appeal of an adverse decision, they should be given an opportunity to apply their expertise to correct their own errors before review in the courts. When an enabling statute specifically requires exhaustion, courts have no choice but to apply the doctrine. However, in exceptional cases, courts may not require exhaustion of administrative remedies if the complainant can show that following such procedure would cause irreparable damage.

The *ripeness* doctrine holds that until an agency makes a final decision and develops an adjudication or rulemaking record sufficient to enable a court to comprehend the nature of the problem, the case is not "ripe" for review. By avoiding premature judicial review, the doctrine prevents courts from entangling themselves in abstract disagreements over administrative policies and protects agencies from judicial interference until administrative decisions have been finalized. For example, an appeal to a court challenging a *proposed* agency rule that has not been *finally* adopted would not be "ripe" for review.

[34]405 U.S. 727 (1972).

General Standards for Judicial Review

Case law supports the conclusion that courts in reviewing agency actions will apply the following general standards and principles:

1. Where the purpose of the agency is to discharge a function essential to the operation of government (such as collection of taxes), judicial review is usually less extensive than where the purpose is control of private business.
2. Where agency action is primarily legislative in character, review is less searching than where the action is primarily judicial.
3. Normally, the greater the experience of the agency (Interstate Commerce Commission, for example), the greater is the confidence displayed by the courts in that agency's determinations.
4. The more abbreviated the administrative procedure, the more likely are the courts to question whether the agency has eliminated fundamental rights and safeguards.

Summary

Like the legislatures and the courts, administrative agencies may be given the power to determine private rights and obligations by making rules and deciding cases. The large number of agencies, the wide scope of their powers, and the great volume of their rules and decisions give some indication of the impact of the action of an agency on modern business.

Administrative law is any law concerning the powers and procedures of administrative agencies, including the law governing judicial review of administrative action. Administrative law does not include the substantive law produced by agencies, which is better classified as tax law, labor law, or the like.

A variety of reasons account for the trend toward administrative regulation. Among them are: (1) the need for expertness in certain fields of regulation; (2) the desire to achieve greater uniformity, continuity, and flexibility in regulation than can be achieved through strictly legislative and judicial means; and (3) the demand of the public for speedy, simple, and inexpensive legal procedures.

Resort to the administrative process as a means of regulation has raised important constitutional issues. Two of these are now well settled. The concentration of quasi-legislative and quasi-judicial power in the hands of an executive agency is no longer held to be incompatible with the doctrine of separation of powers. It is equally well recognized that, under proper safeguards, legislatures may delegate some of their power to administrative agencies.

Statutes that form a framework within which federal agencies operate include: Administrative Procedure Act, Federal Register Act, Freedom of Information Act, Government-in-the-Sunshine Act, and Federal Privacy Act of 1974. Quasi-legislative agency rulemaking can follow formal, informal, or hybrid procedures. Quasi-executive agency functions include issuing licenses and permits, investigating, prosecuting, and advising. The Fourth Amendment generally prohibits warrantless administrative searches of homes and business except where there is a pervasively regulated industry. Agencies can decide to prosecute or not to prosecute a violation by seeking civil or criminal sanctions.

Although most adjudications are informal, an agency may also use formal "on-the-record" proceedings which are sometimes mandated by the enabling statute. In both formal rulemaking and adjudication, the traditional procedural rights of cross-examination, subpoena of witnesses, and exclusion of hearsay evidence have been substantially limited. Although the chief safeguard against agency abuse is judicial review, statutes prohibit it in some disputes. Judicial review is governed by the Constitution, statutes such as the APA, and court decisions. The right to obtain review is limited by the doctrines of standing, exhaustion, and ripeness.

Review Questions

1 Define **(a)** administrative agency; **(b)** administrative law; and **(c)** administrative process.

2 In the text, seven reasons are given for the marked trend toward, and the development of administrative regulation. Which three reasons seem most important today? Why?

3 What evidence is there of the current importance of administrative regulation?

4 **(a)** What is the purpose of the American doctrine of separation of powers? **(b)** What constitutional limit is there on legislative delegations of power to administrative agencies?

5 Which is the most effective regulatory tool, rulemaking or adjudication? Why?

6 What are the main characteristics of **(a)** formal **(b)** informal, and **(c)** hybrid rulemaking?

7 **(a)** What factfinding procedural techniques traditionally used in the courts have been restricted or eliminated in administrative factfinding? **(b)** What justification is there for such restriction?

8 **(a)** Explain the quasi-executive functions of agencies. **(b)** Which do you think is most important? Why? **(c)** What sanctions can agencies impose for violation of their regulations?

9 When does the Fourth Amendment permit warrantless administrative searches and inspections?

10 How does the "due process" clause of the Constitution affect informal agency adjudications?

11 **(a)** Under what circumstances may courts remand, modify, or reverse a decision of an administrative agency? **(b)** What is the purpose of the "substantial evidence rule"? In complying with this rule, what evidence must the federal courts and perhaps the state courts consider? **(c)** What is the function of the courts in reviewing administrative decisions? **(d)** What policy considerations determine the extent of such review?

12 Choose a profession or business that you may enter, and summarize what and how administrative agencies might regulate it.

Case Problems

1 The Economic Stabilization Act of 1970 provided that "The President is authorized to issue such orders and regulations as he may deem appropriate to stabilize prices, rents, wages, and salaries at levels not less than those prevailing on May 25, 1970" and further authorized the President to "delegate the performance of any function under this title to such officers, departments and agencies of the United States as he may deem appropriate." On August 15, 1971, President Nixon issued Executive Order 11615, establishing a 90-day price-wage freeze at levels no greater than the highest rates pertaining to a substantial volume of actual transactions by the seller of goods or services as of a specified base period preceding August 15. The order also established the Cost of Living Council, "which shall act as an agency of the United States." The meat cutters union and major meat-packing companies had agreed on a general wage increase of 25 cents per hour in April 1970, effective September 16, 1971, after the "freeze" order. The union brought an action against John B. Connally, who as Secretary of the Treasury was Chairman of the Cost of Living Council, claiming that the act was an unconstitutional delegation of legislative power to the President in violation of the general constitutional principle of separation of powers and in contravention of Article I, Section 1 of the Constitution, which provides: "All legislative Powers herein granted shall be vested in a Congress of the United States." The union's suit sought an injunction restraining enforcement of the act. Was the act an unconstitutional delegation of legislative power?

2 In 1966, Congress established the National Highway Traffic Safety Administration (NHTSA), which in 1970 issued a rule, Standard 208, requiring car manufacturers to phase in by 1984 their choice of either of two "passive restraint" systems: (1) seat belts, or (2) airbags under the dashboard that would inflate automatically upon rapid deceleration before collision. In 1982, when it was learned that manufacturers had opted for the less-expensive seat belts in 99 percent of the new cars, the NHTSA held notice-and-comment hearings on its proposal to rescind Standard 208. At the hearing no evidence was received on the efficacy of airbag technology. NHTSA then rescinded Standard 208, thus requiring neither seat belts nor airbags, stating as its reasons that (1) seat belts were ineffective because many drivers detached them, and (2) since 99 percent of cars had seat belts, the effectiveness of airbags was lost. State Farm Mutual Auto Ins. Co. petitioned for review under APA Sec. 706. The Court of Appeals held that the rescission of Standard 208 was "arbitrary and capricious," and appeal was then taken to the U.S. Supreme Court. **(a)** Should NHTSA's order rescinding Standard 208 be set aside? **(b)** Does State Farm Insurance Co. have standing to sue? Why or why not?

3 By notice in the *Federal Register*, the Federal Communications Commission (FCC) proposed rules governing applications for licenses for AM clear-channel broadcasting to foreign areas such as Canada and Mexico. The notice stated that the FCC intended to adopt a policy (previously followed in other types of license cases) of granting preference to nonprofit minority-owned stations. During the comment period, National Black Media Coalition, a nonprofit organization, filed a statement applauding the FCC's proposed rule that would apply the minority preference policy when considering applications for the proposed new licenses. After the close of the comment period, FCC, relying on maps and internal studies that were neither referred to in the notice nor available for inspection during the comment period, adopted a rule which abandoned the minority-preference policy. Review was sought in the Circuit Court of Appeals on the ground that the rule was "arbitrary and capricious" because National Black Media was denied the opportunity to see the maps and studies and to comment on the soundness of the FCC methodology and conclusions. Decision?

4 Responding to a nationally publicized "Baby Doe" incident in which a court refused to override a parental decision not to authorize surgery on a handicapped infant, who died 6 days after birth, the Department of Health and Human Services (HHS) issued regulations addressed to state child-care agencies that disbursed federal funds and to hospitals receiving such funds. HHS stated that the regulations were not relevant to the Baby Doe incident because refusal to treat a handicapped child whose parents refuse consent is obviously not discrimination on the basis of handicap. The regulations required the state agencies and hospitals to: (1) post informational notices about the rights of handicapped children, (2) expedite access to records, and (3) expedite compliance actions. The rules also commanded state agencies to "prevent instances of unlawful medical neglect of handicapped infants." In addition, the rules established detailed procedures and forms relating to health care for handicapped infants. After notice-and-comment procedures, the rules were issued in reliance on Section 504 of the Rehabilitation Act of 1973 which provides: "No otherwise qualified handicapped individual shall, solely by reason of his handicap, be excluded from participation in, be denied the benefits of, or be subjected to discrimination under any program or activity receiving Federal financial assistance." There was no evidence in the administrative record that any state agencies or hospitals using federal funds had withheld medical care on the basis of handicap in violation of Sec. 504. The American Hospital Association filed suit in the Federal District Court contending that HHS's rules were arbitrary and capricious. The District Court and Court of Appeals agreed, and appeal was taken to the Supreme Court. Decision?

5 Following the nuclear accident with Unit No. 2 at Three Mile Island in March 1979, the Nuclear Regulatory Commission (NRC) shut down Unit No. 1. In May 1983, the NRC scheduled a meeting to discuss restart of Unit No. 1. NRC sought to close the meeting pursuant to Exemption 10 of the Government-in-the-Sunshine Act. Exemption 10 permits exclusion of the public from portions of meetings that involve a formal agency decision or adjudication of an issue before the agency. The discussion of the formal agency adjudication aspects would have required only a fraction of the total time of the meeting. The Philadelphia *Inquirer* challenged NRC's attempt to close the entire meeting, and the district court held that the commission could properly close the entire meeting to the public without segregating the discussion that was exempt from the Sunshine Act from discussions of other issues. The newspaper contended that when only a small fraction of topics to be discussed are exempt, the agency cannot rely on this fact to close an entire meeting, even if discussion of the exempt topic might come up at various points throughout the meeting. Can NRC close the entire meeting?

6 Customs officers boarded a sailboat near the coast of Louisiana, asked to see the vessel's documents, and while examining them, one of the officers smelled burning marijuana. Looking through the open hatch, he saw burlap-wrapped bales that proved to be 5,800 pounds of marijuana, and arrested the two men aboard. After jury trial and conviction of various drug smuggling laws, the Court of Appeals reversed the judgment, finding that the boarding of the vessel was an illegal administrative search under the Fourth Amendment because there was "no reasonable suspicion of a law violation." A federal statute, which simply reworded the original statute passed by the First Congress in 1790, provides: "Any officer of the customs may at any time go aboard any vessel at any place within the customs waters and examine the documents and papers." The Government appealed the case to the Supreme Court. Decision?

7 Death row inmates in several states requested that the Federal Trade Commission (FTC) exercise its statutory authority to investigate or commence an enforcement action against the manufacturers of the lethal drugs used in executions. The Court of Appeals (D.C. Circuit) held that the FTC's decision not to investigate or enforce should be set aside as "arbitrary and capricious," and appeal was taken to the Supreme Court. Decision?

8 Goldman, an Orthodox Jew and an ordained rabbi, was an officer in the Air Force serving as a clinical psychologist. He wore a yarmulke (skullcap) while on duty indoors. After warnings that he would be subject to court martial if he continued wearing the skullcap indoors in violation of regulations, Goldman sued the Secretary of Defense, claiming that the Air Force regulation abridged his First Amendment right to free exercise of religion. The District Court agreed, but the Court of Appeals reversed, holding that the Air Force's interest in uniformity justified strict enforcement of its regulations. Appeal was taken to the Supreme Court. Did the Air Force rule prohibiting wearing headgear indoors violate Goldman's First Amendment rights?

9 Dow Chemical Co. operated a 2,000-acre chemical manufacturing facility which was heavily secured against entry on the ground. The Environmental Protection Agency (EPA) hired an aerial photographer to take pictures of the plant from legal airspace, without obtaining a legal search warrant. Dow sued, and the District Court enjoined EPA from using the photographs or taking additional pictures. The Court held that the aerial search violated Dow's Fourth Amendment rights. The Court of Appeals reversed, finding that the use of aerial photography was within the general investigative authority of the EPA, and that Dow did not have a reasonable expectation of privacy from the air with respect to those parts of its facility which were not enclosed in buildings. The case was appealed to the Supreme Court. Did the aerial search violate Dow's Fourth Amendment rights?

10 Fraser, a high school student, spoke at an assembly of 600 students, nominating a friend for student government office. The entire speech referred to the candidate in terms of sexual metaphor, e.g., "a man who will go to the very end—even the climax for each and every one of you." The next day, one of the teachers found it necessary to forgo a portion of the scheduled lesson in order to discuss the speech with the class. A high school rule prohibited conduct which "interferes with the educational process, including the use of obscene, profane language. . . ." Before the speech, Fraser discussed it with two teachers who told him it was inappropriate. Fraser was suspended from school for two days. A school district hearing examiner affirmed the discipline. Fraser sued the school district in the Federal District Court, which awarded him damages, holding that the sanctions violated his rights under the First and Fourteenth Amendments. The Court of Appeals affirmed, rejecting the argument that the speech had a disruptive effect on the school and that it had an interest in protecting students from lewd language at a school assembly. Appeal to the Supreme Court raised the question: Did the school district enforcement of its rule deprive Fraser of his constitutional rights? Decision?

CHAPTER 45

Introduction to Antitrust Law; the Sherman Act

The term "antitrust law" refers to a broad system of federal and state law that seeks to promote business competition and to prohibit monopoly power. "Monopoly" literally means "a single seller." Monopoly power may therefore be defined as the power of a single large seller to use predatory means to exclude competitors from a market or to fix prices at arbitrarily high levels. Underlying antitrust law is a fundamental precept of capitalism: Scarce resources can be allocated most efficiently to satisfy consumer wants at the lowest price through a competitive free enterprise system. Such a system is incompatible with monopoly power and the high prices that result from the abuse of such power.

Perhaps unknowingly, each one of us is affected by antitrust law. It applies to manufacturing and service industries that produce over 70 percent of the national income and distribute their products to national markets. The prices we pay for the things we buy each day are often lower because of antitrust law. There is virtually no nationwide industry that has not been involved with antitrust suits.

The first part of this chapter traces briefly the origin of antimonopoly sentiment in the English common law and the early development of antitrust law in the United States. The rest of the chapter examines the Sherman antitrust statute and the interpretive court decisions that have developed an organized body of law aimed at anticompetitive behavior. Chapter 46 will then look at the three other major antitrust statutes—the Clayton Act, Robinson-Patman Act, and Federal Trade Commission Act—and their impact on business today.

Development of Antitrust Law

The Rise of Trusts in the United States

Rapid industrial expansion and growth of national markets after the Civil War encouraged large corporations to form industrial combines, or trusts, to fix prices, control production, divide markets, and freeze out competitors. The type of trust most commonly used was easily formed: Each corporation would cause a majority of its stockholders to transfer their shares to a board of trustees which included a representative from each company that was a party to the combine. The board of trustees would then issue trust certificates to the stockholders in exchange for their shares. These certificates gave the owners the right to any dividends declared by the trustees out of the pooled earnings of the combine.

With a majority of the outstanding shares of each member corporation firmly in hand, the board of trustees of the trust could control the election of the directors of each member company in the trust. The anticompetitive policies and practices of the trust could then be uniformly imposed upon all of the member corporations in the combine. At the same time, each of these companies retained its separate identity and remained autonomous on all management decisions other than those involving the monopolistic policies of the combine.

Enactment of Laws to Promote Competition

During the last quarter of the nineteenth century, trusts began controlling railroads as well as production and distribution of fuel oil, sugar, whiskey, and other commodities. The "captains of industry" who operated these trusts became ruthless. They cut prices below the cost of production in areas where small competitors operated, and after forcing them out of business, boosted prices to monopoly levels. A monopolistic industry with no competitors would also dictate low wages to workers immigrating by the millions from Europe or drifting to the cities because free western land was no longer available. Railroads charged high rates to helpless farmers by using various devices, including secret rebates to powerful shippers. In one way or another, the monopolists exploited the three groups constituting a majority of the American population—workers, farmers, and consumers.

Responding to a public outcry for regulation and reform a few state legislatures enacted "antitrust" laws aimed at restricting the monopolies. Hence, the term "antitrust" referred to trusts created by competitors who pooled their economic resources and transferred decision making to a trustee. Today, however, antitrust legislation is not limited to trusts but regulates a wide variety of practices which have the same anticompetitive effect. These include industrial combinations arising from devices such as holding companies, corporate mergers, interlocking directorates, formal or informal agreements between companies, or cooperative understandings between members of a trade association.

Since the activities of the trusts were nationwide in scope, it is not surprising that state antitrust legislation was largely ineffective. Similarly, the common law, based upon case precedents, was ineffective for three reasons: (1) Although the common law was quick enough to condemn outright monopolies, the courts (functioning in a laissez-faire environment) were hesitant to strike them down. (2) Although certain unfair competitive practices and agreements were illegal at common law, they could be attacked in the courts only when one of the parties brought suit, which seldom occurred. There was no legal basis for either the general public or government to attack unfair competition, and no statute absolutely prohibiting it. (3) Since the common law could be applied only within a particular state jurisdiction, state courts were ineffective in dealing with interstate abuses of the trusts.

Responding to the rising clamor for national corrective regulation, Congress enacted the Interstate Commerce Act (1887), directed against abuses of the railroads. Soon this was followed by the Sherman Antitrust Act (1890), aimed at the anticompetitive practices of the industrial trusts and monopolies. These two major legislative milestones reflect two distinct approaches to government's problem of dealing with monopoly: (1) Recognize it as socially necessary—as in the case of a railroad or public utility—and *regulate* the prices it charges at a level that is fair to the consumer and yields a reasonable rate of return to the company. (2) Recognize the monopoly as socially undesirable—for example, a petroleum cartel—and either break it into a number of small competing firms or stop it from becoming a monopoly. This is the approach Congress took in adopting the Sherman Act and later the Clayton Act, Federal Trade Commission Act, and Robinson-Patman Act. Today, federal antitrust law is founded upon these four basic statutes that regulate competition in interstate commerce. Most states have laws patterned after the federal model to deal with the intrastate dimension.

The Sherman Act

The significance of the Sherman Act was recently stated by the U.S. Supreme Court:

> Antitrust laws in general, and the Sherman Act in particular, are the Magna Carta of free enterprise. They are as important to the preservation of economic freedom and our free-enterprise system as the Bill of Rights is to the protection of our fundamental personal freedoms. And the freedom guaranteed each and every business, no matter how small, "is the freedom to compete—to assert with vigor, imagination, devotion, and ingenuity whatever economic muscle it can muster."[1]

Purpose and Scope of the Act

Purpose. An immediate aim of the Sherman Act was to satisfy public demand for a curb on the anticompetitive practices of John D. Rockefeller's oil empire. The broad congressional purpose was to promote competition by slowing down the trend toward concentration in industry. Another major congressional objective was to create a broad federal court jurisdiction for the development of a new body of federal antitrust law that could reflect common law principles without being bound by them.

Scope. The two basic sections of the Sherman Act[2] are:

> 1 Every contract, combination in the form of trust or otherwise, or conspiracy, in restraint of trade or commerce among the several states, or with foreign nations, is hereby declared to be illegal. . . .
>
> 2 Every person who shall monopolize, or attempt to monopolize, or combine or conspire with any other person or persons, to monopolize any part of the trade or commerce among the several States, or with foreign nations, shall be deemed guilty of a felony. . . .

The conspicuous absence of any wording defining key terms such as "restraint of trade," "combination," and "monopolize" left to the judiciary the

[1] *United States v. Topco Associates, Inc.*, 405 U.S. 596 (1972).
[2] 15 U.S.C.A., Secs. 1–7.

task of developing the legal meaning of these words on a case-by-case basis. Since the Sherman Act was passed as an exercise of Congressional power to regulate interstate commerce, there remained for court clarification this important question: At what point does a local contract restraining trade substantially affect interstate commerce so as to violate the Sherman Act?

Although Sections 1 and 2 were purposely vague in some respects, they were clear in others. Both sections provide that violations are punishable as crimes. Both sections are *proscriptive* rather than *prescriptive,* that is, they tell business (in vague language) what they *cannot* do, rather than what they can do. Initially, the Act created no administrative agency to implement its provisions with regulations, or to consult with business persons and respond to their inquiries. The need for such an agency was eventually met in 1914 with the creation of the Federal Trade Commission.

Enforcement of the Act

The provisions of the Sherman Act as well as other federal antitrust laws are enforced by private or governmental civil suits. In addition, the government may initiate criminal proceedings against violators.

Private Actions; Standing to Sue. Most antitrust cases in the federal courts are commenced by private parties, not the government. Special statutes authorize private enforcement by empowering any person "injured in his business or property by reason of anything forbidden in the antitrust laws"[3] to bring a *private action* to recover treble damages plus reasonable attorney's fees. Private litigants may also ask the court to grant injunctive relief against violations.[4] Damage awards in recent cases have been very substantial. For example, in *Trans World Airlines, Inc. v. Hughes,*[5] the damage award was $137 million after trebling, and attorney's fees totaled $7.5 million.

In order to prevail in a private treble damage suit, the plaintiff must have standing to sue, that is, be able to prove that: (1) the defendant violated the antitrust laws, (2) the violation was a substantial or direct cause of an injury to the plaintiff which can be measured with some certainty in money terms, and (3) the defendant's illegal act affected activities of the plaintiff that are under the protective umbrella of the antitrust laws.

In determining whether a plaintiff has standing to sue, the central focus of the courts is upon the *directness* of the injury suffered by the plaintiff as a result of the defendant's wrongful antitrust violation. To illustrate, the courts have determined that damage was so indirect that the following plaintiffs were held not to have standing under the antitrust laws: shareholders suing derivatively on behalf of their injured corporation, creditors of a corporation allegedly injured by antitrust violations, a partner (as opposed to the partnership) suing for injuries to the partnership, suppliers suing for sales losses because of injury to a customer, franchisors suing to recover lost profits caused by injuries to franchisees, and an indirect purchaser-owner of a building whose contractor purchased blocks from suppliers allegedly charging monopolistic prices.[6]

Government Enforcement. The Sherman Act makes available to the federal government a wide variety of powerful enforcement tools:

1 Under Sections 1 and 2, as amended, restraints and monopolies are declared to be felonies, subject to criminal prosecution. Violators are punishable by a fine of up to $1 million against a corporation or $100,000 against an individual or 3 years imprisonment, or both. The Justice Department's current policy is to proceed criminally if a company engages in "hard core" violations such as "price fixing, bid rigging, market and territorial allocation schemes, and various predatory practices."[7] The department's recent emphasis on criminal enforcement is illustrated by the fact that in 1978 businessmen spent more time in jail for price fixing than in the previous 89 years since the Sherman Act was passed. The Department of-

[3]Section 4 of the Clayton Act, 15 U.S.C., Sec. 15.
[4]15 U.S.C., Sec. 26.
[5]409 U.S. 363 (1973).

[6]*Kaufman v. Dreyfus Fund,* 434 F.2d 727 (3rd Cir. 1970); *Loeb v. Eastman Kodak Co.,* 183 F.704 (1910); *Hauer v. Bankers Trust N.Y. Corp.,* 65 F.R.D. 1 (1974); *Milk Producers v. Bergjans Farm Dairy, Inc.,* 368 F.2d 679 (1966); *Nationwide Auto Appraiser Serv. Inc. v. Ass'n of Cas. & Sur. Cos.,* 382 F.2d 925 (1967); *Illinois Brick Co. v. State of Illinois,* 431 U.S. 720 (1977).
[7]Department of Justice *Release,* October 21, 1978, p. 4.

ten permits companies engaged in lesser offenses to enter nolo contendere (no contest) pleas. Such pleas result in a judgment against the defendant that is not admissible to prove the defendant's liability in any subsequent civil suit, for example, a suit filed by a private party.

2 Section 4 of the Sherman Act also empowers the Department of Justice to bring a *civil action for injunction* against a violation of any provision of the Act.[8] Courts have used their power to restrain violations in a variety of ways, including ordering a defendant to divest itself of ownership of another company ("divestiture"), dissolution of a corporation, or divorcement and cessation by a company from conducting operations that would restrain trade.

3 Property being transported in interstate or foreign commerce pursuant to a contract or conspiracy that violates Section 1 is subject to *seizure and forfeiture* to the United States.

4 Recent legislation authorizes each state's *attorney general to commence civil* treble damage actions, in the name of the state, seeking recovery for antitrust injury to its residents.[9] This legislation was intended to permit recovery by a state attorney general on behalf of large numbers of consumers. However, the Supreme Court's ruling in *Illinois Brick* that only direct purchasers from a violator have standing to sue, raises doubts as to how extensively the new legislation will be used.

Proving "Commerce" Jurisdiction under Sections 1 and 2. Under the Constitution, Congress can regulate only interstate commerce, not intrastate commerce. Therefore, Congress provided in the Sherman Act that federal courts are without jurisdiction to decide an antitrust case unless the restraint has a significant impact on interstate or foreign commerce.

[8] 15 U.S.C., Sec. 4.

[9] 15 U.S.C., sec. 15c (1976), amending Section 4 of the Clayton Act, See *Illinois Brick Co. v. Illinois*, 431 U.S. 720 (1977).

Interstate commerce. Either of two tests is used to meet the interstate commerce jurisdiction required by the Sherman Act:

1 Did the activities occur within the *flow of commerce?* The "flow of commerce" test applies only if a restraint is imposed directly upon goods or services while moving in interstate commerce. Consequently, under this test the volume or size of the restraint may be relatively small.[10]

2 Even though the activities occurred wholly intrastate, did they have a substantial and adverse *effect* on commerce? Thus, a wholly intrastate activity will meet the jurisdictional requirement if it substantially affects interstate commerce and is not merely inconsequential or remote.[11] "The test of jurisdiction is not that the acts complained of affect a business engaged in interstate commerce, but that the conduct complained of affects the interstate commerce of such business."[12]

In practice, a relatively small amount of direct or indirect interstate activity will be held by the courts to "substantially affect" interstate commerce. Thus, Sherman Act jurisdiction under the "effect on commerce" theory has been held to apply to a manufacturer's agreement with wholesalers to boycott a single local retailer, thereby reducing the manufacturer's shipments in interstate commerce,[13] and to a beet producers' agreement to fix beet prices to local processing refineries which in turn ship sugar in interstate commerce.[14]

The following recent decision of the U.S. Supreme Court illustrates the application of both the "flow of commerce test" and the "effects upon commerce test" in determining a Sherman Act jurisdiction.

[10] *United States v. Yellow Cab Co.*, 332 U.S. 218 (1947).

[11] *Northern Cal. Pharmaceutical Ass'n v. United States*, 306 F.2d 379 (9th Cir. 1962).

[12] *C.A. Page Publishing Co. v. Work*, 178 F. Supp. 184 (S.D. Cal. 1959).

[13] *Klor's Inc. v. Broadway-Hale Stores, Inc.*

[14] *Mandeville Island Farms, Inc. v. American Crystal Sugar Co.*, 334 U.S. 219 (1948).

CASE 45.1 McLain v. Real Estate Board of New Orleans · 444 U.S. 232 (1980)

FACTS Treble damage private antitrust class action was instituted by McLain and other real estate vendors (petitioners) against an association of real estate brokers in New Orleans (respondents) alleging that they had conspired to fix prices (brokers' commissions) in violation of Section 1 of the Sherman Act. The trial court's dismissal of the complaint for lack of "commerce" jurisdiction was affirmed by the Court of Appeals, and petitioners appealed to the Supreme Court.

OPINION BURGER, Chief Justice. The allegations of the complaint pertinent to establishing federal jurisdiction are: (1) that the activities of the respondents are "within the flow of interstate commerce and have an effect upon that commerce"; (2) that the services of respondents were employed in connection with the purchase and sale of real estate by "persons moving into and out of the Greater New Orleans area"; (3) that respondents "assist their clients in securing financing and insurance involved with the purchase of real estate in the Greater New Orleans area," which "financing and insurance are obtained from sources outside of Louisiana and move in interstate commerce into the State of Louisiana through the activities" of the respondents; and (4) that respondents have engaged in an unlawful restraint of "interstate trade and commerce in the offering for sale and sale of real estate brokering services."... Petitioners advance two independent theories to support federal jurisdiction: (1) that respondents' activities occurred within the stream of interstate commerce; and (2) that even if respondents' activities were wholly local in character they depended upon and affected the interstate flow of both services and people.... It can no longer be doubted... that the jurisdictional requirement of the Sherman Act may be satisfied under either the "in commerce" or the "effect on commerce" theory.

Since the financing depended on a valid and insured title, in *Goldfarb v. Virginia State Bar* [421 U.S. 773] we concluded that title examination [by lawyers] was "an integral part" of the interstate transaction of obtaining financing for the purchase of residential property and, because of the "inseparability" of the attorneys' services from the title examination process, we held that the legal services were in turn an "integral part of an interstate transaction." By placing the *Goldfarb* holding on the available ground that the activities of the attorneys were within the stream of interstate commerce, Sherman Act jurisdiction was established.

It is clear that an appreciable amount of commerce is involved in the financing of residential property in the Greater New Orleans area and in the insuring of titles to such property. The presidents of two of the many lending institutions in the area stated in their deposition testimony that those institutions committed hundreds of millions of dollars to residential financing during the period covered by the complaint. The testimony further demonstrated that this appreciable commercial activity has occurred in interstate commerce. Funds were raised from out-of-state investors and from interbank loans obtained from interstate financial institutions. Multistate lending institutions took mortgages insured under federal programs which entailed interstate transfers of premiums and settlements. Mortgage obligations physically and constructively were traded as financial instruments in the interstate secondary mortgage market. Before making a mortgage loan in the Greater New Orleans area, lending institutions usually, if not always, required title insurance, which was furnished by interstate corporations.

To establish federal jurisdiction in this case, there remains only the requirement that respondents' activities which allegedly have been infected by a price-fixing conspiracy be shown "as a matter of practical economics" to have a not insubstantial effect on the interstate commerce involved. It is clear, as the record shows, that the function of re-

CASE 45.1 Continued

spondent real estate brokers is to bring the buyer and seller together on agreeable terms. . . . Ultimately, whatever stimulates or retards the volume of residential sales, or has an impact on the purchase price, affects the demand for financing and title insurance; those two commercial activities that on this record are shown to have occurred in interstate commerce. Where, as here, the services of respondent real estate brokers are often employed in transactions in the relevant market, petitioners at trial may be able to show that respondents' activities have a not insubstantial effect on interstate commerce.

JUDGMENT We therefore conclude that it was error to dismiss the complaint at this stage of the proceedings. The judgment of the Court of Appeals is vacated and the case is remanded for further proceedings consistent with this opinion.

Foreign commerce. Restraints which affect the flow of services or goods imported into or exported from the United States meet the jurisdictional requirement of "commerce . . . with foreign nations." Once such foreign jurisdiction is established, the Sherman Act will apply to activities of U.S. citizens or foreign nationals, within the United States or within a foreign country, and before or after the goods actually flow in commerce. Generally, the Sherman Act will not be enforced against an act of a foreign nation or its authorized agent. However, the Foreign Sovereign Immunities Act of 1976[15] applies the Sherman Act to "commercial activities" of a foreign state which have a "direct effect" in the United States.

Proving Conspiracy under Section 1. The words "contract, combination . . . or conspiracy" clearly require proof that at least *two* persons agreed to act in concert so as to restrain trade. Courts have used "combination" and "conspiracy" interchangeably[16] and because it is often impossible to obtain direct evidence of a contract, combination, or conspiracy to restrain trade, circumstantial evidence is sufficient.[17] For example, where a dealers' association distributed to its members a list of wholesalers who sold directly to consumers and the members ceased to deal with the listed wholesalers, a conspiracy to boycott was inferred[18]

Consciously parallel behavior, that is, uniform business conduct by competitors who are aware of each other's actions, would seem to be circumstantial evidence from which an agreement could be inferred. However, standing alone, it is generally insufficient to prove a conspiracy.[19] The doctrine of conscious parallelism was probably extended to its furthest limit in *Interstate Circuit, Inc. v. U.S.*[20] where motion picture distributors and exhibitors were accused of conspiring to impose minimum admission prices on competing exhibitors. Although there was no direct testimony that the defendant distributors and exhibitors had conspired, communicated with each other, or ever met, the Supreme Court affirmed the conviction and said: "Acceptance by competitors without previous agreement of an invitation to participate in a plan, the necessary consequence of which, if carried out, is restraint of interstate commerce is sufficient to establish an unlawful conspiracy under the Sherman Act."

In the later *Theatre Enterprises* case,[21] the plaintiff film exhibitor claimed a conspiracy among the defendant distributors to refrain from leasing films to him. Defendants produced evidence showing why each, acting separately and not in concert, had refused to deal with the plaintiff. The Supreme Court, in affirming a jury verdict for the defendants, said:

> To be sure, business behavior is admissible circumstantial evidence from which the fact finder may infer agreement. But this court has never held that proof of

[15] 38 U.S.C. Secs. 1602–1611.

[16] *Perma Life Mufflers, Inc. v. International Parts Corp.*, 392 U.S. 134 (1968).

[17] *United States v. General Motors Corp.*, 384 U.S. 127 (1966).

[18] *Eastern States Retail Lumber Dealers' Ass'n v. United States*, 234 U.S. 600 (1914).

[19] *FTC v. Lukens Steel Co.*, 454 F. Supp. 1183 (D.D.C., 1978).

[20] 306 U.S. 208 (1939). See also *Theatre Enterprises.*

[21] *Theatre Enterprises, Inc. v. Paramount Film Distrib. Corp.*, 346 U.S. 537 (1954).

parallel business behavior conclusively establishes agreement, or, phrased differently, that such behavior itself constitutes a Sherman Act offense. Circumstantial evidence of consciously parallel behavior may have made heavy inroads into the traditional judicial attitude toward conspiracy; but "conscious parallelism" has not read conspiracy out of the Sherman Act entirely.

Conscious parallelism, together with evidence of exchange of pricing data at meetings or through correspondence, can be enough to infer a conspiracy.[22] A corporation is a separate legal person, and, because it can act only through its agents, it is incapable of conspiring with its officers or employees. Hence, any such "conspiracy" does not meet the two-actor requirement of Section 1. Similarly, wholly owned subsidiaries cannot conspire among themselves or with the parent corporation.[23] Under well-established doctrines of criminal conspiracy, a convicted defendant is liable for all the acts of his or her co-conspirators. As long as a defendant remains active in the conspiracy, he or she is liable for the actions of others which occur before or after the defendant's participation.

Whether a conspiracy can be inferred from conscious parallel pricing activities in an industry is a jury question. In *Esco Corp. v. United States,*[24] the court, in affirming a jury verdict of criminal liability for violating Section 1 by conspiring to fix prices, said:

> It is well recognized law that any conspiracy can ordinarily only be proved by inferences drawn from relevant and competent circumstantial evidence, including the conduct of the defendants charged. A knowing wink can mean more than words. Let us suppose five competitors meet on several occasions, discuss their problems, and one finally states—"I won't fix prices with any of you, but here is what I am going to do—put the price of my gidget at X dollars; now you all do what you want." He then leaves the meeting. Competitor number two says—"I don't care whether number one does what he says he's going to do or not; nor do I care what the rest of you do, but I am going to price my gidget at X dollars." Number three makes a similar statement—"My price is X dollars." Number four says not one word. All leave and fix "their" prices at "X" dollars.
>
> We do not say the foregoing illustration compels an inference in this case that the competitors' conduct constituted a price-fixing conspiracy, including an agreement to so conspire, but neither can we say, as a matter of law, that an inference of no agreement is compelled. As in so many other instances, it remains a question for the trier of fact.

Court Interpretations of Section 1

The Supreme Court's initial response to the Sherman Act was to strip it of its vitality by narrow interpretation. Only 5 years after passage of the act, the Court held that its provisions did not apply to a trust of sugar manufacturers in Pennsylvania because they were not engaged in "interstate commerce" within the meaning of the act.[25] The Court reasoned that even though the sugar would eventually be shipped in interstate commerce, the manufacture of it was purely a local activity.

Commencing in 1897, the court flip-flopped in the other direction, holding to a strict literal interpretation that Section 1 prohibited *every* restraint of trade.[26] Such a rigid interpretation could be used to invalidate every normal business deal by arguing that it restrains trade because the contractually obligated parties are no longer free to deal with others. Retreat from this arbitrary position was inevitable. It came with the Court's decision in the landmark case, *Standard Oil Company of New Jersey v. United States.*[27]

The Rule of Reason. In *Standard Oil,* the Court rejected its earlier position that *all* contracts in restraint of trade were prohibited by the Sherman Act and applied what has come to be called the *Rule of Reason.* The Court ruled that the Congressional intent was to prohibit only those contracts that *unreasonably* restrained trade. This rule of reason—that is, the process of determining if a defendant's conduct is sufficiently anticompetitive to constitute an "unreasonable restraint"—is very much a part of antitrust law today in Section 1 cases.

The Doctrine of Per Se Unreasonableness. The question yet remained: If firms combine to fix

[22]*Gainsville Utilities Dept. v. Florida Power & Light Co.*, 573 F.2d 292 (5th Cir. 1978).

[23]*Copperweld Corp. v. Independence Tube Corp.*, 104 S. Ct. 2731 (1984).

[24]*Esco Corp. v. United States,* 340 F.2d 1000 (9th Cir. 1965).

[25]*United States v. E.C. Knight Co.*, 156 U.S. 1 (1895).

[26]*United States v. Trans-Missouri Freight Ass'n,* 166 U.S. 290 (1897).

[27]221 U.S. 1 (1911).

prices at *reasonable* levels, does such action nevertheless constitute an *unreasonable* restraint of trade under Section 1? The Supreme Court has answered this question in the affirmative, holding that certain actions are per se illegal. In *United States v. Trenton Potteries Co.*,[28] Justice Stone, speaking for the Court, said:

> The aim and result of every price-fixing agreement, if effective, is the elimination of one form of competition. *The power to fix prices, whether reasonably exercised or not, involves power to control the market and to fix arbitrary and unreasonable prices.* The reasonable price fixed today may through economic and business changes become the unreasonable price of tomorrow. Once established, it may be maintained unchanged because of the absence of competition secured by the agreement for a price reasonable when fixed. *Agreements which create such potential power may well be held to be in themselves ["per se"] unreasonable or unlawful restraints, without the necessity of minute inquiry whether a particular price is reasonable as fixed and without placing on the government in enforcing the Sherman Law the burden of ascertaining from day to day whether it has become unreasonable through the mere variation of economic conditions.* [Emphasis added.]

Certain types of restrictive agreements are so inherently anticompetitive that it can be said as a *matter of law* that they unreasonably restrain trade and are therefore illegal under Section 1 of the act. If an activity is illegal per se, proof of that activity is sufficient to establish its anticompetitive nature, and it is not necessary to present evidence that the activity unreasonably restrained trade. Obviously, it takes less effort to establish a per se violation than is required in other Section 1 cases, where proof must be presented that the restraint is unreasonable. Thirty years after *Trenton,* the Supreme Court summarized the nature of per se violations as follows:

> There are certain agreements or practices which because of their pernicious effect on competition and lack of any redeeming virtue are conclusively presumed to be unreasonable and therefore illegal without elaborate inquiry as to the precise harm they have caused or the business excuse for their use. This principle of *per se* unreasonableness not only makes the type of restraints which are proscribed by the Sherman Act more certain to the benefit of everyone concerned, but it also avoids the necessity for an incredibly complicated and prolonged economic investigation into the entire history of the industry involved, as well as related industries, in an effort to determine at large whether a particular restraint has been unreasonable—an inquiry so often wholly fruitless when undertaken. . . .[29]

It is only after considerable experience with certain business relationships that courts classify them as per se violations of the Sherman Act.[30] Joint activities in interstate commerce that are regularly recognized as per se violations include horizontal price fixing, vertical price fixing, restricting production, horizontal division of customers or geographical markets, concerted refusals to deal (group boycotts), promoting reciprocal dealing arrangements, tying contracts, as well as other restraints. Generally, all kinds of anticompetitive restraints that are not per se violations are judged under the "rule of reason" to determine if the particular restraint is unreasonable and therefore unlawful.

Horizontal price fixing. When two or more competitors at the same level—such as two manufacturers, two wholesalers, or two retailers—agree to establish a minimum or maximum price or to charge a set price for a product, the result is a *horizontal price-fixing* agreement. Such an agreement by its very nature eliminates price competition and is the most common per se violation of the antitrust law. Once the prosecution has proved the existence of horizontal price fixing, it is no defense to argue that it was necessary to prevent "ruinous competition," "financial disaster," or the "evils of price cutting." Additionally, the fact that the prices fixed are equal to the fair market price or are otherwise reasonable is considered irrelevant.

The case which follows illustrates an unlawful horizontal price-fixing agreement.

[28] 273 U.S. 392 (1927).

[29] *Northern Pac. Railway Co. v. United States,* 356 U.S. 1 (1958). In the period between *Trenton* and *Northern Pacific Railway,* the only notable departure from per se rules was in *Appalachian Coals, Inc. v. United States,* 288 U.S. 344 (1933), during the emergency conditions of the Great Depression, when many sick industries, including bituminous coal, were trying to avoid failure by entering into price-fixing and market allocation agreements. The Court held that the coal producers' agreement was not an undue restraint of trade under the Sherman Act.

[30] *United States v. Topco Associates, Inc.,* 405 U.S. 596 (1972).

CASE 45.2 Catalano, Inc. v. Target Sales · 446 U.S. 635 (1980)

FACTS A class action by beer retailers (plaintiffs) in the Fresno, California, area, sought treble damages and injunctive relief against a group of wholesalers (defendants) alleging that they had horizontally conspired and agreed to eliminate the industry practice of granting short-term trade credit to the retailers on beer purchases. A violation of Section 1 of the Sherman Act was alleged. The trial court denied plaintiffs' motion requesting that the court declare that defendants' conduct amounted to a per se violation, and the plaintiff appealed. The Court of Appeals (9th Circuit) held that a horizontal agreement among competitors to fix credit terms does not necessarily contravene the antitrust laws, and certiorari was granted by the U.S. Supreme Court.

OPINION PER CURIAM. According to the Petition, prior to the agreement wholesalers had competed with each other with respect to trade credit, and the credit terms for individual retailers had varied substantially. After entering into the agreement, respondents uniformly refused to extend any credit at all. . . . In *Broadcast Music, Inc. v. Columbia Broadcasting System, Inc.*, 441 U.S. 1 (1979), we said:

> In construing and applying the Sherman Act's ban against contracts, conspiracies, and combinations in restraint of trade, the Court has held that certain agreements or practices are so "plainly anticompetitive" and so often "lack any redeeming virtue" that they are conclusively presumed illegal without further examination under the rule of reason generally applied in Sherman Act cases.

A horizontal agreement to fix prices is the archetypal example of such a practice. It has long been settled that an agreement to fix prices is unlawful *per se.* It is no excuse that the prices fixed are themselves reasonable. In *United States v. Socony-Vacuum Oil Co.*, 310 U.S. 150 (1940) we held that an agreement among competitors to engage in a program of buying surplus gasoline on the spot market in order to prevent prices from falling sharply to be unlawful without any inquiry into the reasonableness of the program, even though there was no direct agreement on the actual prices to be maintained. In the course of that opinion, the Court made clear that

> the machinery employed by a combination for price-fixing is immaterial. Under the Sherman Act a combination formed for the purpose and with the effect of raising, depressing, fixing, pegging, or stabilizing the price of a commodity in interstate or foreign commerce is illegal *per se.*

. . . It is virtually self-evident that extending interest-free credit for a period of time is equivalent to giving a discount equal to the value of the use of the purchase price for that period of time. . . . An agreement to terminate the practice of giving credit is thus tantamount to an agreement to eliminate discounts, and thus falls squarely within the traditional *per se* rule against price fixing. . . . Under the reasoning of our cases, an agreement among competing wholesalers to refuse to sell unless the retailer makes payment in cash either in advance or upon delivery is "plainly anticompetitive." Since it is merely one form of price fixing, and since price fixing agreements have been adjudged to lack any "redeeming virtue," it is conclusively presumed illegal without further examination under the rule of reason.

JUDGMENT Accordingly, the judgment of the Court of Appeals is reversed, and the case is remanded for further proceedings consistent with this opinion. It is so ordered.

Vertical price fixing. If a manufacturer sells to a wholesaler (or a wholesaler sells to a retailer) on condition that the buyer will not resell the product below a set minimum price, or on condition that the buyer will only resell at a stated fixed price, the contract is called a *vertical price-fixing agreement.* This process, whereby a seller at one level of the chain of distribution fixes the resale price terms of a buyer at a different level, is also called *resale price maintenance.* Until 1937, the Supreme Court held that resale price maintenance contracts in interstate commerce were per se violations of Section 1 even though the buyer's state legislature had enacted a *fair trade* law permitting such contracts. However, in that year Congress enacted the Miller-Tydings Act exempting resale price maintenance contracts from the Sherman law *if* there was a fair trade law in effect in the buyer's state. Since most states had enacted fair trade laws, the effect of the Miller-Tydings Act was to make most resale price maintenance agreements legal.[31]

In 1976, Congress repealed the Miller-Tydings Act with the result that resale price maintenance in interstate commerce once again constituted a per se violation of Section 1. Today, such vertical price-fixing agreements are unlawful to the same extent as prior to 1937. Thus, it is a violation of the Sherman Act for a manufacturer to establish suggested retail prices and then refuse to sell to wholesalers that are selling to retailers who do not observe such prices. However, it is still lawful for a seller to establish suggested resale prices and to *unilaterally* announce that it will refuse to sell to its immediate customers who do not maintain such prices.[32] This "Colgate exception" rests on the theory that since Section 1 requires two or more actors in order to conspire, a single seller's unilateral announcement that it will sell only to dealers who follow its suggested resale prices cannot violate the law because there is no concerted action—only the seller's unilateral action.

There is an important distinction between vertical price fixing and other vertical nonprice restraints. Generally, vertical restraints not involving price fixing—for example, a manufacturer's allocation of market territory among franchised retailers—are subject to the rule of reason, and are not per se violations.

Restricting production. Competitive theory holds that many producers competing with each other will maximize production at minimum prices. However, if producers combine and agree to fix prices, the effort cannot be effective unless the producers also agree to restrict production and sales. Since price fixing and manipulation of production are closely interrelated, an agreement to manipulate production to achieve an anticompetitive objective is a per se violation.[33]

Dividing markets or customers. It is illegal per se for *horizontal* competitors (that is, at the same level) to geographically apportion market territory among themselves, to allocate customers while agreeing not to solicit each other's customers, or to divide product markets.[34] However, *vertical* division of markets or customers is *not* a per se violation, and courts evaluate such arrangements under the rule of reason, as illustrated by the *Sylvania* decision below. Here the test of reasonableness is whether the procompetitive effect of the restraint on interbrand competition outweighs the anticompetitive effect of eliminating intrabrand competition. *Sylvania* is also a good illustration of how the Supreme Court will reverse itself when it is convinced that its earlier rule is unsound.

[31]However, South Carolina remains the only state with a "fair trade" resale price maintenance law in effect.

[32]*United States v. Parke, Davis & Co.*, 362 U.S. 29 (1960); *United States v. Colgate & Co.*, 250 U.S. 300 (1919); *FTC v. Beech-Nut Packing Co.*, 257 U.S. 441 (1922).

[33]*United States v. Addyston Pipe & Steel Co.*, 85 F. 271 (6th Cir. 1898); *Hartford-Empire Co. v. United States*, 323 U.S. 386 (1945).

[34]*United States v. Topco Associates, Inc., supra,* note 30, p. 966.

CASE 45.3 Continental TV, Inc. v. GTE Sylvania, Inc. • 433 U.S. 36 (1977)

FACTS Continental TV (plaintiff) held a franchise from GTE Sylvania (defendant), a manufacturer of television sets, to sell its TV products. GTE marketed its products through a

CASE 45.3 Continued

limited number of franchised retailers, who were restricted to selling only from the locations at which they were franchised. The franchise agreements did not establish exclusive territory, and Sylvania retained sole discretion to increase the number of retailers in an area in light of the success or failure of existing retailers in developing their market. Sylvania's franchise program increased its market share of national television sales from 1 percent in 1962 to 5 percent in 1965. Continental was one of Sylvania's more successful franchise retailers in the San Francisco area. When Sylvania refused Continental's request for a franchise to open another retail outlet in Sacramento, Continental announced it intended to proceed without a franchise. Sylvania then terminated Continental's San Francisco franchise.

Thereupon Continental sued Sylvania for treble damages, alleging that the franchise location restrictions were a per se violation of Section 1 of the Sherman Act. The trial court relied on *Schwinn & Co. v. U.S.*, 388 U.S. 365, which held that vertical market restraints imposed by sellers were per se violations of Section 1, regardless of the reasonableness of such restraints. Accordingly, the jury was instructed that once Sylvania had parted with title to its products any attempt to control their resale, including the location restriction on dealers, was a violation of Section 1 of the Sherman Act, regardless of the reasonableness of the restriction. Based on those instructions, the jury awarded plaintiff $1,774,515 damages, and Sylvania appealed. The Court of Appeals reversed, stating that the sales location limitation clause should be judged under the rule of reason and that the provision did not constitute a per se violation. Continental appealed to the Supreme Court.

OPINION

POWELL, Associate Justice. In the present case, it is undisputed that title to the televisions passed from Sylvania to Continental. Thus, the *Schwinn per se* rule applies unless Sylvania's restriction on location falls outside *Schwinn's* prohibition against a manufacturer attempting to restrict a "retailer's freedom as to where and to whom it will resell the products." As the Court of Appeals conceded, the language of *Schwinn* is clearly broad enough to apply to the present case. Unlike the Court of Appeals, however, we are unable to find a principled basis for distinguishing *Schwinn* from the case now before us.

Both Schwinn and Sylvania sought to reduce but not to eliminate competition among their respective retailers through the adoption of a franchise system. The Schwinn franchise plan included a location restriction similar to the one challenged here. These restrictions allowed Schwinn and Sylvania to regulate the amount of competition among their retailers by preventing a franchisee from selling franchised products from outlets other than the one covered by the franchise agreement.

Sylvania argues that if *Schwinn* cannot be distinguished, it should be reconsidered. Although *Schwinn* is supported by the principle of *stare decisis,* we are convinced that the need for clarification of the law in this area justifies reconsideration....

The market impact of vertical restrictions is complex because of their potential for a simultaneous reduction of intrabrand competition and stimulation of interbrand competition. Significantly, the Court in *Schwinn* did not distinguish among the challenged restrictions on the basis of their individual potential for intrabrand harm or interbrand benefit.... The pivotal factor was the passage of title: All restrictions were held to be *per se* illegal where title had passed, and all were evaluated and sustained under the rule of reason where it had not....

Vertical restrictions reduce intrabrand competition by limiting the number of sellers of a particular product competing for the business of a given group of buyers. Location restrictions have this effect because of practical constraints on the effective marketing area of retail outlets. Although intrabrand competition may be reduced, the ability of retailers to exploit the resulting market may be limited both by the ability of consumers to travel to other franchised locations and, perhaps more importantly, to purchase the competing

CASE 45.3 Continued

products of other manufacturers. None of these key variables, however, is affected by the form of the transaction by which a manufacturer conveys his products to the retailers.

Vertical restrictions promote interbrand competition by allowing the manufacturer to achieve certain efficiencies in the distribution of his products. These "redeeming virtues" are implicit in every decision sustaining vertical restrictions under the rule of reason. Economists have identified a number of ways in which manufacturers can use such restrictions to compete more effectively against other manufacturers. For example, new manufacturers and manufacturers entering new markets can use the restrictions in order to induce competent and aggressive retailers to make the kind of investment of capital and labor that is often required in the distribution of products unknown to the customer. Established manufacturers can use them to induce retailers to engage in promotional activities or to provide service and repair facilities necessary to the efficient marketing of their products. Service and repair are vital for many products, such as automobiles and major household appliances....

We conclude that the distinction drawn in *Schwinn* between sale and nonsale transactions is not sufficient to justify the application of a *per se* rule in one situation and a rule of reason in the other.... Certainly, there has been no showing in this case, either generally or with respect to Sylvania's agreements, that vertical restrictions have or are likely to have a "pernicious effect on competition" or that they "lack... any redeeming virtue." Accordingly, we conclude that the *per se* rule stated in *Schwinn* must be overruled. In so holding we do not foreclose the possibility that particular applications of vertical restrictions might justify *per se* prohibition under *Northern Pac. R. Co.* But we do make clear that departure from the rule of reason standard must be based upon demonstrable economic effect rather than—as in *Schwinn*—upon formalistic line drawing.

In sum, we conclude that the appropriate decision is to return to the rule of reason that governed vertical restrictions prior to *Schwinn.* When anticompetitive effects are shown to result from particular vertical restrictions they can be adequately policed under the rule of reason, the standard traditionally applied for the majority of anticompetitive practices challenged under Section 1 of the Act.

JUDGMENT Accordingly, the decision of the Court of Appeals is affirmed.

Although the *Sylvania* court held that vertical nonprice restrictions are to be judged under the rule of reason, it also noted that horizontal restrictions and vertical resale price maintenance would remain per se illegal. The District Court on remand granted Sylvania's motion for summary judgment, holding that the sales location clause did not constitute an unreasonable restraint of trade, since it stimulated competition and enabled Sylvania to increase its market share by a method that was least restrictive of competition (461 F. Supp. 1046, 1978).

After *Sylvania,* in the following decision, the U.S. Supreme Court established a standard for the kind of evidence that a plaintiff must produce in order to prove under the rule of reason that a vertical nonprice restraint has violated Section 1 of the Sherman Act.

CASE 45.4 Monsanto Co. v. Spray-Rite Service Corp. · 104 S. Ct. 1464 (1984)

FACTS Spray-Rite (plaintiff) distributed chemical herbicides, including those manufactured by Monsanto Company (defendant). Monsanto's share was 28 percent of the corn herbicide market and 19 percent of the soybean herbicide market. After Spray-Rite had been a distributor of these products for 10 years, Monsanto announced that they would appoint distributors for one-year terms and would renew them each year after evaluating whether

CASE 45.4 Continued

the distributor: (1) concentrated on retail sales, (2) used salespersons trained in application of Monsanto's products, and (3) was fully exploiting the market in the assigned territory. In 1968 Monsanto declined to renew Spray-Rite's distributorship. In 1972 Spray-Rite sued Monsanto under Section 1 of the Sherman Act. It alleged that Monsanto and some distributors conspired to fix resale prices. The jury awarded $10.5 million in damages (after trebling). The Court of Appeals affirmed, and Monsanto appealed.

OPINION

POWELL, Justice. This case presents a question as to the standard of proof required to find a vertical price-fixing conspiracy in violation of Section 1 of the Sherman Act. . . .

This Court has drawn two important distinctions that are at the center of this and any other distributor-termination case. First, there is the basic distinction between concerted and independent action—a distinction not always clearly drawn by parties and courts. Section 1 of the Sherman Act requires that there be a "contract, combination . . . or conspiracy" between the manufacturer and other distributors in order to establish a violation. 15 U.S.C. § 1. Independent action is not proscribed. A manufacturer of course generally has a right to deal, or refuse to deal, with whomever it likes, as long as it does so independently. *United States v. Colgate & Co.*, 250 U.S. 300, (1919); cf. *United States v. Parke, Davis & Co.*, 362 U.S. 29, (1960). . . .

The second important distinction in distributor-termination cases is that between concerted action to set prices and concerted action on nonprice restrictions. The former have been per se illegal since the early years of national antitrust enforcement. See *Dr. Miles Medical Co. v. John D. Park & Sons Co.*, 220 U.S. 373 (1911). The latter are judged under the rule of reason, which requires a weighing of the relevant circumstances of a case to decide whether a restrictive practice constitutes an unreasonable restraint on competition. See *Continental T.V., Inc. v. GTE Sylvania Inc.*, 433 U.S. 36 (1977). . . .

Nevertheless, it is of considerable importance that independent action by the manufacturer, and concerted action on non-price restrictions, be distinguished from price-fixing agreements. . . .

On a claim of concerted price-fixing, the antitrust plaintiff must present evidence sufficient to carry its burden of proving that there was such an agreement. If an inference of such an agreement may be drawn from highly ambiguous evidence, there is a considerable danger that the doctrines enunciated in *Sylvania* and *Colgate* will be seriously eroded.

The flaw in the evidentiary standard adopted by the Court of Appeals in this case is that it disregards this danger. Permitting an agreement to be inferred merely from the existence of complaints, or even from the fact that termination came about "in response to" complaints, could deter or penalize perfectly legitimate conduct. As Monsanto points out, complaints about price-cutters "are natural—and from the manufacturer's perspective, unavoidable—reactions by distributors to the activities of their rivals." Such complaints, particularly where the manufacturer has imposed a costly set of nonprice restrictions, "arise in the normal course of business and do not indicate illegal concerted action." . . .

Thus, something more than evidence of complaints is needed. There must be evidence that tends to exclude the possibility that the manufacturer and nonterminated distributors were acting independently. . . . [T]he antitrust plaintiff should present direct or circumstantial evidence that reasonably tends to prove that the manufacturer and others had a conscious commitment to a common scheme designed to achieve an unlawful objective.

Applying this standard to the facts of this case, we believe there was sufficient evidence for the jury reasonably to have concluded that Monsanto and some of its distributors were parties to an "agreement" or "conspiracy" to maintain resale prices and terminate price-cutters. In fact there was substantial *direct* evidence of agreements to maintain prices. There was testimony from a Monsanto district manager, for example, that Monsanto on at least two occasions in early 1969, about five months after Spray-Rite was terminated, approached price-cutting distributors and advised that if they did not main-

CASE 45.4 Continued tain the suggested resale price, they would not receive adequate supplies of Monsanto's new corn herbicide. . . .

JUDGMENT We conclude that the Court of Appeals applied an incorrect standard to the evidence in this case. The correct standard is that there must be evidence that tends to exclude the possibility of independent action by the manufacturer and distributor. That is, there must be direct or circumstantial evidence that reasonably tends to prove that the manufacturer and others had a conscious commitment to a common scheme designed to achieve an unlawful objective. Under this standard, the evidence in this case created a jury issue as to whether Spray-Rite was terminated pursuant to a price-fixing conspiracy between Monsanto and its distributors. The judgment of the court below is affirmed.

Jointly refusing to deal—group boycotts. In the absence of any purpose to create or maintain a monopoly, one may freely exercise his or her own independent discretion to deal or not deal with another party. Nevertheless, joint action for the purpose of restricting a competitor's access to markets or sources of supply are per se violations of Section 1. Examples of illegal per se group boycotts include refusals to sell, refusals to buy,[35] picketing by a trade association to force retailers to remove a competitor's product, joint cancellation of advertising in a local newspaper in order to eliminate competition against the sole remaining newspaper,[36] and an agreement between member teams of a sports association that they will not negotiate with prospective players until 4 years after graduation from high school.[37]

[35]*United States v. Hilton Hotels Corp.*, 467 F.2d 1000 (9th Cir. 1972).
[36]*Greenspun v. McCarran*, 105 F. Supp. 662 (D. Nev. 1952).
[37]*Denver Rockets v. All-Pro Management, Inc.*, 325 F. Supp. 1049 (C.D. Cal. 1971).

In *Klor's Inc. v. Broadway-Hale Stores, Inc.*,[37a] plaintiff Klor's, a retail appliance store, brought an antitrust action against its next-door competitor, Broadway-Hale, ten national appliance manufacturers and their distributors, claiming they entered into a group conspiracy not to sell to Klor's. The Supreme Court held such actions to be an unlawful group boycott prohibited by Sections 1 and 2 that were "not to be tolerated merely because the victim is just one merchant whose business is so small that his destruction makes little difference to the economy." The Court added: "The Sherman Act has consistently been read to forbid all contracts and combinations which tend to create a monopoly, whether the tendency is a creeping one or one that proceeds at a full gallop." Not all group boycotts are per se violations of Section 1. If coercion is not present, or where the anticompetitive impact of a particular group practice is not obvious, the joint activity will be evaluated by the courts under the rule of reason. The following case, involving a group of dentists who collectively refused to perform certain services, is illustrative.

[37a]359 U.S. 207 (1959).

CASE 45.5 FTC v. Indiana Federation of Dentists · 90 L. Ed.2d 445 (1986)

FACTS A group of dentists, comprising a large majority of their profession in two cities, formed a supposed "union," the Indiana Federation of Dentists. The Federation then adopted a "work rule" which required member dentists to withhold x-rays requested by insurance carriers for use in evaluating patients' claims for reimbursement for dental care. The Federal Trade Commission (FTC), after a full evidentiary trial-type hearing, issued a cease-

CASE 45.5 Continued

and-desist order against further union organizing efforts. The FTC found that the work rule was an unreasonable horizontal restraint of trade in violation of Section 1 of the Sherman Act. Any such violation of Section 1 automatically is a violation of Section 5 of the Federal Trade Commission Act and constitutes an unfair method of competition. The Court of Appeals vacated the FTC's order on the ground that it was not supported by substantial evidence, and the FTC appealed to the Supreme Court which rendered the following unanimous decision.

OPINION

WHITE, Justice. The issue is whether the Commission erred in holding that the Federation's policy of refusal to submit x-rays to dental insurers for use in benefits determinations constituted an "unfair method of competition".... Under the... "substantial evidence" standard for review of agency factfinding, the court must accept the Commission's findings of fact if they are supported by "such relevant evidence as a reasonable mind might accept as adequate to support a conclusion." Universal Camera Corp. v. NLRB, 340 U.S. 474.... The relevant factual findings are that the members of the Federation conspired among themselves to withhold x-rays requested by dental insurers for use in evaluating claims for benefits, and that this conspiracy had the effect of suppressing competition among dentists with respect to cooperation with the requests of the insurance companies. As to the first of these findings there can be no serious dispute: abundant evidence in the record reveals that one of the primary reasons... for the Federation's existence was the promulgation and enforcement of the so-called "work rule" against submission of x-rays in conjunction with insurance claim forms....

The Commission's findings that "in the absence of... concerted behavior, individual dentists would have been subject to market forces of competition, creating incentives for them to... comply with the requests of patients' third-party insurers," finds support not only in common sense and economic theory, upon both of which the FTC may reasonably rely, but also in record documents, including newsletters circulated among Indiana dentists, revealing that Indiana dentists themselves perceived that unrestrained competition tended to lead their colleagues to comply with the insurers' requests for x-rays. Moreover, there was evidence that outside of Indiana, in States where dentists had not collectively refused to submit x-rays, insurance companies found little difficulty in obtaining compliance by dentists with their requests. A "reasonable mind" could conclude on the basis of this evidence that competition for patients, who have obvious incentives for seeking dentists who will cooperate with their insurers, would tend to lead dentists in Indiana (and elsewhere) to cooperate with requests for information by their patients' insurers.

The Commission's finding that such competition was actually diminished where the Federation held sway also finds adequate support in the record....

The policy of the Federation with respect to its members' dealings with third-party insurers resembles practices that have been labeled "group boycotts": the policy constitutes a concerted refusal to deal on particular terms with patients covered by group dental insurance. Although this Court has in the past stated that group boycotts are unlawful per se, we decline to resolve this case by forcing the Federation's policy into the "boycott" pigeon-hole and invoking the per se rule.... The category of restraints classed as group boycotts is not to be expanded indiscriminately, and the per se approach has generally been limited to cases in which firms with market power boycott suppliers or customers in order to discourage them from doing business with a competitor—a situation obviously not present here. Moreover, we have been slow to condemn rules adopted by professional associations as unreasonable per se.... Thus, as did the FTC, we evaluate the restraint at issue in this case under the Rule of Reason rather than a rule of per se illegality.

Application of the Rule of Reason to these facts is not a matter of any great difficulty. The Federation's policy takes the form of a horizontal agreement among the participating dentists to withhold from their customers a particular service that they desire—the for-

CASE 45.5 Continued

warding of x-rays to insurance companies along with claim forms. While this is not price fixing as such, no elaborate industry analysis is required to demonstrate the anticompetitive character of such an agreement. A refusal to compete with respect to the package of services offered to customers, no less than a refusal to compete with respect to the price term of an agreement, impairs the ability of the market to . . . [provide] desired goods and services to consumers at a price approximating the marginal cost of providing them. Absent some countervailing procompetitive virtue—such as, for example, the creation of efficiencies in the operating of a market or the provision of goods and services—such an agreement limiting consumer choice by impeding the ordinary give and take of the market place, cannot be sustained under the Rule of Reason. No credible argument has been advanced for the proposition that making it more costly for the insurers and patients who are the dentists' customers to obtain information needed for evaluating the dentists' diagnoses has any such procompetitive effect. . . . The Federation is not entitled to preempt the working of the market by deciding for itself that its customers do not need that which they demand. . . .

The factual findings of the Commission regarding the effect of the Federation's policy of withholding x-rays are supported by substantial evidence, and those findings are sufficient as a matter of law to establish a violation of Section 1 of the Sherman Act, and hence, Section 5 of the Federal Trade Commission Act. Since there has been no suggestion that the cease-and-desist order entered by the Commission to remedy this violation is itself improper for any reason distinct from the claimed impropriety of the finding of a violation, the Commission's order must be sustained.

JUDGMENT The judgment of the Court of Appeals is accordingly reversed.

The following case is an excellent summary of the principles of Sherman Act Section 1 law that have been discussed up to this point. In its opinion, the Court: (1) discusses the difference between judging anticompetitive behavior under the rule of reason or as a per se violation; (2) considers whether the National Football League is a "single actor" and therefore incapable of conspiring to violate Section 1; (3) discusses whether the NFL combine involves horizontal or vertical restraints, or both; and (4) points out the necessity of weighing the procompetition effect of interbrand competition between football clubs, against the anticompetitive effect of an agreement that reduces intrabrand competition, in determining whether Section 1 has been violated.

CASE 45.6 Los Angeles Memorial Coliseum Com'n v. NFL · 726 F.2d 1381 (9th Cir. 1983)

FACTS In 1978, the Los Angeles Rams' owner decided to leave the Los Angeles Coliseum and move the team to the stadium in Anaheim, California. In searching for a new National Football League tenant, the Coliseum was blocked by Rule 4.3 of the NFL Constitution. The rule required three-fourths approval of 28 member teams before a team could relocate in "home territory" of another team, which term was defined as a radius of 75 miles from the corporate limits of the city in which a club is located and for which it plays its home games. The Coliseum made a tentative agreement with the Oakland Raiders to relocate in Los Angeles. The proposed move failed to obtain the necessary three-fourths vote of the NFL. The Coliseum commissioners and the Oakland Raiders (plaintiffs) then com-

CASE 45.6 Continued

menced suit under Section 1 of the Sherman Act, claiming that Rule 4.3 was an unlawful restraint of trade. The trial court considered the NFL's argument that it was a "single entity" and therefore not capable of conspiring under the "single actor" rule, and held that the league was not a "single entity." The jury returned a verdict of liability and awarded the Raiders $34.6 million and the Coliseum $14.4 million (after trebling), and the NFL appealed.

OPINION

J. BLAINE ANDERSON, Circuit Judge. Section 1 literally prohibits every agreement, conspiracy, or other concerted activity in restraint of trade. Since Congress could not have intended that courts invalidate "every" such agreement, most restraints are analyzed under the so-called "rule of reason." *Standard Oil of New Jersey v. United States,* 221 U.S. 1. The rule of reason requires the factfinder to decide whether under all the circumstances of the case the agreement imposes an unreasonable restraint on competition.

Standard Oil, however, reconciled the earlier categorical prohibition with its own rule of reason by declaring that some restraints remain inherently unreasonable. When judicial experience with a particular kind of restraint enables a court to predict with certainty that the rule of reason will condemn that restraint, the court will hold that the restraint is per se unlawful. See *United States v. Topco Associates, Inc.,* 405 U.S. 596 (1972).... In the present case, the district judge found that the unique nature of the business of professional football made application of a per se rule inappropriate.

A. Single Entity

The NFL contends the league structure is in essence a single entity, akin to a partnership or joint venture, precluding application of Sherman Act Section 1 which prevents only contracts, combinations or conspiracies in restraint of trade. The Los Angeles Coliseum and Raiders reject this position and assert the League is composed of 28 separate legal entities which act independently....

NFL rules have been found to violate Section 1 in other contexts. Most recently, the Second Circuit analyzed the NFL's rule preventing its member-owners from having ownership interests in other professional sports clubs. *North American Soccer League v. National Football League,* 670 F.2d 1249, 1257–1259 (2d Cir.). It recognized the cooperation necessary among league members, even characterizing the NFL as a joint venture, but nonetheless applied rule of reason analysis and found the cross-ownership rule violated Section 1. Other courts have held the League rules governing player contracts violate Section 1 of the Sherman Act. *Smith v. Pro Football, Inc.,* 593 F.2d 1173 (D.C. Cir. 1978);...

Cases applying the single entity or joint venture theory in other business areas also contradict the NFL's argument. As stated by the Supreme Court:

> Nor do we find any support in reason or authority for the proposition that agreements between legally separate persons and companies to suppress competition among themselves and others can be justified by labelling the project a "joint venture." Perhaps every agreement and combination in restraint of trade could be so labeled.

...It is true the NFL clubs must cooperate to a large extent in their endeavor in producing a "product"—the NFL season culminating in the Super Bowl. The necessity that otherwise independent businesses cooperate has not, however, sufficed to preclude scrutiny under Section 1 of the Sherman Act....

Our inquiry discloses an association of teams sufficiently independent and competitive with one another to warrant rule of reason scrutiny under Section 1 of the Sherman Act. The NFL clubs are, in the words of the district court, "separate business entities whose products have an independent value." The member clubs are all independently owned....

In addition to being independent business entities, the NFL clubs do compete with one another off the field as well as on to acquire players, coaches, and management per-

CASE 45.6 Continued

sonnel. In certain areas of the country where two teams operate in close proximity, there is also competition for fan support, local television and local radio revenues, and media space.

These attributes operate to make each team an entity in large part distinct from the NFL. It is true that cooperation is necessary to produce a football game. However, as the district court concluded, this does not mean, "that each club can produce football games only as an *NFL* member."...

For the foregoing reasons, we affirm the district court's rejection of the NFL's single entity defense....

B. Rule of Reason

To establish a cause of action, plaintiff must prove these elements: (1) An agreement among two or more persons or distinct business entities; (2) which is intended to harm or unreasonably restrain competition; (3) and which actually causes injury to competition....

On the one hand, [the NFL] can be viewed simply as an organization of 28 competitors, an example of a simple horizontal arrangement. On the other, and to the extent the NFL can be considered an entity separate from the team owners, a vertical relationship is disclosed. In this sense the owners are distributors of the NFL product, each with its own territorial division. In this context it is clear that the owners have a legitimate interest in protecting the integrity of the League itself. Collective action in areas such as League divisions, scheduling and rules must be allowed, as should other activity that aids in producing the most marketable product attainable. Nevertheless, legitimate collective action should not be construed to allow the owners to extract excess profits. In such a situation the owners would be acting as a classic cartel.

On its face, Rule 4.3 divides markets among the 28 teams, a practice presumed illegal, but, as we have noted, the unique structure of the NFL precludes application of the per se rule. Instead, we must examine Rule 4.3 to determine whether it reasonably serves the legitimate collective concerns of the owners or instead permits them to reap excess profits at the expense of the consuming public.

1. Relevant Market

The NFL contends it is entitled to judgment because plaintiffs failed to prove an adverse impact on competition in a relevant market.... In the antitrust context, the relevant market has two components: the product market and the geographic market. Product market definition involves the

> process of describing those groups of producers which, because of the similarity of their products, have the ability—actual or potential—to take significant amounts of business away from each other. A market definition must look at all relevant sources of supply, either actual rivals or eager potential entrants to the market.

Two related tests are used in arriving at the product market: first, reasonable interchangeability for the same or similar uses; and second, cross-elasticity of demand, an economic term describing the responsiveness of sales of one product to price changes in another. Similar considerations determine the relevant geographic market, which describes the "economically significant" area of effective competition in which the relevant products are traded.

The claims of the Raiders and the L.A. Coliseum, respectively, present somewhat different market considerations. The Raiders attempted to prove the relevant market consists of NFL football (the product market) in the Southern California area (the geographic market). The NFL argues it competes with all forms of entertainment within the United States, not just Southern California. The L.A. Coliseum claims the relevant market is

CASE 45.6 Continued

stadia offering their facilities to NFL teams (the product market) in the United States (the geographic market). The NFL agrees with this geographic market, but argues the product market involves cities competing for all forms of stadium entertainment, including NFL football teams. . . .

The critical question is whether the jury could have determined that Rule 4.3 reasonably served the NFL's interest in producing and promoting its product, i.e., competing in the entertainment market, or whether Rule 4.3 harmed competition among the 28 teams to such an extent that any benefits to the League as a whole were outweighed. As we find below, there was ample evidence for the jury to reach the latter conclusion.

2. The History and Purpose of Rule 4.3

The NFL has awarded franchises exclusive territories since the 1930s. In the early days of professional football, numerous franchises failed and many changed location in the hope of achieving economic success. League members saw exclusive territories as a means to aid stability, ensuring the owner who was attempting to establish an NFL team in a particular city that another would not move into the same area, potentially ruining them both. . . .

That the purpose of Rule 4.3 was to restrain competition among the 28 teams may seem obvious and it is not surprising the NFL admitted as much at trial. . . .

3. Ancillary Restraints and the Reasonableness of Rule 4.3

. . . [The ancillary restraint] doctrine teaches that some agreements which restrain competition may be valid if they are "subordinate and collateral to another legitimate transaction and necessary to make that transaction effective." . . .

We assume, with no reason to doubt, that the agreement creating the NFL is valid and the territorial divisions therein are ancillary to its main purpose of producing NFL football. The ancillary restraint must then be tested under the rule of reason, *id.*, the relevance of ancillarity being it increases the probability that the restraint will be found reasonable. As we have already noted, the rule of reason inquiry requires us to consider the harms and benefits to competition caused by the restraint and whether the putative benefits can be achieved by less restrictive means.

The competitive harms of Rule 4.3 are plain. Exclusive territories insulate each team from competition within the NFL market, in essence allowing them to set monopoly prices to the detriment of the consuming public. The rule also effectively forecloses free competition among stadia such as the Los Angeles Coliseum that wish to secure NFL tenants. The harm from Rule 4.3 is especially acute in this case because it prevents a move by a team into another existing team's market. If the transfer is upheld, direct competition between the Rams and Raiders would presumably ensue to the benefit of all who consume the NFL product in the Los Angeles area. . . .

[A] factor in determining the reasonableness of an ancillary restraint is the "possibility of less restrictive alternatives" which could serve the same purpose. Here, the district court correctly instructed the jury to take into account the existence of less restrictive alternatives when determining the reasonableness of Rule 4.3's territorial restraint. Because there was substantial evidence going to the existence of such alternatives, we find that the jury could have reasonably concluded that the NFL should have designed its "ancillary restraint" in a manner that served its needs but did not so foreclose competition. . . .

It is true, as the NFL claims, that the antitrust laws are primarily concerned with the promotion of *intrabrand* competition. To the extent the NFL is a product which competes with other forms of entertainment, including other sports, its rules governing territorial division can be said to promote interbrand competition. Under this analysis, the terri-

CASE 45.6 Continued

torial allocations most directly suppress intrabrand, that is, NFL team versus NFL team, competition. A more direct impact on intrabrand competition does not mean, however, the restraint is reasonable. The finder of fact must still balance the gain to interbrand competition against the loss of intrabrand competition. Here, the jury could have found that the rules restricting team movement do not sufficiently promote interbrand competition to justify the negative impact on intrabrand competition.

To withstand antitrust scrutiny, restrictions on team movement should be more closely tailored to serve the needs inherent in producing the NFL "product" and competing with other forms of entertainment. An express recognition and consideration of those objective factors espoused by the NFL as important, such as population, economic projections, facilities, regional balance, etc., would be well advised. Fan loyalty and location continuity could also be considered....

JUDGMENT The judgment finding the NFL liable to the Los Angeles Coliseum and the Raiders, and enjoining the NFL from preventing the Raiders from relocating in Los Angeles is Affirmed.

[The U.S. Supreme Court denied certiorari November 5, 1984, leaving the circuit court's decision as final.]

Reciprocal dealing. Sometimes a company buys large quantities of goods from a supplier who also needs the products of the company it supplies. For example, an automobile manufacturer may buy large quantities of steel from a supplier whose nationwide selling organization regularly needs automobiles. If the automobile manufacturer uses its purchasing power leverage to coerce the steel supplier to buy its automobiles, the arrangement is called "reciprocal dealing" or "reciprocity." Reciprocity arising from coercion or even a "voluntary" reciprocal buying arrangement in which one of the parties departs from the usual criteria of product selection (quality, price, service, time of delivery), can be a per se violation of Section 1 of the Sherman Act. Key factors considered by the courts in determining whether reciprocity is illegal per se include: the relative size and purchasing volume of the parties; the existence of power to exert "leverage" pressure on a supplier, regardless of whether the leverage was actually used in a purchasing agreement; and the maintenance of facilities such as a "trade relations department" to exert purchasing power coercion.

Other per se violations. There are other joint per se restraints that occur less frequently than those discussed. For example, collusive bidding ("bid rigging") includes agreements to select one from the group to make the lowest bid while the others refrain from bidding, comparing bids prior to submission, creating a bid depository where competitors compare bids and fix the bid price, or splitting of profits made by the successful bidder. In addition, arrangements to refrain from advertising prices, and most tying contracts are per se unreasonable restraints.

In order to establish an unlawful tying arrangement, three elements must be proved: (1) the scheme in question involves two distinct items and provides that one (the tying product) may not be obtained unless the other (the tied product) is also purchased; (2) the tying product possesses sufficient economic power appreciably to restrain competition in the tied product market; and (3) a "not insubstantial" amount of commerce is affected by the arrangement. It has been held that a trademark can be a tying product. Tying contracts may also violate the Clayton Act, discussed in the next chapter.

In the following case, the U.S. Supreme Court explains factors which determine when a "tying" case is judged as a per se violation, when it is judged under the rule of reason, and the necessity of proof of market power over the tying product in order to establish a Sherman Act Section 1 violation.

CASE 45.7 Jefferson Parish Hosp. Dist. No. 2 v. Hyde · 80 L. Ed.2d 2 (1984)

FACTS In 1977, Edwin Hyde (plaintiff), a certified anesthesiologist, applied for admission to the medical staff of East Jefferson Hospital. The application was denied because of a contract between the hospital and Roux & Associates, a group of anesthesiologists, which provided that Roux would perform all anesthesiological services required by the hospital's patients. Hyde then filed suit, claiming that the contract was an unlawful tying arrangement and a per se violation of Section 1 of the Sherman Act. The district court denied relief, finding that the anticompetitive consequences of the contract were minimal and outweighed by benefits in the form of improved care. The Court of Appeals reversed, holding that the contract was illegal per se and the hospital appealed.

OPINION STEVENS, Justice. . . . It is clear . . . that every refusal to sell two products separately cannot be said to restrain competition. If each of the products may be purchased separately in competitive market, one seller's decision to sell the two in a single package imposes no unreasonable restraint on either market, particularly if competing suppliers are free to sell either the entire package or its several parts. For example, we have written that "if one of a dozen food stores in a community were to refuse to sell flour unless the buyer also took sugar it would hardly tend to restrain competition if its competitors were ready and able to sell flour by itself." . . . Buyers often find package sales attractive; a seller's decision to offer such packages can merely be an attempt to compete effectively—conduct that is entirely consistent with the Sherman Act. . . .

Our cases have concluded that the essential characteristic of an invalid tying arrangement lies in the seller's exploitation of its control over the tying product to force the buyer into the purchase of a tied product that the buyer either did not want at all, or might have preferred to purchase elsewhere on different terms. When such "forcing" is present, competition on the merits in the market for the tied item is restrained and the Sherman Act is violated. . . .

Accordingly, we have condemned tying arrangements when the seller has some special ability—usually called "market power"—to force a purchaser to do something that he would not do in a competitive market. . . . When "forcing" occurs, our cases have found the tying arrangement to be unlawful.

Thus, the law draws a distinction between the exploitation of market power by merely enhancing the price of the tying product on the one hand, and by attempting to impose restraints on competition in the market for a tied product, on the other. When the seller's power is just used to maximize its return in the tying product market, where presumably its product enjoys some justifiable advantage over its competitors, the competitive ideal of the Sherman Act is not necessarily compromised. But if that power is used to impair competition on the merits in another market, a potentially inferior product may be insulated from competitive pressures. This impairment could either harm existing competitors or create barriers to entry of new competitors in the market for the tied product, and can increase the social costs of market power by facilitating price discrimination, thereby increasing monopoly profits over what they would be absent the tie. . . .

Per se condemnation—condemnation without inquiry into actual market conditions—is only appropriate if the existence of forcing is probable. Thus, application of the per se rule focuses on the probability of anticompetitive consequences. Of course, as a threshold matter there must be a substantial potential for impact on competition in order to justify per se condemnation. If only a single purchaser were "forced" with respect to the purchase of a tied item, the resultant impact on competition would

CASE 45.7 Continued

not be sufficient to warrant the concern of antitrust law. It is for this reason that we have refused to condemn tying arrangements unless a substantial volume of commerce is foreclosed thereby. . . .

Once this threshold is surmounted, per se prohibition is appropriate if anticompetitive forcing is likely. For example, if the government has granted the seller a patent or similar monopoly over a product, it is fair to presume that the inability to buy the product elsewhere gives the seller market power. . . . Any effort to enlarge the scope of the patent monopoly by using the market power it confers to restrain competition in the market for a second product will undermine competition on the merits in that second market. . . .

The same strict rule is appropriate in other situations in which the existence of market power is probable. When the seller's share of the market is high, or when the seller offers a unique product that competitors are not able to offer, the Court has held that the likelihood that market power exists and is being used to restrain competition in a separate market is sufficient to make per se condemnation appropriate. . . .

[T]he hospital's requirement that its patients obtain necessary anesthesiological services from Roux combined the purchases of two distinguishable services in a single transaction. Nevertheless, the fact that this case involves a required purchase of two services that would otherwise be purchased separately does not make the Roux contract illegal. As noted above, there is nothing inherently anticompetitive about packaged sales. Only if patients are forced to purchase Roux's services as a result of the hospital's market power would the arrangement have anticompetitive consequences. If no forcing is present, patients are free to enter a competing hospital and to use another anesthesiologist instead of Roux. . . .

Seventy per cent of the patients residing in Jefferson Parish enter hospitals other than East Jefferson. Thus East Jefferson's "dominance" over persons residing in Jefferson Parish is far from overwhelming. The facts that a substantial majority of the parish's residents elect not to enter East Jefferson means that the geographic data does not establish the kind of dominant market position that obviates the need for further inquiry into actual competitive conditions. . . .

In order to prevail in the absence of per se liability, plaintiff has the burden of proving that the Roux contract violated the Sherman Act because it unreasonably restrained competition. That burden necessarily involves an inquiry into the actual effect of the exclusive contract on competition among anesthesiologists. This competition takes place in a market that has not been defined. The market is not necessarily the same as the market in which hospitals compete in offering services to patients; it may encompass competition among anesthesiologists for exclusive contracts such as the Roux contract and might be statewide or merely local. There is, however, insufficient evidence in this record to provide a basis for finding that the Roux contract, as it actually operates in the market, has unreasonably restrained competition. . . .

JUDGMENT In sum, all that the record establishes is that the choice of anesthesiologists at East Jefferson has been limited to one of four doctors who are associated with Roux and therefore have staff privileges. . . . There is no evidence that the price, the quality, or the supply or demand for either the "tying product" or the "tied product" involved in this case has been adversely affected by the exclusive contract between Roux and the hospital. . . . Indeed, . . . the record tells us very little about the market for the services of anesthesiologists. Yet that is the market in which the exclusive contract has had its principal impact. There is simply no showing here of the kind of restraint on competition that is prohibited by the Sherman Act. Accordingly, the judgment of the Court of Appeals is reversed and the case is remanded to that court for further proceedings consistent with this opinion.

Decline of the Per Se Doctrine. The previous five cases (45.3–45.7) reflect the growing reluctance of the Supreme Court to decide antitrust cases under the per se analysis and the Court's increasing tendency to judge borderline restraints under the rule of reason. This trend reflects the influence of antitrust scholars from the University of Chicago. Thus, the "Chicago School" emphasis on *economic efficiency* as the chief standard for judging antitrust challenges is reflected in the Court's refusal to apply per se analysis to an out-and-out price-fixing agreement between composers and a broadcasting company. Instead, the Court judged the agreement under the rule of reason, found that it would increase economic efficiency, and held it not to be a violation of Sherman Section 1.[38]

Proving Monopolization under Section 2

Three distinct offenses are listed in Section 2: to "monopolize, or attempt to monopolize, or combine or conspire . . . to monopolize" any part of interstate or foreign commerce. Unlike the prohibitions of Section 1, which always require at least two actors, a violation of Section 2 can result from a *single firm's* outright acquisition of a monopoly position or attempt to monopolize. However, a Section 2 violation can also result from a plurality of actors as, for example, when two companies combine or conspire to monopolize. It should be further noted that two companies can conspire to restrain trade so as to violate Section 1 but not Section 2, because the amount of trade they are restraining is not sufficient to constitute a monopoly or an attempt to monopolize their industry. On the other hand, any conspiracy or combination to monopolize necessarily is a conspiracy in restraint of trade, which also violates Section 1. Two elements are necessary to establish criminal or civil liability for monopolization under Section 2:

1 The *acquisition of monopoly power,* that is, the power to control prices or exclude competitors in a relevant market.
2 Deliberateness or a *general intent to monopolize.*

A thorough comprehension of these complex concepts requires an understanding of the basic principles of economics as well as antitrust law.[39]

Monopoly Power in a Relevant Market. Courts consider many factors in determining whether a firm has the monopoly power to control prices or exclude competitors in a relevant market. They are: (1) the size of the market share, (2) whether the size of the firm was achieved through "natural growth" or by acquiring competitors, (3) the number of competitors and their financial strength, (4) whether the defendant engaged in unlawful exclusionary practices to prevent entry into the market by potential competitors, and (5) the extent to which the defendant used unduly coercive tactics to suppress competition.[40] The most important of these factors is the size of the market share. Although there are no judicially approved precise formulas, 80 percent or more of the market is generally considered to constitute market power and 50 percent or less is insufficient evidence that such power exists. If a defendant has 50 to 80 percent of the market share, courts will then examine the other factors more closely in order to decide whether the defendant has market power.[41]

A key question in Section 2 cases is: "What is a relevant market?" Generally, it consists of (1) the geographic area of effective competition in which a particular product is traded and (2) the market area for other substitute products with which the particular product is interchangeable. In the language of economists (who are often used as expert witnesses in antitrust cases), product interchangeability is referred to as *cross-elasticity of demand,* that is, the degree to which users of product A will shift to buying product B in response to a drop in the price of B. If the number of users of product A that shift to purchasing B is relatively high, it is said that A and B have a high degree of cross-elasticity of demand or (in the terminology of the courts) a high degree of interchangeability.

The terms "monopoly power," "relevant market," and "cross-elasticity of demand" were ap-

[38]*Broadcast Music, Inc. v. Columbia Broadcasting System, Inc.*, 441 U.S. 1 (1979).

[39]See Ernest Gellhorn, *Antitrust Law and Economics,* West Publishing Co., St. Paul, 1986.

[40]*United States v. Aluminum Co. of America,* 148 F.2d 416 (2nd Cir. 1945).

[41]*Yoder Bros. Inc. v. California-Florida Plant Corp.*, 537 F.2d 1347 (5th Cir. 1976).

plied by the Supreme Court in the leading case of *United States v. du Pont de Nemours and Company,*[42] in which the United States brought a Section 2 civil action charging du Pont with monopolizing the cellophane industry. During the period involved, du Pont produced almost 75 percent of the cellophane in the United States, but cellophane constituted less than 20 percent of all "flexible packaging material" sales. The central question was: Does the "relevant market" include only the product cellophane, or is cellophane competing in a larger market of "flexible packaging materials" (such as Saran, foil, and wax paper) that are interchangeable?

The trial court found that du Pont cellophane was competing in the larger market and that the interchangeable products in that market had a high degree of cross-elasticity of demand. Pointing out that du Pont furnished less than 7 percent of wrappings for bakery products, 25 percent for candy, 32 percent for snacks, and 35 percent for meat and poultry, the trial court concluded that du Pont did not have monopoly power in the flexible packaging material market. In upholding this decision, the Supreme Court said:

> The "market" which one must study to determine when a producer has monopoly power will vary with the part of commerce under consideration. The tests are constant. That market is composed of products that have reasonable interchangeability for the purposes for which they are produced—price, use, and qualities considered. While the application of the tests remains uncertain, it seems to us that du Pont should not be found to monopolize cellophane when that product has the competition and interchangeability with other wrappings that this record shows.

General Intent to Monopolize. Deliberate conduct, the probable result of which is to obtain monopoly, meets the "general intent" requirement necessary to establish Section 2 liability. Obviously, if a firm acquires monopoly power while restraining trade in violation of Section 1, it has also clearly violated Section 2. Intent to monopolize is proved if it can be shown that the single firm engaged in predatory activities such as injuring actual competitors, excluding potential competitors, erecting barriers to entry into the market ("limit pricing"), and refraining from maximizing profits until competitors are driven out of the market ("predatory pricing").

An across-the-board price set at or above marginal cost should not ordinarily form the basis for an antitrust violation, but setting prices below marginal cost may well form the basis for such a violation. It has been held that average variable cost can be used as evidence of marginal cost, in determining whether a setting of price forms the basis of an antitrust violation.[43] Proof of an *attempt to monopolize* is sufficient when it is shown that the defendant employed "methods, means and practices which would, if successful, accomplish monopolization, and which, though falling short, nevertheless approach so close as to create a dangerous probability of it."[44]

Conduct That Is Not Monopolization; Oligopoly. Monopoly power may be lawfully obtained through superior business acumen or product, or as the result of historic accident and by natural, as distinguished from predatory, means. A defendant firm that has acquired monopoly power in this manner will argue (usually without success) that its monopoly position was "thrust upon" it and that its market dominance did not come about as the result of any wrongful conduct under Section 2. In the *du Pont* case discussed earlier, the Supreme Court, in illustrating a lawful monopoly, said:

> A retail seller may have in one sense a monopoly on certain trade because of location, as an isolated country store or filling station, or because no one else makes a product of just the quality or attractiveness of his product. . . .

However, in the leading cases[45] involving the "thrust upon" defense to monopolization, the defendant was found to be liable, because of predatory practices that accompanied the firm's growth to monopoly power.

In the absence of concerted action to fix prices or engage in other anticompetitive conduct, the "thrust upon" or "historic accident" defense to a Section 2 monopolization charge is probably available to most firms in *oligopolistic industries.* Economists use the term "oligopoly" (literally, "a few

[42]351 U.S. 377 (1956).

[43]*Janich Bros. Inc. v. American Distilling Co.,* 570 F.2d 848 (9th Cir. 1977).

[44]*American Tobacco Co. v. United States,* 221 U.S. 106 (1911).

[45]*United States v. Aluminum Co. of America,* 148 F.2d 416 (2nd Cir. 1945); *United States v. Grinnell Corp.,* 384 U.S. 563 (1966).

sellers") to refer to an industry in which a small number of firms account for substantially all of that industry's output. For example, one study conducted by Congress showed that three or less companies in the United States held a market share of 75 percent or more for aluminum, automobiles, telephone equipment, typewriters, cigarettes, soap, cereal, and many other kinds of products.

Concentration in American industry often arose because of historical accident, ownership of a valuable patent, or natural growth up to the point where a few firms found themselves participating in what is sometimes called a "shared monopoly." The mere size of a firm that grew in this manner is not, of itself, a violation of Section 2. However, if one or more firms in an oligopoly jointly participate in predatory activity that presents a probability of creating monopoly power, Section 2 has been violated. In the *Eastman Kodak* case below, which the court described as "one of the largest and most significant private antitrust suits in history," the court focused on present legal elements that must be proved to establish liability for monopolization under Section 2.

CASE 45.8 Berkey Photo, Inc. v. Eastman Kodak Co. · 603 F.2d 263 (2nd Cir. 1979)

FACTS Berkey Photo, Inc. (plaintiff), a supplier of photofinishing services, sought treble damages under both Sections 1 and 2 of the Sherman Act from Eastman Kodak Co. (defendant). Berkey charged, among other things, that Eastman had willfully acquired and exercised monopoly power in the film, color print paper, and camera markets in violation of Section 2 of the Sherman Act, causing it to lose sales in the markets for these products. The jury returned a treble damage verdict which, with attorney's fees, exceeded $87 million, from which Eastman Kodak appealed.

The appellate court confirmed four relevant product markets, each nationwide in scope: (1) The film market in which Kodak had monopoly power, annual sales since 1952 always exceeding 82 percent of the nationwide volume on a unit basis, and 88 percent of revenues. (2) The still camera market, in which Kodak was dominant, with no less than 61 percent of industry annual unit sales from 1954 to 1973. This success was due largely to introduction in 1972 of the small 110 "Pocket Instamatic," which could be loaded only with a special cartridge containing a newly developed film, Kodacolor II. (3) Photofinishing services and photofinishing equipment, furnished by Kodak's Color Print and Processing Laboratories (CP&P), accounting for only 10 percent of the market in 1976, the remainder going to the 600 independent photofinishers in the United States. (4) Color photographic paper, with Kodak's market share dropping from 94 percent in 1968 to 67 percent in 1975.

Berkey contended that, in violation of the Sherman Act, Section 2, Kodak exercised monopoly power by (a) designing the Kodacolor II film in the special cartridge so that the buyers of the camera could buy only Kodak film, thus foreclosing competitors in the film market, and (b) introducing a new film requiring special new developing equipment, thereby foreclosing independent photofinishers from the developing business; and that (c) Kodak's failure to "predisclose" the 110 Pocket Instamatic to competitors foreclosed them from making competing film that was compatible with the 110 design or "format."

OPINION KAUFMAN, Circuit Judge. To millions of Americans, the name Kodak is virtually synonymous with photography.... Snapshots may be taken with a Kodak camera, on Kodak film, developed by Kodak's CP&P, and printed on Kodak photographic paper. The firm has rivals at each stage of this process, but in many of them it stands, and has long stood, dominant....

Monopoly Power

Kodak, then, is indeed a titan in its field, and accordingly has almost inevitably invited attack under § 2 of the Sherman Act. Section 2... is aimed primarily not at improper

CASE 45.8 Continued

conduct but at a pernicious market structure in which the concentration of power saps the salubrious influence of competition. Indeed, there is little argument over the principle that existence of monopoly power—"the power to control prices or exclude competition"—is the primary requisite to a finding of monopolization. The Supreme Court has informed us that "monopoly power, whether lawfully or unlawfully acquired, may itself constitute an evil and stand condemned under § 2 even though it remains unexercised." *U.S. v. Griffith,* 334 U.S. 100.... If a finding of monopoly power were all that were necessary to complete a violation of Section 2, our task in this case would be considerably lightened. Kodak's control of the film and color paper markets clearly reached the level of a monopoly. And, while the issue is a much closer one, it appears that the evidence was sufficient for the jury to find that Kodak possessed such power in the camera market as well. But our inquiry into Kodak's liability cannot end there.

Requirement of Anticompetitive Conduct

Thus, while proclaiming vigorously that monopoly power is the evil at which Section 2 is aimed, courts have declined to take what would have appeared to be the next logical step—declaring monopolies unlawful per se unless specifically authorized by law.... Thus, Judge Hand, in *U.S. v. Aluminum Co. of America,* 148 F.2d 416,... having stated that "Congress did not condone 'good trusts' and condemn 'bad' ones; it forbade all," declared with equal force, "The successful competitor, having been urged to compete, must not be turned upon when he wins." Hand, therefore, told us that it would be inherently unfair to condemn success when the Sherman Act itself mandates competition. Such a wooden rule, it was feared, might also deprive the leading firm in an industry of the incentive to exert its best efforts. Further success would yield not rewards but legal castigation.... The key to analysis, it must be stressed, is the concept of market power.... The mere possession of monopoly power does not *ipso facto* condemn a market participation. But to avoid the proscription of § 2, the firm must refrain at all times from conduct directed at smothering competition.

Attempt to Monopolize Camera Market

There is little doubt that the evidence supports the jury's implicit finding that Kodak had monopoly power in cameras.... [According to Berkey] Kodak persistently refused to make film available for most formats other than those in which it made cameras. Since cameras are worthless without film, this policy effectively prevented other manufacturers from introducing cameras in new formats.... For eighteen months after its introduction, Kodacolor II was available only in the 110 format. Thus it followed that any consumer wishing to use Kodak's "remarkable new film" had to buy a 110 camera. Since Kodak was the leading—and at first the only—manufacturer of such devices, its camera sales were boosted at the expense of its competitors. For the reasons explained below, we do not believe any of these contentions is sufficient on the facts of this case to justify an award of damages to Berkey. We therefore reverse this portion of the judgment.

Predisclosure

We hold that... as a matter of law, Kodak did not have a duty to predisclose information about the 110 system to competing camera manufacturers.... A firm may normally keep its innovations secret from its rivals as long as it wishes, forcing them to catch up on the strength of their own efforts after the new product is introduced. It is the possibility of success in the marketplace, attributable to superior performance, that provides the incentives on which the proper functioning of our competitive economy rests. If a firm that has engaged in the risks and expenses of research and development were required in all circumstances to share with its rivals the benefits of those endeavors, this incentive would

CASE 45.8 Continued

very likely be vitiated. . . . The first firm, even a monopolist, to design a new camera format has a right to the lead time that follows from its success. The mere fact that Kodak manufactured film in the new format as well, so that its customers would not be offered worthless cameras, could not deprive it of that reward.

Restriction of Kodacolor II to the 110 Format

For eighteen months after the 110 system introduction, Kodacolor II was available only in the 110 format. Berkey asserts . . . that since consumers were led to believe that Kodacolor II was superior to Kodacolor X, they were more likely to buy Kodak 110, rather than a Berkey camera, so that the new film could be used. . . . We shall assume *arguendo* that Kodak violated Section 2 of the Sherman Act if its decision to restrict Kodacolor II to the 110 format was not justified by the nature of the film but was motivated by a desire to impede competition in the manufacture of cameras capable of using the new film. This might well supply the element of coercion we found lacking in the previous section. . . .

But to prevail, Berkey must prove more, for injury is an element of a private treble damages action. Berkey must, therefore, demonstrate that some consumers who would have bought a Berkey camera were dissuaded from doing so because Kodacolor II was available only in 110 format. This it had failed to establish. The record is totally devoid of evidence that Kodak or its retailers actually attempted to persuade customers to purchase the Pocket Instamatic because it was the only camera that could use Kodacolor II, or that, in fact, any consumers did choose the 110 in order to utilize the finer-grained film. . . .

Film and Color Paper Claims

. . . Excessive prices, maintained through exercise of a monopolist's control of the market, constituted one of the primary evils that the Sherman Act was intended to correct. . . . But unless the monopoly has bolstered its power by wrongful actions, it will not be required to pay damages merely because it is prices may later be found excessive. Setting a high price may be a use of monopoly power, but its not in itself anticompetitive. . . . If a firm has taken no action to destroy competition it may be unfair to deprive it of the ordinary opportunity to set prices at a profit-maximizing level.

JUDGMENT [The Court remanded the issue of monopolization of film and color paper with instructions for the trial court to receive further evidence as to whether Kodak had exercised coercion or engaged in anticompetitive conduct that would render its monopoly pricing wrongful and unlawful. The trial court's judgment was reversed as to the $45,750,000 treble damages award to Berkey for lost profits arising from Kodak's introduction of the 110 camera. All other portions of the judgment were also reversed and the case was remanded for new trial.]

Summary

The Sherman Act was passed to promote competition, retard concentration in industry, and create a broad federal court jurisdiction to develop a new body of antitrust law. The Act's two basic provisions are: Section 1, which prohibits contracts or conspiracies in restraint of trade; and Section 2, which prohibits monopolization. The Sherman Act is enforced: (1) By civil treble damages suits brought by those private parties who have "standing" to sue, that is, whose injury is causally and directly linked to the defendant's wrongful antitrust conduct. (2) By the government in a civil suit for injunction and damages, or in a criminal proceeding punishable by fine up to $1 million against a corporation or $100,000 against an individual, or 3 years imprisonment, or both. If a defendant is permitted to enter a nolo contendere plea, the result is a judgment against the defendant that is not admissible to prove liability in any subsequent civil suit by a private party such as a competitor of the defendant. (3) By seizure and forfeiture to the United States of property being transported in interstate commerce pursuant to a conspiracy that violates Section 1.

To establish a violation of Section 1 or 2 of the Sherman Act, interstate or foreign "commerce" jurisdiction must be proved by showing that the defendant's activities either (1) occurred within the *flow of commerce* or (2) had a substantial and adverse *effect on commerce,* even though such effect is produced indirectly by intrastate activity. An additional element that must be proved in all cases is *intent* to contract, combine, or conspire (Section 1) or to monopolize (Section 2). However, intent may be inferred by circumstantial evidence. With few exceptions, consciously parallel behavior, standing alone, is insufficient to prove a conspiracy.

In the *Standard Oil* case, the Supreme Court held that Congress intended by Section 1 to prohibit only those contracts that *unreasonably* restrain trade. Under this "Rule of Reason," if a restraint was reasonable, it was lawful. Most Section 1 cases are judged under this rule of reason. However certain agreements or practices have such a deadly effect on competition that they are conclusively presumed to be unreasonable and therefore illegal without the necessity of proof or unreasonableness. Such agreements, called per se violations, include horizontal and vertical price fixing (resale price maintenance), restriction of production, division of markets or customers, refusal to deal (group boycotting), reciprocal dealing arrangements, and most tying contracts. However, vertical nonprice restraints, such as allocation of market territory to franchised retailers, are judged under the rule of reason.

To prove a violation of Section 2, the plaintiff must show: (1) The defendant acquired monopoly power, that is, the power to control prices or exclude competitors in a relevant market. In determining a relevant market, courts first define the *product* (e.g., paint or automotive paint) and then define the geographic area of effective competition in which the product, as well as any interchangeable substitute product, is traded. (2) The defendant had a general intent to monopolize, that is, engaged in deliberate conduct the probable result of which is to obtain monopoly. This is shown by predatory activities such as injuring or excluding competitors, erecting barriers to entry, or adopting "predatory pricing" policies.

Monopoly power may be obtained lawfully if superior business acumen or historic accident thrust upon the defendant a monopoly position. This "thrust upon" defense is usually not successful because predatory practices are found to have accompanied the firm's growth. However, if there is no predatory activity, most firms in oligopolistic industries can successfully avail themselves of this defense.

Review Questions

1 Explain the meaning of "antitrust law."

2 What economic forces led to enactment of antitrust laws in the United States?

3 Explain how the trust device can be used to achieve control of a number of corporations.

4 What was the most significant major objective of Congress in passing the Sherman Act?

5 The Sherman Act prohibits what activities in Section 1? In Section 2?

6 Name three methods of enforcing the Sherman Act. Which is the most commonly used?

7 **(a)** What is meant by "standing to sue"? **(b)** What test do the courts use to determine if a plaintiff has "standing"?

8 How does the doctrine of per se unreasonableness relate to the rule of reason? Of what advantage is it to a plaintiff to prove a per se violation of the Sherman Act?

9 Explain **(a)** vertical price fixing, **(b)** resale price maintenance, **(c)** the Miller-Tydings Act, and **(d)** state fair-trade laws.

10 Is it a violation of the Sherman Act to divide markets or customers **(a)** horizontally? **(b)** vertically? If so, is the violation judged under the rule of reason or as a per se violation?

11 What factors do courts consider in determining whether a firm has the monopoly power to control prices or exclude competition in a relevant market?

12 What evidence is considered relevant by courts in proving intent to monopolize?

13 **(a)** What is meant by "oligopoly"? **(b)** How is it possible to achieve monopoly power lawfully?

Case Problems

1 Unions filed a Sherman Act Section 1 suit against Employers, a multi-employer association. Unions sought treble damages, claiming that Employers coerced certain third parties as well as Employers' members to enter into relationships with nonunion contractors and subcontractors and thus adversely affect the trade of unionized firms and of Unions' business activities. Employers argued that Unions had no standing to sue under the antitrust laws. The district court dismissed the case, the circuit court of appeals reversed the decision, and Employers appealed to the U.S. Supreme Court. Did Unions have standing to sue?

2 Checker Corp. manufactured taxicabs. It entered into a contract with Yellow Cab Co. and other cab operating companies in New York, Chicago, Pittsburgh, and Minneapolis whereby they agreed to buy their cabs exclusively from Checker. The agreement only involved purchase of 5,000 cabs in the four cities. Collectively these purchases constituted a very small percentage of all cabs bought in the United States. The government, in a civil action against the Checker Corp. and the Yellow Cab Co., charged them with violating Section 1 of the Sherman Act. The trial court dismissed the complaint for failure to state facts showing that the transaction affected interstate commerce, and the United States appealed. Decision?

3 In Richmond, Virginia, 35 of 38 savings and loan associations used the "escrow accounting method" for tax and insurance prepayments advanced by mortgage borrowers. Eight of these firms had changed to the escrow method from the "capitalization method" within the previous 3 years. Brown, a borrower, brought an action against the savings and loan associations alleging violations of Section 1 of the Sherman Act. Brown noted that lending institutions must pay more interest on borrowers' advances under the capitalization method and its elimination was therefore an economic motive for conspiring to use the escrow method. Brown also claimed that parallel behavior of the associations established intent to restrain trade. Although most of the defendant firms belonged to the same trade association, there was no evidence that they had exchanged information on accounting methods. Did the defendant savings and loan associations engage in a conspiracy in violation of Section 1?

4 Copperweld, Inc.'s wholly owned subsidiary, Regal, Inc., manufactured steel tubing. XYZ, Inc., a newly formed competitor of Regal, ordered a tube mill from Yoder. Copperweld sent Yoder a letter threatening suit unless Yoder refused to fill the order of XYZ, Inc., and Yoder voided the order. XYZ, Inc. sued Copperweld, Regal, and Yoder, alleging their conduct was an unlawful group boycott in violation of Section 1 of the Sherman Act. The jury returned a verdict of $7.5 million against Copperweld and Regal, for conspiring against XYZ, Inc., but found that Yoder was not a part of the conspiracy. Copperweld and Regal appealed, claiming that a parent and its wholly owned subsidiary corporation are a "single entity" and as such are not capable of "conspiring" in violation of Section 1. Are Copperweld and Regal a single entity?

5 Paper Companies was a group of 10 manufacturing firms that accounted for 90 percent of the shipments of corrugated containers from plants in the southeastern United States. From 1955 to 1963, these firms regularly exchanged price information among themselves, but no agreements to adhere to a price schedule were made. When a seller requested and received price information from a competitor, it affirmed its willingness to furnish such information in return. Frequently, after two competitors exchanged price information, they would quote the same price to a buyer. The exchange of price information had the effect of stabilizing prices within a fairly narrow range, but with supply exceeding demand in the container market, prices drifted downward over an 8-year period. Did Paper Companies violate the price-fixing prohibition of Section 1 of the Sherman Act?

6 Chicken Delight, a fast food franchising company in interstate commerce, required its franchise to purchase certain essential cooking equipment, dry-mix food items, and trademark-bearing packaging exclusively from Chicken Delight, as a condition of getting a franchise and trademark license. A class action suit was filed against Chicken Delight, alleging violation of Section 1 of the Sherman Act for an unlawful tying arrangement. Chicken Delight claimed that the trademark and franchise license were not separate and distinct from the equipment, food items, and packaging, but that all of these constituted an integrated franchise system to be treated as a combined sale. Was the franchise system an unlawful tying arrangement?

7 In 1981, NCAA adopted a plan for television college football games for its member institutions. The plan was designed to reduce the adverse effect of live television upon football game attendance. The plan limited the total number of televised intercollegiate football games and the total number of games any one college could televise, and prohibited any NCAA member from selling television rights except in accordance with the plan. NCAA then made separate agreements with ABC and CBS television networks for the right to televise the games.

The University of Oklahoma and other universities that were members of NCAA formed College Football Association (CFA) and contracted with NBC for a more liberal number of televised games and increased revenues. NCAA then threatened disciplinary action against its members who had also joined CFA. The University of Oklahoma and other CFA universities sued NCAA, claiming violations of the Sherman Act, Section 1. The trial court rejected NCAA's contention that it was a joint venture and therefore a single entity not capable of conspiracy. The trial court, applying the rule of reason further found live college football television "to be relevant market" and held that competition had been unlawfully restrained by (1) NCAA fixing prices for particular broadcasts, (2) exclusive contracts with ABC and CBS which amounted to a group boycott of all other potential television broadcasting competitors, and (3) the NCAA plan which placed an artificial limit on production of televised college football. The circuit court held that these three practices were per se violations of Section 1. **(a)** Was NCAA a "single entity" joint venture? **(b)** Should the case be judged under the rule of reason, or by per se standards? **(c)** Decision?

CHAPTER 46

The Clayton, Robinson-Patman, and Federal Trade Commission Acts

In the 25 years following the Sherman Act of 1890, there was growing criticism of its shortcomings. Small business objected that the act focused on breaking up monopolies after they were formed, and did little or nothing to stop anticompetitive practices in their beginning stages. Labor unions claimed that, contrary to the intent of Congress, injunctions authorized by the act for use against monopolistic business practices had been twisted by court interpretation into a powerful tool to suppress organized labor's only weapons—strikes, pickets, and boycotts. Other critics argued that the general and vague language of the act and conflicting court interpretations of the rule of reason made it difficult or impossible for firms to know precisely what conduct was prohibited. Still others argued that the Sherman Act had done little to arrest the growing trend toward concentration in American industry.

Responding to these objections, Congress enacted the Clayton Act in 1914. At the same time, the Federal Trade Commission Act was passed, creating the Federal Trade Commission (FTC) to administer certain portions of the antitrust laws. The first three parts of this chapter survey the scope and effect of these acts as well as the Robinson-Patman Act of 1936, which amended the Clayton Act. The last part of the chapter reviews various exemptions to the antitrust laws and discusses recent trends and policy developments.

The Clayton Act

Purpose and Scope of the Clayton Act

The Clayton Act[1] was enacted to prohibit four types of anticompetitive business practices involving interstate commerce: price discrimination (Section 2), exclusive dealing and tying contracts (Section 3), anticompetitive corporate mergers (Section 7), and interlocking directorates (Section 8). The underlying philosophy of the Clayton Act was to strike at monopolistic practices in their *incipiency*. Thus, in each section, the particular conduct under attack was declared unlawful if it *tended* "to substantially lessen competition."

The Act authorized *civil sanctions*, most notably private treble damage suits against violators. In addition, Section 11 empowers the FTC to enforce the Act with cease-and-desist orders, and both the FTC and the Justice Department were given authority to sue for injunctive relief against violations. Since the Act focused on practices that would *tend* to substantially lessen competition, it is obvious that it dealt with *probable* (rather than certain) injury. For this reason, no criminal penalties were initially imposed against violators. However, the Robinson-Patman Act amendments to Section 2 of the Clayton Act, dis-

[1] 15 U.S.C., Secs. 12–27.

cussed later in this chapter, now provide for criminal sanctions.

Section 2—Price Discrimination. Section 2, as amended, prohibits discrimination in prices charged different purchasers of commodities—if such discrimination tends to substantially lessen competition or to create a monopoly—unless the price differential is justified by a difference in the "grade, quality, or quantity of the commodity sold," or is justified by the cost of selling or transporting the goods or by the need to meet competition. Two important exceptions are: (1) Any seller can refuse to sell to a buyer if such refusal is not designed to restrain trade and (2) a seller can change his prices in response to market conditions such as deterioration of perishable goods, obsolescence of seasonal goods, distress sales under court process, or sales in discontinuance of business.

Section 2 was meant to put a stop to the practice of using *territorial or local price discrimination* as a means of eliminating competitors. For example, the Standard Oil Company of New Jersey in the early 1900s would force a local competing firm out of business by selling oil below the price Standard charged in other territories as well as below the cost of the competing firm. Section 2 was strengthened by the Robinson-Patman Act amendments, discussed later in this chapter.

Section 3—Exclusive Dealing and Tying Contracts. Section 3 applies to exclusive dealing contracts, that is, to sales of goods on condition that the buyer will not "use or deal in" the goods of a competitor of the seller. Such sales are prohibited if they will "substantially lessen competition or tend to create a monopoly in any line of commerce." The most typical form of exclusive dealing is an agreement between a supplier and distributor which prohibits the distributor from dealing in goods of the supplier's competitors. Such agreements should be distinguished from an *exclusive distributorship,* in which a supplier agrees to deal with a single distributor in a given territory. Another common exclusive dealing arrangement is a *requirement contract,* which provides that the buyer will obtain all of its requirements of a product from a single supplier. Exclusive distributorships and requirement contracts are illegal only if they have an anticompetitive effect.

In addition to the Department of Justice, other groups of potential private plaintiffs who might claim a Section 3 violation are: (1) Buyers or lessees under exclusive dealing arrangements that preclude them from buying or leasing on more favorable terms elsewhere and (2) competitors of the seller (or lessor) who are foreclosed from the buyer's (or lessee's) market because of the exclusive dealing arrangement. Section 3 also prohibits "tying contracts." A tying contract is one in which a seller (or lessor) will sell (or lease) a product (the "tying" product) only on condition that the buyer (or lessee) also purchase (or lease) a second distinct product which is not desired (the "tied" product). Tying contracts are discussed in detail later in this chapter.

Clayton Section 3 and Sherman Section 1 compared. It was noted in Chapter 45 that Section 1 of the Sherman Act also prohibits exclusive dealing and tying contracts. Both statutes apply to an agreement between seller and buyer that forecloses competitors from a substantial share of the market. However, the two acts differ in the following ways:

1 The Clayton Act applies only to the lease or sale of "goods, wares, merchandise, machinery, supplies, or other commodities," but the Sherman Act applies to a broader range of activity including real estate transactions and services such as advertising.
2 The Clayton Act applies to a person who acts "in the course of such commerce"; the Sherman Act is much broader, covering acts which are in the "flow of interstate commerce" as well as those that "affect interstate commerce."
3 The Clayton Act requires only a showing that the exclusive dealing arrangement might *tend* to create a monopoly or lessen competition, whereas the Sherman Act is much narrower in this respect as the arrangement must actively and unreasonably restrain trade to be unlawful.

Because of these differences, a plaintiff might prevail in a Section 3 case under the Clayton Act but not have sufficient evidence to prevail under the stricter language of Section 1 of the Sherman Act.

Tests of competitive effect of exclusive dealing. To determine if an exclusive dealing contract will substantially lessen competition or tend to create a monopoly in an action under the Clayton Act, the court first defines the relevant market and then attempts to measure the effect of the exclusive dealing arrangement on competition in that market. This approach is the same as that used in cases under Section 1 of the Sherman Act. Two tests have been used by the courts to measure competitive effect: (1) the "quantitative substantiality" test and (2) the "qualitative substantiality" test.

Under the *quantitative* test, if the exclusive dealing contract covers a *substantial quantity of the relevant market,* it is held to substantially lessen competition and there is no need for further inquiry into other economic competitive factors. The quantitative test was first applied in *Standard Oil Company of California v. U.S.,*[2] in which Standard was charged with violating Section 3 of the Clayton Act because its contracts with 537 distributors required them to purchase all of their requirements from Standard. The Supreme Court held that Standard had violated Section 3 because its contracts covered a sufficient share of the market so as to substantially lessen competition. The Court rejected Standard's argument that consideration should be given to such qualitative economic factors as evidence that competition had flourished despite use of requirement contracts, the duration of such contracts, and their reasonableness in relation to the legitimate needs of the industry. It was reasoned that the evaluation of such data placed too great a burden on the judiciary. The decision has been criticized because Standard's 6.7 percent relevant market share would hardly seem enough to permit a sole defendant to substantially lessen competition as required by the court's "quantitative" test. The test now appears to be used primarily to evaluate exclusive dealing contracts when the defendant dominates the relevant market.

In *Tampa Electric Co. v. Nashville Coal Co.,*[3] the Supreme Court departed from the quantitative test used in *Standard Oil* and required a *qualitative economic evaluation* of the anticompetitive effect of a contract to supply a power utility's coal requirements. The Court held that such evaluation should consider the relative market strength of the parties, the volume of trade involved in the contract compared with the total volume in the relevant market, the probable immediate and future effect of the contract on competition, and whether it continued to flourish despite the restrictive agreement. After weighing these factors, the Court held that the exclusive contract to supply Tampa's coal requirements for 20 years did not violate Section 3, and was not anticompetitive in its effect.

It is uncertain whether the quantitative or qualitative test will be used in a particular case. However, the qualitative test seems to be favored in those cases where the seller does not dominate the market and where there is a relatively small percentage of competitors' business being cut out of the market (referred to as "market foreclosure") because of the exclusive dealing contract. In such cases, courts have permitted the defendant to try to prove the reasonableness of exclusive dealing by showing that it mutually benefited the parties in such ways as ensuring the buyer a source of supply at a fixed price or providing the seller with a sure outlet as well as fixed selling costs.[4]

Tying contracts. Generally, the tests of legality of tying arrangements are the same regardless of whether the plaintiff brings its action under Section 1 of the Sherman Act or Section 3 of the Clayton Act. Unlike other forms of exclusive dealing which are judged under the rule of reason, tying contracts are almost always held to be per se violations when the plaintiff has shown: (1) that the seller has sufficient economic power with respect to the tying product to appreciably restrain free competition in the market for the tied product[5] and (2) that the tying arrangement affects a "not insubstantial amount of commerce."[6] However, after the plaintiff has made out such a prima facie case, the tying arrangement may be justified by the defendant showing that it is a small company trying to break into the market or that the arrangement was necessary to protect a firm's goodwill.[7]

Requisites of tying contracts. A tying arrangement is not unlawful unless the tying and tied products are distinct. In deciding this issue under either Clayton or Sherman, courts consider such factors

[2]337 U.S. 293 (1949).
[3]365 U.S. 320 (1961).

[4]*American Motors Inns, Inc. v. Holiday Inns, Inc.,* 521 F.2d 1230 (3d Cir. 1975).
[5]*Northern Pac. Ry. v. United States,* 336 U.S. 1 (1958).
[6]*United States Steel Corp. v. Fortner Enterprises, Inc.,* 429 U.S. 610 (1977).
[7]*United States v. Jerrold Electronic Corp.,* 187 F. Supp. 545 (E.D. Pa. 1960), aff'd 365 U.S. 567 (1961).

as whether the products are priced separately, are physically separate, or have separate markets, and whether consumers view them as separate items. For example, in *Times-Picayune Publishing Co. v. U.S.*,[8] the Supreme Court held that a newspaper's refusal to sell advertising in its morning edition unless the advertiser also purchased space in the afternoon edition was not an unlawful tying contract because the products were identical and the markets were the same. On the other hand, in *Siegel v. Chicken Delight, Inc.*,[9] the court held that two distinct products were involved where the franchise agreement required the franchisee to purchase exclusively from Chicken Delight paper cups and supplies (the "tied" product). The court considered the franchisee's right to use the franchisor's trademark (the "tying" product) as separate and distinct, and concluded that the tying agreement was unlawful.

An illegal tying arrangement does not require that the *same party* offer both the tying product and the tied product. A violation occurs if the offeror of the tying product has some economic interest in the tied product, such as a contractual benefit arising from the tied product or stock ownership in the company manufacturing it. Since the Clayton Act applies only to "goods, wares and merchandise," courts have held that *both* the tying and tied products must fall into these personal property categories in order for it to be a Clayton Section 3 violation. Inasmuch as the Sherman Act jurisdiction is not restricted to such categories, a sale of electricity tied to light bulbs might be a violation of Section 1 of the Sherman Act but could not possibly violate Section 3 of the Clayton Act.

Section 7—Corporate Mergers. As amended by the Celler-Kefauver Act of 1950, this "antimerger section" prohibits the acquisition by one business of the *stock* or *assets* of another firm "where in any line of commerce in any section of the country, the effect... may be substantially to lessen competition, or to tend to create a monopoly." However, a firm may purchase corporate stock for investment, provided there is no attempt or motive to lessen competition. Likewise, a corporation is permitted to form a subsidiary to carry on a part of its business when the effect of such formation is not to substantially lessen competition. Today, proposed corporate mergers may be challenged by both the FTC and the Department of Justice. However, since 1981, the Department has filed 60 percent fewer antitrust suits, including merger challenges.

Since 1950, a very substantial body of case law has developed from the growing number of private suits attacking proposed mergers under Section 7. However, since 1980 many major merger cases have been resolved by out-of-court settlement with the result that there are few recent decisions of the Supreme Court clarifying when, and under what circumstances, a merger violates Section 7.

The Antitrust Improvement Act of 1976 required corporations with sales or assets exceeding $100 million to give advance notice to the Department of Justice and the Federal Trade Commission of any acquisition of a corporation with sales or assets of $10 million or more. In addition, the Antitrust Procedural Improvement Act of 1980 strengthened the investigative and enforcement powers of the Department of Justice.

Relevant market under Section 7. Chapter 45 discussed the importance of defining a firm's "relevant product and geographic market" in a Sherman Section 2 monopolization case. These concepts are equally basic to any analysis of a merger under Clayton Section 7. In a proposed merger, a narrowly defined product or geographic market will result in a greater anticompetitive effect. Conversely, a broadly defined product line or geographic market will result in a smaller adverse effect on competition. Therefore, the entire issue of the probable anticompetitive effect of a merger often depends upon the relevant "product" and "geographic" market definitions that the trial court accepts. The Supreme Court in the landmark *Brown Shoe*[10] case developed an elaborate test for defining relevant product markets for purposes of Section 7 mergers. First, the product line ("line of commerce") must be defined, and then the relevant geographic market for that product ("section of the country"). Up to this point the approach is similar to that used in Section 2 cases under the Sherman Act discussed in Chapter 45. However, in defining the relevant geographic market the Court outlined two further

[8] 345 U.S. 594 (1953).
[9] 448 F.2d 43 (9th Cir. 1971).

[10] *Brown Shoe Co. v. United States*, 370 U.S. 294 (1962).

steps that must be taken: (1) Define the "outer boundary market" using criteria similar to those used in monopolizing cases, and then (2) further define *geographic submarkets* within those outer boundaries using the following "practical indicia": the industry or public recognition of the submarket as a separate economic entity, the product's peculiar characteristics and uses, unique production facilities, distinct customers, distinct prices, sensitivity to price changes, and specialized vendors. Once these submarkets are defined, the Court said, "it is necessary to examine the effects of a merger in each such economically significant submarket to determine if there is a reasonable probability that the merger will substantially lessen competition. If such a probability is found to exist, the merger is proscribed." Similarly, the Court said there can be *product submarkets* as well as geographic submarkets. In this case the product (shoes) was further broken down into submarket categories—men's, women's, and children's shoes.

The Court then applied these principles to the facts of the merger between the Brown and Kinney shoe companies. Both were manufacturers who also operated retail outlets. Thus, the merger was vertical as well as horizontal. The "outer boundary market" was found to be the entire nation, and a geographic submarket was determined to be "every city of 10,000 or more population and its immediate surrounding area" in which both a Kinney and a Brown store were located. Basing its analysis primarily upon a review of market shares of the two companies before the merger, the Court held that both the vertical and horizontal aspects of the merger violated Section 7 of the Clayton Act. In the wake of *Brown Shoe,* courts have not consistently applied its "practical indicia," but most frequently the uses of the product and its interchangeability from the viewpoint of buyers have been the criteria.

The definition of the product line is also crucial to the outcome of a Section 7 merger. For example, in the leading case of *United States v. E. I. du Pont de Nemours & Co.*,[11] the government charged du Pont with a violation of Section 7 by reason of its acquisition of 23 percent of the stock of General Motors (GM). Du Pont sold paint to GM as well as to many industrial users other than auto manufacturers. The case turned on whether du Pont's product line was paint in general or automotive paint. If paint in general, GM's purchases were foreclosing competitors of du Pont from only 3.5 percent of the total industrial paint market, an inconsequential amount. On the other hand, if du Pont's product line was *automotive* paint, GM's purchases were 24 percent of total automotive uses. The Supreme Court held that the "line of commerce" was automotive paint, thus greatly exaggerating the impact of the merger upon du Pont's competitors. Having adopted the narrower product line definition, it was then easy for the Court to conclude that the merger foreclosed a substantial share (24 percent) of the market, and that the stock acquisition was unlawful.

Substantial lessening of competition. After determining the relevant product line and geographic market and submarkets, the plaintiff in a Section 7 case must prove, and the court must find, that the effect of the merger "may be substantially to lessen competition, or to tend to create a monopoly." Generally, the approach of the FTC and Department of Justice, as well as the courts, is to examine market concentration as measured by market share percentages of the merging firms before and after the merger. Since the percentage-of-market-share allowed depends on whether the merger is horizontal, vertical, or conglomerate, each type of merger must be evaluated separately.

Horizontal mergers arise from the combination of two firms at the same level, such as two manufacturers, two wholesalers, or two retailers. Where such mergers result in a significant increase in concentration as measured by market share, they are likely to be challenged by the Department of Justice. The Department, which has primary enforcement responsibility with respect to mergers and acquisitions, published its amended *Merger Guidelines* in 1984. These guidelines utilize a statistical test for determining whether to challenge horizontal mergers, i.e., the Herfindahl-Hirschman Index (HHI).

Under the HHI formula, the postmerger market shares of each firm in the relevant market are squared and the squares are added. If the postmerger HHI total for all firms in the relevant market is under 1,000, the merger is not likely to be questioned; it if is between 1,000 and 1,800 it is more

[11]353 U.S. 586 (1957).

likely to be challenged, particularly if (1) the remaining market is highly concentrated, (2) there is a continuing trend in the industry toward concentration, or (3) there are unusually high entry barriers to potential competitors. If the HHI is above 1,850, the market is considered concentrated and the merger is likely to be challenged.

Consider, for example, a proposed merger of 2 firms in a relevant market of 20, each having a 5 percent market share. The premerger HHI is $20 \times 5^2 = 500$. The postmerger HHI is $18 \times 5^2 = 450$ plus $1 \times 10^2 = 100$ for a total of 550. Since the HHI total is only 550, the merger is not likely to be challenged. Moreover, even at HHI totals of up to 1,800, mergers increasing the market's HHI by less than 100 points are unlikely to be challenged.

The Department of Justice as well as the FTC consider factors other than HHI calculations in making a final determination whether to challenge a merger. For example, if the largest firm is double the size of the next largest and has 35 percent or more of the market, the guidelines indicate that such firm's proposed merger, even with a firm having only a 1 percent market share, will be challenged. In addition, other nonmarket share factors will be considered. These include an inquiry into whether (1) there is a trend in the industry toward concentration, (2) the acquiring firm has a previous record of expansion by way of merger acquisitions, (3) the target firm has been an exceptionally competitive influence in the market, and (4) *most* of the firms in the market have historically engaged in anticompetitive activities such as exchanging price information, following a "delivered price" system, collusively eliminating product differentiation through development of uniform product standards, or engaging in other horizontal "cooperation" such as price fixing or agreeing to divide customers or territory.

With some exceptions, the *Merger Guidelines* are also followed by the FTC. In general, the new guidelines indicate that these enforcement agencies have relaxed their scrutiny of vertical and conglomerate mergers. Since 1982 some of the largest mergers of giant corporations in the nation's history have taken place. Although corporate combinations may violate Sections 1 and 2 of the Sherman Act, most challenges are made under Section 7 of the Clayton Act, since it is easier to prove a case under that section.

If one of the merging firms faces the clear probability of being a *failing company* and it has made a good faith effort toward being acquired by a firm that would not produce anticompetitive effects (for example, a conglomerate, discussed below), then the merger will ordinarily not be challenged. Generally, the Department of Justice will not accept as justification for a horizontal merger the claim that it will produce economies or improve efficiency unless there is clear and convincing evidence that it will do so. Section 7 of the Clayton Act was applied to a horizontal merger in the *Von's Grocery* case which follows.

CASE 46.1 United States v. Von's Grocery Co. · 384 U.S. 270 (1966)

FACTS Civil action by the United States charging that the acquisition by Von's Grocery Company of its direct competitor Shopping Bag Food Stores, both large retail grocery companies in Los Angeles, California, violated Section 7 of the Clayton Act. The sole question was whether the District Court properly concluded that the government had failed to prove a violation of Section 7. The facts are stated in the opinion.

OPINION BLACK, Associate Justice. From 1948 to 1958 the number of Von's stores in the Los Angeles area practically doubled from 14 to 27, while at the same time the number of Shopping Bag's stores jumped from 15 to 34. During that same decade, Von's sales increased fourfold and its share of the market almost doubled while Shopping Bag's sales multiplied seven times and its share of the market tripled. . . . In addition the findings of the District Court show that the number of owners operating single stores in the Los Angeles retail grocery market decreased from 5,365 in 1950 to 3,818 in 1961. . . . During roughly the same period, from 1953 to 1962, the number of chains with two or more

CASE 46.1 Continued

grocery stores increased from 96 to 150. While the grocery business was being concentrated into the hands of fewer and fewer owners, the small companies were continually being absorbed by the larger firms through mergers.... These facts alone are enough to cause us to conclude contrary to the District Court that the Von's Shopping Bag merger did violate § 7. Accordingly, we reverse.

...To arrest [the] "rising tide" toward concentration into too few hands and to halt the gradual demise of the small businessman, Congress decided to clamp down with vigor on mergers. [By the Celler-Kefauver amendment] it both revitalized § 7 of the Clayton Act by "plugging its loophole" and broadened its scope...[By using terms] in § 7 which look not merely to the actual present effect of a merger but instead to its effect upon future competition, Congress sought to preserve competition among many small businesses by arresting a trend toward concentration in its incipiency before that trend developed to the point that a market was left in the grip of a few big companies....

The facts of this case present exactly the threatening trend toward concentration which Congress wanted to halt. The number of small grocery companies in the Los Angeles retail grocery market had been declining rapidly before the merger and continued to decline rapidly afterwards. This rapid decline in the number of grocery store owners moved hand in hand with a large number of significant absorptions of the small companies by the larger ones. In the midst of this steadfast trend toward concentration, Von's and Shopping Bag, two of the most successful and largest companies in the area, jointly owning 66 grocery stores, merged to become the second largest chain in Los Angeles. This merger cannot be defended on the ground that one of the companies was about to fail or that the two had to merge to save themselves from destruction by some larger and more powerful competitor. What we have on the contrary is simply the case of two already powerful companies merging in a way which makes them even more powerful than they were before.

Von's primary argument is that the merger between Von's and Shopping Bag is not prohibited by § 7 because the Los Angeles grocery market was competitive before the merger, has been since, and may continue to be in the future. Even so, § 7 requires not merely an appraisal of the immediate impact of the merger upon competition, but a prediction of its impact upon competitive conditions in the future; this is what is meant when it is said that the amended § 7 was intended to arrest anticompetitive tendencies in their incipiency.... Congress passed the Celler-Kefauver Act to prevent such a destruction of competition. Our cases...have faithfully endeavored to enforce this congressional command. We adhere to them now.

JUDGMENT Reversed and remanded.

In recent years there has been a growing number of horizontal mergers of banks. These are subject to the Bank Merger Acts of 1960 and 1966, which require that mergers involving national banks receive prior approval of the Comptroller of Currency, and mergers of member state banks must be approved by the Federal Reserve Board. Since most banks are insured by the Federal Deposit Insurance Corporation, approval of that agency is also required. When the appropriate regulatory agency is reviewing proposed mergers, it must consider anticompetitive effects as well as public convenience and need for banking service. If approved, such proposed mergers may still be challenged by the Department of Justice, in which case the principles and standards of Sherman Sections 1 and 2 as well as Clayton Section 7 are applicable. The Department challenged a proposed merger in *United States v. Philadelphia National Bank,*[12] where the postmerger market share was 30 percent of the relevant market. The Supreme Court held that the proposed

[12] 374 U.S. 321 (1963). *United States v. Marine Bancorporation, Inc.*, 418 U.S. 602 (1974).

merger would result in excessive concentration and should be enjoined as a violation of the antitrust laws. The Supreme Court has also held that a bank proposing to merge with a target bank in a different city is *not* a potential entrant into that market if state banking laws prohibit the acquiring bank from de novo entry by way of opening a branch.

Vertical mergers arise when a firm at one level, such as a manufacturer, acquires a firm at a different level, such as wholesaler or a supplier. In contrast to horizontal mergers, vertical mergers generally do not increase concentration. Regardless of whether such mergers arise from an acquisition that is "backward" into a supplying market—for example, a wholesaler acquiring a manufacturer—or "forward" into a purchasing market, competition can be adversely affected in a number of ways. Suppose for example, as in *Brown Shoe* discussed earlier, two shoe manufacturers acquire two retail shoe store chains. First, suppliers of one of the merged manufacturers may be foreclosed from selling in that market. Second, the merged retail stores can no longer compete among manufacturers for the purchase of shoes for distribution in their outlets. Third, competing shoe manufacturers are foreclosed from distributing their shoes through the two merged retail chains. Fourth, potential manufacturers and retailers may be discouraged from entering the field and competing because of the postmerger market power of the combined firms. The new merger guidelines evaluate vertical and conglomerate mergers on the basis of whether a significant share of the market will be foreclosed to competition. If so, other anticompetitive factors will be scrutinized, such as the existence of barriers to entry which restrict a potential competitor's equal access to potential customers or to potential suppliers. Similarly, the government will review whether the industry as well as the acquiring company reflect a trend toward vertical integration.

Conglomerate mergers arise where there is no visible relation between the business of two uniting firms. Conglomerate mergers experienced an explosive growth in the 1960s. The Department of Justice defines such mergers as any merger that is neither horizontal nor vertical. The Department also classifies as "conglomerate" a *market extension merger* or a *product extension merger*. A market extension merger takes place if the two firms sell the same product in different geographic markets. The *Falstaff* case (Case 46.2) is illustrative. A *product extension merger* arises when the product of the target firm is in the same general category as the products of the acquiring firm, but they do not directly compete with such products. Two types of conglomerate mergers likely to be challenged because of their anticompetitive effect are: mergers creating a danger of reciprocal buying and mergers involving a potential entrant into the market.

The *potential entrant doctrine* holds that the forbidden anticompetitive effect may exist if one of the two merging firms is a potential entrant into the market. Prohibiting such a merger not only increases the chances that the potential entrant will stimulate competition by actually entering the market, but the mere fact that it is "on the edge of the market" has a stimulating effect on competition between firms that are already there. The potential entrant doctrine may be applied to a horizontal merger, as in *Falstaff* (Case 46.2), or to a large conglomerate firm that could potentially enter a new product market. Antitrust policy is concerned that market dominance may result from merger with a powerful conglomerate because: (1) its strength may enable it to sell below cost in a product or geographic market and drive out weaker competitors; (2) economies of scale may enable it to eliminate smaller competitors by underpricing them even without selling below cost; (3) the danger of reciprocal buying is increased, foreclosing suppliers from competing to meet the needs of either merging firm; (4) barriers to entry are potentially increased; and (5) it has the potential for accelerating the trend toward concentration in industry with all the social ills associated with such concentration.

On the other hand, the anticompetitive effects of conglomerate mergers are not readily visible or measurable. Since by definition the firms are in separate markets, the merger cannot *directly* affect competition, and the postmerger number of competitors in the market of both the acquiring firm and the target company remains the same as before. Moreover, in the absence of reciprocal dealing between the merged firms, neither suppliers nor purchasers are foreclosed from continuing to compete in the marketplace.

Conflicting court decisions, the cost and complexity of gathering economic data relevant to a merger, wide differences among experts in interpreting such data, the absence of rigid criteria—all these factors make the outcome of a planned merger very uncertain.

CASE 46.2 United States v. Falstaff Brewing Corporation · 410 U.S. 526 (1973)

FACTS Civil action was filed under Section 7 of the Clayton Act by the United States to enjoin Falstaff Brewing Corp., the nation's fourth largest brewer, from acquiring a firm which was the largest seller of beer in New England. In 1963, Falstaff extended its geographic market into New England by acquiring the Narragansett Brewing Company. Prior to 1965, Falstaff had no beer sales in the New England area, although of the three largest brewers in the nation that did *not* sell beer in New England, Falstaff's brewery was the closest to that market. While beer sales in New England increased approximately 9.5 percent in the 4 years preceding the acquisition, the eight largest sellers increased their share of these sales from approximately 74 to 81.2 percent. The parties agreed that the relevant product market was beer and the six New England states composed the geographic market. The number of brewers operating plants in this market decreased from thirty-two in 1935 to eleven in 1957 and to six in 1964.

After trial, the district court upheld the merger and rejected the government's contention that Falstaff at the time of the acquisition was a potential entrant into the New England market and that the merger deprived that market of additional competition Falstaff would have provided. The court also found that Falstaff's management had consistently decided not to attempt to enter the New England market unless it could acquire an existing company with a strong distribution system such as that possessed by Narragansett. The government appealed directly to the Supreme Court.

OPINION WHITE, Associate Justice. Section 7 of the Clayton Act forbids mergers in any line of commerce where the effect may be substantially to lessen competition or tend to create a monopoly. The section proscribes many mergers between competitors in a market.... Suspect also is the acquisition by a company not competing in the market but so situated as to be a potential competitor and likely to exercise substantial influence on market behavior. Entry through merger by such a company, although its competitive conduct in the market may be the mirror image of that of the acquired company, may nevertheless violate § 7 because the entry eliminates a potential competitor exercising present influence on the market.

In the case before us, Falstaff was not a competitor in the New England market, nor is it contended that its merger with Narragansett represented an entry by a dominant market force. It was urged, however, that Falstaff was a potential competitor so situated that its entry by merger rather than *de novo* violated § 7. The District Court, however, relying heavily on testimony of Falstaff officers, concluded that the company had no intent to enter the New England market except through acquisition and that it therefore could not be considered a potential competitor in that market. Having put aside Falstaff as a potential *de novo* competitor, it followed for the District Court that entry by a merger would not adversely affect competition in New England.

The District Court erred as a matter of law. The error lay in the assumption that because Falstaff, as a matter of fact, would never have entered the market *de novo,* it could in no sense be considered a potential competitor. More specifically, the District Court failed to give separate consideration to whether Falstaff was a potential competitor in the sense that it was so positioned on the edge of the market that it exerted beneficial influence on competitive conditions in that market.

The specific question with respect to this phase of the case is not what Falstaff's internal company decisions were but whether, given its financial capabilities and conditions

CASE 46.2 Continued

in the New England market, it would be reasonable to consider it a potential entrant into that market. Surely, it could not be said on this record that Falstaff's general interest in the New England market was unknown; and if it would appear to rational beer merchants in New England that Falstaff might well build a new brewery to supply the northeastern market then its entry by merger becomes suspect under § 7. The District Court should therefore have appraised the economic facts about Falstaff and the New England market in order to determine whether in any realistic sense Falstaff could be said to be a potential competitor on the fringe of the market with likely influence on existing competition....

JUDGMENT We remand this case to the District Court to make the proper assessment of Falstaff as a potential competitor.

Section 8—Interlocking Directorates. Section 8 attacked the potential anticompetitive effects of interlocking directorates by providing that "no person at the same time shall be a director in any two or more corporations, if any one of them has capital, surplus, and undivided profits aggregating more than $1 million" and if it would constitute a violation of the antitrust laws should competition between the corporations be eliminated. Inasmuch as one legal test is whether a hypothetical merger of the two companies would tend to reduce competition with other firms, there often is sufficient cross-elasticity (interchangeability) of demand for the products of two apparently noncompeting companies to prohibit the same director from serving on both boards. For example, in *United States v. Sears, Roebuck & Co.*,[13] the government sued under Section 8 to enjoin a director from serving on the board of Sears and B. F. Goodrich. Both companies competed in retail sales of refrigerators, washers, automotive supplies, and TV sets. The court found that the two companies were competitors and, in ordering the director's resignation, said:

> Since a price fixing or division of territory agreement would eliminate competition between them, and since such an agreement would *per se* violate at least one of the provisions of the antitrust laws, namely § 1 of the Sherman Act, it follows that § 8 forbids defendant to be a director of both corporations.

In recent years, the hazard of a Section 8 violation coupled with the growing popularity of derivative[14] suits by stockholders against directors for negligence or breach of duty has discouraged corporations from recruiting as an outside director an officer-director of another corporation. However, in one area—interlocking directorates between banks and insurance companies—the recent decision of the U.S. Supreme Court in the following case will undoubtedly encourage such practices.

[13] 111 F. Supp. 14 (S.D.N.Y. 1953).

[14] Derivative suits are defined and explained in Chapter 42.

CASE 46.3 Bankamerica Corp. v. United States · 76 L. Ed.2d 456 (1983)

FACTS The United States brought suit against ten corporations and five directors, asserting that interlocking directorates between banks and insurance companies violated Section 8 of the Clayton Act, which provides: "no person at the same time shall be a director in any two or more corporations, any one of which has capital, surplus, and undivided profits aggregating more than $1,000,000, engaged in whole or in part in commerce, other than banks, ... if such corporations are competitors."

The district court granted summary judgment for the corporations and dismissed the suit, interpreting the statute as prohibiting only interlocks between two corporations,

CASE 46.3 Continued

neither of which is a bank. The court of appeals reversed, holding that Section 8 barred all interlocking directorates between banks and competing nonbanking corporations, and Bankamerica Corporation appealed.

OPINION

BURGER, Chief Justice. The starting point, as always, is the language of the statute. The narrow question here is whether the fourth paragraph of Section 8 of the Clayton Act bars interlocking directorates involving a bank and a nonbanking corporation with which it competes. The language of the statute is unambiguous in prohibiting interlocking directorates between "two or more corporations . . . other than banks." The most natural reading of this language is that the interlocked corporations must all be corporations "other than banks." It is self-evident that a bank and a nonbanking corporation are not both corporations "other than banks." Thus, the fourth paragraph of Section 8 by its express terms does not prohibit interlocking directorates between a bank and a competing nonbanking corporation. . . .

In rejecting the Government's present interpretation of Section 8, we by no means depart from our long-held policy of giving great weight to the contemporaneous interpretation of a challenged statute by an agency charged with its enforcement. But the Government does not come to this case with a consistent history of enforcing or attempting to enforce Section 8 in accord with what it urges now. On the contrary, for over 60 years, the Government made no attempt, either by filing suit or by seeking voluntary resignations, to apply Section 8 to interlocks between banks and nonbanking corporations, even though interlocking directorates between banks and insurance companies were widespread and a matter of public record throughout the period. . . .

In the circumstances of this case, the Government's failure for over 60 years to exercise the power it now claims under Section 8 strongly suggests that it did not read the statute as granting such power. . . .

It is not surprising that for more than a half century literally thousands of citizens in the business world have served as directors of both banks and insurance companies in reliance on what was universally perceived as plain statutory language. . . .

JUDGMENT

The judgment of the Court of Appeals is reversed.

Private Enforcement of the Clayton Act

Hostile Takeovers. The last decade has witnessed a growing number of unfriendly mergers. These are usually accomplished by a *tender offer*, submitted to the shareholders of the target company by the acquiring person or firm. Although premerger notification of tender offers must be given to the FTC and the Department of Justice where the assets and annual sales of the merging firms meet or exceed standards prescribed in the FTC rules, neither agency has opposed unfriendly takeovers in the courts to the extent that private firms have sued to prevent such mergers. Often, the plaintiff is the target company of a hostile tender offer, and files a frivolous suit as a defensive or delaying tactic with no reasonable expectation of proving that the merger would significantly increase concentration in the industry or adversely affect competition. Management of the target firm may file such suit in order to pressure the hostile "raiders" into raising the tender offering price, or in order to buy time during which they can encourage a friendly takeover offer by some other buyer (often referred to as a "white knight"). However, with advance planning, a target firm can invoke other techniques that are probably more effective in blocking a takeover attempt. These include amending the bylaws to require supermajority (e.g., 90 percent) stockholder approval of a tender offer or staggered terms for directors, making it more difficult for the raiders to acquire control of the board; or borrowing at the bank and using the proceeds to buy treasury stock, thereby increasing the voting power of the remaining insiders' "control" shares so as to defeat a vote on the takeover proposal.

Private Treble Damage Actions. Competitors often sue horizontally merging firms, claiming that the postmerger effect will be an anticompetitive violation of Section 7. Clayton Act Sections 4 and 16 authorize persons or firms who suffer business injury arising from a violation of the antitrust laws to bring a civil suit for treble damages plus attorney's fees, and for an injunction restraining the merger or other anticompetitive conduct. However, in 1977 the Supreme Court's "Brunswick" rule restricted private plaintiffs' treble damage suits under Section 4 by requiring that the plaintiff must prove *antitrust injury,* that is, *injury that flows from the defendant's conduct which the antitrust laws were intended to prevent.* In the following case, the Supreme Court held that a plaintiff seeking to enjoin a merger under Section 16 must still allege and prove such antitrust injury under Section 4.

CASE 46.4 Cargill, Inc. v. Monfort of Colorado, Inc. · 93 L. Ed.2d 427 (1986)

FACTS Monfort of Colorado, Inc. (plaintiff), the nation's fifth-largest beef packer brought an action under § 16 of the Clayton Act, against Cargill, Inc. and its wholly owned subsidiary, Excel Corporation, the nation's second-largest packer (defendants), seeking to enjoin a proposed horizontal merger between Excel and Spencer Beef. After the acquisition, Excel would still be the second-largest packer, but would command a market share almost equal to that of the largest packer. At trial, Excel moved to dismiss on the ground that Monfort had failed to show that it would suffer antitrust injury. The trial court held that Monfort's claim that a postmerger "price-cost squeeze" would "severely narrow" its profit margins constituted a claim of antitrust injury, and enjoined the merger. On appeal, Excel argued that Monfort's claim of lost profits due to a "price-cost squeeze" was nothing more than an allegation of losses due to vigorous competition, and that losses from competition do not constitute antitrust injury. The Court of Appeals affirmed the trial court's decision, and Excel appealed to the Supreme Court.

OPINION BRENNAN, Justice. This case presents two questions: whether a plaintiff seeking relief under § 16 must prove a threat of antitrust injury, and, if so, whether loss or damage due to increased competition constitutes such injury. . . . This case requires us to decide, at the outset, a question we have not previously addressed: whether a private plaintiff seeking an injunction under § 16 of the Clayton Act must show a threat of antitrust injury. To decide the question, we must look first to the source of the antitrust injury requirement, which lies in a related provision of the Clayton Act, § 4. . . .

In *Brunswick Corp. v. Pueblo Bowl-O-Mat, Inc.*, 429 U.S. 477 (1977), we held that plaintiffs seeking treble damages under § 4 must show more than simply an "injury causally linked" to a particular merger; instead, "plaintiffs must prove *antitrust* injury, which is to say injury of the type the antitrust laws were intended to prevent and that flows from that which makes the defendants' acts unlawful." The plaintiffs in Brunswick did not prove such injury. The plaintiffs were three of the ten bowling centers owned by a relatively small bowling chain. The defendant, one of the two largest bowling chains in the country, acquired several bowling centers located in the plaintiffs' market that would have gone out of business but for the acquisition. The plaintiffs sought treble damages under § 4, alleging as injury "the loss of income that would have accrued had the acquired centers gone bankrupt" and had competition in their markets consequently been reduced. We held that this injury, although causally related to a merger alleged to violate § 7, was not an antitrust injury, since "it is inimical to the antitrust laws to award damages" for losses stemming from continued competition. This reasoning in Brunswick was consistent with

CASE 46.4 Continued

the principle that "the antitrust laws were enacted for the protection of *competition,* not *competitors.*"...

The wording concerning the relationship of the injury to the violation of the antitrust laws in each section is comparable. Section 4 requires proof of injury "by reason of anything forbidden in the antitrust laws"; § 16 requires proof of "threatened loss or damage by a violation of the antitrust laws."... Sections 4 and 16 are thus best understood as providing complementary remedies for a single set of injuries. Accordingly, we conclude that in order to seek injunctive relief under § 16, a private plaintiff must allege threatened loss or damage "of the type the antitrust laws were designed to prevent and that flows from that which makes defendants' acts unlawful." We therefore turn to the question of whether the proposed merger in this case threatened Monfort with antitrust injury....

Monfort's... claim is that after the merger, Excel would lower prices to some level at or slightly above its costs in order to compete with other packers for market share. Excel would be in a position to do this because of the multiplant efficiencies its acquisition of Spencer would provide. To remain competitive, Monfort would have to lower its prices; as a result, Monfort would suffer a loss in profitability, but would not be driven out of business. The question is whether Monfort's loss of profits in such circumstances constitutes antitrust injury.

To resolve the question, we look again to *Brunswick v. Pueblo Bowl-O-Mat....* The loss of profits to the competitors in Brunswick was not of concern under the antitrust laws, since it resulted only from continued competition.... Brunswick holds that the antitrust laws do not require the courts to protect small businesses from the loss of profits due to continued competition, but only against the loss of profits from practices forbidden by the antitrust laws. The kind of competition that Monfort alleges here, competition for increased market share, is not activity forbidden by the antitrust laws. It is simply, as petitioners claim, vigorous competition. To hold that the antitrust laws protect competitors from loss of profits due to such price competition would, in effect, render illegal any decision by a firm to cut prices in order to increase market share. The antitrust laws require no such perverse result....

We hold that a plaintiff seeking injunctive relief under § 16 of the Clayton Act must show a threat of antitrust injury, and that a showing of loss or damage due merely to increased competition does not constitute such injury. The record below does not support a finding of antitrust injury, but only of threatened loss from increased competition....

JUDGMENT The judgment of the Court of Appeals is reversed and the case remanded for further proceedings consistent with this opinion.

It is so ordered.

The Robinson-Patman Act

In the 20 years that followed the Clayton Act, certain defects appeared which required remedial legislation. Large grocery, drug, and other chain stores were able to use their buying power and to employ various devices to purchase goods at lower prices than their smaller competitors. These devices included receiving payments in lieu of brokerage fees, purchasing through a wholly owned subsidiary that masqueraded as a "wholesaler," and receiving larger advertising and promotional allowances than were given to smaller competitors. In some cases, suppliers sold to chain stores at lower prices than they charged the wholesalers who distributed to the small retail outlets. In the midst of the Great Depression, the outcry of small retailers and wholesalers against the chain stores eventually reached Congress. It passed the Robinson-Patman Act in 1936.[15]

[15] 15 U.S.C., Sec. 13.

Purpose and Scope of the Robinson-Patman Act

Purpose. The primary aim of the Robinson-Patman Act was to limit the buying power of large chain stores and other buyers so as to prevent them from coercing suppliers to furnish discriminatory concessions on prices or services and thereby to prevent such buyers from gaining an unfair advantage over their smaller competitors. Since the act is enforceable against sellers as well as buyers that participated in discriminatory discounts, a secondary objective was to discourage sellers from offering such discounts.

Critics contend that these goals have not been effectively realized. They argue that enforcement has been mostly against small sellers or against buyers engaged in genuine competition, and that fear of prosecution has led sellers to substitute price uniformity for price competition. The complexity of the statute has also made it difficult and costly to establish a violation, with the result that FTC enforcement has been reduced to a trickle in recent years and the Supreme Court rarely accepts appeals from lower courts requesting interpretation of the act. Nevertheless, the act is still on the books, numerous private treble damages suits are founded upon it, and it continues to have a nationwide impact on pricing decisions of manufacturers, wholesalers, and retailers.

Scope. The Robinson-Patman Act amended Section 2(a) of the Clayton Act to provide:

> That it shall be unlawful for any person engaged in commerce, in the course of such commerce, either directly or indirectly, to discriminate in price between different purchasers of commodities of like grade and quality, where either or any of the purchases involved in such discrimination are in commerce, where such commodities are sold for use, consumption, or resale within the United States or any . . . other place under the jurisdiction of the United States, and where the effect of such discrimination may be substantially to lessen competition or tend to create a monopoly in any line of commerce, or to injure, destroy, or prevent competition with any person who either grants or knowingly receives the benefit of such discrimination, or with customers of either of them: *Provided,* That nothing herein contained shall prevent differentials which make only due allowance for differences in the cost of manufacture, sale or delivery resulting from the differing methods or quantities in which such commodities are to such purchasers sold or delivered: . . . *And provided further,* That nothing herein contained shall prevent persons . . . from selecting their own customers in bona fide transactions and not in restraint of trade: *And, provided further,* That nothing herein contained shall prevent price changes from time to time in response to changing conditions affecting the market for or the marketability of the goods concerned, such as but not limited to actual or imminent deterioration of perishable goods, obsolescence of seasonal goods, distress sales under court process or sales in good faith in discontinuance of business in the goods concerned.

Court Interpretation of the Robinson-Patman Act

Proving "Commerce" Jurisdiction. A person charged with a violation of Section 2(a) of the Robinson-Patman Act must be "engaged in interstate, as distinguished from intrastate commerce." In other words, the transaction must involve two or more states. For example, the act applies to a seller in one state who sells to a buyer in the same state at a favorable price but sells to a competing buyer in another state at a discriminatory higher price. Thus, Section 2(a) of the Robinson-Patman Act, by requiring that one of the two transactions must be "in the course" of interstate commerce, imposes a narrower "commerce" test than the Sherman Act test which includes intrastate transactions that substantially *affect* interstate commerce as well as those that are actually in interstate commerce.

Proving Discrimination. To establish price discrimination under Section 2(a) of the Robinson-Patman Act it must be shown that (1) in the "course of commerce" there were (2) two or more sales of (3) commodities (as distinguished from services) which were (4) of like grade or quality to (5) two or more purchasers (6) about the same time, involving (7) discriminatorily different prices which (8) may injure competition. The act does not apply to retail sales, because normally such sales do not injure competition between businesses. There is no violation if a discriminatory price is quoted but the buyer refuses to accept it, inasmuch as a sale is not completed. Likewise, there is no violation if the two sales occur at substantially different times. The allowable time span between sales varies with the durability or perishability of the goods and the volatility of their market. Thus the sale of 100 boxes of bolts to two different buyers 2 weeks apart at different prices might be considered as having occurred at substantially the same time, but if the boxes had contained perishable tomatoes, the sale would probably be treated as having occurred at different times.

Since the act applies to a seller dealing with *different* purchasers there is no violation if the seller sells at uniform prices to bona fide independent distributors who resell to their customers. Section 2(a) of the Act refers to "commodities" and not services. Therefore, discriminatory pricing of electricity, lease rentals, broadcasting network time, or terms of bank loans are not prohibited. Such practices, however, might violate provisions of the Sherman Act or the Federal Trade Commission Act, discussed later in this chapter.

Proving Commodities Are of Like Grade and Quality. Obviously a price differential based upon differences in grade is not discriminatory—large eggs appropriately sell for more than small. Unfortunately, in a specific case, determining whether the goods are of like grade and quality is not always as easy as classifying eggs. For example, the Supreme Court has held that if a seller produces a certain kind of canned milk, the fact that a private label is placed on its cans that are sold to a chain store does not make it different from its cans which bear a major advertising brand label.[16] However, even where the products have the same brand, if there is an actual difference in grade or quality, the seller may charge whatever different prices he chooses, regardless of whether those differentials are proportionate to the differences in the seller's costs. Clearly, the seller who establishes various prices based upon differences in grade and quality is not engaging in price discrimination under the act if all buyers are given the same opportunities to purchase.

Proving Injury to Competition. Section 2(a) of the Robinson-Patman Act does not render price discrimination automatically illegal but applies only if the plaintiff can prove that the price differentials may "tend to create a monopoly in any line of commerce, or to injure, destroy, or prevent competition. . . ." The act is aimed at preventing probable injury to competitors of the seller (*primary line injury*), to buyers (*secondary line injury*), to customers of buyers (*tertiary line injury*), and even to competitors of the buyer's customer (*fourth line injury*). For example, in *Perkins v. Standard Oil Company of California*,[17] Standard sold gasoline at a favored price to another oil company, Signal. Signal resold to its subsidiary Western Hyway, which in turn sold to its subsidiary Regal, whose sales at cut-rate prices caused injury to Regal's competitor Perkins. The Court of Appeals termed Regal's harm to Perkins "fourth level injury" and held that since Section 2(a) quoted above suggests only three levels of injury, Perkins was not entitled to recover under the act. The Supreme Court reversed, and in ruling for Perkins pointed out that "the competitive harm done him by Standard is certainly no less because of the presence of an additional link in this particular distribution chain."

Two customers situated in different geographic markets are clearly not competing. Hence, they cannot suffer competitive injury if one of them receives a favored price from a discriminating supplier. For example, if a manufacturer sells a can opener to a retailer in Boston for $1.00 and to a retailer in Seattle for $1.25, although the latter price is discriminatory, it has not injured the retailer in Seattle who is not competing with the retailer in Boston. However, if such discrimination injures other manufacturers who are competing with the *seller*, Section 2 would be violated.

Competitive injury generally does not result when a supplier sells at different prices to buyers who are differentiated *by function*. For example, a supplier of tires may sell at a given price to wholesalers of replacement tires but sell at a lower price to an automobile manufacturer who markets the tires as part of an automobile in a different functional distribution system. Courts assume that since the buyers perform different functions, they are not competing with each other; therefore, the price differentials cannot injure competition. The decisive test in cases involving functional discounts is: Does the price differential have a significant anticompetitive effect? Functional discounts commonly exist because of cost savings. A seller's charge per unit will be less to the wholesaler who purchases a carload than to the retailer who buys only a few items. Even if the amount of the functional discount is significantly higher than the cost savings, the FTC

[16]*FTC v. The Borden Co.*, 383 U.S. 637 (1966).

[17]89 S.Ct. 1871 (1969).

has been reluctant to challenge such discounts unless there is a clear anticompetitive effect.

Defenses to Liability under the Act

Sellers use two principal defenses to avoid liability under the Robinson-Patman Act: (1) that their price differentials are justified under Section 2(a) by "differences in the cost of manufacture, sale, or delivery resulting from the differing methods or quantities" involved, and (2) that lowering the "price or furnishing of services or facilities... was made in good faith to meet an equally low price of a competitor.... " The burden of proving a defense rests upon the person claiming it.

Cost Justification. Section 2(a) permits a seller accused of discrimination because of the lower price charged large chain stores as opposed to small retailers to defend itself by showing that economies realized in large-quantity sales justify the lower per-unit selling price. The seller who deals with a very large number of customers obviously cannot establish different cost-reflecting prices for each customer. Instead, customers may be grouped for pricing purposes according to their dollar-volume of purchases and the seller's costs are then averaged for each group. The FTC as well as the courts accept such cost averaging provided that the different classes are not established in such an arbitrary manner that they result in discrimination.

An arbitrary cost-averaging system was used in *United States v. Borden Co.*[18] Borden distributed milk at 8.5 percent discount to two large grocery chains, but sold to independent grocers at discounts ranging from 5.5 percent down to nothing. In a price discrimination suit under Section 2(a) Borden defended on the ground that lower costs from quantity purchases by the chains justified the lower prices charged. In support of its claim, Borden submitted data which had classified the independent into four groups with the two chains in a fifth group. However, some independents had larger volumes than the chain stores. Average cost computed for each group tended to support the differences in discounts. The Supreme Court held that the grouping of purchasers according to whether they were chain stores or independents (rather than classifying them on the basis of cost-saving factors such as volume of purchases) was an arbitrary and illegal price discrimination.

Generally, discounts based upon the customer's annual volume of purchases cannot be defended on the ground that they are justified by cost savings to the seller. A 10 percent discount on the purchase price of a single carload delivery of 100,000 units obviously involves a cost saving. The same discount to a buyer who annually purchases the same quantity, but in 20 shipments, is obviously not based upon cost savings. The more probable explanation is that the seller designed the annual discount to attract a larger market share.

The cost defense has been widely criticized for the enormous complexity involved in determining and defining "cost" as well as the uncertainty arising from disagreement among experts as to the accounting standards to be used in interpreting cost data. The Supreme Court has noted the "elusiveness of cost data," and the Attorney General has described the cost justification defense as "illusory." Because the defense has rarely been successful, it is generally considered to be a poor investment of accounting time and legal expense.

Meeting Competition. Section 2(b) provides that when a seller has been shown to have charged a discriminatory price, it may rebut the prima facie case thus made by showing that his lower price or the furnishing of services or facilities to any other purchaser or purchasers was made in good faith to meet an equally low price of a competitor, or the services or facilities furnished by a competitor.

This "meeting competition" defense is not available to a seller who knowingly goes below the standard of meeting the competitor's price by undercutting it. Nor can the defense be claimed by a seller who knowingly meets an unlawful discriminatory price quoted by a competitor. However, a seller is permitted to make a good faith competitive price reduction to retain an old customer, and may also quote the same price in order to take a new customer away from a competitor.[19] The seller must be prepared to show reasonable reliance on the buyer's representations as to the low prices quoted by competitors. However, the *buyer* who lies about competitors' low prices may be violating Section 2(f) by inducing and receiving an illegal discriminatory price from the seller.

[18]370 U.S. 460 (1962).

[19]*Sunshine Biscuits, Inc. v. FTC*, 306 F.2d 48 (7th Cir. 1962).

CASE 46.5 Falls City Industries v. Vanco Beverage · 75 L. Ed.2d 174 (1983)

FACTS Vanco Beverage, Inc. (plaintiff), a wholesaler distributor of beer, sued Falls City Industries, Inc. (defendant), a brewery, for alleged price discrimination in violation of Section 2(a) of the Clayton Act, as amended by the Robinson-Patman Act. It was alleged that the brewery sold its beer to Vanco as a wholesale distributor in Vanderburgh County, Indiana, at a higher price than it charged the only wholesale distributor in Henderson County, Kentucky. The two counties formed a single metropolitan area across the state line. Under Indiana law, brewers were required to sell to all Indiana wholesalers at a single price, Indiana wholesalers were prohibited from selling to out-of-state retailers, and Indiana retailers were not permitted to purchase beer from out-of-state wholesalers. The district court held that Vanco had established a prima facie case of price discrimination, finding that although Vanco and the brewer's Kentucky wholesaler did not sell to the same retailers, they competed for the sale of the brewery's beer to consumers of beer from retailers in the market area; that the defendant brewery's pricing policy resulted in lower retail prices for its beer in Kentucky than in Indiana, that many customers living in the Indiana portion of the market ignored Indiana law to purchase the brewery's beer more cheaply from Kentucky retailers, and that the defendant's pricing policy thus prevented plaintiff from competing effectively with the defendant brewery's Kentucky wholesaler and caused plaintiff lost sales.

The defendant brewery presented a "meeting competition" defense under Section 2(b), which provides that a defendant may rebut a prima facie showing of illegal price discrimination by establishing that its lower price to any purchaser "was made in good faith to meet the equally low price of a competitor." The court reasoned that instead of reducing its prices to meet those of a competitor, the brewery had created the discriminatory price disparity by increasing its prices and by raising prices to Indiana wholesalers more than it had raised Kentucky prices.

The court further found that instead of adjusting its prices on a customer-by-customer basis to meet competition from other brewers, the defendant had charged a single price throughout each state and that the higher Indiana price was not set in good faith but instead was raised solely to allow defendant brewery to follow other brewers to enhance its profits. The court of appeals affirmed, and defendant brewery appealed to the U.S. Supreme Court.

OPINION BLACKMUN, Justice. The United States Court of Appeals... has concluded that the "meeting-competition" defense of § 2(b) is available only if the defendant sets its lower price on a customer-by-customer basis and creates the price discrimination by lowering rather than by raising prices. We conclude that § 2(b) is not so inflexible.... This Court consistently has held that the meeting-competition defense "at least requires the seller, who has knowingly discriminated in price, to show the existence of facts which would lead a reasonable and prudent person to believe that the granting of a lower price would in fact meet the equally low price of a competitor." *United States v. United States Gypsum Co.* 438 U.S. 422 (1978). The seller must show that under the circumstances it was reasonable to believe that the quoted price or a lower one was available to the favored purchaser or purchasers from the seller's competitors. Neither the District Court nor the Court of Appeals addressed the question whether Falls City had shown information that would have led a reasonable and prudent person to believe that its lower Kentucky price would meet competitors' equally low prices there; indeed, no findings whatever were made regarding competitors' Kentucky prices, or the information available to Falls City about its competitors' Kentucky prices.

Instead, the Court of Appeals reasoned that Falls City had otherwise failed to show that its pricing "was a good faith effort" to meet competition. The Court of Appeals

CASE 46.5 Continued

considered it sufficient to defeat the defense that the price difference "resulted from price increases in Indiana, not price decreases in Kentucky,"..., and that the higher Indiana price was the result of Falls City's policy of following the Indiana prices of its larger competitors in order to enhance its profits. The Court of Appeals also suggested that Falls City's defense failed because it adopted a "general system of competition," rather than responding to individual situations....

On its face, § 2(b) requires more than a showing of facts that would have led a reasonable person to believe that a lower price was available to the favored purchaser from a competitor. The showing required is that the "lower price... *was made* in good faith to *meet*" the competitor's low price....

The District Court found that Falls City's prices rose in Indiana in response to competitors' price increases there; it did not address the crucial question whether Falls City's Kentucky prices remained lower in response to competitors' prices in that State....

Here, however, the persistent interstate price difference could well have been attributable, not to Falls City, but to extensive state regulation of the sale of beer. Indiana required each brewer to charge a single price for its beer throughout the State, and barred direct competition between Indiana and Kentucky distributors for sales to retailers. In these unusual circumstances, the prices charged to Vanco and other wholesalers in Vanderburgh County may have been influenced more by market conditions in distant Gary and Fort Wayne than by conditions in nearby Henderson County, Ky.... A separate pricing structure might well have evolved in the two States without collusion, notwithstanding the existence of a common retail market along the border. Thus, the sustained price discrimination does not itself demonstrate that Falls City's Kentucky prices were not a good faith response to competitors' prices there.

Section 2(b) does not require a seller, meeting in good faith a competitor's lower price to certain customers, to forgo the profits that otherwise would be available in sales to its remaining customers. The very purpose of the defense is to permit a seller to treat different competitive situations differently. The prudent businessman responding fairly to what he believes in good faith is a situation of competitive necessity might well raise his prices to some customers to increase his profits, while meeting competitors' prices by keeping his prices to other customers low....

According to Vanco, the Robinson-Patman Act permits price discrimination only if its purpose is to retain a customer. We agree that a seller's response must be defensive, in the sense that the lower price must be calculated and offered in good faith to "meet not beat" the competitor's low price. Section 2(b), however, does not distinguish between one who meets a competitor's lower price to retain an old customer and one who meets a competitor's lower price in an attempt to gain new customers. Such a distinction would be inconsistent with that section's language and logic, would not be in keeping with elementary principles of competition, and would in fact foster tight and rigid commercial relationships by insulating them from market forces....

Section 2(b) specifically allows a "lower price... to any purchaser or purchasers" made in good faith to meet a competitor's equally low price. A single low price surely may be extended to numerous purchasers if the seller has a reasonable basis for believing that the competitor's lower price is available to them.... Once again, this inquiry is guided by the standard of the prudent businessman responding fairly to what he reasonably believes are the competitive necessities.

A seller may have good reason to believe that a competitor or competitors are charging lower prices throughout a particular region. In such circumstances, customer-by-customer negotiations would be unlikely to result in prices different from those set according to information relating to competitors' territorial prices. A customer-by-customer requirement might also make meaningful price competition unrealistically expensive for smaller firms such as Falls City, which was attempting to compete with larger national breweries in 13 separate States....

CASE 46.5 Continued

In summary, the meeting-competition defense requires the seller at least to show the existence of facts that would lead a reasonable and prudent person to believe that the seller's lower price would meet the equally low price of a competitor; it also requires the seller to demonstrate that its lower price was a good faith response to a competitor's lower price. . . .

JUDGMENT Accordingly, the judgment of the Court of Appeals is vacated, and the case is remanded for further proceedings consistent with this opinion.

Both the courts and the FTC have consistently denied the defense of meeting competition to sellers whose products, because of intrinsic superior quality or intense public demand, normally command a price higher than that usually received by sellers of competitive goods. For example, the defense was denied when the price of Lucky Strikes was dropped to the level of a "poorer grade of cigarettes."[20] Similarly, the seller cannot use the defense by meeting the price quoted by the competitor for goods in a larger quantity than that furnished the seller.

The Supreme Court has held that the "meeting competition" defense is not available to a supplier who charges a discriminatorily low price to assist a selected retail dealer in matching the price of another *retail competitor* engaged in a price war.[21] This conclusion was reached by interpreting "equally low price of a competitor" as used in Section 2(b) to mean "equally low price of a competitor of the seller." The Court reasoned that "to allow a supplier to intervene and grant discriminatory price concessions designed to enable its customer to meet the lower price of a retail competitor who is unaided by his supplier would discourage rather than promote competition. . . . To permit a competitor's supplier to bring his often superior economic power to bear narrowly and discriminatorily to deprive the otherwise resourceful retailer of the very fruits of his efficiency and convert the normal competitive struggle between retailers into an unequal contest between one retailer and the combination of another retailer and his supplier is hardly an element of reasonable and fair competition."

[20] *Porto Rican American Tobacco Co. v. American Tobacco Co.*, 30 F.2d 234 (2d Cir. 1929).
[21] *FTC v. Sun Oil Co.*, 371 U.S. 505 (1963).

Prohibited Indirect Price Discrimination

Obviously a supplier who wishes to engage in illegal price discrimination could evade Section 2(a) by charging uniform prices to all customers while secretly paying a phony "brokerage" commission to a favored buyer's agent or by paying such buyer a fictitious "promotional allowance." The following three subsections were included in the Robinson-Patman Act for the purpose of preventing such indirect price discrimination.

Unlawful Brokerage. Section 2(c) of the Robinson-Patman Act establishes an independent per se prohibition of certain kinds of "kickbacks" to favored customers:

> It shall be unlawful for any person . . . to pay or grant, or to receive or accept, anything of value as a commission, brokerage, or other compensation, or any allowance or discount in lieu thereof, except for services rendered in connection with the sale or purchase of goods, wares, or merchandise, either to the other party to such transaction or to an agent, representative, or other intermediary therein where such intermediary is acting in fact for or in behalf, or is subject to the direct or indirect control, of any party to such transaction, other than the person by whom such compensation is so granted or paid.

The section expressly prohibits a seller from paying brokerage to an intermediary who acts for or in behalf of the buyer, or under the buyer's control. Since Section 2(c) creates a per se violation, it is unnecessary to show that the unlawful brokerage payment was injurious to competition. Courts have interpreted the section to prohibit buyers and their brokers from receiving compensation for "brokerage" services rendered to *sellers* in connection with a sale. The effect of these decisions, which also reflect the policy of the FTC, is to eliminate the phrase "except for services rendered" from the subsection, with the result that brokerage payments by the seller to the buyer or buyer's broker for any reason are absolutely prohibited.

An unusual interpretation of Section 2(c) arose in *Rangen, Inc. v. Sterling Nelson & Sons,*[22] where a seller paid a bribe to a state purchasing agent to influence the sale. The court held that an injured competitor was entitled to bring a treble damage suit under Section 2(c). Decisions of the courts include commercial bribes to agents of buyers as violations of Section 2(c) where the effect of such bribes is to injure competition.

Following passage of the Robinson-Patman Act, large buyers argued that their purchasing organization had saved the seller its ordinary brokerage expense and that, therefore, a price reduction to them was lawful because it was justified by cost savings to the seller. A number of courts have rejected this argument, but other decisions have recognized a distinction between bona fide cost savings to the seller and brokerage. For example, in *Central Retailer-Owned Grocers, Inc. v. FTC,*[23] Central operated as a purchasing agent that consolidated orders from member retail grocers, and purchased at quantity discounts from suppliers. Central paid suppliers, and billed the members at slightly higher prices, the difference representing its operating cost. Any profits were distributed as dividends to the members in proportion to their purchases. Government counsel showed that the amount of price reductions Central obtained from the suppliers was nearly the same as the brokerage commissions paid by the suppliers to other buyers, and claimed that Central was in effect functioning as a broker in violation of Section 2(c). The FTC agreed, but the court in setting aside the Commission's order, held that Central was functioning not as a broker, but as a buyer, and that the discounts obtained were justified by cost savings arising from quantity purchases.

Discriminatory Payments and Services. Sellers often promote the sale of their products by furnishing their customers with services such as advertising, give-away samples, merchandise displays, and demonstrations. Alternatively, sellers may pay their customers to engage in promotional activities. It follows that a seller desiring to evade the prohibition of a direct price discrimination under Section 2(a) might attempt to discriminate indirectly by making payments or furnishing services to different buyers on unequal terms. Subsections 2(d) and (e) of the Robinson-Patman Act as interpreted by the courts make it a per se violation for a seller to engage in either discriminatory payments or services. Therefore it is no defense that the discrimination did not injure competition or that it was justified by cost savings to the seller.

Section 2(d) which relates to *payments by the seller* to a customer for promotional services, provides:

> That it shall be unlawful for any person engaged in commerce to pay or contract for the payment of anything of value to or for the benefit of a customer of such person in the course of such commerce as compensation or in consideration for any services or facilities furnished by or through such customers in connection with the processing, handling, sale or offering for sale of any products or commodities manufactured, sold, or offered for sale by such person, unless such payment or consideration is available on proportionately equal terms to all other customers competing in the distribution of such products or commodities.[24]

Section 2(e) applies to *services furnished by the seller* to a customer:

> That it shall be unlawful for any person to discriminate in favor of one purchaser against another purchaser or purchasers of a commodity bought for resale, without or with processing, by contracting to furnish or furnishing, or by contributing to the furnishing of, any services or facilities connected with the processing, handling, sale, or offering for sale of such commodity so purchased upon terms not accorded to all purchasers on proportionately equal terms.

Courts have interpreted the "meeting competition" defense of Section 2(b) as also applying to Sections 2(d) and (e). Thus a supplier accused of making advertising payments to a favored buyer on unequal terms with other customers can defeat liability by showing that the payment was necessary to meet a similar advertising payment offered by the supplier's competitor. Likewise, apparent inconsistencies in Section 2(d) and (e) have been

[22] 351 F.2d 851 (9th Cir. 1965).
[23] 319 F.2d 410 (7th Cir. 1963).

[24] 15 U.S.C., Sec. 13(d).

harmonized by the courts, and for all practical purposes the sections are construed similarly. For example, Section 2(d) requires the seller who pays a favored customer for promotional services to offer proportionately equal payments to other *competing customers.* Although the corresponding phrase used in Section 2(e) is "all purchasers," the courts have interpreted it to mean "competing customers"—the same as in Section 2(d).[25] However, "competing customers" has been held to also include those purchasing for resale from the seller's customer. Thus, in *FTC v. Fred Meyer, Inc.*,[26] where a seller offered promotional allowances to direct-buying retailers, it was required to extend proportionally equal allowances to nondirect-buying competing retailers who purchased through intermediaries.

Courts have interpreted the requirement of two contemporaneous sales transactions for purposes of Sections 2(d) and (e) in the same manner as that requirement has been interpreted with respect to Section 2(a). Similarly, the courts have required customers to handle products of the seller "of like grade and quality" in order to claim equality. The standard used is the same as that under Section 2(a). Thus, a supplier of Canadian bacon who made promotional payments to a buyer was held not to have violated Section 2(d) by refusing to make proportional payment to other buyers who distributed different pork products of the seller.[27]

The requirement of both sections that the seller who provides payments or services to a customer must make them "available on proportionally equal terms" to all other competing customers has been frequently interpreted by the courts. The seller must go beyond merely complying with the request of competing customers for like treatment by actually notifying them of the availability of payments or services on a proportional basis.

A seller is not excused from the obligation of making payments or services available to the favored buyer's competitors simply because the size or type of their operations is not adaptable to the seller's promotional plan. For example, if a seller offers payments to those buyers who promote the seller's goods by radio advertising, a buyer in a rural area where advertising is not practical would not have the benefit of the discount. Therefore, to avoid the possibility of a Section 2(d) violation, the seller is required to broaden the promotion plan to include alternate forms of advertising such as newspapers or handbills.

Diversity and flexibility in the seller's promotional plan are also necessary to meet the statutory requirement that the payments or services be on "proportionately equal terms." For example, in *State Wholesale Grocers v. Great Atlantic & Pacific Tea Co.*,[28] suppliers of A&P purchased from A&P advertising space in *Woman's Day,* a magazine that A&P owned, published, and distributed in its nationwide chain of stores. In a treble damages action, the court held that although the suppliers were not violating Section 2(e) because they were not furnishing any services or facilities, they were violating Section 2(d) by paying A&P for services without making similar payments available on proportionately equal terms to competitors of A&P. It was immaterial that these competitors had no magazine in which the defendant suppliers could also have purchased advertising space. The suppliers could nevertheless have made proportionately equal cash payments to A&P's competitors for use in other promotional advertising media such as newspapers. Suppliers' uncertainty as to the legality of particular promotional allowance programs was significantly reduced when the FTC published its useful and authoritative *Guides for Advertising Allowances and Other Merchandising Payments and Services.*[29]

Buyer Inducement of Discrimination. Section 2(f) provides:

> That it shall be unlawful for any person engaged in commerce, in the course of such commerce, knowingly to induce or receive a discrimination in price which is prohibited by this section.

Since the subsection refers only to a buyer who has induced or received a discriminatory *price,* it does not apply to a buyer who induces promotional allowances or services that are forbidden by Sections 2(d) and (e). However, Section 5 of the FTC Act has been interpreted to prohibit as an unfair method of competition such a buyer inducement and receipt of discriminatory promotional benefits. Courts

[25] *FTC v. Simplicity Pattern Co.*, 360 U.S. 55 (1959).
[26] 390 U.S. 341 (1968).
[27] *Atlanta Trading Corp. v. FTC,* 258 F.2d 365 (2d Cir. 1958).
[28] 258 F.2d 831 (7th Cir. 1938).
[29] 16 CFR, Sec. 240 (1969, amended in 1972).

have held that *scienter* is a necessary element of a violation of Section 2(f), that is, the buyer must know that he is receiving a lower price than that which the seller is charging other customers.

The Federal Trade Commission Act

Purpose and Scope of the FTC Act

Simultaneously with the passage of the Clayton Act in 1914, Congress enacted the Federal Trade Commission Act.[30] This act created the Federal Trade Commission (FTC), a bipartisan agency to provide day-to-day enforcement of the antitrust laws. The Commission was specifically charged with enforcement of Sections 2, 3, 7, and 8 of the Clayton Act. Section 5 of the FTC Act conferred upon the FTC broad authority to proceed against "unfair methods of competition" and "unfair or deceptive acts or practices."[31] In enacting Section 5, Congress recognized the limitless ingenuity of businesspersons to circumvent existing laws by developing anticompetitive practices that were not specifically forbidden by the antitrust statutes. Therefore, the FTC was given comprehensive authority to prosecute any practice that it considered anticompetitive, subject to final review by the courts. In exercising this broad authority, the FTC considers whether the particular practice (1) offends public policy; (2) is immoral, unethical, oppressive, or unscrupulous; or (3) causes substantial injury to consumers, particularly with respect to their purchases of the necessities of life. Courts have also interpreted Section 5 as conferring upon the FTC the nonpenal power to enforce against *any* violation of antitrust laws. However, private treble damages suits cannot be brought under Section 5.

[30] 15 U.S.C., Secs. 41–58.

[31] This phrase was added by the Wheeler-Lea amendments in 1938.

Extension of FTC Power

Since 1914, many statutes have extended the FTC's jurisdiction into the area of consumer protection. These statutes, as well as the manner in which the FTC conducts enforcement hearings, issues cease-and-desist orders, and promulgates trade regulation rules that have the force of law, have been discussed in Chapter 44. The case below illustrates the broad discretion which the FTC is authorized to exercise in prosecuting "unfair methods of competition" that are not specifically prohibited by the Sherman Act or the Clayton Act.

CASE 46.6 FTC v. Sperry and Hutchinson Co. · 405 U.S. 233 (1972)

FACTS The FTC (plaintiff) issued a cease-and-desist order against defendant Sperry and Hutchinson Co. (S&H), a leading seller of trading stamps, restraining continuation of its policy of commencing suit against trading stamp exchanges that would trade "gold stamps" for Sperry's green stamps or pay cash for S&H green stamps. This arrangement enabled the housewife to consolidate various types of stamps into one kind which could then be exchanged for merchandise, but S&H objected to such exchanges on the ground that they lessened consumer patronage of its franchised retailers and decreased its stamp business. During the period from 1957 to 1965, Sperry threatened or filed more than 250 suits against unauthorized stamp exchanges, or against unauthorized purchase of stamps by firms that did not have an S&H franchise. Many of these suits successfully urged that trading exchanges were wrongfully interfering with contracts between S&H and its franchisees or infringing on trademark rights. S&H contended that its activities were not subject to Section 5 of the FTC Act. The FTC appealed from an adverse judgment of the court of appeals.

OPINION WHITE, Associate Justice. In reality, the question is a double one: First, does Section 5 empower the Commission to define and proscribe an unfair competitive practice, even

CASE 46.6 Continued

though the practice does not infringe either the letter or the spirit of the antitrust laws? Second, does Section 5 empower the Commission to proscribe practices as unfair or deceptive in their effect upon consumers regardless of their nature or quality as competitive practices or their effect on competition? We think the statute, its legislative history, and prior cases compel an affirmative answer to both questions. . . .

Legislative and judicial authorities alike convince us that the Federal Trade Commission does not arrogate excessive power to itself if, in measuring a practice against the elusive, but congressionally mandated standard of fairness, it, like a court of equity, considers public values beyond simply those enshrined in the letter or encompassed in the spirit of the antitrust laws.

JUDGMENT [Note: The effect of the decision was to sustain the FTC's theory that its authority under Section 5 was to be interpreted broadly. The Supreme Court specifically held that unfair competitive practices are not limited to those that have anticompetitive effect, nor are unfair practices in commerce confined to purely competitive behavior.]

National Cooperative Research Act—Joint Ventures between Competitors

Joint Ventures and JRDVs

With increasing frequency, competitors form joint ventures, particularly *joint research and development ventures* (JRDVs). In legal effect, a JRDV is a partnership, often between two corporations—one American and one foreign, for the purpose of research, development, and international marketing of a product.

National Cooperative Research Act

In order to encourage the formation of JRDVs by reducing fear and uncertainty of their possible violation of antitrust laws, Congress enacted the National Cooperative Research Act in 1984. The Act defines JRDVs to include pure and applied research and marketing of the resulting products or technologies through licensing agreements. Firms planning a JRDV are required to give advance notice to the Federal Trade Commission and the Justice Department. Responding to growing criticism of treble-damages-plus-attorney fees that the antitrust laws award, the Act only allows *single* damage awards and further provides that if the JRDV wins the suit, it may recover its attorney fees from the unsuccessful challenger.

The Act spells out that any alleged antitrust liability is to be judged under the rule of reason, and not under per se analysis (discussed in Chapter 45). Judging JRDVs under the rule of reason would require examination of the *procompetitive* effect of increasing *interbrand competition* with other competing firms. For example, the economic efficiency of a JRDV may make possible lower and more competitive prices, particularly in world markets. This procompetitive effect of the venture is then weighed against the *anticompetitive* effect of eliminating competition between the two firms. For example, if the JRDV decided to establish monopolistic prices far above the combined marginal cost of the two firms' products, the effect would be clearly anticompetitive, and under the rule of reason, would probably be held to violate the Sherman Act.

Antitrust Exemptions and Extraterritoriality

It has been estimated that approximately one-fourth of America's national income originates in sectors of the economy that are exempt from antitrust laws.

Exemptions from antitrust law may be of two types: "express" or "implied." Express exemptions are found in the antitrust statutes or in regulatory statutes for certain industries, particularly public utilities. Since antitrust law reflects a national policy of major importance to the competitive economic system, courts interpret it liberally so as to give it the broadest possible coverage. Conversely, antitrust exemptions are construed very strictly so as to limit their applicability as much as possible. Implied exemptions arise from court interpretations that are necessary to reconcile conflicts between antitrust law and other statutes or the Constitution. An example is the Noerr-Pennington doctrine discussed below.

Express Exemptions

Labor Organizations. Section 6 of the Clayton Act attempted to exempt labor unions from the antitrust laws, and Section 20[32] granted unions relief from some injunctions. Nevertheless, the use of federal court injunctions against unions under the Sherman Act was not effectively limited until the Norris-La Guardia Act of 1932.[33] A labor union's immunity from antitrust law is confined to a "labor dispute" as defined in that act. A union will also lose its exempt status if its primary intent is to restrain trade, or if it conspires with nonlabor groups to monopolize. In a landmark case,[34] a union, electrical contractors, and the suppliers in New York City all agreed that (1) contractors would hire union labor and buy only from the suppliers and (2) suppliers would sell only in New York to contractors who hired union labor. The Supreme Court held that the arrangement was an unlawful conspiracy under Section 1 of the Sherman Act. In denying the union's claim of exemption, the court said: "When the unions participated with a combination of business men who had complete power to eliminate all competition among themselves and to prevent all competition from others, a situation was created not included within the exemptions of the Clayton and Norris-La Guardia Acts."

The "labor" exemption of the Clayton Act has been held not to apply to organizations representing learned professions, primarily because the members are usually independent contractors, not employees. Thus a county bar association's publication of a "minimum fee schedule"[35] and a ban on competitive bidding by a professional engineer's association[36] have been held to be nonexempt violations of the antitrust laws. Even professional sports are subject to the Sherman Act, with the notable exception of baseball.[37]

Agricultural Cooperatives. Section 6 of the Clayton Act and Section 1 of the Capper-Volstead Act[38] establish an exemption for farmers' cooperative associations that are formed to market agricultural products. Like the labor exemption, the agricultural exemption is lost if the organization combines with outside firms to restrain trade.[39]

Patents and Copyrights. Federal legislation enacted under constitutional authority[40] expressly confers limited monopoly privileges on those who invent or publish. Although such rights inherently conflict with the antitrust objective of promoting competition, they are recognized in order to encourage innovative inventions and creative publications. Patents and copyrights are limited monopolies in the sense that the products or writings that have benefited from the special privileges granted must nevertheless compete in the market with similar or related products.

Generally, courts have resolved the conflict between the competition objective of the Sherman Act and the monopoly objectives of patent laws by interpreting patent and copyright privileges narrowly and by overruling any attempt of the owners to extend and expand such privileges into familiar areas of anticompetitive behavior. For example, in *Morton Salt Co. v. G. S. Suppiger Co.*,[41] Suppiger owned a patent on a machine used in the canning industry for depositing predetermined amounts of

[32]29 U.S.C., Sec. 52.

[33]29 U.S.C., Secs. 101–115; *United States v. Hutcheson*, 312 U.S. 219 (1941).

[34]*Allen Bradley Co. v. Local Union No. 3, International Brotherhood of Electrical Workers*, 325 U.S. 797 (1945).

[35]*Goldfarb v. Virginia State Bar*, 421 U.S. 733 (1975); see also *Boddicker v. Arizona State Dental Ass'n*, 549 F.2d 626 (9th Cir. 1977). In that case a local dental association's requirement that membership was conditional upon the dentist's maintaining membership also in the national association was held to be subject to Sherman Act jurisdiction and not protected by the "learned profession" exemption. The case was remanded for trial on the issue of whether the arrangement was an unlawful tie-in.

[36]*United States v. Nat'l Soc'y of Professional Engineers*, 404 F. Supp. 457; aff'd 55 L. Ed.2d 637 (1978).

[37]*Toolson v. New York Yankees, Inc.*, 346 U.S. 356 (1953).

[38]7 U.S.C., Secs. 291–292.

[39]*Case-Swayne Co. v. Sunkist Growers, Inc.*, 389 U.S. 384 (1967).

[40]U.S. Constitution, Art. 1, Sec. 8, clause 8.

[41]314 U.S. 488 (1942).

salt in tablet form to the contents of cans. It licensed the use of the machine to canneries on condition that they use the patented machines only with tablets that were sold by Suppiger. Morton claimed these were unlawful tying contracts that tended to lessen competition in violation of Section 3 of the Clayton Act. The Supreme Court struck down the tying contract. Sidestepping the issue of whether Section 3 was violated, the Court reached its decision on the ground that it is against public policy for a court of equity to lend its aid to protect a patent monopoly when the owner is misusing it as an "effective means of restraining competition with its sale of an unpatented article." This *patent misuse doctrine* prohibits the owner from obtaining an injunction against infringement as long as the patent is being used in an anticompetitive manner that is outside the scope of the granted patent.

Implied Exemptions

Regulated Enterprises; The Parker Doctrine. In addition to the express statutory exemptions from antitrust law already discussed, federal statutes expressly provide limited exemption for many industries affected with the public interest. For example, insurance carriers may exchange information in establishing their rates without violating the Sherman Act. Broader exemptions are extended to industries regulated under federal law such as telephone, airlines, railroads, television and radio broadcasting, interstate pipeline, stock and grain exchanges, and ocean shipping. Nevertheless, there has been a continuing trend toward deregulation and encouragement of competition.

The majority of industries which affect the public interest are regulated by commissions established by state law. A broad implied exemption for such "state action" was established by the Supreme Court in *Parker v. Brown,*[42] where a raisin packer sued under the Sherman Act to enjoin the California Director of Agriculture from carrying out a statutory price-fixing program to market raisins. The program involved pro rata restrictions on sales, first proposed by the producers but modified and established by the state. In holding that this "state action" was exempt from the antitrust laws, the Court said:

> The prorate program here was never intended to operate by force of individual agreement or combination. It derived its authority and its efficacy from the legislative command of the state and was not intended to operate or become effective without that command. . . . True, a state does not give immunity to those who violate the Sherman Act by authorizing them to violate it or by declaring that their action is lawful. Here, although the organization of a prorate zone is proposed by the producers, and a prorate program, approved by the Commission, must also be approved by referendum of the producers, it is the state, acting through the Commission, which adopts the program and which enforces it with penal sanctions, in the execution of a governmental policy.

In recent cases, the court has further clarified *Parker.* Thus, in the *Goldfarb* case referred to in note 35 in this chapter, the Court held that a minimum lawyer's fee schedule approved by the state bar (an arm of the judicial branch of government) was nevertheless subject to the Sherman Act. The Court stated: "The fact that the State Bar is a state agency for some limited purposes does not create an antitrust shield that allows it to foster anticompetitive practices for the benefit of its members." The Court's current view is that a company affecting the public interest such as a utility can appropriately have its natural monopoly powers regulated by the state and simultaneously be required to comply with antitrust standards to the extent that it engages in business activity in the competitive sector of the economy.

When a sovereign state delegates to a subdivision of government, such as an incorporated city, the power to enact local ordinances, do such local laws constitute "state action" so as to qualify for antitrust exemption under the Parker doctrine? The problem arises frequently when municipal ordinances grant exclusive franchises to local taxicab, water, and other companies. In general, such ordinances are not exempt from antitrust scrutiny because courts view them as acts of cities, not as "acts of the State," unless a state statute deals specifically with the activity involved. Recently, Congress has been urged to amend the antitrust law to allow cities the same immunity from antitrust prosecution that the Parker doctrine gives to states.

Active state authorship of regulatory policy for an industry combined with "active supervision" of

[42] 317 U.S. 341 (1943).

that policy by the state or its administrative agency is sufficient to exempt the industry from antitrust action. On the other hand, passive state control (for example, the mere "rubber stamping" with state approval of a price-fixing scheme primarily authored by an industry association, coupled with little or no ongoing state review of the regulatory program) will not qualify for antitrust exemption. This distinction is discussed by the U.S. Supreme Court in the following case.

CASE 46.7 324 Liquor Corp. v. Duffy · 93 L. Ed.2d 667 (1987)

FACTS Section 101-bb of New York's Alcoholic Beverage Control Law (ABC Law) required wholesalers to file ("post") monthly price schedules with the State Liquor Authority. Retailers were required to charge at least 112 percent of the "posted" wholesale price for liquor, but wholesalers were permitted to sell to retailers at less than the "posted" price. 324 Liquor Corporation, a retailer, sold bottles of liquor for less than 112 percent of the posted bottle price resulting in suspension of its license and a fine of $1,000. The corporation sought relief on the ground that the law violated Section 1 of the Sherman Act. The New York trial and appellate courts denied relief, and the corporation appealed to the Supreme Court.

OPINION POWELL, Justice. In *California Retail Liquor Dealers Assn. v. Midcal Aluminum, Inc.*, 445 U.S. 97 (1980), we invalidated a California statute requiring all producers, wholesalers, and rectifiers of wine to file fair trade contracts or price schedules with the State. Midcal establishes the framework for our analysis of New York's liquor pricing system.

The "threshold question," in this case as in Midcal, is whether the State's pricing system is inconsistent with the antitrust laws. Section 101-bb imposes a regime of resale price maintenance on all New York liquor retailers. Resale price maintenance has been a per se violation of § 1 of the Sherman Act since the early years of national antitrust enforcement. . . . The New York statute, moreover, applies to *all* wholesalers and retailers of liquor. We have noted that industry resale price maintenance also may facilitate cartelization. . . .

The antitrust violation in this case is essentially similar to the violation in Midcal. It is true that the wholesalers in Midcal were required to adhere to a single fair trade contract or price schedule for each geographical area. Midcal therefore involved horizontal as well as vertical price fixing. Although the horizontal restraint in Midcal may have provided an additional reason for invalidating the statute, our decision in Midcal rested on the "vertical control" of wine producers, who held "the power to prevent price competition by dictating the prices charged by wholesalers." The California statute was invalidated because "it mandated resale price maintenance, an activity that has long been regarded as a per se violation of the Sherman Act. We hold that ABC Law § 101-bb is inconsistent with § 1 of the Sherman Act.

In *Parker v. Brown*, 317 U.S. 341 (1943), the Court held that the Sherman Act does not apply "to anticompetitive conduct of a State acting through its legislature." *Parker v. Brown* rests on principles of federalism and state sovereignty. . . . At the same time, "a state does not give immunity to those who violate the Sherman Act by authorizing them to violate it, or by declaring that their action is lawful." Our decisions have established a two-part test for determining immunity under *Parker v. Brown*. First, the challenged restraint must be "one clearly articulated and affirmatively expressed as state policy"; second, the policy must be "actively supervised by the State itself." . . . New York's liquor pricing system meets the first requirement. The state legislature clearly has adopted a policy of resale price maintenance. Just as clearly, however, New York's liquor pricing system is not actively supervised by the State. As in Midcal, the State "simply authorizes

CASE 46.7 Continued

price setting and enforces the prices established by private parties." New York "neither establishes prices nor reviews the reasonableness of the price schedules." New York "does not monitor market conditions or engage in any pointed reexamination of the program." Each wholesaler sets its own "posted" prices; the State does not control month-to-month variations in posted prices. . . . The State has displaced competition among liquor retailers without substituting an adequate system of regulation. The national policy in favor of competition cannot be thwarted by casting such a gauzy cloak of state involvement over what is essentially a private price-fixing arrangement.

The New York Court of Appeals concluded that § 101-bb "was expressly designed to preserve competition in New York's retail liquor industry by stabilizing the retail market and protecting the economic position of small liquor retailers." . . . In Midcal, we found nothing in the record to suggest that California's wine pricing system actually helped sustain small retailers. . . . Our Midcal opinion cites evidence that states with "fair trade laws" not unlike ABC Law § 101-bb actually had higher rates of firm failure, and slower rates of growth of small retail stores, than free trade states in the years between 1956 and 1972. The only relevant evidence in the record indicates that the number of retail liquor outlets in New York continued to decline between 1970 and 1979. We are unwilling to assume on the basis of this record that § 101-bb has the effect of protecting small retailers.

In this case, as in Midcal, the State's unsubstantiated interest in protecting small retailers "simply is not of the same stature as the goals of the Sherman Act." . . .

JUDGMENT We therefore reverse the judgment of the New York Court of Appeals and remand the case for further proceedings not inconsistent with this opinion. It is so ordered.

Lobbying: The Noerr-Pennington Exemption. The First Amendment right of citizens to petition the government has been interpreted by courts to impliedly exempt from the antitrust laws lawful lobbying to obtain legislative or executive action, even if it is intended to restrain trade or eliminate competition. However, this "Noerr-Pennington exemption"[43] is lost if lobbying is used as a sham to cover other activities that directly restrain trade.

Extraterritoriality of Antitrust Laws

Generally, agreements by American firms to divide world markets, assign export quotas, or fix prices overseas are subject to the antitrust laws. Beginning in the 1940s, the Department of Justice sought to break up large international cartels of American and foreign companies dominating markets for such commodities as magnesium alloys, matches, titanium compounds, and roller bearings. Enforcement has focused primarily on foreign activity by American or foreign firms that has a serious anticompetitive effect within the United States, but increasing attention is now being given by the Department as well as by private plaintiffs to the extraterritorial (outside of the United States) anticompetitive activities of multinational corporations.

Effect of Antitrust Law on American Competition Abroad. American antitrust policy conflicts sharply with the view of many other free-world nations which hold that antitrust notions should be discarded in the highly competitive areas of world trade. The United States is virtually alone among major trading nations in the extent to which it imposes a variety of antitrust restrictions on exporters who wish to combine to penetrate foreign markets.

In contrast with American efforts to give antitrust laws extraterritorial effect, many foreign governments openly encourage export cartels by offering antitrust exemption, outright subsidies, or tax incentives. Such foreign export monopolies put at a disadvantage American medium and small firms which are prevented by the antitrust laws from combining to meet world competition. The extent to

[43] *Eastern Railroad Presidents Conference v. Noerr Motor Freight, Inc.*, 365 U.S. 127 (1961); *United Mine Workers v. Pennington*, 381 U.S. 657 (1965).

which joint research and development ventures (JRDVs), discussed earlier in this chapter, will improve this situation remains to be seen. The problem is aggravated by recent expansion of trade with state-controlled, centrally planned nonmarket economies, such as those of the Soviet bloc. These nations usually deal through a state trading agency which can use its superior bargaining power to play American firms off against each other. The negotiating ability of state trading monopolies is actually strengthened by the United States antitrust laws which prohibit American sellers from exchanging price information. Foreign competitors unrestricted by antitrust considerations can obviously bargain much more effectively with such state-controlled agencies.

Webb-Pomerene and Export Trading Company Acts. In token recognition of the competitive disadvantage of American firms in world markets, Congress in 1918 passed the Webb-Pomerene Export Trade Act[44] exempting from the Sherman Act an export trade association provided it does *not* (1) restrain trade within the United States, (2) restrain exports by domestic competitors of the association, and (3) engage in domestic activity that will lessen competition or fix prices in the United States. The very few trade associations that have been organized under the act account for only 3 percent of total American exports.

Failure of the act to stimulate exports is due to business uncertainty as to the scope of the exemption, delay in obtaining necessary clearances from the Justice Department, and failure of the act to cover export *services.*

In an effort to correct these deficiencies and to improve the bargaining position of American sellers in international markets, Congress enacted the Export Trading Company Act of 1982.[45] It authorizes the Commerce and Justice Departments to establish antitrust standards that will be applied to export trading companies and to certify that a particular applicant meets those standards. Eligibility for certification is based on four antitrust criteria, namely, that there be no (1) substantial lessening of competition in the United States, (2) unreasonable upward pressure on prices in the United States, (3) unfair methods of competition, and (4) resale or consumption of exported goods within the United States. A certificate holder has complete immunity from U.S. antitrust laws except for civil lawsuits for injunctive relief and actual damages. However, the plaintiff must show that the trading entity violated the specific standards of the act. Furthermore, in such civil suits there is a presumption of compliance by the defendant trading company, and if the court finds that it complied with the antitrust standards, the plaintiff may be required to reimburse costs of suit and reasonable defense and attorney fees.

The new act does not repeal the Webb-Pomerene Act. It includes services whereas the Webb Act applies to commodities only. The new act also provides exemption from the antitrust laws generally, including Section 5 of the FTC Act, as well as state antitrust laws. The Webb Act, on the other hand, only provides exemption from the Sherman Act and from that part of Section 7 of the Clayton Act which refers to stock acquisition.

Foreign Trade Antitrust Improvements Act. Enacted at the same time as the Export Trading Company Act was a companion bill, the Foreign Trade Antitrust Improvements Act,[46] the key provisions of which are contained in Title IV. The main purpose of Title IV was to free American businesses from excessive antitrust regulation of their export activities and overseas joint ventures. To achieve this goal, Congress attempted to codify and define the extraterritorial reach of the antitrust laws that had been reflected in two landmark court decisions: *Timberlane*[47] and *Mannington Mills.*[48] The *Timberlane* court established an "effects" test of jurisdiction over international antitrust cases. This required the trial court to make a preliminary ruling based upon three factors. First, the court should decide if the conduct had some *effect* on United States commerce. Second, the court should determine whether the conduct was of a type or magnitude cognizable as a violation of antitrust law. Third, the court should decide whether to abstain from asserting jurisdiction for reasons of *comity,* that

[44] 15 U.S.C. Secs. 61–66.
[45] 15 U.S.C. Secs. 4001–4021.

[46] 15 U.S.C. Secs. 6(a)(1), 45(a)(3)(A).
[47] *Timberlane Lumber Co. v. Bank of America,* 549 F.2d (9th Cir. 1976).
[48] *Mannington Mills, Inc. v. Congoleum Corp.,* 595 F.2d 1287 (3rd Cir. 1979).

is, respect for the sovereignty of other nations. The "effects test" of *Timberlane* was supplemented by the *Mannington Mills* court, which listed ten factors to be considered in balancing United States and foreign government interests for the purpose of deciding whether to abstain from exercising jurisdiction for reasons of comity.

Essentially, Title IV reflects the "effects-balancing" standards of *Timberlane-Mannington Mills* with the result that U.S. courts in a proper case can abstain from exercising jurisdiction in deference to foreign sovereign interests. Under Title IV, there is no antitrust jurisdiction over conduct affecting wholly foreign commerce. It is also clear that only United States exporters that suffer injury are entitled to file suit, not foreign competitors. In addition, Title IV exempts conduct which is unimportant because of its negligible magnitude or which produces effects that the antitrust laws were not designed to prevent.

The act has been criticized for the following reasons. (1) It does not modify existing case law or expand antitrust exemption sufficiently to stimulate American export trade. (2) It deals primarily with *exporters'* antitrust exemption; it does *not* reach the major source of conflict between the United States and foreign countries, which arises from foreign conduct and transnational cartels involving *imports* that affect American competition. (3) Because of comity, it does not deal with commercial activities of foreign states that affect American domestic competition.

Responding to this criticism, the Justice Department in 1988 issued long-awaited new *Guidelines* which shield most foreign investors and American-foreign joint ventures from antitrust enforcement actions unless such international business ventures have a direct, substantial, and reasonably forseeable anticompetitive effect on consumers in the United States. The new guidelines also stress that patents, licenses, and other intellectual property rights—previously assumed to conflict with antitrust laws and promote monopolies—now will be considered procompetitive by the Justice Department, because they encourage the efficient development of innovative technology. Although federal or state courts are not bound by the guidelines, nevertheless they give antitrust enforcers greater leeway to rely on diplomatic, foreign policy, considerations of comity, and other noneconomic factors to allow certain activities by foreign companies doing business in the United States. For example, the guidelines suggest that in the future, the Justice Department will be less likely to challenge voluntary quotas, or export restraints by foreign manufacturers, even when they are instigated by a foreign government. This new approach recognizes the inconsistency of antitrust challenge to such controls at a time when the United States is actively negotiating to have foreign governments adopt export restraints.

Recent Trends and Policy Conflicts in Antitrust Law

Trends in Antitrust Law

Since 1981, there have been several important developments involving a noticeable shift in the direction of governmental antitrust enforcement. Three such trends will be discussed.

Increased Emphasis on Economic Analysis. The Department of Justice's antitrust division has steadily increased reliance on economic analysis following the establishment of the Economic Policy Office in 1973. Since then, its policy conclusions have been increasingly influential in deciding whether to commence a particular enforcement action. As a result, there have been virtually no actions against vertical mergers, violations of the Robinson-Patman Act, and no criminal resale price maintenance or conglomerate merger cases have been prosecuted. In many areas, the division's analysis has reflected the growing influence of the "trust-the-market" principles of the Chicago school of economics. Many traditional notions of anticompetitive behavior have been reexamined and reevaluated as imprecise, unreliable, or even procompetitive. For example, the Chicago school holds that many vertical mergers, tying arrangements, joint ventures among competitors, vertical price and nonprice restraints, and even some horizontal mergers may actually encourage competition. Conclusions emerging from careful economic analysis were a major factor that led enforcement attorneys to dismiss as "unwinnable" the antitrust suit against IBM in 1983. In the same year, economic analysis played a major role in the settlement of the 9-year-old AT&T case leading to the world's largest corporation divesting itself of local telephone companies.

Decrease in Antitrust Enforcement Suits. In 1983 and 1984, there was a decrease of approximately 60 percent in the number of antitrust enforcement actions commenced by the FTC and the Department of Justice. Coincidentally, for several years prior to 1983, approximately 60 percent of the antitrust actions were overturned by the appellate courts. Thus, it appears that the antitrust enforcement agencies are moving in the direction of being careful not to sue where suing would be inappropriate. In addition, the new revised 1984 *Merger Guidelines* contained such specific economic formulas for defining markets, computing market share, and determining market power that they fostered more self-regulation by industry with the result that fewer enforcement actions against merging companies were necessary. However, critics of the new guidelines contend that some of the market data are difficult for businesses to gather. For example, to determine elasticity of demand requires measuring the substitutability of products. It is difficult to obtain reliable data that would determine what price level for yo-yos would force buyers to turn to hoola hoops as an alternative.

Increase in Mergers. Another noticeable trend in recent years is a significant increase in mergers and joint ventures. In 1984, there were 2,543 mergers, including eight takeovers of over $1 billion each, mostly in the petroleum industry. The 100 largest mergers involved firms employing 4.5 million people—approximately 4 percent of the nation's workforce. Undoubtedly, the increase in mergers was a result of the more specific 1984 *Merger Guidelines.* In defense of this increase, the FTC has cited statistics to show that the trend of concentration in America over the past several decades remains virtually unchanged.

In 1984, the FTC signed a consent decree permitting a joint venture between General Motors and Toyota. The decree provided that the scope of the joint venture would not be enlarged and that the companies would not exchange competitively sensitive information. The FTC has stated that permitting this joint venture of unprecedented size was justified because (1) production of more and smaller cars meant lower consumer prices and (2) the joint venture represented an important experiment to see whether Japanese management and innovative techniques were adaptable to a U.S. company in the setting of unionized labor. Earlier, in 1983, Justice's antitrust division announced that the government did not plan to challenge a joint venture between major jet engine producers of the United States, England, Japan, West Germany, and Italy. Thus, "world market" economic analysis has won acceptance within the antitrust enforcement agencies. Lack of competition was traditionally viewed as a function of the number of firms in a given market. The new standard for international joint ventures now appears to be: Even very large combines are proper if it can be shown that fewer companies can produce cheaper products.

Conflicts in Antitrust Law

The influence of the Chicago school of economics on antitrust enforcement has stirred controversy, particularly on the issue of whether resale price maintenance should continue to be judged as a per se violation. In addition, there are conflicting views among antitrust lawyers as to whether treble damages are appropriate in "rule of reason" cases.

Resale Price Maintenance—Good or Bad? The central question over which this controversy rages is whether consumers are better served if manufacturers can dictate prices that retailers charge. Stanford University's Professor William Baxter, head of the antitrust division from 1981 to 1983, argued that retailers should be able to provide consumer services (for example, instruction in how to use a computer) without fear that the customer will get a "free ride" by using the service and then buying the product at a nearby discount outlet. Baxter contended that resale price maintenance promotes general consumer interests by eliminating the free rider who creates economic inefficiency. In any event, Baxter argued that resale price maintenance cases should be judged under the "rule of reason" and not as per se violations.

Opponents of resale price maintenance contend that it increases the price all consumers pay for a product, and if it is widely used by manufacturers, it may lead to anticompetitive horizontal price fixing. These critics further hold that because resale price maintenance is inherently bad, it should continue to be prosecuted as a per se violation. Since the *Sylvania* (Case 45.3) decision held that nonprice vertical restraints should be judged under the rule of reason, it is possible that courts may reexamine vertical price restraints with a view to judging them also under the rule of reason.

"Detrebling" Damages; Other Conflicts. After the court or jury determines the damage an antitrust plaintiff has suffered from the anticompetitive actions of the defendant, the law has provided for trebling of damages in all cases. Recently, many experts, including Professor Baxter, have argued that only actual damages without trebling should be awarded in cases decided under the rule of reason. It is argued that since rule-of-reason cases are decided on the basis of whether particular conduct unreasonably restrains competition, they obviously do not involve the same degree of wrong as per se violations. Therefore, it is contended that the treble damage award should be confined to per se violations. Other conflicting theories that have not, as yet, been resolved include proposals to permit more interlocking directorates, to allow antitrust violators to pay only their share of damages and to sue the other codefendants for the balance, and to eliminate jury trials in antitrust cases on the ground that the issues are too complex for lay juries to understand.

Summary

The Clayton Act of 1914 was passed to strike at anticompetitive and monopolistic practices in their incipiency. The act prohibits price discrimination (Section 2 as amended by the Robinson-Patman Act), exclusive dealing and tying contracts (Section 3), mergers (Section 7), and interlocking directorates (Section 8). The act also requires that the prohibited activities must occur "in the course of commerce" and the actor must be "engaged in commerce"—a much narrower "commerce" definition than that used in the Sherman Act.

In all cases, the prohibited conduct must "tend to substantially lessen competition, or to create a monopoly." In applying this standard of exclusive dealing and tying contracts, courts use one of two tests: (1) The "quantitative substantiality" test which is met if the contract covers a substantial quantity of the relevant market, and (2) the "qualitative substantiality" test which judges the contract's anticompetitive effect by examining qualitative factors such as relative market strength of the parties, the probable immediate and future effect of the contract on competition, and whether it continued to flourish despite the restrictive agreement.

Most tying contracts are held to be per se violations when it is shown that (1) the seller has market power with respect to the tying product, and (2) the arrangement affects a "not insubstantial amount of commerce." For a tying arrangement to be unlawful, the tying and tied products must both be distinct *commodities,* inasmuch as the Clayton Act does not apply to services or real estate transactions. In contrast, the Sherman Act applies to a tie-in between a service (e.g., electric power) and a commodity (e.g., light bulbs).

Section 7, as amended by the Celler-Kefauver Act of 1950, prohibits acquisition by one corporation of the stock or assets of another if it would tend to substantially lessen competition or tend to create a monopoly. In evaluating the anticompetitive effect of a merger, the definition of "relevant market" is important. To determine this, courts first define the product and then the relevant geographic market for that product. The relevant geographic market is further subdivided into (1) the "outer boundary market" and (2) one or more submarkets, using economic criteria established by case law. Finally, the court examines whether there is a reasonable probability that the merger will substantially lessen competition in each of the submarkets.

To determine if a merger will substantially lessen competition, the government and the courts examine market concentration as measured by market share percentages, using different percentage-of-market-share guidelines, depending on whether the merger is horizontal, vertical, or conglomerate. Under the "potential entrant" doctrine, the forbidden anticompetitive effect will be found to exist if one of the two merging firms is a potential entrant into the market. The doctrine has the effect of encouraging a firm to expand by branching de novo into a market rather than by merging with a firm already in that market.

The Clayton Act is enforced by private civil treble damages suits and by administrative proceedings instituted by the FTC, usually seeking a cease-and-desist order against conduct prohibited by the act. Corporations and their directors and agents who violate any penal provision of the antitrust laws are also subject to criminal prosecution. In private civil suits, the plaintiff must prove injury that flows from the defendant's conduct which the antitrust laws were intended to prevent.

The purpose of the Robinson-Patman Act, which amended the Clayton Act, was to prevent large chain stores from using their buying power to coerce suppliers into furnishing discriminatory services or prices, and thus to prevent such buyers from gaining an unfair advantage over smaller competitors. Section 2(a) of the Robinson-Patman Act prohibits price discrimination between different purchasers of commodities of like grade and quality in the "course of commerce" if the effect may be to substantially lessen competition or tend to create a monopoly. To constitute a violation, the transaction must involve two or more states, two or more sales of commodities (not services) to two or more purchasers at about the same time, at discriminatorily different prices, which injure competition. The act is aimed at preventing injury to competitors of the seller (primary line injury), to buyers (secondary line injury), to customers of buyers (tertiary line injury), and to competitors of the buyer's customer (fourth line injury).

Sellers charged with Robinson-Patman violations may assert two defenses: (1) that price differentials were justified by differences in costs and (2) that prices were lowered in good faith to meet an equally low price of a competitor.

To prevent circumvention of the Robinson-Patman Act, Sections 2(c) through 2(e) prohibit sellers from paying favored buyers unlawful "brokerage" or "kickbacks," or from discriminating by providing favored buyers with services or promotional allowances not available to other customers on "proportionately equal terms." Section 2(f) prohibits *buyers* from knowingly inducing or receiving a discrimination in price.

The Federal Trade Commission Act of 1914 created the FTC and conferred upon it broad jurisdiction to enforce Sections 2, 3, 7, and 8 of the Clayton Act and prevent "unfair methods of competition" and "unfair or deceptive acts or practices." The Supreme Court has held that such practices are not limited to those that have an anticompetitive effect, nor are such practices confined to purely competitive behavior.

The National Cooperative Research Act encourages joint research and development ventures (JRDVs), which must give advance notice to the FTC and Justice Department, must be judged under the rule of reason, and are subject only to single (not treble) damage awards in antitrust suits.

Exemptions to antitrust law are express, such as those for labor organizations, agricultural cooperatives, and owners of patents or copyrights. Generally, the Supreme Court has interpreted these exemptions narrowly. Implied exemptions arise from court interpretations, such as the *Parker* doctrine. As modified by later decisions, this doctrine holds that state regulatory action is immune from the antitrust laws. However, a firm may be regulated by the state in some areas and simultaneously be required to comply with antitrust standards in other areas involving business activity in the competitive sector of the economy. Another implied exemption from antitrust law, the *Noerr-Pennington* rule, exempts lawful lobbying from the antitrust laws, even if it is intended to restrain trade or eliminate competition.

Agreements by American firms to divide world markets, as well as foreign activity by American or foreign firms that has a serious anticompetitive effect within the United States, are subject to the antitrust laws. The Webb-Pomerene Export Trade Act exempted export trade associations from the antitrust laws, but uncertainty as to the extent of that exemption has discouraged formation of such associations. To correct this deficiency, Congress enacted the Export Trading Company Act of 1982 and the Foreign Trade Antitrust Improvements Act.

Review Questions

1 **(a)** What shortcomings of the Sherman Act did the Clayton Act attempt to correct? **(b)** In your opinion, how effective have Sections 2, 3, 7, and 8 of the Clayton Act been in correcting the defects of the Sherman Act?

2 **(a)** Define exclusive dealing and tying contracts. **(b)** How does an exclusive dealing contract differ from an exclusive distributorship? **(c)** Compare and contrast Section 1 of the Sherman Act and Section 3 of the Clayton Act with respect to (i) the "commerce" jurisdictional requirements and (ii) the products or services covered.

3 Explain how the competitive effect of exclusive dealing and tying arrangements is measured under **(a)** the "quantitative substantiality" test and **(b)** the "qualitative substantiality" test.

4 **(a)** Are violations of the Clayton act civil or criminal offenses, or both? **(b)** What different classes of plaintiffs commence proceedings for violations of the Clayton Act, and what remedies does the act provide for each kind of plaintiff?

5 **(a)** What business practices led to the Robinson-Patman amendment to Section 2 of the Clayton Act? **(b)** What was the primary aim of the Robinson-Patman Act? **(c)** In broad terms, explain the scope of the Robinson-Patman Act. **(d)** What are the eight elements of a violation of Section 2(a) of the Robinson-Patman Act?

6 Under the Robinson-Patman Act, when are the following commodities "of like grade and quality"? **(a)** Identical goods bearing different brand labels. **(b)** Goods of different quality bearing identical brand labels.

7 Explain how the "cost justification" defense to a Robinson-Patman price discrimination charge is affected by: **(a)** classifying customers into groups and averaging costs for each group; **(b)** averaging costs of annual purchases of customers who purchase the same quantity but for whom the number of shipments differ.

8 **(a)** Why and in what manner does the Robinson-Patman Act prevent indirect price discrimination? **(b)** Is it necessary to show that an unlawful brokerage payment injured competition in order to establish a violation of Section 2(c) of the Robinson-Patman Act? **(c)** Can the seller's payment of a bribe to the purchasing agent of a customer violate the Robinson-Patman Act?

9 **(a)** Is it a per se violation for a seller to engage in discriminatory payments or services to the buyer? **(b)** Can a seller accused of making advertising payments to a buyer on unequal terms with other customers in violation of Section 2(d) of the Robinson-Patman Act assert as a defense that such payments were necessary to "meet competition"?

10 **(a)** What is meant by the Robinson-Patman provision that the seller who provides payments or services to a customer must make them "available on proportionally equal terms"? **(b)** What practical problems face a seller trying to comply with the provision quoted in **(a)**, and how can those problems be resolved?

11 If a buyer knowingly induces the seller to pay him a discriminatory promotional allowance, has the buyer violated the Robinson-Patman Act?

12 **(a)** What groups are expressly exempted from the antitrust laws? **(b)** What limits have court decisions placed upon these exemptions?

13 Under the *Parker* doctrine, as modified by later decisions of the courts, how extensive must "state action" be in order to be exempt from the antitrust law?

14 **(a)** To what extent is extraterritorial effect given to the antitrust laws? **(b)** What factors arising from the antitrust laws place American firms at a competitive disadvantage in world markets?

15 **(a)** What is meant by "comity"? **(b)** How do the Export Trading Company Act of 1982 and the Foreign Trade Antitrust Improvements Act affect U.S. foreign commerce, and how do these acts relate to antitrust law?

Case Problems

1 The Principes' family corporation operated two McDonald's franchises in Virginia. When they acquired each of their franchises to use the McDonald trade name, the transaction was similar to all McDonald franchise arrangements. The Principes were required to pay a $10,000 license fee, a $15,000 security deposit (in exchange for a 20-year non-interest-bearing note) plus 2.2 percent of gross receipts as royalties plus 8 percent as rent on their lease of the land and building. The building was built and owned by McDonald's affiliated subsidiary corporation. The Principes sued McDonald's under the antitrust laws, contending that McDonald's was selling not one but three distinct products: the franchise, the lease, and the security deposit note. They argued (citing *Siegel v. Chicken Delight, Inc.*) that this was an unlawful tying arrangement, because they were required to lease the land and building for each of their franchises. McDonald's argued that (1) they expertly selected land and built fast-food restaurant buildings at an average cost of $450,000; (2) that this eliminates risk and high investment cost for the franchisees, so that they could be selected for their management potential rather than their real estate expertise or wealth; (3) the system keeps McDonald's distinctly architectured restaurants in the company so that they can be operated perpetually; and (4) the practice of building and owning their locations and franchising the food preparation system was part of an integrated marketing plan. Was McDonald's franchising system an unlawful tying arrangement?

2 Five cemeteries (Cemetery Group) followed a pattern of selling burial lots only on condition that the buyer also purchase a grave marker from or through the cemetery as well as the services necessary to install the marker. Moore, a gravestone manufacturer, brought a private antitrust action alleging that these arrangements were unlawful tie-ins under Section 3 of the Clayton Act and Section 1 of the Sherman Act. Cemetery Group claimed that cemetery lots and gravemarkers must necessarily be sold as a single product and that they are not two distinct products. As justification for the joint sale of lots and markers, they also claimed that such sales were necessary to retain neatness and aesthetic quality control of the cemetery grounds. The trial court entered judgment for the defendants, and Moore appealed.

Assume that there is sufficient interstate commerce involved to meet the "commerce" jurisdictional requirement, and that a noncompetitive higher price is charged by Cemetery Group for gravemarkers because of their market power over cemetery lots. **(a)** Are cemetery lots sold with gravemarkers and installation services distinct products? **(b)** Is there a possible violation of either Section 3 of the Clayton Act or Section 1 of the Sherman Act arising from a tying arrangement? **(c)** Assuming for argument that the sale of lots and gravemarkers is a tie-in, is it justified in order to promote goodwill of customers who may be favorably impressed with neatness and aesthetic appearance of the cemetery?

3 Bank A (acquiring bank) proposed to acquire Bank T (target bank). The Bank Merger Act required the regulatory banking agency (FDIC) to evaluate the merger according to antitrust standards under Section 7 of the Clayton Act. The "line of commerce" (product market) was demand deposits. However, a dispute arose as to the "section of the country" (geographic market). The uncontradicted survey of Banks A and T showed that Bank A had 91 percent of its demand deposits in the southern half of Pike County and 6 percent in the northern half. Bank T had 95 percent of its demand deposits in the northern half and 3 percent in the southern half. There was strong competition from other banks in the northern half of Pike County. There was good freeway access to all parts of the county, but the evidence showed that small demand depositors tend to bank near their residences.

Banks A and T claimed that the northern and southern halves of the county were separate geographic markets. The FDIC ruled that all of Pike County was the geographic market and denied the merger as anticompetitive. FDIC also held that the merger should not be approved because if Bank A remained a separate entity in the southern half of Pike County, it would be an "actual potential entrant" into the northern half and would therefore have a procompetitive effect on the entire county. However, the evidence showed that it was not viable for Bank A to enter the northern half by establishing branches because of the strong competition already there. Banks A and T filed suit seeking to set aside the FDIC ruling. **(a)** What is the appropriate "geographic market"? **(b)** Should the FDIC ruling be set aside and the merger approved?

4 Brunswick manufactured large Mercury outboard motors which accounted for 26 percent of the American market that was concentrated in only four firms. It also sold Mercury motors throughout the world. Yamaha distributed outboard motors manufactured by Sanshin (both were Japanese corporations) throughout the world except the United States, where Yamaha distributed only motorcycles and snowmobiles. Brunswick and Yamaha signed a joint venture agreement whereby: (1) Yamaha sold to Brunswick half of the controlling stock of Sanshin, (2) Sanshin would manufacture Mariner, a new line of *small* outboard motors, selling all its output to Yamaha which authorized Brunswick as its exclusive distributor to sell Mariner motors in the United States, with Yamaha selling the rest of the output under its own brand name exclusively in Japan, (3) Brunswick was precluded from marketing Mariner in Japan, and Yamaha from doing so in America (except through Brunswick as its distributor), (4) Brunswick could market its large Mercury motors throughout the world, but Yamaha could not sell Mercury or Brunswick's other non-joint-venture products anywhere except in Japan, (5) Brunswick and Yamaha agreed to limit competition between themselves in Europe and South America, and not to attempt distribution through each other's dealers in those markets, and (6) Brunswick was barred from manufacturing any product competitive with those of Yamaha.

The FTC found that the joint venture violated Clayton Sections 7 and 5. It ordered the parties to rescind the agreement, whereupon Brunswick and Yamaha petitioned the Court of Appeals for review. FTC argued that first, the agreement eliminated Yamaha as a potential entrant that could reasonably be expected to compete in the highly concentrated American outboard market and that the agreement thus tended to substantially lessen competition in violation of Section 7; second, that items (4) through (6) above were forms of unfair competition that violated Section 5 of the Act. Did the merger violate either Sections 7 or 5, or both?

5 State Bank, based in Seattle, together with Seattle 1st Bank, were the two largest in Washington, holding 51 percent of the State's total deposits. State Bank proposed to acquire Trust Bank, based 280 miles to the east in Spokane (the relevant market). Trust Bank, with eight branches, had 19 percent of the deposits in Spokane, while the two other largest local banks held 74 percent of the deposits in that market. The Federal Reserve and Federal Deposit Insurance Corporation recommended against the merger because of the concentration in commercial banking in Washington as a whole, as well as in the Spokane market, and the United States sued to enjoin the merger as a violation of Section 7 of the Clayton Act. State law prohibited a state bank from establishing a *branch* in any city outside the city where its principal office is located. The trial court held that State Bank was not a potential entrant into the Spokane market because the law prohibited State Bank from opening a branch 280 miles from its main office in Seattle. The Court also found that State Bank's de novo entry into the Spokane market through acquisition of a small "toehold" bank in Spokane was economically unfeasible. The Government appealed to the Supreme Court, arguing that even though State Bank was not a potential entrant, the merger should be set aside solely on the ground that it would eliminate the prospect for long-term deconcentration of an oligopolistic market; that such deconcentration in theory might result if State Bank was forbidden to enter except through a de novo acquisition by merger of a small existing "toehold" bank in Spokane. Did the proposed bank merger violate Section 7 of the Clayton Act?

6 JLG, Inc. manufactured self-lifting work platforms. Burr, under a distributorship agreement in effect 1976 through 1978, purchased and resold JLG platforms. While this agreement was in effect, JLG in 1977 offered Burr a new distributorship agreement, the effect of which would be to sell platforms to Burr at less favorable prices than JLG was selling to other platform distributors who were competing with Burr. Burr refused to enter into the proposed new distributorship agreement, continued to purchase platforms under the existing agreement, and brought suit against JLG under Section 2(a) of the Robinson-Patman amendment to the Clayton Act, claiming price discrimination. JLG argued that since Burr never signed the proposed new contract or bought platforms under its terms, Burr cannot be one of at least two "purchasers" required by Robinson-Patman to constitute a price discrimination. Was JLG liable for unlawful price discrimination?

7 A&P, a grocery chain, asked its long-time supplier, Borden Co., to supply it with "private label" (as opposed to "brand label") milk. A&P refused Borden's initial offering price and solicited other offers from competitors, resulting in a lower offer from one of Borden's competitors. A&P told Borden that its offer "was not even in the ball park" and that a $50,000 reduction in its offer wouldn't be "a drop in the bucket." Borden then, in good faith, submitted a new offer lower than the competitor's offer, and A&P accepted. Borden did not know that its new offer was, in fact, lower than the competitor's offer.

The FTC charged A&P with misleading Borden by failing to inform it that its second offer was better than its competitor's offer, and thus with violating Section 2(f) of the Robinson-Patman Act by knowingly inducing or receiving price discrimination from Borden. A&P argued that it could not be liable for inducing discrimination because Borden's price, although below that charged to other customers, was cut in order to "meet competition," and since Borden could not be liable under Sections 2(a) and (b) for discrimination, A&P could not be liable under Section 2(f). The FTC contended that A&P is liable even though Borden had the "meeting competition" defense. Is A&P liable for knowingly inducing price discrimination?

8 Southern Motor Carriers Rate Conference, an association of motor common carriers that operated rate bureaus in four states on behalf of their members, submitted joint rate proposals to the public service commissions in each state for approval or rejection. A proposed rate became effective if each state took no action within a specified time. If a hearing was scheduled, a rate would become effective only after affirmative commission approval. The State Public Service Commissions in the four states thus exercised ultimate authority and control over all intrastate rates. This collective rate making was authorized, *but not compelled*, by the states in which the rate bureaus operated. Every common carrier was free to submit individual rate proposals to the Public Service Commissions. The United States filed suit to enjoin the rate bureau's activities as an unlawful conspiracy in violation of Section 1 of the Sherman Act. The rate bureaus argued that their conduct was exempt from the antitrust laws under the "state action" doctrine. The District Court's summary judgment for the Government was affirmed by the Court of Appeals, and the rate bureaus appealed to the Supreme Court. Were the rate-fixing activities of the motor carriers' rate bureaus exempt from the antitrust laws?

9 Trucking Unlimited, a group of highway carriers, commenced suit under Section 1 of the Sherman Act against Cal Motor Associates, a group of competing motor carriers. The complaint alleged that Cal Motor Associates instituted proceedings before California and federal courts as well as agencies regulating the trucking industry to resist and defeat applications by Trucking Unlimited to acquire operating rights or to transfer those rights. It was further claimed that Cal Motor Associates instituted actions without probable cause and regardless of the merits of the cases, in order to discourage and prevent Trucking Unlimited from having meaningful access to the administrative agencies and the courts, all for the purpose of putting Trucking Unlimited out of business and to monopolize the highway common carrier business. Cal Motor Associates claimed that under the *Noerr* doctrine, they had a First Amendment right to petition government through the courts and that, regardless of their purpose, they were immune from Sherman Act liability. Assuming Trucking Unlimited's claims are true, is Cal Motor Associates exempt from Sherman Act liability under the *Noerr* doctrine?

CHAPTER 47

Law of Labor and Employment

Law regulates every aspect of the employer-employee relationship. State and federal statutes, case law, and administrative agency regulations govern employment from its beginning to its termination, and even beyond, into retirement.

This chapter examines the employer-employee relationship and each of the major areas of employment regulation. They are: labor-management relations; equal employment opportunity; wages and hours; workers' compensation; occupational safety and health; and income security and retirement.

Employer-Employee Relationship

All state and federal labor laws apply to the employer-employee relationship. Therefore, a critical question concerning the applicability of any labor law is: Does the relationship of employer and employee exist or is the relationship that of employer and independent contractor? The distinction between the two kinds of relationships, discussed in Chapter 32, is sometimes difficult to draw. Nevertheless, employers must make the distinction correctly because if a person is an employee, the employer must comply with the employment laws discussed in this chapter. Whether a person is an employee or an independent contractor will be determined by the appropriate administrative agency or court at the time it considers whether the employer has failed to comply with a given employment law. Such agency or court will base its decision on the right-of-control test and other factors treated in Chapter 32.

Labor-Management Relations

By the mid-nineteenth century, employees in the United States had begun to unionize in an effort to overcome the superior power of employers and to improve wages and working conditions. Legislatures and courts were intent on protecting America's developing industry, however, and initially viewed unions with hostility. Courts first held union organizing to be a criminal conspiracy; later, they viewed activities such as strikes and picketing as civil wrongs for which unions must answer in damages. Federal courts in particular aided employers in their efforts to prevent unionizing by issuing injunctions to stop strikes and picketing and by enforcing "yellow dog" contracts in which employees promised not to join a labor union.

The Norris-LaGuardia Act

Concerned by the violence and lost productivity associated with growing industrial strife, Congress in 1932 enacted the Norris-LaGuardia Act.[1] The act declared a national policy of government neutrality toward employees' organizing efforts and restricted the circumstances in which federal courts could issue injunctions in labor disputes. It also prohibited federal courts from enforcing "yellow dog" contracts.

The National Labor Relations Act

By 1935, continued industrial conflict and economic disruption had convinced Congress of the need to go beyond neutrality. In the belief that collective action increases employees' bargaining power and produces compromise instead of conflict, Congress enacted the National Labor Relations Act.[2] The act, which is also called the Wagner Act after its chief sponsor, extends legal protection to employees' unionizing efforts and encourages their collective, rather than individual, action.

The Wagner Act's key provision, Section 7, guarantees employees the right "to form, join, or assist labor organizations, to bargain collectively through representatives of their own choosing, and to engage in other concerted activities for the purpose of collective bargaining or other mutual aid or protection..." Section 8 bolsters that guarantee by prohibiting certain employer "unfair labor practices." They include:

1 Interfering with workers' rights to organize as guaranteed in Section 7 [Section 8(a)(1)]; for example, it is an unfair labor practice for an employer to adopt a rule prohibiting

[1] 29 U.S.C. Sec. 101.
[2] 29 U.S.C. Sec. 151.

employees from soliciting union membership on employer property during nonworking hours.

2 Dominating an employee organization or contributing financial support to it [Section 8(a)(2)];
3 Discriminating against employees for the purpose of discouraging or encouraging union membership [Section 8(a)(3)];
4 Discriminating against employees who have given testimony or filed charges under the act [Section 8(a)(4)]; and
5 Refusing to bargain in good faith with employee representatives (ordinarily unions) [Section 8(a)(5)].

Section 9 sets out the procedures for employee selection of a bargaining representative. The Wagner Act also established a new administrative agency, the National Labor Relations Board (NLRB), to oversee the selection process, investigate charges of unfair labor practices, and prosecute where necessary. The NLRB has the authority to adjudicate charges and impose remedies such as cease-and-desist orders, reinstatement, and back pay, but must look to the federal courts of appeal to enforce its orders.

A continuing problem for the NLRB and the courts has been to determine when an employee's activity is "concerted," rather than individual, and therefore entitled to the protection of the Wagner Act. The following case is illustrative.

CASE 47.1 NLRB v. City Disposal Systems, Inc. · 104 S. Ct. 1505 (1984)

FACTS James Brown, a truck driver employed by defendant City Disposal Systems, Inc., was discharged when he refused to drive a truck that he honestly and reasonably believed to be unsafe because of faulty brakes. The collective bargaining agreement which his union had negotiated provided that defendant would not require employees to drive unsafe vehicles and the employees who refused to do so would not be in violation of the agreement unless their refusal was unjustified. Brown did not mention the collective bargaining agreement when he refused to drive a certain truck, was discharged, and filed an unfair labor practice charge with the NLRB.

The NLRB, applying the rule which it had established in the earlier case of *Interboro Contractors, Inc.* (1966), held that Brown's refusal constituted "concerted activity" protected by Section 7 and that his discharge was therefore an unfair labor practice under Section 8(a)(1) of the Act. It ordered Brown reinstated with back pay. The Court of Appeals, finding that Brown's action was taken solely on his own behalf and thus was not a concerted activity within Section 7, denied enforcement of the NLRB's order. The NLRB appealed to the Supreme Court.

OPINION BRENNAN, J. . . . The term "concerted activity" is not defined in the Act but it clearly enough embraces the activities of employees who have joined together in order to achieve common goals. . . . What we must elucidate is the precise manner in which particular actions of an individual employee must be linked to the actions of fellow employees in order to permit it to be said that the individual is engaged in concerted activity. . . .

Although one could interpret the phrase, "to engage in concerted activities," to refer to a situation in which two or more employees are working together at the same time and the same place toward a common goal, the language of Section 7 does not confine itself to such a narrow meaning. In fact, Section 7 itself defines both joining and assisting labor organizations—activities in which a single employee can engage—as concerted activities. . . .

The invocation of a right rooted in a collective-bargaining agreement is unquestionably an integral part of the process that gave rise to the agreement. That process—beginning with the organization of a union, continuing into the negotiation of a collective-bargaining agreement, and extending through the enforcement of the agreement—is a single, collective activity. Obviously, an employee could not invoke a right grounded in

CASE 47.1 Continued

a collective-bargaining agreement were it not for the prior negotiating activities of his fellow employees. Nor would it make sense for a union to negotiate a collective-bargaining agreement if individual employees could not invoke the rights thereby created against their employer. Moreover, when an employee invokes a right grounded in the collective-bargaining agreement, he does not stand alone. Instead, he brings to bear on his employer the power and resolve of all his fellow employees. When, for instance, James Brown refused to drive a truck he believed to be unsafe, he was in effect reminding his employer that he and his fellow employees, at the time their collective-bargaining agreement was signed, had extracted a promise from City Disposal that they would not be asked to drive unsafe trucks. He was also reminding his employer that if it persisted in ordering him to drive an unsafe truck, he could reharness the power of that group to ensure the enforcement of that promise. It was just as though James Brown was reassembling his fellow union members to reenact their decision not to drive unsafe trucks. A lone employee's invocation of a right grounded in his collective-bargaining agreement is, therefore, a concerted activity in a very real sense. . . .

JUDGMENT The NLRB's *Interboro* doctrine recognizes as concerted activity an individual employee's reasonable and honest invocation of a right provided for in his collective-bargaining agreement. We conclude that the doctrine constitutes a reasonable interpretation of the Act. Accordingly, we accept the Board's conclusion that James Brown was engaged in concerted activity when he refused to drive truck No. 244. We therefore reverse the judgment of the Court of Appeals and remand the case for further proceedings consistent with this opinion. . . .

The Taft-Hartley Act

Under the protection afforded by the Wagner Act, the balance of power between employers and employees began to shift in favor of unions. Moreover, the NLRB came under criticism as possessing too much authority and displaying an anti-employer bias. To curb union and NLRB excesses, Congress in 1947 enacted the Labor Management Relations Act,[3] or Taft-Hartley Act, which significantly amended the Wagner Act.

The Taft-Hartley Act did not take away any of the protection guaranteed unions by the Wagner Act; instead it added new protections for employers and for individual employees. One addition was a guarantee of free speech for employers which permits them to state their opinions freely and to campaign actively against union organizing of their employees. Section 7 was amended to provide employees the right to refrain from engaging in the activities enumerated in the section. The Taft-Hartley Act also amended Section 8 to establish union unfair labor practices. They include:

1 Restraining or coercing employees in the exercise of rights guaranteed in Section 7 [8(b)(1)(A)]; for example, it is an unfair labor practice for a union to intimidate nonstrikers who seek to enter a struck plant.
2 Discriminating against employees or causing employers to discriminate against employees for reasons other than nonpayment of dues [8(b)(2)]; for example, it is an unfair labor practice for a union to cause the discharge of an employee who offers to pay dues and fees of the union, but refuses to apply for membership or attend meetings.
3 Refusing to bargain in good faith with employers [8(b)(3)];
4 Engaging in secondary boycotts, that is, pressuring one employer to stop doing business with another employer with whom the union has a dispute [8(b)(4)];
5 Imposing excessive initiation fees [8(b)(5)];
6 Forcing an employer to pay for work not performed (featherbedding) [8(b)(6)]; and
7 Striking, picketing, or boycotting for an illegal purpose. Illegal purposes include forcing an employer to bargain with a union

[3] 29 U.S.C. Sec. 141.

other than the one which has been certified as the representative of his employees or forcing an employer to assign work to one union rather than another [8(b)(4) and 8(b)(7)].

The Taft-Hartley Act reduced the authority of the NLRB by empowering federal courts of appeals to review and overturn NLRB unfair labor practice decisions. It also separated the NLRB's prosecutorial and adjudicatory functions, which under the Wagner Act had been combined.

The Taft-Hartley Act created a Federal Mediation and Conciliation Service to assist employers and unions in voluntarily resolving disputes. It also established an 80-day "cooling-off period" to delay strikes which the President believes pose a danger to national safety or welfare.

The Landrum-Griffin Act

Congress further amended the Taft-Hartley Act by passing the Labor Management Reporting and Disclosure Act, (LMRDA), or Landrum-Griffin Act,[4] in 1959. The LMRDA intended to promote democracy and fairness in internal union affairs after Congressional hearings revealed serious corruption and abuses in labor union conduct. The act established a "bill of rights" for union members and imposed financial reporting and disclosure requirements upon unions and union officials. It also added new union unfair labor practices, including a prohibition on "hot cargo contracts," that is, agreements whereby employers promise not to handle, use, or deal in the goods of nonunion employers. Such contracts, although a type of secondary pressure, had not been precluded by the Taft-Hartley Act, which prevented unions from inducing *employees,* but not *employers,* to engage in secondary boycotts.

Coverage of the National Labor Relations Act and Amendments

The National Labor Relations Act and amendments ("the Acts") apply, with certain exceptions, to employers engaged in business affecting interstate commerce. Railroads and interstate airlines, which are governed by the Railway Labor Act,[5] are excluded, as are local, state, and federal government employers. The protection of the Acts extends to "employees" but employees are defined to exclude certain groups. Among them are: supervisors, independent contractors, agricultural laborers, and domestic servants.

[4] 29 U.S.C. Sec. 153.

[5] 45 U.S.C. Sec. 151.

Major Issues in Labor-Management Relations

Selection of a Bargaining Representative. The Acts' procedures for employee selection of a bargaining representative permit employers and employees to agree voluntarily upon representation. However, employers ordinarily resist union demands for recognition. In that event, upon a proper showing of employee interest (30 percent of affected employees), unions seeking to represent employees, or the employees themselves, petition the NLRB to conduct a secret ballot election. In such elections, employees may vote "no union," for a union, or may choose between unions if more than one is attempting to represent them.

The initial task for the NLRB when an election is requested is to determine the "appropriate bargaining unit," that is, the group of employees who will be allowed to vote and who will be represented by the union if one is elected. The NLRB then sets the date for an election and employers and unions have an opportunity to campaign. Both employers and unions must refrain from committing unfair labor practices in the course of the election campaign. The free speech guaranty of the Taft-Hartley Act generally permits free expression of opinions about unions so long as employers do not make a "threat of reprisal or force or promise of benefit" for the purpose of persuading workers to join or not join a union. Such pre-election interference with workers' free choice is an unfair labor practice under Section 8(a)(1). The NLRB also asserts authority to set aside elections, to order bargaining despite election results, or to mandate bargaining where there has been no election when it considers that unfair labor practices during the campaign have precluded a fair election.

The Duty to Bargain. If employees vote against a union, no new organizing effort can be initiated for at least a year. If employees select a union, the employer and union must then bargain in good faith over wages, hours, and working conditions. Good faith bargaining does not mean that the employer and union must agree; either party can resort to such economic weapons as strikes or lockout if their genuine efforts to reach agreement fail. Furthermore, the NLRB cannot impose an agreement upon the parties when their bargaining is unsuccessful.

The Acts require good faith bargaining over "wages, hours, and other terms and conditions of employment." Such matters, which are called "mandatory" subjects of bargaining, are extensive; they incorporate all forms of compensation and all working conditions which concern the employment relationship. Fringe benefits such as vacation pay and profit-sharing plans are mandatory subjects, for example, as are matters ranging from shift starting time to grievance procedures and work rules. To refuse to bargain or to make a unilateral decision concerning a mandatory subject is to commit a Section 8(a)(5) or 8(b)(3) unfair labor practice.

Other subjects are "permissive," that is, the parties may bargain about them but they need not. Either party can take unilateral action concerning such subjects and neither can resort to economic weapons to persuade the other respecting them. Matters which are not essentially related to employment, for example, those which are managerial or entrepreneurial in nature, are permissive subjects. As the following case illustrates, however, distinguishing between mandatory and permissive subjects remains one of the most crucial but difficult problems under the Acts.

CASE 47.2 First National Maintenance Corporation v. NLRB · 101 S. Ct. 2573 (1981)

FACTS First National Maintenance Corporation (plaintiff) engaged in the business of providing maintenance services for commercial customers. It had a contract to do maintenance for a nursing home. As a result of a dispute with the home over the size of its fee, plaintiff terminated the contract and discharged its employees. Upon learning of plaintiff's intention to discharge its employees, the union which represented them requested a delay for the purpose of bargaining, but plaintiff refused to bargain. The union then filed an unfair labor practice charge against plaintiff, alleging violation of its duty to bargain in good faith. The NLRB upheld the charge and ordered plaintiff to reinstate the employees if it reached an agreement to resume work at the nursing home, or to offer the employees equivalent jobs at other facilities if it did not. The Court of Appeals affirmed, and the employer appealed to the Supreme Court.

OPINION BLACKMUN, J. . . . Must an employer, under its duty to bargain in good faith "with respect to wages, hours, and other terms and conditions of employment," negotiate with the certified representative of its employees over its decision to close a part of its business? . . .

Although parties are free to bargain about any legal subject, Congress has limited the mandate or duty to bargain to matters of "wages, hours, and other terms and conditions of employment." . . . Congress deliberately left the words "wages, hours, and other terms and conditions of employment" without further definition, for it did not intend to deprive the Board of the power further to define those terms in light of specific industrial practices.

Nonetheless, in establishing what issues must be submitted to the process of bargaining, Congress had no expectation that the elected union representative would become an equal partner in the running of the business enterprise in which the union's members are employed. Despite the deliberate open-endedness of the statutory language, there is an undeniable limit to the subjects about which bargaining must take place. . . .

Some management decisions, such as choice of advertising and promotion, product type and design, and financing arrangements, have only an indirect and attenuated impact on the employment relationship between employer and employee. Other manage-

CASE 47.2 Continued

ment decisions, such as the order of succession of layoffs and recalls, production quotas and work rules are almost exclusively an aspect of the relationship between employer and employee. The present case concerns a third type of management decision, one that had a direct impact on employment, since jobs were inexorably eliminated by the termination, but had as its focus only the economic profitability of the contract with [the nursing home], a concern under these facts wholly apart from the employment relationship. This decision, involving a change in the scope and direction of the enterprise, is akin to the decision whether to be in business at all, "not in [itself] primarily about conditions of employment, though the effect of the decision may be necessarily to terminate employment." *Fibreboard Paper Products. v. NLRB,* 379 U.S. 488 (1964). At the same time, this decision touches on a matter of central and pressing concern to the union and its member employees: the possibility of continued employment and the retention of the employees' very jobs. . . .

A union's interest in participating in the decision to close a particular facility or part of an employer's operations springs from its legitimate concern over job security. . . . The union's practical purposes in participating, however, will be largely uniform: it will seek to delay or halt the closing. No doubt it will be impelled, in seeking these ends, to offer concessions, information, and alternatives that might be helpful to management or forestall or prevent the termination of jobs. It is unlikely, however, that requiring bargaining over the decision itself, as well as its effects, will augment this flow of information and suggestions.

Moreover, the union's legitimate interest in fair dealing is protected by Section 8(a)(3), which prohibits partial closings motivated by antiunion animus, when done to gain an unfair advantage. Under Section 8(a)(3) the Board may inquire into the motivations behind a partial closing. An employer may not simply shut down part of its business and mask its desire to weaken and circumvent the union by labeling its decision "purely economic."

Thus, although the union has a natural concern that a partial closing decision not be hastily or unnecessarily entered into, it has some control over the effects of the decision and indirectly may ensure that the decision itself is deliberately considered. It also has direct protection against a partial closing decision that is motivated by an intent to harm a union.

Management's interest in whether it should discuss a decision of this kind is much more complex and varies with the particular circumstances. If labor costs are an important factor in a failing operation and the decision to close, management will have an incentive to confer voluntarily with the union to seek concessions that may make continuing the business profitable. At other times, management may have great need for speed, flexibility, and secrecy in meeting business exigencies. It may face consequences that hinge on confidentiality, the timing of a plant closing, or a reorganization of the corporate structure. The publicity incident to the normal process of bargaining may injure the possibility of a successful transition or increase the economic damage to the business. The employer also may have no feasible alternative to the closing, and even good-faith bargaining over it may be both futile and cause the employer additional loss. . . .

We conclude that the harm likely to be done to an employer's need to operate freely in deciding whether to shut down part of its business purely for economic reasons outweighs the incremental benefit that might be gained through the union's participation in making the decision, and we hold that the decision itself is not part of Section 8(d)'s "terms and conditions," over which Congress has mandated bargaining.

JUDGMENT The judgment of the Court of Appeals, accordingly, is reversed and the case is remanded to the court for further proceedings consistent with this opinion.

Equal Employment Opportunity

Title VII

A major achievement of the civil rights movement of the 1950s and 1960s was passage of the federal Civil Rights Act of 1964. The act broadly prohibits discrimination on the basis of race, color, religion, sex or national origin in accommodation, education, and economic opportunity; Title VII of the act prohibits discrimination in employment.[6]

Title VII applies to all employers of fifteen or more employees whose business affects interstate commerce; to labor unions that have fifteen or more members or operate a hiring hall; and to employment agencies. As amended in 1972, it also covers state, federal, and local employees.

Congress created the Equal Employment Opportunity Commission (EEOC) to administer and enforce Title VII. Headed by a five-member group appointed by the President, the EEOC has the authority to issue binding regulations and nonbinding guidelines. It also investigates, conciliates, and prosecutes alleged violations of the act.

Although the EEOC may itself initiate investigations, most EEOC actions begin with the filing of a complaint by an individual who believes that he or she, or the group that he or she represents, has been illegally discriminated against. The EEOC conducts an investigation, and if it concludes that Title VII has been violated, attempts to conciliate the matter. If the case cannot be resolved, the EEOC may initiate a discrimination lawsuit in federal district court. Typically, however, it issues a "right to sue" letter to the complaining party, who is then free to pursue federal court action on his or her own.

Discrimination in "employment" encompasses far more than hiring; Title VII bars employers from discriminating on the enumerated bases with respect to compensation, job assignment, promotion, transfer, discharge, and any other "term, condition or privilege" of employment. Unions are prohibited from discriminating not only in membership but in grievance representation and in referral for employment and apprenticeship programs. Employment agencies cannot discriminate in making referrals, in interviewing, or in advertising.

Proof of Discrimination. Discrimination that violates Title VII consists of treating an employee or group of employees differently *because of* the employee's race, color, religion, sex, or national origin. It is not illegal discrimination to treat employees differently; to promote a white male over a white male is to discriminate between them but is not illegal because that discrimination is not prohibited by Title VII. Even to promote a white male over a black female does not violate Title VII unless the reason for the discrimination is a prohibited one such as the woman's race or sex.

Illegal discrimination may be established in either of two ways. "Disparate treatment" discrimination is proved when a plaintiff shows that he or she has been treated differently than a person not of his or her race, color, religion, sex, or national origin who is in similar circumstances. A black male who was terminated for excessive absences, for example, would establish "disparate treatment" if he showed that his employer did not terminate a white male who had a similar attendance and work record.

Because it is virtually impossible to prove the real motive for an employment decision, courts allow plaintiffs to prove disparate treatment discrimination indirectly. In a series of decisions beginning with *McDonnell Douglas Corp. v. Green,*[7] the Supreme Court articulated the requirements for indirect proof of disparate treatment. First the plaintiff must establish a prima facie case. To do that in a discharge case, for example, the plaintiff must show that he or she is a member of one of the groups protected by Title VII and that prior to discharge, he or she was capable of performing the job. Next, the defendant must offer a legitimate non-discriminatory reason for its actions. If it fails to do so, the plaintiff wins. If the defendant does provide such a reason, the plaintiff must prove that it was a pretext to mask an illegal motive.

The second theory of discrimination, "disparate impact," is used to show illegal discrimination in the imposition of a seemingly neutral job requirement or test that has a disproportionate effect on members of a particular group. For example, the requirement that an applicant for a job possess a

[6] 42 U.S.C. 2000(e).

[7] 411 U.S. 792 (1973).

minimum height or weight has been found to disproportionately exclude women and certain minorities from job opportunities. When such requirements are not really necessary to performance of the job in question, they violate Title VII. This principal of "job-relatedness" was first articulated by the Supreme Court in the landmark case, *Griggs v. Duke Power.*[8] The company in that case restricted employment in its higher-paying departments to persons holding high school diplomas. Plaintiffs, a group of black employees, proved that such a requirement had a disproportionately negative effect on blacks who, at that time in that area, were significantly less likely than whites to possess high school diplomas. The court held that the requirement was illegal because it was not related to the jobs in question nor required by business necessity. The Court stated:

> Nothing in the Act precludes the use of testing or measuring procedures; obviously they are useful. What Congress has forbidden is giving these devices and mechanisms controlling force unless they are demonstrably a reasonable measure of job performance. Congress has not commanded that the less qualified be preferred over the better qualified simply because of minority origins. Far from disparaging job qualifications as such, Congress has made such qualifications the controlling factor, so that race, religion, nationality, and sex become irrelevant. What Congress has commanded is that any tests used must measure the person for the job and not the person in the abstract.

Major Issues under Title VII. One of the most difficult issues under Title VII is "affirmative action programs," which give preference in employment decisions to women and minorities. Title VII's prohibition of discrimination is perfectly neutral; it protects whites as well as blacks, men as well as women. Nevertheless, Title VII clearly was enacted to correct historical inequities in the treatment of women and minorities, and affirmative action is considered to be a valuable tool for rectifying past wrongs. Courts have imposed affirmative action as a remedy for proven violations of Title VII, and many employers and unions also have instituted it voluntarily in order to head off discrimination lawsuits.

The conflict between Title VII's duty not to discriminate and affirmative actions' preferences for victims of past discrimination, which adversely affects white males, is evident, however. Although the courts have not as yet offered a resolution, they have addressed the problem in the so-called reverse discrimination cases. In *Regents of the University of California v. Bakke,*[9] a white male sued for race discrimination under the Equal Protection Clause when the University of California medical school rejected his application for admission but accepted sixteen blacks whose credentials were inferior to his. The Supreme Court held that quota systems that make race the *sole* criterion for a preference are illegal in the absence of a finding of past discrimination but that race may be considered in a university's admissions process. *United Steelworkers of America v. Weber*[10] involved a provision of the collective bargaining agreement between the Steelworkers and Kaiser Aluminum & Chemical Corporation, which reserved 50 percent of the openings in Kaiser's training programs for blacks. Brian Weber, a white male employee, sued under Title VII for reverse discrimination when less senior blacks were accepted ahead of him into a training program. The Supreme Court held that while Title VII forbids the federal government from *requiring* preferential treatment, it does not prohibit voluntary affirmative action to abolish traditional patterns of race discrimination. Although the Court declined to draw the line between permissible and impermissible affirmative action, it indicated that Kaiser's plan was acceptable because it was voluntary, temporary, and did not abrogate preexisting rights or create an absolute bar to advancement of whites. In *Firefighters Local Union No. 1784 v. Stotts,*[11] however, the Supreme Court did establish a clear limit on affirmative action when it held that a district court could not order a city to depart from its seniority system in a layoff in order to preserve the positions of blacks recently hired pursuant to an affirmative action plan. The plan had been voluntarily entered into by the city and did not contain a provision for overriding white employees' seniority. The district court did not have the power under the mantle of "affirmative action" to invent such an override, the Court ruled. At present, then, it is clear from the cases that voluntary affirmative action in some form is legally permissible but that

[8] 401 U.S. 424 (1971).

[9] 438 U.S. 265 (1978).
[10] 433 U.S. 193 (1979).
[11] 467 U.S. 561 (1984).

given the conflict between affirmative action and nondiscrimination, courts will continue to establish and enforce limits on the use of the doctrine. The Supreme Court provided significant guidance to legal affirmative action in 1987. In *Johnson v. Transportation Agency, Santa Clara County,*[12] the Court held that a county agency did not violate Title VII by taking a female's sex into account and promoting her over a male employee with a higher test score. This was because the decision was made pursuant to an affirmative action plan directing that sex or race be considered as a factor for purposes of remedying underrepresentation of women and minorities in traditionally segregated job categories and because the plan did not necessarily eliminate the rights of male employees. In validating the county's decision and plan, the Court indicated that an employer need not prove actual prior discrimination but only conspicuous imbalance in a traditionally segregated job category in order to establish a legal affirmative action plan. It also signalled that affirmative action in the form of a moderate case-by- case approach to effect gradual improvement is fully consistent with Title VII.

In *U.S. v. Paradise,*[13] the Court ratified an affirmative action plan fashioned by a district court that required 50 percent of promotions of new state trooper corporals to be awarded to blacks until approximately 25 percent of the corporal rank was composed of blacks. The plan was challenged as a violation of the Fourteenth Amendment equal protection clause, but the Court held that plan was justified by the compelling governmental interest in eradicating discriminatory exclusion of blacks and was narrowly tailored to serve that purpose. Thus, even quantified goals may be appropriate in some circumstances. Given the conflict between affirmative action and nondiscrimination, it is certain that courts will continue to consider the limits on appropriate affirmative action. Nevertheless, it is clear that voluntary affirmative action in some form is legally permissible and that the doctrine represents a permanent feature of American discrimination law.

Religious discrimination is another special problem arising under Title VII. The act prohibits discrimination because of religion but, often, to treat all employees alike is to discriminate against persons whose religious beliefs require out-of-the-ordinary considerations. Problems often arise, for example, for persons whose religion forbids work after sundown on Friday, when work is scheduled on a Saturday. The courts have resolved this problem by requiring "accommodation" of religious beliefs, which means that employers must make a reasonable effort to work around an employee's religious requirements. In *Trans World Airlines, Inc. v. Hardison,*[14] however, the Supreme Court held that employers need not make accommodation which contravenes a collective bargaining agreement or requires more than a minimal expense.

Pregnancy has also raised a special issue under Title VII. In *General Electric v. Gilbert,*[15] a group of women employees sued their employer for sex discrimination because the company's disability plan excluded from coverage disability related to pregnancy while covering all other disabilities. The Supreme Court held that the plan merely excluded one type of physical condition and did not discriminate because of sex. Congress reacted by passing the Pregnancy Discrimination Act as a new section of Title VII. The act provides that "the terms 'because of sex' or 'on the basis of sex' include but are not limited to, because of or on the basis of pregnancy, childbirth, or related medical conditions; and women affected by pregnancy, childbirth, or related medical conditions shall be treated the same for all employment related purposes... as other persons not so affected...." Accordingly, employer programs such as disability or leave plans that treat pregnancy differently from other conditions violate Title VII. Subsequent to passage of the act, the Supreme Court held in *Newport News Shipbuilding & Dry Dock Co. v. EEOC*[16] that an employer's health plan which provided less extensive pregnancy-related hospitalization benefits for spouses of male employees than for female employees discriminated against male employees in violation of Title VII.

Another issue raised by Title VII is sexual harassment, which is defined by the EEOC as any unwelcome sexual conduct that "has the purpose or effect of unreasonably interfering with an individual's work performance or creating an intimidating, hostile, or offensive work environment." Such harass-

[12] 107 S. Ct. 1442 (1987).
[13] 107 S. Ct. 1053 (1987).

[14] 432 U.S. 63 (1977).
[15] 429 U.S. 125 (1979).
[16] 462 U.S. 669 (1983).

ment is now held by courts to constitute illegal sex discrimination. Liability usually arises when a supervisor or other agent of an employer makes advances or demands for sexual favors in return for job benefits.

As the Supreme Court held in the first sexual harassment case to come before it, however, sexual harassment in violation of Title VII also can occur when harassment creates a hostile or abusive work environment.

CASE 47.3 Meritor Savings Bank v. Vinson · 106 S. Ct. 2399 (1986)

FACTS Mechelle Vinson, a female employee of Meritor Savings Bank was allegedly subjected to sexual harassment by Sidney Taylor, her male supervisor. Vinson claimed that Taylor subjected her to sexual demands to which she allegedly submitted out of fear she would lose her job. After she was terminated for unrelated reasons, Vinson sued both Taylor and the bank, claiming that her supervisor's conduct violated Title VII. The District Court ruled in favor of the supervisor and the bank, holding (1) that the employee had not made out a case of sexual discrimination because any relationship that might have existed had been voluntary and had never been made a condition of the employee's continued employment or advancement and (2) that the bank could not be held liable for the supervisor's alleged actions because it had not received any notice about his supposed offensive conduct. The Court of Appeals for the D.C. Circuit reversed and remanded, holding that an infringement of Title VII is not necessarily dependent upon the victim's loss of employment or promotion, that the voluntariness of the alleged sexual relationship was immaterial, and that an employer is liable for sexual harassment of a subordinate by a supervisor regardless of whether the employer knew or should have known about the harassment.

OPINION REHNQUIST, J.... Plaintiff argues, and the Court of Appeals held, that unwelcome sexual advances that create an offensive or hostile working environment violate Title VII.... Defendant contends instead that in prohibiting discrimination with respect to "compensation, terms, conditions, or privileges" of employment, Congress was concerned with what defendant describes as "tangible loss" of "an economic character," not "purely psychological aspects of the workplace environment."...

We reject defendant's view. First, the language of Title VII is not limited to "economic" or "tangible" discrimination. The phrase "terms, conditions or privileges of employment" evinces a congressional attempt to "'strike at the entire spectrum of disparate treatment of men and women'" in employment....

Second, in 1980 the EEOC issued guidelines specifying that "sexual harassment," as there defined, is a form of sex discrimination prohibited by Title VII.... Relevant to the charges at issue in this case, the guidelines provide that sexual misconduct constitutes prohibited "sexual harassment," whether or not it is directly linked to the grant or denial of an economic quid pro quo, where "such conduct has the purpose or effect of unreasonably interfering with an individual's work performance or creating an intimidating, hostile, or offensive working environment."

In concluding that so called "hostile environment" (i.e., non quid pro quo) harassment violates Title VII, the EEOC drew upon a substantial body of judicial decisions and EEOC precedent holding that Title VII affords employees the right to work in an environment free from discriminatory intimidation, ridicule and insult....

Since the guidelines were issued, courts have uniformly held, and we agree, that a plaintiff may establish a violation of Title VII by proving that discrimination based on sex has created a hostile or abusive work environment....

CASE 47.3 Continued

[The] District Court's conclusion that no actionable harassment occurred might have rested on its earlier "finding" that "[i]f [plaintiff] and Taylor did engage in an intimate or sexual relationship . . . , that relationship was a voluntary one." But the fact that sex-related conduct was "voluntary," in the sense that complainant was not forced to participate against her will, is not a defense to a sexual harassment suit brought under Title VII. The gravamen of any sexual harassment claim is that the alleged sexual advances were "unwelcome." While the question whether particular conduct was indeed unwelcome presents difficult problems of proof and turns largely on credibility determinations committed to the trier of fact, the District Court in this case erroneously focused on the "voluntariness" of respondent's participation in the claimed sexual episodes. The correct inquiry is whether respondent by her conduct indicated that the alleged sexual advances were unwelcome, not whether her actual participation in sexual intercourse was voluntary. . . .

Although the District Court concluded that plaintiff had not proved a violation of Title VII, it nevertheless went on to consider the question of the bank's liability. Finding that "the bank was without notice" of Taylor's alleged conduct, and that notice to Taylor was not the equivalent of notice to the bank, the court concluded that the bank therefore could not be held liable for Taylor's alleged actions. The Court of Appeals took the opposite view, holding that an employer is strictly liable for a hostile environment created by a supervisor's sexual advances, even though the employer neither knew nor reasonably could have known of the alleged misconduct. The court held that the supervisor, whether or not he possesses the authority to hire, fire, or promote, is necessarily an "agent" of his employer for all Title VII purposes, since "even the appearance" of such authority may enable him to impose on his subordinates. . . .

This debate over the appropriate standard for employer liability has a rather abstract quality about it given the state of the record in this case. We do not know at this stage whether Taylor made any sexual advances toward respondent at all, let alone whether those advances were unwelcome, whether they were sufficiently pervasive to constitute a condition of employment, or whether they were "so pervasive and so long continuing . . . that the employer must have become conscious of [them]."

We therefore decline the parties' invitation to issue a definitive rule on employer liability, but we do agree with the EEOC that Congress wanted courts to look to agency principles for guidance in this area. While such common-law principles may not be transferable in all their particulars to Title VII, Congress' decision to define "employer" to include any "agent" of an employer, surely evinces an intent to place some limits on the acts of employees for which employers under Title VII are to be held responsible. For this reason, we hold the Court of Appeals erred in concluding that employers are always automatically liable for sexual harassment by their supervisors. For the same reason, absence of notice to an employer does not necessarily insulate that employer from liability. . . .

In sum, we hold that a claim of "hostile environment" sex discrimination is actionable under Title VII, [and] that the District Court's findings were insufficient to dispose of respondent's hostile environment claim. . . . As to employer liability, we conclude that the Court of Appeals was wrong to entirely disregard agency principles and impose absolute liability on employers for the acts of their supervisors, regardless of the circumstances of a particular case.

JUDGMENT Accordingly, the judgment of the Court of Appeals reversing the judgment of the District Court is affirmed, and the case is remanded for further proceedings consistent with this opinion.

Other Sources of Employment Discrimination Law

Although Title VII of the 1964 Civil Rights Act is the principal equal employment opportunity law, the duty not to discriminate arises from other sources as well.

Age Discrimination in Employment Act. In 1967, Congress passed the Age Discrimination in Employment Act,[17] which protects employees over the ages of 40 from discrimination on the basis of age. Administered by the EEOC, the act applies to employers, unions, and employment agencies. It covers the same job decisions and is proved in essentially the same way as discrimination under Title VII.

Equal Pay Act. The Equal Pay Act of 1963[18] addresses only the narrow issue of discrimination in compensation because of sex. It was enacted to end the common practice of paying women less than men working the same jobs and mandates "equal pay for equal work" regardless of sex. "Equal" means "substantially equal," not identical. Equal work means work requiring substantially similar "skill, effort, and responsibility" that is performed under similar working conditions. Thus, under the act, male and female flight attendants must be paid the same (with certain permissible differences for non-sex-related factors such as seniority or merit) but male truck drivers and female secretaries need not be. The Equal Pay Act is enforced by the EEOC, and violations of the act are also a type of sex discrimination actionable under Title VII. Plaintiffs sometimes prefer to bring Equal Pay Act claims, however, because, among other reasons, the statute of limitations is longer on Equal Pay Act claims, the claimant need not go through administrative procedures but may go directly to court, and the Equal Pay Act allows recovery of back wages plus an equal amount as a penalty.

The Equal Pay Act does not require "equal pay for *comparable* work." This "pay equity" or "comparable worth" theory, which has attracted considerable attention, holds that certain jobs have traditionally been underpaid because they have been held largely by women. Advocates of comparable worth payment argue that to continue to pay such positions less than jobs that are different (and thus not addressed by the Equal Pay Act) but that require no more skill, effort, or responsibility than less well-paid "women's jobs" is to commit illegal sex discrimination. The Supreme Court has not yet resolved the question. In *County of Washington v. Gunther,*[19] however, the Court at least opened the door to the comparable worth theory by holding that sex discrimination claims under Title VII are not limited to those recognized by the Equal Pay Act, and that sex discrimination in compensation could exist even where the jobs being compared are not substantially equal as required by the Equal Pay Act.

Federal Contractors' Legislation. Other acts impose equal employment obligations on federal contracts, that is, persons or companies having contracts to supply goods and services to the federal government. Executive Order 11246 requires contractors and subcontractors to refrain from discrimination and also to take affirmative action to advance women and minorities. The Rehabilitation Act of 1973, as amended, prohibits discrimination against handicapped individuals by federal agencies and contractors and requires affirmative action to advance such persons in employment.

State Laws. Many states have enacted employment discrimination laws similar to federal laws. Some state laws are even more stringent; California, for example, prohibits discrimination not only on the bases enumerated in Title VII, but also on the bases of marital status, physical handicap, medical condition, and age over 40 (i.e., with no upper limit). In states that have an enforcement agency similar to the EEOC, the EEOC will ordinarily "defer," that is, permit the state agency to conduct the investigation and conciliation effort. If the state does not do so in a timely fashion, the EEOC will assert jurisdiction or issue a "right to sue" letter to the complaining party.

A major issue arising recently under the Rehabilitation Act of 1973 and state laws prohibiting discrimination on the basis of handicap is whether or not Acquired Immune Deficiency Syndrome (AIDS) is a protected handicap. Thus far, a number of antidiscrimination agencies have

[17]29 U.S.C. Sec. 621.
[18]29 U.S.C. Sec. 49.

[19]452 U.S. 161 (1981).

formally declared that AIDS-based discrimination violates their state handicap discrimination statutes. While cases specifically addressing the question of AIDS discrimination have been working their way through the courts, the Supreme Court essentially settled the issue in the following case which involved tuberculosis rather than AIDS.

CASE 47.4 School Board of Nassau County v. Arline · 107 S. Ct. 1123 (1987)

FACTS Gene Arline, an elementary schoolteacher who had contracted and recovered from tuberculosis 20 years earlier suffered a series of relapses and was discharged solely because of her disease. She filed an action against her employer, the school board, in federal District Court alleging that her susceptibility to tuberculosis made her a "handicapped individual" entitled to the protection of Section 504 of the Rehabilitation Act of 1973, which prohibits discrimination against an "otherwise qualified handicapped individual" in federally funded programs. She alleged that because the risk that she would infect her students was minimal, she was "otherwise qualified" for her job and the board's action violated Section 504. The District Court ruled in favor of the school board, holding that a contagious disease such as tuberculosis is not a "handicap" within the meaning of the Rehabilitation Act. The Eleventh Circuit Court of Appeals, however, held that persons with contagious diseases are within the coverage of Section 504 and accordingly reversed the judgment of the District Court and remanded for further proceedings as to whether the risk of transmitting the infection to others precluded the teacher from being "otherwise qualified for her job."

OPINION BRENNAN, J. . . . In enacting and amending the Act, Congress enlisted all programs receiving federal funds in an effort "to share with handicapped Americans the opportunities for an education, transportation, housing, health care, and jobs that other Americans take for granted." To that end, Congress not only increased federal support for vocational rehabilitation, but also addressed the broader problem of discrimination against the handicapped by including Section 504, an antidiscrimination provision patterned after Title VII of the Civil Rights Act of 1964. . . .

To combat the effect of erroneous but nevertheless prevalent perceptions about the handicapped, Congress expanded the definition of "handicapped individual" so as to preclude discrimination against "[a] person who has a record of or is regarded as having, an impairment [but who] may at present have no actual incapacity at all." . . .

Allowing discrimination based on the contagious effects of a physical impairment would be inconsistent with the basic purpose of Section 504, which is to ensure that handicapped individuals are not denied jobs or other benefits because of the prejudiced attitudes or the ignorance of others. By amending the definition of "handicapped individual" to include not only those who are actually physically impaired, but also those who are regarded as impaired and who, as a result, are substantially limited in a major life activity, Congress acknowledged that society's accumulated myths and fears about disability and disease are as handicapping as are the physical limitations that flow from actual impairment. Few aspects of handicap give rise to the same level of public fear and misapprehension as contagiousness. Even those who suffer or have recovered from such noninfectious diseases as epilepsy or cancer have faced discrimination based on the irrational fear that they might be contagious. The Act is carefully structured to replace such reflexive reactions to actual or perceived handicaps with actions based on reasoned and medically sound judgments: the definition of "handicapped individual" is broad, but only those individuals who are both handicapped *and* otherwise qualified are eligible for relief. The fact that *some* persons who have contagious diseases may pose a serious health threat to others under certain circumstances does not justify excluding from the coverage of the Act *all* persons with actual or perceived contagious diseases. Such exclusion would mean

CASE 47.4 Continued

that those accused of being contagious would never have the opportunity to have their condition evaluated in light of medical evidence and a determination made as to whether they were "otherwise qualified." Rather, they would be vulnerable to discrimination on the basis of mythology—precisely the type of injury Congress sought to prevent. We conclude that the fact that a person with a record of a physical impairment that is also contagious does not suffice to remove that person from coverage under Section 504.

The remaining question is whether Arline is otherwise qualified for the job of elementary schoolteacher. To answer this question in most cases, the District Court will need to conduct an individualized inquiry and make appropriate findings of fact. Such an inquiry is essential if Section 504 is to achieve its goal of protecting handicapped individuals from deprivations based on prejudice, stereotypes, or unfounded fear, while giving appropriate weight to such legitimate concerns as avoiding exposing others to significant health and safety risks....

Because of the paucity of factual findings by the District Court, we, like the Court of Appeals, are unable at this stage of the proceedings to resolve whether Arline is "otherwise qualified" for her job. The District Court made no findings as to the duration and severity of Arline's condition, nor as to the probability that she would transmit the disease. Nor did the court determine whether Arline was contagious at the time she was discharged, or whether the school board could have reasonably accommodated her. Accordingly, the resolution of whether Arline was otherwise qualified requires further findings of fact.

We hold that a person suffering from the contagious disease of tuberculosis can be a handicapped person within the meaning of Section 504 of the Rehabilitation Act of 1973, and that respondent Arline is such a person. We remand the case to the District Court to determine whether Arline is otherwise qualified for her position.

JUDGMENT The judgment of the Court of Appeals is affirmed.

Wage and Hour Laws

In addition to union-management relations and equal employment opportunity, state and federal laws regulate employees' wages, hours, and working conditions.

Fair Labor Standards Act

The basic federal law, the Fair Labor Standards Act of 1938 (FLSA),[20] establishes a federal minimum wage, mandates extra pay for overtime work, and regulates the employment of children. It applies to all employers whose business affects interstate commerce, but it exempts certain employees from its minimum wage and overtime provisions. These include executive, administrative, and professional employees, outside salespersons, and the employees of certain small retail establishments and farms. State and local employees are in most cases exempt from the act.

Congress periodically adjusts the minimum wage rate, which was fixed at $3.35 per hour as of 1987. Employers must pay employees at least that amount per hour for the 40 hours in a workweek. Overtime hours, that is, hours in excess of 40 per week, must be compensated at 1½ times the employee's regular rate of pay, whether that rate is minimum wage or higher. In the calculation of hours worked, employers must include all hours "suffered or permitted to be worked," not just those formally scheduled.

The child labor provisions of the FLSA are designed to protect minors from dangerous or unduly rigorous working conditions and to ensure that they have an opportunity to pursue their education. The act, with certain limited exceptions, altogether prohibits the employment of children under the age of 14 and forbids the employment of children under 18 in hazardous occupations.

The FLSA is enforced by the Department of Labor. Employers who violate the minimum wage and

[20] 29 U.S.C. Sec. 201.

overtime provisions of the act must pay injured employees all back wages due, with an additional, equal, sum as liquidated damages. Willful violations of any of the act's provisions are punishable by fines and even imprisonment. The following case, which resulted in a $10 million judgment, one of the highest ever obtained under the FLSA, illustrates a number of violations of the act.

CASE 47.5 Donovan v. Hudson Stations, Inc. · 26 WH Cases 795 (D.C. Kans. 1983)

FACTS Plaintiff Secretary of Labor sued Hudson Stations, Inc., and related corporate entities (defendants) to enjoin them from violating the minimum wage, overtime, and record-keeping provisions of the FLSA and to recover back wages and liquidated damages due as a result of such violations. Defendants operated approximately 260 gasoline stations in thirty-five states. The majority of defendants' stations had two shifts per day; the station manager worked the morning shift, and the attendant worked the afternoon shift. Managers were required to perform certain duties, such as verifying pump readings, setting out equipment, and counting cash before they began their shift. They were expected to count inventory, prepare bank deposits, and perform similar duties at the end of each shift and were expected to compile weekly price surveys and make bank deposits on their day off. Managers were paid by salary until a certain date after which they were converted to hourly workers. Once they began to be paid by the hour, they were paid for an additional one-half hour per day for postshift activities, but their other activities were never compensated.

Attendants were also required to perform duties before and after their shifts. They received an additional 15 minutes pay per day, but evidence revealed that it took longer than 15 minutes to do the required tasks. In addition, attendants were required to pay out of their own pockets or paychecks any cash shortages that occurred during their shifts. Shortages occurred as a result of improper change making, "drive-offs," and uncollectable checks and credit card charges.

The defendant kept no records of shortages paid by attendants nor of the actual time worked by managers and attendants before and after shifts. In investigating the case, the Department of Labor mailed out thousands of questionnaires to current and former employees and conducted over 500 depositions of those who responded to the questionnaire. Data obtained from the depositions were used to calculate weighted and unweighted averages for amounts of shortages collected from attendants and for time off the clock worked by both attendants and managers and to create a formula for determining the amount of back pay owed each employee. The Department of Labor assessed back pay and liquidated damages in the amount of $10 million, and defendants appealed.

The court held, among other things, that:

1. Defendants' requirement that employees repay shortages was unlawful and violated FLSA since it reduced some employees' pay below the minimum wage and resulted in failure to pay overtime at the required rate for others;
2. Defendants' failure to pay managers and attendants for work performed before and after shifts violated the act by not compensating them for all hours worked and resulting in compensation below the minimum wage for some employees and failure to pay overtime for others;
3. Defendants violated the record-keeping provisions of the act by failing to record deductions from employees' pay and hours worked; and
4. The Department of Labor's formula for determining the amount owed was appropriate.

OPINION O'CONNER, C. J. . . . We further hold that defendants' actions in violation of the Act were committed knowingly, not merely negligently or accidentally, with at least a general

CASE 47.5 Continued

awareness of the requirements of the law. We are not persuaded by defendants' argument that they were in good faith trying to comply with the provisions of the Act. Willfulness for purposes of the Act does not mean that the employer must know his conduct violates the Act. The employer must merely be aware that the Act is "in the picture" so that they are aware of the possible application of the Act to their employees. The defendants were no strangers to Fair Labor Standards Act violations if for no other reason because of previous injunctions issued against them. Knowing the risk involved, the defendants continued the same illegal practices. Their acts were willful. . . .

JUDGMENT It follows, that in addition to back wages, each present and former employee is entitled to liquidated damages in an amount equal to the amount calculated to be due him or her in accordance with the formula suggested by plaintiff. . . .

Other Wage and Hour Laws

Several other laws regulate the wages, hours, and working conditions of employees engaged in government projects. The Davis-Bacon Act[21] requires the payment of "prevailing wages," that is, wages equivalent to those paid under local collective bargaining agreements, to employees engaged in federally financed construction projects. The Walsh-Healy Government Contracts Act[22] and the Service Contract Act[23] extend similar provisions to the employees of employers contracting to furnish goods and services to the federal government.

Many states have also enacted wage and hour laws. Though in the main quite similar to federal laws, they sometimes cover additional groups such as state and local employees or impose more stringent requirements such as overtime pay for hours worked in excess of 8 per day.

Workers' Compensation

Before enactment of workers' compensation laws, employees who were injured in the workplace or who contracted job-related diseases received no monetary compensation unless they could establish their employer's negligence. Negligence was often difficult to prove, however, and lawsuits were expensive.

To rectify these problems, the states passed workers' compensation laws. The laws reimburse employees for losses sustained because of work-related injury or disease regardless of who, if anyone, was at fault. Such losses include the costs of medical care, lost income, and rehabilitation expenses. The laws also provide for continuing benefit payments to the spouses and children of workers who die from occupational disease or injury.

Workers' compensation laws apply to virtually all industrial and service employees as well as state and local government employees. The major exclusions from coverage are of agricultural, domestic, and casual employees who may be working for more than one employer or whose work is sporadic.

The expense of workers' compensation is borne by employers, who ordinarily meet their obligation through purchase of insurance from private carriers. A handful of states, however, require employers to participate in a state-administered insurance fund that apportions costs based on claim experience. Almost all states also allow employers to "self-insure," that is, to establish according to state regulations a reserve fund from which claims are paid. Ordinarily, however, only large employers with many employees can afford to elect this method.

Occupational Safety and Health

Unlike workers' compensation statutes, which are designed to reimburse employees once workplace inju-

[21] 40 U.S.C. Sec. 276(a).
[22] 41 U.S.C. Sec. 35.
[23] 41 U.S.C. Sec. 35.

ries have occurred, safety and health laws are intended to prevent injuries and promote job safety. The basic federal legislation is the Occupational Safety and Health Act (better known as OSHA), which Congress enacted in 1970. OSHA's coverage is broad: It applies to virtually all private sector employees with the exception of atomic energy workers and employees of very small agricultural enterprises. It does not apply to state and local government employees, however, nor to employees already regulated by specialized safety laws such as the Maritime Safety Act or the Coal Mine Safety Act.

OSHA takes a comprehensive approach to workplace safety. It mandates the development of detailed health and safety standards by the Occupational Safety and Health Administration (also known as OSHA) of the Department of Labor. OSHA is authorized to enforce such standards through complaint, inspection, and investigation procedures. The act also established the National Institute for Occupational Safety and Health, which conducts research, makes recommendations for development of standards, and provides education and training in the safety field. Finally, the act encourages states to develop their own standards; when the Department of Labor approves a state safety and health plan, it relinquishes its jurisdiction to the state.

OSHA places employers under the general duty to provide a workplace free from "recognized hazards" that are causing or may cause death or serious physical harm. Recognized hazards include, for example, undue exposure to toxic substances or inoperable safety equipment. Employers must also conform to specific standards, such as those relating to workplace air quality and noise levels. In addition, they must keep detailed records of job-related injuries, post annual summaries of the records, and report serious accidents to OSHA.

Acting on complaints by employees or on its own initiative, OSHA may conduct unannounced workplace inspections to determine compliance with the requirements of the act. In *Marshall v. Barlow's, Inc.*,[24] the Supreme Court held that a search warrant is required for such inspections if the employer demands it. The proof required to obtain such a warrant, however, is mere "reasonable basis" for inspection of a particular workplace. Employee complaints or a high employer or industry accident rate, among other things, constitute "reasonable basis."

If the investigation reveals violations, the inspector will direct immediate correction of those conditions which can be corrected easily. For other violations, OSHA will issue a citation that states the nature of the violation and fixes a date by which it must be corrected. OSHA may assess penalties up to $1,000 for each violation. Whether or not penalties will be assessed, and their amount, is determined by such factors as the seriousness of the violation, the size of the enterprise, the employer's good faith, and its record of violations. Penalties as high as $10,000 can be assessed for repeated or willful violations. Employers are able to contest both citations and penalties, first to an administrative law judge and then to the Occupational Safety and Health Review Commission. If the employer remains dissatisfied with the outcome, it can seek review by a federal circuit court of appeals.

The act also imposes responsibilities upon employees, who can be discharged for failure to comply with OSHA standards. OSHA protects employees' rights as well: Employees may not be discharged or discriminated against for filing a complaint, testifying, or exercising any other right under the act. Employees also have the right, under an OSHA regulation, to refuse to perform a task they reasonably believe to pose a serious risk of injury or death. The regulation's validity was established in the following case.

[24]See Chapter 44, Case 44.2.

CASE 47.6 Whirlpool Corp. v. Marshall · 445 U.S. 1 (1980)

FACTS The Secretary of Labor promulgated a regulation that employees have the right under OSHA to refuse to perform assigned tasks where they have a reasonable fear of death or serious injury and a belief that no less drastic alternative is available. Two employees of

CASE 47.6 Continued

defendant Whirlpool Corporation refused to comply with their foreman's order to climb out on a mesh screen (through which an employee previously had fallen to his death) to retrieve objects which had fallen there. They were ordered to punch out immediately, their pay for the remainder of the day was docked, and reprimands were placed in their personnel files. The Secretary of Labor brought suit against Whirlpool claiming that its actions toward the two employees constituted discrimination in violation of the act. Both the District Court and the Court of Appeals found the employees' acts to be justified under the regulation, but the District Court concluded that the regulation was invalid. The Court of Appeals reversed and remanded, but Whirlpool appealed to the Supreme Court.

OPINION STEWART, J. . . . The question before us is whether this interpretative regulation constitutes a permissible gloss on the Act by the Secretary, in light of the Act's language, structure, and legislative history. Our inquiry is informed by an awareness that the regulation is entitled to deference unless it can be said not to be a reasoned and supportable interpretation of the Act.

To accomplish [its] basic purpose, the legislation's remedial orientation is prophylactic in nature. The Act does not wait for an employee to die or become injured. It authorizes the promulgation of health and safety standards and the issuance of citations in the hope that these will act to prevent deaths or injuries from ever occurring. . . .

Moreover, the Secretary's regulation can be viewed as an appropriate aid to the full effectuation of the Act's "general duty" clause. The clause provides that "[e]ach employer . . . shall furnish to each of his employees employment and a place of employment which are free from recognized hazards that are causing or are likely to cause death or serious physical harm to his employees." As the legislative history of this provision reflects, it was intended itself to deter the occurrence of occupational deaths and serious injuries by placing on employers a mandatory obligation independent of the specific health and safety standards to be promulgated by the Secretary. Since OSHA inspectors cannot be present around the clock in every workplace, the Secretary's regulation ensures that employees will in all circumstances enjoy the rights afforded them by the "general duty" clause.

The regulation thus on its face appears to further the overriding purpose of the Act and rationally to complement its remedial scheme. . . .

JUDGMENT Accordingly, the judgment of the Court of Appeals is affirmed.

Income Security and Retirement

Social Security

During the Great Depression, Congress enacted the Social Security Act of 1935 in an effort to relieve the financial insecurity of retired and unemployed workers. Subsequent legislation created programs for disabled employees and added benefits for the families of retired, disabled, and deceased workers.

Old Age, Survivors, and Disability Insurance

One component of the current social security package is the Old Age, Survivors and Disability Insurance Program (OASDI) established by the Federal Insurance Contributions Act (FICA). Both employers and employees contribute under this program to help pay for loss of income on retirement or disability. The tax was set in 1988 at 7.15% percent of the employee's wages up to $43,800. Both the rate and the maximum income on which it is collected will rise in the future.

Retirement benefits are based on an employee's record of employment. A "fully insured" worker, who is entitled to the maximum monthly benefit, is one who has worked at least 40 quarters (10 years). Retirement benefits are payable to retired workers who are at least 62 years old. Their spouses and divorced spouses who are 62 years old, or caring for a child, and dependent children or grandchildren are also eligible to receive payments equal to a certain percentage of the worker's benefits.

Employees who are unable to engage in substantial gainful employment are eligible for disability benefits if they have been disabled for 5 months and the disability is likely to continue at least 12 months. Disability benefits are also payable to the employee's spouse and minor children. Moreover, spouses, dependent parents, and children of a deceased worker are entitled to a small lump-sum death benefit and to monthly payments under the same conditions as those paid to families of retired or disabled workers.

The FICA taxes paid by employers and employees also go to fund the national program of medical and health insurance known as Medicare. The program provides persons over 65 and certain persons under 65 who are disabled with insurance for hospital costs and for supplementary medical costs such as doctor's office visits.

Unemployment Compensation

The Social Security Act of 1935 also imposed a tax on employers' payrolls to finance a program that provides compensation for temporarily unemployed workers. Over the years, the states have taken over major responsibility for such programs so that employers now pay only a small portion of the tax to the federal government and the remainder to the state.

Unemployment taxes are computed as a fixed percentage, called the "contribution rate," of the wages that employers pay. Although the rate is ordinarily about 3 percent of the employer's payroll, in many states it varies according to the employer's "experience rating," that is, its record of creating unemployment among its employees.

Benefits are usually calculated as a percentage of the employee's average wage in a stated period prior to unemployment. Ordinarily, unemployed workers can receive payments for a maximum of 26 weeks, although the federal government will fund half of the payments for an additional period up to 13 weeks if general unemployment reaches a prescribed level. States impose different criteria for eligibility but often refuse benefits to employees who are on strike, who quit their jobs without cause, or who are discharged for misconduct. States also ordinarily require the recipient to be available and actively searching for work in order to receive benefits.

Private Benefit Plans

Many employers offer employee benefit plans in addition to those provided by social security programs. Because of serious abuses in the funding, management, and qualification requirements of many such plans, Congress in 1974 enacted the Employee Retirement Income Security Act (ERISA). The act mandates disclosure of relevant information to employees and imposes government reporting requirements. ERISA also protects employees against inadequate financing, mismanagement, discrimination among classes of employees, and divestiture of earned benefits. In addition, ERISA prohibits employers from imposing unreasonable participation rules.

Summary

In an effort to promote industrial peace, Congress between 1930 and 1960 passed a series of acts designed to equalize the bargaining power of employees and employers. With the Norris-LaGuardia Act, Congress prohibited federal courts from issuing injunctions against union activity. With the National Labor Relations (Wagner) Act, Congress declared a clear national policy in favor of collective activity by employees and established significant protection for such activity. The Taft-Hartley and the Landrum-Griffin Acts balanced the growing power of unions by imposing restraints on their actions and on the conduct of their internal union affairs.

Advocacy of civil rights in the 1960s led to the passage of the Civil Rights Act of 1964. Title VII of the Act prohibits discrimination in employment because of race, color, religion, sex, or national origin. Ordinarily proved by either the "disparate treatment" or "disparate impact" theories, employment discrimination is prohibited with respect to hiring, compensation, discharge, and any other "term, condition, or privilege" of employment. Other equal employment opportunity legislation prohibits discrimination on the basis of age (Age Discrimination in Employment Act) and discrimination in compensation because of sex (Equal Pay Act) and requires affirmative action by federal contractors respecting women and minorities (EO 11246) and the handicapped (Rehabilitation Act).

Congress also regulates the wages and hours of employees. The Fair Labor Standards Act establishes a minimum wage and requires overtime pay for hours worked in excess of 40 per week. In addition, it regulates the hours and working conditions of minors. The Davis-Bacon, Walsh-Healy Government Contracts, and Service Contract Acts regulate the wages of workers employed on government-financed construction projects and involved in fulfilling contracts to furnish goods and services to the government.

Worker's compensation laws reimburse employees for losses from work-related disease and accidents, and provide benefits to the spouses and families of workers who die from occupational disease or injury. Such laws provide for payment to injured workers from insurance policies or funds regardless of fault.

Workplace safety is the concern of the Occupational Health and Safety Act. That act requires employers to maintain a safe working environment and to conform to safety standards. The Occupational Safety and Health Administration (OSHA) enforces the act, and the National Institute for Occupational Safety and Health helps develop standards and provides safety education.

"Social security" consists of several programs designed to assure some measure of financial security to retired and temporarily unemployed workers and their families. The Old Age, Survivors and Disability Insurance Program provides benefits to retired and disabled workers through a program financed by employer and employee contributions. The program also finances Medicare, which provides insurance for hospital and other medical costs for disabled persons and persons over age 65. Unemployment compensation is financed by a payroll tax paid by employers. It provides weekly benefits, usually a portion of the employee's previous monthly wages, for temporarily unemployed workers. Private benefit plans are regulated by the Employee Retirement Income Security Act.

Review Questions

1 What was the purpose of the Norris-LaGuardia Act?

2 **(a)** What was the objective of the National Labor Relations (Wagner) Act? **(b)** By what means did Congress attempt to accomplish this objective?

3 **(a)** In what ways did the Taft-Hartley Act change the Wagner Act? **(b)** What did the Landrum-Griffin Act add?

4 **(a)** What are unfair labor practices? **(b)** Give five examples.

5 Distinguish between "mandatory" and "permissive" subjects of bargaining.

6 Define "discrimination in employment."

7 Explain the difference between "disparate treatment" and "disparate impact" discrimination.

8 **(a)** What is the difference between Title VII's duty not to discriminate and affirmative action? **(b)** What is "reverse discrimination"? **(c)** Is affirmative action legally permissible? Explain.

9 **(a)** Distinguish between "equal pay for equal work" and "equal pay for comparable work." **(b)** Which is legally mandated?

10 **(a)** What obligations does the Occupational Safety and Health Act impose on employers? **(b)** How are they enforced?

11 **(a)** What are the components of "social security"? **(b)** How is each financed and what benefits does each provide?

Case Problems

1 During the course of an election campaign, Exchange Parts Co. sent its employees a letter which noted the "empty promises of the Union" and "the fact that it is the company that puts things in your envelope." The company also announced that a previously promised additional holiday could be taken on the employee's birthday, that a new vacation schedule would be implemented so that employees could extend their vacations by sandwiching them between two weekends, and that there would be a new system for calculating holiday overtime that would result in increased wages. Did the company commit an unfair labor practice and, if so, what type?

2 Jerry Floyd, a sample motor builder for Emerson Electric Company, habitually spent considerable time meandering around the plant collecting parts for his sample motors and chatting with other employees about fishing and other non-work-related topics. Supervisors in a number of departments complained about Floyd's unrestricted activities, and when numerous warnings failed to change his behavior, he was discharged. Immediately before his discharge the company was engaged in a union election campaign; Floyd was a union supporter and the company was aware of his position. Did the company commit an unfair labor practice by discharging Floyd and, if so, what type?

3 After an election campaign, the General Drivers Union became the bargaining representative for the Otis Massey Company's production and maintenance employees. Bargaining between the company and the union resulted in a tentative agreement for a wage increase. The union representative told the company's employees that the raise would not become effective until the contract was signed and that the contract would not be signed until 80 percent of the employees signed union membership applications and check-off dues authorizations, which are agreements providing automatic payroll deductions of union dues. Sixty-two of the company's eighty-three employees joined the union and signed check-off authorizations. Did the union commit an unfair labor practice and, if so, what type?

4 Litton Systems, Inc., had a company policy that it would not employ persons who had been arrested several times for other than minor traffic offenses. The policy applied to all applicants regardless of race. Gregory, a black, applied for employment as a sheet metal mechanic and was hired. When he disclosed the fact that he had been arrested on fourteen different occasions, Litton withdrew its offer. Gregory claimed a violation of Title VII in that Litton's seemingly neutral policy had the effect of denying black applicants an equal opportunity for employment. At trial, Gregory proved, among other things, that blacks are arrested substantially more frequently than whites in proportion to their numbers. What must Litton prove to negate the inference of discrimination? How did the court rule and why?

5 Berrel Matthews, Emily Hampton, Isabel Slack, and Sharon Murphy were employees in the bonding and coating department of Havens Industries. Although their work ordinarily involved only light cleanup, one day their supervisor told them to suspend production and begin a general cleanup of the bonding and coating department. The cleanup involved extremely hard and possibly dangerous work such as cleaning light fixtures and scraping the floor, which was caked with hardened resin. The supervisor excused Sharon Murphy, who was white and had less seniority than the others, who were black, and called in another employee, Kathleen Hale, who was also black, to perform the cleanup work. When the four employees refused, they were discharged. Did Havens discriminate illegally against the employees because of their race?

6 Ronald Philbrook was a schoolteacher and a member of a church whose tenets require members to refrain from secular employment during designated holy days, a practice that caused him to miss approximately 6 days of school per year. Under the collective bargaining agreement between the school board and Philbrook's union, teachers were granted 3 days annual leave for observance of religious holidays but were not permitted to use for religious observance any accumulated sick leave, 3 days of which were normally available for other "necessary personal business." Accordingly, Philbrook had to either work or take unpaid leave for 3 additional religious holidays. When the school board rejected Philbrook's repeated requests to use personal business leave for the extra religious days or to receive full pay while bearing the cost of a substitute himself, Philbrook filed suit alleging that the school board had failed to reasonably accommodate his religious observance. How did the Supreme Court rule, and why?

7 John Chadbourne, a quality control analyst with Raytheon Company, was hospitalized and diagnosed as having AIDS. Although his physician indicated that he could return to work, Raytheon refused to permit him to return because of its concern that Chadbourne's coworkers might be at risk of contracting AIDS. Although Chadbourne died the following year, his estate filed a complaint with the California Fair Employment and Housing Commission alleging that Raytheon had violated California's handicap discrimination law. Is AIDS a physical handicap entitled to protection under the state discrimination statute and did Raytheon violate the law by refusing to reinstate Chadbourne?

8 Mary McKee, a female employee of McDonnell Douglas Technical Services Company, worked as part of a team with a male employee, Huckestein, preparing a materials test data handbook. Huckestein was responsible for the computer system and the generation, collection, and dissemination of computer reports. McKee was originally responsible for encoding the data, but when Huckestein left, she took over the data collection portion of his job but not the computer-related activities that had occupied the major portion of his time. When McKee discovered that she was being paid less than Huckestein had been, she claimed a violation of the Equal Pay Act. Was the act violated? Why or why not?

9 Security officers and housekeeping employees of Mercy Hospital were required to change into uniforms on the hospital's premises. The employees were required to wear their uniforms while at work but were not permitted to wear their uniforms to work. Does the Fair Labor Standards Act require compensation for the time spent changing clothes?

10 Osborne Enterprises, Inc., was charged with an OSHA violation when an employee working on a scaffold four floors above the ground fell to his death during a gust of wind. The employer proved that it provided safety belts on its scaffolds, that it had a work rule requiring their use, that it held safety meetings stressing the importance of safety belt requirements, and that it terminated employees for noncompliance with the rules. Did the employer violate OSHA?

ETHICS IN PRACTICE

The ethical quality of an act cannot be determined without considering the social or legal context within which the act occurred. The major regulatory statutes reflect legislative policy choices that most of the informed public seem to accept as reasonable and right. The Sherman Act controlling monopolistic practices, the Federal Trade Commission Act forbidding unfair and deceptive trade practices, the National Labor Relations Act banning unfair labor practices, and many other state and federal statutes set legal standards of business conduct that are consistent with most people's ideas of ethical behavior. If a person or business commits an unlawful act commonly accepted as wrongful, there is little doubt about the ethical quality of the act—it is both illegal and unethical.

Assessing ethical quality is not so easy where an act or practice is not expressly identified as against the law. Much law is stated in general terms so that administrative agencies and courts can apply it to a variety of suspect business practices that might later develop. Sometimes an act is not forbidden by law, yet is offensive because it violates nonlegal ethical standards. Then the question is whether the offensive practice should be made illegal. Some practices have harsh consequences; these practices may be ethical or unethical, depending on the surrounding circumstances.

Many problems in previous parts have involved the kind of ethical dilemma described in Chapter 2—a person caught up in conflicting norms feels pressure to violate law or ethics or to help others do so. The problems for this part have more to do with the way people use, apply, or evade the law than with the social pressures inducing their conduct. In these problems, all taken from news accounts of actual happenings, your objective should be to evaluate the ethical quality of the action taken. Are the actors conducting themselves ethically or not?

Problems in Ethics

1 Railco, a railway company, believes it has too many railroad clerks on its workforce. The current union contract allows Railco to reduce the number of clerks up to 4 percent overall, but requires Railco to "buy out" each clerk's position with 1 year's severance pay. Railco is willing to continue the buy-outs, but wants a much greater reduction in clerk positions than the union contract allows. To save jobs, the union refuses to agree to more buy-outs. Apparently in an attempt to get workers to pressure the union for broader buy-outs, Railco has put clerks in various former lunchrooms throughout the system with nothing to do but read company rules and timetables.

2 After more than 20 years of service, and 10 months before retirement, John was dismissed from the FBI for refusing an order to investigate peace groups whose views he shared. A devout Roman Catholic and committed pacifist, John said he struggled with the request to investigate Silo Plowshares and Veterans Fast for Life, groups suspected of vandalizing military facilities in Chicago. The FBI contends it fired John for insubordination and for violating his oath of office when he refused to investigate the groups because of his personal, religious, and human beliefs.

3 The Salvation Army fired Jamie for using its copy machine to copy satanic rituals. She brought suit for reinstatement and damages. A U.S. district judge held that the Salvation Army violated her constitutional right to freedom of religion when it fired her because she practices witchcraft. The judge said the Salvation Army cannot discriminate against witches, because it receives federal funds for some programs.

4 U.S. Customs inspectors found a marijuana pipe in the glove compartment of Cheryl's car. Under the government's "zero tolerance" antidrug policy, Custom's officials seized her $6,000 Chrysler Laser Turbo and told her she was welcome to try to buy it back at an auction of confiscated vehicles. Cheryl was not charged with a drug violation and says that she has an affidavit to show the pipe was not hers.

5 U.S. gun manufacturers want to market plastic handguns—the kind that are lethal weapons but don't show up on metal detectors at airports and other security checkpoints. Several members of Congress have proposed legislation banning or limiting the manufacture, sale, or import of plastic guns. The National Rifle Association has vigorously opposed all attempts to ban them, but has recently conceded that some regulation might be acceptable. One Senator, a leading supporter of the NRA, has proposed a ban on plastic guns that do not have enough metal in them to be detected when security machines are set at their highest level. Critics of this proposal say that metal detectors set at maximum levels will detect such small amounts of metal that 90 percent of airport passengers will have to be searched. They prefer a bill banning guns containing less than 8.5 ounces of metal. The Justice Department originally supported the 8.5-ounce limit, but has recently spoken in favor of the bill proposed by the NRA-supporting Senator.

6 A restaurant critic writing for a newspaper under an assumed name allegedly gave a bad review of a good restaurant, mistaking a fine loin of veal for a veal patty, complaining about the restaurant's *bagna cauda* (an elegant oil-and-anchovy dip) because he was expecting a more pedestrian dip, and incorrectly suggesting that its Bolognese sauce was tomato based and flavored with cheese when it was actually a pork sauce flavored with a little tomato. Complaining that the inaccurate reviews cost her business to drop 15–20 percent, the owner asked the state Restaurant Association to seek legislation requiring the licensing of restaurant critics through the Department of Consumer Protection. The proposed license requirements include experience in food-service operation and management, graduation from a recognized culinary arts degree program, or a combination of at least 6 years of experience and formal training. "Licensing opinions is kind of silly," said the critic. Neither he nor the newspaper would reveal his real name.

7 In 1975, the Boston fire department rejected identical twins Phillip and Paul for employment because of poor exam scores. On their applications, they identified themselves as white candidates, but scored only 57 percent and 69 percent on the exam, well short of the 82 percent required of whites. In 1977 they applied again, this time declaring that they were black, and were hired. The department was under pressure to hire more minority fire fighters, and under a court-ordered affirmative-action plan, the lower scores were overlooked for minorities. Ten years later, never having been officially questioned about their race, the twins were listed among black fire fighters proposed for promotion to lieutenant. The fire commissioner thought the twins were white; suspicions aroused, he asked the state department of personnel administration to check out their status. Informed of the investigation, a black city council member asked, "How could twins with Irish names, Caucasian features and no black identification from any perspective get onto the force and stay on without collusion?" The twins claimed that they did not learn they were black until 1976 when their mother discovered a sepia photograph of a pale-looking woman she said was their black great-grandmother. After an investigation, the twins were fired. The mayor recently disclosed that at least five other fire fighters will be asked to prove they are not white.

PART TWELVE

International Business Law

CHAPTER 48
Legal Aspects of International Business Transactions

CHAPTER 48

Legal Aspects of International Business Transactions

Introduction to International Business Transactions

International business transactions involve the sale or exchange of goods or services across national borders. In the simplest form, one business may import products from another country in exchange for money. In a more complex form, an international business transaction might entail shipment of raw materials from one country to another, with eventual return of manufactured products or parts of products for sale in the originating country.

Growing Importance of International Business Transactions

American international trade has increased spectacularly in the last 30 years. Virtually every major business considers foreign countries as potential markets for its products or services, or as sources from which it can import materials and products. Efficient international transportation and communication, availability of cheap foreign raw materials and labor, less strict environmental and business regulation as well as attractive tax incentives are some of the factors which account for this phenomenon.

Today American business is engaged in huge volumes of trade with Japan and member nations of the European Economic Community (EEC) as well as with many other nations. Since World War II, the American economy has become increasingly dependent on international trade. Between 1970 and 1986, exports from the United States increased from $43 billion to $217 billion, while imports increased from $40 billion to $370 billion. The monetary difference between net imports and exports, referred to as the *balance of payments,* is now an important index by which national economic well-being is measured.

No serious student of business or economics can ignore the growing importance of international business transactions. A basic understanding of the legal environment in which international business is conducted is therefore essential.

Overview of International Business Transactions

Suppose that a business enterprise decides to enter into business transactions which cross international borders. What problems arise? First, consider the mechanics of the transactions. International trade may involve businesspersons who speak different languages and adhere to different business customs. How can an American business assure itself that the products which it orders from abroad will be shipped on time and conform to contractual specifications? If products are exported abroad, how can a business assure itself of payment? If payment is in a foreign currency, how is exchange into American dollars to be accomplished, and what are the implications of fluctuating exchange rates?

Another major area of concern is how to resolve disputes when international business transactions do not go as planned. Who should arbitrate or adjudicate such disputes, where should they be resolved, and according to the laws of what country?

The answers to such problems are found in a network of international business laws including those drawn from various sovereign nations, as well as laws established through regional trade communities such as the EEC (also known as the "European Common Market"), and laws resulting from treaties between sovereign nations. This chapter will examine some of the common legal problems encountered in international business dealings, and some principles of international business law through which these problems are resolved.

Alternative Business Approaches to International Trade

A firm entering foreign trade must consider alternative methods of engaging in international transactions. If the sale of products is the objective, investment in foreign markets might be limited to direct sales efforts, or a seller might arrange for a distributor or licensee (franchisee) in a foreign country to make sales in exchange for some percentage of profit or income. An even more intensive form of investment is a joint venture with a foreign business partner. Since many nations restrict business ownership by foreigners to less than majority control, joint venture arrangements often involve a 49 percent ownership by a foreign investor and 51 percent by a business entity in the host country. Certain types of joint venture agreements may violate American antitrust laws (see Chapter 46).

The most extensive form of foreign business investment occurs when a company establishes a wholly owned foreign subsidiary. Firms that do so can exercise a great deal of control over production and marketing in the foreign market. Any business established to move goods, information, money, people, and/or services across national borders, is referred to as a *multinational enterprise.*

Commonly, an expanding multinational enterprise develops foreign trade through a sequence of stages such as those described above. First, it simply exports goods to foreign markets through direct sales efforts. Next, it establishes a sales organization or other marketing arrangement on foreign soil. Eventually, the enterprise develops foreign production capabilities, first by licensing the use of its patents and later by establishing its own manufacturing capabilities. From a legal perspective, different types of problems arise depending on the degree of investment.

Direct Sales

When an American exporter enters into an agreement to sell goods abroad, there are substantial risks concerning delivery and payment, especially if the foreign importer is one unfamiliar to the exporter. Only to the extent that such risks can be controlled will the transaction appear worthwhile.

Irrevocable Documentary Letters of Credit.

Risks of nonpayment or nondelivery are customarily minimized by involving banks located in each country. For example, suppose that a French importer wishes to purchase a shipment of computers from an American manufacturer. The American seller may be unwilling to contract with a foreign stranger unless there is some assurance that the buyer will pay for the goods. Initially, the French importer contacts a local *issuing bank* that has a "correspondent" working relationship with a *confirming* bank located in the United States near the American exporter. The importer contracts with the issuing bank for an *irrevocable documentary letter of credit,* in which the issuing bank agrees to pay the purchase price to the American confirming bank when it presents certain specified documents evidencing ownership of the goods. When the confirming bank presents these documents, the issuing bank is contractually bound to pay the purchase price to the confirming bank, and this obligation is separate and independent from the contract between the exporting seller and the importing buyer.

The documents normally required include a *bill of lading* (proof that the exporter has delivered the goods for shipment), proof of insurance, a commercial invoice setting out the terms of the purchase, and a certificate showing that the goods are cleared by customs for export. After the importer has paid in French francs for the letter of credit, the issuing bank sends it to the American exporter who may now ship the goods knowing payment can be obtained by presenting the proper documents to the local confirming bank. The goods specified in the contract are delivered by the exporter for shipment in exchange for the documents specified in the irrevocable documentary letter of credit.

The exporter then takes the documents to the correspondent bank, which "confirms" that the documents are in proper order and makes payment to the exporter in American dollars. The "confirming bank" then sends the documents to the importer's issuing bank in exchange for payment from the issuing bank. Finally, the documents are delivered by the issuing bank to the importer, who uses them to claim the delivered goods.

The overall effect of using irrevocable documentary letters of credit is to reduce both the risk of nonpayment for goods (the exporter's risk) and the risk of nondelivery of goods (the importer's risk).

Delays between time of shipment and time of payment are also reduced. Each party, the exporter and the importer, relies upon contractual rights between itself and a local bank, rights that may be asserted and determined within each party's own country. The international contractual risks are assumed in large measure by the two banks that have an established working relationship doing international business.

When international legal disputes arise concerning documentary letters of credit, they are generally resolved with reference to the International Chamber of Commerce's Uniform Customs and Practices for Documentary Credits (UCP), a widely adopted written set of rules by which parties to international contracts frequently agree to be bound. Within the United States, applicable laws relating to documentary letters of credit may also be found in Article 5 of the Uniform Commercial Code.

Choice-of-Law, Choice-of-Forum Clauses in Contracts. The parties to an international business contract often decide by agreement how, when, and where disputes over the contract will be resolved and who will resolve them. *Choice-of-law clauses* are agreements between the contracting parties that in the event of a dispute, each party will be governed by the law of the specified jurisdiction. For example, suppose an American exporter anticipates a dispute about the quality of toys shipped to a Dutch buyer. If American law seems favorable to American exporters, the seller may negotiate for a choice-of-law clause in the contract, under which both parties agree to be governed by applicable American laws in the event of a dispute. In a similar vein, *choice-of-forum clauses* in a contract settle the question of *where* legal issues will be resolved if a dispute arises. Choice-of-forum clauses are important because the costs of defending a legal action can be high if a party must travel to a distant forum.

Arbitration Clauses. The parties to an import-export contract may agree to be bound by *arbitration* in the event of a dispute. Arbitration, discussed in Chapter 3, is a process by which contractual disputes are resolved by an agreed-upon third party or tribunal other than a court. Arbitration is often faster and less costly than the courts as a means of resolving disputes. A choice-of-forum clause may specify an arbitration forum that is neutral and require that the expenses of arbitration be shared equally between the parties or be borne by the nonprevailing party. The following case illustrates the importance of an arbitration clause in establishing how an international business dispute will be resolved.

CASE 48.1 Mitsubishi Motors v. Soler Chrysler-Plymouth · 87 L. Ed.2d 444 (1985)

FACTS Mitsubishi Heavy Industries, Inc., a Japanese corporation and Chrysler International, SA (Chrysler), a Swiss corporation wholly owned by Chrysler Corporation, formed a joint venture company, Mitsubishi Motors Corporation (plaintiffs), to distribute through Chrysler dealers outside of the United States vehicles manufactured by Mitsubishi and bearing Chrysler and Mitsubishi trademarks. In 1979, Soler Chrysler-Plymouth (defendant), an automobile dealer incorporated in Puerto Rico, and Chrysler entered into a Distributor Agreement that provided for the sale by Soler of Mitsubishi-manufactured vehicles within a designated area in Puerto Rico. On the same date, Chrysler, Soler, and Mitsubishi entered into a Sales Agreement providing for direct sales of Mitsubishi products to Soler and the terms of such sales. Paragraph VI of the Sales Agreement, labeled "Arbitration of Certain Matters," provided:

> All disputes, controversies or differences which may arise between [Mitsubishi] and [Soler] out of or in relation to . . . this Agreement or for the breach thereof, shall be finally settled by arbitration in Japan in accordance with the rules and regulations of the Japan Commercial Arbitration Association.

CASE 48.1 Continued

Initially, Soler maintained brisk sales of Mitsubishi-manufactured vehicles, but following a slump in the new-car market in 1981, Soler requested Mitsubishi to delay or cancel shipment of several orders. A year later Soler disclaimed any responsibility for failing to sell cars under its contract. Mitsubishi brought suit in the United States in Puerto Rico under the federal Arbitration Act and the Convention on the Recognition and Enforcement of Foreign Arbitral Awards, seeking an order to compel arbitration in accord with paragraph VI of the Sales Agreement. Soler counterclaimed against Mitsubishi and Chrysler, alleging numerous breaches of contract and conspiracy to divide markets in restraint of trade, thereby violating the Sherman Act. The District Court ordered Soler to arbitrate, even as to the antitrust claims. The Court of Appeals reversed the judgment insofar as it had ordered submission of Soler's antitrust claims to arbitration, and appeal was taken to the Supreme Court.

OPINION

BLACKMUN, Justice. We granted certiorari primarily to consider whether an American court could enforce an agreement to resolve antitrust claims by arbitration when that agreement arises from an international transaction.... Soler reasons that, because it falls within a class for whose benefit the federal and local antitrust laws and dealers' acts were passed, but the arbitration clause at issue does not mention these statutes or statutes in general, the clause cannot be read to contemplate arbitration of these statutory claims.

We do not agree, for we find no warrant in the Arbitration Act for implying in every contract... a presumption against arbitration of statutory claims.... The "liberal federal policy favoring arbitration agreements,"... manifested by the Act as a whole, is at bottom a policy guaranteeing the enforcement of private contractual arrangements: the Act simply "creates a body of federal substantive law establishing and regulating the duty to honor an agreement to arbitrate."

There is no reason to depart from these guidelines where a party bound by an arbitration agreement raises claims founded on statutory rights.... Of course, courts should remain attuned to well-supported claims that the agreement to arbitrate resulted from the sort of fraud or overwhelming economic power that would provide grounds "for the revocation of any contract." 9 USC 2; *The Bremen v. Zapata Off-Shore Co.*, 407 U.S. 1 (1972). But, absent such compelling considerations, the Act itself provides no basis for disfavoring agreements to arbitrate statutory claims.

... By agreeing to arbitrate a statutory claim, a party does not forgo the substantive rights afforded by the statute; it only submits to their resolution in an arbitral, rather than a judicial, forum. It trades the procedures and opportunity for review of the courtroom for the simplicity, informality, and expedition of arbitration. We... conclude that concerns of international comity, respect for the capacities of foreign and transnational tribunals, and sensitivity to the need of the international commercial system for predictability in the resolution of disputes requires that we enforce the parties' agreement, even assuming that a contrary result would be forthcoming in a domestic context.... [We] recognize the utility of forum-selection clauses in international transactions.

[T]he party may attempt to make a showing that would warrant setting aside the forum-selection clause—that the agreement was "[a]ffected by fraud, undue influence, or overweening bargaining power;" that "enforcement would be unreasonable and unjust;" or that proceedings "in the contractual forum will be so gravely difficult and inconvenient that [the resisting party] will for all practical purposes be deprived of his day in court." *The Bremen*, 407 U.S. at 12.... But absent such a showing—and none was attempted here—there is no basis for assuming the forum inadequate or its selection unfair.

The international arbitral tribunal... is bound to effectuate the intentions of the parties. Where the parties have agreed that the arbitral body is to decide a defined set of claims which includes, as in these cases, those arising from the application of American

CASE 48.1 Continued antitrust law, the tribunal therefore should be bound to decide that dispute in accord with the national law giving rise to the claim.

JUDGMENT Accordingly, we require this representative of the American business community to honor its bargain, by holding this agreement to arbitrate "enforce[able] in accord with the explicit provisions of the Arbitration Act." The judgment of the Court of Appeals is affirmed in part and reversed in part, and the cases are remanded for further proceedings consistent with this opinion.

Distributorships and Licensing Arrangements

An American business enterprise that decides to invest in more than just direct sales may enter into licensing, franchising, or distributorship arrangements with a business associate in a foreign country. A *distributorship* is an arrangement by which an exporting business agrees to market its products through the sales efforts of a foreign-based distributor. If the distributor obtains the exclusive right to market the product in exchange for sharing profits with the exporting enterprise, the arrangement is called an *exclusive distributorship.* Exclusive distributorships do not violate American antitrust laws because they do not affect competition within the United States or impair efforts of other American exporters to market their products abroad. However, such arrangements should be carefully scrutinized since they may run afoul of antitrust laws in other countries.

One distributorship arrangement that may be challenged under American antitrust laws is an *exclusive dealing* arrangement, in which the foreign distributor agrees not to distribute the products of any competing manufacturer. If, for example, a West German distributor has substantial control of the West German market for personal computers and agrees to deal exclusively in the products of a particular American manufacturer over a substantial time period, other American manufacturers would be foreclosed from the market and antitrust violations under American law could be asserted.

Licensing or *franchising* occurs where a business that owns certain production technology or patent rights to an innovative product or manufacturing technique sells the right to use that technology or patent to an enterprise in another country. The foreign enterprise usually agrees to pay royalties in exchange for the license to use the technology or patent. Licensing is the major means of transferring technology across national borders. Because licensing can be used to limit competition among products that require the same manufacturing technology, license agreements may also be subject to antitrust scrutiny.

Transnational Business Corporations

Corporations that establish wholly owned foreign affiliates are known as *transnational business corporations,* and the fact that they are not subject to only one jurisdiction can be advantageous. Through the use of choice-of-law clauses in contracts, such corporations choose the jurisdiction that is most favorable to current business objectives. Likewise, transnational business corporations can maximize tax advantages by controlling inventory buildups and sales prices among subsidiaries in different host countries.

For example, a transnational corporation with an affiliate in a country that taxes profits heavily or restricts the removal of profits may ship goods and services to that affiliate at a charge that already includes a reasonable profit. The apparent business expenses for the foreign affiliate are then deducted by it in computing taxable net profits. In this way, the transnational corporation maximizes expenses in the jurisdiction where taxes are high and takes profits in the jurisdiction where taxes are low. Transnational corporations also exert powerful influence in negotiating labor contracts. For example, if labor costs in one country become excessive, a transnational business can relocate and hire in a different country where the costs are less expensive. In short, because only one jurisdiction scrutinizes the activities of transnational corporations, many competitive advantages are available to them.

Flexibility gives transnational business corporations the capacity to take greater investment risks and to efficiently match capital and technology to optimize production efforts. However, transnational business corporations can sometimes be insensitive to the impact of business policies on the host country's local environment, economy, and culture. Local employees and their families can be devastated by a business decision to move production elsewhere where costs are less expensive. Balance is required in planning transnational corporate activities so that the host countries' citizens as well as businesses may share in the benefits of international trade. In extreme instances of insensitivity or exploitation, a transnational business corporation may provoke restrictive or retaliatory measures by the host country's regulatory authorities.

Sovereign Regulation of International Trade

National governments seek to regulate international trade for a variety of reasons. One key reason is to prevent foreign exporters from gaining unfair trade advantages by flooding local markets with competitive products priced below the cost of domestic manufacturing. In addition, many developing nations promote economic growth by offering cheap land, tax benefits, or monopoly privileges to foreign firms who will bring in new industries and technologies. Such programs also provide a greater selection of products to a developing nation's consumers. Most nations also regulate international trade to further their national security. For example, a country may prohibit imports of military weapons and at the same time subsidize domestic firms to manufacture them. Most nations prohibit the export of military technologies or products that might compromise their national defenses.

The regulation of international trade may also promote important foreign policies. For example, the United States has an antiboycott law that prohibits its businesses from cooperating with an Arab boycott of Israel or advancing Arab boycotters' abilities to discriminate against foreign companies that do business with Israel. In 1987, the Commerce Department charged Sara Lee Corp. with violations of this law arising out of its attempts to register its L'eggs panty-hose trademark in Kuwait and other Arab countries. Sara Lee Corp. denied the charges, asserting that the information which it provided to Arab countries concerning its business operations was already public information that was provided only to protect its trademark overseas and without intent to assist the Arab boycott. The accusations, if proved, could result in fines totaling as much as $2.4 million. In the United States, such cases are decided by an administrative law judge. Earlier in 1987 the Commerce Department imposed a $381,000 civil penalty on NCR Corp. for alleged violations by its foreign subsidiaries of the same law. NCR Corp. neither admitted nor denied the allegations, but agreed to pay the penalty. These cases highlight the importance of learning about the following sovereign laws that regulate international trade.

Regulation of Imports

A domestic government's regulation of imports usually reflects a balancing of policies designed to protect local business from foreign firms that may have competitive advantages and policies designed to bolster the quantity and quality of products available to local consumers. For example, the importation of Japanese automobiles and motorcycles into the United States initially created unfavorable competitive pressures on American manufacturers while at the same time making a wider variety of products available to the American consumer. Eventually, the American government responded to the concerns of American businesses by introducing import controls and inducing self-restraints by Japanese firms to achieve a more desirable balance in the impact of imported vehicles on American business and consumers.

Product Controls. Regulation of imports by a sovereign nation takes a variety of forms. One of the most direct is the enactment of *tariffs,* or import duties, on foreign products. A variety of nontariff barriers may also be imposed. These include *import bans* that totally prohibit the product; *import quotas* that restrict the quantity of a given product that may be imported into a country; the imposition of safety or other manufacturing standards, for example, requiring seat belts or prohibiting certain food additives in products shipped into a country; and complex customs procedures that must be complied with in order for the product to gain entry into the country. Other more indirect barriers to the successful marketing of imported products include government subsidies to local producers that create or help sustain a local competitive price advantage.

In order to enter the United States, products from another country must pass through customs inspections, a process ensuring compliance with whatever import regulations are imposed. Customs officials must classify goods for purposes of determining whether or not tariffs apply. Classifying goods for import can sometimes be difficult. For example, a set of wooden bookends might be characterized as an "art object," "forest product," or, simply, "personal belonging." Which characterization applies determines which tariffs and other regulations apply. After a good is classified by customs officials, it must be "valued" by determining the "transaction value" or price actually paid for the merchandise (including certain incidental import costs) when it was sold for exportation to the United States. *Classification* and *valuation* together are used to determine the amount of any import duties to be paid. Another determination that must be made by customs officials is a product's "country of origin." Again, import restrictions may vary depending on the country of origin. The general *rule of origin* is that a product is said to originate in a particular country if it is wholly the growth, product, or manufacture of that country or has been substantially transformed into a new and different article while in a particular country.

Many countries impose special tariffs or other restrictions on products that are "dumped" into the country of importation at a price below what would be charged for the same product in the country of origin. *Dumping* is sometimes used to undermine a competitor's market position. In the United States, the Anti-Dumping Act of 1921 helps to counteract dumping by providing for the imposition of special *antidumping duties.* A similar type of protective duty, called a *countervailing duty,* is imposed on imports that have been subsidized by the country of origin through "export subsidies" aimed at creating an unfair advantage in the targeted foreign market.

The United States International Trade Commission, created by Congress in 1916, conducts investigations to determine whether unfair methods of competition or unfair acts are being committed in the importation of articles into the United States. Such investigations are initiated by petition from a business claiming to be harmed. The following case illustrates the Commission's function in investigating a claimed violation of import regulations under the Trade Agreements Act of 1979 within the United States.

CASE 48.2 Budd Company Railway Division v. United States · 507 F. Supp. 997 (1980)

FACTS Budd Company Railway Division (plaintiff) assembled rail passenger cars and manufactured rail car components and parts at its plant in Philadelphia. Budd petitioned the United States International Trade Commission (Commission) to conduct an antidumping investigative proceeding, and alleged that it was being injured by the importation from Italy and Japan of rail passenger cars and component parts from Italy and Japan that were then sold at less than fair value. The Commission made a preliminary determination of "No Reasonable Indication of Material Injury" whereupon Budd brought an action in the U.S. District Court challenging the Commission's findings as "arbitrary, capricious, an abuse of discretion, or not otherwise in accordance with law." In addition, Budd asked the Court to make an affirmative determination of material injury with respect to the products that the Commission had investigated.

OPINION BOE, Judge. . . . A reviewing court must consider whether the decision was based on a consideration of the relevant factors and whether there has been a clear error of judgment. . . .

CASE 48.2 Continued

The preliminary determination by the Commission must be "based upon the best information available to it at the time of the determination." Although recognizing the restrictions placed upon an investigation by virtue of a 45-day time limitation, Congress has prescribed a thorough investigation.

...From the provisions of the Trade Agreements Act of 1979, it appears clear that Congress anticipates that the Commission take an active role in obtaining information prior to its determination.

...[T]he court now directs its attention to the record of the administrative proceedings. Examination thereof clearly indicates the correctness of the Commission's negative finding with respect to the material injury resulting from the importation of *finished rail passenger cars*.... [However, it does not] appear from the record before the Court that the Commission has made a thorough investigation required of it by statute with respect to: (1) the sources, volume and prices of the components and parts contemplated to be imported in connection with the contracts in question, and (2) the domestic suppliers of like components and parts in the United States, and (3) the material injury or threat of material injury resulting thereto by reason of such importations.

From the findings of fact and the administrative record before the court, it would appear that there has been a lack of due diligence by the Commission in seeking information available to it in the absence of such evidence having been presented by any of the parties to the investigative proceeding.

...It must be emphasized that [the Act] does not limit "the best information available" to that furnished by the petitioner or by any party-in-interest to the proceedings. It is clear that all information that is accessible or may be obtained, from whatever its source may be, must be reasonably sought by the Commission. It is only in this manner that the Commission can comply with the intended congressional mandate to conduct a "thorough investigation."

JUDGMENT In view of the foregoing, the court is compelled to remand the instant proceedings to the Commission for further consideration of the best information which would have been available at the time of the original investigation....

Intellectual Property Controls. The transfer of information or technology across national borders is governed by laws concerning patents, trademarks, copyrights, and the like. Each nation has its own laws regulating information and technology transfers. For example, information that is legally protected by a patent in one country is not necessarily protected in another country unless there is some treaty agreement providing for recognition of the patent across national boundaries.

Patents are grants by a government of the right to exclude others from making, using, or selling a properly registered invention without permission. Under United States law, a patent preserves a patentee's exclusive rights for a period of 17 years, thus allowing an opportunity for profits to be earned from a successful patented idea.[1] Although a patent has the potential to eliminate competition, its purpose is to encourage inventors and businesses to invest the time and money needed to develop new technology and improved products. The domestic law of each country establishes procedures for obtaining a patent. In countries where patent laws are not enforced, manufacturers from other countries may find their patented technology or products being "pirated" or copied without permission.

Trademarks are words, names, or symbols that distinguish an enterprise's goods from those manufactured or sold by others. As with patents, trademarks are protected by domestic laws limited to a given country's jurisdiction. In the United States, trademarks are governed by federal laws.[2] In certain instances the protections afforded by American trademark laws have been extended to apply to

[1]35 U.S.C. 154.

[2]15 U.S.C. 1127.

the activities of a foreign licensee of an American business.[3]

Regulation of Exports

National governments may also restrict the export of goods into other countries. Because sales abroad are advantageous for domestic businesses, government export controls are generally used only in special instances and after careful policy deliberation.

Government Licensing of Export Activities. In general, the export activities of business enterprises are subject to licensing by the domestic national government. In the United States, export licenses are obtained by application to the Secretary of Commerce. Enforcement of export controls and export licensing is the responsibility of customs officials at the point of departure. Aside from a complete ban on the export of certain products, export controls may take the form of export quotas or of export duties that must be paid prior to the goods leaving the jurisdiction.

Controls on the Export of Technology and Scarce Resources. In the United States, the Export Administration Act of 1979 limits the use of export controls to special instances, (1) where exports will significantly contribute to the military potential of another country with a result detrimental to national security, (2) where restrictions are necessary to significantly further the foreign policy of the United States or fulfill international treaty obligations, or (3) where restrictions are necessary to protect the domestic economy from an excessive drain of scarce materials.

One current concern of the United States government is the export of high technology to the Soviet Union. In a recent case brought under the Export Administration Act, Digital Equipment Corporation, an American manufacturer, agreed to pay $1.1 million to settle a claim filed against it by the Commerce Department. The Commerce Department alleged that Digital sold advanced computer equipment through a West German subsidiary to a West German citizen who had previously been denied American export privileges for illegally reshipping American high-technology goods to the Soviet Union. This case demonstrates the reach of American export controls and the potentially high costs of allegedly violating export control laws.

[3]See *Wells Fargo & Co. v. Wells Fargo Express Co.*, 556 F.2d 406 (9th Cir. 1977).

Regulation of Money across International Borders

An American business that purchases goods from abroad must ultimately pay in the local currency of the foreign exporter. A unique aspect of international business transactions concerns the means by which parties to an international transaction are paid in local currency. A related monetary concern that affects profitability is fluctuation during the course of a business transaction in the relative value of currencies between countries.

Countries with small or developing economies may establish official exchange rates for their currency in relation to other currencies and enforce the established rate through licensing requirements and by requiring mandatory currency exchanges through the central bank.

Trade with countries that do not fix an official rate of exchange creates the risk that profits may be reduced by fluctuations in the currency exchange rate between the time a transaction price is agreed upon and the time payment is actually made. For example, an American importer agrees to pay a given amount in francs for a shipment of French wine. At the time the contract is entered, 1 American dollar is worth 9 French francs. By the time payment is due under the contract, the exchange rate has changed so that 1 dollar is now worth 8 francs. The American importer must now spend more dollars to obtain the francs needed to pay the French wine exporter than was contemplated at the time the contract was agreed upon. The additional expense, due solely to fluctuating currency rates, may convert an anticipated profit into a loss. A business can protect itself against disadvantageous fluctuations by entering into a contract with a local bank that deals in foreign exchange for delivery of whatever francs are needed on the date payment is due. The risk of fluctuating exchange rates is thus passed on to the bank which routinely handles foreign exchange transfers.

Other monetary concerns arise where foreign countries place limits or conditions on the removal of business earnings by foreign investors. The general purpose of such laws is to discourage foreign investors from exploiting a given country's resources or market potential without leaving behind some of the benefits derived from the opportunity to do business. Some countries place absolute limits on the percentage of a foreign enterprise's investment that may be *repatriated,* or returned to the country of origin. Other countries levy graduated taxes on repatriated earnings, taxing higher amounts of earnings more heavily. Transnational corporations that are restricted by currency control laws from freely transferring and exchanging currencies across national borders can sometimes circumvent such restrictions by swapping currencies with another transnational corporation in the same country that has a similar but reverse need for the currency of another nation.

The Foreign Corrupt Practices Act (F.C.P.A.) was enacted by the United States government in 1977 as one means of requiring American businesses to account for expenditures made in the pursuit of international business. The F.C.P.A. requires American businesses to keep financial records that will accurately reflect the disposition of assets and assure that expenditures are in accordance with management's authorization. Key criminal provisions of the F.C.P.A. prohibit any American business or its agents from giving or paying "anything of value" to "any foreign official for the purpose of influencing any act or decision of such official." Businesses may be fined up to $1 million and individuals may be fined up to $10,000 and imprisoned for up to 5 years for violating the statute.

The F.C.P.A. antibribery provisions are viewed by some international businesses as an effort to impose American business ethics on trade in foreign countries where different ethical standards may prevail. For instance, payment of "bribes" to foreign officials may be a commonly accepted way of obtaining or retaining business in a foreign country. In such contexts, the F.C.P.A. may be viewed as creating competitive disadvantages for United States firms by making such payments illegal. On the other hand, American courts have interpreted the F.C.P.A. antibribery provisions as a legislative effort to avoid "a decline of foreign esteem for the United States" by discouraging suspicious activities by American business enterprises and requiring full accountability and disclosure of expenditures abroad.[4]

Extraterritoriality of Sovereign Business Regulations

How far can an American business enterprise expect the reach of its own country's laws or the laws of other countries in which it is operating to extend? It is a widely accepted principle of international law that one country can assert and enforce its laws in the territory of another country only with the permission of the other country. Nevertheless, American courts have taken the view that "... if Congress has expressly prescribed a rule with respect to conduct outside the United States, even one going beyond the scope recognized by ... foreign relations laws, a United States court would be bound to follow the Congressional direction unless this would violate the due process clause of the Fifth Amendment."[5] Attempts by the United States or other governments to assert laws governing international business transactions beyond their own borders have met with resistance from other nations.

Antitrust. American courts have attempted to assert United States antitrust laws beyond the boundaries of the United States (see Chapter 46). In the area of antitrust law, disputes over the efforts of American courts to assert jurisdiction abroad have met with retaliatory legislation. For example, the United Kingdom has enacted legislation that forbids English courts from enforcing antitrust judgments of American courts. This "clawback" legislation, called the Protection of Trading Interests Act (1980), is in apparent retaliation against perceived overreaching by United States courts. The British legislation also provides that a suit can be brought in English courts to recover any punitive damages levied by American courts as the result of antitrust claims.

The United States Congress took steps to clarify the extraterritorial scope of antitrust laws by enacting the Foreign Trade Antitrust Improvements Act of 1982. That act limits the extraterritorial application of antitrust laws to situations where conduct has a

[4]*Clayco Petroleum Corp. v. Occidental Petroleum Corp.*, 712 F.2d 404 (9th Cir. 1983).

[5]*Leasco Data Processing Equipment Corp. v. Maxwell,* 468 F.2d 1326, 1334 (2nd Cir. 1972).

direct, substantial, and reasonably foreseeable effect on import or export activities in the United States.

Taxes; Contractual Obligations. In addition to the extraterritorial application of American antitrust legislation, the United States has also asserted laws pertaining to taxation by claiming the right to inspect records held abroad by foreigners who do business in the United States. A further example of extraterritorial reach occurred in 1982 when, pursuant to authority granted in the Export Administration Act of 1979, the Commerce Department tried to compel European companies to dishonor contractual obligations to the Soviet Union to supply materials manufactured in the United States for use in the Soviet Union's Siberian-European oil pipeline.

Forum Non Conveniens. In some circumstances involving transnational business activities, disputes may arise that can be brought before the court of more than one jurisdiction. For example, where a corporation has a home office in the United States and is sued over alleged misconduct in a foreign country, jurisdiction may rest with a court in the United States because that is the corporation's residence, but jurisdiction may also rest with a court in the foreign country because the alleged misconduct occurred there. The common law doctrine of *forum non conveniens* permits a court to dismiss an action where it is determined that the action, although jurisdictionally sound, would be better adjudicated elsewhere. The burden rests upon the party challenging the forum to demonstrate relevant private or public interest factors which mitigate against accepting the litigation. The following case illustrates application of the doctrine of *forum non conveniens* in an international business context involving noncontractual issues.

CASE 48.3 In re Union Carbide Corporation Gas Plant Disaster · 634 F. Supp.842 (S.D.N.Y. 1986)

FACTS On December 3, 1984 the most tragic industrial disaster in history occurred in Bhopal, India. Located there was a chemical plant owned and operated by Union Carbide India Limited ("UCIL"), incorporated under Indian law in 1934, with 50.9% of its stock being owned by defendant, Union Carbide Corporation which was incorporated in New York. At the request of the Government of India, UCIL's Bhopal plant manufactured pesticides, using a highly toxic gas known as methyl isocyanate (MIC). On the night of the tragedy, for reasons yet undetermined, large quantities of MIC leaked from the plant and prevailing winds blew the deadly gas into overpopulated squatter huts near the plant and into the city, causing death of an estimated 2100 persons, injuring over 200,000 people, killing livestock, and damaging crops.

In March, 1985, the Indian Parliament enacted the Bhopal Gas Leak Disaster Act ("Bhopal Act"), which provided that the Government of India had the exclusive right to represent Indian plaintiffs in India and elsewhere in connection with the tragedy. In April 1985 the Union of India (plaintiff) filed a complaint with the U.S. District Court setting forth consolidated claims for relief on behalf of all Indian plaintiffs. In September 1985 the Central Government of India framed a plan for the registration and processing of claims arising from the disaster, and over 487,000 claims were filed. Defendant Union Carbide (the New York parent corporation) moved to dismiss the action on the grounds of forum non conveniens.

OPINION KEENAN, District Judge. The doctrine of *forum non conveniens* allows a court to decline jurisdiction, even when jurisdiction is authorized by a general venue statute. In support of its position that the consolidated action... should be transferred to a more convenient forum within the Union of India pursuant to this doctrine, Union Carbide relies on the United States Supreme Court's decision in *Gulf Oil Corp. v. Gilbert,* 330 U.S. 501 (1947) and *Piper Aircraft Co. v. Reyno,* 454 U.S. 235 (1981).... *Gilbert* and *Piper* are the touch-

CASE 48.3 Continued

stones in sorting out and examining the contentions of both sides to this motion on the various factors bearing on convenience.

. . . At this juncture, it would be appropriate to discuss the presumptions on a *forum non conveniens motion.* A plaintiff's choice of forum is entitled to great deference when the forum chosen is the home of the plaintiff. This presumption is based on the fact that the choice of the home forum indicated a reasonable assumption that the choice was convenient. . . . Conversely, when the plaintiff is foreign, this assumption is much less reasonable. Because the central purpose of any *forum non conveniens* inquiry is to ensure that the trial is convenient, a foreign plaintiff's choice of the United States forum deserves less deference than would be accorded a United States citizen's choice.

1. Preliminary Considerations

At the outset, the court must determine whether there exists an alternative forum. Ordinarily, this requirement will be satisfied when the defendant is "amenable to process" in the other jurisdiction. . . . A court engaged in the inquiry regarding the existence and adequacy of an alternative forum should not hinge its decision on an unfavorable change in the law. A change of forum might frequently involve an unfavorable change of law for foreign defendants. Consequently, if the unfavorable change in law were a major factor in the analysis, the American courts, which are already extremely attractive to foreign plaintiffs, would become even more attractive. The flow of litigation into the United States would increase and further congest already crowded courts. . . . Of course, if the remedy provided by the alternative forum is so clearly inadequate or unsatisfactory that it is no remedy at all, the unfavorable change in law may be given substantial weight; the district court may conclude that dismissal would not be in the interests of justice. Plaintiffs' preliminary concern, regarding defendant's amenability to process in the alternative forum, is more than sufficiently met in the instant case . . . Union Carbide is definitely amenable to process in India.

This Court acknowledges that delays and backlog exist in Indian courts, but United States courts are subject to delays and backlog too . . . However, the Bhopal Act permits the cases to be treated "speedily, effectively, equitably and to the best advantage of the claimants." . . . This Court is persuaded that the most significant, urgent and extensive litigation ever to arise from a single event could be handled through special judicial accommodation in India, if required.

To sum up the discussion to this point, the Court determines that the Indian legal system provides an adequate alternative forum for the Bhopal litigation. . . . Differences between the two legal systems, even if they inure to plaintiffs' detriment, do not suggest that India is not an adequate alternative forum. . . . The inquiry now turns to a weighing of the public and private interest factors.

2. Private Interest Concerns

. . . [T]he private interest factors in this case weigh strongly in favor of dismissal. The first example of a private interest consideration . . . is "relative ease of access to sources of proof." . . . Union Carbide argues that virtually all of the evidence which will be relevant at a trial in this case is located in India. . . . In the aggregate, it appears to the Court that most of the documentary evidence concerning design, training, safety and start-up, in other words, matters bearing on liability, is to be found in India.

Gilbert teaches a second important consideration . . . , the "availability of compulsory process for attendance of willing, and the cost of obtaining attendance of unwilling, witnesses." . . [M]ost witnesses whose testimony would relate to questions of causation and liability are in India.

The third private interest factor articulated in *Gilbert* is the ease of arranging for a view of the premises around which the litigation centers. . . . An Indian court is in a far better position than this Court to direct and supervise such a viewing should one ever be required . . .

CASE 48.3 Continued

3. Public Interest Concerns

The *Gilbert* Court articulated certain factors which affected the interests of non-parties to a litigation to be considered in the context of the doctrine of *forum non conveniens*. . . . The Court expressly identified a few factors:

> Administrative difficulties follow for courts when litigation is piled up in congested centers instead of being handled at its origin. Jury duty is a burden that ought not to be imposed upon the people of a community which has no relation to the litigation . . . There is a local interest in having local controversies decided at home. There is an appropriateness, too, in having . . . a forum that is at home with the . . . law that must govern the case.

. . . The substantial administrative weight of this case should be centered on a court with the most significant contacts with the event. Thus, a court in Bhopal, rather than New York, should bear the load.

In addition . . . [t]he taxpayers of this State should not be compelled to assume the heavy financial burden attributable to the cost of administering the litigation contemplated when their interest in the suit and the connection of its subject matter . . . is so ephemeral. Administrative concerns weigh against retention of this case.

. . . The specific American interests allegedly to be served by this Court's retention of the case include the opportunity of creating precedent which will "bind all American multinationals henceforward." . . . The incremental deterrence that would be gained if this trial were held in an American court is likely to be insignificant. The American interest in this accident is simply not sufficient to justify the enormous commitment of judicial time and resources that would inevitably be required if the case were to be tried here.

The Indian government, which regulated the Bhopal facility, has an extensive and deep interest in ensuring that its standards for safety are complied with . . . It would be sadly paternalistic, if not misguided, of this Court to attempt to evaluate the regulations and standards imposed in a foreign country.

The Court concludes that the public interest of India in this litigation far outweighs the public interest of the United States. This litigation offers a developing nation the opportunity to vindicate the suffering of its own people within the framework of a legitimate legal system. This interest is of paramount importance.

An Indian court . . . would be better able to apply the controlling law than would this United States Court, or a jury working with it. This public interest factor also weighs in favor of dismissal on the grounds of *forum non conveniens.*

JUDGMENT Therefore, the consolidated case is dismissed on the grounds of *forum non conveniens* under the following conditions that Union Carbide shall consent to submit to the jurisdiction of the courts of India. . . . So ordered.

Foreign Government Takeovers of Foreign Investments

From a business perspective, the most onerous form of government action with respect to a foreign investment is an actual takeover of the business by the government of the country in which the investment is located. Careful evaluation must precede investment where a government is perceived as unstable and susceptible to overthrow. In other countries, even though overthrow of the government may not be likely, a change in political control can result in radical changes in attitudes toward foreign investment. *Nationalization* is a general term that refers to the conversion of privately owned businesses into governmentally owned businesses. Nationalization of foreign-owned business is most likely to occur in unstable developing countries.

Expropriation; Confiscation. When a sovereign government takes over a business enterprise that belongs to foreign investors without adequately compensating them for the value of their investment, the result is referred to as an *expropriation.* Expropriation may be "legal" insofar as the actions taken by the foreign government comply procedurally with established law in the foreign country and serve a valid public purpose. The real issue for the business investor is whether or not the compensation paid by the expropriating government is "just" relative to the size of the investment. A governmental taking of a private business that neither serves a proper public purpose nor is justly compensated is referred to as a *confiscation.* Confiscations violate the generally adhered to principles of international law, whereas expropriations do not.

A transnational business enterprise that wishes to challenge the legality of a confiscation or dispute the amount of compensation received in an expropriation of its capital investment may face a losing battle because of two key doctrines of international law: the doctrine of sovereign immunity and the act of state doctrine.

Doctrine of Sovereign Immunity. The doctrine of sovereign immunity prohibits the domestic courts of one country from asserting jurisdiction over the acts of another country's government within that government's own territorial borders. The domestic courts of one country may, in certain instances, exercise jurisdiction over the acts of another sovereign government if the government is acting out of a commercial or business interest similar to any business enterprise. However, if the foreign government's acts are official acts with an expressed public or governmental purpose and not a commercial interest, courts will tend to apply the doctrine of sovereign immunity to raise a jurisdictional bar. The practical effect of this doctrine is that one who feels wronged by an expropriation or confiscation of business assets by a foreign government may fail to convince the courts within his or her home jurisdiction that there is a proper basis to exercise jurisdiction over the acts of the foreign government.

The general trend in the United States is toward finding exceptions to the doctrine of sovereign immunity. However, the Foreign Sovereign Immunities Act (1976) narrows the doctrine by excluding certain categories of action by foreign governments. Once a basis for jurisdiction over a foreign country's acts is alleged under the act, the burden of proof is upon the foreign country to demonstrate that immunity under the doctrine should still be granted.[6] The following case illustrates a current application of the doctrine of sovereign immunity under the act.

[6] *Matter of SEDCO, Inc.*, 543 F. Supp. 561 (S.D.Tex., 1982).

CASE 48.4 Texas Trading & Milling Corp. et al. v. Federal Republic of Nigeria · 647 F.2d 300 (1981)

FACTS KAUFMAN, Irving R., Circuit Judge. These four appeals grow out of one of the most enormous commercial disputes in history, and present questions which strike to the very heart of modern international economic order. An African nation [Nigeria], developing at breakneck speed by virtue of huge exports of high-grade oil, contracted to buy huge quantities of Portland cement, a commodity crucial to the construction of its infrastructure. It overbought, and the country's docks and harbors became clogged with ships waiting to unload. Unable to accept delivery of the cement it had bought, the nation repudiated its contracts. In response to suits brought by disgruntled suppliers, it now seeks to invoke sovereign immunity. For the ruling principles here, we must look to a new and vaguely worded statute, the Foreign Sovereign Immunities Act of 1976 ("FSIA"). Accordingly, we find that the defense of sovereign immunity is not available in any of these four cases.

OPINION In structure, the FSIA is a marvel of compression. Within the bounds of a few tersely-worded sections, it purports to provide answers to three crucial questions in a suit against a foreign state: the availability of sovereign immunity as a defense, the presence of subject matter jurisdiction over the claim, and the propriety of personal jurisdiction over the defendant.

CASE 48.4 Continued

[More specifically,] a foreign state shall not be immune from the jurisdiction of the courts of the United States or of the States in any case in which the action is based upon a commercial activity carried on in the United States by a foreign state; or upon an act performed in the United States in connection with a commercial activity of the foreign state elsewhere; or upon an act outside the territory of the United States in connection with a commercial activity of the foreign state elsewhere [if] that act causes a direct effect in the United States. If the activity is not "commercial" but, rather, is "governmental," then the foreign state is entitled to immunity and "original jurisdiction" is not present.

. . . A "commercial activity" means either a regular course of commercial conduct or a particular commercial transaction or act. The commercial character of an activity shall be determined by reference to the nature of the course of conduct or particular transaction or act, rather than by reference to its purpose. If "commercial activity" is present, and if it bears the relation to the United States required, then the foreign state is "not entitled to immunity," and the district court has subject matter jurisdiction over the claim.

Unfortunately, the definition of "commercial" is the one issue on which the Act provides almost no guidance at all.

The first source [of guidance] is statements contained in the legislative history itself. The second source for interpreting the phrase "commercial activity" is the "very large body of case law which exist[ed]" in American law upon passage of the Act in 1976. Finally, current standards of international law concerning sovereign immunity add content to the "commercial activity" phrase of the FSIA.

Under each of these three standards, Nigeria's cement contracts qualify as "commercial activity." Nigeria's activity here is in the nature of a private contract for goods. Its purpose—to build roads, army barracks, whatever—is irrelevant.

JUDGMENT The district court ordered the complaint dismissed for lack of jursidiction. That order is reversed, and the case is remanded.

Act-of-State Doctrine. The doctrine of sovereign immunity precludes a domestic court from judging the actions of a foreign government because of a lack of jurisdiction. By comparison, the act-of-state doctrine applies in situations where a domestic court has jurisdiction to consider the validity of foreign acts of state but chooses to abstain from ruling through a self-imposed exercise of judicial restraint. The act-of-state doctrine is based on the recognition that interference in the acts of a foreign government within *its* own territory by the courts of another nation may impair international relations between the countries and their respective citizens. In short, the validity of a foreign act of state in certain circumstances is a political question not cognizable in our courts.

The reluctance of one country's courts to sit in judgment on the acts of another country that occur within that country's own territory is a matter of *comity,* a voluntary recognition by the courts of the sovereignty of another country, resulting in a deliberate decision not to exercise jurisdiction. The following case illustrates differences between the doctrine of sovereign immunity and the act-of-state doctrine.

CASE 48.5 Allied Bank International v. Banco Credito Agricola de Cartago · 566 F. Supp. 1440 (1983)

FACTS GRIESE, District Judge. The essential facts are not in dispute. Plaintiff is a bank chartered with its principal place of business in New York. As a result of certain banking transac-

CASE 48.5 Continued

tions which need not be described in detail, the three defendant Costa Rican banks in 1976 executed a series of promissory notes payable to Plaintiff.

Payments were made on schedule until 1981. In that year Costa Rica was encountering a serious economic crisis. In response, the Costa Rican government imposed restrictions upon foreign exchange transactions. On November 6, 1981 the President of Costa Rica and the Ministry of Finance published an Executive Decree preventing any institution in Costa Rica from making payment on an external debt. Subsequently, the Central Bank notified each of the defendant banks that they would not be permitted to make external debt repayments pending resolution of the entire Costa Rican external debt situation. This effectively blocked all further payments on the promissory notes by defendant banks to plaintiffs.

There is no question about the fact that defendant banks have defaulted on debts due to Allied and the other syndicate banks.

However, various defenses are raised. All three defendants deny subject matter jurisdiction, asserting sovereign immunity. They also raise the defense of the act of state doctrine.

OPINION

The sovereign immunity issue is covered by statute—*i.e.*, the Foreign Sovereign Immunities Act of 1976. It is quite clear that the execution of the promissory notes, upon which this action is based, was a commercial activity within the meaning of the statute. It follows that the action is not barred by the doctrine of sovereign immunity.

A different question arises by virtue of the fact that the payment of the notes was prevented by certain directives of the Central Bank of Costa Rica, and of the President and Ministry of Finance of that country. This question is whether the governmental acts preventing payment of the notes fall within the act of state doctrine.

Even where the defense of sovereign immunity does not apply, nevertheless the act of state doctrine may prevent recovery. The act of state doctrine is designed to avoid judicial action which would impinge upon the foreign relations of the United States.

The Second Circuit has summarized the principal factors relied upon in the decisions for justifying application of the act of state doctrine—*i.e.*, where a court is asked to judge a foreign government's conduct under ambiguous principles of international law; where the challenged governmental conduct was public rather than commercial in nature, and where its purpose was to serve an integral governmental function; and where the executive branch of the United States Government has stated its view regarding the propriety of applying the act of state doctrine or regarding the validity of the foreign governmental action in question.

The crucial factor in the instant case is that the conduct of the Costa Rican government which *prevented payment* of the notes was public in nature, rather than commercial, and its purpose was to serve a governmental function.

A judgment in favor of Allied in this case would constitute a judicial determination that defendants must make payments contrary to the directives of their government. This puts the judicial branch of the United States at odds with policies laid down by a foreign government on an issue deemed by that government to be of central importance. Such an act by this court risks embarrassment to the relations between the executive branch of the United States and the Government of Costa Rica.

JUDGMENT

. . . Allied's motion for summary judgment is denied.

Overseas Private Investment Corporation (OPIC). American business investors who wish to hedge against the possibility of expropriation or confiscation of foreign investments by host governments may be able to insure against such risks through government-backed insurance. The Overseas Private Investment Corporation was created in 1969 as an agency of the United States with authority to insure American citizens' and corporations' private investments abroad. However, OPIC insurance is only available for new investments, and an applicant who seeks insurance must not take any binding action toward investing abroad without first obtaining approval of OPIC and the host country. OPIC insurance is available only for investments in countries that have signed bilateral investment guarantee treaties with the United States. However, there are more than 100 countries in which investments can qualify for OPIC insurance coverage.

Transnational Regulation of International Trade

Beyond the sovereign laws of nations that apply to international trade, international business activities in most countries are subject to a range of transnational business regulations. Transnational business regulations have developed largely through the formation of multinational regional trade communities and through various forms of international trade agreements and treaties.

Multinational Regional Trade Communities

The last three decades have seen the emergence of regional trade communities as important regulatory authorities for the conduct of international trade. *Regional trade communities* are organizations of countries that adopt and adhere to common trade policies and rules among member nations. The EEC is the most developed regional trade community, as evidenced in part by the fact that the EEC has transnational rule-making authority that is binding on member nations irrespective of national sentiments within member countries. Other significant regional trade communities are the Association of Southeast Asian Nations, formed in 1967 by Indonesia, Malaysia, the Philippines, Singapore, and Thailand; and the Andean Common Market, which was established in 1969 and now includes the countries of Bolivia, Colombia, Ecuador, Peru, and Venezuela. Additional regional trade communities have appeared among groups of African nations, Caribbean nations, and Arab oil-producing nations.

General Purposes. Regional trade communities share similar objectives. One common objective is to establish uniform trade regulations and tariff policies between member nations to promote expansion of trade and economic growth. Other objectives include establishing uniform trade policies relative to nonmember nations and obtaining favorable tariff or other concessions from nonmember nations by combining to form powerful economic bases from which to negotiate. Regional trade communities have also established judicial systems to resolve disputes arising from the treaty which created the community.

Each regional community has a central administrative authority and a representative body composed of designees from member nations that formulate common points of agreement among member nations. Community policies are carried out in a variety of ways. For example, the Association of Southeast Asian Nations has focused principally on instituting tariff reductions for goods transferred among member states, rather than on creating protective external tariffs. By comparison, the Andean Common Market has emphasized common external tariffs and extensive regulation of foreign investment within the region. Foreign investment in some industries is excluded altogether, and existing foreign-owned enterprises are now being required to reduce foreign ownership to a minority control position within a specified number of years. Furthermore, all direct foreign investment must be registered and the repatriation of annual profits or monies acquired through obligatory sales of majority interests by foreign investors is restricted.

European Economic Community (EEC) as an Example. The EEC was established in 1957 and its members now include Belgium, Denmark, France, Greece, Ireland, Italy, Luxembourg, Netherlands, Spain, the United Kingdom, and West Germany. The EEC countries are a powerful economic force with a combined annual gross product in excess of $2.8 trillion. The EEC is crucial to American business because as an economic unit it is the largest importer of American products in the world.

Organizational structure of EEC. A "Commission" that includes representatives from each member nation—but who operate independently of member nations—performs executive functions for the community. The Commission proposes legislation that is submitted to a "Council of Ministers" for possible adoption. The Council of Ministers is composed of appointed representatives of member nations and is empowered to act on proposals from the Commission, although it may not initiate proposals. A third body, the "Assembly" or European Parliament, also serves an important role. Members of the Assembly are elected directly by citizens of member states. The Assembly has the power to supervise the Commission and to inquire of the Council of Ministers. It has the authority to censure the Commission, in which event all Commissioners are required to resign.

The Commission and the Council of Ministers are each empowered to issue regulations, directives, or decisions that are binding upon member nations and their citizens. These rules are promulgated to carry out the purposes of the EEC as expressed in the treaties that created the community.

In addition to the above organizational components, there is a Court of Justice that interprets and applies the treaties that created the EEC. The Court of Justice also adjudicates questions of authority arising between the component bodies that legislate and govern the EEC. The Court of Justice plays a key role because its rulings become law for all member states, and national courts are required to implement and adhere to decisions by the Court of Justice. Where a conflict between community law and domestic law occurs, community law prevails. This principle is referred to as the "supremacy of European law." Furthermore, rules established by appropriate EEC authority or by decision of the Court of Justice apply directly to citizens of member nations. This principle is referred to as the doctrine of "direct effect." No ratification is required by national governmental authority, and citizens may invoke EEC law directly in national courts of member nations.

Effects of EEC laws on international business transactions. As with other regional trade communities, the EEC has promoted the free movement of goods, labor, and money services across national borders of member nations. Common tariff policies have been adopted toward nonmember states. In addition, numerous laws affecting business have been harmonized among member nations.

Articles 85 and 86 of the Treaty of Rome are among the most crucial provisions of the EEC that have implications for nonmember businesses engaged in commerce with member nations or their citizens. Article 85(1) prohibits all agreements which may affect trade between member states and which have as their objective or potential effect the prevention, restriction, or distortion of competition within the Common Market.

With limited exceptions or "exemptions," agreements that violate Article 85 are null and void and may result in large fines. For example, exclusive dealing arrangements that substantially affect the position of third parties could be held to be violations of Article 85 and could subject a licensee or distributee to costly sanctions. Article 85 expressly prohibits price fixing, limiting or controlling production or marketing, applying unequal terms to parties that give the same consideration, or requiring contract terms that have no connection in normal commercial usage to the subject matter of the contract.

An American business that enters into agreements in violation of Article 85 or 86 may find its actions will become the subject of a commission ruling or Court of Justice decision. The fact that one of the parties to a prohibited agreement is located in a nonmember country does not necessarily preclude applicability. For example, in *J. R. Geigy, AG v. Commission* (Court of Justice, July 14, 1972), the Court found a nonresident parent company liable for acts of a wholly owned subsidiary within the EEC, where the subsidiary's acts were dictated by the parent corporation. Similarly, in the *Continental Can* case (Court of Justice, February 21, 1973) a foreign parent company was held liable for the acquisition activities of a subsidiary that was domiciled within the EEC, where those activities violated Article 86. Any judgment entered within the EEC pursuant to Article 85 or 86 is enforceable by the national courts of any EEC member nation with which the American firm is doing business.

Negative clearance. It is possible for a business enterprise to obtain a formal opinion *in advance* as to whether a planned business activity would violate Article 85 or 86. The EEC Commission is authorized to issue declarations of "negative clearance" or formal certifications, based on the facts provided, that there are no grounds to assert a violation of Article 85 or 86. Businesses that contemplate questionable activities can thus avoid liability by learning ahead of time whether or not the Commission views such activities as prohibited.

International Trade Agreements

In addition to the important regulatory authority of multinational regional trade communities, businesses engaged in international trade need to be aware of applicable international trade agreements. Such trade agreements may exist among many different nations (multilateral agreements) or simply between one nation and another (bilateral treaties).

General Agreement on Tariffs and Trade. A significant example of a multilateral agreement is the General Agreement on Tariffs and Trade (GATT), which includes over eighty participating nations. The basic aim of GATT is to reduce barriers to international trade by reaching common agreement on such matters as import fees, customs, quantitative restrictions, subsidies, antidumping, and countervailing duties. The general effect of GATT provisions has been to promote even dealing among participating nations. Any advantage, favor, privilege, or immunity granted by one nation to another is automatically extended to other participating nations. Quantitative trade restrictions (import or export) by a nation are to be applied in like fashion to all other participating nations, rather than in a discriminatory manner.

GATT recognizes and makes provisions for circumstances in which participating nations may need to suspend or partially suspend cooperation under the Agreement, as, for example, when considerations of vital national interests or national security, or other exceptional circumstances arise.

The GATT has sponsored periodic multinational trade negotiations or "rounds" that have helped to advance the common objectives of promoting freer movement of goods among countries. Since the inception of GATT, tariff barriers to trade among participating nations have been reduced by approximately 70 percent in comparison with those existing two decades before. In addition, there has been substantial progress in lessening nontariff trade barriers and promoting nondiscrimination between domestically produced goods and imported goods. Future "rounds" are expected to focus on the international transfer of services, a rapidly expanding area of the international economy.

Convention on Contracts for the International Sale of Goods. On January 1, 1988 the United States joined nine other nations in adopting a significant new written agreement called the United Nations Convention on Contracts for the International Sale of Goods (CISG). The CISG developed out of a diplomatic conference that was organized by the United Nations General Assembly and met in Vienna in 1980. The conference, attended by sixty-two nations representing all sectors of the world community, concluded nearly 50 years of study and efforts toward the development of a uniform law on the international sale of goods. Thus far, the CISG has also been adopted by Argentina, China, Egypt, France, Hungary, Italy, Lesotho, Syria, Yugoslavia, and Zambia. Because of widespread participation in developing the CISG it is expected that many other countries will ratify it during the next few years and it will become the international sales law of the future.

The CISG creates a substantive law to govern the formation of international sales contracts and the rights and obligations of the buyer and seller. The CISG applies to transactions where the buyer and seller of goods are each located in a participating different country that has adopted the Convention, and where the contract between them does not specify applicable law. Individual buyers and sellers have a choice whether their transaction will fall under the Convention; if the parties to such a contract specify that other law will apply, then the Convention will not apply. If only one country has ratified the Convention and a dispute arises between buyer and seller in which conflict of law is an issue, the Convention may apply if the conflict of law rules are resolved in favor of the party whose country has ratified the Convention. For example, if a sales contract dispute arises between a buyer in the United States and a seller in the Philippines and a judge in the United States finds that U.S. laws are applicable where the parties did not specify a choice of law, then the judge would apply the CISG.

The Convention does not apply to consumer transactions. Also, it does not provide a basis for determining the validity of a contract, the effect of the transaction on the title in the goods, nor liability for death or personal injury caused by the goods. For example, a contractual dispute arising out of claimed defects in the quality of manufactured goods sold by an Italian exporter to a United States importer would fall within the CISG. However, a tort claim arising out of personal injuries caused to the U.S. importer by a claimed defect in the manufactured goods would not fall within the CISG. Again, these principles apply only in the absence of a contrary agreement by the parties.

In many respects, the Convention is similar to the Uniform Commercial Code (U.C.C.) in its approach. Like the U.C.C., the CISG attempts to give full effect to the intention of the parties, consistent with the normal expectations of other business enterprises in the same trade. The Convention gives rise to a presumption that the parties have intended to follow normal trade usage and course of dealing practices. The Convention also provides that in the absence of a contrary agreement, the goods being traded are fit for the purpose intended, or fit for any particular use known to the seller or otherwise contemplated by the parties.

As a practical matter, monetary compensation for damages is the main remedy provided for by the CISG, although in specific instances other remedies such as specific performance (requiring a party to fulfill the original promises), rejection of goods, or a reduction of price (a "self help" remedy sometimes available to the buyer) may be applicable. The CISG emphasizes completing performance of a contract: a party may avoid a contract altogether only if there has been a fundamental breach by the other party. Both the CISG and the U.C.C. grant the seller the same basic right to cure a breach, before or after the time for performance. Also like the U.C.C., the CISG limits recovery to foreseeable losses which the nonbreaching party could not reasonably avoid. The overall objective is to put the damaged party in the same position she or he would have been in if the other party had fully performed.

In overview, the CISG represents a significant and potentially far-reaching improvement in the laws governing international sales of goods. In addition to affecting trade activities that cross sovereign borders, international treaties cover activities such as extracting minerals from the seabed (United Nations Conference on Law of the Sea) and operating commercial telecommunications satellites (Outer Space Treaty of 1967).

Bilateral Treaties. Bilateral treaties between the United States and other individual countries are another source of international business regulation. While a discussion of specific treaties is beyond the scope of this chapter, it is noteworthy that such agreements often provide specific protections for businesses engaged in international trade. Particularly important are agreements that one nation's citizens will be accorded rights in the courts of the other nation to the same extent as resident citizens of that nation.

The Treaty Section of the Office of Legal Affairs in the United Nations Secretariat registers and publishes treaties and international agreements affecting business. Since 1946, the UN Secretariat has published over 30,000 international treaties that directly or indirectly affect international business.

Summary

International business law concerns business transactions that cross international boundaries. A variety of problems are encountered by the business enterprises dealing in foreign countries. First, decisions must be made concerning the type and extent of business activity, with the alternatives ranging from direct sales, franchising or licensing, to joint ventures, or the establishment of wholly owned subsidiaries by transactional business corporations. International transactions require special arrangements to assure each party of delivery and payment. Issuing and correspondent banks can facilitate such assurances by handling the transfer of documents and payment of money in local currency.

Each nation imposes laws and regulations on international business transactions. Regulation of imports affects tangible products as well as intellectual property such as patents and trademarks. Customs officials who enforce applicable laws must classify imports by type and determine value and country of origin in order to properly apply import laws. Export controls include licensing requirements and controls on the export of technology and scarce resources.

Sovereign nations also regulate the flow of money across international borders. Business enterprises must examine the extraterritorial reach of sovereign laws to determine whether planned activities will be subject to regulation by the home country's laws. In situations where foreign investments are nationalized through confiscation or expropriation, recourse through the courts may be limited by the doctrine of sovereign immunity or the act-of-state doctrine. Government-sponsored insurance through OPIC is one means of controlling risk in foreign investment.

In addition to the laws of sovereign nations, regional trade communities composed of multiple nations have an important regulating effect on international trade. The European Economic Community (EEC) is the most developed of such regional trade communities. Rules adopted by the EEC are binding on member nations as well as their citizens and may result in liability to investors located in nonmember nations. Articles 85 and 86 of the Treaty of Rome are particularly far-reaching provisions.

Multilateral trade agreements such as the General Agreement on Tariffs and Trade (GATT) play a significant role in regulating international trade. The Convention on Contracts for the International Sale of Goods, effective January 1, 1988, is a uniform law of international sales widely adopted by major industrial countries of the world. Bilateral treaties that provide mutual assurances to the citizens of agreeing nations are also important to international business.

Review Questions

1 What does the term "balance of payments" refer to and why is it significant?

2 What business considerations are relatively unique to international trade?

3 What are "choice-of-law" and "choice-of-forum" clauses in business contracts, and how can they be used to advantage in the context of international trade?

4 How important are arbitration clauses in international business contracts? Explain.

5 Define and differentiate "exclusive distributorships" and "exclusive dealing." What are the antitrust implications of each type of arrangement?

6 What advantages may a transnational business corporation exercise over other forms of multinational enterprise in order to minimize labor costs and taxes and maximize profits?

7 What economic and other purposes are served by regulating international trade?

8 To what extent do patents and trademarks afford international protection to their holders?

9 What similarities and differences are there in the policies that underlie the regulation of imports versus exports?

10 What advantages might a country gain by restricting the transfer of currencies across its borders?

11 How far can an American business enterprise expect the reach of its own country's laws to extend?

12 What considerations in the doctrine of *forum non conveniens* may limit the extraterritorial reach of United States courts?

13 Define and differentiate "expropriation" and "confiscation."

14 What principal objectives are sought through multinational regional trade communities?

15 How has the General Agreement on Tariffs and Trade (GATT) affected the volume and nature of international business transactions? What influence is GATT likely to exert in the future?

16 Describe the main features of the Convention on Contracts for the International Sale of Goods. Under what circumstances will the Convention apply?

Case Problems

1 Company A wishes to assure that it will receive prompt full payment in American dollars for goods it has agreed to ship to Company B, a foreign purchaser. How can Company B provide the assurance that Company A seeks?

2 Country A expropriates the property of a business that is incorporated in Country A but whose principal shareholders are residents of Country B. The corporation is made an instrumentality of Country A. The shareholders file suit in Country B to recover lost proceeds from the corporation. Will the court in Country B proceed to rule on the merits of the case? What reasoning may the court use to justify its decision?

3 Universe Tankships, defendant, chartered a cargo ship which was used to transport wheat from the United States to Egypt. Plaintiff Ministry of Supply, Cairo, the purchaser of the wheat, found that the wheat was damaged upon its arrival in Cairo and halted the discharge of the cargo for 81 days. Plaintiff then filed an action for cargo damages against defendant in the U.S. District Court having jurisdiction where the contract arose. Defendant counterclaimed for losses that it alleged occurred because plaintiff wrongfully halted offloading of the wheat. It is conceded that plaintiff is an "agency or instrumentality" of Egypt within the meaning of the Foreign Sovereign Immunities Act of 1976. Plaintiff argues that defendant's counterclaim is barred on the ground of sovereign immunity. What decision is the District Court likely to reach on the issue of whether the counterclaim is barred, and why?

4 A British supplier of electric massage appliances contracted with a German importer wherein the German importer became the sole distributor of its appliances in France and West Germany. Subsequently, the German importer entered into a separate agreement with a French distributor wherein the French distributor became the sole distributor of the electric massage appliances in France. The French distributor began selling the appliances, but when other similar massage instruments appeared in French markets, the French distributor broke its agreement with the German distributor. The German distributor then sued for damages resulting from the French distributor's alleged breach of contract. The French distributor answered, claiming that its agreement with the German distributor was null and void because it violated Article 85, paragraph 1, of the Treaty of Rome and thus could not be a basis for claiming damages. Does the Treaty of Rome apply to the facts in this case? If so, which party will prevail? Why?

5 Deepsouth Packing Company and Laitram Corporation each held patents on machines that devein shrimp. Laitram's patent prevented Deepsouth from selling its machines in the United States. However, Deepsouth began selling its machines outside the United States. Laitram sued, asserting that its patent rights should apply to halt Deepsouth's actions abroad. Which party is likely to prevail, and why?

ETHICS IN PRACTICE

International business is perhaps the most difficult area in which to develop and apply consistent standards of business ethics. Differences in language, customs, traditions, and religions of the societies that compose the trading nations account for the wide divergence of ethical principles encountered throughout the world. For example, in many third world countries it is common for high-ranking officials to ask for and receive secret payments in exchange for directing government business to a particular firm or facilitating the flow of goods across a border. To these officials and to much of the population, such payoffs are customary and well within the bounds of ethical business practices.

This view contrasts sharply with ethical standards in the United States. Here, commercial bribery is thought to have so many harmful effects as to be difficult to justify morally. For one thing, if corporate executives were allowed to disburse secret funds for bribes, they would have no accountability to the shareholders and would be in a position to misappropriate corporate funds for their own use. Moreover, if it is acceptable to pay bribes to foreign governmental officials, it might also be acceptable to bribe foreign customers and to receive return bribes in the form of kickbacks from foreign suppliers. Business decisions might turn on the size of the bribe rather than the quality of goods and services, and consumers here and abroad would face increased costs and danger to their health and safety. Bribe-related misappropriations by executives of large American corporations became such a problem that Congress in 1977 enacted the Foreign Corrupt Practices Act, discussed in Chapter 43.

Some foreign business practices are so traditional and time-honored that to ignore them would amount to a breach of ethics. For example, it is widely recognized that Japanese businesspersons negotiating a contract rarely close a deal at the first meeting, but prefer to consider the offer and subsequent counteroffers in a series of meetings. An impatient American who insists on concluding a deal in a single prolonged negotiating session may be considered offensive for violating such a deeply ingrained custom. Diverse religious practices pose similar problems. For example, Brazil is a predominantly Catholic country with many religious holidays that are widely observed. It would be inefficient and perhaps offensive for an American routinely to schedule business conferences on such days.

The laws of a country establish mandatory standards of business conduct. However, business practices that do not violate the law may nevertheless create ethical dilemmas and undesirable repercussions. "Dumping" excess inventory at below-cost prices into a foreign market may violate that country's law. Even if the country does not prohibit dumping, the practice can have a highly disruptive impact on prices, sales, and production of local competitors in the importing country, which then may impose retaliatory governmental import restrictions. Another form of dumping—the export to unregulated foreign markets of dangerous or defective products banned from sale in the United States—raises serious questions of business ethics and corporate social responsibility.[7] This kind of dumping is especially troublesome where the banned products are sent to developing countries whose populations are unaware of the danger or unable to cope with it.

The following problems illustrate some ethical dilemmas typical of international business transactions.

Problems in Ethics

1 Computek, an American manufacturer, has an inventory of 10,000 of last year's Model 10 computers which it will not be able to sell in the United States because its

[7]Frank B. Cross & Brenda J. Winslett, "'Export Death': Ethical Issues and the International Trade in Hazardous Products," 25 *American Business Law Journal* 487 (1987).

new Model 11 is about to be released on the American market. Computek has an offer from a German distributor to buy the computers at a price 50 percent below cost. This price will enable the German distributor to sell the computers at prices 60 percent cheaper than prices charged by local competitors for German computers of like quality. Recently, German legislators have increasingly clamored for import quotas, higher tariffs, and other restrictive trade measures aimed at American imports. Computek's management has good reason to believe that its sale, amounting to more than $10 million, will trigger enactment of restrictive legislation. Computek predicts that such legislation would close Germany's doors to Computek products, adversely affect thousands of American exporters of other manufactured goods, and fuel retaliatory trade legislation by the United States Congress. What ethical norms should Computek consider in deciding whether to accept the German buyer's offer?

2 Pharmatek has spent over $2 million in research on a drug antidote for AIDS (acquired immune deficiency syndrome). Medical experimentation with 100 patients has indicated the drug is reasonably effective. However, the Food and Drug Administration has mandated 2 years of further testing because there is not sufficient data to evaluate the side effects of the drug. Until investigation of the side effects is complete, the FDA will not certify the drug, thus precluding sales in the United States for 2 years. Namibia and its neighboring African nations have fewer governmental restrictions on the introduction of medicines and drugs, and it is legal for Pharmatek to manufacture and distribute its product there. Pharmatek is considering whether it should invest $2 million in a manufacturing laboratory in Namibia and widely advertise its drug among African nations that will permit its use. Although most of these nations do not compile reliable statistics, Pharmatek estimates that 500,000 people will die in Africa from AIDS each year that a cure is not found. Pharmatek's management believes, on the basis of Pharmatek's limited medical research, that the drug has no harmful side effects. With regard to Pharmatek's plan to manufacture, advertise, and distribute the drug in Africa, what ethical considerations should management take into account?

3 Eli Lily manufactures Spike, a herbicide that destroys coca bushes, the source of illegal cocaine. In cooperation with the Peruvian government, the United States government wishes to buy a large quantity of Spike to spread on 120 square miles of coca bushes in the Andes' Huallaga Valley, the world's number one source of cocaine. Lily fears that if it permits export of its product to Peru, it may become subject to suits such as those against the makers of Agent Orange, alleging that Agent Orange caused cancer in people who came into contact with it. Lawsuits and adverse publicity might arise if local workers in Peru come into contact with Spike or if it is improperly applied. Dow Chemical manufactures another herbicide, Garlon-4, that also destroys coca bushes. Dow shares Lily's concern that misapplication of the product could raise complex environmental and health controversies in a tropical country where the herbicide had not previously been used. Each company fears potential terrorist reprisals if its product is sold and used to eradicate lucrative coca crops that belong to large organized-crime syndicates. Neither company believes that the profit on the sale would justify the potential risks. With proper application, both products have been used safely in the United States to kill brush along utility rights-of-way. The managements of Lily and Dow recognize the importance of the war on drug trafficking, but refuse to sell the herbicides to the government. **(a)** Does the concept of "corporate social responsibility" (see Ethics in Practice for Part Ten) require Lily and Dow to sell their products for drug eradication in Peru? **(b)** Suppose that the U.S. or the Peruvian government would be willing to indemnify Lily and Dow for any losses resulting from herbicide-related lawsuits. Would this fact change your assessment of their corporate social responsibility? **(c)** The U.S. government has threatened to take away Lily's patent for Spike and give it to a more cooperative firm. Although the legality of such a move is in doubt, Lily could incur substantial costs in defending against the government's action. Is the government acting ethically in making the threat?

4 John and Sara are vice presidents of Oilco, each receiving annual salaries of over $200,000 plus substantial fringe benefits. After the Arab oil embargo in 1979, they learned that Oilco's chairman had made payments of millions of dollars to intermediaries who had ties with the leader of an oil-rich foreign country to help the company obtain crude oil from that country. John and Sara (a lawyer) believe that the payments violated the Foreign Corrupt Practices Act and the Racketeer Influenced and Corrupt Organizations Act (RICO). They also believe, however, that if they "blow the whistle" on the chairman, Oilco will fire them. If fired, they are unlikely to find employment at the high salaries they receive from Oilco, since prospective employers might be reluctant to hire "whistleblowers." Because they were engaged in other activities that made it impossible for them to participate in the bribery, they believe that if the chairman is prosecuted, neither of them will be implicated. Furthermore, if the chairman is convicted, one of them might be in line for promotion to the position of chairman. **(a)** Should John and Sara report the chairman's activity to the federal authorities? **(b)** Would your answer be different if you knew that exposure of the chairman's activities would eventually cost Oilco millions of dollars in fines and penalties?

APPENDIXES

1
Excerpts from the U. S. Constitution

2
Uniform Commercial Code

3
Uniform Partnership Act

4
Uniform Limited Partnership Act (1976),
with 1985 Amendments

5
Revised Model Business Corporation Act
(1984), as Amended

APPENDIX 1
Excerpts from the U. S. Constitution

ARTICLE I

Section 8. The Congress shall have power to lay and collect taxes, duties, imposts and excises, to pay the debts and provide for the common defence and general welfare of the United States; but all duties, imposts and excises shall be uniform throughout the United States:

To borrow money on the credit of the United States:

To regulate commerce with foreign nations, and among the several states, and with the Indian tribes:

To establish an uniform rule of naturalization, and uniform laws on the subject of bankruptcies throughout the United States:

To coin money, regulate the value thereof, and of foreign coin, and fix the standard of weights and measures:

To provide for the punishment of counterfeiting the securities and current coin of the United States:

To establish post-offices and post-roads:

To promote the progress of science and useful arts, by securing for limited times to authors and inventors the exclusive right to their respective writings and discoveries:

To constitute tribunals inferior to the supreme court:

. . . And to make all laws which shall be necessary and proper for carrying into execution the foregoing powers, and all other powers vested by this constitution in the government of the United States, or in any department or officer thereof.

Section 9. . . . No *ex post facto* law shall be passed.

. . . No tax or duty shall be laid on articles exported from any state.

Section 10. No state shall enter into any treaty, alliance, or confederation; . . . pass any . . . *ex post facto* law, or law impairing the obligation of contracts. . . .

ARTICLE III

Section 1. The judicial power of the United States, shall be vested in one supreme court, and in such inferior courts as the Congress may, from time to time, ordain and establish. The judges, both of the supreme and inferior courts, shall hold their offices during good behavior, and shall, at stated times, receive for their services a compensation, which shall not be diminished during their continuance in office.

Section 2. The juducial power shall extend to all cases, in law and equity, arising under this constitution, the laws of the United States, and treaties made, or which shall be made under their authority; to all cases affecting ambassadors, other public ministers and consuls; to all cases of admiralty and maritime jurisdiction; to controversies to which the United States shall be a party: to controversies between two or more states, between a state and citizens of another state, between citizens of different states, between citizens of the same state, claiming lands under grants of different states, and between a state, or the citizens thereof, and foreign states, citizens or subjects.

In all cases affecting ambassadors, other public ministers and consuls, and those in which a state shall be party, the supreme court shall have original jurisdiction. In all the other cases before-mentioned, the supreme court shall have appellate jurisdiction, both as to law and fact, with such exceptions, and under such regulations as the Congress shall make.

The trial of all crimes, except in cases of impeachment, shall be held by jury; and such trial shall be held in the state where the said crimes shall have been committed; but when not committed within any state, the trial shall be at such place or places as the Congress may by law have directed.

ARTICLE IV

Section 1. Full faith and credit shall be given in each state to the public acts, records and judicial proceedings of every other state. . . .

AMENDMENT I

The first 10 Amendments, called the "Bill of Rights," were ratified and adopted December 15, 1791.)

Congress shall make no law respecting an establishment of religion, or prohibiting the free exercise thereof; or abridging the freedom of speech or of the press; or the right of the people peaceably to assemble, and to petition the government for a redress of grievances.

AMENDMENT IV

The right of the people to be secure in their persons, houses, papers, and effects, against unreasonable searches and seizures, shall not be violated, and no warrants shall issue but upon probable cause, supported by oath or affirmation, and particularly describing the place to be searched, and the persons or things to be seized.

AMENDMENT V

No person shall be held to answer for a capital or other infamous crime unless on a presentment or indictment of a grand jury, except in cases arising in the land or naval forces, or in the militia, when in actual service, in time of war or public danger; nor shall any person be subject for the same offence to be twice put in jeopardy of life or limb; nor shall be compelled in any criminal case to be a witness against himself, nor be deprived of life, liberty, or property, without due process of law; nor shall private property be taken for public use without just compensation.

AMENDMENT VI

In all criminal prosecutions, the accused shall enjoy the right to a speedy and public trial, by an impartial jury of the state and district wherein the crime shall have been commmitted, which district shall have been previously ascertained by law, and to be informed of the nature and cause of the accusation; to be confronted with the witnesses against him; to have compulsory process for obtaining witnesses in his favor, and to have the assistance of counsel for his defence.

AMENDMENT XIII (Ratified 1865)

Section 1. Neither slavery nor involuntary servitude, except as a punishment for crime whereof the party shall have been duly convicted, shall exist within the United States, or any place subject to their jurisdiction.

AMENDMENT XIV (Ratified 1868)

Section 1. All persons born or naturalized in the United States, and subject to the jurisdiction thereof, are citizens of the United States and of the state wherein they reside. No state shall make or enforce any law which shall abridge the privileges or immunities of citizens of the United States; nor shall any state deprive any person of life, liberty, or property without due process of law; nor deny to any person within its jurisdiction the equal protection of the law.

AMENDMENT XVI (Ratified 1913)

The Congress shall have the power to lay and collect taxes on incomes, from whatever source derived, without apportionment among the several States, and without regard to any census of enumeration.

APPENDIX 2
Uniform Commercial Code*

ARTICLE 1: GENERAL PROVISIONS

Part 1: Short Title, Construction, Application and Subject Matter of the Act

§1-101. Short title. This act shall be known and may be cited as Uniform Commercial Code.

§1-102. Purposes; Rules of Construction; Variation by Agreement.

(1) This Act shall be liberally construed and applied to promote its underlying purposes and policies.

(2) Underlying purposes and policies of this Act are

(a) to simplify, clarify and modernize the law governing commercial transactions;

(b) to permit the continued expansion of commercial practices through custom, usage and agreement of the parties;

(c) to make uniform the law among the various jurisdictions.

(3) The effect of provisions of this Act may be varied by agreement, except as otherwise provided in this Act and except that the obligations of good faith, diligence, reasonableness and care prescribed by this Act may not be disclaimed by agreement but the parties may be agreement determine the standards by which the performance of such obligations is to be measured if such standards are not manifestly unreasonable.

(4) The presence in certain provisions of this Act of the words "unless otherwise agreed" or words of similar import does not imply that the effect of other provisions may not be varied by agreement under subsection (3).

(5) In this Act unless the context otherwise requires

(a) words in the singular number include the plural, and in the plural include the singular;

(b) words of the masculine gender include the feminine and the neuter, and when the sense so indicates words of the neuter gender may refer to any gender.

§1-103. Supplementary General Principles of Law Applicable. Unless displaced by the particular provisions of this Act, the principles of law and equity, including the law merchant and the law relative to capacity to contract, principal and agent, estoppel, fraud, misrepresentation, duress, coercion, mistake, bankruptcy, or other validating or invalidating cause shall supplement its provisions.

§1-104. Construction Against Implicit Repeal. This Act being a general act intended as a unified coverage of its

 The 1972 version of Article 9 and the 1977 version of Article 8 appear in this appendix.

subject matter, no part of it shall be deemed to be impliedly repealed by subsequent legislation if such construction can reasonably be avoided.

§1-105. Territorial Application of the Act; Parties' Power to Choose Applicable Law.

(1) Except as provided hereafter in this section, when a transaction bears a reasonable relation to this state and also to another state or nation the parties may agree that the law either of this state or of such other state or nation shall govern their rights and duties. Failing such agreement this Act applies to transactions bearing an appropriate relation to this state.

(2) Where one of the following provisions of this Act specifies the applicable law, that provision governs and a contrary agreement is effective only to the extent permitted by the law (including the conflict of laws rules) so specified:

Rights of creditors against sold goods. Section 2-402.

Applicability of the Article on Bank Deposits and Collections. Section 4-102.

Bulk transfers subject to the Article on Bulk Transfers. Section 6-102.

Applicability of the Article on Investment Securities. Section 8-106.

Perfection provisions of the Article on Secured Transactions. Section 9-103.

§1-106. Remedies to Be Liberally Administered.

(1) The remedies provided by this Act shall be liberally administered to the end that the aggrieved party may be put in as good a position as if the other party had fully performed but neither consequential or special nor penal damages may be had except as specifically provided in this Act or by other rule of law.

(2) Any right or obligation declared by this Act is enforceable by action unless the provision declaring it specifies a different and limited effect.

§1-107. Waiver or Renunciation of Claim or Right After Breach. Any claim or right arising out of an alleged breach can be discharged in whole or in part without consideration by a written waiver or renunciation signed and delivered by the aggrieved party.

§1-108. Severability. If any provision or clause of this Act or application thereof to any person or circumstances is held invalid, such invalidity shall not affect other provisions or applications of the Act which can be given effect without the invalid provision or application, and to this end the provisions of this Act are declared to be severable.

§1-109. Section Captions. Section captions are parts of this Act.

Part 2: General Definitions and Principles of Interpretation

§1-201. General Definitions. Subject to additional definitions contained in the subsequent Articles of this Act which are applicable to specific Articles or Parts thereof, and unless the context otherwise requires, in this Act.

(1) "Action" in the sense of a judicial proceeding includes recoupment, counterclaim, set-off, suit in equity and any other proceedings in which rights are determined.

(2) "Aggrieved party" means a party entitled to resort to a remedy.

(3) "Agreement" means the bargain of the parties in fact as found in their language or by implication from other circumstances including course of dealing or usage of trade or course of performance as provided in this Act, (Section 1-205 and 2-208). Whether an agreement has legal consequences is determined by the provisions of this Act, if applicable; otherwise by the law of contracts (Section 1-103). (Compare "Contract".)

(4) "Bank" means any person engaged in the business of banking.

(5) "Bearer" means the person in possession of an instrument, document of title, or certificated security payable to bearer or indorsed in blank.

(6) "Bill of lading" means a document evidencing the receipt of goods for shipment issued by a person engaged in the business of transporting or forwarding goods, and includes an airbill. "Airbill" means a document serving for air transportation as a bill of lading does for marine or rail transportation, and includes an air consignment note or air waybill.

(7) "Branch" includes a separately incorporated foreign branch of a bank.

(8) "Burden of establishing" a fact means the burden of persuading the triers of fact that the existence of the fact is more probable than its non-existence.

(9) "Buyer in ordinary course of business" means a person who in good faith and without knowledge that the sale to him is in violation of the ownership rights or security interest of a third party in the goods buys in ordinary course from a person in the business of selling goods of that kind but does not include a pawnbroker. All persons who sell minerals or the like (including oil and gas) at wellhead or minehead shall be deemed to be persons in the business of selling goods of that kind. "Buying" may be for cash or by exchange of other property or on secured or unsecured credit and includes receiving goods or documents of title under a pre-existing contract for sale but does not include a transfer in bulk or as security for or in total or partial satisfaction of a money debt.

(10) "Conspicuous": A term or clause is conspicuous when it is so written that a reasonable person against whom it is to operate ought to have noticed it. A printed heading in capitals (as: NON-NEGOTIABLE BILL OF LADING) is conspicuous. Language in the body of a form is "conspicuous" if it is in larger or other contrasting type or color. But in a telegram any stated term is "conspicuous". Whether a term or clause is "conspicuous" or not is for decision by the court.

(11) "Contract" means the total legal obligation which results from the parties' agreement as affected by this Act and any other applicable rules of law. (Compare "Agreement".)

(12) "Creditor" includes a general creditor, a secured creditor, a lien creditor and any representative of creditors, including an assignee for the benefit of creditors, a trustee in

bankruptcy, a receiver in equity and an executor or administrator of an insolvent debtor's or assignor's estate.

(**13**) "Defendant" includes a person in the position of defendant in a cross-action or counterclaim.

(**14**) "Delivery" with respect to instruments, documents of title, chattel paper, or certificated securities means voluntary transfer of possession.

(**15**) "Document of title" includes bill of lading, dock warrant, dock receipt, warehouse receipt or order for the delivery of goods, and also any other document which in the regular course of business or financing is treated as adequately evidencing that the person in possession of it is entitled to receive, hold and dispose of the document and the goods it covers. To be a document of title a document must purport to be issued by or addressed to a bailee and purport to cover goods in the bailee's possession which are either identified or are fungible portions of an identified mass.

(**16**) "Fault" means wrongful act, omission or breach.

(**17**) "Fungible" with respect to goods or securities means goods or securities of which any unit is, by nature or usage of trade, the equivalent of any other like unit. Goods which are not fungible shall be deemed fungible for the purposes of this Act to the extent that under a particular agreement or document unlike units are treated as equivalents.

(**18**) "Genuine" means free of forgery or counterfeiting.

(**19**) "Good faith" means honesty in fact in the conduct or transaction concerned.

(**20**) "Holder" means a person who is in possession of a document of title or an instrument or a certificated investment security drawn, issued or indorsed to him or to his order or to bearer or in blank.

(**21**) To "honor" is to pay or to accept and pay, or where a credit so engages to purchase or discount a draft complying with the terms of the credit.

(**22**) "Insolvency proceedings" includes any assignment for the benefit of creditors or other proceedings intended to liquidate or rehabilitate the estate of the person involved.

(**23**) A person is "insolvent" who either has ceased to pay his debts in the ordinary course of business or cannot pay his debts as they become due or is insolvent within the meaning of the federal bankruptcy law.

(**24**) "Money" means a medium of exchange authorized or adopted by a domestic or foreign government as part of its currency.

(**25**) A person has "notice" of a fact when

(**a**) he has actual knowledge of it; or

(**b**) he has received a notice or notification of it; or

(**c**) from all the facts and circumstances known to him at the time in question he has reason to know that it exists.

A person "knows" or has "knowledge" of a fact when he has actual knowledge of it. "Discover" or "learn" or a word or phrase of similar import refers to knowledge rather than to reason to know. The time and circumstances under which a notice or notification may cease to be effective are not determined by this Act.

(**26**) A person "notifies" or "gives" a notice or notification to another by taking such steps as may be reasonably required to inform the other in ordinary course whether or not such other actually comes to know of it. A person "receives" a notice or notification when

(**a**) it comes to his attention; or

(**b**) it is duly delivered at the place of business through which the contract was made or at any other place held out by him as the place for receipt of such communications.

(**27**) Notice, knowledge or a notice or notification received by an organization is effective for a particular transaction from the time when it is brought to the attention of the individual conducting that transaction, and in any event from the time when it would have been brought to his attention if the organization had exercised due diligence. An organization exercises due diligence if it maintains reasonable routines for communicating significant information to the person conducting the transaction and there is reasonable compliance with the routines. Due diligence does not require an individual acting for the organization to communicate information unless such communication is part of his regular duties or unless he has reason to know of the transaction and that the transaction would be materially affected by the information.

(**28**) "Organization" includes a corporation, government or governmental subdivision or agency, business trust, estate, trust, partnership or association, two or more persons having a joint or common interest, or any other legal or commercial entity.

(**29**) "Party", as distinct from "third party", means a person who has engaged in a transaction or made an agreement within this Act.

(**30**) "Person" includes an individual or an organization (See Section 1-102).

(**31**) "Presumption" or "presumed" means that the trier of fact must find the existence of the fact presumed unless and until evidence is introduced which would support a finding of its non-existence.

(**32**) "Purchase" includes taking by sale, discount, negotiation, mortgage, pledge, lien, issue or re-issue, gift or any other voluntary transaction creating an interest in property.

(**33**) "Purchaser" means a person who takes by purchase.

(**34**) "Remedy" means any remedial right to which an aggrieved party is entitled with or without resort to a tribunal.

(**35**) "Representative" includes an agent, an officer of a corporation or association, and a trustee, executor or administrator of an estate, or any other person empowered to act for another.

(**36**) "Rights" includes remedies.

(**37**) "Security interest" means an interest in personal property or fixtures which secures payment or performance of an obligation. The retention or reservation of title by a seller of goods notwithstanding shipment or delivery to the buyer (Section 2-401) is limited in effect to a reservation of a "security interest". The term also includes any interest of a buyer of accounts or chattel paper, which is subject to Article 9. The special property interest of a buyer of goods on identification of such goods to a contract for sale under Section 2-401 is not a "security interest", but a buyer may also acquire a "security interest" by complying with Article 9. Unless a lease or consignment is intended as security, reservation of title thereunder is not a "security interest" but a consignment is in any event subject to the provisions on consignment sales (Section 2-326). Whether a lease is intended as security is to be determined by the facts of each case; however, (a) the inclusion of an option to purchase does not of itself make the lease one intended for security, and (b) an agreement that upon compliance with the terms of the lease the lessee shall become or has the option to become the owner of the property for no additional consideration or for a nominal consideration does make the lease one intended for security.

(**38**) "Send" in connection with any writing or notice means to deposit in the mail or deliver for transmission by any other usual means of communication with postage or cost of transmission provided for and properly addressed and in the case of an instrument to an address specified thereon or otherwise agreed, or if there by none to any address reasonable under the circumstances. The receipt of any writing or notice within the time at which it would have arrived if properly sent has the effect of a proper sending.

(**39**) "Signed" includes any symbol executed or adopted by a party with present intention to authenticate a writing.

(**40**) "Surety" includes guarantor.

(**41**) "Telegram" includes a message transmitted by radio, teletype, cable, any mechanical method of transmission, or the like.

(**42**) "Term" means that portion of an agreement which relates to a particular matter.

(**43**) "Unauthorized" signature or indorsement means one made without actual, implied or apparent authority and includes a forgery.

(**44**) "Value". Except as otherwise provided with respect to negotiable instruments and bank collections (Sections 3-303, 4-208 and 4-209) a person gives "value" for rights if he acquires them

(**a**) in return for a binding commitment to extend credit or for the extension of immediately available credit whether or not drawn upon and whether or not a chargeback is provided for in the event of difficulties in collection; or

(**b**) as security for or in total or partial satisfaction of a pre-existing claim; or

(**c**) by accepting delivery pursuant to a pre-existing contract for purchase; or

(**d**) generally, in return for any consideration sufficient to support a simple contract.

(**45**) "Warehouse receipt" means a receipt issued by a person engaged in the business of storing goods for hire.

(**46**) "Written" or "writing" includes printing, typewriting or any other intentional reduction to tangible form. As amended 1962 and 1972.

§1-201. General Definitions (1977 Amendments).

Subject to additional definitions contained in the subsequent Articles of this Act which are applicable to specific Articles or Parts thereof, and unless the context otherwise requires, in this Act:

* * *

(**5**) "Bearer" means the person in possession of an instrument, document of title, or certificated security payable to bearer or indorsed in blank.

* * *

(**14**) "Delivery" with respect to instruments, documents of title, chattel paper, or certificated securities means voluntary transfer of possession.

* * *

(**20**) "Holder" means a person who is in possession of a document of title or an instrument or a certificated investment security drawn, issued, or indorsed to him or his order or to bearer or in blank.

* * *

§1-202. Prima Facie Evidence by Third Party Documents.

A document in due form purporting to be a bill of lading, policy or certificate of insurance, official weigher's or inspector's certificate, consular invoice or any other document authorized or required by the contract to be issued by a third party shall be prima facie evidence of its own authenticity and genuineness and of the facts stated in the document by the third party.

§1-203. Obligation of Good Faith. Every contract or duty within this Act imposes an obligation of good faith in its performance or enforcement.

§1-204. Time; Reasonable Time; "Seasonably".

(1) Whenever this Act requires any action to be taken within a reasonable time, any time which is not manifestly unreasonable may be fixed by agreement.

(2) What is a reasonable time for taking any action depends on the nature, purpose and circumstances of such action.

(3) An action is taken "seasonably" when it is taken at or within the time agreed or if no time is agreed at or within a reasonable time.

§1-205. Course of Dealing and Usage of Trade.

(1) A course of dealing is a sequence of previous conduct between the parties to a particular transaction which is fairly to be regarded as establishing a common basis of understanding for interpreting their expressions and other conduct.

(2) A usage of trade is any practice or method of dealing having such regularity of observance in a place, vocation or trade as to justify an expectation that it will be observed with respect to the transaction in question. The existence and scope of such a usage are to be proved as facts. If it is established that such a usage is embodied in a written trade code or similar writing the interpretation of the writing is for the court.

(3) A course of dealing between parties and any usage of trade in the vocation or trade in which they are engaged or of which they are or should be aware give particular meaning to and supplement or qualify terms of an agreement.

(4) The express terms of an agreement and an applicable course of dealing or usage of trade shall be construed wherever reasonable as consistent with each other; but when such

construction is unreasonable express terms control both course of dealing and usage of trade and course of dealing controls usage of trade.

(5) An applicable usage of trade in the place where any part of performance is to occur shall be used in interpreting the agreement as to that part of the performance.

(6) Evidence of a relevant usage of trade offered by one party is not admissible unless and until he has given the other party such notice as the court finds sufficient to prevent unfair surprise to the latter.

§1-206. Statute of Frauds for Kinds of Personal Property Not Otherwise Covered.

(1) Except in the cases described in subsection (2) of this section a contract for the sale of personal property is not enforceable by way of action or defense beyond five thousand dollars in amount or value of remedy unless there is some writing which indicates that a contract for sale has been made between the parties at a defined or stated price, reasonably identifies the subject matter, and is signed by the party against whom enforcement is sought or by his authorized agent.

(2) Subsection (1) of this section does not apply to contracts for the sale of goods (Section 2-201) nor of securities (Section 8-319) nor to security agreements (Section 9-203).

§1-207. Performance or Acceptance Under Reservation of Rights. A party who with explicit reservation of rights performs or promises performance or assents to performance in a manner demanded or offered by the other party does not thereby prejudice the rights reserved. Such words as "without prejudice", "under protest" or the like are sufficient.

§1-208. Option to Accelerate at Will. A term providing that one party or his successor in interest may accelerate payment or performance or require collateral or additional collateral "at will" or "when he deems himself insecure" or in words of similar import shall be construed to mean that he shall have power to do so only if he in good faith believes that the prospect of payment or performance is impaired. The burden of establishing lack of good faith is on the party against whom the power has been exercised.

§1-209. Subordinated Obligations. An obligation may be issued as subordinated to payment of another obligation of the person obligated, or a creditor may subordinate his right to payment of an obligation by agreement with either the person obligated or another creditor of the person obligated. Such a subordination does not create a security interest as against either the common debtor or a subordinated creditor. This section shall be construed as declaring the law as it existed prior to the enactment of this section and not as modifying it. Added 1966.

Note: *This new section is proposed as an optional provision to make it clear that a subordination agreement does not create a security interest unless so intended.*

ARTICLE 2: SALES

Part 1: Short Title, General Construction and Subject Matter

§2-101. Short Title. This Article shall be known and may be cited as Uniform Commercial Code—Sales.

§2-102. Scope; Certain Security and Other Transactions Excluded From This Article. Unless the context otherwise requires, this Article applies to transactions in goods; it does not apply to any transaction which although in the form of an unconditional contract to sell or present sale is intended to operate only as a security transaction nor does this Article impair or repeal any statute regulating sales to consumers, farmers or other specified classes of buyers.

§2-103. Defintions and Index of Definitions.

(1) In this Article unless the context otherwise requires

(a) "Buyer" means a person who buys or contracts to buy goods.

(b) "Good faith" in the case of a merchant means honesty in fact and the observance of reasonable commercial standards of fair dealing in the trade.

(c) "Receipt" of goods means taking physical possession of them.

(d) "Seller" means a person who sells or contracts to sell goods.

(2) Other definitions applying to this Article or to specified Parts thereof, and the sections in which they appear are:

"Acceptance". Section 2-606.
"Banker's credit". Section 2-325.
"Between merchants". Section 2-104.
"Cancellation". Section 2-106(4).
"Commercial unit". Section 2-105.
"Confirmed credit". Section 2-325.
"Conforming to contract". Section 2-106.
"Contract for sale". Section 2-106.
"Cover". Section 2-712.
"Entrusting". Section 2-403.
"Financing agency". Section 2-104.
"Future goods". Section 2-105.
"Goods". Section 2-105.
"Identification". Section 2-501.
"Installment contract". Section 2-612.
"Letter of Credit". Section 2-325.
"Lot". Section 2-105.
"Merchant". Section 2-104.
"Overseas". Section 2-323.
"Person in position of seller". Section 2-707.
"Present sale". Section 2-106.
"Sale". Section 2-106.
"Sale on approval". Section 2-326.
"Sale or return". Section 2-326.
"Termination". Section 2-106.

(3) The following definitions in other Articles apply to this Article:

"Check". Section 3-104.

"Consignee". Section 7-102.
"Consignor". Section 7-102.
"Consumer goods". Section 9-109.
"Dishonor". Section 3-507.
"Draft". Section 3-104.

(4) In addition Article 1 contains general definitions and principles of construction and interpretation applicable throughout this article.

§2-104. Definitions: "Merchant"; "Between Merchants"; "Financing Agency".

(1) "Merchant" means a person who deals in goods of the kind or otherwise by his occupation holds himself out as having knowledge or skill peculiar to the practices or goods involved in the transaction or to whom such knowledge or skill may be attributed by his employment of an agent or broker or other intermediary who by his occupation holds himself out as having such knowledge or skill.

(2) "Financing agency" means a bank, finance company or other person who in the ordinary course of business makes advances against goods or documents of title or who by arrangement with either the seller or the buyer intervenes in ordinary course to make or collect payment due or claimed under the contract for sale, as by purchasing or paying the seller's draft or making advances against it or by merely taking it for collection whether or not documents of title accompany the draft. "Financing agency" includes also a bank or other person who similarly intervenes between persons who are in the position of seller and buyer in respect of the goods (Section 2-707).

(3) "Between merchants" means in any transaction with respect to which both parties are chargeable with the knowledge or skill of merchants.

§2-105. Definitions: Transferability; "Goods"; "Future" Goods; "Lot"; "Commercial Unit".

(1) "Goods" means all things (including specially manufactured goods) which are movable at the time of identification to the contract for sale other than the money in which the price is to be paid, investment securities (Article 8) and things in action. "Goods" also includes the unborn young of animals and growing crops and other identified things attached to realty as described in the section on goods to be severed from realty (Section 2-107).

(2) Goods must be both existing and identified before any interest in them can pass. Goods which are not both existing and identified are "future" goods. A purported present sale of future goods or of any interest therein operates as a contract to sell.

(3) There may be a sale of a part interest in existing identified goods.

(4) An undivided share in an identified bulk of fungible goods is sufficiently identified to be sold although the quantity of the bulk is not determined. Any agreed proportion of such a bulk or any quantity thereof agreed upon by number, weight or other measure may to the extent of the seller's interest in the bulk be sold to the buyer who then becomes an owner in common.

(5) "Lot" means a parcel or a single article which is the subject matter of a separate sale or delivery, whether or not it is sufficient to perform the contract.

(6) "Commercial unit" means such a unit of goods as by commercial usage is a single whole for purposes of sale and division of which materially impairs its character or value on the market or in use. A commercial unit may be a single article (as a machine) or a set of articles (as a suite of furniture or an assortment of sizes) or a quantity (as a bale, gross, or carload) or any other unit treated in use or in the relevant market as a single whole.

§2-106. Definitions: "Contract"; "Agreement"; "Contract for Sale"; "Sale"; "Present Sale"; "Conforming" to Contract; "Termination"; "Cancellation".

(1) In this Article unless the context otherwise requires "contract" and "agreement" are limited to those relating to the present or future sale of goods. "Contract for sale" includes both a present sale of goods and a contract to sell goods at a future time. A "sale" consists in the passing of title from the seller to the buyer for a price (Section 2-401). A "present sale" means a sale which is accomplished by the making of the contract.

(2) Goods or conduct including any part of a performance are "conforming" or conform to the contract when they are in accordance with the obligations under the contract.

(3) "Termination" occurs when either party pursuant to a power created by agreement or law puts an end to the contract otherwise than for its breach. On "termination" all obligations which are still executory on both sides are discharged but any right based on prior breach or performance survives.

(4) "Cancellation" occurs when either party puts an end to the contract for breach by the other and its effect is the same as that of "termination" except that the cancelling party also retains any remedy for breach of the whole contract or any unperformed balance.

§2-107. Goods to Be Severed From Realty: Recording.

(1) A contract for the sale of minerals or the like (including oil and gas) or a structure or its materials to be removed from realty is a contract for the sale of goods within this Article if they are to be severed by the seller but until severance a purported present sale thereof which is not effective as a transfer of an interest in land is effective only as a contract to sell.

(2) A contract for the sale apart from the land of growing crops or other things attached to realty and capable of severance without material harm thereto but not described in subsection (1) or of timber to be cut is a contract for the sale of goods within this Article whether the subject matter is to be severed by the buyer or by the seller even though it forms part of the realty at the time of contracting, and the parties can by identification effect a present sale before severance.

(3) The provisions of this section are subject to any third party rights provided by the law relating to realty records, and the contract for sale may be executed and recorded as a document transferring an interest in land and shall then constitute notice to third parties of the buyer's rights under the contract for sale.

Part 2: Form, Formation and Readjustment of Contract

§2-201. Formal Requirements; Statute of Frauds.

(1) Except as otherwise provided in this section a contract for the sale of goods for the price of $500 or more is not enforceable by way of action or defense unless there is some writing sufficient to indicate that a contract for sale has been made between the parties and signed by the party against whom enforcement is sought or by his authorized agent or broker. A writing is not insufficient because it omits or incorrectly states a term agreed upon but the contract is not enforceable under this paragraph beyond the quantity of goods shown in such writing.

(2) Between merchants if within a reasonable time a writing in confirmation of the contract and sufficient against the sender is received and the party receiving it has reason to know its contents, it satisfies the requirements of subsection (1) against such party unless written notice of objection to its contents is given within 10 days after it is received.

(3) A contract which does not satisfy the requirements of subsection (1) but which is valid in other respects is enforceable

(a) if the goods are to be specially manufactured for the buyer and are not suitable for sale to others in the ordinary course of the seller's business and the seller, before notice of repudiation is received and under circumstances which reasonably indicate that the goods are for the buyer, has made either a substantial beginning of their manufacture or commitments for their procurement; or

(b) if the party against whom enforcement is sought admits in his pleading, testimony or otherwise in court that a contract for sale was made, but the contract is not enforceable under this provision beyond the quantity of goods admitted; or

(c) with respect to goods for which payment has been made and accepted or which have been received and accepted (Sec. 2-606.)

§2-202. Final Written Expression: Parol or Extrinsic Evidence.

Terms with respect to which the confirmatory memoranda of the parties agree or which are otherwise set forth in a writing intended by the parties as a final expression of their agreement with respect to such terms as are included therein may not be contradicted by evidence of any prior agreement or of a contemporaneous oral agreement but may be explained or supplemented

(a) by course of dealing or usage of trade (Section 1-205) or by course of performance (Section 2-208); and

(b) by evidence of consistent additional terms unless the court finds the writing to have been intended also as a complete and exclusive statement of the terms of the agreement.

§2-203. Seals Inoperative. The affixing of a seal to a writing evidencing a contract for sale or an offer to buy or sell goods does not constitute the writing a sealed instrument and the law with respect to sealed instruments does not apply to such a contract or offer.

§2-204. Formation in General.

(1) A contract for sale of goods may be made in any manner sufficient to show agreement, including conduct by both parties which recognizes the existence of such a contract.

(2) An agreement sufficient to constitute a contract for sale may be found even though the moment of its making is undetermined.

(3) Even though one or more terms are left open a contract for sale does not fail for indefiniteness if the parties have intended to make a contract and there is a reasonably certain basis for giving an appropriate remedy.

§2-205. Firm Offers. An offer by a merchant to buy or sell goods in a signed writing which by its terms gives assurance that it will be held open is not revocable, for lack of consideration, during the time stated or if no time is stated for a reasonable time, but in no event may such period of irrevocability exceed three months; but any such term of assurance on a form supplied by the offeree must be separately signed by the offeror.

§2-206. Offer and Acceptance in Formation of Contract.

(1)Unless otherwise unambiguously indicated by the language or circumstances

(a) an offer to make a contract shall be construed as inviting acceptance in any manner and by any medium reasonable in the circumstances;

(b) an order or other offer to buy goods for prompt or current shipment shall be construed as inviting acceptance either by a prompt promise to ship or by the prompt or current shipment of conforming or nonconforming goods, but such a shipment of nonconforming goods does not constitute an acceptance if the seller seasonably notifies the buyer that the shipment is offered only as an accommodation to the buyer.

(2) Where the beginning of a requested performance is a reasonable mode of acceptance an offeror who is not notified of acceptance within a reasonable time may treat the offer as having lapsed before acceptance.

§2-207. Additional Terms in Acceptance or Confirmation.

(1) A definite and seasonable expression of acceptance or a written confirmation which is sent within a reasonable time operates as an acceptance even though it states terms additional to or different from those offered or agreed upon, unless acceptance is expressly made conditional on assent to the additional or different terms.

(2) The additional terms are to be construed as proposals for addition to the contract. Between merchants such terms become part of the contract unless:

(a) the offer expressly limits acceptance to the terms of the offer;

(b) they materially alter it; or

(c) notification of objection to them has already been given or is given within a reasonable time after notice of them is received.

(3) Conduct by both parties which recognizes the existence of a contract is sufficient to establish a contract for sale although the writings of the parties do not otherwise establish a contract. In such case the terms of the particular contract consist of those terms on which the writings of the parties agree, together with any supplementary terms incorporated under any other provisions of this Act.

§2-208. Course of Performance or Practical Construction.

(1) Where the contract for sale involves repeated occasions for performance by either party with knowledge of the nature of the performance and opportunity for objection to it by the other, any course of performance accepted or acquiesced in without objection shall be relevant to determine the meaning of the agreement.

(2) The express terms of the agreement and any such course of performance, as well as any course of dealing and usage of trade, shall be construed whenever reasonable as consistent with each other; but when such construction is unreasonable, express terms shall control course of performance and course of performance shall control both course of dealing and usage of trade (Section 1-205).

(3) Subject to the provisions of the next section on modification and waiver, such course of performance shall be relevant to show a waiver or modification of any term inconsistent with such course of performance.

§2-209. Modification, Rescission and Waiver.

(1) An agreement modifying a contract within this Article needs no consideration to be binding.

(2) A signed agreement which excludes modifcation or rescission except by a signed writing cannot be otherwise modified or rescinded, but except as between merchants such a requirement on a form supplied by the merchant must be separately signed by the other party.

(3) The requirements of the statute of frauds section of this Article (Section 2-201) must be satisified if the contract as modified is within its provisions.

(4) Although an attempt at modification or rescission does not satisfy the requirements of subsection (2) or (3) it can operate as a waiver.

(5) A party who has made a waiver affecting an executory portion of the contract may retract the waiver by reasonable notification received by the other party that strict performance will be required of any term waived, unless the retraction would be unjust in view of a material change of position in reliance on the waiver.

§2-210. Delegation of Performance; Assignment of Rights.

(1) A party may perform his duty through a delegate unless otherwise agreed or unless the other party has a substantial interest in having his original promisor perform or control the acts required by the contract. No delegation of performance relieves the party delegating of any duty to perform or any liability for breach.

(2) Unless otherwise agreed all rights of either seller or buyer can be assigned except where the assignment would materially change the duty of the other party, or increase materially the burden or risk imposed on him by his contract, or impair materially his chance of obtaining return performance. A right to damages for breach of the whole contract or a right arising out of the assignor's due performance of his entire obligation can be assigned despite agreement otherwise.

(3) Unless the circumstances indicate the contrary a prohibition of assignment of "the contract" is to be construed as barring only the delegation to the assignee of the assignor's performance.

(4) An assignment of the "the contract" or of "all my rights under the contract" or an assignment in similar general terms is an assignment of rights and unless the language or the circumstances (as in an assignment for security) indicate the contrary, it is a delegation of performance of the duties of the assignor and its acceptance by the assignee constitutes a promise by him to perform those duties. This promise is enforceable by either the assignor or the other party to the original contract.

(5) The other party may treat any assignment which delegates performance as creating reasonable grounds for insecurity and may without prejudice to his rights against the assignor demand assurances from the assignee (Section 2-609).

Part 3: General Obligation and Construction of Contract

§2-301. General Obligations of Parties. The obligation of the seller is to transfer and deliver and that of the buyer is to accept and pay in accordance with the contract.

§2-302. Unconscionable Contract or Clause.

(1) If the court as a matter of law finds the contract or any clause of the contract to have been unconscionable at the time it was made the court may refuse to enforce the contract, or it may enforce the remainder of the contract without the unconscionable clause, or it may so limit the application of any unconscionable clause as to avoid any unconscionable result.

(2) When it is claimed or appears to the court that the contract or any clause thereof may be unconscionable the parties shall be afforded a reasonable opportunity to present evidence as to its commercial setting, purpose and effect to aid the court in making the determination.

§2-303. Allocation or Division of Risks. Where this Article allocates a risk or a burden as between the parties "unless otherwise agreed", the agreement may not only shift the allocation but may also divide the risk or burden.

§2-304. Price Payable in Money, Goods, Realty, or Otherwise.

(1) The price can be made payable in money or otherwise. If it is payable in whole or in part in goods each party is a seller of the goods which he is to transfer.

(2) Even though all or part of the price is payable in an interest in realty the transfer of the goods and the seller's

obligations with reference to them are subject to this Article, but not the transfer of the interest in realty or the transferor's obligations in connection therewith.

§2-305. Open Price Term.

(1) The parties if they so intend can conclude a contract for sale even though the price is not settled. In such a case the price is a reasonable price at the time for delivery if

(a) nothing is said as to price; or

(b) the price is left to be agreed by the parties and they fail to agree; or

(c) The price is to be fixed in terms of some agreed market or other standard as set or recorded by a third person or agency and it is not so set or recorded.

(2) A price to be fixed by the seller or by the buyer means a price for him to fix in good faith.

(3) When a price left to be fixed otherwise than by agreement of the parties fails to be fixed through fault of one party the other may at his option treat the contract as cancelled or himself fix a reasonable price.

(4) Where, however, the parties intend not to be bound unless the price be fixed or agreed and it is not fixed or agreed there is no contract. In such a case the buyer must return any goods already received or if unable so to do must pay their reasonable value at the time of delivery and the seller must return any portion of the price paid on account.

§2-306. Output, Requirements and Exclusive Dealings.

(1) A term which measures the quantity by the output of the seller or the requirements of the buyer means such actual output or requirements as may occur in good faith, except that no quantity unreasonably disproportionate to any stated estimate or in the absence of a stated estimate to any normal or otherwise comparable prior output or requirements may be tendered or demanded.

(2) A lawful agreement by either the seller or the buyer for exclusive dealing in the kind of goods concerned imposes unless otherwise agreed an obligation by the seller to use best efforts to supply the goods and by the buyer to use best efforts to promote their sale.

§2-307. Delivery in Single Lot or Several Lots. Unless otherwise agreed all goods called for by a contract for sale must be tendered in a single delivery and payment is due only on such tender but where the circumstances give either party the right to make or demand delivery in lots the price if it can be apportioned may be demanded for each lot.

§2-308. Absence of Specified Place for Delivery. Unless otherwise agreed

(a) The place for delivery of goods is the seller's place of business or if he has none his residence; but

(b) in a contract for sale of identified goods which to the knowledge of the parties at the time of contracting are in some other place, that place is the place for their delivery; and

(c) documents of title may be delivered through customary banking channels.

§2-309. Absence of Specific Time Provisions; Notice of Termination.

(1) The time for shipment or delivery or any other action under a contract if not provided in this Article or agreed upon shall be a reasonable time.

(2) Where the contract provides for successive performances but is indefinite in duration it is valid for a reasonable time but unless otherwise agreed may be terminated at any time by either party.

(3) Termination of a contract by one party except on the happening of an agreed event requires that reasonable notification be received by the other party and an agreement dispensing with notification is invalid if its operation would be unconscionable.

§2-310. Open Time for Payment or Running of Credit; Authority to Ship Under Reservation. Unless otherwise agreed

(a) payment is due at the time and place at which the buyer is to receive the goods even though the place of shipment is the place of delivery; and

(b) if the seller is authorized to send the goods he may ship them under reservation, and may tender the documents of title, but the buyer may inspect the goods after their arrival before payment is due unless such inspection is inconsistent with the terms of the contract (Section 2-513); and

(c) if delivery is authorized and made by way of documents of title otherwise than by subsection (b) then payment is due at the time and place at which the buyer is to receive the documents regardless of where the goods are to be received; and

(d) where the seller is required or authorized to ship the goods on credit the credit period runs from the time of shipment but post-dating the invoice or delaying its dispatch will correspondingly delay the starting of the credit period.

§2-311. Options and Cooperation Respecting Performance.

(1) An agreement for sale which is otherwise sufficiently definite (subsection (3) of Section 2-204) to be a contract is not made invalid by the fact that it leaves particulars of performance to be specified by one of the parties. Any such specification must be made in good faith and within limits set by commercial reasonableness.

(2) Unless otherwise agreed specifications relating to assortment of the goods are at the buyer's option and except as otherwise provided in subsections (1) (c) and (3) of Section 2-319 specifications or arrangements relating to shipment are at the seller's option.

(3) Where such specifications would materially affect the other party's performance but is not seasonably made or where one party's cooperation is necessary to the agreed performance of the other but is not seasonably forthcoming, the other party

(a) is excused for any resulting delay in his own performance; and

(b) may also either proceed to perform in any reasonable manner or after the time for a material part of his own performance treat the failure to specify or to cooperate as a breach by failure to deliver or accept the goods.

§2-312. Warranty of Title and Against Infringement; Buyer's Obligation Against Infringement.

(1) Subject to subsection (2) there is in a contract for sale a warranty by the seller that

(a) the title conveyed shall be good, and its transfer rightful; and

(b) the goods shall be delivered free from any security interest or other lien or encumbrance of which the buyer at the time of contracting has no knowledge.

(2) A warranty under subsection (2) will be excluded or modified only by specific language or by circumstances which give the buyer reason to know that the person selling does not claim title in himself or that he is purporting to sell only such right or title as he or a third person may have.

(3) Unless otherwise agreed a seller who is a merchant regularly dealing in goods of the kind warrants that the goods shall be delivered free of the rightful claim of any third person by way of infringement or the like but a buyer who furnishes specifications to the seller must hold the seller harmless against any such claim which arises out of compliance with the specifications.

§2-313. Express Warranties by Affirmation, Promise, Description, Sample.

(1) Express warranties by the seller are created as follows:

(a) Any affirmation of fact or promise made by the seller to the buyer which relates to the goods and becomes part of the basis of the bargain creates an express warranty that the goods shall conform to the affirmation or promise.

(b) Any description of the goods which is made part of the basis of the bargain creates an express warranty that the goods shall conform to the description.

(c) Any sample or model which is made part of the basis of the bargain creates an express warranty that the whole of the goods shall conform to the sample or model.

(2) It is not necessary to the creation of an express warranty that the seller use formal words such as "warrant" or "guarantee" or that he have a specific intention to make a warranty, but an affirmation merely of the value of the goods or a statement purporting to be merely the seller's opinion or commendation of the goods does not create a warranty.

§2-314. Implied Warranty: Merchantability; Usage of Trade.

(1) Unless excluded or modified (Section 2-316), a warranty that the goods shall be merchantable is implied in a contract for their sale if the seller is a merchant with respect to goods of that kind. Under this section the serving for value of food or drink to be consumed either on the premises or elsewhere is a sale.

(2) Goods to be merchantable must be at least such as

(a) pass without objection in the trade under the contract description; and

(b) in the case of fungible goods, are of fair average quality within the description; and

(c) are fit for the ordinary purposes for which such goods are used; and

(d) run, within the variations permitted by the agreement, of even kind, quality and quantity within each unit and among all units involved; and

(e) are adequately contained, packaged, and labeled as the agreement may require; and

(f) conform to the promises or affirmations of fact made on the container or label if any.

(3) Unless excluded or modified (Section 2-316) other implied warranties may arise from course of dealing or usage of trade.

§2-315. Implied Warranty: Fitness for Particular Purpose.

Where the seller at the time of contracting has reason to know any particular purpose for which the goods are required and that the buyer is relying on the seller's skill or judgment to select or furnish suitable goods, there is unless excluded or modified under the next section an implied warranty that the goods shall be fit for such purpose.

§2-316. Exclusion or Modification of Warranties.

(1) Words or conduct relevant to the creation of an express warranty and words or conduct tending to negate or limit warranty shall be construed wherever reasonable as consistent with each other; but subject to the provisions of this Article on parol or extrinsic evidence (Section 2-202) negation or limitation is inoperative to the extent that such construction is unreasonable.

(2) Subject to subsection (3), to exclude or modify the implied warranty of merchantability or any part of it the language must mention merchantability and in case of a writing must be conspicuous, and to exclude or modify any implied warranty of fitness the exclusion must be by a writing and conspicuous. Language to exclude all implied warranties of fitness is sufficient if it states, for example, that "There are no warranties which extend beyond the description on the face hereof."

(3) Notwithstanding subsection (2)

(a) unless the circumstances indicate otherwise, all implied warranties are excluded by expressions like "as is", "with all faults" or other language which in common understanding calls the buyer's attention to the exclusion of warranties and makes plain that there is no implied warranty; and

(b) when the buyer before entering into the contract has examined the goods or the sample or model as fully as he desired or has refused to examine the goods there is no implied warranty with regard to defects which an examination ought in the circumstances to have revealed to him; and

(c) an implied warranty can also be excluded or modified by course of dealing or course of performance or usage of trade.

(4) Remedies for breach of warranty can be limited in accordance with the provisions of this Article on liquidation or limitation of damages and on contractual modification of remedy (Sections 2-718 and 2-719).

§2-317. Cumulation and Conflict of Warranties Express or Implied. Warranties whether express or implied shall be construed as consistent with each other and as cumulative but if such construction is unreasonable the intention of the parties shall determine which warranty is dominant. In ascertaining that intention the following rules apply:

(a) Exact or techinical specifications displace an inconsistent sample or model or general language of description.

(b) A sample from an existing bulk displaces inconsistent general language of description.

(c) Express warranties displace inconsistent implied warranties other than an implied warranty of fitness for a particular purpose.

§2-318. Third Party Beneficiaries of Warranties Express or Implied.

Note: *If this Act is introduced in the Congress of the United States this section should be omitted. (States to select one alternative.)*

Alternative A—A seller's warranty whether express or implied extends to any natural person who is in the family or household of his buyer or who is a guest in his home if it is reasonable to expect that such person may use, consume or be affected by the goods and who is injured in person by breach of the warranty. A seller may not exclude or limit the operation of this section.

Alternative B—A seller's warranty whether express or implied extends to any natural person who may reasonably be expected to use, consume or be affected by the goods and who is injured in person by breach of the warranty. A seller may not exclude or limit the operation of this section.

Alternative C—A seller's warranty whether express or implied extends to any person who may reasonably be expected to use, consume or be affected by the goods and who is injured by breach of the warranty. A seller may not exclude or limit the operation of this section with respect to injury to the person of an individual to whom the warranty extends. As amended 1966.

§2-319. F.O.B. and F.A.S. Terms.

(1) Unless otherwise agreed the term F.O.B. (which means "free on board") at a named place, even though used only in connection with the stated price, is a delivery term under which

(a) when the term is F.O.B. the place of shipment, the seller must at that place ship the goods in the manner provided in this Article (Section 2-504) and bear the expense and risk of putting them into the possession of the carrier; or

(b) when the term is F.O.B. the place of destination, the seller must at his own expense and risk transport the goods to that place and there tender delivery of them in the manner provided in this Article (Section 2-503);

(c) when under either (a) or (b) the term is also F.O.B. vessel, car or other vehicle, the seller must in addition at his own expense and risk load the goods on board. If the term is F.O.B. vessel the buyer must name the vessel and in an appropriate case the seller must comply with the provisions of this Article on the form of bill of lading (Section 2-323).

(2) Unless otherwise agreed the term F.A.S. vessel (which means "free alongside") at a named port, even though used only in connection with the stated price, is a delivery term under which the selller must

(a) at his own expense and risk deliver the goods alongside the vessel in the manner usual in that port or on a dock designated and provided by the buyer; and

(b) obtain and tender a receipt for the goods in exchange for which the carrier is under a duty to issue a bill of lading.

(3) Unless otherwise agreed in any case falling within subsection (1) (a) or (c) or subsection (2) the buyer must seasonably give any needed instructions for making delivery, including when the term is F.A.S. or F.O.B. the loading berth of the vessel and in an appropriate case its name and sailing date. The seller may treat the failure of needed instructions as a failure of cooperation under this Article (Section 2-311). He may also at his option move the goods in any reasonable manner preparatory to delivery or shipment.

(4) Under the term F.O.B. vessel or F.A.S. unless otherwise agreed the buyer must make payment against tender of the required documents and the seller may not tender nor the buyer demand delivery of the goods in substitution for the documents.

§2-320. C.I.F. and C.&F. Terms.

(1) The term C.I.F. means that the price includes in a lump sum the cost of the goods and the insurance and freight to the named destination. The term C.&F. or C.F. means that the price so includes cost and freight to the named destination.

(2) Unless otherwise agreed and even though used only in connection with the stated price and destination, the term C.I.F. destination or its equivalent requires the seller at his own expense and risk to

(a) put the goods into the possession of a carrier at the port for shipment and obtain a negotiable bill or bills of lading covering the entire transportation to the named destination; and

(b) load the goods and obtain a receipt from the carrier (which may be contained in the bill of lading) showing that the freight has been paid or provided for; and

(c) obtain a policy or certificate of insurance, including any war risk insurance, of a kind and on terms then current at the port of shipment in the usual amount, in the currency of the contract, shown to cover the same goods covered by the bill of lading and providing for payment of loss to the order of the buyer or for the account of whom it may concern; but the seller may add to the price the amount of the premium for any such war risk insurance; and

(d) prepare an invoice of the goods and procure any other doucments required to effect shipment or to comply with the contract; and

(e) forward and tender with commercial promptness all

the documents in due form and with any indorsement necessary to perfect the buyer's rights.

(3) Unless otherwise agreed the term C. & F. or its equivalent has the same effect and imposes upon the seller the same obligations and risks as a C.I.F. term except the obligation as to insurance.

(4) Under the term C.I.F. or C. & F. unless otherwise agreed the buyer must make payment against tender of the required documents and the seller may not tender nor the buyer demand delivery of the goods in substitution for the documents.

§2-321. C.I.F. or C. & F.: "Net Landed Weights"; "Payment on Arrival"; Warranty of Condition on Arrival. Under a contract containing a term C.I.F. or C. & F.

(1) Where the price is based on or is to be adjusted according to "net landed weights", "delivered weights", "out turn" quantity or quality or the like, unless otherwise agreed the seller must reasonably estimate the price. The payment due on tender of the documents called for by the contract is the amonut so estimated, but after final adjustment of the price a settlement must be made with commercial promptness.

(2) An agreement described in subsection (1) or any warranty of quality or condition of the goods on arrival places upon the seller the risk of ordinary deterioration, shrinkage and the like in transportation but has no effect on the place or time of identification to the contract for sale or delivery or on the passing of the risk of loss.

(3) Unless otherwise agreed where the contract provides for payment on or after arrival of the goods the seller must before payment allow such preliminary inspection as is feasible; but if the goods are lost delivery of the documents and payment are due when the goods should have arrived.

§2-322. Delivery "Ex-Ship".

(1) Unless otherwise agreed a term for delivery of goods "ex-ship" (which means from the carrying vessel) or in equivalent language is not restricted to a particular ship and requires delivery from a ship which has reached a place at the named port of destination where goods of the kind are usually discharged.

(2) Under such a term unless othewise agreed

(a) the seller must discharge all liens arising out of the carriage and furnish the buyer with a direction which puts the carrier under a duty to deliver the goods; and

(b) the risk of loss does not pass to the buyer until the goods leave the ship's tackle or are otherwise properly unloaded.

§2-323. Form of Bill of Lading Required in Overseas Shipment; "Overseas".

(1) Where the contract contemplates overseas shipment and contains a term C.I.F. or C. & F. or F. O.B. vessel the seller unless otherwise agreed must obtain a negotiable bill of lading stating that the goods have been loaded on board or, in the case of a term C.I.F. or C. & F., received for shipment.

(2) Where in a case within subsection (1) a bill of lading has been issued in a set of parts, unless otherwise agreed if the documents are not to be sent from abroad the buyer may demand tender of the full set; otherwise only one part of the bill of lading need be tendered. Even if the agreement expressly requires a full set

(a) due tender of a single part is acceptable within the provisions of this Article on cure of improper delivery (subsection (1) of Section 2-508); and

(b) even though the full set is demanded, if the documents are sent from abroad the person tendering an incomplete set may nevertheless require payment upon furnishing an indemnity which the buyer in good faith deems adequate.

(3) A shipment by water or by air or a contract contemplating such shipment is "overseas" insofar as by usage of trade or agreement it is subject to the commercial, financing or shipping practices characteristic of international deep water commerce.

§2-324. "No Arrival, No Sale" Term. Under a term "no arrival, no sale" or terms of like meaning, unless otherwise agreed,

(a) the seller must properly ship conforming goods and if they arrive by any means he must tender them on arrival but he assumes no obligation that the goods will arrive unless he has caused the nonarrival; and

(b) where without fault of the seller the goods are in part lost or have so deteriorated as no longer to conform to the contract or arrive after the contract time, the buyer may proceed as if there had been casualty to identified goods (Section 2-613).

§2-325. "Letter of Credit" Term; "Confirmed Credit".

(1) Failure of the buyer seasonably to furnish an agreed letter of credit is a breach of the contract for sale.

(2) The delivery to seller of a proper letter of credit suspends the buyer's obligation to pay. If the letter of credit is dishonored, the seller may on seasonable notification to the buyer require payment directly from him.

(3) Unless otherwise agreed the term "letter of credit" or "banker's credit" in a contract for sale means an irrevocable credit issued by a financing agency of good repute and, where the shipment is overseas, of good international repute. The term "confirmed credit" means that the credit must also carry the direct obligation of such an agency which does business in the seller's financial market.

§2-326. Sale on Approval and Sale or Return; Consignment Sales and Rights of Creditors.

(1) Unless otherwise agreed, if delivered goods may be returned by the buyer even though they conform to the contract, the transaction is

(a) a "sale on approval" if the goods are delivered primarily for use, and

(b) a "sale or return" if the goods are delivered primarily for resale.

(2) Except as provided in subsection (3), goods held on approval are not subject to the claims of the buyer's creditors until acceptance; goods held on sale or return are subject to such claims while in the buyer's possession.

(3) Where goods are delivered to a person for sale and such person maintains a place of business at which he deals in goods of the kind involved, under a name other than the name of the person making delivery, then with respect to claims of creditors of the person conducting the business the goods are deemed to be on sale or return. The provisions of this subsection are applicable even though an agreement purports to reserve title to the person making delivery until payment or resale or uses such words as "on consignment" or "on memorandum". However, this subsection is not applicable if the person making delivery

(a) complies with an applicable law providing for a consignor's interest or the like to be evidenced by a sign, or

(b) establishes that the person conducting the business is generally known by his creditors to be substantially engaged in selling the goods of others, or

(c) complies with the filing provisions of the Article on Secured Transactions (Article 9).

(4) Any "or return" term of a contract for sale is to be treated as a separate contract for sale within the statute of frauds section of this Article (Section 2-201) and as contradicting the sale aspect of the contract within the provisions of this Article on parol or extrinsic evidence (Section 2-202).

§2-327. Special Incidents of Sale on Approval and Sale or Return.

(1) Under a sale on approval unless otherwise agreed

(a) although the goods are identified to the contract the risk of loss and the title do not pass to the buyer until acceptance; and

(b) use of the goods consistent with the purpose of trial is not acceptance but failure seasonably to notify the seller of election to return the goods is acceptance, and if the goods conform to the contract acceptance of any part is acceptance of the whole; and

(c) after due notification of election to return, the return is at the seller's risk and expense but a merchant buyer must follow any reasonable instructions.

(2) Under a sale or return unless otherwise agreed

(a) the option to return extends to the whole or any commercial unit of the goods while in substantially their original condition, but must be exercised seasonably; and

(b) the return is at the buyer's risk and expense.

§2-328. Sale by Auction.

(1) In a sale by auction if goods are put up in lots each lot is the subject of a separate sale.

(2) A sale by auction is complete when the auctioneer so announces by the fall of the hammer or in other customary manner. Where a bid is made while the hammer is falling in acceptance of a prior bid the auctioneer may in his discretion reopen the bidding or declare the goods sold under the bid on which the hammer was falling.

(3) Such a sale is with reserve unless the goods are in explicit terms put up without reserve. In an auction with reserve, the auctioneer may withdraw the goods at any time until he announces completion of the sale. In an auction without reserve, after the auctioneer calls for bids on an article or lot, that article or lot cannot be withdrawn unless no bid is made within a reasonable time. In either case a bidder may retract his bid until the auctioneer's announcement of completion of the sale, but a bidder's retraction does not revive any previous bid.

(4) If the auctioneer knowingly receives a bid on the seller's behalf or the seller makes or procures such a bid, and notice has not been given that liberty for such bidding is reserved, the buyer may at his option avoid the sale or take the goods at the price of the last good faith bid prior to the completion of the sale. This subsection shall not apply to any bid at a forced sale.

Part 4: Title, Creditors and Good Faith Purchasers

§2-401. Passing of Title; Reservation for Security; Limited Application of This Section. Each provision of this Article with regard to the rights, obligations and remedies of the seller, the buyer, purchasers or other third parties applies irrespective of title to the goods except where the provision refers to such title. Insofar as situations are not covered by the other provisions of this Article and matters concerning title become material the following rules apply:

(1) Title to goods cannot pass under a contract for sale prior to their identification to the contract (Section 2-501), and unless otherwise explicitly agreed the buyer acquires by their identification a special property as limited by this Act. Any retention or reservation by the seller of the title (property) in goods shipped or delivered to the buyer is limited in effect to a reservation of a security interest. Subject to these provisions and to the provisions of the Article on Secured Transactions (Article 9), title to goods passes from the seller to the buyer in any manner and on any conditions explicitly agreed on by the parties.

(2) Unless otherwise explicitly agreed title passes to the buyer at the time and place at which the seller completes his performance with reference to the physical delivery of the goods, despite any reservation of a security interest and even though a document of title is to be delivered at a different time or place; and in particular and despite any reservation of a security interest by the bill of lading

(a) if the contract requires or authorizes the seller to send the goods to the buyer but does not require him to deliver them at destination, title passes to the buyer at the time and place of shipment; but

(b) if the contract requires delivery at destination, title passes on tender there.

(3) Unless otherwise explicitly agreed where delivery is to be made without moving the goods.

(a) if the seller is to deliver a document of title, title passes at the time when and the place where he delivers such documents; or

(b) if the goods are at the time of contracting already identified and no documents are to be delivered, title passes at the time and place of contracting.

(4) A rejection or other refusal by the buyer to receive or

retain the goods, whether or not justified, or a justified revocation of acceptance revests title to the goods in the seller. Such revesting occurs by operation of law and is not a "sale".

§2-402. Rights of Seller's Creditors Against Sold Goods.

(1) Except as provided in subsections (2) and (3), rights of unsecured creditors of the seller with respect to goods which have been identified to a contract for sale are subject to the buyer's rights to recover the goods under this Article (Section 2-502 and 2-716).

(2) A creditor of the seller may treat a sale or an identification of goods to a contract for sale as void if as against him a retention of possession by the seller is fraudulent under any rule of law of the state where the goods are situated, except that retention of possession in good faith and current course of trade by a merchant-seller for a commercially reasonable time after a sale or identification is not fraudulent.

(3) Nothing in this Article shall be deemed to impair the rights of creditors of the seller

(a) under the provisions of the Article on Secured Transactions (Article 9); or

(b) where identification to the contract or delivery is made not in current course of trade but in satisfaction of or as security for a pre-existing claim for money, security or the like and is made under circumstances which under any rule of law of the state where the goods are situated would apart from this Article constitute the transaction a fraudulent transfer or voidable preference.

§2-403. Power to Transfer; Good Faith Purchase of Goods; "Entrusting".

(1) A purchaser of goods acquires all title which his transferor had or had power to transfer except that a purchaser of a limited interest acquires rights only to the extent of the interest purchased. A person with voidable title has power to transfer a good title to a good faith purchaser for value. When goods have been delivered under a transaction of purchase the purchaser had such power even though

(a) the transferor was deceived as to the identity of the purchaser, or

(b) the delivery was in exchange for a check which is later dishonored, or

(c) it was agreed that the transaction was to be a "cash sale", or

(d) the delivery was procured through fraud punishable as larcenous under the criminal law.

(2) Any entrusting of possession of goods to a merchant who deals in goods of that kind gives him power to transfer all rights of the entruster to a buyer in ordinary course of business.

(3) "Entrusting" includes any delivery and any acquiescence in retention of possession regardless of any condition expressed between the parties to the delivery or acquiescence and regardless of whether the procurement of the entrusting or the possessor's disposition of the goods have been such as to be larcenous under the criminal law.

(4) The rights of other purchasers of goods and of lien creditors are governed by the Articles on Secured Transactions (Article 9), Bulk Transfers (Article 6) and Documents of Title (Article 7).

Part 5: Performance

§2-501. Insurable Interest in Goods; Manner of Identification of Goods.

(1) The buyer obtains a special property and an insurable interest in goods by identification of existing goods as goods to which the contract refers even though the goods so identified are non-conforming and he has an option to return or reject them. Such identification can be made at any time and in any manner explicitly agreed to by the parties. In the absence of explicit agreement identification occurs

(a) when the contract is made if it is for the sale of goods already existing and identified;

(b) if the contract is for the sale of future goods other than those described in paragraph (c), when goods are shipped, marked or otherwise designated by the seller as goods to which the contract refers;

(c) when the crops are planted or otherwise become growing crops or the young are conceived if the contract is for the sale of unborn young to be born within twelve months after contracting or for the sale of crops to be harvested within twelve months or the next normal harvest season after contracting whichever is longer.

(2) The seller retains an insurable interest in goods so long as title to or any security interest in the goods remains in him and where the identification is by the seller alone he may until default or insolvency or notification to the buyer that the identification is final substitute other goods for those identified.

(3) Nothing in this section impairs any insurable interest recognized under any other statute or rule of law.

§2-502. Buyer's Right to Goods on Seller's Insolvency.

(1) Subject to subsection (2) and even though the goods have not been shipped a buyer who has paid a part or all of the price of goods in which he has a special property under the provisions of the immediately preceding section may on making and keeping good a tender of any unpaid portion of their price recover them from the seller if the seller becomes insolvent within ten days after receipt of the first installment on their price.

(2) If the identification creating his special property has been made by the buyer he acquires the right to recover the goods only if they conform to the contract for sale.

§2-503. Manner of Seller's Tender of Delivery.

(1) Tender of delivery requires that the seller put and hold conforming goods at the buyer's dispostion and give the buyer any notification reasonably necessary to enable him to take delivery. The manner, time and place for tender are determined by the agreement and this Article, and in particular

(a) tender must be at a reasonable hour, and if it is of goods they must be kept available for the period reasonably necessary to enable the buyer to take possession; but

(b) unless otherwise agreed the buyer must furnish facilities reasonably suited to the receipt of the goods.

(2) Where the case is within the next section respecting shipment tender requires that the seller comply with its provisions.

(3) Where the seller is required to deliver at a particular destination tender requires that he comply with subsection (1) and also in any appropriate case tender documents as described in subsections (4) and (5) of this section.

(4) Where goods are in the possession of a bailee and are to be delivered without being moved

(a) tender requires that the seller either tender a negotiable document of title covering such goods or procure acknowledgement by the bailee of the buyer's right to possession of the goods; but

(b) tender to the buyer of a non-negotiable document of title or of a written direction to the bailee to deliver is sufficient tender unless the buyer seasonably objects, and receipt by the bailee of notification of the buyer's rights fixes those rights as aginst the bailee and all third persons; but risk of loss of the goods and of any failure by the bailee to honor the non-negotiable document of title or to obey the direction remains on the seller until the buyer has had a reasonable time to present the document or direction, and a refusal by the bailee to honor the document or to obey the direction defeats the tender.

(5) Where the contract requires the seller to deliver documents

(a) he must tender all such documents in correct form, except as provided in this Article with respect to bills of lading in a set (subsection (2) of Section 2-323); and

(b) tender through customary banking channels is sufficient and dishonor of a draft accompanying the documents constitutes non-acceptance or rejection.

§2-504 Shipment by Seller. Where the seller is required or authorized to send the goods to the buyer and the contract does not require him to deliver them at a particular destination, then unless otherwise agreed he must

(a) put the goods in the possession of such a carrier and make such a contract for their transportation as may be reasonable having regard to the nature of the goods and other circumstances of the case; and

(b) obtain and promptly deliver or tender in due form any document necessary to enable the buyer to obtain possession of the goods or otherwise required by the agreement or by usage of trade; and

(c) promptly notify the buyer of the shipment.

Failure to notify the buyer under paragraph (c) or to make a proper contract under paragraph (a) is a ground for rejection only if material delay or loss ensues.

§2-505. Seller's Shipment under Reservation.

(1) Where the seller has identified goods to the contract by or before shipment:

(a) his procurement of a negotiable bill of lading to his own order or otherwise reserves in him a security interest in the goods. His procurement of the bill to the order of a financing agency or of the buyer indicates in addition only the seller's expectation of transferring that interest to the person named.

(b) a non-negotiable bill of lading to himself or his nominee reserves possession of the goods as security but except in a case of conditional delivery (subsection (2) of Section 2-507) a non-negotiable bill of lading naming the buyer as consignee reserves no security interest even though the seller retains possession of the bill of lading.

(2) When shipment by the seller with reservation of a security interest is in violation of the contract for sale it constitutes an improper contract for transportation within the preceding section but impairs neither the rights given to the buyer by shipment and identification of the goods to the contract nor the seller's powers as a holder of a negotiable document.

§2-506. Rights of Financing Agency.

(1) A financing agency by paying or purchasing for value a draft which relates to a shipment of goods acquires to the extent of the payment or purchase and in addition to its own rights under the draft and any document of title securing it any rights of the shipper in the goods including the right to stop delivery and the shipper's right to have the draft honored by the buyer.

(2) The right to reimbursement of a financing agency which has in good faith honored or purchased the draft under commitment to or authority from the buyer is not impaired by subsequent discovery of defects with reference to any relevant document which was apparently regular on its face.

§2-507. Effect of Seller's Tender; Delivery on Condition.

(1) Tender of delivery is a condition to the buyer's duty to accept the goods and, unless otherwise agreed, to his duty to pay for them. Tender entitles the seller to acceptance of the goods and to payment according to the contract.

(2) Where payment is due and demanded on the delivery to the buyer of goods or documents of title, his right as against the seller to retain or dispose of them is conditional upon his making the payment due.

§2-508. Cure by Seller of Improper Tender or Delivery; Replacement.

(1) Where any tender or delivery by the seller is rejected because non-conforming and the time for performance has not yet expired, the seller may seasonably notify the buyer of his intention to cure and may then within the contract time make a conforming delivery.

(2) Where the buyer rejects a non-conforming tender which the seller had reasonable grounds to believe would be acceptable with or without money allowance the seller may if he seasonably notifies the buyer have a further reasonable time to substitute a conforming tender.

§2-509. Risk of Loss in the Absence of Breach.

(1) Where the contract requires or authorizes the seller to ship the goods by carrier

(a) if it does not require him to deliver them at a

particular destination, the risk of loss passes to the buyer when the goods are duly delivered to the carrier even though the shipment is under reservation (Section 2-505); but

(b) if it does require him to deliver them at a particular destination and the goods are there duly tendered while in the possession of the carrier, the risk of loss passes to the buyer when the goods are there duly so tendered as to enable the buyer to take delivery.

(2) Where the goods are held by a bailee to be delivered without being moved, the risk of loss passes to the buyer

(a) on his receipt of a negotiable document of title covering the goods; or

(b) on acknowledgement by the bailee of the buyer's right to possession of the goods; or

(c) after his receipt of a non-negotiable document of title or other written direction to deliver, as provided in subsection (4) (b) of Section 2-503.

(3) In any case not within subsection (1) or (2), the risk of loss passes to the buyer on his receipt of the goods if the seller is a merchant; otherwise the risk passes to the buyer on tender of delivery.

(4) The provisions of this section are subject to contrary agreement of the parties and to the provisions of this Article on sale on approval (Section 2-327) and on effect of breach on risk of loss (Section 2-510).

§2-510. Effect of Breach on Risk of Loss.

(1) Where a tender or delivery of goods so fails to conform to the contract as to give a right of rejection the risk of their loss remains on the seller until cure or acceptance.

(2) Where the buyer rightfully revokes acceptance he may to the extent of any deficiency in his effective insurance coverage treat the risk of loss as having rested on the seller from the beginning.

(3) Where the buyer as to conforming goods already identified to the contract for sale repudiates or is otherwise in breach before risk of their loss has passed to him, the seller may to the extent of any deficiency in his effective insurance coverage treat the risk of loss as resting on the buyer for a commercially reasonable time.

§2-511. Tender of Payment by Buyer; Payment by Check.

(1) Unless otherwise agreed tender of payment is a condition to the seller's duty to tender and complete any delivery.

(2) Tender of payment is sufficient when made by any means or in any manner current in the ordinary course of business unless the seller demands payment in legal tender and gives any extension of time reasonably necessary to procure it.

(3) Subject to the provisions of this Act on the effect of an instrument on an obligation (Section 3-802), payment by check is conditional and is defeated as between the parties by dishonor of the check on due presentment.

§2-512. Payment by Buyer Before Inspection.

(1) Where the contract requires payment before inspection non-conformity of the goods does not excuse the buyer from so making payment unless

(a) the non-conformity appears without inspection; or

(b) despite tender of the required documents the circumstances would justify injunction against honor under the provisions of this Act (Section 5-114).

(2) Payment pursuant to subsection (1) does not constitute an acceptance of goods or impair the buyer's right to inspect or any of his remedies.

§2-513. Buyer's Right to Inspection of Goods.

(1) Unless otherwise agreed and subject to subsection (3), where goods are tendered or delivered or identified to the contract for sale, the buyer has a right before payment or acceptance to inspect them at any reasonable place and time and in any reasonable manner. When the seller is required or authorized to send the goods to the buyer, the inspection may be after their arrival.

(2) Expenses of inspection must be borne by the buyer but may be recovered from the seller if the goods do not conform and are rejected.

(3) Unless otherwise agreed and subject to the provisions of this Article on C.I.F. contracts (subsection (3) of Section 3-221), the buyer is not entitled to inspect the goods before payment of the price when the contract provides

(a) for delivery "C.O.D." or on other like terms; or

(b) for payment against documents of title, except where such payment is due only after the goods are to become available for inspection.

(4) A place or method of inspection fixed by the parties is presumed to be exclusive but unless otherwise expressly agreed it does not postpone identification or shift the place for delivery or for passing the risk of loss. If compliance becomes impossible, inspection shall be as provided in this section unless the place or method fixed was clearly intended as an indispensable condition failure of which avoids the contract.

§2-514. When Documents Deliverable on Acceptance; When on Payment. Unless otherwise agreed documents against which a draft is drawn are to be delivered to the drawee on acceptance of the draft if it is payable more than three days after presentment; otherwise, only on payment.

§2-515. Preserving Evidence of Goods in Dispute. In furtherance of the adjustment of any claim or dispute

(a) either party on reasonable notification to the other and for the purpose of ascertaining the facts and preserving evidence has the right to inspect, test and sample the goods including such of them as may be in the possession or control of the other; and

(b) the parties may agree to a third party inspection or survey to determine the conformity or condition of the goods and may agree that the findings shall be binding upon them in any subsequent litigation or adjustment.

Part 6: Breach, Repudiation and Excuse

§2-601. Buyer's Rights on Improper Delivery. Subject to the provisions of this Article on breach in installment contracts

(Section 2-612) and unless otherwise agreed under the sections on contractual limitations of remedy (Sections 2-718 and 2-719), if the goods or the tender of delivery fail in any respect to conform to the contract, the buyer may

(a) reject the whole; or

(b) accept the whole; or

(c) accept any commercial unit or units and reject the rest.

§2-602. Manner and Effect of Rightful Rejection.

(1) Rejection of goods must be within a reasonable time after their delivery or tender. It is ineffective unless the buyer seasonably notifies the seller.

(2) Subject to the provisions of the two following sections on rejected goods (Section 2-603 and 2-604),

(a) after rejection any exercise of ownership by the buyer with respect to any commercial unit is wrongful as against the seller; and

(b) if the buyer has before rejection taken physical possession of goods in which he does not have a security interest under the provisions of this Article (subsection (3) of Section 2-711), he is under a duty after rejection to hold them with reasonable care at the seller's disposition for a time sufficient to permit the seller to remove them; but

(c) the buyer has no further obligations with regard to goods rightfully rejected.

(3) The seller's rights with respect to goods wrongfully rejected are governed by the provisions of this Article on Seller's remedies in general (Section 2-703).

§2-603. Merchant Buyer's Duties as to Rightfully Rejected Goods.

(1) Subject to any security interest in the buyer (subsection (3) of Section 2-711), when the seller has no agent or place of business at the market of rejection a merchant buyer is under a duty after rejection of goods in his possession or control to follow any reasonable instructions received from the seller with respect to the goods and in the absence of such instructions to make reasonable efforts to sell them for the seller's account if they are perishable or threaten to decline in value speedily. Instructions are not reasonable if on demand indemnity for expenses is not forthcoming.

(2) When the buyer sells goods under subsection (1), he is entitled to reimbursement from the seller or out of the proceeds for reasonable expenses of caring for and selling them, and if the expenses include no selling commission then to such commission as is usual in the trade or if there is none to a reasonable sum not exceeding ten per cent on the gross proceeds.

(3) In complying with this section the buyer is held only to good faith and good faith conduct hereunder is neither acceptance nor conversion nor the basis of an action for damages.

§2-604. Buyer's Options as to Salvage of Rightfully Rejected Goods. Subject to the provisions of the immediately preceding section on perishables if the seller gives no instructions within a reasonable time after notification of rejection the buyer may store the rejected goods for the seller's account or reship them to him or resell them for the seller's account with reimbursement as provided in the preceding section. Such action is not acceptance or conversion.

§2-605. Waiver of Buyer's Objections by Failure to Particularize.

(1) The buyer's failure to state in connection with rejection a particular defect which is ascertainable by reasonable inspection precludes him from relying on the unstated defect to justify rejection or to establish breach

(a) where the seller could have cured it if stated seasonably; or

(b) between merchants when the seller has after rejection made a request in writing for a full and final written statement of all defects on which the buyer proposes to rely.

(2) Payment against documents made without reservation of rights precludes recovery of the payment for defects apparent on the face of the documents.

§2-606. What Constitutes Acceptance of Goods.

(1) Acceptance of goods occurs when the buyer

(a) after a reasonable opportunity to inspect the goods signifies to the seller that the goods are conforming or that he will take or retain them in spite of their nonconformity; or

(b) fails to make an effective rejection (subsection (1) of Section 2-602), but such acceptance does not occur until the buyer has had a reasonable opportunity to inspect them; or

(c) does any act inconsistent with the seller's ownership; but if such act is wrongful as against the seller it is an acceptance only if ratified by him.

(2) Acceptance of a part of any commercial unit is acceptance of that entire unit.

§2-607. Effect of Acceptance; Notice of Breach; Burden of Establishing Breach After Acceptance; Notice of Claim or Litigation to Person Answerable Over.

(1) The buyer must pay at the contract rate for any goods accepted.

(2) Acceptance of goods by the buyer precludes rejection of the goods accepted and if made with knowledge of a nonconformity cannot be revoked because of it unless the acceptance was on the reasonable assumption that the non-conformity would be seasonably cured but acceptance does not of itself impair any other remedy provided by this Article for nonconformity.

(3) Where a tender has been accepted

(a) the buyer must within a reasonable time after he discovers or should have discovered any breach notify the seller of breach or be barred from any remedy; and

(b) if the claim is one for infringement or the like (subsection (3) of Section 2-312) and the buyer is sued as a result of such a breach he must so notify the seller within a reasonable time after he receives notice of the litigation or be barred from any remedy over for liability established by the litigation.

(4) The burden is on the buyer to establish any breach with respect to the goods accepted.

(5) Where the buyer is sued for breach of a warranty or other obligation for which his seller is answerable over

(a) he may give his seller written notice of the litigation. If the notice states that the seller may come in and defend and that if the seller does not do so he will be bound in any action against him by his buyer by any determination of fact common to the two litigations, then unless the seller after seasonable receipt of the notice does come in and defend he is so bound.

(b) if the claim is one for infringement or the like (subsection (3) of Section 2-312) the original seller may demand in writing that his buyer turn over to him control of the litigation including settlement or else be barred from any remedy over and if he also agrees to bear all expense and to satisfy any adverse judgment, then unless the buyer after seasonable receipt of the demand does turn over control the buyer is so barred.

(6) The provisions of subsection (3), (4) and (5) apply to any obligation of a buyer to hold the seller harmless against infringement or the like (subsection (3) of Section 2-312).

§2-608. Revocation of Acceptance in Whole or in Part.

(1) The buyer may revoke his acceptance of a lot or commercial unit whose non-conformity substantially impairs its value to him if he has accepted it

(a) on the reasonable assumption that its non-conformity would be cured and it has not been seasonably cured; or

(b) without discovery of such non-conformity if his acceptance was reasonably induced either by the difficulty of discovery before acceptance or by the seller's assurances.

(2) Revocation of acceptance must occur within a reasonable time after the buyer discovers or should have discovered the ground for it and before any substantial change in condition of the goods which is not caused by their own defects. It is not effective until the buyer notifies the seller of it.

(3) A buyer who so revokes has the same rights and duties with regard to the goods involved as if he had rejected them.

§2-609. Right to Adequate Assurance of Performance.

(1) A contract for sale imposes an obligation on each party that the other's expectation of receiving due performance will not be impaired. When reasonable grounds for insecurity arise with respect to the performance of either party the other may in writing demand adequate assurance of due performance and until he receives such assurance may if commercially reasonable suspend any performance for which he has not already received the agreed return.

(2) Between merchants the reasonableness of grounds for insecurity and the adequacy of any assurance offered shall be determined according to commercial standards.

(3) Acceptance of any improper delivery or payment does not prejudice the aggrieved party's right to demand adequate assurance of future performance.

(4) After receipt of a justified demand failure to provide within a reasonable time not exceeding thirty days such assurance of due performance as is adequate under the circumstances of the particular case is a repudiation of the contract.

§2-610. Anticipatory Repudiation. When either party repudiates the contract with respect to a performance not yet due the loss of which will substantially impair the value of the contract to the other, the aggrieved party may

(a) for a commercially reasonable time await performance by the repudiating party; or

(b) resort to any remedy for breach (Section 2-703 or Section 2-711), even though he has notified the repudiating party that he would await the latter's performance and has urged retraction; and

(c) in either case suspend his own performance or proceed in accordance with the provisions of this Article on the seller's right to identify goods to the contract notwithstanding breach or to salvage unfinished goods (Section 2-704).

§2-611. Retraction of Anticipatory Repudiation.

(1) Until the repudiating party's next performance is due he can retract his repudiation unless the aggrieved party has since the repudiation cancelled or materially changed his position or otherwise indicated that he considers the repudiation final.

(2) Retraction may be by any method which clearly indicates to the aggrieved party that the repudiating party intends to perform, but must include any assurance justifiably demanded under the provisions of this Article (Section 2-609).

(3) Retraction reinstates the repudiating party's rights under the contract with due excuse and allowance to the aggrieved party for any delay occasioned by the repudiation.

§2-612. "Installment Contract"; Breach.

(1) An "installment contract" is one which requires or authorizes the delivery of goods in separate lots to be separately accepted, even though the contract contains a clause "each delivery is a separate contract" or its equivalent.

(2) The buyer may reject any installment which is non-conforming if the non-conformity substantially impairs the value of that installment and cannot be cured or if the non-conformity is a defect in the required documents; but if the non-conformity does not fall within subsection (3) and the seller gives adequate assurance of its cure the buyer must accept that installment.

(3) Whenever non-conformity or default with respect to one or more installments substantially impairs the value of the whole contract there is a breach of the whole. But the aggrieved party reinstates the contract if he accepts a non-conforming installment without seasonably notifying of cancellation or if he brings an action with respect only to past installments or demands performance as to future installments.

§2-613. Casualty to Identified Goods. Where the contract requires for its performance goods identified when the contract is made, and the goods suffer casualty without fault of either party before the risk of loss passes to the buyer, or in a proper case under a "no arrival, no sale" term (Section 2-324) then

(a) if the loss is total the contract is avoided; and

(**b**) if the loss is partial or the goods have so deteriorated as no longer to conform to the contract the buyer may nevertheless demand inspection and at his option either treat the contract as avoided or accept the goods with due allowance from the contract price for the deterioration or the deficiency in quantity but without further right against the seller.

§2-614. Substituted Performance.

(1) Where without fault of either party the agreed berthing, loading, or unloading facilities fail or an agreed type of carrier becomes unavailable or the agreed manner of delivery otherwise becomes commercially impracticable but a commercially reasonable substitute is available, such substitute performance must be tendered and accepted.

(2) If the agreed means or manner of payment fails because of domestic or foreign governmental regulation, the seller may withhold or stop delivery unless the buyer provides a means or manner of payment which is commercially a substantial equivalent. If delivery has already been taken, payment by the means or in the manner provided by the regulation discharges the buyer's obligation unless the regulation is discriminatory, oppressive or predatory.

§2-615. Excuse by Failure of Presupposed Conditions. Except so far as a seller may have assumed a greater obligation and subject to the preceding section on substituted performance:

(**a**) Delay in delivery or non-delivery in whole or in part by a seller who complies with paragraphs (b) and (c) is not a breach of his duty under a contract for sale if performance as agreed has been made impracticable by the occurrence of a contingency the non-occurrence of which was a basic assumption on which the contract was made or by compliance in good faith with any applicable foreign or domestic governmental regulation or order whether or not it later proves to be invalid.

(**b**) Where the causes mentioned in paragraph (a) affect only a part of the seller's capacity to perform, he must allocate production and deliveries among his customers but may at his option include regular customers not then under contract as well as his own requirements for further manufacture. He may so allocate in any manner which is fair and reasonable.

(**c**) The seller must notify the buyer seasonably that there will be delay or non-delivery and, when allocation is required under paragraph (b), of the estimated quota thus made available for the buyer.

§2-616. Procedure on Notice Claiming Excuse.

(1) When the buyer receives notification of a material or indefinite delay or an allocation justified under the preceding section he may by written notification to the seller as to any delivery concerned, and where the prospective deficiency substantially impairs the value of the whole contract under the provisions of this Article relating to breach of installment contracts(Section 2-612), then also as to the whole,

(**a**) terminate and thereby discharge any unexecuted portion of the contract; or

(**b**) modify the contract by agreeing to take his available quota in substitution.

(2) If after receipt of such notification from the seller the buyer fails so to modify the contract within a reasonable time not exceeding thirty days the contract lapses with respect to any deliveries affected.

(3) The provisions of this section may not be negated by agreement except in so far as the seller has assumed a greater obligation under the preceding section.

Part 7: Remedies

§2-701. Remedies for Breach of Collateral Contracts Not Impaired. Remedies for breach of any obligation or promise collateral or ancillary to a contract for sale are not impaired by the provisions of this Article.

§2-702. Seller's Remedies on Discovery of Buyer's Insolvency.

(1) Where the seller discovers the buyer to be insolvent he may refuse delivery except for cash including payment for all goods theretofore delivered under the contract, and stop delivery under this Article (Section 2-705).

(2) Where the seller discovers that the buyer has received goods on credit while insolvent he may reclaim the goods upon demand made within ten days after the receipt, but if misrepresentation of solvency has been made to the particular seller in writing within three months before delivery the ten day limitation does not apply. Except as provided in this subsection the seller may not base a right to reclaim goods on the buyer's fraudulent or innocent misrepresentation of solvency or of intent to pay.

(3) The seller's right to reclaim under subsection (2) is subject to the rights of a buyer in ordinary course or other good faith purchaser under this Article (Section 2-403). Successful reclamation of goods excludes all other remedies with respect to them. As amended 1966.

§2-703. Seller's Remedies in General. Where the buyer wrongfully rejects or revokes acceptance of goods or fails to make a payment due on or before delivery or repudiates with respect to a part or the whole, then with respect to any goods directly affected and, if the breach is of the whole contract (Section 2-612), then also with respect to the whole undelivered balance, the aggrieved seller may

(**a**) withhold delivery of such goods;

(**b**) stop delivery by any bailee as hereafter provided (Section 2-705);

(**c**) proceed under the next section respecting goods still unidentified to the contract;

(**d**) resell and recover damages as hereafter provided (Section 2-706);

(**e**) recover damages for non-acceptance (Section 2-708) or in a proper case the price (Section 2-709);

(f) cancel.

§2-704. Seller's Right to Identify Goods to the Contract Notwithstanding Breach or to Salvage Unfinished Goods.

(1) An aggrieved seller under the preceding section may

(**a**) identify to the contract conforming goods not already identified if at the time he learned of the breach they are in his possession or control;

(b) treat as the subject of resale goods which have demonstrably been intended for the particular contract even though those goods are unfinished.

(2) Where the goods are unfinished an aggrieved seller may in the exercise of reasonable commercial judgment for the purposes of avoiding loss and of effective realization either complete the manufacture and wholly identify the goods to the contract or cease manufacture and resell for scrap or salvage value or proceed in any other reasonable manner.

§2-705. Seller's Stoppage of Delivery in Transit or Otherwise.

(1) The seller may stop delivery of goods in the possession of a carrier or other bailee when he discovers the buyer to be insolvent (Section 2-702) and may stop delivery of carload, truckload, planeload or larger shipments of express or freight when the buyer repudiates or fails to make a payment due before delivery or if for any other reason the seller has a right to withold or reclaim the goods.

(2) As against such buyer the seller may stop delivery until

(a) receipt of the goods by the buyer; or

(b) acknowledgement to the buyer by any bailee of the goods except a carrier that the bailee holds the goods for the buyer; or

(c) such acknowledgement to the buyer by a carrier by reshipment or as warehouseman; or

(d) negotiation to the buyer of any negotiable document of title covering the goods.

(3)

(a) To stop delivery the seller must so notify as to enable the bailee by reasonable diligence to prevent delivery of the goods.

(b) After such notification the bailee must hold and deliver the goods according to the directions of the seller but the seller is liable to the bailee for any ensuing charges or damages.

(c) If a negotiable document of title has been issued for goods the bailee is not obliged to obey a notification to stop until surrender of the document.

(d) A carrier who has issued a non-negotiable bill of lading is not obliged to obey a notification to stop received from a person other than the consignor.

§2-706. Seller's Resale Including Contract for Resale.

(1) Under the conditions stated in Section 2-703 on seller's remedies, the seller may resell the goods concerned or the undelivered balance thereof. Where the resale is made in good faith and in a commercially reasonable manner the seller may recover the difference between the resale price and the contract price together with any incidental damages allowed under the provisions of this Article (Section 2-710), but less expenses saved in consequence of the buyer's breach.

(2) Except as otherwise provided in subsection (3) or unless otherwise agreed resale may be at public or private sale including sale by way of one or more contracts to sell or of identification to an existing contract of the seller. Sale may be as a unit or in parcels and at any time and place and on any terms but every aspect of the sale including the method, manner, time, place and terms must be commercially reasonable. The resale must be reasonably identified as referring to the broken contract, but it is not necessary that the goods be in existence or that any or all of them have been identified to the contract before the breach.

(3) Where the resale is at private sale the seller must give the buyer reasonable notification of his intention to resell.

(4) Where the resale is at public sale

(a) only identified goods can be sold except where there is a recognized market for a public sale of futures in goods of the kind; and

(b) it must be made at a usual place or market for public sale if one is reasonably available and except in the case of goods which are perishable or threaten to decline in value speedily the seller must give the buyer reasonable notice of the time and place of the resale; and

(c) if the goods are not to be within the view of those attending the sale the notification of sale must state the place where the goods are located and provide for their reasonable inspection by prospective bidders; and

(d) the seller may buy.

(5) A purchaser who buys in good faith at a resale takes the goods free of any rights of the original buyer even though the seller fails to comply with one or more of the requirements of this section.

(6) The seller is not accountable to the buyer for any profit made on any resale. A person in the position of a seller (Section 2-707) or a buyer who has rightfully rejected or justifiably revoked acceptance must account for any excess over the amount of his security interest, as hereinafter defined (subsection (3) of Section 2-711).

§2-707. "Person in the Position of a Seller".

(1) A "person in the position of a seller" includes as against a principal an agent who has paid or become responsible for the price of goods on behalf of his principal or anyone who otherwise holds a security interest or other right in goods similar to that of a seller.

(2) A person in the position of a seller may as provided in this Article withhold or stop delivery (Section 2-705) and resell (Section 2-706) and recover incidental damages (Section 2-710).

§2-708. Seller's Damages for Non-acceptance or Repudiation.

(1) Subject to subsection (2) and to the provisions of this Article with respect to proof of market price (Section 2-723), the measure of damages for non-acceptance or repudiation by the buyer is the difference between the market price at the time and place for tender and the unpaid contract price together with any incidental damages provided in this Article (Section 2-710), but less expenses saved in consequence of the buyer's breach.

(2) If the measure of damages provided in subsection (1) is inadequate to put the seller in as good a position as performance would have done then the measure of damages is the profit (including reasonable overhead) which the seller would have made from full performance by the buyer, together with any incidental damages provided in this Article (Section 2-710), due

allowance for costs reasonably incurred and due credit for payments or proceeds of resale.

§2-709. Action for the Price.

(1) When the buyer fails to pay the price as it becomes due the seller may recover, together with any incidental damages under the next section, the price

(a) of goods accepted or of conforming goods lost or damaged within a commercially reasonable time after risk of their loss has passed to the buyer; and

(b) of goods identified to the contract if the seller is unable after reasonable effort to resell them at a reasonable price or the circumstances reasonably indicate that such effort will be unavailing.

(2) Where the seller sues for the price he must hold for the buyer any goods which have been identified to the contract and are still in his control except that if resale becomes possible he may resell them at any time prior to the collection of the judgment. The net proceeds of any such resale must be credited to the buyer and payment of the judgment entitles him to any goods not resold.

(3) After the buyer has wrongfully rejected or revoked acceptance of the goods or has failed to make a payment due or has repudiated (Section 2-610), a seller who is held not entitled to the price under this section shall nevertheless be awarded damages for non-acceptance under the preceding section.

§2-710. Seller's Incidental Damages. Incidental damages to an aggrieved seller include any commercially reasonable charges, expenses or commissions incurred in stopping delivery, in the transportation, care and custody of goods after the buyer's breach, in connection with return or resale of the goods or otherwise resulting from the breach.

§2-711. Buyer's Remedies in General; Buyer's Security Interest in Rejected Goods.

(1) When the seller fails to make delivery or repudiates or the buyer rightfully rejects or justifiably revokes acceptance then with respect to any goods involved, and with respect to the whole if the breach goes to the whole contract (Section 2-612), the buyer may cancel and whether or not he has done so may in addition to recovering so much of the price as has been paid

(a) "cover" and have damages under the next section as to all the goods affected whether or not they have been identified to the contract; or

(b) recover damages for non-delivery as provided in this Article (Section 2-713).

(2) Where the seller fails to deliver or repudiates the buyer may also

(a) if the goods have been identified recover them as provided in this Article (Section 2-502); or

(b) in a proper case obtain specific performance or replevy the goods as provided in this Article (Section 2-716).

(3) On rightful rejection or justifable revocation of acceptance a buyer has a security interest in goods in his possession or control for any payments made on their price and any expenses reasonably incurred in their inspection, receipt, transportation, care and custody and may hold such goods and resell them in like manner as an aggrieved seller (Section 2-706).

§2-712. "Cover"; Buyer's Procurement of Substitute Goods.

(1) After a breach within the preceding section the buyer may "cover" by making in good faith and without unreasonable delay any reasonable purchase of or contract to purchase goods in substitution for those due from the seller.

(2) The buyer may recover from the seller as damages the difference between the cost of cover and the contract price together with any incidental or consequential damages as hereinafter defined (Section 2-715), but less expenses saved in consequence of the seller's breach.

(3) Failure of the buyer to effect cover within this section does not bar him from any other remedy.

§2-713. Buyer's Damages for Non-Delivery or Repudiation.

(1) Subject to the provisions of this Article with respect to proof of market price (Section 2-723), the measure of damages for non-delivery or repudiation by the seller is the difference between the market price at the time when the buyer learned of the breach and the contract price together with any incidental and consequential damages provided in this Article (Section 2-715), but less expenses saved in consequence of the seller's breach.

(2) Market price is to be determined as of the place for tender or, in cases of rejection after arrival or revocation of acceptance, as of the place of arrival.

§2-714. Buyer's Damages for Breach in Regard to Accepted Goods.

(1) Where the buyer has accepted goods and given notification (subsection (3) Section 2-607) he may recover as damages for any non-conformity of tender the loss resulting in the ordinary course of events from the seller's breach as determined in any manner which is reasonable.

(2) The measure of damages for breach of warranty is the difference at the time and place of acceptance between the value of the goods accepted and the value they would have had if they had been as warranted, unless special circumstances show proximate damages of a different amount.

(3) In a proper case any incidental and consequential damages under the next section may also be recovered.

§2-715. Buyer's Incidental and Consequential Damages.

(1) Incidental damages resulting from the seller's breach include expenses reasonably incurred in inspection, receipt, transportation and care and custody of goods rightfully rejected, any commercially reasonable charges, expenses or commissions in connection with effecting cover and any other reasonable expense incident to the delay or other breach.

(2) Consequential damages resulting from the seller's breach include

(a) any loss resulting from general or particular requirements and needs of which the seller at the time of contracting had reason to know and which could not reasonably be prevented by cover or otherwise; and

(b) injury to person or property proximately resulting from any breach of warranty.

§2-716. Buyer's Right to Specific Performance or Replevin.

(1) Specific performance may be decreed where the goods are unique or in other proper circumstances.

(2) The decree for specific performance may include such terms and conditions as to payment of the price, damages, or other relief as the court may deem just.

(3) The buyer has a right of replevin for goods identified to the contract if after reasonable effort he is unable to effect cover for such goods or the circumstances reasonably indicate that such effort will be unavailing or if the goods have been shipped under reservation and satisfaction of the security interest in them has been made or tendered.

§2-717. Deduction of Damages From the Price The buyer on notifying the seller of his intention to do so may deduct all or any part of the damages resulting from any breach of the contract from any part of the price still due under the same contract.

§2-718. Liquidation or Limitation of Damages; Deposits.

(1) Damages for breach by either party may be liquidated in the agreement but only at an amount which is reasonable in the light of the anticipated or actual harm caused by the breach, the difficulties of proof of loss, and the inconvenience or nonfeasibility of otherwise obtaining an adequate remedy. A term fixing unreasonably large liquidated damages is void as a penalty.

(2) Where the seller justifiably withholds delivery of goods because of the buyer's breach, the buyer is entitled to restitution of any amount by which the sum of his payments exceeds

(a) the amount to which the seller is entitled by virtue of terms liquidating the seller's damages in accordance with subsection (1), or

(b) in the absence of such terms, twenty per cent of the value of the total performance for which the buyer is obligated under the contract or $500, whichever is smaller.

(3) The buyer's right to restitution under subsection (2) is subject to offset to the extent that the seller establishes

(a) a right to recover damages under the provisions of this Article other than subsection (1), and

(b) the amount or value of any benefits received by the buyer directly or indirectly by reason of the contract.

(4) where a seller has received payment in goods their reasonable value or the proceeds of their resale shall be treated as payments for the purposes of subsection (2); but if the seller has notice of the buyer's breach before reselling goods received in part performance, his resale is subject to the conditions laid down in this Article on resale by an aggrieved seller (Section 2-706).

§2-719. Contractual Modification or Limitation of Remedy.

(1) Subject to the provisions of subsections (2) and (3) of this section and of the preceding section on liquidation and limitation of damages,

(a) the agreement may provide for remedies in addition to or in substitution for those provided in this Article and may limit or alter the measure of damages recoverable under this Article, as by limiting the buyer's remedies to return of the goods and repayment of the price or to repair and replacement of non-conforming goods or parts; and

(b) resort to a remedy as provided is optional unless the remedy is expressly agreed to be exclusive, in which case it is the sole remedy.

(2) Where circumstances cause an exclusive or limited remedy to fail of its essential purpose, remedy may be had as provided in this Act.

(3) Consequential damages may be limited or excluded unless the limitation or exclusion is unconscionable. Limitation of consequential damages for injury to the person in the case of consumer goods is prima facie unconscionable but limitation of damages where the loss is commercial is not.

§2-720. Effect of "Cancellation" or "Rescission" on Claims for Antecedent Breach. Unless the contrary intention clearly appears, expressions of "cancellation" or "rescission" of the contract or the like shall not be construed as a renunciation or discharge of any claim in damages for an antecedent breach.

§2-721. Remedies for Fraud. Remedies for material misrepresentation or fraud include all remedies available under this Article for non-fraudulent breach. Neither rescission or a claim for rescission of the contract for sale nor rejection or return of the goods shall bar or be deemed inconsistent with a claim for damages or other remedy.

§2-722. Who Can Sue Third Parties for Injury to Goods. Where a third party so deals with goods which have been identified to a contract for sale as to cause actionable injury to a party to that contract

(a) right of action against the third party is in either party to the contract for sale who has title to or a security interest or a special property or an insurable interest in the goods; and if the goods have been destroyed or converted a right of action is also in the party who either bore the risk of loss under the contract for sale or has since the injury assumed that risk as against the other;

(b) if at the time of the injury the party plaintiff did not bear the risk of loss as against the other party to the contract for sale and there is no arrangement between them for disposition of the recovery, his suit or settlement is, subject to his own interest, as a fiduciary for the other party to the contract;

(c) either party may with the consent of the other sue for the benefit of whom it may concern.

§2-723. Proof of Market Price: Time and Place.

(1) If an action based on anticipatory repudiation comes to trial before the time for performance with respect to some or all of the goods, any damages based on market price (Section 2-708 or Section 2-713) shall be determined according to the price of such goods prevailing at the time when the aggrieved party learned of the repudiation.

(2) If evidence of a price prevailing at the times or places described in this Article is not readily available the price prevailing within any reasonable time before or after the time described or at any other place which in commercial judgment

or under usage of trade would serve as a reasonable substitute for the one described may be used, making any proper allowance for the cost of transporting the goods to or from such other place.

(3) Evidence of a relevant price prevailing at a time or place other than the one described in this Article offered by one party is not admissible unless and until he has given the other party such notice as the court finds sufficient to prevent unfair surprise.

§2-724. Admissibility of Market Quotations. Whenever the prevailing price or value of any goods regularly bought and sold in any established commodity market is in issue, reports in official publication or trade journals or in newspapers or periodicals of general circulation published as the reports of such market shall be admissible in evidence. The circumstances of the preparation of such a report may be shown to affect its weight but not its admissibility.

§2-725. Statute of Limitations in Contracts for Sale.

(1) An action for breach of any contract for sale must be commenced within four years after the cause of action has accrued. By the original agreement the parties may reduce the period of limitation to not less than one year but may not extend it.

(2) A cause of action accrues when the breach occurs, regardless of the aggrieved party's lack of knowledge of the breach. A breach of warranty occurs when tender of delivery is made, except that where a warranty explicitly extends to future performance of the goods and discovery of the breach must await the time of such performance the cause of action accrues when the breach is or should have been discovered.

(3) Where an action commenced within the time limited by subsection (1) is so terminated as to leave available a remedy by another action for the same breach such other action may be commenced after the expiration of the time limited and within six months after the termination of the first action unless the termination resulted from voluntary discontinuance or from dismissal for failure or neglect to prosecute.

(4) This section does not alter the law on tolling of the statute of limitations nor does it apply to causes of action which have accrued before this Act becomes effective.

ARTICLE 3: COMMERCIAL PAPER

Part 1: Short Title, Form and Interpretation

§3-101. Short Title. This Article shall be known and may be cited as Uniform Commercial Code—Commercial Paper.

§3-102. Definitions and Index of Definitions.

(1) In this Article unless the context otherwise requires

(**a**) "Issue" means the first delivery of an instrument to a holder or a remitter.

(**b**) An "order" is a direction to pay and must be more than an authorization or request. It must identify the person to pay with reasonable certainty. It may be addressed to one or more such persons jointly or in the alternative but not in succession.

(**c**) A "promise" is an undertaking to pay and must be more than an acknowledgement of an obligation.

(**d**) "Secondary party" means a drawer or endorser.

(**e**) "Instrument" means a negotiable instrument.

(2) Other definitions applying to this Article and the sections in which they appear are:

"Acceptance". Section 3-410.
"Accommodation party". Section 3-415.
"Alteration". Section 3-407.
"Certificate of deposit". Section 3-104.
"Certification". Section 3-411.
"Check". Section 3-104.
"Definite time". Section 3-109.
"Dishonor". Section 3-507.
"Draft". Section 3-104.
"Holder in due course". Section 3-302.
"Negotiation". Section 3-202.
"Note". Section 3-104.
"Notice of dishonor". Section 3-508.
"On demand". Section 3-108.
"Presentment". Section 3-504.
"Protest". Section 3-509.
"Restrictive Indorsement". Section 3-205.
"Signature". Section 3-401.

(3) The following definitions in other Articles apply to this Article:

"Account". Section 4-104.
"Banking Day". Section 4-104.
"Clearing house". Section 4-104.
"Collecting bank. Section 4-105.
"Customer". Section 4-104.
"Depositary Bank". Section 4-105.
"Documentary Draft". Section 4-104.
"Intermediary Bank". Section 4-105.
"Item". Section 4-104.
"Midnight deadline". Section 4-104.
"Payor bank". Section 4-105.

(4) In addition Article 1 contains general definitions and principles of construction and interpretation applicable throughout this Article.

§3-103. Limitations on Scope of Article.

(1) This Article does not apply to money, documents of title or investment securities.

(2) The provisions of this Article are subject to the provisions of the Article on Bank Deposits and Collections (Article 4) and Secured Transactions (Article 9).

§3-104. Form of Negotiable Instruments; "Draft"; "Check"; "Certificate of Deposit"; "Note".

(1) Any writing to be a negotiable instrument within this Article must

(**a**) be signed by the maker or drawer; and

(**b**) contain an unconditional promise or order to pay a sum certain in money and no other promise, order, obligation or power given by the maker or drawer except as authorized by this Article; and

(c) be payable on demand or at a definite time; and

(d) be payable to order or to bearer.

(2) A writing which complies with the requirements of this section is

(a) a "draft" ("bill of exchange") if it is an order;

(b) a "check" if it is a draft drawn on a bank and payable on demand.

(c) a "certificate of deposit" if it is an acknowledgement by a bank of receipt of money with an engagement to repay it;

(d) a "note" if it is a promise other than a certificate of deposit.

(3) As used in other Articles in this Act, and as the context may require, the terms "draft", "check", "certificate of deposit" and "note" may refer to instruments which are not negotiable within this Article as well as to instruments which are so negotiable.

§3-105. When Promise or Order Unconditional.

(1) A promise or order otherwise unconditional is not made conditional by the fact that the instrument

(a) is subject to implied or constructive conditions; or

(b) states its consideration, whether performed or promised, or the transaction which gave rise to the instrument, or that the promise or order is made or the instrument matures in accordance with or "as per" such transaction; or

(c) refers to or states that it arises out of a separate agreement or refers to a separate agreement for rights as to prepayment or acceleration; or

(d) states that is drawn under a letter of credit; or

(e) states that it is secured, whether by mortgage, reservation of title or otherwise; or

(f) indicates a particular account to be debited or any other fund or source from which reimbursement is expected; or

(g) is limited to payment out of a particular fund or the proceeds of a particular source, if the instrument is issued by a government or governmental agency or unit; or

(h) is limited to payment out of the entire assets of a partnership, unincorporated association, trust or estate by or on behalf of which the instrument is issued.

(2) A promise or order is not unconditional if the instrument

(a) states that it is subject to or governed by any other agreement; or

(b) states that it is to be paid only out of a particular fund or source except as provided in this section. As amended 1962.

§3-106. Sum Certain.

(1) The sum payable is a sum certain even though it is to be paid

(a) with stated interest or by stated installments; or

(b) with stated different rates of interest before and after default or a specified date; or

(c) with a stated discount or addition if paid before or after the date fixed for payment; or

(d) with exchange or less exchange, whether at a fixed rate or at the current rate; or

(e) with costs of collection or an attorney's fee or both upon default.

(2) Nothing in this section shall validate any term which is otherwise illegal.

§3-107. Money.

(1) An instrument is payable in money if the medium of exchange in which it is payable is money at the time the instrument is made. An instrument payable in "currency" or "current funds" is payable in money.

(2) A promise or order to pay a sum stated in a foreign currency is for a sum certain in money and, unless a different medium of payment is specified in the instrument, may be satisfied by payment of that number of dollars which the stated foreign currency will purchase at the buying sight rate for that currency on the day on which the instrument is payable or, if payable on demand, on the day of demand. If such an instrument specifies a foreign currency as the medium of payment the instrument is payable in that currency.

§3-108. Payable on Demand. Instruments payable on demand include those payable at sight or on presentation and those in which no time for payment is stated.

§3-109. Definite Time.

(1) An instrument is payable at a definite time if by its terms it is payable

(a) on or before a stated date or at a fixed period after a stated date; or

(b) at a fixed period after sight; or

(c) at a definite time subject to any acceleration; or

(d) at a definite time subject to extension at the option of the holder, or to extension to a further definite time at the option of the maker or acceptor or automatically upon or after a specified act or event.

(2) An instrument which by its terms is otherwise payable only upon an act or event uncertain as to time of occurrence is not payable at a definite time even though the act or event has occurred.

§3-110. Payable to Order.

(1) An instrument is payable to order when by its terms it is payable to the order or assigns of any person therein specified with reasonable certainty, or to him or his order, or when it is conspicuously designated on its face as "exchange" or the like and names a payee. It may be payable to the order of

(a) the maker or drawer; or

(b) the drawee; or

(c) a payee who is not maker, drawer or drawee; or

(d) two or more payees together or in the alternative; or

(e) an estate, trust or fund, in which case it is payable to the order of the representative of such estate, trust or fund or his successors; or

(f) an office, or an officer by his title as such in which case it is payable to the principal but the incumbent of the office or his successors may act as if he or they were the holder; or

(g) a partnership or unincorporated association, in which case it is payable to the partnership or association and may be indorsed or transferred by any person thereto authorized.

(2) An instrument not payable to order is not made so payable by such words as "payable upon return of this instrument properly indorsed."

(3) An instrument made payable both to order and to bearer is payable to order unless the bearer words are handwritten or typewritten.

§3-111. Payable to Bearer. An instrument is payable to bearer when by its terms it is payable to

(a) bearer or the order of bearer; or

(b) a specified person or bearer; or

(c) "cash" or the order of "cash", or any other indication which does not purport to designate a specific payee.

§3-112. Terms and Omissions Not Affecting Negotiability.

(1) The negotiability of an instrument is not affected by

(a) the omission of a statement of any consideration or of the place where the instrument is drawn or payable; or

(b) a statement that collateral has been given to secure obligations either on the instrument or otherwise of an obligor on the instrument or that in case of default on those obligations the holder may realize on or dispose of the collateral; or

(c) a promise or power to maintain or protect collateral or to give additional collateral; or

(d) a term authorizing a confession of judgment on the instrument if it is not paid when due; or

(e) a term purporting to waive the benefit of any law intended for the advantage or protection of any obligor; or

(f) a term in a draft providing that the payee by indorsing or cashing it acknowledges full satisfaction of an obligation of the drawer; or

(g) a statement in a draft drawn in a set of parts (Section 3-801) to the effect that the order is effective only if no other part has been honored.

(2) Nothing in this section shall validate any term which is otherwise illegal. As amended 1962.

§3-113. Seal. An instrument otherwise negotiable is within this Article even though it is under a seal.

§3-114. Date, Antedating, Postdating.

(1) The negotiability of an instrument is not affected by the fact that it is undated, antedated or postdated.

(2) Where an instrument is antedated or postdated the time when it is payable is determined by the stated date if the instrument is payable on demand or at a fixed period after date.

(3) Where the instrument or any signature thereon is dated, the date is presumed to be correct.

§3-115. Incomplete Instruments.

(1) When a paper whose contents at the time of signing show that it is intended to become an instrument is signed while still incomplete in any necessary respect it cannot be enforced until completed, but when it is completed in accordance with authority given it is effective as completed.

(2) If the completion is unauthorized the rules as to material alteration apply (Section 3-407), even though the paper was not delivered by the maker or drawer; but the burden of establishing that any completion is unauthorized is on the party so asserting.

§3-116. Instruments Payable to Two or More Persons. An instrument payable to the order of two or more persons

(a) if in the alternative is payable to any one of them and may be negotiated, discharged or enforced by any of them who has possession of it;

(b) if not in the alternative is payable to all of them and may be negotiated, discharged or enforced only by all of them.

§3-117. Instruments Payable With Words of Description. An instrument made payable to a named person with the addition of words describing him

(a) as agent or officer of a specified person is payable to his principal but the agent or officer may act as if he were the holder;

(b) as any other fiduciary for a specified person or purpose is payable to the payee and may be negotiated, discharged or enforced by him;

(c) in any other manner is payable to the payee unconditionally and the additional words are without effect on subsequent parties.

§3-118. Ambiguous Terms and Rules of Construction. The following rules apply to every instrument:

(a) Where there is doubt whether the instrument is a draft or a note the holder may treat it as either. A draft drawn on the drawer is effective as a note.

(b) Handwritten terms control typewritten and printed terms, and typewritten control printed.

(c) Words control figures except that if the words are ambiguous figures control.

(d) Unless otherwise specified a provision for interest means interest at the judgment rate at the place of payment from the date of the instrument, or if it is undated from the date of issue.

(e) Unless the instrument otherwise specifies two or more persons who sign as maker, acceptor or drawer or indorser and as a part of the same transaction are jointly and severally liable even though the instrument contains such words as "I promise to pay."

(f) Unless otherwise specified consent to extension authorizes a single extension for not longer than the original period. A consent to extension, expressed in the instrument, is binding on secondary parties and accommodation makers. A holder may not exercise his option to extend an instrument over the objection of a maker or acceptor or other party who in accordance with Section 3-604 tenders full payment when the instrument is due.

§3-119. Other Writings Affecting Instrument.

(1) As between the obligor and his immediate obligee or any

transferee the terms of an instrument may be modified or affected by any other written agreement executed as a part of the same transaction, except that a holder in due course is not affected by any limitation of his rights arising out of the separate written agreement if he had no notice of the limitation when he took the instrument.

(2) A separate agreement does not affect the negotiability of an instrument.

§3-120. Instruments "Payable Through" Bank. An instrument which states that is is "payable through" a bank or the like designates that bank as a collecting bank to make presentment but does not of itself authorize the bank to pay the instrument.

§3-121. Instruments Payable at Bank.

Note: *If this Act is introduced in the Congress of the United States this section should be omitted. (States to select either alternative.)*

Alternative A—A note or acceptance which states that it is payable at a bank is the equivalent of a draft drawn on the bank payable when it falls due out of any funds of the maker or acceptor in current account or otherwise available for such payment.

Alternative B—A note or acceptance which states that it is payable at a bank is not of itself an order or authorization to the bank to pay it.

§3-122. Accrual of Cause of Action.

(1) A cause of action against a maker or an acceptor accrues

(a) in the case of a time instrument on the day after maturity;

(b) in the case of a demand instrument upon its date or, if no date is stated, on the date of issue.

(2) A cause of action against the obligor of a demand or time certificate of deposit accrues upon demand, but demand on a time certificate may not be made until on or after the date of maturity.

(3) A cause of action against a drawer of a draft or an indorser of any instrument accrues upon demand following dishonor of the instrument. Notice of dishonor is a demand.

(4) Unless an instrument provides otherwise, interest runs at the rate provided by law for a judgment

(a) in the case of a maker, acceptor or other primary obligor of a demand instrument, from the date of demand;

(b) in all other cases from the date of accrual of the cause of action. As amended 1962.

PART 2: Transfer and Negotiation

§3-201. Transfer: Right to Indorsement.

(1) Transfer of an instrument vests in the transferee such rights as the transferor has therein, except that a transferee who has himself been a party to any fraud or illegality affecting the instrument or who as a prior holder had notice of a defense or claim against it cannot improve his position by taking from a later holder in due course.

(2) A transfer of a security interest in an instrument vests the foregoing rights in the transferee to the extent of the interest transferred.

(3) Unless otherwise agreed any transfer for value of an instrument not then payable to bearer gives the transferee the specifically enforceable right to have the unqualified indorsement of the transferor. Negotiation takes effect only when the indorsement is made and until that time there is no presumption that the transferee is the owner.

§3-202. Negotiation.

(1) Negotiation is the transfer of an instrument in such form that the transferee becomes a holder. If the instrument is payable to order it is negotiated by delivery with any necessary indorsement; if payable to bearer it is negotiated by delivery.

(2) An indorsement must be written by or on behalf of the holder and on the instrument or on a paper so firmly affixed thereto as to become a part thereof.

(3) An indorsement is effective for negotiation only when it conveys the entire instrument or any unpaid residue. If it purports to be of less it operates only as a partial assignment.

(4) Words of assignment, condition, waiver, guaranty, limitation or disclaimer of liability and the like accompanying an indorsement do not affect its character as an indorsement.

§3-203. Wrong or Misspelled Name. Where an instrument is made payable to a person under a misspelled name or one other than his own he may indorse in that name or his own or both; but signature in both names may be required by a person paying or giving value for the instrument.

§3-204. Special Indorsement; Blank Indorsement.

(1) A special indorsement specifies the person to whom or to whose order it makes the instrument payable. Any instrument specially indorsed becomes payable to the order of the special indorsee and may be further negotiated only by his indorsement.

(2) An indorsement in blank specifies no particular indorsee and may consist of a mere signature. An instrument payable to order and indorsed in blank becomes payable to bearer and may be negotiated by delivery alone until specially indorsed.

(3) The holder may convert a blank indorsement into a special indorsement by writing over the signature of the indorser in blank any contract consistent with the character of the indorsement.

§3-205. Restrictive Indorsements. An indorsement is restrictive which either

(a) is conditional; or

(b) purports to prohibit further transfer of the instrument; or

(c) includes the words "for collection", "for deposit", "pay any bank", or like terms signifying a purpose of deposit or collection; or

(d) otherwise states that it is for the benefit or use of the indorser or of another person.

§3-206. Effect of Restrictive Indorsement.

(1) No restrictive indorsement prevents further transfer or negotiation of the instrument.

(2) An intermediary bank, or a payor bank which is not the depositary bank, is neither given notice nor otherwise affected by a restrictive indorsement of any person except the bank's immediate transferor or the person presenting for payment.

(3) Except for an intermediary bank, any transferee under an indorsement which is conditional or includes the words "for collection", "for deposit", "pay any bank", or like terms (subparagraphs (a) and (c) of Section 3-205) must pay or apply any value given by him for or on the security of the instrument consistently with the indorsement and to the extent that he does so he becomes a holder for value. In addition such transferee is a holder in due course if he otherwise complies with the requirements of Section 3-302 on what constitutes a holder in due course.

(4) The first taker under an indorsement for the benefit of the indorser or another person (subparagraph (d) of Section 3-205) must pay or apply any value given by him for or on the security of the instrument consistently with the indorsement and to the extent that he does so he becomes a holder for value. In addition such taker is a holder in due course if he otherwise complies with the requirements of Section 3-302 on what constitutes a holder in due course. A later holder for value is neither given notice nor otherwise affected by such restrictive indorsement unless he has knowledge that a fiduciary or other person has negotiated the instrument in any transaction for his own benefit or otherwise in breach of duty (subsection (2) of Section 3-304).

§3-207. Negotiation Effective Although It May Be Rescinded.

(1) Negotiation is effective to transfer the instrument although the negotiation is

(a) made by an infant, a corporation exceeding its powers, or any other person without capacity; or

(b) obtained by fraud, duress or mistake of any kind; or

(c) part of an illegal transaction; or

(d) made in breach of duty.

(2) Except as against a subsequent holder in due course such negotiation is in an appropriate case subject to rescission, the declaration of a constructive trust or any other remedy permitted by law.

§3-208. Reacquisition. Where an instrument is returned to or reacquired by a prior party he may cancel any indorsement which is not necessary to his title and reissue or further negotiate the instrument, but any intervening party is discharged as against the reacquiring party and subsequent holders not in due course and if his indorsement has been cancelled is discharged as against subsequent holders in due course as well.

Part 3: Rights of a Holder

§3-301. Rights of a Holder. The holder of an instrument whether or not he is the owner may transfer or negotiate it and, except as otherwise provided in Section 3-603 on payment or satisfaction, discharge it or enforce payment in his own name.

§3-302. Holder in Due Course.

(1) A holder in due course is a holder who takes the instrument

(a) for value; and

(b) in good faith; and

(c) without notice that it is overdue or has been dishonored or of any defense against or claim to it on the part of any person.

(2) A payee may be a holder in due course.

(3) A holder does not become a holder in due course of an instrument:

(a) by purchase of it at judicial sale or by taking it under legal process; or

(b) by acquiring it in taking over an estate; or

(c) by purchasing it as part of a bulk transaction not in regular course of business of the transferor.

(4) A purchaser of a limited interest can be a holder in due course only to the extent of the interest purchased.

§3-303. Taking for Value. A holder takes the instrument for value

(a) to the extent that the agreed consideration has been performed or that he acquires a security interest in or a lien on the instrument otherwise than by legal process; or

(b) when he takes the instrument in payment of or as security for an antecedent claim against any person whether or not the claim is due; or

(c) when he gives a negotiable instrument for it or makes an irrevocable commitment to a third person.

§3-304. Notice to Purchaser.

(1) The purchaser has notice of a claim or defense if

(a) the instrument is so incomplete, bears such visible evidence of forgery or alteration, or is otherwise so irregular as to call into question its validity, terms or ownership or to create an ambiguity as to the party to pay; or

(b) the purchaser has notice that the obligation of any party is voidable in whole or in part, or that all parties have been discharged.

(2) The purchaser has notice of a claim against the instrument when he has knowledge that a fiduciary has negotiated the instrument in payment of or as security for his own debt or in any transaction for his own benefit or otherwise in breach of duty.

(3) The purchaser has notice that an instrument is overdue if he has reason to know

(a) that any part of the principal amount is overdue or that there is an uncured default in payment of another instrument of the same series; or

(b) that acceleration of the instrument has been made; or

(c) that he is taking a demand instrument after demand has been made or more than a reasonable length of time after its issue. A reasonable time for a check drawn and payable within the states and territories of the United States and the District of Columbia is presumed to be thirty days.

(4) Knowledge of the following facts does not of itself give the purchaser notice of a defense or claim

(a) that the instrument is antedated or postdated;

(b) that it was issued or negotiated in return for an executory promise or accompanied by a separate agreement, unless the purchaser has notice that a defense or claim has arisen from the terms thereof;

(c) that any party has signed for accommodation;

(d) that an incomplete instrument has been completed, unless the purchaser has notice of any improper completion;

(e) that any person negotiating the instrument is or was a fiduciary;

(f) that there has been default in payment of interest on the instrument or in payment of any other instrument, except one of the same series.

(5) The filing or recording of a document does not of itself constitute notice within the provisions of this Article to a person who would otherwise be a holder in due course.

(6) To be effective notice must be received at such time and in such manner as to give a reasonable opportunity to act on it.

§3-305. Rights of a Holder in Due Course. To the extent that a holder is a holder in due course he takes the instrument free from

(1) all claims to it on the part of any person; and

(2) all defenses of any party to the instrument with whom the holder has not dealt except

(a) infancy, to the extent that it is a defense to a simple contract; and

(b) such other incapacity, or duress, or illegality of the transaction, as renders the obligation of the party a nullity; and

(c) such misrepresentation as has induced the party to sign the instrument with neither knowledge nor reasonable opportunity to obtain knowledge of its character or its essential terms; and

(d) discharge in insolvency proceedings; and

(e) any other discharge of which the holder has notice when he takes the instrument.

§3-306. Rights of One Not Holder in Due Course. Unless he has the rights of a holder in due course any person takes the instrument subject to

(a) all valid claims to it on the part of any person; and

(b) all defenses of any party which would be available in an action on a simple contract; and

(c) the defenses of want or failure of consideration, non-performance of any condition precedent, non-delivery, or delivery for a special purpose (Section 3-408); and

(d) the defense that he or a person through whom he holds the instrument acquired it by theft, or that payment or satisfaction to such holder would be inconsistent with the terms of a restrictive indorsement. The claim of any third person to the instrument is not otherwise available as a defense to any party liable thereon unless the third person himself defends the action for such party.

§3-307. Burden of Establishing Signatures, Defenses and Due Course.

(1) Unless specifically denied in the pleading each signature on an instrument is admitted. When the effectiveness of a signature is put in issue

(a) the burden of establishing it is on the party claiming under the signature; but

(b) the signature is presumed to be genuine or authorized except where the action is to enforce the obligation of a purported signer who has died or become incompetent before proof is required.

(2) When signatures are admitted or established, production of the instrument entitles a holder to recover on it unless the defendant establishes a defense.

(3) After it is shown that a defense exists a person claiming the rights of a holder in due course has the burden of establishing that he or some person under whom he claims is in all respects a holder in due course.

Part 4: Liability of Parties

§3-401. Signature.

(1) No person is liable on an instrument unless his signature appears thereon.

(2) A signature is made by use of any name, including any trade or assumed name, upon an instrument, or by any word or mark used in lieu of a written signature

§3-402. Signature in Ambiguous Capacity. Unless the instrument clearly indicates that a signature is made in some other capacity it is an indorsement.

§3-403. Signature by Authorized Representative.

(1) A signature may be made by an agent or other representative, and his authority to make it may be established as in other cases of representation. No particular form of appointment is necessary to establish such authority.

(2) An authorized representative who signs his own name to an instrument

(a) is personally obligated if the instrument neither names the person represented nor shows that the representative signed in a representative capacity;

(b) except as otherwise established between the immediate parties, is personally obligated if the instrument names the person represented but does not show that the representative signed in a representative capacity, or if the instrument does not name the person represented but does show that the representative signed in a representative capacity.

(3) Except as otherwise established the name of an organization preceded or followed by the name and office of an authorized individual is a signature made in a representative capacity.

§3-404. Unauthorized Signatures.

(1) Any unauthorized signature is wholly inoperative as that

of the person whose name is signed unless he ratifies it or is precluded from denying it; but it operates as the signature of the unauthorized signer in favor of any person who in good faith pays the instrument or takes it for value.

(2) Any unauthorized signature may be ratified for all purposes of this Article. Such ratification does not of itself affect any rights of the person ratifying against the actual signer.

§3-405. Impostors; Signature in Name of Payee.

(1) An indorsement by any person in the name of a named payee is effective if

(a) an impostor by use of the mails or otherwise has induced the maker or drawer to issue the instrument to him or his confederate in the name of the payee; or

(b) a person signing as or on behalf of a maker or drawer intends the payee to have no interest in the instrument; or

(c) an agent or employee of the maker or drawer has supplied him with the name of the payee intending the latter to have no such interest.

(2) Nothing in this section shall affect the criminal or civil liability of the person so indorsing.

§3-406. Negligence Contributing to Alteration or Unauthorized Signature. Any person who by his negligence substantially contributes to a material alteration of the instrument or to the making of an unauthorized signature is precluded from asserting the alteration or lack of authority against a holder in due course or against a drawee or other payor who pays the instrument in good faith and in accordance with the reasonable commercial standards of the drawee's or payor's business.

§3-407. Alteration.

(1) Any alteration of an instrument is material which changes the contract of any party thereto in any respect, including any such change in

(a) the number or relations of the parties; or

(b) an incomplete instrument, by completing it otherwise than as authorized; or

(c) the writing as signed, by adding to it or by removing any part of it.

(2) As against any person other than a subsequent holder in due course

(a) alteration by the holder which is both fraudulent and material discharges any party whose contract is thereby changed unless that party assents or is precluded from asserting the defense;

(b) no other alteration discharges any party and the instrument may be enforced according to its original tenor, or as to incomplete instruments according to the authority given.

(3) A subsequent holder in due course may in all cases enforce the instrument according to its original tenor, and when an incomplete instrument has been completed, he may enforce it as completed.

§3-408. Consideration. Want or failure of consideration is a defense as against any person not having the rights of a holder in due course. (Section 3-305), except that no consideration is necessary for an instrument or obligation thereon given in payment of or as security for an antecedent obligation of any kind. Nothing in this section shall be taken to displace any statute outside this Act under which a promise is enforceable notwithstanding lack or failure of consideration. Partial failure of consideration is a defense pro tanto whether or not the failure is in an ascertained or liquidated amount.

§3-409. Draft Not an Assignment.

(1) A check or other draft does not of itself operate as an assignment of any funds in the hands of the drawee available for its payment, and the drawee is not liable on the instrument until he accepts it.

(2) Nothing in this section shall affect any liability in contract, tort or otherwise arising from any letter of credit or other obligation or representation which is not an acceptance.

§3-410. Definition and Operation of Acceptance.

(1) Acceptance is the drawee's signed engagement to honor the draft as presented. It must be written on the draft, and may consist of his signature alone. It becomes operative when completed by delivery or notification.

(2) A draft may be accepted although it has not been signed by the drawer or is otherwise incomplete or is overdue or has been dishonored.

(3) Where the draft is payable at a fixed period after sight and the acceptor fails to date his acceptance the holder may complete it by supplying a date in good faith.

§3-411. Certification of a Check.

(1) Certification of a check is acceptance. Where a holder procures certification the drawer and all prior indorsers are discharged.

(2) Unless otherwise agreed a bank has no obligation to certify a check.

(3) A bank may certify a check before returning it for lack of proper indorsement. If it does so the drawer is discharged.

§3-412. Acceptance Varying Draft.

(1) Where the drawee's proffered acceptance in any manner varies the draft as presented the holder may refuse the acceptance and treat the draft as dishonored in which case the drawee is entitled to have his acceptance cancelled.

(2) The terms of the draft are not varied by an acceptance to pay at any particular bank or place in the United States, unless the acceptance states that the draft is to be paid only at such bank or place.

(3) Where the holder assents to an acceptance varying the terms of the draft each drawer and indorser who does not affirmatively assent is discharged. As amended 1962.

§3-413. Contract of Maker, Drawer and Acceptor.

(1) The maker or acceptor engages that he will pay the instrument according to its tenor at the time of his engagement or as completed pursuant to Section 3-115 on incomplete instruments.

(2) The drawer engages that upon dishonor of the draft and

any necessary notice of dishonor or protest he will pay the amount of the draft to the holder or to any indorser who takes it up. The drawer may disclaim this liability by drawing without recourse.

(3) By making, drawing or accepting the party admits as against all subsequent parties including the drawee the existence of the payee and his then capacity to indorse.

§3-414. Contract of Indorser; Order of Liability.

(1) Unless the indorsement otherwise specifies (as by such words as "without recourse") every indorser engages that upon dishonor and any necessary notice of dishonor and protest he will pay the instrument according to its tenor at the time of his indorsement to the holder or to any subsequent indorser who takes it up, even though the indorser who takes it up was not obligated to do so.

(2) Unless they otherwise agree indorsers are liable to one another in the order in which they indorse, which is presumed to be the order in which their signatures appear on the instrument.

§3-415. Contract of Accommodation Party.

(1) An accommodation party is one who signs the instrument in any capacity for the purpose of lending his name to another party to it.

(2) When the instrument has been taken for value before it is due the accommodation party is liable in the capacity in which he has signed even though the taker knows of the accommodation.

(3) As against a holder in due course and without notice of the accommodation oral proof of the accommodation is not admissible to give the accommodation party the benefit of discharges dependent on his character as such. In other cases the accommodation character may be shown by oral proof.

(4) An indorsement which shows that it is not in the chain of title is notice of its accommodation character.

(5) An accommodation party is not liable to the party accommodated, and if he pays the instrument has a right of recourse on the instrument against such party.

§3-416. Contract of Guarantor.

(1) "Payment guaranteed" or equivalent words added to a signature mean that the signer engages that if the instrument is not paid when due he will pay it according to its tenor without resort by the holder to any other party.

(2) "Collection guaranteed" or equivalent words added to a signature mean that the signer engages that if the instrument is not paid when due he will pay it according to its tenor, but only after the holder has reduced his claim against the maker or acceptor to judgment and execution has been returned unsatisfied, or after the maker or acceptor has become insolvent or it is otherwise apparent that it is useless to proceed against him.

(3) Words of guaranty which do not otherwise specify guarantee payment.

(4) No words of guaranty added to the signature of a sole maker or acceptor affect his liability on the instrument. Such words added to the signature of one of two or more makers or acceptors create a presumption that the signature is for the accommodation of the others.

(5) When words of guaranty are used presentment, notice of dishonor and protest are not necessary to charge the user.

(6) Any guaranty written on the instrument is enforcible notwithstanding any statute of frauds.

§3-417. Warranties on Presentment and Transfer.

(1) Any person who obtains payment or acceptance and any prior transferor warrants to a person who in good faith pays or accepts that

(a) he has a good title to the instrument or is authorized to obtain payment or acceptance on behalf of one who has a good title; and

(b) he has no knowledge that the signature of the maker or drawer is unauthorized, except that this warranty is not given by a holder in due course acting in good faith

(i) to a maker with respect to the maker's own signature; or

(ii) to a drawer with respect to the drawer's own signature, whether or not the drawer is also the drawee; or

(iii) to an acceptor of a draft if the holder in due course took the draft after the acceptance or obtained the acceptance without knowledge that the drawer's signature was unauthorized; and

(c) the instrument has not been materially altered, except that this warranty is not given by a holder in due course acting in good faith

(i) to the maker of a note; or

(ii) to the drawer of a draft whether or not the drawer is also the drawee; or

(iii) to the acceptor of a draft with respect to an alteration made prior to the acceptance if the holder in due course took the draft after the acceptance, even though the acceptance provided "payable as originally drawn" or equivalent terms; or

(iv) to the acceptor of a draft with respect to an alteration made after the acceptance.

(2) Any person who transfers an instrument and receives consideration warrants to his transferee and if the transfer is by indorsement to any subsequent holder who takes the instrument in good faith that

(a) he has a good title to the instrument or is authorized to obtain payment or acceptance on behalf of one who has a good title and the transfer is otherwise rightful; and

(b) all signatures are genuine or authorized; and

(c) the instrument has not been materially altered; and

(d) no defense of any party is good against him; and

(e) he has no knowledge of any insolvency proceeding instituted with respect to the maker or acceptor or the drawer of an unaccepted instrument.

(3) By transferring "without recourse" the transferor limits the obligation stated in subsection (2) (d) to a warranty that he has no knowledge of such a defense.

(4) A selling agent or broker who does not disclose the fact that he is acting only as such gives the warranties provided in this section, but if he makes such disclosure warrants only his good faith and authority.

§3-418. Finality of Payment or Acceptance. Except for recovery of bank payments as provided in the Article on Bank Deposits and Collections (Article 4) and except for liability for breach of warranty on presentment under the preceding section, payment or acceptance of any instrument is final in favor of a holder in due course, or a person who has in good faith changed his position in reliance on the payment.

§3-419. Conversion of Instrument; Innocent Representative.

(1) An instrument is converted when

(a) a drawee to whom it is delivered for acceptance refuses to return it on demand; or

(b) any person to whom it is delivered for payment refuses on demand either to pay or to return it; or

(c) it is paid on a forged indorsement.

(2) In an action against a drawee under subsection (1) the measure of the drawee's liability is the face amount of the instrument. In any other action under subsection (1) the measure of liability is presumed to be the face amount of the instrument.

(3) Subject to the provisions of this Act concerning restrictive indorsements a representative, including a depositary or collecting bank, who has in good faith and in accordance with the reasonable commercial standards applicable to the business of such representative dealt with an instrument or its proceeds on behalf of one who was not the true owner is not liable in conversion or otherwise to the true owner beyond the amount of any proceeds remaining in his hands.

(4) An intermediary bank or payor bank which is not a depositary bank is not liable in conversion solely by reason of the fact that proceeds of an item indorsed restrictively (Sections 3-205 and 3-206) are not paid or applied consistently with the restrictive indorsement of an indorser other than its immediate transferor.

Part 5: Presentment, Notice of Dishonor and Protest

§3-501. When Presentment, Notice of Dishonor, and Protest Necessary or Permissible.

(1) Unless excused (Section 3-511) presentment is necessary to charge secondary parties as follows:

(a) presentment for acceptance is necessary to charge the drawer and indorsers of a draft where the draft so provides, or is payable elsewhere than at the residence or place of business of the drawee, or its date of payment depends upon such presentment. The holder may at his option present for acceptance any other draft payable at a stated date;

(b) presentment for payment is necessary to charge any indorser;

(c) in the case of any drawer, the acceptor of a draft payable at a bank or the maker of a note payable at a bank, presentment for payment is necessary, but failure to make presentment discharges such drawer, acceptor or maker only as stated in Section 3-502(1)(b).

(2) Unless excused (Section 3-511)

(a) notice of any dishonor is necessary to charge any indorser;

(b) in the case of any drawer, the acceptor of a draft payable at a bank or the maker of a note payable at a bank, notice of any dishonor is necessary, but failure to give such notice discharges such drawer, acceptor or maker only as stated in Section 3-502(1) (b).

(3) Unless excused (Section 3-511) protest of any dishonor is necessary to charge the drawer and indorsers of any draft which on its face appears to be drawn or payable outside of the states, territories, dependencies and possessions of the United States, the District of Columbia and the commonwealth of Puerto Rico. The holder may at his option make protest of any dishonor of any other instrument and in the case of a foreign draft may on insolvency of the acceptor before maturity make protest for better security.

(4) Notwithstanding any provision of this section, neither presentment nor notice of dishonor nor protest is necessary to charge an indorser who has indorsed an instrument after maturity. As amended 1966.

§3-502. Unexcused Delay; Discharge.

(1) Where without excuse any necessary presentment or notice of dishonor is delayed beyond the time when it is due

(a) any indorser is discharged; and

(b) any drawer or the acceptor of a draft payable at a bank or the maker of a note payable at a bank who because the drawee or payor bank becomes insolvent during the delay is deprived of funds maintained with the drawee or payor bank to cover the instrument may discharge his liability by written assignment to the holder of his rights against the drawee or payor bank in respect of such funds, but such drawer, acceptor or maker is not otherwise discharged.

(2) Where without excuse a necessary protest is delayed beyond the time when it is due any drawer or indorser is discharged.

§3-503. Time of Presentment.

(1) Unless a different time is expressed in the instrument the time for any presentment is determined as follows:

(a) where an instrument is payable at or a fixed period after a stated date any presentment for acceptance must be made on or before the date it is payable;

(b) where an instrument is payable after sight it must either be presented for acceptance or negotiated within a reasonable time after date or issue whichever is later;

(c) where an instrument shows the date on which it is payable presentment for payment is due on that date;

(d) where an instrument is accelerated presentment for payment is due within a reasonable time after the acceleration;

(e) with respect to the liability of any secondary party presentment for acceptance or payment of any other instrument is due within a reasonable time after such party becomes liable thereon.

(2) A reasonable time for presentment is determined by the nature of the instrument, any usage of banking or trade and the facts of the particular case. In the case of an uncertified check which is drawn and payable within the United States and which is not a draft drawn by a bank the following are presumed to be reasonable periods within which to present for payment or to initate bank collection:

(a) with respect to the liability of the drawer, thirty days after date or issue whichever is later; and

(b) with respect to the liability of an indorser, seven days after his indorsement.

(3) Where any presentment is due on a day which is not a full business day for either the person making presentment or the party to pay or accept, presentment is due on the next following day which is a full business day for both parties.

(4) Presentment to be sufficient must be made at a reasonable hour, and if at a bank during its banking day.

§3-504. How Presentment Made.

(1) Presentment is a demand for acceptance or payment made upon the maker, acceptor, drawee or other payor by or on behalf of the holder.

(2) Presentment may be made

(a) by mail, in which event the time of presentment is determined by the time of receipt of the mail; or

(b) through a clearing house; or

(c) at the place of acceptance or payment specified in the instrument or if there be none at the place of business or residence of the party to accept or pay. If neither the party to accept or pay nor anyone authorized to act for him is present or accessible at such place presentment is excused.

(3) It may be made

(a) to any one of two or more makers, acceptors, drawees or other payor; or

(b) to any person who has authority to make or refuse the acceptance or payment.

(4) A draft accepted or a note made payable at a bank in the United States must be presented at such bank.

(5) In the cases described in Section 4-210 presentment may be made in the manner and with the result stated in that section. As amended 1962.

§3-505. Rights of Party to Whom Presentment Is Made.

(1) The party to whom presentment is made may without dishonor require

(a) exhibition of the instrument; and

(b) reasonable identification of the person making presentment and evidence of his authority to make it if made for another; and

(c) that the instrument be produced for acceptance or payment at a place specified in it, or if there be none at any place reasonable in the circumstances; and

(d) a signed receipt on the instrument for any partial or full payment and its surrender upon full payment.

(2) Failure to comply with any such requirement invalidates the presentment but the person presenting has a reasonable time in which to comply and the time for acceptance or payment runs from the time of compliance.

§3-506. Time Allowed For Acceptance or Payment.

(1) Acceptance may be deferred without dishonor until the close of the next business day following presentment. The holder may also in a good faith effort to obtain acceptance and without either dishonor of the instrument or discharge of secondary parties allow postponement of acceptance for an additional business day.

(2) Except as a longer time is allowed in the case of documentary drafts drawn under a letter of credit, and unless an earlier time is agreed to by the party to pay, payment of an instrument may be deferred without dishonor pending reasonable examination to determine whether it is properly payable, but payment must be made in any event before the close of business on the day of presentment.

§3-507. Dishonor; Holder's Right of Recourse; Term Allowing Re-Presentment.

(1) An instrument is dishonored when

(a) a necessary or optional presentment is duly made and due acceptance or payment is refused or cannot be obtained within the prescribed time or in case of bank collections the instrument is seasonably returned by the midnight deadline (Section 4-301); or

(b) presentment is excused and the instrument is not duly accepted or paid.

(2) Subject to any necessary notice of dishonor and protest, the holder has upon dishonor an immediate right of recourse against the drawers and indorsers.

(3) Return of an instrument for lack of proper indorsement is not dishonor.

(4) A term in a draft or an indorsement thereof allowing a stated time for re-presentment in the event of any dishonor of the draft by nonacceptance if a time draft or by nonpayment if a sight draft gives the holder as against any secondary party bound by the term an option to waive the dishonor without affecting the liability of the secondary party and he may present again up to the end of the stated time.

§3-508. Notice of Dishonor.

(1) Notice of dishonor may be given to any person who may be liable on the instrument by or on behalf of the holder or any party who has himself received notice, or any other party who can be compelled to pay the instrument. In addition an agent or bank in whose hands the instrument is dishonored may give notice to his principal or customer or to another agent or bank from which the instrument was received.

(2) Any necessary notice must be given by a bank before its midnight deadline and by any other person before midnight of the third business day after dishonor or receipt of notice of dishonor.

(3) Notice may be given in any reasonable manner. It may be oral or written and in any terms which identify the instrument and state that it has been dishonored. A misdescription which does not mislead the party notified does not vitiate the notice. Sending the instrument bearing a stamp, ticket or writing

stating that acceptance or payment has been refused or sending a notice of debit with respect to the instrument is sufficient.

(4) Written notice is given when sent although it is not received.

(5) Notice to one partner is notice to each although the firm has been dissolved.

(6) When any party is in insolvency proceedings instituted after the issue of the instrument notice may be given either to the party or to the representative of his estate.

(7) When any party is dead or incompetent notice may be sent to his last known address or given to his personal representative.

(8) Notice operates for the benefit of all parties who have rights on the instrument against the party notified.

§3-509. Protest; Noting for Protest.

(1) A protest is a certificate of dishonor made under the hand and seal of a United States consul or vice consul or a notary public or other person authorized to certify dishonor by the law of the place where dishonor occurs. It may be made upon information satisfactory to such person.

(2) The protest must identify the instrument and certify either that due presentment has been made or the reason why it is excused and that the instrument has been dishonored by nonacceptance or nonpayment.

(3) The protest may also certify that notice of dishonor has been given to all parties or to specified parties.

(4) Subject to subsection (5) any necessary protest is due by the time that notice of dishonor is due.

(5) If, before protest is due, an instrument has been noted for protest by the officer to make protest, the protest may be made at any time thereafter as of the date of the noting.

§3-510. Evidence of Dishonor and Notice of Dishonor. The following are admissible as evidence and create a presumption of dishonor and of any notice of dishonor therein shown:

(a) a document regular in form as provided in the preceding section which purports to be a protest;

(b) the purported stamp or writing of the drawee, payor bank or presenting bank on the instrument or accompanying it stating that acceptance or payment has been refused for reasons consistent with dishonor;

(c) any book or record of the drawee, payor bank, or any collecting bank kept in the usual course of business which shows dishonor, even though there is no evidence of who made the entry.

§3-511. Waived or Excused Presentment, Protest or Notice of Dishonor or Delay Therein.

(1) Delay in presentment, protest or notice of dishonor is excused when the party is without notice that it is due or when the delay is caused by circumstances beyond his control and he exercises reasonable diligence after the cause of the delay ceases to operate.

(2) Presentment or notice or protest as the case may be is entirely excused when

(a) the party to be charged has waived it expressly or by implication either before or after it is due; or

(b) such party has himself dishonored the instrument or has countermanded payment or otherwise has no reason to expect or right to require that the instrument be accepted or paid; or

(c) by reasonable diligence the presentment or protest cannot be made or the notice given.

(3) Presentment is also entirely excused when

(a) the maker, acceptor or drawee of any instrument except a documentary draft is dead or in insolvency proceedings instituted after the issue of the instrument; or

(b) acceptance or payment is refused but not for want of proper presentment.

(4) Where a draft has been dishonored by nonacceptance a later presentment for payment and any notice of dishonor and protest for nonpayment are excused unless in the meantime the instrument has been accepted.

(5) A waiver of protest is also a waiver of presentment and of notice of dishonor even though protest is not required.

(6) Where a waiver of presentment or notice of protest is embodied in the instrument itself it is binding upon all parties; but where it is written above the signature of an indorser it binds him only.

Part 6: Discharge

§3-601. Discharge of Parties.

(1) The extent of the discharge of any party from liability on an instrument is governed by the sections on

(a) payment or satisfaction (Section 3-603); or

(b) tender of payment (Section 3-604); or

(c) cancellation or renunciation (Section 3-605); or

(d) impairment of right of recourse or of collateral (Section 3-606); or

(e) reacquisition of the instrument by a prior party (Section 3-208); or

(f) fraudulent and material alteration (Section 3-407); or

(g) certification of a check (Section 3-411); or

(h) acceptance varying a draft (Section 3-412); or

(i) unexcused delay in presentment or notice of dishonor or protest (Section 3-502).

(2) Any party is also discharged from his liability on an instrument to another party by any other act or agreement with such party which would discharge his simple contract for the payment of money.

(3) The liability of all parties is discharged when any party who has himself no right of action or recourse on the instrument

(a) reacquires the instrument in his own right; or

(b) is discharged under any provision of this Article, except as otherwise provided with respect to discharge for impairment of recourse or of collateral (Section 3-606).

§3-602. Effect of Discharge Against Holder in Due Course. No discharge of any party provided by this Article is effective against a subsequent holder in due course unless he has notice thereof when he takes the instrument.

§3-603. Payment or Satisfaction.

(1) The liability of any party is discharged to the extent of his payment or satisfaction to the holder even though it is made with knowledge of a claim of another person to the instrument unless prior to such payment or satisfaction the person making the claim either supplies indemnity deemed adequate by the party seeking the discharge or enjoins payment or satisfaction by order of a court of competent jurisdiction in an action in which the adverse claimant and the holder are parties. This subsection does not, however, result in the discharge of the liability

(a) of a party who in bad faith pays or satisfies a holder who acquired the instrument by theft or who (unless having the rights of a holder in due course) holds through one who so acquired it; or

(b) of a party (other than an intermediary bank or a payor bank which is not a depositary bank) who pays or satisfies the holder of an instrument which has been restrictively indorsed in a manner not consistent with the terms of such restrictive indorsement.

(2) Payment or satisfaction may be made with the consent of the holder by any person including a stranger to the instrument. Surrender of the instrument to such a person gives him the rights of a transferee (Section 3-201).

§3-604. Tender of Payment.

(1) Any party making tender of full payment to a holder when or after it is due is discharged to the extent of all subsequent liability for interest, costs and attorney's fees.

(2) The holder's refusal of such tender wholly discharges any party who has a right of recourse against the party making the tender.

(3) Where the maker or acceptor of an instrument payable otherwise than on demand is able and ready to pay at every place of payment specified in the instrument when it is due, it is equivalent to tender.

§3-605. Cancellation and Renunciation.

(1) The holder of an instrument may even without consideration discharge any party

(a) in any manner apparent on the face of the instrument or the indorsement, as by intentionally cancelling the instrument or the party's signature by destruction or mutilation, or by striking out the party's signature; or

(b) by renouncing his rights by a writing signed and delivered or by surrender of the instrument to the party to be discharged.

(2) Neither cancellation or renunciation without surrender of the instrument affects the title thereto.

§3-606. Impairment of Recourse or of Collateral.

(1) The holder discharges any party to the instrument to the extent that without such party's consent the holder

(a) without express reservation of rights releases or agrees not to sue any person against whom the party has to the knowledge of the holder a right of recourse or agrees to suspend the right to enforce against such person the instrument or collateral or otherwise discharges such person, except that failure or delay in effecting any required presentment, protest or notice of dishonor with respect to any such person does not discharge any party as to whom presentment, protest or notice of dishonor is effective or unnecessary; or

(b) unjustifiably impairs any collateral for the instrument given by or on behalf of the party or any person against whom he has a right of recourse.

(2) By express reservation of rights against a party with a right of recourse the holder preserves

(a) all his rights against such party as of the time when the instrument was originally due; and

(b) the right of the party to pay the instrument as of that time; and

(c) all rights of such party to recourse against others.

Part 7: Advice of International Sight Draft

§3-701. Letter of Advice of International Sight Draft.

(1) A "letter of advice" is a drawer's communication to the drawee that a described draft has been drawn.

(2) Unless otherwise agreed when a bank receives from another bank a letter of advice of an international sight draft the drawee bank may immediately debit the drawer's account and stop the running of interest pro tanto. Such a debit and any resulting credit to any account covering outstanding drafts leaves in the drawer full power to stop payment or otherwise dispose of the amount and creates no trust or interest in favor of the holder.

(3) Unless otherwise agreed and except where a draft is drawn under a credit issued by the drawee, the drawee of an international sight draft owes the drawer no duty to pay an unadvised draft but if it does so and the draft is genuine, may appropriately debit the drawer's account.

Part 8: Miscellaneous

§3-801. Drafts in a Set.

(1) Where a draft is drawn in a set of parts, each of which is numbered and expressed to be an order only if no other part has been honored, the whole of the parts constitutes one draft but a taker of any part may become a holder in due course of the draft.

(2) Any person who negotiates, indorses or accepts a single part of a draft drawn in a set thereby becomes liable to any holder in due course of that part as if it were the whole set, but as between different holders in due course to whom different parts have been negotiated the holder whose title first accrues has all rights to the draft and its proceeds.

(3) As against the drawee the first presented part of a draft drawn in a set is the part entitled to payment, or if a time draft to acceptance and payment. Acceptance of any subsequently presented part renders the drawee liable thereon under subsection (2). With respect both to a holder and to the drawer

payment of a subsequently presented part of a draft payable at sight has the same effect as payment of a check notwithstanding an effective stop order (Section 4-407).

(4) Except as otherwise provided in this section, where any part of a draft in a set is discharged by payment or otherwise the whole draft is discharged.

§3-802. Effect of Instrument on Obligation for which It Is Given.

(1) Unless otherwise agreed where an instrument is taken for an underlying obligation

(a) the obligation is pro tanto discharged if a bank is drawer, maker or acceptor of the instrument and there is no recourse on the instrument against the underlying obligor; and

(b) in any other case the obligation is suspended pro tanto until the instrument is due or if it is payable on demand until its presentment. If the instrument is dishonored action may be maintained on either the instrument or the obligation; discharge of the underlying obligor on the instrument also discharges him on the obligation.

(2) The taking in good faith of a check which is not postdated does not of itself so extend the time on the original obligation as to discharge a surety.

§3-803. Notice to Third Party. Where a defendant is sued for breach of an obligation for which a third person is answerable over under this Article he may give the third person written notice of the litigation, and the person notified may then give similar notice to any other person who is answerable over to him under this Article. If the notice states that the person notified may come in and defend and that if the person notified does not do so he will in any action against him by the person giving the notice be bound by any determination of fact common to the two litigations, then unless after seasonable receipt of the notice the person notified does come in and defend he is so bound.

§3-804. Lost, Destroyed or Stolen Instruments. The owner of an instrument which is lost, whether by destruction, theft or otherwise, may maintain an action in his own name and recover from any party liable thereon upon due proof of his ownership, the facts which prevent his production of the instrument and its terms. The court may require security indemnifying the defendant against loss by reason of further claims on the instrument.

§3-805. Instruments Not Payable to Order or to Bearer. This Article applies to any instrument whose terms do not preclude transfer and which is otherwise negotiable within this Article but which is not payable to order or to bearer, except that there can be no holder in due course of such an instrument.

ARTICLE 4: BANK DEPOSITS AND COLLECTIONS

Part 1: General Provisions and Definitions

§4-401. Short Title.—This Article shall be known and may be cited as Uniform Commercial Code—Bank Deposits and Collections.

§4-102. Applicability.

(1) To the extent that items within this Article are also within the scope of Articles 3 and 8, they are subject to the provisions of those Articles. In the event of conflict the provisions of this Article govern those of Article 3 but the provisions of Article 8 govern those of this Article.

(2) The liability of a bank for action or non-action with respect to any item handled by it for purposes of presentment, payment or collection is governed by the law of the place where the bank is located. In the case of action or non-action by or at a branch or separate office of a bank, its liability is governed by the law of the place where the branch or separate office is located.

§4-103. Variation by Agreement; Measure of Damages; Certain Action Constituting Ordinary Care.

(1) The effect of the provisions of this Article may be varied by agreement except that no agreement can disclaim a bank's responsibility for its own lack of good faith or failure to exercise ordinary care or can limit the measure of damages for such lack of failure; but the parties may by agreement determine the standards by which such responsibility is to be measured if such standards are not manifestly unreasonable.

(2) Federal Reserve regulations and operating letters, clearing house rules, and the like, have the effect of agreements under subsection (1), whether or not specifically assented to by all parties interested in items handled.

(3) Action or non-action approved by this Article or pursuant to Federal Reserve regulations or operating letters constitutes the exercise of ordinary care and, in the absence of special instructions, action or non-action consistent with clearing house rules and the like or with a general banking usage not disapproved by this Article, prima facie constitutes the exercise of ordinary care.

(4) The specification or approval of certain procedures by this Article does not constitute disapproval of other procedures which may be reasonable under the circumstances.

(5) The measure of damages for failure to exercise ordinary care in handling an item is the amount of the item reduced by an amount which could not have been realized by the use of ordinary care, and where there is bad faith it includes other damages, if any, suffered by the party as a proximate consequence.

§4-104. Definitions and Index of Definitions.

(1) In this Article unless the context otherwise requires

(a) "Account" means any account with a bank and includes a checking, time, interest or savings account;

(b) "Afternoon" means the period of a day between noon and midnight;

(c) "Banking day" means that part of any day on which a bank is open to the public for carrying on substantially all of its banking functions;

(d) "Clearing house" means any association of banks or other payors regularly clearing items;

(e) "Customer" means any person having an account with a bank or for whom a bank has agreed to collect items and includes a bank carrying an account with another bank;

(f) "Documentary draft" means any negotiable or non-negotiable draft with accompanying documents, securities or other papers to be delivered against honor of the draft;

(g) "Item" means any instrument for the payment of money even though it is not negotiable but does not include money;

(h) "Midnight deadline" with respect to a bank is midnight on its next banking day following the banking day on which it receives the relevant item or notice or from which the time for taking action commences to run, whichever is later;

(i) "Properly payable" includes the availability of funds for payment at the time of decision to pay or dishonor;

(j) "Settle" means to pay in cash, by clearing house settlement, in a charge or credit or by remittance, or otherwise as instructed. A settlement may be either provisonal or final;

(k) "Suspends payments" with respect to a bank means that it has been closed by order of the supervisory authorities, that a public officer has been appointed to take it over or that it ceases or refuses to make payments in the ordinary course of business.

(2) Other definitions applying to this Article and the sections in which they appear are:

"Collecting bank". Section 4-105
"Depositary bank". Section 4-105.
"Intermediary bank". Section 4-105.
"Payor bank". Section 4-105.
"Presenting bank". Section 4-105.
"Remitting bank". Section 4-105.

(3) The following definitions in other Articles apply to this Article:

"Acceptance". Section 3-410.
"Certificate of deposit": Section 3-104
"Certification". Section 3-411.
"Check". Section 3-104.
"Draft". Section 3-104.
"Holder in due course". Section 3-302.
"Notice of dishonor". Section 3-508.
"Presentment". Section 3-504.
"Protest". Section 3-509.
"Secondary party". Section 3-102.

(4) In addition Article 1 contains general definitions and principles of construction and interpretation applicable throughout this Article.

§4-105. "Depositary Bank"; "Intermediary Bank"; "Collecting Bank"; "Payor Bank"; "Presenting Bank"; "Remitting Bank". In this Article unless the context otherwise requires:

(a) "Depositary bank" means the first bank to which an item is transferred for collection even though it is also the payor bank;

(b) "Payor bank" means a bank by which an item is payable as drawn or accepted;

(c) "Intermediary bank" means any bank to which an item is transferred in course of collection except the depositary or payor bank;

(d) "Collecting bank" means any bank handling the item for collection except the payor bank;

(e) "Presenting bank" means any bank presenting an item except a payor bank;

(f) "Remitting bank" means any payor or intermediary bank remitting for an item.

§4-106. Separate Office of a Bank. A branch or separate office of a bank [maintaining its own deposit ledgers] is a separate bank for the purpose of computing the time within which and determining the place at or to which action may be taken or notices or orders shall be given under this Article and under Article 3. As amended 1962.

Note: (*The brackets are to make it optional with the several states whether to require a branch to maintain its own deposit ledgers in order to be considered to be a separate bank for certain purposes under Article 4. In some states "maintaining its own deposit ledgers" is a satisfactory test. In others branch banking practices are such that this test would not be suitable.*

§4-107. Time of Receipt of Items.

(1) For the purpose of allowing time to process items, prove balances and make the necessary entries on its books to determine its position for the day, a bank may fix an afternoon hour of 2 P.M. or later as a cut-off hour for the handling of money and items and the making of entries on its books.

(2) Any item or deposit of money received on any day after a cut-off hour so fixed or after the close of the banking day may be treated as being received at the opening of the next banking day.

§4-108. Delays.

(1) Unless otherwise instructed, a collecting bank in a good faith effort to secure payment may, in the case of specific items and with or without the approval of any person involved, waive, modify or extend time limits imposed or permitted by this Act for a period not in excess of an additonal banking day without discharge of secondary parties and without liability to its transferor or any prior party.

(2) Delay by a collecting bank or payor bank beyond time limits prescribed or permitted by this Act or by instructions is excused if caused by interruption of communication facilities, suspension of payments by another bank, war, emergency conditions or other circumstances beyond the control of the bank provided it exercises such diligence as the circumstances require.

§4-109. Process of Posting. The "process of posting" means that usual procedure followed by a payor bank in determining to pay an item and in recording the payment including one or more of the following or other steps as determined by the bank:

(a) verification of any signature;

(b) ascertaining that sufficient funds are available;

(c) affixing a "paid" or other stamp;

(d) entering a charge or entry to a customer's account;

(e) correcting or reversing an entry or erroneous action with respect to the item. Added 1962.

Part 2: Collection of Items: Depositary and Collecting Banks

§4-201. Presumption and Duration of Agency Status of Collecting Banks and Provisional Status of Credits; Applicability of Article; Item Indorsed "Pay Any Bank".

(1) Unless a contrary intent clearly appears and prior to the time that a settlement given by a collecting bank for an item is or becomes final (subsection (3) of Section 4-211 and Sections 4-212 and 4-213) the bank is an agent or sub-agent of the owner of the item and any settlement given for the item is provisional. This provision applies regardless of the form of indorsement or lack of indorsement and even though credit given for the item is subject to immediate withdrawal as of right or is in fact withdrawn; but the continuance of ownership of an item by its owner and any rights of the owner to proceeds of the item are subject to rights of a collecting bank such as those resulting from outstanding advances on the item and valid rights of setoff. When an item is handled by banks for purposes of presentment, payment and collection, the relevant provisions of this Article apply even though action of parties clearly establishes that a particular bank has purchased the item and is the owner of it.

(2) After an item has been indorsed with the words "pay any bank" or the like, only a bank may acquire the rights of a holder

(a) until the item has been returned to the customer initiating collection; or

(b) until the item has been specially indorsed by a bank to a person who is not a bank.

§4-202. Responsibility for Collection; When Action Seasonable.

(1) A collecting bank must use ordinary care in

(a) presenting an item or sending it for presentment; and

(b) sending notice of dishonor on non-payment or returning an item other than a documentary draft to the bank's transferor [or directly to the depositary bank under subsection (2) of Section 4-212] (*see note to Section* 4-212) after learning that the item has not been paid or accepted, as the case may be; and

(c) settling for an item when the bank receives final settlement; and

(d) making or providing for any necessary protest; and

(e) notifying its transferor of any loss or delay in transit within a reasonable time after discovery thereof.

(2) A collecting bank taking proper action before its midnight deadline following receipt of an item, notice or payment acts seasonably; taking proper action within a reasonably longer time may be seasonable but the bank has the burden of so establishing.

(3) Subject to subsection (1) (a), a bank is not liable for the insolvency, neglect, misconduct, mistake or default of another bank or person or for loss or destruction of an item in transit or in the possession of others.

§4-203. Effect of Instructions. Subject to the provision of Article 3 concerning conversion of instruments (Section 3-419) and the provisions of both Article 3 and this Article concerning restrictive indorsements only a collecting bank's transferor can give instructions which affect the bank or constitute notice to it and a collecting bank is not liable to prior parties for any action taken pursuant to such instructions or in accordance with any agreement with its transferor.

§4-204. Methods of Sending and Presenting; Sending Direct to Payor Bank.

(1) A collecting bank must send items by reasonably prompt method taking into consideration any relevant instructions, the nature of the item, the number of such items on hand, and the cost of collection involved and the method generally used by it or others to present such items.

(2) A collecting bank may send

(a) any item direct to the payor bank;

(b) any item direct to any non-bank payor if authorized by its transferor; and

(c) any item other than documentary drafts to any non-bank payor, if authorized by Federal Reserve regulation or operating letter, clearing house rule or the like.

(3) Presentment may be made by a presenting bank at a place where the payor bank has requested that presentment be made. As amended 1962.

§4-205. Supplying Missing Indorsement; No Notice from Prior Indorsement.

(1) A depositary bank which has taken an item for collection may supply any indorsement of the customer which is necessary to title unless the item contains the words "payee's indorsement required" or the like. In the absence of such a requirement a statement placed on the item by the depositary bank to the effect that the item was deposited by a customer or credited to his account is effective as the customer's indorsement.

(2) An intermediary bank, or payor bank which is not a depositary bank, is neither given notice nor otherwise affected by a restrictive indorsement of any person except the bank's immediate transferor.

§4-206. Transfer Between Banks. Any agreed method which identifies the transferor bank is sufficient for the item's further transfer to another bank.

§4-207. Warranties of Customer and Collecting Bank on Transfer or Presentment of Items; Time for Claims.

(1) Each customer or collecting bank who obtains payment or acceptance of an item and each prior customer and collecting bank warrants to the payor bank or other payor who in good faith pays or accepts the item that

(a) he has a good title to the item or is authorized to obtain payment or acceptance on behalf of one who has a good title; and

(b) he has no knowledge that the signature of the maker or drawer is unauthorized, except that this warranty is not given by any customer or collecting bank that is a holder in due course and acts in good faith

(i) to a maker with respect to the maker's own signature; or

(ii) to a drawer with respect to the drawer's own

signature, whether or not the drawer is also the drawee; or

(**iii**) to an acceptor of an item if the holder in due course took the item after the acceptance or obtained the acceptance without knowledge that the drawer's signature was unauthorized; and

(**c**) the item has not been materially altered, except that this warranty is not given by any customer or collecting bank that is a holder in due course and acts in good faith

(**i**) to the maker of a note; or

(**ii**) to the drawer of a draft whether or not the drawer is also the drawee; or

(**iii**) to the acceptor of an item with respect to an alteration made prior to the acceptance if the holder in due course took the item after the acceptance, even though the acceptance provided "payable as originally drawn" or equivalent terms; or

(**iv**) to the acceptor of an item with respect to an alteration made after the acceptance.

(**2**) Each customer and collecting bank who transfers an item and receives a settlement or other consideration for it warrants to his transferee and to any subsequent collecting bank who takes the item in good faith that

(**a**) he has a good title to the item or is authorized to obtain payment or acceptance on behalf of one who has a good title and the transfer is otherwise rightful; and

(**b**) all signatures are genuine or authorized; and

(**c**) the item has not been materially altered; and

(**d**) no defense of any party is good against him; and

(**e**) he has no knowledge of any insolvency proceeding instituted with respect to the maker or acceptor or the drawer of an unaccepted item.

In addition each customer and collecting bank so transferring an item and receiving a settlement or other consideration engages that upon dishonor and any necessary notice of dishonor and protest he will take up the item.

(**3**) The warranties and the engagement to honor set forth in the two preceding subsections arise notwithstanding the absence of indorsement or words of guaranty or warranty in the transfer or presentment and collecting bank remains liable for their breach despite remittance to its transferor. Damages for breach of such warranties or engagement to honor shall not exceed the consideration received by the customer or collecting bank responsible plus finance charges and expenses related to the item, if any.

(**4**) Unless a claim for breach of warranty under this section is made within a reasonable time after the person claiming learns of the breach, the person liable is discharged to the extent of any loss caused by the delay in making claim.

§4-208. Security Interest of Collecting Bank in Items, Accompanying Documents and Proceeds.

(**1**) A bank has a security interest in an item and any accompanying documents or the proceeds of either

(**a**) in case of an item deposited in an account to the extent to which credit given for the item has been withdrawn or applied;

(**b**) in case of an item for which it has given credit available for withdrawal as of right, to the extent of the credit given whether or not the credit is drawn upon and whether or not there is a right of charge-back; or

(**c**) if it makes an advance on or against the item.

(**2**) When credit which has been given for several items received at one time or pursuant to a single agreement is withdrawn or applied in part the security interest remains upon all the items, any accompanying documents or the proceeds of either. For the purpose of this section, credits first given are first withdrawn.

(**3**) Receipt by a collecting bank of a final settlement for an item is a realization on its security interest in the item, accompanying documents and proceeds. To the extent and so long as the bank does not receive final settlement for the item or give up possession of the item or accompanying documents for purposes other than collection, the security interest continues and is subject to the provisions of Article 9 except that

(**a**) no security agreement is necessary to make the security interest enforceable (subsection (1) (b) of Section 9-203); and

(**b**) no filing is required to perfect the security interest; and

(**c**) the security interest has priority over conflicting perfected security interests in the item, accompanying documents or proceeds.

§4-209. When Bank Gives Value for Purposes of Holder in Due Course. For purposes of determining its status as a holder in due course, the bank has given value to the extent that it has a security interest in an item provided that the bank otherwise complies with the requirements of Section 3-302 on what constitutes a holder in due course.

§4-210. Presentment by Notice of Item Not Payable by, Through or at a Bank; Liability of Secondary Parties.

(**1**) Unless otherwise instructed, a collecting bank may present an item not payable by, through or at a bank by sending to the party to accept or pay a written notice that the bank holds the item for acceptance or payment. The notice must be sent in time to be received on or before the day when presentment is due and the bank must meet any requirement of the party to accept or pay under Section 3-505 by the close of the bank's next banking day after it knows of the requirement.

(**2**) Where presentment is made by notice and neither honor nor request for compliance with a requirement under Section 3-505 is received by the close of business on the day after maturity or in the case of demand items by the close of business on the third banking day after notice was sent, the presenting bank may treat the item as dishonored and charge any secondary party by sending him notice of the facts.

§4-211. Media of Remittance; Provisional and Final Settlement in Remittance Cases.

(**1**) A collecting bank may take in settlement of an item

(**a**) a check of the remitting bank or of another bank on

any bank except the remitting bank; or

(b) a cashier's check or similar primary obligation of a remitting bank which is a member of or clears through a member of the same clearing house or group as the collecting bank; or

(c) appropriate authority to charge an account of the remitting bank or of another bank with the collecting bank; or

(d) if the item is drawn upon or payable by a person other than a bank, a cashier's check, certified check or other bank check or obligation.

(2) If before its midnight deadline the collecting bank properly dishonors a remittance check or authorization to charge on itself or presents or forwards for collection a remittance instrument of or on another bank which is of a kind approved by subsection (1) or has not been authorized by it, the collecting bank is not liable to prior parties in the event of the dishonor of such check, instrument or authorization.

(3) A settlement for an item by means of a remittance instrument or authorization to charge is or becomes a final settlement as to both the person making and the person receiving the settlement

(a) if the remittance instrument or authorization to charge is of a kind approved by subsection (1) or has not been authorized by the person receiving the settlement and in either case the person receiving the settlement acts seasonably before its midnight deadline in presenting, forwarding for collection or paying the instrument or authorization,—at the time the remittance instrument or authorization is finally paid by the payor by which it is payable;

(b) if the person receiving the settlement has authorized remittance by a non-bank check or obligation or by a cashier's check or similar primary obligation of or a check upon the payor or other remitting bank which is not of a kind approved by subsection (1) (b),—at the time of the receipt of such remittance check or obligation; or

(c) if in a case not covered by sub-paragraphs (a) or (b) the person receiving the settlement fails to seasonably present, forward for collection, pay or return a remittance instrument or authorization to it to charge before its midnight deadline,—at such midnight deadline.

§4-212. Right of Charge-Back or Refund.

(1) If a collecting bank has made provisional settlement with its customer for an item and itself fails by reason of dishonor, suspension of payments by a bank or otherwise to receive a settlement for the item which is or becomes final, the bank may revoke the settlement given by it, charge back the amount of any credit given for the item to its customer's account or obtain refund from its customer whether or not it is able to return the items if by its midnight deadline or within a longer reasonable time after it learns the facts it returns the item or sends notification of the facts. These rights to revoke, charge-back and obtain refund terminate if and when a settlement for the item received by the bank is or becomes final (subsection (3) of Section 4-211 and subsections (2) and (3) of Section 4-213).

[(2) Within the time and manner prescribed by this section and Section 4-301, an intermediary or payor bank, as the case may be, may return an unpaid item directly to the depositary bank and may send for collection a draft on the depositary bank and obtain reimbursement. In such case, if the depositary bank has received provisional settlement for the item, it must reimburse the bank drawing the draft and any provisional credits for the item between banks shall become and remain final.]

Note: *Direct returns is recognized as an innovation that is not yet established bank practice, and therefore, Paragraph 2 has been bracketed. Some lawyers have doubts whether it should be included in legislation or left to development by agreement.*

(3) A depositary bank which is also the payor may charge-back the amount of an item to its customer's account or obtain refund in accordance with the section governing return of an item received by a payor bank for credit on its books. (Section 4-301).

(4) The right to charge-back is not affected by

(a) prior use of the credit given for the item; or

(b) failure by any bank to exercise ordinary care with respect to the item but any bank so failing remains liable.

(5) A failure to charge-back or claim refund does not affect other rights of the bank against the customer or any other party.

(6) If credit is given in dollars as the equivalent of the value of an item payable in a foreign currency the dollar amount of any charge-back or refund shall be calculated on the basis of the buying sight rate for the foreign currency prevailing on the day when the person entitled to the charge-back or refund learns that it will not receive payment in ordinary course.

§4-213. Final Payment of Item by Payor Bank: When Provisional Debits and Credits Become Final; When Certain Credits Become Available for Withdrawal.

(1) An item is finally paid by a payor bank when the bank has done any of the following, whichever happens first:

(a) paid the item in cash; or

(b) settled for the item without reserving a right to revoke the settlement and without having such right under statute, clearing house rule or agreement; or

(c) completed the process of posting the item to the indicated account of the drawer, maker or other person to be charged therewith; or

(d) made a provisional settlement for the item and failed to revoke the settlement in the time and manner permitted by statute, clearing house rule or agreement.

Upon a final payment under subparagraphs (b), (c) or (e) the payor bank shall be accountable for the amount of the item.

(2) If provisional settlement for an item between the presenting and payor banks is made through a clearing house or by debits or credits in an account between them, then to the extent that provisional debits or credits for the item are entered in accounts between the presenting and payor banks or between the presenting and successive prior collecting banks seriatim, they become final upon final payment of the item by

the payor bank.

(3) If a collecting bank receives a settlement for an item which is or becomes final (subsection (3) of Section 4-211, subsection (2) of Section 4-213) the bank is accountable to its customer for the amount of the item and any provisional credit given for the item in an account with its customer becomes final.

(4) Subject to any right of the bank to apply the credit to an obligation of the customer, credit given by a bank for an item in an account with its customer becomes available for withdrawal as of right

(a) in any case where the bank has received a provisional settlement for the item—when such settlement becomes final and the bank has had a reasonable time to learn that the settlement is final;

(b) in any case where the bank is both a depositary bank and a payor bank and the item is finally paid,—at the opening of the bank's second banking day following receipt of the item.

(5) A deposit of money in a bank is final when made but, subject to any right of the bank to apply the deposit to an obligation of the customer, the deposit becomes available for withdrawal as of right at the opening of the bank's next banking day following receipt of the deposit.

§4-214. Insolvency and Preference.

(1) Any item in or coming into the possession of a payor or collecting bank which suspends payment and which item is not finally paid shall be returned by the receiver, trustee or agent in charge of the closed bank to the presenting bank or the closed bank's customer.

(2) If a payor bank finally pays an item and suspends payments without making a settlement for the item with its customer or the presenting bank which settlement is or becomes final, the owner of the item has a preferred claim against the payor bank.

(3) If a payor bank gives or a collecting bank gives or receives a provisional settlement for an item and thereafter suspends payments, the suspension does not prevent or interfere with the settlement becoming final if such finality occurs automatically upon the lapse of certain time or the happening of certain events (subsection (3) of Section 4-211, subsections (1) (d), (2) and (3) of Section 4-213).

(4) If a collecting bank receives from subsequent parties settlement for an item which settlement is or becomes final and suspends payments without making a settlement for the item with its customer which is or becomes final, the owner of the item has a preferred claim against such collecting bank.

Part 3: Collection of Items: Payor Banks

§4-301. Deferred Posting; Recovery of Payment by Return of Items; Time of Dishonor.

(1) Where an authorized settlement for a demand item (other than a documentary draft) received by a payor bank otherwise than for immediate payment over the counter has been made before midnight of the banking day of receipt the payor bank may revoke the settlement and recover any payment if before it has made final payment (subsection (1) of Section 4-213) and before its midnight deadline it

(a) returns the item; or

(b) sends written notice of dishonor or nonpayment if the item is held for protest or is otherwise unavailable for return.

(2) If a demand item is received by a payor bank for credit on its books it may return such item or send notice of dishonor and may revoke any credit given or recover the amount thereof withdrawn by its customer, if it acts within the time limit and in the manner specified in the preceding subsection.

(3) Unless previous notice of dishonor has been sent an item is dishonored at the time when for purposes of dishonor it is returned or notice sent in accordance with this section.

(4) An item is returned:

(a) as to an item received through a clearing house, when it is delivered to the presenting or last collecting bank or to the clearing house or is sent or delivered in accordance with its rules; or

(b) in all other cases, when it is sent or delivered to the bank's customer or transferor or pursuant to his instructions.

§4-302. Payor Bank's Responsibility for Late Return of Item. In the absence of a valid defense such as breach of a presentment warranty (subsection (1) of Section 4-207), settlement effected or the like, if an item is presented on and received by a payor bank the bank is accountable for the amount of

(a) a demand item other than a documentary draft whether properly payable or not if the bank, in any case where it is not also the depositary bank, retains the item beyond midnight of the banking day of receipt without settling for it or, regardless of whether it is also the depositary bank, does not pay or return the item or send notice of dishonor until after its midnight deadline; or

(b) any other properly payable item unless within the time allowed for acceptance or payment of that item the bank either accepts or pays the item or returns it and accompanying documents.

§4-303. When Items Subject to Notice, Stop-Order, Legal Process or Setoff; Order in Which Items May be Charged or Certified.

(1) Any knowledge, notice or stop-order received by, legal process served upon or setoff exercised by a payor bank, whether or not effective under other rules of law to terminate, suspend or modify the bank's right or duty to pay an item or to charge its customer's account for the item, comes too late to so terminate, suspend or modify such right or duty if the knowledge, notice, stop-order or legal process is received or served and a reasonable time for the bank to act thereon expires or the setoff is exercised after the bank has done any of the following:

(a) accepted or certified the item;

(b) paid the item in cash;

(c) settled for the item without reserving a right to revoke the settlement and without having such right under statute, clearing house rule or agreement;

(**d**) completed the process of posting the item to the indicated account of the drawer, maker or other person to be charged therewith or otherwise has evidenced by examination of such indicated account and by action its decision to pay the item; or

(**e**) become accountable for the amount of the item under subsection (1) (d) of Section 4-213 and Section 4-302 dealing with the payor bank's responsibility for late return of items.

(**2**) Subject to the provisions of subsection (1) items may be accepted, paid, certified or charged to the indicated account of its customer in any order convenient to the bank.

Part 4: Relationship between Payor Bank and its Customer

§4-401. When Bank May Charge Customer's Account.

(**1**) As against its customer, a bank may charge against his account any item which is otherwise properly payable from that account even though the charge creates an overdraft.

(**2**) A bank which in good faith makes payment to a holder may charge the indicated account of its customer according to

(**a**) the original tenor of his altered item; or

(**b**) the tenor of his completed item, even though the bank knows the item has been completed unless the bank has notice that the completion was improper.

§4-402. Bank's Liability to Customer for Wrongful Dishonor. A payor bank is liable to its customer for damages proximately caused by the wrongful dishonor of an item. When the dishonor occurs through mistake liability is limited to actual damages proved. If so proximately caused and proved damages may include damages for an arrest or prosecution of the customer or other consequential damages. Whether any consequential damages are proximately caused by the wrongful dishonor is a question of fact to be determined in each case.

§4-403. Customer's Right to Stop Payment; Burden of Proof of Loss.

(**1**) A customer may by order to his bank stop payment of any item payable for his account but the order must be received at such time and in such manner as to afford the bank a reasonable opportunity to act on it prior to any action by the bank with respect to the item described in Section 4-303.

(**2**) An oral order is binding upon the bank only for fourteen calendar days unless confirmed in writing within that period. A written order is effective for only six months unless renewed in writing.

(**3**) The burden of establishing the fact and amount of loss resulting from the payment of an item contrary to a binding stop payment order is on the customer.

§4-404. Bank Not Obligated to Pay Check More Than Six Months Old. A bank is under no obligation to a customer having a checking account to pay a check, other than a certified check, which is presented more than six months after its date, but it may charge its customer's account for a payment made thereafter in good faith.

§4-405. Death or Incompetence of Customer.

(**1**) A payor or collecting bank's authority to accept, pay or collect an item or to account for proceeds of its collection if otherwise effective is not rendered ineffective by incompetence of a customer of either bank existing at the time the item is issued or its collection is undertaken if the bank does not know of an adjudication of incompetence. Neither death nor incompetence of a customer revokes such authority to accept, pay, collect or account until the bank knows of the fact of death or of an adjudication of incompetence and has reasonable opportunity to act on it.

(**2**) Even with knowledge a bank may for 10 days after the date of death pay or certify checks drawn on or prior to that date unless ordered to stop payment by a person claiming an interest in the account.

§4-406. Customer's Duty to Discover and Report Unauthorized Signature or Alteration.

(1) When a bank sends to its customer a statement of account accompanied by items paid in good faith in support of the debit entries or holds the statement and items pursuant to a request for instructions of its customer or otherwise in a reasonable manner makes the statement and items available to the customer, the customer must exercise reasonable care and promptness to examine the statement and items to discover his unauthorized signature or any alteration on an item and must notify the bank promptly after discovery thereof.

(**2**) If the bank establishes that the customer failed with respect to an item to comply with the duties imposed on the customer by subsection (1) the customer is precluded from asserting against the bank

(**a**) his unauthorized signature or any alteration on the item if the bank also establishes that it suffered a loss by reason of such failure; and

(**b**) an unauthorized signature or alteration by the same wrongdoer on any other item paid in good faith by the bank after the first item and statement was available to the customer for a reasonable period not exceeding fourteen calendar days and before the bank receives notification from the customer of any such unauthorized signature or alteration.

(**3**) The preclusion under subsection (2) does not apply if the customer establishes lack of ordinary care on the part of the bank in paying the item(s).

(4) Without regard to care or lack of care of either the customer or the bank a customer who does not within one year from the time the statement and items are made available to the customer (subsection (1)) discover and report his unauthorized signature or any alteration on the face or back of the item or does not within 3 years from that time discover and report any unauthorized indorsement is precluded from asserting against the bank such unauthorized signature or indorsement or such alteration.

(**5**) If under this section a payor bank has a valid defense against a claim of a customer upon or resulting from payment of an item and waives or fails upon request to assert the defense the bank may not assert against any collecting bank or other prior party presenting or transferring the item a claim based upon the unauthorized signature or alteration giving rise to the customer's claim.

§4-407. Payor Bank's Right to Subrogation on Improper Payment. If a payor bank has paid an item over the stop payment order of the drawer or maker or otherwise under circumstances giving a basis for objection by the drawer or maker, to prevent unjust enrichment and only to the extent necessary to prevent loss to the bank by reason of its payment of the item, the payor bank shall be subrogated to the rights

(**a**) of any holder in due course on the item against the drawer or maker; and

(**b**) of the payee or any other holder of the item against the drawer or maker either on the item or under the transaction out of which the item arose; and

(**c**) of the drawer or maker against the payee or any other holder of the item with respect to the transaction out of which the item arose.

Part 5: Collection of Documentary Drafts

§4-501. Handling of Documentary Drafts; Duty to Send for Presentment and to Notify Customer of Dishonor. A bank which takes a documentary draft for collection must present or send the draft and accompanying documents for presentment and upon learning that the draft has not been paid or accepted in due course must seasonably notify its customer of such fact even though it may have discounted or bought the draft or extended credit available for withdrawal as of right.

§4-502. Presentment of "On Arrival" Drafts. When a draft or the relevant instructions require presentment "on arrival", "when goods arrive" or the like, the collecting bank need not present until in its judgment a reasonable time for arrival of the goods has expired. Refusal to pay or accept because the goods have not arrived is not dishonor; the bank must notify its transferor of such refusal but need not present the draft again until it is instructed to do so or learns of the arrival of the goods.

§4-503. Responsibility of Presenting Bank for Documents and Goods; Report of Reasons for Dishonor; Referee in Case of Need. Unless otherwise instructed and except as provided in Article 5 a bank presenting a documentary draft

(**a**) must deliver the documents to the drawee on acceptance of the draft if it is payable more than three days after presentment; otherwise, only on payment; and

(**b**) upon dishonor, either in the case of presentment for acceptance or presentment for payment, may seek and follow instructions from any referee in case of need designated in the draft or if the presenting bank does not choose to utilize his services it must use diligence and good faith to ascertain the reason for dishonor, must notify its transferor of the dishonor and of the results of its effort to ascertain the reasons therefor and must request instructions.

But the presenting bank is under no obligation with respect to goods represented by the documents except to follow any reasonable instructions seasonably received; it has a right to reimbursement for any expense incurred in following instructions and to prepayment of or indemnity for such expenses.

§4-504. Privilege of Presenting Bank to Deal With Goods; Security Interest for Expenses.

(**1**) A presenting bank which, following the dishonor of a documentary draft, has seasonably requested instructions but does not receive them within a reasonable time may store, sell, or otherwise deal with the goods in any reasonable manner.

(**2**) For its reasonable expenses incurred by action under subsection (1) the presenting bank has a lien upon the goods or their proceeds, which may be foreclosed in the same manner as an unpaid seller's lien.

ARTICLE 5: LETTERS OF CREDIT

§5-101. Short Title. This Article shall be known and may be cited as Uniform Commercial Code—Letters of Credit.

§5-102. Scope.

(**1**) This Article applies

(**a**) to a credit issued by a bank if the credit requires a documentary draft or a documentary demand for payment; and

(**b**) to a credit issued by a person other than a bank if the credit requires that the draft or demand for payment be accompanied by a document of title; and

(**c**) to a credit issued by a bank or other person if the credit is not within subparagraphs (a) or (b) but conspicuously states that it is a letter of credit or is conspicuously so entitled.

(**2**) Unless the engagement meets the requirements of subsection (1), this Article does not apply to engagements to make advances or to honor drafts or demands for payment, to authorities to pay or purchase, to guarantees or to general agreements.

(**3**) This Article deals with some but not all of the rules and concepts of letters of credit as such rules or concepts have developed prior to this act or may hereafter develop. The fact that this Article states a rule does not by itself require, imply or negate application of the same or a converse rule to a situation not provided for or to a person not specified by this Article.

§5-103. Definitions.

(**1**) In this Article unless the context otherwise requires

(**a**) "Credit" or "letter of credit" means an engagement by a bank or other person made at the request of a customer and of a kind within the scope of this Article (Section 5-102) that the issuer will honor drafts or other demands for payment upon compliance with the conditions specified in the credit. A credit may be either revocable or irrevocable. The engagement may be either an agreement to honor or a statement that the bank or other person is authorized to honor.

(b) A "documentary draft" or a "documentary demand for payment" is one, honor of which is conditioned upon the presentation of a document or documents. "Document" means any paper including document of title, security, invoice, certificate, notice of default and the like.

(c) An "issuer" is a bank or other person issuing a credit.

(d) A "beneficiary" of a credit is a person who is entitled under its terms to draw or demand payment.

(e) An "advising bank" is a bank which gives notification of the issuance of a credit by another bank.

(f) A "confirming bank" is a bank which engages either that it will itself honor a credit already issued by another bank or that such a credit will be honored by the issuer or a third bank.

(g) A "customer" is a buyer or other person who causes an issuer to issue a credit. The term also includes a bank which procures issuance or confirmation on behalf of that bank's customer.

(2) Other definitions applying to this Article and the sections in which they appear are:

"Notation of Credit". Section 5-108.

"Presenter". Section 5-112(3).

(3) Definitions in other Articles applying to this Article and the sections in which they appear are:

"Accept" or "Acceptance". Section 3-410.

"Contract for sale". Section 2-106.

"Draft". Section 3-104

"Holder in due course". Section 3-302.

"Midnight deadline". Section 4-104.

"Security". Section 8-102.

(4) In addition, Article 1 contains general definitions and principles of construction and interpretation applicable throughout this Article.

§5-104. Formal Requirements; Signing.

(1) Except as otherwise required in subsection (1)(c) Section 5-102 on scope, no particular form of phrasing is required for a credit. A credit must be in writing and signed by the issuer and a confirmation must be in writing and signed by the confirming bank. A modification of the terms of a credit or confirmation must be signed by the issuer or confirming bank.

(2) A telegram may be a sufficient signed writing if it identifies its sender by an authorized authentication. The authentication may be in code and the authorized naming of the issuer in an advice of credit is a sufficient signing.

§5-105. Consideration. No consideration is necessary to establish a credit or to enlarge or otherwise modify its terms.

§5-106. Time and Effect of Establishment of Credit.

(1) Unless otherwise agreed a credit is established

(a) as regards the customer as soon as a letter of credit is sent to him or the letter of credit or an authorized written advice of its issuance is sent to the beneficiary; and

(b) as regards the beneficiary when he receives a letter of credit or an authorized written advice of its issuance.

(2) Unless otherwise agreed once an irrevocable credit is established as regards the customer it can be modified or revoked only with the consent of the customer and once it is established as regards the beneficiary it can be modified or revoked only with his consent.

(3) Unless otherwise agreed after a revocable credit is established it may be modified or revoked by the issuer without notice to or consent from the customer or beneficiary.

(4) Notwithstanding any modification or revocation of a revocable credit any person authorized to honor or negotiate under the terms of the original credit is entitled to reimbursement for or honor of any draft or demand for payment duly honored or negotiated before receipt of notice of the modification or revocation and the issuer in turn is entitled to reimbursement from its customer.

§5-107. Advice of Credit; Confirmation; Error in Statement of Terms.

(1) Unless otherwise specified an advising bank by advising a credit issued by another bank does not assume any obligation to honor drafts drawn or demands for payment made under the credit but it does assume obligation for the accuracy of its own statement.

(2) A confirming bank by confirming a credit becomes directly obligated on the credit to the extent of its confirmation as though it were its issuer and acquires the rights of an issuer.

(3) Even though an advising bank incorrectly advises the terms of a credit it has been authorized to advise, the credit is established as against the issuer to the extent of its original terms.

(4) Unless otherwise specified the customer bears as against the issuer all risks of transmission and reasonable translation or interpretation of any message relating to a credit.

§5-108. "Notation Credit"; Exhaustion of Credit.

(1) A credit which specifies that any person purchasing or paying drafts drawn or demands for payment made under it must note the amount of the draft or demand on the letter or advice of credit is a "notation credit".

(2) Under a notation credit

(a) a person paying the beneficiary or purchasing a draft or demand for payment from him acquires a right to honor only if the appropriate notation is made and by transferring or forwarding for honor the documents under the credit such a person warrants to the issuer that the notation has been made; and

(b) unless the credit or a signed statement that an appropriate notation has been made accompanies the draft or demand for payment the issuer may delay honor until evidence of notation has been procured which is satisfactory to it but its obligation and that of its customer continue for a reasonable time not exceeding thirty days to obtain such evidence.

(3) If the credit is not a notation credit

(a) the issuer may honor complying drafts or demands for

payment presented to it in the order in which they are presented and is discharged pro tanto by honor of any such draft or demand;

(**b**) as between competing good faith purchasers of complying drafts or demands the person first purchasing has priority over a subsequent purchaser even though the later purchased draft or demand has been first honored.

§5-109. Issuer's Obligation to Its Customer.

(**1**) An issuer's obligation to its customer includes good faith and observance of any general banking usage but unless otherwise agreed does not include liability or responsibility

(**a**) for performance of the underlying contract for sale or other transaction between the customer and the beneficiary; or

(**b**) for any act or omission of any person other than itself or its own branch or for loss or destruction of a draft, demand or document in transit or in the possession of others; or

(**c**) based on knowledge or lack of knowledge of any usage of any particular trade.

(**2**) An issuer must examine documents with care so as to ascertain that on their face they appear to comply with the terms of the credit but unless otherwise agreed assumes no liability or responsibility for the genuineness, falsification or effect of any document which appears on such examination to be regular on its face.

(**3**) A non-bank issuer is not bound by any banking usage of which it has no knowledge.

§5-110. Availability of Credit in Portions; Presenter's Reservation of Lien or Claim.

(**1**) Unless otherwise specified a credit may be used in portions in the discretion of the beneficiary.

(**2**) Unless otherwise specified a person by presenting a documentary draft or demand for payment under a credit relinquishes upon its honor all claims to the documents and a person by transferring such draft or demand or causing such presentment authorizes such relinquishment. An explicit reservation of claim makes the draft or demand non-complying.

§5-111. Warranties on Transfer and Presentment.

(**1**) Unless otherwise agreed the beneficiary by transferring or presenting a documentary draft or demand for payment warrants to all interested parties that the necessary conditions of the credit have been complied with. This is in addition to any warranties arising under Articles 3, 4, 7 and 8.

(**2**) Unless otherwise agreed a negotiating, advising, confirming, collecting or issuing bank presenting or transferring a draft or demand for payment under a credit warrants only the matters warranted by a collecting bank under Article 4 and any such bank transferring a document warrants only the matters warranted by an intermediary under Articles 7 and 8.

§5-112. Time Allowed for Honor or Rejection; Withholding Honor or Rejection by Consent; "Presenter".

(**1**) A bank to which a documentary draft or demand for payment is presented under a credit may without dishonor of the draft, demand or credit

(**a**) defer honor until the close of the third banking day following receipt of the documents; and

(**b**) further defer honor if the presenter has expressly or impliedly consented thereto. Failure to honor within the time here specified constitutes dishonor of the draft or demand and of the credit [except as otherwise provided in subsection (4) of Section 5-114 on conditional payment].

Note: *The bracketed language in the last sentence of subsection (1) should be included only if the optional provisions of Section 5-114(4) and (5) are included.*

(**2**) Upon dishonor the bank may unless otherwise instructed fulfill its duty to return the draft or demand and the documents by holding them at the disposal of the presenter and sending him an advice to that effect.

(**3**) "Presenter" means any person presenting a draft or demand for payment for honor under a credit even though that person is a confirming bank or other correspondent which is acting under an issuer's authorization.

§5-113. Indemnities.

(**1**) A bank seeking to obtain (whether for itself or another) honor, negotiation or reimbursement under a credit may give an indemnity to induce such honor, negotiation or reimbursement.

(**2**) An indemnity agreement inducing honor, negotiation or reimbursement

(**a**) unless otherwise explicitly agreed applies to defects in the documents but not in the goods; and

(**b**) unless a longer time is explicitly agreed expires at the end of ten business days following receipt of the documents by the ultimate customer unless notice of objection is sent before such expiration date. The ultimate customer may send notice of objection to the person from whom he received the documents and any bank receiving such notice is under a duty to send notice to its transferor before its midnight deadline.

§5-114. Issuer's Duty and Privilege to Honor; Right to Reimbursement

(**1**) An issuer must honor a draft or demand for payment which complies with the terms of the relevant credit regardless of whether the goods or documents conform to the underlying contract for sale or other contract between the customer and the beneficiary. The issuer is not excused from honor of such a draft or demand by reason of an additional general term that all documents must be satisfactory to the issuer, but an issuer may require that specified documents must be satisfactory to it.

(**2**) Unless otherwise agreed when documents appear on their face to comply with the terms of a credit but a required document does not in fact conform to the warranties made on negotiation or transfer of a document of title (Section 7-507) or of a certificated security (Section 8-306) or is forged or fraudulent or there is fraud in the transaction

(**a**) the issuer must honor the draft or demand for payment if honor is demanded by a negotiating bank or other holder of the draft or demand which has taken the draft or demand under the credit and under circumstances which would make it a holder in due course (Section 3-302) and in an appropriate case would make it a person to whom a document of title has been duly negotiated (Section 7-502) or a bona fide purchaser of a certificated security (Section 8-302); and

(**b**) in all other cases as against its customer, an issuer acting in good faith may honor the draft or demand for payment despite notification from the customer of fraud, forgery or other defect not apparent on the face of the documents but a court of appropriate jurisdiction may enjoin such honor.

(**3**) Unless otherwise agreed an issuer which has duly honored a draft or demand for payment is entitled to immediate reimbursement of any payment made under the credit and to be put in effectively available funds not later than the day before maturity of any acceptance made under the credit.

[(**4**) When a credit provides for payment by the issuer on receipt of notice that the required documents are in the possession of a correspondent or other agent of the issuer

(**a**) any payment made on receipt of such notice is conditional; and

(**b**) the issuer may reject documents which do not comply with the credit if it does so within three banking days following its receipt of the documents; and

(**c**) in the event of such rejection, the issuer is entitled by charge back or otherwise to return to the payment made.]

[(5) In the case covered by subsection (4) failure to reject documents within the time specified in sub-paragraph (b) constitutes acceptance of the documents and makes the payment final in favor of the beneficiary.]

Note: *Subsections (4) and (5) are bracketed as optional. If they are included the bracketed language in the last sentence of Section 5-112(1) should also be included.*

§5-115. Remedy for Improper Dishonor or Anticipatory Repudiation.

(**1**) When an issuer wrongfully dishonors a draft or demand for payment presented under a credit the person entitled to honor has with respect to any documents the rights of a person in the position of a seller (Section 2-707) and may recover from the issuer the face amount of the draft or demand together with incidental damages under Section 2-710 on seller's incidental damages and interest but less any amount realized by resale or other use or disposition of the subject matter of the transaction. In the event no resale or other utilization is made the documents, goods or other subject matter involved in the transaction must be turned over to the issuer on payment of judgment.

(**2**) When an issuer wrongfully cancels or otherwise repudiates a credit before presentment of a draft or demand for payment drawn under it the beneficiary has the rights of a seller after anticipatory repudiation by the buyer under Section 2-610 if he learns of the repudiation in time reasonably to avoid procurement of the required documents. Otherwise the beneficiary has an immediate right of action for wrongful dishonor.

§5-116. Transfer and Assignment.

(**1**) The right to draw under a credit can be transferred or assigned only when the credit is expressly designated as transferable or assignable.

(**2**) Even though the credit specifically states that it is nontransferable or nonassignable the beneficiary may before performance of the conditions of the credit assign his right to proceeds. Such an assignment is an assignment of an account under Article 9 on Secured Transactions and is governed by that Article except that

(**a**) the assignment is ineffective until the letter of credit or advice of credit is delivered to the assignee which delivery constitutes perfection of the security interest under Article 9; and

(**b**) the issuer may honor drafts or demands for payment drawn under the credit until it receives a notification of the assignment signed by the beneficiary which reasonably identifies the credit involved in the assignment and contains a request to pay the assignee; and

(**c**) after what reasonably appears to be such a notification has been received the issuer may without dishonor refuse to accept or pay even to a person otherwise entitled to honor until the letter of credit or advice of credit is exhibited to the issuer.

(**3**) Except where the beneficiary has effectively assigned his right to draw or his right to proceeds, nothing in this section limits his right to transfer or negotiate drafts or demands drawn under the credit.

§5-117. Insolvency of Bank Holding Funds for Documentary Credit.

(**1**) Where an issuer or an advising or confirming bank or a bank which has for a customer procured issuance of a credit by another bank becomes insolvent before final payment under the credit and the credit is one to which this Article is made applicable by paragraphs (a) or (b) of Section 5-102(1) on scope, the receipt or allocation of funds or collateral to secure or meet obligations under the credit shall have the following results:

(**a**) to the extent of any funds or collateral turned over after or before the insolvency as indemnity against or specifically for the purpose of payment of drafts or demands for payments drawn under the designated credit, the drafts or demands are entitled to payment in preference over depositors or other general creditors of the issuer or bank; and

(**b**) on expiration of the credit or surrender of the beneficiary's rights under it unused any person who has given such funds or collateral is similarly entitled to return thereof; and

(**c**) a charge to a general or current account with a bank if specifically consented to for the purpose of indemnity against or payment of drafts or demands for payment drawn under the designated credit falls under the same rules as if the funds had been drawn out in cash and then turned over with specific instructions.

(**2**) After honor or reimbursement under this section the customer or other person for whose account the insolvent bank has acted is entitled to receive the documents involved.

ARTICLE 6: BULK TRANSFERS

§6-101. Short Title. This Article shall be known and may be cited as Uniform Commercial Code—Bulk Transfers.

§6-102. "Bulk Transfers"; Transfers of Equipment; Enterprises Subject to This Article; Bulk Transfers Subject to This Article.

(1) A "bulk transfer" is any transfer in bulk and not in the ordinary course of the transferor's business of a major part of the materials, supplies, merchandise or other inventory (Section 9-109) of an enterprise subject to this Article.

(2) A transfer of a substantial part of the equipment (Section 9-109) of such an enterprise is a bulk transfer if it is made in connection with a bulk transfer of inventory, but not otherwise.

(3) The enterprises subject to this Article are all those whose principal business is the sale of merchandise from stock, including those who manufacture what they sell.

(4) Except as limited by the following section all bulk transfers of goods located within this state are subject to this Article.

§6-103. Transfers Excepted From This Article. The following transfers are not subject to this Article:

(1) Those made to give security for the performance of an obligation;

(2) General assignments for the benefit of all the creditors of the transferor, and subsequent transfers by the assignee thereunder;

(3) Transfers in settlement or realization of a lien or other security interests;

(4) Sales by executors, administrators, receivers, trustees in bankruptcy, or any public officer under judicial process;

(5) Sales made in the course of judicial or administrative proceedings for the dissolution or reorganization of a corporation and of which notice is sent to the creditors of the corporation pursuant to order of the court or administrative agency;

(6) Transfers to a person maintaining a known place of business in this State who becomes bound to pay the debts of the transferor in full and gives public notice of that fact, and who is solvent after becoming so bound;

(7) A transfer to a new business enterprise organized to take over and continue the business, if public notice of the transaction is given and the new enterprise assumes the debts of the transferor and he receives nothing from the transaction except an interest in the new enterprise junior to the claims of creditors;

(8) Transfers of property which is exempt from execution. Public notice under subsection (6) or subsection (7) may be given by publishing once a week for two consecutive weeks in a newspaper of general circulation where the transferor had its principal place of business in this State an advertisement including the names and addresses of the transferor and transferee and the effective date of the transfer.

§6-104. Schedule of Property, List of Creditors.

(1) Except as provided with respect to auction sales (Section 6-108), a bulk transfer subject to this Article is ineffective against any creditor of the transferor unless:

(a) The transferee requires the transferor to furnish a list of his existing creditors prepared as stated in this section; and

(b) The parties prepare a schedule of the property transferred sufficient to identify it; and

(c) The transferee preserves the list and schedule for six months next following the transfer and permits inspection of either or both and copying therefrom at all reasonable hours by any creditor of the transferor, or files the list and schedule in (a public office to be here identified).

(2) The list of creditors must be signed and sworn to or affirmed by the transferor or his agent. It must contain the names and business addresses of all creditors of the transferor, with the amounts when known, and also the names of all persons who are known to the transferor to assert claims against him even though such claims are disputed. If the transferor is the obligor of an outstanding issue of bonds, debentures or the like as to which there is an indenture trustee, the list of creditors need include only the name and address of the indenture trustee and the aggregate outstanding principal amount of the issue.

(3) Responsibility for the completeness and accuracy of the list of creditors rests on the transferor, and the transfer is not rendered ineffective by errors or omissions therein unless the transferee is shown to have had knowledge.

§6-105. Notice to Creditors. In addition to the requirements of the preceding section, any bulk transfer subject to this Article except one made by auction sale (Section 6-108) is ineffective against any creditor of the transferor unless at least ten days before he takes possession of the goods or pays for them, whichever happens first, the transferee gives notice of the transfer in the manner and to the persons hereafter provided (Section 6-107).

§6-106. Application of the Proceeds. In addition to the requirements of the two preceding sections:

(1) Upon every bulk transfer subject to this Article for which new consideration becomes payable except those made by sale at auction it is the duty of the transferee to assure that such consideration is applied so far as necessary to pay those debts of the transferor which are either shown on the list furnished by the transferor (Section 6-104) or filed in writing in the place stated in the notice (Section 6-107) within thirty days after the mailing of such notice. This duty of the transferee runs to all the holders of such debts, and may be enforced by any of them for the benefit of all.

(2) If any of said debts are in dispute the necessary sum may be withheld from distribution until the dispute is settled or adjudicated.

[(3) If the consideration payable is not enough to pay all of the said debts in full distribution shall be made pro rata.]

Note: *This section is bracketed to indicate division of opinion as to whether or not it is a wise provision, and to suggest that this is a point on which State enactments may differ without serious damage to the principle of uniformity.*

In any State where this section is omitted, the following parts of sections, also bracketed in the text, should also be omitted, namely:

Section 6-107(2) (e).
6-108(3) (c).
6-109(2).

In any State where this section is enacted, these other provisions should be also.

Optional Subsection (4)

[(**4**) The transferee may within ten days after he takes possession of the goods pay the consideration into the (specify court) in the county where the transferor had its principal place of business in this state and thereafter may discharge his duty under this section by giving notice by registered or certified mail to all the persons to whom the duty runs that the consideration has been paid into that court and that they should file their claims there. On motion of any interested party, the court may order the distribution of the consideration to the persons entitled to it.]

Note: *Optional subsection (4) is recommended for those states which do not have a general statute providing for payment of money into court.*

§6-107. The Notice.

(**1**) The notice to creditors (Section 6-105) shall state:

(**a**) that a bulk transfer is about to be made; and

(**b**) the names and business addresses of the transferor and transferee, and all other business names and addresses used by the transferor within three years last past so far as known to the transferee; and

(**c**) whether or not all the debts of the transferor are to be paid in full as they fall due as a result of the transaction, and if so, the address to which creditors should send their bills.

(**2**) If the debts of the transferor are not to be paid in full as they fall due or if the transferee is in doubt on that point then the notice shall state further:

(**a**) the location and general description of the property to be transferred and the estimated total of the transferor's debts;

(**b**) the address where the schedule of property and list of creditors (Section 6-104) may be inspected;

(**c**) whether the transfer is to pay existing debts and if so the amount of such debts and to whom owing;

(**d**) whether the transfer is for new consideration and if so the amount of such consideration and the time and place of payment; [and]

[(**e**) if for new consideration the time and place where creditors of the transferor are to file their claims.]

(**3**) The notice in any case shall be delivered personally or sent by registered or certified mail to all the persons shown on the list of creditors furnished by the transferor (Section 6-104) and to all other persons who are known to the transferee to hold or assert claims against the transferor.

Note: *The words in brackets are optional. See Note under § 6-106.*

§6-108. Auction Sales; "Auctioneer".

(**1**) A bulk transfer is subject to this Article even though it is by sale at auction, but only in the manner and with the results stated in this section.

(**2**) The transferor shall furnish a list of his creditors and assist in the preparation of a schedule of the property to be sold, both prepared as before stated (Section 6-104).

(**3**) The person or persons other than the transferor who direct, control or are responsible for the auction are collectively called the "auctioneer". The auctioneer shall:

(**a**) receive and retain the list of creditors and prepare and retain the schedule of property for the period stated in this Article (Section 6-104);

(**b**) give notice of the auction personally or by registered or certified mail at least ten days before it occurs to all persons shown on the list of creditors and to all other persons who are known to him to hold or assert claims against the transferor; [and]

[(**c**) assure that the net proceeds of the auction are applied as provided in this Article (Section 6-106).]

(**4**) Failure of the auctioneer to perform any of these duties does not affect the validity of the sale or the title of the purchasers, but if the auctioneer knows that the auction constitutes a bulk transfer such failure renders the auctioneer liable to the creditors of the transferor as a class for the sums owing to them from the transferor up to but not exceeding the net proceeds of the auction. If the auctioneer consists of several persons their liability is joint and several.

Note: *The words in brackets are optional. See Note under § 6-106.*

§6-109. What Creditors Protected; [Credit for Payment to Particular Creditors].

(**1**) The creditors of the transferor mentioned in this Article are those holding claims based on transactions or events occurring before the bulk transfer, but creditors who become such after notice to creditors is given (Sections 6-105 and 6-107) are not entitled to notice.

[(**2**) Against the aggregate obligation imposed by the provisions of this Article concerning the application of the proceeds (Section 6-106 and subsection (3) (c) of 6-108) the transferee or auctioneer is entitled to credit for sums paid to particular creditors of the transferor, not exceeding the sums believed in good faith at the time of the payment to be properly payable to such creditors.]

Note: *The words in brackets are optional. See Note under § 6-106.*

§6-110. Subsequent Transfers. When the title of a transferee to property is subject to a defect by reason of his non-compliance with the requirements of this Article, then:

(**1**) a purchaser of any of such property from such transferee who pays no value or who takes with notice of such non-compliance takes subject to such defect, but

(**2**) a purchaser for value in good faith and without such notice takes free of such defect.

§6-111. Limitation of Actions and Levies. No action under this Article shall be brought nor levy made more than six months after the date on which the transferee took possession of the goods unless the transfer has been concealed. If the transfer has been concealed, actions may be brought or levies made within six months after its discovery.

ARTICLE 7: WAREHOUSE RECEIPTS, BILLS OF LADING AND OTHER DOCUMENTS OF TITLE

Part 1: General

§7-101. Short Title. This Article shall be known and may be cited as Uniform Commercial Code—Documents of Title.

§7-102. Definitions and Index of Definitions.

(1) In this Article, unless the context otherwise requires:

(a) "Bailee" means the person who by a warehouse receipt, bill of lading or other document of title acknowledges possession of goods and contracts to deliver them.

(b) "Consignee" means the person named in a bill to whom or to whose order the bill promises delivery.

(c) "Consignor"means the person named in a bill as the person from whom the goods have been received for shipment.

(d) "Delivery order" means a written order to deliver goods directed to a warehouseman, carrier or other person who in the ordinary course of business issues warehouse receipts or bills of lading.

(e) "Document" means document of title as defined in the general definitions in Article 1 (Section 1-201).

(f) "Goods" means all things which are treated as movable for the purposes of a contract of storage or transportation.

(g) "Issuer" means a bailee who issues a document except that in relation to an unaccepted delivery order it means the person who orders the possessor of goods to deliver. Issuer includes any person for whom an agent or employee purports to act in issuing a document if the agent or employee has real or apparent authority to issue documents, notwithstanding that the issuer received no goods or that the goods were misdescribed or that in any other respect the agent or employee violated his instructions.

(h) "Warehouseman" is a person engaged in the business of storing goods for hire.

(2) Other definitions applying to this Article or to specified Parts thereof, and the sections in which they appear are:

"Duly negotiate". Section 7-501.

"Person entitled under the document". Section 7-403(4).

(3) Definitions in other Articles applying to this Article and the sections in which they appear are:

"Contract for sale". Section 2-106.

"Overseas". Section 2-323.

"Receipt" of goods. Section 2-103.

(4) In addition Article 1 contains general definitions and principles of construction and interpretation applicable throughout this Article.

§7-103. Relation of Article to Treaty, Statute, Tariff, Classification or Regulation. To the extent that any treaty or statute of the United States, regulatory statute of this State or tariff, classification or regulation filed or issued pursuant thereto is applicable, the provisions of this Article are subject thereto.

§7-104. Negotiable and Non-Negotiable Warehouse Receipt, Bill of Lading or Other Document of Title

(1) A warehouse receipt, bill of lading or other document of title is negotiable

(a) if by its terms the goods are to be delivered to bearer or to the order of a named person; or

(b) where recognized in overseas trade, if it runs to a named person or assigns.

(2) Any other document is non-negotiable. A bill of lading in which it is stated that the goods are consigned to a named person is not made negotiable by a provision that the goods are to be delivered only against a written order signed by the same or another named person.

§7-105. Construction Against Negative Implication. The omission from either Part 2 or Part 3 of this Article of a provision corresponding to a provision made in the other Part does not imply that a corresponding rule of law is not applicable.

Part 2: Warehouse Receipts: Special Provisions

§7-201. Who May Issue a Warehouse Receipt; Storage Under Government Bond.

(1) A warehouse receipt may be issued by any warehouseman.

(2) Where goods including distilled spirits and agricultural commodities are stored under a statute requiring a bond against withdrawal or a license for the issuance of receipts in the nature of warehouse receipts, a receipt issued for the goods has like effect as a warehouse receipt even though issued by a person who is the owner of the goods and is not a warehouseman.

§7-202. Form of Warehouse Receipt; Essential Terms; Optional Te-ms.

(1) A warehouse receipt need not be in any particular form.

(2) Unless a warehouse receipt embodies within its written or printed terms each of the following, the warehouseman is liable for damages caused by the omission to a person injured thereby:

(a) the location of the warehouse where the goods are stored;

(b) the date of issue of the receipt;

(c) the consecutive number of the receipt;

(d) a statement whether the goods received will be delivered to the bearer, to a specified person, or to a specified person or his order;

(e) the rate of storage and handling charges, except that where goods are stored under a field warehousing arrangement a statement of that fact is sufficient on a non-negotiable receipt;

(f) a description of the goods or of the packages containing them:

(g) the signature of the warehouseman, which may be made by his authorized agent;

(h) if the receipt is issued for goods of which the warehouseman is owner, either solely or jointly or in common with others, the fact of such ownership; and

(i) a statement of the amount of advances made and of liabilities incurred for which the warehouseman claims a lien or security interest (Section 7-209). If the precise amount of such advances made or of such liabilities incurred is, at the time of the issue of the receipt, unknown to the warehouseman or to his agent who issues it, a statement of the fact that advances have been made or liabilities incurred and the purpose thereof is sufficient.

(3) A warehouseman may insert in his receipt any other terms which are not contrary to the provisions of this Act and do not impair his obligation of delivery (Section 7-403) or his duty of care (Section 7-204). Any contrary provisions shall be ineffective.

§7-203. Liability for Non-Receipt or Misdescription. A party to or purchaser for value in good faith of a document of title other than a bill of lading relying in either case upon the description therein of the goods may recover from the issuer damages caused by the non-receipt or misdescription of the goods, except to the extent that the document conspicuously indicates that the issuer does not know whether any part or all of the goods in fact were received or conform to the description, as where the description is in terms of marks or labels or kind, quantity or condition, or the receipt or description is qualified by "contents, condition and quality unknown," "said to contain" or the like, if such indication be true, or the party or purchaser otherwise has notice.

§7-204. Duty of Care; Contractual Limitation of Warehouseman's Liability.

(1) A warehouseman is liable for damages for loss of or injury to the goods caused by his failure to exercise such care in regard to them as a reasonably careful man would exercise under like circumstances but unless otherwise agreed he is not liable for damages which could not have been avoided by the exercise of such care.

(2) Damages may be limited by a term in the warehouse receipt or storage agreement limiting the amount of liability in case of loss or damage, and setting forth a specific liability per article or item, or value per unit of weight, beyond which the warehouseman shall not be liable; provided, however, that such liability may on written request of the bailor at the time of signing such storage agreement or within a reasonable time after receipt of the warehouse receipt be increased on part or all of the goods thereunder, in which event increased rates may be charged based on such increased valuation, but that no such increase shall be permitted contrary to a lawful limitation of liability contained in the warehouseman's tariff, if any. No such limitation is effective with respect to the warehouseman's liability for conversion to his own use.

(3) Reasonable provisions as to the time and manner of presenting claims and instituting actions based on the bailment may be included in the warehouse receipt or tariff.

(4) This section does not impair or repeal . . .

Note: *Insert in subsection (4) a reference to any statute which imposes a higher responsibility upon the warehouseman or invalidates contractual limitations which would be permissible under this Article.*

§7-205. Title Under Warehouse Receipt Defeated in Certain Cases. A buyer in the ordinary course of business of fungible goods sold and delivered by a warehouseman who is also in the business of buying and selling such goods takes free of any claim under a warehouse receipt even though it has been duly negotiated.

§7-206. Termination of Storage at Warehouseman's Option.

(1) A warehouseman may on notifying the person on whose account the goods are held and any other person known to claim an interest in the goods require payment of any charges and removal of the goods from the warehouse at the termination of the period of storage fixed by the document, or, if no period is fixed, within a stated period not less than thirty days after the notification. If the goods are not removed before the date specified in the notification, the warehouseman may sell them in accordance with the provisions of the section on enforcement of a warehouseman's lien (Section 7-210).

(2) If a warehouseman in good faith believes that the goods are about to deteriorate or decline in value to less than the amount of his lien within the time prescribed in subsection (1) for notification, advertisement and sale, the warehouseman may specify in the notification any reasonable shorter time for removal of the goods and in case the goods are not removed, may sell them at public sale held not less than one week after a single advertisement or posting.

(3) If as a result of a quality or condition of the goods of which the warehouseman had no notice at the time of deposit the goods are a hazard to other property or to the warehouse or to persons, the warehouseman may sell the goods at public or private sale without advertisement on reasonable notification to all persons known to claim an interest in the goods. If the warehouseman after a reasonable effort is unable to sell the goods he may dispose of them in any lawful manner and shall incur no liability by reason of such disposition.

(4) The warehouseman must deliver the goods to any person entitled to them under this Article upon due demand made at any time prior to sale or other disposition under this section.

(5) The warehouseman may satisfy his lien from the proceeds of any sale or disposition under this section but must hold the balance for delivery on the demand of any person to whom he would have been bound to deliver the goods.

§7-207. Goods Must Be Kept Separate; Fungible Goods.

(1) Unless the warehouse receipt otherwise provides, a warehouseman must keep separate the goods covered by each receipt so as to permit at all times identification and delivery of those goods except that different lots of fungible goods may be commingled.

(2) Fungible goods so commingled are owned in common by the persons entitled thereto and the warehouseman is severally liable to each owner for that owner's share. Where because of overissue a mass of fungible goods is insufficient to meet all the receipts which the warehouseman has issued against it, the persons entitled include all holders to whom overissued receipts have been duly negotiated.

§7-208. Altered Warehouse Receipts. Where a blank in a negotiable warehouse receipt has been filled in without authority, a purchaser for value and without notice of the want of authority may treat the insertion as authorized. Any other unauthorized alteration leaves any receipt enforceable against the issuer according to its original tenor.

§7-209. Lien of Warehouseman.

(1) A warehouseman has a lien against the bailor on the goods covered by a warehouse receipt or on the proceeds thereof in his possession for charges for storage or transportation (including demurrage and terminal charges), insurance, labor, or charges present or future in relation to the goods, and for expenses necessary for preservation of the goods or reasonably incurred in their sale pursuant to law. If the person on whose account the goods are held is liable for like charges or expenses in relation to other goods whenever deposited and it is stated in the receipt that a lien is claimed for charges and expenses in relation to other goods, the warehouseman also has a lien against him for such charges and expenses whether or not the other goods have been delivered by the warehouseman. But against a person to whom a negotiable warehouse receipt is duly negotiated a warehouseman's lien is limited to charges in an amount or at a rate specified on the receipt or if no charges are so specified then to a reasonable charge for storage of the goods covered by the receipt subsequent to the date of the receipt.

(2) The warehouseman may also reserve a security interest against the bailor for a maximum amount specified on the receipt for charges other than those specified in subsection (1), such as for money advanced and interest. Such a security interest is governed by the Article on Secured Transactions (Article 9).

(3)

(a) A warehouseman's lien for charges and expenses under subsection (1) or a security interest under subsection (2) is also effective against any person who so entrusted the bailor with possession of the goods that a pledge of them by him to a good faith purchaser for value would have been valid but is not effective against a person as to whom the document confers no right in the goods covered by it under Section 7-503.

(b) A warehouseman's lien on household goods for charges and expenses in relation to the goods under subsection (1) is also effective against all persons if the depositor was the legal possessor of the goods at the time of deposit. "Household goods" means furniture, furnishings and personal effects used by the depositor in a dwelling.

(4) A warehouseman loses his lien on any goods which he voluntarily delivers or which he unjustifiably refuses to deliver. (As amended in 1966.)

§7-210. Enforcement of Warehouseman's Lien.

(1) Except as provided in subsection (2), a warehouseman's lien may be enforced by public or private sale of the goods in block or in parcels, at any time or place and on any terms which are commercially reasonable, after notifying all persons known to claim an interest in the goods. Such notification must include a statement of the amount due, the nature of the proposed sale and the time and place of any public sale. The fact that a better price could have been obtained by a sale at a different time or in a different method from that selected by the warehouseman is not of itself sufficient to establish that the sale was not made in a commercially reasonable manner. If the warehouseman either sells the goods in the usual manner in any recognized market therefor, or if he sells at the price current in such market at the time of his sale, or if he has otherwise sold in conformity with commercially reasonable practices among dealers in the type of goods sold, he has sold in a commercially reasonable manner. A sale of more goods than apparently necessary to be offered to insure satisfaction of the obligation is not commercially reasonable except in cases covered by the preceding sentence.

(2) A warehouseman's lien on goods other than goods stored by a merchant in the course of his business may be enforced only as follows:

(a) All persons known to claim an interest in the goods must be notified.

(b) The notification must be delivered in person or sent by registered or certified letter to the last known address of any person to be notified.

(c) The notification must include an itemized statement of the claim, a description of the goods subject to the lien, a demand for payment within a specified time not less than ten days after receipt of the notification, and a conspicuous statement that unless the claim is paid within that time the goods will be advertised for sale and sold by auction at a specified time and place.

(d) The sale must conform to the terms of the notification.

(e) The sale must be held at the nearest suitable place to that where the goods are held or stored.

(f) After the expiration of the time given in the notification, an advertisement of the sale must be published once a week for two weeks consecutively in a newspaper of general circulation where the sale is to be held. The advertisement must include a description of the goods, the name of the person on whose account they are being held, and the time and place of the sale. The sale must take place at least fifteen days after the first publication. If there is no newspaper of general circulation where the sale is to be held, the advertisement must be posted at least ten days before the sale in not less than six conspicuous places in the neighborhood of the proposed sale.

(3) Before any sale pursuant to this section any person claiming a right in the goods may pay the amount necessary to satisfy the lien and the reasonable expenses incurred under this section. In that event the goods must not be sold, but must be retained by the warehouseman subject to the terms of the receipt and this Article.

(4) The warehouseman may buy at any public sale pursuant to this section.

(5) A purchaser in good faith of goods sold to enforce a warehouseman's lien takes the goods free of any rights of persons against whom the lien was valid, despite noncompliance by the warehouseman with the requirements of this section.

(6) The warehouseman may satisfy his lien from the proceeds of any sale pursuant to this section but must hold the balance, if any, for delivery on demand to any person to whom he would have been bound to deliver the goods.

(7) The rights provided by this section shall be in addition to all other rights allowed by law to a creditor against his debtor.

(8) Where a lien is on goods stored by a merchant in the course of his business the lien may be enforced in accordance with either subsection (1) or (2).

(9) The warehouseman is liable for damages caused by failure to comply with the requirements for sale under this section and in case of willful violation is liable for conversion. As amended in 1962.

Part 3: Bills of Lading: Special Provisions

§7-301. Liability for Non-Receipt or Misdescription; "Said to Contain"; "Shipper's Load and Count"; Improper Handling.

(1) A consignee of a non-negotiable bill who has given value in good faith or a holder to whom a negotiable bill has been duly negotiated relying in either case upon the description therein of the goods, or upon the date therein shown, may recover from the issuer damages caused by the misdating of the bill or the non-receipt or misdescription of the goods, except to the extent that the document indicates that the issuer does not know whether any part or all of the goods in fact were received or conform to the description, as where the description is in terms of marks or labels or kind, quantity, or condition or the receipt or description is qualified by "contents or condition of contents of packages unknown", "said to contain", "Shipper's weight, load and count" or the like, if such indication be true.

(2) When goods are loaded by an issuer who is a common carrier, the issuer must count the packages of goods if package freight and ascertain the kind and quantity if bulk freight. In such cases "shipper's weight, load and count" or other words indicating that the description was made by the shipper are ineffective except as to freight concealed by packages.

(3) When bulk freight is loaded by a shipper who makes available to the issuer adequate facilities for weighing such freight, an issuer who is a common carrier must ascertain the kind and quantity within a reasonable time after receiving the written request of the shipper to do so. In such cases "shipper's weight" or other words of like purport are ineffective.

(4) The issuer may by inserting in the bill the words "shipper's weight, load and count" or other words of like purport indicate that the goods were loaded by the shipper; and if such statement be true the issuer shall not be liable for damages caused by the improper loading. But their omission does not imply liability for such damages.

(5) The shipper shall be deemed to have guaranteed to the issuer the accuracy at the time of shipment of the description, marks, labels, number, kind, quantity, condition and weight, as furnished by him; and the shipper shall indemnify the issuer against damage caused by inaccuracies in such particulars. The right of the issuer to such indemnity shall in no way limit his responsibility and liability under the contract of carriage to any person other than the shipper.

§7-302. Through Bills of Lading and Similar Documents.

(1) The issuer of a through bill of lading or other document embodying an undertaking to be performed in part by persons acting as its agents or by connecting carriers is liable to anyone entitled to recover on the document for any breach by such other persons or by a connecting carrier of its obligation under the document but to the extent that the bill covers an undertaking to be performed overseas or in territory not contiguous to the continental United States or an undertaking including matters other than transportation this liability may be varied by agreement of the parties.

(2) Where goods covered by a through bill of lading or other document embodying an undertaking to be performed in part by persons other than the issuer are received by any such person, he is subject with respect to his own performance while the goods are in his possession to the obligation of the issuer. His obligation is discharged by delivery of the goods to another such person pursuant to the document, and does not include liability for breach by any other such persons or by the issuer.

(3) The issuer of such through bill of lading or other document shall be entitled to recover from the connecting carrier or such other person in possession of the goods when the breach of the obligation under the document occurred, the amount it may be required to pay to anyone entitled to recover on the document therefor, as may be evidenced by any receipt, judgment, or transcript thereof, and the amount of any expense reasonably incurred by it in defending any action brought by anyone entitled to recover on the document therefor.

§7-303. Diversion; Reconsignment; Change of Instructions.

(1) Unless the bill of lading otherwise provides, the carrier may deliver the goods to a person or destination other than that stated in the bill or may otherwise dispose of the goods on instructions from

(a) the holder of a negotiable bill; or

(b) the consignor on a non-negotiable bill notwithstanding contrary instructions from the consignee; or

(c) the consignee on a non-negotiable bill in the absence of contrary instructions from the consignor, if the goods have arrived at the billed destination or if the consignee is in possession of the bill; or

(d) the consignee on a non-negotiable bill if he is entitled as against the consignor to dispose of them.

(2) Unless such instructions are noted on a negotiable bill of lading, a person to whom the bill is duly negotiated can hold the bailee according to the original terms.

§7-304. Bills of Lading in a Set.

(1) Except where customary in overseas transportation, a bill of lading must not be issued in a set of parts. The issuer is liable for damages caused by violation of this subsection.

(2) Where a bill of lading is lawfully drawn in a set of parts, each of which is numbered and expressed to be valid only if the goods have not been delivered against any other part, the whole of the parts constitute one bill.

(3) Where a bill of lading is lawfully issued in a set of parts and different parts are negotiated to different persons, the title of the holder to whom the first due negotiation is made prevails as to both the document and the goods even though any later holder may have received the goods from the carrier in good faith and discharged the carrier's obligation by surrender of his part.

(4) Any person who negotiates or transfers a single part of a

bill of lading drawn in a set is liable to holders of that part as if it were the whole set.

(5) The bailee is obliged to deliver in accordance with Part 4 of this Article against the first presented part of a bill of lading lawfully drawn in a set. Such delivery discharges the bailee's obligation on the whole bill.

§7-305. Destination Bills.

(1) Instead of issuing a bill of lading to the consignor at the place of shipment a carrier may at the request of the consignor procure the bill to be issued at destination or at any other place designated in the request.

(2) Upon request of anyone entitled as against the carrier to control the goods while in transit and on surrender of any outstanding bill of lading or other receipt covering such goods, the issuer may procure a substitute bill to be issued at any place designated in the request.

§7-306. Altered Bills of Lading. An unauthorized alteration or filling in of a blank in a bill of lading leaves the bill enforceable according to its original tenor.

§7-307. Lien of Carrier.

(1) A carrier has a lien on the goods covered by a bill of lading for charges subsequent to the date of its receipt of the goods for storage or transportation (including demurrage and terminal charges) and for expenses necessary for preservation of the goods incident to their transportation or reasonably incurred in their sale pursuant to law. But against a purchaser for value of a negotiable bill of lading a carrier's lien is limited to charges stated in the bill or the applicable tariffs, or if no charges are stated then to a reasonable charge.

(2) A lien for charges and expenses under subsection (1) on goods which the carrier was required by law to receive for transportation is effective against the consignor or any person entitled to the goods unless the carrier had notice that the consignor lacked authority to subject the goods to such charges and expenses. Any other lien under subsection (1) is effective against the consignor and any person who permitted the bailor to have control or possession of the goods unless the carrier had notice that the bailor lacked such authority.

(3) A carrier loses his lien on any goods which he voluntarily delivers or which he unjustifiably refuses to deliver.

§7-308. Enforcement of Carrier's Lien.

(1) A carrier's lien may be enforced by public or private sale of the goods, in block or in parcels, at any time or place and on any terms which are commercially reasonable, after notifying all persons known to claim an interest in the goods. Such notification must include a statement of the amount due, the nature of the proposed sale and the time and place of any public sale. The fact that a better price could have been obtained by a sale at a different time or in a different method from that selected by the carrier is not of itself sufficient to establish that the sale was not made in a commercially reasonable manner. If the carrier either sells the goods in the usual manner in any recognized market therefor or if he sells at the price current in such market at the time of his sale or if he has otherwise sold in conformity with commercially reasonable practices among dealers in the type of goods sold he has sold in a commercially reasonable manner. A sale of more goods than apparently necessary to be offered to ensure satisfaction of the obligation is not commercially reasonable except in cases covered by the preceding sentence.

(2) Before any sale pursuant to this section any person claiming a right in the goods may pay the amount necessary to satisfy the lien and the reasonable expenses incurred under this section. In that event the goods must not be sold, but must be retained by the carrier subject to the terms of the bill and this Article.

(3) The carrier may buy at any public sale pursuant to this section.

(4) A purchaser in good faith of goods sold to enforce a carrier's lien takes the goods free of any rights of persons against whom the lien was valid, despite noncompliance by the carrier with the requirements of this section.

(5) The carrier may satisfy his lien from the proceeds of any sale pursuant to this section but must hold the balance, if any, for delivery on demand to any person to whom he would have been bound to deliver the goods.

(6) The rights provided by this section shall be in addition to all other rights allowed by law to a creditor against his debtor.

(7) A carrier's lien may be enforced in accordance with either subsection (1) or the procedure set forth in subsection (2) of Section 7-210.

(8) The carrier is liable for damages caused by failure to comply with the requirements for sale under this section and in case of willful violation is liable for conversion.

§7-309. Duty of Care; Contractual Limitation of Carrier's Liability.

(1) A carrier who issues a bill of lading whether negotiable or non-negotiable must exercise the degree of care in relation to the goods which a reasonably careful man would exercise under like circumstances. This subsection does not repeal or change any law or rule of law which imposes liability upon a common carrier for damages not caused by its negligence.

(2) Damages may be limited by a provision that the carrier's liability shall not exceed a value stated in the document if the carrier's rates are dependent upon value and the consignor by the carrier's tariff is afforded an opportunity to declare a higher value or a value as lawfully provided in the tariff, or where no tariff is filed he is otherwise advised of such opportunity; but no such limitation is effective with respect to the carrier's liability for conversion to its own use.

(3) Reasonable provisions as to the time and manner of presenting claims and instituting actions based on the shipment may be included in a bill of lading or tariff.

Part 4: Warehouse Receipts and Bills of Lading: General Obligations

§7-401. Irregularities in Issue of Receipt or Bill or Conduct of Issuer. The obligations imposed by this Article on an issuer apply to a document of title regardless of the fact that

(a) the document may not comply with the requirements of this Article or of any other law or regulation regarding its issue, form or content; or

(b) the issuer may have violated laws regulating the conduct of his business; or

(c) the goods covered by the document were owned by the bailee at the time the document was issued; or

(d) the person issuing the document does not come within the definition of warehouseman if it purports to be a warehouse receipt.

§7-402. Duplicate Receipt or Bill; Overissue. Neither a duplicate nor any other document of title purporting to cover goods already represented by an outstanding document of the same issuer confers any right in the goods, except as provided in the case of bills in a set, overissue of documents for fungible goods and substitutes for lost, stolen or destroyed documents. But the issuer is liable for damages caused by his overissue or failure to identify a duplicate document as such by conspicuous notation on its face.

§7-403. Obligation of Warehouseman or Carrier to Deliver; Excuse.

(1) The bailee must deliver the goods to a person entitled under the document who complies with subsections (2) and (3), unless and to the extent that the bailee establishes any of the following:

(a) delivery of the goods to a person whose receipt was rightful as against the claimant;

(b) damage to or delay, loss or destruction of the goods for which the bailee is not liable [, but the burden of establishing negligence in such cases is on the person entitled under the document];

Note: *The brackets in (1) (b) indicate that State enactments may differ on this point without serious damage to the principle of uniformity.*

(c) previous sale or other disposition of the goods in lawful enforcement of a lien or on warehouseman's lawful termination of storage;

(d) the exercise by a seller of his right to stop delivery pursuant to the provisions of the Article on Sales (Section 2-705);

(e) a diversion, reconsignment or other disposition pursuant to the provisions of this Article (Section 7-303.) or tariff regulating such right;

(f) release, satisfaction or any other fact affording a personal defense against the claimant;

(g) any other lawful excuse.

(2) A person claiming goods covered by a document of title must satisfy the bailee's lien where the bailee so requests or where the bailee is prohibited by law from delivering the goods until the charges are paid.

(3) Unless the person claiming is one against whom the document confers no right under Sec. 7-503(1), he must surrender for cancellation or notation of partial deliveries any outstanding negotiable document covering the goods, and the bailee must cancel the document or conspicuously note the partial delivery thereon or be liable to any person to whom the document is duly negotiated.

(4) "Person entitled under the document" means holder in the case of a negotiable document, or the person to whom delivery is to be made by the terms of or pursuant to written instructions under a non-negotiable document.

§7-404. No Liability for Good Faith Delivery Pursuant to Receipt or Bill. A bailee who in good faith including observance of reasonable commercial standards has received goods and delivered or otherwise disposed of them according to the terms of the document of title or pursuant to this Article is not liable therefor. This rule applies even though the person from whom he received the goods had no authority to procure the document or to dispose of the goods and even though the person to whom he delivered the goods had no authority to receive them.

Part 5: Warehouse Receipts and Bills of Lading: Negotiation and Transfer

§7-501. Form of Negotiation and Requirements of "Due Negotiation".

(1) A negotiable document of title running to the order of a named person is negotiated by his indorsement and delivery. After his indorsement in blank or to bearer any person can negotiate it by delivery alone.

(2)

(a) A negotiable document of title is also negotiated by delivery alone when by its original terms it runs to bearer.

(b) When a document running to the order of a named person is delivered to him the effect is the same as if the document had been negotiated.

(3) Negotiation of a negotiable document of title after it has been indorsed to a specified person requires indorsement by the special indorsee as well as delivery.

(4) A negotiable document of title is "duly negotiated" when it is negotiated in the manner stated in this section to a holder who purchases it in good faith without notice of any defense against or claim to it on the part of any person and for value, unless it is established that the negotiation is not in the regular course of business or financing or involves receiving the document in settlement or payment of a money obligation.

(5) Indorsement of a non-negotiable document neither makes it negotiable nor adds to the transferee's rights.

(6) The naming in a negotiable bill of a person to be notified of the arrival of the goods does not limit the negotiability of the bill nor constitute notice to a purchaser thereof of any interest of such person in the goods.

§7-502. Rights Acquired by Due Negotiation.

(1) Subject to the following section and to the provisions of Section 7-205 on fungible goods, a holder to whom a negotiable document of title has been duly negotiated acquires thereby:

(a) title to the document;

(b) title to the goods;

(c) all rights accruing under the law of agency or estoppel, including rights to goods delivered to the bailee after the document was issued; and

(d) the direct obligation of the issuer to hold or deliver the goods according to the terms of the document free of any defense or claim by him except those arising under the terms of the document or under this Article. In the case of a delivery order the bailee's obligation accrues only upon acceptance and the obligation acquired by the holder is that the issuer and any indorser will procure the acceptance of the bailee.

(2) Subject to the following section, title and rights so acquired are not defeated by any stoppage of the goods represented by the document or by surrender of such goods by the bailee, and are not impaired even though the negotiation or any prior negotiation constituted a breach of duty or even though any person has been deprived of possession of the document by misrepresentation, fraud, accident, mistake, duress, loss, theft or conversion, or even though a previous sale or other transfer of the goods or document has been made to a third person.

§7-503. Document of Title to Goods Defeated in Certain Cases.

(1) A document of title confers no right in goods against a person who before issuance of the document had a legal interest or a perfected security interest in them and who neither

(a) delivered or entrusted them or any document of title covering them to the bailor or his nominee with actual or apparent authority to ship, store or sell or with power to obtain delivery under this Article (Section 7-403) or with power of disposition under this Act (Sections 2-403 and 9-307) or other statute or rule of law; nor

(b) acquiesced in the procurement by the bailor or his nominee of any document of title.

(2) Title to goods based upon an unaccepted delivery order is subject to the rights of anyone to whom a negotiable warehouse receipt or bill of lading covering the goods has been duly negotiated. Such a title may be defeated under the next section to the same extent as the rights of the issuer or a transferee from the issuer.

(3) Title to goods based upon a bill of lading issued to a freight forwarder is subject to the rights of anyone to whom a bill issued by the freight forwarder is duly negotiated; but delivery by the carrier in accordance with Part 4 of this Article pursuant to its own bill of lading discharges the carrier's obligation to deliver.

§7-504. Rights Acquired in the Absence of Due Negotiation; Effect of Diversion; Seller's Stoppage of Delivery.

(1) A transferee of a document, whether negotiable or non-negotiable, to whom the document has been delivered but not duly negotiated, acquires the title and rights which his transferor had or had actual authority to convey.

(2) In the case of a non-negotiable document, until but not after the bailee receives notification of the transfer, the rights of the transferee may be defeated

(a) by those creditors of the transferor who could treat the sale as void under Section 2-402; or

(b) by a buyer from the transferor in ordinary course of business if the bailee has delivered the goods to the buyer or received notification of his rights; or

(c) as against the bailee by good faith dealings of the bailee with the transferor.

(3) A diversion or other change of shipping instructions by the consignor in a non-negotiable bill of lading which causes the bailee not to deliver to the consignee defeats the consignee's title to the goods if they have been delivered to a buyer in ordinary course of business and in any event defeats the consignee's rights against the bailee.

(4) Delivery pursuant to a non-negotiable document may be stopped by a seller under Section 2-705, and subject to the requirement of due notification there provided. A bailee honoring the seller's instructions is entitled to be indemnified by the seller against any resulting loss or expense.

§7-505. Indorser Not a Guarantor for Other Parties. The indorsement of a document of title issued by a bailee does not make the indorser liable for any default by the bailee or by previous indorsers.

§7-506. Delivery Without Indorsement: Right to Compel Indorsement. The transferee of a negotiable document of title has a specifically enforceable right to have his transferor supply any necessary indorsement but the transfer becomes a negotiation only as of the time the indorsement is supplied.

§7-507. Warranties on Negotiation or Transfer of Receipt or Bill. Where a person negotiates or transfers a document of title for value otherwise than as a mere intermediary under the next following section, then unless otherwise agreed he warrants to his immediate purchaser only in addition to any warranty made in selling the goods

(a) that the document is genuine; and

(b) that he has no knowledge of any fact which would impair its validity or worth; and

(c) that his negotiation or transfer is rightful and fully effective with respect to the title to the document and the goods it represents.

§7-508. Warranties of Collecting Bank as to Documents. A collecting bank or other intermediary known to be entrusted with documents on behalf of another or with collection of a draft or other claim against delivery of documents warrants by such delivery of the documents only its own good faith and authority. This rule applies even though the intermediary has purchased or made advances against the claim or draft to be collected.

§7-509. Receipt or Bill: When Adequate Compliance With Commercial Contract. The question whether a document is adequate to fulfill the obligations of a contract for sale or the conditions of a credit is governed by the Articles on Sales (Article 2) and on Letters of Credit (Article 5).

Part 6: Warehouse Receipts and Bills of Lading: Miscellaneous Provisions

§7-601. Lost and Missing Documents.

(1) If a document has been lost, stolen or destroyed, a court may order delivery of the goods or issuance of a substitute document and the bailee may without liability to any person comply with such order. If the document was negotiable the claimant must post security approved by the court to indemnify any person who may suffer loss as a result of non-surrender of the document. If the document was not negotiable, such security may be required at the discretion of the court. The court may also in its discretion order payment of the bailee's reasonable costs and counsel fees.

(2) A bailee who without court order delivers goods to a person claiming under a missing negotiable document is liable to any person injured thereby, and if the delivery is not in good faith becomes liable for conversion. Delivery in good faith is not conversion if made in accordance with a filed classification or tariff or, where no classification or tariff is filed, if the claimant posts security with the bailee in an amount as least double the value of the goods at the time of posting to indemnify any person injured by the delivery who files a notice of claim within one year after the delivery.

§7-602. Attachment of Goods Covered by a Negotiable Document. Except where the document was originally issued upon delivery of the goods by a person who has no power to dispose of them, no lien attaches by virtue of any judicial process to goods in the possession of a bailee for which a negotiable document of title is outstanding unless the document be first surrendered to the bailee or its negotiation enjoined, and the bailee shall not be compelled to deliver the goods pursuant to process until the document is surrendered to him or impounded by the court. One who purchases the document for value without notice of the process or injunction takes free of the lien imposed by judicial process.

§7-603. Conflicting Claims; Interpleader. If more than one person claims title or possession of the goods, the bailee is excused from delivery until he has had a reasonable time to ascertain the validity of the adverse claims or to bring an action to compel all claimants to interplead and may compel such interpleader, either in defending an action for nondelivery of the goods, or by original action, whichever is appropriate.

ARTICLE 8: INVESTMENT SECURITIES

Part 1: Short Title and General Matters

§8-101. Short Title. This Article shall be known and may be cited as Uniform Commercial Code—Investment Securities.

§8-102. Definitions and Index of Definitions

(1) In this Article, unless the context otherwise requires:

(a) A "certificated security" is a share, participation, or other interest in property of or an enterprise of the issuer or an obligation of the issuer which is

(i) represented by an instrument issued in bearer or registered form:

(ii) of a type commonly dealt in on securities exchanges or markets or commonly recognized in any area in which it is issued or dealt in as a medium for investment; and

(iii) either one of a class or series or by its terms divisible into a class or series of shares, participations, interest, or obligations.

(b) An "uncertificated security" is a share, participation, or other interest in property or an enterprise of the issuer or an obligation of the issuer which is

(i) not represented by an instrument and the transfer of which is registered upon books maintained for that purpose by or on behalf of the issuer;

(ii) of a type commonly dealt in on securities exchanges or markets; and

(iii) either one of a class or series or by its terms divisible into a class or series of shares, participations, interests, or obligations.

(c) A "security" is either a certificated or an uncertificated security. If a security is certificated, the terms "security" and "certificated security" may mean either the intangible interest, the instrument representing that interest, or both, as the context requires. A writing that is a certificated security is governed by this Article and not by Article 3, even though it also meets the requirements of that Article. This Article does not apply to money. If a certificated security has been retained by or surrendered to the issuer or its transfer agent for reasons other than registration of transfer, other temporary purpose, payment, exchange, or acquisition by the issuer, that security shall be treated as an uncertificated security for purposes of this Article.

(d) A certificated security is in "registered form" if

(i) its specifies a person entitled to the security or the rights it represents, and

(ii) its transfer may be registered upon books maintained for that purpose by or on behalf of the issuer, or the security so states.

(e) A certificated security is in "bearer from" if it runs to bearer according to its terms and not by reason of any indorsement.

(2) A "subsequent purchaser" is a person who takes other than by original issue.

(3) A "clearing corporation" is a corporation registered as a "clearing agency" under the federal securities laws or a corporation:

(a) at least 90 percent of whose capital stock is held by or for one or more organizations, none of which other than a national securities exchange or association, holds in excess of 20 percent of the capital stock of the corporation, and each of which is

(i) subject to supervision or regulation pursuant to the provisions of federal or state banking laws or state insurance laws,

(ii) a broker or dealer or investment company registered under the federal securities laws, or

(iii) a national securities exchange or association registered under the federal securities laws; and

(b) any remaining capital stock of which is held by individuals who have purchased at or prior to the time of their taking office as directors of the corporation and who have purchased only so much of the capital stock as is necessary to permit them to qualify as directors.

(4) A "custodian bank" is a bank or trust company that is supervised and examined by state or federal authority having supervision over banks and is acting as custodian for a clearing corporation.

(5) Other definitions applying to this Article or to specified Parts thereof and the sections in which they appear are:

"Adverse claim".	Section 8-302.
"Bona fide purchaser".	Section 8-302.
"Broker".	Section 8-303.
"Debtor".	Section 9-105.
"Financial intermediary".	Section 8-313.
"Guarantee of the signature".	Section 8-402.
"Intial transaction statement".	Section 8-408.
"Instruction".	Section 8-308.
"Intermediary Bank".	Section 4-105.
"Issuer".	Section 8-201.
"Overissue".	Section 8-104.
"Secured Party".	Section 9-105.
"Security Agreement".	Section 9-105.

(6) In addition Article 1 contains general definitions and principles of construction and interpretation applicable throughout this Article.

§8-103. Issuer's Lien. A lien upon a security in favor of an issuer thereof is valid against a purchaser only if:

(a) the security is certificated and the right of the issuer to the lien is noted conspicuously thereon; or

(b) the security is uncertificated and a notation of the right of the issuer to the lien is contained in the initial transaction statement sent to the purchaser or, if his interest is transferred to him other than by registration of transfer, pledge, or release, the initial transaction statement sent to the registered owner or the registered pledgee.

§8-104. Effect of Overissue; "Overissue".

(1) The provisions of this Article which validate a security or compel its issue or reissue do not apply to the extent that validation, issue, or reissue would result in overissue; but if:

(a) an identical security which does not constitute an overissue is reasonably available for purchase, the person entitled to issue or validation may compel the issuer to purchase the security for him and either to deliver a certificated security or to register the transfer of an uncertificated security to him, against surrender of any certificated security he holds; or

(b) a security is not so available for purchase, the person entitled to issue or validation may recover from the issuer the price he or the last purchaser for value paid for it with interest from the date of his demand.

(2) "Overissue" means the issue of securities in excess of the amount the issuer has corporate power to issue.

§8-105. Certificated Securities Negotiable; Statements and Instructions Not Negotiable; Presumptions.

(1) Certificated securities governed by this Article are negotiable instruments.

(2) Statements (Section 8-408), notices, or the like, sent by the issuer of uncertificated securities and instructions (Section 8-308) are neither negotiable instruments nor certificated securities.

(3) In any action on a security:

(a) unless specifically denied in the pleadings, each signature on a certificated security, in a necessary indorsement, on an initial transaction statement, or on an instruction, is admitted;

(b) if the effectiveness of a signature is put in issue, the burden of establishing it is on the party claiming under the signature, but the signature is presumed to be genuine or authorized;

(c) if signatures on a certificated security are admitted or established, production of the security entitles a holder to recover on it unless the defendant establishes a defense or a defect going to the validity of the security;

(d) if signatures on an initial transaction statement are admitted or established, the facts stated in the statement are presumed to be true as of the time of its issuance; and

(e) after it is shown that a defense or defect exists, the plaintiff has the burden of establishing that he or some person under whom he claims is a person against whom the defense or defect is ineffective (Section 8-202).

§8-106. Applicability. The law (including the conflict of law rules) of the jurisdiction of organization of the issuer governs the validity of a security, the effectiveness of registration by the issuer, and the rights and duties of the issuer with respect to:

(a) registration of transfer of a certificated security;

(b) registration of transfer, pledge, or release of an uncertificated security; and

(c) sending of statements of uncertificated securities.

§8-107. Securities Transferable; Action for Price.

(1) Unless otherwise agreed and subject to any applicable law or regulation respecting short sales, a person obligated to transfer securities may transfer any certificated security of the specified issue in bearer form or registered in the name of the transferee, or indorsed to him or in blank, or he may transfer an equivalent uncertificated security to the transferee or a person designated by the transferee.

(2) If the buyer fails to pay the price as it comes due under a contract of sale, the seller may recover the price of:

(a) certificated securities accepted by the buyer:

(b) uncertificated securities that have been transferred to

(**7**) Nothing in this Article shall be construed to affect the liability of the registered owner of a security for calls, assessments, or the like.

§8-208. Effect of Signature of Authenticating Trustee, Registrar, or Transfer Agent.

(**1**) A person placing his signature upon a certificated security or an initial transaction statement as authenticating trustee, registrar, transfer agent, or the like, warrants to a purchaser for value of the certificated security or a purchaser for value of an uncertificated security to whom the initial transaction statement has been sent, if the purchaser is without notice of the particular defect, that:

(**a**) the certificated security or initial transaction statement is genuine;

(**b**) his own participation in the issue or registration of the transfer, pledge, or release of the security is within his capacity and within the scope of the authority received by him from the issuer; and

(**c**) he has reasonable grounds to believe that the security is in the form and within the amount the issuer is authorized to issue.

(**2**) Unless otherwise agreed, a person by so placing his signature does not assume responsibility for the validity of the security in other respects.

Part 3: Transfer

§8-301. Rights Acquired by Purchaser

(**1**) Upon transfer of a security to a purchaser (Section 8-313), the purchaser acquires the rights in the security which his transferor had or had actual authority to convey unless the purchaser's rights are limited by Section 8-302 (4).

(**2**) A transferee of a limited interest acquires rights only to the extent of the interest transferred. The creation or release of a security interest in a security is the transfer of a limited interest in that security.

§8-302. "Bona Fide Purchaser"; "Adverse Claim"; Title Acquired by Bona Fide Purchaser.

(**1**) A "bona fide purchaser" is a purchaser for value in good faith and without notice of any adverse claim:

(**a**) who takes delivery of a certificated security in bearer form or in registered form, issued or indorsed to him or in blank;

(**b**) to whom the transfer, pledge or release of an uncertificated security is registered on the books of the issuer; or

(**c**) to whom a security is transferred under the provisions of paragraph (c) (d) (i), or (g) of Section 8-313(1).

(**2**) "Adverse claim" includes a claim that a transfer was or would be wrongful or that a particular adverse person is the owner of or has an interest in the security.

(**3**) A bona fide purchaser in addition to acquiring the rights of a purchaser (Section 8-301) also acquires his interest in the security free of any adverse claim.

(**4**) Notwithstanding Section 8-301(1), the transferee of a particular certificated security who has been a party to any fraud or illegality affecting the security, or who as a prior holder of that certificated security had notice of an adverse claim, cannot improve his position by taking from a bona fide purchaser.

§8-303. "Broker". "Broker" means a person engaged for all or part of his time in the business of buying and selling securities, who in the transaction concerned acts for, buys a security from, or sells a security to, a customer. Nothing in this Article determines the capacity in which a person acts for purposes of any other statute or rule to which the person is subject.

§8-304. Notice to Purchaser of Adverse Claims.

(**1**) A purchaser (including a broker for the seller or buyer, but excluding an intermediary bank) of a certificated security is charged with notice of adverse claims if:

(**a**) the security, whether in bearer or registered from, has been indorsed "for collection" or "for surrender" or for some other purpose not involving transfer; or

(**b**) the security is in bearer form and has on it an unambiguous statement that it is the property of a person other than the transferor. The mere writing of a name on a security is not such a statement.

(**2**) A purchaser (including a broker for the seller or buyer, but excluding an intermediary bank) to whom the transfer, pledge, or release of an uncertificated security is registered is charged with notice of adverse claims as to which the issuer has a duty under Section 8-403(4) at the time of registration and which are noted in the initial transaction statement sent to the purchaser or, if his interest is transferred to him other than by registration of transfer, pledge, or release, the initial transaction statement sent to the registered owner or the registered pledge.

(**3**) The fact that the purchaser (including a broker for the seller or buyer) of a certificated or uncertificated security has notice that the security is held for a third person or is registered in the name of or indorsed by a fiduciary does not create a duty of inquiry into the rightfulness of the transfer or constitute constructive notice of adverse claims. However, if the purchaser (excluding an intermediary bank) has knowledge that the proceeds are being used or the transaction is for the individual benefit of the fiduciary or otherwise in breach of duty, the purchaser is charged with notice of adverse claims.

§8-305. Staleness as Notice of Adverse Claims. An act or event that creates a right to immediate performance of the principal obligation represented by a certificated security or sets a date on or after which a certificated security is to be presented or surrendered for redemption or exchange does not itself constitute any notice of adverse claims except in the case of a transfer:

(**a**) after one year from any date set for presentment or surrender for redemption or exchange; or

(**b**) after 6 months from any date set for payment of money against presentation or surrender of the security if funds are available for payment on that date.

§8-306. Warranties on Presentment and Transfer of Certificated Securities; Warranties of Originators of Instructions.

(1) A person who presents a certificated security for registration of transfer or for payment or exchange warrants to the issuer that he is entitled to the registration, payment, or exchange. But, a purchaser for value and without notice of adverse claims who receives a new, reissued, or re-registered certificated security on registration of transfer or receives an initial transaction statement confirming the registration of transfer of an equivalent uncertificated security to him warrants only that he has no knowledge of any unauthorized signature (Section 8-311) in a necessary indorsement.

(2) A person by transferring a certificated security to a purchaser for value warrants only that:

(a) his transfer is effective and rightful;

(b) the security is genuine and has not been materially altered; and

(c) he knows of no fact which might impair the validity of the security.

(3) If a certificated security is delivered by an intermediary known to be entrusted with delivery of the security on behalf of another or with collection of a draft or claim against delivery, the intermediary by delivery warrants only his own good faith and authority, even though he has purchased or made advances against the claim to be collected against the delivery.

(4) A pledgee or other holder for security who redelivers a certificated security received, or after payment and on order of the debtor delivers that security to a third person makes only the warranties of an intermediary under subsection (3).

(5) A person who originates an instruction warrants to the issuer that:

(a) he is an appropriate person to originate the instruction; and

(b) at the time the instruction is presented to the issuer he will be entitled to the registration of transfer, pledge, or release.

(6) A person who originates an instruction warrants to any person specially guaranteeing his signature (subsection 8-312 (3)) that:

(a) he is an appropriate person to originate the instruction; and

(b) at the time the instruction is presented to the issuer

(i) he will be entitled to the registration of transfer, pledge, or release; and

(ii) the transfer, pledge, or release requested in the instruction will be registered by the issuer free from all liens, security interests, restrictions, and claims other than those specified in the instruction.

(7) A person who originates an instruction warrants to a purchaser for value and to any person guaranteeing the instruction (Section 8-312(6)) that:

(a) he is an appropriate person to originate the instruction;

(b) the uncertificated security referred to therein is valid; and

(c) at the time the instruction is presented to the issuer

(i) the transferor will be entitled to the registration of transfer, pledge, or release;

(ii) the transfer, pledge, or release requested in the instruction will be registered by the issuer free from all liens, security interests, restrictions, and claims other than those specified in the instruction; and

(iii) the requested transfer, pledge, or release will be rightful.

(8) If a secured party is the registered pledgee or the registered owner of an uncertificated security, a person who originates an instruction of release or transfer to the debtor or, after payment and on order of the debtor, a transfer instruction to a third person, warrants to the debtor or the third person only that he is an appropriate person to originate the instruction and at the time the instruction is presented to the issuer, the transferor will be entitled to the registration of release or transfer. If a transfer instruction to a third person who is a purchaser for value is originated on order of the debtor, the debtor makes to the purchaser the warranties of paragraphs (b), (c)(ii) and (c)(iii) of subsection (7).

(9) A person who transfers an uncertificated security to a purchaser for value and does not originate an instruction in connection with the transfer warrants only that:

(a) his transfer is effective and rightful; and

(b) the uncertificated security is valid.

(10) A broker gives to his customer and to the issuer and a purchaser the applicable warranties provided in this section and has the rights and privileges of a purchaser under this section. The warranties of and in favor of the broker acting as an agent are in addition to applicable warranties given by and in favor of his customer.

§8-307. Effect of Delivery Without Indorsement; Right to Compel Indorsement. If a certificated security in registered form has been delivered to a purchaser without a necessary indorsement he may become a bona fide purchaser only as of the time the indorsement is supplied; but against the transferor, the transfer is complete upon delivery and the purchaser has a specifically enforceable right to have any necessary indorsement supplied.

§8-308. Indorsements; Instructions.

(1) An indorsement of a certificated security in registered form is made when an appropriate person signs on it or on a separate document an assignment or transfer of the security or a power to assign or transfer it or his signature is written without more upon the back of the security.

(2) An indorsement may be in blank or special. An indorsement in blank includes an indorsement to bearer. A special indorsement specifies to whom the security is to be transferred, or who has power to transfer it. A holder may convert a blank indorsement into a special indorsement.

(3) An indorsement purporting to be only of part of a certificated security representing units intended by the issuer to be separately transferable is effective to the extent of the indorsement.

(4) An "instruction" is an order to the issuer of an uncertifi-

cated security requesting that the transfer, pledge, or release from pledge of the uncertificated security specified therein be registered.

(5) An instruction originated by an appropriate person is:

(a) a writing signed by an appropriate person; or

(b) a communication to the issuer in any form agreed upon in a writing signed by the issuer and an appropriate person.

If an instruction has been originated by an appropriate person but is incomplete in any other respect, any person may complete it as authorized and the issuer may rely on it as completed even though it has been completed incorrectly.

(6) "An appropriate person" in subsection (1) means the person specified by the certificated security or by special indorsement to be entitled to the security.

(7) "An appropriate person" in subsection (5) means:

(a) for an instruction to transfer or pledge an uncertificated security which is then not subject to a registered pledge, the registered owner; or

(b) for an instruction to transfer or release an uncertificated security which is then subject to a registered pledge, the registered pledgee.

(8) In addition to the persons designated in subsections (6) and (7), "an appropriate person" in subsections (1) and (5) includes:

(a) if the person designated is described as a fiduciary but is no longer serving in the described capacity, either that person or his successor;

(b) if the persons designated are described as more than one person as fiduciaries and one or more are no longer serving in the described capacity, the remaining fiduciary or fiduciaries, whether or not a successor has been appointed or qualified;

(c) if the person designated is an individual and is without capacity to act by virtue of death; incompetence, infancy, or otherwise his executor, administrator, guardian, or like fiduciary;

(d) if the persons designated are described as more than one person as tenants by the entirety or with right of survivorship and by reason of death all cannot sign the survivor or survivors;

(e) a person having power to sign under applicable law or controlling instrument; and

(f) to the extent that the person designated or any of the foregoing persons may act through an agent, his authorized agent.

(9) Unless otherwise agreed, the indorser of a certificated security by his indorsement or the originator of an instruction by his origination assumes no obligation that the security will be honored by the issuer but only the obligations provided in Section 8-306.

(10) Whether the person signing is appropriate is determined as of the date of signing and an indorsement made by or an instruction originated by him does not become unauthorized for the purposes of this Article by virtue of any subsequent change of circumstances.

(11) Failure of a fiduciary to comply with a controlling instrument or with the law of the state having jurisdiction of the fiduciary relationship, including any law requiring the fiduciary to obtain court approval of the transfer, pledge, or release, does not render his indorsement or an instruction originated by him unauthorized for the purposes of this Article.

§8-309. Effect of Indorsement Without Delivery. An indorsement of a certificated security, whether special or in blank, does not constitute a transfer until delivery of the certificated security on which it appears or, if the indorsement is on a separate document, until delivery of both the document and the certificated security.

§8-310. Indorsement of Certificated Security in Bearer Form. An indorsement of a certificated security in bearer form may give notice of adverse claims (Section 8-304) but does not otherwise affect any right to registration the holder possesses.

§8-311. Effect of Unauthorized Indorsement or Instruction. Unless the owner, or pledgee has ratified an unauthorized indorsement or instruction or is otherwise precluded from asserting its ineffectiveness:

(a) he may assert its ineffectiveness against the issuer or any purchaser, other than a purchaser for value and without notice of adverse claims, who has in good faith received a new, reissued, or re-registered certificated security on registration of transfer or received an initial transaction statement confirming the registration of transfer, pledge, or release of an equivalent uncertificated security to him; and

(b) an issuer who registers the transfer of a certificated security upon the unauthorized indorsement or who registers the transfer, pledge, or release of an uncertificated security upon the unauthorized instruction is subject to liability for improper registration (Section 8-104).

§8-312. Effect of Guaranteeing Signature, Indorsement or Instruction.

(1) Any person guaranteeing a signature of an indorser of a certificated security warrants that at the time of signing:

(a) the signature was genuine;

(b) the signer was an appropriate person to indorse (Section 8-308); and

(c) the signer had legal capacity to sign.

(2) Any person guaranteeing a signature of the originator of an instruction warrants that at the time of signing:

(a) the signature was genuine;

(b) the signer was an appropriate person to originate the instruction (Section 8-308) if the person specified in the instruction as the registered owner or registered pledgee of the uncertificated security was, in fact, the registered owner or registered pledgee of such security, as to which fact the signature guarantor makes no warranty;

(c) the signer had legal capacity to sign; and

(d) the taxpayer identification number, if any, appearing on the instruction as that of the registered owner or registered pledgee was the taxpayer identification number of the signer or of the owner or pledgee for whom the signer was acting.

(3) Any person specially guaranteeing the signature of the originator of an instruction makes not only the warranties of a signature guarantor (Subsection (2)) but also warrants that at the time the instruction is presented to the issuer:

(a) the person specified in the instruction as the registered owner or registered pledgee of the uncertificated security will be the registered owner or registered pledgee; and

(b) the transfer, pledge, or release of the uncertificated security requested in the instruction will be registered by the issuer free from all liens, security interests, restrictions, and claims other than those specified in the instruction.

(4) The guarantor under subsections (1) and (2) or the special guarantor under subsection (3) does not otherwise warrant the rightfulness of the particular transfer, pledge, or release.

(5) Any person guaranteeing an indorsement of a certificated security makes not only the warranties of a signature guarantor under subsection (1) but also warrants the rightfulness of the particular transfer in all respects.

(6) Any person guaranteeing an instruction requesting the transfer, pledge, or release of an uncertificated security makes not only the warranties of a special signature guarantor under subsection (3) but also warrants the rightfulness of the particular transfer, pledge, or release in all respects.

(7) No issuer may require a special guarantee of signature (subsection (3)), a guarantee of indorsement (subsection (5)), or a guarantee of instruction (subsection (6)) as a condition to registration of transfer, pledge, or release.

(8) The foregoing warranties are made to any person taking or dealing with the security in reliance on the guarantee, and the guarantor is liable to the person for any loss resulting from breach of the warranties.

§8-313. When Transfer to Purchaser Occurs: Financial Intermediary as Bona Fide Purchaser; "Financial Intermediary".

(1) Transfer of a security or a limited interest (including a security interest) therein to a purchaser occurs only:

(a) at the time he or a person designated by him acquires possession of a certificated security;

(b) at the time the transfer, pledge, or release of an uncertificated security is registered to him or a person designated by him:

(c) at the time his financial intermediary acquires possession of a certificated security specially indorsed to or issued in the name of the purchaser;

(d) at the time a financial intermediary, not a clearing corporation, sends him confirmation of the purchase and also by book entry or otherwise identifies as belonging to the purchaser

(i) a specific certificated security in the financial intermediary's possession;

(ii) a quantity of securities that constitute or are part of a fungible bulk of certificated securities in the financial intermediary's possession or of uncertificated securities registered in the name of the financial intermediary; or

(iii) a quantity of securities that constitute or are part of a fungible bulk of securities shown on the account of the financial intermediary on the books of another financial intermediary;

(e) with respect to an identified certificated security to be delivered while still in the possession of a third person, not a financial intermediary, at the time that person acknowledges that he holds for the purchaser;

(f) with respect to a specific uncertificated security the pledge or transfer of which has been registered to a third person, not a financial intermediary, at the time that person acknowledges that he holds for the purchaser;

(g) at the time appropriate entries to the account of the purchaser or a person designated by him on the books of a clearing corporation are made under Section 8-320;

(h) with respect to the transfer of a security interest where the debtor has signed a security agreement containing a description of the security, at the time a written notification, which, in the case of the creation of the security interest, is signed by the debtor (which may be a copy of the security agreement) or which, in the case of the release or assignment of the security interest created pursuant to this paragraph, is signed by the secured party, is received by

(i) a financial intermediary on whose books the interest of the transferor in the security appears:

(ii) a third person, not a financial intermediary, in possession of the security, if it is certificated;

(iii) a third person, not a financial intermediary, who is the registered owner of the security, if it is uncertificated and not subject to a registered pledge; or

(iv) a third person, not a financial intermediary, who is the registered pledgee of the security, if it is uncertificated and subject to a registered pledge;

(i) with respect to the transfer of a security interest where the transferor has signed a security agreement containing a description of the security, at the time new value is given by the secured party; or

(j) with respect to the transfer of a security interest where the secured party is a financial intermediary and the security has already been transferred to the financial intermediary under paragraphs (a), (b), (c), (d), or (g), at the time the transferor has signed a security agreement containing a description of the security and value is given by the secured party.

(2) The purchaser is the owner of a security held for him by a financial intermediary, but cannot be a bona fide purchaser of a security so held except in the circumstances specified in paragraphs (c), (d)(i), and (g) of subsection (1). If a security so held is part of a fungible bulk, as in the circumstances specified in paragraphs (d)(ii) and (d)(iii) of subsection (1), the purchaser is the owner of a proportionate property interest in the fungible bulk.

(3) Notice of an adverse claim received by the financial

intermediary or by the purchaser after the financial intermediary takes delivery of a certificated security as a holder for value or after the transfer, pledge, or release of an uncertificated security has been registered free of the claim to a financial intermediary who has given value is not effective either as to the financial intermediary or as to the purchaser. However, as between the financial intermediary and the purchaser the purchaser may demand transfer of an equivalent security as to which no notice of adverse claim has been received.

(4) A "financial intermediary" is a bank, broker, clearing corporation or other person (or the nominee of any of them) which in the ordinary course of its business maintains security accounts for its customers and is acting in that capacity. A financial intermediary may have a security interest in securities held in account for its customer.

§8-314. Duty to Transfer, When Completed.

(1) Unless otherwise agreed, if a sale of a security is made on an exchange or otherwise through brokers:

(a) the selling customer fulfills his duty to transfer at the time he:

(i) places a certificated security in the possession of the selling broker or of a person designated by the broker;

(ii) causes an uncertificated security to be registered in the name of the selling broker or a person designated by the broker;

(iii) if requested, causes an acknowledgment to be made to the selling broker that a certificated or uncertificated security is held for the broker; or

(iv) places in the possession of the selling broker or of a person designated by the broker a transfer instruction for an uncertificated security, providing the issuer does not refuse to register the requested transfer if the instruction is presented to the issuer for registration within 30 days thereafter; and

(b) the selling broker, including a correspondent broker acting for a selling customer, fulfills his duty to transfer at the time he:

(i) places a certificated security in the possession of the buying broker or a person designated by the buying broker;

(ii) causes an uncertificated security to be registered in the name of the buying broker or a person designated by the buying broker;

(iii) places in the possession of the buying broker or of a person designated by the buying broker a transfer instruction for an uncertificated security, providing the issuer does not refuse to register the requested transfer if the instruction is presented to the issuer for registration within 30 days thereafter; or

(iv) effects clearance of the sale in accordance with the rules of the exchange on which the transaction took place.

(2) Except as provided in this section and unless otherwise agreed, a transferor's duty to transfer a security under a contract of purchase is not fulfilled until he:

(a) places a certificated security in form to be negotiated by the purchaser in the possession of the purchaser or of a person designated by the purchaser;

(b) causes an uncertificated security to be registered in the name of the purchaser or a person designated by the purchaser; or

(c) if the purchaser requests, causes an acknowledgment to be made to the purchaser that certificated or uncertificated security is held for the purchaser.

(3) Unless made on an exchange, a sale to a broker purchasing for his own account is within subsection (2) and not within subsection (1).

§8-315. Action Against Transferee Based Upon Wrongful Transfer.

(1) Any person against whom the transfer of a security is wrongful for any reason, including his incapacity, as against anyone except a bona fide purchaser, may:

(a) reclaim possession of the certificated security wrongfully transferred;

(b) obtain possession of any new certificated security representing all or part of the same rights:

(c) compel the origination of an instruction to transfer to him or a person designated by him an uncertificated security constituting all or part of the same rights; or

(d) have damages.

(2) If the transfer is wrongful because of an unauthorized indorsement of a certificated security, the owner may also reclaim or obtain possession of the security or a new certificated security, even from a bona fide purchaser, if the ineffectiveness of the purported indorsement can be asserted against him under the provisions of this Article on unauthorized indorsements (Section 8-311).

(3) The right to obtain or reclaim possession of a certificated security or to compel the origination of a transfer instruction may be specifically enforced and the transfer of a certificated or uncertificated security enjoined and a certificated security impounded pending the litigation.

§8-316. Purchaser's Right to Requisites for Registration of Transfer, Pledge, or Release on Books. Unless otherwise agreed, the transferor of a certificated security or the transferor, pledgor, or pledgee of an uncertificated security on due demand must supply his purchaser with any proof of his authority to transfer, pledge, or release or with any other requisite necessary to obtain registration of the transfer, pledge, or release of the security; but if the transfer, pledge, or release is not for value, a transferor, pledgor, or pledgee need not do so unless the purchaser furnishes the necessary expenses. Failure within a reasonable time to comply with a demand made gives the purchaser the right to reject or rescind the transfer, pledge, or release.

§8-317. Creditors' Rights.

(1) Subject to the exceptions in subsections (3) and (4), no attachment or levy upon a certificated security or any share or other interest represented thereby which is outstanding is valid

until the security is actually seized by the officer making the attachment or levy, but a certificated security which has been surrendered to the issuer may be reached by a creditor by legal process at the issuer's chief executive office in the United States.

(2) An uncertificated security registered in the name of the debtor may not be reached by a creditor except by legal process at the issuer's chief executive office in the United States.

(3) The interest of a debtor in a certificated security that is in the possession of a secured party not a financial intermediary or in an uncertificated security registered in the name of a secured party not a financial intermediary (or in the name of a nominee of the secured party) may be reached by a creditor by legal process upon the secured party.

(4) The interest of a debtor in a certificated security that is in the possession of or registered in the name of a financial intermediary or in an uncertificated security registered in the name of a financial intermediary may be reached by a creditor by legal process upon the financial intermediary on whose books the interest of the debtor appears.

(5) Unless otherwise provided by law, a creditor's lien upon the interest of a debtor in a security obtained pursuant to subsection (3) or (4) is not a restraint on the transfer of the security, free of the lien, to a third party for new value; but in the event of a transfer, the lien applies to the proceeds of the transfer in the hands of the secured party or financial intermediary, subject to any claims having priority.

(6) A creditor whose debtor is the owner of a security is entitled to aid from courts of appropriate jurisdiction, by injunction or otherwise, in reaching the security or in satisfying the claim by means allowed at law or in equity in regard to property that cannot readily be reached by ordinary legal process.

§8-318. No Conversion by Good Faith Conduct. An agent or bailee who in good faith (including the observance of reasonable commercial standards if he is in the business of buying, selling, or otherwise dealing with securities) has received certificated securities and sold, pledged, or delivered them or has sold or caused the transfer or pledge of uncertificated securities over which he had control according to the instructions of his principal, is not liable for conversion or for participation in breach of fiduciary duty although the principal had no right so to deal with the securities.

§8-319. Statute of Frauds. A contract for the sale of securities is not enforceable by way of action or defense unless:

(a) there is some writing signed by the party against whom enforcement is sought or by his authorized agent or broker, sufficient to indicate that a contract has been made for sale of a stated quantity of described securities at a defined or stated price;

(b) delivery of a certificated security or transfer instruction has been accepted, or transfer of an uncertificated security has been registered and the transferee has failed to send written objection to the issuer within 10 days after receipt of the initial transaction statement confirming the registration, or payment has been made, but the contract is enforceable under this provision only to the extent the delivery, registration, or payment;

(c) within a reasonable time a writing in confirmation of the sale or purchase and sufficient against the sender under paragraph (a) has been received by the party against whom enforcement is sought and he has failed to send written objection to its contents within 10 days after its receipt; or

(d) the party against whom enforcement is sought admits in his pleading, testimony, or otherwise in court that a contract was made for the sale of a stated quantity of described securities at a defined or stated price.

§8-320. Transfer or Pledge Within Central Depository System.

(1) In addition to other methods, a transfer, pledge, or release of a security or any interest therein may be effected by the making of appropriate entries on the books of a clearing corporation reducing the account of the transferor, pledgor, or pledgee and increasing the account of the transferee, pledgee, or pledgor by the amount of the obligation, or the number of shares or rights transferred, pledged, or released, if the security is shown on the account of a transferor, pledgor, or pledgee on the books of the clearing corporation; is subject to the control of the clearing corporation; and

(a) if certificated,

(i) is in the custody of the clearing corporation, another clearing corporation, a custodian bank or a nominee of any of them; and

(ii) is in bearer form or indorsed in blank by an appropriate person or registered in the name of the clearing corporation, a custodian bank, or a nominee of any of them; or

(b) if uncertificated, is registered in the name of the clearing corporation, another clearing corporation, a custodian bank, or a nominee of any of them.

(2) Under this section entries may be made with respect to like securities or interests therein as a part of a fungible bulk and may refer merely to a quantity of a particular security without reference to the name of the registered owner, certificate or bond number, or the like, and, in appropriate cases, may be on a net basis taking into account other transfers, pledges, or releases of the same security.

(3) A transfer under this section is effective (Section 8-313) and the purchaser acquires the rights of the transferor (Section 8-301). A pledge or release under this section is the transfer of a limited interest. If a pledge or the creation of a security interest is intended, the security interest is perfected at the time when both value is given by the pledgee and the appropriate entries are made (Section 8-321). A transferee or pledgee under this section may be a bona fide purchaser (Section 8-302).

(4) A transfer or pledge under this section is not a registration of transfer under Part 4.

(5) That entries made on the books of the clearing corporation as provided in subsection (1) are not appropriate does not affect the validity or effect of the entries or the liabilities or

obligations of the clearing corporation to any person adversely affected thereby.

§8-321. Enforceability, Attachment, Perfection, and Termination of Security Interests.

(1) A security interest in a security is enforceable and can attach only if it is transferred to the secured party or a person designated by him pursuant to a provision of Section 8-313(1).

(2) A security interest so transferred pursuant to agreement by a transferor who has rights in the security to a transferee who has given value is a perfected security interest, but a security interest that has been transferred solely under paragraph (i) of Section 8-313(1) becomes unperfected after 21 days unless, within that time, the requirements for transfer under any other provision of Section 8-313(1) are satisfied.

(3) A security interest in a security is subject to the provisions of Article 9, but:

(a) no filing is required to perfect the security interest; and

(b) no written security agreement signed by the debtor is necessary to make the security interest enforceable, except as otherwise provided in paragraph (h), (i), or (j) of Section 8-313(1).

The secured party has the rights and duties provided under Section 9-207, to the extent they are applicable, whether or not the security is certificated, and, if certificated, whether or not it is in his possession.

(4) Unless otherwise agreed, a security interest in a security is terminated by transfer to the debtor or a person designated by him pursuant to a provision of Section 8-313(1). If a security is thus transferred, the security interest, if not terminated, becomes unperfected unless the security is certificated and is delivered to the debtor for the purpose of ultimate sale or exchange or presentation, collection, renewal, or registration of transfer. In that case, the security interest becomes unperfected after 21 days unless, within that time, the security (or securities for which it has been exchanged) is transferred to the secured party or a person designated by him pursuant to a provision of Section 8-313(1).

Part 4: Registration

§8-401. Duty of Issuer to Register Transfer, Pledge, or Release.

(1) If a certificated security in registered form is presented to the issuer with a request to register transfer or an instruction is presented to the issuer with a request to register transfer, pledge, or release, the issuer shall register the transfer, pledge, or release as requested if:

(a) the security is indorsed or the instruction was originated by the appropriate person or persons (Section 8-308);

(b) reasonable assurance is given that those indorsements or instructions are genuine and effective (Section 8-402);

(c) the issuer has no duty as to adverse claims or has discharged the duty (Section 8-403);

(d) any applicable law relating to the collection of taxes has been complied with; and

(e) the transfer, pledge, or release is in fact rightful or is to a bona fide purchaser.

(2) If an issuer is under a duty to register a transfer, pledge, or release of a security, the issuer is also liable to the person presenting a certificated security or an instruction for registration or his principal for loss resulting from any unreasonable delay in registration or from failure or refusal to register the transfer, pledge, or release.

§8-402. Assurance that Indorsements and Instructions Are Effective.

(1) The issuer may require the following assurance that each necessary indorsement of a certificated security or each instruction (Section 8-308) is genuine and effective:

(a) in all cases, a guarantee of the signature (Section 8-312(1) or (2)) of the person indorsing a certificated security or originating an instruction including, in the case of an instruction, a warranty of the taxpayer identification number or, in the absence thereof, other reasonable assurance of identity:

(b) if the indorsement is made or the instruction is originated by an agent, appropriate assurance of authority to sign;

(c) if the indorsement is made or the instruction is originated by a fiduciary, appropriate evidence of appointment or incumbency;

(d) if there is more than one fiduciary, reasonable assurance that all who are required to sign have done so; and

(e) if the indorsement is made or the instruction is originated by a person not covered by any of the foregoing, assurance appropriate to the case corresponding as nearly as may be to the foregoing.

(2) A "guarantee of the signature" in subsection (1) means a guarantee signed by or on behalf of a person reasonably believed by the issuer to be responsible. The issuer may adopt standards with respect to responsibility if they are not manifestly unreasonable.

(3) "Appropriate evidence of appointment or incumbency" in subsection (1) means:

(a) in the case of a fiduciary appointed or qualified by a court, a certificate issued by or under the direction or supervision of that court or an officer thereof and dated within 60 days before the date of presentation for transfer, pledge, or release; or

(b) in any other case, a copy of a document showing the appointment or a certificate issued by or on behalf of a person reasonably believed by the issuer to be responsible or, in the absence of that document or certificate, other evidence reasonably deemed by the issuer to be appropriate. The issuer may adopt standards with respect to the evidence if they are not manifestly unreasonable. The issuer is not charged with notice of the contents of any document obtained pursuant to this paragraph (b) except to the extent that the contents relate directly to the appointment or incumbency.

(4) The issuer may elect to require reasonable assurance beyond that specified in this section, but if it does so and, for a purpose other than that specified in subsection (3)(b), both requires and obtains a copy of a will, trust, indenture, articles of co-partnership, by-laws, or other controlling instrument, it is charged with notice of all matters contained therein affecting the transfer, pledge, or release.

§8-403. Issuer's Duty as to Adverse Claims.

(1) An issuer to whom a certificated security is presented for registration shall inquire into adverse claims if:

(a) a written notification of an adverse claim is received at a time and in a manner affording the issuer a reasonable opportunity to act on it prior to the issuance of a new, reissued, or re-registered certificated security, and the notification identifies the claimant, the registered owner, and the issue of which the security is a part, and provides an address for communications directed to the claimant; or

(b) the issuer is charged with notice of an adverse claim from a controlling instrument it has elected to require under Section 8-402(4).

(2) The issuer may discharge any duty of inquiry by any reasonable means, including notifying an adverse claimant by registered or certified mail at the address furnished by him or, if there be no such address, at his residence or regular place of business that the certificated security has been presented for registration of transfer by a named person, and that the transfer will be registered unless within 30 days from the date of mailing the notification, either:

(a) an appropriate restraining order, injunction, or other process issues from a court of competent jurisdiction; or

(b) there is filed with the issuer an indemnity bond, sufficient in the issuer's judgment to protect the issuer and any transfer agent, registrar, or other agent of the issuer involved from any loss it or they may suffer by complying with the adverse claim.

(3) Unless an issuer is charged with notice of an adverse claim from a controlling instrument which it has elected to require under Section 8-402(4) or receives notification of an adverse claim under subsection (1), if a certificated security presented for registration is indorsed by the appropriate person or persons the issuer is under no duty to inquire into adverse claims. In particular:

(a) an issuer registering a certificated security in the name of a person who is a fiduciary or who is described as a fiduciary is not bound to inquire into the existence, extent, or correct description of the fiduciary relationship; and thereafter the issuer may assume without inquiry that the newly registered owner continues to be the fiduciary until the issuer receives written notice that the fiduciary is no longer acting as such with respect to the particular security;

(b) an issuer registering transfer on an indorsement by a fiduciary is not bound to inquire whether the transfer is made in compliance with a controlling instrument or with the law of the state having jurisdiction of the fiduciary relationship, including any law requiring the fiduciary to obtain court approval of the transfer; and

(c) the issuer is not charged with notice of the contents of any court record or file or other recorded or unrecorded document even though the document is in its possession and even though the transfer is made on the indorsement of a fiduciary to the fiduciary himself or to his nominee.

(4) An issuer is under not duty as to adverse claims with respect to an uncertificated security except:

(a) claims embodied in a restraining order, injunction, or other legal process served upon the issuer if the process was served at a time and in a manner affording the issuer a reasonable opportunity to act on it in accordance with the requirements of subsection (5);

(b) claims of which the issuer has received a written notification from the registered owner or the registered pledgee if the notification was received at a time and in a manner affording the issuer a reasonable opportunity to act on it in accordance with the requirements of subsection (5);

(c) claims (including restrictions on transfer not imposed by the issuer) to which the registration of transfer to the present registered owner was subject and were so noted in the initial transaction statement sent to him; and

(d) claims as to which an issuer is charged with notice from a controlling instrument it has elected to require under Section 8-402(4).

(5) If the issuer of an uncertificated security is under a duty as to an adverse claim, he discharges that duty by:

(a) including a notation of the claim in any statements sent with respect to the security under Sections 8-408(3), (6), and (7); and

(b) refusing to register the transfer or pledge of the security unless the nature of the claim does not preclude transfer or pledge subject thereto.

(6) If the transfer or pledge of the security is registered subject to an adverse claim, a notation of the claim must be included in the initial transaction statement and all subsequent statements sent to the transferee and pledgee under Section 8-408.

(7) Notwithstanding subsections (4) and (5), if an uncertificated security was subject to a registered pledge at the time the issuer first came under a duty as to a particular adverse claim, the issuer has no duty as to that claim if transfer of the security is requested by the registered pledgee or an appropriate person acting for the registered pledgee unless:

(a) the claim was embodied in legal process which expressly provides otherwise;

(b) the claim was asserted in a written notification from the registered pledgee;

(c) the claim was one as to which the issuer was charged with notice from a controlling instrument it required under Section 8-402(4) in connection with the pledgee's request for transfer; or

(d) the transfer requested is to the registered owner.

§8-404. Liability and Non-Liability for Registration.

(1) Except as provided in any law relating to the collection of taxes, the issuer is not liable to the owner, pledgee, or any other person suffering loss as a result of the registration of a transfer, pledge, or release of a security if:

(a) there were on or with a certificated security the necessary indorsements or the issuer had received an instruction originated by an appropriate person (Section 8-308); and

(b) the issuer had no duty as to adverse claims or has discharged the duty (Section 8-403).

(2) If an issuer has registered a transfer of a certificated security to a person not entitled to it, the issuer on demand shall deliver a like security to the true owner unless:

(a) the registration was pursuant to subsection (1);

(b) the owner is precluded from asserting any claim for registering the transfer under Section 8-405(1); or

(c) the delivery would result in overissue, in which case the issuer's liability is governed by Section 8-104.

(3) If an issuer has improperly registered a transfer, pledge, or release of an uncertificated security, the issuer on demand from the injured party shall restore the records as to the injured party to the condition that would have obtained if the improper registration had not been made unless:

(a) the registration was pursuant to subsection (1); or

(b) the registration would result in overissue, in which case the issuer's liability is governed by Section 8-104.

§8-405. Lost, Destroyed, and Stolen Certificated Securities.

(1) If a certificated security has been lost, apparently destroyed, or wrongfully taken, and the owner fails to notify the issuer of that fact within a reasonable time after he has notice of it and the issuer registers a transfer of the security before receiving notification, the owner is precluded from asserting against the issuer any claim for registering the transfer under Section 8-404 or any claim to a new security under this section.

(2) If the owner of a certificated security claims that the security has been lost, destroyed, or wrongfully taken, the issuer shall issue a new certificated security or, at the option of the issuer, an equivalent uncertificated security in place of the original security if the owner:

(a) so requests before the issuer has notice that the security has been acquired by a bona fide purchaser;

(b) files with the issuer a sufficient indemnity bond; and

(c) satisfies any other reasonable requirements imposed by the issuer.

(3) If, after the issue of a new certificated or uncertificated security, a bona fide purchaser of the original certificated security presents it for registration of transfer, the issuer shall register the transfer unless registration would result in overissue, in which event the issuer's liability is governed by Section 8-104. In addition to any rights on the indemnity bond, the issuer may recover the new certificated security from the person to whom it was issued or any person taking under him except a bona fide purchaser or may cancel the uncertificated security unless a bona fide purchaser or any person taking under a bona fide purchaser is then the registered owner or registered pledgee thereof.

§8-406. Duty of Authenticating Trustee, Transfer Agent, or Registrar.

(1) If a person acts as authenticating trustee, transfer agent, registrar, or other agent for an issuer in the registration of transfers of its certificated securities or in the registration of transfers, pledges, and releases of its uncertificated securities, in the issue of new securities, or in the cancellation of surrendered securities:

(a) he is under a duty to the issuer to exercise good faith and due diligence in performing his functions; and

(b) with regard to the particular functions he performs, he has the same obligation to the holder or owner of a certificated security or to the owner or pledgee of an uncertificated security and has the same rights and privileges as the issuer has in regard to those functions.

(2) Notice to an authenticating trustee, transfer agent, registrar or other agent is notice to the issuer with respect to the functions performed by the agent.

§8-407. Exchangeability of Securities.

(1) No issuer is subject to the requirements of this section unless it regularly maintains a system for issuing the class of securities involved under which both certificated and uncertificated securities are regularly issued to the category of owners, which includes the person in whose name the new security is to be registered.

(2) Upon surrender of a certificated security with all necessary indorsements and presentation of a written request by the person surrendering the security, the issuer, if he has no duty as to adverse claims or has discharged the duty (Section 8-403), shall issue to the person or a person designated by him an equivalent uncertificated security subject to all liens, restrictions, and claims that were noted on the certificated security.

(3) Upon receipt of a transfer instruction originated by an appropriate person who so requests, the issuer of an uncertificated security shall cancel the uncertificated security and issue an equivalent certificated security on which must be noted conspicuously any liens and restrictions of the issuer and any adverse claims (as to which the issuer has a duty under Section 8-403(4)) to which the uncertificated security was subject. The certificated security shall be registered in the name of and delivered to:

(a) the registered owner, if the uncertificated security was not subject to a registered pledge; or

(b) the registered pledgee, if the uncertificated security was subject to a registered pledge.

§8-408. Statements of Uncertificated Securities.

(1) Within 2 business days after the transfer of an uncertificated security has been registered, the issuer shall send to the new registered owner and, if the security has been transferred subject to a registered pledge, to the registered pledgee a written statement containing:

(a) a description of the issue of which the uncertificated

security is a part;

(b) the number of shares or units transferred;

(c) the name and address and any taxpayer identification number of the new registered owner and, if the security has been transferred subject to a registered pledge, the name and address and any taxpayer identification number of the registered pledgee;

(d) a notation of any liens and restrictions of the issuer and any adverse claims (as to which the issuer has a duty under Section 8-403(4)) to which the uncertificated security is or may be subject at the time of registration or a statement that there are none of those liens, restrictions, or adverse claims; and

(e) the date the transfer was registered.

(2) Within 2 business days after the pledge of an uncertificated security has been registered, the issuer shall send to the registered owner and the registered pledgee a written statement containing:

(a) a description of the issue of which the uncertificated security is a part;

(b) the number of shares or units pledged;

(c) the name and address and any taxpayer identification number of the registered owner and the registered pledgee;

(d) a notation of any liens and restrictions of the issuer and any adverse claims (as to which the issuer has a duty under Section 8-403(4)) to which the uncertificated security is or may be subject at the time of registration or a statement that there are none of those liens, restrictions or adverse claims; and

(e) the date the pledge was registered.

(3) Within 2 business days after the release from pledge of an uncertificated security has been registered, the issuer shall send to the registered owner and the pledgee whose interest was released a written statement containing:

(a) a description of the issue of which the uncertificated security is a part;

(b) the number of shares or units released from pledge;

(c) the name and address and any taxpayer identification number of the registered owner and the pledgee whose interest was released;

(d) a notation of any liens and restrictions of the issuer and any adverse claims (as to which the issuer has a duty under Section 8-403(4)) to which the uncertificated security is or may be subject at the time of registration or a statement that there are none of those liens, restrictions or adverse claims; and

(e) the date the release was registered.

(4) An "initial transaction statement" is the statement sent to:

(a) the new registered owner and, if applicable, to the registered pledgee pursuant to subsection (1);

(b) the registered pledgee pursuant to subsection (2); or

(c) the registered owner pursuant to subsection (3).

Each initial transaction statement shall be signed by or on behalf of the issuer and must be identified as "Initial Transaction Statement."

(5) Within 2 business days after the transfer of an uncertificated security has been registered, the issuer shall send to the former registered owner and the former registered pledgee, if any, a written statement containing:

(a) a description of the issue of which the uncertificated security is a part;

(b) the number of shares or units transferred;

(c) the name and address and any taxpayer identification number of the former registered owner and of any former registered pledgee; and

(d) the date the transfer was registered.

(6) At periodic intervals no less frequent than annually and at any time upon the reasonable written request of the registered owner, the issuer shall send to the registered owner of each uncertificated security a dated written statement containing:

(a) a description of the issue of which the uncertificated security is a part;

(b) the name and address and any taxpayer identification number of the registered owner;

(c) the number of shares or units of the uncertificated security registered in the name of the registered owner on the date of the statement;

(d) the name and address and any taxpayer identification number of any registered pledgee and the number of shares or units subject to the pledge; and

(e) a notation of any liens and restrictions of the issuer and any adverse claims (as to which the issuer has a duty under Section 8-403(4)) to which the uncertificated security is or may be subject or a statement that there are none of those liens, restrictions, or adverse claims.

(7) At periodic intervals no less frequent than annually and at any time upon the reasonable written request of the registered pledgee, the issuer shall send to the registered pledgee of each uncertificated security a dated written statement containing:

(a) a description of the issue of which the uncertificated security is a part;

(b) the name and address and any taxpayer identification number of the registered owner;

(c) the name and address and any taxpayer identification number of the registered pledgee;

(d) the number of shares or units subject to the pledge; and

(e) a notation of any liens and restrictions of the issuer and any adverse claims (as to which the issuer has a duty under Section 8-403(4)) to which the uncertificated security is or may be subject or a statement that there are none of those liens, restrictions, or adverse claims.

(8) If the issuer sends the statements described in subsections (6) and (7) at periodic intervals no less frequent than quarterly, the issuer is not obliged to send additional statements upon request unless the owner or pledgee requesting them pays to the issuer the reasonable cost of furnishing them.

(9) Each statement sent pursuant to this section must bear a conspicuous legend reading substantially as follows: "This statement is merely a record of the rights of the addressee as of the time of its issuance. Delivery of this statement, of itself, confers

no rights on the recipient. This statement is neither a negotiable instrument nor a security."

ARTICLE 9: SECURED TRANSACTIONS; SALES OF ACCOUNTS AND CHATTEL PAPER

Part 1: Short Title, Applicability and Definitions

§9-101. Short Title. This Article shall be known and may be cited as Uniform Commercial Code —Secured Transactions.

§9-102. Policy and Subject Matter of Article.

(1) Except as otherwise provided in Section 9-104 on excluded transactions, this Article applies:

(a) to any transaction (regardless of its form) which is intended to create a security interest in personal property or fixtures including goods, documents, instruments, general intangibles, chattel paper or accounts; and also

(b) to any sale of accounts or chattel paper.

(2) This Article applies to security interests created by contract including pledge, assignment, chattel mortgage, chattel trust, trust deed, factor's lien, equipment trust, conditional sale, trust receipt, other lien or title retention contract and lease or consignment intended as security. This Article does not apply to statutory liens except as provided in Section 9-310.

(3) The application of this Article to a security interest in a secured obligation is not affected by the fact that the obligation is itself secured by a transaction or interest to which this Article does not apply.

Note: *The adoption of this Article should be accompanied by the repeal of existing statutes dealing with conditional sales, trust receipts, factor's liens where the factor is given a non-possessory lien, chattel mortgages, crop mortgages, mortgages on railroad equipment, assignment of accounts and generally statutes regulating security interests in personal property.*

Where the state has a retail installment selling act or small loan act, that legislation should be carefully examined to determine what changes in those acts are needed to conform them to this Article. This Article primarily sets out rules defining rights of a secured party against persons dealing with the debtor; it does not prescribe regulations and controls which may be necessary to curb abuses arising in the small loan business or in the financing of consumer purchases on credit. Accordingly there is no intention to repeal existing regulatory acts in those fields by enactment or re-enactment of Article 9. See Section 9-203(4) and the Note thereto.

§9-103. Perfection of Security Interests in Multiple State Transactions.

(1) Documents, instruments and ordinary goods.

(a) This subsection applies to documents and instruments and to goods other than those covered by a certificate of title described in subsection (2), mobile goods described in subsection (3), and minerals described in subsection (5).

(b) Except as otherwise provided in this subsection, perfection and the effect of perfection or non-perfection of a security interest in collateral are governed by the law of the jurisdiction where the collateral is when the last event occurs on which is based the assertion that the security interest is perfected or unperfected.

(c) If the parties to a transaction creating a purchase money security interest in goods in one jurisdiction understand at the time that the security interest attaches that the goods will be kept in another jurisdiction, then the law of the other jurisdiction governs the perfection and the effect of perfection or non-perfection of the security interest from the time it attaches until thirty days after the debtor receives possession of the goods and thereafter if the goods are taken to the other jurisdiction before the end of the thirty-day period.

(d) When collateral is brought into and kept in this state while subject to a security interest perfected under the law of the jurisdiction from which the collateral was removed, the security interest remains perfected, but if action is required by Part 3 of this Article to perfect the security interest,

(i) if the action is not taken before the expiration of the period of perfection in the other jurisdiction or the end of four months after the collateral is brought into this state, whichever period first expires, the security interest becomes unperfected at the end of that period and is thereafter deemed to have been unperfected as against a person who became a purchaser after removal;

(ii) if the action is taken before the expiration of the period specified in subparagraph (i), the security interest continues perfected thereafter;

(iii) for the purpose of priority over a buyer of consumer goods (subsection (2) of Section 9-307), the period of the effectiveness of a filing in the jurisdiction from which the collateral is removed is governed by the rules with respect to perfection in subparagraphs (i) and (ii).

(2) Certificate of title.

(a) This subsection applies to goods covered by a certificate of title issued under a statute of this state or of another jurisdiction under the law of which indication of a security interest on the certificate is required as a condition of perfection.

(b) Except as otherwise provided in this subsection, perfection and the effect of perfection or non-perfection of the security interest are governed by the law (including the conflict of laws rules) of the jurisdiction issuing the certificate until four months after the goods are removed from that jurisdiction and thereafter until the goods are registered in another jurisdiction, but in any event not beyond surrender of the certificate. After the expiration of that period, the goods are not covered by the certificate of title within the meaning of this section.

(c) Except with respect to the rights of a buyer described

in the next paragraph, a security interest, perfected in another jurisdiction otherwise than by notation on a certificate of title, in goods brought into this state and thereafter covered by a certificate of title issued by this state is subject to the rules stated in paragraph (d) of subsection (1).

(d) If goods are brought into this state while a security interest therein is perfected in any manner under the law of the jurisdiction from which the goods are removed and a certificate of title is issued by this state and the certificate does not show that the goods are subject to the security interest or that they may be subject to security interests not shown on the certificate, the security interest is subordinate to the rights of a buyer of the goods who is not in the business of selling goods of that kind to the extent that he gives value and receives delivery of the goods after issuance of the certificate and without knowledge of the security interest.

(3) Accounts, general intangibles and mobile goods.

(a) This subsection applies to accounts (other than an account described in subsection (5) on minerals) and general intangibles and to goods which are mobile and which are of a type normally used in more than one jurisdiction, such as motor vehicles, trailers, rolling stock, airplanes, shipping containers, road building and construction machinery and commercial harvesting machinery and the like, if the goods are equipment or inventory leased or held for lease by the debtor to others, and are not covered by a certificate of title described in subsection (2).

(b) The law (including the conflict of laws rules) of the jurisdiction in which the debtor is located governs the perfection and the effect of perfection or non-perfection of the security interest.

(c) If, however, the debtor is located in a jurisdiction which is not a part of the United States, and which does not provide for perfection of the security interest by filing or recording in that jurisdiction, the law of the jurisdiction in the United States in which the debtor has its major executive office in the United States governs the perfection and the effect of perfection or non-perfection of the security interest through filing. In the alternative, if the debtor is located in a jurisdiction which is not a part of the United States or Canada and the collateral is accounts or general intangibles for money due or to become due, the security interest may be perfected by notification to the account debtor. As used in this paragraph, "United States" includes its territories and possessions and the Commonwealth of Puerto Rico.

(d) A debtor shall be deemed located at his place of business if he has one, at his chief executive office if he has more than one place of business, otherwise at his residence. If, however, the debtor is a foreign air carrier under the Federal Aviation Act of 1958, as amended, it shall be deemed located at the designated office of the agent upon whom service of process may be made on behalf of the foreign air carrier.

(e) A security interest perfected under the law of the jurisdiction of the location of the debtor is perfected until the expiration of four months after a change of the debtor's location to another jurisdiction, or until perfection would have ceased by the law of the first jurisdiction, whichever period first expires. Unless perfected in the new jurisdiction before the end of that period, it becomes unperfected thereafter and is deemed to have been unperfected as against a person who became a purchaser after the change.

(4) Chattel paper.

The rules stated for goods in subsection (1) apply to a possessory security interest in chattel paper. The rules stated for accounts in subsection (3) apply to a non-possessory security interest in chattel paper, **but the security interest may not be perfected by notification to the account debtor.**

(5) Minerals.

Perfection and the effect of perfection or non-perfection of a security interest which is created by a debtor who has an interest in minerals or the like (including oil and gas) before extraction and which attaches thereto as extracted, or which attaches to an account resulting from the sale thereof at the wellhead or minehead are governed by the law (including the conflict of laws rules) of the jurisdiction wherein the wellhead or minehead is located.

§9-103. Perfection of Security Interests in Multiple State Transactions *(1977 Amendments).*

* * *

(3) Accounts, general intangibles and mobile goods.

(a) This subsection applies to accounts (other than an account described in subsection (5) on minerals) and general intangibles (other than uncertificated securities) and to goods.

* * *

(6) Uncertificated securities.

The law (including the conflict of laws rules) of the jurisdiction of organization of the issuer governs the perfection and the effect of perfection or non-perfection of a security interest in uncertificated securities.

§9-104. Transactions Excluded From Article. This Article does not apply

(a) to a security interest subject to any statute of the United States to the extent that such statute governs the rights of parties to and third parties affected by transactions in particular types of property; or

(b) to a landlord's lien; or

(c) to a lien given by statute or other rule of law for services or materials except as provided in Section 9-310 on priority of such liens; or

(d) to a transfer of a claim for wages, salary or other compensation of an employee; or

(e) to a transfer by a government or governmental subdivision or agency; or

(f) to a sale of accounts, or chattel paper as part of a sale of the business out of which they arose, or an assignment of accounts or chattel paper which is for the purpose of collection only, or a transfer of a right to payment under a contract to an assignee who is also to do the performance under the contract or a transfer of a single account to an assignee in whole or partial satisfaction of a preexisting indebtedness; or

(g) to a transfer of an interest in or claim in or under any policy of insurance, except as provided with respect to proceeds (Section 9-306) and priorities in proceeds (Section 9-312); or

(h) to a right represented by a judgment (other than a judgment taken on a right to payment which was collateral); or

(i) to any right of set-off; or

(j) except to the extent that provision is made for fixtures in Section 9-313, to the creation or transfer of an interest in or lien on real estate, including a lease or rents thereunder; or

(k) to a transfer in whole or in part of any claim arising out of tort; or

(l) to a transfer of an interest in any deposit account (subsection (1) of Section 9-105), except as provided with respect to proceeds (Section 9-306) and priorities in proceeds (Section 9-312).

§9-105. Definitions and Index of Definitions.

(1) In this Article unless the context otherwise requires:

(a) "Account debtor" means the person who is obligated on an account, chattel paper or general intangible;

(b) "Chattel paper" means a writing or writings which evidence both a monetary obligation and a security interest in or a lease of specific goods, but a charter or other contract involving the use or hire of a vessel is not chattel paper. When a transaction is evidenced both by such a security agreement or a lease and by an instrument or a series of instruments, the group of writings taken together constitutes chattel paper;

(c) "Collateral" means the property subject to a security interest, and includes accounts and chattel paper which have been sold;

(d) "Debtor" means the person who owes payment or other performance of the obligation secured, whether or not he owns or has rights in the collateral, and includes the seller of accounts or chattel paper. Where the debtor and the owner of the collateral are not the same person, the term "debtor" means the owner of the collateral in any provision of the Article dealing with the collateral, the obligor in any provision dealing with the obligation, and may include both where the context so requires;

(e) "Deposit account" means a demand, time savings, passbook or like account maintained with a bank, savings and loan association, credit union or like organization, other than an account evidenced by a certificate of deposit;

(f) "Document" means document of title as defined in the general definitions of Article 1 (Section 1-201), and a receipt of the kind described in subsection (2) of Section 7-201);

(g) "Encumbrance" includes real estate mortgages and other liens on real estate and all other rights in real estate that are not ownership interests.

(h) "Goods" includes all things which are movable at the time the security interest attaches or which are fixtures (Section 9-313), but does not include money, documents, instruments, accounts, chattel paper, general intangibles, or minerals or the like (including oil and gas) before extraction. "Goods" also includes standing timber which is to be cut and removed under a conveyance or contract for sale, the unborn young of animals, and growing crops.

(i) "Instrument" means a negotiable instrument (defined in Section 3-104), or a security (defined in Section 8-102) or any other writing which evidences a right to the payment of money and is not itself a security agreement or lease and is of a type which is in ordinary course of business transferred by delivery with any necessary indorsement or assignment;

(j) "Mortgage" means a consensual interest created by a real estate mortgage, a trust deed on real estate, or the like;

(k) An advance is made "pursuant to commitment" if the secured party has bound himself to make it, whether or not a subsequent event of default or other event not within his control has relieved or may relieve him from his obligation.

(l) "Security agreement" means an agreement which creates or provides for a security interest;

(m) "Secured party" means a lender, seller or other person in whose favor there is a security interest, including a person to whom accounts or chattel paper have been sold. When the holders of obligations issued under an indenture of trust, equipment trust agreement or the like are represented by a trustee or other person, the representative is the secured party;

(n) "Transmitting utility" means any person primarily engaged in the railroad, street railway or trolley bus business, the electric or electronics communications transmission business, the transmission of goods by pipeline, or the transmission or the production and transmission of electricity, steam, gas or water, or the provision of sewer service.

(2) Other definitions applying to this Article and the sections in which they appear are;

"Account". Section 9-106.
"Attach". Section 9-203.
"Construction mortgage". Section 9-313 (1).
"Consumer goods". Section 9-109 (1).
"Equipment". Section 9-109 (2).
"Farm products". Section 9-109 (3).
"Fixture". Section 9-313.
"Fixture filing". Section 9-313.
"General intangibles". Section 9-106.
"Inventory". Section 9-109 (4).

"Lien creditor". Section 9-301 (3).
"Proceeds". Section 9-306 (1).
"Purchase money security interest". Section 9-107.
"United States". Section 9-103.

(3) The following definitions in other articles apply to this Article:

"Check". Section 3-104.
"Contract for sale". Section 2-106.
"Holder in due course". Section 3-302.
"Note". Section 3-104.
"Sale". Section 2-106.

(4) In addition Article 1 contains general definitions and principles of construction and interpretation throughout this Article.

§9-105. Definitions and Index of Definitions *(1977 Amendments).*

(1) In this Article unless the context otherwise requires:

* * *

(i) "Instrument" means a negotiable instrument (defined in Section 3-104), or a certificated security (defined in Section 8-102) or . . .

* * *

§9-106. Definitions: "Account"; "General Intangibles". "Account" means any right to payment for goods sold or leased or for services rendered which is not evidenced by an instrument or chattel paper, whether or not it has been earned by performance. "General intangibles" means any personal property (including things in action) other than goods, accounts, chattel paper, documents, instruments, and money. All rights to payment earned or unearned under a charter or other contract involving the use or hire of a vessel and all rights incident to the charter or contract are accounts.

§9-107. Defintions: "Purchase Money Security Interest". A security interest is a "purchase money security interest" to the extent that it is

(a) taken or retained by the seller of the collateral to secure all or part of its price;

(b) taken by a person who by making advances or incurring an obligation gives value to enable the debtor to acquire rights in or the use of collateral if such value is in fact so used.

§9-108. When After-Acquired Collateral Not Security for Antecedent Debt. Where a secured party makes an advance, incurs an obligation, releases a perfected security interest, or otherwise gives new value which is to be secured in whole or in part by after-acquired property his security interest in the after-acquired collateral shall be deemed to be taken for new value and not as security for an antecedent debt if the debtor acquires his rights in such collateral either in the ordinary course of his business or under a contract of purchase made pursuant to the security agreement within a reasonable time after new value is given.

§9-109. Classification of Goods; "Consumer Goods"; "Equipment"; "Farm Products"; "Inventory". Goods are

(1) "consumer goods" if they are used or bought for use primarily for personal, family or household purposes;

(2) "equipment" if they are used or bought for use primarily in business (including farming or a profession) or by a debtor who is a non-profit organization or a governmental subdivision or agency or if the goods are not included in the definitions of inventory, farm products or consumer goods;

(3) "farm products" if they are crops or livestock or supplies used or produced in farming operations or if they are products of crops or livestock in their unmanufactured states (such as ginned cotton, wool-clip, maple syrup, milk and eggs), and if they are in the possession of a debtor engaged in raising, fattening, grazing or other farming operations. If goods are farm products they are neither equipment nor inventory;

(4) "inventory" if they are held by a person who holds them for sale or lease or to be furnished under contracts of service or if he has so furnished them, or if they are raw materials, work in process or materials used or consumed in a business. Inventory of a person is not to be classified as his equipment.

§9-110. Sufficiency of Description. For the purposes of this Article any description of personal property or real estate is sufficient whether or not it is specific if it reasonably identifies what is described.

§9-111. Applicability of Bulk Transfer Laws. The creation of a security interest is not a bulk transfer under Article 6 (see Section 6-103).

§9-112. Where Collateral Is Not Owned by Debtor. Unless otherwise agreed, when a secured party knows that collateral is owned by a person who is not the debtor, the owner of the collateral is entitled to receive from the secured party any surplus under Section 9-502 (2) or under Section 9-504 (1), and is not liable for the debt or for any deficiency after resale, and he has the same right as the debtor

(a) to receive statements under Section 9-208;

(b) to receive notice of and to object to a secured party's proposal to retain the collateral in satisfaction of the indebtedness under Section 9-505;

(c) to redeem the collateral under Section 9-506;

(d) to obtain injunctive or other relief under Section 9-507 (1); and

(e) to recover losses caused to him under Section 9-208 (2).

§9-113. Security Interests Arising Under Article on Sales. A security interest arising solely under the Article on Sales (Article 2) is subject to the provisions of this Article except that to the extent that and so long as the debtor does not have or does not lawfully obtain possession of the goods

(a) no security agreement is necessary to make the security interest enforceable; and

(b) no filing is required to perfect the security interest; and

(c) the rights of the secured party on default by the debtor are governed by the Article on Sales (Article 2).

§9-114. Consignment.

(1) A person who delivers goods under a consignment which is not a security interest and who would be required to file under this Article by paragraph (3) (c) of Section 2-326 has

priority over a secured party who is or becomes a creditor of the consignee and who would have a perfected security interest in the goods if they were the property of the consignee, and also has priority with respect to identifiable cash proceeds received on or before delivery of the goods to a buyer, if

(**a**) the consignor complies with the filing provision of the Article on Sales with respect to consignments (paragraph (3) (c) of Section 2-326) before the consignee receives possession of the goods; and

(**b**) the consignor gives notification in writing to the holder of the security interest if the holder has filed a financing statement covering the same types of goods before the date of the filing made by the consignor; and

(**c**) the holder of the security interest receives the notification within five years before the consignee receives possession of the goods; and

(**d**) the notification states that the consignor expects to deliver goods on consignment to the consignee, describing the goods by item or type.

(**2**) In the case of a consignment which is not a security interest and in which the requirements of the preceding subsection have not been met, a person who delivers goods to another is subordinate to a person who would have a perfected security interest in the goods if they were the property of the debtor.

Part 2: Validity of Security Agreement and Rights of Parties Thereto

§9-201. General Validity of Security Agreement. Except as otherwise provided by this Act a security agreement is effective according to its terms between the parties, against purchasers of the collateral and against creditors. Nothing in this Article validates any charge or practice illegal under any statute or regulation thereunder governing usury, small loans, retail installment sales, or the like, or extends the application of any such statute or regulation to any transaction not otherwise subject thereto.

§9-202. Title to Collateral Immaterial. Each provision of this Article with regard to rights, obligations and remedies applies whether title to collateral is in the secured party or in the debtor.

§9-203. Attachment and Enforceability of Security Interest; Proceeds; Formal Requisities.

(**1**) Subject to the provisions of Section 4-208 on the security interest of a collecting bank and Section 9-113 on a security interest arising under the Article on Sales, a security interest is not enforceable against the debtor or third parties with respect to the collateral and does not attach unless

(**a**) the collateral is in the possession of the secured party pursuant to agreement, or the debtor has signed a security agreement which contains a description of the collateral and in addition, when the security interest covers crops growing or to be grown or timber to be cut, a description of the land concerned; and

(**b**) value has been given; and

(**c**) the debtor has rights in the collateral.

(**2**) A security interest attaches when it becomes enforceable against the debtor with respect to the collateral. Attachment occurs as soon as all of the events specified in subsection (1) have taken place unless explicit agreement postpones the time of attaching.

(**3**) Unless otherwise agreed a security agreement gives the secured party the rights to proceeds provided by Section 9-306.

(**4**) A transaction, although subject to this Article, is also subject to . . . . *, and in the case of conflict between the provisions of this Article and any such statute, the provisions of such statute control. Failure to comply with any applicable statute has only the effect which is specfied therein.

Note: *At * in subsection (4) insert reference to any local statute regulating small loans, retail installment sales and the like.*

The foregoing subsection (4) is designed to make it clear that certain transactions, although subject to this Article, must also comply with other applicable legislation.

This Article is designed to regulate all the "security" aspects of transactions within its scope. There is, however, much regulatory legislation, particularly in the consumer field, which supplements this Article and should not be repealed by its enactment. Examples are small loan acts, retail installment selling acts and the like. Such acts may provide for licensing and rate regulation and may prescribe particular forms of contract. Such provisions should remain in force despite the enactment of this Article. On the other hand if a retail installent selling act contains provisions on filing, rights on default, etc., such provisions should be repealed as inconsistent with this Article except that inconsistent provisions as to deficiencies, penalities, etc., in the Uniform Consumer Credit Code and other recent related legislation should remain because those statutes were drafted after the substantial enactment of the Article and with the intention of modifying certain provisions of this Article as to consumer credit.

§9-203. Attachment and Enforceability of Security Interest; Proceeds; Formal Requisites *(1977 Amendments).*

(**1**) Subject to the provisions of Section 4-208 on the security interest of a collecting bank, Section 8-321 on security interests in securities and Section 9-113 on a security interest arising under the Article on Sales, a security interest in not enforceable against the debtor or third parties with respect to the collateral and does not attach unless:

(**a**) the collateral is in the possession of the secured party pursuant to agreement, or the debtor has signed a security agreement which contains a description of the collateral and in additon, when the security interest covers crops growing or to be grown or timber to be cut, a description of the land concerned;

(**b**) value has been given; and

(**c**) the debtor has rights in the collateral.

* * *

§9-204. After-Acquired Property; Future Advances.

(1) Except as provided in subsection (2), a security agree-

ment may provide that any or all obligations covered by the security agreement are to be secured by after-acquired collateral.

(2) No security interest attaches under an after-acquired property clause to consumer goods other than accessions (Section 9-314) when given as additional security unless the debtor acquires rights in them within ten days after the secured party gives value.

(3) Obligations covered by a security agreement may include future advances or other value whether or not the advances or value are given pursuant to commitment (subsection (1) of Section 9-105).

§9-205. Use or Disposition of Collateral Without Accounting Permissible. A security interest is not invalid or fraudulent against creditors by reason of liberty in the debtor to use, commingle or dispose of all or part of the collateral (including returned or repossessed goods) or to collect or compromise accounts or chattel paper, or to accept the return of goods or make repossessions, or to use, commingle or dispose of proceeds, or by reason of the failure of the secured party to require the debtor to account for proceeds or replace collateral. This section does not relax the requirements of possession where perfection of a security interest depends upon possession of the collateral by the secured party or by a bailee.

§9-206. Agreement Not to Assert Defenses Against Assignee; Modification of Sales Warranties Where Security Agreement Exists.

(1) Subject to any statute or decision which establishes a different rule for buyers or lessees of consumer goods, an agreement by a buyer or lessee that he will not assert against an assignee any claim or defense which he may have against the seller or lessor is enforceable by an assignee who takes his assignment for value, in good faith and without notice of a claim or defense, except as to defenses of a type which may be asserted against a holder in due course of a negotiable instrument under the Article on Commercial Paper (Article 3). A buyer who as part of one transaction signs both a negotiable instrument and a security agreement makes such an agreement.

(2) When a seller retains a purchase money security interest in goods the Article on Sales (Article 2) governs the sale and any disclaimer, limitation or modification of the seller's warranties.

Amended in 1962.

§9-207. Rights and Duties When Collateral is in Secured Party's Possession.

(1) A secured party must use reasonable care in the custody and preservation of collateral in his possession. In the case of an instrument or chattel paper reasonable care includes taking necessary steps to preserve rights against prior parties unless otherwise agreed.

(2) Unless otherwise agreed, when collateral is in the secured party's possession

(a) reasonable expenses (including the cost of any insurance and payment of taxes or other charges) incurred in the custody, preservation, use or operation of the collateral are chargeable to the debtor and are secured by the collateral;

(b) the risk of accidental loss or damage is on the debtor to the extent of any deficiency in any effective insurance coverage;

(c) the secured party may hold as additional security any increase or profits (except money) received from the collateral, but money so received, unless remitted to the debtor, shall be applied in reduction of the secured obligation;

(d) the secured party must keep the collateral indentifiable but fungible collateral may be commingled;

(e) the secured party may repledge the collateral upon terms which do not impair the debtor's right to redeem it.

(3) A secured party is liable for any loss caused by his failure to meet any obligation imposed by the preceding subsections but does not lose his security interest.

(4) A secured party may use or operate the collateral for the purpose of preserving the collateral or its value or pursuant to the order of a court of appropriate jurisdiction or, except in the case of consumer goods, in the manner and to the extent provided in the security agreement.

§9-208. Request for Statement of Account or List of Collateral.

(1) A debtor may sign a statement indicating what he believes to be the aggregate amount of unpaid indebtedness as of a specified date and may send it to the secured party with a request that the statement be approved or corrected and returned to the debtor. When the security agreement or any other record kept by the secured party identifies the collateral a debtor may similarly request the secured party to approve or correct a list of the collateral.

(2) The secured party must comply with such a request within two weeks after receipt by sending a written correction or approval. If the secured party claims a security interest in all of a particular type of collateral owned by the debtor he may indicate that fact in his reply and need not approve or correct an itemized list of such collateral. If the secured party without reasonable excuse fails to comply he is liable for any loss caused to the debtor thereby; and if the debtor has properly included in his request a good faith statement of the obligation or a list of the collateral or both, the secured party may claim a security interest only as shown in the statement against persons misled by his failure to comply. If he no longer has an interest in the obligation or collateral at the time the request is received he must disclose the name and address of any successor in interest known to him and he is liable for any loss caused to the debtor as a result of failure to disclose. A successor in interest is not subject to this section until a request is received by him.

(3) A debtor is entitled to such a statement once every six months without charge. The secured party may require payment of a charge not exceeding $10 for each additional statement furnished.

Part 3: Rights of Third Parties; Perfected and Unperfected Security Interests; Rules of Priority

§9-301. Persons Who Take Priority Over Unperfected Security Interests; Right of "Lien Creditor".

(1) Except as otherwise provided in subsection (2), an unperfected security interest is subordinate to the rights of

(a) persons entitled to priority under Section 9-312;

(b) a person who becomes a lien creditor before the security interest is perfected;

(c) in the case of goods, instruments, documents, and chattel paper, a person who is not a secured party and who is a transferee in bulk or other buyer not in ordinary course of business, or is a buyer of farm products in ordinary course of business, to the extent that he gives value and receives delivery of the collateral without knowledge of the security interest and before it is perfected;

(d) in the case of accounts and general intangibles, a person who is not a secured party and who is a transferee to the extent that he gives value without knowledge of the security interest and before it is perfected.

(2) If the secured party files with respect to a purchase money security interest before or within ten days after the debtor receives possession of the collateral, he takes priority over the rights of a transferee in bulk or of a lien creditor which arise between the time the security interest attaches and the time of filing.

(3) A "lien creditor" means a creditor who has acquired a lien on the property involved by attachment, levy or the like and includes an assignee for benefit of creditors from the time of assignment, and a trustee in bankruptcy from the date of the filing of the petition or a receiver in equity from the time of appointment.

(4) A person who becomes a lien creditor while a security interest is perfected takes subject to the security interest only to the extent that it secures advances made before he becomes a lien creditor or within 45 days thereafter or made without knowledge of the lien or pursuant to a commitment entered into without knowledge of the lien.

§9-302. When Filing Is Required to Perfect Security Interest; Security Interests to Which Filing Provisions of This Article Do Not Apply.

(1) A financing statement must be filed to perfect all security interests except the following:

(a) a security interest in collateral in possession of the secured party under Section 9-305;

(b) a security interest temporarily perfected in instruments or documents without delivery under Section 9-304 or in proceeds for a 10 day period under Section 9-306;

(c) a security interest created by an assignment of a beneficial interest in a trust or a decedent's estate;

(d) a purchase money security interest in consumer goods; but filing is required for a motor vehicle required to be registered; and fixture filing is required for priority over conflicting interests in fixtures to the extent provided in Section 9-313;

(e) an assignment of accounts which does not alone or in conjunction with other assignments to the same assignee transfer a significant part of the outstanding accounts of the assignor;

(f) a security interest of a collecting bank (Section 4-208) or arising under the Article on Sales (see section 9-113) or covered in subsection (3) of this section;

(g) an assignment for the benefit of all the creditors of the transferor, and subsequent transfers by the assignee thereunder.

(2) If a secured party assigns a perfected security interest, no filing under this Article is required in order to continue the perfected status of the security interest against creditors of and transferees from the original debtor.

(3)) The filing of a financing statement otherwise required by this Article is not necessary or effective to perfect a security interest in property subject to

(a) a statute or treaty of the United States which provides for a national or international registration or a national or international certificate of title or which specifies a place of filing different from that specified in this Article for filing of the security interest; or

(b) the following statutes of this state; [[list any certificate of title statute covering automobiles, trailers, mobile homes, boats, farm tractors, or the like, and any central filing statute*.]]; but during any period in which collateral is inventory held for sale by a person who is in the business of selling goods of that kind, the filing provisions of this Article (Part 4) apply to a security interest in that collateral created by him as debtor; or

(c) a certificate of title statute of another jurisdiction under the law of which indication of a security interest on the certificate is required as a condition of perfection (subsection (2) of Section 9-103).

(4) Compliance with a statute or treaty described in subsection (3) is equivalent to the filing of a financing statement under this Article, and a security interest in property subject to the statute or treaty can be perfected only by compliance therewith except as provided in Section 9-103 on multiple state transactions. Duration and renewal of perfection of a security interest perfected by compliance with the statute or treaty are governed by the provisions of the statute or treaty; in other respects the security interest is subject to this Article.

§9-302. When Filing is Required to Perfect Security Interest; Security Interests to Which Filing Provisions of This Article Do Not Apply *(1977 Amendments).*

(1) A financing statement must be filed to perfect all security interests[s] except the following:

* * *

(f) a security interest of a collecting bank (Section 4-208) or in securities (Section 8-321) or arising under the Article on Sales (see Section 9-113) or covered in subsection (3) of this section;

* * *

§9-303. When Security Interest Is Perfected; Continuity of Perfection.

(1) A security interest is perfected when it has attached and when all of the applicable steps required for perfection have been taken. Such steps are specified in Section 9-304, 9-305 and 9-306. If such steps are taken before the security interest attaches, it is perfected at the time when it attaches.

* **Note:** It is recommended that the provisions of certificate of title acts for perfection of security interests by notation on the certificates should be amended to exclude coverage of inventory held for sale.

(2) If a security interest is originally perfected in any way permitted under this Article and is subsequently perfected in some other way under this Article, without an intermediate period when it was unperfected, the security interest shall be deemed to be perfected continuously for the purposes of this Article.

§9-304. Perfection of Security Interest in Instruments, Documents, and Goods Covered by Documents; Perfection by Permissive Filing; Temporary Perfection Without Filing or Transfer of Possession.

(1) A security interest in chattel paper or negotiable documents may be perfected by filing. A security interest in money or instruments (other than instruments which constitute part of chattel paper) can be perfected only by the secured party's taking possission, except as provided in subsections (4) and (5) of this section and subsections (2) and (3) of Section 9-306 on proceeds.

(2) During the period that goods are in the possession of the issuer of a negotiable document therefor, a security interest in the goods is perfected by perfecting a security interest in the document, and any security interest in the goods otherwise perfected during such period is subject thereto.

(3) A security interest in goods in the possession of a bailee other than one who has issued a negotiable document therefor is perfected by issuance of a document in the name of the secured party or by the bailee's receipt of notification of the secured party's interest or by filing as to the goods.

(4) A security interest in instruments or negotiable documents is perfected without filing or the taking of possession for a period of 21 days from the time it attaches to the extent that it arises for new value given under a written security agreement.

(5) A security interest remains perfected for a period of 21 days without filing where a secured party having a perfected security interest in an instrument, a negotiable document or goods in possession of a bailee other than one who has issued a negotiable document therefor

(a) makes available to the debtor the goods or documents representing the goods for the purpose of ultimate sale or exchange or for the purpose of loading, unloading, storing, shipping, transshipping, manufacturing, processing or otherwise dealing with them in a manner preliminary to their sale or exchange, but priority between conflicting security interests in the goods is subject to subsection (3) of Section 9-312; or

(b) delivers the instrument to the debtor for the purpose of ultimate sale or exchange or of presentation, collection, renewal or registration of transfer.

(6) After the 21 day period in subsections (4) and (5) perfection depends upon compliance with applicable provisions of this Article.

§9-304. Perfection of Security Interest in Instruments, Documents, and Goods Covered by Documents; Perfection by Permissive Filing; Temporary Perfection Without Filing or Transfer of Possession *(1977 Amendments)*.

(1) A security interest in chattel paper or negotiable documents may be perfected by filing. A security interest in money or instruments (other than certificated securities or instruments which constitute part of chattel paper) can be perfected only by the secured party's taking possession, except as provided in subsections (4) and (5) of this section and subsections (2) and (3) of Section 9-306 on proceeds.

* * *

(4) A security interest in instruments (other than certificated securities) or negotiable documents is perfected without filing or the taking of possession for a period of 21 days from the time it attaches to the extent that it arises for new value given under a written security agreement.

(5) A security interest remains perfected for a period of 21 days without filing where a secured party having a perfected security interest in an instrument (other than a certificated security), a negotiable document or goods in possession of a bailee other than one who has issued a negotiable document therefor:

* * *

(b) delivers the instrument to the debtor for the purpose of ultimate sale or exchange or of presentation, collection, renewal, or registration of transfer.

(6) After the 21 day period in subsections (4) and (5) perfection depends upon compliance with applicable provisions of this Article.

§9-305. When Possession by Secured Party Perfects Security Interest Without Filing. A security interest in letters of credit and advices of credit (subsection (2) (a) of Section 5-116), goods, instruments, money, negotiable documents or chattel paper may be perfected by the secured party's taking possession of the collateral. If such collateral other than goods covered by a negotiable document is held by a bailee, the secured party is deemed to have possession from the time the bailee receives notification of the secured party's interest. A security interest is perfected by possession from the time possession is taken without relation back and continues only so long as possession is retained, unless otherwise specified in this Article. The security interest may be otherwise perfected as provided in this Article before or after the period of possession by the secured party.

§9-305. When Possession by Secured Party Perfects Security Interest Without Filing *(1977 Amendments)*. A security interest in letters of credit and advices of credit (subsection (2)(a) of Section 5-116), goods, instruments (other than certificated securities), money, negotiable documents, or chattel paper may be perfected by the secured party's taking possession of the collateral. If such collateral other than goods covered by a negotiable document is held by a bailee, the secured party is deemed to have possession from the time the bailee receives notification of the secured party's interest. A security interest is perfected by possession from the time possession is taken without relation back and continues only so long as possession is retained, unless otherwise specified in this Article. The security interest may be otherwise perfected as provided in this Article before or after the period of possession by the secured party.

§9-306. "Proceeds"; Secured Party's Rights on Disposition of Collateral.

"Proceeds" includes whatever is received upon the sale, exchange, collection or other disposition of collateral or proceeds. Insurance payable by reason of loss or damage to the collateral is proceeds, except to the extent that it is is payable to a person other than a party to the security agreement. Money, checks, deposit accounts, and the like are "cash proceeds". All other proceeds are "non-cash proceeds".

(**2**) Except where this Article otherwise provides, a security interest continues in collateral notwithstanding sale, exchange or other disposition thereof unless the disposition was authorized by the secured party in the security agreement or otherwise, and also continues in any identifiable proceeds including collections received by the debtor.

(**3**) The security interest in proceeds is a continuously perfected security interest if the interest in the original collateral was perfected but it ceases to be a perfected security interest and becomes unperfected ten days after receipt of the proceeds by the debtor unless

(**a**) a filed financing statement covers the original collateral and the proceeds are collateral in which a security interest may be perfected by filing in the office or offices where the financing statement has been filed and, if the proceeds are acquired with cash proceeds, the description of collateral in the financing statement indicates the types of property constituting the proceeds; or

(**b**) a filed financing statement covers the original collateral and the proceeds are identifiable cash proceeds; or

(**c**) the security interest in the proceeds is perfected before the expiration of the ten day period.

Except as provided in this section, a security interest in proceeds can be perfected only by the methods or under the circumstances permitted in this Article for original collateral of the same type.

(**4**) In the event of insolvency proceedings instituted by or against a debtor, a secured party with a perfected security interest in proceeds has a perfected security interest only in the following proceeds:

(**a**) in identifiable non-cash proceeds and in separate deposit accounts containing only proceeds;

(**b**) in identifiable cash proceeds in the form of money which is neither commingled with other money nor deposited in a deposit account prior to the insolvency proceedings;

(**c**) in identifiable cash proceeds in the form of checks and the like which are not deposited in a deposit account prior to the insolvency proceedings; and

(**d**) in all cash and deposit accounts of the debtor in which proceeds have been commingled with other funds, but the perfected security interest under this paragraph (d) is

(**i**) subject to any right of set-off; and

(**ii**) limited to an amount not greater than the amount of any cash proceeds received by the debtor within ten days before the institution of the insolvency proceedings less the sum of (**i**) the payments to the secured party on account of cash proceeds received by the debtor during such period and (**ii**) the cash proceeds received by the debtor during such period to which the secured party is entitled under paragraphs (a) through (c) of this subsection (**iv**).

(**5**) If a sale of goods results in an account or chattel paper which is transferred by the seller to a secured party, and if the goods are returned to or are repossessed by the seller or the secured party, the following rules determine priorities:

(**a**) If the goods were collateral at the time of sale, for an indebtedness of the seller which is still unpaid, the original security interest attaches again to the goods and continues as a perfected security interest if it was perfected at the time when the goods were sold. If the security interest was originally perfected by a filing which is still effective, nothing further is required to continue the perfected status; in any other case, the secured party must take possession of the returned or repossessed goods or must file.

(**b**) An unpaid transferee of the chattel paper has a security interest in the goods against the transferor. Such security interest is prior to a security interest asserted under paragraph (a) to the extent that the transferee of the chattel paper was entitled to priority under Section 9-308.

(**c**) An unpaid transferee of the account has a security interest in the goods against the transferor. Such security interest is subordinate to a security interest asserted under paragraph (a).

(**d**) A security interest of an unpaid transferee asserted under paragraph (b) or (c) must be perfected for protection against creditors of the transferor and purchasers of the returned or repossessed goods.

§9-307. Protection of Buyers of Goods.

(**1**) A buyer in ordinary course of business (subsection (9) of Section 1-201) other than a person buying farm products from a person engaged in farming operations takes free of a security interest created by his seller even though the security interest is perfected and even though the buyer knows of its existence.

(**2**) In the case of consumer goods a buyer takes free of a security interest even though perfected if he buys without knowledge of the security interest, for value and for his own personal, family or household purposes unless prior to the purchase the secured party has filed a financing statement covering such goods.

(**3**) A buyer other than a buyer in ordinary course of business (subsection (1) of this section) takes free of a security interest to the extent that it secures future advances made after the secured party acquires knowledge of the purchase, or more than 45 days after the purchase, whichever first occurs, unless made pursuant to a commitment entered into without knowledge of the purchase and before the expiration of the 45 day period.

§9-308. Purchase of Chattel Paper and Instruments.

A purchaser of chattel paper or an instrument who gives new value and takes possession of it in the ordinary course of his business has priority over a security interest in the chattel paper or instrument

(a) which is perfected under Section 9-304 (permissive filing and temporary perfection) or under Section 9-306 (perfection as to proceeds) if he acts without knowledge that the specific paper or instrument is subject to a security interest; or

(b) which is claimed merely as proceeds of inventory subject to a security interest (Section 9-306) even though he knows that the specific paper or instrument is subject to the security interest.

§9-309. Protection of Purchasers of Instruments and Documents. Nothing in this Article limits the rights of a holder in due course of a negotiable instrument (Section 3-302) or a holder to whom a negotiable document of title has been duly negotiated (Section 7-501) or a bona fide purchaser of a security (Section 8-301) and such holders or purchasers take priority over an earlier security interest even though perfected. Filing under this Article does not constitute notice of the security interest to such holders or purchasers.

§9-309. Protection of Purchasers of Instruments, Documents and Securities ***(1977 Amendments).*** **Nothing in this Article limits the rights of a holder in due course of a negotiable instrument (Section 3-302) or a holder to whom negotiable document of title has been duly negotiated (Section 7-501) or a bona fide purchaser of a security (Section 8-302) and such holders or purchasers take priority over an earlier security interest even though perfected. Filing under this Article does not constitute notice of the security interest to such holders or purchasers.**

§9-310. Priority of Certain Liens Arising by Operation of Law. When a person in the ordinary course of his business furnishes services or materials wıtn respect to goods subject to a security interest, a lien upon goods in the possession of such person given by statute or rule of law for such materials or services takes priority over a perfected security interest unless the lien is statutory and the statute expressly provides otherwise.

§9-311. Alienability of Debtor's Rights: Judicial Process. The debtor's rights in collateral may be voluntarily or involuntarily transferred (by way of sale, creation of a security interest, attachment, levy, garnishment or other judicial process) notwithstanding a provision in the security agreement prohibiting any transfer or making the transfer constitute a default.

§9-312. Priorities Among Conflicting Security Interests in the Same Collateral.

(1) The rules of priority stated in other sections of this Part and in the following sections shall govern when applicable: Section 4-208 with respect to the security interests of collecting banks in items being collected, accompanying documents and proceeds; Section 9-103 on security interests related to other jurisdictions; Section 9-114 on consignments.

(2) A perfected security interest in crops for new value given to enable the debtor to produce the crops during the production season and given not more than three months before the crops become growing crops by planting or otherwise takes priority over an earlier perfected security interest to the extent that such earlier interest secures obligations due more than six months before the crops become growing crops by planting or otherwise, even though the person giving new value had knowledge of the earlier security interest.

(3) A perfected purchase money security interest in inventory has priority over a conflicting security interest in the same inventory and also has priority in identifiable cash proceeds received on or before the delivery of the inventory to a buyer if

(a) the purchase money security interest is perfected at the time the debtor receives possession of the inventory; and

(b) the purchase noney secured party gives notification in writing to the holder of the conflicting security interest if the holder had filed a financing statement covering the same types of inventory (i) before the date of the filing made by the purchase money secured party, or (ii) before the beginning of the 21 day period where the purchase money security interest is temporarily perfected without filing or possession (subsection (5) of Section 9-304); and

(c) the holder of the conflicting security interest receives the notification within five years before the debtor receives possession of the inventory; and

(d) the notification states that the person giving the notice has or expects to acquire a purchase money security interest in inventory of the debtor, describing such inventory by item or type.

(4) A purchase money security interest in collateral other than inventory has priority over a conflicting security interest in the same collateral or its proceeds if the purchase money security interest is perfected at the time the debtor receives possession of the collateral or within ten days thereafter.

(5) In all cases not governed by other rules stated in this section (including cases of purchase money security interests which do not qualify for the special priorities set forth in subsections (3) and (4) of this section), priority between conflicting security interests in the same collateral shall be determined according to the following rules:

(a) Conflicting security interests rank according to priority in time of filing or perfection. Priority dates from the time a filing is first made covering the collateral or the time the security interest is first perfected, whichever is earlier, provided that there is no period thereafter when there is neither filing nor perfection.

(**b**) So long as conflicting security interests are unperfected, the first to attach has priority.

(**6**) For the purposes of subsection (5) a date of filing or perfection as to collateral is also a date of filing or perfection as to proceeds.

(**7**) If future advances are made while a security interest is perfected by filing or the taking of possession, the security interest has the same priority for the purposes of subsection (5) with respect to the future advances as it does with respect to the first advance. If a commitment is made before or while the security interest is so perfected, the security interest has the same priority with respect to advances made pursuant thereto. In other cases a perfected security interest has priority from the date the advance is made.

§9-312. Priorities Among Conflicting Security Interests in the Same Collateral *(1977 Amendments).*

(**7**) If future advances are made while a security interest is perfected by filing, the taking of possession, or under Section 8-321 on securities, the security interest has the same priority for the purposes of subsection (5) with respect to the future advances as it does with respect to the first advance. If a commitment is made before or while the security interest is so perfected, the security interest has the same priority with respect to advances made pursuant thereto. In other cases a perfected security interest has priority from the date the advance is made.

* * *

§9-313. Priority of Security Interests in Fixtures.

(**1**) In this section and in the provisions of Part 4 of this Article referring to fixture filing, unless the context otherwise requires

(**a**) goods are "fixtures" when they become so related to particular real estate that an interest in them arises under real estate law

(**b**) a "fixture filing" is the filing in the office where a mortgage on the real estate would be filed or recorded of a financing statement covering goods which are or are to become fixtures and conforming to the requirements of subsection (5) of Section 9-402

(**c**) a mortgage is a "construction mortgage" to the extent that it secures an obligation incurred for the construction of an improvement on land including the acquisition cost of the land, if the recorded writing so indicates.

(**2**) A security interest under this Article may be created in goods which are fixtures or may continue in goods which become fixtures, but no security interest exists under this Article in ordinary building materials incorporated into an improvement on land.

(**3**) This Article does not prevent creation of an encumbrance upon fixtures pursuant to real estate law.

(**4**) A perfected security interest in fixtures has priority over the conflicting interest of an encumbrancer or owner of the real estate where

(**a**) the security interest is a purchase money security interest, the interest of the encumbrancer or owner arises before the goods become fixtures, the security interest is perfected by a fixture filing before the goods become fixtures or within ten days thereafter, and the debtor has an interest of record in the real estate or is in possession of the real estate; or

(**b**) the security interest is perfected by a fixture filing before the interest of the encumbrancer or owner is of record, the security interest has priority over any conflicting interest of a predecessor in title of the encumbrancer or owner, and the debtor has an interest of record in the real estate or is in possession of the real estate; or

(**c**) the fixtures are readily removable factory or office machines or readily removable replacements of domestic appliances which are consumer goods, and before the goods become fixtures the security interest is perfected by any method permitted by this Article; or

(**d**) the conflicting interest is a lien on the real estate obtained by legal or equitable proceedings after the security interest was perfected by any method permitted by this Article.

(**5**) A security interest in fixtures, whether or not perfected, has priority over the conflicting interest of an encumbrancer or owner of the real estate where

(**a**) the encumbrancer or owner has consented in writing to the security interest or has disclaimed an interest in the goods as fixtures; or

(**b**) the debtor has a right to remove the goods as against the encumbrancer or owner. If the debtor's right terminates, the priority of the security interest continues for a reasonable time.

(**6**) Notwithstanding paragraph (a) of subsection (4) but otherwise subject to subsections (4) and (5), a security interest in fixtures is subordinate to a construction mortgage recorded before the goods become fixtures if the goods become fixtures before the completion of the construction. To the extent that it is given to refinance a construction mortgage, a mortgage has this priority to the same extent as the construction mortgage.

(**7**) In cases not within the preceding subsections, a security interest in fixtures is subordinate to the conflicting interest of an encumbrancer or owner of the related real estate who is not the debtor.

(**8**)) When the secured party has priority over all owners and encumbrancers of the real estate, he may, on default, subject to the provisions of Part 5, remove his collateral from the real estate but he must reimburse any encumbrancer or owner of the real estate who is not the debtor and who has not otherwise agreed for the cost of repair of any physical injury, but not for any diminution in value of the real estate caused by the absence of the goods removed or by any necessity of replacing them. A person entitled to reimbursement may refuse permission to remove until the secured party gives adequate security for the performance of this obligation.

§9-314. Accessions.

(**1**) A security interest in goods which attaches before they are installed in or affixed to other goods takes priority as to the goods installed or affixed (called in this section "accessions") over the claims of all persons to the whole except as stated in subsection (3) and subject to Section 9-315(1).

(2) A security interest which attaches to goods after they become part of a whole is valid against all persons subsequently acquiring interests in the whole except as stated in subsection (3) but is invalid against any person with an interest in the whole at the time the security interest attaches to the goods who has not in writing consented to the security interest or disclaimed an interest in the goods as part of the whole.

(3) The security interests described in subsections (1) and (2) do not take priority over

(a) a subsequent purchaser for value of any interest in the whole; or

(b) a creditor with a lien on the whole subsequently obtained by judicial proceedings; or

(c) a creditor with a prior perfected security interest in the whole to the extent that he makes subsequent advances

if the subsequent purchase is made, the lien by judicial proceedings obtained or the subsequent advance under the prior perfected security interest is made or contracted for without knowledge of the security interest and before it is perfected. A purchaser of the whole at a foreclosure sale other than the holder of a perfected security interest purchasing at his own foreclosure sale is a subsequent purchaser within this section.

(4) When under subsections (1) or (2) and (3) a secured party has an interest in accessions which has priority over the claims of all persons who have interests in the whole, he may on default subject to the provisions of Part 5 remove his collateral from the whole but he must reimburse any encumbrancer or owner of the whole who is not the debtor and who has not otherwise agreed for the cost of repair of any physical injury but not for any diminution in value of the whole caused by the absence of the goods removed or by any necessity for replacing them. A person entitled to reimbursement may refuse permission to remove until the secured party gives adequate security for the performance of this obligation.

§9-315. Priority When Goods are Commingled or Processed.

(1) If a security interest in goods was perfected and subsequently the goods or a part thereof have become part of a product or mass, the security interest continues in the product or mass if

(a) the goods are so manufactured, processed, assembled or commingled that their identity is lost in the product or mass; or

(b) a financing statement covering the original goods also covers the product into which the goods have been manufactured, processed or assembled. In a case to which paragraph (b) applies, no separate security interest in that part of the original goods which has been manufactured, processed or assembled into the product may be claimed under Section 9-314.

(2) When under subsection (1) more than one security interest attaches to the product or mass, they rank equally according to the ratio that the cost of the goods to which each interest originally attached bears to the cost of the total product or mass.

§9-316. Priority Subject to Subordination. Nothing in this Article prevents subordination by agreement by any person entitled to priority.

§9-317. Secured Party Not Obligated On Contract of Debtor. The mere existence of a security interest or authority given to the debtor to dispose of or use collateral does not impose contract or tort liability upon the secured party for the debtor's acts or omissions.

§9-318. Defenses Against Assignee; Modification of Contract After Notification of Assignment; Term Prohibiting Assignment Ineffective; Identification and Proof of Assignment.

(1) Unless an account debtor has made an enforceable agreement not to assert defenses or claims arising out of a sale as provided in Section 9-206 the rights of an assignee are subject to

(a) all the terms of the contract between the account debtor and assignor and any defense or claim arising therefrom; and

(b) any other defense or claim of the account debtor against the assignor which accrues before the account debtor receives notification of the assignment.

(2) So far as the right to payment or a part thereof under an assigned contract has not been fully earned by performance, and notwithstanding notification of the assignment, any modification of or substitution for the contract made in good faith and in accordance with reasonable commercial standards is effective against an assignee unless the account debtor has otherwise agreed but the assignee acquires corresponding rights under the modified or substituted contract. The assignment may provide that such modification or substitution is a breach by the assignor.

(3) The account debtor is authorized to pay the assignor until the account debtor receives notification that the amount due or to become due has been assigned and that payment is to be made to the assignee. A notification which does not reasonably identify the rights assigned is ineffective. If requested by the account debtor, the assignee must seasonably furnish reasonable proof that the assignment has been made and unless he does so the account debtor may pay the assignor.

(4) A term in any contract between an account debtor and an assignor is ineffective if it prohibits assignment of an account or prohibits creation of a security interest in a general intangible for money due or to become due or requires the account debtor's consent to such assignment or security interest.

Part 4: Filing

§9-401. Place of Filing; Erroneous Filing; Removal of Collateral.

First Alternative Subsection (1)

(1) The proper place to file in order to perfect a security interest is as follows:

(a) when the collateral is timber to be cut or is minerals or the like (including oil and gas) or accounts subject to subsection (5) of Section 9-103, or when the financing statement is filed as a fixture filing (Section 9-313) and the collateral is goods which are or are to become fixtures, then in the office where a mortgage on the real estate would be filed or recorded;

(**b**) in all other cases, in the office of the [[Secretary of State]]

Second Alternative Subsection (1)

(**1**) The proper place to file in order to perfect a security interest is as follows:

(**a**) when the collateral is equipment used in farming operations, or farm products, or accounts or general intangibles arising from or relating to the sale of farm products by a farmer, or consumer goods, then in the office of the . . . . in the county of the debtor's residence or if the debtor is not a resident of this state then in the office of the . . . . in the county where the goods are kept, and in addition when the collateral is crops growing or to be grown in the office of the . . . . in the county where the land is located;

(**b**) when the collateral is timber to be cut or is minerals or the like (including oil and gas) or accounts subject to subsection (5) of Section 9-103, or when the financing statement is filed as a fixture filing (Section 9-313) and the collateral is goods which are or are to become fixtures, then in the office where a mortgage on the real estate would be filed or recorded;

(**c**) in all other cases, in the office of the

Third Alternative Subsection (1)

(**1**) The proper place to file in order to perfect a security interest is as follows:

(**a**) when the collateral is equipment used in farming operations, or farm products, or accounts or general intangibles arising from or relating to the sale of farm porducts by a farmer, or consumer goods, then in the office of the . . . . . . in the county of the debtor's residence or if the debtor is not a resident of this state then in the office of the . . . . . . in the county where the goods are kept, and in addition when the collateral is crops growing or to be grown in the office of . . . . . . in the county where the land is located;

(**b**) when the collateral is timber to be cut or is minerals or the like (including oil and gas) or accounts subject to subsection (5) of Section 9-103, or when the financing statement is filed as a fixture filing (Section 9-313) and the collateral is goods which are or are to beome fixtures, then in the office where a mortgage on the real estate would be filed or recorded;

(**c**) in all other cases, in the office of the . . . . . and in addition, if the debtor has a place of business in only one county of this state, also in the office of . . . . . . of such county, or, if the debtor has no place of business in this state, but resides in the state, also in the office of . . . . . . of the county in which he resides.

Note: *One of the three alternatives should be selected as subsection (1).*

(**2**) A filing which is made in good faith in an improper place or not in all of the places required by this section is nevertheless effective with regard to any collateral as to which the filing complied with the requirements of this Article and is also effective with regard to collateral covered by the financing statement against any person who has knowledge of the contents of such financing statement.

(**3**) A filing which is made in the proper place in this state continues effective even though the debtor's residence or place of business or the location of the collateral or its use, whichever controlled the original filing, is thereafter changed.

Language in double brackets is Alternative Subsection (3).

[[(**3**) A filing which is made in the proper county continues effective for four months after a change to another county of the debtor's residence or place of business or the location of the collateral, whichever controlled the original filing. It becomes ineffective thereafter unless a copy of the financing statement signed by the secured party is filed in the new county within said period. The security interest may also be perfected in the new county after the expiration of the four-month period; in such case perfected dates from the time of perfection in the new county. A change in the use of the collateral does not impair the effectiveness of the original filing.]]

(**4**) The rules stated in Section 9-103 determine whether filing is necessary in this state.

(**5**) Notwithstanding the preceding subsections, and subject to subsection (3) of Section 9-302, the proper place to file in order to perfect a security interest in collateral, including the fixtures, of a transmitting utility is the office of the [[Secretary of State]]. This filing constitutes a fixture filing (Section 9-313) as to the collateral described therein which is or is to become fixtures.

(**6**) For the purposes of this section, the residence of an organization is its place of business if it has one or its chief executive office if it has more than one place of business.

Note: *Subsection (6) should be used only if the state chooses the Second or Third Alternative Subsection (1).*

§9-402. Formal Requisites of Financing Statement; Amendments; Mortgage as Financing Statement.

(**1**) A financing statement is sufficient if it gives the names of the debtor and the secured party, is signed by the debtor, gives an address of the secured party from which information concerning the security interest may be obtained, gives a mailing address of the debtor and contains a statement indicating the types, or describing the items, of collateral. A financing statement may be filed before a security agreement is made or a security interest otherwise attaches. When the financing statement covers crops growing or to be grown, the statement must also contain a description of the real estate concerned. When the financing statement covers timber to be cut or covers minerals or the like (including oil and gas) or accounts subject to subsection (5) of Section 9-103, or when the financing statement is filed as a fixture filing (Section 9-313) and the collateral is goods which are or are to become fixtures, the statement must also comply with subsection (5). A copy of the security agreement is sufficient as a financing statement if it contains the above information and is signed by the debtor. A carbon, photographic or other reproduction of a security agreement or a financing statement is sufficient as a financing statement if the security agreement so provides or if the original has been filed in this state.

(2) A financing statement which otherwise complies with subsection (1) is sufficient when it is signed by the secured party instead of the debtor if it is filed to perfect a security interest in

(a) collateral already subject to security interest in another jurisdiction when it is brought into this state, or when the debtor's location is changed to this state. Such a financing statement must state that the collateral was brought into this state or that the debtor's location was changed to this state under such circumstances; or

(b) proceeds under Section 9-306 if the security interest in the original collateral was perfected. Such a financing statement must describe the original collateral; or

(c) collateral as to which the filing has lapsed; or

(d) collateral acquired after a change of name, identity or corporate structure of the debtor (subsection (7)).

(3) A form substantially as follows is sufficient to comply with subsection (1):

Name of debtor (or assignor) . . . .
Address . . . .
Name of secured party (or assignee). . . . .
Address . . . .

1. This financing statement covers the following types (or items) of property:
(Describe) . . . .

2. (If collateral is crops) The above described crops are growing or are to be grown on:
(Describe Real Estate) . . . .

3. (If applicable) The above goods are to become fixtures on *(Describe Real Estate) . . . . . and this financing statement is to be filed [[for record]] in the real estate records. (If the debtor does not have an interest of record) The name of a record owner is. . . . .

4. (If products of collateral are claimed) Products of the collateral are also covered.

(use whichever is applicable)
. . . .
Signature of Debtor (or Assignor)
. . . .
Signature of Secured Party (or Assignee)

(4) A financing statement may be amended by filing a writing signed by both the debtor and the secured party. An amendment does not extend the period of effectiveness of a financing statement. If any amendment adds collateral, it is effective as to the added collateral only from the filing date of the amendment. In this Article, unless the context otherwise requires, the term "financing statement" means the original financing statement and any amendments.

(5) A financing statement covering timber to be cut or covering minerals or the like (including oil and gas) or accounts subject to subsection (5) of Section 9-103, or a financing statement filed as a fixture filing (Section 9-313) where the debtor is not a transmitting utility, must show that it covers this type of collateral, must recite that it is to be filed [[for record]] in the real estate records, and the financing statement must contain a description of the real estate [[sufficient if it were contained in a mortgage of the real estate to give constructive notice of the mortgage under the law of this state]]. If the debtor does not have an interest of record in the real estate, the financing statement must show the name of a record owner.

(6) A mortgage is effective as a financing statement filed as a fixture filing from the date of its recording if (a) the goods are described in the mortgage by item or type, (b) the goods are or are to become fixtures related to the real estate described in the mortgage, (c) the mortgage complies with the requirements for a financing statement in this section other than a recital that it is to be filed in the real estate records, and (d) the mortgage is duly recorded. No fee with reference to the financing statement is required other than the regular recording and satisfaction fees with respect to the mortgage.

(7) A financing statement sufficiently shows the name of the debtor if it gives the individual, partnership or corporate name of the debtor, whether or not it adds other trade names or the names of partners. Where the debtor so changes his name or in the case of an organization name, identity or corporate structure that a filed financing statement becomes seriously misleading, the filing is not effective to perfect a security interest in collateral acquired by the debtor more than four months after the change, unless a new appropriate financing statement is filed before the expiration of that time. A filed financing statement remains effective with respect to collateral transferred by the debtor even though the secured party knows of or consents to the transfer.

(8) A financing statement substantially complying with the requirements of this section is effective even though it contains minor errors which are not seriously misleading.

Note: *Language in double brackets is optional.*

Note: *Where the state has any special recording system for real estate other than the usual grantor-grantee index (as, for instance, a tract system or a title registration or Torrens system) local adaptations of subsection (5) and Section 9-403(7) may be necessary. See Mass. Gen. Laws Chapter 106, Section 9-409.*

§9-403. What Constitutes Filing; Duration of Filing; Effect of Lapsed Filing; Duties of Filing Officer.

(1) Presentation for filing of a financing statement and tender of the filing fee or acceptance of the statement by the filing officer constitutes filing under this Article.

(2) Except as provided in subsection (6) a filed financing statement is effective for a period of five years from the date of filing. The effectiveness of a filed financing statement lapses on the expiration of the five year period unless a continuation statement is filed prior to the lapse. If a security interest perfected by filing exists at the time insolvency proceedings are commenced by or against the debtor, the security interest remains perfected until termination of the insolvency proceedings and thereafter for a period of sixty days or until expiration of the five year period, whichever occurs later. Upon lapse the

security interest becomes unperfected, unless it is perfected without filing. If the security interest becomes unperfected upon lapse, it is deemed to have been unperfected as against a person who became a purchaser or lien creditor before lapse.

(3) A continuation statement may be filed by the secured party within six months prior to the expiration of the five year period specified in subsection (2). Any such continuation statement must be signed by the secured party, identify the original statement by file number and state that the original statement is still effective. A continuation statement signed by a person other than the secured party of record must be accompanied by a separate written statement of assignment signed by the secured party of record and complying with subsection (2) of Section 9-405, including payment of the required fee. Upon timely filing of the continuation statement, the effectiveness of the original statement is continued for five years after the last date to which the filing was effective whereupon it lapses in the same manner as provided in subsection (2) unless another continuation statement is filed prior to such lapse. Succeeding continuation statements may be filed in the same manner to continue the effectiveness of the original statement. Unless a statute on dispostion of public records provides otherwise, the filing officer may remove a lapsed statement from the files and destroy it immediately if he has retained a microfilm or other photographic record, or in other cases after one year after the lapse. The filing officer shall so arrange matters by physical annexation of financing statements to continuation statements or other related filings, or by other means, that if he physically destroys the financing statements of a period more than five years past, those which have been continued by a continuation statement or which are still effective under subsection (6) shall be retained.

(4) Except as provided in subsection (7) a) filing officer shall mark each statement with a file number and with the date and hour of filing and shall hold the statement or a microfilm or other photographic copy thereof for public inspection. In addition the filing officer shall index the statements according to the name of the debtor and shall note in the index the file number and the address of the debtor given in the statement.

(5) The uniform fee for filing and indexing and for the stamping a copy furnished by the secured party to show the date and place of filing for an original financing statement or for a continuation statement shall be $ . . . . if the statement is in the standard form prescribed by the . . . . . and otherwise shall be $ . . . ., plus in each case, if the financing statement is subject to subsection (5) of Section 9-402, $ . . . . The uniform fee for each name more than one required to be indexed shall be $ . . . . The secured party may at his option show a trade name for any person and an extra uniform indexing fee of $ . . . . shall be paid with respect thereto.

(6) If the debtor is a transmitting utility (subsection (5) of Section 9-401) and a filed financing statement so states, it is effective until a termination statement is filed. A real estate mortgage which is effective as a fixture filing under subsection (6) of Section 9-402 remains effective as a fixture filing until the mortgage is released or satisfied or record or its effectiveness otherwise terminates as to the real estate.

(7) When a financing statement covers timber to be cut or covers minerals or the like (including oil and gas) or accounts subject to subsection (5) of Section 9-103, or is filed as a fixture filing, [[it shall be filed for record and]] the filing officer shall index it under the names of the debtor and any owner of record shown on the financing statement in the same fashion as if they were the mortgagors in a mortgage of the real estate described, and, to the extent that the law of this state provides for indexing of mortgages under the name of the mortgagee, under the name of the secured party as if he were the mortgagee, thereunder, or where indexing is by description in the same fashion as if the financing statement were a mortgage of the real estate described.

Note: *In states in which writings will not appear in the real estate records and indices unless actually recorded the bracketed language in subsection (7) should be used.*

§9-404. Termination Statement.

(1) If a financing statement covering consumer goods is filed on or after . . . ., then within one month or within ten days following written demand by the debtor after there is no outstanding secured obligation and no commitment to make advances, incur obligations or otherwise give value, the secured party must file with each filing officer with whom the financing statement was filed, a termination statement to the effect that he no longer claims a security interest under the financing statement, which shall be identified by file number. In other cases whenever there is no outstanding secured obligation and no commitment to make advances, incur obligations or otherwise give value, the secured party must on written demand by the debtor send the debtor, for each filing officer with whom the financing statement was filed, a termination statement to the effect that no longer claims a security interest under the financing statement, which shall be identified by file number. A termination statement signed by a person other than the secured party of record must be accompanied by a separate written statement of assignment signed by the secured party of record complying with subsection (2) of Section 9-405, including payment of the required fee. If the affected secured party fails to file such a termination statement as required by this subsection, or to send such a termination statement within ten days after proper demand therefor he shall be liable to the debtor for one hundred dollars, and in addition for any loss caused to the debtor by such failure.

(2) On presentation to the filing officer of such a termination statement he must note it in the index. If he has received the termination statement in duplicate, he shall return one copy of the termination statement to the secured party stamped to show the time of receipt thereof. If the filing officer has a microfilm or other photographic record of the financing statement, and of any related continuation statement, statement of assignment and statement of release, he may remove the originals from the files at any time after receipt of the termination statement, or if he has no such record, he may remove them from the files at any time after one year after receipt of the termination statement.

(3) If the termination statement is in the standard form prescribed by the . . . . . , the uniform fee for filing and indexing the termination statement shall be $. . . . . , and otherwise shall be $. . . . . , plus in each case an additional fee of $. . . . . for each name more than one against which the termination statement is required to be indexed.

Note: *The date to be inserted should be the effective date of the revised Article 9.*

§9-405. Assignment of Security Interest; Duties of Filing Officer; Fees.

(1) A financing statement may disclose an assignment of a security interest in the collateral described in the financing statement by indication in the financing statement of the name and address of the assignee or by an assignment itself or a copy thereof on the face or back of the statement. On presentation to the filing officer of such a financing statement the filing officer shall mark the same as provided in Section 9-403(4). The uniform fee for filing, indexing and furnishing filing data for a financing statement so indicating an assignment shall be $. . . . . if the statement is in the standard form prescribed by the . . . . and otherwise shall be $. . . . . plus in each case an additional fee of $. . . . . for each name more than one against which the financing statement is required to be indexed.

(2) A secured party may assign of record all or part of his rights under a financing statement by the filing in the place where the original financing statement was filed of a separate written statement of assignment signed by the secured party of record and setting forth the name of the secured party of record and the debtor, the file number and the date of filing of the financing statement and the name and address of the assignee and containing a description of the collateral assigned. A copy of the assignment is sufficient as a separate statement if it complies with the preceding sentence. On presentation to the filing officer of such a separate statement, the filing officer shall mark such separate statement with the date and hour of the filing. He shall note the assignment on the index of the financing statement, or in the case of a fixture filing, or a filing covering timber to be cut, or covering minerals or the like (including oil and gas) or accounts subject to subsection (5) of Section 9-103, he shall index the assignment under the name of the assignor as grantor and, to the extent that the law of this state provides for indexing the assignment of a mortgage under the name of the assignee, he shall index the assignment of the financing statement under the name of the assignee. The uniform fee for filing, indexing and furnishing filing data about such a separate statement of assignment shall be $. . . . . if the statement is in the standard form prescribed by the . . . . . and otherwise shall be $. . . . . , plus in each case an additional fee of $. . . . . for each name more than one against which the statement of assignment is required to be indexed. Notwithstanding the provisions of this subsection, an assignment of record of a security interest in a fixture contained in a mortgage effective as a fixture filing (subsection (6) of Section 9-402) may be made only by an assignment of the mortgage in the manner provided by the law of this state other than this Act.

(3) After the disclosure or filing of an assignment under this section, the assignee is the secured party of record.

§9-406. Release of Collateral; Duties of Filing Officer; Fees. A secured party of record may by his signed statement release all or a part of any collateral described in a filed financing statement. The statement of release is sufficient if it contains a description of the collateral being released, the name and address of the debtor, the name and address of the secured party, and the file number of the financing statement. A statement of release signed by a person other than the secured party of record must be accompanied by a separate written statement of assignment signed by the secured party of record and complying with subsection (2) of Section 9-405, including payment of the required fee. Upon presentation of such a statement of release to the filing officer he shall mark the statement with the hour and date of filing and shall note the same upon the margin of the index of the filing of the financing statement. The uniform fee for filing and noting such a statement of release shall be $. . . . . if the statement is in the standard form prescribed by the . . . . . and otherwise shall be $. . . . . , plus in each case an additional fee of $. . . . . . . for each name more than one against which the statement of release is required to be indexed.

§[[9-407. Information From Filing Officer.]]

[[(1) If the person filing any financing statement, termination statement, statement of assignment, or statement of release, furnishes the filing officer a copy thereof, the filing officer shall upon request note upon the copy the file number and date and hour of the filing of the original and deliver or send the copy to such person.

[[(2) Upon request of any person, the filing officer shall issue his certificate showing whether there is on file on the date and hour stated therein, any presently effective financing statement naming a particular debtor and any statement of assignment thereof and if there is, giving the date and hour of filing of each such statement and the names and addresses of each secured party therein. The uniform fee for such a certificate shall be $. . . . . if the request for the certificate is in the standard form prescribed by the [[Secretary of State]] and otherwise shall be $. . . . . Upon request the filing officer shall furnish a copy of any filed statement or statement of assignment for a uniform fee of $. . . . . per page.]]

Note: *This section is proposed as an optional provision to require filing officers to furnish certificates. Local law and practices should be consulted with regard to the advisability of adoption.*

§9-408. Financing Statements Covering Consigned or Leased Goods. A consignor or lessor of goods may file a financing statement using the terms "consignor," "consignee," "lessor," "lessee" or the like instead of the terms specified in Section 9-402. The provisions of this Part shall apply as appropriate to such a financing statement but its filing shall not of itself be a factor in determining whether or not the consignment or lease is intended as security (Section 1-201(37)). However, if it is determined for other reasons that the consignment or lease is so intended, a security interest of the consignor or lessor which attaches to the consigned or leased goods is perfected by such filing.

Part 5: Default

§9-501. Default; Procedure When Security Agreement Covers Both Real and Personal Property.

(1) When a debtor is in default under a security agreement, a secured party has the rights and remedies provided in this Part and except as limited by subsection (3) those provided in the security agreement. He may reduce his claim to judgment, foreclose or otherwise enforce the security interest by any available judicial procedure. If the collateral is documents the secured party may proceed either as to the documents or as to the goods covered thereby. A secured party in possession has the rights, remedies and duties provided in Section 9-207. The rights and remedies referred to in this subsection are cumulative.

(2) After default, the debtor has the rights and remedies provided in this Part, those provided in the security agreement and those provided in Section 9-207.

(3) To the extent that they give rights to the debtor and impose duties on the secured party, the rules stated in the subsections referred to below may not be waived or varied except as provided with respect to compulsory disposition of collateral (subsection (3) of Section 9-504 and Section 9-505) and with respect to redemption of collateral (Section 9-506) but the parties may by agreement determine the standards by which the fulfillment of these rights and duties is to be measured if such standards are not manifestly unreasonable:

(a) subsection (2) of Section 9-502 and subsection (2) of Section 9-504 insofar as they require accounting for surplus proceeds of collateral;

(b) subsection (3) of Section 9-504 and subsection (1) of Section 9-505 which deal with disposition of collateral;

(c) subsection (2) of Section 9-505 which deals with acceptance of collateral as discharge of obligation;

(d) Section 9-506 which deals with redemption of collateral; and

(e) subsection (1) of Section 9-507 which deals with the secured party's liability for failure to comply with this Part.

(4) If the security agreement covers both real and personal property, the secured party may proceed under this Part as to the personal property or he may proceed as to both the real and the personal property in accordance with his rights and remedies in respect of the real property in which case the provisions of this Part do not apply.

(5) When a secured party has reduced his claim to judgment the lien of any levy which may be made upon his collateral by virtue of any execution based upon the judgment shall relate back to the date of the perfection of the security interest in such collateral. A judicial sale, pursuant to such execution, is a foreclosure of the security interest by judicial procedure within the meaning of this section, and the secured party may purchase at the sale and thereafter hold the collateral free of any other requirements of this Article.

§9-502. Collection Rights of Secured Party.

(1) When so agreed and in any event on default the secured party is entitled to notify an account debtor or the obligor on an instrument to make payment to him whether or not the assignor was theretofore making collections on the collateral, and also to take control of any proceeds to which he is entitled under Section 9-306.

(2) A secured party who by agreement is entitled to charge back uncollected collateral or otherwise to full or limited recourse against the debtor and who undertakes to collect from the account debtors or obligors must proceed in a commercially reasonable manner and may deduct his reasonable expenses of realization from the collections. If the security agreement secures an indebtedness, the secured party must account to the debtor for any surplus, and unless otherwise agreed, the debtor is liable for any deficiency. But, if the underlying transaction was a sale of accounts or chattel paper, the debtor is entitled to any surplus or is liable for any deficiency only if the security agreement so provides.

§9-503. Secured Party's Right to Take Possession After Default. Unless otherwise agreed a secured party has on default the right to take possession of the collateral. In taking possession a secured party may proceed without judicial process if this can be done without breach of the peace or may proceed by action. If the security agreement so provides the secured party may require the debtor to assemble the collateral and make it available to the secured party at a place to be designated by the secured party which is reasonably convenient to both parties. Without removal a secured party may render equipment unusable, and may dispose of collateral on the debtor's premises under Section 9-504.

§9-504. Secured Party's Right to Dispose of Collateral After Default; Effect of Dispositon.

(1) A secured party after default may sell, lease or otherwise dispose of any or all of the collateral in its then condition or following any commercially reasonable preparation or processing. Any sale of goods is subject to the Article on Sales (Article 2). The proceeds of disposition shall be applied in the order following to

(a) the reasonable expenses of retaking, holding, preparing for sale or lease, selling, leasing and the like and, to the extent provided for in the agreement and not prohibited by law, the reasonable attorneys' fees and legal expenses incurred by the secured party;

(b) the satisfaction of indebtedness secured by the security interest under which the disposition is made;

(c) the satisfaction of indebtedness secured by any subordinate security interest in the collateral if written notification of demand therefor is received before distribution of the proceeds is completed. If requested by the secured party, the holder of a subordinate security interest must seasonably furnish reasonable proof of his interest, and unless he does so, the secured party need not comply with his demand.

(2) If the security interest secures an indebtedness, the secured party must account to the debtor for any surplus, and, unless otherwise agreed, the debtor is liable for any deficiency. But if the underlying transaction was a sale of accounts, or chattel paper, the debtor is entitled to any surplus or is liable for any deficiency only if the security agreement so provides.

(3) Disposition of the collateral may be by public or private proceedings and may be made by way of one or more contracts. Sale or other disposition may be as a unit or in parcels and at any time and place and on any terms but every aspect of the disposition including the method, manner, time, place and terms must be commercially reasonable. Unless collateral is perishable or threatens to decline speedily in value or is of a type customarily sold on a recognized market, reasonable notification of the time and place of any public sale or reasonable notification of the time after which any private sale or other intended dispostion is to be made shall be sent by the secured party to the debtor, if he has not signed after default a statement renouncing or modifying his right to notification of sale. In the case of consumer goods no other notification need be sent. In other cases notification shall be sent to any other secured party from whom the secured party has received (before sending his notification to the debtor or before the debtor's renunication of his rights) written notice of a claim of an interest in the collateral. The secured party may buy at any public sale and if the collateral is of a type customarily sold in a recognized market or is of a type which is the subject of widely distributed standard price quotations he may buy at private sale.

(4) When collateral is disposed of by a secured party after default, the disposition transfers to a purchaser for value all of the debtor's rights therein, discharges the security interest under which it is made and any security interest or lien subordinate thereto. The purchaser takes free of all such rights and interests even though the secured party fails to comply with the requirements of this Part or of any judicial proceedings

(a) in the case of a public sale, if the purchaser has no knowledge of any defects in the sale and if he does not buy in collusion with the secured party, other bidders or the person conducting the sale; or

(b) in any other case, if the purchaser acts in good faith.

(5) A person who is liable to a secured party under a guaranty, indorsement, repurchase agreement or the like and who receives a transfer of collateral from the secured party or is subrogated to his rights has thereafter the rights and duties of the secured party. Such a transfer of collateral is not a sale or disposition of the collateral under this Article.

§9-505. Compulsory Disposition of Collateral; Acceptance of the Collateral as Discharge of Obligation.

(1) If the debtor has paid sixty per cent of the cash price in the case of a purchase money security interest in consumer goods or sixty per cent of the loan in the case of another security interest in consumer goods and has not signed after default a statement renouncing or modifying his rights under this Part a secured party who has taken possession of collateral must dispose of it under Section 9-504 and if he fails to do so within ninety days after he takes possession the debtor at his option may recover in conversion or under Section 9-507(1) on secured party's liability.

(2) In any other case involving consumer goods or any other collateral a secured party in possession may, after default, propose to retain the collateral in satisfaction of the obligation. Written notice of such proposal shall be sent to the debtor if he has not signed after default a statement renouncing or modifying his rights under this subsection. In the case of consumer goods no other notice need be given. In other cases notice shall be sent to any other secured party from whom the secured party has received (before sending his notice to the debtor or before the debtor's renunciation of his rights) written notice of a claim of an interest in the collateral. If the secured party receives objection in writing from a person entitled to receive notification within twenty-one days after the notice was sent, the secured party must dispose of the collateral under Section 9-504. In the absence of such written objection the secured party may retain the collateral in satisfaction of the debtor's obligation.

§9-506. Debtor's Right to Redeem Collateral. At any time before the secured party has disposed of collateral or entered into a contract for its disposition under Section 9-504 or before the obligation has been discharged under Section 9-505(2) the debtor or any other secured party may unless otherwise agreed in writing after default redeem the collateral by tendering fulfillment of all obligations secured by the collateral as well as the expenses reasonably incurred by the secured party in retaking, holding and preparing the collateral for disposition, in arranging for the sale, and to the extent provided in the agreement and not prohibited by law, his reasonable attorneys' fees and legal expenses.

§9-507. Secured Party's Liability for Failure to Comply With This Part.

(1) If it is established that the secured party is not proceeding in accordance with the provisions of this Part disposition may be ordered or restrained on appropriate terms and conditions. If the disposition has occurred the debtor or any person entitled to notification or whose security interest has been made known to the secured party prior to the disposition has a right to recover from the secured party any loss caused by a failure to comply with the provisions of this Part. If the collateral is consumer goods, the debtor has a right to recover in any event an amount not less than the credit service charge plus ten per cent of the principal amount of the debt or the time price differential plus 10 per cent of the cash price.

(2) The fact that a better price could have been obtained by a sale at a different time or in a different method from that selected by the secured party is not of itself sufficient to establish that the sale was not made in a commercially reasonable manner. If the secured party either sells the collateral in the usual manner in any recognized market therefor or if he

sells at the price current in such market at the time of his sale or if he has otherwise sold in conformity with reasonable commercial practices among dealers in the type of property sold he has sold in a commercially reasonable manner. The principles stated in the two preceding sentences with respect to sales also apply as may be appropriate to other types of disposition. A disposition which has been approved in any judicial proceeding or by any bona fide creditors' committee or representative of creditors shall conclusively be deemed to be commercially reasonable, but this sentence does not indicate that any such approval must be obtained in any case nor does it indicate that any disposition not so approved is not commercially reasonable.

ARTICLE 10: EFFECTIVE DATE AND REPEALER

[omitted]

ARTICLE 11: EFFECTIVE DATE AND TRANSITION PROVISIONS

[omitted]

APPENDIX 3
Uniform Partnership Act

Part I Preliminary Provisions

§1. Name of Act. This act may be cited as Uniform Partnership Act.

§2. Definition of Terms. In this act, "Court" includes every court and judge having jurisdiction in the case.

"Business" includes every trade, occupation, or profession.

"Person" includes individuals, partnerships, corporations, and other associations.

"Bankrupt" includes bankrupt under the Federal Bankruptcy Act or insolvent under any state insolvent act.

"Conveyance" includes every assignment, lease, mortgage, or encumbrance.

"Real property" includes land and any interest or estate in land.

§3. Interpretation of Knowledge and Notice.

(1) A person has "knowledge" of a fact within the meaning of this act not only when he has actual knowledge thereof, but also when he has knowledge of such other facts as in the circumstances shows bad faith.

(2) A person has "notice" of a fact within the meaning of this act when the person who claims the benefit of the notice:

(a) States the fact to such person, or

(b) Delivers through the mail, or by other means of communication, a written statement of the fact to such person or to a proper person at his place of business or residence.

§4. Rules of Construction.

(1) The rule that statutes in derogation of the common law are to be strictly construed shall have no application to this act.

(2) The law of estoppel shall apply under this act.

(3) The law of agency shall apply under this act.

(4) This act shall be so interpreted and construed as to effect its general purpose to make uniform the law of those states which enact it.

(5) This act shall not be construed so as to impair the obligations of any contract existing when the act goes into effect, nor to affect any action or proceedings begun or right accrued before this act takes effect.

§5. Rules for Cases Not Provided for in This Act. In any case not provided for in this act the rules of law and equity, including the law merchant, shall govern.

Part II Nature of Partnership

§6. Partnership Defined.

(1) A partnership is an association of two or more persons to carry on as co-owners a business for profit.

(2) But any association formed under any other statute of this state, or any statute adopted by authority, other than the authority of this state, is not a partnerhsip under this act, unless such association would have been a partnership in this state prior to the adoption of this act; but this act shall apply to limited partnerships except in so far as the statutes relating to such partnerships are inconsistent herewith.

§7. Rules for Determining the Existence of a Partnership. In determining whether a partnership exists, these rules shall apply:

(1) Except as provided by section 16 persons who are not partners as to each other are not partners as to third persons.

(2) Joint tenancy, tenancy in common, tenancy by the entireties, joint property, common property, or part ownership does not of itself establish a partnership, whether such co-owners do or do not share any profits made by the use of the property.

(3) The sharing of gross returns does not of itself establish a partnership, whether or not the persons sharing them

have a joint or common right or interest in any property from which the returns are derived.

(4) The receipt by a person of a share of the profits of a business is prima facie evidence that he is a partner in the business, but no such inference shall be drawn if such profits were received in payment:

(a) As a debt by installments or otherwise,

(b) As wages of an employee or rent to a landlord,

(c) As an annuity to a widow or representative of a deceased partner,

(d) As interest on a loan, though the amount of payment vary with the profits of the business,

(e) As the consideration for the sale of a good-will of a business or other property by installments or otherwise.

§8. Partnership Property.

(1) All property originally brought into the partnership stock or subsequently acquired by purchase or otherwise, on account of the partnership, is partnership property.

(2) Unless the contrary intention appears, property acquired with partnership funds is partnership property.

(3) Any estate in real property may be acquired in the partnership name. Title so acquired can be conveyed only in the partnership name.

(4) A conveyance to a partnership in the partnership name, though without words of inheritance, passes the entire estate of the grantor unless a contrary intent appears.

Part III Relations of Partners to Persons Dealing with the Partnership

§9. Partner Agent of Partnership as to Partnership Business.

(1) Every partner is an agent of the partnership for the purpose of its business, and the act of every partner, including the execution in the partnership name of any instrument, for apparently carrying on in the usual way the business of the partnership of which he is a member binds the partnership, unless the partner so acting has in fact no authority to act for the partnership in the particular matter, and the person with whom he is dealing has knowledge of the fact that he has no such authority.

(2) An act of a partner which is not apparently for the carrying on of the business of the partnership in the usual way does not bind the partnership unless authorized by the other partners.

(3) Unless authorized by the other partners or unless they have abandoned the business, one or more but less than all the partners have no authority to:

(a) Assign the partnership property in trust for creditors or on the assignee's promise to pay the debts of the partnership,

(b) Dispose of the good-will of the business,

(c) Do any other act which would make it impossible to carry on the ordinary business of a partnership,

(d) Confess a judgment,

(e) Submit a partnership claim or liability to arbitration or reference.

(4) No act of a partner in contravention of a restriction on authority shall bind the partnership to persons having knowledge of the restriction.

§10. Conveyance of Real Property of the Partnership.

(1) Where title to real property is in the partnership name, any partner may convey title to such property by a conveyance executed in the partnership name; but the partnership may recover such property unless the partner's act binds the partnership under the provisions of paragraph (1) of section 9, or unless such property has been conveyed by the grantee or a person claiming through such grantee to a holder for value without knowledge that the partner, in making the conveyance, has exceeded his authority.

(2) Where title to real property is in the name of the partnership, a conveyance executed by a partner, in his own name, passes the equitable interest of the partnership, provided the act is one within the authority of the partner under the provisions of paragraph (1) of section 9.

(3) Where title to real property is in the name of one or more but not all the partners, and the record does not disclose the right of the partnership, the partners in whose name the title stands may convey title to such property, but the partnership may recover such property if the partner's act does not bind the partnership under the provisions of paragraph (1) of section 9, unless the purchaser or his assignee, is a holder for value, without knowledge.

(4) Where the title to real property is in the name of one or more or all the partners, or in a third person in trust for the partnership, a conveyance executed by a partner in the partnership name, or in his own name, passes the equitable interest of the partnership, provided the act is one within the authority of the partner under the provisions of paragraph (1) of section 9.

(5) Where the title to real property is in the names of all the partners a conveyance executed by all the partners passes all their rights in such property.

§11. Partnership Bound by Admission of Partner. An admission or representation made by any partner concerning partnership affairs within the scope of his authority as conferred by this act is evidence against the partnership.

§12. Partnership Charged with Knowledge of or Notice to Partner. Notice to any partner of any matter relating to partnership affairs, and the knowledge of the partner acting in the particular matter, acquired while a partner or then present to his mind, and the knowledge of any other partner who reasonably could and should have communicated it to the acting partner, operate as notice to or knowledge of the partnership, except in the case of a fraud on the partnership committed by or with the consent of that partner.

§13. Partnership Bound by Partner's Wrongful Act. Where, by any wrongful act or omission of any partner acting in the ordinary course of the business of the partnership or with the authority of his co-partners, loss or injury is caused to any person, not being a partner in the partnership, or any penalty is incurred, the partnership is liable therefor to the same extent as the partner so acting or omitting to act.

§14. Partnership Bound by Partner's Breach of Trust. The partnership is bound to make good the loss:

(a) Where one partner acting within the scope of his apparent authority receives money or property of a third person and misapplies it; and

(b) Where the partnership in the course of its business receives money or property of a third person and the money or property so received is misapplied by any partner while it is in the custody of the partnership.

§15. Nature of Partner's Liability. All partners are liable

(a) Jointly and severally for everything chargeable to the partnership under sections 13 and 14.

(b) Jointly for all other debts and obligations of the partnership; but any partner may enter into a separate obligation to perform a partnership contract.

§16. Partner by Estoppel.

(1) When a person, by words spoken or written or by conduct, represents himself, or consents to another representing him to any one, as a partner in an existing partnership or with one or more persons not actual partners, he is liable to any such person to whom such representation has been made, who has, on the faith of such representation, given credit to the actual or apparent partnership, and if he has made such representation or consented to its being made in a public manner he is liable to such person, whether the representation has or has not been made or communicated to such person so giving credit by or with the knowledge of the apparent partner making the representation or consenting to its being made.

(a) When a partnership liability results, he is liable as though he were an actual member of the partnership.

(b) When no partnership liability results, he is liable jointly with the other persons, if any, so consenting to the contract or representation as to incur liability, otherwise separately.

(2) When a person has been thus represented to be a partner in an existing partnership, or with one or more persons not actual partners, he is an agent of the persons consenting to such representation to bind them to the same extent and in the same manner as though he were a partner in fact, with respect to persons who rely upon the representation. Where all the members of the existing partnership consent to the representation, a partnership act or obligation results; but in all other cases it is the joint act or obligation of the person acting and the persons consenting to the representation.

§17. Liability of Incoming Partner. A person admitted as a partner into an existing partnership is liable for all the obligations of the partnership arising before his admission as though he had been a partner when such obligations were incurred, except that this liability shall be satisfied only out of partnership property.

Part IV Relations of Partners to One Another

§18. Rules Determining Rights and Duties of Partners. The rights and duties of the partners in relation to the partnership shall be determined, subject to any agreement between them, by the following rules:

(a) Each partner shall be repaid his contributions, whether by way of capital or advances to the partnership property and share equally in the profits and surplus remaining after all liabilities, including those to partners, are satisfied; and must contribute towards the losses, whether of capital or otherwise, sustained by the partnership according to his share in the profits.

(b) The partnership must indemnify every partner in respect of payments made and personal liabilities reasonably incurred by him in the ordinary and proper conduct of its business, or for the preservation of its business or property.

(c) A partner, who in aid of the partnership makes any payment or advance beyond the amount of capital which he agreed to contribute, shall be paid interest from the date of the payment or advance.

(d) A partner shall receive interest on the capital contributed by him only from the date when repayment should be made.

(e) All partners have equal rights in the management and conduct of the partnership business.

(f) No partner is entitled to remuneration for acting in the partnership business, except that a surviving partner is entitled to reasonable compensation for his services in winding up the partnership affairs.

(g) No person can become a member of a partnership without the consent of all the partners.

(h) Any difference arising as to ordinary matters connected with the partnership business may be decided by a majority of the partners; but no act in contravention of any agreement between the partners may be done rightfully without the consent of all the partners.

§19. Partnership Books. The partnership books shall be kept, subject to any agreement between the partners, at the principal place of business of the partnership, and every partner shall at all times have access to and may inspect and copy any of them.

§20. Duty of Partners to Render Information. Partners shall render on demand true and full information of all things affecting the partnership to any partner or the legal representative of any deceased partner or partner under legal disability.

§21. Partner Accountable as a Fiduciary.

(1) Every partner must account to the partnership for any benefit, and hold as trustee for it any profits derived by him without the consent of the other partners from any transaction connected with the formation, conduct, or liquidation of the partnership or from any use by him of its property.

(2) This section applies also to the representatives of a deceased partner engaged in the liquidation of the affairs of the partnership as the personal representatives of the last surviving partner.

§22. Right to an Account. Any partner shall have the right to a formal account as to partnership affairs:

(a) If he is wrongfully excluded from the partnership business or possession of its property by his co-partners,

(b) If the right exists under the terms of any agreement,

(c) As provided by section 21.

(d) Whenever other circumstances render it just and reasonable.

§23. Continuation of Partnership beyond Fixed Term.

(1) When a partnership for a fixed term or particular undertaking is continued after the termination of such term or particular undertaking without any express agreement, the rights and duties of the partners remain the same as they were at such termination, so far as is consistent with a partnership at will.

(2) A continuation of the business by the partners or such of them as habitually acted therein during the term, without any settlement or liquidation of the partnership affairs, is prima facie evidence of a continuation of the partnership.

Part V Property Rights of a Partner

§24. Extent of Property Rights of a Partner. The property rights of a partner are (1) his rights in specific partnership property, (2) his interest in the partnership, and (3) his right to participate in the management.

§25. Nature of a Partner's Right in Specific Partnership Property.

(1) A partner is co-owner with his partners of specific partnership property holding as a tenant in partnership.

(2) The incidents of this tenancy are such that:

(a) A partner, subject to the provisions of this act and to any agreement between the partners, has an equal right with his partners to possess specific partnership property for partnership purposes; but he has no right to possess such property for any other purpose without the consent of his partners.

(b) A partner's right in specific partnership property is not assignable except in connection with the assignment of rights of all the partners in the same property.

(c) A partner's right in specific partnership property is not subject to attachment or execution, except on a claim against the partnership. When partnership property is attached for a partnership debt the partners, or any of them, or the representatives of a deceased partner, cannot claim any right under the homestead or exemption laws.

(d) On the death of a partner his right in specific partnership property vests in the surviving partner or partners, except where the deceased was the last surviving partner, when his right in such property vests in his legal representative. Such surviving partner or partners, or the legal representative of the last surviving partner, has no right to possess the partnership property for any but a partnership purpose.

(e) A partner's right in specific partnership property is not subject to dower, curtesy, or allowances to widows, heirs, or next of kin.

§26. Nature of Partner's Interest in the Partnership. A partner's interest in the partnership is his share of the profits and surplus, and the same is personal property.

§27. Assignment of Partner's Interest.

(1) A conveyance by a partner of his interest in the partnership does not of itself dissolve the partnership, nor, as against the other partners in the absence of agreement, entitle the assignee, during the continuance of the partnership, to interfere in the management or administration of the partnership business or affairs, or to require any information or account of partnership transactions, or to inspect the partnership books; but it merely entitles the assignee to receive in accordance with his contract the profits to which the assigning partner would otherwise be entitled.

(2) In case of a dissolution of the partnership, the assignee is entitled to receive his assignor's interest and may require an account from the date only of the last account agreed to by all the partners.

§28. Partner's Interest Subject to Charging Order.

(1) On due application to a competent court by any judgment creditor of a partner, the court which entered the judgment, order, or decree, or any other court, may charge the interest of the debtor partner with payment of the

unsatisfied amount of such judgment debt with interest thereon; and may then or later appoint a receiver of his share of the profits, and of any other money due or to fall due to him in respect of the partnership, and make all other orders, directions, accounts and inquiries which the debtor partner might have made, or which the circumstances of the case may require.

(2) The interest charged may be redeemed at any time before foreclosure, or in case of a sale being directed by the court may be purchased without thereby causing a dissolution:

(a) With separate property, by any one or more of the partners, or

(b) With partnership property, by any one or more of the partners with the consent of all the partners whose interests are not so charged or sold.

(3) Nothing in this act shall be held to deprive a partner of his right, if any, under the exemption laws, as regards his interest in the partnership.

Part VI Dissolution and Winding Up

§29. Dissolution Defined. The dissolution of a partnership is the change in the relation of the partners caused by any partner ceasing to be associated in the carrying on as distinguished from the winding up of the business.

§30. Partnership not Terminated by Dissolution. On dissolution the partnership is not terminated, but continues until the winding up of partnership affairs is completed.

§31. Causes of Dissolution. Dissolution is caused:

(1) Without violation of the agreement between the partners,

(a) By the termination of the definite term or particular undertaking specified in the agreement,

(b) By the express will of any partner when no definite term or particular undertaking is specified,

(c) By the express will of all the partners who have not assigned their interests or suffered them to be charged for their separate debts, either before or after the termination of any specified term or particular undertaking,

(d) By the expulsion of any partner from the business bona fide in accordance with such a power conferred by the agreement between the partners;

(2) In contravention of the agreement between the partners, where the circumstances do not permit a dissolution under any other provision of this section, by the express will of any partner at any time;

(3) By any event which makes it unlawful for the business of the partnership to be carried on or for the members to carry it on in partnership;

(4) By the death of any partner;

(5) By the bankruptcy of any partner or the partnership;

(6) By decree of court under section 32.

§32. Dissolution by Decree of Court.

(1) On application by or for a partner the court shall decree a dissolution whenever:

(a) A partner has been declared a lunatic in any judicial proceeding or is shown to be of unsound mind,

(b) A partner becomes in any other way incapable of performing his part of the partnership contract,

(c) A partner has been guilty of such conduct as tends to affect prejudicially the carrying on of the business,

(d) A partner willfully or persistently commits a breach of the partnership agreement, or otherwise so conducts himself in matters relating to the partnership business that it is not reasonably practicable to carry on the business in partnership with him,

(e) The business of the partnership can only be carried on at a loss,

(f) Other circumstances render a dissolution equitable.

(2) On the application of the purchaser of a partner's interest under sections 27 or 28:

(a) After the termination of the specified term or particular undertaking,

(b) At any time if the partnership was a partnership at will when the interest was assigned or when the charging order was issued.

§33. General Effect of Dissolution on Authority of Partner. Except so far as may be necessary to wind up partnership affairs or to complete transactions begun but not then finished, dissolution terminates all authority of any partner to act for the partnership,

(1) With respect to the partners,

(a) When the dissolution is not by the act, bankruptcy or death of a partner; or

(b) When the dissolution is by such act, bankruptcy or death of a partner, in cases where section 34 so requires.

(2) With respect to persons not partners, as declared in section 35.

§34. Right of Partner to Contribution from Co-Partners after Dissolution. Where the dissolution is caused by the act, death or bankruptcy of a partner, each partner is liable to his co-partners for his share of any liability created by any partner acting for the partnership as if the partnership had not been dissolved unless

(a) The dissolution being by act of any partner, the partner acting for the partnership had knowledge of the dissolution, or

(b) The dissolution being by the death or bankruptcy of a partner, the partner acting for the partnership had knowledge or notice of the death or bankruptcy.

§35. Power of Partner to Bind Partnership to Third Persons after Dissolution.

(1) After dissolution a partner can bind the partnership except as provided in paragraph (3).

(a) By any act appropriate for winding up partnership affairs or completing transactions unfinished at dissolution;

(b) By any transaction which would bind the partnership if dissolution had not taken place, provided the other party to the transaction

(I) Had extended credit to the partnership prior to dissolution and had no knowledge or notice of the dissolution; or

(II) Though he had not so extended credit, had nevertheless known of the partnership prior to dissolution, and, having no knowledge or notice of dissolution, the fact of dissolution had not been advertised in a newspaper of general circulation in the place (or in each place if more than one) at which the partnership business was regularly carried on.

(2) The liability of a partner under paragraph (1b) shall be satisfied out of partnership assets alone when such partner had been prior to dissolution

(a) Unknown as a partner to the person with whom the contract is made; and

(b) So far unknown and inactive in partnership affairs that the business reputation of the partnership could not be said to have been in any degree due to his connection with it.

(3) The partnership is in no case bound by any act of a partner after dissolution

(a) Where the partnership is dissolved because it is unlawful to carry on the business, unless the act is appropriate for winding up partnership affairs; or

(b) Where the partner has become bankrupt; or

(c) Where the partner has no authority to wind up partnership affairs; except by a transaction with one who

(I) Had extended credit to the partnership prior to dissolution and had no knowledge or notice of his want of authority; or

(II) Had not extended credit to the partnership prior to dissolution, and, having no knowledge or notice of his want of authority, the fact of his want of authority has not been advertised in the manner provided for advertising the fact of dissolution in paragraph (1bII).

(4) Nothing in this section shall affect the liability under section 16 of any person who after dissolution represents himself or consents to another representing him as a partner in a partnership engaged in carrying on business.

§36. Effect of Dissolution on Partner's Existing Liability.

(1) The dissolution of the partnership does not of itself discharge the existing liability of any partner.

(2) A partner is discharged from any existing liability upon dissolution of the partnership by an agreement to that effect between himself, the partnership creditor and the person or partnership continuing the business; and such agreement may be inferred from the course of dealing between the creditor having knowledge of the dissolution and the person or partnership continuing the business.

(3) Where a person agrees to assume the existing obligations of a dissolved partnership, the partners whose obligations have been assumed shall be discharged from any liability to any creditor of the partnership who, knowing of the agreement, consents to a material alteration in the nature or time of payment of such obligations.

(4) The individual property of a deceased partner shall be liable for all obligations of the partnership incurred while he was a partner but subject to the prior payment of his separate debts.

§37. Right to Wind Up. Unless otherwise agreed the partners who have not wrongfully dissolved the partnership or the legal representative of the last surviving partner, not bankrupt, has the right to wind up the partnership affairs; provided, however, that any partner, his legal representative or his assignee, upon cause shown, may obtain winding up by the court.

§38. Rights of Partners to Application of Partnership Property.

(1) When dissolution is caused in any way, except in contravention of the partnership agreement, each partner, as against his co-partners and all persons claiming through them in respect of their interests in the partnership, unless otherwise agreed, may have the partnership property applied to discharge its liabilities, and the surplus applied to pay in cash the net amount owing to the respective partners. But if dissolution is caused by expulsion of a partner, bona fide under the partnership agreement and if the expelled partner is discharged from all partnership liabilities, either by payment or agreement under section 36(2), he shall receive in cash only the net amount due him from the partnership.

(2) When dissolution is caused in contravention of the partnership agreement the rights of the partners shall be as follows:

(a) Each partner who has not caused dissolution wrongfully shall have,

(I) All the rights specified in paragraph (1) of this section, and

(II) The right, as against each partner who has caused the dissolution wrongfully, to damages for breach of the agreement.

(b) The partners who have not caused the dissolution wrongfully, if they all desire to continue the business in the same name, either by themselves or jointly with others, may do so, during the agreed term for the partnership and for that purpose may possess the partnership property, provided they secure the payment by bond approved by the court, or pay to any partner who has caused the dissolution wrongfully, the value of his interest in the partnership at the dissolution, less any damages recoverable under clause (2aII) of this section, and in like manner indemnify him against all present or future partnership liabilities.

(c) A partner who has caused the dissolution wrongfully shall have:

(I) If the business is not continued under the provisions of paragraph (2b) all the rights of a partner under paragraph (1), subject to clause (2aII), of this section,

(II) If the business is continued under paragraph (2b) of this section the right as against his co-partners and all claiming through them in respect of their interests in the partnership, to have the value of his interest in the partnership, less any damages caused to his co-partners by the dissolution, ascertained and paid to him in cash, or the payment secured by bond approved by the court, and to be released from all existing liabilities of the partnership; but in ascertaining the value of the partner's interest the value of the good-will of the business shall not be considered.

§39. Rights Where Partnership Is Dissolved for Fraud or Misrepresentation. Where a partnership contract is rescinded on the ground of the fraud or misrepresentation of one of the parties thereto, the party entitled to rescind is, without prejudice to any other right, entitled,

(a) To a lien on, or a right of retention of, the surplus of the partnership property after satisfying the partnership liabilities to third persons for any sum of money paid by him for the purchase of an interest in the partnership and for any capital or advances contributed by him; and

(b) To stand, after all liabilities to third persons have been satisfied, in the place of the creditors of the partnership for any payments made by him in respect of the partnership liabilities; and

(c) To be indemnified by the person guilty of the fraud or making the representation against all debts and liabilities of the partnership.

§40. Rules for Distribution. In settling accounts between the partners after dissolution, the following rules shall be observed, subject to any agreement to the contrary:

(a) The assets of the partnership are:

(I) The partnership property,

(II) The contributions of the partners necessary for the payment of all the liabilities specified in clause (b) of this paragraph.

(b) The liabilities of the partnership shall rank in order of payment, as follows:

(I) Those owing to creditors other than partners,

(II) Those owing to partners other than for capital and profits,

(III) Those owing to partners in respect of capital,

(IV) Those owing to partners in respect of profits.

(c) The assets shall be applied in order of their declaration in clause (a) of this paragraph to the satisfaction of the liabilities.

(d) The partners shall contribute, as provided by section 18 (a) the amount necessary to satisfy the liabilities; but if any, but not all, of the partners are insolvent, or, not being subject to process, refuse to contribute, the other partners shall contribute their share of the liabilities, and, in the relative proportions in which they share the profits, the additional amount necessary to pay the liabilities.

(e) An assignee for the benefit of creditors or any person appointed by the court shall have the right to enforce the contributions specified in clause (d) of this paragraph.

(f) Any partner or his legal representative shall have the right to enforce the contributions specified in clause (d) of this paragraph, to the extent of the amount which he has paid in excess of his share of the liability.

(g) The individual property of a deceased partner shall be liable for the contributions specified in clause (d) of this paragraph.

(h) When partnership property and the individual properties of the partners are in possession of a court for distribution, partnership creditors shall have priority on partnership property and separate creditors on individual property, saving the rights of lien or secured creditors as heretofore.

(i) Where a partner has become bankrupt or his estate is insolvent the claims against his separate property shall rank in the following order:

(I) Those owing to separate creditors,

(II) Those owing to partnership creditors,

(III) Those owing to partners by way of contribution.

§41. Liability of Persons Continuing the Business in Certain Cases.

(1) When any new partner is admitted into an existing partnership, or when any partner retires and assigns (or the representative of the deceased partner assigns) his rights in partnership property to two or more of the partners, or to one or more of the partners and one or more third persons, if the business is continued without liquidation of the partnership affairs, creditors of the first or dissolved partnership are also creditors of the partnership so continuing the business.

(2) When all but one partner retire and assign (or the representative of a deceased partner assigns) their rights in partnership property to the remaining partner, who continues the business without liquidation of partnership affairs, either alone or with others, creditors of the dissolved partnership are also creditors of the person or partnership so continuing the business.

(3) When any partner retires or dies and the business of the dissolved partnership is continued as set forth in paragraphs (1) and (2) of this section, with the consent of the retired partners or the representative of the deceased partner, but without any assignment of his right in partnership property, rights of creditors of the dissolved partnership and of the creditors of the person or partnership continuing the business shall be as if such assignment had been made.

(4) When all the partners or their representatives assign their rights in partnership property to one or more third persons who promise to pay the debts and who continue the business of the dissolved partnership, creditors of the dissolved partnership are also creditors of the person or partnership continuing the business.

(5) When any partner wrongfully causes a dissolution and the remaining partners continue the business under the provisions of section 38(2b), either alone or with others, and without liquidation of the partnership affairs, creditors of the dissolved partnership are also creditors of the person or partnership continuing the business.

(6) When a partner is expelled and the remaining partners continue the business either alone or with others, without liquidation of the partnership affairs, creditors of the dissolved partnership are also creditors of the person or partnership continuing the business.

(7) The liability of a third person becoming a partner in the partnership continuing the business, under this section, to the creditors of the dissolved partnership shall be satisfied out of partnership property only.

(8) When the business of a partnership after dissolution is continued under any conditions set forth in this section the creditors of the dissolved partnership, as against the separate creditors of the retiring or deceased partner or the representative of the deceased partner, have a prior right to any claim of the retired partner or the representative of the deceased partner against the person or partnership continuing the business, on account of the retired or deceased partner's interest in the dissolved partnership or on account of any consideration promised for such interest or for his right in partnership property.

(9) Nothing in this section shall be held to modify any right of creditors to set aside any assignment on the ground of fraud.

(10) The use by the person or partnership continuing the business of the partnership name, or the name of a deceased partner as part thereof, shall not of itself make the individual property of the deceased partner liable for any debts contracted by such person or partnership.

§42. Rights of Retiring or Estate of Deceased Partner When the Business Is Continued. When any partner retires or dies, and the business is continued under any of the conditions set forth in section 41 (1, 2, 3, 5, 6), or section 38(2b) without any settlement of accounts as between him or his estate and the person or partnership continuing the business, unless otherwise agreed, he or his legal representative as against such persons or partnership may have the value of his interest at the date of dissolution ascertained, and shall receive as an ordinary creditor an amount equal to the value of his interest in the dissolved partnership with interest, or, at his option or at the option of his legal representative, in lieu of interest, the profits attributable to the use of his right in the property of the dissolved partnership; provided that the creditors of the dissolved partnership as against the separate creditors, or the representative of the retired or deceased partner, shall have priority on any claim arising under this section, as provided by section 41(8) of this act.

§43. Accrual of Actions. The right to an account of his interest shall accrue to any partner, or his legal representative, as against the winding up partners or the surviving partners or the person or partnership continuing the business, at the date of dissolution, in the absence of any agreement to the contrary.

Part VII Miscellaneous Provisions

§44. When Act Takes Effect. This act shall take effect on the. . . . . day of. . . . . one thousand nine hundred and. . . . .

§45. Legislation Repealed. All acts or parts of acts inconsistent with this act are hereby repealed.

APPENDIX 4

Uniform Limited Partnership Act (1976), with 1985 Amendments

ARTICLE I

General Provisions

§101. Definitions. As used in this Act, unless the context otherwise requires:

(1) "Certificate of limited partnership" means the certificate referred to in Section 201, and the certificate as amended or restated.

(2) "Contribution" means any cash, property, services rendered, or a promissory note or other binding obligation to contribute cash or property or to perform services, which a partner contributes to a limited partnership in his capacity as a partner.

(3) "Event of withdrawal of a general partner" means an event that causes a person to cease to be a general partner as provided in Section 402.

(4) "Foreign limited partnership" means a partnership formed under the laws of any state other than this State and having as partners one or more general partners and one or more limited partners.

(5) "General partner" means a person who has been admitted to a limited partnership as a general partner in accordance with the partnership agreement and named in the certificate of limited partnership as a general partner.

(6) "Limited partner" means a person who has been admitted to a limited partnership as a limited partner in accordance with the partnership agreement and named in the certificate of limited partnership as a limited partner.

(7) "Limited partnership" and "domestic limited partnership" mean a partnership formed by 2 or more persons under the laws of this State and having one or more general partners and one or more limited partners.

(8) "Partner" means a limited or general partner.

(9) "Partnership agreement" means any valid agreement, written or oral, of the partners as to the affairs of a limited partnership and the conduct of its business.

(10) "Partnership interest" means a partner's share of the profits and losses of a limited partnership and the right to receive distributions of a partnership assets.

(11) "Person" means a natural person, partnership, limited partnership (domestic or foreign), trust, estate, association, or corporation.

(12) "State" means a state, territory, or possession of the United States, the District of Columbia, or the Commonwealth of Puerto Rico.

§102. Name. The name of each limited partnership as set forth in its certificate of limited partnership:

(1) shall contain without abbreviation the words "limited partnership";

(2) may not contain the name of a limited partners unless (i) it is also the name of a general partner or the corporate name of a corporate general partner, or (ii) the business of the limited partnership had been carried on under that name before the admission of that limited partner;

(3) may not be the same as, or deceptively similar to, the name of any corporation or limited partnership organized under the laws of this State or licensed or registered as a foreign corporation or limited partnership in this State; and

(4) may not contain the following words [here insert prohibited words].

§103. Reservation of Name. . . .

§104. Specified Office and Agent. Each limited partnership shall continuously maintain in this State:

(1) an office, which may but need not be a place of its business in this State, at which shall be kept the records required by Section 105 to be maintained; and

(2) an agent for service of process on the limited partnership, which agent must be an individual resident of this State, a domestic corporation, or a foreign corporation authorized to do business in this State.

§105. Records to Be Kept.

(a) Each limited partnership shall keep at the office referred to in Section 104(1) the following:

(1) a current list of the full name and last known business address of each partner, separately identifying the general partners (in alphabetical order) and the limited partners (in alphabetical order);

(2) a copy of the certificate of limited partnership and all certificates of amendment thereto, together

with executed copies of any powers of attorney pursuant to which any certificate has been executed;

(3) copies of the limited partnership's federal, state, and local income tax returns and reports, if any, for the three most recent years;

(4) copies of any then-effective written partnership agreements and of any financial statements of the limited partnership for the three most recent years; and

(5) unless contained in a written partnership agreement, a writing setting out:

(i) the amount of cash and a description and statement of the agreed value of the other property or services contributed by each partner and which each partner has agreed to contribute;

(ii) the times at which or events on the happening of which any additional contributions agreed to be made by each partner are to be made;

(iii) any right of a partner to receive, or of a general partner to make, distributions to a partner which include a return of all or any part of the partner's contribution; and

(iv) any events upon the happening of which the limited partnership is to be dissolved and its affairs wound up.

(b) Records kept under this section are subject to inspection and copying at the reasonable request and at the expense of any partner during ordinary business hours.

§106. Nature of Business A limited partnership may carry on any business that a partnership without limited partners may carry on except [here designate prohibited activities].

§107. Business Transactions of Partner with Partnership Except as provided in the parntership agreement, a partner may lend money to and transact other business with the limited partnership and, subject to other applicable law, has the same rights and obligations with respect thereto as a person who is not a partner.

ARTICLE 2

Formation: Certificate of Limited Partnership

§201. Certificate of Limited Partnership.

(a) In order to form a limited partnership, a certificate of limited partnership must be executed and filed in the office of the Secretary of State. The certificate shall set forth:

(1) the name of the limited partnership;

(2) the address of the office and the name and address of the agent for the service of process required to be maintained by Section 104;

(3) the name and the business address of each general partner;

(4) the latest date upon which the limited partnership is to dissolve; and

(5) any other matters the general partners determine to include therein.

(b) A limited partnership is formed at the time of the filing of the certificate of limited partnership in the office of the Secretary of State or at any later time specified in the certificate of limited partnership if, in either case, there has been substantial compliance with the requirements of this section.

§202. Amendment to Certificate.

(a) A certificate of limited partnership is amended by filing a certificate of amendment thereto in the office of the Secretary of State. The certificate shall set forth:

(1) the name of the limited partnership;

(2) the date of filing the certificate; and

(3) the amendment to the certificate.

(b) Within 30 days after the happening of any of the following events, an amendment to a certificate of limited partnership reflecting the occurrence of the event or events shall be filed:

(1) the admission of a new general partner;

(2) the withdrawal of a general partner; or

(3) the continuation of the business under Section 801 after an event of withdrawal of a general partner.

(c) A general partner who becomes aware that any statement in a certificate of limited partnership was false when made or that any arrangements or other facts described have changed, making the certificate inaccurate in any respect, shall promptly amend the certificate.

(d) A certificate of limited partnership may be amended at any time for any other proper purpose the general partners determine.

(e) No person has any liability because an amendment to a certificate of limited partnership has not been filed to reflect the occurrence of any event referred to in subsection (b) of this section if the amendment is filed within the 30-day period specified in subsection (b).

(f) A restated certificate of limited partnership may be executed and filed in the same manner as a certificate of amendment.

§203. Cancellation of Certificate. A certificate of limited partnership shall be canceled upon the dissolution and the commencement of winding up of the partnership or at any other time there are no limited partners. A certificate of cancellation shall be filed in the office of the Secretary of State and set forth:

(1) the name of the limited partnership;

(2) the date of filing of its certificate of limited partnership;

(3) the reason for filing the certificate of cancellation;

(4) the effective date (which shall be a date certain) of cancellation if it is not to be effective upon the filing of the certificate; and

(5) any other information the general partners filing the certificate determine.

§204. Execution of Certificates.

(a) Each certificate required by this article to be filed in the office of the Secretary of State shall be executed in the following manner:

(1) an original certificate of limited partnership must be signed by all general partners;

(2) a certificate of amendment must be signed by at least one general partner and by each other general partner designated in the certificate as a new general partner; and

(3) a certificate of cancellation must be signed by all general partners;

(b) Any person may sign a certificate by an attorney-in-fact, but a power of attorney to sign a certificate relating to the admission, of a general partner must specifically describe the admission.

(c) The execution of a certificate by a general partner constitutes an affirmation under the penalties of perjury that the facts stated therein are true.

§205. Execution by Judicial Act. If a person required by Section 204 to execute any certificate fails or refuses to do so, any other person who is adversely affected by the failure or refusal, may petition the [designate the appropriate court] to direct the execution of the certificate. If the court finds that it is proper for the certificate to be executed and that any person so designated has failed or refused to execute the certificate, it shall order the Secretary of State to record an appropriate certificate.

§206. Filing in Office of Secretary of State.

(a) Two signed copies of the certificate of limited partnership and of any certificates of amendment or cancellation (or of any judicial decree of amendment or cancellation) shall be delivered to the Secretary of State. A person who executes a certificate as an agent or fiduciary need not exhibit evidence of his or her authority as a prerequisite to filing. Unless the Secretary of State finds that any certificate does not conform to law, upon receipt of all filing fees required by law he or she shall:

(1) endorse on each duplicate original the word "Filed" and the day, month and year of the filing thereof;

(2) file one duplicate original in his or her office; and

(3) return the other duplicate original to the person who filed it or his or her representative.

(b) Upon the filing of a certificate of amendment (or judicial decree of amendment) in the office of the Secretary of State, the certificate of limited partnership shall be amended as set forth therein, and upon the effective date of a certificate of cancellation (or a judicial decree thereof), the certificate of limited partnership is canceled.

§207. Liability for False Statement in Certificate. If any certificate of limited partnership or certificate of amendment or cancellation contains a false statement, one who suffers loss by reliance on the statement may recover damages for the loss from:

(1) any person who executes the certificate, or causes another to execute it on his behalf, and knew, and any general partner who knew or should have known, the statement to be false at the time the certificate was executed; and

(2) any general partner who thereafter knows or should have known that any arrangement or other fact described in the certificate has changed, making the statement inaccurate in any respect within a sufficient time before the statement was relied upon reasonably to have enabled that general partner to cancel or amend the certificate, or to file a petition for its cancellation or amendment under Section 205.

§208. Scope of Notice. The fact that a certificate of limited partnership is on file in the office of the Secretary of State is notice that the partnership is a limited partnership and the persons designated therein as general partners are general partners, but it is not notice of any other fact.

§209. Delivery of Certificates to Limited Partners. Upon the return by the Secretary of State pursuant to Section 206 of a certificate marked "Filed", the general partners shall promptly deliver or mail a copy of the certificate of limited partnership and each certificate of amendment or cancellation to each limited partner unless the partnership agreement provides otherwise.

ARTICLE 3

Limited Partners

§301. Admission of Limited Partners.

(a) A person becomes a limited partner:

(1) at the time the limited partnership is formed; or

(2) at any later time specified in the records of the limited partnership for becoming a limited partner.

(b) After the filing of a limited partnership's original certificate of limited partnership, a person may be admitted as an additional limited partner:

(1) in the case of a person acquiring a partnership interest directly from the limited partnership, upon compliance with the partnership agreement or, if the partnership-agreement does not so provide, upon the written consent of all partners; and

(2) in the case of an assignee of a partnership interest of a partner who has the power, as provided in Section 704, to grant the assignee the right to become a limited partner, upon the exercise of that power and compliance with any conditions limiting the grant or exercise of the power.

§302. Voting. Subject to Section 303, the partnership agreement may grant to all or a specified group of the limited partners the right to vote (on a per capita or other basis) upon any matter.

§303. Liability to Third Parties.

(a) Except as provided in subsection (d), a limited partner is not liable for the obligations of a limited partnership unless he or she is also a general partner or, in addition to the exercise of his or her rights and powers as a limited partner, he or she participates in the control of the business. However, if the limited partner participates in the control of the business, he or she is liable only to persons who transact business with the limited partnership reasonably believing, based upon the limited partner's conduct, that the limited partner is a general partner.

(b) A limited partner does not participate in the control of the business within the meaning of subsection (a) solely by doing one or more of the following:

(1) being a contractor for or an agent or employee of the limited partnership or of a general partner or being an officer, director, or shareholder of a general partner that is a corporation;

(2) consulting with and advising a general partner with respect to the business of the limited partnership;

(3) acting as surety for the limited partnership or guaranteeing or assuming one or more specific obligations of the limited partnership;

(4) taking any action required or permitted by law to bring or pursue a derivative action in the right of the limited partnership;

(5) requesting or attending a meeting of partners;

(6) proposing, approving, or disapproving, by voting or otherwise, one or more of the following matters:

(i) the dissolution and winding up of the limited partnership;

(ii) the sale, exchange, lease, mortgage, pledge, or other transfer of all or substantially all of the assets of the limited partnership;

(iii) the incurrence of indebtedness by the limited partnership other than in the ordinary course of its business;

(iv) a change in the nature of the business;

(v) the admission or removal of a general partner;

(vi) the admission or removal of a limited partner;

(vii) a transaction involving an actual or a potential conflict of interest between a general partner and the limited partnership or the limited partners;

(viii) an amendment to the partnership agreement or certificate of limited partnership; or

(ix) matters related to the business of the limited partnership not otherwise enumerated in this subsection (b), which the partnership agreement states in writing may be subject to the approval or disapproval of limited partners;

(7) winding up the limited partnership pursuant to Section 803; or

(8) exercising any right or power permitted to limited partners under this [Act] and not specifically enumerated in this subsection (b).

(c) the enumeration in subsection (b) does not mean that the possession or exercise of any other powers by a limited partner constitutes participation by him or her in the business of the limited partnership.

(d) A limited partner who knowingly permits his or her name to be used in the name of the limited partnership, except under circumstances permitted by Section 102(2), is liable to creditors who extend credit to the limited partnership without actual knowledge that the limited partner is not a general partner.

§304. Person Erroneously Believing Himself or Herself Limited Partner.

(a) Except as provided in subsection (b), a person who makes a contribution to a business enterprise and erroneously but in good faith believes that he or she has become a limited partner in the enterprise is not a general partner in the enterprise and is not bound by its obligations by reason of making the contribution, receiving distributions from the enterprise, or exercising any rights of a limited partner, if, on ascertaining the mistake, he or she:

(1) causes an appropriate certificate of limited partnership or a certificate of amendment to be executed and filed; or

(2) withdraws from future equity participation in the enterprise by executing and filing in the office of the Secretary of State a certificate declaring a withdrawal under this section.

(b) A person who makes a contribution of the kind described in subsection (a) is liable as a general partner to any third party who transacts business with the enterprise (i) before the person withdraws and an appropriate certificate is filed to show withdrawal, or (ii) before an appropriate certificate is filed to show that he [or she] is not a general partner, but in either case only if the third party actually believed in good faith that the person was a general partner.

§305. Information. Each limited partner has the right to:

(1) inspect and copy any of the partnership records required to be maintained by Section 105; and

(2) obtain from the general partners from time to time upon reasonable demand (i) true and full information regarding the state of the business and financial condition of the limited partnership, (ii) promptly after becoming available, a copy of the limited partnership's federal, state and local income tax returns for each year, and (iii) other information regarding the affairs of the limited partnership as is just and reasonable.

ARTICLE 4

General Partners

§401. Admission of Additional General Partners. After the filing of a limited partnership's original certificate of limited partnership, additional general partners may be admitted as provided in writing in the partnership agreement or, if the partnership agreement does not provide in writing for the admission of additional general partners, with the written consent of all partners.

§402. Events of Withdrawal. Except as approved by the specific written consent of all partners at the time, a person ceases to be a general partner of a limited partnership upon the happening of any of the following events:

(1) the general partner withdraws from the limited partnership as provided in Section 602;

(2) the general partner ceases to be a member of the limited partnership as provided in Section 702;

(3) the general partner is removed as a general partner in accordance with the partnership agreement;

(4) unless otherwise provided in writing in the partnership agreement, the general partner: (i) makes an assignment for the benefit of creditors; (ii) files a voluntary petition in bankruptcy; (iii) is adjudicated a bankrupt or insolvent; (iv) files a petition or answer seeking for himself or herself any reorganization, arrangement, composition, readjustment, liquidation, dissolution or similar relief under any statute, law, or regulation; (v) files an answer or other pleading admitting or failing to contest the material allegations of a petition filed against him or her in any proceeding of this nature; or (vi) seeks, consents to, or acquiesces in the appointment of a trustee, receiver, or liquidator of the general partner or of all or any substantial part of his or her properties;

(5) unless otherwise provided in writing in the partnership agreement, [120] days after the commencement of any proceeding against the general partner seeking reorganization, arrangement, composition, readjustment, liquidation, dissolution or similar relief under any statute, law, or regulation, the proceeding has not been dismissed, or if within [90] days after the appointment without his or her consent or acquiescence of a trustee, receiver, or liquidator of the general partner or of all or any substantial part of his or her properties, the appointment is not vacated or stayed or within [90] days after the expiration of any such stay, the appointment is not vacated;

(6) in the case of a general partner who is a natural person,

(i) his or her death; or

(ii) the entry by a court of competent jurisdiction adjudicating him or her incompetent to manage his or her person or estate;

(7) in the case of a general partner who is acting as a general partner by virtue of being a trustee of a trust, the termination of the trust (but not merely the substitution of a new trustee);

(8) in the case of a general partner that is a separate partnership, the dissolution and commencement of winding up of the separate partnership;

(9) in the case of a general partner that is a corporation, the filing of a certificate of dissolution, or its equivalent, for the corporation or the revocation of its charter; or

(10) in the case of an estate, the distribution by the fiduciary of the estate's entire interest in the partnership.

§403. General Powers and Liabilities. (a) Except as provided in this Act or in the partnership agreement, a general partner of a limited partnership has the rights and powers and is subject to the restrictions of a partner in a partnership without limited partners. (b) Except as provided in this Act, a general partner of a limited partnership has the liabilities of a partner in a partnership without limited partners to persons other than the partnership and the other partners. Except as provided in this Act or in the partnership agreement, a general partner of a limited partnership has the liabilities of a partner in a partnership without limited partners to the partnership and to the other partners.

§404. Contributions by General Partner. A general partner of a limited partnership may make contributions to the partnership and share in the profits and losses of, and in distributions from, the limited partnership as a general partner. A general partner also may make contributions to and share in profits, losses, and distributions as a limited partner. A person who is both a general partner and a limited partner has the rights and powers, and is subject to the restrictions and liabilities, of a general partner and, except as provided in the partnership agreement, also has the powers, and is subject to the restrictions, of a limited partner to the extent of his or her participation in the partnership as a limited partner.

§405. Voting. The partnership agreement may grant to all or certain identified general partners the right to vote (on a per capita or any other basis), separately or with all or any class of the limited partners, on any matter.

ARTICLE 5

Finance

§501. Form of Contribution. The contribution of a partner may be in cash, property, or services rendered, or a promissory note or other obligation to contribute cash or property or to perform services.

§502. Liability for Contribution.

(a) A promise by a limited partner to contribute to the limited partnership is not enforceable unless set out in a writing signed by the limited partner.

(b) Except as provided in the limited partnership agreement, a partner is obligated to the limited partnership to perform any enforceable promise to contribute cash or property or to perform services, even if he or she is unable to perform because of death, disability, or any other reason. If a partner does not make the required contribution of property or services, he or she is obligated at the option of the limited partnership to contribute cash equal to that portion of the value, as stated in the partnership records required to be kept pursuant to Section 105, of the stated contribution that has not been made.

(c) Unless otherwise provided in the partnership agreement, the obligation of a partner to make a contribution or return money or other property paid or distributed in violation of this Act may be compromised only by consent of all the partners. Notwithstanding the compromise, a creditor of a limited partnership who extends credit, or otherwise acts in reliance on that obligation after the partner signs a writing which reflects the obligation, and before the amendment or cancellation thereof to reflect the compromise, may enforce the original obligation.

§503. Sharing of Profits and Losses. The profits and losses of a limited partnership shall be allocated among the partners, and among classes of partners, in the manner provided in writing in the partnership agreement. If the partnership agreement does not so provide in writing, profits and losses shall be allocated on the basis of the value, as stated in the partnership records required to be kept pursuant to Section 105, of the contributions made by each partner to the extent they have been received by the partnership and have not been returned.

§504. Sharing of Distributions. Distributions of cash or other assets of a limited partnership shall be allocated among the partners, and among classes of partners in the manner provided in writing in the partnership agreement. If the partnership agreement does not so provide in writing, distributions shall be made on the basis of the value, as stated in the partnership records required to be kept pursuant to Section 105, of the contributions made by each partner to the extent they have been received by the partnership and have not been returned.

ARTICLE 6

Distribution and Withdrawal

§601. Interim Distributions. Except as provided in this Article, a partner is entitled to receive distributions from a limited partnership before his or her withdrawal from the limited partnership and before the dissolution and winding up thereof to the extent and at the times or upon the happening of the events specified in the partnership agreement.

§602. Withdrawal of General Partner. A general partner may withdraw from a limited partnership at any time by giving written notice to the other partners, but if the withdrawal violates the partnership agreement, the limited partnership may recover from the withdrawing general partner damages for breach of the partnership agreement and offset the damages against the amount otherwise distributable to him or her.

§603. Withdrawal of Limited Partner. A limited partner may withdraw from a limited partnership at the time or upon the happening of events specified in writing in the partnership agreement. If the agreement does not specify in writing the time or the events upon the happening of which a limited partner may withdraw or a definite time for the dissolution and winding up of the limited partnership, a limited partner may withdraw upon not less than six months' prior written notice to each general partner at his or her address on the books of the limited partnership at its office in this State.

§604. Distribution Upon Withdrawal. Except as provided in this Article, upon withdrawal any withdrawing partner is entitled to receive any distribution to which he or she is entitled under the partnership agreement and, if not otherwise provided in the agreement, he or she is entitled to receive, within a reasonable time after withdrawal, the fair value of his or her interest in the limited partnership as of the date of withdrawal based upon his or her right to share in distributions from the limited partnership.

§605. Distribution in Kind. Except as provided in writing in the partnership agreement, a partner, regardless of the nature of his or her contribution, has no right to demand and receive any distribution from a limited partnership in any form other than cash. Except as provided in writing in the partnership agreement, a partner may not be compelled to accept a distribution of any asset in kind from a limited partnership to the extent that the percentage of the asset distributed to him or her exceeds a percentage of that asset which is equal to the percentage in which he or she shares in distributions from the limited partnership.

§606. Right to Distribution. At the time a partner becomes entitled to receive a distribution, he or she has the status of, and is entitled to all remedies available to, a creditor of the limited partnership with respect to the distribution.

§607. Limitations on Distribution. A partner may not receive a distribution from a limited partnership to the extent that, after giving effect to the distribution, all liabilities of the limited partnership, other than liabilities to partners on account of their partnership interests, exceed the fair value of the partnership assets.

§608. Liability upon Return of Contribution.

(a) If a partner has received the return of any part of his or her contribution without violation of the partnership agreement or this Act, he or she is liable to the limited partnership for a period of one year thereafter for the amount of the returned contribution, but only to the extent necessary to discharge the limited partnership's liabilities to creditors who extended credit to the limited partnership during the period the contribution was held by the partnership.

(b) If a partner has received the return of any part of his or her contribution in violation of the partnership agreement or this Act, he or she is liable to the limited partnership for a period of six years thereafter for the amount of the contribution wrongfully returned.

(c) A partner receives a return of his or her contribution to the extent that a distribution to him or her reduces his or her share of the fair value of the net assets of the limited partnership below the value as set forth in the partnership records required to be kept pursuant to Section 105, of his or her contribution which has not been distributed to him or her.

ARTICLE 7

Assignment of Partnership Interests

§701. Nature of Partnership Interest. A partnership interest is personal property.

§702. Assignment of Partnership Interest. Except as provided in the partnership agreement, a partnership interest is assignable in whole or in part. An assignment of a partnership interest does not dissolve a limited partnership or entitle the assignee to become or to exercise any rights of a partner. An assignment entitles the assignee to receive, to the extent assigned, only the distribution to which the assignor would be entitled. Except as provided in the partnership agreement, a partner ceases to be a partner upon assignment of all his or her partnership interest.

§703. Rights of Creditor. On application to a court of competent jurisdiction by any judgment creditor of a partner, the court may charge the partnership interest of the partner with payment of the unsatisfied amount of the judgment with interest. To the extent so charged, the judgment creditor has only the rights of an assignee of the partnership interest. This Act does not deprive any partner of the benefit of any exemption laws applicable to his or her partnership interest.

§704. Right of Assignee to Become Limited Partner.

(a) An assignee of a partnership interest, including an assignee of a general partner, may become a limited partner if and to the extent that (i) the assignor gives the assignee that right in accordance with authority described in the partnership agreement or (ii) all other partners consent.

(b) An assignee who has become a limited partner has, to the extent assigned, the rights and powers, and is subject to the restrictions and liabilities, of a limited partner under the partnership agreement and this Act. An assignee who becomes a limited partner also is liable for the obligations of his or her assignor to make and return contributions as provided in Articles 5 and 6. However, the assignee is not obligated for liabilities unknown to the assignee at the time he or she became a limited patner.

(c) If an assignee of a partnership interest becomes a limited partner, the assignor is not released from his or her liability to the limited partnership under Sections 207 and 502.

§705. Power of Estate of Deceased or Incompetent Partner. If a partner who is an individual dies or a court of competent jurisdiction adjudges him or her to be incompetent to manage his or her person or his or her property, the partner's executor, administrator, guardian, conservator, or other legal representative may exercise all the partner's rights for the purpose of settling his or her estate or administering his or her property, including any power the partner had to give an assignee the right to become a limited partner. If a partner is a corporation, trust, or other entity and is dissolved or terminated, the powers of that partner may be exercised by its legal representative or successor.

ARTICLE 8

Dissolution

§801. Nonjudicial Dissolution. A limited partnership is dissolved and its affairs shall be wound up upon the happening of the first to occur of the following:

(1) at the time specified in the certificate of limited partnership;

(2) upon the happening of events specified in writing in the partnership agreement;

(3) written consent of all partners;

(4) an event of withdrawal of a general partner unless at the time there is at least one other general partner and the written provisions of the partnership agreement permit the business of the limited partnership to be carried on by the remaining general partner and that partner does so, but the limited partnership is not dissolved and is not required to be wound up by reason of any event of withdrawal, if, within 90 days after the withdrawal, all partners agree in writing to continue the business of the limited partnership and to the appointment of one or more additional partners if necessary or desired; or

(5) entry of a decree of judicial dissolution under Section 802.

§802. Judicial Dissolution. On application by or for a partner the [designate the proper court] court may decree dissolution of a limited partnership whenever it is not reasonably practicable to carry on the business in conformity with the partnership agreement.

§803. Winding Up. Except as provided in the partnership agreement, the general partners who have not wrongfully dissolved a limited partnership, or, if none, the limited partners, may wind up the limited partnership's affairs; but the [designate the proper court] court may wind up the limited partnership's affairs upon application of any partner, his or her legal representative, or assignee.

§804. Distribution of Assets. Upon the winding up of a limited partnership, the assets shall be distributed as follows:

(**1**) to creditors, including partners who are creditors, to the extent permitted by law, in satisfaction of liabilities of the limited partnership other than liabilities for distributions to partners under Section 601 or 604;

(**2**) except as provided in the partnership agreement, to partners and former partners in satisfaction of liabilities for distributions under Section 601 or 604; and

(**3**) except as provided in the partnership agreement, to partners first for the return of their contributions and secondly respecting their partnership interests, in the proportions in which the partners share in distributions.

ARTICLE 9

Foreign Limited Partnerships

§901. Law Governing. Subject to the Constitution of this State, (i) the laws of the state under which a foreign limited partnership is organized govern its organization and internal affairs and the liability of its limited partners, and (ii) a foreign limited partnership may not be denied registration by reason of any difference between those laws and the laws of this State.

§902. Registration. . . .

§903. Issuance of Registration. . . .

§904. Name. A foreign limited partnership may register with the Secretary of State under any name, whether or not it is the name under which it is registered in its state of organization, that includes without abbreviation the words "limited partnership" and that could be registered by a domestic limited partnership.

§905. Changes and Amendments. . . .

§906. Cancellation of Registration. . . .

§907. Transaction of Business without Registration.

(**a**) A foreign limited partnership transacting business in this State may not maintain any action, suit, or proceeding in any court of this State until it has registered in this State.

(**b**) The failure of a foreign limited partnership to register in this State does not impair the validity of any contract or act of the foreign limited partnership or prevent the foreign limited partnership from defending any action, suit, or proceeding in any court of this State.

(**c**) A limited partner of a foreign limited partnership is not liable as a general partner of the foreign limited partnership solely by reason of having transacted business in this State without registration.

(**d**) A foreign limited partnership, by transacting business in this State without registration, appoints the Secretary of State as its agent for service of process with respect to [claims for relief] [causes of action] arising out of the transaction of business in this State.

§908. Action by [Appropriate Official.] The [designate the appropriate official] may bring an action to restrain a foreign limited partnership from transacting business in this State in violation of the Article.

ARTICLE 10

Derivative Actions

§1001. Right of Action. A limited partner may bring an action in the right of a limited partnership to recover a judgment in its favor if general partners with authority to do so have refused to bring the action or if an effort to cause those general partners to bring the action is not likely to succeed.

§1002. Proper Plaintiff. . . .

§1003. Pleading. . . .

§1004. Expenses. . . .

ARTICLE 11

Miscellaneous

§1101. Construction and Application. . . .

§1102. Short Title. This Act may be cited as the Uniform Limited Partnership Act.

§1103. Severability. . . .

§1104. Effective Date, Extended Effective Date and Repeal. . . .

§1105. Rules for Cases Not Provided for in This Act. In any case not provided for in this Act the provisions of the Uniform Partnership Act govern.

§1106. Savings Clause. . . .

APPENDIX 5

Revised Model Business Corporation Act (1984), as Amended*

CHAPTER 1. GENERAL PROVISIONS

Subchapter A. Short Title and Reservation of Power

§1.01. Short Title. This Act shall be known and may be cited as the "[name of state] Business Corporation Act."

§1.02. Reservation of Power to Amend or Repeal. The [name of state legislature] has power to amend or repeal all or part of this Act at any time and all domestic and foreign corporations subject to this Act are governed by the amendment or repeal.

Subchapter B. Filing Documents

§1.20–§1.30. [Procedure for filing articles of incorporation and other documents with Secretary of State, filing fees, etc.]

§1.40. Act Definitions. In this Act:

(1) ...

(2) "Authorized shares" means the shares of all classes a domestic or foreign corporation is authorized to issue.

(3) ...

(4) "Corporation" or "domestic corporation" means a corporation for profit, which is not a foreign corporation, incorporated under or subject to the provisions of this Act.

(5) ...

(6) "Distribution" means a direct or indirect transfer of money or other property (except its own shares) or incurrence of indebtedness by a corporation to or for the benefit of its shareholders in respect of any of its shares. A distribution may be in the form of a declaration or payment of a dividend; a purchase, redemption, or other acquisition of shares; a distribution of indebtedness; or otherwise.

(7) ...

(8) "Employee" includes an officer but not a director. A director may accept duties that make him also an employee.

(9) ...

(10) "Foreign corporation" means a corporation for profit incorporated under a law other than the law of this state.

(11)–(16)...

(17) "Principal office" means the office (in or out of this state) so designated in the annual report where the principal executive offices of a domestic or foreign corporation are located.

(18) ...

(19) "Record date" means the date established under chapter 6 or 7 on which a corporation determines the identity of its shareholders for purposes of this Act....

(20) "Secretary" means the corporate officer to whom the board of directors has delegated responsibility under section 8.40(c) for custody of the minutes of the meetings of the board of directors and of the shareholders, and for authenticating records of the corporation.

(21) "Share" means the unit into which the proprietary interests in a corporation are divided.

(22) "Shareholder" means the person in whose name shares are registered in the records of a corporation or the beneficial owner of shares to the extent of the rights granted by a nominee certificate on file with a corporation.

(23) ...

(24) "Subscriber" means a person who subscribes for shares in a corporation, whether before or after incorporation.

(25) ...

(26) "Voting group" means all shares of one or more classes or series....

§1.41. Notice.—

(a) Notice under this Act must be in writing unless oral notice is reasonable under the circumstances.

(b)–(g)...

§1.42. Number of Shareholders.—

(a) For purpose of this Act, the following identified as a shareholder in a corporation's current record of shareholders constitutes one shareholder.

*Portions of the Act are omitted since they are essentially procedural and not necessary to an understanding of chapters 39–43.

(**1**) three or fewer coowners;

(**2**) a corporation, partnership, trust, estate, or other entity;

(**3**) the trustees, guardians, custodians, or other fiduciaries of a single trust, estate, or account.

(**b**) . . .

CHAPTER 2. INCORPORATION

§2.01. Incorporators.—One or more persons may act as the incorporator or incorporators of a corporation by delivering articles of incorporation to the secretary of state for filing.

§2.02. Articles of Incorporation.—

(**a**) The articles of incorporation must set forth:

(**1**) a corporate name for the corporation that satisfies the requirements of section 4.01;

(**2**) the number of shares the corporation is authorized to issue;

(**3**) the street address of the corporation's initial registered office and the name of its initial registered agent at that office; and

(**4**) the name and address of each incorporator.

(**b**) The articles of incorporation may set forth:

(**1**) the names and addresses of the individuals who are to serve as the initial directors;

(**2**) provisions not inconsistent with law regarding:

(**i**) the purpose or purposes for which the corporation is organized;

(**ii**) managing the business and regulating the affairs of the corporation;

(**iii**) defining, limiting, and regulating the powers of the corporation, its board of directors, and shareholders;

(**iv**) a par value for authorized shares or classes of shares;

(**v**) the imposition of personal liability on shareholders for the debts of the corporation to a specified extent and upon specified conditions; and

(**3**) any provision that under this Act is required or permitted to be set forth in the bylaws.

(**c**) The articles of incorporation need not set forth any of the corporate powers enumerated in this Act.

§2.03. Incorporation.—

(**a**) Unless a delayed effective date is specified, the corporate existence begins when the articles of incorporation are filed.

(**b**) The secretary of state's filing of the articles of incorporation is conclusive proof that the incorporators satisfied all conditions precedent to incorporation except in a proceeding by the state to cancel or revoke the incorporation or involuntarily dissolve the corporation.

§2.04. Liability for Preincorporation Transactions.—All persons purporting to act as or on behalf of a corporation, knowing there was no incorporation under this Act, are jointly and severally liable for all liabilities created while so acting.

§2.05. Organization of Corporation.—

(**a**) After incorporation:

(**1**) if initial directors are named in the articles of incorporation, the initial directors shall hold an organizational meeting, at the call of a majority of the directors, to complete the organization of the corporation by appointing officers, adopting bylaws, and carrying on any other business brought before the meeting;

(**2**) if initial directors are not named in the articles, the incorporator or incorporators shall hold an organizational meeting at the call of a majority of the incorporators:

(**i**) to elect directors and complete the organization of the corporation; or

(**ii**) to elect a board of directors who shall complete the organization of the corporation.

(**b**) Action required or permitted by this Act to be taken by incorporators at an organizational meeting may be taken without a meeting if the action taken is evidenced by one or more written consents describing the action taken and signed by each incorporator.

(**c**) An organizational meeting may be held in or out of this state.

§2.06. Bylaws.—

(**a**) The incorporators or board of directors of a corporation shall adopt initial bylaws for the corporation.

(**b**) The bylaws of a corporation may contain any provision for managing the business and regulating the affairs of the corporation that is not inconsistent with law or the articles of incorporation.

§2.07. Emergency Bylaws.—. . .

CHAPTER 3. PURPOSES AND POWERS

§3.01. Purposes.—

(**a**) Every corporation incorporated under this Act has the purpose of engaging in any lawful business unless a more limited purpose is set forth in the articles of incorporation.

(**b**) A corporation engaging in a business that is subject to regulation under another statute of this state may incorporate under this Act only if permitted by, and subject to all limitations of, the other statute.

§3.02. General Powers.—Unless its articles of incorporation provide otherwise, every corporation has perpetual duration and succession in its corporate name and has the same powers as an individual to do all things necessary or convenient to carry out its business and affairs, including without limitation power:

(**1**) to sue and be sued, complain and defend in its corporate name;

(2) to have a corporate seal, which may be altered at will, and to use it, or a facsimile of it, by impressing of affixing it or in any other manner reproducing it;

(3) to make and amend bylaws, not inconsistent with its articles of incorporation or with the laws of this state, for managing the business and regulating the affairs of the corporation;

(4) to purchase, receive, lease, or otherwise acquire, and own, hold, improve, use, and otherwise deal with, real or personal property, or any legal or equitable interest in property, wherever located;

(5) to sell, convey, mortgage, pledge, lease, exchange, and otherwise dispose of all or any part of its property;

(6) to purchase, receive, subscribe for, or otherwise acquire; own, hold, vote, use, sell, mortgage, lend, pledge, or otherwise dispose of; and deal in and with shares or other interests in, or obligations of, any other entity;

(7) to make contracts and guarantees, incur liabilities, borrow money, issue its notes, bonds, and other obligations (which may be convertible into or include the option to purchase other securities of the corporation), and secure any of its obligations by mortgage or pledge of any of its property, franchises, or income;

(8) to lend money, invest and reinvest its funds, and receive and hold real and personal property as security for repayment;

(9) to be a promoter, partner, member, associate, or manager of any partnership, joint venture, trust, or other entity;

(10) to conduct its business, locate offices, and exercise the powers granted by this Act within or without this state;

(11) to elect directors and appoint officers, employees, and agents of the corporation, define their duties, fix their compensation, and lend them money and credit;

(12) to pay pensions and establish pension plans, pension trusts, profit sharing plans, share bonus plans, share option plans, and benefit or incentive plans for any or all of its current or former directors, officers, employees, and agents;

(13) to make donations for the public welfare or for charitable, scientific, or educational purposes;

(14) to transact any lawful business that will aid governmental policy;

(15) to make payments or donations, or do any other act, not inconsistent with law, that furthers the business and affairs of the corporation.

§3.03. Emergency Powers.—...

§3.04. Ultra Vires.—

(a) Except as provided in subsection (b), the validity of corporate action may not be challenged on the ground that the corporation lacks or lacked power to act.

(b) A corporation's power to act may be challenged:

(1) in a proceeding by a shareholder against the corporation to enjoin the act;

(2) in a proceeding by the corporation, directly, derivatively, or through a receiver, trustee, or other legal representative, against an incumbent or former director, officer, employee, or agent of the corporation; or

(3) in a proceeding by the Attorney General under section 14.30.

(c) In a shareholder's proceeding under subsection (b)(1) to enjoin an unauthorized corporate act, the court may enjoin or set aside the act, if equitable and if all affected persons are parties to the proceeding, and may award damages for loss (other than anticipated profits) suffered by the corporation or another party because of enjoining the unauthorized act.

CHAPTER 4. NAME

§4.01. Corporate Name.—

(a) A corporate name:

(1) must contain the word "corporation," "incorporated," "company," or "limited," or the abbreviation "corp.," "inc.," "co.," or "ltd.," or words or abbreviations of like import in another language; and

(2) may not contain language stating or implying that the corporation is organized for a purpose other than that permitted by section 3.01 and its articles of incorporation.

(b)–(d)...

(e) This Act does not control the use of fictitious names.

§4.02. Reserved name.—...

§4.03. Registered Name. [of foreign corporation.]...

CHAPTER 5. OFFICE AND AGENT

§5.01. Registered Office and Registered Agent.— Each corporation must continuously maintain in this state:

(1) a registered office that may be the same as any of its places of business; and

(2) a registered agent, who may be:

(i) an individual who resides in this state and whose business office is identical with the registered office;

(ii) a domestic corporation or not-for-profit domestic corporation whose business office is identical with the registered office; or

(iii) a foreign corporation or not-for-profit foreign corporation authorized to transact business in this state whose business office is identical with the registered office.

§5.02. Change of Registered Office or Registered Agent.—. . .

§5.03. Resignation of Registered Agent.—

(a) A registered agent may resign his agency appointment by signing and delivering to the Secretary of State for filing the signed original and two exact or conformed copies of a statement of resignation. The statement may include a statement that the registered office is also discontinued.

(b)–(c). . .

§5.04. Service on Corporation.—

(a) A corporation's registered agent is the corporation's agent for service of process, notice, or demand required or permitted by law to be served on the corporation.

(b) If a corporation has no registered agent, or the agent cannot with reasonable diligence be served, the corporation may be served by registered or certified mail, return receipt requested, addressed to the secretary of the corporation at its principal office. Service is perfected under this subsection at the earliest of:

(1) the date the corporation receives the mail;

(2) the date shown on the return receipt, if signed on behalf of the corporation; or

(3) five days after its deposit in the United States Mail as evidenced by the postmark, if mailed postpaid and correctly addressed.

(c) This section does not prescribe the only means, or necessarily the required means, of serving a corporation.

CHAPTER 6. SHARES AND DISTRIBUTIONS

Subchapter A. Shares

§6.01. Authorized Shares.

(a) The articles of incorporation must prescribe the classes of shares and the number of shares of each class that the corporation is authorized to issue. If more than one class of shares is authorized, the articles of incorporation must prescribe a distinguishing designation for each class, and prior to the issuance of shares of a class the preferences, limitations, and relative rights of that class must be described in the articles of incorporation. All shares of a class must have preferences, limitations, and relative rights identical with those of other shares of the same class except to the extent otherwise permitted by section 6.02.

(b) The articles of incorporation must authorize (1) one or more classes of shares that together have unlimited voting rights, and (2) one or more classes of shares (which may be the same class or classes as those with voting rights) that together are entitled to receive the net assets of the corporation upon dissolution.

(c) The articles of incorporation may authorize one or more classes of shares that:

(1) have special, conditional, or limited voting rights, or no right to vote, except to the extent prohibited by this Act;

(2) are redeemable or convertible as specified in the articles of incorporation (i) at the option of the corporation, the shareholder, or another person or upon the occurrence of a designated event; (ii) for cash, indebtedness, securities, or other property; (iii) in a designated amount or in an amount determined in accordance with a designated formula or by reference to extrinsic data or events;

(3) entitle the holders to distributions calculated in any manner, including dividends that may be cumulative, noncumulative, or partially cumulative;

(4) have preference over any other class of shares with respect to distributions, including dividends and distributions upon the dissolution of the corporation.

(d) The description of the designations, preferences, limitations, and relative rights of share classes in subsection (c) is not exhaustive.

§6.02. Terms of Class or Series Determined by Board of Directors.—

(a) If the articles of incorporation so provide, the board of directors may determine, in whole or part, the preferences, limitations, and relative rights (within the limits set forth in section 6.01) of (1) any class of shares before the issuance of any shares of that class or (2) one or more series within a class before the issuance of any shares of that series.

(b) Each series of a class must be given a distinguishing designation.

(c) All shares of a series must have preferences, limitations, and relative rights identical with those of other shares of the same series and, except to the extent otherwise provided in the description of the series, with those of other series of the same class.

(d) . . .

§6.03. Issued and Outstanding Shares.—

(a) A corporation may issue the number of shares of each class or series authorized by the articles of incorporation. Shares that are issued are outstanding shares until they are reacquired, redeemed, converted, or cancelled.

(b) The reacquisition, redemption, or conversion of outstanding shares is subject to the limitations of subsection (c) of this section and to section 6.40.

(c) At all times that shares of the corporation are outstanding, one or more shares that together have unlimited voting rights and one or more shares that together are entitled to receive the net assets of the corporation upon dissolution must be outstanding.

§6.04. Fractional Shares.—

(a) A corporation may:

(1) issue fractions of a share or pay in money the value of a share;

(2) arrange for disposition of fractional shares by the shareholders;

(3) issue scrip in registered or bearer form entitling the holder to receive a full share upon surrendering enough scrip to equal a full share.

(b)–(d) . . .

Subchapter B. Issuance of Shares

§6.20. Subscription for Shares Before Incorporation.—

(a) A subscription for shares entered into before incorporation is irrevocable for six months unless the subscription agreement provides a longer or shorter period or all the subscribers agree to revocation.

(b) The board of directors may determine the payment terms of subscriptions for shares that were entered into before incorporation, unless the subscription agreement specifies them. A call for payment by the board of directors must be uniform so far as practicable as to all shares of the same class or series, unless the subscription agreement specifies otherwise.

(c) Shares issued pursuant to subscriptions entered into before incorporation are fully paid and nonassessable when the corporation receives the consideration specified in the subscription agreement.

(d) If a subscriber defaults in payment of money or property under a subscription agreement entered into before incorporation, the corporation may collect the amount owed as any other debt. Alternatively, unless the subscription agreement provides otherwise, the corporation may rescind the agreement and may sell the shares if the debt remains unpaid more than 20 days after the corporation sends written demand for payment to the subscriber.

(e) A subscription agreement entered into after incorporation is a contract between the subscriber and the corporation subject to section 6.21.

§6.21. Issuance of Shares.—

(a) The powers granted in this section to the board of directors may be reserved to the shareholders by the articles of incorporation.

(b) The board of directors may authorize shares to be issued for consideration consisting of any tangible or intangible property or benefit to the corporation, including cash, promissory notes, services performed, contracts for services to be performed, or other securities of the corporation.

(c) Before the corporation issues shares, the board of directors must determine that the consideration received or to be received for shares to be issued is adequate. That determination by the board of directors is conclusive insofar as the adequacy of consideration for the issuance of shares relates to whether the shares are validly issued, fully paid, and nonassessable.

(d) When the corporation receives the consideration for which the board of directors authorized the issuance of shares, the shares issued therefore are fully paid and nonassessable.

(e) The corporation may place in escrow shares issued for a contract for future services or benefits or a promissory note, or make other arrangements to restrict the transfer of the shares, and may credit distributions in respect of the shares against their purchase price, until the services are performed, the note is paid, or the benefits received. If the services are not performed, the note is not paid, or the benefits are not received, the shares escrowed or restricted and the distributions credited may be canceled in whole or part.

§6.22. Liability of Shareholders.—

(a) A purchaser from a corporation of its own shares is not liable to the corporation or its creditors with respect to the shares except to pay the consideration for which the shares were authorized to be issued (section 6.21) or specified in the subscription agreement (section 6.20).

(b) Unless otherwise provided in the articles of incorporation, a shareholder of a corporation is not personally liable for the acts or debts of the corporation except that he may become personally liable by reason of his own acts or conduct.

§6.23. Share Dividends.—

(a) Unless the articles of incorporation provide otherwise, shares may be issued pro rata and without consideration to the corporation's shareholders or to the shareholders of one or more classes or series. An issuance of shares under this subsection is a share dividend.

(b) Shares of one class or series may not be issued as a share dividend in respect of shares of another class or series unless (1) the articles of incorporation so authorize, (2) a majority of the votes entitled to be cast by the class or series to be issued approve the issue, or (3) there are no outstanding shares of the class or series to be issued.

(c) If the board of directors does not fix the record date for determining shareholders entitled to a share dividend, it is the date the board of directors authorizes the share dividend.

§6.24. Share Options.—A corporation may issue rights, options, or warrants for the purchase of shares of the corporation. The board of directors shall determine the terms upon which the rights, options, or warrants are issued, their form and content, and the consideration for which the shares are to be issued.

§6.25. Form and Content of Certificates.—

(a) Shares may but need not be represented by certificates. Unless this Act or another statute expressly provides otherwise, the rights and obligations of shareholders are identical whether or not their shares are represented by certificates.

(b) At a minimum each share certificate must state on its face:

(1) the name of the issuing corporation and that it is organized under the law of this state;

(2) the name of the person to whom issued; and

(3) the number and class of shares and the designation of the series, if any, the certificate represents.

(c) If the issuing corporation is authorized to issue different classes of shares or different series within a class, the designations, relative rights, preferences, and limitations applicable to each class and the variations in rights, preferences, and limitations determined for each series (and the authority of the board of directors to determine variations for future series) must be summarized on the front or back of each certificate. Alternatively, each certificate may state conspicuously on its front or back that the corporation will furnish the shareholder this information on request in writing and without charge.

(d) Each share certificate (1) must be signed (either manually or in facsimile) by two officers designated in the bylaws or by the board of directors and (2) may bear the corporate seal or its facsimile.

(e) If the person who signed (either manually or in facsimile) a share certificate no longer holds office when the certificate is issued, the certificate is nevertheless valid.

§6.26. Shares Without Certificates.—

(a) Unless the articles of incorporation or bylaws provide otherwise, the board of directors of a corporation may authorize the issue of some or all of the shares of any or all of its classes or series without certificates. The authorization does not affect shares already represented by certificates until they are surrendered to the corporation.

(b) Within a reasonable time after the issue or transfer of shares without certificates, the corporation shall send the shareholder a written statement of the information required on certificates by section 6.25(b) and (c), and, if applicable, section 6.27.

§6.27. Restriction on Transfer of Shares and Other Securities.—

(a) The articles of incorporation, bylaws, an agreement among shareholders, or an agreement between shareholders and the corporation may impose restrictions on the transfer or registration of transfer of shares of the corporation. A restriction does not affect shares issued before the restriction was adopted unless the holders of the shares are parties to the restriction agreement or voted in favor of the restriction.

(b) A restriction on the transfer or registration of transfer of shares is valid and enforceable against the holder or a transferee of the holder if the restriction is authorized by this section and its existence is noted conspicuously on the front or back of the certificate or is contained in the information statement required by section 6.26(b). Unless so noted, a restriction is not enforceable against a person without knowledge of the restriction.

(c) A restriction on the transfer or registration of transfer of shares is authorized:

(1) to maintain the corporation's status when it is dependent on the number or identity of its shareholders;

(2) to preserve exemptions under federal or state securities law;

(3) for any other reasonable purpose.

(d) A restriction on the transfer or registration of transfer of shares may:

(1) obligate the shareholder first to offer the corporation or other persons (separately, consecutively, or simultaneously) an opportunity to acquire the restricted shares;

(2) obligate the corporation or other persons (separately, consecutively, or simultaneously) to acquire the restricted shares;

(3) require the corporation, the holders of any class of its shares, or another person to approve the transfer of the restricted shares, if the requirement is not manifestly unreasonable;

(4) prohibit the transfer of the restricted shares to designated persons or classes of persons, if the prohibition is not manifestly unreasonable.

(e) For purposes of this section, "shares" includes a security convertible into or carrying a right to subscribe for or acquire shares.

§6.28. Expense of Issue.—A corporation may pay the expenses of selling or underwriting its shares, and of organizing or reorganizing the corporation, from the consideration received for shares.

Subchapter C. Subsequent Acquisition of Shares by Shareholders and Corporation

§6.30. Shareholders' Preemptive Rights.—

(a) The shareholders of a corporation do not have a preemptive right to acquire the corporation's unissued shares except to the extent the articles of incorporation so provide.

(b)–(c) . . .

§6.31. Corporation's Acquisition of its Own Shares.—

(a) A corporation may acquire its own shares and shares so acquired constitute authorized but unissued shares.

(b) If the articles of incorporation prohibit the reissue of acquired shares, the number of authorized shares is reduced by the number of shares acquired, effective upon amendment of the articles of incorporation.

(c) The board of directors may adopt articles of amendment under this section without shareholder action, and deliver them to the secretary of state for filing. . .

Subchapter D. Distributions

§6.40. Distributions to Shareholders.—

(a) A board of directors may authorize and the corporation may make distributions to its shareholders subject to restriction by the articles of incorporation and the limitation in subsection (c).

(b) If the board of directors does not fix the record date for determining shareholders entitled to a distribution (other than one involving a purchase redemption, or other acquisition of the corporation's shares), it is the date the board of directors authorizes the distribution.

(c) No distribution may be made if, after giving it effect:

(1) the corporation would not be able to pay its debts as they become due in the usual course of business; or

(2) the corporation's total assets would be less than the sum of its total liabilities plus (unless the articles of incorporation permit otherwise) the amount that would be needed, if the corporation were to be dissolved at the time of the distribution, to satisfy the preferential rights upon dissolution of shareholders whose preferential rights are superior to those receiving the distribution.

(d) The board of directors may base a determination that a distribution is not prohibited under subsection (c) either on financial statements prepared on the basis of accounting practices and principles that are reasonable in the circumstances or on a fair valuation or other method that is reasonable in the circumstances.

(e)–(g) . . .

CHAPTER 7. SHAREHOLDERS

Subchapter A. Meetings

§7.01. Annual Meeting.—

(a) A corporation shall hold annually at a time stated in or fixed in accordance with the bylaws a meeting of shareholders.

(b) Annual shareholders' meetings may be held in or out of this state at the place stated in or fixed in accordance with the bylaws. If no place is stated in or fixed in accordance with the bylaws, annual meetings shall be held at the corporation's principal office.

(c) The failure to hold an annual meeting at the time stated in or fixed in accordance with a corporation's bylaws does not affect the validity of any corporate action.

§7.02. Special Meeting.—

(a) A corporation shall hold a special meeting of shareholders;

(1) on call of its board of directors or the person or persons authorized to do so by the articles of incorporation or bylaws; or

(2) if the holders of a least 10 percent of all the votes entitled to be cast on any issue proposed to be considered at the proposed special meeting sign, date, and deliver to the corporation's secretary one or more written demands for the meeting describing the purpose or purposes for which it is to be held.

(b) If not otherwise fixed under sections 7.03 or 7.07, the record date for determining shareholders entitled to demand a special meeting is the date the first shareholder signs the demand.

(c) Special shareholders' meetings may be held in or out of this state at the place stated in or fixed in accordance with the bylaws. If no place is stated or fixed in accordance with the bylaws, special meetings shall be held at the corporation's principal office.

(d) Only business within the purpose or purposes described in the meeting notice required by section 7.05(c) may be conducted at a special shareholders' meeting.

§7.03. Court-Ordered Meeting.—

(a) The [name or describe] court of the county where a corporation's principal office (or, if none in this state, its registered office) is located may summarily order a meeting to be held:

(1) on application of any shareholder of the corporation entitled to participate in an annual meeting if an annual meeting was not held within the earlier of 6 months after the end of the corporation's fiscal year or 15 months after its last annual meeting; or

(2) on application of a shareholder who signed a demand for a special meeting valid under section 7.02 if:

(i) notice of the special meeting was not given within 30 days after the date the demand was delivered to the corporation's secretary; or

(ii) the special meeting was not held in accordance with the notice.

(b) The court may fix the time and place of the meeting, determine the shares entitled to participate in the meeting, specify a record date for determining shareholders entitled to notice of and to vote at the meeting, prescribe the form and content of the meeting notice, fix the quorum required for specific matters to be considered at the meeting (or direct that the votes represented at the meeting constitute a quorum for action on those matters), and enter other orders necessary to accomplish the purpose or purposes of the meeting.

§7.04. Action Without Meeting.—

(a) Action required or permitted by this Act to be taken at a shareholders' meeting may be taken without a meeting if the action is taken by all the shareholders entitled to vote on the action. The action must be evidenced by one or more written consents describing the action taken, signed by all the shareholders entitled to vote on the action, and delivered to the corporation for inclusion in the minutes or filing with the corporate records.

(b) If not otherwise determined under section 7.03 or 7.07, the record date for determining shareholders entitled to take action without a meeting is the date the first shareholder signs the consent under subsection (a).

(c) A consent signed under this section has the effect of a meeting vote and may be described as such in any document.

§7.05. Notice of Meeting.—

(a) A corporation shall notify shareholders of the date, time, and place of each annual and special shareholders' meeting no fewer than 10 nor more than 60 days before the meeting date. Unless this Act or the articles of incorporation require otherwise, the corporation is required to give notice only to shareholders entitled to vote at the meeting.

(b) Unless this Act or the articles of incorporation require otherwise, notice of an annual meeting need not include a description of the purpose or purposes for which the meeting is called.

(c) Notice of a special meeting must include a description of the purpose or purposes for which the meeting is called.

(d) If not otherwise fixed under section 7.03 or 7.07, the record date for determining shareholders entitled to notice of and to vote at an annual or special shareholders' meeting is the day before the first notice is delivered to shareholders.

§7.06. Waiver of Notice.—

(a) A shareholder may waive any notice required by this Act, the articles of incorporation, or bylaws before or after the date and time stated in the notice. The waiver must be in writing, be signed by the shareholder entitled to the notice, and be delivered to the corporation for inclusion in the minutes or filing with the corporate records.

(b) A shareholder's attendance at a meeting:

(1) waives objection to lack of notice or defective notice of the meeting, unless the shareholder at the beginning of the meeting objects to holding the meeting or transacting business at the meeting;

(2) waives objection to consideration of a particular matter at the meeting that is not within the purpose or purposes described in the meeting notice, unless the shareholder objects to considering the matter when it is presented.

§7.07. Record Date.—

(a) The bylaws may fix or provide the manner of fixing the record date for one or more voting groups in order to determine the shareholders entitled to notice of a shareholders' meeting, to demand a special meeting, to vote, or to take any other action. If the bylaws do not fix or provide for fixing a record date, the board of directors of the corporation may fix a future date as the record date.

(b)–(d) . . .

Subchapter B. Voting

§7.20. Shareholders' List for Meeting.—

(a) After fixing a record date for a meeting, a corporation shall prepare an alphabetical list of the names of all its shareholders who are entitled to notice of a shareholders' meeting. The list must be arranged by voting group (and within each voting group by class or series of shares) and show the address of and number of shares held by each shareholder.

(b) The shareholders' list must be available for inspection by any shareholder, beginning two business days after notice of the meeting is given for which the list was prepared and continuing through the meeting, at the corporation's principal office or at a place identified in the meeting notice in the city where the meeting will be held. A shareholder, his agent, or attorney is entitled on written demand to inspect and, subject to the requirements of section 16.02(c), to copy the list, during regular business hours and at his expense, during the period it is available for inspection.

(c)–(d) . . .

(e) Refusal or failure to prepare or make available the shareholders' list does not affect the validity of action taken at the meeting.

§7.21. Voting Entitlement of Shares.—

(a) Except as provided in subsection (b) and (c) or unless the articles of incorporation provide otherwise, each outstanding share, regardless of class, is entitled to one vote on each matter voted on at a shareholders' meeting. Only shares are entitled to vote.

(b) Absent special circumstances, the shares of a corporation are not entitled to vote if they are owned, directly or indirectly, by a second corporation, domestic or foreign, and the first corporation owns, directly or indirectly, a majority of the shares entitled to vote for directors of the second corporation.

(c) Subsection (b) does not limit the power of a corporation to vote any shares, including its own shares, held by it in a fiduciary capacity.

(d) . . .

§7.22. Proxies.—

(a) A shareholder may vote his shares in person or by proxy.

(b) A shareholder may appoint a proxy to vote or otherwise act for him by signing an appointment form, either personally or by his attorney-in-fact.

(c) An appointment of a proxy is effective when received by the secretary or other officer or agent authorized to tabulate votes. An appointment is valid for 11 months unless a longer period is expressly provided in the appointment form.

(d) An appointment of a proxy is revocable by the shareholder unless the appointment form conspicuously states that it is irrevocable and the appointment is coupled with an interest. . . .

(e) The death or incapacity of the shareholder appointing a proxy does not affect the right of the corporation to accept the proxy's authority unless notice of the death or incapacity is received by the secretary or other officer or agent authorized to tabulate votes before the proxy exercises his authority under the appointment.

(f)–(h) . . .

§7.23. Shares Held by Nominees. . . .

§7.24. Corporation's Acceptance of Votes.—

(a) If the name signed on a note, consent, waiver, or proxy appointment corresponds to the name of a shareholder, the corporation, if acting in good faith, is entitled to accept the vote, consent, waiver, or proxy appointment and give it the effect as the act of the shareholder.

(b)–(e). . .

§7.25. Quorum and Voting Requirements for Groups.

§7.26. Action by Single and Multiple Voting Groups....

§7.27. Greater Quorum or Voting Requirements.—
(a) The articles of incorporation may provide for a greater quorum or voting requirement for shareholders (or voting groups of shareholders) than is provided for by this Act.

(b) An amendment to the articles of incorporation that adds, changes, or deletes a greater quorum or voting requirement must meet the same quorum requirement and be adopted by the same vote and voting groups required to take action under the quorum and voting requirements then in effect or proposed to be adopted, whichever is greater.

§7.28. Voting for Directors; Cumulative Voting.—
(a) Unless otherwise provided in the articles of incorporation, directors are elected by a plurality of the votes cast by the shares entitled to vote in the election at a meeting at which a quorum is present.

(b) Shareholders do not have a right to cumulate their votes for directors unless the articles of incorporation so provide.

(c) A statement included in the articles of incorporation that "[all] [a designated voting group of] shareholders are entitled to cumulate their votes for directors" (or words of similar import) means that the shareholders designated are entitled to multiply the number of votes they are entitled to cast by the number of directors for whom they are entitled to vote and cast the product for a single candidate or distribute the product among two or more candidates.

(d) Shares otherwise entitled to vote cumulatively may not be voted cumulatively at a particular meeting unless:

(1) the meeting notice or proxy statement accompanying the notice states conspicuously that cumulative voting is authorized; or

(2) a shareholder who has the right to cumulate his votes gives notice to the corporation not less than 48 hours before the time set for the meeting of his intent to cumulate his votes during the meeting....

Subchapter C. Voting Trust and Agreements

§7.30. Voting Trusts.—...

§7.31. Voting Agreements.—
(a) Two or more shareholders may provide for the manner in which they will vote their shares by signing an agreement for that purpose....

(b) A voting agreement created under this section is specifically enforceable.

Subchapter D. Derivative Proceedings

§7.40. Procedure in Derivative Proceedings.—...

CHAPTER 8. DIRECTORS AND OFFICERS

Subchapter A. Board of Directors

§8.01. Requirement for and Duties of Board of Directors.—
(a) Except as provided in subsection (c), each corporation must have a board of directors.

(b) All corporate powers shall be exercised by or under the authority of, and the business and affairs of the corporation managed under the direction of, its board of directors, subject to any limitation set forth in the articles of incorporation.

(c) A corporation having 50 or fewer shareholders may dispense with or limit the authority of a board of directors by describing in its articles of incorporation who will perform some or all of the duties of a board of directors.

§8.02. Qualifications of Directors.—
The articles of incorporation or bylaws may prescribe qualifications for directors. A director need not be a resident of this state or a shareholder of the corporation unless the articles of incorporation or bylaws so prescribe.

§8.03. Number and Election of Directors.—
(a) A board of directors must consist of one or more individuals, with the number specified in or fixed in accordance with the articles of incorporation or bylaws.

(b) If a board of directors has power to fix or change the number of directors, the board may increase or decrease by 30 percent or less the number of directors last approved by the shareholders, but only the shareholders may increase or decrease by more than 30 percent the number of directors last approved by the shareholders.

(c) The articles of incorporation or bylaws may establish a variable range for the size of the board of directors by fixing a minimum and maximum number of directors. If a variable range is established, the number of directors may be fixed or changed from time to time, within the minimum and maximum, by the shareholders or the board of directors. After shares are issued, only the shareholders may change the range for the size of the board or change from a fixed to a variable-range size board or vice versa.

(d) Directors are elected at the first annual shareholders' meeting and at each annual meeting thereafter unless their terms are staggered under section 8.06.

§8.04. Election of Directors by Certain Classes of Shareholders.—
If the articles of incorporation authorize dividing the shares into classes, the articles may also authorize the election of all or a specified number of directors by the holders of one or more authorized classes of shares. A class (or classes) of shares entitled to elect one or more directors is a separate voting group for purposes of the election of directors.

§8.05. Terms of Directors Generally.—

(**a**) The terms of the initial directors of a corporation expire at the first shareholders' meeting at which directors are elected.

(**b**) The terms of all other directors expire at the next annual shareholders' meeting following their election unless their terms are staggered under section 8.06.

(**c**) A decrease in the number of directors does not shorten an incumbent director's term.

(**d**) The term of a director elected to fill a vacancy expires at the next shareholders' meeting at which directors are elected.

(**e**) Despite the expiration of a director's term, he continues to serve until his successor is elected and qualifies or until there is a decrease in the number of directors.

§8.06. Staggered Terms for Directors.—If there are nine or more directors, the articles of incorporation may provide for staggering their terms by dividing the total number of directors into two or three groups, with each group containing one half or one-third of the total, as near as may be. In that event, the terms of directors in the first group expire at the first annual shareholders' meeting after their election, the terms of the second group expire at the second annual shareholders' meeting after their election, and the terms of the third group, if any, expire at the third annual shareholders' meeting after their election. At each annual shareholders' meeting held thereafter, directors shall be chosen for a term of two years or three years, as the case may be, to succeed those whose terms expire.

§8.07. Resignation of Directors.—

(**a**) A director may resign at any time by delivering written notice to the board of directors, its chairman, or to the corporation.

(**b**) A resignation is effective when the notice is delivered unless the notice specifies a later effective date.

§8.08. Removal of Directors by Shareholders.—

(**a**) The shareholders may remove one or more directors with or without cause unless the articles of incorporation provide that directors may be removed only for cause.

(**b**) If a director is elected by a voting group of shareholders, only the shareholders of that voting group may participate in the vote to remove him.

(**c**) If cumulative voting is authorized, a director may not be removed if the number of votes sufficient to elect him under cumulative voting is voted against his removal. If cumulative voting is not authorized, a director may be removed only if the number of votes cast to remove him exceeds the number of votes cast not to remove him.

(**d**) A director may be removed by the shareholders only at a meeting called for the purpose of removing him and the meeting notice must state that the purpose, or one of the purposes, of the meeting is removal of the director.

§8.09. Removal of Directors by Judicial Proceeding.—

(**a**) The [name or describe] court of the county where a corporation's principal office (or, if none in this state, its registered office) is located may remove a director of the corporation from office in a proceeding commenced either by the corporation or by its shareholders holding at least 10 percent of the outstanding shares of any class if the court finds that (1) the director engaged in fraudulent or dishonest conduct, or gross abuse of authority or discretion, with respect to the corporation and (2) removal is in the best interest of the corporation.

(**b**) The court that removes a director may bar the director from reelection for a period prescribed by the court.

(**c**) If shareholders commence a proceeding under subsection (a), they shall make the corporation a party defendant.

§8.10. Vacancy on Board.—

(**a**) Unless the articles of incorporation provide otherwise, if a vacancy occurs on a board of directors, including a vacancy resulting from an increase in the number of directors:

(**1**) the shareholders may fill the vacancy;

(**2**) the board of directors may fill the vacancy; or

(**3**) if the directors remaining in office constitute fewer than a quorum of the board, they may fill the vacancy by the affirmative vote of a majority of all the directors remaining in office.

(**b**)–(**c**) . . .

§8.11. Compensation of Directors.—Unless the articles of incorporation or bylaws provide otherwise, the board of directors may fix the compensation of directors.

Subchapter B. Meetings and Action of the Board

§8.20. Meetings.—

(**a**) The board of directors may hold regular or special meetings in or out of this state.

(**b**) Unless the articles of incorporation or bylaws provide otherwise, the board of directors may permit any or all directors to participate in a regular or special meeting by, or conduct the meeting through the use of, any means of communication by which all directors participating may simultaneously hear each other during the meeting. A director participating in a meeting by this means is deemed to be present in person at the meeting.

§8.21. Action Without Meeting.—

(**a**) Unless the articles of incorporation or bylaws provide otherwise, action required or permitted by this Act to be taken at a board of directors' meeting may be taken without a meeting if the action is taken by all members of the board. The action must be evidenced by one or more written consents describing the action taken, signed by each director, and included in the minutes or filed with the corporate records reflecting the action taken.

(b)–(c)...

§8.22. Notice of Meeting.—

(**a**) Unless the articles of incorporation or bylaws provide otherwise, regular meetings of the board of directors may be held without notice of the date, time, place, or purpose of the meeting.

(**b**) Unless the articles of incorporation or bylaws provide for a longer or shorter period, special meetings of the board of directors must be preceded by at least two days' notice of the date, time, and place of the meeting. The notice need not describe the purpose of the special meeting unless required by the articles of incorporation or bylaws.

§8.23. Waiver of Notice.—

(**a**) A director may waive any notice required by this Act, the articles of incorporation, or bylaws before or after the date and time stated in the notice. Except as provided by subsection (b), the waiver must be in writing, signed by the director entitled to the notice, and filed with the minutes or corporate records.

(**b**) A director's attendance at or participation in a meeting waives any required notice to him of the meeting unless the director at the beginning of the meeting (or promptly upon his arrival) objects to holding the meeting or transacting business at the meeting and does not thereafter vote for or assent to action taken at the meeting.

§8.24. Quorum and Voting.—

(**a**) Unless the articles of incorporation or bylaws require a greater number, a quorum of a board of directors consists of:

(**1**) a majority of the fixed number of directors if the corporation has a fixed board size; or

(**2**) a majority of the number of directors prescribed, or if no number is prescribed the number in office immediately before the meeting begins, if the corporation has a variable-range size board.

(**b**) The articles of incorporation or bylaws may authorize a quorum of a board of directors to consist of no fewer than one-third of the fixed or prescribed number of directors determined under subsection (a).

(**c**) If a quorum is present when a vote is taken, the affirmative vote of a majority of directors present is the act of the board of directors unless the articles of incorporation or bylaws require the vote of a greater number of directors.

(**d**) ...

§8.25. Committees.—

(**a**) Unless the articles of incorporation or bylaws provide otherwise, a board of directors may create one or more committees and appoint members of the board of directors to serve on them. Each committee may have two or more members, who serve at the pleasure of the board of directors.

(**b**)–(**c**) ...

(**d**) To the extent specified by the board of directors or in the articles of incorporation or bylaws, each committee may exercise the authority of the board of directors under section 8.01.

(**e**) A committee may not, however:

(**1**) authorize distributions;

(**2**) approve or propose to shareholders action that this Act requires be approved by shareholders;

(**3**) fill vacancies on the board of directors or on any of its committees;

(**4**) amend articles of incorporation pursuant to section 10.02;

(**5**) adopt, amend, or repeal bylaws;

(**6**) approve a plan of merger not requiring shareholder approval;

(**7**) authorize or approve reacquisition of shares, except according to a formula or method prescribed by the board of directors; or

(**8**) authorize or approve the issuance or sale or contract for sale of shares, or determine the designation and relative rights, preferences, and limitations of a class or series of shares, except that the board of directors may authorize a committee (or a senior executive officer of the corporation) to do so within limits specifically prescribed by the board of directors.

(**f**) The creation of, delegation of authority to, or action by a committee does not alone constitute compliance by a director with the standards of conduct described in section 8.30.

Subchapter C. Standards of Conduct

§8.30. General Standards for Directors.—

(**a**) A director shall discharge his duties as a director, including his duties as a member of a committee:

(**1**) in good faith;

(**2**) with the care an ordinarily prudent person in a like position would exercise under similar circumstances; and

(**3**) in a manner he reasonably believes to be in the best interest of the corporation.

(**b**) In discharging his duties a director is entitled to rely on information, opinions, reports, or statements, including financial statements and other financial data, if prepared or presented by:

(**1**) one or more officers or employees of the corporation whom the director reasonably believes to be reliable and competent in the matters presented;

(**2**) legal counsel, public accountants, or other persons as to matters the director reasonably believes are within the person's professional or expert competence; or

(**3**) a committee of the board of directors of which he is not a member if the director reasonably believes the committee merits confidence.

(**c**) A director is not acting in good faith if he has knowledge concerning the matter in question that makes reliance otherwise permitted by subsection (b) unwarranted.

(d) A director is not liable for any action taken as a director, or any failure to take any action, if he performed the duties of his office in compliance with this section.

§8.31. Director Conflict of Interest.—

(a) A conflict of interest transaction is a transaction with the corporation in which a director of the corporation has a direct or indirect interest. A conflict of interest transaction is not voidable by the corporation solely because of the director's interest in the transaction if any one of the following is true:

(1) the material facts of the transaction and the director's interest were disclosed or known to the board of directors or a committee of the board of directors and the board of directors or committee authorized, approved, or ratified the transaction;

(2) the material facts of the transaction and the director's interest were disclosed or known to the shareholders entitled to vote and they authorized, approved, or ratified the transaction; or

(3) the transaction was fair to the corporation.

(b) For purposes of this section, a director of the corporation has an indirect interest in a transaction if (1) another entity in which he has a material financial interest or in which he is a general partner is a party to the transaction or (2) another entity of which he is a director, officer, or trustee is a party to the transaction and the transaction is or should be considered by the board of directors of the corporation.

(c) For purposes of subsection (a)(1), a conflict of interest transaction is authorized, approved, or ratified if it receives the affirmative vote of a majority of the directors on the board of directors (or on the committee) who have no direct or indirect interest in the transaction, but a transaction may not be authorized, approved, or ratified under this section by a single director. If a majority of the directors who have no direct or indirect interest in the transaction vote to authorize, approve, or ratify the transaction, a quorum is present for the purpose of taking action under this section. The presence of, or a vote cast by, a director with a direct or indirect interest in the transaction does not affect the validity of any action taken under subsection (a)(1) if the transaction is otherwise authorized, approved, or ratified as provided in that subsection.

(d) For purposes of subsection (a)(2), a conflict of interest transaction is authorized, approved, or ratified if it receives the vote of a majority of the shares entitled to be counted under this subsection. Shares owned by or voted under the control of a director who has a direct or indirect interest in the transaction, and shares owned by or voted under the control of an entity described in subsection (b)(1), may not be counted in a vote of shareholders to determine whether to authorize, approve, or ratify a conflict of interest transaction under subsection (a)(2). The vote of those shares, however, is counted in determining whether the transaction is approved under other sections of this Act. A majority of the shares, whether or not present, that are entitled to be counted in a vote on the transaction under this subsection constitutes a quorum for the purpose of taking action under this section.

§8.32. Loans to Directors.—

(a) Except as provided by subsection (c), a corporation may not lend money to or guarantee the obligation of a director of the corporation unless:

(1) the particular loan or guarantee is approved by a majority of the votes represented by the outstanding voting shares of all classes, voting as a single voting group, except the votes of shares owned by or voted under the control of the benefited director; or

(2) the corporation's board of directors determines that the loan or guarantee benefits the corporation and either approves the specific loan or guarantee or a general plan authorizing loans and guarantees.

(b) The fact that a loan or guarantee is made in violation of this section does not affect the borrower's liability on the loan.

(c) This section does not apply to loans and guarantees authorized by statute regulating any special class of corporations.

§8.33. Liability for Unlawful Distributions.—

(a) A director who votes for or assents to a distribution made in violation of section 6.40 or the articles of incorporation is personally liable to the corporation for the amount of the distribution that exceeds what could have been distributed without violating section 6.40 or the articles of incorporation if it is established that he did not perform his duties in compliance with section 8.30. In any proceeding commenced under this section, a director has all of the defenses ordinarily available to a director.

(b) A director held liable under subsection (a) for an unlawful distribution is entitled to contribution:

(1) from every other director who could be liable under subsection (a) for the unlawful distribution; and

(2) from each shareholder for the amount the shareholder accepted knowing the distribution was made in violation of section 6.40 or the articles of incorporation.

(c) . . .

Subchapter D. Officers

§8.40. Required Officers.—

(a) A corporation has the officers described in its bylaws or appointed by the board of directors in accordance with the bylaws.

(b) . . .

(c) The bylaws or the board of directors shall delegate to one of the officers responsibility for preparing minutes of the directors' and shareholders' meetings and for authenticating records of the corporation.

(d) The same individual may simultaneously hold more than one office in a corporation.

§8.41. Duties of Officers.—Each officer has the authority and shall perform the duties set forth in the bylaws or, to the extent consistent with the bylaws, the duties prescribed by the board of directors or by direction of an officer authorized by the board of directors to prescribe the duties of other officers.

§8.42. Standards of Conduct for Officers.—

(a) An officer with discretionary authority shall discharge his duties under that authority:

(1) in good faith;

(2) with the care an ordinarily prudent person in a like position would exercise under similar circumstances; and

(3) in a manner he reasonably believes to be in the best interests of the corporation.

(b) In discharging his duties an officer is entitled to rely on information, opinions, reports, or statements, including financial statements and other financial data, if prepared or presented by:

(1) one or more officers or employees of the corporation whom the officer reasonably believes to be reliable and competent in the matters presented; or

(2) legal counsel, public accountants, or other persons as to matters the officer reasonably believes are within the person's professional or expert competence.

(c) ...

(d) ...

§8.43. Resignation and Removal of Officers.—

(a) An officer may resign at any time by delivering notice to the corporation....

(b) A board of directors may remove any officer at any time with or without cause.

§8.44. Contract Rights of Officers.—

(a) The appointment of an officer does not itself create contract rights.

(b) An officer's removal does not affect the officer's contract rights, if any, with the corporation. An officer's resignation does not affect the corporation's contract rights, if any, with the officer.

Subchapter E. Indemnification

§8.50. Subchapter Definitions.—...

§8.51. Authority to Indemnify.—

(a) Except as provided in subsection (d), a corporation may indemnify an individual made a party to a proceeding because he is or was a director against liability incurred in the proceeding if:

(1) he conducted himself in good faith; and

(2) he reasonably believed:

(i) in the case of conduct in his official capacity with the corporation, that his conduct was in its best interests; and

(ii) in all other cases, that his conduct was at least not opposed to its best interests; and

(3) in the case of any criminal proceeding, he had no reasonable cause to believe his conduct was unlawful.

(b) ...

(c) The termination of a proceeding by judgment, order, settlement, conviction, or upon a plea of nolo contendere or its equivalent is not, of itself, determinative that the director did not meet the standard of conduct described in this section.

(d) A corporation may not indemnify a director under this section:

(1) in connection with a proceeding by or in the right of the corporation in which the director was adjudged liable to the corporation; or

(2) in connection with any other proceeding charging improper personal benefit to him, whether or not involving action in his official capacity, in which he was adjudged liable on the basis that personal benefit was improperly received by him.

(e) ...

§8.52. Mandatory Indemnification.—Unless limited by its articles of incorporation, a corporation shall indemnify a director who was wholly successful, on the merits or otherwise, in the defense of any proceeding to which he was a party because he is or was a director of the corporation against reasonable expenses incurred by him in connection with the proceeding.

§8.53. Advance for Expenses....

§8.54. Court-ordered Indemnification....

§8.55. Determination and Authorization of Indemnification....

§8.56. Indemnification of Officers, Employees, and Agents.—Unless a corporation's articles of incorporation provide otherwise:

(1) An officer of the corporation who is not a director is entitled to mandatory indemnification under section 8.52, and is entitled to apply for court-ordered indemnification under section 8.54, in each case to the same extent as a director.

(2)–(3) ...

§8.57. Insurance....

§8.58. Application of Subchapter....

CHAPTER 9 [RESERVED]

CHAPTER 10. AMENDMENT OF ARTICLES OF INCORPORATION AND BYLAWS

Subchapter A. Amendment of Articles of Incorporation

§10.01. Authority to Amend.—

(a) A corporation may amend its articles of incorporation at any time to add or change a provision that is required or permitted in the articles of incorporation or to delete a provision not required in the articles of incorporation. . . .

(**b**) A shareholder of the corporation does not have a vested property right resulting from any provision in the articles of incorporation, including provisions relating to management, control, capital structure, dividend entitlement, or purpose or duration of the corporation.

§10.02. Amendment by Board of Directors.—Unless the articles of incorporation provide otherwise, a corporation's board of directors may adopt one or more amendments to the corporation's articles of incorporation without shareholder action [under certain limited conditions.]. . .

§10.03–§10.08. [Concern amendment of articles of incorporation; voting on amendments by voting groups; amendment before issuance of shares; articles and restated articles of incorporation and amendment pursuant to reorganization.]

§10.09. Effect of Amendment. An amendment to articles of incorporation does not affect a cause of action existing against or in favor of the corporation, a proceeding to which the corporation is a party, or the existing rights of persons other than shareholders of the corporation. An amendment changing a corporation's name does not abate a proceeding brought by or against the corporation in its former name.

Subchapter B. Amendment of Bylaws

§10.20. Amendment by Board of Directors or Shareholders.—

(**a**) A corporation's board of directors may amend or repeal the corporation's bylaws unless:

(**1**) the articles of incorporation or this Act reserve this power exclusively to the shareholders in whole or part;

(**2**) . . .

(**b**) A corporation's shareholders may amend or repeal the corporation's bylaws even though the bylaws may also be amended or repealed by its board of directors.

§10.21. Bylaw Increasing Quorum or Voting Requirement for Shareholders.—

(**a**) If authorized by the articles of incorporation, the shareholders may adopt or amend a bylaw that fixes a greater quorum or voting requirement for shareholders (or voting groups of shareholders) than is required by this Act. . . .

(**b**) A bylaw that fixes a greater quorum or voting requirement for shareholders under subsection (a) may not be adopted, amended, or repealed by the board of directors.

§10.22. Bylaw Increasing Quorum or Voting Requirement for Directors.—

(**a**) A bylaw that fixes a greater quorum or voting requirement for the board of directors may be amended or repealed.

(**1**) . . .

(**2**) if originally adopted by the board of directors, either by the shareholders or by the board of directors.

(**b**)–(**c**) . . .

CHAPTER 11. MERGER AND SHARE EXCHANGE

§11.01. Merger.—

(**a**) One or more corporations may merge into another corporation if the board of directors of each corporation adopts and its shareholders (if required by section 11.03) approve a plan of merger.

(**b**) The plan of merger must set forth. . .

§11.02. Share Exchange. . . .

(**a**) A corporation may acquire all of the outstanding shares of one or more classes or series of another corporation if the board of directors of each corporation adopts and its shareholders (if required by section 11.03) approve the exchange.

(**b**) The plan of exchange must set forth. . .

(**c**)–(**d**) . . .

§11.03. Action on Plan. . . .

§11.04–§11.07. [concerns merger of subsidiary; articles of merger; effect of merger; merger with foreign corporation.]

CHAPTER 12. SALE OF ASSETS

§12.01. Sale of Assets in Regular Course of Business and Mortgage of Assets.—

(**a**) A corporation may, on the terms and conditions and for the consideration determined by the board of directors:

(**1**) sell, lease, exchange, or otherwise dispose of all, or substantially all, of its property in the usual and regular course of business;

(**2**) mortgage, pledge, dedicate to the repayment of indebtedness (whether with or without recourse), or otherwise encumber any or all of its property whether or not in the usual and regular course of business; or

(**3**) transfer any or all of its property to a corporation all the shares of which are owned by the corporation.

(**b**) Unless the articles of incorporation require it, approval by the shareholders of a transaction described in subsection (a) is not required.

§12.02. Sale of Assets Other Than in Regular Course of Business.—

(**a**) A corporation may sell, lease, exchange, or otherwise dispose of all, or substantially all, of its property (with or without the good will), otherwise than in the usual and regular course of business, on the terms and conditions and for the consideration determined by the corporation's board of directors, if the board of directors proposes and its shareholders approved the proposed transaction.

(b)–(g) ...

CHAPTER 13. DISSENTERS' RIGHTS

Subchapter A. Right to Dissent and Obtain Payment for Shares

§13.01. Definitions.— In this chapter...

§13.02. Right to Dissent.—

(a) A shareholder is entitled to dissent from, and obtain payment of the fair value of his shares in the event of, any of the following corporate actions:

(1) consummation of a plan of merger to which the corporation is a party (i) if shareholder approval is required for the merger by section 11.03 or the articles of incorporation and the shareholder is entitled to vote on the merger or (ii) if the corporation is a subsidiary that is merged with its parent under section 11.04;

(2) consummation of a plan of share exchange to which the corporation is a party as the corporation whose shares will be acquired, if the shareholder is entitled to vote on the plan;

(3) consummation of a sale or exchange of all, or substantially all, of the property of the corporation other than in the usual and regular course of business, if the shareholder is entitled to vote on the sale or exchange, including a sale in dissolution, but not including a sale pursuant to court order or a sale for cash pursuant to a plan by which all or substantially all of the net proceeds of the sale will be distributed to the shareholders within one year after the date of sale;

(4) an amendment of the articles of incorporation that materially and adversely affects rights in respect of a dissenter's shares...

§13.03. Dissent by Nominees and Beneficial Owners....

Subchapter B. Procedure for Exercise of Dissenters' Rights

§13.20–§13.28. [concern notice, demand for payment, and procedures related to dissenters' rights.]

Subchapter C. Judicial Appraisal of Shares

§13.30–§13.31. [Court action and costs.]

CHAPTER 14. DISSOLUTION

Subchapter A. Voluntary Dissolution

§14.01. Dissolution by Incorporators or Initial Directors.—A majority of the incorporators or initial directors of a corporation that has not issued shares or has not commenced business may dissolve the corporation....

§14.02. Dissolution by Board of Directors and Shareholders.—

(a) A corporation's board of directors may propose dissolution for submission to the shareholders.

(b) For a proposal to dissolve to be adopted:

(1) the board of directors must recommend dissolution to the shareholders unless the board of directors determines that because of conflict of interest or other special circumstances it should make no recommendation and communicates the basis for its determination to the shareholders; and

(2) the shareholders entitled to vote must approve the proposal to dissolve as provided in subsection (e).

(c) The board of directors may condition its submission of the proposal for dissolution on any basis.

(d) The corporation shall notify each shareholder, whether or not entitled to vote, of the proposed shareholders' meeting in accordance with section 7.05. The notice must also state that the purpose, or one of the purposes, of the meeting is to consider dissolving the corporation.

(e) Unless the articles of incorporation or the board of directors (acting pursuant to subsection (c)) require a greater vote or a vote by voting groups, the proposal to dissolve to be adopted must be approved by a majority of all the votes entitled to be cast on that proposal.

§14.03. Articles of Dissolution.—...

§14.04. Revocation of Dissolution.—...

§14.05. Effect of Dissolution.—

(a) A dissolved corporation continues its corporate existence but may not carry on any business except that appropriate to wind up and liquidate its business and affairs, including:

(1) collecting its assets;

(2) disposing of its properties that will not be distributed in kind to its shareholders;

(3) discharging or making provision for discharging its liabilities;

(4) distributing its remaining property among its shareholders according to their interests; and

(5) doing every other act necessary to wind up and liquidate its business and affairs.

(b) Dissolution of a corporation does not:

(1) transfer title to the corporation's property;

(2) prevent transfer of its shares or securities, although the authorization to dissolve may provide for closing the corporation's share transfer records;

(3) subject its directors or officers to standards of conduct different from those prescribed in chapter 8;

(4) change quorum or voting requirements for its board of directors or shareholders; change provisions for selection, resignation, or removal of its directors or officers or both; or change provisions for amending its bylaws;

(5) prevent commencement of a proceeding by or against the corporation in its corporate name;

(6) abate or suspend a proceeding pending by or against the corporation on the effective date of dissolution; or

(7) terminate the authority of the registered agent of the corporation.

§14.06–§14.07. [concern known and unknown claims against dissolved corporations.]

Subchapter B. Administrative Dissolution

§14.20–§14.23. [concern grounds and procedures for administrative dissolution; reinstatement; appeal of denial of reinstatement.]

Subchapter C. Judicial Dissolution

§14.30. Grounds for Judicial Dissolution.—The [name or describe court or courts] may dissolve a corporation:

(1) in a proceeding by the attorney general if it is established that:

(i) the corporation obtained its articles of incorporation through fraud; or

(ii) the corporation has continued to exceed or abuse the authority conferred upon it by law;

(2) in a proceeding by a shareholder if it is established that:

(i) the directors are deadlocked in the management of the corporate affairs, the shareholders are unable to break the deadlock, and irreparable injury to the corporation is threatened or being suffered, or the business and affairs of the corporation can no longer be conducted to the advantage of the shareholders generally, because of the deadlock;

(ii) the directors or those in control of the corporation have acted, are acting, or will act in a manner that is illegal, oppressive, or fraudulent;

(iii) the shareholders are deadlocked in voting power and have failed, for a period that includes at least two consecutive annual meeting dates, to elect successors to directors whose terms have expired; or

(iv) the corporate assets are being misapplied or wasted;

(3) in a proceeding by a creditor if it is established that:

(i) the creditor's claim has been reduced to judgment, the execution on the judgment returned unsatisfied, and the corporation is insolvent; or

(ii) the corporation has admitted in writing that the creditor's claim is due and owing and the corporation is insolvent; or

(4) in a proceeding by the corporation to have its voluntary dissolution continued under court supervision.

§14.31–§14.40. [concern procedures for judicial dissolution, decree, receivership, and transfer of assets.]

CHAPTER 15. FOREIGN CORPORATIONS

Subchapter A. Certificate of Authority

§15.01. Authority to Transact Business Required.—

(a) A foreign corporation may not transact business in this state until it obtains a certificate of authority from the secretary of state.

(b) The following activities, among others, do not constitute transacting business within the meaning of subsection (a):

(1) maintaining, defending, or settling any proceeding;

(2) holding meetings of the board of directors or shareholders or carrying on other activities concerning internal corporate affairs;

(3) maintaining bank accounts;

(4) maintaining offices or agencies for the transfer, exchange, and registration of the corporation's own securities or maintaining trustees or depositaries with respect to those securities;

(5) selling through independent contractors;

(6) soliciting or obtaining orders, whether by mail or through employees or agents or otherwise, if the orders require acceptance outside this state before they become contracts;

(7) creating or acquiring indebtedness, mortgages, and security interests in real or personal property;

(8) securing or collecting debts or enforcing mortgages and security interests in property securing the debts;

(9) owning, without more, real or personal property;

(10) conducting an isolated transaction that is completed within 30 days and that is not one in the course of repeated transactions of a like nature;

(11) transacting business in interstate commerce.

(c) The list of activities in subsection (b) is not exhaustive.

§15.02. Consequences of Transacting Business Without Authority.—

(a) A foreign corporation transacting business in this state without a certificate of authority may not maintain a proceeding in any court in this state until it obtains a certificate of authority.

(b) The successor to a foreign corporation that transacted business in this state without a certificate of authority and the assignee of a cause of action arising out of that business may not maintain a proceeding based on that cause of action in any court in this state until the foreign corporation or its successor obtains a certificate of authority.

(c) A court may stay a proceeding commenced by a foreign corporation, its successor, or assignee until it determines whether the foreign corporation or its successor requires a certificate of authority. If it so determines, the court may further stay the proceeding until the foreign corporation or its successor obtains the certificate.

(d) A foreign corporation is liable for a civil penalty of $_____ for each day, but not to exceed a total of $_____ for each year, it transacts business in this state without a certificate of authority. The attorney general may collect all penalties due under this subsection.

(e) Notwithstanding subsections (a) and (b), the failure of a foreign corporation to obtain a certificate of authority does not impair the validity of its corporate acts or prevent it from defending any proceeding in this state.

§15.03–§15.04. [concern application for certificate of authority and for amended certificate.]

§15.05. Effect of Certificate of Authority.—

(a) A certificate of authority authorizes the foreign corporation to which it is issued to transact business in this state subject, however, to the right of the state to revoke the certificate as provided in this Act.

(b) A foreign corporation with a valid certificate of authority has the same but no greater rights and has the same but no greater privileges as, and except as otherwise provided by this Act is subject to the same duties, restrictions, penalties, and liabilities now or later imposed on, a domestic corporation of like character.

(c) This Act does not authorize this state to regulate the organization or internal affairs of a foreign corporation authorized to transact business in this state.

§15.06–§15.10. [concern corporate name of foreign corporation; its registered office and agent; service of process upon a foreign corporation.]

Subchapter B. Withdrawal

§15.20–§15.32. [concern withdrawal and revocation of certificate of authority of foreign corporation; promoters; appeal.]

CHAPTER 16. RECORDS AND REPORTS

Subchapter A. Records

§16.01. Corporate Records.—

(a) A corporation shall keep as permanent records minutes of all meetings of its shareholders and board of directors, a record of all actions taken by the shareholders or board of directors without a meeting, and a record of all actions taken by a committee of the board of directors in place of the board of directors on behalf of the corporation.

(b) A corporation shall maintain appropriate accounting records.

(c) A corporation or its agent shall maintain a record of its shareholders, in a form that permits preparation of a list of the names and addresses of all shareholders, in alphabetical order by class of shares showing the number and class of shares held by each.

(d) A corporation shall maintain its records in written form or in another form capable of conversion into written form within a reasonable time.

(e) A corporation shall keep a copy of the following records at its principal office:

(1) its articles or restated articles of incorporation and all amendments to them currently in effect;

(2) its bylaws or restated bylaws and all amendments to them currently in effect;

(3) resolutions adopted by its board of directors creating one or more classes or series of shares, and fixing their relative rights, preferences, and limitations, if shares issued pursuant to those resolutions are outstanding;

(4) the minutes of all shareholders' meetings, and records of all action taken by shareholders without a meeting, for the past three years;

(5) all written communications to shareholders generally within the past three years, including the financial statements furnished for the past three years under section 16.20;

(6) a list of the names and business addresses of its current directors and officers; and

(7) its most recent annual report delivered to the secretary of state under section 16.22.

§16.02–§16.04. [concern inspection of corporate records by shareholders.]

Subchapter B. Reports

§16.20–§16.21. [concern reports to shareholders.]

§16.22. Annual report for Secretary of State....

CHAPTER 17. TRANSITION PROVISIONS

§17.01–§17.06. [concern application of Act; savings provisions; severability; effective date.]

GLOSSARY

Abatement In the law of wills, a required reduction or nonpayment of a gift stated in a will. In real estate law, putting a stop to a nuisance.

Acceleration clause A provision in a promissory note permitting the maker to make, or a holder to have, payment before the stated due date.

Acceptance An offeree's manifestation of assent to the terms of an offer, needed for a contract to arise. Also, *in the law of sales:* a buyer's act of taking as the buyer's own property the particular goods covered by a contract, whether by words or by action or silence when it is time to speak. Also, *in the law of commercial paper,* a drawee's act of writing the word "accepted" across the face of a draft (or the word "certified" across the face of a check), or signing on the face of the instrument, and thereby becoming a primary party to the instrument. Also, *in the law of bankruptcy,* an agreement by a class of creditors (or holders of ownership interests) to a plan for satisfaction of claims against the debtor's estate. A class accepts by means of a vote.

Accession In general, coming into possession of a right; in the law of sales, goods that are installed in or affixed to other goods.

Accommodation party A person who signs an instrument for the purpose of lending his or her name (credit) to another party to the instrument.

Accommodation surety See *Surety.*

Accord and satisfaction The reaching of a new agreement and the performance of it or the acceptance of it by both parties as a substitute for the original contract. Usually associated with settlement of a disputed claim or unliquidated debt.

Account receivable (account) A right to payment for goods sold or leased or for services rendered.

Acknowledgment Certification by a notary public as to the identity of a person who signs a document.

Adhesion contracts See *Contract of adhesion.*

Administrative agency A government office, department, board, bureau, or commission, (other than legislatures and courts) with power to make rules and regulations concerning private rights and duties.

Administrative law The law concerning the powers and procedures of administrative agencies, including the law governing judicial review of administrative action.

Administrative Procedure Act A federal law generally establishing the manner in which federal administrative agencies operate.

Administrator In estate or inheritance law: a person or entity, not designated by a decedent's will, appointed by a court to administer a decedent's estate.

Admitted to probate The determination of a court that a will is valid.

Affirmation (to affirm) The ratification of an act, statement, or promise; used primarily to express agreement to be held to a voidable transaction, as the affirmance or ratification of a minor's voidable contract or the ratification by a principal of an agent's voidable action on the principal's behalf.

After-acquired property clause A clause in a security agreement that gives a creditor a security interest in both present and future assets of the debtor instead of a security interest only in specific assets on hand at the creation of the secured transaction.

Agency A relationship in which one person acts for or represents another by the latter's authority; where one person acts for another either in the relationship of principal and agent, master and servant, or employer and employee.

Agent A person authorized by another to act for him or her; one entrusted with another's business.

Aggressor corporation A corporation which attempts, either through a friendly or an unfriendly action, to gain control of a public corporation, called the "target corporation."

Agreement A mutual assent; a contract embodies the agreement of the parties; however, frequently a contract is loosely called an agreement.

Allowed claim In bankruptcy law, a valid claim against the debtor's estate. An allowed claim will be paid to the extent that funds are available.

All-risk contract An insurance policy which indemnifies the insured against property loss resulting from any peril except those specifically excluded by the insurance contract.

Amicus curiae A "friend of the court," not a party to a lawsuit, who, with permission of a court, files a brief (usually in a matter of broad public interest) suggesting a rationale for solution of a legal question.

Annuity A contractual device for systematically using up (liquidating) an existing fund; a type of contract sold by some life insurance companies.

Anticipatory breach of contract Repudiation of a contract obligation before performance is due.

Apparent authority The authority which, though not actually granted, the principal knowingly permits an agent to exercise or which the principal holds the agent out as possessing.

Appellant One who files an appeal.

Appellee The party opposite the appellant. Usually, the party who won at the trial level.

Arbitrager (or arbitrageur) An individual who buys and sells shares, not for investment, but to take advantage of anticipated short movements in the cost of the security; he or she frequently takes advantage of temporary small differences in the price of a security on different stock exchanges.

Arbitration A nonjudicial method of resolving civil disputes, informal and voluntary in most cases.

Arraignment The reading by a judicial officer of an information or indictment to an accused in a criminal case and asking how he or she pleads.

Articles of incorporation A legal document, filed with a designated state official, that meets the requirements of the state's incorporation statute before a person or persons can commence doing business as a corporation. The articles, sometimes called "corporate charter," provide the framework within which the corporation must operate.

Artisan A skilled craftsperson, such as a carpenter, mechanic, or tailor. An "artisan's lien" is the right of one who repairs goods of another to keep possession of the goods until the repair charges are paid.

Assignee A person to whom an assignment is made.

Assignment A transfer of rights, usually of contract rights.

Assignment for the benefit of creditors A voluntary transfer, under state law, by a debtor of all her or his available property to a trustee for distribution to the debtor's creditors in exchange for their promises to release the debtor from further liability. Also called a "general assignment."

Assignor The maker of an assignment.

Assumpsit A common law form of action to recover damages for breach of contract.

Attachment Seizure of a debtor's property, generally at the start of a lawsuit, through legal process to protect a creditor's claim.

Attachment of a security interest In the law of secured transactions, the name given to the process of creating (agreeing to) a security interest in personal property and of making it enforceable against the debtor.

Authority The power of an agent to affect the legal relations of a principal by acts done in accordance with the principal's manifestations of consent.

Authority by estoppel Authority that is not actual, but is apparent only, being imposed on the principal because the conduct of the principal has been such as to mislead a third party, so that it would be unjust to let the principal deny it.

Automatic stay A suspension of legal action. In bankruptcy law, a suspension of legal action (other than the bankruptcy proceeding itself) until the bankruptcy case is over or until the stay is vacated by the bankruptcy court.

Bail Security given to guarantee the presence of an accused at a criminal hearing or trial.

Bailment A transaction in which the possessor of personal property (bailor) puts someone else (bailee) in possession for a limited purpose, such as for repair or for storage.

Bankruptcy A process under federal law whereby the nonexempt assets of a debtor, incapable of paying his or her debts, are distributed to creditors, and the debtor, if honest, is discharged from liability for most remaining unpaid debts.

Bear An individual who believes the price of shares will go down; contrasted with a "bull" who believes the price will rise.

Bearer document of title Similar to bearer commercial paper. See *Commercial paper*.

Bearer paper See *Commercial paper*.

Bequest A gift by will of personal property.

Bilateral contract A contract in which the parties make promises to each other. See also *Unilateral contract.*

Bill of exchange A draft.

Bill of lading A document of title issued by a railroad or other carrier that lists the goods accepted for transport and that sometimes states the terms of the shipping agreement. See *Document of title.* A *through bill* of lading is one issued by a carrier for transport of goods over its own lines for a certain distance, and then over connecting lines to the destination. A *destination bill* of lading is one to be issued at the destination point instead of sending point so that the documents will be available when the goods arrive.

Bill of Rights The First Ten Amendments to the Constitution of the United States. The Bill of Rights confers a number of rights intended to protect individuals from federal governmental oppression.

Blue-sky laws State statutes that protect investors against fraudulent schemes by regulating the issuance, sale, and/or transfer of securities.

Board of directors One or more persons elected and authorized by the shareholders of a corporation to manage the corporation and its affairs.

Bona fide In or with good faith.

Bond In corporation financing, a certificate or other evidence of long-term debt obligating the corporation to pay the holder a fixed rate of interest on the principal at regular intervals and to pay the principal on a stated maturity date. In criminal law, a guarantee that the accused will be present at a hearing or trial.

Boycott A combination to abstain from or to prevent dealings with a person or an organization as a means to influence the settlement of a labor dispute.

Breach The breaking of a promise, a duty, or an obligation, as a breach of contract.

Bribery Improperly attempting to influence an action, generally of a public servant, by offering money or other favors.

Bulk sale The sale of a whole stock in trade of a business.

Bull See *Bear.*

Burden of proof In law, the degree of proof necessary to sustain a verdict or judgment, in criminal cases, beyond a reasonable doubt, in civil cases by a preponderance of the evidence.

Bylaws Self-made regulations or rules adopted by a corporation to regulate and govern its internal actions and affairs.

C&F (CF) An abbreviation meaning that the price includes in a lump sum the cost of goods and the cost of freight to the named destination.

Call A demand of payment, either in installments or portions, made upon subscribers of shares by directors of a corporation. Also, a negotiable option contract under which the bearer has the right to buy a certain number of shares of stock at an agreed price before a fixed date.

Callable preferred shares Preferred shares which a corporation may "call back" or redeem at a fixed date and price established when they are issued.

Carrier An individual or a business firm engaged in transporting passengers or goods for hire. A *common carrier* offers its services to the public and must carry goods for all who apply, as long as there is room and no legal excuse for refusing. A *private carrier* carries goods only for those persons with whom the carrier chooses to contract.

Case law The accumulated body of court decisions that form an important part of the law of a particular subject.

Cash surrender value A dollar value of an insurance policy, generated from premium payments that exceed the amount needed to pay claims against and expenses of the insurer. The excess payments are retained and invested by the insurer, and the accumulation is held in a *legal reserve fund.*

Cause of action Legal basis for a lawsuit.

Caveat emptor A Latin phrase meaning "let the buyer beware."

Cease-and-desist order A command from an administrative agency to stop a challenged practice. A cease-and-desist order is similar to an injunction.

CEO The "chief executive officer" of a corporation; usually its president or chairperson of the board of directors.

Certificate of deposit A written acknowledgment by a bank of the receipt of a specified amount of money held subject to the depositor's order in accordance with the certificate's terms; a type of promissory note issued by a bank in exchange for a deposit of money.

Certificate of incorporation A document, issued by some states, that grants an organization permission to do business as a corporation.

Certified check A check that has been accepted by the drawee bank. See *Acceptance.*

Certiorari A formal request by a higher court to a lower court to transmit to it the record of a case so that it can be heard on appeal.

Chancery A *court of equity.* See *Equity.*

Charging order A court order granting a creditor a right to a partner's interest in a partnership.

Charter An instrument by which the state creates a corporation and confers on it the right, power, and authority to do business under the corporate form. The term "charter" is sometimes used to refer to the articles of incorporation.

Chattel A term often used to refer to movable, tangible things which are not firmly attached to real property.

Chattel mortgage A writing evidencing a secured transaction in personal property; i.e., a mortgage evidencing both a monetary obligation and a security interest in personal property. The debtor has possession of the property, but the creditor has, as his or her security interest, title to the property or, in some states, a lien (claim) against it.

Chattel paper A writing which evidences both a monetary obligation and a security interest in specific goods.

Check A draft drawn on a bank payable on demand; a written order addressed to a bank by a party who has money on deposit, directing the bank to pay on presentment, to the party named in the check or to bearer or order, a specified sum of money.

CIF An abbreviation meaning that the price includes in a lump sum the cost of goods and the cost of insurance and freight to the named destination.

Civil law In the United States, that law under which a person (the plaintiff) may sue another (the defendant), e.g., in a lawsuit involving a contract or tort, to obtain redress for a wrong committed by the defendant. The expression "civil law" is also used to describe those legal systems (e.g., that of the French) whose law is centered around a comprehensive legislative code.

Class action shareholder suit An action brought against a corporation by one or more of its shareholders on behalf of themselves and other shareholders similarly situated.

Clearinghouse A place where banks exchange checks and drafts drawn on each other and thereby settle their daily balances.

Close corporation A corporation whose stock is held by one stockholder or by a relatively small group of stockholders who actively participate in its management. The stock is generally subject to restrictions on transfer and is not publicly traded.

COD An abbreviation of "collect on delivery."

Codicil An amendment to a formal or holographic will.

Cognovit note A promissory note containing a confession-of-judgment clause.

Coinsurance A method used by property insurers to prevent customers who underinsure commercial property from receiving disproportionately larger benefits than those who insure near the full value of their property.

Collateral Something of value that can be converted into cash by a creditor if the debtor defaults.

Collusive bidding Bid-rigging. An agreement for one of a group of bidders to make a low bid while the others refrain from bidding or bid higher amounts; to compare bids prior to submission; to create a bid depository where competitors compare bids and fix the bid price; or to split profits made by a successful bidder.

Commercial bribery Improperly attempting to gain advantage in a commercial transaction by offering money or other favors.

Commercial impracticability A basis upon which a party to a contract may be excused from performance obligations. The essence of commercial impracticability is an unexpected occurrence which seriously impairs a party's ability to perform.

Commercial paper Negotiable instruments payable in money; negotiable drafts, checks, notes, and certificates of deposit; called *bearer paper* if it can be negotiated by delivery alone; called *order paper* if, in addition to delivery, an endorsement is required for negotiation.

Commercial unit An amount of goods that in business practice is treated as a single whole for purposes of sale and whose division would materially impair its value or character (e.g., a machine, a bale of cotton, a carload of wheat).

Commingled goods Goods that are combined with and are indistinguishable from others to form a single mass or product.

Common law In England, a body of law *common* to the whole population, produced primarily by the efforts of judges in various parts of England to harmonize their decisions with those of judges in other parts of the country.

Common stock (shares) A class of corporate stock which gives the holder a right to vote in elections of its directors, to receive dividends, and, upon dissolution of the corporation, to receive a pro rata share of its assets, subordinate to the rights of preferred stock, if any.

Community property A system whereby a husband and wife jointly own property earned by either during the marriage.

Compensated surety See *Surety.*

Compensatory damages Damages awarded to a plaintiff to compensate him or her for harm suffered, such as medical bills or lost profits. In tort cases, it includes general damage for embarrassment, pain, or suffering. See also *Punitive damages.*

Complainant A party who brings an action in equity.

Complete integration See *Integration.*

Composition agreement An arrangement between a debtor and two or more creditors whereby the debtor agrees to turn his or her assets over to the creditors, and the creditors agree to accept their pro rata portions in full satisfaction of their claims.

Composition plan In bankruptcy law, a plan for the adjustment or settlement of debt in which the debtor pays creditors less than 100 percent of their claims on a pro rata basis for each class of claims. In contrast, under an *extension plan,* the debtor pays the full amount, but over a longer period than originally agreed.

Condition A qualification or limitation of a grant or of an agreement.

Conditional sale contract A contract evidencing a secured transaction in which a buyer of goods receives possession of them and the seller-creditor retains title to them until the buyer makes payment.

Conditional surety See *Surety.*

Confession-of-judgment clause A provision in a promissory note or other instrument authorizing the holder to have an attorney enter a judgment in court, without a trial, against the maker or drawer if the instrument is not paid when due, even though the failure to pay may be justified.

Confirmation In bankruptcy law, the act of the bankruptcy court in approving a plan of reorganization or some other plan for the adjustment or settlement of debt.

Conforming goods In the law of sales, goods that are in accordance with the seller's obligations under the contract of sale.

Conscious parallelism In antitrust law, uniform pricing or other business conduct by competitors not acting in concert but who are aware of one another's actions.

Consent order An order of an administrative agency under which a person agrees to discontinue a challenged practice. Under a consent order the respondent does not admit any violation of law.

Consequential damages In general, a loss or injury which does not result directly or follow immediately from the act of a party but nonetheless is a consequence or result of the act. In the law of sales, a loss resulting from the buyer's general or particular requirements and needs of which the seller, at the time of contracting, had reason to know and which could not reasonably be prevented by cover or otherwise; injury to person or property proximately resulting from any breach of warranty. See also *Compensatory damages, Punitive damages.*

Consideration In contract law, a bargained-for legal detriment incurred by the promisee in exchange for a promise.

Consignment A transfer of possession of property for the purpose of transportation or sale. The consignor retains title to (ownership of) the property until it is sold.

Conspiracy An unlawful combination between two or more persons or corporations to do an illegal act or to accomplish a lawful end through illegal means; it may be a civil wrong *and* a criminal offense.

Construction As applied to a statute, the process of discovering and explaining the legal effect which the statute is to have. "Construing" a statute may involve interpreting unclear language, but it mainly involves such tasks as determining the purpose or policy of the statute, deciding how the provisions of a complex statute are related, and deciding to what specific people or things the statute applies.

Construction mortgage A mortgage used to finance new residential or commercial building. See *Mortgage.*

Constructive notice A notice, knowledge of which, pursuant to law, is charged to a party whether it was actually received or not; generally given by means of publication in a newspaper of general circulation.

Constructive trust A device imposed by a court of equity to compel one who unfairly holds a property interest to convey that interest to another to whom it justly belongs.

Consumer goods Tangible personal property normally used for personal, family, or household purposes.

Consumer product As used in the Magnuson-Moss Warranty Act, any tangible personal property that is distributed in commerce and that is normally used for personal, family, or household purposes, including any such property intended to be attached to or installed in any real property.

Contempt of court Failure to comply with a personal order or direction of a court.

Contract A promise or set of promises for the breach of which the law gives a remedy or for the performance of which the law in some way recognizes as a duty. In the law of sales, a contract consists of the total legal obligation that results from the parties' agreement, as that agreement is affected by the UCC and by any other applicable rules of law. *Contract* should be distinguished from *agreement*. See also *Implied contract*.

Contract for deed See *Land contract*.

Contract of adhesion A contract in which a party, usually the buyer, has no meaningful choice with regard to some or all the terms of the contract, e.g., an insurance contract.

Contract for sale See *Sale (of goods)*.

Contract to sell See *Sale (of goods)*.

Contribution In the law of suretyship, a payment owed by one cosurety to another on account of the first cosurety's payment of the principal debtor's debt. In the law of torts, the amount a joint tortfeasor is obligated to pay another tortfeasor in order to equalize their obligations to the victim.

Conversion Wrongful exercise of dominion and control over, or seriously interfering with, the possession or ownership of the personal property of another.

Convertible preferred shares Shares of preferred stock which may be exchanged at the option of the holder for shares in another series or class issued by the same corporation.

Corporate opportunity doctrine A doctrine that prohibits a person who has a fiduciary relation to a corporation from seizing a business opportunity which rightfully belongs to the corporation.

Corporation A legal entity created by authority of a statute as an artificial person whose rights, obligations, and liabilities are separate and distinct from those of its shareholders.

Corporation by estoppel A legal phrase meaning that a defectively formed corporation is not permitted to assert as a defense to an action against it that the corporation was not properly formed.

Cosurety See *Surety*.

Course of dealing In the law of sales, a pattern of prior business transactions (not just the performance of one transaction) which can establish a background for the interpretation of the immediate transaction.

Course of performance In the law of sales, the carrying out of a particular transaction. There can be no course of performance unless there are repeated occasions for performance, such as several deliveries of coal to be made pursuant to a single contract of sale.

Court of Claims A special court created by Congress for the purpose, among others, of hearing and determining contract claims against the United States; now named the "U.S. Court of Claims."

Cover A buyer's arrangement for the purchase of goods in substitution for goods which the seller failed to deliver.

Cumulative voting A system, permitted by many state statutes, whereby a shareholder can cast all of his or her votes (shares owned multiplied by the number of directors to be elected) for one candidate.

Cure The act of correcting a defective tender or delivery of goods.

D&O Insurance Policy generally paid by a corporation insuring its directors and officers from personal liability against claims for negligence, failure to exercise proper business judgment, and breach of fiduciary obligations, but not against defalcations.

Damages Money compensation for a wrong—e.g., a money payment for breach of a contract. See also *Compensatory damages*, *Consequential damages*, and *Punitive damages*.

Dealer A person engaged in the business of buying goods or other property such as real estate for resale to final customers.

Dealer-merchant As used in this book, the kind of merchant who deals in goods of the kind involved in the transaction between the dealer-merchant seller and the buyer. See *Merchant*.

Debenture An unsecured corporate bond.

Debit In commercial paper law, to charge against a customer's bank account; also, a charge against an account.

Debtor-in-possession In a Bankruptcy Code business reorganization, the debtor or the management of a corporate debtor that stays in possession of the firm who has the duties of a bankruptcy trustee.

Debtor's estate In the law of bankruptcy, the various property interests either owned by the debtor at the commencement of a bankruptcy case or recoverable for the estate by the trustee in bankruptcy from someone other than the debtor.

Decedent A person who has died.

Deceit (action for deceit) An action at law based upon a misrepresentation or concealment by which one deceives another who has no means of detecting the fraud, to the injury and damage of such person. Used interchangeably with *fraud.*

Deductible A specified amount of loss that an insured must absorb before being entitled to payment from an insurer.

Deep-rock doctrine In bankruptcy law, the rule which subordinates inequitable claims filed by controlling shareholders of a bankrupt corporation to the claims of general or trade creditors. The name is taken from the name of the corporation involved in the case where the rule was enunciated.

De facto corporation An organization that operates as a corporation, whose organizers have made an unsuccessful attempt in "good faith" to comply with the state enabling statutes. Only the state can challenge the existence of a de facto corporation.

Defendant A party against whom a court action is brought.

Defense A circumstance or reason put forward by a defendant to defeat the claim of the plaintiff or to defeat a criminal charge. In the law of commercial paper, defenses are personal or real. A *personal defense* is not good against a holder in due course. A *real defense* is good against anyone, including a holder in due course.

De jure corporation A corporation that has all the legal characteristics of a corporation and whose incorporators have substantially complied with the enabling statute of the state of incorporation.

Delectus personae In Latin, "choice of persons." A phrase used in partnership law to express the right of any partner to accept or reject a new member to the partnership.

Delegatee See *Delegation.*

Delegation The authorizing, by a person under a duty of performance, of another person to render the required performance. The person who does the authorizing is the *delegator.* The person authorized to carry out the performance is the *delegatee.*

Delegator See *Delegation.*

Demise As used in law, a transfer of real property or of an interest in real property, usually in connection with a lease.

Demurrer A document, filed by the defendant in a lawsuit, by which the defendant challenges the court's jurisdiction or the legal sufficiency of the plaintiff's complaint. Usually a form of pleading which admits the facts alleged but asserts that they do not constitute a cause of action.

De novo From the beginning; a new start, as "trial de novo."

Derivative suit An action filed in the corporate name by one or more shareholders to enforce a corporate cause of action.

Destination bill of lading See *Bill of lading.*

Destination contract A contract in which the seller is required to make delivery at the point of destination.

Detour A slight deviation by an employee from a prescribed route while traveling on authorized work.

Devise A gift by will of real property.

Directed verdict A verdict entered for either the plaintiff or the defendant, not as a result of jury deliberation, but as a result of the judge ordering the entry. A directed verdict is ordered only if the facts are so clear that the jury could not reasonably reach a verdict for the other party.

Disaffirmance The setting aside or avoiding of a contract or obligation which can be avoided legally.

Discharge To extinguish an obligation, whether by performance or otherwise. The termination of a contractual obligation.

Discharge hearing In bankruptcy, a proceeding that a debtor must attend before being granted a discharge from debts.

Disclaimer A denial, especially a denial that a warranty was made or is effective; or a denial of liability for fraud, negligence, etc.

Discount In a general sense, to sell for less than face value. In banking, the taking of interest in advance.

Dishonor Refusal or failure to pay or to accept a negotiable instrument that has been properly presented for payment or acceptance.

Dissolution In corporation law, the termination of a corporation by legislative act, by judicial decree, by voluntary action of the shareholders, or by expiration of the period of time for which the corporation was formed. With reference to a partnership, dissolution is a preparatory step to its termination.

Dividends Distribution from corporate assets (usually earned surplus), made on a pro rata basis to shareholders of a designated class of stock, as authorized by the corporation's board of directors. Also, *in the law of insurance,* the difference between (1) the premium charged for a policy plus earnings from investing the premium and (2) the lower amount justified by the actual loss and expense experience of the insurer. An insurance dividend may be viewed as a refund of a part of the premium initially charged for the insurance.

Dock receipt See *Document of title.*

Dock warrant See *Document of title.*

Document of title A writing that is treated as adequately evidencing that the person in possession of it is entitled to receive, hold, and dispose of the document and the goods it covers. Documents of title include *bills of lading, dock warrants, dock receipts,* and *warehouse receipts.*

Domestic corporation A corporation which is doing business in the state of incorporation.

Dormant partner A partner who does not represent the partnership to the public. Also called a *silent* or *secret* partner.

Double jeopardy A second prosecution after a prior prosecution for the same offense, transaction, or omission.

Dower The right of a widow to a portion of her deceased husband's estate. Most states now provide for a forced or elective share instead.

Draft A type of commercial paper commanding the drawee to pay a sum of money. A *time draft* is payable at a specified future time; a *demand draft* is payable on demand of the holder any time.

Drawee The person, bank, or firm that is ordered by the drawer of a draft or check to make payment to a payee.

Drawer The person, bank, or firm that issues a draft or check and thereby orders the drawee to make payment to the payee.

Due negotiation In the law of documents of title, the kind of transfer of a document of title that confers upon the transferee the right to have the document and the goods it represents free from any defenses of prior owners and of warehousers and carriers.

Due process The administration of law in accordance with rules and forms which have been established for the protection of private rights. *Procedural due process* requires a fair hearing or the right to one. *Substantive due process* requires that laws not be arbitrary, unreasonably discriminatory, or demonstrably irrelevant to the matter which the law purports to govern.

Duress Any wrongful or illegal coercion, by threat or other means, that overcomes the free will or judgment of a person and induces the person to do something he or she otherwise would not do.

Electronic funds transfer A process in which banking transactions are accomplished by means of computers.

Emancipation In contract law, a status wherein a minor may enter into contracts and assumes responsibility for his or her own support.

Embezzlement The wrongful appropriation of property by a person to whom it has been entrusted.

Enabling legislation A statute expressing in general terms the powers and purposes of an administrative agency.

Engagement In commercial paper law, a promise imposed by law.

Enforceable contract One for the breach of which the law gives a remedy.

Enjoin "Prohibit." An order of a court, entered at the request of a plaintiff, which "enjoins" (prohibits) the defendant from carrying on certain conduct.

Entrustment In the law of sales, the act of putting goods into the possession of a merchant who deals in goods of that kind.

Equal dignities rule The requirement that an agent's authority must be in writing if his or her act requires a writing.

Equitable decree An order of a court of equity.

Equitable remedies The relief given by a court of equity.

Equity A body of law developed by the English courts of chancery to supplement the rigid common law of the time. The courts of chancery developed new remedies and flexible procedures for cases where the remedy at law (damages) was inadequate. The word "equity" implies fairness and a wise discretion in the formulation and application of equitable remedies. Also, an ownership interest in property.

Equity financing Raising money by a corporation through the sale of shares of stock. See also *Equity securities.*

Equity securities Shares of capital stock representing a shareholder's proportionate ownership interest in the corporation as a whole.

Escrow In general, a system whereby a neutral third party acts as a depository of money or documents to be transferred from one party to another upon completion of agreed conditions.

Estoppel A bar to alleging or denying facts in court.

Exculpatory clause See *Disclaimer.*

Executed contract One that has been fully performed by both parties.

Execution (of judgment at law) The process of procuring a writ of execution from the clerk of court and having the sheriff seize the defendant's property and sell it to satisfy the judgment.

Executive committee In a corporation, a committee composed entirely of directors who are authorized by majority vote of the board of directors to make corporate management decisions (not involving extraordinary transactions) during intervals between board meetings.

Executor A person or entity, named in a will, appointed by a probate court to administer a deceased testator's estate and to carry out the testator's wishes expressed in his or her will concerning the disposition of his or her property.

Executory contract One in which neither party has rendered the promised performance.

Exemplary damages See *Punitive damages.*

Exemptions In bankruptcy law, property that an individual debtor may preserve free from the claims of creditors.

Exoneration An act freeing another from blame; the discharge of an obligation.

Experience rating In insurance, the process of adjusting the premium to reflect, for renewal years, the actual loss experience of the insured.

Ex post facto law A law imposing a criminal sanction upon a person for an act that, when committed, was not criminal. Ex post facto laws are unconstitutional.

Express authority The authority explicitly given by a principal to an agent, either in writing or orally.

Express contract One in which the terms of the contract are stated in words, either written or spoken.

Express powers In constitutional law, the powers specifically named by a constitution. The Constitution of the United States specifically grants certain powers (called "express" or "enumerated" powers) to the federal government. In corporation law, those powers are set forth in articles of incorporation or in a statute.

Express warranty See *Warranty.*

Ex rel. Abbreviation for *ex relationi,* meaning "upon relation" or information. Legal proceedings instituted by an attorney general (or another proper person) in the name and behalf of the state.

FAS Free alongside a vessel.

FOB (fob) Free on board.

Face value The nominal value of a security as expressed on its face, e.g., the par value of a share of stock or the amount due and payable on a bond, according to its terms.

Featherbedding The requirement, through union pressure, that an employer hire unnecessary employees, assign unnecessary work, or limit production.

Felony A serious criminal offense.

Fiction An assumption of law that something that is or may be false is true. It is a legal fiction to say that a corporation is a person.

Fictitious name A counterfeit, feigned, or pretended name taken by a person, differing in some essential particular from his or her true name; a name adopted to identify a business concern. Sometimes called a "dba" (doing business as).

Fiduciary An obligation of trust or confidence.

Fiduciary relationship A relation between persons of such a character that trust and confidence are reposed in the other who must exercise the utmost degree of fairness and good faith.

Field warehousing A secured transaction for the financing of business inventory. The inventory used as collateral is segregated in a fenced-off area of the borrower's premises and is placed under the control of an independent warehouse.

Financing statement A writing that is filed in the public records to give notice of the creditor's security interest in collateral.

Firm offer In the law of sales, a written offer in which the offeror, a merchant, promises to hold the offer open, usually for a certain period of time.

Fixture An article that was personal property but which has been attached to real property with the intent that it become a permanent part of the real property.

Fixture filing See *Perfection.*

Floating lien A security interest in both present and future assets of the debtor instead of a security interest only in specific assets on hand at the creation of the secured transaction. Floating liens are created by the use of *after-acquired property clauses.*

Forced (elective) share The portion of a deceased spouse's estate to which the surviving spouse is entitled by law. Most states grant this rather than dower.

Foreclosure A procedure by which encumbered (mortgaged) property is sold upon the debtor's default, in satisfaction of the debt.

Foreign corporation A corporation that is doing business in a state other than the state of incorporation.

Form A printed document, generally with blank spaces to be filled in. Also, in the law of contracts, the style of language used—the wording of the contract.

Formal contract A contract to which the law gives special effect because of the form used in creating it; e.g., a negotiable instrument such as a check is a formal contract because to create a negotiable instrument, a person must use a particular form or style of language.

Four-corner rule In the law of commercial paper, the rule that whether an instrument is unconditional is to be determined solely by what is expressed on the face of the instrument.

Franchise A contract in which the owner (franchisor)of intangible property such as a trademark or trade name, authorizes another (franchisee) to use such property in the operation of a business within described territory.

Fraud An intentional, false representation or concealment of material fact intended to induce another to act, justifiably relied on by the other to his or her injury. See also *Deceit.*

Fraudulent transfer In bankruptcy law, a transfer of property by the debtor within 1 year preceding bankruptcy, where the debtor was insolvent when the transfer was made and where the debtor received less than a reasonable equivalent value for the transfer. A fraudulent transfer can also occur in other than bankruptcy situations. Also called a "fraudulent conveyance."

Freeze-out A course of action taken by the holders of the majority shares of a close corporation designed to force a minority shareholder to sell his or her interest in the corporation on terms favorable to the majority shareholders.

Frolic A substantial deviation by an employee from a prescribed route while traveling on authorized work.

Full warranty A written consumer product warranty that meets the four minimum standards or requirements of the Magnuson-Moss Warranty Act.

Fungible Equivalent. Goods are fungible if by their nature or by usage of trade one unit is the equivalent of any other unit.

Future-advances clause A clause in a security agreement that permits the collateral of the debtor to be used to secure future loans.

Future goods Goods which are not both existing and identified to the contract for their sale.

Garnishment A legal procedure by means of which a creditor acquires money or other property of a debtor where the property is in the hands of some other person, such as a bank or an employer. "Property" includes a debt owed to a debtor, such as wages due from an employer.

General creditor In bankruptcy law, an unsecured creditor.

General lien A lien that entitles a creditor to keep the debtor's property until all debts owed the creditor as a result of the general course of business between creditor and debtor have been paid. See also *Specific lien.*

General partners The members of a limited partnership who are in charge of the partnership affairs; they are liable to third parties for the partnership debts.

General partnership See *Partnership.*

Going and coming rule A principal's freedom from liability for an employee's actions while the latter is going to or from work.

Golden parachute A contract which grants extraordinary benefits to a top executive in the event the company is taken over and the executives are either forced to leave or voluntarily leave the company.

Good faith In the law of sales, honesty in fact in the conduct or transaction concerned. With regard to a merchant, good faith is honesty in fact and the observance of reasonable commercial standards of fair dealing in the trade.

Goodwill The expectation of a continuance of customers and profits enjoyed because of the manner in which a business has been conducted.

Grab law Law, usually state law, that permits unpaid creditors to seize and sell the property of the debtor.

Grace period Extra time to carry out a legal duty. In the law of secured transactions, an amount of time, beyond the usual time given, to file or otherwise perfect a security interest.

Graded rate In property insurance, a reduced premium rate that is applied when a person approaches insuring his or her property for full value. Graded rates reflect the fact that there are more partial than full losses and are a means, seldom used, for assuring that people who underinsure their property receive no more indemnity per dollar of premiums than do people who insure for full value.

Grantee One to whom a grant is made. In property law, the person to whom real property is granted and conveyed.

Grantor One who transfers property, or a right, to another (the grantee).

Gratuitous agent An agent who serves without pay.

Gratuitous surety See *Surety*.

Gravaman The heart or essence of a matter.

Greenmail A premium payment by a target company to purchase the company's shares held by a corporation raider in exchange for his or her promise not to attempt a takeover bid.

Ground for relief Generally, the basis of a lawsuit; the conduct of a debtor that triggers the applicability of the Bankruptcy Code if creditors who are entitled to do so choose to invoke it.

Group boycott A joint refusal to deal. Joint action for the purpose of restricting a competitor's access to markets or sources of supply.

Group insurance Insurance in which the insurer undertakes to insure every person in the group without regard to the insurability of individuals within it. The insurer issues one detailed *master contract* to the group policyholder but only brief certificates to individual members of the group. Many group policies are experience rated.

Guarantor One who guarantees the obligation of another. In the law of commercial paper, a signer who adds "payment guaranteed" or equivalent words to the signature and thereby promises that if the instrument is not paid when due, he or she will pay it without insisting on resort to any other party.

Hearsay evidence Statements, made in court by a witness, not having personal knowledge or observation but who merely repeats of what he or she has heard others say.

Heir Under modern practice, a person who inherits from another real or personal property or an interest in such property. Formerly, one who inherits by virtue of the laws of descent and distribution.

Holder A person who is in possession of an instrument drawn, issued, or indorsed to him or her or to his or her order or to bearer or in blank.

Holder in due course A *holder* who takes an instrument for value, in good faith, and without notice that it is overdue or that it has been dishonored or that there is any defense against or claim to it on the part of any person.

Holographic will A will in the testator's own handwriting, signed and dated. Recognized in most states as a valid will.

Horizontal merger A combination of two or more firms who are competitors in the marketplace. See also *Vertical merger*.

Identification In the law of sales, the act of designating goods as the subject of a particular contract of sale.

Illusory Deceptive; an illusory promise appears to be promissory in its terms but actually promises nothing because the promisor retains the choice of performing or nonperforming.

Impairment In bankruptcy law, the adverse impact of a plan of reorganization that gives a claimant less than the full value of his or her claim or interest.

Implied contract A contract in which the terms are wholly or partly inferred from conduct or from surrounding circumstances.

Implied powers In *constitutional law*, powers that are not specifically named but which are necessary and proper for carrying out the express powers. In *corporation law*, powers not specifically set out in a statute or charter but necessary and proper for carrying out the corporation's express powers. In *agency law*, the implied authority of an agent.

Implied warranty See *Warranty*.

Incontestability An inability, imposed by law or by contract, of an insurer to avoid a policy for concealment, breach of warranty, or misrepresentation. Also, a noncontest clause in a will.

Incorporation The process (as established in state statutes) by which a corporation is formed.

Incorporator A person who organizes a corporation by signing and filing the articles of incorporation with the designated officer of the state.

Indemnification (to indemnify) The compensation or payment of a damage another sustains. In legal terms, it may also mean to give security against the possibility of future damage or loss; for instance, an insurance company undertakes to *indemnify* its policyholders against loss.

Indemnity Reimbursement for loss.

Indemnity principle The theory that in the event of casualty an insured should be limited to reimbursement (indemnity) for loss actually suffered, because insurance is a system for distributing losses and not for generating a profit for insureds. The principle is especially applicable in liability, property, and health insurance.

Independent contractor One who, exercising an independent employment, contracts to do certain work according to his or her own methods and without being subject to the control of an employer except as to the results to be accomplished.

Indictment An accusation in writing found and presented by a grand jury that a person named in the indictment has done some act or has been guilty of some omission which by law is a public offense.

Indorsement A signature customarily found on the back of commercial paper; made by a person other than a maker, a drawer, or an acceptor; and ordinarily resulting in secondary liability on the instrument. An indorsement is in-blank or special, nonrestrictive or restrictive, *and* unqualified or qualified. A *special indorsement* maintains the order character of an order instrument or gives order character to a bearer instrument. A *restrictive indorsement* specifies a use to which the proceeds of the instrument must be put. A *qualified indorsement* protects the indorser from liability on the instrument but not for liability for breach of warranty.

Informal contract One for which the law does not prescribe a particular form in order for the contract to be enforceable.

Information In criminal law, a formal accusation of crime similar to an indictment but preferred (made) by a competent prosecuting official, such as a district attorney, instead of by a grand jury.

Infraction A minor wrong, usually not a criminal offense.

Inheritance Something obtained by operation of law from a person who dies without leaving a valid will and, under modern usage, by virtue of the provisions of a will.

Injunction An equitable remedy in which a court orders a person to do or to refrain from doing something.

In pari delicto The common law principal that a court will not entertain a cause of action between two people who are equally at fault.

In re In the matter of; regarding. The title of a judicial proceeding as, *In re Smith,* in which there are no adversary parties. Commonly used in bankruptcy and estate proceedings.

Insanity A mental derangement due to a disease of the mind. An insane person is without legal competence to enter into a contract or to make a will; proof of insanity may free an accused person from responsibility for a criminal act. Tests for insanity differ in contract law, probate law, and criminal law.

Inside director A corporation director who also holds a management position in the company.

Insider trading A purchase or sale of a corporation's securities based upon inside or advance company information.

Insolvency laws State laws under which a troubled debtor may make arrangements with creditors for full or partial payment, or the postponement of payment, of her or his debts.

Insurable interest A financial stake in property or in someone's life that will justify the person who has that stake in insuring the property or life.

Insurance A contractual means of transferring and distributing the risk of financial loss.

Integration A written statement being the final expression of the parties to an agreement. *Complete integration:* a written complete and exclusive statement of all the contract terms. *Partial integration:* a written final expression only of the contract terms included in the writing, other contract terms existing outside the writing.

Inter alia Among other things.

Interlocking directorates A practice in which members of the board of directors of one corporation also serve as directors of other corporations that do business with one another.

Interpretation The process of discovering and explaining the meaning of any unclear language—e.g., of a statute or a contract. See *Construction.*

Interpretive rule An administration regulation, without the force of law, setting out the agency's opinion as to the meaning of the law it administers.

Interstate commerce Commercial intercourse, communication, transportation of persons or property between or among two or more states of the Union.

Inter vivos Between the living; from one living person to another. Where property passes by conveyance, the transaction is said to be inter vivos, to distinguish it from a transfer by will effective upon death.

Intestacy laws Laws governing the passage of title to property when a person dies without a will. Also called "laws of intestate succession."

Intestate Without making a will. Also, an intestate: a person who dies without leaving a valid will.

Intrastate Activity or territory that is wholly within a single state of the Union.

Intra vires Within the power of a person or corporation; within the scope of express or implied powers or authority.

Ipso facto By the fact itself; by the mere fact.

Issue A legal question to be decided by a court. Under the laws of *descent and distribution,* all persons who have descended from a common ancestor; also, the child or children of an individual and of their children. In the law of *commercial paper,* the act of putting a negotiable instrument such as a check into circulation; issuance of a negotiable instrument, a document of title, or some other commercial document.

Jingle rule The rule of partnership law that the creditors of partners have first claim to assets of the partners and that creditors of the partnership have first claim to the partnership assets. This rule has been modified by the Bankruptcy Code for situations to which the Code applies.

Joint and several liability The liability of the various defendants is joint and several when a plaintiff, at his or her option, may sue and establish liability of persons separately, or sue all of them together. For example, if a tort is committed against a plaintiff victim by several tortfeasors, they have joint and several liability and the plaintiff may sue only one, or elect to sue all of them.

Joint tortfeasors Includes: (1) persons who have acted together by agreement for the purpose of injuring another; and (2) persons who have acted independently but have caused a single indivisible injury.

Joint venture A business owned and managed by two or more persons to accomplish a single objective.

Judgment In law, the decision of a court.

Judgment creditor A party in whose favor a judgment for money is rendered.

Judgment debtor A party against whom a judgment for money is rendered.

Judgment nowithstanding the verdict ("judgment n.o.v.") A judgment entered by a judge for the losing party in a jury trial, thus refusing the verdict of the jury. The trial judge will overrule the jury only if there is no substantial evidence to support their decision.

Judgment rate A rate of interest, established by statute, to be applied by the courts to judgments for damages where interest is an element of damages.

Jurisdiction The power of a court to hear and decide cases.

Jurisprudence The philosophy of law; the science which treats of the principles of law and legal relations, a body of law.

Laches See *Statute of limitations.*

Land contract A long-term credit arrangement under which a seller of real estate transfers some ownership rights to the buyer but retains a security interest in the property until it is paid for. Also called *contract for deed* or *installment land contract.*

Larceny The unlawful taking and carrying away of the property of another with the intent to deprive the owner of it permanently.

Law merchant The old law of merchants, developed to supplement the common law.

Lease A rental agreement in which the *lessor* conveys to the *lessee* the right to use the lessor's personal or real property, usually in exchange for a payment of money.

Legacy A bequest (gift by will) of money.

Legal entity An entity, other than a natural person, existing in contemplation of law and having the legal rights and duties of a separate person, e.g., a corporation.

Legal fiction See *Fiction.*

Legal reserve fund See *Cash surrender value.*

Legislative rule A regulation, promulgated by an administrative agency, having the force of law.

Letter of credit A written promise by a bank or another person (the "issuer") made at the request of a customer of the issuer that the issuer will honor drafts or other demands for payment upon the customer's compliance with the conditions specified in the letter of credit; a letter of credit may be either revocable or irrevocable.

Level premium A life insurance premium fixed at a certain amount for the duration of the contract. The premium is larger than needed to pay claims and expenses during the early years of the contract. The excess is invested to provide funds to pay increasingly frequent future claims.

Leveraged buyout The purchase of all of the shares of stock of a corporation, generally by some members of the top management of the corporation itself, together with others. The transaction entails the purchasers borrowing the necessary funds and pledging all of the assets of the corporation purchased as security for the loan.

Libel Defamation expressed by print, writing, pictures, or signs.

Lien A claim or charge against property. A lien may be created by contract or imposed by law to secure, for example, the claims of mechanics or other artisans for work done on property, or to secure the claim of a government for unpaid taxes.

Limited partnership A partnership consisting of one or more general partners, responsible as ordinary partners, by whom the business is conducted, and one or more limited partners, who are not liable for the debts of the partnership beyond the funds contributed, and who do not participate in the firm's management.

Limited warranty A written consumer product warranty that does not conform with the standards imposed by the Magnuson-Moss Warranty Act for a full warranty.

Liquidated damages An amount of money established by a contract as a remedy for its breach.

Liquidation proceeding A bankruptcy proceeding, the object of which is to convert the debtor's nonexempt assets into cash, to distribute it in accordance with the scheme of distribution provided by the Bankruptcy Code, and to grant the honest debtor a discharge from most of the remaining debts.

"Long-arm" statute A statute conferring jurisdiction over out-of-state defendants.

Majority shareholders Shareholders who collectively own a majority of the voting shares of a corporation and who exercise control over the corporation by electing directors, amending articles, and making decisions on extraordinary transactions. Often used to describe one who controls a majority of votes by means of proxies.

Mandamus "We command." A command issued by a court of competent jurisdiction to an inferior court, corporation, or person.

Master An employer who has the right to control the physical performance of an employee's (servant's) work.

Master contract In group insurance, the detailed insurance policy held by the group policyholder, to be contrasted with the brief certificate held by each member of the group.

Master limited partnership A limited partnership established with many limited partnership interests which are traded on a securities exchange.

Material alteration Any significant change in an instrument which affects or may possibly affect the rights of the parties interested in the document.

Mechanic's lien See *Lien*.

Meeting of creditors In bankruptcy law, a gathering at which creditors elect a trustee to oversee the distribution of a bankrupt's estate and to decide other matters regarding the bankruptcy.

Merchant In the law of sales, a person who deals in goods of the kind involved in the transaction. Also, a person who by occupation holds himself or herself out as having knowledge or skill peculiar to the practices or goods involved in the transaction, and a person to whom such knowledge or skill may be attributed by his or her employment of an intermediary who by occupation holds himself or herself out as having such knowledge or skill.

Merger In corporation law, the absorption of one corporation by another; the latter acquires all the assets and assumes all the liabilities of the "target" corporation which then ceases to exist.

Midnight deadline Midnight of the banking day following the banking day on which a bank receives an item for collection.

Minor A person under the age at which the law recognizes a capacity to contract, to vote, or to purchase intoxicating liquor. The age of "majority" to contract, 21 at common law, is now 18 in many states.

Minority shareholders Shareholders whose collective voting rights are insufficient to elect a corporation's board of directors or otherwise control management decisions.

Miranda warning A statement by an arresting officer to an individual in custody as to his or her rights with respect to answering police questions.

Mirror-image rule In the common (general) law of contracts, the requirement that for a contract to arise, the acceptance must correspond exactly to ("mirror") the offer. In the law of sales, the mirror-image rule has largely been abandoned.

Misdemeanor A criminal offense less serious than a felony.

M'Naghten rule A test of insanity used in criminal cases by many courts; also known as the right and wrong test.

Model Business Corporation Act A model statute designed by the America Law Institute and the American Bar Association to meet the changing needs of modern business and to encourage greater uniformity in state laws governing the incorporation and operation of corporations. (See Appendix 5.)

Monopoly power In antitrust law, the power to fix prices, exclude competitors, or control the market in a given geographical area.

Mortgage A secured transaction in real estate in which the creditor has an interest in the real estate to secure payment of the debt. See *Secured transaction, Chattel mortgage.*

Motion to strike A request by a litigant that a court delete the whole or part of a pleading.

NLRB The National Labor Relations Board, established to hear disputes between labor and management, and to supervise worker elections of a union as bargaining agent.

Necessaries Suitable food, clothing, education, medical service, and place of residence in view of the rank, position, and mode of living of an individual.

Negotiable document of title Similar to *Negotiable instrument.*

Negotiable form The style of language required by law for creating a negotiable instrument or document.

Negotiable instrument A document such as a check or a promissory note which, because of its language, confers more than the usual rights of collection on a person who qualifies as or otherwise has the rights of a holder in due course. See *Commercial paper.*

Negotiation With reference to contracts, the exploring or discussing through oral or written communication of the terms and conditions of a contract preliminary to the making of a final contract. With reference to commercial paper, the *transferring* of a negotiable instrument to another.

Nolo contendere A plea to a criminal charge which neither admits nor denies guilt. Such a plea cannot be used as an admission of guilt for purposes of a related civil suit.

Nominal consideration In contract law, an amount stated which is not bargained for by the parties but simply inserted to give the transaction the appearance of legality. Usually $1.

Nominal damages A trifling sum awarded to a plaintiff who wins a case and receives a judgment but who is unable to prove any harm or loss.

Nonconforming goods Goods that differ from what was ordered under a sales contract.

Nonconforming tender An offer of performance that differs from the performance called for by a sales contract. See *Tender* and *Performance.*

Nonprofit corporation A corporation that is formed for charitable, religious, educational, or fraternal purposes. No part of its income may be distributed to members, and assets can only be distributed to members when the corporation is dissolved.

No-par stock Authorized stock to which "no par" value is assigned by the articles of incorporation. Upon issuance, the directors fix the per-share subscription price, but the amount is not stated on the certificate.

Note A promissory note.

Notice A legal notification received by a party either directly or indirectly through an agent or as otherwise provided by law. *Actual notice* is information actually received. *Constructive notice* is information a person is charged by law with having received even if he or she has not actually been made aware of it, as where an announcement has been published in a newspaper of general circulation but is not read by the person or persons upon whom such announcement is legally binding.

Novation The extinguishment of a party's obligation (e.g., a debt) through an agreement between the old obligor, a new obligor, and the obligee for the substitution of the new obligor for the old one.

n.o.v. (non obstante veredicto) "Notwithstanding the verdict." A judgment entered by order of a court for the losing party although there has been a verdict for the other party. See *Judgment notwithstanding the verdict.*

Nullity Nothing; an act or proceeding which is of no legal force or effect.

OSHA The Occupational Safety and Health Act of 1970 which is implemented by the Department of Labor. The Act is intended to force employers to maintain safe and healthful working conditions.

Obligee A person to whom an obligation or duty is owed.

Obligor A person who owes a duty to someone else—i.e., a person who has an obligation to perform.

Offer A statement or other conduct by which the offeror confers upon the offeree a legal power to accept the offer and thereby to create a contract.

Open term Some aspect or detail of a contract which the parties have not agreed upon but have, instead, left undecided.

Option An offer for which the offeree pays (or gives other valuable consideration) to keep the offer open for a stated period of time. Sometimes called "option contract."

Order document of title Similar to order commercial paper. See *Commercial paper.*

Order for relief A term sometimes used to describe an order promulgated by a court of equity. In bankruptcy law, a formal court ruling or declaration that an alleged debtor is insolvent.

Output contract A contract in which one party agrees to purchase the total production of the other party. Also, a contract in which the seller agrees to sell his or her total production to the other party.

Pari delicto Parties who are equally at fault.

Parol evidence rule The legal doctrine preventing the use of prior or contemporaneous oral statements or writings as evidence to contradict or change the terms of a signed integrated contract.

Partner A member of a general or limited partnership; may be either a general partner or a limited partner.

Partner by estoppel A nonpartner who acquires a partner's liability to a third party who relied upon the nonpartner's assertion (or the assertion of a member of a partnership) that the nonpartner is in fact a partner. Also called "ostensible partner."

Partnership A form of business organization owned and managed by two or more parties.

Partnership at will A partnership without any fixed term of existence.

Par-value stock Shares of corporation stock assigned a fixed value by the articles of incorporation or by its board of directors; being the minimum price for which each share can be sold by the corporation. The par value is printed on each stock certificate.

Payee One to whom payment is due or made. See also *Promissory note* and *Draft.*

Penal damages A harsh monetary penalty provided for by a contract, to coerce the performance of the contract. Penal damages clauses are not enforceable because the amount of damages provided for is not related to actual damages caused by breach of the contract.

Per capita Literally, "by the head." In inheritance laws, a method of distribution of the estate of a decedent where the persons designated are to receive equal shares, taking in their own right.

Per curiam By the court. Opinion of the whole court, as contrasted with an opinion written by one justice.

Perfection In the law of secured transactions, the process by which a security interest is made enforceable against subsequent lien creditors and certain other persons having a right in the collateral.

Perfect tender rule A rule of law, often relaxed by the UCC, that a buyer may elect to reject goods if the goods or the tender of delivery fails in any respect to conform to the contract.

Performance The carrying out of a legal obligation; the performance of a contract or a contractual promise.

Peril A cause of loss such as fire, flood, theft, or vandalism.

Per se In and of itself; inherently.

Personal defense See *Defense.*

Personal property floater A type of property insurance that applies to movable property, whatever its location.

Per stirpes A method of distribution of the estate of a decedent whereby heirs take the shares their respective deceased ancestor (e.g., parent, grandparent, etc.) would have taken if he or she had been living. Also called "right of representation."

Piercing the corporate veil The process whereby a court disregards the separateness of the corporation from its shareholders and holds them liable for wrongful conduct that injures third parties.

Plaintiff A party who brings a civil suit.

Plea bargain A plea of guilty to a lesser charge in exchange for an agreed punishment or for the recommendation by the prosecutor to the judge of a lesser punishment than may have been imposed for the offense originally charged.

Pleading A formal statement in a lawsuit setting out a cause of action or defense.

Pledge A transaction in which a debtor gives possession of the debtor's personal property to the creditor as security for repayment of a loan.

Poison pill A tactic adopted by a target company to defeat a takeover attempt by making its shares very high priced or otherwise unattractive to a corporate raider.

Pooling A process of treating as a single group a large number of individual risks of a certain kind so that the total loss likely to be sustained by the group of insureds can be accurately estimated.

Possessory lien A lien (charge against property) that is effective only as long as the bailee retains possession of the property subject to the charge.

Posting In banking, the decision to pay an item and the recording of payment.

Power The ability to do any act; in agency law, the *authority* to do an act which the grantor might himself or herself lawfully perform; an authority by which one person enables another to do some act for him or her; a person may have the "power" to act but not the "right" to do so.

Predatory pricing In antitrust law, the prohibited practice of refraining from maximizing profits until competitors are driven out of the market.

Preempt To take exclusive control, as where the federal government, in accordance with the Constitution, expressly denies the states the right to regulate an activity, or enacts a comprehensive scheme of regulation which by implication precludes state regulation.

Preemptive right The right of a stockholder to preserve his or her proportionate stock interest by purchasing shares of a new issue ahead of others.

Preference In bankruptcy law, a transfer of property by the debtor that enables an unsecured creditor to receive a greater percentage of his or her claim against the debtor than the creditor would have received in a distribution of the debtor's assets pursuant to a Chapter 7 liquidation.

Preferential transfer See *Preference.*

Preferred stock A class of stock that has superior rights to dividends and, upon dissolution of the corporation, to corporate assets.

Preincorporation subscription An offer, before a corporation is incorporated, to buy its shares when they are issued; see also *Stock subscription.*

Presentment The act of producing a negotiable instrument and demanding its payment or acceptance.

Present sale See *Sale.*

Pretermitted In inheritance law, a child or other descendant not mentioned or provided for in a testator's will and who had not been otherwise provided for by the testator. Also, sometimes used to designate a spouse who is not provided for in a will.

Price discrimination In antitrust law, a practice whereby a seller charges two or more buyers different prices for an identical product or service.

Prima facie Latin phrase meaning, "on the face of it"; evidence sufficient to support a conclusion.

Primary party A signer of a negotiable instrument who is liable for payment immediately and unconditionally when the instrument comes due. To be contrasted with a *secondary* party, whose liability is conditional because it normally does not arise until after presentment, dishonor, and notice of dishonor.

Primogeniture An English system whereby the eldest son had the exclusive right to inherit the estate of his ancestor. Not used in the United States.

Principal In agency law, the party (disclosed, partially disclosed, or undisclosed) primarily responsible for an obligation incurred by an agent.

Priority claim In bankruptcy law, an allowed, unsecured claim that is, by statute, to be paid before claims of lower rank may be paid. The Bankruptcy Code lists seven classes of priority claims.

Private corporation A profit or nonprofit corporation organized by individuals, as opposed to one formed by the government.

Private law Law dealing with the relationships among private persons and organizations.

Privity of contract A relationship that exists between contracting parties because of the contract. A person usually must be in privity of contract in order to bring suit on it. However, the absence of privity of contract between a manufacturer and a remote purchaser of goods is not ordinarily a good defense to a suit brought against the manufacturer by a purchaser on the ground of negligence or breach of warranty.

Probate The act or process of proving the validity of a will; also, the name generally given to all proceedings within the jurisdiction of a probate court.

Procedural due process See *Due process.*

Procedural law That law which specifies the formal steps to be followed in enforcing or asserting rights, duties, privileges, or immunities; also called "adjective" law.

Procedural rule An administrative regulation without the force of law, establishing the process by which the public may deal with the issuing agency.

Proceeds Money or other property received as a result of the sale or other disposition of property.

Professional corporation A corporation which certain professional people, such as doctors, lawyers, or accountants, may establish for their practices to obtain corporate tax benefits.

Promise A manifestation of intention to act or to refrain from acting in a specified way, so made as to justify a promisee in understanding that a commitment has been made.

Promissory estoppel A doctrine or rule of law that prevents (estops) a promisor from avoiding liability.

Promissory note A type of commercial paper in which the maker promises to pay the payee a sum of money at a future time or on demand, usually with interest.

Promoter A person who plans and takes necessary action, including soliciting subscriptions for the purchase of shares of stock, in organizing a corporation.

Promulgate To announce officially; to make known publicly as important or obligatory.

Proof of claim A document by which a creditor seeks payment from the debtor's estate, or from the estate of a deceased person.

Pro rata Proportionate.

Pro rata share Where funds are insufficient to pay a class of bankruptcy claims in full, the percentage of the claim that each creditor of that class will receive.

Prospectus An instrument containing corporate information required by the SEC to be furnished to a prospective purchaser of the corporation's registered securities offered to the public for sale.

Protest A certificate of dishonor signed and sealed by an authorized public official such as a United States consul or a notary public. See *Dishonor*.

Proxy A person who is authorized by another person to represent or act for her or him at a meeting. With reference to corporations, a person authorized to vote a shareholder's shares at a shareholders' meeting. The term is used also to mean the writing that authorizes a person to vote the shares of another at a shareholders' meeting.

Public corporation A corporation created for governmental purposes by any agency or subdivision of state or federal government.

Public defenders Attorneys paid out of public funds to defend individuals who cannot afford to hire legal counsel in criminal cases.

Public law Law dealing with the organization of government and with the relation of the government to the people.

Puffing See *Sales puffing*.

Punitive damages Damages awarded against a defendant as punishment for outrageous conduct or to set an example for other wrongdoers; also called exemplary damages. See also *Compensatory damages*.

Purchase-money security interest (PMSI) A security interest taken or retained by a seller or other financer in financing the purchase or leasing of the collateral.

Purchaser In the ordinary sense, a buyer. In its technical sense, as under the UCC, a person who takes property by sale, negotiation, mortgage, gift, or any other voluntary transaction creating an interest in property.

Qualified indorsement See *Indorsement*.

Quash To cancel or annul.

Quasi Resembling, possessing some of the attributes of something else. An administrative agency may have a quasi-judicial and a quasi-legislative function. In its *quasi-judicial* function it hears and disposes of disputes in the manner of a court. In its *quasi-legislative* function it makes rules and regulations of relatively general application, in the manner of a legislature.

Quasi contract A restitutionary remedy for an obligation imposed by law, intended to prevent the unjust enrichment of a person upon whom a benefit has been conferred.

Quasi-judicial See *Quasi*.

Quasi-legislative See *Quasi*.

Quasi-public corporation A profit corporation privately organized for purposes which affect the public interest to an extent requiring special state or federal regulation, e.g., a bank or an insurance company.

Quiet title A proceeding filed for the purpose of establishing one's ownership of property.

Quorum The number of qualified persons (usually a majority of the entire body) required to be present at a meeting in order to conduct business. With reference to corporations, the minimum number of qualified persons (shares represented in person or by proxy) required to conduct business lawfully at a shareholders' meeting.

Ratable Proportional.

Ratification Confirmation of a prior act or promise.

Reaffirmation An agreement by a debtor to pay a debt that has been discharged in bankruptcy.

Real defense See *Defense*.

Recognizance In criminal law, a personal assurance or promise to be present for trial, called "giving one's own recognizance."

Redemption The exercise by a corporation of a right to buy back outstanding shares at a fixed price.

Reformation A contractual remedy in which a court rewrites or corrects a written contract so that it accurately reflects the bargain of the parties.

Reimbursement Repayment.

Reinsurance A contractual arrangement in which an insurance company transfers a part of the group risk it has assumed to another insurer called a "reinsurer."

Release A legally binding contract to give up a right held by the releasing party.

Relevant market The geographic area of effective competition in which a particular product as well as other interchangeable products are traded.

Remand To send back; usually the sending back of a court record or case by a higher court to the court from which a decision, an order, or a judgment originated, for the purpose of having the originating court take the action dictated by the higher court.

Remedy A means, such as court action, by which a violation of a right is prevented or is compensated for; legal redress.

Reorganization In bankruptcy, a proceeding by means of which a financially troubled firm may stay in business while it undergoes a process of financial rehabilitation that may involve a discharge from the firm's debts. Also, restructuring a corporation's organization.

Replevin An action taken to recover possession of goods.

Requirements contract A contract in which one party agrees to purchase from the other party all of certain goods or services which the purchasing party needs in his or her business.

Resale price maintenance In antitrust law, the practice of a seller fixing the resale price terms of the buyer at a lower level in the chain of distribution. This practice is also known as *Vertical price-fixing.*

Rescission (to rescind) The setting aside or avoiding of a contract, a transaction, or any obligation that can be set aside legally. Used primarily with reference to the avoidance of an agreement, such as the repudiation of a contract by one of the parties to it.

Res ipsa loquitur A Latin expression meaning "the thing (or incident) speaks for itself." Under the doctrine of *res ipsa loquitur,* the defendant may be required to prove that he or she was *not* negligent where the injury-causing instrumentality was completely within the control of the defendant.

Respondeat superior A maxim meaning "Let the master answer." The doctrine under which a master (employer) can be held liable for the wrongful acts of his or her servant (employee) performed within the scope of employment.

Restitution In the law of contracts, compensation for or the return of partial performances. In general, the return of a thing.

Resulting trust A trust relationship imposed by a court of equity to carry into effect the presumed intentions of the parties.

Restrictive endorsement See *Indorsement.*

Reverse To overturn or set aside a judgment, order, or decree previously entered by a court.

Revocation Annulling, cancelling, or rescinding an act, as to revoke a will or an offer.

Risk of loss In the law of sales, the danger that goods will be lost, stolen, destroyed, or damaged.

Rider An attachment to an insurance policy that modifies the contract in some way.

Rule of reason In antitrust law, the rule that conduct which unreasonably restrains trade is illegal.

Sale (of goods) The passing of title to goods from the seller to the buyer in return for a consideration, i.e., the price. In a *present sale,* title passes at the time the sales transaction is entered into. In a *contract to sell,* title passes to the buyer at some future time. Article 2 of the UCC covers both present sales and contracts to sell. The term *contract for sale* includes present sales and contracts to sell.

Sale on approval A sale of goods in which the buyer is not obligated until the buyer accepts, that is, approves, the goods.

Sale or return A transaction in which the buyer of goods purchases them for resale but has a right to return to the seller any unsold goods.

Sales puffing Exaggeration and opinion (short of actual fraud) by a seller intended to induce a sale.

Sanction A punishment. However, sanction may also mean "approval."

Scienter A necessary element of the tort of fraud and deceit which requires the plaintiff to prove that at the time false representations were made, the defendant knew they were false or had a reckless disregard as to whether they were true or false. Scienter is a necessary element required to be proved in most violations of federal antitrust and securities laws.

Scope of employment The general nature and conditions of the work for which an employee is hired.

Seasonably In a timely manner.

Secondary boycott Economic pressure by employees of one firm against another firm with whom those employees have no dispute.

Secondary party See *Primary party.*

Secret lien A claim against the property of another person, the acquisition of which is unknown to the general public because the claim has not been filed in the public records or otherwise has not been made known to the public.

Secured transaction Any arrangement made by agreement of the parties for the purpose of providing a creditor with a backup source of payment if the debtor defaults. In a *surety* arrangement, a person or a firm makes a backup promise to pay the debt in the event that the debtor defaults. In a *secured transaction in personal property*, personal property is the collateral and may be sold in the event of the debtor's default.

Secured transaction in real property See *Mortgage.*

Security An investment in a common enterprise in which the investor usually profits solely from the efforts of others. If the investment is in a corporation, it is usually evidenced by a stock or bond certificate issued in bearer or registered form.

Security agreement An agreement between the debtor and the creditor that the creditor is to have a security interest in the collateral. Unless the creditor is to possess the collateral, the security agreement must be in writing.

Security interest Some interest in property, such as possession or title, which a creditor retains or acquires to secure the payment of a debt.

Separation of powers In constitutional law, the doctrine that each branch of government (judicial, legislative, executive) should be allowed to exercise its constitutional prerogatives without undue interference by the other branches.

Servant A person employed to perform work or services for another, whose physical conduct in the performance of the work or service and the means by which it will be accomplished are subject to the control of the person (generally called a "master" or "employer") for whom it is being performed.

Set off The right of each party to a contract or litigation to require payment or performance from the other party based upon some other dealing with that party.

Settlement option Any of several ways of receiving the proceeds of a life insurance policy upon its maturity.

Shareholder A person who owns a proportionate ownership interest in a corporation; usually such ownership is evidenced by a stock certificate.

Share of stock An equity security that represents a proportionate ownership interest in a corporation including the rights which the shareholder has in the management, profits, and assets of the corporation.

Shelter provision The provision of the Uniform Commercial Code that gives holders through a holder in due course the same freedom from claims and defenses that a holder in due course enjoys. The shelter provision reflects the principle that a person may assign whatever rights she or he has.

Shipment contract A contract in which the seller is required or authorized to send goods to the buyer but is not required to deliver them at a particular destination.

Shop right privilege The right of an employer to use without payment of royalties an invention conceived by an employee in the course of employment or through use of the employer's facilities, the employee not having been hired to perform such work.

Shortswing transactions Those transactions under Section 16 of the Securities Exchange Act of 1934, in which a director, an officer, or a beneficial owner of more than 10 percent of any class of nonexempt securities buys and sells (or sells and buys) the company's securities within a 6-month period. The profits from such transactions belong to the corporation.

Slander Defamation expressed verbally; oral defamation.

Small claims court A court authorized to hear, in simplified proceedings, cases involving small sums usually no more than $500.

Special indorsement See *Indorsement.*

Specification A clear and accurate description of the technical requirements for a material, product, or service to be purchased, including the procedure for determining that the requirements have been met.

Specific lien A lien that entitles a creditor to retain possession of an item of property for only the one debt involved in the immediate transaction. Also called a "special" or "particular" lien. See also *General lien.*

Specific performance An equitable remedy under which a person is entitled to a contractual performance rather than to money damages for breach of the contract, as, for example, a court order to convey title to specific property. Specific performance is granted where the remedy at law (damages) is inadequate.

Specified perils contract An insurance policy which indemnifies the insured against loss caused by specified perils.

Standing In antitrust law, a doctrine requiring the plaintiff to prove that the defendant's violation was a substantial or direct cause of the plaintiff's injury which can be measured with some certainty in money terms, and that the defendant's illegal act affected legally protected activities of the plaintiff.

Stare decisis To abide by, or adhere to. A doctrine that precedents set by decisions in previous cases are to be followed in later cases involving the same point unless there is a compelling reason to depart from precedent.

Stated capital That portion of the issuance price of the outstanding shares of stock that is set aside in the capital stock account.

Statute of frauds A law providing that certain classes of contracts are unenforceable unless in writing, signed by the party to be charged for its breach (or signed by his or her authorized agent).

Statute of limitations A statute prescribing time limitations on certain described causes of action or criminal prosecutions; i.e., declaring that no suit shall be maintained on such causes of action unless brought within a specified period of time after the right accrued. A statute of limitations applies to the remedy at law. In equity there is also a limit (called "laches") on the time that a person has to bring suit. Under the equitable principle of laches, suit is barred if not brought with a *reasonable* time.

Stock certificate A certificate issued by a corporation to a named person as owner of a given number of shares of stock in the corporation. The certificate is written evidence of the owner's proportionate equity interest in the corporation.

Stock split The issuance to a shareholder of additional shares of stock, without cost, at some ratio of new shares to old shares as established by the board of directors.

Stock subscription A contract whereby a person agrees to purchase a specified number and class of shares of a new stock issue.

Stop-payment order The instruction by a drawer of a check to the drawee not to pay a certain check.

Straight bankruptcy See *Liquidation proceeding.*

Strict liability in tort A liability imposed by the law regardless of the care or skill of the defendant, as, for example, when injury results from a defective product or from an ultrahazardous activity. The liability is called "strict" because the plaintiff need not prove fault (negligence or intent).

Subchapter S corporation A corporation which complies with Subchapter S of the Internal Revenue Code. It may have no more than thirty-five stockholders and is taxed as though it were a partnership.

Subcontract An agreement with a contracting party to perform all or part of the work the latter is required to perform under a contract. The party who undertakes a subcontract is called a "subcontractor."

Subrogation The act or process of substituting one person for another so that the first acquires the legal rights of the second. In the law of suretyship, a surety's right to be substituted for or to take over the rights of the creditor (whom the surety has paid) against the debtor. The surety who has the right of subrogation is called the "subrogee."

Substantial performance In contract law, a doctrine that permits a party to a contract to recover damages even if that party has not fully performed. For performance to be substantial, there must be only minor departures from full performance.

Substantive due process See *Due process.*

Substantive law That law which is concerned with the recognition of rights, duties, privileges, and immunities (as contrasted with that law which is concerned with procedure).

Subsurety See *Surety.*

Sum certain In the law of negotiable instruments, an amount payable that is sufficiently calculable for an instrument to be classified as a negotiable instrument.

Summary Short, abbreviated, as a summary hearing before an administrative agency.

Surety A person who, by contract or by operation of law, is liable for the debt, default, or miscarriage of another. A *gratuitous* (voluntary or accommodation) *surety* receives consideration for acting as a surety, but does not receive a monetary payment. *Cosureties* share the burden of the principal debtor's default. In a *subsuretyship,* however, one of the sureties must alone be ultimately responsible for payment of the debt. *A conditional surety is not liable until the creditor first makes a reasonable attempt to exhaust the creditor's remedies against the debtor.*

Target corporation A corporation over which another entity seeks to gain control.

Tenancy in partnership The manner in which the legal title to partnership property is held.

Tender An offer of performance by one party to a contract which, if unjustifiably refused, places the other party in default and permits the party making the tender to exercise remedies for breach of contract.

Tender offer The offer by a corporation or person to purchase the shares of stock from shareholders of a "target corporation" in exchange for money or other securities. A tender offer is most commonly used to acquire voting control of the target corporation.

Tenor In the law of negotiable instruments, the amount originally intended. Where the face amount of a stolen negotiable instrument has been raised without the consent of the maker, a holder in due course ordinarily may enforce the instrument only in accordance with its original tenor.

Testamentary capacity The capability to make a valid will.

Testamentary intent The intent to direct the transfer of property, effective upon death.

Testate A person who dies leaving a will is said to die testate.

Testator, Testatrix A person who makes a will.

Third-person beneficiary In the law of contracts, a person who is not a party to a contract but who is intended to receive benefits from it.

Through bill of lading See *Bill of lading.*

Time draft See *Draft.*

Title Ownership; in the law of secured transactions, "title" is often used to describe a security interest, an interest in property less extensive than ownership. See *Security interest.*

Tort A civil wrong, other than breach of contract, for which a court may award damages.

Trademark A word, symbol, device, or design affixed to or placed upon an article or its container to identify an article offered for sale.

Trade name A name used in trade to designate a particular business.

Trade regulation rule A legislative rule with the force of law promulgated by the Federal Trade Commission regulating business practices.

Transaction Any act of conducting business. Broader than the word "contract," the word "transaction" includes "gift," "lease," "sale," "mortgage," and "bailment."

Traveler's check A three-party draft purchased from a bank or another firm and carried instead of cash.

Treasury stock Stock issued by a corporation but subsequently reacquired by the corporation and not canceled. May be reissued.

Trial de novo A new trial held in an appellate court.

Trust A relationship involving an obligation arising out of a confidence reposed in a person, for the benefit of another, to apply property or services faithfully according to such confidence. A trust arises when property is given to one person with direction that it be used and applied for the benefit of another.

Trustee in bankruptcy A bankruptcy official responsible for collecting, liquidating, and distributing the debtor's estate.

Turnover In bankruptcy law, the act of delivering to the trustee in bankruptcy property that belongs to the debtor's estate.

Tying contract A contract in which a seller sells a product only on condition that the buyer also purchases a distinct second product which is not desired.

Ultrahazardous activity An activity that necessarily involves a risk of serious harm, which risk cannot be eliminated by the exercise of utmost care. Also called an "abnormally dangerous activity."

***Ultra vires* act** A corporate act or action that is beyond the scope of authority and powers conferred upon the corporation by law or by the articles of incorporation.

Unconscionable Conduct (not necessarily amounting to fraud, misrepresentation, or duress) that results in the oppression or unfair surprise of one contracting party by the other.

Undue influence The overcoming of the free will of a person by unfair persuasion, usually involves misuse of a position of confidence or relationship.

Unenforceable contract A contract that the law will not enforce by direct legal proceedings but may recognize in some indirect way as creating some duty of performance.

Uniform state laws A draft of law prepared by the National Conference of Commissioners on Uniform State Laws and submitted to all states for adoption. When adopted, such a law is amended to meet individual state needs.

Unilateral contract A contract in which one party makes a promise; the other party must perform an act to enforce the contract. See also *Bilateral contract.*

Usage of trade In the law of sales, any practice or method of dealing having such regularity of observance in a place, vocation, or trade as to justify an expectation that it will be observed with respect to the transaction in question.

Usury The charging of any rate of interest in excess of that permitted by law.

Value In the law of *sales, secured transactions,* and *documents of title,* any promise or other consideration sufficient to support a simple contract. In the law of *commercial paper, performed* consideration.

Verification A person's statement, signed under penalty of perjury, that facts recited in a document are true and correct.

Vertical merger A combination in which a firm at one level acquires a firm at a different level, e.g., a manufacturer acquiring a wholesaler.

Vertical price fixing See *Resale price maintenance.*

Vest To become established, to take effect, giving an immediate, fixed right of present or future enjoyment.

Vicarious act An act performed or exercised by one party for another. In agency law, an agent's or a servant's act which may bind the principal or master.

Void Of no effect whatsoever.

Voidable A condition where a party has the option of avoiding a contract.

Voidable contract A contract that a party may enforce or set aside (avoid) as that person wishes.

Void contract An attempt at contracting which never produced a contract because some essential contractual element was missing.

Wanton act A malicious and unjustifiable act; a heedless and reckless disregard for another's rights; careless of the consequences.

Warehouse A building or other enclosed area used to hold goods temporarily or for an indefinite time. A *public warehouse* stores goods for any member of the public who seeks and pays for the storage service. A *private warehouse* stores goods only for those persons with whom it chooses to contract.

Warehouser A person or firm engaged in the business of receiving and storing goods for hire.

Warehouse receipt See *Document of title.*

Warranty A statement, promise, or other representation that a thing has certain qualities or that the seller has title to the thing. Also, an obligation imposed by law that a thing will have certain qualities. An *express warranty* is made by means of a statement or other affirmation of fact; an implied warranty is one that is imposed by law. In the law of sales a *warranty of merchantability*, whether express or implied, assures the recipient that the goods are of fair, average quality. A sales *warranty of fitness for a particular purpose* assures the buyer that the goods are fit for the buyer's particular purpose. In the law of commercial paper, there are two kinds of warranties: *transfer warranties* and *presentment warranties.*

Warranty of fitness See *Warranty.*

Warranty of merchantability See *Warranty.*

Warranty of title See *Warranty.*

White knight An entity which, at the request of a target corporation, takes over the target company in order to foil an unfriendly takeover attempt.

Will In estate or inheritance law, a declaration of a person's wishes as to how his or her property will be disposed of, to take effect after death. Until death, a will is said to be ambulatory and may be revoked.

Winding up A necessary step after the dissolution of a partnership, during which the partnership assets are gathered in, all its debts are paid, and distribution of the remainder is made to the partners.

With reserve In auctions, an expression indicating that the auctioneer, on behalf of the owner, reserves the right to withdraw the goods from bidding.

Without reserve In auctions, an expression indicating that the owner of the goods will sell them to the highest bidder no matter how low the bid is.

Worker's Compensation Law A law enacted in all states which establishes systems for the payment of compensation to workers who are injured in or suffer a disease as a result of their employment.

Writ A writing, issued by a court or other competent tribunal and directed to the sheriff or to some other officer for the purpose of carrying out an order or sentence of the court.

Writ of execution See *Execution.*

INDEX